Mantle Fielding's

Dictionary Of

AMERICAN PAINTERS
SCULPTORS
& ENGRAVERS

*New Completely
Revised, Enlarged
and Updated Edition*

Published By
APOLLO

Edited by Glenn B. Opitz

Thanks to –
everyone who helped on this monumental project,
especially the staff: Cindy Spano, Shari Hubner,
Judy Dym, Pam Shott, Christopher Melley, Patty
Carey, Steve Clark, Maria Moustakas-Petersen,
Barbara Hosie, Mary Kay Maley, Chris Lettieri,
Vincent Porter and Norman Posel.

Thanks to IBM and Lise Paulin-Perry who wrote
the original computer program for this work.

Special thanks to Henry Holt and Bob Bahssin for
their continued support and encouragement.

Dedicated to –
my Mom and Dad, who guided and aided me through
all my life's endeavors, and my children, Adam and
Nancy, who put up with my short temper during this
undertaking.

Printed in the United States of America
SECOND PRINTING, OCTOBER 1984

APOLLO BOOK
391 South Road   Poughkeepsie, N.Y.   12601
800-431-5003   N.Y.S. ONLY 800-942-8222
914-452-0660

FOREWORD

The editors of this volume have drawn upon Mantle Fielding's Dictionary of American Painters, Sculptors and Engravers to create an efficient reference tool for anyone seeking information about American artists who worked during the 18th, 19th and 20th centuries. The entries are not intended to be anything more than introductory; they serve instead as a guide to further study.

Fielding's 1926 Dictionary was first reprinted in 1965 when James F. Carr compiled a 92-page addendum of corrections and additions to entries that appeared in the original work. Nine years later Modern Books and Crafts, Incorporated, enlarged the Dictionary, adding 2,500 two-line entries, but this version proved to be of limited value because it contained only the most basic kind of information. The present editors eliminated most of these shortcomings by expanding the scope of the work to include the names of 1,000 living contemporary artists and the names of numerous others - no longer living - whose names were omitted from the earlier editions.

Now, for the first time in more than 50 years, the records and accomplishments of over 10,000 major and minor professional artists appear in a single up-to-date volume that is certain to be useful to researchers, collectors, curators, art dealers, or anyone else seeking biographical information.

The editors have achieved uniformity in their presentation by taking some entries directly from Fielding's original work and they have expanded others to include schooling, collections, date and place of birth, and date of death, or at least the individual's last known address. The entries are neither popular in tone nor do they assume specialized knowledge. They give, as far as reasonably possible, a central body of fairly well-established facts in terse, compact statements and make no attempt to supply complete lists of an artist's achievements.

Bringing together such an extensive reference work is a tremendous undertaking, and yet is merely a beginning. The publisher has already made plans to produce a multi-volume edition that will extend the range of this volume to include national and regional professional artists whose names have all but disappeared from print. He should be commended for making available to the layman and the scholar such a useful and important contribution to the literature of American art.

Wichita State University   Martin H. Bush
Kansas   Director
June 1983   Edwin A. Ulrich Museum

ADDENDUM

When our edition of <u>Mantle Fielding's</u>
<u>Dictionary</u> <u>of American Painters</u>, <u>Sculptors</u>
<u>and Engravers</u> went to press in June 1983, a
number of important artists were omitted.
The limitations of time and space caused some
omissions; others, unfortunately, resulted
from inexcusable oversight. In a few cases,
even the computer let us down and lost a
biography too late in the process for correction.

This addendum of 52 names was prepared to
fill in the more important gaps. The artists
range from William Michael Harnett and
Whistler to Jackson Pollock and Andy Warhol.
Other artists will be included in future
specialized volumes, such as our <u>Dictionary</u>
<u>of American Sculptors</u>, due January 1984,
which will have over 5,000 names not in the
revised <u>Fielding</u>.

Glenn B. Opitz
Publisher

AVERY, MILTON.

Painter. Born in Altmar, NY, March 7, 1893. Studied at Conn. League of Art Students, briefly 1913, with C. N. Flagg. Exhibited at numerous New York City galleries, including P. Rosenberg and Co., Bertha Schaefer Gallery, Knoedler and Co., Grace Borgenicht (many in the 1950's); Baltimore Museum of Fine Arts; Boston Museum of Fine Arts; Museum of Modern Art; Philadelphia Art Alliance; American Federation of Arts, NYC (retro.); Carnegie; Pennasylvania Academy of Fine Arts; Art Institute of Chicago; Corcoran; Whitney; Albright, Buffalo, NY; many more. Awards: Logan prize, Art Institute of Chicago, 1929; Atheneum prize, Conn. Academy of Fine Arts, 1930; Baltimore Water-color Club, first prize, 1949; Boston Arts Festival, second prize, 1948; ART:USA:59, NYC. In collections of Addison Gallery, Andover, Mass.; Baltimore; Brandeis Univ.; Brooklyn; Albright-Knox; Dayton Art Institute; Houston Museum of Fine Arts; Atlanta (GA) Art Association; Metropolitan Museum of Art; Museum of Modern Art; Newark; Penna. Academy of Fine Arts; Philadelphia Museum of Art; Tel-Aviv; Whitney; Walker; many more. Died in NYC January 3, 1965.

BARD, JAMES.

Marine painter. Born in Chelsea, NYC, 1815. Twin brother of John Bard, both of whom were self-taught and specialized in depicting steamboats of the Hudson River and NYC. James worked to scale. Over 300 of their paintings are recorded. Work is represented in the collections of the NY State Historical Assoc., Cooperstown, NY; Mariner's Museum, Newport News, VA; Peabody Museum, Salem, Mass.; Brooklyn Museum, NY; Shelburne Museum, Shelburne, VT; and the Wadsworth Athenaeum, Hartford, CT. His first painting is dated 1827; his last known attributed painting is dated 1897. He died at White Plains, NY, March 26, 1897.

BARD, JOHN.

Marine painter. Born in Chelsea, New York City, 1815. Twin brother of James Bard. Self-taught. Worked with his brother until 1849. Their work is very similar and difficult to distinguish; both artists used the signature "J. Bard" at different times. Works are represented in the Brooklyn Mus., NY; NY State Historical Association, Cooperstown, NY; Mariner's Museum, Newport News, VA; Peabody Museum, Salem, MA; Shelburne Museum, Shelburne, VT; and Wadsworth Athenaeum, Hartford, CT. Died on Blackwell's Island, Oct. 18, 1856.

BLUEMNER, OSCAR.

Painter. Born in Preuzlau, Germany, 1867. Emigrated to Chicago in 1893. Before he left Germany, he won a royal medal for a painting of an architectural subject, 1892. Came to Chicago to seek work at the World's Columbian Exposition, in 1893. In 1900, his Beaux-Arts design won the competition for the Bronx Courthouse. Made a trip abroad in 1912. Noted for his paintings after 1912; especially "Old Canal Port," 1914, at the Whitney Museum of American Art, NYC. Died in 1938.

BLUME, PETER.

Painter. Born in Russia, Oct. 27, 1906. Came to US in 1911; later became a US citizen. Studied at the Educational Alliance School of Art, 1919-24; Beaux-Arts Institute of Design; and the Art Students' League. Exhibited: Boston Museum of Fine Arts; Whitney Mus. of Am. Art; Metropolitan Museum of Art; Mus. of Modern Art; others. First attracted notice by his painting in 1931 called "South of Scranton," held now by the Museum of Modern Art, which won him the prize at the Carnegie International Exhibition of Painting in 1934. Another celebrated work is his "The Eternal City," 1937, held now at the Museum of Modern Art, a piece inspired by his experience of Italy under rule of Mussolini, 1932-33. Blume also painted government sponsored murals for post offices in Geneva, New York, 1941, and Canonsburg, PA; also a mural in the Courthouse in Rome, GA, 1941. Artist-in-residence at the American Academy in Rome. Many of his paintings deal with Italian themes. Member: National Academy of Design; National

1

Institute of Arts and Letters; and the American Academy of Arts and Letters. Address in 1982, Rte 1, Box 140, Sherman, CT.

BOREN, JAMES ERWIN.
Painter. Born in Waxahachie, TX, Sept. 26, 1921. Studied at the Kansas City Art Inst. and School of Design, B.F.A. and M.F.A.; Univ. of Kansas City. Exhibited: National Cowboy Hall of Fame, 1969; Texas Art Gallery, Dallas, 1969-81; Cowboy Artists of America, National Cowboy Hall of Fame, 1970-72; Whitney Museum, Cody, Wyoming, 1973; and others. Awards: Excellence Award, from the Society of Technical Writers and Publishers, 1964; nine gold and eight silver awards, from Cowboy Artists of America (secretary-treasurer, 1969-70; president, 1973-74 and 1979-80). Works executed in watercolor and oil. Address in 1982, P.O. Box 533 Clifton, TX.

BRISCO, FRANKLIN D.
Marine painter. Born in Baltimore, MD, 1844. Exhibited: Penn. Academy of Fine Arts in 1863; and at the Brooklyn Art Association, in 1873. Died in Philadelphia, PA, 1903.

BURLIUK, DAVID.
Painter. Born in Kharkov, Ukraine, July 22, 1882. Studied at art schools in Kazan, 1898-1902, Odessa, 1911, Munich, Moscow, 1914; Bayerische Akademie der Schonen Kunst, Munich; Academie des Beaux-Arts, Paris. Came to US in 1922. In collections of Boston Mus. of Fine Arts; Brooklyn Mus.; Met. Mus. of Art; Whitney; Phillips Gallery, Washington, DC; Yale University. Exhibited in Russia, 1904, 1907; Societe Anonyme, J. B. Neumann Gal., Morton Gallery, Dorothy Paris Gallery, Leonard Hutton Gallery, all NYC; Galerie Maeght, Der Blaue Reiter, Paris; Brooklyn; Phila.; others. Co-founder of Futurist art movement in Russia, 1911; art magazine Color Rhyme, 1930; founder-member of Der Blaue Reiter and Der Sturm groups, 1910-14. Died in Southampton, NY, January 15, 1967.

BUTTERSWORTH, JAMES EDWARD.
Marine painter. Born in England in 1817. Pupil of his father, the painter Thomas Buttersworth. Came to US c. 1845/47, settling in West Hoboken, New Jersey. Painted for N. Currier and Currier and Ives, who published his work, approximately 1847-1865. Exhibited at American Art-Union 1850-52. Represented in US Naval Acad. Museum, Annapolis; Bath Marine Museum, ME; Newark Museum, NJ; Yale Centre for British Art; Mariner's Museum, Newport News, VA; Museum of the City of NY; Portland Museum of Art, ME; VA Museum of Fine Arts, Richmond; Peabody Museum of Salem; Butler Institute, Youngstown, Ohio; others. He painted ships in NY Harbor, yachts, steamships, warships; also painted landscapes and portraits. Died in West Hoboken, NJ, March 2, 1894.

CORNELL, JOSEPH.
Sculptor. Born in Nyack, NY, 1903. Studied at Phillips Acad. at Andover, MA. Settled in NYC, 1929. Exhibited at Peggy Guggenheim's "Art of this Century" Gallery (1944-45); Egan Galleries (1947-53); Stable Gallery (1953); and Allen Frumkin Gallery (1953), Chicago. Associated with the Julien Levy Galleries, exhibiting there from 1932-42. Many of his works are now held by the Hirschhorn Museum. Died in 1973.

COZZENS, FREDERIC SCHILLER.
Marine painter. Born in New York City, October 11, 1846. Attended Rensselaer Polytechnic Institute, Troy, New York, 1864-67; no information available on course of study. He was painting in New York City by 1874; from mid-1870's to 1898, his illustrations appeared in New York's Daily Graphic and Harper's Weekly. Most famous work is series of watercolors for Kelley's American Yachts: Their Clubs and Races, published by Scribner's in 1884. Did book and magazine illustrations until about 1906: Yachts and Yachting, Outing magazine (1886-87), Rushton's Portable Canoes (1891), The Rudder magazine (1903, 06); 24 paintings for Our Navy: Its Growth and Achievements were reproduced as

chromolithographs by American Publishing Co., Hartford. Also executed many paintings; from 1870 through 1920, he depicted every match in America's Cup, held off NY Harbor. Also painted fishing vessels and scenes, and warships. Painted scenes of North Amer. Indians, 1920, 21. First major exhibit, Mystic Seaport Mus., 1983. In many private collections; Mariner's Mus. (Newport News, VA), MIT, NY Yacht Club, Peabody Museum of Salem (MA), US Coast Guard Acad., Kennedy Galleries (NYC). Died in NYC August 29, 1928.

CRAWFORD, RALSTON.
Painter, lithographer, and photographer. Born in St. Catharines, Ontario, Canada, 1906. Lived in Buffalo between 1910-26. Studied art at the Otis Art Inst., in Los Angeles, CA; Phila. Acad. of Fine Arts, 1927-30; Academie Colarossi; and Academie Scandinave, Paris, 1932-33. Also worked at the Walt Disney studio, 1926. First photographic works were photos of New Orleans, 1937-38. Worked in lithography, 1951-52, in Paris. Characteristic work of his painting is his "Grain Elevators from the Bridge," 1940, at the Whitney Museum of American Art, NYC.

DIEBENKORN, RICHARD.
Painter. Born in Portland, OR, April 22, 1922. Studied at Stanford Univ., 1940-43; Univ. of California, 1943-44; California School of Fine Arts, 1946; Univ. of New Mexico, M.A., 1952. Exhibited five times at the Whitney Museum of American Art, 1955-70; one-man shows include the DeYoung Memorial Museum, in San Francisco, 1963; Jewish Museum, 1965; and the Los Angeles County Museum, Los Angeles, 1969 and 72; Venice Biennale, 1968; 20th National Print Exhibit, 1977; plus numerous others. Awards: Albert M. Bender fellowship, 1946; Gold Medal, Penn. Academy of Fine Arts, 1968; Purchase prize, Olivet College, 1968. Member: American Academy of Arts and Letters. Taught: Professorship in art, University of Calif., Los Angeles, 1966-73. Early work, realism; later work abstract expressionism, such as "Woman in a Window," 1957,

at the Albright-Knox Art Gal., Buffalo, NY. Authored a book on drawing in 1965. Address in 1982, c/o Knoedler Gallery, 19 East 70th St., NYC.

GRAVES, MORRIS.
Painter. Born in Fox Valley, OR, August 28, 1910. Exhibited at Seattle Art Museum; Willard Art Gallery, NYC, 1942-78; Detroit Art Institute; L.A. Co. Museum; Art Institute of Chicago; Museum of Modern Art; National Academy of Design, NYC; and others. Received Guggenheim Foundation Fellowship, 1946; Blair Prize, Art Institute of Chicago, 1948; Windsor Award (Duke and Duchess of Windsor), 1957. In collections of Seattle Art Museum; Museum of Modern Art; Phillips; Whitney; Metropolitan Museum of Art. Honorary member of American Watercolor Society. Works in oil and tempera. Address in 1982, c/o Willard Gallery, NYC.

GROOMS, RED.
Sculptor. Born Charles Rogers Grooms, in Nashville, TN, 1937. Studied at the Art Inst. of Chicago; Peabody College for Teachers, Nashville, TN; Hans Hofmann School, NYC; and the New School for Social Research. Became involved in non-verbal spontaneous theatrical presentations called "Happenings," with Claes Oldenberg, Jim Dine, and Allan Kaprow, New York City. One of his better known "happenings" was entitled "Burning Building," 1959. Permanent works of his are assemblages of groups of objects, which in turn make environments such as his "Loft on 26th Street," 1965-66, at the Hirschhorn Museum. Collections of his works are at Rutgers University and the Art Inst. of Chicago. Exhibited: Art Institute of Chicago, 1966; Museum of Modern Art, New York City, 1966; Guggenheim Museum, New York City, 1972; one-man shows were held at Ft. Worth Art Museum, in Texas, 1976; "Discount Store," Southern University of NY, Purchase, 1978; University of Miami, 1980. Co-authored a book with Allan Kaprow titled Assemblage, Environments and Happenings, 1965. Address in 1982, Marlborough Gallery Inc., 40

3

West 57th St., NYC.

GROSS, CHAIM.
Sculptor. Born March 17, 1904, in Kolomea, East Austria. Came to USA in 1921. Studied: Kunstgewerbe Schule; Educational Alliance, NYC; Beaux-Arts Inst. of Design, with Elie Nadelman; Art Students' League, with Robert Laurent. Work: Ain Harod; Andover (Addison Gal.); Baltimore Mus. of Art; Bezalel Museum; Boston Mus. of Fine Arts; Brooklyn Mus.; Art Institute of Chicago; Jewish Museum; Met. Mus. of Art; Mus. of Modern Art; Penn. Acad. of Fine Arts; Phila. Mus. of Art; Queens Coll.; Reed Coll.; Rutgers Univ.; Smith Coll.; Tel-Aviv; Whitney Mus.; Walker; Worcester Art Mus.; Butler; and many others, including commissions for Main P.O. Wash., DC; FTC Bldg., Wash., DC; Hadassah Hospital, Jerusalem; Temple Shaaray Tefila, NYC; and others. Exhibited: Boyer Gal., Phila., 1935; Boyer Gal., NYC, 1937; AAA Gal., NYC, 1942, 69; Youngstown (Butler); Jewish Mus.; Duveen-Graham Gal., NYC; Whitney Mus.; Sculptors Guild Annuals; Penn. Academy of Fine Arts; American Fed. of Arts; Am. Painting and Sculpture, Moscow, 1959; Mus. of Modern Art; Smithsonian; NY World's Fair, 1964-65. Awards: L. C. Tiffany Grant, 1933; Paris World's Fair, 1937, Silver Medal; Mus. of Modern Art, Artists for Victory, $3,000 Second Prize, 1942; Boston Arts Festival, Third Prize for Sculpture, 1954; Penn. Acad. of Fine Arts, Hon. Men., 1954; Audubon Artists, prize for Sculpture, 1955; Nat. Inst. of Arts and Letters, Award of Merit Medal, 1963. Member: Sculptors Guild (President); Artists Equity; Federation of Modern Painters and Sculptors; Nat'l. Inst. of Arts and Letters. Taught: Educational Alliance, NYC; New School for Social Research; Mus. of Modern Art. Address in 1982, NYC.

HARNETT, WILLIAM MICHAEL.
Still life painter. Born in Ireland in 1848. Family moved to Phila. Harnett practiced engraving in Phila. from 1865. In 1871 he moved to NYC. Studied at National Academy and Cooper Union in NYC. Returned to Philadelphia in 1876; studied at Penna. Academy of Fine Arts. In 1880, went to London to study; visited Frankfort, stayed in Munich, studying Old Masters, from 1881-1885. Returned to US via Paris and London, arriving in NYC in April 1886. He exhibited at Paris Salon c. 1885. Subjects of his first pictures, exhibited in 1875, were fruit and vegetables; from about 1876 he turned to other subjects such as beer mugs, tobacco, books, musical instruments, writing materials, money, skulls. His work is in collections of Addison Gallery, Andover, MA; Art Museum, Wichita, KS; Columbus Gallery of Fine Arts; Butler Institute, Youngstown, OH; Fine Arts Museum of San Fran.; Met. Museum of Art, NYC; Graves Art Gallery, Sheffield, Eng.; Museum of Fine Arts, Boston. He died in 1892.

HELD, AL.
Painter. Born in NYC, Oct. 12, 1928. Studied at Art Students' League, 1948-49; Academie de la Grande Chaumiere, 1949-52. Exhibited: Guggenheim Museum, 1966; Jewish Museum, 1967; Documenta IV, Kassel, West Germany, 1968; one-man shows at the San Francisco Museum of Art and the Corcoran Gallery of Art, 1968; Whitney Museum of Art, NYC, 1971; Emmerich Gallery, Zurich, Switzerland, 1977; numerous others. Taught art at Yale Univ., 1962-78; as an adjunct of painting, 1978. Awards: Logan Medal, from the Art Institute, Chicago, 1964; Guggenheim Foundation Fellowship, 1966. Commissioned by NY State to paint 90-foot wide "Albany Mural" in the Empire State Plaza, Albany, NY. Address in 1982, Dept. of Painting and Printmaking, Yale University School of Art, New Haven, CT.

HIRSCHFIELD, MORRIS.
Primitive painter. Born in Russia-Poland in 1872. Produced religious sculpture at early age. Emigrated to US in 1890; lived in Brooklyn, NY. Worked in ladies' garment shop, later had own highly successful business. Not active again artistically until 1937. First one-man exhibition organized in 1943 for

4

Museum of Modern Art; work shown in numerous expositions in US and Europe. In collections of Museum of Modern Art; Sidney Janis Gal.; private collections. Brooklyn Museum has photos of 74 of his 77 paintings. Considered one of the greatest primitive painters. Died in Brooklyn, NY, July 26, 1946.

HUDSON, GRACE CARPENTER.
Painter. Born in Potter Valley, California, in 1865. Studied at Hopkins Art Inst., San Francisco, 1878. Won Alvord Gold Medal for figure drawing, San Francisco Art Assoc., 1880. She exhibited paintings of Indians in women's dept. of California state building, Chicago World's Columbian Expo., 1893. Made field trips to Hawaii to paint native children; to Oklahoma to paint Pawnee tribe. Went to Europe in 1905. Settled permanently in Ukiah, Calif. In collections of Field Mus., Chicago (Pawnee tribe paintings); Oakland (California) Museum; National Gallery of Art, Washington, DC; others. She concentrated on studying and painting the Pomo Indians of Mendocino County, California. Died in 1937.

JACKSON, HARRY ANDREW.
Sculptor and painter. Born in Chicago, IL, April 18, 1924. Studied at the Art Inst., 1931-38, with Ed Grigware in Cody, WY, 1938-42, with Hans Hofmann at the Brooklyn Mus. Art Sch., 1946-48. Exhibited: Nat'l. Collection of Fine Arts, Wash., DC; Nat'l. Acad. of Design, NYC, 1964, 65, 67, 68, and 70; Nat'l. Cowboy Hall of Fame, Oklahoma City, 1966 and 70-72; a retrospective of works was held at the Buffalo Bill Historical Center, Cody, WY, 1981. Awards: Samuel Finley Breese Morse Gold Medal from the National Academy of Design, 1968 and the silver medal, from the Nat'l. Cowboy Hall of Fame, 1971. Member: Cowboy Artists of America; National Sculpture Society; Am. Artists Professional Lg.; Bohemian Club; National Acad. of Western Art; and the National Acad. of Design. He was official combat artist for the US Marine Corps, 1944-45; the youngest combat artist in World War II. He is the author of a volume entitled Lost Wax Bronze Casting, 1972. Subject matter of his works draws upon the life of the American West and his own experience as a cowboy. Address in 1982, P.O. Box 2836, Cody, WY.

JACOBSEN, ANTONIO NICOLO GASPARO.
Marine painter. Born in Copenhagen, Denmark, Nov. 2, 1850; son of a violin maker. Studied art at the Royal Acad., in Copenhagen, although these studies ended abruptly with the advent of the Franco-Prussian War in 1871, when he fled to America to avoid conscription. In NYC he decorated iron safes and painted the ships of the Old Dominion Steamship Line. Moved to West Hoboken, NJ, in 1880, where he continued to specialize in steamer portraits. Later in his life, his daughter, Helen, may have aided him in painting cloud and sky backgrounds in many of his paintings. He is said to be the most prolific of all American marine painters and is well represented in the Mass. State House, Boston, MA; India House, NYC; Mariner's Mus., Newport News, VA; Mystic Seaport Mus., Mystic, CT; Nation Scheepvaart-museum, Antwerp, Belgium; Peabody Mus., Salem, MA; Phila. Maritime Mus., Phila., PA; Museo Civico Navale, Genoa-Pegli, Italy; and the Seamen's Bank for Savings. Jacobsen died February 2, 1921.

JOHNS, JASPER.
Sculptor and painter. Born in Augusta, GA, May 15, 1930; grew up in Allendale and Sumpter. Studied at University of South Carolina, 1947-48. Works: "The Critic Sees," 1961; "Double White Map," 1965, which sold at an auction in NY for $240,000, highest price ever paid at that time for a 20th century American piece of art; "Book," 1957, and "Drawer," 1957, which are examples of the attachment of objects to paintings; represented in Mus. of Modern Art; Whitney; Albright-Knox; Paris, Mus. of Modern Art; Victoria & Albert, London. Exhibited: Retrospective, San Francisco Mus. of Modern Art, 1978; Mus. of Modern Art, NY, 1968, 70, and 72; Univ. of California,

Irvine, 1969; Mus. of Contemporary Art, Chicago, 1971-72; Seattle Art Museum, Washington, 1973; Art Inst. of Chicago, 1974; numerous other group and one-man shows, some of which were held at the Gallery d'Arte del Noviglio, in Milan, 1959, the Galerie Rive Droite in Paris, and the Whitechapel Gallery, London, 1964. Executed numerous sculpted objects consisting of mass produced pieces such as beer cans, flashlights, and lightbulbs. Address in 1982, c/o Leo Castelli, 420 W. Broadway, NYC.

LANE, FITZ HUGH.
Painter and lithographer. Born in Gloucester, MA, Dec. 19, 1804. No formal art training until 1832 when apprenticed to lithographing firm of William S. and John Pendleton, Boston. In 1845 formed own litho firm with John W. A. Scott. In the 1840's he turned increasingly to oil painting. Returned to Gloucester in 1848. His paintings were primarily of that city and environs and the Maine coast; also of NY Harbor, Baltimore, Porto Rico (St. John's). Subjects were harbor views, wharf scenes, sailing and steamships, landscapes. Exhibited frequently in Gloucester, Boston, Albany (NY), and NYC. Many works purchased and sold by American Art-Union. Most of his works are in collections of Cape Ann Historical Association, Gloucester, MA; Karolik Collection, Museum of Fine Arts, Boston. Also represented in Butler Inst., Youngstown, Ohio; Shelburne (VT) Museum; Mariner's Museum, Newport News, VA; RI School of Design; Richmond (VA) Museum of Fine Arts; Newark (NJ) Museum; Farnsworth Mus., Rockland, ME; Berry-Hill Galleries, NYC; others, including private collections. Died in Gloucester, MA, Aug. 18, 1865.

LEAVITT, EDWARD C.
Painter. Born in 1842. Exhibited at the National Academy of Design in New York City, 1875. His specialty was fruit and flower still life oil paintings, often in conjunction with opulent backgrounds of highly polished tables, costly antiques, etc.; rich in color, sharp detail.

Most celebrated works characteristic of the artist are those of the 1880's to early 1890's. 1892 marks a rapid decline in quality of his work. Died in Providence, Rhode Island, November 20, 1904.

LEBDUSKA, LAWRENCE H.
Painter. Born in Baltimore, MD, September 1894. Studied in Leipzig, Germany, and with Fleider, Schneider, Swoboda. In collections of Museum of Modern Art, New York City; Whitney, New York City; Newark (NJ) Museum; Albright Art Gallery, Buffalo, New York; Univ. of Arizona. Exhibited at the Art Center of New York in 1926; other galleries in New York City and nationally; Brandenmeyer Gallery, Buffalo, New York. Received award at Leipzig International Art Exposition, 1912. Member of Audubon Artists. Paints in the Primitive style. Address in 1953, 230 East 52nd St., NYC.

LINDNER, RICHARD.
Painter. Born in Hamburg, West Germany, 1901. Raised in Nuremberg. Studied at the Hamburg School of Fine and Applied Arts in 1922 and the Academy of Fine Arts in Munich, 1924. In 1933, he left for Paris, emigrating to the US in 1941, where he illustrated for Vogue magazine 1941-50. Taught at Pratt Inst., NYC, 1951-65. Characteristic of his work are his "The Meeting," 1953, Museum of Modern Art; and "Rock-Rock," 1963, Dallas Museum. Painting subjects concentrate on women, precocious children, and men. Died in 1978.

MACDONALD-WRIGHT, STANTON.
Painter. Born in Charlottesville, VA, July 8, 1890. Studied at the Sorbonne; Beaux-Arts, Colarossi, and Julian Academies, Paris; Art Students' League with W. T. Hedges, J. Greenbaum. Founded Synchromist movement in Paris with Morgan Russell, 1913. Taught at Univ. of California, 1942-50; Fulbright Exchange Professor, Japan, 1952-53; others. In collections of Boston Museum of Fine Arts; Brooklyn; Carnegie; Art Institute of Chicago; Corcoran; Denver; Detroit Art Institute; L.A. County Museum of Art; Met. Mus. of Art; Mus. of

Modern Art; Phila.; Toledo; Santa Barbara; Whitney; Walker; others. Exhibited at Photo-Secession, NYC, 1917; Stendahl Gallery, Los Angeles; Duveen-Graham Gallery, NYC; L.A. County Museum; Salon d'Automne, Paris; The Synchromists, Munich and Paris, 1913; Met. Museum of Art; Brooklyn; others. Died in 1973. Address in 1971, Pacific Palisades, California.

MELROSE, ANDREW.
Landscape painter. Born in 1836. Had studio in West Hoboken and Guttenberg, NJ, during 1870's and 80's. Executed paintings of views in North Carolina, Hudson River Valley, Berkshires, New York City, Cornwall (England), Lake Killarney (Ireland), Tyrolese Alps. He died February 23, 1901, in West New York, New Jersey.

MOHOLY-NAGY, LAZLO.
Sculptor, painter, and photographer. Born July 29, 1895, Bacsbarsod, Hungary; came to US in 1937. Studied: University of Budapest, 1913-14, LLB. Work: Art Institute of Chicago; Dayton Art Institute; Detroit Institute; Los Angeles Co. Museum of Art; Museum of Modern Art; San Francisco Museum of Art; Guggenheim. Exhibited: Stedelijk; Brno, Czechoslovakia; Hamburg; Mannheim; Cologne; Budapest (Nat'l.); Stockholm (Nat'l.); The London Gal., London, 1937; Harvard Univ., 1950; Zurich, 1953; Kunst Kabinett Klihm, 1956, 59, 62, 66; Kleemann Gal., NYC, 1957; Dusseldorf, 1961; Eindhoven, 1967; Guggenheim; Art Institute of Chic.; Whitney Museum; Yale Univ.; The Machine as Seen at the End of the Mechanical Age, Museum of Modern Art, 1968, and others. Taught: Staatliche Bauhaus, Berlin, 1922; founding collaborator, with Gyorgy Kepes and Robert Wolff, of the Inst. of Design, Chicago, 1938-42; Director of the New Bauhaus, Chicago. Designed for State Opera and the Piscator Theatre, Berlin, 1928. Died Nov. 24, 1946, Chicago, IL.

PASSUNTINO, PETER ZACCARIA.
Sculptor and printmaker. Born in Chicago, IL, February 18, 1936. Studied at Art Inst. of Chicago,

scholarships, 1954-58; Oxbow School of Painting, summer, 1958. Exhibited: Corcoran Museum, Washington, DC; Knowlton Gallery, New York, 1976; Gallery K, Wash., DC, 1976; Joseph Gallery, New York; Gallery 187, Englewood, NJ; Art Latitude, NJ, 1979; and numerous others. Awards: Fulbright Fellowship, 1963-64; and a Guggenheim Award, 1971. Address in 1982, 530 La Guardia Place, NYC.

POLLOCK, JACKSON.
Painter. Born in Cody, Wyoming, January 28, 1912. Family settled in Southern California in 1925. Studied at Manual Arts High School, Los Angeles, 1925-29; Art Students' League of New York, with Thomas Benton, 1929-31. Settled in New York City in 1935. Worked in Federal Arts Project, 1938-42. Exhibited at McMillan Gallery, New York City, 1940; Peggy Guggenheim's Art of This Century Gallery, New York City, 1943; Betty Parson's Gallery, New York City, yearly 1943-50; Venice Biennale, 1950; Sidney Janis Gallery, New York City, 1952; Museum of Modern Art. In collections of Peggy Guggenheim (shown in Venice, Florence, Milan, Amsterdam, Brussels, Zurich, 1948); Museum of Modern Art; San Francisco Museum of Art; others. Died August 11, 1956, Easthampton, LI, NY.

POONS, LARRY.
Painter. Born in Tokyo, Japan, Oct. 1, 1937. Studied at the Boston Museum of Fine Arts School, 1958. Exhibited: Art Institute of Chicago, 1966; Corcoran Gallery of Art, 1967; Carnegie Institute, 1967; Documenta IV, Kassel, West Germany, 1968; Whitney Museum of American Art Annual, 1968 and 72; and the Whitney Biennial, 1973; plus numerous others. Taught: NY Studio School, 1967. Authored a book titled The Structure of Color, 1971. Address in 1982, 831 Broadway, New York City.

RAUSCHENBERG, ROBERT.
Painter and photographer. Born in Port Arthur, Texas, October 22, 1925. Studied at Kansas City Art Institute and School of Design, 1946-47; Academie Julian, 1947; Black Mountain College, with Josef

Albers, 1948-49; Art Students' League of NY, with Vaclav Vytlacil, Morris Kantor, 1949-50. Exhibited at Museum of Modern Art, 1968; Milwaukee Art Center, 1968; Whitney, New York City, annuals 1969, 1970, 1973; Guggenheim; Copenhagen; Baltimore; Munich; Tate, London; Pompidou Center, Paris; numerous other group and solo shows in US and abroad. Received Grand Prix d'Honneur, 13th International Exhibition of Graphic Art, Ljubljana, Yugos.; gold medal, Oslo; Officer of the Order of Arts and Letters, France; others. In collections of Albright-Knox, Buffalo; Whitney; White Museum, Cornell University; Tate; Museum of Modern Art; many others. Address in 1982, c/o Leo Castelli Gallery, NYC.

RIVERS, LARRY.
Sculptor and painter. Born in New York City, 1923. Studied at Juilliard School of Music, New York City, 1944-45; Hofmann Sch.; New York Univ., 1947-48. Works: Brooklyn Museum; Art Institute of Chicago; Corcoran; Kansas City (Nelson); Met. Mus. of Art; Museum of Modern Art; Minneapolis Inst.; New Paltz SUNY; Parrish; Tate; Utica; Victoria and Albert Mus.; Whitney. Exhibitions: Tibor de Nagy Gallery, New York City; Martha Jackson Gallery, New York City; Dwan Gallery, New York City; Galerie Rive Droite, 1962; Gimpel Fils Ltd., London; Marlborough-Gerson Gallery, Inc., New York City; Whitney; Mus. of Modern Art; Sao Paulo; Carnegie; II Inter-American Paintings and Prints Biennial, Mexico City; Seattle World's Fair, 1962; Penn. Acad. of Fine Art; Flint Inst., I Flint Invitational; Herron; San Fran. Mus. of Art; Documenta IV, Kassel; Virginia Mus. of Fine Art; plus many more. Awards: Corcoran, Third Prize, 1954. Professional jazz musician; began sculpture 1953. Rep. by Marlborough Gallery, NYC. Address in 1982, Southampton, NY.

ROESEN, SEVERIN.
Still life painter, porcelain and enamel painter. Born c. 1815 probably in German Rhineland. Came to US in 1848, settled in NYC. About 1857 he went to Phila. and later Harrisburg; in Huntington, PA, in 1860; lived in Williamsport, PA, from at least 1862 for about 10 years. Exhibited a flower painting at Cologne in 1847; work also shown at Maryland Historical Society, Baltimore, 1858; Penna. Academy of Fine Arts, 1863; Brooklyn Art Association, 1873. In 1848, the American Art-Union in NYC purchased works by Roesen. Date of death uncertain; references show a death date of 1871, but Gerdts in Painters of the Humble Truth mentions a painting executed by Roesen in 1872.

ROSENQUIST, JAMES.
Painter. Born in Grand Forks, ND, Nov. 29, 1933. Studied at the Minneapolis School of Art in 1948, at the University of Minnesota, with Cameron Booth, from 1952 to 54, and at Art Students' League, in 1955. From 1954-60, he worked as a billboard painter. Involved with the Aspen Institute of Humanist Studies, in Colorado, Eastern philosophy and history, 1965. Exhibited: Six Painters and the Object, Solomen R. Guggenheim Museum, NYC, 1963; Mixed-Media, 1963 and Kid Stuff, 1971, at the Albright-Knox Art Gallery, Buffalo, NY; American, 1963, Around the Automobile, 1965, The 1960's, 1967, and Works from Change, 1974, all at the Museum of Modern Art, New York City; Whitney Museum of Art, New York City; Documenta IV, Kassel, West Germany, in 1968; Los Angeles County Museum of Art, 1971; Portland Art Center, OR, 1973; and others. Taught: Visiting lecturer at Yale University, New Haven, Conn., 1964. First fine art piece he painted was "Zone," 1961; in 1963, painted a mural for the New York World's Fair. Another work is "F-111," 1964-65, a work which is 86 feet wide and shows the fuselage of an airliner which is broken up by smaller pictures such as images of spaghetti, a lightbulb, and a child's face. Works are in oil. Address in 1982, Leo Castelli Gallery, 420 West Broadway, NYC.

ROSZAK, THEODORE.

Sculptor. Born in Poznan, Poland, May 1, 1907. Studied at Columbia University, 1925-26; Chicago Art Institute School, 1922-29, with John W. Norton, Boris Ainsfeld; Nat'l. Acad. of Design, 1925-26, with C. W. Hawthorne. Works: Baltimore Mus. of Art; Art Inst. of Chicago; Cleveland Mus. of Art; U. of Illinois; Industrial Mus., Barcelona; Mus. of Modern Art; U. of Michigan; Penn. Acad. of Fine Art; Guggenheim; Sao Paulo; Smithsonian; Tate; Whitney; Walker; University of Wisconsin; Yale University; plus commissions including, MIT (spire and bell tower); American Embassy, London; New Pub. Health Lab, New York City. Exhibitions: Albany Institute; Artists' Gallery, NYC; Julien Levy Gal., NYC; Pierre Matisse Gal., NYC; XXX Venice Biennial, 1960; Art Institute of Chicago Annuals, 1931, 32, 35, 37, 38, 41; Whitney Annuals, 1932-38, 1941, 57, 58, 59, 62, 1964-68, and retro., 1956; Museum of Modern Art; Penna. Academy of Fine Art; American Federation of Arts; Documenta I & II, Kassel, West Germany, 1955, 59; Brussels World's Fair, 1958; Carnegie; National Institute of Arts and Letters; Tate; Cleveland Museum of Art. Awards: World's Fair, Poland, 1929, Silver Medal; Art Institute of Chicago, Joseph N. Eisendrath Prize, 1934; Art Institute of Chicago, Logan Medal, 1947, 51; I Sao Paulo Biennial, 1951; Tate, International Unknown Political Prisoner Competition, 1953; PAFA, George D. Widener Memorial Gold Medal, 1958; Art Institute of Chicago, Campana Prize, 1961; Ball State Teachers College, Griner Award, 1962; elected to the Nat'l. Institute of Arts and Letters; Century Assn., Medal for Sculpture. Member: Commission of Fine Arts, Wash., DC (appointed for 1963-67); Advisory Committee on the Arts, US State Department (appointed for 1963-67); National Council on Art and Government. Taught: Chicago Art Institute School, 1927-29; Design Laboratory, New York City, 1938-40; Sarah Lawrence College, 1940-56; lectured at many museums and universities. Died in 1981.

Address in 1970, One St. Lukes Place, NYC.

SEGAL, GEORGE.

Sculptor. Born in NYC, Nov. 26, 1924. Studied at NYU, 1950, BS; Rutgers University, 1963, MFA Works: Stedelijk; Albright; Charlotte (Mint); Art Inst. of Chicago; Mus. of Modern Art; Newark Museum; Ottawa (National); Stockholm (National); Toronto; Whitney; Walker. Exhibitions: Hansa Gallery, NYC; Ileana Sonnabend Gallery, Paris; Sidney Janis Gallery, NYC; Toronto, 1967 (three-man, with Jim Dine, Claes Oldenburg); Boston Arts Festival, 1956; Jewish Museum; Whitney; American Federation of Arts; VII & IX Sao Paulo Biennials, 1963, 67; Stockholm (National), American Pop Art; Corcoran Biennial; Palais des Beaux-Arts, Brussels, 1965; Guggenheim; Rhode Island Sch. of Design, Recent Still Life, 1966; Art Inst. of Chicago; Walker; Los Angeles Co. Museum of Art, American Sculpture of the Sixties; Museum of Modern Art, the 1960's; Carnegie; Trenton State, Focus on Light. Awards: Walter K. Gutman Found. Grant, 1962; Art Inst. of Chicago, First Prize, 1966. Rep. by Sidney Janis Gallery, New York City. Address in 1982, S. Brunswick, NJ.

SELTZER, OLAF CARL.

Painter. Born in Copenhagen, Denmark, August 14, 1877. Studied at Technical Inst. of Copenhagen. Came to Great Falls, Montana, in 1892. Worked on a ranch; apprentice machinist for Great Northern Railroad; worked as Railroad and locomotive repairman until 1926. Met Charles Russell, who taught and encouraged him. Stayed in New York City, 1926 and 27, studying paintings in museums and galleries. Executed over 2,500 oils and water colors, largely of Western subjects. In collections of Gilcrease Institute of Art, Tulsa, OK; Montana Historical Society; Great Falls Clinic, Montana; Harmsen Collection. Died in Great Falls, Montana, in December, 1957.

SLOANE, ERIC.

Illustrator and writer. Born in

NYC, February 27, 1910. Studied at Art Students' League, NYC; School of Fine Arts, Yale University; NY School of Fine and Applied Art. Represented in Sloane Museum of Early American Tools, Kent, Conn.; commissions including Willett's Memorial at American Museum of Natural History, NYC, National Air and Space Museum in Washington, DC, others. Received gold medal, Hudson Valley Art Assoc., 1964; Freedom Foundation Award, 1965; gold medal, National Academy of Design. Author and illustrator of many books, including Skies and the Artist, Return to Taos, Reverence for Wood, I Remember America, and many more. Member of National Academy of Design, Salmagundi Club, Lotos Club, others. Address in 1982, Cornwall Bridge, CT.

SMITH, DAVID.
Sculptor. Born in Decatur, Indiana, in 1906. Studied at Ohio Univ., 1924; Art Students' League, 1926-30, with John Sloan, Jan Matulka. Works: Baltimore Museum of Art; Brandeis Univ.; Carnegie; Cincinnati Art Mus.; Art Inst. of Chicago; Detroit Inst.; Met. Mus. of Art; Mus. of Modern Art; Univ. of Mich.; Univ. of Minn.; San Fran. Mus. of Art; St. Louis City; Utica; Whitney; Walker. Exhibitions: The Willard Gallery, NYC; Kalamazoo Inst.; Walker; Buchholz Gallery, NYC; Cooling Gallery, London; Utica; Tulsa (Philbrook); The Kootz Gallery, NYC; Cincinnati Art Mus.; Otto Gerson Gallery, NYC; Everett Ellin Gallery, Los Angeles; Harvard Univ.; Tate; Guggenheim; XXIX Venice Biennial, 1958; Sao Paulo, 1959; Documenta II & III, Kassel, West Germany, 1959, 64; Whitney; Art Inst. Chicago; Carnegie; Mus. Modern Art. Awards: Guggenheim Found. Fel., 1950, 51; Brandeis University, Creative Arts Award, 1964. Taught: Sarah Lawrence Coll., 1948; Univ. of Arkansas, 1953; Indiana Univ., 1954; Univ. of Miss., 1955. Died May 5, 1965, Bennington, VT.

SMITH, TONY.
Sculptor. Born in South Orange, New Jersey, 1912. Studied at the Art Students' League, 1934-35; New Bauhaus, Chicago, for architectural study, in 1937-38; architectural apprentice of Franklin Lloyd Wright, 1938-40. Gave up architecture for sculpture in 1960, of geometric forms. His works concentrate on unifying architecture, painting, and sculpture, exemplified by his "Gracehoper" (1961), the cubic piece "Black Box" (1962) and "The Snake is Out" (1962). Later pieces include his "Smoke," based on a space grid. Noted for his cave-like sculpture executed for 1970 World's Fair at Osaka, Japan. Exhibited: Wadsworth Atheneum, Hartford, CT, 1964, 67, and 74; Phila. Inst. of Contemp. Art, 1967; Whitney Museum of Am. Art Annual, 1970-73; Metro. Museum of Art, NY, 1970; Los Angeles Co. Museum of Art, 1971; San Francisco Museum of Art, 1971; Seattle Art Museum Pavilion, Washington, 1973; Cleveland Museum of Art, 1974; Painting and Sculpture Today, 1974, Indianapolis Museum of Art, 1974; Art Inst. of Chicago, 1974; Walker Art Center Minneapolis, 1974; Art Inst. of Chicago, 1974; New Orleans Museum of Art, LA, 1976; and others. Taught: New York Univ., 1946-50; at Cooper Union, Pratt Inst., Bennington College, and Hunter College from 1962. Associated with Barnett Newman, Clyfford Still, Jackson Pollock, and Mark Rothko.

TANGUY, YVES.
Painter and printmaker. Born in Paris, France, January 5, 1900. Came to US in 1939. In collections of Albright-Knox, Buffalo; Art Institute of Chicago; Wadsworth Atheneum, Hartford; Metropolitan Museum of Art; Museum of Modern Art; Whitney; Phila. Exhibited at Galerie Surrealiste, Paris, 1928; Galerie des Cahiers d'Art, Paris, 1935, 47; Stanley Rose Gallery, Hollywood, 1935; Julien Levy Galleries, NYC, 1936; Guggenheim Jeune Gallery, London; Wadsworth Atheneum; Pierre Matisse Gallery, NYC, 1939, 42, 43, 45, 46, 50, 63; San Francisco Museum of Art; Luxembourg, Paris; Kunsthalle, Basel, Switzerland; Museum of Modern Art (retro.); Art Institute of Chicago; Whitney; and many other galleries in US and Europe. Died in Woodbury, Conn., Jan. 15, 1955.

WALKER, WILLIAM AIKEN.
Portrait and genre painter. Born in Charleston, South Carolina, 1838, where at the age of twelve, he exhibited his first works. Studied later in Duesseldorf, West Germany. Spent most of his life in Charleston, although he executed some work in Florida and Louisiana which was lithographed by Currier and Ives in 1880's. Died January 3, 1921, in Charleston, South Carolina.

WARHOL, ANDY.
Painter and craftsman. Born in Cleveland, Ohio, August 8, 1931. Studied at Carnegie Institute of Technology. Exhibited at Museum of Modern Art (The 1960's), 1967; Documenta VI, Kassel, Germany; Milwaukee Art Center; Baltimore Museum of Art; Art Institute of Chicago; Whitney and Metropolitan Museum of Art, New York City; plus many more. Received Sixth Film Cult Award, 1964; Los Angeles Film Festival Award, 1964. In collections of Albright-Knox, Buffalo; L.A. County Museum of Art; Museum of Modern Art; Whitney, New York City; Walker Art Center, Minneapolis; others. Member of Film Co-op. Represented by Leo Castelli Gallery, New York City. Address in 1982, Andy Warhol Enterprises, New York City.

WESSELMANN, TOM.
Painter. Born in Cincinnati, Ohio, February 23, 1931. Studied art at the Art Academy of Cincinnati and at Cooper Union in New York City in late 1950's. Exhibited: One-man shows at the Green Gallery, 1962, 64, and 65; Sidney Janis Gallery, New York City, 1966, 68, 70, 72, 74, 76, 79, 80; and at the Ehrlich Gallery, 1979; group shows at the Museum of Contemporary Art, in Chicago, Illinois, 1969; De Cordova Museum, Lincoln, Massachusetts, 1969; numerous others. Early work was in collages; many depicting interior domestic scenes. Many of his works are interspersed with depictions of the female nude; often as sex objects, emphasizing breasts, mouths, and genitalia. Address in 1982, RD1, Box 36, Long Eddy, NY.

WHISTLER, JAMES ABBOTT McNEILL.
Painter, etcher and lithographer. Born in Lowell, Massachusetts, July 11, 1834. Raised in Lowell and in Russia, where father was employed. Returned to United States in 1849. At West Point Military Academy 1851-54. Traveled to Europe in 1855 to pursue artistic career. Settled in Paris, entered studio of Gleyre, became acquainted with Degas, Bracquemond, Legros, Faintin-Latour, and other well-known artists, poets and critics. Executed the "Little French Set" of etchings published in 1858. In London from 1859. Visited Valparaiso 1865-66, where he painted several pictures of the harbor. Returned to Chelsea, where he painted "The Thames in Ice," "The Last of the Thames;" pictures showing Japanese influence--"La Princesse du Pays de la Porcelaine," "The Golden Screen," "The Little White Girl," "Symphony in White No. 3," "The Balcony." Went to Venice in 1879, where he executed etchings and pastels. Returned to Chelsea in 1880. On subsequent travels in Europe and North Africa he worked largely in pastel, watercolor, and graphic media. Lived in Paris again, 1893-95; returned to England. Exhibited at the Royal Acad., London; Salon des Refuses, Paris, 1863; gallery in Pall Mall, 1874, Grosvenor Gal., 1877, Fine Art Society's Gal., 1880, 81, 95, Dowdeswells' Gal., 1883, 84, 86, all in London; Working Women's Col., Queen's Square, 1888; Goupil's Gal., London, 1892. In collections of Taft Mus., Cincinnati, OH; National Gal. of Art, Wash., DC; Detroit Inst.; Louvre, Paris; decorations for Peacock Room (1876-77), Freer Gal. of Art, Wash., DC; Met. Mus., NYC. Elected member of Royal Soc. of British Artists, 1884, president 1890; first pres. of Internat'l. Soc. of Sculptors, Painters, and Gravers, 1898; Officer of Legion of Honor of France; member of Societe Nationale des Artistes Francais; Commander of the Order of the Crown of Italy; Chevalier of the Order of St. Michael of Bavaria; honorary member of Royal Academies of Bavaria, Dresden, St. Luke in Rome. Died in London, July 17, 1903.

WHORF, JOHN.
Painter and watercolorist. Born in Winthrop, Mass., January 10, 1903. Studied under Charles Hawthorne, later studied at the Academy of Boston. Member of American Watercolor Society, 1948-58. Work included in exhibition, "200 Years of Watercolor Painting in America," at the Metropolitan Museum of Art, 1966-67. Represented at the Brooklyn Museum, New York City. Exhibited at the National Academy of Design, 1945-56, 58-59. Awarded an honorary MA Degree from Harvard, in 1938. Subjects include harbor, yachting, and beach scenes; landscapes; ducks; and interiors. Died in Provincetown, MA, in 1959.

WIEGENHORST, OLAF.
Painter. Born in Denmark, April 30, 1899. Self-taught. Exhibited: Cowboy Hall of Fame, Oklahoma City, 1974, San Diego Fine Art, Calif., 1980, Tucson Art, AZ, 1981, and Gilcrease, Tulsa, OK. Noted for cowboy paintings in oil. Address in 1982, Bluff Place, El Cajon, CA.

WIMAR, CHARLES.
(or Karl Ferdinand). Painter. Born in Sieburg, near Bonn, West Germany, February 20, 1828. Emigrated to US in 1843. Studied under Leon Pomarede 1846-51 in St. Louis, also apprenticed to him on a trip up the Mississippi River. Trained in Duesseldorf, Germany, 1851-56, studying under Emanuel Gottlieb Leutze. Returned to St. Louis where he made at least three trips up the Missouri River for artistic material. Painting subjects were of American Indians, hunting, war scenes, of Buffalo, of wide, highly panoramic plains views. Celebrated works are his "Indians Pursued by American Dragoons," 1853, Noonday Club, St. Louis; "Indians Aproaching Fort Benton," 1859, Washington Univ., St. Louis. Also executed some portrait pictures and in 1861 painted mural decorations in the rotunda of the St. Louis Court House, those murals being almost completely destroyed. Four Am. sketchbooks have been preserved and approximately fifty of his finished works have been identified. Took many photographs of American Indians. Died in St. Louis, Nov. 28, 1862.

WYETH, JAMES BROWNING (JAMIE).
Painter. Born in Wilmington, Delaware, July 6, 1946. Studied with Carolyn Wyeth and with his father, Andrew Wyeth; received honorary DFA, Elizabethtown Col. In collections of Smithsonian, Washington, DC; Museum of Modern Art; Joslyn Art Museum, Omaha; Delaware Art Museum, Wilmington; others. Exhibited at Knoedler Gallery, NYC; Penna. Academy of Fine Arts, 1980; Amon Carter Museum, Forth Worth, Texas, 1981; others. Member of National Academy of Design, NYC; Am. Watercolor Society; National Endowment for the Arts. Works in oil and watercolor. Address in 1982, c/o Frank Fowler, Lookout Mountain, Tenn.

PREFACE TO NEW EDITION

This dictionary is published in the same vein as Mantle Fielding's original Dictionary of American Painters, Sculptors and Engravers: as a compilation of biographical information from a multitude of sources in one comprehensive volume. Some entries are exactly the same as the original, since no new information has been found. Many entries have been expanded to include more information such as birth place and date, schooling, collections, awards, date of death, etc. Of special importance in this work is the addition of biographies of over 1,000 living artists, as well as many modern artists no longer living and not included in the original edition of Fielding. The bulk of the new entries, over 6,000, are primarily 19th and early 20th century artists. This is the area which most researchers have become interested in.

As Fielding wrote in the preface to his own dictionary, no claim is made that the list of American artists included here is complete. Although we have drawn from numerous sources, including resumes solicited from artists, some names have, inevitably, been omitted through the limitations of time and space. This volume is, however, intended to be one step in a multi-volume reference work projected to include many more American artists in all media, ranging from those of international stature to those whose artistic contributions are significant regionally. The compilation of a comprehensive dictionary of this kind is, thus, a continuing process.

Fielding's dictionary, published in 1926, has never been so extensively updated and enlarged. In 1965, James F. Carr, New York, reprinted the dictionary with a 93-page addendum correcting and supplementing only the original biographical entries; no new names were added. This edition is now out of print. In 1974, Modern Books and Crafts, Inc., Connecticut, reprinted the original edition and added a 31-page index of 2,500 names but with only two-line entries.

In using our new edition, the reader will note that many entries include an address in 1926 or 1929. Those for 1926 are from Fielding's original dictionary; those for 1929 are from the American Art Annual of 1929, reprinted in 1982 as the Dictionary of American Artists, 19th and 20th Century. It was decided to include these addresses, as well as information about travel in the U.S. and abroad, for their research value in confirming an artist's work.

Inspiration to undertake this project came from the recognition that a significant need exists for a primary source of concise biographies of major and minor professional American artists from the 18th, 19th, and 20th centuries. It is my hope that this dictionary will provide dealers, collectors, and researchers of American painting, sculpture, and graphics with a valuable and useful resource.

In continuing to meet this objective in subsequent volumes, I welcome not only additional accurate biographical information about these and other American artists, but also correction of any mistakes which may be discovered. Corrections will then be made in later editions. While every effort has been made to record accurately and completely all information contained herein, any liability resulting from any errors or omissions is disclaimed.

Realization of this first volume in the project has been made possible by the efforts of the researchers, editors, and proofreaders who have worked with me, and the unfailing patience of the displaywriter operators (thank God for IBM), to all of whom I extend my gratitude.

Glenn B. Opitz

CITY AND STATE ABBREVIATIONS

AK - Alaska
AL, Ala. - Alabama
AR, Ark. - Arkansas
AZ, Ariz. - Arizona
CA, Calif. - California
Chic. - Chicago
CO, Colo. - Colorado
CT, Conn., Ct. - Connecticut
CZ - Canal Zone
DC - District of Columbia
DE, Del. - Delaware
FL, Fla. - Florida
GA, Ga. - Georgia
HI - Hawaii
IA, Ia. - Iowa
ID, Id. - Idaho
IL, Ill. - Illinois
IN, Ind. - Indiana (Ind. - also Indianapolis)
KS, Kans. - Kansas
KY, Ky. - Kentucky
LA, La. - Louisiana
L.A. - Los Angeles (also LA)
MA, Mass. - Massachusetts
MD, Md. - Maryland
ME, Me. - Maine
MI, Mich. - Michigan
MN, Minn. - Minnesota
MO, Mo. - Missouri
MS, Miss. - Mississippi
MT, Mont. - Montana
NC, N.C. - North Carolina
ND, N.D., N. Dak. - North Dakota
NE, Neb., Nebr. - Nebraska
NH, N.H. - New Hampshire
NJ, N.J. - New Jersey
NM, N.M., N. Mex. - New Mexico
NO, N.O. - New Orleans
NV, Nev. - Nevada

NY, N.Y. - New York
NYC - New York City
NYS - New York State
OH, Oh. - Ohio
OK, Okla. - Oklahoma
OR, Ore. - Oregon
PA, Penn., Penna. - Pennsylvania
Phila. - Philadelphia
RI, R.I. - Rhode Island
SC, S.C. - South Carolina
SD, S.D. - South Dakota
S.F., S. Fran., San Fran., San F. - San Francisco
TN, Tenn. - Tennessee
TX, Tex. - Texas
UT, Ut. - Utah
VA, Va. - Virginia
VT, Vt. - Vermont
WA, Wash. - Washington
WI, Wis., Wisc. - Wisconsin
WV, W.V., W. Va. - West Virginia
WY, Wyo. - Wyoming

ABBREVIATIONS

AA - Art Association (preceded by place name)
AAA - Allied Artists of America; American Art Association
AAS - American Art Society
AC - Art Club (preceded by place name)
Acad. - Academy, Academie
ACC - Arts and Crafts Club (preceded by place name)
ACD - Art Center College of Design
ADC - Art Directors' Club
AEF - American Expeditionary Force
AFA - American Federation of Arts
AFAS - American Fine Arts Society, New York
A. Fellowship - Artists' Fellowship, Inc. (formerly A. Aid S.)
A. Fund S. - Artists' Fund Society, New York
AG - Artists Guild (preceded by place name)
AI - Art Institute (preceded by place name)
AIA - American Institute of Architects
AIC - Art Institute of Chicago
AI Graphic A. (AIGA) - American Institute of Graphic Arts
AL - Artists' League (preceded by place name)
Alliance - Art Alliance of America
Allied AA - Allied Artists of America
Am., Amer. - American
Am. Acad. A.L. - American Academy of Arts and Letters
Am. APL - American Artists Professional League
ANA - Associate National Academy of Design, New York
Ann., ann. - annual
AP - Associated Press
arch., archit. - architect, architecture, architectural
ASL of NY (ASL NY, NY ASL) - Art Students' League of New York
A.S. Min P. - American Society of Miniature Painters, New York
Assn., Asso., Assoc. - Association, Associate
auth. - author
Ave. - Avenue
AWCS - American Water Color Society, New York
AWCW - Art Workers' Club for Women, New York
AWS - American Watercolor Society
Bd. - Board
Bibliog. - Bibliography

bldg. - building
Boston GA - Guild of Boston Artists
Boston SA - Boston Society of Architects (Chapter AIA)
Boston SAC - Boston Society of Arts and Crafts
Boston SWCP - Boston Society of Water Color Painters
BPC - Brush and Palette Club (preceded by place name)
Brit. - Britain, British
Brooklyn S. Min. P. - Brooklyn Society of Miniature Painters
Buffalo SA - Buffalo Society of Artists
Calif. AC - California Art Club
Calif. PM - Print Makers' Society of California
Calif. PS - California Painters and Sculptors
Calif. SE - Calif. Society of Etchers
Calif. WCS - California Water Color Society
Can., CN - Canada, Canadian
CCAD - Columbus College of Art and Design
CCNY - City College of New York
Century Assoc. - Century Association of New York
Char. C. - Charcoal Club, Baltimore
Chicago AD - Chicago Academy of Design
Chicago AFA - Chicago Academy of Fine Arts
Chicago Gal. A. - Chicago Galleries Association
Chicago NJSA - Chicago No-Jury Society of Artists
Chicago PS - Painters and Sculptors of Chicago
Chicago SAC - Chicago Society of Arts and Crafts
Chicago SE - Chicago Society of Etchers
Chicago S. Min. P. - Chicago Society of Miniature Painters
CI - Carnegie Institute, Pittsburgh, PA
Cleveland Arch. C. - Cleveland Architectural Club
Co. - Company, County
Col., Coll. - College, Collegiate, Collection(s)
Columbus PPC - Columbus Pen and Pencil Club
comn. - commission(s)
comp. - competition
Cong. - Congress
Conn. AFA - Connecticut Academy of Fine Arts, Hartford
contemp. - contemporary
Contemporary - Contemporary Group
Copley S. - Copley Society of Boston
corp. - corporate, corporation(s)
coun. - council
Ct. - Court
Ctr. - Center
CU - Cooper Union
Czech. - Czechoslovakia
Detroit S. Women P. - Detroit Society of Women Painters
Dir. - Director

Dr. - Drive
EAA - Eastern Arts Association
East. - Eastern
Eng. - England, English (also engineer, engineering)
Eur., Europ. - Europe, European
Exh., Exhib. - Exhibit(s), Exhibition(s)
Exp., Expo. - Exposition(s)
FA - Fine Arts
FAS - Famous Artists School
Fellowship PAFA - Fellowship of the Pennsylvania Academy of the
                  Fine Arts
Fed., Fedn. - Federation
FIT - Fashion Institute of Technology
FR, Fr. - France, French
GA - Guild of Artists (preceded by place name)
GAG - Graphic Artists Guild
Gal. - Gallery(ies)
GB - Great Britain
GCSA - Grand Central School of Art
Gen., Gen'l. - General
Ger. - Germany, German
GFLA - Artists Guild of the Authors' League of America, New York
Grand Cent. AG - Grand Central Art Galleries
Hartford ACC - Hartford Arts and Crafts Club
hist. - history
hon. - honorable, honorary
Hoosier Salon - Hoosier Salon, Chicago
illus., illustr. - illustration, illustrator
incl. - including
indust. - industry(ies), industrial
inst. - institute, institution
int., inter., int'l. - international
Inter. Soc. A.L. - International Society of Arts and Letters (also
                   given as Soc. Inter. des Beaux Arts et des
                   Lettres)
Inter. Soc. SPG - International Society of Sculptors, Painters and
                  Gravers
KCAI - Kansas City Art Institute
LC - Library of Congress
lect. - lecturer
lib., libr. - library
lit. - literary, literature
lith., litho. - lithograph, lithographer
MacD. C. - MacDowell Club, New York
mem. - member, membership(s)
men. - mention
Mex. - Mexico

Minneapolis AL - Minneapolis Artists' League
MMA (Met. Mus. Art) - Metropolitan Museum of Art, New York
mod. - modern
Modern AA - Modern Artists of America, New York
MOMA - Museum of Modern Art, New York
munic. - municipal
Municipal AS - Municipal Art Society (preceded by place name)
Mural P. - National Society of Mural Painters, New York
mus. - museum(s), musee, museo
Mystic SA - Society of Mystic (Conn.) Artists
NA - National Academy of Design, New York (Academicians)
NAC - National Arts Club, New York
NAD - National Academy of Design, New York (used chiefly for
      school)
nat., nat'l. - national (also natural)
Nat. Gal. - National Gallery, Washington, D.C.
Nat. Inst. A.L. - National Institute of Arts and Letters
NA Women PS - National Association of Women Painters and
                  Sculptors, New York
New Eng. - New England
New Haven BPC - New Haven Brush and Palette Club
New Haven PCC - New Haven Paint and Clay Club
New Soc. A. - New Society of Artists, New York
NJSA - No-Jury Society of Artists (preceded by place name)
NL Am. Pen Women - National League of American Pen Women
N.O. - New Orleans
NOAA - Art Association of New Orleans
NO ACC - New Orleans Arts and Crafts Club
North Shore AA - North Shore Arts Association, Gloucester, Mass.
NSS - National Sculpture Society, New York
NY Arch. Lg. - Architectural League of New York
NYPL - New York Public Library
NYSC - New York Society of Craftsmen
NYSWA - New York Society of Women Artists
NYU - New York University
NYWCC - New York Water Color Club
Ohio WCS - Ohio Water Color Society, Columbus
PAFA - Pennsylvania Academy of the Fine Arts, Philadelphia
Paris AAA - American Art Association of Paris
Paris Groupe PSA - Groupe des Peintres et Sculpteurs Americains de
                  Paris
Paris Women's AAA - Paris American Women's Art Association
Paris SAP - Paris Society of American Painters
Pa. S. Min. P. - Pennsylvania Society of Miniature Painters
Pastelists - Society of Pastelists, New York
PBC - Pen and Brush Club of New York
PCC - Paint and Clay Club (preceded by place name)

Phila. ACG - Arts and Crafts Guild of Philadelphia
Phila. Alliance - Art Alliance of Philadelphia
Phila. Sketch C. - Philadelphia Sketch Club
Phila. Soc. AL - Philadelphia Society of Arts and Letters
Photo. Sec. - Photo-Secession, New York
PI - Pratt Institute, Brooklyn, New York
Pittsburgh AA - Associated Artists of Pittsburgh
Pittsburgh AS - Pittsburgh Art Society
Plastic C. - Plastic Club of Philadelphia
PM - Print Maker's Society (preceded by place name)
port. - portrait(s)
Port. P. - National Association of Portrait Painters, New York
P.-P. - Panama-Pacific
PPC - Pen and Pencil Club (preceded by place name)
pres. - present, president
prof. - professor, profession, professional
Providence HC - Providence Handicraft Club
PS - Painters and Sculptors (preceded by place name)
PSD - Parsons School of Design
PS Gallery Assoc. - Painters' and Sculptors' Gallery Association,
                    New York
ptg., ptgs. - painting(s)
ptr. - painter
publ. - published, publisher, publication(s)
RISD - Rhode Island School of Design
Rd. - Road
RD - Rural Delivery
rep. - represented, representative
Rome Acad. Alumni - Alumni Association American Academy in Rome
RSA - Royal Scottish Academician
SA - Society of Artists (preceded by place name)
SAA - Society of American Artists, New York
SAC - Society of Arts and Crafts (preceded by place name)
Salma. C. - Salmagundi Club, New York
Scarab C. - Scarab Club, New York
Sch. - School(s)
sci. - science
SCWP - Society of Water Color Painters (preceded by place name)
SE - Society of Etchers (preceded by place name)
SFA - Society of Fine Arts (preceded by place name)
SI (S of I) - Society of Illustrators
S. Indp. A. - Society of Independent Artists
S. Min. P. - Society of Miniature Painters (preceded by place
                name)
SMPF West - Society of Men who Paint the Far West
Soc. - Society
SPNY - Society of Painters, New York

SSAL - Southern States Art League
St. - Street, Saint
St. Louis AG - St. Louis Artists' Guild
SVA - Society of Visual Arts
Switz. - Switzerland
S. Women P. - Society of Women Painters (preceded by place name)
2x4 Soc. - Two by Four Society, St. Louis
tech., techn. - technology, technical, technique
Ten Am. P. - Ten American Painters
Ten Phil. P. - Ten Philadelphia Painters
TID - The Institute of Design
UCLA - University of California at Los Angeles
univ. - university(ies)
US - United States
USA - United States Army
USAF - United States Air Force
USMC - United States Marine Corps
USN - United States Navy
Vet. - Veteran(s)
var. - various
Wash. - Washington, DC
WCC - Water Color Club (preceded by place name)
WCS - Water Color Society (preceded by place name)
West. - Western
Wilmington SFA - Wilmington Society of Fine Arts
Wis. PS - Wisconsin Painters and Sculptors
Woman's AC - Woman's Art Club (preceded by place name)
WW I - World War I
WW II - World War II
Yugos., Yugosl. - Yugoslavia

AACH, HERB.
Painter and writer. Born Cologne, Ger., March 24, 1923; US citizen. Pupil, Art Acad., Cologne; Pratt Inst.; Stanford U.; Escuela di Pintura Y Escultura, Mex.; Brooklyn Mus. Art Sch. Exhibited at Acad. of Arts and Letters; Martha Jackson Gal., NYC; Albright-Knox Mus. Taught at Pratt; Brooklyn Mus.; Skowhegan Sch. Rep. by Martha Jackson and Aaron Berman Galleries in NYC.

AARONS, GEORGE.
Sculptor. Born in Lithuania Apr. 6, 1896; US citizen. Pupil of Mus. of FA Sch., Boston; Beaux-Arts Inst. of Design, NYC. In collections of Art Mus., Ein Harod, Israel; Fitchburg (MA) Art Mus.; Mus. de St. Denis, France; others. Exhib. at Phila. Mus.; Inst. of Contemp. Art, Boston; Whitney; MIT. Member of NSS. Living in Gloucester, MA, in 1976; died in 1980.

ABADI, FRITZIE.
Painter and sculptor. Born in Aleppo, Syria; US citizen. Pupil of ASL NY; and Tschacbasov, NY. In collections of Butler Inst.; Slater Mem. Mus. Exhib. at Carnegie; Lib. of Congr.; Butler Inst. Awards from Nat. Assn. Women Artists; Am. Soc. Contemp. Artists. Rep. by Phoenix Gal., NYC. Living in NYC.

ABANY, ALBERT CHARLES.
Painter, printmaker and teacher. Born in Boston, Mass., March 30, 1921. Study: School of Mus. of Fine Arts, Boston, Longstreth Scholar, 1942, diploma, 1948; Tufts Univ., BS educ., 1949. Exhib.: Carl Siembab Gal., Boston; Clark Univ.; Northeastern Univ.; Wessell Lib., Tufts Univ.; Art Inst., Boston. Teaching: Boston Center for Adult Education, 1949-51; Art Institute of Boston 1965-75; Brockton Art Center, MA, 1975-77; others. Media: Oil, graphics, mixed media. Address in 1982, 42 MacArthur Rd., Natick, MA.

ABBATE, PAOLA S.
Sculptor and lithographer. Born in Italy, 1884. Educated there and in the United States. Member of International Fine Arts Society. Works: Dante monument, Newburgh, NY, and at Providence, R.I. Bust collection in Newark, NJ. Bust of Enrico Caruso in New York. Address in 1926, 1931 Broadway, New York City.

ABBATT, AGNES DEAN.
Painter. Born 1847; died 1917. Elected member of National Academy, 1902. Studied Art at Cooper Union and the National Academy of Design. Painted in oils and water-colors, also wax modelling. She painted landscapes, coast scenes, and flowers. Medal at Cooper Union, and first prize in oil painting at San Antonio, Texas. Address in 1926, New York.

ABBE, ELFRIEDA MARTHA.
Sculptor, engraver and illustrator. Born in Washington, DC, in 1919. Studied: Cornell University and Syracuse University. Awards: Cornell University, 1938, 1940; Tiffany Foundation Fellowship, 1948. Work: World's Fair, New York, 1939; Memorial panels, Ellis Room, Wiegand Herbarium, 1953 and Mann Library, 1955, Cornell University and Boston Museum of Fine Arts.

ABBEY, EDWIN AUSTIN.
Painter, illustrator and mural decorator. Born in Philadelphia, 1852; died in London, 1911. He studied at the Penna. Academy of Fine Arts. His "King Lear" is at the Metropolitan Museum, NY, and his "Quest of the Holy Grail" at the Boston Public Library. His illustrations for Shakespeare's Works, Herrick's Poems, and "She Stoops to Conquer" are among his best known illustrations. Elected member of National Academy, 1902. See "Life of Edwin Abbey", by E. V. Lucas. 2 vols., London. Died in 1911.

ABBEY, IVA L.
Painter. Born in Chester, Conn., in 1882. Pupil of Hale, Benson, and C. J. Martin. Member of Hartford Art Society. Address in 1926, Wilkes-Barre Institute, Wilkes-Barre, Penna.

ABBOT, SAMUEL NELSON.
Illustrator. Born in Illinois, 1874. He studied in Paris under

1

Laurens and Constant. His first illustration assignment was for Hart Schaffner and Marx, where he continued to design and illustrate their fashion catalogues for the next 25 years. During this period he also did illustration for Ladies' Home Journal, The Saturday Evening Post and Collier's. Died in 1953.

ABBOTT, ANNE FULLER.
Painter. Born Brandon, VT. Pupil of Chase; Douglas Volk; Francis Jones; ASL of NY; Corcoran Art School; NAD. Member: Wash. AC; Wash. WCC; AFA; PBC. Work: "Yeomanette," Navy Department, Washington, DC. Director of the Abbott School of Fine and Commercial Art, Washington, DC. Address in 1929, 1624 H. St. N.W.; h. 1028 Connecticut Ave., Washington, D.C.

ABBOTT, ELEANORE PLAISTED.
Painter. Born at Lincoln, Maine, 1875; married Yarnall Abbott. Pupil of Penna. Academy of Fine Arts, Phila., and Simon and Cottet in Paris. Member: Phila. WCC; Plastic C.; Felloswhip PAFA. Address in 1926, The Gladstone, 11th and Pine Sts., Philadelphia. Died 1935.

ABBOTT, EMILY.
Painter. Born in Minneapolis, Minnesota in 1900. Studied: University of Minnesota; Minneapolis School of Art. Awards: Minnesota State Fair, 1937; Minneapolis Institute of Art, 1938, 1944. Collections: Walker Art Center. Exhibited mostly in the Minneapolis area.

ABBOTT, FRANCIS R.
Painter. Pupil of the Penna. Academy of Fine Arts, and the Julian Academy in Paris. He was born in Philadelphia and was an Artist Member of the Art Club for twenty years. He died in Philadelphia in 1925.

ABBOTT, W. H.
Sculptor. Address in 1926, 46 Greenwich Ave., NY.

ABBOTT, YARNALL.
Painter. Born in Philadelphia, 1870. Pupil of Thos. Anschutz at Penna. Academy of Fine Arts and Collin and Courtois in Paris. Exhibited at the Penna. Academy of the Fine Arts, 1924-25. Address in 1926, 1612 Latimer Street, Philadelphia, PA. Died 1938.

ABDY, ROWENA MEEKS.
Painter and illustrator. Born in Austria, 1887, of American parents. Came to San Francisco, California, and studied under Arthur F. Mathews. Awarded medal by California Museum of Art, 1920. Exhibited water-color "Old Fashioned Room" at Penna. Academy of Fine Arts, Phila., 1924. Address in 1926, 1050 Lombard Street, Russian Hill, San Francisco, California. Died 1945.

A'BECKET, MARIA J. C.
Landscape painter. Born in Portland, Maine. Studied in the White Mountains with Homer Martin in 1865, and in 1875-78 with William Hunt in Boston. She also spent a summer painting in France with Daubigny. She died in New York, September 6th, 1904. She exhibited in Boston, Baltimore, Philadelphia and Washington.

ABEL, LOUISE.
Sculptor. Born at Mt. Healthy, Ohio, in 1894. Pupil of Barnhorn, Meakin, and Wessel. Exhibited portrait statuettes at the annual exhibition of the Penna. Academy of Fine Arts, 1924. Address in 1926, North Bend Road, Mt. Healthy, Ohio.

ABEL, M.
Painter. Exhibited at Cincinnati Museum in 1925. Address in 1926, 939 Richmond Street, Cincinnati, Ohio.

ABERNETHIE.
An early American engraver of maps, Masonic prints and book plates who worked in Charleston, SC, about 1780.

ABRAHAMSEN, CHRISTIAN.
Painter and illustrator. Born in Norway, 1887. Represented in Chicago Art Institute by "Winter."

ABRAMOFSKY, ISRAEL.
Painter and etcher. Born Kiev, Russia, Sept. 10, 1888. Pupil of Jean Paul Laurens, Joseph Berges. Member: Salon Artist, France. Award: Hon. mention, Salon Artist, 1928. Work: "Winter Scene on Mt. Blanc," Luxembourg Galleries, Paris, France; "Street Scene, Paris," Museum, Jaffe, Jerusalem; "Fountain of the Luxembourg Garden," Toledo Museum of Art. Address in 1926, 78 Quai de La Rapee, Paris, France; h. 1616 Adams St., Toledo, Ohio.

ABRAMOVITZ, ALBERT.
Painter. Member of Society of Independent Artists. Address in 1926, 336 East 17th Street, New York.

ABRAMOVITZ, CARRIE.
Sculptor. Born: new York City in 1913. Studied: Brooklyn College and Columbia University. Lived in Paris 1962-63. Awards: Morrison medal, Oakland Museum in 1960. Exhibited: Mostly in San Francisco area.

ABRAMS, ELEANOR.
Painter. Born in Karns City, PA. Pupil of Elliott Daingerfield and Henry B. Snell. Address in 1926, 10 East 9th Street, New York.

ABRAMS, LUCIAN.
Painter. Born at Lawrence, Kansas, 1870. Pupil of Laurens, Constant, and Whistler in Paris. Member of Society of Independent Artists. Represented by "Sandy Bay," Dallas Art Association. Address in 1926, Lyme, Conn. Died 1941.

ABRAMSON, ROSALIND.
Painter and etcher. Born in Norfolk, VA, 1901. Pupil of Art Students' League of New York under Bridgman, Henri, Bellows, and DuMond. Address in 1926, 59 West 59th Street, New York, or 706 Riverside Drive, New York.

ACHERT, FRED.
Painter. Member Cincinnati Art Club. Address in 1926 10 East 3d Street, Cincinnati, Ohio.

ACHESON, ALICE S(TANLEY).
Painter and illustrator. Born Charlevoix, Mich., August 12, 1895. Pupil of Howard Smith and Richard Meryman. Illustrated "New Roads in Old Virginia." Address in 1926, 2805 P St., Washington, DC; summer, Harewood Farm, Sandy Spring, MD.

ACHESON, GEORGINA ELLIOTT.
Miniature and water-color artist. Exhibited at the Penna. Academy of Fine Arts, Philadelphia, 1924-25. Address in 1926, Ardsley on Hudson, New York City.

ACKER, HERBERT V(AN) BLARCOM.
Painter. Born Pasadena, Calif., October 4, 1895. Pupil of Cecilia Beaux, Frank V. DeMond. Member: Pasadena SA; NAC; AFA. Address in 1926, 8320 Fountain Ave., Hollywood, Calif.

ACKERS, CHARLES.
Sculptor. Born in 1835 near Hollis, ME. He went to Rome in 1855 to study art with his brother Benjamin Paul Ackers, also a sculptor. Died in New York in 1906.

ACKERSON, F(LOYD) G(ARRISON).
Painter. Born Portage, Kalamazoo Co., Mich., Jan. 1, 1883. Pupil at Carnegie Tech. Art School. Member: Pittsburgh AA. Award: 2nd prize Pittsburgh AA., 1920. Address in 1929, 103 Colonial Apts., Wilkinsburg, PA.

ADAM, DAVID LIVINGSTON.
Portrait painter. Born in Glasgow, Scotland, in 1883; died in Chicago, Ill., 1924. He studied in Glasgow, Brussels, and the Art Institute of Chicago. He was a member of the Palette and Chisel Club, The Chicago Society of Artists, and the Alumni of the Art Institute of Chicago. In 1920 he was awarded a gold medal by the Palette and Chisel Club.

ADAM, WILBUR G.
Painter and illustrator. Born Cincinnati, Ohio, July 23, 1898. Pupil of Duveneck, L. H. Meakin, James R. Hopkins, H. H. Wessel, C. A. Lord. Member: Tiffany Foundation; Cincinnati AC. Award: Augustus S. Peabody prize, AIC, 1925. Address in 1929, Malabry Court, 675 North Michigan Ave., Chicago, Ill.

ADAM, WILLIAM.
Painter of landscapes. Born in England, studied at Glasgow and Paris. Address in 1926, 450 Central Ave., Pacific Grove, California.

ADAMS, BERTRAND R.
Taxidermist. Born November 29, 1907, Webster City, Iowa. Studied Taxidermy with local taxidermist 1925; enrolled in a commercial art correspondence course, 1928; entered University of Iowa, where he majored in art and economics, 1934; began work on Iowa State College Library murals as assistant, under Public Works of Art Project. Has worked in most mediums, with exception of lithography and fresco. Has prepared plaster casts for bronze tablets and modelled heads.

ADAMS, CHARLES PARTRIDGE.
Painter of landscapes. Born 1858, at Franklin, Mass. Self-taught. Member: Denver AC; Laguna AA, (life). Awards: Gold Medal, National Mining and Industrial Exp., Denver; hon. mention, Pan-Am. Exp., Buffalo, 1901. Work: In State University, Boulder, Colo.; Normal School, Greeley, Colo.; Kansas City, MO; San Diego, Calif.; Woman's Club, and Denver Art Association, Denver, Colo. Address in 1926, 3935 Dalton Ave., Los Angeles, California.

ADAMS, CHAUNCEY M.
Painter, etcher and teacher. Born Unadella Forks, NY. Mar. 28, 1895. Pupil of Daniel Garber, PAFA. Member: Utica ASL. Work: "The Willows", Converse College, Spartanburg, SC. Address in 1929, Chamber of Commerce, Utica, NY.; summer, Unadilla Forks, NY.

ADAMS, DUNLAP.
Engraver. Working in Philadelphia in 1764. He engraved on gold, silver, copper and brass, and seems to have been more of a silversmith and die sinker than a copper-plate engraver. See announcement in "Pennsylvania Gazette" for September 6, 1764.

ADAMS, HERBERT.
Sculptor. Born Jan. 28, 1858, in Concord, VT. Studied at Mass. Institute of Technology, pupil of Mercie at Paris. Elected member of National Academy, 1899. Taught at Pratt. His portrait statues are very fine; his William Cullen Bryant, in the park behind the Public Library, NY, the seated figures of Marshall and Ranney at the Cleveland Court House, and the McMillan Fountain, Washington, DC, are among his best known works. His portrait busts of Miss DeFanti, Miss duPont, and his bas-relief of Choate at the Union League Club of N.Y. are also well known. Address in 1926, 131 West 11th St., New York. Died in 1945.

ADAMS, J. HOWARD.
Painter. Member of Providence Art Club. Address in 1926, 1217 Turks Head Bldg., Providence, RI.

ADAMS, JOHN OTTIS.
Painter of landscapes. Born 1851 at Amitz, Ind. Pupil of John Parker, London, and Loefftz in Munich. Among his works: "Summer Afternoon" at Richmond, Ind.; also "The Road to Town," "The Pool" and "Late Autumn." Address in 1926, The Hermitage, Brookville, Ind.

ADAMS, JOHN WOLCOTT.
Born 1874, Worcester, Mass. Student of Art Mus., Boston; Art Students' League, New York. Began work in New York, 1899; illustrator of books, poems, etc., for Harper's, Scribner's, Century and other magazines. Illustrator: Hoosier Romance (by James Whitcomb Riley), 1910; known for drawings in connection with old songs, Colonial incidents, etc. Address in 1926, 360 West 22d Street, New York City.

ADAMS, JOSEPH ALEXANDER.
Born 1803 in New Germantown, NJ. An early American wood engraver, largely self-taught. He was elected an Associate member of the National Academy of Design in 1841. His Bible illustrations are well known, his "Last Arrow" was engraved in 1837 for the New York Mirror. He also worked for the "Treasury of Knowledge" and other publications. See "History of Wood Engraving in America," by W. J. Linton. Died Sept. 16, 1880 in Morristown, NJ.

ADAMS, KATHERINE LANGHORNE.
Painter. Born Plainfield, New Jersey. Member of the Association of Women Painters and Sculptors, New York. Exhibited: "Gloss of Satin and Glimmer of Silk," "The Blue House." Address in 1926, 142 East 18th Street, New York.

ADAMS, KENNETH M.
Painter and graphic artist. Born August 6, 1897, Topeka, Kansas. Studied Art under George M. Stone, 1916; at Chicago AI, 1916; ASL of NY in 1919 under Bridgman, Speicher and Sterne; and at Summer Art School, Woodstock, NY, under Dasburg. In 1921 went to France and spent some months in Paris in various sketch classes. Painted landscapes in south of France, later returning to Paris. Spent some months in Italy studying frescoes of Giotto, Piero della Francesca and Masaccio. In 1924 painted in Taos, New Mexico. Revisited France, but soon returned to Southwest. In 1934, worked under Public Works of Art Project. Has exhibited in national exhibitions and held several one-man shows. Work owned by Los Angeles Museum; Mulvane Art Museum, Topeka, Kansas; University of New Mexico; Honolulu Academy of Fine Arts; Kansas State Agricultural College; San Francisco Art Museum. Awards: Hon. Men. for oil painting, Denver (Colo.) Museum, 1928; Hon. Men. for Graphic arts, Denver, 1930; 1st Hon. Men., 4th Exh. of Am. Litn., Print Club of Phila.; Purchase Prize, New Mexico AL, 1932; Clark Prize and Hon. Men., Corcoran Gallery. Died in 1966.

ADAMS, LINDA.
Graphics. Born in Massachusetts in 1948. Studied: Worcester Art Museum; Boston University School of Fine Arts. She has exhibited mostly in the Boston area. Noted for life-size representational nudes of women.

ADAMS, MARJORIE NICKLES.
Painter. Born: Shippensburg, Pennsylvania. Studied: Shippensburg Teachers College; Philadelphia Museum School of Industrial Art; Pennsylvania Academy of Fine Arts; Chester

Springs Academy of Fine arts. Awards: fellowship, Pennsylvania Academy of Fine Arts, 1922, 1923. Cresson traveling scholarship for study in Europe, 1924; Philadelphia Plastic Club, 1929. Collections: In the United States and abroad.

ADAMS, NORMAN.
Illustrator. Born in Walla Walla, Washington, 1933. He was trained at the ACD. In 1960 his first illustration, watercolor, ran on the cover of Today's Living in the Herald Tribune magazine section. He has since done covers for Sports Afield, Field and Stream, True and Reader's Digest. His editorial work has been published in Holiday and The Saturday Evening Post, among others. A participant in the S of I Annual Exhibitions, he received the Mystery Writers' Raven Award.

ADAMS, PAT.
Painter. Born in Stockton, California July 28, 1928. Studied: University of California. Awards: Fulbright to France, 1956; Yaddo Foundation residency; National Council for the Arts, 1968. Extensive exhibitions throughout the United States and Europe. Collections: Whitney Museum of American Art, New York City; University of Michigan; University of California at Berkeley; University of North Carolina at Greensboro. Media: Oil, isobutyl and methacrylate.

ADAMS, PHILIP.
Painter. Born 1881, in Honolulu. Pupil of Bridgman, Paxton, and Hale. Benson and Woodbury in Boston. Member of Copley Society. Address in 1926, 1310 Massachusetts Ave., Washington, D.C.

ADAMS, WAYMAN.
Portrait painter. Born September 23, 1883, Muncie, Ind. Student of John Herron Art Institute, Indianapolis, 1905-9, also studied in Italy, 1910, Spain, 1912. Elected Associate Member of National Academy, 1926. Among his portraits are Joseph Pennell, Samuel Rabston, Thomas R. Marshall, and Edward W. Redfield, the painter. Member: ANA; Salma. C.; Port. P.; Phila. Sketch C.; Phila.

5

AC; Phila. WCC; Ind. AC; Allied AA; NYWCC; AWCS; NAC; Century C.; Hoosier Salon; AFA. Awards: Proctor portrait Prize, NAD, 1914; Foulke prize, Richmond (Ind.) AA, 1915; Holcomb prize, Herron AI, 1916; Logan Medal, AIC, 1918; Newport AA prize, 1918; Greenough Memorial prize, Newport AA, 1925; Shaffer prize, hoosier Salon, Chicago, 1926; Silver medal, Sesqui-Cent. Exp., Phila., 1926; 1st Altman prize, NAD, 1926; portrait prize, Springfield (Mass.) AA, 1926; Indianapolis star portrait prize, Hoosier Salon, Chicago, 1929. Represented in Herron Art Institute; State Library, Indiana; Harrison Gallery, Los Angeles Museum Lafayette (Ind.), Art Association; Texas Art Association; Nashville Art Association; Harvard University; John Hopkins University; University of Pennsylvania; Indiana University; New York Chamber of Commerce; Indiana State Capitol; Pennsylvania State Capitol; Butler Art Institute; Texas State Capitol; Louisiana State University. Address in 1929, Rodin Studios, 200 West 57th St., New York, NY. Died in 1959.

ADAMS, WINIFRED BRADY.
(Mrs. John Ottis Adams). Painter. Born May 8, 1871, in Muncie, Ind. Studied in Philadelphia at Drexel Inst. and at ASL of NY. Among her works, "Marigolds" at Art Inst. of Indianapolis, and several studies in still life painting. Member: Cin. Woman's AC; Ind. AC; C. L. Wolfe AC; Portfolio C., IndianaPOLIS, Ind.; AFA. Awards: Fine Arts prize, Herron AI, 1926; Buckingham prize, Hoosior Salon, 1926. Address, The Hermitage, Brookville, Ind. Died 1955.

ADAMS, WOODHULL.
Painter. Exhibited oil painting, "At Miss Florence's," Penna. Academy of Fine Arts, Phila., 1924. Address in 1926, Lyme, Conn.

ADDAMS, CLIFFORD ISAAC.
Painter and etcher. Born in 1876. Pupil of Whistler, and studied in Belgium, Holland, Spain, France, Italy, British Isles. Member: Chicago SE; Brooklyn SE. Awards:

Cresson engraving scholarship, PAFA. Exhibited miniatures at Exhibition Academy of Fine Arts for water-colors and miniatures, 1924-25. Works: "Portrait of the Artist's Wife" and "Decoration," Pennsylvania Academy of the Fine Arts, Philadelphia; "Cottages in Wales" and many etchings, Chicago Art Institute. Address in 1926, London, England, and 71 Washington Square, New York.

ADDAMS, INEZ.
(Mrs. Clifford Addams). Painter. Address in 1926, 71 Washington Square, New York.

ADLER, SAMUEL (MARCUS).
Painter. Born in New York City, July 30, 1898. Study: NAD, with Leon Kroll, Charles Louis Hinton. Work: Whitney Mus., New York City; Nat'l. Collection Fine Arts, Smithsonian; Hirshhorn Mus., Wash. DC; Brooklyn Mus.; Munson-Williams-Proctor Ins., Utica, NY; and others. Exhib. PAFA, 1948-68; Univ. of Ill., 1949-71; Met. Mus., New York City, 1950; Whitney Mus., 1951-57; many others. Awards: Scheidt Mem. Prize, PAFA; purchase award, Whitney; Audubon Artists; Ford Foundation; others. Teaching: Visiting Prof. of Art at Univ. of IL, 1959-60; Visiting Prof. of Art at Univ. of IL, 1964; NYU, from 1948; others. Media: Oil, collage. Died Nov. 12, 1979. Address in 1976, 27 E. 22nd St., New York City.

ADNEY, EDWIN TAPPIN.
Artist and illustrator. Born at Athens, Ohio, 1868. Studied at Art Students' League, New York. Illustrated Harper's Weekly and Collier's Weekly. Died 1950.

ADOLPHE, ALBERT JEAN.
Painter and mural decorator. Born 1865 in Phila. Studied with Gerome and Whistler in Paris; De Vriendt, Antwerp; Eakins, Phila. School of Ind. A. Member: Alumni Assn. School of Ind. A., Phila.; Graphic Sketch C. Awards: Hon. mention, Columbian Exp., Chicago 1894; hon. mention, Paris Salon, 1899; gold medal, Phila. AC, 1904; Stotesbury Prize, Phila., 1916,

6

"Americanization Through Art" Exhibition; Hon. mention, Phila. AC, 1921. Work: Decorations in Marlborough-Blenheim Hotel, Atlantic City, NJ, and for steamships "St. Louis" and "St. Paul." Instructor at the La France Art Institute, Philadelphia. Address in 1926, 2616 Montgomery Ave., Philadelphia, PA. Died 1940.

ADOMEIT, GEORGE G(USTAV), Painter. Born Germany, Jan. 15, 1879. Pupil of F. C. Gottwald. Member: Cleveland SA; Al Graphic A.; Cleveland Print C.; AFA. Awards: Prize, Ohio State Fair, 1922; prize, Cleveland Museum of Art, 1923, 1927. Address in 1929, Caxton Bldg.; h. 2054 East 102nd St., Cleveland, Ohio.

ADRIANCE, MINNIE H. Painter. Member of Society of Independent Artists. Address in 1926, 51 East 53d Street, New York City.

AGAM, YAACOV. Painter, sculptor, multi-media artist and lecturer. Born Israel, 1928. Studied at Bezalel School of Art, Jerusalem. Went to Paris, 1951. Deeply influenced by Hebrew conception that reality cannot be represented in a graven image, seeks to create an image which cannot be seen completely at any one time. Has expressed these concepts in monumental architectural works: "Jacob's Ladder," ceiling of Nat'l. Conv. House, Jerusalem; "Double Metamorphosis II," MOMA, NY; mural for passenger ship "Shalom;" visual environment, Civic Center at Leverkusen, 1970; Environmental Salon, Elysee Palace, Paris, 1972 which includes all the walls, kinetic ceiling, moving transparent colored doors and a kinetic tapestry on the floor; mural, President's Mansion, Jerusalem, 1972; monumental musical fountain, Paris, 1977; mural, Eye Foundation Hospital, Birmingham, Ala., 1982. One-man shows: Craven Gallery, Paris, 1953, (first one-man show of kinetic art); Marlborough-Gerson Gallery, NY, 1966; Tel Aviv Mus., 1973; Gallery Attali opening in Paris, first worldwide presentation of video researches by Agam, 1974; Jewish Museum, NY, 1975; Janus Gal., Wash. DC, 1977; S. African Nat'l. Gal., 1977; and many other solo and group shows, US and abroad. Group shows: First group show of kinetic movement, Galerie Denise Rene, Paris, 1955; Gallery Attali, Paris, 1976. Retrospectives: Nat'l. Mus. Mod. Art, Paris, 1972; exhib. traveled to Stedelijk Mus., Amsterdam, 1972, and Dusseldorfs Kunsthalle, 1973. Awards: First prize for creative research, Biennial, Sao Paulo, 1963; Chevalier de l'Ordre des Arts et Lettres, 1974; Honorary Doctorate of Philosophy, Tel Aviv U., 1975; Medal of Council of Europe, 1977. Guest-lecturer, theory of advanced visual communication, Harvard Univ., 1968. Died in 1953.

AGATE, ALFRED. Miniature painter. Born Feb. 14, 1812. Brother of Frederick S. Agate. He received his instruction from the artist Thomas S. Cummings. Elected Associate Member of National Academy. Died Jan. 5, 1846 in Wash., DC.

AGATE, FREDERICK S. Painter. Born 1807, in Sparta, Westchester Co., NY. He first studied art with the engraver Rollinson, and later with John R. Smith and S. F. B. Morse. He painted an excellent portrait of Rollinson, also of the actor Forrest as "Metamora." He was elected an Associate of the National Academy of Design and an Academician in 1826. Died May 1, 1844 in Sparta, NY.

AHL, HENRY HAMMOND. Painter. Born at East Hartford, Conn., in 1869. Pupil of Alexander Wagner and Gerome. Among his works, "In the Shadow of the Cross" at Washington, DC; "Sunset Glow" at Art Museum, Springfield, Mass., "Sunset Hour" at Portland, Maine, and "Sunset" at Worcester Art Museum. He has also done mural painting in Jamaica Plain, Boston, and in Providence, RI. Address in 1926, 12 Harcourt Street, Boston, Mass.

AHLGREN, ROY B.
Printmaker and instructor. Born in Erie, PA, July 6, 1927. Study: Erie (PA) Tech. Sch.; Villa Maria College; Univ. of Pittsburgh, BS ed.; Penn State Univ. Work: US Info. Agency, Wash. DC; Butler Art Inst., Youngstown, OH; etc. Comn.: Serigraphs, Assn. Am. Artists, NYC; WQLN Publ. TV; others. Exhibitions: National Academy of Design Annual, NY. Penna. Academy of Fine Arts, 1969 Nat'l Exh. of Prints, Library of Congress; Silvermine Guild Print Exh; Int'l. Exh; Graphic Art, Frechen, Ger.; others. Awards: Merit, 4th Miami Int'l. Graphic Biennial; etc. 21 national and regional prizes. Teaching: Tech. Memorial HS, Erie, PA, 1970. Member: Boston Printmakers; Phila. Print Club; World Print Council, San Francisco. Media: Serigraph. Address in 1982, 1012 Boyer Rd., Erie, PA.

AHRENS, ELLEN WETHERALD.
Painter of portraits and miniatures, illustrator. Born 1859 in Baltimore, MD. Member of Penna. Society of Miniature Painters. Awarded prizes at Penna. Academy of Fine Arts and Carnegie Institute, Pittsburgh. Address in 1926, Lansdowne, PA. Died 1953.

AID, GEO. C.
Miniature painter, etcher. Born 1872, in Quincy, Ill. Medal at St. Louis Exposition, 1904. Pupil of Laurens, and Benjamin Constant, in Paris. Address in 1926, 3660 Blaine Ave., St. Louis, MO. Died 1938.

AIKEN, CHARLES A.
Mural painter. Born 1872 in Georgia, VT. Pupil of Boston Museum of Fine Arts School. Exhibited water colors, Penna. Academy of Fine Arts, Phila., 1925. Address in 1926, 57 West 57th Street, New York. Died 1965.

AIKEN, ROBERT.
Sculptor. Exhibited in 1920 the "Elizabeth Watrous Medal" at the Penna. Academy of Fine Arts, Phila. Elected member of National Academy, 1914. Address in 1926, 162 West 11th Street, New York.

AIKMAN, WALTER MONTEITH.
Artist. Born 1857, New York. Studied engraving in NY under Frank French and J. G. Smithwick, drawing and painting under Boulanger and Lefebvre, Paris. Work and Awards: Medal for engraving, Paris Exp., 1889, and Chicago Exp., 1893; Exhibited at Paris, 1900; silver medal for original engravings on wood, Buffalo Exp., 1901; wood and copper engravings at Carnegie Inst., Pittsburgh and NY Public Library. Address in 1926, 133 Macon Street, Brooklyn, NY.

AIMAN, PEARL.
Painter. Exhibited "Fishing Pier, Provincetown," at Penna. Academy of Fine Arts, 1920. Address in 1926, East Willow Grove Ave., Chestnut Hill, Phila., PA.

AITKEN, PETER.
Wood engraver. Born June 16, 1858, Dundas, Can. Studied engraving under Timothy Cole several years, visited Europe 1887 and 1891, and studied in Paris, 1895. Awarded medal, Chicago Expn., 1893, and exhibited Paris Expn., 1900. Address in 1926, Hart Street, Brooklyn, NY. Died in 1912.

AITKEN, ROBERT INGERSOLL.
Sculptor. Born May 8, 1878, in San F. Studied Mark Hopkins Inst. of Art, San F., and under Arthur F. Matthews and Douglas Tilden. Prof. sculpture, Mark Hopkins Inst. of Art (U. of Cal.), 1901-4. Taught at ASL. Directed Schools of NA. Among important works are busts of Mme. Modjeska, Douglas Tilden, Dr. J. L. York; monuments to William McKinley, at St. Helena, Cal., 1902, Berkeley, Cal., 1902; bust of Charles J. Dickman, Charles Rollo Peters, 1902; McKinley Monument, Golden Gate Park, San F., 1903. Also designs of $50 gold coin issued by US Govt. in commemoration of the expn. Burritt Memorial, New Britain, CT. Helen Foster Barnet Prize, NAD; Medal of Honor (gold) Arch. League, NY, for sculpture, 1915; silver medal for sculpture, Panama-Pacific International Expn., 1915. Worked in Paris, 1904-7, Instr. Nat. Acad. Schs. Sculpture Class. NA sec. Nat. Sculpture Soc.

Address in 1926, 154 West 55th Street, NYC. Died Jan. 3, 1949.

AITKEN, ROBERT.
Engraver and illustrator. Born 1734, in Scotland; died 1802, in Philadelphia. Aitken issued the Pennsylvania Magazine in 1776, and engraved the vignette on the title page after a design by Pierre E. duSimitiere, and a number of the illustrations; among the latter were some of the first views of military operations in the revolution ever engraved.

AKAWIE, THOMAS FRANK.
Painter. Born in New York City, Feb. 22, 1935. Study: Los Angeles City College, 1953-56; Univ. of Calif., Berkeley, BA 1959, MA 1963. Work: Milwaukee Art Center, Wis.; Ithaca College; Oakland Mus., Calif.; Williams College; private collections. Exhib.: 1969 annual, Whitney, NYC, 1969; San Fran. Mus. of Mod. Art, 1976; Nat'l. Collection of Fine Arts, Smithsonian, 1977; La Jolla Mus. (Calif.) of Art, 1967; Calif. Palace of Legion of Honor, San Fran., 1972; San Jose Museum, 1977; Japan, 1978; and others. Awards: Anne Downey Mus. Invit., Calif.; Jack London Art Exhib., Oakland, Calif.; others. Teaching: San Fran. Art Inst.; others. Address in 1982, Berkeley, Calif.

AKELEY, CARL ETHAN.
Sculptor. Born 1864, in Claredon, NY. Member of National Sculpture Society Works. Animal studies in Brooklyn Institute, and American Museum of Natural History.

AKERS, BENJAMIN PAUL.
Sculptor. Born July 10, 1825, in Westbrook, ME. Studied painting in Portland, ME, and in 1894, studied plaster coating with Carew. Made his first visit to Europe, visiting Florence, Italy, where he remained during the year 1852, and studied under Powers. His second visit abroad was made in 1854. Among his works are: "Peace," "Una and the Lion," "Girl Pressing Grapes," "Isaiah," "Schiller's Diver," "Reindeer," "The Lost Pearl Diver," "St. Elizabeth of Hungary,"

"Milton," "Diana and Endymion"; portrait busts of Tilton, Longfellow, Samuel Appleton, Edward Everett, Prof. Cleveland, Gerrit Smith, Sam Houston, and Justice John McLean. According to some biographers, he was called Paul because of his religiosity. Died May 21, 1861, in Philadelphia.

AKERS, CHARLES.
Sculptor. Born in Hollis, Maine, Oct. 15, 1836. He also worked as a crayon portrait draughtsman. His studio was in New York, 1860-69. In 1875 he was working in Waterbury, Conn., and in 1879 he had returned to New York. Died Sept. 16, 1906, in New York City.

AKERS, GARY.
Painter. Born Pikeville, KY, Feb. 22, 1951. Study: Morehead (KY) State University, BA, 1972; MA, 1974. One-man exhibition: Claypool-Young Art Gallery, Morehead, KY, 1978. Exhibitions: KY Water Color Soc., 1978, 1981; Am. Water Color Soc., NY, 1979, 1982; Nat'l. Acad. Galleries, NYC, 1979, 1982; So. Water Color Soc., Denton, TX, 1979, and Ashville, NC, 1983; 4th Invitational Water Color Exhib., Springfield (Ill.), AA, 1980; AAA, NY, 1981, 1982. Awards: Grant, Greenshields Foundation, Montreal, Canada, 1976; Friends of KY WC Soc. award 1978. Included in Am. WCS 115th traveling exhib. Media: Egg tempera, water color. Dealer: McBridge Gallery, 117 Main St., Annapolis, MD. Gary Akers Art Studio, Union, KY, opened 1980.

AKIN, JAMES.
Born 1773, in Charleston, South Carolina. His earliest engraved work is found in Drayton's "Views of South Carolina," Charleston, SC, 1802. In 1804 he was working in Salem, Mass.; in 1808 he returned to Phila., where he drew caricatures, and engraved book plates. He also published prints in connection with William Harrison, Jr. Died July 16, 1846, in Philadelphia.

AKIN, LOUIS.
Painter. Was born 1868, in Portland, ME; died 1913, in Flagstaff, Arizona. He studied in

New York City under Chase and DuMond. His specialty was painting the life of the American Indian, and the American Museum of Natural History in New York commissioned him to decorate their room devoted to Indians of the Southwest.

AKIN, MRS.
She is supposed to have been the wife of James Akin, and engraved membership certificates. Her work was done in Newburyport, Mass., in 1806-08.

ALAJALOV, CONSTANTIN.
Illustrator. Born in Rostov-on-the-Don, he was brought up in pre-revolutionary Russia and by the age of 15 was illustrating a book of poetry by Baudelaire as well as the Lives of Savanarola. He attended the University of Petrograd, enjoyed a brief stay as a court painter and was a member of their new artists' guild. Having fled from Constantinople, Alajalov arrived in New York in 1923 and found work painting murals for Russian cabarets. Three years later he began a 20-year relationship with The New Yorker doing cover art and in 1945 he began working for The Saturday Evening Post, in addition to illustrating children's books.

ALBEE, GRACE THURSTON ARNOLD.
(Mrs. Percy F. Albee). Painter. Born Scituate, RI, July 28, 1890. Pupil of R. I. School of Design; Paul Bornet in Paris. Work: Linoleum cut, "Willows at Straitsmouth," Rhode Island School of Design Museum, Providence. Address in 1929, 7 Rue Campagne Premiere, Paris, France.

ALBEE, GRACE.
Engraver. Born in Scituate, Rhode Island, in 1890. Study: Rhode Island School of Design and with Paul Bornet in Paris. Awards: NAD; Providence Art Club; Society of American Graphic Artists, 1951; Connecticut Academy, 1955, 1958; Hunterdon County Art Center, 1958; Boston Printmakers; Audubon Art; Artists fellowship. Work: Met. Mus. of Art; NYC; Carnegie Institute; Cleveland Museum of Art; Okla. Agricultural and

Mechanical College; John Herron Art Institute; Rhode Island School of Design; Library of Congress; National Museum, Stockholm; National Academy of Design; Philadelphia Museum of Art; Cleveland Printmakers Club; Marblehead Art Association; New York Public Library; Newark Public Library; Boston Public Library; Culver Military Academy; National Muesum, Israel; Collection of King Victor Emmanuel, Italy.

ALBEE, PERCY F.
Painter. Born 1883, in Bridgeport, Conn. Pupil of Penna. Academy of Fine Arts and Providence School of Design. Address in 1926, 235 Benefit Street, Providence, RI. Died in 1959.

ALBERS, ANNI.
Designer, graphic artist, weaver and teacher. Born in Berlin, Germany, June 12, 1899. US citizen. Study: Bauhaus, Weimar, Germany, dipl. Hon doctorates: Maryland Col. of Art, 1972; York Univ., Toronto, 1973; Phila. Coll. of Art, 1976; Univ. of Hartford, 1978. Work: Met. Mus. of Art; MOMA; Monmouth (NJ) Mus.; Art Inst. of Chicago; Univ. of Calif. at Riverside; and others. Comn.: Memorial to Nazi victims; comn. by List Family for Jewish Mus.; Ark Curtain, Dallas. Exhib.: MOMA; Brooklyn Mus., NY; Katonah Gallery, NY; Univ. of Hartford Art Sch.; Queens Coll. Library, NY; Monmouth (NJ) Mus.; Univ. of Calif., Riverside; Carnegie Inst., Yale Univ. Art Gal; and others. Awards: Phila. Coll. of Art, 1962; Tamarind Lithog. Workshop Fellow, Los Angeles, 1964; gold medal, American Craft Council, 1981. Teaching: Black Mtn. College, 1933-49; lecturer at univ. and museums. Author: Anni Alber: On Designing, Wesleyan Univ. Press, 1962, 71; On Weaving, same press, 1965, 72; Anni Albers: Pre-Columbian Mexican Miniatures, Praeger, 1970. Media: Textile. Address in 1982, 808 Birchwood Dr., Orange, CT.

ALBERS, JOSEF.
Painter, printmaker and teacher. Born in Bottrop, Germany, March 19, 1888. US citizen. Study: Royal

Art Sch., Berlin; Art Acad., Munich; Bauhaus, Weimar, Ger. Work: Met. Mus. Art; Guggenheim; MOMA; Whitney; Chicago Art Inst. Comn.: brick mural, Harvard Univ., 1950; glass mural, Time & Life Bldg., NYC, 1961; plastic mural, Pan Am Bldg., NYC, 1963; Rochester Inst. Tech., 1969; Yale Univ. Art Bldg. Exhib.: Homage to the Square, MOMA, S. Am., & US travelling show 1964-66; Los Angeles Co. Mus., 1966; Kunsthalle, Dusseldorf, Ger., 1970; Princeton Univ. Art Mus., 1971; Met. Mus. Art, 1971-72. Teaching: Bauhaus, Weimar, Dessau and Berlin, 1923-33; Black Mtn. College, NC, 1933-46; Yale Univ., 1950-60. Awards: Commander's Cross, Order of Merit, Ger. Fed. Rep., 1968; Fine Arts Medal, Am. Inst. Architects, 1975; Ford Found. Grant. Mem.: Am. Abstract Artists; Am. Inst. Graphic Arts; Print Council of Am.; Nat'l. Inst. Arts and Letters. Bibliog.: Extensive. Author: Interaction of Color, Yale Univ., 1963; Formulation: Articulation, Abrams, 1972; others. Died in 1976. Address in 1976, 808 Birchwood Dr., Orange, CT.

ALBERT, CALVIN.
Sculptor. Born Nov. 19, 1918, in Grand Rapids, Mich. Studied at Grand Rapids Art Gallery With Otto Bach; Art Inst. of Chicago; Inst. of Design, Chicago with Moholy-Nagy, Gyorgy Kepes; Archienko Sch. of Sculpture. Taught at Inst. of Design, Chicago, and at NYU and Brooklyn; with Pratt Inst. since 1949. Work: Whitney; Jewish Mus.; Art Inst. of Chicago; Brooklyn Mus.; Met. Mus. of Art; Detroit Inst. of Arts; Colby College. Exhib.: G. Borgenight Gallery, NYC; Jewish Mus., NYC; MOMA; The Tate, London; Grand Rapids; Stable Gallery; Benson Gallery. Awards: Fulbright, 1957; Tiffany grant; Guggenheim fellowship, Detroit Inst.; Audubon Artists, NYC.

ALBERT, E. MAXWELL.
Painter. Born 1890, in Chicago, Ill. Pupil of Art Students League of New York. Address in 1926, New Canaan, NY.

ALBERT, ERNEST.
Painter. Born 1857, in Brooklyn, NY. Pupil of Brooklyn Art School. Elected Associate, National Academy of Design. Address in 1926, New Canaan, Conn. Died in 1946.

ALBERTS, JOHN B.
Painter. Born 1886, at Louisville, KY. Pupil of Cincinnati Art Academy.

ALBRECHT, CLARENCE JOHN.
Sculptor, lecturer and teacher. Born Waverly, IA, Sept. 28, 1891. Pupil of H. R. Dill, James A. Wehn, Charles Eugene Tefft. Works: Grizzly Bear Group, Calif. Academy of Sciences; Sea Lion Group, American Museum of Natural History; Deer, Bear and Goat groups, State Museum, Univ. of Washington. Address in 1929, American Museum of Natural History, New York, NY.

ALBRIGHT, ADAM EMORY.
Artist. Born 1862, at Monroe, Wis. Student of Art Inst. of Chicago, 1881-3; Pa. Acad. Fine Arts, Philadelphia, 1883-6; Munich and Paris, 1887-8. Painter of Am. country children; exhibited at Chicago Exp., in 1893, and later in New York, Philadelphia, Boston, Washington, Chicago, Paris Salon. Member Soc. Western Artists; Fellowship of PAFA; Chicago Soc. Artists (pres., 1915-16); Chicago WCC (dir., pres.), Chicago Acad. Design; Am. Water Color Soc., New York. Member Am. Federation of Arts. Died in 1957. Address in 1926, Hubbard Woods, Ill.

ALBRIGHT, GERTRUDE PARTINGTON.
Painter. Born in England. Among her paintings, the "Portrait of an Actress," owned by the city of San Francisco, is the best known. Address in 1926, 737 Buena Vista Ave., San Francisco, Cal.

ALBRIGHT, H. OLIVER.
Painter. Born 1876 in Mannheim, Germany. Member of San Francisco Art Association. Address in 1926, 737 Buena Vista Ave., San Francisco, Cal.

ALBRIGHT, HENRY JAMES.

11

Painter and sculptor. Born 1887, in Albany, NY. Pupil of Wm. St. Hohn Harper, John F. Carlson, and C. W. Hawthorne. Died in 1951. Address in 1926, Albany, New York.

ALBRIGHT, IVAN LE LORRAINE.
Painter, sculptor and lithographer. Born in North Harvey, Ill., Feb. 20, 1897. Studied at Ecole Regionale Beaux-Arts, Nantes, 1919; Arti Inst. Chic., 1920-23, 1977; NAD, NYC, 1924; PAFA; and others. In collections of Nat'l. Gallery, Wash., DC; Met. Mus. of Art, MOMA, Guggenheim, Whitney, in NYC; others. Exhibited at Carnegie Inst.; NY and Brussels World's fairs; MOMA; Art Inst. of Chic.; Corcoran Gallery, Wash., DC; NAD and Whitney, NYC; and many more. Awards: Hon. mention, Art Inst. of Chic., 1926, ans Shaffer prize, 1928; medal, painting, 1942, and Met. Mus. prize, 1952, at Met. Mus. of Art; Silver medal, Corcoran Gallery, 1955; others. Member of Nat'l. Inst. of Arts and Letters; Am. WC Soc.; Am. Acad. Arts and Letters; Academician, NAD; fellow, PAFA. Currently represented by Kennedy Galleries, NYC, Albright Studios in Warrenville, Ill., in 1929. Living in Woodstock, VT, in 1982.

ALBRIGHT, MALVIN MARR.
Painter and sculptor. Born Chicago, Ill., Feb. 20, 1897. Studied at Art Inst. of Chicago; PAFA; Beaux Arts Inst. of Design, NYC; with Albin Polasek, Charles Gafly. Work: San Diego (Calif.) Fine Arts Gallery; Cocroran Gallery, Wash., DC; Toledo (Ohio) Mus. of Art; Butler Inst., Youngstown, Ohio; PAFA; and others. Exhibited at NAD, Whitney, MOMA, all in New York City; PAFA; Carnegie Inst.; and more. Awards: Fountain prize, Chic. Daily News, 1922; Jenkins prize, Art Inst. of Chic., 1929; Altman prize, NAD, 1942-62; Corcoran Silver Medal; Dana Medal, PAFA, 1965; and others. Member: Fellow, PAFA; Art Inst. of Chic. Alumni; Laguna Beach AA; NAD; fellow, Royal Soc. of Arts; Int'l. Inst. of Arts and Letters; Nat'l. Sculpture Soc.; and others. Albright Studio in Warrenville,

Ill., in 1929. Address in 1982, Chicago, Ill.

ALBRIZZIO, CONRAD A.
Draughtsman. Born, October 20, 1894, NYC 1911. Studied architectural drawing, Cooper Union night classes, 1911; Beaux Arts under Frederick Hirons, 1918; NY ASL under Luks and DuMond, 1923; Also studied in Paris, learned fresco in Rome, Italy under Paperi and encanstic in Pompy; American Assembly and Fontainebeeau School, France. Worked during studies as draftsman in New Orleans, 1919, and designer in NY. Work: Frescoes, Governor's reception room and court rooms, Louisiana State Capitol, 1932; Murals for Richmond Hill High School, under Public works of Art project, and church of St. Cecilia, Detroit, MI. Organized Fresco Guild. Taught fine Arts, Louisiana St. U., Baton Rouge, 1936.

ALCOTT, ABIGAIL MAY.
Painter. Born July 26, 1840 in Concord, Mass. Studied at Boston School of Design and abroad. Her professional life was spent in Boston, London, and Paris. Illustrator for books of her sister, Louisa May Alcott, author of Little Women and other classics. Best known for still life compositions. She exhibited in America and Europe. Died 1889 in Paris, France.

ALDRICH, F(RANK) H(ANDY).
Painter, illustrator, craftsman, lecturer, and teacher. Born Wauseon, Ohio, Mar. 29, 1866. Pupil of Metcalf, Twachtman, Knaufft. Member: Toledo Artklan. Custodian of Ancient Books and Manuscripts, Toledo Museum of Art. Address in 1929, Toledo Mus. of Art.

ALDRICH, GEORGE AMES.
Painter and etcher. Born 1872, in Worcester, Mass. Address in 1926, 155 East Ohio Street, Chicago, Ill. Died in 1941.

ALDRIDGE, ADELE.
Painter/graphics. Studied: Silvermine College of Art; Parsons School of Design; Chicago Art Institute. Exhibitions: Bodley

12

Gallery, New York City, 1970; Metamorphosis Gallery, Ridgefield, Connecticut, 1971; Three Interpretations of the I Ching, Greenwich Library, 1972. Currently working on interpreting the I Ching in 64 separate portfolios of seven prints each.

ALEXANDER, A(RTHUR) H(ADDEN).
Etcher, landscape artist. Born Decatur, Ill., Oct. 27, 1892. Member: Am. Soc. Ldscp. A.; Cleveland SA; Cleveland Print C. Address in 1929, 4500 Euclid Ave.; h. 2572 Kemper Road, Cleveland, Ohio.

ALEXANDER, CLIFFORD GREAR.
Painter, illustrator and teacher. Born 1870, in Springfield, Mass. Pupil of School of Boston Museum of Art. Address in 1926, 6 Upland Road, Faneuil Station, Brighton, Mass.

ALEXANDER, COSMO.
Born c. 1724. Scottish painter who visited this country in 1770 and remained in Newport, RI, for a year or so, and then went to South Carolina and then to Edinburgh. He died shortly after reaching home. He painted portraits of Dr. William Hunter's family of Newport, and a number of his countrymen residing in this country. On his return to Scotland he took young Gilbert Stuart with him. Died Aug. 25, 1772.

ALEXANDER, FRANCIS.
Born Feb. 3, 1800 in Connecticut. Began painting in water color, and studied under Alexander Robinson in New York. Later he went to Providence, and then opened his studio in Boston, where he had many sitters, the most famous being Daniel Webster, of whom he painted several excellent portraits. In 1831 he visited Europe, finally settling in Florence, where he remained until his death. Alexander wrote a short autobiography published in Dunlap's "History." He went to New York for a brief period in 1820 and again the following year for study. He then went to Boston with a letter to Gilbert Stuart from John Trumbull, where he advanced rapidly in his painting under Stuart's influence. In 1831 he first visited Italy. He did not in his final years continue his profession as an artist. He drew on stone the earliest attempts at portrait lithography in America. For full account see Boston Magazine, 1825. He painted Charles Dickens, Benjamin R. Curtis, John Odin, Baron Stow, Mrs. Fletcher Webster and Master Lord, and many others. Died March 27, 1880.

ALEXANDER, JACQUES.
Painter. Born Berlin, Germany, Dec. 15, 1863. Pupil of Laurens and Constant in Paris. Member: Soc. of Deaf Artists. Address in 1929, 436 Fort Washington Ave., New York, NY.

ALEXANDER, JOHN WHITE.
Artist. Born 1856, in Allegheny City, PA; died in 1915 in New York City. Educated in the schools of his native city, he early manifested a talent for sketching and at sixteen went to New York, where he soon obtained employment with Harper & Brothers as an illustrator. In 1877 he went abroad and studied at the Munich Royal Gallery and later in Venice, Florence, Holland and Paris. On his return to this country in 1881 he won immediate recognition as a portrait painter; many eminent men, including Walt Whitman, Joseph Jefferson, Oliver Wendell Holmes, John Burroughs, Grover Cleveland and Robert Louis Stevenson, sat for him. In 1891 he went to Europe for his health and during the course of his travels made a series of portraits of distinguished authors. Three of his portraits of women were accepted by the Paris Salon of 1893, marking the beginning of his international reputation and winning him election as an associate of the Societe Nationale des Beaux Arts. He also achieved distinction in mural painting. The six decorative panels representing "The Evolution of the Book," which adorn the Congressional Library, were done by him in 1895. Later he painted the titanic series of murals surrounding the grand staircase of the Carnegie

13

Institute, Pittsburgh, and in 1906 was engaged to do a series depicting "The Industrial Development of Pennsylvania" for the State Capitol, which he never completed. He was one of the most active members of the National Academy of Design, and its president from 1909 until shortly before his death. Among his painting, "The Pot of Basil," painted in 1856, is owned by the Boston Museum of Fine Arts. "The Blue Bowl" is owned by the Rhode Island School of Design. His portrait of the Norwegian painter Thaulow is owned by the Penna. Fairmount Park, Wilstach Collection.

ALEXANDER, JULIA STANDISH.
Sculptor, craftsman, writer and teacher. Born Springfield, Mass. Pupil of ASL of NY; Victor Brenner. Member: Alliance; NYSC; AFA. Director, Art and Craft Dept., Heckscher Foundation for Children, New York City.

ALEXANDER, MARIE DAY.
Painter. Born Greenfield, Oct. 21, 1887. Pupil of Augustus Vincent Tack. Member: Springfield AL; North Shore AA; NA Women PS. Work: "Green River in Autumn," Mass. Federation of Women's Clubs, Boston.

ALEXANDER, MARY LOUISE.
Sculptor, writer and teacher. Pupil of Meakin, Duveneck, Barnhorn, Grafly, Nowottny. Member: Cincinnati Women's AC; MacDowell Soc., Cincinnati; PBC. Work: Vincent Nowottny tablet, Cincinnati Art Academy. Address in 1929, 28 Alexandra Bldg.; h. 2238 Gilbert Ave., Cincinnati, Ohio.

ALEXANDER, NINA.
Painter and illustrator. Born in Auburn, Kansas. Pupil of Penna. Academy of Fine Arts. Student under Chase, and under Henri and Brangwyn in London. Address in 1926, 1315 Clifton Street, Washington, DC.

ALFANO, VICENZO.
Italian sculptor. Exhibited in 1902 at the Sculpture Society in New York, "Cicerone."

ALGER, JOHN HERBERT.
Painter. Born 1879 in Boston, Mass. Member of the Society of Independent Artists. Address in 1926, 210 East 17th Street, New York.

ALKE, STEPHEN.
Painter. Born in 1874. Exhibited landscapes in the annual exhibition of Cincinnati Museum, 1925. Address in 1926, New Richmond, Ohio. Died in 1941.

ALLAIRE, LOUISE.
Painter. Member of National Association of Women Painters and Sculptors. Address in 1926, 646 St. Marks Ave., Brooklyn, New York.

ALLAN, MRS. CHARLES BEACH.
Painter. Born 1874 in Detroit, Mich. Address in 1926, 542 Park Ave., Kansas City, MO.

ALLEN, ANNE HUNTINGTON
(Mrs. Thomas W. Allen). Painter. Born New York, 1858. Student, Cooper Institute, pupil of Wyatt Eaton, and Carolus Duran. Address in 1926, 230 Southern Ave., Mt. Auburn, Cincinnati, Ohio.

ALLEN, CHARLES CURTIS.
Painter. Born Dec. 13, 1886. Instructor in water color painting, Worcester Art Museum. Exhibited at Penna. Academy of Fine Arts, Philadelphia, 1925. Address in 1926, 41 Commonwealth Ave., Chestnut Hill, Mass. Died in 1950.

ALLEN, COURTNEY.
Illustrator, etcher and craftsman. Born Norfolk, VA, Jan. 16,1896. Pupil of C. W. Hawthorne, C. C. Curran, Felix Mahony, W. H. W. Bicknell. Member: New Rochelle AA; Beachcombers C.

ALLEN, FRANK (LEONARD).
Painter, lecturer, and teacher. Born in Portland, Maine, Nov. 14, 1884. Pupil of Tarbell, Major, Deman Ross, Henry B. Snell. Member: Salma. C.; Yonkers AA.; AWCS; Artist's Fund Society; Alliance; Artists Fellowship. Director, Boothbay Studios Summer School of Art. Address in 1929, Pratt Inst.; 220A Willoughby Ave.,

14

Brooklyn, NY; summer, Boothbay Studios, Boothbay Harbor, ME.

ALLEN, FREDERICK WARREN.
Sculptor and teacher. Born North Attleboro, Mass., May 5, 1888. Pupil of Pratt, Lanouski, Bartlett. Member: Boston GA; Boston SS; NSS; Concord AA. Work: "Toreo" at PAFA, 1924; in Boston Mus. of FA; Boston AC; Boston City Hall; New Eng. Historic General Soc.; Met. Mus., NY; Boston Public Library; Trinity Church; Concord Museum; WWI Vet. Mem., Mt. Hope Cem., Boston; and others. Instructor, Museum of Fine Arts Schools, Boston. Address in 1929, 27 Mechanic St., Roxbury, Mass.; h. Elm St., Concors, Mass.; summer, Bartlett's Harbor, N. Haven, ME.

ALLEN, GREGORY SEYMOUR.
Sculptor. Born in Orange, NJ, July 8, 1884. Pupil of G. Borglum and H. N. Bushbrown. Major work in LA Museum of Art.

ALLEN, GRETA.
Portrait painter. Born in Boston. Pupil of DeCamp and Benson. Member of Copley Society. Address in 1926, 755 Boylston Street, Boston.

ALLEN, HAROLD A.
Painter. Exhibited water colors at the Penna. Academy Exhibition, 1925. Address in 1926, 142 Oakdale Ave., Pawtucket, RI.

ALLEN, HAZEL LEIGH.
Sculptor. Born Morrilton, Ark., Dec. 8, 1892. Pupil of AIC and Ferdinand Koenig. Member: SSAL. Address in 1929, 644 Murray Ave., Milwaukee, Wis.

ALLEN, JAMES E.
Painter, etcher, and illustrator. Born Louisiana, MO, Feb. 23, 1894. Pupil of Harvey Dunn, Nicholas Fechin. Member: SI; Arch. LA; Salma C. Address in 1929, 49 East 9th St., New York, NY; h. 41 Mayhew Ave., Larchmont, NY.

ALLEN, JOEL.
Engraver. Born 1755 at Farmington, Conn. He engraved plates for "Maynard's" edition of Josephus, pub. 1792. Died 1825 in Middletown, Conn.

ALLEN, LOUISE.
(Mrs. Louise Allen Hobbs.). Sculptor. Born Lowell, Mass. Studied RI School of Design and Boston Museum Fine Arts. Member: NA Women PS; Copley S.; NSS; Boston SS; North Shore AA; Providence AC. Exhibited at PAFA Nat. Academy, New York; Art Inst. Chicago; Albright Galleries, Buffalo; Museum Fine Arts, Providence, RI; represented in Cleveland Museum. Works includs: World War Memorial, East Greenwich, RI; World War Tablet. Gloucester, Mass.; memorial tablet Bancroft Hall, Annapolis, MD; also ideal bronzes, portraits, etc. Address in 1926, 45 Charles Street, Boston Mass.

ALLEN, LUTHER.
Engraver. Born at Enfield, Conn., June 11, 1780; died at Ithaca, NY, Nov. 27, 1821. He was the son of Moses Allen of Enfield, Conn., a soldier in the Revolution. Luther Allen married Sally P. Abbe on November 17, 1802, and soon after that date removed to Ithaca, NY, where he is referred to as an engraver, portrait painter, and a musician of some ability. The only engravings of Luther Allen noted are a quarto mezzotint portrait of the Rev. Stephen Williams, D. D., a view of New Port, NJ, and a book-plate engraved by him, either for his father, Moses Allen, or for a brother by the same name.

ALLEN, MARGARET N(EWTON).
Painter and sculptor. Born Lincoln, Mass., Dec. 3, 1894. Pupil of Frederick Allen, Charles Grafly, Bela Pratt. Member: Boston SS. Award: First prize, Junior League, Boston, 1929. Work: Medallion, Frigate "Constitution," US Navy; War Memorial, Cohasset, Mass.

ALLEN, MARION BOYD.
(Mrs. William A. Allen). Painter. Born in Boston, Mass., Oct. 23, 1862. Pupil of Tarbell and Benson, at School of Boston Museum of Fine Arts. Member: Copley S.; Conn. AFA; NAC; NA Women PS; PBC; Buffalo SA. Almros: Hon. Men., Conn. AFA, 1915, 1921; People's Prize, Newport AA, 1919; Hudson Prize, Conn. AFA, 1920; Fellowship prize, Buffalo

SAC, 1920; and others. Specialty portraiture and landscapes. Address in 1926, Fenway Studios, Boston, Mass.

ALLEN, MARY COLEMAN.
Painter. Born Troy, OH, Aug. 9, 1888. Pupil of Duveneck. Miniatures exhibited at Penna. Academy of Fine Arts, Philadelphia, 1924. Member of American Society of Miniature Painters. Address in 1926, 125 East 10th Street, New York City.

ALLEN, MARY G(ERTRUDE).
Painter and sculptor. Born Mendota, Ill., Oct. 7, 1869. Pupil of Anna Hills. Member: Seattle AI. Work: "Portrait of Narcissa Prentiss Whitman," Prentiss Hall, Whitman College, Walla Walla, Wash.; frieze, convalescent childrens ward, Everett General Hospital, Everett, Wash. Address in 1929, Lake Stevens, Wash.

ALLEN, MRS. P(EARL) W(RIGHT).
(Mrs. J. G. Allen). Painter and teacher. Born Kossuth, Miss., Apr. 9, 1880. Pupil of Anna Hills, Walter Gotz, John F. Carlson. Member: Muskogee AC; Okla. AA. Works: "Laguna Beach" and "Sunlit Rocks," Muskogee Public Library; in conjunction with Nola Jean Sharp, Baptistry Painting, First Baptist Church, Muskogee; First Baptist Church, Bristow; First Christian Church, Bristow, Okla. Address in 1929, 1412 Baltimore St., Muskogee, Okla.

ALLEN, SARAH LOCKHART.
Miniature painter. Also drew portraits in crayon. Born in Salem, Mass., Aug. 12, 1793. In Felt's "Annals of Salem" there is the following note under the year 1820: "Portraits of full size are executed by Miss Sarah Allen in crayons. She is a native of this City." Died July 11, 1877 in Salem.

ALLEN, THOMAS B.
Illustrator. Born in Nashville, Tennessee in 1928. He studied at Vanderbilt University and received his BFA from the AIC. His work has appeared in Esquire, Sports Illustrated, McCall's, Life, Redbook and Playboy. He has also

done illustrations for CBS, Harper & Row and Signet Classics. Gold medals have been awarded to him by the New York ADC and the S of I. Fron 1958 to 1964 he taught at the SVA in New York.

ALLEN, THOMAS.
Born in St. Louis, 1849. Studied in France and Germany and exhibited at the Salon in Paris and the National Academy of Design in 1877. Awarded medals Boston and Buffalo. Among his paintings are "Maplehurst at Noon," "Toilers of the Plains," "Upland Pastimes," and "Moonlight Landscapes." The Boston Museum of Fine Arts owned his "Portals of the Mission of San Jose, Texas." He was elected an Associate Member of the National Academy. Died 1924.

ALLEN, WILLARD
Painter. Born in Woodstock, NY, 1860. Pupil of Academy of Fine Arts, Philadelphia, PA, under Chase and Carlesen. Address in 1926, Woodstock, New York.

ALLEN & GAW.,
Engravers who signed a "Chart of Boston Harbor, Surveyed in 1817." It was published by John Melish in Philadelphia in 1819. The Gaw of the above firm was R. M. Gaw, who was employed by Peter Maverick of Newark, New Jersey, in 1829.

ALLER, GLADYS.
Painter. Born in Springfield, Massachusetts in 1915. Studied: Otis Art Institute; Choninard Art Institute; Art Students League and with George Grosz. Awards: California Watercolor Socity, 1936; Los Angeles Museum of Art, 1942. Work: Metropolitan Museum of Art.

ALLERDICE, SAMUEL.
Engraver. Was a pupil and later a partner of Robert Scot of Philadelphia. He engraved many copper-plates for book illustrations. Scot and Allerdice made many of the plates for Dobson's edition of Rees' Encyclopedia, published in Philadelphia, 1794-1803.

ALLIS, C. HARRY.
Painter. Born Dayton, Ohio.

16

Studied at Detroit Museum of Art. Exhibited "November in the Ozarks" at National Academy of Design, 1925. Address in 1929, 15 Gramercy Park, New York. Died in 1938

ALLISON, W(ILLIAM) M(ERIE).
Illustrator. Born Kansas, Jan. 27, 1880. Pupil of John Herron Art Inst., and Chicago Art Academy. Member: SI. Illustrated "Heroes of Liberty" and "Women in American History," published by The Bobbs-Merrill Co. Specialty, historical and western subjects. Address in 1929, 118 East 28th St., New York: h. 8916 Cherokee Ave., Hollis, LI, NY.

ALLSTON, WASHINGTON.
Painter. A South Carolinian, born at Waccanaw, on November 5, 1779, was sent to Rhode Island as a child, his native climate not agreeing with him. He was educated at Harvard, and returned to South Carolina, where he painted some religious compositions. In 1801 he went with Malbone to England and studied under West at the Royal Academy. In the following year he exhibited three pictures at Somerset House and sold one of them. Three years later he accompanied Vanderlyn to France, reveling there in the art treasures Napoleon had accumulated from all Europe, and developing the richness of color that came to characterize many of his paintings. He visited Italy, came back to America and married, and again in 1811 returned to England, taking with him S. F. B. Morse as a pupil. After a few years he returned home, a success on both sides of the ocean. He died at Cambridge, Mass., July 9, 1843. His "Uriel in the Sun" and "Jacob's Dream" are owned in England. His best known paintings in the United States are "Jeremiah," "Belshazzar's Feast" and "Witch of Endor." Among his portraits, Wm. Ellery Channings; Sam'l T. Coleridge and his self-portrait are owned by the Boston Museum of Fine Arts. The "Dead Man Revived" is in the Penna. Academy of Fine Arts, Philadelphia. See "Life and Letters of Washington Allston," by Jared B. Flagg. Also see "Artist Biographies," Allston. (Boston 1879.). Died in 1843.

ALLWELL, STEPHEN S.
Sculptor. Born in Baltimore, MD, Oct. 15, 1906. Study: MD Inst., Baltimore. Work: Metromedia Permanent Collection private collections, including commissions. Exhibitions: Miniature Painters, Sculptors and Gravers Soc., Wash., DC, 1967-71. Awards: Miniature Painters, Sculptors and Gravers Soc., 1969; etc. Mem.: Artists Equity Assn.; MD Federation of Art; Rehoboth Art Lg.; and others. Address in 1982, 803 Evesham Avenue Baltimore, MD.

ALTEN, MATHIAS J.
Painter. Born in Germany, 1871. Pupil of Constant, Laurens, and Whistler in Paris. Member of Grand Rapids, (Mich.) Art Association. Address in 1926, 1593 E. Fulton Street, Grand Rapids, Michigan. Died in 1938.

ALTMANN, AARON.
Painter. Born San Francisco, Cal., 1872. Student of Constant, Laurens, and Gerome, Paris. Address in 1926, 2298 Green Street, San Francisco, California.

ALTORFER, GLORIA FINCH.
Painter and designer. Born in Peoria, Ill., April 19, 1931. Study: Bradley Univ., BA; with H. Kosak, R. Weidenaar. Exhibitions: Greater Fall River Art Assn., MA, 1970; Miniature Painters, Sculptors and Gravers Soc., Wash. DC, 1970; 73rd Annual Nat'l. Exhib. for Prof. Women, Catharine Lorillard Wolfe Art Club, NAD, NYC, 1970; and others. Mem.: Ill. Art Lg.; Fine Arts Soc.; Peoria (Ill.) Art Guild; others. Teaching: Private and studio classes, YMCA and galleries. Int. designer, E. G. Lehmann Assns. Media: Acrylic, oil, watercolor, collage. Dealer: Collectors Upstairs Gallery Lakeview Ctr., 1125 W. Lake St., Peoria, Ill. Address in 1976, 2923 W. Vassar Ct., Peoria, Ill.

ALTSCHULER, FRANZ.
Illustrator. Born in Mannheim, Germany, 1923. He was educated in

New York City at CU and TID. His professional career began in 1951 and he has since illustrated over 30 books. The recipient of awards in New York and Chicago, he has shown his work in galleries in Denver and Baltimore. His illustrations have been used as posters for the Chicago newspapers as well as for major magazines, including Palyboy and Skeptic.

ALTVATER, CATHERINE THARP.
Painter. Born in Little Rock, Arkansas, July 26, 1907. Study: Grand Central Sch. of Contemp. Arts and Crafts; Art League of Long Island, with F. Spradling, E. Whitney; Nat'l. Acad. of Fine Arts, with Mario Cooper, Ogden Pleissner, Louis Bouche, Robert Phillips. Work: Many private collections and museums in US, Europe, Japan, Canada, and South America. Exhibitions: National Academy of Design; National Arts Club; Royal Water Color Soc., London; Audubon Artists, Metropolitan Museum of Art; Mexico City Museum; numerous one-man shows and traveling exhibits. Awards: Over 70 awards including 20 first prizes. Mem.: Am. Watercolor Society; Nat'l. Art League; Allied Artists of America. Media: Watercolor. Rep.: Lord & Taylor, 39th & 5th Avenue, New York, NY. Address in 1982, 505 Douglas St., New Smyrna Beach, Fla.

ALVAREZ, MABEL.
Painter. Born in Hawaii. Studied: with Cahill and McBurney. Awards: California Exposition, San Diego, 1916; California Art Club, 1918, 1919, 1933. Federation of Women's Club, 1923; Laguna Beach Art Association, 1928; Ebell Club, 1933-35; Honolulu Printmakers, 1939; Oakland Art Gallery, 1838; Madonna Festival, Los Angeles, 1954. Palos Verdes Annual, 1957. Collections: Honolulu Art Academy; San Joaquin Museum; University of Southern California.

AMANS, JACQUES.
Painter. Born in 1801, died in Paris in 1888. Painted portraits in New Orleans from 1828 till 1856. Address in 1838, 163 Royal Street; 1840, 184 Royal Street; 1854-56, Bienville and Customhouse Streets.

AMATEIS, EDMUND R.
Sculptor. Born in Rome, Italy, Feb. 7, 1897. Son of Louis Amateis. Pupil of Beaux-Arts Inst. of Design and Julian Academy in Paris. Member: Alumni Assn. American Acad. in Rome; NSS; NY Arch. L.; AFA. Award: Prix de Rome, 1921 to 1924; Avery prize, Arch. L., 1929. Work: Sculptured groups for Baltimore War Memorial; Metopes for Buffalo Historical Building, colossal relief for Rochester Times-Union. Address in 1926, 126 East 75th Street, New York.

AMATEIS, LOUIS.
Born in Turin, Italy, December 13, 1855; died in West Falls Church, VA, March 16, 1913. Educated in the schools of Turin, and a graduate of the Institute of Technology and the Academy of Fine Arts of Turin, where he was awarded a gold medal upon his graduation. His first sculptural work of importance was a bas-relief purchased by a committee of sculptors for the Art Gallery of Turin. In a competition he was awarded the commission for the sculptural decorations for the Palace of Fine Arts of Turin. In 1884 he came to the United States and became a naturalized citizen of this country. He was the founder of the School of Architecture and Fine Arts of the Columbian University, Washington, DC, and a member of the National Sculpture Society. Among his works are many portraits busts, and the bronze doors in the Capitol, Washington, DC.

AMEIJIDE, RAYMOND.
Illustrator. Born in Newark, New Jersey, 1924. He attended PI. After a seven-year stint at Ross Advertising he went free-lance and later formed AKM Studio. His paper sculpture and felt constructions have appeared in Art Direction and Graphis as well as being shown at the ADC and the S of I of New York.

AMEN, WILL RICE.
Painter. Exhibited water colors at

18

the Penna. Academy of Fine Arts, Philadelphia, 1925. Address in 1926, 17 Gramercy Park, New York.

AMENT, ROBERT SELFE.
Painter and etcher. Born in New York, 1879. Pupil of Ward, Chase and Henri. Address in 1926, 2380 Grand Avenue, New York City.

AMES, DANIEL.
New York miniature painter, active from 1841-1852.

AMES, EZRA.
Portrait painter. Born May 5, 1768 in Framingham, MA. Little is known of his life excepting that he commenced work as a coach painter in Albany. Later he turned his attention to portrait painting, and gained recognition in 1812, by a portrait of Gov. Geo. Clinton, exhibited at the Penna. Academy of Fine Arts. For many years after this he painted in Albany and Western New York, painting most of the New York legislators. He also painted miniatures. Died Feb. 23, 1836 in Albany, NY.

AMES, FRANCIS.
(Mrs. Linwood P. Ames). Painter. Born Massina, NY, 1868. Pupil of Chase, New York, also studied in Paris. Specialty: portraiture. Address in 1926, "The Twinpike," Fort Plain, New York.

AMES, JOSEPH ALEXANDER.
Portrait painter. Born 1816 in Roxbury, MA. Elected an Associate of National Academy of Design in 1869 and Academician, 1870; had his studio in Boston, Baltimore and later in New York. He also studied in Rome. His best known work is "The Death of Webster," which has been engraved. His portraits of Prescott, Geo. Southward, Ristori, Gazzaniga, Felton and his portrait of Brady are at the Metropolitan Museum. Died Oct 30, 1872 in New York City.

AMES, JULIUS R.
Born in 1801 in Albany, NY. He was a son of Ezra Ames, the portrait and miniature painter. Julius Ames worked in Albany, New York, and

flourished from 1834 to 1850. Died June 5, 1850 in Albany.

AMES, MAY.
Painter, teacher, lecturer, and etcher. Born in Cleveland, Ohio. Pupil Cleveland School of Art, RI School of Design, Johonnot, and abroad. Member: Women's Art Club of Cleveland; Cleveland School of Art Alumni A.; Buffalo SA; Ohioborn Women A. Address in 1926, 9315 Miles Ave., Cleveland, Ohio. Died in 1946.

AMES, SARAH FISHER CLAMPITT.
(Mrs. Ames). Sculptor. Born in Lewes, Delaware, Aug. 13, 1817, and died in Washington, DC, March 8, 1901. Studied art in Boston, and Rome, Italy. She was the wife of Joseph Ames, portrait painter. She was personally acquainted with President Lincoln and her bust of him is considered excellent. Among her other portrait busts are General Grant and Ross Winans.

AMICK, ROBERT WESLEY.
Painter and illustrator. Born in Canon City, Colo., in 1879. Pupil of Art Students' League, New York. Address in 1926, 63 Washington Square, New York. Died in 1969.

ANACREON, JOAN.
Painter. Studied: Pratt Institute, New York; Rowayton Art Center; The Wooster Community Art Center; The Wooster Commuinty Art Center. Exhibitions: Women in the Arts Show, Community Church Gallery, New York City; The Stamford Museum; Women's Interarts Co-op. Collections: Van Summer and Weigold, New York City; Hamilton Press, Danbury, Connecticut; Connecticut Savings Bank, New Haven, Connecticut.

ANCORA, PIETRO.
Italian painter and drawing-master. Had an art school and gave instructions in drawing in Philadelphia early in 1800; he taught John Neagle.

ANDERSEN, ROY H.
Illustrator. Born in Chicago, in 1930. He studied at the Academy of Fine Arts and the ACD. Associated with Jack O'Grady's Studio for a

number of years, he came to New York in 1976. His illustrations have appeared in National Geographic, Boy's Life, Sports Illustrated and Ladies' Home Journal. He is a member of the S of I, and his work has been selected for its Annual Exhibitions; it has also been exhibited at the ADCs of Tucson and Washington and is part of the permanent collection of the LC.

ANDERSON, ABRAHAM ARCHIBALD.
Artist. Born in New Jersey, 1847. Studied painting under Cabanel, Bonnat, Carmon, Godin and Collin. Exhibited Paris Salon, Universal Expn., Paris, 1899, etc. Work: portraits of Gen. O. O. Howard, Gov. Morgan, H. B. Claflin, Thomas A. Edison, Bishop Cleveland Coxe, Elihu Root, Charles Stewart Smith, John Wanamaker, etc., also "Morning after the Ball," "The Convalescent," "Neither Do I Condemn Thee," etc. Address in 1926, 80 West 40th Street, New York.

ANDERSON, ALEXANDER.
Born in New York City, Jan. 21, 1775; died in Jersey City, NJ, April 18, 1870. Anderson early became interested in copperplate engraving and was self-taught; but, yielding to the wishes of his family, he studied medicine, and in 1796 was graduated from the Medical Department of Columbia College as an MD. He was again engraving on copper in New York in 1797, and the next year he permanently abandoned medicine for the burin. He engraved a number of copperplates and attained very considerable proficiency in that branch of his art. In 1820 Dr. Anderson became interested in the wood-engravings of Bewick and his followers, and he so much improved upon the work of his predecessors in this country that he is generally recognized as the Father of Wood-Engraving in the United States. His use of the "white line" in wood-engraving was successful and effective. He made many pencil and wash drawings and painted portraits. The New York Historical Society has a small portrait painted by him in 1820.

See "Life and Works of Alexander Anderson" by Frederick M. Burr, and a "Memorial of Alexander Anderson," by Benjamin J. Lossing.

ANDERSON, CARL (THOMAS)
Painter, illustrator and etcher. Born Madison, Feb. 14, 1865. Pupil at Penn. Museum and Sch. of Ind. Art. Member: Am. Artists P. L. Work: Illustrations in "Life," "Judge," "Saturday Evening Post," "Colliers Weekly," "The American Kennel Gazette"; author "Dusty, the Story of a Dog and his Adopted Boy"; animated cartoons for the screen. Address in 1929, 834 Prospect Pl., Madison, Wis. Died in 1948.

ANDERSON, DOROTHY V.
Painter. Born in Oslo, Norway. Pupil of AIC; W. M. Chase. Member: AIC Alumni; Chicago AG; Chicago AC; S. Indp. A.; San Diego FAS. Awards: Fine Arts Building Prize, Chicago AG, 1918; first, second and third prizes, Illinois Artists, Springfield. Represented in Vanderpoel Memorial Collection, G. W. Tilton School, Chicago; Elks Club, Los Angeles, Women's Club, Hollywood, Calif. Address in 1926, 3130 Palmer Square, Chicago, Ill.

ANDERSON, ELLEN G.
Painter and illustrator. Born in Lexington, VA. Pupil of Charles Guerin; studied also in Paris. Address in 1926, 39 Charles Street, New York.

ANDERSON, ELMER G.
Painter. Exhibited a "Landscape," at the Penna. Academy of Fine Arts, Philadelphia, 1920. Address in 1926, 2545 North Chadwick Street, Philadelphia.

ANDERSON, F. W.
Painter, sculptor, and craftsman. Born Sweden, Aug. 28, 1896. Member: Brooklyn PS; Brooklyn SA; Scandinavian Am. A. Address in 1929, 169 Seventh Ave., Brooklyn, NY.

ANDERSON, FREDERIC A.
Illustrator. Exhibited at the Penna. Academy of Fine Arts, 1922. Address in 1926, 1520 Chestnut Street, Philadelphia.

ANDERSON, G. ADOLPH.
Painter. Born Rochester, Minn., May 21, 1877. Pupil of Robert Henri, Julian Academy. Member of National Arts Club, New York; Wash. AC; AFA. Address in 1926, 522 Franklin Ave., Ridgewood, New Jersey.

ANDERSON, GENEVIEVE DILLAYE.
Painter. Born in Avon, New York in 1900. Studied: Skidmore College; Columbia University; Hillyer College; University of Guadalajara, Mexico; University of Hawaii; Alfred University, New York. Award: Connecticut Watercolor Society, 1944.

ANDERSON, GEORGE M.
Painter. His water color at Pas Christian was loaned to the Cincinnati Museum by Mrs. Larz Anderson for their 33d Annual Exhibition, 1925.

ANDERSON, HEATH.
Painter and illustrator. She was born San Francisco, Jan. 1, 1903. Pupil of Calif. Sch. of Arts and Crafts; Geneve Rixford Sargeant. Member: All Arts C., Berkeley; Calif. S. Women A. Awards: Hon. mention, State Exhibition, Santa Cruz, 1928; 1st prize, Nat'l. American Humane Assoc., 1928.

ANDERSON, HELGE.
Painter. Exhibited at Penna. Academy of the Fine Arts, Philadelphia, 1921. Address in 1926, 152 Huntingdon Ave., Boston, Mass.

ANDERSON, HENDRIK CHRISTIAN.
Sculptor. Born Bergen, Norway, 1872. Brought to United States in infancy, settling at Newport, RI, 1873; studied art and architecture at Boston, Paris, Naples, Rome. Prin. works: "Fountain of Life," "Fountain of Immortality," "Jacob Wrestling with the Angel," "Study of an Athlete," etc.

ANDERSON, HUGH.
Engraver. Born 1790 in Scotland. Listed in the Philadelphia Directory from 1811 to 1824. He engraved a number of plates for S. F. Bradford's Philadelphia edition of the Edinburgh Encyclopedia. He also engraved portraits and book illustrations. Died in 1830.

ANDERSON, KARL.
Painter. Born in Oxford, Ohio, Jan. 13, 1874. Student of Chicago Art Institute and Colarossi Academy in Paris. Painted in Holland, Italy and Madrid. Elected Member of National Academy of Design. Also illustrated for many publications. Among his works, "The Idlers," "Sisters," "Apple Gatherers," and "The Heirloom." Address in 1926, Westport Conn. Died in 1956.

ANDERSON, LYMAN MATTHEW.
Illustrator. Born in Chicago in 1907. He was educated at the AIC, GCSA and in private classes under Walter Biggs, Pruett Carter and Harvey Dunn. Acceptance in the 1939 Art Directors Club Annual started his career. He did a great many dry brush illustrations for the pulps until 1935 when he produced a syndicated strip for three years. Though his work appeared in major publications, he was most active in the field of advertising art until 1963 when he became an instructor for the FAS. He is a Life Member of both the S of I and Joint Ethics Committee.

ANDERSON, MARTINUS.
Painter and illustrator. Born in Peru, Ind., 1878. Pupil of Herron Art Institute, Indianapolis. He also did mural decorations in City Hospital, Indianapolis. Address in 1926, 135 West 44th Street, New York.

ANDERSON, OSCAR.
Painter. Born in Sweden in 1873. Pupil of Charles N. Flagg, Hartford. Address in 1926, 78 Rocky Neck Avenue, Gloucester, Mass.

ANDERSON, PERCY E.
Illustrator. Member: Salma. C. Address in 1929, Westport, Conn.; 58 East 56th St., New York, NY.

ANDERSON, PETER BERNARD.
Sculptor. Born in Sweden in 1898. Pupil of J. K. Daniels. Address in 1926, 959 Lombard Street, St. Paul, Minn.

ANDERSON, RAYMOND H.
Painter. Born at Bradford, Penna.,
in 1884. Pupil of Stevenson Art
School. Address in 1926, R. D. No.
1, Saltsburg Road, Verona, Penna.

ANDERSON, RONALD.
Painter and illustrator. Born at
Lynn, Mass., in 1886. Student at
Chicago Art Inst. Pupil of Eric
Pape. Address in 1926, 54 West
37th Street, New York.

ANDERSON, RUTH A.
(Mrs. Sam'l Temple). Painter.
Born in Carlisle, Penna. Pupil of
Penna. Academy of Fine Arts.
Member of National Association of
Women Painters and Sculptors, and
the Fellowship of the Penna.
Academy of Fine Arts. Address in
1926, 53 Charles Street, Boston,
Mass.

ANDERSON, RUTH BERNICE.
Painter. Born in Indianapolis,
Indiana in 1914. Studied: John
Herron Art Institute. Awards:
Allied State Exhibition, Tucson,
Arizona, 1937; L. S. Ayers and
Company award, 1954; Edward
Gallahue prize, 1955. Work: Daily
Memorial Collection, Indiana
University; DePauw University.

ANDERSON, TENNESSEE M(ITCHELL).
Sculptor. Born Jackson, Mich.
Member: AC of Chicago; Chicago
NJSA; Romany C. Address in 1929,
153 East Erie St., Chicago, Ill.

ANDERSON, WILLIAM.
Born c. 1834 in IN. About 1855
this excellent engraver of
portraits and landscapes was
working for the engraving firm of
C. A. Jewett & Co. of Cincinnati,
Ohio. Much of his work will be
found in the Ladies' Repository,
published in that city.

ANDERTON, G.
Engraver. Born in London about
1826, he was engraving in the
United States as early as 1850. He
was in the employ of J. M. Butler
of Philadelphia and was a good
engraver of portraits in both the
stipple and mezzotint manner. Died
c. 1890.

ANDRADE, MARY FRATZ.
Painter, illustrator and teacher.

Born Philadelphia. Pupil of Robert
Vonnoh, Henry Thouron, Thomas
Anshutz and Mucha in Paris.
Member: Fellowship PAFA; Phila.
Alliance; Art Teachers A. of Phila.
Address in 1929, Studioshop, Old
York Road; h. 503 West Ave.,
Jenkintown, PA.

ANDREW, JOHN.
Wood engraver. Born 1815 in Hull,
England. Working for publishers in
New York and Boston from 1850.
Died in Boston in 1870.

ANDREW, RICHARD.
Portrait painter. Born in Ireland.
Exhibited at the Penna. Academy of
Fine Arts, Philadelphia, 1921.
Pupil of Laurens and Gerome in
Paris. Mural painting in State
House, Boston. Address in 1926,
Fenway Studios, Boston, Mass.

ANDREWS, AMBROSE.
Portrait painter in oils and
miniature. Flourished 1824-59.
From 1829 to 1831 he was in Troy,
New York. He later moved to St.
Louis and then to New York. He
painted a portrait of Gen'l Sam.
Houston.

ANDREWS, ELIPHALET F.
Painter. Born at Steubenville,
Ohio, June 11, 1835. Portrait and
general painter; studied in Paris
under Bonnat. Director of Corcoran
Art School for twenty-five years.
He painted several portraits
hanging in the White House,
including those of Martha
Washington, Dolly Madison,
Jefferson and others. He died in
Washington, DC, March 1915.

ANDREWS, HELEN FRANCIS.
Painter. Born in Farmington,
Conn., in 1872. Pupil of Art
Students' League, New York.
Student of Laurens and Constant in
Paris. Address in 1926, Westover
School, Middlebury, Conn.

ANDREWS, J. W.
Painter. Born in Newtonville,
Mass., in 1879. Pupil of DuMond,
Hamilton, and DeCamp. Address in
1926, Yonkers, New York.

ANDREWS, JOSEPH.
Engraver. Born in Hingham, Mass.

22

1806, he was apprenticed to Abel Bowen, a wood engraver of Boston, and learned copper plate engraving from Hoogland. In 1835 he went to London and studied under Goodyear, and in Paris he engraved the head of Franklin by Duplessis. Returning to the United States he engraved many fine portraits and did considerable work for the book publishers. His portrait of Washington after Stuart is one of his best plates; he also engraved "Plymouth Rock in 1620." He died in 1873. For a life of this engraver and a list of his work see Pennsylvania Magazine for 1908, "Joseph Andrews and His Engravings," by Mantle Fielding.

ANDREWS, MRS. M. MINNIGERODE.
Painter and illustrator. Born in Richmond, VA, 1869. Pupil of Andrews and Chase. Represented by portraits owned by University of Virginia. Address in 1926, 1232 Sixteenth Street, Washington, DC.

ANGAROLA, ANTHONY.
Painter. Born in Chicago, 1893. Pupil of Minneapolis School of Art. He exhibited paintings at Academy of Fine Arts, Philadelphia, 1921, and Carnegie Institute, Pittsburgh, PA. Address in 1926, 1318 Rosedale Avenue, Chicago, Ill.

ANGELA, EMILIO.
Sculptor. Born in Italy, 1889. Studied at Cooper Union, Art Students' League, National Academy of Design, and was pupil of A. A. Weinman. Membership, National Sculpture Society, American Federation of Fine Arts. Works: "Goose Boy," "Barking Seals," "Boxer," "Goose Girl," "Baby Angela." Address in 1926, 558 Broome Street, New York City.

ANGULO, CHAPPIE.
Painter and illustrator. Born March 3, 1928. US citizen. Study: Los Angeles City Col.; U. of Calif., Los Angeles; Kahn Art School; Esmeralda, Inst. Nac. Bellas Artes, Mex. City; London Art Center. Work: Mus. Cultures, Mex. City; Art Mus., Chilpantzingo Guerrero, Mex. Comn.: Nat. Mus. of Anthropology, Moneda, Mex., 1957,

1958; Ballet Nacional, Mexico, 1959. One-man shows: Olympic Cult. Prog., 1969; Mus. Fronterizo, Juarez, Mex., 1971; La Ciudadela, Monterrey, 1974; Gentes y Lugares Mus. de las Cult., Mex; retrospective, Museo Las Culturas, Mex., 1976; others. Exhib.: La Mujer en la Plastica Bellas Artes, Mex., Anglo Mexicano, 1981. Mem.: La Muerte-Unam. Illustrations: "Teotihuacan-un autoretrato cultural," 1964; "Relieves de Chalcatzingo;" "The Cuauhnahuac Museum-A Hist. Recompilation;" "A Guide to Chalcatzingo;" "Arqueology Zunes;" and others. Media: Fiber, paper; acrylic, oil. Address in 1982, Cuernavaca, Morelos, Mex.

ANKENEY, JOHN SITES.
Painter. Born at Xenia, Ohio, in 1870. Pupil of Twachtman, Chase and Saint Gaudens; also studied in Paris. Address in 1926, 906 Conley Ave., Columbia, MO. Died in 1946.

ANNABLE, GEORGE O.
Sculptor. Born about 1829. He had a studio in the Hoppin Building in Providence, and in 1850 cut a cameo portrait of Dr. Nathan B. Crocker, the rector of St. John's Church. The following account from the Providence Journal of January 18, 1851, gives us an idea of Annable's work and ambition: "With respect to the medallion heads and cameos by Mr. George O. Annable, of Providence, the committee heartily concur in the general expression of opinion. They are excellent; and considering the youth of the artist and the short time which has passed since his first work was produced-remarkably so." In 1852 cameos were exhibited by Annable and were described as "capital likenesses and finely executed." He received a silver medal, the highest premium for portrait busts in marble and cameos. Besides the portraits of Dr. Chapin, Mr. Chapin, and Dr. Crocker, Annable cut a cameo likeness of James S. Lincoln, the portrait painter, who in exchange painted Annable's portrait. This cameo portrait of Lincoln was in the possession of Mrs. Joseph T. A. Eddy of Hingham. Annable's cameo portraits were cut in shell and were usually about an

inch and a half tall. Died April 22, 1887 in Brooklyn, NY.

ANNAN, ABEL H.
Painter. Member of Washington (DC) Watercolor Club. Address in 1926, Carnegie Studios, West 57th Street, New York.

ANNAN, ALICE H.
Painter. Born in New York. Member of Art Students' League, pupil of Snell, and Ben Foster. Address in 1926, Carnegie Studios, West 57th Street, New York City.

ANNELLI, FRANCESCO.
He painted historic compositions, portraits and miniatures. Very little of his work is known. He flourished in New York from 1841 to 1878.

ANNIN, WILLIAM B.
This engraver was a pupil of Abel Bowen of Boston; he was working for him in 1813. As early as 1823 he was associated with George Girdler Smith. The firm of Annin & Smith did a general engraving business and were for some time also engaged in lithography in Boston.

ANSBACHER, JESSIE.
Painter. Portrait of Miss Tait. Exhibited at Penna. Academy of Fine Arts, Philadelphia, 1921. Pupil of William Chase, Joseph Pennell and Auerbach-Levy. Address in 1926, 1 West 81st Street, New York City. Died in 1964.

ANSHUTZ, THOMAS POLLOCK.
Painter and teacher. Born Newport, Kentucky, October 5, 1851; died, Fort Washington, Pennsylvania, June 16, 1912. Pupil of National Academy of Design, PAFA and of Doucet and Bouguereau, Paris. Awards: Gold Medal of Honor, PAFA 1909. Lippincott Prize, PAFA, 1909. Member of Fellowship, and also of Faculty, of PAFA; Philadelphia WCC; New York WCC. Elected an Associate Member, NAD, 1910. Represented in collection of PAFA.

ANTHONY, ANDREW VARICK STOUT.
Artist. He was born Dec. 4, 1835 in New York City, and studied drawing and engraving under the best teachers. Anthony was an original member of the American Water Color Society. His illustrations for the works of Whittier, Longfellow and Hawthorne are of considerable merit. He passed part of his professional life in New York and California, but settled in Boston in 1878. He died July 2, 1906 in West Newton, MA.

ANTHONY, CAROL.
Illustrator. Born in New York, 1943. Educated at Stephens College, Missouri, and graduated from RISD. An exhibition of her three-dimensional figures at the Museum of Contemporary Crafts was the beginning of a successful career leading to assignments for Redbook, Vintage Books and The New York Times. Her intriguing characters often develop from a prop as simple as a pair of old shoes. Her work is part of the Hirshhorn collection in Washington and the Museum of New Orleans. A member of the S of I, she works out of her home in Greenwich, Connecticut.

APEL, BARBARA JEAN.
Printmaker and educator. Born in Falls City, Nebraska June 16, 1935. Studied: Kansas City Art Institute, Missouri; University of Illinois, Urbana. Awards: Lincoln College, Illinois, 1966; Springfield Art League Annual, Massachusetts, 1968; Boston Printmakers, 1974. Collections: Worcester Fine Arts Museum; The University of Wisconsin; The University of Illinois. Exhibitions: Surreal Images, De Cordova Mus., Lincoln, MA, '68; Boston Vis. Artists' Group Show, NY, 76 and many others. Address in 1980, 235 Rawson Road, Brookline, MA.

APEL, CHARLES P.
Painter. Born in Brooklyn, New York, in 1857. Pupil of Chase and Mora. Address in 1926, 57 Eby Place, East Orange, New Jersey.

APEL, MARIE.
Sculptor. Born in England, 1888. Member of National Association of Women Painters and Sculptors.

24

Work: Langdon Memorial Augusta, Ga., and Hodges Memorial, St. Paul's, Baltimore, MD. Address in 1926, 3 Washington Square, New York.

APPEL, KAREL.
Painter and sculptor. Born in Amsterdam, Holland, April 25, 1921. Study: Royal Academy of Fine Arts, Amsterdam, 1940-43. Work: Tate Gallery, London; MOMA, NYC; Stedelijk Mus., Amsterdam; Mus. of Fine Arts, Boston. Comn.: Numerous in Amsterdam, Rotterdam, The Hague, Holland. Exhib.: Studio Fachetti, Paris, 1954; Stedelijk Mus., Amsterdam, 1962; Guggenheim Foundation Works, NYC, 1969; Kunsthalle, Basel, Switz., 1969; Canadian museums, 1972-73; retrospectives in Mexico City, Caracas, Venez., Bogota, Colombia, Germany and Holland. Awards: UNESCO Prize, Int. Biennale, Venice, 1954; Int'l. Ptg. Prize, 5th Sao Paulo Biennale, 1959; 1st Prize, Ptg., Guggenheim Int'l. Exhib., NYC, 1960. Media: Acrylic; aluminum and wood. Address in 1982, c/o Martha Jackson Gallery, NYC.

APPEL, MARINNE.
Painter. Born in New York in 1913. Studied: Woodstock School of Painting. Awards: Keith Memorial, Woodstock Art Association, 1938; Carville, Louisiana, 1940; Dutchess County Fair, 1935. Collections: Metropolitan Museum of Art; Marine Hospital, Carville, Louisiana; United States Post Office, Middleporte, New York and Wrangell, Alaska.

APPLEGATE, FRANK G.
Sculptor. Born in Atlanta, Ill., in 1882. Studied under Frederick and Grafly and in Paris under Verlet. Exhibited water colors at Penna. Academy of Fine Arts, Philadelphia, 1925. Address in 1926, Santa Fe, New Mexico.

APPLETON, ELIZA B.
(Mrs. Everard Appleton). Sculptor. Born in 1882. Studied with M. Ezekiel in Rome. Address in 1926, 42 Pleasant Street, Rumford, RI.

APPLETON, THOMAS G.
Art patron and painter. Born in

Boston, March 31, 1812. He studied in America and England. He exhibited many paintings on his return from Egypt in Boston that attracted much attention. He was deeply interested in the Boston Museum of Fine Arts. Died April 17, 1884 in New York City.

ARAKAWA, (SHUSAKU).
Painter. Born July 6, 1936, in Tokyo, Japan. In New York City since 1959. Work: In private collections; MOMA, NYC; Basel Mus., Switz.; Japan Nat'l. Mus., Tokyo; others. Exhib.: Museum of Mod. Art; Nat. Mus., Tokyo, 1958; Schmela Gallery in Dusseldorf; Kennedy Center for Perf. Arts, Wash., DC; Met. Mus. of Art, 1974; U. of Wisconsin; Toronto; many other international exhibits. Awards: DAAD Fellowship, West Berlin. Address in 1982, 124 W. Houston St., NYC.

ARBEIT, ARNOLD A.
Painter. Born in New York City, Oct. 1, 1916. Work: Columbus Museum, Columbus, GA; numerous private collections. Comn.: Ptg., Lobby, 20 Vesey St. Bldg., New York City, 1960. Exhibitions: Cooper Union Art School, NY, 1966-67; Isaac Delgado Museum, New Orleans; Esperanto Gallery, NYC, 1967; Scarsdale Gallery, many years. Awards: Beaux Arts Inst. of Design F. B. Morse Medal for Des.; Cert. of Honor for Des. NYSA; Armstrong Memorial Medal. Mem.: Am. Inst. Architects; Mil. Gov't. Assn. Monuments, Fine Arts and Archives; etc. Teaching: Cooper Union, architecture, 1947-64; City College, NY, architecture, 1964-68. Media: Oil, watercolor. Address in 1976, Scarsdale Gallery.

ARCHAMBAULT, ANNA MARGARETTA.
Portrait and miniature painter. Born in Philadelphia. Pupil of PAFA, and Julian Academy. Painted miniature of Warren G. Harding, at White House, Washington. Also Mrs. Jasper O. Nicolls, Master William Jasper Nicolls, and Mrs. William I. Moseley. Member: PA S. Min. P.; Fellowship PAFA; Plastic C.; Phila. Alliance; Fairmount Park AA.

Address in 1926, 1714 Chestnut Street, Philadelphia.

ARCHER, DOROTHY BRYANT.
Painter and teacher. Born in Hampton, Virginia, April 18, 1919. Study: Richmond Prof. Inst.; Kansas City Art Inst., with Wilbur Niewald; Honolulu Acad. of Art, with John Young. Exhibitions: Honolulu Academy of Arts, Hawaii, 1962; Laguna Gloria Museum, Austin, Texas, 1965; Inst. Relaciones Culturales, Chihuahua, Mex., 1969; El Paso Museum of Art, El Paso, Texas, 1971, 73, 74. Awards: El Paso Art Assn., 1970; El Paso Mus. Art award, 1973. Teaching: Staff Instructor, El Paso Museum of Art; national acrylic workshop. Media: Acrylic, oil. Address in 1980, 8717 Marble Drive, El Paso, Texas.

ARCHER, JAMES.
Engraver. He did the majority of the large plates illustrating "Hinton's History of the United States" published in Boston in 1834.

ARCHIPENKO, ALEXANDER.
Painter, sculptor, illustrator, etcher, artist, craftsman, and teacher. Born Kiev, Ukraine, May 30, 1887. Studied at Ecole des Beaux-Arts, Kiev, 1902-1905. Exhib. in Moscow, 1906; at Salons in Paris, where he arrived in 1908; and in major cities in Europe and US until his death. Travelled to Berlin, 1920-23; came to US in 1924. Founded Ecole d'Art in NY, 1924; also taught at ASL. Invented "animated painting," known as "Archipentura;" figured significanty in Cubist movement in his early years. In collections of Guggenheim, NYC; Mus. of Mod. Art, Paris; and others. Died Feb. 25, 1964. Address in 1929, 16 West 61st St.; h. 44 West 57th St., New York, NY; summer, Woodstock, NY.

ARENSBACH, HARAL.
Artist. Exhibited water color paintings at the Academy of Fine Arts, 1921-25. Address in 1926, 121 North 21st Street, Philadelphia, PA.

ARMBRUSTER, A. E.
Scenic Painter. Member of League

of Columbus Artists. Address in 1926, 3102 North High Street, Columbus, Ohio.

ARMFIELD, MAXWELL.
Painter and illustrator. Born in England. Studied abroad. He did mural painting, and illustrated for Century and other magazines. Address in 1926, 104 West 40th Street, New York City.

ARMINGTON, CAROLINE H(ELENA).
Painter and etcher. Born Brampton, Ontario, Canada, Sept. 11, 1875. Pupil of Julian Academy in Paris, Member: AFA; Chicago SE; Societe Nationale des Beaux Arts; Societe de la Gravure Originale en Noir; Societe des Gravures Francais. Work: "St. Pol-de-Lyon," painting purchased by French Government. Etchings in the New York Public Library; the Library of Congress, Washington; Luxembourg and Petit Palais, Paris; British Museum and South Kensington Museum, London; National Gallery, Ottawa, and Art Gallery, Toronto, Canada; Cleveland Museum; Syracuse Museum, Dayton Art Institute; Bibliographie de Belgique, Brussels. Address in 1929, 70 Blvd. du Montparnasse (XIVeme), Paris, France. Died in 1939.

ARMINGTON, FRANK M(ILTON).
Painter and etcher. Born Frodwich, Ontario, Canada, July 28, 1876. Pupil of Jean Paul Laurens and Henri Royer at Julian Academy in Paris. Member: Societe Nationale de la Gravure Originale en Noir. Work: "Portrait of Yetta Rianza," "La Vallee a Bizy" and "Pont Louis Philippe, Paris," Luxembourg Gallery, Paris; "La Rue Royale, Pluie." Address in 1929, 70 Blvd du Montparnasse, (XIVeme), Paris, France. Died in 1941.

ARMS, ANNELI.
Born New York City, 1935. Study: BA, Painting and Sculpture, U. of Mich., 1958; scholarship, ASL NY, Morris Kantor, 1956-58. Exhibitions: Solo: Camino Gallery, NYC, 1962; Studio, Greene St., 1968; Benson Gal., Bridgehampton, NY, 1971; Phoenix Gal., NYC, 1978, 81, 83; Westtown Art Center, PA,

1978; Edw. Wms. College, Fairleigh-Dickinson U., 1981; Hudson Highlands Mus., Cornwall, NY, 1983. 3-Person: Avant-Garde Gal., NYC, 1959; Camino Gal., NYC, 1960; Phoenix Gal., NYC, 1977. Other: Detroit Inst. of Art, 1955; Riverside Mus., NYC, 1959, 60; U. of Mich., Rackham & Slusser Galleries, 1955-56, 59, 75; Miami Mus. of Mod. Art, 1960; 2nd Int'l Pan-Pac., Tokyo, 1961-62; Benson Gal., Bridgehampton, NY, 1974, 77, 82-83; Heckscher Mus., Huntington, NY, 1975; Guild Hall, East Hampton, NY, 1977-80; Landmark Gal., NYC, 1977-78; OIA Constructs Exhib., NYC, 1978; Ingber Gal., NYC, 1978-79, 1983; Sculpturesites, Amagansett, NY, 1981-82; Thorpe Intermedia Gal., Sparkill, NY, 1981-82. Reviewed in Art News, 1960, 62, 68; Arts, 1978, 81; NY Times, 1959, 78, 81, 82. Media: Oil; polyurethane, wire and acrylic sculpture; monoprint etching. Address in 1983, 113 Greene St., New York City.

ARMS, JOHN TAYLOR.
Etcher. Born in Washington, DC, in 1887. Trained as an architect, in 1919 he devoted himself to the graphic arts. His aquatints were most successful. Pupil of Ross Turner, D. A. Gregg, Felton Brown and Despradelles. Member: Calif. PM; Royal Soc. Canadian Painter-Etchers; Salma. C.; Chicago SE; Brooklyn SE; Print S. of England; Wash. WCC; North Shore AA; AA of Newport; Springfield AA; Boston AC; S. Indp. A; AFA; Associe de la Societe des Beaux Arts (France); Baltimore WCC; Cleveland Print C.; Century A. Work in Congressional Library; Brooklyn Museum; U. S. National Museum; Peabody Museum, Salem; British Museum; Toronto Art Gallery; Cleveland Museum; Delgado Museum, New Orleans; Bibliotheque Nationale, Paris; Musee de Rouen (France). Address in 1929, Greenfield Hill, Fairfield, Conn. Died in 1953.

ARMSTRONG, ARTHUR.
Portrait, landscape and historic painter. Born 1798 in Manor Township, Lancaster County. In 1820 he opened a studio in Marietta, Lancaster County, and there began his career as artist and teacher. In 1849 he opened a studio and gallery for exhibition of paintings in Mechanics' Institute, Lancaster, and later had a large studio on Orange Street, Lancaster, built by himself and with the second story fitted up as a gallery to exhibit paintings. He painted there some very large canvasses, "Hamlet and Ophelia" and the "Assassination of Caesar." At some time in his career he resorted to "pot-boilers," painting signs and banners, and made and gilded frames. One silk banner which was painted for the Washington Fire Company of Louisville, Kentucky, represented the Washington Family under the portico of their mansion at Mount Vernon, with the Potomac dotted with sails seen in the background. He was a prolific painter, and while many of his works are in the vicinity of Lancaster, others are widely scattered. Died June 18, 1851.

ARMSTRONG, BARBARA.
Painter. Born in Bellaire, Ohio, 1896. Pupil of Hamilton E. Field. Address in 1926, Ogunquit, Maine.

ARMSTRONG, DAVID MAITLAND.
Painter. Born April 15, 1836 in Danskammer, NY. Graduate of Trinity College. He was an early member of the American Artists Society, founded in 1877, and was elected an Associate Member in 1906 of the National Academy of Design. He died in 1918.

ARMSTRONG, ESTELLE MANON.
Painter. Member of National Association of Women Painters and Sculptors and exhibited at 33d Annual (1924). Address in 1926, 603 Bloomfield Avenue, Nutley, NJ.

ARMSTRONG, HELEN MAITLAND.
Mural painter and designer. Born in Florence, Italy, 1869. Student of Art Students' League, New York. Address in 1926, Maitland Armstrong Co., 58 West 10th Street, New York.

ARMSTRONG, SAMUEL JOHN.
Painter and illustrator. Born Denver, Colorado, 1893. Address in

27

1926, Steilacoorn Lake, Pierce Co., Washington.

ARMSTRONG, VOYLE N.
Painter and illustrator. Born in Dobbin, West Virginia, Nov. 26, 1891. Pupil of Duveneck at Cincinnati Art Academy. Member: Cincinnati AC; SSAL. Address in 1926, 717 North 1st Street, Bedford, Ind.

ARMSTRONG, WILLIAM G.
Engraver, portrait painter in water color, and portrait draughtsman. Born 1823, Montgomery Co., PA. Lived in Philadelphia. Armstrong was a pupil of Longacre in Philadelphia, drew small portraits and finally became a line engraver. He engraved several portraits for Longacre's "National Portrait Gallery." He also devoted a large part of his professional life to bank-note engravings. Died in 1890.

ARMSTRONG, WILLIAM T. L.
Painter and artist. Born Belfast, Ireland, Sept. 10, 1881. Member: AIA; NY Arch. Lg.; Society of Beaux-Arts Architects; AWCS; NYWCC. Work: Milwaukee (Wis.) County General Hospital; Nurley (NJ) Public Library; Grace Episcopal Church, Nutley, NJ; Brooklyn Presbyterian Church. Associate in Design, School of Architecture, Columbia University; instructor, architecture, NY University. Address in 1929, 122 East 25th St., New York, NY; h. 603 Bloomfield Ave., Nutley, NJ. Died 1934.

ARNO, PETER.
Illustrator. Born in New York City, 1904. He was a student at Yale University from 1922 to 1924, but had no formal art training at the time. 1925 marked the beginning of his long-standing relationship with The New Yorker, where his cartoons and covers appeared with great frequency. The consummate New Yorker, he brought his style and wit to his books of cartoons: Dearie, Peter Arno's Parade and Peter Arno's Circus. Died in 1968.

ARNOLD, CLARA MAXFIELD.
Painter. Born East Providence, RI,

1879. Member of Providence Art Club. Specialty flower and fruit paintings. Address in 1926, 22 Highland Avenue, East Providence, RI.

ARNOLD, HARRY.
Painter. Born in England. Member of the Society of Independent Artists. Address in 1926, 208 Gillette Avenue, Waukeegan, Ill.

ARNOLD, JOHN K.
Portrait painter. Born in 1834; died in 1909. He painted the portraits of many prominent men of the state of Rhode Island.

ARONSON, DAVID.
Sculptor and painter. Born in Shilova, Lithuania, Oct. 28, 1923. US citizen. Study: Sch. of Mus. of Fine Arts, Boston, with Karl Zerbe, 1945; Nat'l. Soc. of Arts and Letters Grant, 1958; Guggenheim Fellow, 1960. Work: Atlanta Univ.; Mus. of Fine Arts, Boston; Bryn Mawr; Art Inst. of Chicago; Whitney Mus.; Met. Mus. of Art; Smithsonian Inst. Exhib.: Met. Mus of Art, MOMA, Whitney, NYC; Zappeion, Athens; Musee d'Arte Moderne, Paris; 1964 Worlds Fair, and others. Awards: Boston Inst. of Contemp. Art, 1944; Boston Arts Festival, 1952-54; NAD, 1973-75. Teaching, Boston Mus. of Fine Arts School, 1943-54; Boston Univ., 1954-63. Media: Bronze. Address in 1982, Sudbury, MA.

ARONSON, SANDA.
Born NYC, Feb. 29, 1940. Study: SUNY Oswego, BS, 1960; with Jose DeCreeft, Paul Pollaro, New School for Soc. Research, NYC; Tulane U., New Orleans; ASL NY. Exhibitions: Women Self Image, Women's Interart Center, NYC, 1974; Women Showing/Women Sharing, US Mil. Acad., West Point, NY, 1975; Works on Paper, Brooklyn Mus., NY, 1975; Exhib. for Women Artists, Manhattan Comm. College for Performing Arts, 1975; travelling show, Fairleigh Dickinson U., Chatham Col., SUNY Binghamton, 1976; Four Artists, Women in the Arts Foundation, NYC, 1976; Nine/Plus or Minus, US Mil. Acad., 1977, and Arsenal Gal. of NYC, 1978; NY/Artists Equity Assn.,

NYC, 1980; Artists in Res. Gal., NYC, invit. show, 1981. Awards: Hon. mention, Sculpture, Women Showing/Women Sharing, US Mil. Acad., West Point, NY, 1975. Member: Women in the Arts Found., Bd. Mem.-at-large, NYC, 1975-76; NY Artists Equity Assn. Commission: Handprinted editions, woodcuts by Clem Haupers, 1982. Publ.: Frontispiece, Hear the Wind Blow, John Beecher, Int'l. Publishers, NYC, 1968, woodcut. Teaching: Artist-in-Residence, NY Found. for the Arts, 1977-79. Media: Clay, pen & ink drawing, woodcut. Address in 1983, 70 West 95th St., NYC.

ARP, HILDA.
Work: Norfolk Museum, Norfolk, VA; Wagner College, NY; collections in the US and Europe. Exhibitions: Brooklyn Museum; Norfolk Museum; Musee de Cognac, France; Int. Exh., Cannes, France. Art Positions: Dir. of the Colorama Gal., NY; NY World's Fair 1965. Address in 1970, 4516-7th Avenue, Brooklyn, NY.

ARPA, JOSE.
Painter. Born in Spain, 1868. Exhibited water color painting at the Penna. Academy of the Fine Arts, Philadelphia, 1925. Address in 1926, 418 Oakland Street, San Antonio, Texas.

ARTER, CHARLES J.
Painter. He died in Alliance, Ohio, in 1923. He had his studios in Venice, London and New York. He painted many people of distinction and was decorated by the King and Queen of Italy for portraits he had made of them.

ARTHUR, ROBERT.
Painter. Born in Philadelphia, 1850, he died in New York, 1914. His early work was mainly decorative, and his later work was largely marine painting. He was a close friend of Robert Louis Stevenson; his studio was at Ogunquit, Maine.

ARTHURS, STANLEY MASSEY.
Mural painter. Born in Kenton, Del., 1877. Pupil of Howard Pyle. Among his works, "Landing of

DeVries," at Delaware College, Newark, Delaware, "The Crusaders" at the State Capitol, Dover, Delaware. Address in 1926, 1305 Franklin Street, Wilmington, Delaware.

ARTIS, WILLIAM ELLISWORTH.
Ceramist and teacher. Born Washington, NC, Feb. 2, 1914. Study: Alfred Univ.; Syracuse Univ.; Chadron State College; Penn. State Univ. Work: Walker Art Ctr., Minneapolis; IBM; Slater Mem. Mus., Norwich, CT; Nat'l. Portrait Gallery, Wash. DC; others. Comn.: Chadron State College. Exhib.: Nat'l. Sculpture Soc.; Whitney Mus. of Am. Art; Colleges and Universities. Awards: Rosenwald Fellow, 1947; nine Purchase Awards, Atlanta Univ., 1944-65. Teaching: Prof. Art, Mankato State College, Minn. Mem.: Am. Ceramic Soc.; Nat'l. Sculpture Soc.; etc. Rep.: Gallery 500 Mankata, Minn. Died in 1977. Address in 1976, Sch. of Arts and Sci., Mankato State College, Minn.

ARTZYBASHEFF, BORIS.
Illustrator. Born in Kharkov, Russia, 1899. He received his art training at the Prince Tenisheff School in St. Petersburg. In 1919 he fled to the United States, where he worked as an engraver's apprentice while illustrating books by Balzac and Aesop. A long-standing relationship with Time magazine resulted in his production of over 200 covers. Among a number of citations awarded him was the prestigious Newberry Medal. Died 1965.

ASANGER, JACOB.
Painter and etcher. Born in Bavaria in 1887. Member of Society of Independent Artists. Address in 1926, 12 East 15th Street, New York City.

ASCHER, MARY.
Painter and printmaker. Born in Leeds, England. US citizen. Study: NY School of Applied Design for Women; Hunter College; ASL; with Will Barnet, Vaclav Vytlacl, Morris Kantor. Work: Ein Harod Museum, Israel; Nat'l Collection of Fine Arts, Smithsonian Inst., Wash.

DC; Norfolk Museum of Fine Arts; US Nat'l Museum of Sport, NYC; Butler Inst. of Am. Art, Youngstown, many public and private collections. Comn.: 12 Women of the Old Testament and Apocrypha, Wizo Bldg., Tel Aviv. Exhib.: Exch. Exhib. with Japanese Women Artists, 1960; with Argentine Artists, 1963; Silvermine Guild, New England Ann., 1967; 30 year Retro., Nat'l. Arts Club, NYC, 1973; Met. Mus. of Art, 1979; etc. Awards: Huntington Hartford Foundation Fellowship, 1960; Medal of Honor, Nat'l Painters & Sculp. Soc.; Nat'l Assn. of Women Artists; Nat'l League of Am. Penwomen, Prof. Art; Int'l. Women's Year Award, 1975-76; First prize-oil, Womanart Gallery, NYC, 1977; and others. Mem.: Royal Soc. of Arts, fellow, London; Am. Soc. of Contemp. Artists; ASL (life); Nat'l. Assn. Women Artists; Chaplain, Nat'l. Soc. Arts and Letters (Empire State); etc. Author: Twelve Women of the New Testament and Early Church, with 25 portfolios; and more. Media: Oil, watercolor, prints. Address in 1982, 116 Central Park South, New York, NY.

ASHBROOK, PAUL.
Painter. Born in New York, 1867. He exhibited in oil, water color and etching at the Cincinnati Museum, 1925. Address in 1926, No. 2 Hedgerow Lane, Cincinnati, Ohio.

ASHE, EDMUND M.
Painter, illustrator and teacher. Member: NYWCC; SI, 1901; Pittsburgh AA. Address in 1929, care of Carnegie Institute of Technology, Pittsburgh, PA; Westport, Conn.

ASHFORD, PEARL J.
Painter and illustrator. Born in Phila., PA. Study: Pratt Inst., NY; Tyler Sch. of Art, Temple Univ.; with Morris Blackburn, Phoebe Shih. Exhib.: 1st NY Int'l. Art Show, NY Coliseum, 1970; Plastic, Women's Art Club, Phila., 1971; Int'l. Art Show, Rotunda Gallery, London, 1972; Urban League Guild Ann., Phila., 1972, 74; Gallerie Paula Insel, NY, Ann. Group Show, 1976, 77. Awards: Second prize for Geraniums

(painting), Willingboro Art Alliance, 1973. Mem.: Nat'l. Forum Prof. Artists; Equity Assn. Illustrator-general, US Army Ord., Phila., 1955-60. Media: Oil, watercolor. Address in 1980, 2400 Chestnut St., Apt. 1007, Phila., PA.

ASHLEY, CLIFFORD WARREN.
Painter. Born in New Bedford, Mass., 1881. Pupil of Howard Pyle. Among his works, "The Whaling Industry," "Outfitting the Whaler." Address in 1926, 31 Eighth Street, New Bedford, Mass.

ASHLEY, WILLIAM JOHN.
Born in England in 1868. He was successful as a landscape painter. He died at Mt. Vernon, NY, October, 1921, having lived and painted for the previous ten years in this country.

ASMAR, ALICE.
Painter and printmaker. Born in Flint, Mich. Study: Lewis and Clark College; with Edward Melcarth, Archipenko, Univ. of Wash., MFA; Woolley Fellow, Ecole Nat. Superieure des Beaux-Arts, Paris, with M. Souverbie; Huntington Hartford Found. residence fellowships, 1961-64. Work: Franklin Mint, PA; Smithsonian Inst.; Public Interest Mus., Gabrova, Bulgaria; etc. Comn.: Jos. Magnin's, 1964; Security Pacific Int'l. Bank, NYC, 1970; lithographs, Artists Profusions, NYC, 1980; others in US and abroad. Exhib.: West Assn. of Art Museum Circulating Banner Exhib., 1970-72; West 79/The Law, Minn. Museum of Art, 1979-80; Portland (OR) Art Museum, 1979-80; other one-person and group shows. Awards: Menzione Onorevole, Biennale Delle Regione, 1968-69; purchase award, Seattle Art Mus.; 1st prize Southern Calif. Expos. Mem.: Am. Federation of Arts; Artists Equity; and others. Eng. draftsman, Boeing Aircraft, 1952-54; engraver, Nambe Mills, Santa Fe, NM, 1968-present. Media: Casein, oil, india ink, lithograph. Rep.: Hatfield Dalzell Galleries, Los Angeles; Gallery G Fine Arts, Wichita, KS. Address in 1982, 1125 N. Screenland Dr., Burbank, CA.

TCHISON, JOSEPH ANTHONY.
Sculptor. Born Washington, Feb. 12, 1895. Pupil of George Julian Zolnay, Richard Edwin Brooks. Work: "Round the World Flight Memorial," National Museum, Washington; allegorical frieze, Cleveland Public Auditorium. Address in 1929, Belasco Theatre; 1262 - 21st St., Washington, DC.

ATHERTON, EZRA.
Miniature painter. Mentioned in the Boston directories for 1841-1842.

ATHERTON, JOHN.
Illustrator. Born in Brainerd, Minnesota, 1900. He studied art at the College of the Pacific and the School of Fine Arts in San Francisco. His advertising and editorial illustrations led to a One-Man Show in New York in 1936. He was an award winner in the 1943 Artists for Victory show for his piece, Black Horse, which is now owned by the Metropolitan Museum of Art. His first job was a cover for the Saturday Evening Post and later he produced three of their Franklin anniversary covers. A founding member of the FAS. Died in New Brunswick, Canada 1952, while on a fishing trip.

ATHEY, RUTH.
See Vivash.

ATKINS, ALBERT HENRY.
Sculptor. Born Milwaukee, Wis., 1899. Studied at Cowles Art School, Boston, 1896-98; Academie Julien and Academie Colorossi, Paris, 1898-1900. Mem. faculty, RI School of Design, Dept. of Sculpture, from 1909. Member: Nat. Sculpture Soc., Architectural League of NY, Copley Society of Boston, American Art Assn. (Paris), Provident Art Club. Prin. works: Copenhagen Memorial Fountain, City of Boston; Lapham Memorial, Milwaukee, Wis.; Architectural sculptures, Christ Church, Ansonia, Conn., All Saints Church, Dorchester, Mass.; also portraits, ideal sculptures, etc. Exhibited at NAD (New York), PAFA, Philadelphia, Albright Galleries (Buffalo), Art Inst. (Milwaukee). Address in 1926, 162 West 11th Street, New York City. Died in 1951.

ATKINS, FLORENCE ELIZABETH.
Sculptor. Born in Louisiana. Exhibited "Frogs," "Rabbit," at the Penna. Acad. of the Fine Arts, Philadelphia, 1921. Address in 1926, 1040 Bush Street, San Francisco, California. Died in 1946.

ATKINSON, E. MARIE.
See Mrs. A. Hull.

ATKINSON, LEO F.
Painter. Born at Sunnyside, Washington, Sept. 23, 1896. Pupil of Seattle Art Club. Mural paintings in Columbian Theatre, Baton Rouge, La., and American Theatre, Bellingham, Washington. Represented at Seattle Fine Arts Gallery, "On Cedar Drive." Address in 1926, 1122 36'th St., Seattle, Washington.

ATROBUS, JOHN.
Painter. Died in Detroit, Michigan, October 18, 1908. He had lived in Chicago, and Washington, DC.

ATWOOD, JESSE.
Philadelphia portrait painter in 1860. He painted several portraits of President Lincoln.

ATWOOD, JR.
Was a map engraver working in Philadelphia about 1840.

ATWOOD, WILLIAM E.
Painter. Born at Killinoly, Conn. Member of National Arts Club, New York. Address in 1926, East Gloucester, Mass.

AUDUBON, JOHN JAMES.
Born April 26, 1785, Haiti, West Indies; died in January 27, 1851, New York City. The celebrated ornithologist and artist Audubon was the son of Captain Jean Audubon and a Creole woman named Rabin. He was legally adopted in France by both his father and his father's legal wife, Anne Moynet Audubon. He was in America from 1804 to 1805, visiting France in 1806. It was probably at this time that he received the instruction in drawing

from Louis David of which he speaks in his "Journal." In 1807 he returned to America. He traveled extensively in United States and Canada, making notes and drawings for his "Birds of North America" and "Quadrupeds of North America." John James Audubon came to New York in August 1824, Sully having given him letters to Stuart, Allston and Trumbull. At this time Audubon met John Vanderlyn and stood to him for the figure of Vanderlyn's portrait of General Jackson. Audubon visited Meadville, Penna., in 1824, and while in that city painted several portraits. Late in 1824, he went to Louisiana. He remained in the South until May 1826, when he again started to Europe, landing at Liverpool on July 21. Was in Eng. for much of time between 1826-39. He was at once invited to show his drawings at the Royal Academy. He made several trips to the United States between 1829 and 1839. See "Life of Audubon," edited by his widow, "Audubon, the Naturalist," by F. H. Herrick; also Scribner's for March, 1893.

AUDUBON, VICTOR GIFFORD.
Son of John J. Audubon, was born June, 1809, in Louisville, KY. He was elected in 1864 an Academician of the National Academy in New York. His brother, J. W. Audubon, was elected as associate member of the National Academy in 1847. Died Aug. 1862 in New York City.

AUERBACH-LEVY, WILLIAM.
Painter and etcher. Born in Russia, Feb. 14, 1889. Pupil of NAD; Julian Academy in Paris under Laurens. Member: ANA, 1926; Salma. C.; Chicago SE. Awards: Mooney traveling scholarship, NAD, 1911; first figure prize, Chicago SE, 1914; bronze medal, P.-P. Exp., San F., 1915; Logan prize ($25), Chicago SE, 1918; third Hallgarten prize, NAD, 1921; bronze medal, Calif. PM, 1923; Shaw prize ($100), Salma C., 1923; 2nd Lewis caricature prize ($100), PAFA, 1924; Isaac N. Maynard prize ($100) for portrait, NAD, 1925; Isidor prize, Salma. C., 1925; prize, Jewish Centre Exhib., 1926; Lewis first prize (caricature), PAFA, 1927; Fellow, Guggenheim Mem.

Foundation, 1928. Represented in AIC; Worcester Museum; New York Public Library; Carnegie Institute of Pittsburgh; "Corner of my Studio." Detroit Institute of Arts. Address in 1929, 46 Washington Sq., South, New York, NY.

AUGUR, HEZEKIAH.
Born Feb. 21, 1791 in New Haven, Conn. The son of a shoemaker. He was self-taught, his artistic studies being carried out in New Haven, Conn. His modeling and carving were excellent; his group "Jephthah and his Daughter" is in the Yale College Gallery. He died in New Haven, January 10, 1858.

AULT, GEORGE COPELAND.
Painter. Born in Cleveland, Ohio, 1891. Member of Society of Independent Artists. Address in 1926, 11 Charles Street, New York, NY. Died Dec. 30, 1948.

AUNIO, IRENE.
Painter. Born in Finland 1919. Studied: Art Students' League. Awards: National Association of Women Artists, 1952, 1958; Pen and Brush Club, 1953; Ranger purchase prize, National Academy of Design, 1953; Catherine L. Wolfe Art Club, 1955, 1957; Art Students' League, Johnson Merit Scholarship, 1954-55; Michael Engel award, 1958. Collections: Art Students League; National Academy of Design; Seton Hall University.

AUNSPAUGH, V(IVIAN) L(OUISE).
Painter, lecturer, and teacher. Born Bedford, VA. Pupil of Fitz and Twachtman; Weld in Rome; Mucha in Paris. Founder and director of Aunspaugh Art School, Dallas, Tex. Address in 1929, 3405 Bryan St., Dallas, Tex.

AUS, CAROL.
Painter. Born Norway, March 27, 1878. Pupil of Julian Academy, Paris, France. Work: Portrait of Governor Scofield, State Capitol, Madison, Wisc.; portraits in courthouses and libraries in Fort Wayne, Ind. and Madison, Wisc. Address in 1929, 2635 Hampden Court, Chicago, Ill. Died in 1934.

32

AUSTIN, CHARLES P.
Painter. Born in Denver, Colo., 1883. Pupil of Twachtman in New York and Castelluche, Paris. Address in 1926, San Juan Capistrano, California.

AUSTRIAN, BEN.
Painter. Died in Kempton, Penna., Dec. 9, 1921. He was self-taught and first achieved distinction in depicting barnyard subjects and later for landscapes. He also had a studio at Palm Beach, Florida.

AUSTRIAN, FLORENCE H(OCHSCHILD).
(Mrs. Charles Robert Austrian). Painter. Born Baltimore, MD, Sept. 8, 1889. Pupil of Hugh Breckenridge, John Sloan, Charles Hawthorne and Leon Kroll. Member: AFA. Address in 1929, 1417 Eutaw Pl., Baltimore, MD.

AUTH, ROBERT R.
Painter and printmaker. Born in Bloomington, Illnois, Oct. 27, 1936. Study: Ill. Wesleyan Univ., BFA; Wash. State U., MFA. Work: Salt Lake Art Center; Washington State University; others. Exhib.: Intermountain Painting and Sculpture, Salt Lake Art Center, 1969; Springville Mus. of Art, Utah, 1972; others. Awards: Intermountain Ptg. and Sculpture, 4th Biennial award, 1969; Allied Arts Council Artist of Year award, 1972. Art Positions: Boise High School, 1961; bd. dir., Boise Art Gallery, 1969; etc. Mem.: Idaho Art Assn.; Boise Art Assn. Medium: Acrylic. Rep.: Brown's Gallery, Boise, Idaho. Address in 1982, 530 Hillview Drive Boise, Idaho.

AVAKIAN, JOHN.
Painter and teacher. Born in Worcester, MA. Study: Yale Univ. School of Art and Architecture, BFA, MFA; Boston Mus. School. Work: Bucknell University Coll.; Kansas State University; Western Mich. University; others. Exhibitions: "New Talent" DeCordova Museum, Mass., 1965; 38th International Printmakers Exhib., Seattle Art Mus., 1967; Worcester (MA) Art Mus., solo, 1971; others. Awards: Boston Museum, Travel Grant '69; Providence Art Club, 1968; Art Patrons Lg. of Mobile

award, 1972; Mem.: Col. Art Assn. of America; Boston Visual Artists Union. Teaching: Worcester (MA) Art Mus. School, from 1965. Mt. Ida Jr. College, 1965-pres. Media: Acrylic, serigraph. Rep.: Assn. Am. Artists, NYC. Address in 1982, 43 Morse St. Sharon, Mass.

AVENT, MAYNA TREANOR.
(Mrs. Frank Avent). Painter. Born Nashville, Tenn., Sept. 17, 1868. Pupil of Julian Academy and Lasar in Paris. Member: Nashville AA; SSAL. Award: Gold medal, Nashville AA. Address in 1929, 2811 Belmont Blvd., Nashville, Tenn.

AVERY, HOPE.
Painter. Exhibited portrait of Mr. Baker, in 33d Annual Exhibition of National Association of Women Painters and Sculptors, 1924. Address in 1926, Pittsford, VT.

AVERY, MILTON.
Painter. Born in 1893. Pupil of Charles Noel Flagg. Member: Conn. AFA; S. Indp. A; Salons of Amer. Award: Atheneum prize, Conn. AFA, 1929. Address in 1929, 1931 Broadway, New York, NY. Died in 1965.

AVEY, MARTHA.
Painter, craftsman and teacher. Born Arcola, Ill. Pupil of J. H. Vanderpoel; Martha Walter; Cecilia Beaux; Maurice Braun; AIC; NY School of Fine and Applied Art; Am. School of Art, Fontainebleau, France. Member: Okla. AA; North Shore AA; SSAL. Represented John H. Vanderpoel Art Assn., Okla. Art League. Head of Art Department, Oklahoma City University. Address in 1929, Oklahoma City University; 1325 North Kentucky St., Oklahoma City, Okla. Died in 1943.

AVINOFF, A(NDREW N.).
Painter and etcher. Born in Russia, Feb. 1, 1884. Studied in Russia. Member: NY WCC. Director, Carnegie Museum. Address in 1929, Napanoch, NY. Died in 1948.

AVISON, GEORGE.
Painter and illustrator. Born Norwalk, Conn., May 6, 1885. Pupil of William M. Chase, Robert Henri,

33

etc. Member: GFLA; Silvermine GA. Illustrated "Pirate Tale from the Law," published by Little, Brown and Co.; "Lost Ships and Lonely Seas," published by Century Co., "Jimmy Makes the Varsity," Bobbs Merrill Co.

AYER, J(AMES) C.
Painter. Born Lowell, Mass., Oct. 13, 1862. Pupil of Cullen Yates, New York, L. Cohen Michel, Paris. Member: NY Physicians AC; Nassau Co. AL. Address in 1929, 2 West 67th St., New York, NY; Glen Cove, NY.

AYLWARD, IDA.
(Mrs. W. J. Aylward). Painter, illustrator and craftsman. Born Fairport, NY. Pupil of Kenyon Cox; Howard Pyle; Edmund Tarbell. Work: Mosaic glass window, Madison Ave. M. E. Church, New York; six mosaic glass windows, Pro- Cathedral of St. John, Milwaukee, Wis.; illustrations for "Woman's Home Companion." Address in 1929, Longview Rd., Port Washington, LI, NY.

AYLWARD, WILLIAM J.
Painter and illustrator. Born in Milwaukee, Wis., 1875. Pupil of Howard Pyle. Exhibited at the Paris Salon, 1924, and National Academy of Design, New York, 1925. Address in 1926, 51 West 10th Street, New York City.

AZADIGIAN, MUNUEL.
Painter. Exhibited "Still Life" at Penna. Academy of the Fine Arts, Philadelphia, 1921. Address in 1926, 1834 North Darien Street, Philadelphia, PA.

AZARA, NANCY.
Painter and sculptor. Born in New York City Oct. 13, 1939. Studied: Finch College, New York; Art Students' League, sculpture with J. Havannes, Painting and drawing with E. Dickinson, 1964-67. Lester Palakov Studio of Stage Design, New York City; The Art Students League, New York City. Exhibitions: Douglass College, Rutgers University, Newark, New Jersey, 1972; Cornell University, 1973; Ocean County College, New Jersey, 1974. One-woman shows, Women

Series, Douglas College Library, 1972, Orgn. of Independent Aritists, NY, 1977. Teaching: Lectured on art, Brooklyn Col., 1973-75, NY Feminist Art Inst. Main medium; woodcarvings. Address in 1980, 46 Great Jones St. New York, NY.

AZUMA, NORIO.
Painter and serigrapher. Born in Kii-Nagashima-cho, Japan, Nov. 23, 1928. Study: Kanazana Art College, Japan, BFA; Chouinard Art Inst., Los Angeles; ASL. Work: Whitney Museum; Philadelphia Museum of Art; Art Institute of Chicago; Smithsonian Institution, Nat'l Coll. of Fine Arts; Brooklyn Museum. Exhibitions: 28th Biennial of Corcoran Gallery, 1963; Original Graphics, Grenchen, Switz., 1964; Mus. Mod. Art, Tokyo, 1965; 1966 Annual of Whitney Museum of American Art; Phila. Mus. of Art, 1972. Awards: International Print Exhibition, Seattle, Wash., 1960; Soc. of Am. Graphic Artists Exh., 1968; Boston Printmakers, 1970. Mem.: Soc. Am. Color Prints; Print Club; Soc. Am. Graphic Artists; Print Council of Am. Medium: Oil. Rep.: Associated American Artists, NYC Azuma Gallery, NYC. Address in 1982, 276 Riverside Dr., NYC.

AZZI, MARIUS A.
Sculptor. Exhibited statuettes at the Penna. Academy of the Fine Arts, Philadelphia, 1921. Address in 1926, 120 West 11th Street, New York.

34

B., J. W.
These initials as "J. W. B. del. et sc." are signed to a quarto line print representing an engagement between the Georgia militia under Gen. John Floyd and a force of Creek Indians at Antossee, Ala.

B., S. P.
Engraver. The initials "S.P.B." are signed to a heading of the fire insurance policy of "The Mutual Assurance Society against Fire in Virginia." There is no indication of date but the work would suggest about the year 1825.

B., W.
These initials "W.B. 1825" are signed to a number of plates illustrating "Pug's Tour through Europe," Published in Baltimore about 1826.

BAAR, STANFIELD MARION.
Painter. Born in NYC, Sept. 22, 1895. Pupil of Johansen and Henri. Member: NA Women PS; MacD. C. Address in 1929, 310 West 80th St., NYC.

BABCOCK, DEAN.
Painter. Born in Canton, IL, Jan. 14, 1888. Pupil of John Vanderpoel, Robert Henri and Helen Hyde. Member: Denver AA; AFA. Address in 1929, Longs Peak, Colorado.

BABCOCK, E(LIZABETH) J(ONES).
(Mrs. J. W. Babcock II). Painter and illustrator. Born Keokuk, IA, July 19, 1887. Pupil of Duveneck and Chase. Member: NA of Women Painters and Sculptors; Guild of Free Lance Artists. Illustrator for Scribner's, Harper's, etc. Address in 1929, 172 East 71st, NYC. Died Sept. 13, 1963.

BABCOCK, RICHARD.
Mural painter. Born in Denmark, 1887. Member of Art Students' League, NY. Address in 1926, Woodland Road, Pittsburgh, PA. Died 1954.

BABCOCK, WILLIAM P.
Painter. Born in Boston in 1826; died in 1899, in Bois d'Arcy, France. Studied under Conture in

Paris. Boston Museum of Fine Arts have: "The Red Hat," "Susanna and the Elders," "Still Life," "Fish," and "Landscape, with Figures."

BABOT, AMY W.
Painter. Exhibited at Penna. Academy of Fine Arts, 1924. Address in 1926, 72 Chestnut St., Boston, Mass.

BABSON, R.
Engraver of stipple portraits. About 1860 he was apparently in the employ of Joseph Andrews of Boston as we find plates signed "Eng'd at J. Andrews by R. Babson."

BACH, FLORENCE JULIA.
Painter and sculptor. Born Buffalo, NY, June 24, 1887. Member of Art Students' League. Pupil of William M. Chase and Du Mond. Represented in the Buffalo Fine Arts Academy. Address in 1926, 1110 Elmwood Ave., Buffalo, NY.

BACHELER, FRANCES HOPE.
Painter and teacher. Born Lebanon, Conn., in 1889. Member of Hartford Art Club. Address in 1926, 39 Hopkins St., Hartford, Conn.

BACHER, OTTO HENRY.
Painter, etcher, and illustrator. He was born in Cleveland, Ohio, in 1856. Pupil of Duveneck, in Cincinnati; and of Duvan, Boulanger, and Lefebvre in Paris. He spent some time with Whistler in Venice. He died in New York in 1909, having received many honors and medals. He was an Associate of the National Academy of Design.

BACHER, WILL LOW.
Painter and etcher. Born Bronxville, NY, Jan. 9, 1898. Pupil of George Bridgman and G. Maynard. Member: MacD. C.; Salma. C. Address in 1929, Rock Tavern, Orange Co., NY.

BACHMAN, MAX.
Sculptor. Born 1862. Died in New York City, Jan. 13, 1921. He designed the allegorical figures of the continents for the Pulitzer Building in New York City.

BACHMURA, BARBARA LEE.
Painter. Born in Detroit, MI, in
1925. Studied: Wayne Univ.; Univ.
of Mexico; Mexican Art Workshop;
University of Oslo. Award:
Fulbright Award, 1952.
Collections: Wayne University;
Denison University; Motive
Magazine; Vanderbilt Hospital;
Nashville Art Guild, Tennessee;
Crandall Art Gal., Alliance, Ohio.

BACHOFEN, MAX ALBIN.
Painter. Born Neubrunen,
Switzerland, Aug. 25, 1903. Pupil
of Paul Bough Travis. Awards:
Hon. mention for landscape,
Cleveland, 1927; first prize for
landscape, Cleveland, 1928; hon.
mention for landscape, Cleveland,
1929. Work: "Sun Shine in New
Hungary," City of Cleveland.
Address in 1929, Castroville, Tex.;
h. R.F.D. No. 1, Alliance, Ohio;
summer, 11340 Mayfield Rd.,
Cleveland, Ohio.

BACKSTROM, FLORENCE J.
Painter and designer. Born in NY.
Study: Cooper Union with V.
Perard; ASL, NY, with Robert Bev.
Hale, Frank Reilly. Exhibitions:
Smithsonian Inst., Wash. WCC;
Miniature Painters and Sculptors
Soc.; American Artists Prof. League
Cherry Blossom Festival, Wash., DC;
Diamond Jubilee Art Students
League; PAFA. Awards: Garden
State Plaza Gold Cup and many other
first prizes and awards. Teaching:
Teacher adult classes, Bergenfield
H.S., NJ; private classes. Member:
ASL (life); Am. APL; NJ Painters
and Sculptors Soc. Media:
Watercolor. Address in 1976, 84
Carletondale Road Ringwood, NJ.

BACKUS, J(OSEFA) C(ROSBY).
Painter. Born Brooklyn, NY, Oct.
13, 1875. Member: AFA. Work:
"Young Lincoln", Vardy School,
Tennessee. Address in 1929, 2416
Tracy Pl., Washington, DC; summer,
Beech Hill, Dublin, NH.

BACON, CHARLES ROSWELL.
Painter. Born in New York, 1868.
Pupil of Constant, Lefebvre and
Collin in Paris. Paintings in
Union Trust Co., New York. He died
October 9, 1913 in New York City.

BACON, GEORGE.
An excellent music-engraver working
in the city of Philadelphia about
1815. The firm was Bacon & Hart,
and Bacon was a near relative of
the senior member of the firm.

BACON, HENRY.
Painter. Born in Haverhill,
Massachusetts, 1839; died Cairo,
Egypt, March 13, 1912. Painted in
oils and water colors. Made a
specialty of Egyptian subjects.
Visited Paris in 1864, where he
became a pupil of the Ecole des
Beaux Arts and of Cabanel; and in
1866-67 studied under Edouard Frere
at Ecouen. Represented at the
Corcoran Art Gallery by "The
Nile-Evening" (water color) and in
Boston Museum of Fine Arts by "On
Shipboard."

BACON, IRVING R.
Painter. Born in Fitchburg, Mass.,
1875. Pupil of William M. Chase in
New York; Carl von Marr and
Heinrich von Zugel in Munich.
Work: "Village Street Scene "
Louisville Assóc.; "The Little Old
Man of the Woods " D & C. Steamer,
Detroit; "The Conquest of the
Prairie " Book Tower Bldg.,
Detroit. Address in 1926, Redford,
Michigan. Died 1962.

BACON, KATE L.
See Kate B. Bond.

BACON, PEGGY.
Painter. Born in Ridgefield, Conn.
Pupil of James Lie. Member of
Society of Independent Artists.
Address in 1926, 152 West 55th
Street, New York.

BADGER, JAMES W.
Miniature painter working in Boston
from 1845 to 1846.

BADGER, JOHN C.
Crayon portrait artist. Born c.
1822 in NH. Exhibited at the
Pennsylvania Academy in 1855 and
must not be confused with Joseph W.
Badger who painted miniatures in
New York from 1832 to 1838, nor
with the two artists who painted
portraits in Boston. Thomas Badger
lived there from 1836 to 1859 and
James W. Badger lived there from
1845 to 1846.

BADGER, JOSEPH W.
Miniature painter, working in New York 1832-1838.

BADGER, JOSEPH.
Painter. Born 1708 in Charleston, Mass. He died in Boston, and was an early colonial portrait painter. His work was not as good as Copley, Smibert and Feke. An excellent life of Joseph Badger with a description of about a hundred of his portraits was written by Laurence Park and published by the Massachusetts Historical Society, Dec. 1917. His work is owned by Worcester Art Museum, Bowdoin College and many private collections in Boston. Died 1765.

BADGER, THOMAS.
Miniature painter. Born Dec. 1792 in MA. Working in Boston from 1836 to 1859. Died Feb. 3, 1868 in Cambridge, MA.

BAEHR, FRANCINE.
Painter and etcher. Born Chicago, Ill., July 21, 1898. Member: Art Alliance; MacDowell Club. Address in 1929, 170 East 78th St., New York, NY; summer, Westport, Conn.

BAER, HERBERT M.
Painter and engraver. Born in New York, 1879. Honorable mention at Paris Salon 1905. Address in 1926, 655 Fifth Ave., New York.

BAER, JO.
Painter. She is known for her minimalist paintings. First major showings of her minimal paintings in the 1960's in New York City.

BAER, LILIAN.
Sculptor. Born New York City, 1887. Student of Art Students' League, pupil of Jas. E. Fraser and K. H. Miller. Works: "The Dance," "Specialty Statuettes." Address in 1926, 601 Madison Ave., New York City.

BAER, WILLIAM JACOB.
Artist. Born Cincinnati, Jan. 29, 1860. Pupil of Munich Royal Academy, 1880. Received 4 medals, and one of his works being purchased by the Directors for the Academy. Painted pictures in genre and portraits in oil and taught

1885-92; then confined himself to miniature painting, of which art he is a pioneer of the modern school. Awarded 1st medal for miniatures and ideal paintings, New York, 1897; 1st class medals, Paris Exp. Among his better known works in miniature are: "Aurora," "The Golden Hour," "Summer," "Daphne," "Nymph," "In Arcadia," "Madonna with the Auburn Hair," "Primavera." Treas., Am. Soc. of Miniature Painters; ANA 1913. Address in 1926, West 59th Street, New York. Died in 1941.

BAERER, HENRY.
Sculptor. Born in Kirchlim, Germany in 1837, he came to the United States as a young man. Among his best known works are his statue of Beethoven in Central Park, General Fowler in Fort Green Park, and General Warren in Prospect Park, Brooklyn. He died in New York in 1908. He was a member of the National Sculpture Society.

BAHLS, RUTH (KATHERINE).
Painter. Born Lafayette, March 23, 1901. Pupil of William Forsyth. Address in 1929, 502 Perrin Ave., Lafayette, Ind.

BAHNC, SALCIA.
Painter, sculptor, etcher, and teacher. Born Dukla, Austrian Poland in 1898. Work: "Torso," Arts Club, Chicago, Ill. Address in 1929, 1218 East 53rd St., Chicago, Ill.

BAILEY, C. FOSTER.
Painter. Was awarded honorable mention, Carnegie Institute, 1923.

BAILEY, HARRY LEWIS.
Painter, illustrator, and etcher. Born St. Louis, MO, Dec 2. 1879. Pupil of St. Louis School of Fine Arts. Member: Calif. AC; Calif. PM. Address in 1926, 175 North Almont Dr., Beverly Hills, Calif.

BAILEY, HENRIETTA D(AVIDSON).
Painter, craftswoman, and teacher. Born New Orleans, LA. Pupil of Newcomb Art Schools, New Orleans; Arthur W. Dow in New York. Member: NOAA; Baltimore Handcraft C. Represented in Delgado Museum, New

37

Orleans, LA; City Art Museum, St. Louis. Address in 1929, Newcomb Pottery, Audubon Pl. and Plum St.; h. 3315 De Soto St., New Orleans, LA.

BAILEY, HENRY LEWIS.
Etcher. Member of Print Makers Society of California. Address in 1926, Mortgage Guarantee Bldg., Los Angeles, California.

BAILEY, HENRY TURNER.
Illustrator, craftsman, teacher, writer and lithographer. Born in Mass., 1865. Student of Mass. Normal Art School. Member: Cleveland AA; College AA; Cleveland SA; Cleveland AIA; AFA. Was Dean of the Cleveland School of Art 1917 and the John Huntington Polytechnic Inst., Cleveland, 1919. Represented in Vanderpoel AA. Address in 1926, Cleveland School of Art, Cleveland.

BAILEY, JAMES E(DWARD).
Painter. Born Baltimore, MD, Dec. 13, 1885. Member: AL of Phila.; Graphic Sketch C. Awards: prizes, Wanamakers, Phila., 1915-16; gold medal, World Fair Poster, Chicago, 1923. Address in 1929, 1933 West Norris St., Philadelphia, PA; summer, 117 East St., Easton, MD.

BAILEY, LA FORCE.
Painter and artist. Born Joliet, Ill., Apr. 17, 1893. Pupil of William M. Hekking; John L. Frazier; Charles W. Hawthorne. Member: AIA; Provincetown AA; Wash. WCC: Scarab C. Address in 1929, Architectural Bldg., University of Illinois; H. 205 West University Ave., Urbana, Ill.; summer, care of Gray Inn, Provincetown, Mass.

BAILEY, MINNIE M.
Painter, illustrator. Born in Oberlin, Kans., in 1890. Address in 1926, 3908 Swiss Ave., Dallas, Tex.

BAILEY, R. O.
Painter. Member: Cleveland SA. Address in 1929, 2114 East 96th St., Cleveland, Ohio.

BAILEY, VERNON HOWE.
Artist. Born in Camden, NJ, April 1, 1874. Student PA Mus. Sch. of Art, and PA Acad. Fine Arts, Philadelphia. Studied in London and Paris. Staff artist, Philadelphia Times, 1892-4; Boston Herald, 1894-01-spl. artist for latter at coronation of Edward VII; artist contbr. to Graphic, Mail and Express, London, 1902, and after to leading Am. mags., The Studio London. Exhibited at PAFA, Philadelphia, 1891; Architectural League, New York, 1903-12. Represented in permanent collections, Detroit Mus. of Art, Minn. State Art Soc., St. Paul. Illustrator: "Lady Baltimore," "Charleston, the Place and Its People," "The Story of Harvard," etc. Mem. Soc. of Illustrators. Address in 1926, The Players, 16 Gramercy Park, New York, NY.

BAILEY, WALTER A.
Painter, illustrator, and etcher. Born Wallula, Wyandotte Co., Kan., Oct. 17, 1894. Pupil of Charles A. Wilimovsky and John D. Patrick. Member: Kansas City SA. Address in 1929, care of the "Kansas City Star;" h. 3864 East 60th St., Kansas City, MO.

BAILLY, JOSEPH A.
Sculptor. Born in Paris in 1825. Came to Philadelphia and followed his occupation of carving on wood and marble. Later became instructor at the Penna. Academy of Fine Arts. He produced a statue of Washington that was placed in front of the Philadelphia state-house (1896), also portrait busts of Gen. Grant and Gen. Meade. Died June 15, 1883 in Phila., PA.

BAIN, HARRIET F.
Painter. Born Kenosha, Wis. Pupil of John Vanderpoel; E. A. Webster; Collin; Garrido. Member: Wis. PS; Chicago AC; Provincetown AA; Salons of America. Represented in Vanderpoel Art Assn. Collection, Chicago. Address in 1929, 112 East 10th St., New York, NY; h. 6328 7th Ave., Kenosha, Wis.

BAIN, LILIAN PHERNE.
Painter, sculptor, etcher, and teacher. Born Salem, Ore. Pupil

of F. V. Du Mond, Guy Rose, Joseph Pennell. Member: Pennell Graphic AS. Address in 1929, 140 East 92nd St., New York, NY; summer, 6520 - 62nd St., Portland, Ore.

BAINS, ETHEL FRANKLIN BETTS.
Illustrator and painter. Member: Fellowship PAFA, Phila. WCC. Award: Bronze medal. P.-P. Exp., San F., 1915. Exhibited at PAFA, 1922. Address in 1929, 1018 Westview St.; 104 Harvey St., Germantown, Philadelphia, PA.

BAIRD, EUGENE Q(UENLIN).
Painter. Born Straits Settlements, Asia, May 6, 1897. Pupil of Pratt Inst.; ASL of NY; Jane Peterson. Member: NYWCC; Art Director's C. Address in 1929, 98 Newfield St., East Orange, NJ.

BAIRNSFATHER, A. L.
Painter and illustrator. Born 1883. Member: Salma. C.; NAC. Address in 1929, 119 East 19th St.; 53 West 37th St., New York, NY; Rockport, Mass.

BAISDEN, FRANK.
Painter. Born 1904. Exhibited at the Penna. Academy Annual Water Color Exhibition, Philadelphia, 1925. Address in 1926, Care of Penna. Academy of the Fine Arts, Philadelphia.

BAKER, ADELAIDE CLARISSA.
Painter and craftswoman. Born Cleveland. Pupil of George Elmer Browne; Max Bohm, Cleveland School of Art. Member: Washington Art Center; Cleveland AA; Cleveland School of Art Alumni. Address in 1929, 1437 East 115th Street, Cleveland, Ohio.

BAKER, BRYANT.
Sculptor. Born in London, July 8, 1881. Pupil of London Royal Acad. of Arts. Member: Fellow, Royal Society of British Sculptors; AFA. Arrived 1916 in US. Among his works are "Snowden Andrews Memorial" at Winchester, VA, "Edward Wright Memorial," Austin, Texas, and busts of President Wilson, Senator Lodge, Gen'l March, Gen'l Pershing and Hon. Herbert Hoover. Address in 1926, 154 West 55th Street, New York City.

BAKER, BURTIS.
Painter. Exhibited 1921 at Penna. Academy of the Fine Arts, and in 1923 at Carnegie Inst. with "Interior with Figure." Address in 1926, Fenway Studios, Boston, Mass.

BAKER, CATHERINE (ISABELLE).
Painter and teacher. Born 1905 in Columbus. Pupil of Alice Schille. Member: Columbus AL. Award: Hon. Mention, Columbus Art League, 1928. Address in 1929, 2590 Glenmour Ave., Columbus, Ohio.

BAKER, CHARLES.
Painter. Born in 1844. He was the son of Charles Baker, one of the founders of the Art League. His home was in Brooklyn, NY, and he died at Hague, Lake George, NY. Died Aug. 19, 1906, in Hague, Lake George, NY.

BAKER, DORIS WINCHELL.
Painter. Born: Washington, DC, in 1905. studied: Chouinard Institute of Art; Otis Art Institute. Awards: Art in National Defense, 1943, Palos Verdes, California, 1955; Women Painters of the West, 1941, 1946, 1949.

BAKER, ELIZABETH GOWDY.
Portrait painter. Born in Xenia, OH, 1860. Specialized in children's portraits in water color. Student of New York School of Art, and Penna. Academy of Fine Arts. Studied also in Rome, Florence, and Paris. Address in 1926, 24 Gramercy Park, New York. Died Oct. 11, 1927.

BAKER, ELLEN KENDALL.
Painter. Born in New York State; she lived for years in Buffalo, New York. She married Harry Thompson, the English artist, and exhibited in the Paris salons and at many exhibitions in this country. Died in Chalfant, St. Giles, England in 1913.

BAKER, FREDERICK VAN VLIET.
Artist and teacher. Born in New York, Nov. 6, 1876. Educated, Pratt Inst., Brooklyn, Ecole des Beaux Arts, Courtois in, Paris. Instr. in life drawing, painting and composition, Pratt Inst.

Exhibited in salons, Paris, 1901-2-3; also at Ghent, Vienna, Chicago, New York, etc. Address in 1926, 39 West 67th Street, New York.

BAKER, GEORGE A.
Portrait painter. Born in New York City, 1821; died there 1880. His first portrait work was in miniature painting, but he soon became an excellent portrait artist; he studied in Europe. Elected to the National Academy in 1851. Noted for his portraits of women and children. His portrait of the artist John F. Kensett is in the Metropolitan Museum, New York, and an Ideal Head is in the Corcoran Gallery, Washington, DC.

BAKER, GEORGE HERBERT.
Painter. Born in Muncie, Ind., Feb. 14, 1878. Studied at Cin. AA. Member: Richmond Art Assoc.; Indiana Artists' Club; S. Indp. A.; Wayne County S. Indp. A. Address in 1926, 605 Main St., Richmond, Ind.

BAKER, GEORGE O.
Painter and illustrator. Born in Mexico, MO, 1882. Pupil of Laurens, and Miller in Paris. Address in 1926, Care of Chas. E. Johnson, 941 Glengyle Place, Chicago.

BAKER, GRACE M.
Painter and teacher. Born Annawan, Ill., Oct. 18, 1876. Pupil of AIC. Member: Nat. Educational A; Western AA; College AA of Am. Head of Art Dept., Colorado State Teachers' College. Address in 1929, Guggenheim Hall, Colorado State Teachers' College, Greeley, Colo.

BAKER, GRACE.
Painter. Born in Riverdale, New York. Study: Finch College; with William Oden-Waller. Exhib.: Art Graphic Gallery, one-man show; Chrysler Mus., Norfolk, VA; UN Postage Stamp Design Comp. Awards: Todd Ctr. Arts Fest.; Peninsula Arts Assn.; etc. Mem.: Am. APL; etc. Media: Oil. Address in 1980, P.O. Box 2962, Williamsburg, Virginia.

BAKER, HORACE.
Wood engraver. Born Nov. 12, 1833, in in North Salem, NY. He studied engraving in his brother's firm in Boston, of which he afterwards became a partner. For many years he was connected with the engraving department of Harper's Magazine. Died March 2, 1918, in Greatneck, LI, NY.

BAKER, I. H.
A good engraver of stipple portraits working in Boston, about 1860.

BAKER, JOHN.
Engraver. He designed and etched in line a large plate of the "Battle of Bunker's Hill." About 1832, he also executed two separate plates of "Washington Crossing the Delaware."

BAKER, JOSEPH E.
Etcher and caricature illustrator. He was a native of Boston and drew many of the caricatures of the Civil War period.

BAKER, M. K. (MISS).
Painter. Born in New Bedford, Mass. Specialty, figure painting and portraits. Works have been at Boston Art Club and New York Academy of Design.

BAKER, MARIA MAY.
Painter. Born in Norfolk, VA, 1890. Pupil of Penna. Academy of Fine Arts and Corcoran Art Gallery. Member: Norfolk SA. Work: "Open the Gates as high as the Sky," Norfolk SA. Address in 1926, 408 Raleigh Ave., Norfolk, VA.

BAKER, MARTHA SUSAN.
Miniature painter. Born Dec. 25, 1871 in Evansville, Ind. Also painted in oil and water color, and has did some mural work. Pupil of Chicago Art Institute. Died Dec. 21, 1911, in Chicago, Ill.

BAKER, MARY FRANCES.
Painter. Born in New Orleans, LA, in 1879. Student of Penna Academy of Fine Arts; Newcomb Art School. Member: New Orleans Art Assn. Award: Silver medal, New Orleans Art Assn. Address in 1926, 2263

Carondelet Street, New Orleans, LA. Died 1943.

BAKER, P(ERCY) BRYANT.
Sculptor. Born in London, Eng., 1881. Graduated Royal Academy Arts, London, 1910. Executed bust and heroic statue of King Edward VII; bust of Prince Olav of Norway; also busts of many notable persons in Eng. Exhibited at Royal Academy, London (medals 1910), Paris Salon, Corcoran Art Gallery, Washington, etc. Member Royal Soc. British Sculptors. Came to United States 1915. Address in 1926, 100 Chestnut Street, Boston, Mass.

BAKER, ROBERT P.
Sculptor. Born London, June 29, 1886. Studied in England. Member: NSS; Salma. C. Address in 1929, Woods Hole, Mass.

BAKER, S(AMUEL) B(URTIS).
Painter. Born Boston, Sept, 29, 1882. Pupil of Major, De Camp and Edward H. Barnard. Member: Boston AG; Salma. C.; Wash. AC; Wash. SA. Awards: 2nd William A. Clark prize ($1,500), and Corcoran medal, 1922; bronze medal, Sesqui-Centennial Exposition, Phila., 1929. Work: "The Black Mantilla," Macon Art Inst., Macon, GA; Portraits in the Massachusetts State House and Girls High School, Boston; Harvard Law School, Cambridge, Mass.; Pinkerton Academy, Derry, NH; New Hampshire State House; US Marine Corps headquarters, Washington, DC; VA. Theological Seminary, Alexandria; seven portraits in Boston schools; portrait in Lawrence School, Brookline, Mass.; Framingham (Mass.), Normal School; National Academy of Design, NY. Instructor at Corcoran School of Art; Asst. Professor, Dept. of Arts and Sciences, George Washington University, Washington. Died 1967.

BAKER, SARAH MARIMDA.
Painter. Born Memphis, Tenn., Mar. 7, 1899. Pupil of Hugh Breckenridge; Arthur Charles; Andre L'hote. Member: Fellowship PAFA; Wash. SA. Award: Fellowship gold medal, PAFA, 1926. Work: Altar decoration, St. John's Church, McLean, VA. Address in 1929, McLean, VA.

BAKER, WILLIAM BLISS.
Painter. Born 1859. Died at about the age of thirty, but painted some excellent landscapes.

BAKER, WILLIAM H.
Painter. Born in 1825; died in Brooklyn, NY, Mar. 29, 1875. He was brought up in mercantile pursuits in New Orleans; he devoted his spare time to the study of art and became a portrait and genre painter. He had a studio from 1853 to 1861 at 123 Canal Street; moved to New York in 1865, where he taught art and painted portraits and ideal subjects. He was a conscientious artist. Among his works, "Cupid Disarmed," "Floral Offering," "Red Riding Hood," and "Morning Glories."

BAKERVILLE, CHARLES, JR.,
Illustrator. Born Raleigh, NC, Apr. 16, 1869. Member: GFLA. Work: Illustrations for Scribner's, Life, Judge, Theatre, Vogue, Vanity Fair, Harpers Bazaar, etc., also lacquer screens and murals. Address in 1929, 113 East 34th St., New York, NY.

BAKKE, LARRY.
Painter and teacher. Born in Vancouver, BC, Jan. 16, 1932. Study: Univ. Wash., BA, MFA; Syracuse Univ., PhD., with L. Schmeckebier. Work: Syracuse University Collection, Everett College and private collections. Exhibitions: U. New Mex.; Watercolor Soc., NYC, annual; other univ. galleries. Awards: Watercolor, Seattle Art Museum; Painting, Spokane-Northwest; Kinorn Gallery, Seattle; Center Show-Syracuse, NY. Teaching: Univ. Victoria, 1958-71; Everett College, 1959-63; Syracuse Univ.; from 1963; and more. Media: Oil, collage. Address in 1982, Syracuse, NY.

BAKOS, JOSEPH G.
Painter, sculptor and teacher. Born Buffalo, NY, 1891. Pupil of J. E. Thompson. Address in 1926, Old Palace, Santa Fe, New Mexico. Died 1977.

BALANO, PAULA HIMMELSBACH.
(Mrs. Cosme Balano). Painter and illustrator. Born in Leipzig,

Germany, May 10, 1878. Pupil of Penna. Academy of Fine Arts under Chase and of Mucha in Paris. Awarded gold medal for her work in water color. Work in fellowship PAFA collection. Member of the Phila. Sch. of Design for Women. Address in 1926, 54 Linden Ave., Landsdowne, Penna.

BALCH, VISTUS.
Engraver. Born in Williamstown, Mass., in 1799; he died at Johnstown, NY, in 1884. Balch worked in Utica, Albany, and New York; he engraved a number of book illustrations, and several plates for the New York Mirror. About 1825 Balch drew on stone a portrait of Dr. Samuel L. Mitchell, for Imbert, who was the pioneer lithographer of New York City.

BALCOM, LOWELL LEROY.
Painter, illustrator and etcher. Born in Kansas City, MO, 1887. Studied at Kansas City Art Inst.; pupil of J. D. Patrick. Member of the GFLA. Represented in Kansas City Public Lib. Painted officers' portraits, WWI; visited Virgin Islands; travelled Orient and Mediterranean on commission from US Shipping Board; editorial work appeared in "American Legion," "Hearst's International." Member: Silvermine Guild. Address in 1926, 136 65th Street, New York. Died 1938.

BALDAUGH, ANNI.
(Mrs. Von Westrum). Miniature painter. Born in Holland, 1886. Pupil of Arendsen in Holland, Zasehke in Vienna, von Kunowsky in Munich. Member: Conn. AFA; Beaux-Arts, Paris; Bookplate Assn. Inst.; San Diego FAS; Calif. WCC. Awards: Gold medal, Los Angeles Museum, 1922; Water color prize, Phoenix, Ariz., 1923; exhibited the miniature of the "Washburn Children" at Miniature Exhibition, Penna. Academy of the Fine Arts, Philadelphia, 1924. Balch prize Calif., Soc. Minn. Painters, 1929. Address in 1926, Los Angeles, California.

BALDREY, HAYNSWORTH.
Sculptor and etcher. Born Cortland, NY, Aug. 24, 1885. Pupil

of C. T. Hawley, Charles Grafly, Ephriam Keyser. Member: AFA; Balto. WCC; Handicraft C. of Balto. Awards: Rinehart prize, Baltimore, 1908, 1909, 1910. Address in 1929, Newton, NJ.

BALDRIDGE, CYRUS LEROY.
Illustrator, painter and writer. Born in Alton, NY, 1889. Pupil of Frank Holme. Illustrated "I Was There," "The Spy," by Cooper, 1924 edition (Minton Balch & Co.); "Turn to the East," by, Caroline Singer, 1926 (Minton Balch & Co.) Member: GFLA. Address in 1926, Harmon-on-Hudson, NY.

BALDWIN, BARBARA.
Sculptor. Born: Portland, Maine, in 1914. Studied: Portland School of Fine Arts; Pennsylvania Academy of Fine Arts; National Academy of Design; Art Students League. Collections: Deering High School, Portland, Maine; Worlds Fair, New York, 1939; Pathe News.

BALDWIN, BURTON CLARKE.
Illustrator. Born in Danville, Ill., 1891. Pupil of Chicago Academy of Fine Arts. Member: Palette and Chisel C. Address in 1926, 805 Junior Terrace, Chicago, Ill.

BALDWIN, GEORGE.
Painter. A native of Thompson, Conn., born about 1818. He received a common school education and went to Norwich where he studied portraiture. George Baldwin painted many portraits of men prominent in his native state of Connecticut.

BALDWIN, JOSEPHINE K(NIGHT).
Painter. Born Harrisburg, July 4, 1888. Pupil of PAFA. Member: Harrisburg AA. Address in 1929, 236 North Second St., Harrisburg, PA.

BALDWIN, WILLIAM.
Born c. 1808. Flourished 1827-1846. New Orleans miniature painter.

BALFOUR, HELEN.
Painter and illustrator. Born July 11, 1857, in England. Member of California Art Club. Illustrated

42

"Sunset Highways." Address in 1926, 310 Mt. Washington Drive, Los Angeles, California.

BALINK, HENDRICUS C.
Painter and etcher. Born 1882. Exhibited landscapes entitled "The Portuguese Hill" and "Gloucester" at Penna. Academy of the Fine Arts, Philadelphia, 1921. Address in 1926, West Monument Street, Baltimore, MD. Died 1963.

BALL, CAROLINE PEDDLE.
Sculptor. Born in Terre Haute, Ind., 1869. Pupil of Augustus St. Gaudens and Kenyon Cox, New York. Honorable mention Paris Expn., 1900; sculptor of figure of "Victory" in quadriga on the US bldg., at Paris Expn., 1900; memorial corbels, Grace Church, Brooklyn; memorial fountains at Flushing, LI, and Auburn, NY. Address in 1926, Westfield, NJ. Died 1938.

BALL, L. CLARENCE.
Landscape painter. Born July 4, 1858 in Mt. Vernon, Ohio. Member of Chicago Society of Artists. His specialty was landscapes with cattle and sheep. Died October 10, 1915, in South Bend, IN.

BALL, LINN B.
Painter and illustrator. Born in Milwaukee, Wis., in 1891. Member: GFLA; Soc. of Ills. Address in 1926, 163 West 23d Street, New York.

BALL, ROBERT.
Painter and illustrator. Born in Kansas City, MO, in 1890. Pupil of Richard Miller in Paris and Brittany. Award: OH Dean Prize, Artists of Kansas City, 1915. Mural decorations in State Capitol, Jefferson, MO. Address in 1926, 9 West 47th Street, New York.

BALL, RUTH NORTON.
Sculptor. Born in Madison, Wis. Pupil of Liberty Tadd in Philadelphia. Represented in City Art Museum, St. Louis. Address in 1926, Indian Arts Bldg., San Diego, California.

BALL, THOMAS
Sculptor. Born in Charlestown, MA, June 1819. His art studies began with silhouette-cutting, miniature and portrait painting. After 1851 he devoted himself to sculpture. His prominent works are the Wash. monument in Boston, Forrest as "Coriolanus," Emancipation Group, Wash. For his life see "My Three Score Years and Ten," by Thomas Ball, Boston, 1891. Died Dec. 11, 1911 in Monclair, NJ.

BALL, THOMAS WATSON.
Painter. Born in New York City, 1863. Pupil of Art Students' League, New York. Studied with Beckwith and Mowbray. He has also done mural decorations. Ceiling decoration in Chapel of the Intercession, NYC; ceiling decoration in Trinity Chapel of the Intercession, NYC. Address in 1926, Old Lynne, Conn. Died 1934.

BALLANTINE, EDWARD J.
Painter. Born in Scotland in 1885. Member of the Society of Independent Artists. Address in 1926, 36 Grove Street, New York.

BALLANTYNE, KENNETH M.
Painter, illustrator and etcher. Born Gisborne, New Zealand, Jan. 27th, 1886. Pupil of C. F. Goldie. Member: SI. Address in 1929, 22 West 49th St.; h. 1 Oakmere Drive, Baldwin's, LI, NY.

BALLATOR, JOHN R.
Painter. Born, February 7, 1909; Portland, Oregon. 1928; Studied painting and sculpture at Universtiy of Oregon under Kenneth Hudson and Harry Camden. 1929; Entered Yale School of Fine Arts. Studied sculpture under Robert G. Eberhart, and painting under Edwin C. Taylor, Eugene Savage and Deane Keller. 1934; B.B.A. from Yale. Collaborated in executing seven panel mural in oil for Nathan Hale School, New Haven, Connecticut, under Public Works of Art Project, having at different times about seven assistants. In October, supervised a mural undertaking for Franklin High School, Portland, Oregon, consisting of one panel in oil and two over-door panels in tempera. Has painted number of

43

portraits and pictures for private individuals, receiving commissions both in the East and in Portland, Oregon.

BALLIN, HUGO.
Artist. Born New York, 1879. Studied at Art Students' League, New York, and in Rome and Florence. Awarded Scholarship Art Students' League; Shaw Prize Fund, 1905; Thomas B. Clarke Prize, 1906; Architectural League Medal, 1906 and 1907. Elected Associate Member of National Academy. Specialty, mural decorations. Works: executive chamber, Madison, Wis.; Room in home of Oliver Gould Jennings, NY City, and E. D. Brandegee of Boston; decorative pictures in many pvt. collections; also represented in National Museum, Washington, DC; Montclair Museum, NJ; Ann Mary Memorial, RI; etc. Address in 1926, 662 Lexington Ave., New York. Died Nov. 27, 1956, in CA.

BALLING, OLE P. H.
Painter. Born April 1828 in Norway. A painter of the Civil War, his "Heroes of the Republic," a group of twenty-seven Union generals on horseback, has been much praised. Died May 1, 1906.

BALLINGER, H(ARRY) R(USSELL).
Illustrator. Born in Port Townsend, Wash., 1892. Pupil Maurice Braun, Art Students' League of NY, and Harvey Dunn. Illustrations for Cosmopolitan, Good Houskeeping, Saturday Evening Post, McClure's, etc. Address in 1926, Studio, 1947 Broadway; Home, 15 West 67th Street, New York, NY.

BALLOU, BERTHA.
Painter. Born in Hornby, New York in 1891. Studied: Randolph-Macon Woman's College, Art Students League; Corcoran gallery of Art; Boston Museum of Fine Arts School. Collections: Eastern Washington Historical Museum; Spokane Public Library; Spokane County Courthouse; Washington State College; First Federal Savings Loan Bank, Spokane.

BALLOU, P. IRVING.
Painter. Exhibited water colors at the Penna. Academy of the Fine

Arts, Philadelphia, 1925. Address in 1926, 1015 Prospect Place, Brooklyn, NY.

BAMA, JAMES ELLIOTT.
Illustrator. Born in the Bronx, New York, 1926. He attended the High School of Art and Design and the ASL as a pupil of Frank Reilly. His career began in 1949 and has included illustrations for hundreds of books and magazines such as the Saturday Evening Post, Argosy and Reader's Digest, as well as posters for a number of advertising firms. His artwork has been shown in galleries across the country and is part of the permanent collections in many museums. He retired from illustration in 1971 to live and work as a Western painter in Wyoming. The results of his efforts were recently recorded in a book, Paintings by Jim Bama, published by Ballantine Books.

BAMBOROUGH, WILLIAM.
Miniature painter. An Englishman, who worked on portraits in 1830 at Shippenport.

BANASEWICZ, IGNATIUS.
Painter and etcher. Born Leningrad, Russia, Dec. 5, 1903. Pupil of W. A. Levy; A. Ostrowsky; Clinton Peters; C. C. Curran. Member: Brooklyn SE; Salons of Am.; S. Indp. A.

BANCROFT, HESTER.
Painter. Exhibited National Academy of Design, 1925. Address in 1926, Ithaca, New York.

BANCROFT, MILTON HERBERT.
Painter. Born at Newton, Mass., 1867. Student Mass. State Normal Art School, 1883-6; continued studies irregularly at PAFA; Supt. Schools and instr. in PA. Academy Fine Arts, 1892-4; studied in Colorossi, Delacluse and Julien Academies, Paris, 1894-9. Exhibited in Societe des Artists Francais, and in all large exhibitions of New York, Philadelphia, Boston, Washington and Chicago. Specialty, portraits; also executed mural decorations for Court of the Seasons, Panama-Pacific Expn., San Francisco. Instr. Mechanics Inst.,

New York. Address in 1926, 58 W. 57th Street, New York, NY.

BANKSON, G(LEN) P(EYTON).
Painter and craftsman. Born Mount Hope, Wash., Sept. 7, 1890. Self-taught. Work: Murals in Fidelity National Bank, Spokane; mantel-piece, University of Idaho, Moscow. Address in 1929, 824½ Riverside Ave.; South 222 Lacey St., Spokane, Wash.

BANNERMAN, J.
Engraver. He produced two portraits of Franklin, one in line and the other in stipple, about 1800; they were published in the "Works of Franklin" and are rather crude.

BANNERMAN, WILLIAM W.
Engraver of book illustrations for the publishers in Baltimore, MD. He etched in a rather crude manner a series of full-length portraits of statesmen for the United States Magazine and Democratic Review in 1840-45. Died c. 1846.

BANNING, WILLIAM J.
Painter. Born in Conn., in 1810. Pupil of National Academy under Sam'l Waldo. His specialty was portrait painting. He exhibited in the National Academy of Design in 1840 and 1841. He died in 1856.

BANNISTER, EDWARD M.
Artist. Born in St. Andrews, New Brunswick, in 1833. He studied art at the Lowell Institute in Boston, and spent the greater part of his professional life there. In 1871 he moved to Providence, RI. He contributed regularly to the Boston Art Club exhibitions. His picture "Under the Oaks" was awarded a first-class medal at the centennial exhibition of 1876 in Philadelphia. Died Jan. 9, 1901.

BANNISTER, ELEANOR CUNNINGHAM.
Painter. Born in New York, NY. Pupil of Whittaker in Brooklyn; Constant and Lefebvre in Paris. Member: Brooklyn Society of Artists. Work: "Portrait of Rev. R. S. Storrs," Brooklyn Museum. Died 1939. Address in 1929, 109 Cambridge Place, Brooklyn, NY.

BANNISTER, JAMES.
Engraver. Was born in England in 1821. He came to New York at an early age and was apprenticed in the engraving establishment of A. L. Dick in New York. He also became interested in bank-note work, but his chief production was portraits for book-illustrations. Died Oct. 11, 1901 in Brooklyn, NY.

BANVARD, JOHN.
Painter. Born in 1815 and died in 1891. Educated in New York schools. At an early age he supported himself with selling his pictures in New Orleans. He painted a panorama of the Mississippi River that was exhibited in this country and abroad. He also painted the picture from which the first chromo made in America was taken. It was entitled "The Orison" (New York, 1861).

BARANCEANU, BELLE.
Painter. Born Chicago, Illinois in 1905. Studied at Minneapolis School of Art and in Chicago. Pupil of Richard Lahey, Morris Davidson, Cameron Booth and Anthony Angarola. Painted and taught in Chicago, where she was member of Chicago Society of Artists and served on Board of Directors, Chicago No-Jury Society of Artists. Has exhibited at Art Institute of Chicago, Los Angeles Museum, Kansas City Art Institute, John Herron Art Institute of Indianapolis, Nebraska Art Association, Des Moines, and San Diego Fine Arts Gallery. Has painted four murals, including one in Palace of Education, Balboa Park, and one, which was executed in true fresco in the San Diego Fine Arts Gallery Garden.

BARBEE, HERBERT.
Sculptor, son of William R. Barbee the sculptor. He studied in Florence.

BARBEE, WILLIAM R.
Sculptor of Virginia. Born Jan. 17, 1818 in Luray, VA. His famous "Fisher Girl" belonged to Mrs. A. T. Stuart of New York City. Died June 16, 1868.

BARBER, ALICE.
Painter. Born in Illinois.
Studied: Indiana Univ.
Exhibitions: Univ. of Texas at
Austin; Corcoran Gallery,
Wash., DC; American Women's Show in
Hamburg, Germany. Collections:
Museum of Modern Art, New York
City; Whitney Museum of American
Art, New York City; San Francisco
Museum of Art, California.

BARBER, CHARLES E.
Engraver. Born in London in 1840;
he came to this country early in
his career. Studied with his
father, Wm. Barber. In 1869 he was
appointed assistant engraver in the
United States Mint in Philadelphia.
His best work is found in the
medals struck for Presidents
Garfield, Arthur, and the Great
Seal of the United States. Died
Feb. 19, 1917, in Philadelphia, PA.

BARBER, JOHN WARNER.
Engraver. Born 1798. He was
apprenticed to Abner Reed, who was
then established as a bank-note
engraver. Reed soon turned his
attention to engraving historical
scenes, both on copper and wood.
Barber engraved on wood the
illustrations for "Easy Lessons in
Reading" and the "History of New
England." His engraving
establishment was in New Haven,
Conn. See "Linton's Wood
Engraving." Died June 22, 1885 in
New Haven, CT.

BARBER, WILLIAM.
Engraver. Born in London, May 2,
1807 in London, Eng. came to US in
1853. became silver-plate engraver
and later Chief Engraver of US Mint
(1869-1879). Died Aug. 31, 1879 in
Phila.

BARCLAY, EDITH LORD.
Painter. Exhibited "The May
Basket" at 33d Annual of National
Association of Women Painters and
Sculptors. Address in 1926, 229
Williamsburg Ave., Brooklyn, NY.

BARCLAY, JAMES EDWARD.
Portrait painter. Born 1846. At
one time occupied a studio in this
city, during which time his
portrait of Mr. S. H. Kauffman was
painted from life. Died 1903.

BARCLAY, McCLELLAND.
Painter, illustrator. Born St.
Louis, MO, 1891. Pupil of H. C.
Ives, George R. Bridgman, Thomas
Fogarty. Member: Art Students'
League of New York; Chicago Art
Club; Art Service League, Chicago.
Awards: Navy poster prize,
Committee on National Preparedness,
1917; first prize U.S.M.C.
Recruiting poster; first prize for
allegorical painting of Commerce of
Chicago from Chicago Association of
Commerce. Died 1943. Address in
1929, 730 Fifth Ave., 350 East 57th
St., New York, NY.

BARD, JOELLEN.
Painter. Born in Brooklyn, New
York, June 19, 1942. Studied:
Pratt Institute with Gabriel
Laderman, Dore Ashton and Robert
Goodenough; Brooklyn College;
Syracuse University. Exhibitions:
The Brooklyn Museum, the Little
Gallery, 1973; Gallery 91, 1974;
Gallery 26, 1975. Address in 1980,
Pleiades Gallery, 152 Wooster St.,
New York, NY.

BARD, SARA (FORESMAN).
Painter and teacher. Born Slippery
Rock, PA. Pupil of Henry B. Snell,
George Pearse Ennis, Sigourd Skou.
Member: NA Women PS; AWCS; NYWCC;
Wash. WCC. Awards: Prize, NYWCC,
1928; prize, Balto. WCC, 1928;
Lloyd C. Griscom prize, NYWCC,
1929; Clemant Studebaker prize,
Hoosier Salon, Chicago, Ill., 1929.
Address in 1929, 40 West St. Joe
St., Indianapolis, Ind.

BARENSFELD, MARK.
Illustrator. Born in Cleveland,
1947. He attended Ohio University
and Memphis State. His career
began with an illustration for St.
Anthony's Messenger in 1970 and his
illustrations have since appeared
in Cincinnati Magazine and Writer's
Digest. He has produced posters
for Ohio universities and his works
have been shown at several Ohio
museums and Art Directors' Clubs.

BARGER, RAYMOND GRANVILLE.
Sculptor. Born in Brunswick, MD,
Aug. 27, 1906. Study:
Carnegie-Mellon Univ., BA;
Winchester Fellow, Europe; Yale
Univ., BFA; Spec. Acad. Rome, 2

years. Comn.: Column of Perfection, H. J. Heinz Co., NY Worlds Fair, 1939; J.C. Penney, NYC, 1965; J. Mitchelle Collection, NYC, 1968; Bicentennial Bronze, 1975-76. Awards: Title of Cavaliere - San Marino, Italy. Teaching: RI Sch. of Des., 1939-40; Cooper Union, New York, NY, 1940-45. Mem.: Nat'l. Sculpt. Soc., NYC; Arch. Lg. of NY. Media: Welded bronze, wood and stone. Address in 1980, The Mill, Carversville, PA.

BARHYDT, JEAN K.
(Mrs. George Weed Barhydt). Painter. Born Brooklyn, NY, 1868. Pupil of G. A. Thompson. Member: National Academy Women Painters and Sculptors; Conn. Association of Fine Arts. Address in 1926, The Belnord, 548 Orange Street, New Haven, Conn.

BARILE, XAVIER J.
Painter, illustrator, etcher. Born in Italy, March 18, 1891. Pupil of Chapman, Mora, Sloan, and Dodge. Member: Art Students' League of New York and the Kit Kat C. Address in 1929, 7 W. 14th St., h. 2126 Hughes Avenue, New York, NY.

BARKER, ALBERT WINSLOW.
Illustrator, writer, lecturer, etcher and teacher. Born Chicago, Ill., in 1874. Director of Art Education, Public Schools, City Bldg., Wilmington, Del.; Watch Hill, RI; Maylon, PA. Pupil of PAFA; Phila. School of Industrial Art. Member: Wilmington SFA; Phil. PC. Died in 1947.

BARKER, KATHERINE.
Painter. Born Pittsburgh, PA, 1891. Pupil of Breckenridge, Anshutz, Carlson, Hale, Beaux, and Vonnoh. Member: Fellowship, PAFA. Address in 1926, The Avondale, 39th and Locust Streets, Philadelphia, PA.

BARKER, M.
Miniature painter, working in New York about 1820.

BARKLEY, BRUCE E.
Illustrator. Born in New York City, 1950. He attended the ASL

and received his BFA from the School of Visual Arts. A pupil of Steven Kidd, Jack Potter and Robert Weaver, he had his first illustration, Boston Tea Party, published in 1973. His work is owned by the United States Department of Interior, USAF, Walsh Galleries in Yonkers and the Pentagon.

BARKSDALE, GEORGE (EDWARD).
Painter. Born Charlotte County, VA, Aug., 13, 1869. Pupil of William L. Shepherd, Herman Sodersten, PAFA. Member: SI; SSAL. Born 161 School Rd., Malvern Hills, Asheville, NC.

BARLOW, JOHN NOBLE.
Painter. Born 1861 in Manchester Eng. He was a member of the Providence Art Club, and is represented by three landscapes in the Rhode Island School of Design. Died March 24, 1917 in St. Ives, Cornwall, England.

BARLOW, MYRON.
Born in 1873 in Ionia, Mich. Pupil of Art Institute Chicago, and Ecole des Beaux Arts in Paris. Exhibited in Salon. Member of the Paris American Artists' Association. Works: "Mother's Love," Penna. Academy of Fine Arts; "Pecheuse," Detroit Museum of Art. Address in 1926, 362 Woodland Ave., Detroit, Mich.

BARNARD, EDWARD HERBERT.
Painter. Born July 10, 1855 in Belmont, MA. Studied at Boston Museum of Fine Arts, and with Boulanger and Collin in Paris. Awarded many honorable mentions and medals. Address in 1926, 603 Belmont Street, Belmont, Mass. Died April 16, 1909 in Westerly, MA.

BARNARD, ELINOR M.
(Mrs. Manuel Komroff). Painter. Born Kensington, London, England, Aug. 29, 1872. Member: National Academy of Women Painters and Sculptors. Specialty, portraits in water color. Address in 1926, 601 Madison Ave., New York, NY.

47

BARNARD, GEORGE GREY.
Sculptor. Born in Bellefonte, PA,
1863. Studied at Art Institute of
Chicago, Ecole Nationale des Beaux
Arts, 1884-5-6-7. Exhibited in
Paris Salon, 1894. Awarded Gold
Medal Paris Expn., 1900. Prof.
Sculpture, Art Students' League,
NY; Associate Member of National
Academy. Works include:
"Brotherly Love," "Norway," "Two
Natures" (Metropolitan Museum, New
York), "The God Pan" (in Central
Park), "The Boy," group, "Brotherly
Love in Norway," "The Hewer," "Urn
of Life" (19 figures in marble),
group, "Brotherhood in Suffering,"
"Despair and Hope," "Youth,"
"Mother and Angel," "Lone Woman,"
"Prodigal Son and Father," great
group, "Adam and Eve," relief (22
ft. high), "Labor and Rest,"
"Christ," group of "Baptism," "Love
and Labor," "The Brothers," family
group of 4 figures; PA Capitol.
Address in 1926, 454 Fort
Washington Ave., NYC. Died April
24, 1938 in NYC.

BARNARD, JOSEPHINE W.
Painter. Born in Buffalo, NY,
1869. Pupil of Dow, Snell and
Carlson. Address, 117 Waverly
Place, NY, or 26 Middagh Street,
Brooklyn, NY.

BARNARD, W. S.
Born c. 1809 in CT. Engraver of
book illustrations, working in New
York about 1845. He was associated
with A. L. Dick and was probably in
his employ in his engraving
establishment. Other engravings
are signed "Tuthill & Barnard, Sc."

BARNES, BURT.
Painter, illustrator, writer, and
teacher. Born Manitowoc, Wisc.,
June 30, 1879. Pupil of AIC.
Member: Wisc. PS. Award: Water
Color prize, Milwaukee, 1925.
Work: "Under the Viaduct" and "The
Lagoon," Milwaukee Art Institute,
Milwaukee, Wisc. Address in 1929,
528 Clyde Ave., Wauwatosa, Wisc.

BARNES, ERNEST HARRISON.
Landscape painter and teacher.
Born Portland, NY, 1873. Exhibited
at National Academy of Design,
1925. Pupil of Art Students'
League, Howe Foote, Charles H.

Davis and Henry R. Poore New York.
Teacher of freehand drawing and
painting, Univ. of Mich. Address
in 1926, Detroit, Mich.

BARNES, GERTRUDE JAMESON.
(Mrs. Henry N. Barnes.). Painter.
Born at Tyngsboro, Mass., 1865.
Pupil of Minneapolis School of Fine
Arts. Specialty, landscapes.
Work: "In the Orchard," "Trees by
the Sea." Address in 1926, 1812
Emerson Ave., Minneapolis, Minn.

BARNES, HIRAM PUTNAM.
Artist, illustrator. Born in
Boston, 1857. Public school
education; studied drawing and
painting with Fernand Lungren and
F. Childe Hassam. Began as engraver
making designs for Waltham Watch
Co., also engraved on wood; became
illustrator for leading Boston
publishers. Exhibited water colors
Boston Art Club. Address in 1926,
Waltham, Mass.

BARNES, JOHN P.
Painter. Exhibited pastels at the
Annual Water Color Exhibition at
the Penna. Academy of Fine Arts,
Philadelphia, 1922. Address in
1926, 518 Parker Ave.,
Collingsdale, Penna.

BARNET, WILL.
Painter and printmaker. Born in
Beverly, MA, May 25, 1911. Work:
In the permanent collections of the
Metropolitan Museum of Art, the
Museum of Modern Art, the Whitney
Museum of American Art, The
Guggenheim Museum, New York; The
Corcoran Gallery of Art,
Washington; the Pennsylvania
Academy of Fine Arts, Philadelphia;
the Museum of Fine Arts, Boston.
Exhibitions of his prints:
Associated American Artists in
1972, 79, 82. Taught at the Art
Students League from 1934-78, at
Cooper Union from 1944-77, and he
continues to teach at the
Pennsylvania Academy of Fine Arts.
Academician, NAD, 1982; Am. Acad.
of Arts and Letters, 1982. Living
in New York City.

BARNETT, EUGENE A.
Illustrator, painter, sculptor,
etcher and writer. Born Atlanta,
GA, March 18, 1894. Pupil of

Edward Penfield. Member: SI. Address in 1929, 522 Fifth Ave.; 1 West 67th St., New York, NY.

ARNETT, TOM P.
Painter. Exhibited oil painting entitled "Old Coal Pocket" at Penna. Academy of the Fine Arts, Philadelphia, 1921. Student of Paul Carnoyer. Born in St. Louis, MO, in 1870. Address in 1926, Lindell Boulevard, St. Louis, Missouri.

ARNEY, ALICE PIKE.
Painter and writer. Born Cincinnati, Ohio, in 1860. Pupil of Carolus Duran and Whistler. Represented by portraits of Whistler (used in illustrating) and of Natalie Barney, owned by the French Government. Address in 1926, Studio House, Washington, DC.

ARNEY, FRANK A.
Painter. Born Union Springs, NY, Dec. 7, 1862. Work: "Gray Day" and "April Morning," Syracuse Museum of Fine Arts. Address in 1929, 4 Howard St., Auburn, NY.

ARNEY, JOHN STEWART.
Landscape painter. Born 1869. He exhibited a collection of Scottish and American landscapes at the Ehrich Galleries, New York, in 1924. He died in New York City, Nov. 22, 1925, in his 57th year.

ARNEY, MARIAN GREENE.
(Mrs. W. Pope Barney). Painter and architect. Born St. Paul, Minn. Pupil of Cecilia Beaux, Violet Oakley, Emil Carlsen, Phillip Hale, Pearson. Member: Fellowship PAFA; Phila. Alliance; Print C. Address in 1929, "Wychwood," Moylan, PA.

ARNHORN, CLEMENT JOHN.
Sculptor. Born in Cincinnati, Ohio, in 1857. Pupil of Rebisso in Cinncinatti; Bouguereau, Peuch, Mercie, Ferrier and Julian Acad. in Paris. Studied at Academie Julien in Paris. Salon Medals and honorable mention. Member of National Sculpture Society, Cincinnati Art club. Works; Fountain figures, Hartford, Conn., and Prince George Hotel, New York; "Magdalen," Cincinnati Art Museum.

Address in 1926, Art Museum, Cincinnati, Ohio. Died 1935.

BARNITZ, MYRTLE TOWNSEND.
Painter, sculptor, craftsman, writer and teacher. Born Greensburg, PA. Pupil of Charles Francis Browne, Thomas Hovenden, Thomas Eakins, William Gilchrist, Thomas P. Anshutz, Hugh Breckenridge. Member: Fellowship PAFA; Chicago NJSA. Work: "Help Belgium" and "Boy Scout." Red Cross, Chicago. Address in 1929, Glen View, Ill.

BARNS, CORNELIA.
Painter and illustrator. Born in New York, 1888. Pupil of Twachtman and Chase. Illustrated for the "Liberator." Address in 1926, Morgan Hill, California.

BARNUM, EMILY KEENE.
Painter. Born in New York, 1874. Pupil of Vibet in Paris and Irving Wiles in New York. Member of Art Students' League, New York. Founder and editor of "The Swiss Monthly," published at Lausanne. Specialty is water colors. Address in 1929, Les Tourelles, Mousquines 2, Lansanne, Switzerland.

BARNUM, J. H.
Painter and illustrator. Member: GFLA; SI. Address in 1929, Silvermine, Norwalk, Conn.

BARONE, ANTONIO.
Painter. Born 1889. Member of Oakland Art Association, Oakland, Calif. Awarded Gold Medal, Philadelphia Art Club, 1917. Exhibited "Grazia" at the Carnegie Institute, 1920, and "Lady with Muff" at the Penna. Academy of the Fine Arts, 1921. Address in 1926, 771 Lexington Ave., New York City.

BARR, PAUL E.
Painter, writer, lecturer, and teacher. Born near Goldsmith, Ind., Nov. 25, 1892. Pupil of AIC. Member: Tipton AA; S. Indp. A.; Chicago AC; Indiana AC; Hoosier Salon; AFA. Work in Goldsmith Public Schools. Died 1953.

BARR, WILLIAM.
Painter and illustrator. Born in Scotland, April 26, 1867. Among

49

his works "Paisley Cross," portrait of Provost Peter Eadie, and portrait of Thomas Boyle at City Hall, San Francisco. Address in 1926, 311 Lyon Street, San Francisco, Calif. Died 1933.

BARRALET, JOHN JAMES.
Painter and engraver. Born in Ireland, 1747. He died in Philadelphia, 1815. He painted portraits, engraved a few plates, painted landscapes in water color, and designed a number of plates for other engravers.

BARRATT, LOUISE BASCOM.
Illustrator. Member: SI. Address in 1929, 2 West 67th St., New York, NY.

BARRATT, THOS. E.
Miniature painter. Born c. 1814 in Eng. Flourished 1837-1854, Philadelphia. May have been a relative of Edward Barratt, who painted miniatures in Dublin in 1790.

BARRATT, WATSON.
Illustrator and mural painter. Born in Salt Lake City, Utah, in 1884. Pupil of Howard Pyle and Henri. Represented by "Canton Street" in Corcoran Art Gallery, and mural painting in Burham Library, Art Institute, Chicago. Address in 1926, 330 West 39th St., New York.

BARRET, LAURA A.
Painter. Member: Society of Independent Artists, National Arts Club, 15 Gramercy Park, New York, NY.

BARRETT, ELIZABETH HUNT.
(Mrs. Edward N. Barrett). Painter. Born New York, NY, 1863. Pupil of NAD. Address, Amherst, VA.

BARRIE, ERWIN (S.).
Painter. Born Canton, Ohio, June 3, 1886. Pupil AIC. Member: Chicago AC; Business Men's AC of Chicago. Address in 1926, 1188 Asbury Ave., Hubbard Woods, Ill.

BARRINGTON, AMY L.
Painter. Born Jersey City, NJ; pupil of Cox, Brush, and Chase. Member: National Academy of Women

Painters and Sculptors. Lecture and wrote in magazines on interior decoration, art objects, an archaeology. Address in 1926, 308 Broadway, New York, NY.

BARRON.
A little-known genre painter note in Tuckerman's "Book of the Artists."

BARRY, CHARLES A.
Born July, 1830 in Boston Portrait and genre painter. Amon, his best remembered work wa "Motherless," "Evangeline," and head of the poet Whittier. H flourished in Boston, 1851-1859 Died 1892.

BARRY, EDITH C(LEAVES).
Painter. Born in Boston, Mass Studied in New York and France Member: National Academy of Wome Painters and Sculptors; Conn Academy of Fine Arts; Society o Independent Artists; Art Students League of New York.

BARRY, GERARD M.
Painter. Born in County Cork Ireland, 1864. Began to study ar at Paris, France, in 1885, at th Academie Julien, and studied unde Le Febre, Boulanger, and Carolu Duran. Exhibited in the Pari Salons of 1885 and 1886, and at th Royal Academy, London, England, i 1887. Came to the United States i 1888, and after remaining for 1 months returned to study unde Carmon. Returned to United States

BARRY, JOHN J(OSEPH).
Etcher. Born Hamilton, Ontario Canada, 1885. Pupil of Ernes Haskell; Joseph Pennell; Fran Short in London. Member California Society of Etchers Calif. Print-Makers. Address i 1926, Burton Arms Apts., 680 Witme Street, Los Angeles, Calif.

BARSE, GEORGE RANDOLPH, JR.
Artist. Born Detroit, 1861 Studied art at Ecole des Beaux Art and Academie Julien, Paris 1879-85; pupil of A. Cabanel Boulanger and Lefebvre. Academ prize, Paris, France, 1882; Ne England prize, Boston, 1885; 1s prize Nat. Acad. Design, 1895

50

Academy of National Arts, 1898; National Academy, 1899. Member: Architectural League of New York. Work: Eight panels in Library of Congress, Wash., DC; Represented in the Vanderpoel Art Assn. Collection, Chicago. Address in 1926, Katonah, NY. Died 1938.

BARTH, EUGENE F(IELD).
Painter, sculptor, illustrator and teacher. Born St. Louis, Mar. 4, 1904. Pupil of Fred C. Carpenter. Member: ASL of NY. Award: Halsey Ives prize, St. Louis Artists Guild, 1928. Address in 1929, 311 Queen Anne Rd., Reaneck, NJ; summer, 3925 South Compton Ave., St. Louis, MO.

BARTHOLDI, FREDERIC AUGUSTE.
French sculptor. Born in 1834. Known in this country from his gigantic statue of "Liberty Enlightening the World" on Bedloes Island in New York harbor. He was a commissioner in 1876 of the French government, at the Centennial Exposition in Philadelphia. His statue of "Lafayette Arriving in America" is in Union Square, New York. Died 1904.

BARTHOLOMEW, EDWARD SHEFFIELD.
Sculptor. Born in Connecticut in 1822. He studied in Italy. A collection of his work is in Hartford, Conn. His full-length statue of Washington belonged to Noah Walker and his "Eve Repentant" to Jos. Harrison of Philadelphia. He died in Naples in 1858.

BARTLE, GEORGE P.
Wood engraver. Born in 1853. He studied wood engraving with H. H. Nichols. Much of his best work was done for the Century Magazine. He died in 1918.

BARTLE, SARA N(ORWOOD).
Miniature painter. Born Washington, DC. Pupil of Carroll Beckwith, Art Students' League of NY; Art Students' League of Washington. Address in 1926, 2300 18th Street, Washington, DC.

BARTLETT, DANA.
Painter, illustrator, and teacher. Born Ionia, Mich., Nov. 19, 1878.

Pupil ASL of NY and William M. Chase; Coussens in Paris. Member: Calif. AC; Calif. WCS; Decorative AS; Laguna Beach AA; Painters and Sculptors C. Represented in Sacramento (Calif.) State Library; "Nocturne" and "California Landscape," Los Angeles Museum of Art; Southwest Museum; "The Lake of Enchantment," Huntington Collection, San Gabriel, Calif.; "California," permanent collection, Los Angeles Public Library; "California Landscape," Lafayette Park Branch, Los Angeles Public Library; "The Blue Hill," Gardena School Coll.; "Seven Poplars," Hollywood High School; "Pacific Coast," Garfield High School, Los Angeles; "Venetian Boats," permanent print department, Public Library, Boston, Mass. Illustrations for "The Bush Aflame." Address in 1929, 101 South Virgil Ave., Los Angeles, Calif. Died 1957.

BARTLETT, ELIZABETH M. P.
Painter and teacher. Member: Society of Independent Artists. Pupil of Comins; Breckenridge; Naum Los in Rome. Address in 1926, 136 Hemenway Street, Boston, Mass.

BARTLETT, FREDERIC CLAY.
Artist. Born at Chicago, June 1, 1873. Educated, Harvard School, St. Paul's School, Concord, NH, Royal Academy Art Munich, Germany, and studied art in Paris under Collin, Aman-Jean, Whistler, etc. Professionally engaged as artist in mural decorations in Council Chamber of Chicago City Hall. Address in 1926, The Players, 16 Gramercy Park, New York. Died 1953.

BARTLETT, MADELEINE ADELAIDE.
Painter, craftsman and writer. Born in Woburn. Pupil of Cowles Art School, and Henry H. Kitson. Specialty, small bas-reliefs. Exhibited portraits at Penna. Academy of the Fine Arts, 1924. Address in 1926, Boyleston Street, Boston, Mass.

BARTLETT, PAUL WAYLAND.
Sculptor and painter. Born New Haven, Conn., 1865. Went to France in childhood. Pupil of Cavelier and Rodin. Represented by statue

of General Joseph Warren in Boston, equestrian statue of Lafayette in Louvre, Paris, statue of Columbus in Washington. Elected member of National Academy of Design, 1917. Painting "The Pond above the Sea" at Carnegie Institute, 1923. Also in collections of MMA; Hartford State Capitol and Library of Congress. Died Sept. 20, 1925 in Paris, France.

BARTLETT, PAUL.
Painter. Born Taunton, Mass., July 8, 1881. Pupil of John Sloan. Member: S. Indp. A. Awards: Hon. mention, Chicago SA, 1919. Work: "Landscape," Cincinnati Museum, Cincinnati, O.; "Landscape," Luxemburg Museum, Paris, France. Address in 1929, 1965 East 60th St., New York, NY.

BARTLETT, TRUMAN H.
Sculptor, teacher. Born Dorset, VT, 1835. Pupil of Fremiet in Paris. Work: "Wells," bronze statue, Hartford, Conn.; "Benedict," cemetery monument, Waterbury, Conn.; "Clark," cemetery monument, Hartford, Conn.; many busts and statuettes. Writings: "Life of Dr. William Rimmer," "Physiognomy of Abraham Lincoln." He died in 1923.

BARTOL, E. H. (MISS).
Painter. A disciple of William M. Hunt, who had her studio in Boston.

BARTON, DONALD B(LAGGE).
Painter. Born Fitchburg, Aug. 23, 1903. Pupil of Michael Jacobs, Philip Hale, A. T. Hibbard, Gifford Beal, Hans Hoffman. Member: NYWCC; North Shore AA; Rockport AA; Gloucester SA. Address in 1929, 61 Fox St., Fitchburg, Mass.; summer, Rockport, Mass.

BARTON, LOREN ROBERTA.
Painter and Etcher. Born Oxford, Mass. Member of California Art Club. Her dry point of Geo. Arliss as Disraeli, and her study of the Spaniards of California are well known. Address in 1926, 993 South Wilton Place, Los Angeles, Calif.

BARTON, RALPH.
Painter and illustrator. Born Kansas City, MO, 1891. Worked for "Kansas City Star;" moved to New York City in 1910, where he did satirical drawings, caricatures for "Harper's Weekly," "Puck" "Judge," "Liberty," Vanity Fair," The New Yorker." Anita Loos' Gentlemen Prefer Blondes and his own Science in Rhyme Without Reason and God's Country. Died in 1931.

BARTOO, CATHERINE R.
Born Williamsport, Penna. Pupil of Henri and Mora. Address in 1926, 102 Oak Street, Binghamton, NY.

BASING, CHARLES.
Painter. Born in Australia in 1865. Pupil of Bougereau. Executed museum decorations in Columbia College, New York, and Carnegie Institute, Pittsburgh. Address in 1926, 163 Clymer Street, Brooklyn, NY.

BASKIN, LEONARD.
Painter, sculptor and graphic artist. Born in New Brunswick, NJ, Aug. 15, 1922. Moved to Brooklyn, NY, 1929. Studied at NYU, 1939-41; apprenticed to sculptor M. Glickman; Yale School of Fine Arts, 1941-43; Tiffany Found. Fellow, 1947; New School for Soc. Research, AB, 1949, DFA, 1966; Academie de la Grande Chaumiere, Paris, 1949; Academia di Belle Arti, Florence, 1950. Illustrated Auguries of Innocence by Wm. Blake, in 1959. In collections of MOMA, Met. Mus. of Art, Brooklyn Mus., Nat'l. Gallery in Wash., Fogg Art Museum; other in US and abroad. Exhibited at New Sch. for Social Research, 1967; Sao Paulo, Brazil; Mus. of Mod. Art, Paris; and others in US and abroad. Received Guggenheim Found. Fellowship, 1953; medal, Am. Inst. of Graphic Artists, 1965; Medal, Nat'l. Inst. of Arts and Letters, 1969; and others. Taught at Smith College, 1953-74. Mem., Nat'l. Inst. of Arts and Letters; Am. Inst. of Graphic Artists. Represented by Kennedy Galleries, NYC. Address in 1982, Lurley Near Tiverton, Devon, England.

BASSETT, REVEAU MOTT.
Painter. Born 1897. Exhibited at National Academy of Design, New York, 1925. Member: Dallas AA;

SSAL. Address in 1926, Dallas, Texas.

ASSETT, W. H.
Engraver. His plates occur in "The Poetical Works of John Trumbull," Published in Hartford, Conn., in 1820, the designs being by E. Tisdale.

ASSFORD, WALLACE.
Painter and illustrator. Born St. Louis, MO, Jan. 2, 1900. Pupil of Wuerpel, Carpenter, Gleeson, Goetch, George Elmer Browne, and the St. Louis School of FA. Member: Alliance. Address in 1929, Louderman Bldg.; h. 6 Shaw Pl., St. Louis, MO; summer, Provincetown, Mass.

ASTIAN, LINDA.
Painter. Born in Ayer, Mass., Nov. 7, 1940. Studied at Antioch College, Ohio; Boston Mus. School; NYU, Ph D art educ. Head, dept. of art educ., School of Visual Arts, NYC. Work in collections of Port Authority of NY and NJ; UN Children's Fund, Readers' Digest, and others. Exhibited at SOHO 20 Gallery, Ellen Sragow Gallery, Jane Baum Gallery, others in NYC; Durmont-Landis Gallery, New Brunswick, NJ; and other locations. Member of SOHO 20 Gallery. Works depict flowers; media include oil, watercolor, painting on silk. Living in New York City in 1983.

ATCHELDER, MRS. E. B. L.
See Evelyn Longman.

ATCHELOR, CLARENCE DANIEL.
Illustrator. Member: SI. Address in 1929, 12 West 8th St.; 226 Fifth Ave., New York, NY. Died 1977.

ATE, RUTLEDGE.
Painter. Born 1891. Exhibited portrait at Annual Exhibition of the National Academy of Design, 1925. Address in 1926, Brooklyn, NY.

ATEMAN, CHARLES.
Painter. Born in Minneapolis in 1890. Pupil of Art Students' League of New York. Address in 1926, Woodstock, Ulster Co., NY.

BATEMAN, JOHN.
Sculptor. Born Cedarville, NJ, 1887. Studied at PAFA; also studied in Paris. Pupil of Charles Grafly. Works: One hundred year Anniversary Fountain and Soldier's Memorial Fountain, Doylestown, PA; large group machinery and three historical bas relief panels for Penna. Bldg. Sesqui-Centennial Exposition, Phila. Address in 1926, 230 Park Ave., Haddonfield, NJ.

BATEMAN, WILLIAM.
Engraver on "stone, steel, silver, and copper." Is known only from his advertisement in the New York Mercury for Dec. 1, 1774.

BATES, BERTHA DAY (MRS.).
Painter and illustrator. Born Aug. 20, 1875. Pupil of Howard Pyle. Member: Plastic C. Born in Philadelphia in 1875. Address in 1926, Chestnut Hill, Philadelphia.

BATES, DEWEY.
Painter. Born 1851. Specialized in landscape painting, portraiture, genre. He studied in Paris, under Gerome.

BATES, EARL KENNETH
Painter. Born 1895. Exhibited oil paintings "The Waning Year" and "The Hills of Pennsylvania" in the Penna. Academy of the Fine Arts, Philadelphia, 1921, also 1924. "Experience," Beach Memorial Collection, Conn. State College; "Boundaries, "Penn. Academy of the FA. He was born in Haverhill, Mass., in 1895. Pupil of Penna. Academy of Fine Arts. Address in 1926, North 21st Street, Philadelphia; Studio, Hopewell, NJ.

BATES, GLADYS (BERGH).
Painter and illustrator. Born London, England, of American parents, July 19, 1898. Pupil of New York School of Fine and Applied Art; Felicie Waldo Howell; Howard Giles. Member: Alliance; NA Women PS; North Shore AA; Cath. L. Wolfe AC. Died 1944.

BATES, JOHN EVERTS.
Painter and teacher. Born Brooklyn, NY; Dec. 22, 1891. Pupil of Henry Lee McFee. Address in

53

1929. Architects Bldg.; h. 1412 Pontiac Rd., Ann Arbor, Mich.

BATHER, GEORGE.
Engraver. Born in England, he came to the United States in 1851. He was employed in book illustrating in New York by J. C. Buttre & Co. His son, George Bather, Jr., was employed by the same firm. Died in Brooklyn in 1890.

BATHER, W. T.
An engraver of portraits in a mixed and rather mechanical manner, working in Chicago in 1897, and residing in Brooklyn, NY. He was probably a son of the engraver George Bather.

BATHURST, CLYDE C.
Sculptor. Born in Mount Union, Penna., 1883. Pupil of Grafly at Penna. Academy of Fine Arts. Address in 1926, 20th and Cherry Streets, Philadelphia. Died 1938.

BATTLES, D. BLAKE.
Painter, craftsman, and teacher. Born Wellington, Ohio, Dec. 25, 1887. Pupil of Henry Keller, F. C. Gottwald, Herman Matzen. Member: Cleveland SA. Address in 1929, Art and Color Section, General Motors Corp'n, Detroit, Mich.

BAUER, THEODOR.
Sculptor. Exhibited at the National Sculpture Society in New York.

BAUER, WILLIAM.
Painter, illustrator and craftsman. Born in St. Louis, MO, in June 13, 1888. Awarded 1921 prize for landscapes. Represented in Kansas City Art Inst. Address in 1926, 709 Pine Street, St. Louis, MO.

BAUGHMAN, MARY B.
Sculptor. Born in Richmond, VA. Pupil of Colarossi Academy. Address in 1926, 521 West Grace Street, Richmond, Virginia.

BAULCH, A. V.
Engraver. Did some excellent line engraving for the Appletons of New York in 1869, after designs by F. O. C. Darley.

BAUM, WALTER EMERSON.
Painter and illustrator. Born in Penna., Dec. 14, 1884. Pupil of PAFA, T. Trego and PAFA. Exhibited at the PAFA, 1924. Address in 1926, Sellersville, Bucks County, PA. Died July 12, 1956 in PA.

BAUMANN, GUSTAVE.
Engraver, painter and illustrator. Born in Germany, 1881. Awarded gold medal for engraving at San Francisco, 1915. Member: Chicago SA; Cliff Dwellers; Calif. P.M. Awards: Gold Medal for engraving. Represented in the Vanderpoel art Assoc. Collection, Chicago. Address in 1926, 140 Canyon Road, Santa Fe, NM. Died 1971.

BAUMBER, JULIUS H.
Portrait painter. Born in Germany in 1848, he came to America in 1869, and died in Chicago in 1917.

BAUS, S(IMON) (PAUL).
Painter. Born in Indianapolis Sept. 4, 1882. Pupil of Adams Forsyth and Stark. Member: Ind. SS; Hoosier Salon. Awards: First Wanamaker prize, Philadelphia, 1909; Holcomb prize ($100) Indianapolis Art Assoc., 1919; Indianapolis Art Assn. prize, 1921 hon. mention in portraiture, Chicago Exhibition of American Painters and Sculptors, 1923; Foulke prize, Richmond, Ind. AA 1924; Studebaker prize for portraiture, Hoosier Salon Chicago, 1925; Muncie AL prize Hoosier Salon, Chicago, 1926; Griffiths prize, Hoosier Salon, Chicago 1927; Kittle portrait prize, Hoosier Salon, Chicago 1928. Represented in John Herron Art Inst., and the Richmond Art Gallery, Richmond, Ind. Address in 1929, 47 Union Trust Bldg., 110 East Market St., h. 26 de Quincy St., Indianapolis, Ind

BAUSMAN, MARIAN D.
See Mrs. Otis L. Walker

BAXTER, BERTHA E.
Painter. Exhibited oil paintings "Evening Tide" and "Sails Drying" at the Penna. Academy of Fine Arts 1921, Philadelphia, and "Down by the Sea" at National Academy, NY

54

1925. Address in 1926, Gramercy Park, New York City.

AXTER, ELIJAH, JR.
Painter. Born in Hyannis, Mass., Sept. 1, 1849. Studied in the Antwerp Academy from 1871-73, after that his studio was in Providence, RI. Painted landscapes with figures, and occasional fruit and flower pieces. He exhibited at the Boston Art Club and the Academy of Design in New York. Address in 1929, "The Rocks," Ocean Ave.; h. Ocean Ave., Newport, RI.

AXTER, MARTHA WHEELER.
Miniature painter. Born at Castleton, VT, in 1869. Pupil of Penna. Academy of Fine Arts and Art Students' League of New York; also studied in Paris and Venice. Represented by "The Girl in Red," at Penna. Academy Fine Arts in 1924. "Lieut. L. E. Bray, UAN," Nat. Gallery, Wash.; "Girl with Black Hat, "Museum of History, Science and Art, Los Angeles; Late and Fifth Earl of Chichester," Staumer Park Collection, England. Address, Santa Barbara, Calif. Died 1955.

AYARD, CLIFFORD ADAMS.
Painter and etcher. Member of the Associated Artists of Pittsburgh. Curator of Exhibitions, Carnegie Inst., 1921-1922. He exhibited "The Road to Ripples," at the Carnegie Institute, Pittsburgh, PA. Address in 1929, 433 Thirtieth Ave., McKeesport, Penna.

AYARD, ELEANOR.
Painter. Member: NA Women PS. Address in 1929, 44 Morningside Dirve; 411 West 114th St., New York, NY.

AYHA, EDWIN F.
Illustrator. Member: Fellowship PAFA. Address in 1929, Glenside, PA.

AYLINSON, A. S.
Painter. Born in Moscow, Russia Jan. 6, 1882. Pupil of Robert Henri. Member of Society of Independent Artists. Represented in Newark Museum and Public Library and New York Univ. Address in

1926, 1947 Broadway, New York. Died 1950.

BAYLISS, LILLIAN.
Miniature painter.

BAYLOR, EDNA ELLIS.
(Mrs. Armistead K. Baylor). Painter. Born Hartford, Conn., May 9, 1882. Pupil of Boston Art Museum, Frank Benson, Edmund Tarbell, Ross Turner, Henry Rice. Member: NAC; North Shore AA; Springfield AL; Nat'l. Lg. Amer. Pen Women; Amer. Artists Prof. Lg; Copley S. Award: First hon. mention, Nat'l. Lg. Amer. Pen Women, New York, 1929. Address in 1929, 15 Park Ave., New York, NY; summer, Ipswich, Mass.

BAYLOS, ZELMA.
Painter, sculptor, lithographer and writer. Born in Hungary. Pupil of Will Low. Painted portrait of General Geo. R. Dyer, also "Spirit of Democracy" owned by the American Red Cross. "Reflections after Sunset," Standish Hall, NY. Address in 1929, 1 East 47th St., New York, NY.

BAYMAN, LEO.
Sculptor. Exhibited a portrait at the Penna. Academy of Fine Arts, Philadelphia, 1920. Address in 1926, 10 East 14th Street, New York.

BEACH, CHESTER.
Sculptor. Born San Francisco, Calif., May 23, 1881. Pupil of Verlet and Roland in Paris; studied in Rome. Member: NA 1924; AM Acad. AL; NY Arch. Lg.; NSS; American Numismatic Society; NAC; New Soc. A; AFA. Awards: Gold medal, Julian Academy, 1905; Barnett prize, NAD, 1907; silver medal P.-P. Exp., San F., 1915; 1st prize NAC, 1923; gold medal, Architectural League, NY, 1924; Potter Palmer gold medal ($1,000), AIC, 1925; gold medal and prize, NAC, 1926. Works: Three large groups on the Main Tower, Court of Abundance, P.-P. Exp.; "The Sacred Fire," Academy of Arts and Letters; marble reredos, St. Mark's Church, New York; "Cloud Forms," Brooklyn Museum; marble portrait head, Art Institute of Chicago; "Dawn,"

55

Cleveland Art Museum; "Beyond," California Palace of the Legion of Honor, San Francisco; "Spirit of the Barnard Greek Games," Barnard College; "Fountain of the Waters and Signs of Zodiac," terrace, Gallery of Fine Arts, Cleveland, Ohio; "Surf," Newark Art Museum; bronze, "Service," with marble figures in relief, Messages of Peace and War, American Telephone and Telegraph Building, New York; portraits of Peter Cooper, Asa Gray, Eli Whitney, S. F. B. Morse, Hall of Fame, New York; Henry Fairfield Osborn, Am. Museum of Natural History, New York; Augustus Juilliard, Juilliard Musical Foundation, New York; Adolph Lewisohn, Lewisohn Stadium, New York; U. S. Coins, Monroe-Adams half dollar, Lexington-Concord half dollar, Hawaiian dollar. Died 1956. Address in 1929, 207 East 17th St., New York, NY.

BEACHAM, NOBLE F.
Painter. Exhibited water color at the Penna. Academy of the Fine Arts, Philadelphia, 1925. Address in 1926, Lansdowne, Penna.

BEACHAM, OLIVER C(ONLEY).
Painter and etcher. Born Xenia, Ohio, Oct. 4, 1862. Member: Dayton SE; Dayton Fine AG; Am. APL. Address in 1929, 215 Oakwood Ave., Dayton, Ohio.

BEAL, GIFFORD.
Painter. Born in New York City, 1879. Pupil of William Chase, Du Mond, and Ranger. Elected Associate Member of National Academy 1908, and Academician 1914. Represented at Metropolitan Museum by "Mayfair" and "The Albany Boat;" at Chicago Institute by "A Puff of Smoke." Also at Syracuse Museum and San Francisco Art Institute. Address in 1926, 230 West 59th Street, New York. Died Feb. 5, 1956 in New York City.

BEAL, REYNOLDS.
Painter. Born in New York City, Oct. 11, 1867. Pupil of William Chase, and studied in Europe, especially at Madrid. Elected Associate Member of National Academy, 1909; also member of New York Water Color Club. Address in

1929, 80 Middle Street, Glouster MA. Died 1951.

BEALES, ISAAC B.
Painter. Born Great Yarmouth England, 1866. Pupil of E. J Poynter, Woodhouse Stubbs. Addres in 1926, 356 Harrison Ave. Hasbrouck Heights, NJ.

BEALS, GERTRUDE.
See Mrs. Frank B. A. Bourne.

BEAMES, S(TEPHEN).
Sculptor and teacher. Born Multan India, March 3, 1869. Pupil o Boston School of Fine Arts an Crafts; Albin Polasek; Beaux-Art Inst. of Design in New York. Work War Memorial, Evanston, Ill. sculpture for Chicago Theologica Seminary. Instructor: Rockfor College, Rockford, Ill. Address i 1929, 1608 Ridge Ave., Evanston IL.

BEAN, CAROLINA VAN HOOK.
(Mrs. Algernon H. Binyon) Painter, writer, and teacher. Bor Washington, DC. Pupil of Harr Thompson, Paris; Chase, New York John S. Sarent, London. Member National Academy of Women Painter and Sculptors. Address in 1926-301 O Street, Washington, DC.

BEARD, ADELIA BELLE.
Artist. Born Painesville, Ohio Went to New York; studied drawin at Cooper Union and Art Students League; portrait painting wit Wyatt Eaton and William Chase Taught classes in drawing an painting; exhibited at Nationa Academy Design; illustrated book and magazines. Died Feb. 16, 192 in Flushing, NY.

BEARD, DANIEL CARTER.
("Dan Beard"). Painter an illustrator. Born Cincinnati, OH June 21, 1850; son of James Henr Beard, NA Pupil of Sartain an Beckwith at ASL of NY. Member: SI Ind. SS; ASL (hon.). Specialty animals and illustrating books o outdoor life; cartoonist, historia Americana. Illustrated fo Cosmopolitan, Harpers, Century Scribners, Life, Puck, Judge an works of Mark Twain. Address i 1929, Suffern, NY. Died 1941.

56

BEARD, FRANK.
The third son of the artist James Henry Beard was a special artist for Harper & Bros. during the Civil War. He was for a time Professor of Fine Arts in Syracuse University. Born in Cincinnati OH in 1842. Died Sept. 28, 1905 in Chicago, IL.

BEARD, GEORGE.
Miniature painter. Flourished 1840, Cincinnati, Ohio.

BEARD, HENRY.
The second son of the artist James Henry Beard. He painted genre subjects in oil and water colors and made designs for many of Prang's publications.

BEARD, JAMES HENRY.
Painter. Born in 1812 in Buffalo, New York, died at Flushing, LI. He lived in Cincinnati during the earlier part of his life at a time when he devoted himself almost exclusively to portrait painting. He is known to have made portraits of Henry Clay, and Presidents John Q. Adams, Taylor, and Wm. H. Harrison. He came to New York in 1846 and was one of the originators and charter members of the Century Club. In his later years he devoted his time chiefly to animal painting. In 1872 he was elected a full member of the New York School of Design.

BEARD, LINA.
Illustrator. Born Cincinnati, Ohio. Sister of Daniel C. Beard. Pupil of Cooper Union and ASL of NY. Author and illustrator, with her sister Adelia, of "Little Folks Handy Book," etc. Address in 1929, Flushing, NY.

BEARD, WILLIAM HOLBROOK.
Born in Painesville, Ohio, April 13, 1824. Began his career as a traveling portrait painter after some instruction from his elder brother, James H. Studio in Buffalo, NY, 1850. Went to Europe in 1857. Studied and painted in Dusseldorf, Switzerland, Italy and France. Settled in New York City, 1860. National Academy 1862. Represented at Chicago Art Institute by "The Bear's Temperance Question." Died Feb. 20, 1900 in New York City.

BEATTY, JOHN WESLEY.
Painter and etcher. Born Pittsburgh, PA, 1851. Pupil of Royal Bavarian Academy, Munich. Has been represented at several exhibitions. Member of jury on painting, Columbian Exp., Chicago, 1893; National Advisory Board, Paris Exp., 1900; Fine Arts Committee Pan-American Exp., Buffalo, 1901; National Advisory Committee, St. Louis Exp., 1904; International Jury of Awards, Panama-Pacific International Exp., San Francisco, 1915. Member: Pittsburgh Art Society; Pittsburgh Photographers' Society; Royal Society of Arts, London. Director Department of Fine Arts, Carnegie Institute, Pittsburgh. Represented by "Plymouth Hills," at National Gallery, Washington, DC. Address in 1926, Richland Lane, Pittsburgh, PA. Died Sept. 29, 1924 in Clifton Springs, NY.

BEAU, JOHN ANTHONY.
Engraver and chaser. He was a drawing teacher and a silver-plate engraver and advertised in the New York Journal for Dec. 13, 1770.

BEAUCHAMP, ROBERT.
Painter. Born Nov. 19, 1923, in Denver, Colo. Study: Colo. Springs Fine Arts Center and Univ. of Denver; Hans Hofmann School of Fine Arts; BFA from Cranbrook in Michigan. Taught at Brooklyn College and School of Vis. Arts. Work: Carnegie. Inst.; Denver Art Museum; Whitney; Met. Mus. of Art; private collections. Exhib.: Tanager, Green, Hansa, March Galleries, NYC; MOMA; Whitney; Carnegie Inst.; AIC; others. Awards: Fullbright, 1959; Guggenheim Fellowship, 1974. Address in 1982, c/o Knowlton, New York City.

BEAULEY, WILLIAM JEAN.
Painter. Born Joliet, Ill., Sept. 15, 1874. Pupil of Henri and Maratta in New York; Yvon in Paris. Member: New York Arch. League; Philadelphia Art Club; Art Fund Society. Award: Arch. League

57

prize awarded 1912. Represented in Vanderpoel AA Collection, Chicago. Address in 1929, 16 Gramercy Park, New York.

BEAUMONT, ARTHUR.
Painter. Born Bradford, Eng., April 7, 1879. Pupil of Bouguereau in Paris; Olsson in London. Member: Society of Independent Artists, United Scenic Artists' Association. Award: Gold medal Julien Academy, Paris, 1905. Address in 1926, 112 Rhine Ave., Stapleton, NY. Died 1956.

BEAUMONT, HENRIETTA (E.).
Painter and teacher. Born York, England, Feb. 19, 1881. Pupil of H. Locke in England; A. J. Bagdanove in New York. Member: NA Women PS. Address in 1929, 112 Rhine Ave., Stapleton, SI, NY.

BEAUMONT, LILIAN A(DELE).
Painter. Born Jamaica Plain, Mass. Pupil of School of Boston Museum of Fine Arts under Benson, Tarbell and Philip Hale. Member Copley Society. Died 1922. Address in 1926, 23 Alveston Street, Jamaica Plain, Boston, Mass.

BEAUX, CECILIA.
Painter and teacher. Born 1863 in Philadelphia. Pupil of Wm. Sartain, the Julien School and the Lazar School, Paris. Awarded the Mary Smith Prize, PA Academy Fine Arts, 4 times; gold medal, Philadelphia Art club; Dodge Prize National Academy of Design. Represented at PA Academy Fine Arts; Toledo Art Museum; Metropolitan Museum, New York; Brooks Memorial Gallery, Memphis; John Herron Art Institute, Indianapolis. Exhibited at Champs de Mars, 1896; National Academy, 1902; Societaire des Beaux Arts of American Federation of Arts. Address in 1926, Gloucester, Mass.; (Dec.-May) 132 E. 19th Street, New York, NY. Died 1942.

BEAVER, PEGGY.
Sculptor. Born in Greensboro, North Carolina in 1931. Studied: University of North Carolina at Greensboro; University of South Carolina, Columbia. Awards: South Carolina Craftsmen, 1973; Bigelow Sanford Award of Merit, Guild of South Carolina Artists, 1973; Dutch Folk Art Association, 1974. Collections: Middle Tennessee State University, Murfreesboro; University of South Carolina; Associated Distributing Company, Columbia, South Carolina.

BEBIE, W.
Portrait and landscape painter, who flourished about 1845. His work is not well known; an excellent portrait-group of a lady and her two daughters is in the Gallery of the Minneapolis Institute of Arts.

BECHDOLT, JACK.
Painter. Exhibited water color at Annual Exhibition of Penna. Academy, 1922. Address in 1926, 404 West 20th Street, New York City, NY.

BECHER, ARTHUR E.
Painter, pupil of Louis Mayer and Howard Pyle. Born in Germany, 1877. Address in 1926, Hopewell Junction, NY.

BECK, CAROL H.
Portrait painter. Born in Philadelphia PA in 1859. She was a pupil of Penna. Academy of Fine Arts; also studied in Dresden and Paris. Among her best known portraits are "Governor Patterson" for the State Capitol, and her brother, "Hon James M. Beck." Died Oct. 15, 1908, in Philadelphia.

BECK, GEORGE.
An American landscape painter. Born in 1748 or 1750 in England and died in 1812 in Kentucky. He was the first painter who worked beyond the Alleghenies.

BECK, J. AUGUSTUS.
Painter and sculptor. Born in 1831 in Lititz, PA. Died c. 1915 Student of H. Powers and Thomas Crawford in Italy. The Penna. Historical Soc. has several copies of portraits that were made by this artist from original pictures. Independence Hall also has several copies by this artist.

BECK, MINNA McLEOD
Painter. Born in Atlanta, GA, 1878. Pupil of Arthur Dow in New

58

York. Head of Art Dept., Alabama College, Montevallo, Alabama. Address in 1926, 121 Chestnut Street, Harrisburg, Penna.

BECK, RAPHEL.
Painter, sculptor, and illustrator. Studied at Julien Academy in Paris. Address in 1926, 78 Delaware Ave., Buffalo, NY.

BECK, ROSEMARIE.
(Rosemarie Beck Phelps). Painter and educator. Study: Oberlin College; Columbia Univ.; NYU. Work: Whitney Mus. of Am. Art, New York City; Vassar College Art Gallery, Poughkeepsie, NY; SUNY New Paltz; Hirshhorn Collection, Wash., DC; Nebr. Art Mus. Exhib.: PAFA; Nat'l. Inst. Arts and Letters; Whitney Mus. of Am. Art; Art Institute of Chicago; one-man shows at Peridot Gallery and Poindexter Gallery, NYC. Awards: Ingram-Merrill Grant, 1967 and 79. Teaching: Vassar College, 1957-58, 61-62 and 63-64'; Middlebury College, 1958-60 and 63; Queens College, from 1968. Media: Oil. Rep.: Ingber Gallery, New York City.

BECK, WALTER.
Mural painter. Born Dayton, Ohio, March 11, 1864. Studied in Munich pupil of Gysis and Loefftz. Work: Murals, City Hall, Cincinnati; "Life of Christ" in Art Museum of Brooklyn; and 80 Civil War Portraits in National Gallery, Washington, DC. Address in 1926, "Innisfree," Millbrook, NY.

BECKER, FREDERICK.
Painter. Born at Vermillion, SD, March 24,1888. Pupil of H. Breckenridge and Daniel Garber. His paintings, the "Gray Day" and "After the Shower," are in the Gallery of University of Oklahoma. "Cliffs at Laguna," Oklahoma City Art League; mural decoration, First Christian Church, Oklahoma City. Address in 1926, 511 East 7th Street, New York.

BECKER, MAURICE.
Painter and cartoonist. Born in Russia, 1889. Pupil of Robert Henri and Home Boss. Exhibited drawing at 1913 Armory Show.

Address in 1926, Tioga, Tioga County, Penna.

BECKHOFF, HARRY.
Illustrator. Born in Perth Amboy, New Jersey, 1901. He studied art under Harvey Dunn and George Bridgman at the ASL and GCSA. In 1925 he began his career at Country Gentleman and has since worked for Collier's, American, Woman's Home Companion, Reader's Digest and others. His illustrations have been published in several books and exhibited at the Grand Central Art Galleries.

BECKINGTON, ALICE.
Painter and teacher. Born St. Louis, July 30, 1868. Studied Art Students' League, New York; Academie Julien, Paris; and with Charles Lazar, Paris. Has exhibited at Paris Salons, and Paris Expn., 1900, Society of American Artists; honorable mention, Buffalo Expn., 1901; bronze medal, St. Louis Expn., 1904. A founder and president of American Society Miniature Painters. Work: Miniature, "Mrs. Beckington," Met. Museum of Art, NY. Address in 1926, 156 Carnegie Hall, New York. Died 1942.

BECKMAN, JESSIE MARY.
Painter and teacher. Born Upper Sandusky, Ohio. Pupil of Meakin, Satler, Chase, Henri, Webster, Colarossi Academy, Paris. Member: Calif. AC; West Coast AC; MacDowell C. of Allied Arts. Awards: Prizes for portraits, Tri State Fair. Address in 1929, 2401 West Sixth St., Los Angeles, Calif.; summer, Laguna Beach, Calif.

BECKMAN, WILLIAM.
Painter. Born in Minnesota. Studied at Univ. of Minnesota, philos. and anthrop.; graduated from State Univ. at St. Cloud; graduate work at Univ. of Iowa, completed 1969. Moved to NYC in 1969. Exhibitions at Allan Stone Gallery, NYC; AT&T, Basking Ridge, NJ; Allan Frumkin Gallery, NYC; others. Works are chiefly portraits and landscapes, in oil or pastel. Also makes "trompe l'oeil" boxes. Currently living in New York City.

BECKWITH, ARTHUR.
Painter. Born in London Jan. 24, 1860. Among his paintings "Sunlight and Shadow" is in Golden Gate Park Museum, and "Foggy Morning on the Coast" in San Francisco Gallery. Address in 1926, 438 Montgomery Block, San Francisco, California. Died 1930.

BECKWITH, HENRY.
Engraver. Born in England. His best work is of animals after paintings by Landseer; he also engraved landscapes after American artists. He was working in New York 1842-43.

BECKWITH, JAMES CARROLL.
Painter. Born Hannibal, MO, 1852. Pupil of Carolus Duran and Ecole des Beaux Arts in Paris. Honorable mention Paris Exp., 1889; gold medal, Atlanta Exp., 1895; bronze medal, Paris Exp., 1900; gold medal, Charleston Exp., 1902; National Academy, 1894. Member: American Water Color Society; Art Students' League, New York; National Institute Arts and Letters. Specialty, portraits and genre pictures. Represented by "The Blacksmith" at National Museum, Washington, DC. Portrait Mrs. R. H. McCurdy, Academy Exhibition, 1789. Portrait Capt. Jos. Lentilhon, Paris Salon, 1889. His works include "Judith" and the "Falconer" sent to the Paris Exposition of 1878. Died Oct. 24, 1917 in New York City.

BEDFORD, CORNELIA E.
Illustrator and writer. Born New York City, June 17, 1867. Pupil of School of Industrial Art of the Pennsylvania Academy of the Fine Arts, Phila. Author and illustrator of "Views and Interviews in Germany." Dresden correspondent of New York Herald, published in Paris. Address in 1929, Girard Trust Co., Philadelphia, PA; Hotel Continental, Dresden A, Germany. Died 1935.

BEDFORD, HENRY EDWARD.
Painter, sculptor, writer, and lithographer. Born Brooklyn, March 3, 1860. Pupil of William Anderson; Heatherly Art School in London.

Member: Salma. C. Address in 1926, 2744 Broadway, New York.

BEDORE, SIDNEY NELSON.
Sculptor. Born in Stephenson, Mich., March 5, 1883. Pupil of Beaux-Arts Institute of Design, New York. Work: Theodore Roosevelt monument, Benton Harbor, Mich., Fountain at T. Roosevelt School, Chicago. Address in 1926, Midway Studios, Chicago, Ill. Died 1955.

BEEBE, DEE.
Painter and teacher. Born New Orleans, LA. Member of National Association of Women Painters and Sculptors. Pupil of Chase, Cox, Snell in New York; Duveneck in Cincinnati. Address in 1926, 18 Gramercy Park, New York.

BEECHER, HILDA.
Painter. Exhibited at National Association of Women Painters and Sculptors, 1924. Address in 1926, 939 Eighth Ave., New York.

BEEK, ALICE DENGLEY.
Painter, writer and lithographer. Born in Providence, RI, in June 17, 1876. Pupil of Puvis de Chavannes. Paris. Grand prize and gold medal at Seattle Exposition, 1909. Address in 1926, 1310 North 5th Street, Tacoma, Wash.

BEEKMAN, HENRY RUTGERS.
Painter and etcher. Born in New York City, 1880. Pupil of Hawthorne, Bredin and Lathrop. He exhibited his etching "The Gallery" at the Penna. Academy of Fine Arts, Philadelphia, 1924. Address in 1926, 38 East 76th Street, New York. Died 1938.

BEERS, ALEXANDER R.
Painter. Born in Titusville, 1882. Student of Art Institute, Chicago. Address in 1926, Auditorium Theatre, Chicago.

BEERY, ARTHUR O.
Painter. Born in Marion, Ohio, March 4, 1930. Work: Butler Institute of American Art, Youngstown, Ohio; Erie Art Center, Erie, PA; J. M. Katz Collection. Exhibitions: PA Academy of Fine Arts 1968 Annual; Galerie 8, Erie,

PA, 2nd Nat'l Watercolor; one-man show Ruth Sherman Gallery, NYC; Columbus Art League, Columbus, Ohio; Contemp. Am. Art, Paris; etc. Awards: Butler Inst. of American Art; Columbus Ohio Art Fest. Address in 1982, c/o Cernuschi Galleries, NYC.

EEST, ALBERT VAN.
Born in Holland in 1820. In 1845 he came to New York, where he made a reputation as a marine and landscape painter and teacher. He lived mainly in Boston and New York. Among his pupils were William Bradford and R. Swain Gifford. He died in 1860, in NYC.

EHAR, ELY MAXIM.
Painter and illustrator. Born France, Aug. 15, 1890. Exhibited water colors at the Penna. Academy of the Fine Arts, Philadelphia, 1925. Pupil of John F. Carlson and C. W. Hawthorne. Illustrations for newspapers and magazines. Address in 1926, 880 West 181st Street, NY.

EHNCKE, NILE J(URGEN).
Painter. Born Oshkosh, June 4, 1893. Member: Balto WCC; Wisc. PS. Director, Oshkosh Public Museum. Address in 1929, 123 Mt. Vernon St., Oshkosh, WI.

EIN, CHARLES W.
Painter. Born New Orleans, Aug. 1, 1891. Studied in New York. Member: New Orleans ACC. Address in 1929, 510 Lowerline St., New Orleans, LA.

ELASKI, STEPHEN J.
Born, March 25, 1909. Enrolled in International Correspondence Schools, Scranton, Pennsylvania. Studied at Vesper George School of Art in Boston. Won a school scholarship for free tuition for one year, and later won a foreign scholarship for three months study at Fontainebleau School, France. Studied with Jean Despujols, Andre Strauss and Gaston Balande. Work includes group of murals for foyer, Bellows Falls High School; large mural executed for the American Legion, Bellows Falls; and a number of paintings commissioned by various private individuals. Died in New York City.

BELAUME, J.
Seal engraver. In 1825 this name as "J. Belume Sculpt." appears on a dry-point etching in New Orleans, on a print representing the triumphal arch erected to commemorate the visit of General Lafayette to New Orleans.

BELCHER, HILDA.
Painter and illustrator. Born in Pittsford, Vermont, Sept. 20, 1881. Studied: NY School of Art; with Chase, Henri, Bellows and Luks. Awards: Strathmore Competition, 1908; NY Watercolor Club, 1909, 1915; American Watercolor Society, 1918; National Academy of Design, 1926, 1931; Penn. Academy of Fine Arts, 1932; Brown-Bieglow Company, 1925; Phila. Watercolor Club, 1935; Middlebury College, 1941. Collections: Montclair Museum of Art; Museum of Fine Arts of Houston; Wood Museum of Art; High Museum of Art; Dumbarton House, Washington, DC; Vassar College; Laurence Museum, Williamstown, Masschusetts; American Unitarian Association Headquarters, Boston, Massachusetts; Pennsylvania Academy of Fine Arts; Newark, New Jersey, Museum of Art; Maryland Institute.

BELCHER, MARTHA WOOD.
Painter, etcher, teacher. Born in England, 1844. Pupil of Cooper Institute, New York; Flugen, Lietzenmeyer, and Lindenschmidt in Munich. Member of National Association of Women Painters and Sculptors; New York Water Color Club Association. Address in 1926, Van Dyke Studios, 939 Eighth Ave., New York.

BELKNAP, ZEDEKIAH.
Portrait painter. Born in 1781 in Vermont. Graduated from Dartmouth College 1807, and died in Weathersfield, VT in 1858.

BELL, CLARA LOUISE
Painter. Born Newton Falls, Ohio, 1886. Pupil of Edith P. Stevenson, Cleveland School of Art, Art Students' League of New York. Award: Penton medal for miniature painting, Cleveland Museum, 1919. Address in 1926, 3226 Euclid Ave., Cleveland, Ohio.

BELL, EDITH (MARION).
Painter and teacher. Born Cushing, IA. Pupil of Charles A. Cumming, George W. Maynard, Francis C. Jones, Ivan G. Olinsky, Richard Miller. Member: Iowa AG. Awards: First prize, annual exhibit of Des Moines Artists, Women's Club, Des Moines, 1916; gold medal, Women's Club, Des Moines, 1925, 1926. Represented in the F. L. Owen Collection, Des Moines, IA. Address in 1929, 317 Physics Bldg.; h. 1338 - 22nd St., Des Moines, IA.

BELL, EDWARD AUGUST.
Painter. Born in New York, Dec. 18, 1862. Pupil of National Academy of Design and Bavarian Royal Academy, Munich. Member of Art Students' League. Elected an Associate Member of the National Academy of Design. Represented in Art Association, Indianapolis; Cincinnati Museum; Smith College. Work: "Ready for a Walk," Art Assn., Indianapolis; "The Statuette," Cincinnati Museum;" "The Rose," Smith College, Northampton, MA. Address in 1926, 226 West 59th Street, New York.

BELL, WENONAH.
Painter. Born Trenton, SC. Pupil of PAFA; H. Hofmann of Munich. Member: Fellowship PAFA. Awards: Mary Smith prize, PAFA, 1926; first prize, Georgia-Alabama Artists Exhibition, Nashville, Tenn., 1926. Represented in the Virginia High School, Bristol, VA. Address in 1929, Greenville, GA.

BELLEW, FRANK HENRY TEMPLE.
Born in 1828 in India. Came to US in 1850. Illustrator for Harper Bros., also drew caricatures for the magazines. In 1866 he issued a book on the "Art of Amusing." His son, F. P. W. Bellew ("Chip"), illustrated for Life. Died June 29, 1888 in New York City.

BELLOWS, ALBERT F.
Landscape and genre painter. Born in Milford, Mass., 1829. Studied in Paris and Antwerp Royal Academy. Painted in England and Wales. Associate member of National Academy, 1859; National Academy, 1861. Died in 1883. "A Village Scene" (New England?), signed A. F.

Bellows, 1876. Lent by W. T. Carrington, Art Institute, Chicago. "Forest Life," painted in 1860. Owned by New York Public Library.

BELLOWS, GEORGE WESLEY.
Painter, lithographer, cartoonist, portrait painter. Born in Columbus, Ohio, Aug. 12, 1882. Studied in New York School of Art, under Robert Henri. Elected an associate member of National Academy in 1908, and Academician in 1918. Among his work: "Riverfront," "Gramercy Park," "Ringside Seats," "Crucifixion," and many portraits. Represented in Metropolitan Museum, Penna. Academy of Fine Arts and Brooklyn Museum. He was one of the founders of the Soc. of Independent Artists. Died Jan. 8, 1925 in New York City.

BELMONT, IRA JEAN.
Painter. Born in Kaunas Lithunia in 1885. Studied: Konigsberg, Paris, New York. Collections: Brooklyn Museum; University of Georgia; Tel-Aviv Museum, Israel; Crocker Collection, San Francisco; Musee du Jeu de Plume, Paris; Denver Museum of Art; Heckscher Foundation. Exhibited widely nationally and internationally.

BELSEN, JACOBUS.
Painter, printmaker and sculptor. Born in Patkino, Russia, in 1870. Studied at St. Petersburg (Leningrad) Academie. Professor at Craftsman School, St. Petersburg; positions at Alexander Lyceum Univ. for Architects and Engineers Craft School of Imperial Society for the Benefit of Arts. Created murals for Humanistisches Gymnasium, stained glass windows for Hotel d'Europe, St. Petersburg other works for churches, public and private bldgs.; also painted landscape watercolors, created woodcuts representing Russian aristocracy. Fled to Germany in 1917 or 18, arriving in July 1919 In Berlin he worked in metal blockprint, oils, painted miniatures, designed furniture for architects Friedmann and Weber became a sculptor, and created caricatures and political cartoon for newspapers, magazines, some published in Hanfstaengel's Hitle

62

in the Caricature of the World. Also published Russian Winter Pictures, Figures of the Russian Revolution, Illustration of Norwegian and Finnish Tales, Illustrations of Russian Children's Tales; plus a monogram of his work by F. Paul Schmidt (Ottens, Berlin). In 1924 and 1931, travelled to Holland and the East to sketch. Fled Germany in 1936, arriving in New York City. Commissioned by Met. Opera Co. to paint clouds, water, fire effects on mica for special stage effects. Died Sept. 12, 1937.

BELZONS, M.
French miniature painter working in Charleston, SC, was the first instructor of Thomas Sully in 1799, whose sister he married. Dunlap notes "he was a very poor painter." He flourished about 1779 in Charleston, SC.

BEMELMANS, LUDWIG.
Illustrator. Born in Austria, 1898. He studied in Germany until 1914; he then emigrated to the United States where he became a citizen four years later. Besides doing magazine illustations for The New Yorker, Vogue and Holiday, he worked extensively in book illustration. As an author and artist he produced the Madeline series beginning in 1939. Very popular in the 1930's he illustrated such books as My War with the United States and Life Class. Died 1962.

BEMENT, ALON.
Painter, photographer and teacher. Born Ashfield, Mass., Aug. 15, 1878. Pupil of Boston Museum School; Bonnat and Constant in Paris; Naas School, Sweden; Ecole Des Beaux Arts, Paris. Prof. of Fine Arts, Teachers Coll., Columbia University, since 1906. Instructor, College of City of New York. Director, Maryland Institute, Baltimore. Address in 1926, 210 West 59th Street, New York, NY, or care of Maryland Institute, Baltimore, MD.

BEMIS.
Painter. Flourished about 1850. The Worcester Art Museum owns a "View in Worcester or Vicinity."

BEMUS, MARY B.
Painter, teacher. Born Leicester, New York, Aug. 17, 1849. Pupil of L. M. Wiles. Address in 1926, 401 S. Hope Street, Los Angeles, Calif., 2130 Emerson Ave., Santa Barbara, Calif.

BENBRIDGE, HENRY.
Portrait painter and miniature artist. Born in Phila., 1743; painting as early as 1758. Went to Italy in 1759 to study with Battoni and Mengs. On his way to Italy he stopped in London long enough to paint portraits of Dr. Franklin (at Carnegie Inst.) and Rev. Thomas Coombs. Benbridge painted many portraits in the South. He died in 1812. His work has frequently been attributed to Copley. He lived for years in Charleston, SC.

BENDA, RICHARD R.
Painter and collage artist. Study: Chic. Acad. Fine Arts, Art Inst. Chic. Work: Illinois Bell Telephone; Borg-Warner, Chicago; Illinois Bar Center; Columbia College, Chicago, Ill.; Immaculate Conception Church, Chicago, Ill.; St. John's Church, Brooklyn, NY; Temple B'rith Sholom, Springfield, Ill.; Rod McKuen, the Episcopal Bishop of Chicago and many private collections. Exhibitions: Knickerbocker Artists, NYC; Arts Club, Chicago; B. Russell Centenary, London; and more. Awards: Annual Knickerbocker Artists Exbn., Grumbacher; Union League Club Exbn., Purchase Award; Nat'l Soc. of Painters in Casein, First Award; Slidell Nat'l Art Exbn., 1st Award. Mem.: Audubon Artists Soc., NYC; Arts Club, Chic. Media: Acrylic, collage. Address in 1982, c/o Verzyl Gallery, Northport, NY.

BENDA, WLADYSLAW T.
Illustrator. Born in Poznan, Poland, in 1873. Studied at Krakow College of Technology and Art; Vienna. Came to New York in 1900; illustrated for magazine, book publishers. Painted East European

scenes such as A Russian Grandmother's Wonder Tales, Scribner's, 1906. Also worked as a designer, creating the highly decorative Benda Masks worn by actors. Member: Arch. League, 1916; Player's Club, 1905. Mural Painter Award: silver medal, at Panama and Pacific Exposition. Died 1948. Address in 1926, 140 Wadsworth Ave., 1 Gramercy Park, New York, NY.

BENDELL, MARILYN.
Painter and instructor. Born in Grand Ledge, Mich., Sept. 19, 1921. Study: Am. Acad. Art; with Arnold Turtle and Pierre Nuytens. Work: Hadley School for Blind, Winnetka, Ill.; Huntington Mus. Fine Arts, W. VA. Comn.: Portrait, Hellen Keller, Hadley Sch.; and others. Exhibitions: 3-man show, Chicago Galleries; Select Group Oelschlaeger Gal., Sarasota, Fla.; One-man show Florida Fed of Art, Debary. Elected member Royal Soc. of Arts, London, England; Academic Artists, Springfield, Mass. Media: Oil. Address in 1982, 6832 Pine, Longboat Key, Florida.

BENDER, RUSSELL THURSTON.
Illustrator. Born in Chicago, 1895. Pupil of Chicago Academy of Fine Arts. Member: Palette and Chisel Club. Address in 1926, 333 South Dearborn Street; Home, 2717 Jackson Blvd., Chicago, Ill.

BENEDICT, J. B.
Painter. Exhibited water color landscape at Annual Exhibition Penna. Academy of Fine Arts, 1922. Address in 1926, 1669 Broadway, Denver, Colorado.

BENEDUCE, ANTIMO.
Painter. Born Italy, March 28, 1900. Pupil of Cleveland School of Art. Exhibited water colors in annual exhibition of Water Colors, Penna. Academy of Fine Arts, Philadelphia, 1925. Address in 1926, 1959 East 73d Street, Cleveland, Ohio.

BENEKER, GERRIT A.
Painter and illustrator. Born Grand Rapids, Mich., Jan. 26, 1882. Pupil of John Vanderpoel and Frederick Richardson in Chicago; F. V. Du Mond, Henry Reuterdahl in New York; Charles W. Hawthorne in Provincetown. Member: Provincetown Art Association; Cleveland Art Students' Association. Award: New York Herald Easter prize, 1905; Scarab Club 3d prize, Detroit, 1916; Penton medal for industrial painting, Cleveland Museum, 1919. Represented in permanent collection of Provincetown Art Association, and Grand Rapids Central High School; Youngstown Museum of Art. Author of Victory Liberty Loan Poster, "Sure, We'll Finish the Job." Address in 1926, Provincetown, Mass.

BENGELSDORF, ROSALIND.
Painter. Born April 30, 1916, in New York City. Studied at the Art Students' League with Anne Goldthwaite, George Bridgman, John Steuart Curry and Raphael Soyer; Arnot School of Art; New York School on 57th St. with Hans Hofmann. Employed as art teacher by the WPA Fed. Art Proj. in 1935-36. Married avant-garde painter George Byron Browne. Changed her emphasis to art critic and columnist in 1947. Ed. Assn. for Art News until 1972. She lives in New York City.

BENGLIS, LYNDA.
Painter and sculptor. Born in Lake Charles, Louisiana, October 25, 1941. Studied: Newcomb College; Tulane Univ. with Ida Kohlmeyer, Pat Travigno, Zolton Buki; and Harold Carney. Awards: Yale-Norfolk in 1963 and Max Beckman Scholarship, Brooklyn Museum, in 1965. She has exhibited widely throughout the United States. Address in 1980, Paula Copper Gallery, 155 Wooster St., New York, NY.

BENGOUGH, WILLIAM.
Painter and illustrator. Born Whitby, Ontario, Canada, Oct. 14, 1863. Pupil of Ontario Society of Artists, Toronto; ASL of NY. Member: NAC. Work: Figure illustrations for "Harper's," "Longon Graphic" and "Collier's;" portrait painting and drawings for "Cyclopaedia of American

64

Biography". Address in 1929, Kiamesha, NY.

BENJAMIN, CHARLES HENRY.
Painter, sculptor, writer and lecturer. Born Maine, Aug. 29, 1856. Self-taught. Member Art League, Los Angeles, AFA. Address in 1929, 2215 Lewis Ave., Altedena, CA.

BENJAMIN, LUCILE JULLIN.
Painter. Born at Genesco, Ill., in 1876. Pupil of John Vanderpoel and Art Institute of Chicago. She painted under the name of Lucile Joullin. She died in San Francisco, Calif., on June 5, 1924. Represented by the "Algerian Slave," in the Bohemian Club, San Francisco, Calif.

BENJAMIN, SAMUEL GREENE WHELLER.
Marine painter. Born in Argos, Greece Feb. 13, 1837. Graduated from Williams College in 1859, became a member of Boston Art Club, which owns his painting "Daybreak off the Corbiere." He died in Burlington, VT, in 1914.

BENN, BEN.
Painter. Born in Russia, Dec. 27, 1884. Pupil at National Academy of Design. His portrait of Judge J. Planken in Muncipal Court House, New York; "Still Life," Kroeller Collection, The Hague, Holland. Address in 1926, 244 East 23d Street, New York. Died 1983.

BENNERS, ETHEL ELLIS DE TURCK.
Painter. Pupil of Wm. F. Chase, Cecilia Beaux. Member: PAFA, Phila. Alliance, NA Women PS, College Art Assoc.

BENNETT, BELLE.
Sculptor. Born in New York City in 1900. She studied under Solon Borglum, and at the School of American Sculpture. Address in 1926, 152 East 63d Street, New York.

BENNETT, EMMA DUNBAR.
(Mrs. Harrison Bennett). Sculptor. Born in New Bedford, Mass. Pupil of British Academy in Rome. Address in 1926, Cochituate, Mass.

BENNETT, EMMA-SUTTON (CARTER).
Painter, illustrator and etcher. Born Aug. 26, 1902, in Albany, GA. Pupil of Hayley Lever; ASL of NY. Member: ASL of NY; Three Arts C; Salons of America. Specialty, drypoints, etchings and book covers for magazines. Address in 1929, 613 Jackson St., Albany, GA.

BENNETT, FRANCIS I.
Painter. Born in Philadelphia, March 8, 1876. Pupil of Anshutz, Chase, and Henri. Address in 1926, 72 Whitford Ave., Nutley, NJ.

BENNETT, FRANKLIN.
Painter and etcher. Born Greenport, Jan. 5, 1908. Pupil of ASL of NY. Member: NAC; New Rochelle AA; Amer. Artists Prof. Lg. Award: Mortimer L. Schiff purchase prize ($100), NAC, 1928. Work: "Maine Woods", National Arts Club, New York. Address in 1929, care of The Holt Gallery, 630 Lexington Ave., New York, NY; summer, Greenport, LI, NY.

BENNETT, HARRY R.
Illustrator. Born in Lewisboro, New York. He studied at the AIC and American Academy of Art. His first illustration appeared in Woman's Day in 1950, but most of his work since then has been for book publishers, as demonstrated by the 982 paperback covers he has illustrated over the last 20 years. His works have been shown at the NYPL, the New York Historical Society and several Annual Exhibitions of the S of I.

BENNETT, PHILOMENE.
Painter and editor. Born in Lincoln, NE, Jan. 2, 1935. Studied: Univ. of Nebraska. Awards: Mid-American Exhibition, Nelson Gallery, Kansas City, Missouri, 1956 and 1962. Collections: Hallmark Collection, Kansas City; Missouri Historical Society, Columbia, Missouri; Univ. of Nebraska, Lincoln. Media: Oil and acrylic. Address in 1980, 616 Central St., Kansas City, MO.

BENNETT, REGINALD (OSBORN).
Painter and teacher. Born Devils Lake, ND, Feb. 20, 1893. Pupil of J. P. Wicker; J. Despujols; Othon

65

Friesz. Member: Scarab Club. Address in 1929, Scarab Club, 217 Farnsworth; h. 645 Merrick, Detroit, Mich.

BENNETT, RICHARD.
Wood Engraver. Born Ireland, July 22, 1899. Pupil of Walter Isaacs, Ambrose Patterson. Illustrations for N.Y. Times Magazine, Bookman, Theatre Arts Monthly, Forum, Survey and Graphic. England and Ireland - Twelve Woodcuts - published by the University of Washington in 1927; "Winter," "Donkey Stable, Clovelly," "Thomas Hardy's Cottage," Baltimore Museum.

BENNETT, RUTH M.
Painter and craftsman. Born Momence, Ill., Feb. 11, 1899. Pupil of George Bridgman, John Carlson, E. Vysedal, R. Shraeder, Armin Hansen. Member: Calif. AC; Younger Painters C. Awards: Hon. mention, Calif. AC Exh., Los Angeles Museum, 1925; hon. mention, Pomona Fair, 1926; Minnie Tingle prize ($200), Calif. AC, 1926; hon. mention, Fine Arts Gallery of San Diego, 1927. Address in 1929, 5449 Sunset Blvd.; h. 1746 McCadden Pl., Hollywood, Calif.

BENNETT, WILLIAM JAMES.
Born in England, 1789, he died in New York, 1844. He came to that city in 1816 as a landscape painter in water color and an engraver in aquatint. He was elected an associate member of the National Academy of Design in 1827 and an Academician in 1828; for some years he was the curator of the Academy.

BENNEY, ROBERT L.
Painter and illustrator. Born in New York City in 1904. Study: Cooper Union; NAD; Grand Central Art Sch.; ASL; with Harry Wickey, Frank Nankivell, Harry Sternberg, Harvey Dunn. Work: Corcoran Gallery; de Young Museum, Calif.; IBM; Chrysler Coll.; USAF, US Navy, US Army, U.S.M.C.; Mariners Museum, VA; etc. Comn.: Readers Digest; Vietnam combat art, U.S.M.C. Exhibitions: National Gallery, Wash., DC; Metropolitan Museum; Brooklyn Museum; de Young Museum, San Francisco; Corcoran Gallery; Carnegie Institute; and many others. Teaching: Pratt Institute; School of Visual Arts; Dutchess Community College. Awards: Phila. Museum of Art 1st Award; USAF official artist; Certif. of Commendation, USN. Mem.: Soc. Illustrators; Artists Equity Assn.; ASL (life); Artists and Writers Assn.; Appraisers Assn. of Am. Media: Oil, acrylic, tempera, watercolor, etching, aquatint. Address in 1982, 50 West 96 St., New York City.

BENSELL, GEORGE. F.
Portrait and genre painter. Born 1837, died in 1879. Flourished 1855-1868, Philadelphia.

BENSON, EUGENE.
Painter and art critic. Born in 1839 in Hyde Park, NY. He was best known for his writing and was considered the best art critic in America. He was most successful in his portraits, elected to the Artists' Fund in 1861. In 1873 Mr. Benson went abroad for study and resided there. Among his works are "Bazaar at Cairo," "Slaves Tower," "Reverie," "Ariadne," and "Strayed Maskers."

BENSON, FRANK WESTON.
Painter and etcher of portraits, interiors, birds and landscapes with figures; also teacher. Born, Salem, Massachusetts, March 24, 1862. Pupil of Boston Museum School; Boulanger and Lefebvre, in Paris. Temple Gold Medal, Penna. Academy of the Fine Arts, 1908; Harris Silver Medal, Art Institute of Chicago, 1909; Palmer Medal and Prize, Art Institute of Chicago, 1910; Associate National Academy, 1897; National Academy, 1905; Ten American Painters; National Institute of Arts and Letters. Represented by "My Daughter," in Corcoran Art Gallery and "Still Life Decoration," Art Institute of Chicago. Died in 1951.

BENSON, JOHN HOWARD.
Painter, sculptor, etcher, craftsman, and teacher. Born Newport, RI, July 6, 1901. Pupil of NAD; ASL of NY under Joseph Pennell. Member: Newport AA; ASL of NY. Address in 1929, 29 Thames St.; h. 20 Ayrault St., Newport, RI.

ENSON, JOHN P.
Painter. Born Salem, Mass., Feb 8.
1865. Member: AFA; Boston GA.
Work: Eight murals of the Sea and
Sealife, Hall of Ocean Life, New
York City; ten murals, Early Ships
of New England, Providence
Institution For Savings,
Providence, RI. Address in 1929,
Kittery, ME.

ENSON, LESLIE LANGILLE.
Illustrator. Born at Mahone, NS,
Mar. 15, 1885. Pupil of School of
Boston Museum of Fine Arts, Erie
Pape School, Fenway School.
Member: GFLA. Address in 1926,
602 West 190th Street, New York.

BENTLEY, JOHN W.
Painter. Born in Patterson, NJ,
Jan. 3, 1880. Pupil of Bridgeman,
Du Mond, and Henri. Member: AFA;
Salfolo SA, 1921. Address in 1926,
Woodstock, Ulster Co., NY.

BENTON, HARRY STACY.
Painter and illustrator. Born
Saratoga Springs, NY, Oct. 11,
1877. Pupil of AIC. Member:
Salma. C. 1905. Address in 1929,
South Norwalk, Conn.

BENTON, SUZANNE.
Sculptor and art writer. Born Jan.
21, 1936. Studied: Queens
College, New York City; Columbia
University; Brooklyn College;
Brooklyn Mus. Art Sch.; Silvermine
Awards: The International Susan B.
Anthony Hall of Fame; Grant from
the Connecticut Commission on the
Arts. Exhib.: Metal Masks
Sculpture for the Performing Arts,
Lincoln Ctr.; Touching Ritual,
Wadsworth Atheneum; many others in
US and abroad. Creates metal masks
for narrative theatre; mask rituals
examining stories and ancient
tales, such as Sarah and Hagar,
from Genesis. Address in 1980, 22
Donnelly Drive, Ridgefield, CT.

BENTON, THOMAS HART.
Painter, lithographer, illustrator.
Born 1889. Studied at AIC and
Academie Julian in Paris. Taught
at ASL (1926-35), and at Kansas Art
Inst. (1930-41). Exhibited at PAFA.
Work: U. of Indiana; Whitney; New
School for Soc. Research. Address

in 1926, 102 East 29th St., New
York City.

BENTZ, JOHN.
Painter, etcher and teacher. Born
Columbus, Ohio. Pupil of Robert
Blum; Kenyon Cox; W. M. Chase.
Member: ASL of NY; PA S. Min. P.;
Am. S. Min. P. Address in 1929,
171 Lakeview Ave., Leonia, NJ.

BENZ, LEE R.
Painter and printmaker. Born in
Neponset, Ill. Study: Bradley
Univ., BA and MA; Salzburg Col.,
Austria. Exhib.: Prix de Paris;
Bradley Univ.; West Ill. Univ.;
Colorprint, USA; Springfield (Ill.)
Art Mus. Awards: Printmaking Salon
of 50 states award, NYC, etc.
Mem.: Nat'l. Soc. Lit. and Arts;
Int'l. Soc. of Artists; etc.
Media: Intaglio, collagraph,
watercolor. Address in 1982, 1125
Fon Du Lac Dr., East Peoria, Ill.

BENZIGER, AUGUST.
Portrait painter. Born at
Einsiedein, Switzerland, 1867. Art
Studies, Royal Academy, Vienna,
Academie Julien and Ecole des Beaux
Arts, Paris. Engaged as portrait
painter, 1891; painted portraits of
Presidents McKinley, Roosevelt and
Taft; of Popes Leo XIII and
Benedict XV; President Diaz,
Mexico; Sir Stuart Knill, Lord
Mayor of London; Leon Bourgeois,
Prime Minister of France;
Presidents Hauser, Forrer and
Deucher, of Switzerland; J.
Pierpont Morgan, Robert S.
Brookings, St. Louis, Charles F.
Brooker, Charles M. Schwab;
Cardinals Gibbons, Farley, and
O'Connell, and many other notables,
United States and abroad. Address
in 1926, Villa Gutenberg, Brunnen,
Switzerland; 140 W. 57th Street,
New York, NY.

BERDANIER, PAUL F.
Painter, etcher, and illustrator.
Born Frackville, PA, March 7, 1879.
Pupil of Charles Hope Provost in
New York; Gustave Wolff and School
of Fine Arts in St. Louis; Albert
Gihon in Paris. Member: 2x4 Soc.;
AL Nassau Co., NY. Awards: 2nd
Prize, Thumb Box Exhibition, St.
Louis Art League, 1919; 1st Prize,
Missouri State Fair, Sedalia, MO,

67

1920; St. Louis Chamber of Commerce Prize, St. L. AG, 1920; 2nd prize, Missouri State Fair, Sedalia, 1922. Represented in permanent collection of Jefferson Memorial, St. Louis; and by landscape "Sur la Canal a Morte," permanent collection, Art Museum, Moret, France. Designer of historical costumes and stage settings. Address in 1929, 57-86th St., Jackson Heights, NY.

BERDICK, VERONICA.
Painter. Born in Chicago, Illinois, in 1915. Studied: Art Institute of Chicago. Awards: Renaissance Society; Art Institute of Chicago; Northwest Printmakers; Pennsylvania Library of Congress(2 purchase awards); Huntington Hartford Study grant, 1955. Collections: Art Inst. of Chic.; Lib. of Congress; NY Public Lib.; Mus. of Lyon, France; Bibliotheque Nat'le., Paris; Victoria and Albert Mus., London.

BERG, GEORGE LOUIS.
Painter. Born Oct. 27, 1870, McGregor, Iowa. Pupil of Art Students' League, New York. Member: Salmagundi Club; Guild of Seven Arts, Darien, CT; Hinckley Art Gallery; NY Fed. of Women's Clubs. Address in 1926, Stony Creek, Conn. Died July, 1941 in CA.

BERGE, EDWARD.
Sculptor. Born in Baltimore, MD 1876; he died Oct. 12, 1924 in Baltimore. He studied in Baltimore, and in Paris under Verlet and Rodin. He was a member of the National Sculpture Society. Represented by Watson Monument, Baltimore; "Pieta," St. Patrick's Church, Washington; and the Gist Memorial, Charleston, SC.

BERGER, C(HARLES) F.
Painter. His full-length portrait of President Polk with his hand extended is signed C. F. Berger.

BERGER, MARIE.
Painter and printmaker. Born in Fort Worth, Texas. Study: Texas Christian University; St. Louis School of Fine Art, Washington Univ., Missouri. Exhib.: Bateau Lavar Gallery, Rome; Rassagna permanente d'arte contemporanea, Veterbo, Italy; Oklahoma Art Mus.; Wittie Mus., Texas; Fort Worth Art Mus., Texas; Laguna Gloria, Austin, Texas. Awards: Benedictine Award, NY; Texas Fine Arts Jurors Award. Mem.: Reg'l. dir., Texas Fine Arts Assn.; Texas WC Soc. Media: Oil, acrylic, watercolor; etching, lithograph, collograph. Currently living in Texas.

BERGER, WILLIAM MERRITT.
Illustrator. Born Union Springs, NY, Feb. 14, 1872. Pupil of William M. Chase; George DeForest Brush; Bashet. Work: Illustrations for "Scribner's." Address in 1929, 534 West 147th St., New York, NY.

BERGLUND, HILMA L. G.
Painter. Born Stillwater, Minn., Jan. 23, 1886. Pupil St. Paul School of Art; Handicraft Guild, Minneapolis. Member: Artists' Society, St. Paul, Minn. Address in 1926, 1860 Feronia Ave., St. Paul, Minn.

BERGMAN, FRANK.
Born. August 6, 1898. Studied at National Academy, Vienna, for seven years. Exhibited at Kuenstlerhaus, Vienna. Worked with Josef Urban and Willy Pogany, New York. Has exhibited at Architectural League, New York; Chicago Art Institute; Los Angeles Museum; Palace of Legion of Honor, San Francisco; and annual exhibitions of San Francisco Art Association. Work includes mural executed under Public Works of Art Project; murals for San Francisco Board of Education; two well-known steamships (won in local competition); and for a number of buildings in San Francisco, including the Sir Francis Drake Hotel, the San Jose Pacific Loan Associations and a number of other prominent buildings.

BERKAN, OTTO.
Portrait painter. Born in 1834. He lived in Philadelphia for many years, many of his pictures being in the Catholic Cathedral of that

city. He died in his studio at Passaic, NJ, on Oct. 3, 1906.

BERKEY, JOHN CONRAD.
Illustrator. Born in Edgley, North Dakota, 1932. His work has included advertising, editorial posters, calendars and book covers. He has been an illustrator for the past 20 years.

BERKMAN-HUNTER, BERNECE.
Painter. Born in Chicago, Illinois. Studied: Art Institute of Chicago; New School for Social Research; Hunter College; Columbia University. Award: Seattle Art Museum, 1946. Collections: Evansville State Hospital; Kelly High School, Chicago; Art Institute of Chicago; Carnegie Institute; Seattle Art Museum; University of Iowa; University of Michigan. Exhibited extensively throughout the United States.

BERKOWITZ, HENRY.
Painter and designer. Born in Brooklyn, NY, Feb. 5, 1933. Study: Brooklyn Mus. Art Sch. with Sidney Simon; Workshop Sch. of Advertising and Ed. Art; NY Sch. Visual Arts. Work: Gutenberg Mus., Ger. Exhibitions: Brooklyn Museum; Lever House; Burr Gallery; Galleries Raymond Duncan, Paris; Art Fest., Tours, France; many more. Awards: Merit, NY Coliseum; Am. Vet. Soc. for Artists; Palmas de Oro, Int. Art Fest., Pans, etc. Address in 1982, 11701 NW 29th Manor, Sunrise, Fla.

BERMAN, EUGENE.
Painter and designer. Born Nov. 4, 1899, in St. Petersburg, Russia. Studied in Russia, Switzerland, France, Italy, Germany. Awarded Guggenheim Fellowship (1947 and 1949). Designed scenery, costumes for the Met, City Center Opera, Ballet Russe de Monte Carlo, La Scala, and Sadler's Wells Ballet. Work in collections of Met. Mus. of Art; MOMA; Vassar College, Poughkeepsie, NY; Wash. Univ.; Phil. Museum of Art; Smith College; Mus. Fine Arts, Boston; Wadsworth Atheneum, Hartford; Musee d'Art Moderne, Paris; Graphische Sammlung Albertina, Vienna. Died Dec. 15. 1972.

BERMAN, HARRY G.
Painter in oils and water colors. Born Phila, PA, June 1, 1900. Pupil of PAFA. Fellowship Penna. Academy of Fine Arts, 1924. Works: "Late Afternoon Winter, The Waterfall." Address in 1926, North 15th Street, Philadelphia.

BERMAN, SAUL.
Painter. Born Russia, March 18, 1899. Pupil of Charles Hawthorne. Worked in Brooklyn, NY; and Provincetown, Mass.

BERNARD, EDWARD H.
Painter. Born in Belmont, Mass., in 1855; died in 1909. Student of Boston Museum of Fine Arts.

BERNARD, FRANCISCO.
Nothing is known of this artist except that he painted portraits and landscapes of merit in New Orleans at intervals from 1848 until 1867, having a studio in the latter year at 146 Customhouse Street.

BERNATH, SANDOR.
Painter. Born in Hungary in 1892. Pupil of National Academy of Design. Member of New York Water Color Club. Address in 1926, 341 West 22d Street, New York.

BERNEKER, LOUIS F(REDERICK).
Painter. Born Clinton, MO. Pupil of St. Louis School of Fine Arts; Laurens in Paris. Member: NYWCC; AWCS; Allied AA; Salma. Club; NAC (life); NYSP. Work: Murals in church of St. Gregory the Great, New York City; Chicago Theatre, Chicago; Public School No. 60, Bronx, NY; Dallas (Tex.) Art Association. Instructor, Mechanics Institute.

BERNEKER, MAUD F(OX).
Painter. Born Memphis, Tenn., April 11, 1882. Pupil of NAD. Member: NA Women PS; Allied AA. Address in 1929, 53 East 59th St., New York, NY; summer, 65 East Main St., East Gloucester, Mass.

BERNEY, THERESA.
Painter and illustrator. Born Baltimore, Dec. 4, 1904. Pupil of Henry A. Roben, C. H. Walther, C. W. Hawthorne. Member: Balto. WCC;

MD Inst. Alumni Assoc. Address in 1929, 2400 Linden Ave., Baltimore, MD.

BERNINGHAUS, J. CHARLES.
Painter. Born St. Louis, MO, May 19, 1905. Awards: Hon. mention, St. Louis Artists Guild. 1926; hon. mention, St. Louis Art League, 1925, 1926. Address in 1929, Taos. NM.

BERNINGHAUS, OSCAR E.
Painter, illustrator. Born St. Louis, Oct 2, 1874. Pupil of St. Louis School of Fine Arts. Member: Salma Club and the Taos Students' Association. Awards: Dolph prize, St. Louis, 1907; share of Chicago Fine Arts Bldg. prize; Chamber of Commerce prize. Works: Two lunettes, Jefferson City, MO, State Capitol Bldg.; "Winter in the West," City Art Museum, St. Louis; and in various libraries and schools. Specialty, Western subjects. Address in 1926, Clayton, Missouri. Died April 27, 1952.

BERNSTEIN, GERDA MEYER.
Painter. Born in Hagen, Germany, in 1925. Studied: London, England; Art Institute of Chicago. Awards: Parke-Bernet Gallery; New Horizon Exhibition, 1975. Exhibitions: Roosevelt University; Old Orchard Art Festival; Springfield Museum, 1975; ARC Gallery, Chicago, Illinois.

BERNSTEIN, THERESA F.
Painter and printmaker. Born in Philadelphia, Pennsylvania. Studied: Philadelphia School of Design; Pennsylvania Academy of Fine Arts; Art Students League. Awards: Philadelphia Plastic Club; French Institute of Art and Science; National Association of Women Artists, 1949, 1951, 1955; Society of American Graphic Artists, 1953; Library of Congress (purchase prize), 1953; North Shore Art Association; American Color Printmakers Society. Collections: Art Institute of Chicago; Library of Congress; Boston Museum; Princeton University; Harvard University; Dayton Art Institute; Whitney Museum of American Art; Bezalel Museum, Jerusalem; Tel-Aviv

and Ain Harod Museum, Israel; Metropolitan Museum of Art. Address in 1980, 54 W 74th St., New York, New York.

BERNSTROM, VICTOR.
Wood engraver. Born in Stockholm, Sweden in 1845. Worked in London on the staff of the Grafic; he came to New York and became associatee with the Harpers. He joined the Society of American Wood Engravers, and received a medal at the Columbian Exposition, Chicago, in 1893, and at the Pan-American and Buffalo Expositions. Later he devoted his time to landscapes in water colors. He died in Europe or March 13, 1907.

BERRY, CAROLYN.
(Carolyn Berry Becker). Painter and writer. Born in Sweet Springs, Missouri, June 27, 1930. Studied: Christian College for Women, University of Oklahoma; University of Missouri. Awards: University of Missouri, 1950; Yakima, Washington, 1974; Monterey Peninsula Museum of Art, 1974. Collections: Brandeis University; Marist College; Albrecht Gallery, St. Joseph, Missouri; Monterey Peninsula Museum of Art. Address in 1980, 78 Cuesta Vista, Monterey, CA.

BERRY, WILSON REED.
Painter, illustrator, lithographer and teacher. Born Indiana, April 22, 1851. Work: "Dominion Parliament Bldgs. at Ottowa, owned by King of Gt. Britain. Address in 1929, 216½ Fourth St.; h. Island Home, Logansport, Ind.

BERRYMAN, CLIFFORD KENNEDY.
Illustrator and lithographer. Born Versailles, KY, April 2, 1869. Author "Cartoons of 58th House of Representatives"; originator of "Teddy Bear." On staff of Washington Evening Star since 1907. Died in 1949. Address in 1926, 1754 Euclid St., NW, Washington, DC. Died Dec. 11, 1949.

BERSON, ADOLPHE.
Painter. Born San Francisco, Calif. Pupil of Lefebvre and Robert- Fleury in Paris. Address

70

in 1926, 1037 Fillmore Street, San Francisco, Calif.

BERT, CHARLES H.
Painter. Born in Milwaukee, Wis., 1873. Pupil of Cincinnati Art Academy, and Art Students' League of New York, also Julien Academy, Paris. Address in 1926, Lyme, Conn.

BERTHELSEN, JOHANN.
Painter. Born in Copenhagen, Denmark, in July 25, 1883. Member: AWCS. Address in 1929, Rodin Studios, 200 W. 57th St., New York, NY.

BERTSCH, FRED S.
Designer. Born in Michigan in 1879. Pupil of AIC. Member: Palette and Chisel Club. Address in 1926, 15 East Huron Street; Home, 1629 Granville Ave., Chicago, Ill.

BERZEVIZY, J(ULIUS).
Painter. Born Hormonna, Hungary, Dec. 14, 1875. Pupil of Conrad Svestka. Member: Rochester AC; Buffalo SA; The Geneseeans. Address in 1929, 356 Maryland St., Buffalo, NY.

BESSIRE, DALE P(HILLIP).
Painter. Born Columbus, Ohio, May 14, 1892. Member: Indiana AC; Brown Co. Art Gallery Assn.; Hoosier S. Patrons Assn. Address in 1929, Nashville, Ind.

BEST, EDWARD S.
Engraver. Born in London in 1826, he came to this country about 1850 and received employment in J. M. Butler's publishing establishment in Philadelphia. His best engraved plate is "Washington at Valley Forge" after the painting by C. Scheussele. Died in 1865.

BETSBERG, ERNESTINE.
Painter. Born in Bloomington, Illinois, in 1909. Studied: Art Institute of Chicago. Awards: Raymond Traveling fellowship; Art Institute of Chicago. Exhibited extensively in the United States, Japan, France and Italy.

BETTIS, CHARLES HUNTER.
Illustrator, designer. Born in Texas in 1891. Pupil of AIC. Member: Palette and Chisel, Chicago Arch., T Square, and Palette Clubs. Address in 1926, 127 North Dearborn Street; Home, 1429 Sherwin Ave., Chicago, Ill.

BETTS, ANNA WHELAN.
Illustrator, painter, teacher. Born in Philadelphia. Pupil of Howard Pyle, and of Vonnoh. Member: Philadelphia Water Color Club. Award: bronze medal, P.-P. Expn. Work: Illustrations in color for Century, Harper's and other magazines.

BETTS, E. C.
Landscape painter. Born in Hillsdale, Mich., in 1856, he died in Denver, Colo., 1917. His best known painting was "The Valley of the Housatonic."

BETTS, EDWIN D.
Painter. Born in 1847. He was the father of Louis Betts, and several other members of the family are artists. His best known work is an idealized "Birth of Christ." Died Feb. 1915, in Chicago, IL.

BETTS, LOUIS.
Portrait painter. Born in Little Rock, Ark., 1873. Pupil of his father, E. D. Betts, Sr., Wm. Chase; AIC. Member: Academy of National Arts, 1912; National Academy, 1915. Works: "William M. R. French" and "Apple Blossoms." Art Institute of Chicago. Died in 1961. Address in 1926, 19th St., New York.

BEVERIDGE, KUHNE.
Sculptor. Born Springfield, Ill., 1877. Pupil of William Rudolph O'Donovan, NY. Exhibited at National Academy of New York; Royal Academy London; Salon Champs de Mars, Paris; Paris Expn., 1900. Hon. mention, Paris, 1900.

BEVIN, ALICE CONKLIN.
Born East Hampton, Conn., Aug. 21, 1898. Pupil of Philip Hale, Charles Hawthorne, George Bridgman and Froul Du Mond. Address in 1929, Grue Leon Bonnat, Paris.

BEWLEY, MURRAY P.
Painter. Born Fort Worth, Tex., June 19, 1884. Pupil of AIC; Chase, Beaux and Henri in New York. Member: Paris American Arts Association; Salma. C. Awards: Hon. mention, Paris Salon, 1910; first prize Salma. C., 1921. Works: "Buds," and "Portrait of Mrs. Percy V. Pennybacker," Ft. Worth (Tex.) Museum, and in the Pennsylvania Academy of the Fine Arts, Philadelphia.

BEYER, GEORGE ALBERT.
Painter, illustrator and designer. Born Minneapolis, Aug. 30, 1900. Award: Minneapolis Inst. of Arts, 1925. Address in 1929, 215 Northwestern Bldg. South Minneapolis, Minn.

BIAFORA, ENEA.
Sculptor. Born in Italy, 1892; came to New York in 1914. Exhibited at National Academy, New York, 1922.

BICKFORD, NELSON N.
Painter. Born in 1846. Died 1943. Specialty, animal painting. Address in 1926, New York City.

BICKNELL, ALBION HARRIS.
Painter. Born March 18, 1873 in Turner, ME. Died April 23, 1915 in Malden, Maine. He painted chiefly portraits and historical subjects. His portrait work included "Lincoln," "Webster," and "Horace Mann." Two of his historical paintings are "Lincoln at Gettysburg" and the "Battle of Lexington."

BICKNELL, EVELYN M.
Painter. Born in New York, 1857. Address in 1926, 18 West 27th Street, New York.

BICKNELL, FRANK ALFRED.
Painter. Born Augusta, ME, 1866. Died in 1905. Pupil of Julien Academy in Paris under Bouguereau and Robert-Fleury. Member: AAA of Paris; NA; National Arts Club, New York; Chicago Water Color Society. Taught at Carngie Inst. of Technology, Pittsburgh. Work: "October Morning," Nat. Gallery, Wash., DC; "Maintain Laurel, "Montclair, NJ; "Pirate's Cove,"

Denver Art Museum; "November," Boston Art Club. Specialty, landscapes. Address in 1926, Old Lyme, Conn.

BICKNELL, WILLIAM HARRY WARREN.
Etcher. Born in Boston, Mass., July 12, 1860. Pupil of Otto Grundmann and Boston Museum School. Member: Copley S. 1880; Chicago SE; Boston SE; Provincetwon AA. Award: Bronze medal, St. Louis Exp., 1904. Represented in Art Institute of Chicago; Rochester Memorial Art Gallery; Boston Museum of Fine Arts; New York Public Library; Congressional Library, Washington, DC. Address in 1926, Arlington Street, Winchester, Mass.

BIDDLE, GEORGE.
Painter. Born, January 19, 1885; Philadelphia, PA. Educated at Groton School and Harvard College, receiving A.B. in 1908 and LLD in 1911. Studied one year at Julian's Academy, Paris, and two years at PAFA. Served two years during World War; was in action at Second Battle of Marne, St. Mihiel, Meuse Argonne; became Acting Assistant Chief of Staff, First Army Corps. Wrote and illustrated "Green Island," Coward McCann, 1930. Published articles in Scribner's, Creative Arts, Am. Mag. of Art, Parnassus, and The Arts. Paintings owned by Whitney Museum, NY; PAFA; Dallas Museum. Work in Kaiser Friederich Museum, Berlin; Museo D'Arte Moderna, Venice; Chicago Art Inst.; Boston Museum; John Herron Art Inst.; Calif. Palace of Legion of Honor; Public Library, NYC; MOMA, NYC. Former Vice-Pres., Soc. of Painters, Sculptors and Gravers; Pres., Soc. of Mural Painters. 1936, Studied with Ole Nordmark.

BIERSTADT, ALBERT.
Painter. Born Jan. 7, 1830, in Duesseldorf, Germany Landscape painter. Brought by his parents in 1831 to New Bedford, Mass., where his youth was spent. Began painting in oils in 1851; returned to Duesseldorf in 1853, and studied four years there and in Rome. On his return to the United States in 1857 he made a sketching tour in the Rocky Mountains, and from this and other visits to the West

gathered materials for his most important pictures. He again visited Europe 1867, 1878 and 1883. Elected National Academy, 1860. Legion of Honor, 1867. Medals: Austria, Germany, Bavaria and Belgium, and various orders. Represented in the Metropolitan Museum, New York, and Corcoran Art Gallery of Washington, DC and The Hermitage, St. Petersburg, Russia. Died in 1902. Died Feb. 18, 1902 in New York City.

IESEL, CHARLES.
Painter. Born New York City, Oct. 20, 1865. Member of the Art Club of Providence, RI. Died 1945. Address in 1926, 30 East Ontario, Street, Chicago, Ill.

IESEL, H. FRED.
Painter and illustrator. Born in Philadelphia, 1903. Pupil of the Rhode Island School of Design. Address in 1926, 5249 Calumet Ave., Chicago.

IESTER, ANTHONY.
Portrait and landscape painter. Born in Cleves, Germany, in 1840; he came to American early in life; died March 26, 1917, in Madisonville, Ohio. He was a member of the Cincinnati Art Club. He painted portraits of Archbishop Purcell and Bishop Henri, and decorations in St. John's Church, Lewisburg, KY.

IGELOW, CONSTANCE.
Painter. Exhibited in Annual Water Color Exhibition, Penna. Academy of the Fine Arts, Philadelphia, 1925. Address in 1926, Provincetown, Mass.

IGELOW, DANIEL FOLGER.
Landscape painter. Born in 1823, in Peru, IN. He was a friend of the portrait painter, G. P. A. Healy, and with him organized the Academy of Design; later it became the Art Institute of Chicago. He died in Chicago in July, 1910.

IGELOW, FOLGER ALLEN.
Painter. Born in Chicago in 1868, he died there in 1891.

BIGELOW, I. W. (or JAMES W.)
Portrait painter. His portrait of Miss Lillian Pullen, of White Plains, was painted about 1840, exhibited in New York.

BIGELOW, OLIVE.
Painter. Born in Mountain Station, NJ in 1886. Studied: Art Students League and in Paris, France. Awards: Royal Drawing Society, London, 1902, 1904; Newport Art Assoc., 1901. Collections: Providence Mus.; Vienna Military Mus.; Norwich Mus. of Art, England; Naval Mus., Annapolis; NY Historical Society; St. John's Hospital, London; St. Elizabeth's Hospital, London; Palmella Palace, Portugal; Portuguese Embassy, London; Vassar Coll., NY Oakwood School, Poughkeepsie, NY; Chinese Embassy, Wash., DC. She has designed covers for Vogue, Harper's Weekly and other magazines. Also known for her condensed version of King James, Old and New Testaments "Olive Pell Bible" 1952-55, now in 6th edition.

BIGGS, WALTER.
Illustrator. Born 1866, in Elliston, VA. Studied at Chase School, NYC, with Edward Penfield, Lucius Hitchcock, Robert Henri. Illustrations in Harper's, Scribner's, The Century, Ladies' Home Journal, Good Housekeeping, McCall's, Cosmopolitan. Taught at ASL, Grand Central School of Art. Elected to Hall of Fame by Soc. of Illus., 1963. Died in 1968.

BIGOT, TOUSSAINT FRANCOIS.
Painter. Born France 1794. Settled in New Orleans in 1816. Painted mostly landscapes and portraits; in 1841 he had a studio at 45 St. Philip Street, New Orleans, LA. Died 1869.

BILL, CARROLL.
Painter. Exhibited water colors at the Annual Water Color Exhibitions, at Penna. Academy of Fine Arts, Philadelphia, 1922. Address in 1926, 132 Riverway, Boston, Mass.

BILL, SALLY CROSS.
(Mrs. Carroll Bill). Painter and teacher. Born Lawrence, Mass.

Pupil of DeCamp and Ross Turner in Boston. Member: PA S. Min. P.; NYWCC; Am. S. Min. P.; G. Boston A. Award: Silver medal for miniatures, P.-P. Exp. San. F., 1915. Work: Murals in three steamers of Bethlehem Ship Co.; Elks Bldg., Boston, and St. James Church, New Bedford (in collaboration with Carroll Bill); represented in Philadelphia Museum of Art, and Woman's City Club, Boston, Mass. Address in 1929, 132 Riverway, Boston, MA.

BILLIAN, CATHEY.
Painter and instructor. Born: Chicago, Illinois, Feb. 24, 1946. Studied: University of Arizona; Temple University; The Art Students League; The Art Institute of Chicago. Exhibitions: Northern Arizona University, 1969; Larry Aldrich Museum of Contemporary Art, Ridgefield, Connecticut, 1974; Hudson River Museum, 1975. Address in 1980, 456 Broome St., New York, NY.

BILLINGS, A.
Engraver. His work was chiefly book-plates and some crude book-illustrating; his book-plate for Richard Varick, an officer in the Revolution, and Mayor of New York in 1801, is signed "A Billing, Sculpt."

BILLINGS, EDWIN T.
Portrait painter. Born in 1893. He painted a portrait of Stephen Salisbury that is signed and dated 1885. Several of his paintings are owned by the Worester Art Museum, Worcester, Mass. Died Oct., 1893 in Dorchester, Mass.

BILLINGS, JOSEPH.
Engraver, on silver plate; was also a silversmith and watchmaker. According to a proclamation of 1770, he was a forger and counterfeiter of bills of credit of the Province of Pennsylvania.

BILLINGS, MARY HATHAWAY.
Painter. Born Brooklyn, NY. Pupil of Rhoda Holmes Nicholls, Cullen Yates. Pape, Whittaker. Member: NAC; Brooklyn SA. Address in 1926, 373 Grand Avenue, Brooklyn, NY: Round Hill. Northampton, MA.

BILLOUT, GUY R.
Illustrator. Born in Decize France, in 1941, he studied art a the Ecole des arts Appliques fo four years. He has received tw Gold Medals from the S of I sinc 1969, when his first illustratio appeared in New York Magazine Esquire, Redbook, Ms., McCall's Money, Town and Country and Vogu have all published his charmin illustrations.

BILOTTI, S(ALVATORE) F.
Sculptor. Born in Italy, Feb. 3 1879. Member of National Sculptur Society. Exhibited at the Penna Academy of the Fine Arts, 1924 Address in 1926, New York City, No 9 Macdougal Alley.

BINGHAM, GEO. CALEB.
Portrait and genre painter. Bor 1811 in VA. Friend of Cheste Harding, the artist. He went t Duesseldorf in 1857, and in 187 was made professor of art in th University of Missouri at Columbia Missouri. Died July 7, 1879, i Kansas City, MO.

BINNS, ELSIE.
Sculptor. Exhibited at Penna Academy of Fine Arts, Philadelphia 1924. Address in 1926, Alfred, NY

BINON.
Sculptor, who exercised his art i Boston in 1820. He was educated i France and studied art there. Whe in Boston he executed a bust o John Adams, of considerable merit he was an early instructor of th sculptor, Horatio Greenough.

BIRCH.
Engraver. In 1789 a portrait wa published of "Mr. Tho. Gurney" signed "Birch Sculp." It is wel engraved in line; it occurs in a Essay on The System of Short Hand, written by Thomas Sarjeant.

BIRCH, B.
Flourished 1784. Portrai draughtsman in crayons, sea engraver, and miniature painter He inserted an advertisement in th N.Y. Packet, 1784, "Likenesses ar painted in crayon at one guine. each, with elegant oval, gil

74

frames included." By B. Birch from London.

IRCH, GERALDINE.
(Mrs. G. R. Duncan). Painter and etcher. Born Forest Row, Sussex, England, Nov. 12, 1883. Pupil of Desvallieres, Menard, Prinet in Paris; W. W. Russell. Member: Calif. PM; Calif. AC; AFA. Work: "The Bookworm," State Library, Sacramento; "Aubrey and his Hen," Oakland Art Gallery; "The Sacred Garden," San Juan Capistrano Mission; etching, State Library, Sacramento, Calif. Address in 1929, 1550 Garfield Ave., Pasadena, Calif.

IRCH, REGINALD B.
Illustrator. Studied in Paris, Antwerp, Munich. Noted for pen-and-ink drawings for children's books such as Little Lord Fauntleroy in 1886. Illustrated for many magazines. Active in later years in Massachusetts. Born in London, 1856; came to America, 1872. Died there in 1943. Address in 1926, Box 636, Dover, NJ.

IRCH, THOMAS.
Artist. Born in London in 1779, son of William Birch, and emigrated to the US in 1793. He established himself in Philadelphia about the year 1800, and commenced the painting of profile likenesses. A visit, made in a pilot-boat, to the capes of the Delaware, in the year 1807, turned his attention to marine views, in the delineation of which he acquired a high reputation. During the war of 1812, he executed a series of historical paintings, representing the naval victories of the US. He also painted many landscapes, which are highly prized, particularly those representing snow scenes. His views of Philadelphia are excellent. He died in 1851, aged seventy-two years.

IRCH, WILLIAM.
Born in Warwickshire, England, 1755; died in Philadelphia, 1834. Birch was an enamel painter and engraver; for a time he was working in Bristol, and in 1788-91 he was engraving prints and publishing them at Hampstead Heath, near London, and he was later living in London. In 1794 he came to Philadelphia with a letter of introduction from Benjamin West to the Hon. William Bingham, and in that city he painted landscapes in water colors and miniatures in enamel; among the latter were several portraits of Wash. done after the Stuart head. The earlier engraved work of Birch was executed in stipple and was much more finished than that published in this country. His one known portrait, that of Mrs. Robinson, engraved after a portrait by Sir Joshua Reynolds, belongs to this period and is an excellent piece of work. In 1791 he published in London a quarto volume entitled "Delicies de la Grande Bretagne," a collection of views of places in the neighborhood of London, and well done in stipple. His reputation as an American engraver is founded upon his Views of Philadelphia, drawn and engraved in 1798-1800 in connection with his son Thomas Birch, later well known as a landscape and marine painter. In 1808 he also issued a smaller series showing the country seats of the United States. These views are now chiefly valued for their historical interest. His Philadelphia views were republished by him in 1802 and again republished by Robert Desilon in 1841. Extracts from an unpublished autobiography of William Birch are published in Anne Hollingsworth Wharton's "Heirlooms in Miniatures."

BIRDSALL, AMOS, JR.
Painter. Exhibited "The Coast" at the Penna. Academy of Fine Arts, Philadelphia, 1921. Born in New Jersey, 1865. Address in 1926, Melrose Park, Penna.

BIRDSEYE, DOROTHY CARROLL.
Painter. Born New York City. Pupil of George Bridgman, Hugh Breckenridge. Member: North Shore AA; Fellowship PAFA. Address in 1929, 11 West 90th St., New York, NY; summer, Gloucester, Mass.

BIRELINE, GEORGE.
Painter. Born Aug. 12, 1923, in
Peoria, Ill. Studied at Bradley
Univ. (BFA) and U. of North
Carolina (MA). Taught at School of
Design, NC State, 1957-75. In
collections of NC Mus.;
Prentice-Hall, Inc., NJ;
Fayetteville Mus. of Art; Fed.
Reserve Bank, Richmond, VA.
Exhibited at PAFA, 1950; NC Mus. of
Art; LA County Mus.; Butler Inst.
in Youngstown, Ohio; Southeastern
Center for Contemp. Art,
Winston-Salem, 1979. Received
awards from NC Mus. of Art, Ford
Foundation, Winston-Salem Gallery
of Fine Arts, Guggenheim, and Nat.
Council on Arts Grant. Works in
oil, watercolor, colored pencil.
Living in Raleigh, NC, in 1982.

BIRGE, MARY THOMPSON.
Painter. Born in NY, 1872. Pupil
of Yale School of Fine Arts.
Address in 1926, 1914 North
Penna. Street, Indianapolis, Ind.

BIRGE, PRISCILLA.
Photographic media. Studied:
Putney School, Vermont; Brown
University; University of
California, Elisha Benjamin Andrews
Scholar, 1955, 1956. Exhibitions:
Lucien Labaudt Gallery, San
Francisco, 1965; Brown University,
Providence, Rhode Island, 1975;
Joan Peterson Gallery, Boston,
1975. Collections: E. B. Crocker
Art Gallery, Sacramento,
California; Joslyn Art Museum,
Omaha, Nebraska; Pembroke College,
Providence, Rhode Island.

BIRMELIN, ROBERT.
Painter and dragtsman. Born Nov.
7, 1933, in Newark, NJ. Studied at
Cooper Union, ASL, Yale (BFA, MFA),
and U. of London. Taught at Yale;
at Queens College since 1964. In
collections of Brooklyn Mus.;
Whitney; Addison Gallery; MOMA;
Mus. of Art, San Fran.; and Chase
Manhattan Bank. Exhibited at Am.
Fedn. of Arts, 1960; Silvermine
Guild, 1960; Whitney; MOMA; PAFA;
Nat'l. Inst. of Arts and Letters.
Awarded Fulbright, 1960; Am. Acad.
fellowship; Schiedt Prize, PAFA;
Nat'l. Inst. Arts and Letters;
Tiffany Grants. Address in 1982,
Leonia, NJ.

BIRNBAUM, MEG.
Illustrator. Born in Greenwich,
Connecticut, 1952. She studied for
two years in Massachusetts at the
Montserrat School of Visual Art and
Vesper George School of Visual Art.
She began free-lance illustrating
in 1972 with a piece in Of
Westchester Magazine and presently
works for The Real Paper in
Cambridge, Massachusetts. Her
artwork has been shown at the Beaux
Arts Gallery, Mamaroneck Artist
Guild Gallery and in the Annual
Exhibition of the S of I.

BIRREN, JOSEPH P.
Painter and lithographer. Born in
Chicago, studied in Philadelphia,
New York, Paris; and Munich.
Member: Chicago AC (life); Palette
and Chisel C.; AIC Alumni Assoc.;
Chicago PS, and others. Exhibited
at the Penna. Academy of the Fine
Arts, Philadelphia, 1924. Address,
49 Elm Street, Chicago, Ill.

BISBEE, JOHN.
Artist and lithographer. He is
recorded by Dunlap as a good
draughtsman.

BISBING, H. SINGLEWOOD.
Painter. Born in 1849 in Phila.
Studied at PA and in Paris, and
Brussels. Lived abroad. Exhibited
in the Paris Salon, and at PAFA.
Died in 1933.

BISCHOFF, ELMER NELSON.
Born July 9, 1916, in Berkeley,
Calif. BA, Univ. Cal/Berkeley,
1938, and MA, 1939. In collections
of Whitney; Oakland Art Museum;
MOMA; Art Inst. of Chicago; San
Francisco Mus. Art. Exhibited at
Tate Gallery, London; Osaka World's
Fair (1970); Carnegie Inst; Whitney
and others. Awarded Ford Foundation
grant, 1959; award from Art Inst.
of Chicago, 1964. Teaching, San
Fran. Art Inst.; Univ. of
California, Berkeley, from 1963.
Address in 1982, Berkeley, Calif.

BISCHOFF, ILSE M(ARTHE).
Illustrator and etcher. Born New
York, NY, Nov. 21, 1903. Pupil of
Joseph Pennell; George Buchner.
Member: ASL of NY. Award:
Boericke prize, Phila. PC, 1927.

76

Address in 1929, 27 Mt. Morris Pk., West, New York, NY.

BISHOP,
A little-known portrait and genre painter, working about 1850.

BISHOP, HUBERT.
Painter and etcher. Born in Norwalk, Conn., in 1869. Address in 1926, 87 East Ave., Norwalk, Conn.

BISHOP, ISABEL.
(Mrs. Harold G. Wolfe). Painter and etcher. Born March 3, 1902, in Cincinnati, Ohio. Studied at Wicker Art School, Detroit; NY School of Applied Design for Women; Art Students League, NYC; Moore Inst., Hon. DFA. Taught at Yale; Art Students League, and Skowhegan School, Maine. In collections of Boston Mus. of Fine Art; Whitney; Met. Mus. of Art; Philips Mem. Gallery, Wash., DC; Victoria and Albert Mus., London; Herron Mus. of Art, Indianapolis; the Newark Mus.; Munson-Williams-Proctor Inst., Utica, NY. Exhibited at Berkshire Museum; Whitney; Midtown Galleries, NYC; Venice Biennials; and others. Awards from Am. Artists Group, etching; Nat'l. Acad. of Design; Corcoran Gallery of Art, Wash., DC. Mem.: Am. Soc. of Graphic Artists; Nat'l. Arts Club; Audubon Artists; Royal Society of Arts, London. Address in 1982, 355 W. 246th St., New York City.

BISHOP, RICHARD E(VETT).
Etcher. Born Syracuse, NY, May 30, 1887. Graduated from Cornell University, studied at Graphic Sketch Club, and with Ernest D. Roth. Specialty, bird studies; his "Canada Geese" was awarded the Charles Lea prize, in Philadelphia, 1924. Address in 1926, Springback Lane, Mt. Airy, Penna.

BISHOP, THOMAS.
Miniature painter. Born 1753 and died 1840. He lived in London and Paris, and came to Philadelphia about 1811; he took a studio in Germantown, PA and painted miniatures. One of his enamels of a Venus was much admired. He exhibited at the Penna. Academy in 1811.

BISONE, EDWARD GEORGE.
Painter. Born in Buffalo, NY, Nov. 19, 1928. Study: Univ. of Buffalo, with Seymour Drumlevitsch. Exhibitions: Nat'l Academy of Design; Albright-Knox Art Gal., Buffalo; plus many others. Mem.: Artists Equity Assn.; Nat'l. Soc. Lit. and Arts. Media: Mixed. Address in 1982, Cheektowaga, NY.

BISPHAM, HENRY COLLINS.
Born in Philadelphia, 1841. He studied there with William T. Richards, and later with Otto Weber in Paris. He died in 1882. "The Lion Sultan," signed "H. C. Bispham Paris 1879," exhibited at the Salon, 1879, and Royal Academy, 1880, was presented in 1883 to Penna. Academy of Fine Arts, Philadelphia.

BISSELL, EDGAR J.
Painter. Born in Aurora, Ill., 1856. Studied in Boston, Mass., and with Boulanger and Lefebvre in Paris. Address in 1926, 3016 Bartold Ave., St. Louis, MO.

BISSELL, GEORGE EDWIN.
Sculptor. Born New Preston, Litchfield Co., Conn., Feb. 16, 1839. Died Aug. 30, 1920 in Mt. Vernon, NY. In marble business with his father and brother at Poughkeepsie, NY, 1866; studied art, Paris, Rome and Florence. Public monuments and statues: Soldiers' and Sailors' Monument, and statue Col. Chatfield, Waterbury, Conn.; portrait statue Gen. Horatio Gates on Saratoga Battle Monument; Chancellor John Watts and Col. Abraham de Peyster, New York; Abraham Lincoln, Edinburgh, Scotland; Chancellor James Kent, Congressional Library; bronze statues Admiral Farragut and Gen. Sherman; statue of Lincoln, Clermont, IA; marble bust and bronze statuette in Metropolitan Museum, New York.

BISTTRAM, EMIL.
Born, April 7, 1895. 1906; came to America; was naturalized as US citzen. Studied in night classes, National Academy of Design, Cooper Union and New York School of Fine and Applied Art. Became commercial artist, and opened an art service

which employed from eighteen to twenty men. Was Associate Instructor, New York School of Fine and Applied Art, and later taught for five years at Master Institute, Roerich Museum, New York. 1931; Won Guggenheim Fellowship award for study of fresco abroad. Worked for short time with Diego Rivera in Mexico. 1932; Founded Taos School of Art, Taos, New Mexico.

BITTENBENDER, BEN.
Painter. Exhibited "Twilight, Susquehanna Valley" at Annual Exhibition of National Academy of Design, New York, 1925. Address in 1926, Nescopeck, Penna.

BITTER, KARL T.
He came to America in 1889, after studying in Vienna at the School of Applied Arts. Member of NIAL, NAD, and Pres. of NSS at the time of his death. Works: Statue of Gen'l Sigel, Riverside Drive, NYC; panels in Trinity Church Gates, NYC; figures in facade of MMA; statue of Dr. William Pepper, Phila.; statue of facade of Brooklyn Mus.; statues on Vanderbilt and Rockefeller estates; and the battle group for Dewey Arch, NYC. See "Karl Bitter, A Biography," by Schevill, pub. in Chicago, 1917. Died in 1915.

BITTINGER, CHARLES.
Artist. Born Wash., June 27, 1879. Student Mass. Institute Tech., 1897-99; Ecole des Beaux Arts, Paris, 1901-5. Has exhibited at Paris Salon; Societie Nationale des Beaux Arts; NY, Phila., Washington, etc.; medal St. Louis Expn., 1904; 2d Hallgarten prize, National Academy Design, 1909; Clark prize, same, 1912; silver medal, San Francisco Expn., 1915; 1st prize, Duxbury Art Assn., 1919. Elected Associate Member of National Academy. Address in 1926, 1 West 81st Street, New York.

BIXBEE, WILLIAM JOHNSON
Painter, illustrator, and teacher. Born Aug. 31, 1850. Died July 14, 1921 in Lynn, MA. He was secretary of the Boston Society of Water Color Artists. Designer of the seal of the city of Lynn. His painting of "Morning" has been exhibited.

BJORKMAN, OLAF.
Sculptor. Born in Scandinavia in 1886. Died in 1946. Among his best known works: "Beethoven," "The Titan," and heads of Lincoln, and Edgar Allen Poe. Address in 1926, New York.

BJURMAN, ANDREW.
Sculptor, craftsman, and teacher. Born in Sweden, Apr. 4, 1876. Member: Calif. AC; S. Calif. S. G. Awards: Bronze medal, San Diego Exp., 1915; second prize, California Liberty Fair, 1918; popular prize, Southwest Museum, 1923; hon. mention, Los Angeles Museum, 1924; first prize, Pomona, Calif., 1924 and 1927; hon. mention, Los Angeles Museum, 1927; gold medal, Southwest Exposition, Long Beach, Calif., 1928. Address in 1926, 834 South Garfield Ave., Alhambra, California.

BLACK, ELEANOR SIMMS.
(Mrs. Robert M. Black). Painter. Born in Washington, DC, 1872. Exhibited at the Penna. Academy of the Fine Arts, 1924. Pupil of Corcoran School. Address in 1926, 3732 Dawson Street, Pittsburgh, PA. Died 1949.

BLACK, KATE ELEANOR.
Painter. Born London, 1855. Pupil of Cincinnati Academy. Member: Cincinnati Woman's Art Club. Award: Bronze medal, Provincial Exhibition, New Westminster, British Columbia, Canada. Address in 1926, 4168 Forest Ave., South Norwood, Ohio. Died Dec. 14, 1924.

BLACK, LISA.
Painter. Born in Lansing, Michigan, in June 19, 1934. Studied: University of Paris, Sorbonne; University of Michigan. Awards: Rowayton Arts Center, 1971; New Rochelle Art Association, 1971; Springfield Museum National Annual, Time-Life Building; Smithsonian Magazine. Exhib.: New Haven Paint and Clay Club Art Exhib. CT, 1971 and 1972. Media: Acrylic.

BLACK, MARY C. W.
(Mrs. Clarence A. Black). Painter.
Born Poughkeepsie, NY. Pupil of W.
L. Lathrop, Art Students' League of
New York, Mora and Glenn Newell.
Member: National Academy of Women
Painters and Sculptors; California
Art Club; National Art Club;
Society of Independent Artists.
Address in 1926, "El Cerrito,"
Santa Barbara, California.

BLACK, MRS. NORMAN I.
Painter. Born Providence, RI,
1884. Pupil of Eric Pape School,
Boston; Julien Academy in Paris;
studied in Munich. Member:
Providence Art Club. Address in
1926, 414 West 154th Street, New
York.

BLACK, NORMAN I.
Painter and illustrator. Born in
Chelsea, Mass., Nov. 8, 1883.
Pupil of Eric Pape School, Boston;
Julien Academy and Beaux Arts,
Paris. Address in 1926, 414 West
154th Street, New York, NY.

BLACK, OLIVE P(ARKER).
Painter. Born Cambridge, Mass.,
July 22, 1868. Pupil of H. Bolton
Jones, Chase, Art Students' League
of New York, and National Academy
of Design in New York. Member:
National Academy of Women Painters
and Sculptors. Address in 1926, 242
West 56th Street, New York.

BLACK, WILLIAM THURSTON.
Flourished 1850-1851, Phila. and
NY. Portrait painter and portrait
draughtsman in pastel and crayon.

BLACKBURN, JOSEPH.
He was born and trained in Great
Britain, and painted in this
country from 1754 to 1762. His
portraits were painted in Bermuda
in 1753. From 1754 to 1761 he was
working in Boston. There are about
eighty portraits by Blackburn in
America, most of them signed. He
painted a number of his figures
"knee-length" with rather awkwardly
posed legs. His portrait of Thomas
Dering and his wife Mary are owned
by the Metropolitan Museum.
Theodore Atkinson, Jr., owned by
the Rhode Island School of Design,
and Col. Theodore Atkinson, owned
by the Worcester Art Museum. The

Boston Museum of Fine Arts own the
portrait of Jonathan Simpson and
his wife Margaret.

BLACKBURN, M(ORRIS) ATKINSON.
Painter and engraver. Born
Philadelphia, Oct. 13, 1902. Pupil
of PAFA. Member: Fellowship PAFA.
Address in 1929, 211 Oakmont Ave.,
Oakmont, Delaware Co., PA.

BLACKMAN, CARRIE HORTON.
(Mrs. George Blackman). Painter.
Born Cincinnati, Ohio. Pupil of
St. Louis School of Fine Arts;
Chaplin in Paris. Specialty,
children's portraits.

BLACKMAN, WALTER.
Painter. Born in New York.
Studied in Paris under Gerome.
Exhibited with the Society of
American Painters in 1878 and in
the Paris Salon of the same year.

BLACKMORE, ARTHUR E(DWARD).
Painter. Born Bristol, England,
Feb. 8, 1854, and died Dec. 15,
1921. Pupil of South Kensington
Museum, London. Member: Arts Aid
Society; Art Fund Society; NY
Architectural League, 1914;
Washington Art Club; and Society of
Independent Artists. Executed many
mural decorations.

BLACKSHEAR, ANNE LAURA E(VE).
Painter, illustrator, lithographer
and teacher. Born Augusta, GA,
Oct. 30, 1875. Pupil of Twachtman,
Chase, Gifford, Breckenridge,
Garber. Member: Athens AA; Ga.
AA; SSAL. Work: Portrait of
President Spence, Piedmont College,
Demorest, GA. Bulletin "Charts for
Visual Instruction in Extension
Work," owned by the Georgia State
College of Agriculture. Lectures,
"Rediscovered Principles of Greek
Design," "Delineation and Aid in
Education" and "Class Room Practice
in Design," owned by the Georgia
Education Association. Writer and
director of pageants and plays
staged for the GA. State College of
Agriculture and the University of
GA. Summer School. Address in
1929, Georgia State College of
Agriculture; h. 165 Willcox Park,
Athens, GA.

BLACKSTONE, HARRIET.
Painter. Born New Hartford, NY.
Pupil of Julien Academy in Paris;
Chase Summer Schools; Pratt
Institute, Brooklyn. Member:
Chicago Society of Artists;
American Women's Art Association,
Paris. Represented in Vincennes
Art Association; San Francisco
Museum; National Gallery of Art,
Washington. Died in 1939. Address
in 1929, 222 West 23rd St., NYC.

BLACKWELL, GARIE.
Illustrator. Born in Los Angeles
in 1939, she attended the Chouinard
Art Institute for three years. Her
first illustration was done for
Seventeen in 1967 and she has since
worked for Cosmopolitan, Ladies'
Home Journal, Mademoiselle and
Allied Chemical Corporation. She
is now working in Cambridge,
Massachusetts, and researching the
possible health hazards to artists
resulting from the use of certain
products used in the profession.

BLAGDEN, ALLEN.
Painter and printmaker. Born in
Salisbury, Conn., Feb. 21, 1938.
Studied at Cornell Univ., BFA;
travelled in Egypt and Greece for a
year; summer painting fellowship,
Yale Univ. Work at Garvan
Collection, Peabody Mus., New
Haven, Conn.; Berkshire Mus.,
Pittsfield, Mass. Exhibited at
Silvermine Guild Artists; St.
Gaudens Mus., NH; Wadsworth
Atheneum; Albright-Knox Gallery,
Buffalo, NY; others. Received
Allied Artists Award, 1963; NAD;
Century Club Art Prize, 1971.
Member: Century Assn., NYC.
Address in 1982, Salisbury, Conn.

BLAINE, NELL.
Painter. Born in Richmond, VA,
July 10, 1922. Study: Richmond
Prof. Inst., 1939-42; Hans Hoffman
School of Fine Arts, 1942-43,
Atelier 17, etching and engraving
with Wm. S. Hayter 1945; New School
for Soc. Research, 1952-53. Work:
Whitney Museum of Art, NY; Virginia
Museum of Fine Arts; MOMA; Met.
Mus. of Art; murals in Tishman
Bldg., NYC; plus numerous public
and private collections.
Exhibitions: Art in the White
House Program; Corcoran Gallery;

MOMA, NY; Museum of Modern Art,
Rome; Palais de Beaux-Arts de la
Ville de Paris; and many other
group and one-man shows in USA and
abroad. Awards: VA Mus., Fine
Arts Fellowship; Guggenheim Fellow;
Nat'l Endowment award. Mem.:
Artists Equity Assn. Media: Oil
and watercolor. Rep.: Fischbach
Gal., NYC. Address in 1982, 210
Riverside Drive, NYC.

BLAIR, CARL RAYMOND.
Painter and art dealer. Born in
Atchison, Kansas, Nov. 28, 1932.
Study: Univ of Kans., BFA 1956;
Kans. City Art Inst.; Sch. of
Design, MFA 1957. Work: Greenville
College, Greenville, Ill.; Old
Dominion College, Norfolk, VA; SC
State Art Collection; etc.
Exhibitions: International
Platform Assoc., Wash. DC; 33rd
Butler Ann.; others. Awards:
State, regional and national.
Media: Oil. Address in 1982, 1
Oakleaf Rd, Greenville, SC.

BLAIR, E. R.
Illustrator. Member: Cleveland
SA. Address in 1929, 2248 Euclid
Ave., Cleveland, Ohio.

BLAKE, DONALD.
Illustrator. Born Tampa, Fla.,
1889. Pupil of Henry McCarter.
Award: Cresson Traveling
Scholarship. Member of Fellowship
Penna. Academy of Fine Arts.
Address in 1926, 244 West 14th
Street, New York.

BLAKE, JAMES HENRY.
Painter, illustrator and teacher
Born in Boston, Mass., July 8,
1845. Pupil of Hollingsworth and
Rimmer in Boston; Moore in
Cambridge. President Cambridge Art
Circle. Specialty, scientific
subjects. Address in 1926, 117 Elm
Street, West Somerville, Mass.

BLAKE, PETER.
Illustrator. Born 1932. Presently
living and illustrating in
Somerset, England, he has worked
for Standard Oil Company and Exxon
Corporation. His work has been
exhibited in The Tate and other
major galleries.

80

LAKE, WILLIAM W.
Engraver of business buildings, working in NY in 1848; he then had his work rooms at 167 Broadway.

LAKELOCK, RALPH (ALBERT).
Landscape painter. Born Oct. 15, 1847 in New York City. Son of Dr. R. A. Blakelock, who intended him to pursue med. career. Blakelock was self-taught, going west to study Am. Indians. Paintings were noted for rich, vibrant color. Awarded first Hallgarten Prize in 1899, and hon. men. (1892) from PA. After a change in his style, his work was no longer popular, until after his death. Work: "From St. Ives to Lelant" (St. Louis Mus.); and at Whitney and MMA. Died Aug. 9, 1919 in a mental hospital, after suffering extreme poverty.

LAKELY, JOYCE C.
Painter. Born in New Orleans, LA, July 1, 1929. Study: Delgado Art Mus.; S. Georgia College; with Bill Hendrix, John Pellew, Zoltan Szabo, Edmond Fitzgerald. Comn.: Presby. Church, Hendersonville, NC; Pardee Hosp, Hendersonville; and more. Exhibitions: Hendrix Gal., St. Simons Island, Georgia; Butler Inst. Am. Art, Youngstown, OH; others in US and London. Mem.: Nat. Lg. Pen Women. Media: Oil. Address in 1980, Route 1, Zirconia, North Carolina.

LAMEUSER, SISTER MARY FLEURETTE.
Painter and teacher. Born in Skokie, Ill. Study: Art Inst. of Chicago; Univ. of Colo.; Columbia Univ.; Clarke College, BA; State Univ. Iowa, MA; Georgio Cini Found. and Fellow, Venice; watercolor with Noel Quinn, Edgar Whitney. Exhibitions: Wichita Art Museum and others, including commissions for Sisters of Charity, Wichita. Awards: Wichita (KS) Women Artists; Kans. Watercolor award. Mem.: Artists Guild of Wichita; Kansas Watercolor Soc.; etc. Media: Watercolor, oil. Rep.: Wichita Art Museum, Kansas. Address in 1982, 8506 E. Central, Wichita, Kansas.

LANC, ANTHONY.
French artist. Painting in Philadelphia, noted in the directory shortly after 1800 as a "Profile Portrait Painter."

BLANCHARD, ELIZA H.
Portrait and miniature painter. Flourished 1843-1846, Providence, RI.

BLANCHARD, WASHINGTON.
Miniature painter. Born 1808. Portrait of Wm. Ellery Channing exhibited at Boston Athereum in 1834. Painted John C. Calhoun and Henry Clay.

BLANCHING, C.
Painter. Portraits of Revolutionary patriots at Independence Hall, Philadelphia.

BLANEY, DWIGHT.
Painter. Born in Brookline, Mass., Jan. 24, 1865. Exhibited at Penna. Academy of the Fine Arts, Philadelphia, 1921. He works in both oil and water colors. Member: Copley S., 1892; Boston GA. Represented in Cleveland Mus. of Art. Address in 1926, 308 Fenway, Boston, Mass.

BLANKE, ESTHER.
Painter and craftwoman. Born Chicago, Ill., Feb. 2, 1882. Pupil of Chicago Art Inst., studied in London and Munich. Member: Chicago AG; Cordon Club. Address in 1926, 1200 Steinway Hall, 64 East Van Buren Street; Home, 418 Deming Place, Chicago, Ill.

BLANKE, MARIE ELSA.
Painter. Born in Chicago. Pupil of Chicago Art Inst., and studied in Munich and London. Member: Chicago Society of Artists; Chicago Art Club. Instructor in art, Lewis Institute, Chicago. Address in 1929, 1236 N. Dearborn St., Chicago, Ill.

BLASHFIELD, EDWIN HOWLAND.
Artist. Born New York, Dec. 15, 1848. Studied Paris, 1867, under Leon Bonnat, also receiving advice from Gerome and Chapu; exhibited at Paris Salon, yearly, 1874-79, 1881, 1892; also several years at Royal Academy, London; returned to America, 1881; has exhibited genre pictures, portraits and decorations. Among his paintings

are "Christmas Bells" and "Angel with Flaming Sword." Decorated great Central Dome, Library of Congress; decorative panel, Bank of Pittsburgh. Elected member of Academy in 1888. Author, with Mrs. Blashfield, of "Italian Cities;" editor, with Mrs. Blashfield and A. A. Hopkins, of Vasari's "Lives of the Painters"; author, "Mural Painting in America," 1914. Address in 1926, Carnegie Hall, New York City.

BLASY, ALEXANDER.
Sculptor. Exhibited at Penna. Academy of Fine Arts, 1924. Address in 1926, 31 Bank Street, New York.

BLAU, DANIEL.
Painter, etcher and teacher. Born Dayton, Ohio, Feb. 2, 1894. Pupil of Art Academy of Cincinnati; Dayton Art Inst. Member: Dayton SE. Address in 1929, Dayton Art Inst.; h. 27 Yale Ave., Dayton, Ohio.

BLAUVELT, CHARLES F.
Painter. Born in New York in 1824, he was elected an Academician of the National Academy in New York in 1859. He died April 16, 1900 in Greenwich, CT. Represented in Wilstach Collection in Fairmount Park, Philadelphia.

BLAZEY, LAWRENCE E.
Painter and teacher. Born Cleveland, April 6, 1902. Member: Cleveland SA. Address in 1929, Carnegie Hall, 1221 Huron Rd.; h. 2017 Bunts Rd., Cleveland, Ohio.

BLEIL, CHARLES GEORGE.
Painter and etcher. Born in San Francisco, Dec. 24, 1893. Among his works are "Autumn Road" and the "Green House" at California Artists' Gallery. Member: San F. AA; Calif. SE. Awards: First prize graphic arts, San Francisco Art Assoc., 1924.

BLENNER, CARLE JOAN.
Painter. Born Richmond, VA, Feb 1, 1864. Educated Marburg, Germany, and special course, Yale; 6 years at Julien Academy, Paris. Exhibited Paris Salon, 1887-8-9-91; Chicago Exposition, 1893; medal at

Boston, 1891; Hallgarten Prize National Academy of Design, 1899 represented at exhibitions in Ne York since 1889; bronze medal St Louis Expn., 1904. Address i 1926, 58 W. 57th Street, New York.

BLOCH, ALBERT.
Painter, etcher, writer, lecture and teacher. Born St. Louis, MO Aug. 2, 1882. Studied at the St Louis School of Fine Arts an abroad. Represented in Phillip Memorial Gallery, Washington, DC Address in 1926, School of Fin Arts, University of Kansas.

BLOCH, JULIUS T(HIENGEN).
Painter. Born in Germany, May 12 1888. Studied at Penna. Academy o Fine Arts. Exhibited at Penna Academy of Fine Arts, 1924. Work "Tulips and Anemones," Penna. Acad of FA. Address in 1926, 10 Sout 18th St., Philadelphia.

BLOCH, LUCIENNE.
Painter. Born Jan. 5, 1909, i Geneva. In 1917 she and her famil moved to US. Studied at Clevelan School of Art 1924-25; Paris wit Antoine Bourdelle and Andre Lhote anatomy and drawing classes at th Ecole Nat. des Beaux Arts Assisted Diego Rivera in 1932-34 a Det. Inst. of Arts, Rockefeller Ctr. and New Worker's School in Ne York City. One of her assignment on the WPA project, entitled "Th Evolution of Music," at the Musi Room of George Washington Hig School in Upper Manhattan, wa warmly received.

BLOCK, ADOLPH.
Sculptor. Born New York City, Ja 29, 1906. Pupil of Hermon MacNeil; Edward F. Sanfor Gregory; A. Stirling Calder; Edwa McCartan; Beaux- Arts Inst. Design in New York; Fontainebles School of Fine Arts, Paris. Awar Third Award, National Aeronaut Trophy Competition; prize, Ot Elevator Dial design competitio Tiffany Foundation Fellowshi Architects silver medal, Beaux Ar Institute, 1926; Fontainebles Fellowship, 1927; Paris Priz Beaux-Arts Institute, 192 Address in 1929, 1103 Lebanon St Bronx, New York, NY.

82

LOCK, HENRY.
Painter, illustrator, etcher and teacher. Born Lithuania, March 11, 1875. Pupil of ASL of NY. Member: Plainfield AA. Address in 1929, 1103 Lebanon St., New York, NY; summer, 200 Third St., Dunellin, NJ.

LOCK, JOYCE.
Painter and calligrapher. Born in Chicago, Ill. Study: Univ. Calif. at LA; Columbia Univ. Teachers College; Tenshin Calligraphy Institute, Tokyo, with Kakei Fujita. Exhibitions: Ann. Callig. Exhib., Nihon Shodo Bijutsuin, Tokyo 1963 to 80; Yokohama Shodo Renmei, 1968-75; and others in Japan and US. Awards: Nihon Shodo Bijutsuin, Tokyo; Yokohama Shodo Renmei. Teaching: Yokohama, Japan, 1960-79; US and Italy. Mem.: Nat'l. Ed. Assn.; Am. Assn. of Univ. Women. Media: Sumi ink, dyes. Address in 1982, 360 Alcatraz Ave., Oakland, CA.

LONDEL, JACOB D.
Portrait painter. Born 1817 and died 1877. He was elected an Associate Member of the National Academy in 1854.

LONDHEIM, ADOLPHE W.
Painter, etcher, illustrator and teacher. Born in Maryland, Oct. 16, 1888. Pupil of Maryland Institute, and Penna. Academy of Fine Arts. Represented in Chicago Art Institute, California Public Library, and State House, MO. Address in 1926, Provincetown, MA.

LOODGOOD, ROBERT FANSHAWE.
Painter, sculptor, illustrator, etcher and teacher. Born New York, Oct. 5, 1848. Pupil of NAD; ASL of NY. Member: Salma. C.; Calif. SE; NAC. Address in 1929, 64 East 56th St; 112 Park Ave., New York, NY; summer, Setauket, LI, NY.

LOOMER, H. REYNOLDS.
Painter. Born in New York, studied in Paris, and exhibited in the Salon of 1877.

LOSSOM, DAVID J.
Illustrator. Born in Chicago, 1927, the son of illustrator Earl Blossom. He studied at the Yale School of Fine Arts and ASL under Reginald Marsh. In 1947 he became an art director at the J. Walter Thompson advertising agency, but upon publication of his first illustration in 1961, he turned his talents to painting and drawing. Since that time he has illustrated several books and his work has appeared in The Saturday Evening Post, McCall's, Good Housekeeping and Outdoor Life. He received Awards of Excellence from the S of I Annual Exhibitions in 1962 and 1963 and the Hamilton King Award in 1972.

BLOSSOM, EARL.
Illustrator. Born 1891 in Siloam Springs, Missouri, he attended the AIC in 1920 and began his career drawing men's fashions, illustrating for the Chicago American newspaper and working on staff for Charles Daniel Frey Studio. He later worked for Pete Martin of The Saturday Evening Post where he began his inventive and often humorous style of fiction illustration. When Martin left the Post, Blossom moved to Collier's and subsequently appeared in True, Bluebook, Liberty and American Legion Magazine, among others. His work was seen in many ADC Annual Shows and is part of the collection of the New Britain Museum of American Art. His son, David, is presently a successful illustrator in New York.

BLUM, ALEX A.
Etcher and painter. He exhibited dry point etchings at the Penna. Academy of Fine Arts in the exhibition of 1924. Address in 1926, 1520 Chestnut Street, Philadelphia.

BLUM, JUNE.
Painter and curator. Born Dec. 10, 1939. Studied: Brooklyn College, New York; Brooklyn Museum Art School; The New School; Pratt Graphic Art Center. Exhibitions: Fleisher Memorial Art Gallery, Philadelphia Museum, 1974; Bronx Museum, "Year of the Woman," New York, 1975; Queens Museum, "Sons and Others, Women See Men," New York City, 1975. She is represented in the collection of Brooklyn

College.   Membership: Women's
Caucus for Art; Col. Art Assoc. of
Am; Artists' Equity Assoc. Media:
Oil.

BLUM, ROBERT FREDERICK.
Painter, illustrator, and mural
decorator. Born July 9, 1857 in
Cincinnati, Ohio, and died June 8,
1903, in New York City. He worked
in oil and pastel and studied
lithography and etching. He
traveled in Europe and in Japan and
did much illustrating. Blum
painted many Japanese street
scenes, his "The Amega" being in
the Metropolitan Museum, NY. He
also executed the long wall-panels
for the old Mendelssohn Glee Club
Hall in New York City. Elected
Member of National Academy, 1893.

BLUM, ZEVI.
Illustrator. Born in Paris, 1933.
He received a degree in
architecture from Cornell
University in 1957. After several
years as a practicing architect, he
began a career in illustration and
is presently acting chairman of the
Fine Arts Department at Cornell. A
book illustrator with works
published by Doubleday and Pantheon
Books, he is a frequent contributor
to the Op-Ed page of The New York
Times. Intellectual Digest,
Rolling Stone and Atlantic Monthly
have also used his work.

BLUME, MELITA.
Landscape painter. Born in
Germany. Pupil of Art Students'
League of New York. Nat. Acad,
Munich. Address in 1926,
Brookhaven, LI, NY.

BLUMENSCHEIN, EARNEST L.
Painter. Born at Pittsburgh, May
26, 1874. Pupil Art Students'
League and Academy Julien, Paris;
illustrator for Century,
Scribner's, McClure's, Harper's,
American, and other magazines and
books. Chiefly engages in portrait
work. Elected Associate Member of
the National Academy, 1910.
Represented in Cincinnati Art
Museum; Harrison Collection, Los
Angeles Art Museum; Kansas City
Library; Wichita Museum; Pratt
Institute, Brooklyn; Dayton Art
Institute; Ft. Worth Museum of Art;
Milwaukee Institute; five murals,
Missouri State Capitol, Jefferson
City; National Museum, Washington,
DC; NAC, New York; Brooklyn Museum;
Toronto Art Gallery. Address in
1926, Taos, New Mexico.

BLUMENSCHEIN, HELEN GREENE.
Painter. Born in New York City in
1909. Awards: New Mexico and
Arizona State Fairs. Collections:
New York Public Library; Library of
Congress; Newark Public Library;
Carnegie Institute; Cincinnati
Museum Association.

BLUMENSCHEIN, MARY SHEPARD GREENE.
(Mrs. E. L. Blumenschein). Painter
and sculptor. Born in New York
pupil of Herbert Adams in New York
and Collin in Paris. Elected an
Associate Member of Nationa
Academy of Design in 1913
Represented in Brooklyn Mus. of Art
and Sciences. Member: ANA, 1913
NA Women PS; S.I., 191
(association). She was awarded
third medal in the Paris Salon
1900; second medal, Paris Salon
1902; silver medal, St. Loui
Exposition, 1904; Julia Sha
Memorial ($300), NAD 1915. Address
in 1926, Taos, New Mexico.

BLUMENTHAL, M(OSES) L(AURENCE).
Illustrator and teacher. Bor
Wilmington, NC, July 13, 1879
Studied at Pennsylvania Museu
School, and in Munich. Member
Guild of Free Lance Artists
Philadelphia Sketch Club
Illustrated for Saturday Evening
Post, The Ladies' Home Journal
Collier's, McClure's, Scribner's
etc. Instructor in illustration
Graphic Sketch Club, Philadelphia
Pennsylvania.

BLYTH, BENJAMIN.
Engraver and portrait draughtsma
in pastel. Born 1746, Salem
Mass.; died after 1787. The son o
Samuel Blyth. He was admitted t
the Essex Lodge of Masons in Sale
on March 1, 1781. In Felt'
"Annals of Salem" under the dat
1769, there is the following entry
"Benjamin Blyth draws crayons a
his father's house in the grea
street leading to Marblehead.
Many of his portraits are extant i
the old families of New York. Hi
only work as an engraver is foun

84

in a Mezzotint Allegorical
Composition entitled "Sacred to
Liberty, or an Emblem of Ye Rising
Glory of Ye American States" signed
"Cole del-Blyth Facit." On the
portrait of Martha Washington
engraved by John Norman his name
appears "B. Blythdel."

BLYTHE, DAVID GILMOUR.
Painter. Born near East Liverpool,
Ohio, in 1815. Apprenticed at age
16 to a Pittsburgh woodcarver; no
formal art training. Became an
itinerant portrait painter. Lived
in Uniontown, Pennsylvania, for
five years from about 1847, where
he carved an eight-foot statue of
Gen. Lafayette, commissioned for
dome of co. court house, and
painted a 300-foot panorama of
western Pennsylvania. During his
artistic career he worked in
portraiture, sculpture, historical
panoramas, theatrical scenery, and
lithography. He became best known
for his satirical genre paintings
of 19th century society.
Represented by Kennedy Galleries,
New York City; Carnegie Institute,
Rochester Museum, Brooklyn museum,
and National Baseball Museum,
Cooperstown (NY). Died in 1865.

BOARDMAN, RICHARD A.
Collector and admenistrator. Born
in Philadelphia, Pennsylvania, June
18, 1940. He studied at the Ecole
des Louvre, Sorbonne in Paris,
1961, Brown University, AB, 1962,
John Hopkins School of Advanced
International Studied, Bologna,
1973. He was a Special Assistant
Director at the Corcoran Gallery,
Washington, DC, 1974-1975; the Fine
Arts Advisor at the International
Communications Agency, Washington,
DC, 1975. He was awarded the
Special Commendation from the
United States Information Agency,
1978. Memberships include the
Friends of Corcoran (board member);
New Museum (advisory board);
Friends of List Art Center, Brown
University (advisory board).
Collections of his work are
included in the African and
Oriental art and furniture;
contemporary American Art; Haitian
painting and met꤯l work. Address
in 1980, 2236 Decatur Pl NW
Washington, DC.

BOARDMAN, ROSINA COX.
Painter. Born in New York City.
Studied: Art Students League;
Chase School of Art with William
Chase, DuMond and Mora. Awards:
Boardman prize, New York;
Pennsylvania Society of Miniature
Painters, 1949; American Society of
Miniature Painters, 1952; Nat'l.
Assn. of Women Artists, 1932, 58;
Los Angeles Soc. of Miniature
Painters; Boston Museum of Fine
Arts. Collections: Metropolitan
Museum of Art; Brooklyn Museum;
City Art Museum of St. Louis;
Corcoran Gallery of Art; Fairmont
Museum of Art, Philadelphia.

BOBBS, RUTH PRATT.
Painter. Born Indianapolis, Ind.,
Sept. 3, 1884. Pupil of Wm. M.
Chase. Member: National Art Club;
National Academy Women Painters and
Sculptors; Pen and Brush Club;
Indiana Art Club. Work: "The
Spanish Shawl," Herron Art
Institute, Indianapolis. Address
in 1926, 10 Gramercy Park, New
York.

BOCK, CHARLES PETER.
Painter. Born in Germany, 1872.
Pupil of Art Institute of Chicago;
Simon in Paris. Member: Dallas
Painters; Overland Landscape
Outfit. Work: "Where Sand and
Water Meet," Dallas Public Library.
Address in 1926, Manvel, Texas.

BOCK, RICHARD W.
Sculptor. Born in Germany, July
16, 1865; came to America at age of
five. Pupil Schafer, Berlin
Academy; Falguiere, Ecole des Beaux
Arts, Paris. Work: Illinois State
Soldiers' and Sailors' Monument at
Shiloh; Lovejoy monument at Alton,
Ill.; bronze group on Public
Library at Indianapolis; Soldiers'
Monument at Chickamauga, for
Lancaster, PA. Address in 1926,
The Gnomes, River Forest, Ill.

BODGAR, WILLIAM F. JR.,
Sculptor. Born at Salem, NJ, 1893.
Pupil of Penna. Academy of Fine
Arts. Exhibited at Penna. Academy
of Fine Arts, Philadelphia.
Address in 1926, Hadonfield, NJ;
summer, Provincetown, Mass.

85

BODMER, KARL.
Painter and etcher. Born 1809 in Switzerland. He traveled in America in 1832. He made water color sketches of his travels, also executed the copper plates in the atlas published in Maximilian's "Journey through North America" (1838-1842).

BODO, SANDOR.
Painter, sculptor, and conservator. Born in Szamosszeg, Hungary, Feb. 13, 1920; US citizen. Study: College of Fine and Applied Arts, Budapest, Hungary. Commissions: Bronze reliefs, Hungarian Reformed Fedn. of Am.; portrait of Andrew Jackson, Royal Palace, Copenhagen. Exhibitions: Nat'l. Housing Ctr., Wash., DC; Smithsonian Inst.; Tenn. Fine Art Ctr., Nashville; Butler Inst. of Am. Art, Youngstown, Ohio; Nat'l. Acad. Galleries, NYC; others. Awards: Am. APL gold medal, watercolor; Nat'l. Arts Club, NY, gold medals, sculpt. and oil ptg.; Smithsonian Inst.; others. Mem.: Nat'l. Arts Club; Am. APL (fellow); Allied AA. Works in oil, watercolor, bronze. Address in 1982, Nashville, Tenn.

BOEBINGER, CHARLES WILLIAM.
Painter, illustrator, teacher. Born Cincinnati, Ohio, June 17, 1876. Pupil of Cincinnati Art Academy; Art Students' League of New York. Member: Western Drawing and Manual Teachers' Association. Address in 1926, Walnut and Central Parkway, Cincinnati, Ohio.

BOECKMAN, CARL L.
Painter. Born Christiania, Norway. Studied at Christiania, Copenhagen and Munich. Award: Silver medal for portrait, Columbian Exposition, Chicago, 1893. Work: "Battle of Killdeer Mountain," Capitol, St. Paul, Minn. Address in 1929, 3500 - 3rd Ave., South Minneapolis, MN.

BOERICKE, JOHANNA MAGDALENE.
Painter and sculptor. Born in Philadelphia Feb. 13, 1868. Pupil of PAFA, studied in Rome and Paris. Address in 1926, 5932 Overbrook Ave., Philadelphia.

BOGARDUS, JAMES.
Engraver and diesinker. Born 1800 in Catskill, NY. He was a skillful mechanic and invented a machine for producing bank-notes from separate dies. He died in 1874 in NYC.

BOGARDUS, MRS. JAMES.
Miniature painter. Was born in 1804, and died in 1879. She exhibited portraits at the National Academy, New York, 1842 to 1846.

BOGART, GEORGE HIRST.
Landscape painter. Born New York in 1864. Pupil of the National Academy of Design; also studied in Paris. Elected an associate member of the National Academy in 1899; also member of the Society of American Artists. Represented at Metropolitan Museum, NY, by "Moonlight," at Corcoran Art Gallery by "Sunset," and at Brooklyn Institute by "Dordrecht." He died in New York City in 1944.

BOGDANOVE, ABRAHM JACOBI.
Painter and teacher. Born Minsk, Russia, Aug. 11, 1887. Pupil at National Academy under Marnard and F. C. Jones. Member: Society Independent Artist League of New York. Work: Mural decoration in Hebrew Sheltering Guardian Society, Pleasantville, NY; two mural decorations in the Brooklyn Commercial High School. Address in 1926, 145 East 23d Street, New York, NY.

BOGEN, BEVERLY.
Painter. Born in Jersey City, NJ. Study: Syracuse Univ.; ASL; Pratt Graphic Art Ctr.; with Victor Perard, Benton Spruance, Harry Sternberg, Leo Manso. Work: More than 500 private collections, US and abroad; Bank of VA, Wash., DC. Exhibitions: Silvermine Guild Ann.; Allied Artists, Nat'l. Acad Galleries, NYC; Yellow Hse. Gal. Huntington, NY; others. Mem. Artists Equity Assn.; Am. Fedn. of Arts. Works in acrylic. Address in 1976, Jericho, NY.

BOGER, FRED.
Painter and illustrator. Born Baltimore, MD, Oct. 12, 1857. Pupil of Frank Duveneck in Cincinnati. Member: Cincinnat

86

Art Club. Work: "Judge Alphonso Taft," Superior Court, Hamilton County, Ohio; portraits of George B. Cox and August Herrman at Blaine Club, Cincinnati, Ohio. Address in 1926, 2440 Jefferson Ave., S. Norwood, Ohio.

BOGGS, FRANK M.
Born in Springfield, Ohio, 1855, lived in Paris. Studied at the Ecole des Beaux Arts and under Gerome in Paris; "A Rough Day, Harbor of Honfleur, France" is owned by Boston Museum of Fine Arts. Died Aug. 11, 1926 in Meudon, France.

BOGLE, JAMES.
Portrait painter. Born in South Carolina in 1817. He moved to New York in 1836, where he studied under Morse. He was elected an Associate of the National Academy in 1850, and an Academician in 1861. He painted many portraits in the south, Calhoun, Clay, Webster; his portraits of John Dix and Henry Raymond were among his later works. He died in 1873 in Brooklyn, NY.

BOHLAND, GUSTAV.
Sculptor. Born Austria, Jan. 26, 1897. Pupil of A. A. Weinman; Cooper Union; NAD; Beaux Arts Inst. of Design. Address in 1929, 637 Madison Ave., New York, NY.

BOHM, C. CURRY.
Painter. Born Nashville, Tenn., Oct. 19, 1894. Pupil of AIC; Edward F. Timmins. Member: Palette and Chisel C., Chicago; Brown County SA; Hossier Salon; Ill. AFA; Amer. Artists Prof. Lg. Award: Municipal Art League prize ($100) Palette and Chisel Club. Address in 1929, Palette and Chisel Club, 1012 North Dearborn St.; h. 4121 North Lincoln St., Chicago Ill.

BOHM, MAX.
Painter. Born in Cleveland, Ohio, in 1868. Travelled to Europe 1886, studied at Julien School, Paris, with Constant, Lefebvre, Boulanger, Mosler, and others; travelled in Eng., Holland, Ger., Italy, and France to study works of the Old Masters. In collections of the Nat'l. Gallery, Wash., DC; San

Diego Mus., Calif.; Wichita Art Mus., Kans.; Luxembourg Mus., Paris; Met. Mus. of art, New York City; Butler Inst., Youngstown, Ohio; Smithsonian, Wash., DC; and many others, including private collections, in US, France, England. Exhibited at Paris Salon from 1888; Royal Academy, London; Met. Mus. of Art, Brooklyn Mus., NYC; Luxembourg Gallery, Paris; National Gallery, Wash., DC; Macbeth and Grand Central Galleries, NYC; others, including retrospective, Castellane Galleries, NYC. Awarded Gold Medal, Salon of 1898, Paris; Gold Medal, Panama-Pacific International Exposition, San Francisco, 1915; Clark prize, Figure composition, NAD, 1917; and many others. Opened school of painting, Etaples, France, in 1895; continued school in London during winters; ceased teaching in 1911 to concentrate on own painting. Lived in France, England, and briefly in the US until he settled near NYC in 1919. Elected National Academician, 1920; member, Arch. Lg.; vice pres., Nat'l. Mural Painters Soc.; life member, Nat'l. Arts Club. Died in Provincetown, MA, in 1923 where he had become one of the early forces in creation of art colony there.

BOHNERT, HERBERT.
Painter and illustrator. Born Cleveland, Ohio, 1888. Pupil Cleveland School of Art. Address in 1926, 2258 Euclid Ave., Cleveland, Ohio.

BOHROD, AARON.
Born, November 21, 1907; Chicago Ill. Studied two years at Chicago Art Institute; two years at Art Students' League, New York, under John Sloan, Boardman Robinson and Kenneth Hayes Miller. 1936; Won Guggenheim Fellowship award in creative painting. Work owned by Chicago Art Institute and Whitney Museum of American Art, New York. Awards: Clyde M. Carr Prize, 1933; Joseph Eisendrath Prize, 1934; William H. Tuthill Prize, 1934; Watson F. Blain Prize, 1935; Chicago Artists' Prize, 1935.

87

BOILEAU, PHILIP.
Painter. Born in Quebec, Canada in
1864, he died   New York   Jan.
18, 1917. He lived in Baltimore
for some years and painted many
pictures of fashionable women.

BOIT, EDWARD DARLEY.
Painter in water colors. Born in
1840, he graduated from Harvard in
1863 and died April 22, 1916. He
was an intimate friend of John S.
Sargent and held several joint
water color exhibitions with him in
Boston and New York. Represented
in Boston Museum of Fine Arts by
forty water color paintings.

BOIX, RICHARD.
Painter. Exhibited in Philadelphia
in 1921. Address in 1926, 49 West
8th Street, New York.

BOLANDER, KARL S.
Painter. Born in Marion, OH, May
3, 1893. Pupil of Dow and Walter
Sargent, Ensign, MacGilvary, Walter
Beck, Lemos, Ohio State Univ.,
Pratt Inst., Berkshire Summer
School of Art, Univ. of Chicago.
Member: Columbus AL; Ohio WCS;
Eastern AA; Western AA; Assn. Art
Mus. Directors. Instructor in
Applied Arts School, Chicago,
Snow-Froehlich School of Industrial
Art, NY Director, Fort Wayne Art
School and Mus., 1922-26; director
and lecturer, FA Department, Ohio
State Fair; Director, Columbus
Gallery of Fine Arts and Columbus
Art School. Address in 1929, 478
East Broad St., Columbus, Ohio.

BOLEN, JOHN GEORGE
This engraver's work is unknown
except for an armorial book-plate
of Charles M. Connolly, signed "J.
G. Bolen, 104 B'way."

BOLINSKY, JOSEPH ABRAHAM.
Sculptor. Born in NYC, Jan. 17,
1917. Study: Columbia Univ.;
Stourbridge College of Art, Eng.;
Skowhegan Sch. of Ptg. and Sculpt.,
with Jose de Creeft; Iowa Univ.
Work: Newark (NJ) Mus.; Mus. of
Art, Tel-Aviv, Israel numerous
others. Comn.: Synagogue,
Waterloo, Iowa; Temple Sinai,
Amherst, NY; and more.
Exhibitions: Columbia Univ.;
Gallery West, Buffalo, NY; Brock

Univ., Can.; Rome; others. Awards:
des Moines Art Ctr.; Albright-Knox
Art Gallery, Buffalo, NY; Rochester
Fest., Religious Art; others.
Professor of Fine Arts, SUNY
Buffalo, sculpture; others. Works
in bronze and stone. Address in
1982, Tonawanda, NY.

BOLLES, IDA RANDALL.
Painter. Pupil of George C.
Hopkins, Duveneck, ASL of
Washington, Corcoran AS. Member:
Laguna Beach AA. Award: Purchase
prize, comp. ex. Southern Calif.
Orange Assoc., 1923. Specialty,
marines. Address in 1929, Laguna
Beach, Calif.

BOLMAN, CAROLINE.
Amateur miniature painter,
flourished in Philadelphia about
1827. Exhibited miniature of
Madame Murat, Penna. Academy, 1827.

BOLMAR, CARL P(IERCE).
Painter, illustrator and writer.
Born Aug. 28, 1874. Pupil of PAFA;
Spring Garden Inst. Member:
Topeka AG. Art critic and staff
artist for the Topeka State
Journal. Illustrated "Overland
Stage to California," and books by
Margaret Hill McCarter. Address in
1929, Topeka State Journal, 800
Kansas Ave.; h. 1726 West St.,
Topeka, Kan.

BOLMER, M. DeFORREST.
Landscape painter. Born 1854 in
Yonkers, NY. He died July 7, 1910.
His painting "Cold and Gray" was
sold in auction at New York, 1923.

BOLTON, J. B.
Engraver of letters and script. He
was located in Boston, Mass., in
1841 and worked in connection with
D. Kimberly.

BOLTON, ROBERT FREDERICK.
Painter, illustrator, etcher and
craftsman. Born in New York City
March 19, 1901. Studied with
Curran, Maynard and Bridgman.
Pupil of Charles C. Curran; Francis
C. Johen; Edwin H. Blashfield; Ivan
Olinsky. Work: Series of mural
decorations, Consolidated Gas Co.
NY; series of decorative panels, NY
Winter Garden Theatre. Address in

88

1926, 502 West 139th Street, New York.

BOMAR, BILL.
Painter. In collections of Ft. Worth (TX) Art Ctr. Mus.; Brooklyn Mus.; Guggenheim; Houston Fine Arts Mus.; others. Exhibitions at Wayne Gallery, NYC, and many others. Address in 1970, 222 W. 23rd St., NYC.

BONA-PARTE.
This fictitious signature appears on a crude portrait of James Madison. The portrait is printed from the plate of Benjamin Rush, engraved by James Akin; this is a case of the engraver Akin disclaiming his own work.

BONAR, T.
Engraver of stipple portraits. About 1850 he was working for the Methodist Book Room. About the same time the firm of Bonar and Cummings were producing portraits for the Methodist Magazine.

BOND, KATE LEE BACON.
Painter and teacher. Born Topeka, Kan., Nov. 18, 1890. Pupil of AIC. Member: Chicago SA; Chicago S. Min. P. Address in 1929, 899 Ash St., Winnetka, Ill.

BOND, ORIEL E.
Painter and illustrator. Born in Altus, Okla., July 18, 1911. Study: Rockford College, with Marquis Reitzel, Einar Lunquist, Alice McCurry. Work: Private collections only. Exhibitions: Rockland (Ill.) Art Assn., 1956-63; Am. APL, NYC, 1971, 72; others. Chief artist, J. L. Clark Mfg. Co., Rockford, Ill., 1938-77. Mem.: Am. APL; Nat'l. Soc. of Literature and Arts. Works in oil, polymer. Address in 1982, Roscoe, Ill.

BONE, HENRY.
An English miniaturist of note. Likely to have painted in America, as portraits of prominent Americans by him are known.

BONEVARDI, MARCELO.
Painter and sculptor. Born May 13, 1929, in Buenos Aires, Argentina. In US since 1958. Studied architecture, painting, sculpture at Univ. of Cordoba. In collections of MOMA; Ciba-Geigy Corp.; Brooklyn Mus.; NYU; Tel Aviv; U.N.; Univ. of Texas; and Moderno Mus. in Buenos Aires. Exhibited at Argentinian Galleries; Pan Am. Union, Wash., DC; Latow Gallery, NYC; Center for Inter-Am. Relations, NYC, 1980. Awards: Guggenheim fellowship, 1958, 58; New School for Soc. Research 1964, 65; Bienal, Sao Paulo. Address in 1982, 799 Greenwich St., NYC.

BONFIELD, GEORGE R.
Marine and landscape painter. Born in England in 1802; came to Philadelphia as a youth and became a stone carver. Encouraged by Joseph Bonaparte of Bordentown, NJ, became one of the leading marine painters of America. An early member of the Penna. Academy of Fine Arts; he died in Philadelphia in 1898. Represented in Wilstach Collection, Fairmount Park, Philadelphia.

BONGART, SERGEI R.
Painter and teacher. Born in Kiev, Russia. Study: Kiev Art Academy. Work: National Academy of Design; Kiev Academy of Fine Arts, Russia; Charles and Emma Frye Art Museum, Seattle; Theater Museum, Kiev, Russia; Laguna Beach Art Assn. Gallery; Cerritos College, Norwalk, Conn.; Sacramento State Art Collection; others in US and abroad. Exhibitions: Metropolitan Museum of Art, NY; National Academy of Design; Museum of Russian Art, Kiev, Russia; American Water Color Society; M. H. De Young Memorial Museum, San Fran., Calif.; and many other group and one-man shows. Awards: Gold medal, Am. APL, NY, 1959; silver medal, Am. Watercolor Society, 1969; Watercolor USA, 1974. Teaching: Founder and Instructor Sergei Bongart School of Art, Santa Monica, Calif., from 1949. Mem.: NAD; Nat'l. Acad. Western Art; Am. Watercolor Soc.; Royal Soc. of Arts; Society of Western Art. Media: Oil, acrylic. Address in 1982, Santa Monica, Calif.

BONHAM, HORACE.
Genre painter. Born West Manchester, Penna., 1835; died

89

1892. Pupil of Bonnat, in Paris. Represented by "Nearing the Issue at the Cockpit," at the Corcoran Gallery, Washington, DC.

BONSALL, ELIZABETH F.
Painter. Born in Philadelphia in 1861. Pupil of Penna. Academy of Fine Arts, under Eakins and Howard Pyle. Studied in Paris under Collin and Courtois. Represented at Penna. Academy of Fine Arts by "Hot Milk" (purchased 1897). Address in 1926, 3430 Walnut Street, Philadelphia.

BONSALL, MARY W.
Painter and illustrator. Has exhibited miniatures at the Penna. Academy of Fine Arts. Born at Fernwood, Penna. Pupil of Cecilia Beaux, Chase, and Vonnoh. Address in 1926, 3430 Walnut Street, Philadelphia.

BONTA, ELIZABETH B.
Painter. Born in Syracuse, NY. Received medal for water color, "The Pale Moon," St. Paul Institute, 1916. Address in 1926, 290 Adelphi Street, Brooklyn, NY.

BOOG, CARLE MICHEL.
Painter. Born in Switzerland, June 27, 1877. Pupil of Art Students' League of New York and of Bonnat in Paris. Drawings in Historical Museum, Bennington, VT. Address in 1926, 206 Parkville Ave., Brooklyn, NY.

BOOGAR, WILLIAM F. JR.
Painter and sculptor. Born Salem, NJ, Aug. 12, 1893. Pupil of Charles Hawthorne; PAFA. Address in 1929, Wahington and Atlantic Aves., Haddonfield, NJ; summer, Provincetown, Mass.

BOONE, CORA.
Painter. Exhibited water colors at Annual Exhibition of Water Colors, 1922, Penna. Academy of fine Arts, Philadelphia. Address in 1926, Oakland, Calif.

BOOTH, CAMERON.
Painter. Born Erie. PA, Mar. 11, 1892. Pupil of H. M. Walcott; Andre L'hote, Paris; Hans Hofmann, Munich. Awards: John Quincy Adams Foreign Traveling Scholarship, AIC,

1917; first prize, Minnesota State AS, 1922; first prize, Twin City Artists, 1925 and 1926. Work: "Horses," Pennsylvania Academy of the Fine Arts, Philadelphia; "Early Mass," Newark Museum Association, Newark, NJ. Address in 1926, 2525 - 5th Ave. S., Minneapolis, Minn.

BOOTH, EUNICE ELLENETTA.
Painter and teacher. Born Goshen, NH. Pupil of Mass. School of Art, Boston; NY School of Fine and applied Art; Handicraft Guild, Minneapolis, under Batchelder; William Chase; Julian Academy and Academie Delecluse in Paris. Member: College AA of America; Calif. State AA. Director, Dept. of Graphic Arts and Prof. of Drawing and Painting, College of the Pacific. Address in 1929, Weber Hall, College of the Pacific, Stockton, Calif.; summer, Norton, Mass. Died 1942.

BOOTH, FRANKLIN.
Illustrator. Born in Carmel, Indiana, in 1874. Copied intricate wood and steel engravings from magazines in pen-and-ink. In 1925, published book of 60 drawings in the decorative style he often used to illuminate poetry and articles. Member: SI 1911; Salma C. Died in 1943. Address in 1929, 58 West 57th St., New York, NY.

BOOTH, HANSON.
Painter and illustrator. Born at Noblesville, Ind., May 19, 1886. Pupil of Bridgman in New York, also Vanderpoel. Work: Illustrations for Harper's Monthly. Address in 1926, Woodstock, Ulster County, NY.

BOOTH, JAMES SCRIPPS.
Painter and sculptor. Born in Detroit, Mich., May 31, 1888. He studied in Europe. Member of California Art Club. Address in 1926, 836 South El Molina Ave. Pasadena, Calif.

BOOTH, T. DWIGHT.
Engraver. Said to have been born in Albany, NY. He was for a time engaged in bank-note work, but is chiefly known for illustrating for the publishing firm of G. P. Putnam and Co. of New York.

90

OOTT, ELIZABETH.
Painter. Born in Cambridge, Mass.
She studied in Europe. Some of her
paintings were exhibited in Boston
in 1877, and in 1878 she exhibited
"Head of a Tuscan Ox" and "Old Man
Reading." At the National Academy
Exhibition of 1886 she had
"Hydrangeas" and "Old Woman
Spinning."

ORCHARDT, NORMAN.
Illustrator. Born Brunswick, GA,
Jan. 21, 1891. Pupil of John
Vanderpoel and John Norton.
Member: GFLA. Works:
Illustrations for Century Co.;
Harper's Bros.; Collier's; etc.
Address in 1929, 82 West 12th St.,
New York, NY.

ORDEWISCH, FERDINAND F.
Etcher and illustrator. Born
Kettlersville, Ohio, June 2, 1889.
Pupil of Bridgman, Fogarty and
Mora. Member: Dayton SE; ASL.
Address in 1929, 4001 East Third
St., Dayton, Ohio.

ORDLEY, JOHN BEALE.
Portrait painter. Born in "Wye
Island," Talbot County MD, in 1800.
He was the grandson of Judge
Bordley. After a period of legal
study in Philadelphia, Bordley took
up painting. He worked in
Baltimore from 1834-51, appearing
in the directories variously as
John Beale Bordley, Beale Boardley,
and Peale Boardley. He exhibited
at the National Academy in 1843 as
B. Boardley, and at the Penna.
Academy in 1832. After 1851
Bordley retired to a farm in
Harford County, MD, where he
continued to paint. He later moved
to Bel Air and then to Baltimore,
where he died in 1882.

ORDLEY, JUDGE JOHN BEALE.
Artist. Born February 11, 1727,
and spent the greater part of his
life in Maryland. Jurist,
agricultural experimenter and
publicist, founder of the
Philadelphia Society for Promoting
Agriculture, amateur artist. He was
an early patron of Charles Willson
Peale, and shared a painting- room
in Phila. with him in 1776. In
1791 he moved to Philadelphia,
where he was prominent as a
promoter of agricultural
improvements. He died on January
26, 1804. His drawing of
wheat-harvesting in Maryland in
1787 is owned by the Philadelphia
Society for Promoting Agriculture.

BOREIN, EDWARD.
Etcher of Western life. Born in
California, Oct. 21, 1872. His
work is well known for its truth as
well as artistic merit. He is a
member of the Print Makers' Society
of California and Art Students'
League of New York City. Pupil
Hopkins' Art Sch., San Francisco.
Address in 1926, El Patio, Santa
Barbara, Calif. Died May 19, 1945
in CA.

BORG, CARL OSCAR.
Painter. Born in Sweden March 3,
1879. Self-taught. Member of
California Art Club. Represented
in University of California, and
Golden Gate Museum, LA Museum and
LA Public Library. Address in
1926, Santa Barbara, Calif. Died
May 8, 1947.

BORGLUM, GUTZON.
(John Gutzon de la Mothe Borglum).
Born Mar. 25, 1867, near Bear Lake,
Idaho. Studied with Virgil
Williams and William Keith in
Kansas. Went to Paris in 1890 and
studied at Ecole des Beaux-Arts.
Taught at ASL. Member of APSS; AL
and Societe des Beaux-Arts. In
collections of MMA; and LA Mus.
Work: Apostles for Cathedral of
St. John the Divine, NYC; Sheridan
monument, Wash., DC. Head of
Lincoln, the Capitol in Wash., DC.
Memorials to Lee (Stone Mt., GA);
James McConnell (U. of VA); and war
memorial in Newark, NJ. Statue of
Thomas Paine (Paris). Best known
for Heads of the Presidents on
Mount Rushmore, DS. Died March 6,
1941 in New York City.

BORGLUM, SOLON H(ANNIBAL).
Sculptor. Born Dec. 22, 1868, in
Ogden, Utah. Studied with his
brother, Gutzon Borglum; at Cin.
Art Acad.; and with Fremiet and
Puech in Paris. Member of NSS and
NA (1911). In collections of MMA;
Detroit Inst.; Univ. of Iowa;
Cincinnati and Nat. Gallery of
Canada. Works: Statue of Gen'l

Gordon (Atlanta, GA); Soldiers and Sailors Monument (Danbury, CT); statues "Inspiration" and "Aspiration;" and 8 colossal portrait Busts of Civil War generals. Died Jan. 31, 1922, in Stamford, CT.

BORGORD, MARTIN.
Painter and sculptor. Born Norway, 1869. Pupil of Laurens in Paris. Member: Allied Art Association; Paris American Art Association; St. Lucas Society, Amsterdam, Holland. Award: medal, Paris Salon, 1905. Work: "Laren Weaver," Carnegie Institute, Pittsburgh. Address in 1926, care of Salmagundi Club, 47 Fifth Ave., New York, NY.

BORIE, ADOLPHE.
Artist. Born Philadelphia, 1877. Studied Penna. Academy of Fine Arts, Royal Academy, Munich, Bavaria. Awards: Carol Beck gold medal, Penna. Academy Fine Arts, 1910; silver medal, San Francisco Expn., 1915; Isaac N. Maynard prize, National Academy of Design, 1917. Fellow, Penna. Academy of Fine Arts. Member: National Society Portrait Painters. Died 1934, in Philadelphia. Address in 1926, 4100 Pine Street, Philadelphia, PA.

BORKMAN, GUSTAF.
Wood engraver. Born in Sweden, 1842; died Feb. 19, 1921 in Brooklyn New York. Worked for the Graphic, Harper's Weekly, and for Harper's Monthly.

BOROCHOFF, (IDA) SLOAN.
Painter. US citizen. Study: High Mus. of Art, 1939; Univ. of Georgia, 1939-40; GA State Univ., 1940; Chic. Sch. of Interior Decorating, 1966; Atlanta Art Inst., 1968. Work in Georgia collections. Exhib.: Many in Georgia, including Atlanta Art Mus.; High Mus.; GA State College; others. Has held numerous art-related positions in design and artistic direction in Georgia. Address in 1982, Atlanta, Georgia.

BORONDA, LESTER D.
Painter. Born in Nevada, 1886. Exhibited at the Penna. Academy of

Fine Arts, 1924. Address in 1926, 131 Waverly Place, New York City.

BORST, GEORGE H.
Sculptor. Born Philadelphia, Feb. 9, 1889. Pupil of Charles Grafly, Albert Laessle; Itallo Vagnetti in Florence, Italy. Member: Alliance, AFA, Fellowship PAFA, Amer. Artists Prof. Lg. Awards: Stewartson prize and Stimson prize, PAFA, 1927. Address in 1929, 312C Market St., Philadelphia, PA; h. 201 Walnut Ave., Wayne, PA; summer, East Hebron, NH.

BORZO, K(AREL).
Painter. Born Hertogenbosch, Holland, April 3, 1888. Self taught. Member: Seattle Art Inst. Award: First prize, Washington State Fair, 1928. Address in 1929, 3025 East Madison St., Seattle, Wash.

BOSE, NEAL.
Painter, illustrator and etcher. Born Columbia, Tenn., May 22, 1894. Pupil of Leopold Seyffert; Audubon Tyler and Leon Kroll. Member: GFLA. Specialty, advertising illustration. Address in 1929, Wrigley Bldg., 410 North Michigan Blvd., Chicago, Ill.; h. 836 Hinman Ave., Evanston, Ill.

BOSLEY, FREDERICK ANDREW.
Born at Lebanon, NH, Feb. 24, 1881. Pupil of the Museum of Fine Arts School, Boston. Represented by "The Dreamer." Signed "F. Bosley, 1911." Owned by Boston Museum of Fine Arts. Address in 1926, 162 Newbury Street, Boston.

BOSS, HOMER.
Painter. Born 1882; died 1956. Exhibited at 1913 Armory Show and at Philadelphia in 1921. Address in 1926, 37 West 16th St., NY.

BOSTICK, ALMA.
Piatner and teacher. Born Monroe, LA, Oct. 1, 1891. Pupil of Catherine Critcher; E. Ambrose Webster. Member: Wash. SA; SSAL. Instructor Critcher School of Painting. Specialty, portraits. Address in 1929, 604 Copley Courts, 1514 Seventeenth St., NW, Washington, DC.

92

BOSTON, FREDERICK J(AMES).
Painter. Born Bridgeport, Conn.,
1855. Pupil of Whittaker in
Brooklyn; Carolus Duran in Paris.
Member: Brooklyn Society of
Artists. Address in 1926, Carnegie
Hall, New York City.

BOSTON, JOSEPH H.
Painter. Born Bridgeport, Conn.
Associate Member of the National
Academy of Design and the Brooklyn
Art Club, New York. Member of the
Allied Artists of America, New
York. Representation, Brooklyn
Institute of Arts and Sciences, New
York. Died in New York City in
1954. Address in 1926, Carnegie
Hall, NY.

BOSWORTH, WINIFRED.
Painter and etcher. Born Elgin,
Ill., 1885. Studied at Boston
Museum of Fine Arts; Art Students'
League of New York; Laurens in
Paris; Eisengruber in Munich.
Member: Chicago Water Color Club;
Society of Independent Artists.
Address in 1926, Woodland, Elgin,
Ill.

BOTH, ARMAND.
Painter and illustrator. Born in
Portland, Maine, in 1881; died in
New York, Feb. 1, 1922. Studied in
Boston, and with Laurens in Paris.
Illustrator for magazines and
books.

BOTH, WILLIAM C.
Illustrator. Born Chicago, Ill.,
Feb. 18, 1880. Pupil of J. Francis
Smith and Laurens. Member:
Palette and Chisel C. Address in
1929, Meyer Both Co., 1935 South
Michigan Ave.; h. 6714 Bennett
Ave., Chicago, Ill.

BOTKE, CORNELIUS.
Painter. Born Leenwarden, Holland,
July 6, 1887. Pupil of Chris Le
Beau. Member: Chicago Society of
Artists. Awards: Fine Arts Bldg.
Prize, 1918; Hon. mention for
landscapes, American Exhibition,
Chicago, 1921. Work: "The Golden
Tree," Public School, Chicago; "The
Last Snow," Oak Park High School;
"Lifting Clouds," Public Library,
Ponca City, Okla.

BOTKE, JESSIE ARMS (MRS.).
Painter and illustrator. Born
Chicago, Ill., 1883. Pupil of
Johansen, Woodbury and Herter.
Member: Chicago Society of
Artists. Awards: Englewood
Woman's Club prize, 1917; bronze
medal, Peoria Society of Allied
Arts, 1918; medal Chicago Society
of Artists, 1919. Work: "White
Swans," Municipal Gallery, Chicago;
mural decoration for Ida Noyes'
Hall, Univ. of Chicago; "Geese,"
Chicago Art Institute. Address in
1926, Carmel-by-the-Sea Calif.

BOTTUME, GEO. F.
Painter. Born in Baltic, Conn.,
1828. Painted many portraits in
the eastern part of the state. He
was still living in Springfield,
Mass., in 1878.

BOUCHE, LOUIS.
Born March 18, 1896 in New York
City. 1910 to 1915; Studied in
Paris with Desvailliers, Lucien
Simon, Prinet and Bernard Naudin;
Ateliers- Colarossi, La Grande
Chaumiere and L'Ecole des Beaux
Arts. 1915 to 1916; Studied at Art
Students' League, New York, with Du
Mond and Luis Mora. Exhibited in
American and European shows and
held one- man exhibitions. Work
owned by New York University
Gallery of Living Art, Phillips
Memorial Gallery, Whitney Museum of
American Art, Ferdinand Howald
Collection and private collectors.
Executed decorations for Radio City
Music Hall, New York City, and
various private residences.
Member: Society of Painters,
Sculptors and Gravers, and member
of the National Society of Mural
Painter.

BOUCHE, MARIAN WRIGHT.
Painter. Born New York, Dec. 8,
1895. Pupil of Henry Matisse and
Walt Kuhn. Member: Penguin Club,
Society of Independent Artists.
Address in 1926, care of Daniel
Gallery, 2 West 47th Street, New
York, NY.

BOUCHE, RENE ROBERT.
Illustrator. Born in Prague,
Czechoslovakia, in 1906. He
studied briefly at the universities
of Munich and Paris. He was a

93

frequent contributor to Vogue, which assigned him to paint an editorial series on the 1948 Republican and Democratic conventions. Best known for the fluid elegance of his drawings, he greatly influenced future styles and modes of fashion illustration.

BOUCHER, GRAZIELLA V.
Painter and writer. Born Detroit, Mich., Oct. 31, 1906. Specialty, paintings of animals. Feature writer for newspapers and magazines. Director Nat. Pub. Campaigns and Art exhibitions.

BOUDIER.
Engraver of portraits in the same style as St. Memin. He was evidently of French birth and probably was only in this country for a short time, as only one plate of his is known and that was engraved in Philadelphia.

BOUGHTON, GEORGE H.
Painter. Born Norwich England, 1833. Lived for years in New York City. His specialty was landscapes. Boughton was elected a member of the National Academy of Design in 1871; he died in London, England Jan. 19, 1905. Represented at Boston Museum of Fine Arts by "Sea Breeze."

BOUGUEREAU, ELIZABETH JANE GARDINIER.
Born in Exeter, NH, 1837. Studied in Paris and married her teacher, W. A. Bouguereau; she survived him, dying Jan. 1922 in St. Cloud France. Her specialty was ideal figure-pieces. She received a medal at the Philadelphia Centennial in 1876.

BOULTON, JOSEPH I.
Sculptor. Born in Ft. Worth, Texas, 1896. Member of League of American Artists. Exhibited at the Penna. Academy of Fine Arts, Philadelphia, 1924. Address in 1926, 424 West 20th Street, New York City, NY.

BOUNTHEAU, HENRY BRINTNELL.
Miniature painter. Born 1797 in Charleston, VA. He painted a miniature of a descendant of the patriotic family of Manigault of South Carolina. Died Jan. 31, 1877 in Charleston.

BOURDON, DAVID.
Portrait painter and musician flourishing about 1810, Pittsburgh, PA.

BOURKE-WHITE, MARGARET.
Photographer. Born June 14, 1906, in New York City, Margaret White studied at Columbia Univ., Univ. of Michigan, and Cornell Univ., where she graduated in 1927. In 1929 to 1933 she was an associate editor for Fortune magazine. Several extensive tours of the Soviet Union resulted in the picture-and-text books Eyes on Russia, 1931, Red Republic, 1934, and U.S.S.R., a Portfolio of Photographs, 1934. In 1936 she became a member of the original staff of Life magazine. She remained an editor for 33 years and contributed photographs and photo-essays. In 1939 travelled extensively in Europe, the Near East and the Soviet Union (where in 1941 she photographed Josef Stalin in the Kremlin), covered political and military events. 1942 she became the first woman to be accredited as a war correspondent to the US Army. Accompanied Gen. George S. Patton's Third Army into Germny in 1944, where she recorded on film the opening of Buchenwald and other concentration camps. Ohter books of her photographs and text included Shooting the Russian War, 1942, They Called It Purple Heart Valley, 1944, Dear Fatherland, Rest Quietly, 1946, and Halfway to Freedom: A Study of the New India, 1949. Later published works included A Report on the American Jesuits, 1956, volume of autobiography, Portrait of Myself, 1963. Died in Stamford, CT, on August 27, 1971.

BOURNE, GERTRUDE BEALS.
(Mrs. Frank A. Bourne). Painter. Specialty, water colors. Member of National Association of Women Paitners and Sculptors. Address in 1926, 130 Mt. Vernon Street, Boston.

BOURQUIN, J. E.
Painter, Yonkers, NY.

BOUTELLE, DE WITT CLINTON.
Painter. Born in Troy, 1820, and died 1884. He early came under the influence of Cole and Durand. After painting in New York and Philadelphia, he moved to Bethlehem, Penna. He painted a portrait of Asa Packer, presented to Lehigh University. He was elected an associate to the National Academy in 1853, and a member of the Pennsylvania Academy in 1862.

BOUTWOOD, CHARLES E.
Painter. Born in England, naturalized in United States 1892.

BOUTWOOD, CHARLES EDWARD.
Painter and teacher. Born in England. Pupil of Royal Academy in London; later studied in Paris. Member: Chicago SA; Chicago WCC. Award: Silver medal, Chicago SA, 1913. Represented in Vanderpoel Art Asso. collection, Chicago. Address in 1929, care of F. A. Bryden and Co., Chicago, Ill.

BOUVE, ELISHA W.
Engraver and lithographer (of Bouve and Sharp, who had their lithographic establishment at Graphic Court, Boston, Mass.). Born in Boston 1817, and died there April 13, 1897. He printed many rare views of Boston, as well as the scarce, colored print representing S. S. Britannia leaving her dock.

BOUVE, ROSAMOND SMITH.
Painter. Member: Boston GA; Conn. AFA; NA Women PS. Award: Bronze medal, P.-P. Expo., San F., 1915. Address in 1929, 334 East 57th St., New York, NY.

BOWDISH, EDWARD ROMAINE.
Painter, illustrator, and etcher. Born Richfield Springs, NY, May 26, 1856. Pupil of his father and August Schwabe. Member: Yonkers AA; AFA. Address in 1929, Skaneateles, NY.

BOWDITCH, MARY O.
Sculptor. Exhibited at the Penna. Academy of Fine Arts, Philadelphia, 1920. Address in 1926, 16 Arlington Street, Boston, Mass.

BOWDOIN, HARRIETTE.
Painter and illustrator. Born in Mass. Pupil of Elliott Dangerfield. Address in 1926, 1947 Broadway, NY.

BOWEN, ABEL.
Engraver. Born in Sand Lake Village, Greenbush, NY, 1790; died in Boston, 1850. Bowen was engraving upon wood as early as 1811, and in August, 1812, he was in business as a printer in Boston. In 1816 Bowen published in Boston "The Naval Monument," illustrated by copper and woodcut views of naval combats, a number of which were engraved by Bowen himself. He was certainly engraving upon copper in 1817 in both line and stipple; in 1821 he was in business with Alexander McKensie, a copperplate printer, and in 1825 he published Shaw's "History of Boston," illustrated by Bowen. He illustrated an edition of the lectures of Sir Astley Paston Cooper, published by Pendleton, who established the first lithographic press in Boston. Mr. W. G. Linton, in his "History of Wood Engraving in America," says that in 1834 Abel Bowen in association with the Wood-engravers Alonzo Hartwell and John C. Crossman, established the American Engraving and Printing Co. This company later became the "Boston Bewick Co.," the publishers of the American Magazine, a publication devoted to the encouragement of wood-engraving in America. The two volumes of this magazine contain about 500 woodcuts, generally coarse and crude in execution. In 1836 their printing establishment was burned down and the company failed.

BOWEN, ALEXANDER.
Painter. Born in New York in 1875. Pupil of Penna. Academy of Fine Arts. Address in 1926, Salmagundi Club, 45 Fifth Ave., New York.

BOWEN, BENJAMIN JAMES.
Painter. Born in Boston, Feb. 1, 1859. Studied abroad, studio in Paris. Pupil of Lefebvre and Robert Fleury in Paris. Exhibited in the Salon, and in America.

95

BOWEN, JOHN.
Engraver of maps, and some rather crude stipple portraits and illustrations. He was working in Philadelphia 1810-19.

BOWEN, THOMAS.
Portrait painter. He died in 1790.

BOWER, LUCY SCOTT.
Painter and writer. Born Rochester, IA, 1864. Pupil of Robert-Fleury, Lefebvre, Simon and Menard in Paris. Member: NYSA; North Shore AA; AN. Women PS; PBC. Award: Gold prize, Arc-en-Ciel Exhibition, Paris, France, 1917; prize ($100) exhibition artist members Nat. L. Amer. Pen Women, 1929. Work: "The Knitters," Museum of Vitre, France; "The Red Roofs," Pen and Brush Club, New York; "Fishermen Mending Nets," Long Branch Club of the New Jersey Federation of Women's Clubs, "Port of La Rochelle," Museum, Warrenton, NC. Author of poems, "In a Minor Vein." Address in 1929, care of the Pen and Brush Club, 16 East 10th St., NYC. Died in 1934.

BOWER, MAURICE L.
Illustrator. Member: SI. Address in 1929, 1520 Chestnut St., Philadelphia, PA.

BOWERS, EDWARD.
Painter in oils, and crayon portrait draughtsman. Born in Maryland in 1822. He was working in Philadelphia in 1855-58.

BOWES, JOSEPH.
Engraver in line and stipple and architect. He was living in Philadelphia as early as 1796. His work appears in the American Universal Magazine and the Monthly Magazine of Philadelphia.

BOWES, JULIAN.
Sculptor. Born in New York City in 1893. Author of "Proportions of the Ideal Human Figure" and "The Lost Canon of Polykleitos." Address in 1926, 7 Macdougal Alley, NY.

BOWLER, JOSEPH JR.
Illustrator. Born in Forest Hills, New York, in 1928. He started working at Cooper Union Studios in

1948. His first published illustration was for Redbook in 1949. He was acclaimed Artist of the Year in 1967 by the AG in New York, and his work appears at the Sanford Low Collection and the Hartford Museum. He has illustrated for all the major magazines and currently all his covers and illustrations are portraits.

BOWMAN, DOROTHY.
Painter ans serigrapher. Born in Hollywood, CA, Jan. 20, 1927. Studied: Chouinard Art Institute; Jepson Art Institute. Awards: Los Angeles County Fair, 1952, 1953; National Serigraph Society, 1952; Brooklyn Museum, 1954; Library of Congress, 1954; University of Illinois, 1956; Boston Printmakers, 1956, 1958; California Artists, 1957; Wichita, Kansas, 1957. Collections: New York Public Library; Immaculate Heart College, Los Angeles; Brooklyn Museum; Crocker Art Gallery, Sacramento, California; Metropolitan Museum of Art; Library of Congress; San Jose State College; Boston Museum of Fine Arts; Rochester Memorial Art Gallery; University of Wisconsin. Address in 1980, Los Angles, CA.

BOWMAN, F. G.
According to Dunlap a painter by this name was born in Pennsylvania and had a studio in Boston. He was said to have exhibited in the early days of the Boston Athenaeum, and was working in Maryland about 1800.

BOWNE, J. C.
A line engraver of this name made a number of landscape plates for Peterson's Magazine of Philadelphia about 1854.

BOYCE, RICHARD A(UDLEY).
Painter, illustrator, etcher and craftsman. Born Brooklyn, NY, July 24, 1902. Pupil of O'Neil and Pennel. Member: S. Indp. A. Address in 1929, 598 Prospect St., Ridgewood, NJ; summer, 4710 Fifteenth St., N.W., Washington, DC.

BOYCE, RICHARD.
Sculptor. Born June 11, 1920, in NYC. Studied at Boston Mus.

School, with Paige fellowship in painting, Bartlett grant in sculpture. Taught at the school, at Boston Univ., and now at UCLA. In private collections, and in Rhode Island Sch. of Design Mus.; Wellesley; Harvard; Whitney; Hirshhorn Foundation, Wash. DC; Exhibited at the B. Mirski Gallery, Boston, 1952; Swetzoff Gallery, Boston; Art Inst. of Chicago; PAFA; Landau Gallery, NYC; Smithsonian Inst.; European travelling exhib.; the Whitney; and others. Living in Santa Monica, CA, in 1976.

BOYD, BYRON BEN.
Born Jan. 22, 1889, Wichita, KS. Attended public schools, Denver, CO. Studied painting in high school under Jean Manheim, and under various instructors in schools and universities. Univ. of Colorado for three years; Northwestern Univ. for one year, receiving A.B. Four years later received M.A. in architecture from Columbia Univ. 1914. Moved to Des Moines. Became designer in architectural firm. 1916; Organized firm of Boyd and Moore and practiced architecture for fourteen years, building some of most important stuctures in Iowa. During World War headed division designing submarine bases, Navy Dept., Bureau of Yards and Docks. Attended National Academy for two seasons, later studying with Henry Leith Ross and Henry Hensche. Painted during extended trips to Europe, Africa and the Near East. Has exhibited in galleries and museums in NYC, Boston, Phila., Wash., Chicago and in most national exhibitions.

BOYD, EVERETT C.
Painter. Exhibited a "Grey Day" at Cincinnati Museum, Annual Exhibition of 1925. Address in 1926, 1322 Arlington Street, Cicinnati, Ohio.

BOYD, FISKE.
Born Philadelphia, PA in 1895. 1913-16; Studied at PAFA under Grafley, Garber, Pearson and Breckinridge. 1921-24; Studied at Art Students' League, NY, under John Sloan, Boardman Robinson and Kenneth Hayes miller. Has held one-man exhibitions in leading galleries in New York and Boston. Painted landscapes under Public Works of Art Project. Awarded Woodblock Prize, Philadelphia Print Club, 1931. Represented by woodcuts and etchings in Print Collection of Metropolitan Museum; Whitney Museum of American Art; New York Public Library; Boston Museum of Fine Arts; John Herron Art Institute, Indianapolis; Addison Gallery of American Art, Andover, Massachusetts; paintings in Phillips Memorial Gallery, Washington, DC; Whitney Musuem of American Art; Newark Musuem. Was one of the painters exhibiting regularly with the group which came into prominence soon after the famous "Armory" show.

BOYD, JOHN.
Engraver of stipple portraits and book-illustrations for the Phila. publishers from 1811- 1827.

BOYD, RUTHERFORD.
Illustrator. Member: Salma. C. Address in 1929, 112 Prospect St., Leonia, NJ.

BOYD, WILLIAM.
Painter and artist. Born Glasgow, Scotland, Aug. 24, 1882. Studied in Paris. Member: Pitts. AA; FAIA. Award: Water color prize, Pitts. AA, 1921. Address in 1929, 1213 Empire Bldg., Pittsburgh, PA; h. Edgeworth, Sewickley, PA; summer, Medomak, Lincoln Co., ME.

BOYDEN, DWIGHT FREDERICK.
Landscape painter. Born in Boston, 1865. Pupil of Boulanger in Paris. Gold medal of Paris Salon, 1900. Address in 1926, Algonquin Club, Boston, Mass.

BOYER, HELEN KING.
Engraver. Born in Pittsburgh, PA, in 1919. Studied: With Boyd Hanna, Wilfred Readio and Samuel Rosenberg. Awards: Society of American Graphic Artists, 1943; Library of Congress, 1943; Tiffany Foundation grant, 1949; New Jersey Federation of Women's Club, 1952, 1953, 1954. Collections: Library of Congress; Carnegie Institute;

97

Metropolitan Museum of Art; Henning Company, 1955.

BOYER, RALPH.
Painter, etcher and illustrator. Born Camden, NJ, July 23, 1879. Pupil of Anshutz, Breckenridge, Beaux and Chase. Member: NY Arch Lg.; Salma. C.; Fellowship PAFA. Specialty, portrait painting. Address in 1929, Westport, Conn.

BOYLE, CHARLES WASHINGTON.
Painter. Born in New Orleans, LA. Pupil of Art Students' League of New York. Represented by "Afternoon Light" Delgado Museum, and "Oak on Bayou" New Orleans Art Association. Died Feb. 9, 1925, in New Orleans, LA.

BOYLE, FERDINAND THOMAS LEE.
Painter. Born in Ringwood, England, 1820, and died 1906. He came to this country in childhood and studied painting under Inman. He settled in St. Louis in 1855, and organized the Western Academy of Art. In 1866, he came to New York, where he painted portraits of Chas. Dickens, Archbishop Hughes, Gen'l Grant (Union League Club of Brooklyn), Edgar Allan Poe and other celebrities. For many years he was professor at Brooklyn Institute of Art.

BOYLE, JOHN J.
Sculptor. Born Jan. 12, 1852,in New York City. He began life as a stonecarver and studied at the Penna. Academy of Fine Arts. He was elected an Associate of the National Academy. Represented by the "Alamo" in Lincoln Park, Chicago, and "Plato" in the Library of Congress. In 1902 he moved to New York City, where he died on Feb. 10, 1917.

BOYLE, SARAH YOCUM McFADDEN.
(Mrs. Frederick A. Boyle). Miniature painter. Born in Germantown, PA. Studied at Drexel Institute. Pupil of Howard Pyle. Exhibited at the Penna. Academy of Fine Arts in 1924-25. Address in 1926, 94 South Munn Ave., Orange NJ.

BOYNTON, G. W.
Engraver of maps, apparently located in Boston in 1842.

BOYNTON, GEORGE RUFUS.
Painter. Born at Pleasant Grove, Wis., 1928. Student National Academy Design (medalist), and Art Students' League, and under Walter Shirlaw, C. Y. Turner and J. G. Brown, New York. Portraits are hung in Union League Club; 7th Regt. Armory; 71st Regt. Armory; New York Yacht Club; Larchmont Yacht Club; US District Court, etc. Has painted portraits of Gen. F. D. Grant, Gen. Alexander S. Webb, Gen. Stewart L. Woodford, Gen. James Grant Wilson. Address in 1926, 58 W. 57th Street, New York, NY.

BOYNTON, RAY.
Born Iowa, 1883. 1904; Studied at Chicago Academy of Fine Arts under William P. Henderson, John W. Norton and W. J. Reynolds. 1913; Moved to Spokane, Washington, where he did first mural decoration in that city. 1914; Moved to Calif. 1917; Made first experiments in fresco. Has taught drawing and painting at University of California since 1920, and fresco at Cali. School of Fine Arts, San Fran., since 1927. Work: Council Chamber, Spokane City Hall; lunette for dining room in a San Francisco hotel; ceiling in Mills College, Oakland, Calif.; and frescos and murals for various private and public buildings, including Calif. School of Fine Arts, University of Calif. Faculty Club, and Coit Memorial. Exhibited continously for many years.

BOZZO, FRANK EDWARD.
Illustrator. Born in Chicago, IL in 1937. He was a pupil of Robert Shore and Eugene Karlin at SVA with classmates Paul Davis and Paul Giovanopoulos. In 1959 Harper's magazine gave him his first assignment, a pen and ink drawing which accompanied the article How Much Poison Are You Breathing? He has illustrated a number of children's books and worked for most major periodicals, including Playboy, Equire, Seventeen, and New York Magazine. Some of the organizations that have given his

98

awards are the S of I, the ADC's of New York, Chicago, and Detroit, AIGA and the Society of Publication designers. His work hangs in many private collections.

BRABAZON, THOMAS.
Painter. Member of the Connecticut Academy of fine Arts, Hartford. Address in 1926, 21 Pavilion Street, Hartford, Conn.

BRACH, PAUL HENRY.
Painter. Born March 13, 1924, in NYC. BFA and MFA from State Univ. of Iowa. In collections of St. Louis Museum; Smith College; MOMA, Whitney; and private collections. Exhibited at Castelli Gallery, NYC; Dwan Gallery, LA; MOMA; Baltimore; Corcorcan Gallery, Wash., DC; Whitney; NY; Lerner-Heller Gallery; many more. Awarded Tamarind Fellowship, 1964. Taught at Univ. of Missouri; New School for Social Research, NYC; NYU; Parsons Sch. of Design; Cooper Union; Cornell Univ.; Univ. of CA, San Diego; dean, Calif. Inst. of Art, 1969-75; chairman, arts div.; Forham Univ. at Lincoln Ctr. Living in NYC in 1982.

BRACKEN, CLIO HINTON.
Sculptor. (Mrs. Wm. B. Bracken). Daughter of Lucy Brownson Hinton, and cousin of Roland Hinton Perry studied with Chapu, Carpeaux, and A. Saint-Gaudens. Resided in Boston and Conn. Had studio in New York City. Work: Statues of Gen. Fremont in Cal.; bust of Gen. Pershing. Died Feb. 12, 1925 in New York City.

BRACKEN, JULIA M.
Sculptor. Her best known work "Illinois Welcoming the Nations," a souvenir of the Columbian Exposition, stands in bronze in the capitol at Springfield, Ill. Considered a leading western woman sculptor by her contemporaries.

BRACKER, M. LEONE.
Illustrator. Born in Cleveland, Ohio, in 1885. He was best known for his World War I posters, particularly Keep 'em Smiling. Accidential drowning caused his death in Rye, New Hampshire, in 1937.

BRACKET, H. V. (MISS).
Engraver. Probably the earliest woman engraver in the United States. Her name appears on a large Bible plate of "Ruth and Boaz," published in 1816.

BRACKETT, EDWARD A.
Sculptor. Born in Vassalboro, Maine, in 1819. Work: Portrait busts, among which are "President Harrison," "W. C. Bryant," "Wendell Phillips." His group of the "Shipwrecked Mother" is at Mount Auburn, and another of his groups was purchased by the Boston Athenaeum.

BRACKETT, WALTER M.
Painter. Born 1823 in Unity, ME, and died March 8, 1919, in Boston. A native of Maine, he painted portraits and fancy heads; and made a specialty of game fish.

BRACKMAN, ROBERT.
Painter. Born 1898 in Odessa, Russia. In US since 1908. Studied in San F. and at NAD under Bellows and Henri. Taught at ASL. Member of ASL; NA; Audubon Soc.; CT Acad.; Allied Artist of Am. and AWCS. He exhibited "Life and Still-Life" in Annual Exhibition of National Academy of Design, 1925. Address in 1926, 67 West 52d Street, New York.

BRACOUY, LEOPOLD.
Sculptor. Has exhibited in many exhibitions.

BRADBURY, C. EARL.
Painter and illustrator. Born at North Bay, NY, May 21, 1888. Pupil of Laurens and Academie Julien, Paris. Exhibited at Academy of Fine Arts, Philadelphia, 1924. Address in 1926, 610 So. Prairie Street, Champaign, Ill.

BRADDOCK, E(FFIE) F(RANCES).
Sculptor. Born Philadelphia, PA, May 13, 1866. Member: AFA; Fellowship PAFA; Plastic C. Address in 1929, 406 Third Ave., Warren, PA.

BRADFIELD, ELIZABETH P.
Sculptor. Exhibited at National Academy of Design, 1925. Address in 1926, Pontiac, Mich.

BRADFORD, FRANCIS S(COTT).
Painter. Born Appleton, Wis., Aug.
17, 1898. Pupil of NAD. Member:
NY Arch. Lg. (asso.), 1924; Mural
P. Award: Prix de Rome, American
Academy in Rome, 1923; Mooney
Traveling Scholarship, NAD, 1923.
Address in 1929, 1947 Broadway, New
York, NY.

BRADFORD, WILLIAM.
American marine painter with
specialty of Arctic Scenes. Born
in New Bedford, Mass., 1830.
Self-taught but influenced by Van
Beest, whose studio at Fairhaven he
shared for two years. Accompanied
several exploring expeditions
towards the North Pole. Died 1892
in New York City. "Arctic Whaler
Homeward Bound," signed "Wm.
Bradford, NY," is in Chicago Art
Institute.

BRADISH, ALVAH.
Portrait painter. Born September
4, 1806, in Geneva, New York. He
is noted in Dunlap as painting
portraits in Detroit. Died April
20, 1901 in Detroit, MI.

BRADLEY, CAROLYN G(ERTRUDE).
Painter, illustrator and craftsman.
Born Richmond, Ind. Pupil of
Victor Julius, William Forsyth,
Henry B. Snell, Herron Art Inst.
Member: Alumni Herron Art Inst.;
Indiana AC; Richmond Palette C; NA
Women PS; NYWCC; AWCS (assn.);
Cincinnati WAC. Represented,
permanent collection Richmond Art
Association. Address in 1929, 215
North 16th St., Richmon, Ind.

BRADLEY, SUSAN H.
Landscape painter. Born Boston,
1851. Pupil of Thayer, Edward
Boit, Chase, and School of Boston
Museum. Member: Philadelphia
Water Color Club; Boston Water
Color Club; New York Water Color
Club; Society of Independent
Artists. Represented in Herron Art
Institute, Indianapolis. Address in
1926, 20 Brimmer Street, Boston,
Mass.

BRADLEY, WILL (WILLIAM H.).
Illustrator. Born Boston, Mass.,
July 10, 1868. Member: SI 1910;
NY Arch. Lg. 1914 (assn.); Players,
1905. Art director "Collier's

Magazine," 1907-09, and of "Good
Housekeeping," 1911-13;
"Metropolitan," 1914-16; "Century,"
1914-16. Author and illustrator of
"Toymaker to the King" and "The
Wonder Box." Address in 1926
Short Hills, NJ.

BRADSHAW, GEORGE A.
Etcher and teacher. Born Trenton
NJ. Pupil of John Ward Stimson and
the Trenton School of Industria
Arts. Member: Brooklyn SE
Chicago SE; North Shore AA
Address in 1926, School o
Industrial Arts, West State and
Willow Sts.; h. Hutchinson Rd.
Trenton, NJ.

BRADSTREET, EDW. D.
Painter. Born in Meriden, Conn.
1878; died there Jan. 14, 1921
Member of Connecticut Academy o
Fine Arts.

BRADT, DELPHINE.
Painter. Exhibited flower-piece
at the Penna. Academy of Fine Arts
Philadelphia, 1924. Address i
1926, 1820 Spruce Street
Philadelphia.

BRADWAY, FLORENCE DOLL.
Painter. Born in Philadelphia Oct
16, 1898. Exhibited at Penna
Academy of Fine Arts, Philadelphia
1924. Address in 1926
Philadelphia Art Alliance Bldg.

BRAINARD, ELIZABETH H.
Portrait painter. Born i
Middleboro, and after studying i
Boston went to Italy. On he
return to this country she had he
studio in New York and Boston
Several of her portraits are owne
by Boston College; she died i
Boston in 1905.

BRAMNICK, DAVID.
Painter. Born Kishineff, Russia
1894. Pupil of the Penna. Academ
of the Fine Arts, Philadelphia
Work in Graphic Sketch Club
Address in 1926, Mark Bldg., 72
Walnut St., Philadelphia, PA.

BRANCH, GROVE R.
Painter, teacher. Instructor o
Jewelry Department, School of th
Worcester Museum; also a
Commonwealth School of Art

Boothbay Harbor, ME. Director of Manual Arts, Worcester Academy. Member: Arts and Crafts Society of Boston. Address in 1926, 64 Fruit St., Worcester, Mass.

BRANCHARD, EMILE (PETER).
Painter. Born New York, NY in 1881. Member: Society of Independent Artists. Address in 1926, 61 South Washington Square, New York, NY. Died in 1938.

BRANDEGEE, ROBERT B.
Painter. Born in Berlin, Conn., 1848. He studied in Paris at the Ecole des Beaux Arts. He painted portraits and landscapes, also executed a number of notable mural decorations. Died March 5, 1922 in Farmington, CT.

BRANDNER, KARL C.
Painter and etcher. Born Berwyn, Jan. 17, 1898. Pupil of AIC; Chicago AFA; Detroit School of Art. Member: Palette and Chisel C; Hoosier Salon; Austin, Oak Park and River Forest AL; Ill. AFA. Award: Hon. mention, Austin, Oak Park and River Forest AL, 1929. Work: "Old Red Mill," State Museum of Fine Arts, Springfield, Ill.; "June," Plymouth High School, Plymouth, Ill. Address in 1929, 1219 Kenilworth Ave., Berwyn, Ill.

BRANDON, WARREN EUGENE.
Painter. Born in San Fran., Calif., Nov. 2, 1916. Study: Milligan College; with Raymond Brose, Jack Feldman, Jack Davis, Eliot O'Hara. Work: Didrichsen Art Found., Helsinki; plus commissions. Exhibitions: Frye Museum, Seattle; Victoria Museum, Brit. Columbia; de Young Mus.; San Fran., Knickerbocker Nat'l. Ann., NYC; etc. Awards: Elected Life Fellow of the Royal Soc. of Artists, one of four Americans; etc. Media: Oil, acrylic. Living in San Fran. in 1976; died in 1977.

BRANDT, CARL L.
Painter and sculptor. Born in Holstein, Germany, 1831, he came to America in 1852. He painted portraits of John Jacob Astor, Mr. and Mrs. William Astor, and many other prominent people. He was elected a member of the National Academy of Design in 1872. He died Jan. 20, 1905 in Savannah, GA.

BRANDT, REXFORD ELSON.
Born in San Diego, Calif., Sept. 12, 1914. Study: Univ. Calif.; Berkeley; Stanford Univ. Work: San Diego Fine Arts Gal.; Currier Gallery, Andover, NH; NAD Galleries, NYC; and more; plus numerous commissions. Exhibitions: Int'l. Watercolor Exhib., Chic. Art Inst., 1936 and 1937; Calif. Palace of Legion of Honor, San Fran.; 1940 and 1960; Nat'l. Gallery, Wash., DC; Royal Soc. Painters in WC, London; Am. WC Ann. 1960-75; plus many more. Awards: NAD Ann., 1968 and 1970; Am. WC Soc., 1970; others. Mem.: Am. WC Soc.; NAD; etc. Rep.: Challis Galleries, Laguna Beach, Calif. Address in 1982, 405 Goldenrod, Corona Del Mar, CA.

BRANNAN, SOPHIE MARSTON.
Painter. Born Mountain View, Cal. Pupil of Mark Hopkins Institute of Art, San Francisco; studied in Paris. Member: National Association of Women Painters and Sculptors. Represented in Nat. Acad. of Design, New York; Corcoran Gallery, Wash., DC; Art Inst. of Chicago and many others. Address in 1926, 27 West 67th St., New York, NY.

BRANNAN, WILLIAM PENN.
Painter. He opened his studio in Cincinnati, OH; about 1840 and became known as a portrait painter. Died 1866 in Cincinnati.

BRANNIGAN, GLADYS.
(Mrs. Robt. A.). Painter. Born in Hingham, Mass. Pupil of Corcoran Art School, Washington, DC. Member of National Association of Women Painters and Sculptors. Exhibited at Penna. Academy of Fine Arts, Philadelphia, 1924. Address in 1926, 145 West 55th St., New York City. Died in 1944.

BRANSOM, PAUL.
Painter and illustrator. Born Washington, DC, 1885. Member: Society of Illustrators, 1911; New York Zoological Society. Illustrated: "The Call of the Wild," "The Wind in the Willows,"

"Neighbors Unknown," "The Feet of the Furtive," "Hoof and Claw," "The Sandman's Forest," "The Sandman's Mountain," "Over Indian and Animal Trails," "More Kindred of the Wild," "The Secret Trails," "Children of the Wild," etc. Address in 1926, Green Lake PO, Fulton Co., NY.

BRANSON, LLOYD.
Painter. Born in 1861, he died in Knoxville, Tenn., on June 12, 1925.

BRANTLY, BEN(JAMIN) (D.).
Painter and teacher. Born Little Rock, Ark. Pupil of Maryland Inst.; St. Louis School of Fine Arts. Member: St. Louis AL; NO AA; SSAL; FAC of Ark. Awards: First prizes for water color and oil, Arkansas State Fair, 1923-24-25. Work: Landscape, "Southern Memories," Scottish Rite Consistory, Little Rock; mural, Baptist Church, Little Rock. Address in 1929, 501 East 8th St., Little Rock, Ark.

BRASZ, ARNOLD F(RANZ).
Painter, sculptor, illustrator and etcher. Born in Polk County, Wis., 1888. Pupil of Minneapolis School of Fine Arts; Henri in New York. Member: Wis. "Painters and Sculptors." Address in 1926, 189 Main St., Oshkosh, Wis.

BRAUGHT, ROSS EUGENE.
Painter. Born in Carlisle, PA, in Aug. 6, 1898. Pupil of Penna. Academy of Fine Arts. Exhibited landscape, "Provincetown," at Penna. Academy of Fine Arts, Philadelphia, 1924. Work: "In the Valley," "Dear Chestnut." Address in 1926, Carlisle, Penna.

BRAUN, CORA FISHER.
Painter. Born Jordon, Minn., 1885. Pupil of Garber, Hale, Joseph Pearson, Breckenridge, Chase, Blashfield and Beaux. Acting Associate Professor of Art, University of Nebraska; Acting Assistant Professor of Art, Ohio State University; Director, Dept. of Applied and Fine Arts, University of Tennessee. Address in 1926, Department of Fine and Applied Arts, University of Tennessee, Knoxville, Tenn.

BRAUN, M(AURICE).
Painter. Born Nagy Bittse, Hungary, Oct. 1, 1877. Pupil of E. M. Ward, Maynard and Francis C. Jones at National Academy of Design in New York. Member: California Art Club. Represented in Municipal Collection, Phoeniz, Ariz.; San Diego Museum. Awards: Hallgarten prize, National Academy of Design; gold medal, Panama-California Exp., San Diego, 1910; gold medal, Panama-California Int. Exp., San Diego, 1916. Address in 1926, Point Loma, California.

BRAUNER, OLAF.
Painter. Born in Norway, Feb. 9, 1869. Pupil of Benson and Tarbell in Boston; Professor of Painting at Cornell University since 1900. Portraits in Kimball Library, Randolph, VT. Sculptor of "Dane Memorial" in Brookline, Mass. Painted altarpiece, Church of Our Saviour, Chicago, Ill. Address in 1926, Cornell University, Ithaca, NY.

BRAUNHOLD, LOUIS.
Etcher. Member of Chicago Society of Etchers. Address in 1926, 3 North Dearborn St., Chicago, Ill.

BRAXTON, WILLIAM ERNEST.
Painter and illustrator. Born in Wash., DC, Dec. 10, 1878. Member of League of New York Artists, and Society of Independent Artist.

BRAYMER, L. E.
Illustrator. Born Chicago, Ill. June 2, 1901. Member: Palette and Chisel C.; Phila. AC. Address in 1929, 804 Pine St.; h. 1826 Spruce St., Philadelphia, PA.

BRCIN, JOHN DAVID.
Sculptor. Born Serbia, Aug. 15 1899. Pupil of Chicago AI under Albin Polasek. Member: AFA, Chicago Gal. A. Awards: Bryan Lathrop European Travelling Scholarship (AIC); Certificate o Merit, (AIC); Shaffer Prize (AIC) French Memorial gold medal (AIC) Spaulding prize, Hossier Salon Work: Portrait bust of Judge Gary Commercial Club, Gary, Ind. memorial relief of Newton Mann First Unitarian Church, Omaha, Neb

Memorial Relief of Benjamin Franklin Lounsbury, Washington Blvd. Hospital, Chicago, Ill. Address in 1929, 4 East Ohio St., Chicago, Ill.

BRECK, GEORGE WILLIAM.
Artist. Born Washington, DC, 1863, and died Nov. 22, 1920 in Flushing, NY. Studied Art Students' League, NY; first winner Lazarus Scholarship for study of mural painting (offered through Metropolitan Museum) and thereby became student of American Academy Fine Arts, Rome, Italy. Director Academy of Fine Arts, Rome. Located in New York, 1910. Mural decorations, University of VA; Watertown, NY. Member: Century Club; Architectural League of New York; National Society of Mural Painters; Municipal Art Society.

BRECK, JOSEPH.
Painter and illustrator. Awarded gold medal for painting, Minnesota State Art Society, 1916. Address in 1926, Metropolitan Museum of Art, New York.

BRECKENRIDGE, HUGH H(ENRY).
Painter. Born Leesburg, 1870. Pupil of Penna. Academy of Fine Arts and of Bouguereau, Ferrier and Doucet in Paris. Member: New York Water Color Club; Philadelphia Water Color Club; Art Club of Philadelphia. Instructor in Penna. Academy of Fine Arts since 1894. Member of Municipal Art Jury of Philadelphia. Awards: Hon. mention Paris Exp., 1900; gold medal Fellowship PAFA, 1920, etc. Work: Portraits in University of PA and in Art Club, Philadelphia. "Still Life," San Francisco Art Museum; Court House, Reading, PA; State Normal School, West Chester, PA, etc. Elected Associate Member of National Academy of Design. Address in 1926, Fort Washington, Penna.

BREDIN, C(HRISTINE) S.
Painter and illustrator. Pupil of Cincinnati Art Academy, and Colarossi in Paris. Address in 1926, 5450 Delancey St., Philadelphia.

BREDIN, R. SLOAN.
Painter. Born in Butler Co., PA, Sept. 9, 1881. Pupil of Chase, Du Mond, and Beckwith. Elected Associate of National Academy. Among his works, "Midsummer" and "By the River." Address in 1926, New Hope, PA. Died in 1933.

BREGLER, CHARLES.
Painter and sculptor. Born in Philadelphia. Studied at the Penna. Academy of Fine Arts. Pupil of Thomas Eakins. Address in 1926, 4935 North 11th St., Philadelphia.

BREGY, EDITH.
Painter. Born in Phila. Studied at PAFA, pupil of Beaux and Carlsen. Represented at Herron Art Inst., Indianapolis, Ind., by "Pink Roses." Exhibited at PAFA, Phila., 1924. Address in 1926, 1627 Sansom St., Philadelphia, PA.

BREHM, GEORGE.
Illustrator. Born in Indiana, 1878. Pupil of Twachtman, Bridgman, DuMond at ASL. Well known for depiction of children in everyday life. Assignments for "Reader's Magazine," published by Bobbs-Merrill Co.; illustrated for "The Saturday Evening Post," "Delineator." Died in 1966. Address in 1926, 15 West 67th St., New York.

BREHM, WORTH.
Illustrator. Born in Indianapolis in 1883. His career was lauched by Outing Magazine, which first bought his drawings. He is perhaps best known for his illustration of Adventures of Tom Sawyer and Huckleberry Finn, which were published by Harper's. He produced an abundance of artwork for Cosmopolitan, Good Housekeeping and The Saturday Evening Post. Died in 1928.

BREIDVIK, MONS.
Painter, illustrator, etcher, craftsman, writer, lecturer and teacher. Born Sogn, Norway, Jan. 15, 1881. Pupil of Erik Werenskiold, Hariet Backer. Member: S. Indp. A; Scandinavian Amer. A. Award: Norwegian National League prize, Chicago,

1926. Work: "Children Bathing," "The Artists Mother," and "The Princess," Brooklyn Museum, Brooklyn, NY. Address in 1929, 867 Union St., Brooklyn, NY.

BREIN, JOHN DAVID.
Sculptor. Born in Servia in 1899. Exhibited at Penna. Academy of Fine Arts, Philadelphia, 1924. Address in 1926, 4 East Ohio St., Chicago, Ill.

BREITMAYER, M. V.
Etcher. Exhibited etchings at the Annual Water Color Exhibition, 1922, Penna. Academy of Fine Arts, Philadelphia. Address in 1926, Pomona, New York.

BREMER, ANNE.
Painter and mural decorator. Born in San Francisco and died there Nov. 1923. Pupil of Art Students' League of New York, and member of the San Francisco Art Association. She is represented by mural panels in many of the cities in California.

BREMER, HESTER.
Sculptor. Born Alsace, July 8, 1887. Pupil of Hudler; Murdach; AIC. Member: Chicago SA. Award: Eisendrath prize, AIC, 1922. Address in 1929, 6016 Ellis Ave., Chicago, Ill.

BRENDEL, BETTINA.
Painter. Born in Luneburg, Germany; US citizen. Study: Hamburg, Germany. BA 1940; Kunstschule Schmilinsky, Hamburg, 1941-42; Landes Hochschule Bildende Kunste, Hamburg, 1945-47, with Erich Hartmann; Univ. So. Calif., 1955-58; New Sch. for Soc. Research, 1968-69. Work: Pasadena Art Museum; San Francisco Museum; Santa Barbara Museum of Art; Mr. & Mrs. Joseph Hazen, NYC; Mr. Michael Tapie, Paris, France, etc. Exhibitions: Int'l. Center, Turin, Italy; Los Angeles County Museum; Spectrum Gallery, NYC; Esther Robles Gallery, LA; San Francisco Museum; Santa Barbara Museum; others. Awards: Long Beach Museum of Art; San Francisco Museum of Art; La Jolla Art Center. Media: Acrylic. Author, The Painter and the New Physics; also research on

relation of theoretical physics to the arts. Living in New York City in 1970; address in 1982, Los Angeles, Calif.

BRENNAN, ALFRED LAURENS.
Painter and illustrator. Born 1853; died in New York, 1921. He worked in pen and ink, and water colors.

BRENNER, VICTOR DAVID.
Sculptor and medalist. Born in Shavely, Russia in 1871; came to New York 1890. Represented by medals in Metropolitan Museum, New York, and Luxembourg, Paris. Died on April 5, 1924 in NYC.

BRENNERMAN, GEORGE W.
Painter and illustrator. Born in New York in 1856. He studied with Chase and Duveneck in Munich Landscapes and animals, especially horses in action, were his favorite subjects. He died in New York on Feb. 4, 1906.

BRETT, HAROLD M.
Painter and illustrator. Born Middleboro, Mass., Dec. 13, 1880. Pupil of Walter Appleton Clark, H Siddons Mowbray, and Howard Pyle Member: Boston Art Club. Address in 1926, Fenway Studios, 30 Ipswich St., Boston, Mass.

BREUER, HENRY J.
Landscape painter. Born in Philadelphia in 1860. He has painted many California views Address in 1926, Lone Pine, Iny County, Calif.

BREUL, HAROLD G(UENTHER).
Illustrator. Born 1889. Pupil of Henry McCarter. Awarded Cresso Scholarship, P. A. F. A Illustrated for Collier's an McGraw-Hill publications. Address in 1926, 57 West 10th St., New York City, NY.

BREULL, HUGO.
Painter. Born in Saalfeld German on May 27, 1854. Pupil of Willia M. Chase in New York, and o Boulanger and Lefebvre in Paris His studio was in Providence, RI He died on Aug. 7, 1910 i Providence.

BREVOORT, JAMES RENWICK.
Landscape painter. Born in Westchester County, NY, in 1832. Studied with Thomas Cummings; also sketched in England, Holland and Italy. Elected an associate member of National Academy in 1861 and full member 1863. Among his pictures "English Moor" (1882), "New England Scene," and "Morning in Early Winter." He died on Dec. 15, 1918 in Yonkers, NY.

BREWER, ADRIAN L(OUIS).
Painter. Born St. Paul, Minn., Oct. 2, 1891. Pupil of N. R. Brewer. Member: Minneapolis Art club. Awards: Bronze medal St. Paul Institute, 1917; silver medal for oils, St. Paul Institute, 1918. Work: "In a Bluebonnet Year," Latus Club, NY; "Portrait of Senatro Joe T. Robinson, State Capitol, Little Rock, Ark.; "Ozark Valley in the Autumn," Municipal Art Gallery, Little Rock. Address in 1926, 448 River Blvd., St. Paul, Minn.

BREWER, ALICE HAM.
(Mrs. F. Layton). Miniature painter. Born Chicago, Ill., March 14, 1872. Pupil Art Students' League of New York; Art Institute of Chicago. Address in 1926, 241 Midland Ave., Montclair, NJ.

BREWER, B(ESSIE) M(ARSH).
Painter, illustrator, etcher and teacher. Born Toronto, June 1, 1883. Pupil of Henri, Pennell, Sloan, and Chase. Address in 1929, Quintard Bldg., 140 Atlantic Sq.; h. Long Ridge Rd.; summer, Box 1123, Stamford, Conn.

BREWER, MARY LOCKE.
Painter. Studied in Rome in 1911, under Signor Tanni, and later in Paris under Henri, Martin and Ernest Laurent. Among her best known pictures are "The Lagoon" in Jackson Park, Chicago, "The Sun Dial," "The Seine Boat," and "High and Dry."

BREWER, NICHOLAS RICHARD.
Painter. Born in Olmstead County, Minn., 1857. Pupil of D. W. Tryon and Charles Noel Flagg in New York. Member: Chicago Society of Artists, 1891. Represented in

Collection of portraits of governors of Rhode Island, Wisconsin, South Dakota and Minnesota; state portrait collections of Maine, Iowa, North Dakota; Salmagundi Club, New York; Art Institute of Chicago.

BREWSTER, ANNA RICHARDS.
(Mrs. William T. Brewster). Painter, illustrator and sculptor. Born Germantown, PA, April 3, 1870. Pupil of Dennis Bunker and H. Siddons Mowbray in America; Constant and Laurens in Paris. Member: National Academy of Women Painters and Sculptors. Award: Dodge prize National Academy of Design, 1889. Address, Hartsdale, NY.

BREWSTER, EDMUND.
Philadelphia portrait and landscape painter, working there about 1818.

BREWSTER, EUGENE V.
Painter. Born Bayshore, NY., 1870. Self-taught. Salmagundi Club. Address in 1926, 175 Duffield St., Brooklyn, New York. Home, Roslyn, NY.

BREWSTER, GEORGE T(HOMAS).
Sculptor. Born Kingston, Mass., Feb. 24, 1862. Pupil of Mass. State Normal Art School; Ecole des Beaux Arts, under Du Mond; and of Mercie in France. Member National Sculpture Society, 1898; Instructor RI School of Design, 1892-93. Instructor at Cooper Union since 1900. Work: Portraits of "Thomas R. Proctor," Utica, New York; "J. Carroll Beckwith," Library of New York University; "Robert E. Lee," for Hall of Fame, New York City; "J. S. Sherman," Utica, NY; "Indiana," crowning statue at Indianapolis; "Hope," crowning statue, State House, Providence, RI; Mural Portrait tablets of Judge Andrews and Judge Bischoff, Supreme Court, New York, NY. Address in 1926, Tottenville, Staten Island, NY.

BREWSTER, JOHN.
Portrait painter in oils and miniatures, born 1766, flourishing in Boston about 1802.

105

BRICHER, ALFRED THOMPSON.
Marine painter. Born in
Portsmouth, NH, on April 10, 1837.
He was elected an Associate Member
of the NAD in 1879, also of the
American Water Color Society. He
died in Staten Island, NY, in 1908.
He painted "Rocky Shore, Off
Shelter Island," and "Grand Manan,
Monhegan Island." Died Sept. 30,
1908, in Staten Island.

BRIDGE, EVELYN.
Miniature painter and etcher. Born
Chicago, Ill. Pupil of Ethel Coe,
Fursman and Senseney. Member:
Chicago AG; AIC Alumni. Address in
1929, 218 East Huron St.; 619 North
Michigan Blvd., Chicago, Ill.;
summer, Provincetown, Mass.

BRIDGES, CHARLES.
An Englishman, painted in Virginia
from 1730 to 1750. Most of the
portraits in the South attributed
to Sir Godfrey Kneller were by
Bridges. He painted as late as
1750. Many of his portraits are
extant and almost always, in case
of women, may be known by a lock of
hair resting on or in front of the
shoulder. Bridges was trained in
the British School, and shows by
his work the influence of Lely and
Kneller. Portrait of Mrs. John
Page, in the collection at William
and Mary College.

BRIDGES, FIDELIA.
Artist. Born in Salem, Mass. May
19, 1835. Moved to Brooklyn, 1854,
and to Philadelphis, 1859, where
she studied art under William T.
Richards. Has painted and exhibited
many noteworthy landscapes; earlier
work principally in oil; later work
mostly in water colors. Academy of
National Arts, 1869. Member of
American Water Color Society. Died
in New Canaan CT, March 1924.

BRIDGMAN, FREDERIC ARTHUR.
Artist. Born at Tuskegee, Ala.,
1847. apprentice in American Bank
Note Co., New York; meanwhile
studied in Brooklyn Art School and
National Academy of Design; pupil
under J. L. Gerome at the Ecole des
Beaux Arts, Paris; had studio in
Paris, occasionally visiting New
York. Painter of figure, and of
oriental and archaeological

pictures. Elected member of
National Academy in 1881.
Represented at Corcoran Art Gallery
of Washington, DC., by "Procession
of the Sacred Bull, Apis-Osiris."
The Art Institute of Chicago has
"Awaiting His Master," "Cafe in
Cairo," "A Street in Algiers," and
"The Neighbors." Address in 1926,
5 Impasse de Guelma, Paris, France.
Died January 13, 1928, in Rouen,
France.

BRIDGMAN, GEORGE B.
Painter, teacher, writer and
lecturer. Born Bing, County of
Monk, Canada, Nov. 5, 1864. Pupil
of Gerome, Boulanger. Author:
Bridgman's Constructive Anatomy;
Bridgman's Life Drawing; Bridgman's
Book of Hundred Hands. Instructor
at Art Students League of New York.
Address in 1926, 8 Park Place,
Pelham, NY. Died Dec. 16, 1943, in
NYC.

BRIDPORT, GEORGE.
Painter. Brother of Hugh Bridport.
He was associated with his brother
as instructor in an Art School in
Philadelphia in 1818. He also did
the ceiling decorations in the old
Hall of the House of
Representatives in Washington
burned by the British in 1814. He
died in Havana, Cuba, in 1819.

BRIDPORT, HUGH.
Painter and miniaturist. Born in
London, 1794, and died
Philadelphia, c. 1868. He was
induced by Thomas Sully to come to
this country in 1816. He opened a
drawing-academy in 1817, in
Philadelphia. He was one of the
instructors of the deaf-mute
lithographer, Albert Newsam
Bridport gained a great reputation
in Philadelphia as a portrait
painter. The Penna. Academy o
Fine Arts has a collection of seve
miniatures by Bridport; he als
painted a number of oil portraits.

BRIDWELL, HARRY L.
Painter. Born in Leesburg, Ohio
in 1861. Member Cincinnati Ar
Club. Address in 1926, 28
McCormick Place, Cincinnati, Ohio.

106

BRIGGS, AUSTIN.
Illustrator. Born in Humboldt, Minnesota, in 1909. He studied at the Wicker Art School and briefly at Detroit City College. At age 16, he went to work in a studio doing Rickenbaker Auto advertisements, as well as local editorial work for the Dearborn Independent. Two years later he came to NY and soon after appeared in Collier's. During the Depression he was able to do some movie posters for Fox Studios and attend the ASL. From the 1940's on, his work drew acclaim in The Saturday Evening Post, Redbook, and Cosmopolitan. A Gold Medal winner in the S of I exhibitions, he is a member of their Hall of Fame. A constant innovator, he was always ahead of his imitators. Having lived most of his life in Connecticut, he moved to Paris, where he died in 1973.

BRIGGS, CLARE A.
Cartoonist. Member: SI. Address in 1929, care NY Tribune, NY; Wykagyl Park New Rochelle, NY.

BRIGHAM, CLARA RUST.
(Mrs. W. E. Brigham). Painter and craftsman. Born Cleveland, Ohio, July 25, 1879. Pupil of Blanche Dillaye, William Brigham. Member: Prov. AC; Needle and Bobbin Club; Handicraft Club, Providence; AFA. Director: Industrial Dept., Federal Hill House. Address in 1929, 460 Rochambeau Ave., Providence, RI.

BRIGHAM, W. COLE.
Painter, craftsman and teacher. Born Baltimore, MD, Jan. 11, 1870. Pupil of ASL of NY. Member: ASL of NY Specialty, marine mosaics. Address in 1929, Oak Lodge, Shelter Island Heights, Suffolk Co., NY.

BRIGHAM, WILLIAM EDGAR.
Painter and illustrator. Born North Attleboro, Mass., in 1885. Pupil Henry Hunt Clark and Denman Ross. Address in 1926, 460 Rochambeau Ave., Providence, RI.

BRINDESI, OLYMPIO.
Sculptor. Born in Italy, 1897. Pupil of Chester Beach. Exhibited at Penna. Academy of Fine Arts,
Philadelphia, 1924. Address in 1926, 207 East 17th St., New York City, NY.

BRINGHURST, ROBERT PORTER.
Sculptor. Born at Jerseyville, Ill., 1855. Studied at St. Louis School of Fine Arts and at Ecole des Beaux Arts, Paris; died March 22, 1925 in University City, MO. Principal works: "Awakening Spring," Art Institute, Chicago; "Kiss of Immortality," destroyed at Portland Fair; statue of General Grant, City Hall Park, St. Louis; Minnesota's monument at Gettysburg; Pennsylvania's monument at Shiloh.

BRINKERHOFF, ROBERT MOORE.
Illustrator. Born in Toledo, Ohio, May 4, 1879. Pupil of Art Students' League, New York. Colarossi Academy in Paris. Member: SI 1912. Illustrations in Saturday Evening Post, Red Book, etc. Author of short story series, "Dear Mom"; "Little Mary Mixup in Fairyland" (Duffield), 1926. Cartoons in New York Evening World, Evening Mail, etc. Studied in Florence and Paris. Address in 1926, 50 West 67th St., New York.

BRINLEY, DANIEL P.
Landscape painter. Born in Newport, RI, March 8, 1879. Pupil of ASL of NY; studied in Florence and Paris. Member: NAC (life); MacD. C.; N.Y. Arch Lg; Mural P.; Silvermine GA.; PS Gallery Asso. Work: Decoration for Y. M. C. A. Convention Bldg., 1919; decorations for the Hudson Motor Car Bldg., New York, NY; Borglum Memorial, New Canaan, Conn; Maillard's Restaurant, Chicago; decoration war maps, Liberty Memorial, Kansas City; stained glass windows, Fordham Lutheran Church, New York. Died July 30, 1963.

BRINTON, CAROLINE P.
Born in Pennsylvania. Student at the Penna. Academy of Fine Arts. Address in 1926, Androssan Park, West Chester, Penna.

BRISTOL, JOHN BUNYAN.
Painter. Born in Hillsdale, NY, 1826. Pupil of Henry Ary, in Hudson, NY. He became an Associate of the National Academy in 1861,

and an Academician in 1875. His landscapes received medals in the Exhibitions at Philadelphia in 1876 and Paris in 1889. He died Aug. 31, 1909 in NYC.

BRITT, RALPH M.
Painter. Born in Winchester, Ind., July 19, 1895. Pupil of William Forsyth. Works: "Melting Snow," "Wood Cutters," and "November Weather." Address in 1926, 456 West South St., Winchester, Ind.

BRITTON, EDGAR.
Born, April 15, 1901, Kearney, Nebraska. 1921; First worked with small group in Cedar Rapids, Iowa, drawing and painting landscapes. Moved to Chicago; spent several years studying and working with Edgar Miller, using many mediums. Executed series of nine panels in tempera for Deerfield-Shields High School, Highland Park, Illinois, under Public Works of Art Project, and six frescoes for Bloom Township High School, Chicago Heights, IL. Exhibited at Chicago Art Institute, Whitney Museum of American Art and Brooklyn Museum, New York.

BRITTON, JAMES.
Painter, illustrator and engraver. Born in Hartford, Conn., in 1878. Pupil of C. N. Flagg, and Geo. de F. Brush. Represented at Morgan Museum at Hartford, Conn., by portrait of William G. Bunce. Address in 1926, Holbein Studios, 107 West 13th St., New York City, NY.

BROBECK, CHARLES I.
Born in Columbus, Ohio, in 1888. Pupil of Columbus Art School and Detroit School of Fine Arts. Address in 1926, 893 Locburn Ave., Columbus, Ohio.

BROCK, EMMA L.
Illustrator. Born in Fort Shaw, Mont., in 1886. Pupil of George Bridgman. Address in 1926, Fort Snelling, Minn.

BROCKMAN, ANN.
Born, Alameda, California; 1898. Studied at Art Students' League, New York, with John Sloan and Gifford Beal. Has exhibited extensively.

BRODEAU, ANNA MARIA.
Amateur miniature painter. Born 1775, Phila. Died 1865, Wash.

BRODERSON, MORRIS.
Painter. Born on Nov. 4, 1928, in Los Angeles, CA. Studied at Pasadena Art Mus. with de Erdetey Jepson Art Inst. and UCLA. Travelled Orient. In collections of Whitney; Stanford Univ.; S.F. Mus. of Art; Kalamazoo Inst. of Art; Yale; Mus. of Fine Arts, Boston; Hirshhorn Collection, Washington DC; and others. Exhibited at de Young Mem. Mus., San Fran. Staempli Gallery, NYC; Carnegie Inst. Int'l.; NAD Annual; Minn. Mus., St. Paul; and others. Awards from "Art in America" magazine; L.A. County Mus.; the Whitney and Phil. Art Directors Club. Reviewed in Time Magazine; Christian Science Monitor; the NY Times. Address in 1982, c/o Ankrum Gallery, Los Angeles, CA.

BRODERSON, ROBERT.
Painter. Born in West Haven, Connecticut, July 6, 1920. B.A. from Duke University, Durham, North Carolina, 1950; M.F.A. State College of Iowa, Iowa City, 1952. Recipient of a grant from the National Institute of Arts and Letters, New York, in 1962; a fellowship from the John Simon Guggenheim Memorial Foundation in 1964; a Summer Research Grant from Duke University. Taught at Duke University. Awards: Childe Hassam Fund Foundation; Gallery of Fine Arts, Winston-Salem, 1949; Des Moines Art Fund Foundation; Gallery of Fine Arts, Winston-Salem, 1949; Des Moines Art Center, 1951; North Carolina State Art Society, Raleigh, 1953; Eastern Illinois University, Charleston, 1954; Atlanta Art Association Galleries, 1958, 1960. Exhibitions: Mint Museum of Art, Charlotte; Allied Arts, Durham; North Carolina State Art Society, Raleigh; Catherine Viviano Gallery, New York; Atlanta Art Association Galleries; PAFA; Butler Institute of American Art, Youngstown; The Metropolitan Museum of Art, New York; The Corcoran Gallery of Art, Whitney Museum; The Museum of Modern Art, New York.

others. In collections of Wadsworth Atheneum; Whitney; Nat'l. Inst. of Arts and Letters; others. Living in Raleigh, NC.

RODHEAD, GEORGE H(AMILTON). Painter. Born in Boston, Mass., 1860. Member of Rochester Art Club. Address in 1926, 194 Harvard St., Rochester, NY.

RODIE, HOWARD. Illustrator. Born in Oakland, California, in 1916. He studied at the California School of Fine Arts. He earned fame doing reportage during World War II in which, as an enlisted man, he worked for Yank Magazine. His drawings of the Pacific battles were most striking, as were his later sketches in Korea and Vietnam. His work as a staff artist in San Francisco eventually led to a weekly feature in the Associated Press with assignments such as the Watergate hearings.

RODY, LILY. Painter. Born in Budapest, Hungary, in 1905. Studied: With Leopold Herman; Hungarian Art Academy; Colarossi Academy in Paris. Exhibitions: Museum of Modern Art, New York City, 1962-64; International Drawing Exhibition, Rijeka Museum, Yugoslavia, 1970; Whitney Museum of American Art, 1972; New York Cultural Center, 1973.

RODY, NANCY. Painter. Born Chicago, IL, Dec. 1, 1949. Study: MOMA children's classes, 1961-64; High School of Performing Arts, 1964-67; Carnegie Mellon U., 1967-69; Royal Acad. of Dramatic Art, London, 1970-72; ASL of NY, 1978-80. Shows: The Montauk Club, Brooklyn, solo, 1982; Muse Gallery, Clearwater, IL, group, 1981; Keane Mason Gallery, NYC, group, 1983. Comn.: Portraits of King Hassan Durani I of Afghanistan, King Amanullah, and Mohammed Ali; auctioned and proceeds donated to refugee relief, Afghanistan. Media: Oil, watercoor, pastel, charcoal, pen and ink. Address in 1983, 1653 President St., Brooklyn, NY.

BRODZKY, H(ORACE). Painter, illustrator and etcher. Born Melbourne, Austraila, 1885. Studied in Melbourne and London. Member: Allied Artists' Association, London. Address in 1926, 141 East 27th St., NYC.

BROEDEL, MAX. Illustrator. Born June 8, 1870, in Leipzig, Germany. Pupil of Leipzig Academy of Fine Arts. Associate professor of art as applied to medicine, Johns Hopkins University.

BROEMEL, CARL WILLIAM. Painter. Born Cleveland, OH, Sept. 5, 1891. Pupil of H. G. Keller, Cleveland, OH; Robert Engels in Munich. Member: Cleveland SA. Awards: first prize for water colors, Cleveland Museum of Art, 1924 and 1925; second prize, 1926. Work: "Air and Sunshine" and "St. George, Bermuda," Cleveland Museum of Art; "Royal Palms, Barbados," Brooklyn Museum. Address in 1929, 849 Hanna Bldg.; h. 3471 Warren Road, Cleveland, OH.

BROKAW, IRVING. Painter. Born NYC, March 29, 1871. Pupil of Bouguereau, Ferrier, Julien Academy. Member: S. Ind. A; Salons of America. Work: "The Skating Girl" Luxembourg Mus., Paris. Address in 1926, 522 Fifth Ave., New York, NY.

BROMWELL, ELIZABETH HENRIETTA. Painter. Born in Charleston, Ill. Studied in Denver and Europe. Member: Denver Art Association. Address in 1926, 646 Williams Parkway, Denver, Colo.

BROOK, ALEXANDER. Painter. Born New York, July 14, 1898. Member: Society of Independent Artists. Address in 1926, care of Mrs. C. R. Bacon, Ridgfield, Conn.

BROOKE, RICHARD NORRIS. Artist. Born at Warrenton, VA, 1874; died 1920. Studied Penna. Academy of Fine Arts, and under Bonnat and Constant, Paris, France. Vice-principal Corcoran School of Art; President Society Washington Artists. Member: American

Federation of Arts; Council Washington Society Fine Arts. Represented at Corcoran Art Gallery of Washington, DC., by "A Pastoral Visit" and "Incoming Tide."

BROOKINS, JACOB BODEN.
Sculptor and consultant. Born in Princeton, MO, August 28, 1935. Studied at Boise Jr. College; Univ. of Ore., BS (ceramics) MFA (metalsmithing and sculpture). Exhib.: Mus. Northern Ariz., 1977-79. Teaching: Instr. jewelry, Univ. Ore, 1967-68; instu. sculptures, Northern Ariz. Univ., 1969-75; instr. ceramics, Yavasai Col, 1979-80. Address in 1980, Cosnino Found Res Ctr. RR, 1 Box 430 Flagstaff, AZ.

BROOKS, A(LDEN) F(INNEY).
Painter and sculptor. Born West Williamsfield, Ohio, April 3, 1840. Pupil of Edwin White in Chicago; Carolus-Duran in Paris. Member: Chicago SA. Awards: Yerkes prize, Chicago SA, 1892; Ill. State Fair prize, 1895. Work: "Boys Fishing," Union Club, Chicago; "Gen. George H. Thomas" and "Judge Kirk Hawes," Public Library, Chicago; "Gov. Jon. R. Tanner," Capitol, Springfield, Ill.; "Isaac Elwood" and "James Glidden," State Normal School, De Kalb, Ill.; "Vice-Pres. Sandison," State Normal School, Terre haute, Ind.; Vanderpoel Art Asso. Collection, Chicago. Adderss in 1929, 4357 St. Lawrence Ave., Chicago, Ill.; summer, Hilaire Cottage, R.F.D. No. 2, Fennville, Mich.

BROOKS, ADELE R(ICHARDS).
Painter, craftsman, writer and teacher. Born Buffalo, KS, Sept. 22, 1873. Pupil of Simon; Mme. La Forge; Richard Miller; Henry Snell; Hough Breckenridge; NY School of Fine and Applied Art; Pratt Inst.; Art Inst. of Chic. Member: Western AA; St. Louis A. Lg; S. Indp. A.; AFA. Work: "Cahokia Mounds," and "Red Mound," owned by the Univ. of Ill.; "Monks Mound," Phillips Academy, Andover, Mass. Specialty, Miniatures on ivory, landscapes and craftwork. Address in 1929, 4411 McPherson Ave., St. Louis, MO.

BROOKS, AMY.
Painter, illustrator. Born Boston Mass. Pupil of Boston Mus. School Illustrated own books, such as "The Dorothy Dainty Books," "The Rand Books," and "At the Sign of the Three Birches." Address in 1926, Colliston Road, Brookline, Mass.

BROOKS, ARTHUR D.
Painter. Born Cleveland, May 23 1877. Pupil of Henry Keller Member: Cleveland SA. Award Second prize in decoration Cleveland Museum of Art, 1926 Address in 1929, 11936 Carlton Road, Cleveland, Ohio; summer Chatham, Mass.

BROOKS, CAROLINE SHAWK.
Sculptor and modeller. Born in Cincinnati, 1840. First known by her modelling in butter exhibited in Paris World's Fair, 1878. She subsequently opened her studio in New York and executed portrait marbles of Garfield, Geo. Eliot Thomas Carlyle, and a portrait group of five figures representing "Mrs. Alicia Vanderbilt and Family."

BROOKS, CORA S(MALLEY).
Painter. Pupil of Phila. Sch. of Design for women, Daingerfield, Snell. Member: NAC.; N. A. Women PS; Plastic C.; Phila. Sch. of design Alumni; Phila. Alliance; Ter Philadelphia P.; AFA. Awards: Hon. mention, Plastic C., 1920; 1st hon. mention, N. A. Women PS., 1922. Represented in Pennsylvania State College, permanent collection of Phila. School of Design Alumnae Assn., and permanent collection of the Twentieth Century Club, Lansdowne, PA. Address in 1926, North Lansdowne Ave., Lansdowne, PA.; summer, Boothbay Harbor, ME.

BROOKS, ERICA M(AY).
Painter, sculptor, illustrator, craftsman, writer, lecturer and teacher. Born London, England, July 9, 1894. Pupil of Myra K. Hughes, Norman Charles Woodbury. Member: NA Women PS; PBC; Nat'l. Lg. of Am. Pen Women. Award: Hon. mention, Nat'l. Lg. of Am. Pen Women, New York, 1928. Address in 1929, 38 Union Sq., East 16th St., New York, NY.

ROOKS, HENRY H(OWARD).
Painter. Born Bedford, Mass., Feb 8, 1898. Pupil of W. M. Paxton. Member: Boston GA; AFA. Address in 1929, Concord, Mass.

ROOKS, ISABEL.
Painter. Born "Cloverdale," Baltimore. Pupil of Hugh Newell, Rhoda Holmes Nicholas and A.P.C. de Haas. Exhibited in Annual Water Color Exhibition at Penna. Academy of the Fine Arts, Philadelphia, 1925. Specialty, water colors. Address in 1926, 1506 Park Ave., Baltimore, MD.

ROOKS, JAMES.
Painter. Born on Oct. 18, 1906, in St. Louis, MO. Studied at So. Methodist Univ.; Dallas Art Inst., with Martha Simkins; ASL, with Kimon Nicolaides, Boardman Robinson; private study with Wallace Harrison. Taught at Columbia, Pratt, Yale, American Acad. in Rome, Cooper Union. In collections of Yale; MOMA; Fordham; Wadsworth Atheneum; Met. Mus. of Art; Guggenheim; Tate Gallery, London; and others. Exhibited at Peridot Gallery, NYC, 1950-53; Kootz Gallery, NYC; Whitney; Sidney Janis Gallery, NYC; Carnegie; Guggenheim; Brandeis; The Tate; MOMA; many more. Awards from Carnegie Inst.; Art Inst. of Chicago; Ford Foundation; Guggenheim Found.; Fellowship, 1967; others. Living in East Hampton, NY, in 1976.

ROOKS, LOU.
Illustrator. Born in Abington, PA, in 1944. He has won awards from Art Directors' Clubs of New York and Philadelphia and the Amer. Inst. of Graphic Arts. He illustrated for Oui, Viva, National Lampoon and Scholastic's Bananas, for whom he illustrated the poster The World's Gone Bananas in 1977.

BROOKS, RICHARD EDWIN.
Sculptor. Born in Braintree, Mass., 1865. Art instruction received in the studios of T. H. Bartlett, Boston, Mass., and Jean Paul Aube and Antonin Injalbert, Paris. Among his works are: Busts of Gov. William E. Russell (bronze) and Col. Gardener Tufts (marble),

Boston Statehouse; O. W. Holmes, 1897; and Gen. F. A. Walker, Boston Public Library. Awards: Honorable mention, Paris Salon, 1895. Is also represented by statues of Charles Carroll and John Hanson in Statuary Hall, Capitol Bldg., Washington, DC. He died May 2, 1919 in Boston, MA.

BROOKS, RICHARD.
Born, Haverhill, MA; 1894. Spent early life in Montana. Attended Virginia Military Institute. Studied at Boston museum School, five years; Art Students' League, New York; and various night classes in drawing. Served twenty months in France during World War. Worked for commercial paitners, assisted mural painters, and did some easel painting. 1929-33; Worked and studied abroad. Exhibited in National Academy and Architectural League Shows, New York. Work includes decoration of public buildings in New York, Montreal and the Middle West; collaborated with Eric Gugler, Architect, on maps and ceiling decorations, State Board of Education Building, Harrisburg, Pennsylvania.

BROOKS, SAMUEL.
Medallist, miniature, and profile painter, flourishing in Boston in 1790.

BROOME, ISAAC.
Sculptor. Born May 16, 1835 in Valcartier, Quebec. In 1938, arrived in Phila. Studying at PAFA. Worked with Hugh Cannon. Member of PA. Exhibited at PA, Wash. Art Assoc, and won award at Phila. Cetn. Expo of 1876. Specialty: Ceramics. In collection of PA. Died May 1922 in Trenton, NJ.

BROSS, ALBERT L. JR.
Painter. Born in Newark, NJ, June 29, 1921. Studied: ASL with DuMond, Bridgeman, and McNulty. Work: Wpringville Art Museum, Utah; New Jersey State Museum; Roebling Collection; others. Exhibitions: Nat'l. Arts Club Print Show, NYC, 1972; Acad. Artists Assn., Springfield, MA, 1972; others. Awards: Newark Museum; Hudson Vallery Art Assn; Montclair Museum; Springfield,

Mass., Art Museum; others. Mem.: ASL (life); Hudson Valley Art Assn.; Acad. Artists Assn.; others. Media: Oil. Address in 1982, New Vernon, NJ.

BROUN, AARON.
Illustrator. Born London, England, 1895. Pupil New York School of Design, Beaux Arts Society. Member: American Bookplate Society; Society of Poster Friends; Alliance. Address in 1926, Pocono Bldg., 229 4th Ave., New York City, NY.

BROWERE, ALBURTIS DELL ORIENT.
Painter. Born March 17, 1814 in Tarrytown, NY. Son of John Henri Isaac Browere, the artist who made life-masks of Jefferson, Gilbert Stuart, and other prominent Americans. Browere painted still life and landscapes, esp. mining scenes in Cal. Exb. at Am. Acad., AAU and NA. Died Feb. 17, 1887 in Catskill, NY.

BROWERE, JOHN HENRI ISAAC.
Sculptor and painter. Born in New York City, 1792; died 1834 in NYC. Pupil of Archibald Robertson. He also studied in Italy. On his return to America he modelled several busts, and perfected a method of making casts from the living model. Died 1834 in NYC.

BROWN, ABBY MASON.
Miniature painter. Flourished 1800-1822. She painted a miniature portrait of C. F. Herreshoff, Newport, RI.

BROWN, ABIGAIL K(EYES).
(Mrs. Roy H. Brown). Painter. Born Rockford, Mar. 29, 1891. Pupil of Marques E. Reitzel, Carl Krafft, William Owen. Member: Rockford AA; Oak Park, Austin and River Forest AL. Awards: Hon. mention, 1926, first prize for landscape, 1927, prize for most original composition, 1928, Rockford AA. Work: "Open Water," Illinois Academy of Fine Arts, Chicago, Ill. Address in 1929, 620 John St., Rockford, Ill.

BROWN, AGNES.
Born at Newburyport, Mass. Wife of J. Appleton Brown. Specialty oil landscapes, flowers; and cats. Exhibited at the Boston Art Club.

BROWN, ALICE VAN VECHTEN.
Painter. Born Hanover, NH, 1862. Pupil of Art Students' League of NY. Professor of Art, Wellesley College, since 1897. Author with William Rankin of "Short History of Italian Painting."

BROWN, ARTHUR WILLIAM.
Illustrator. Born Hamilton, Canada, Jan. 26, 1881. Pupil of Siddons Mowbray, Kenyon Cox, Walter Appleton Clark, F. V. DuMond, at ASL. Member: SI; GFLA. Illustrated "Seventeen," "The Magnificent Ambersons" and "Alice Adams," all by Booth Tarkington. Also illustrated for F. Scott Fitzgerald, O'Henry. Illustrator for Saturday Evening Post and other major magazines. Was on staff of the "Saturday Evening Post." Spent most of his life in New York City where he died in 1966. Address in 1926, 116 West 87th St.; h. 29 West Eng Ave., New York, NY.

BROWN, BENJAMIN C.
Landscape painter and etcher. Born in Marion, Ark. Pupil of Paul Harney and John Fry, in St. Louis; Laurens and Benjamin Constant in Paris. Awards: Bronze medal for etching, Panama Pacific Exp., San Francisco, 1915. Represented in Oakland Art Gallery; Public Library, Pasadena, Calif.; British Museum; Smithsonian Institute, Washington, DC. Illustrations in Saturday Evening Post and other magazines. Was on staff of Sat. Eve. Post. Address in 1926, 120 N. El Molino Ave., Pasadena, Calif.

BROWN, BENJAMIN.
Engraver. The earliest known plate signed by B. Brown is an excellent stipple portrait of Sir Philip Francis, the frontispiece to "The Identity of Junius," by John Taylor, published in New York in 1812. Line illustrations to botanical work, also published in New York, signed "B. Brown Sc. New York." The New York directory for 1819 contains the name of "Benjamin Brown, engraver and printer of bookplates, maps, visiting-cards

112

etc., in the first style of elegance." The name only appears for this one year. Died in 1942.

ROWN, BOLTON (COLT).
Painter and etcher. Born Dresden, NY, 1865. Died 1936. Instructor, Cornell University; Head of Art Dept., Leland Stanford University. Work:; "The Bather," National Arts Club, New York; "Monterey Fishing Village Indianapolis Art Association; "Sifting Shadows" and "Farmhouse in Winger," Brooklyn Institute Museum; 1913 Armory Show; lithographs in Brooklyn Museum and New York Public Library. Address in 1926, National Arts Club, 15 Gramercy Park, New York, NY.

ROWN, BRUCE ROBERT.
Painter and sculptor. Born in Philadelphia, PA, July 25, 1938. Studied: Tyler school of Art, Temple Univ., BFA 1962, MFA 1964. Work: Museum of Fine Arts, Savannah, Georgia; Erie Summer Festival; Am. Academy of Arts. Exhibitions: PAFA National; American Academy of Arts and Letters, NY; Butler Institute, Youngstown, Ohio; Am. Acad. Arts and Letters, New York City; Int'l. Exhib., Beaumont, TX; plus more. Awards: Carnegie Inst.; Ford Foundation; Hallmark Co. purchase award; am. Acad. Arts and Letters. Teaching: Monroe Comm. Coll. of the State Univ. of NY in Rochester. Mem.: Artists Equity Assn. NY; So. Sculptors Assn.; Rochester Print Club. Media: Oil. Address in 1982, 17 Sedgewick Dr., Honeoye, NY.

ROWN, CAROLOON ACKERMAN.
(Mrs. Egbert Guernsey Brown). Painter. Born New York City. Pupil of ASL. of NY and M. Seymour Bloodgood. Member: Brooklyn SA. Address in 1929, 445 Macon St., Brooklyn, NY.

ROWN, CHARLES V.
Portrait painter. Son of J. Henry Brown, born in Philadelphia in 1848. Pupil of Thos. Eakins, and Prof. Schussele, at the Pennsylvania Academy of Fine Arts.

BROWN, CHARLOTTE HARDING.
(Mrs. James A. Brown). Illustrator. Born Newark, NJ, Aug. 31, 1873. Pupil of Philadelphia School of Design for Women. Member of Fellowship PAFA; Phila. WCC; Plastic C. Awards: Silver medal, Woman's Exp., London, 1900; silver medal, St. Louis Exp., San Francisco, 1915. Also illustrated for The Century. Address in 1926, Smithtown, LI, NY.

BROWN, DOROTHY H.
Painter. Member of Providence Art Club. Address in 1926, Arlington Ave., Providence, RI.

BROWN, ETHEL P.
Painter and illustrator. Born in Wilmington, Del. Pupil of Twachtman and Howard Pyle. Student at the PAFA. Address in 1926, Frederica, Delaware.

BROWN, FRANCIS F.
Painter and teacher. Born in Glassboro, NJ., in 1891. Pupil of J. Ottis Adams and William Forsyth; John Herron Art Inst. Represented in Richmond Art Gallery and Herron Art Institute. Address in 1926, 126 W. 7th St., Richmond, VA.

BROWN, FRANK.
Painter. Born Beverly, Mass., April 21, 1876. Pupil of Julian Academy in Paris. Member: AWCS; Salma. C; Societe Internationale d'Aquarellistes, Paris. Work: "Ponte del Cavallo-Venise," French National Museums; "Gitanes a la foire de Seville," Wanamaker Collection, New York. Address in 1929, 47 Fifth Ave., NYC; 6 bis Villa Brune (XIV) Paris, France.

BROWN, G.
Two portraits were exhibited at the Penna. Academy in Oct. 28, 1847. They were miniatures by G. Brown and may be the work of the English artist by that name who exhibited at the Royal Academy from 1825 to 1839.

BROWN, GEORGE BACON.
Painter, born in Ogdensburg, NY, 1893. Pupil of Chicago Art Institute. Also painted mural

113

decorations. He died in 1923 in Mankato, MN.

BROWN, GEORGE LORING.
Born in Boston, Mass., 1814; died at Malden, Mass., 1889. Brown was originally apprenticed to Abel Bowen, wood-engraver, and woodcuts are found signed by him. Studied in Rome 1853-55 and became a landscape painter. His work upon copper is a series of admirably produced etchings of views of Rome, in 1860. He returned to America as a landscape painter. His "View at Amalfi" is in the Metropolitan Museum of New York. He was a pupil of Isabey in Paris.

BROWN, GLENN MADISON.
Painter and etcher. Born in Hartford, Conn., in 1854, died 1932. Member of Art Students' League of New York, and Julien Academy, Paris. Pupil of Laurens and Colarossi.

BROWN, GRACE EVELYN.
Painter and illustrator, also writer of poems, articles and essays. Born Beverly, Mass., in Nov. 24, 1873. Pupil of Joseph De Camp, Albert H. Munsel and Vesper L. George. Address in 1926, Trinity Bldg., 168 Dartmouth St., Boston, Mass.

BROWN, HAROLD HAVEN.
Artist. Born Malden, Mass., 1869. Studied Ecole des Beaux Arts, Paris, under Gerome, and Academy Julien, Paris, under Laurens. Became director of Art Museum, and teacher in School of Art, of The John Herron Art Institute, Indianapolis, in 1913.

BROWN, HARRISON B.
Marine painter and landscapist. Born in Maine in 1831. His best known paintings were of Casco Bay, Maine. He died in England on March 10, 1915., where he had been living for several years, in March, 1915.

BROWN, HARRISON PAUL.
Painter. Born in Waterloo, Ind., 1889. Member of Indiana Art Club. Address in 1926, 42 Macomb St., Mt. Clemens, Michigan.

BROWN, HENRY B.
Born in Portland Maine, in 1839 and died 1860. Landscape an marine painter. Best known pictur is "On the Coast of Maine. Exhibited in England and America.

BROWN, HENRY I.
Miniature painter. Flourished i Boston, 1844-1851.

BROWN, HENRY KIRKE.
Sculptor. Born in 1814 in Mass Beginning as a portrait painter, h early took up sculpture, and afte five years' study in Italy established himself in New York Work: "Washington" in Unio Square, NY; "Lincoln" in Unio Square, NY; "General Scott" an "Nathaniel Greene," Stanton Square Washington, DC. Elected Member o National Academy in 1851. Die July 10, 1886 in Newburgh, NY.

BROWN, HORACE.
Painter. Born at Rockford, Ill. on Oct. 23, 1876. Pupil of Joh Carlson and Johansen. Member o the Allied Artists of America Exhibited landscapes at PAFA Philadelphia, 1924, and at the Ar Institute of Chicago. Address i 1926, Springfield, VT.

BROWN, HOWARD V.
Painter and illustrator. Bor Lexington, KY, Jluy 5, 1878 Student of Art Students' League o New York. Address in 1926, 13 West 23d St., New York.

BROWN, HOWELL C(HAMBERS).
Etcher. Born Little Rock, Ark. July 28, 1880. Member of th California Society of Etchers Specialty, western scenes of th Indian country; "Edge of th Desert". Represented in the Museur of History Sc. and Art, Lo Angeles, CA. Address in 1926 Molino Ave., Pasadena, Calif.

BROWN, IRENE.
Painter and sculptor. Bor Hastings, Michigan. Pupil o William M. Chase. Member o National Association of Wome Painters and Sculptors. Address Llemellyn Park, West Orange, NJ.

114

ROWN, J.
This name, as engraver, is signed to a Biblical plate published in New York about 1810, but nothing else of his work has been found.

ROWN, JAMES FRANCIS.
Painter. Born at Niagara Falls, NY. Pupil of NAD, New York, and of Collin and Bouguereau in Paris. Address in 1926, 51 West 10th St., New York City, NY.

ROWN, JOHN APPLETON.
Painter of apple orchards. Born in West Newbury, Mass. July 24, 1844, and died on Jan. 8, 1902 in NYC. He came to Boston in 1865, where he opened his first studio; in 1867 he went to Paris for study. Exhibited frequently in the Salon in Paris, and had exhibitions of his landscape and figure work in the US. Several of his landscapes are in the collection of the Museum of Fine Arts in Boston. Elected Associate Member of National Academy in 1896.

ROWN, JOHN GEORGE.
Genre painter. Born Durham, England, Nov. 11, 1831; died Feb. 8, 1913 in New York City. Studied first at Newcastle-on-Tyne, then at Edinburgh Academy, and in 1853 at the schools of the National Academy of Design, New York. Elected Associate National Academy 1862, and to the National Academy in 1863. Represented in Metropolitan Museum, NY, and Corcoran Art Gallery, Washington, DC.

ROWN, JOHN HENRY.
Painter. Born in Lancaster, 1818. In 1836 he studied of painting under Mr. Arthur Armstrong. In 1839 he went into business for himself in the same line as that followed by Mr. Armstrong, viz., portrait, historical, landscape, sign and fancy painting, to which he also added miniature painting on ivory. In the fall of 1845 he moved to Philadelphia, where he continued to follow the choice of his profession until his death, in 1891. He painted a miniature on ivory of Abraham Lincoln at Springfield, Ill., 1860, at the request of Judge John M. Read of Philadelphia. The miniature was in possession of Hon. Robert T. Lincoln.

BROWN, LAURENCE.
According to the Selectmen's Records of the Town of Boston, July 31st, 1701, "Laurence Brown, a Limner, was granted admittance to this Towne."

BROWN, LILIAN CUSHMAN.
(Mrs. Charles Lyman Brown). Painter, teacher and lithographer. Member of Art Students' League of New York. Address in 1926, 8 Ellsworth Terrace, Pittsburgh, PA.

BROWN, LYDIA M.
Painter and teacher. Born Watertown, NY. Pupil of ASL of NY. Member: New Orleans AA; New Orleans ACC; SSAL.

BROWN, MARGARETTA (GRATZ).
Painter. Born St. Louis. Pupil of E. Ambrose Webster. Member: St. Louis AG; Provincetown AA. Address in 1929, Provincetown, Mass.; h. 421 Lake Ave., St. Louis, MO.

BROWN, MATHER.
Portrait painter. Born in Massachusetts, 1761. Was the son of a noted clock-maker. Studied in London under Benjamin West. His portraits were in the manner of Gilbert Stuart and West. He was appointed portrait painter to the Duke of York, and painted George III and others of the Royal family. He is also said to have painted miniatures while in the US. His portraits are owned by the National Portrait Gallery, London, and in collections in America. Among his portraits are Mrs. James Madison, William V. Murray, John Howard, and his self-portrait once owned by Mrs. Frederick L. Gay. Died in 1831 in London.

BROWN, PAMELA V.
Miniature painter. Exhibited portrait miniatures at Exhibition of Miniatures, Penna. Academy of Fine Arts, Philadelphia, 1922-25. Address in 1926, 51 West 12th St., New York City, NY., or Woodstock, New York.

BROWN, ROY.
Landscape painter and illustrator. Born Decatur, Ill., 1879. Pupil of ASL of NY; Rafaelli and Menard in Paris. Member: Academy of National Artists, etc. Work: "The Dunes," Art Institute of Chicago; "Landscape," Northwestern Univ., Evanston, ill.; "Pines and Poplars," National Arts Club, New York. Elected Associate Member of National Academy. Died in 1956. Address in 1926, 45 Washington Square, NY. Died May 15, 1956.

BROWN, SONIA F.
(Mrs. Gordon Brown). Painter, sculptor and teacher. Born Moscow, Russia, Jan. 11, 1890. Studied in Europe. Member: NY Soc. Women A (Pres. 1927). Address in 1929, 6 McDougal Alley; h. 70 West 11th St., New York, NY; summer, Siasconset, Mass.

BROWN, THOMAS E.
Painter. Born Wilmington, NC, May 31, 1881. Pupil of Corcoran School of Art, Washington; Fred Wagner, PAFA, W. Lester Stevens, Edgar Nye. Member: Wash. SA; Wash. WCC; SSAL; AFA. Award: First prize landscape, Society Washington Artists medal, 1928. Address in 1929, 3358 - 18th St., NW, Washington, DC.

BROWN, URIEL or URIAH.
According to Dunlap, a portrait painter of that name was working in Salem, Mass., in 1805.

BROWN, WALTER FRANCIS.
Painter, illustrator. Born Providence, RI, Jan. 10, 1853. Pupil of Gerome and and Bonnat in Paris. Member: Providence Art Club. Work: "The Acropolis" and "The Parthenon," Hay Library, Providence. Illustrated "A Tramp Abroad," by Mark Twain, "Roger Williams," by Charles Miller. Address in 1926, Palazzo da Mula, San Vio 725, Venice, Italy.

BROWN, WALTER.
A little-known genre painter, best known for his miniatures; he was the son of John Henry Brown, the Lancaster artist.

BROWN, WILLIAM ALDEN.
Landscape painter. Born Providence, March 15, 1877. Pupil of E. M. Bannister; RI School of Design. Member: Providence Art Club; Providence Water Color Club. Work: "Beside Still Waters," Pen and Pencil Club, Providence, RI; "The Oaks," Alpha Delta Psi Fraternity, RI State College, Kingston, RI. Address in 1926, 120 Dora St., Providence, RI.

BROWN, WILLIAM MASON.
Landscape and still-life painter. Born in Troy, New York, 1828. Studied with local artist for several years then moved to Newark, NJ. "Fruit and Art Objects," signed "W. M. Browne," purchased 1889, Penna. Academy of Fine Arts. Died Sept. 6, 1898 in Brooklyn, NY.

BROWNBACK, LOUIS U.
Painter, landscapes and harbor scenes. Represented in Brooklyn Museum by "The Harbor." Address in 1926, 7 East 12th St., New York.

BROWNE, ALDIS B.
Born, August 2, 1907; Washington, DC 1928. Entered Yale School of Fine Arts, studying under Taylor, Savage and York; spent one year in tempera class. 1934; B.F.A. from Yale. Worked under Public Works of Art Project. Did two panels for Fairhaven Junior High School in collaboration with Vincent Mondo. Interested in water color, imaginative composition and decoration. His work further includes portraits which have been carried out in various mediums.

BROWNE, BELMORE.
Painter. Born Tomkinsville, SI, New York, 1880. Pupil of Chase and Carroll Beckwith; under Julien in Paris. Member: Society of American Animal Painters and Sculptors. Represented in National Gallery, Washington.

BROWNE, FRANCES E.
Painter. Member: Cincinnati Woman's Art Club. Address in 1926, 11 "The Westminster," Walnut Hills, Cincinnati, Ohio.

BROWNE, GEORGE ELMER.
Born Gloucester, Mass., May 6, 1871. Studied at School of Drawing and Painting, Museum of Fine Arts, and Cowles Art School, Boston; Julien Academy, Paris, under Lefebvre and Robert-Fleury. Member: Artists' Fund Society; American Art Association, Paris. Associate member of National Academy of Design, New York. Work: "The White Cloud," and "Edge of the Grove," Toledo Museum; "The Wain Team," National Gallery, Washington; "The Port Douarnenez, Brittany," Art Institute, Chicago; "Coast of Brittany," Montclair (NJ) Museum; "Autumn in Finistere," Omaha (Neb.) Public Library; "Evening in Brittany," Erie (PA) Art Club; "La Guidecca," Union League Club, Chicago; "The Church, Montreuil," Kansas Univ.; "After the Rain," Milwaukee Art Inst.; "Moonrise in Holland," Univ. Club, Milwaukee, "Les Contrabandiers," Harrison Gal., Los Angeles Museum of History, Science and Art; "Bait Sellers of Cape Cod," purchased by French Govt. from Salon of 1904; "Afternoon Sottomarina," Luxembourg, Paris; "The Golden Hour," purchased by Ranger Fund, NAD, 1929. 9 lithographs, New York Public Library, represented in Museum of Montpellier, France; Hotel de Ville, Cahors, France. Instructor of drawing and painting, West End School of Provincetown, Mass., and Met. Art School, NY. Decorated by French Government 1925, and made Officer of Public Instruction and Fine Arts. Address in 1926, 58 West 57th St., NY.

BROWNE, HAROLD PUTNAM.
Painter. Born Danvers, Mass., April 27, 1894. Son of George Elmer Browne. Pupil of Caro-Delvaille at Colarossi Academy; of Jean Paul Laurens and Paul Albert Laurens at Julien Academy in Paris; Heymann at Munich; George Elmer Browne and F. Luis Mora in New York. Professor, School of Fine Arts, University of Kansas. Address in 1926, School of Fine Arts, University of Kansas, Lawrence, Kans.

BROWNE, LEWIS.
Illustrator, writer and lecturer. Born London, Eng., June 24, 1897. Award: Prize, AI Graphic A, 1926. author and illustrator of "Stranger Than Fiction" (Macmillan), 1925; "The Story of the Jews" (Jonathan Cape, Ltd.), 1926; "This Believing World" (Macmillan), 1926. Address in 1929, 60 Fifth Ave., New York, NY; summer, Westport, Conn.

BROWNE, MARGARET F.
Painter. Born in Boston, MA, in 1884. Studied: Massachusetts Normal Art School; Boston Museum of Fine Arts School; also with Frank Benson and Joseph De Camp. Awards: North Shore Art Association, 1925; Brooklyn Museum, 1928; Ogunquit Art Center, 1941; Rockport Art Association, 1955; Connecticut Academy of Fine Arts. Collections: Massachusetts Institute of Technology; Boston University; Harvard University; Bureau of Standards, Washington, DC; Buckley School, New York; Powers School Boston; Driscoll School, Brookline, Massachusetts.

BROWNE, MATILDA.
(Mrs. Frederick Van Wyck). Painter and teacher. Born in Newark, NJ, 1869. Pupil of C. M. Dewey, H. S. Bisbing and Julien Dupre. Member: National Academy Women Painters and Sculptors. Awards: Hon mention, Columbian Expo., Chicago. Address in 1926, 142 East 18th St., NY.

BROWNELL, CHAS. DE WOLF.
Landscape and still life painter. Born in Providence, RI, 1822. Studied in Hartford, Conn. In 1860 moved to New York; studied abroad 1861 to 1867 and afterwards settled in Bristol, RI. Painted many pictures of the Connecticut Valley.

BROWNELL, MATILDA A.
Painter. Born May 8, 1869, New York. Pupil of Chase and MacMonnies. Represented in Yale Univ., Barnard College. Awards: Hon. Mention, Columbia Exp., Chicago, 1893. Address in 1926, 1110 Carnegie Studios; Home, 322 West 56th St., New York.

117

BROWNELL, ROWENA P.
Painter. Member Providence Art Club. Address in 1926, 368 Thayer St., Providence, RI.

BROWNING, AMZIE D(EE).
Painter, illustrator, craftsman, writer and teacher. Born Kent, Wash., Feb 29, 1892. Pupil of George T. Heuston. Member: Tacoma Fine AA. Address in 1929, 932 Commerce St.; h. 5044 South Union Ave., Tacoma, Wash.

BROWNING, COLLEEN.
Painter. Born in Country Cork, Ireland, in 1929; US citizen. Studied at Slade Scho. of Art, London, scholarship. In collections of Detroit Art Inst.; Butler Art Inst; Columbia (SC) Mus.; Wichita (KS) Art Mus.; others. Has exhibited at Little Gallery, London, 1949; contemp. annual, Whitney, 1951-63; Art Inst. of Chicago, 1954; annuals, NAD, NYC, 1957-78; solos, Kennedy Galleries, 1968, 72, 76, 79, 82; others. Has received awards in Figure Composition, Stanford Univ., 1956; 2nd prize, oils, Butler Inst., 1960, 74; Obrig prize, NAD, 1970. Taught at City College, NY, 1960-76; NAD, 1979-81. Member of Audubon Artists; Academician, NAD. Paints in oil. Represented by Kennedy Galleries, NYC. Living in NYC.

BROWNING, G. W(ESLEY).
Painter and illustrator. Born Salt Lake City, 1868. Member: Society Utah Artists. Awards: First prize for water color, Utah Art Institute. Illustrations on nature study. Address in 1926, 730 Third Ave., Salt Lake City, Utah.

BROWNLOW, C(HARLES).
Painter. Born in England, 1863. Pupil of J. W. Whymper. Address in 1926, 435 Hansberry St., Philadelphia, PA.

BROWNLOW, WILLIAM J(ACKSON).
Illustrator. Born Elmira, NY, Jan. 22, 1890. Pupil of Bridgman, Fogarty and Dufner. Member: Cleveland SA; Cleveland Print C. Address in 1929, 416-417 Cleveland Clinic Bldg., Euclid at 93rd St.; h. 3296 Grenway Road, Shaker Heights, Ohio.

BROWNSCOMBE, JENNIE (AUGUSTA).
Painter. Born Honesdale, PA, 1850 Pupil of L. E. Wilmarth, NAD; Henry Mosier in Paris. Work: "First Thanksgiving," Museum of Pilgrim Hall, Plymouth, Mass. "The Peace Ball," Newark Museum. Specialty, historical figure subjects. Address in 1926, 96 Fifth Ave. NYC.

BRUBAKER, JON O.
Painter and illustrator. Born in Dixon, Ill., Oct. 5, 1875. Pupil of Bridgman and Julien. Address in 1926, 32 West 47th St., New York City.

BRUCE, BLANCHE CANFIELD.
Painter and lecturer. Born Wells, Minn., Sept. 29, 1880. Pupil of Charles W. Hawthorne, Susan Ricker Knox, Hayley Lever and AIC. Member; AIC Alumni; Terre Haute PBC; Hossier Salon. Works: "Sand Dune Group," Natural History Museum, Chicago; "Trees in Sunlight," Indiana State Normal Terre Haute. Specialty, landscape Address in 1929, 2108 North 10th St., Terre Haute, Ind.

BRUCE, EDWARD.
Painter. Born Dover Plains, NY in 1879. Exhibited in the Cincinnat Museum Annual Exhibition of 1925 Work: "A Sawoie Farm," Luxembourg Gallery, Paris, France. Address in 1926, Care of Scott & Fowles, New York.

BRUCKNER, C. W.
Portrait painter. Portrait of Gen'l Robert E. Lee, signed and dated 1865.

BRUEN, R. C.
Engraver. He was apprenticed to Maverick and Durand. After his apprenticeship he drowned in the Hudson River. He engraved book-illustrations, published by Wm. Durell of New York about 1820.

BRUESTLE, BERTRAM G.
Painter, sculptor, writer, lecturer and teacher. Born New York City April 24, 1902. Pupil of NAD Address in 1929, 424 East 57th St. New York, NY; summer, Lyme, Conn.

RUESTLE, GEORGE M.
Landscape painter. Born in NY,
1872. Pupil of ASL of NY. Studied
in Paris. Represented by "Afternoon
Landscape," in Gibbes Mus.,
Charleston, SC, and "Brown
Hillside," Reading Mus., PA.
Address in 1926, 132 E. 23d St.,
NY.

RUFF, CHARLES OLIVER.
Bruff advertised in the
New York Mercury of 1770, and
possible earlier, as a goldsmith
and jeweler. In 1775 he added an
engraving department to his
business, then established at the
sign of "The Teapot, Tankard and
Ear-ring," between Maiden Lane and
Crown Street, near the Fly Market;
and he adds to his notice, "Where
he engraves all sorts of arms,
crests, cypher & fancies, in the
neatest manner and greatest
expedition, with heads of Lord
Chatham, Shakespeare, Milton,
Newton, etc., with Mason's arms and
all emblems of Liberty."

RULS, MICHELSON GODHART DE.
Probably chief engraver doing
business in NY in the period
1759-64; though Elish Gallaudet was
engraving in that city as early as
1759. Engraved book-plates, maps
and views. The earliest work was
well executed "Plan of Niagara with
the Adjacent Country, surrendered
to the English Army under the
Command of Sir Will'm Johnson,
Bart., on the 28th of July 1759."
The New York Mercury, for May 3,
1762, stated this plan and a
companion plate were to be
published by subscription by
"Michael de Bruls, Engraver and an
Inhabitant of this City." The
second plate was "A Plan of the
Landing, Encampment and Attack
against Fort Niagara, on Lake
Ontario. The plans were engraved
"on two large copperplates" and
"would form a print 2 ft. 11 in. by
1 ft. 1 in." Although presumed both
plates were published, the second
plate is unknown.

RUMBACK, LOUISE UPTON.
Painter. Born Rochester, NY.
Pupil of W. M. Chase. Member of
National Association of Women

Painters and Sculptors. Address in
1926, 118 East 19th St., New York.

BRUMIDI, CONSTANTINO.
Painter. Born in Rome, 1805. Died
in Washington, DC, in 1880. He
came to this country in 1852, and
was naturalized in Washington, DC.
The rapid progress of the Capitol
extension under the superintendency
of Capt. Meigs suggested to him the
idea that the solid construction of
this national building required a
superior style of decoration in
real fresco, like the Roman
palaces. Meigs accepted the service
of Brumidi. "The committee room on
Agriculture, in the south wing of
the Capitol, was painted in 1885 as
the first specimen of real fresco
introduced in America."

BRUNDAGE, WILLIAM TYSON.
Painter. Born in New York, 1849.
He was a pupil of Walter Shirlaw at
the Art Students' League, New York.
His specialty was marine subjects.
He died in February 6, 1923.

BRUNNER, FREDERICK SANDS.
Illustrator. Born in Boyertown,
PA, in July 27, 1886. Pupil of
Herman Deigendesch. Address in
1926, 6033 Webster St.,
Philadelphia, PA.

BRUNNER-STROESSER, RUTH.
Illustrator. Born in Pittsburgh,
PA, in 1944. She attended the Ivy
School of Professional Art and has
since had exhibitions and received
awards in the Pittsburgh area,
including the Pittsburgh ADC and
the humane Society. Her
illustrations have appeared in
Fortune, Newsweek, Time, Sports
Illustrated and local Pittsburgh
magazines, as well as in
exhibitions at the Carnegie Museum
and Three Rivers Art Festival.

BRUNTON, RICHARD.
Engraver and diesinker. He
advertised in 1781 in the
American Journal
and Daily Advertiser of Providence,
RI. A memoir of Richard Brunton,
by A. C. Bates, librarian of the
Connecticut Historical Society at
Hartford, states that he was
imprisoned for making counterfeit

money. Died Sept. 8, 1832 in Groton, CT.

BRUSH, GEORGE DE FOREST.
Painter. Born Shelbyville, Tennessee, 1855. Figure painter and painter of Indian subjects. Pupil of the National Academy of Design, and of Gerome in Paris. Awards: First Hallgarten Prize, National Academy of Design, 1888; Medal, Columbian Exposition, Chicago, 1893; Temple Gold Medal, Pennsylvania Academy of the Fine Arts, Philadelphia, 1897; Gold Medal, Paris Exposition, 1900. Elected Society of American Artists, 1880; Associate National Academy, 1888; National Academy, 1901. Work: "In the Garden," and Henry George," Met. Mus. of NY; "Mother and Child," Corcoran Gallery, Wash; "Portrait of a Lady," Carnegie Inst., Pitt., PA; "Mother and Child," Museum of Fine Art, Boston; "The Moose Chase," Nat. Gallery, Wash. "Young Violinist," Worcester Art Museum. Address in 1926, Studio, New York and Dublin, NH. Died 1941, Hanover, NH.

BRYANT, EVERETT LLOYD.
Painter. Born in Galion, Ohio, Nov. 13, 1864. Pupil of Couture in Paris, Herkomer in London, and Anshutz, Chase and Breckenridge in Philadelphia. Member of the Penna. Academy of Fine Arts. Specialty, flower painting and mural painting. Work: "Asters," Penn. Acad. of the F.A., Phil.; "A Study," St. Paul Inst. Address in 1926, Care of Alley and Trask, 52 East 53d St., New York City.

BRYANT, HENRY.
Painter and engraver. Born in East Hartford, Conn., 1812. Painted portraits and landscapes; in 1837 he was elected an Associate Member of the National Academy of Design. He died in 1881 in Hartford, CT.

BRYANT, MAUD DREIN.
Painter. Born in Wilmington, Del., in May 11, 1880. Studied at Penna. Academy of Fine Arts under Anshutz, Chase and Breckenridge; also at Colarossi Academy in Paris. Work: "Calendula and Aster," Penn. Acad. of FA; "Pomons and Doll,"

Fellowship PAFA; Phila. Address in 1926, Hendricks, Penna.

BRYANT, NANNA MATHEWS.
Sculptor. Exhibited at Academy of Fine Arts, Philadelphia, 1924. Address in 1926, 94 Beacon St., Boston, Mass.

BRYANT, WALLACE.
Portrait painter. Born in Boston, Mass. Pupil of Constant, Laureny, Robert-Fleury and Bouguereau in Paris. Address in 1926, Cosmos Club, Washington, DC.

BUBERL, CASPER.
Sculptor. Born 1834 in Bohemia. Died Aug. 22, 1899, in NYC.

BUCHANAN, ELLA.
Sculptor. Born in Canada. Member of the Chicago Society of Artists. Work: "Martha Baker Memorial," Chicago; "Pete" and "Dry Water Hole." Address in 1926, 1539 North Edgemont St., Los Angeles, Calif.

BUCK, CHARLES C.
Painter and sculptor. Born in New York City. Pupil of Emil Carlsen. Address in 1926, 495 East 188th St., New York City.

BUCK, CLAUDE.
Painter. Born New York City, July 3, 1890. Pupil of Emil Carlsen, DeForest Brush, Francis Jones. Member: Chicago PS. Awards: Prize $400, 1926, $300, 1927, $1,000, 1928, chicago Galleries Assn.; Shaffer prize, AIC, Chicago, 1929. Address in 1929, 563 Lawrence Ave., Chicago, Ill.

BUCK, EMMA G.
Painter and sculptor. Member of Chicago Art Club. Born in Chicago, Ill., in 1888. Work: Wisconsin Perry's Centennial Medal. Address in 1926, 1732 North Shore Ave., Chicago, Ill.

BUCK, WILLIAM H.
Painter of landscapes. Born in Norway in 1840, died in New Orleans, 1888. Studied under Clague and also in Boston; opened a studio as a professional painter in 1800 at 26 Carondelet St., New Orleans, where he remained until

120

his death. Many of his paintings are of the Louisiana Landscape.

BUCKLIN, WILLIAM SAVERY.
Painter. Born in Phalanx, NJ., 1851. Member of Art Students' League, New York. Mural paintings in Library, Westminster, Mass. Address in 1926, Riverside, Conn. Died May 3, 1928, in Phalanx, NJ.

BUDD, CHARLES JAY.
Painter and illustrator. Born S. Schodack, Rensselaer County, NY, 1859. Pupil of P. A. F. A. under Eakins; Art Students' League of New York. Member: Philadelphia Sketch Club. Specialty, children's books. Died April 25, 1926 in NYC.

BUDD, D(ENISON) M.
Illustrator. Born Burlington, IA, June 10, 1893. Pupil of AIC. Member: SI; NY Art Directors C. Specialty, drawings for advertising. Address in 1929, 247 Park Ave., New York, NY; h. 163 Radford St., Yonkers, NY.

BUDD, KATHERINE COTHEAL.
Painter and illustrator. Pupil of William M. Chase. Address in 1926, 527 Fifth Ave., New York, NY.

BUDDINGTON, JONATHAN.
Painting portraits in New York City about 1798 to 1812.

BUDELL, ADA.
Painter and illustrator. Born Westfield, NJ, June 19, 1873. Pupil of Art Students' League of New York. Member: National Association of Women Painters and Sculptors. Illustrated numerous books for children. Address in 1926, 76 Washington Place, New York, NY.

BUDELL, HORTENSE.
Landscape Painter. Born Lyons, France. Exhibited at National Association of Women Painters and Sculptors in 1924. Address in 1926, 627 Fourth Ave., Westfield, NJ.

BUDWORTH, WILLIAM S(YLVESTER).
Painter. Born Brooklyn, NY, Sept. 22, 1861. Self-taught. Awards: Silver medals, American Art Society, Philadephia, 1902 and

1903. Work in Rochester Museum, NY. Address in 1926, 615 South Eighth Ave., Mt. Vernon, NY.

BUEHLER, LYTTON (BRIGGS).
Painter. Born Gettysburg, 1888. Pupil of PAFA. Member: Fellowship PAFA. Award: European traveling scholarship, PAFA, 1908. Work: "Portrait Major Richardson" in Canandaigua, NY, Public Library. Address in 1926, 346 W. 58th St., New York, NY.

BUEHR, KARL ALBERT.
Painter. Born in Germany. Studied in England, France and Holland. Pupil of Art Institute, Chicago. Awards: Bronze medal, St. Louis Exp., 1904; Hon. mention, Paris Salon, 1910; silver medal, Chicago Society of Artists, 1914. Associate Member of National Academy of Design. Address in 1926, 1727 Chase Ave., Chicago, Ill.

BUEHR, MARY G. HESS.
(Mrs. Karl Albert Buehr). Miniature painter. Born in Chicago, Ill. Studied in Holland and in France. Pupil of Art Institute, Chicago. Address in 1926, 1727 Chase Ave., Chicago Ill.

BUELL, ABEL.
Engraver. Born in 1742 in CT. Engraver on silver plate and type metal. It is said he was imprisoned for having altered a Colonial note. He engraved a plan of Boston, published by Romans in 1775, and a diploma-plate for Yale College prior to 1775. Died March 10, 1822 in New Haven, CT.

BUERGERNISS, CARL.
Painter. Member: Fellowship Penna. Acad. of Fine Arts. Address in 1926, 2819 West Girard Ave., Philadelphia. PA.

BUFF, CONRAD.
Mural painter. Born Switzerland, Jan. 15, 1886. Studied in Munich. Member: Calif. AC; Chicago Gal. A. Awards: Mrs. Henry E. Huntington prize, Los Angeles Museum, 1925; award for best display of paintings, Sacramento State Fair, Calif., 1924; first Fine Arts Prize, San Diego Museum, 1926.

Work: "Romance," William Penn Hotel, Whittier, Calif., six murals, Church of Latter Day Saints. Los Angeles. Calif. Address in 1929, 1225 Linda Rosa St., Eagle Rock, Los Angeles, Calif.

BUFFORD, JAMES A.
Engraver. About 1850 he engraved upon copper, and published a few views of Boston. Later he is listed as a lithographer with an office at No. 313 Washington St., Boston, Mass. His work was chiefly on the covers of sheet music.

BUFFUM, KATHARINE G.
Illustrator. Born Providence, RI, Sept 2, 1884. Pupil of P. A. F. A. Work: Illustrated "The Secret Kingdom," "Mother Goose in Silhouette," "Silhouettes to Cut in School," "Songs of Schooldays," etc. Specialty, silhouettes. Died Jan. 1922 in Phila., PA.

BULL, CHARLES LIVINGSTON.
Illustrator and painter. Born New York State, 1874. Pupil of Harvey Ellis and M. Louise Stowell; studied at Phila. Art Sch. Member: New York Water Color Club; National Art Club. Worked as taxidermist, Nat'l. Mus., Wash., DC. Well known for animal illustrations such as Under the Roof of the Jungle, his collection of stones and drawings based on trip to Guiana. Worked for US Biological Survey banding birds and drawing preservation posters, chiefly of Am. eagle. Died in 1932. Address in 1926, Oradell, NJ.

BULL, MARTIN.
Engraver. Born 1744 and died 1825. Engraver of early American bookplates. He was probably born in Farmington, Conn. Bull engraved the book-plate for the Monthly Library of Farmington, Conn.

BULLARD, MARION R.
Painter. Born Middletown, NY. Exhibited "The Apple Tree" at Penna. Academy of Fine Arts, Philadelphia, 1920. Wrote and illustrated "The Sad Garden Toad"; "The Someraulting Rabbitt" (Dutton), 1927; "Travels of Sammiethe Turtle," and "The Cow Next Door," 1928 and 1929. Address in 1926, Woodstock, New York.

BULLARD, OTIS A.
Portrait, genre, historical, and panoramic painter. Born in Howard, NY, on February 25, 1816; died in New York City, October 13, 1853. He received instruction in portrait painting from the Hartford artist, Philip Hewins. In 1840 he was at Amherst (Mass.), painting portraits of the family of Emily Dickinson. Bullard exhibited at the National Academy (1842-53) and at the American Art Union (1847-48), but his chief work was a panorama of New York City, painted with the assistance of several other artists between 1846 and 1850.

BUMSTEAD, ETHEL QUINCY.
Painter. Born London, England, 1873. Pupil of Boston Museum School, of Abbot Graves and of A. Buhler. Member: Copley Society, 1893. Address in 1926, 12 Berkeley St., Cambridge, Mass.

BUNCE, WILLIAM GEDNEY.
Landscape painter. Born in Hartford, Conn. Sept 19, 1840, and died Nov. 5, 1916 in Hartford. Studied with William Hart. In 1867 he sailed to Europe, where lived in Paris. Member National Academy of Design. Among his works are "Watch Hill, RI," "Sautucket, New England," and "Venetian Night." He was noted for his landscpaes.

BUNDY, GILBERT.
Illustrator. Born in Centralia, Illinois, in 1911. He spent his childhood in Oklahoma and Kansas. As a teenager he worked in an engraving house in Kansas City. Before coming to New York in 1929, where his first cartoons appeared in Life and Judge. Editorial illustrations for Esquire in the 1930's led to advertising work for such clients as Munsingwear and Cluett Peabody. During World War II he reported on the Pacific theater for King Features Syndicate.

BUNDY, JOHN ELWOOD.
Landscape painter. Born Guilford County, NC, May 1, 1853. Awards: Holcomb prize, Herron Art

122

Institute, 1917. Member Richmond Art Association. Work: "Blue Spring" and "Old Farm in Winter," Public Gallery, Richmond, Ind.; "Wane of Winter" and "Beech Woods in Winter," Art Association of Indianapolis. Address in 1926, 527 West Main St., Richmond, Ind.

BUNKER, DENNIS M.
Painter. Born in New York City in 1861, he died in Boston in 1890. Pupil of National Academy of Design in New York, and Herbert and Gerome in Paris. The portrait of his wife is in the Metropolitan Museum, NY. "Jessica," painted in 1890, is owned by the Boston Museum of Fine Arts, and "The Mirror" by the Philadelphia Art Club. His specialty was portraying feminine charm in portrait and figure paintings.

BUNN, KENNETH.
Sculptor. Born in Denver, CO. Apprentice at Smithsonian Inst., Wash., DC, 1953, 54; worked in Denver with taxidermist Coleman Jonas; operated own business producing sculpture for commercial clients and wax museum, until late 1960's. Exhibited at dealer Sandra Wilson's gallery in Santa Fe, NM, and Denver, CO; Kennedy Galleries and Graham Gallery, NYC; National Academy; Forrest Fenn Galleries, Santa Fe; Stremmel Galleries, Reno, Nevada; Mongerson Gallery, Chicago; Bishop Galleries, Scottsdale, Arizona. Ellected Associate of NAD, 1973, and member, Nat'l. Sculpture Society, 1973; member of Natl. Acad. of Western Art and Society of Animal Artists. Received Barnett Prize and an Award of Merit in competition.

BUNN, WILLIAM L.
Born, May 29, 1910; Muscatine, Iowa. 1933; B.A. in Graphic and Plastic Arts, University of Iowa. 1934; Made summer tour with own Punch and Judy Puppet Theatre in rural Iowa and Missouri, performing in town squares, sketching meanwhile. Returned to University of Iowa; became Graduate Assistant in Dramatic Arts. Engaged for two years in art and technical activities of University Theatre; studied mural design under Grant

Wood. Held Carnegie Fellowship in Art; assisting in designing frescoes for University theatre.

BUNNER, RUDOLPH F.
Painter and illustrator. Member: New York Water Color Club. Address in 1926, Ridgefield, Conn.; or Great Kills, SI., New York.

BUNT.
A little-known landscape painter, has only left a record of his name as painting landscapes.

BUONGIORNO, DONATUS.
Mural painter. Born Solofra, Italy, 1865. Pupil of Roil Institute of Fine Arts, Naples. Work: "Apotheosis of the Evangelist," in Church of St. Leonard of the Franciscan Fathers, Boston, Mass.; "St. Charles Borromeo," in Church of Sacred Heart, Boston; "Fall of the Angels," in Church of St. Peter, Boston. Address in 1926, Maddaloni, Caserta, Italy.

BURBANK, ADDISON BUSWELL.
Illustrator and writer. Born Los Angeles, Calif., June 1, 1895. Studied Art Institute of Chicago, and Grande Chaumiere, Paris. Member: Cliff Dwellers, Chicago; GFLA; SI. Address in 1929, 120 East 39th St., New York, NY.

BURBANK, E(LBRIDGE) A(YER).
Painter. Born Harvard, Ill., 1858. Pupil of Academy of Design in chicago; Paul Nauen in Munich. From 1897 made portraits of over 125 types of North American Indians. Represented in Field Museum and Newberry Lib., Chicago, and Smithsonian Inst., Wash., DC.

BURCHFIELD, CHARLES E.
Painter. Born in Ashtabula Harbor, Ohio, in 1893. Won scholarship to study at Nat'l. Acad. of Design; also studied at Rhode Island Sch. of Design and Cleveland Art School. Had first important one-man show in NYC in 1920; major retrospective, Whitney Mus., 1956. Elected member of Nat'l. Inst. of Arts and Letters in 1943. Became known for his American scene paintings; depicted sites west of the Alleghenies, in

123

Ohio and Western NYS. Acknowledged interest in 1920's American realist writers such as Sherwood Anderson, Willa Cather, Sinclair Lewis; and Oriental art, particularly Hiroshige and Hokusai. Worked chiefly in watercolor. Died in 1967. Represented by Kennedy Galleries, NYC.

BURCHFIELD, CHARLES S.
Painter. Born in Ohio in April 9, 1893. Pupil of Cleveland School of Art. Address in 1926, 459 Franklin St., Buffalo, NY.

BURD, CLARA MILLER.
Painter and illustrator. Born in New York; studied there and in Paris. Member: GFLA. Illustrated in "In Memoiran," and numerous children's books; designed covers for magazines; painted portraits of children; designed and executed numerous memorial windows. Address in 1926, 18 West 34th St., New York City.

BURDICK, HORACE ROBBINS.
Portrait painter. Born in East Killingly, Conn., Oct. 7, 1844. Pupil of Boston Museum School. His portraits are in crayon and oil. Member of Boston Art Club. Address in 1926, 16 Park Ave., Malden, Mass.

BURGDORFF, FERDINAND.
Painter. Born in Cleveland, Ohio, Nov. 7, 1881. Student at Cleveland School of Art. Represented at Memorial Museum, San Francisco, by "Old Wharf," "Grand Canyon," Cleveland Museum of Art; and "Venus," at the Hotel del Monte, Del Monte, Calif.

BURGER, I., JR.
In the New York Magazine for May 1790, a plate of well-engraved music is signed "Burger Jun. Sc." This may have been a son or relative of the John Burger silversmith of New York, with whom Cornelius Tiebot served his apprenticeship about 1790. One of the plates is signed as "printed by I. Burger, Jun'r." This is probably the music engraver noted above.

BURGESS, ALICE L.
Painter. Born in St. Louis, MO, 1880. Pupil of W. M. Chase; A Shands, Anton Fabres, Kenneth H. Miller and W. L. Lathrop. Address in 1926, 1268 Quinnipiac Ave., New Haven, Conn.

BURGESS, GELETT.
Illustrator and writer. Born Boston, Mass., Jan. 30, 1866. Member: SI. Illustrator and author of "Lady Mechante," "The Burgess Nonsense Book," the "Goop" books, etc. Address in 1929, 203 Blvd. Raspail, Paris, France; h. 16 Gramercy Park, New York, NY.

BURGESS, HENRIETTA.
Painter, craftsman, writer, lecturer and teacher. Born Auburn, Calif., May 14, 1897. Pupil of Wong of Tsing Hua, Peiping, China. Member: Northwest PM; Seattle AI. Specialty, Oriental design, symbolism and textiles. Address in 1929, Grover Cleveland High School, Seattle, Wash.; h. Alderwood Manor, Wash.

BURGESS, IDA J.
Painter. Born in Chicago, Ill. Pupil of Chase and Shirlaw in New York, and Mason in Paris. Executed decorations and mural painting. Work: "Youth Engquiring of the Sphinx," "The Libation Purer," "THe Law," "Inspiration," mural decorations in the Orington Lunt, Lib., NW. Univ., Evanston, IL. Designed many stained glass windows and has written on the subject. Address in 1926, Washington Square, New York and Woodstock, NY.

BURGESS, RUTH PAYNE.
(Mrs. John W. Burgess). Artist. Born in Montpelier, VT. Studied at ASL of NY, and in Germany and Italy, Ex. Pres. of Art Students' League; Patron of Met. Mus. of Art, NY; member of Providence WCC. Painted portraits of Hon. A. B. Hepburn, Judge Pierson, Professor March, Dr. Daniel Bliss and his Royal Highness, Prince August William. Address in 1926, Rhode Island Ave., Newport, RI.

BURGIS, WILLIAM.
Engraver. His work was chiefly in line, though he did attempt

124

mezzotint engraving. He was a publisher of American maps and views as early as 1717. Burgis also published views of the College at Cambridge, Mass., and of the New Dutch Church in New York.

BURINE.
This name as "Burine sc." is signed to a large sheet of "shells," Engraved for Resse's Encyclopedia published by S. F. Bradford Philadelphia, 1805 to 1818.

BURKE, FRANCES.
Painter. Resided in Richmond, Virginia. She made several copies of the Washington portrait painted by William Joseph Williams in 1792. It was owned by the Masonic Lodge of Alexandria, VA, and shows Washington in Masonic Dress. The copy of this picture in the Philadelphia Masonic Hall was made by Miss Burke from the original painting.

BURKE, MAY CORNELLA.
Painter and illustrator. Born Brooklyn, NY, Aug. 30, 1903. Pupil of F. R. Bruger. Member: SI. Address in 1929, 430 Greenwich St.; h. 1086 Ocean Ave., Brooklyn, NY.

BURKE, ROBERT E.
Painter, lecturer and teacher. Born Winsted, Conn., Sept. 14, 1884. Pupil of Pratt Inst., Brooklyn, NY. Member: College AA; Brown County (Ind.) AA. Professor of Fine Arts, Indiana University. Address in 1929, 1220 Atwater Ave., Bloomington, Ind.; summer, Nashville, Ind.

BURKERT, NANCY EKHOLM.
Illustrator. Born in 1933 in Sterling, CO. Studied art at Univ. of Wis. Noted for Illust. of children's books. Work: Illust. Carlson's Jean-Claude's Island (1963), Andersen's The Nightingale (1965), and John Updike's A Child's Calendar (1965).

BURKHARD, HENRI.
Painter. Born New York City, Feb. 17, 1892. Pupil of ASL of NY; Julian Academy, Colarossi Academy and Grand Chaumiere in Paris. Address in 1929, 35 Jane St., New York, NY; h. 54 Hawthorne Terrace, Leonia, NJ.

BURKO, DIANE.
Painter, graphic artist and teacher. Born in New York City Sept. 24, 1945. Studied: Skidmore College; University of Pennsylvania. Awarded the Scott Paper Company Award in "Earth Space Art 73. Exhibitions: Wm. Penn. Memorial Museum, Harrisburg, Pennsylvania, 1971; Philadelphia Museum of Art-Fleischer Art Memorial, 1972; Bronx Museum of the Arts, "Year of the Women", 1975; Phil. Art Alliance, 1973; Pennsylvania Academy of FA, 1980; "Objects and...," Univ. Mass., Amherst, 1973. Media: Oil, acrylics, pencil drawing.

BURLEIGH, CHARLES C.
Painter. Born in Pennsylvania in 1848, he lived in Plainfield, Conn., as a young man and later painted portraits at Northampton, Mass.

BURLEIGH, SYDNEY R(ICHMOND).
Born in Little Compton, RI, 1853. Pupil of Laurens in Paris. Among his pictures, "Landscape," "Luxembourg Garden." Address in 1926, "Fleur-de-Lys," Providence, RI.

BURLIN, PAUL.
Artist. Born in New York City, 1886. Studied New York, and London, England. Landscape, mural and figure painter; spent much time in the Southwest; exhibited at Salon des Independents, Paris, and annual exhibitions in U. S. Associate member of Societe International des Arts et Lettres, Salon D'Automne, Paris. Address in 1926, 106 West 57th St., New York City.

BURLIN, RICHARD.
Miniature painter. Flourished 1845-1863, New York. He also painted small portraits in oils.

BURLING, GILBERT.
Painter in oil and water colors. Born in 1843, he died in 1875. He excelled in the portrayal of game birds. His last works exhibited in 1875, "Normandy Sketches," "Beach

125

below East Hampton, LI," "Canadian Lake," and the "Old Harness-Maker."

BURLINGAME, CHARLES A.
Painter and illustrator. Born at Bridgeport, Conn., 1860. Pupil of Edward Moran. Address in 1926, Nanuet, New York.

BURLINGAME, SHEILA.
Painter and sculptor. Born Kansas, April 15, 1894. Pupil of AIC; ASL of NY. Member: St. Louis AG; St. Louis AL; AFA. Awards: First prize, St. Louis AL, 1922; gold medal, Kansas City AI, 1922; hon. mention, St. Louis AL, 1926; first prize, St. Louis AG, 1927; second prize, St Louis AL, 1927; hon. mention, St. Louis AG, 1928. Work: Woodcuts for St. Louis Post Dispatch, 1923-24; twenty-three woodcuts for "From the Days Journey," by Harry Burke, 1924.

BURNAP, DANIEL.
Engraver. His chief work was on brass clockfaces. He was working in East Windsor, Conn., before 1800.

BURNHAM, ANITA WILLETS.
(Mrs. Alfred Newton Burnham). Painter, craftsman, writer, lecturer and teacher. Born Brooklyn, NY, Aug. 22, 1880. Pupil of Chase, Freer, Vanderpoel, Du Mond, Cecilia Beaux, John Johansen, Castellucho in Paris Lawton Parker, etching under Ralph Pearson, ASL of NY, PAFA. Member: The Cordon, Chicago; Chicago AC; Chicago SA; Ill. AFA; North Shore AA. Awards: First water color prize, 1903 and 1905, and Goodman prize, 1916, AIC. Work: School frieze, Chicago Public School; painting in Children's Hospital, Chicago; altar decoration, All Angels Church, Chicago. Address in 1929, 1407 Tower Road, Hubbard Woods, Ill.

BURNHAM, ROGER NOBLE.
Sculptor, lithorgrapher and teacher. Born in Boston, Mass., in 1876. Work: Four Colossal figures, City Hall Annex, Boston; panels on main doors, Forsyth Dental Infirmary for Children, Boston; "Uncle Remus" memorial tablet, Atlanta; medallion, "Johann Earnest Perabo," Boston Art Museum;

Carrington Mason Memorial, Memphia; figure of Centaur, head of Athena and Tritons on Germanic Art Museum, Harvard. Instructor in School of Architecture, Harvard University, 1912 to 1917. Address in 1926, 5 Garden Terrace, Cambridge, Mass.

BURNHAM, WILBUR HERBERT.
Painter, craftsman, writer and lecturer. Born Boston, MA, Feb. 4, 1887. Studied at MA Art School, and abroad. Member: Boston AC; Boston Arch. C.; Soc. of Arts and Crafts, Boston; AFA. Works: Chancel War Mem. window, Central M. E. Church, Lawrence, Mass.; channel window, Trinity M. E. Church, Springfield, MA; transept window, Church of Our Saviour, Middleboro, MA; War Mem. window, St. Paul's Episcopal Church, Peabody, MA; clerestory window, St. John's Cathedral, Denver, Colo.; aisle windows, Princeton U. Chapel; window, St. Mary's Church, Detroit; clerestory windows, First Presbyterian Church, Jamestown, NY. Address in 1929, Fenway Bldg., Boylston St., Boston, MA; h. 14 Overlook Rd., Melrose Highlands, MA.

BURNS, BONNIE PHELPS.
Painter, designer and teacher. Study: Berkshire Community College; North Adams State College. Work: The gallery, Williamstown; The Gallery, Stockbridge, MA; collections in US and abroad. Ehib.: Boston Globe Art Exhib.; Univ. of Chic. Art Exhib.; Berkshire Art Assn. Exhib.; Williams College; Fox Hollow Festival; Int'l. Artists in Watercolor Competition; many more. Commercial Design Work: Pine Cobble Summer School, 1976-83; Schaeffer-Eton Co., Inc., Pittsfield, MA; H. George Caspari Co., Inc., NYC. Awards: Northern Berkshire Painting Award, 1968; Waterford Crystal Expressive Design Competition, 1980; Strathmore-Hallmark Competition First Prize; and others. Teaching: Pine Cobble Summer School and private lessons, drawing and watercolor. Media: Watercolor.

Address in 1983, 79 Linden St., Williamstown, MA.

BURNS, JOSEPHINE.
Painter. Born in Wales, Great Britian July 2, 1917. Studied: Cooper Union; the Art Students' League, New York City. Exhibitions: The National Academy of Design; Audubon Artists; National Arts Club. Collections: C. W. Post College Museum; Oklahoma Museum; The Lanza Corporation, NJ. One-woman show, Alonzo Gallery, NY, 1966; Comm. Gallery, Brooklyn Mus., 1976 and 1977. Address in 1980, 248 Garfield Pl., Brooklyn, NY.

BURNSIDE, CAMERON.
Painter. Born in England, July 23, 1887. Studied in Paris. Paintings owned by French Government. Exhibited at the Penna. Academy of Fine Arts, Philadelphia, 1924. Official painter to American Red Cross in France 1918-19. Address in 1926, 7637 Thirty-First St., Washington, DC.

BURPEE, WILLIAM P(ARTRIDGE).
Painter. Born in Rockland, Maine, in April 13, 1846. Represented in Boston Art Club, Springfield Museum, and Rockland Public Library. Work: "Gloucester-Evening," Boston Art Club; "Almond and Olive," "Springfield Museum;" "Vulcan's Forge," Rockland Pub. Library. Address in 1926, 43 Park St. Rockland Maine.

BURR, FRANCES.
(Mrs. Frances Burr Ely). Painter and sculptor. Born Boston, Mass., Nov. 24, 1890. Pupil of Chase and Hawthorne. Member: AFA; ASL of NY; NA Women PS; Mural P. Specialty, Panels in gesso relief, painted. Address in 1929, 148 East 65th St., New York, NY.

BURR, G(EORGE) BRAINERD.
Painter. Born Middletown, Conn. Pupil of Berlin and Munich Academies FA; Art Students' League of New York; Colarossi Academy in Paris. Member: Allied Art Association. Address in 1926, Old Lyme, Conn.

BURR, GEORGE ELBERT.
Etcher and water colorist. Born Cleveland, Ohio. His plates for his etchings and aquatints are generally small and his work shows the miniaturist's precise delicacy. Illustrations for the Metropolitan Museum Collection. Address in 1926, Denver, Colorado.

BURR-MILLER, CHURCHILL.
Sculptor. Born in 1904. Exhibited portrait bust at PAFA in 1914. Lived in Wilkes-Barre, PA.

BURRAGE, MILDRED G(IDDINGS).
Painter. Born Portland, ME, May 18, 1890. Pupil of Richard Miller. Member: International Art Union, Paris. Address in 1926, Kennebunkport, ME.

BURRELL, LOUISE.
Painter. Born London, England. Pupil of Herkomer. Member: California Art Club. Address in 1926, 1189 West Adams St., Los Angeles, California.

BURROUGHS, BRYSON.
Artist. Born Hyde Park, Mass., Sept. 8, 1869. After general education, studied at Art Students' League, New York, where he won Chanler Scholarship, 1891; also studied in Paris with Puvis de Chavannes and in Florence. Engaged professionally as artist since 1889; silver medal, Buffalo Expn., 1901; Pittsburgh Expn., 1903; 3d prize, Worcester Expn., 1904; Curator of paintings, Metropolitan Museum Art, New York. Member: Association of National Artists. Work: "Danae in the Tower," Brooklyn Museum; "The Consolation of Ariadne," Metropolitan Museum, New York; "The Fishermen," Chicago Art Inst.; "The Princess and the Swineherd," Denver Art Museum; "The Age of Gold," Newark Museum Association; "Hippocrene," Luxembourg, Paris. Address in 1926, Metropolitan Museum, New York City, NY. Died 1934.

BURROUGHS, EDITH WOODMAN.
(Mrs. Bryson Burroughs). Sculptor. Born Oct. 20, 1871 in Riverdale, NY. Studied at ASL and in Paris with Injalbert. Traveled in Europe. Member of NA (1913), and NSS. Works: Bust of John La Farge

127

and "At the Threshhold" (MMA) and "Fountain of Youth." Died Jan. 16, 1916 in LI.

BURROWS, HAROLD L.
Painter and etcher. Born in Salt Lake City in 1889. Pupil of Young and Henri. Address in 1926, 469 Fifth Ave., New York.

BURT, BEATRICE MILLIKEN.
Miniature painter. Born New Bedford, Mass., 1893. Pupil of Delecluse and Mme. Laforge in Paris; Mrs. Lucia F. Fuller, Mrs. Elsie Dodge Pattee and Miss Welch in New York.

BURT, CHARLES.
Born in Scotland 1823. He came to New York in 1836. He was employed for a time by A. L. Dick of that city, and engraved and etched a number of portraits and book illustrations. His later work was bank-note engraving. For some years he was one of the chief engravers for the Treasury Department at Washington, DC. Several of his larger plates were made for the American Art Union in 1851-52. Died in 1892 in Brooklyn, NY.

BURT, LOUIS.
Painter. Born in New York, NY, July 20,1900. Pupil of Henri, George Bellows, John Sloan. Awards: Hon. mention, MacDowell Club, 1916-17-18. Address in 1926, 3835 White Plains Ave., Bronx, New York, NY.

BURT, MARY THEODORA.
Painter. Born Philadelphia. Pupil of PAFA; Julien Academy in Paris. Member: Plastic Club, Philadelphia. Address in 1926, 1203 Walnut St., Philadelphia, PA.

BURTIS, MARY E(LIZABETH).
Painter. Born Orange, NJ, 1878. Pupil of Mme. Christine Lumsden. Member: Society of Independent Artists. Address in 1926, 406 Claredon Place, Orange, NJ.

BURTON, S(AMUEL) C(HATWOOD).
Painter, sculptor, illustrator and etcher. Born Manchester, England, Feb. 18, 1881. Pupil of Laurens in Paris; Lanteri in London. Member:

Beachcombers' Club, Provincetown; Chicago Society of Etchers; Art Masters of England. Awards: Third prize for painting, 1917; second prize for etching, Minneapolis Institute, 1921. Professor of painting and lecturer on art, University of Minnesota.

BURTON, VIRGINIA LEE.
Author and illustrator. Born August 30, 1909, in Newton Centre, MA. She studied at the California School of Fine Arts; Boston Museum School. In 1929 she became a sketch artist for the Boston Transcript. In 1937 she published her first book, a children's story written, designed, and illustrated by herself and entitled Choo. In 1939 she published Mike Mulligan and His Steam Shovel, in 1941 Calico, The Wonder Horse, and in 1942 The Little House, which won the Caldecott Medal for best illustrated children's book of the year. She also illustrated Song of Robin Hood by A. B. Malcolmson, 1947, and an edition of Hans Christian Andersen's The Emperor's New Clothes, 1949. During the 1940s she taught graphic design and organized the Folly Cove Designers. She died on October 15, 1968, in Boston.

BUSBEE, JACQUE.
Painter. Born in Raleigh, NC, in 1870. Student of National Academy of Design, and Art Students' League, New York. Painted a number of portraits; later became interested in pottery.

BUSCH, CLARENCE F(RACIS).
Painter. Born Phila., PA, Aug. 28, 1887. Exhibited "Nude," Annual Exhibition of the National Academy of Design, 1925. Address in 1926, 58 West 57th St., New York.

BUSENBARK, E. J.
Painter. Member: Guild of Free Lance A. Address in 1926, 117 East 27th St., New York, NY.

BUSENBENZ-SCOVILLE, V(IRGINIA).
Painter and etcher. Born Chicago, April 26, 1896. Pupil of W. J. Reynolds in Chicago; Ehrilict in Munich. Member: Chicago Ag; Chicago SE; GFLA. Work: Screen in

128

Lake Shore Athletic Club, Chicago; "Old Sailor," Bibliotheque Nationale, Paris. Address in 1929, 14 East 75th St., New York, NY; Salisbury, Conn.

BUSEY, NORVAL H.
Painter. Born in Christiansburg, VA, 1845. Studied in Paris under Bouguereau. Member: Salma Club. Address in 1926, 39 West 67th St., New York, NY.

BUSH, AGNES S(ELENE).
Painter. Born Seattle, Washington. Pupil of Ella S. Bush and Paul Morgan Gustin. Address in 1926, 529 Belmont, North, Seattle, Washington.

BUSH, ELLA SHEPARD.
Miniature painter. Born Galesburg, Ill. Pupil of J. Alden Weir, Kenyon Cox, Robert Henri, Theodore W. Thayer. Member: Painters, Sculptors, Miniature Painters; Art Students League of New York; California Art Club; Seattle Fine Arts Society. Award: Prize, Seattle Fine Arts Society, 1920.

BUSH, JOSEPH H.
Painter. Born 1794 in Frankfort, KY. At seventeen he became a student of Thomas Sully in Philadelphia. Studio at Frankfort but spent winters at Natchez and New Orleans. He painted Gen'l Zachary Taylor, Gov. John Adair, Judge Thos. B. Monroe and Gen. Martin D. Hardin. He died in Lexington KY in 1865.

BUSH, NORTON.
Painter. Born in Rochester, NY, 1834. He became a student of Jasper F. Cropsey in New York. Among his works are "Lake Tahoe," "Summit of the Sierras," and "Lake Nicaragua." In 1874 he was elected a member of the San Francisco Art Association, and in 1878 a director. Died in 1894, in San Francisco, CA.

BUSH-BROWN, HENRY KIRKE.
Sculptor. Born Ogdensburg, NY, April 21, 1857. Studied art at National Academy of Design. Pupil of Henry Kirke Brown; studied art in Paris and Italy 1886-9. Prominent works: Equestrian

Statues Gen. G. G. Meade and Gen. John F. Reynolds, Gettysburg, PA; statues "Justinian," Appellate Court, New York; "Indian Buffalo Hunt," Chicago Expn., 1893; equestrian statue Gen. Anthony Wayne for Valley Forge, PA; memorial architecture, Stony Point, NY; The Lincoln Memorial, Gettysburg, 1911; Union Soldiers' Monument, Charleston, W. VA, 1912; equestrian statue, Gen. John Sedgwick, Gettysburg, PA. Member: National Sculpture Society, Architectural League. Address in 1926, 1729 G St., Washington, DC.

BUSH-BROWN, MARGARET LESLEY.
(Mrs. Henry Kirke Bush-Brown). Portrait painter. Born in Philadelphia, May 19, 1857. Pupil of Penna. Academy of Fine Arts, and Julien Academy in Paris. Represented by portraits of Lincoln, Lee, and Professor Lesley. Also painted miniatures. Address in 1926, 1729 G. St., Washington, DC.

BUTENSKY, JULES L.
Sculptor. Born in Russia, 1871. Pupil of Mercie and Boucher in Paris. Among his works are "Universal Peace" at the Metropolitan Museum, New York, "Exile" at the White House, Washington, DC, and "Goliath," group at Hebrew Institute, Chicago, Ill. Address in 1926, Ramah, Romona, Rockland County, New York.

BUTLER.
Engraver of Baltimore. Engraving of a man and a lion signed "Butler Sc. Balto." was published prior to 1835.

BUTLER, ANDREW R.
Pianter and etcher. Born Yonkers, NY, May 15, 1896. Pupil of Frank DuMond, Eugene Speicher, F. Luis Mora, Joseph Pennell.

BUTLER, EDWARD BURGESS.
Painter. Born in Lewistown, ME, in 1853. Pupil of F. C. Peyraud. Member of Chicago Art Club. Among his works "Misty Morning," City of Chicago; "October Mist," Chicago Art League; "California Wheat," Los Angeles Museum; and Cleveland Museum of Art, "Early Springs."

129

Address in 1926, 1608 Monroe Bldg., Chicago, Ill. Died February 20, 1928, in Pasadena, Calif.

BUTLER, EDWARD SMITH.
Painter. Born in Cincinnati, 1848. Member of the Cincinnati Art Club. Address in 1926, 1001 Chapel St., Walnut Hill, Cincinnati, Ohio.

BUTLER, FRANK.
Painter. Exhibited in Annual Water Color Exhibition at Penna. Academy of the Fine Arts, Philadelphia, 1925. Address in 1926, Care of A. R. Thayer, 126 Moss Ave., Boston, Mass.

BUTLER, GEORGE BERNARD.
Portrait painter. Born Feb. 8, 1838 in New York. Pupil of Thomas Hicks, and of Couture. Served in the Civil War. In 1873 he was elected a member of the National Academy, his last painting being exhibited there in the year of his death. Represented in the Metropolitan Museum by "The Gray Shawl." He died in May 4, 1907 at Croton Falls, NY.

BUTLER, HELEN SHARPLESS.
Painter. Born in West Chester, PA. Pupil of Chase and Anshutz. Member of Fellowship of Penna. Academy of Fine Arts.

BUTLER, HOWARD RUSSELL.
Painter. Born New York, 1856. Honorable mention Paris Salon, 1886, medals Paris Expn., 1889. Elected Associate member of National Academy, 1898, and Academician, 1902. Member of New York Water Color Club. Died in 1934. Address in 1926, Santa Barbara, California, and Princeton, NJ.

BUTLER, J. M.
Engraver, or rather a publisher of prints, as there is no evidence that he engraved himself. He was active in Philadelphia about 1850.

BUTLER, M.
Working in Boston 1821, he engraved in line five humorous copperplate illustrations for "The Songster's New Pocket Companion, etc.," published by T. Swan, Boston, 1821. This may be the same Butler who was

working in Baltimore at a somewhat later date.

BUTLER, MARY.
Painter. Born in Philadelphia. Pupil of Chase, Henri and Redfield. Member of Fellowship of Penna. Academy of Fine Arts, Philadelphia. Among her paintings "Goatfell Mountain," Penna. Academy of Fine Arts, Philadelphia; "Ogonquit Dunes," West Chester State Normal School; and "Maine Headlands," Williamsport High School. Address in 1926, 2127 Green St., Philadelphia, PA.

BUTLER, THEODORE E.
Painter. Born in 1876; died in 1937. Member of Society of Independent Artists. Address in 1926, 75 Washington Place, New York, NY.

BUTTERWORTH, A. H.
He engraved the frontispiece and vignette title page for "The Life and Adventures of Robinson Crusoe," published by Silas Andrews, Hartford, NJ, about the year 1828.

BUTTON, ALBERT PRENTICE.
Painter and illustrator. Born in Lowell, Mass., 1872. Pupil of Boston Art Club. Address in 1926, 44 Boyleston St., Boston, Mass.

BUTTRE, JOHN CHESTER.
Engraver. Born 1821 and died 1893. He did portrait painting, but soon became a line engraver of reputation, and established an extensive engraving business in New York.

BUZBY, ROSELLA T.
Painter and illustrator. Born in Philadelphia in 1867. Pupil of Penna. Academy of Fine Arts. Address in 1926, Fuller Building, 10 South 18th St., Philadelphia, PA.

BYE, ARTHUR E.
Painter and teacher. Born in Philadelphia, 1885. Pupil of John Carlson; studied in Paris. Member of Art Alliance, Philadelphia. Address in 1926, Langhorne, Philadelphia.

130

YER, SAMUEL.
Painter. Born in Poland, 1886.
Pupil of Art Institute of Chicago,
Ill. Address in 1926, 439 South
Halstead St., Chicago.

YERS, EVELYN.
Painter. Exhibited water colors at
PAFA, Philadelphia, 1922. Address
in 1926, 1102 Bagby St., Houston,
Texas.

YERS, MARYHELEN.
Painter and teacher. Born Seattle,
March 23, 1902. Pupil of Andre
L'hote in Paris. Member: Seattle
SFA. Address in 1929, University
of Washington; h. 1651 Windemere
Dr., Seattle, Wash.

YFIELD, N.
Portrait painter. Born in Boston,
1677, and probably the son of
Nathaniel and Deborah Byfield.
Portrait of Richard Middleton,
signed and dated 1713.

YRAM, RALPH SHAW.
Painter and illustrator. Born in
Philadelphia, 1881. Member of
Philadelphia Sketch Club. Address
in 1926, Lena and Church Lane,
Germantown, Philadelphia.

YRD, HENRY.
Portrait painter. Lived in New
Orleans in the 40's and 50's;
travelling portrait painter unitl
1867. Died in 1883.

YRNE,, ELLEN A(BERT).
Painter. Born Fort Moultrie, SC,
1858. Pupil of Corcoran School of
Art in Washington; William M.
Chase; Simon and Menard in Paris.
Member: Society of Washington
Artists.

YRUM, RUTHVEN H(OLMES).
Painter and teacher. Born Grand
Junction, Mich., July 10, 1896.
Pupil of AIC. Member: Ind. AC;
Hossier Salon; Anderson SA; Terre
Haute AL. Awards: Second prize for
still life, Indiana State Fair,
1928; second prize, figure
composition, third in landscape,
Indiana State Fair, 1929. Work:
"The Old Timer," Richmond Art
association, Richmond, Ind.
"Portrait of Mr. J. C. Black," High
School, Anderson, Ind. Address in

1929, 520 Eagle St., Terre Haute,
Ind.; h. 419 Union Ave., Anderson,
Ind.

131

CABALLERO, EMILIO.
Painter and educator. Born in
Newark, NJ, July 5, 1917. Studied
at Amarillo Coll.; W. TX State U.;
Columbia U. Exhibited at 104th
Ann. Am. WCS Exhib., NY; 9th Ann.
Southwestern Exhib., Prints &
Drawings, Dallas, TX; many others.
Prof., W. TX State U., from 1949.
Member Royal Soc. of GB (fellow).
Works, watercolor and enamel.
Address in 1982, Amarillo, TX.

CABLE, MAXINE ROTH.
Sculptor. Born Phila, PA. Studied
at Tyler Sch. of FA; Corcoran Sch.
of Art; Am. U. with Hans Hofmann.
Work at Allied Chem. Corp., NYC;
Nat. Acad. of Science, Wash., DC;
Wolf Trap Farm Performing Arts, VA.
Exhib. at Corcoran; Morgan Gal.,
and Gal. Ten, Wash., DC; others.
Received Sculpture Award, Corcoran;
1st prize ptg., Smithsonian Inst.
Address in 1982, Bethesda, MD.

CABOT, AMY W.
Painter. Member: NA Women PS;
Boston MA. Address in 1929, 72
Chestnut Street, Boston, MA.

CADE, J. J.
Engraver. Was born in Canada. He
was a good engraver of portraits
and worked for the New York
publishers. In 1890 he was living
in Brooklyn, NY.

CADMUS, EGBERT.
Painter. Born Bloomfield, NJ, May
26, 1868. Pupil of Charles E.
Moss, C. Y. Turner, E. M. Ward and
Robert Henri. Member: AWCS
(assoc.); AFA. Address in 1929, 150
West 95th Street, New York, NY.
Died in 1939.

CADMUS, PAUL.
Painter and engraver. Born New
York City, December 17, 1904.
Pupil of Francis C. Jones, William
Auerbach Levy and Charles C.
Curran. Member: Tiffany Foundation
AG; Brooklyn SE. Award:
Fellowship, Tiffany Foundation.
Address in 1929, 150 West 95th
Street, New York, NY.

CADORIN, ETTORE.
Sculptor. Born in Venice, Italy,
March 1, 1876. Studied in Venice.
Member: NSS. Award: First medal,

Royal Academy, Venice. Work: Tw
colossal statues, St. Mark'
Square, Venice; Wagner memorial
Venice; war memorial, Edgewater
NJ. Address in 1929, Sant
Barbara, CA. Died June 18, 1952.

CADWALDER, LOUISE.
Painter and craftsman. Bor
Cincinnati, Ohio. Pupil c
Carlson; William M. Chase; Joh
Rich Cahill; Winold Reiss; Ralp
Johonnot; Rudolph Scaeffer; ASL c
NY; Cincinnati Art Acad. Member
San Francicso S. Women A; Bostc
SAC; Alliance. Address in 192°
3120 Eton Ave., Berkeley, CA.

CADY, EDWIN A. (MRS.)
Painter. Member: Providence Ar
Club; Providence Water Color Club
Address in 1926, Warren, RI.

CADY, HENRY N.
Painter. Born Warren, RI, July 8
1849. Pupil of NAD. Member
Providence AC. Address in 1929, 8
Union Street, Warren, RI.

CADY, WALTER HARRISON.
Illustrator. Born Gardner, MA
June 17, 1877. Member: Salma. C.
SI 1911; AWCS; NY Arch. L.; Nort
Shore AA; GFLA; NYWCC. Illustrate
Rackety Packety, Queen Silve
Bell, The Spring Cleaning, The Cos
Lion, by Frances Hodgson Burnett
etc.; contributor to Life, St
Nicholas, Saturday Evening Post
Country Gentleman, Ladies Hom
Journal, etc. Author of Cale
Cottontail and other children'
stories. Died in 1970.

CAESAR, DORIS.
Sculptor. Born, New York City i
1893. Studied: Art Students Lg
Archipenko School of Art. Work
Addison Gallery of American Art
Chapel of Our Redeemer, Chappaqua
NY; Conn. College; Dayton Inst. o
Art; Fort Worth Art Assoc.; Phila
Mus. of Art; Minneapolis Inst. o
Art; Newark Mus. of Art; Univ. c
Iowa; Univ. of Minn.; Utica Publi
Library; Wadsworth Atheneum
Whitney Mus. of Am. Art; PAFA
Wellesley College; Atlanta Ar
Center; Erhard Weyhe, whos
collection of Caesar's sculptur
was shown at Weyhe Gallery, Ne
York City. Media: Bronze. Die

c. 1971. Rep.: Randall Galleries, Ltd., New York City.

\FARELLI, MICHELE A.
Painter. Born in 1889. Member: Society Independent Artists. Address in 1926, 24 West 60th Street, New York, NY.

\FFERTY, JAMES H.
Painter. Born in Albany, in 1819. Portrait and still life painter. He became an Academician, National School of Design, in 1853. His most notable paintings are "My Girl" "Brook Trout," and several studies of "Fish." With K. M. Wiles painted a graveyard scene from Hamlet. Died Sept. 7, 1869.

\GE, ROBERT FIELDING.
Painter and sculptor. Born Charlotte Co., Virginia, Oct. 7, 1923. Study: De Bourgos Sch. of Art, Wash., DC; Salisbury School of Art, Rhodesia; Am. Student and Arts Lg., Paris. Exhibitions: Contemporary Gallery of Art, Wash, DC; Smithsonian Inst.; National Gallery of Rhodesia, Norfolk Museum of Art; others. In collections of commercial and private organizations in US, France and Africa. Works: "Free Form", and "Moby Dick." Address in 1976, South Boston, Virginia.

\HAN, SAMUEL GEORGE.
Illustrator. Member: SI. Address in 1929, 644 Riverside Drive, New York, NY. Died in 1974.

\HILL, ARTHUR JAMES.
Painter and illustrator. Born in San Francisco, 1879. Pupil of California Art School. Member: California Artists' Association; Bohemian Club, San Francisco. Work: "Governor Hiram Johnson of California," State Capitol, CA; "Congressman Kent of California," "Templeton Crocker" in Crocker Art Gallery, Sacramento; "Chief Justice Irwin," Bohemian Club, San Francisco. Address in 1926, San Anselmo, California.

\HILL, KATHARINE KAVANAUGH.
Painter. Born Four Oaks, Kentucky. Pupil of Wm. V. Cahill and S. MacDonald Wright. Member: Phoenix FAA. Award: First prize for still life, AZ State Fair, 1926. Address in 1929, 562 South New Hampshire Ave., Los Angeles, CA, summer, 708 Heard Bldg., Phoenix, AZ.

CAHILL, WILLIAM VINCENT.
Painter. Born Syracuse, NY. Pupil of Howard Pyle. Member of Art Students League of New York. Professor of drawing and painting, University of Kansas, 1918 -19. Work: "Thoughts of the Sea," Museum of History, Science and Art, Los Angeles; "Summer," Municipal Collection, Phoenix, Arizona. He died in Chicago, Aug. 1924.

CAIN.
An American portrait painter who flourished about 1760 in Maryland.

CALDER, ALEXANDER (MILNE).
Sculptor. Born Alberdeen, Scotland, 1846, and died June 14, 1923 in Phila. Pupil of John Rhind in Edinburgh. Studied in England; came to United States in 1868. Pupil of PAFA under J. A. Bailly and Thomas Eakins. Work: Equestrian statue of Gen. George G. Meade in Fairmount Park, Philadelphia, PA; colossal statue of William Penn, and groups on City Hall, Philadelphia, PA.

CALDER, ALEXANDER STIRLING.
Sculptor and painter. Born Phila., PA, Jan. 11, 1870; son of Alexander Milne Calder. Pupil of PAFA; Chapu and Falguiere in Paris. Member: ANA 1906; NA 1913; NASS, 1896; AC Phila.; SAA 1905; NY Municipal AS; NY Arch. Lg., 1910; Century Assoc.; Players'; Nat. Inst., AL; NAC (life); Port. P.; New SA. Instructor NAD; ASL of NY. Had studio in NYC after 1908. Awards: Gold medal, AC Phila., 1893; hon. mention, Pan-Am. Exp., Buffalo, 1901; silver medal, St. Louis Exp., 1904; Lippincott prize, PAFA, 1905; grand prize, Alaska-Yukon-Pacific Exp., 1909; designer's medal, San F. CA, 1915; silver medal, Sesqui-Centennial Exp., Phila., 1926. Work: Statues of Witherspoon, Marcus Whitman and Davies, Presbyterian Bldg., Phila.; Marble sun dial, Fairmount Park, Phila.; monumental archways, Throop Inst., Pasadena, CA; Lea Mem.,

133

Laurel Hill Cemetary, Phila; Fountain of Engergy, etc., P.-P. Exp., San F., 1915; "The Star," Herron Art Inst., Indianapolis; "Washington Group," Washington Arch., NY, NY; Depew mem. fountain, Indianapolis, IN, "The Island," Viscaya, Fla. Represented in permanent collection; PA Acad.; St. Louis Mus. of Art; Franklin Inn Club; and Smithsonian Inst. grounds, Washington, DC; Metropolitan Mus., New York, NY; Reading Mus.; Telfair Acad., Savannah, GA. Acting Chief, Dept. of Sculpture, P.-P. Exp., San F., 1915. Address in 1929, 11 E. 14'th St., New York, NY.

CALDER, ALEXANDER.
Sculptor. Born in Philadelphia, PA, July 22, 1898. Study: Stevens Inst. of Technology, ME 1919; ASL, 1923-26, with George Luks, Guy du Bois, Boardman Robinson, John Sloan. Work: MOMA, Met. Mus. of Art, NYC; Wadsworth Atheneum; Mus. of Western Art, Moscow, USSR; Phila. Mus. of Art; others. Comn.: Gen. Motors Corp., 1954; NY International Airport, 1958; UNESCO, Paris, 1958; many others. Exhib.: In leading museums throughout, US and abroad. Awards: First prize sculpture, Int'l. Exhib of Contemp. Painting & Sculpture, Pittsburgh, 1958; gold medal award, Nat'l. Inst. of Arts & Letters, 1971; Commander, Fr. Legion of Honor, 1973. Mem.: Nat'l Inst. Arts and Letters. Died in 1976. Address in 1976, RFD Painter Hill Road, Roxbury, CT.

CALDER, JOSEPHINE ORMOND.
Painter. Member: National Academy of Women Painters and Sculptors. Address in 1926, 1861 Parkwood Avenue, Toledo, OH.

CALDER, RALPH M.
Painter. Born Philadelphia, PA, 1884. Pupil of Penna. Academy of Fine Arts. Address in 1926, Care Paul Chalfin, 597 Fifth Avenue, New York, NY.

CALEWAERT, LOUIS H.S.
Painter, etcher, and sculptor. Born Detroit, Mich., 1894. Pupil of Detroit School of Fine Arts under Wicker, and in Italy, Sicily,

France and Belgium. Member: Chicago Society of Etchers. Work: Toledo Museum of Art. Address in 1926, 4316 Greenwood Avenue, Chicago, IL.

CALHOUN, FREDERIC D.
Painter. Born Minneapolis, MN, 1883. Pupil of Art Students' League of New York; Minneapolis School of Art. Member: Minneapolis Art Club.

CALIGA, ISAAC HENRY.
Painter. Born Auburn, IN, March 24, 1857. Pupil of William Lindenschmidt, studied in Munich. Member: S. Indp. A. Work: "Portrait of H. F. Waters," New England Historical and Genealogical Society; "Portrait of Matthew Robson," Salem (MA) YMCA; "James B. Colgate," New York Chamber of Commerce; "Gov. Alexander H. Rice," MA State House; "Rev. Alfred W. Putnam," Danvers, MA, Historical Society. Address in 1929, Provincetown, MA.

CALKINS, LORING GARY.
Engraver and teacher. Born Chicago, IL, June 11, 1884. Pupil of Vanderpoel; Charles Francis Brown; Freer. Member: AIC Alumni Assoc.; ASL of Chicago. Illustrated "Land and Sea Mammals of Middle America and West Indies." Represented in Field Columbian Museum. Address in 1929, 10 Avalon Rd., Waban, MA. Died in 1960.

CALLE, PAUL.
Illustrator. Born in New York City in 1928. He studied at PI for four years. Following his first illustration for Liberty Magazine in 1947, he produced many campaigns for major advertising agencies. He has recorded the NASA space program beginning with the Mercury Program and in 1975 he covered the Apollo-Soyuz training team Assignments for commemorative United States postal stamps followed and his works are in collections of the Phoenix Art Museum, NASA and the Northwest Indian Center in Spokane. A Hamilton King Award winner, he has also exhibited illustrations and

134

won awards in the S of I Annual Exhibitions.

CALLENDER, BENJAMIN.
Engraver. Born March 16, 1773, in Boston, MA. His engraved work chiefly consists of maps and charts. He was engraving for Boston publishers as early as 1796. Callender engraved some of the maps in the "American Gazetteer" by Jedediah Morse, Boston, 1897. Died Feb. 22, 1856.

CALLENDER, JOSEPH.
Born in Boston, MA, 1751; died there Nov. 10, 1821, and was buried in the Old Granary Burying Ground. He was the son of Eleazer Callender and Susanna Hiller. Joseph Callender was employed for some time as a die-sinker for the Massachusetts Mint. With Paul Revere, he engraved a number of line-plates for the "Royal American Magazine", published in Boston in 1774.

CALLERY, MARY.
Born June 19, 1908 in NYC. Studied at NY ASL and with Jacques Loutchansky in Paris, where she lived many years. Was commissioned to create work for NYC Schools and Lincoln Center. Exhibited at Brussels World's Fair, 1958; MOMA; Virginia Mus. of Fine Arts; Knoedler & Co., NYC; Salon de Tuileries, Paris. In collections of MOMA; Toledo Mus. of Art; Cinn. Art Museum; S. F. Museum of Art; Wadsworth Atheneum; and Alcoa. Died in Paris, February 12, 1977.

CALOGERO, EUGENE D.
Illustrator. Born in New York City in 1932. He attended the School of Industrial Arts in 1950 and had his first piece published in 1951. He has since illustrated several posters, most recently a poster for the Smithsonian Inst. His works have received many awards from the AIGA, the ADC, Type Designers Club and the Society of Magazine and Publication Designers.

CALVERLY, CHARLES.
Sculptor. Born Nov. 1, 1833, in Albany, NY. Educated in Albany, NY, became an Associate National Academy of Design in 1872, and of a full member in 1875. Executed many groups and figures; especially known for his portrait busts in bronze of Horace Greeley, John Brown, Peter Cooper, and Elias Howe. Died Feb. 24, 1914 in Essex Falls, NJ.

CALVERT, BERTHA W.
Painter. Born in Nashville, TN, in 1885. Specialty, ivory miniatures. Address in 1926, Fourth Avenue and Union Street, Nashville, TN.

CALVERT, E.
Painter. Born in England, 1850. Painted portraits in Mercer University, Lake Geneva, WI. Address in 1926, 238 Fourth Avenue, Nashville, TN.

CALVERT, PETER R.
Painter. Born in England, 1855. Pupil of John Sowden. Specialty, ivory miniatures. Address in 1926, Fourth Avenue and Union Street, Nashville, TN.

CALYO, NICOLINO.
Painter. Born in 1799. Italian portrait and miniature painter. In 1837 he lived in New York with other refugees, among them Napoleon III. He died there Dec. 9, 1884. (see NY Tribune, December 14, 1884).

CAMERON, EDGAR SPIER.
Painter and writer. Born Ottawa, Ill., May 26, 1862. Pupil of Chicago Academy of Design; ASL of NY; Cabanel, Constant and Laurens in Paris. Member: Cliff Dwellers. Awards: Silver medal, Paris Exp., 1900; Grower prize, AIC 1909; Butler Purchase prize, AIC 1914; Carr prize, AIC, 1914; Rosenwald purchase prize, AIC, 1917; Carr prize, AIC, 1917; Officier, Beaux Arts et Instruction Publique, Paris, 1920; purchase prize ($500), Municipal AL of Chicago, 1926, prize ($200), Chicago Gallery Assoc., 1927. Work: In Chicago Historical Soc.; Chicago Union League Club; Supreme Court Library, Springfield, IL; "Youth and Moonlight," Chicago Commission purchase, City Hall, 1915; "Cabaret Breton," Art Institute of Chicago; mural decoration, Genesee Co. Court House, Flint, Mich. Address

in 1929, 10 East Ohio Street, Chicago, IL. Died in 1944.

CAMERON, ELIZABETH WALLACE.
Painter and teacher. Born in Woodland, PA. Pupil of Christian Walter, Ossip Linde and Hugh Breckenridge. Member: Pitts. AA; Pitts. Teachers Assoc. Address in 1929, 4145 Windsor Street, Squirrel Hill, Pittsburgh, PA.

CAMERON, MARIE GELON.
Painter. Born Paris, France. Pupil of Moreau de Tours, Cabanel, Laurens and Constant in Paris; AIC. Awards: Prize, AIC, 1902; Julius Rosenwald purchase prize, AIC, 1922. Represented in Historical Society, Chicago; portrait, "Maj. Gen. Joseph B. Sanborn," First Regiment Armory, Chicago; portraits of "Judges Cutting and Kohlsaat," Cook Co. Probate Court. Address in 1929, 10 East Ohio Street, Chicago, IL.

CAMERON, WILLIAM ROSS.
Illustrator, writer and engraver. Born in New York City, June 14, 1893. Pupil of F. L. Meyer, Xavier Martinez, Nahl, E. Spencer Mackey, Martin Griffin. Studied in London and Paris. Member: San F. AA: CA SE; Roxburgh C. Address in 1929, 55 Borica Street, Ingleside Terraces, San Francisco, CA.

CAMFFERMAN, MARGARET GOVE.
Painter. Born in Rochester MN in 1895. Pupil of Henri. Award: Hon. mention, Seattle FAS, 1921. Address in 1929, "Brackenwood," Langley, Washington.

CAMFFERMAN, PETER MARENUS.
Painter. Born in the Hague, Holland, February 6, 1890. Pupil of Robert Koehler and MacDonald-Wright. Member: S. Indp. A. Address in 1929, "Brackenwood" Langley, Washington. Died in 1957.

CAMINS, JACQUES JOSEPH.
Painter and printmaker. Born Odessa, Russia, Jan. 1, 1904; US citizen. Study: Paris; ASL; with Jean Liberty and Byron Browne; Pratt Graphics Ctr., with Matsubara Naoka and Carol Summer. Work: Isreal Museum, Jerusalem; The Negev Museum; Memorial Art Museum Czechoslovakia; Hebrew University Jerusalem; Cooper-Hewitt Mus.; an others. Exhibitions: Nationa Academy Galleries, NYC; Cryp Gallery, Columbia University Provincetown, MA, Art Assn.; etc Mem.: Artists Equity Assn. Provincetown (MA) Art Assn; ASL etc. Media: Oil. Address in 1982 1065 98th St., Studio G, Bay Harbo Islands, Fla.

CAMMEYER, W.
Engraver, working in Albany, NY about 1812. He engraved a numbe of book-illustrations.

CAMPBELL.
An American portrait painter, sai to have flourished about 1776 Washington writes at that date of portrait painted of himself, bu states that he never saw th artist.

CAMPBELL, ANNA BARRAND.
Miniature painter. Born in Nelso County, VA, 1879. Pupil of Ar Students' League of New York, an Corcoran Art Gallery, Washington DC. Address in 1926, 1977 Biltmor Street, Washington, DC. Died Marc 24, 1927, in NYC.

CAMPBELL, BLENDON REED.
Painter and illustrator. Born St Louis, MO, July 28, 1872. Pupil o Constant, Laurens and Whistler i Paris. Member: SI 1905; Pari AAA; NY Arch. Lg. 1911. Award Third prize, Paris AAA 1900 Represented in Chicago Ar Institute, Smithsonian Institut and Witchita AA. Address in 1929 3 Washington Square, North, Ne York, NY.

CAMPBELL, C. ISABEL.
Painter and sculptor. Bor Brooklyn, NY. Pupil of Phila School of Design for Women Member: Plastic C.; AFA. Award Silver medal for miniature mode and mural decorations Sesqui-Centennial Exposition Phila., 1926. Work: Miniatur models and mural decorations Commercial Museum. Address i 1929, Commercial Museum, 34th an Spruce Sts.; h. 6156 Webster St. Philadelphia, PA.

CMPBELL, CORA A.
Painter, etcher, and teacher. Born in Philadelphia in 1873. Pupil of J. Frank Copeland; Charles W. Hawthorne; Earl Horter; Henry Pitz. Member: Plastic C.; Phila. Alliance; AFA. Address in 1929, 2231 N. 22nd St., Philadelphia.

CMPBELL, DOROTHY BOSTWICK.
Painter, sculptor. Born March 26, 1899, in NYC. She studied with Eliot O'Hara, Washington, DC and Marilyn Bendell, Corteg, FL. Work: Cooperstown Art Association, both group and one-man shows, 1965; Sarasota Art Association, FL and Pioneer Gallery, Cooperstown; Corteg Art Sch, FL, 1972. Awarded First Prize for Watercolor, Cooperstown Art Association, 1965. Member of American Art League; American Federation of the Arts. Address in 1980, 4315 Mangrove Pl., Sarosota, FL.

CMPBELL, EDMUND S.
Painter. Born in Freehold, NJ, in 1884. Pupil of Mass. Inst. of Technology; Ecole des Beaux Arts. Member of Associated Artists of Pittsburgh; Chic. Soc. of Artists; NY WC Club; Am. WC Soc. Exhibited water color paintings at Penna. Academy of Fine Arts, 1922. Died in 1950. Address in 1926, Care of Chicago Art Institute. Died in 1950.

CMPBELL, ELIZABETH.
Painter. Born in 1893 in Iowa Falls, Iowa. Studied with Alexander Nepote, at Marian Hartwell's School of Design, San Fran.; and San Fran. Art Inst., one year scholarship. Taught privately. Received grant from Montalva Foundation, Cal. Exhibited at Cal. Palace, San Fran.; Louis Terah Haggin Mem. Galleries, Stockton; and San Fran. Museum of Art. Living in San Francisco in 1965.

CMPBELL, FLOY.
Painter, illustrator, writer, teacher and lecturer. Born Kansas City, MO, September 30, 1875. Pupil of ASL of NY; Colarossi Academy, Garrido, and Cottet in Paris. Member: Kansas City SA. Represented in Jefferson College,

Philadelphia. Author and illustrator of "Girls in Camp Aready." Address in 1929, Kansas City, MO.

CAMPBELL, HARRIET DUNN.
Painter, sculptor, and teacher. Born Columbus, Ohio, August 16, 1873. Pupil of Robert Henri; William M. Chase; Arthur W. Dow; Kenneth Millier; George Bridgman; Charles Hawthorne. Member: Columbus AL; Ohio WCS; Ohio-Born Women Painters. Awards: Hon. mention for oil, 1920, 1921, for water color, 1923, Columbus Art League; hon. mention, Ohio State Fair, 1922; Robert Wolf water color prize, Columbus Art League, 1927. Address in 1929, 1780 W. 1st Avenue, Columbus, Ohio; summer, Huron, Ohio.

CAMPBELL, HELENA EASTMAN OGDEN.
Painter, writer, and teacher. Born Eastman, Georgia. Pupil of William M. Chase and Robert Henri School in New York; Grande Chaumiere School in Paris. Member: National Aacademy of Women PS; S. Indp. A.; Alliance; Municipal Art Committee, New York; SSAL. Work: Portrait of Rt. Rev. Frederick F. Reese, Bishop of Georgia, owned by the Diocese of Georgia; portrait of Henry Carr Pearson in Horace Mann School, Columbia University, New York; portrait of Pres. William F. Quillian, owned by Wesleyan College, Macon, Georgia; portrait sketch of Prof. William H. Kilpatrick of Teachers College, Columbia University, owned by Mercer University, Macon, Georgia. Address in 1929, 419 W. 119th St., The Kingscote, New York City.

CAMPBELL, HEYWORTH.
Painter, writer, lecturer, teacher. Born Philadelphia, Pennsylvaina, June 20, 1886. Member: Grolier C.; Salma. C.; Art Directors' C.; Advertising Club. Specialty, advertising art. Address in 1929, care of Batten Barton, Durstine and Osborn, 383 Madison Ave.; h. 325 East 72nd Street, New York, NY; summer, Oakland, New Jersey.

CAMPBELL, ISABELLA GRAHAM.
(Mrs. Henry Munroe Campbell, Jr.) Painter. Pupil of Chase and

Bourdelle. Member: Detroit S. Women P. Address in 1929, "Greystone," Klingle Road, Washington, DC.

CAMPBELL, KENNETH.
Sculptor and painter. Born April 14, 1913, in West Medford, MA. Studied at MA Sch. of Art, with E. Major, C. Darlin, R. Andrews, W. Porter; Nat'l. Academy of Design, with L. Kroll, G. Beal; ASL, with Arthur Lee. Taught at Erskine School, Boston; Silvermine, New Canaan; Queens College, Columbia University; and others. Received awards from Longview Foundation (NYC - 1962); Ford Foundation; Audubon; and 1965 fellowship, Guggenheim. Exhibited at Stable Gallery, NYC; Art Inst. of Chicago; Whitney; PAFA; others. In collections of Dillard University (New Orleans); Whitney; Walker Art Center (Minn.), and private collections. Member: ASL; Sculptors Guild; Audubon Artists; Boston S. Indep. A. Address in 1976, 79 Mercer St., New York City.

CAMPBELL, ORLAND.
Portrait painter. Born Chicago, IL, November 28, 1890. Pupil of Henry McCarter; Penna. Acad. of the Fine Arts. Member: Century Club. Work: "Anna Bartlett Warner," U.S.M.A. Museum, West Point, NY; "Davis Rich Dewey," Walker Memorial Hall, Cambridge, MA; "Dr. Miller," Walker Memorial Hall, Cambridge, MA; "Blewett Lee," University of Chicago. Died in 1972. Address in 1929, 21 MacDougal Alley, New York, NY. Died in 1972.

CAMPBELL, ROBERT.
Engraver. Working in Philadelphia about 1806 - 1831.

CAMPBELL, SARA WENDELL.
Painter and illustrator. Born St. John, N. B., Canada. Pupil of Eric Pape, Chase, Penfield and Miller. Member: GFLA; SI. Specialty, story illustration and advertising in magazines. Address in 1929, 1 West 67th Street, NYC. Died in 1960.

CAMPBELL, WANDS.
Painter. Exhibited in the 1925 Annual Exhibition of the National

Academy of Design. Address i 1926, Athens, PA.

CAMPOLI, COSMO P.
Sculptor. Born in South Bend Indiana, March 21, 1922. Study Art Inst. of Chicago, grad. 195C Anna Louise Raymond travelin fellow to Italy, France, Spain 1950-52. Work: MOMA, NYC Richmond Mus., VA; Unitaria Church, Chicago; many privat collections. Exhib.: New Image of Man, MOMA, 1959; US Info. Agenc Show, Moscow & Petrograd; Chicag Sch. Exhib., Galerie du Dragone Paris; sculpture exhib., Spoletc Italy; 30-year retro., Mus Contemp. Art, Chicago, 1971; plu many more. Awards: Bronze medal Deleg. Nat'l. Educ. - Frisica Madrid, 1969; Automotive Assn. c Spain award, 1969; etc. Teaching Contemp. Art Workshop, Chicagc 1952-pres.; Inst. of Desigr Illinois Inst. of Technology 1953-pres. Address in 1982, 115 East 54th, Chicago, IL.

CANADE, VINCENT.
Painter. Born Albanese, Italy 1879. Self-taught. Represented i Phillips Memorial Gallery Washington, DC. Address in 1929 care of E. Weyhe, 794 Lexingtc Ave., New York, NY.

CANDEE, GEO. EDWARD.
Painter. Born in New Haven, CT. 1838. Pupil of Joseph Kyle in Ne Haven, and also studied in Italy Painted landscapes, portraits ar figure pieces.

CANE, ALICE NORCROSS.
Painter and teacher. Bo Louisville. Pupil of Charle Hawthorne, James Hopkins, V. Deering Perrine, Jonas Lie Member: Louisville AA; Louisvil AC; Louisville Handicraft C Address in 1929, Cortlandt Hote Louisville, Kentucky; summe Provincetown, MA.

CANNON, BEATRICE.
Painter. Born in Louisville, K in 1875. Pupil at Art Institute c Chicago. Address in 1926, 11 East 61st Street, New York.

138

ANNON, FLORENCE V.
Painter. Born in Camden, NJ. Studied: Phila. Mus. School of Industrial Art; PAFA; Grande Chaumiere, Paris. Awards: Cresson traveling scholarships, PAFA, 1928, 1929; Toppan Award, 1930; Northwest Printmakers, 1933; Nat'l Assn. of Women Artists, 1936; Southern Printmakers, 1937; Plastic Club, 1943; fellowship, PAFA; Camden High School, Camden, NJ. Collections; PAFA; Phila. Art Alliance; Harcum Junior College, Bryn Mawr, PA; Phila. Museum of Art; Woodmere Art Gallery; Northwest Printmakers; Southern Printmakers.

ANNON, HUGH.
Sculptor. Born in Ireland, he settled in Phila. and there did considerable modelling and carving. Pennsylvania, c. 1814.

ANTER, ALBERT M.
Painter. Born at Norma, Salem County, NJ, 1892. Member of Fellowship of the Penna. Academy of Fine Arts, Philadelphia. Among his best known paintings are "Virginia Road," and "Landscape" at the Graphic Sketch Club Gallery. Address in 1926, 721 Walnut Street, Philadelphia, PA.

ANTIN, KATHLEEN MARIE.
Printmaker. Born in 1951. Study: Univ. of New Hampshire. Work: Phila. Public Library; Decordova Mus.; Fairbanks Mus.; Fed. Reserve Bank of Phila.; various corporations; commissions by New Hampshire Graphics Society, President and Mrs. Derek Bok of Harvard Univ., the Franklin Mint, Collector's Guild. Exhib.: 23rd Berkshire Mus. Exhib.; 2nd US Int'l. Graphics Annual; Boston Printmakers 30th Annual Exhib.; 39th Annual Exhib. of Miniature Painters, Sculptors, and Engravers Soc. of Wash., DC. Awards: Helen Slottman Graphics Award, Pen & Brush Club, NYC. Currently living in Vermont.

ANTRALL, HARRIET M.
Painter. Born near Springfield, IL. Pupil of Pratt Institute, Dow, Woodbury, Townsley, Poore, Van Laer. Member: Western Arts Association; St. Louis AG;

Springfield AA; AFA. Co-editor with J. C. Boudreau of "Art in Daily Activities," Mentzer Bush Co. Address in 1926, 853 Grand Blvd. Springfield, IL.

CAPELLANO, ANTONIO.
Sculptor, possibly a pupil of Canova. As early as 1815 he was in New York, going from that city to Baltimore, MD, at the request of Max Godefroy, the architect of the Battle Monument of that city. Prior to his work on the Battle Monument, Capellano secured a commission for the execution of two panels in bas-relief upon the front of St. Paul's Church, of which Robert Cary Long was the architect. These two works, "Moses with the Tables of the Law" and "Christ Breaking Bread," were executed for the sum of $1,000 and completed before he began the Battle Monument. In September, 1817, Capellano, writing from Baltimore to James Madison at Montpelier, solicited a commission for a marble bust of James Madison, an arrangement which he was unable to complete. Capellano was then employed as a sculptor at the Capitol. In 1827 he offered to execute a statue of Washington for the Washington Monument at Baltimore. Rembrandt Peale met Capellano while in Baltimore in 1815, and again in the Boboli Gardens in Florence in 1830, when the latter resided there.

CAPERS, HAROLD HARPER.
Painter and illustrator. Born Brooklyn, NY, April 21, 1899. Pupil of F. Tadema, J. Allen St. John and Wellington Reynolds. Member: GFLA. Specialty, commercial art and advertising. Address in 1929, 30 North Michigan Avenue; h. 1345 Kenilworth Avenue, Chicago, IL.

CAPLAN, JERRY L.
Sculptor. Born Pittsburgh, PA, Aug. 9, 1922. Study: Carnegie-Mellon Univ.; ASL; Univ. NC. Work: Raleigh State Art Gallery, NC; Westinghouse Corp.; many private collections. Comn.: Friendship Fed. Plaza, Pittsburgh; Westinghouse Ceramic Div., Derry, PA; Kossman Assocs., Pittsburgh; Rockwell Corp., Pittsburgh; others.

Exhib: Butler Inst. Am. Art, Youngstown, Ohio, 1955-75; Carnegie Inst., 1971; others. Awards: Soc. of Sculptors; Associated Artists of Pgh. Annual; Kent State U. Invitational Sculp. Show; others. Teaching: Chatham Coll.; Professor in Art at Rochester Institute of Tech., Temple U., Carnegie Mellon U. and others. Media: Terra-cotta. Address in 1982, Pittsburgh, PA.

CAPOLINO, JOHN JOSEPH.
Painter. Born in Philadelphia, PA, Feb. 22, 1896. Studied with Henry McCarter at the PAFA, and abroad. Member: Fellowship PAFA. Awards: Two European traveling scholarships, PAFA, 1924. Work: Fourteen mural decorations. "History of the U.S. Marine Corps." in the US Marine Corps bldg., Philadelphia, PA. Address in 1929, 1515 Arch Street; h. 1646 South 13th Street, Philadelphia, PA.

CARAVIA, THALIA FLORA.
Painter. Exhibited at Annual Exhibition of the National Academy of Design in 1925. Address in 1926, Paterson, NJ.

CARBEE, SCOTT CLIFTON.
Painter. Born Concord, VT, April 26, 1860. Pupil of Hugo Breul in Providence; Bouguereau and Ferrier in Paris, Ma Bohm in Florence. Founder and director, Fine Arts Dept., University of Vermont Summer School, Burlington, VT. Address in 1929, director of Scott Carbee School of Art, Massachusetts Avenue, at Boylson Street; h. Massachusetts Chambers, Boston, MA.

CARDELLI, GEORGIO.
Sculptor and painter. Born in Italy, 1791, in 1816 he came to New York. About 1818 he was commissioned by Trumbull the artist to model busts of himself his wife. He turned his attention to portrait painting and did considerable work in New England. Cardelli worked for some time on the decorations for the Capitol in Washington, DC.

CARDOSO, ANTHONY A.
Painter. Born in Tampa, Fla., Sept. 13, 1930. Study: Univ. of Tampa; Art Inst. of Minn.; U. of Southern Fla. Work: Minn. Mus. o Art, St. Paul; and others. Comn. Sports Authority, Tampa Stadiu office; many others in schools an institutions in Tampa, Florida Exhibitions: Duncan Gallery, NY Paris; Smithsonian Inst; Brussel Int'l.; Accademia Italia Exhib. Terme, Italy; many more. Awards Latham Foundation Int'l Smithsonian XXII Biennial; Prix d Paris Award 1970; Gold medal, Acad Italia Exhib.; etc. Mem.: Florid Arts Council; Tampa Realist Artists; etc. Media: Oil acrylic. Address in 1982, 32C Nassau Street, Tampa, Florida.

CAREW, BERTA.
Painter. Born in Springfield, MA 1878. Pupil of Blashfield, Mowbra and Chase in New York; Carlandi i Rome; Mme. Richarde in Paris Member National Academy Wome Painters and Sculptors. Address i 1926, Care Kidder, Peabody Co., 1 Wall Street, New York City.

CAREY, CONSTANCE BEDDOE.
Painter. Born Birmingham, England Pupil of ASL of NY. Member Plastic C. Address in 1929, 24 South 51st Street, Philadelphia PA.

CAREY, HENRY.
Early to mid-century American "Landscape and Cattle."

CAREY, PEYTON.
At the Exhibition of Earl Engraving in America, held at th Museum of Fine Arts, Boston, 1904 a seal of the University of Georgi was shown. A note says that thi seal was designed and cut by "Mr Peyton Carey, a graduate of 1810."

CAREY, ROSALIE MACGILL.
Painter and engraver. Born i Baltimore, MD, June 8, 1898. Pupi of C. Y. Turner, H. McCarter, H Breckenridge, Friez, F. Leger Ozenfant, and Andre L'hote Member: Balto., WCC; S. Indp. A of NY, and of Balto. Address i 1929, Riderwood, Baltimore, MD.

CARIANI, VERALDO J.
Painter. Born in Italy in 189] Pupil of National Academy c Design, and Art Students League o

140

New York. Address in 1926, 148 Bemis Place, Springfield, MA.

ARIATA, GIOVANNI.
Sculptor. Born in Rome in 1865, he lived for some years in New York and died there in 1917. He made the bronze medalion presented to Gen'l Joffre.

ARIO, MICHAEL.
The American Weekly Mercury, Philadelphia, July 8-15, 1736, advertises the arrival from London of "Michael Cario, Jeweller." After detailing his various wares, in the form of rings, button for sleeves, snuff boxes, etc., he adds the following: "N.B. The said Michael Cario buys all sorts of old Diamonds, or any other Stones, and performs all sorts of Engraving Work, either in Gold or Silver."

ARIOLA, ROBERT J.
Painter and sculptor. Born in Brooklyn, NY, March 28, 1927. Study: Pratt Inst. Art School; Pratt Graphic Ctr. Work: Fordham Univ.; Topeka Public Library; and various church, school and private collections. Comn.: St. Gabriel's Church, Oakridge, NJ; Walker Mem. Baptist Church, Bronx, NY; Mt. St. Mary Cemetary, Queens, NY. Exhibitions: Corcoran Gal.; PA Acad.; NAD; Boston Museum; Silvermine, Guild; others. Awards: John F. Kennedy Cultural Ctr. Awd.; Grumbacher Award; Silvermine Guild; etc. Mem.: Prof. Artists Guild; Cath. Fine Arts Society (honorary). Media: Painting - acrylic; sculpture - electric arc and gas welded metals. Address in 1982, Merrick, NY.

ARL, KATHARINE AUGUSTA.
Artist. Born in New Orleans. Studied art under Bouguereau and Gustave Courtois, Paris. Painted portrait of Empress Dowager of China; also "At the Mirror," "Cupid and Psyche," "Iris", etc. Member: Societe Nationale des Beaux Arts, Paris; Internation Society Women Painters, London. Member International Jury of Fine Arts, International Jury of Applied Arts, St. Louis Expn., 1904. Orders of Double Dragon and Manchu Flaming Pearl, China, etc. Died in 1938.

CARLES, ARTHUR BEECHER.
Painter. Born 1882. Member: Fellowship PAFA. Awards: Harris bronze medal ($300), AIC 1913; silver medal, P.-P. Exp., San F., 1915; Lippincott prize, PAFA, 1917; Stotesbury prize, PAFA 1919; Logan medal and prize, $1,500, AIC, 1928. Work: "An Actress as Cleopatra," Pennsylvania Academy of the Fine Arts, and at MMA. Died June 18, 1952.

CARLES, SARAH.
Painter. Exhibited at Penna. Academy of Fine Arts, Philadelphia, 1924. Address in 1926, 2007 Girard Avenue, Philadelphia, PA.

CARLETON, CLIFFORD.
Illustrator. Born Brooklyn, NY 1867. Pupil of Arts Students League of New York under Mowbray. Member Society of Illustrators 1901. Illustrated: "Pembroke," by Julian Ralph; "Their Wedding Journey," by Howells. Address in 1926, 52 West 94th Street, New York, NY. Died in 1946.

CARLIN, JOHN.
Born June 15, 1813 in Philadelphia. A deaf mute, graduate of the Penna. Institution for the Deaf and Dumb, 1825. Studied drawing under J. R. Smith and portrait painting under John Neagle; went to London, 1838, and made studies from the antiques in the British Museum; afterwards became a pupil of Paul Delaroche in Paris; returned to America, 1814, taking up his permanent residence in New York, and devoting himself to miniature painting for many years until interfered with by the progess of photography. After that his attention was turned to landscape and genre subjects, and the painting of portraits in oil. Loan Ex. Philadelphia, 1887. Died April 23, 1891 in NYC.

CARLISLE, MARY HELEN.
Painter. Born in Grahamstown, South Africa. Member National Academy of Painters and Sculptors. Award: McMillin prize, National Academy of Women Painters and Sculptors, 1914. Address in 1926, 24 West 40th Street, New York, NY. Died March 17, 1925 in NYC.

CARLSEN, DINES.
Born in New York, NY 1901. Pupil of Emil Carlsen. Award: Third Hallgarten prize, National Academy of Design, 1919. Elected an Associate Member of National Academy. Work: "The Brass Kettle," Corcoran Gallery of Art, Washington DC. Address in 1926, 43 East 50th Street, New York, NY. Died in 1966.

CARLSEN, EMIL.
Painter. Born in Copenhagen, Denmark, 1853; came to United States in 1872. Elected Associate Member of National Academy, 1904; Academician, 1906. Work: "The Open Sea" and "Still Life," Metropolitan Museum, New York; "Moonlight on the Kattegat," Albright Art Gallery, Buffalo; "Morning," Rhode Island School of Design, Providence; "The South Stand," National Gallery, Washington; "The Lazy Sea," Brooklyn Institute Museum; "Summer Clouds," Pennsylvania Academy of the Fine Arts, Philadelphia; "Moonlight on a Calm Sea," Corcoran Gallery of Art, Washington, DC. Died Jan. 2, 1932. Address in 1926, 43 East 59th Street, New York, NY.

CARLSEN, FLORA BELLE.
Painter and sculptor. Born in Cleveland, OH, March 7, 1878. Pupil of F. C. Jones; Du Bois; Matzen; Solon Borglum; Lentelli. Member: NA Women PS. Address in 1929, 300 East 163rd Street, NYC.

CARLSEN, JOHN H.
Painter and etcher. Born Arendal, Norway, 1875. Member: Palette and Chisel Club; Chicago Society of Artists. Address in 1926, 5230 West Congress Street, Chicago, IL.

CARLSON, CHARLES.
Painter. Born Eskilstuna, Sweden, Jan. 16, 1866. Self-taught. Member: Salons Am.; Scandinavian Am. A. Address in 1929, 606 Carlton Avenue, Brooklyn, NY.

CARLSON, EDWARD W.
Painter. Born Chicago, May 4, 1883. Pupil of AIC. Member: Chicago SA; Hoosier Salon; Swedish Amer. AA. Awards: Prize Hoosier Salon, Chicago, 1928; prize, Swedish American Art Association, Chicago, 1929. Address in 1929, 7413 Evans Avenue, Chicago, IL.

CARLSON, JEAN.
Illlustrator. Born in Burlington, Vermont, in 1952. She attended the University of Vermont and RISD. In 1975 she won third place in the ! of I Annual Student Scholarhsip Competition and has won various awards at New England Art Shows. She is presently teaching art at South Burlington High School in Vermont.

CARLSON, JOHN FABIAN.
Landscape painter, and teacher. Born in Sweden, 1875. Member: ANA 1911; NA 1925; NY WCC; AWCS; Salma. C.; Wash. WCC; Conn. AFA; PS Gal. Assoc.; NAC; Fellowship PAFA. Awards: Vezin and Isidor prizes, Salma. C., 1912; silver medal, Wash. SA, 1913, silver medal, P.-P. Exp., San F., 1915; Carnegie prize, NAD, 1918; Shaw water color prize, 1923, and Isidor prize, Salma. C. 1925; Ranger Fund purchase prize, NAD, 1923. Work: "Woods in Winter," Corcoran Gallery, Washington, DC; "Woodland Response," Toledo Mus.; "Passing Winter," Oberlin Col., Oberlin, O.; "Morning Mists," Brooks Mem. Gal., Memphis, TN; "Autumn Beeches," Public Art Gal., Dallas, Texas; "Winter Dream Days," Art Assoc. Lincoln Neb.; "Winter Rigor," Toledo Club, Toledo, O.; "Forest Pool," Fort Worth Art Assoc.; "Winter Beeches," Randolph Macon Women's College, Lynchburg, VA. Author of "Elem. Principles of Landscape Painting." Died in 1945.

CARLSON, MARGARET GODDARD.
Painter. Born Plainsfield, NJ 1882. Member: National Academy of Women Painters and Sculptors. Address in 1926, Woodstock, NY.

CARLSON, MARGARET MITCHELL.
Illustrator. Born Deming, WA 1892. Address in 1926, 39 Throckmorton Avenue, Mill Valley CA.

142

CARLTON, HARRY.
Painter. Born Brooklyn, June 9,
1895. Pupil of ASL of NY. Member:
Scandinavian Am. A.; Salons Am.
Address in 1929, 62 Washington
Square, New York, NY; h. 606
Carlton Avenue, Brooklyn, NY.

CARMEN, EVA L.
Miniature painter. Member: PA S.
Min. P.; NA Women PS. Address in
1929, 939 Eighth Avenue, NYC.

CARMICHAEL, DONALD RAY.
Painter. Born Elnora, Indiana,
Dec. 26, 1922. Study: Herron Art
Inst.; Univ. of TN; with John
Taylor, David Friedenthal, NY; with
Edwin Fulwider, Ford Times, Garo
Antreasian, New Mexico. Work:
Cheekwood Fine Arts Ctr.,
Nashville; Enjay Chemical, New
Jersey; Dyersburg Public Library,
TN; and other public and private
coll. Comn.: Numerous in Jackson,
TN. Exhibitions: Lynn Kottler
Gal., NYC; 23rd Grand Prize Int'l.,
Deauville, France, and Palace of
Fine Arts, Rome; Water Color USA,
Springfield, Art Mus.; etc.
Awards: Hoosier Salon; Enjay
Chemical National, purchase award;
TN Arts Commission, purchase award.
Mem.: Artists Equity Assn.; Tenn.,
Watercolorist; So. WC Soc; Tenn. Wc
Soc. Media: Watercolor, oil.
Address in 1982, Tarble Art Ctr.,
Eastern IL Univ., Charleston, IL.

ARMIENCKE, JOHN HERMANN.
Painter. Born in Germany, Feb. 9,
1810. He came to America in 1848
and settled in Brooklyn. He was an
early member of the Brooklyn
Academy and of the Artists' Fund
Society of New York. Yale owns
"Poughkeepsie Iron Works." Belongs
to the Hudson River School of
Painting. Died in 1867.

ARNELL, ALTHEA J.
Painter and illustrator. Member of
the Plastic Club, Philadelphia.
Address in 1926, 1907 North 7th
Street, Philadelphia, PA.

ARNELL, JAMES L.
Painter. Member of the Society of
Independent Artists. Address in
1926, 80 Columbia Heights,
Brooklyn, NY.

CARPENTER, A. M.
Painter, craftsman, and teacher.
Born Jan. 4, 1887. Pupil of D. C.
Smith. Member: Western AA; College
AA. Work: "Judean Hills and Mount
Hermon," First Baptist Church,
Abilene, Texas. Address in 1929,
Fine Arts Bldg., Simmons
University, Abilene, Texas.

CARPENTER, B.
Carpenter was a line-engraver of
landscapes and buildings,
apparently working in Boston in
1855.

CARPENTER, BERNARD V.
Painter and teacher. Born Foxboro,
MA. Studied in Europe. Pupil of MA
Normal Art School, Boston. Member:
Buffalo SA. Head of Dept. of
Design, School of Fine Arts,
Buffalo Fine Arts Academy. Address
in 1929, The Algon, 76 Johnson
Park, Buffalo, NY; summer,
Nantucket, MA. Died in 1936.

CARPENTER, ELLEN MARIA.
Born Nov. 23, 1836 in Killingly,
CT. She visited Europe and studied
in Paris under Lefebve and Fleury.
Among her works are "The Yosemite
Valley" and numberous portraits.
Died 1909.

CARPENTER, FLETCHER H.
Painter and teacher. Born
Providence, RI, June 27, 1879.
Pupil of Ernest Major. Graduate of
MA Art School, Boston. Member:
Rochester AC. Address in 1929, 97
Middlesex Road, Rochester, NY.

CARPENTER, FRANCIS BICKNELL.
Painter. Born in Homer, NY, Aug.
6, 1830. In 1844 he became a pupil
of Sanford Thayer at Syracuse, NY.
In 1851 he removed to New York City
and painted portraits of many
prominent people: Lincoln,
Fillmore, Greeley, Asa Packer,
Lieut. Gov. Woodford, Ezra Cornell,
Geo. Wm. Curtis, James Russel
Lowell, Lewis Gass and many others.
His most celebrated work, "The
Emancipation Proclamation," was
exhibited in the large cities in
1864 - 1865 and was later in the
House of Representatives,
Washington, DC. Died May 23, 1900
in NYC.

CARPENTER, FRED GREEN.
Painter. Born in Nashville, TN, 1882. Art study at St. Louis School of Fine Arts and later in Julien Academie, Paris. Pupil of Lucien Simon and Richard Miller. Instructor, drawing and printing, St. Louis School of Fine Arts. Represented in permanent collection of St. Louis City Art Museum, and John Herron Institute, Indianapolis, and Penna. Academy of Fine Arts. Honorable mention par droit, Salon des Artistes Francais, Paris, 1910; silver medal, Panama Exp., San Francisco, 1915. Member: Society Western Artists. Address in 1926, Washington University, St. Louis, MO.

CARPENTER, HELEN K.
Illustrator. Born in Philadelphia, 1881. Pupil of Penna. Academy of Fine Arts under Chase, Breckenridge and Anshutz. Address in 1926, 75 West 55th Street, New York.

CARPENTER, HORACE T.
Pupil of Penna. Academy of Fine Arts, and member of League of American Artists, New York. Portrait painter, and specialized in copies of early American historical pictures.

CARPENTER, MILDRED BAILEY.
Painter and illustrator. Born St. Louis, MO, June 19, 1894. Pupil of St. Louis School of Fine Arts. Member St. Louis AG. Address in 1929, 416 Woodlawn, Webster Groves, MO; summer, Wyalusing, Wis.

CARR, ALICE R.
Sculptor. Born in Roanoke, VA, 1899. Pupil of C. Stirling Calder. Member of Art Students League of New York. Address in 1926, 934 State Street, Santa Barbara, CA.

CARR, GENE.
Illustrator. Born in New York, 1881. Was illustrator on staff of "New York World" and other papers from 1903. Address in 1926, "The World," New York City.

CARR, J. GORDON.
Painter and architect. Born in Batavia, NY, Feb. 20, 1907. Study: MIT, BS architecture; Howard U.; with Gordon Grat, Herb Olsen, and

John Pike. Work: Grand Centra Galleries, NYC; Silvermine Artist Guild; Navy Dept., Wash. DC; an others. Exhibitions: NAD; AWS Knickbocker Artists, NYC; one-ma shows at Grand Central Ar Galleries, NYC; and many others Awards: Salmagundi Club; Alvor mem. award, Hudson Valley Ar Assn.; John Kellam award, N. Engl Artists exhib., Silvermine Guild Mem.: Am. WC Soc.; Silvermin Guild, Hudson Valley Art Assn. Salmagundi Club; CT WC Soc. Media Watercolor. Address in 1976, 4 Beechcroft Road, Greenwich, CT.

CARR, MICHAEL C.
Painter and engraver. Born in Sa Francisco, CA, 1881. Pupil o Wilson Steer, Fred Brown and Gordo Craig. Awarded Slade Scholarship Address in 1926, 711 Missour Avenue, Columbia, MO.

CARRIGAN, WILLIAM L.
Painter. Born San Francisco, CA. 1868. Pupil of Emil Carlsen Address in 1926, Falls Village, CT Died 1939.

CARROLL, HARRIET I.
Painter and teacher. Born Erie PA, 1872. Pupil of Birge Harrison John Carlson, Hugh Breckenridge; N School of Applied Design for Women Member: Erie AC; AFA. Address i 1929, 401 Peach Street, Erie, PA.

CARROLL, JOHN WESLEY.
Painter. Born Wichita, Kansas August 14, 1892. Pupil of Fran Duveneck. Taught at ASL, an Detroit Society of Arts and Crafts Award: Harris silver medal an prize ($500), AIC, 1927 Guggenheim Fellow. Work "Agatha," Pennsylvania Academy o the Fine Arts; "Lady in Blue, Harrison Gallery, Los Angele Museum. Address in 1929 Woodstock, NY. Died in 1959.

CARROTHERS, GRACE NEVILLE.
Painter. Born: Abington, Indiana Studied: with John Carlson Anthony Thieme. Awards: Oklahom State Exhib., 1938. Collections New York Public Library; Gibbes Ar Gallery, Charleston, Sout Carolina; Nat'l Gallery of Art British Museum; Library o

144

Congress; Royal Ontario Museum, Toronto; Bibliotheque Nationale, Paris, France; Philbrook Art Center.

ARRUTHERS, ROY.
Illustrator. Born in South Africa in 1938. He studied art there for many years at Port Elizabeth Technical College. Beginning his career in London with an illustration for Woman's Mirror in 1966, he has since had illustrations published in Redbook, Ladies Home Journal, New York, Playboy and Oui. His works are in the collections of the Ponce Museum and the Galeria de las Americas in Puerto Rico.

ARRY, MARION KATHERINE.
Painter and lithographer. Born Newport, RI, Jan. 31, 1905. Pupil of John R. Frazier. Member: Newport AA. Work: "The Constellation," Museum of the Rhode Island School of Design, Providence. Address in 1929, Art Association of Newport, Bellevue Avenue; h. 12 Friendship Street, Newport, RI.

ARSON, C. W.
This man was a line-engraver of maps and vignettes, located in Albany, NY, in 1843.

ARSON, FRANK.
Painter. Born Waltham, MA, Sept. 8, 1881. Pupil of MA Normal Art School; Fenway School; ASL of. NY. Member: Copley S.; Providence WCC; Provincetown AA; Boston AC; Berkeley Lg. of FA. Award: First Schneinder Prize, Boston Art Club, 1924. Work: "Cedar and Palmettos," Boston Art Club; "Provincetown," Berkeley Lg. of FA; "Arboretum," John Vanderpoel Art Association, Chicago. Director, Provincetown School of Art. Address in 1929, 168 Dartmouth Street, Boston, MA; summer, "Anchorite," 11 Conwell Street, Provincetown, MA., winter, Hamilton, Bermuda.

ARSPECKEN, GEORGE LOUIS.
Painter. Born in Pittsburgh, PA, July 27, 1884. Studied at Carnegie Institute, and abroad. Awarded first prize in 1902 at Worcester

Art Museum. He died July 15, 1905 in Burlington, IA.

CARTER, A. HELENE.
Illustrator. Born Toronto, Canada in 1887. Member: GFLA; SI Illustrated, "Three of Salu," "The Little Misogynists." Address in 1929, 112 West 11th Street, New York, NY. Died in 1960.

CARTER, CHARLES MILTON.
Painter, writer, and teacher. Born North Brookfield, MA, Dec. 9, 1853. Pupil of MA Normal Art School in Boston. Studied in European schools. Member: Boston AC; Denver AC; Ex-Director of Art Public Schools of Denver; former State Supervisor of Drawing for MA; Hon. Pres., US Section, International Congress for the Teaching of Drawing, Paris Exp., 1900; International Jury of Awards, Dept. of Education, St. Louis Exp., 1903; delegate, Dept. of Interior to Art Congress, London, 1908. Author of "Some European Art Schools;" "Arts, Denver Public Schools." Died in 1929.

CARTER, CLARENCE HOLBROOK.
Painter. Born Portsmouth, OH, March 26, 1904. Pupil of Henry G. Keller, William J. Eastman, Paul B. Travis, Hans Hoffman. Member: Cleveland Art Center. Awards: Third prize for portrait, Ninth annual exhibition of work by Cleveland artists and craftsmen, Cleveland Museum of Art, 1927; 1st prize for water color, 3rd prize for figure composition, Cleveland Museum of Art, 1928. Work: "The Patient Cow," water color, and "A Women of the Sabines," oil, Cleveland Museum of Art; water color, "Sommer Bros. Stoves and Hardware," Brooklyn Institute of Arts and Sciences, Brooklyn, NY.

CARTER, DENNIS MALONE.
Born in Ireland, 1827. He was accompanied by his parents to America in 1839. He painted portraits and historical pictures. He settled in New York City and was one of the original members of the Artists's Fund Society, founded in 1859. He painted "Washington's Reception" (to Alex. Hamilton after his marriage to the daughter of

Gen'l Schuyler) and numerous portraits. Died July 6, 1881 in NYC.

CARTER, MARY MELN.
(Mrs. James Newman Carter.) Miniature painter, and craftsman. Born Philadelphia, Aug. 16, 1864. Pupil of Carl Weber and C. Faber Fellows. Member: Plastic C.; Phila. Alliance; AFA. Address in 1929, "Westover," Chadds Ford, Del. Co., PA; 1832 Spruce Street, Philadelphia, PA.

CARTER, PRUETT A.
Illustrator. Born in Lexington, Missouri, in 1891. He was reared on an Indian reservation until his family moved to California where he attended the Los Angeles Art School. His first job was with the NY American and he later worked at the Atlanta Georgian. Moving closer to his chosen field, he became art editor for Good Housekeeping where he gave himself his first magazine illustration assignment. He moved to California in 1930, mailing his finished pieces to such NY publications as Woman's Home Companion, Ladies Home Journal and McCall's. His tasteful illustrations showed his particular understanding of women, whom he portrayed as gentle and elegant without pretension. Greatly respected by his students, he taught at the GCSA in New York and Chouinard Art Institute in Los Angeles. Died in 1955.

CARTOTTO, ERCOLE.
Painter and teacher. Born Valle Mosso, Piemonte, Italy, Jan. 26, 1889. Pupil of Bosley, Paxton, Benson, Tarbell, Hale. Member: Alumni, School of the Museum of Fine Arts, Boston; Florida Soc. A. and S.; AFA. Awards: Second Hallgarten prize, NAD, 1919; Jones prize, Balto. WCC, 1924. Work: "Mater Divina Gratia," The Vatican; "Portrait of Dr. H. C. Jones," Johns Hopkins University, Baltimore, MD; "beatrice," "Portrait of Wm. A. Burnet," and "Harmony in Blue and Rose," Amherst, (MA), Art Gallery; "Mary Catherine" and "Portrait of Marion Ryder," MMA New York; "Profile," San Diego Art Gallery; "Reveries,"

Cleveland Museum of Art; "Portrai of President Calvin Coolidge, "Portrait of Judge William H Moore," "Portrait of Prof. Joh Mason Tyler," Amherst College "Portrait of Dr. H. Hitchcock, Alpha Delta Phi, Amherst MA "Portrait of Attorney General Jot G. Sargent" and "Portrait o Justice Harlan F. F. Stone, Department of Justice, Washington DC; "Portrait of President Calvi Coolidge," Phi Gamma Delta Clut New York; "Portrait of C. N Pratt," Pratt Institute, Brooklyn "Portrait of Dean Frederick J. F Woodbridge," Columbia University New York. Died Oct. 3, 1946.

CARTWRIGHT, ISABEL BRANSON.
Painter. Born Coatesville, PA Sept. 4, 1885. Pupil c Daingerfield, Henry B. Snell, am Frank Brangwyn. Member: Phila Alliance; Plastic C.; NA Women PS AFA. Awards: European Fellowshi from Philadelphia School of Desigr 1906; Phila. AC Gold Medal fc water color, 1906; hon. mentior Buffalo SA, 1920; hon. mentior Plastic C., Phila.; 1921; Max Smith prize, PAFA, 1923; firs prize ($1,500), cotton-field scene San Antonio AL, competitiv exhibition, 1928; fourth pri. ($1,750), wild flowers, San Antoni AL, competitive exh., 192 Represented in permanent collecti of Philadelphia School of Desi Alumnae Association. Address 1929, The Studios, 2107 Walnu Street, Philadelphia, PA.

CARUGATI, ERALDO.
Illustrator. Born in Milan, Ital in 1921. He was educated at ti Scuola Superiore D'arti Applica for four years and began his care in Italy in 1948, producing ma posters until 1970. He illustrate for the Enciclopedia dei Ragazzi 1965 and in the United States h done work for Playboy, Oui, Skept and Psychology Today. His wor are in the collection of tl Oklahoma Historical Society.

CASARIN, ALEXANDER.
Painter and sculptor. Born Mexico and educated in Franc Studied with Messonier. Served Franco-Prussian War. Beca

interested in sculpture and came to the United States. Specialty was portrait busts. Died May 26, 1907 in NYC.

ASE, ELIZABETH.
Painter, illustrator, teacher and designer. Born Philadelphia, Sept. 29, 1867. Pupil of Weir, Metcalf, Brush, Low, Chase. Member: C. L. Wolfe AC. In charge of fashion department, Gatchel and Manning; for 5 years fashion artist on "Women's Wear." Address in 1929, 330 West 15th Street, New York, NY.

ASEAU, CHARLES HENRY.
Painter, and illustrator. Born Boston, MA, 1880. Pupil of Boston Museum School of Fine Arts; Denman Ross. Address in 1929, 133 East 34th Street, New York, NY.

ASELLAS, FERNANDO.
Sculptor. Born 1842 in Valencia, Spain. Came to US in 1876. He designed a statue of Columbus and other decorations for the St. Louis Exposition. He was President of the American Sculptor Society. Died Feb. 12, 1925 in NYC.

ASER, ETTORE.
Painter and etcher in Venice, 1880. Pupil of de Maria in Venice, he went to Boston, MA, in 1908. Exhibited Penna. Academy of Fine Arts, 1924. Address in 1926, 1931 Broadway, New York, NY. Died in 1944.

ASEY, F. DeSALES.
Illustrator. Member Society of Illustrators. Address in 1926, Care of Life Publishing Co., 598 Madison Avenue, New York, NY.

ASEY, JOHN J.
Illustrator and painter. Born in San Francisco, 1878. Pupil of Tarbell and Benson in Boston; Laurens, Julien and Lazar in Paris. Address in 1926, 278 West 11th Street, New York, NY.

ASEY, L. W.
Painter. Member Society of Washington Artists. Address in 1926, Stoneleigh Court, Washington, DC.

CASH, HAROLD CHENEY.
Sculptor. Born Chattanooga, TN, Sept. 26, 1895. Pupil of Beaux Arts Inst. of Design, New York. Address in 1929, 6 Rue Aumont Thieville, Paris XVII, France.

CASILAER, JOHN W.
Engraver and painter. Born June 25, 1811 in NY. At the age of 15 apprenticed to the engraver Peter Maverick, and after a time he became an excellent line engraver; his large plate of "A Sibyl," after the painting by Daniel Huntington, was an admirable example of pure line work. Having studied banknote engraving under Maverick and A.B. Durand, he was engaged in that business for some yrs., and about 1854 he became a member of the banknote engraving firm of Carpenter, Casilaer and Co., of NY. Studied painting in Europe in 1840, and by 1857, Casilaer had become a landscape painter of reputation. He was an Associate of the National Academy in 1835, and a full Academician in 1851. The Metropolitan Museum owned his "View of the Catskills," painted 1891; and the Corcoran Gallery of Washington, DC owned his painting of Lake George. Member of the Hudson River School of Painting. Died Aug. 17, 1893 in Saratoga, NY.

CASON, MERRILL.
Illustrator. Born in Marshall, Texas, in 1929. He worked for 15 years doing display, television, graphic design and illustration in Oklahoma City. Presently a free-lance illustrator in NY, he has taught in a number of schools and has had One-Man Shows in Texas, Oklahoma and Missouri. His Artwork has been selected to hang in several S of I Annual Exhibitions.

CASSATT, MARY.
Figure painter and etcher. Born 1845 in Pittsburgh, PA. Pupil of PAFA. Elected Associate of NAD, 1910; Legion of Honor, 1904. Miss Cassatt was associated with the modern French School of Monet, Renoir, Pissario and Degas. She has exhibited in the Paris Salon after 1872; her paintings are from child life, many of her groups being "Mother and Baby." Her work

147

is represented in the principal American Museums. Died June 14, 1926 in Paris, France.

CASSELL, JOHN HARMON.
Cartoonist. Born in Nebraska City, Neb., 1873. Pupil of AIC. Member: SI, 1905; Salma. C.; GFLA. Address in 1929, "Evening World," Park Row; h. 2 West 67th Street, New York, NY.; Silvermine, CT. Died c. 1960.

CASSIDY, I. D. GERALD.
Painter and illustrator. Born 1879 in Cincinnati, OH. Pupil of Cincinnati Academy; National Academy of Design of New York. Work: Decorations on Indian Arts Building, San Diego, CA; decorations "Last of the Indians," Hotel Gramatan, Bronxville, NY; "Reflections," Freer Collection, Washington, DC. Address in 1926, 541 El Canimo del Canon, Santa Fe, NM. Died in 1934.

CASSIDY, LAURA E.
Painter. Member: Cincinnati Woman's AC; Calif. WCS. Address in 1929, 6426 Desmond Avenue, Madisonville, OH.

CASTANIS, MURIEL.
(Julia Brunner). Sculptor. Born in Sept. 26, 1926. Self-taught. Exhibitions: Women Artists at SOHO, New York City; "Feminine Perceptions," Buffalo State University, NY; "Unmanly Art," Suffolk Museum; Portland Museum of Art, Maine. Collections: Andrew Dickson White Museum, NY; Joe and Emily Lowe Museum, Florida. Media: Cloth and resins. Address in 1980, 444 Sixth Ave., New York, NY.

CASTANO, GIOVANNI.
Painter and sculptor. Born Italy, October 2, 1896. Pupil of School of the Boston Museum of Fine Arts; Philip L. Hale, Lesley P. Thompson, Huger Elliot, F. M. Lamb, Henry James. Member: Soc. AC, Brockton; Boston AC; Cincinnati AC. Awards: Hon. mention, PAFA, 1918; hon. mention, Springfield AA, 1926. Work includes: "Threataning, Springfield AA. Address in 1929, Highland and Dorchester Aves.; h. 293 Dorchester Ave.; Cincinnati, OH.

CASTELLO, EUGENE.
Painter. Born in Philadelphia, PA 1851. Pupil of Penna. Academy o. the Fine Arts, under Eakins Represented in Historical Societ' of PA; University of PA Correspondent, American Art News The Studio, London.

CASTELLON, FEDERICO.
Painter and printmaker. Born i 1914 in Almeria, Spain, and came t the US in 1921. Self-taught Awarded a fellowship from th Ministry of State of the Spanis Republic. Participated in th Exhibition of Spanish Artists including Picasso, Gris, and Miro held at the Cite de Universitaire Paris, 1935. Won numerous award including two Guggenhei Fellowships; the Nat'l Inst. o Arts and Letters Grant an membership; First prize from th Lib. of Congress; and Membership i the Nat'l Acad. More than fort one-man shows work is in th permanent collections of most majo American museums. A retrospectiv of his prints was held at AAA i 1978. Died in 1971.

CASTERTON, EDA NEMOEDE.
Minature painter. Born Brillion WI, April 14, 1877. Pupil o Virginia Reynolds, Lawton S. Parke and Chicago Academy of Fine Arts Minneapolis School of Fine Arts AIC; Chicago School o Illustration; Ralph Clarkson Students' Hostel, Paris. Member Am., Chicago, and PA S. Min. F Awards: Hon. mention International Art Union, Paris 1907 and 1908; silver medal, P.-F Exp., San F., 1915; bronze medal Sesqui-Centennial Expositior Phila., 1926. Address in 1929 Fine Arts Bldg.; 1915 Berteau Ave. Chicago, Ill.

CASTILEDEN, GEORGE F(REDERICK).
Painter, illustrator, etcher, ar craftsman. Born Canterbury, Kent England, December 4, 1861. Pupi of Sidney Cooper. Member: NOACC SSAL. Work: Mural in Hot Sprim Sanitarium, Coffeeville, Kansa Address in 1929, Andrew Jacks Building, 622 St. Peter Street, N Orleans, LA.

148

CASTLE, MONTAGUE.
Painter. Member: Mural Painters.
Address, 247 West 36th Street, NYC.

CASTRO-CID, ENRIQUE.
Born 1937 in Santiago, Chile. Came
to US after attending University of
Chile. Awarded Guggenheim in 1964.
Exhibited in Santiago; Pan Am.
Union, Wash. DC. (1961); Feigen
galleries in NYC, Chicago, and L.A.
(1964); Carnegie; Inst. of Comtemp
Arts, Wash. DC. In collections of
Guggenheim; MOMA, and in private
collections.

CASWELL, EDWARD C.
Illustrator. Born New York City,
Sept. 12, 1879. Pupil of Francis
C. Jones. Member: GFLA. Works:
Illustrated "Old New York," by
Edith Wharton; "Coasting Down
East," by Ethel Hueston and Edward
C. Caswell; the "Patty" books, by
Carolyn Wells; "Viola Gwyn," by
George Barr McCutcheon; "Spanish
Towns and People" and "Towns and
People of Modern Germany" by Robert
M. McBride; illustrated for Vickery
and Hill publications; illustrated
and decorated "The Corsairs of
France," Norman. Address in 1929,
402 West 22nd Street, New York, NY;
h. Yonkers, NY.

CATALANO, GUISEPPI.
Etcher. Member of Chicago Society
of Etchers. Address in 1926,
Chiesannova, Province of Trapani,
Sicily.

CATLIN, GEORGE.
Painter. Born in Wilkes-Barre, PA.
Catlin was noted for his portraits
of American Indians. He lived and
painted in Louisiana in the late
1840's and early 1850's. His
collection of painting of Indians
was in the United States National
Museum of Washington, DC. Died
Dec. 23, 1872 in Jersey City, NJ.

CATTON, CHARLES.
Painter. Born Dec. 30, 1756 in
London, England. Painter of genre
and still-life. Died April 24,
1819 in New Paltz, NY.

CAULDWELL, LESLIE GIFFEN.
Artist. Born in New York, 1861.
Studied art in Julien Academy,

Paris 1884. Pupil of Boulanger,
Lefebvre, Carolus-Durant. Had
pictures admitted to Paris Salon,
1886 and 1888; also Paris Expn.
1889; Salon, Champs de Mars,
1890-96; also to Society British
Artists, and Royal Academy, London.
Exhibited at Liverpool and Berlin,
and at NAD, and SAA, New York;
kater exhibited his painting in
various American cities and at
World's Fair. Died in 1941.
Specialty, portraits in pastel.
Address in 1926, 58 West 57th
Street, New York.

CAUSICI, ENRICO.
Born in Verona, Italy. Sculptured
the "Washington" for the monument
at Baltimore, and several subjects
for Congress at Washington. He
died in Havana. He modelled an
equestrian statue of Washington at
New York; it was erected in 1826.

CAVACOS, EMMANUEL A.
Sculptor and painter. Born Island
of Kythera, Greece, Feb. 10, 1885.
Pupil of Ephraim Keyser in
Baltimore; Jules Coutan and V.
Peter in Paris. Member: Balt. WCC;
Assoc. des Anciens Eleves de
l'Ecole Nationale des Beaux-Arts de
Paris; Inst. Social de
l'Enseignement. Awards: Rinehart
Paris Scholarship, 1911-1915; hon.
mention, Paris Salon 1913; silver
medal, Int. Exp. Dec. Arts, Paris
1925; "Officier de l'Academie,"
French Gov't, 1927. Works:
"Aspiration," Enoch Pratt Free
Library; "Penseur," Peabody
Institute, Baltimore; "Grief,"
Collection of Queen of Roumania.
Address in 1929, S Rug Laarey,
Paris, France.

CAVANAGH, J. ALBERT.
Painter. Member: Salma. Club.
Address in 1926, 25 East 26th
Street, New York, NY.

CAVERLEY, CHARLES.
Sculptor. Born in Albany, 1833.
Pupil of E. D. Palmer in Albany.
He was elected to the National
Academy in 1871. He is represented
in the Metropolitan Museum of New
York by a bust of Robert Burns. He
died in Essex Falls, NJ in 1914.

149

CAWEIN, KATHRIN.
Etcher. Born: New London, CT, in
1895. Studied: ASL. Awards:
Society of American Graphic
Artists, 1936; Village Art Center,
1944; National Association of Women
Artists, 1947; Pleasantville
Woman's Club, 1949, 1953;
Westchester Museum of Art; St.
Mark's Church, Van Nuys, Calif.

CECERE, ADA RASARIO.
Painter. Born New York City.
Pupil ASL; NAD. Member: Alliance;
AFA. Address in 1929, 412 West 33rd
Street; h. 344 West 28th Street,
New York, NY.

CECERE, GAETANO.
Sculptor. Born New York, NY, Nov.
26, 1894. Pupil of H. A. MacNeil
and Beaux-Arts Institute of Design.
Member: NSS, NY Arch. Lg.; NY
Municipal A. S. Awards; American
Academy in Rome scholarship, 1920;
Helen Foster Barnett prize, NAD,
1924; hon. mention, Chicago Art
Inst., 1927; prize, Garden C. of
Am., 1929. Work: Art in Trades
Club medal for School Art League of
New York; John F. Stevens Monument,
Montana; pediment group, Stambaugh
Auditorium, Youngtown, OH; war
memorials at Plainfield, NJ;
Princeton, NY, and Astoria, LI, NY;
Commemorative medal. Princeton
University.

CERRACCHI, ENRICO FILIBERTO.
Sculptor. Born in Italy, 1880;
came to America in 1900, and
settled at Houston, Texas.
Principal works: Monument to John
A. Wharton, State Capitol, Austin,
Texas; "The American Doughboy" for
Italian Government. Address in
1926, 705 Harold Street, Houston,
Texas.

CERRACCHI, GUISEPPE.
Born July, 1751 in Corsica. An
Italian sculptor, who arrived in
Philadelphia in 1791. He executed
a bust of Washington, and also made
portraits of Jefferson, Clinton,
Hamilton, Jay Benson, and Paul
Jones. His portrait painted in
miniature by Trumbull was in Yale
Museum. On returning to France he
was guillotined for his
conspiracies against Napoleon.

Died Jan. 30, 1802 in Paris,
France.

CERUTTI-SIMMONS, TERESA.
Etcher and writer. Born
Sarigliano, Italy. Pupil of J.
McNeil, Whistler, Will Simmons.
Member: Brooklyn SE. Address in
1929, New Milford, 3, CT.

CHACE, DOROTHEA.
Painter and sculptor. Born
Buffalo, NY, Feb. 3, 1894. Pupil
of the Art School of the Albright
Art Gallery ASL of NY. Instructor
of Art at Bennett School,
Millbrook. Address in 1929, 6 East
15th Street, New York, NY.

CHADEAYNE, ROBERT OSBORNE.
Painter and teacher. Born
Cornwall, Dec. 13, 1897. Pupil of
C. K. Chatterton, George Lux, John
Sloan, George Bridgman. Member:
Columbus AL. Awards: John Lambert
purchase prize, PAFA, 1919; Norman
Wait Harris bronze medal and cash
prize, AIC, 1920; 1st prize,
Columbus AL, 1928, 1929. Work:
"Back Yards," Lambert Collection,
PAFA, Philadelphia, PA. Address in
1929, Columbus Gallery of Fine
Arts, East Broad Street; h. 20
Marshall Ave., Columbus, OH; summer
Cedar Lane, Cornwall, NY.

CHADWICK, ARCH D.
Painter, craftsman, and teacher
Born Ovid, NY, May 18, 1871. Pupil
of Ithaca Conservatory of Music and
Art. Member: AFA. Scenic artist
and designer in theatrical and
motion picture studio productions
Instructor, Scenic Art. Ithaca
Conservatory of Music and
Affiliated Schools. Address in
1929, 945 Cliff Street, Ithaca, NY

CHADWICK, CHARLES WESLEY.
Engraver. Born in
Red-Hook-on-the-Hudson, NY, 1861
Studied wood- engraving under
Frederick Jeungling, William
Miller. Work appeared mostly in
Century Magazine and
Scribner's Magazine; engaged in
finishing and engraving half-ton
plates. Exhibited at Paris Expn.
1900. Awards: Bronze medal
Buffalo Expn., 1901; St. Louis
Expn., 1904; silver medal, Panama
Expn., San Francisco, 1915. Ha

150

Lectured on wood-engraving. Address in 1926, 137 East 150th Street New York. Died in 1948.

CHADWICK, WILLIAM.
Painter. Exhibited at Penna. Academy of Fine Arts, 1924. Address in 1926, Blackhall, Lyme, CT.

CHAFFEE, OLIVER HOLBERT.
Painter. Born in Detroit, MI, 1881. Pupil of Wm. M. Chase, Robt. Henri and Miller. Address in 1926, 141 East 21st Street, New York City. Died in 1944.

CHALFANT, JEFFERSON DAVID.
Painter. Born in PA, 1846. Pupil of Bouguereau and Lefebvre in Paris. Address in 1926, "Ashley," Wilmington, DE. Died in 1931.

HALFIN, PAUL.
Mural painter. Born in New York City, 1874. Awarded Lazarus Scholarship for mural painting, 1905. Address in 1926, 597 Fifth Avenue, New York.

HALMERS, HELEN AUGUSTA.
Painter. Born New York City, March 29, 1880. Pupil of Henry A. Loop, NA.; William J. Whittemore and Irving Wiles. Member: Laguna Beach AA. Work: "Maker of Tales: An Impression of Robert Louis Stevenson," Stevenson Memorial, Saranac Lake, NY. Address in 1929, "Trailsend," Laguna Beach, CA; summer, Camp Running Waters, Bear Lake, CA.

HAMBELLAN, RENE PAUL.
Sculptor and architect. Born in 1893. Studied with Solon Borglum. Collaborated with Solon Borglum on dedication panel, Pershing Stadium, Vincennes, France; and with Grosvenor Atterbury on sculptural panels, Russell Sage Foundation Bldg. New York. Designed John Newbury medal for American Library Association. Address in 1929, Care of Grosvenor Atterbury, 139 East 53rd Street, New York, NY. Died in 1955.

HAMBERLAIN, ARTHUR B.
Painter. Born Kitchner, Ontario, Canada, Jan. 18, 1860. Member of Rochester Art Club. Address in

1926, 16 Gladstone Street, Rochester, NY.

CHAMBERLAIN, JUDITH.
Painter. Born in San Francisco, CA, in 1893. Pupil of Max Weber. Address in 1926, 728 Montgomery Street, San Francisco, CA.

CHAMBERLAIN, NORMAN S(TILES).
Painter and teacher. Born Grand Rapids, MI, March 7, 1887. Pupil of Mathias Alten and Alson Clark. Member: CA PS; Laguna Beach AA. Award: Mrs. Henry Huntington prize, Los Angeles Museum of History, Science and Art, 1923. Work: "Adobe Flores," Los Angeles Museum. Address in 1929, Laguna Beach, CA. Died in 1961.

CHAMBERLAIN, SAMUEL.
Etcher, writer, and teacher. Born Cresco, IA, Oct. 28, 1895. Pupil of Edouard Leon in Paris, Malcolm Osborne in London. Member: Chicago SE. Awards: Hon. mention, Paris Salon, 1925; Medaille de Bronze, Paris Salon, 1928. Author of "Domestic Architecture in Rural France" and "Tudor Homes of England." Address in 1929, Rue Jean Dolent; care of Guaranty Trust Co., 3 rue des Italiens, Paris, France. Died in 1975.

CHAMBERLIN, EDNA W.
Sculptor. Exhibited "The Muff" at the Penna. Academy of Fine Arts Philadelphia, 1925. Address in 1926, Hobart Avenue, Summit, NJ.

CHAMBERLIN, FRANK TOLLES.
Mural painter, sculptor, etcher, and teacher. Born San Francisco, CA March 10, 1873. Pupil of D. W. Tryon in Hartford; George de Forest Brush and George Bridgman at ASL of NY Member: Mural P.; Guild of Bookworkers; NY Arch. Lg., 1913; MacDowell Memorial Assoc.; CA AC; Beaux Arts (hon.); Pasadena FAC; Los Angeles Museum Patrons Assoc.; AFA. Awards: Lazarus Scholarship in mural painting, American Academy in Rome, 1909-1912; Fellowship American Academy in Rome, 1913; Aver prize, NY Arch. Lg. 1914; first prize and commission for mural panel, 1915. Represented in Peabody Inst., Baltimore, New Rochelle (NY) Public Library and

Detroit Art Institute. Instuctor, University of Southern California and Chouinard School of Arts, Los Angeles. Address in 1929, 223 South Catalina Avenue, Pasadena, CA. Died in 1961.

CHAMBERLIN, HELEN.
Illustrator. Born Grand Rapids, MI. Pupil of AIC. Member: Ill. Acad. of FA; South Side AA; Art Institute Alumni Assoc. Specialty, juvenile illustration. Address in 1929, Auditorium Tower, 56 East Congress Street, h. 4640 Lake Park Avenue, Chicago, IL.

CHAMBERS, C. BOSSERON.
Painter, illustrator, and teacher. Born St. Louis, MO, May 1882. Pupil of Louis Schultze at the Berlin Academy; Alois Hrdliezka at the Royal Academy of Vienna. Member: Salma. C.; SI; Alliance. Work: Decoration and altar pieces in St. Ignatius' Church, Chicago; portraits in Missouri Historical Soc., St. Louis, and Osceola Club, St. Augustine, Fla.; illustrated "Quentin Durwood," by Sir Walter Scot (Scribner's).

CHAMBERS, CHARLES EDWARD.
Illustrator. Born in Ottumwa, IN. Pupil of AIC, and ASL of New York. Member: SI, 1912; Salma. C., 1915; GFLA. Award: Shaw prize, Salma. C., 1918. Illustrated for Harper's Magazine. Address in 1926, Waldo Avenue, Riverdale-on-Hudson, NY.

CHAMBERS, HALLIE WORTHINGTON.
Painter. Born Louisville, Oct. 27, 1881. Pupil of A. Margarett Archambault and Hugh Breckenridge. Member: North Shore AA; Louisville AC; Louisville AA. Awards: Prize for still life, Kentucky State Fair, 1921; prizes for landscape, marine and flowers, 1923, and prize for best group of paintings (ivory miniatures), Kentucky State Fair, 1924. Address in 1929, 100 East Main Street; h. "Kenwood Hill," Louisville, KY.

CHAMBERS, R.
Engraver, about 1820-26. His best work is a bust of Thomas Jefferson, in an oak-garlanded circle, heading a facsimle of a letter written by

Jefferson to R. C. Weightman, Mayor of Baltimore dated June 24, 1826.

CHAMBERS, ROBERT WILLIAM.
Painter. Born in Brooklyn, 1865. Student in Julien Academy, Paris, 1886-93. First Exhibited in Salon 1889. Illustrator for Life Truth, Vogue, etc. Address in 1926, 4. East 83d Street, New York.

CHAMBERS, WILLIAM.
Illustrator. Born in Chicago in 1940. He graduated from the American Academy of Art in 1961 and later attended Northeastern Illinois Univ. His art career began in 1965 with an educational book illustration; he has since been a frequent contributor to Ballantine Books and Playboy Press. He has produced several posters and his illustrations have been accepted for the S of I Annual Exhibitions and the AG shows o. Chicago.

CHAMPLAIN, DUANE.
Sculptor. Born in Black Mountain NC, in 1889. Student of Ar. Students' League of New York. Address in 1926, 509 West 161s Street, New York.

CHAMPLIN, ADA BELLE.
Painter. Born in St. Louis, MO. Pupil of Art Institute, Chicago and Art Student's League, New York. Address in 1926, 640 Prospec Avenue, Pasadena, CA. Died c. 1954.

CHAMPNEY, BENJAMIN.
Painter. Born Nov. 17, 1817 in Ne. Hampshire. Worked on Litho. with Pendleton firm in Boston. Studie. in Europe then returned to paint landscapes. Member: Boston A (pres.). Died Dec. 11, 1909 i. Woburn, MA.

CHAMPNEY, JAMES WELLS.
Painter. Born in Boston, in 1843. Pupil of Lowell Institute, h. studied wood-engraving. In 186. went to Europe, studying in Pari. and Antwerp. Returned and opene. his studio in Boston. He painte. genre subjects in oil and pastel. Elected an Associate Member o. National Academy in 1882. He die. in 1903.

CHANDLER, GEORGE W.
Etcher. Born in Milwaukee, WI.
Pupil of Julien Academy in Paris.
Work in the Petit-Palais, Paris,
Victoria and Albert Museum, London,
and Congressional Library,
Washington, D.C.

CHANDLER, HELEN C.
Painter, illustratior and etcher.
Born in Wellington, Kansas, in
1881. Pupil of MacMonnies and Birge
Harrison. Member of San Francisco
Art Association. Address in 1926,
543 North Heliotrope Drive, Los
Angeles, CA.

CHANDLER, WINTHROP.
Painter. Born April 6, 1747.
Early American portrait painter,
who studied art in Boston. Several
of his portraits are preserved in
Woodstock and Thompson, CT, and in
Worcester and Petersham, MA. Died
July 29, 1790 in Woodstock, CT.

CHANLER, ROBERT W.
Painter. Born New York City, Feb.
22, 1872. Pupil of Ecole des
Beaux-Arts, Paris. Member: NY
Arch. Lg., 1914 (Assoc.); Mural P.;
S. Indp. A. Work: "Porcupine,"
screen, Metropolitan Museum, NY;
"Giraffes," Luxembourg Museum,
Paris. Address in 1929, 147 East
19th Street, New York, NY. Died in
1930.

CHAPEL, GUY MARTIN.
Painter. Born in Detroit, MI, in
1871. Pupil of Art Institute,
Chicago. Address in 1926, 3919
North Kenneth Avenue, Chicago, IL;
summer, Fox Lake, Ill.

CHAPIN, ARCHIBALD B.
Illustrator and cartoonist. Born
at Mt. Vernon, OH, in 1875.
Address in 1926, 435 Clay Avenue,
Kirkwood, MO.

CHAPIN, CORNELIA VAN AUKEN.
Sculptor. Born: Waterford, CT, in
1893. Studied: in Paris with
Hernandez. Awards: National
Association of Women Artists, 1936;
Paris International, 1937; American
Artists Professional League, 1939;
Pen and Brush Club, 1942-1945;
Meriden, CT, 1951. Collections:
Cathedral St. John the Divine, NY;
Rittenhouse Square, Philadelphia;

International Business Machines;
Dumbarton Oaks, Washington, DC;
Brookgreen Gardens, SC; Corcoran
Gallery of Art; Brooklyn Mus.;
Springfield Art Museum; PAFA;
National Zoological Gardens,
Washington, DC.

CHAPIN, HENRY.
An artist of that name was said to
be painting pictures in America,
flourishing towards the late 18th
or early 19th centuries.

CHAPIN, JAMES ORMSBEE.
Painter. Born in West Orange, NY,
July 9, 1887. Pupil of Antwerp
Royal Academy and Society of
Independent Painters of America.
Address in 1926, 232 West 14th
Street, New York City.

CHAPIN, JOSEPH HAWLEY.
Painter. Born Hartford, Ct., Nov.
9, 1869. Pupil of Charles Noel
Flagg. Member: AI Graphic Arts;
Art Directors C.; Players; SI;
Century Assoc. Art Director,
Charles Scribner's Sons. Died in
1939.

CHAPIN, LUCY GROSVENOR.
Painter and teacher. Born
Syracuse, NY. Pupil of Baschet
Merson, Collin and Prinet in Paris.
Member: AA Syracuse; Nat'l Lg. Am.
Pen Women; AFA. Award: Hiram Gee
Fellowship in painting. Works:
Portraits of Chief Justices Ezekiel
Whitman and Prentiss Mellen, in
State Gallery, Capitol, Augusta,
ME; Portrait of Bishop Eveland,
Dickinson Seminary, Williamsport,
PA. Address in 1929, 410 W. Y.
Foote Bldg.; 947 Lancaster Ave.,
Syracuse, NY. Died in 1939.

CHAPIN, WILLIAM.
Engraver. Born in Phila., PA, Oct.
17, 1802. William Chapin was a
lineal descendant of Deacon Samuel
Chapin, who settled at Springfield,
CT, in 1642. In 1817 William
Chapin was apprenticed to John
Vallance of the engraving firm of
Tanner, Vallance, Keany & Co., of
Philadelphia. He remained with
this firm until 1822, when he began
business for himself as an
engraver. In December of the same
year he made a contract with the
Baltimore publisher, Fielding

Lucas, and in 1824 he accepted a similar engagement with a New York firm. About 1827 Mr. Chapin turned his attention to projecting and engraving maps, and in time he established an extensive map business in New York. Chapin's large map of the United States is said to be the first map engraved upon steel in this country. In 1838 Mr. Chapin became much interested in the education of the blind, and in 1840 he permanently abandoned engraving and map publishing to become principal of institutions for the Blind in Columbus, and later Phila. Work to which he was to devote the reminder of his life. Died Sept. 20, 1888 in Phila., PA.

CHAPLIN , CARLTON THOEDORE.
Painter and illustrator. Born in New London, OH, in 1860. Student of National Academy, Art Students' League of New York and Julien Academy in Paris. Specialty, marines and landscapes. Represented in Brooklyn Institute by "Gloucester Harbor" and at Toledo Museum by "Rocky Coast." He died in 1925.

CHAPLIN, CHRISTINE.
Painter. Born in Bangor, ME, in 1842. Studied in London, Paris. Specialty: painting wild flowers in water color.

CHAPLIN, ELISABETH.
Painter. Born Fontainbleau, France. Member: Societe Nationale des Beaux-Arts. Awards: Gold medal from the Minister of Public Instruction, Rome; traveling scholarship from the French State; silver medal from the City of Florence. Works: "Mia Sorella," Galerie Moderne, Florence; "Demeter and Persephone," owned by the French Government; "Vendange," owned by the City of Paris. Address in 1929, 111 Avenue Victor Hugo, Paris, France; h. Villa Chaplin, San Domenico di Fiesole, Florence, Italy.

CHAPLIN , JAMES.
Painter. Address in 1926, Care of Seattle Fine Arts Society, Seattle, WA.

CHAPLIN, MARGARET.
Painter. Member: National Academy of Women Painters and Sculptors. Address in 1926, 346 West 22d Street, New York, NY.

CHAPMAN, CHARLES SHEPARD.
Painter. Born in Morristown, NY, 1879. Pupil of Chase and W. Appleton Clark. Member: Salma. Club; Academy of National Artists. Elected an Associate Member of the National Academy. Awards: First Shaw prize, Salmagundi Club; Saltus gold medal, National Academy of Design. Work: "In the Deep Woods," Metropolitan Museum, New York. Address in 1929, 156 Sylvan Avenue, Leonia, NJ or Salmagundi Club, NYC. Died in 1962.

CHAPMAN, CONRAD WISE.
Painter. Born 1842 in Rome, Italy. Son and pupil of the artist John Gadsby Chapman. When the Civil War started he joined the Confederate troops and made many pictures of army life. After the war he lived in Virginia where he died. His painting of "Fort Sumter" was in Richmond, with a collection of his paintings of the war. Died in 1910.

CHAPMAN, CYRUS DURAND.
Painter. Born Irvington, NJ, 1856. Pupil of Wilmarth and J. G. Brown in New York; Cormon and Constant in Paris. Address in 1926, 332 Wisconsin Avenue, Washington, DC. Died in 1918.

CHAPMAN, ESTHER I. E. MCCORD.
Painter. Born Richardson CO, Neb. Pupil of Corcoran School of Art. Member: Wash. WCC. Address in 1929, 1600 Q Street, Washington, DC.

CHAPMAN, JOHN GADSBY.
Painter and engraver. Born Dec. 8, 1808 in Alexandria, VA. Little of Mr. Chapman's early life is known other than that he studied art in Italy and in 1836 opened a studio in NY. For sometime thereafter he was largely employed by the Harper Bros. and by others as a designer for book-illustrations, as a wood-engraver, and an etcher after his own designs. He did not engrave upon copper in line or

154

stipple. In 1848 Mr. Chapman returned to Italy and devoted himself entirely to painting, maintaini ing a studio in Rome until his death. Two of Mr. Chapman's sons, Conrad Wise and John Linton Chapman, were painters and artist etchers. A daughter, Mary Chapman, married Count Cerovitch, one time private secretary to Victor Emanuel, King of Italy. John Gadsby Chapman had his studio for several years in Wash., DC, during which period he painted "The Baptism of Pocahontas" for the rontunda of the Capitol. Died Nov. 28, 1889 in Brooklyn, NY.

CHAPMAN, KENNETH MILTON.
Painter. Born Ligonier, IN, 1875. Pupil of Art Institute of Chicago; New York Art Students' League. Work: Three murals, Museum of New Mexico; illustrator of works on Natural Sciences; writer and lecturer on Indian Art. Address in 1926, Museum of New Mexico. Died c. 1968.

CHAPMAN, MINERVA JOSEPHINE.
Painter. Born Altmar, NY, December 6, 1858. Pupil of AIC and Annie Shaw; Robert-Fleury, Bouguereau, Bourtois and Chas. Lazar in Paris. Assoc. Soc. Nat. des Beaux-Arts, Paris, 1906. Member: CA S. Min. P. Awards: Two gold medals, San Diego (CA) Exp., 1915 and 1916; first prize, California Society of Miniature Painters, 1929. Work: "Brittany Woman," miniature owned by the French Government. Address in 1929, Stanford Univerisity, CA; 420 Amherst Street, Palo Alto, CA.

CHAPMAN, W. E.
Painter. Address in 1926, 18 East 90th Street, New York, NY.

CHARD, LOUISE CABLE.
Painter. Member: Society Independent Artists. Address in 1926, 54 Melrose Place, Montclair, NJ.

CHARD, WALTER G(OODMAN).
Sculptor. Born Buffalo, NY, April 20, 1880. Pupil of Charles Grafly; School of the Museum of Fine Arts, Boston; Beaux Arts Institute of Design. Address in 1926, Fenway Studios, Ipswich Street, Boston, MA.

CHARLES, H.
He signed a number of copper-plates published in Philadelphia in 1810. As William Charles did not establish himself in Philadelphia until 1816, he cannot be connected with him.

CHARLES, SAMUEL M.
Miniature painter. Flourished about 1836. Worked: Portrait, "Andrew Jackson" (miniature), signed "S. M. Charles."

CHARLES, WILLIAM.
Engraver. Died in Philadelphia, 1820. Born 1776 in Edinburgh, Scotland. Came to New York in 1801, and in 1807 was established there as an engraver and publisher at "Charles Repository of Arts." The directories of Philadelphia locate him in that city from 1816 to 1820, inclusive; he was in business there as copper-plate engraver, as a bookseller and as a publisher and stationer. Engraved in line-stipple, and in aquatint. Best known for series of caricatures, chiefly of events connected with the War of 1812, or with local politics. These war etchings were issued in 1813, with S. Kennedy. Died in Philadelphia, Aug. 24, 1820.

CHARLOT, JEAN.
Painter. Born: Paris, France, in 1898. Studied: Lycee Condorcet, Paris. Awards: Guggenheim fellowship, 1945-1947; Grinnell College, 1946; St. Mary's College, 1956; Yale University, 1948; Los Angeles County Fair, 1949, Honolulu Acad. of Art. Collections: Museum of Modern Art; Rochester Memorial Art Gallery; Dallas Museum of Fine Arts; San Francisco Museum of Art; Metropolitan Museum of Art; Art Inst. of Chicago; San Diego Fine Arts Society; University of Georgia Fine Arts Building; Arizona State College; Univ. of Hawaii; churches in Hawaii, Notre Dame, Indiana, and Lincoln Park, Michigan; murals, Des Moines Fine Arts Ctr.; St. Catherine's Church, Kauai; Hawaiian Village Hotel, Waikiki; St. Leonard Friary, Centerville, Ohio.

155

CHARMAN, LAURA B.
Sculptor. Member: Fellowship Penna. Academy of Fine Arts. Address in 1926, Magnolia, NJ.

CHARMAN, MONTAGUE.
Painter. Exhibited water colors at Annual Exhibition of Water Colors at PAFA, Philadelphia, 1925. Address in 1926, 615 Walnut Avenue, Syracuse, NY.

CHARMATZ, WILLIAM.
Illustrator. Born in New York City in 1925. He attended the High School of Industrial Art with Henry Wolf and Helmut Krone. Beginning his career in 1946 with pen and ink illustrations for Harper's Bazaar, he has since worked for several magazines and illustrated many books, including The Cat's Whiskers, The Little Duster, Endeerments and Horse Bus Stop.

CHARPENTIER, AUGUSTE.
A French-American portrait painter. Born in Paris, 1815, and died in Besancon in 1880. He was a pupil of Ingres and exhibited in the Paris Salon of 1833. He lived and had his studio for many years in New Orleans, where he painted numerous fine portraits.

CHASE, ADELAIDE COLE.
Portrait painter. Born in Boston, 1868, daughter of the artist J. Foxcroft Cole. Pupil of Tarbell in Boston, and Carolus Duran in Paris. Elected an Associate of the National Academy of Design, 1906. Represented by "The Violinist" in the Boston Museum of Fine Arts. Died in 1944.

CHASE, CLARENCE M(ELVILLE).
Painter. Born Auburn, ME, July 13, 1871. Pupil of George B. Gardner and Carl Gordon Cutler. Member: Copley S.; East Gloucester SA; New Indp. S., Boston. Address in 1929, 268 Savin Hill Avenue, Boston, 25, MA.

CHASE, EDWARD L.
Illustrator. Address in 1926, Woodstock, NY.

CHASE, ELLEN WHEELER.
Painter. Born Faribault, MN. Studied in Buffalo, New York City,

Boston, under Tarbell, and Rene Menard and Lucien Simon in Paris. Member: Buffalo Society of Artists. Address in 1926, The Meyer Studios, 1110 Elmwood Avenue, Buffalo, NY. Died Aug. 1, 1948.

CHASE, ELSIE ROWLAND.
Painter, illustrator, etcher, writer and craftsman. Born Saratoga Springs, NY, Feb. 10, 1863. Pupil of Yale School of Fine Arts. Member: Hartford Art Club; NAC; Society of Independent Artists; New Haven PCC; AFA. Address in 1926, 165 Grove Street, Waterbury, CT. Died in 1937.

CHASE, FRANK SWIFT.
Painter and teacher. Born St. Louis, MO, March 12, 1886. Member: Allied AA; Salma. C.; CT AFA; Woodstock AA. Awards: Richard Greenough Memorial prize, Newport AA, 1921; Peabody prize, Chicago A. Lg., 1922. Work: "Morning Shadows," South Carolina Art Association, Charleston, SC; "Landscape," Mechanics Institute, Rochester, NY. Address in 1929, Woodstock, NY. Died in 1958.

CHASE, HARRY.
Born in Woodstock, VT, 1852, and died 1889. He studied at The Hague, and in Paris. On his return he opened his studio in New York. He was elected an associate of the National Academy in 1883. His principal work: "The Harbor of New York," at the Corcoran Art Gallery; "Low Tide," "Outbound Whaler;" "The North River," and "Bringing the Fish Ashore."

CHASE, JESSIE KALMBACK.
Landscape painter. Born Bailey's Harbor, WI, Nov. 22, 1879. Pupil AIC and Frederick Fursman. Member WI Painters and Sculptors; Madison AG. Award: Hon. mention Milwaukee Art Inst., 1925; Madison Art Guild prize, Milwaukee Art Inst., 1928. Address in 1929, 200 Adams Street, Madison, WI.

CHASE, JOSEPH CUMMINGS.
Portrait painter. Born Kents Hill ME, 1878. Studied art at Pratt Institute, New York; Penna Academy Fine Arts; Academie Julien Paris, under Jean Paul Laurens

156

Exhibited in Paris Salon; won 1st and 2d prizes, Grunwald poster competition, Paris 1904. As war artist, painted at the front 142 portraits of officers of A.E.F., including General Pershing and staff; also many "Doughboys" who had been cited for extraordinary heroism in action, and several officers of the Allies, including Marshal Foch. Address in 1926, 22 West 23d Street, NY. Died in 1965.

CHASE, MARION MONKS.
Painter. Born Boston, MA, in 1874. Pupil of G. L. Noyes. Address in 1926, 144 Brattle Street, Cambridge, MA.

CHASE, SIDNEY MARCH.
Painter, illustrator, and writer. Born Haverhill, MA June 19, 1877. Pupil of Woodbury, Tarbell, Pyle and Pape. Member: Salma. C.; North Shore AA. Address in 1929, 4 Mt. Vernon Street, Haverhill, MA. Died in 1957.

CHASE, SUSAN BROWN.
Painter. Born St. Louis, MO. Pupil H. B. Snell, C. E. Messer, Bertha Perrie, R. E. James, Chester Springs Summer School. Member: Wash. WCC; NA Women PS; S. Wash. A. Address in 1929, care of the Arts C., 2017 I Street, N.W. Wash., DC.

CHASE, WENDALL W.
Painter and etcher. Born in Foxcroft, ME, in 1875. Pupil of Geo. L. Noyes and Hawthorne. Address in 1926, 9-A Park Square, Boston, MA.

CHASE, WILLIAM MERRITT.
Painter. Born Nov. 1, 1849 in Franklin, IN. A pupil of B. F. Hayes, of Indianapolis, he was a local portrait painter for a time, but came East to study under J. O. Eaton and in the schools of the Acad. in NY. In 1872 he went to Munich. His masters there were Alexander Wagner and Karl Von Piloty. Taught at ASL. Mr. Chase was for 10 yrs. pres. of the society of Am. Artists, and was most successful with his work in portraiture; his "Carmencita" and his "James McNeil Whistler" were owned by the Met. Mus. of NY. The Cleveland Mus. owned "Alice in Her

Grandmother's Gown" and his portrait of Miss Dora Wheeler. Elected a Member of the NA in 1890. Died Oct. 25, 1916 in NYC.

CHATTERTON, C. K.
Painter and teacher. Born in Newburgh, NY, Sept. 19, 1880. Study: NY School of Art under W. M. Chase, Rbt. Henri, Luis Mora, Kenneth Hayes. His paintings combine plein-air tradition with forthrightness about homely subject matter, chiefly in Hudson Valley and Maine. Work: Brooklyn Mus.; Nat'l Coll. of FA (Smithsonian Inst.); Sheldon Mus., Omaha, Neb.; Hackley Gal., Muskegan, MI; Canajoharie (NY) Gal.; Taylor Hall Art Gal., Vassar Coll., Poughkeepsie, NY; private collections. One-man shows: Wildenstein Gal., Macbeth Gal., Chapellier Galleries, NYC. Group shows: Carnegie Inst's. Int'l. exhibitions; Corcoran Gal. of Art, Wash. DC; Toledo Mus. of FA; PAFA; Albright Galleries, Buffalo; NAD, NYC; Art Inst. of Chic.; Rhode Island School of Design. Member: Salma. C.; Chicago WCC. Award: Isidor prize, Salma. C., 1913. In 1910, painting "Snow Clad Town" included in first showing of US Art in So. America. In 1926, painting "Clinton Square, Newburgh" was selected for Tri-Nat'l. Exhib. sent abroad under sponsorship of Wildenstein Gallery. Teaching: Artist-in-Residence, Vassar College, 1915; Professor Emeritus of Art, Vassar, retired 1948. Died New Paltz, NY, July 2, 1973.

CHEFFETZ, ASA.
Painter, illustrator, and etcher. Born Buffalo, New York, August 16, 1897. Pupil of Philip Hale, Ivan Olinsky, William Auerbach-Levy. Award: Eyre gold medal, PAFA, 1928. Address in 1929, 484 White Street, Springfield Massachusetts. Died in 1965.

CHENEY, JOHN.
Engraver. Born Oct. 20, 1801 at South Manchester, CT. Line engraver of small heads and book illustrations working as an engraver in Boston in 1829. In 1833 he went to Europe to study art, supporting himself there by

157

engraving for American publishers. Died Aug. 20, 1885 in his home town.

CHENEY, MARY MOULTON.
Painter, designer, and teacher. Born Minneapolis, MN. Graduate of Univ. of Minnesota; School of Boston Mus. of FA. Pupil of Denman W. Ross, George Elmer Browne. Award: Hon. mention, MN State Fair, 1917. Director, Minneapolis School of Art, 1917-1926. Address in 1929, 1912 South Third Avenue, Minneapolis, MN.

CHENEY, RUSSELL.
Painter. Born South Manchester, CT, Oct. 16, 1881. Pupil of Kenyon Cox, Chase, Woodbury, ASL of NY; Laurens in Paris. Member: CT AFA; Colorado Springs AS; Century C. Work: "Skungimaug Morning," Morgan Memorial Museum, Hartford, CT; "Ute Pass," San Francisco Museum of Art; "Colleone," Newark Museum Association. Address in 1929, 22 Forest Street, South Manchester, CT. Died in 1945.

CHENEY, SETH WELLS.
Painter and engraver. Born Nov. 26, 1810 at South Manchester, CT. In 1829 S. W. Cheney joined his brother, John Cheney, in Boston, and with him learned to engrave. He accompanied John Cheney to Europe in 1833, and studied in Paris under Isabey, Delaroche, and other French masters. Seth W. Cheney returned home in 1834, He again went to Europe in 1837 and resumed his art studied in France, Italy and Germany. In 1841 he opened a studio in Boston and began to draw portraits in crayon, and he was first among American artists to effectively work in "black and white." His line-engravings are comparatively few in number. His life was written by Ednah D. Cheney, and published in Boston, 1881. A memorial exhibition of the work of John and Seth Wells Cheney at the Boston Museum in 1893 included 338 engravings, paintings, drawings and two or three objects of sculpture. Died Sept. 10, 1856 in South Manchester, CT.

CHERMAYEFF, IVAN.
Illustrator. Born in London, England, in 1932. Studied at Harvard Univ.; the Inst. of Design in Chicago; BFA Yale Univ., School of Art and Architecture. His many clients have included IBM, Philip Morris USA, Westinghouse Electric Corp., and others. Vice-president of Yale Art Association and a member of the Yale Council Committee on Art and Architecture, Industrial Designers Society of America, Archi. Lg. of NY and the Alliance Graphique Internationale. He is author of Observations on American Architecture published by The Viking Press in 1972.

CHERNEY, MARVIN.
Painter. Born in Baltimore, MD, in 1925. Studied drawing at Maryland Inst. of Art; scholarship, School of Art Studies, NYC. Initially influenced by work of German Expressionists Kokoschka, Kollwitz; also work of Titian, Rembrandt; travelled to France, Italy for five months. Lived and worked in NYC. Painted portraits and still lifes; worked primarily in oil, lithography, painting in oil on paper. Received many prizes and awards. Died in 1967. Represented by Kennedy Galleries, NYC.

CHERRY, EMMA RICHARDSON.
Painter, teacher and lecturer. Born Aurora, IL, Feb. 28, 1859. Pupil of ASL of NY; Chase; Cox; McCarter; Breckenridge; Zanetti Zilla in Venice; Merson, Andre L'Hote, Julien Academy in Paris. Member: ASL of NY; Denver AA; Houston AL; San Antonio AL. Awards: Gold medal, Westerm Art. Assoc., Omaha; landscape prize, SSAL, Birmingham; still life prize, Nashville, TN; portrait prize, Austin, TX. Work: In Elizabet Ney Museum, Austin, TX; Soc. of Civil Engineers Club, New York City; San Antonio Art League; Houston Art Museum; Denver Art Museum. Director, Texas Fine Arts Association. Address in 1929, 608 Fargo Avenue, Houston, Texas; care of American Express, 11 Rue Scribe, Paris, France.

CHERRY, KATHRYN E.
Painter and teacher. Born Quincy, IL in 1880. Pupil of St. Louis Art School, NY Art School, Richard Miller and Hugh Breckenridge; studied abroad. Member: St. Louis AG; Chicago AC; NA Women PS; North Shore AA; Rockport AS; PBC; 8 Women P. of Phila.; Atlan. C. (hon.); Chicago Galleries Assoc.; AFA. Awards: St. Louis A. Lg. ($500), 1919, Hugo Kohler Landscape prize, St. Louis AG, 1920; John Liggett Scott memorial prize, St. Louis AG, 1921; Kansas City Art Institute gold medal, for painting 1922; purchase prize ($350), St. Louis Chamber of Commerce, 1923; hon. mention, Phila. Artists Week Ex., 1923; hon. mention, NA Women PS, 1923; Bixby landscape prize, St. Louis, 1924; hon. mention, NA Women PS, 1927; prize ($200), Chicago Gal. A., 1927. Work: "Inner Harbor," and "Nisbit Hills," St. Louis High Schools; also represented in Soldan High School; Principia Academy, St. Louis; South Eastern Missouri State Teachers College, Cape Girardeau; Laura Davidson Sears Academy of Fine Arts Club, Quincy, IL. Address in 1929, 5504 Delmar Street, St. Louis, MO; summer, East Gloucester, MA.

CHESKIN, L(OUIS).
Painter and teacher. Born Russia, Feb. 17, 1907. Pupil of F. Tkatch; Frederic M. Grant. Member: Ill. AFA; Chicago NJSA. Address in 1929, 25 East Superior Street; h. 3576 Lyndale Street, Chicago, IL.

CHESNEY, LETITIA.
Painter, craftsman, and teacher. Born Louisville, KY, Feb. 14, 1872. Pupil of Natilia Sawyer Bentz, Paul Sawyer. Member: Seattle AI. Work: "Daniel Boone," Historical Society, Kentucky State House, Louisville; "Shawondassee," Queen Anne Hill Branch Library, Seattle, WA. Address in 1929, Winslow, Bainbridge Island, WA.

CHESNEY, MARY.
Painter, craftsman, and teacher. Born Louisville, KY, Jan. 6, 1872. Pupil of Mary Harbough. Award: First prize, North West Independent Salon, 1928. Address in 1929, Winslow, Bainbridge Island, WA.

CHESSE, RALPH.
Painter. Born New Orleans, Jan. 6, 1900. Member: Oakland AA; Modern Gallery Group. Award: Second Anne Bremer prize, San Francisco Art Association, 1928. Address in 1929, 7 Blackstone Ct., San Francisco, CA.

CHICAGO, JUDY.
Painter and writer. Born in Chicago, Illinois in July 20, 1939. Until 1970 she exhibited under the name of Judy Gerowitz. Studied: UCLA and received her MA 1964. She is currently involved in the development of teaching methods for the education of young women in the arts. Exhib.: Jewish Mus., NY, 1966; Whitney Mus. Am. Art, 1970; MMA, 1979. Address in 1980, 1651 B. 18th St., Santa Monica, CA.

CHICHESTER, CECIL.
Painter, illustrator, and teacher. Born New York City, April, 8, 1891. Pupil of Maratta and Birge Harrison. Instructor, Art Students Lg. of NY, and Woodstock School of Landscape Painting. Address in 1929, Woodstock, Ulster Co., NY.

CHILD, EDWIN BURRAGE.
Painter. Born Gouverneur, NY, May 29, 1868. Studied art ASL, New York, of 1891, and was a pupil of John La Farge. Asst. of John La Farge in glass work and mural painting for several years. Exhibited regularly in Society of American Artists, and National Academy of Design, and other important annual exhibitions. Illustrator of many articles in Scribner's and other perodicals and contributor to magazines. Later engaged chiefly in portrait painting. Address in 1926, 42 West 93d Street, New York, NY. Died in 1937.

CHILD, LOUIS.
Portrait painter, working in New York about 1800. His portrait of Micah Hawkins is inscribed on back of canvas, "Retouched from memory by Wm. S. Mount, 1856."

CHILD, THOMAS.
Early American portrait painter, noted as being in Boston in 1688. Died Nov. 10, 1706.

159

CHILDS, BENJAMIN F.
Wood engraver. Born at Cambridge, 1814, and died 1863. In 1850 he became superintendent of engraving for the Tract Society. He engraved the illustrations after drawings by Darley for Irving's "Knickerbocker's History of New York," published by Wiley and Putnam of New York, in 1853.

CHILDS, CEPHAS G.
Engraver. Born in Bucks Co., PA, 1793; died in Philadelphia, 1871. Childs was taught to engrave by Gideon Fairman in Philadelphia. Childs issued his "Views of Philadelphia" in 1826-33, many of these being engraved by himself. After a visit to Europe, he associated himself with the artist Henry Inman, under the firm name of Childs & Inman. This firm, which was in existence from 1831 to 1835, brought P. S. Duval from Europe and placed him at the head of the lithographic department; this added to their general engraving business. Inman drew upon the stone himself, and their deaf and dumb apprentice, Albert Newsam, executed some of his best work for the firm of Childs & Inman, and became the foremost lithographic artist of his day. About 1845 Childs abandoned engraving and interested himself in newspaper work in Philadelphia. Along with Walter Colton he was one of the editors of The Commerical Herald, John R. Walker being the publisher. He was afterward commercial editor of The North American, published by Thomas R. Newbold. Childs was a soldier in the War of 1812.

CHILDS, LILLIAN E.
Miniature painter. Born in Little Silver, NJ. Pupil of William M. Chase in New York and Art Institute of Chicago. Address in 1926, 85 Washington Place, New York City.

CHILLMAN, JAMES JR.
Painter, artist, writer and teacher. Born in Philadelphia, PA, Dec. 24, 1891. Pupil of P.-P. Cret. George Walter Dawson. Member: AIA; Amer. A. of Museums; SSAL; AFA. Award: Fellowship in architecture, American Acad. in Rome, 1919; water color prize, SS Art League, 1926.

Author of articles on architecture in "Journal AIA", "Memories of American Academy in Rome." Address in 1929, Museum of Fine Arts of Houston; h. 2242 Stanmore Drive, River Oaks, Houston, Texas; summer, School of Fine Arts, University of Pennsylvania, Philadelphia, PA.

CHILTON, WILLIAM.
Painter. Born in Washington, DC. Dec. 15, 1856. Pupil of Washington ASL. Member: S. Wash. A.; Wash. WCC; Wash. AC; AFA. Address in 1929, 1961 Biltmore Street, N.W. Washington, DC. Died in 1939.

CHIMES, THOMAS.
Painter. Born in Philadelphia, Pennsylvania, in 1921. Studied at the Art Students League of New York. Taught at the Drexel Institute of Technology in Philadelphia. Exhibitions: Avant Garde Gallery, Bodley Gallery, and The Museum of Modern Art, New York. Work in private collections.

CHISOHN, MARY B.
Painter. Exhibited at National Association of Women Painters and Sculptors, 1924. Address in 1926, 1337 Lexington Avenue, New York.

CHITTENDEN, ALICE BROWN.
Painter and teacher. Born Brockport, NY, Oct. 14, 1860. Pupil of CA School of Fine Arts under Virgil Williams. Member: AFA. Awards: Gold medal for flower painting, San F. Exp. of Art and Industries, 1891; silver medals, Lewis-Clark Exp., Seattle, 1909. Work: Portrait, Rt. Rev. William Ford Nicholls, Bishop of CA, in Episcopal Divinity School, San Francisco; six portraits for CA Society of Pioneers. Instructor of Art, Sarah Dix Hamlin School; member of Faculty, CA School of Fine Arts, San Francisco. Address in 1929, 1351 Sutter Street, San Francisco, CA. Died in 1934.

CHIVERS, HERBERT CHELSEY.
Painter, sculptor, etcher, artist, and writer. Born Windsor, England. Pupil of Luks, Sloan, Robinson, Lever, Young, Preissig and Pennell. Address in 1929, 16 Morningside Avenue, New York, NY.

160

CHORLEY, JOHN.
Line-engraver of portraits and book- illustrations, working in Boston as early as 1818. Upon a well-executed Bible print the name is signed "I. P. Chorley Sc."

CHOUINARD, NELBERT MURPHY.
Painter, and designer. Born Montevideo, MN, Feb 9, 1880. Pupil of Arthur Dow, Ernest Batchelder, Ralph Johonnot, and of Pratt Institute. Member: CA AC; Alliance. Director of the Chouinard School of Art of Los Angeles. Address in 1929, 2606 West Eighth Street, Los Angeles, CA; 1114 Garfield Avenue, South Pasadena, CA. Died in 1969.

CHRISTENSEN, INGEBORG.
Painter, writer, lecturer, and teacher. Born Chicago. Pupil of Pauline Palmer; AIC. Member: Chicago AC; Chicago PS; Alumni AIC. Award: Municipal Art League prize, AIC, 1925. Work: "Pals," John Marshall High School, Chicago. Address in 1929, Studio 21, 4 East Ohio Street; h. 5357 Wayne Ave., Chicago, IL.

CHRISTENSEN, RALPH A.
Painter, craftman, etcher, writer, lecturer, and teacher. Born in Chicago, IL, April 4, 1886. Pupil of Vanderpoel, Ufer, Mucha. Member: Alumni AIC; AFA; CA AC. Address in 1929, Boudeman Bldg., 122 West South Street, h. R. 4 Pomeroy Park; summer, 1133 Reycraft Drive, Kalamazoo, MI. Died in 1961.

CHRISTIE, RUTH VIANCO.
Painter, craftsman, and teacher. Born Rochester, Aug. 23, 1897. Pupil of Mechanics Inst. Member: Rochester AC. Awards: Second Wiltsie water color prize, 1917; first Wiltsie water color prize, 1918. Address in 1929, 74 Harding Road, Rochester, NY.

CHRISTY, HOWARD CHANDLER.
Illustrator and portrait painter. Born in Morgan County, Ohio, 1873. In his youth studied under Chase, NY, ASL. He was employed as an illustrator on Harper's and Scribner's magazines. His reporting on the Spanish-American war from Cuba for the latter publication brought much acclaim. He later devoted his time to painting portraits; among his best known pictures are the portrait of Mrs. William Randolph Hearst of New York, of Secretary of State Hughes, Crown Prince Humbert of Italy, Amelia Earhart, and others. His masterpiece is "Signing of the Constitution," Rotunda, US Capitol. Address in 1926, Hotel des Artistes, West 67th Street, New York City. Died March 3, 1952.

CHRYSSA, VARDEA.
Sculptor and painter. Born: Athens, Greece, in 1933. Studied: Grande Chaumiere, Paris and in California. Collections: Museum of Modern Art; Whitney Museum of American Art; Albright-Knox Art Gallery, Buffalo, NY; and The Solomon R. Guggenheim Museum. Actively exhibiting in major galleries during the 1960's. Living in New York City.

CHUBB, T. Y.
Engraver. About 1860 Chubb was an engraver of portraits in mezzotint and worked for the book publishers.

CHUBBUCK, THOMAS M.
Engraver of portraits and landscapes in line and stipple. He was located in Springfield, MA.

CHURBUCK, LEANDER M.
Painter. BOrn Wareham, MA, Feb. 19, 1861. Pupil of Copley S. and Boston Art Students' Assoc. Member: Copley S. 1905; Brockton AL. Awards: Gold medal, Dallas Exp. 1903; first prize for water colors, Denver Exp. 1909. Work: "On the Cape Ann Shore," "In Old Marblehead," Municipal Gallery, Brockton, MA; copy of L'hermette's "Friend of the Humble," Library, Brockton, MA. Address in 1929, 270 Green Street, Brockton, MA.

CHURCH, ANGELICA SCHUYLER.
Sculptor, and craftsman. Born Scarborough-on-Hudson, NY, April 11, 1878. Pupil of NY School of Applied Design; Alphonse Mucha. Member: Alliance; NYSC. Work: Statue of the Savior, Calvary Church, NY; Mark Twain portrait tablet, at his boyhood home,

161

Hannibal, MO; Seal of Bienville D'Hiberville, LA State Library, New Orleans; four miniature medallions, LA State Museum, New Orleans; "The Rescue," equestrian group, in action, New York City Police Department. Address in 1929, 212 Spring Street, Ossining-on-Hudson, NY.

CHURCH, CHARLES F.
Painter. Member: Chicago SA; GFLA. Represented in the Vanderpoel Art Assoc. Collection, Chicago. Address in 1929, 64 East Lake Street; 9244 South Winchester Ave.; London Guarantee Bldg., Chicago, IL.

CHURCH, FREDERICK EDWIN.
Painter. Born Hartford, CT, May 4, 1826. Landscape painter. Pupil of Thomas Cole at Catskill, where he worked for several years before opening a studio in New York. Was elected a member of the National Academy of Design in 1849. Traveled in South Labrador and the West Indies, and in 1868 made his first trip through Europe, which also extended to Palestine. Received a second-class medal at the Paris Exposition, 1867. His best known work is "The Falls of Niagara," owned by the Corcoran Gallery of Art; also the "Aurora Borealis." Died April 7, 1900 in NYC.

CHURCH, FREDERICK STUART.
Painter. Born 1842, Grand Rapids, MI. Pupil of Chicago Academy of Design, L.E. Wilmarth, Walter Shirlaw, National Academy of Design and Art Students' League of New York. Silver medal, St. Louis Exp., 1904. Painter in oil and water color, illustrator and etcher. Elected to National Academy, 1885. Member: AWCS; New York Etching Club; Society of Illustrators, New York. Studio, New York. Work: "Moonrise," Metropolitan Museum, New York. Hudson River School of Painting. Died Feb. 18, 1923 in NYC.

CHURCHILL, ALFRED VANCE.
Painter, and teacher. Born Oberlin, OH, Aug. 14, 1864. Pupil of Julian Academy in Paris. Member: Union Internationale des

Beaux Arts; College AA; North Shore AA. Dir. Art Dept., Iowa College, 1891-93; Dir. Art Dept. Teachers College, Columbia Univeristy, New York, 1897-1905; lecturer, Johns Hopkins University, Baltimore, 1902-03; University of Chicago, 1914, 1916 and 1917; Professor of the History and Interpretation of Art, Smith College, Northampton, MA, after 1907; Director, Smith College Museum of Art, after 1920; editor, Smith College Art Museum Bulletin. Address in 1929, Smith College Museum of Art; h. 38 Franklin Street, Northampton, MA. Died in 1949.

CHURCHILL, FRANCIS G.
Painter, illustrator and etcher. Born in New Orleans in 1876. Pupil of Cincinnati Academy. Address in 1926, Canal-Commercial Building, New Orleans, LA.

CHURCHILL, LETHA E.
Painter. Address in 1926, 3919 Wyandotte Street, Kansas City, MO.

CHURCHILL, WILLIAM WORCESTER.
Painter. Born in Jamaica Plains, MA, in 1858, and lived in Boston. Pupil of Bonnat in Paris. "Leisure" (Girl dressed in white), signed and dated 1910, in Boston Museum of Fine Arts Collection. Address in 1926, Fenway Studios, Boston, MA. Died Feb. 15, 1926 in Wash., DC.

CHURCHMAN, E. MENDENHALL.
Painter. Born Brooklyn, NY. Pupil of Penna. Academy of Fine Arts, Tarbell and Benson in Boston. Member: Fellowship Penna. Academy of Fine Arts; Plastic Club; Society of Independent Artists. Address in 1926, Union Lane, Brielle, NJ. Died in 1939.

CHWAST, SEYMOUR.
Designer and illustrator. Born Aug. 18, 1931, in NYC. Studied at Cooper Union under Leon Friend. Work: Mus. of Mod. Art, NY; Greengrass Gal., NYC. Exhibitions: The Louvre, Paris, France, 1971; Lincoln Ctr., NYC; Brooklyn Mus.; Art Mus., Amsterdam; throughout Italy. Teaching: Instr. design and illustr., Cooper Union, 1975. Known for his numerous poster

designs as well as animated commercials, book and children's book designs. Received many awards from ADC, AIGA, Cooper Union. Address in 1982, c/o Push Pin Studios, 67 Irving Place, New York, NY.

CIAMPAGLIA, CARLO.
Painter. Born in Italy, March 8, 1891. Pupil of Cooper Union; NAD. Member: Allied AA; Arch. Lg of NY; NS Mural P. Award: American Academy in Rome Scholarship, 1920. Instructor, Cooper Union Art School. Address in 1929, 1193 Broadway, New York, NY. Died in 1875.

CIARDIELLO, JOSEPH G.
Illustrator. Born in Staten Island in 1953, he graduated from PSD in 1974, having illustrated for the Parsons Catalogue while still a student. He has illustrated books, including The Great Houdini and Buffalo Bill, as well as major magazines. He won a National Parks Purchase Prize in 1974 and his work is part of the collection of Mauro Graphics in Staten Island.

CIAVARRA, PIETRO.
Sculptor. Born Philadelphia, PA, June 29, 1891. Pupil of Charles Grafly, Guiseppe Donato, Charles T. Scott, PAFA, Philadelphia School of Industrial Art. Member: Fellowship PAFA; AFA. Represented in Fellowship of the Pensylvania Academy of the Fine Arts and Samuel Fleisher Galleries. Address in 1929, 2036 Rittenhouse Street; h. 440 W. Queen Lane, Germantown, Philadelphia, PA.

CICERI, EUGENE M.
Painter, working in New Orleans about 1850.

CICERO, CARMEN LOUIS.
He was born 1926 in Newark, NJ. Earned B.S. Newark State Col. Studied under Motherwell. Taught at Sarah Lawrence, now at Montclair State Col. Awarded Guggenheim (1957 & 1963); Ford Foundation Purchase Prize, (1965). Exhibited at Newark Museum; Brooklyn Museum; MOMA; Whitney; Art Inst. of Chicago; PAFA; University of Colorado. In collections of Guggenheim; Univeristy of Michigan; MOMA; Art Gallery of Toronto; Worcester Art Museum; and Whitney.

CIMINO, H(ARRY).
Wood engraver, and illustrator. Born in Marion, IN, Jan. 24, 1898. Pupil of AIC; ASL of NY. Illustrated: "Gifts of Fortune," by Tomlinson (Harper); "Sutter's Gold," by Cendrars (Harper); "The King's Henchman," by Millay (Harper). Address in 1929, 2 East 23rd Street; h. 102 East 22nd Street, New York, NY; summer, Falls Village, CT.

CIMIOTTI, GUSTAVE.
Painter. Born New York, Nov. 10, 1875. Pupil of ASL of NY under Mowbray, Cox, J. Alden Weir and Robert Blum; Constant in Paris. Member: Salma. C., 1908; Grand Cent. AG; Montclair AA. Address in 1929, 51 West 10th Street, New York, NY.

CIRINO, ANTONIO.
Painter, craftman, writer, and teacher. Born Serino, Italy, March 23, 1889. Pupil of A. W. Dow. Member: Rockport AA; Providence AC; Springfield AL; North Shore AA; Eastern AA: Salma. C. Award: Prize Springfield Art League, 1926. Author of "Jewelry Making and Design." Address in 1929, 108 Vinton Street, Providence, RI, summer, Granite Street, Rockport, MA.

CITRON, MINNA WRIGHT.
Painter and printmaker. Born Oct. 15, 1896. Studied painting at the Brooklyn Inst. of Arts and Sc. with Benjamin Kopman; commercial art at the NY School for Applied Design of Womens 1925-27; Art Students League with Kenneth Hayes Miller, H. Sternberg, and K. Nicolaides. Exhib.: Solo at Brownwell-Lawbertson Gallery in 1932; "Feminaries," Midtown Cooperative Galleries, 1935. Address in 1982, 145 Fourth Ave., New York, New York.

CLAGHORN, JOSEPH C.
Painter, etcher, and teacher. Born Philadelphia, Sept. 4, 1869. Pupil of Anshutz; PAFA. Member: S. Wash. A; Fellowship PAFA; Landscape

Club of Wash. Instructor in arts and crafts, Central High School, Washington. Address in 1929, Cabin John, MD.

CLAPP, WILLIAM HENRY.
Painter, etcher, and teacher. Born Montreal, Canadain 1879. Pupil of Jean Paul Laurens. Member: Royal Canadian Academy; CA AC; Montreal AC; Oakland AL; Pen and Pencil C., Montreal. Work: Canadian National Gallery; Montreal Art Gallery; Oakland Art Gallery; Montreal Arts Club and in possession of various Provincial Governments of Canada. Director, Oakland Municipal Art Gallery. Address in 1929, Oakland Art Gallery, Civic Auditorium, Oakland, CA. Died in 1954.

CLARK.
As "Clark Sculpt" this man signed three copperplates of buildings in Lancaster, PA. The work was evidently done between 1813 and 1820.

CLARK, ADELE.
Painter. Pupil of D. J. Connah, Kenneth Hayes Miller, Henri and Chase. Member: Richmond Art Club. Work: "Portrait of R. A. Dunlop," Richmond Chamber of Commerce.

CLARK, ALLAN.
Sculptor. Born June 8, 1896 in Missoula, MT. Studied at Puget Sound College. Pupil of Polasek at Art Institute of Chicago; Japanese and Chinese Masters. Member of National Sculpture Society, and Society of Independent Artists. Taught at Beaux-Arts Inst. Traveled in Orient. Painted in Santa Fe, NM. Work: Bronze statue, "The Antelope Dance," marble bust, "Mme. Galli-Curci." In collections of MMA; Honolulu Acad. of Arts; Whitney and Seattle. Address in 1926, 436 West 24th New York. Died in 1950.

CLARK, ALSON SKINNER.
Painter, illustrator, craftman, etcher, and teacher. Born Chicago, March 25, 1876. Pupil of Simon, Cottet, Whistler, Mucha and Merson in Paris; Chase in New York. Member: Paris AAA; Chicago SA; Allied AA; Chicago Cliff Dwellers; Calif. PM; Calif. AA; Laguna Beach

AA. Awards: Bronze medal, St. Louis Exp. 1904; Cahn prize, AIC, 1906; bronze medal, P.-P. Exp., San F., 1915; hon. mention, Los Angeles Museum, 1922; Grand Museum prize, Southwest Museum, Los Angeles, 1923; Huntington prize, Los Angeles Museum, 1924. Work: Municipal commission purchase; "The Coffee House," Art Institute of Chicago; lithographs in Hackley Gallery, Muskegon, MI, Victoria Museum, London; Union League C., and Univerisity C., Chicago; Municipal collection, Watertown, NY; State Library, Sacramento, CA; curtains, New Community Theater, Pasadena; murals, Carthay Circle Theatre, Los Angeles; murals, First Nat. Bank, Pasadena; panels, Town Club, Pasadena. Represented in Pasadena High School collection of paintings; Woman's Athletic Club, Los Angeles; Chic. Athletic Club, Chicago. Died 1949.

CLARK, ALVIN.
Painter and engraver. Born March 8, 1804 in Ashfield, MA. He was an engraver and was employed for a short time in Boston, where he made watercolors and India ink portraits. He also painted in Providence, RI, New York and Fall River, MA. In 1835, at forty years of age, Clark became interested in telescopes and made the first achromatic lenses manufacured in this country. Died Aug. 19, 1877 in Cambridge, MA.

CLARK, C. H.
Painter. Pupil of Julian and Delecluse Academies in Paris. Address in 1926, 432 Baldwin Street, Meadville, PA.

CLARK, ELIOT C(ANDEE).
Painter, teacher, lecturer, and writer. Born New York, March 27, 1883; son of Walter Clark, Member: ANA, 1917, NAC; SPNY; AWCS; Allied AA; Conn. AFA; Salma. C.; Int. Soc. AL; MacD.C.; A. Fund S.; NYWCC. Awards: Third Hallgarten prize, NAD, 1912; Ranger purchase prize, NAD, 1922; Edgar B. Davis prize, San Antonio, Texas, 1929. Work: "March," Maryland Institute, Baltimore; "Santa Maria delle Salute," Bloomington (Ind.) Art Assoc.; "Rolling Country," owned by

164

estate of Woodrow Wilson; "Winds of Destiny," Dayton Museum; "Autumn Twilight," Fort Worth (Texas) Museum; "Golden Autumn," Woman's Forum, Wichita Falls; "Landscape," NAC. Teacher, Art Students League, 1912- 1914. Author "Alexander Wyant"; "J. Francis Murphy"; "John Twachtman"; "Theodore Robinson," and writer for art magazines. Address in 1929, Kent, CT. Died in 1980.

CLARK, ELIZABETH L.
Painter. Member: Balto. WCC. Address in 1929, 1025 North Calvert Street, Baltimore, MD.

CLARK, ELSIE S.
Painter. Born in Providence, RI, 1881. Studied in Paris. Address in 1926, Rodin Studios, 200 West 57th Street, New York.

CLARK, EMELIA M. GOLDSWORTHY.
Painter and teacher. Born Platteville, WI, June 3, 1869. Pupil of AIC; Otis Art Inst., Los Angeles; Pratt Inst.; Dow, Forsyth, Snell, Freer, Batchelder, Mannheim, Fursman, Vanderpoel and Townsley. Member: Calif. AC; West Coast Arts, Inc.; Calif. WCS; MacDowell C. of Allied Arts; Artland C. Formerly art director Western State Normal College, Kalamazoo, Mich. Author and art editor "Public School Methods," Chicago. Address in 1929, 114 West 42nd Street, Los Angeles, CA. Died c. 1955.

CLARK, FREEMAN.
Painter. Born Holly Springs, MI. Pupil of Chase; Wiles; ASL of NY; NY School of Art; Shinnicock School of Art. Represented in Riverside Branch Public Library, New York, NY. Address in 1929, Freeman Place, Holly Springs, MI.

CLARK, HARRIETTE A.
Miniature painter. Born in Depere, WI, 1876. Pupil of Laurens and Blaschet in Paris. Painted Miniatures of Ex-President Diaz and Madame Diaz. Address in 1926, 27 West 67th Street, New York City, NY.

CLARK, HERBERT F.
Painter and illustrator. Born Holyoke, MA, 1876. Pupil of Rhode Island School of Design, Providence, RI, and the School of the Corcoran Art Gallery, Washington, DC. Specialty, landscapes. Address in 1926, 3034 R Street, NW, Washington, DC.

CLARK, JAMES L(IPPITT).
Sculptor, craftsman, and lecturer. Born Providence, RI, Nov. 18, 1883. Pupil of RI School of Design. Traveled Africa, Europe, and Orient. Member: Animal PS. NY Zoological S. and NSS. In collections of Mus. Nat. History; RISD; Ohio State U. and Nat. Mus., Wash., DC. Address in 1929, 705 Whitlock Ave., Bronx, NY; care of the American Museum of Natural History, 77th Street and Central Park; h. 40 West 77th Street, New York, NY. Died in 1957.

CLARK, JAMES.
Engraver. In 1840, James Clark was an engraver of bank-notes, cards, etc., with an establishment at 67 Broadway, New York City.

CLARK, JOHN DEWITT.
Sculptor. Born Kansas City, Missouri. Study: Kansas City Art Inst.; San Diego State Col.; with Lowell Houser, Everett Jackson, John Dirks. Work: The Mexican North Am. Cultural Inst., Mexico; Palomar College; Southwestern College; La Jolla Mus. of Contemp. Art. Exhibitions: Findlay Gallery, NY; Eleven Calif. Sculptors, Western Museum Assn.; Santa Barbara West Coast Invitational; San Diego Fine Arts Gallery; Mex. - North Am. Cult. Inst., Mexico City. Media: Black granite, bronze. Address in 1982, c/o Art Dept. Southwestern College, Chula Vista, CA.

CLARK, MATT.
Illustrator. Born in Coshocton, Ohio, in 1903. He was educated at the National Academy Art School in New York. College Humor published his first illustration in 1929 which led to a career with The Saturday Evening Post and other major magazine of the time. He was well known for his watercolor and pen and ink drawings of the early West, with particular attention to horses and cowboys.

165

CLARK, ROLAND.
Painter and etcher. Born New
Rochelle, NY, April 2, 1874.
Address in 1929, 49 West 12th
Street; h. 37 Madison Ave., New
York, NY; summer, "Breezewood,"
Peconic P.O., NY. Died in 1957.

CLARK, ROY C.
Landscape painter. Born Sheffield,
MA, April 3, 1889. Pupil of Edgar
Nye; Irving Wiles; William Judson.
Member: S. Indp. A.; Wash.
Landscape C; Wash. SA; Wash. WCC.
Address in 1929, 144 Uhland
Terrace, Washington, DC; summer, 8
Pine Street, Pittsfield, MA.

CLARK, SARAH L.
Painter, illustrator, and teacher.
Born Philadelphia, PA, Aug. 22,
1869. Pupil of Chase and Carlson;
PAFA. Specialty, pathological and
surgical drawings. Address in
1929, 642 North 42nd Street,
Philadelphia, PA. Died in 1936.

CLARK, VIRGINIA KEEP.
Portrait painter. Born New
Orleans, LA, Feb. 17, 1878. Pupil
of William Forsyth, J. C. Beckwith,
Howard Pyle. Member: NA Women PS.
Address in 1929, 4 East 66th
Street, New York, NY; summer,
"Windy Meadow," Oyster Bay," LI,
NY.

CLARK, WALTER.
Landscape painter. Born in
Brooklyn, March 9, 1848. Pupil of
Innes. He became an Associate of
the National Academy in 1898 and an
Academician in 1909. Among his
paintings were "In Early Leaf," and
"Gloucester Harbor." He died March
12, 1917 in Bronxville, NY.

CLARK, WILLIAM BULLOCK (MRS).
Painter. Member: Baltimore WCC.
Address in 1929, 3 Upland Road,
Baltimore, MD.

CLARKE, FREDERICK BENJAMINE.
Sculptor. Born Mystic, CT in 1874.
Pupil of Augustus Saint-Gaudens.
Member: Beaux-Arts Inst. of Des.
Address in 1929, 304 East 44th
Street, New York, NY. Died in
1943.

CLARKE, JOHN L.
Painter. Exhibited, Penna.
Academy of Fine Arts, Philadelphia,
1924. Address in 1926, 46 Bayley
Avenue, Yonkers, NY.

CLARKE, RENE.
Painter and illustrator. Member:
NYWCC; Phila. WCC. Address in
1929, 46 Bayley Avenue, Yonkers,
NY; 250 Fifth Avenue, New York, NY.

CLARKE, THOMAS SHIELDS.
Sculptor and painter. Born 1860 in
Pittsburgh, PA. Studied painting
and sculpture at Ecole des Beaux
Arts, Paris, and in Rome and
Florence, for 11 years. Exhibited
works and won many medals at
London, Madrid, Berlin, Paris,
Chicago Exp., and at Exp. of San
Francisco and Atlanta, GA. He
executed many large works in bronze
and marble for New York, San
Francisco, Chicago, and other
cities. Pictures in Museums of
Boston and Philadelphia. Academy
of National Artists. Member:
Royal Society of Arts, London;
National Sculpture Society;
Metropolitan Museum of Art;
American Museum Natural History;
Architectual League. Among his
best known paintings is the "Night
Market, Morocco," owned by the
Philadelphia Art Club. Died Nov.
15, 1920 in NYC.

CLARKE, THOMAS.
Engraver. The name of this
engraver in the stipple manner
first appears in 1797, when he was
engraving portraits and subject
plates of the American Universal
Magazine of Philadelphia, and
illustrations for an edition of
"Telemachus," published by David
Longworth of NY. He was apparently
in both cities in this year, as he
signed his plates respectively, "T.
Clarke, Sculp.," Phila., 1779, and
"engraved by Thos. Clarke, NY."
Clarke was engraving in New York at
least as late as 1800.

CLARKSON, RALPH ELMER.
Portrait painter and teacher. Born
Amesbury, MA, Aug. 3, 1861. Pupil
of School of Boston Museum; Julian
Academy under Lefebvre and
Boulanger in Paris. Member: ANA
1910; Chicago SA; Municipal Art Lg.

of Chicago; NYWCC; Port. P.; AFA; Chicago WCC; Chicago PA; Municipal Art Commission; Chicago AC. Instructor, AIC. Awards: Cahn prize, AIC 1909, hors concours (jury of awards), P.-P. Exp., San F., 1915. Work: "A Daughter of Armenia," Art Institute of Chicago. Address in 1929, 410 South Michigan Avenue; h. 255 Dearborn Street, Chicago, IL; summer, Oregon, IL. Died in 1942.

CLASSEN, WILLIAM M.
Engraver. This name is signed to a few well-engraved line-plates of Buildings and book-illustrations as "Wm. M. Classen, Eng. No. 1 Murry Street, Corner of B. Way" (New York). The apparent date of these plates is about 1840-50. On one plate seen, the name is signed "J. M. Classen Sc.," though the work seems to be the same.

CLAUS, MAY AUSTIN.
Painter. Born in Berlin, NY, Aug. 18, 1882. Pupil of School of Boston Museum and of W. A. J. Claus. Member: PA S. Min. P. Address in 1929, 410 Boylston Street, Boston, MA; summer, Provincetown, MA.

CLAUS, WILLIAM A. J.
Portrait painter. Born Maintz, Germany, June 14, 1862. Pupil of Grundmann in Boston; Julian Academy in Paris; Henri Quyton in Belgium. Work: "Old Pioneer," Boston Art Club; "Gov. Greenhalge," State House, Boston; "Carl Faelten," Faelten Hall, Boston; "Dr. Eben Tourjee," N.E. Convervatory, Potsdam College, Potsdam, NY; altar peices at the Chruch of St. Francis de Sales, Boston; portraits of prominent natives painted in India, 1884 to 1887. Director, Claus Art School. Address in 1929, 410 Boylston Street, Boston, MA.

CLAY, EDWARD WILLIAMS.
Engraver. Born April 9, 1799 in Phila., PA. Clay is said to have been a midshipman under Commodore Perry, but he later studied law and was admitted to the Phila. bar in 1825. He had, however, a decided leaning toward art; he drew some of the plates engraved for Child's "Views of Philadelphia," and he drew upon stone for the lithographing firm of Childs & Inman. Clay was a merciless caricaturist, and some of his lampoons of fellow-citizens are said to have caused him much personal inconvenience. In the Philadelphia directories of 1835-36 his profession is given as "Artist." He engraved several fairly well- executed plates in the stipple manner, the best of these being a portrait of the Rev. Joseph Eastburn. His caricatures were etched. Died Dec. 3, 1837, in NYC.

CLAY, MARY F. R.
Painter. Member: Fellowship PAFA; NA Women PS; North Shore AA; Plastic C. Award: Kohnstamm prize ($250), AIC, 1925. Address in 1929, 1734 Pine Street, Philadelphia, PA. Died in 1939.

CLAYPOOLE, JAMES.
Painter. Was the earliest native artist of Pennsylvania. He was born in Philadelphia, 1720, and died in the West Indies about 1796. He was the son of Joseph Claypoole of Philadelphia and his wife, Edith Ward. Joseph Claypoole was the First Warden of Christ Church, Philadelphia, and was "Concerned in the promoting and assisting of the building of Christ Church, and contributed much toward it." Joseph Claypoole, the artist's father, was born in 1677, and died before May 3, 1744. He was the son of James Claypoole, friend of Penn, Patentee of PA, and Register General of the Colony. The first James Claypoole was a wealthy merchant. His son Joseph, father of the artist, was also a man of wealth, as he was a large property owner in Philadelphia. James Claypoole painted portraits in Philadelphia before 1750; little is known of his paintings, but he was the instructor of his nephew, Mathew Pratt, whose autobiographical notes state that he was apprenticed "To my uncle James Claypoole, limner and portrait painter in general" in 1749. His work shows that he was guided by a painter of no mean acquirements. Claypoole abandoned art for public life and was High Sheriff of Philadelphia during the

Revolutionary War. His daughter, Elizabeth, married Timothy Matlack, the soldier and patriot of Phila., whose portrait was painted by Charles Willson Peale. His daughter Mary married James Peale, the artist, brother of Charles Willson Peale, and his cousin John Claypoole was the husband of the celebrated Betsy Ross. There is a portrait inscribed on the back of the canvas "Margaret Allen drawn and colored by Claypoole, Philadelphia, 1746." Charles Willson Peale in a letter, mentions "James Claypoole," whose painting he examined at his home in Philadelphia in 1762.

CLEAVER, ALICE.
Painter and teacher. Born Racine, WI, April 11, 1878. Pupil of Vanderpoel, Chase, Beaux, Biloul; Lucien Simon in Paris. Member: Lincoln AG: Omaha SFA. Award: John L. Webster prize, Omaha SFA, 1922. Address in 1929, Falls City, NE.

CLEAVES, MURIEL MATTOCKS.
Illustrator, and teacher. Born Hastings, NE. Pupil of M. C. Carr, John S. Ankeney, Birger Sandzen, AIC. Member: Kansas City SA; Alliance. Awards: Second and third prizes, water colors, Pueblo, 1922; hon. mention, Kansas City AI, 1923. Address in 1929, 1848 Wahington Avenue., New York, NY. Died in 1947.

CLELAND, THOMAS MAITLAND.
Painter, illustrator, and writer. Born New York, NY, Aug. 18, 1880. Member: Boston SAC. Awards: Medal, Boston SAC, 1920; 2 gold medals and bronze medal, Am. Inst. of Graphic A., 1920. Address in 1929, 70 Fifth Avenue, New York, NY; h. Route 2, Danbury, CT. Died in 1964.

CLEMENS, ISAAC.
Engraver. The New York Gazette, 1776, contains the following advertisement: "Isaac Clemens, Engraver (who lately arrived with his Majesty's Fleet from Boston, in New England) informs the Gentlemen of the Navy and Army and the Public in general, that he now carries on the Engraving Business at his shop near the French Church, 1 King Street, New York." This advertisement disappears in a very short time, and Mr. Clemens probably went back to England, as nothing more is known about him.

CLEMENT, EDWARD H.
Painter. Born in Chelsea, MA, 1843. Pupil of Boston Art Students' Association.

CLEMENTS, GABRIELL de VEAUX.
Painter and teacher. Born in Philadelphia, PA, 1858. Pupil of Robert-Fleury and Bouguereau in Paris. Member: Fellowship PAFA; Wash. WCC; S. Wash. A.; Chicago SE; North Shore AA; Charleston EC. Awards: Second Toppan prize, PAFA; Mary Smith prize, PAFA. 1895. Work: Painting in St. Patrick's Church, Washington, DC; Mural paitings; St. Paul's Chapel, Baltimore; St. Matthews Church, Sparrow Point, MD; etchings in National Museum, Washington, DC. Address in 1929, 1673 Columbia Road, Washington, DC; summer, Lanesville, Gloucester, MA. Died March 26, 1948.

CLEMENTS, GEORGE HENRY.
Painter. Member: New York Water Color Club. Born in Louisiana. Landscape and genre painter. He exhibited a portrait of Frank Duveneck at Cincinnati Museum in 1925. Address in 1926, 33 West 67th Street, New York City, NY. Died in 1935.

CLEMENTS, ROSALIE.
Painter. Born Washington, DC Jan. 5, 1878. Pupil of E. F. Andrews in Washington; F. Luis Mora and Thomas Fogarty in New York. Member: PBC; S. Indp. A. Address in 1929, Wiccopee, Hopewell Junction, Dutchess Co., NY.

CLEPHANE, LEWIS PAINTER.
Painter. Born Washington DC, Feb. 8, 1869. Pupil of Birge Harrison; Alexander Robinson in Holland. Member: S. Wash. A.; Wash. AC; S. Indp. A.; AFA. Address in 1929, 1824 Ontario Place, Washington, DC.

CLEVENGER, SHOBAL V.
Sculptor. He was born Oct. 22 1812 near Middleton, OH. Largely self-taught, he executed many bust

168

of prominent men, and was enabled to go abroad for study. Died Sept. 1843 at Sea.

CLIFFORD, JUDY DEAN.
Illustrator. Born in Orange, California, in 1946. She attended the Univ. of Wash. in Seattle and studied art at the Acad. of Art in San Fran. for four years. Her career began with a series for the Simpson Lee Paper Co., and she has since won awards at the Western ADC Show and exhibited in the S of I Annual Exhibitions in New York and Los Angeles. She has worked for magazines and produced posters for Levi's and the San Fran. Ballet.

CLIFTON, ADELE ROLLINS.
Painter, illustator, etcher, writer and teacher. Born Brooklyn, NY, July 27, 1875. Pupil of Alexander W. Dow; William M. Chase. Member: Plastic C; Phila. Alliance. Address in 1929, 1830 Rittenhouse Square, Philadelphia, PA; summer, Whitefield, NH.

CLIME, WINFIELD SCOTT.
Painter. Born Philadelphia, PA, Nov. 7, 1881. Pupil of Corcoran Art School, Washington; ASL of NY. Member: S. Wash. A.; Wash, WCC; Wash. AC; Landscape C., Washington; NAC; Salma. C. Allied AA; AFA; Tiffany Foundation. Represented in the Los Angeles Museum of Art. Address in 1929, Old Lyme, CT. Died in 1958.

CLINEDINST, BENJAMIN WEST.
Painter. Born Woodstock, VA, Oct. 14, 1859. Studied at Ecole des Beaux Arts, Paris. Pupil of Cabanel and Bonnat. Specialty, genre pictures and portraits; illustrator of books. Painted portraits of Theodore Roosevelt, Admiral Peary, Gen. Curtis Lee, Edward Echols, Gen. E. W. Nichols. Elected Member of the National Academy of Design, 1898. Awards: Evans prize, AWCS, 1900; silver medal, Pan-Am. Exp., Buffalo, 1901; silver medal, Charleston Exp., 1902. Address in 1926, Pawling, NY. Died Sept. 12, 1931 in Pawling, NY.

CLIVE, RICHARD R.
Painter. Born in NYC, Jan. 8, 1912. Study: NAD; NYU; with Dan Greene, Harold Wolcott. Work: Navy Combat Art Collection; Municipal Coll., Ossining, NY; Arts and Sci. Ctr., Nashua, NH; others, including commissions for Navy. Exhibitions: Salma. C., Annual, 1961-82; Am. Artists Professional Lg.; Am. Veterans Soc. of Artists; Naval Art Coop, 1963-72; Stevens Inst. of Technology; etc. Awards: New Rochelle Art Assn., portrait and graphics; Am. Legion, Lt. Breng award; Miniature Art Soc. of NJ. Mem.: Salma. C. (hon.); Am. APL; Acad. Artists Assn.; Pastel Soc. of America; etc. Media: Oil, pastel, watercolor. Address in 1982, 29 Holly Street, Yonkers, NY.

CLIVETTE , MERTON.
Painter, sculptor, etcher, writer, lecturer, and teacher. Born in Wisconsin, June 11, 1868. Pupil of Chase, La Farge, Twachtman, ASL of NY.; Rodin in Paris. Address in 1929, 92 Fifth Avenue, New York, NY; h. 1020 West 56th Street, Kansas City, MO.

CLOAR, CARROLL.
Painter. Born in Earle, Ark., Jan. 18, 1913. Study: Southwestern at Memphis, BA; Memphis Acad. of Arts; ASL, MacDowell fellow, 1940. Work: Met. Mus. of Art, MOMA, Whitney, NYC; Brooks Mem. Art Gallery, Memphis; Hirshhorn Mus., Wash., DC. Exhib.: Pittsburgh Int'l.; Whitney Annual; PAFA; Brooks Mem. Art Gallery, Memphis; others. Awards: Guggenheim Fellow, 1946; Am. Acad. of Arts and Letters Prize, 1967; Southwestern College, 1977. Rep.: Forum Gallery, NYC. Address in 1982, Memphis, TN.

CLONNEY, JAMES GOODWYN.
Genre and miniature artist. Born Jan. 28, 1812 in Liverpool, England. He started painting minatures in New York, 1834, and exhibited in the National Academy, 1841-1852. Also exhibited at PA. He was elected an Associate Member of the National Academy in 1867. Died Oct. 7, 1867 in Binghamton, NY.

169

CLOPATH, HENRIETTE.
Painter. Born in Switzerland.
Award: Gold medal, University of
Okla., 1916. Writer and lecturer
on modern painting. Address in
1926, Chalet Art Studio.

CLOSSON, WILLIAM BAXTER PALMER.
Painter and engraver. Born
Thetford, VT, 1848. Pupil of
Lowell Inst.; travelled in Europe.
Followed engraving on wood,
1872-94; then painted in pastel and
oil. Awards for wood engraving:
Gold, silver, and bronze medals;
silver medal, Paris Expn., 1889;
medal, Columbian Expn., Chicago.
Member: Boston Art Club; Copley
Society; Society Wash. Artists;
Union Internationale des Beaux Arts
et des Lettres. See "History of
Wood Engraving in America," by W.
J. Linton. Address in 1926,
Newton, MA. Died May, 1926.

CLOUGH, JANE B.
Sculptor. Born Chicago, IL, March
30, 1881. Pupil of Solon Borglum,
Mahonri Young, J. E. and Laura
Fraser, Anna V. Hyatt. Member:
NSS (life); Kansas City SA.
Address in 1929, 1 West 67th
Street, New York, NY; h. 1020 West
56th Street, Kansas City, MO.

CLOVER, LEWIS P. Jr.
Born in New York, Feb. 20, 1819.
He studied painting and engraving
under Asher B. Durand. He had his
studio for some years in New York
and Baltimore. Exhibited at AAU
and NA. Later he entered the church
and afterward the priesthood.
Among his paintings are "The
Rejected Picture," "The Idle Man,"
and "The Phrenologist." Died Nov.
9, 1896 in NYC.

CLOVER, PHILIP.
Portrait painter. Born in 1842.
He was formerly of Columbus, OH,
but painted many Chicago
politicians. Works: "Fatima", and
"The Criminal." He died in 1905.

CLUSMANN, WILLIAM.
Painter. Born in North Laporte,
IN, 1859. Pupil of Benczur at
Royal Academy in Munich. Member:
Chicago Society of Artists; Chicago
Water Color Club. Awards: Hon.

mention, Stuttgart, Germany, 1885.
Died Sept. 28, 1927 in Chicago, IL.

CLUTE, BEULAH MITCHELL.
Painter, illustrator, and lecturer.
Born Rushville, IL, March 24, 1873.
Pupil of ASL of NY; AI Chicago.
Member: Artists Guild, Chicago;
AIC Alumni Assoc.; Cal. Book Plate
Soc. Designer for the Three
Redwoods Studio, Berkeley.
Specialty, bookplates and
illuminated parchments. Address in
1929, 2614 Channing Way, Berkeley,
CA.

CLUTE, CARRIE E(LISABETH).
Painter, etcher, and teacher. Born
Schenectady, NY, July 3, 1890.
Pupil of Henry B. Snell. Members
AWSC; PBC; NA Women PS. Address in
1929, 67 Bedford Street, New York,
NY; summer, Rhinebeck, NY.

CLUTE, WALTER MARSHALL.
Painter and illustrator. Born in
Schenectady, New York, Jan. 9,
1870. He was a pupil of the Art
Students' League of New York, and
of Constant and Laurens in Paris.
He received the 1910 prize of Art
Institute of Chicago, and was
vice-president of the Society of
Western Artists at the time of his
death. Died Feb. 13, 1915 in North
Cucamonga, CA.

CLYMER, EDWIN SWIFT.
Painter. Brn Cincinnati, Ohio,
1871. Pupil of PAFA. Member
Phila. Sketch C.; Phila. WCC. Work
in Reading, PA, Museum of Art
Address in 1929, Lanesville P.O.
Gloucester, MA.

CLYMER, JAMES FLOYD.
Painter. Born in 1893. Exhibited
Penna. Academy of Fine Arts, 1924
Philadelphia. Address in 1926
Provincetown, MA.

CLYMER, JOHN.
Illustrator. Born in Ellensburg
Washington, 1907. He studied in
Vancouver and Port Hope, Canada, as
well as in Wilmington and New York
He illustrated several Chrysler
advertisements before painting a
cover for The Saturday Evening Post
in 1947. In addition to
illustrations in many major
magazines, he has had specia

assignments for a number of Canadian publications and the Marine Corps.

OALE, GRIFFITH B.
Illustrator. Born in Baltimore in 1890, he studied art in both Paris and Munich. His career as a muralist and portrait artist was interrupted by World War II, during which time he founded the Navy's Combat Artists Corps and served as a Lieutenant Commander. His murals can be seen in public buildings in New York City and his portraits of famous Americans are in the collections of Johns Hopkins University and the Maryland Historical Society. Died in 1950.

OALE, GRIFFITH BAILEY.
Painter. Born Baltimore MD, May 21, 1890. Studied with M. Heymann, Munich; Richard Miller and Laparra in Paris; and in Italy and Spain. Member: Charcoal C.; Mural P. Work: "Portrait of Cardinal Mercier," Maryland Historical Society; portraits in Johns Hopkins University; murals, Lee Higginson & Co., New York; New York Athletic Club. Address in 1929, 125 West 11th Street, New York, NY.

OAN, C. ARTHUR.
Painter, writer, and lecturer. Born Ottawa, IL, Dec. 16, 1867. Author of "History of an Appearance." "Southnumberland's Yule Tide," "The Fragrant Note Book" "Proportional Form," etc. Lecturer on art and archaeology. Address in 1929, Piermont Avenue, Nyack, NY.

OAN, FRANCES CHALLENOR.
Painter and illustrator. Born East Orange, NJ, Pupil of Heny B. Snell and E. M. Scott; Metropolitan Art School. Ilustrator of "The Fragrant Note Book," etc. Designer and painter of stage settings. Address in 1929, Piermont Avenue, Nyack, NY.

OAN, HELEN E.
Painter. Born Byron, NY. Pupil of Art Student's League of New York; Frederick Freer and William E. Chase. Member: California Art Club. Award: Medals for oil and water color, Alaska-Yukon-Pacific

Exposition, Seattle, 1909; medal and diploma, San Diego Exp., 1915. Address in 1926, 204 North Burlington Avenue, Los Angeles, CA.

COAST, OSCAR REGAN.
Painter. Born Salem, OH, 1851. Studied with Yewell, Thomas Hickes and Faller in Paris and Rome. Member: Salma. C., 1897; Wash. AC; Santa Barbara AC; ADA. Specialty, landscapes. Address in 1929, 802 Union Title Bldg.; h. 418 East 19th Street, Indianapolis, IN. Died in 1931.

COBB, CYRUS.
Portrait painter. Born at Malden, MA, Aug. 6, 1834. His career for about twenty years was identical with that of his twin brother, Darius Cobb. He painted portraits of Rev. A. P. Peabody, Dr. Appleton and others, but devoted himself to the law, which was his profession. He died Jan. 29, 1903 in Allston, MA.

COBB, DARIUS.
Portrait painter. Born at Malden, MA, Aug. 6, 1834. Twin brother of Cyrus Cobb, with whom he studied and worked until 1870. They worked near Boston. He painted portraits, some landscapes and figure pieces; he also cut several busts in marble. Lectured on art. Died April 23, 1919 in Newton Upper Falls, MA.

COBB, GERSHAM.
A book-plate engraver working about 1800. Worked in Boston at later date. He was most probably an American, as the only plate signed by him is of the pictorial type, with an American eagle bearing an oval frame, once containing a name, later carefully erased; there is a scratchy landscape at the base.

COBB, KATHERINE M.
Painter. Born Syracuse, Jan. 5, 1873. Pupil of Charles Hawthorne; Carlson; Webster. Member: PBC; Associated Artists of Syracuse. Address in 1929, 602 Comstock Avenue, Syracuse, NY.

COBER, ALAN E.
Illustrator. Born in New York City in 1935. He began law studies at

the University of Vermont until he returned to NY to attend SVA. His reputation as a top line and half-tone artist grew as his work appeared in books and magazines. The pen and ink drawing from his book The Forgotten Society, published by Dover Press, have been exhibited in galleries and museums nationwide. Named Artist of the Year in 1965 by the AG, he has received five Gold Medals, four Awards of Excellence and the Hamilton King Award from the S of I as well as two Gold Medals from the ADC. In addition, The New York Times has twice placed his children's books on their 10-Best list. President of the Illustrators Workshop, he collects folk art.

COBURN, FREDERICK WILLIAM.
Illustrator, and writer. Born Nashua, NH, Aug. 6, 1870. Pupil of ASL of Washington, DC, and NY. Member: Copley S.; Lowell AA; Concord AA. Address in 1929, 722 East Merrimack Street, Lowell, MA. Died in 1953.

COCHRAN, ALLEN D.
Painter. Born Cincinnati, OH, Oct. 23, 1888. Pupil of Kenyon Cox and Birge Harrison. Member: Salma. C. Address in 1929, Woodstock, NY.

COCHRANE, CONSTANCE.
Painter and teacher. Born Pensacola, Florida. Pupil of Elliot Daingerfield and Henry B. Snell. Member: Phila. School of Design for Women Alumnae; NA Women PS; Phila. AL: Ten Phila. P.; AFA. Represented in Twentieth Century Club, Lansdowne, PA; Bywood Public School, Upper Darby, PA. Address in 1929, 7103 Pennsylvania Avenue, Bywood, Upper Darby, PA.

COCHRANE, JOSEPHINE G.
Painter. Member: NA Women PS; Conn. AFA. Address in 1929, 123 West Monument Street, Baltimore, MD.

COCKCROFT, EDITH V.
Painter. Born in Brooklyn, NY, 1881. Member of National Association of Women Painters and Sculptors. Address in 1926, 17 East 39th Street, New York City.

COCKRELL, DURA (BROKAW).
Painter, craftman, writer, lecturer, and teacher. Born Liscomb, Iowa, Feb. 16, 1877. Pupil of William M. Chase and Kenneth Hayes Miller. Member: Ft. Worth AA; Ft. Worth Painters Club. Award: Bronze medal, Woman's Forum, Dallas, TX, 1919; silver medal, Dallas Woman's Forun, 1926. Head of art dept, Texas Christian University. Fort Worth, 1900-1924; head of art dept. William Woods College, from 1925. Address in 1929, William Woods College, Fullton, MO.

COCONIS, CONSTANTINOS (TED).
Illustrator. Born in Chicago in 1937. He spent a year at the American Academy of Art and three months at the AIC, before the appearance of his first illustration in Sunset in 1954. His distinctive style and intricate technique have earned him a reputation resulting in the publication of his work by almost every major magazine, including Redbook, Cosmopolitan, Playboy and Time, as well as by many publishers such as Fawcett, The Viking Press and Random House. Among his advertising assignments are movie campaigns and record covers. An award winner in the S of I Annual Exhibitions, he owns and drives formula race cars.

CODEZO, THOMAS.
Spanish-American painter. Born in Havanna in 1839. Studied in Paris with Henri Regnault. He came to the United States in 1869; worked in oil, and crayon.

CODMAN, EDWIN E.
Painter. Member of Providence Art Club. Address in 1926, 166 Ontario Street, Providence, RI.

COE, ETHEL LOUISE.
Painter, illustrator, lecturer, writer, and teacher. Born Chicago, IL. Pupil of AIC; Hawthorne and Sorolla. Member: Chicago PS; Chicago AC; Cordon C.; Chicago GC; NAC. Award; Young Fortnightly prize, AIC 1911. Work: In Sioux City Art Museum; Vanderpoel AA Collection, Chicago. Director, Dept. of Art, Sarah Lawrence

College, Bronxville, New York. Lecturer, AIC and Clubs. Address in 1929, care of Art Institute, Chicago, IL; 1223 Elmwood Avenue, Evanston, IL. Died 1938.

COE, THEODORE DEMEREST.
Painter. Born Suffern, NY, April 13, 1866. Pupil of John Twachtman and Carlo Rossi Academy in Paris. Member: Boston AC. Address in 1929, East Sandwich, MA.

COFFEE, THOMAS M.
English sculptor; modelled small portrait busts of merit. He resided in Charleston.

COFFEE, WILL.
Painter. Exhibited water colors at Annual Exhibition of Water Colors at Penna. Academy of Fine Arts, Philadelphia, 1925. Address in 1926, 729 Walnut Street, Philadelphia.

COFFIN, GEORGE ALBERT.
Marine painter. He was born 1856, and died Feb. 3, 1922 in NYC.

COFFIN, ROBERT P. TRISTRAM.
Illustrator, writer, lecturer, and teacher. Born Brunswick, ME, March 18, 1892. Illustrations for "Crowns and Cottages," Yale University Press; "An Attic Room," Doubleday, Doran & Co.; pen and ink illustrations for "The Forum" and "The Bookman." Address in 1929, Aurora-on-Cayuga, NY; summer, Pennellville, Brunswick, ME.

COFFIN, SARAH TABER.
Painter. Born Vassalboro, ME, June 1, 1844. Pupil of Dr. Rimmer, R. Swain Gifford, W. Sartain, Frank Duveneck and Charles Woodbury; ASL of NY under C.Y. Turner, and Ross Turner in Boston. Member: Copley S; North Shore AA. Work: In Moses Brown School, Providence, RI. Address in 1929, Chestnut Hill, MA.

COFFIN, W. HASKELL.
Painter. Studied at Corcoran Art School, Washington, DC, and in Paris. Member: SI. Died 1941. Address in 1926, 80 West 40th Street, New York City.

COFFIN, WILLIAM ANDERSON.
Landscape and figure painter. Born in Allegheny, PA, in 1855. Studied in New York and Paris. Elected an Associate Member of the National Academy of Design in 1898, and National Academy in 1912. Represented in Collection of Metropolitan Museum, New York, and National Collection at Washington, DC. Died Oct. 26, 1925 in NYC.

COGDELL, JOHN STEPHANO.
Sculptor and painter. Born Sept. 19, 1778 in Charleston, SC. He was largely self-taught, but received some help from Washington Allston, and studied abroad. About 1820 to 1850 modelled a few busts of distinguished Americans. Died Feb. 25, 1847.

COGSWELL, RUTH McINTOCH.
Illustrator and teacher. Born Concord, NH, Aug. 17, 1885. Pupil of Yale School of Fine Arts; Henry B. Snell. Member: New Haven PCC; New Haven BPC. Address in 1929, 301 Alden Avenue, New Haven, CT.

COGSWELL, WILLIAM.
Painter. Born in Fabius, NY, 1819. He died in Pasadena, CA, 1903. He was practically self-taught as a portrait painter. He resided at times in NY, Phila., Chicago, St. Louis, and Calif. His list of portraits include: Presidents Lincoln, Grant and McKinley. His "President Grant and Family" was in the Nat. Gal., and the portraits of Gen'l Grant and Salmon P. Chase were in the Capitol, Wash., DC.

COHEN, GEORGE.
Born 1919 in Chicago, IL. Educated at the School of the Art Inst. (Chicago-BFA) at Drake Univeristy and at University of Chicago. Taught at Northwestern since 1948. Awards from Art Inst., and Copley Foundation (1956). ExhIbited at Bordelon Gallery (Chicago - 1950); Alan Gallery, NYC; Feigen galleries in Chicago, LA and NYC; MOMA; Carnegie; SF Museum of Art. In collections of Lipman Foundation, and in many private collections.

COHEN, HY.
Painter. Born London, England, June 13, 1901. Pupil of NAD;

William Starkweather. Address in 1929, 991 Carroll Street, Brooklyn, NY.

COHEN, ISABEL.
Painter. Born, Charleston, SC, April 12, 1867. Pupil of Elliott Daingerfield and Henry S. Rittenberg in NY; Joseph Noel, Rome, Italy; British Acad. of Art. Member: NA Women PS; PBC; NAC; Yonkers AC: Springfield AA; SSAL; AA of Charleston. Awards: Prize, St. Louis Exp.; first portrait prize, Charleston Exp. Address in 1929, The Colonial Studios, 39 West 67th Street, New York, NY; h. Gilbes Art Bldg., Meeting Street, Charleston, SC.

COHEN, KATHERINE M.
Sculptor and painter. Born in Philadelphia, 1859. Pupil of PAFA, ASL, NY under Augustus Saint Gaudens, and of Mercie in Paris. Among her best known works: Statue of General Beaver, bronze of Abraham Lincoln, "Dawn of Thought," and "Vision of Rabbi Ben Ezra." She died in Philadelphia in 1924.

COHEN, LEWIS.
Painter. American. Born June 27, 1857 in London. Pupil of Alphonse Legros, J. Watson Nicholl, and A. S. Cope. Elected an Associate Member of the National Academy. He painted "Puente San Martin, Toledo." Died 1915 in New York.

COHEN, NESSA.
Sculptor. Born 1885 in New York City. Pupil of James S. Fraser. Among her work "Sunrise," Havana, Cuba, and groups of Indians of the Southwestern United States. Exhibited, PAFA, Philadelphia, 1924. Address in 1926, 1143 Lexington Avenue, New York City. Died Aug. 4, 1915 in NYC.

COHILL, CHARLES.
A portrait painter born in 1812 in PA. A painting of a Shakespearean character was shown in Philadelphia at Barr & Co. in 1923. It was inscribed on the back of the canvas "Charles Cohill, 1838."

COINER, CHARLES TOUCEY.
Painter. Born Santa Barbara, CA, August 21, 1898. Address in 1929,

271 East Meehan Avenue, Mt. Airy, Philadelphia, PA.

COLBURN, ELEANOR R.
Painter. Born in Dayton, OH, in 1866. Pupil of Art Institute of Chicago. Among her paintings "An Offshore Wind" was owned by the Chicago Art Institute. Address in 1926, 3028 Michigan Avenue, Chicago, IL. Died in 1939.

COLBY, GEORGE W.
Painter and illustrator. Exhibited at the Penna. Academy of Fine Arts, Philadelphia, 1922, pastel, "Study of a Woodcock." Address in 1926, 25 Cedar Street, Malden, MA.

COLBY, HOMER WAYLAND.
Illustator, etcher, and craftman. Born North Berwick, ME, April 30, 1874. Pupil of George H. Bartlett. Illustrations for "Classic Myths" (Gayley); "Virgil's Aeneid" (Kittredge); "English and American Literature" (Long); "Ancient History" (Myers); "Stories of Heroism" (Mace); "Civilization in Europe" (Schapiro and Morris). Address in 1929, 66 Maynard Street, Arlington, MA. Died in 1950.

COLBY, JOSEPHINE WOOD.
Painter. Born in New York, NY, Jan. 26, 1862. Pupil of ASL of NY; NAD; Will Low, Carroll Beckwith, William Sartain, John W. Alexander. Member: NYWCC; NY Soc. C.; NAC (life); SPNY. Work in Pennsylvania Academy of the Fine Arts, Phila.; Walker Gallery, Liverpool, England; Manchester Art Gallery, England. Address in 1929, The Tamaracks, Andover, NJ.

COLE, ALPHAEUS PHILEMON.
Painter. Born Jersey City Heights, NY, July 12, 1876. Pupil of Constant and Laurens in Paris. Member: Conn. AFA; NYWCC; Salma. C.; AWCS; Allied AA; NY Soc. P.; ADA; NAC (life). Awards: Hon. mention, Pan-Am Exp., Buffalo, 1901; hon. mention, Conn. AFA, 1919; Isidor prize, Salma. C., 1926. Work: "Dr. Richard Whitehead," Historical Society, Raleigh, VA, and University of Virginia; "Mrs. Isaac Gates," Huntington Library, Oneonta, NY; "Mr. Manning," Chamber of Commerce,

New York. Address in 1929, 33 West 67th Street, New York, NY.

COLE, ANNIE ELIZABETH.
Painter. Born Providence, RI, Dec. 9, 1880. Pupil of Corcoran School of Art, Washington, DC. Member: Wash. WCC. Address in 1929, 2941 Tilden Street, N.W., Washington, DC.

COLE, CHARLES OCTAVIUS.
Portrait painter. Born July 1, 1814, in MA. He was working in New Orleans, LA, about 1835.

COLE, EMILY BECKWITH.
Sculptor. Born New London, CT, 1896. Pupil of Louis Gudebrod. Address in 1926, 220 Beacon Street, Hartford, CT.

COLE, FRANCES.
Watercolorist. Born: St. Louis, MO, Sept. 2, 1910. Studied: Antioch College; Univ. of Mich.; Univ. of Dayton. Exhibited at Watercolor Soc., NYC; Nat'l. Acad. of Design Galleries, NYC; and throughout the US. Living in Phoenix, Arizona.

COLE, GEORGE TOWNSEND.
Painter. Born in California. Pupil of Bonnat in Paris. Address in 1929, 1103 El Centro Avenue, Los Angeles, California.

COLE, JACQUES MOYSE DUPRE.
Afterwards know as Moses D. Cole. Was born in France, in 1783. He came to Newburyport, MA, from the West Indies with his father in 1795, and on the death of his father he took the name of Moses Dupre Cole. He remained in Newburyport where he painted many portraits.

COLE, JESSIE DUNCAN SAVAGE.
Painter. Born Pass Christian, MA, 1858. Pupil of Wyatt Eaton; John La Farge. Died Oct. 27, 1940. Address in 1926, 81 Wickes Avenue, Nepperham, Yonkers, NY.

COLE, JOSEPH FOXCROFT.
Painter. Born in ME, Nov. 9, 1837. He studied abroad and was a pupil of Charles Jacque in 1867. He exhibited in the Salon, 1866-67-73-74, and the Royal

Academy of 1875. Represented in the Boston Museum of Fine Arts. Died May 2, 1892 in Winchester, MA.

COLE, JOSEPH GREENLEAF.
Painter. Born in Newburyport c. 1803, son of Moses D. Cole. After studying with his father a few years, he established himself in Boston where he died in 1858. He painted portrait of Geo. R. T. Hewes, belonging to the Bostonian Society, and hanging for years in the Old State House, Boston.

COLE, MARGARET WARD.
Sculptor. Born Haslington, England in 1874. Pupil of Injalbert and Rollard in Paris. Member: Allied AA. Work: Memorial tablet of Dr. Clinton L. Bagg, Metropolitan Hospital, Welfare Island, New York City. Address in 1926, 33 West 67th Street, New York, NY; summer, R.F.D., Lower Montville, NJ.

COLE, THOMAS.
Landscape painter. Born Feb. 1, 1801 in England. In 1819 his father, James Cole, emigrated to Am. and settled in Ohio where he studied the rudiments of his art; later Thomas studied abroad, but lived the greater part of his life in New York City. Elected Member of National Academy in 1826. He is represented by the "Catskill" in the Metropolitan Museum, New York, and in the Corcoran Museum, Washington, by "The Departure and the Return." Hudson River School of painting. Died Feb. 1848 near Catskill, NY.

COLE, THOMAS CASILAER.
Portrait painter. Born Staatsburgh-on-Hudson, NY, July 23, 1888. Pupil of Tarbell, Benson and Hale at Boston Museum of Fine Arts School; Julian Academy under Baschet and Laurens in Paris. Address in 1929, Hotel Chelsea, 222 West 23rd Street, New York, NY.

COLE, TIMOTHY.
Wood-engraver. Born London, England, 1852. Burned out by Chicago fire of 1871; returned to New York; entered employment of Century Magazine (then Scribner's); went to Europe to engrave the Old Masters, 1883; finished 1st Italian

175

series, 1892; Dutch and Flemish series, 1896; English series, 1900; Spanish series, 1907; French series, 1910; engraved "Old Italian Masters." Awards: Honorable mention, Society of Sculptors, Painters and Engravers, London; National Academy, 1908. Member: American Academy Arts and Letters; honorable mention, Brotherhood of Engravers of Chicago. Represented in Carnegie Institute, Pittsburgh, and City Art Museum, St. Louis; Chicago Art Institute; Metropolitan Museum; Boston Art Museum; Washington National Gallery, etc. Died 1931. Address in 1926, Ferris Lane, Poughkeepsie, New York.

COLE, VIRGINIA THURMAN.
Painter and teacher. Born Columbus OH, Pupil of George Elmer Browne; Alice Schill; Columbus Art School. Member: Ohio WCS, Columbus AL. Address in 1929, 389 Library Park, South, Columbus, OH.

COLEMAN, CHARLES CARYL.
Painter. Born Buffalo, NY, Apr. 25, 1840. Studied in Paris and Rome. Member: ANA 1865; Players C.; NAC; London AC. Awards: Bronze medal, Columbian Exp., Chicago, 1893; silver medal, Pan Am. Exp., Buffalo, 1901. Work: "Early Moonlight - Capri," "The Antiquary," and "The Capri Girl," Buffalo Fine Arts Acad.; "Vesuvius from Pompeii," and "Music in the Moonlight," Detroit Inst.; "Oil Press, Anacapri-Capri," and "In the Garden of Villa Castello," Buffalo Academy of Fine Arts; "The Return from the Crucifixion" and Vesuvius Eruption of 1906," Brooklyn Mus.; "Christ Walking on the Sea," Seamen's Inst. of NY, the drawings for which are in the St. Louis Mus.; "A Decorative Pane" and "A View of the Castello of Capri," Louisville Mus. of FA. Address in 1929, Villa Narcissus, Island of Capri, Italy; and "The Players," 16 Gramercy Park, New York, NY. Died Dec. 4, 1928 in Capri, Italy.

COLEMAN, GLENN O.
Painter. Born Springfield, OH, July 18, 1887. Pupil of Henri. Member: S. Indp. A; Whitney Studio C; New Soc. A. Award: Third prize, Carnegie Institute, 1928. Work: Manetta Lane," Luxembourg Museum; "Coenties Slip," Newark Museum, Newark, NJ. Address in 1929, Glenco Studios, 414 National Blvd., Long Beach, LI, NY. Died May, 1932 in Long Beach, NY.

COLEMAN, RALPH PALLEN.
Illustrator. Born Philadelphia PA, June 27, 1892. Pupil of the Philadelphia School of Ind. Art. Illustrated "The Man with Three Names" and "Drums of Jeopardy" by McGrath; "The Loring Mystery" and "Sir John Dering," by Jeffery Farnol; "The Panther," by Richard Washburn Child; "A Speaking Likeness," by Julian Street; "Nobody's Man," by Oppenheim, etc.; and for many magazines. Address in 1929, 234 Walnut Street, h. 20. Rodman Avenue, Jenkintown, PA. Died in 1968.

COLEMAN, SAMUEL Jr.
Painter. Born in Portland, ME March 4, 1832. He moved to New York and became a pupil of Asher B. Durand. He studied in France and Spain. He became an associate member of the National Academy in 1860, and a full member in 1862. He was a founder of the American Society of Painters in Water Colors. Among his works are "Bay of Gibraltar, " "Market Day in Brittanny," and "The Arab Burying-Ground." Died March 26, 1920 in New York City.

COLES, ANN CADWALLADER.
Painter. Born Columbia, SC, 1882. Pupil of C. A. Whipple, A. V. Tack and F. Luis Mora. Member: Society of Independent Artists. Work: "Gen. M. C. Butler," Confederate Museum, Richmond, VA. Address in 1926, 164 Waverly Place, New York, NY.

COLES, JOHN JR.
Born c. 1778. Son of John Coles, heraldic painter, a student with Frothingham under Gilbert Stuart. He painted portraits from 1807 to 1820 in Boston. His scenes were always on panels w. lead color b.g. Died Sept. 6, 1854 in Charlestown, MA.

COLETTI, JOSEPH ARTHUR.
Sculptor. Born in Italy, Nov. 5, 1898. Pupil of John Singer Sargent. Member: NSS; Arch. Lg. of NY. Work: Chapel of St. George's School, Newport, RI; Tympanum, Mercersburg Academy, Mercersburg, PA; Eugene Dodd Medal, Harvard, Architectural School and Edward W. Bok gold medal, Harvard Advertising Award, Cambridge, MA, Coolidge Memorial, Widener Library, Harvard Univerisity, Cambridge, MA. Address in 1929, 295 Huntington Avenue, Boston MA, h. 18 Verchild Street, Qunicy, MA. Died in 1973.

COLL, JOSEPH CLEMENT.
Illustrator. Born June 2, 1881 in Phila. PA. Exhibited at PAFA, 1922. Pen and Ink Drawings. Died Oct. 19, 1921 in Phila.

COLLARD, W.
Line-engraver of portraits, working for the magazines about 1840-45.

COLLAS, LOUIS ANTOINE.
Painter. Born 1775 in Bordeaux, France. Painted miniatures and larger portraits in oil in and about New Orleans, from 1820 til 1828. He was listed in the directory, 1822, as "portrait and miniature painter, 44 St. Peter Street." Nothing is recorded of him after 1828.

COLLES, GERTRUDE.
Painter. Born Morristown, NJ, 1869. Pupil of Laurens in Paris; George de Forest Brush and B. R. Fitz in New York. Work: "Former Senator Jacob Miller," State House, Trenton, NJ. Address in 1926, 939 Eighth Avenue, NYC. Died in 1957.

COLLES, JOHN.
Profile miniature painter. Born 1751. Flourished 1778-1780, New York. His advertisement is recorded in the New York Gazette for May 10, 1780. Died 1807.

COLLIDGE, BERTHA.
Miniature painter. Born Lynn, Mass., Aug., 1880. Pupil of Boston Museum School under Tarbell and Benson; Bourgeois in Paris; Grueber in Munich. Member: Soc. de La Min., Paris; PA Soc. Min. P.

Address in 1929, 133 East 40'th St., NY. Died in 1934.

COLLIER, CHARLES MYLES.
Marine painter. Born in Hampton, VA, in 1836. Died Sept. 14, 1908 in Gloucester, MA.

COLLIER, ESTELLE E(LIZABETH).
Painter and writer. Born Chicago, IL, Aug. 1, 1881. Pupil of F. W. Southworth. Member: Tacoma FAA. Several awards received at Washington State Fairs. Work: "Lake Cachelus, Washington," Stadium High School, Tacoma, Wash.; "The Resolute," Seattle, (Wash.) Yacht Club. Address in 1929, R. 1, Box 267, South Tacoma, Wash.

COLLIER, JOHN.
Illustrator. Born in Dallas, Texas, in 1948. He attended Central College in Kansas for two years. He began illustrating Christmas cards in 1967. His career has blossomed in NY as illustrations for Redbook and McCall's have won him Gold Medals and an Award of Excellence at the Annual Exhibitions of the S of I. He has had exhibitions in Oklahoma City, Little Rock, Tulsa and New York.

COLLIER, NATE.
Illustrator. Born Orangeville, IL, Nov. 14, 1883. Pupil of J. H. Smith and G. H. Lockwood. Member: SI. Work: Illustrations for The Saturday Evening Post; Life; Judge; The Country Gentleman; Ladies' Home Journal; Bystander; Passing Show; London Opinion; London Humorist; McNaught Newspaper Syndicate of New York; and the "Illiterate Digest," by Will Rogers. Address in 1929, 140 Paulin Blvd., Leonia, NJ. Died in 1961.

COLLINS, FRANK H.
Painter and teacher. Director of drawing, elementary public schools of New York. Address in 1929, 500 Park Avenue, New York, NY.

COLLINS, FRED L.
Illustrator. Born Prince Adward Island, Jan. 1, 1876. Pupil of Hamilton Art School; S. J. Ireland. Member: Columbus PPC (Secy-treas from 1903). Manage Art Dept.,

Bucher Engraving Co. Address in 1929, Franklin Avenue, Columbus, Ohio; summer, Ancaster, Ont., Canada.

COLLINS, JULIA ALICE.
Painter. Born Savannah, GA. Pupil of the Telfair Academy, Savanna, GA; St. Louis School of Fine Arts. Awards: Three first prizes and two second prizes for portraits in the Tri-State Expositions of 1921 and 1923. Works: The Fourteen Stations of the Cross in the John Flannery Memorial Chapel, St. Joseph's Hospital, Savannah, GA. Address in 1929, 217 Gordon Street, East, Savannah, GA; summer, 81 Charlotte Street, Asheville, NC.

COLLINS, MARJORIE S.
Miniature painter. Exhibited portrait miniatures at Penna. Academy of Fine Arts, Philadelphia, 1922. Address in 1926, 701 Nottingham Road, Wilmington, DE.

COLLINS, MARY SUSAN.
Painter, craftsman, and teacher. Born Bay City, MI, June 1, 1880. Pupil of Museum of Fine Arts, Boston; Columbia University; SAL of NY. Member: Cleveland AA; Cleveland Woman's AC; AFA. Awards: First prize for batik, Cleveland Museum, 1921; third prize for landscape, Clev. Mus., 1922; Penton Medal, 1921; 1st prize for landscape painting, 1924, at the Cleveland Museum of Art; Prize Gal. Assoc., 1927; first prize ($200), Chic. oil, still life, Cleveland; "Primrose," Cleveland Museum of Art. Address in 1929, 1816 Wellesley Ave., East Cleveland, Ohio.

COLLINS, WALTER.
Painter, illustrator, lecturer, and teacher. Born Dayton, OH, Sept. 26, 1870. Pupil of Julian and Colarossi Acad. in Paris; Hyman's School of Illustration, Munich; Martz Weinholdt, Walter Thor, Royal Acad. in Munich; Adolf von Menzel in Berlin; Cincinnati Art Academy. Member: SSAL; Tampa Art Inst. Address in 1929, Lykes Hall, 302 North Boulevard, Tampa, FL; h. Seffner, FL.

COLLOW, JEAN.
Painter. She exhibited water colors in Cincinnati Museum i 1925. Address in 1926, Art Academy Cincinnati.

COLLVER, ETHEL BLANCHARD.
Painter. Born Boston, MA. Pupi of Tarbell, Benson, and Hale i Boston; Academie, Colarossi Naudin, Guerin, in Paris. Member Copley Society, 1901. Address i 1926, Fenway Studios, 12 Commonwealth Avenue, Boston, MA Died in 1955.

COLMAN, R. CLARKSON.
Painter. Born Elgin, IL, Jan 26 1884. Studied in Chicago, and wit Laurens and Julian in Paris Member: Calif. AC; San Diego Ar Guild; Laguna Beach AA. Awards Texas Cotton Place Exposition 1910; gold medal, Riverside Fair 1917; popular prize, Laguna Beac Assoc. 1920, 1922; cash prize Sacramento State Fair, 1920 Represented in Public Lib., Ajo Arizona; Public Lib., Waco, Texas Santa Monica Woman's Club; three murals, Junior H.S., Santa Ana, CA Address in 1929, Studio-by-the-Se Laguna, Beach, CA.

COLSON, FRANK V.
Painter, illustrator, etcher, an teacher. Born Boston, Oct. 24 1894. Pupil of Boston Museum o Fine Arts School. Member: Nort Shore AA; Boston SE. Instructor North Shore Summer School of Art Address in 1929, 98 Everett Street East, Boston, MA.

COLT, MARTHA COX.
Painter, sculptor, and teacher. Born Harrisburg, PA. Pupil o Phila. School of Design for Women PAFA; NY School of Art. Member Harrisburgh AA. Work: Bronze bus of Dr. Charles Hatch Ehrenfeld York Collegiate Institute, York PA. Addresss in 1929, 26 Sout Queen Street, York, PA; summer, 12 South Beeson Ave., Uniontown, PA.

COLT, MORGAN.
Painter. Born in Summit, NY, 1876 Member of Rochester Art Club Address in 1926, New Hope, PA Died April 12, 1926.

178

COLTMAN, ORA.
Painter and sculptor. Born Shelby, OH, 1860. Pupil of ASL of NY; Julian Academy in Paris; Magidey Schule, Munich. Member: Cleveland SA. Address in 1929, 11415 Mayfield Road, Cleveland, OH.

COLTON, MARY RUSSELL FERRELL.
Landscape and portrait painter. Born Louisville, KY, March 25, 1889. Pupil of Daingerfield; Henry B. Snell; Phila. School of Design for Women. Member: Phila. WCC; Plastic C.; Wash. WCC; Phila. Alliance; Aquarellists; NA Women PS; NYWCC; AWCS; AFA. Address in 1929, Llanfair and Wister Roads, Ardmore, PA.

COLWELL, ELIZABETH.
Painter, etcher, illustrator, and craftman. Born in Michigan in 1881. Pupil of Vanderpoel and Olson-Nordfeldt in Chicago. Member: Chicago SE; NY, SE; Chicago Cordon C. Award: Hon. mention, P.-P. Exp., San F., 1915. Represented in Print Dept., Chicago Art Institute. Designer of typeface called "Colwell Hand Letter," put out by American Type Foundry Co. Address in 1929, 1373 East 57th Street, Chicago, IL.

COLYER, VINCENT.
Painter. Born 1825 in Bloomingdale, NY. In 1849 he was elected an associate of the National Academy. Before the Rebellion he painted "Freedom's Martyr," representing the burial of Barber by John Brown. He also painted a number of Indian pictures from sketches he had made in the West. He was born in New York, but lived most of his life in Connecticut. Died July 12, 1888 near Darien, CT.

COMAN, CHARLOTTE BUELL.
Painter of landscapes. Born at Waterville, NY, 1833. Pupil of James Brevoort in New York, and Vernier in Paris. Elected an Associate Member of National Academy of Design in 1910. Represented in Metropolitan Museum, New York, and National Gallery, Washington, DC. She died in Yonkers New York, Nov. 11, 1924.

COMBS, FRANCES HUNGERFORD.
Painter. Member: Wash. WCC. Address in 1929, The Wellinton, 3820 Kanawha Street, Washington, DC.

COMEGYS, GEORGE H.
Painter. Born in Maryland. Died in the PA Hospital for the Insane, in Philadelphia. He was a pupil of Neagle and member of Board of the Artists' Fund Society in 1845. Work: "The Ghost Story", "Little Plunderers", Penna. Academy of Fine Arts.

COMES, MARCELLA RODANGE.
Painter. Born Pittsburgh, Sept. 3, 1905. Pupil of Giovanni Romagnoli. Member: Associated Artists of Pittsburgh. Award: Art Society prize for best portrait, Associated Artists of Pittsburgh, 1929. Address in 1929, 3242 Beechwood Blvd., Pittsburgh, PA.

COMINS, ALICE R.
Painter. Member: Concord AA; NA Women PS. Address in 1929, care Old Colony Trust Co., 22 Boylston Street, Boston, MA; Carmel, California; Cape Neddick, ME.

COMINS, EBEN F.
Portrait painter, lecturer, and teacher. Born Boston, MA in 1875. Pupil of Beaux-Arts in Paris, Denman Ross and Art Museum School in Boston. Member: Boston S. Indp. A.; Boston AC; Copley S.; Boston SWCP; CT AFA; Wash. AC; X Painters of Wash.; AFA. Awards: Hon. mention, CT AFA, 1919; first prize, Hartford Exhibition, 1921. Address in 1929, 1611 Connecticut Avenue, Washington, DC; summer, East Gloucester, MA.

COMSTOCK, ANNA BOTSFORD.
Naturalist and illustrator. Born near Otto, Cattaraugus County, New York, on September 1, 1854. Attended schools in her native town and the Chamberlain Inst. and Female College. In 1879-1881, when her husband chief entomologist in the US Department of Agriculture, she was formally appointed his assistant and prepared the drawings for his Report of the Entomologist (on citrus scale insects) of 1880. She studied wood engraving at

Cooper Union, New York City, in order to prepare illustrations for her husband's Introduction to Entomology, 1888. In 1888 she was one of the first four women admitted to Sigma XI, national honor society for the sciences. She made engravings for the more than 600 plates in Prof. Comstock's Manual for the Study of Insects, 1895, and for Insect Life, 1897, and How to Know the Butterflies, 1904. Her engravings were also widely exhibited in major expositions and won several prizes. Books written and illustrated by herself included Ways of the Six-Footed, 1903, How to Keep Bees, 1905, Confessions to a Heathen Idol, a novel, 1906, The Handbook of Nature Study, which went through more than two dozen editions, 1911, The Pet Book, 1914, and Trees at Leisure, 1916. She was a contributing editor for Nature-Study Review in 1905-1917 and editor in 1917-1923 and was on the staff of Country Life in America. In 1923 she was chosen one of the twelve greatest living American women in a poll by the League of Women Voters. She died in Ithaca, New York, on August 24, 1930.

COMSTOCK, ENOS B(ENJAMIN).
Painter, illustrator, and writer. Born Milwaukee, Dec. 24, 1879. Pupil John H. Vanderpoel, Frederick W. Freer. Author and illustrator of "Tuck-Me-In Stories," "When Mother Lets Us Tell Stories," "Fairy Frolics," etc. Illustrated "She and Allan," "When the World Shook," "The Ancient Allan," etc. Address in 1929, 178 Highwood Avenue, Leonia, NJ. Died in 1945.

COMSTOCK, FRANCES BASSETT.
Painter, sculptor, and illustrator. Born Elyria, OH, Oct. 16, 1881. Pupil of Gari Melchers, Frederick W. Freer and John Vanderpoel. Member: NYWCC. Address in 1929, 178 Highwood Avenue, Leonia, NJ.

CONACHER, JOHN C.
Illustrator. Lived from 1876 to 1947. Though classically trained, he developed a style, full of comic detail, which appeared in his many pen and ink drawings for magazines

in the early 1900's. Everybody's and Judge published his illustrations and his work for the Seaboard National Bank advertisements was selected for the ADC Annuals of Advertising Art.

CONANT, ALBAN JASPER.
Painter. Born Chelsea, Sept. 24, 1821. Painted portraits of Lincoln, Sherman, Anderson at Sumter; judges of Ct. of Appeals and Supreme Ct. of US, and cabinet secretaries; 4 portraits of Henry Ward Beecher, Dr. James McCosh, Bishop H. C. Potter, "Burial of De Soto," etc. Author: "Footprints of Vanished Races in the Mississippi Valley," My Acquaintance with Abraham Lincoln," etc. Died Feb. 3, 1915 in NYC.

CONANT, MARJORIE.
Painter. Born Boston, MA, Sept. 14, 1885. Pupil of Hale, Benson and Tarbell. Member: Atlanta AA; NA Women PS. Address in 1929, 6 Peachtree Place, N.W., Atlanta, GA.

CONARD, GRACE DODGE.
Painter, craftsman, and teacher. Born Dixon, IL, April 10, 1885. Pupil of AIC. Member: Chicago ASL; Chicago AG. Instructor, AIC. Address in 1929, Art Institute, Chicago; h. 297 Keystone Avenue, River Forest, IL.

CONARROE, GEORGE W.
Born in 1803 and died 1882. He was a portrait painter in Philadelphia about 1825. A self-portrait of the artist is owned by the PA Historical Society in Philadelphia. In 1829 he exhibited paintings in the PA Academy of Fine Arts. At that time he was living in Salem, NJ. He then lived in Philadelphia, until his death.

CONDAK, CLIFFORD ARA.
Illustrator. Born in Haverhill, MA, in 1930. He attended the Institute of Applied Arts and Sciences and the New School for Social Research in New York City. His first illustration, a tempera, appeared in Therapeutic Notes, a Parke, Davis and Company publication, in 1954. Since then his pieces have appeared in publications such as Seventeen,

180

Nugget, Playboy and Sports Illustrated. His artwork and illustrations have been shown at the Museum of Modern Art in NY, Gallery of Modern Art in Washington, DC, and San Francisco Museum of Modern Art.

CONDIT, CHARLES L. (MRS.)
Painter, craftsman, and teacher. Born Perryburg, OH, Nov. 29, 1863. Pupil of Maud Mason. Member: Texas FAS; Austin AL. Specialty, conventional decoration of china. Address in 1929, 2308 San Antonio Street, Austin, Texas.

CONDON, GRATTAN.
Illustrator. Born Eugene, OR, June 10, 1887. Pupil of Los Angeles School of Art and Design; Los Angeles ASL; Walter Biggs. Illustrated for the "Ladies' Home Journal" and the "Saturday Evening Post." Address in 1929, 15 West 67th Street, New York, NY.

CONE, JOSEPH.
Engraver in both stipple and line, was chiefly engaged upon portrait work. Joseph Cone was engraving over his own name in Philadelphia, 1814-19, inclusive. In the period 1820-24 he was engraving prints and publishing them in Baltimore, MD. He also worked for Boston publishers, and in 1829-30 his name reappears in the Philadelphia directories as an "Engraver."

CONE, MARVIN D.
Painter and teacher. Born Cedar Rapids, Oct. 21, 1891. Pupil of AIC; Ecole des Beaux-Arts, Montpellier, France. Work: "Cloud Bank," Cedar Rapids Art Association. Address in 1929, 1721 Fifth Avenue, Cedar Rapids, IA. Died in 1964.

CONGDON, ADAIRENE VOSE.
Painter. Born in New York City. Pupil of Art Students' League of New York. Represented in Petit Palace, Paris, Library of Congress, New York Public Library, and Boston Art Club. Address in 1926, Villa Vose Studios, Campbell, NY.

CONGDON, THOMAS RAPHAEL.
Painter and etcher. Born in Addison, NY, in 1862. Pupil of Art Students' League of New York, also studied in Paris. Represented by prints in Library of Congress, New York Public Library, and Boston Art Club. Died Nov. 15, 1917 in Boston, MA.

CONKLING, MABEL.
Sculptor. Born in Boothbay, ME, Nov. 17, 1871. Studied in Paris under Bouguereau and Collin until 1899. In 1900 she studied sculpture under MacMonnies. Work: "The Lotus Girl," "Song of the Sea," and portrait reliefs of Dr. George Alexander, Mrs. James A. Garland, and Hope Garland. Address in 1926, 22 West 9th Street, New York.

CONKLING, PAUL.
Sculptor. Born in New York City, 1871. Pupil of MacMonnies. His specialty was portraiture. Address in 1926, 5 McDougal Alley, New York.

CONLEY, SARAH WARD.
Painter, sculptor, illustrator, artist, craftsman, writer and teacher. Born Nashville, TN, Dec. 21, 1861. Pupil of Bouguereau, Julian and F. A. Bridgman in Paris; Ferrari in Rome. Member: Nashville AA. Work: Woman's Bulding, Centennial Exp., Nashville, TN; mural decorations in Battle Creek Sanitarium. Address in 1929, 2104 West End Avenue, Nashville, TN.

CONLON, GEORGE.
Sculptor. Born in Maryland in 1888. Pupil of Injalbert and Bartlett in Paris. Address in 1926, 1230 St. Paul Street, Baltimore, MD.

CONN, JAMES.
Engraver and writing-master at Elizabethtown, NJ, advertised in 1771 his "intention to teach writing, arithmetic, mathematics, geography," etc., and adds to his notice the following: "Futhermore, the said Conn at leisure hours, engraves Shop Bills, Bills of Parcels, Bills of Exchange, or any kind of Writing for the Rolling-Press, in the neatest Manner."

CONNAWAY, JAY HALL.
Painter. Born Liberty, IN, Nov. 27, 1893. Member: ASL of NY; Allied AA; Salma. C. Work: "Winter," Herron Art Institute, Indianapolis, IN; "The Everlasting Cliffs," permanent collection, Springfield (IL) High School. Award: Hallgarten prize ($200), NAD, 1926. Address in 1929, care of The Macbeth Gallery, 15 East 57th Street, New York, NY. Died in 1970.

CONNELL, EDWIN D.
Painter. Born New York, NY, Sept. 3, 1859. Pupil of Bouguereau, Robert-Fleury and Julien Dupre in Paris. Member: Societe Internationale des Beaux-Arts; Paris AAA. Awards: Hon. mention, Paris Salon, 1899; medal, second class, Orleans Exp., 1905; first class medal, Toulouse Exp., 1908; silver medal, P.-P. Exp., San F., 1915. Work: "Cattle," Toledo Museum of Art. Address in 1929, 56 Rue de Sevres, Clamart, France.

CONNELLY, EUGENE L.
Painter. Member Pittsburgh Academy of Artists. Address in 1926, Davis Theatre, Pittsburgh, PA.

CONNELLY, MARC.
Illustrator. Member: Society of Illustrators. Address in 1926, 159½ East 83d Street, New York, NY.

CONNELLY, PIERRE FRANCIS.
Born in Southern City, 1840. He was taken to England as a child. He studied painting in France, and sculpture in Italy. In 1876 he visited the United States and exhibited in the Centennial at Philadelphia.
Died in 1902.

CONNER, CHARLES.
Landscape painter. Born in Richmond, IN, in 1857. His best known canvas was "Wet Night in February," shown at St. Louis Exposition. Died Feb. 14, 1905 in Richmond.

CONNER, JEROME.
Sculptor. Born in Ireland, Oct. 12, 1875. Self-taught. Member: S. Wash. A. Work: Bronze tablet, "Nuns of the Battlefield,"
Washington, DC. Address in 1929, 322 North Carolina Avenue, S.E., Washington, DC.

CONNER, JOHN RAMSEY.
Painter. Born Radnor, PA in 1867. Pupil of PAFA. Award: Bronze medal, P. P. Exp., San F., 1915; silver medal, Sesqui-Centennial Exposition, Philadelphia, 1926. Work: "The Fisherman," Pennsylvania Academy of Fine Arts, Philadelphia; "Under the North Light," Des Moines Assoc. of Fine Arts; "A Cottage Interior," California C., Los Angeles. Address in 1929, 1718 East Ocean Blvd., Long Beach, California. Died Sept. 12, 1952.

CONNICK, CHARLES J.
Craftsman, and draftsman. Born in Springboro, PA, Sept. 27, 1875. Studied in Pittsburgh, Boston, England and France. Member: Mural P.; Boston SAC; Boston Arch. C.; Boston AC; Boston SA (hon.); AFA. Awards: Gold medal, P.-P. Exp., San F., 1915; Logan medal, AIC, 1917; Soc. of Arts and Crafts medal, Boston, 1920; American Institute of Architects, craftsmanship medal, 1925. Work: Stained glass windows in Fourth Presbyterian Church, Chicago; Chapel and Synod House St. John the Divine Cathedral Seattle, Wash.; All Saints' Church, Peterboro, NH; Christ Church, Glendale, Ohio; St. John's Chruch, Beverly Farms, MA; Trinity College Chapel, Washington, DC; St. Agatha's Church, Philadelphia, PA. Represented in Vanderpoel AA Collection, Chicago. Address in 1929, 9 Harcourt Street, Boston MA, h. 157 Webster Street, West Newton, MA. Died in 1945.

CONNY, JOHN.
Engraver. Born 1655 in Boston. Was a prominent gold and silversmith, of Boston, at least as early as 1700. The MSS. Archives of MA, under date of March 12, 1702-3, note the indebtedness of the Colony "To John Conny for graving 3 Plates for Bills of Credit," and on Nov. 26, 1706, the same records show that, to prevent counterfeiting, the plate for the bills was to be provided with, "eight blazons and put on by the engraver." This MA currency of 1702 included little

182

more than the engraved script and the seal of the Colony, and the earlier bills of 1690 approach it so closely in general design and execution, especially in the character of the decoration at the top of the note, that there is a strong possibility that both plates were made by the same man. If this assumption were correct, John Conny would be the first American engraver upon copper on record. Died 1722 in Boston.

CONRADS, CARL H.
Sculptor. Born in Germany, 1829, came to New York in 1860. He served in the Union Army. Among his works are statues of Alexander Hamilton, Central Park; "Gen'l Thayer," West Point; and "Daniel Webster" for the Capitol at Washington. He has resided in Hartford, CT, after 1866.

CONREY, LEE F.
Illustrator. Born St. Louis, MO, 1883. Pupil of St. Louis School of Fine Arts. Member: Soceity of Illustrators. Illustrations for Cosmopolitan, McClure's, Munsey's Magazines.

CONROW, WILFORD S(EYMOUR).
Painter, lecturer, and writer. Born South Orange, NJ, June 14, 1880. Pupil of Jean-Paul Laurens, Morisset, P. Tudor-Hart, Hambidge. Member: Slama. C.; Wash. AC; NYSC.; Art Center, New York; Barnard C; Brooklyn SA; Grolier C; Cosmos; Century; Am. APL. Work: "Portrait of Cephas Brainerd," Y.M.C.A., New York City; Portraits of Henry Clay Cameron, Karl A. Langiotz, Howard Crosby Butler, Princeton University, Princeton, NJ; Portrait of Dr. Wm. H. Dall, Cosmos Club, Washington, DC; mural painting of George Washington, George Washington Life Insurance Co. Building., Charleston, W. VA,; Portraits of Prof. Wm. H. Goodyear, Brooklyn Museum; Dr. Charles R. Gillett, Dr. Charles Cuthbert Hall, Dr. Francis Brown, Union Theological Seminary, New York; Gov. J. Franklin Fort, State House, Trenton, NJ. Address in 1929, 130 Carnegie Hall; 154 West 57th Street, New York, NY. Died Nov. 24, 1957 in NYC.

CONROY, GEORGE I.
Painter. Member: Salma. Club. Address in 1926, 793 Gravesend Avenue, Brooklyn, NY.

CONSTANT, GEORGE.
Painter, illustrator, etcher, and teacher. Born Aijon, Greece, April 18, 1892. Pupil of Charles Hawthorne, George Bellows, R. Davy, Wolcott. Member: Dayton SE; S. Indp. A. Address in 1929, 51 West 8th Street, New York, NY, summer, 867 N. Dearborn Street, Chicago. Died in 1978.

CONSTANT, MARJORIE.
Painter. Exhibited at National Association of Women Painters and Sculptors, New York, 1924. Address in 1926, Duxbury, MA.

CONTENT, DAN.
Illustrator. Born in 1902. He received training at PI and the ASL. A pupil of Dean Cornwell, his illustrations for various adventure stories reflected Cornwell's teachings. His editorial work appeared in Cosmopolitan, Good Housekeeping, Liberty, Ladies Home Journal, Collier's and McCall's as early as 1923. He taught at the Workshop School of Art in the 1940's.

CONTI, GINO EMILIO CESARA.
Painter and etcher. Born Lucca, Barga, Italy, July 18, 1900. Pupil of R.I. School of Design; Ecole des Beaux-Arts, Fontainebleau, France. Member: Arch. Lg. of NY; Prov. AC; Prov. WCC. Work: "French School Boy," Rhode Island School of Design Museum; mural decorations, Corvese Hospital, Providence, RI. Address in 1929, 50 rue Vercingetorix, Paris, France; h. 504 Broadway, Providence, RI.

CONVERSE, LILLY S.
Painter. Born Petrograd, 1892. Pupil of Kenneth Hayes Miller. Address in 1926, Rue Desbordes, Valmore, Paris, France.

CONWAY, JOHN SEVERINUS.
Painter and sculptor. Born at Dayton, Ohio, in 1852. Pupil of Conrad Diehl, Jules Lefebvre and Boulanger in Paris. Work: Mural decorations in Chamber of Commerce,

Milwaukee. Sculptor for Soldiers' Monument, Milwaukee. Address in 1925, Tenafly, NJ, P.O. 231. Died Dec. 25, 1925 in Tenafly, NJ.

CONWAY, WILLIAM JOHN
Painter and sculptor. Born in St. Paul, Oct. 26, 1872. Pupil of Colarossi Academy under Collin, Courtois and Prinet in Paris. Member: Whistler Club; Art Workers' Guild; Minnesota State Art Soc.; Artists' Soc., St. Paul Inst. Address in 1929, 1394 Lincoln Avenue, St. Paul, MN.

COOK, CHARLES B.
Painter. Exhibited "Mountain Building" at the Penna. Academy of Fine Arts, 1924. Address in 1926, Woodstock, New York.

COOK, DANIEL.
Painter. Born Cincinnati, 1872. Pupil of Nicholas Gysis, Cincinnati Art Academy. Member: Munich Art Club; Cincinnati Art Club. Instructor at University of Cincinnati. Work: "A Rainy Day," University of Cincinnati; mural decorations, Cincinnati Music Hall. Address in 1926, 104 Saunders Street, Cincinnati, OH.

COOK, FRANCES KERR.
Illustrator. Born West Union, Iowa. Pupil of AIC; Chicago AFA. Member: ASL; AIC Alumni. Work: Illustrated "Today's Stories of Yesterday," "Red and Gold Stories," "The Alabaster Vase" cover designs and illustrations for books of Scott, Foresman and Co., A. Flannagan and Co., Albert Whitman and Co.; illustrations for "Youth's Companion," "Child Life," "Little Folks," "Woman's Home Companion," "Designer," "Craftsman," "McCalls." Specialty, illustration of children's stories. Address in 1929, 200 River Bluff Road, Elgin, IL.

COOK, HOWARD (NORTON).
Illustrator and etcher. Born Springfield, July 16, 1901. Pupil of ASL of NY. Award: Hon. mention for woodcut, Philadelphia Print Club, 1929. Represented by etchings and woodcuts in the print collection of the Metropolitan Museum of Art, New York, Fogg Art Museum, Harvard University, Cambridge, MA; Baltimore Museum of Art, Baltimore, MD. Address in 1929, Rue Du Vallonnet, Cagnes-sur-mer, Alpes-Maritimes, France; h. 100 Washington Road, Springfield, MA.

COOK, ISABEL VERNON.
Painter. Born Brooklyn, NY. Pupil of Art Students' League of New York and Chase; Blanche and Simon in Paris. Member: National Academy of Women Painters and Sculptors. Address in 1926, 39 West 67th Street, New York, NY.

COOK, JOHN A.
Painter. Born Gloucester, MA, March 14, 1870. Pupil of DeCamp, E. L. Major and Douglas Volk. Member: S. Indp. A.; North Shore AA; Boston AC; New Haven PPC; AFA. Address in 1929, 16 Sayward Street; h. 8 Highland Street; summer 67 E Point Road, Gloucester, MA. Died in 1936.

COOK, MAY ELIZABETH.
Sculptor. Born Chillicothe, Ohio Dec. 1881. Pupil of Paul Bartlett, Ecole des Beaux-Arts and Colarossi Academy in Paris. Member Columbus Lg. of Artists; AM Ceramic Soc. (assoc.); Plastic C. NA Women PS; Alliance; Phila Alliance; Gallery FA, Columbus AFA; Union Internationale des Beaux-Arts des Lettres, Paris Represented in Carnegie Library Columbus, OH.; Ohio State University, Columbus, Ohio National Museum, Washington, DC memorial panels, Colorado Springs Chillicothe, Ohio; war work, wa models from life masks fo reconstruction among wounded soldiers. Address in 1929, 1550 Clifton Avenue; h. 1546 Richmond Avenue, Columbus, Ohio.

COOK, PAUL RODDA
Painter. Born Salina, Kansas, Aug. 17, 1897. Pupil of H. D. Pohl Birge Harrison, H. D. Murphy Member: SSAL; San Antonio AL Amer. Artists Prof. Lg. Awards First prize, Waco Cotton Palace 1st prize, San Angelo, 2nd prize Lockhart State Fair and hon mention, Davis Competition, all in

1929. Address in 1929, 409 West Park Avenue, San Antonio, TX.

COOK, T. B.
Engraver. In 1809-16 T. B. Cook was engraving portraits in stipple for Wm. Durell and other book publishers of New York.

COOK-SMITH, JEAN BEMAN.
Painter and sculptor. Born in New York, March 26, 1865. Pupil of Art Institute of Chicago; Chase. Studied in Holland, France and Italy. Member: National Academy of Women Painters and Sculptors. Work: "The Maya Frieze," San Diego Museum, CA. Address in 1926, Jamaica, Long Island, New York.

COOKE, ABIGAIL W.
Painter. Pupil of Rhode Island School of Design. Member of Providence Art Club. Address in 1926, 15 Pitman Street, Providence, RI.

COOKE, CHARLES H.
Painter. Born Toledo, Ohio, July 31, 1859. Pupil of AIC. Member: Palette and Chisel C.; AIC Alumni Assoc.; S. Indp. A.; Chicago NJSA; Am. APL; Ill. Acad. FA. Address in 1929, 6329 Glenwood Avenue, Chicago, IL.

COOKE, EDNA.
Illustrator. Born in Philadelphia, 1891. Pupil of Breckenridge and McCarter at the Penna. Academy of Fine Arts. Address in 1926, Care of 235 South 11th Street, Philadelphia.

COOKE, GEORGE.
Engraver and portrait-painter. Born in St. Mary County, MD, March 1793. He studied art in Europe in 1826-30, and established himself in New York on his return to this country. It is not known that this man ever attempted to engrave, and the plates signed by George Cooke as "engraver", are too well done to be ascribed to any prentice hand. Died in 1849.

COOKE, JESSIE DAY.
Painter, illustrator, and teacher. Born Atchison, Kansas, May 16, 1872. Pupil of Vanderpoel, Freer, Pauline Dohn. Member: Alumni

Assoc. AIC; Chicago NJSA; Ill. Acad. FA; Am. APL. Address in 1929, 6329 Glenwood Avenue, Chicago, IL.

COOKE, JOSEPH.
Engraver. In the Pennsylvania Gazette, Philadelphia, 1789, Joseph Cooke advertises himself as goldsmith, jeweler and hair-worker. Advertises "Church, State or County Seals, Coats of Arms, and all manner of Engraving on steel, silver, gold, or metal, executed in the best manner and at the lowest prices."

COOKINS, JAMES.
Landscape painter. Born in Terre Haute, IN, 1825. After study abroad he opened his studio in Cincinnati in 1861, but finally settled in Chicago, IL.

COOKMAN, CHARLES EDWIN.
Painter. Born in Columbus, OH, in 1856; died in 1913.

COOLEY, GARY.
Illustrator. Born in Jackson, Michigan, in 1947. He studied for four years at the Society of Arts and Crafts. Since 1969, when he entered the field of illustration doing black and white art for Detroit newpapers, his work has appeared in books, magazines and posters. The Graphic Artists Guild of Detroit has awarded him three Gold Medals and he received a First Honor from the 1973 Ace Awards in Pittsburgh.

COOLIDGE, DAVID W.
Painter. Born in Lincoln, Neb. Study: Drake Univ.; with John Falter; PAFA; Tyler Sch. Art, Rome. Work: US Nat'l. Bank, Omaha; Arthur Anderson & Co., Phila. Exhibitions: Wm. Penn. Mem. Mus., Harrisburg, PA; Hazleton (PA) Art Mus.; Phila. WC Club Ann., Phila. Art Alliance, etc. Mem.: Phila. WC Club; assoc. mem., Am. WC Soc. Media: Watercolor, oil. Address in 1982, Box 359, Bryn Mawr, PA.

COOLIDGE, JOHN.
Painter, illustrator, and writer. Born Pennsylvania, Dec. 6, 1882. Pupil of Chase, Cecilia Beaux, T. P. Anshutz; J. Francis Smith.

185

Member: Calif. AC. Address in 1929, 930 Central Bldg.; h. 3459 S. Arlington Avenue, Los Angeles, CA. Died in 1934.

COOLIDGE, MOUNTFORT.
Painter. Born in Brooklyn, NY, in 1888. Pupil of Robert Henri. Address in 1926, 126 Pennsylvania Street, Brooklyn, New York. Died in New York.

COONSMAN, NANCY.
Sculptor. Born at St. Louis, MO, in 1888. Pupil of Zolnay and Grafly. Address in 1926, 6171 Delmar Blvd., St. Louis, MO.

COOPER, ALICE.
Sculptor. Born in Denver, CO. Among her best known works, "Summer Breeze," "Dancing Fawn," and "Frog Girl."

COOPER, B. Z.
Painter. Exhibited water colors at Penna. Academy of the Fine Arts, Philadelphia, 1922. Address in 1926, 1947 Broadway, New York.

COOPER, COLIN CAMPBELL.
Painter. Born Philadelphia. Pupil of PAFA; Julian and Delecluse Academies in Paris. Member: ANA 1908, NA 1912; NYWCC; AC Phila; Phila. WCC; AWCS; Fellowship PAFA; Lotos C.; NAC; SPNY; AFA. Specialty - Street scenes. Awards: Bronze medal, Atlanta Exp., 1895; Wm. T. Evans prize, AWCS, 1903; Senan prize, PAFA, 1904; gold medal, ACP, 1905; silver medal, Buenos Aires Exp., 1910; Beal prize, NYWCC, 1911; gold medal for oil painting and silver medal for water colors, P.-P. Exp., San F., 1915; Hudnut prize, NYWCC, 1918; Lippincott prize, PAFA, 1919. Work: "Broad Street, New York," Cincinnati Museum; "The Flatiron, New York," Dallas (TX) Art Association; "Grand Basin, World's Fair," and "The Plaza, New York," St. Louis Museum of Fine Arts; "Basilika, Quebec," Boston Art Club; "Procession at Bruges," Art Club of Philadelphia; "The Rialto," Lotos Club, New York; "Broadway in War Time," PAFA, Philadelphia; "Fifth Avenue, New York," owned by the French Government; "Lotos Pool, El Encanto, Santa Barbara," Reading

Museum. Address in 1929, 222 West 59th Street, New York, NY; Santa Barbara, California. Died Nov. 6, 1937.

COOPER, ELIZABETH.
Sculptor. Born in Dayton, OH, 1901. She made a specialty of animals. Address in 1926, Stamford, CT.

COOPER, EMMA LAMPERT.
Painter. Born Nunda, NY. Studied New York, Cooper Union, and Art Students' League, and with Miss Agnes D. Abbatt in water colors; later went abroad several times for study in Paris and to sketch in Holland, Italy, etc. Member: NY WCC; AWCS; NA Women PS New York Society of Painters; (pres.) Women's Art Associaton of Canada; Philadelphia Water Color Club. Died July 30, 1920 in Pittsfield, NY.

COOPER, FRED G.
Illustrator. Born McMinnville, OR, Dec. 29, 1883. Member: SI, 1910; Salma. C.; Al Graphic A.; Phila. Sketch C.; GFLA. Illustrations for "Collier's" "Life," "Liberty." Cartoonist and advertising designer. Theater posters for Food Administration. Originator of the Cooper Letter. Address in 1929, care of Life, 598 Madison Avenue; h. 101 West 55th Street, New York, NY. Died in 1962.

COOPER, JAMES.
miniature painter. Flourished in Philadelphia, 1855. He exhibited at the Penna. Academy in 1855.

COOPER, MARGARET MILLER.
Painter. Born Terryville, CT, March 4, 1874. Pupil NAD; PAFA at Chester Springs, PA; Henry B. Snell; Guy Wiggins. Member: NA (Assoc.); NA Women PS; AFA; CT AFA Address in 1929, 169 Vine Street, New Britain, CT; summer, Lyme, CT.

COOPER, MARIO RUBEN.
Painter, sculptor and illustrator. Born in Mexico City, Nov. 26, 1905. Study: Otis Art Inst., Los Angeles, 1924; Chouinard Art Sch., Los Angeles, 1925; Grand Central Art Sch., NYC, 1927-37; Columbia Univ.; with F. Tolles Chamberlin

186

Louis Trevisco, Pruett Carter, Harvey Dunn. Work: Met. Mus. of Art; Butler Inst.; NASA; and others. Commissions for USAF: ptg. of Atlas ICBM, planes, capitals of Europe; invited by Nat'l. Gal. to doucment Apollo 10 & 11 flights. Exhibitions worldwide. Illustrations in Collier's, Woman's Home Companion, American, Cosmopolitan. Head, team of artists to Japan, Korea, Okinawa, USAF, 1956, and to Japan, 1957; art consultant, USAF, 1960; teacher, ASL, from 1957, and at NAD Sch. of FA, City College NY, 1961-68, and GCSA. Received Audubon Artists Guild Medal of Hon., 1974; Samuel F. B. Morse Gold Medal, NAD; Am. WC Soc. High Winds Medal, 1979, 81. Member, Am. WC Soc; Audubon Artists; NAD; hon. mention Royal WC Soc. of Great Brit.; Cent. Assn.; Nat'l. Sculpt. Soc. Works in watercolor. Address in 1982, 1 W. 67th St., New York City.

COOPER, PEREGRINE F.
Painter. He worked in oil portraits, miniatures, also drawing in pastels. He flourished in Philadelphia from 1840 to 1890. In 1863 he published a book on miniature painting. He exhibited for a number of years at the Pennsylvania Academy of the Fine Arts, Philadelphia.

COOPER, PETER.
Painter. Painted a view of Philadelphia; The records of the "Philadelphia City Council" read: "Peter Cooper, painter, was admitted a freeman of the city in May 1717."

COOTES, FRANK GRAHAM.
Painter and illustrator. Born Staunton, VA, April 6, 1879. Pupil of Kenneth Hayes Miller, Robert Henri and F. V. Du Mond in New York. Member: SI 1910. Illustrations for "The Shepherd of the Hills," etc. Designed covers for magazines. Address in 1929, 50 West 67th Street, New York, NY. Died in 1960.

COPE, MARGARETTA PORTER.
Painter. Born Philadelphia, Feb. 17, 1905. Pupil of A. Margaretta Archambault and PAFA. Address in

1929, 1928 Panama Street; h. 2418 Spruce Street, Philadelphia, PA; summer, 839 Kearney Avenue, Cape May City, NJ.

COPELAND, ALFRED BRYANT.
Painter. Born in Boston, 1840. He studied abroad and on returning to this country he became professor in the University of St. Louis. He later opened his studio in Paris, exhibited in the Salon, and sent a collection of his paintings to Boston. He died Jan. 30, 1909 in Boston, MA.

COPELAND, CHARLES.
Painter. Born Thomaston, ME, 1858. Engaged as illustrator and painter in water color; exhibited at Society American Artists; Penna. Academy Fine Arts; Boston Art Club, etc. Member: Boston Art Club, Boston Society Water Color Painters. Address in 1926, 110 Tremont Street, Boston, MA.

COPELAND, JOSEPH FRANK.
Painter, craftsman, and teacher. Born St. Louis, MO, Feb. 21, 1872. Member: Phila. Sketch C.; Phila. WCC; Phila. Alliance. Instructor Pennsylvania Museum School of Industrial Art. Address in 1929, 320 South Broad Street, Philadelphia, PA; h. 58 Forest Avenue, Drexel Hill, PA.

COPELAND, M. BAYNON.
Portrait painter. Born El Paso, Texas. Pupil of Kenyon Cox in New York; Ferdinand Humbert and R. Miller in Paris; Shanon in London. Address in 1929, 73 Longridge Road, S.W. 5, London, England.

COPLEY, JOHN SINGLETON.
Portrait painter. Born in Boston, July 3, 1738. This famous American portrait painter was the stepson of the English portrait painter and mezzotint engraver Peter Pelham, who died in Boston in 1751. On May 22, 1748, his first wife having died, Pelham married Mary Singleton Copley, the widow of Richard Copley and the mother of the subject of his sketch. John Singleton Copley doubtless received instructions from his step-father in both portrait painting and in engraving. As evidence of the latter statement

there exists a small but creditably executed mezzotint plate of the Rev. Mr. William Welsted of Boston in New England. This plate is signed "J.S. Copley pinxt. et fecit." William Welsted died 1753, and this plate was probably engraved soon after this date. He sent over to London, for exhibition at the Royal Academy in 1760, a picture of "The Boy and the Flying Squirrel." In 1775 after a successful career as a portrait painter in Boston he established himself in London. His masterpieces, "The Death of Major Pierson," and "The Death of Lord Chatham" are both in the Nat'l Acad. See "Life of John Singleton Copley," by Augustus T. Perkins. Also "The Life and Works of John Singleton Copley," by Frank W. Bayley. The Boston Mus. of Fine Arts owns his portraits of Samuel Adams, Gen'l Jos. Warren, Mrs. Warren, John Quincy Adams, and "Watson and the Shark." Died Sept. 9, 1815 in London, England.

COPPEDGE, FERN ISABELL.
Painter. Born Decatur, IL, July 28, 1888. Pupil of William M. Chase, John Carlson, and ASL of NY; AIC; PAFA. Member: NA Women PS; Plastic C.; Phila. Alliance; Fellowship PAFA; ASL of NY; Ten Phila. P.; North Shore AA; Gloucester SA. Awards: H. O. Dean prize, Artists of Kansas City and vicinity, 1927; E. Shield prize, 1918; hon. mention, NA Women PS, 1922; first prize, Plastic Club, 1924; silver medal, Kansas City AI, 1924. Work: "The Thaw," Detroit Institute of Art; "Winter on the Schuylkill," Pennsylvania State Capitol; "Snow Covered Hills," PAFA; "From the Hill Top," American Embassy, Rio de Janeiro, Brazil; "The Frozen Canal," DeWitt Museum, San Antonio, TX; "A Village on the Delaware," Thayer Museum, Kansas University, Lawrence, Kansas. Address in 1929, 4011 Baltimore Avenue, Philadelphia, PA; summer; Lumberville, Bucks Co., PA.

COPPINI, POMPEO.
Sculptor. Born Moglia, Italy, May 19, 1870. Pupil of Augusto Rivalta in Florence; came to America in 1896; citizen of United States in 1901. Represented in the United States by 36 public monuments, 16 portrait statues and about 75 portrait busts, and in Mexico City by the Washington Statue, gift from Americans to Mexico. Address in 1929, 210 West 14th Street, New York, NY; h. 7244 Boston Post Road, Pelham Manor, NY. Died Sept. 27, 1957, in San Antonio, Texas.

CORAM, THOMAS.
Portrait and landscape painter. He was born in Bristol, England, April 25, 1757. He came to Charleston, SC, at an early age. He was a self-taught artist and attempted engraving (see "Stauffer's American Engravers"). Died May 2, 1811 in Charleston, SC.

CORBETT, EDWARD M.
Born August 22, 1919 in Chicago, IL. Studied at Cal. School of Fine Arts, S.F. Taught there and at S.F. State Teachers College; UC/Berkeley, Mount Holyoke (1953-62); Santa Barbara. Received Rosenberg fellowship (1951), and award from Nat. Inst. of Arts and Letters. Exhibited at Art Inst. of Chicago; Riverside Museum, NYC; G. Borgenicht Gallery, NYC MOMA; Tulane; Whitney, others. In collections of the Tate, Newark Museum; Bankers Trust; Whitney, MOMA, and many others, incl. private collections. Died June 6, 1971 in MA.

CORBETT, GAIL SHERMAN.
Sculptor. Born in Syracuse, NY. Pupil of Augustus Saint Gaudens. Awards: Honorable mention for sculpture, and bronze medal for medals, Panama Pacific Expn. Work: "Hamilton White Memorial" and "Kirkpatrick Fountain," Syracuse, NY; bronze doors, Auditorium and Municipal Building, Springfield, MA; Springfield medal, Boston Museum. Address in 1926, 443 West 21st Street, New York City, NY. Died in 1952.

CORCOS, LUCILLE.
Painter and illustrator. Born in New York City in 1908. Studied: Art Students Lg. Awards: Pepsi-Cola, 1944; Grumbacher award, 1956. Collections: Whitney Museum of American Art; US Gypsum Company;

Upjohn Pharmaceutical Company; Columbia Broadcasting System; Museum of Art, Tel-Aviv; mural, North Shore Hospital, Manhassets, New York; Life Magazine; mural, Waldorf-Astoria, New York. Her first illustration assignments came in 1929 from Conde Nast's Vanity Fair. She became well known for her children's book illustrations, including Grimm's Fairy Tales, published by Limited Editions Club, and Ungskah and Oyaylee. Died in 1973.

CORISH, JOSEPH R.
Painter. Born Somerville, MA, April 9, 1909. Study: Boston Univ.; Harvard Univ.; Bridgewater State College. Work: US Naval Acad. Mus.; US Naval War College; state capitols; foreign embassies; ships of US, Brit., Japan, Ger., Spain and Portugal. Exhibitions: Boston Museum of Fine Arts; Busch Reisinger Museum; Jordan Exhib. of Contemp. N. Eng. Artists; Harvard, Yale, Boston U., Conn. College; museums in US, Germany, Spain, Norway, and Japan. Mem.: Am. Soc. of Marine Artists; Salmagundi Club; Am. APL; also US Navy Combat Artist; lecturer at Harward, Univ. of Conn. and others. Media: Oil. Address in 1982, Somerville, MA.

CORNE, MICHAEL FELICE.
Italian marine and portrait painter in oil. Born 1752 on Elba, came to US in 1799. He also drew portraits in India ink, several being in Essex Institute at Salem, MA. During the War of 1812 he painted a series of naval engagements. Died July 10, 1845 in Newport, RI.

CORNELIUS, MARTY.
Painter and illustrator. Born in Pittsburgh, Pennsylvania in 1913. Studied: Carnegie Inst.; and with Reginald Marsh, Alexander Kostellow. Awards: Association Art Pittsburgh, 1939, 1945, 1953; Martin Leisser School of Design, 1946-1949; Butler Institute of American Art, 1948; Corcoran Gallery of Art, 1941, 1947; others. Collections: Pittsburgh Public Schools; MOMA, NYC; others. Exhib. at Whitney, NYC; Corcoran, Wash., DC; Carnegie, from 1937; Pal. of

Legion of Hon., San Fran.; others. Died in 1979.

CORNER, THOMAS C.
Painter. Born Baltimore, MD, 1865. Pupil of Weir and Cox in New York; Lefebvre and Constant in Paris. Member: Charcoal Club. Represented in Virginia State Library, Richmond, by portrait of Gov. F. W. Mackey Holliday, painted in 1897. Died in 1938.

CORNETT, ROBERT FRANK.
Painter. Born Lafayette, LA, July 27, 1867. Pupil of George Essig; Corcoran School of Art. Member: S. Wash. A.; Wash. Landscape C. Address in 1929, 2944 Taver Street, N.W., Woodridge, DC.

CORNOYER, PAUL.
Painter. Born St. Louis, MO, 1864. Pupil of Lefebvre, Constant and Louis Blanc in Paris. Work: "After the Rain," Brooklyn Institute Museum; "Madison Square," Art Association, Dallas, Texas; St. Louis Art Museum; "Rainy Day, Columbus Circle," Newark Art Association. Died June 17, 1923 in East Gloucester, MA.

CORNWELL, DEAN.
Illustrator. Born Louisville, KY, March 5, 1892. Pupil of Harvey Dunn; Charles S. Chapman. Member: SI; GFLA; Players C.; Chelsea Arts C., London; London Sketch C; Salma. C.; Arch. L. of NY. Awards: First Illustration prize, Wilmington SFA, 1919 and 1921; two awards of merit, AIC Alumni, 1922; Isidor water color prize, Salma. C., 1927. Illustrated: "Torrent," "Kindred of the Dust," "Rivers End," "Valley of Silent Men," "Find the Women," "The Desert Healer," "The Garden of Peril," "Never the Twain Shall Meet," "The Enchanted Hill," "Exquisite Perdita." Author of "City of the Great King," (Cosmopolitan Book Corp.). Address in 1929, 206 East 33rd Street, New York, NY; Mamaroneck, NY. Died in 1960.

CORNWELL, MARTHA JACKSON.
Sculptor and painter. Born West Chester, Jan. 29, 1869. Studied at Philadelphia School of Design, and Art Students' League of New York;

189

and with Saint Gaudens, H. Siddons Mowbray and George deForest Brush. Member: ASL of NY; Fellowship PAFA. Specialty, portrait bronzes. Exhibited at Penna. Academy of Fine Arts, Philadelphia, 1924. Deied before 1926.

CORNWELL, WILLIAM CARYL.
Painter. Born Lyons, NY Aug. 19, 1851. Pupil of Lefebvre, Boulanger, and Julian Acad., Paris. Member: Salma. C.; NAC; AFA. Inventor of the Cornwell luminos. Address in 1929, 434 Lafayette Street, New York, NY.

CORSON, KATHERINE LANGDON.
(Mrs. Walter H. Corson). Landscape painter and illustrator. Born Rochdale, England. Pupil of Emil Carlsen, H. Bolton Jones and F. C. Jones in New York. Member: National Academy of Women Painters and Sculptors: Fellowship Penna. Academy of Fine Arts; Plastic Club. Award: Medal, Atlanta Expn., 1895. Work: "Across the Cove," Hamilton Club. Died Feb. 12, 1937.

CORTIGLIA, NICCOLO.
Painter and teacher. Born New York City, April 7, 1893. Pupil of William Forsyth; Academy of Arts, Florence Italy. Member: Florence, (Italy) SFA. Award: First prize, Florence, Italy, "Primaverile," 1920. Address in 1929, 900 Coal Exchange Bldg.; h. 61 West Union Street, Wilkesbarre, PA.

CORTRIGHT, HAZEL PACKER.
Painter. Member: Plastic Club. Address in 1926, St. Martin's, Philadelphia, PA; Saunderstown, RI.

CORWAINE, AARON H.
Born in Kentucky Aug. 31, 1802; died in Philadelphia in July, 1830. Studied with Thomas Sully. His studios in Phila. and later in Cincinnatti.

CORWIN, CHARLES ABEL.
Painter. Born in Newburgh, NY, Jan. 6, 1857. Pupil of Frank Duveneck. Member: Chicago SA; Salma. C. 1905; Bronx AG. Awards: Cahn prize, AIC 1900; hon. mention, Chicago SA; participant in Fine Arts Bldg. prize, AIC 1914. Work in Piedmont Gallery, Berkeley, CA.

Address in 1929, Salmagundi Club 47 Fifth Ave.; 2486 Grand Concourse, New York, NY. Died in 1938.

CORWIN, SOPHIE M.
Sculptor and painter. Born: New York. Studied at ASL; Nat'l. Acad. School of Fine Arts; Hoffman Sch.; Archipenko School; Phillips Ga. Art Sch., Wash., DC, with Karl Knaths; NYU. Awards: Phillips Gallery of Art, Washington, DC; Creative Art Gallery. Collection: New York University. Exhib.: Corcoran Gallery; Baltimore Mus.; NYU; Capricorn Gallery, NYC; others. Living in Yonkers, NY.

CORY, KATE T.
Painter. Born in Illinois in 1861. Pupil of Cooper Union and Art Students' League of New York. Member: National Academy Women Painters and Sculptors; Society of Independent Artists. Represented by collection of pictures in the Smithsonian Institute, Washington, DC. Address in 1926, Prescott, Arizona. Died in 1958.

COSIMINI, ROLAND FRANCIS.
Painter and illustrator. Born Paris, France, May 1, 1898. Pupil of Richard Andrews and Ernest L. Major. Decorations and publicity for Raymond & Whitcomb Co.; illustrations and jacket designs for Houghton Mifflin Co. Address in 1929, 28 St. Botolph Studios, Boston, MA.

COSTA, HECTOR.
Painter and sculptor. Born, Caltanessetta, Italy, March 6, 1903. Pupil of Prior, Hinton, Olinsky and Ellerhusen. Member: PAFA; ASL. Award: Bronze medal, first prize, design, Italian-American Art Exhib. 1928. Address in 1929, 162 East 84th Street, New York, NY.

COSTAGGINI, FILIPPO.
Painter. Born in Rome, Italy, 1839; died at Upper Falls, Baltimore County, MD, April 15, 1904. Began his artistic career in Rome, where he won distinction as an historical painter. He came to America in 1870 and engaged in the painting of historical and religious pictures, as well as

portraits, among his notable portraits being one of the late Senator Justin S. Morrill, of Vermont. His works can be found in the large cathedrals and churches of the US, especially in NY, Phila., and Baltimore. He was given the commission to complete the historical frieze in the Rotunda of the Capitol representing American History, commenced by Constantino Brumidi. The work of Costaggini began at the three Indians in the group, representing Penn's Treaty, and continued the historical events in chronological order to the period of the Discovery of Gold in California, this being two thirds of the frieze. He died before completing the work.

COSTELLO, VAL.
Painter. Member: Calif. AC; Calif. WCS; Laguna Beach AA. Address in 1929, 518 West 53rd Street, Los Angeles, CA.

COSTIGAN, IDA.
Sculptor. Born in Germany in 1894. Exhibited at Penna. Academy of Fine Arts, Philadelphia, 1924. Address in 1926, Orangeburg, NY.

COSTIGAN, JOHN E.
Painter. Born Providence, RI, Feb. 29, 1888. Self-taught. Member: ANA, 1926; NA, 1928; AWCS; NYWCC; Salma. C.; Allied AA; Am. Soc. Animal PS; Guild of American Painters; NAC. Awards: Third Hallgarten prize, NAD, 1920; Isidor prize, Salma. C. 1920; Peterson purchase prize, AIC, 1922; Charles E. Kramer purchase prize, 1923; Vezin prize ($200), Salma. C., 1923; W. H. Tuthill purchase prize, AIC, 1924; Shaw purchase prize ($1,000), Salma. C., 1924; Saltus medal, NAD, 1925; medal ($300), NAC, 1925; bronze medal, Sesq. Expos., 1926; Logan medal ($1,500), AIC, 1927; Clark prize ($300), NAD, 1927; second Altman, NAD, 1927; Plimton ($100), Salma. C., 1928; Speyer ($300), NAD, 1928; Lloyd Griscom P.-P., WCC, 1928; Mrs. Julius Rosenwald prize ($500), Grand Cent. Art Gallery Members' Exp., 1928; John McGowan P.-P. WC Exhib., 1929. Represented in Art Institute, Chicago; Duncan Phillips Gallery, Los Angeles Museum;

Vanderpoel AA Collection, Chicago; Delgado Museum, New Orleans; Museum, Nashville, TN; RI School of Design; Conn. Agricultural College; NAC Collection; Salma. C. Thumb Box Collection; Montclair Museum. Address in 1929, care of Grand Central Galleries, 15 Vanderbilt Avenue, New York, NY, Orangeburg, NY. Died in 1972.

COTHARIN, KATE LEAH.
Painter. Born Detroit, MI, Oct. 27, 1866. Pupil of J. M. Dennis in Detroit. Member: Copley S. Represented in Springfield Art Museum. Specialty, pastel landscapes in miniature. Address in 1929, 279 Dartmouth Street, Boston, MA; summer, Rockport, MA.

COTHER, DOROTHY McVEY.
Painter and teacher. Born Crossville, TN. Pupil of M. L. Weatherford, Henry B. Snell, Pratt Institute; Ecole des Beaux Arts, Fontainebleau. Member: NA Women PS; L. C. Tiffany Foundation. Awards: Holland prize, AWCS and NYWCC, 1926; Memorial Fellowship Award ($1,000), AA of Pratt Institute, 1927. Address in 1929, 309 Washington Avenue, Brooklyn, NY.

COTTON, JOHN WESLEY.
Painter, etcher, and lecturer. Born Ontario, Canada, Oct. 29, 1868. Pupil of E. Marsden Wilson in London; AI Chicago. Member: Ontario SA; Chicago SE; Calif. PM; Calif. AC; Calif. WCC; Calif. PS. Awards: DeWolf prize, Chicago SE, 1915; hon. mention for etchings, P.-P. Exp., San F., 1915; gold medal, Pac. Southwest Expos., Long Beach, 1928; hon. mention, PS Club, Los Angeles, 1928. Etchings in: New York Public Library; Congressional Library, Washington; Art Institute of Chicago; National Gallery, Ottawa; Art Museum, Toronto; State Library, Sacramento, Calif.; Oakland Public Library; Los Angeles Art Museum. Address in 1929, Glendale, CA. Died in 1931.

COTTON, WILLIAM HENRY.
Portrait painter. Born Newport, RI, July 22, 1880. Studied Cowles Art School, Boston, under Andreas Anderson and Joseph De Camp, also

Julien Academy, Paris, under Jean Paul Laurens. Exhibited at National Academy of Design, New York; Corcoran Art Gallery, Wash.; Art Institute, Chicago; PAFA; St. Louis Art Museum; Carnegie Institute, Pittsburgh, etc. Award: First Hallgarten prize, NAD, 1907. Has painted portraits of Honorable Willard Bartlett, George Barr McCutcheon, Harrison Rhodes, Miss Chrystal Herne; mural painting in the Capitol Theatre, NY; represented in the exhibition of American Artists at Luxembourg Museum, at the invitation of the French Gov't, Academy of National Artists; a founder National Association Portrait Painters. Member: Newport Art Association. Address in 1926, 132 East 19th Street, New York City, NY. Died in 1958.

COUARD, ALEXANDER P.
Painter. Born in New York City, 1891. Pupil of George Bridgman and F. V. DuMond. Address in 1926, R. D. 42, Norwalk, Ct.

COUDERT, AMALIA KUSSNER.
Miniature painter. Born 1876. Painted King Edward, Czar and Czarina, Cecil Rhodes, and many of the English aristocracy.

COUGHLIN, MILDRED MARION.
Etcher. Born Pennsylvania, July 16, 1895. Pupil of M. Waltner; Beaux Arts School of Design in Paris. Member: Brooklyn SE; Chicago SE. Address in 1929, Roslyn Estates, L.I., NY.

COULON, GEORGE DAVID.
Portrait painter, born c. 1823 in France. Studio at 103 Conde Street in 1850, and continued to paint in New Orleans for fifty years. His last residence, given shortly before his demise, was at 1536 North Claiborne Street. Died in 1904.

COULTER, MARY J.
Painter, etcher, craftsman, and lecturer. Born Newport, KY. Pupil of Cincinnati Art Academy under Duveneck, Nowottny and Meakin, AI Chicago; Lionel Walden and C. W. Hawthorne; studied in Florence, Italy. Member: San F. AA;

Provincetown AA; Chicago SE; Calif. SE; Calif. PM; AFA; San Diego AG; Santa Barbara AG; North Shore AA. Awards: Silver medal for pottery and overglaze at the Lewis and Clark Exp., Portland, OR, 1905; Atlan Ceramic prize, AI Chicago, 1909; bronze medal for porcelain, bronze medal for jewerly and hon. mention for textiles, P.-P. Exp., San F., 1915. Represented in Art Institute of Chicago; Cooke Collection, Honolulu, HI; Commercial Club and Fitzhugh Collection, San Francisco; Metropolitan Museum of Art, New York; Boston Museum of Fine Arts; University Club, San Diego; Charles M. Lea Collection, Phila.; Print Dept., New York Public Library, Los Angeles Public Library, and Library of Congress, Washington; one hundred and sixty-eight prints on the "S.S. Malolo," Matson Navigation Co., San Francisco. Asst. Director, Fine Arts Gallery of San Diego, 1926; Director and Curator, North Shore Arts Association of Gloucester, 1927. Address in 1929, "de la Guerra Studios," Santa Barbara, CA.

COUPER, B. KING. (MRS.)
Painter and sculptor. Born Augusta, GA, Feb. 23, 1867. Pupil of Chase, Daingerfield, Du Mond, Breckenridge and Cox. Member: North Shore AA; Atlanta AA; SSAL; NA Women PS. Represented in permanent collection, Spartanburg, NC. Address in 1929, Montreat, NC.

COUPER, WILLIAM.
Sculptor. Born Norfolk, VA, Sept. 20, 1853. Pupil of Thomas Ball and Cooper Inst. in New York; studied in Munich and Florence, where he lived 22 years. Member: NSS; NY Arch. Lg. Award: Bronze medal, Pan AM. Exp. Buffalo, 1901. Work: "A Crown for the Victor," Art Museum Montclair, NJ; statues, Henry W. Longfellow and Dr. John Witherspoon, Washington, DC; Capt. John Smith, Jamestown Island, VA; Morris K. Jesup, Natural History Museum and John D. Rockefeller, Rockefeller Institute, New York; John A. Roebling, City Park, Trenton, NJ; Tirteen heroic portrait busts of Scientists, foyer Natural History Museum, New York. Address in 1929,

14 Berkeley Place, Montclair, NJ. Died in 1942.

COURSEN, LOUISE.
Painter and writer. Born Canton, IL, Feb. 26, 1866. Pupil of AIC; Minneapolis AI. Member: S. Indp. A; Salons of America; Chicago NJSA. Specialty, exhibit talks. Address in 1929, 123 South Adams Street, Lewiston, IL.

COURTENEY, LEO.
Block printer. Born Hutchinson, KS, Aug. 11, 1890. Pupil of C. A. Seward. Member: Wichita AA; Wichita AG. Address in 1929, 502 Butts Bldg.; h. 342 North Volutsia Ave., Wichita, Kansas.

COURTRIGHT, ROBERT.
Born October 20, 1926 in Sumter, SC. Studied at St. John's College, Annapolis (1943-5), Am. Art School, NYC, and Art Students League. Lived in France. Works in collage art. Exhibited at New Gallery, NYC (many since 1951); Galerie du Fleuve, Paris (1963); MOMA; Smithsonian; and MMA. In collections of Wadsworth; Phillips collection, Washington, DC; MMA and many private collections.

COUSE, EANGER IRVING.
Painter. Born Saginaw, MI, Sept. 3, 1866. Pupil of NAD in New York; Bouguereau, Robert-Fleury and Ecole des Beaux-Arts in Paris. Member: ANA 1902; Lotos C. (life); NAC (life); Taos SA; SPNY; Allied AA; AFA. Awards: Shaw prize for black and white at Salma. C., 1890; 2nd Hallgarten prize, NAD, 1900; Proctor prize, Salma. C. 1900; hon. mention, Paris Exp., 1900; hon. mention, Pan-Am. Exp., Buffalo, 1901; 1st Hallgarten prize, NAD 1902; Osborne competition prize ($500) 1903; 2 bronze medal, St. Louis Exp., 1904; Lotos C. Purchase prize, 1910; Isidor Gold Medal, NAD 1911; Carnegie prize ($500), NAD 1912; silver medal, P.-P. Exp., San F., 1915; Altman prize, NAD, 1916; Isidor prize ($100), Salma C. 1917; Ranger Fund purchase prize, NAD, 1921; Lippincott prize, PAFA, 1921. Specialty, Indians. Work: "Elkfoot," Nat. Gal., Washington; "The Forest Camp," Brooklyn Institute Museum; "Medicine Fires," Dallas (TX) Museum; "Under the

Trees," Smith College, Northhampton, MA; "The Tom Tom Maker," Lotos Club, New York; "Sheep at Evening," St. Paul, (MN) Museum; decoration, "Adoration of the Shepherds," Grace Church, Harrisburg, PA; "Shappanagons, Chippewa Chief," and "San Juan Pottery," Detroit Inst.; "Song of the Flute," NAC, NY; "Indian Courtship," Art Museum, Montclair, NJ; "Indian Love Song," Brooklyn Inst. Museum; "Making Pottery," Ft. Worth (TX) Museum; "The Peace Pipe," Metropolitan Museum, New York, NY; "A Vision of the Past," "Making Medicine" and "The Water Shrine," Butler Art Institute, Youngstown, OH; "Wild Turkey Hunters," Santa Barbara (CA) Museum; "Shrine of the Rain Gods," Toledo Museum; "Apache Water Bottle," Nashville, (TN) Museum; "Sacred Birds," Cleveland Museum; "The Waterfall," Milwaukee Art Inst.; three lunettes, Missouri State Capitol, Jefferson City, MO; "Indian Moonlight," San Diego Museum. Address in 1929, Taos, N.M. Died in 1936.

COUTTS, GORDON.
Painter. Born in Scotland, 1880. Pupil of Lefebvre in Paris. Address in 1926, 406 Pacific Avenue, Piedmont, California. Died 1937.

COUTURIER, HENRI.
Portrait painter. Born in Holland. He is said to have painted a portrait of Frederick Philipse (owner of Philipse manor, Yonkers) in New Orange in 1674. He resided for some years in Delaware, where he became councillor or Burgomaster of the Province. He died in 1684 in Eng. Some of his portraits are signed by the monogram of the artist.

COVELL, MARGARET.
A little-known portrait and genre painter.

COVERT, JOHN.
Painter. Exhibited "Resurrection" and "Temptation of St. Anthony" at Exhibition of "Paintings Showing the Later Tendencies in Art," at the Penna. Academy of Fine Arts, 1921. Address in 1926, 15 West

29th Street, New York City. Died in 1960.

COVEY, ARTHUR SINCLAIR.
Painter and etcher. Born Bloomington, IL, June 13, 1877. Pupil of Vanderpoel, Karl Marr, Frank Brangwyn. Member: ANA; Salma. C.; Mural P.; Arch. Lg. of NY. Awards: First, second and third Shaw prizes, Salma. C., 1910, 1911, 1912; bronze medal for etching, P.-P. Exp., San F., 1915; medal for decorative painting, NY, Arch. L., 1925. Works: "The Spirit of the Prairies" and three mural panels, Wichita Public Library; "The Great Wheel," etching in Library of Congress; mural decorations, Orange Hospital; "Spirit of Modern Industry," Administration Bldg., Kohler Co., Kohler, WI; 13 decorative mural paintings, Memorial Hall Administration Bldg., The Norton Co., Worcester, MA. Address in 1929, 115 East 40th Street, New York, NY; Torrington, CT. Died in 1960.

COVINGTON, WICKLIFFE C(OOPER).
Painter and teacher. Born Shelby County, KY, July 2, 1867. Pupil of Kenyon Cox, William M. Chase; ASL of NY. Member: Louisville AA; SSAL; AFA; Miss. State AA; Carmel AA. Work: "Flower Study," Louisville Art Association Collection. Address in 1929, Bowling Green, KY; summer, Carmel, CA. Died in 1938.

COWAN, R. GUY.
Sculptor and craftsman. Born East Liverpool, OH, Aug. 1, 1884. Pupil of N.Y.S. School of Ceramics. Member: Am. Ceramic Soc.; Cleveland SA. Awards: 1st prize for pottery, 1917, and Logan medal for applied design, 1924, Art Inst. of Chicago; 1st prize for pottery, Cleveland Museum, 1925. Address in 1929, care of Cowan Pottery, Rocky River, OH, h. 1499 Cohasset Avenue, Lakewood, OH.

COWAN, SARAH EAKIN.
Miniature painter. Born 1875. Member: NA Women PS; Am. S. Min. P.; PA S. Min. P.; PBC. Address in 1929, 125 East 10th Street; 35 West 10th Street, New York, NY. Died in 1958.

COWELL, JOSEPH G(OSS).
Painter and sculptor. Born Peoria, IL, Dec. 4, 1886. Pupil of Bridgman, DuMond, Tarbell and Benson; Laurens in Paris. Member: Boston AC, Boston Arch. C. Work: Murals in Universalist Church, YMCA, Peoria, IL; theater, Holyoke, MA; theatres in Boston, and Tower Theatre, Phila.; stained glass windows, St. Mary's Cathedral, Peoria, IL; War Memorial flagstaff base, Wrentham, MA; murals in churches in Boston, Nashua, NH, Whitman, MA, Bridgeport, CT; murals, altars, screens and altar figures, St. Mary's Cathedral, Peoria, IL, and St. James Church, New York. Associate Director, Designers Art School, Boston. Address in 1929, 196 Dartmouth Street, Boston, MA, h. Wrentham, MA.

COWEN, A. MARIAN.
Painter. Member: Pitts. AA. Address in 1929, 5818 Rippey Street, E.E., Pittsburgh, PA.

COWLES, EDITH V.
Painter and illustrator. Born Farminton, Ct., 1874. Pupil of John T. Niemeyer; Bruneau and Mme. Laforge in Paris. Illustrated: "House of Seven Gables," by Hawthorne; "Old Virginia," by Thomas Nelson Page; "Friendship," by Emerson. Has five stained glass windows in St. Michael's Church, Brooklyn. Director of Craft Work at the "Lighthouse for the Blind." Address in 1926, 152 West 57th Street, New York, NY.

COWLES, GENEVIEVE A(LMEDA).
Painter, illustrator, craftman, writer, and lecturer. Born Farmington, CT, Feb. 23, 1871. Pupil of Niemeyer and Brandegee. Work: Mural of the "Charge to St. Peter," Conn. State Prison; windows of the seven parables, Grace Church, NY; Altar piece, St. Peter's Church, Springfield, MA; stained glass windows in honor Eliezer Ben Jehvdah, Talpioth, Palestine. Illustrated "The House of the Seven Gables," "Litte Folk Lyrics," and for Scribner's and McClure's. Author

194

of "The Prisoners and their Pictures," McClure's, 1922; "The Camouflage of Crime," Psychology Magazine. Lecturer on the prison question and on Palestine. Address in 1929, 123 East 28th Street, New York, NY.

COWLES, MILDRED.
Painter. Born in Farmington, CT, 1876. Pupil of Yale Art School. Address in 1926, 102 West 57th Street, New York, NY.

COWLES, RUSSELL.
Painter. Born Algona, IA, Oct. 7, 1887. Pupil of NAD; ASL of NY. Member: NAC; Century Assn. Award: American Academy in Rome Fellowship, 1915-1920; Harris silver medal ($500), AIC, 1925. Address in 1929, care of the Century Association, 7 West 43rd Street, New York, NY. Died in 1978.

COX, ALBERT SCOTT.
Painter and illustrator. Born Randolph, ME, 1863. Studied at Academy, Paris. Painter of figures and landscapes; much illustrating and many caricatures.

COX, ALLYN.
Painter. Born New York, June 5, 1896. Pupil of his father, Kenyon Cox; NAD; George Bridgman. Member: NY Arch. Lg.; Mural P. Awarded: Fellowship American Academy in Rome, 1916. Work: Overmantel in Public Library, Windsor, VT. Address in 1929, 123 East 63rd Street; 130 East 67th Street, New York, NY.

COX, CHARLES BRINTON.
Sculptor. Born in Philadelphia. His modeling of animals shows beauty and power. He died in 1905.

COX, DOROTHY E.
Painter. Exhibited at Penna. Academy of Fine Arts, Philadelphia, 1924. Address in 1926, 107 South Front Street, Harrisburg, PA.

COX, GEORGE J.
Sculptor. Exhibited "The Zodiac" at Annual Exhibition of National Academy of Design, 1925, New York. Address in 1926, 509 West 121st Street, New York.

COX, JAMES.
Artist. Born in England, 1751, and died 1834. He came to this country as a young man and settled in Philadelphia where he was the fashionable drawing-master for many years. He collected over 5,000 volumes on the fine arts which he sold to the Library Co. of Philadelphia; he did much to advance the arts in that city. He excelled in flower painting.

COX, KENYON.
Painter. Born Warren, Ohio, Oct. 27, 1856. Pupil of Carolus Duran and Gerome in Paris. Awards: Second Hallgarten prize, NAD, 1889; Temple silver medal, PAFA, 1891; medal of honor for mural paintings, NY Architectural League, 1909; Isidor medal, NAD, 1910; National Academy, 1903. Member: Mural Painters; National Institute and American Academy of Arts and Letters. Specialty, portraits, figure pieces, mural decoration; also illustrator, teacher and writer. Died March 17, 1919 in NYC.

COX, LOUISE HOWLAND KING.
Painter. Born San Francisco, CA, June 23, 1865. Pupil of NAD; ASL under Kenyon Cox in New York. Member: ANA 1902; SAA 1893; Mural P. 1919. Awards: Third Hallgarten prize, NAD, 1896; bronze medal, Paris Exp., 1900; silver medal, Pan-Am. Exp., Buffalo, 1901; Shaw Memorial prize, SAA, 1903; silver medal, St. Louis Exp., 1904. Specialty, children's portraits. Work: "May Flowers," National Gallery, Washington. Address in 1929, 130 East 67th Street, New York, NY. Died Dec. 11, 1945.

COX, LYDA MORGAN.
Painter, craftsman, and teacher. Born Depere, WI, May 15, 1881. Pupil of Cullen Yates, Gottwald, Johonnot; Cleveland School of Art. Member: Seattle FAS; Woman's AC of Cleveland; S. Indp. A.; Western Traveling Artists. Award: Second hon. mention, Seattle FAS, 1923. Work: Wall decorated tile in the Cleveland Orphan Asylum. Address in 1929, 8333 - 46th Avenue, South, Seattle, Wash.; summer, 1887

195

Hillside Avenue, East, Cleveland, OH.

COX, PALMER.
Illustrator. Born in Quebec, Canada, in 1840. In 1875 he settled in New York, where he followed his artistic and literary pursuits. His illustrated work was well known. Died July 24, 1924 in Quebec, Canada.

COX-McCORMACK, NANCY.
Sculptor. Born Nashville, TN, Aug. 15, 1885. Pupil of Victor Holm, St. Louis; Charles Mulligan, Chicago. Member: NA Women PS; Chic. AC; Cordon C; Nashville AA. Work: "Harmony," Nashville Mus.; Carmack Memorial, Nashville; bronzes of Rev. John Cavanaugh, Univ. of Notre Dame, South Bend, IN; Dean Craven Laycock, Dartmouth College, Hanover, NH; Perkins Memorial, Perkins Observatory, Wesleyan Univ., Delaware, OH; "H. E. Benito Mussolini," The Capital, Rome, copy in FA Mus., Phila.; "Senator Giaccomo Boni," Compedoglio, Rome; Primo de Rivera, Madrid, Spain. Address in 1929, 28 East 11th Street, New York, NY.

COXE, R. CLEVELAND.
Painter and engraver. Born Baltimore, MD, 1855. Pupil of Bonnat and Gerome in Paris. Address in 1926, 1320 Fifth Avenue, Seattle, Washington.

COY, ANNA.
Painter and teacher. Born Rockford, IL. Pupil of Chase, Henri and Alexander Robinson. Member: Rockford AA; Am. APL. Work: Portrait of the first president of Rockford Womans Club. Address in 1929, 127 No. 3d Street, Rockford, IL.

COY, C. LYNN.
Sculptor. Born Chicago, IL, Oct. 31, 1889. Pupil of AIC; F. C. Hibbard; Albin Polasek, Lorado Taft. Member: Alumni AIC; Chicago SA; IL AFA. Work: George H. Munroe Memorial, Joliet, IL. Represented in Vanderpoel AA Collection, Chicago. Address in 1929, Brookfield, IL.

COYLE.
Painter and designer; came to New York from England. He died in New York City in 1824.

COYLE, JAMES.
Painter. He was elected a member of National Academy of Design, New York, in 1826. He died in New York City July 22, 1828.

COYNE, ELIZABETH K(ITCHENMAN).
Painter. Born Philadelphia, PA. Pupil of Leopold Seyffert and Cecilia Beaux. Member: Fellowship PAFA; Phila. Alliance; AFA. Award: Cresson Traveling Scholarship, PAFA. Work: "Along the Neshaminy," Lambert Collection, Penn. Academy of the Fine Arts. Address in 1929, Wall Bldg., 1716 Chestnut Street; h. 508 Spring Ave., Elkins Park, Philadelphia, PA.

COYNE, JOAN JOSEPH.
Painter, sculptor, craftsman, and writer. Born Chicago, IL, June 16, 1895. Pupil of George Mulligan, Leonard Crunelle and Albin Polasek. Member: Chicago SA; S. Indp. A. Address in 1929, 209 Pelham Road, Germantown, Philadelphia, PA.

COYNE, WILLIAM VALENTINE.
Painter, illustrator, and etcher. Born New York, Feb. 14, 1895. Pupil of Henri, Beaux Arts Inst. Member: S. Indp. A.; Beaux-Arts Inst. Represented in the New York Public Library. Illustrations for "New York Evening Post," "The Bookman." Address in 1929, 123 East 88th Street, New York, NY.

CRAFT, KINUKO YAMABE.
Illustrator. Born in Japan in 1940. She spent four years at the Kanazawa Municipal College of Fine Arts and one and a half years at the AIC. The winner of various awards and selected to show her work in S of I Annual Exhibitions, she has had assignments from Psychology Today, Science Research Associates and Scott, Foresman and Company. She currently lives and works in Chicago.

CRAIG, ANDERSON.
Painter and teacher. Born Iowa City, IA, April 15, 1904. Pupil of Randall Davey. Director, Experimental School of Art. Address in 1929, 20 West Eighth Street, New York, NY.

CRAIG, ANNA BELLE.
Painter. Born Pittsburgh, PA, March 13, 1878. Pupil of Pittsburgh School of Design; ASL of NY, Chase, Shirlaw, Henry G. Keller, Martin G. Borgord, and Howard Pyle. Member: Pittsburgh AA; Cordova C. of Women P., Pittsburgh. Illustrated in "Harper's," "St. Nicholas," "Metropolitan," and books for children. Address in 1929, Penn Col. for Women, Woodland Road; h. 5806 Walnut Street, Pittsburgh, PA.

CRAIG, CHARLES.
Painter. Born Morgan County, OH, 1846. Educated Penna. Academy of Fine Arts, Philadelphia. Painter of Indians, cowboys, plains, and mountains. Exhibited at American Water Color Society, New York; Denver, 1883; Minneapolis Expn., 1886-8; St. Louis, 1889; Omaha, 1894-6. Awards: Honorable mention, Western Artists' Association. Represented by Indian paintings in many fine private collectons in US and abroad. Address in 1926, Colorado Springs, CO. Died in 1931.

CRAIG, EMMETT J(UNIUS).
Sculptor. Born DeWitt, MO, March 3, 1878. Pupil of Merrill Gage and Wallace Rosenhomer. Member: Kansas City SA. Awards: Silver medal, 1924, and bronze medal, 1925, Kansas City Art Inst. Address in 1929, 723 Argyle Building; McMillian Building; h. 44 West Concord Street, Kansas City, MO.

CRAIG, ISAAC EUGENE.
Painter. Born near Pittsburgh, in 1830. After studying art in Phila. he went to Paris. He returned to this country in 1855, but returned to Europe some ten years later. He painted a portrait of Joel T. Hart, the Kentucky sculptor, and some striking views of Venice.

CRAIG, THOMAS BIGELOW.
Painter. Born in Philadelphia, 1849. Exhibited at PAFA, and NAD. Represented at the Boston Art Club and Pennsylvania Academy of Fine Arts. Elected Associate Member of National Academy. Died 1924 in Woodland, New York.

CRAIG, WILLIAM.
Born in Dublin, Ireland, 1829; in 1863 he settled in this country. He was one of the original members of the American Society of Water Color Painters. Among his paintings "Mount Washington," "Hudson River, near West Point" and many landscapes of preculiar transparency in coloring. He died in 1875 in Lake George, NY.

CRAM, ALLEN G(ILBERT).
Painter, illustrator, and teacher. Born Washington, DC, Feb. 1, 1886. Pupil of William Chase, Charles H. Woodbury. Member: Santa Barbara AL. Award: Ruth Payne Burgess prize, Art Association of Newport, 1914. Work: "A Lady in Fiesta Costume," Court House, Santa Barbara. Illustrations for "Old Seaports of the South," "Fifth Avenue," "Greenwich Village" (Dodd Mead). Address in 1929, 2317-A Rancheria Street; h. 124 Oceana Avenue, Santa Barbara, CA. Died in 1947.

CRAMER, FLORENCE BALLIN.
Painter. Born Brooklyn, NY in 1884. Pupil of DuMond, Brush and Harrison. Member: NA of Women PS. Address in 1926, 163 East 72d Street, New York, NY.

CRAMPTON, ROLLIN McNEIL.
Painter and illustrator. Born New Haven, CT, March 9, 1886. Pupil of Thomas Benton, Yale Art School, ASL of NY. Work: "Portrait of Frau Busnell" in Union League Club. Address in 1929, Madison, CT. Died in 1970.

CRANCH, CAROLINE A.
Painter. Daughter of Christopher P. Cranch, and pupil of her father and the Cooper Institute of New York, under William Hunt. Specialty, figurepieces. Address in 1926, Cambridge, MA.

CRANCH, CHRISTOPHER PEARSE.
Painter. Born in Alexandria, VA, on March 8, 1813. Studied abroad, returned to NY and in 1864 was elected a member of the NA. He later moved to Cambridge, MA. He was a portrait, landscape and still life painter. The son of Wm. Cranch, Chief Justice of the US circuit court of the Dist. of Columbia, he studied divinity at Harvard and was a Unitarian minister until he turned to painting in 1842. Published a volume of poems in 1844. Among his paintings are "Washington Oak, at Newburg, NY;" "Venice" and "Forest of Fountainebleau," Represented in the Boston Mus. of FA. He died Jan. 20, 1892 in Cambridge, MA.

CRANCH, JOHN.
Portrait painter. Born in Wash., DC, Feb. 2, 1807. Student of King, Harding, and Sully, he commenced painting portraits in Wash., DC in 1829. In 1830 he studied in Italy, and in 1834 returned to this county, where he painted many portraits and original compositions. He was elected an Associate of the National Academy in 1853. He was the brother of Christopher Pearse Cranch. Died Jan. 1, 1891 in Urbana, OH.

CRANDELL, BRADSHAW.
Illustrator. Born in Glens Falls, NY in 1896. He was educated at Wesleyan Univ. and the AIC. In 1921 his first cover appeared on Judge, marking the beginning of his career which concentrated on cover design. His art graced the front of such magazines as Collier's, Redbook, American, Ladies Home Journal and The Saturday Evening Post. For 12 years in the 1930's and 1940's he worked on Cosmopolitan covers doing a series of pastels of beautiful women, often using Hollywood stars for models. He was a member of the Dutch Treat Club, the Artists and Writers Association and the S of I. Died in 1966.

CRANE, ANN.
Painter. Born in New York City. Pupil of Twachtman in New York and of Merson in Paris. Died Jan. 26 1948. Address in 1926, Arcade Bronxville, NY.

CRANE, BRUCE.
Landscape painter. Born New York, NY, Oct. 17, 1857. Pupil of A. H. Wyant. Member: ANA 1897; NA 1901; SAA 1881; AWCS; A. Fund S.; Salma C. 1888; Lotos C.; Union Internationale des Beaux-Arts et des Lettres; NAC. Awards: Webb prize, SAA 1897; bronze medal Paris Exp., 1900; Inness medal, NAD 1901; silver medal, Pan.-Am. Exp. Buffalo, 1901; silver medal Charleston Exp., 1902; gold medal St. Louis Exp., 1904; third prize C.I. Pittsburgh 1909; Saltus medal NAD 1912; silver medal, P.-P. Exp. San F., 1915; Shaw prize ($500) Salma. C., 1917; Ranger Purchase Fund, NAD, 1919. Work: "Autumn Uplands," Metropolitan Museum, New York; "November Hills," Carnegie Institute, Pittsburgh; "Autumn," National Gallery, Washington; "March," Brooklyn Institute Museum; "Autumn Hills," Montclair (NJ) Gallery; "Springtime," Peabody Institute, Baltimore; "November Hillsides," Corcoran Gallery, Washington, DC; "Last of Winter," Fort Worth (TX) Museum; "Autumn Meadowland," Hackley Art Gallery, Muskegon, MI; "December Uplands," Syracuse, (NY) Museum of Art; "The Wilderness," Museum, Oshkosh, WI. Address in 1929, Studio Arcade, Bronxville, NY. Died in 1937.

CRANE, FREDERICK.
Painter of mountain scenery. Born in Bloomfield, NJ, in 1847. He was awarded the bronze medal in 1904 on the St. Louis Exposition. He died in New York City, Jan 25, 1915. Represented in Worcester Art Museum by "London from the Thames."

CRANE, WILBUR.
Painter. Born New York City, Dec. 18, 1875. Pupil of William M. Chase, Robert Henri. Member: Salma. C.; Arch. Lg.; New Rochelle AS. Address in 1929, 167 Broadway, New York, NY; h. 6 Ormond Place, New Rochelle, NY; summer, Lake Hill, Ulster Co., NY.

198

RANK, JAMES H.
Illustrator. Member: GFLA.
Address in 1929, Interlaken, Asbury
Park, NJ.

RASKE, LEONARD.
Sculptor. Born in London, 1882, he
came to America in 1910 and made
his home in Boston and Gloucester.
Address in 1926, 22 Street Botolph
Studios, Boston, MA. Died in 1950.

RATZ, BENJAMIN ARTHUR.
Painter.   Born   Shanesville,
Tuscarawas Co., OH, May 1, 1886.
Pupil of George Elmer Browne;
Julian in Paris. Member: Toledo
Artklan;   Provincetown   AA;
Beachcombers Club; Springfield (IL)
AA; Salma. C; AFA. Address in
1929, 2150 Parkwood Ave., Toledo
OH; summer, Provincetown, MA. Died
c. 1951.

RAWFORD, ARTHUR ROSS.
Painter   and   craftsman.   Born
Marilla, Manistee Co., MI, July 29,
1885. Pupil of Chicago Academy of
FA under W. J. Reynolds and W. P.
Henderson. Member: ASL of Chicago
(life).   Manager   of   Crawford
Decorating Co. Specialty, landscape
and decorative painting. Address
in 1929, Jaruis Avenue, Niles, IL.

RAWFORD, BRENETTA HERMANN.
Painter, illustrator, and teacher.
Born Toledo, OH, Oct. 27, 1875.
Pupil of ASL of NY; Colarossi and
Carmen Academies in Paris. Member:
Am. S. Min. P.; NA Women PS.
Address   in   1929,   41   "The
Enclosure," Nutley, NJ; care of
Guaranty Trust Co., Paris, France.

RAWFORD, EARL STETSON.
Painter. Born Philadelphia, PA,
June 6, 1877. Studied at School of
Industrial Art, Philadelphia, PA;
PAFA;   Delacluse   and   Julien
Academies;   Ecole   Nationale   des
Beaux Arts, Paris; also in Munich,
London, Rome, Florence and Venice.
Connected with School of Applied
Design for Women, NY, 1912-17.
Portrait   painter   and   mural
decorator, also designer of stained
glass windows in various churches;
mural work in US Gov't Bldgs., San
Francisco.   Fellow   of   Society
American Illustrators; member of
National   Association   Portrait

Painters. Address in 1926, "The
Enclosure," Nutley, NJ.

CRAWFORD, ESTHER MABEL.
Painter, craftman, and teacher.
Born Atlanta, GA, April 23, 1872.
Pupil of Whistler, Dow, Beck.
Member: Calif. AC; West Coast
Arts. Award: Bronze medal, San
Diego Exp., 1915. Address in 1929,
716 North Avenue 66, Los Angeles,
CA.

CRAWFORD, THOMAS.
Sculptor. Born March 22, 1814 in
NYC. In 1835 he went to Rome, and
studied with Thorwaldsen. His best
known works are the bronze doors
and   work   on   the   Capitol   at
Washington,   DC;   the   equestrian
statue of Washington at Richmond,
VA; and his statue of Adam and Eve.
His   son   was   Francis   Marion
Crawford, the well-known author.
Died Oct. 10, 1857 in London.

CRAWFORD, WILL.
Illustrator. Born in Washington,
DC, in 1869. He was a self-taught
artist who worked on staff for the
Newark Daily Advertiser and the
Sunday Call while still in his
teens. He illustrated for the New
York World before establishing a
studio with John Marquand and
Albert Levering, later to be shared
by Charles M. Russell. He was a
successful free-lancer for Life,
Munseys, Puck and Cosmopolitan,
after which he worked in Hollywood
as an expert on Indian costumes.
Died in 1944.

CRAWLEY, IDA JOLLY.
Painter, writer, and lecturer.
Born Pond Creek, London Co., E. TN,
Nov. 15, 1867. Pupil of Corcoran
Art School; Johannes Oertell in
Germany; Sir Frederic Massi in
Paris. Member: Amer. A. Union,
Paris; AFA; AA Kenilworth Inn
Galleries, Asheville. Awards:
Gold medal, Appalachian Exp.,
Knoxville; silver medal, East TN
Art Assoc.; loving cup and bronze
medal, Kenilworth Inn Galleries;
Asheville (NC) Gal. Work: 15
paintings, 1st Nat'l Bank,
Champaign, Ill.; two paintings in
Gayosa Hotel, Memphis, TN; painting
in University School, Memphis; two
paintings,   University,

Fayetteville, Ark.; twenty-five painting, Crawley Museum of Art and Archaeology, Asheville; painting, City Hall, Asheville; 30 paintings, William Collection, Hot Springs, Ark. Director, William Collection, Hot Springs Ark., President, Crawley Museum of Art and Arch., Asheville, NC. Address in 1929, 31 Park Avenue, Asheville, NC.

CRAWLEY, JOHN.
Painter. Born in England, 1784, he was brought over to this country by his parents when very young and settled at Newark, NJ. He studied with the artist Savage. Crawley painted portraits at Philadelphia and exhibited at the first opening of the Penna. Academy of Fine Arts.

CRAWLEY, JOHN JR.
Draughtsman. Son of the artist is recorded in Dunlap's "History of Art" as an excellent draughtsman, much interested in lithography. He was engaged at Endicott's and Swett's lithographic establishment and executed some beautiful specimens of work on the title pages of the music of that day.

CREAL, JAMES PIRTLE.
Painter and etcher. Born Franklin, KY, Sept. 5, 1903. Pupil of Walter Ufer. Member: Louisville AA. Award: Purchase prize, Speed Memorial Museum, Louisville, 1927. Work: "New Mexico," public schools, Louisville, KY. Address in 1929, 1927 West 10th Street, Los Angeles, CA; h. Altawood, Anchorage, KY; summer, 521 South Coronado Street, Los Angeles, CA. Died in 1934.

CREIFELDS, RICHARD.
Painter. Born New York City, May 26, 1853. Pupil of NAD; Barth, Wagner and the Royal Academy in Munich. Works: Altar piece, St. Andrews Church, equestrian portrait of Col. Daniel Appleton, 107th Regiment Armory and portrait of William B. Dana, Chamber of Commerce, all in New York City; portrait of Judge Brown, Court of Appeals, Albany, NY; portrait of W. H. English, Montauk Club, Brooklyn, NY. Address in 1929, Broadway Studios, 70th St. and Broadway; h.

209 West 107th Street, New York NY. Died in 1939.

CRENIER, HENRI.
Sculptor. Born Paris, France, Dec 17, 1873. Pupil of Falguiere, an Ecole des Beaux-Arts, Paris Member: NSS, 1912; NY Arch. Lg. 1913. Awards: Hon. mention, P.-P Exp., San F., 1915. Work: "Bo and Turtle," Metropolitan Museum o Art; pediments and caryatides, Cit Hall, San Francisco; Fenimor Cooper Memorial, Scarsdale, NY "Boys and Turtle," Mt. Verno Place, Baltimore, MD. Address i 1929, Shore Acres, Mamaroneck, NY.

CRESSON, MARGARET FRENCH.
Sculptor. Born Concord, MA, Aug 3, 1889. Pupil of Daniel C. Frencl and Abastenia St. L. Eberle Member: NSS; NA Women PS; AFA Grand Central AG; Wash. SA Awards: Shaw memorial prize, NAD 1927; hon. mention, Junior L Exhib., 1928; hon. mention, S Wash. A., 1929. Work: Portrai bust of "President James Monroe, National Museum, Wash., DC; bronz bust of "Daniel C. French," Trasl Foundation, Saratoga Springs, NY bronze relief of "F. F. Murdock, MA State Normal School; bronz relief of "Willaim E. Barker, YWCA, Wash., DC; bronze memorial t Mrs. Alvin Klein, St. Paul' Church, Stockbridge, MA; Baro Serge A. Korff Memorial prize Georgetown School of Foreig Service; bust, Com. Richard E Byrd, Corcoran Gallery, Washington and may portrait busts and relief in private hands. Address in 1929 1727-19th Street, Washington, DC summer, Glendale, MA. Died i 1973.

CRESSY, SUSAN.
Painter. Award: Hon. mention, W. PS, 1922. Address in 1929 222-18th Street, Milwaukee, WI.

CREW, MAYO.
Painter, illustrator, craftman, an teacher. Born Memphis, TN, Jun 30, 1903. Pupil of Clar Schneider; Newcomb School of Art ASL of NY. Member: Memphis AA. Awards: First prizes in wate color, pottery and design, Memphi Tri-State Fair Address in 1929,

200

295 South Bellevue Blvd. h. 1512 Court Avenue, Memphis, TN.

RIMI, ALFREDO DIGIORGIO.
Painter. Born San Fratello, Messina, Italy, Dec. 1, 1900. Pupil of NAD. Member: Louis Comfort Tiffany Foundation; Arch. Lg. of NY. Address in 1929, 9 West 14th Street, New York, NY; h. 1962 Pilgrim Avenue, Bronx, NY.

RISP, ARTHUR WATKINS.
Mural painter. Born Hamilton, Canada, April 26, 1881. Pupil of ASL of NY. Member: Associate, National Academy of Design, New York; NY Socia. Lg. 1911; Mural P.; Players' C.; NYWCC; AWCS; Allied AA; NYSC; Century A. Awards: Collaborative prize, NY Arch. Lg., 1914; bronze medal, P.-P. Exp., San F., 1915; first Hallgarten prize, NAD, 1916; gold medal, NY Arch. Lg., 1920. Work: "Hamlet," "As You Like It," "Taming of the Shrew," and four allegorical paintings in Belasco Theatre, NY; two allegorical lunettes, The Playhouse, NY; two mural paintings in Robert Treat Hotel, Newark, NJ; mural panel, Mark Twain Hotel, Elmira, NY; picture in Nat. Gal., Ottawa, Canada; mural decoration for auditorium of Greenwich House, NY; wall hanging for Hotel Du Pont, Wilmington, DE; picture for Canadian War Records; mural paintings, Houses of Parliament, Ottawa, Canada; "The Garden Party," owned by Edward, Prince of Wales; decorations in Mt. Vernon (NY) High School; Clover Garden Dance Hall; Peddie School, Hightstown, NJ. Formerly Instructor at ASL of NY; Cooper Institute; Beaux Art School of Design; NAD. Address in 1929, 308 East 51st Street, New York, NY.

RISSEY, THOMAS HENRY.
Painter. Born Stamford, CT, 1875. Pupil of George Bridgman, Walter Florian, Edward Dufner. Member: Society of Independent Artists; New York Society of Artists. Address in 1926, Powers Street, New Canaan, Ct.

RITCHER, CATHERINE CARTER.
Painter and teacher. Born Westmoreland Co., VA in 1868.

Pupil of Cooper Union; Corcoran Art School; Richard Miller and Charles Hoffbauer in Paris. Member: S. Wash. A.; Wash. WCC; NA Women PS; Provincetown AA; Sail Loft C.; Wash. AC; Taos SA; SSAL. Award: Bronze medal, Wash. AC, 1914, 1922. Represented in Boston Arts Club. Address in 1929, 1 Dupont Circle; 3 St. Matthews' Alley; h. 1836 S Street, N.W., Washington, DC.

CRITTENDEN, ELIZABETH C.
Painter. Exhibited at National Association of Women Painters and Sculptors, New York, 1924. Address in 1926, 76 North 30th Street, Flushing, LI, NY.

CROASDALE, E.
Portrait painter. He painted a portrait of Abraham Lincoln, and on the back of the canvas is inscribed "Painted by E. Croasdale, and retouched by S. J. Ferris, 1863."

CROCKER, J. DENISON.
Landscape and portrait painter. He was born in Salem, Ct., Nov. 25, 1823. With exception of some instruction from Charles Lanman, he was self-taught.

CROCKER, MARION E.
Painter. Born Boston, MA. Pupil of Tarbell in Boston; Kenyon Cox in New York; Constant and Laurens in Paris; George Hitchcock in Holland. Member: Copley S., 1888. Address in 1929, 40 Webster Place, Brookline, MA.

CROCKER, MARTHA E.
Painter. Born South Yarmouth, MA, May 3, 1883. Pupil of Benson, Tarbell, Cottet, Simon and Hawthorne. Member: NA Women PS; Boston S. Indp. A; Provincetown AA. Address in 1929, 107 Fenway Studios, 30 Ipswich Street, Boston, MA; h. Channing Place, Cambridge, MA; summer, Provincetown, Cape Cod, MA.

CROCKER, W. H.
Painter. Born in New York City, 1856. Pupil of Robert Vonnoh and Charles Rosen. Address in 1926, 50 Hamilton Terrace, New York, NY.

CROM, LILLIAN HOBBES.
Painter. Member: Fellowship Penna. Academy of Fine Arts. Address in 1926, Schwenksville, PA.

CROMARTY, MARGARET A.
Painter and designer. Born Canada, Aug. 7, 1873. Pupil of Scranton School of Design. Member: Pensacola AC. Awards: First prize for water color, Pensacola Tri-County Fair 1911; 1st prize for tapestry, Lagrange, Ind., 1923. Address in 1929, 314 South Fla Blanca Street, Pensacola, FL.

CROMWELL, JOANE.
Painter, illustrator, and teacher. Born Lewistown, IL. Pupil of AIC; Anna A. Hills. Member: Laguna Beach AA. Work: "Driver's Point," Laguna Beach Chamber of Commerce; "The Emerald Pool," Cal-Acres Co., Los Angeles; "Beyond the Arch," Laguna Beach Art Gallery. Address in 1929, 1900 Parry Avenue, Laurel Canyon, Hollywood, CA.

CRON, NINA NASH.
Miniature painter. Born Spokane, Wash., April 28, 1883. Pupil of Elsie Dodge Pattee, Mabel Welch and Amelia Fuller. Address in 1929, 3302 KcKinley Street, Wash., DC.

CRONENWETT, CLARE.
Engraver. Address in 1926, 641 O'Farrell Street, San Francisco, CA.

CRONYN, RANDOLPH E.
Painter. Born New York City, Feb. 25, 1901. Pupil of Edmund Greacen, John Costigan, George Pearse Ennis. Member: Salma. C.; NAC; New Rochelle AA. Address in 1929, 6 Minetta Street, New York, NY; summer, 210 Lyncroft Road, New Rochelle, NY.

CROOKS, FORREST C.
Illustrator. Born Goshen, IN, Oct. 1, 1893. Pupil of George Sotter and Arthur Sparks. Illustrated for Scribner's Pictorial Review, Collier's Weekly, Woman's Home Companion, Century. Address in 1926, Carversville, PA.

CROOME, WILLIAM.
Wood engraver; was a pupil of Bowan's. He illustrated a number

of books. Later in life he gave hi time to designing bank-notes. H is also said to have been a ver good painter in water colors. Se "History of Wood Engraving i America," by W. J. Linton.

CROPSEY, JASPER F.
Painter. Born Feb. 18, 1823 a Rossville, LI, New York. Pupil o National Academy of Design in Ne York City; traveled in Europe. A first an architect; later painte landscapes, chiefly Hudson Rive scenery, including landscape owened by the Metropolitan Museum New York. Elected member o National Academy in 1851. Hudso River School of painting. Die June 22, 1900 in Hastings, Ne York.

CROSBY, KATHARINE VAN RENSELLAER.
Sculptor and teacher. Bor Colorado Springs, CO, Sept 1, 1897 Pupil of Jess M. Lawson. Member NA Women PS; S. Indp. A. Addres in 1929, 222 East 71st Street, Ne York, NY; summer, Tuxedo Park, NY.

CROSBY, PERCY L.
Painter and illustrator. Born i 1891. Member: SI; Salma. C. Bes known for comic strip "Skippy" His work, executed almos exclusively in black and whit line, hung in Paris, Rome an Luxembourg Galleries. Address i 1929, 54 East 59th Street, 131 Eas 93rd Street, New York, NY. Died i New York City, 1964.

CROSS, A. B.
This engraver of landscapes was pupil of A. L. Dick in 1840. He i said to have abandoned engravir early in his life for some othe business.

CROSS, AMY.
Painter and teacher. Bor Milwaukee, WI, April 5, 185(Pupil of Cooper Inst., R. Swai Gifford, William Sartain and ASL (NY; Hague Academy under Fri(Jansen, Jacob Maris and Albei Neuhuys in Holland; Julian Acader in Paris. Member: NYWCC; AF(Awards: Silver medal at Hagt Academy, 1893; silver meda] Atlanta Exp., 1895; bronze meda] Charleston Exp., 1902. Address :

202

1929, 15 West 67th Street, New York, NY.

ROSS, ANSON KENT.
Painter, teacher, and writer. Born Lawrence, MA, Dec. 6, 1862. Pupil of MA Normal Art School. Member: AFA; Boston AC; Copley S. (hon.) Awards: Bronze medal, MA Charitable Merchanics Assoc., Boston, 1892. Received medal, P.-P. Exposition, San Francisco, 1915, for new vision training method of teaching drawing and painting. Author of several books on art education. Director of classes in drawing and painting, Home Study Dept., Columbia University; Director, The Vision Training Art School, Boothbay Harbor, ME. Address in 1929, Boothbay Harbor, ME. Died in 1944.

ROSS, P. F.
Engraver. Born in Sheffield, England; died in Philadelphia in 1856. Cross was a die-sinker and served in that capacity in the Mint of England before he came to Philadelphia about 1845, and became an assistant to James B. Longacre, chief engraver of the U. S. mint. Cross engraved the adverse of the Ingraham medal.

ROSS, SALLY.
Painter. Born Lawrence, MA. Pupil of De Camp and Ross Turner in Boston. Member: Penna. Society of Miniature Painters; New York Water Color Club. Address in 1926, 120 Riverway, Boston, MA.

ROSSMAN, ABNER.
Painter. Born St. Johnsbury, VT, June 14, 1847. Pupil of William Hart in New York; F. W. Moody in London. Member: Chicago Water Color Club. Address in 1926, 658 Woodland Park, Chicago, IL.

ROSSMAN, WILLIAM HENRY.
Painter and etcher. Born New York, NY, Aug. 7, 1896. Pupil of Henri, Lie, Bridgman and Hawthorne. Member: Salma. C.; ASL of NY. Represented in the NY Stock Exchange, Hotel Barclay and the Harvey School, New York; College of William and Mary and in the Wythe Museum, Williamsburg. Address in

1929, Colonial Studios, 39 West 67th Street, New York, NY.

CROUCH, EMILY H.
Painter. Member: Providence Water Color Club. Address in 1926, 102 George Street, Providence, RI.

CROWE, AMANDA MARIA.
Sculptor. Born in Cherokee, North Carolina, in 1928. Studied: Art Institute of Chicago; Instituto Allende San Miguel, Mexico; De Paul University, Chicago. Awards: John Quincy Adams traveling scholarship, Art Institute of Chicago, 1952; Art Institute of Chicago, scholarship, 1946. Collections: Container Corporation of America; Cherokee Indian School in North Carolina; Museum of the Cerokee Indian, North Carolina.

CROWELL, MARGARET.
Illustrator, painter, and sculptor. Born in Philadelphia, PA. Pupil of Penna. Academy of Fine Arts. Member: Fellowship Penna. Academy of Fine Arts. Address in 1926, Avondale, PA.

CROWN, JOHN.
Painter. Member: GFLA. Address in 1929, 303 Fifth Avenue; 381 Fourth Avenue, New York, NY.

CROWNINSHIELD, FREDERIC.
Painter. Born Boston, Nov. 27, 1845. Studied art, France and Italy. Specialty, mural painting and stained glass windows; also landscape in oils and water colors. Instructor of drawing and painting, Museum of Fine Arts, Boston, 1879-85. Director, American Academy in Rome. Academy of National Arts. Member: National Society Mural Painters; National Institute Arts and Letters. The Boston Museum of Fine Arts owned his "Perugia," painted 1911, "Taormina," 1913, and "Capri Cliff," 1916. Elected Associate Member of National Academy in 1905. Died Sept. 3, 1918 in Capri, Italy.

CRUMB, CHARLES P.
Sculptor. Born Bloomfield, MO, Feb. 9, 1874. Pupil of O'Neill, Verlet, Barnard, Taft, Lanteri, Bringhurst, Grafly. Address in 1929, 723 Walnut St., Phila., PA;

203

h. 42 Beechwood Drive, Beechwood Park, Delaware Co., PA.

CRUMB, R.
Illustrator. Born in the eastern United States in 1945. His interest in comic art began at the age of eight when he wrote, drew and sold his own comic books. A self-taught artist, he has had his work published in many books and magazines. His book Fritz the Cat was the basis for the popular animated movie and his Mr. Natural appeared weekly in the Village Voice. Presently living in California, he works for such comic book publishers as Print Mint and Last Gasp.

CRUMBLING, WAYNE K.
Painter. Exhibited at Penna. Academy of Fine Arts, Philadelphia, 1920. Address in 1926, Wrightville, PA.

CRUMP, LESLIE.
Painter, illustrator, and teacher. Born Saugerties, NY, Jan. 7, 1894. Pupil of F. Luis Mora, Charles S. Chapman, Julian Academy in Paris. Member: NYWCC; Brooklyn WCC; ASL of NY. Address in 1929, 503 Central Avenue, Cranford, NJ. Died in 1962.

CRUMPACKER, GRACE DAUCHY.
Painter. Born Troy, NY, Oct. 4, 1881. Pupil of AIC. Member: Hoosier Salon, Artists League of Northern Ind. Award: Prize, Artists League of Northern Indiana, South Bend, 1929. Address in 1929, 1121 Riverside Drive, South Bend, Ind.; summer, R. F. D. No. 1, Wanatah, Ind.

CRUNELLE, LEONARD.
Sculptor. Born Lens, France, July 8, 1872. Pupil of Lorado Taft and AIC. Member: Chicago SA; Cliff Dwellers Club; State Art Commission; Chicago PS. Awards: Medal and diploma, Atlanta Exp., 1895; special prize, AIC, 1904; bronze medal and diploma, St. Louis Exp., 1904; Chicago SA medal, AIC, 1911. Work: "Squirrel Boy," Art Institute of Chicago. Address in 1929, 6016 Ellis Avenue, h. 2034 East 73d Street, Chicago, IL. Died in 1944.

CRUZ, RAYMOND.
Illustrator. Born in New York City, in 1933. He studied art for five years at Cooper Union and PI. His first illustration was published in 1964 for the New York Graphic Society. Besides working for Seventeen and McCall's, he has illustrated several books for Atheneum Press and Four Winds Press. His works have been exhibited at the Museum of Contemporary Crafts in Houston and the S of I Annual Exhibitions.

CSAKANY, GABRIEL S.
Illustrator. Born in Budapest, Hungary, in 1938. He emigrated to Canada in 1956, attended the Toronto College of Art and studied under local professionals as an apprentice. He has had several magazine assignments in the United States and in Canada. As a designer and illustrator, he has won awards in Canada, the United States and Germany.

CSOSZ, JOHN.
Painter and etcher. Born Hungary, Oct. 2, 1897. Pupil of Gottwald and Keller. Member: Cleveland SA. Work: "End of a Perfect Day," Public School Collection; portrait, Dr. Henderson, Memorial Library; mural decorations, Holy Ghost Church, Cleveland, OH; "Atlanta," University Club, Akron, OH. Address in 1929, 14918 Superior Road, Cleveland, Ohio.

CUCUEL, EDWARD.
Painter and illustrator. Born San Francisco, CA, Aug. 6, 1875. Pupil of Constant, Laurens and Gerome in Paris; Leo Putz in Munich. Member: Soc. Nat. des Beaux-Arts (Assoc.) Paris; Isaria and Aussteller Verbund Munchner Kunstler, Der Ring, Munich. Award: Silver medal, P.-P. Exp., San F., 1915. Represented in Detroit Art Inst.; Birkenhead Museum Liverpool. Work: "The Art of Edward Cucuel," by Baron von Ostini, with 100 plates; "Color Plates of Edward Cucuel," E. W. Savory, Ltd., Publishers; "Color plates by Stehli Freres, Zurich" (Zehrfeld and Co., Leipzig Amalthea Pub. Co., Vienna). Address in 1929, 1 West 67th Street; h. 575 Riverside Dr., NY; 5

204

Klarstrasse, Munich, Germany; 16 Kreuzplatz, Zurich, Switzerland; 19 Rue Vavin, Paris, France.

CULBERTSON, JOSEPHINE M.
Painter, etcher, and teacher. Born Shanghai, China, May 4, 1852. Pupil of William M. Chase, Authur W. Dow, George H. Smillie. Member: San Francisco S. Women A; Carmel AA; Laguna Beach AA; Berkeley Lg. FA. Award: Hon. mention, Alaska Yukon Exposition, Seattle, Wash., 1909. Address in 1929, cor. Lincoln and 7th Sts.; Box 53, Carmel, CA.

CULBERTSON, LINN.
Painter and teacher. Born Princeton, IA, Sept. 29, 1890. Pupil of Charles Atherton Cumming. Awards: First prize ($100), Des Moines Women's Club, 1914; gold medal, Des Moines Women's Club, 1922, and bronze, 1924; silver medal, 1928, and purchase prize, 1929, Des Moines Women's Club. Address in 1929, 1131-22d Street, Des Moines, IA.

CULBERTSON, QUEENIE.
Painter and illustrator. Born San Angelo, Texas. Pupil of Frank Duveneck; William Del. Dodge. Member: Cincinnati Woman's AC. Address in 1929, 4120 Forest Avenue, Norwood, Cincinnati, Ohio.

CULIN, ALICE MUMFORD.
Painter. Born Philadelphia, PA, Jan. 30, 1875. Pupil of Joseph De Camp, Carl Newman and Robert Henri. Awards: Mary Smith prize, PAFA 1906 and 1910; bronze medal, P.-P. Exp., San Francisco, 1915. Address in 1929, 137 West 12th Street, New York, NY.

CULTER, RICHARD.
Illustrator. Member: SI. Address in 1929, Ridgefield, CT, 211 Secor Lane, Pelham Manor, NY.

CUMING, BEATRICE LAVIS.
Painter. Born Brooklyn, NY, March 25, 1903. Pupil of Henry B. Snell. Member: NYWCC; NA Women PS; AWCS; Allied AA. Address in 1929, 245 Fulton Street, Brooklyn, NY. Died in 1975.

CUMMENS, LINDA.
(Linda Talaba Cummens). Sculptor

and graphic artist. Born Detroit, MI, July 15, 1943. Studied: Illinois Wesleyan University; Southern Illinois University. Awards: Birmingham, Michigan Art Assoc., 1963; Royal Oak Art Assoc., Michigan, 1966; Ball State University, 1975. Collections: Henry Ford Traveling Print Collection; J. L. Hudson Collection, Grosse Point, Michigan; McLean County Bank, Bloomington, Illinois. Address in 1980, Deerfield, IL.

CUMMING, CHARLES ATHERTON.
Painter, lecturer, and teacher. Born in Illinois, March 31, 1858. Pupil of Boulanger at Julian Academy, Lefebvre and Constant in Paris. Member: Iowa AA; College AA of America. Founder and Director, Cumming School of Art, Des Moines; and head of department of Graphic and Plastic Arts,State Univerisity, Iowa City, IA; founder, Iowa Art Guild. Work: Mural painting, "Departure of the Indians from Fort Des Moines," in Polk County Court House; portraits in the State Historical Gallery, Des Moines, IA; portraits, Memorial collection, State Univ. of Iowa, Iowa City; landscapes in Des Moines Woman's Club Gallery and Cedar Rapids Gallery of Art Association. Author of "Classification of the Arts of Expression," "The White Man's Art Defined," "The Psychology of the Symbolic Pictorial Arts" and "My Creed." Address in 1929, The Cumming School of Art, Des Moines, IA; h. P.O. Box 345, San Diego, CA. Died in 1932.

CUMMINGS, MELVIN EARL.
Sculptor. Born Salt Lake City, Utah, 1876. Student of Mark Hopkins Art Institute, San Francisco; pupil of Douglas Tilden. Executed numerous statues in and around San Francisco, notably 11 ft. statue of Robert Burns, Golden Gate Park; also Conservatory Fountain; National Monument to Commodore Sloat, Monterey, CA, etc. Instructor of modeling, University of CA, 1904. Member: San Francisco Art Association. Address in 1926, 3966 Clay Street, San Francisco.

205

CUMMINGS, THOMAS SEIR.
Painter. Born in Bath, England, Aug. 26, 1804, he came to America at an early age and became one of the most successful miniature painters in the country. He was one of the founders of the National Academy in 1826 and an early vice-president. Among his many beautiful portraits are those of Miss O'Bryan, Mrs. Cummings, Henry Inman and Mr. Hatch. Died Sept. 24, 1894 in Hackensack, NJ.

CUNNINGHAM, JOE.
Writer, cartoonist, and lecturer. Born Philadelphia, PA, June 22, 1890. Member: PPC; Amer. Assoc. Cartoonists and Caricaturists. Designer of "Coat of Arms" for the U.S. Tank Corps. Creator of "Rufus McGoofus" the cartoon calendar. Address in 1929, Philadelphia Record; Melrose Park, Philadelphia, PA.

CUNNINGHAM, MILDRED C.
Painter. Born St. Paul, MN, Aug. 23, 1898. Pupil of Charles A. Cumming. Member: Iowa AG; Ill. AFA; All-Ill. SFA; Rockford AA. Address in 1929, 1718 Camp Avenue, Rockford, IL.

CUNNINGHAM, ROBERT MORRIS.
Illustrator. Born in Herington, Kansas, in 1924. He attended the University of Kansas, KCAI and ASL. His first illustration was done for American Cyanamid Company in the 1960's. The recipient of Gold Medals in 1966 and 1967 from the S of I, he has shown his paintings at the Brooklyn Museum and the Smithsonian Inst. of Washington, DC.

CUPRIEN, FRANK W.
Painter. Born Brooklyn, NY, 1871. Pupil of Carl Webber in Philadelphia; ASL of NY; studied in Munich, Dresden, Leipzig, Italy and Paris. Member: Leipzig AA; Calif. AC; Laguna Beach AA; Dallas AA; Denver AA; Munich P.; SSAL; New Haven PCC; PSC of Los Angeles. Awards: Gold medal, Berliner Ausstellung; silver medal, Galveston, TX, 1913; silver medal, San Diego Exp. 1915; silver medal, San Diego Exp., 1916; hon. mention, Phoenix (Ariz.) State Fair, 1916; bronze medal, Sacramento State

Fair, 1918; prize, Sacramento fair 1920; popular prize, Laguna Beach Art Assoc., 1921; Skidmore priz ($50), Laguna Beach AA, 1922; prize ($100) Pac. Southwest Exp., Lon Beach, CA; Prize ($100), Lagun Beach AA, 1928. Work: "Homewar Bound," del Vecchio Gallery Leipzig. Address in 1929, Th Viking Studio, Laguna Beach, CA Died June 21, 1948.

CUREL-SYLVESTRE, ROGER.
Painter. Born Nice, France, 1884 Pupil of A. Stevens and Noel Member: Societe Royale des Beau Arts, Bruxelles (Assoc.); Salons o America. Work: "Autumn, Milwaukee Art Inst. Address i 1929, 1 rue Charles Dickens, Paris France.

CURRAN, CHARLES COURTNEY.
Painter. Born Hartford, KY, Feb 13, 1861. Pupil of Cincinnat School of Design; ASL and NAD i New York; Julian Academy unde Constant, Lefebvre and Doucet i Paris. Member: ANA 1888; NA 1904 NYWCC; AWCS; SAA 1888; Salma. C. Lotos (life); NAC (life); Allie AA; MacD. C. Awards: Thir Hallgarten prize, NAD, 1888; hon mention, Paris Salon, 1890; Clar Prize, NAD, 1893; silver medal Atlanta Exp., 1895; Medal Columbian Exp., Chicago, 1893 second Hallgarten prize, NAD, 1895 hon. mention, Paris Exp., 1900 silver medal, Pan-Am. Exp. Buffalo, 1901; Carnegie prize, SAA 1904; silver medal, St. Louis Exp. 1904; first Corcoran prize, S Wash. A., 1905; Altman prize ($1,000), NAD, 1919. Work "Perfume of the Roses," Nationa Gallery, Washington; "The Breez Day," Pennsylvania Academy Philadelphia; "The Golden Hour, Museum of Art, Columbus; "Noo Sunshine," Art Association Richmond, IN; "The Jungfrau" an "The Swimming Pool," Toledo (OH Museum of Art; "Children Catchin Minnows," Buffalo (NY) Fine Art Academy; "Imprisoned Jewel," Ar Museum, Montclair, NJ; "The Hawk, San Antonio Art Museum; "Th Carnelian Necklace," Fort Worth Ar Museum; "Pine Needles an Sunlight," Dallas Art Association "Rita," Witte Memorial Museum, Sa

206

Antonio, TX; "Cathedral Interior, Verona," Metropolitan Museum. Address in 1929, 39 West 67th Street, NYC. Died in 1942.

URRIER, CHARLES.
Lithographer. Born 1818. Brother of Nathaniel (of Currier & Ives, 1862-1901), had a lithographic establishment for years at 33 Spruce Street, New York City. He did a large amount of work on the sheet music illustrations of the day. Died Jan. 4, 1887.

URRIER, CYRUS BATES.
Painter and illustrator. Born Marietta, OH, Dec. 13, 1878. Pupil of Julian Academy, Bouguereau, Constant, Mucha, Paris. Member: Salma. C. Address in 1929, 1347 Lucile Avenue, Los Angeles, CA. Died c. 1951.

URRIER, JOSEPH FRANK.
Painter. Born Nov. 21, 1843. He is represented in the permanent collection in Herron Art Gallery, IN, and the St. Louis Museum. He studied in Munich, and in 1878 sent to the Society of American Artists "A Bohemian Beggar," and two landscapes. Died in Jan. 1909.

URRIER, NATHANIEL.
Lithographer. Born March 27, 1818 in Roxbury, MA. The firm of Currier and Ives, 1862 - 1901, issued for years lithographic portraits, views and pictorial records of sporting events and other happenings. For a number of years in the 1850's and 60's work in lithographic stone crowded out the wood block. Currier productions were often crudely executed, but some very beautiful prints did come from his presses. The shooting, fishing and racing prints furnish us today with a pictured idea of American sports of the period, which is of great interest to the modern sportsman. Died Nov. 20, 1888 in NYC.

URRIER, WALTER BARRON.
Painter, etcher, craftsman, writer, lecturer, and teacher. Born Springfield, MA, May 3, 1879. Pupil of Dow, Eben Comins, Kenyon Cox. Member: Calif. AC; Calif.

PM; Laguna Beach AA; Santa Monica AA. Award: First prize Annual Art Exhib., Santa Monica AA. Work: "California the Golden," "The Land of the Afternoon" and "Dalton Canyon," Lincoln High School, Los Angeles; "Sunset Glow from Bigbear," "The Phantom," "Sunrise in San Leandro Hills," Exposition Park Galleries, Los Angeles; "California," Cecil B. de Mille Home for Girls, Hollywood, CA. Writer and lecturer on Art Education. Head of Fine and Vocational Art Depts., Lincoln High School, Los Angeles, CA. Director Currier Creative Art School, Santa Monica, CA. Address in 1929, 432 - 15th Street, Santa Monica, CA. Died in 1934.

CURRY, JOHN STEUART.
Painter. Born in 1897 in Kansas. Studied at the Art Inst. of Kansas; Art Institute of Chicago; Geneva College; and the Studio of Schoukhaieff in Paris. Taught at the University of Wisconsin, Cooper Union and at the Art Students League. Second Prize from the Carnegie International Exhibition in 1933, the Pennsylvania Acad. of Fine Arts Gold Medal in 1941, and the $3,000 Prize in the Artists for Victory Exhibition at the Metropolitan Museum of Art in 1941. Died in 1946.

CURTIS, CALVIN.
Painter. Born in Stratford, CT, 1822. He began his studies under Daniel Huntington in 1841, also working at the Academy of Design. His work was largely portrait painting. In a limited degree he extended his work to landscapes.

CURTIS, CONSTANCE.
Painter. Born Washington. Pupil of Art Students' League of New York, and William M. Chase. Exhibited Paris Expn., 1900; St. Louis Expn., 1904. Pres. Art Workers' Club for Women. Member: Art Students' League; Women Painters and Sculptors. Address in 1926, 1199 Park Avenue, New York, NY. Died in 1959.

CURTIS, ELIZABETH.
Painter. Born New York, NY. Pupil of Twachtman and Chase. Member: PBC; AFA. Address in 1929, 127

207

East 10th Street; 399 Park Avenue, New York, NY; summer Watertown, NY.

CURTIS, GEORGE.
Painter. Born in Southampton, England, in 1859. Pupil of Legros; Benjamin Constant. Member: Society of Independent Artists. Represented in Musee de Melun; large mural paintings in the Church Villemomble. Address in 1926, 5 West 16th Street, New York. Died in 1943.

CURTIS, IDA MAYNARD.
Painter. Born Lewisburg, PA, in 1860. Pupil of Hawthorne, Ross, Maynard, Simon, Jolley. Member: San Diego AA; Laguna Beach AA; Carmel AA; Provincetown AA; NAC. Award: Landscape prize, Catherine L. Wolfe C., 1923. Address in 1929, care Back Bay Branch of Old Colony Trust Co., Boston, MA; R.F.D. No. A, Box 60, Carmel, Calif.

CURTIS, LELAND.
Painter. Born Denver, Colo., Aug. 7, 1897. Member: Calif. AC; Artland C; PSC of Los Angeles; AFA; Am. APL. Awards: Bronze medal, PSC of Los Angeles, 1924; cash prize, Calif. State Fair, 1926; Los Angeles Co. Fair, 1926; silver medal, PSC of Los Angeles, 1928. Work: "Sierra Gold," Artland Club, Los Angeles; "The Everlasting Mountains," permanent collection, Hollywood Athletic Club; "High Sierras," purchased by City of Los Angeles, 1929. Address in 1929, 560 South New Hampshire Street; h. 3871 South Hobart Blvd., Los Angeles, CA.

CURTIS, NATHANIEL CORTLANDT.
Painter, architect, writer, lecturer, and teacher. Born Smithville, NC, Feb. 8, 1881. Pupil of William R. Ware. Member: AIA; N.O. AA; Arts and Crafts Club of N.O. Designed buildings for Alabama Polytechnic Inst., Auburn, Ala. Author: "Architectural Graphics," "Architectural Composition." Address in 1929, 1105 Hibernia Bldg.; h. 1423 Calhoun Street, New Orleans, LA.

CURTIS, SIDNEY.
Painter. Member: Salmagundi Club. Address in 1926, 112 Hicks Street, Brooklyn, New York.

CURTIS, WILLIAM FULLER.
Painter, illustrator, and craftsman. Born Staten Island, NY, Feb. 25, 1873. Pupil of Julius Rolshoven, Lefebvre and Robert-Fleury in Paris. Awards: Third Corcoran prize, S. Wash. A., 1902; first Corcoran prize, Wash. WCC, 1903; silver medal, St. Louis Exp., 1904. Work: Panels for altar for Church of St. Michael and All Angels, Geneseo, NY; decorative panels, Cosmos Club, Washington, DC. Address in 1929, Ashfield, MA.

CURTIS-BROWN, MARY SEYMOUR.
Painter. Born Norwalk, CT, July 28, 1888. Pupil of Albert Sterner. Member: NAC. Address in 1929, Whitney Point, NY; h. Peck Farm, Lisle, NY.

CUSHING, HOWARD GARDINER.
Portrait painter. Born in Boston, 1869. He studied for five years in Paris at the Julien Academy; was also pupil of Laurens and Constant. Represented at Metropolitan Museum, New York, by portrait of Mrs. Ethel Cushing. He exhibited "A Woman in White," "Woman in Silver Dress," and "Sunlight." He also painted a series of murals for Mrs. H. P. Whitney's studio, on Long Island. Elected Associate Member of National Academy in 1906. Died April 26, 1916 in NYC.

CUSHMAN, ALICE.
Landscape painter. Born Philadelphia, Sept. 27, 1854. Pupil of NAD in New York, Ross, Turner in Boston. Member: Plastic C.; Phila. WCC; Fellowship PAF. (assoc.). Award: Woman's Exposition of the Carolinas, 1897. Specialty, water colors. Address in 1929, 919 Pine Street, Philadelphia, PA.

CUSHMAN, GEORGE H.
Engraver and painter. Born June 5, 1814 in Windham, CT. Cushman was pupil of Asaph Willard, the Hartford engraver, and became an admirable line-engraver of landscapes and book illustrations. He was chiefly known as a miniature painter. Died Aug. 3, 1876 in Jersey City, NJ.

CUSHMAN, HENRY.
Sculptor and craftsman. Born London, England, Dec. 16, 1859. Work: Carved ivory cup, Windsor Castle. Specialty, carved wood and stonework. Address in 1929, 4823 Genevieve Avenue, Los Angeles, CA.

CUSHMAN, THOMAS HASTINGS.
Born at Albany, NY, June 6, 1815. He was apprenticed in the engraving establishment of A. L. Dick in New York. He is well known as a bank-note engraver. Died Nov. 7, 1841 in Albany, NY.

CUSTIS, ELEANOR PARKE.
Painter. Born Washington, DC, 1897. Pupil of Corcoran Art School, Henry B. Snell. Member: Wash. WCC; S. Wash. A.; NA Women PS; Wash. AC; PBC; NYWCC; AWCS; AFA. Address in 1929, 626 East Capitol Street, Washington, DC.

CUSUMANO, STEFANO.
Born Febuary 5, 1912, in Tampa, Florida. Studied at Met. Art School, NYC; Cooper Union; and with Arthur Schwieder. Taught at Cooper Union, NYU, and Cornell. Awarded Ford Foundation Purchase Award (1962), Am. Acad. Arts and Letters award (1962, 1968, 1971). Exhibited at Montross Gallery, NYC (1942); George Binet Gallery (1946-50); Oregon State University; Tampa Art Inst.; Terry Dintenfass (1967); MOMA; Corcoran, Washington, DC. In collections of Newark Museum; Whitney; Nat. Gal. (Washington, DC); Brooklyn Mus.; Johns Hopkins; University of Illinois; Florida State University and others. Died November 18, 1975.

CUTLER, CARL GORDON.
Painter. Born Newtonville, MA, Jan. 3, 1873. Pupil of Boston Museum School; Constant and Laurens in Paris. Member: Boston AC; Copley S.; Boston SWCP; (assoc.) NYWCC. Address in 1929, Fenway Studios, Boston, MA; h. 24 Central Avenue, Newtonville, MA. Died in 1945.

CUTLER, JERVIS.
Engraver. Born Sept. 19, 1768 in Martha's Vineyard, MA. In 1812 he engraved, on copper, illustrations for a book, including the earliest view of Cincinnati. Died June 25, 1846 in Evansville, IN.

CZERMANSKI, ZOLZISLAW.
Illustrator. Born in Krakow, Poland, in 1900. He became a pupil of the famous Polish caricaturist Kazimierz Sichulski and later had his first exhibit, Caricatures of Personalities of the Arts, held in the Tatra mountains. He moved to Paris to study art with Fernand Leger and there began his career as a painter of everyday Parisian life. In 1931 he was invited to the US to work for the newly founded magazine Fortune. His paintings have appeared in Warsaw, Paris, London, Geneva, Vienna, New York, Washington, and Philadelphia. Died in 1970.

DABO, LEON.
Landscape and mural painter, writer, and lecture. Born Detroit, MI, July 9, 1868. Pupil of Daniel Vierge, Pierre Galland, Ecole des Beaux-Arts and Julian Academy in Paris. Member: Pastellists; Hopkin C. of Detroit; NAD; Allied Artists, London, England; Royal Society of Arts and Sciences, London, England; Les Mireilles, Avigon, France; Les Amis des Arts, Arles, France; Societe des Amis du Louvre, Paris, France; School Art League of NY; Brooklyn SA; PS ; Mural P.; Three Arts C. Cincinnati. In collections of: MMA; Luxembourg Mus., Paris; National Gallery, Washington, DC; Imperial Museum of Art, Tokyo, Japan; National Gallery, Ottawa, CN; Boston; Brooklyn; Herron Art Inst., Indianapolis; St. Louis; Detroit; Toledo; Mus. of Art, Montclair, NJ; Poland Springs (ME) Mus.; Art Assoc., Milwaukee; Art Assoc. Muncie, IN; Hackley Art Gal., Muskegon, MI; Art Assoc., Saginaw, MI; Nat. Arts Club, NY; Arbuckle Inst., Brooklyn, NY; Baltimore, MD; Newark, NJ; Mus. of Art, Fort Worth, TX; Beloit College, Beloit, Wisc.; Delgado Museum, New Orleans; Memorial Art Gal., Rochester, NY; Reading Art Gal., Reading, PA; Mus. of Art, Minneapolis, MN; Mus. Avignon, France; Montreal Art Assoc.; Tuskogee Inst, Ala.; Mus. of Lyons, France; Mural "Ascension," ceiling-triforium gallery (16 panels) and altar (4 panels) church of St. John the Baptist, Brooklyn, NY; ten historical paintings, Flower Mem. Lib., Watertown, NY. Address in 1929, 222 West 22nd Street, NYC.

DABO, THEODORE SCOTT.
Painter. Born in New Orleans, LA, 1877. Painting in Ecole des Arts Paris; traveled extensively and studied painting independently. Ceased painting 1890, owing to irreconcilable views of teachers and his own ideas; studied natural law and optics, and made discoveries in atmosphere, luminosity and vibration that have since made his paintings quoted; returned to New York 1900, and entered various exhibitions;

subsequently, exhibitions a London, Paris and elsewhere Address in 1926, Billancour (Seine), France.

DABOUR, JOHN.
Artist. Born in Smyrna, Asia, i 1837. Pupil of Academy of Fin Arts in Paris. Fifteen years o his professional life were spent i the United States paintin portraits which are found in th principal cities in the Unite States, but chiefly in Baltimore MD. Among his most prominen sitters were Archbishop Spaulding Senator Cameron, Senator Davis an Governor Groome of Maryland. H died in NY in 1905.

DAGGET, MAUD.
Sculptor. Born Kansas City, MO Feb. 10, 1883. Pupil of Lorad Taft. Member: Calif. AC. Award Silver medal, Pan. Calif. Exp., Sa Diego 1915. Work: Fountain, Hote Raymond, Pasadena; drinkin fountain; medallion and Memoria Fountain, "Castelar St. Crech Building," City of Los Angeles "Peter Pan Frieze," Pasadena Publi Library; Bertha Harton Orr Memoria Fountain, Occidental College, Lo Angeles; Four works, Am. Exhib. o Sculpture, NSS, San Francisco 1929. Address in 1929, 725 Sout Catalina Ave., Pasadena, CA.

DAGGETT, ALFRED.
Line engraver of portraits, an bank-note vignettes, was the uncl and the first preceptor of th American artist J. F. Kensett Daggett was born in New Haven, CT 1799, and died there 1872. He wa a member of the engraving firms c Daggett and Ely, and Daggett Hinman and Co. The work signed t these firm names, however, i usually executed in stipple.

DAGGY, RICHARD S.
Painter, illustrator, and etcher Born Chatham, NJ, Feb. 17, 189; Pupil of Augustus S. Dagg Member: Silvermine Guild c Artists; Darien Guild of the Sev Arts; S. Indp. A. Address in 192! Seir Hill, Norwalk, CT.

DAHLER, WARREN.
Painter. Born Helena, Mont., 1887. Pupil of NY School of Art and NAD. Member: Mural P. Award: Prize collaborative competition, NY. Arch. Lg., 1915. For three years director of painting at the Herter Looms, New York. Address in 1929, 69 Tiemann Place, New York, NY.

DAHLGREEN, CHARLES W.
Landscape painter, etcher, and teacher. Born Chicago, Sept. 8, 1864. Pupil of AIC. Member: ASL of Chicago; Art Service League; Chicago PS; Chicago SE; Chicago Gal. A. Awards: Hon. mention, P.-P. Exp., San F., 1915; Rosenwald and Carr prizes, AIC, 1919; Chicago Municipal Art Lg. purchase prize, 1920; first prize for landscape in oil, Indiana Hoosier Salon, 1925 and landscape prize, 1928; purchase prize, Chicago Gal. A., 1927 and 1928. Represented: Library of Congress, Wash., DC and Smithsonian Inst.; Chicago AG; Inter. Soc. AL; Museum of History, Science and Art, Los Angeles; Vanderpoel AA Collection, Chicago; and NY Public Lib.. Address in 1929, 409 North Cuyler Ave., Oak Park, IL.

DAILEY, CHUCK.
Painter and museologist. Born in Golden, CO, May 25, 1935. Studied: Univ. Colorado; western Europe 1962-63. Work: Vincent Price Collection, CA; Museum of New Mexico, permanent collection, Santa Fe. Exhibitions: Fine Arts Museum of NM; U. of Colo. Mus.; Gallery 5, Santa Fe; others. Awards: Biennial Exhibition Museum of NM, New Mexico State Fair. Art positions: Curator, Exhibitions Division, Museum of New Mexico; has managed numerous exhibitions; teaches exhibition arrangement. Mem.: NM Assn. of Mus.; Am. Indian Mus. Assn; Am. Assn. of Mus., etc. Media: Acrylic. Address in 1982, 412 Sosaya Lane, Santa Fe, NM.

DAILY, EVELYNNE B.
Painter and printmaker. Born Indianapolis, IN, Jan. 8, 1903. Studied: Herron Sch. of Art of Indiana U.; The Bauhaus; Butler U. Exhibitions: Brooklyn Mus.; Chicago Art Inst.; NAD. Her work is in the collection of the Library of Congress, Washington, DC.

DAINGERFIELD, ELLIOTT.
Painter, illustrator, teacher, writer and lecturer. Born Harper's Ferry, VA, March 26, 1859; came to NY in 1880. Studied in NY. Member: ANA, 1902; NA, 1906; NYWCC; SAA, 1903; Lotos C.; NAC. Awards: Silver medal, Pan-Am. Exp., Buffalo, 1901; Clarke prize, NAD, 1902. Work: "Christ Stilling the Tempest," and "Slumbering Fog," Metropolitan Museum, NY; "Storm Breaking Up," Toledo Museum; "The Child of Mary," National Gallery, Washington; "The Midnight Moon," Brooklyn Inst. Museum; mural decorations in Lady Chapel of Church of St. Mary the Virgin, NY; "An Arcadian Huntress" and "Swirling Mists," City Art Mus., St. Louis; "The Valley of the Dragon," Chicago Art Inst.; "Sunset Hour," "West Glow," Butler Art Inst, Youngstown, OH; "Little Town of Bethlehem," Harrison Gallery, Los Angeles Museum. Address in 1929, 222 West 59th Street, New York, NY.

DAINGERFIELD, MAJORIE.
Sculptor. Born in New York City. Studied: School of Am. Sculpture; Grand Central School of Art; and with James Fraser, Edmond Amateis, and Solon Borglum. Award: Pen & Brush Club, 1956. Collections: School of Tropical Medicine, San Juan, Puerto Rico; Hobart College, Geneva, NY; Queens College, Charlotte, NC; Georgetown University. She is perhaps best known for her statuette-emblem for Girl Scouts of America.

DAINTY, S.
This man was engraving landscapes in mixed manner, about 1840, in Philadelphia. John Dainty was a copperplate printer in Philadelphia, working as early as 1817, and this S. Dainty may have been his son.

DALAND, KATHARINE
Illustrator. Born in Boston, MA, 1883. Illustrated "Lyrics of Eliza," and many other books.

DALE, BENJAMIN M.
Illustrator. Member: SI. Address in 1929, 15 West 37th Street, New York, NY; 111 Meteor St., Forest Hills, LI, NY.

DalFABBRO, MARIO.
Sculptor. Born in Cappella Maggiore, Italy, Oct. 6, 1913; US citizen. Studied: Inst. Indust. Art, Venice; Magistero Art, Venice. Work: Kemerer Mus., Bethlehem, PA; Mus. Art, Sci, & Indust., Bridgeport, CT; Allentown (PA) Art Mus. Exhibitions: Triennial International of Milan, Italy; Allentown (PA) Art Mus.; New Engl. Exhib., Silvermine Guild; Mus. of Art, Sci., and Indust., Bridgeport, CT; etc. Awards: Sculpture, first prize, City of Vittorio Veneto, Italy; first prize, sculpture, Lehigh Art Alliance; and others. Mem.: Int'l Acad. Tommaso Campanella, Rome; Silvermine Guild. Media: Wood. Address in 1982, 67 Sherman Ct., Fairfield, CT.

DALLAM, ELIZABETH FORBES.
Painter and teacher. Born Philadelphia, PA, Feb. 9, 1875. Pupil of Anshutz, Breckenridge, and McCarter. Awards: Two European traveling scholarships, PAFA. Member: Fellowship PAFA; North Shore AA. Address in 1929, 2224 Pine St., Philadelphia, PA; summer, Rocky Neck, Gloucester, MA.

DALLIN, CYRUS E(DWIN).
Sculptor and writer. Born Springville, Utah, Nov. 22, 1861. Pupil of Chapu and Dampt in Paris. Member: ANA 1912; NSS 1893; NY Arch. Lg.; AC Phila., 1895; Boston AC; St. Botolph C., 1900; Royal Soc. of Arts, London; Boston GA; Boston SS; AFA. Instructor, MA Normal Art School. Awards: hon. mention, Paris Salon 1890; first class medal and diploma, Columbian Exp., Chicago, 1893; silver medal, MA. Charitable Mechanics Association, 1895; silver medal, Paris Exp., 1900; silver medal, Pan-Am. Exp., Buffalo, 1901; gold medal, St. Louis Exp., 1904; third class medal, Paris Salon, 1909; gold medal, P.-P. Exp., San F., 1915. Work: Lincoln Park, Chicago; Library of Congress Washington; Salt Lake City; Fairmount Park, Phila.; "Soldiers and Sailors Monument," Syracuse NY; marble relief "Julia War Howe," Museum of Fine Arts, Boston Arlington, MA; "Alma Mater, Wash. Univ., St. Louis, MO; Kansa City, MO; Cleveland School of Art Plymouth, MA; Provincetown, MA Storrow Memorial Lincoln, MA Address in 1929, 69 Oakland Ave. Arlington Heights, MA.

DALLISON, KEN.
Illustrator. Born in Hounslow Middlesex, England, in 1933. H attended the Twickenham School o Art for two years. He began hi career in 1956 with Liberty i Toronto, Canada. He lived in M for many years and as a free-lanc illustrator won several award including a Gold Medal from the of I. Presently he lives nea Toronto with his wife and fou children and is represented in th Ontario Gallery of Art.

DALRYMPLE, AMY FLORENCE.
Landscape painter. Born Boston Studied at Massachusetts Normal Ar School; and in Italy. Member Boston SAC; Copley S. Address i 1929, Blue Ship Studio; h. 27 1 Wharf, Boston, MA.

DALRYMPLE, LUCILE STEVENSON.
Painter. Born Sandusky, OH, c Oct. 19, 1882. Pupil of AIC, a J. Francis Smith Acad., Chicago Member: Cordon C; AIC Alumni Chicago S. Min. P.; South Side A Renaissance Soc. U. of C; AFA; AFA. Work: Portrait of "Mr. J. Gillick," director's room, Unio Station, Chicago; "I. C. Elston Elston Bank, Crawfordsville, I "Betsey Gates Mills," Betsey Mill Club, Marietta, OH; portrait Presidents of Wabash College, D J. F. Tuttle, Dr. G. S. Burrough Dr. William P. Kane, Dr. George Mackintosh, Dr. Charles Whit Theodore H. Ristine, in Truste Room, Wabash Colleg Crawfordsville, Indiana; Dr. Alfr Tyler Perry, Marietta Colleg Marietta, OH. Miniature, "Youth purchased by IL AFA, for Permane Gallery, Springfield, IL. Addre in 1929, Fine Arts Bldg.; h. 47 Drexel Blvd., Chicago, IL; summe

212

"Marais du Cygne," R. D. No. 1, Port Clinton, OH.

DALSTROM, GUSTAF O(SCAR).
Painter. Born Gothland, Sweden, Jan. 18, 1893. Pupil of AIC; George Bellows; Randall Davey. Member: Chicago SA; Chicago NJSA. Address in 1929, 645 Kemper Place, Chicago, IL.

DALTON, E.
Miniature painter, who flourished in 1827 in Philadelphia.

DALY, MATT A.
Painter. Born Cincinnati, OH, on Jan. 13, 1860. Pupil of Duveneck, Noble and Lutz. Member: Cincinnati AC.; Am. APL. Represented in Cincinnati Art Museum; University of Cincinnati. Address in 1929, Apts. 7 and 9, 127 East 3rd St., Norwood, OH.

DAMINAKES, CLEON.
Painter and etcher. Born Berkeley, CA. Member: Calif. SE; Chicago SE. Award: Logan medal, Chicago SE, 1922. Work: Mural decorations, Berkeley High School Auditorium. Address in 1929, 11 West 52nd St., New York, NY; h. 327 Lenox Ave., Oakland, Calif.

DAMMAT, WILLIAM T.
Painter. Born at New York, 1853. Pupil of Munich Academy, and Munkacsy. Represented by "The Woman in Red" and "The Contrabandist" in the Luxembourg Museum, Paris; "A Quartette," Metropolitan Museum, New York; "Eva Haviland," Boston Museum. Address in 1926, 45 Avenue de Villiers, Paris.

DAMROSCH, HELEN T(HERESE).
See Tee-Van, Mrs. John.

DANA, CHARLES E.
Painter. Specialty, water colors. Born in Pennsylvania in 1843, he received the gold medal of the Philadelphia Art Club for his water colors in 1891. He died in Philadelphia in 1924.

DANA, WILLIAM PARSONS WINCHESTER.
Painter. Born Boston, 1833. Went to sea in early life; studied art Ecole des Beaux Arts, and under Le Poittevin, Paris, 1854-62. Had studio in NY 1862-70, residing abroad since 1870. Member of Academy of National Artists 1862; National Academy 1863. Painted marine, landscape, and figure pictures. Received medals at Paris International Expn., 1878 and 1889; 1st prize marine painting at Penna. Academy of Fine Arts 1881. Address in 1926, 57 Onslow Gardens, London, S.W., England.

DANAHER, MAY.
Painter, craftsman, and teacher. Born La Grange, TN. Pupil of PAFA, Hugh Breckenridge and George Elmer Browne. Member: SSAL; Miss. AA.; North Shore AA; S. Indp. A., NY; AFA. Awards: First prizes for miniature on china, enamel vase and gold brooch, second prizes for collection and landscape in oil, Tri-State Fair, Memphis, TN; first prizes for collection of oils, 1923, 1924; second prizes for flower paintings and portraits, Arkansas State Fair. Director, Fine Arts Club, Little Rock. Address in 1929, 2022 Izard St., Little Rock, AR.

DANBY, J.
"Paulson's Advertiser," Philadelphia, May 29, 1822, contains the advertisement of "J. Danby, Engraver in General, from London." This notice says that he engraves on "Gold, Silver, Copper, Brass, Wood, etc. in a superior manner," but no signed work by Danby is known to Fielding in 1926.

DANDO, SUSIE MAY.
Painter and teacher. Born Odell, IL, on Sept. 6, 1873. Pupil of William L. Judson in California. Member: Calif. AC.; Laguna Beach AA.; West Coast Arts. Award: Silver medal, Panama-Calif. Exp., San Diego, 1915. Address in 1929, 126 Brooks Ave., Venice, CA.

DANFORTH, MARIE.
See Mrs. Page.

DANFORTH, MOSELY ISAAC.
Engraver. Born Hartford, CT, in 1800; died in New York in 1862. In 1818 Dangorth was an apprentice to Asaph Willard of the Graphic Company, of Hartford, and he became a meritorious line-engraver of

213

portraits and bank-note vignettes. He established himself in business in New Haven in 1821, but soon after moved to New York. Danforth was one of the founders of the Drawing Association of 1825, and of the National Academy of Design in 1826. Danforth went to London in 1827 and remained there about 10 yrs. and some of his largest and best plates were engraved in that city. Upon his return to NY he became interested in bank-note engraving as a business. He was a member of the firm of Danforth, Underwood & Co. about 1850; about 1858 this firm was merged into the American Banknote Co., and he was vice-president of the latter company at the time of his death. While abroad in 1827 he began to study art at the Royal Academy in London. He was chiefly successful as a painter in water colors, and some of his sketches became very popular and brought high prices.

DANIEL, LEWIS C.
Illustrator and etcher. Born New York on Oct. 23, 1901. Pupil of Harry Wickey. Work: "He That is Without Sin Among You Let Him First Cast a Stone at Her," La Bibliotheque Nationale. Address in 1929, 119 West 57th St.; h. 506 Fort Washington Ave., New York, NY.

DANIELE, FRANCESO.
Painter. Exhibited water colors in Annual Exhibition at Penna. Academy of Fine Arts, Philadelphia, 1925. Address in 1926, 2021 Randon Road, Cleveland, OH.

DANIELI, FIDEL ANGELICO.
Painter and art critic. Born in Ironwood, MI, June 15, 1938. Pupil of Pasadena City Col., Leonard Edmondson; UCLA, Jan Stussy, Wm. Brice. Lives and exhibits in CA.

DANIELL, WILLIAM SWIFT (or DANIEL).
Painter. Born San Francisco, CA, on April 26, 1865. Pupil of Julian, Delecluse and Vitti Academies and Laurens in Paris. Member: Calif. AC.; Laguna Beach AA.; Beach Combers, Provincetown, MA. Address in 1929, Daniell Studio, Laguna Beach, CA.

DANIELS, E(LMER) H(ARLAND).
Sculptor and craftsman. Born Owosso, MI, on Oct. 23, 1905. Pupil Myra Richards, Edward McCarten, Williams, Amateis, Derejenski, Flanagan. Award: Prize for portrait, Indiana State Fair, 1928. Address in 1929, 310 Euclid Ave., Westfield, NJ.

DANIELS, J. B.
Painter. Born NYC, 1846. Pupil of Lindsay. Member: Cincinnati Art Club. Address in 1926, 619 Walnut Street, Cincinnati, Ohio.

DANIELS, JULIA.
Illustrator. Member: SI. Address in 1929, 145 East 47th Street, New York, NY.

DANIELSON, PHYLLIS I.
Painter. Born in 1932. Studied: Ball State Univ.; Michigan State Univ.; Indiana University. Exhibitions: Mint Museum of Art, Charlotte, North Carolina, 1971; Matrix Gallery, Bloomington, Indiana, 1971; South Bend Art Center, Indiana, 1975. Media: Fabric. Living in Grand Rapids, MI.

DANNER, SARA KOLB.
(Mrs. W. M. Danner, Jr.). Painter. Born New York City on Oct. 2, 1894. Pupil of Phila. School of Design for Women, MA Normal Art School, G. L. Noyes Henry Snell. Member: Chicago SA.; IN AC.; Phila. Alliance; IL AFA; All-Ill. SFA; Santa Barbara AL. Address in 1929, Las Tunas Road, Santa Barbara, CA.

DARBY, HENRY F.
An American portrait painter, born about 1831. From 1853 to 1859 he resided in NY and Brooklyn, and painted portraits exhibited at the National Academy of Design. His grief at the loss of his wife in 1859 caused him to abandon his profession, and live in England. His last exhibited portraits were "Henry Clay" and "John Calhoun," and these paintings are in the Capitol at Washington, DC.

DARBY, J. G.
This name, as engraver, is signed to a view of Niagara Falls, and to a map of the region about the

214

falls, both published in Buffalo, NY, 1838.

DARLEY, EDWARD H.
Philadelphia portrait painter, and a brother of F.O.C. Darley the illustrator. He painted a portrait of the poet, Edgar Allen Poe.

DARLEY, FELIX O. C.
Illustrator and draughtsman. Born in Philadelphia 1822 and died 1888. He soon became known as an accomplished pen and ink artist; his fine drawings in outline for Irving, Cooper, and other authors place him in the front rank of the illustrators. Darley traveled in Europe and made many sketches and drawings, also a few compositions in color.

DARLEY, JOHN CLARENDON.
Portrait painter, exhibiting in Philadelphia between 1830 and 1840. Represented in loan exhibition of Penna. Academy in 1887.

DARLING, JAY NORWOOD.
(J. N. Ding). Illustrator. Born Norwood, MI, on Oct. 21, 1876. Member: NAC; SI. Cartoonist for Des Moines Register, New York Herald Tribune. Address in 1929, 2320 Terrace Road, Des Moines, IA.

DARNAULT, FLORENCE MALCOLM.
Sculptor. Born in New York City in 1905. Studied: Radcliffe College; National Acad. of Design; Art Students League; and in Europe. Awards: Pen & Brush Club; National Art Club. Collections: City College of NY; US Naval Acad.; Am. Inst. of Engineers; Whitehead Metals Company; NY University Medical School; American Telephone & Telegraph Company; Harvard University; Army Officers Club, Governor's Island, NY; Statue, Mexico City; Colombian Government, Cartagena, Colombia.

DARRAGH, MARIAN R. A.
Miniature painter. Exhibited at the Annual Miniature Exhibition of the Penna. Academy of Fine Arts, Philadelphia, 1925. Address in 1926, 1830 Mannning Street, Philadelphia, PA.

DARRAH, MRS. S. T.
Painter. A native of PA, her professional life was spent in Boston. She painted landscapes and marines. Among her paintings are "Rocks at Manchester, MA" and "Gathering Kelp." She died in Boston in 1881.

DASBURG, ANDREW (MICHAEL).
Painter. Born Paris, France, on May 4, 1887. Pupil of Cox, Harrison, and Henri. Member: New Mexico P. Award: Second prize, Pan-Am. Exhib., Los Angeles, CA, 1925. Address in 1929, Santa Fe, NM.

D'ASCENZO, MYRTLE GOODWIN.
(Mrs. Nicola D'Ascenzo). Painter. Born North Tunbridge, VT, Dec. 31, 1864. Pupil of PA School of Industrial Art. Member: Phila. WCC; Plastic C. Address in 1929, 425 West Price Street, Germantown, PA.

D'ASCENZO, NICOLA.
Painter and craftsman. Born Torricella, Italy, Sept. 25, 1871. Pupil of Mariani and Jacovacci in Rome. Member: Fellowship PAFA; T. Sq. C.; Phila. Sketch C.; NY Arch. Lg. 1902; Mural P.; AC Phila.; Phila. A. Crafts. G.; NAC; AIA (hon); AFA. Awards: Columbian Exp., Chicago 1893; gold medal, T. Sq. C. prize Americanization through Art. Exhib., Phila., 1916; gold medal, Arch. L. of NY, 1925; gold medal, Alumni Assn. of the Penn. Museum and School of Industrial Art. Work: Stained glass, St. Thomas PE Church, NY; mural decoration, Municipal Bldgs., Springfield, MA; stained glass, Wash. Memorial Chapel, Valley Forge; Mosaic frieze, Cooper Library, Camden, NJ; stained glass, chapel at Mercersburg, PA; great west window, chapel at Princeton U. Specialty, mural decoration and stained glass and Mosaics. Address in 1929, 1602 Summer St.; h. 425 W. Price St., Germantown, PA.

DATZ, ABRAHAM MARK.
Painter. Born Russia on Oct. 27, 1891. Pupil of Arthur Crisp; Ivan Olinsky. Member: Salons Am.; S. Indp. A. Address in 1929, 38 Union Sq., New York, NY.

215

DAUB, MATTHEW.
Painter. Born in NYC. Studied at
Pratt; BA in painting, Southern IL
Univ., Carbondale. Work at St.
Louis (MO) Neurological Inst.;
Dobrick Gallery, Chicago; others.
Solo exhibitions at Far Gallery,
NYC; Signet Fine Arts/Kemp Gallery,
St. Louis; Dobrick Gallery,
Chicago, 1983; and Evansville (IN)
Museum of Arts and Sciences.
Selected for the Am. Watercolor
Society's 111th Annual; the 46th
National Midyear Show at the Butler
Inst., Youngstown, OH; Watercolor
USA. Works in watercolor.
Currently living in Illinois.

DAUGHERTY, JAMES HENRY.
Painter, illustrator, and engraver.
Born Asheville, NC, 1886. Pupil of
Frank Brangwyn; also Penna. Academy
of Fine Arts. Member: Mural
Painters; Modern Artists of
America; New York Architectural
League. Work: Murals in State
Theatre, Cleveland; decoration in
Safety Institute, New York;
recruiting posters for US Navy.
Address in 1926, 59 South
Washington Square, New York, NY.

DAUGHERTY, NANCY LAURIENE.
Painter, illustrator, writer,
lecturer, and teacher. Born
Kittanning, on June 21, 1890.
Pupil of Irving Wiles, Douglas
Connah, Frank A. Parsons; Simon and
Billeau in Paris. Represented in
Federal Court, Pittsburgh, PA;
Armstrong Co. Court of
Pennsylvania. Address in 1929, 130
Vine Street, Kittanning, PA.

DAVENPORT, E(DITH) FAIRFAX.
Painter. Born Kansas City. Pupil
of Collin, Laurens, and Ecole des
Beaux Arts in Paris. Member:
SSAL; New Orleans AA; North Shore
AA; AFA. Awards: Medal of Queen
Elizabeth of Belgium for war
poster; Press prize, SSAL, 1925.
Work: Portrait,"Achille Perretti,"
Cabildo, New Orleans, LA; portrait
"Helen R. Parsons," Public Library
Bldg., Kansas City, MO. Address in
1929, Zellwood, Orange Co., Fla.;
15 East 38th St., New York, NY.

DAVENPORT, HENRY.
Painter, lecturer, and teacher.
Born Boston, MA, on April 1, 1882.

Pupil of Ecole des Beaux Arts,
Dechenaud, Charles Hawthorne,
George Elmer Browne. Member:
Paint and Clay Club; S. Indp. A.
Address in 1929, 7 Cite Martignac,
rue de Grenelle, Paris, France.

DAVENPORT, JANE.
(Mrs. Reginald G. Harris).
Sculptor. Born Cambridge, MA, on
Sept. 11, 1897. Pupil of Stirling
Calder, Antonio Bourdelle, and
Jacques Louchansky. Member: ASL
of NY; S. Indp. A.; AFA. Work:
"Erbiah," American University
Union, Paris, France; Wall
Fountain, The Biological
Laboratory, Cold Spring Harbor;
Tablet (low relief), Buckley
School, NYC; Statue, Carnegie
Institution, Washington, DC; Medal,
George Lane Nichols, Buckley
School, NYC. Address in 1929, Cold
Spring Harbor, LI, NY.

DAVEY, RANDALL.
Painter. Member: Portrait
painter; S. Indp. A.; New SA;
Painter- Graver's S; Indp. S.; New
Mexico SA; Kansas City SA; Taos SA.
Awards: Second Hallgarten prize,
NAD 1915; hon. mention, P.-P. Exp.
San F. 1915; hon. mention, P.-P.
Exp., San F. 1915. Work: Art
Inst. of Chicago; Kansas City Art
Inst.; Corcoran Gallery, Wash., DC;
Cleveland Museum; Detroit Institute
of Arts; Santa Fe Museum of Art and
Archeology. Address in 1929, 2
West 14th St., New York, NY; Santa
Fe, NM.

DAVIDSON, CLARA D.
(Mrs. Simpson). Painter and
illustrator. Born St. Louis, MO
Jan. 16, 1874. Pupil of ASL and
Dow in New York; Blanche and Mucha
in Paris. Member: NA Women PS.
CT AFA; CT SA; Silvermine GA. Work
in Art Museum, Rockford, IL
Address in 1929, 3 Park St.
Norwalk, CT.

DAVIDSON, FLORENCE A.
Painter. Born Baltimore County
MD, on Aug. 30, 1888. Pupil o
AIC; ASL of NY.; School of th
Boston Museum of Fine Arts
Member: NA Women PS; PBC
Catherine Lorillard Wolfe AC; Ne
Rochelle AA; Balto. WCC. Awards
Gertrude Hoyt water color prize

216

1926, and Mary Landon portrait prize, 1927, Catherine Lorillard Wolfe AC, New York. Address in 1929, 261 West 22nd St., New York, NY.

DAVIDSON, GEORGE.
Painter. Born Butka, Russian Poland on May 10, 1889. Pupil of F. C. Jones and Douglas Volk. Member: Mural P.; Arch. L. of NY. Award: Medal of Honor for mural painting, Arch. L. of NY, 1926. Work: Decorations for Barnard College; ten panels, Palm Room, Hotel Mt. Royal, Montreal; two historical paintings, Buffalo Savings Bank, Buffalo, NY. Instructor, mural painting, Cooper Union, NY. Address in 1929, 11 East 14th Street, New York, NY.

DAVIDSON, HARRY.
Wood engraver. Born in Philadelphia in 1857, he went to New York in 1878 and entered the employ of the Century Company. He died in New York in 1924.

DAVIDSON, JO.
Sculptor. Born in New York in 1883. Designed US War Industries badge; designed heroic group for French Gov't to commemorate first victory of the Marine; made bust of President Wilson, 1916; selected to make bronze busts of leaders of the Allies. Address in 1926, 23 Macdougal Alley, New York, NY.

DAVIDSON, MORRIS.
Painter. Born Rochester, NY, on Dec. 16, 1898. Pupil of AIC, Harry Walcott. Member: Provincetown AA. Address in 1929, 76 Horatio St., New York, NY; summer, Provincetown, MA.

DAVIDSON, OSCAR L.
Painter. Born in 1875; died in Indianapolis, IN, in 1922. He was a member of Society of Indiana Artists, and of the Indiana Illustrators' Club. He made a specialty of reproducing historic ships.

DAVIDSON, ROBERT.
Sculptor. Born Indianapolis, IN, on May 13, 1904. Pupil of Myra R. Richards, Albinn Polasek, A. Iannelli, Edmond R. Amateis, and R.

A. Baillie. Member: IN AA.; Chicago AA. Awards: First prizes Indiana State Fair, 1923 and 1924. Grand Prize, 1928; Art Assoc. prize, Herron Art Inst., Indianapolis, 1925 and 1928; Spaulding first prize, Hoosier Salon, Chicago, 1927; Muncie Star prize, H. S. Chicago, 1928. Work: "Asam," owned by the Colony Artists Association of Chicago; Portrait Busts, Mr. and Mrs. S. E. Raub, Raub Memorial Library, Indianapolis; Peace and War reliefs, exterior Shortridge High School, Indianapolis; bronze medal, IN S. of Arch.; Linton A. Cox Memorial Tennis trophy, Hawthorne Tennis Club, Indianapolis; many portrait heads privately owned. Address in 1929, 1722 N. Delaware St., Indianapolis, IN.

DAVIES, ARTHUR BOWEN.
Painter. Born at Utica, New York, in Sept. 26, 1862. He studied in the Art Institute of Chicago, and in New York. Specialty, landscapes with figures. Represented in Metropolitan Museum and Chicago Institute. One-man show at Macbeth Gal., NYC, 1896. Awarded Silver Medal, ptg. Pan Am. Expo., Buffalo, 1901; hon. mem. Carnegie Inst., 1913. Important in collection of Europe art and founding of MOMA, NYC. Died in 1928. Address in 1926, 53 West 39th Street, New York.

DAVIES, CHARLES WILLIAM.
Engraver. Born at Whitesboro, NY, 1854. Davies learned to engrave upon copper and steel in Utica, NY, was in partnership with his preceptor for two years, and then went into business for himself in Syracuse, NY. He was burned out after a short time; and after working at his business in various places, in 1881 he established himself in Minneapolis, MN, as the pioneer engraver of that city. No signed work of this engraver is known to the writer.

DAVIES, THEODORE PETER.
Printmaker and painter. Born in Brooklyn, NY, Oct. 9, 1928. Studied: Sch. of Mod. Photography, NYC, in 1952; ASL, with George Grosz, Harry Sternberg, 1957-60,

John Sloan, merit scholar, 1958. Work: Photograms, MOMA, NYC; woodcuts, Nat'l. Gallery of Art, Wash., DC, and Phila. Mus. Art; ASL; etc. Exhib.: Print Club of Phila. Annual; Silvermine Guild Annual; Boston Printmakers Ann; MOMA; SUNYA; others. Awards: Hon. men., Boston Printmakers; Creative Artists Public Service Fellowship in Graphics, 1973-74. Mem.: ASL (life); Print Council of Am.; Print Club of Phila.; Jamaica Art Mobilization; etc. Media: Wooodcut, serigraph. Address in 1982, Hollis, NY.

DAVIESS, MARIA T.
Painter. Born in Harrodsburg, KY, 1872. Pupil of Blanche, Mucha, and Delecluse. Member of the Nashville Art Club. Died in 1924 at Acklen Avenue, Nashville, TN.

DAVIS, CECIL CLARK (MRS.).
Painter. Born Chicago on July 12, 1877. Member: Chicago SA; Chicago AC; Colony Club; NA Women PS; AFA. Award: Portrait prize, Municipal AL, 1918; gold medal, Salon, Rio de Janeiro, 1920; gold medal, Phila. AC., 1925; portrait prize, NA Women PS., 1926. Address in 1929, 7 West 51st Street, h. 969 Park Ave., New York, NY; summer, Marion, MA.

DAVIS, CHARLES H(AROLD).
Landscape painter. Born Amesbury, MA, on Jan, 1856. Pupil of Otto Grundmann and Boston Mus. School; Boulanger and Lefebvre in Paris. Member: SAA 1886; ANA 1901, NA 1906; Copley S. Lotos C; NAC; Mystic SA; AFA. Awards: Gold medal, American Art Assoc., New York, 1886; hon. mention, Paris Salon, 1887; $2,000 prize, Am. Art Assoc., NY, 1887; silver medal paris Exp., 1889; hors concours, Paris Salon; Palmer prize, AIC, 1890; medal Mass. Charitable Mechanics Assoc., Boston, 1890; medal Columbian Exp., Chicago, 1893; grand gold medal, Paris Exp., 1900; Lippincott prize, PAFA, 1901; S. Wash. A, 1902; silver medal, St. Louis Exp., 1904; Harris bronze medal ($300), AIC, 1914; gold medal, P.-P. Exp., San F., 1915; Altman prize ($1,000), NAD, 1917; Sesnan gold medal, PAFA, 1919; second W.

A. Clark prize ($1,500), and Corcoran silver medal, Corcoran Gallery, Washington, 1919; Saltus medal, NAD, 1921. Work: MMA; Corcoran Gallery; Carnegie Inst.; Boston Art Museum, Worcester, MA; Nat. Gal. Wash., DC; PAFA: AIC; Hackley Art Gal. , Muskegon, MI; Minneapolis; St. Louis; Syracuse; Butler; Bruce Art Museum, Greenwich, CT; and Harrison collection, LA. Address in 1929, Mystic, CT.

DAVIS, CHARLES PERCY.
Painter, illustrator, craftsman, and teacher. Born Iowa City, IA. Pupil of Chase and Beckwith in NY; Bouguereau, Ferrier and Robert-Fleury in Paris. Member: Boston SAC. Curator, City Art Museum since 1914. Address in 1929, City Art Museum, St. Louis, MO.

DAVIS, CORNELIA CASSADY.
Painter. Born 1870, died 1920. Pupil of Cincinnati Art Academy. She is represented in London by her portrait of President Wm. McKinley. She also painted pictures of American Indian life.

DAVIS, EARL R.
Painter. Born Jan. 17, 1886. Member: Providence AC; Providence WCC; S. Indp. A.; AFA. Address in 1929, P. O. Box 1532, Providence, RI.

DAVIS, EMMA EARLENBAUGH.
(Mrs. William John Davis.). Painter and illustrator. Born Altoona, PA, on Sept. 8, 1891. Pupil of Walter Everett, J. Frank Copeland, and Daniel Garder. Member: Phila. Alliance. Work: Illustrations for "Ladies Home Journal," "Saturday Evening Post," "Country Gentlemen,". Illustrated, "Ann of Sea Crest High," "Romee Ann Sophomore," "Romee Ann Junior". Address in 1929, 144 Edgehill Road, Bala-Cynwyd, PA.

DAVIS, FLOYD MacMILLAN.
Illustrator. Born in 1896. While still very young he began illustrating for small advertising firms. He is known for his depiction of southern people and he illustrated books by such famous authors as William Faulkner, Glenn

218

Allan and Sigmar Byrd. During World War II, he was a correspondent-artist for the War Department and many of his paintings were reproduced in Life magazine. His war paintings are owned by the Pentagon, and over the years he won several ADC Medals. Died in 1966.

DAVIS, GLADYS ROCKMORE.
Painter. Born in New York City in 1901. Studied: Art Institute of Chicago with John Norton. Awards: Corcoran Gallery of Art, 1939; Art Institute of Chicago, 1937; Virginia Museum of Fine Arts, 1938; Pennsylvania Academy of Fine Arts, 1938, gold medal, 1952; National Academy of Design, 1944, gold medal, 1955; Pepsi-Cola, 1946. Collections: Metropolitan Museum of Art; PAFA; Nebraska Art Assn.; Toledo Mus. of Art; Butler Art Inst.; Swope Art Gallery; Cranbrook Acad. of Art; Dayton Art Inst.; Nelson Gal. of Art; Univ. of Arizona; Univ. of Nebraska; Baltimore Mus. of Art; Kent State University; Miami Univ.; Atlanta Museum of Art; Davenport Municipal Museum; Birmingham Museum of Art; Encyclopaedia Britannica Collection.

DAVIS, HALLIE.
Painter. Exhibited at the Pennsylvania Academy of Fine Arts in 1924. Address in 1926, 1620 Summer Street, Philadelphia, PA.

DAVIS, JACK.
Illustrator. Born in Atlanta, GA, in 1924. He attended the University of Georgia and studied at the ASL. His first illustration was published in the Georgia Tech Yellow Jacket, a humor magazine. His distinctive caricatures have been seen in many TV film spots and movie posters for the major studios as well as in Time, TV Guide, Audubon, Ladies Home Journal and Life.

DAVIS, JOHN PARKER.
Wood engraver. Born on March 17, 1832. His work appeared in the American Art Review and Harper's Monthly. Among his best engravings is "Eager for the Fray" after Shirlaw. See "History of Wood Engraving in America" by W. J. Linton. He was one of the founders of the Society of American Wood Engravers. Died in 1910, and was the last Secretary of the Society of American Wood Engravers.

DAVIS, LEONARD M.
Landscape painter. Born Winchendon, MA, May 8, 1864. Pupil of Art Students' League of NY; Julian Academy under Laurens, Lefebvre and Benjamin-Constant, and of Ecole des Beaux-Arts in Paris. Member: American Federation of Artists. Specialty, since 1898, Alaska scenes. Award: Silver medal for 127 Alaska paintings, P.-P. Exp., San F., 1915. Work: Washington State Art Assoc. Mus., Seattle; "Peril Straits," Municipal Art Gal. Seattle, Wash.; "The Aurora Borealis," Museum of New Mexico, Santa Fe, NM; "The Edward Prince Ranch, Alberta, Canada," "The Edward Prince Ranch and the Canadian Rockies," "From Mt. Prince of Wales," "The Trout's Paradise on the Royal Ranch of Canada," purchased by the Prince of Wales for St. James Palace, London, England; 23 paintings of The Edward Prince Ranch, purchased by the Canadian Gov't for the Mus. of The Public Archives of Canada. Address in 1929, care of NY Camera Club, 121 West 68th St., NY.

DAVIS, PAUL.
Illustrator. Born in Cetrahoma, OK in 1938. He came to NY and studied with Robert Weaver, Tom Allen and George Tacherny at SVA. His first illustration was published in Playboy and he then joined Push Pin Studios with Milton Glaser and Seymour Chwast. In 1975 and 1976 the Paul Davis Exhibition was shown in Japan at a number of art museums. He has received more than 50 awards of distinctive merit for typography, design and illustration.

DAVIS, RONALD WENDEL.
Painter and printmaker. Born June 29, 1937, in Santa Barbara, CA. Studied at U. of Wyoming; San Fran. Art Inst.; Yale U.-Norfolk Summer School on grant, 1962. Awarded grant from Nat. Endowment for the Arts, 1968. Exhibited S. F. Arts

219

Festival, 1961-3; Bienal in Argentina; Stanford U.; J. Hellman Gallery, 1972; U. of Nevada; Whitney Mus.; Corcoran Biennial, 1975; others. In collections of MOMA; L.A. County Mus.; Albright-Knox, Buffalo; Tate; others. Living in Malibu, CA, in 1982.

DAVIS, STARK.
Painter. Born Boston, MA, May 13, 1885. Member: Palette and Chisel C. of Chicago; Chicago PS; Chicago Gal. A. Work: Overmantel decoration, office of the President, Bell Telephone Co., NY. Award: Eisendrath prize, AIC, 1924. Address in 1929, 1012 North Dearborn St. Chicago, IL; Flossmoor, IL.

DAVIS, STUART.
Painter, illustrator, and teacher. Born Philadelphia, PA, on Dec. 7, 1894. Pupil of Robert Henri. Member: Modern AA; Brooklyn S. A. Represented by "In Cuba," Harrison Gallery, Los Angeles Museum, and in collections of: Albright; MMA; Cranbrook Acad. of Art; Whitney; LA; and PAFA. Address in 1929, 356 West 22nd Street, New York, NY; summer, 51 Mt. Pleasant Ave., East Gloucester, MA.

DAVIS , W. TRIPLETT.
Painter and illustrator. Born in Washington, DC. Pupil of Corcoran Gallery School of Arts, and of Lucien Powell. Member: Society Washington Artists. Address in 1926, 3521 13th Street, N.W., Washington, DC.

DAVIS, WARREN B.
Painter. Awards: Inness prize 1905; Evans prize 1906; Isidor prize 1911. Address in 1926, 7 East 42d Street, New York City.

DAVIS, WILL.
Painter, etcher, craftsman, and teacher. Born Boston, MA, on April 7, 1879. Pupil of De Camp, Tarbell, Benson. Member: Copley S; AFA; North Shore AA. Address in 1929, 18A, 53 Aldworth St., Jamaica Plain, MA.

DAVIS, WILLIAM STEEPLE.
Marine painter, etcher, and writer Born in Orient, NY, on May 7, 1884 Member: Brooklyn SA; AFA. Work Etchings in print collection of th Toledo Museum of Art; block print and one etching, Los Angeles Museu of History, Science and Art Address in 1929, Orient, LI, NY.

DAVISON, L(UCIEN) A(DELBERT).
Painter, writer, lecturer, an teacher. Born Clay, NY, June 15 1872. Pupil of College of Fin Arts, Syracuse. Member: S. Indp A. Address in 1929, 325 East 31s St., NYC; h. Waverly Pl., Syracuse NY; summer, Brewerton, NY.

DAVISSON, H(OMER) G(ORDON).
Painter and teacher. Bor Blountsville, IN, on April 14 1866. Pupil of PAFA; Corcora School of Art in Washington; ASL o NY; Szbe School in Munich Director, Fort Wayne Art School 1911-1917. Member: Brown Co. AGA Indiana AC, Hoosier Salon. Award Indiana University prize, Hoosie Salon, Chicago, 1927. Represente in the Hamilton Club, Brooklyn Public Libraries at Marion, Tipto and Peru, IN; Fort Wayne Ar Museum, Fort Wayne Women's Club and numerous private collections Address in 1929, Fort Wayne, IN.

DAVOL, JOSEPH B.
Painter. Born Chicago, IL, 1864 Pupil of Benjamin Constant an Laurens in Paris. Member Fellowship, Penna. Academy Fin Arts. Died in 1923.

DAWES, DEXTER B.
Painter. Born Englewood on Jun 15, 1872. Pupil of ASL of NY Member: New Haven PSS; NAC Address in 1929, 221 Lydecke Street, Englewood, NJ.

DAWES, E(DWIN) M.
Painter. Born Boone, IA, April 21 1872. Self-taught. Member Calif. AC. Awards: Hon. mentio 1909, gold medal 1913, second awar 1914, all given by Minnesota State Art Society; bronze medal, St. Pau Inst., of Art, 1915. Works: "By the River," State Art Society, St Paul, MN; "Dawn in Sweet Gras Mountains," Public Library,

Owatonna, MN; "Channel to the Mills," Minneapolis Institute. Address in 1929, Fallon, Nevada.

DAWES, H. M.
Book-plate engraver. Was probably a member of the Massachusetts family of that name. He engraved a book-plate for Rev. Wm. Emerson (1769-1811), the father of Ralph Waldo Emerson. Dawes must thus have been working prior to 1811.

DAWKINS, HENRY.
One of the earlier engravers in the American Colonies, described himself engraver and silversmith. In New York by 1754, he engraved a book-plate for Burnet, an attorney. In 1775 Dawkins advertised in the New York Mercury that he had set up business opposite the Merchants Coffee House in New York. Worked with James Turner in Phila. in 1758, and in 1761, engraved a music book published by James Lyon. Remained in Philadelphia until 1774, when he returned to NY. Dawkins was chiefly occupied in the production of book-plates, bill-heads, map ornamentation, etc. This work is executed in line. His large plate of Nassau Hall, at Princeton, is probably his best work, and his one known portrait plate is that of Benjamin Lay, an eccentric Quaker of Phila., the latter plate being poorly engraved.

DAWLEY, HERBERT M.
Sculptor and writer. Born Chillicothe, OH, March 15, 1880. Pupil of ASL of Buffalo, NY. Member: Buffalo SA. Award: Fellowship prize, 1915, Buffalo SA. Address in 1929, Chatham, NJ.

DAWSON, ARTHUR.
Painter. Born in England in 1857, he studied at South Kensington Schools; in 1857 he came to this country. He was a founder of the Chicago Society of Artists. He had charge of the restoration of the pictures belonging to the Public Library, New York, and the United States Military Academy at West Point, New York. He died at Richmond, VA, in 1922.

DAWSON, DIANE.
Illustrator. Born in Galveston, TX, in 1952. She attended Stephens College and RISD, studying under Tom Sgouros. She graduated from the SVA in 1975 and began her career that year with illustrations for Ginn and Company. She has illustrated several children's books and the cartoon strip Burdseed for Scholastic's Bananas.

DAWSON, GEORGE WALTER.
Painter and teacher. Born Andover, MA, on March 16, 1870. Pupil of MA Normal Art School in Boston; PAFA. Member: Phila. WCC; Fellowship PAFA; Phila. Alliance; T. Sq. C.; NYWCC; Chicago WCC; AFA. Professor of Drawing at Univ. of PA. Specialty, landscapes and flowers. Address in 1929, Dept. of Architecture, Univ. of Penn.; h. Univ. Dormitories, West Phila., PA.

DAWSON, JOHN W(ILFRED).
Painter and craftsman. Born Chicago, IL, on Aug. 23, 1888. Pupil of William Rice, Arthur Dawson, and Julian Academy, Paris. Member: Providence AC. Address in 1929, 3 Church Lane, Wickford, RI.

DAWSON-WATSON, D.
Painter, engraver, and teacher. Born London, England, July 21, 1864; came to US in 1893; settled in St. Louis 1904. Pupil of Mark Fisher in Steyning, England; Carolus Duran, Chartran, Collin, Aime Morot and Leon Glaize in Paris. Member: St. Louis AG; St. Louis Art League; 2x4 Soc. Awards: Silver medal, Lewis and Clark Exp., Portland, OR, 1905; silver and gold medals, Sedalia, MO; three first prizes and one second, Illinois State Fair, 1916; National prize ($5,000), Texas Wildflower Competitive Exhibition, 1927; special first prize, Nashville AA, 1927; hors concours, Texas Wildflower Competitive Exhibition, 1928; first and fifth prizes, Texas Wildflower Competitive Exhibition, 1929; popularity prize, Southern States Art League, 1929. Work: "Light Breeze," painting and also mezzotint, City Art Museum, St. Louis; "The Open Book," decorative panel, Wichita High School; "Rainbow in Winter," Central High

School and Barr Branch Library, St. Louis; Oakland (CA) Museum; Library, Houston, TX; "The Wheatfield," Springfield (IL) Art Assoc.; "Grand Canyon," St. Louis Club; "The Glory of the Morning," Lotus Club, NY. Teacher in St. Louis School of Fine Arts, 1904 - 1915. Author and director of pageant at Brandsville, MO, 1916. Director, San Antonio Art Guild, 1918-19. Art director, Missouri Centennial. Art director, St. Louis Industrial Exhib., 1920. Art director, City of St. Louis Homecoming of Soldiers. Art director, designer and scenic constructor of the St. Louis Junior Players, 1920-23. Address in 1929, The Bright School, 4th and Nacogdoches St., h. 1118 North St. Mary's St., San Antonio, TX. Died in 1939.

DAY, BERTHA C.
See Mrs. D. M. Bates.

DAY, FRANCIS.
Painter. Born LeRoy, NY, on Aug. 12, 1863. Pupil of ASL of NY; Ecole des Beaux-Arts, Herbert and Merson in Paris. Member: SAA 1891; ANA 1906; Salma. C. 1888. Award: Third Hallgarten prize, NAD 1895. Work: "Fairyland," Art Museum, Montclair, NJ. Address in 1929, Lanesboro, MA.

DAY, JOHN.
Painter. Born May 27, 1932, in Malden, MA. Studied at Yale Univ., BFA 1954, MFA 1956; with Josef Albers, Burgoyne Diller, James Brooks. Taught at Univ. of Bridgeport, CT; William Patterson College, NJ, since 1970. In collections of Lyman Allyn Mus., CT; MOMA; Met. Mus. of Art; Montclair (NJ) Art Mus.; and others. Exhibited at Lyman Allyn Mus.; Whitney; Found. Maeght, St. Paul de Vence, France; Mus. Pompidou, Paris; Contemp. Arts Assoc., Houston; Parrish Art Mus., Southampton, NY; and others. Received Ford Foundation purchse award; fellowships to MacDowell colony, 1960-64; First prize Silvermine Guild Artists, 1969. Address in 1982, 22 E. 89th St., NYC.

DAY, MABEL K.
Painter. Born Yarmouth, Nova Scotia, on July 7, 1884. Pupil of Robert Henri, Kenneth Hayes Miller, Henry Snell, and Homer Boss. Member: Pittsburgh AA. Awards: 1st prize Pittsburgh AA., 1913; prize for best picture by a woman, Pittsburgh AA., 1923; second prize, Pittsburgh, AA., 1927. Address in 1929, Union College, Schenectady, NY; summer, Lake Annis, Nova Scotia, Canada.

DAY, WOERDEN.
Painter and printmaker. Born in Columbus, OH, June 11, 1916. Studied: Randolph-Macon College; Art Students League; and with Maurice Sterne and Stanley William Hayter. Awards: Traveling Fellowship, Virginia Museum of Fine Arts, 1940-1942; Guggenheim Fellowship, 1951-1952; Rosenwald Fellowship, 1942-1944; Norfolk Museum of Art, 1944; Corcoran Art Museum, 1948; Brooklyn Museum, 1949, 1950. Collections: Virginia Museum of Fine Arts; National Gallery of Art; Museum of Modern Art; University of MN; Bradley University; Brooks Mem. Gal.; Library of Congress; Corcoran Art Museum; Yale University; University of Louisville; Metropolitan Museum of Art; Brooklyn Museum of Art; Mills College. Media: Sculpture; printmaking in wood, collage drawing. Address in 1980, Studios 21/28, 427 Bloomfield Ave., Montclair, NJ.

DAYTON, F. E.
Illustrator. Member: SI. Address in 1929, 33 West 67th St.; 259 West 11th Street, New York, NY.

DAYTON, HELENA SMITH.
Illustrator. Member: SI. Address in 1929, 33 West 67th Street; 259 West 11th St., New York, NY.

DEAKIN, EDWIN.
Painter. Born in England in 1840. He came to America, and settled in Berkeley, CA. His specialty was the Spanish Missions.

DEAN, ELIZABETH M.
Painter. Born Cambridge, MA. Pupil of Ludovici in London, and

Lazar in Paris; Duveneck and H. D. Murphy in Boston. Member: Copley Society, 1896. Address in 1926, 107 Winthrop Street, Roxbury, MA.

DEAN, GRACE RHOADES.
Sculptor, etcher, printmaker, and litographer. Born in Cleveland, OH, on Jan. 15, 1878. Pupil of Cleveland School of Art; Kenyon Cox; Arthur W. Dow; and studied in Munich. Member: NA Women PS; Cleveland Woman's AC; Toledo Athena Soc.; OH WCS; AFA; Dayton SE. Wards: Prize for etching, Toledo Art Mus., 1918; second prize for landscape decoration, 1920 and first water color prize, 1924, Toledo Federation of Art Societies; prize, Ohio State Fair, 1922. Address in 1929, 1064 Oakwood Ave., Toledo, OH.

DEAN, J(AMES) ERNEST.
Painter, etcher, and teacher. Born East Smithfield, PA, on Feb. 23, 1871. Pupil of Twachtman, Beckwith, Chase, and McCarter; Brockhoff, and Groeber in Munich. Member: Toledo Artklan. Address in 1929, 1064 Oakwood Ave., Toledo, OH.

DEANE, L(ILLIAN) REUBENA.
Miniature painter. Born Chicago, on Sept. 24, 1881. Pupil of AIC; J. Wellington Reynolds and Virginia S. Reynolds. Address in 1929, 1446 Stanely Ave., West Hollywood, Los Angeles, CA.

DEARBORN, NATHANIEL.
Engraver. Born in New England, 1786. Died in South Roadway, MA, 1852. Nathaniel was the son of Benjamin Dearborn, a man of some scientific attainments. At an early age he was apprenticed to Abel Bowen, in Boston, to learn wood engraving; and in 1814 Dearborn was in business for himself as an engraver on wood, with an office on School Street, Boston. He also engraved upon copper, in the stipple manner, a few portraits and views, of little merit. Dearborn published several books: among them "The American Text-book for making Letters"; "Boston Notions"(1848); "Reminiscences of Boston and a Guide through the City and its Environs" (1851); and a "Guide through Mount Auburn."

DEARTH, HENRY GOLDEN.
Painter. Born in Bristol, RI, 1864. He spent most of his professional life in Paris. He painted landscapes and figures. Is represented at Metropolitan Museum by "Cornelia;" "The Old Church at Montreuil" is in the National Gallery at Washington, DC, and the "Black Hat" at Art Institute, Indianapolis. Elected an Associate of the National Academy of Design, 1902; Academician in 1906. He died in New York City, March 27, 1867.

DEAS, CHARLES.
Painter. Born in Philadelphia in 1818; grandson of Ralph Izard. Visits to the Penna. Academy, and Sully's painting-room fostered his artistic propensities. He was also a great sportsman and traveled among the Indians, his best know work being his painting of Indian character. Elected Associate Member of the National Acadmey of Design in 1829. He died in 1867.

DeBECK, WILLIAM MORGAN.
Cartoonist, caricurist, and writer. Born Chicago, on April 16, 1890. Pupil Chicago AFA. Member: SI; Author's L; Club Ormesson, Paris. Work: In over 300 newspapers US and foreign. Originator of Barney Google and Spark Plug, Parlor Bedroom and Sink, Bughouse Fables. Address in 1929, King Features Syndicate, 2 Columbus Circle, New York, NY. Died in 1942.

DeBEET, CORNELIUS.
Painted a number of landscapes in Baltimore, MD, in 1812; he also painted fruit and flower pieces.

DEBEREINER, GEORGE.
Painter, etcher, and craftsman. Born Arzberg, Germany, on Sept. 28, 1860. Studied AIC; Holland and Germany. Member: Cincinnati AC. Work: Mural "Labor and Commerce," Union Savings Bank, Cincinnati, OH, and murals in Elk Club, Indianapolis, IN. Died in 1939. Address in 1929, 347 Wood Ave., Clifton, Cincinnati, Ohio.

DeBEUKELAER, LAURA HALLIDAY.
Sculptor. Born Cincinnati, OH, 1885. Pupil of Cincinnati Art Academy; St. Louis School of FA. Member: Cincinnati Woman's Art Club. Work: State Normal School, Geneseo, NY; Washburn College, Topeka, KS. Address in 1926, 1346 College Avenue, Topeka, Kansas.

DEBONNET, M(AURICE) G.
Painter and writer. Born Paris, France, on Dec. 24, 1872. Member: Brooklyn S. Modern A.; Brooklyn WCC; NYWCC; AWSC: Nassau Co. AL; Am. APL; Salma. C. Died in 1946. Address in 1929, 4340-215th St., Bayside, NY.

DeBOTTON, JEAN PHILIPPE.
Painter and sculptor. A French and US citizen. Studied: Ecole Beaux-Arts, Paris; Sorbonne, Paris; Rollins College; with Antoine Bourdelle, George Braque, Jules Romains. Work: Met. Mus., NY, Chester Dale Collection; Nat'l Mus. of Modern Art, Paris; Wallraff-Richards Mus., Germany; Musee du Luxembourg, Paris; Museum of Art, Atlanta; Fogg Museum, Harvard; and many other museums in Geneva, France, Vienna, US. Comn.: French gov't. commissions; H. M. King George VI coronation; Am. at War, City of San Fran.; plus others. Exhibitions: Carnegie; Knoedler & Wildenstein Galleries, NYC & Paris; many others. Awards: Grand prix, Salon Honneur Beaux-Arts, Fr. Gov't; many more. Teaching: Acad. Montmartre Paris; NYC. Mem.: Salon Automne Paris; Salon Mod. Paris; Salon France Novelle; Am. Federation of Arts. Died in 1978. Address in 1976 was 930 Fifth Avenue, New York, NY.

DeBOYEDON, O(SCAR) H(UGH).
Sculptor and craftsman. Born Porto Alegre, Brazil, on June 13, 1882. Pupil of Bourdelle in Paris. Member: Boston SAC. Address in 1929, care of Ainslie Galleries, 677 Fifth Ave., New York, NY; 54 Via Montebello, Florence, Italy; 9 rue de l'Universite, Paris, France.

DeBRA, MABEL MASON.
Painter, illustrator, and teacher. Born Milledgeville, OH, on Oct. 24, 1899. Pupil of Henry B. Snell,

Will S. Taylor, and Walter Beck. Member: NYWCC; Wash. WCC; Ohio WCS; Columbus AL. Award: Robert Wolfe water color prize, Columbus Art League, 1929. Work: Mural, "Crystal Springs," Ohio State Archeological Museum. Address in 1929, Dept. of Fine Arts, Ohio State University; h. 2084 Neil Ave., Columbus, Ohio.

DeBREHAN, MARCHIONESS.
Miniature painter. The Marchioness De Brehan was the sister of Count de Moustier, French minister to the United States. She visited Mount Vernon in 1788 with her brother, and painted several profile miniatures of George Washington and Nelly Custis.

DeCAMBREY, LEONNE.
Painter, craftmans, teacher, lecturer, and writer. She was born Southern Sweden, on March 7, 1877. Pupil of Alfred Jansson, Walter Sargent, Vanderpoel, etc. Member: Chicago NJSA.; Chicago AA. Author of "Lapland Legends" and "A Girl in Sweden". Specialty color pyschology. Address in 1929, 6582 Sheridan Road, Chicago, IL.

DeCAMP, JOSEPH RODEFER.
Painter. Born at Cincinnati, OH, 1858. Pupil of Duveneck at Cincinnati Academy; Royal Academy; Royal Academy in Munich; Florence, and Italy. Died in 1923. Represented in Wilstach Collection, Philadelphia, by "The New Gown;" Cincinnati Museum, by "Woman Drying her Hair;" Portrait of "Dr. Horace Howard Furness" at Pennsylvania Academy of Fine Arts; Portrait of "Frank Duveneck" at Cincinnati Museum; "Daniel Merriman" at Worcester Museum.

DECKER, JOSEPH.
Painter. Born in Germany, 1853; came to United States in 1867. Studied in the schools of the National Academy of Design and abroad. He died in Brooklyn, NY, in 1924.

DECKER, MRS. E. BENNET.
Miniature painter and illustrator. Born Washington, DC, on Feb. 28, 1869. Pupil of William H. Whittemore in miniature painting.

224

Member: Wash. AC. Microscopic drawings for Smithsonian Institution and the National Museum, Washington, DC. Address in 1929, 3111 Hawthorne St., N. W. Washington, DC.

DECKER, RICHARD.
Illustrator, cartoonist and designer. Born in 1907. He studied at the Philadelphia Museum School of Industrial Art. In 1939 he illustrated an Evening Bulletin series and was a regular contributor to The New Yorker and advertisers in the Philadelphia area. He designed sets for seven major plays for Connecticut Playmakers, Inc.

DeCORDOBA, MATHILDE.
Painter and etcher. Born in New York City. Pupil of Whittenmore, Cox, and Mowbray in New York, and Aman-Jean in Paris. Represented by prints in Luxembourg, Paris and Library of Congress, Washington, DC. Address in 1926, "The Rembrant," 152 West 57th Street, New York.

DeCOSSEY, EDWIN.
Illustrator. Member: SI. Address in 1929, Care of Hanff-Metzger, Inc., 95 Madison Ave., New York, NY.

DeCOUX, JANET.
Sculptor. Born in Niles, MI. Studied: Carnegie Institute; New York School of Industrial Design; Rhode Island School of Design; Art Inst. of Chicago. Awards: Guggenheim Fellowship, 1938-39, 1939-40; Widener medal 1942; Carnegie award; Nat'l. Sculpt. Society; Am. Acad. of Arts and Letters, grant. Collections: College of New Rochelle; United States Post Office, Girard, PA; St. Mary's Church, Manhasset, NY; Society of Medalists; Sacred Heart School, Pittsburgh; St. Vincent's, Latrobe, PA; St. Scholastica, Aspinwall, PA; Crucifixion Group, Lafayette, NJ; altar, St. Margaret's Hospital Chapel, Pittsburgh; Christ King Church of Advent, Pittsburgh; doors, St. Ann, Palo Alto, California; Charles Martin Hall Memorial, Thompson, Ohio; Brookgreen Gardens, South

Carolina. Address in 1980, Gibsonia, PA.

DeCREEFT, JOSE.
Sculptor. Born in Guadalajara, Spain, Nov. 27, 1884; US citizen; settled in NYC. Studied at Academie Julien, 1906; Maison Greber, 1911-14. In collections of Whitney; Met. Mus. of Art; Phila. Mus. of Art; Miro Foundation, Barcelona; others. Commissions in Puy de Dome, France, soldier war mem.; Mallorca, Spain, 200 stone sculptures; Central Pk., NYC, Alice in Wonderland bronze group; Bronx (NY) Municip. Hosp.; Bellevue (NY) Hosp. Exhibitions at Paris Salons 1919-28; Ford Found. Traveling Show, US, 1959-60; Festival of Arts, White House, DC, 1965; New School Art Ctr., 1974; Kenneth Gal., NYC, 1979; traveling retrospective, 1980, 81, Spain; others. Received Widener Mem. gold metal, PAFA; 1945; Brevoort - Eyckemeyer prize, Columbia Univ.; others. Taught at New School for Soc. Research, 1932-39, 57-65; ASL. Member of Audubon Artists; Fellow, Nat'l Sculptor Soc.; Academician, NAD; founding member, Sculptors Guild. Media: Lead, marble, quartz, ebony, onyx, marble, wood, terra-cotta, serpentine. Represented by Kennedy Galleries in NYC.

DEELEY, S.
Engraver. All that is know to the writer of this man is that he engraved in line, a fairly well-executed plate showing the "New Hampshire Granite Ledge at Concord, NH." The plate is sign "C. Deeley Sc., Boston." The apparent date is about 1835-40.

DEEM, GEORGE.
Painter. Born Aug. 18, 1932, in Vincennes, IN. BFA from School of Chicago Art inst., with Paul Wieghardt and Boris Margo; also studied calligraphy, Christian symbolism, and drawing and painting for one year at St. Meinard Archabbey. Lived in Eng. and Italy. Taught at School of Visual Arts, NYC; Leicester Polytech., Eng.; Univ. of Penn. In collections of Neue Galerie, Aachen, Ger.; U. of Rochester;

Oberlin; Indianapolis Mus. Art; Albright-Knox Gallery, Buffalo, NY; others. Exhibited at Allan Stone Gallery, NYC; Art Inst. of Chicago; MOMA; Albright-Knox Buffalo; Corcoran; MMA; Whitney; PAFA; others. Awarded: MacDowell Colony Fellowship (1977). Rep.: Allan Stone Gallery, NYC. Address in 1982, 10 W. 18th St., NYC.

DeFOE, ETHELLYN BREWER.
(Mrs. Louis DeFoe). Miniature painter. Born in New York City. Pupil of Whittemore and Mowbray in New York. Member: NA Women PS. Address in 1929, 250 West 88th Street, New York, NY.

DeFOREST, CORNELIUS WORTENDYKE (MRS.). See Julie Morrow.

DeFOREST, GRACE EMILY BANKER.
Painter, illustrator, and teacher. Born on Dec. 5, 1897. Pupil of Joseph W. Gies; John P. Wicker; and Francis P. Paulus. Member: Detroit S. Women P; Am. APL. Address in 1929, 610 Parkview Manor, Apt. 404, Jefferson Ave., and Parkview, Detroit, MI.

DeFOREST, LOCKWOOD.
Landscape painter, arch., and writer. Born in NY, on June 23, 1850. Pupil of Corrode in Rome; F. E. Church in NY. Member: ANA 1891, NA 1898; A. Fund A.; Artists Aid S.; NY Arch. Lg.; NY Soc. C.; Boston SAC; Century Assoc.; NAC; AFA. Founded Assoc. Artists with L. C. Tiffany and Mrs. C. Wheeler, 1878. Awards: Medal, for Indian Carvings, Colonial Exp., London, 1886; medal, Columbian Exp., Chicago, 1893; bronze medal, St. Louis Exp., 1904. Founded workshops at Ahmedabad, India, for revival of woodcarving. Work: "The Rameseum Thebes," Smith College, Northampton, MA; "Mission Canyon, Santa Barbara," Herron Art Inst., Indianapolis. Published "Indian Domestic Architecture," 1885; "Illustrations of Design," 1912. Died April 4, 1932 in Santa Barbara, CA. Address in 1929, 1815 Laguna St., Santa Barbara, CA.

DeFOREST, ROY.
Painter. Born Feb. 11, 1930, in North Platte, NE. MA from S. F.

State College (1958). Also attended Cal. School of Fine Arts. In collection of S. F. Mus. of Art; Oakland Mus.; Joslyn (Omaha) Art Mus; MOMA; Whitney; others. Exhibited at East and West Gallery, S. F. (1955, 58); S.F. Mus. of Art; Whitney; Albright-Knox; Reed College; Wash. State Univ.; and many galleries, incl. Hansen-Fuller (1971-8) and Alberta (Can.) Inst., Calgary, (1974). Received Nat'l Endowment of Arts Award (1972) and others. Rep.: Hansen-Fuller Gallery, San Fran.; Allan Frumkin Gallery, NYC. Address in 1982, Port Costa, California.

DeFRANCA, MANUEL J.
Painter. One of the original members of the Artists' Fund Society of Philadelphia; member of its Council 1835-36; Controller 1837. Painted portrait of Mrs. Sartain (John) in 1836.

DeFRANCISCI, ANTHONY.
Sculptor. Born in Italy, on June 13, 1887. Pupil of George T. Brester, James E. Fraser, and A. A. Weinman in NY. Member: NSS; NY Arch. Lg.; American Numismatic Soc. (Assoc.); Allied AA. Award: Saltus medal, American Numismatic Soc., NY, 1927. Represented: Cincinnati Museum; Numismatic Soc. Galleries; Met. Museum, NY; Union Square Memorial, NY. Instructor at Columbia Univ. Address in 1929, 154 West 57th St.; h. 500 West 114th St., New York, NY; summer, Towaco, NJ. Died in 1964.

DeGAVERE, COR.
Painter. Born Batavia, Java, of Dutch parents, on Jan. 25, 1877. Pupil of Janssen and Guerin. Member: Santa Cruz AL; West Coast Arts; San Francisco SWA; Berkeley AL. Address in 1929, 452 East Cliff Drive, Seabright, Santa Cruz, CA.

DeGROOT, ADRIAAN M.
Portrait painter. Born in Holland in 1870. His portrait of Col Roosevelt is owned by The Outlook New York. Address in 1926, 9 Fifth Avenue, New York.

DeHASS, M. F. H.
Marine painter. Born in Rotterdam in 1832. He came to New York, and during the Civil War painted several naval actions for Admiral Farragut. He was elected a member of the National Academy in 1867; he died in 1895. His "Rapids above Niagara" was exhibited at the Paris Exposition of 1878.

DeHAVEN, FRANKLIN.
Landscape painter. Born Bluffton, IN, on Dec. 26, 1856. Pupil of George H. Smillie in NY. Member: ANA, 1902; NA 1920; Salma. C. 1899; NAC; Allied AA. Awards: Inness prize, Salma. C., 1900; Show prize, Salma. C., 1901; hon. mention, Pan-Am. Exp., Buffalo, 1901; silver medal, Charleston Exp., 1903; silver medal, St. Louis Exp., 1904; Vezin prize, 1916; silver medal and cash prize, NAC, 1921; Plimpton prize, Salma. C., 1925. Work: "The Gleaming" and "Indian Camp near Custer," Brooklyn Inst. Museum; "Castle Creek Canyon, South Dakota," National Gallery, Washington, DC; "Silvery Waters," Butler Art Inst., Youngstown, Ohio. Died Jan. 10, 1934 in NYC. Address in 1929, 257 West 86th St., New York, NY.

DEHN, ADOLPH (ARTHUR).
Lithographer. Born Waterville, MN, on Nov. 22, 1895. Pupil of MN Art School, ASL of NY. Represented in British Museum; Metropolitan Museum; Minnapolis Museum. Died in 1968. Address in 1929, 98 Joralemon St., Brooklyn, NY; summer, Waterville, MN.

DEHNER, DOROTHY.
Sculptor and printmaker. Born in Cleveland, OH, in 1908. Studied at UCLA; Skidmore College, BS; ASL, with Nicolaides, K. H. Miller, Jan Matulka; Atelier 17, NYC; Yaddo Found. Fellow, 1971. In collections of Met. Mus. of Art; MOMA; Seattle Art Mus; commission, bronze wall sculpture, Rockefeller Ctr., NYC; others. Exhibited at Whitney Mus.; MOMA; Hirshhorn, Wash. DC; Guggenheim; Carnegie Inst.; Dallas Mus. of Contemp. Art; San Fran. Mus. of Art; LA Co. Mus. of Art; others. Awarded Tamarind Lithography Inst. Artists in Res.,

1970-71; Sculpture Prize, Art USA, 1968; others. Mem. of Sculptor's Guild; Federation of Mod. Painters and Sculptors; Artists Equity Inst. Works in bronze and wood. Rep.: Associated Am. Artists, NYC; Parsons-Dreyfuss, NYC. Address in 1982, 33 Fifth Ave., New York City.

DEHNER, WALTER LEONARD.
Painter, landscaper, and teacher. Born Buffalo, NY, on Aug. 13, 1898. Pupil of ASL of NY at Woodstock, and PAFA. Director of Art University of Puerto Rico. Address in 1929, Whitehouse, Ohio.

DEIGAN, JAMES THOMAS.
Illustrator. Born in Monongahela, PA, in 1934. He was educated at Temple University and Carnegie Institute of Technology. A resident of Pittsburgh for many years, he has been awarded prizes from the ADC there.

DEIGENDESCH, HERMAN F.
A painter, etcher, and teacher. He was born in Philadelphia in 1858, and was a pupil of the Munich Academy. For many years he was an instructor at the School of Industrial Art in Philadelphia. He was a member of the Philadelphia Society of Etchers. Represented at Independence Hall, Philadelphia, by his copy of the portrait of "John Hart" by Copley. He died at Southampton, PA, May 9, 1921.

DEIKE, CLARA L.
Painter and teacher. Born Detroit, MI. Pupil of H. G. Keller; F. C. Gottwald; H. H. Breckenridge; Herr Hans Hofmann in Munich. Member: Woman's AC, Cleveland; Cor Ardens, Chicago. Awards: 2nd prize, Cleveland Museum, 1922; 1st prize and 1st hon. mention, Cleveland Museum, 1923; 2nd prize, Cleveland Museum of Art, 1925; 3rd prize, Cleveland Museum, 1926; hon. mention group drawings, 1927, and first prize, Cleveland Museum, 1928. Work: "Italian Fishing Boats, Gloucester, MA," and "Through the Trees," Central High School, Cleveland; "Flowers," Public School Art Collection, Cleveland Board of Education. Address in 1929, 1309 West 111th St. Cleveland, Ohio.

DeIVANOWSKY, SIGISMUND.
Painter, illustrator, architect, and writer. Born Poland, on April 17, 1874. Pupil of Petrograd Academy; Constant, Laurens, and Cormon in Paris. Member: Petrograd Academy; SI. Awards: Gold medal, Petrograd Academy; silver medal, Societe des Artists, Paris. Series of heroines of the stage and heroines of fiction for "Century Magazine." Illustrated for the "Ladies Home Journal". Address in 1929, Westfield, NJ; summer, Martha's Vineyard, MA.

DeKAY, HELENA.
(Mrs. R. Watson Gilder). She exhibited since 1874 flower-pieces and decorative panels at the National Academy of Design. In 1878 she exhibited the "Young Mother" and "The Last Arrow" (figure-piece).

DeKOONING, WILLEM.
Painter. Born in Rotterdam, Holland, April 24, 1904. Studied: Acad. Beelende Kunsten ed Technische Wetenschappen, Amsterdam, 1916-24. Work: Art Inst. of Chic.; Met. Mus. of Art, MOMA, Whitney in NYC; Walker Art Ctr., Minneapolis, MN; plus others. Comn.: Murals, NY World's Fair, 1939; French Line Pier (with Fernand Leger), NYC. Exhib.: Melbourne Nat'l., 1967; Frankfurter Kunstverein, Kimpass, NYC, 1968; Stedelijk Mus. retrospective, Amsterdam, 1968; MOMA retrospective 1968, exhib. 1969; Whitney, Am. Art Annual, 1969 & 70; Carnegie Inst., 1979; many others. Awards: Logan medal, Art Inst. of Chic.; President's medal; Mellon prize; others. Teaching: Black Mtn. College, 1948; Yale Univ., 1950-51. Mem.: Nat'l Inst. Arts and Letters. Address in 1982, c/o Fourcade Droll Inc., 36 E. 75th St., NYC.

DeKOSENKO, STEPAN.
Sculptor and draftsman. Born in Tiflis, Caucasus, Russia, 1865. Pupil of Ecole des Art Decorative, Paris. Member: Salmagundi Club; National Sculpture Society; MacDowell C; Arch. Lg. of NY. Designer in decorative art.

Address in 1929, 50 West 67th Street, h. 18 East 40th Street, New York, NY.

DeKRUIF, HENRI G(ILBERT).
Painter and etcher. Born Grand Rapids, MI, on Feb. 17, 1882. Pupil of Gifford Beal, F. Luis Mora, Frederick Richardson, DuMond, Vanderpoel, and Ernest Haskel. Member: California AC; Los Angeles Modern AS; Laguna Beach AA; ASL of NY; California PM.; California WCS; Group of Eight. Awards: $100, Los Angeles County Fair, 1923; first prize, Southern California Painters and Sculptors, Los Angeles Museum, 1925; cash honorarium, Pan-Am Exhibit of oil paintings, Los Angeles Museum, 1926; first prize for water colors, Orange Co. Fair, 1925. Represented in permanent collection of Los Angeles Museum. Address in 1929, 2324 Miramar St. Los Angeles, CA. Died in 1944.

DeKRYZANOVSKY, ROMAN.
Painter. Born Balta, Russia, 1885. Pupil of E. Renard, E. Tournes and P. Gouzguet. Member: Scarab Club, Detroit. Work: "Kismet," Detroit Institute of Arts. Address in 1926, 48 Adams Avenue, West Detroit, MI.

DeLAMOTTE, CAROLINE J(ONES).
(Mrs. Octave John DeLamotte.). Painter and teacher. Born Pikesville, MD, on Sept. 3, 1889. Pupil of C. Y. Turner, Ephraim Keyser, and Charles H. Webb. Awards: First prize for charcoal drawing and first prize for watercolor, LA State Fair, Shreveport, LA, 1917; first prize for charcoal portrait, first prize for original design, and first prize for watercolor collection at Donaldsonville, LA, 1917. Work: In M. E. Church, Le Compte, Louisiana. Address in 1929, McNary, Arizona.

DeLAND, CLYDE OSMER.
Illustrator and painter. Born Union City, PA, on Dec. 27, 1872. Pupil of Drexel Inst. under Howard Pyle in Philadelphia. Member: Phila. Alliance. Work: Painting, "First American Flag," City of Somerville, MA; "First Continental

Congress," Carpenters' Hall, Philadelphia; "The first Steamboat," "The First Automobile," "The First Street Railway," National Museum, Washington, DC; illustrated, "The Count's Snuffbox," etc. Address in 1929, 603 Baker Bldg., 1520 Chestnut Street, h. 22 N. St. Bernard Street, Philadelphia, PA. Died in 1947.

DELANEY, JOSEPH.
Painter and writer. Born Knoxville, TN, Sept. 13, 1904. Studied: ASL with Thomas Denton, Alexander Brook, 1929-35; NYU, writing, with Horace Coohn; also with George Bridgman. Work: Huntington Hartford Collection; Truman Library, Independence, MO; Nat'l. Gallery, Smithsonian, Wash. DC; NYC Museum; others. Exhibitions: Metropolitan Museum; Brooklyn Museum; Riverside Museum; Krashauer Gallery; ACA Art Gallery; Whitney Museum; Studio Museum, Harlem, NYC; others. Awards: Rosenwald Fellowship; Greenwich Village Art Center. Art Positions: Instr., researcher WPA Fed. Art Project, 1934-40; researcher, Am. Wing, Met. Mus of Art, 1936-39. Media: Oil. Address in 1982: PO Box 383, New York City.

DELANEY, JOSEPH E.
This man was a line engraver of portraits and landscape, working for the magazines about 1850.

DELANO, ANNITA.
Painter, writer, lecturer and teacher. Born Hueneme, Calif., on Oct. 2, 1894. Member: Calif. AC: Calif. WCS. Award: Henry E. Huntington prize ($250), Los Angeles Museum. Work: "Virgins of the Red Rocks," Los Angeles Museum. Address in 1929, Univeristy of California at Los Angeles; h. 2332½ Miramar Street, Los Angeles, CA.

DELANOY, ABRAHAM JR.
Painter. Born in New York, probably in 1740, and died in the same city about 1786. He visited England about 1766 to 1769, and was instructed for a time by West. There is a reference to his being in London, in a letter from Charles Willson Peale, published in John Sartain's "Reminiscences of a Very Old Man," where he mentions going with West in 1769, to the rooms of Mr. Delanoy, who expected soon to "return to his native place, New York". One of the students in the painting by Pratt, "The American School," is supposed to be Abraham Delanoy. Dunlap mentions several portraits of members of the Beekman family by this painter, and he himself remembered the man from 1780 to 1783 in "the sear and yellow leaf both of life and fortune; consumptive and poor, his only employment being sign-painting." In 1772 he painted a portrait of Peter Livingston (1737-1794).

DeLAP, TONY.
Sculptor. Born in Oakland, CA, Nov. 4, 1927. Studied: Menlo Jr. College, CA; Calif. College of Arts and Crafts, Oakland; Claremont Graduate School, Claremont, CA. In collections of Whitney; Walker Art Inst., Minneapolis; MOMA; Tate Gallery, London; others. Exhib. at Whitney; Jewish Mus., NYC; L.A. Co. Mus. of Art; La Jolla (CA) Mus. of Art; Art Inst. of Chic.; others. Awarded Am. Federation of Arts & Ford Found. Grants, Artists in Res. Program; Neallie Sullivan Award, San Fran. Art Inst.; L.A. Dept. of Airports, First prize, sculpture. Fine arts lecturer, U. Calif., Davis; prof., U. Calif Irvine, from 1965. Rep. by Janus Gal., Venice, Calif.; Rbt. Elkon Gal., NYC. Address in 1982, Del Mar, CA.

DELBOS, JULIUS (M.).
Painter, etcher, and teacher. Born London, July 22, 1879. Member: AWCS; NYWCC; Soc. of Graphic A.; Old Dudley Art Society, London; Salma. C., NAC. Exhibited at National Academy of Design, NY, 1925. Address in 1929, Salmagundi Club, 47 Fifth Ave., New York, NY.

DELBRIDGE, THOMAS JAMES.
Painter, etcher, craftsman, and teacher. Born Atlanta, on Sept. 16, 1894. Pupil of Charles Hawthorne. Member: NAC; Alliance; L. C. Tiffany Foundation. Award: Fellowship, L. C. Tiffany Foundation, 1922; first water color prize, NAC, Junior Exhib., 1928.

Work: "Indian Still Life," Tiffany Foundation. Address in 1929, National Arts Club, 15 Gramercy Park, New York, NY.

DeLEON, AMANDA.
Painter. Born in Madrid, Spain, in 1908. Studied: San Jose de Tarbes Convent, Caracas, Venzuela. Collections: Musee d'Art Moderne, Paris; National Gallery Modern Art, Rome; Glasgow Art Gallery, Scotland; Museum Modern Art, Barcelona; Musee de Beaux Arts, Lausanne; Municipal Gallery Modern Art, Dublin; Municipal Gallery Modern Art, Genoa; Art Gallery of Toronto, Canada; Denver Museum of Art; Butler Art Inst.; University of California; Museum of Modern Art, Sao Paulo, Brazil; National Gallery of Modern Art, New Delhi, India; National Museum of Modern Art, Tokyo; Municipal Art Museum, Dusseldorf, Germany; Neue Galerie de Stadt Linz, Austria; Hamburger Kunsthalle, Germany.

DeLESLIE, ALEXANDER.
Painter, lecturer, and teacher. Born Moscow, Russia, Dec. 14, 1892. Pupil of Bridgeman, Bellows, and Maynard. Author of: "How France built her Cathedral" (Harpers); "A Childhood in Brittany" (Century). Art director, Stirling Press, NY. Instructor in Design, Mechanics Inst., New York. Address in 1929, Springfield Gardens, LI, NY; summer, Longmeadow, MA.

DELLA-VOLPE, RALPH.
Painter and educator. Born in NJ, May 10, 1923. Study: NAD; ASL. Work: NY Cultural Center; ASL; Wichita (KS) AA; Lib. of Congress, Pennell Coll.; Chase Manhattan Bank Coll.; Treasury Bldg., Wash., DC; Slater Mus., Norwich, CT One-man shows: Berkshire Mus., Pittsfield, MA; Artists Gal., NYC, 1959; Babcock Gal., NYC, 1960,62,63; The Gal., West Cornwall, CT, 1974; Anderson (IL) Fine Art Center, 1975; Wolfe St. Gal., Wash., DC, 1974, 77; retrospective, Columbia (SC) Mus. of Art, 1975; and many others. Group shows: PAFA; Lib. of Congress; Nat'l Inst. of Arts and Letters, NYC; Parke-Bernet Gal., NYC; Butler Art Inst. Ann., Youngstown, OH; Contemp. Gal., NYC;

Wadsworth Atheneum, Hartford, CT; Soc. of Am. Etchers, Chicago, IL; Brooklyn Mus. NY; Corcoran Gal., Wash., DC; MOMA Lending Lib.; Am. Color Print Soc., Phila., PA; and many others. Awards: MacDowell Fellowship, 1963; purchase award, Lib. of Congress; Wichita (KS) AA; NY ASL; hon. mention, Wash. WCC; Nat'l Vet. Art Exhib.; drawing prize, Berkshire Mus.; finalist, Nat'l Inst. Arts & Letters, 1963, 64. Teaching: Chairman, prof., Art Dept, artist in res., Bennett College, Millbrook, NY, 1949-77; prof. drawing/painting, Marist College, Poughkeepsie, from 1977. Style: Realistic and abstract landscapes, figures, and portraits. Address in 1982, South Road, Box 51, Millbrook, NY.

DELLEKER, GEORGE.
With the profession of "engraver" appended, this name appears in the Philadelphia directories from 1817-24, inclusive. He was possibly engraving in that city earlier than the first-named date, as we find portraits of naval heroes of the War of 1812 executed by him, and evidently intended for popular distribution. He was later associated with the engraver G. H. Young, under the firm name of Delleker & Young, in the general engraving business in Philadelphia,

DELLENBAUGH, FREDERICK SAMUEL.
Painter. Born in McConnelsville, Ohio, 1853. Pupil of Carolus Duran and Acadmie Julien, Paris. Engaged in art and literary pursuits; librarian American Geographical Soceity, 1909-11; artist and topographer with Major Powell's 2d expedition down Colorado River 1871-3; with Harriman expedition to Alaska and Siberia 1899; voyages to Iceland, Spitzbergen, Norway, West Indies and S. A. 1906; several personal expeditions to the Southwest in early days.

DelMAR, FRANCES.
Painter, teacher, writer and lecturer. Born Washington, DC. Pupil of Collin, Fleury, and Bouguereau in Paris; Rolshoven in London. Work: Mural decorations at Caroline Rest (hospital), Hartsdale, NY; paintings of New

Zealand and South Sea Islands for the American Museum of Natural History. Author of "A Year Among the Maoris" (London). Died May 8, 1957 in NYC. Address in 1929, Barnard Club, 221 West 57th Street, New York, NY.

DelMUE, M(AURICE) (AUGUST).
Painter. Born Paris, France, on Nov. 4, 1878. Member: San Francisco Art Association; American Artists Professional League. Award: Silver medal, Panama Pacific Exp., San Francisco, 1915. Work: "Late Afternoon in the Sierras," Comparative Museum of Art; "West Winds," Golden Gate Park Museum, San Francisco, CA; "Forest Knolls," Walters Collection, San Francisco. Address in 1929, Forest Knolls, Marin Co, Calif.

DELNOCE, LUIGI.
Engraver. Born in Italy; died in New York about 1888. Delnoce was an admirable engraver of book-illustrations, appearing in New York publications of 1855-60; but he was chiefly engaged in bank-note work.

DelPIATTA, BEGNI.
Sculptor. Exhibition at the Pennsylvania. Acadmy of Fine Arts, Philadelphia, in 1924. Address in 1926, 125 West 11th Street, New York.

DELSON, ELIZABETH.
Painter and printmaker. Born in New York, NY, Aug. 15, 1932. Studied: Smith College; Hunter College; Pennsylvania Academy of Fine Arts. Awarded the Audubon Artists Medal of Honor for Graphics. Exhibited in several NY galleries and is in the for-sale collection of Associated American Artists and the Landmarks Collection. Media: Oils on 3 dimensional surfaces; etchings. Address in 1980, 625 Third St., Brooklyn, NY.

DeLUCE, PERCIVAL
Painter. Born in New York, 1847, and died 1914. Pupil of Antwerp Academy, Joseph Portaels, Brussels; Sonnat, Paris. Specialty, portrait and genre painting; exhibited at all principal exhibitions, especially in New York. Silver medal, S. C. Inter-State Expn.; Academy of National Artists. Member: American Water Color Society, Artists' Fund Society, S.C.

DeLUNA, FRANCIS P.
Sculptor. Born New York, on Oct. 6, 1891. Pupil of Herman A. McNeil. Member: NSS; Arch. Lg. of NY. Address in 1929, 128 East 23rd Street, New York, NY.

DelVALLE, HELEN.
Painter. Studied: The Art Inst. of Chicago; PAFA. Awards: Chicago, NLAPW, 1971, 1973; Municipal Art Lg. of Chicago, 1973. Exhibitions: Chicago Public Library, 1969; American Society of Artists, 1973; Balzekas Museum, Chicago, 1973. Past-president of the American Society of Artists. Her work is included in collections throughout the world.

DeMAINE, HARRY.
Painter. Born Liverpool, England on Dec. 23, 1880. Pupil of Castellucho in Paris; F. V. Burridge in London. Member: Salma. C.; AWCS.; NYWCC. Address in 1929, care of Salmagundi Club, 47 Fifth Ave., New York, NY.

DeMANCE, HENRI.
Painter. Born Hamburg, Germany, on Oct. 5, 1871. Pupil of Lenbach. Member: S. Indp. A. Work: "Portrait of a Man," "Grapes of the Hudson," Schiller Museum, Marbach. Address in 1929, 332 East 69th Street, New York, NY; summer, Sorento, Italy. Died in 1948.

DeMARIS, WALTER.
Illustrator. Born Cedarville, NJ, Aug. 24, 1877. Pupil of ASL of NY. Address in 1929, 34 Pierce St., New Rochelle, NY.

DeMERS, JOSEPH.
Illustrator. Born in San Diego, CA, in 1910. He attended the Chouinard Art School and, as a fine artist, exhibited work at the Museum of Modern Art in 1933. After ten years as a production illustrator for Warner Brothers Studios, he became a successful

231

book publisher in California. Ultimately, he moved to NY in the late 1940's to work at Cooper Studio. His free-lance work was seen in The Saturday Evening Post, Ladies Home Journal and McCall's. Good business sense prompted him, Coby Whitmore and Joe Bowler to form a corporation through which they retained world rights for the many European reprints to their artwork. His paintings have been shown and are owned by many museums and galleries. A member of the S of I, he currently runs a gallery on Hilton Head Island in South Carolina.

DEMETRIOS, GEORGE.
Sculptor. Exhibited at the Pennsylvania Academy of Fine Arts, Philadelphia, in 1924. Address in 1926, 4 Harcourt Street, Boston, MA.

DeMILHAU, ZELLA.
Etcher. Born New York City, on April 3, 1870. Pupil of ASL of NY. Member: NAC; NA Women PS; Phila. Print C; Chicago SE; Calif. PM. Represented in NY Public Library; National Museum, Washington, DC; Brooklyn Museum. Address in 1929, Southhampton, LI, NY.

DEMILLIERE.
Portrait painter in oils and miniatures. Flourished in New York, 1796.

DEMING, ADELAIDE.
Landscape painter. Born Litchfield, CT, on Dec. 12, 1864. Pupil of ASL of NY; Pratt Inst., Chase, Lathrop, Dow, and Snell. Member: NA Women PS; New Haven PSS: NYWCC; CT AFA. Awards: Beal prize, NYWCC, 1908; Burgess prize, NY Woman's AC, 1908. Represented in Litchfield Public Library and Pratt Inst. Address in 1929, Litchfield, CT.

DEMING, E(DWIN) W(ILLARD).
Painter, sculptor, and illustrator. Born Ashland, OH, on Aug. 26, 1860. Pupil of ASL of NY; Lefebvre and Boulanger in Paris. Member: Mural P.; Wash. AC; (life) NAC. Specialty, Indian and animal subjects. Awards: Silver medal, AAS, 1892; bronze medal, St. Louis

Exp., 1904; bronze medal for sculpture, P.-P. Exp., San F., 1915. Work: Two mural paintings, Morris High School, NYC; "Braddock's Defeat" and "Discovery of Wisconsin," mural decorations, Wis. Historical Soc., Madison, Wis. "The Fight" and "Mutual Surprise," two bronzes, Metropolitan Museum, New York; "The Watering Place," "Pueblo Buffalo Dance" and "Sioux War Dance," Art Museum, Montclair, NJ; "Mourning Brave," National Museum, Washington, DC; also represented in American Museum of Natural History, New York, Heye Foundation, Explorers Club, National Arts Club and Montifeore Home for Crippled Children. Died in 1942. Address in 1929, 15 Gramercy Park, NYC.

DeMOLL, MARY HITCHNER.
(Mrs. Carl DeMoll). Illustrator. Member: Fellowship PAFA; Plastic, C. Address in 1929, 135 Rutger's Ave., Swarthmore, PA; 282 West Rittenhouse St., Germantown, Philadelphia, PA.

DEMUTH, CHARLES.
Painter. Born Lancaster, PA, 1883. Pupil of PAFA; studied in Paris. Member: Fellowship PAFA. Award: Silver medal, Sesqui-Centennial Exp., Phila., 1926. Represented by water colors in the Metropolitan Museum of Art, New York; Art Inst. of Chicago; Fogg Art Museum; Cambridge, MA; Brooklyn Museum; Cleveland Museum; Rochester Museum; Barnes Foundation, Merion, PA; Phillips Memorial Gallery, Wash., DC; Harrison Gallery, Los Angeles Museum. Died in 1935. Address in 1929, Lancaster, PA.; care of Daniel Gallery, 600 Madison Ave., New York, NY.

DeNESTI, ADOLFO.
Sculptor. Exhibited "Dancing Faun" at Penna. Academy of Fine Arts, 1914. Address in 1926, 3919 Irivng Street, Philadelphia.

DENGLER, FRANK.
Sculptor. Born in Cincinnati, Ohio, in 1853. He studied abroad, and on his return to this country was for a time instructor in modelling in the Boston Museum. He resigned in 1877, and moved to

Covington, KY, and afterwards to Cincinnati. Among his works are "Azzo and Melda," and an ideal head of "America," and several portrait busts.

DeNIKE, MICHAEL NICHOLAS.
Sculptor and writer. Born in Regina, Sask., Can., Sept. 14, 1923; US citizen. Studied: NAFA; with Jean de Marco, Carl Schmitz. Comn.: Young St. Francis (bronze), St. Davids, Kinnelon, NJ; and more. Exhib: NAD, NYC; 1964; Audubon Artists, 1965; Knickerbocker Artists, 1965; Nat'l Sculpture Soc. Ann., 1966; Am. APL, 1974; etc. Awards: Dr. Ralph Weiler award, NAD, 1964; Alfred Artists of Am. award, 1975; etc. Mem.: Am. APL. Media: Wood, stone. Address in 1982, 2343 Hamburg Tpke, Wayne, NJ.

DENISON, HAROLD (THOMAS).
Painter, illustrator, and etcher. Born Richmond, MI, Sept. 17, 1887. Pupil of Art Students League, NY; Chic. Academy of Fine Arts. Specialty, etchings, water colors and illustration. Member: SI; Salma. C. Died in 1940. Address in 1929, Boston Corners, NY.

DENMAN, HERBERT.
Painter. Born in New York in 1855. Student at the Art Students' League, New York, and with Carolus Duran in Paris. His "Trio" received Honorable Mention at the Paris Salon 1886. He decorated Mr. Fred. Vanderbilt's Ball Room. He died in California in 1903.

DENNING, CHARLOTTE.
Miniature painter. Flourished about 1834, Plattsburg, New York.

DENNIS, CHARLES W(ARREN).
Portrait painter and illustrator. Born New Bedford, on Feb. 25, 1898. Pupil of Harold Brett, Howard E. Smith, and Frederick Bosley. Member: S. Indp. A.; Boston, AC; Business Men's AC of Boston. Address in 1929, 1269 Great Plain Ave., Needham, MA.

DENNIS, MORGAN.
Illustrator and etcher. Born Boston, MA, on Feb. 27, 1891. Pupil of W. H. W. Bicknell.

Member: Beachcombers; North Shore AA; New Haven PCC. Illustrated "The Champion," "Themselves," "What's Up," and "The Black Watch." Address in 1929, 412 Eighth Ave.; h. 258 West Fourth St., New York, NY; summer, Provincetown, MA.

DENNISON, DOROTHY, BUTLER.
Painter. Born in Beaver, PA, on Feb. 13, 1908. Awards: Cresson European Traveling Scholarship; Butler Inst. of American Art; Ohio State Fair. Collections: PAFA; Columbus Art Gallery; Canton Art Inst.; Marine Midland Bank; Lawrence Fleishman; Olsen Foundation. Address in 1980, 915 Walker Mill Road, Poland, OH.

DENNISON, GEORGE AUSTIN.
Painter and sculptor. Born in New Boston, Illinois, 1873. Exhibited sculptured enamels in the Louvre Museum, Paris. Address in 1926, Cathedral Oaks, Alma, CA.

DENNISON, LUCY.
Painter. Born Youngstown, on April 5, 1902. Pupil of Butler AI; James R. Hopkins, and Daniel Garber. Member: Youngstown S. Women A; Mahoning SP. Address in 1929, Women's City Club, Wick Ave.; h. 33 Scott St., Youngstown, Ohio.

DENNY, MILO B.
Painter. Born Waubeek, IA, April 21, 1887. Pupil of AIC; NY ASL; Cornell Coll. School of Art. Address in 1929, 901 Chateau Ave., Cincinnati, OH; summer, Taos, NM.

DENSLOW, DOROTHEA HENRIETTA.
Sculptor and teacher. Born New York City, on Dec. 14, 1900. Pupil of ASL of NY. Member: CT AFA; AFA. Work: Fountain sculpture. (Richmond, VA); Bas-relief, and Beth Moses Hosp., NYC. Address in 1929, 937 Park Place, Brooklyn, NY; summer, Perry Mansfield School, Steamboat Springs, CO.

DePEYSTER, GERARD BEEKMAN.
Several portraits of the DePeyster family in the collection of the New York Historical Society, and are painted by Gerald Beekman DePeyster.

233

DERCUM, ELIZABETH.
Painter. Exhibited at the Pennsylvania Academy of Fine Arts, Philadelphia, in 1924. Address in 1926, 1719 Walnut Street, Philadelphia.

DERGANS, LOUIS S.
Painter. Born Laiback, Austria, on Nov. 4, 1890. Pupil of Richard S. Meryman and S. Burtis Baker; California School of Fine Arts. Member: S. Wash. A; Wash. Landscape C; Wash. Art Club; American Federation of Arts. Specialty, portraits. Address in 1929, "The Lombardy," 2019 Eye St., NW, Washington, DC.

DeRIBCOWSKY, DEY.
Marine painter. Born at Rustchuk, Bulgaria, on Oct. 13, 1880. Studied in Paris, Florence and Petrograd. Member: Art Association of Newport; Buenos Aires Society of Fine Arts. Awards: Gold medal, Petrograd, 1902; gold medal, Uruguay Exhibition, Montevideo, 1908; gold medal, Rio de Janeiro Exp., 1909; Kuznezoff prize, Odessa, 1909; Orloff prize, Moscow, 1910; first prize, Sofia National Gallery, 1910; first grand prize, Southwestern Int. Fair and Exp., El Paso, Texas, 1924. Inventor of the Medium "Reflex." Work: "Aurora Bureale," Museum Alexander III, Petrograd; "Winter Sunset at Volga," Tretiacof Gallery, Moscow; "After Glow at Yalta," Odessa Museum; "President William," Uruguay Museum Montevideo; "Pres. Quintana," Buenos Aires Museum; "The Fleet," National Palace, Montevideo; "Brazilian High Sea Fleet," National Palace, Rio de Janeiro; "Balantia," Governor's Palace, Barbadoes; "Monterey at Moonlight," "Grand Canyon," Manchester (NH) Memorial.

DeROSE, ANTHONY LEWIS.
Painter. Born in New York City in 1803. He studied under J. R. Smith, and was an early student at the National Academy School. He was elected an Academician in 1833, his specialty being portraiture and historical composition. He died in New York in 1836.

DERRICK, WILLIAM R(OWELL).
Painter and craftsman. Born San Francisco, CA. Pupil of Bonnat, Boulanger and Lefebvre in Paris. Member: ANA; NAC; CT AFA; Lotos C.; Chicago AG; SPNY. Awards: Prize ($100), CT AFA, 1916. Work: "The Plaza," National Gallery, Washington. Address in 1929, 58 West 57th Street, New York, NY.

DERUJINSKY, GLEB, W.
Painter, sculptor, lecturer, and teacher. Born Smolensk, Russia, on Aug. 13, 1888. Pupil of Verlet, Injalbert in France and of the Russian Academy. Member: NSS; NY Arch. L. Award: Silver medal, Encouragement of Art, Petrograd, 1909; gold medal, Sesqui-Centennial Expo., Phila., 1926. Work: "Theodore Roosevelt," Roosevelt Memorial House, NY, "Thompsons Trophy," National Fencing Society. In collections of MMA; Cranbrook and San Diego FA Gallery. Address in 1929, 39 West 67th Street, NYC.

DESCH, FRANK H.
Painter. Born Philadelphia, PA, on Feb. 19, 1873. Pupil of Chase and Hawthorne and of Biloul, Paris. Member: Allied AA; Fellowship PAFA; Salma. C.; Provincetown AA. Awards: F. A. Thompson prize and $1,000 purchase prize, Salmagundi Club, 1924. Work: "The Blue Chinese Coat," Butler Art Inst., Youngstown, OH; "La Robe de Boudoir," Salmagundi Club, NY; "Alice in Wonderland," Bloomington Art Association, Bloomington, IL. Died in 1934. Address in 1929, Provincetown, MA.

DESSAR, LOUIS PAUL.
Painter. Born Indianapolis, IN, on Jan. 22, 1867. Pupil of NAD in NY; Bouguereau, Robert-Fleury and Ecole des Beaux-Arts in Paris. Member: SAA 1898; ANA 1900, NA 1906; Salma. C. 1895; Lotos C.; A. Fund S. Awards: Third class medal, Paris Salon, 1891; medal Columbian Exp., Chicago, 1893; hon. mention, CI Pittsburgh, 1897; second Hallgarten prize, NAD 1899; first Hallgarten prize, NAD 1900; bronze medal, Paris Exp., 1900; silver medal Pan-Am. Exp., Buffalo, 1901; silver medal Charleston Exp., 1902. Work: "Return to the Fold" and "The

Watering Place," National Gallery, Washington; "Wood Cart," Metropolitan Museum, NY; "Early Morning" and "Evening at Longpre," Art Museum, Montclair, NJ. Died on Feb. 14, 1952. Address in 1929, 58 West 57th St., Lotos Club, 110 West 57th St., 331 West 24th St., New York, NY; summer, Becket Hill, Lyme, CT.

DESVARREAUX-LARPENTEUR, JAMES.
Painter. Born Baltimore, MD, on Oct. 20, 1847. Pupil of Van Marcke and Ecole des Beaux-Arts in Paris. Award: Gold medal, Alaska Yukon Exp., 1909. Specialty, landscapes with cattle or sheep. Address in 1929, 26 rue de Fleurus, VI, Paris, France.

DETHLOFF, PETER H(ANS).
Painter. Born Barnsdorf, Germany, on Sept. 8, 1869. Pupil of William Gaethe and Christian von Schneidau; Calif. Art Inst. Awarded three first prizes at Utah State Fair Association. Work: Fresco ceiling, St. Mary's Academy Chapel, Salt Lake City, Utah. Address in 1929, 1555 North Harvard Blvd., Hollywood, Calif.

DeTHULSTRUP, THURE.
Painter and illustrator. Member: SI 1901 (hon.); AWCS; Century Assoc.; GFLA. Awards: Hon. mention for drawings, Pan-Am. Exp., Buffalo, 1901. Address in 1929, 1060 Amsterdam Ave; 33 West 67th St., New York, NY.

DETWILLER, F(REDERICK) K(NECHT).
Painter, illustrator, etcher, and artist. Born Easton, PA, on Dec. 31, 1882. Pupil of Ecole des Beaux Arts, Paris; Inst. di Belle Arti, Florence; Columbia University, NY. Member: Paris Am. Students C.; Paris AAA; Brooklyn WCC; AFA; Allied AA; Philadelphia SE; Artists Fellowship, Inc.; Lotos C; CT AFA; Guild of Am. Painters; Philadelphia Print C.; Salma. C.; S. Indp. A.; Brooklyn SE; Brooklyn S. Mod. A.; Salons of Am. (Dir. 1922-25). Award: Medal, Soc. of Beaux Arts Arch., NY, 1910; Shaw prize for etching, Salma. C., 1920. Represented in the Nat. Gal.; Lib. of Congress; Smithsonian Inst., Wash.; Imperial War Mus., London;

Print Div., NY Pub. Lib.; Peabody Mus., MA; CT State Lib., Hartford; Farnsworth Art Mus., Wellesley College, MA; Vanderpoel Art Assn. Coll., Chicago; Lafayette College, Easton, PA; Bibliotheque Nat., Paris, France. Died in Sept. 1953. Address in 1929, Carnegie Hall, 56th St. and 7th Ave., NY.

DeVEAUX, JACQUES MARTIAL.
Born in 1825, and died in 1891. Painted portraits.

DeVEAUX, JAMES.
Born in Charleston, SC, in 1812. In 1829 he visited Philadelphia and received help and instruction from Henry Inman and Thomas Sully. In 1836 he visited Europe for study, returning to America in 1838 where he painted many portraits, his portrait of his friend, Col. John S. Manning, of South Carolina, painted in Clarendon, SC, about 1839, being one of his best. He died in Rome 1844. (See life of James DeVeaux in "Artists of America" by C. E. Lester, New York, 1846.)

DEVILLE, J.
Portrait painter who had a studio about 1840 to 1855. Address in 1926, 66 Saint Ann Street, New Orleans.

DEVINE, BERNARD.
Painter. Born in Portland, ME, in 1884. Pupil of Bridgman in New York and Laurens in Paris. Member of the Paris American Artists' Association. Address in 1926, Williard, ME.

DeVOLL, F. USHER.
Painter. Born Providence, RI., Dec. 15, 1873. Pupil of RI School of Design; Chase, Hawthorne, Henri, Mowbray; Laurens in Paris. Member: Providence AC; Salma. C.; Providence WCC; CT AFA; Wash. AC; AFA. Award: Silver medal, P.-P. Exp., San F., 1915. Work: "Autumn Landscape," and "NY Waterfront Winter," RI School of Design, Providence; "Spring," Art Club, St. Johns, New Brunswick; "Winter in New England," Delgado Mus. New Orleans, LA; "Winter in the Berkshires," Newcomb College, New Orleans, LA; "Studies of New York

Street and Harbor Scenes," Milwaukee Art Inst.; "Twixt Day and Night Madison Sq., NY" Vanderpoel Art Assn., Chicago. Address in 1929, 19 Arcade Building, Providence, RI.

DeVOS, FLORENCE M(ARIE).
Painter. Born Cook Co., IL, on Oct. 13, 1892. Pupil of Henry Mattson. Address in 1929, P. O. Box 287, Woodstock, NY.

DEWEY, CHARLES (MELVILLE).
Landscape painter. Born Lowville, NY, July 16, 1849. Pupil of Carolus- Duran in Paris. Member: ANA 1903, NA 1907; Nat. Inst. A. L.; Lotos C.; NAC. Awards: Silver medal, Pan-Am. Exp., Buffalo, 1901; silver medal, Pan-Am. Exp., Buffalo, 1901; silver medal, St. Louis Exp., 1904. Work: "Edge of the Forest," Corcoran Gallery, Washington; "The Grey Robe of Twilight," Fine Arts Academy, Buffalo; "The Harvest Moon" and "The Close of Day," Nat. Gallery, Washington; "Old Fields," PA Academy, Phila. "Amagansett from the Fields," "Evening Landscape" and "November Sunset," Brooklyn Inst. Museum; "The Valley Road," Art Museum, Monclair, NJ; Homeward," Minneapolis Inst. of Arts; "The Sun Shower," Metropolitan Museum of Art, New York. Address in 1929, 222 West 23d Street, New York, NY.

DEWEY, CHARLES S.
Painter. Born in Cadiz, Ohio, in 1880. Member of Chicago Society of Artists. Address in 1926, 2708 Lake View Avenue, Chicago.

DEWEY, JULIA H.
(Mrs. Charles M.). Painter and illustrator. Born in Batavia, NY. Member of National Association of Women Painters and Sculptors. Address in 1926, 222 West 23d Street, New York City, NY.

DEWEY, KENNETH FRANCIS.
Illustrator. Born in Brooklyn, NY, in 1940. He studied under Robert Weaver and Phil Hays at the SVA. His first illustration was done for a magazine in Phoenix, AZ, in 1967. Three years later he wrote and illustrated a book entitled Onyamarks. His illustrations have been selected to appear in the S of I Annual Exhibitions of 1974, 1975 and 1976.

DEWEY, S.
Silhouettist and miniature painter. Flouished 1800-1810 in Baltimore. There was a Silas Dewey, a portrait painter, in Baltimore, 1814-1815.

DEWING, FRANCIS.
Engraver. A Boston newspaper heralds the arrival of this early American engraver in New England as follows: "Boston, July 30, 1716. Lately arrived from London, Francis Dewing, who Engraveth and Printeth Copper Plates, Likewise Coats of Arms and Cyphers on Silver Plate. He likewise Cuts neatly in wood and Printeth Callicoes". In 1722, Dewing engraved and printed a large map of "The Town of Boston in New England, By John Bonner, 1722, Aetatis Suae 60". The plate is signed as "Engraved and Printed by Fra. Dewing, Boston N. E. 1722. Sold by Captain John Bonner and William Price, against ye Town House where may be had all sorts of Prints, Maps etc."

DEWING, MARIA OAKEY.
Painter. Born at New York, 1857. Studied at National Academy, New York, and under John LaFarge and Thomas Couture. Specialties are figures, flower pieces and portraits. Address in 1926, 12 West 8th Street, New York City.

DEWING, T(HOMAS) W(ILMER).
Painter. Born Boston, May 4, 1851. Pupil of Boulanger and Lefebvre in Paris. Member: ANA 1887, NA 1888; Ten American Painters; Nat. Inst. A. L. Specialty, small figures. Awards: Clarke prize, NAD 1887; silver medal, Paris Exp., 1889; gold medal, Pan-Am. Exp., Buffalo, 1901; gold medal, St. Louis Exp., 1904; gold medal, International Exp., Munich, 1905; Lippincott prize, PAFA, 1906; first medal, CI. Pittsburgh, 1908. Work: "Summer," Nat. Gal. Wash; twenty-two oil paintings, two screens, one silver point, a pastel, Freer Collection, National Gallery, Wash. D.C.: "The Recitation," and "Lady in Green and Gray," Art Inst., Chicago; "The

Letter," "Tobit and the Angel," and "Girl at Desk," Metropolitan Mus., New York; "Lady with a Mask," Corcoran Gal. Wash. DC; "Writing a Letter," Toledo Mus.; "Lady with a Macaw," Fine Arts Acad., Buffalo; "Lady in Gold," Brooklyn Inst. Museum; "Lady in Gray," RI School of Design, Providence; "Lady in Yellow," "Lady in Green," and "Lady with Lute," City Art Museum, St. Louis; "Lady in Black and Rose," Carnegie Inst. Pittsburgh; "A Musician," Luxembourg Museum, Paris. Died on Nov. 5, 1938 in NYC. Address in 1929, 12 West 8th Street, New York, NY.

DeWITT, JEROME PENNINGTON.
Painter, illustrator, craftsman, lecturer, and teacher. Born Newark, NJ, May 27, 1885. Pupil of G. A. Williams; G. Lunger; Pratt Inst. under Prellwitz, Beck, Moschcowitz and Paddock. Member: Art Centre of the Oranges. Instructor, Fawcett Art School, Newark, NJ; Hunter College, NY; Newark College of Technology; Berkshire Summer School of Art; Cartaret Academy, Orange, NJ. Address in 1929, Van Dyck Studios, 939 8th Ave., Cor. 56th St., New York, NY; h. 94 Berkeley Ave., Bloomfield, NJ.

DeWOLF, WALLACE L.
Painter, etcher, and writer. Born Chicago, IL, on Feb. 24, 1854. Self-taught. Member: ACI; Chicago, SA; Municipal A. Lg.; Chicago SE; Calif. AC; Calif PM; Chicago Art Commission; Chicago PS; Los Angeles PS; Pasadena SA; AFA. Work: "Lake Louise," Springfield Art Assoc.; "Coast Scene, Santa Barbara," Union League Club, Chicago; "Hermit Range," Glacier, B. C. South Park Commission; "Mojave Desert" and "Among the Redwoods," Art Inst. of Chicago. Represented in Vanderpoel AA. Collection, Chicago. Died in 1930. Address in 1929, 105 West Monroe St., Chicago, IL.

DEXTER, HENRY.
Sculptor. Born New York State on Oct. 11, 1806. Died in Cambridge, MA, on June 23, 1876. Among his portrait busts are those of Charles Dickens, Longfellow, Agassiz, Henry Wilson and Anson Burlingame. His statues include "The Backwoodsman," "The Cushing Children," "Gen'l Jos. Warren at Bunker Hill," and "Nymph of the Ocean".

DEXTER, MARY L.
Painter. Member: Society Independent Artists. Address, 526 Astor Street, Milwaukee, WI.

DeYOUNG, H(ARRY) A(NTHONY).
Landscape painter and teacher. Born Chicago, IL, Aug. 5, 1893. Pupil of AIC, F. de Forrest Schook and John W. Norton; Edward Lake at University of Illinois. Member: Chicago Gal. A.; Chicago PSA; All-Ill . SA; San Antonio AA. Former instructor, Glenwood Sketch classes; National Academy of Art, Chicago, and Midwest Summer School of Art, Coloma, MI.; Founder and Director, San Antonio Acad. of Art. Awards: Fine Arts Bldg., Purchase Prize ($500), AIC, 1925; hon. mention, AIC, 1925; members prize ($200), Chicago Gallery of Art, 1927; hon. mention ($100), Davis Comp., San Antonio, Texas, 1929. Represented in Chicago Public Schools. Died in 1956. Address in 1929, Pabst Galleries, 222 Losoya St., San Antonio, Texas.

DeZAYAS, G(EORGE).
Illustrator. Born Mexico City, Mexico, on Nov. 30, 1895. Pupil of Jean Paul Laurens in Paris. Illustrations in "Collier's," "The Mentor." Illustrated "Strange Bedfellows" and "How to Get Rid of a Woman." Address in 1929, 15 West 51st St., New York, NY.

DEZAYAS, MARIUS.
Portrait painter. Exhibited at the "Exhibition of Paintings Showing the Later Tendencies in Art," at the Penna. Academy of Fine Arts, Philadelphia, 1921. Address in 1926, 549 Fifth Avenue, New York City.

DHAEMMERS, ROBERT AUGUST.
Sculptor. Born in Luverne, MN, Nov. 24, 1926. Studied: Calif. College of Arts and Crafts. Work: First Christ Lutheran Church, Burlingame, CA; Mills College; others. Comn.: Jerrys Rest., San Leandro, CA; First Lutheran Church;

science complex, Mills College; Holy Cross Hosp., San Leandro; others. Exhibitions: NY Mus. of Contemporary Crafts; Addison Gal. of Amer. Art, NY; de Young Mus., San Fran., CA; San Fran. Art Mus.; Brigham Young Univ.; etc. Awards: Gold medal, sculpture, Oakland Mus. of Art; first prize, metal work, CA State Fair; Mills College faculty research grant. Teaching: Mills College, Oakland, CA, 1957-1980. Mem.: West. Assn. Schools & Colleges; Accrediting Comn. Colleges & Univs.; others. Media: Metal, stainless steel, galvanized painted steel; etching, lithography, silk screen. Address in 1982, Mills Coll., Oakland, CA.

DIAMOND, HARRY O.
Illustrator. Born in Los Angeles in 1913. He attended Los Angeles City College in 1932 and 1933 and Chouinard Art Inst. in 1934 and 1935. He has received numerous awards as both illustrator and art director. His first published illustration was done for Westways magazine in Los Angeles in 1932 and he is presently the art director at Exxon Corporation.

DIAMONDSTEIN, DAVID.
Painter, illustrator, craftsman, and writer. Born in Kurenitz, Vilna Province, Russia, on April 14, 1883. Pupil of Robert Henri, Jerome Myers, Sigismund de Ivanowsky. Member: S. Indp. A. Author of "Spirit of the Storm and other Poems." Address in 1929, 2347 Pitkin Ave., Brooklyn, NY.

DIBBLE, THOMAS (REILLY) (JR).
Painter. Born Haddonfield, NJ, April 19, 1898. Pupil of Van Deering Perrine. Member: Palisade AA; AFA. Address in 1929, 4 Dean St.; h. 25 East Demarest Ave., Englewood, NJ.

DIBONA, ANTHONY.
Sculptor. Born Quincy, MA, on Oct. 11, 1896. Pupil of Philip L. Hale, and Charles Grafly, L. P. Thompson, Bela Pratt, and School of the Museum of FA, Boston; also American Acad. in Rome and Paris. Member: Boston AC and Boston SS;

Gloucester SA; North Shore AA. Work: Portrait of Thomas Allen, School of the Boston Museum of Fine Arts; Fountain, War Memorial, Woburn, MA. Address in 1929, 9 Larry St., West Quincy, MA.

DICK, ALEXANDER L.
Engraver. Born in Scotland about 1805. He was a pupil of Robert Scott, a reputable engraver of Edinburgh; he came to the US in 1833 and in time established an extensive engraving business in New York City. He employed many engravers, and since all plates issued from his business bore his name, it is practically impossible to identify his individual work.

DICK, G. R.
Painter. Born in New York, NY, 1889. Pupil of George Bridgman. Address in 1926, 818 Madison Avenue, New York, NY.

DICK, JAMES, T.
Artist . Born in 1834 and died 1868. He was the son of A. L. Dick the engraver. James T. Dick was one of the originators of the Brooklyn Art School and a founder of the Academy of Design. Among his best efforts are "Cooling Off," "Leap Frog", and "At Mischief".

DICKEY, ROBERT L(IVINGSTON).
Illustrator. Born Marshall, MI, on May 27, 1861. Pupil of J. Francis Smith and AIC. Member: SI; The Players, Creator of "Mr. and Mrs. Beans" in Saturday Evening Post; "Buddie and His Friends," Metropolitan Newspaper Serivce. Died in 1944. Address in 1929, Hotel Chelsea, 222 West 23rd St., New York, NY; winter, St. Petersburg, Florida.

DICKINSON, ANSON.
Portrait painter in oils and miniatures. Born Litchfield, CT, in 1780. He was a brother of the artist Daniel Dickinson. In 1811 he was considered the best miniature painter in New York; in 1818 he went to Canada, and in 1840 settled in New Haven, CT. He worked for a time in Boston. He died in 1852 at New Haven, CT.

DICKINSON, DANIEL.
Painter. Born in 1795 and died after 1840. He was a portrait painter in oils and miniatures, and was a contemporary of Jocelyn in New Haven, CT. He moved to Philadelphia in 1820 and in 1830 he started painting in oils. He was a brother of Anson Dickinson. He exhibited six miniatures at the Penna. Academy 1827-1831, several being after paintings by Sully.

DICKINSON, EDWIN W.
Painter and teacher. Born Seneca Falls, NY, on Oct. 11, 1891. Pupil of DuMond, Chase, Hawthorne. Address in 1929, 46 Pearl St. Provincetown, MA.

DICKINSON, PRESTON.
Painter. Born NY, 1891. Pupil of ASL of NY. Award: Bronze medal, Sesqui-Centennial Expo., Phila., 1926. Represented in Mus. of Art, Cleveland, Ohio; Brooklyn Mus.; Albright Gallery, Buffalo, NY; Fogg Museum, Cambridge, MA; Omaha; Hartford; Philips Mem. Gal., Wash., DC. Died in 1930 in Spain. Address in 1929, care of Daniel Gallery, 600 Madison Ave., New York, NY.

DICKINSON, SIDNEY E(DWARD).
Painter. Born Wallingford, CT, on Nov. 28, 1890. Pupil of Bridgeman, Volk and Chase. Member: NA; NAC; Century C; Allied AA. Awards: Third Hallgarten prize, NAD, 1917; Philadelphia prize, PAFA, 1923; popular prize, Corcoran Gallery, Washington, DC., 1924; Carol Beck gold medal, PAFA, 1924; first Hallgarten prize, NAD, 1924. Work: "Self Portrait," Corcoran Gallery, Washington; "Unrest," Chicago Art Inst.; "The Young Painter," "The Black Cape," City Art Museum, St. Louis; Portrait of the Artist, Houston Museum, Houston, TX. Instructor ASL of NY, 1920-21; NAD Art Schools, 1928. Address in 1929, 78 West 55th Street, NYC.

DICKMAN, CHARLES J(OHN).
Painter. Born Demmin, Germany, on May 14, 1863. Pupil of Laurens and Constant in Paris. Member: San F. AA. Mural decoration in Syndicate Bldg., Oakland Calif. Mural decoration, Steamship Co. Offices,

San Francsico, CA. Died in 1943. Address in 1929, 628 Montgomery St.; h. Bohemian Club, Post and Taylor Sts., San Francisco, CA.

DICKSON, H. E.
Painter. Exhibited water colors at the Annual Exhibition of Water Colors at the Penna. Academy, Philadelphia, 1925. Address in 1926, Pugh Street, State College, Penna.

DIEDERICH, (WILHELM) HUNT.
Sculptor and artist. Born Hungary, on May 3, 1884. Member: Salon d'Automme, Paris, and Salon des Tuileries. Award: Gold medal, Arch. League, pottery, 1927. Address in 1929, care of Milch Gallery, 108 West 57th St., New York, NY; summer, Cagues A. M. France; Burgthaun, Bavaria.

DIEDRICKSEN, THEODORE.
Etcher and illustrator. Born New Haven, on May 30, 1884. Pupil of Yale School of Fine Arts; Baschet and Gervais in Paris. Member: New Haven PCC. Instructor in drawing, Yale School of Fine Arts, New Haven, CT. Address in 1929, 24 Wilkins St., Hamden, CT.

DIELMAN, ERNEST B.
Painter. Born New York City, 1893. Pupil of Volk. Address in 1926, 154 West 55th Street, New York City, NY.

DIELMAN, FREDERICK.
Painter, illustrator, craftsman, etcher, and teacher. Born Hanover, Germany, on Dec. 25, 1847; came to the US in childhood. Pupil of Diez at the Royal Academy in Munich. Member: ANA 1881, NA 1883; AWSC; SAA 1905; SI (hon.) 1910; Mural P.; Nat. Inst. AL; Century Assoc.; Salma. C. (hon); Pres. NAD, 1899-1910; Pres. Fine Arts Fed. of NY, 1910 to 1915. Professor of Art in the College of the City of NY, 1903-18. Director, Art Schools of Cooper Union. Work: Two mosaic panels, "Law" "History," Library of Congress, Washington, DC; mosaic panel, "Thrift," Albany (NY) Savings Bank; six mosaics in Iowa State Capitol, Des Moines; seven paintings, "Star" Office, Washington, DC. Died in 1935.

Address in 1929, 41 West 10th St., New York, NY; h. Ridgefield, CT.

DIEMAN, CLARE SORENSEN.
Sculptor. Born Indianapolis, IN. Pupil of AIC. Work: Collaborating with architects in architectonic sculpture; forty-five models, Denver National Bank; models for Gulf Bldg., Houston, Texas. Address in 1929, 1018 Second National Bank Bldg., Houston, Texas.

DIERINGER, ERNEST.
Painter. Born July 6, 1932, in Chicago, IL. Studied at Art Inst. of Chicago on Nat. Scholastic Scholarship, 1950-4. Taught at Hyde Park Center, 1958. Work: Montana Hist. Society. Exhibited: Wells St. Gallery, Chicago, 1959; Art Gallery in Toronto; Art Inst. of Chicago; L.A. County Museum.

DIETERICH, LOUIS P.
Portrait painter. Born in Germany, 1842. Address in 1926, 347 North Charles Street, Baltimore, MD.

DIETERICH, WALDEMAR F(RANKLIN).
Portrait painter, illustrator, and teacher. Born Baltimore, MD, Nov. 10, 1876. Pupil of Constant, L'Hermite and Laurens in Paris. Member: Charcoal C., Baltimore, ASL of NY. Instructor, Maryland Inst., Baltimore. Address in 1929, 347 North Charles St.; h. 4403 Kathland Ave., Baltimore, MD.

DIETRICH, GEORGE A(DAMS).
Painter, sculptor, illustrator, and teacher. Born Clark County, IN, April 26, 1905. Pupil of Charlott . Partridge, Garolomo Picolli, Viola Norman; Layton School of Art; AIC. Member: Wisc. PS; Hoosier Salon. Awards: Culver Military Acad. prize ($200), Hoosier Salon, 1927; Clement Studebaker water color prize ($100). Hoosier Salon and the Currie Monon prize ($100), Hoosier Salon, 1928; Milwaukee Art Inst. Medal and $50 for sculpture Wisc. PS, 1929. Address in 1929, Layton School of Art, 428 Jefferson St.; winter 367 Lake Drive., Milwaukee, Wisc.; h. Bordon, IN.

DIETSCH, C. PERCIVAL.
Sculptor. Born New York City, on May 23, 1881. Member: Alumni Amer. Acad. in Rome; N SS 1910; NY Arch. Lg. 1911. Awards: Rinehart Scholarship in sculpture, American Acad. in Rome, 1906 - 1909; hon. mention. P.-P. Exp. San F., 1915. Work: Besso Memorial Monument in Rome; panels for Rice Inst., Houston, Texas; "Athlete," Peabody Inst., Baltimore. Address in 1929, Saybrook Park, Saybrook, CT; 330 Peruvian Ave., Palm Beach, Florida.

DiFILIPPO, ANTONIO.
Sculptor. Exhibited at the PAFA, Philadelphia, in 1924. Address in 1926, 126 East 75th Street, New York.

DIGGS, ARTHUR.
Painter. Born Columbia, MO, on Nov. 16, 1888. Pupil of AIC. Member: Chicago AL. Award: Eames MacVeagh prize, Chicago AL. Address in 1929, 1239 West 109th St. Chicago, IL.

DILLAWAY, THEODORE M.
Painter, writer, lecturer, and teacher. Born Sommerville, MA in 1874. Pupil of MA NAS; Delacluse Acad., Paris. Member: Phila. Sketch C; Phila. Alliance; AFA. Works: "Autumn in the Fells" and "Spring in the Fells," O. W. Holmes School, Boston; "Bald Mr., N. H.," John Story Jenks School, Phila.; "Spring Blossoms," Hackett School, Phila.; "Boothbay Harbor Scene," LaFrance Inst., Phila. Author; "Decoration of School and Home," Milton Bradley Co.; "American Renaissance Craft and Picture Texts for Teachers," Brown Robertson Co. Director of Art, Philadelphia Public Schools. Address in 1929, Dept. of Art Education, Grant Bldg., 17th and Pine Sts., Philadelphia, PA; h. 332 Wellesley Road, Mt. Airy, Philadelphia; summer Acad. of Fine Arts Country School Chester Springs, PA.

DILLAYE, BLANCHE.
Painter, illustrator, and etcher. Born Syracuse, NY. Pupil of PAFA; etching under Stephen Parrish; painting under Garrido in Paris. Member: NYWCC; Phila. WCC;

240

Fellowship PAFA; Plastic C.; NA Women PS; Phila AC. Awards: Silver medal for etching, Atlanta Exp. 1895; silver medal, AAS 1902; sivler medal for etchings, International Exp., at Lorient, France, 1903; gold medal for water color, Conservation Exp., Knowville, TN, 1913. Work: "Still Evening in the Little Street," W. C. Art Collection Univ. of Syracsue, NY; "Arrangement in Green" (oil), Syracuse Museum of Fine Arts. Address in 1929, 24 South 17th St., Philadelphia, PA.

DILLON, FRANK H.
Painter. Born Evanston, IL, on Oct. 11, 1886. Pupil Art Inst., Chicago. Member: GFLA. Address in 1929, 180 N. Michigan Ave., Chicago, IL; h. 1108 Spruce St., Winnetka, IL; summer, Glen Haven, MI.

DILLON, LEO AND DIANE.
Illustrators. Born in the same year, 1933, Leo in NY and Diane in CA, they studied together at PSD and SVA in NY under John Groth and Leo Leonni. As a team they have illustrated many children's books, including The Hundred Penny Box, 1974, Why Mosquitoes Buzz in People's Ears, 1975 and Ashante to Zulu, 1976. Their illustrations have appeared in Ladies Home Journal, The Saturday Evening Post and others. Their work has been exhibited at Gallery 91 in Brooklyn, and they often travel to schools on the East Coast as guest speakers.

DiMEO, DOMINICK.
Painter and sculptor. Born Feb. 1, 1927, in Niagara Falls, NY. BA from Art Inst. of Chicago; MA from U. of Iowa (1953). Awarded Guggenheim Mem. Foundation Fellowship in Graphics, 1972-73. In collections of Whitney; U. of Mass., Amherst; Art Inst. of Chicago; others. Exhibited at Albright-Knox; Buffalo, NY; Art Inst. of Chic.; Whitney Mus.; Int'l Drawing Comp., Barcelona; and others.

D'IMPERIO, DOMINIC.
Sculptor. Born Italy, on Aug. 31, 1888. Pupil of Grafley and Leasoly. Membership: PAFA;

Phila. Alliance. Award: Bronze medal, Spring Garden Inst., 1916. Work: "Sincler Memorial," Church of St. James, Phila.; "Pan," Graphic Sketch C. Phila. Address in 1929, 1523 Chestnut St., Philadelphia, PA, h. 3419 Emerson St., Holmesburg, Philadelphia, PA.

DINE, JAMES.
Painter and sculptor. Born in Cincinnati, OH, June 16, 1935. Studied: Univ. of Cincinnati; Boston Mus. School. Work: The Museum of Modern Art, NYC; Tate Gallery, London; Stedelijk Mus., Amsterdam; Whitney, NYC; Albright-Knox, Buffalo, NY. Exhibitions: Guggenheim, NYC, 1963; Venice Biennial, 1964; Whitney Mus., NYC, 1966; Milwaukee Art Ctr., 1979; many more. Awards: Harris silver medal & prize, Art Inst., Chicago. Address in 1982, c/o The Pace Gallery, NYC.

DINNEEN, ALICE.
Painter. Born in New York City in 1908. Studied: New York School Applied Design for Women; Art Students League; with Furlong. Collections: Carville, Louisiana; La Fortaliza, San Juan, Puerto Rico; New York Hospital; mural, United States Post Office, Warrenton, NC; Corbin, Kentucky; Department of Labor, Washington, DC.

DINNERSTEIN, HARVEY.
Illustrator. Born in Brooklyn, NY, in 1928. He attended Tyler Art School of Temple University for four years. His first illustration to be published was for a medical advertisement, followed by many assignments for advertising and editorial clients. He has illustrated several books, including Tales of Sherlock Holmes, Remember the Day and At the North Wind. Since 1946, when he won the Conde Nast Award, he has received numerous awards and his paintings are in the collections of major museums and universities throughout the United States.

DIRK, NATHANIEL.
Painter. Born Brooklyn, NY, on Dec. 21, 1895. Pupil of Max Weber, Kenneth H. Miller, Boardman

Robinson. Member: S. Indp. A.; ASL of NY. Died in 1961. Address in 1929, 15 East 14th St., New York, NY.

DISMUKES, MARY ETHEL.
Painter, craftsman, writer, and lecturer. Born Pulaski, TN. Pupil of ASL of NY; Twachtman, Kenyon Cox, Loeb and Carleton. Member: New Orleans AA; Miss. AA; Gulf Coast AA; Nashville AA; SSAL; New Orleans ACC. Awards: First Nat'l Bank of Biloxi gold medal, Gulf Coast AA., 1927; first prize for painting of place of historic interest in MI, first and second prizes for pictorial photography and second prize for flower study, State Fed. of Women's Clubs, Jackson, 1927; first prize, State Fair, Jackson, 1926; first prize, Guild Coast Fair, Gulfport, 1926; prizes at District and State Convention M. F. W. C., for most popular picture and best colored photographs. Died in 1952. Address in 1929, 113 Lameuse St., Biloxi, MI.

DiSUVERO, MARK.
Painter and sculptor. Born in Shanghai, China. Studied at University of California. In collections of Wadsworth Atheneum; NYU. Exhibited at AIC; Peace Tower, Los Angeles; Am. Sculpture of the Sixties, Los Angeles Co. Museum; Whitney; San Fran. Museum of Art; 20th National Print Exhib.; etc. Received Longview Found. Grant; Walter K. Gutman Found. Grant; AIC Award. Living in NYC in 1982.

DIX, CHARLES T.
Artist. Born in Albany in 1838, died in Rome 1873. Served on his father's staff in the Civil War. Later he won a name for his marine and landscape painting. In 1866-67 he exhibited at the Royal Academy, London. His "Sunset at Capri" is a spirited study of sea and shore.

DIX, EULABEE.
(Mrs. Alfred Le Roy Becker). Miniature painter. Born Greenfield, IL, on Oct. 5, 1879. Pupil of St. Louis School of Fine Arts. Studied in NY, London and Paris. Member: PA. S. Min. P.; A.

S. Min. P.; NA Women PS. Address in 1929, 58 West 57th St., New York, NY; care Morgan and Co., 1 Place Vendome, Paris, France.

DIXEY, GEORGE.
Sculptor. Son of John Dixey, a English sculptor; was born i Philadelphia and studied under hi father. He executed "Theseu Finding his Father's Sword," "Sain Paul on the Island of Malta," an "Theseus and the Wild Boar". Die c. 1854.

DIXEY, JOHN.
Sculptor. An Irishman; settled i Philadelphia towards the close o the eighteenth century, and di some modelling and stone cutting His "Hercules and Hydra" an "Ganymede" were much admired. Th figures of "Justice" on the Ne York City Hall are by him. Died i 1820.

DIXEY, JOHN V.
Sculptor and painter. The younges son of the English sculptor wa born in Philadelphia and receive instruction from his father. I 1819 he modelled "St. John writin the Revelations." He also painte several landscapes in oil that wer exhibited at the gallery of th National Academy of Design.

DIXON, FRANCIS S(TILLWELL).
Painter. Born New York City, c Sept. 18, 1879. Pupil of ASL c NY. Member: Allied AA; CT AFA. Salma. C. Work: "The Leanir Tree," Morgan Memorial, Hartfor CT. Died in 1962. Address i 1929, 241 Franklin Place, Flushin NY.

DIXON, MABEL E(ASTMAN).
Painter. Born Auburn, IA. Pup of Arthur W. Dow, Andre Strauss Member: IA. AC. Work: "Th Vaiduct, Moret," Fontainebles Museum, Fontainebleau, France Address in 1929, 4330 Harwo Drive, Des Moines, IA.

DIXON, MAYNARD.
Mural painter and illustrato Born Fresno, CA, Jan. 24, 187. Self taught. Member: San F. A Bohemian C.; Southwest Societ Painters of the West; Club Bea

242

Arts; Chicago al. A; Commonweath C; Oakland AL Specialty, western life and scenes. Work: Decorations for dining salons SS Silver State and SS Sierra; Murals for "Room of the Dons," Mark Hopkins Hotel, San Francisco (Frank van Sloun collaborating); mural, Technical High School, Oakland, Calif.; panel "India," Oakland Theatre; South Wall Main Reading Room, California State Library, Sacramento; "Legend of Earth and Sun," dining room, Arizona Biltmore, Phoenix, Ariz. Died in Nov., 1946. Address in 1929, 728 Montgomery St.; h. 1637 Taylor St., San Francisco, CA.

DOBLER, MAUD A.
(Mrs. Geroge Dobler). Painter and teacher. Born Rockford, IL, on Feb. 3, 1885. Pupil of Marquis E. Reitzel, Carl Krafft, and H. A. Oberteuffer. Member: Rockford AA; Austin, Oak Park and River Forest AL; IL. AFA; All-Ill. SFA. Award: First hon. mention, Rockford Art Assoc., 1929. Address in 1929, 1507 Harlem Blvd., Rockford, IL.

DOBSON, MARGARET (ANNA).
Painter and teacher. Born Baltimore, MD, on Nov. 9, 1888. Pupil of PAFA under Weir, Vonnoh, Breckenridge, Garber, Pearson, and Cecilia Beaux; Baudouin and St. Hurbert in fresco decoration. Member: Md. Inst. Alumni A.; Provincetown AA. Represented in Mississippi Art Collection and Syracuse Art Museum; fresco decoration in Hospital of St. Vincent de Paul at Fontainebleau, an din the Fontainebleau Palace, France.

DODD, MARK DIXON.
Painter and etcher. Born in St. Louis, MO, 1888. Pupil of Art Students' League of New York. Address in 1926, 106 Columbus Heights, Brooklyn, NY.

DODD, SAMUEL.
Engraver. Born in Bloomfield, NJ, 1797; he died in Aug. 7, 1862. He was little known. The only signed plate of Samual Dodd is a portrait of "Washington in Uniform" (Hart, 690) signed "S, Dodd Set. New Ark".

The plate was probably engraved about 1820.

DODGE, CHESTER L.
Painter and illustrator. Born Salem, ME, on May 21, 1880. Studied at RI School of Design and ASL of NY. Member: Providence AC; Providence WCC. Instructor at RI. School of Design. Address in 1929, The Fleur- de-Lys, 7 Thomas St.; h. 29 Waterman St., Providence, RI.

DODGE, FRANCES F.
(Mrs. A. C. Dodge). Landscape painter and etcher. Born Lansing, MI, Nov. 22, 1878. Pupil of Duveneck, Meakin, Wessel, Joseph Pennel. Member: NA Women PS; Chic. South Side AA; Cincinnati Woman's AC. Address in 1929, 5844 Stoney Island Ave. Chicago, IL.

DODGE, JOHN WOOD.
Miniature painter. Born on Nov. 4, 1807 and died on Dec. 16, 1893. His portrait miniature of General Jackson executed in 1842 was engraved for the postage stamp of 1863. He was elected an associate member of the National Academy of Design in 1832.

DODGE, OZIAS.
Painter and etcher. Born in Morrisville, VT, in 1868. Pupil of Yale School of Fine Arts and under Gerome in Paris. Represented by etchings in Congressional Library, Art Institute Chicago, and New York Public Library. He died in 1925.

DODGE, W., DeLEFTWICH.
Mural painter. Born Liberty, VA, on March 9, 1867. Studied in Munich and with Gerome in Paris. Member: Mural P. Award: Gold medal, prize Fund Exhib., NY, 1886; third medal, Paris Exp., 1889; medal, Columbian Exp., Chicago, 1893. Work: Majestic Theatre, Boston; Empire Theatre, NY; Acad. of Music, Brooklyn; Orpheum Theatre, Kansas City, MO; hotels Astor, Algonquin, Devon and Waldorf-Astoria, NY; "Ambition," ceiling in Library of Congress, Wash.; Mosaics, Hall of Records, NY; mural paintings, Panama-Pacific Exp., San Francisco, 1915; 5 mural paintings, Teachers College, Cedar Falls, IA; 21 mural paintings, Flag

243

Room, Albany, NY; Memorial panel, Kenosha Co. Court House, Wis. Died in 1935. Address in 1929, 52 West 9th Street, New York, NY.

DODSON, RICHARD W.
Engraver. Born in Cambridge, MD, Feb. 5, 1812; died in Cape May, NJ, 1867. Dodson was an excellent line-engraver of portraits and book-illustrations. He was pupil of the Philadelphia engraver James B. Longacre, and he made some of the best portraits in the National Portrait Gallery, Published by Longacre & Herring. Dodson is said to have abandoned engraving for another business in 1845. Died on July 25, 1867.

DODSON, SARAH PAXTON BALL.
Landscape and figure painter. Born Philadelphia, PA, 1847; died Brighton, England, 1906. Pupil of M. Schussele, in Philadelphia; later in Paris; of Evariste Vital Luminais and Jules Lefebvre; also criticisms by Boutet de Monvel. Was an exhibitor at the Paris Salon.

DOELGER, FRANK
Painter. Member: Society of Independent Artists. Address in 1926, 430 Irving Avenue, Brooklyn, NY.

DOHANOS, STEVAN.
Illustrator and painter. Born in Lorain, OH in 1907. He attended the Cleveland School of Art, after which he embarked on a long, successful career. His first assignment was a watercolor done for McCall's in 1934 and within four years he had won an Award for Distinctive Merit from the ADC of NY. From 1943 to 1959, his tightly rendered paintings, usually depicting everyday incidents in small town America, appeared on over 120 covers of The Saturday Evening Post. He has also designed 25 United States postage stamps and his artwork is owned by the Whitney Museum of Art in New York City. A founding faculty member of the FAS, he was elected to the S of I's Hall of Fame in 1971. Address in 1982, Westport, CT.

DOHERTY, MRS. LILLIAN C.
Painter. Pupil of Corcoran Schoo of Art, Washington, DC; Rhoda H Nicholis; C. W. Hawthorne; als studied in Europe. Member Washington Society of Artists Address in 1926, 12 Rhode Islan Avenue, N.W. Washington, DC.

DOHN, PAULINE.
See Mrs. Rudolph.

DOKE, SALLIE GEORGE.
(Mrs. Fred Doke). Painter. Bor Keachie, LA. Pupil of Cincinnat Academy and Chicago Academy of Fin Arts. Member: Society o Independent Artists. Award: Gol medal at Dallas, 1916. Address i 1926, Lometa, Texas.

DOLAN, ELIZABETH HONOR.
Painter, illustrator, and teacher Born in Fort Dodge, IA, on May 20 1887. Pupil of La Montague, St Hubert; Paul Baudoin; F. Luis Mora George Bridgman; Thomas Fogarty Work: Mural decorations, Morril Hall, State Museum, Lincoln, NE Address in 1929, Room 315 Liberty Bldg.; h. 1608 E. St., Lincoln, NE

DOLE, MARGARET FERNALD.
Painter. Born Melrose, MA, on May 5, 1896. Pupil of School MFA Boston; FA Course, Radcliffe Coll. Charles Woodbury, and Philip L Hale. Member: Providence AC; AFA Address in 1929, 133 Prospect St. Providence, RI; summer, Hause Heights, Orleans, MA.

DOLE, WILLIAM.
Painter. Born in Angola, IN, Sept 2, 1917. BA from Olivet College Mich.; MA from U. Calif., Berkeley 1947; studied with Moholy-Nagy an Gyorgy Kepes. Taught at Berkeley U. Calif., Santa Barbara, since 1949. In collection of Walker Art Center, Minneapolis; Santa Barbar Mus. of Art; PAFA; Fogg Art Mus. Boston; others. Exhibited at d Young Mus., San Fran.; Staempfl Gallery, NYC, 1974, 76, 78, 80 Hirshhorn Collection, Wash., DC and others. Received Art Awar from Am. Acad. and Inst. of Arts Letters, 1978. Works in collage Rep. in NYC, Staempfli Gal.; in Lo Angeles, Mekler Gal.Address i

1982, Dept. of Art, Univ. of Calif., Santa Barbara.

*OLINSKY, NATHAN.
Painter and teacher. Born in Russia, on Aug. 9, 1889. Pupil of NAD. Member: Salma. C.; NY Arch. Lg.; Mural P. Address in 1929, 9 East 12th St., New York, NY; 709 Willoughby Ave., Brooklyn, NY; summer, Hunter, NY.

*OLPH, JOHN HENRY.
Painter. Born on April 18, 1835. Elected a Member of the National Academy in 1898. He died in Sept. 28, 1903. Represented at Penna. Academy of Fine Arts by his portrait of the artist , Charles Loring Elliott. His specialty was the painting of cats and dogs.

)OMBECK, BLANCHE M.
Sculptor. Born in New York City in 1914. Studied: Graduate Training School of Teachers; with Zeitlin and Amino. Awards: Fellowship, MacDowell Colony, 1957; Huntington Hartford Foundation, 1958. Collections: Brooklyn Museum; Randolph-Macon Woman's College. Address in 1980, Hancock, NH.

)OMVILLE, PAUL.
Painter and teacher. Born Hamilton, Canada, on June 16, 1893. Pupil of PAFA; School of Fine Arts, Univ. of PA. Member: Phila. Alliance; T-Square C., Phila.; Mural P.; (assoc.) Arch L. of NY. Work: Murals in Mutual Trust Company of Phila.; St. Luke's Church, Germantown, PA; Seamens Church Inst., Phila. Asst. Professor of drawings, Univ. of Penna. School of Fine Arts. Head of Dept. of Interior Decoration, Phila. School of Design for Women. Address in 1929, 2037 Moravian St., Philadelphia, PA; summer, Woodstock, Ulster Co., NY.

*ONAHEY, JAMES H(ARRISON).
Illustrator, craftsman, writer, lecturer, and cartoonist. Born Westchester, OH, on April 8, 1875. Pupil of Cleveland School of Art. Member: Cleveland AA. Address in 1929, "Plain Dealer," Cleveland, OH; h. Aurora, OH.

DONAHEY, WILLIAM.
Painter. Born in Westchester, Ohio, 1883. Artist for children's papers, magazines, and books. Died c. 1953. Address in 1926, 2331 Cleveland Avenue, Chicago, IL.

DONAHUE, WILLIAM HOWARD.
Painter. Born NYC, on Dec. 21, 1881. Pupil of Henry R. Poore and E. L. Warner. Member: Brooklyn S. Modern A.; Allied A.; The NY Group; Salma. C.; Nanuet PS. Address in 1929, Lyme, CT; 47 Fifth Ave., NYC.

DONALDSON, ALICE WILLITS.
Painter, illustrator, and craftsman. Born in Illinois, Sept. 28, 1885. Pupil of Cincinnati Acad.; PA Mus. School. Member: NYWCC; Alliance; GFLA; AM. Union Dec. Artists and Craftsmen. Address in 1929, 313 West 20th St., New York, NY.

DONATI, ENRICO.
Painter and sculptor. Born in Milan, Italy, Feb. 19, 1909; US citizen. Studied at Univ. of Pavia, Italy; ASL, 1940; New Sch. for Social Research. In collections of Albright-Knox Art Gal., Buffalo, NY; MOMA; Whitney; Baltimore Mus; Corning Glass, NY; Univ. of Mich.; others. Exhibited at Carnegie Int'l. Exhibits, 1945-61; MOMA; Guggenheim; Whitney; PAFA; Staempfli Gallery, NYC; and others, including museums in Rome, Milan, Brussels, Munich, Sao Paulo. Served on advisory bd., Brandeis Univ.; Yale Univ. president's council on arts & architecture; others. Also taught at Yale, 1962-72. Rep. by Staempfli Gal., NYC. Address in 1982, 222 Central Park S., NYC.

DONATO, GUISEPPE.
Sculptor. Born Maida, Calabria, Italy, on March 14, 1881. Pupil of Phila. Industrial Art School under Grafly and J. Liberty Tadd and PAFA under Grafly; Ecole des Beaux-Arts; Julian and Colarossi Academies in Paris. Member: NSS 1909; NY Arch. Lg.; Paris AA; Union Internationale des Beaux-Arts et des Lettres; Fellowship PAFA. Awards: Stewardson scholarship, PAFA, 1900 (first time awarded); Cresson European scholarship, PAFA,

1903-1905 (First time awarded).
Work: "The Quaker," City Hall,
Phila. and in PA Acad. of the Fine
Arts. Died in 1965. Address in
1929, 716 Walnut Street, 501 South
Broad Street; h. 1512 South 9th
St., Phila. PA.

DONDO, MATHURIN M.
Painter, writer, lecturer, and
teacher. Born on March 8, 1884.
Pupil of Hawthorne, Henri, Bellows,
and Schumacher. Member: Berkeley
Lg. FA; S. Indp. A. Address in
1929, University of California,
Berkeley, CA.

DONEY, THOMAS.
Engraver. This capital engraver of
portraits in mezzotint came to
Canada from France, and after
working for some time in Illinois
and Ohio, he established himself in
business in NY about 1845. Doney
engraved a number of meritorious
portrait plates for the Democratic
Review and other NY and Phila.
periodicals.

DONIPHAN, DORSEY.
Painter and teacher. Born
Washington, DC, on Oct. 8, 1897.
Pupil of Tarbell, R. S. Meryman,
Burtis Baker, and A. R. James,
Corcoran School of Art; and School
of the Mus. of Fine Art, Boston.
Member: S. Wash. A.; Am. APL.
Address in 1929, 1462 Harvard St.,
N.W. Washington, DC.

DONLEVY, ALICE H.
Painter and illustrator. Born
Manchester, England, 1846. Pupil
of Women's Art School of Cooper
Union, New York. Address in 1926,
308 East 173d Street, Bronx, New
York, NY.

DONLON, LOUIS J.
Painter. Member: Conn. Academy of
Fine Arts. Address in 1926, Care
of Connecticut Academy of Fine
Arts, 904 Main Street, Hartford,
CT.

DONLY, EVA BROOK.
Painter. Born in Simcoe, Ontario,
CN, on April 30, 1867. Pupil of F.
M. Bellsmith and John Ward Stimson.
Member: NYWCC; NAC; Gamut Club; NA
Women PS; Pen and Brush C.; Wash.
AC; Lyceum Club of London; Wash.

WCC; Brooklyn SA: AFA. Award:
Hon. mention for water color, NA
Women PS, 1923; first prize for
water colors, Great Western Fair,
London, 1926 and 1927. Works:
"Arrival of U-Boat Deutschland at
Norfolk, VA," owned by United
States Government; "Elba Beach,
Bermuda," "Beach Lake Erie,"
National Gallery, Ottawa, CN.
Address in 1929, Simcoe, Ontario,
CN.

DONNESON, SEENA.
Printmaker and sculptor. Born in
New York City. Studied: Pratt
Institute; The Art Students League,
New York City. Awards: Edward
MacDowell Foundation, 1963-64;
Tarmarind Lithography Workshop,
1968; and ten national competition
awards. She has exhibited in
twenty-five museums, galleries, and
universities throughout the United
States. Collections: Finch
College, New York; Norfolk Museum,
Virginia; Museum of Modern Art, New
York; Los Angeles County Museum of
Art, CA; plus many others. Media:
Clay, handmade paper, heavily
embossed collographs and etching.
Rep. by Assoc. Am. Artists and
Grippi Gal. in NYC. Living and
working in NYC.

DONOGHUE, JOHN.
Sculptor. Born in Chicago in 1853.
Pupil of Academy of Design; also
studied in Paris. Principal work:
"Young Sophicles" (1885), "Hunting
Nymph" (1886), and "St. Paul," at
Congressional Library, Washington,
DC. Died in July of 1903.

DONOHO, GAINES RUGER.
Landscape painter. Born in Church
Hill, MI, in 1857. He died in New
York City, 1916. Pupil of Art
Students' League in New York; also
studied in Paris. Represented in
Brooklyn Institute Museum by "La
Marcellerie".

DONOHUE, WILLIAM H.
Painter. He exhibited at Annual
Exhibition, Academy of Design, New
York, 1925. Address in 1926,
Nanuet, New York.

DOOLITTLE, AMOS.
Engraver. Born in Cheshire, CT,
1754; died in New Haven, CT, 1832.

Doolittle learned early to engrave upon metal. His artist friend Ralph Earle made some rather curious drawings of the engagement at Lexington and Concord, and these, Doolittle engraved on copper and published in New Haven in 1775. Doolittle engraved a considerable number of portraits, views, Bible illustrations, book-plates, etc., all executed in line. Mr. Barber credits Doolittle with engraving the first historical plates done in America. Mr. Barber overlooked Paul Revere's plate of the Boston Massacre, published in 1770, and Romans' "Exact View of the Late Battle at Charleston," which was published in Philadelphia in September 1775, or about three months before the appearance of Doolittle's views of Lexington and Concord.

DOOLITTLE, EDWIN S.
Painter. Born in Albany, 1843. He had a studio in 1867 in New York; in 1868 he went to Europe for study. In 1869 he painted his "Shadow of a Great Rock in a Weary Land". His painting comprised landscapes and marine subjects. Mr. Doolittle also executed illustrations for books, and has designed book covers. He died in 1900.

DOOLITTE, HAROLD L.
Etcher. Born Pasadena, CA, on May 4, 1883. Member: Chicago SE; Brooklyn SE; Calif. SE.; Calif. PM; AFA. Prints owned by Los Angeles Museum; Calif. State Library; Art Inst., Chicago. Address in 1929, 1520 Rose Villa St., Pasadena, CA.

DOOLITTLE, SAMUEL.
Engraver. A "Goodwin" book-plate, signed "S. D. Sct. 1804," is assigned to this name in the descriptive catalogue of the late exhibition of early American engravings held under the auspices of the Museum of Fine Arts, in Boston.

DOOLITTLE & MUNSON.
Engravers. This firm was engraving portraits, bank-notes, etc., in 1842, in Cincinnati, OH. The second member of this firm may have been S. B. Munson, living, earlier,

in New Haven. Some good line work of about this period, signed "A. Doolittle Sc.," may be the work of the first member of this firm. The work referred to is too well done to have been engraved by Amos Doolittle, of New Haven, and this latter Amos died in 1832. A view of the engraving establishment of Doolittle & Munson is to be found in a work entitled "Cincinnati in 1842," published in that city. The sign shown calls them "bank note engravers."

DOONER, EMILIE ZECKWER.
(Mrs. Richard T. Dooner). Painter and etcher. Born Philadelphia, on Aug. 31, 1877. Studied at PAFA and abroad. Member: Fellowship PAFA; Plastic C.; Phila. Alliance; Print C. Address in 1929, 523 Kenilworth Road, Merion, PA.

DOONER, RICHARD T.
Painter and teacher. Born Philadelphia, on May 19, 1878. Pupil of Anshutz and Thouron. Member: Phila. Art Week Assoc.; Phila. Alliance;
Phila. Park AA.; Fellowship PAFA; Phila. Print C; AFA. Awards: Gold medals at expositions in Dresden, 1909; Parks 1910; Budapest, 1912; Royal Photographic Society of Great Britain, 1923; International gold medal, American Arts and Crafts Assoc., 1923. Address in 1929, 1822 Chestnut St., Philadelphia, PA; h. Merion, PA.

DORAN, ROBERT C.
Painter and etcher. Born Dallas, Texas, 1889. Pupil of Kenneth Hayes Miller in New York. Address in 1926, 304 West 52d Street, New York, NY.

DORNE, ALBERT.
Illustrator. Born in New York City in 1904. He learned his trade, after leaving school at an early age, by taking odd jobs in art studios and advertising agencies. He worked under Saul Tepper in NY while supporting himself as a clerk and a professional boxer. He started his career with sheet music cover illustrations; rose to the top of his profession, receiving the Horatio Alger Award for his achievement. His superb

draftsmanship and strong compositions were seen in most major magazines in the 1930's and 1940's. He was President of the S of I, founding director of the FAS and Co-founder of the Code of Ethics and Fair Practices. He received an honorary degree from Adelphi University and the First Gold Medal from the NY ADC for his distinguished career. Died in 1965.

DORSEY, JOHN SYNG.
Born in Philadelphia on Dec. 23, 1783; died there on Nov. 12, 1818. This eminent American surgeon published, in 1813, his "Elements of Surgery," "with plates by John Syng Dorsey, M.D." These plates are etched and sometimes finished in stipple; they are excellently done. Dr. Dorsey also etched several good book-plates.

DOSKOW, ISRAEL.
Painter and illustrator. Born Russia, on Nov. 30, 1881. Pupil of PAFA. Member: Salma. C.; SI. Address in 1929, 150 East 41st Street; 219 East 39th St.; 452 Fifth Ave., New York, NY.

DOTY, ROY.
Illustrator. Born in Chicago, IL, in 1922. He received his art training at CCAD. After service with US Army in World War II, when he worked with Yank and Stars and Stripes, he began his free-lance career. His illustrations have appeared in over 50 books and in advertising and editorial journals. Two of his longstanding clients are Consumer Reports and Popular Science. His work, ranging in style from decorative to cartoon, has also been seen in advertisements for Macy's, The Bowery Savings Bank and in the comic strip Laugh-In based on the TV series.

DOUGAL, W. H.
Engraver. Born in New Haven, CT, about 1808; was living in Washington, DC, in 1853. Mr. Alfred Jones says that his name was originally Macdougal, and he was so known for a time, but for some reason he later dropped the "Mac". He was a good engraver of landscapes and portraits, latter being executed in a mixed manner. In 1853 he was in the employ of the US Treasury Dept. at Washington, DC.

DOUGHERTY, LOUIS R.
Sculptor. Born Philadelphia, 1874. Pupil of Penna. Academy of Fine Arts, and Drexel Institute. Member: The Scumblers, Philadelphia; Fellowship Penna. Academy of Fine Arts. Address in 1926, 27 Norwood Avenue, Stapleton, NY.

DOUGHERTY, PARK C.
Painter. Born Philadelphia, PA, 1867. Pupil of Penna. Academy of Fine Arts; Julien Academy in Paris. Member: Art Club, Philadelphia; Fellowship Penna. Academy of Fine Arts, 1916. Address in 1926, 49 Boulevard du Montpernasse, Paris, France.

DOUGHERTY, PAUL.
Marine painter. Born Brooklyn, NY, on Sept. 6, 1877. Studied alone in Paris, London, Florence, Venice, and Munich. Member: SAA 1905; ANA 1906, NA 1907; Nat. Inst. A. L.; Lotos C.; Salma. C. 1907; AWCS; Century Assoc.; NAC; New Soc. A. Award: Osborne prize ($500) 1905; second prize, CI Pittsburgh, 1912; Inness goldmedal, NAD, 1913; gold medal, P. P. Exp., San F., 1915; Carnegie prize, NAD 1915; Altman prize ($1,000) NAD 1918. Work: "The Land and the Sea." Corcoran Gal. Wash.; "Flood Tide," Carnegie Inst., Pitts.; "Moonlight Cove," Toledo Museum; "Sun and Storm." Nat. Gal, Wash.; "Autumn Oaks," Brooklyn Inst. Mus.; "Storm Quiet," Chicago Art Inst. "Oct. Sea." "The Road to Cayey," and "Lake Louise," Metropolitan Mus., NY; "A Freshening Gale," Buffalo Fine Arts Acad.; "Spring in the Hills," Art Mus., Montclair, NJ; "Coast of Cornwall," Memorial Art Gal. Rochester, NY; "In a Golden Light," Hackley Gal. Muskegon, MI; "After the Gale," City Art Museum, St Louis; "Moonlit Surf," Minneapolis Inst.; "Sun and Surf," Omaha (NE) Museum; five paintings in Philips Memorial Gal., Washington, DC Died in 1947. Address in 1929, 1

East 10th St.; 7 West 43rd St.; 943 Lexington Ave., New York, NY.

DOUGHTY, THOMAS.
Lanscape painter. Born in Philadelphia on July 19, 1793; died in New York on July 22, 1856. Self-taught. represented at the Metropolitan Museum by "On the Hudson" and "A River Glimpse".

DOUGLAS, CHESTER.
Painter and craftsman. Born Lynn, on Oct. 6, 1902. Pupil of John Sharman. Address in 1929, 233 Lynnfield St., Lynn, MA.

DOUGLAS, HALDANE.
Painter and etcher. Born Pittsburgh, PA, on Aug. 13, 1893. Pupil of Armin Hansen. Member: Calif. AC; Calif. PS; Laguna Beach AA; Calif. PSC. Award: Hon. mention, Pomona, 1925. Address in 1929, 212 South Catalina St., Los Angeles, CA; 704 Alpine Drive, Beverly, CA; summer, Monterey, Calif.

DOUGLAS, HAROLD.
Painter. Member: Ct. AFA; Salma. C. Address in 1929, Farmington, CT.

DOUGLAS, LAURA GLENN.
Painter. Born in Winnsboro, SC. Studied: College for Women, Columbia, SC; Corcoran School of Art; Art Students League; NAD with Hawthorne; and abroad. Awards: Metropolitan Musem of Art, 1926; Art Institute of Chicago, 1942. Collections: Rochester Memorial Art Gallery; Gibbes Art Gallery; United States Treasury Department, Washington, DC. United States Post Office, Camilla, GA.

DOUGLAS, LUCILLE SINCLAIR.
Painter and illustrator. Born Tuskogee, AL. Pupil of ASL of NY, Lucien Simon, Richard Miller, and ALexander Robinson in Paris; studied in Spain and Holland. Member; Soceite des Artistes Independentes, Paris; NA Women PS; SSAL. Work: Illustrated "The Autobiography of a Chinese Dog," by Florence Ayscough (Houghton Mifflin). Address in 1929, care of Millie Higgins Smith, 489 Park Ave., New York; American Woman's

Club, 66 Synchwan Road, Shanghai, China.

DOUGLAS, WALTER.
Painter. Born Cincinnati, OH, on Jan. 14, 1868. Pupil of Chase, NAD, and Aslin, NY. Member: AWCS; Salma. C., 1904; Art Center of the Oranges. Work: "In the Shade," Dallas (TX) Art Association. Specialty, poultry. Address in 1929, 264 West 19th St., New York, NY; summer, Block Island, RI.

DOULBERRY, FRANK R.
Painter. Member: Artists Guild of the Author's League of America, New York. Address in 1929, 145 East 42nd St., New York, NY.

DOULL, MARY ALLISON.
Miniature painter, craftsman, and teacher. Born Prince Edward Island, Canada. Pupil of C. Y. Turner, National Academy of Design in NY; Julian Acad. in Paris. Member: PBC.; Catherine Lorillard Wolfe C.; NY. Soc. Ceramic Art. Address in 1929, 150 East 34th St. 77 Irving Place, NY, NY; summer, Cap Traverse, Prince Edward Island, Canada.

DOVE, ARTHUR G.
Painter and illustrator. Born Canandaigua, NY, on Aug. 2, 1880. Work: "Golden Storm," and "Waterfall," Phillips Memorial Gallery; "Cow," "Rain," and "Fishing Nigger," Intimate Gallery, New York, NY. Address in 1929, Halesite, NY.

DOVE, LEONARD.
Illustrator. He was a frequent contributor of cartoons and covers to The New Yorker in the 1940's and 1950's. He worked in pen and ink and watercolor.

DOW, ARTHUR WESLEY.
Painter. Born 1857, in Ipswich, MA. Studied art in Boston and at Paris. Pupil of Boulanger and Lefebvre. Pictures in Salon, Paris, 1886-87. Instructor of Art, Pratt Institute, Brooklyn, 1895-1904; instructor of Composition at Art Students' League, New York, 1897-1903. Member: Society of Independent

Artists; American Federation Arts. Died in 1922.

DOW, LELIA A.
Painter, craftsman, and teacher. Born Cooksville, Wis., on April 2, 1864. Pupil of AIC; John Vanderpoel; F. W. Fursman. Member: Madison AG.; Wis. PS; AFA. Address in 1929, 301 Forest St., Madison, Wisc.

DOWIATT, DOROTHY.
Painter. Born Pittsburgh, PA, on Oct. 9, 1903. Pupil of Edouard Vysekal; E. Roscoe Shrader. Member: Calif. AC; Younger Painters C. (Pres.). Awards: First prize for figure composition and 2nd prize for still life, Arizona State, Fair, 1928. Address in 1929, 421 North Greenleaf Ave., Whittier, CA.

DOWNES, J(OHN) IRELAND HOWE.
Landscape painter. Born Derby, CT, in 1861. Pupil of Yale School of Fine Arts and J. Alden Weir; Merson in Paris. Member: New Haven PCC.; CT AFA; Rockport AA. Work: "Destruction of SS. Emden off the Cocos Island, War Memorial Collection, National Gallery, Washington, DC. Died on Oct. 16, 1933. Address in 1929, 254 Lawrence St.; h. 345 Whitney Ave., New Haven, CT.

DOYLE, ALEXANDER.
Sculptor. Born in Steubenville, Ohio, 1857, and died in 1922. He studied sculpture in Florence and Rome. Returned to the US in 1878. Among his works are: Bronze equestrian statue of Gen. Albert Sidney Johnston; bronze statue of Gen. Robert E. Lee; marble statue of Margaret Haugherty, for New Orleans, LA; National Revolutionary Monument, Yorktown, VA; bronze statue of Gen. Philip Schuyler, Saratoga, NY; marble statue of Gen. Garfield, Cleveland, OH; bronze statue of Gen. James R. Steedman, Toledo, OH; marble statue of Senator Benjamin H. Hill, Atlanta, GA ; bronze statue of Horace Greeley, NY; bronze statue and monument to Henry W. Grady, Atlanta, GA; and statues of Benton, Blair, and Kenna, in Statuary Hall, Capitol.

DOYLE, MARGARET BYRON.
(Mrs. John Chorley). She was a daughter of W.M.S. Doyle, and became the wife of John Chorley the engraver. She painted many excellent portraits in Boston between 1820 and 1830.

DOYLE, WILLIAM M. S.
Portrait painter. Born in Boston, MA, in 1796. Was the son of a British army officer who was stationed there. He associated as a young man with Daniel Bowen the silhouettist, at the "Bunch of Grapes Tavern," and in 1805 the Boston directory states he was a "miniature painter". He died in 1828 and at that time was proprietor of the Columbian Museum in Boston. Among his portraits are those of Gov. Caleb Strong, Isaiah Thomas and John Adams. Died May, 1828.

DRABKIN, STELLA.
Painter. Born in New York City in 1906. Studied: NAD; Phila. Graphic Sketch Club, with Earl Horter. Awards: American Color Printmaker Society, 1944; Phila. Printmaker Club, 1955. Collections: PAFA; Phila. Museum of Art; Nat'l. Gal. of Art; Metropolitan Museum of Art; PA State College; Library of Congress; Atwater Kent Museum; Tel-Aviv Museum, Israel, Bazalel Museum, Jerusalem.

DRADDY, JOHN G.
Sculptor. Born in 1833. He executed many notable church altars including the August Daly altar, and the "Coleman Memorial" in St. Patrick's Cathedral, New York City. He died in Italy, 1904.

DRAKE, WILL H.
Painter and illustrator. Born in New York, 1856. Pupil of Julien Academy under Constant and Doucet. Elected Associate Member of National Academy, 1902. Specialty, animals. Address in 1926, 362 West 9th Street, Los Angeles, CA.

DRAYTON, EMILY.
See Mrs. J. Madison Taylor.

DRAYTON, G(RACE) G(EBBIE).
Illustrator and sculptor. Born Philadelpha, PA, on Oct. 14, 1877.

Member: Fellowship PAFA; Alliance; SI; GFLA. Author and illustator of "Fido," "Kitty Puss" and other children's books. Originator of Campbell's Soup Kids. Address in 1929, 145 East 52nd St., New York, NY.

DRAYTON, JOSEPH.
Engraver of landscape in aquatint, and an expert print colorist. At least as early as 1820 he was working in Phildelphia. He was later employed for some years as a draftsman in one of the Government departments in Washington. Drayton engraved a few book illustrations in line.

DREIER, KATHARINE SOPHIE.
Painter, writer, and lecturer. Born Brooklyn, NY, on Sept. 10, 1877. Pupil of Walter Shirlaw. Member: Societe Anonyme (founder and pres.). Work: "The Good Shepherd," St. Paul's School, Garden City, LI; "Mother and Child," pastel, Houston Museum of Fine Arts. Translator of, with critical essay, "Personal Recollections of Van Gogh," by Elizabeth D. Van Gogh, 1913; Western Art and The New Era or An Introduction to Modern Art," (Brentano) 1923. Special Catalog, Intern'l. Exhib. Modern Art, Brooklyn Museum, with Foreword and 104 biographical sketches, 1926. Died in 1952. Address in 1929, 88 Central Park, West, New York, NY.

DREIFOOS, BYRON G(OLDING).
Painter and teacher. Born Philadelphia, on Jan. 30, 1890. Pupil of Fawcett School of Industrial Arts. Member: Art Centre of the Oranges; APL. Address in 1929, 268 So. Centre St., Orange, NJ.

DRENNAN, VINCENT J(OSEPH).
Painter and writer. Born New York, on Jan. 5, 1902. Pupil of NAD; Cooper Union. Address in 1929, 1044 East 36th St., Brooklyn, NY.

DRESHER, A.
Dresher was a landscape engraver of little merit, working in New York about 1860.

DRESSLER, BERTHA MENZIER.
See Menzler-Peyton.

DREWES, WERNER.
Painter, printmaker, teacher. Born in Canig, Ger., July 27, 1899; US citizen, 1936. Studied: Charlottenburg Techn.-Hochschule, Berlin; Stuttgart Sch. Arch.; Stuttgart Sch. Arts & Crafts; Weimar Staatliches Bauhaus, with Johannes Itten, Paul Klee, 1921-22; travelled to Italy and Spain to study Old Masters, 1923; Dessau Staatliches Bauhaus, with Wassily Kandinsky, Lyonel Feininger, 1927-28. Work: MOMA; Met. Mus. Art, NYC; Guggenheim Mus. Art, NYC; Brooklyn Mus. of Art, NY; Boston Mus. FA; Wadsworth Atheneum, Hartford, CT; Yale Univ. Art Gal.; Nat'l Gal. of Art, Wash. DC; Nat'l Mus. of Am. Art; Art Inst. Chicago; Cleveland Mus. of Art; Achenbach Found. for Graphic Arts, San F.; Mus. in Frankfurt, Cologne, Hamburg, Karlsruhe, Stuttgart, Berlin, Paris, London & Jerusalem. One-man shows: Cleveland Mus. Art, 1961; Achenbach Found., San F., 1962; Wash. U., St. Louis, 1965; Nat'l Collection Fine Arts, Wash. DC, 1969; Wash. U., St. Louis, 1979; AAA, NY, 1983; other shows in US and abroad. Teaching: Columbia U., 1937-40; Inst. of Des., Chicago, 1946; prof. design & dir. first yr. prog., School of FA, Wash. U., St. Louis, 1946 - 65. Member: Founding member, Am. Abstract Artists, NY, 1937 - 1946; Wash. Soc. Printmakers. Awards: Plexiglass Sculpture Competition, MOMA, 1939; painting "Autumn Harvest," St. Louis City Art Mus., 1959; Media: Oil, watercolor, woodcut. Rep.: Assoc. Am. Artists, 653 Fifth Ave., NYC; Princeton (NJ) Gallery of FA, 9 Spring St. Address in 1982, 11526 Links Drive, Reston, VA.

DREXEL, FRANCIS MARTIN.
Painter and banker. Born in Dornbirn, Austrian Tyrol, 1792; died in Phila., 1863. After studying in Italy, came to America to settle in Phila. He achieved success as a portrait painter, taking up his residence at the southwest corner of Sixth and Chestnut Streets, where he

established his studio. After several years, hearing that South America offered a profitable field for an ambitious artist, he sailed for Valparaiso. On his return home he brought with him a large collection of curiosities for Peale's Museum, then in the State House. Having accumulated some capital, he decided to settle down and become a broker, in order to open a career for his sons. In this field he made an auspicious beginning in Louisville, KY, but on his wife's desire to return to Phila. he opened an office on Third Street, below Market, on January 1, 1838, the beginning of the noted house of Drexel & Co.

DREYER, MARGARET WEBB.
Painter. Born in East St. Louis, IL, in 1917. Awards: Houston Artists Annual; Texas Watercolor Society. Collections: Inst. of International Education; Witte Museum; Thomas P. Creaven. Media: Acrylic, watercolor. Address in 1980, 4713 San Jacinto, Houston, TX.

DREYFOUS, FLORENCE.
Painter. Born New York, NY. Pupil of Robert Henri. Member: NYS. Women A. Address in 1929, 235 West 102nd Street, New York, NY.

DREYFUS, ISIDORA C.
Miniature painter and teacher. Born Santa Barbara, CA, on Aug. 8, 1896. Pupil of Delecluse, Mme. de Billemont-Chardon and Sonia Routchine. Address in 1929, 60 East 42nd Street, New York, NY; h. Santa Barbara, CA.

DREYFUSS, ALBERT.
Painter, writer, and sculptor. Born New York, NY, 1880. Pupil of George Gray Barnard, Harper, Twatchman, DuMond, Pratt Inst. ASL of NY. Member: Salons of Amer. Work: Arsenal Park Memorial, Pittsburgh, PA; awarded Pioneer Monument for Albion, Orlean Co., NY, 1911. Assisted in the studios of R. Hinton Perry, Tonette and Victor Ciani on sculpture of public buildings and monuments. Contributor of art criticism and essays to newspapers and magazines.

Address in 1929, 232 West 14th St., New York, NY.

DRIGGS, ELSIE.
Painter. Born Hartford, CT. Pupil of ASL of NY; Maurice Sterne in Italy. Member: NY. S. Women A. Address in 1929, care of Daniel Gallery, 600 Madison Ave., NYC.

DROGSETH, EINSTEIN OLAF.
Painter. Exhibited "Rough Country" at PAFA, 1920. Address in 1926, 190 Beniteau Avenue, Detroit, Michigan.

DRUMMOND, A(RTHUR) A.
Painter and illustrator. Born Toronto, on May 28, 1891. Pupil of C. M. Manly. Member: AWCS; Canadian Soc. of Graphic A. Address in 1929, 63 Inglewood Drive, Toronto, CN.

DRUMMOND, (I. G.).
Painter and sculptor. Born in Edmonton, Alberta, Canada, April 11, 1923; US citizen. Studied: PAFA; Univ. of PA; with George Harding. Work: Commissions for NY World's Fair Trade Ctr., 1963-64; Aeromatic Travel Corp., 1969; AC Camera, Grand Central Sta.; Ahi Ezer Synagogue, Brooklyn, 1971, many more. Exhibitions: PAFA, 1950; Silvermine Guild, 1964; East Hampton Gal., NY, 1968-69; Art Image, Manhattan, 1969-70. Media: Colored concrete and wire lathe. Address in 1980, Astoria, NY.

DRURY, HERBERT R.
Painter. Born Cleveland, OH, on Aug. 21, 1873. Pupil of Carlson and DuMond. Member: Cleveland SA. Address in 1929, Drury Lane, Willoughby, OH.

DRURY, HOPE CURTIS.
(Mrs. William H. Drury). Painter. Born Pawtucket, RI, on June 14, 1889. Pupil of RI Sch. of Design. Member: Providence AC; Providence WCC. Address in 1929, Paradise Road, Newport, RI.

DRURY, JOHN. H.
Painter. Born in Wash., DC, on June 30, 1816. A follower of the French school and pupil of T. Couture of Paris. Member, Chic. Acad. of Design; spent most of his professional life in Chic.

DRURY, WILLIAM H.
Marine painter. Born Fitchburg, MA, on Dec. 10, 1888. Pupil of RI School of Design; Boston Museum of Fine Arts School; Tarbell and Woodbury. Member: Providence AC; Providence WCC; Newport AA.; Brooklyn SE; California PM. Award: Gillespie prize, Newport AA, 1916. Represented in RI School of Design; National Gallery of Art Washington; the Brooklyn Museum; California State Library. Address in 1929, St. George's School; Paradise Rd., Newport, RI.

DRYDEN, HELEN.
Illustrator and draftsman. Born Baltimore, MD, on Nov. 26, 1887. Pupil of Penn. Academy of Fine Arts. Member: S. Indp. A.; SI, 1914 (assoc); GFLA; Alliance; AFA. Award: Second prize ($500), Newark poster competition, 1915. Designed covers for magazines, posters, stage costumes, and scenery. Address in 1929, 9 East 10th St., New York, NY.

DRYFOOS, NANCY P.
Sculptor. Born in New Rochelle, NY. Studied: Sarah Lawrence College; Columbia University; ASL. Awards: National Art Club, 1947; New Jersey Painters and Sculptors Society, 1950, 1957; Village Art Center, 1950; Westchester Arts & Crafts Guild, 1950, 1951; Knickerbocker Artists, 1953, 1958; National Association of Women Artists, 1953; Hudson Valley Art Assn., 1953; Silvermine Guild, 1954; Brooklyn Society of Art, 1955. Media: Marble and terra cotta.

DRYSDALE, ALEXANDER JOHN.
Painter and illustrator. Born in Marietta, GA, on March 2, 1870. Pupil of Paul Poincy in New Orleans; ASL of NY, under Curran and DuMond. Member: New Orleans AA. Award: Gold medal, New Orleans AA, 1909. Represented in Delgado Museum, New Orleans and Louisiana State Museum. Address in 1929, 320-322 Exchange Place; h. 1323 Louisiana Ave., New Orleans, LA.

DUBOIS, CHARLES E.
Landscape painter. Born in New York, 1847. He studied in Paris; also painted in Venice and Rome. Among his paintings, "Willows at West Hampton" and "Palisades, Hudson River," were exhibited at the Phila. Exposition. His "Evening at East Hampton" was in the Exhibition of Society of American Artists in 1878. He died in 1885.

DuBOIS, GUY PENE.
Painter and writer. Born Brooklyn, NY, on Jan 4, 1884. Pupil of Chase, DuMond and Henri. Taught at ASL. Member: New Soc. A.; NIAL and NA. Work: "The Doll and the Monster," Metropolitan Museum; two paintings in Phillips Memorial Gallery, Washington. Died in 1958. Address in 1929, Kraushaar, 680 Fifth Ave., New York, NY.; summer, Garnes, par Dampierre, Seine et Oise, France.

DUBOURJAL, SAVINIEN EDME.
Painter in oils and miniatures. He was born in Paris on Feb. 12, 1795, and died there on Dec. 8, 1853. Pupil of Girodet. He exhibited at the Salon in 1814. In 1846 he was working in Boston and 1847 to 1850 he was in New York, where he exhibited frequently at the National Academy of Design Exhibitions. He was a friend of the artists G.P.A Healy; see the "Life of Healy" by Healy's daughter.

DuBRAU, GERTRUD (MARGARETE).
Painter, illustrator, craftsman, and teacher. Born in Germany, on June 1, 1889. Pupil of Maryland Inst., Baltimore, and Royal Academy, Leipzig, Germany. Member: S. Indp. A. Work: Murals in Masonic Temple, Cumberland, MD; "Entry of Gen. Braddock into Fort Cumberland, 1754," "Gen. Washington Reviewing Troops at Fort Cumberland, 1794." City Hall Rontunda, Cumberland, MD; "Tea Burning at Bridgeton, NJ" New Cumberland Hotel, Bridgeton, NJ. Manager, DuBrau Art Studio. Address in 1929, Piedmont and Columbia Avenues, Cumberland, MD.

DUBUFE, CLAUD MARIE.
French portrait painter, who had his studio in New Orleans, LA, about 1837, and painted portraits of many of the members of the Old French Families of Louisiana. Born in Paris, Oct., 1790, he studied under David. He died in 1864. His portraits painted when in the United States are remarkable for their forceful character and their firm, strong modeling.

DUBUQUE, EDWARD W(ILLIAM).
Painter and teacher. Born Moosup, CT, on Nov. 5, 1900. Pupil of Heintzelman; Gorguet, Laurens and Bauduin in Paris. Member: Providence AC. Work: "In Memoriam" (in collaboration with Auguste F. Gorguet), Morris H.S., NY; 3 panels in Seaman's Bank, NY (in collaboration with Ernest Peixotto); pure fresco, Chancel of Christ Church, Birmingham, MI (in collaboration with Katherine McEwen), redecorated St. Joseph's Church, North Grosvenordale, CT. Address in 1929, 31 Vicksburg St., Providene, RI.

DUCASSE, MABEL LISLE.
(Mrs. C. J. Ducasse). Painter. Born in Colorado, in 1895. Pupil of Walter Isaacs, F. DuMond, Will S. Taylor, George Bridgeman, Luis Mora, Charles Chapman and Yasushi Tanaka. Member: Providence WCC. Awards: Third prize, 1919, first prize, 1924 and second prize, 1925, Seattle SFA. Address in 1929, 261 Benegit St., Providence, RI.

DUCHE, THOMAS SPENCE.
Born in Philadelphia in 1763. He went to England and studied painting under Benjamin West, and while there he painted the portrait of Bishop Seabury now at Trinity College, Hartford, CT. He also painted a portrait of Bishop Provost, which is owned by the New York Historical Society. He died in England in 1790.

DUCLORY, LEPELITIER.
Portrait painter; a creole of Martinique, West Indies. He came to New Orleans in the first half of the nineteenth century, and remained there about ten years, painting portraits.

DUDENSING, BIBI.
Painter. Born in San Francisco, on Feb. 1901. Pupil of Richard Miller, Louis Wilson, Colarossi and Julian Academies in Paris. Member: S. Indp. A.; NAC. Award: Gold medal, Paris, 1914; hon. mention, AIC. Address in 1929, 119 East 19th St., New York, NY; care of Victor Charreton, 8 Blvd. Chicey, Paris, France.

DUDENSING, F. VALENTINE.
Painter. Born in San Francisco, CA, 1901. Member: Society of Independent Artists. Address in 1926, 116 East 19th Street, New York, NY.

DUDENSING, RICHARD.
Engraver of portraits and landscape, in stipple and in line. Came to the US from Germany about 1857. About 1880 he established a book publishing house in New York which is still in existence. He died on Sept. 4, 1899 during a visit to the old home in Germany.

DUDLEY, DOROTHY.
Painter. Born in Somerville, MA, on Dec. 23, 1892. Pupil of Henry B. Snell. Member: NA Women PS. Award: Prize for landscape, NA Women PS., 1927. Address in 1929, 83 State St., Brooklyn, NY.

DUDLEY, FRANK V.
Painter and lecturer. Born Delavan, WI, 1868. Studied at Chicago Art Inst. Member: AIC Alumni Assoc.; Chicago AC; Chicago AG; Chicago PS; Union Internationale des Beaux Arts et des Lettres, Paris. Awards: Chicago Municipal Art League prize, 1907; Municipal Art League purchase prize, 1914; Butler purchase prize, ACI, 1915; Cahn Prize, AIC, 1919; Logan Medal and Prize, AIC, 1921; prize ($300), Chicago Gal. A., 1927, Chicago Art Inst. Collection; Municipal collction of Owatona, MN; collection of Cedar Rapids Art Assoc.; Public School collections of St. Louis and Chicago. Address in 1929, 6356 Greenwood Ave., Chicago, IL; summer, Chesterton, IN.

DUER, DOUGLAS.
Painter. Member: Society of
Illustrator. Address in 1926, 51
West 10th Street, Brooklyn, NY.

DUER, HENRIETTA A.
Painter. Pupil of S. Edwin
Whiteman, Coutois Castaign and
Giradot. Member: Balto. Mus. of A;
Balto. WCC; North Shore AA; Am.
APL. Address in 1929, Sudbrook
Park, Baltimore Co., MD.

DUESBERG, OTTO.
Painter. Member: Society of
Independent Artists. Address in
1926, 10 Eldert Street, Brooklyn,
NY.

DUFFIELD, EDWARD.
Engraver, and a clock and
watch-maker of Philadelphia. Born
in 1730, and died 1805. He was
also a diesinker and engraver of
medals. He engraved the silver
medal presented to Col. John
Armstrong, in 1756, as a memorial
of the destruction of the Indian
village of Kittanning by Armstrong;
he also made the dies for the
medals prepared in 1762 for
distribution among the Indians, by
The Friendly Association for
Preservation of Peace among the
Indians. The dies for this latter
medal cost 15L; they were cut upon
punches fixed in a socket, and the
impression was made by the stroke
of the sledge-hammer.

DUFFY, EDMUND.
Illustrator. Born in Jersey City,
NH, 1899. Pupil of ASL of NY
and studied in Paris. Cartoonist
for "The Baltimore Sun." Address
in 1929, care of the Baltimore Sun;
h. 901 Cathedral St., Baltimore,
MD.

DUFFY, RICHARD H.
Sculptor. Born New York, NY, 1881.
Pupil of ASL of NY; Mercie in
Paris. Died in 1953. Address in
1926, 9 East 55th Street, New York,
NY.

DUFNER, EDWARD.
Painter. Born Buffalo, NY, on Oct.
5, 1872. Pupil of ASL of Buffalo,
under Bridgman; ASL of NY, under
Mowbray; Whistler and Laurens, in
Paris; Studied in Spain and Italy.
Member: ANA 1910; NA, 1929; NYWCC;

AWCS; Salma. C. 1908; Paris AAA;
Lotos C; NAC; Allied AA; Patron
Montclair Art Mus. Awards:
Albright prize and scholarship,
1893, Buffalo Fine Arts Acad.; hon
mention and Fist Wanamaker prize,
Paris AAA, 1899; bronze medal,
Pan-Am. Exp., Buffalo, 1901; hon.
mention, Paris Salon, 1902;
Fellowship prize, Soc. of Artists,
Buffalo, 1904; Silver medal, St.
Louis Exp., 1904; Evans prize, AWCS
1909; Julius Levy prize, Peabody
Inst., 1921; Walter Lippincott
prize, PAFA, 1924; gold medal,
National Art Competition New York,
1925. Work: "In the Studio,"
Buffalo Fine Arts Academy; "By the
Window," Milwaukee Art Soc.;
"Meadow Brook," Rochelle Public
Library; "End of the Day," Art
League, Deymour, IN; "Gladys by the
Window," Lotos Club, NY; "Song of
the Thrush," National Arts Club,
NY; "Youth Fort Worth Mus.;
"Sunlight a Joy," Montclair Art
Mus; "Margaret by the Window,"
permanent Coll. National Acad. of
Design. Instructor, ASL of
Buffalo, 1903 to 1906; ASL of NY,
1908 to 1917; Carnegie Inst. Tech.
Pittsburgh, 1920. Address in 1929,
939 Eighth Ave., New York, NY.

DUGGAN, PETER PAUL.
Painter. Born in Ireland. He came
to America in 1810, and settled in
New York, where he taught in the
New York Academy. He drew a head
of Washington Allston for the
American Art Union Medal. He later
left America and went to England,
and finally to Paris, where he died
in 1861.

DUGGAR, MRS. MARIE R.
Sculptor. She died in St. Louis,
MO, in 1922. She made a specially
of bas-relief portraits of
children.

DULIN, JAMES HARVEY.
Painter and etcher. Born in Kansas
City, MO, on Oct. 24, 1883. Pupil
of AIC; Laurens, Naudin, Avy in
Paris. Address in 1929, 9 Rue des
Acacias, Paris, France; h. 1330
Sheridan road, Wilmette, IL.

DULL, CHRISTIAN L(AWTON).
Painter. Born in Phila., PA, on
May 24, 1902. Pupil of Daniel

255

Garber, George Harding. Member: Phila. Alliance; Amer. Artists Prof. Lg. Work: "Studio Reflected," Smedley Junior High School, Philadelphia. Address in 1929, 5853 Willows Ave., Philadelphia, PA.

DULL, JOHN J.
Painter and architect. Born Phila. PA, 1862. Pupil of PAFA. Member: Fellowship PAFA; T. Sq. C.; Phila. Sketch C.; Phila. WCC; AFA. Award: Gold medal, Plastic C., 1903. Address in 1929, 1524 Chestnut St., 5853 Willows Ave., Phila., PA.

DUMLER, M(ARTIN) G(EORGE).
Painter. Born in Cincinnati, OH, on Dec. 22, 1868. Pupil of Edward H. Potthast, M. Rettig, and R. Busebaum. Member: Salma. C.; Cincinnati AC. Address in 1929, 127 East 3rd St.; h. 1607 Dexter Ave., Cincinnati, OH.

DUMMER, H. BOYLSTON.
Painter, illustrator, and teacher. Born in Rowley, MA, in Oct. 19, 1878. Pupil of Eric Pape, George Noyes, Ambrose Webster, and John Carlson. Member: Salma. C.; North Shore AA; Boston S. Indp. A; Rockport AA. Work: Illustrated nature books for Ginn and Co.; World Book Co.; American Book, Co. Address in 1929, 6 Mill Lane, Rockport, MA.

DUMMER, JEREMIAH.
Portrait painter. A noted goldsmith and engraver of Boston in the seventeenth century; son of Richard and Frances Curr Dummer of Newbury, and the father of William Dummer, acting governor of Massachusetts from 1723 to 1728. Jeremiah Dummer was born in 1645, and died in 1718. The portraits of himself and his wife are the property of direct descendants of the heirs of Samuel Dummer of Wilmington, MA. On the back of the self-portrait of Jeremiah Dummer is inscribed: "Jeremiah Dummer pinx. Del in Anno 1691. Mei Effigles, Aetat 46".

DUMMETT, LAURA DOW.
Painter, draftsman, and teacher. Born in Allegheny, PA, on Aug. 17,

1856. Pupil of Pittsburgh School of Design for Women; Julian Academy and Desgoffe in Paris. Member Pittsburgh, AA. Address in 1929, Glendora, Chews P.O., Glocester Co., NJ.

DuMOND, F(RANK) V(INCENT).
Painter, illustrator, and teacher. Born Rochester, NY, 1865. Pupil of Boulanger, Lefebvre, and Constant in Paris. Member: SAA 1905; ANA 1900, NA 1906; ASL of NY; NY Arch. Lg. 1904; Mural P.; Lotos C.; Salma. C. 1900; Century Assoc.; Players C.; Rochester AC; Yonkers AA. Awards: Third class medal, Paris Salon, 1890; gold medal, Boston, 1892; gold medal, Atlanta Exp., 1895; silver medals ofr painting and for illustration, Pan-Am Exp., Buffalo, 1901; silver medal, St. Louis Exp., 1904; hors concours (jury of awards), P.-P. Exp., San F., 1915. Director, Dept. of Fine Arts, Lewis and Clark Exp., Portland, 1905. Instructor at ASL of NY. Work: "At the Well," Public Gallery, Richmond, IN; Two murals in San Francisco Public Library. Died Feb. 6, 1951 in NYC. Address in 1929, 27 West 67th St., New York, NY; Grassy Hill, Lyme, CT.

DuMOND, HELEN SAVIER.
(Mrs. F. V. DuMond). Painter. Born in Portland, OR, on Aug. 31, 1872. Pupil of ASL, Robert Brandegee and F. V. DuMond in NY; Collin and Merson in Paris. Member: NAC (life); Art Workers C; Catherine Lorillard Wolfe AC. Address in 1929, 27 West 67th St., New York, NY.

DUNBAR, DAPHNE FRENCH.
Lithographer and painter. Born in Port Colban, Canada, in 1883. Studied: Boston Museum of Fine Art School; with Ross, Zerbe, and Kenneth H. Miller. Awards: San Diego, California, 1941; Institute of Modern Art, Boston, 1945. Collections: Colorado Springs Fine Art Center; Boston Museum of Fine Art; Addison Gallery of American Art; Los Angeles Museum of Art; Detroit Inst. of Art; Library of Congress.

DUNBAR, HAROLD.
Painter and illustrator. Born in Brockton, MA, on Dec. 8, 1882. Pupil of MA Normal Art School under E. L. Major, DeCamp and Tarbell; Colarossi in Paris. Member: Boston SWCP; Boston AC; NYWCC; Copley S.; Concord AA; AWCS. Award: Hon. mention, AWCS, 1917. Work: "Spring Evening," Boston Art Club; "Portrait of Arthur Gilman," Radcliffe College; "Portrait of Gov. Woodbury," State House, Vermont; "The Morning Letter," Municipal collection, McPherson, Kansas; "Portrait of Chief Justice Watson," Supreme Court, VT; portraits of Buechner Family, Buechner Hospital, Youngstown, OH. Director, Chatham Summer School of Painting, Cape Cod, MA. Address in 1929,Box 494 Chatham, MA.

DUNBAR, ULRIC STONEWALL.
Sculptor. Born London, Oct., 1862. Professionally engaged as sculptor since 1880. Has received medals and diplomas; executed over 150 portrait busts, principally of prominent men, for US Capitol and Corcoran Gal. of Art, Wash.; bronze statue of late Gov. Alex R. Shepherd for front of new Municipal Bldg., Wash. Address in 1926, 1517 H. Street, N.W. Wash., DC.

DUNBIER, AUGUSTUS WILLIAM.
Painter, teacher, and lecturer. Born in Osceola, NE, on Jan. 1, 1888. Pupil of Royal Acad., Dusseldorf; and AIC. Member: Omaha SA; Salma. C.; S. Indp. A. Awards: Hon. mention, Northwestern Ex., 1918; C. N. Dietz prize ($100), Nebraska Ex., 1922. Work: "Clouds," in Public Library, Omaha. Address in 1929, Education Dept. YMCA, Omaha, NE.

DUNCAN, FLORIDA.
Painter. She was born near London, Ontario, Canada. Self-taught. Member: NYWCC; Wash. WCC. Address in 1929, Provincetown, MA.

DUNCAN, FREDERICK (ALEXANDER).
Painter, illustrator, and writer. Born in Texarkana, AR, on May 11, 1881. Pupil of George Bridgman. Address in 1929, 70 West 68th Street, New York, NY.

DUNCAN, G(ERALDIN) R(OSE).
See Birch, Geraldin.

DUNCAN, JEAN.
Painter, craftsman, and teacher. Born in St. Paul, MN, on Dec. 26, 1900. Pupil of George Bridgman, Clarence Chatterton and Charles Hawthorne. Member: St. Paul ASL; S. Indp. A. Award: Second prize, Minneapolis Art Inst., 1925. Address in 1929, 482 Laurel Ave., St. Paul, MN.

DUNCAN, WALTER JACK.
Illustrator. Born Indianapolis, IN, 1881. Student of Art Students' League of New York. Pupil of John Twachtman. Began with Century Magazine, 1903; sent to England by Scribner's, 1905; became connected with McClure's, 1907; with Harper's 1912-13. Illustrated books by Booth Tarkington, Robert C. Holliday, Christopher Morley, etc. Died in 1941. Address in 1926, 7 East 8th Street, New York, NY.

DUNDAS, VERDE VAN. V.
Sculptor. Born in Marlin, TX, 1865. Pupil Lorado Taft. Member of the Chicago Art League. Address in 1926, 630 Orchestra Hall, Chicago, IL.

DUNKERLEY, JOSEPH.
Miniature painter, who flourished 1784 and 1785 in Boston, MA. He advertised in the Independent Chronicle, Boston, December 1784, saying that he "Still carries on his Profession of Painting in Miniatures at his house in the North Square".

DUNLAP, HELENA.
Painter. Born Los Angeles, CA. Pupil of PAFA: L'hote in Paris. Member: San F. AA. Awards: Gold and silver medals, Panama-Calif. Exp., San Diego, 1915; silver medal, San Francisco AA, 1919. Represented in San Diego Fine Arts Gallery and the Los Angeles Museum. Address in 1929, 750 South Windsor Blvd., Los Angeles, Calif., and care of Lefebvre- Foinet, 19 Rue Vavin, Paris, France.

DUNLAP, WILLIAM.
Painter and engraver. Born in Perth Amboy, NJ, on Feb. 18, 1766. He died in New York on Sept. 28, 1839. In 1784 Dunlap went to London to study art with Benjamin West, and as early as 1783 he had made a crayon portrait from life of George Washington. He engraved a portait of the actor Wignell in the character of Darby. He painted a number of portraits, settled in New York, and was elected president of the National Academy of Design. The Metropolitan Museum owns his portraits of Mr. and Mrs. John A. Conant. He was the author of the "History of the Arts of Design, in the United States" (1834).

DUNLAP, ZOE F.
Miniature painter. Born in Cincinnati, Ohio, 1872. Pupil of Cincinnati Academy; also studied in Paris. Address in 1926, Dunlap Villa, 2210 Upland Palce, Cincinnati, Ohio.

DUNN, ALAN (CANTWELL).
Painter. Born in Belmar, NJ, on Aug. 11, 1900. Pupil of NAD. Fontainebleau School of FA, France; visiting fellow Amer. Acad. in Rome, 1923-24. Member: NYWCC; Tiffany Foundation; AWCS (assoc.). Lithographer on sociological and humorous subjects for "New Yorker" and other magazines and newspapers. Address in 1929, 418 West 144th St., 228 Madison Ave., NYC.

DUNN, CHARLES A. R.
Painter. Born in Washington, DC, on Dec. 9, 1895. Pupil of Edgar Nye and C. W. Hawthorne. Member: S. Wash. A. Wash. WCC; Wash. Lndsp. C; Ten Painters of Wash. Award: First prize, S. Wash. A., 1925. Address in 1929, 3810 Eighth St., N. W., Washington, DC.

DUNN, DELPHINE.
Painter, craftsman, and teacher. Born in Rushville, IN. Pupil of Artus Van Briggle, Arthur Dow, Daniel Garber, H. Breckenridge, and L. Soutter in Paris. Member: Indiana AC; Columbus A. Lg. Professor of art history and art director, Otterbein College, Westerville, OH. Address in 1929, Lambert Hall, College Ave.; h. 58 College Ave., Westville, OH; summer, Gloucester, MA.

DUNN, E. B.
Painter and sculptor. Born Rochester, NY, 1859. Pupil of Hiram Powers in Sculpture, and in painting of Wiles. Address in 1926, 435 West 199th Street, New York.

DUNN, HARVEY HOPKINS.
Illustrator and draftsman. Born in Philadelphia, July 9, 1879. Pupil of Univ. of PA; PAFA; PSIA: Denman Ross at Harvard Univ. Member: GFLA; AI of Graphic A; Phila. Alliance; Fellowship PAFA; Phila. Sketch C; Amer. Soc. of Illustrators; The Stowaways, NY; AFA. Awards: First prize, Poster Competition, Jewelry Fashion Show, Phila., 1918; first prize, Poster Competition, Phila. Chapter AIA and the T-Square Club, 1927; first prize, cover design competition, "World's Work" (Doubleday Page and Co.), 1926; first hon. mention. Shakespeare Bookplate Competition, AI of Graphic A., 1925; fourth prize, Symbol Competition, Lord and Taylor, NY, 1926. Work: "La Fayette," trade mark for La Fayette Motor Car Co.; "Alexander Medallion," trade mark for Alexander Bos.; memorial to George W. Wells, Pres. Am. Optical Co., replica in Smithsonian Inst., Wash., DC; "Servant to the Home," trade mark delineation, Hoover Suction Sweeper Co.; permanent cover design, "International Studio,"; "The Gardens of Kijkuit," book designed for John D. Rockefeller; trade mark design, General Motors Export Co.; bulletin for Phillips Memorial Gallery, Wash., DC; cover design "Journal of Heredity," Wash., DC. Address in 1929, 33 West 42nd St., New York, NY; 44 Westview Ave., Mount Airy, Philadelphia, PA.

DUNN, HARVEY T.
Painter, illustrator, and teacher. Born in Manchester, SD, on March 8, 1884. Pupil of AI Chicago and Howard Pyle. Member: SI 1913; Salma. C.; GFLA. Opened school with Chas. Chapman in Leonia, NJ, in 1906; later taught at ALS and Grand Central School of Art, NYC.

Worked for all major magazines; officical war artist during World War I. Represented in Smithsonian Inst. Int'l. Art Gallery, Nat'l. Gallery, Wash., DC. Address in 1929, Tenafly, NJ.

DUNN, LOUISE M.
Painter. Born East Liverpool, OH, 1875. Pupil of H. G. Keller and Cleveland SA; AFA. Award: Second prize for water color, Cleveland Mus., 1923. Address in 1929, 1541 Crawford Road, Cleveland, OH.

DUNNEL, E. G.
Engraver. He was a student in the National Academy of Design, in New York, in 1837, and in that year he secured the third prize for drawing. He became a good engraver of landscape and book illustrations, and in 1847 he was in the employ of Rawdon, Wright, and Hatch, an engraving firm of New York. Soon after this latter date he is said to have abandoned engraving for the pulpit.

DUNNEL, WILLIAM N.
This clever engraver in line and stipple was one of the many pupils of A. L. Dick, of New York. Dunnel was engraving for the magazines about 1845, but he contracted bad habits and disappeared.

DUNSMORE, JOHN WARD.
Painter. Born near Cincinnati, OH, Feb. 29, 1856. Pupil of Cincinnati Art Acad.; Couture in Paris. Member: ANA; NY Arch. Lg., 1903; Salma. C., 1903; Boston AC, 1881; AWCS, A. Fund S; Cincinnati AC; AFA. Award: Medal, MA Charitable Mechanics Assoc., Boston, 1881; Evans prize, Salma. C.; 1914. Director, Detroit School of Arts, 1890-94. Work: "Macbeth," Ohio Mechanics Inst., Cincinnati; "All's Fair in Love and War," Lassell Seminary, Auburndale, MA. Represented in Salmagundi Club and National Academy of Design, NY; Cincinnati Art Museum. Specialties, historical subjects and portraits. Address in 1929, 96 Fifth Ave., New York, NY.

DUNTON, W. HERBERT.
Painter and writer. Born Augusta, ME, Aug. 28, 1878. Pupil of

Andreas M. Anderson, DeCamp, F. V. DuMond, William L. Taylor, Ernest L. Blumenschein, and Leon Gaspard. Member: AFA; Salma C.; S. Indp. A.; Springfield AA. Awards: Gold medal, Nashville, 1927; hon. mention, San Antonio, 1928; cash prize, Pac. Southeastern Expos., 1929; cash prize, San Antonio, 1929. Work: "The Navajo Country," " Witte Memorial Museum of Fine Arts, San Antonio; "My Children," Mus. of New Mexico, Santa Fe; "Breakfast of the Grizzly Hunters," U. Club, Akron, O.; "The Shower" and "The Emigrants," Santa Fe Railroad; Murals; "First Train Arriving at Tipton, 1858," "Pony Express Leaving St. Joseph, 1861," "Emigrants Leaving Westport over Santa Fe Trail-1850," Missouri State Capitol, Jefferson City, MO, Specialty, paintings of the West. Address in 1929, Taos, Taos Co., New Mexico.

DUNWIDDIE, CHARLOTTE.
Sculptor and patron. Born in Strasbourg, France, in 1907. Studied: Wilhelm Otto Academy of Art, Berlin; Mariano Benlluire y Gil, Spain, and in Buenos Aires. Award: Pen & Brush Club, 1958. Collections: Marine Corp Museum, Washington, DC; Church of the Good Shepherd, Lima, Peru; Throne Room of the Cardinal's Palace, Buenos Aires; Bank of Poland, Buenos Aires; Church of Santa Maria, Cochabamba, Bolivia.

DUPAS, JEAN-THEODORE.
Illustrator. Born in Bordeaux, France, in 1882. He studied under Carolus-Duran and A. Besnard. A member of the Artists of France, he won the Prix de Rome in 1910 and, in 1941, received the Chevalier de la Legion d'honneur from the French Art Institution. Some of his best known works are Les Pigeons Blanc, Le Judgement de Paris, La Paix and Les Antilopes. When he came to the United States, he worked for Cheney Brothers Silk Company doing advertising and fashion illustration.

DUPHINEY, WILFRED I(SRAEL).
Painter, illustrator, and teacher. Born Central Falls, RI, Sept. 16, 1884. Pupil of ASL of NY; W. C.

Loring and Albert F. Schmitt. Member: Prov. AC.; Prov. WCC. Works: Portrait of Bishop Hickey in Providence, RI; portrait ex-Mayor John Lamay, Central Falls, RI; portraits ex-Gov. J. San Souci, Ex-Gov. William S. Flynn and Hon. Roy Rawlings, Speaker of the House, State House, Providence; portrait of Mayor James E. Dunne, City Hall, Providence. Illustrations for magazines. Address in 1929, Fleur-de-lis Bldg, 7 Thomas Stret, Providence, RI.

DUQUE, FRANCIS.
Painter. Born in 1832. Studied in Paris and Rome. He came to the United States about 1865 and became a popular portrait painter. He died in New York City in 1915.

DURAND, ASHER BROWN.
Engraver and painter. Born in 1796; died in 1886. Durand's father was a watchmaker and in his father's shop he acquired some knowledge of the elementary process of engraving. In 1812 he was apprenticed to the engraver Peter Maverick, and in 1817 he became a partner of his preceptor, under the firm name of Maverick & Durand. The reputation of Asher B. Durand as an engraver in pure line was established by his large plate of the "Declaration of Independence," after the painting by John Trumbull. His "Musidora," engraved in 1825, was also one of his important plates of this period, and his portrait work has never been surpassed in excellence by an American engraver. For a time he was interested in the business of bank-note engraving in 1925, in connection with his brother Cyrus Durand, and in the same year he was a member of the firm of Durand, Perkins and Co. About 1836, A. B. Durand abandoned engraving for the brush and palette, and he soon became as famous as a painter of landscapes as he had been as an engraver; and to this branch of art he devoted the remainder of his life. In 1895 the Grolier Club, of NY, published a very full check-list of the engraved work of Asher B. Durand. He was a charter member and very active in the affairs of the National Academy and

was president from 1845 to 1861. His biography was written by John Durand. Durand painted the portraits of Edward Everett, Gouverneur Kemble, Christian Gobrecht, and many other prominent men. The New York Historical Society has a set of the early Presidents painted by Durand from originals by Gilbert Stuart. The Metropolitan Museum owns his "Judgement of God" and five of his landscapes. Durand has been called the "Father of American Landscape Painting."

DURAND, CYRUS.
Engraver. Born in Jefferson, NJ on Feb. 27, 1787; died at Irvington, NJ, on Sept. 18, 1868. He was the elder brother of Asher B. Durand. In 1814 Cyrus Durand was in business as a silversmith in Newark, NJ. He was a most ingenious mechanic, and among his earlier inventions was a machine constructed for Peter Maverick, then of Newark, for ruling straight and wavy lines in connection with bank-note work. This was the first of a long series of improvements and inventions intended for use in notes, and Cyrus Durand is credited with having made the first American geometrical lathe. Though not an engraver himself, Cyrus Durand devoted his life to the invention and perfection of machinery used in bank-note work, and his services were so important in this connection that his name can not be omitted from the present record.

DURAND, JOHN.
Engraver. Two well-engraved vignettes on the title-pages of the works of William Cowper and Thomas Gray, published in New York by R. & W. A. Bartow, but undated, are signed "Engraved by J. Durand." In answer to a query, Mr. John Durand, of Nice, Italy, and son of Asher B. Durand, writes that these vignettes were engraved by John Durand, a younger brother of A. B. Durand, who died about 1820, aged twenty-eight years. Mr. Durand says that his father always maintained that his brother John was the most talented member of the family at the time of his death.

DURAND, WILLIAM.
This nephew of A. B. Durand was a man of very considerable mechanical ability. He was engraving for note work in New York in 1850.

DURANT, J. WALDO.
Portrait painter. Born in the West Indies in 1774; died in Philadelphia in 1832. The Worcester Art Museum owns a portrait of John Waldo, signed by Durant and dated 1791.

DURKEE, HELEN WINSLOW.
(Mrs. C. J. Mileham). Miniature painter. Born New York, NY. Pupil of ASL of NY, Chase, DuMond, George Bridgeman and Mora. Member: PA. S. Min. P.; NA Women PS; A.S. Min. P. Award: C. D. Smith Memorial prize, Baltimore Water Color Club, 1921. Address in 1929, 350 East 57th St., New York, NY.

DURLACHER, RUTH.
Painter. Born in Springfield, MA, in 1912. Studied: Ecole des Beaux-Arts, Fontainebleau; Yale School of Fine Arts with Rathbone, York and Keller. Awards: Brush & Palette Club, Meriden, CT; Scarsdale Art Association. Collections: School for the Deaf, New York; Springfield Hospital; Government House, Nassau, British West Indies (Portrait of Princess Margaret).

DURRIE, GEORGE H.
Painter. Born in New Haven, CT, 1820. He was a pupil of Jocelyn, and painted portraits, but was better known for his farm-scenes. He died in 1863. The Yale Art School owns his "Winter in the Country".

DURRIE, JOHN.
Painter. In 1818 John Durrie was born in Hartford, CT. He passed most of his life at New Haven, CT, and painted landscapes and a few portraits.

DUSHINSKY, JOSEPH.
Painter. Exhibited at Annual Exhibition of Water Colors at the Penna. Academy of Fine Arts, Philadelphia, 1925. Address in 1926, 64 East 88th Street, New York City.

DuSIMITIERE, PIERRE EUGENE.
Artist, antiquary and naturalist. Born in Geneva, Switzerland, about 1736, and died in Philadelphia in 1784. In 1768 he was elected a member of the American Philosophical Society, and in 1777 one of the curators of the society. He designed the vignette for the title page of Aitkin's Pennsylvania Magazine in 1775, and the frontispiece for the United States Magazine in 1779. He painted portraits in oils and miniature, also maps and views. See "Memoir of DuSimitiere" in the Pennsylvania Magazine. His collection of manuscripts, drawings, and broadsides is in the Philadelphia Library Co., Philadelphia.

DUSTIN, SILAS S.
Landscape painter. Born in Richfield, OH. Pupil of NAD and William M. Chase. Member: A. Fund S.; Salma. C.; Laguna Beach AA.; Calif. AC. Represented in Seattle Museum of Art; Portland, OR, Museum of Art; Berkshire Athenaeum and Museum, Pittsfield, MA. Address in 1929, Bryson Bldg., 2nd and Spring St., Los Angeles, CA.

DUTHIE, JAMES.
He was born in England and was taught there to engrave. Duthie was engraving book-illustrations on steel in New York in 1850-55. Some of his best line work appears in the illustrations of an edition of Cooper's works, published in New York in 1860.

DUVAL, AMBROSE.
Flourished 1827 to 1830 in New Orleans, LA, as a miniature painter. His miniature of Gov. William C. C. Caliborne of Louisiana has often been reproduced and copied. It is signed "A. Duval." He also painted Lelande de Ferrier.

DUVAL, P. S.
Lithographer. He was first in the employ of Cephas G. Childs in Philadelphia, and afterwards became his successor. In 1850 his firm executed the title for "Godey's"; their card read "P.S. Duval's

Lithographic and Color Printing Establishment."

DUVALL, FANNY E(LIZA).
Painter and teacher. Born Port Byron, NY. Pupil of Sartain in NY; Mlle. Olga de Boznanska and F. Auburtin in Paris. Member: Ca AC; West Boast Arts, Incorporated; Laguna Beach AA; AFA. Awards: Bronze medal, Lewis and Clarke Centennial Exp., 1905; gold medal, Alaska-Yukon-Pacific Exp. 1909. Work: "Large Rose," Jonathan Club, Los Angeles; "Pont Neuf, Paris," Friday Morning Club, Los Angeles; "Sycamore Tree in Spring," Ruskin Art Club, Los Angeles. Address in 1929, 4547 Marmion Way, Los Angeles, CA.

DUVENECK, FRANK.
Painter, sculptor, etcher and teacher. He was born at Covington, KY, in 1848, and received his early training at a monastery near Pittsburgh. He also studied in Munich. He was made a National Academician in 1906, and was a member of the Society of American Artists of NY, Cincinnati Art Club, and the National Institute of Arts and Letters. He died 1919. Represented at the Cincinnati Museum Association; Art Association of Indianapolis; Pennsylvania Academy of Fine Arts, Philadelphia; National Gallery of Art, Washington, DC. Died in 1916 in Ohio.

DUVIVIER AND SON.,
Portrait painters, flourishing in Philadelphia about 1796. Their advertisement in Claypoole's "American Daily Advertiser," Philadelphia, is as follows; "Academy of Drawing and Painting, Duvivier & Son, No. 12 Strawberry Street, between Second & Third Streets., Near Market, Philadelphia."

DUYCKINCK, EVERT 1st.
Portrait painter, who came to New Amsterdam in 1638 from Holland. He is described as a limner, painter, glazier, and burner of glass. Born in 1621, he died in 1702. In 1693 he painted the portrait of Stephanus Van Cortland, Mayor of New York City in 1677.

DUYCKINCK, EVERT 3d
Portrait painter. Born in 1677 and died in 1727. He painted in 1725 the portrait of his cousin Ann Sinclair Crommelin. He is also said to have painted a portrait of Lieut-Governor William Stoughton. The Duyckincks were the most important family of painters in Colonial America.

DUYCKINCK, GERARDUS.
Portrait painter. Born 1695; died 1742. He was the son of Gerret Duyckinck. He was admitted as freeman of the city in 1731, and there described as a limner.

DUYCKINCK, GERRET.
Portrait painter of the early Dutch families in New York State. Born 1660; died about 1710. He painted Anne Van Cortland, who married Stephen de Lancey in 1700. The portrait is signed and dated "Gt. Duyckinck, 1699."

DWIGGINS, W(ILLIAM) A(DDISON).
Illustrator and writer. Born in Martinsville, OH, on June 19, 1880. Address in 1929, Fenway Studios, Boston, MA; h. Hingham Center, MA.

DWIGHT, JULIA S.
Painter. Born Hadley, MA, 1870. Pupil of Tryon and Tarbell in Boston; Brush in New York. Address in 1926, 1651 Beacon Street, Brookline, MA.

DWIGHT, MABEL.
Painter and lithographer. Born in Cincinnati, OH, on Jan. 29, 1876. Pupil of Arthur Mathews. Work: Lithographs in Metropolitan Musem; Museum of Fine Arts, Boston; Cleveland Museum of Art; Art Inst. of Chicago; Victoria and Albert Museum, London; Bibliotheque Nationale, Paris. Address in 1929, 34 Grove St., New York, NY.

DYE, CLARKSON.
Painter. Born San Francisco, CA, 1869. Pupil of Virgil Williams, Burridge, Michelson, etc. Work: Mural decorations in Cathedral of Los Angeles, Durango, Mexico; Grand Opera House, Waco, Texas. Address in 1926, 2595 Union Street, San Francisco, CA.

262

DYER, AGNES. S. (MRS.).
Painter. Born San Antonio, TX,
1887. Pupil of Julian Onderdonk,
Arthur Dow, John Carlson, and Art
Students' League of New York.
Address in 1926, 483 North Grove
Street, East Orange, NJ.

DYER, CHARLES GIFFORD.
Painter. Born in Chicago, 1846.
Graduated from US Naval Academy and
served in Civil War, but resigned,
from ill health, and studied art in
Paris. Among his works, "St.
Mark's Venice," "Venice at Birth of
Day," and "Among the Domes of St.
Mark's".

DYER, H. ANTHONY.
Landscape painter and lecturer.
Born in Providence, on Oct. 23,
1872. Studied in Holland and
France. Member: Providence AC;
Providence WCC; Boston SWCP; AFA;
Newport AA. Work: "The Road that
Leads them Home," water color,
Corcoran Gallery, Washington, DC;
"Marine," Providence RI, Art Club;
"The Jungfrau," watercolor,
permanent collecton RI School of
Design. Address in 1929, 170
Blackstone Blvd., Providence, RI.

DYER, H(ARRY) W.
Painter and illustrator. Born in
Portland, ME, on Nov. 16, 1871.
Pupil of Chas. L. Fox in Portland,
Frank W. Benson, and Ross Turner in
Boston; Voitz Preissig and ASL of
NY; Despradelle. Award: 2nd prize
Beaux Arts, 1896. Address in 1929,
90 Morningside Drive, New York, NY;
East Stroudsburg, PA.

DYER, NANCY A.
Painter. Born in Providence, RI,
in Oct. 20, 1903. Pupil of RI
School of Design; studied in Paris.
Member: Prov. WCC; Prov. AC;
Newport AA. Represented in
Providence Art Club, Providence,
RI. Address in 1929, 170
Blackstone Blvd., Providence, RI.

263

EAKINS, MRS. THOMAS.
Mrs. Eakins copied and restored Sully's portrait of Dr. Philip Syng Physick at the University in 1889.

EAKINS, THOMAS COWPERTHWAIT.
Painter. Born in Phila., July 25, 1844. Studied in the Ecole des Beaux Arts under Gerome and the sculptor Du Mond. Returned to Amer., taught life classes, lectured in anatomy, and became prof. of painting, and dir. of schools at PAFA. Painted portraits and early Amer. domestic life, sporting scenes and incidents in the lives of fishermen and cowboys. His works include composition portraits of Dr. D. Hayes Agnew and Prof. Gross in their clinics; "William Rush Carving an Allegorical Figure of the Schuylkill," and "The Cruxifixion," the latter in Overbrook Seminary. Assisted his pupil, Samuel Murray, in modelling figures of prophets adorning Witherspoon Bldg.; modelled two reliefs for Trenton Battle monument, and the horses of Grant and Lincoln on the Soldiers' and Sailors' monument at Brooklyn. His paintings won awards. Member: NA. Memorial exhib., 150 ptgs., PAFA, 1917-18. Died June 25, 1916.

EARHART, JOHN FRANKLIN.
Landscape painter. Born in OH, March 12, 1853. Member: Cincinnati AC. Award: Landscape prize ($100), Cincinnati AC, 1903. Address in 1929, Fernbank, Cincinnati, Ohio.

EARL, JAMES.
Painter. Born in Mass., May 1, 1761. Brother of Ralph Earle. He painted portraits in Charleston, and died suddenly of yellow fever on Aug. 18, 1796. His portrait of Charles Pinckney is owned by the Worcester Art Museum.

EARL, RALPH ELEASER.
Painter. Son of Ralph Earl, the well-known portrait painter, who died in 1801. Ralph Jr. was born in England, c. 1785, while his father was studying art in that country, and came to the United States with him when he was a child. He studied first with his father, and then went to London in 1809, where he continued his art studies, and to Paris in 1814. He returned from Europe in 1815, arriving in Georgia. From there he went to Tennessee, where he married Miss Caffery, a niece of General Andrew Jackson. He painted in New Orleans and died there Sept. 16, 1838. He was buried at the "Hermitage."

EARL (or EARLE), RALPH.
Painter of portraits and historical scenes. Born in Leicester, Mass., May 11, 1751. He was the author of "Four Scenes of the Battle of Lexington," and was present at the famous march. Amos Doolittle later engraved the subjects. After the war he went to London, where he studied with Benjamin West. He returned to America in 1786. Died in Bolton, Conn., Aug. 16, 1801. (Also signed "Earle.")

EARL (or EARLE), THOMAS.
A little-known American painter who lived at Cherry Valley, Mass. Born 1737, and died 1819. He was a cousin of Ralph Earl, the artist, gunmaker, and soldier of the Revolutionary War. He painted portraits in Connecticut in 1775 and in Charleston, SC, in 1792. His full-length portrait of Dr. Dwight and his wife are in Copley's manner with black shadows.

EARLE, AUGUSTUS.
Artist, and son of James Earle, was admitted as a student at the Royal Academy in 1793. From 1815 to 1832 he traveled in North and South America. When in New York he spent his time with Thomas Cummings the well-known painter of miniatures. Died in 1838.

EARLE, CORNELIA.
Painter and teacher. Born Huntsville, Ala., Nov. 25, 1863. Pupil of G. L. Noyes. Member: Columbia AA; Southern SAL; Carolina AA; North Shore AA. Award: First prize, Columbia AA, 1922. Address in 1929, 1703 Laurel St., Columbia, SC.

264

EARLE, EDWIN.
Painter. Born Somerville, Mass., Dec. 9, 1904. Pupil of Mass. Sch. of Art; ASL of NY; Pruett Carter. Address in 1929, 51 West 16th St., NYC; summer, Derby Line, VT.

EARLE, ELINOR.
Painter. Born Phila. Pupil of PAFA. Member: Plastic C.; Fellowship PAFA; Phila. Alliance. Award: Mary Smith prize, PAFA, 1902; bronze medal, St. Louis Exp., 1904. Address in 1929, 8840 Stenton Ave., Chestnut Hill, Philadelphia, PA.

EARLE, J.
He was engraving portraits in Philadelphia in 1876, in connection with James R. Rice.

EARLE, LAWRENCE CARMICHAEL.
Painter. Born New York City, Nov. 11, 1845; died at Grand Rapids, Nov. 20, 1921. He studied in Munich, Florence and Rome. He was an Associate of the NAD, and a member of the American Water Color Society; Artists' Fund Society; Art Institute of Chicago (honorary); and the NY WCC. Represented in the Art Institute of Chicago, and in the Chicago National Bank. He made a specialty of portraits.

EARLE, OLIVE.
Painter. Born London, Dec. 27, 1888. Work: "Marine Life," Trade Development Board, Bermuda. Address in 1929, 416 West 20th St., New York, NY; summer, Jefferson Valley, NY.

EAST, NATHANIEL S., JR.
Designer and sculptor. Born in Delaware Co., PA, Mar. 21, 1936. Studied at Phila. College of Art; with Herman Cohen. In collections of Glassboro College, NJ; Univ. City Arts Lg., Phila.; Phila. Sch. System; Bell Telephone Co., Phila. Exhibited at Allentown, PA; Antonio Souza Gallery, Mexico City, 1969; Grabar Gal., Phila., 1968; Nat'l. Forum of Prof. Artists, Phila.; etc. Received Nat'l. Ornamental & Misc. Metals Assn. awards, 1978, 80. Mem., Univ. City Arts Lg.; Nat'l. Forum of Prof. Artists; etc.

Author and teacher. Works in pre-used metal objects. Address in 1982, Hatfield, PA.

EASTMAN, CHARLOTTE FULLER.
Painter. Born in Norwich, CT. Studied at PAFA; ASL; Art Inst. of Chicago; Boston Mus. of Fine Arts School; and with Wayman Adams.

EASTMAN, RUTH.
Illustrator. Member: Society of Illustrators, New York; Artists Guild of the Authors' League of America. Address in 1929, 80 West 40th St., New York, NY.

EASTMAN, SETH.
Painter. Born in Brunswick, Maine, Jan. 24, 1808. He graduated from the Military Academy at West Point in 1831, and taught drawing there from 1830-40. He was afterwards stationed with his regiment in the Western states, where he became greatly interested in the Indians. Nine paintings of Indian life and 17 paintings of U. S. forts are in the Capitol Bldg., Washington, DC. He died Aug. 31, 1875, in Wash., DC.

EASTMAN, W(ILLIAM) JOSEPH.
Painter, craftsman, writer and teacher. Born Nov. 14, 1888. Member: Cleveland SA; Cleveland AA. Award: First prize, Penton medal, Cleveland Museum of Art, 1919. Died in 1950. Address in 1929, 1868 East 82nd St., Cleveland, Ohio.

EASTON, LINWOOD.
Etcher. Born Portland, ME, May 17, 1892. Pupil of Albert E. Moore, Alexander Bower. Member: Salma. C.; Portland SA. Died 1939. Address in 1929, 518 Brighton Ave., Portland, ME.

EASTWOOD, R(AYMOND) J(AMES).
Painter and teacher. Born Bridgeport, Conn., May 25, 1898. Pupil of F. V. DuMond, W. S. Kendall, E. C. Taylor. Member: ASL of NY; Provincetown AA. Address in 1929, 317 East Administration Bldg.; h. 1135 Ohio St., Lawrence, Kans.; summer, 53 Sedgwick St., Bridgeport, Conn.

265

EATON, CHARLES FREDERICK.
Painter. Born in Providence, RI,
1842. Lived in Europe until 1886;
settled in Santa Barbara, 1886;
occupied in painting, wood carving
and landscape architecture; made
rare collection of antique carved
furniture and tapestries. An
advocate of the Arts and Crafts
movement in America. Address in
1926, Santa Barbara, Calif.

EATON, CHARLES HARRY.
Painter. Born Dec. 13, 1850, and
died Aug. 4, 1901. First exhibited
at NAD, NY. Gold medal at the
Philadelphia Art Club, 1900,
exhibiting "The Willows." Elected
an Associate Member of the National
Academy of Design in 1893. He
exhibited "The Willows" at the
Paris Exposition in 1889, and at
the World's Fair, Chicago, in 1893.

EATON, CHARLES WARREN.
Landscape painter. Born Albany,
NY, Feb. 22, 1857. Pupil of NAD
and ASL of NY. Member: AWCS;
NYWCC; Salma. C. 1897; A. Fund S.;
Lotos C. Awards: Hon. mention,
Paris Exp., 1900; Proctor prize,
Salma. C., 1901; silver medal,
Charleston Exp., 1902; Inness
prize, Salma. C., 1902; Shaw prize,
Salma. C., 1903; gold medal, Phila.
AC, 1903; Inness gold medal, NAD
1904; silver medal, St. Louis Exp.,
1904; gold medal, Paris Salon,
1906; silver medal, Buenos Aires
Exp., 1910. Work: "Dunes at
Knocke, Belgium," Cincinnati
Museum; "Gathering Mists," National
Gallery, Washington; "Connecticut
Pines," B'klyn Ins. Museum; "The
Strip of Pines," Art Museum,
Montclair, NJ; "Snow Scene" and
"Landscape," Hackley Gallery,
Muskegon, Mich.; "The Tall Pines,"
Nashville, Tenn., Museum; "An
Autumnal Mood," Arnot Art Gallery,
Elmira, NY. Died Sept. 10, 1937.
Address in 1929, 63 Monroe Pl.,
Bloomfield, NJ.

EATON, HUGH McDOUGAL.
Painter and illustrator. Born in
Brooklyn, NY, in 1865. Pupil of
Cox and Chase. Specialty,
illustrations and lead block
prints. Died Sept. 14, 1924, at
Halsey St., Brooklyn, NY.

EATON, JOSEPH ORIEL.
Painter. Born Feb. 8, 1829, i
Licking Co., Ohio. Genre an
portrait painter in oil and wate
colors. He was an Associate of th
National Academy, and a member o
the Society of Painters in Wate
Colors. He visited Europe in 1873
Exhibited at National Academy i
1868, "View on Hudson." He died i
New York on Feb. 7, 1875.

EATON, LOUISE HERRESHOFF.
Painter. Born Providence. Pupi
of Mary C. Wheeler; Constant
Laurens and Collin in Paris
Member: Providence AC; Providenc
WCC; North Shore AA; Gloucester SA
Address in 1929, 11 Charles Fiel
St., Providence, RI; summer, Eas
Gloucester, Mass.

EATON, MARGARET FERNIE.
(Mrs. Hugh M. Eaton). Painter
illustrator and craftsman. Bor
Leamington, England, April 22
1871. Pupil of J. B. Whittaker i
Brooklyn; ASL of NY under Cox an
Mowbray. Member: NY WCC; ASL o
NY (life). Address in 1929, 33
Halsey St., Brooklyn, New York, NY
summer, "The Fircone," Montville
NJ.

EATON, WILLIAM S(YLVESTER).
Painter and etcher. Born i
Waltham, Mass., Dec. 12, 1861
Member: S. Indp. A; Salma. C.
PBC. Address in 1929, Eaton Bldg.
Jermain Ave.; h. The Terrace, Sa
Harbor, LI, NY.

EATON, WYATT.
Painter. Born in Philipsburg
Canada, in 1849; died in Newport
RI, in 1896. Figure and portrai
painter. Pupil of J. O. Eaton, th
National Academy of Design, an
later of Gerome at the Ecole de
Beaux Arts. He was the first
secretary of the Society o
American Artists. He painte
"Ariadne," and is represented a
the Boston Museum of Fine Arts b
"Mother and Child."

EBBELS, VICTORIA.
Painter. Born in Hasbrouc
Heights, NJ, in 1900. Pupil o
George Luks and Robert Henri
Member of the Society o
Independent Artists. Address i

266

1926, 1213 Carrier St., Denton, Texas.

EBERBACH, ALICE KINSEY.
Painter. Born in Philadelphia, June 16, 1872. Pupil of Courtois, Girardot, Henri, Chase. Member: Fellowship PAFA. Address in 1929, 441 West Safford St., Germantown, Philadelphia, PA.

EBERHARD, ROBERT GEORGE.
Sculptor and teacher. Born Geneva, Switzerland, June 28, 1884. Pupil of MacNeil, Mercie, Carlier, Peter, Rodin. Member: Societe des Artistes Francais; Artistes du Cher; New Haven PCC. Head of Department of Sculpture at Yale Univ. Work: War Memorial tablets, White Plains (NY) High School; flagstaff base, Public School No. 9, Brooklyn; war memorial, Rosedale, NY. Address in 1929, 154 West 55th St., New York, NY.

EBERLE, ABASTENIA St. LEGER.
Sculptor. She was born in Webster City, IA, April 6, 1878. Pupil of ASL of NY; George Grey Barnard. Member: ANA; NSS; Allied AA; AFA. Awards: Bronze medal, St. Louis Exp., 1904; Barnett prize, NAD 1910; bronze medal, P.-P. Exposition, San Francisco, 1915; prize Garden C. of Am., 1929. Work: "Girl on Roller Skates" and "Mowgli," Metropolitan Museum, New York; "Windy Doorstep," Worcester Art Museum; Peabody Art Inst., Baltimore; Newark Museum and Carnegie Inst., Pittsburgh; "Little Mother," Chicago Art Institute; "The Dancer," Venice, Italy, and Twentieth Century Club, Buffalo, NY; "Rag Time," Toledo Art Museum; "Hurdy Gurdy," Detroit Institute; general excellence trophy, "Iron Man," Pacific and Asiatic Fleet. Died Feb. 26, 1942, in New York City. Address in 1929, 204½ West 13th St., New York, NY.

EBERT, CHARLES H.
Painter. Born Milwaukee, Wis., July 20, 1873. Pupil of Cincinnati Art Academy; ASL of NY; Julian Academy in Paris. Member: Greenwich SA; Salma. C.; Lyme AA; Wis. PS. Awards: Bronze medal, Buenos Aires Exp., 1910; silver medal, P.-P. Exp., San F., 1915;

Milwaukee Sentinel prize, 1927. Address in 1929, Lyme, Conn.; summer, Monhegan Island, ME.

EBERT, MARY ROBERTS.
(Mrs. Charles H. Ebert). Painter and craftsman. Born Titusville, PA, Feb. 8, 1873. Pupil of ASL of NY; Twachtman; Hunt in Boston. Member: AWCS; N.A. Women P.S. Address in 1929, Lyme, Conn.; summer, Monhegan Island, ME.

EBY, KERR.
Illustrator. Born in Japan in 1889. The son of Canadian Methodist missionaries, he came to America at age 18 to study at PI and the ASL. He produced a very popular volume entitled War, from his sketches of France in World War I, which was published by Yale University Press in 1936. He spent most of World War II in the Pacific where he produced many sketches. Other illustrations of his appeared in books and magazines such as Life and The Century. An extensive collection of his work is housed at the New York Public Library. Died in 1946.

ECHERT, FLORENCE.
Painter and craftsman. Born Cincinnati, Ohio. Pupil of Cincinnati AA; ASL of NY; W. M. Chase. Member: Cincinnati Woman's AC. Address in 1929, The Valencia, 276 St. George St., St. Augustine, Fla.; summer, "Little Chalet," Intervale, White Mountains, NH.

ECKE, BETTY TSENG YU-HO.
See Tseng Yu-Ho.

ECKFORD, JESSIEJO.
Painter. Born Dallas, Texas, Nov. 21, 1895. Pupil of Aunspaugh Art School, Hale Bolton, Frank Reaugh, and Felicie Waldo Howell. Member: Dallas Art Assoc.; S. Indp. A.; Highland Park SA; SSAL; Tex. S. FA; AFA. Awards: Bronze medal, 1916, gold medal, 1919, Dallas Woman's Forum Exhibit; prize, Davis wildflower comp., San Antonio. Address in 1929, Wallnut Hill Lane, Dallas, Texas.

ECKSTEIN, JOHN.
Portrait painter, modeler and engraver. Born in Germany 1750 and

died 1817. In proposals for a "Representation of a Monument of Gen. Washington," he is referred to as "formerly historical painter and statuary to the King of Prussia." His name was in Phila. directories of 1796-97 and 1805-06 as "Limner and Statuary;" 1811-16 was listed as "Engraver." Was still painting and engraving in 1822. Eckstein's few portrait plates are inscribed "Painted and Engraved by John Eckstein," and executed in comb. of stipple and roulette work, hard in effect. In 1806 he modeled statue of Washington for above proposed monument, and engraved the plate of that subject for the Soc. of the Cincinnatus. In 1809 he engraved illustrations for Freneau's poems, pub. by Lydia R. Bailey, of Phila. Although German, should not be confused with Johannes Eckstein, a German portrait painter and engraver in mezzotint, who died in London 1798.

EDDY, HENRY B.
Illustrator. Born New York, NY, Sept. 16, 1872. Member: SI 1914; New Rochelle AA. Died in 1935. Address in 1929, care of N.Y. Sunday American, 2 Duane St., New York, NY; h. Mamaroneck, NY.

EDDY, HENRY S(TEPHENS).
Painter. Born Rahway, NJ, Dec. 31, 1878. Pupil of Volk, Cox, Twachtman, ASL of NY, Alphonse Mucha and Geo. E. Browne. Member: Salma. C.; Beachcombers of Provincetown; Artists Fellowship; A. Fund S.; Provincetown AA; Guild of Am. Painters; Allied AA; Westfield AA; Amer. Assn. of Museums; Lotos C; Plainfield AA; New Haven PCC; Phila. Alliance; Am. APL; AFA. Work: "In from the Nets," Milwaukee Art Inst.; "St. Michaels at Passaic," Reid Memorial Library, Passaic, NJ; "Finse in June," Arnot Art Gallery, Elmira; "A Nantucket Doorway," Junior Art League of Miss Hutchinson's School, Memphis, Tenn.; "Cranford River," Free Public Library, Cranford, NJ; "Winter," Westfield High School; "The Path through the Woods," First National Bank, Plainfield, NJ; "Ravello, Italy," Lotos Club, NY.

Died in 1944. Address in 1929, Springfield Road, Westfield, NJ.

EDDY, ISAAC.
Engraver. Born in Weathersfield, VT, Feb. 17, 1777. He engraved some crude plates for the "First Vermont Edition of a Bible," published at Windsor, VT, by Merifield & Cochran. Mentioned as an engraver, or possibly as a land-surveyor. Was probably connected with Pendleton's engraving establishment in Boston. Died July 25, 1847, in Waterford, NY.

EDDY, JAMES.
Engraver. Born May 29, 1806, was living in Providence, RI, 1881. He was a good engraver of portraits in the stipple manner, and was working as early as 1827 to 1830 in Boston. Died May 18, 1888, in Providence.

EDDY, OLIVER TARBELL.
Engraver. A folio map of New Hampshire with an inset view of Bellows Falls engraved in line is signed "O. T. Eddy, engraver, Walpole (N.H.) Aug. 1817."

EDDY, SARAH JAMES.
Sculptor. Born Boston in 1851. Exhibited portrait bust of Samuel S. Fleisher, at the Penna. Academy of Fine Arts, Philadelphia, 1914. Address in 1926, Bristol Ferry, RI.

EDELSON, MARY BETH.
Mixed Media, lecturer and conceptual artist. Studied: The Art Institute of Chicago; DePauw University; New York University. Awarded a National Endowment Grant, 1973. Exhibitions: Indianapolis Museum of Art, formerly John Herron Museum, 1968; Corcoran Gallery of Art, Washington, DC, 1973; Ringling Mus. of Art, Sarasota, FL, 1974. Collections: Corcoran Gallery of Art; Joe Cantor Collection; Sheldon Swope Gallery. Media: Conceptual works, sculpture, photos, books, performance art, drawings, posters. Address in 1980, 110 Mercer Street, New York, NY.

EDENS, ANNETTE.
Painter, craftsman and teacher.
Born Guemos, Wash., April 16, 1892.
Pupil of Dow, Hawthorne. Member:
Seattle FAS. Address in 1929,
University of Washington, Seattle,
Wash.; summer, Eldridge Farm,
Bellingham, Wash.

EDERHEIMER, RICHARD.
Portrait painter. Born Frankfort,
Germany, 1878. Died 1934 in New
York. Member: League of New York
Artists; Society of Independent
Artists. Address in 1926, 18 East
57th St., New York.

EDGERLY, MIRA.
See Korzybska.

EDHOLM, C(HARLTON) L(AWRENCE).
Painter, illustrator and writer.
Born Omaha, Neb., Mar. 21, 1879.
Pupil of Ludwig Herterich in
Munich. Address in 1929, 7 Main
St., Dobbs Ferry, NY.

EDMISTON, ALICE R.
Painter. Born Monroe, Wis. Pupil
of AIC; ASL of NY and studied in
Paris. Award: Prize ($100), Omaha
SFA, 1923. Represented in
Vanderpoel AA. Collection, Chicago.
Address in 1929, 1900 South 40th
St., Lincoln, Neb.

EDMOND, ELIZABETH.
Sculptor. Born 1887 in Portland,
ME. Exhibited at the PAFA,
Philadelphia, 1914. Died June 22,
1918, in Pasadena, Calif.

EDMONDS, ESTHER TOPP.
Painter. Born in New York City,
1888. Daughter of A. Edmonds, She
began her art studies with her
father, subsequently studied at
Cooper Union and Art Students'
League of NY, graduated with
honors. After completing her
studies, she became associated with
her father. In 1910 he opened a
studio in Columbia, SC, where she
continued to work with him. After
his death, she continued her
profession of portrait painter, and
painted portraits of many prominent
men.

EDMONDS, FRANCIS WILLIAM.
Painter. Born in Hudson, NY, Nov.
22, 1806. He was a genre painter

who had little art education. He
was employed as a cashier in a New
York bank. In 1840 he was elected
a member of the National Academy.
He died Feb. 7, 1863, in New York
City.

EDMONDSON, WILLIAM JOHN.
Painter. Born Norwalk, Ohio, 1868.
Pupil of Academy of the Fine Arts,
Phila., under Vonnoh and Chase;
Julian Academy, Paris, under
Lefebvre; Aman-Jean Academy, Paris.
Member: Fellowship PAFA; Cleveland
SA; Cleveland AA. Awards: Second
Toppan prize, PAFA; European
traveling scholarship, PAFA; first
prize, figure painting; popular
vote prize and Penton medal,
Cleveland Museum of Art, 1919; 1st
prize for decorative and mural
painting, Cleveland Museum, 1923.
Work in: Delgado Art Museum, New
Orleans; Cleveland Museum; Western
Reserve University; Society for
Savings, Cleveland; Fellowship
PAFA, Philadelphia; State House,
Columbus, Ohio; Municipal
Collection, Cleveland. Address in
1929, 2362 Euclid Ave., Cleveland,
Ohio; h. 2812 Scarborough Rd.,
Cleveland Heights, Ohio.

EDMUNDSON, CAROLYN.
Painter. Born in Pittsburgh, PA,
1906. Studied: Carnegie
Institute, College of Fine Arts;
Columbia University. Awards:
Nevada Art Association, 1952;
Society Western Art, 1954.
Collections: Nevada State Museum,
Carson City; still life paintings,
advertising illustrations for
Cannon Mills, Forstmann Woolens,
Yardleys of London and many others.

EDROP, ARTHUR (NORMAN).
Painter and illustrator. Born
Birmingham, England, May 15, 1884.
Pupil of Whittaker in Boston.
Member: Phila. Sketch C.; SI; Art
Directors C. Illustrator for
"Life," "Collier's Weekly," "Ladies
Home Journal," etc. Specialty,
Advertising art. Address in 1929,
"Topping," Hilaire Rd., St.
David's, PA.

EDSTROM, DAVID.
Sculptor, writer, lecturer and
teacher. Born Hvetlanda, Sweden,
March 27, 1873. Pupil of Borjison,

Royal Acad., Stockholm; Injalbert in Paris. Member: Los Angeles PS; So. Calif. Sculptors C.; Scandinavian Artists of NY; Calif. PSC. Award: Silver medal World's Fair, St. Louis, 1904. Work: "Soldiers Monument," Ottumwa, Iowa; "Isis" and "Nepthys," Masonic Temple, Washington, DC; War memorial relief, Montreal, Canada; Statue of Judge G. F. Moore, Scottish Rite Temple, Dallas, Tex.; "Athlete," National Museum, Stockholm, Sweden; "Cry of Poverty," "Caliban," "Portrait of Baron Beck-Friis" and "Portrait of Dr. Romdahl" in Gothenburg Museum, Sweden; reliefs in the Faehrens Gallery, Stockholm; "Portrait of the Crown Prince of Sweden," and "Portrait of Princess Patricia of Connaught," in the Royal Palace, Stockholm; Statue of "Gen. P. Cochran," Dallas, Tex.; Statue, M. H. Whittier, Los Angeles; Strickland Memorial, Dallas, Tex.; "The Hunchback," "Caliban," "February," "Peasant," "Old Italian Soldier," "Two Souls," "Grotesque," "Ernest Thiel," "Prometheus," National Museum, Stockholm. Died in 1938. Address in 1929, Hollywood Plaza Hotel, Los Angeles, Calif.

EDWARDS, EDWARD B.
Painter, illustrator and draughtsman. Born Columbia, PA, Feb. 8, 1873. Studied in Paris and Munich. Member: NY Arch. Lg., 1892; A.L. Graphic A.; Salma. C.; GFLA.

EDWARDS, ELLENDER MORGAN.
Graphic artist and photographer. Born in Hagerstown, MD. Studied: The Maryland Institute of Art; George Washington University, Washington, DC; ASL. Awards: Rockville, Maryland N.L.A.P.W.; Shepherd College, West Virginia; Waterford Foundation, Inc., Virginia. Exhibitions: University of Arizona; De Young Museum, California; Montgomery College, Maryland. Address in 1980, Rockville, MD.

EDWARDS, GEORGE WHARTON.
Painter, illustrator and writer. Born Fair Haven, CT, in 1869. Studied in Antwerp and in Paris.

Member: NYWCC; AWCS; (life) NAC; SI; Am. Inst. of Arts and Letters; PS. Awards: Bronze and silver medals, Boston, 1884 and 1890; bronze medal, Pan-Am. Expo., Buffalo, 1901, for painting, and hon. mention for drawing; silver medal, Charleston Expo., 1902; medal, Barcelona, Spain, 1902; medal of King Albert, 1920; Golden Palms of French Acad., 1921; Knight Chevalier, Legion d'Honneur, France, for "Eminent Services in Art," 1925; Knight Chevalier, Order de la Couronne Belge, for "Distinction in Art," 1927; Royal Order of Knight Chevalier (Isabella) from Alfonso XIII, Spain, 1928, for eminent distinction in Art. Manager art dept. at Collier's 1898-1903; Amer. Bank Note Co. since 1904. Work: Mural decoration, "Henrik Hudson," U.S. Miltary Acad; illustrated Austin Dobson's "Sun Dial"; "Old English Ballads," "The Last Leaf," by O. W. Holmes, etc. Author of "Alsace-Lorraine," "Vanished Towers and Chimes of Flanders," "Vanished Halls and Cathedrals of France," "Holland of Today," "Belgium, Old and New," "Paris," "London," "Spain," "Rome." Died in 1950. Address in 1929, Greenwich, Conn.

EDWARDS, HARRY C.
Painter and illustrator. Born Philadelphia, PA, Nov. 29, 1868. Pupil of Adelphi College, Brooklyn, under J. B. Whittaker; Art Students' League of New York under Mowbray. Member: Brooklyn Society of Artists. Illustrated "The Gun Brand," "Blackwater Bayou," etc. Died in Brooklyn, NY, May 9, 1922.

EDWARDS, KATE F(LOURNOY).
Painter. Born Marshallville, GA, in 1877. Pupil of AIC; and Simon in Paris. Member: The Cordon, Chicago; Atlanta AA; Atlanta FAC; Atlanta Studio Club. Awards: 1st prize, Southeastern Fair Expo., 1916, Atlanta, GA; 1st prize, Atlanta AA, 1921. Work: Portraits of Judge Barbour, property of U.S. Gov., Wash., DC; Gov. Slaton, property of State of Georgia; Senator A. S. Clay, Georgia State Capitol; Jos. Clisby, Clisby Sch., Macon, GA; Gov. M. B. Wellborn, Fed. Reserve Bank, Atlanta; Dr. I.

S. Hopkins and Dr. William H. Emerson, Georgia Sch. of Technology, Atlanta; Judge Cincinnatus Peeples, Fulton Co. Courthouse, Altanta; Dean Robert J. Sprague, Rollins College, Winter Park, FL; Dr. John E. White, Wake Forest College, NC; George Muse, Geo. Muse Clothing Co., Atlanta; Stanley M. Hastings, O'Keefe Junr. High School, Atlanta, GA. Address in 1929, Pershing Point Apts., Atlanta, GA.

EDWARDS, ROBERT.
Painter and illustrator. Born Buffalo, NY, Oct. 4, 1879. Pupil of ASL of Buffalo; ASL of NY; Chase School; Eric Pape School and Cowles School in Boston. Member: SI, 1910; Salons of Am.; S. Indp. A. Illustrated "Eve's Second Husband;" Composed "The Song Book of Robert Edwards." Died in 1948. Address in 1929, 144 Macdougal St., New York, NY.

EDWARDS, SAMUEL ARENT.
Engraver. Born in 1862 in Somersetshire, England, living in New York in 1905. Mr. Edwards was a student at the Kensington Art School in 1877-81, and was then taught to engrave in mezzotint by Appleton, Josey & Alais, of London. He first exhibited examples of his engraving in the Royal Academy in 1885. In 1890 Mr. Edwards came to the United States, established himself in New York, and made book illustrations, portraits, and subject plates. He successfully revived the art of printing in colors from mezzotinto plates, and deservedly achieved a reputation. His color plates were issued without touching up with water colors, as was often the custom in prints of this description. Died in 1935.

EDWARDS, THOMAS.
Silhouettist, and portrait painter in oils and miniatures. Flourished 1822-56 in Boston, Mass. He was a frequent exhibitor in the early years of the Boston Athenaeum, and also contributed drawings to the first lithographic press in Boston, established in 1825 by the Pendleton Brothers.

EDWARDS, WILLIAM ALEXANDER.
Illustrator. Born in NYC in 1924. Studied: Whitney Art School in Manor Haven under Alfred Freundeman. His first published illustration was a cover, entitled Big Nickelodeon, for Bantam Books. Since 1962, he has illustrated for magazines and books, the most notable being his covers for Herman Hesse's novels Demian, Steppenwolf, and Magister Ludi: The Glass Bead Game. A prolific portrait artist, he has had work exhibited in galleries in Bridgeport and Waterbury, CT.

EDWIN, DAVID.
Engraver. Born in Bath, England, in Dec. 1776. He was a son of John Edwin, an English actor. David Edwin was apprenticed to a Dutch engraver, Jossi, who was residing in England, but who returned to Holland, with Edwin. Edwin disagreed with his master and went to Philadelphia in 1797. He found a friend and employer in T. B. Freeman, for whom he engraved the title-page for "Scotch Airs," by Benjamin Carr. He was later assistant to Edward Savage. Lack of tools, poor quality of obtainable plates and rude printing led him to totally change his method completely. For 30 years he was the most prolific workman in America. Failing health and overwork impaired his sight, and about 1830 he ceased work. In 1835 he became treasurer of the newly formed "Artists' Fund Society of Philadelphia," and also received a bequest from a friend which made his last years comfortable. These details are from a biographical sketch in "Catalogue of the Engraved Work of David Edwin," by Mantle Fielding, Philadelphia, 1905. His engravings were in stipple and were beautifully finished. Among his best known plates are Thomas McKean, Thomas Jefferson, Dolly Madison, and a number of General Washington. Died in Phila., Feb. 22, 1841.

EGGELING, HERMAN.
Painter and teacher. Born New York, NY, Aug. 17, 1884. Pupil of Bridgman and Sloan. Member: Bronx AG. Illustrated "Encyclopedia of

Foods," by Artemas Ward. Specialty, landscape painting. Address in 1929, 106 Pleasant Ave., Tuckahoe, NY.

EGGEMEYER, MAUDE KAUFMAN.
Painter. Born New Castle, Ind., Dec. 9, 1877. Pupil of J. E. Bundy; Gifford Beal; Cincinnati Art Academy. Member: Chicago Gal. A; Ind. AC; Richmond Palette C.; Cincinnati Women's AC. Awards: Beaumont Parks prize, Hoosier Salon, 1924; Crilly prize, Hoosier Salon, 1927; Salon Patrons Assn. prize, 1928. Address in 1929, "Twin Oaks," Richmond, Ind.

EGGERS, GEORGE WILLIAM.
Lithographer, writer and lecturer. Born Dunkirk, NY, Jan. 31, 1883. Pupil of Pratt Institute. Member: Chic. AC; Denver Cactus Club; Worcester C; Assn. Art Mus. Dir. Director Worcester Museum of Art. Died in 1958. Address in 1929, 76 West St., Worcester, Mass.

EGGLESTON, BENJAMIN.
Painter. Born Belvidere, Minn., Jan. 22, 1867. Pupil of Minneapolis School of Fine Arts under Douglas Volk and studied in Paris. Member: Brooklyn AC; Brooklyn WCC; Salma. C.; 1903; Brooklyn SA; Allied A.A.; PS; AFA; Scandinavian Am. A. Died in Feb., 1937. Address in 1929, 164 East 22nd St., Brooklyn, NY; summer, West Stockbridge, Mass.

EGGLESTON, EDWARD M.
Painter and illustrator. Born Ashtabula, Ohio, Nov. 22, 1887. Pupil of John N. Piersche, Albert Fowley, Alice Schilly, Harvey Dunn. Member: GFLA; SI. Address in 1929, 59 West 35th St., NYC, h. 109-61-198th St., Hollis, Long Is., NY; summer, Twin Lakes, Conn.

EHNINGER, JOHN WHETTEN.
Painter. Born July 22, 1827, in New York. He studied abroad and afterwards painted a number of genre studies of American life. His best known paintings are "New England Farmyard," "Yankee Peddler," "Lady Jane Grey." He also produced illustrations in outline and a series of etchings. Elected a member of the National Academy in 1860. Died Jan. 22, 1889, in Saratoga, NY.

EICHHOLTZ, JACOB.
Painter. Born Nov. 2, 1776, of an old family of German origin in Lancaster, Penn. He was an expert coppersmith who developed a talent for portrait drawing. Early in the century he was aided by visiting artists, and when Thos. Sully visited Lancaster, before his departure for Europe in 1809, he directed him to the instruction of Gilbert Stuart in Boston. He took with him his best known portrait (of Nicholas Biddle, with the US Bank in the background.) He later settled in Phila. as a portrait painter for 10 years. In the style of Sully and Stuart, he painted over 250 portraits and some landscapes and historical groups, between 1810 and his death in 1842. Among his subjects were Chief Justices Marshall and Gibson; Governors Shulze, Porter and Ritner; Attorneys Gen. Elder, Franklin and Champneys; Nicholas Biddle and many of the foremost people of his day in Phila., Baltimore, Harrisburg and Lancaster.

EILERS, EMMA.
Painter and craftsman. Born New York. Pupil of ASL of NY under Cox, Chase, Mowbray, Beckwith and Du Mond. Member: ASL of NY; NY Woman's AC. Address in 1929, 751 St. Marks Ave., Brooklyn, New York, NY; summer, Littleworth Lane, Sea Cliff, LI, NY.

EILSHEMIUS, L(OUIS) M(ICHEL).
Painter, illustrator, craftsman and writer. Born Laurel Hill, Arlington, NJ, Feb. 4, 1864. Pupil of Schenker, Robert C. Minor, Van Luppen, Julian in Paris. Member: Modern AA; AFA; Salons of America; Societe Anonyme. Died in 1941. Address in 1929, 118 East 57th St., New York, NY.

EIMER, ELSA.
Painter. Member: S. Indp. A. Address in 1929, 209 East 19th St., New York, NY.

272

EINSEL, NAIAD.
Illustrator. Born in Phila. in 1927. Graduated from PI in 1947, beginning her career the next year with an illustration for Seventeen. Since 1950, her work has appeared in many major magazines and in exhibitions at the S of I, ADC and Greengrass Gallery. Among her many poster assignments was the Westport Bicentennial Quilt in 1976 which she designed and which 33 Westport women hand-stitched, under the guidance of J. L. McCabe.

EINSEL, WALTER.
Illustrator. Born in NY in 1926. Attended PSD and graduated from the ASL and the Brooklyn Museum School. In 1953, his first work was published in The New York Times Magazine. He has since illustrated many magazines and books. His pen and ink and three-dimensional artwork has been exhibited at the Museum of Contemporary Crafts, Montreal Expo, and the Fairtree and Greengrass Galleries in NY.

EISENBACH, DOROTHY L.
Painter and teacher. Born Lafayette, Ind. Pupil of William Forsyth, Felicie Waldo Howell. Award: J. I. Holcomb prize ($100), Indiana Artists Exhibition, 1929. Address in 1929, John Herron Art Institute, Indianapolis, Ind.; h. 627 Owen St., Lafayette, Ind.

EISENLOHR, E. G.
Painter, lecturer and teacher. Born Cincinnati, Ohio, Nov. 9, 1872. Pupil of R. J. Onderdonk and F. Reaugh in Texas; Academy Karlsruhe, Germany, under G. Schoenleber. Member: Salma. C; AFA. Work: "The Sentinel of the Canyon," Dallas Public Art Gallery; Elizabeth Ney Mus., Austin, Tex. Author of "Study and Enjoyment of Pictures," "Tendencies in Art and Their Significance," "Landscape Painters." Died in 1961. Address in 1929, 324 Eads Ave., Station A, Dallas, Tex.

ELAND, JOHN SHENTON.
Painter, illustrator and etcher. Born Market Harborough, England, March 4, 1872. Pupil of Sargent. Member: AFA. Medalist of the Royal Academy, England. Represented by

etching in Brooklyn Museum. Died in 1933. Address in 1929, 205 West 57th St., New York, NY.

ELDER, ARTHUR J(OHN).
Painter, etcher, teacher and craftsman. Born London, England, March 28, 1874. Pupil of Walter Sickert, Theodore Roussel, Charles Huard, David Muirhead, James Pryde. Member: Chelsea AC; Junior Art Workers Guild, London. Award: Medal, Crystal Palace, London, 1901. Died c. 1951. Address in 1929, Westport, Conn.

ELDER, JOHN ADAMS.
Painter of portraits and battle subjects. Born Fredericksburg, VA, Feb. 3, 1833. In his early youth he was a cameo carver. Pupil of the Duesseldorf Academy and of Emanuel Leutze. Won prize at Duesseldorf Academy. He painted portraits of General Robert Edward Lee and General T. J. Jackson. Died Feb. 24, 1895.

ELDRED, L. D.
Marine artist and etcher. Was born in Fairhaven, Mass. He studied in Julien Studio in Paris. On his return to this country he opened his studio in Boston, where his work has been much sought after.

ELDRIDGE.
Engraver. A line engraving of a residence, "Hickory Grove," is signed as "Drawn by J. Collins, Engraved by Eldrige." It is a good work and appears in "The Miscellaneous Writings of Samuel J. Smith, of Burlington, NJ," Philadelphia, 1836.

ELDRIDGE, CHARLES W.
Miniature painter. Born in New London, Conn., in Nov., 1811. He lived for years in Hartford, Conn. He also painted many miniatures in the South. He was a member for years of the old firm of miniature painters, Parker & Eldridge. Died in 1883.

ELIA, ALBERT.
Illustrator. Born in Beirut, Lebanon, in 1941. Studied for five years at the Beaux Arts in Paris and PSD in NY. Mademoiselle published his first illustration in

1964 and he has since worked for Harper's *Bazaar*, *The New York Times*, and *Seventeen*. Since 1970, he has been involved in film and photography.

ELKINS, HENRY ARTHUR.
Painter. Born in Vershire, VT, in 1847. He moved to Chicago in 1856 and taught himself to paint. Among his pictures are "Mount Shasta," "New Eldorado," and the "Crown of the Continent." Died in Colorado 1884.

ELLERHUSEN, F(LORENCE) COONEY.
Painter and teacher. Born Canada. Pupil of Chase, Vanderpoel; AIC; ASL of NY; George Luks. Member: Allied AA; NA Women PS. Died in 1950. Address in 1929, 939-8th Ave., New York, NY; summer, Towaco, NJ.

ELLERHUSEN, ULRIC H(ENRY).
Sculptor and teacher. Born in Germany, April 7, 1879; came to America at age of 15. Pupil of AIC; Lorado Taft; ASL of NY; Karl Bitter. Member: NSS 1912; NY Arch. Lg. 1914; Beaux-Arts Inst. of D. (hon.), 1916; Allied AA; AFA. Awards: First prize in competition for medal for St. Louis Art Lg.; medal of honor for Sculpture, NY. Arch. Lg., 1929. Work: "Contemplation," "Wonderment," "Meditation" and "Frieze of Garland Bearers," exterior decorations, Fine Arts Bldg. San F.; Schwab Mem. Fountain, Yale University Campus, New Haven, CT; medal for St. Louis Art Lg.; Penna Mem. medal to employees of the Penna. R. R. in military service; Peace monument and allegorical portraits of "Confucius," "Columbus," "Pocahontas," and "Douglass," Elmwood Park, East Orange, NJ; 3 reliefs illustrating "Life of Douglass," F. Douglass Mem. Home, Wash., DC; Edward Austin Abbey II, Mem., U. of Penna.; portrait of Very Rev. Walter G. Moran, St. Vincent Ferrer Church, NY; Communion Rail, Church of St. Gregory the Great, NY; The People's Home Journal medal; portrait of Prof. Alexander Smith, U. of Chicago; St. Michael Relief, St. Mary's College, Notre Dame, Ind.; "The March of Religion," South

Front Chapel, U. of Chicago; also "Morning," "Evening," "Prophet," "Priest," "Learning," "Science," portraits of "Bach," "Wilson," "Roosevelt." Exterior of Christ Church, Cranbrook, Mich.; buttress finial statues of Guttenberg, Pasteur, W. Wright, Penan, Pere Marquette, Phillips Brooks, Bishop Williams, Bishop Page, Dr. Samuel Marquis. "They came and stood at the Cross," (John and Mary); Church of the Heavenly Rest, NY Symbolism, main entrance, "Moses" and "St. John Baptist." Died in 1957. Address in 1929, 939 Eighth Ave.; 16 East 23rd St., New York NY; Towaco, NJ.

ELLERTSON, HOMER E.
Painter and illustrator. Born River Falls, Wisc., Dec. 23, 1892 Pupil of Pratt Inst., Brooklyn, NY M. de la Cluse, Naudin and Miller in Paris. Member: Scandinavian American SA; SSAL; AFA. Work "The Encore" and "The Ebro," Phillips Memorial Gallery Washington, DC. Died in 1935 Address in 1929, "El-Taarn," Tryon NC.

ELLICOTT, HENRY JACKSON.
Sculptor. Born in Anne Arundel County, MD, 1848; died in Washington, DC, Feb. 11, 1901 Studied drawing at the National Academy of Design; also studied under Brumidi, Powell, and Leutze.

ELLIOT, GEORGE.
A little-known American portrait painter born in 1776; he died in 1852. His portrait of Mr. Van Dusen, of Connecticut, was signed He was said to have been an Academician, but the published lists of the National Academy of Design do not note his name.

ELLIOTT, BENJAMIN F.
Landscape and portrait painter Born Sept. 26, 1829, in Middletown Conn. He painted many portraits for Kellogg Brothers, in Hartford He died Sept. 6, 1870.

ELLIOTT, CHARLES LORING.
Portrait painter. Born in Scipio NY, Oct. 12, 1812. He came to New York City about 1834, and became the pupil of John Trumbull. I

274

1846 he was elected a member of the National Academy of Design. He was said to have painted more than seven hundred portraits of prominent men of his time. His portraits are in all the prominent galleries. He died in Albany, NY, Aug. 25, 1868.

ELLIOTT, ELIZABETH SHIPPEN GREEN. (Mrs. Huger Elliott). Illustrator. Born Philadelphia, PA. Pupil of PAFA and of Howard Pyle. Member: Phila. WCC; NYWCC; SI (assoc.) 1903; Fellowship PAFA; Plastic C; Providence AC; Concord AA; Phila. Alliance; AFA. Awards: Second Corcoran prize, Wash. WCC, 1904; bronze medal, St. Louis Exp., 1904; Mary Smith prize, PAFA, 1905; Beck prize, Phila. WCC, 1907; silver medal, P.-P. Exp., San F., 1915. Work: Magazine and Book Illustrations; exclusively on staff Harpers Magazine, 1902-11; illustrated edition Lambs Tales from Shakespeare, 1922; Old Country House, 1902; Aurelie, 1912; "The Book of the Little Past," 1908; Riverland, 1904; Rebecca Mary, 1905; A Daughter of the Rich, 1924; Bred in the Bone, 1925, Little Hop Skippel, 1926; Bryn Mawr Coll. May Day Program, 1924 and 1928. Address in 1929, 114 East 90th St., New York, NY.

ELLIOTT, HANNAH. Painter, miniature painter, illustrator and teacher. Born Atlanta, GA, Sept. 29, 1876. Studied in America and Europe. Award: Third prize for Miniature, All Southern Exhibition, Charleston, SC., 1921. Address in 1929, 2036-13th Ave., South, Birmingham, Ala.

ELLIOTT, JOHN. Painter. Born in England, 1858. Student in Julien's Academy. Pupil of Carolus Duran, Paris; Jose di Villegas at Rome. Subjects, chiefly portraits and mural decorations, some of the more notable in America being "The Vintage," frieze and ceiling in house of Mrs. Potter Palmer, Chicago; "The Triumph of Time," ceiling decoration in Boston Public Library; "Diana of the Tides," mural painting in new National

Museum, Washington. Represented in permanent collection of Old State House, Boston, and collection of H. M. the Dowager Queen of Italy. Died May 26, 1925.

ELLIS, EDMUND L(EWIS). Painter, etcher and artist. Born Omaha, Neb., Oct. 30, 1872. Pupil of G. B. Post; McKim, Mead and White. Member: NY Arch. Lg.; Bronz AG; NSS; AIA; AFA. Work: Marble reredos and Church decorations, St. James Protestant Episcopal Church, Fordham, and interiors of Park Central Hotel, New York City. Address in 1929, 25 West 43rd St.; h. 2341 Andrews Ave., New York, NY.

ELLIS, EDWIN M. Born 1841. This engraver of portraits and landscape, working both in stipple and in line, was in business in Philadelphia in 1844. Died in 1895.

ELLIS, FREMONT F. Painter, etcher and teacher. Born Virginia City, Mont., Oct. 2, 1897. Pupil of ASL of NY. Member: Calif. AC; Santa Fe Art Club; Los Cinco Pintores. Address in 1929, Camino del Monte Sol, Santa Fe, NM.

ELLIS, GEORGE B. Engraver. In 1821 Ellis was a pupil of the Philadelphia engraver Francis Kearny, and in 1825-37, inclusive, he was in business for himself in the same city. His name disappears from the Philadelphia directories in 1838. Ellis first attracted attention as an engraver by his excellent copies of English engravings, which he made for an edition of "Ivanhoe." He produced some very good portraits, but his best work is found among his small "Annual" plates.

ELLIS, HARRIET. Painter and draughtsman. Born Springfield, Mass., April 4, 1886. Pupil of Hawthorne, Mabel Welch, Johonnot, Albertus Jones, Cecilia Beaux, Pratt Inst. Member: NA Women PS; Springfield AL; Springfield AG. Specialty: Portraits in oil, sepia-pencil, silhouette. Address in 1929, 158 Sherman St., Springfield, Mass.

275

ELLIS, JOSEPH BAILEY.
Sculptor and teacher. Born North Scituate, Mass., May 24, 1890. Pupil of Albert H. Munsell, Bela Pratt; Peter and Injalbert in Paris. Member: Copley S.; Boston Arch. C.; Pittsburgh AA; Salma. C. Died Jan. 24, 1950. Address in 1929, College of Fine Arts, Carnegie Inst. of Technology; h. 5546 Pocusset St., Pittsburgh, PA; summer, Boothbay, Maine.

ELLIS, MAUDE MARTIN.
Painter and illustrator. Born Watseka, Ill., Feb. 7, 1892. Pupil of J. Wellington Reynolds. Address in 1929, Beil Bldg., 19 East Pearson St., Chicago, Ill.

ELLIS, SALATHIEL.
A painter of cameo likenesses. Born in 1860. Flourished 1845-46 in New York.

ELLIS, WILLIAM H.
Line-engraver. He was a good line-engraver of landscape and book illustrations. His work appears in Philadelphia publications of 1845-47.

ELLSWORTH, JAMES SANFORD.
Miniature painter. Born in Windsor, Conn., in 1802. Moved to the West. He painted "A Wounded Grecian Racer," and made several copies of Gilbert Stuart's full-length portrait of Washington; one being in the Wadsworth Gallery. Died in Pittsburgh, PA, in 1874.

ELMENDORF, STELLA.
See Stella E. Tylor.

ELMORE, ELIZABETH TINKER.
Painter, etcher and writer. Born Clinton, Wis., Aug. 7, 1874. Pupil of William Merritt Chase, Charles Mielatz; George De Forest Brush, and portrait study in Rome, Italy. Member: NA Women PS.; PBC.; Catherine Lorillard Wolfe Club. Awards: First prize for portrait, 1918; first prize for etching, 1919, Catherine Lorillard Wolfe Art Club. Specialty, marines, portraits and etchings. Died in 1933. Address in 1929, 17 East 67th St., New York, NY.

ELOUIS, JEAN PIERRE HENRI.
(Henry Elouis). Painter. Born in Caen, France, Jan. 20, 1755. He studied art under the French painter Jean Barnard Restout and went to London in 1783. Exhibited at the Royal Academy 1785-87. At the beginning of the French Revolution emigrated to Baltimore. Charles Wilson Peale met him in 1791 at Annapolis, and calling him "Mr. Louis," mentions that "he paints in a new style." In 1792 Elouis moved to Phila. and his name appears in the Directories for 1793 as "limner, 201 Mulberry St." He remained in Phila. until 1799, where he taught drawing to Eleanor Custis and painted miniatures of Washington and Mrs. Washington. Elouis travelled the U.S., Mexico, and South America. Returned in 1807 to France. His portraits are noted for their simplicity and directness. Died in Caen on Dec. 23, 1840.

ELSHIN, JACOB, ALEXANDROVITCH.
Painter and illustrator. Born in Leningrad, Russia, Dec. 30, 1891. Pupil of Zemin, Roussanoff, Andriev, Dimitrieff. Member: Seattle AI; Seattle AG. Work: Stage setting "Chinese Street Scene," "Buddhist Temple Scene," Seattle Civic auditorium; "Ruins of Troy," Cornish School of Art and Music, Seattle; settings for "Theatre Russe de Miniature," "Chopiniana Ballet" and "Danse Macabre Ballet," Metropolitan Theatre, Seattle. Address in 1929, 1326 Sixth Ave.; h. 517 27th Ave., South, Seattle, Wash.

ELWELL, FRANCIS EDWIN.
Sculptor. Born in Concord, Mass., June 15, 1858; he died in Darien, Conn., Jan. 23, 1922. He was a pupil of Daniel French, and also studied in Paris. His works include "Dickens and Little Nell," in Philadelphia; "The Flag" at Vicksburg, Miss.; Equestrian statue of General Hancock at Gettysburg, Penn.; and "The New Life" at the PAFA, Philadelphia.

ELWELL, JOHN H.
Etcher and draughtsman. Born Marblehead, Mass., March 10, 1878. Pupil of Vesper L. George, Reuben

276

Carpenter, Evening Art School, Boston. Member: Boston AC. Specialty, designing, etching and engraving Ex Libris labels. Address in 1929, 30 Bromfield St., Boston, Mass.; h. 33 Brewster Rd., Newton Highlands, Mass.; summer, Naugus Head, Marblehead, Mass.

ELY, A.
Engraver. Ely engraved the script title-page, the music, and a curious "musical" vignette for "The Songster's Assistant, etc.," by T. Swan, Suffield, Conn.; printed by Swan and Ely. The work is undated but is probably c. 1800. The only copy known is in the Watkinson Library, Hartford, Conn.

ELY, RICHARD.
Illustrator. Born in Rochester, NY, in 1928. Attended the Kunst Akademie in Munich and studied under Jack Potter at SVA. He has worked for magazines and publishing companies since the 1950's and his works are in the collections of the NY Pub. Lib., the private collection of the late Princess Grace of Monaco, and the Museum of Afro-American Heritage in Phila. His paintings of Elizabeth Rethberg and George Cehanovsky hang in the Founder's Hall of the Metropolitan Opera House in New York.

EMEREE, BERLA LYONE.
Painter and teacher. Born Witchita, Kan., Aug. 7, 1899. Pupil of Frank B. A. Linton; Jose Arpa. Member: SSAL; San Antonio AG; El paso AG. Awards: Three blue ribbons, Kendall County Fair, Boerne, Tex., 1926, 1927. Work: "New Mexico Ranch Life," State Museum, Santa Fe., NM; "On the River, San Antonio," Carnegie Public Library, Fort Worth, Tex. Address in 1929, 2315 Byron St., El Paso, Tex.

EMERSON, ARTHUR W(EBSTER).
Painter, illustrator, etcher and teacher. Born Honolulu, Hawaii, Dec. 5, 1885. Pupil of John C. Johansen; ASL of NY. Member: ASL of NY; Salons of America; AFA; Berkeley Lg. FA. Address in 1929, 139 South School St., Honolulu, Hawaii.

EMERSON, CHARLES CHASE.
Illustrator and painter. Member: Society of Illustrators, 1912; Boston Art Club. Died in 1922.

EMERSON, EDITH.
Painter. Born Oxford, Ohio, 1888. Pupil of AIC; PAFA and Violet Oakley. Member: Fellowship PAFA; Phila. Print C; Phila. Alliance; Mural P.; Phila. WCC; Alumni AIC. Work: Mural decorations in the Little Theatre, Philadelphia; Roosevelt memorial window, Temple Keneseth Israel, Philadelphia, PA; Moorestown Trust Co., Moorestown, NJ. Represented in the Pennsylvania Academy of the Fine Arts; Vanderpoel AA. Collection, Chicago; illustrations in "Asia" and "The Century." Address in 1929, "Lower Cogslea," St. George's Rd., Mt. Airy, Philadelphia, PA.

EMERSON, W. C.
Painter and architect. Member: Chicago SA; Chicago WCC; NYWCC; New Canaan SA. Award: Englewood Club prize. Address in 1929, New Preston, Conn.; New Canaan, Conn.

EMERTON, JAMES H.
Illustrator. Born Salem, Mass., 1847. Member: Copley Society 1894. Illustrated zoological publications. Specialty, Amer. spiders. Address in 1929, Fenway Studios, 30 Ipswich St., Boston, Mass.

EMMES, THOMAS.
The earliest known attempt of a portrait engraved upon copper by an American engraver is the work of Thomas Emmes, of Boston. This is a portrait of the Rev. Increase Mather, and appears as a frontispiece to "The Blessed Hope, etc.," published in Boston, New England, 1701, by Timothy Green for Nicholas Boone. The plate itself is a very rough attempt at a copy of a London portrait engraved either by Sturt or Robert White, and is little more than scratched upon the copper in nearly straight lines; it has a strongly cross-hatched background. The plate is signed "Tho. Emmes Sculp. Sold by Nicholas Boone 1701."

EMMET, ELLEN G.
See Mrs. Rand.

EMMET, LESLIE.
Painter. Exhibited at the National Association of Women Painters and Sculptors, New York, 1924. Address in 1926, Salisbury, Conn.

EMMET, LYDIA FIELD.
Portrait painter and illustrator. Born New Rochelle, NY, Jan. 23, 1866. Pupil of Chase, Mowbray, Cox and Reid in New York; Bouguereau, Collin, Robert-Fleury and MacMonnies in Paris. Member: ANA 1909, NA 1912; ASL of NY; NYWCC; Portrait painter; Conn. AFA; NA Women PS; AFA. Awards: Bronze medal, Columbian Exp., Chicago, 1893; bronze medal, Atlanta Exp., 1895; hon. mention, Pan-Am. Exp., Buffalo, 1901; silver medal, St. Louis Exp., 1904; Shaw prize, SAA, 1906; Proctor prize, NAD, 1907; Clarke prize, NAD, 1909; hon. mention, City of Pittsburgh, 1912; Bok prize (first award), PAFA, 1915; popular prize, Corcoran Gall. of Art, Wash., 1917; Maynard portrait prize, NAD, 1918; Hudson prize, Conn., AFA, 1919; popular prize, Newport AA, 1921; popular prize, Newport AA, 1923; Phila. prize, PAFA, 1925. Died Aug. 16, 1952. Address in 1929, 535 Park Ave., NYC; summer, Stockbridge, MA.

EMMET, ROSINA.
See Mrs. Sherwood.

EMMONS, ALEXANDER HAMILTON.
Portrait painter. Born in East Haddam, Conn., on Dec. 12, 1816. He painted in oil, and executed numerous miniatures. In 1843 he opened his studio in Hartford. His only absence for any length of time from this country was an extended trip through Europe to study the work of the old masters. He finally settled in Norwich, Conn., where he died in 1879.

EMMONS, C(HANSONETTA) S(TANLEY).
Miniature painter and craftsman. Born Kingfield, ME, Dec. 30, 1858. Pupil of Enneking and Alice Beckington. Member: Boston SAC. Represented in SAC collection, Boston Museum and Museum of Fine Arts, Newport, RI. Died in 1937.

Address in 1929, 21 Bennington St., Newton, Mass.

EMMONS, DOROTHY STANLEY.
Painter and etcher. Born Roxbury, Mass., June 14, 1891. Pupil of Woodbury, G. E. Browne, G. A. Thompson, Aldro T. Hibbard, and G. L. Noyes. Member: New Haven PCC; Am. APL. Address in 1929, 2 Bennington St., Newton, Mass.

EMMONS, NATHANIEL.
Painter. Born in Boston, 1704. A little-known American painter of considerable merit. He painted a portrait of Judge Sewall (engraved by Pelton). William Clarke, Andrew Oliver and Rev. John Lowel (painted 1728). He died May 19 1740, in Boston.

EMORY, HOPPER.
Illustrator and etcher. Born Baltimore, MD, May 8, 1881. Member: Balto. Charcoal C. Address in 1929, 17 East 22nd St. Baltimore, MD; summer, Towson, MD.

ENDEWELT, JACK.
Illustrator. Born in NYC in 1935 Studied under Jack Potter an Daniel Schwartz at SVA where he ha been an instructor of boo illustration and drawing sinc 1968. He has illustrate educational books as well as man covers for Dell and Avon, and hi work has often been included in th S of I Annual Exhibitions.

ENDRES, LOUIS J.
Painter. Exhibited at Cincinnat Art Museum in 1925. Address i 1926, 4206 Ballard Ave. Cincinnati.

ENGEL, RICHARD DRUM.
Painter and writer. Bor Washington, DC, Dec. 25, 1889 Largely self taught. Studied i France. Member: Soc. Wash. A Address in 1929, 806 Farragut St. N.W., Washington, DC.

ENGELMANN, C. F.
Engraver. An elaborate, curiousl designed, and crudely engrave Birth and Baptismal Certificate published about 1814, is signe "Eng. and sold by C. F. Engleman on Pennsmount near Reading, PA.

The design closely follows similar work emanating from the community of Seventh Day Baptists at Ephrata, Lancaster Co., PA, which is in the vicinity of Reading.

ENGLAND, PAUL GRADY.
Painter and teacher. Born in Hugo, Okla., Jan. 12, 1918. Study: Carnegie Institute of Technology; Univ. of Tulsa; ASL, 1943-46; Zadkine Studio, Paris, 1948- 49. Work: New York Public Lib. Print Collection; Philbrook Art Center, Tulsa, Okla.; Staten Island Museum; State Collection, Oklahoma City; and others. Exhibitions: Pa. Academy of Art; Library of Congress; Grand Central Moderns, NYC; Philbrook Art Ctr., Tulsa; and others. Awards: Philbrook Art Center, Tulsa; Smithtown Arts Council, Long Island; etc. Teaching: Hofstra U., 1959-present. Mem.: ASL, NY. Media: Oil. Address in 1982, Rocky Point, NY.

ENGLE, BARBARA.
Painter, graphic artist, jeweler. Born in Grandin, ND. Studied at Honolulu Academy of Arts, Honolulu; Chouinard Art Institute, Los Angeles, California; Otis Art Institute, Los Angeles. Exhibitions: Pasadena Art Museum, California, 1959; Objects, U.S.A., Touring Show, 1969; Foundry Gallery, Honolulu, Hawaii, 1975. Collections: Honolulu Academy of Arts; State Foundation on Culture and Arts, Hawaii; Department of Education, Hawaii. Media: Oil. Address in 1980, 2231 Noah Street, Honolulu, HI.

ENGLE, H(ARRY LEON).
Landscape painter. Born Richmond, Ind., 1870. Pupil of Art Inst. of Chicago. Member: Palette and Chisel C.; Chicago PS. Award: Palette and Chisel Club prize, 1917. Work: "Old Lyme Road," purchased by Chicago Art Commission, 1914. "Laurel Blossoms," Long Beach (Calif.) Public Library. Address in 1929, 1544 Arthur Ave., Chicago, Ill.; summer, Yorkville, Ill.

ENGLE, NITA.
Illustrator. Born in Marquette, MI, in 1925. Attended Northern Michigan Univ. and the AIC. After nine years as an art director in a Chicago agency, she decided to start free-lancing. She began illustrating children's books at Chicago Text publishers and later for such magazines as Reader's Digest and Playboy. A member of the AWS, she has exhibited in Ill., Mich., Calif., and England.

ENGLER, ARTHUR.
Engraver. Born Jersey City, NJ, 1885. Pupil of Francis Clarke. Address in 1926, 150 Nassau St., New York, NY.

ENGLERT, GEORGE.
Painter. Self-taught artist. He is a current member of the American Watercolor Society, Allied Artists of America, Audubon Artists, National Society of Painters in Casein and Acrylic, Rockport Art Association, and other numerous memberships. He has won almost a hundred awards in national shows. Principal medium: acrylic. Currently resides in Tivoli, NY.

ENGLISH, FRANK F.
Painter. Born in Louisville, KY, in 1854. Pupil of Penna. Academy of Fine Arts; he also studied in England. Address in 1926, Point Pleasant, Bucks County, Penna.

ENGLISH, MABEL BACON PLIMPTON.
(Mrs. J. L. English). Painter. Born Hartford, Conn., Feb. 18, 1861. Pupil of Chase and D. W. Tryon. Member: Hartford AS; Hartford AC; Conn. AFA; Hartford Arts and Crafts C. Address in 1929, 210 Fern St., Hartford, Conn.; summer, Weekapaug, RI.

ENGLISH, MARK F.
Illustrator. Born in Hubbard, TX, in 1933. Attended the Univ. of Texas for one year before going to Los Angeles to study under John LaGatta at the ACD. His first job was in Detroit in an advertising studio and soon his editorial illustrations were appearing in Redbook, Ladies' Home Journal, and McCall's. He has been awarded many medals from the S of I where he is

currently a member. Named Artist of the Year in 1969 by the AG, he received awards from several ADCs in the U.S. He has been a contributor to the National Park Service Art Program and has exhibited at the Brandywine Gallery.

ENNEKING, JOHN JOS.
Painter. Born in Ohio, on Oct. 4, 1841. He came to Boston in 1865. In 1872 he went abroad to study, and afterwards returned to this country and settled in Boston. His landscapes and cattle pictures have decided merit. His "Hillside" is in the Boston Museum of Fine Arts, and "Autumn in New England" is owned by the Worcester Art Museum. Died Boston, MA, Nov 16, 1916.

ENNEKING, JOSEPH ELIOT.
Painter. Born Hyde Park, Mass. Pupil of De Camp, Benson and Tarbell in Boston. Member: Boston AC; Copley S.; Salma. C.; Conn, AFA. Died in 1916. Address in 1929, 17 Webster Square, Hyde Park, Mass.; summer, Mystic, Conn.

ENNIS, GEORGE PEARSE.
Painter and craftsman. Born St. Louis, MO, 1884. Pupil of Chase. Member: Salma. C.; AWCS; Allied AA; A. Aid S.; NY Arch. Lg.; NYWCC; Guild of Amer. Painters; A. Fund S.; NYSP; Aquarellists; Boston AC. Awards: Shaw prize, Salma. C., 1922; Kramer purchase prize, AIC.; Isidor prize, Salma. C., 1923 and 1925; William Church Osborn prize, 1926; R. Horace Gallatin prize, 1927. Work: 15 large canvases, 31 pencil drawings (material gathered Steel Co.) executed at direction of Ordinance Dept. US Govt., 1917-18. Three Victory windows in NY Military Acad.; mem. windows, NY Athletic Club; Church of All Nations, NYC; mural decorations and stained glass windows, Unitarian Ch., Eastport, ME; Presbyterian Ch., Cornwall, NY; Calvary Methodist Ch., Bronx, NY; First Bapist Ch., Jamaica, LI, NY. Represented at the Art Inst. of Chicago; U. of Arkansas, Fayetteville. Died in 1936. Address in 1929, 67 West 87th St., NY; summer, Eastport, ME.

ENNIS, GLADYS ATWOOD.
Block printer. Born Natick, Mass. Pupil of Henry B. Snell; George Pearse Ennis. Member: AWCS; NYWCC; Three Arts C; NA Women PS. Address in 1929, 67 West 87th St., New York, NY; summer, Eastport, ME.

ENOS, CHRIS.
Photographer and art administrator. Born in California Aug. 21, 1944. Studied: Foothill College, Los Altos, CA; San Francisco State University; San Francisco Art Institute. Exhib.: Photography and Film Center West, Berkeley, CA, 1972; Focus II Gal., NYC, 1974; Bibliotheque Nationale, Paris, France, 1975. Collections: San Francisco Museum of Art, California; San Francisco Art Institute, CA; Fogg Museum, Harvard University, Cambridge, MA. Address in 1980, P.O. Box 507, Boston, MA.

ENOS, RANDALL.
Illustrator. Born in New Bedford, MA, in 1936. Studied at Boston Museum for two years. He began illustrating for Harper's and has since worked for many other major magazines. He illustrated the children's book It's Not Fair in 1976 as well as other books for Simon and Schuster and Harper & Row. He has done a considerable amount of film animation for NBC as well as for other companies, winning an award at the Cannes Film Festival in France.

ENQUIST, MARY B.
Sculptor. Member: Wash. WCC. Address in 1929, 111 14th St., N.E., Washington, DC.

ENRIGHT, WALTER.
Illustrator. Born Chicago, Ill. July 3, 1879. Pupil of AIC. Member: SI 1910; Players; NYAC. Award: Harmon Cartoon, 1929. Address in 1929, 1 West 67th St., New York, NY.

ENSIGN, RAYMOND P.
Draughtsman, lecturer and teacher Born River Falls, Wisc., Aug. 4 1883. Pupil of Pratt Institute and Ralph Robertson. Member: Western AA; AFA; Fed. Council on Art Ed.; EAA. Award: Medal, Cleveland Society of Artists, 1921

Director, Newark School of Fine and Industrial Art; Director, Berkshire Summer School of Art. Address in 1929, Newark School of Fine and Industrial Art, 55 Academy St., Newark, NJ; summer, Berkshire Summer School of Art, Monterey, Mass.

ENTE, LILY.
Sculptor, painter, printmaker. Born May 20, 1905. Works mostly in black and white marble. Exhibitions: Riverside Museum, New York; Stable Gallery, New York; University of Illinois. Collections: Phoenix Art Museum; Riverside Museum; Safad Museum, Israel. Address in 1980, 400 Riverside Drive, New York, NY.

ENTZING-MILLER, T. M.
Born in 1804. This man was a designer for engravers, and an engraver of portraits in line. He did good work and was located in Philadelphia and in New York in 1850-55. Died 1855 in New York.

EPPENSTEINER, JOHN J(OSEPH).
Painter and illustrator. Born St. Louis, MO, Feb. 14, 1893. Pupil of St. Louis School of Fine Arts. Member: St. Louis AG; St. Louis A. Lg.; St. Louis Two-by-Four SA. Awards: First landscape prize, 1923, and prize for best small painting, 1924 and 1926, St. Louis Artists Guild; bronze medal, Midwestern Artists' Exh., Kansas City Art. Inst., 1927; first modern painting prize ($100), St. Louis AG., 1928; bronze medal for black and white, Kansas City AI, 1929; first prize, black and white ($250) Post Dispatch, 1929. Address in 1929, 3831 Nebraska Ave., St. Louis, MO.

ERBAUGH, RALPH (WALDO).
Painter. Born Peru, Miami Co., Ind., June 29, 1885. Member: S. Indp. A.; Chicago No-Jury Society of Artists. Address in 1929, "The Avon," 6109 Dorchester Ave., Chicago, Ill.

ERDMANN, R(ICHARD) FREDERICK.
Painter. Born Chillicothe, Ohio, Feb. 12, 1894. Pupil of L. H. Meakin, James Hopkins, Herman Wessel, Paul Jones, Charles Curran,

Frank DuMond, George Luks, Frank Duveneck. Address in 1929, 405 South Cornell St., Albuquerque, NM.

ERICKSON, CARL O. A.
Illustrator. Born in Joliet, IL, in 1891. Studied for two years at the Chicago Acad. of Arts and began his career working for dept. stores in Chicago (Marshall Field and Lord and Thomas) as well as for advertisers. Arriving in NYC in 1914, he continued doing advertising illus. until 1920 when he began a very successful career as a fashion artist. Shortly thereafter he moved to Paris where for 20 years he reigned supreme in the fashion field. His elegant illus., often the final draft of 20 or more preliminary sketches, first appeared in Vogue in 1923. He returned to America in 1940, after the Nazi takeover of France, to continue his work for Conde Nast.

ERICSON, DAVID.
Painter. Born Motala, Sweden, April 15, 1873. Pupil of Chase, Whistler and Prinet. Member: Provincetown AA; Paris AAA. Awards: Silver medal, St. Louis Exposition, 1904; hon. mention, Carnegie Institute, International Exp., 1904; 1st prize, Minnesota Art Exp., St. Paul, 1911. Work: "Nativity," Duluth Art Assn.; "Moonlight, Provincetown," La Crosse Art Asso.; "Barley Field, Etaples," Commercial Club, Duluth. Address in 1929, care of the American Express Co., 11 Rue Scribe, Paris, France.

ERLA, KAREN.
Painter and printmaker. Born Pittsburgh, PA, Nov. 17, 1942. Study: Carnegie Inst. of Technology; Boston Univ.; CA State College; Geo. Wash. Univ., DC; Pratt Inst; Parsons School of Design. Work: IBM; Reuben Donnelly Co. Exhibitions: Corcoran Gallery, Wash. DC; New School for Social Research, NYC; Saddle River (NJ) Group; Multi-Cultural Arts Inst., San Diego, CA; NJ Printmaking Society (mono print etchings); Cork Gal., Avery Fisher Hall, Lincoln Center, NYC; Manhattanville College (solo).

Rep.: Phoenix Gallery, 30 W. 57th St., NYC; Rye (NY) Art Center. Technique: Collage, mixed media, etching, monoprint, other. Address in 1983, Old Orchard St., North White Plains, NY.

ERLANGER, ELIZABETH N.
Painter. Born in Baltimore, MD, 1901. Studied: with Ralph M. Pearson, Umberto Romano, Liberte and Hans Hofmann. Awards: National Association of Women Artists, 1952, 1953, 1956; Brooklyn Society of Art, 1953, 1955, 1958; Village Art Center, 1953, 1955, 1956. Collections: Florida Southern College; Univ. of Maine; Colby College; NY Public Library; Evansville, IN, Museum of Art.

ERSKINE, H(AROLD) (PERRY).
Sculptor. Born Racine, Wis., June 5, 1879. Pupil of Ecole des Beaux-Arts, Paris. Member: Beaux Arts Soc. and Century C., New York. Died in 1951. Address in 1929, 251 East 61st St., New York, NY; summer, Roxbury, Conn.

ERTZ, BRUNO.
Painter. Born Manitowoc, Wis., March 1, 1873. Self taught. Painted birds and insects. Address in 1929, 701 South 16th St., Manitowoc, Wis.

ERTZ, EDWARD (FREDERICK).
Painter, illustrator, etcher and teacher. Born Canfield, Tazewell Co., Ill., March 1, 1862. Pupil of Lefebvre, Constant and Delance in Paris. Member: Royal Soc. of British Artists; Soc. of Arts, London; Imperial Arts League; British WCS; Essex AC; Aberdeen AG; Societe Inter. d'Aquarellistes, Paris; Societe des Cinquante; Union Inter. des Beaux-Arts; Chicago SE; Chicago AG; Cal. SE. Awards: Diploma of honor, Inter. Exp., St. Etienne; gold medal, Exp. d'Angiers; grand prix, Inter. Exp., Rouen, France; medal, Soc. des Amis des Arts de la Somme, 1899; medal, Ville d'Elboeuf, France; two awards, Bristol (Eng.) Arts and Crafts; medal AAS Phila., 1902; medal, Festival of Arts and Letters, London, 1927. Work: "The Gardener," Alexander Palace Mus.,

London; "Spanish Water Carrier," Public Gall. Liverpool; Print Dept., Library of Congress, Wash., DC, and Calif. State Library; NY Pub. Library; Boston Mus. of Fine Arts; "The Vacation Girl," "Sunset, Grand Canyon," American Consulate, London; "Normandy Cider Mill," Alexander Palace Museum, London. Address in 1929, Pulborough, Sussex, England.

ESCHERICH, MRS. ELSA F.
Painter. Born Davenport, IA, March 20, 1888. Pupil of Vanderpoel, Hawthorne and Walcott. Member: Calif. AC; West Coast Arts, Inc.; Los Angeles AL. Address in 1929, 3333 North Marengo Ave., Pasadena, Calif.

ESHERICK, WHARTON H(ARRIS).
Painter, sculptor and wood engraver. Born Philadelphia, PA, July 15, 1887. Pupil of Chase, Beaux and Anshutz. Member: Phila. Alliance; Phila. AC. Died in 1970. Address in 1929, Paoli, PA.

ESKRIDGE, ROBERT LEE.
Painter, etcher and draughtsman. Born Philipsburg, PA, Nov. 22, 1891. Pupil of Los Angeles College of Fine Arts; AIC; Chicago Academy of Fine Arts; George Senseney. Member: Chicago SE; Brooklyn SE; Chicago AC. Awards: Bronze medal for water color, Pan.-Cal. Exp., San Diego, 1915; Martin B. Cahn prize, AIC, 1928. Address in 1929, Philipsburg, PA; 115 East Chestnut St., Chicago, Ill.; Coronado Beach, Calif.

ESSIG, GEORGE EMERICK.
Painter and illustrator. Born in Philadelphia, Sept. 2, 1838. Pupil of Edward Moran and James Hamilton. Student at Penna. Academy of Fine Arts, Philadelphia. Specialty, marines. Address in 1926, Ventnor, Atlantic City, NJ.

ESTABROOK, FLORENCE C.
Painter and teacher. Born Sewell, Mass. Pupil of School of the Museum of Fine Arts, Boston. Member: Lg. of Amer. Pen and Brush Women. Address in 1929, 1230 Eleventh St., NW, Washington, DC.

ESTE, FLORENCE.
Painter. Born in Cincinnati, Ohio, in 1860. Her water colors won the PAFA prize, 1925. Died April 25, 1926, in Paris France. Address in 1926, Paris, France.

ETTER, DAVID RENT.
Born in Philadelphia, 1807; he lived there until his death in 1881. He was interested in the city and state politics. An artist of fair ability, best known for his copies of Gilbert Stuart's paintings. The city of Philadelphia owns his copy of the Stuart-Washington "Lansdowne" portrait.

ETTL, ALEX J.
Sculptor. Born Fort Lee, NJ, Dec. 12, 1898. Pupil of his father, John Ettl, and Robert Aitken. Work: "Katrina Trask Memorial," Yaddo, Saratoga Springs, NY; Wolf and Jacobs Memorial, Friars' Club, New York City; marble bench historical site, Hackensack, NJ; sculpture, Pennsylvania Bldg., Phila., PA. Address in 1929, 180 Thirteenth Ave., New York, NY; h. 115 Kingsley St., Leonia, NJ.

ETTL, JOHN.
Sculptor. Born Budapest, Hungary, Aug. 1, 1872. Studied in Budapest and Vienna. Work: "Abraham Lincoln," State Arsenal, New York; "War Memorial," East Rutherford, NJ; sculpture in Place of Justice, Berne, Switzerland; Soldiers Monument, Haverstraw; "Chief Oratam," Bergen County Historical Society; sculpture, Pennsylvania Bldg., Phila., PA. Died in 1940. Address in 1929, 180 Thirteenth Ave., New York, NY; h. 115 Kingsley St., Leonia, NJ.

EUWER, ANTHONY HENDERSON.
Illustrator. Born in Allegheny, Penna., in 1877. Illustrated many American and English periodicals and papers. Address in 1926, 508 Aspen Road, Portland, Oregon.

EVANS, ANNE.
Painter. Member: Denver AC; AFA. Address in 1929, 1320 Hannock St., Denver, Colo.

EVANS, DeSCOTT.
Born in Wayne Co., Ind., 1847. He studied in Paris, returned to Cleveland and became instructor and codirector in the Academy of Fine Arts there. He was very skillful in painting draperies. He painted numerous portraits, and among his genre paintings are "The first Snow-Storm," "Grandma's Visitors," and "Day before the Wedding." He died July 4, 1898, at sea.

EVANS, DULAH MARIE.
See Dulah Evans Krehbiel.

EVANS, EDWIN.
Painter and teacher. Born Lehi, Utah, Feb. 2, 1860. Pupil of Laurens, Lefebvre and Benjamin-Constant in Paris. Died in 1946. Address in 1929, 1261 Emerson Ave., Salt Lake City, Utah.

EVANS, ELIZABETH H.
Painter. Exhibited at National Association of Women Painters and Sculptors. Address in 1926, 204 Clay St., Baltimore, MD.

EVANS, GRACE (LYDIA).
Painter and teacher. Born Pittston, PA, Feb. 19, 1877. Pupil of PAFA under Chase, Anshutz and Breckenridge; Drexel Inst. Member: Phila. Alliance; Fellowship PAFA; Conn. AFA. Work: Portrait of Dr. Francis March, March H.S., Easton, PA. Specialty, portraits. Address in 1929, 1551 Shakespeare Ave., NYC; 510 Presser Bldg, 1714 Chestnut St.; h. 218 - 32nd St., Phila., PA.

EVANS, GRACE FRENCH.
Painter. Born Davenport, IA. Pupil of Hermon More, Kenneth Hayes Miller. Member: AFA; NA Women PS; Woodstock AA. Address in 1929, 20 Forest Rd., Davenport, IA; summer, Woodstock, NY.

EVANS, JESSIE BENTON.
Painter, etcher and teacher. Born Akron, OH, March 24, 1866. Pupil of AIC and W. M. Chase in Chic.; Zanetti Zilla in Venice. Member: Chic. SA; Chic. AC; Phoenix AC; AFA Salvator Rosa, Naples. Awards: 1st prize landscape, 1913 and 1923 and 2nd portrait prize, 1923, Arizona State Fair. Works: "On the way to

McDowel," Municipal coll.; "Morning," Country Club, Phoenix, Ariz.; "On the Verde River" and "Gray Day," Arizona Club. Represented in the College Club, Chicago; Public School Art Societies, Chicago, Phoenix and Mesa, Ariz; Vanderpoel AA. Collection, Chicago; Art Institute, Akron, Ohio. Died in 1954. Address in 1929, 1517 East 61st St., Chicago, Ill.; winter, Scottsdale, Ariz.

EVANS, JOHN T.
Flourished in 1809, in Philadelphia, as a landscape, portrait and miniature painter. He exhibited his miniatures and water colors at the Penna. Academy of the Fine Arts.

EVANS, JOHN W(ILLIAM).
Wood engraver. Born Brooklyn, March 27, 1855. Pupil of P. R. B. Pierson. Awards: Bronze medal, Pan-Am. Exp., Buffalo, 1901; bronze medal, St. Louis Exp., 1904; silver medal, P.-P. Exp., San F., 1915. Represented in NY Public Library; Carnegie Institute; Brooklyn Inst. of Arts and Sciences. Address in 1929, 4 Carlton Place, Baldwin, LI, NY.

EVANS, MARGARET.
Painter, craftsman, lecturer and teacher. Born Youngstown, Ohio. Pupil of Birge Harrison and John Carlson at the ASL of NY, Woodstock; Columbia Univ., Arthur Dow; sp. course in Europe. Director of the Butler Art Institute. Address in 1929, care of Butler Art Institute; h. 810 Glenwood Ave., Youngstown, Ohio.

EVANS, RAY O.
Illustrator. Born in Columbus, Ohio, 1887. Made illustrations for daily papers and Puck. Address in 1926, The Columbus Dispatch, Columbus, Ohio.

EVANS, RUDULPH.
Sculptor. Born Washington, DC, Feb. 1, 1878. Pupil of Falguiere and Rodin. Member: ANA, 1919; NA, 1929; Paris AA; Allied AA; National Institute of Arts and Letters, 1926. Awards: Bronze medal, Paris Salon, 1914; Watrous gold medal,

NAD, 1919. Work: Marble portrait, Gen. Bolivar, Bureau American Republics, Washington; statue James Pierce, New York; bronze portrait, John Greenleaf Whittier, Hall of Fame, New York; Jean Webster McKinney Memorial, Greenwich, Conn.; Kiernan Memorial, Green Bay, Wis.; Woolley Memorial, Detroit, Mich.; bronze portrait, Joseph French Johnson, NY University. Decorated by King Victor Emanuel for Exhib. in Rome. Statue acquired by French Government for Luxembourg; "The Golden Hour," Metropolitan Museum, New York. Died in 1960. Address in 1929, 71 Washington Pl., New York, NY.

EVANS, W. G.
A map designed to illustrate the geography of the Heavens is fantastically designed by E. H. Burnett, and is engraved by W. G. Evans. It was published at Hartford, Conn., in 1835.

EVENS, THEODORE A.
A good line map of Cincinnati published in 1838 is signed as "Drawn & Engraved by T. A. Evens."

EVERDELL.
This name as "Everdell Sct. 1816" is signed to a business card, in line and script. It is an advertisement of the business of "Elijah Lewis, Saddle, Harness & Trunk Maker," New York, 1816.

EVERETT, ELIZABETH (RINEHART).
Painter, sculptor, illustrator, etcher and craftsman. Born Toledo, Ohio. Pupil of Walter Isaacs. Awards: Sweepstake prize, 1926; first prize, 1927, 1928, Western Washington Fair. Address in 1929, 602 36th Ave., North, Seattle, Wash.

EVERETT, FLORENCE.
Painter and teacher. Born Ontario, Canada. Member: St. Louis AS; St. Louis AG. Address in 1929, Harris Teachers College, Park and Theresa Aves., St. Louis, MO; 3935 Castleman Ave., St. Louis, MO.

EVERETT, HERBERT EDWARD.
Sculptor and teacher. Born Worcester, Mass. Pupil of Boston Museum School; Julian Academy in

Paris; PAFA. Member: Phila. WCC. Died in 1935. Address in 1929, 1632 Latimer St., Philadelphia, PA.

EVERETT, JOS(EPH) A(LMA) F(REESTONE).
Painter, etcher, lecturer and teacher. Born Salt Lake City, Jan. 7, 1884. Pupil of J. T. Harwood. Member: Utah Art Colony. Work: "Boats, Oakland, Calif.," "Street in Winter" and "Rainy Day," Utah Art Institute, Salt Lake City. Died in 1945. Address in 1929, 610 Union Pacific Bldg.; h. 240 South 11th East, Salt Lake City, Utah.

EVERETT, LOUISE.
Painter and sculptor. Born Des Moines, IA, April 9, 1899. Pupil of Fursman, Hawthorne, Julia Bracken Wendt, Otis Art Inst.; Fontainebleau School of Fine Arts, 1925; Julian Academy in Paris, 1926. Member: Calif. AC; Laguna Beach AA; West Coast Arts. Awards: Second prize, West Coast Arts, 1923; marine prize, Laguna Beach AA, 1923; silver medal, sculpture, Pac. Southwest Exposition, 1928. Address in 1929, 980 South Manhattan Pl., Los Angeles, Calif.

EVERETT, MARY O.
(Mrs. H. G. Everett). Painter. Born Mifflinburg, PA, 1876. Pupil of Hawthorne, Chase. Member: Calif. AC; Laguna Beach AA; West Coast Arts; AFA. Awards: Second prize ($50), 1909, and first prize ($100), 1910, Des Moines Women's Club. Died in 1948. Address in 1929, 980 South Manhattan Place, Los Angeles, Calif.; summer, Laguna Beach, Calif.

EVERETT, RAYMOND.
Painter, sculptor, artist and teacher. Born Englishtown, NJ, Aug. 10, 1885. Pupil of Howard Pyle, Denman, Rosa. Member: Texas FAA; SSAL; AIA. Award: Silver medal, SSAL, San Antonio, 1929. Represented in Detroit Public Library; Elisabet Ney Museum, Austin, Tex.; Univ. of Colorado Museum. Professor of drawing and painting, University of Texas. Address in 1929, 917 West 31st St., Austin, Tex.

EVERGOOD, PHILIP (HOWARD FRANCIS).
Painter. Born Oct. 26, 1901, in NYC. Studied at Slade School, London; under von Schlegell and Luks at ASL, NYC, and in France under Andre Lhote. Taught privately and at Iowa State Teachers College. Awards from Art Inst. of Chicago; PAFA; Carnegie Inst., others. Exhibited internationally. In collections of Santa Fe, NM; Syracuse U.; MOMA; IBM; Boston Mus. of FA; Carnegie; Arizona State; Geelong Gal., Australia; the Grolier Club, Wadsworth Atheneum; Baltimore Mus. Died March 11, 1973. Address in 1929, Martinsville, NJ.

EVERS, IVAR EILS.
Painter. Born in Sweden, 1866. Pupil of Napoleon Caesar in Sweden; De Camp in Boston; Twachtman in New York. Member: Society of Independent Artists. Address in 1926, Tillson, Ulster County, New York.

EVERS, JOHN.
Miniaturist and painter of theatre scenery. Born Aug. 17, 1797, in Newtown, LI. He was a founder of the National Academy of Design. Died May 3, 1884, in Hempstead, LI.

EXILIOUS, JOHN G.
Engraver. This reputable line engraver of landscape and buildings was working in Philadelphia in 1810-14. He was, in 1810, one of the founders of the Society of Artists, in Philadelphia, but nothing more is known about him. His largest and best plate is a view of the Pennsylvania Hospital, engraved in 1814 after his own drawings.

EYRE, LOUISA.
Sculptor. Born Newport, RI, Jan. 16, 1872. Pupil of Augustus Saint Gaudens. Member: Phila. ACG; Penn. Mus. and Sch. Ind. Art; Philadalphia Alliance. Work: Tablet to Gen. George Sykes for Memorial Hall, West Point, NY. Died in 1953. Address in 1929, 1003 Spruce St., Philadelphia, PA.

EZEKIEL, MOSES.
Sculptor. Born Richmond, VA, Oct. 28, 1844. Graduated VA. Military

Institute, 1866; studied anatomy at
Medical College of VA; removed to
Cincinnati, 1868; visited Berlin,
Germany, 1869, where he studied at
Royal Academy of Art, and under
Prof. Albert Wolf. Admitted to
Society of Artists, Berlin, on the
merits of his colossal bust of
Washington, and was first foreigner
to win the Michael Beer prize. The
Jewish order, "Sons of the
Covenant," commissioned him in 1874
to execute a marble group
representing "Religious Liberty,"
for Centennial Exhibition, later in
Fairmount Park, Philadelphia.
Among his productions are busts of
Liszt, Cardinal Hohenlohe, Eve,
Homer, David, Judith; "Christ in
the Tomb;" statue of Mrs. Andrew D.
White for Cornell University;
"Faith," Cemetery, Rome; "Madonna,"
for Church, Tivoli; "Apollo and
Mercury," in Berlin, etc. Died in
Rome, Italy, March 27, 1917.

FABER, LUDWIG E.
Painter and etcher. Born in Philadelphia, Oct. 21, 1855. Studied at Penna. Academy of the Fine Arts. Painted portraits and miniatures. Died May 16, 1913, in Philadelphia.

FABIAN, LYDIA DUNHAM.
Painter. Born Charlotte, MI, March 12, 1857. Pupil of the ASL of NY; AIC; Ossip Linde and Henry Henshall. Member: Santa Fe Society of Artists; Alumni of the Chicago Art Institute. Address in 1929, 3918 Lake Park Ave., Chicago, IL.

FABRI, RALPH.
Painter, etcher and teacher. Born Budapest, Hungary, April 23, 1894. Pupil of Royal Hungarian Academy of Fine Arts. Address in 1929, 45 Washington Sq., South, New York, NY.

FACKERT, OSCAR WILLIAM.
Painter and illustrator. Born Jersey City, NJ, July 29, 1891. Pupil of Schook, Grant, Gottwald, Bentley. Member: Palette and Chisel C. Awards: First prizes, 1923 and 1925, and second prize, 1924, Northern Indiana Exhibition; hon. mention, Midwest Exhibition, Kansas City AI, 1924. Work: Mural decoration in the Oliver Hotel, South Bend, IN Address in 1929, 1558 Juneway Ter., Chicago, IL.

FAGG, KENNETH S.
Painter, illustrator and etcher. Born Chicago, IL, May 29, 1901. Pupil of Pennell, Bridgman, Du Mond, Garber, Vysekal. Member: ASL of NY. Address in 1929, 3926 Packard St., Sunny Side, LI, NY

FAGGI, ALFEO.
Sculptor. Born Florence, Italy, Sept. 11, 1885. Pupil of Accademia Belle Arts, Florence. Member: Salons of America. Work: War Memorial "Pieta" and fourteen reliefs "Stations of the Cross," St. Thomas Church, Chicago; "The Doubting St. Thomas," Chapel at the University of Chicago; life-size figure of St. Francis, Museum of Santa Fe, NM; bronze head of Japanese poet, Art Institute of Chicago; Head of Noguchi, Phillips Memorial Gallery, Washington, DC;

Statue of Eve, Arts Club of Chicago; bronze door, episodes in life of St. Francis, University of Chicago. Address in 1929, Woodstock, NY.

FAGNANI, JOSEPH.
Sculptor and portrait painter. Born in Naples, Dec. 24, 1819; died in New York, May 22, 1873. He came to America in 1851 and lived in New York. His painting of the "Nine Muses," in the Metropolitan Museum of Art, New York, attracted much attention, as well-known American beauties had served as models.

FAHNESTOCK, WALLACE WEIR.
Painter. Born Harrisburg, PA, Jan. 15, 1877. Pupil of Chase, Mowbray, DuMond and Dow. Member: Salma. C.; Painters of So. Vermont. Work: "Wilderness Music," B. and B. Academy, Manchester, VT; "Late Afternoon," Boston City Club. Address in 1929, Dorset, VT.

FAIG, FRANCES WILEY.
Painter. Pupil of Duveneck, Grover, and Hawthorne. Member: MacD. C. of Cincinnati; Cin. Woman's AC. Work: Mural decorations in Engineering Library, University of Cincinnati. Address in 1929, 3345 Whitfield Ave., Clifton, Cincinnati, OH.

FAILLE, C(HARLES) A(RTHUR).
Painter, etcher and lecturer. Born Detroit, MI, Feb. 17, 1883. Self-taught. Member: Calif. AC. Work: "The Hum of the Mill," Society of Fine Arts, Omaha, NE. Address in 1929, 1854 Ft. Stockton Dr., San Diego, CA; 396 Blenheim Road, Columbus, OH.

FAIR, ROBERT.
Painter. Born in Ireland in 1847, he came to America in 1876 and established himself in New York City. He later moved to Philadelphia and painted several pictures of note, some of which gained places in the Pennsylvania Academy of Fine Arts. He died in Philadelphia in May 1907.

FAIRBANKS, AVARD TENNESON.
Sculptor. Born Provo, UT, March 2, 1897. Pupil of ASL of NY under James E. Fraser; Beaux-Arts in

Paris, under Injalbert; Fellow, Guggenheim Memorial Foundation, 1927. Member: NSS; AFA. Work: "The Indian," "The Pioneer," Salt Lake City Public Schools; monument "The Blessing of Joseph" and fountain in honor of Hawaiian motherhood, Laie, T.H.; "Doughboy of Idaho," Service Memorial, Oregon Agricultural College, Corvallis; "Old Oregon Trail Marker" and "War Memorial," Jefferson High School, Portland, OR; bronze doors, U.S. National Bank, Portland, OR; "Fountain of Aphrodite," Washburne Gardens, Eugene, OR; Memorial to the Pioneer Mothers, Vancouver, WA; the Three Witnesses Memorial, Salt Lake City; Tabernacle Door for Altar, St. Mary's Cathedral, Eugene, OR; "Heat and Power," Power House, University of Oregon. Address in 1929, University of Oregon, Eugene, OR.

FAIRBANKS, FRANK PERLEY.
Painter and architect. Born Boston, 1875, died 1939. Pupil of Tarbell and De Camp in Boston. Member: NY Arch. Lg. 1913; Mural P.; Fellow American Academy in Rome. Awards: Sears prize and Page traveling scholarship from the Boston Museum of Fine Arts; Academy at Rome scholarship, 1909-12; annual professor in the School of Fine Arts of the Amer. Academy in Rome, 1922; professor in charge of the School of Fine Arts, 1923. Work: Public Library, St. Paul, Minn.; University of Cincinnati, Memorial Apse, Tivoli-on-the-Hudson etc. Address in 1929, American Academy in Rome, Porta San Pancrazio, Rome, Italy.

FAIRBANKS, J. LEO.
Painter, etcher and teacher. Pupil of Julian Academy, Paris. Member: Associated Artists of Salt Lake City; Utah A. Inst; Salt Lake City Art Commission; Salt Lake City Planning Commission; Corvallis, OR, City Planning Commission; Bd. Governors Pac. AA; Oregon AA. Designed and assisted in executing sculpture frieze on Morman Temple, Hawaii; mural paintings, Salt Lake Temple; Library Building, Oregon State College; State War Memorial, Idaho. Director of Art in public schools of Salt Lake City for several years. Head of Dept. of Art and Rural Architecture, Oregon State College. Address in 1929, Oregon State College, Corvallis, OR.

FAIRBANKS, JOHN B.
Painter and teacher. Born Payson, UT, Dec. 27, 1855; died in 1940. Pupil of Constant, Lefebvre and Laurens in Paris. Member: Paris AA; S. Utah A.; Assoc. Artists Salt Lake City. Awards: First prize, Utah State Fair, 1899; first prize for marine, Utah State Fair, 1913; second prize for marine, Utah State Fair, 1917; second prize for landscape, Utah State Fair, 1918; first, second and third prizes, Utah State Fair, 1920; first prize, Payson High School Exhibit, 1926. Address in 1929, Springdale, Mouth of Zion Canyon, UT.

FAIRCHILD, (CHARLES) WILLARD.
Illustrator. Born Marinette, WI, Nov. 18, 1886. Pupil of Chicago AFA; ASL of NY. Member: SI; Art Directors C. Address in 1929, care Batten, Barton, Justine and Osborn, 383 Madison Ave.; h. 1 West 67th St., New York, NY.

FAIRCHILD, LOUIS.
Engraver. Born in Farmington, Conn., in 1800; was living in New York in 1840. Fairchild learned to engrave with Asaph Willard, in New Haven, and became an etcher and line-engraver of landscape. He also painted portraits in miniature and excelled in that branch of art, though he did little work as a painter. Died c. 1840.

FAIRCHILD, MARY.
See Mrs. Will H. Low.

FAIRCHILD, MAX.
Painter. Exhibited at the National Association of Women Painters and Sculptors, New York, 1924. Address in 1929, 58 West 57th St., NY.

FAIRCHILD, MAY.
(Mrs. Charles Nelson Fairchild). Portrait and miniature painter. Born Boston, MA. Pupil of Cowles Art School in Boston; ASL of NY; John F. Carlson. Member: NA Women PS; PBC; ASL of NY; Brooklyn Min. S.; C. L. Wolfe AC. Taught

miniature painting at ASL of NY. Work; "Miss Evelyn Hall," Northfield (MA) School; "Col. Livingston," State Normal School, Plattsville, WI. Address in 1929, Rhinebeck, NY.

FAIRFAX, D. R.
Portrait painter, who flourished early in the nineteenth century. The collection of paintings at Independence Hall, Philadelphia, has a portrait of Johnston Blakeley, 1781-1814, painted by D. R. Fairfax.

FAIRMAN, DAVID.
A brother of Gideon Fairman. He is mentioned as an engraver, though none of his work has been found. David was born in 1782 and died in Philadelpia, Aug. 19, 1815. His obituary refers to him as "A respectable Artist."

FAIRMAN, GIDEON.
Engraver. Born in Newtown, CT, June 26, 1774. Died in Philadelphia, March 18, 1827. In 1796 he opened an office in Albany as an engraver, and in 1810 he moved to Philadelphia and became a member of the bank note engraving firm of Murray, Draper, Fairman & Co. About 1824 he entered into partnership with Cephas G. Childs, and in 1826 he was a member of the firm of Fairman, Draper, Underwood & Co.

FAIRMAN, RICHARD.
Born in 1788. Died in Philadelphia, 1821. Mr. C. Gobrecht says that Richard was a brother of Gideon Fairman, and in 1820 he was working in the establishment of the latter engraver. He was engraving subject plates in line in Philadelphia as early as 1812.

FALCONER, JOHN M.
Painter and etcher. Born in Edinburgh, Scotland, May 22, 1820. He came to America in 1836, and became an honorary member of the National Academy in 1856. He painted in oils and water colors; etched on copper from his own works and designs of other artists. Died March 12, 1903, in New York City.

FALLS, CHARLES BUCKLES.
Illustrator. Born Fort Wayne, IN, Dec. 10, 1874; died in 1959. Member: SI, 1909; GFLA; Mural P. Award: Beck prize, Phila. WCC, 1918. Work: Illustrated "An Alphabet Book," by Rachel Field (Doubleday, Page & Co.); "The East Window," by Bert Leston Taylor (Knopf). Address in 1929, 2 East 23d St., New York, NY.

FALLS, D(e) W(ITT) C(LINTON).
Painter and illustrator. Born New York, Sept. 29, 1864. Pupil of Walter Satterlee. Specialty, military subjects, portraits, comic illustrating. Address in 1929, 449 Park Ave., New York, NY.

FALTER, JOHN PHILIP.
Illustrator. Born in Plattsmouth, NE, Feb. 28, 1910. Studied: Kansas City Art Institute and in NY at the ASL. Beginning his career in 1929 at Youth Magazine, he has since illustrated for many major magazines and book publishers, including Macmillan and Reader's Digest. He served in the Navy in World War II as a special artist, producing some 180 posters. A member of the Player's Club, the Philadelphia Sketch Club and S of I, he was elected to the latter's Hall of Fame in 1976.

FANNING, RALPH.
Painter, artist, writer, lecturer and teacher. Born New York, Nov. 29, 1889. Pupil of Cornell and Univ. of IL. Member: Ohio Soc. WCP; Columbus A. Lg. Lecturer for Bureau of University Travel. Professor of History of the Fine Arts, Ohio State University. Address in 1929, Dept. of Fine Arts, Ohio State Univ., Columbus, OH.; summer, Riverhead, LI, NY.

FANNING, SOLOMON.
Painter. Born in Preston, CT, in 1807. In 1833 he went to New York and studied portrait painting, and in 1840 he settled in Norwich, CT, where he practiced his profession. His portraits were said to have been good likenesses.

FANNING, WILLIAM S(ANDERS).
Painter and artist. Born Detroit, May 10, 1887. Pupil of Francis

Paulus, Joseph Gies, John P. Wickes, Othon Friesz, Jean Marchand. Address in 1929, 5470 Trumbull Ave., Detroit, MI.

FANSHAW, SAMUEL RAYMOND.
Miniature painter. Born Dec. 21, 1814, in New York City. He exhibited at the National Academy from 1841 to 1847. He was elected an Associate of the Academy in 1881. Died Dec. 15, 1888, in New York City.

FARINA, PASQUALE.
Painter. Born Naples, Italy, Nov. 2, 1864. Studied at the Academy of Fine Arts, Naples. Directed manufacture of artistic ceramics and a class in sculpture at "Aversa," near Naples, Italy, 1885-87. Professor of drawing and perspective in the Normal School for Girls, at Tucuman, Argentine Republic, 1888-90. In 1890, founded a school of drawing, painting and sculpture at Tucuman. Member: Phila. Art Alliance; Fellowship PAFA; S. Indp. A.; AFA; Am. APL; Fairmount Park Association; Fairmount Art Assn. Award: Bronze medal, World's Fair, Chicago, 1893. Represented by: Allegorical painting of Italy in Council Hall, Atessa, Italy; National Museum, Buenos Aires, Argentina. Expert on "Old Masters" work. Address in 1929, 1350 South 51st St., Philadelphia, PA.

FARIS, BEN(JAMIN) HOWARD.
Painter. Born July 21, 1862; died 1935. Pupil of Cincinnati Academy. Member: Cincinnati AC. Specialty, newspaper art. Address in 1929, "Com.-Tribune"; h. Newlands Hotel, Cincinnati, OH.

FARJEON, ELIOT EMANUEL.
Portrait painter. Born in New York City. Studied at Cooper Union; NAD; ASL of NY; with Bonnat, Bouguereau, Robert-Fleury and Lefebvre in Paris. Member: Pittsburgh AA. Address in 1929, Rosenbaum Bldg., Pittsburgh, PA.

FARLEY, R(ICHARD) B(LOSSOM).
Painter. Born Poultney, VT, Oct. 24, 1875. Pupil of Whistler, Chase, Cecilia Beaux. Member: AFA, Salma. C.; Fellowship PAFA;

Phila. Sketch C.; Phila. Alliance. Awards: Fellowship prize, PAFA, 1912; gold medal, Phila. AC., 1912; fourth W. A. Clark prize ($500), Corcoran Gallery, 1914; silver medal, P.-P. Exp., San F., 1915. Work: "Morning Mists," Pennsylvania Academy of the Fine arts; "Fog," Corcoran Gallery, Washington, DC.; "Blue and Gold," "The Passing Cloud," Reading (PA.) Museum. Address in 1929, 1520 Chestnut St., Philadelphia, PA.

FARLINGER, JAMES S(HACKELTON).
Painter. Born Buffalo, NY, July 8, 1881. Address in 1929, 99 Claremont Ave., Verona, NJ; summer, 88 Mary St., Pembroke, Ontario, Canada.

FARLOW, HARRY.
Painter. Born Chicago, IL, April 11, 1882. Pupil of Duveneck, Benson, and Tarbell. Member: Salma. C., MacD. C. Portraits in Hunter College, Lawyers' Club, Yale Club, Board of Education, Princeton Club, Calumet Club, New York; Manufacturers' Club, and Neff College, Philadelphia. Address in 1929, 55 Continental Ave., Forrest Hills, NY.

FARMER, BIRGITTA MORAN.
(Mrs. Thomas P. Farmer). Miniature painter. Born Lyons, NY; died 1939. Pupil Syracuse Univ.; Academie de la Grande Chaumiere, Paris. Member: AFA; Penn. S. Min. P.; NA Women PS. Address in 1929, 912 North Alvord St. Syracuse, NY.

FARMER, JOHN.
Engraver. Born Feb. 9, 1798, in Half Moon, Saratoga County, NY. Farmer was educated near Albany, NY, and taught school in that city. In 1821 he moved to Michigan, became a surveyor, and drew the first published map of Michigan. He later published a number of maps of Michigan, Wisconsin, Lake Superior, Detroit, etc. It is stated that he engraved most of these maps. Held many important city offices in Detroit. Died March 24, 1859, in Detroit, MI.

FARNDON, WALTER.
Painter. Born in England, March 13, 1876. Pupil of NAD under Edgar

M. Ward. Member: ANA, 1928; Salma. C.; AWCS; NYWCC; Allied A. A.; NYSP. Award: Turnbull prize, Salma. C., 1919; Paul H. Hammond prize, AWCS, 1925; Vezin prize, Salma C., 1926; Isidor prize, Salma. C., 1929. Address in 1929, Douglaston, Long Island, NY.

FARNHAM, ALEXANDER.
Painter and writer. Born in Orange, New Jersey, May 5, 1926. Study: ASL, with George Bridgman, W. C. McNulty, Frank Vincent DuMond; also with Van Dearing Perrine and Anne Steel Marsh. Work: Newark Art Museum; The National Arts Club; James A. Michener Collection; Harkness Collection; others. Comn.: Murals, Naval Repair Base, New Orleans, 1945; pewter plate design, Washington Crosses the Del., Franklin Mint, 1976; and many more, 1945-76. Exhibitions: National Academy of Design, 1960; Museum of Fine Arts, Springfield, Mass., 1965-67; Montclair Art Museum, 1966; Newark Museum, 1968. Awards: Noyes Award, Montclair Art Mus.; Newark Mus. Invit.; Summit (NJ) Art Ctr. Nat'l. Exhib., 1981; Art Positions: Artist for U.S. Navy, 1945- 46. Mem.: Assoc. Artists of NJ; Hunterdon Art Ctr. Media: Oil. Auth.: Tool Collectors Handbook; Architectural Patterns, Subject for the Artists Brush. Address in 1982, Stockton, NJ.

FARNHAM, SALLY JAMES.
(Mrs. Paulding Farnham). Sculptor. Born in Ogdensburg, NY, Nov. 26, 1876. Studied at Wells College. Work: Equestrian statue of Gen. Bolivar, New York, NY; War memorial, Fultonville, NY; Statue of Sen. Clark, Corcoran; Soldiers and Sailors Monument, Ogdensburg, NY, and frieze in Pan Am Bldg, Wash. DC. Died April 28, 1943, in New York City. Address in 1929, 57 West 57th St., New York, NY.

FARNSWORTH, JERRY.
Painter. Born Dalton, GA, Dec. 31, 1895. Pupil of C. W. Hawthorne, Clinton Peters. Member: Provincetown AA; Salma. C.; Wash. AC.; Wash. SA; Ten Painters of Wash. Awards: Second prize, Wash. SA, 1924; third Hallgarten prize,

NAD, 1925; Hallgarten prize ($100), NAD, 1927; Golden State prize ($500), Grand Cent. Gal., 1928. Work: "Helen," Delgado Museum, New Orleans; "Three Churches," Penn. Academy of the Fine Arts, 1929. Address in 1929, North Truro, MA.

FARNSWORTH, MRS. JERRY.
See Helen Sawyer.

FARNUM, HERBERT CYRUS.
Painter. Born Gloucester, RI, Sept. 19, 1866. Pupil of RI School of Design; Julian Academy in Paris. Member: Providence AC; Providence WCC. Work: "Flood Tide," Rhode Island School of Design. Address in 1929, Olney Ave., North Providence, RI.

FARNUM, ROYAL B(AILEY).
Art designer, writer, lecturer and teacher. Born Somerville, MA, June 11, 1884. Pupil of Massachusetts Normal Art School. Member: Fed. Council on Art Education; Eastern Arts Assn.; Boston AC; Design and Industries Assn. of Great Britain; Mass. Art Teachers A.; Inter. Fed. A. Tea; AFA. Author of "Present Status of Drawing and Art in the Elementary and Secondary Schools in the United States," 1914, for the Bureau of Education, Washington; "Manual Arts in New York State," 1917; "Decoration for Rural Schools," Cornell Leaflet, 1914; "Syllibi on Drawing and Art;" Practical Drawing Books--Art Education Series," 1924; "Education Thru Pictures," 1928. Writer of Articles on art education in various magazines. On editorial staff, Practical Drawing Co., Dallas, TX. Educational Director, Rhode Island School of Design. Address in 1929, Rhode Island School of Design, 11 Waterman St., Providence, RI.

FARNUNG, HELEN M.
Painter and etcher. Born in Jersey City, NJ, in 1896. Pupil of Art Students' League, New York. Address in 1926, 413 West 147th St., New York.

FARNY, HENRY.
Born in Ribeauville, Alsace, 1847. He came to this country in 1853, and later lived in Cincinnati. In

291

1867 he worked for Harper Bros. in New York, illustrating their publications; he visited Europe, and in Rome met Regnault, who gave him employment. He returned to America in 1870. Died Cincinnati, OH, on Dec. 24, 1916.

FARRAR, HENRY.
Painter and etcher in oil and water colors. Born March 23, 1843, in England. He attained distinction as a landscape painter. His principal works are "On the East River," "November Day," "A Hot Day." Member of the New York Etching Club and the American Society of Painters in Water Colors. Died Feb 24, 1903, in Brooklyn, NY.

FARRAR, THOMAS CHARLES.
Painter. Born in England, 1838. He came to America in 1858, and served in the Union Army during the Civil War. He was the brother of Henry Farrar. Among his works exhibited at the National Academy in New York were "Twilight on the Hudson," "Sunset," and "Coming through the Lock." Died in 1901.

FARRELL, A. T.
Illustrator. Member: SI. Address in 1929, 1910 Forster Ave., Brooklyn, NY.

FARRELL, KATHERINE LEVIN.
(Mrs. Theo. P. Farrell). Painter and etcher. Born Philadelphia, PA; died in 1951. Pupil of School of Design, School of Industrial Art and of PAFA. Member: Plastic C.; Fellowship PAFA; Phila. Alliance; NA Women PS. Awards: Silver medal, 1922, and gold medal, 1923, Plastic Club. Represented in Pennsylvania State College Art Gallery; Trenton AA. Address in 1929, 330 South 43rd St., Philadelphia, PA.

FARRINGTON, KATHERINE.
Painter in St. Paul, MN, in 1877. Pupil of De Camp, and Art Students' League of New York. Address in 1926, 483 Field Point Road, Greenwich, CT.

FARROW, W(ILLIAM) M(cKNIGHT).
Painter, etcher, writer, lecturer and teacher. Born Dayton, OH,

April 13, 1885. Pupil of AIC. Member: Alumni AIC; All-Ill. SFA; Chicago Art Lg. Awards: Eames MacVeagh prize for etching, Chicago Art League, 1928; Charles S. Peterson prize, Chicago Art League, 1929. Work: "Christmas Eve," Woman's Club, Western Springs, IL; "Mother Nature's Mirror," Phillips Junior High School, Chicago; portrait of Abraham Lincoln, Stewart Community House, Gary, IN. Address in 1929, Art Institute of Chicago; h. 6038 South Racine Ave., Chicago, IL.

FASANO, CLARA.
Sculptor. Born in Castellaneta, Italy in 1900. Studied: Cooper Union Art School; Art Students' League; Adelphi College, Brooklyn, NY. Awards: National Association of Women Artists, 1945, 1950; Audubon Art, 1952; National Institute of Arts and Letters, 1952 Medal of Honor, 1956; Scholarship abroad, 1922-1923. Exhibitions at the Whitney Mus. of Am. Art, NY; Met. Mus. of Art; Nat. Academy of Designs, NY; PA Academy of FA, Phil. Collections: United States Post Office, Middleport, OH; Technical High School, Brooklyn, NY; Port Richmond High School, Staten Island, NY. Taught sculpture at the Indust. and FA Sch. of NY and Adult Ed., 1946-56; Manhattanville Col., 1956-66. Address in 1980 Nat. Academy of Design, 1083 Fifth Ave., New York, NY.

FASOLINO, TERESA.
Illustrator. Born in Port Chester, NY, in 1946. Attended the SVA where she studied under Robert Weaver. She also attended PI and ASL. Her career began at Ingenue and she has worked for Travel and Leisure, Playboy, Redbook, and The New York Times.

FASSETT, CORNELIA ADELE STRONG.
Painter. Born Nov. 9, 1831, in Owasco, NY. Daughter of Judge Strong. Studied abroad under Meissonier, and moved to Washington, DC, in 1875. Her large portrait of the Supreme Justices in 1876 was exhibited at the Centennial. Painted many portraits of men and women in public life of

Washington. She had eight children. Several of her paintings are in the Capitol Bldg., Washington, DC. Died Jan. 4, 1898, in Wash., DC.

FASSETT, TRUMAN E.
Painter and teacher. Born Elmira, NY, May 9, 1885. Pupil of Boston Museum School; Richard Miller; Lucien Simon. Member: Salma. C.; NAC; AFA. Address in 1929, 47 Washington Square, South, New York, NY; h. Woodmere, LI, NY.

FAULKNER, BARRY.
Mural painter. Born Keene, July 12, 1881. Pupil of Abbott H. Thayer and George de F. Brush. Member: ANA, 1926; Mural P.; NY Arch. Lg., 1911; Nat'l Inst. of Arts and Letters; NAD (assn.). Awards: American Academy in Rome Scholarship, 1908-1911; medal of honor for painting, NY Arch. Lg., 1914. Work: Panels in foyer of Washington Irving High School, New York City; Pictorial Maps in Cunard Bldg., New York, NY; Eastman School of Music, Rochester; decorations in University of Illinois Library. Address in 1929, 319 East 72nd St., New York, NY, and 61 Summer St., Keene, NH.

FAULKNER, HERBERT WALDRON.
Painter, illustrater, engraver, writer and lecturer. Born Stamford, CT, Oct. 8, 1860. Pupil of ASL of NY under Beckwith and Mowbray; Collin in Paris. Member: Salma. C., 1897; Syndicat de la Presse Artistique. Award: Hon. mention, Pan-Am. Exp., Buffalo, 1901. Work: "Gondolier's Kitchen," Dallas (Tex.) Art Association; "Palace on Grand Canal," St. Louis Museum; "Une Fete qui finit mal," Minneapolis Museum; "San Georgio, Venice, at Sunset," Herron Art Institute, Indianapolis. Died in 1940. Address in 1929, Washington, CT.

FAUST, DORBERT C.
Painter. Exhibited a water color at Cincinnati Museum, 1925. Address in 1926, 552 Mt. Vernon Road, Newark, OH.

FAWCETT, GEORGE.
Illustrator and etcher. Born London, April 8, 1877. Studied in England. Member: Canadian Soc. PE; Chicago SE. Work: Three etchings, National Gallery, Ottawa, Canada. Address in 1929, 828 Valencia Ave., Coral Gables, FL; h. Old Branchville Rd., Ridgefield, CT.

FAWCETT, ROBERT.
Illustrator. Born in London in 1903. Moved to Canada as a child and in 1924, after studying at the Slade School of Art, London, began his career in NY. He went on to produce illustrations for magazines and advertising clients, as well as to paint murals for the Commonwealth Institute and to write a book on the art of drawing, demonstrating his superb draftsmanship and mastery of composition. His intricate, atmospheric illustrations were published in Look, Collier's, and The Saturday Evening Post, appearing in the latter for the first time in 1945. A founding faculty member of the FAS, he was President of the Westport Artists and later elected to the S of I Hall of Fame. Died in 1967.

FAXON, WILLIAM BAILEY.
Painter. Born Hartford, CT, 1849. Pupil of Jacquesson de la Chevreuse. Member; SAA 1892; ANA 1906; AFAS; A. Aid S.; Century Assoc. Address in 1929, 7 West 43rd St., New York, NY.

FAY, NELLIE.
Painter. Born Eureka, CA, 1870. Pupil of Arthur F. Mathews and Emil Carlsen. Address in 1926, 1612 Washington St., San Francisco, CA.

FeBLAND, HARRIET.
Painter/constructionist. Born in New York City. Studied: The Art Students' League, New York; Pratt Institute; New York University. Exhibitions: Hudson River Museum, Yonkers, NY; Silvermine Guild, New Canaan, CT; Huntington Hartford Museum, New York City. Collections: Cincinnati Art Museum, OH; Westchester County Court House, White Plains, NY; Tweed Gallery, University of Minnesota. Taught at

NY Univ., 1960-62; Harriet FeBland's Advan. Painters Workshop, Pelham, NY, 1962. Media: Acrylic, sculpture in steel, plexiglass, marble, wood. Address in 1980, E. 63rd Street, Apt. 408, New York, NY.

FECHIN, NICOLAI IVANOVICH.
Painter. Born Kazan, Russia, Nov. 28, 1881. Pupil of Repin. Member: Imperial Academy of F.A., Petrograd, Russia. Awards: First prize Imperial Academy of Fine Arts, Petrograd, 1908; Proctor Prize, NAD, 1924. Works: "Kapustinga," Imperial Academy of Fine Arts, Petrograd; "Nude," Kuingi Galleries, Petrograd; "Self Portrait," Museum of Kazan, Russia; "Isabella," Albright Art Gallery, Buffalo, NY; "Lillian Gish as Romola," Art Institute of Chicago. Address in 1929, 2 West 67th St., New York.

FEDERE, MARION.
Collage and drawing. Born in Vienna, Austria. Studied: Vienna, Austria; Brooklyn Mus.; Seide's Workshop; San Miguel De Allende, Instituto, Mex.; Pratt Graphic Center. Exhibitions: Village Art Center; NAD; Brooklyn Mus.; Brandeis Univ. 19th Ann. Drawing Award, Village Art Ctr., 1964; Floyd Bennett Field 1st Prize, 1st Place Prof. Awards, 1969; Contemp. Awards, Am. Soc. of Contemp. Artists, 1981. Address in 1980, 2277 E. 17th St. Brooklyn, NY.

FEHRER, OSCAR.
Portrait painter. Born New York City in 1872. Studied in New York, Paris and Munich. Member: Allied AA; Salma. C.; NAC (life), Brooklyn SA; Brooklyn PS. Represented in Memorial Hall City Library, Lowell, MA. Address in 1929, care of the National Arts Club, 15 Gramercy Park, New York, NY; h. Lyme, CT.

FEININGER, LYONEL.
Painter and printmaker. Born: Elizabeth, NJ in 1871. Studied at the Berlin Acad.; in Paris attended classes at Colarossi. Newspaper illustrator in Berlin, Chicago and Paris. Taught painting and graphic

arts at the Bauhaus in Dessau. A member of the Exhibition Group, the Blau Vier, which included Klee, Kandinsky, and Jawlensky. Retrospective exhib. Nat'l. Gal. Berlin 1931. First major show in held in 1944 at Museum of Modern Art. Died in 1956.

FEITELSON, LORSER.
Painter. Born 1898 in Savannah, GA. Studied in New York City and Paris. Taught at Art Center School in LA. Exhibited at Cal. Palace (SF) 1928-29; S. F. Mus. of Art; Scripps College; MOMA (1936-37); Brooklyn, Mus.; MMA; L.A. County Mus.; Whitney, and abroad. In collections of Brooklyn; MOMA; San Francisco Mus. of Art; Long Beach Mus. of Art; The Art Inst. of Chicago, 1947; Univ. of IL, 1950,'51,'52; The Met Mus. of Art, 1953; many private collections. Died May 24, 1978.

FEKE, ROBERT.
Early American portrait painter. Born c. 1707 at Oyster Bay, Long Island. Married Eleanor Cozzens in 1742 at Newport, RI. Worked there and in Boston, New York and Philadelphia. The earliest date on his painting is 1741, and the latest is 1748. Made several sea trips; was possibly captured and taken to Spain. Went to Bermuda. His portraits are in Harvard University and the Redwood Library, Newport, RI. Portraits of the Bowdoins owned by Bowdoin College, Brunswick, ME. The Rhode Island School of Design has his "Pamela Andrews," and the Cleveland Museum owns his portrait of Charles Apthorp. Died in 1750 in Bermuda.

FELCH.
This name is signed to some poorly executed landscape work published in 1855, with no indication of place.

FELDMAN, BARUCH M.
Painter. Born in Russia, 1885. Pupil of Anshutz. Member: Fellowship, Penna. Academy of Fine Arts. Address in 1926, 320 Harmony St., Philadelphia, PA.

FELDMAN, CHARLES.
Painter, writer and lecturer. Born Lublin, Russia, Jan. 27, 1893. Pupil of NAD; Robert Henri; George Bellows. Member: Salons of America; S. Indp. A. Address in 1929, 66 West 9th St., New York, NY; summer 123 Beach 86th St., Rockaway Beach, NY.

FELDMAN, HILDA.
Painter, craftsman and teacher. Born Newark, NJ, Nov. 22, 1899. Pupil of Ida Wells Stroud, Anna Fischer. Member: NA Women PS. Address in 1929, 507 Richmond Ave., Maplewood, NJ.

FELKER, RUTH KATE.
(Mrs. W. D. Thomas). Painter. Born St. Louis, MO, May 16, 1889. Pupil of School of Architecture at Washington University and St. Louis School of Fine Arts; ASL of NY; Society of Beaux-Arts Architects; studied in Europe. Member: Soc. of Ancients of St. Louis; Wash. Univ. Arch. Soc. (hon.); St. Louis AG. Awards: Mallinckrodt prize, St. Louis AG, 1915, 1916, 1917, 1919.. Work: Mural decoration in St. John's Hospital, St. Louis. Paintings in St. Louis Art League Gallery. Address in 1929, 7530 Harter Ave., Richmond Hgts., St. Louis Co., MO.

FELLOWS, ALBERT P.
Painter and etcher. Born Selma, Ala., 1864. Pupil of School of Industrial Art and of Drexel Inst., Philad.; PAFA; ASL of NY. Member: Phil. Soc. of Etchers; Phila. Sketch C.; Phila. Print C. Address in 1929, 112 South 52nd St., Philadelphia, PA; h. 127 Chatham Rd., Stonehurst, Del. Co., PA.

FELLOWS, CORNELIA FABER.
(Mrs. A. P. Fellows). Portrait painter. Born Philadelphia. Pupil of Penna. Academy of Fine Arts, and Drexel Institute. Member: Fellowship, Penna. Academy of Fine Arts; Plastic Club. Address in 1926, 3203 Summer St., Philadelphia, PA.

FELLOWS, LAWRENCE.
Illustrator. Born in Ardmore, PA, in 1855. Attended the Philadelphia Academy of Fine Arts, followed by studies in England and France. Upon his return he did many humorous drawings for Judge and Life. His tasteful line drawings, utilizing large areas of white space, were suited to fashion illustration and appeared often in Vanity Fair, Apparel Arts, and Esquire. He was best known for his Kelly-Springfield Tire advertisements in the 1920's. Died in 1964.

FELTON, ROBERT.
Engraver, and one of the early American die-sinkers, according to the Colonial Records of Pennsylvania. At a meeting of the Governor's Council, held in Philadelphia, 1663, Charles Pickering and others were accused of coining silver "in imitation of Spanish pieces with too great an alloy of copper in it." From the minutes of the trial it appears that Robert Felton testified that he "made the Seals and the bills, viz-the Spanish Bills." He further speaks of the "Stamping of New Bills" and "Striking on the Stamp;" and he says he worked several weeks in "Cutting the Seals."

FENDERSON, ANNIE M.
(Mrs. Mark Fenderson). Painter. Born Spartansburg, PA. Member: NA Women PS; Pa. S. Min. P. Specialty, miniatures. Address in 1929, 144 West 23rd St., New York, NY.

FENDERSON, MARK.
Illustrator. Member: SI 1913. Address in 1929, 144 West 23d St., New York, NY.

FENN, HARRY.
Painter, illustrator and engraver. Born in England on Sept. 14, 1845. In 1864 he came to America. He was a founder of the American Water Color Society, the Society of Illustrators, and the Salmagundi Club. Specialty: landscapes. Died Montclair, NJ, April 21, 1911.

FENNER, MAUDE RICHMOND.
(Mrs. Albert Fenner). Painter, craftsman and writer. Born Bristol, RI, May 24, 1868. Pupil of Burleigh, Mathewson and RI School of Design. Member: Providence AC; Providence WCC.

Address in 1929, 78 Oriole Ave., Providence, RI.

FENTON, BEATRICE.
Sculptor. Born Philadelphia, PA, July 12, 1887. Pupil of School of Industrial Art, Phila., and PAFA. Member: Fellowship PAFA; Plastic C.; Phila. Alliance; NA Women PS. Awards: Stewardson sculpture prize, PAFA, 1908; Cresson Traveling scholarship, PAFA, 1909-10; hon. mention, P.-P. Exp., San F., 1915; hon. mention, Plastic C., 1916; Widener medal, PAFA, 1922; Fellowship prize, PAFA, 1922; Shillard silver medal, Plastic C., 1922; bronze medal, Sesqui-Centennial Exposition, Phila., 1926. Represented in permanent collection, Philadelphia Art Club; "Seaweed Fountain," Fairmount Park, Philadelphia; Charles M. Schmitz Memorial, Academy of Music; "Fairy Fountain," Wister Park, Philadelphia. Address in 1929, 1523 Chestnut St.; h. 1319 Spruce St., Philadelphia, PA.

FENTON, HALLIE CHAMPLIN.
Painter and teacher. Born St. Louis, MO, Oct. 1880. Pupil of Jacques Blanche in Paris. Member: NA Women PS. Died in 1935. Address in 1929, Sagamore Park, Bronxville, NY.

FENTON, JOHN WILLIAM.
Painter and teacher. Born Conewango Valley, NY, July 6, 1875. Pupil of NY School of Fine and Applied Art; Cullen Yates and Howard Giles. Member: Salma. C.; New Rochelle AA. Award: First hon. mention, New Rochelle AA, 1923; E. Irving Hanson prize, 1927, New Rochelle AA. Work: "Bittersweet," Literary Digest cover. Teacher of Art in New York City High Schools. Died in 1939. Address in 1929, 244 State St., East Westport, CT; summer, "Fenton Farms," Conewango Valley, Catteraugus Co., NY.

FERG, FRANK X.
Painter. Member: Penna. Academy of Fine Arts. Address in 1926, 6026 Webster St., Philadelphia, PA.

FERGUSON, ALICE L. L.
(Mrs. H. G. Ferguson). Painter. Born Washington, DC. Pupil of

Corcoran School in Washington; and of Hawthorne and Breckenridge. Member: Wash. WCC; S. Wash. A; SSAL; NA Women PS; AFA. Address in 1929, 2330 California St., Washington, DC.

FERGUSON, DOROTHY H.
Painter and etcher. Born Alton, IL, Dec. 9, 1896. Pupil of Charles Hawthorne. Award: First prize, St. Louis Artists Guild, 1928. Work: "Goin' Home," Public Schools, St. Louis, MO. Address in 1929, 628 East 15th St., Alton, IL; summer, care of Provincetown Art Association, Provincetown, MA.

FERGUSON, DUNCAN.
Sculptor. Born Shanghai, China, Jan. 1, 1901. Pupil of A. H. Atkins, Robert Laurent. Member: S. Indp. A; Salons of America. Work: "Anatol" and "Mimi," Newark Museum, Newark, NJ. Address in 1929, 11 Minetta St., New York, NY.

FERGUSON, EDWARD L.
Engraver. Born in Illinois in 1859. He lived in New York; his specialty was steel engraving. He died in New York City in 1915.

FERGUSON, ELEANOR M.
Sculptor. Born Hartford, June 30, 1876. Pupil of C. N. Flagg in Hartford; D. C. French, G. G. Barnard and ASL of NY. Member: Conn. AFA. Address in 1929, 847 Prospect Ave.; 123 Vernon St., Hartford, CT.

FERGUSON, ELIZABETH F.
Illustrator. Born in Omaha, NE, 1884. Pupil of Penna. Academy of Fine Arts. Address in 1926, 1039 Fine Arts Bldg., Chicago, IL.

FERGUSON, HENRY.
Painter. Born 1842. Elected an Associate member of the National Academy in 1884. He died in 1911 in New York. His painting "In Venice" was exhibited in the Centennial of the National Academy in 1925.

FERGUSON, LILLIAN.
Painter and craftsman. Born Windsor, Ont., Canada, Aug. 18, 1877. Pupil of Lefebvre and Julian Academy in Paris; Alexander

296

Robinson in Holland; William Chase. Member: Calif. AC; Laguna Beach AA; San Diego FAS; West Coast Arts, Inc. Award: Cash prize, Calif. State Fair, Sacramento, 1926; Tingle Memorial Fund prize, West Coast Arts, Inc., Los Angeles, 1926. Address in 1929, 1841 No. Highland Ave., Hollywood, CA.

FERGUSON, NANCY MAYBIN.
Painter. Born Philadelphia, PA. Pupil of Elliott Daingerfield, Hugh Breckenridge, William M. Chase and Charles Hawthorne. Member: Fellowship PAFA; Phila. Alliance; NA Women PS; Provincetown AA.; Alumnae Asson. Phila. School of Design for Women. Awards: European Fellowships from the Phila. School of Design and the PAFA; Mary Smith prize, PAFA, 1916; hon. mention, NA Women PS; second and first Toppan prize, Schools of PAFA; gold medal, exhibition Fellowship PAFA, 1929. Work in the Pennsylvania Academy of the Fine Arts, Philadelphia; Barnes Collection, Overbrook, PA; Public Museum and Art Gallery, Reading, PA. Address in 1929, 53 West Tulpehecken St., Philadelphia, PA; summer, Provincetown, MA.

FERGUSON, WILLIAM HUGH.
Etcher. Born Reading, PA, 1905. Exhibited at the Annual Exhibition of Water Colors at the PAFA, Philadelphia, 1925. Died Reading in 1964. Address in 1926, Perkiomen Ave., Reading, PA.

FERNALD, HELEN E(LIZABETH).
Painter, writer and lecturer. Born Baltimore, MD, Dec. 24, 1891. Pupil of ASL of NY. Member: Plastic C.; Phila. Alliance; Am. Oriental S. Author of articles and lectures on Chinese art. Address in 1929, The University Museum, Philadelphia, PA; h. 27 Central Ave., Bryn Mawr, PA; summer, 44 Amity St., Amherst, MA.

FERNBACH, A(GNES) B.
Etcher. Born New York City, June 29, 1877. Pupil of ASL of NY; Cooper Union; NY School of Applied Design for Women; Alphonse Mucha and Ernest Haskell. Member:

Brooklyn SE. Address in 1929, 320 West 89th St., New York, NY.

FERNE, HORTENSE T.
Painter and etcher. Born New York, NY. Pupil of Chase, Hawthorne, Browne, Wagner and Auerbach-Levy; Breckenridge; NAD; School of Industrial Art, Phila. Member: Phila. Alliance; Print C.; AWCS; (sec.-treas.) Phila. SE; North Shore AA; Art Centre, NY; (Chm.) New Group Phila. A.; Plastic C.; NA Women PS. Award: First hon. mention, Plastic C., 1927. Work: "Indian Study" and "White Cloud," Lanape Club, Philadelphia; Cardinal portrait, Rome; Republican Club, New York. Address in 1929, 10 South 18th St.; 1901 Walnut St., Philadelphia, PA.

FERNIE, MARGARET.
See Mrs. Hugh Eaton.

FERNOW, BERNICE PAUAHL ANDREWS.
(Mrs. B. E. Fernow, Jr.). Painter. Born Jersey City, NJ, Dec. 17, 1881. Pupil of Olaf M. Brauner and Theodora Thayer. Member: ASL of NY; A.S. Min. P. Specialty: Portraits and miniatures. Address in 1929, Clemson College, SC.

FERRARI, FEBO.
Sculptor. Born Pallanza, Italy, Dec. 4, 1865. Pupil of Royal Academy, Turin. Member: New Haven PCC. Specialty, architectural sculpture. Address in 1929, Onahill Cottage, Short Beach, CT.

FERRER, VERA L.
Miniature painter. Born New York, NY, Jan 13, 1895. Pupil of Lucia Fairchild Fuller and J. B. Whitaker; NAD. Member: NA Women PS. Address in 1929, Little Neck, NY.

FERRIS, BERNICE BRANSON.
(Mrs. Warren W. Ferris). Illustrator. Born Astoria, IL. Pupil of J. C. Leyendecker, F. Goudy, Lawton Parker; Chicago AI; Chicago Academy of F.A. Member: Lincoln AG; Wash. AC. Died in 1936. Address in 1929, Russell Rd., Alexandria, VA.

FERRIS, EDYTHE.
(Mrs. Raynond H. Ferris). Painter,
illustrator and teacher. Born
Riverton, NJ, June 21, 1897. Pupil
of Philadelphia School of Design
for Women. Member: Phila.
Alliance; Philadelphia School of
Design for Women, Alumnae; AFA.
Address in 1929, 3741 Locust St.,
Philadelphia, PA.

FERRIS, JEAN LEON GEROME.
Historical painter. Born
Philadelphia, Aug. 8, 1863. Pupil
of S. J. Ferris and Christian
Schuessele in Philadelphia;
Bouguereau and Gerome in Paris.
Member: A. Fund S. of Phila.;
Phila. SE, 1881; Phila. AC, 1890.
Loan collection of seventy
paintings of American History,
Museum of Independence Hall,
Philadelphia. Died in 1930.
Address in 1929, 8 No. 50th St.,
Philadelphia, PA.

FERRIS, STEPHEN JAMES.
Portrait painter. Born in
Plattsburg, NY, Dec. 25, 1835. He
received the Fortuny prize for the
best portrait of the artist in
Rome, 1876. He painted about 2000
portraits and made a number of
etchings. He died in Philadelphia,
July 9, 1915.

FERRIS, STEPHEN JR.
Etcher and crayon portrait
draughtsman. Flourished 1857-60,
Phila. He was a close friend of the
engraver John Sartain of Phila.

FERRIS, WARREN W(ESLEY).
Painter and illustrator. Born
Rochester, NY, June 22, 1890.
Pupil of John Norton; AIC; Le Mans
in France. Member: Wash. AC;
Wash. WCC. Award: First prize,
Decorative Art League, New York,
1923. Address in 1929, Russell
Rd., Alexandria, VA.

FERRISS, HUGH.
Illustrator, architect designer.
Born St. Louis, MO, July 12, 1889.
Pupil Sch. FA, St. Louis; Arch.
Sch. Washington Univ. Member: NY
Arch. Lg.; NYAG. Illustrations for
"Harpers," "Century," "Pencil
Points," "Monitor," "Arts and
Decoration," "McCalls," etc.
Contr. article on "Architectural

Rendering," Encyclopaedia
Brittannica, 1929. Consultant to
Arch. Comm. World's Fair, Chicago,
of 1933; Spec. Lecturer on Design
and Illustration, Columbia (1926);
Yale (1928); U. of Penn. (1928);
Hon. Master of Arch., Wash. U.
(1928). Address in 1929, 101 Park
Ave., New York, NY.

FERRY, ISABELLE H.
Painter and teacher. Born
Williamsburg, MA. Pupil of Tryon,
Henri, Bouguereau, Boutet de
Monvel, Fleury, etc. Member:
Springfield, MA, Art Lg.; Conn.
AFA; Holyoke A. Lg. Died in 1937.
Address in 1929, Skye Studio,
Boothbay Harbor, ME; h. 189 East
St., Easthampton, MA.

FETERS, W. T.
A crudely done stippled portrait of
the Rev. John Davenport, of
Connecticut, is signed "W. T.
Feters," though this may be a
mistake of the letter-engraver for
Peters. The plate has no
indication of its origin, and the
only reasons for ascribing it to an
American are the poor quality of
the work and the fact that the
subject is American. The date of
publication is about 1820.

FETSCHER, CHARLES W.
Painter and architect. Member:
Soc. Deaf A. Address in 1929, 323
Guion Ave., Richmond Hill, LI, NY.

FETTE, HENRY GERHARD.
Portrait painter in oils and
miniature. Flourished in Boston,
1842-51.

FIELD, EDWARD LOYAL.
Landscape painter. Born Jan 4,
1856, in Galesburg, IL, and died
March 22, 1914, in New York City.
He also painted in water color.

FIELD, ERASTUS SALISBURY.
Painter. Born 1805 in Leverett,
MA. Self-taught; briefly a student
of Samuel F. B. Morse in 1824.
Field was an itinerant painter
painting portraits in W. Mass. and
Conn. In 1845 and 1847 works were
exhibited at Am. Inst. of NYC.
Died in 1900.

298

FIELD, HAMILTON EASTER.
Painter and etcher. Born in Brooklyn, 1873; died there, 1922. Pupil in Paris of Gerome, Collin, Courtois, Fantin-Latour, and Lucien Simon. He was also an art editor, writer and teacher.

FIELD, LOUISE BLODGETT.
Painter. Born in Boston. Pupil of Ross Turner, Fred D. Williams, William Morris Hunt and Tomasso Juglaris in Boston. Member: Boston WCC; Copley S., 1896. Address in 1929, 32 Cottage St., Wellesley, MA.

FIELD, MARY.
(Mrs. Herman Field). Painter and craftsman. Born Stoughton, MA, Jan. 14, 1864. Pupil of AIC. Member: Chicago SA; Chicago AC. Award: Bronze medal, Alaska Yukon Pacific Exp., Seattle, 1909; prize for portrait, Chicago AC, 1918. Address in 1929, 4826 Kimbark Ave., Chicago, IL.

FIELD, ROBERT.
Portrait painter and engraver. Probably born in Gloucester, England, and came to NY c. 1793. Went to Halifax, after painting very good miniatures in Boston, Phila., Baltimore, and NY. Field was in Phila., 1795, and on August 1st he published his portrait of Washington in NYC. He engraved stipple portraits of Washington, Jefferson, Hamilton and Shakespeare; but was chiefly occupied in painting miniatures. Subjects of miniatures include Washington and Jefferson, after Stuart, Charles Carroll of Carrollton, both of the latter engraved by Longacre and William Cliffton, and J. E. Harwood, engraved by Edwin. Painted portraits of Mrs. Allen, of Boston, and Mrs. Thornton, of Wash., DC. About 1808 Field moved to Halifax, Nova Scotia, to paint portraits; there he engraved at least one large plate, a full-length portrait of Governor-General Sir John Coape Sherbrooke, published in Halifax in 1816. He painted this and several Governors for the Government House in Halifax. A number of Field's portraits in that city were those of Bishop Charles Ingles, now in

the National Gallery in London, and portraits of Adam Dechezean, John Lawson, Michael Wallace, and William Bowie, of Halifax. He probably returned to England for a short time, as Algernon Graves, in his "Dictionary of Artists," mentions R. Field as "a portrait painter of Halifax, NS." He later went to Jamaica. In a letter of Field's, in the Pennsylvania Historical Society, addressed to Robert Gilmor, Jr., Baltimore, Field refers to the Robertson portrait of Washington which he engraved "with some ornaments to surround and make it more interesting." Died Aug. 9, 1819, in Jamaica.

FIELDING, MANTLE.
Architect, designer and author of books relating to painting and engraving. Born in New York, 1865. Member of Philadelphia Art Club, and Penna. Academy of Fine Arts. Author of American Engravers, and "Gilbert Stuart, and his portraits of Washington." Address in 1926, 520 Walnut St., Philadelphia, PA.

FIELDS, FREDERICA HASTINGS.
3-Dimensional Stained Glass artist and glass engraver. Born in Philadelphia, PA, Jan. 10, 1912. Studied: Wellesley College; The Art Students League, NY; Awards: Corcoran Gallery of Art, 1955, 1956; Sixth International Exhibition of Ceramic Arts, 1957. Collections: Washington Cathedral, Washington, DC; Greenwich Library, CT; Y.M.C.A., Greenwich, CT.

FIELDS, MITCHELL.
Sculptor. Born in Rumania, Sept. 28, 1900. Member: Sculptors and Modellers of Am. Address in 1929, 1931 Broadway, New York, NY.

FILKOSKY, JOSEFA.
Sculptor. Born in Westmoreland City, PA, June 15, 1933. Study: Seton Hall College; Carnegie-Mellon Univ.; Cranbrook Academy of Art; Art Inst. of Chicago, Summer Sculpture Seminar. Work: Commissions for Taubman Corp., Southfield, PA; Oxford Merchandise Mart, Monroeville, PA; Everson (PA) Museum. Exhibitions: Art Image in All Media, NYC, 1970; Indiana

Univ., 1972; Bertha Schaefer Gallery, NYC, 1973 (all solos); Pittsburgh Plan for Art, 1971, 73, 75; Sculpture in the Fields, Storm King Art Center, 1974-76; Sculpture on Shoreline Sites, Roosevelt Island, NY, 1979-80. Awards: Three Rivers Purchase Prize, 1972; Assoc. Artists of Pittsburgh Award, 1976. Teaching: Prof. of Art, Seton Hall, 1956-Present. Mem.: Assoc. Artists of Pittsburgh; Pittsburgh Plan for Art. Media: Aluminum, Plexiglass. Address in 1982, Seton Hall College, Greensburg, PA.

FILMER, JOHN.
Engraver and book illustrator.

FINCH, ELINOR G.
Miniature painter. Exhibited portrait miniatures at the Penna. Academy of the Fine Arts, Philadelphia, 1922. Address in 1926, 22 Terrace Park, Spokane, WA.

FINCKEN, JAMES H(ORSEY).
Engraver and etcher. Born Bristol, England, May 9, 1860. Member: Phila. Sketch C.; Phila. Alliance; Phila. Print C.; AFA. Address in 1929, 1012 Walnut St.; h. 909 South Saint Bernard St., Philadelphia, PA. Died in 1943.

FINE, PERLE.
Painter. Born in Boston, MA, May 1, 1908. Studied with Hans Hofmann and printmaking with William Hayter. Collections: Whitney Museum of American Art; Smith College Museum; Rutgers University; Munson-Williams-Proctor Institute; Los Angeles Museum of Art; Guggenheim Museum of art; The Miller Company Collection; Brandeis University; Brooklyn Museum. Exhibited at Carnegie Inst., Pittsburgh; Art of the Century, Peggy Guggenheim Gallery, NY; Geometric Abstraction in Am. and Nature in Abstractions Whitney Mus. of Am. Art, NY. Media: Oil, acrylic, wood collage, and collage. Address in 1980, 538 Old Stone Highway, The Springs, NY.

FINK, DENMAN.
Painter and illustrator. Born Springdale, PA, Aug. 29, 1880. Pupil of Benson, Hale and Walter A.

Clark. Member: SI. Illustrated "Mace's History of United States;" "The Barrier" and "The Lost Girl," by Rex Beach; "Post Borders," by Mary Austen, etc. Illustrations for "Harper's," "Scribner's," "Century," etc. Address in 1929, Haworth, NJ.

FINK, FREDERICK.
Genre and portrait painter. Born Dec. 28, 1817 in Little Falls, NY. Studied under Morse. The subjects of the few pictures he lived to execute are "An Artist's Studio," "The Shipwrecked Mariner," "The Young Thieves," "A Negro Woodsawyer," and a portrait of W. S. Parker, painted when the artist was eighteen years old. Fink died Jan. 23, 1849.

FINK, SAMUEL.
Illustrator. Born in NYC, in 1916. Studied: NAD and ASL in the mid-1930's. His first work appeared in The New York Times in 1938. He has spent most of his career at Young and Rubicam as an art director and is author and illustrator of the book 56 Who Signed for E.P. Dutton. He is represented in the collection of the Brooklyn Museum.

FINKELNBURG, AUGUSTA.
Painter. Born Fountain City, WI. Pupil of AIC; Pratt Inst., Brooklyn; studied in Paris, Italy, Holland and England and with Robert Reid, Willard Metcalf, Henry B. Snell, Herbert Adams and Arthur W. Dow. Awards: Three first prizes at Missouri State Fair. Member: St. Louis AG; St. Louis AL. Work: Landscape St. Louis High Schools. Address in 1929, Kimmswick, MO.

FINN, HENRY JAMES.
Miniature painter, actor and author. Born June 17, 1787, in Sydney, NS, Canada. Painted miniatures in Boston, 1833. Died Jan. 13, 1840.

FINNEY, BETTY.
Painter. Born in Sidney, Australia in 1920. Studied: Royal Art Society, Sydney; Academie des Beaux-Arts, Brussels; Otis Art Institute; also with Paul Clemens, Ejnar Hansen and Normal Rockwell.

300

Awards: Scholarship, Royal Art Society, Sydney; Los Angeles, Stacy award, 1952; Traditional Art Show, Hollywood, 1955; Friday Morning Club.

FINTA, A(LEXANDER).
Sculptor. Born Turkeve, Hungary, June 12, 1881. Member: AFA. Work: Marble bust of his Eminence Cardinal Hayes, Metropolitan Museum of Art, New York; bronze portrait of Count Apponyi, National Museum of Budapest, Hungary; "Strength," granite monument, City of Rio de Janeiro, Brazil; 30-foot high marble War Monument, City of Nyitra, Czechoslovakia; 15-foot high granite War Monument, City of Maniga, Czechoslovakia; 12-foot high marble monument of Adolf Merey, City of Budapest, Hungary; monument of Honveds, City of Hatvan, Hungary, etc. Address in 1929, 8 West 13th St., New York, NY.

FIRESTONE, I(SADORE) L(OUIS).
Painter, illustrator and teacher. Born in Austria-Hungary, April 13, 1894. Pupil of Carnegie Inst. of Tech., Pittsburgh; NY Evening School of Ind. A.; ASL of NY. Member: Pittsburgh AA. Address in 1929, 148 East 34th St., New York, NY; h. 246 Dinwiddie St., Pittsburgh, PA.

FISCHER, ANTON OTTO.
Painter and illustrator. Born Munich, Bavaria, Feb. 23, 1882. Pupil of Jean Paul Laurens, Julian Academy, Paris. Member: SI; AFA. Illustrated for "Harper's Weekly," "Saturday Evening Post," "Everybody's Life," and Scribner's. Best known for marine paintings; author, illus. of Fo'cs'le Days, publ. by Scribner's. Died in 1962. Address in 1929, 164 Elmendorf St., Kingston, NY; summer, Shandaken, Ulster Co., NY.

FISCHER, H.
Painter. Member: Society of Independent Artists. Address in 1926, 48 West 90th St., New York, NY.

FISCHER, J. F.
Work: Portrait of Albert Pike, born in 1809 and died 1891.

American lawyer, author, and Confederate commissioner appointed to treat with the Indians. Half length to left, long white locks and white beard. Size 29½ in. x 23½ in. Signed "J. F. Fischer." Sold American Art Association, NY, Dec., 1921.

FISCHER, MARTIN.
Painter, writer and lecturer. Born Kiel, Germany, Nov. 10, 1879. Member: Duveneck Soc. of Painters; Cincinnati AC. Work: Murals, Physiological Laboratories, College of Medicine and Assembly Hall, College of Pharmacy, Cincinnati, OH. Address in 1929, College of Medicine, Eden Ave.; h. 2236 Auburn Ave., Cincinnati, OH.

FISCHER, MARY ELLEN SIGSBEE.
(Mrs. Anton O. Fischer). Illustrator. Born New Orleans, LA, Feb. 26, 1876. Member: SI (assoc.), 1912. Address in 1929, 402 Albany Ave., Kingston, NY; Shandaken, Ulster Co., NY.

FISHER, A. HUGH.
Painter, etcher and writer. Born London, Feb. 8, 1867. Pupil of Jean Paul Laurens, Benjamin Constant, Sir Frank Short. Member: Chicago SE; Calif. PM; Royal Soc. of Painter Etchers. Represented in Washington Public Library, Washington, DC; British Museum, National Art Gallery of Victoria, London. Address in 1929, The Print Corner, Hingham Center, Mass.; h. 46 Aldridge Rd. Villas, Bayswater, London, England.

FISHER, ALVAN.
American portrait and genre painter. Born Aug. 9, 1792, in Needham, MA. In 1825 he visited Europe for study and travel. He established his studio in Boston, where he painted many portraits. One of his best works is a portrait of Spurzheim painted from recollection in 1832. Died in Feb. 1863 in Dedham, MA.

FISHER, ANNA S.
Painter. Born Cold Brook, NY. Member: ANA; AWCS; NYWCC; NA Women PS; SPNY.; Allied AA. Awards: National Arts Club prize, NA Women PS, 1919; Harriet B. Jones prize,

Balto. WCC., 1922. Work: "The Orange Bowl," National Academy of Design, New York, NY. Died in 1942. Address in 1929, 939 Eighth Ave., New York, NY.

FISHER, BUD.
Cartoonist. Born in 1885. Address in 1926, 258 Riverside Drive, New York.

FISHER, EMILY KOHLER.
Painter. Member: Fellowship, Penna. Academy of Fine Arts. Address in 1926, Manheim Apartments, Queen Lane, Germantown, Philadelphia.

FISHER, FLAVIUS J.
Portrait painter. Born 1832 in Virginia. He studied in Philadelphia; also abroad. In Washington he painted portraits of many prominent people; also some landscapes. He died May 9, 1905, in Washington, DC.

FISHER, GEORGE V.
Painter. Member: Society of Independent Artists. Address in 1926, 858 52d St., New York, NY.

FISHER, HARRISON.
Illustrator. Born Brooklyn, NY, July 27, 1875. Studied in San Francisco. Member: SI 1911. Illustrated "The Market Place," by Harold Frederic; "Three Men on Wheels," by Jerome K. Jerome; for "Life," etc. Died in 1934 in New York City. Address in 1929, 80 West 40th St., New York, NY.

FISHER, HUGH ANTOINE.
Landscape painter. Born 1867; died in 1916 in Almeda, California. He was the father of the illustrator Harrison Fisher.

FISHER, HUGO MELVILLE.
Painter. Born Brooklyn, Oct. 20, 1876. Pupil of Whistler, Laurens, Constant in Paris. Member: Paris AAA. Address in 1929, 344 West 28th St., New York, NY.

FISHER, IRMA.
Exhibited water colors at the Exhibition of the Penna. Academy of Fine Arts, 1925, in Philadelphia. Address in 1926, 7621 Star Ave., Cleveland, OH.

FISHER, JOHN.
The Journals of the Continental Congress, under date of June 26, 1773, note "that there is due to John Fisher, for re-newing two copper-plates for loan-office certificates, and making two letters in the device of the thirty dollar bills, 20 dollars."

FISHER, LEONARD EVERETT.
Illustrator. Born in NY, June 24, 1924. Attended Yale Univ. and received a Pulitzer Prize for Painting in 1950. His illustrations for over 200 children's books have earned him many awards. The designer of ten U.S. postage stamps, he has produced a poster series of the bicentennial and of great composers in 1976. Many museums have exhibited his works, which are also in the collections of the LC, NAD, New Britain Museum of American Art and several universities. He has been on the faculty of the Paier School and Dean of the Whitney Art School.

FISHER, VAUDREY.
Painter. Born Staffordshire, England, 1889. Pupil of von Herkomer; Castellucho; Brangwyn. Address in 1926, 1730 Broadway, New York, NY.

FISHER, WILLIAM EDGAR.
Illustrator and designer. Born Wellsville, NY, Oct. 24, 1872. Pupil of AIC; Cornell Univ. Member: A. Bookplate S.; Salma. C. On "Judge" Editorial Staff; Art Director, William Green Printing Co. Specialty, bookplate designs. Address in 1929, 627 West 43rd St.; h. 611 West 136th St., New York, NY.

FISHER, WILLIAM MARK.
Landscape painter. Born in Boston, 1841. Studied at the Lowell Institute, Boston, and in Paris. He was elected an Associate of the Royal Academy in 1913. He died in London in 1923. Represented at Boston Museum of Fine Arts by "Road to Menil," painted in 1869.

FISK, EDWARD.
Landscape painter. Exhibited at the "Exhibition of Paintings

302

Showing the Later Tendencies in Art," at the Penna. Academy of the Fine arts, Philadelphia, 1921. Address in 1926, Care of Daniel Galleries, New York City.

FISKE, CHARLES ALBERT.
Painter. Born in MA, 1837. He graduated from Dartmouth College, lived in New York City, and exhibited at the National Academy of Design. He died May 13, 1915, in Greenwich, CT.

FISKE, GERTRUDE.
Painter and etcher. Born Boston, April 16, 1879. Pupil of Tarbell, Benson, Hale and Woodbury. Member: ANA; Boston GA; NA Women PS; Boston SE; Concord AA; Conn. AFA.; New Haven PCC; AFA. Awards: Silver medal, P.-P. Exp., San F., 1915; Hudson prize, Conn. AFA, 1918; Samuel Bancroft, Jr., prize, Wilmington, SFA, 1921; Thomas B. Clarke prize, NAD, 1922; Shaw Memorial prize, NAD, 1922; Clerici prize, NA Women PS, 1925; figure prize, New Haven PCC, 1925; Clarke prize, NAD, 1925; prize, Springfield AL, 1925; Conn. Acad. Flagg prize, 1925; portrait prize, Conn. AFA, 1926; New Haven PCC prize, 1929. Address in 1929, 132 Riverway, Boston, MA.

FISKEN, JESSIE.
Painter. Born in Row, Scotland, 1860. Pupil of Glasgow School of Art. Address in 1926, 1607 Minot Ave., Seattle, WA.

FITCH, BENJAMIN HERBERT.
Painter. Born Lyons, NY, 1873. Self-taught. Member: Rochester Art Club; Rochester Society of Artists. Address in 1926, 217 West 33d St., Philadelphia, PA.

FITCH, JOHN.
Engraver. Born in South Windsor, CT, Jan. 21, 1743; died in Bardstown, KY, July 2, 1798. Also inventor of the steamboat, he was apprenticed to a clock-maker at an early age. After some service in the Revolutionary War as a gunsmith he was appointed a deputy-surveyor by the State of Virginia in 1780. In 1785 Fitch made a map of the northwest country for explorers, based on maps of Hutchins and Morrow and his own explorations. This he crudely engraved on copper, hammered out and printed on a press of his manufacture. According to his advertisement in the Pennsylvania Packet of 1785, he sold it for "A French crown," and he apparently disposed of a considerable number. With $800 raised he formed a steamboat company in 1787, and built a 60-ton boat.

FITCH, JOHN LEE.
Born in Hartford, CT, 1836; died in 1895. He studied abroad, and spent his professional life in Hartford and New York City. He was an Associate of the National Academy and Treasurer of the Artists' Fund Society of New York. His works include "In the Woods," "Gill Brook Willows on the Croton," "Near Carmel, NY."

FITE, MRS. FRANK E.
See Anne Merriman Peck.

FITLER, MRS. W. C.
See Claude Raguet Hirst.

FITLER, WILLIAM C.
Painter. Born Cincinnati, OH, c. 1897. Specialty, landscapes in water color. Studio in New York City. Died c. 1926.

FITSCH, EUGENE C(AMILLE).
Painter and etcher. Born Alsace, France, Dec. 11, 1892. Pupil of Mahonri Young, Frank V. DuMond; Joseph Pennell; Albright Art School; ASL of NY; Beaux Arts School of Sculpture. Member: S. Indp. A.; ASL of NY; Alliance. Instructor of the Graphic Arts, Art Students League of New York. Address in 1929, 143 West 4th St., New York, NY; summer, Grassy Hill, Lyme, CT.

FITTS, CLARA ATWOOD.
(Mrs. F. W. Fitts). Illustrator. Born Worcester, MA, Oct. 6, 1874. Pupil of School of the Boston Museum of Fine Arts. Member: Copley S; AFA. Work: Altarpiece, three panels, St. John's Church, Roxbury, MA. Illustrated books for children, etc. Address in 1929, 40 Linwood St., Roxbury, MA.

FITZ, BENJAMIN RUTHERFORD.
Painter. Born in 1855 in New York.
Pupil of National Academy and Art
Students' League from 1877 to 1881;
studied in Munich under Loefftz and
returned to America in 1884. He
died in Peconic, LI, NY, in 1891.
He was a member of the Society of
American Artists and is represented
in the Metropolitan Museum, New
York.

FITZ, GRACE RANDOLPH.
Painter and sculptor. Born in New
York City. She was a pupil of
Alden Weir and Augustus Saint
Gaudens. She died in New York,
Jan. 1917.

FITZER, KARL H.
Painter and illustrator. Born
Kansas City, May 4, 1896. Member:
Kansas City SA. Work: pastel
paintings; designer of fine year
books. Address in 1929, 700 Graphic
Arts Bldg.; h. 7341 Terrace, Kansas
City, MO.

FITZGERALD, HARRINGTON.
Landscape and marine painter. Born
in Philadelphia, April 5, 1847.
Pupil of Fortuny and Gerome in
Paris; George Nicholson in
Philadelphia. Member: Fairmount
Park AA; Phila. Sketch C.; Pen and
Pencil C., Phila.; Newspaper
Artists' Assn.; A.A.S., Artist
member, Art Jury Philadelphia,
1908-12. Awards: Gold medal, AAS,
1902; bronze medal, Charleston
Exp., 1902. Represented in
Smithsonian Institution and
National Gallery of Art, Wash., DC;
Albright Art Gallery, Buffalo;
Detroit Museum of Art; Commercial
Museum, Phila.; State College,
Penn., etc. Died in 1930. Address
in 1929, 918 Spruce St.,
Philadelphia, PA.

FITZGERALD, PITT L(OOFBOURROW).
Painter and illustrator. Born
Washington C.H., O., Oct. 3, 1893.
Pupil of PAFA and N. C. Wyeth.
Member: Columbus PPC; Columbus AL.
Died in 1971. Address in 1929, 515
Grove Ave., Columbus, OH.

FITZPATRICK, DANIEL ROBERT.
Cartoonist. Born Superior, WI,
March 5, 1891. Pupil of AIC.
Member: St. Louis AG. Awards:

Lewis first caricature prize, PAFA,
1924; Pulitzer cartoon prize;
Harmon-Survey prize. Address in
1929, Post-Dispatch Bldg, 12th and
Olive St.; h. 5624 Cabanne Ave.,
St. Louis, MO.

FITZPATRICK, JOHN C.
Painter, illustrator and writer.
Born Washington, DC, Aug. 10, 1876.
Pupil of ASL of NY. Member: Wash.
WCC; Washington AC. Address in
1929, 135 A Street, NE, Washington,
DC.

FITZPATRICK, JOHN KELLY.
Painter and teacher. Born
Wetumpka, AL, Aug. 15, 1888. Pupil
of AIC. Member: NOAA; SSAL.
Awards: Special mention, SSAL,
Houston, TX, 1926; popular prize
($75), State Fair, Montgomery, AL,
1927. Work: "Portrait of Gov.
Parsons" and "Pioneer Cabin," State
of Alabama. Address in 1929,
Wetumpka, AL.

FJELDE, PAUL.
Sculptor and teacher. Born
Minneapolis, MN, Aug. 12, 1892.
Pupil of Minneapolis School of Fine
Arts; ASL of NY; Ecole des
Beaux-Arts, New York; Royal
Academy, Copenhagen; Academy de la
Grande Chaumiere, Paris. Taught at
Carnegie Inst. (1928) and at Pratt.
Work: Lincoln monument, Oslo,
Norway; monument of Col. H. C. Heg,
Madison, WI; decorations for
Washington School, McKeesport, PA.
Address in 1929, 49 West 57th St.,
New York, NY; h. 95 Woodruff Ave.,
Brooklyn, NY.

FLACK, ARTHUR W.
Painter. Born in San Francisco,
1878. Pupil of Rochester Fine Arts
Institute; also studied in London
and Paris. Address in 1926, Atlas
Building, Rochester, NY.

FLAGG, CHARLES NOEL.
Portrait painter. Born in
Brooklyn, Dec. 25, 1848; died in
Hartford, CT, Nov. 10, 1916. He
studied for years in Paris. His
principal portraits were of Mark
Twain, Charles Dudley Warner, and a
series of seven governors of
Connecticut. He was elected an
Associate of the National Academy
in 1908.

FLAGG, GEORGE WHITING.
Painter. Nephew of Washington Allston, born in New Haven, CT, June 26, 1816, he spent his childhood in South Carolina. In 1830 he went to Boston as a portrait painter. He was assisted by Luman Reed, patron of art and artists, and many of his works are to be found in the Reed collection (New York Historical Society). In 1851 he was elected a member of the National Academy of New York. Represented at the New York Historical Society by the "Wood-chopper's Boy," "Match Girl," "Lady and Parrot," and "The Nun." He died Jan. 5, 1897, in Nantucket, MA.

FLAGG, H. PEABODY.
Painter. Born Somerville, MA, 1859. Pupil of Carolus-Duran in Paris. Member: NY Arch. Lg. 1899; Boston AC; Salma. C. 1904. Work: Two historical paintings in Flower Memorial Library, Watertown, NY. Address in 1929, 26 East 23rd St., New York, NY.

FLAGG, HENRY C.
Marine painter. Nephew of Washington Allston, and brother of George W. Flagg, was born in New Haven, CT, on Dec. 10, 1811. He painted many marines and later joined the United States Navy. Died Aug. 23, 1862, in Jamestown, NY.

FLAGG, J(AMES) MONTGOMERY.
Painter and illustrator. Born Pelham Manor, NY, June 18, 1877. Pupil of ASL of NY; Herkomer in England; Victor Marec in Paris. Member: SI, 1911; Lotos C.; GFLA. Illustrations for "Liberty," "Cosmopolitan," "College Humor" and other magazines; "City People," "Kitty Cobb" and books of satire; travel book-"Boulevards all the Way-Maybe." Collection of drawings published as "The Well-Knowns." Appointed military artist for New York State in World War I and made forty-six posters, which were used for U.S. Government. Died in 1960. Address in 1929, 108 West 57th St.; 1 West 64th St., New York, NY.

FLAGG, JARED BRADLEY.
Painter. A younger brother of Geo. W. Flagg, the artist. Born in New Haven, CT, 1820. He studied with his brother and also received some instruction from his uncle, Washington Allston. He afterwards became a minister in the Episcopal Church. He painted many portraits and was active in the work of the Yale Art Gallery at New Haven. Elected a Member of the National Academy of New York in 1849. He died on Sept. 25, 1899.

FLAGG, JOSIAH (JR.).
Miniaturist. Born c. 1763. Flourished in Boston about 1783. He advertised in the Boston Gazette, Feb. 10, 1783. "Copying of Miniature Painting in Hair."

FLAGG, JOSIAH.
Engraver. Born c. 1737. Charles E. Goodspeed, of Boston, notes the following book as containing 70 pages of copper-plate music engraved by Josiah Flagg--"Sixteen Anthems, collected from Tan'sur Williams, Knapp, Ashworth & Stephenson, etc. Engraved and printed by Josiah Flagg, and sold by him at his house near the Old North Meeting House and at his shop in Fish Street. Also by the Booksellers in Boston, New England." Died in 1795.

FLAGG, MONTAGUE.
Painter. Born in 1842 in Hartford, CT; died Dec. 24, 1915, in NYC. Pupil of Jacquesson de la Chevreuse in Paris. Most of his professional life was spent in New York. Elected a member of the NA in 1910. He painted "Portrait of My Wife." The figure is seen to the waist; the hair is parted and drawn over the ears; she wears a simple black dress, slightly open at the throat. Painting owned by the Metropolitan Musem of Art, New York.

FLANAGAN, JOHN.
Sculptor. Born Newark, NJ, in 1865. Pupil of Saint Gaudens in NY; Chapu and Falguiere in Paris. Member: ANA 1911; NSS 1902; NY Arch. Lg. 1914; Conn. AFA; Salma. C.; Am. Numismatic Soc.; SI; New Soc. A. Awards: Silver medal, Paris Exp., 1900; silver medal,

Pan-Am. Exp., Buffalo, 1901; silver medal, St. Louis Exp., 1904; medal of honor for section of medals, P.-P. Exp., San F., 1915; Saltus medal, American Numismatic Soc., 1921; Chevalier of the Legion of Honor, 1927. Work: Clock Library of Congress, Wash., DC; bronze relief, "Antique Education," Free Pub. Lib., Newark, NJ; tinted marble relief "Aphrodite," Knickerbocker Hotel, New York, NY; bronze memorial portrait of Samuel Pierpont Langley, Smithsonian Institution, Wash., DC; Bulkley memorial, Aetna Life Insurance Bldg., Hartford, CT; Alexander memorial medal for School Art League of New York, 1915. Represented in medal collections of the Luxembourg, Paris; Museum of Ghent, Belgium; Metropolitan Museum of Art and American Numismatic Society of New York; Chicago Art Institute; Carnegie Institute, Pittsburgh; Newark Art Museum; war medal for the town of Marion, MA; medal for the Garden Club of America; "Medaille de Verdun," voted by Congress, and presented by the President of the United States to the City of Verdun. Died March 28, 1952. Address in 1929, 133 West 79th St.; 638 West End Ave.; 1931 Broadway, New York, NY.

FLANAGAN, JOHN RICHARD.
Illustrator. Born in Sydney, Australia, in 1895. He was an apprentice to a lithographer while studying art. He came to the U.S. and worked on Everyweek magazine, illustrating Chinese stories, soon establishing himself as an authority on the Orient. His illustrations also appeared in Blue and Collier's. Working almost exclusively in pen and ink, both in color and black and white, he later decided to design stained glass windows. He served as a instructor at New York Academy of Arts for many years. Died in 1964.

FLANIGEN, JEAN NEVITT.
Painter. Born Athens, GA, Feb. 7, 1898. Pupil of Wagner, Breckenridge, Garber, McCarter and Pearson; PAFA. Member: Fellowship PAFA; SSAL. Represented in Fellowship PAFA Collection. Art

editior of University of Georgia Annual. Address in 1929, 424 Prince Ave., Athens, GA.

FLECK, JOSEPH A.
Painter. Born Vienna, Austria, Aug. 25, 1892. Pupil of Vienna FA. Member: IL Acad. AFA; Taos S. Awards: Bronze medal, Kansas City AS, 1923; Rosenwald prize ($300), AIC, 1927; prize (figure) Phoenix, AZ, 1928; silver medal, K.C.A.I., 1929. Work: "Indian Motherhood," Kansas City Public Library; "Little Wolf," St. Joseph Art Collection, St. Joseph, MO; portrait of General Paxton, Confederate Museum, Richmond, VA; "Their Domain," Wesleyan College, Salina, Kan.; "Survivors," Fort Worth Art Museum, Fort Worth, TX. Address in 1929, Taos, NM.

FLEISHBEIN, FRANCOIS.
Portrait painter. Born in Germany c. 1804. Came to New Orleans in 1833. He had a studio at 135 Conde Street, New Orleans, from 1840 to 1860.

FLEISHER, LILLIAN B.
Painter. Exhibited at the Pennsylvania Academy of Fine Arts, Philadelphia, in 1924. Address in 1926, 237 Wyncote Road, Jenkintown, PA.

FLEMING, H(ENRY) S(TEWART).
Painter, illustrator, sculptor and craftsman. Born Philadelphia, July 21, 1863. Pupil of Lefebvre and Benjamin-Constant in Paris. Member: SI 1901. Address in 1929, 1 Broadway, New York, NY; Eton College, Scardsale, NY.

FLEMMING, JEAN ROBINSON.
(Mrs. Ralston Flemming). Painter. Born Charleston, SC, Sept. 22, 1874. Pupil of Elliott Daingerfield, H. B. Snell, John Carlson, F. S. Chase, Castelluche. Member: Carolina AA; Jackson AA; Southern SAL; Norfolk SA. Address in 1929, York Apts., 429 West York St.; Talbot Bldg., 105 West Main St., Norfolk, VA.; summer, Virginia Beach, VA.

FLERI, JOSEPH C.
Sculptor. Born Brooklyn, NY, May 20, 1889. Member: NSS; Arch. Lg.

of NY. Work: "Crucifixion and Twelve Apostles," Holy Cross Church, Philadelphia, PA. Address in 1929, 110 West 54th St., New York, NY.

FLETCHER, ANNE.
Painter and teacher. Born Chicago, IL, June 18, 1876. Pupil of Hawthorne, Bridgman, ASL of NY; Simon and Lasar in Paris. Work: Paintings and decorations in the Confederate Museum, Governor's Mansion, U.S. District Court, Westmoreland Club, Richmond, VA; University of Virginia, Charlottesville. Address in 1929, 211 East Franklin St., Richmond, VA.

FLETCHER, CALVIN.
Painter, craftsman, writer, lecturer and teacher. Born Provo, UT, June 24, 1882. Pupil of Pratt Institute; Columbia University; AIC; Central School Arts and Crafts in London; Colarossi and Biloul in Paris; Morse in Chicago. Award: First prize, Utah State Fair Assoc. Work: Two murals in L. D. S. Temple at Logan, Utah. Former President UT Art Institute. Address in 1929, Utah Agricultural College; h. 166 South 4th East, Logan, UT.

FLETCHER, FRANK MORLEY.
Painter, craftsman, writer, lecturer and teacher. Born Whiston, Lancashire, England, April 25, 1866. Pupil of Cormon in Paris. Member: Art Worker's Guild and Graver-Printer's Society, London; Calif. P.M. Awards: Medals for oil painting, World's Columbian Exposition, Chicago, 1893, and for prints, Milan International, 1906. Works: Woodblock prints in British Museum and Victoria and Albert Museum, London, and in galleries at Dresden and Budapest and the Boston Museum of Fine Arts. Author of text book on woodblock printing. Director Santa Barbara School of the Arts. Address in 1929, 2626 Puesta del Sol. Santa Barbara, CA.

FLETCHER, G(ILBERT).
Illustrator and block printer. Born Mankato, MN, March 24, 1882. Pupil of PAFA. Work: "Ship at Wave Crest," Metropolitan Museum of Art; "The Village," Newark Museum of Art; illustrations for "Ladies' Home Journal." Address in 1929, Towners, NY.

FLETCHER, GODFREY B.
Painter. Born at Watsonville, CA, Dec. 16, 1888. Pupil of Armin Hansen. Frequently worked in water color. Died in Dec. 1923, at Watsonville, CA.

FLEURY, ALBERT.
Mural painter. Born in Havre, France, 1848. Member of Chicago Water Color Club. Address in 1926, 1133 North Dearborn St., Chicago, IL.

FLISHER, EDITH E.
Painter, craftsman and teacher. Born Cleveland, OH, Sept. 26, 1890. Pupil of PAFA. Member: Nashville AA; Nashville Des. Club. Work: "Portrait of Gov. Tom Rye," State Capitol, Nashville; "Portrait of Dr. J. A. Crook," Union Univ., Jackson, Tenn. Address in 1929, 167 Eighth Ave., North; h. 8 West End Apartments, Nashville, TN.

FLOEGEL, ALFRED E.
Painter. Born Leipzig, Germany, Sept. 4, 1894. Pupil of C. C. Curran, F. C. Jones, Ivan G. Olinsky; NAD; Beaux-Arts Inst. of Design; American Academy in Rome. Member: Arch. Lg. of NY; Mural P. Work: Decoration on organ doors, Church, Cranbrook, MI; stained glass windows, Church, Kalamazoo, MI. Address in 1929, 160 Fifth Ave., New York, NY; h. 5906 Woodbine St., Brooklyn, NY.

FLOET, LYDIA.
Painter. Exhibited at National Association of Women Painters and Sculptors, New York, 1925. Address in 1926, Wilton, CT.

FLORANCE, EUSTACE LEE.
Painter. Born in Philadelphia. Member: St. Botolph C; Wash. AC. Address in 1929, 10 Frisbie Pl., Cambridge, MA; 1090 Washington St., Dorchester, MA.

FLORENTINO-VALLE, MAUDE RICHMOND.
Painter and illustrator. Pupil of Art Students' League of New York, under Cox, Chase, Brush and

Beckwith; Academie Julien under Lefebvre, Constant and Beaury-Sorel, in Paris. Address in 1926, 1136-1140 Corona St., Denver, CO.

FLORIAN, WALTER.
Painter. Born 1878 in New York City; died there, April 1, 1909. Pupil of Metropolitan Museum Art School under Twachtman and Herbert Morgan; Art Students' League of New York; Julien and Colarossi in Paris. He painted Jozef Israels, Dutch painter, life size; seated figure, with palette and brushes held in his left hand; a characteristic pose, painted in Israels' studio. Signed: "Walter Florian." Owned by the Metropolitan Museum, New York.

FLORIMONT, AUSTIN.
Portrait draughtsman in crayon, and miniature painter. Flourished in Philadelphia, 1781.

FLORSHEIM, RICHARD A.
Painter and printmaker. Born in Oct. 25, 1916, in Chicago, IL. Studied at the U. of Chicago; Mus. of Mod. Art and the Met. Mus. of Art, NY; Musee Nationale d'Art Moderne, in Paris, France. Works were exhibited in Rijksakademie, Amsterdam, Holland, 1968; Art Inst. of Chicago, 1970; National Acad. of Design, NY, 1972. Taught as inst. of painting at the Layton Sch. of Art in Milwaukee, 1949-50; at the Contemporary Art Workshop, Chicago, 1952-63. Various awards include the Chicago Newspaper Guild Artists, 1959 and the Pennell Fund Award, Libr. of Congress, 1956. He is a member of the National Acad. of Design; Soc. of Am. Graphic Artists; Audobon Soc. of Artists, among others. Major media were oil and lithography. Lived in Chicago, Illinois. Died in 1979.

FLOWER, SHERWOOD.
Painter. Born Oakwood, Cecil County, MD, 1878. Address in 1926, Evesham Ave., Baltimore, MD.

FOGARTY, THOMAS.
Illustrator. Born New York, 1873. Pupil of ASL of NY under Mowbray, Beckwith. Member: SI 1901; Salma. C. 1908. Illustrated "The Making

of an American," by Riis; "On Fortune's Road," by Will Payne, etc. Taught at ASL, 1903-1922; pupils included Norman Rockwell. Works in collections of Met. Mus. of Art, NYC; Brooklyn Mus., NY. Died in 1938. Address in 1929, 38 East 22d St., New York, NY.

FOLAWN, THOMAS JEFFERSON.
Painter. Born Youngstown, OH. Pupil of C. S. Niles, CO Sch. F. A.; van Waeyenberge in Paris; J. M. Waloft in NY. Member: Denver Art Asso.; Brush and Pencil Club, St. Louis; S. Indp. A.; Boulder AA; AAPL; Boulder AG. Award: Hon. mention, oil painting, Springville, UT, AA. Died in 1934. Address 1929, 1805 Marine St., Boulder, CO; summer, Santa Fe, NM.

FOLEY, MARGARET.
Sculptor. Biographers differ as to where Margaret Foley, (Margaret E. Foley) was born. Some give her birthplace as Vermont, others as New Hampshire. Largely self-taught. Worked in Boston and later went to Rome. Some of her works were exhibited at the Centennial Exposition at Philadelphia in 1876. Tuckerman wrote of her that she "achieves new and constant success in her relievos." Her medallions of William and Mary Howitt, of Longfellow, and of William Cullen Bryant, and her ideal statues of Cleopatra, of Excelsior, and of Jeremiah are considered to be the best specimens of her cameo work. The cameo portrait of William Cullen Bryant, in the New York Historical Society, is said to be cut by Margaret Foley. She died in 1877 at Meran in the Austrian Tyrol.

FOLGER, L.
Portraits signed "L. Folger" are found in the southern states; one known to Mantle Fielding author was so signed, and dated 1837.

FOLINSBEE, JOHN FULTON.
Painter. Born Buffalo, NY, March 14, 1892. Studied with Birge Harrison, John F. Carlson and Du Mond. Member: ANA, 1919; NA, 1928; Salma. C.; Allied AA; Conn. AFA; NAC. Awards: Third

Hallgarten prize, NAD, 1916; second Hallgarten prize, NAD, 1917; Greenough memorial prize, Newport AA, 1917; hon. mention, AIC, 1918; hon. mention, Conn. AFA, 1919; Isidor prize, Salma. C., 1920; Carnegie prize, NAD, 1921; J. Francis Murphy prize, NAD, 1921; 3rd Wm. A. Clark prize and Corcoran bronze medal, Corcoran Gallery, 1921; 3rd prize, NAC, 1922; hon. mention, Phila. AC, 1922; 1st Hallgarten prize, NAD, 1923; Phila. Sketch Club medal, 1923; Charles Noel Flagg prize, Conn. Academy of the Fine Arts, 1924; purchase prize, Phila. Art Club, 1924; Plimpton prize, Salma. C., 1924; Gedney Bunce prize, Conn. AFA., 1925; Thompson prize, Salma. C., 1926; bronze medal, Sesqui-Centennial Expo., Phila., 1926; Murphy prize, NAD, 1926. Represented in Syracuse (NY) Museum of Fine Arts; Corcoran Gallery, Wash.; Nat. Arts Club, NY; Grand Rapids Art Assn.; Phila. Art Club; RI School of Design, Providence; Public Museum and Art Gallery, Reading, PA. Address in 1929, New Hope, PA.

FOLSOM, MRS. C. A.
Born in New York City Dec. 27, 1812. Flourished in New York, 1837-38, painting miniatures. Died Feb. 1899, Westfield NJ.

FOLTZ, LLOYD C(HESTER).
Painter and etcher. Born Brown Co., KS, Sept. 24, 1897. Pupil of Chicago AFA. Member: Wichita AG; Calif. PM. Address in 1929, Western Lithograph Bldg.; h. 1320 Woodrow Ave., Wichita, KS.

FOLWELL, SAMUEL.
Born c. 1767; died in Phila., 1813. Possibly from New England. Engraved bookplates in 1792 for residents of New Hampshire. In 1798 came to Phila. as min. painter, silhouette cutter; "worker in hair." Conducted a school in Phila. Few examples of his work have been seen, and his 2 portraits are a combination of aquatint and stipple, pleasing in effect, though showing an unpracticed hand. His studio in 1795 was at No. 2 Laetitia Court, and he exhibited portraits that year at the "Columbianum" in Phila.

Profile portrait of Geo. Washington, owned by Penn. Hist. Soc., is inscribed "S. Folwell, Pinxt. 1795," and is said to have been taken from life on a public occasion, the Pres. being unaware of the fact. It is drawn on paper, painted in India ink, with certain lights touched in, and declared at the time a correct likeness. Reproduced on wood and published in Watson's "Annals and Occurrences of NYC and State in the Olden Time," 1846.

FON, W. W.
Painter. Exhibited water colors at Exhibition at Penna. Academy of Fine Arts, Philadelphia, 1922. Address in 1926, Care of Penna. Academy of Fine Arts, Philadelphia.

FOOTE, MARY ANNA HALLOCK.
(Mrs. Arthur De Wint Foote). Painter and engraver. Born in Milton, NY, Nov. 19, 1847, where she continued to live. Attended Poughkeepsie Female Collegiate Seminary. Studied at the Cooper Institute, and with William J. Linton, the wood engraver. Many of her illustrations were published by Scribner & Co. The Worcester Art Museum owns a pencil drawing, "Spring Whistles." Died in 1938.

FOOTE, WILL HOWE.
Painter and teacher. Born Grand Rapids, MI, June 29, 1874. Pupil of AIC; ASL of NY; Julian Academy in Paris under Laurens and Constant. Member: ANA 1910; Salma. C.; Lyme AA; Grand Rapids AA; Century C. Awards: Hon. mention, Pan-Am. Exp., Buffalo, 1901; third Hallgarten prize, NAD 1902; bronze medal, St. Louis Exp., 1904; silver medal, P.-P. Exp., San F., 1915; Eaton purchase prize, Lyme AA, 1926. Died in 1965. Address in 1929, Old Lyme, CT.

FORBELL, CHARLES.
Illustrator. Member: Salma. C.; GFLA. Address in 1929, Park Lane, Douglas Manor, LI, NY.

FORBES, BART JOHN.
Illustrator. Born in Altus, OK, in 1939. Studied under John LaGatta at the ACD and also attended the

Univ. of North Carolina. He has received 34 Certificates of Merit from the S of I Annual Exhibitions. His first illustration was done for Bell Helicopter in Dallas, TX, in 1965. Periodicals such as McCall's, TV Guide, Saturday Review, Time, Redbook, Penthouse, and Money have published his illustrations.

FORBES, EDWIN.
Painter and etcher. Was born in New York, 1839. At first he devoted himself to animal painting. During the Civil War he was a special artist of Frank Leslie's Illustrated Newspaper. His studio was in Brooklyn, and from 1878 he devoted himself to landscape and cattle pictures. In 1877 he was elected an Honorary Member of the London Etching Club. He died March 6, 1895, in New York City.

FORBES, HELEN (KATHARINE).
Painter. Born San Francisco, Feb. 3, 1891. Pupil of Van Sloun, Hansen, Groeber and L'hote. Member: San F. AA; San F. S. Women A; Palo Alto AC. Address in 1929, 712 Montgomery St., San Francisco, CA; summer, 1151 University Ave., Palo Alto, CA.

FORBES, LIONEL C. V.
Painter. Born in Australia in 1898. Member of California Water Color Society. Address in 1926, Los Angeles, CA.

FORCE, CLARA G.
Miniature painter. Born Erie, PA, Nov. 30, 1852. Pupil of Lucia F. Fuller, Alice Beckington, Maria Strean, Mabel Welsh, Elsie D. Pattee, Theodora Thayer, Du Mond, Seyffert. Member: Calif. S. Min. P.; Calif. AC. Represented in Art Gallery, Erie Public Library, Woman's Club, Erie, PA. Died in 1939. Address in 1929, 1800 East Mountain St., Pasadena, CA.

FORD, J. W. NEILSON.
Painter. Pupil of Leonce Rabillon in Paris; Hugh Newell in New York; B. West Clinedinst in Philadelphia; J. W. Jackson in England; Lippish in Berlin. Address in 1926, 1124 Calvert St., Baltimore, MD.

FORD, L. W. NEILSON.
(Mrs. Wm. B. Ford). Painter. Born Baltimore, MD. Pupil of Leonce Rabillon; Hugh Newell; B. West Clinedinst; Henry Snell; William Nickerson; Fred Jackson, Manchester, England; Richard Luy, Vienna; Colarossi Academy, Paris. Member: Baltimore WCC; Plastic C. Died in 1931. Address in 1929, Woodbrook, Govans P.O., MD.

FORD, LOREN.
Painter. She was born in New York City, Jan. 23, 1891. Pupil of George Bridgman; Frank DuMond. Member: A.W.A.; Mural P. Address in 1929, Ford Farm, Milton Rd., Rye, NY.

FORD, RUTH VANSICKLE.
Painter. Born in Aurora, IL, Aug. 8, 1897. Studied: Chicago Academy of Fine Arts; Art Students' League; with George Bellows, Guy Wiggins and John Carlson. Awards: Art Institute of Chicago, 1931; Chicago Woman's Aid, 1932; Connecticut Academy of Fine Arts, 1932; Professional Art Show, Springfield, IL, 1958. Collections: Aurora College; Valparaiso Indiana University. Exhibited a one-man show, Chicago Art Inst., 1934; Watercolor USA, Springfield, 1962-63; Nat. Academy of Design; Chicago Art Inst. and many more. Media: Watercolor and oil. Address in 1980, 69 Central Ave. Aurora, IL.

FORESMAN, ALICE C(ARTER).
Miniature painter and teacher. Born Darien, WI, July 24, 1868. Pupil of Lucia Fairchild Fuller and Elsie Dodge Pattee. Member: Calif. S. Min. P.; West Coast Arts, Inc. Address in 1929, 7002 Hawthorn Ave., Los Angeles, CA; summer, 893 East 28th St., North, Portland, OR.

FORINGER, A(LONZO) E(ARL).
Mural painter and illustrator. Born Kaylor, Armstrong Co., PA, Feb. 1, 1878. Pupil of H. S. Stevenson in Pittsburgh; Blashfield and Mowbray in New York. Member: Mural P.; NY Arch. Lg. 1911; AFA. Award: Third prize ($300), Newark poster competition, 1915. Work: 11 panels, Council Chamber, City

Hall, Yonkers, NY; Baptistry and Organ Walls, Church of the Savior, Philadelphia; panel, County Court House, Mercer, PA; panel, House of Representatives, Utah State Capitol; two panels, Kenosha Co. Court House, Kenosha, WI; bank note designer for European and Canadian banks; Red Cross War poster "The Greatest Mother in the World;" and the post-war poster "Still the Greatest Mother in the World;" 4 panels in the Home Savings and Loan Company Bldg., Youngstown, O. Illustrations for "Scribner's" and other magazines. Address in 1929, Saddle River, NJ.

ORKNER, EDGAR.
Painter. Born Richmond, IN. Pupil of C. Beckwith, Irving Wiles, F. DuMond, ASL of NY. Member: Seattle Art Institute; Chicago Gallery Association; Hoosier AP Association, Chic. Awards: First prize, Hoosier Salon, 1916; Owsley prize, Hoosier Salon, 1917; first prize, Seattle FAS, 1918, 1923. Address in 1929, 319 White Bldg.; 2615 East Cherry St., Seattle, WA.

ORMAN, ALICE.
Painter. Born in NYC, June 1, 1931. Study: ASL, NYC, Sat. classes with Ethel Katz, 1944-48; Cornell Univ., BA 1952; Mex. Art Workshop, Taxco, summer 1950; Brooklyn Mus. Art Sch., summer 1951; NYU, fall 1952; ASL, NYC, with Harry Sternberg, Morris Kantor, 1954-56. Work: J. Walter Thompson Co.; Cornell U.; Inst. for Rehabilitation, Houston. One-Man Shows: Camino Gallery, NYC, 1960, 62; Phoenix Gallery, NYC, 1966, 68, 71, 74, 76; Marist College, Poughkeepsie, NY, 1965, 68, 73; Kornblee Gallery, NYC, 1977, 79; etc. others. Exhibitions: Whitney, 1960; Kornblee Gallery, D'Arcy Gallery, NYC; Contemp. Arts Mus., Houston; Butler Inst. Biann., 1972; "Tenth Street" Exhibition, NYC; Westmoreland Co. Mus. of Art, Greensburg, PA, "New American Still Life"; others. Awards: Nat'l. Stud. Assn. Reg'l. Awards; Daniel Schnackenberg Merit Scholar, ASL, 1955-56. Visiting Prof. of Art, Vassar College, 1980-81; free lance writer. Represented by Kornblee

Gallery, NYC. Address in 1983, Poughkeepsie, NY.

FORMAN, HELEN.
Etcher. Born London, England, June 9, 1892. Pupil of Allen Philbrick; AIC. Member: Calif. AC; San Francisco AA. Address in 1929, Art Dept., Chicago Public Library; h. 1360 East 49th St., Chicago, IL.

FORMAN, KERR S(MITH).
Painter and illustrator. Born Jacksonville, IL, Oct. 26, 1889. Pupil of John Douglas Patrick, Charles A. Wilimovsky. Member: Iowa AC; Des Moines Sketch C. Awards: Prize, Des Moines Women's Club, 1925; gold medal, Des Moines Women's Club, 1929. Work: "Silent Mesas," Des Moines Women's Club. Address in 1929, 308 Insurance Exchange Bldg.; h. 213 Argonne Apts., Des Moines, IA.

FORREST, IAN B.
Engraver and painter. Born in Aberdeenshire, Scotland, about 1814; died in Hudson County, NJ, in 1870. Forrest was an apprentice to the London engraver Thomas Fry, and he remained in his employ until he was induced to come to Philadelphia in 1837 to engrave for the National Portrait Gallery. He later turned to miniature painting. Forrest was a good engraver of portraits in the stipple manner; but some of his best work is found in the form of small fancy heads and vignettes.

FORSBERG, ELMER A.
Painter, lecturer and teacher. Born Gamlakarleby, Finland, July 16, 1883. Pupil of AIC. Member: Chicago PS; Cliff Dwellers; Swedish C. Address in 1929, The Art Institute of Chicago; h. 3730 Rokeby St., Chicago, IL; summer, Covington, MI.

FORSTER, JOHN.
Lithographer. Born in 1825. Worked with the firm Kimmel & Forster, executed a number of lithographs of the Civil War period. Died in 1900.

FORSYTH, CONSTANCE.
Painter, illustrater, etcher and teacher. Born Indianapolis, Aug. 18, 1903. Pupil of William

Forsyth, George Harding, Henry McCarter. Award: Prize, Hoosier Salon, Chicago, 1928. Address in 1929, 15 South Emerson Ave., Indianapolis, IN; summer, Winona Lake, IN.

FORSYTH, WILLIAM.
Painter and teacher. Born Hamilton Co., OH, in 1854. Pupil of Royal Academy in Munich under Loefftz, Benczur, Gysis and Lietzenmeyer. Member: Art Assoc. of Indianapolis; AWCS. Instructor Herron Art Inst. Awards: Medal Munich, 1885; silver medal for water color and bronze medal for oil, St. Louis Exp., 1904; bronze medal, Buenos Aires Exp., 1910; Fine Arts Bldg. prize ($500), SWA 1910; bronze medal for oil and silver medal for water colors, P.-P. Exp., San F., 1915; Foulke prize, Richmond, Ind., 1923; Holcomb prize, 1924, and Landon prize, 1925, Ind. AA. Work: "Autumn at Vernon," "The Constitutional Elm-Corydon," "Close of a Summer Day," "Still Life," "Old Market Woman" and "In October," Art Assoc., Indianapolis; "Autumn Roadside," and "The Smoker," Public Gallery, Richmond, Ind.; flower piece, Brooklyn Mus.; Vanderpoel AA. Collection, Chicago. Died in 1935. Address in 1929, 15 South Emerson Ave., Irvington, IN.

FORSYTHE, (VICTOR) CLYDE.
Painter. Born Orange, CA, Aug. 24, 1885. Pupil of L. E. Garden Macleod; Frank Vincent DuMond. Member: Salma. C.; California A.C.; Allied AA; Painters of the West. Award: Bronze medal, Painters of the West, 1927. Author of poster used in Fifth Victory Liberty Loan, "And They Thought We Couldn't Fight." Address in 1929, 520 North Almansor St., Alhambra, California.

FORT, MARTHA F(ANNIN).
See Anderson, Mrs. Frank Hartley.

FORTUNATO, NANCY.
Painter and teacher. Born IL, Nov. 29, 1941. Study: Art Inst., Chic., IL; Ed Whitney, AWS; Zoltan Szabo, R. E. Wood, AWS; & others. Work: Amoco Oil; Eddie Bauer's; Pres.

Libr. Coll., Wash. DC. One-person shows; Botanical Gdns., IL; others. Exhib: Am. Watercolor Soc., NY, 111th Annl.; Nat'l Lg. of Am. Pen Women, NY; Sumi-e Soc. Nat'ls; Les Etoiles, Paris; other nat'l watercolor shows. Teaching: Illinois District 211 Adult Ed., 1972-pres.; U. of IL, Chic.; state workshops. Awards: Artists in Watercolor Comp., London, 1978; Am. Artists 1st Nat'l Art Comp., NY, 1979; M. Grumbacher Award, Int'l Soc. of Artists Show, Foothills Art Center, CO, 1979; Nat'l Miniature Show, top awards, 1978-79. Mem: Sumi-e Soc. of Am.; AWS; Old Watercolor Soc. and Soc. of Italic Handwriting, Eng. Media: Watercolor. Address in 1983, 249 N. Marion St., Palatine, IL.

FORTUNE, E. CHARLTON.
Painter. She was born Marin Co., CA, 1885. Studied at St. John's Wood School of Art in London; ASL of NY under F. V. Du Mond, Mora and Sterner. Member: Calif. AC; San Francisco AA; NY ASL; Soc. of Scottish A. Awards: Silver medal P.-P. Exp., San F., 1915; silver medal, Panama-Calif., Exp., San Diego, 1915; honorary prize, San. F. AA, 1916; Emanuel Waiter purchase prize, San Francisco AA, 1920; silver medal, Societe des Artistes Francais, Paris, 1924; first prize, Calif. State Fair, 1928. Address in 1929, The Studio, High St., Monterey, CA.

FOSDICK, GERTRUDE CHRISTIAN.
(Mrs. J. W. Fosdick). Painter, sculptor and writer. Born in Middlesex Co., VA, April 19, 1862. Pupil of Julian Academy in Paris under Bouguereau and Lefebvre. Member: Pen and Brush C.; North Shore AA; Allied AA. Address in 1929, 33 West 67th St., New York, NY; summer "The Nutshell," Sugar Hill, NH.

FOSDICK, J(AMES) WILLIAM.
Mural painter, craftsman and writer. Born Charlestown, MA, Feb. 13, 1858. Pupil of Boston Museum School; Julian Academy in Paris under Boulanger, Lefebvre and Collin. Member: NY Arch. Lg. 1890; Mural P.; Copley S. 1904; NY Soc. C.; NAC; Lotos C. Specialty,

312

mural decorations, both in paint and in fire etching. Work: "Veneration of St. Joan of Arc," National Gallery, Washington; "Decorative Portrait Louis XIV," Pennsylvania Academy, Philadelphia. Decorations in National Arts Club; Lotos C.; St. Louis Museum; "Pentaptych of the Life of St. Joan of Arc," Church of St. Joan of Arc, Jackson Heights, LI, NY; Reredos, St. Johns Church, Montclair, NJ; Stations of Cross, Church of Immaculate Conception, Waterbury, CT. Died 1937. Address in 1929, 33 West 67th St., New York, NY; summer, Sugar Hill, NH, and Gloucester, MA.

FOSSETTE, H.
Was an engraver of landscape, working in New York about 1850, after drawings by A. Dick.

FOSTER, ALAN.
Illustrator. Born Fulton, NY, Nov. 2, 1892. Cover designs for "The Saturday Evening Post," "Collier's," "American Boy." Address in 1929, 367 Fulton St.; h. 155 Henry St., Brooklyn, NY.

FOSTER, ARTHUR TURNER.
Painter and teacher. Born Brooklyn, NY, in 1877. Self taught. Member: Artland C; Los Angeles PSC; Calif. WCS. Address in 1929, 2509 West 7th St., Los Angeles, CA.

FOSTER, BEN.
Landscape painter and art writer. Born North Anson, ME, 1852. Student of Abbott H. Thayer in New York; Morot and Merson in Paris. Awards: Carnegie prize, National Academy of Design, New York, 1906; Inness gold medal, National Academy of Design, 1909. Elected Society of American Artists, 1897; Associate, National Academy, 1901; National Academy, 1904; New York Water Color Club; American Water Color Society, New York; Century Association; National Institute of Arts and Letters. Died Jan. 28, 1926, in New York. Address in 1926, 119 East 19th St., New York.

FOSTER, CHARLES.
Painter. Born North Anson, ME, July 4, 1850. Pupil of Cabanel,

Ecole des Beaux-Arts and Jacquesson de la Chevreuse in Paris. Member: Conn. AFA. Died in 1931. Address in 1929, Farmington, CT.

FOSTER, ELIZABETH H(AMMOND).
Painter. Born St. Paul, MN, March 5, 1900. Pupil of Minneapolis Institute of Art, and of Carl L'hote in Paris; Hans Hofman in Munich. Awards: Third prize, Minnesota State Fair; hon. mention, Minnesota State AS. Address in 1929, 117 Farrington Ave., St. Paul, MN; summer, Otisville, MN.

FOSTER, ENID.
Sculptor. Born San Francisco, CA, Oct. 28, 1896. Pupil of Chester Beach. Work: "Three Fates," Mt. View Cemetery Association, Oakland, CA; "Reuniting of Souls," Mausoleum, Oakland; memorial pool to Sarah B. Cooper, Golden Gate Park, San Francisco. Address in 1929, 312 Sheridan Avenue, Piedmont, Calif.

FOSTER, GRACE.
Painter and teacher. Born Wolfe City, TX, March 9, 1879. Pupil of Elia J. Hobbs, Zella Webb, Frank Reaugh. Member: SSAL. Address in 1929, 2905 Polk St., Greenville, TX; summer, 825 Victoria St., Abilene, TX.

FOSTER, JOHN.
Born in Dorchester, MA, 1648. In 1667 Foster graduated from Harvard; in 1675 he established the first printing office in Boston. Foster was the first engraver of a portrait in this country, of whom there is any record. This is a wood-block portrait of the Rev. Richard Mather, and one of the three known impressions has written on it, in an almost contemporaneous hand, "Johannes Foster, Sculpt." This impression was found in the New York Public Library, as the frontispiece to a life of Richard Mather published in Cambridge, New England, in 1670. Another copy of this portrait, framed, is in the possession of the Massachusetts Historical Society. It has the name of Richard Mather printed upon it in type, but has no indication of the engraver. Dr. Samuel A. Green, of the Massachusetts

Historical Society, has made a close study of Foster as the possible engraver of this portrait. Foster is also credited with having engraved the rude woodcut map of New England issued with Rev. W. Hubbard's narrative of the troubles with the Indians in New England, published by John Foster in Boston in 1677. Died Sept. 9, 1681, in Boston.

FOSTER, O. L.
Painter. Born Ogden, IN, May 12, 1878. Pupil of Laura A. Fry, Harry Leith-Ross. Address in 1929, 24 Littleton St., Lafayette, IN.

FOSTER, RALPH L.
Illustrator and designer. Born Providence, May 20, 1881. Pupil of RI School of Design; ASL of NY. Member: Providence AC; Vice-President and Art Director, Livermore Knight Co. Address in 1929, care of Livermore & Knight Co., 42 Pine St.; h. 268 President Ave., Providence, RI.

FOSTER, W(ILLIAM) F.
Illustrator. Member: SI, 1910; Salma. C. Award: Clarke prize ($300), NAD, 1926. Address in 1929, 15 West 67th St.; care of Salmagundi Club., 47 Fifth Ave., New York, NY.

FOTE, MARY.
Painter and illustrator. Member: NA Women PS; New Haven PCC; Port. P. Work: "Portrait of an Old Lady," Art Institute of Chicago. Address in 1929, 3 Washington Square, North, New York, NY.

FOULKES, LLYN.
Painter. Born Nov. 17, 1934 in Yakima, WA. Studied at Central Wash. State Col. (1953); University Wash. (Seattle) and Calif. Inst. of the Arts. Taught at UCLA, and Art Center School in L.A. Exhibited at L.A. County Mus. (1968); Pomona College; S.F. Mus. of Art; Pasadena; Willarn Gallery (1975); Contemp. Gallery in Chicago (1978); Corcoran Biennial (1975). In collections of MOMA; L.A. County Mus. of Art; Stanford U.; UCLA and Pasadena, and many private collections.

FOURNIER, ALEXIS J(EAN).
Painter, illustrator and lecturer. Born St. Paul, MN. Pupil of Laurens, Constant, Harpignies and Julian Academy in Paris. Member: Buffalo SA; Buffalo AC; Toledo Art Klan; Minneapolis A. Lg.; Paris AAA; Cliff Dwellers; NAC; AFA. Awards: Gold and silver medals, Minn. Industrial Soc.; Hengerer prize, Buffalo, 1911; hon. mention, Chicago AG, 1917. Work: "Clearing After a Storm," Vanderbilt Univ., Nashville, Tenn.; "The Haunts and Homes of the Barbizon Masters," twenty oil paintings. Represented in Minneapolis Inst.; St. Paul Lib.; Detroit Art Insitute; PA Historical Soc.; Congressional Lib. Print Dept.; Woman's Club of Minneapolis; Progress Club, South Bend, Ind.; Public Library and Erie Co. Trust Co. Bank, East Aurora, NY; "A France Sky," Hackley Art Gallery, Muskegon, MI; Kenwood C., Chicago; Minneapolis Club and Library. Address in 1929, 142 East Elder St., South Bend, Ind.; 150 Walnut St., East Aurora, NY.

FOWLE, EDWARD A.
This man was a landscape engraver, working in line in Boston in 1843, and in New York a little later.

FOWLER, CARLTON C.
Painter. Born New York, NY, March 19, 1877. Pupil of Academie Julian and Caro-Delvaille. Member: NAC; Salma. C. Award: Hon. mention, Pan-American Exp., Buffalo, 1901. Died in 1930. Address in 1929, 47 Fifth Ave.; 15 West 67th St., New York, NY.

FOWLER, EVA(NGELINE).
Painter, writer, lecturer and teacher. Born Kingsville, OH, in 1885. Pupil of ASL of NY; PAFA; Delaye and Carl in France. Member: Dallas AA. Awards: Gold medal, Cotton Centennial, New Orleans, 1885; Saint-Gaudens bronze medal, World's Columbian Exposition, Chicago, 1893. Died in 1934. Address in 1929, Binkley Hall, Kidd Key College, Sherman, TX.

FOWLER, FRANK.
Portrait painter. Born July 12, 1852, in Brooklyn, New York, and died August 18, 1910 in New Canaan

Connecticut. Studied at Ecole des Beaux Arts. Member of Society of American Artists, and National Academy of Design, 1899. He exhibited a portrait at the Society of American Artists in New York in 1878; he also did some work in fresco.

FOWLER, TREVOR THOMAS.
Portrait painter. Born 1830. His studio was at No. 10 St. Charles St., New Orleans. Died New Orleans, 1871.

FOWLER.
Philadelphia portrait painter, living in Germantown about 1860. Painted a portrait of Miss Anna Howell of Philadelphia about 1860.

FOX, FONTAINE.
Cartoonist. Born in 1884. Member: SI. Address in 1929, care of Wheeler Syndicate, 373 Fourth Ave., New York, NY; 1 Park Ave., Manhasset, LI, NY.

FOX, GILBERT.
According to Wm. Dunlap, Fox was born in London, England, about 1776. He was apprenticed to the London engraver Thomas Medland and was asked to come to Philadelphia in 1795 by James Trenchard. Fox engraved a few portraits and book illustrations for Philadelphia publishers and later became a teacher of drawing in a women's academy there. Dunlap says that he eloped with one of his pupils, lost his position, and went on the stage; the Philadelphia directory of 1798 lists his name as "A Comedian." It was for Gilbert Fox that Joseph Hopkinson wrote "Hail Columbia," and Fox sang it for the first time at his benefit, in 1798. Died c. 1806.

FOX, LORRAINE.
Illustrator. Born in Brooklyn, NY, in 1922. Published her first illustration, a gouache, in Better Homes and Gardens in 1951. She went to PI and the Brooklyn Museum Art School where she studied under Will Burtin and Reuben Tam. She was a lecturer and teacher at PSD in NYC and a faculty member at the FAS. She had numerous illustrations published in most of the well known magazines and won Gold Medals from the S of I and the Philadelphia ADC. Died in 1976.

FOX, MARGARET M. TAYLOR.
(Mrs. George L. Fox). Painter, illustrator, etcher, and teacher. Born Philadelphia, July 26, 1857. Pupil of Peter Moran, T. P. Anshutz. Illustrated "The Deserted Village," "The Traveller," "English Poems," published by J. B. Lippincott Co.; "Historic Churches of America." Address in 1929, Silver Spring P.O., Linden, MD.

FOX, MORTIMER J.
Painter. Born New York, Oct. 2, 1874. Address in 1929, Carnegie Hall; h. 888 Park Ave., New York, NY; summer, "Foxden," Peekskill, NY.

FOY, EDITH GELLENBECK.
Painter. Born Cincinnati, OH, Oct. 9, 1893. Pupil of Wessel, Meakin, Hopkins, Weis. Member: Cincinnati Woman's AC. Address in 1929, 6322 Grandvista Ave., Cincinnati, OH.

FOY, FRANCES M.
Painter, illustrator and etcher. Born Chicago, IL, April 11, 1890. Pupil of George Bellows; AIC. Member: Chicago SA; Chicago NJSA. Address in 1929, 645 Kemper Place, Chicago, IL.

FOYSTER, JERRY.
Painter. Born in Albany, New York, in 1932. Studied at the University of Buffalo, New York. Group Exhibitions: The Contemporary Arts Center, Cincinnati, 1964; at the Bianchini Gallery, New York, 1964; and at the Leo Castelli Gallery, New York, 1964.

FRAIN, N(ELLIE) M.
Painter and medical illustrator. Born Furnessville, IN, June 25, 1887. Pupil of AIC. Illustrated: "Pathology of the Mouth," by Moorehead and Dewey; "Dental Histology," by Frederick Brogue Noyes; "Tuberculosis of Lymphatic System" by Walter B. Metcalf; "Surgical Anatomy," by Eycleschymer; "Bastin's College Botany," by W. B. Day; "Histology," by Prentiss Arey; "Physical Exercises for Invalids and Convalescents," by Edward H.

Ochsner. Address in 1929, College of Dentistry, University of Ill., 1838 West Harrison St.; h. 53 West Burton Pl., Chicago, IL.

FRAME, ROBERT.
Painter. Born July 31, 1924, in San Fernando, CA. Earned B.A. from Pomona College in 1948; MFA (Claremont Grad. Sch.) 1951. Taught at Pasadena City Col., Pasadena School of Fine Arts and UCLA. Awards from National Academy of Design, New York, 1950; Cal. State Fair; Pasadena Art Museum; Guggenheim fellowship (1957-58); Calif. Invitational Exhibit (1961). Exhibited at Scripps Col.; San Diego State Col.; Otis Art Inst, LA; S. F. Mus. of Arts; Carnegie; and Santa Barbara Mus. In collections of National Academy of Design; Pasadena Art Mus.; Santa Barbara Art Mus.; and many private collections.

FRANCE, EURILDA LOOMIS.
Painter, illustrator and teacher. Born Pittsburgh, PA, March 26, 1865. Pupil of Julian Academy, Carolus Duran and Ami Morot in Paris. Member: Buffalo SA; Phila. Alliance; New Haven PCC; New Haven BPC; AFA. Died in 1931. Address in 1929, 562 Orange St., New Haven, Conn.; summer, R. F. D. 2, Scarboro, ME.

FRANCE, JESSE LEACH.
Painter and illustrator. Born in Cincinnati, OH, in 1862. Pupil of Carolus-Duran, Paris. Address in 1926, 78 Pearl St., New Haven, CT.

FRANCES, HARIETTE ANTON.
Painter/graphics. Born in San Francisco, CA in 1927. Studied: San Francisco Art Institute; California School of Fine Art; University of the Pacific. Awards: James D. Phelan Award, 1965; Marin Society of Artists, 1973-75; San Francisco Women Artists, 1975. Collections: Aschenbach Foundation for Graphic Arts at the California Palace of the Legion of Honor, San Francisco; Fresno Arts Center. Exhibited at the De Young Mus., San Francisco, 1963; Calif. Printmakers, 1971; Bicentennial Exhibit, Mus. of Mod. Art, San Francisco, 1976. Media:

Lithography and acrylic. Address in 1980, 105 Rice Lane, Lark Spur, CA.

FRANCIS, GEORGE.
Painter. Born in Hartford, CT, in 1790, and died there in 1873. He studied drawing under Benjamin West, and coloring with Washington Allston. His father was a carriage builder and he had to carry on the business after his father's death. He designed the ornamental work for sleighs and carriages, and occasionally painted a portrait or landscape.

FRANCIS, HELEN I.
See Mrs. H. F. Hodge.

FRANCIS, JOHN F.
Painter. Born in 1808 in Phila. Practised portrait painting in Schuylkill County, and elsewhere; came to Philadelphia and devoted himself to painting fruit pieces, many of which were sold from the exhibition rooms of the Art Union 1844-1850. He painted a portrait in 1838 of William R. Smith of Philadelphia, which was exhibited in the Loan Ex. at Penna. Academy of Fine Arts in 1887. Died Nov. 15, 1886, in Jeffersonville, PA.

FRANCIS, VIDA HUNT.
Illustrator. Born in Philadelphia in 1892. Illustrated "Bible of Amethens," "Cathedrals and Cloisters of the South of France," etc. Address in 1926, Hillside School, Norwalk, CT.

FRANCIS, WILLIAM C.
Architect and decorator. Born Buffalo, NY, May 21, 1879. Pupil of Buffalo ASL; Columbia Univ. School of Arch. Member: Alumni Academy in Rome; Buffalo SA. Award: Fellowship prize, Buffalo SA, 1918. Address in 1929, 64 Pearl St., Buffalo, NY; h. 15 Upper Croton Ave., Ossining, NY.

FRANCISCO, J. BOND.
Painter. Born Cincinnati, OH, Dec. 14, 1863. Pupil of Fechner in Berlin; Nauen Schule in Munich; Bouguereau, Robert-Fleury and Courtois in Paris. Member: Laguna Beach Assn.; S. Calif. AC; Los

Angeles P and SC. Address in 1929, 1401 Albany St., Los Angeles, CA.

FRANK, BENA VIRGINIA.
Painter, etcher, teacher and lecturer. Born Norfolk, VA, May 31, 1900. Pupil of Cooper Union; ASL of NY; studied abroad. Member: SSAL; Gloucester SA; Allied AA; Salons of America. Work: Portraits of Prof. and Mrs. Horace Esterbrook, University of Maine. Address in 1929, 230 East 15th St., New York, NY.

FRANK, GERALD A.
Painter. Born Chicago, Nov. 22, 1888. Pupil of Reynolds and Ufer in Chicago; Hawthorne, Webster and Nordfeldt in Provincetown, Mass. Member: Chicago PS; Chicago AC; Chicago AG; AIC. Alumni; North Shore AA. Awards: Chicago AG Fine Arts prize, 1919; prize, AIC, 1921; Muncipal A. Lg. prize ($100), AIC, 1922; Peterson purchase prize, AIC, 1922. Represented in AIC; Municipal collection, Chicago. Address in 1929, Tree Studio Bldg., 4 E. Ohio St., Chicago, IL; summer, Box 8 Clifton, MA.

FRANKENBURG, ARTHUR.
Illustrator. Member: SI. Address in 1929, 1947 Broadway; 33 West 67th St., New York, NY.

FRANKENSTEIN, JOHN.
Sculptor. Born c. 1816 in Germany. Worked in Cincinnati. A number of casts show masterly handling of the clay. Died April 16, 1881, in NYC.

FRANKENTHALER, HELEN.
Painter. Born Dec. 28, 1928, in New York City. B. A. from Bennington College, 1949. Honor degrees from Radcliffe and Amherst. Taught at NYU, Yale, Princeton and Hunter. Awarded I Biennale (Fr.) 1959, National Conf. Christians and Jews, 1978, Bennington Alum. Award, 1979. Exhibited in Milan, London, and at MMA, Guggenheim, Whitney, Museum of Fine Arts (Boston). In collections of MMA, MOMA, Whitney, Cooper Hewitt, Guggenheim, Cleveland, and Art. Inst. (Chicago).

FRANKLIN, CHARLOTTE WHITE.
Painter and sculptor. Born in Phila., PA, 1923. Studied at Tyler Art Sch., Temple Univ. BA, 1945, BS (education), 1946, MFA, 1947; Inst. San Miguel Allende, Univ. Guanajuato, 1957; Mexico City College, 1958; Univ. of Madrid, 1968. Award: Fulbright Fellowship; Phila. Board of Education fellowship to Univ. of Madrid and Rome; Les Beaux Arts Exhib., Phila. Media: Oil. Address in 1980, 24th and Franklin Parkway, Phila., PA.

FRANKLIN, DWIGHT.
Painter and sculptor. Born New York, NY, Jan. 28, 1888. Member: Am. Assoc. of Museums. Work in American Museum of Natural History; Newark Public Library; Metropolitan Museum; Children's Museum, Brooklyn; Cleveland Museum; University of Illinois; French War Museum. Specialty, miniature groups for museums, usually of historical nature. Address in 1929, care of The Coffee House, 54 West 45th St., New York, NY.

FRANKLIN, KATE MANN.
Painter, craftsman, writer, lecturer and teacher. Born Flushing, NY. Pupil of Arthur Wesley Dow. Member: NA Women PS. Contributor, magazine articles; Lecturer, Brooklyn Museum and Metropolitan Museum of Art; Instructor, Cornell SS of Art. Address in 1929, Eagle Nest Lane, Flushing, LI, NY; summer, South Bristol, ME.

FRANTZ, MARSHALL.
Illustrator. Born Kiev, Russia, Dec. 26, 1890. Pupil of Walter Everett. Member: GFLA; SI. Illustrations for: "Saturday Evening Post," "Cosmopolitan," "Harper's Bazaar," "Good Housekeeping," "McCalls," "Ladies Home Journal," "American," "Red Book," "Colliers," "Liberty." Address in 1929, 939 Eighth Ave., New York, NY.

FRANZEN, AUGUST.
Portrait painter. Born Norrkoping, Sweden, 1863. Pupil of Dagnan-Bouveret in Paris. Member: SAA 1894; ANA 1906; NA 1920; Century C; Lotos C. Awards: Medal Columbian

Exp., Chicago, 1893; bronze medal, Paris Exp., 1900; hon, mention, Pan-Am. Exp., Buffalo, 1901; gold medal, AAS, 1902; portrait prize, NAD, 1924. Work: "Yellow Jessamines," Brooklyn Institute Museum; "William H. Taft," Yale University; "Admiral Robley Evans," National Gallery, Washington, DC; Toledo Museum of Art, Toledo, Ohio. Died in 1938. Address in 1929, 222 West 59th St., New York, NY.

FRANZONI, CARLO.
Sculptor. Born 1789 in Carrara, Italy. Represented in the Capitol in Wash., DC. Died May 12, 1819 in Wash. DC.

FRANZONI, GIUSEPPE.
Sculptor. Born c. 1780 in Carrara, Italy. Represented in the Capitol in Wash., DC. Died April 6, 1815, in Wash., DC.

FRASCONI, ANTONIO M.
Illustrator and Painter. Born in Apr. 28, 1919, in Montevideo, Urguay. Studied at the Art Students League; New Sch. for Soc. Research. Work: Met. Mus. of Art; MOMA; FA Mus., Montevideo; Bibliot. Nat'l., Paris; Arts Council of GB, London . Exhib. at PAFA, Smithsonian, etc. Teaching: SUNY Purchase. Awarded scholarships from the ASL; Nat. Inst. of Arts and Letters and Conn. Comn. of the Arts. Received top prize for book illust. from the Limited Editions Club in NY. Rep.: Wehye and Dintenfass Galleries, NYC. Living in Norwalk, Conn.

FRASER, CHARLES.
Portrait painter in miniature and oils. Born Aug. 20, 1782, Charleston, SC. He entered Charleston College about 1792, graduated in 1798, studied in a law office until 1800, and then devoted himself for a time to art, probably encouraged by the example of his friend Malbone. He lived in Charleston most of his life except for a few visits to Boston, New York, and Columbia, South Carolina. In 1857 his friends and admirers formed an exhibition of more than three hundred examples of his work. (See the excellent illustrated article by Miss Alice R. H. Smith in "Art in America," 1915, and "Early American Portrait Painters in Miniature," by Bolton.) Died Oct. 5, 1860, in Charleston.

FRASER, DOUGLASS.
Painter. Born Vallejo, CA, Dec. 29, 1885. Pupil of Arthur Matthews at Mark Hopkins Inst. of Art; ASL of NY; Du Mond and Hawthorne. Member: Carmel AA; Bohemian C, San Fran.; AFA. Work: "Monterey Cypress Trees," Crew's Reading Room, U.S. Battleship "California;" "Greenwood Oaks," Library, Elk's Club, Vallejo, CA; two mural panels--"The Bringing of Talents to Beauty," Bohemian Club, San Francisco; "Sunny Hills," Mrs. Isadore Grigsby Memorial, George Washington Junior High Sch., Vallejo, CA; "California Oaks," library Business Men's Club, Portland, Ore.; "Ships of the Navy, Old and New," Mare Island Golf Club; "Donner Lake, U.S. Submarine S-29. Address in 1929, 203 Sacramento St., Vallejo, CA; forwarding address, Bohemian Club, San Francisco, CA.

FRASER, JAMES EARLE.
Sculptor. Born Winona, MN, Nov. 4, 1876. Pupil of Falguiere in Paris. Member: ANA 1912; NA 1917; N. Inst. A.L.; NSS 1907; Port. P.; National Commission of Fine Arts; New Soc. A; NAC. Awards: First prize, Paris AAA, 1898; medal Edison competition, 1906; gold medal for sculpture and gold medal for medals, P.-P. Exp., San F., 1915. Knighted in Swedish order of Vasa. Represented by medals in Metropolitan Museum, New York; Ghent Museum and Rome; bust Ex-Pres. Roosevelt, Senate Chamber, Capitol, Wash.; Fine Arts Academy Buffalo; statue of Bishop Potter in Cathedral of St. John the Divine, NY; "End of the Trail," City of San F.; Buffalo nickel; U.S. Victory Medal; John Hay Memorial, Cleveland; "Alexander Hamilton," south entrance U.S. Treasury, Wash.; "Victory Figure," Bank of Montreal; "Canadian Soldier," Bank of Montreal, Winnipeg. Instructor, ASL of NY 1906-11. Died in 1953. Address in 1929, 328 East 42nd St., New York.

318

FRASER, LAURA GARDIN.
(Mrs. James E. Fraser). Sculptor. Born Chicago, IL, Sept. 14, 1889. Pupil of James E. Fraser. Member: ANA, 1924; NSS; NA Women PS. Awards: Helen Foster Burnet prize, NAD, 1916; Shaw Memorial prize, NAD, 1919; Saltus gold medal, NAD, 1924; Saltus gold medal, Amer. Numismatic Society, 1926. Work: Wadsworth Atheneum; Elks Bldg, Chicago; and Grant memorial half dollar and gold dollar. Died in 1966. Address in 1929, 328 East 42nd St., New York, NY.

FRASER, MALCOLM.
Illustrator. Born Montreal, Canada, April 19, 1868. Pupil of ASL of NY, under Wyatt Eaton; Julian Academy in Paris under Boulanger and Lefebvre. Member: Salma. C. 1897. Illustrated "Richard Carvel," "Caleb West," etc. Died in 1949. Address in 1929, care of Salmagundi Club, 47 Fifth Ave., New York, NY; h. Brookhaven, NY.

FRAZEE, JOHN.
Sculptor. Born in Rahway, NJ, July 18, 1790. He was apprenticed as a youth to a country bricklayer, William Lawrence. His first work with the chisel was carving his employer's name upon the tablet of a bridge, constructed by Lawrence over Rahway River at Bridgetown, in 1808. In 1814 he formed a partnership with a former apprentice, and established a stonecutting business at New Brunswick. In 1818 he moved to New York, and with his brother William opened a marble shop in Greenwich Street. From that time until 1825 he made tombstones and mantels. His portrait bust of John Wells, old St. Paul's Church, Broadway, New York, is probably the first marble bust made in this country by a native American. A number of busts were executed by Frazee in 1834, seven of which are in the Boston Athenaeum. Died Feb. 24, 1852, in Crompton Mills, RI.

FRAZER, HARLAND.
Painter. Member: St. Louis AG. Awards: Mallinckrodt portrait prize, 1921, and first figure prize, 1922, St. Louis AG. Address

in 1929, 2 West 67th St., New York, NY.

FRAZER, OLIVER.
Painter. Born in Fayette County, KY, Feb. 4, 1808. He was the son of Alexander Frazer, an Irish patriot. His father died while Oliver was very young. His uncle, Rbt. Frazer, assumed charge of his education. He early showed signs of great artistic talent, and his uncle placed him under the tuition of Kentucky's great artist, M. H. Jouett. Later he was sent to Phila. and studied with T. Sully. After his course in Phila., he spent 4 years studying in Europe, attending the art schools of Paris, Florence, Berlin and London. When he returned to US he opened a studio in Lexington. Frazer devoted himself principally to portraits, his group-portrait of his wife and children, and portraits of Col. W. R. McKee, Chief Justice George Robertson, M. T. Scott, J. T. Hart, the famous sculptor, and H. Clay being among his works. Many critics say his portrait of Clay is the finest ever painted of that man. Died near Lexington, KY, Feb. 9, 1864.

FRAZIER, CHARLES.
Sculptor. Born 1930 in Morris, OK. Studied at Chouinard Art Inst., L.A. 1948-49 & 1952-6. Also resided in Italy. Work: La Jolla's and L.A. Museum, and many private collections. Exhib.: La Jolla, Ellin Gallery, L.A.; Kornblee Gal., NYC; L.A. County Mus.; PAFA; Dwan Gallery, L.A.; Art Inst. of Chi.; Pasadena Art Mus. Awards: La Jolla Art Center, 1962; Long Beach Mus. of Art, 1963.

FRAZIER, JOHN R. (MRS.).
See Stafford, Mary.

FRAZIER, JOHN R(OBINSON).
Painter and teacher. Born Stonington, CT, July 29, 1889. Pupil of RI School of Design, and C. W. Hawthorne. Member: Phila. WCC; Providence AC; NYWCC; Providence WCC. Awards: Phila. WCC. Prize, 1920; Dana gold medal, Phila. WCC, 1921; Harriet B. Jones prize, Balto. WCC, 1922; Logan purchase prize, AIC, 1922; Kansas

City Art Institute purchase prize, 1923. Represented in RI School of Design, Chicago Art Institute and Brooklyn Museum. Address in 1929, Rhode Island School of Design, Providence, RI.

FRAZIER, KENNETH.
Painter. Born Paris, France, June 14, 1867. Pupil of Herkomer in England; Constant, Doucet and Lefebvre in Paris. Member: SAA 1893; ANA 1906; Century Assoc. Award: Bronze medal, Pan-Am. Exp., Buffalo, 1901. Died Aug. 31, 1949. Address in 1929, 7 West 43rd St., New York, NY; Garrison-on-Hudson, NY.

FRAZIER.
Nothing known of him except that he flourished about 1793, in Norfolk, VA, and painted a number of portraits.

FRECHETTE, MARIE MARGUERITE.
Painter. Born Ottawa, Canada, 1884. Pupil of Kenyon Cox, Charles Hawthorne; Mme. LaFarge in Paris. Member: Union Internationale des Beaux Arts et des Lettres. Work: Ten historical portraits for Chateau Frontenac, Quebec. Address in 1926, 67 Somerset St., West Ottawa, Canada.

FREDENTHAL, DAVID.
Painter. Born in Detroit, Michigan, in 1914. Studied art at Cass Technical High School, Detroit, with Mary Davis. Studied works of Masaccio, Michelangelo, Rembrandt, Daumier; strongly influenced by work of Brueghel. Exhibited pencil drawings at Young Artists' Market, Detroit, 1933; all sold. Won Museum of Modern Art Traveling Fellowship to Europe. Received commissions including WPA Mural, Detroit Post Office; drawings of New England plants for defense purposes; artist correspondent for Life Magazine during WWII. First important show on East Coast at Whitney Museum, NYC, 1947. Received many awards and had many successful exhibitions. Worked in oil, watercolor. Died in 1958. Represented by Kennedy Galleries, NYC.

FREDER, FREDERICK C(HARLES).
Painter. Born Monroe, Orange Co., NY, July 4, 1895. Pupil of Charles Curran, Francis Jones, Ivan Olinsky, NAD, Fernand Cormon and Angel Zarraga, Ecole des Beaux Arts, Paris; also studied Germany, Italy, Spain. Member: Salma C. Award: Pulitzer prize ($1,500), Columbia University, 1920. Work: "Before the Walls of Kairouan, Tunisia," Fine Arts Gallery, San Diego, Calif. Address in 1929, 646 East 241st St., New York, NY.

FREDERICK, EDMUND.
Illustrator. Born Philadelphia, PA, April 2, 1870. Studied at PAFA. Member: SI 1910. Worked in New York for the "World" and "The Morning American." Illustrated books by Elinor Glyn, Robert W. Chambers, Joseph C. Lincoln, etc. Address in 1929, 330 West 58th St., New York, NY; 322 Fenimore St., Brooklyn, NY.

FREDERICK, FRANK F(ORREST).
Painter, craftsman, teacher, writer and lecturer. Born Methuen, MA, Oct. 21, 1866. Pupil of Mass. Normal Art School; Royal College of Art, London. Director, Trenton School of Industrial Arts. Address in 1929, School of Industrial Arts, Trenton, NJ.

FREDERICK, JOHN L.
Engraver. Born c. 1798. Frederick was an engraver of buildings and book illustrations, in business in Philadelphia from 1818 until 1845. As he was engraving for Collins' Quarto Bible, published in New York in 1816, it is probable that he came from that city to Philadelphia. His one known portrait, that of the Rev. Joseph Eastburn, is an attempt in stipple, and is poorly done. He is said to have died in Philadelphia in 1880-81.

FREDERICKS, ALFRED.
Wood Engraver and illustrator of books.

FREEDLANDER, ARTHUR R.
Painter and teacher. Born in New York in 1875. Pupil of Twachtman and Mowbray in New York; Cormon in Paris. Member: Salma. C., 1905;

Guild of American Painters. Award: Isidor portrait prize, Salma. C., 1915, Director, Martha's Vineyard School of Art. Died in 1940. Address in 1929, 1 West 67th St.; 220 West 59th St., New York, NY.

FREEDLEY, ELIZABETH C.
Painter. Exhibited at Annual Exhibition of Pennsylvania Academy of Fine Arts, Philadelphia, 1924, and at National Association of Women Painters and Sculptors. Address in 1926, New Hope, Pennsylvania.

FREEDMAN, RUTH.
Painter. Born in Chicago, Illinois, 1899. Pupil of Chicago Academy of Fine Arts. Address in 1926, Seattle, Washington, 1001 Seaboard Bldg.

FREELAND, ANNA C.
Painter. Born in 1837; died in 1911. She painted figure and historical scenes; her "William the Conqueror" is signed and dated "1886," and is owned by the Worcester Art Museum.

FREELON, ALLAN (RANDALL).
Painter, etcher and teacher. Born Philadelphia, PA, Sept. 2, 1895. Pupil of Pennsylvania Museum School of Industrial Art; Earl Horter, Hugh Breckenridge. Member: Alumni Association, Pennsylvania Museum School of Art; Philadelphia Art Teachers A; Eastern AA; AFA; North Shore AA. Supervisor Art Education, Philadelphia Public Schools. Address in 1929, 2220 Catherine St., Philadelphia, PA; summer, c/o Hugh Breckenridge, East Gloucester, MA.

FREEMAN, E. O.
This good line-engraver of historical subjects was working for Boston publishers about 1850.

FREEMAN, FLORENCE.
Sculptor. Born in Boston, MA, 1836. After study with Richard Greenough, she went abroad and studied with Hiram Powers. She executed several bas-reliefs of Dante, and many portrait busts She died after 1876.

FREEMAN, GEORGE.
Miniature painter. Born April 21, 1789, at Spring Hill, CT. In 1813 he went abroad for study and remained in London and Paris for twenty-four years. He painted on ivory and porcelain, and was honored by being allowed to paint Queen Victoria and Prince Albert, from life. He returned to the US in 1837 and died in Hartford, CT, on March 7, 1868. He painted miniatures of President Tyler, Mrs. Sigourney, Mr. and Mrs. Nicholas Biddle, Mr. and Mrs. James Brown, and Mrs. J. W. Wallace.

FREEMAN, H. A. L.
Sculptor. Wife of the artist James E. Freeman. Born in 1826. For many years she had her studio in Rome. A "Group of Children," also the "Culprit Fay," of Drake's poem, were modelled with skill by Mrs. Freeman.

FREEMAN, JAMES EDWARD.
Painter. Born in Nova Scotia in 1808. He was brought to the US in 1810. He studied in NYC and entered the School of the NA. He later studied abroad, and had his studio in Rome. His best known paintings are "The Beggars," "Italian Peasant Girl," "The Bad Shoe," "Girl and Dog on the Campagna," and "The Mother and Child." His self-portrait was shown in the Centennial Exhibition of the NAD, NY, 1925. Elected a Member of the NA in 1833. He died Nov. 21, 1884 in Rome.

FREEMAN, JANE.
Painter and teacher. Born in England, Feb. 11, 1883. Pupil of Chase, Du Mond, Henri, George E. Browne, Frank Fairbanks, Hawthorne, Bredin, Cooper Union; Academy de la Grand Chaumiere in Paris. Member: NA Women PS. Awards: Popular vote prize, Art and Industries Exhib., Hotel Astor, NY, 1928; water color prize, NA Women PS, 1928. Died in 1963. Address in 1929, 160 Carnegie Hall, NY; summer, Provincetown, MA.

FREEMAN, MARGARET (LIAL).
Illustrator. Born Cornwall-on-Hudson, NY, May 13,

321

1893. Pupil of Eric Pape; Richard Miller, Troy, and Margaret West Kinney. Illustrated: "The Story of a Wonder Man," by Ring Lardner (Scribner); "Father's First Two Years," Fairfax Downey (Minton, Balch & Co.); "Italian Fairy Tales," by Capuana (Dutton); "The Frantic Young Man," by Charles Samuels (Coward, McCann); "American Folk Tales," edited by Rachel Field (Scribner); "Jane's Father," by Dorothy Aldis (Minton, Balch and Co.). Address in 1929, 177 MacDougal St., New York, NY.

FREEMAN, MARION.
Painter. Exhibited at the National Academy of Design, 1925. Address in 1926, 123 Waverly Place, New York.

FREEMAN, W. H.
Engraver. Very little is known about this engraver or his work beyond the fact that he was a fairly good engraver of line plates, and worked for New York and Baltimore publishers in 1815 and 1816. In Mr. Stauffer's work he notes that Freeman engraved a number of plates for a quarto Bible that was published in New York in 1816. Freeman also engraved "The Washington Monument at Baltimore," which was published by John Horace Pratt in 1815, in a rare publication on the laying of the corner stone of Washington Monument.

FREER, FREDERICK WARREN.
Painter. Born in Chicago June 16, 1849; died there March 7, 1908. He was elected an Associate member of the National Academy of Design, and a member of the American Water Color Society. He was president of the Chicago Academy of Design.

FRENCH, ALICE HELM.
(Mrs. William M. R. French). Painter. Born Lake Forest, IL, March 17, 1864. Pupil of AIC. Member: AFA. Represented in St. Louis Mus.; Beloit Col. Art Museum; Doshisha College, Kyoto, Japan; Vanderpoel AA. Collection, Chicago; Colegio Internacional, Gaudalajara, Mexico. Address in 1929, 37 Glen Road, Williamstown, MA.

FRENCH, DANIEL C(HESTER).
Sculptor. Born Exeter, NH, April 20, 1850. Pupil of Wm. Rimmer in Boston; J. Q. A. Ward in NY; Thomas Ball in Florence. Member: ANA 1900, NA 1901; NSS 1893; SAA 1882; NY Arch. Lg. 1890; AIA (cor.) 1896; Acad. San Luca, Rome; NAC; Century Assoc.; Nat. Inst. A.L.; Am. Acad. A.L.; Concord A.A. Member Nat. Commission of Fine Arts 1910-15. Awards: third class medal, Paris Salon, 1892; medal of honor, Paris Exp., 1900; medal of honor for sculpture, NY Arch. Lg. 1912; medal of honor, P.-P. Exp., San F., 1915; gold medal of honor, Nat. Inst. AL, 1918. Work: "Death and the Sculptor," memorial to Martin Milmore, Boston; "The Minute Man," Concord, MA; "Abraham Lincoln," for Lincoln, Neb.; "Continents," NY Custom House; "Gen. Devens," equestrian statue (in collaboration with E. C. Potter), Worcester, Mass.; "Jurisprudence" and "Commerce," Fed. Bldg., Cleveland; "Quadriga," State Capitol, St. Paul, Minn.; "Alma Mater," Columbia University, NY; Parkman Memorial Boston; "Mourning Victory," memorial to Melvin brothers in Concord, Mass., and replica and "Memory," Metropolitan Mus., NY; bust of Emerson, Art Museum, Montclair, NJ; "Spirit of Life," Trask Memorial, Saratoga, NY; "Sculpture" on exterior of St. Louis Museum; "Study of a Head," Fine Arts Academy, Buffalo; "Statue of Emerson," Concord, Mass.; "Lafayette Monument," Brooklyn, NY; "Lincoln" in the Lincoln Memorial, Monument to First Division, Dupont Fountain, and "The Sons of God Saw the Daughters of Men that they were Fair," Corcoran Gallery, all in Washington, DC; White Memorial Fountain, Boston, Mass.; War Memorial, Milton, Mass; War Memorial, St. Paul's School, Concord, NH. Died Oct. 7, 1931. Address in 1929, 12 West 8th St., h. 36 Gramercy Park, New York, NY; summer, Glendale, MA.

FRENCH, EDWIN DAVIS.
Engraver. Born in North Attleborough, MA, June 19, 1851. In 1869 he began engraving on silver with the Whiting Manfg. Co., and he moved with that

establishment to NY in 1876. Studied drawing and painting at the Art Students' League of NY, under William Sartain in 1883-86; later on the board of that organization until 1891, serving as pres. in 1890-91. In 1894 he began designing and engraving book-plates and similar work on copper, and achieved a well-deserved reputation. He designed and engraved 245 bookplates, chiefly for private owners; also many for clubs and pub. institutions. Among the latter may be noted the beautiful plates designed and engraved for the Grolier Club, Union League, and Metropolitan Museum of Art of NY; Dean Hoffman Lib., etc. For the Society of Iconophiles he engraved their first publication, a series of views of historical NY buildings, and he made a number of title-pages and certificate plates. Moved his studio to Saranac Lake in 1897. Died Dec. 8, 1906, in New York City.

FRENCH, FRANK.
Painter. Born Loudon, NH, May 22, 1850. Mainly self-taught. Member: ANA, 1923; Soc. of American Wood Engravers; Salma. C.; A. Fund S. Awards: bronze medal, Centennial Exp., Philadelphia, 1876; medal, Columbian Exp., Chicago, 1893; silver medal for wood engravings, Pan- Am. Exp., Buffalo, 1901; gold medal for wood engraving, St. Louis Exp., 1904. Died in 1933. Address in 1929, "The Sycamores," Reeds Ferry, NH.

FRERICHS, WILLIAM CHARLES A.
Painter. Born in Ghent, Belgium in 1829. Came to New York. In 1854 he became instructor in various art schools. He died March 16, 1905, in Tottenville, LI, NY.

FRESHMAN, SHELLEY A.
Illustrator. Born in NYC, in 1950. Attended PI for four years, studying under David Byrd and Alvin Hollingsworth. She began her career with a poster for the off-Broadway production Geese and illustrated the book Cricket for Bobbs-Merrill in 1975. Her works have appeared in the S of I 1975 and 1976 Annual Exhibitions.

FREUND, H(ARRY) LOUIS.
Painter. Born Clinton, Sept. 16, 1905. Pupil of Ankeney, Carpenter, Goetsen, Wuerpel. Member: Delta Phi Delta. Awards: Wayman Crow medal, St. Louis, 1927; second portrait award, St. Louis Artists Guild, 1929. Address in 1929, St. Louis School of Fine Arts, St. Louis, MO; h. Clinton, MO.

FREY, ERWIN F.
Sculptor and teacher. Born Lima, OH, April 21, 1892. Pupil of C. J. Barnhorn, James Fraser, Henri Bouchard, Paul Landowski. Member: NSS; Columbus AL. Award: Honorable mention, Paris Salon, 1923; hon. mention, AIC, 1925. Work: Beatty Memorial, Springfeld, OH; Madonna and Child, Lamme Engineering Medal, Ohio State University. Address in 1929, Hayes Hall, Ohio State University; h. 4837 Ofentangy Blvd., Beechwood, Columbus, OH.

FREY, GRACE EGGERS.
Sculptor. Exhibited a portrait in the Cincinnati Museum in 1925. Address in 1926, 1801 E. Rich St., Columbus, OH.

FRIEDLANDER, LEO.
Sculptor. Born New York City, 1889. Pupil of ASL of NY; Ecole des Beaux Arts of Paris and Brussels. Member: NSS; Alumni, Amer. Acad. in Rome; NY Arch Lg. Awards: Amer. Acad. in Rome Fellowship, 1913-16; Helen Foster Barnett Prize, NAD, 1918 and 1924; hon. mention, AIC, 1920; silver medal, Sesqui-Centennial Exposition, Phila., 1926. Work: Sculptures on Washington Memorial Arch, Valley Forge, PA, 1912; figures on altar of St. Thomas' Church, Frankfort, PA; colossal heads of Beethoven and Bach, Eastman School of Music, Rochester, NY; 3 colossal figures, entrance Masonic Temple, Detroit, MI; 28 Allegorical life-sized bas-reliefs, National Chamber of Commerce, Washington, DC; 3 life-sized, allegorical figures, Ann Arbor, Univ. of Mich. Museum; "Bacchante," Metropolitan Museum of Art; 8 Allegorical figures for Baptismal Font, Cranbrook Church, Mich.; 3-6 ft. figures "The Three Wise Men,"

chapel, Berkeley, CA; bronze doors and allegorical column caps, Goldman Memorial, Congregational Cemetery, Bor. of Queens, NY; entire sculptures for Epworth Euclid M. E. Church, Cleveland, OH; designed the seal for the New York Building Congress; three marble reliefs, American Bank and Trust Co., Philadelphia, PA; eight marble Metopes, Lee Higginson Bank, New York City; Cent. pediment, Museum, City of New York, 1929; all sculptures for facades, Jefferson Co. Court House, Birmingham, Ala., 1929-30; bronze relief, and two stone reliefs, main entrance, Genessee Valley Trust Co., 1929-30; all exterior figurative sculpture, Grosse Pointe Church, Grosse Pointe, MI, 1929-30. Address in 1929, 207 East 61st St., New York, NY.

FRIEDMAN, ARNOLD.
Painter. Born New York City, 1879. Pupil of ASL of NY; Robert Henri. Address in 1929, 53 Baylie St., Corona, LI, NY.

FRIEDMAN, MARVIN.
Illustrator. Born in Chester, PA, Sept. 26, 1930. Attended the School of Art at the Philadelphia Museum. He studied under Henry C. Pitz, Albert Gold, and Benjamin Eisenstat and has illustrated books such as Chewing Gum published by Prentice-Hall in 1976, Pinch by the Atlantic Monthly Press in 1976, and Can Do Missy by Follet in 1975. Work: Playboy Collection, Chicago; Ford Motor Co., Dearborne, IL; Nat. Broadcasting Co. Coll., NY. Exhib. at Phila. Mus. of Art, Pittsburgh Mus. Brandywine Mus. Delaware.

FRIES, CHARLES ARTHUR.
Painter, illustrator and teacher. Born Hillsboro, OH, Aug. 14, 1854. Studied at Cincinnati Art Academy. Member: San Diego AG; Laguna Beach AA; La Jolla AA; Calif. AC. Awards: Silver medal, Seattle FAS., 1911; silver medal, P.-P. Exp., 1915. Represented in San Diego Fine Arts Gal. Died in 1940. Address in 1929, 2843 E Street; h. 2876 F. St., San Diego, CA.

FRIESEKE, FREDERICK CARL.
Painter. Born Owosso, MI, April 7, 1874. Pupil of AIC; ASL of NY; Constant, Laurens and Whistler in Paris. Member: ANA 1912, NA 1914; Soc. Nat. des Beaux-Arts, Paris; Paris AA; Inter. Soc. AL; NYWCC; Chevalier of the Lg. of Honor, France. Awards: Silver medal, St. Louis Exp., 1904; gold medal, Munich, 1904; fourth W. A. Clark prize ($500), Corcoran AG 1908; temple gold medal, PAFA 1913; grand prize, P.-P. Exp., San F., 1915; Harris silver medal and prize ($500), AIC 1916; Wm. M. R. French Gold Medal, AIC, 1920; Potter Palmer Gold Medal ($1,000), AIC, 1920; Edw. B. Butler prize ($100), AIC, 1920; gold medal, Phila, AC, 1922. Work: "Before the Mirror," Luxembourg Museum, Paris; "The Toilet," Metropolitan Museum, New York; "The Open Window," "On the Bank" and "The Toilet," Art Institute, Chicago; "Garden in June," "Wooden Bridge," Minneapolis Institute of Arts; "Nude" and "The Hammock," Telfair Academy, Savannah, GA; "Girl Sewing" and "Autumn," Modern Gallery, Venice, Italy; Museum of Odessa; "The Sun Bath," Museum of Fine Arts, Syracuse, NY, and "Torn Lingerie," Art Museum, St. Louis; "Under the Willows," Cincinnati Museum; "Memories," Toledo Museum; "The Bird Cage," New Britain (Conn.) Institute; "The Blue Gown," Detroit, Mich. Inst.; "Dressing Room" and "Peace,"Corcoran Art Gallery, Washington; "Golden Locket," Cincinnati Museum; "Lady in Rose," Arts and Crafts Guild, New Orleans, LA; "Lady in Pink," Lincoln, Nebr., Museum; "Before the Window," Cedar Rapids Art Assoc.; "Blue Curtains," "Truth," and "Nude," Harrison Gallery, Los Angeles Mus. of History, Science and Art. Died in 1939. Address in 1929, care of Macbeth Galleries, 15 East 57th St., NYC; and 64 Rue du Cherche Midi, Paris, France.

FRIETSCH, CHARLOTTE G.
Painter, writer and teacher. Born WI, Jan. 18, 1896. Member: S. Indp. A.; Salons of Amer. Awards: Second prize and hon. mention for design, Alliance. Address in 1929, 253 West 85th St., New York, NY;

summer, "Pine Rest," Brunswick Gardens, Spotswood, NJ.

FRISCHKE, ARTHUR.
Painter. Born New York City, June 25, 1893. Pupil of NAD and Cooper Union. Member: Bronx AG; Am. APL. Address in 1929, 656 Eagle Ave., New York, NY.

FRISHMUTH, HARRIET W.
Sculptor. Born in Philadelphia on Sept. 17, 1880. Studied: with Rodin and Injalbert in Paris; in New York with Borglum; National Sculpture Society; Academician of National Academy of Design. Awards: National Academy of Design, 1922. Collections: Metropolitan Museum of Art; Los Angeles Museum of Art; Museums in Ohio, New Hampshire, Georgia, New Jersey; John Herron Art Institute.

FRITZ, HENRY EUGENE.
Painter, etcher, writer, lecturer and teacher. Born in Germany, Oct. 12, 1875. Pupil of George Bridgman, Robert Blum, George Maynard, C. Y. Turner, Arthur W. Dow, NAD; Beaux Art Inst.; ASL, New York. Member: Eastern AA.; Salons of America; New Rochelle AA. Award: Hon. mention New Rochelle AA, 1922. Address in 1929, 4 Poplar Ave., Chester Park, Pelham, NY.

FROELICH, PAUL.
Painter. Exhibited at Annual Exhibition of Penna. Academy of Fine Arts, Philadelphia, 1924, and Water Color Exhibition, 1925. Address in 1926, 1703 Tioga St., Philadelphia.

FROLICH, FINN HAAKON.
Sculptor. Born Norway, Aug. 13, 1868. Pupil of Ernest Barrias, Augustus Saint Gaudens, D. C. French. Member: Southern Calif. Sculptors Guild; Norse Studio Club; Calif PS. Award: Silver medal, Paris Exp., 1900. Work: Monuments to James Hill and Edward Grig, Seattle; monument to Jack London, Honolulu; Tower of Legends, Forest Lawn Cemetery, Los Angeles. Died in 1947. Address in 1929, 6426 Sunset Bldg.; 612 North Van Ness Ave., Hollywood, CA.

FROMEN, AGNES VALBORG.
Sculptor. Born Waldermasvik, Sweden, Dec. 27, 1868. Pupil of AIC under Lorado Taft. Member: Chicago SA; AIC Alumni. Awards: Prize Municipal Art League of Chicago, 1912; Swedish Exhibition, 1912; second and third for frieze of Illinois State Fair Building, 1914; prizes at Swedish American Exhibition, 1917, 1919 and 1924. Work: "The Spring," Art Institute of Chicago; "Bust of Washington Irving," Washington Irving School, Bloomington, IL; memorial fountain in Englewood High School; memorial tablet in Hyde Park Church of Christ, Chicago; Memorial Fountain, Oxford, OH. Address in 1929, 6016 Ellis Ave., Chicago, IL.

FROMKES, MAURICE.
Painter. Born Feb. 19, 1872. Pupil of NAD under Ward and Low. Member: ANA, 1927; Salma. C.; Allied AA; AFA. Award: Isidor portrait prize, Salma. C., 1908; Diploma of Honor, International Exposition of Fine Arts, Bordeaux, France, 1927. Work: Painting at Delgado Museum, New Orleans; "Portrait," Newcomb College, New Orleans; "Madonna of the Road," National Museum of Modern Arts, Madrid; "Jacinta and her Family," Albright Gallery, Buffalo; "A Spanish Mother," Rhode Island School of Design; "Little Carmen of the Hills," Duncan Phillips Memorial Gallery, Washington, DC; "Adoration of Pepito," Randolph-Macon Women's College, Lynchburg, VA. Died in 1931 in Paris. Address in 1929, 51 West 10th St.; 108 West 57th St., New York, NY.

FROMUTH, CHARLES H(ENRY).
Marine painter. Born Philadelphia, PA, Feb. 23, 1861. Pupil of PAFA under Thomas Eakins. Member: Fellowship Pennsylvania Academy of Fine Arts; Assoc. Soc. Nat. des Beaux-Arts; Paris; London Pastel Soc.; Soc. Des Peintres de Marine, Paris; Berlin Secession Soc. of Painters (cor.). Awards: Second class gold medal, International Exp., Munich, 1897; silver medal, Paris Exp., 1900; gold medal, St. Louis Exp., 1904. Represented in Museums of Wellington and Christ

325

Church, New Zealand; Museum of Quimper, France. Died in 1937. Address in 1929, Concarneau, Finistere, France.

FROST, ANNA.
Painter, lithographer and teacher. Born Brooklyn. Pupil of C. W. Hawthorne, George Senseney, H. B. Snell, Hugh Breckenridge, Bolton Brown. Member: Brooklyn WCS.; NA Women PS; North Shore AA; PBC. Address in 1929, 152 Henry St., Brooklyn, NY.

FROST, ARTHUR BURDETT.
Illustrator. Born in Philadelphia, Jan. 17, 1851, he began illustrating early. Studied at PAFA (part-time) and in London, but primarily self-taught. In 1877 he went to England and returned in 1878. Hon. mention, Paris Expo., 1909. Illustrated "Uncle Remus," "Tom Sawyer" and "Mr. Dooley." Wrote and illustrated own books. Died June 22, 1928, in Pasadena, CA.

FROST, JOHN.
Painter and illustrator. Born Philadelphia, May 14, 1890. Pupil A. B. Frost. Member: Calif. AC., Calif. PS.; Pasadena SA. Awards: Hon. mention, Southwest Museum, 1921; landscape prize, Southwest Museum, Los Angeles, 1922; 2nd prize and popular prize, Southwest Museum, 1923, gold medal, Calif. PS., 1924. Address in 1929, 284 Madeline Drive, Pasadena, CA.

FROST, JULIUS H.
Painter and teacher. Born Newark, NJ, July 11, 1867. Self-taught. Member: S. Indp. A; Salons of America. Died in 1934. Address in 1929, 452 East 136th St., New York, NY; summer, 1318 Ridge Pl., S.E., Washington, DC.

FROTHINGHAM, JAMES.
Portrait painter. Born in Charleston, Mass., 1786. Coach painter; later he received some instruction from Gilbert Stuart and finally became his pupil. Frothingham painted portraits in Boston, Salem, New York and Brooklyn. Elected Member of National Academy of Design in 1831. His copies of Stuart's "Washington"

are excellent, and his original portraits have fine coloring at times, resembling his master's work in color and composition. A number of his portraits were owned by the City of New York, and hung in the Old Court House. Died Jan. 6, 1864, in New York City.

FROTHINGHAM, SARAH C.
Miniature painter. Born in 1821. Daughter of James Frothingham, NA. She exhibited at the National Academy, 1838-42. Died July 20, 1861, in New York City.

FRUEH, (ALFRED J.).
Painter and illustrator. Born Lima, OH, 1880. Member: Society of Independent Artists. Best known for cartoon caricatures. Contributed to "New Yorker." Lived most of life in NYC. Died in 1968.

FRY, GEORGIA TIMKEN.
Painter. Wife of the painter John H. Fry. She was born in St. Louis in 1864, and was a pupil of Harry Thompson, Aime Morot, Schenck and Cazin in Paris. She was a member of the National Association of Women Painters and Sculptors; Society of New York Artists; Society of Women Artists. She is represented by "Return of the Flock," at the Boston Art Club. She made a specialty of landscapes with sheep. She died in China in 1921.

FRY, JOHN H.
Painter. Born in IN. Pupil of Boulanger and Lefebvre in Paris. Member: Union Lg. C.; Paris AA; A. Fund S; Salma. C., 1902; SPNY; Wash. AC; AFA. Died Feb. 24, 1946. Address in 1929, 200 West 57th St., New York, NY.

FRY, M(ARY) H(AMILTON).
Illustrator and cartoonist. Born Salem, MA, April 18, 1890. Pupil of Boston Museum School. Member: Boston SAC; Copley S. Address in 1929, 106 Winthrop St., Cambridge, MA.

FRY, SHERRY E(DMUNDSON).
Sculptor. Born Creston, IA, Sept. 29, 1879. Pupil of AIC under Taft; MacMonnies in Paris. Member: ANA 1914; NSS 1908; NY Arch. Lg. 1911.

326

Awards: Hon. mention, Paris Salon, 1906; medal, Salon, 1908; Am. Acad. at Rome scholarship 1908-11; silver medal, P.-P. Exp., San F., 1915; Watrous gold medal, NAD, 1917; hon. mention, AIC., 1921; Wm. M. R. French gold medal, AIC, 1922. Work: Statue, "Indian Chief," Oskaloosa, IA; "Au Soleil," fountain, Toledo Museum of Art; "The Dolphin," fountain, Mt. Kisco, NY; "The Turtle," fountian, Worcester, MA; fountain for St. George, SI, NY; Capt. Abbey, Tompkinsville, CT; pediment, H. C. Frick house, New York City; pediment, Clark Mausoleum, Los Angeles; Statue of Ira Allen, U. of VT. Address in 1929, Century Club, 7 West 43rd St., New York, NY; Roxbury, CT.

FUCHS, BERNARD.
Illustrator. Born in O'Fallon, IL, in 1932. Studied at the School of Fine Art at Washington Univ. His career started in Detroit, where he produced illustrations for automobile advertisements. This success brought him recognition and assignments from such magazines as Redbook, Lithopinion, and Sports Illustrated. Elegance and craftsman- ship are constants of the innovative style that have earned him many awards and prompted the AG to name him Artist of the Year in 1962. A Hamilton King Award winner, he is the youngest member of the S of I Hall of Fame. As a faculty member of the Illustrators Workshop, he is passing on the knowledge that has made him a continuing influence in American illustration.

FUCHS, EMIL.
Painter, sculptor and etcher. Born in Vienna, Aus., in 1886; died in New York in 1929. Represented in Metropolitan Museum, Cleveland Museum, and designer of medal for Hudson-Fulton Exhibition. Address in 1926, 80 West 40th St., New York.

FUECHSEL, HERMAN.
Painter. Born in Brunswick, Germany, Aug. 1833, he came to America in 1858, and was a member of the Artists' Fund Society of New

York. He died Sept. 30, 1915, in New York City.

FUERST, SHIRLEY M.
Mixed Media. Born in Brooklyn, NY, June 3, 1928. Studied: Hunter College; Brooklyn Museum Art School; Pratt Center for Contemporary Printmaking; Art Students' League, New York City. Awards: Village Art Center, 1963; Enjay Art Competition, 1966; National Association of Women Artists, 1970. Exhibitions: "Unmanly Art", Suffolk Museum, 1972; Brooklyn Museum; Riverside Museum. She was a founding member of "Floating Gallery," a women's artist group. Publ.: Author, Health Hazards In Art, 1975. Address in 1980, 266 Marlborough Road, Brooklyn, NY, 11226.

FUERTES, LOUIS AGASSIZ.
Painter. Born at Ithaca, NY, 1874. Painter of birds since 1896. Illustrated: "Birding on a Broncho," 1896; "Citizen Bird," 1897; "Songbirds and Water Fowl," 1897; "Birdcraft Birds of the Rockies," 1902; "Handbook of Birds of Western United States"; "Coues' Key to North American Birds," 1903; "Handbook of Birds of Eastern United States;" plates for "Report of NY State Game, Forest and Fish Commission;" "Birds of New York;" several series in National Geographic Magazines. Permanent work: Habitat groups, American Museum Natural History, New York; 25 decorative panels for F. F. Brewster, New Haven, CT; birds of New York at State Museum, Albany. Died in Unadilla NY, Aug. 1900. Address in 1926, Cornell Heights, Ithaca, NY.

FUHR, ERNEST.
Illustrator. Born 1874 in New York. Member: SI; GFLA. Died 1933 in Westport, CT. Address in 1929, Westport, CT.

FULLER, GEORGE.
Born at Deerfield, MA, Jan. 17, 1822. Studied in Boston, New York, London and Continental Europe. First known as a portrait painter. Elected Associate of the National Academy of Design, 1857. Original

327

Member of Society of American Artists. Since his death the exhibition of his later works has placed him in the front rank of American colorist and painters of original inspiration. He painted "Fedalma" (the Spanish gypsy), "Nydia" (the blind girl in Bulwer's "Last Days of Pompeii"); also represented at Corcoran Gallery, Washington, by "Lorette." Died March 21, 1884, in Brookline, MA.

FULLER, HENRY B(ROWN).
Painter. Born Deerfield, MA, Oct. 3, 1867; son of George Fuller. Pupil of Cowles Art School in Boston under Bunker; Cox and Mowbray at ASL of NY; Collin in Paris. Member: SAA 1902; ANA 1906. Awards: Bronze medal, Pan-Am. Exp., Buffalo, 1901; Carnegie prize, NAD 1908; silver medal, P.-P. Exp., San F., 1915. Work: "Illusions," National Gallery, Washington. Died in 1934. Address in 1929, 113 Berkeley St., Cambridge, MA; summer, Deerfield, MA.

FULLER, LUCIA FAIRCHILD.
Miniature painter. Born in Boston, 1872. Pupil of Art Students' League of New York under William M. Chase and H. Siddons Mowbray. Engaged professionally as painter from 1889, chiefly doing miniatures. Bronze medal, Paris Expn., 1900; silver medal, Buffalo Expn., 1901. Member: American Society of Miniature Painters; Penna. Society of Miniature Painters; New York Water Color Club, etc. Died in Madison, WI, May 22, 1924.

FULLER, MARY.
(Mary Fuller McChesney). Sculptor. Born in Wichita, KS, Oct. 20, 1922. Studied: University of California in Berkeley; California Faience Company of Berkeley. Awarded the Merit of Honor, San Francisco Arts Festival, 1971. Exhibitions: Syracuse Museum, New York; San Francisco Museum of Art; San Francisco Women's Center. Commission: California Medical Center and the San Francisco General Hospital. Awarded first prize for Ceramic Sculpture, Pacific Coast Ceramic Assn. 1947

and 1949; Merit Award, San Francisco Art Festival, 1971; National Endowment Arts art critic grant, 1975. Medium: Concrete. Also noted for her writing of short stories, novels, and articles on art. Address in 1980, 2955 Sonoma Mountain Road, Petalumn, CA.

FULLER, META W.
See Warrick.

FULLER, R(ALPH) B(RIGGS).
Painter and illustrator. Born Capac, MI, March 9, 1890. Member: Salma. C. Humorous drawings in "Life," "Judge," "Liberty," "Saturday Evening Post," "American Magazine," etc. Address in 1929, 170 Ames Ave., Leonia, NJ summer, West Boothbay Harbor, ME.

FULLER, RICHARD HENRY.
Painter. Born at Bradford, NH, in 1822, he was chiefly self-taught. He died in 1871 at Chelsea, MA. He is represented in the Boston Museum of Fine Arts by his painting "Near Chelsea," painted in 1847.

FULLER, SUE.
Sculptor and printmaker. Born in Pittsburgh, PA, in 1914. Studied: Carnegie Institute; Columbia University. Awards: Association of Artists Pittsburgh, 1941, 1942; Northwest Printmakers, 1946; Philadelphia Printmakers Club, 1944, 1946, 1949; Tiffany Foundation Fellowship, 1947; National Institute of Arts and Letters, 1950; New York State Fair, 1950; Guggenheim Fellowship, 1948. Collections: New York Public Library; Library of Congress; Harvard University Library; Carnegie Institute; Whitney Museum of American Art; Ford Foundation; Art Institute of Chicago; Museum of Modern Art; Brooklyn Museum; Metropolitan Museum of Art; National Academy of Design; Baltimore Museum of Art; Philadelphia Museum of Art; Seattle Art Museum. Media: Plastic and string. Address in 1980, P.O. Box 1580, Southampton, NY.

FULLER-LARGENT, LYDIA.
Painter, craftsman, lecturer and teacher. Born CA. Pupil of Calif. School of Fine Arts; Rudolph

328

Schaeffer, Ralph Johonnot. Member: PAA; Calif. Women A. Address in 1929, Moulder Bldg., Page and Gough Sts.; h. 1450 Taylor St., San Francisco, CA.

FULTON, A(GNES) FRASER.
Painter, sculptor and designer. Born Yonkers, NY, March 10, 1898. Pupil of Dow, Martin, Bement, Upjohn. Member: Yonkers A.A. Award: Hon. mention, "House Beautiful" cover contest. Address in 1929, Teachers' College, Columbia Univ., New York, NY; h. 218 Park Ave., Yonkers, NY.

FULTON, C(YRUS) J(AMES).
Painter. Born Pueblo, CO, June 26, 1873. Pupil of H. F. Wentz and A. H. Schroff. Work: "Sky-Line Trail," Eugene Chamber of Commerce. Died in 1949. Address in 1929, 1192 Jefferson St., Eugene, OR.

FULTON, ROBERT.
Artist, inventor, successful introducer of the steamboat. Born in Little Britain township, Lancaster County, PA, Nov. 14, 1765. Came to Phila. in 1872 as a portrait painter, within 4 years he earned enough to establish his widowed mother on a small farm clear of debt. He then went to London to study under Benjamin West, after establishing himself in Devonshire under the patronage of men of wealth. In 1794 he became a member of the family of Joel Barlow, author of "The Columbiad," in Paris, where he painted the first panorama exhibited in the French capital. In 1797 he began experiments in submarine navigation and torpedo warfare. As early as 1803 he had, with the financial assistance of Chancellor Livingston, launched a steamboat on the Seine, which sank, though a partial success later achieved encouraged him to build the famous "Clermont," which, in 1807, set out on her historic voyage to Albany. Died in NY Feb. 24, 1815.

FUNK, WILHELM HEINRICH.
Painter. Born Hanover, Germany, 1866. Studied at Art Students' League of New York, and in museums of Spain, Holland, France, Italy and Germany. Came to America 1885;

first attracted attention by a pen-portrait of Edwin Booth, the actor. He became the pen and ink artist on the staff of the New York Herald; also contributed to Scribner's Magazine, Century, Harper's, Judge and Truth; he devoted his attention to portrait painting. Address in 1926, 80 West 40th St., New York.

FURLONG, CHARLES (WELLINGTON).
Painter, illustrator, writer and lecturer. Born Cambridge, MA, Dec. 13, 1874. Pupil of Ecole des Beaux Arts, Bouguereau, Jean Paul Laurens. Member: Boston Art School Alumni Assoc.; Salma. C.; Boston AC. Award: Prix de concours, Academie Julian, Paris. Illustrations for Bailey's Encyclopedia of Horticulture; "Harper's;" "Scribners;" "The Gateway to the Sahara." Address in 1929, 333 Beacon St., Boston, MA; summer, Pendleton, OR.

FURLONG, THOMAS.
Painter, craftsman, illustrator, writer, lecturer and teacher. Born St. Louis. MO. Pupil of ASL of NY; John Vanderpoel, Max Weber. Member: ASL of NY. Work: Altar piece, Tryptich, St. Vincent de Paul's Church, Brooklyn, NY; two altar pieces, St. Bridgid's Church, Queens, New York City. Lectures at New York University on "Free Hand Drawing and Applied Art." Author of "Form: Its Analysis and Synthesis" and "Design and Its Structural Basis." Address in 1929, 3 Washington Sq., North, New York, NY; summer, Golden Heart Farm, Bolton Landing on Lake George, NY.

FURNASS, JOHN MASON.
Painter and engraver. Born on March 4, 1763, in Boston, MA. He was the nephew of the engraver Nathaniel Hurd, who bequeathed him his engraving tools. Furnass engraved book-plates and certificates for the Massachusetts Loan Society. In 1785 he was painting portraits in Boston, and in 1834 the Boston Athenaeum exhibited two copies by him of paintings by Teniers. He painted two portraits of John Venal, the old schoolmaster of Boston. Died at Dedham, MA, June 22, 1804.

FURNESS, WILLIAM HENRY, JR.
Painter. Born in Philadelphia,
1827. Son of Rev. William H.
Furness. He drew many excellent
portraits in crayon, and painted a
number of portraits of well-known
Philadelphians in oils. His work
in crayon stood next to Cheney. He
painted Charles Sumner, Lucretia
Mott, Rev. Dr. Barnes, Hamilton
Wilde, Mrs. Lathrop and Miss
Emerson. Died in 1867.

FURSMAN, FREDERICK.
Painter. Born El Paso, IL, Feb.
15, 1874. Pupil of AIC; Julian
Academy, Jean Paul Laurens and
Raphel Collin, in Paris. Member:
Cliff Dwellers; Chicago SA; Chicago
Gal. A. Awards: Cahn prize
($100), AIC, 1911; Frank prize
($150), 1923; Chicago SA, silver
medal, AIC, 1924. Work: "In the
Garden," Museum of Art, Toledo, OH.
Director, Summer School of
Painting, Saugatuck, MI. Address
in 1929, Saugatuck, MI.

FURST, FLORENCE WILKINS.
(Mrs. F. E. Furst). Painter. Born
Delavan, Wisc. Pupil of Lucy
Hartrath, Marquis Reitzell, Madame
Armand Oberteuffer. Member:
Rockford AA; Ill. AFA, All-Ill.
SFA.; AFA. Works: "Still Life,"
State permanent collection,
Centennial Building, Springfield,
Ill. Address in 1929, 819 West
Stephenson St., Freeport, Ill.

FURST, MORITZ.
Engraver. Born at Bosing, Hungary,
1782, he was living in New York in
1834. Engraver of dies for coins
and medals. In 1807 Mr. Joseph
Clay, U.S. Consul at Leghorn, asked
Furst to come to the United States,
as die-sinker in the U.S. Mint at
Philadelphia; in this capacity he
engraved the dies for a large
number of Congressional medals
awarded to heroes of the War of
1812. Also engaged in business, as
he advertised in 1808 as "Engraver
of Seals and Dye-Sinker on Steel
and other metals," in Phila. in
business in Phila. as late as
September, 1820.

G., L.
The initials of this unknown engraver appear upon a reversed copy of a caricature originally etched by William Charles, of Phila. Also signed as "L. G. Sculpt." on a map of Sacketts Harbour, by Patrick May, published and sold by Partick May in Bristol, CT. This map is copyrighted in 1815, indicating the date of the work.

GAADT, GEORGE S.
Illustrator. Born in Erie, PA, in 1941. Studied: Columbus College of Art and Design. Since his first illustration, a silk-screen, appeared in 1961, he has received over 60 awards in many cities in the U.S. In addition to corporate advertising work and editorial illustration for many major magazines, he has also done children's books for Macmillan. His work has been shown in galleries in Columbus, OH, Pittsburgh, PA, and at the S of I.

GABAY, ESPERANZA.
Painter. Born New York City. Pupil of Kenyon Cox, Walter Shirlaw. Member: NA Women PS. Award: Emerson McMillan Prize, NA Women PS, 1917; hon. mention, NAC, 1925. Address in 1929, 136 West 91st St., New York, NY; summer, Sheffield, MA.

GABRIEL, GABRIELLE.
Painter and craftswoman. Born Germantown, PA, Dec. 24, 1904. Pupil of Daniel Garber, Hugh Breckenridge. Member: Fellowship PAFA; Plastic C. Address in 1929, 4523 Sansom St., Philadelphia, PA; summer, Stone Harbor, NJ

GADBURY, HARRY L(EE).
Painter, illustrator and etcher. Born Greenfield, OH, June 5, 1890. Pupil of Buchler, Meekin, Wessel, Duveneck. Member: Dayton SE. Address in 1929, 11 Westminster Apts., Dayton, OH.

GADE, JOHN.
Painter. Born Tremont, NY, Oct. 24, 1870. Self taught. Member: S. Indp. A.; Salons of America; Chicago NJSA; Buffalo Salon IA.

Address in 1929, 108 Stewart St., Floral Park, LI, NY.

GAER, FAY.
Sculptor and craftswoman. Born London, England, April 7, 1899. Pupil of Ralph Stacpoole, Leo Lentelli. Member: ASL of NY. Address in 1929, 391 North Baldwin Ave., Sierra Madre, CA.

GAERTNER, CARL F.
Painter, illustrator, etcher and teacher. Born Cleveland, OH, April 18, 1898. Pupil of Cleveland School of Art; F. N. Wilcox and H. G. Keller. Member: Cleveland SA. Awards: Second prize, 1922, first prize, 1923, and first prize, 1924, Cleveland Museum of Art. Exhibited Annual Exhib. of PAFA, 1924. Works: "The Ripsaw," Cleveland Museum of Art; "The Furnace," Midday Club of Cleveland and mural--War Memorial in Kenyon College. Died Nov. 1952. Address in 1929, 401 Prospect-Fourth Bldg., Cleveland, OH; h. 3325 Greenway Rd., Shaker Village, OH.

GAERTNER, LILLIAN V.
Painter, illustrator, etcher and craftswoman. Born New York City, July 5, 1906. Pupil of Joseph Hoffmann, Ferdinand Schmutzer. Member: Mural P; Arch. Lg. of NY; AFA. Work: Murals in Montmartre Club, Palm Beach, Fla.; Ziegfeld Theatre, New York; original sketch Ziegfeld Theatre, Vienna Museum; Metropolitan Opera Costume Designs, Vienna Museum, Chicago, IL. Address in 1929, 312 West 101st St., New York, NY

GAETANO, NICHOLAS.
Illustrator. Born in Colorado Springs, Colorado, he attended ACD. Art Direction magazine published his cover in 1965 and since 1970 his editorial work has appeared in many magazines including New Times, Travel and Leisure, Contempo, and Newsday. With advertising and book illustration to his credit, he has received numerous awards from the AIGA, ADC and S of I. He has produced posters for the Open Gallery in Los Angeles which has exhibited his work.

331

GAG, WANDA HAZEL.
Artist and author. Born in New Ulm, Minn., on March 11, 1893. Entered the ASL, where she studied under John Sloan and other noted teachers. A show of her drawings, lithographs, and woodcuts at the Weyhe Gallery in NYC in 1926 brought her first recognition as a serious artist. Represented in the Museum of Modern Art's 1939 exhibition of "Art in Our Time." She wrote and illustrated Millions of Cats, 1928. Other books for children included The Funny Thing, 1929, Snippy and Snappy, 1931, A.B.C. Bunny, 1933, Gone Is Gone, 1935, and Nothing at All, 1941. She also translated and illustrated Tales from Grimm, 1936, Snow White and the Seven Dwarfs, 1938, Three Gay Tales of Grimm, 1943, and More Tales from Grimm, 1947. Growing Pains: Diaries and Drawings for the Years 1908-1917, 1940, was a memoir based on her journals. Died in NYC on June 27, 1946.

GAGE, G(EORGE) W(ILLIAM).
Painter and illustrator. Born Lawrence, MA, Nov. 14, 1887. Pupil of Hale, Benson and Pyle. Member: GFLA. Designed covers for leading magazines, and illustrated numerous books. Instructor of book illustrations, New York Evening School of Industrial Art. Died Aug. 7, 1957, in New York City. Address in 1929, 61 Poplar St., Brooklyn, NY.

GAGE, HARRY L.
Painter, draughtsman and teacher. Born Battle Creek, MI, Nov. 1887. Pupil of AIC. Member: AFA; AI Graphic A. Secretary, Bartlett Orr Press, New York; Asst. Typographic Director, Mergenthaler Linotype Co., Brooklyn; Pres., Wm. H. Denny Co., New York. Address in 1929, 49 Brunswick Rd., Montclair, NJ.

GAGE, MERRELL.
Sculptor, lecturer and teacher. Born Topeka, KS, Dec. 26, 1892. Pupil of ASL of NY; Beaux Arts and Henri School of Art. Member: Calif. AC; Calif. PS. Award: Gold medal, Kansas City Art Institute, 1921; gold medal and Way Side Colony prize, Pac. Southwest Exp., 1928; hon. mention Los Angeles

Museum, 1929. Works: Lincoln Memorial and Billard Memorial, owned by the State of Kansas; Police Memorial and American Legion Memorial Fountains, Kansas City; Bar Association Memorial, Jackson Co., MO; Santa Monica World Flight Memorial; Childrens Fountain, La Jolla Public Library; Figures of "Agriculture" and "Industry," Calif. State Bldg., Los Angeles; "John Brown" and "The Flutist," Mulvane Museum, Topeka, KS. Address in 1929, 456 Mesa Rd., Santa Monica, CA.

GAGE, ROBERT M.
Sculptor. His bronze statue of Lincoln stands in the State House Grounds, Topeka. Address in 1926, 1031 Filmore Ave., Topeka, KS.

GAINS.
Nothing is known of this painter, except that the portrait of Rev. James Honyman, executed by Samuel Oakey of Newport in 1774, records the portrait as painted by "Gains," probably a local artist. Honyman was pastor of Trinity Church, Newport, RI, from 1704 to 1750. The painting hangs in the vestry of Old Trinity Church, Newport, RI.

GAIR, SONDRA BATTIST.
Painter. Studied: School of Education, NY Univ., NYC; Univ. of Texas, Austin, TX; Univ. of Maryland, College Park Maryland; The American Univ., Wash., DC. Awards: Wash. Watercolor Society, 1971-1972; Carnegie Institute Exhibit, Penn., 1962; National Watercolor Society, 1969.

GALE, CHARLES F.
Painter. Born in Columbus, OH, in 1874; died in 1920.

GALE, GEORGE (ALBRET).
Painter, illustrator and etcher. Born Bristol, RI, Nov. 16, 1893. Pupil of RI School of Design. Member: Providence WCC; RI School Design Alumni; Newport AA; RI Shipmodel S. Represented in RI School of Design Museum. Illustrated for "Scribner's" and "Yachting." Address in 1929, 25 Pearse Ave., Bristol, RI.

332

GALE, WALTER RASIN.
Painter, illustrator, lecturer and teacher. Born Worton Manor, Kent County, MD, Jan. 17, 1878. Pupil of Maryland Inst.; Charcoal C. School of Art and various art courses at Johns Hopkins Univ., Univ. of Chicago and NY Univ. Member: Arch. Inst. of A.; Eastern AA; College AA of Amer.; Balto WCC. Instructor, Art Dept., Baltimore City College. Died in 1959. Address in 1929, Baltimore City College; h. 233 West Lanvale St., Baltimore, MD.

GALLAGHER, GENEVIEVE.
Painter and teacher. Born Baltimore, MD, Jan. 19, 1899. Pupil of Henry Roben, Hugh Breckenridge, Leon Kroll and John Sloan. Award: Baltimore Municipal Art Society Prize, 1921. Address in 1929, 4212 Pennhurst Ave., Baltimore, MD.

GALLAGHER, SEARS.
Painter and etcher. Born in Boston, April 30, 1869. Pupil of Tomasso Juglaris in Boston; Laurens and Constant in Paris. Member: Boston GA; Boston SWCP; Chicago SE; Cal. SE; Boston SE; Concord AA; Brooklyn SE; AFA. Award: Logan prize for etching, AIC, 1922; silver medal for etching, Tenth Inter. Exhib. Print MS, Calif., 1929. Etchings in Boston Museum of FA; Art Institute of Chicago; NY Pub. Lib.; Brooklyn Museum; Library of Congress. Died in 1955. Address in 1929, 755 Boylston St, Boston, MA; h. West Roxbury, MA.

GALLAGHER.
An Irishman who painted portraits in Philadelphia about 1800; he also painted signs and other pictures. In 1807 he was employed in New York as a scene painter by Thomas A. Cooper, but he was not a success. In 1798 he painted a standard for the First Philadelphia Volunteer Cavalry, commanded by Capt. McKean.

GALLAND, JOHN.
Engraver. Born April 30, 1809. The name of John Galland, "engraver," appears in the Philadelphia directories for 1796-1817, inclusive. He engraved in the stipple manner with little

effect. Probably his most ambitious work is a large portrait of Washington done after a similar plate by David Edwin. A number of portraits and historical plates executed by Galland are to be found in a history of France published by James Stewart, Philadelphia, 1796-97. Died Oct. 11, 1847.

GALLAUDET, EDWARD.
Born in Hartford, CT, 1809; died there, 1847. He was the son of Peter Wallace Gallaudet, merchant. Edward Gallaudet was probably apprenticed to one of the several engraving establishments in Hartford; he then worked in Boston with John Cheney. Gallaudet was a reputable line engraver, his best work appearing in the Annuals of 1835-40. A miniature portrait of Edward Gallaudet was owned by his nephew, Mr. E. M. Gallaudet, principal of the Gallaudet College for the Deaf and Dumb, at Washington, DC.

GALLAUDET, ELISHA.
Born in New Rochelle, NY, about 1730. Elisha Gallaudet was the second son of Dr. Peter Gallaudet. Gallaudet was in business in New York as an engraver, as he advertised in the New York Mercury of March 5, 1759. In this issue appear proposals for printing by subscription, "Six Representations of Warriors who are in the Service of their Majesties, the King of Great Britain and the King of Prussia. Designed after life with a Description as expressed in the Proposals." Besides early bookplates his only known engraving was a portrait of the Rev. George Whitfield, issued as a frontispiece to a "Life of Whitfield," published by Hodge & Shober, New York, 1774. This plate was poorly engraved, and evidently a copy of an English print. Died in 1805 in New York City.

GALLI, STANLEY W.
Illustrator. Born in San Fran., Calif., in 1912. Did a number of odd jobs in Nevada and Calif. before enrolling in the Calif. School of Fine Arts, and later studied at the ACD. He worked briefly in a San Fran. studio and

333

later as a free-lance illustrator. He has had assignments for magazines including Country Gentleman, Sports Afield, McCall's, and True. Among his clients are Random House and United Airlines, for which he illustrated a series of posters in the 1960's. His works are in the collections of the USAF and the Baseball Hall of Fame.

GALLISON, HENRY HAMMOND.
Landscape painter. Born in Boston on May 20, 1850. Studied in Paris, pupil of Bonnefoy. Represented in Boston Museum of Fine Arts by "The Golden Haze" and "The Morning Shadow." He died in Cambridge, MA, on Oct. 12, 1910.

GALLO, FRANK.
Sculptor. Born in 1933 in Toledo, OH. Earned B.F.A. from Toledo, Mu. School (1954); M.F.A. from U. of Iowa (1959). Taught at U. of IL since 1960. Rec. Awards from Des Moines Art Center; Contemp. Arts Center, Cinn.; Guggenheim fellowship (1966). Exhibited at Toledo Mus. of Art (1955); Gillman Galleries of NYC and Chicago; PAFA; Whitney; Art Inst. of Chicago; Louisiana State U; Puch Gallery, NYC; Time, Inc. In collections of MOMA; Colorado State U.; Baltimore Mus. of Art; Princeton; and many private collections.

GALLUP, JEANIE.
See Mrs. Mottet.

GALT, ALEXANDER.
Sculptor. Born June 26, 1827, in Norfolk, VA. He studied abroad. Among his works are many portrait busts; bust of Jefferson Davis was executed from actual measurements. Died Jan. 19, 1863, in Richmond, VA.

GALT, CHARLES FRANKLIN.
Painter. Born St. Louis, 1884. Pupil of St. Louis School of Fine Arts and of Richard Miller. Address in 1926, 4021 Washington Ave., St. Louis, MO.

GAMBERLING, GRACE THORP.
Painter. Exhibited at the Pennsylvania Academy of Fine Arts, Philadelphia, in 1924. Address in 1926, Cynwyd, PA.

GAMBLE, JOHN MARSHALL.
Painter. Born Morristown, NJ, Nov. 25, 1863. Pupil of San Francisco School of Design; Academie Julian, Laurens and Constant in Paris. Member: San F., AA; Santa Barbara AL; AFA. Award: Gold medal, Alaska- Yukon-Pacific Exp., 1909. Represented in Museum of Art, Auckland, NZ; Park Museum, San Francisco. Address in 1929, 813½ State St.; h. 2518½ Castillo St.; P.O. Box 313, Santa Barbara, CA.

GAMBLE, ROY C.
Painter. Born June 12, 1887. Pupil of Detroit Fine Arts Academy; ASL of NY; Julian in Paris. Member: Scarab C. Awards: Second Hopkin prize for painting, Scarab C., Detroit, 1914; gold medal, 1920, Scarab C.; Herbert Munio prize, MI, Artists Exh., 1926; Founders prize, Detroit Art Inst., 1928. Work in Pennsylvania Academy of the Fine Arts; "Freckles," Detroit Art Institute. Address in 1929, 5726 14th St.; 83 Fort St., West, Detroit, MI.

GAMMELL, R(OBERT) H(ALE) IVES.
Painter. Born Providence, RI, Jan. 7, 1893. Pupil of William M. Paxton. Member: AFA; Providence AC; Boston GA. Work: Decorations, hemicycle of Toledo Museum of Art; Women's Club, Fall River, MA; Public Library, Newark, NJ. Address in 1929, 22 St. Rotolph St., Boston, MA; h. 170 Hope St., Providence, RI; summer, Provincetown, MA.

GANDOLA, P(AUL) M(ARIO).
Sculptor, architect and craftsman. Born Besano, Italy, Aug. 15, 1889. Pupil of Milan Academy of Fine Art. Member: Cleveland SA; Cleveland Sculptors S. Address in 1929, 12208-10 Euclid Ave.; care The Cleveland Society of Artists, 2022 East 88th St., Cleveland, OH.

GANDOLFI, MAURO.
Engraver. Born in Bologna, Italy, in 1764; died there in 1834. This master engraver in line, and a pupil of the famous Giuseppe Longhi, was probably the first of the really prominent European engravers to visit the United States professionally, although he

334

never engraved here. Dunlap tells us that he came to the United States under a contract to engrave, for $4,000, Col. Trumbull's large plate of the "Declaration of Independence."

GANIERE, GEORGE ETIENNE.
Sculptor and teacher. Born Chicago, IL, April 26, 1865. Pupil of AIC. Member: Chicago SA; Alumni AIC. Award: Shaffer prize, AIC, 1909. Work: "Baby Head" in John Vanderpoel Memorial Collection; "Lincoln" at Lincoln Memorial School, Webster City, IA, and at Burlington, Wis.; "Lincoln Fountain." Lincoln Highway, Chicago, IL; "Gen. Anthony Wayne," equestrian statue Fort Wayne, IN; "Lincoln" and "Douglas," Chicago Hist. Society; "Lincoln," IL. Historical Society; "Lincoln," Grand Army Memorial Hall, Chicago; Hately Memorial," Highland Park, IL; "Lincoln Memorial," Starved Rock, State Park. IL; "Dr. Frank W. Gunsaulus Memorial," Chicago; "Head of Lincoln," "Meditation," Milwaukee Art Institute; "The Debator," Omaha Society of Fine Arts; "Head of Lincoln," Morgan Park, IL; "Tecumseh," "Little Turtle," Chicago Historical Society; "The Toilers," "Awakening Soul" and ideal figure, "Innocence," Fine Arts Gallery, De Land, FL. Former instructor in Sculpture Dept., Chicago Art Inst. Director and instructor, Dept. of Sculpture, Stetson University, De Land, Fla. Died in 1935. Address in 1929, Glenwood, FL.

GANNAM, JOHN.
Illustrator. Born in Lebanon, in 1897. Spent his early years in Chicago and at age 14 he became the family breadwinner. One of his many odd jobs was in an engraving studio where he began his artistic training in 1926 he moved to Detroit where for four years he worked in an art studio. Coming to NY in 1930, he quickly found assignments, at Woman's Home Companion and later Good Housekeeping, Ladies' Home Journal and Cosmopolitan. His advertising illustrations were in high demand and although he used all media, his most prolific work was done in watercolor. A member of the AWS, NAD, and S of I, he worked most of his life from his studio on West 67th Street. He is a member of the Illustrators Hall of Fame. Died in 1965.

GANO, KATHARINE V.
Painter. Born in Cincinnati in 1884. Pupil of Duveneck. Address in 1926, Southern Railway Bldg., Cincinnati, OH.

GARBER, DANIEL.
Painter and teacher. Born N. Manchester, IN, April 11, 1880. Pupil of Cincinnati Art Academy under Nowottny; PAFA under Anshutz. Member: ANA 1910; NA 1913; NAC; Salma. C. since 1909. Awards: Cresson scholarship PAFA, 1903; first Hallgarten prize, NAD 1909; hon. mention, ACP 1910; hon. mention, CI Pittsburgh 1910; fourth Clark prize, Corcoran Gal. 1910; Lippincott prize, PAFA 1911; Palmer prize ($1,000), AIC 1911; second W. A. Clark prize ($1,500) and silver Corcoran medal, 1912; gold medal P.-P. Exp., San F., 1915; Altman prize ($500), NAD, 1915; Shaw prize, Salma. C., 1916; NAD, 1915; Shaw prize, Salma. C., 1916; Morris prize, Newport AA, 1916; Altman prize ($1,000), NAD, 1917; Stotesbury prize, PAFA, 1918; Temple gold medal, PAFA, 1919; 1st W.A. Clark prize and gold medal, Corcoran Gallery, 1921; Locust medal, PAFA, 1923; third prize ($500), Carnegie Inst., 1924; first Altman prize ($1,000), National Academy of Design, 1927; gold medal of honor Penn. Academy of Fine Arts, 1929. Work: "April Landscape," and "South Room--Green Street," Corcoran Gallery, Washington; "Winter--Richmont," Cincinnati Museum; The Hills of Byram" and "Towering Trees," Art Institute, Chicago, IL; "September Fields," City Art Museum, St. Louis; "Midsummer Landscape," University of Missouri; "March," Carnegie Institute, Pittsburgh; "Down the River, Winter," Mus. of Art and Science, Los Angeles; represented in Ann Mary Brown Memorial, Providence; National Arts Club, New York; St. Paul Institute of Art; Pennsylvania Academy of the

Fine Arts; Detroit Institute; Wilstach collection, Memorial Hall, Philadelphia; Phillips Gallery, Washington; Locust Club, Philadelphia Albright Gallery, Buffalo; Swarthmore College, Swarthmore, PA; National Gallery, Washington, DC; Art Association, Topeka, Kansas; Metropolitan Museum of Art, New York. Died in 1958. Address in 1929, Lumberville, Bucks Co., PA.

GARBER, VIRGINIA WRIGHT.
Painter, lecturer and teacher. Pupil of Chase; Constant in Paris. Member: Fellowship PAFA; Plastic C.; PA Sch. Ind. A. Alumni A. Address in 1929, Bryn Mawr, PA.

GARCIA, J. TORRES.
Painter. Exhibited at the PAFA, 1921, at "Exhibition of Paintings Showing the Later Tendencies in Art." Address in 1926, 4 West 29th St., New York.

GARDEN, FRANCIS.
Engraver. The Boston Evening Post, 1745, contains the following advertisement: "Francis Garden, engraver from London, engraves in the newest Manner and at the cheapest Rates, Coats-of-Arms, Crests or Cyphers on Gold, Silver, Pewter or Copper. To be heard of at Mr. Caverly's Distiller, at the South End of Boston." "N.B. He will wait on any Person, in Town or Country, to do their work at their own House, if desired; also copperplate printing performed by him." No work of any kind signed by Garden was known to Fielding in 1926.

GARDIN, ALICE TILTON.
Painter. Born in 1859. Member: NA Women PS. Address in 1929, care J. E. Fraser, 328 East 42nd St.; 3 MacDougal Alley, New York, NY.

GARDIN, LAURA.
(Mrs. James E. Fraser). Sculptor. Born in Chicago, IL, 1889. Pupil of James E. Fraser. Member: National Sculptors' Society; National Academy of Women Painters and Sculptors. Awards: Helen Foster Barnett prize, National Academy of Design, 1916; Shaw

memorial prize, National Academy of Design, 1919. Address in 1926, 3 MacDougal Alley, New York, NY.

GARDINER, ELIZA D(RAPER).
Painter, engraver and teacher. Born Providence, RI, Oct. 29, 1871. Pupil of RI School of Design. Member: Providence AC; Providence WCC; Calif. PM. Represented in Detroit Institute; Springfield Public Library; Providence AC, and Philadelphia Print Club; Bibliotheque Nationale, Paris. Address in 1929, 2139 Broad St., Providence, RI.

GARDINER, FREDERICK M(ERRICK).
Painter, etcher and writer. Born Sioux Falls, SD, June 27, 1887. Pupil of Edourd Leon in Paris; Phillip L. Hale. Member: Phila. PC. Address in 1929, Valley St., Beverly Farms, MA; h. Contoocook, NH; summer, Schooner "Evanthia II", care of Theodore Chadwick, 19 Congress St., Boston, MA.

GARDNER, CHARLES REED.
Painter, illustrator and etcher. Born Phila., Aug. 17, 1901. Pupil of Thornton Oakley, Herbert Pullinger. Member: Phila. Print C. Work: Cover and end paper for "Peder Victorious" (Harper Bros.); cover in Baltimore Museum of Art; covers for "Ecstasy of Thomas DeQuincy" (Doubleday Doran); "The Lost Child" (Longman, Green and Co.); "The Garden of Vision" (Cosmopolitan). Address in 1929, 522 Walnut St., h. 2029 North Carlisle St., Philadelphia, PA; summer, 137 South Spruce St., Lititz, PA.

GARDNER, DONALD.
Illustrator. Member: GFLA; SI. Address in 1929, 12 Park Ave., North, Bronxville, NY.

GARDNER, FRED.
Painter and architect. Born Syracuse, NY, April 16, 1880. Pupil of Pratt Institute, Brooklyn; ASL of NY. Member: S. Indp. A. Address in 1929, 110 Columbia Heights, Brooklyn, NY; summer, Spring Valley, NY.

GARDNER, GERTRUDE G(AZELLE).
Painter and teacher. Born Fort Dodge, IA. Pupil of Henry B. Snell; Pratt Inst.; Fontainebleau Sch. FA, France. Member: NA Women PS; AFA. Address in 1929, 195 Union St., Flushing, LI, NY; summer, Boothbay Harbor, ME.

GARESCHE, MARIE R.
Painter, writer and lecturer. Born St. Louis, MO, July 29, 1864. Pupil of Jules Machard and Henry Mosler. Member: St. Luke AS, (founder). Author of "Art of the Ages." Address in 1929, 4930 Maryland Ave.; h. 3622 West Pine Blvd., St. Louis, MO; summer, "Ravinedge," Douglas, MI.

GARNER, CHARLES S., JR.
Painter. Born 1890. Exhibited at Annual Exhibition of the Penna. Academy of Fine Arts, Philadelphia, 1924. Died 1933 in New Hope, PA. Address in 1926, 320 Harmony St., Philadelphia.

GARNER, FRANCES C.
Painter. Exhibited at the Water Color Exhibition of the Penna. Academy of the Fine Arts, Philadelphia, 1925. Address in 1926, 320 Harmony St., Philadelphia.

GARNSEY, ELMER E(LLSWORTH).
Painter. Born Holmdel, Monmouth Co., NJ, Jan. 24, 1862. Pupil of Cooper Union, ASL, George Maynard and Francis Lathrop in New York. Member: Mural P; AIA (hon.), 1899; Century Assoc.; A. Aid S. AFA. Awards: Bronze designer's medal, Columbian Exp., Chic., 1893; hon. mention and silver medal for mural decorations, Paris Exp., 1900. Work: General color schemes--Library of Congress, Wash.; Public Library, Boston; Public Library, St. Louis; Library of Columbia Univ., New York; Memorial Hall, Yale University, New Haven; State Capitol, St. Paul, MN; State Capitol, Des Moines, IA; State Capitol, Madison, WI; U.S. Customs House, New York; Richardson Memorial Library, City Art Museum, St. Louis. Specialty, mural and landscape painting. Died in 1946. Address in 1929, care of Fifth Avenue Bank, 530 Fifth Ave., NYC.

GARNSEY, JULIAN E(LLSWORTH).
Mural painter. Born New York City, Sept. 25, 1887. Pupil of ASL of NY; Jean Paul Laurens in Paris. Member: Calif. AC; Calif. WCS; Los Angeles Arch. C. Arch. Lg. of NY; Los Angeles PS. Award: Honor award in fine arts, Southern Calif. Chapter, Amer. Inst. of Architects, 1927. Work: Decoration of Library and Auditorium, University of Calif., Los Angeles; decorations in Los Angeles Public Library, Hawaiian Electric Company, Honolulu; Union Depot, Ogden, UT; Bridges Art Museum, San Diego, CA; Del Monte Hotel, Del Monte, CA. Address in 1929, 3305 Wilshire Blvd.; h. 657 North Mariposa Ave., Los Angeles, CA; summer, Hermosa Beach, CA.

GARRETSON, ALBERT M.
Painter and illustrator. Born Buffalo, NY, Oct. 12, 1877. Pupil of Laurens in Paris. Award: Inness bookplate prize, Salma. C., 1912. Address in 1929, Publicity Division, Metropolitan Life Insurance Co., 1 Madison Ave., New York; h. Beechurst, LI, NY.

GARRETSON, DELLA.
Painter. Born Logan, OH, April 12, 1860. Pupil of Detroit Art Museum; NAD; ASL of NY. Address in 1929, Dexter, MI; summer, Ogunquit, ME.

GARRETT, ANNA.
Illustrator. Member: Plastic Club, Wilmington SFA; Fellowship PAFA. Address in 1929, Lansdowne, PA; 1609 Broome St., Wilmington, DE.

GARRETT, ANNE SHAPLEIGH.
Painter. Exhibited at the Pennsylvania Academy of Fine Arts, Philadelphia, in 1924. Address in 1926, 1609 Broome Street, Wilmington, DE.

GARRETT, CLARA PFEIFER.
(Mrs. Edmund A. Garrett). Sculptor. Born Pittsburgh, PA, July 26, 1882. Pupil of St. Louis School of Fine Arts; Ecole des Beaux-Arts; Mercie and Bourdelle in Paris. Awards: Bronze medal, Louisiana Purchase Exp., St. Louis, 1904; hon. mention, NSS, 1905; sculpture prize, Artists' Guild of

St. Louis, 1915; St. Louis Art Lg. Prize, 1916. Work: "Boy Teasing Turtle," Metropolitan Museum, New York City; "McKinley," City of St. Louis; "Children at Play," 50 ft. frieze, Eugene Field School, St. Louis. Address in 1929, 439 North Bedford Drive, Beverly Hills, CA.

GARRETT, EDMUND HENRY.
Painter, illustrator and etcher. Born in Albany, NY, 1853. Studied at Academie Julien, Paris; pupil of Jean Paul Laurens, Boulanger and Lefebvre, Paris. Medal at Boston, 1890. Exhibitor at Paris Salon and principal exhibitions in America. Died 1929 in Nedham, MA. Address in 1926, 142 Berkeley St., Boston, MA.

GARRETT, JOHN W. B.
Portraits, signed "J. W. B. Garrett," have been found in the southern states; one so signed is dated 1852.

GARRETT, THERESA A.
Etcher. Born June 8, 1884. Member: Chicago SE; GFLA. Address in 1929, 410 South Michigan Ave., Chicago, IL.

GARRIS, PHILIP.
Illustrator. Born in Maryland in 1951. He received no formal art training. In 1976, the S of I awarded him a Gold Medal for his Grateful Dead album cover. He also illustrated concert posters for Bill Graham and the 1976 album cover for Kingfish. He is presently living in Sausalito, California.

GARRISON, EVE.
Painter. Born in Boston, MA. Studied: Art Institute of Chicago. Award: Gold Medal, Corcoran Gallery of Art, 1933. Collections: Univ. of Illinois; United States Treasury Department, Wash., DC.

GARRISON, JOHN L(OUIS).
Painter and illustrator. Born Cincinnati, OH, June 14, 1867. Pupil of Nowottny and Goltz. Member: Columbus PPC. Address in 1929, 179 Clinton Place Ave., Columbus, OH

GARRISON, ROBERT.
Sculptor. Born Fort Dodge, IA, May 30, 1895. Pupil of PAFA; Gutzon Borglum. Work: 2 Bronze Mountain Lions for State Office Bldg. of Colorado, Denver; two seal fountains, Voorhees Memorial; Daly Memorial; Fairmount Cemetery; Athena, Morey High School; Overseas Memorial Tablet, Post Office, Denver; Mosher Memorial, Rochester, NY; sculpture on Riverside Baptist Church, New York City; terra cotta decorations on South Side High School. Nat'l Jewish Infirmary, and Midland Bldg., Denver, CO; sculpture on Boston Ave. M.E. Church, Tulsa, OK. Died in 1945. Address in 1929, Chappell House, Denver, CO; 125 West 55th St., New York, NY.

GARSTIN, ELIZABETH W(ILLIAMS).
Sculptor. Born New Haven, Jan. 12, 1897. Pupil of Eberhard; Yale Art School. Member: New Haven PCC; AFA. Address in 1929, 155 Whitney Ave.; h. 54 Lincoln St., New Haven, CT; summer, Salisbury, CT.

GARVEY, JOSEPH M.
Painter. Born in New York, 1877. Pupil of William M. Chase. Member of Society of Independent Artists. Address in 1926, Alpine, NJ.

GARY, LOUISA M(ACGILL).
Painter. Born Baltimore, Dec. 19, 1888. Member: Balto. WCC. Address in 1929, "Upsandowns," Catonsville, MD.

GASPARD, LEON.
Painter. Born Vitebsk, Russia, 1882. Studied at Academie Julien, Paris, France. Came to U.S. 1916. Exhibited in Belgium; Salon d'Artistes Francaise; Salon d'Autumn, Paris; also in New York, Philadelphia, Chicago, New Orleans, etc. Awarded gold medal, National Academy, Russia. Honorable mention, Salon Francaise. Clubs: Russian (Moscow), Salmagundi, New York. Died in 1964. Address in 1926, 108 West 57th St., New York.

GASSER, HENRY MARTIN.
Painter. Born in Newark, NJ, Oct. 31, 1909. Study: Newark Sch. of Fine & Indust. Art; ASL, with Robert Brackman, John R. Grabach.

338

Work: Met. Mus. of Art, NYC; Phila. Mus. of Art; Newark (NJ) Mus.; Dept. of War, Wash. DC; Nat'l Gal., Smithsonian, Wash. DC. Exhib.: NAD, 1971 & 75; Am. WC Soc., 1971 & 75; others. Awards: Hall- garten Prize, NAD, 1943; Phila. Watercolor Club, 1945; American Watercolor Society, 1969; Allied Artists Gold Medal; plus various awards from Audubon Artists, Conn. Academy, Salamagundi. Teaching: Newark School of Fine & Industl. Art, Dir., 1946-54; ASL, 1964-70. Mem.: NAD; Am. WC Soc.; Phila. WC Club; Audubon Artists; AAA. Media: Watercolor. Address in 1982, So. Orange, NJ.

AST, MICHAEL CARL.
Painter. Born in Chicago, IL, June 11, 1930. Study: School of Art Institute, Chicago, BFA 1952; Univ. of the Americas, Mex., MFA 1960. Exhibits: Wash. WC Assn., 66th Ann. Nat. Exhib., Smithsonian Inst., 1963; Metrop. Area Exhib., Howard Univ., Wash., DC, 1970; Soc. Wash. Artists Ann. Exhibs., Smithsonian Inst., 1963 & 64; Mickelson Gallery, Wash., DC., 1966; Foundry Gallery, Wash., DC, 1980; etc. Positions: Museum technician, Nat'l. Mus. Hist. & Technology, 1961- 1964; Museum 1964; museum specialist, Nat'l. Coll. Fine Arts, Smithsonian, 1969-71. Mem.: Artists Equity Assn.; College Art Assn. Media: Polymer, oil. Address in 1982, 5730 First St., S., Arlington, VA.

ATEWOOD, MAUD FLORANCE.
Painter. Born on Jan. 8, 1934. Studied: Women's College, Univ. of North Carolina; Ohio State Univ. Awards: National Academy of Arts and Letters, 1972. Collections: Mint Museum, Charlotte, NC; Coca Cola Company, Atlanta, GA. Address in 1980, Box 42, Yanceyville, NC.

ATHMAN, THOMAS.
Painter. Born in Chicago, IL, in 1946. Studied at Chic. Acad. of Fine Art, BFA; painting with Gustav Likan, Chicago, 1967-68; Mayfair College, Loop College, YMCA, Roosevelt Univ., Northeastern Univ., all in Chicago. Work owned by numerous galleries in Illinois,

Indiana, Iowa, Ohio, including Raffles, Inc., in Chicago, Atlanta and London. Exhibited at Chicago Academy of Fine Art, 1966; Univ. of Illinois Medical Center, 1969, Linda Graves Gal., 1974, Mary Bell Galleries, 1981, 82, 83, all in Chicago; Krasl Art Center, St. Joseph, MI, 1983; Muskegon (MI) Mus. of Art, 1983. Awarded First Prize, ptg., Chic. Acad., 1967, 68; scholarship, Chic. Acad., 1967, 68; Beckman Mem. Scholarship, Brooklyn Mus., NY, 1969. Represented by Mary Bell Galleries, Chicago. Address in 1983, Elmwood Park, IL.

GATTER, OTTO JULES.
Painter and illustrator. Born in Philadelphia, 1892. Pupil of Penna. Academy of Fine Arts. Illustrates for Scribner's, Cosmopolitan and McClure's. Died July 5, 1926. Address in 1926, 1530 Wallace St., Philadelphia.

GAUGENGIGL, I(GNAZ) M(ARCEL).
Painter. Born Passau, Bavaria, July 29, 1855; came to United States in 1880. Pupil of Academy of Munich. Member: SAA 1895; ANA 1906; Copley S. (hon.); Boston GA. Awards: Medal, New Orleans Exp.; medal, Mass. Charitable Mechanics' Assoc. Work: "An Amateur," RI School of Design, Providence, "Une Question Difficile," Metropolitan Museum of Art; "Scercando," Boston Museum of Art. Died Aug. 3, 1932, in Boston. Address in 1929, 5 Otis Place, Boston, MA.

GAUK, JAMES.
The New York directories for 1795-1804 contain this name as "Engraver."

GAUL, ARRAH LEE.
(Mrs. A. L. G. Brennan). Painter. Member: Plastic C.; AWCS; NA Women PS. Address in 1929, Spruce and Sixteenth Sts.; Ludlow Bldg., 34 South 16th St., Philadelphia, PA.

GAUL, GILBERT.
Painter. Born in Jersey City, NJ, in 1855. Pupil of J. G. Brown, of the National Academy. His extensive study of the soldier's career supplemented his academic training, insight, and feeling for dramatic composition. "Charging

the Battery" and "Wounded to the Rear" are among the best of his episodic compositions, and these have equally interesting, if less animated companion pieces in a host of subjects which depict the excitement and the picturesque features of army scenes on the plains of the far West. For "Charging the Battery" he was awarded a medal at Paris Exposition, 1889. In 1882 was elected National Academician. Died in 1919 in New York.

GAULEY, ROBERT D(AVID).
Painter and teacher. Born Carnaveigh, County Monaghan, Ireland, March 12, 1875; came to U.S. in 1884. Pupil of D. W. Ross in Cambridge; Benson and Tarbell in Boston; Bouguereau and Ferrier in Paris. Member: ANA 1908; NYWCC; AWCS. Awards: Bronze medal, Paris Exp., 1900; hon. mention, Pan-Am. Exp., Buffalo, 1901; "Hors Concours," Charleston, SC, Exp., 1902; bronze medal, St. Louis Exp., 1904; Isidor prize, Salma. C., 1907; Clarke prize, NAD, 1908; third prize, Appalachian Exp., Knoxville, TN, 1910; Isidor portrait prize, Salma. C. 1912; silver medal, P.-P. Exp., San F., 1915. Work: "The Fur Muff," National Gallery, Wash., DC; "Hon. Nathaniel Macon," Capitol, Wash., DC; "Peter Toft Mem. Portrait," Kolding, Denmark; "A Holland Lady," Pub. Lib., Watertown, NY; "Copy of a Fresco Found at Medurn, now in the Mus. at Gizeh, Egypt," "Mediterranean Coast," "Naples," "Amalfi," "Azores," "Coast of Sardinia," "Coast of Crete," "Fountain, Rome," "Mount Vesuvius from the Bay of Naples, Museum of Fine Arts, Boston; Harvard University, Dept. of Fine Arts, Cambridge. Died in 1943. Address in 1929, 26 Oakland St., Watertown, MA.

GAUSTA, HERBJORN.
Painter. Born in Norway, 1854. Pupil of Royal Academy of Munich. Member: Minneapolis Art League. Address in 1926, 1706 Elliott Ave., Minneapolis, MN.

GAVALAS, ALEXANDER BEARY.
Painter. Born in Limerick Ireland, Jan. 6, 1945. Famil moved to US in 1947. Grew up i Wash. Heights, NYC. Study: Schoo of Arts and Design, diploma 1963 Manhattanville College, 1969-71 Largely self- taught in art studied paintings of Old Masters influenced by Hudson Rive locations and the Cloisters, NYC Exhibitions: Landscape painting and drawings, Queens College Ar Center, City U. of NY, 1983 exhibit first traveled to For Wayne Mus. of Art; Marycres College Ebert Art Gall., Davenport IA; Arnot Art Mus., Elmira, NY Has also exhibited at Krasl Ar Center, St. Jos., MI; Tweed Mus of Art, Duluth, MN; Western I (Macomb) Univ. Style: Landscape classical realism. Media: Pen ink, oil. Rep: Eric Galleries, 6 East 57th St., NYC. Address i 1983, Long Island City, NY.

GAVIN, VERNONA E.
Painter. She was born in Ea Claire, March 4, 1891. Pupil o Gerrit V. Sinclair, Emily Groom Member: Wis. PS. Award: Florenc B. Fawsett prize ($100), Milwauke Art Institue, 1929. Address i 1929, 587 Marshall St.; h. 1544 23 St., Milwaukee, WI; summer, 85 Grand Ave., East, Eau Claire, WI.

GAVIT, JOHN E.
Engraver. Born Oct. 29, 1817, i New York. Gavit learned hi business in Albany, NY, where h established an engraving, printin and lithographing business. H later became interested i bank-note work, and in 1855 h assisted in organizing the America Bank Note Co. in New York. Afte serving as secretary, he wa elected president in 1866, and hel the office until his death. Die Aug. 25, 1874, in Stockbridge, MA.

GAW, ROBERT M.
Engraver. Born in New Jersey i 1829. Probably in employ of Pete Maverick in Newark, NJ, in 182 Executed portrait and architectura engravings in line.

GAY, EDWARD.
Painter. Born April 25, 1837, in
Dublin, Ireland. He came to
America in 1848; began to study art
under Lessing and Schirmer at
Karlsruhe, Germany. Specialty,
landscapes. He received the
Metropolitan prize for the picture
"Broad Acres," presented to the
Metropolitan museum of Art, New
York; later works are: "Washed by
the Sea," "Atlantis," "The
Suburbs," in Tewksberry Collection,
New York; "Where Sea and Meadow
Meet," Governor's Mansion, Albany,
NY. Elected Associate Member
NA 1868; NA, 1907. Died in 1928.
Address in 1926, 434 South 2d Ave.,
Mt. Vernon, NY.

GAY, GEORGE HOWELL.
Painter. Born Milwaukee, WI, Aug.
2, 1858. Pupil of Paul Brown and
Henry A. Elkins in Chicago.
Settled in New York in 1889.
Specialty, marines and landscapes.
Died in 1931. Address in 1929, 100
Kraft Ave., Bronxville, NY.

GAY, INKWORTH ALLAN.
Landscape painter. Born Aug. 18,
1821, in West Hingham, MA. He
studied with Robert W. Weir, and
later in Paris. Represented by
landscapes in the Boston Museum.
He was a brother of the artist
Walter Gay. Died Feb. 23, 1910, in
MA.

GAY, WALTER.
Painter. Born Hingham, MA, Jan.
22, 1856. Pupil of Bonnat in
Paris, Member: ANA 1904; AFA;
Societe Nouvelle; Nat. des
Beaux-Arts; Societe de la Peinture
a l'Eau; Royal Society Water
Colors, Brussels; Nat. Inst. A. L.
Member executive committee Societe
des Amis du Louvre, Paris; National
Inst. of Arts and Letters;
Committee des Amis du Musee de
Luxembourg, Paris; Committee des
Amis de Versailles. Awards: Hon.
mention, Paris Salon, 1885; third
class medal, Paris Salon 1888; gold
medal, Vienna, 1893; gold medals,
Antwerp and Munich, 1894; gold
medal, Berlin and Budapest, 1895;
silver medal, Paris Exp., 1900;
silver medal, Pan-Am. Exp.,
Buffalo, 1901; Chevalier of the
Legion of Honor 1894, officer 1906.

Commander, Legion of Honor, 1927.
Work: Seven pictures bought by the
French Government; "White and Blue"
and "Las Cigarreras," Luxembourg
Museum, Paris; "Interior of Palazzo
Barbaro," Boston Museum of Fine
Arts; "Chez Helleu," Pennsylvania
Academy, Philadelphia; "The
Spinners" and portrait of W. H.
Huntington, Metropolitan Museum,
New York; "Benedicite," Museum at
Amiens, France; represented at
Buffalo, NY; Providence, RI;
Carnegie Institute, Pittsburgh, PA;
Pinacotheque, Munich; "Interior of
Petit Trianon," RI School of
Design, Providence; "The Green
Salon," Metropolitan Museum of Art,
New York; "Interior, Chateau du
Breau (La Commode)," Art Institute
of Chicago; "Interior-Musee Correr,
Venice," Metropolitan Museum of
Art, New York; "La Console," Palace
of the Elysee, Paris; represented
in Boston Museum of Fine Arts;
Detroit Institute of Arts. Died in
1937. Address in 1929, 11 Rue de
l'Universite, Paris, France;
summer, Le
Breau-par-Dammarie-les-Lys, Seine
et Marne, France.

GAYLOR, (SAMUEL) WOOD.
Painter, etcher and lecturer. Born
Stamford, CT, Oct. 7, 1883. Pupil
NAD. Member: Penguins; Modern
Artists of America; Salons of
America; Brooklyn S. Modern A.
Address in 1929, 10 Vannest Place,
New York, NY.

GEARHART, FRANCES H(AMMEL).
Engraver and etcher. Born in
Illinois. Member: Calif. PM; AFA.
Prints in Toronto Museum; Rhode
Island School of Design; Los
Angeles Museum; Chicago Art School;
Smithsonian Institution,
Washington; Delgado Museum, New
Orleans; State Library, Sacramento,
CA. Address in 1929, 18 West
California St.; h. 595 South Fair
Oaks Ave., Pasadena, CA.

GEARHART, MAY.
Etcher and teacher. Born Henderson
Co., IL. Pupil of Walter Shirlaw,
Rudolph Schaeffer, B. C. Brown, A.
W. Dow, AIC, San Francisco School
FA. Member: Chicago SE; Calif.
PM. Work: "Rim of the World" and
"North of 64," Los Angeles Museum;

341

etching in Calif. State Library, Sacramento; etching in Smithsonian Institution, Washington, DC. Supervisor of Art, Los Angeles City Schools. Address in 1929, 595 South Fair Oaks Ave., Pasadena, CA.

GEBHART, PAUL.
Designer. Born Greenville, PA, Jan. 2, 1890. Pupil, Cleveland SA. Member: Cleveland SA. Address in 1929, 1101 Citizens Bldg., Cleveland, Ohio; h. 41 Sagamore Rd., R. F. D. No. 4, Willoughby, OH.

GEDDENS, GEORGE.
Painter. Born in Bedford, England, in 1845. By profession an actor, he practiced painting in his leisure hours. He studied in California and at the National Academy schools in New York. His studio was in New York City. Among his works, "Twilight" was exhibited at the National Academy in 1878, and "Noontide" and "Eventide" at the Brooklyn Art Association.

GEER, GRACE WOODBRIDGE.
Portrait painter and teacher. Born Boston, July 25, 1854. Pupil of Mass. Normal Art School, F. H. Tompkins, Triscott, Tarbell, Vonnoh and Lowell Inst. Member: AG; Nat. Lg. Am. Pen. W.; Copley S. 1900. Represented by portrait at International Institute for Girls, Madrid, Spain; Girls' High School, Boston. Died 1938 in Boston. Address in 1929, 12 Pinckney St., Boston, MA.

GEERLINGS, GERALD KENNETH.
Painter. Born 1897. Exhibited water colors at the Exhibition of Water Colors at the Penna. Academy of Fine Arts, Philadelphia, 1925. Address in 1926, 148 Central Ave., Flushing, Long Island, NY.

GEISEL, THEODORE (DR. SEUSS)
Illustrator. Born in Springfield, Mass., in 1904. Studied art at Dartmouth College, Oxford Univ. and traveled extensively in Europe. He wrote several screenplays and won the Academy Award in 1951 for his animated cartoon Gerald McBoing-Boing. In 1954 he went to Japan as a foreign correspondent for Life and later received an

Honorary Doctorate of Humane Letters. He has illustrated over ten picture books and is currently working on elementary school readers. Some of his most famous illustrated books are If I Ran the Circus, Scrambled Eggs Supper and On Beyond Zebra, published by Random House. A number of his books have been translated into animated television programs.

GEISSMANN, ROBERT.
Illustrator. Born in New Washington, Ohio, in 1909. Studied art at Ohio State Univ. before serving with the Air Force in World War II as an art director with a film unit. He continued his illustration and design career in NY after the war, but maintained ties with the service as director of the USAF Art Program. An active member of the S of I, he was Presendinet from 1953 to 1955. In 1967, he helped found the NY GA and served as its president for many years. Died in 1976.

GELERT, JOHANNES SOPHUS.
Sculptor. Born in Denmark, 1852 came to the United States in 1887 and died in New York City, Nov. 4 1923. He was a member of the National Sculpture Society Represented by Haymarket Monument Chicago; Gen. Grant in Galena, IL in the Art Institute, Chicago, and museums in Denmark.

GELLENBECK, ANN P.
Painter. Born Shakopee, Minn Member: Tacoma Fine Arts Asso.; S Indp. A; Chicago NJSA; AFA Address in 1929, 4415 North 8t St., Tacoma, Wash.

GELLERT, EMERY.
Painter. Born Budapest, Hungary July 24, 1889. Pupil of Papp Kriesch, Ignace and Geza Udvary Member: "Feszek," Hungarian AC Award: Prize, Cleveland Museum 1925. Work: "The Life of Joseph, The Temple, Cleveland, OH; "Hear of Jesus," St. Margaret's Church Cleveland, OH; "Christ' Resurrection" and "Moses Receive the Ten Commandments, Greek-Cathedral Church, Detroit Mich. Address in 1929, 3920 Eucli Ave., Cleveland, OH.

342

GELLERT, HUGO.
Painter and illustrator. Born Budapest, Hungary, May 3, 1892. Pupil of NAD. Work: Mural decorations at the Workers Center, Union Square, NY. Address in 1929, Buckhout Rd., White Plains, NY.

GELON, MARIE MARTHA J.
See Mrs. Edgar Cameron.

GENDROT, FELIX ALBERT.
Painter and sculptor. Born Cambridge, MA, April 28, 1866. Pupil of Mass. Normal Art School, Boston; Julian Academy in Paris under Laurens and Constant; sculpture with Puech and Verlet. Member: Boston AC; Paris AAA; Copley S; AFA. Address in 1929, Buena Vista St., Roxbury, MA.

GENIN, JOHN.
Born in France, 1830; died in New Orleans, 1895. He had a studio as portrait, historical and genre painter at 150 Canal Street in 1876; he resided and painted in New Orleans for the next twenty years, and at the time of his death had a studio at 233 Royal Street.

GENIN, SYLVESTER.
Painter. Born in Ohio, Jan. 22, 1822. With comparatively little training, he had a remarkable talent for composition. His painting of historical art had a spirited style. Died April 4, 1850, in Kingston, Jamaica.

GENTH, LILLIAN.
Painter. Born Phila. Pupil of Phila. School of Design for Women under Elliott Daingerfield; Whistler in Paris. Member: ANA 1908; Assoc. Fellowship PAFA; NAC; R. Soc. Arts, London; Inter. Soc. AL; Allied AA. Awards: Mary Smith prize, PAFA 1904; Shaw mem., NAD 1908; bronze medal, Buenos Aires Exp., 1910; first Hallgarten prize, NAD 1911; bronze medal, NAC 1913. Work: "Depths of the Woods" and "Adagio," Nat. Gallery, Wash.; "Springtime," Metropolitan Mus., NY; "The Lark," Engineers' Club, NY; "The Bird Song," Carnegie Inst., Pittsburgh; "Pastoral," Brooklyn Inst. of Arts and Sciences; "Venice" and "In Normandy," Phila. Art Club; and in Detroit (MI) Club; Grand Rapids (MI) Art Assoc.; Muncie (IN) Art Assoc.; Rochester (NY) Museum; National Arts Club, NY; Cremer Collection, Dortsmund, Germany; Nashville AA; Dallas AA; Des Moines AA; Newark Mus. Assoc. Died March 28, 1953, in NYC. Address in 1929, 50 Central Park West, NY.

GENTHE, ARNOLD.
Illustrator. Born Berlin, Germany, Jan. 8, 1869. Award: Gold medal, Paris, 1928. Illustrated "Old Chinatown," "The Book of the Dance," "Impressions of Old New Orleans," "Isadora Duncan," "The Yellow Jacket" (Geo. C. Hazleton and Benrimo), "Sanctuary" (Percy MacKaye). Died in 1942. Address in 1929, 41 East 49th St.; h. 443 East 58th St., New York, NY.

GENTLE, EDWARD.
Painter, illustrator, craftsman and teacher. Born Chicago, IL, July 20, 1890. Self taught. Works: Cover designs for "Compton's Pictured Encyclopedia" and "Our Wonder World." Address in 1929, Garden Studio Ohio, 3 East Ontario St., Chicago, IL; Country studio, Grand Ave. and Ruby St., Franklin Park, IL.

GEORGE, DAN.
Sculptor. Born in Lake George, NY, July 5, 1943. Studied: State Univ. NY, Albany; ASL, 1968-73; Academie v Schonekunsten, Antwerp, 1970-71; Henry Schenckenberg Merit Scholar, ASL, 1972- 73. Work: Hyde Collection, Glens Falls, NY; Manhattan Laboratory Mus., NYC; Sculpture Space, Utica, NY. Comn.: Stewart-Scott Assoc., Poughkeepsie, NY; site project, Lake George, NY. Exhib: Lowe Art Gallery, Syracuse, NY, 1978; Prospect Mtn. Sculpture Show, Lake George, 1979; Usden Gallery, Bennington College, VT, 1979; Sculpture at Columbia Plaza, Wash., DC, 1980; and others. Awards: Grant, NYS Council on the Arts, 1978; Collaborations in Art, Sci. & Technology, 1978. Media: Cast metals. Address in 1982, 64 W. 21st St., NYC.

GEORGE, THOMAS.
Painter. Born July 1, 1918, in New
York City. Earned B.A. from
Dartmouth (1940); studied at Art
Students League and at Chaumiere,
Paris. Awards: Rockefeller grant
to Far East; and awards from
Brooklyn Mus.; and the Whitney
(1962-63). Exhibited at Carnegie;
MOMA; Dartmouth; Whitney; Korman
Gallery, NYC; Contemp. Gallery,
NYC; PAFA; Corcoran Gallery Wash.,
DC. Commissioned by US Olympic and
Kennedy Galleries for poster. In
collections of Dartmouth; Brooklyn
Mus.; Albright Knox Gallery;
Whitney; Library of Congress; Wash.
(DC) Gallery of Mod. Art; MOMA;
Guggenhein; and the Tate.

GEORGE, VESPER LINCOLN.
Painter and teacher. Born Boston,
MA, June 4, 1865. Pupil of
Constant, Lefebvre and Doucet in
Paris. Member: Boston AC; NY
Arch. Lg.; Mural P.; North Shore
AA. Director, Vesper George School
of Art, Boston. Died 1934 in
Boston, Mass. Address in 1929, 116
Charles St., Boston; h. West
Gloucester, MA.

GEORGI, EDWIN.
Illustrator. Born in 1896. Began
his art training in an advertising
agency and later free-lanced for
many companies, including Hartford
Fire Insurance Co., Crane Paper,
and Yardley and Co. His editorial
work appeared in most major
magazines, The Saturday Evening
Post being a frequent user of his
paintings of beautiful women. He
worked most of his life from his
studio in Norwalk, CT. Died in
1964.

GERARDIA, HELEN.
Painter. Born in Ekaterinislav,
Russia, in 1903. Studied:
Brooklyn Museum; ASL; and with Hans
Hofmann, Charles Seide, Adam Garret
and Nahum Tschacbasov. Awards:
Boston Society of Independent
Artists, 1952, 1956, 1957; Village
Art Center, 1952, 1954, 1955;
Fellowship Research Studios,
Maitland, FL, 1952-1953; Fellowship
Yaddo Found., 1955; Woodstock Art
Assoc., 1956; Abraham Lincoln High
School; National Association of
Women Artists, 1958. Collections:

Univ. of Illinois; Smith College;
Univ. of Maine; Dartmouth College;
Colby College; Lincoln High School;
Yeshiva College; Butler Art
Institute; Research Studios Art
Center; Cincinnati Museum Assoc.;
Fogg Museum of Art. Address in
1980, 490 West End Ave., 4C, NY,
NY.

GERE, NELLIE HUNTINGTON.
Landscape painter, interior
decorator and teacher. Born
Norwich, CT, 1859. Pupil of A.
Chicago; John Vanderpoel; Frederick
Freer; Pratt Inst., Brooklyn;
Ispwich Summer School under Dow
Member: Chicago ASL; Arthur Dow A
Associate professor of Fine Art and
lecturer on staff of Univ
Extension, University California
Southern Branch, Los Angeles
Author of "Outline on Picture Study
in the Elementary School." Address
in 1929, 529 North Alexandria Ave.
Los Angeles, CA.

GERHARDT, KARL.
Sculptor. Born in Boston, MA
1853. He was largely self-taught
but was sent to Paris to study art
He afterward exhibited in th
Salon. Executed portrait busts o
many prominent men, and statues o
Gen. Putnam at Brooklyn, Natha
Hale at Hartford, Conn., and Gen
Gouveneur K. Warren at Gettysburg
PA. Died in 1940.

GERITZ, FRANZ.
Painter, etcher, craftsman, writer
lecturer and teacher. Born
Hungary, April 16, 1895. Pupil o
Nahl, Van Sloun; Martinez. Member
Alumni Calif. School AC; Calif. PM
Oakland AA. Instructor of bloc
cutting and printing, Univ. o
Calif. Extension Division. Died i
1945. Address in 1929, 701-B Nort
Belmont Ave., Los Angeles, CA
summer R. F. D., Box 114, Berkeley
CA.

GERLACH, GUSTAVE.
Sculptor. Pupil of Karl Bitter
and sculptor of the colossa
personification of "Minnesota."

GERMAN, JOHN D.
Miniature painter. Flourished i
New York in 1837.

GERNHARDT, HENRY F.
Painter and etcher. Born Des Moines, IA, June 30, 1872. Pupil of Charles Noel Flagg. Member: Conn. AFA. Address in 1929, Framingham, MA.

GERRER, ROBERT GREGORY.
Painter and teacher. Born Alsace, France, July 23, 1867. Pupil of Ortiz, Nobile, Gonnella, and Galliazzi. Member: AFA. Work: "Portrait of Pope Pius X," in the Vatican, Rome; portrait of Dr. J. B. Murphy, Wightman Memorial Gallery, Notre Dame, IN. Address in 1929, St. Benedict and Kickapoo Sts., Shawnee, OK.

GERRY, SAMUEL LANCASTER.
Portrait painter in oils and miniatures. Born May 10, 1813, in Boston. He was President of the Boston Art Club in 1858. Works: "The Old Man of the Mountain," "The Artist's Dream," and "Bridal Tour of Priscilla and John Alden." Also painted landscapes. He died 1891 at Roxbury, MA.

GERSTEN, GERRY N.
Illustrator. Born in NYC, in 1927. Attended the High School of Music and Art and Cooper Union Art School. He studied under the painter Robert Gwathmey and fellow classmates included Milton Glaser, Seymour Chwast, Reynold Ruffins, and Edward Sorel. His first illustration was done for Sudler and Hennessey, Inc. in 1951. He illustrates for Playboy, Esquire, Harper's Time, McCall's, True magazine and others. In 1975 the NY State Lottery poster was executed by this illustrator. Noted for his humorous caricatures, he is profiled in Idea Magazine, North Light, and in the book The Art of Humorous Illustration. He is an active member of the S of I and his work has appeared often in their Annual Exhibitions.

GERSTENHEIM, LOUIS.
Painter. Born in Poland, 1890. Pupil of National Academy of Design. Member of the Society of Independent Artists. Address in 1926, 344 East 57th St., New York.

GERSTLE, MIRIAM ALICE.
Painter, illustrator and etcher. Born San Francisco, CA, March 9, 1898. Work: Mural Decorations in Royal Links Hotel, Cromer, England; Royal Bath Hotel, Bournemouth, England. Address in 1929, 37 Hamilton Terrace, St. John's Wood, London, N.W. 8, England.

GERSTLE, WILLIAM L(EWIS).
Painter. Born San Francisco, Jan. 28, 1868. Pupil of George Weiss, ASL of NY; San Francisco School of Fine Arts. Member: San Francisco AA; AFA. Address in 1929, 716 Montgomery St.; h. 310 Sansome St., San Francisco, CA.

GEST, J(OSEPH) H(ENRY).
Painter. Born Cincinnati, 1859. Member: NAC; Cin. Municipal AC. Director Cincinnati Museum; President Rookwood Pottery; member Nat. Gallery of Art Comm. Address in 1929, Art Museum Eden Park; h. 2144 Grandin Road, Cincinnati, OH.

GETCHELL, EDITH LORING.
Etcher. Born in Bristol, PA. Pupil of Penna. Academy of Fine Arts. Her etchings are in the Library of Congress, Wash., DC; Boston Mus. of FA, Worcester Art Museum, MA; and Walters Collection, Baltimore, MD. Address in 1926, 6 Linden St., Worcester, MA.

GETTIER, C. R.
Illustrator. Member: Char. C. Address in 1929, Tudor Hall, Baltimore, MD.

GETTIER, G. WILMER.
Landscape painter. Born Baltimore, MD, Feb. 23, 1877. Studied in Baltimore and Munich, and under S. E. Whitman. Member: Char. C.; Baltimore Alliance; Fine Arts C., Baltimore. Address in 1929, 855 North Howard St.; h. 1019 West Lanvale St., Baltimore, MD.

GETZ, ARTHUR.
Painter. Born in 1913, in Passaic, NJ. Studied at Pratt Inst. Painted murals for the WPA Fed. Art Proj. in 1939-42. Contr. to The New Yorker. He also painted under the name of Arthur Kimmel. Illust. Hamilton Duck, 1972.

GETZ, PETER.
He was a silversmith and jeweler of Lancaster, PA, in the last quarter of the eighteenth century. He was a "self-taught mechanic of singular ability," says Wm. Barton in his life of David Rittenhouse. In 1792 Getz was a candidate for the position of Chief Coiner and Engraver to the newly organized mint in Philadelphia, but the place was given to the engraver Robert Scott.

GIBALA, LOUISE.
Painter. Born in Allegheny, PA. Awards: American Artists Professional League; National Art League; Low Ruins Gallery, Tubac, Arizona. Collections: Christ Lutheran Church, Little Neck, NY; Dutch Reformed Church, Flushing, NY. Exhibitions: NA Gal.; Smithsonian Gal.; Lever House.; etc.

GIBBS, GEORGE.
Painter and illustrator. Born New Orleans, LA, March 8, 1870. Pupil of Corcoran School and ASL in Washington, DC. Member: S. Wash. A.; Wash. WCC; AFA; Phila. Alliance; Phila. AC. Author and illustrator of "American Sea Fights," "Tony's Wife," "The Yellow Dove," and twenty- five other novels and historical tales. Address in 1929, 1520 Chestnut St., Philadelphia, PA; h. Rosemont, PA.

GIBSON, CHARLES DANA.
Painter and illustrator. Born Roxbury, MA, Sept. 14, 1867. Pupil of ASL, NY; George Post, architect, at St. Gaudens. Member: ANA; SI 1902; AI Graphic A.; Nat. Inst. AL; Port. P.; GFLA; AFA. Author and illustrator of "Education of Mr. Pipp." "Sketches in London;" "The Social Ladder;" "A Widow;" "The Americans." He illustrated for "Life" magazine, "Cosmopolitan," and "Collier's" for many years. Acquired the original "Life" mag., served as editor. Died Dec. 23, 1944, in New York City. Address in 1929, Life Pub. Co., 598 Madison Ave,; Carnegie Studios; h. 127 East 73d St., New York, NY.

GIBSON, FREDERICK (MRS.).
See Kremelberg, Mary.

GIBSON, LYDIA.
Painter and illustrator. Born New York City, Dec. 29, 1891. Pupil of Fraser, Bourdelle, Guerin, Varnum, Poor. Member: S. Indp. A; Salons of Am. Address in 1929, Mt. Airy Rd., Croton-on-Hudson, NY.

GIBSON, THOMAS.
Miniature painter. Notice of his death published in the Morning Star of New York City of December 27th, 1811: "Thomas Gibson, painter, died December 23, 1811."

GIBSON, WILLIAM HAMILTON.
Artist and illustrator. Born in Sandy Hook, CT, 1850. He worked on the "Art Journal" and "Picturesque America." He was a member of the New York Water Color Society, and exhibited his work after 1872. He died in 1896 in Washington, DC.

GICHNER, JOANNA E.
Sculptor. Born in Baltimore in 1899. Pupil of Grafly. Address in 1926, 1516 Madison Ave., Baltimore, MD.

GIDDENS, PHILIP H(ARRIS).
Etcher. Born Cuthbert, GA, Oct. 15, 1898. Pupil of Ecole Nationale des Beaux-Arts, Paris. Member: Brooklyn SE; Chicago SE; Arch. Lg. of NY. Awards: Hon. mention, Grand Salon, Paris, 1923; first prize, Southern Artists Exhibition, Nashville, TN, 1925. Address in 1929, 7 MacDougal Alley; h. 95 Park Ave., New York, NY.

GIDDINGS, ALBERT F.
Painter and etcher. Born in Brenham, TX, 1883. Pupil of Art Institute of Chicago; Frederick W Freer. Decoration in Wendel Phillips High School, Chicago Address in 1926, Hotel Del Prado 1400 East 59th St., Chicago, IL.

GIDDINGS, FRANK A.
Painter and etcher. Born Hartford CT, 1882. Pupil of Chase. Member Conn. Academy of Fine Arts Address in 1926, 74 Webster St. Hartford, CT.

GIDEON, SAMUEL EDWARD.
Painter, artist, writer, lecture and teacher. Born Louisville, KY Dec. 9, 1875. Pupil of Ros

Turner, L'Ecole des Beaux Arts, Fontainebleau, France, Gorguet, Duquesne, Despradelle. Member: Texas FAA; Southern SAL; AIA; Laguna Beach AA. Address in 1929, Univ. of Texas; 2514 Pearl St., Austin, TX.

GIEBERICH, O(SCAR) H.
Painter and etcher. Born New York City, March 25, 1886. Pupil of ASL of NY; Charles Hawthorne. Member: Salma. C.; Paris Groupe PSA. Work: "B. P. Ciboure," Brooklyn Museum of Art . Address in 1929, 25 rue du Montparnasse, Paris, France; h. 1716 Ocean Ave., Brooklyn, NY.

GIES, JOSEPH W.
Painter. Born in Detroit. Pupil of Bouguereau and Robert-Fleury in Paris; Royal Academy in Munich. Work: "Lady in Pink" and "Portrait of Robert Hopkins," Detroit Institute. Address in 1926, 14 West Adams Ave., Detroit, MI.

GIESBERT, EDMUND.
Painter, illustrator, lecturer and teacher. Born Neuwied, Germany, June 1, 1893. Pupil of AIC. Member: Chicago PS; Chicago SA. Award: F. G. Logan medal and $500, AIC, 1929. Address in 1929, 6022 Woodlawn Ave., Chicago, IL.

GIESE, AUGUSTUS F.
Painter. Member: Society of Independent Artists. Address in 1926, 1852 Jerome Ave., New York, NY.

GIFFEN, LILIAN.
Painter, writer, lecturer and teacher. Born New Orleans, LA. Member: Balto. WCC; Washington AC; Phila. Alliance; North Shore AA; NA Women PS; Rockport AA; Gloucester SA; SSAL; New Orleans AA; AFA. Awards: Membership prize, Balto. WCC, 1925; prize for painting, League of American Pen Women, Baltimore, 1926. Address in 1929, 1004 North Charles St., Baltimore, MD; summer, East Gloucester, MA.

GIFFORD, FRANCES ELIOT.
Painter. Born New Bedford, MA, 1844. Received art Education in Cooper Institute, New York, and in Boston, under S. L. Gerry. Painter

of birds with landscapes; also magazine illustrator.

GIFFORD, ROBERT GREGORY.
Painter, illustrator and writer. Born West Medford, MA, Dec. 10, 1895. Pupil of Boston Museum School. Member: Duxbury AA; Rockford AA. Award: Second place, School of Amer. Academy in Rome competition, 1922. Work: "America's oldest Department Store," Gallery of the Duxbury His. Assoc.; "Portrait of J. Fisler," Manufacturers' Club, Philadelphia. Illustrates own stories. Designer of bookplates, stage sets, etc. Address in 1929, Fenway Studios, Boston, MA; h. Box 166, Duxbury, MA.

GIFFORD, ROBERT SWAIN.
Landscape painter and etcher. Born at Island of Naushon, MA, Dec. 23, 1840. He learned the rudiments of his art from Albert Van Beest, a Dutch marine painter at New Bedford, MA. Moved to Boston in 1864 and two years later settled in New York. First exhibited in 1864 at the National Academy of Design, of which he was elected an Associate in 1867, and an Academician in 1878. Traveled extensively, painting in Oregon and California in 1869, and later in Europe Algiers, and Egypt. Member of the Society of American Artists; American Water Color Society; National Arts Club; Society of London Painters; Royal Society of Painters and Etchers, London. Painted "Near the Ocean," and is represented at the Corcoran Gallery by "October on Massachusetts Coast." Died Jan. 15, 1905, in New York.

GIFFORD, SANFORD ROBINSON.
Painter. Born at Greenfield, NY, July 10, 1823. Graduate of Brown University, 1842. Pupil of J. R. Smith and the National Academy of Design, New York. Elected National Academician, 1854. Studied in Paris and Rome, 1855-57; traveled also in Italy, Greece, Syria, Egypt and through the Rocky Mountains. He was one of the first American painters to depart from the conventions of the old school and create a broader and higher style.

347

A Hudson River School artist. He painted "The Villa Malta," "Sunset on the Lake," "Near Palermo." Represented at the Corcoran Gallery, Washington, DC, by "Ruins of the Parthenon." Died Aug. 24, 1880, in New York.

GIFFUNI, FLORA BALDINI.
Painter. Born in Naples, Italy, Oct. 26, 1919. Study: NYU, BFA 1942; Teachers College, Columbia Univ., MFA 1945; Universities of Madrid, Pisa, Instituto d'Allende, NY School of Interior Design, ASL. Work: NY City Hall (portrait, Mayor V. Impelliteri); Columbus Club (portrait, Judge DiFalco); colleges; private collections. Awards: Am. Artists Professional Lg., Lever House National, NY.; Nat'l Art Lg.; Pastel Society of America; Salmagundi; and many others. Mem.: Fellow, Am. Artists Professional Lg.; honorary member, Salma. C.; founder, pres., Pastel Society of Am.; life member, ASL; Accademia di Belle Arte, Parma, Italy; and others. Teaching: Adults, teenagers, Flora Baldini Giffuni Art Studio. Media: Pastel. Rep.: Reyn Gallery, NYC. Address in 1983, 180-16 Dalny Road, Jamaica Estates, NY.

GIGNOUX, F. REGIS.
Landscape and historical painter. Born in Lyon, France, in 1816. He came to America in 1844. Elected National Academician in 1851. Lived in Brooklyn, NY; in US to 1870. His best known landscapes are "Niagara Falls," "Virginia in Indian Summer," "Mount Washington," and "Spring." He died Aug. 6, 1882, in Paris.

GIHON, A(LBERT) D(AKIN).
Landscape painter and teacher. Born Portsmouth, NH, Feb. 16, 1866. Pupil of Eakins in Philadelphia; Constant, Laurens and Ecole des Arts Decoratifs in Paris. Member: Fellowship PAFA. Awards: Second prize, Paris AAA, 1900; first prize, Paris AAA, 1901. Represented in Luxembourg. Address in 1929, 59 Avenue de Saxe, Paris, France.

GIHON, CLARENCE MONTFORT.
Painter. Born Phila., 1871. Pupil of Chase and Cox in NY; Laurens and Constant in Paris. Died 1929 in Paris. Address in 1926, 51 Blvd. St. Jacques, Paris, France.

GIKAS, CHRISTOPHER.
Stained glass artist. Born: Lincoln, NE, Jan. 26, 1926. Study: OK State Univ.; Univ. of NM, stained glass with Hans Tatschl. Work: Oklahoma State U.; Museum of NM, Santa Fe; Univ. of NM Albuquerque, NM. Comn.: Vietnam Monument, Cannon AFB, NM, and East. NM Univ. Exhibitions: University of NM Gallery. Awards: East. NM Univ. Faculty Award, 1969. Teaching: W. Tex. State Univ., 1955-62; East. NM Univ., from 1962. Mem.: NM Arts Council. Media: Stained glass. Address in 1982, Portales, NM.

GILBERT, ARTHUR HILL.
Painter and teacher. Born Chicago, IL, June 10, 1894. Member: Calif. AC; Carmel AA; Salma. Club; Laguna Beach AA. Awards: Hon. mention, Laguna Beach AA, 1921; third prize, Orange Co. Exhib., 1921, and second prize, 1928; prize, Sacramento State Fair, 1922; hon. mention, Painters of the West, 1927; hon. mention Springville, Utah Annual, 1927; second Hallgarten, NAD, 1929. Work: "Mexican Weavers," "Spirit of Rubidoux," "Church Tower," Mission Inn Public Galleries, Riverside, CA. Address in 1929, Carmel by the Sea, Monterey County, CA.

GILBERT, CAROLINE.
Etcher, designer, craftswoman, teacher. Born Pardeeville, WI, Jan. 12, 1864. Pupil of Arthur Dow. Member: St. Paul Inst. Artists' S. Awards: 2nd etching prize and 1st prize for lithography, MN State Fair, 1920; 2nd prize in painting Twin City Exhibit, 1922. Address in 1929, Mechanic Arts High School; h. 8 Arundel St., St. Paul, MN; summer, 204 Lake Ave., White Bear, MN.

GILBERT, CHARLES ALLAN.
Illustrator and painter. Born Hartford, CT, 1873. Pupil of Art Students' League of New York;

Constant and Laurens in Paris. Illustrated "Women of Fiction;" "A Message from Mars." Died 1929 in New York. Address in 1926, 251 East 61st St., New York, NY.

GILBERT, CLYDE LINGLE.
Painter. Born in Medora, IN, Oct. 15, 1898. Study: School of Applied Art, Battle Creek, MI; Nat'l. Acad. of Commercial Art, Chicago; Studio of Fine Arts, Brazil, IN. Work: Private collections. Exhibitions: Howe Military School, Ind, 1949; Wawasee Art Gallery, Ind., 1949; Battle Creek Sanitarium, Mich., 1966; French Lick Hotel, Ind, 1966. Awards: Irwin D. Wolf, Gold Medal, Packaging, 1938; others. Art Positions: Designer, American Coating Mills, Inc. Mem.: Indiana Federation of Art Clubs. Media: Oil, watercolor. Address in 1982, 139 Riverview Ave., Elkhart, IN.

GILBERT, GROVE SHELDON.
Born in Clinton, NY, Aug. 5, 1805. In 1834 he settled in Rochester, NY. He devoted himself to portraiture. In 1848 he was elected an honorary member of the National Academy of Design of New York. He died March 23, 1885.

GILBERT, SARAH.
Painter of flowers and several figure pieces. She was a student of the Cooper Institute, and for years had her studio in New Haven, CT, and exhibited at the New Haven Art Building.

GILBERT, SHARON.
Sculptor. Born in NYC in 1944. Studied: The Cooper Union; The Skowhegan School of Painting and Sculpture; Brooklyn Museum. Exhibitions: Columbia Univ. NY, 1971; State Univ. of NY at Albany, 1972; Whitney Museum, Art Resources Center, NY, 1974.

GILBERTSON, CHARLOTTE.
Painter. Born in Boston, MA. Studied: Boston Univ.; The Art Students' League, and Pratt Graphics in NYC; Studied with Fernand Leger in Paris. Exhibitions: Galerie Mai, Paris, France, 1949; Bodley Gallery, NYC, 1971 "Along the Yukon"; Iolas

Gallery, NYC, 1972. Media: Oil and acrylic. Address in 1981, Old Schoolhouse Rd., Harwich Port, MA.

GILCHRIST, EMMA S.
Painter. Member: Carolina AA; SSAL. Died 1929 in Charleston, SC. Address in 1929, care Gibbes Memorial Art Gallery; 140 Broad St.; 4 Savage St., Charleston, SC.

GILCHRIST, W. WALLACE.
Painter. Born 1879. Studied at Penna. Academy of Fine Arts, and in Munich, Paris and London. Awards: Third Hallgarten prize, National Academy of Design, 1908; gold medal, Washington, DC, Society Artists, 1914. Work: "The Model's Rest," at Cincinnati Museum. Died Nov. 4, 1926, in Brunswick, ME. Address in 1926, Brunswick, ME.

GILDEMEISTER, CHARLES.
Lithographer and painter. Born Oct. 11, 1820, in Bremen, Germany. Signed a "View of the Narrows" and a "View of the Hudson River, from Fort Lee." Published by Seitz in 1851. Died Feb. 8, 1869.

GILDER, ROBERT F(LETCHER).
Painter. Born Flushing, NY, Oct. 6, 1856. Pupil of August Will in NY. Work: "Where Rolls the Broad Missouri," University Club, Omaha; "Sunshine and Shadow," Omaha Friends of Art Assoc.; "Winter Morning," St. Paul Inst.; "Desert Clouds," Philip Payne Memorial, Amherst College; "Arizona Desert" and "San Gabriel Canyon, Calif.," Omaha Public Library; "Among the Hemlocks," State Normal School, Wayne, NE; "October at Wake Robin," State Normal School, Kearney, Neb.; "October in Nebraska," South Omaha Public Library; "Winter Afternoon," Lincoln High School, Council Bluffs, IA; "Autumn Colors," High School, Lincoln, NE; "Head of Mill Hollow, Fontenelle Forest," Public Library, Fremont, NE; and others in Omaha schools. Died in 1940. Address in 1929, Omaha World-Herald, South Side Office; 2318 N St., Omaha, NE; h. Wake Robin, Sarpy Co., NE.

GILDERSLEEVE, BEATRICE.
(Mrs. C. C. Gildersleeve). Painter and craftswoman. Born San

Francisco, CA, Jan. 28, 1892. Member: San Francisco S. Women A; Santa Cruz AL. Address in 1929, Felton, Santa Cruz Co., CA.

GILE, SELDEN CONNOR.
Painter and etcher. Born Stow, ME, March 20, 1877. Pupil of Perham Nahl, Frank Van Sloun, Spencer Macky, W. H. Clapp. Member: Soc. of Six, Oakland AL, Am. Artist Prof. Lg. Award: Prize, Santa Cruz, CA, 1929. Died in 1947. Address in 1929, Belvedere, CA; h. 7027 Chabot Rd., Oakland, CA.

GILES, CHARLES T.
Engraver. Born Aug. 25, 1827, in New York, living in Brooklyn, NY, in 1900. This reputable line-engraver of landscape and historical subjects began work in New York in 1847, and was practicing his profession as late as 1898.

GILES, HOWARD.
Painter, illustrator and teacher. Born Brooklyn, NY, Feb. 10, 1876. Pupil of Jay Hambidge; ASL of NY under Mowbray. Member: ANA; AWCS; A. Fund S.; AI Graphic A; Philadelphia AC; NAC (life); GFLA; Century Association; Philadelphia WCC. Awards: Shaw Purchase Prize ($500), Salma. C., 1915; Shaw illustration prize, Salma. C., 1915; Beck prize, Phila. WCC, 1917; Inness gold medal, NAD, 1918; hon. mention Chicago Art Institute, 1918; Silver medal ($1,000), Carnegie Inst., 1921; Water Color Purchase Prize, AIC, 1921; bronze medal, Sesqui-Centennial Expo., Phila., 1926; Phila. WC. prize, 1928. Represented in Pennsylvania Academy of the Fine Arts; Chicago Art Institute; Brooklyn Museum; Museum of Fine Arts, Boston; Fogg Museum, Harvard University; Fine Arts Gallery, San Diego, CA; Denver Art Museum. Died in 1955. Address in 1929, 35 West 14th St., New York, NY; h. Forest Hill, NJ.

GILKISON, MRS. A. H.
Painter. Member: Pittsburgh Artists' Association. Address in 1926, 226 West Swissvale Ave., Pittsburgh, PA.

GILL, DeLANCEY.
Painter. Born 1859 in Chester, SC. Member: S. Wash. A. Address in 1929, Rutland Cts., Washington, DC.

GILL, PAUL LUDWIG.
Painter and illustrator. Born New York, March 14, 1894. Pupil of PAFA, George Harding, Henry McCarter, Fred Wagner, Daniel Garber; Academy Colarossi, Paris. Member: Phila. WCC; Sketch C.; Fellowship PAFA; AWCS; NYWCC; Phila. Alliance. Awards: Cresson Travelling Fellowship PAFA, 1922-23; prize, Balto. WCC, 1926; Tuthill purchase prize, Chicago, 1926; silver medal, Sesqui-Centennial Expo., Phila., 1926; purchase prize, NYWCC, 1927; Phila. WC prize 1927; William Church Osborne prize, NY, 1928. Represented in Brooklyn Museum; La France Institute, Phila. Instructor, Phila. School of Design for Women. Died in 1938. Address in 1929, Wynnewood, PA.

GILL, S. LESLIE.
Painter. Born Valley Falls, RI, May 12, 1908. Pupil of John R. Frazier, Charles W. Hawthorne. Work: "Ice Plant," Rhode Island School of Design Museum, Providence. Address in 1929, 172 Linwood Ave., Providence, RI.

GILL, SUE MAY (WESTCOTT).
Painter. Born Sabinal, TX, Jan. 14, 1890. Pupil of Hugh Breckenridge, Daniel Garber, Henry McCarter, Fred Wagner, Joseph Pearson, Julian Acad., Paris. Member: Phila. Alliance; Fellowship PAFA. Specialty, portraits. Address in 1929, 34 South 17th St., Phila., PA; h. Wynnewood, PA.

GILLAM FREDERICK, VICTOR and T. BERNA
Illustrators for Harper's Weekly and other papers and magazines. They were born in England in 1867. Came to US and settled in NY. Their work suggests the work of Tenniel. Frederick died Jan. 29, 1920.

GILLAM W(ILLIAM), C(HARLES) F(REDERIC
Painter, etcher, artist and craftsman. Born Brighton, England, Oct. 14, 1867. Member: Calif. SE. Work: Hambrook House, Sussex,

350

England; Provincial Normal School, Victoria, B.C.; Queen Mary High School, Vancouver, B.C.; St. Paul's Episcopal Church, Burlingame, CA. Address in 1929, 1401 Broadway; h. 1143 El Camino Real, Burlingame, CA.

GILLESPIE, GEORGE.
Painter. Member: Pittsburgh Artists' Association. Address in 1926, 711 Penn Ave., Pittsburgh, PA.

GILLESPIE, JESSIE.
Illustrator. Born Brooklyn, NY. Pupil of PAFA. Illustrations for "Pictorial Review," "Girl Scouts," and Keystone Publishing Co. Address in 1929, 5909 Wayne Ave., Germantown, Philadelphia, PA; summer, Henryville, Monroe Co., PA.

GILLESPIE, JOHN.
Painter. Born Malta, OH, May 15, 1901. Pupil of School of the Columbus Gallery of FA. Member: Columbus A. Lg.; Ohio WCS. Award: Walter A. Jones water color prize, 1924, at Columbus Art League. Superv. of Art, Columbus Junior Acad., and Columbus Acad. Address in 1929, 54 South Garfield Ave., Columbus, OH; summer, McConnellsville, OH.

GILLESPIE, W.
Engraver. Engraving on steel in Pittsburgh, PA, about 1845. He made a line map of Pittsburgh and vicinity, "Designating the portion destroyed by fire April 10, 1845," It is signed as "Eng'd by W. Gillespie."

GILLETTE, L(ESTER) A.
Painter and teacher. Born Columbus, OH, Oct. 5, 1855. Pupil of Hill, Williams, Chase, Jacobs, Carlson and AIC. Member: Topeka AG; Miami AA; Gloucester SA; AFA. Address in 1929, 717 Fillmore St., Topeka, KS.

GILLIAM, MARGUERITE HUBBARD.
Painter and teacher. Born Boulder, CO. Member: Fellowship PAFA. Award: Bronze medal, Kansas City AI, 1925. Addres in 1929, White Rock Lane, Boulder, CO.

GILLINGHAM, EDWIN.
A map of Boston and its vicinity, made from an actual survey by John G. Hales, is signed "Edwin Gillingham Sc."

GILMAN, J. W.
Engraver. He engraved the music and words in "The American Harmony, or Royal Melody Complete, etc.," in 2 volumes, by "A. William Tan'sur, Senior, Musico Theorico," and by "A. Williams, Teacher of Pasalmody in London." The book was "Printed and Sold by Daniel Bayley, at his House next Door to St. Paul's Church, Newbury-Port, 1771." A study of the "Gilman Geneology" implies that he was John Ward Dilman, born in Exeter, MA, 1741, who died there in 1823. The only record of his career is that he was postmaster of Exeter for 40 years.

GILMORE, ADA.
Painter and wood engraver. Born in Kalamazoo, MI, 1882. Studied with Henri in NY; Art Institute of Chicago; and in Paris. Work: "Parasols," purchased by Municipal Art Commission, Chicago. Address in 1926, Provincetown, MA.

GILPIN, CHARLES ARMOUR.
Painter. Born Cumberland, MD, Oct. 7, 1867. Pupil of PAFA. Member: Pittsburgh AA; AFA. Work: "Relic of 1824," owned by Hundred Friends of Pittsburgh Art. Address in 1929, Hotel Judson, 53 Washington Sq., New York, NY.

GIMBER, STEPHEN H.
Painter, engraver and lithographer. Born in England in 1810, where he learned to engrave. Was working at his profession in New York by 1830; in 1832-33 his name is associated on plates with that of A. L. Dick, NYC. His name is found in the New York directories until 1842. Moved to Philadelphia as an engraver and lithographer, after 1856. Gimber was a good portrait engraver in stipple and mezzotint, and his early subject plates are in line; he also drew portraits upon stone, and printed miniatures. He died in Philadelphia in 1862.

351

GIMBREDE, JOSEPH NAPOLEON.
Born at West Point, NY, in 1820. Son of Thomas Gimbrede. Learned to engrave with his uncle, J. F. E. Prud'homme. J. N. Gimbrede was in business as an engraver in New York in 1841-45, producing portraits and subject plates. He was later a stationer with an establishment under the Metropolitan Hotel, 588 Broadway, New York.

GIMBREDE, THOMAS.
Engraver. Born in France in 1781; died at West Point, NY, Oct. 25, 1832. Gimbrede came to the United States in 1802 as a miniature painter; he was engraving some excellent portraits in the stipple manner for the New York publishers John Low and William Durell as early as 1810. In 1816 he had an office at 201 Broadway, New York. He did a considerable amount of work for the Philadelphia magazines, The Port Folio and The Analectic. On January 5, 1819, he was appointed drawing-master at the Military Academy at West Point, and was there until his death. He continued to engrave and publish portrait plates as late as 1831. He was a brother-in-law of J. F. E. Prud'homme. Also engraved portraits in stipple.

GIMENO, P(ATRICIO).
Painter, lecturer and teacher. Born Arequipa, Peru, SA, Dec. 25, 1865. Pupil of M. Rosas and Valencia in Spain. Member: Okla. Art League. Award: $500 prize for Allegorical Painting awarded by Okla. City R. R. Co. Work: Portrait of Pres. Pierola in Gov. Palace, Lima, Peru. Address in 1929, 807 Jenkins Ave., Norman, OK.

GINSBERG, RUTH PLACE.
Tapestry. Studied: New School for Social Research; Syracuse Univ. Exhibitions: Southern Illinois Univ., 1969; The AIC, 1970; Albright-Knox Gallery, Buffalo, NY, 1974. Commissions: Temple B'Nai Amoona, St. Louis; Law Offices of Moldover, Strauss & Hertz, NYC. Collections: The AIC; Federal Reserve Bank of Memphis.

GINSBURG, A.
Painter. Member: PS. Address in 1929, Bible House, New York, NY.

GINTHER, MARY PEMBERTON.
See Mrs. M. P. G. Heyler.

GINTHER, WALTER K(ARL).
Painter and etcher. Born Winona, MN, April 3, 1894. Pupil of Vaclav Vytlacil, Cameron Booth, R. F. Lahey and E. Dewey Albinson. Awards: First prize, student competition, 1922, and first prize, 1924 and 1926, MN State Fair; special mention, MN State AS, 1923. Address in 1929, 407 East 7th St., Winona, MN

GIORDANO, JOAN M.
Painter. Born in Staten Island, NY, in 1939. Awards: Museum of Modern Art.

GIOVANOPOULOS, PAUL A.
Illustrator. Born in Kastoria, Greece, in 1939. He came to America on scholarship to attend NYU School of Fine Art, and later SVA, studying under Robert Weaver. His career began with magazine illustrations for Seventeen in 1960. His children's book illustrations have won several awards from The New York Times and his artwork has been shown at the S of I Annual Exhibitions. New York, Baltimore, Philadelphia, and Washington have shown his work. He has been an instructor at Parsons School of Design and SVA.

GIRARDET, P.
Engraver. A well-engraved line and stipple plate was published in New York in 1857 entitled "Winter Scene in Broadway." The plate is signed as engraved by "P. Girardet" from a painting by H. Sebron. His works may not have been executed in the US. The names of the engraver and painter are French, and though the scene is laid in NY, the plate may have been made abroad.

GIRARDIN, FRANK J.
Landscape painter. Born in Kentucky, 1856. Pupil of Cincinnati Art Academy. Represented by "The Hillside" and "Lingering Snow" in Public Gallery,

352

Richmond, Ind. Address in 1926, Redondo Beach, CA.

GIRAULT, LOUIS.
Miniature painter. He was flourishing in NY in 1798.

GIRSCH, FREDERICK.
Engraver and etcher. Born March 31, 1821 in Germany. Received some instruction from a local artist, Carl Seeger. Earned some money by portrait painting, and his portrait of a Princess attracted attention. A sufficient sum was raised by subscription to enable him to study at the Royal Academy of Darmstadt. Settled in NY, having learned to etch and to engrave in line. First work in this country was done for the then New Yorker Criminal Zeitung. As was then the custom, this publication issued "premium" engravings, and Girsch engraved two of these--"Die Helden der Revolution" the "Niagara Falls." He improved in the quality of his line work and made portraits for publishers of NYC. It was as a bank-note engraver that he did his best work and achieved a reputation. Engraved "De Soto Discovering the Mississippi" on the back of one of the early bank-notes; the head of "Liberty" and portrait of Washington on fractional currency; engraved, in etching and line, a large plate, "Grandma's Toast," which was excellent; "The Gypsy Girl," executed for "his own pleasure," about the same time, is in pure line, and probably as meritorious a plate as was ever engraved by him. Died Dec. 18, 1895, in Mt. Vernon, NY.

GIULIANI, VIN.
Illustrator. Born in NYC in 1930. Attended PI. He started as an industrial designer, but he became best known for his assemblage technique using wood shapes. Both his editorial illustrations for Seventeen, McCall's Redbook, and Time and his advertising work for Scovill Manufacturing, Exxon, and Corporate Annual Reports earned him a reputation as a fine craftsman. His illustrations were selected for several Annual Exhibitions at the S of I. Died in 1976.

GIUSTI, ROBERT G.
Illustrator. Born in Zurich, Switzerland in 1937. Attended Tyler School of Fine Art and Cranbrook Academy of Art until 1961. His artwork was first published in 1956 in American Girl and more recently in McCall's, Redbook, Fortune, Idea, and Penthouse. He also illustrated many book covers and promotional posters. Exhibits of his work were held at the Cranbrook Museum of Art and the Greengrass Gallery in New York.

GLACKENS, WILLIAM J.
Painter and illustrator. Born Philadelphia, March 13, 1870. Pupil of PAFA and studied in Europe. Member: ANA 1906; SI 1902; SAA 1905; Am. PS; Port. P.; Society Independent Artists; Los Angeles Modern AS; New Soc. A; Paris Groupe PSA. Awards: Gold medal for drawings at Pan-Am. Exp., Buffalo, 1901; silver medal for painting and bronze for illustration, St. Louis Exp., 1904; hon. mention, CI Pittsburgh, 1905; bronze medal, P.-P. Exp., San F. 1915. Work: "Luks at Work," Harrison Gallery, Los Angeles Museum. Drawings in Metropolitan Museum, New York; Minneapolis Institute of Arts. Died in 1938 in New York City. Address in 1929, care Kraushaar Galleries, 680 Fifth Ave.; Daniel Gallery, 600 Madison Ave., h. 10 West 9th St., New York, NY.

GLADDING, K. C.
Engraver. Several rather poorly engraved "Rewards of Merit" are signed "K. C. Gladding Sc." There is no indication of the place of origin, other than that the plates are undoubtedly American. Judging from the "bank-note" ornamentation the date of the plates is about 1825-30.

GLAMAN, EUGENIE FISH.
Painter and etcher. She was born in St. Joseph, MO, 1873. Pupil of AIC; Simon, Cottet and Fremiet in Paris; Frank Calderon, Briton Reviere, London. Member: Chic. PS; Chicago WCC; Alumni Asso. AIC.; Chicago ASL; Chicago SE. Awards: Bronze medal, St. Louis Exp., 1904;

Butler Purchase prize ($200), AIC, 1913. Work: purchased by Chicago Municipal Commission. Represented in Vanderpoel AA. Collection, Chicago; etchings, permanent coll., State Museum and State Library, Springfield, IL. Specialty, animal subjects. Died in 1956. Address in 1929, 2850 Lexington St., Chicago, IL.

GLARNER, FRITZ.
Painter. Born July 20, 1899, in Zurich, Switzerland. Studied at Ac. of Fine Arts, Naples. In America after 1936. Won Corcoran award in 1957. Exhibited at Kootz Gallery NYC (1945); Cal. Palace (1950); WMA (1950-55); Carnegie; Seattle's World Fair (1962); U. of Penn (1971); MOMA; Corcoran, many others here and abroad. Painted Time Life building mural, NYC (1960). In collections of Brandeis, Florida State U.; Yale; Chase Manhattan Bank; NYU; MOMA; Rockefeller Inst.; Mus. Fine Arts, Boston and Smithsonian. Died Sept. 18, 1972, in Switzerland.

GLASER, JOSEPHINE.
Painter. Born New York City, May 6, 1901. Pupil of Eugene Savage, Ernest Peixotto, Bridgman, Curran, Du Mond, Gorguet, St. Hubert, etc. Member: Alliance; ASL of NY. Award: Tiffany Foundation Fellowship. Work: Three portraits at Georgetown University, Washington, DC; "Flower Study," Tiffany Foundation, Oyster Bay, NY; altar piece, Church of Our Lady of Martyrs, Auriesville, NY. Address in 1929, 135 West 84th St., NYC.

GLASER, MILTON.
Illustrator. Born in NYC in 1929. Attended Cooper Union Art School with classmates Edward Sorel, Seymour Chwast and Reynold Ruffins. He was awarded a Fulbright Scholarship to study etching with the late Giorgio Morandi in Italy in 1952. A co-founder of Push Pin Studios, former design director and Chairman of the Board at New York Magazine and designer of Village Voice, he co-authored The Underground Gourmet and is a faculty member of the SVA. He is also the designer of the Childcraft

store and the decorative programs for the World Trade Center. His distinctive work has earned him many awards, including a Gold Medal from the S of I and the honor of a One-Man Show at the Museum of Modern Art.

GLASS, JAMES WILLIAM.
Painter. Born in 1825. Became a student of Huntington, and afterwards painted in England for a number of years. He was particularly successful in his drawing of horses, and an equestrian portrait of the Duke of Wellington brought him into prominence. Died Dec. 22, 1855, in New York City.

GLASS, SARAH KRAMER.
Painter. Born in Troy, OH, Nov. 7, 1885. Pupil of Bertha Menzler Peyton; ASL of NY; Grand Central School of Art. Member: NA Women PS; North Shore AA; Gloucester SA. Address in 1929, 107 Mt. Pleasant Ave., East Gloucester, MA.

GLEASON, J. DUNCAN.
Painter and etcher. Born Watsonville, CA, Aug. 3, 1881. Pupil of DuMond, Vanderpoel. Member: Calif. AC; Laguna Beach AA; Los Angeles PSC; Long Beach AA. Died in 1959. Address in 1929, 2411 Edgemont Glen, Los Angeles, CA.

GLEESON, ADELE S.
Sculptor. Born in St. Louis, MO, 1883. Student of St. Louis School of Fine Arts. Address in 1926, 115 Edwin Ave., Kirkwood, MO.

GLEESON, C(HARLES) K.
Painter and etcher. Born St. Louis, MO, March 5, 1878. Pupil of Theo. Steinlen; St. Louis School of Fine Arts; ASL of NY; Colarossi Academy in Paris. Member: Chicago SE; St. Louis AG. Work in: Herron Art Institute, Indianapolis; Worcester Art Museum; Chicago Art Institute; St. Louis Museum of Fine Arts; New York Public Library; Library of Congress, Washington, DC; Toledo Art Museum. Address in 1929, 115 Edwin Ave., Kirkwood, MO.

GLEESON, JOSEPH MICHAEL.
Painter. Born in Dracut, MA, 1861.
Went to Munich to study art, 1885,
and afterward made many trips to
Europe, studying in France and
Italy. Settled in New York as
painter and illustrator of animal
life. Writer about animal life for
magazines. Address in 1926,
Newfoundland, NJ.

GLENNY, ALICE RUSSELL.
(Mrs. John Glenny). Painter and
sculptor. Born Detroit, MI, 1858.
Pupil of Chase in NY; Boulanger in
Paris. Member: Buffalo SA; ASL of
Buffalo; NA Women PS. Award:
Prize for mural decoration, Buffalo
Historical Soc. Address in 1929,
Raymond House, 17 Holland St.,
Kensington, W. London, England;
1150 Amherst St., Buffalo, NY.

GLINTENKAMP, HENDRICK.
Painter, sculptor and illustrator.
Born Augusta, NJ, Sept. 10, 1887.
Pupil of Robert Henri; NAD. Work:
Series of twelve woodblock prints,
Victoria and Albert Museum, London,
England; group of seven woodblock
prints, Public Library, New York;
group of three woodblock prints,
Baltimore Museum of Art, Baltimore,
MD. Died in 1946. Address in
1929, 9 East 17th St., New York,
NY.

GLOETZNER, JOSEPHINE P.
Painter and draufhtsman. Born
Washington, DC. Member:
Washington WCC; S. Wash. A.;
Kunstlerinen Verein, Munich.
Address in 1929, 1526 Corcoran St.;
1228 M St., N.W., Washington, DC.

GLOVER, DeLAY.
Engraver. Born 1823. Glover was
an engraver of portraits and
subjects in line and in stipple.
He was located in New York in
1850-55. Died in 1863.

GLOVER, DeWITT CLINTON.
Engraver. Born in DeRuyter,
Madison County, NY, in 1817; died
there Jan. 3, 1836. He was the son
of Daniel and Rhoda (Gage) Glover
and the brother of De Lay and Lloyd
Glover. He early attempted
engraving on wood and steel and to
perfect himself in the art he
entered the office of J. & W.

Casilear in New York, where he made
rapid progress; but he died at the
age of nineteen.

GLOVER, LLOYD.
Engraver. Born in DeRuyter,
Madison County, NY, in 1825; he was
living in 1859. He was the son of
Daniel Glover, and the brother of
De Lay Glover, also an engraver.
Lloyd Glover was taught to engrave
under a Boston master and for
several years he was the head of
the New England branch of the Bank
Note Engraving firm of Danforth,
Wright & Co. of New York. He
finally abandoned engraving for
commerical pursuits, residing at
Lynn, MA. He was said to be a man
of decided literary and artistic
attainments.

GLUECKMAN, JOAN.
Painting/Tapestry. Studied: Wayne
State Univ.; UCLA; Univ. of
Michigan; Detroit Institute of
Arts. Exhibitions: SOHO 20
Gallery, NYC; Hobart & William
Smith Colleges "The Eye of Woman",
1974; Women's Interart Center's
"Erotic Garden," NYC. Initiated
and Organized Artists' Cooperative,
Feminist Gallery, SOHO 20, NYC. She
also helped organize and set up the
Women's Interart Center.

GNOLI, DOMENICO.
Illustrator. Born in Rome, in
1932. Lived for many years in
Majorca, Spain. Self-taught, at
age 18 he was designing sets for
the Old Vic theater and began his
career as a portrait and graphic
artist with exhibits in Rome and
Brussels. His works have appeared
in many magazines including
Playboy, Sports Illustrated, and
Holiday and he has written several
children's books. Since his death
in NY in 1970 at the age of 37, his
works have been acquired by
National Gallery in the U.S. Died
in 1970.

GOATER, JOHN.
Illustrator and engraver. He
worked on the
Illustrated American News.

GOBRECHT, CHRISTIAN.
Engraver and die-sinker. Born Dec.
23, 1785, in Hanover, York County,
PA; died in Phila., July 23, 1844.

Apprenticed to a clockmaker of Manheim, Lancaster County, PA. He learned engraving and die-sinking, and by 1810 had engraved a creditable portrait of Washington for J. Kingston's "New American Biographical Dictionary," published in Baltimore. About 1811 he moved to Phila. and while engaged in sinking dies for medals and work of that type he furnished a few good portrait plates for the publishers there. Work: Franklin Inst. medal of 1825, after a design by Thomas Sully; portrait medal of Charles Willson Peale; the Seal of St. Peter's Church, Phila. In 1836 appointed draughtsman and die-sinker to U.S. Mint in Phila. Designed and made dies for the dollar of 1836. In 1840 succeeded William Kneass as chief engraver to Mint, until his death. Dies made by Gobrecht are esteemed for their artistic excellence. Was original inventor of the medal-ruling machine, a device whereby medals, etc., could be engraved directly from the relief face, and a plate thus prepared for reproduction on paper.

GODDARD, RALPH (BARTLETT).
Sculptor. Born Meadville, PA, June 18, 1861. Pupil of NAD and ASL of NY; Dampt in Paris. Member: NSS 1899. Work: Statuettes of Carlyle and of Tennyson and bronze portrait medallions, Metropolitan Museum, New York; "Premiere Epreuve," Detroit Institute; Statue of Gutenberg, Hoe Building, New York. Died April 25, 1936. Address in 1929, 290 Broadway, New York, NY; and Madison, CT.

GODEFROID, F.
Painter. Father of another artist of that name. In 1807 he painted a portrait of merit of M. Fortin, master of a Masonic Lodge, in the Louisiana State Museum. In 1809 he had a studio in South Burgundy Street, near Canal Street, New Orleans.

GODEFROY, LOUIS.
Painter. In the New Orleans directory of 1824 as "a painter, with his studio at 139 Tehoupitoulas street," and in 1830 at "31 Poydras, corner of Tehoupitoulas street."

GODWIN, ABRAHAM.
Engraver. Born July 16, 1763, in what is now Paterson, NJ; died there Oct. 5, 1835. Enlisted in a New York regiment as fife major; served until the close of the Revolutionary War, when he became an apprentice to A. Billings, an indifferent engraver of book-plate, etc., located in New York. As an engraver Godwin apparently issued but few signed plates, and his work was not of high quality.

GODWIN, FRANK.
Illustrator. Born Washington, DC, Oct. 20, 1889. Pupil of Corcoran School of Art. Member: SI; Darien G. of Seven Arts. Address in 1929, Riverside, CT; summer, Lake Skaneateles, Skaneateles, NY.

GODWIN, KARL.
Painter, illustrator, etcher and teacher. Born Walkerville, Canada, Nov. 19, 1893. Pupil of Charles W. Hawthorne, Sigurd Skou. Member: Salma. C; Allied AA. Address in 1929, 360 East 55th St.; Salmagundi Club, 47 Fifth Ave., New York, NY.

GOETSCH, GUSTAV F.
Painter, etcher and teacher. Born Minneapolis, March 15, 1877. Pupil of Koehler in Minneapolis; Chase and Beckwith in New York; Blanche and Julian in Paris. Member: SFA; St. Louis AG; Chicago SE; Calif. SE; St. L. AL; 2 x 4 Soc. Awards: First prize ($100) for painting, Minneapolis AI; hon. mention, St. Paul Inst., 1917; first prize for best work of art, and first prize, thumb box exhibition, St. L. AL, 1918, 1920, 1922; first prize for best work of art, and first prize for pastel, St. L. AG, 1918; gold medal, Kansas City AI, 1924; first prize, Missouri State Fair, 1924; first prize, second prize and hon. mention, St. Louis AG, 1926; first prize St. Louis AL, 1926, hon. mention, Kansas City AI, 1927. Work in: City Art Museum, St. Louis; Minneapolis Inst. of Arts; Chicago Art Institute; and Worcester Art Museum. Address in 1929, 20 Elm Ave., Glendale, MO; School of Fine

Arts, Washington University, St. Louis, MO.

GOFF, SUDDUTH.
Painter. Born Eminence, KY, Aug. 6, 1887. Pupil of Meakin, Nowottny, Benson, Bosley and Hale; Cincinnati Art Academy (Duveneck School); School of Boston Museum of Fine Arts. Member: Alumni Boston School of Museum of Fine Arts; Louisville AC. Award: First prize and gold medal in painting, Art Colony Exhibiton, Louisville, 1924. Work: Portrait in Kentucky State Capitol, Frankfort; portrait, Standard Sanitary Mfg. Co.; Pittsburgh; portrait owned by KY State Federation of Women's Clubs, Lexington Public Library; portrait owned by KY W.C.T.U. in State Historical Bldg.; portrait of Ex-Governor McCreery in Richmond, KY, City Hall; portraits in Paris, KY, and Lexington, KY, City Hall Instructor, American Academy of Art, Chicago, IL. Address in 1929, American Academy of Art, Chicago, IL.

GOHL, EDWARD HEINRICH.
Painter. Born in Harrisburg, PA, 1862. Pupil of Constant, Laurens, Bashet and Schommer in Paris. Address in 1926, Pearson Bldg., Auburn, NY.

GOLBIN, ANDREE.
Painter. Born in Leipzig, Germany in 1923. Studied: in Switzerland with Henri Bercher; NY School of Fine and Applied Arts; ASL; Hans Hofmann School of Art. Awards: National Assoc. of Women Artists, 1950; Grumbacher prize, Laurel Gallery, 1950.

GOLD, ALBERT.
Illustrator. Born in Philadelphia, in 1916. Studied under Henry C. Pitz at the Philadelphia College of Art where he is now a professor. He joined the Army in 1943, the year his first illustration appeared in Yank. Examples of the artwork he did as an Army War Artist can be seen in the James Jones New Anthology of World War II Art, published by Grosset and Dunlap. His illustrations have appeared in Holiday, The Lamp, and in many children's books. His work, which has received many awards, has been shown at the Metropolitan Museum of Art, the New Britain Museum of American Art, and the Philadelphia Art Museum.

GOLDBECK, WALTER DEAN.
Painter, sculptor and etcher. Born in St. Louis, MO, 1882. Award: Cahn honorable mention, Art Institute of Chicago, 1911. Died in 1925.

GOLDBERG, REUBEN LUCIUS.
Illustrator. Born San Francisco, CA, July 4, 1883. Cartoonist on "Evening Mail" since 1907. Member: SI. Died in 1970. Address in 1929, care of McNaught Syndicate, Times Bldg.; "Evening Mail," 25 City Hall Place, New York, NY.

GOLDIE, JAMES L.
Painter. Born in Dorchester, MA, in 1892. Member of Conn. Academy of Fine Arts, Springfield, MA. Address in 1926, 284 Oakland St., Springfield, MA.

GOLDNER, JANET.
Sculptor. Born in Wash., DC, 1952. Study: Asgard Sch., Hurup Thy, Denmark, 1971; Penland Sch., NC, 1972; Experiment in Int'l. Living, indp. study of arts in West Africa, 1973; Antioch Col., BA Art, 1974; NYU, MA Sculpture, 1981. Work: Terry Gal., Sudbury, MA; Rockrose Devel. Corp., NYC; many priv. coll. and commissions. Outdoor sculpture: Austerlitz, NY, 1981; Bethesda, MD, 1981, 82; Wilton, CT, 1982. One-person shows: Stamford Mus., CT, 1977; 80 Wash. Sq. E. Gal. NYC 1978, 80; Phoenix Gal. NYC, 1983. Exhib.: Concord Art Assoc., MA, 1975; Worcester Craft Center, MA; Bell Gal., Greenwich, CT, 1977; Phoenix Gal., NYC, 1981, 82; Cable Artists, NYC, 1982. Award: Millay Colony for the Arts, NY; Ossabow Island Proj., GA; VA Center for the Creative Arts, Sweet Briar; Yaddo, Saratoga Springs, NY. Media: Fibers, wire mesh, copper, wire, metal, found objects. Address in 1983, 77 Bleecker St., NYC.

GOLDSBOROUGH, NANNIE COX.
Died Nov. 1923 in Eastland MD. She painted a number of portraits and exhibited at the Paris Salons.

GOLDSTEIN, GLADYS HACK.
Painter. Born in Newark, OH, in 1918. Studied: Maryland Inst.; Penn. State Univ.; Columbia Univ. Awards: Penn. State Univ., 1954; Berney Mem. award, Maryland, 1956; Nat. Lg. of Amer. Pen Women, 1956; Rulon-Miller award, Baltimore, 1957. Collections: Penn. State Univ.; Univ. of Arizona; Univ. of Penn.; Baltimore Mus. of Art. Media: Acrylics, oil, watercolor. Address in 1980, 2002 South Rd., Baltimore, MD.

GOLDSTEIN, MILTON.
Printmaker. Born in Holyoke, MA, Nov. 14, 1914. Study: ASL, 1946-49; with Harry Sternberg, Morris Kantor, Will Barnet; Guggenheim Fellow, 1950. Work: Phila. Mus. of Art; Met. Mus. of Art & MOMA, NYC; Brooklyn Mus., NY; Smithsonian Nat'l. Mus., Wash., DC. Comn.: Collection of etchings, Int'l. Graphics Society, NYC, 1952; Collection of Etchings, 1954. Exhib.: Library of Congress, 1948; Smithsonian Inst., 1955; Brooks Mem. Mus. Mus., Memphis, TN, 1959; Am. Printmakers in Italy, Boston Publ. Lib., 1960; Queens College, NY, 1964; Brooklyn (NY) Mus., 1977. Awards: 1st and purchase award, Phila. Art Mus., 1952; 1st and purchase award, Nat'l. Print Show, West, NM Univ., 1971. Teaching: Adelphi Univ., 1953-present. Mem.: Soc. Am. Graphic Artists; Fellow Royal Soc. of Arts, London; Am. Color Print Soc., etc. Address in 1982, Bayside, NY 11364.

GOLDSWORTHY, EMELIA M.
Painter. Born in Platteville, WI, 1869. Pupil of Art Institute of Chicago, and of Otis Art Institute, Los Angeles, CA. Address in 1926, Art Director, Western States Normal School, Kalamazoo, MI.

GOLDTHWAIT, G. H.
This man, apparently a bank-note engraver, was working in Boston in 1842. There is a "Miniature County Map of the United States, Drawn, Engraved and Published by G. H.

Goldthwait, Boston 1842." The map is embellished with a border of small views of public buildings and natural scenery.

GOLDTHWAITE, ANNE.
Painter and etcher. Born Montgomery, AL, in 1875. Pupil of NAD under Mielatz in New York; Academie Moderne in Paris. Member: NA Women PS; NYWCC; Eclectics; Calif. P.M.; Brooklyn SE; SPNY. Awards: McMillin landscape prize, ($100), NA Women PS, 1915; bronze medal for etching, P.-P. Exp., San F., 1915. Work in Library of Congress, Washington, DC; Metropolitan Museum of Art; New York Public Libary; Musee du rue Spontini, Paris; Brooklyn Museum; Bibliotheque Nationale, Paris. Address in 1929, 112 East 10th St., New York, NY.

GOLINKIN, J(OSEPH) W(EBSTER).
Painter, illustrator and lithographer. Born Chicago, IL, Sept. 10, 1896. Pupil of AIC; ASL of NY. Address in 1929, 55 East 59th St., New York, NY.

GOLTZ, WALTER.
Painter and teacher. Born Buffalo, NY, June 20, 1875. Award: Bronze medal, Sesqui-Centennial Exposition, Phila., 1926. Address in 1929, Woodstock, NY.

GOLUB, LEON ALBERT.
Painter. Born IN Chicago, IL, in 1922. Received his Bachelor's degree, history of art, University of Chicago in 1942; Master of Fine Arts from The School of The Art Institute of Chicago in 1950. Taught at the University of Chicago, University of Indiana, and Northwestern University. Exhibitions: Wittenborn and Company, New York, 1952; Institute of Contemporary Arts, London, 1957; Hanover Gallery, London, 1962, 1964. Group Exhibitions: The Solomon R. Guggenheim Museum, New York, 1954; Museum of Art, Carnegie Institute, Pittsburgh, 1955; University of Illinois, Champaign-Urbana, 1957, 1961, 1963; The Museum of Modern Art, New York, 1960, 1962; Tate Gallery, London, 1963; Kassel, Germany, 1964; Prix Marzotto, Italy, 1964. In

collections of Art Inst. of Chicago, MOMA; private and corporate owners. Living in NYC.

GOLUB, LEON.
Painter. Born Jan. 23, 1922, in Chicago. Earned BA at U. of Chic. (1942) and MFA at Inst. of Chic. (1950). Taught at U. of Chic.; Univ. of Indiana; Northwestern. Awarded grant from Ford Found. in 1960; Florsheim prize at annual exhib.; Art Inst. of Chicago (1954); award at Biennal, Mexico City, 1962. Exhibited at Pasadena (1956); Frumkin Gallery; Temple Univ.; Carnegie; MOMA; Guggenheim; S. F. Mus. of Art; U. of Ill.; the Tate; PAFA; Colgate U.; Sch. of Visual Arts, NYC. In collections of MOMA; Art Inst. of Chic.; Chase Manhattan Bank; University of Calif.; University of Texas; Kent State and Tel Aviv.

GONZALES, BOYER.
Painter. Born Houston, TX. Pupil of Wm. J. Whittemore in New York; Walter Lansil in Boston; ASL; Birge Harrison at Woodstock, NY; studied in Holland, Paris and Florence; painted with Winslow Homer. Member: NYWCC; Salma. C.; NAC; SSAL; Texas FAA. Awards: Arthur Evarts gold medal, Dallas, 1921; gold medal, Dallas, 1924; hon. mention, SSAL., 1926. Represented in Galveston Art League; Municipal Schools of Galveston; Delgado Museum, New Orleans, LA. Address in 1929, 3327 Avenue O, Galveston, TX; summer, Woodstock, NY.

GOOD, B(ERNHARD) STAFFORD.
Painter and illustrator. Born England, Jan. 7, 1893. Pupil of AIC, George Bellows, N.C. Wyeth. Illustrated "The Children of the New Forest," by Captain Marryat (Scribner's). Illustrations in "Scribner's Magazine." Address in 1929, Folcroft, PA.

GOOD, MINNETTA.
Painter and craftsman. Born New York City. Pupil of F. Luis Mora and Cecilia Beaux. Member: NA Women PS. Died in 1946. Address in 1929, 335 East 31st St., NYC; summer, Middle Valley, NJ.

GOODALL, ALBERT GALLATIN.
Engraver. Born in Montgomery, AL, Oct. 31, 1826. In 1844 he went to Havana and learned copperplate engraving. He moved to Philadelphia in 1848 and commenced to engrave bank-notes on steel. Later was with a New York company which became, in time, the American Bank Note Co. Goodall was president of this company for the last twelve years of his life. Died in New York City Feb. 19, 1887.

GOODELMAN, AARON J.
Sculptor, illustrator, etcher, lecturer and teacher. Born in Russia, April 1, 1890. Pupil of G. T. Brewster; J. Injalbert. Member: Plastic C.; S. Indp. A. Awards: Bronze medal, Soc. Beaux Arts Arch., 1914, 1915, 1916. Work: Portrait bust of Ansky, Classic Theatre; "The Golem," Gabel's Theatre; "Sholem Alachem," Sholem Alachem Folks' Institute; "Relief," Hospital for Joint Diseases; all in New York. Illustrated for "Kinter Journal" and "Kinter Land." Address in 1929, 25 East 14th St., New York, NY; summer, Hurleyville, NY.

GOODING, WILLIAM C.
Portrait painter. Born in 1775. In the Ontario Messenger, published in Canandaigua, NY, 1815, Mr. William C. Gooding advertised to do "Portrait and Miniature Painting." Died in 1861.

GOODMAN, CHARLES.
Engraver. Born in Philadelphia 1796; died there Feb. 11, 1835. Pupil of David Edwin, and a good engraver in the stipple manner. Goodman and his fellow apprentice, Robert Piggot, founded the firm of Goodman & Piggot and produced a considerable number of portraits, etc., in Philadelphia.

GOODMAN, WALTER.
Painter. Born in England in 1838. He resided in Cuba for five years. He was in the United States in 1870. He devoted himself to portrait painting, and also did illustrating.

GOODRICH, J(AMES) H(ARRY).
Painter. Born Colon, St. Joseph
Co., MI, Nov. 29, 1878. Pupil of
Gies in Detroit; Freer in Chicago.
Member: Nashville AA; Southern
SAL. Awards: Carnegie Scholarship
to Harvard Univ., 1928, 1929.
Instructor in art, George Peabody
College for Teachers, Nashville,
TN; head of art department, Fisk
University. Address in 1929, Route
3, Hamilton Rd., Nashville, TN.

GOODRIDGE, SARAH.
Miniature artitst. Was born in
Massachusetts in 1788. She early
showed a love of art, but did not
have the means to study. Largely
self-taught, it was not till about
1812 that she went to Boston and
began painting miniatures; here she
was introduced to Gilbert Stuart,
who gave her the only real
instruction she ever received. Her
miniature of Stuart is in the
Metropolitan Museum, New York;
others are owned by the Boston
Museum and private collectors.
Memoir of Sarah Goodridge is in
Mason's "Life and Works of Gilbert
Stuart." Died in 1853.

GOODWIN, ALICE HATHAWAY HAPGOOD.
(Mrs. Harold Goodwin, Jr.).
Painter. Born Hartford, CT, Nov.
5, 1893. Pupil of Hugh H.
Breckenridge, Emil Carlsen, Violet
Oakley. Member: Fellowship PAFA.
Work: Reredos, Episcopal Church,
Castleton, VT. Address in 1929,
118 Walnut St., Jenkintown, PA.

GOODWIN, ARTHUR CLIFTON.
Painter and illustrator. Born in
Portsmouth, NH, 1866. Exhibited at
Annual Exhibition of PAFA,
Philadelphia, 1924. Address in
1926, 139 West 54th St., New York.

GOODWIN, FRANCES M.
Sculptor. Born in Newcastle, IN.
She studied art in Indianapolis,
IN, and later at the Chicago Art
Institute, where she became
interested in modeling, and
abandoned her intention of becoming
a painter for sculpture. She
studied at the Art Students'
League, New York, with D. C. French
as instructor. Except as stated
she was self-taught. Among her
works are: Statue representing

Indiana, for Columbian Exposition;
bronze bust of Capt. Everett,
Riverhead Cemetery, New York;
marble bust of Schuyler Colfax,
Senate gallery; bust of Robert Dale
Owen for the State House at
Indianapolis, IN. Died 1929 in
Newcastle IN.

GOODWIN, GILBERTA D(ANIELS).
Painter. Born Burlington, VT, Aug.
20, 1888. Pupil of John F. Weir,
Edwin Taylor, G. A. Thompson, Hayes
Miller. Member: NYWCC; New Haven
PCC; Conn. Soc. of Painters.
Address in 1929, 120 West 11th St.,
New York, NY.

GOODWIN, HELEN M.
Painter. Born New Castle, IN.
Pupil of Hoffbauer and Mme. La
Forge in Paris; Hawthorne. Member:
Indiana AC; Provincetown AA;
American Woman's AA, Paris; Hoosier
Salon. Awards: First prize,
miniature, Hoosier Salon, Marshall
Field Galleries, 1925. Works:
"The Lone Sentinel," Public School,
New Castle; "Sierra Madre,
California," Spiceland Academy of
Indiana; "The Old Bible," Public
Library, New Castle. Address in
1929, 320 South Main St.; summer,
Oak Hill Lodge, New Castle, IN.

GOODWIN, MYRTLE.
See Mrs. Nicola D'Ascenzo.

GOODWIN, PHILIP RUSSELL.
Painter and illustrator. Born in
Norwich, CT, 1882. Pupil of RI
School of Design; Howard Pyle; Art
Students' League of New York. His
editorial work appeared in many
magazines and he had exhibitions in
New York at the Hammer, Kennedy and
Latendorf Galleries. Died in 1935.
Address in 1926, Grove and Louis
Sts., Mamaroneck, NY.

GOOSSENS, JOHN.
Painter. Born Norway, MI, Aug. 27,
1887. Pupil of Royal Academy of
Antwerp, Belgium; Frederick Poole;
George Oberteuffer; AIC. Member:
Alumni AIC; Ill. AFA. Awards: Two
blue ribbons, Aurora, 1927; two red
ribbons, Aurora, 1928; hon.
mention, Springfield, IL, 1928.
Address in 1929, 1624 North Shore
Ave., Chicago, Ill.; summer, care

360

of Charles Treve, R.D. No. 1, Aurora, IL.

GORDON, ELIZABETH.
Sculptor. Born in St. Louis, MO, in 1913. Studied: The Lenox School; sculpture with Walter Russell, Edmondo Quattrocchi. Awards: Brooklyn War Memorial Competition, 1945; Catherine L. Wolfe Artist Club, 1951, 1958; Pen and Brush Club, 1954; National Academy of Design, 1956; gold medal, Hudson Valley Art Assoc., 1956; Pen and Brush Club, 1957. Collections: The Lenox School, NY; Aircraft Carrier "U.S.S. Forrestal"; James L. Collins Parochial School, TX; Woodstock Cemetary; Kensico Cemetery, NY; James Forrestal Research Center, Princeton Univ.

GORDON, EMELINE H.
(Mrs. Beirne Gordon). Painter and teacher. Born Boston, MA, June 25, 1877. Pupil of Tarbell, Frank Benson, Eliot Clark. Member: Savannah AC. Address in 1929, 304 East Huntingdon St., Savannah, GA; summer, North Hatley, Canada.

GORDON, FREDERICK CHARLES.
Painter. Born at Cobourg, Ont., 1856; died March 20, 1924, in High Orchard, NJ. Studied at ASL, of NY and Julien and Colarossi Academies, Paris. Began work 1882, at Toronto, Can., and came to U.S. in 1886; painter of portraits, landscapes and genre. Later devoted his attention chiefly to decorative drawings for publications. In collection of Boston Mus. and private collectors.

GORDON, LEON.
Painter. Born Bonsor, Russia, May 25, 1889. Pupil of AIC, ASL of NY; Julian Academy, Paris; Kunst Academy, Vienna. Member: Salma. C.; SI. Address in 1929, 80 W. 40th St., New York, NY; 11 Rue Schoelcher, Paris, France.

GORE, THOMAS H.
Painter and draughtsman. Born Baltimore, MD, Oct. 1, 1863. Studied with Duveneck. Member: Cincinnati AC. Died in 1937.

Address in 1929, 211 Pleasant St., Covington, KY.

GOREY, EDWARD.
Illustrator. Born in 1929. A graduate of Harvard in 1950, he worked briefly in a publishing house and began his free-lance career in 1953. Aside from many editorial assignments for The New York Times, Esquire, and Holiday, he has illustrated several children's books, of which the first was entitled Unstrung Harp. In the early 1950's he illustrated the Henry James novels for Anchor Books and has since published many albums of drawings. Presently living in Barnstable, Mass., he has had exhibitions in Minneapolis and New York.

GORKY, ARSHILE.
Painter. Born 1905 in Khorkom Vari Haiyotz Dzor, Armenia. Emigrated in 1920 to US. He studied at the Polytechnic Inst., in Tilfis, 1916-18; New Sch. of Design, Boston, 1923; Grand Central Sch., NYC, 1925-31. Exhibitions were held at the Guild Art Gallery in NYC, 1932, 1935, 1936; Mellon Gallery, Phila., 1934, and many others. In collections of the Univ. of Arizona; Albright-Knox Gallery, Buffalo, NY; Oberlin College. Died July 21, 1948, in Sherman, CT.

GORSON, AARON HARRY.
Painter. Born in Russia, July 2, 1872; came to America in 1889. Pupil of PAFA; Julian Academy, Constant and Laurens in Paris. Member: Pittsburgh AA; Brooklyn AS; Alliance. Represented in Newark Museum Association; American Art Museum, Worcester, MA; Heckscher Park Art Museum, Huntington, LI, NY. Died Oct. 11, 1933, in New York City. Address in 1929, 6 West 28th St.; 1995 Creston Ave., New York, NY.

GOSHORN, JOHN THOMAS.
Painter. Born near Independence, IA, 1870. Pupil of Art Institute of Chicago, and Smith Art Academy. Address in 1926, 512 Washington Bank Bldg., Pittsburgh, PA.

GOSS, JOHN.
Painter and illustrator. Born
Lewiston, ME, Sept. 19, 1886.
Member: Boston AC; AWCS. Died c.
1963. Address in 1929, Fenway
Studios, 30 Ipswich St., Boston,
MA; h. Walpole, MA.

GOSSELIN, LUCIEN H.
Sculptor. Born Whitefield, NH,
Jan. 2, 1883. Pupil of Verlet,
Bouchard, Landowski, and Mercie.
Member: Societe Libre des Artistes
Francais. Award: Hon. mention,
French Artists Salon, 1913.
Address in 1929, 52 Rue
Vercingetorix, Paris, France; 1061
Elm St.; h. 135 Amory St.,
Manchester, NH.

GOTH, MARIE.
Painter. Born in Indianapolis, IN.
Studied: Art Students' League,
with DuMond, Chase, and Mora.
Known chiefly as a portrait
painter. Awards: Evansville,
Indiana Museum of Art and History,
1939; Indiana Art Club, 1935, 1939,
1944, 1945, 1956; Brown County Art
Gallery, 1933; Hoosier Salon, 1926,
1929, 1932, 1934, 1942, 1945, 1946,
1948, 1949, 1951, 1952, 1957, 1958;
NAD, 1931. Collections: Hanover
College; Franklin College, Purdue
Univ; Indiana Univ; Butler College;
John Herron Art Institute; Florida
State Univ. Honeywell Memorial
Community Center, Wabash, Indiana;
John Howard Mitchell House, Kent,
England.

GOTHELF, LOUIS.
Painter. Born Russia, April 6,
1901. Pupil of Ivan Olinsky, G. W.
Maynard, NAD, J. Wellington
Reynolds, AIC. Member: Rockford
AA; Artklan; United Scenic A.,
Chicago. Work: "Portrait of
Scholem Alachem," Jewish
Educational Bldg., Toledo. Art
director, Orpheum Theatre,
Rockford, IL. Address in 1929, 119
Floyd St., Toledo, OH.

GOTTHOLD, FLORENCE W(OLF).
(Mrs. Frederick Gotthold). Painter
and craftswoman. Born
Uhrichsville, OH, Oct. 3, 1858.
Pupil of B. R. Fitz, H. Siddons
Mowbray and H. G. Dearth. Member:
NY Pen and Brush C.; MacD. C.;
Greenwich SA; NA Women PS;

Silvermine GA; Gld. of Book
Workers; Wilton SA. Died in 1930.
Address in 1929, 67 West 52nd St.,
New York, NY; summer, Wilton, CT.

GOTTLIEB, ADOLF.
Painter. Born March 14, 1903, in
NYC. Studied at the Art Students'
League, 1919, with John Sloan and
Robert Henri; Parsons Sch. of
Design, 1923. In 1944-45, was
president of Fed. of Mod. Painters.
Taught at the Pratt Inst., 1958;
UCLA, 1958. Awarded Dudensing Nat.
Competition, 1929; U.S. Treasury
Dept., Mural Competition, 1939;
Brooklyn Museum First Prize, 1944.
Exhibitions: Dudensing Gallery,
NYC, 1930, Uptown Gallery NYC
1934; Gallerie Handschen, Basel,
1961.

GOTTWALD, F(REDERICK) C(ARL).
Painter and teacher. Born in 1860.
Pupil of ASL of NY; Royal Academy,
Munich. Member: Cleveland SA.
Work: "The Umbrian Valley, Italy,"
Cleveland Museum. Instructor at
Cleveland School of Art. Died in
1941. Address in 1929, Cleveland
School of Art, Cleveland, OH.

GOUDY, FRED W.
Type designer, craftsman, writer,
lecturer and teacher. Born
Bloomington, IL, March 8, 1865.
Member: Grolier C.; Amer. Inst.
Graphic A.; Stowaways. Awards:
Bronze medal, St. Louis Exp., 1904;
gold medal, Amer. Inst. Graphic A.;
gold medal, AIA.; Friedsam gold
medal, NY Arch. L. Author "The
Alphabet," and "Elements of
Lettering," published by Mitchell
Kennerly, New York, and John Lane,
London, and editor of "Arts
Typographica." Instructor, Art
Students' League, New York;
University of New York. Died in
1947. Address in 1929,
Marlboro-on-Hudson, NY.

GOULD, CARL FRELINGHUYSEN.
Painter, architect, lecturer and
teacher. Born New York City, Nov.
24, 1873. Pupil of William Sartain;
Ecole des Beaux Arts; M. Victor
Laloux. Member: Beaux-Arts
Architects; Seattle Fine Arts Soc.;
AIA; NY Arch. Lg. Work: Campus
Bldgs., University of Washington;
New Seattle Times Bldg.; formerly

362

Head of Department of Architecture, University of Washington. Address in 1929, 710 Hoge Bldg.; h. 1058 East Lynn St., Seattle, WA; summer, Bainbridge Island, WA.

GOULD, THOMAS RIDGEWAY.
Sculptor. Born in Boston, Nov. 5, 1818. He studied with Seth Cheney. His two colossal heads of "Christ" and "Satan" were exhibited at the Boston Athenaeum in 1863. His most celebrated statue was the "West Wind;" among his portrait busts are those of Emerson, Seth Cheney, and the elder Booth. He died Nov. 26, 1881, in Florence, Italy.

GOULD, WALTER.
Painter. Born in Philadelphia in 1829, he studied under J. R. Smith and Thomas Sully. He became a member of the Artists' Fund Society of Phila. His subjects are generally oriental, a reminiscence of his travels in Egypt and Asia. He visited Constantinople and painted pictures of many important persons there. Died Jan. 18, 1893, in Florence, Italy.

GOULET, LORRIE.
(Lorrie J. de Creeft). Sculptor. Born in Riverdale, NY, Aug. 17, 1925. Studied at Inwood Pottery Studios, 1932-36, with Amiee Voorhees; Black Mountain College, NC, with Joseph Albers; sculpture with Jose de Creeft, 1943-44. In collections of Hirshhorn, Wash. DC; NJ State Mus.; others, including commissions for NY Public Library; Bronx Munic. Hosp.; Bronx Police and Fire Sta. Exhibited at Clay Club Sculpture Center, NYC, 1948, 55; Am. Fedn. of Arts, 1963; World Trade Fairs, Algiers, Barcelona, Zagreb, 1964; Contemp. Gallery, NYC, 1959, 62, 66, 68; Kennedy Galleries, NYC, 1971, 73-75, 78, 80; many more. Taught at MOMA, 1957-64; New Sch. for Soc. Research, 1961-75; ASL, 1981; others. Received First Sculpt. Prize, Norton Gallery, 1949, 50, and Westchestr Art Soc., 1964; Soltan Engel Mem. Award, Audubon Artists, 1967. Member of Sculptors Guild; Audubon Artists; founding mem., Visual Artists and Galleries Assn.; Nat'l. Comm. on Art Educ.; others. Works in wood, stone,

ceramics. Represented by Kennedy Galleries, NYC. Address in 1982, 241 W. 20th St., NYC.

GOVE, ELMA MARY.
Portrait artist in crayons and oils. She was working in New York in 1851-55.

GRABACH, JOHN R.
Painter. Born Newark, NJ, in 1886. Pupil of ASL of NY. Member: North Shore AA; AFA. Awards: Peabody prize, AIC, 1924; Sesnan gold medal, PAFA, 1927; Preston Harrison prize, Los Angeles Museum. Work: "Wash Day in Spring," AIC; "The Steel Rainbow," Vanderpoel AA, Chicago. Address in 1929, 915 Sanford Ave., Irvington, NJ.

GRAD, BARBARA.
Painter/graphics. Born in 1951. Studied: The School of the Art Institute of Chicago. Exhibitions: Allan Frumkin Gallery, Chicago, IL, 1973; Suburban Fine Arts Center, Highland Park, IL, 1974; Northern Illinois Univ., DeKalb, IL, 1975. She is represented in the collections of The Art Institute of Chicago Museum.

GRAF, CARL C.
Painter. Born Sept. 24, 1890. Pupil of Herron Art Inst., Indianapolis, IN, and Cincinnati Academy. Member: Ind. AC; Nashville A. Colony. Died in 1947. Address in 1929, 43 Union Trust Bldg., Indianapolis, IN; Nashville, IN.

GRAFLY, CHARLES.
Sculptor. Born Dec. 3, 1862, in Philadelphia. Pupil of Penna. Academy of Fine Arts, and Chapu and Dampt, Paris. Member of International Jury of Awards, St. Louis Expn., 1904; Instructor in Sculpture, Penna. Academy of Fine Arts, since 1892. Represented in permanent collections of Penna. Academy of Fine Arts; Detroit Art Museum; St. Louis Museum; Carnegie Institute, Pittsburgh; Boston Museum. Member of Municipal Art Jury, Philadelphia National Academy, 1906. Member: National Institute Arts and Letters; National Sculpture Society; Architectural League; Philadelphia

Art Club. Executed much notable work in busts, life size; colossal figures and portrait and ideal figures, and groups, largely in bronze. George D. Widener gold medal, 1913; Watrous gold medal, National Academy 1918. Address in 1926, 20th and Cherry Sts., Philadelphia, PA. Died May 5, 1929, in Phila.

GRAFSTROM, RUTH SIGRID.
Illustrator. Born in Rock Island, Illinois, in 1905. Studied at the AIC and the Colarossi Academy in Paris. A fashion artist for Vogue from 1930 to 1940, she later worked for Delineator, Cosmopolitan and Woman's Home Companion. She won many awards and citations from the NY ADC and the S of I, of which she had been a member.

GRAFTON, ROBERT WADSWORTH.
Painter. Born in Chicago, IL, Dec. 19, 1876. Pupil of AIC; Julian Academy in Paris; studied in Holland and England. Awards: Mary T. R. Foulke, prize, Richmond AA, 1910 and 1919; Leroy Goddard prize, Hoosier Salon, Chicago. Member: Chicago PS; Palette and Chisel C.; Chicago AC; Chicago AG. Work in Delgado Museum and New Orleans Art Assoc., New Orleans; La Fayette Art Assoc.; Union Lg. C., Chicago; Northwestern Univ; Purdue Univ.; Earlham College; Public Art Gallery, Richmond, IN; mural panels in State House, Springfield, IL; Tulane Univ., New Orleans, LA; First National Bank, Ft. Wayne, IN; two portraits, State Library, Indianapolis; portrait, State House, Lansing, MI; portrait Ex-President Collidge, Saddle and Sirloin Club; Mural "Coming of Pioneers," Kansas Wesleyan Univ.; official portrait, Secretary Jardine, Dept. of Agriculture, WA. Died in 1936. Address in 1929, East Coolspring Ave., Michigan City, IN.

GRAHAM, A. W.
Engraver. Born in England, he studied engraving under Henry Meyer, a well-known London engraver. He came to the United States about 1832, and in 1934 he engraved some excellent views for the New York Mirror. He engraved a

few portraits at a later date; but his best work is to be found in the small plates executed for the "Annuals" of 1835-40. Graham was located in Philadelphia in 1838-40, and in 1844-45, according to the directories of that city; he was living in New York in 1869.

GRAHAM, CECILIA B(ANCROFT).
Sculptor. Born San Francisco, CA, March 2, 1905. Pupil of Louis de Jean, Oskar Thiede, Nicolo D'Antino. Address in 1929, 2515 Piedmont Ave.; h. 53 Plaza Dr., Berkeley, CA; summer, Stateline, Lake Tahoe, CA.

GRAHAM, ELIZABETH SUTHERLAND.
Painter. Born New York City. Pupil of NY Sch. of Applied Design for Women; M. Despujols. Member: NA Women PS; Brooklyn SA; Brooklyn S. Min. P. Died in 1938. Address in 1929, 464 Clinton Ave., Brooklyn, NY.

GRAHAM, GEORGE.
Engraver in mezzotint and in stipple. His first work appeared in 1795. Probably located in Philadelphia in 1797. Working for New York publishers in 1804. He designed and apparently engraved a frontispiece for the "Proceedings of the Society of the Cincinnati," published in Boston in 1812, and he was again engraving in Philadelphia in 1813.

GRAHAM, JOHN D.
Painter and sculptor. Born Kiev, Russia, Dec. 27, 1890. Pupil of John Sloan. Work: Sixteen paintings, Phillips Memorial Gallery, Washington, DC; painting, Spencer Kellog collection, New York; five paintings, Ben Hecht collection, New York. Address in 1929, 5 East 57 St., New York, NY; summer, care of American Express Co., 11 Rue Scribe, Paris, France.

GRAHAM, MARGARET NOWELL.
(Mrs. J. L. Graham). Painter. Member: SSAL; AFA. Address in 1929, 625 Summit St., Winston-Salem, NC.

GRAHAM, P. PURDON.
This name, as engraver, is signed to a well-executed line-engraving

of Cadwallader Colden, after a portrait painted by Matthew Pratt, and belonging to the Chamber of Commerce of New York. The work was probably done about 1870-75, but nothing more is known about the engraver.

GRAHAM, PAYSON.
Sculptor and illustrator. She was a member of Art Students' League of New York. Address in 1926, 251 West 81st St., New York.

GRAHAM, ROBERT A(LEXANDER).
Painter and teacher. Born Brooklyn, IA, June 29, 1873. Pupil of ASL of NY; Joseph DeCamp; Twachtman; Bridgman. Member: NYWCC; Salma. C. Specialty, figure and landscape painting. Died in 1946. Address in 1929, 300 East 13th Ave., Denver, CO.

GRAHAM, WILLIAM.
Born in New York, but spent many years in Rome. Painted generally Roman and Venetian landscapes. "Outside the Porto del Popolo, Rome," (signed) "W. Graham, 1874, Rome," exhibited at Penna. Academy of Fine Arts.

GRAMATKY, HARDIE.
Illustrator. Born in Dallas, Texas, in 1907. Attended Stanford Univ. and Chouinard Institute under Pruett Carter. He initiated his career with a 12-page spread for Fortune in 1939, and went on to illustrate for major periodicals such as Collier's, Good Housekeeping, Redbook, and True. Author-illustrator of Little Toot, he is the creator of 12 additional children's books and recipient of 40 watercolor awards. His paintings have been in museums and galleries worldwide as well as part of many permanent collections.

GRANDEE, JOE RUIZ.
Painter and gallery director. Born in Dallas, TX, Nov. 19, 1929. Study: Aunspaugh Art Sch., Dallas. Work: White House, Wash. DC; Xavier Univ. Mus., Cincinnati, OH; Marine Corps Mus., Quantico, VA; others. Comn.: US Borax Co., Hollywood, CA; Portrait, Linda Bird & Chuck Robb, 1967; portrait of Johnny Carson, 1967; portrait of Robert Taylor, US Borax Co. for Rbt. Taylor, 1968; Leander H. McNelly, Tex. Ranger, White House, 1972; and others. Exhib.: Custer Exhib., Amon Carter Mus. of Western Art, Ft. Worth, TX, 1968; Norton Art Gallery Mus., Shreveport, LA, 1971; US Capitol, 1974; others. Awards: First Official Artist of Texas, 1971; Franklin Mint Gold Medal Western Art for Pursuit and Attack, 1974; others. Owner: Joe Grandel Gallery & Mus. of Old West. Media: Oil, ink. Address in 1982, Arlington, TX.

GRANDIN, ELIZABETH.
Painter and craftsman. Born Camden, NJ. Pupil of Henri; Guerin in Paris. Member: MacD. C.; NA Women PS; NYS Women Artists. Address in 1929, 25 East 11th St., New York, NY; h. Annandale, NJ.

GRANER, LUIS.
Portrait, genre and landscape painter of great versatility. Born in Barcelona, Spain, 1867. Came to America in 1910, and lived and painted in New Orleans from 1914 to 1922, at intervals. Received medals at Barcelona, Madrid, Berlin, Paris, and in many other places. In 1904 he was made a member of the "Societe Nationale des Beaux Arts," France. Represented in art museums, Madrid and Barcelona, Spain; Brussels, Belgium; Bordeaux, France; Berlin, Germany; and in the National Museums of Brazil, Chile, Argentina and Uruguay, and in the Papal gallery, Rome.

GRANGER, CAROLINE GIBBONS.
Painter. Exhibited at the Penna. Academy of Fine Arts, Philadelphia, in 1924. Address in 1926, 1016 South 46th St., Philadelphia, PA.

GRANT, BLANCHE C.
Painter, lecturer and writer. Born Leavenworth, KS, in 1874. Pupil of Paxton, Hale, McCarter, Johansen. Award: Hon. mention, St. Paul Inst., 1917. Address in 1929, Taos, NM.

GRANT, CATHARINE (HARLEY).
Painter and teacher. Born Pittsburgh, PA, Jan. 27, 1897.

Pupil of PAFA; Hugh H. Breckenridge. Member: Fellowship PAFA; Phila. Alliance; Plastic C. Specialty, portraits. Died in 1954. Address in 1929, 303 Walnut St.; h. 1809 Pine St., Phila., PA; summer, Bellwood, PA.

GRANT, CHARLES H(ENRY).
Marine painter. Born Oswego, NY, Feb. 6, 1866. Pupil of deHaas, and NAD. Member: San. F. AA; Bohemian Club; Sequoia Club. Work: "Salute to the Flag," Oswego (NY) City Hall; "Safe in Port," Syracuse Museum of Art; "After the Rain," Sequoia Club, San F.; "Arrival of Atlantic Battleship Fleet in Golden Gate, San Francisco, 1908," Memorial Museum, San F.; "They Made the World Safe for Democracy," Bohemian Club, San Francisco; "Arrival Pacific Battle Fleet in Golden Gate, San Francisco, 1919," Bohemian Club; commissioned by Bohemian Club to paint H.M.S. Hood and U.S.S. California; by Citizens Committee of the Chamber of Commerce to paint U.S.S. California; official artist of U.S. Navy on 1925 cruise to Australia. Died in 1939. Address in 1929, Bohemian Club, San Francisco, CA.

GRANT, CLEMENT ROLLINS.
Painter. Born in Freeport, ME, 1849. Studied abroad; on his return to this country, established his studio in Boston and became a member of the Boston Art Club. Specialty: landscape and portrait. Work: "Amy Wentworth," "Marguerita," and a "Normandy Fisherman."

GRANT, FREDERIC M.
Painter, illustrator, etcher and teacher. Born Sibley, IA, Oct. 6, 1886. Pupil of Chase, Miller, Vanderpoel and Snell. Member: Chicago PS; Cliff Dwellers. Awards: Goodman prize, AIC, 1914.; Fine Arts Bldg. prize, Chicago AG, 1916; Cahn prize and Butler prize, AIC, 1917; Municipal AL prize, AIC, 1917; popular prize, Chicago AC, 1918; hon. mention, Chicago AG, 1918; Eisendrath prize, AIC, 1919; Chase prize, Venice, 1918; Municipal AS prize, AIC, 1919; Holmes prize, AIC, 1924; Logan medal ($500), AIC, 1926; Hearst prize ($300), AIC, 1927. Address in 1929, 139 East Ontario St., Chicago, IL.

GRANT, GORDON HOPE.
Painter and illustrator. Born San Francisco, CA, June 7, 1875. Pupil of Heatherley's and Lambeth's Schools, London. Member: AWCS; SI 1911; Salma. C. 1901; Allied AA; NYSP; AFA. Worked on the "San Francisco Chronicle" and "The Examiner." Reports of Boer War, Mexican border conflicts in "Harper's". Paintings of nautical subjects in collections of Met. Mus. of Art; Libr. of Congress. Died in 1962. Address in 1929, 137 East 66th St., New York, NY.

GRANT, ISSAC H.
Painter. Member: Conn. Academy of Fine Arts. Address in 1926, 10 Olds Place, Hartford, CT.

GRANT, J.
A little known portrait painter who was working in Philadelphia in 1829.

GRANT, J. JEFFREY.
Painter. Born 1883. Member: Chicago SA; Chicago PS; GFLA; Chicago Gal. A.; Palette and Chisel C. Award: Business Men's AC prize ($300), AIC, 1926; hon. mention, AIC, 1927. Died in 1960. Address in 1929, 21 East Van Buren St.; 3634 West 22nd St., Chicago, IL.

GRANT, LAWRENCE W.
Painter. Born Cleveland, OH, June 10, 1886. Pupil of Chase in New York; Laurens and Lefebvre in Paris. Member: Salma. C. Address in 1929, Provincetown, MA.

GRANVILLE-SMITH, WALTER.
See Smith, W. Granville.

GRAVATT, SARA H(OFFECKER).
Painter. Born Philadelphia, PA, Aug. 31, 1898. Pupil of George Harding, Henry B. Snell, Joseph Pearson. Member: Fellowship PAFA; Plastic C.; Graphic Sketch C. Address in 1929, 1565 Washington St., Charleston, W. VA; summer, Fairchance, PA.

GRAVES, ABBOTT (FULLER).
Painter. Born Weymouth, MA, April 15, 1859. Pupil of Inst. of Technology, Boston; Cromon, Laurens and Gervais in Paris. Member: ANA, 1926; Boston AC; Copley S.; Salma. C., 1909; Paris AAA (hon.); Allied AA; NAC (life); Artists Fund (hon.). Specialty, paintings of gardens. Award: Medal, Exp. des Beaux Arts, Paris, 1905. Represented in National Arts Club, New York; Art Museum, Portland, ME. Died in 1936. Address in 1929, Kennebunkport, ME.

GRAVES, ELIZABETH EVANS.
Painter, illustrator, craftswoman and teacher. Born Fort Brady, MI, March 13, 1895. Pupil of R. Sloan Bredin, Henry B. Snell, Howard Giles, etc. Member: Wash. SA; Wash. WCC; NA Women PS; Wash. AC. Address in 1929, 3705 Harrison St., NW, Washington, DC.

GRAVES, MARY DE B(ERNIERE).
Painter, illustrator, writer, lecturer and teacher. Born Chapel Hill. Pupil of William Chase; Henry McCarter. Member: SSAL. Awards: Prize, N.C. Federation of Women's Clubs, 1926, and 1929; Silver Cup, Kenilworth Exh., Asheville, NC, 1927. Illustrated in "New York Evening Post;" "The World;" "Tribune;" "Southern Magazine;" "The Ruralist;" "Philadelphia Record;" "Country Life." Address in 1929, 203 Battle Lane, Chapel Hill, NC.

GRAY, CHARLES A.
Painter. Born in Iowa in 1857. Connected with Art Department of Chicago Herald and Tribune. He painted portraits of Presidents McKinley and Garfield, Eugene Field, Opie Read and many others. His portraits of J. Warren Keifer and M. G. Kerr are in the Capitol Bldg., Washington.

GRAY, HARRIET TYNG.
Painter. Born So. Orange, NJ, May 26, 1879. Pupil of DuMond, Beaux, Hawthorne and Howell. Member: Greenwich SA; NA Women PS; AFA. Address in 1929, Rock Ridge, Greenwich, CT.

GRAY, HENRY PETERS.
Painter. Born June 23, 1819, in New York. He began his art studies under Daniel Huntington, P.N.A., in 1839. He went to Europe in 1840 and studied the old masters. On his return in 1842 he was elected a National Academician. From 1869-71, he was president of NA. Painting portraits in New York, with an occasional figure picture, occupied the greater part of his career. "The Origin of Our Flag" was one of the last of his exhibits at the Academy, in 1875. His work shows his sound academic study, and his color is reminiscent of the golden tone of Titian or Correggio. Many of his portraits are cabinet size. He died Nov. 12, 1877, in New York.

GRAY, KATHRYN.
Painter. Born Jefferson Co., KS, 1881. Pupil of ASL of NY; Julian Academy, Paris. Member: Am. APL; Allied Artists of NY; AFA. Died in 1931. Address in 1929, Van Dyke Studios, New York, NY.

GRAY, MARY.
Painter. Member: Allied AA; N.A. Women PS; North Shore AA; NAC; AFA. Address in 1929, 47 Gramercy Park; 59 West 9th St., New York, NY.

GRAY, PERCY.
Painter. Born San Francisco, Oct. 3, 1869. Studied in San Francisco and New York. Member: Bohemian C.; Sequoia C.; San F. AA. Award: Bronze Medal, P.-P. Exp., San F., 1915. Died in 1952. Address in 1929, Monterey, CA.

GRAY, W(ILLIAM) F(RANCIS).
Painter, lecturer and teacher. Born Philadelphia, PA, May 9, 1866. Pupil of PA Museum and PAFA. Member: Phila. AC; Phila. Sketch C.; Art Teachers' Assoc. of Phila.; Fellowship PAFA. Address in 1929, 2014 Mt. Vernon St., Phila., PA.

GRAY & TODD.
This firm was engraving diagrams and script-work in Philadelphia in 1817.

GRAYDON, ALEXANDER.
Author, soldier and limner. Born in Bristol, PA, April 10, 1752. He

served in the revolution, was taken prisoner, was exchanged, and received the appointment of Captain from Congress for raising recruits for the army. In 1811 he published "Memoirs of a Life, chiefly passed in Penna. within the Last Sixty Years." In this he notes his love of drawing and painting. He is known to have copied Stuart's portrait of Washington, painted on glass, similar to those done in China about 1800, but not as well painted. Died May 2, 1818, in Piladelphia.

GRAYHAM, WILLIAM.
Painter. Born in 1832, and died in 1911. His "Rainy Day in Venice" is signed "W. Grayham, Venezia 1885.

GRAYSON, CLIFFORD P(REVOST).
Painter. Born Philadelphia, July 14, 1857. Pupil of PAFA; Gerome and Bonnat; Ecole des Beaux Arts in Paris. Member: Phila. AC; Century Asoc.; Salma. C. Awards: $2,000 prize, American Art Galleries, New York, 1886; Temple gold medal, PAFA, 1887. Work: "Mid-Day Dreams," Corcoran Gallery, Washington; "Rainy Day in Pont Aven," Art Institute, Chicago; "Le Toussaint," Art Club, Philadelphia. Died in 1951. Address in 1929, Box 73, Lyme, CT.

GREACEN, EDMUND W.
Painter and teacher. Born New York, 1877. Pupil of Chase and Du Mond in New York; studied in Europe. Member: ANA; Salma. C., 1910; Soc. des Artistes Independents, Paris; Allied AA; NAC (life); AWCS; PS Gallery Asso. Awards: Shaw Purchase Prize, Salma. C., 1921; NAC prize, 1923. Work: "The Lady in Blue," "Sidonie," Butler Art Institute, Youngstown, Ohio; "Hudson River Twilight," Newark Museum; "The Feather Fan," National Arts Club. President Grand Central School of Art. Died Oct. 4, 1949. Address in 1929, 142 East 18th St., New York, NY.

GREASON, WILLIAM.
Painter. Born St. Mary's, Ontario, Feb. 26, 1884. Pupil of PAFA, Breckenridge, Julian Academy, Boschel and Laurens in Paris.

Member: Scarab C.; Salma. C.; North Shore AA. Award: Hopkin 1st prize, Scarab. C., 1915; gold medal, Scarab. C., 1917. Work: "The D. A. C. at Twilight," Detroit Art Institute. Address in 1929, 1504 Broadway; h. 528 Canfield Ave., East Detroit, MI.

GREATH.
Miniature painter from Sweden who visited Philadelphia and, according to Chas. W. Peale, "painted for his own amusement."

GREATOREX, ELEANOR.
Painter. Born in New York City, 1854. Devoted her time to painting and illustration. Flower paintings frequently exhibited.

GREATOREX, ELIZA PRATT.
Painter. Born Dec. 25, 1820, in Ireland, she came to America in 1836. Pupil of James and William Hart in New York. In 1869 she was elected an Associate of the National Academy, being the first woman to receive that recognition. Her work was in oils, and she also illustrated a number of publications. She died Feb. 9, 1897, in Paris.

GREATOREX, KATHLEEN HONORA.
Painter. Born Hoboken, NJ, 1851. Studied art in New York, Rome and Munich. Besides decorative work and book-illustration, she painted flower pieces, etc., which she has exhibited in the Paris Salon and elsewhere. Awards: Honorable mention, Paris Salon; gold medals, Philadelphia, Chicago and Atlanta Expns. Among her flower pieces she exhibited the panels "Thistles," "Corn," and "Hollyhocks."

GREAVES, WILLIAM A.
Painter. Born in Watertown, NY, 1847, he died in 1900. Studied under Thomas Le Clair, and was a student at the Cooper Institute of New York City. Resided in Utica, NY, for several years and in 1873 moved to Warrentown. Painted portraits of S. J. Randall, G. A. Grow, Matthew S. Quay, Gov. Fenton, and Gov. Beaver. Portraits of Randall and Grow in the Capitol Bldg., Washington, DC.

GREBEL, ALPHONSE.
Painter. Member: Society of Independent Artists. Address in 1926, 174 St. Nicholas Ave., New York, NY.

GRECO, DANIEL.
Painter. Member: Pittsburgh Artists' Association. Address in 1926, 608 Fifth Ave., New Kensington, PA.

GREEN.
An English portrait painter, who arrived in the Colonies about 1750 and painted portraits from then until 1785.

GREEN, BERNARD I.
Painter, etcher and teacher. Born Swerzen, Russia, Feb. 12, 1887. Pupil of Douglas Volk, Francis Jones, Edgar M. Ward and Pressig; NAD; ASL of NY; NY Univ. (art course). Member: NY SE; Chicago AG; Bronz AG; School Art Lg.; Mystic AA. Work: "Girl Reading," Museum of Oakland, CA. Head of art dept., Thomas Jefferson High School, Brooklyn; head of art dept., Yeshivah Rabbi Isaac Elchanan, New York. Died in 1951. Address in 1929, 939 Eighth Ave., NY; h. 259 Montgomery St., Brooklyn, NY.

GREEN, EDITH JACKSON.
Painter. Born Tarrytown, NY, March 22, 1876. Pupil of Twachtman, DeCamp, Raphael Collin. Work: "A Fantasy of Old Providence," Providence Plantation Club. Address in 1929, 74 North Main St.; h. 25 John St., Providence, RI; summer, Old Town, North Attleboro, MA.

GREEN, ELIZABETH SHIPPEN.
See Mrs. Huger Elliott.

GREEN, ERIK H. (Mrs).
Painter. Member: Providence Art Club. Address in 1926, Oldtown, North Attleboro, MA.

GREEN, FLORENCE TOPPING.
(Mrs. Howard Green). Landscape and miniature painter, writer and lecturer. Born London, England, Feb. 23, 1882. Pupil of Cooper Union; R. Swain Gifford, John Carlson. Member: Am. APL; (asso.)

NYWCC; Art Div. Am. Women's Assn., NY; AFA; PBC. Chairman of Arts and Crafts, General Federation of Women's Clubs, 1924-1928; Art Division, 1928-1930. Died in 1945. Address in 1929, 104 Franklin Ave., Long Branch, NJ.

GREEN, FRANK RUSSELL.
Painter. Born Chicago, April 16, 1856. Pupil of Boulanger, Lefebvre, Collin and Courtois in Paris. Member: ANA 1897; AWCS; NYWCC; Salma. C. 1887; Lotos C. Awards: Lotos Fund, NAD 1896; hon. mention, Paris Salon, 1900; Morgan prize, Salma. C. 1903; bronze medal, St. Louis Exp., 1904; Shaw prize, Salma. C. 1908. Died in 1940. Address in 1929, care of Salmagundi Club, 47 Fifth Ave., New York, NY.

GREEN, FRED STUART.
Painter. Born in North Stonington, CT, 1876. Pupil of Rhode Island School of Design. Member of Providence Water Color Club. Address in 1926, "Ye Hollie Studio," Westerly, RI.

GREEN, H(IRAM) H(AROLD).
Painter, illustrator and etcher. Born Paris, Oneida Co., NY, Nov. 15, 1865. Pupil of H. S. Mowbray, Cox, Bridgman. Member: AFA. Award: Albright Prize, Albright Art Academy, 1898. Work: "Grand Canon," owned by the Santa Fe R.R.; "Apache Trail," owned by the Southern Pacific R.R.; "My Soldier," U.S. Government Liberty Loan Poster. Specialty, pictorial maps. Died in 1930. Address in 1929, Fort Erie, Ont., Canada.

GREEN, HAROLD ABBOTT.
Painter. Born Montreal, Canada, Nov. 10, 1883. Pupil of Flagg and Brandegee. Member: Conn. AFA. Awards: Dunham prize, Conn. AFA, 1918. Address in 1929, 284 Asylum St.; h. 50 Ashley St., Hartford, CT.

GREEN, MILDRED C.
Painter, illustrator and teacher. Born Paris, Oneida County, NY, April 18, 1874. Pupil of Bridgman, Hitchcock and Dufner. Member: Buffalo SA; Buffalo Guild of Allied Arts; Buffalo Fine Arts Academy.

Instructor, Life Class, Buffalo School of Fine Arts. Address in 1929, 717 Delaware Ave., Buffalo, NY; summer, Clayville, NY.

GREEN, WILLIAM BRADFORD.
Painter, lecturer and teacher. Born Binghamton, NY, Aug. 1, 1871. Pupil of Chase, Blom and Dow. Member: Conn. AFA; Brooklyn SA; Copley S. Died in 1945. Address in 1929, 133 Steele St., Hartford CT.

GREENAMYER, LEAH J.
Painter, craftswoman, writer, lecturer and teacher. Born Ashtabula, OH, April 17, 1891. Pupil of Cora B. Austin, George S. Krispinsky, Grace Williamson, John Lloyd, Butler Art Institute. Member: Youngstown Art Alliance; Columbus AL; Cleveland Art Center; Mahoning Soc. of Painters; Ohio-Born Women A. Art Editor of Youngstown Sunday Vindicator. Address in 1929, 117 East Warren Ave., Youngstown, OH.

GREENAWALT, FRANK F.
Painter. Member: S. Wash. A.; Wash. AC; Wash. WCC. Address in 1929, 1719 Lanier Pl., Washington, DC.

GREENBAUM, DELPHINE BRADT.
(Mrs. William E. Greenbaum). Painter. Member: Fellowship PAFA. Address in 1929, Box 101, Iloilo, Phila.

GREENBERG, FLORIA.
Painter. Born on March 4, 1932. Studied: Cooper Union Art School, NYC; Yale-Norfolk Art School; The Brooklyn Museum Art School. Exhibition: The Denver Art Museum, 1953; The Josyln Art Museum, Omaha, Nebraska, 1953; Columbia Univ., 1965-1966; 55 Mercer, NYC 1970-1974. Collections: Ms. Lucy R. Lippard and other private collectors. Media: Acrylic and paper works with ink. Address in 1980, 118 E 17th St., NY, NY.

GREENBERG, MAURICE.
Illustrator. Born Milwaukee, WI, in 1893. Pupil of Wisconsin School of Art; AIC. Member: Palette and Chisel C. Award: Municipal AL Prize, Chicago, 1927.

GREENBERG, MORRIS.
Etcher, writer and teacher. Pupil of Birge Harrison and Maynard. Member: Municipal AS; Brooklyn SE; AFA. Died June 22, 1949. Address in 1929, 1183 Dean St., Brooklyn, NY.

GREENE, ALBERT V(AN NESSE).
Painter, illustrator and etcher. Born Jamaica, LI, NY, Dec. 14, 1887. Pupil of Corcoran Gallery, ASL of NY, PAFA, Academie de la Grand Chaumiere in Paris. Member: Phila. Sketch C., Fellowship PAFA; Phila. Alliance; Paris AAA; S. Indp. A.; Salons of America. Award: Second landscape prize, PAFA, 1919. Represented in Collection of Fellowship of PAFA. Address in 1929, 704 South Washington Sq.; Philadelphia Sketch Club, 235 South Camac St., Philadelphia, PA; summer, Chester Springs, PA.

GREENE, E. D. E.
Painter. Born 1823 in Boston. He was elected National Academician of Design, New York, 1858. He painted several beautiful female portraits, remarkable for their exquisite finish. He died June 17, 1879, in New York City.

GREENE, FRED STEWART.
Painter. Born North Stonington, CT, June 23, 1876. Pupil of RI School of Design; ASL of NY. Member: Alumni Assoc., RI School of Design; Providence WCC. Specialty, landscapes. Died in 1946. Address in 1929, Ye Hollie Studio; h. 58 Beach St., Westerly, RI; winter, Quidnesset, Belleview, Marion Co., FL.

GREENE, HERBERT.
Collage and architect. Born in Oneonta, NY, in 1929. Studied at Syracuse University, 1947; University of Oklahoma, a Bachelor of Architecture degree in 1952. Taught at the University of Oklahoma, Norman, and the University of Kentucky, Lexington. Exhibitions: University of Oklahoma, Norman, 1960; and at the Oklahoma Art Center, Oklahoma City. Group Exhibitions: Arizona State University, Tempe, 1961; Kansas State University of Agriculture and

370

Applied Science, Manhattan, 1962; University of Kentucky, Lexington, 1963; J. B. Speed Art Museum, Louisville, 1963. Architect of bldgs. in Houston, TX, and Oklahoma.

GREENE, MARIE ZOE.
Sculptor. Born in 1911. Studied: Radcliffe College; New Bauhaus, Chicago; in France; in Italy. Award: gold medal, Cannes, France, 1969. Collections: Roosevelt Univ., Chicago; Sothwest Missouri State College; Radcliffe College, Roosevelt Univ., Chicago.

GREENE, MARY SHEPARD.
See Mary S. G. Blumenschein.

GREENFIELD, E. J. FORREST.
Painter, craftsman, writer and teacher. Born London, England, June 24, 1866. Pupil of Karl Schearer. Member: S. Indp. A.; Needle and Bobbin Club. Address in 1929, The Willows Studios, Point Pleasant, NJ.

GREENING, HARRY C.
Illustrator and cartoon artist. Born in Titusville, PA, in 1876. Pupil of Art Students' League of New York. Address in 1926, 350 Madison Avenue, New York.

GREENLEAF, BENJAMIN.
Painter. Born Sept. 25, 1786, in Haverhill, MA. A painter of portraits who was working in New England about 1817. Died Oct. 29, 1864, in Bradford, MA.

GREENLEAF, RAY.
Illustrator. Member: SI; Salma. C.; AI Graphic A. Died in 1950. Address in 1929, 50 Union Sq.; 263 West 11th St., New York, NY.

GREENLEAF, RICHARD C(RANCH).
Painter. Born Berlin, Germany, Nov. 15, 1887. Pupil of Collin, Courtois, Simon and Menard in Paris. Address in 1929, Lawrence, LI, NY.

GREENLEAF, VIOLA M.
Illustrator. Member: SI. Address in 1929, 263 West 11th St., New York, NY.

GREENMAN, FRANCES CRANMER.
(Mrs. F. C. Greenman). Painter. Born Aberdeen, SD, June 28, 1890. Pupil of Chase, Benson, Castellucho in Paris. Member: S. Washington A. Awards: Gold medal, Corcoran School, 1908; gold medal, MN State Art Com., 1915; first award, MN Inst. of Arts, 1921 and 1922. Address in 1929, 522 East 89th St., New York, NY.

GREENOUGH, BUHLER.
See Mrs. Hardy.

GREENOUGH, HORATIO.
Sculptor. Born Sept. 6, 1805. He made the design used afterwards for the construction of the Bunker Hill Monument; his colossal statue of "Washington" stands in front of the National Capitol. Died Dec. 18, 1852, in Somerville, MA.

GREENOUGH, JOHN.
Painter. Born Nov. 1801 in Boston, MA. A little known portrait painter who worked about 1840. He painted some excellent portraits. Died in Paris in November, 1852.

GREENOUGH, RICHARD S.
Sculptor. Born in Jamaica Plain, MA, April 27, 1819. He was a younger brother of Horatio Greenough. Worked in Paris. Had a studio in Newport, RI. His statue of Benjamin Franklin is in City Hall Square, NY; and his "Boy and Eagle" is in the Boston Athenaeum. He died April 23, 1904, in Rome.

GREENWOOD, CORA.
Painter and craftsman. Born Waltham, MA, July 11, 1872. Pupil of Denman Ross, Alphonse Mucha. Member: Boston SAC. Address in 1929, 38 Cypress Rd., Wellesley Hills, MA; summer, Annisquam, MA.

GREENWOOD, ETHAN ALLEN.
Painter. Born in 1779 and died in 1856. He studied under Edward Savage. Settled in Boston and succeeded Savage in the ownership of the New England Museum. Greenwood frequently signed and dated his portraits "Greenwood Pinx 18." His portrait of Isaiah Thomas is reproduced in Goodspeed's edition of "Dunlap."

GREENWOOD, JOHN.
Painter and engraver. Born in Boston, New England, in 1727; died at Margate, England, 1792. Son of Samuel Greenwood of Boston and nephew of Prof. Isaac Greenwood, of Harvard. In 1752 he went to Surinam, in a clerical capacity, and from there he went to Holland. In Holland he learned to engrave in the mezzotint manner. In 1763 he established himself in London as a painter and engraver of portraits. Greenwood is sometimes referred to as an early American engraver, but there is no evidence that he ever practiced that art in this country. The portrait of Thomas Prince, engraved by Pelham in Boston in 1750, was painted by John Greenwood. In 1760 he engraved a portrait of himself. Greenwood's American portraits were all painted before 1752. His portrait of Benjamin Pickman of Salem, Mass., is dated 1749. His own portrait was engraved by Pether.

GREENWOOD, JOSEPH H.
Painter. Born in Spencer, MA, 1857. Pupil of R. Swain Gifford in New York. Represented by "Autumn," Worcester Art Museum. Address in 1926, 2 Woodbine St., Worcester, MA.

GREENWOOD, MARION.
Painter and muralist. Born April 6, 1909. Studied at Art Students' League with G. Bridgman, F. V. DuMond and J. Sloan, 1924-28; studied lithography with Emil Ganso and mosaic technique with A. Archipenko at Woodstock, NY, 1929-30; and the Academie Colorossi, Paris. First exhibit was at the Assoc. Am. Artists Gallery, NY, in 1944; elected member of the National Acad. of Design in 1959. Taught U. of TN. (1954-55) and Syracuse U. in 1965. Died in Woodstock, NY as a result of an auto accident.

GREENWOOD, WILLIAM RUSSELL.
Painter and etcher. Born Oxford, IN, June 25, 1906. Pupil of Sister Rufinia; Delle Miller. Member: Lafayette AA; Hoosier Salon; Ind. Acad. of Sciences. Address in 1929, 520 South Ninth St.,

Lafayette, IN; summer, Colorad Springs, CO; Manitou, CO.

GREER, BLANCHE.
Painter, illustrator and decorator Born Eldora, IA, Aug. 9, 1884 Pupil of Chase and Eben F. Comins Member; Phila. WCC; Plastic C Fellowship PAFA; Wash. WCC; Phila Alliance; GFLA. Award: Bec prize, Phila. WCC, 1916. Addres in 1929, 4 Franklin Place, Summit NJ.

GREGORI, LUIGI.
Born in Italy, 1819. He came t the United States in 1874 and wa made Art Director of the Ar Department of the University o Notre Dame, IN. Historical an portrait painter; also successfu in fresco work and miniatures.

GREGORY.
This name, as "Gregory Sc," i signed to a very crude line bibl print, illustrating "Zachariah' Vision." As this print was foun loose, there is no indication o place or date, though the apparen date is within the first quarter o the 19th century.

GREGORY, ANGELA.
Sculptor and educator. Born in Ne Orleans, LA, on Oct. 13, 1903 Studied: NY State College o Ceramics, Alfred, NY; Newcom College of Tulane Univ.; Parson School in Paris and Italy; Grand Chaumiere, Paris; with Antoin Bourdelle. Awards: scholarshi Newcomb College; Southern State Art League, 1930, 1931; Louisian Painters and Sculptors, 1929 Collections: Internationa Business Machines; Delgado Museu of Art; Louisiana State Museum Criminal Courthouse, New Orleans Courthouse, Opelousas, Louisiana Louisiana State Univ.; Louisian Library; La Tour Caree, Septmonts France; Louisiana National Bank Baton Rouge; Charity Hospital, Ne Orleans; Silver-Burdette Publishin Company, NY; Louisiana State Univ. Baton Rouge; St. Gabriel Church St. Gabriel, Louisiana; McDonog monument, Civic Center, 1938 Bienville monument, 1955, Ne Orleans, Loiusiana. Address i

1980, 630 Pine St., New Orleans, LA.

GREGORY, DOROTHY LAKE.
Illustrator and etcher. Born Brooklyn, NY, Sept. 20, 1893. Pupil of Robert Henri, Charles W. Hawthorne. Illustrator of "Early Candlelight Stories" and "Happy Hour Series." Address in 1929, 50 Commercial St., Provincetown, MA.

GREGORY, ELIOT.
Painter and sculptor. Born in New York in 1854. He entered Yale, studied in Rome and Paris and exhibited paintings and sculpture in the Paris Salon. Work: "Soubrette," "Children," "Coquetterie," and portraits of Gen. Cullum, Admiral Baldwin, and Ada Rehan. Died in 1915.

GREGORY, FRANK M.
Born in Mansfield, Tioga County, PA, 1848. He studied at the National Academy of Design in 1871, and subsequently studied at the Art Students' League, and with Walter Shirlaw. Worked in etching and design. In 1888 he illustrated "Faust."

GREGORY, JOHN.
Sculptor. Born London, England, May 17, 1879. Arrived in United States c. 1891. Pupil of ASL of NY; Beaux-Arts, Paris; American Academy, Rome. Member: Beaux-Arts Institute of Design (hon.); NSS; NY Arch. Lg; AFA. Awards: Amer. Acad. in Rome Fellowship, 1912-15; NY Arch. Lg. medal in Sculpture, 1921; hon. mention, AIC, 1921; medal, Concord AA, 1926. Work: "Philomela," Metropolitan Museum; "Launcelot and Sir Ector," Corcoran Gallery, Washington, DC. Died in 1958. Address in 1929, 54 West 74th St., New York, NY.

GREGORY, KATHARINE.
See Crosby.

GREGSON, MARIE E(VANGELINE).
Painter. Born New York City, Dec. 16, 1888. Pupil of Twachtman and Cox. Member: NA Women PS; Am. APL. Specialty, portraits and landscapes. Address in 1929, Auburndale, LI, NY.

GREIMS, MARY HEARN.
(Mrs. Herbert S. Greims). Painter. Born in New York. Pupil of Cooper Union, and George Smillie in New York; Philadelphia School of Design for Women; Penna. Academy of Fine Arts, Philadelphia. Member of the Fellowship of the Penna. Academy of Fine Arts, and National Academy of Women Painters and Sculptors. Address in 1926, Ridgefield.

GREINER, CHRISTOPHER.
Portrait painter in oils and miniatures, flourishing in Philadelphia in 1837. Died in 1864. Portrait of "Daniel Billmeyer" is owned by the Historical Society of Penna.

GRENHAGEN, MERTON.
Portrait painter. Born Orihula, WI. Pupil of Chase in Phila.; Laurens in Paris; Chicago AI. Member: Chicago SA; Wis. PS. Represented in University of Wisconsin, Wisconsin Historical Museum, Wisconsin State Capitol Bldg.; University of Illinois, University of Michigan, Milwaukee Public Library. Address in 1929, Oshkosh, WI.

GRESSEL, MICHAEL L.
Sculptor. Born in Wurzburg, Germany, Sept. 20, 1902; US citizen. Study: Art School, Bavaria, with Arthur Schleglmueng; Beaux Arts Inst. of Design, NYC. Work: Metropolitan Museum of Art, New York; Bruckner Museum, Albion, MI; Nat'l. Theatre & Acad., NYC; Nat'l. Theatre, Wash., DC. Comn: Ivory relief portrait for Gen. Eisenhower, 1962; emblem, Harvard Univ.; Legend of Sleepy Hollow, Monument, Tarrytown, NY; and others. Exhibitions: Hudson Valley Art Assn., White Plains, NY 1946-72; AAA, NAD, 1971; Nat'l. Sculpt. Soc., NY, 1972; and others. Awards: Gold Medal - Hudson Valley Art Assn., 1972; others. Mem.: Hudson Valley Art Assn., dir. from 1952; Nat'l. Sculpture Society. Address in 1982, Gressel Place, Armonk, NY.

GRIBBLE, HARRY WAGSTAFF.
Illustrator. Member: SL. Address in 1929, Inter-Theatre Arts, 42 Commerce St., New York, NY.

GRIDLEY, ENOCH G.
This engraver in both stipple and line was in business in New York in 1803-05 inclusive, and at a later date he was working for Philadelphia publishers. The latest date on his plates is 1818.

GRIFFEN, DAVENPORT.
Painter, lithographer and teacher. Born Millbrook, NY, Oct. 5, 1894. Pupil of John W. Norton. Member: Chicago SA. Awards: Jenkins prize, Chicago Artists Exhibition, Chicago, 1928; Chicago Womens Club prize, Chicago, 1929. Address in 1929, Douglas Arcade, 3569 Cottage Grove Ave., Chicago, IL.

GRIFFIN, J(AMES) M(ARTIN).
Painter, etcher and teacher. Born Cork, Ireland, Feb. 20, 1850. Pupil of James Brenan at School of Art, Cork. Member: WCS of Ireland. Address in 1929, 3342 Chestnut St., Oakland, CA.

GRIFFIN, THOMAS B.
Landscape painter.

GRIFFIN, WALTER.
Painter. Born Portland, ME, 1861. Pupil of Collin and Laurens in Paris. Member: ANA 1912; NA 1922; Allied AA; NYWCC; Paris AAA; Salma. C.; AWCS. Awards: Medal of honor. P.-P. Exp., San F., 1915; Sesnan gold medal, PAFA, 1924. Represented in Memorial Art Gallery, Rochester; Buffalo Fine Arts Academy; Brooklyn Art Museum; Luxembourg Gallery, Paris. Died in 1935. Address in 1929, care of American Express Co., Nice. Alpes-Maritime, France.

GRIFFING, MARTIN.
Painter of profiles in color. Born in 1784, and died in 1859. He worked in Massachusetts, Vermont, and New York.

GRIFFITH, BEATRICE FOX.
(Mrs. Charles F. Griffith). Sculptor and craftswoman. Born Hoylake, Cheshire, England, Aug. 6, 1890. Pupil of Grafly; PAFA. Member: Phila. Alliance; NA Women PS; Fellowship PAFA; Plastic C. Work: Marble portrait of Edith Wynne Mathison, Bennett School, Millbrook, NY; marble portrait,

President Ewing, Lahore Union College, Lahore, India; bronze portrait of Herbert Burke, Valley Forge Historical Soc., Valley Forge Memorial Chapel; 75th Anniversary medal for Women's Medical College, Philadelphia; Nat'l Soc. of Colonial Dames of America medal for Sesqui-Centennial Expo., Phila. 1926; bronze trophy, "Swan Dive," Nat'l A.A.U. Swimming Trophy, 1927; illuminated manuscripts for Board of Education, Phila., Art Alliance, Phila., and Valley Forge Historical Society. Address in 1929, "Lynhurst," Ardmore, PA.

GRIFFITH, CONWAY.
Painter. Member of Laguna Beach Art Association. His specialty was marine and desert scenes. He died at Laguna Beach, CA, in 1924.

GRIFFITH, JULIA S(ULZER).
Painter. Born Chicago. Pupil of AIC; Mulhaupt, Noyes and Breckenridge. Member: North Shore AL; Gloucester SA; Ill. AFA; Chicago NJSA; Chicago SA. Died in 1945. Address in 1929, 1318 Sunnyside Ave.; h. 4223 Greenview Ave., Chicago, IL; summer, Eastern Pt. Rd., Gloucester, MA.

GRIFFITH, LILLIAN.
Painter. Born Philadelphia, PA, July 11, 1889. Pupil of Elliott Daingerfield, Henry B. Snell. Award: Spec. mention, Calif. Art Club exhibition, Exposition Park, Los Angeles, 1928. Adddress in 1929, Bonita Ave., Azusa, CA; summer, 409 East Bay Front, Balboa, CA.

GRIFFITH, LOUIS OSCAR.
Landscape painter and etcher. Born Greencastle, IN, Oct. 10, 1875. Pupil of Frank Reaugh; St. Louis School of Fine Arts; AIC; studied in New York and Paris. Member: Chicago Gal. A.; Indiana SP; Brown Co. Art Gal. A.; Boston AG; Chic. SE; Chic. SPS. Awards: Bronze medal for etching, P.-P. Exp., San F., 1915; gold medal, Palette and Chisel C., 1921; Daughters of Indiana prize, 1924, and Ade prize, 1925, Hoosier Salon, Chicago; San Antonio AL, prize, 1929. Represented in Union League Club of Chicago; "Winter," Chicago

Commission purchase; Delgado Museum, New Orleans, LA; Oakland (Calif.) Museum; Indiana State University Collection; Vanderpoel AA. Collection, Chicago. Died in 1956. Address in 1929, Nashville, IN.

GRIFFITH, NINA K.
Painter. Born in Wausau, WI, in 1894. Studied: Art Institute of Chicago; with Charles Rosen, Wayman Adams, and Victor Higgins. Awards: Art Institute of Chicago, Chicago Galleries Assoc. Collections: Wausau High School; Milwaukee-Downer College; Wellesley College; Illinois Veterans Orphanage.

GRIFFITH, W(ILLIAM) A(LEXANDER).
Painter and lecturer. Born Lawrence, KS, Aug. 19, 1866. Pupil of St. Louis School of Fine Arts; Lefebvre and Constant in Paris. Member: Laguna Beach AA. Awards: Wyman Crow gold medal, St. Louis, 1889; first prize, Orange Co. Fair; first prize Southern Calif. Fair, Riverside, 1928; first prize Calif. Artists, Santa Cruz, 1929. Represented in Mulvane Art Gallery, Topeka, Kansas; State Historical Society, Topeka; State Teachers College, Emporia, Kan.; Thayer Memorial Museum, Lawrence, Kansas; University Club, San Diego, CA, High Schools at Santa Ana, Corona, and Long Beach, CA. Died in 1940. Address in 1929, Laguna Beach, CA.

GRIFFITHS, ELSA CHURCHILL.
Miniature painter. Address in 1926, 1114 9th Ave., West, Seattle, WA.

GRIGWARE, EDWARD T.
Painter and illustrator. Born Caseville, MI, April 3, 1889. Pupil of Chicago AFA. Member: Palette and Chisel O.; Oak Park Lg.; Chicago PS. Awards: Charles Worcester prize, Palette and Chisel C., 1925; Edward Rector prize, Indiana Hoosier Salon, 1925; Art Review Prize, 1926; prize, Circle AL, Chicago, 1927; silver medal, Oak Park Lg., 1928; gold medal, Palette and chisel C., 1928. Address in 1929, 180 North Michigan Ave., Chicago, IL; h. 162 Taylor Ave., Oak Park, IL.

GRILO, SARAH.
Painter. Born in Buenos Aires, Argentina, in 1920. Studied in Madrid and Paris from 1948 to 1950. Group Exhibitions: Stedelijk Museum, Amsterdam, 1952; Museu de Arte Moderna, Rio de Janeiro, 1952, 1963; New Delhi, 1953; Museu de Arte Moderna de Sao Paulo, 1953, 1961; Brussels World's Fair, 1958; Instituto de Arte Contemporaneo, Lima, 1958; Carnegie Institute, 1958; The Art Institute of Chicago, 1959; Museu de Arte Moderna, Bahia, Brazil, 1961. Walker Art Ctr., Minneapolis; many more. Awarded Guggenheim Foundation fellowship, 1962; many prizes. In collections of Stedelijk Mus., Amsterdam; museums in Argentina, Venezuela, Colombia, and Wash., DC. Living in NYC in 1970.

GRIMALDI, WILLIAM.
Miniature painter. Born in England, 1750; died in London in 1830. He worked in Paris from 1777-85, and in London, 1786-1824, exhibited yearly. He is said to have visited the United States about 1794, but it is doubtful if he ever came to this country. A portrait of George Washington in military uniform somewhat similar to the Trumbull type, signed "Grimaldi," was sold in Philadelphia.

GRIMES, FRANCES.
Sculptor. Born Braceville, OH, Jan. 25, 1869. Pupil of Pratt Inst. in Brooklyn, Member: NSS, 1912; NA Women PS; AFA. Awards: Silver medal for medals, P.-P. Exp., San F., 1915; McMillin sculpture prize, NA Women PS, 1916. Work: Overmantel, Washington Irving High School, New York City; "Girl by Pool" and "Boy with Duck," Toledo Museum of Art; Busts of Charlotte Cushman, and Emma Willard, Hall of Fame. Died in 1963. Address in 1929, 229 East 48th St., New York, NY.

GRIMES, JOHN.
Painter. Born in 1799 at Lexington, KY. He studied under Matthew Harris Jouett, who painted his portrait, now owned by the Metropolitan Museum. Grimes painted for some time in Nashville,

375

TN. He painted a portrait of
Charles Wetherill, copied by Thomas
Sully about 1853. He died Dec. 27,
1837, in Lexington, KY.

GRIMSON, MRS. SAMUEL BONARIES.
See Hoffman, Malvina.

GRINAGER, ALEXANDER.
Painter. Born Minneapolis, MN, in
1864. Pupil of Royal Academy,
Copenhagen, Denmark; Laurens and
Constant in Paris; studied also in
Norway, Italy and Sicily. Member:
Allied AA; Salma. C. 1908;
Minneapolis A. Lg.; AFA. Died in
1949. Address in 1929,
"Nordstede," Cedar Lane Road,
Ossining, NY; Mohegan Heights,
Tuckahoe, NY.

GRINNELL, G. VICTOR.
Painter. Member: New Haven PCC;
Conn. AFA; Mystic SA. Address in
1929, 40 East Main St., Mystic, CT.

GRISCOM, LLOYD C(ARPENTER).
Painter. Born Riverton, NJ, 1872.
Pupil of Ezra Winter and George P.
Ennis. Member: AWCS. Address in
1929, 580 Park Ave., New York, NY;
summer, Syosset, LI, NY.

GRISWOLD, CARRIE.
Painter. Born in Hartford, CT.
Studied under Leutze in New York
City. A skilled copyist. She died
in Florida.

GRISWOLD, CASIMIR CLAYTON.
Painter. Born in Delaware, OH,
1834. He studied wood engraving in
Cincinnati, but moved to New York
in 1850. He received some
instruction in painting from a
brother and in 1857 exhibited his
first picture at the National
Academy of Design. Specialty,
landscapes and coast scenes. He
lived in Rome, Italy, 1872-86.
Elected Associate Member of the
National Academy in 1866; National
Academy in 1867. He was one of the
original members of the Artists'
Fund Society. His best pictures
were "December," exhibited in 1864;
"A Winter Morning," 1865; "The Last
of the Ice," 1866. Died June 7,
1918, in Poughkeepsie, NY.

GROLL, ALBERT L(OREY).
Landscape painter. Born New York,
Dec. 8, 1866. Pupil of Gysis and
Loefftz in Munich. Member: ANA
1906, NA 1910; NYWCC; AWCS; A. Fund
S.; Salma. C. 1900; Lotos C; NAC;
Allied AA; SPNY. Awards: Morgan
Prize, Salma. C. 1903; hon.
mention, Munich; Shaw prize, Salma.
C. 1904; silver medal, St. Louis
Exp., 1904; Sesnan medal, PAFA
1906; medals, Buenos Aires and
Santiago Exp., 1910; Inness gold
medal, NAD 1912; silver medal,
P.-P. Exp., San F., 1915. Work:
"No Man's Land--Arizona," Corcoran
Gallery, Wash.; "California
Redwoods" and "Washoe Valley,
Nevada," Brooklyn Inst. Mus.;
"Acoma Valley, New Mexico,"
Nat'l. Gallery, Wash.; "Hopi Mesa,"
Pub. Gallery, Richmond, Ind.;
"Laguna River, New Mexico," Art
Mus., Montclair, NJ; "Silver
Clouds," Metropolitan Mus., NY;
"The Milky Way," Minneapolis
Inst. of Arts; "On the Beach," and
"The Garden of the Gods," Lotos
Club; "Storm Cloud, Arizona," Fort
Worth (TX) Mus.; "In New Mexico,"
Boston Mus.; "Arizona Desert," St.
Louis Mus.; "Passing Shadows,"
National Arts Club, NY; "In
Arizona," St. Paul Museum; "Land of
the Sage Brush," Carnegie Museum,
Pittsburgh. Died in 1952. Address
in 1929, 222 West 59th St., NYC.

GROOM, EMILY.
Painter. Born Wayland, MA, March
17, 1876. Pupil of AIC; Brangwyn
in London. Member: Wis. PS;
Concord AA; NYWCC; NA Women PS;
AWCS; Chic. Gal. Assn. Awards:
Gold Medal, St. Paul Inst., 1917;
hon. mention, Milwaukee Art Inst.,
1918; Medal of honor, Milwaukee Art
Institute, 1920; Fausett prize,
Milwaukee AI, 1925; Shortridge
prize, St. Louis, 1926; Bain prize,
Milwaukee AI, 1926; Wisconsin art
purchase prize, 1928, Milwaukee AI.
Work: "Hillside--November," St.
Paul Inst.; and in Milwaukee Art
Inst. Represented in Vanderpoel
AA. Collection, Chicago. Address
in 1929, Genesee Depot; h. 325
Cambridge Ave., Milwaukee, WI.

GROOME, ESTHER M.
Painter and etcher. Born York
County, PA. Pupil of Fuchs,

376

Castaigne, William M. Chase, Henri and Cecilia Beaux. Member: Fellowship, Penna. Academy of Fine Arts. Address in 1926, Library Bldg., State Normal School, West Chester, PA.

GROOMRICH, WILLIAM.
An English landscape painter, who came to this country about 1800. He settled first in New York and later in Baltimore. He painted a view from Harlem Heights and other views around New York. He exhibited in 1811 at Philadelphia with the Society of Artists, giving his address as Baltimore.

GROOMS, REGINALD L.
Painter and teacher. Born Cincinnati, Nov. 16, 1900. Pupil of Cincinnati Art Acad.; Laurens, Pages and Royer at Julian Academy in Paris. Member: Duveneck SPS; Cincinnati AC. Work: "The Harbor," Hughes High School; "The Tuna Fleet," College High School, Cinncinnati; "The Road to the River." Address in 1929, Germania Bldg., 31 East 12th St.; h. 2211 Fulton Ave., Cincinnati, OH.

GROPPER, WILLIAM.
Painter and illustrator. Born New York, Dec. 3, 1897. Pupil of Henri, Bellows, Giles. Awards: MacDonald prize, 1919, for caricature; Collier prize, 1920, for illustration. Illustrated "Chinese White," "Diary of a Physician," "Munchausen, M.D.," "Literary Spotlight," "The Circus Parade," "The Golden Land," 56 drawings of U.S.S.R. Address in 1929, 50 West 10th St., New York, NY.

GROSBECK, DAN SAYRE.
Painter and illustrator. Address in 1926, care of Foster and Kleiser, 287 Valencia St., San Francisco, CA.

GROSE, HELEN M(ASON).
(Mrs. Howard B. Grose, Jr.). Illustrator. Born Providence, Oct. 8, 1880. Pupil of Frank Benson, Will Foote, Converse Wyeth, Elizabeth Shippen, Green Elliott. Member: Prov. AC. Illustrated: "The House of the Seven Gables," "Rebecca of Sunnybrook Farm," "The

Seven Vagabonds" (Houghton Mifflin Co.); "Jolly Good Times," "Jolly Good Times at School" (Little Brown Co.); "Anna Karenina" (Jacobs and Co.). Address in 1929, 39 Benevolent St., Providence, RI.

GROSH, PETER LEHN.
Born near Mechanicsville, Lancaster County, PA, in 1798. Lived at same village, where he was a general utility artist and painter, as well as fruit and flower grower, until 1857. Painted a number of portraits, most of which were produced between 1820 and 1835. He was a versatile man, practically self-taught, though with much native ability in striking a likeness. He died at Petersburg, 1859. He painted Mr. and Mrs. John Beck; Peter and Samuel Grosh; Mrs. Samuel Grosh; and "King and Jester".

GROSS, ALBERT R.
Painter. Member: Charcoal Club. Address in 1926, 1230 St. Paul St., Baltimore, MD.

GROSS, ALICE.
(Alice Gross Fish). Painter. Born in NYC in 1913. Awards: Allied Artists of America; Westchester Art League; New Rochelle Art Assoc. Collection: Berkshire Museum. Exhibitions: Audubon Artists, NAD; AAA; Knickerbocker Artists. Address in 1980, 16 Sutton Pl., NY, NY.

GROSS, IRENE.
(Irene Gross Berzon). Painter. Born in Germany. Awards: National Assoc. of Women Artists, Bocour Artists colors prize and Goldie Paley prize. Collections: Springfield Museum of Fine Arts, MA; St. Vincent's College, Latrobe, PA. Exhibitions: Silvermine, Audubon Artists, Knickerbocker.

GROSS, J.
This reputable engraver of portraits in stipple was working for the "National Portrait Gallery," published in 1834; probably one of the group of engravers brought to Philadelphia by James B. Longacre. J. D. Gross was engraving portraits in mezzotint about the same time, but

the work is so inferior in execution to the stipple work of J. Gross that it must be executed by another man.

GROSS, JULIET WHITE.
(Mrs. John Lewis Gross). Painter, sculptor, draughtsman and writer. Born Philadelphia, PA. Pupil of Philadelphia School of Design; PAFA; Edouard Leon in Paris. Member: Fellowship PAFA; NA Women PS; Phila. Alliance. Awards: Mary Smith prize, PAFA, 1919; Fellowship PAFA prize, 1920; gold medal, Plastic C., 1925; hon. mention (Societe des Artistes Francais), Paris Salon, 1926. Address in 1929, Sellersville, PA.

GROSS, OSKAR.
Painter. Born in Vienna, Austria, 1871. Pupil of Imperial Royal Academy of Fine Arts, Vienna; studied in Munich and Paris. member: Wiener Kunstler-Genossenschaft; Austrian Artists' Assoc. (hon.); Chicago PS; Cliff Dwellers; Palette and Chisel C. Award: Municipal Art Lg. prize, AIC, 1928. Work: "Dreams of Future," Chicago Municipal Commission purchase; "At The Market," Municipal Gallery, Vienna; "Alonzo Stag," University of Chicago; "Fred Bauman" and "Dankmar Adler," Chicago Chap., AIA. Died Aug. 19, 1963. Address in 1929, 19 East Pearson St., Chicago, IL.

GROSS, RICHARD.
Painter. Was born in Munich in 1848, but came to America as a child. Pupil of National Academy in New York. Among his important pictures was a portrait of "William Chambers," "Old Nuremberg," "The Savant," and "The Lady of Shalott."

GROSS, SYDNEY.
Painter, illustrator, writer and teacher. Born Philadelphia, Jan. 9, 1897. Pupil of Arthur Pope. Member: Phila. Sketch C; Friends of Fogg Art Museum. Author of "A Short Outline of European Painting." Address in 1929, 1109 West Lehigh Ave., Philadelphia, PA.

GROSSMAN, EDWIN BOOTH.
Painter. Born Boston, MA, April 9, 1887. Pupil of W. M. Chase and

Richard Miller. Member: S. Indp. A. Died Feb. 17, 1957, in Poughkeepsie, NY.

GROSSMAN, ELIAS M.
Painter, illustrator and etcher. Born Russia, Jan. 8, 1898. Pupil of Cooper Union and Educational Alliance Art School. Address in 1929, 150 Columbia Hgts., Brooklyn, NY.

GROSSMAN, JOSEPH B.
Painter. Born in Russia, 1888. Pupil of Penna. Academy of Fine Arts. Address in 1926, 152: Chestnut St., Philadelphia.

GROSVENOR, THELMA CUDLIPP.
Illustrator. Born Richmond, VA, Oct. 14, 1891. Studied ASL of NY; St. John's Wood School; Royal Academy Schools, London, England. Member: SI; NYS Women A. Covers for "Vanity Fair," "Town and Country," Illustrations for "Saturday Evening Post," "Harper's," "Century," "McClure's," "Vanity Fair." Address in 1929, 455 East 57th St., New York, NY; summer, Grosvenor Cottage, Washington, CT.

GROTH, JOHN.
Illustrator. Born in Chicago, in 1908. Went to the AIC and the ASL. His first piece, a cartoon, was published in 1930 in Ballyhoo magazine. His ink and wash illustrations appeared in Holiday and Esquire and in several books such as The Grapes of Wrath and War and Peace. Among his many honors are citations from the U.S. Army and USAF as a result of his work as a War Correspondent during World War II, in Korea, Indochina, the Congo, Santo Domingo, and Vietnam. His work has been shown and is owned by many prestigious museums including the Metropolitan Museum of Art and the Museum of Modern Art.

GROVE, DAVID.
Illustrator. Born in Wash., DC, he went to Syracuse Univ. and began a career as a photographer in the early 1960's. He settled in Paris in 1964 as a free-lance illustrator. Returning to the U.S. in 1969, he presently lives in San

Fran. where he is President of the S of I of San Fran. His artwork appears frequently in books for Ballantine, Avon, Dell, Fawcett, and Bantam, earning him awards in Los Angeles and New York.

GROVE, SHELTON GILBERT.
Painter. Born in Clinton, NY, 1805; died in Rochester, 1885. Studied medicine, but gave it up for painting, his work being mostly portraiture.

GROVER, OLIVER DENNETT.
Painter. Born Earlville, IL, 1861. Student of University of Chicago; studied painting at Royal Academy, Munich; Duveneck School, Florence, Italy; and in Paris. Received first Yerkes prize for painting "Thy Will Be Done," Chicago, 1892; executed mural decorations, Branford, Conn., Mem. Library, 1897; Blackstone Mem. Library, Chicago, 1903. His pictures are in many public collections. Elected Associate Member of the National Academy, 1913. Address in 1926, 9 E. Ontario St., Chicago, IL.

GROVES, DOROTHY LYONS.
Painter. Born Condersport, PA. Pupil of John Carlson; Harry Leith-Ross. Member: New Haven PCC; New Haven BPC; Am. APL. Address in 1929, 80 Vista Terrace, New Haven, CT.

GROVES, HANNAH CUTLER.
Painter and teacher. Born Camden, NJ, Dec. 30, 1868. Pupil of William M. Chase and School of Design, Phila. Member: Phila. Alliance; Plastic C. Died in 1952. Address in 1929, Pressor Bldg., 1714 Chestnut St., Philadelphia, PA; h. 237 Hopkins Ave., Haddonfield, NJ.

GROW, RONALD.
Sculptor. Born 1934 in Wooster, OH. Studied at U. of Colorado; earned MA at UCLA. Taught at U. of Mexico since 1962. Work: In private collections. Exhib.: Cal. State Fair, 1961; Long Beach Mus. of Art; U. of New Mexico; Scripps College; Syracuse U.; Downey Mus. of Art, Cal.; UCLA; Brandeis U. Awards: Sculpture, Cal. State Fair, 1961; Long Beach Mus. of Art

and LA and Vicinity Exhib., both 1962.

GRUB, HENRY.
Painter and sculptor. Born in Baltimore, MD, 1884. Pupil of Maynard, Ward and Bridgman. Member: New York Society of Independent Artists. Address in 1926, 53 Greenwich Ave., New York.

GRUELLE, RICHARD B.
Landscape painter. Born in 1851. Among his best known paintings are "The Passing Storm" at Indianapolis Public Library; "A Gloucester Inlet" at the Herron Art Institute; "In Verdure Clad" at Public Gallery, Richmond, IN. He died in Indianapolis in 1915.

GRUENBERG, RUTH.
Painter. Exhibited at the Penna. Academy of Fine Arts, 1922. (Water colors.) Address in 1926, 3211 Oxford St., Philadelphia.

GRUGER, FREDERIC R.
Illustrator. Born in Philadelphia in 1871. Studied at the Pennsylvania Academy of Fine Arts with Wm. Glackens, Maxfield Parrish. First work in "Phila. Ledger;" career associated with magazines, especially "Saturday Evening Post." Address in 1926, 57 West 57th St., New York. Died March 1953 in New York City.

GRUMIEAU, EMILE J(ACQUES).
Painter, illustrator and teacher. Born Gosselies, Hainaut, Belgium, May 17, 1897. Pupil of AIC. Member: Chicago SA. Address in 1929, 149 East Huron St., Chicago, IL; summer, Glenwood, IL.

GRUNEWALD, GUSTAVUS.
Painter. Born Dec. 19, 1805, in Germany. A Pennsylvania German artist who was painting landscapes in Bethlehem, Penna., in 1832. Died Aug. 1, 1878, in Germany.

GRUPPE, C(HARLES) P(AUL).
Painter. Born Picton, Canada, Sept. 3, 1860. Studied in Holland; chiefly self-taught. Member: NYWCC; AWCS; AC Phila.; Salma. C. 1893; NAC; Rochester AC; AFA; Pulchre Studio, The Hague. Awards: Gold medal, Rouen; gold medal, AAS

1902; two gold medals, Paris; silver medals for oils and for water color, St. Louis Exp., 1904; bronze medal, Appalachian Exp., Knoxville, 1910; Tuthill prize, AIC, 1917. Work: "The Old Water Wheel," Brooklyn Institute Museum: "A Dutch Canal," Inst. of Arts, Detroit; National Arts Club, New York; Art Club of Philadelphia; "The Meadow Brooks," National Gallery, Washington, DC; "Homeward Way," Reading (PA), Museum; "It Sure is Jan," Butler Art Institute, Youngstown, OH. Died in 1940. Address in 1929, 1112 Carnegie Hall; h. 138 Manhattan Ave., New York, NY.

GRUPPE, EMILE A(LBERT).
Painter. Born Rochester, NY, Nov. 23, 1896. Pupil of John Carlson, Bridgman, Richard Miller, Charles Chapman. Member: Salma. C. Address in 1929, 138 Manhattan Ave., New York, NY; summer, Reed Studios, Gloucester, MA.

GRUPPE, KARL H(EINRICH).
Painter and sculptor. Born Rochester, NY, March 18, 1893. Son of Charles Gruppe, the painter. Lived childhood in Holland. Returned to U.S. as adult. Pupil of Karl Bitter. Member: NSS; Arch. Lg. of NY. Award: Helen Foster Burnett prize, 1926. Work: Final figure, Italian towers, P.-P. Exp., San F., 1915; Memorial Tablet, City Club, New York; Memorial Tablet, Princeton Charter Club; Portrait Bust, Dean of Adelphi College, Brooklyn, NY, 1929. Address in 1929, 149 Sixth Ave., New York, NY.

GRYGUTIS, BARBARA.
Sculptor and ceramist. Born on Nov. 7, 1946. Studied: Univ. of Arizona, Tucson, AZ; Travel-study in Japan. Awards: Tucson Art Center, AZ, 1968, 1970, 1971, 1975. Exhibitions: Univ. of Arizona Museum of Art, 1971; Graphic Arts Gallery, Tuscon, AZ, 1972; Harlan Gallery, Tucson, 1975. Commissions: Union Bank Branch Office, Tucson; La Placita Shopping Center, Tucson; Navaho County Governmental Complex, Holbrook, AZ (joint project with Charles Hardy).

Media: Clay and glass. Address in 1980, 273 N. Main St., Tucson, AZ.

GSCHWINDT, R.
Painter. He painted some excellent portraits in New Orleans in 1859 and 1860; studio at 82 Camp Street. No date could be found regarding his birth or death.

GUARINA, SALVATOR ANTHONY.
Painter and etcher. Born in Sicily, Italy. Pupil of Whittaker and Blum, and member of the Washington Art Club. Address in 1926, care of Salmagundi Club, New York.

GUDERBROD, LOUIS A(LBERT).
Sculptor. Born Middletown, CT, Sept. 20, 1872. Pupil of Yale Art School; ASL of NY, under Mary Lawrence and Augustus Saint Gaudens; Dampt in Paris. Member: NSS 1902; NY Arch. Lg. 1902; Conn. AFA; New Haven PCC; Lyme AA. Awards: Silver medal, Charleston Exp., 1902; gold medal, Panama-Pacific Exp., San Francisco, CA, 1915. Assistant to Saint Gaudens in Paris. Director of Sculpture, Charleston Exp., 1902. Work: Anderson Prison Monument for New York State at Andersonville, GA; "Henry Clay Work Memorial," Hartford, CT; portrait memorials in Bristol and Meriden public libraries; Weaver High School, Hartford; Grace Hospital, New Haven; Mayflower tablet in State Capitol, Hartford. Address in 1929, 69 Silver St., Meriden, CT.

GUE, DAVID JOHN.
Portrait, landscape and marine painter. Born in Farmington, New York, Jan. 17, 1836. He painted the portraits of Grant, Lincoln and Beecher. He died in Brooklyn, New York, May 1, 1917.

GUERIN, JULES.
Painter and illustrator. Born St. Louis, MO, Nov. 18, 1866. Pupil of Constant and Laurens in Paris. Member: ANA 1916; AWCS; NYWCC; SI 1901; Nat. Inst. AL; The Players; NY Arch. Lg. 1911; Mural P.; NY Art Com.; Beaux Arts Inst. of Design; AFA. Awards: First Yerkes medal, Chicago; hon. mention, Paris Exp., 1900; hon. mention for drawings,

Pan-Am. Exp., Buffalo, 1901; silver medal, St. Louis Exp., 1904; Beck prize, Phila. WCC, 1913; gold medal, P.-P. Exp., San F., 1915. Specialty, architectural subjects and decoration. Director of color, Panama-Pacific Exp., San Francisco, 1915. Painted decorations in Lincoln Memorial, Washington, DC, and Penn. Station, NY; decorations in Federal Reserve Bank, San Francisco; murals in Illinois Merchant's Trust Co., Chicago; Liberty Mem., Kansas City, MO; and Union Trust Co., Cleveland; murals, Terminal Building, Cleveland. Address in 1929, 50 E. 23rd St.; h. 24 Gramercy Park, NY.

GUERNSEY, ELEANOR LOUISE.
Sculptor. Born in Terre Haute, IN, 1878. Pupil of Art Institute of Chicago. Member: Art Students' League of Chicago; Ind. Sculptors' Society. Address in 1926, James Milliken University, Decatur, IL.

GUGLER, FRIDA.
Painter. Born Milwaukee, WI Pupil of AIC; studied in Paris, Munich and Italy. Work: "Landscape," Vanderpoel Memorial Association, Chicago, Ill.; "Landscape," Milwaukee Art Institute, Milwaukee, WI. Address in 1929, 2 Washington Mews, New York, NY.

GUGLIELMO, VICTOR.
Sculptor. Born in Italy. He has assisted Frank Happersburger in his work in San Francisco.

GUILD, FRANK S.
Painter. Member: Philadelphia AC; Phila. Sketch C. Died in 1929. Address in 1929, 721 Walnut St., Philadelphia, PA.

GUILD, LURELLE VAN ARSDALE.
Painter, illustrator and writer. He was born in New York City, Aug. 19, 1898. Pupil of Bridgman. Member: SI; GFLA; A. Directors C. Award: Hon. mention for water color, Art Directors Club, 1924. Works: Illustrations for House and Garden, Country Life, Ladies' Home Journal, McCall's and Designer. Author of "The Geography of American Antiques" (Doubleday, Doran and Co.). Address in 1929, 31 Park Ave., New York, NY; h.

Revonah Manor, Urban St., Stamford, CT.

GUILLETT, MADAME J.
French miniature painter who flourished in New York, 1839-42. She also painted many miniatures in Virginia.

GUINNESS, BENJAMIN MRS.
Painter. Member: National Academy of Women Painters and Sculptors.

GUINZBURG, FREDERIC V(ICTOR).
Sculptor, craftsman, lecturer and teacher. Born New York City, June 18, 1897. Pupil of Victor David Brenner; Ernesto Grazzeri in Rome. Member: NSS (asso.); NY Arch. Lg. Award: Hon. mention, Concord AA, 1924; bronze medal, Sesqui-Centennial, Expo., Phila., 1926. Address in 1929, 21 West 89th St., New York, NY; Chiselhurst Studio, Chappaqua, Westchester Co., NY.

GUISLAIN, J. M.
Painter. Born in Louvain, Belgium, 1882. Address in 1926, 725 West 172d St., New York, NY.

GULDBERG, CHRISTIAN A(UGUST).
Painter and architect. Born Madagascar, April 13, 1879. Member: NY Arch. C; Montclair AA. Address in 1929, 7 St. Luke Pl., Montclair, NJ.

GULLAGER, CHRISTIAN.
Portrait painter. Born March 1, 1759, in Copenhagen, Denmark. He painted excellent portraits in Boston from 1789. He painted portraits of President Washington, Geo. Richards Minot, Col. John May, Rev. James Freeman, Dr. Eliakin Morse, David West, Reb. Ebenezer Morse and Benjamin Goldthwait. His portraits are signed "Gullager." Died Nov. 12, 1826, in Phila.

GULLEDGE, JOSEPHINE.
Painter. Member: Washington Water Color Club. Address in 1926, Fairmount Seminary, Washington, DC.

GULLIVER, MARY.
Painter and teacher. Born Norwich, CT, Sept. 9, 1860. Pupil of Boston Museum of Fine Arts School; Grundmann, Niemeyer, Vonnoh and

Crowninshield; Whistler, Collin, Delance, Callot, Lazar and Prinet in Paris; Delecluse and Colarossi Academies, Paris; studied in England, Holland, Italy, Spain, Germany. Member: Copley S, 1883. Teacher in Drawing and Painting and History of Art, Mary A. Burnham School for Girls, Northampton, MA, for 10 years; head of department of Fine Arts, Rockford College, 1911-1919. Specialty, portrait and genre painting. Address in 1929, 1115 Orange Ave., Eustis, FL.

GUNN, ARCHIE.
Painter, illustrator, etcher and teacher. Born Taunton, Somersetshire, England, Oct. 11, 1863. Pupil of Archibald Gunn, P. Calderon in London. Address in 1929, 120 West 49th St., New York, NY; summer, Inglesea Bungalow, East Rockaway, LI, NY.

GUNN, EDWIN.
Painter. Member: Salmagundi Club, New York. Address in 1926, 252 Mt. Hope Ave., New York, NY.

GURDUS, LUBA.
Painter. Born in Bialystok, Poland in 1914. Studied: Art School, Lausanne, Switzerland; Academy of Art, Warsaw, Poland; Institute of Fine Arts, NY Univ.; in Germany. Award: Warsaw Academy of Art, 1938. Collections: Tel-Aviv, Israel, Municipal College; Howard Univ.; Jewish Museum of NY; Israeli Consulate; Stephen West House, NY.

GUSSOW, BERNARD.
Painter and teacher. Born in Russia, Jan. 2, 1881. Pupil of Bonnat in Paris. Member: S. Indp. A.; Modern Artists of America. Represented in Newark (NJ) Museum; Harrison Gallery, Los Angeles Museum; Barnes Foundation, Phila. Died in 1957. Address in 1929, 108 West 75th St., New York, NY.

GUSTIN, PAUL MORGAN.
Painter, illustrator, etcher and teacher. Born Fort Vancouver, Wash., 1886. Member: PS. Work: Group of murals, Roosevelt High School, Seattle; "Road Through Forest," Art Gallery, University of Washington; "April Afternoon," Washington State College. Address

in 1929, care Grand Central Art Galleries, New York, NY.

GUSTON, PHILIP.
Painter. Born June 27, 1913, in Montreal, Canada. Studied at Otis Art Inst., LA; Hon. D.F.A. from Boston Univ. Taught at University of Iowa, Washington University in St. Louis, NYU, Pratt, Boston University and Brandeis University. Awards: Carnegie Inst. (1945); Guggenheim (1947 & 1968); Ford Foundation Grant (1959); Brandeis Award (1980). Exhibited at University of Iowa; School of Mus. of Fine Arts, Boston; Muson-Williams-Proctor Inst., Utica. In collections of City Art Museum, St. Louis; Philips Collection (Wash., DC); Worchester (MA) Art Mus.; Whitney; MOMA; and Tate Gallery, London.

GUTHERS, CARL.
Painter. Born in Switzerland in 1844. He came to America in 1851, where he received his art training. In 1868 he went to Paris. His work was mural, portrait, and genre subjects. Many portraits in the Minnesota State Capitol; mural paintings in the Library of Congress, Washington, DC. He died in 1907 in Washington, DC.

GUTIERREZ, LOUIS.
Painter and collage. Born 1933 in Oakland, CA. Studied at San Jose State, BA 1957; Instituto San Miguel Allende, Mexico, MFA 1958. Work: San Fran. Mus. of Art; Diablo Valley College; San Jose State Coll. Exhibit.: San Fran. Art Center, 1962-64; CA State Fair, 1960-64; San Fran. Mus. of Art, 1960-64. Awards: San Fran. Art Festival 1962; Art Inst. Annual, San Fran.; Ford Foundation award. Taught at Lincoln U. (CA) and Acad. of Art, S.F. Works in low relief construction.

GUTMAN, ELIZABETH.
Painter. Born Baltimore. Pupil of Breckenridge, H. B. Snell, S. E. Whiteman. Member: Baltimore WCC. Address in 1929, Pikesville, MD.

GUTMANN, BERNHARD.
Painter, etcher and craftsman. Born Hamburg, Germany, Sept. 26,

1869. Studied in Dusseldorf and Karlsruhe, Germany, and in Paris. Member: Allied AA; Salma. C.; Silvermine GA. Died in 1936. Address in 1929, Silvermine (R. F. D. No. 43), New Canaan, CT.

GUY, FRANCIS.
Born in 1760 in England. Arrived 1795 is US. Painted landscapes in Baltimore and Philadelphia about 1800. He was originally a tailor, and was self-taught. His style was crude and harsh. He exhibited a number of drawings and paintings at the Exhibition in 1811 of the Society of Artists in Philadelphia. About 1817 he returned to Brooklyn, NY, where he died Aug. 12, 1820.

GUY, SEYMOUR J.
Painter. Born in England, Jan. 16, 1824. He came to America in 1854 and settled in New York. Pupil of Ambrosino Jerome in London. He was elected a member of the National Academy of Design in 1865. His portrait of the artist Chas. Loring Elliott (1868) is in the Metropolitan Museum. He painted many scenes and incidents drawn from childlife, among them "The Good Sister," "The Little Stranger," and "The Little Orange Girl." He died Dec. 10, 1910, in New York City.

GUYSI, ALICE V.
Painter. Born Cincinnati, OH. Pupil of Colarossi Academy, and of Harry Thompson in Paris. Address in 1926, 209 Longfellow Ave., Detroit, MI.

GUYSI, JEANNETTE.
Painter and craftswoman. Born Cincinnati, OH. Pupil of Colarossi Academy and of Harry Thompson in Paris. Died in 1940. Address in 1926, 209 Longfellow Ave., Detroit, MI.

GWATHMEY, ROBERT.
Painter. Born Jan. 24, 1903, in Richmond, VA. Studied at Maryland Inst. (Baltimore); Penn. Acad. of Fine Arts (Phil.); NC State College, Raleigh. Awards from 48 States Mural Contest (1939); Carnegie; Corcoran Gallery of Art, Wash., DC, (1957). Taught at Carnegie Inst. of Tech, PA; Cooper

Union; Boston Univ. Exhibited at Brooklyn Museum (1932), ACA Gallery (many times 1933-76). In collections of U. of Georgia; Boston Mus. of Fine Arts; IBM; Mus. of Fine Arts, Springfield, MA; Whitney; L.A. County Mus.; Brooklyn Mus.; U. of Texas, Austin; Carnegie; Birmingham Mus. of Art and Museum de Arte Moderna de Sao Paulo, Brazil.

GYBERSON, INDIANA.
Painter. She studied with Chase in LI, NY; and in Paris. In 1912 was working on painting for Salon; suffered eye injury. Later had studio in Chicago, IL. Member: Chicago PS; Chicago Gal. A.; AFA.

GYER, E. H., JR.
Painter and illustrator. Born Tacoma, Oct. 15, 1900. Pupil of G. Z. Heuston. Member: Tacoma FAA. Award: Hon. mention, Tacoma FAA., 1922. Address in 1929, 5811 South Junett St., Tacoma, WA.

GYRA, FRANCIS JOSEPH JR.
Painter. Born in Newport, RI, Feb. 23, 1914. Study: RI School of Design, Dipl.; Parsons Sch. of Design, Paris; Brighton College of Arts & Crafts, Sussex, Eng.; Froebel Inst.; Roehampton, Eng.; Univ. of Hawaii; McNeese State College; Keene State College, BS. Work: Providence (RI) Art Mus.; Tennessee Fine Arts Center. Exhib.: Int. WC Exhib., Art Inst. of Chic., 1938-40; 1st Art Ann., Northern New England, Canaan, NH, 1969; Stratton Arts Festival, VT, 1970; and others. Awards: Art Assn. of Newport, RI, 1938; Eva Gebhard-Gourgand Foundation grants, 1966-72. Teaching: Woodstock (VT) Union & Dist. Schools, 1949- 69; VT State Dept. of Educ., 1954-70; Woodstock (VT) Sch. Dist., from 1969. Mem.: Int'l. Inst. Arts & Letters; others. Address in 1982, Linden Hall, Woodstock, VT.

HAAG, C.
Miniature painter, who flouished in New York about 1848, and exhibited at the National Academy, New York.

HAAG, CHARLES OSCAR.
Sculptor. Born Norrkoping, Sweden, 1867. Pupil of Junghaenel Ziegler and Injalbert. Awards: Bronze and silver medal, first prize, Swedish-American Exhibition. Work: "Cornerstone of the Castle" in Winnetka; "Accord," Metropolitan Museum, New York; series of fountains, among them the "American Fountain," at Johnstown, PA. Sculptor of Symbolic and Poetic Art and series of figures and groups in wood called "the spirits from the woods." Died in 1934.

HAAPANEN, JOHN NICHOLS.
Landscape painter. Born Nyantic, CT, Oct. 13, 1891. Pupil of E. L. Major, W. Felton Brown, A. K. Cross. Member: Boston AC; Copley S. Address in 1929, Boothbay Harbor, ME.

HABBEN, JOSEPH E.
Painter and illustrator. Born Britt, IA, March 25, 1895. Member: ASL of NY. Address in 1929, care of J. M. Forkner, R. R. 2, Anderson, IN.

HABERGRITZ, GEORGE JOSEPH.
Painter and sculptor. Born in NYC, June 16, 1909. Study: NAD; Cooper Union, grad.; Acad. Grande Chaumiere. Work: Butler Mus., Youngstown, Ohio; Safad Mus., Israel; Jewish Mus., London; Purdue Univ.; Wilberforce Univ. Exhib.: Albright Mus., Ptg. Ann., Buffalo, NY, 1938-40; Am. WC Soc. Ann., 1947-49; Nat'l Assn. Painters in Casein, 1947-74; NAD, 1948-51; others in US and Bogata, Colombia. Awards: Gold medal, drawing, NAD, 1938; Grumbacher awards, Nat'l Soc. of Painters in Casein, 1968, 70, 72, 74. Teaching: Dir, Sch. of Continuing Art Educ., 1968 to pres.; lecturer in Africa, So. Pac., India, 1957 to pres.; ASL Instr. in Ptg., 1960-64; Workshop Prof. Artists, 1967 to pres; others. Mem.: Nat'l Soc. of Painters in Casein. Media: Oil wood, metal, collage, found

material. Address in 1982, 150 Waverly Place, NYC.

HACK, GWENDOLYN DUNLEVY KELLEY.
(Mrs. Charles Hack). Painter. Born in Columbus, OH, in 1877. Educated at Art Students' League of NY; in Paris studied under Mesdames Debillement and Gallet. Specialties, miniatures on ivory, pastels, bas-reliefs etc.; painted portraits on ivory, Queen of Italy, 1895, and received decoration; exhibited paintings in Paris Salon; National Academy of Design; Chicago Art Institute; Cincinnati Art Museum and in other cities; also in Nashville and Omaha expositions. Address in 1926, 12 West 93d Street, New York.

HACK, KONRAD F.
Illustrator. Born in Chicago in 1945. He attended the AIC and University of Chicago between 1964 and 1968. He produced movie promotion art and sports advertisements for WGN-TV in Chicago. Serving as a combat artist in Vietnam with the 19th Military History Detachment, he earned the Bronze Star and Army Commendation Medal. Recently he has illustrated books for the Franklin Library and the Hamilton Mint for whom he also designed a set of bicentennial pewter plates.

HACKETT, GRACE EDITH.
Painter, illustrator, and craftsman. Born Boston, Sept. 22, 1874. Pupil of MA. Normal Art School in Boston; H. B. Snell in Europe. Member: Boston SAC; NYWCC; Copley S; Eastern AA; AFA. Supervisor of drawing in public schools, Boston. Died in 1955.

HADEN, ELMER S.
Painter. Born in United States. Pupil of Flameng in Paris. Address in 1926, Nyack, NY.

HADLEY, MARY HAMILTON.
Painter. Address in 1926, 355 Willow Street, New Haven, CT.

HADLEY, PAUL.
Painter and draftsman. Born Indianapolis, IN. Pupil of PA Museum, Phila. Member: Ind. AC; Chicago Gal. A; Hoosier Salon.

Work: Decoration in Eagle's Club, Indianapolis, IN.; design for Indiana flag accepted by the legislature, 1917. Address in 1929, 44 Union Trust Bldg., Indianapolis; h. Mooresville, IN.

HAENEL, WILLIAM M.
Painter and teacher. Born Chicago, April 26, 1885. Pupil of Walter Ufer; Leo Putz in Munich. Member: Chicago AC; GFLA. Award: William Ormonde Thompson prize, AIC, 1928. Address in 1929, 19 Pearson Street, h. 421 St. James Pl., Chicago, IL.

HAFFNER, J. J.
Painter. Member: Boston SWCP. Address in 1929, 26 Hillard Street, Cambridge, MA.

HAFNER, CHARLES ANDREW.
Sculptor. Born Omaha, NE, Oct. 28, 1888. Pupil of Edmund C. Tarbell, F. W. Benson, Philip Hale at School of Museum FA, Boston; James Earle Fraser, ASL, NY; Solon Borglum, Edward McCartan, Beaux Art Inst. Member: NY Arch. Lg.; Allied AA; Artist Fellowship, Inc.; Numismatic S. of NY. Works: Terra cotta pediment, Rivoli Theatre, New York; marble fountain "The Dance," Albee Theatre, Brooklyn, NY; Peter Pan Fountain (bronze), Paramount Theatre, NY; three medals Numismatic Museum, NY.

HAGEN, LOUISE.
Painter, lecturer, and teacher. Born Chicago, IL, March 16, 1888. Pupil of Henri. Member: N. A. Women PS. Lectures on Contemporary American Art illustrated by paintings. Address in 1929, 51 West 10th Street, New York, NY.

HAGENDORN, MAX.
Painter, draftsman, and teacher. Born Stuttgart, Germany. June 27, 1870. Pupil of Faller, Kurtz, Seubert in Stuttgart; Gebhard Fugel in Munich; Royal Academy of Fine and Industrial Arts, Stuttgart. Member: AFA. Award: Prize, St. Louis Exp., 1904. Address in 1929, 46 Bullard Street, Sharon, MA.

HAGER, LUTHER GEORGE.
Illustrator and cartoonist. Born in Terre Haute, IN, in 1885. Died 1945. Address in 1926, 655 Empire Building, Seattle, WA.

HAGGIN, BEN ALI.
Portrait and figure painter. Born in 1882. Associate Member of the National Academy. His charming portrait of Miss Kitty Gordon is now famous, and his portrait of Mary Garden as Thais sold for $25,000. It is in the painting of the nude that he has had his greatest success. Member of National Arts Club, NY; Portrait Painter. Awards: third Hallgarten prize NAD 1909. Died in 1951. Address in 1929, 62 Washington News, NYC; Great Neck, LI and Tannersville, NY.

HAGUE, MAURICE STEWART.
Landscape painter. Born Richmond, Jefferson Co., OH, May 12, 1862. Member: S. Indp. A. Studied medicine 3 yr. before changing to art, with portrait painting and modeling, and beginning landscape painting by 1895. Exhibited at Boston, St. Louis, Minneapolis, Buffalo, Cleveland, and Columbus. Work in Columbus Gallery of Fine Arts, and many private collections.

HAHN, NANCY COONSMAN.
Sculptor. Born St. Louis, MO, Aug. 28, 1892. Pupil of Zolnay and Grafly. Member: St. Louis AG. Work: Missouri State Memorial presented by the State to the French Government; Kinkaid Memorial Fountain and bench ends. City of St. Louis: "Maidenhood" and Reedy Memorial, St. Louis Art Museum; H. H. Culver Memorial, Colver, IN; Barclay Memorial, New London, MO, Doughboy War Memorial, Memphis, TN. Address in 1929, 68 Vandeventer Place, St. Louis, MO.

HAHS, PHILIP B.
Painter. Born in Reading, PA, in 1853. He commenced preparing for a business career in Philadelphia, but employed his leisure in artistic experiments, and about 1872 he joined the Philadelphia Sketch Club. Here Mr. Hahs went on with his studies and also continued to receive instruction from Mr. Thomas Eakins. Mr. Hahs was considered almost unrivalled in technique. He was a regular

contributor to the exhibitions, until at the exhibition of the Phila. Society of Artists in 1881, in which he was represented by a landscape and four genre paintings, he was recognized as the foremost among the young artists of his period. About this time he was attacked by a severe illness, terminating, after some months, in his death, which occurred in Philadelphia, 1882.

HAIDT, JOHN VALENTINE.
Born in Germany in Oct. 4, 1700. He emigrated to America and joined the Moravian Church. A gallery of his portraits and several other pictures are still preserved at Bethlehem, Penna. He died Jan. 18, 1780. Also religious painter.

HAIG, MABEL GEORGE.
Painter. Born Blue Earth, MN., May 31, 1884. Pupil of W. L. Judson, Helena Dunlap, Anna Hills. Member: Laguna Beach AA; Calif. WCS.

HAIGH, ELIZA VOORHIS.
Painter. Born Brooklyn, NY, April 12, 1865. Pupil ASL, New York and Paris. Member: CT AFA. Address in 1929, Winsted, CT.

HAILMAN, JOHANNA K. WOODWELL.
(Mrs. James D. Hailman). Painter. Born Pittsburg, 1871. Member: AFA; NA Women PS; Pittsburgh AA. Awards: Second prize, Pittsburgh AA, 1911; silver medal, P.-P. Exp., San F., 1915. Represented in Fine Arts Dept. Collection, Carnegie Institute, Pittsburgh. Address in 1929, 7010 Penn Ave., Pittsburgh.

HAINES, BOWEN AYLESWORTH.
Painter and illustration. Born in Canada, Dec. 21, 1858. Pupil of Frank Smith and Mrs. Emma Lampert Cooper. Member: Rochester AC. Address in 1929, Hilton, NY.

HAINES, FRED STANLEY.
Etcher. Born 1879. Member: Chicago SE; CA PM. Died 1960. Address in 1929, Thornhill, Ontario, Canada.

HAINES, MARIE BRUNER.
Painter, illustrator, craftman, writer, lecturer, and teacher Born Cincinnati, OH, Nov. 16, 1885

Pupil of Noble, Volk, Francis Jones, DuMond, Dimitri Romanofsky. Member: Southern SAL; TX. FAA. Awards: 1st portrait prize, Southern artists Exhibition, Atlanta, 1917; 1st prize figure painting, Macon, 1920. Represented in Agricultural and Mechanical College, College Station, TX; Museum of New Mexico, Santa Fe, gesso panels; decorations in theatre, Bryan, TX. Specialty, mural decoration in gesso. Address in 1929, College Station, TX; summer Taos, NM.

HAINES, WILLIAM.
This excellent engraver of portraits in the stipple manner was born June 21, 1778. He came from England to Phila. in 1802. He opened a studio at No. 178 Spruce Street, and advertised that he painted portraits in water colors "in a style entirely new in the United States," and his work of this description proves that Haines was a master of this branch of his art. He produced a number of good portrait plates for American publishers, and he also drew for other engravers. Haines returned to England about 1809, as his name disappears from the Philadelphia directory of 1810, and a subject plate engraved by "W. Haines" was published in London in 1809. He died July 24, 1848.

HAKE, OTTO EUGENE.
Painter and illustrator. Born in Germany, Dec. 17, 1876. Pupil of AIC; Morisset at Colarossi's in Paris: Debschitz in Munich. Member: Palette and Chisel C.; Chicago SA; GFLA. Represented in Municipal Art Collection. Address in 1929, 1012 North Dearborn St., Chicago, IL.

HALBERG, CHARLES EDWARD.
Marine painter. Born Gothenburg, Sweden, Jan. 15, 1855. Member: Chicago SA; Swedish-American AS. Ward: Rosenwald purchase prize ($200), AIC 1914. Represented in Stockholm Museum and Gothenburg Museum. Address in 1929, 1114 North Parkside Ave., Austin, IL.

HALBERT, A.
Engraver. He was a nephew of J.F.E. Prud'homme and was probably a pupil of that engraver. In 1825 he was working for the Harper Bros. in New York, and in 1838 he was in the employ of the engraving firm of Rawdon, Wright & Hatch, of the same city. Halbert was a good line engraver of portraits and vignettes; as his signed plates are very few in number he was probably chiefly engaged in bank-note work.

HALBERT, SAMUEL.
Painter. Exhibited paintings at the academy of FA, Phila., 1921, in "Exhibition of Paintings Showing the Later Tendencies in Art" Address in 1926, 128 W. 85th St., New York.

HALE, ELLEN DAY.
Painter. Born Worcester, MA, Feb. 11, 1855; daughter of Rev. Edward Everett Hale. Member: Wash. SA; Wash. WCC; Chicago SE; Charleston EC; North Shore AA; Wash. AC. Award: Third Corcoran prize, S. Wash. A., 1905. Work: "The Lily," St. Paul Institute. Died in 1940.

HALE, GARDNER.
Painter. Born Chicago, Feb. 1, 1894. Member: NY Arch. Lg.; Mural P.; AFA. Work: Fresco in Director!s Room, Ill. Merchants Trust Bank, Chic.; Church, Souverain Moulin, France; and many important works privately owned. Died 1931. Address in 1929, 23 Charlton St., NY; 20 rue Jacob, Paris.

HALE, HELME.
Painter, Sculptor, and teacher. Born Kingston, RI, April 12, 1862. Pupil of ASL of NY; RI School of Design; Chase; Saint-Gaudens; Duveneck; Knowlton. Member: Alumni Assoc. RI. School of Design; North Shore AA; Am. APL; AFA.

HALE, LILIAN WESTCOTT.
(Mrs. Philip L. Hale). Painter. Born Hartford, CT, Dec. 7, 1881. Pupil of Elizabth Stevens, Tarbell and Chase. Member: ANA; CT AFA; Boston GA; Concord AA; Port. P.; AFA. Awards: Bronze medal, Buenos Aires Expostion, 1910; gold medal and medal of honor, P. P. Exp., San. F., 1915; gold medal, Phila.

AC, 1919; Potter Palmer Gold medal, AIC, 1919; Beck gold medal, PAFA, 1923; Julia S. Shaw Memorial prize, NAD, 1924; first Altman prize NAD, 1927. Represented in the collection of the Pennsylvania Academy of the Fine Arts and the Philadelphia Art Club; Metropolitan Museum of Art; Corcoran Gallery; Denver Art Museum; Art Association, Concord, MA; Phillip Memorial Gallery, Washington.

HALE, PHILIP LESLIE.
Painter, teacher, and writer. Born Boston, May 21, 1865; son of Rev. Edward Everett Hale. Pupil of J. Alden Weir in NY. Member: ANA 1917, Phila, AC ; St. Botolph C.; Boston GA; San F. AC.; Fellowship PAFA (assoc.); Eclectics; Port. P.; NAC. Awards: Hon. mention, Pan. - Am. Exp. Buffalo. 1901; bronze medal, St. Louis Exp., 1904, gold medal, Buenos Aires Exp., 1910; Harris silver medal ($500), AIC 1914; hors concurs (jury of awards), P.-P Exp., San F., 1915; Proctor prize, NAD 1916; Lea prize, Phila. WCC, 1916; popular prize, PAFA, 1919. Instructor at Boston Museum School and PAFA. Work: "The Crimson Rambler," PA Phila.; "Spirit of Antique Art," Museum of Montevideo, Uruguay; "Girl with Muff," Corcoran Gallery, Washington, DC; "Girl with Pearls," Philadelphia AC. Died Feb. 2, 1931. Address in 1929, Fenway Studios, 30 Ipswich St., Boston MA; h. Federal Hill, 213 Highland St., Dedham, MA.

HALE, SUSAN.
Painter. Born in Boston, 1834. Specialty, landscape painting in water colors. Exhibited a series of pictures of the White Mountains. Died Sept. 17, 1910 in Matunuck, RI.

HALEY, ROBERT DUANE.
Painter and sculptor. Born Lambertville, NJ, Jan. 6, 1892. Pupil of Kenneth Hayes Miller, George Bridgman, Robert Tolman and John C. Johansen. Address in 1929, 6 West Putnam Avenue, Greenwich CT; 458 State Street, Bridgeport, CT.

HALL, ALFRED BRYAN.
Engraver. Born in Stepney, London, England, in 1842. He was living in New York in 1900. A. B. Hall was a son of H. B. Hall, Sr., and came to New York in 1851. After serving an apprenticeship of seven years with his father, he worked as an engraver with J. C. Buttre, H. Wright Smith, A. H. Ritchie and George E. Perine, all of NY. He was later a member of the firms of H. B. Hall and Sons, and H. B. Hall Sons, until his retirement in 1899.

HALL, ALICE.
Engraver. Born at Halloway, London, England, 1847. She was living in New York in 1900. She was a daughter of H. B. Hall, Sr., and while still young she evinced considerable talent in drawing and etching. She etched portraits of Washington, after Stuart and Trumbull, among her other works.

HALL, ANNE.
Miniature painter. Born in Pomfret, CT, in 1792. When very young she received some instruction in miniature painting from S. King of Newport, who at one time had given lessons in oil painting to Washington Allston; she afterward studied painting in oil with Alexander Robertson in New York, but finally devoted herself to miniature painting. She was an exhibitor at the National Academy of Design in New York, and elected Academician in 1833. Among her best known works are a portrait of a Greek girl, which has been engraved, and a group representing Mrs. Dr. Jay with her infant child. She died in Dec., 1863.

HALL, ARNOLD.
Illustrator. Born Binghamton, March 2, 1901. Pupil of George Bridgman, Charles C. Curran, Frances C. Jones. Illustrated The Swiss Family Robinson (Minton Balch and Co.); "Brackie, the Fool" and "Jataka Tales Out of Old India" (G. P. Putnam's Sons.) Address in 1929, Columbia Height, Brooklyn, NY; summer, 171 Front Street, Binghamton, NY.

HALL, ARTHUR WILLIAM.
Painter. Born Bowie, TX, Oct. 30, 1889. Pupil of AIC. Address in 1929, 38 Drummond Place, Edinburgh, Scotland.

HALL, CHARLES BRYAN.
Engraver. Born in Camden Town, London, Aug. 18, 1840. C. B. Hall was the second son of H. B. Hall, Sr., and he came to NY in Spring, 1851, and commenced his studies under his father. In 1885 he was apprenticed to James Duthie, a landscape engraver then living in Morrisania, NY. After working about five years with George E. Perine, of New York, he started in business for himself as an engraver of portraits. He died in 1896.

HALL, FLORENCE S.
Painter. Born in Grand Rapids, MI. Pupil of AIC, and of Johansen. Member: Chicago Art Students' League. Address in 1926, 63 West Ontario Street, Chicago, IL.

HALL, FRANCES DEVEREUX JONES.
Sculptor and craftsman. Born New Orleans, LA. Pupil of Sophie Newcomb College, New Orleans; Henry McCarter, Howard Pyle, Charles Grafly. Member: Phila Alliance; N.A. Women PS.

HALL, FREDERICK GARRISON.
Painter and etcher. Born Baltimore, MD, April 22, 1879. Pupil of William Paxton and Henri Royer. Member: Brooklyn SE; Boston AG; North Shore AA.; Chic. SE; AFA. Award: Bijur Prize, Brooklyn SE., 1926; Lea prize, Phila. Print Club, 1926; silver medal, Sesqui-Centennial Exposition, Phil., 1926; Eyre gold medal, Philadelphia, 1927. Represented in Cleveland Museum of Art; Print Dept. Library of Congress, Wash., D.C.; Art Inst. of Chicago; Boston Museum of Fine Arts; Bibliotheque Nationale, Paris; Uffizi Gallery, Florence. Died in 1946. Address in 1929, Riverway Studios, 132 Riverway; h. 260 Beacon St., Boston; summer, Eastern Point, Gloucester, MA.

HALL, GEORGE F.
Painter, Arch. Born Providence, RI. Member: Providence AC.

Address in 1929, 80 Union Trust Bldg,; h. 49 Orchard Avenue, Providence, RI.

HALL, GEORGE HENRY.
Painter. Born in Boston, Sept. 25, 1825. He was largely self-taught and began painting in 1842. Elected member of National Academy in 1868. Represented by "Self-portrait," in Brooklyn Museum, painted in 1845; "The Roman Wine Cart," in Boston Museum of Fine Arts, painted in 1851. He died Feb. 17, 1913, in NYC.

HALL, GEORGE R.
Engraver. Born in London, Enlgand, in 1818. He was a brother of H. B. Hall, Sr. George R. Hall commenced engraving under the tuition of his brother, and then worked in London and in Leipzig. He came to NY in 1854, and was first employed by Rawdon, Wright, Hatch & Co., and was later engraving over his own name for the Putnams and other New York publishers.

HALL, HENRY BRYAN Jr.
Engraver. Born in Camden Town, London, England. He was living in New York in 1900. He came to NY with his father in 1850 and served his apprenticeship with his father. In 1858 he went to London and worked under Charles Knight for about one year, and then returned and established himself in the engraving business in NY. He engraved many portraits of generals and officers of the Civil War, and also a number of historical plates, but retired from business in 1899. Among his larger plates are "The Death of Lincoln," and subjects after the painting of J. G. Brown and other American artists.

HALL, HENRY BRYAN.
Engraver. Born in London, England, May 11, 1808; died at Morrisania, NY, April 25, 1884. Hall was a pupil of the London engravers Benjamin Smith and Henry Meyer, and he was later employed by H.T. Ryall, historical engraver to the Queen, to execute the portrait work in the large plate of "The Coronation of Victoria," after the painting by Sir George Hayter. Mr. Hall came to NY in 1850, and soon established a very extensive business as an engraver and publisher of portraits. He had very considerable ability as a portrait painter, and while in London he painted a portrait of Napoleon II, among others; among his portraits painted in the US are those of Thomas Sully and C. L. Elliott. He painted miniature on ivory, and etched a large number of portraits of men prominent in the Colonial and Revolutionary history of this country for a private club of NY and for Philadelphia collectors. He made the drawings in pencil and wash for Dr. Thomas Addis Emmett's series of privately printed "Club" portraits of the signers of the "Declaration of Independence" and of other Revolutionary characters which he also engraved.

HALL, ISABEL HAWXHURST.
Painter, illustrator, and craftsman. Born New York City. Pupil of Henry Prellwitz, Frank Vincent Du Mond, Mrs. Elbert Treganza. Member: NYSC; Am. APL. Work: Illustrated "The Rubaiyat of Omar Khayyam." Designer of numerous church windows. Address in 1929, 23 Sixth Ave; h. 195 West 10th St., NYC.

HALL, JOHN H.
Wood engraver and lithographer. Was born at Cooperstown, NY. Self-taught except for a few lessons from Dr. Anderson. He began to engrave about 1826 and in 1840 he illustrated the "Manual of Ornithology," which contains some of his best work. (See "The History of Wood Engraving in America," by W. J. Linton.) Died in CA in 1849.

HALL, MABEL B.
Painter. Member: Phila. WCC. Address in 1929, 1211 Locust St., Philadelphia, PA.

HALL, NORMA BASSETT.
Painter and teacher. Born Halsey, OR, May 21, 1889. Pupil of AIC; Portland, OR, Art Assoc. School.

HALL, NORMAN.
Illustrator. Born Chicago, Feb. 21, 1885. Member: GFLA. Address

in 1929, 1013 Lake Michigan Bldg.;
180 North Michigan Avenue, Chicago,
IL; h. 171 St. Charles Rd.,
Elmhurst, IL.

HALL, PETER.
Engraver. Born in Birmingham,
England, in 1828. Mr. Hall came to
the US in 1849 and learned to
engrave in the NY establishment of
the American Bank Note Co. His
special work was bank note script
engraving, in which he excelled.
In 1886 he went into business in NY
as a bank-note engraver; later the
firm became Kihn & Hall, and was
later known as of "Kihn Brothers."
His son, Charles A. Hall, was
employed at of the Bureau of
Printing and Engraving, at
Washington, D.C. A well' executed
stipple portrait of Washington,
after the portrait by Mrs. E.
Sharpless, is signed as "Engraved
by P. Hall" and appears as a
frontispiece to the "Memoirs of
Thaddeus Kosciusko." Died July 5,
1895.

HALL, SUSAN.
Sculptor. Member: NA Women PS.
Address in 1929, 130 West 57th
Street, New York, NY.

HALL, THOMAS.
Painter. Born in Sweden, April 23,
1883. Pupil of Freer, Wolcott,
Reynolds. Member: Swedish Soc.,
Chicago; Scandinavian Am. Soc., NY;
Chicago SA; Chiacgo Gal. A.
Awards: Hon. mention, 1920 and
1923, and first prizes for water
colors, 1924 and 1925, Swedish-
American Soc. Work: "Northern
Sunset," Midway Masonic Temple,
Chicago; painting in Englewood
(Chicago) H.S. Address in 1929,
5725 South Wells St., Chicago, IL.

HALL, THOMAS VICTOR.
Painter, sculptor, illustrator, and
teacher. Born Rising Sun, IN, May
30, 1879. Pupil of Nowottny,
Meakin, Duveneck, Art Academy,
Cincinnati. Member: Salma, C.;
KitKat Club; Cincinnati AC. Address
in 1929, 203 West 14th St., NYC.

HALLADAY, MILTON RAWSON.
Illustrator. Born in 1874. Member:
Providence AC; Providence WCC.

Address in 1929, Providence Journal
Co.; Providence, RI.

HALLER, ARLENE.
Sculptor. Born in Newark, NJ, Feb.
17, 1935. Study: Newark State,
1957; self-taught in art. Exhib.:
Newark (NJ) Mus.; Nat'l Acad. of
Design, NYC; Silvermine Guild, New
Canaan, CT; Catherine Lorillard
Wolfe Art Club, NYC; Allied Artists
of Am. Nat'l Arts Club; Rutgers
Univ. (solo); and others. Awards:
Am. Assoc. of Univ. Women;
Catherine Lorillard Wolfe Art Club,
Excalibur award & Harriet Frishmuth
award for traditional sculpture.
Address in 1983, 121 Greenbrook
Rd., North Plainfield, NJ.

HALLER, EMANUEL.
Painter and printmaker. Born in
Newark, NJ, Sept. 7, 1927. Study:
Newark School of Fine & Industrial
Art, Cert., 1949; Pratt Inst., NY.
Work: NJ State Mus., Trenton;
Newark Mus., NJ; Monmouth College,
West Long Branch, NJ; Rosenwald
Collection, Jenkintown, PA; others.
Exhib.: Boston Mus. Fine Arts, MA;
NAD, NYC; PAFA; Phila. Mus. of Art;
Seattle Art Mus.; Squibb Art
Gallery, Princeton, NJ; Wadsworth
Atheneum, Hartford, CT; and others,
including several one-person shows.
Media: Oil, watercolor. Address
in 1983, 121 Greenbrook Road, North
Plainfield, NJ.

HALLETT, HENDRICKS A.
Painter. He was born at
Charlestown, MA, in 1847, and
studied in Antwerp and Paris. He
was well known for his pictures of
various types of ships and of
notable events. A member of the
Boston Society of Water Color
Painters. Awarded a bronze medal
at MA Charitable Mechanics'
Association, Boston, in March 17,
1892. He died in Boston in 1921.

HALLIDAY, MARY HUGHITT.
Painter. Born Cairo, IL, Oct. 31,
1866. Pupil of W. M. Chase,
Charles Lasar, Academie Carmen and
Academie Colarossi in Paris.
Member: Calif. AC; Chicago Gal A;
AFA. Address in 1929, 316 Adelaide
Drive, Santa Monica, CA.

HALLMAN, HENRY THEODORE.
Painter, illustrator, and craftsman. Born Milford Square, PA, Sept. 17, 1904. Pupil of Thornton Oakley. Work: "Christ Entering Jerusalem," "Gethsemane," "Christ Bearing the Cross" and "Miraculous Draft of Fishes," Emmanuel Lutheran Church, Souderton.

HALLOCK, RUTH MARY.
Painter and illustrator. Born Erie, PA. Pupil of AIC; ASL of NY. Member: North Shore AA; PBC; NAC. Died 1945. Address in 1929, 40 Gramercy Park, New York, NY; summer, Gloucester, MA.

HALLOWELL, GEORGE HAWLEY.
Born in Boston in 1871, He studied architecture and painting. His early work was making copies of the old Italian Masters. His specialty was landscapes, of logging scenes and the woods. In 1906 he studied abroad. He worked in both oil and water colors. Pupil of F. W. Benson; E. C. Tarbell; and H. B. Warren. Studio, Boston, MA. Represented in the Boston Museum of Fine Arts. Address in 1926, 229 Park Avenue, Arlington Heights, MA. Died March 26, 1926 in Boston.

HALLOWELL, ROBERT.
Painter and etcher. Born Denver, CO, March 12, 1886. Work: "Afternoon Light," Brooklyn Museum: "Matterhorn," Cleveland Museum; "St. Tropez," "Wild Flowers" and "Rain," Phillips Memorial Gallery, Washington, DC; "Cassio" and "Tranquility," Lewisohn Collection, New York. Address in 1929, 408 West 20th Street, NYC. Died in 1939.

HALPERT, SAMUEL.
Painter. Born Russia, Dec. 25, 1884. Member: New SA; (pres.) S. Indp. A. Detroit; Societare Salon d'Automne, Paris. Represented in the PAFA; Newark Museum; San Francisco Museum; Harrison Gallery, Los Angeles Museum; Phillips Memorial Gallery, Washington, DC; Art School of the Society of Arts and Crafts. Died in 1930. Address in 1929, 47 Watson St., Detroit, MI; summer, Ogunquit, ME.

HALPIN, FREDERICK.
Engraver. Born in Worcester, England, in 1805. He was the pupil of his father, an engraver for one of the Staffordshire potteries. About 1827 Frederick Halpin was located in London, engraving historical subjects and portraits. He came to NY about 1842, and for a time was in the employ of Alfred Jones in that city. He was a good engraver of portraits and book illustrations in stipple. His name is sometimes signed to prints as "F. W. Halpin." Died Feb. 1880, in Jersey City, NJ.

HALPIN, JOHN.
Engraver. He was a brother of Frederick Halpin, and was engraving in St. Petersburg, Russia, before he reached the US, by way of Halifax. About 1850 John Halpin was engraving landscapes and a few portraits for NY publishers as late as 1867. Some few years later he was employed by the Ladies' Repository and the Methodist Book Concern, both of Cincinnati, OH. Also worked in watercolors.

HALSALL, WILLIAM FORMBY.
Painter. Born in Kirkdale, England, March 21, 1841; died Nov., 1919. At the age of 12 he went to sea in the ship "Ocean Rover," of Portsmouth, NH, and followed the sea for seven years. He was in the United States Navy during part of the Civil War, and afterwards became a fresco painter. He was a student in the MA Inst. of Tech., class 1874. After 1877 he painted the following marine pictures: "First Fight of Ironclads, Monitor and Merrimac"' "The Mayflower (Memorial Hall, Plymouth, MA); "Niagara Falls;" "Sheeted Ghost;" "The Winter Passage;" and "When Sleep Falleth on Men."

HALTOM, MINNIE HOLLIS.
Painter and teacher. Born Belton, TX. Pupil of Rolla Taylor; Jose Arpa in Spain; Metropolitan Art School, New York; Xavier Gonzalez. Member: San Antonio AL; SSAL; Am. Salon Painters. Represented in Colorado High School and Main Avenue HS, San Antonio.

HAMANN, CHARLES F.
Sculptor. Member of National
Sculpture Society.

HAMBRIDGE, JAY.
Painter and illustrator. Born in
1867 in Simcoe, Canada; he died in
NYC, Jan. 20, 1924. Pupil of the
Art Students' League in New York
and of William M. Chase. He was
the discoverer of dynamic symmetry.

HAMILTON, DAVID OSBORNE.
Painter, etcher and writer. Born
Detroit, MI, June 19, 1893.
Member: ASL of NY; Brooklyn SE.
Author of Four Gardens - book of
verse published by Yale University
Press in their Younger Poets
Series; Pale Warriors, a novel
(Scribners). Address in 1929, 1505
Astor Street, Chicago, IL; summer,
Huron Mt. Club, Huron Mountain, MI.
Died in 1955.

HAMILTON, EDWARD W. D.
Painter. Born in 1862. He painted
"Canal, Venice." (owned by the
Boston Museum of Fine Arts).

HAMILTON, ETHEL HEAVEN.
Painter and teacher. Born in
Mexico, July 14, 1871. Pupil of
Chase, MacMonnies, Calarossi
School, Paris. Member: NYWCC;
Catherine Lorillard Wolfe AC; Nart.
LG. of Amer. Pen Women (Artists
Member). Died in 1936.

HAMILTON, FRANK O.
Painter. Born in 1923 in Selma, TN.
Earned BA from Standford University
in 1948. Taught at SF Art
Institute. Exhibited at Humboldt
State College (CA); Richmond Art
Center, (both in1959). Also at
Cal. Palace, SF; LA County Museum;
Poindexter Gallery, NYC and in
Toronto.

HAMILTON, FRANK MOSS.
Painter and architect. Born in
Kansas City, MO, June 26, 1930.
Study: With Eliot O'Hara; Stanford
Univ.; Univ. Kansas. Work: Favell
Mus., OR; others. Exhib.: Laguna
Beach Festival of Arts, CA,
1949-68; Franklin Mint Yearly
Western Show, 1974. Awards:
First Awards, Laguna Beach Art
Festival, 1963-65; Franklin Mint
Bicentennial Medal Design, 1972;

others. Media: Watercolor.
Address in 1983, Cambria, CA.

HAMILTON, HAMILTON.
Painter. Born in England, 1847.
He began his career as a portrait
painter at Buffalo, NY, in 1872;
specialty, landscapes. Elected
Associate Member of the National
Academy in 1886; National Academy,
1889. Member of American Water
Color Soc. Represented at the Fine
Arts Academy Buffalo, NY, by "The
Valley of Fountains" and "Sunset
After the Storm." Address in 1926,
Norwalk, CT. Died 1928.

HAMILTON, HILDEGARDE.
Painter. Born in Syracuse, NY, in
1908. Studied: Art Students'
League; John Herron Art Inst.;
Cincinnati Art Acad.; Syracuse
Univ.; Julian Acad., Ecole des
Beaux-Arts, Paris. Collections:
Wesleyan College, GA; Hall of Art,
NY; Evergreen School, Plainfield,
New Jersey; Eaton Gallery, NY;
Nassau, Bahamas.

HAMILTON, J. M. C.
Painter. His work is said to be
similar to that of Alfred Stevens.

HAMILTON, JAMES.
Marine and landscape painter. Born
in Ireland, Oct. 1, 1819; he died
in Philadelphia, March 10, 1878.
He was particularly successful in
his marine views. He also painted
several views of Niagara Falls
which attracted much attention.

HAMILTON, JOHN McLURE.
Portrait painter and illustrator.
Born Philadelphia, PA, Jan. 31,
1853. Pupil of PAFA; Royal Acad.
in Antwerp; Ecole des Beaux-Arts in
Paris. Member: Phila. WCC (hon.):
Fellowship PAFA; AFA; Royal Soc. of
Port. P.; Pastel Soc.; Senefelder
C., London. Awards: Hon. mention,
Paris Salon, 1892; gold medal,
Pan-Am. Exp. Buffalo, 1901; gold
medal, Pan-Am Exp., Buffalo, 1901;
hors concours (jury of awards),
P.-P. Exp., San F. 1915; gold medal
of honor, PAFA, 1918. Work:
"Gladstone at Downing Street."
"Hon. Richard Vaux," "George
Meredith," "William R. Richards,"
"Henry Thouron" and "Cardinal
Manning." Pittsburgh; "Gladstone,"

Luxembourg Museum, Paris; "Prof. Tyndall," "Aislow Ford," "Cosmo Monkhouse," "Ridley Corbet," Nat. Gallery, London. Author of "Men I Have Painted." Died in 1936. Address in 1929, Hermitage, Kingston on Thames, Eng.

HAMILTON, MARIANNA.
Batik and watercolorist. Born: Berkeley, CA, in 1943. Studied: University of California at Santa Barbara; San Francisco Art Inst.; University of Arizona. Exhibitions: San Francisco Museum of Art, CA, 1965; Phoenix Art Museum, AZ, 1967; Monterey Peninsula Museum of Art, CA, 1973.

HAMILTON, MARY W.
Miniature painter. Member: Detroit S. Women P. Address in 1929, 4 Beverly Road, Grosse Pointe, MI.

HAMILTON, NORAH.
Etcher. Born Fort Wayne, IN, 1873. Pupil of Cox in New York: Whistler in Paris. Member: Chicago SE. Address in 1929, Hull House, Chicago, IL.

HAMILTON, ROBERT.
Painter and teacher. Born County Down, Ireland. Studied in London and Paris. Member: Salma. C.; Kit Kat C. Work: Mural in Public School 43, the Bronx New York City. Many portraits and landscapes are privately owned. Address in 1929, 20 West 15th St., NYC; summer, Pontoosuc Studio, Lanesboro, MA.

HAMILTON, WILBUR DEAN.
Painter, illustrator, and craftsman. Born Somerfield, Ohio, 1864. Pupil of Ecole des Beaux-Arts in Paris. Member: Copley S. 1903; Boston GA; St. Botolph Club. Awards: Jordan prize in Boston; medal, Atlanta Exp., 1895; gold medal, P. P. Exp. San Francisco 1915. Work: "Beacon Street, Boston," RI School of Design, Providence. Represented in Boston Museum, Boston University, American Univeristy, John Wesley Memorial Room, Lincoln College, Oxford, England. Instructor at Mass. Normal Art School. Address in 1929, Trinity Court, Dartmouth Street, Boston.

HAMLIN, EDITH.
Painter. Born Oakland, CA, in 1902. Studied: California School of Fine Arts; and with Maynard Dixon. Collections: San Francisco Museum of Art; San Diego Fine Arts Gallery; Mission High School, San Fran., CA; United States Post Office, Tracy, CA; Coit Mem. Tower, San Fran.; Santa Fe RR Ticket Office, Chicago and Los Angeles; Arizona Biltmore Hotel, Phoenix; Plains Hotel, Cheyenne, WY; Jacome's Department Store, Tucscon, AZ; St. Ambrose Church, Tucson, AZ; Old Pueblo Club, Tucson, AZ.

HAMLIN, GENEVIEVE (KARR).
Sculptor and teacher. Born in New York City, July 1, 1896. Pupil of Abastenia St. L. Eberle and Henry Dropsy in Paris. Member: NA Women PS; American Numismatic S. Work: Portrait Medallion of Theodore Roosevelt, Tsing Hua College, Peking, China; medal for Exposition of Women's Arts and Industries. Address in 1929, 39 Claremont Ave., NYC.

HAMLIN, WILLIAM.
Engraver. Born in Providence, RI, Oct. 15, 1772; died there Nov. 22, 1869. Mr. Hamlin established himself in business as a manufacturer and repairer of sextants, quadrants, and such other nautical and mathematical instruments as were used by the navigator. As engraving upon metal was part of his business, he began experimenting upon copper, and his business card of a later date adds to his business proper, that of "Engraving & Copperplate Printing." As an engraver Mr. Hamlin made his own tools and worked practically without instruction. His plates show a somewhat weak mixture of mezzotint and stipple, frequently worked over with the roulette. Good impressions of his plates, however, show that he made the best of his limited opportunities. Mr. Hamlin saw Gen. Washington, on one of his visits to the Eastern States, and the impression made upon the engraver was so strong that his most important plates have Washington for their subject. Considering the Savage portrait as the best likeness, he followed that

artist in his several portraits of Washington; but he also held Houdon's bust in high esteem and in his ninety-first year he engraved Washington after that sculptor. This was his last plate.

HAMM, PHINEAS ELDRIDGE.
Engraver. Born in Philadelphia in 1799; he died there in 1861. Hamm was probably the pupil of a Philadelphia engraver and in 1825-27 he was in business as an engraver in the city. While he usually worked in line, he engraved a few good portraits in stipple.

HAMMARGREN, FRITZ EMANUEL.
Sculptor. Born Orebro, Sweden, April 7, 1892. Pupil of Bourdelle. Member: Scandinavian-American AC. Work: "Leda and the Swan," fountain, and monument to Dr. N. A. Wilson, Orebro, Sweden. Address in 1929, 211 Collens St., Hartford, CT.

HAMMELL, WILL.
Illustrator. Born Trenton, NJ, Aug. 14, 1888. Pupil of William M. Chase, R. Sloan Bredin, Frank V. Dumond. Member: SI; Art Dir. C. Address in 1929, 25 West 45th Street, New York, NY; h. 180 Spring Street, Red Bank, NJ.

HAMMER, JOHN.
Painter. Member: GFLA. Address in 1929, West 12th Street, New York, NY.

HAMMER, TRYGVE.
Sculpture, craftman, and draftsman. Born Arendal, Norway, Sept. 6, 1878. Pupil of Skeibrak, MacNeil, Calder and Solon Borglum. Member: NSS; S. Indp. A.; Brooklyn S. Modern A.; Scandinavian-American A.; Arch. L. of NY; Phil. Art Alliance. Work: Roosevelt Commons Memorial, Tenafly, NJ; memorial window, Crescent Athletic Club, Brooklyn, NY; head of a baby. Newark Museum; "Good Shepherd" memorial tablet Zion Lutheran Church. Brooklyn, NY; Humphrey Memorial Tablet, Stevens Institute, Hoboken, NJ. Died 1947. Address in 1929, 329 Forest Road, Douglaston, LI.

HAMMERSMITH, PAUL.
Painter and etcher. Born Naperville, IL, March 17, 1857. Self-taught. Member: Milwaukee AS; Cal. SE; Chicago SE; Wisconsin PS. Work in: New York Public Library; Newark Public Library. Awards: Bronze medal for etching. St. Paul Inst., 1916; silver medal for etching, St. Paul Inst., 1918. Died in 1937. Address in 1929, 116 Michigan St., h. 567 Belleview Place, Milwaukee, WI.

HAMMITT, CLAWSON S. LAKESPEARE.
Painter. Born in Wilmington, DE, in 1857. Pupil of Eakins and Chase in Philadelphia, and Constant and Lefebvre in Paris. Among his portraits are those of James Latimer and Henry Latimer in the US Capitol, others in State House, Dover, DE, and State College, Newark, Delaware. Died 1927 in Wilmington DE. Address in 1926, 12th and Jefferson Streets, Wilmington, DE.

HAMMOND, ARTHUR J.
Painter. Born Vernon, CT, April 3, 1875. Pupil of Eric Pape, Charles Woodbury and G. L. Noyes. Member: New Haven PPC; AFA; CT. AFA. Award: Hon. mention, CT AFA, 1919. Represented in Lynn. (MA) Public Library. Address in 1929, Rockport, MA.

HAMMOND, GEORGE F.
Painter. Born Boston, MA, Nov. 25, 1855. Pupil of MA. Normal Art School, W. M. Chase, W. L. Sonntag and Walter F. Lansil. Member: Cleveland SA. Address in 1929, 555 Luck Avenue, Zanesville, OH.

HAMMOND, J. T.
A good line engraver of landscapes and subject plates in 1839. Born c. 1820. In that year he was employed in Phila., but later he seems to have moved to St. Louis, MO.

HAMMOND, NATALIE HAYS.
Painter. Born Lakewood, NJ, Jan. 6, 1905. Pupil of Sergei Soudekine. Member: Royal Soc. Min. P., Scultprs and Gravers; Guilford Soc. of England; ADA; NAC; Wash. AC. Address in 1929, 133 East 6th Street, New York, NY; summer, "Lookout Hill," Gloucester, MA.

HAMMOND, RICHARD HENRY.
Painter. Born in Cincinnati, OH, in 1854. Pupil of Noble, Weber and Duveneck. Member of Cincinnati Art Club. Address in 1926, 806 Barr Street, Cincinnati, OH.

HAMPTON, BLAKE.
Illustrator. Born in Poteau, OK, in 1932. He attended North Texas State College where he received his BA. Influenced by his study with Octavio Medellin, a sculptor, he has produced many fine dimensional pieces in addition to his other work. His first illustration was done in 1946 in California and it was entitled How the Froggy Lost His Whoop. The Eisenhower Museum and the John F. Kennedy Library own his artwork.

HAN, SHARRY.
Cartoonist and journalist. Born in San Francisco, CA, Feb. 17, 1957. Study: CA State at LA, 1977; Defense Information School, Dept. of Defense, Navy Journalist/Broadcaster, 1981. Exhib: US Naval History Mus. Cartoons sold to "OMNI" magazine, "Playgirl," the "National Enquirer," "Los Angeles" magazine; cartoons distributed nationwide by McNaught Newspaper Syndicate. Awards: US Navy OPSEC Poster Award; US Navy Chief of Information (CHINFO) Merit Award for a Published Graphic Art. Address in 1983, 1644 W. Little Creek Road #4, Norfolk, VA.

HANATSCEK, H.
Painter. Born Zuaim Moraira, Dec. 19, 1873. Pupil of Griepenkerl, Eisenmenger in Vienna and Munich. Address in 1929, 53 West 72nd Street, New York, NY.

HANCOCK, ADELAIDE D.
Painter. Born Boston, MA. Pupil of Chicago ADA; Eda N. Casterton. Address in 1929, 225 North Michigan Avenue; h. 1120 Hyde Park Blvd. Chicago, IL.

HANCOCK, JOSEPH LANE.
Landscape painter. Born in Chicago, IL, in 1864. Pupil of Art Institute, Chicago. He died in 1925.

HANCOCK, NATHANIEL.
Miniature painter and engraver. He was working in Boston from 1790 to 1802. In 1805 he moved to Salem, MA. His miniature of Colonel William Raymond Lee is in the collection at the Essex Institute, Salem, MA.

HANCOCK, WALKER (KIRTLAND).
Sculptor. Born in St. Louis, MO, June 28, 1901. Study: St. Louis School of Fine Arts; Washington Univ., St. Louis, 1918-20, hon. DFA, 1942; Univ. of WI, 1920; PAFA, 1921-25; American Acad. in Rome. Work: PAFA; Corcoran Gallery, National Gallery of Art, and Nat'l. Portrait Gallery, Washington, DC; and many others. Comm.: Eisenhower Inaugural Medals; PA R. R. War Memorial, PA R. R. Sta., Phila.; Army and Navy Medal; portrait statues of Douglas MacArthur, US Military Academy; John Paul Jones, Fairmount Park, Phila.; James Madison, Library of Congress, Madison Bldg.; Booth Tarkington & Robert Frost, Nat'l Portrait Gal.; Field Service Memorial, Blerancourt, France; bronze bas-relief of Edwin A. Ulrich, The Edwin A. Ulrich Mus., Wichita (KS) State Univ.; and many others. Exhib.: National and international museums and galleries. Positions: Resident Sculptor, Am. Acad., Rome, 1956-57, 1962-63; Sculptor in Charge, Stone Mt. Mem., GA, 1964; Head, Dept. of Sculpture, PAFA, 1929-68. Awards: Widener Gold Medal, PAFA; Fellowship prize, PAFA, 1931; sculpture, NAD, 1949; J. Sanford Saltus medal, Am. Numismatic Society, 1953; Thomas H. Proctor prize, NAD, 1959; Medal of Achievement, Nat'l Sculpture Soc., 1968; Medal of Honor, 1981; and many others. Mem.: Exec. Comm., Am. Acd. in Rome; Nat'l Collection of Fine Arts Comn.; Academician, NAD; Fellow, Nat'l. Sculpt. Soc.; Nat'l Inst. of Arts and Letters; Arch. Lg. of NY; Benj. Franklin Fellow, Royal Soc. of Arts. Media: Bronze, stone. Address in 1982: Gloucester, MA.

HAND, MOLLY WILLIAMS.
Painter, etcher, and teacher. Born Keene, NH, April 29, 1892. Pupil of Daniel Garber, Ralph Pearson,

Hugh Breckenridge, Arthur Carles, George Luks, Robert Henri, John Sloan, Phillip Hale, Frank von der Lancken, Albert Heckman, George Bridgman. Member: Amer. Artists Prof. Lg.; NA Women PS; ASL of NY; Fellowship PAFA; Westfield AA. AFA; Elizabeth SA. Work: "Still Life No. 1," Newark Museum, Newark, NJ. Address in 1929, Carteret Arms, 16 South Broad St., Elizabeth, NJ; h. 246 East Sixth Avenue, Roselle, NJ.

HANDELL, ALBERT GEORGE.
Painter. Born in Brooklyn, NY, Feb. 13, 1917. Studied at ASL; Grande Chaumiere, Paris. In collections of Syracuse U.; Brooklyn Mus., NY; Schenectady Mus., NY; Salt Lake City Mus.; ASL. Exhib. at Berkshire Mus., Pittsfield, MA; ACA Gallery, NYC; Eileen Kuhlik Gallery; group shows at Allied Artists of Am. and Audubon Artists, NY, and many more. Awards: John F. and Anna Lee Stacy Scholarship Fund, 1962-65; Ranger Fund Purchase Prize, Audubon Artists, 1968; Eliz. T. Greenshields Mem. Foundation, 1972. Extensive Bibliog. Member of Allied Artists of Am.; Salma. C.; ASL. Media: Multimedia. Rep. by Eileen Kuhlik Gallery, NYC. Address in 1982, Woodstock, New York.

HANDFORTH, THOMAS SCHOFIELD.
Painter, illustrator, and etcher. Born Tacoma, Sept. 16, 1897. Pupil of Hawthorne; NAD; ASL; Ecole National des Beaux Arts in Paris. Member: Brooklyn SE; Phila. SE; AFA. Awards: Emil Fuchs prize, Brooklyn Society of Etchers, 1927; Charles M. Lea prize, Phila. Print C., 1929. Work: Twenty-one etchings, Metropolitan Museum of Art, New York; Pennsylvania Museum (Etching); NY Public Library (six etchings); Honolulu Academy of Arts (twelve etchings); Bibliotheque Nationale (three etchings); Fogg Art Museum, Cambridge, MA. (six etchings, five drawings.) Represented in "Fine Prints of the Year," 1926-28. Illustrated: Sedonie, by Pierre Coalfleet; Handbook on the Italian Ballet, by Luigi Albertiere; Toutou in Bondage, by Elizabth Coatsworth;

and for the Forum, 1925 to 1929, and Asia Magazine. Died 1948. Address in 1929, The Print Corner, Hingham Center, MA.

HANDLEY, MONTAGUE.
Sculptor. His work includes busts of "Diana," "Bacchus," and "Flora."

HANDVILLE, ROBERT T.
Illustrator. Born in Paterson, NJ, in 1924. He graduated first in his class at PI. He studied under Reuben Tam at the Brooklyn Museum Art School and went to school with Ellsworth Kelly. His first published illustration was done for Elks Magazine in 1948. He has done extensive work for many well-known magazines and publishing houses, and has also been an artist-reporter for Sports Illustrated.

HANE, ROGER.
Illustrator. Born in Bradford, PA, in 1940. He received his training in advertising design and illustration from the Phila. College of Art. Among his many clients were Fortune, NY Magazine, The Times of London, Ladies Home Journal, Time, McCall's, Exxon Corporation, Columbia Records and others. The Swiss magazine Graphis in 1975 published an article on his great insight and imagination in depicting the everyday world. In 1975 he received an Award of Excellence from the S of I as well as being elected Artist of the Year by the AG. Died in 1975.

HANEY, IRENE W.
Painter and teacher. Born Pittsburgh, Feb. 3, 1890. Pupil of Christ Walter. Member: Pitts, AA.; Teachers AC. Address in 1929, 6828 Lyric Street, Pittsburgh, PA.

HANEY, JAMES PARTON.
Painter. Born in NYC April 16, 1869. Pupil of Bell, DuMond and Mucha. Studied with Woodbury. Became art director and teacher. He died March 3, 1923 in NYC.

HANKS, JERVIS F.
Born in New York State in 1799. He moved with his family to Wheeling, West VA, 1817, and found employment there in painting signs. In 1823

he visited Philadelphia, and made some experiments in portrait painting which he continued on his return to Virginia. In 1827 he was in NY and when he could not gain sufficient employment painting portraits, he returned to his sign painting.

HANKS, OWEN G.
Engraver. Born in Troy, NY, in 1838. He studied engraving in the establishment of Rawdon, Wright & Hatch, in New York. He was a capital line engraver, both of portraits and landscapes, and was chiefly employed by the bank-note companies. He died about 1865.

HANLEY, HARRIET CLARK,
Sculptor. Born St. Louis, MO. Work: Monument to George B. Wright, Fergus Fall, MN. Address in 1929, 2411 Blaidsdell Avenue, Minneapolis, MN.

HANLEY, MEREDITH.
Painter. Member: GFLA: Chicago AC. Address in 1929, 5810 Blackstone Avenue, Chicago, IL.

HANLEY, WILLIAM H.
Portrait draughtsman in crayon. He is known to have been working in Boston from 1850 to 1856.

HANLON, LOUIS.
Painter and illustrator. Member: SI. Died c. 1955. Born in 1882. Address in 1929, 9018-107th Street, Richmond Hill, LI, NY; 6525 Germantown Avenue, Philadelphia, PA.

HANNA, THOMAS KING JR.
Painter and illustrator. Born Kansas City, MO, April 10, 1872. Pupil of ASL of NY. Member: SI , 1904; Salma. C.; GFLA. Work in National Art Gallery, Sydney, N.S.W., Australia. Died 1951. Address in 1929, 14 Knollwood Terrace, Caldwell, NJ.

HANNAFORD, ALICE IDE.
(Mrs. Foster Hannaford). Sculptor. Born Baltimore, MD, Aug. 28, 1888. Pupil of Fraser and ASL of NY. Work: "Wigwam Dance," Brooklyn Institute Museum. Address in 1929, 341 Dayton Avenue, St. Paul, MN;

summer, Manitou Island, White Bear, MN.

HANNY, WILLIAM F.
Cartoonist. Born in Burlington, IA, in 1882. Address, Pioneer Press, St. Paul, MN.

HANSELL, GEORGE H.
Portrait painter in oils and miniatures, who flourished 1844-1857 in NY. In 1844 he exhibited a "Miniature of a Little Girl" at the National Academy of Design in New York.

HANSEN, ARMIN CARL.
Painter, etcher, and teacher. Born San Francisco, CA. Oct. 23, 1886. Pupil of Mathews; Grethe at Royal Academy, Stuttgart, Germany. Member: ANA, 1926; San. F. AA; Calif. SE; Salma. C.; Allied AA; Wis. PS; Societe Royale des Beaux-Arts, Brussels. Awards: Prize International Exp., Brussels, 1910; silver medal, Panama-Pacific Exp., 1915; silver medal for drawing and painting, San F. AA. 1919; first Hallgarten prize, NAD, 1920; Los Angeles Chamber of Commerce Prize, Los Angeles Museum, 1923; William Preston Harrison Prize ($100) for etching, International Print Makers, Los Angeles, 1924; gold medal. Painters of the West, 1925; Lea prize, Print Club of Phila., 1927. Represented in Memorial Museum, San Francisco; Los Angeles Museum of History, Science and Art; Palace of Fine Arts, San Francisco; Ranger Fund Purchase, National Academy of Design. Died 1957. Address in 1929, 762 Eldorado Street, h. 621 Cass Street, Monterey, CA.

HANSEN, HANS PETER.
Painter. Born in Denmark in 1881. Member: Kunst Gewerbe Verein. Award: Mention, collaborative competition, New York Architectual League, New York. Address in 1926, 467 West 159th Street, New York, NY.

HANSON, HENRY T.
Painter and illustrator. Born in Chicago, IL, in 1888. Pupil of DuMond, Bridgman, Snell and John Carlsen. Address in 1926, 225 West 39th Street, New York, NY.

HANSON, MAUDE.
Painter. Member: NYWCC; Art Director's Club. Address in 1929, Woodstock, NY.

HAPGOOD, ALICE HATHAWAY.
See Goodwin.

HARARI, HANANIAH.
Painter. Born: Rochester, NY, in 1912. Studied: Syracuse Univ.; Fontainebleau, Paris; with Leger, L'Hote and Gromaire, Paris. Awards: NAD, 1941; Audubon Art, 1945; Art Directors Club, Chicago; Ossining, NY, 1953, 1955, 1957; Mt. Kisco, NY, 1955. Collections: Whitney Museum of American Art; University of Arizona; Philadelphia Museum of Art; Museum of Modern Art; Albright Art Gallery; San Francisco Museum of Art; Rochester Memorial Art Gallery; Iowa State University. Media: Oil. Address in 1980, 34 Prospect Place, Croton-on-Hudson, NY.

HARBESON, GEORGIANA (NEWCOMB) BROWN.
(Mrs. John F. Harbeson). Painter, illustrator, and craftsman. Born New Haven, CT, May 13, 1894. Pupil of Hugh Breckenridge, Joseph T. Pearson, Jr., Dan. Garber, Violet Oakley. Member: Fellowship PAFA; Philadelphia Alliance; Plastic C.; Phila. WCC; NA Women PS. Award: First prize, NA. Women PS., 1926; prize Nat. Textile Design Comp. Art Alliance of Am., 1929. Address in 1929, 110 East 59th Street, New York, NY; h. care Caroline Drum, Westport, CT.

HARCOURT, GEORGE E.
Illustrator. Born Detroit, May 23, 1897. Pupil of John Wicker. Member: Scarab C; Art Founders S. Address in 1929, Parke Davis & Co.; h. 5775 Wabash Avenue, Detroit, MI.

HARDENBERGH, ELIZABETH RUTGERS.
Painter and craftsman. Born New Brunswick, NJ. Pupil of H. B. Snell and Mrs. E. M. Scott. Member: N.A. Women PS; NY WCC; NY Soc. Ceramic A; Allied AA; SPNY; Alliance. Specialty: pottery and painting. Address in 1929, 17 East 62nd Street, New York, NY; summer, Byrdcliffe, Woodstock, Ulster Co., NY.

HARDIE, ROBERT GORDON.
Painter. Born in Brattleboro, VT, on March 29, 1854. Studied at Cooper Institute, and National Academy of Design, New York; with Gerome in Paris. Elected to Society of American Artists in 1897. His portrait of Miss Hariet S. Walker (painted in 1900) is in the Walker Art Gallery, Bowdoin College, Brunswick, ME. He died in Brattleboro, VT, on Jan. 10, 1904.

HARDING, CHARLOTTE.
See Mrs. James A. Brown.

HARDING, CHESTER.
Born at Conway, MA, Sept, 1792. He began life as a peddler in Western New York, painted signs in Pennsylvania, and finally, although entirely self-taught, became a fashionable portrait painter. He lived at various times in St. Louis, Philadelphia, and Boston; he went to London and painted the poet Rogers, the historian Alison, and several members of the Royal Family. Among his American portraits are one of Daniel Webster, owned by the Bar Association of NY; John Randolph, in the Corcoran Gallery, Washington; Charles Carroll of Carrollton. Elected Honorary Member of National Academy in 1828. He died in 1866. (See "Autobiography of Chester Harding, Artist," edited by hs daughter Margaret E. White, Boston, 1890.)

HARDING, GEORGE.
Mural Dec., Illustrator. Born Philadelphia, PA, Oct. 2, 1882. Pupil of PAFA and Howard Pyle and studied abroad. Member: SI; Salma. C.; Phila WCC; Phila. AC: Fellowship PAFA; NY Arch. Lg.; Phila. Alliance; Mural P. Special artists, Harper's Magazine, around the world, 1913. Mural decorations, Hotel Traymore, Atlantic City, NJ; Corn Exchange National Bank, Phila.; Earle Theatre, Phila.; Capitol Theatre, Trenton; Pere Marquette Hotel, Peoria, IL; American Hotel, Allentown, PA; First Nat. Bank, and Germantown Trust Co., Phila; War Dept. Collection, Smithsonian Institution, Washington, DC; Imperial War Museum Library,

London; Library War Museum, Paris. Official artists, A. E. F., 1918. Member of Faculty of the Pennsylvania Academy of the Fine Arts, and Arch. Dept., University of PA. Died 1959. Address in 1929, 128 North Broad Street, Philadelphia, PA.

HARDING, JOHN L.
Portrait painter. Working in New England. His portrait of Mrs. John Lovett is signed "J. L. Harding, 1837" and is owned in Woodstock, CT.

HARDRICK, JOHN W.
Painter and teacher. Born Indianapolis, IN, Sept. 21, 1891. Pupil of William Forsythe, Otto Stark. Member: Indiana AA. Works: Portrait of Evans Wollen, Fletcher Savings and Trust Co.; portrait of George L. Knox and H. L. Sanders, YMCA. Indianapolis; portrait of Bishop Jones, Wilberforce University; portrait of Miss Lackey, Haughville School; portrait of Rev. Lewis, Bethel, AME Indianapolis; "Still Life," School No. 64 Indianapolis. Address in 1929, 46 North Pennsylvania Street, Rm. 314; h. 2908 Meredith Avenue, Indianapolis, IN.

HARDWICK, ALICE R.
(Mrs. Melbourne H. Hardwick). Painter, writer, and teacher. Born Chicago, Jan. 18, 1876. Pupil of DuMond, Birge Harrison, Melbourne H. Hardwick; ASL of NY; studied in Holland and Belgium. Member: Springfield AL; North Shore AA; Copley S; AFA. Address in 1929, 486 Boylston Street, Boston, MA; summer, Annisquam, MA.

HARDWICK, MELBOURNE H.
Painter. Born in Digby Nova Scotia on Sept. 29, 1857. He died in Waverly, MA, 1916. He was a pupil of Triscott, Luyton and Blummers. Represented in Boston Museum of Fine Arts by "Mid-summer." Died Oct. 25, 1916, in Belmont, MA.

HARDY, ANNA E.
Painter. Born in Bangor, ME, Jan. 26, 1839. Pupil of George Jeanin in Paris; Abbott H. Thayer in Dublin, N. H. Specialty, flower painting. Died Dec. 15, 1934, in S. Orrington, ME.

HARDY, BEULAH GREENOUGH.
Painter. Born Providence, RI. Pupil of Collin, Merson, Courtois and Virginia Reynolds in Paris; Sir Charles Holroya in London. Member: Soc. of Miniatures, London; Plastic C.; Phila. Alliance; Phila. PC; AFA. Address in 1929, 336 Meehan Avenue, Mt. Airy, Philadelphia, PA.

HARDY, CHARLES.
Illustrator. Born In England, May 29, 1888. Pupil of E. P. Kinsella. Member: GFLA. Died in 1935. Address in 1929, 43 West 67th Street, New York, NY; Compo Street, Westport, CT.

HARDY, JEREMIAH.
Painter Born Oct. 22, 1800. Pupil of S. F. B. Morse. He painted a portrait of Cyrus Hamlin (seen in profile to left, wearing spectacles), owned by Boston Museum of Fine Arts. He died in 1888. Father of Anna. E. Hardy.

HARDY, WALTER MANLY.
Painter and illustrator. Born at Brewer, ME, in 1877. Pupil of Lazar in Paris; Blum, Brush, Cox, Clark and Bridgman in NY. Address in 1926, 159 Wilson Street, Brewer, ME.

HARE, J. KNOWLES.
Illustrator. Born Montclair, NJ, Jan. 19, 1882. Member: SI. Designer of covers for Saturday Evening Post, American Magazine, etc. Died 1947. Address in 1929, 1 West 67th Street; 27 East 27th Street, New York, NY.

HARE, JEANNETTE R.
Sculptor. Born Antwerp, Belgium, Aug. 24, 1898. Pupil of C. C. Rumsey, A.S. Calder, H. Frischmuth. Member: NA Women PS. Address in 1929, 20 Whitson Street, Forest Hills, LI, NY.; Forest Hills, LI, NY; summer Ogunquit, ME.

HARER, FREDERICK W.
Etcher. Born Uhlerstown, PA, Nov. 15, 1880. Pupil of PAFA under Anshutz and Chase. Award: Balto. WCC. prize, 1921. Represented in Pennsylvania Academy of the Fine

Arts. Address in 1929, Uhlerstown, PA.

HARGENS, CHARLES.
Painter. Born 1893. He exhibited water colors at the Penna. Academy of Fine Arts Water Color Exhibition, Philadelphia, 1925. Address in 1926, 303 Walnut Street, Philadelphia, PA.

HARHBERGER, FLORENCE E.
Painter, illustrator, and teacher. Born Freetown, Cortland Co., NY, Nov. 19, 1863. Pupil of ASL and Cooper Union in New York, under Brush, J. Alden Weir, Shirlaw and Frederick Freer. Member: Utica Art C.; Utica Sketch C. Address in 1929, 223 West Fayette Street, Syracuse, NY.

HARKAVY, MINNA.
Sculptor. Studied at Art Students' League; Hunter College; in Paris with Antoine Bourdelle. Awards: National Association of Women Artists, 1940-1941; National Exhibition of American Science, Metropolitan Museum of Art, 1951; Project award, United States Treasury. Collections: Whitney Museum of American Art; Museum of Modern Art; Musee Municipal, St. Denis, France; Museum of Western Art, Russia; Tel-Aviv, Ain Harod Museum, Israel; United States Post Office, Winchendon, MA. Address in 1980, 2109 Broadway, New York City.

HARKINS, ROBERT.
Miniature painter of Brooklyn, NY. He flourished about 1841.

HARLAN, HAROLD COFFMAN.
Illustrator, etcher and artist. Born Dayton, OH, April 5, 1890. Pupil of Max Seiffert, Carl Howell, ect. Member: AIA; Dayton SE; Dayton AG; Ohio State A. of Arch. Address in 1929, 2905 Salem Avenue, at Benton, Dayton, OH.

HARLAND, MARY.
Painter. Born Yorkshire, Eng., Oct. 8, 1863. Studied in London, Dresden and Paris. Member: Cal. Soc. Min. P. Award: Silver medal, P.-P. Exp., San F., 1915. Address in 1929, 1323 14th Street, Santa Monica, CA.

HARLAND, THOMAS.
Book plate engraver, located for a time in Norwich, CT.

HARLES, VICTOR J.
Painter. Born in St. Louis, MO, in 1894. Pupil of St. Louis School of Fine Arts. Address in 1926, Hanley Road and Canton Avenue, Clayton, MO.

HARLEY, CHARLES RICHARD.
Sculptor. Born in Philadelphia in 1864. Educated at Spring Garden Institute; Penna. Academy of Fine Arts; in Paris at Ecole Nationale des Arts Decorative, Academie Julien, École des Beaux Arts, and under Dampt and Aube; also in NY under St. Gaudens and Martiny; and in Rome and Florence. Professionally engaged as sculptor since 1895. Medal, Buffalo Exposition, 1901. Address in 1926, 709 West 169th Street, New York.

HARLOS, STELLA.
Painter and teacher. Born Milwaukee, Aug. 6, 1901. Pupil of Layton School of Art. G. V. Sinclair, William Owens, Jr. Member: Wis. Soc. AC. Award: Hon. mention, Milwaukee, AI, 1924. Address in 1929, 752 - 24th Street, Milwaukee, WI.

HARLOW, HARRY MERRICK SUTTON.
Painter and craftsman. Born Haverhill, July 19, 1882. Pupil of Eric Pape in Boston. Member: Haverhill SAC. Work: Mural decorations, Trinity Church, Haverhill, MA; St. Martin banner, St. Augustine and St. Martin Mission Church, Boston, MA; panels in Chapel of the Society of the Divine Compassion, New York City; panels in Christ Church, Portsmouth, NH. Specialty, illumination. Address in 1929, 226 Merrimack Street, Lowell, MA; h. 307 Dennett Street, Portsmouth, NH.

HARLOW, LOUIS R.
Water color artists and etcher. Born in Wareham, MA. In 1880 he opened his studio in Boston. His work was very popular with publishers of fine books, his illustrations having color and brilliancy.

400

HARMER, THOMAS C.
Landscape painter. Born Hastings, Eng., April 29, 1865. Pupil of L. H. Meakin, Frank Duveneck. Member Tacoma AS.; Seattle FAS. Address in 1929, 516 North K Street, Tacoma, WA.

HARMES, ELMER E.
Painter and teacher. Born Milwaukee, WI, June 20, 1902. Pupil of George Oberteuffer, Arthur Carles, Henry McCarten, G. Moeller. Member: Wis. PS; Fellowship PAFA; Delta Phi Delta. Awards: Ramborger prize, PAFA, 1924; Bain prize, Wis. PS, 1928. Address in 1929, No. 9, 1000 University Avenue, S. E. Minneapolis, MN.

HARMON, CLIFF FRANKLIN.
Painter. Born in Los Angeles, CA, June 26, 1923. Study: Bisttram School of Fine Art, Los Angeles and Taos, with Emil Bisttram; Black Mtn. College, NC, with Joe Fiore; Taos Valley Art School, with Louis Ribak. Work: Museum of Art, Santa Fe, NM; Oklahoma Art Ctr. Exhibitions: Dallas Museum; NM Museum of Art; Joslyn Museum, Omaha; Bertrand Russell Centennial, London. Awards: NM State Fair; NM Mus.; Phoenix Art Mus. Mem.: Taos Art Assn. Media: Acrylic, watercolor. Address in 1982, Taos, NM.

HARMON, EVELYN SHAYLOR.
Miniature painter. Born 1871. Member: PA. S. Min. P. Exhibited at PAFA in 1925. Address in 1929, 40 Carleton Street, Brookline, MA; 147 Pine Street, Portland, ME.

HARMON, LILY.
Painter, lithographer, and sculptor. Born: New Haven, CT, Nov. 19, 1912. Studied: Yale University School of Fine Art; Art Students League; also in Paris. Collections: Encyclopaedia Britannica; Butler Art Inst.; Tel-Aviv, Ain Harod Museum, Israel; Newark Museum of Art; New York Jewish Community Center, Port Chester. Address in 1980, 151 Central Park W., New York, NY.

HARNETT, WILLIAM M.
Painter of still life. Born in 1848, died in 1892.

HARNISCH, ALBERT E.
Sculptor. Born in Philadelphia, 1843. Pupil of Jos. A. Bailly. He executed the Calhoun Monument and the Barclay family group. He made a specialty of portrait busts; he studied at the Pennsylvania Academy of Fine Arts and later went to Italy for study, residing for eight years in Rome.

HARPER, EDITH W.
Painter. Exhibited at Cincinnati Museum in 1925. Address in 1926, 2119 Alpine Place, Cincinnati, OH.

HARPER, GEORGE COBURN.
Etcher. Born Leetonia, OH, Oct. 23, 1887. Pupil of Cleveland School of Art, ASL of NY. Member: Scarab C. Work: "Christmas Morning," Biblioteque Nationale, Paris; "Mountain Home," Los Angeles Museum of Art, Los Angeles, CA. Died 1962. Address in 1929, 116 Orchard Drive, Northville, MI.

HARPER, MARIAN DUNLAP.
Miniature painter. Studied at AIC and in Paris. Member: Chicago SA; Chicago S. Miniature painter.; Chicago AG. Address in 1929, 578 Washington Avenue,; 847 Grove Street, Glencoe, IL.

HARPER, WILLIAM ST. JOHN.
Painter, etcher and illustrator. He was born at Rhinebeck, NY, Sept. 8, 1851, and first studied in the schools of the National Academy under Professor Wilmarth. Later he was a pupil of William M. Chase and Walter Shirlaw in NY and of MM. Munkacsy and Bonnat in Paris. Mr. Harper was president of the Art Students' League in 1881 and was Associate of the National Academy. Member of the New York Etching Club. In 1892 he was awarded the Clarke Prize at the Academy for his picture called "Autumn." He died Nov. 2, 1910, in NYC.

HARRIS, ALEXANDRINA ROBERTSON.
Miniature painter. Born Aberdeen, Scotland, July 11, 1886. Pupil of Adelphi Art School under Whitaker; ASL of NY; Am. School of Min. Painters. Member: NA Women PS; Brooklyn S. Min. P.; PA Soc. Min. P. Awards: Hon. mention, NA Women PS, 1922; Charlotte Ritchie Smith

Memorial Prize, Balto, WCC., 1922. Address in 1929, 101 Columbia Heights, Brooklyn, New York, NY.

HARRIS, CHARLES GORDON.
Painter. Born Providence, Oct. 17, 1891. Pupil of Stacy Tolman, George A. Hays, H. Cyrus Farnum, RI. School of Design. Member: Prov. AC; Prov. WCC; South County, AA. Address in 1929, 138 Smithfield Road, North Providence, RI.

HARRIS, CHARLES X.
Painter. Born Foxcroft, ME, 1856. Pupil of Cabanel in Paris. Work in: Memorial Hall, Philadelphia; portraits in Manor Hall, Yonkers; Mercantile Library; Lambs' Club, New York; stained glass window, Doylestown, PA; Perce, Quebec, Canada. Address in 1929, 356 Mountain Road, West Hoboken, NJ.

HARRIS, GEORGE EDGERLY.
Painter and etcher. Born Milford Hundred, DE, Oct. 22, 1898. Pupil of NAD; C. C. Curran; Charles X. Harris. Member: Mural P; Salma. C. Work: Portraits in the Manor Hall, Yonkers, NY. Address in 1929, 412 Eighth Avenue, New York, NY. Died before 1940.

HARRIS, JAMES.
A line engraving of a Madonna, well executed and published about 1850, is signed "Ja's Harris, Engraver, 58 Nassau Street, New York." No other plates of this engraver have been seen.

HARRIS, JOSEPH T.
Portrait painter. He exhibited at the Boston Athenaeum in 1833, "A Portrait of a Gentleman."

HARRIS, LOUIS.
Painter and teacher. Born St. Louis, MO, Nov. 7, 1902. Pupil of Kenneth Hayes Miller, Max Weber. Member: ASL of NY. Address in 1929, 331 East 25th Street, NYC.

HARRIS, MARION D.
Painter. Born 1904 in Phila. PA. Exhibited water colors at Annual Exhibition of Water Colors, Penna. Academy of Fine Arts, Philadelphia,

1925. Address in 1926, 920 Madison Avenue, Wilmington, DE.

HARRIS, MRS. REGINALD G.
See Davenport, Jane.

HARRIS, ROBERT G.
Illustrator. Born in 1911 in Kansas City, MO. He studied under Harvey Dunn and George Bridgman. He attended the KCAI, ASL and GCSA in New York. From 1938 to 1960 his illustrations appeared in The Saturday Evening Post, Ladies Home Journal, Redbook, Woman's Home Companion, McCall's and Good Housekeeping. In 1962 he had a one-man show entitled Portraits, which was held at the Phoenix Art Museum in Arizona. He is currently working exclusively on portraits.

HARRIS, SAMUEL.
Engraver. Born in Boston, MA, May 1783. He was drowned in the Charles River, on July 7, 1810. "The Polyanthos," Boston 1812, published a memoir of Samuel Harris, and from this we learn that he was apprenticed at an early age to his relative, the Boston engraver, Samuel Hill, and the first portrait executed by Harris appeared in "The Polyanthos" for 1806. As an engraver Harris worked in both line and in stipple and his plates possess some merit and show great promise.

HARRIS, WILLIAM L.
Mural painter. Born in New York in 1870, he died at Lake George, NY, in 1924. Studied art at Art Students' League, New York, and in Paris at Academie Julien. Worked on decorations for Congressional Library, Washington, DC and collaborated with Francis Lathrop in decorating St. Bartholomew's Church, New York. He also lectured on art subjects. Designed decoration for Church of the Paulist Fathers, New York.

HARRISON, CATHERINE NORRIS.
(See Patterson, Catherine Norris.)

HARRISON, CHARLES.
Engraver. In 1840 he was working as a letter engraver in New York.

HARRISON, CHARLES P.
Engraver. Born in England in 1783, he was the son of Wm. Harrison, Sr., and was brought to Philadelphia by his father in 1794. He was probably a pupil of his father in engraving. From 1806 until 1819 he was in business in Philadelphia as a copperplate printer, but in 1820-22 Harrison combined "engraving" with his printing establishement. In 1823 he was in business in NY; he remained there until 1850 and probably later. Died 1854 in NYC. There is some very good line work signed by C. P. Harrison, but his stipple portrait work is inferior in execution. He also attempted portrait painting with very indifferent success. Charles P. Harrison was the father of Gabrial Harrison, the actor and author, born in Philadelphia in 1818.

HARRISON, DAVID R.
This bank-note engraver was for many years in the employ of the American Bank Note Co., and he continued to engrave until he was nearly ninety years of age.

HARRISON, HENRY.
Painter. Born in England in 1844. He came to America with his parents when six years old and studied under Danl. Huntington and LeClear. He has painted many portraits. His picture of Jonathan Dayton is in the Capitol Building at Wash., DC. He died in 1923 in Jersey City, NJ.

HARRISON, J. P.
Engraver. He is known as the first engraver who practiced west of Alleghenies. He was established in Pittsburgh, PA, in 1817.

HARRISON, JEANNETTE SHEPHERD.
See Loop, Mrs. Henry A.

HARRISON, LOWELL BIRGE.
Painter. Born in Philadelphia in 1854. Pupil of Cabanel in Paris. Elected an Associate Member of the National Academy of Design, NY, in 1902, and to full membership in 1910. Represented by "The Mirror," in Wilstach Collection, Philadelphia; "Glimpse of St. Laurence" at Penna. Academy of Fine Arts; at the Luxembourg Gallery,

Paris. Died 1911 in Woodstock, NY. Address in 1926, Woodstock, NY.

HARRISON, RICHARD.
The name of "Richard Harrison, Engraver" appears in the Philadelphia directories in 1820-22 inclusive, together with that of Richard G. Harrison, noted below. Previous to that time, or in 1814, he was engraving line frontispieces, etc., for F. Lucas & J. Cushing, publishers of Baltimore, Maryland.

HARRISON, RICHARD G.
This line engraver was probably one of the "several sons" of Wm. Harrison, Sr., who came to Philadelphia in 1794. R. G. Harrison was engraving for the "Port Folio" in 1814 and possibly earlier than that for S. F. Bradford's Philadelphia edition of the Edinburgh Encyclopedia of 1805-18. After 1822 he is called "bank-note engraver" in the Philadelphia directories and in this capacity his name appears there continuously until 1845.

HARRISON, RICHARD G. JR.
This younger R. G. Harrison was mezzotint engraver working in Philadelphia about 1860-65, chiefly upon portrait.

HARRISON, SAMUEL.
Engraver. Born in 1789. Westcott, in his "History of Philadelphia," says that Samuel Harrison was a son of William Harrison and that he was a pupil in engraving with his father before 1810, and died on July 18, 1818, aged twenty-nine years. The only example of his work seen is a good line map of Lake Ontario and Western New York, engraved in 1809.

HARRISON, THOMAS ALEXANDER.
Painter. Born Philadelphia, PA, Jan. 17, 1853. Pupil of PAFA; Ecole des Beaux-Arts, Bastien-Lepage and Gerome in Paris. Member: SAA 1885; ANA 1898, NA 1901; AC Phila.; Paris SAC; Fellowship Penna. Acad. of Fine Arts; Century Assoc.; Phila. WCC (hon.); Cercle d'Union Artistique; Soc. Nat. des Beaux-Arts; Royal

403

Inst. of Painters in Oil Colors, London; Soc. of Secessionists, Berlin and Munich (cor.); National Institute of Arts and Letters. Awards: Honorable mention, Paris Salon, 1885; Temple silver medal, PAFA 1887; gold medal, Paris Exp., 1889; second medal, Munich Salon, 1891; medal of honor, Brussels and Ghent 1892; gold medal of honor, PAFA 1894; medals of honor at Vienna and Berlin. Chevalier of Legion of Honor 1889, Officer 1901; Officer of Public Instruction, by French Government. Work: "L'Arcadie" and "Solitude," Luxembourg Museum, Paris; "The Wave," Pennsylvania Academy, Philadelphia; "Crepuscule," Corcoran Gallery, Washington, DC; "Sables et Lune," Quimper Museum, France; "Les Amateurs," Art Institute, Chicago; "Nude," Royal Gallery, Dresden; "A Festival Night," "Boys Bathing," "East Hampton," "Le Grand Mirror" and "Marine," Milstack Gallery, Philadelphia; "Castles in Spain," Metropolitan Museum, New York; "Golden Dunes," St. Paul Institute. Died in 1930. Address in 1929, 6 Rue du Val de Grace, Paris, France; and Century Assoc., 7 West 43d Street, NY; Woodstock, NY; Concarneau, France.

HARRISON, WILLIAM.
Engraver. Born in England; died in Philadelphia, Oct. 18, 1803. William Harrison is said to have been a grandson of John Harrison, the inventor of the chronometer. He learned to engrave in London and was for a time in the employ of the Bank of England; he also engraved maps for the East India Company. In 1794 Wm. Harrison came to Philadelphia "with several sons" under an engagement to engrave for the Bank of Pennsylvania. He remained there until his death.

HARRISON, WILLIAM F.
Born c. 1912 in PA. This excellent letter engraver was in the employ of New York bank-note companies 1831-40.

HARRISON, WILLIAM JR.
Engraver. This son of William Harrison was engraving in line in Philadelphia as early as 1797,

signing himself "W. Harrison, Junior Sculp't." As an engraver his name appears in the Philadelphia directories for 1802-19 inclusive. He was a good portrait engraver in line and also worked in stipple. Very little of his signed work is seen and he was probably chiefly employed by the bank-note engraving companies.

HARRITON, ABRAHAM.
Painter and etcher. Born Bucharest, Romania, Feb. 16, 1893. Pupil of NAD under J. W. Maynard and C. F. Mielatz. Member: S. Indp. A; Salons of Amer. Represented in Oakland (CA) Public Museum. Address in 1929, 3908 Gorman Avenue, Sunnyside, LI, NY.

HARSHE, ROBERT BARTHOLOW.
Painter, etcher, teacher, and writer. Born Salisbury, MO, May 26, 1879. Pupil of AIC; ASL of NY. University of MO; Teachers Col. New York, under Dow; Laszlo in London; Colarossi Academy in Paris. Member: Cal. SE (hon.); Brooklyn SE (hon.); Am. Ceramic S. (hon.) Chicago SI; NY SE; Am. Com. on Three to Internat. Congr. of Art Edn. Paris; Sec. - Treas., Assoc Art Museum Directors, 1917-1922 Chic. AC; Cliff Dwellers C Advisory Council Artistic Relations Section, Lg. of Nations Int. Institute of Intellectual Cooperation. Work in: Luxembourg Museum, Paris; Brooklyn Museum; Harrison Gallery, Los Angeles Museum. Asst. chief Dept. of Fine Arts, Panama-Pac. Exp. San Francisco, 1915; ex-asst. director Dept. of Fine Arts, Carnegie Institute, Pittsburgh, PA. Chevalier Legion of Honor (France) 1925. Director of Art Institute of Chicago. Address in 1929, 31 Belden Avenue, Chicago, IL. Died in 1938.

HART, ALFRED.
Painter. Born in Norwich, CT March 28, 1816, in 1848 he moved to Hartford, CT, and later to the West.

HART, GEORGE OVERBURY.
Painter and etcher. Born Cairo IL, May 10, 1868. Self-taught Member: AWCS; NYWCC; Brooklyn SE

404

Salons of America; S. Indp. A. Awards: Etching prize, Brooklyn SE, 1923-24; first prize, water color, Palisade Art Association, Englewood, NJ, 1924; bronze medal, Sesqui-Centennial Expost., Phila., 1926. Represented in New York Public Library; Metropolitan Museum of Art; Brooklyn Museum; Smithsonian Institution, Washington, DC; Newark Museum; Cincinnati Museum; Memorial Gallery, Rochester, NY; South Kensington and British Museums, London. Died in 1933. Address in 1929, Coytesville, NJ.

HART, JAMES MCDOUGAL.
Landscape painter. Born in Kilmarnock, Scotland, May 10, 1828. He was brought to America in 1831 and apprenticed to a coach painter. In 1851 he went to Dusseldorf, Germany, for a year's study and returning home he settled in New York City. Elected Associate of National Academy in 1857 and National Academy in 1859. Represented at Corcoran Art Gallery, Washington, DC, by "The Drove at the Ford." He died October 24, 1901 in Brooklyn, NY.

HART, JOEL T.
Sculptor. Born Feb 10, 1810, in Clark County, KY. He went abroad for study and spent much of his life in Florence, Italy. He executed several statues of Henry Clay and busts of many prominent men. He died March 12, 1877.

HART, JOHN FRANCIS.
Cartoonist. He was born in Germantown, Philadelphia, in 1867. Died c. 1950. Address in 1926, 169 Hansberry Street, Germantown, Philadelphia.

HART, LEON.
Painter. Exhibited at "Exhibition of Paintings Showing Later Tendencies in Art," Philadelphia, 1921. Address in 1926, 311 West 24th Street, New York City.

HART, LETITIA BONNET.
Painter. Born New York, April 20, 1867. Pupil of her father, James M. Hart; NAD under Edgar M. Ward. Award: Dodge prize, NAD 1898. Work: Miss Mattie Harris, Virginia

College, Roanoke. Exhibited at NA, 1885. Address in 1929, 94 First Place, Brooklyn, New York, NY; summer, Lakeville, CT.

HART, WILLIAM HOWARD.
Painter. Born Fishkill-on-Hudson, NY, 1863. Pupil of ASL and J. Alden Weir in New York; Boulanger and Lefebvre in Paris. Member: Salma. C., 1898; AFA. Address in 1929, 131 East 66th Street, New York, NY.

HART, WILLIAM M.
Painter. Born at Paisley, Scotland, March 31, 1823; died at Mt. Vernon, NY, June 17, 1894. Specialty, landscapes with cattle. Represented at the Metropolitan Museum by "Scene at Napanock" and "Seashore Morning." Elected to National Academy, 1858. Brother of James M. Hart. Hudson River School Artist.

HARTIGAN, GRACE.
Painter. Born: Newark, NJ, March 28, 1922. Studied: Newark College of Engineering; and with Isaac Lane. Her subject matter is usually abstract. Collections: Museum of Modern Art; Metropolitan Museum of Art. Media: Oil on canvas, watercolor collage. Address in 1980, Baltimore, MD.

HARTING, GEORGE W.
Illustrator and painter. Born Little Falls, MN, Dec. 11, 1877. Pupil of Henri, Chase, Mora, Miller and Koehler. Member: SI 1912; Salma. C., 1917; Pictorial Photographers, 1918; contributing member, Pittsburgh Photo Salon. Illustrations for House and Garden, Woman's Home Companion, Vogue, McCalls, Delineator, etc. Address in 1929, 51 West 10th Street, New York, NY.

HARTLEY, JONATHAN SCOTT.
Sculptor. Born in Albany, NY, in 1845. He studied in New England and later in Paris and Italy. His first teacher was Erastus D. Palmer, one of the early American sculptors. He married the daughter of the painter George Inness. He was elected to the National Academy in 1891 and died in New York City on Dec. 6, 1912.

405

HARTLEY, MARSDEN.
Painter. Born Lewiston, ME, 1878. Studied at Cleveland Art School and ASL. Pupil of Nina Waldeck; DuMond; Cox; Luis Mora; Francis Jones; Chase School. Represented in Phillips Memorial Gallery, Washington, DC. Exhibited at PAFA in 1921, at "Exb. of Paintings Showing the Later Tendencies in Art." Died Sept. 2, 1943. Address in 1929, Aix-en-Provence, France; Room 303, 489 Park Avenue, New York, NY.

HARTLEY, RACHEL.
Painter, illustrator, lecturer, and teacher. Born New York, Jan. 4, 1884. Pupil of ASL of NY. Member: ASL of NY; NAC; PBC; Wash. AC; AFA. Work: "Shrimp Gatherers," Museum of Georgetown, British Guiana. Address in 1929, Barn Yard Studio, Southampton, LI, NY; h. 16 East 96th Street, New York, NY.

HARTMAN, BERTRAM.
Painter. Dec. Born Junction City, KS, April 18, 1882. Studied at AIC; Royal Acad., Munich; and in Paris. Member: Chicago SA; AWSC. Died c. 1960. Address in 1929, care of the Montross Gallery, 26 East 56th Street; 267½ West 11th Street, New York, NY.

HARTMAN, REBER S.
Painter. He exhibited water colors at the PAFA, Philadelphia, 1925. Address in 1926, 1316 Spring Garden Street, Philadelphia, PA.

HARTMAN, ROBERT.
Painter. Born Dec. 17, 1926, in Sharon, PA. Educated at University of Arizonia (BFA, MA), Colorado Springs W. Mangravite, Vytlacil, Sander and Woelffer. Taught Texas Tech. College, University Nevada/Reno, University CA. Berkeley (1961). Awarded 1st prize Walter Fund, SF Art Inst. (1967); awards from Tucson Art Center, (1952 & 1957), Butler Inst., Youngstown (1955), Art Center, LaJolla (1962), Int. Young Artists, Tokyo (1967). Exhibited at Kipnis Gallery, Westport, CT. (1954); Whitney Biennial (1973), Baum Gallery (1978) & Cerf Gallery (1980), in SF. In collections of University of Washington; Roswell Mus., New Mexico; Butler Inst., Youngstown; Smithsonian, Colo. Springs Fine Art Center, and Oakland Mus.

HARTMAN, SYDNEY K.
Painter and illustrator. Born in Germany in 1863. Pupil of Laurens and Benjamin Constant in Paris. Address in 1926, 13 West 30th Street, New York, NY.

HARTRATH, LUCIE.
Painter and teacher. Born in Boston. Pupil of Rixens, Courtois and Collin in Paris; Angelo Jauk in Munich, 1906. Studied at ASL in 1896. Member: Chicago PS; Cordon C; Chicago AC; Kunstlerinen Verein Munich; NA Women PS. Awards Butler purchase prize, AIC 1911 Young Fortnightly prize, AIC 1912 Rosenwald purchase prize ($200) AIC 1915; Carr landscape prize, AI 1916: Municipal Art Lg. Purchase Prize; Terre Haute Star Prize ($200), Hoosier Salon, 1925 and 1928; DeFrees prize. Hoosier Salon, 1927; Trikappa prize ($200) Hoosier Salon, 1929. head of Dept of Drawing and paintings Rockfor (IL) College. Address in 1929, East Ohio Street, Chicago, IL.

HARTSON, WALTER C.
Painter. Born in Wyoming, IA, in 1866. Member: New York Water Color Club; Society of Independent Artists. Awards: Bronze medal and honorable mention, Atlanta Exposition, 1895; third Hallgarten prize, National Academy of Design, 1898; first landscape prize Osborne competition, 1904. Address in 1926, Wassaic, Dutchess County NY.

HARTWELL, ALONSO.
Portrait painter in oils, and crayon portrait draughtsman. Born 1805 in Littleton, MA; died Waltham, MA, 1873. Hartwell moved to Boston in 1822, and was apprenticed to a wood engraver and practiced that art professionally from 1826 to 1851. In the latter year he started painting portraits in oils.

HARTWELL, GEORGE KENNETH.
Painter, illustrator, and craftsman. Born Fitchburg, MA, June 6, 1891. Pupil of Frank DuMond, Kenneth Miller, W. R. Leigh. Member: AFA. Died Dec. 13, 1949. Address in 1929, 333 Fourth Avenue; h. 518 Ft. Washington Avenue, New York, NY.

HARTWELL, KENNETH.
Painter. Exhbited water colors at the PAFA, Philadelphia, 1925. Address in 1926, 518 Fort Washington Avenue, New York City.

HARTWICH, HERMAN.
Painter. Born in New York in 1853. He received his first instruction in drawing and painting from his father. Studied Royal Academy, Munich, in 1877 received a medal there. Pupil of Profs. Diez and Loefftz. Specialty: figure, landscapes, portraits, animals, etc. Has painted many subjects in Upper Bacaria in the Tyrol. Made short stays in Paris and Holland, and was painting portraits in the United States, 1893-96. Died 1926.

HARVEY, ELI.
Sculptor, painter, and craftsman. Born Ogden, OH, Sept 23, 1860. Pupil of Cincinnati Academy under Leutz, Noble and Rebisso; Julian Academy in Paris under Lefebvre, Constant and Doucet; Delecluse Academy under Delance and Callot, and Fremiet at the Jardin des Plantes. Member: NSS 1902; NY Arch. Lg. 1903; Paris AAA; Am. Soc. Animal P and S.; Allied AA; Nat. des Beaux Arts; CA. AC: Laguna Beach AA; AFA. Awards: First class gold medal for painting, Paris-Province Exp., 1900; Wanamaker prize for sculpture, Paris AAA, 1900; bronze medal for sculpture, Pan-Am. Exp., Buffalo, 1901; bronze medal St. Louis Exp., 1904; bronze medal P. P. Exp., San F., 1915. Work: "Maternal Caress" and American bald eagle for honor roll, Metropolitan Museum, New York; sculpture for Lion House, New York Zoo; recumbent lions for Eaton Mausoleum; portrait of "Dinah," gorilla, for NY Zoological Society; medal; commemorating entry of the U.S. into the war, for American Numismatic Soceity; Eagles for the Victory Arch, New York; American Elk for BPOE; sculpture for the Evangeline Blashfield Memorial Fountain; Brown Bear Mascot for Brown University, Providence; represented in museums of St. Louis, Liverpool, Newark, Cincinnati; American Museum of National History, and Metropolitan Museum of Art, New York. Died Feb. 10, 1957 in CA. Address in 1929, 333 Fourth Avenue, h. 518 Ft. Washington Avenue, New York, NY.

HARVEY, GEORGE.
Born in England, 1800. Painter of landscapes and miniatures, flourishing 1837 to 1840. In 1836 he painted a miniature from life of Daniel Webster in the Senate Chamber, Washington, DC. Died in England, 1878.

HARVEY, HAROLD LeROY.
Painter and illustrator. Born Baltimore, July 7, 1899. Pupil of Turner, McCarter, Desponjols. Baudouin and others. Member: Carcoal C., Baltimore; Fellowship PAFA; Kit Kat C.; Paris AAA. Address in 1929, 62 West 9th Street, New York, NY; h. 2935 St. Paul Street, Baltimore, MD.

HARVEY, PAUL.
Painter. Born Chicago, IL. Pupil of AIC; Boston Museum School. Member: Boston AC; CA AC. Work: "The Cedars." Boston Art Club. Address in 1929, 268 West 40th Street, New York, NY.

HARVEY, RICHARD D.
Illustrator. Born in Meadville, PA, in 1940. He studied under John LaGatta at the ACD and Phoenix College. Beginning in 1967 with an illustration for Good Housekeeping, he has since illustrated for McCall's, Business Week, Time, Oui, Cosmopolitan and others. Many of his illustrations have been paperback covers for Avon, Dell, Pyramid and Ballantine.

HARVEY, ROBERT.
Painter. Born Dublin, Ireland, May 12, 1868. Pupil of George Smillie. Member: Chicago NJSA; Salons of America. Address in 1929: 10 Sniffen Court, East 36th Street,

New York, NY; summer, 165 Oak Street, Plattsburg, NY.

HARWOOD, BURT S.
Painter. Born in Iowa in 1897. His specialty was painting the Indians of Taos, NM, where he died in 1924.

HARWOOD, JAMES T.
Painter and teacher. Born Lehi, UT, 1860. Pupil of Laurens and Bonnat in Paris. Member: NAC. Head of Art Department, Universtiy of Utah. Specialty, colored etching. Died 1940. Address in 1929, University of Utah; h. 1718 Lake Street, Salt Lake City, UT.

HARWOOD, SABRA B.
Sculptor. Born Brookline, MA, Jan. 18, 1895. Pupil of Bela Pratt and Charles Grafly. Member: Copley S. Address in 1929, 21 Lime Street, Boston, MA.

HASELTINE, HERBERT.
Sculptor. Born Rome, Italy, April 10, 1877. Pupil of Aime Morot. Work: "British Champion Animals," Field Museum, Chicago, IL. Died 1962. Address in 1929, 4 Rue Docteur Blanche;. h. 20 Impasse Raffet, Paris, France.

HASELTINE, JAMES HENRY.
Sculptor. Born in Philadelphia Nov. 2, 1833. He studied in Paris and Rome. Served in the United States Army in Civil War. He executed statue of "America Honoring Her Fallen Brave," owned by Philadelphia Union League Club. He also did portraits of Longfellow, Read, Gen'l Sheridan and Gen'l Merritt. Died Nov. 9, 1907, in Italy.

HASELTINE, WILLIAM STANELY.
Sculptor. Born June 11, 1835, in Phila. Studied in Philadelphia under Webster. Elected an Academician of National Academy of Design, 1861. He had a studio in Rome, and exhibited at the "Centennial," in Philadelphia, 1876. Died Feb. 3, 1900, in Rome, Italy. Brother of J. H. Haseltine.

HASEN, BURT STANLEY.
Painter and printmaker. Born in NYC, Dec. 19, 1921. Study: ASL,

1940, 42, 46, with Morris Kantor Hans Hofmann School of Fine Arts 1947-48; Acad. Grande Chaumiere Paris, 1948-50, with Ossip Zadkine; Accad. Belli Arti, Rome 1959-60. Work: Walker Art Ctr. Minneapolis; Worcester Art Mus. Muhlenberg College, Allentown, PA others. Comn.: Mural, YMHA & YWHA NYC, 1947. Exhib.: Salon Mai Mus. Art Mod., Paris, 1951; Met Mus., NYC, 1953; Berlin Acad. 1956; Whitney, NYC, 1963; Walker Art Ctr., 1966. Awards: Purchase prizes, Emily Lowe Found., 1954 Fulbright Grant to Italy, 1959-66 Teaching: Sch. of Visual Arts 1953-pres.; etc. Media: Oil acrylic. Address in 1982, 7 Dutch St., NYC.

HASHIMOTO, MICHI.
Painter and illustrator. Born Japan, July 10, 1897. Member: C, WCS; Arthur Wesley Dow A. Address in 1929, 1947 Sawtelle Blvd. Sawtelle, CA.

HASKELL, ERNEST.
Painter, lithographer, etcher, and writer. Born Woodstock, CT, Jul 30, 1876. Member: Chicago SE Award: Bronze medal for etchings P. P. Exp., San F., 1915. Also resided in New Milford, CT. Died in Bath, ME, on Nov. 1, 1925.

HASKELL, IDA C.
Painter. Born in California, 1861 Studied in Chicago, Philadelphi, and Paris. Died 1932. Member: N, Women PS. Address in 1929, 23 East 15th Street, New York, NY summer, Brookhaven, LI, NY.

HASLER, WILLIAM N.
Painter and etcher. Born Washington, DC., May 9, 1865 Studied at ASL. Address in 1929 32 Hillside Avenue, Caldwell, NJ.

HASSAM, CHILDE.
Painter and etcher. Born Boston Oct. 17, 1859. Studied in Boston and Paris. Member: ANA 1902; N, 1906; AWCS; NYWCC; Boston AC; Te Am. P.; Munich Secession; Soc. Nat des Beaux-Arts; Nat. Inst. A.L. Am. Acad. A. L. Awards: AC Phila. 1892; Columbian Exp., Chicago 1893; Cleveland Art Assoc. 1893 Temple medal, PADA 1899; Pari

Exp., 1901; Pan- Am. Exp., Buffalo, 1901; St. Louis Exp., 1904; PAFA 1906; Sesnan medal, PAFA 1910; W. A. Clark prize ($2,000) and Corcoran medal, Washington, AWCS, gold medal of honor, PAFA, 1920; gold medal for painting, Phila. AC, 1915; Altman prize ($500), NAD, 1922; Altman prize ($1,000), NAD, 1924; and 1926; gold medal Sesqui-Centennial Expo., Phila., 1926. Died in 1935. Address in 1929, 130 West 57th Street, New York, NY.

HASSELBUSCH, LOUIS.
Painter. Born Philadelphia, Nov. 8, 1863. Pupil of PAFA; Academy Julian under Constant and Lefebvre in Paris; Royal Academy in Munich. Member: Phila. Sketch C. Specialty: portraits. Represented in libraries, universities, etc. Address in 1929, 1009 Lindley Avenue, Logan Station, PA; summer, Edison, Bucks Co., PA. Died before 1940.

HASSELMAN, ANNA.
Painter, lecturer, and teacher. Born Indianapolis, 1873. Pupil of Chase, Hawthorne and Forsyth. Member: Indianapolis AA: Portfolio. Lecturer on art appreciation. Curator of paintings, John Herron Art Institute. Address in 1929, John Herron Art Institute; h. 121 West 41st Street, Indianapolis, IN.

HASSELRIIS, MALTHE C. M.
Painter, illustrator, and craftsman. Born Skive, Denmark, Jan. 16, 1888. Address in 1929, 333 Seventh Avenue, New York, NY; Forest Hills Gardens, LI, NY.

HASTINGS, MARION (McVEY).
Painter. Born Geneva, NY, Jan. 25, 1894. Pupil of Alethea Hill Platt, D. J. Connah, A. H. Hibbard. Member: Seattle FAS. Award: Prize, Yakima, WA, 1929. Address in 1929, 102 Marlborough House; 1220 Boren Avenue, Seattle, WA.

HASWELL, ERNEST BRUCE.
Sculptor, writer, lecturer, and teacher. Born Kentucky, July 25, 1887. Pupil of Barnhorn, Meakin, Dubois. Member: Cin. MacD. S.; Cincinnati AC; Crafters' Guild.

Work: "Spinoza," bas-relief, Hebrew Union College and Spinoza House, The Hague; "Northcott Memorial," Springfield, IL; Cincinnati Museum, Cincinnati MacDowell Society, Rockwood Pottery; St. Coleman's Church, Cleveland; war memorial, Bond Hill, OH; was memorial, Avondale (OH) School; Kuhn Memorial, University School; Portraits of Generals Greene, St. Clair, and Wayner, Greensville, OH; Nippert Memorial, University of Cincinnati Stadium; Jacob Burnett Memorial, Cincinnati; Moorman Memorial, Louisville, KY; Holmes Memorial, Cincinnati, OH. Address in 1929, 148 East 4th Street; h. 3443 Cornell Place, Cincinnati, OH.

HATCH, EMILY NICHOLS.
Painter. Born Newport, RI. Pupil of John Ward Stimson, Chase, and Hawthorne. Member: NA Women PS (Prs. 1922-1926); SPNY, PSC. Award: McMillan prize, NY Woman's AC, 1912. Represented in National Museum, Washington. Address in 1929, 62 Washington Square, New York, NY.

HATCH, GEORGE W.
Engraver. Born about 1805, in Western New York; died at Dobbs Ferry, NY, in 1867. Hatch was one of the first students in the National Academy of Design in 1826, and for a time he was a pupil of A. B. Durand. He was a good line engraver, and in 1830 he was designing and engraving bank-note vignettes in Albany and in New York City. While he engraved portraits, landscape plates and subject plates for the "Annuals," his signed work is not plentiful. A large and well engraved portrait of Washington Irving, published in the New York Mirror in 1832, is signed "Engraved by Hatch and Smillie."

HATCH, L. J.
He was a bank-note engraver in the employ of the Treasury Department, at Washington, DC, about 1875.

HATFIELD, DONALD GENE.
Painter. Born in Detroit, MI, May 23, 1932. Study: Northwestern Mich. College; Mich. State Univ.;

Univ. of Wisc. Work: Montgomery Museum of Art, AL; Tuskegee Inst.; and others. Exhibitions: Birmingham Museum of Art; Chautauqua Art Assn., NY; others. Awards: 11th Dixie Annual; Annual Exhibition of Wisconsin Art; and many others. Mem.: Ala. Art League; AL WC Soc.; Birmingham Art Assn. Media: Watercolor. Address in 1982, Auburn, AL.

HATFIELD, JOSEPH HENRY.
Painter. Born near Kingston, Canada, in 1863. Pupil of Constant, Doucet and Lefebvre in Paris. Awards: Silver medal, MA. Charitable Mechanics Association Boston, 1892; second Hallgarten prize, National Academy of Design, 1896. Work in Boston Art Club. Address in 1926, Canton Junction, MA.

HATFIELD, KARL LEROY.
Painter and etcher. Born Jacksonville, IL, Feb. 19, 1886. Pupil of John Montgomery, Cyril Kay-Scott. Member: SSAL; El Paso AG. Address in 1929, 14 Morehouse Block; h. 1508 Elm Street, El Paso, TX; summer, Chapel Studio, Santa Fe, NM.

HATHAWAY, DR. R.
Portrait artist. He was working in New England in 1793. The lithograph portrait of Col. Briggs Alden is inscribed "Dr. R. Hallaway, del 1793."

HATHAWAY, J.
Miniature painter. Flourishing in Boston about 1833. He exhibited a miniature of a lady at the Boston Athenaeum in 1833.

HATOFSKY, JULIAN.
Painter. Born 1922 in Ellenville, NY. Studied at the Art Students' League, NYC (1946-50); Chaumiere, Paris and Hofmann School of Fine Arts, NYC (1951). Exhibited at Avant Garde Gallery, NYC (1957); Egan Gallery, NYC (1963). In the collections of the Whitney and private collections.

HAUPERS, CLEMENT B.
Painter, craftsman, and teacher. Born St. Paul, MN, March 2, 1900. Pupil of C. S. Wells; Vaclay Vytlacil, Cameron Booth, Robert Hale; Andre L'hote, E. A. Bourdelle, W. Shukhaeff, Colarossi Academy and the Academie de la Grande Chaumiere, Paris. Member: St. Paul AS: MN State AS. Award: Special mention, MN State Fair 1920; first prize, 1925, first prize, 1926, hon. mention, 1926, hon. mention, 1926, MN State Fair. Address in 1929, 783 Randolph Street, St. Paul, MN; summer, Cloverton, Pine Co., MN.

HAUPT, ERIK G.
Painter. Born in Cassel, Germany, in 1891. Pupil of Laurens and Richard Miller in Paris. Address in 1926, Care of the Charcoal Club, 1230 St. Paul Street, Baltimore, MD.

HAUSCHKA, CAROLA SPAETH.
Sculptor. April 29, 1883, in Philadelphia.

HAUSHALTER, GEORGE M.
Painter. Born Portland, ME, Jan. 9, 1862. Pupil of Julian Academy and Ecole des Beaux-Arts. Member: AWCS; Rochester AC. Work: Decorations in St. Andrew's and St. Philip's Church, Rochester, NY. Address in 1929, New Hope, PA.

HAUSMANN, GEORGE E.
Painter. Born St. Louis, MO. Pupil of Chase, Richard Miller, Laurens. Member: GFLA. Work: Mural - "Success Crowning Industry," The Fleishman Co. Address in 1929, 33 West 67th St., New York, NY; summer, Leonia, NJ.

HAVELL, ROBERT JR.
Born Nov. 25, 1793, in Eng. In 1839 the English engraver, Robt. Havell, Jr., arrived in America; his work was well known in "Audubon's Birds of America." He settled on the Hudson soon after his arrival, and died in Tarrytown, Nov. 11, 1878. In 1848 he published his engraving of "West Point from Fort Putnam" after a painting by himself. He also engraved a "View of the City of Hartford," and a number of views of other Am. Cities. An excellent sketch of Robert Havell and Robert Havell, Jr., by Geo. A. Williams, will be found in The Print

410

Collector's Quarterly, Vol. 6, No. 3, 1916. Also painted landscapes.

HAVENS, BELLE.
See Mrs. H. M. Walcott.

HAVILAND, JOHN.
Born in 1792. An English artist and architect who was in Philadelphia soon after 1800. He designed a number of buildings, and started a school for drawing in 1818 with Hugh Bridport, the miniature painter. Died March 28, 1853.

HAVLENA, JARI.
Painter. Born: Grand Forks, ND, in 1923. Studied: Abbott School of Fine Arts, Washington, DC. De Paul University, Chicago; Art Inst. of Chicago; University of Kansas City; and with Robert von Neumann, Max Kahn and Paul Wiegert. Awards: Vandergritt scholarship, Art Inst. of Chicago; Kansas des-Craftsmen, 1954. Collection: Quigley Music Studio, Kansas City.

HAWEIS, STEPHEN.
Painter and etcher. Born in London, England. Pupil of Alphonse Mucha and Eugene Carriere in Paris. Work: Mural decorations in War Memorial Chapel of St. Francis Xavier, Nassau, Stone Ridge Church, New York; painted windows in St. Anselm's Church, Bronx, NY; paintings in Detroit Institute and Toledo Museum. Address in 1926, Nassau, N.P., Bahama Islands, B.W.I.

HAWKINS, BENJAMIN FRANKLIN.
Sculptor. Born St. Louis, MO, June 17, 1896. Pupil of Victor Holm, Leo Lentelli, Lee Lawrie. Member: NSS. Work: "Minerva," University of Michigan, Ann Arbor; sculptural detail, Washington Hall, United States Military Academy, West Point, NY; figures, High School, Little Rock, AR. Address in 1929, 47 East Ninth Street, New York, NY.

HAWKINS, CORNELIUS H.
Portrait and landscape painter. Born near Tupelo, MI, in 1861. Studied in St. Louis School of Fine Arts; in NY, under William Chase. He is represented in the Louisiana

State Museum at New Orleans, and the Alabama State Capitol.

HAWKINS, EDWARD MACK CURTIS.
Painter. Born in New York, Nov. 24, 1877. Pupil of Whistler, Cazin, Monet, and Beardsley. Member: Charcoal C, Binghamton SAC. Awards: Silver medal, Liege, Belgium, 1899-1902; Order of Leopold of Belgium; Iron Crown, Romania. Works: owned by Queen of Romania, King of Serbia and late King Leopold of Belgium. Address in 1929, 120 East State Street, Ithaca, NY; summer, "The Hawk's Nest," Frontinac, NY.

HAWKINS, GRACE MILNER.
Painter and lecturer. Born Bloomington, WI, Oct. 20, 1869. Pupil of H. Siddons Mowbray, Kenyon Cox Twachtman. Member: NAC; ADA; Madison AA. Award: First prize, Midland Empire Fair, Billings, MT, 1925. Work: "The Trout Stream," New Gallery, Hartford, CT. Address in 1929, Drumlinbrow, 1910 Regent Street, Madison, WI; summer, Leafy Lodge, Absarokee, MT.

HAWKINS, MAY PALMER.
(Mrs. Edward M. C. Hawkins). Painter. Born London, Feb. 14, 1879. Pupil of Cadmus, Bernard Meyers, E. M. C. Hawkins, Ward and Stouffer. Member: AFA. Address in 1929, 120 East State Street, Ithaca, NY; summer, "The Hawk's Nest," Frontinac, NY.

HAWKINS, THOMAS WILSON, JR.
Painter. Born in Los Angeles, CA, May 15, 1941. Study: CA State Univ., Long Beach; CA State Univ., Los Angeles. Work: Various collections in CA. Exhib: So. CA Expos, Del Mar, 1967-77; Butler Inst., Youngstown, OH, 1970; Da Vinci Open Art Comp., NYC, 1970; Bertrand Russell Cent., London & Nottingham, Eng., 1973; others. Awards: So. CA Expos, 1967, 70; purchase award, All City Los Angeles Art, Barnsdall, 1977; others. Mem.: Regional assns.; Nat'l Educ. Assn. Address in 1982, Arcadia, CA.

HAWKS, RACHEL MARSHALL.
(Mrs. Arthur W. Hawks). Sculptor and teacher. Born Port Deposit,

MD, March 20, 1879. Pupil of Maryland Institute, Rinehart School of Sculpture under Ephraim Keyser, Charles Pike. Member: Handicraft C. of Baltimore; Maryland Inst. Alumni. Work: Bust of Dr. Basil Gildersleeve, John Hopkins University, Baltimore; numerous garden sculpture- "Boy and Dragon Fly," "Boy and Dolphins," etc. in Administration Bldg., Maryland Casualty Co., Baltimore. Specialty, mural decorations in relief. Address in 1929, Ruxton, Baltimore Co., MD.

HAWLEY, CARL T.
Painter, illustrator, etcher and teacher. Born Montrose, Penn., April 4, 1885. Pupil of ASL of New York; Julian and Colarossi Academies in Paris. Member: ASL of New York; Paris AAA; Paris SE. Award: Silver medal, Sesqui-Centennial. Work: Mural decoration, Court House, Pulaski, New York. Represented in Syracuse Museum. Illustrated, "History in Rhymes and Jingles," "Tanglewood Tales." Address in 1929, 871 Ostrom Avenue, Syracuse, New York; summer, Heart Lake, Penn.

HAWLEY, MARGARET FOOTE.
Miniature painter. Born Guilford, CT, June 12, 1880. Pupil of Corcoran AS; Howard Helmick; Colarossi in Paris. Member: AM. S. Min. P.; PA S. Min. P.; Boston GA; New Haven PCC.; AFA. Awards: Medal of honor, PAFA, 1918; Lea prize ($50), PAFA, 1920; Charlotte Ritchie Smith Memorial prize, Balto. WCC; silver medal, Sesqui-Centennial Exposition, Phila., 1926. Work in: Metropolitan Museum, New York, and Concord Art Association. Address in 1929, 58 West 57th Street, New York, NY.

HAWLEY, THEODOSIA.
Painter. Member: NA. Women PS. Address in 1929, 141 East 40th Street, New York, NY; care of the Concord Art Asso., Concord, MA.

HAWTHORNE, CHARLES WEBSTER.
Painter and teacher. Born in Maine, Jan. 8, 1872. Pupil of NAD and ASL in NY; Chase at Shinnecock, LI. Member: ANA; NA Salma.C. NAC;

Lotos C.; A. Fund S.; Players; Societe Nat. des Beaux-Arts, Paris; AWCS.; NIAL; PP; Salma C. NAD, 1904; Worcester, C. I. Pittsburgh, Buenos Aires Exp. Clarke Isidor gold medal, NAD; PAFA, P.P. Exp., San F., 1915; Concord Lippincott prize, PAFA, 1923; Phila. Expo., 1923; Corcoran Gallery, WA, 1923; Carnegie prize, NAD, gold medal, Sesqui- Centennial Expo., Phila., 1926. In collections of MMA; Corcoran; Syracuse; RI School of Design; Worcester; Buffalo; Detroit; St. Louis; Herron Inst, Indianapolis; Boston; Houston; Toledo; Cincinnati; Hackley Art Museum; Muskegon, MI; Dayton; Fort Worth; NAD; Lotos Club, NYC; Denver; Univ. of IL; Carnegie; Washburn CO; Kansas and Brooklyn. Died Nov. 29, 1930 in Baltimore.

HAY, DE WITT CLINTON.
Engraver. Born in 1819 in or near Saratoga, NY. In 1850 he was an apprentice with Rawdon, Wright, Hatch & Smillie, in New York. He devoted himself to bank-note engraving as a member of the firm of Wellstood, Hanks, Hay & Whiting, of New York. Contemporaries of Hay Attributed the engraving of the small annual plate of "The Oaken Bucket," after the painting by Frederick S. Agate; this plate was signed by his employers, Rawdon, Hatch & Smillie.

HAY, GEORGE AUSTIN.
Painter and filmmaker. Born in Johnstown, PA, Dec. 25, 1915. Study: PAFA; ASL; Nat'l Acad.; Univ. of Rochester; Univ. of Pittsburgh; Columbia Univ.; also with Robert Brackman, Dong Kingman. Work: Univ. of Pittsburgh; NY Public Lib.; Dept. of Army; Lib. of Congress, Met. Mus. of Art, NYC. Exhibitions: Pittsburgh Playhouse; Rochester Memorial Art Gallery; Philharmonic Hall, Lincoln Center, 1965; Riverside Museum, 1970; Carnegie Inst., 1972; Duncan Galleries, NYC, 1973; Am. Painters in Paris 1976, and others. Awards: Prizes in regional exhibitions. Mem.: Am. APL; Fed. Design Council, AAA; others. Media: Oil, watercolor. Address in 1982, Washington, DC.

HAY, STUART.
Painter. Born Sewickly, PA, Feb. 22, 1889. Member: GFLA; AFA. Address in 1929, 242 East 19th Street, New York, NY.

HAY, WILLIAM.
This line engraver of buildings and subjects was working in Philadelphia from 1819 to 1824.

HAY, WILLIAM H.
Engraver. This name is signed to plates found in C. G. Childs' "Views of Philadelphia," published in 1828. Both this man and the William Hay noted above were line engravers of similar subjects and comtemporaries. There is enough difference in their style of work, however, to encourage the belief that they were different men.

HAYDEN, CHARLES H.
Landscape painter. Born in Plymouth, MA, on Aug. 4, 1856; died in Belmont, MA, in 1901. Pupil of the Boston Mus. Sch.; also of Boulanger, Lefebvre and R. Collin, in Paris. Awards: Honorable mention, Paris Exposition, 1889; Jordon prize, Boston, 1895; silver medal, Atlanta Exposition, 1895; bronze medal, Paris Exposition, 1900. Member of Boston Water Color Society. Represented by "The Poplars, Chatham, Massachusetts" at the Corcoran Art Gallery, and "Turkey Pasture," owned by Boston Museum of Fine Arts.

HAYDEN, EDWARD PARKER.
Landscape painter. Died in Haydenville, MA, Feb. 7, 1922.

HAYDEN, ELLA FRANCES.
Painter. Born Boston, MA, March 21, 1860. Pupil of NAD; Delecluse School, Paris National Art School, Munich; Cowles Art School, Boston. Member: Providence AC; Providence WCC. Specialty, landscapes. Address in 1929, 70 Intervale Road, Providence, RI; summer, Pomfret, CT.

HAYDEN, SARA S.
Painter, illustrator, and teacher. Born Chicago. Pupil of AIC; Collin, Merson and Lazar in Paris; Chase and Duveneck. Member: Chicago, SA. Address in 1929, 3319 Michigan Avenue, Chicago, IL.

HAYES, DAVID VINCENT.
Born March 15, 1931 in Hartford, CT. Earned A.B. at U. of Notre Dame (1951), and MFA from Indiana (1955). Awarded Fullbright and Guggenheim (both 1961). Taught at Harvard U. Received awards from Art Inst. of Chicago and Providence Art Festival Commissions executed for Great Southwest Corp. in Atlanta, GA. Exhibited at Smithsonian; Guggenheim; Willard Gal., NYC; Wadsworth; Musee Rodin (Am. Center) Paris. In collections of Dallas Mus; Guggenhiem; Addison Gal.; MOMA; Brooklyn Mus; Houston Mus. of Fine Arts and private collectors.

HAYES, KATHERINE WILLIAMS.
(Mrs. James A. Hayes, Jr.). Painter, illustrator, and teacher. Born Washington, DC, April 5, 1889. Pupil of Enrico Nardi, Robert Logan, Philip Hale, William James, Frederick Bosley. Address in 1929, Wallingford, PA.

HAYES, TUA.
Painter. Born in Anniston, AL. Studied at Converse College; Columbia Univ. Teacher's College; with Henry Lee McFee. Collections: Delaware Art Mus.; University of Delaware; others Exhib.: NAD; Baltimore Mus.; others. Awards: Delaware Art Mus. Mem.: Phila Alliance. Works in oil and watercolor. Lives in Wilmington, DE.

HAYS, AUSTIN.
Sculptor. Born in New York City in 1869. He was the son of the late William J. Hays, and a brother of William J. Hays, the landscape painter. Elected Associate Member of the National Academy. His work was exhibited at the Petit Salon, Paris, and the National Academy of Design, NY. Died July 24, 1915 in White Mts., NH.

HAYS, GEORGE A.
Landscape painter. Born Greenville, NH, Nov. 23, 1854. self-taught. Member: Providence AC; Copley S. 1892; S. Indp. A.; Providence WCC. Specialty:

landscapes with cattle. Address in 1929, Room 42, Woods Bldg., 19 College Street, Providence, RI.

HAYS, HENRY.
This book-plate engraver was an Englishman working in London as early as 1820 at 168 Regent Street. While working on book-plates, Fenshaw says that Hays was located in NY in 1830-55. American book-plates signed by him have been found.

HAYS, PHILIP.
Illustrator. Born in Shreveport, LA, in 1940. He studied with Jack Potter at ACD. Shortly thereafter his free-lance career began in New York with Seventeen magazine, one of his first clients. With many record covers and other advertising work to his credit, he has been awarded medals by the ADC of NY and S of I. Predominantly executed in watercolor, his works have been used by Sports Illustrated, Seagram's Distillers and Columbia Records.

HAYS, WILLIAM J(ACOB.) JR.
Painter. Born Catskill, NY, July 1, 1872. Pupil of NAD in NY; Julian and Colarossi academies in Paris. Member: ANA 1909; Salma. C. 1900; AFA . Award: Shaw prize, Salma, C. 1912. Address in 1929, Millbrook, NY.

HAYS, WILLIAM JACOB SR.
Animal painter. Born in NY, Aug. 8, 1830; died March 13, 1875. He was a pupil of J. R. Smith. Elected an Associate Member of the NAD in 1852. Represented in Corcoran Art Gallery of Washington, DC, by "head" of a Bull-Dog.

HAYWARD, ALFRED.
Painter. Cartoonist. Born in 1883 in Camden, NJ. Pupil of PAFA. Member: Fellowship PAFA; Phila. WCC.; Phila. Sketch C. Phila. AC; NYWCC. Award: Dana gold medal, Phila. WCC, 1919. Address in 1929, 6642 North 18th Street, Philadelphia, PA. Died in 1939.

HAYWARD, BEATRICE BURT.
(Mrs. Caleb Anthony Hayward, Jr.). Miniature painter. Born New Bedford, MA, Dec. 17, 1893. Pupil of Delecluse and Mme. La Farge in Paris, Lucia Fairchild Fuller, Elsie Dodge Pattee and Mabel Welch in New York. Address in 1929, 17 Jenny Lind Street, New Bedford, MA.

HAYWOOD, MARY CAROLYN.
Painter and illustrator. Born Philadelphia, Jan. 3, 1898. Pupil of Violet Oakley, Elizabeth S. F. Elliott, Hugh Breckenridge. Member: Phila Alliance; Fellowship PAFA; Phila. WCC; AFA. Work: Portrait in the Pennsylvania Academy of the Fine Arts. Address in 1929, 2107 Walnut Street, h. 152 W. Wyoming Avenue, Germantown, Philadelphia, PA.

HAZARD, ARTHUR MERTON.
Painter and teacher. Born North Bridgewater, MA, Oct. 20, 1872. Pupil of De Camp; Duveneck; Prinet and Henri Blanc in Paris. Member: St. Botolph C.; Copley S.; CA. AC; Salma. C; Painters of the West. Awards: Medal, MA. Charitable Mechanics' Assoc., 1892. Work: "Israel, the Light of the Nations" mural dec., Temple Israel, Boston; "Canadian War Memorial," Houses of Parliament, Toronto; "Spirit of Service," American Red Cross Museum, Washington, DC; "Not by Might" and "Spirit of the Armistice," National Museum, Washington, DC. Died 1930. Address in 1929, Carnegie Hall, 57th Street, and 7th Avenue, New York, NY.

HAZELETT, SALLY POTTER.
Painter. Born: Evanston, IL, 1924. Studied: Rollins College; Columbia University; University of Louisville; Inst. of Design, Chicago; Illinois Inst. of Technology. Awards: Fulbright award, 1952. Collection: University of Louisville.

HAZELL, FRANK.
Painter and illustrator. Born Hamilton, CT, June 7, 1883. Pupil of ASL of NY, Alphonse Mucha. Member: Slama. C.; SI, NWYCC; Guild of Am. Painters; AWCS; GFLA; NY Arch. Lg. Address in 1929, 321 West 112th Street, New York, NY.

HAZELTINE, FLORENCE.
Painter, craftsman, and teacher.
Born Jamestown, NY, April 28, 1889.
Pupil of Pratt Institute; Fursman,
Watson, Garber, Lever, Henry Snell,
Bell Cady White. Member:
Springfield (IL). AA; WAA. Award:
Mallinkrodt prize, St. Louis AG.;
1924. Address in 1929, 5610
Bartmer Avenue, St. Louis, MO.

HAZELTON, MARY ISAAC BREWSTER.
Painter and teacher. Born Milton,
MA. Pupil of Edmund C. Tarbell.
Member: Copley S.; Boston GA;
Concord AA; CT AFA; AFA. Awards:
First Hallgarten prize, NAD 1896;
Paige traveling scholarship, School
of Boston Mus. of FA, 1899; hon.
mention, Pan-Am. Exp., Buffalo,
1901; bronze medal, P.-P. Exp., San
F., 1915; Popular Prize, New Port
AA, 1916. Work: Decoration for
chancel, Wellesley Hills
Congratn'l. Church, 1912. Address
in 1929, 304 Fenway Studios,
Boston; h. Wellesley Hills, MA.

HAZEN, BESSIE ELLA.
Painter, etcher, and teacher. Born
Waterford, New Brunswick, CT. Pupil
of Columbia U., NY; U. of CA.
Member: CA AC; CA P.M.; West Coast
Arts; CA A. Teachers, Arthur W. Dow
Foundation; Pacific AA. Awards:
Second prize of water color,
Arizona State Fair, 1916; Second
prize for water color and prize for
black and white, Arizona State
Fair, 1917; 2nd prize for water
color, Arizona State Fair, 1919;
first prize for realistic painting,
Art Teachers Asso., Los Angeles,
1924; gold medal for water color,
West Coast Arts, Inc., 1926.
Represented in City Lib.,
Springfield, MA. Died 1946.
Address in 1929, 1042 West 36th
Street, Los Angeles, CA.

HAZEN, FANNIE WILHELMINA.
(Mrs. B. F. Ledford). Painter and
sculptor. Born Murphy's Gulch, CA,
Aug. 27, 1877. Pupil of Hopkins
Inst., San Francisco, and Academie
Moderne, Paris. Address in 1929,
2305 Effie Street, Los Angeles, CA.

HAZELTON, ISAAC BREWSTER.
Painter and illustrator. Born
Boston, Dec. 30, 1875. Pupil of
Tarbell, Benson, De Camp, and W. F.

Brown, Member: GFLA. Address in
1929, 2 East 23rd Street, New York,
NY; h. 33 Rutgers Place, Nutley,
NJ; summer, Isle au Haut, ME.

HAZLEWOOD, PHOEBE W(EEKS).
Painter. Born Ellendale, ND, Dec.
12, 1885. Pupil of Sarah Hayden.
Specialty, glass painting and
silhouette cutting. Address in
1929, Redford Gardens, Sackett
Harbor, NY.

HAZLITT, JOHN.
Born in England in 1767. He
painted portraits in Hingham, MA,
and was working in Salem, MA, in
1782 painting both miniatures and
large portraits in oil. In 1785 he
conducted an Art School in Boston.
He was of English birth and
returned to England in 1787. He
died May 16, 1837.

HAZZARD, SARA.
Miniature painter. Born Jamestown,
NY. Pupil of ASL of NY; William M.
Chase; American School of Miniature
Painting. Member: PA Soc. Min.
P.; N.A. Women PS. Address in
1929, Commodore Hotel, New York,
NY; h. 516 East Second Street,
Jamestown, NY; summer, Lakewood-
on-Chautauqua, NY.

HEADE, MARTIN JOHNSON.
Born August 11, 1819, in Bucks
County, PA. He began his career as
a portrait painter, studied in
Italy, traveled in the west and
then settled in Boston as a
landscape painter. His studio was
later moved to New York. His best
known works are "Off the California
Coast" and his South American
scenes. Died Sept. 4, 1904 in
Florida.

HEALY, GEORGE P.A.
Portrait painter. Born in Boston,
July 15, 1813; died in Chicago in
1894. Began studies in Paris in
1836. Went to Chicago about 1858
where he had a farm of 50 acres.
With his family he went to Europe
and remained a long time in Rome.
His portraits of distinguished
people are numerous. He painted
many portraits in Chicago and
Washington and for Louis Philippe.
He was an honorary member of the
National Academy of Design. (See

"Reminiscences of a Portrait Painter," by George P. A. Healy.) Died June 24, 1894 in Chicago.

HEATH, EDDA MAXWELL.
Painter, illustrator, and teacher. Born Brooklyn, NY. Pupil of Pratt Inst., New York; Wm. M. Chase. Member: Brooklyn SA; Nanuet PS; Yonkers AA; Carmel AA; Am. APL; AFA. Address in 1929, care Babcock Galleries, 5 East 57th Street, New York, NY; h. Rockland Avenue, Park Hill, Yonkers, NY.

HEATH, HOWARD P.
Painter and illustrator. Born Boulder, CO, Oct. 2, 1879. Pupil of AIC; ASL of NY; Frank Nankivell. Member: Salma, C.; SI 1911; NYWCC. Address in 1929, Norwalk, CT.

HEATON, AUGUSTUS G(OODYEAR).
Painter. Born Phila., PA, April 28, 1844. Pupil of Cabanel at Ecole des Beaux-Arts (1863) and of Bonnat (1879) in Paris. Member: Phila. Sketch C.; S. Indp. A.; Salma. C. 1908. Award: Bronze medal, Columbian Exp., Chicago, 1893. Work: "The Recall of Columbus," U.S. Capitol, Washington (engraving on fifty cent postage stamp, Columbian Exp.); "Washington's First Mission," Union League Club, Philadelphia; "Baron Steuben at Valley Forge," War College, Washington; portraits in State Dept. and Navy Dept., Washington, DC; Delaware State House; New York Historical Society; Tulane Univ.; Cornell Univ. "Hardships of Emigration" engraved on ten cent postage stamp, Omaha Exp. Author: "The Heart of David," "Fancies and Thoughts in Verse," "Mint Marks," and "New National Anthem," Died in 1931. Address in 1929, 1400 South Olive Street, West Palm Beach, FL.

HEAVEN, ETHEL R.
See Mrs. Hamilton.

HEBER, CARL AUGUSTUS.
Sculptor. Born Stuttgart, Germany, April 15, 1874. Pupil of AIC; Academie Julian, and Ecole des Beaux Arts, Paris. Member: NSS 1904; Phila. Alliance. Awards: Bronze medal, St. Louis Exp., 1904; bronze medal, P.P. Exp., San F.;

1915. Work: "Pastoral," St. Louis Museum Fine Arts; "Champlain Memorial," Crown Point, NY, "Champlain Statue," Plattsburg, NY; "Schiller Monument," Rochester, NY, "Benjamin Franklin," Princeton University; statue "Valor," New York City; Everett Memorial, Goshen, NY; Soldiers and Sailors Monument, Geneva, IL; World War Memorial, Wausau, WI; "Roman Epic Poetry," Brooklyn Museum Fine Arts; "Herald of the Dawn" erected at Batavia, NY. Died 1956. Address in 1929, 1716 Ludlow Street, Philadelphia; h. 7741 Temple Road, West Oak Lane, Philadelphia, PA.

HEBER, CLAUDIA.
See Smith.

HECHT, VICTOR DAVID.
Painter. Born Paris, France, May 15, 1873. Pupil of ASL of NY; Lefebvre and Robert-Fleury in Paris. Member: Port. P. Address in 1929, 14 East 60th Street, New York, NY.

HECKMAN, ALBERT WILLIAM.
Painter, etcher and designer. Born in 1893 in Meadville, PA. Studied W. Arthur Dow. Member: NYS. Ceramic A; Am. Inst. Graphis A; Alliance. Address in 1929, Woodstock, Ulster Co., NY.

HEDIAN, HELENA.
Painter. Member: Balto. WCC. Address in 1929, 2112 Bolton Avenue, Baltimore, MD.

HEE, MARJORIE WONG.
Painter. Born: Honolulu, HI. Studied: University of Hawaii; Honolulu Acad. of Arts; Columbia University Teachers College; Art Students League. Awards: Hawaii Easter Art Festival; Hawaii Ten Bamboo Studio; Hawaii Watercolor and Serigraph Society Annual. Collections: Castle Memorial Hospital; The Hawaii State Foundation on Culture and the Arts.

HEEBNER, ANN.
See Mrs. McDonald.

HEERMAN, NORBERT.
Painter and writer. Born Frankfort-on-the-Main, Germany, May 10, 1891. Pupil of Reynolds in

Chicago, Fleury in Paris, Corinth in Berlin, Duveneck in Cincinnati. Member: Cincinnati AC; Colorado Springs AS. Work: "The Continental Divide" (mural), Evanston School, Cincinnati; "Cameron's Cone, Colorado," Hughes High School, Cincinnati; "Concetta, Capri Coal Carrier," permanent Collection, Art Museum, Cincinnati, OH. Author of "Frank Duveneck," a biography. Address in 1929, Woodstock, NY.

HEIDEL, EDITH OGDEN.
Sculptor and writer. Born St. Paul, MN. Pupil of Augustus Saint-Gaudens. Member: Wash. AC. Address in 1929, 2829-28th Street, N.W., Washington, DC.

HEIDEMANS, HENRI.
Miniature painter, who flourished in New York about 1841-42.

HEIL, CHARLES EMILE.
Painter, illustrator, and teacher. Born Boston, Feb. 28, 1870. Studied in Boston and Paris. Member: Salma C.; Boston WCC; S. Indp. A.; Boston SWCP; Chicago SE; CA. PM; Bronx AG; Brooklyn SE; AFA. Award: Gold medal for water color, P.-P. Exp., San F., 1915. Represented in Worcester (MA) Art Museum; Malden (MA) Public Library; National Gallery, Washington; New York Public Library; Concord A. A.; Chicago Art Inst.; Cleveland Museum of Art; Milwaukee Art Inst.; Cincinnati Museum; CA State Library; Los Angeles Museum; Print Divison, State Galleries, Munich. Germany; Bibliotheque Nationale Paris. Address in 1929, 43 Arborough Road, Roslindale, MA.

HEIMER, J. L.
Marine painter. He was known for his many excellent paintings of ships.

HEINDEL, ROBERT ANTHONY.
Illustrator. Born in Toledo, OH, in 1938. He is a graduate of the FAS. Since moving to NY, he has done illustrations for Redbook, Ladies Home Jornal, Time, Good Housekeeping and Sports Illustrated. His work has appeared in several books including Psycho, The Grapes of Wrath for the Franklin Library and Sybil, for which he received an Award of Excellence from the S of I. In addition to a One-Man Show in NY, his illustrations have been exhibited in Cleveland and at the Smithsonian Inst. He is a founding faculty member of the Illustrators Workshop.

HEINTZ, MARION.
Painter and craftsman. Born Buffalo, Aug. 16, 1900. Pupil of Buffalo School of Fine Arts. Member: Allied AG. Address in 1929, 80 Hodge Avenue, Buffalo, NY.

HEINTZELMAN, ARTHUR WILLIAM.
Painter, etcher, lecturer, and teacher. Born Newark, NJ, Nov. 22, 1891. Pupil of RI School of Design; studied in Holland, France, Belgium, Spain, England and Scotland. Member: Chicago SE; Providence AC; CA P.M.; CA SE; Salma. C.; AFA; Brooklyn SE; Paris AAA.; Societe Gravure Originale en Noir, Paris; Associee Societe Nationale Des Beaux Arts. Awards: Logan prize AIC, 3 yrs.; Barnett prize, Brooklyn SE, 1920; 1st prize, CA. SE., 1921; Noyes prize, Brooklyn SE, 1924; Lea prize, Print C. Phila., 1925. Etchings in Metropolitan Museum, NY; Chicago Art Inst.; NY Public Library; Milwaukee Art Inst.; L.A. Museum; Rhode Island School of Design; Cincinnati Museum; Corcoran Gallery, Washington, DC; Bibliotheque Nationale, Paris; Victoria and Albert Museum, South Kinsington, London; British Museum, London. Address in 1929, care of Frederick Keppel & Co., 16 East 57th Street, NY; 20-22 Route de la Croix, Le Vesinet (S&O), FR.

HEINZ, CHARLES LLOYD.
Painter and craftsman. Born Shelbyville, IL, Jan. 8, 1885. Pupil of R. M. Root; St. Louis School of FA; Chicago Acad. FA; Miller and Hawthorne, Cape Cod School of Art. Member: IL. AFA; All-Ill. SFA. Awards: Ten first and seven second prizes at Indiana State Fair, Indianapolis; two second prizes, State Fair, Springfield, IL. Died c. 1955. Address in 1929, Shelbyville, IL; summer, Provincetown, MA.

417

HEINZE, ADOLPH.
Painter. Born Chicago, Feb. 5, 1887. Pupil of Buehr, Grant and Snell. Member: Chicago PS; Chicago Gal. A.; All-IL SFA. Awards: Municipal AL. prize, 1927; prize ($200) Chicago Gal. A., 1927. Work: "The Cloud Break," John Marshall High School, Chicago; "Booth Bay Harbor," Downers High School, IL; second prize award for "Mt. Wilbur," presented to America Forks High School, Utah, 1929. Address in 1929, 209 South State Street, Chicago, IL; h. 106 North Main Street, Downers Grove, IL.

HEINZMANN.
See Samilla Love Jameson.

HEITER, MICHAEL M.
Painter and illustrator. Born New York City, Sept, 15, 1883. Pupil of W. L. Taylor, O. Rouland and M. H. Bancroft; Sigurd Skou. Member: GFLA; Bronx AG; S. Indp. A. Address in 1929, 116 West 39th Street, New York, NY; h. Scarsdale, NY.

HEITLAND, WILMOT EMERTON.
Painter and illustrator. Born Superior, WI, July 5, 1893. Pupil of PAFA, Garber, Beaux, Briggs, ect. Member: Phila. WCC; NYWCC; AWCS; Aquarelists; Fellowship PAFA; SI; Darien Guild of the Seven Arts. Awards: Cresson Traveling Scholarship, PAFA, 1913; Art Directors medal, 1921; Dana gold medal, Phila. WCC, 1922; Brown and Bigelow Purchase prize, AIC, 1923; Logan medal, AIC, 1924; prize, Phila. WCC. 1924; prize, Baltimore WCC, 1925; gold medal, Phila. Art Week, 1925. Work: "The Shanty, Tampa Bay" and "The Road to Chester," Art Institute of Chicago; "The Jungle, Santo Domingo" and "San Geromino, S.D.," Brooklyn Museum. Illustrator of "Ambling thorugh Arcadia," by C. H. Towne. Illustrator for Century, Collier's, Woman's Home Companion, McCalls, Cosmopolitan, Delineator, Ladies Home Journal, New Yorker, Liberty, Harper's Bazaar. Instructor of illustration, Art Students' League, New York. Address in 1929, "Buttonwood," Noroton Heights, CT.

HEKKING, WILLIAM M.
Painter, writer, lecturer, and teacher. Born Chelsea, WI, March 10, 1885. Pupil of Laurens; Richard Miller; ASL of NY; Julian Academy, Paris. Member: Salma, C.; AFA. Awards: Gold medal, Kansas City AI., 1922; Huntington prize ($200), Columbus SA, 1924; first prize, Wilmington SA, 1926. Director, Buffalo FAA, Albright Art Gallery. Address in 1929, Albright Art Gallery; h. 2 Saybrook Place, Buffalo, NY; summer, Monhegan Island, ME.

HELBIG, MARGARET A.
Painter and teacher. Born Leesville, VA, Nov. 8, 1884. Pupil of John Carlson, Henry B. Snell. Member: Lynchburg AC. Work: "Phlox," Randolph-Macon Woman's College, Lynchburg, VA. Address in 1929, 701 Floyd Street, Lynchburg, VA.

HELCK, C. P.
Painter. Exhibited at National Academy of Design, New York, in 1925. Address in 1926, 256 West 55th Street, New York.

HELCK, PETER.
Illustrator. Born in NYC in 1893. He studied at the ASL and in England as a pupil of Frank Brangwyn. In 1911 he did advertising art for NY department stores and later editorial illustration for major magazines. His first love was the automobile, and he would often leave his studio in Benton Corners, NY, to take motor trips across Europe. In 1961 he published The Checkered Flag, a collection of his race drawings. A member of the S of I Hall of Fame, he is also a founding faculty member of the FAS.

HELD, ALMA M.
Painter and teacher. Born Iowa, Dec. 16, 1898. Pupil of Charles A. Cumming; NAD. Member: NA Women PS; Iowa AG. Awards: Silver medal, Iowa State Fair and Exposition, 1925; gold medal, Iowa State Fair and Exposition, 1926. Address in 1929, 623 West Eighth Street, Waterloo, IA.

418

HELD, JOHN JR.
Illustrator. Born Salt Lake City, UT, Jan. 10, 1889. Pupil of M. M. Young. Work: Murals, Milton Point Casino; illustrated Adventures of Baron Munschausen, Christopher Columbus, etc. Moved to NYC about 1910. Began his career as sports cartoonist; illustrations of stylized flappers in 1920's, 30's; cartoon strips - "Margie" and "Ra, Ra Rosalie," 1930's. Later concentrated on sculpting and ceramics; artist-in-res., Harvard and Univ. of Georgia. Died 1958. Address in 1929, Westport, CT; Palm Beach, FL.

HELD, PHILIP.
Painter and photographer. Born: NYC, June 2, 1920. Study: ASL, 1938-42 & 46, with Kuniyoshi, Fiene, Blanch, Lee, Vytlacil. School of Art Studies, NYC, with Moses Soyer, 1947-48; Columbia Univ. Teachers Coll., serigraphy with Arthur Young, 1949. Work: Univ. of MA; The Berkshire Museum; Phila. Mus. Lending Lib.; ASL Collection; others. Exhibitions: Berkshire Mus.; PAFA and Phila. Museum; Pleiades Gallery, NYC, 1978 - 80; many more. Awards: Kleinhert Foundation Grant; Sarasota Art Assn; etc. Teaching: Scarborough (NY) School, 1947-52; Fieldstone School, Riverdale, NY, 1952-62; Booker-Bay Haven Sch., Sarasota, FL, 1971-78; etc. Mem.: ASL (life); Woodstock Artists Assn.; FL Art Lg.; etc. Media: Oil. Address in 1982, Sarasota, FL.

HELDER, Z. VANESSA.
Painter. Born: Lynden, WA, in 1904. Studied: Univ. of Wash.; ASL, with Robert Brackman, George Picken and Frank DuMond. Awards: Pacific Coast Painters and Sculptors, 1936, 1939; Women Painters of Wash., 1937; Seattle Art Mus.; Women Painters of the West, 1946; Pen and Brush Club, 1947; Greek Theatre, Los Angeles, 1948; Nat'l Orange Show, 1949; Ramona High School, 1953; Glendale Art Association, 1955; Calif. State Fair, 1949. Collections: Seattle Art Mus.; Newark Mus.; High Museum of Art; IBM; American Acad. of Arts and Letters; Eastern Wash. State College; Lynden Washington Public Libray; Spokane Art and History Museum; Coulee Dam Building; Glendale Art Association.

HELDNER, KNUTE.
Painter, writer, and teacher. Born June 10, 1884. Studied in Sweden, and at AIC and MN. School of FA. Address in 1929, 212 West 1st Street, h. 123 West Superior Street, Duluth, MN.

HELLER, EUGENIE M.
Painter and craftsman. Pupil of J. Alden Weir in New York; Aman-Jean, Grasset, Rodin and Whistler in Paris. Award: Silver medal, Phila. AA., 1903. Address in 1929, 140 West 57th Street, New York, NY.

HELLER, HELEN WEST.
Painter, illustrator, etcher, craftsman, writer, and lithographer. Born 1872, in Rushville, IL. Represented by woodcuts in the Art Gallery, Lindsborg, Kansas; Illinois State Art Gallery, Springfield. Author of poem "Migratory Urge" with text cut in wood. Died 1955. Address in 1929, Wisconsin Hotel, 226 Wisconsin Street, Chicago, IL.

HELLMAN, BERTHA LOUISE.
Painter and teacher. Born La Grange, Jan. 30, 1900; Pupil of Rice Inst.; PAFA. Member: SSAL; Fellowship PAFA. Awards: Prize for black and white drawing, SSAL, Houston, TX, 1925; silver medal, SSAL, San Antonio, 1929. Address in 1929, 1616 Main Street, h. 2402 Jackson Street, Houston, TX; summer, La Grange, TX.

HELM, JOHN F. JR.
Painter, etcher, and teacher. Born Syracuse, NY, Sept. 16, 1900. Pupil of F. Montague, Charman. Member: Balto WCS; North West PM. Address in 1929, Dept. of Archicture; Kansas State Agriculture; Kansas State Agricultural College; h. 1508 Humbodt, Manhattan, KS.

HELMICK, HOWARD.
Painter, etcher, and illustrator. Born in Zanesville, OH, in 1845. Studied in Paris and London. Member of British Artists and Royal Society of Painters and Etchers.

He was a professor of art at Georgetown University. He died at Washington, DC, on April 28, 1907.

HELOK, C. PETER.
Painter, illustrator, and etcher. Born New York City, June 17, 1893. Pupil of W. de Leftwich Dodge, Frank Brangwyn. Member: Salma C.; AWCS. Murals. Address in 1929, 206 East 33d Street, New York, NY; h. 90 Caryl Avenue, Yonkers, NY.

HELWIG, ALBERT METTEE.
Illustrator. Born Baltimore, MD, Sept. 27, 1891. Pupil of C. Y. Turner and Henry B. Snell, and Maryland Inst. School of Art. Member: Charcoal C. Address in 1929, 918 Equitable Bldg. Fayette and Calvert Streets; h. 1223 East North Avenue, Baltimore, MD.

HELWIG, ARTHUR.
Painter. He exhibited the "Black Canyon, Colorado," at the exhibition held at the Cincinnati Museum in 1925. Address in 1926, 323 Elland Circle, Cincinnati, OH.

HEMBERGER, ARMIN BISMARCK.
Illustrator, etcher, and lecturer. Born Scranton, PA, April 1, 1896. Pupil of Maryland Inst.; Max Brodel. Member: New Haven PCC. Medal illustrator, School of Medicine, Yale Univeristy. Address in 1929, School of Medicine, Yale University; h. 10 Prospect Place, New Haven, CT.

HEMING, ARTHUR.
Illustrator and writer. Born Paris, Ontario, Canada, Jan. 17, 1870. Pupil of Frank Brangwyn, Frank V. DuMond. Member: SI; Arts and Letters Club of Toronto. Awards: Gold medal for best work, bronze medal for best illustrations and MacLean prize for illustration, Canadian Society of Graphic Arts, 1926. Represented in Canadian National Gallery; 10 pictures in the Royal Ontario Museum. Author and illustrator- "Spirit Lake," "The Drama of the Forests" and "The Living Forest." Address in 1929, 771 Yonge Street, Toronto, Canada; summer, Old Lyme, CT.

HEMINGWAY, GRACE HALL.
Painter, lecturer, and teacher. Born Chicago, IL, June 15, 1872. Pupil of AIC; Florida Art School; Leon Kroll; Carl Krafft; Karl Buehr; Anna Lee Stacey. Member: Chicago SA; All-Ill. SFA; All-Mich. SFA; Oak Park AL. Address in 1929, 600 North Kenilworth Avenue, Oak Park, IL; summer, "Windemere," Walloon Lake, MI.

HEMPSTEAD, JOSEPH LESLIE.
Painter and etcher. Born Brooklyn, NY, Feb. 3, 1884. Member: Chicago AC. Work: "Lincoln," owned by Illinois State Historical Library; "Coolidge," owned by Former President Coolidge; "Lincoln," "Washington," "Jefferson," "Hamilton" and "Coolidge," Congressional Library, Wash., DC; "Hamilton and "Jefferson," Chicago Historical Society. Address in 1929, Tree Studio Bldg., 10 East Ohio Street, Chicago, IL.

HENDERSON, A. ELIZABETH.
Miniature painter. Born in Ashland, KY, in 1873. Pupil of ASL of New York. Address in 1926, 79 Hamilton Place, NY.

HENDERSON, EVELYN.
Painter. Born Cape Anne, MA. Pupil of Guerin; Le Beau. Member: San Francisco S. Women A; Soc. Internat'l Des Beaux' Arts et Des Lettres. Address in 1929, 133 Marion Avenue, Mill Valley, CA.

HENDERSON, HARRY V. K.
Painter and artist. Born in Poughkeepsie, NY, March 6, 1883. Pupil of Pratt Inst., Brooklyn. Member: AWCS; Arch. Lg. of NY; AIA; Soc. of Beaux-Arts Arch. Address in 1929, 40 West 40th Street; h. 29 West 8th Street, New York, NY.

HENDERSON, HELEN WESTON.
Painter. Born Philadelphia in 1874. Studied at Penna. Academy of Fine Arts, 1892-97; Academie Colarossi, Paris. Art and music editor of Philadelphia North American, 1900-04; art editor Philadelphia Inquirer, 1904-09.

HENDERSON, WILLIAM PENHALLOW.
Mural painter and teacher. Born
Medford, MA, 1877. Pupil of Boston
Museum School under Tarbell.
Holder of Paige traveling
scholarship, Boston Museum School.
Member: Denver AA. Work: "The
Green Cloak;" series of Indian
dance pastels, Art Institute of
Chicago; Marquette and Joliet mural
decorations, High School, Joliet,
IL; "Felipe de los Valles," Denver
Art Association. Died 1943.
Address in 1929, care of the Cliff
Dwellers, Orchestra Hall, Chicago,
IL; Santa Fe, NM.

HENDRICKS, EMMA STOCKMON.
(Mrs. H. G. Hendricks). Painter,
writer, lecturer, and teacher.
Born Solano County, CA, Sept. 1,
1869. Pupil of Mon. Campoin,
Gerald Cassidy, Jose Arpa. Member:
Amarillo AA; SSAL; Texas, FAA; AFA.
Award: First prize, Cotton Palace
Exposition, Waco, TX, 1927. Work:
"Palo Duro Canyon," Library,
Amarillo, TX. Address in 1929,
2212 Polk Street, Amarillo, TX.

HENDRIX, CONNIE SUE.
(Connie Sandage Manus). Painter.
Born: Mt. Ayr, IA, May 30, 1942.
Studied: Drake Univ., Des Moines,
Iowa. Awards: Tennessee
Watercolor Society, 1973; National.
Bank of Commerce, 1973; Central
South Art Exhibition, 1973.
Collections: Foothills Art Center,
Golden, Colorado; Union Planters
National Bank; Commercial and
Industrial Bank. President of the
Tennesse Watercolor Society, 1975.
Address in 1980, 1408 Flamingo St.,
Memphis, TN.

HENGLE, WALTER VANDEN.
Painter. Exhibited water colors at
the PAFA, Philadelphia, 1925.
Address in 1926, 2095 North 63d
Street, Philadephia.

HENKE, BURNARD ALBERT.
Painter and illustrator. Born
Cologne, Germany, April 25, 1888.
Pupil of Guy Rose. Member: CA AC.
Address in 1929, 1497 Sunset
Avenue, Pasadena, CA.

HENKORA, LEO AUGUSTA.
Painter, illustrator, etcher,
lecturer, and teacher. Born

Vienna, Austria, Aug. 10, 1893.
Pupil of Anthony Angarola and
Cameron Booth. Member: S. Indp.
A.; Nat. AA; Am. AP1; AFA. Awards:
First Prize, MN State Fair, 1924;
second prize, portraiture, second
prize, Batik decoration, MN State
Fair, 1928. Address in 1929, 1435
East Franklin Street, h. 3029
Dupont Avenue, S., Minneapolis, MN.

HENNEMAN, VALENTIN.
Painter, sculptor, etcher,
lecturer, and teacher. Born
Oost-Camp, Belgium, July 7, 1861.
Studied in Belgium, Germany, Italy,
France. Work: "The Decline of
Illiteracy in Belgium," "The
Shepherd," "Storm in the North
Sea," "Moonlight of the Atlantic,"
owned by the Belgian Government;
"Liniken Bay," Museum of Bruges;
"View at Southport," City Hall,
Bruges; portrait of Baron L. de Bu
de Westvoorde, City Hall Oost-Camp.
Three hundred portraits of noted
Belgians. Known as the "Snow
Sculptor." Instructor, in portrait,
Bangor Society of Art. Died 1930.
Address in 1929, 199 Main Street,
Bangor, ME; summer, Boothbay
Harbor, ME.

HENNESSY, WILLIAM JOHN.
Painter. Born July 11, 1839, in
Thomastown, Ireland. Entered the
National Academy in 1856, and was
elected an Academician in 1861. He
went to London in 1870. Genre
painting and illustrating were his
chief interest. Among his works,
"On the Sands," "Autumn," "The
Votive Offering," "Flowers of May."
He died Dec. 26, 1917, in NYC.

HENNING, ALBIN.
Illustrator. Born in Oberdorla,
Germany, in 1886. He was raised in
St. Paul, MN. A student of Harvey
Dunn at the AIC, he also attended
the GCSA in NY. Adventure
illustration was his specialty,
resulting in many assignments for
boys' stories in publications such
as American Boy and Boys Life. He
was most remembered, however, for
his exciting paintings of World War
I subjects, some of which appeared
in The Saturday Evening Post.

HENNINGS, E. MARTIN.
Painter. Born in Pennsgrove, NJ, Feb. 5, 1886. Pupil of AIC; Nat. Acad., Munich. Member: AIC; Toas SA.; Chicago PS; Chicago Gal A., Chic. Cliff Dwellers; Salma. C.; AFA Awards: Palette and Chisel Club gold medal, 1916; Englewood Woman's Club prize, Aic, 1916, Clyde M. Carr prize, AIC., 1922; Cahn prize, AIC, 1923; Lippincott prize, PAFA, 1925; Fine Arts Building, AIC, 1926; Isidor medal, NAD., 1926; Ranger purchase, NAD., 1926; Frank prize, AIC, 1927; hon. mention, Paris Salon, 1927; First prize, Texas Wild Flower Competition ($3000), 1929; prize Chic. Gal. Assn., 1929. Repreesentd by "Stringing the Bow," Harrison Gallery, Los Angeles Museum; Chicago Municipal Collection, "Announcements," Temple Collection, PAFA; "Passing By," Museum of Fine Art; Houston, TX; "Drying Nets," State Collection, Springfield, IL. Address in 1929, Tree Studio Bldg., 4 East Ohio Street, Chicago, IL.

HENRI, MRS. ROBERT.
See Organ, Marjorie.

HENRI, PIERRE.
Miniature painter, who flourished in Philadelphia about 1790-1812. He painted Mrs. Beaumont in the character of "The Grecian Daughter," Penna. Academy 1811.

HENRI, ROBERT.
Painter. Born in Cincinnati, June 24, 1865. Studied at Penna. Academy of Fine Arts, Philadephia, 1886-88; Academie Julien and Ecole des Beaux Arts, Paris, 1888-91. He studied without instruction for years, in France, Spain, and Italy. His picture "La Neige" was purchased from the Salon, 1899, by the French Gov't for the Luxembourg Gallery; represented in permanent collections of Carnegie Institute, Pittsburgh; Art Institute, Chicago; Columbus, Ohio, Fine Arts Gallery; New Orleans Art Association; City of Spartanburg, SC; Dallas Art Association; Penna. Acadmey of Fine Arts; Brooklyn Museum of Arts and Sciences; Art Institute, Kansas City; Carolina Art Association, Charleston, SC; Metropolitan Museum of New York; San Francisco Institute. Address in 1926, 10 Gramercy Park, NY. Member of Nat. Acad. ASL, and NIAL. Died in NYC in 1929.

HENRY, ALBERT P.
Sculptor. Born Versailles, KY. His first art work, as a boy, was a carving from marble of an Indian girl holding a dove while a wolf creeps up to snatch the bird from her grasp. He modelled small portrait busts and cast them in iron for door stoppers. At the beginning of the Civil War, young Henry recruited a company of the Fifteenth Kentucky Cavalry. He was captured and taken to Libby Prison. While in prison he devoted much of his time to carving oxen bones used for making soup. He smuggled some from the prison including "The Prisoner's Dream," showing the interior of a cell, an armed sentry at the door, while the prisoner is sleeping on the floor. Following the close of the war he was appointed consul at Anconia, Italy. Prior to his leaving the US he had executed his bust of Henry Clay, now in the Capital at Washington, and a bust of Abraham Lincoln from life, now in the Custom House, in Louisville, KY. He studied in Florence, Italy under Powers and Joel T. Hart. His most ambitious work was an ideal bust of Genevieve. He also made one of Senator Guthrie, of Kentucky, and a bust of Senator Garrett Davis. Died November 6, 1872.

HENRY, COAH.
Painter and teacher. She was born Hamilton, MO, in 1878. Pupil of H. B. Snell. Member: Kansas City SA; N.A. Women PS; AFA. Work: "The Footbridge after Rain," Newark Museum of Art. Address in 1929, 2718 Linwood Blvd., Kansas City, MO.

HENRY, COLONEL OF KENTUCKY.
He modelled a most creditable bust of Lincoln, now in the United States Court Room of Louisville, KY.

HENRY, EDWARD LAMSON.
Born in Charleston, SC, Jan. 12, 1841. Pupil of Penna. Academy of

Fine Arts, and of Gleyre in Paris. Lived in Paris, Rome, and Florence from 1800 to 1863. Sketched and studied with the armies in Virginia during the Civil War. Elected National Academician in 1869. His special gift lay in the line of American genre, and he painted scenes from real life with a keen eye for character. He is represented in the Metropolitan Museum in New York, and the Corcoran Art Gallery, Washington, DC. He died in Ellenville, NY, May 11, 1919.

HENRY, JOHN.
The name of "John Henry, Engraver," appears in the Philadelphia directory for the one year of 1793, and he was engraving well-executed business cards in that city. In 1818 he was working for Baltimore publishers, and in 1828 he was engraving the illustrations for Madame Mothe Guion's "Die Heilige Leibe Gottes," published in Lancaster, PA. He may have had some connection of William Henry of Lancaster, Member of the Continental Congress and prominent in Revolutionary affairs in support of this suggestion we find that a John Henry was a pupil at the Franklin College, in Lancaster, in 1787.

HENSCHE, HENRY.
Painter. Born Chicago, IL, Feb. 20, 1901. Pupil of C. W. Hawthorne. Member: Salma C. Exhibited in the Annual Exhibition (1925) of the NA. Address in 1929, Provincetown, MA.

HENSHAW, ANNE BIGELOW.
Painter and craftsman. Born Providence, RI. Pupil of William C. Loring, Henry Hunt Clark. Member: Providence AC; Newport AA; Boston SAC. Address in 1929, 8 Champlin Street, Newport, RI.

HENSHAW, GLEN COOPER.
Painter. Born Windfall, IN, 1881. Pupil of Bonnat and Jean Paul Laurens in Paris. Address in 1929, 66 West 93rd Street, New York, NY.

HENSHAW, JULIA.
See Mrs. C. N. Dewey.

HENTZ, N. M.
Engraver. A large and very well executed etching of an "American Alligator" appears in Vol. 11 of the Transactions of the American Philosophical Society, Philadelphia, 1825. This plate is signed "N. M. Hentz Del & Sculp." and illustrates an article by Hentz on the American alligator presented to the society on July 21, 1820.

HENWOOD, MARY R.
Miniature painter. She exhibited at the Penna. Acadmey of Fine Arts, Philadelphia, in 1925. Address in 1926, 3219 West Penn Street, Philadelphia.

HEPBURN, CORNELIA.
See Cushman, Mrs. Paul.

HEPBURN, NINA MARIA.
Painter. She exhibited water colors at the Penna. Academy of Fine Arts, Philadelphia, in 1925. Address in 1926, Freehold, NJ.

HERBERT, JAMES D(RUMMOND)
Painter and sculptor. Born New York, Dec. 26, 1896. Pupil of Bridgman, DuMond, Hayes Miller, Lentelli. Member: ASL of NY; NAC. Address in 1929, 434 West 22nd Street, New York, NY.

HERBERT, LAWRENCE.
Engraver. The Pennsylvania Gazette, in 1748, contains the following advertisement: "Engraving on Gold, Silver, Copper, or Pewter, done by Lawrence Herbert, from London, at Philip Syng's, Goldsmith, in Front Street." In 1751 Herbert apparently left Phildelphia, as on August 1st of that year he requested persons having any demands upon him to present them at the home of Peter David, in Second Street, Philadelphia.

HERBST, FRANK C.
Illustrator. Member: SI. Address in 1929, 152 LaFayette Street, Newark, NJ.

HERDLE, GEORGE LINTON.
Painter. Born in Rochester, in 1868. Studied in Holland and in Paris. Member: Rochester Art Club; Rochester Municipal Art Commission.

Director, Memorial Art Gallery of Rochester University. Address: 47 Clinton Avenue, Rochester, NY. Died Sept 22, 1922, in Rochester.

HERFORD, OLIVER.
Illustrator. Illustrated for the Ladies Home Journal. Died 1935. Address in 1929, 142 East 18th Street, New York, NY.

HERGESHEIMER, ELLA SOPHONISBA.
Painter. Born Allentown, PA. Pupil of PAFA under Cecilia Beaux and Chase; Prinet and Mucha in Paris and in Italy and Spain. Member: Fellowship PAFA; Nicholoson A. Lg., Knoxville; NAC; Alliance; AFA. Awarded traveling scholarship, PAFA; hon. mention, Southern SAL, 1922; gold medal for portrait Appalachian Exp., Knoxville, 1910; first prize, TN State Exp., 1924; first prize, SSAL, 1925; first prize for portrait, first prize for still life, and first prize for flower study, TN State Exh., 1916. Director of art schools in TN and KY. Died 1943. Address in 1929, 803½ Board Street, Nashville, TN; summer, 435 Windsor Street, Reading, PA.

HERING, ELSIE WARD.
Sculptor. Born Aug. 29, 1872, in Howard Country, MO; died in NY, Jan. 12, 1923 Studied in Denver, CO. and at ASL. Pupil of Augustus Saint Gaudens. She and her husband became his assistants. Member: Denver Art Club. Work: Schermerhorn memorial font in Chapel of Our Savior, Denver, CO; W.C.T.U. drinking fountain, St. Louis Museum.

HERING, HARRY.
Painter. Born NYC, Jan. 12, 1887. Member: Brooklyn WCC; Alliance; NSS. Address in 1929, 324 East 23rd Street, New York, NY; h. 8507 Norwich Avneue, Jamaica, LI, NY.

HERING, HENRY.
Sculptor. Born New York City, Feb. 15, 1874. Pupil of Augustus Saint-Gaudens. Member: NY Arch. Lg. 1910; NSS 1913; AFA. Awards: Silver medal for medals and bronze medal for sculpture, P.P. Exp., San F. 1915. Work: Civil War Memorial, Yale University, New Haven; Robert Collyer Memorial, Church of Messiah, NYC; Sculpture on Field Museum of Natural History, Chicago; The ten South Pylon groups, "Defense" and "Regeneration," Michigan Ave. Bridge, Chicago; "Pro Patria," Union Station, Chicago, Indiana State War Memorial; Federal Reserve Banks at Dallas, Kansas City, Chicago and Cleveland. Died Jan. 17, 1949 in NYC. Address in 1929, Waldorf Bldg. 10 West 33d Street; h. Hotel White, 37th Street, and Lexington Avenue, New York, NY.

HERMAN, LEONORA OWSLEY.
Painter and etcher. Born Chicago, July 2, 1893. Pupil of Simon, Menard, Helleu, Leon in Paris. Member: Phila. Alliance; Fellowship PAFA. Specialty, decorative murals. Address in 1929, 740 Beacon Lane, Merion, Philadelphia, PA.

HEROLD, DON.
Illustrator. Born in Bloomfield, IN, in 1889. Address in 1926, Bronxville, New York.

HERRICK, HUGH M.
Painter. Born Rocky Ford, CO, May 8, 1890. Pupil of William Forsyth, E. Roscoe Shrader. Member: CA, AC. Address in 1929, 119 South Kingsley Drive, Los Angeles, CA.

HERRICK, MARGARET COX.
Painter. Born San Francisco, CA, June 24, 1865. Pupil of Carlsen, Fred Yates, Arthur Mathews, and Mary C. Richardson; ASL of NY and San Francisco; studied in Europe. Member: San. F. AA. Work: Lunette in YMCA, Oakland, CA; portrait of Rev. J. K. McLean, First Congregational Church; two canvases, Peidmont Community Chruch; Portrait, President Hoover, for Convention, hung in Convention Hall, Kansas City; Portrait Col. Charles Lindbergh, Veteran's Home, Livermore, CA. Specialties, portraits, flowers, still life. Address in 1929, 312 Pacific Avenue, Piedmont, CA.

HERRING, FREDERICK WILLIAM.
Son of the artist James Herring, he was born in New York City in 1821, and studied art with his father and Henry Inman. Devoted his attention to portrait painting. Died Aug. 13, 1899 in NYC.

HERRING, JAMES.
Portrait painter and engraver who was born in London, England, Jan. 12, 1794. His father emigrated the the US in 1804 and settled in NY. He associated himself with. James Longacre in publishing the "National Portrait Gallery." He painted a number portraits and had a studio in Chatham Square, New York. He died October 8, 1867 in Paris.

HERRING, JAMES VERNON.
Painter and teacher. Born Clio, SC, Jan. 7, 1887. Pupil of College of FA, Syracuse Univ. Member: College AA; AFA. Address in 1929, Howard Univ.; h. 2201 Second Street, N. W. Wash., DC; summer, 815 King St., Greensboro, NC.

HERRMANN, MAX.
Painter. Member: Salma. C. Specialty: Cattle and Sheep. Member of Soc. of Animal painters and sculptors of America. Address in 1929, 246 Fulton Street, Brooklyn, NY.

HERSCHEL, S. FRANCES.
(Mrs. Arthur H. Herchel). Painter. Born Boston, MA. Pupil of Henry B. Snell, Jean L. Boyd, Corcoran AS. Member: WA. ECC; Syracuse Allied A. Died in 1937. Address in 1929, P.O. Box 44, Albany, NY.

HERSCHFIELD, HARRY.
Illustrator. Member: SI. Address in 1929, Care of the New York Journal, New York, NY.

HERTER, ADELE.
(Mrs. Albert Herter). Painter. Born in New York, Feb. 27, 1869. Pupil of Courtois in Paris. Member: N. A. Women PS; AFA. Awarded bronze medal, St. Louis Expo., 1904, and hon-mention, Pan-Am. Exp. Buffalo (1901). Died in 1946. Address in 1929, 1324 Garden Street, Santa Barbara, CA; h. East Hampton, LI, NY.

HERTER, ALBERT.
Mural painter and craftsman. Born New York, March 2, 1871. Pupil of ASL of NY under Beckwith; Laurens and Cormon in Paris. Member SAA, 1894; ANA, 1906; AWCS; NYWCC; Mural P; NY Arch. L., 1901; Century Assoc. Awards: Hon. mention, Paris Salon, 1890; medal, Atlanta Exp., 1895; Lippincott prize, PAFA, 1897; hon. mention, Nashville Exp., 1897; Evans prize, AWCS, 1899; bronze medal, Paris Exp., 1900; silver medal, Pan Am. Exp., Buffalo, 1901. Work: Painting, "Two Boys," Metropolitan Museum, NY; "Hour of Despondency," Brooklyn Institute Museum. Specialty, mural paintings and portraits. Died Feb. 15, 1950. Address in 1929, 1324 Garden Street, Santa Barbara, CA; h. East Hampton, LI, NY.

HERTER, CHRISTINE.
Painter. Born Irvington-on-Hudson, NY, Aug. 25, 1890. Pupil of Sergeant Kendall. Member: NYWCC; New Haven PCC; N.A. Women PS; Newport AA; AFA. Awards: Second Hallgarten prize, NAD, 1916; popular vote prize, Newport AA, 1915, prize NAWP, 1922. Address in 1929, Hot Springs, VA.

HERTHEL, ALICE.
Painter. Born St. Louis. Pupil of St. Louis School of Fine Arts; Simon and Anglada-Camarasa in Paris. Member: St. Louis AG; AFA. Address in 1929, 96 Arundel Place, St. Louis, MO.

HERVIEUE, AUGUSTIN JEAN.
Painter. Born near Paris, France, in 1794. He studied in England with Sir Thomas Lawrence. He painted "The Landing of Lafayette," and a portrait of Robert Owen which is owned by the Ohio Historical Society. Exhibited at the Royal Academy, London, 1819 and 1858.

HERZ, NORA.
Sculptor. Born: Hipperholme, England, in 1910. Studied: Pratt Inst. Art School; Sculpture Center; and in Germany. Awards: Village Art Center, 1949, 1951; Montclair Art Museum, 1956; Pen and Brush Club, 1956; Hunterdon County Art Center, 1957; Bamberger Company, 1957, 1958. Collections: Bavarian

National Museum, Munich, Germany; Athens, GA.

HERZEBERG, ROBERT A.
Painter, illustrator, etcher and teacher. Born Germany, May 22, 1886. Pupil of Vanderpoel, H. M. Walcott, A. Mucha, Kenyon Cox. Member: Scarab C. Work: "Ancient Egypt," mural decoration in Tuly High School, Chicago. Director, Detroit School of Applied Art. Address in 1929, Bonstelle Studio Bldg., 3408 Woodward Avenue, h. 425 West Seventh Street, Royal Oak, Detroit, MI.

HERZEL, PAUL.
Sculptor, painter, and illustrator. Born Germany, Aug. 28, 1876. Pupil of St. Louis School of Fine Arts; Beaux-Arts Inst. of Design, New York. Member: NSS (Assoc.); AFA. Awards: Mrs. H. P. Whitney "Struggle" prize, 1915; Barnett prize, NAD, 1915; prize, Garden C. of Am. 1929. Address in 1929, Room 401-2, 400 West 23rd Street, New York, NY.

HERZOG, LEWIS.
Painter. Born Philadelphia, PA, Oct. 15, 1868. Studied in London, Rome, Berlin, Dusseldorf, Munich and Venice. Member: AC Phila.; NAC; Salma. C.; AFA. Awards: Gold medal, Munich; hon. mention, Berlin; bronze medal, St. Louis Exp., 1904. Address in 1929, 390 West End Avenue; 80 West 40th Street, New York, NY; h. Scarsdale, NY.

HESS, EMMA KIPLING.
See Mrs. D. W. Ingersoll.

HESS, HAROLD W.
Painter. Exhibited water colors at the Penna. Academy of Fine Arts, Philadelphia, 1925. Address in 1926, 346 South Smedley Street, Philadelphia.

HESS, MARY G.
See Mrs. Karl A. Buehr.

HESS, SARA M.
Painter and teacher. Born Troy Grove, IL, Feb. 25, 1880. Pupil of Richard Miller, Ossip Linde, AIC; Julian Academy, Paris. Member: NA Women PS; Brooklyn SA: PS; Alumni AIC; New Haven PCC; New Soc. Amer. A., SPNY; PBC. Represented in Public School Collection, Gary, IN; Oshkosh Museum, Oshkosh, WI. Address in 1929, Hillsdale, NJ.

HESSELIUS, GUSTAVUS.
Swedish artist. Born in 1682. He arrived in America (1711) near Wilmington, DE. He painted an altarpiece of the "Last Supper" for the parish Church of St. Barnabas, Prince George's County, MD, in 1721. He was the first organ builder in America. He also painted a number of portraits of Judge William Smith of New York, and his first wife Mary Het. (Signed and dated "G. H. 1729.") He died May 25, 1755.

HESSELIUS, JOHN.
Painter. Born in 1728. He was the son of Gustavus Hesselius, the Swedish artist, and nephew of Samuel Hesselius, the Swedish missionary. He settled in Maryland, and in 1763 he married Mary, only child of Col. Richard Young of Annapolis, MD. His earliest portraits were painted in Philadelphia in 1750; he afterwards painted many portraits in Maryland. He was an early instructor of Charles Willson Peale. Died April 9, 1778.

HETZEL, GEORGE.
Painter. Born in Alsace in 1826. He studied at Dusseldorf, and lived and painted for years at Pittsburgh, PA. Represented in Wilstach Collection, Fairmount Park, Philadelphia. He died in Pittsburgh in 1906.

HEUERMANN, MAGDA.
Painter, illustrator, writer, and lecturer. Born Galesburg, IL, Sept. 10, 1868. Pupil of F. H. C. Sammons and AIC in Chicago; Roth, von Lenbach and Duerr in Munich; Mme. Richard in Paris. Member: Chicago S. Min. P.; Chicago AG; Chicago AC; Chicago Woman's C.; Cordon C.; Schleswig Holstein Kunstlerbund; Chicago SA; AIC Alumni; West Coast A. Lg.; Oak Park A. Lg. Awards: Medals at New Orleans, Philadelphia, Atlanta, Columbian Exp., Chicago, 1893. Author of "How I Paint a Head," and

426

"Miniatures Old and New." Represented in Carnegie Library, Joliet, IL, and in University of Iowa. Address in 1929, Fine Arts Bldg., Chcago, IL; h. 520 Fair Oak Avenue, Oak Park, IL; summer, Palisades Park, MI.

HEUSTIS, EDNA F.
See Mrs. Simpson.

HEUSTIS, LOUISE LYONS.
Portrait painter and illustrator. Born Mobile, AL. Pupil of ASL of NY under Chase of Kenyon Cox; Julian Academy, Lasar and MacMonnies in Paris. Member: NA Women PS.; New port AA. Awards: First prize Brown and Bigelow Nat'l. Compet., 1925; prize Newport AA., 1921, 1928, 1928; prize, Nashville AA, 1926; prize, portrait, Birmingham, AL., 1928. Address in 1929, 228 West 59th Street, New York, NY; summer, Newport, RI.

HEUSTON, FRANK ZELL.
Painter. Born La Crosse, WI, Dec. 14, 1880. Pupil of George Maynard, George Heuston, George Bridgman. Member: NAC. Address in 1929, 3226 Oxford Avenue, New York, NY.

HEWINS, PHILIP.
Portrait and religious painter. Born in Blue Hill, ME, in July, 1806. In 1834 he established his studio in Hartford, CT, where he lived till his death, May 14, 1850. His portraits were considered good likenesses.

HEWITT, EDWIN H.
Artist and painter. Born Red Wing, MN, March 26, 1874. Studied architecture at Paris Ecole des Beaux-Arts under Pascal. Member: Fellow AIA. Awards: Hon. mention for painting, MN State Art Society, 1914; gold medal in architecture. President Metropolitan District Planning Committee. Address in 1929, 1200 Second Avenue, South; h. Silver Ridge Farm, Excelsior, MN.

HEWITT, WILLIAM K.
Portrait painter. Born in New Jersey in 1818. He commenced exhibiting at the Penna. Academy of Fine Arts about 1847. He painted many excellent portraits of

Philadelphians of his day. Died in Philadelphia in 1892.

HEWITT.
This engraver was working for the "Port Folio" and other Philadelphia magazines about 1820. He was an engraver of landscapes in line. J. Hewitt is noted as an engraver of music, published in NY, but without indication of date.

HEWLETT, JAMES MONROE.
Mural painting and architecture. Born Lawrence, LI, NY, Aug. 1, 1868. Pupil of Columbia University, McKim, Mead and White, P.V. Gailand in Paris. Member: AIA; Mural P.; NY Arch. Lg.; AFA. Work: Mural Paintings in Carnegie Technical School, Pittsburgh; Cornell Theatre, Ithaca; Columbia University Club, New York. Architect of Soldiers' and Sailors' monuments in Phila. and Albany, Brooklyn Hospital, Brooklyn Masonic Temple. Died 1941. Address in 1929, 2 West 45th Street, New York, NY; h. Lawrence, LI, NY.

HEYLER, MARY REMBERTON GINTHER.
(Mrs. M. P. Heyler.). Painter, illustrator, craftsman, and writer. Born Phila., PA. Pupil of PAFA. Member: Plastic C.; Fellowship PAFA. Stained glass windows, "St. John on Patmos," Church of the Restoration, Philadelphia; "Peter and John at the Tomb," and angel panels below, St. John's Church Suffolk, CA. Illustrator for magazines and books. Address in 1929, Gable End, Buckingham, PA.

HIBBARD, ALDRO T.
Painter. Born Falmouth, MA, Aug. 25, 1886. Pupil of De Camp, Major and Tarbell. Member: Boston GA; St. Botolph C.; Gloucester AA; Rockport AA. Awards: First prize at Duxbury, 1920; hon. mention, AIC., 1921; first Hallgarten prize, NAD, 1922; Sesnan gold medal, PAFA, 1923; Stotesbury prize, PAFA, 1928; second Altman prize, NAD, 1928. Work: "The Moate Range," National Academy of Design; "Winter," Boston Art Museum; "Hills of Jamaica," Metropolitan Museum, New York; "Ice Pond," purchased by Ranger Fund, NAD, presented to Phillips Academy Collection. Address in 1929, Fenway

Studios, 30 Ipswich Street, Boston, MA; summer School, 71 A. Main Street, Rockport, MA.

HIBBARD, FREDERICK CLEVELAND.
Sculptor. Born Canton, MO, June 15, 1881. Pupil of AIC under Taft. Member: Chic. SA; Cliff Dwellers; Chic PS; AFA. Awards: Hon. mention AIC, 1913; Shaffer prize; AIC, 1914; gold medal, Kansas City AI, 1924. Work: "Mark Twain," Hannibal, MO; "Gen. James Shields," Carrollton, MO.; "The Virginian," Winchester, VA; "U. D. C. Shiloh Memorial," Shiloh National Park, TN; "General Grant," Vicksburg, MI; "Dr. G. V. Black," Lincoln Park, Chicago, IL; "Volney Rogers," Youngstown, OH; "Gen. H W. Lawton," Ft. Wayne, IN; "Soldier and Sailor," Pittsburgh; "Doughboy," McConnellsville, OH; "Tom Sawyer" and "Hucklebury Finn," Hannibal, MO; "Champ Clark," Bowling Green, MO; "Fountains," Stevens Hotel, Chicago. Represented in Vanderpoel AA. Collection, Chicago. Vice President, Municipal Art League, Chicago. Address in 1929, 923 East 60th Street, h. 6209 Ellis Avenue, Chicago, IL.

HIBBEN, HELENE.
Sculptor. Born Indianapolis, Nov. 18, 1882. Pupil of William Forsyth at Herron Art Inst.; Lorado Taft at AIC; James Earle Frazer at ASL of NY. Member: NYSC. Address in 1929, 5433 University Avenue, Indianapolis, IN.

HIBBEN, THOMAS.
Etcher and artist. Born Indianapolis, IN, Oct. 22, 1893. Pupil of William Forsyth, Robinson Locke, Stark, Jaussley and Cret. Address in 1929, 124 East 40th Street, New York, NY.

HIBEL, EDNA.
Painter and lithographer. Born: Boston, MA, on Jan. 15, 1917. Studied: Boston Museum of Fine Arts School; and with Carl Zerbe and Jacovleff. Award: Boston Art Festival, 1956. Collections: Boston Museum of Fine Arts; Harvard University; Norton Gallery of Art. Media: Oil. Address in 1980, Riviera Beach, FL.

HICKEY, ISABEL.
Painter. Born Philadelphia, PA, Oct. 24, 1872. Pupil of Chase, Pyle. PAFA; studied in France, Spain, Italy. Member: Plastic C.; Fellowship PAFA; Phila. Alliance; Phila. Print C.; AFA; Brooklyn SE; President Phila. Art teachers Assn. Supervisor Art Education Phila. Public Schools. Address in 1929, 1931 Wallace Street, Philadelphia, PA.

HICKEY, ROSE VAN VRANKEN.
Sculptor. Born: Passaic, NJ, in 1917. Studied: Pomona College; Art Students League; University of Iowa; and with Bridgman, Zorach and Laurent. Awards: Los Angeles Museum of Art, 1944; Oakland Art Gallery, 1945, 1946; Pasadena Art Inst. 1945, 1951; Joslyn Museum of Art, 1950; Walter Art Center, 1951; Des Moines Art Center, 1953; National Association of Women Artists, 1952.

HICKOK, CONDE WILSON.
Painter. Born Batavia, IL. Pupil of AIC.C. P. Browne. Member: Chicago SA; Chicago AC; AIC Alumni; Hoosier Salon. Work: "In the Window," City of Danville, IL; "The White Dune," Chicago College Club. Address in 1929, 3106 Wenonah Avenue, Berwyn, IL.

HICKOX, ANN LENHARD.
Painter and teacher. Born Phoenixville, PA, June 26, 1893. Pupil of Chester Springs School of Industrial Art; PAFA and Fred Wagner. Member: Eastern AA. Address in 1929, Phoenixville, PA; summer, Weekapaug, RI.

HICKS, AMI MALI.
Painter, craftsman, writer, lecturer, and teacher. Born Brooklyn, NY. Pupil of William M. Chase; studied in Berlin and Paris. Member: Boston SAC; NY Soc. C; Alliance; S. Indp. A. Awards: Hon. mention, World's Fair, Chicago, 1893, and St. Louis tablets in Bowdoin College, ME. Author, "The Craft of Hand-made Rugs" and "Everyday Art" (Dutton). Specialty: theatrical decoration of costumes and material. Address in 1929, 141 East 17th Street, New York, NY.

HICKS, HERBERT.
Painter and illustrator. Born Columbus, OH, June 26, 1894. Pupil of Messer, Brooks, Wagner, Garber, and Harding, Corcoran School of Art; PAFA Chester Spings School; PAFA. Member: Wash. WCC. Address in 1929, John's Bldg., 407 Locust Street, Phila., PA; h. 402 High Street, Clarendon, VA.

HICKS, THOMAS.
Painter. Born in Newton, Bucks County, PA, died Oct. 8, 1890. Began painting at the age of 15. Studied in the Penna. Academy of Fine Arts, Philadelphia, PA, and the Academy of Design, New York. His first important picture, the "Death of Abel," was exhibited in 1841. In 1845 he sailed for Europe, and painted in London, Florence, Rome, and Paris. In Paris he was a pupil of Couture. In 1849 he returned to New York and entered upon a successful career as a portrait painter. Among his works are: Portraits of Dr. Kane, Henry Ward Beecher, William C. Bryant, T. Addison Richards, Bayard Taylor, Oliver Wendell Holmes, Henry W. Longfellow, Harriet Beecher Stowe, Daniel Wesley Middleton in the Capital, at Washington; Mrs. Hick (wife of the artist) in Metropolitan Museum, New York. He was elected a member of the National Academy in 1851. His portrait of Abraham Lincoln is known from the engraving only.

HIGGINS, EUGENE.
Painter and etcher. Born Kansas City, MO, Feb., 1874. Pupil of Julian Academy and L'Ecole des Beaux-Arts in Paris. Member: NA; NYWCC; Brooklyn SE; NAC; AWCS; Salma. C.; AFA. Work: "Tired Out," "Man and the Setting Sun," and etchings, Milwaukee Art Institute; "The Covered Wagon," Harrison Gallery, Los Angeles Museum; etchings in the British Museum, London; NY Public Library; Boston, Brooklyn and Washington Libraries; City Art Museum. St. Louis; Bibliotheque Nationale, Paris. Died in 1958. Address in 1929, 360 West 22nd Street, New York, NY.

HIGGINS, W. VICTOR.
Painter and teacher. Born Shelbyville, IN, June 28, 1884. Pupil of AIC and Academy of Fine Arts in Chicago; Rene Menard and Lucien Simon in Paris; Hans von Hyeck in Munich. Member: ANA; Allied AA.; Chicago SA; Palette and Chisel C.; Chicago Commission for Encouragement of Local Art; Taos Society of Artists; Los Angeles Modern AS. Awards: Gold medal, Palette and Chisel C., 1914; Municipal Art League purchase prize, 1915; Cahn prize ($100), AIC 1915; Butler purchase prize ($200), AIC 1916; Chicago SA medal 1917; Logan medal, AIC 1917; Hearst prize, AIC 1917; Altman prize ($1000), NAD 1918. Work: "Moorland Piper," Terre Haute Art Association; "Moorland Gorse and Bracken," Municipal Gallery, Chicago; mural decorations in Englewood theater, Chicago; "Women of Taos," Santa Fe Railroad; "Juanito and the Suspicious Cat," Union League C., Chicago; "The Bread Jar," City of Chicago; "A Shrine to St. Anthony," collection of Des Moines Assoc. of Fine Arts; "Fiesta Day," Butler Art Inst., Youngstown, OH; "Pueblo of Taos," "Indian at Stream," Los Angeles Museum, etc. Instructor, Chicago Academy of Fine Arts. Address in 1929, 220 South Michigan Avenue, Chicago, IL; summer, Taos, NM.

HIGHWOOD, C.
Painter. He painted a portrait of Henry Clay (1777-1852); half length, seated; body to left; arms folded in front; large collar and cravat. Size 29½ by 39½ inches. Painted from life in NY in 1850. Signed "C. Highwoods." Sold by American Art Association, New York, December, 1921.

HILDEBRANDT, HOWARD LOGAN.
Painter. Born Allegheny, PA, Nov. 1, 1872. Pupil of Ecole des Beaux-Arts under Constant and Laurens in Paris; NAD in New York. Member: ANA; Salma. C. 1899; NYWCC; Lotos C. AWCS; NAC; Pittsburgh AA; Allied AA; S. Indp. A; AFA. Awards: Evans prize, AWCS 1906; first honor, Associated Artists of Pittsburgh, 1911; purchase prize, Salma. C.; gold

medal, Brown and Bigelow, Allied AA. Work: "Cleaning Fish," John Herron Art Institute, Indianapolis; represented in Lotos Club, New York; Butler Art Inst., Youngstown, OH. Address in 1929, 1 West 67th Street, 306 East 51st Street, New York, NY.

HILDEBRANDT, TIM A. and GREG J.
Illustrators. Twin brothers born in Detroit in 1939. They attended Meinzinger's Art School in 1958 and began their career as an illustrating team in 1961 with The Man Who Found Out Why. Together they have produced several books, including Mother Goose, Panda Book, Hippo Book and A Home for Tandy. They also illustrated many book covers and the 1976-1977 J. R. R. Tolkien Calendar for Ballantine.

HILDEBRANT, CORNELIA (ELLIS).
Painter. Born Eau Claire, WI. Pupil of AI Chicago; Augustus Koopman and Virginia Reynolds in Paris. Member: NA Women PS; A.S. Min. P. Address in 1929, 306 East 51st Street, New York, NY; summer, New Canaan, CT.

HILDEBRANT, HOWARD (MRS.).
Mural painter. Born London, England, Sept. 28, 1866. Pupil of Bouguereau, Ferrier, Dagnan-Bouveret, De la Gandara and Jacque in Paris; De Bock and Josef Israels in Holland. Member: St. Lucas Soc. Amsterdam. Holland; Newport AA.; Fla. Soc. Arts and Sciences. Work: Murals, King Cole Hotel, Miami Beach; "Life of Christ" series, St. Stephen's Church, Coconut Grove, FL; Woman's Club, Miami; YWCA.; Miami; Scenery Viking Pageant, Newport, RI, 1922; Asbestos Drop and Stage Scenery, Miami Sr. H.S. Auditorium, 1928. Chariman of Decorative Painting, Architectural Lg. of Greater Miami. Address in 1929, Coconut Grove, FL; summer "Waban-aki," Muscongus, ME.

HILDRETH, SUSAN W.(SUSY).
Painter. Born Cambridge, MA. Pupil of Ross Turner. A. H. Thayer. Member: Allied AA; NY. WCC. Address in 1929, 27 Everett Street, Cambridge, MA. Died in 1938.

HILGENDORF, FRED C.
Painter and craftsman. Born Milwaukee, WI, Dec. 28, 1888. Pupil of Milwaukee School of Fine and Applied Arts. Member: WI. PS; WI. Soc. Applied Arts. Address in 1929, 211 Glen Avenue, Whitefish Bay, Milwaukee, WI.

HILL, ARTHUR TURNBULL.
Painter. Born New York, April 26, 1868. Pupil of Brooklyn Inst. Art School; chiefly self-taught; studied works of George Inness. Member: A. Fund S.; Brooklyn AC; NAD (life); Salma. C. Work: "The Dunes - Amagansett" and "The Marches-Amagansett," Museum of the Brooklyn Institute; "After a Storm," National Gallery, Washington, DC; "Low Tide - Amagansett," National Arts Club, New York. Address in 1929, 33 West 67th Street, New York, NY; Briar Woods, East Hampton, LI, NY.

HILL, CARRIE L.
Painter and teacher. Born Tuscaloosa County, AL. Pupil of Elliott Daingerfield, George Elmer Browne. Member: NA Women PS; SSAL; Birmingham AC. Awards: Gold medal, Mississippi Art Assn., 1925; 1st prize for flower painting, Nashville, Art Assn., 1926. Work: "Foothills of the Pyrenees," Public Library, Birmingham; "Red Roofs," Phillips High School, Birmingham; "New England Landscape," University of Alabama, University. Address in 1929, 1034 South 20th Street, Birmingham, AL.

HILL, CLARA.
Sculptor. Born in MA. Pupil of Augustus Saint-Gaudens; Julian Academy under Puech and Colarossi Academy under Injalbert, in Paris. Member: S. Wash. A; AFA. Award: Grand prize, Seattle Exp., 1909. Represented in Trinity College, Wash., DC; Army Medical Museum, Wash, DC; Woman's Medical College, Phila. Died 1935 in Wash., DC. Address in 1929, care of the Arts Club, 2017 I Street., NW; h. 3620 - 16th Street, NW, Washington, DC.

HILL, J. W.
In Dunlap's History of the Arts" he is recorded as painting landscapes in New York.

HILL, JAMES JEROME II.
Painter, illustrator, and writer.
Born St. Paul, MN, March 2, 1905.
Pupil of Louis W. Hill. Awards:
Gold medal, New Haven PCC 1922,
1923. Mural paintings at St. Paul
Academy. Address in 1929, 260
Summit Avenue, St. Paul, MN;
summer, Del Monte, CA.

HILL, JAMES.
In 1803 James Hill engraved some
crude Bible illustrations published
in Charlestown, MA. He also
engraved a large plate of the
"Resurrection of a Pious Family,"
after the painting by the Enlgish
clergyman, Rev. William Peters.
This was published in Boston,
without date; but the copy of this
print sold in the Clark sale,
Boston, 1901, shows a watermark of
"1792" in the paper, though this
paper may be older than the
impression. It is executed in
stipple, and a large plate of the
same subject was engraved by Thomas
Clarke and published in New York in
1797.

HILL, JOHN HENRY.
Engraver. Son of J. W. Hill, was
born in 1839. He was an etcher of
landscape. Died 1922.

HILL, JOHN WILLIAM.
Born in England, Jan. 13, 1812. He
died in this country in 1879. He
worked in aquatint and lithography.
Later he painted landscapes in
water color and achieved
considerable reputation; he also
drew upon stone for the
lithographers. Son of John Hill.

HILL, JOHN.
Engraver. Born in London in 1770;
died at West Nyack, NY, in 1850.
John Hill engraved in aquatint a
considerable number of plates
published in London, the best of
these being a series of views after
the paintings of J. M. W. Turner,
Loutherberg, and others. Hill came
to New York in the summer of 1816,
but soon moved to Philadelphia, and
remained there until 1824. He
lived in NY from 1824 until 1839.
The first plates executed in the US
by Hill were his small magazine
plates of Hadrill's

Point and York Springs, PA. He
later issued his American
drawing-books, with colored plates;
but his best work is found in "The
Landscape Album," a series of large
aquantint plates of American
scenery, after the paintings by
Joshua Shaw, and published by Hill
and Shaw in Philadelphia in 1820.
His "Hudson River Port Folio" is an
equally good series of still larger
plates; these views on the Hudson
were aquantinted by Hill after
paintings by W. G. Wall. One of
his last plates was a large view of
Broadway, New York, published in
1836. He seems to have retired
from active work soon after this
date.

HILL, MABEL BETSY.
Illustrator. Born Cambridge, MA,
May 7, 1877. Member: GFLA. Work:
Illustrated "Bolenius," "Barnes"
and "The Children's Method,"
Readers and other books for
children. Address in 1929, 436
Fort Washington Avenue, New York,
NY.

HILL, PAMELA E.
Miniature painter. Born May 9,
1803 in Framingham, MA, died in
1860. Exhibited at a number of the
Boston Athenaeum Exhibitions. She
painted miniatures of Mrs. Joel
Thayer, Miss L. B. Vose, Rev. Mr.
Sharp, Rev. Mr. Croswell, and Miss
Walsingham. Her studio in 1834 was
at 28 Somerset Street, Boston.

HILL, PAULINE POLLY KNIPP.
Painter and etcher. Born Ithaca,
NY, April 2, 1900. Pupil of
Jeannette Scott. Work: Etchings,
"St. Cloud" and "Trianon," Syracuse
Museum of Fine Art, Syracuse, NY;
"Barbara," "Montmorency," "On the
Stairway," "Place de la Concorde"
and "St. Cloud," J. B. Speed
Memorial Museum, Louisville, KY.
Address in 1929, 70 bis Rue Notre
Dame des Champs, Paris, France; h.
1003 West Nevada Street, Urbana,
IL.

HILL, PEARL L.
Painter. Born in Lock Haven, PA,
in 1884. Pupil of Penna. Museum
and School of Industrial Art.
Member: Plastic Club; Fellowship,
Penna. Academy of Fine Arts;

Philadelphia Art Alliance. Address in 1926, 10 South 18th Street, Philadelphia, PA.

HILL, POLLY KNIPP.
Etcher and painter. Born: Ithaca, NY, April 2, 1900. Studied: University of Illinois; Syracuse University; and with Hawley, George Hess and Jeannette Scott. Awards: Society of American Graphic Artists, 1929, 1948; Brooklyn Society of Etchers, 1930-1933; Florida Federation of Art, 1933, 1944, 1950; Southern States Art League, 1943; Gulf Coast Group, 1946; Phila. Printmakers Club, 1941; Phila. Sketch Club, 1957; Florida Art Group, 1951; Library of Congress, 1950. Collections: Library of Congress; Tel-Aviv Mus., Israel; Syracuse Mus. of Fine Arts; Metropolitan Mus. of Art; J. B. Speed Memorial Mus. Address in 1980, St. Petersburg, FL.

HILL, ROBERT JEROME.
Painter, illustrator, and teacher. Born Austin, TX. Pupil of ASL of NY; and with Kunz-Meyer. Member: Dallas AA; Texas FAA; SSAL. Curator, Dallas Public Art Gallery. Address in 1929, 805 W. Jefferson Avenue, Dallas, TX.

HILL, S. W.
A little known landscape painter, who also painted fruit-pieces.

HILL, SAMUEL.
Engraver. As early as 1789 Samuel Hill was engraving in Boston, and he made many portraits and engraved early American views for the Massachusetts Magazines, published in that city. In 1803 Hill engraved some Bible plates for the NY Publisher, William Durell. In Russell's Gazette, Boston, 1794, Samuel Hill advertised as engraver and copperplate printer, with a shop at No. 2 Cornhill."

HILL, SARA. B.
Etcher and draftsman. Born Danbury, CT. Pupil of Alphonse Mucha. Member: American Bookplate Soc.; Soc. of Bookplate Collectors and Designers. Represented in print collection of: Metroplitan Museum, NY; Grolier C., New York;

Library of Congress, Wash., DC; Harvard Library, Cambridge; Vassar College, Poughkeepsie; Carnegie Inst. Pittsburgh; National Gallery and Guild Hall, London. Specialty, bookplates. Address in 1929, 135 East 66th Street, New York, NY.

HILL, THOMAS.
Painter. Born Sept. 11, 1829, in England, he came to the United States in 1840 and settled in Taunton, MA. He later removed to Philadelphia and studied in the life class of the Penna. Academy of Fine Arts. He studied in Paris in 1866 and in 1867 opened his studio in Boston. He soon moved to San Francisco. Among his works: "Yosemite Valley"; "Danner Lake"; "The Heart of the Sierras"; "The Yellowstone Canon." He died June 30, 1908.

HILLARD, WILLIAM H.
Painter. Born 1830 he died in Washington, DC, April, in 1905. Among his best known paintings were "The Fight above the Clouds" and a portrait of President Garfield.

HILLBOM, HENRIK.
Painter and craftsman. Born Sweden, April 8, 1863. Pupil of Lefebvre and Constant. Member: CT AFA; New Haven PCC. Silver designer with Wallace Mfg. Co. since 1899. Address in 1929, Wallingford, CT; summer, Lyme, CT.

HILLER, J. JR.
Engraver. A close copy of the Joseph Wright etching of Washington is signed "J. Hiller Ju'r Sculp. 1794." This Hiller portrait has only appeared on the back of playing cards and the few copies known all come from New England. It is possible that this J. Hiller, Jr., was Joseph Hiller, Jr. son of Major Joseph Hiller, an officer in the Revolution and the collector of customs at Salem, MA, in 1789-1802. The younger Hiller was born in Salem, June 21, 1777, and the "Cleveland Genealogy" says that he was lost overboard from a ship off the Cape of Good Hope, on Aug. 22, 1795.

HILLER, LEJAREN A.
Illustrator and painter. Born Milwaukee, WI, July 3, 1880. Pupil of AI Chicago; studied in Paris. Member: SI, 1910; A. I. Graphic A; Art Directors' C; AFA. Illustrator for magazines and advertising. Address in 1929, Underwood and Underwood, Inc., 242 West 55th Street, h. 332 West 28th Street, New York, NY.

HILLES, CARRIE P.
Miniature painter. Exhibited at the Penna. Academy of Fine Arts, Philadelphia, in 1925. Address in 1926, 238 Allen Lane, Germantown, Philadelphia.

HILLIARD, WILLIAM HENRY
Painter. Born in Auburn, NY, in 1836. He studied art in New York City; also studied abroad, and on his return to this country established his studio in Boston. Landscapes and marine views were his specialty, and among his best known works are views of Maine, the White Mountains and the Atlantic Coast, including "Castle Rock"; "Wind against Tide"; "Allatoona Pass, GA." Died in 1905, in Washington, DC.

HILLS, ANNA ALTHEA.
Painter, lecturer, and teacher. Born Ravenna, OH. Pupil of AIC., Cooper Union; Julian in Paris. Member: CA AC; (pres.) Laguna Beach AA; Wash. WCC. Awards: Bronze medal, Panama-CA Exp., San Diego, 1915; Bronze medal, CA State Fair, 1919; landscape prize, Laguna Beach Art Assn., 1922 and 1923; prize Orange Co. Fair, 1925. Address in 1929, Laguna Beach, CA.

HILLS, J. H.
Born in 1814. This line-engraver was working at his profession in Burlington, VT, about 1845-50. His plates were of considerable merit.

HILLS, LAURA COOMBS.
Painter. Born Newburyport, MA, Sept. 7, 1859. Pupil of Helen M. Knowlton; Cowles Art School in Boston; ASL of NY. Member: SAA 1897; ANA 1906; Boston ECC; Copley S. 1892; Boston GA; Am. S. Min. P.; Pa. S. Min. P.; AFA. Awards: Bronze medal, Paris Exp., 1900; 2nd prize Corcoran prize, S. Wash. A.

1901; silver medal, Pan-Am. Exposition, Buffalo, 1901; silver medal, Charleston, Exp., 1902; gold medal, St. Louis Exp. 1904; medal of honor, P.P. Exp., San. F., 1915; medal of honor, PAFA 1916; Lea prize ($100), PAFA, 1920. Work: "Persis," Metropolitan Musuem, NY. Specialty, miniatures and flowers in pastel. Address in 1929, 66 Chestnut Street, Boston, MA; summer, Sawyer Hill, Newburyport, MA.

HILLS, METTA V.
(Mrs. Elijah C. Hills). Painter. Born Orleans, NY, April 1, 1873. Member: San Francisco S. Women A. Address in 1929, 1570 Hawthorne Terrace, Berkeley, CA.

HILLSMITH, FANNIE.
Painter and collage artist. Born: Boston, MA, March 13, 1911. Studied: Boston Museum of Fine Arts School; Art Students League, with Alexander Brook, Sloan and Hayter. Awards: Currier Gallery of Art, 1952; Berkshire Museum, 1956, 1957; Boston Art Festival, 1957; Portland Museum of Art, 1958; Boston Museum of Fine Arts School, Alumni Traveling Scholarship, 1958. Collections: Museum of Modern Art; New York Public Library; Currier Gallery of Art; Fogg Museum of Art; Addison Gallery of American Art; Gallatin Collection. Address in 1980, Second Ave, New York, NY.

HILLYER, WILLIAM.
Portrait painter in oils and miniatures, flourishing in New York 1834-1861. Member of the firm of Miller & Hillyer.

HIMMELSBACH, PAULA B.
See Mrs. Balano.

HINCHMAN, MARGARET S.
Illustrator and painter. Dec. Born Philadelphia. Pupil of Howard Pyle and Kenyon Cox. Member: AFA; Plastic C.; Phila ACG; Phil Alliance; Fellowship PAFA; Print C.; Lg. of AA; La Musee des Arts Decoratifs and Union Centrale des Arts Decoratifs, Paris. Award: Silver medal, Plastic Club, Phila, 1927. Address in 1929, 3635 Chestnut Street, Philadelphia, PA.

HINCKLEY, ROBERT.
Painter. Born 1853 in MA. Studied art in Paris 1864 to 1884. Graduated from Ecole des Beaux Arts. Had a studio in Washington, DC, since 1884, where he painted 350 portraits of eminent Americans. He also was the instructor of the portrait class at the Corcoran Art School for six years. His portraits of Chas. F. Crisp and John E. Rutledge are in the Capitol Building, Washington, DC. Also in collections of Annapolis & West Point. Died June 1, 1941.

HINCKLEY, THOMAS HEWES.
Born in Milton, MA, Nov. 4, 1813. He devoted himself to animal painting. In 1851 he went abroad to study the work of Sir Edwin Landseer and the Flemish masters. He painted two pictures of dogs and game in 1858, which were exhibited at the Royal Academy. Among his early works were a few portraits and landscapes. He died Feb. 15, 1896, in MA.

HINE, CHARLES.
Painter. Born in Bethany, CT, in 1827. Studied with Jared B. Flagg. His work was largely figure-pieces, and his masterpiece was nude figure, "Sleep." He died in New Haven, July 29, 1871.

HINGSTON.
Line-engraver of bill-heads and work of that description, apparently working in Georgetown, near Washington, DC, as he signs his plates "Hingston ft., G. Town." One of his plates is a bill-head for the City Hotel of Alexandria, VA. The work appears to belong to the first quarter of the last century.

HINKELMAN, EDNA WEBB.
(Mrs. Edward Hinkelman). Painter and teacher. Born Cohoes, NY, Feb. 12, 1892. Pupil of C. L. Hinton; Emil Carlsen. Address in 1929, 9 Lansing Avenue, Troy, NY; summer, Navesink, NJ.

HINMAN, DAVID C.
This capital engraver of portraits in stipple was working about 1830-35, both over his own name and as a member of the firm of Daggett, Hinman & Co., of New Haven, CT.

HINOJOSA, ALBINO R.
Illustrator. Born in Atlanta in 1943. He attended Texarkana and East Texas State University, studying under Jack Unruh and Otis Lumpkin. His first published illustration appeared in the Greenville Texas Herald in 1968 and he has since exhibited in Tennessee, Louisiana and NY. He is a member of the S of I of Los Angeles and NY. He lives in Ruston, LA.

HINSCHELWOOD, ROBERT.
Engraver. Born in Edinburgh in 1812. He came to the United States about 1835 and was employed as a landscape engraver by the Harpers and other New York publishers. He also worked for the Ladies' Repository, of Cincinnati, about 1855, and was later, for a long time, in the employ of the Continental Bank Note Co. of New York. Hinschelwood married a sister of James Smillie and many of his landscape plates are engraved after Smillie's drawings.

HINSDALE, RICHARD.
Landscape and genre painter. Born in Hartford, CT, in 1825. He died early in life (1856) when his work was beginning to show great promise.

HINTERMEISTER, HENRY.
Painter and illustrator. Born New York, NY, June 10, 1897. Pupil of Will Taylor, Otto Walter Beck, Anna Fisher. Member: NYWCC; AWCS; Brooklyn SA. Address in 1929, 4622-14th Avenue; h. 7920 Ft. Hamilton Pkway, Brooklyn, New York, NY.

HINTON, CHARLES LOUIS.
Painter, illustator, and sculptor. Born Ithaca, NY, Oct. 18, 1869. Pupil of NAD under Will H. Low; Gerome and Bouguereau, in Paris. Member: ANA 1916. Mural P.; NSS; A. Fellowship; Century C.; NY. Arch. Lg., 1911. Award: Traveling scholarhsip, NAD, 1893. Work: Mural decoration in court house, Wilkes Barrre, PA. Illustrated "Emmy Lou," Etc. Address in 1929,

74 Gard Avenue, Armour Villa Park, Bronxville, NY.

HINTON, MRS. HOWARD.
Sculptor. Pupil of Lant Thompson. She was born in 1834 and died in New York City, on December 19, 1921.

HIOS, THEO.
Painter and graphic artist. Born in Sparta, Greece, Feb. 2, 1910; US citizen. Study: Am. Artists School; ASL; Pratt Inst.; Nat'l Univ. of Athens. Work: Parrish Art Museum, South Hampton, NY; Riverside Mus., NY; Guild Hall Museum, Easthampton, NY; Tel Aviv Museum; Carnegie Inst., Pittsburgh; Nat'l Collection of Fine Arts, Wash., DC; Nat'l. Pinokothiki Mus., Athens, Greece; and others. Exhibitions: Carnegie Institute International; PAFA; Brooklyn Mus., and MOMA, NYC. Awards: Silvermine Guild; Guild Hall, Easthampton, NY; Adolph & Esther Gottlieb Found. Grant $10,000, 1981; and others. Teaching: City College, NYC, 1958-61; Dalton School, NYC, 1962-73; New School for Soc. Research, 1962-pres. Mem.: Federation of Mod. Painters & Sculptors; Audubon Artists. Media: Oil, acrylic, pastel, watercolor. Address in 1982, 136 West 95th Street, New York, NY.

HIRAMOTO, MASAJI.
Painter and sculptor. Born Fukui, Japan, Dec. 8, 1888. Pupil of PA Museum; Columbia University. Member: S. Indp. A.; Japanese AS.; Salons of America; Salon D'Automne, Societe Nationale Des Beaux-Arts, Paris. Work: "The Daibutsu," Columbia University. Asst., Columbia Univeristy, 1918-1920. Address in 1929, Suite 1601, 165 Broadway, New York, NY; h. 24 Rue Greuze, Paris, France.

HIRCH, ALICE.
Painter. Born in 1888. Member: NA Women PS; CT AFA. Died in 1935. Address in 1929, 53 Washington Square, New York, NY.

HIRSCH, JOSEPH.
Painter. Born Philadelphia, PA, April 25, 1910. Studied at Penn. Mus. Sch. for Indust. Art; Phila.

College of Art, 1927-31; with Henry Hensche, Provincetown, and George Luks, NYC. In collections of Whitney; MOMA; Corcoran Gallery, Wash., DC; Boston (MA) Mus. of Fine Arts; Met. Mus. of Art; others, including several commissions. Exhibted at PAFA; NAD; numerous others in US from 1934. Taught at ASL, NYC, 1959-67; others. Received Sch. Art League Prize, drawing, Phila. Sesquicentennial, 1926; munic. scholarship, PA Mus. Sch. for Indust. Art, 1928; PAFA; Altman prizes, NAD, 1959, 67, 78; Purchase Prize, Butler Inst., 1964; Carnegie Prize, 1968; many more. Member, Artists Equity Assn.; NAD; Nat'l. Inst. Arts & Letters. Represented by Kennedy Galleries, NYC. Address in 1980, 90 Riverside Dr., NYC.

HIRSCH, STEFAN.
Painter and teacher. Born Nuremberg, Germany, Jan. 2, 1899. Pupil of Hamilton Easter Field. Member: Modern A. of Amer.; Salons of Amer.; Brooklyn S. Modern A. Work: "Nightscene" Newark Museum, Newark, NJ; "New England Town," Worcester Art Museum, Worcester, MA; "Lower Manhattan," "Farmyard" and "Factory Town," Phillips Memorial Gallery, Washington, DC. Address in 1929, 110 Columbia Heights Brooklyn, NY; h. 135 Central Park, West, New York, NY.

HIRSCHBERG, CARL.
Painter and illustrator. Born in Germany March 8, 1854. Pupil of Art Students' League; also studied in Paris. Specialty, figure painter of genre. Founder of Salmagundi Club. Died in June 2, 1923, in Danbury, CT.

HIRSHFELD, ALBERT.
Illustrator. Born in St. Louis, MO, in 1903. He traveled and studied art in NY, Paris, London and Bali. He started his career at The New Masses, and in 1923 his first pen and ink caricatures appeared in The NY World. His drawing of political, television and, most notably, theater personalities have been published in magazines, books and in The NY Times for over 50 years. Examples of his unique drawings are owned by

the Whitney Museum, Metropolitan Museum of Art and others.

HIRST, CLAUDE RAGUET.
(Mrs. W. C. Fitler). Painter. Born Cincinnati, OH. Pupil of Cincinnati Art Academy under Noble; Agnes D. Abbatt, George Smillie and Charles C. Curran in New York. Member: NA Women PS.; NYW CC. Awards: First hon. mention. Syracuse, 1897; second prize, Syracuse, 1898; hon. mention, NA Women PS 1922 and 1927. Work in: Boston Art Club; Art Club of Philadelphia. Address in 1929, 65 West 11th Street, New York, NY.

HITCHCOCK, DAVID HOWARD.
Landscape painter, sculptor, and illustrator. Born Hawaii, May 15, 1861. Pupil of Virgil Williams; Bouguereau and Ferrier in Paris. Member: Salma. C. 1904; Honolulu AS. Address in 1929, Laniakeal; h. 25 Judd Street, Honolulu, Hawaiian Islands.

HITCHCOCK, GEORGE.
Painter. Born 1850 in Providence, RI. Studied painting in Paris. Exhibited "Tulip-Growing," Paris Salon, 1887. He was fond of painting subjects and places in Holland. Elected an Associate Member of the National Academy. Died Aug. 2, 1913 on Island of Maarken, Holland.

HITCHCOCK, LUCIUS WOLCOTT.
Painter and illustrator. Born West Williamsfield, OH, Dec. 2, 1868. Pupil of ASL of NY; Lefebvre, Constant, Laurens and Colarossi Academy in Paris. Member: SI 1904; Salma, C. 1907; New Rochelle AA. Awards: Silver medal for illustration, Paris, 1900; hon. mention, Pan-Am. Exp., Buffalo, 1901; silver medal for illustration and bronze for painting, St. Louis Exp., 1904. Address in 1929, Premium Point Park, New Rochelle, NY.

HITE, GEORGE H.
Born in Urbana, OH. Painted miniatures and portraits; flourished 1839-61 in New York. Died in 1880.

HITTELL, CHARLES J.
Painter. Born in San Francisco, 1861. Studied in San Francisco School of Design, 1881-83; Royal Academy of Fine Arts, Munich, 1884-88; Academie Julien, Paris, 1892-93. Since 1893 painted Western American subjects, figures and landscapes. His landscapes are in the American Museum of Natural History, New York; and in the Museum of Vertebrate Zoology, Berkeley, CA. Address in 1926, San Jose, Santa Clara County, CA.

HITTLE, MARGARET A.
Painter, illustrator and etcher. Born in 1886. pupil of Art Institute of Chicago. Has executed mural panels in several schools in Chicago, IL. Address in 1926, 55 Arlington Place, Chicago, IL.

HO, TIEN.
Illustrator. Born in Shanghai, China, in 1951. She attended the University of Dublin, Ireland, and the ASL in New York, studying under Marshall Glasier. Her first illustration was an annual report cover, done for Topps Chewing Gum in Feb. 1976. Her work has been shown at the S of I. In addition to being an illustrator, she is a fabric and fashion designer, known professionally as Tien.

HOARD, MARGARET.
Sculptor. Born in Iowa. Pupil, ASL. of NY. Member: L'Union Internationale des Beaux-Arts et des Lettres, Paris, 1914; ASL of NY; NA Women PS. Award: Hon. mention, P.-P. Exp. San F. 1915. Represented in Metropolitan Museum of Art, New York, NY. Died in 1944. Address in 1929, 140 Wadsworth Avenue, NYC in 1879.

HOBAN, FRANK J.
Painter and designer. Born Cincinnati, OH. Member: Palette and Chisel C. Address in 1929, 608 South Dearborn Street; h. 5345 Winthrop Avenue, Chicago, IL.

HOBART, CLARK.
Painter and etcher. Born in Illinois. Pupil of Art Students' League, New York; also studied in Paris. Address in 1926, 1371 Post Street, San Francisco, CA.

HOBART, ELIJAH.
Engraver. Born in England; was killed in battle during the Civil War of 1861-63. As early as 1845 Hobart was engraving in Albany and in New York. He was a good line-engraver of portraits and was at one time apparently in the employ of Joseph Andrews, as we find plates engraved by Hobart under the "direction" of that engraver. Engraved a folio line-plate of "The Landing of the Pilgrims," dedicated to the Pilgrims Society of Plymouth and published by Hobart in 1850, apparently in Boston, MA.

HOBART, GLADYS MARIE.
Painter and teacher. Born Santa Cruz, CA, Aug. 28, 1892. Pupil of J. C. Johansen. Member: Palette and Chisel C. Address in 1929, 1910 Fulton Street, San Francisco, CA.

HOBBIE, HOLLY.
Illustrator. Born in 1944. The early influence of her farm upbringing in Connecticut infused her art with a homespun, fresh quality which captured the hearts of greeting card lovers all over America. Having attended PI and Boston University, she has been employed by the American Greeting Corporation for the past ten years. She has chosen to remain somewhat anonymous, maintaining a quiet life as a wife and mother of three.

HOBER, ARTHUR.
Painter. Born in New York City, 1854. Studied at Art Students' League under Beckwith and later in Paris under Gerome. He contributed to many exhibitions and in 1909 was elected an Associate of the National Academy of Design. He died in 1915.

HODES, SUZANNE.
Painter. Studied: Radcliffe College; Brandeis University; Columbia University. Awards: Kokoschka School, 1959; Brandeis Arts Festival, 1959, 1960; Fulbright Fellowship to Paris, 1963-64; Radcliffe Inst. Fellowship, 1970-72. Exhibitions: Weizman Inst., Israel, 1972; Gund Hall, Harvard Graduate School of Design, 1972. Collections: Fogg Museum, Cambridge, MA; Rose Art Museum, Waltham, MA; City of Salzburg, Austria.

HODGE, HELEN.
Painter and lecturer. Born Topeka, KS. Pupil of Corcoran School of Art in Washington. George M. Stone, George Hopkins. Member: Topeka AG.; Laguna Beach AA.; West Coast Arts. Seven first prizes, Kansas State Fair. Represented in Mulvane Art Museum and in the Woman's Club, Topeka, KS. Address in 1929, 714 Kansas Avenue,; h. 1515 Boswell Avenue, Topeka, KS.

HODGE, R. GAREY.
Painter. Born Moweaqua, IL, July 27, 1937. Study: Eastern IL Univ.; Howard Univ. Summer School, with Wm. Georgenes. Work: Numerous private coll. in IL, WI, IN, & MO. Exhibitions: Tri-State Exhib., Evansville Mus., IN; Mississippi Valley Invitational, State Museum, Springfield, IL; IL Bell Tele. Competition, Chicago; River Roads Exhib., St. Louis; Int'l Biennial Sport Fine Arts, Barcelona, Spain; etc. Awards: NY World's Fair Sculpture Design runner up, 1963; St. Louis, North Side Art Assn.; Grand Prize, US Hockey Hall of Fame. Mem.: Artists Equity Assn.; IL State Mus. Soc.; Springfield Art Assn.; others. Media: Acrylic, graphite, watercolor. Address in 1982, Springfield, IL.

HODGES, STEVE LOFTON.
Painter. Born in Port Arthur, TX, Oct. 9, 1940. Study: Univ. of TX; Lamar Univ.; Univ. of AK. Work: Delgado Mus., New Orleans; Atlanta (GA) Artists Club. Exhib.: Biennial, Delgado Mus., 1971; Galerie Simonne Stern, New Orleanns, 1972; 1st St. Gal., NYC, 1975. Awards: Atlanta Artists Club, 1970; purchase award, Delgado Mus., 1975. Mem.: Coll. Art Assn. Media: Acrylic. Address in 1980, c/o Gallerie Simonne Stern, New Orleans, LA.

HODGIN, MARSTON (DEAN).
Painter. Born Cambridge, OH, Dec. 3, 1903. Pupil of F. F. Brown, R. L. Coars. J.R. Hopkins, Charles

437

Hawthorne; Art Dept., IN University under R. E. Burke and T. C. Steele; Walter Sargent, Univ. of Chicago. Member: IN. AC; Richmond AA; Oxford AC. Awards: Hon. mention. Indiana Painters' Exhibition, 1924-1925; first prize, still life 1925-1926, first prize, portrait, 1927-1928, first prize, landscape, 1928-1929 at Richmond AA Exhib. Work: "On Clear Creek," owned by Morton High School, Richmond, IN. Instructor Fine Arts, Miami University, Oxford, Ohio. Address in 1929, Miami Univeristy, Oxford, OH.

HOECKNER, CARL.
Painter. Born Munich, Germany, Dec. 19, 1883. Studied in Hamburg and Cologne. Member: Chicago SA, "Cor Ardens." Address in 1929, 63 W. Ontario Street, Chicago, IL.

HOERMAN, CARL.
Painter, artist, and craftsman. Born Babenhausen, Bavaria, April 13, 1885. Member: Laguna Beach AA. Awards: Englewood Womens Club prize, AIC, 1927; Logan purchase prize, IL. AFA, Springfield, 1928. Work: "Mount Shasta, CA" State Museum, Springfield, IL. Address in 1929, Saugatuck, MI; h. Highland Park, IL.

HOFF, GUY.
Painter and illustrator. Born Rochester, NY, May 1, 1889. Pupil of Wilcox and DuMond. Award: First Honorable mention, Albright Art Gallery, Buffalo, 1916. Address in 1929, 939 8th Avenue, h. 655 Riverside Drive, New York, NY.

HOFFBAUER, CHARLES.
Painter. Born Paris, France, June 18, 1875. Pupil of Gustave Moreau, F. Flameng and Cormon in Paris. Member: Societe des Artistes Francais; Societe des Artistes Francais; Soceite Internationale; NY Arch. Lg. 1912. Awards: Hon. mention, Paris Salon, 1898; second class medal, Paris salon, 1899; bonze medal, Paris Exp., 1900; Bourse de Voyage, 1902; Prix Rosa Bonheayr, 1902; Prix National du Salon, 1906; Knight of the Legion of Honor. Work: "Les Gueux," Carnegie Rouen; "The Roof Garden," Carnegie Institute, Pittsburgh; "Revolte de Flamands," Memorial Hall, Philadelphia; "Coin de Bataille," Luxembourg, Paris; "Sur les Toits," National Gallery, Sydney, N.S. Wales; mural decorations in Confederate Memorial Hall, Richmond, CA. Died July 26, 1957 in Boston, MA. Address in 1929, 70 dis Rue Notre Dame-des-Champs, Paris, France.

HOFFMAN, BELLE.
Painter and illustrator. Born Garretsville, OH, April 28, 1889. Pupil of Henry Snell; Cleveland School of Art; ASL of NY. Member: NA Women PS; AFA; Cleveland Woman's AC. Award: Second landscape prize, Cleveland Museum, 1923. Address in 1929, 140 West 57th Street, New York, NY.

HOFFMAN, GRACE LeGRAND.
Painter. Born Syracuse, NY, Nov. 11, 1890. Pupil of Arthur Dow, Walter Sargent, James Parton Haney, Despujols, Andre Strauss, Gaston Ballande, and Gorguet. Member: S. Indp. A. Address in 1929, 25 Davis Avenue, New Rochelle, NY.

HOFFMAN, GUSTAVE ADOLPH.
Painter, etcher, and lecturer. Born Cottbus, Brandenburg, Germany, Jan. 28, 1869. Pupil of NAD and Royal Acad. FA, Munich. Represented by a series of etchings in the National Gallery, Berlin; Royal Gallery, Munich; National Gallery, Leipzig; Art Gallery, Frankfurt; British Museum, London; Lenox Library, New York City; two oil portrait, Capitol, Hartford, "Judge Dwight Loomis" and "Judge Joel H. Reed," Superior Court, Rockville, CT. Address in 1929, 5 Laurel Street, Rockville, CT. Died 1945.

HOFFMAN, HARRY LESLIE.
Painter. Born Cressona, PA. Pupil of ASL under DuMond in New York; Julian Academy in Paris. Member: Salma C. 1908; MacD. C.; Allied AA; New Haven PCC; A. Aid S.; Lotus C.; AWCS; NYWCC; Lyme AA; AFA; NY Arch. Lg. Awards: Gold medal, P.P. Exp., San F. 1915; Eaton Purchase prize, Lyme AA, 1924; landscape prize, New Haven PCC, 1925. Represented at Milwaukee and Chicago Art Institute; Boston City Club; National Gallery of Art.

Washington, DC; Oshkosh Public Museum, Oshkosh, WI. Address in 1929, 50 West 67th Street, New York, NY; summer, Old Lyme, CT.

HOFFMAN, HARRY ZEE.
Painter. Born in Baltimore, MD, Dec. 5, 1908. Study: Univ. of MD, 1928; MD Inst. of Fine Arts, 1937; Pratt Inst., 1947; also with Robert Brackman, 1930-40 Aldro T. Hibbard, 1940. Exhibitions: Nat'l Museum, Wash., DC; PAFA; Albany Inst. of History & Art; Audubon Artists, NYC; Enoch Pratt Library; Maryland Inst.; Creative Gallery, NYC; others. Work: Baltimore Community College; Enoch Pratt Film Collection; Baltimore Museum of Art Film Coll. Awards: WC Show, Wash. Co. Art Mus.; Baltimore WC Club Show; others. Teaching: Hoffman School of Art. Mem.: Baltimore WC Club; Wash. WC Soc.; Artists Equity Assn.; Am. APL. Media: Acrylic, oil, watercolor. Address in 1976, Baltimore, MD.

HOFFMAN, MALVINA.
(Mrs. Samuel Bonaries Grimson). Sculptor and painter. Born NYC, June 15, 1887. Pupil of Rodin in Paris; Gutzon Borglum, Herbert Adams and J. W. Alexander in NY. Member: ABA, 1925; Nat. Inst. of Social Sciences; Three Arts Club, NY. (hon); NA Women PS.; Alliance; Painters and Sculptors' Gal. A.; NSS. Awards: Hon. men., Paris, 1911; First prize, "Russian Dancers" exhibit, Paris, 1911; hon. men., for sculpture, P.P. Exp., San F., 1915; Shaw mem'l. prize, NAD, 1917; Widener gold medal, PAFA, 1920; Barnett prize, NAD, 1921; Elizabeth Watrous gold medal, NAD, 1924; Joan of Arc gold medal, NA. Women PS, 1925; hon. mention, Concord AA, 1925. Work: "Russian Bacchanale," Luxembourg Museum, "Bill" Jeu de Paume, annex, Luxembourg Museum, Paris; "Head of Modern Crusader," Metropolitan Museum of Art; "Ivan Mestrovic," "Martinique Woman," "Senegalese Soldier," Brooklyn Mus.; "Pavlowa Mask," Carnegie Inst. Pittsburgh; "Pavlowa Gavotte," Museum of Art, Stockhom; "The Sacrifice," Cathedral of St. John the Divine, NY; "Gervais Elwes," Queen's Hall, London; "Ignace Paderewski," (The

Artist), Academy of Rome; "John Keats," University of Pittsburgh, Pittsburgh, PA; "Anna Pavlowa," mask, Corcoran Gallery of Art. Washington, DC; "Ignace Paderewski" (the Statesman), portrait, purchased for permanent exhibition in US. Represented at American Musuem of Natural History; Detroit Museum of Art; Cleveland Museum; heroic size, stone group, entrance Bush House, London. Decorated with Palmes Academique, France, 1920: Royal Order of St. Sva, III. Yugoslavia, 1921. Address in 1929, 157 East 35th Street, h. 120 East 34th Street, New York, NY. Died in 1966. Hobart College; Springfield Art Museum; Am. Acad. of Arts and Letters; Hackley Art Gallery; Hall of Fame; New York Historical Society; Maryhill Washington Museum; Smith College; International Business Machines; Chapel of the American Military Cemetery, Epinal, France. Joslin Clinic, boston, MA; St. Andrews-by-the-Sea Church, Rye Beach, New Hampshire.

HOFFMAN, POLLY.
(Mrs. Luther Hoffmann). Painter and craftsman. Born Bryan, TX, Feb. 8, 1890. Pupil of Henry B. Snell. Member: SSAL. Awards: First prize. Texas Oklahoma Fair, 1925, 1926, 1927. Address in 1929, 2004 Avondale, Wichita Falls, TX.

HOFFMAN, RICHARD PETER.
Painter. Born in Allentown, PA, Jan. 10, 1911. Study: Mercersborg Acad.; Parsons Sch. of Design. Work: Butler Inst. of Am. Art, Youngstown, OH; Moravian College, Bethlehem; other collections in PA. Exhibitions: Harry Salpeter Gallery, NY; Woodmere Art Gallery, Phila., PA; Allentown Art Museum, PA; Woodmere Art Gallery, Phila.; New Brit. Mus. of Am. Art, CT; and others. Awards: Woodmere Art Gallery, Phila, PA; Casein Award, Knickerbocker Artists, NY; Commercial Civic Center Phila. Award; and more. Address in 1982, Allentown, PA.

HOFFMAN, WILMER.
Sculptor. Born Catonsville, MD, Aug. 1, 1889. Pupil of Charles Grafly and Albert Laessle. Member:

Fellowship PAFA. Award: Cresson traveling scholarship, PAFA, 1922, 1924. Died May 21, 1954. Address in 1929, Ruxton, MD.

HOFFMANN, ARNOLD.
Painter and teacher. Born Russia, Oct. 15, 1886. Studied in Munich. Member: AWCS. Lanscape painter. Exhibited at Annual Ex. of Nat. Acad. of Design in 1925. Address in 1929, 310 Riverside Drive, New York, NY.

HOFFMANN, MAXIMILIAN A.
Sculptor and painter. Born in Trier, Germany, in 1888. Pupil of Milwaukee Art Students' League; Royal Academy, Munich. Member: Chicago Society of Artists. He died in 1922.

HOFFSTETTER, W. A.
Painter. Member: Fellowship PADA; Phila. WCC; Phila, AC. Address in 1929, 721 Walnut Street, Phila., PA; Glenside, PA.

HOFFY, ALFRED.
Born in 1790 in England. Portrait painter, crayon portrait draughtsman and lithographer. Hoffy exhibited at the Pennsylvania Academy for a number of years and was working in Philadelphia, 1840-52.

HOFMAN, HANS O.
Painter and illustrator. Born Saxony Germany, Aug. 20, 1893. Member: S. Indp. A. Illustrations in "The New Yorker." "Chicagoan," "The Nomad," "Plain Talk." Address in 1929, 14 Christopher Street, New York, NY.

HOFTRUP, JULIUS LARS.
Painter. Born in Sweden, Jan. 21, 1874. Self-taught. Member: Buffalo SA; AWCS; NYWCC; Brooklyn S. Modern A; Scandinavian-American A. Award: Gallatin purchase prize, 1925. Represented in Brooklyn Museum; Cleveland Museum; Cedar Rapids Museum; Phillips Memorial Gallery, Washington, DC. Died April 11, 1959 in Elmira, NY. Address in 1929, 400 West 57th Street, New York, NY; h. Munstorp, Pine City, NY.

HOGUE, ALEXANDRE.
Painter, craftman, block printer, and writer. Born Memphis, MO, Feb. 22, 1898. Pupil of Frank Reaugh; Minneapolis AI. Member: SSAL; Highland Park SA, Dallas, TX. Address in 1929, 912 Moreland Street, Dallas, TX; summer, Taos, NM.

HOHNHORST, WILL.
Painter. Member: Cleveland SA. Address in 1929, 3219 Oak Road, Cleveland Heights, Cleveland, OH.

HOIE, HELEN HUNT.
Painter and collage artist. Born: Leetsdale, PA. Studied: Carnegie Tech. Exhibitions: Guild Hall Museum, Award, 1970; Long Island Painter's Show, 1973; Babcock Galleries, New York City, 1974. Address in 1980, E. 67th St., NYC.

HOLBERG, RICHARD A.
Painter and illustrator. Born Milwaukee, WI, March 11, 1889. Pupil of Alexander Mueller; Louis Wilson, E. A. Webster. Member: Salma. C.; WI. PS; Rockport AA; North Shore AA; GFLA. Awards: Hon. mention, WI P.S., 1920; special hon. mention, WI. P.S., 1922. Address in 1929, 131 East 31st Street, New York, NY.

HOLBERG, RUTH LANGLAND.
Painter. Born Milwaukee, WI, Feb. 2, 1891. Pupil of Alexander Mueller, F. F. Fursman, E. A. Webster. Member: WI P.S.; Provincetown AA; Rockport AA; North Shore AA; PW Lg. Address in 1929, 131 East 31st Street, New York, NY.

HOLDEN, CORA MILLET.
Painter and teacher. Born Alexandria, VA, Feb. 5, 1895. Pupil of Cyrus Dallin; Joseph DeCamp; MA School of Art; Cleveland School of Art. Mural decorations "Separation" and "Reunion" war memorials at Goodyear Hall, Akron, OH; "Steel Production." mural decoration, Federal Reserve Bank. Cleveland, OH; series of four mural decorations, Allen Memorial Medical Library, Cleveland, OH. Specialty: portraits and murals. Address in 1929, 2049 Cornell Avenue, Cleveland, OH. Died in 1939.

440

HOLDSWORTH, WATSON.
Painter. Member: Providence WCC. Address in 1929, Orchard Avenue, Graniteville, RI.

HOLLAND, BRAD.
Illustrator. Born in Fremont, OH, in 1944. He presently works in New York and his illustrations are seen frequently on the Op-Ed page of The New York Times. His magazine work for such publications as Playboy, Redbook, Evergreen Review and National Lampoon and his book illustrations for Simon and Schuster have won him two Gold Medals and an Award of Excellence from the S of I Annual Exhibitions. His drawings were part of an American Exhibition at the Louvre in Paris.

HOLLAND, FRANCIS RAYMOND.
Painter. Born Pittsburgh, PA, Jan. 10, 1886. Pupil of ASL of NY. Member: S. Indp. A.; Silvermine Group; CT SA; Pittsburgh AA, 1916. Work: "Marsh House." Darien, CT. Died 1934, NY. Address in 1929, 4415 Warwick Blvd.; h. 4322 Warwick Blvd., Kansas City, MO.

HOLLAND, JOHN JOSEPH.
Scene-painter. Born in London in 1776, he came to Philadelphia in 1706 and worked at the Chestnut Street Theatre. He also painted landscapes in water colors; in 1797 he drew a view of Philadelphia which was engraved by Gilbert Fox. Died December 15, 1820.

HOLLAND, ROBERT A.
Painter and teacher. Born Edgerton, MO, May 6, 1868. Pupil of Cincinnati Art Academy under Duveneck. Member: Kansas City SA; Asso. Art Museum Directors. Ex-director, City Art Museum, St. Louis. Director, Kansas City Art Inst. Address in 1929, 4415 Warwick Blvd.; h. 4322 Warwick Blvd, Kansas City, MO.

HOLLAND, THOMAS.
Landscape artist working in New York about 1800. He exhibited in Philadelphia at the Society of Artists Exhibition in 1811.

HOLLINGSWORTH, ALICE CLAIRE.
Illustrator. Born Indianpolis, Feb. 12, 1907. Pupil of Herron Art School; Circle Art Academy. Address in 1929, 1116 West 30th Street, Indianapolis, IN.

HOLLINGSWORTH, GEORGE.
Painter of landscapes and portraits. Born in Milton, MA, in 1813. He painted a portrait of Captain Fisher of Milton (Owned by the Boston Museum of Fine Arts). He died in 1882 in MA.

HOLLISTER, ANTOINETTE B.
Sculptor. Born Chicago, IL, Aug. 19, 1873. Pupil of AIC; Injalbert and Rodin in Paris. Member: SW. Sc.; Chicago SA. Awards: Hon. mention for Sculpture, P.P. Exp., San. F., 1915; Shaffer prize for sculpture, AIC, Chicago, 1919. Address in 1929, St. Catherine's Richmond, VA.

HOLLOWAY, EDWARD STRATTON.
Illustrator, painter, craftsman, and writer. Born Ashland, Greene Co., NY. Pupil of PAFA. Award: Bronze medal, St. Louis Exp., 1904. Art director, J. B. Lippincott Co.; joint author, The Practical Book of Interior Decoration; Author of The Practical Book of Furnishing of Small House and Apartment; The Practical Book of Learning Decoration and Furniture, and American Furniture and Decoration: Colonial and Federal. Address in 1929, 400 South 15th Street, Philadelphia, PA. Died in 1939.

HOLLOWAY, IDA H(OLTERHOFF).
(Mrs. George C. Holloway). Painter, illustrator, and craftsman. Born Cincinnati. Pupil of Cincinnati Art Academy under Frank Duveneck; Henry B. Snell, and studied in Europe. Member: Cincinnati Woman's AC; MacD.C.; The Crafters C., Cincinnati. Address in 1929, 2523 Ritchie Avenue, East W. H., Cincinnati, OH.

HOLLROCK, GEORGE L.
Painter. Member: GFLA. Address in 1929, 70 Fifth Avenue, NYC.

HOLLYER, SAMUEL.
Engraver. Born Feb. 24, 1826 in London. Died in New York City,

Dec. 29, 1919. Mr. Hollyer was a pupil of the Findens in London. He came to the United States in 1851; but he twice returned to England for periods of two and six years, and finally settled in this country in 1866. Besides engraving Mr. Hollyer was engaged here at different times in lithography, photography and the publishing business. In collection of MMA. An excellent engraver in both line and in stipple. Produced a large number of portraits, landscapes, and historical subjects. Among his larger and best plates are "The Flaw in the Title," "Charles Dickens in His Study" and "The Gleaner."

HOLM, VICTOR S.
Sculptor and teacher. Born Copenhagen, Denmark, Dec. 6, 1876. Pupil of Art Institute of Chicago under Lorado Taft; Philip Martiny in New York. Member: NSS, 1913; St. Louis AG; St. Louis AL; 2 x 4 S. of St. Louis; Municipal Art Com.; Alumni AIC; St. Louis Arch. C. (hon.); Ethical Culture S.; Societe Francaise (hon.). Awards: Silver medal, Missouri State Fair, 1913; Carleton prize ($100), St. Louis AG, 1914, 1916, 1917; honorable mention, P.-P. Exp, San. Fran., 1915; St. Louis AL prize ($300), 1922; silver medal, Midwestern Artists, Kansas City, 1926. Work: Parker Memorial, State University Library, Rolla, MO; Ives Memorial, City Art Museum, St. Louis; Barnes Memorial, Barnes Hospital, St. Louis; Missouri State Monument at Vicksburg, MO; Gov. Carlin Monument, Carrollton, IL; Washington Fischel Monument, Bellefontaine, St. Louis, MO; "Boy With Father's Sword," St. Louis Public Library; decorations on exterior of St. Pius' Church, St. Louis; Waterloo, Iowa, High School; Ft. Dodge High School; "Col. Drieux" monument, New Orleans; Washington University War Memorial, St. Louis; Nelson Memorial Fountain, Le Claire, IL; Musicians Memorial Fountain, Forest Park, St. Louis; Dr. Beaumont Memorial, Beaumont High School, St. Louis; Wayman Crow Memorial, City Art Museum, St. Louis; World War Monument, Maplewood, MO; Emile Zola

Memorial, WMHA, St. Louis; Claude Monet Medal for Two-By- Four Soc., St. Louis; George W. Niedringhaus Memorial, Granite City, IL; Festus Wade Memorial, Mercantile Trust Co., St. Louis; John M. Malany Memorial, Missouri State Capital Building, Jefferson City, MO; "Spirit of St. Louis," Gold Medal given by American Society of Mechanical Engineers for Aviation; Long Memorial, Long Public School, St. Louis, MO. Address in 1929, School of Fine Arts, Washington University, St. Louis, MO. Died in 1935.

HOLMAN, LOUIS ARTHUR.
Illustrator. Born at Summerside, P.E.I., in 1866. Illustrated "Boston, the Place and the People," in 1903, "Boston Common" in 1910; contributor also to Scribner's, Century, Printing Art, etc. Address in 1926, 9A Ashburn Place, Boston MA. Died in 1939.

HOLMBOM, JAMES W.
Painter. Born in Monson, ME, March 3, 1926. Study: Portland (ME) School of Art, with Alexander Bower; University of ME; Inst. Allende, Mexico, with James Pinto and Fred Samuelson. Work: MA & ME corp. collections; Instituto Allende. Exhibitions: Instituto Allende; Galleria San Miguel; UNICEF Invitational; Bertrand Russell Cent., and others. Awards: Portland Art Festival-Purchase Prize. Art Pos.: City Art Dir., Montpelier, VT, 1956-59, and Marblehead, MA, 1959-71; other. Media: Acrylic, oil. Address in 1980, Hancock, ME.

HOLMES, HARRIET MORTON.
(Mrs. J. Garnett Holmes). Etcher. Born Portland, ME. Member: CA Print Makers; CA SE. Address in 1929, R.F.D. 2, Temple, Arizona; 826 North Central Avenue, Phoenix, Arizona.

HOLMES, RALPH.
Painter, illustrator, craftsman, writer, lecturer, and teacher. Born La Grange, IL. Pupil of Art Institute of Chicago; studied in Paris. Member: CA AC; Los Angeles PS. Award: Silver medal, Associated Artists of

Pittsburgh, Carnegie Inst., 1915. Address in 1929, 6553 Colgate, Los Angeles, CA.

HOLMES, RHODA CARLETON.
See Mrs. Nicholls.

HOLMES, WILLIAM H.
Painter. Born Harrison Co., OH, Dec. 1, 1846. Artist to US Geological Survey of the Territories, 1872; Curator, 1906, and Director, 1920, National Gallery of Art. Member: President, Wash. WCC; Hon. President, S. Wash. A.; Wash. Landscape C. (hon.); AFA. Art Edit., "Art and Archaeology." Awards: First Corcoran prize, Wash. WCC 1900; Parsons prize, Wash. WCC 1902. Work: "Midsummer," Corcoran Gallery, Washington, "The Wanderlusters' Rest," Nat'l Gallery of Art, Washington, DC. Address in 1929, National Gallery of Art, Smithsonian Institution; h. Cosmos Club, Washington, DC. Died 1933.

HOLMGREN, R. JOHN.
Painter and illustrator. Born St. Paul, MN, Nov. 27, 1897. Pupil of Bridgman and Woodbury. Member: SI; GFLA. Address in 1929, 412 East 58th Street, New York, NY. Died 1963.

HOLSLAG, EDWARD J.
Painter and mural designer. Born in Buffalo, NY, in 1870. Pupil of National Academy of Design, and of John La Farge. He exhibited portraits and landscapes at the Chicago Art Institute, and is represented by murals in the Congressional Library, Washington, DC, and in many banks, theatres and public buildings. He died in De Kalb, IL, Dec. 10, 1925. He was formerly president of the Palette and Chisel Club.

HOLSMAN, ELIZABETH TUTTLE.
Painter and sculptor. Born Brownville, NE, Sept. 25, 1873. Pupil of AIC. Member: Chicago SI; Chicago AC; Chicago Gal. A. Award: Silver medal, St. Paul Inst., 1916. Work: "Still Waters," Omaha Society of Fine Arts; "Portrait of David Rankin," bronze bas-releif, and "Portrait of Joseph Addison Thompson," Tarkio College, Tarkio,

MO; bronze bas- relief of Dean Reese, Law School, University of Nebraska, Lincoln, NE; war memorial bas-relief "Lieut. Alexander McCornick" in US Destroyer "The McCornick"; war memorial "Victory" with honor roll in Harrison Technical High School, Chicago. Address in 1929, 307 North Michigan Avenue; 1224 East 57th Street, Chicago, IL; summer, Lotus Island, Lauderdale Lakes, WI.

HOLT, MAUD S.
(Mrs. Winfield Scott Holt). Painter. Born Carbondale, IL, Nov. 1, 1866. Pupil of Harry Thompson and Percy Tudor; Hart in Paris; George Elmer Browne; Academie des Grandes Chaumieres. Member: SSAL; Little Rock FAC; Springfield, IL, AA. Awards: First prize for flower paintings, St. Louis Fair, 1890. Represented by portraits in the Arkansas State House; Public Libary, Little Rock; and a landscape in the Boys Club, Little Rock. Address in 1929, 1003 Barber Avenue, Little Rock, AR.

HOLT, PERCY WILLIAM.
Painter. Born Mobile, AL. Pupil of Birge Harrison, John F. Carlson, Charles Rosen. Address in 1929, 2214 Broadway, Galveston, TX; summer, Woodstock, NY.

HOLT, SAMUEL.
Miniature painter. Born in Meriden, CT, in 1801. He lived in Hartford for many years.

HOLTERHOFF, IDA.
See Mrs. George C. Holloway.

HOLTON, LEONARD T.
Illustrator and writer. Born Philadelphia, Sept. 6, 1900. Member: SI; Phila. AG. Address in 1929, 3501 Powelton Avenue, Philadelphia, PA.

HOLTZMAN, IRVING.
Painter. Born Russia, Feb. 16, 1897. Pupil of Cooper Union; NAD. Member: Salons of America; S. Indp. A. Address in 1929, 671 Manida St., New York, NY.

HOLVEY, SAMUEL BOYER.
Sculptor and designer. Born in Wilkes Barre, PA, July 20, 1935.

Study: Syracuse Univ.; Am. Univ. Comn.: Bas-relief mural, WY Valley Country Club, Wilkes Barre, PA, 1962. Exhib.: Corcoran Area Show, Wash., DC; Ann. Wash. Area Sculpture Show; Am. Genius, Corcoran Gallery, etc. Teaching: Design and graphic design, Corcoran School of Art, DC; Univ. of MD, 1967-78. Media: Metal direct contruction, lumia. Address in 1982, Bethesda, MD.

HOLYLAND, C. I.
Engraver. He engraved on copper in New York in 1834. The only plate known is an allegorical frontispiece to "A Defense of Particular Redemption- In four letters to the Baptist Minister," New York, 1834. He signed his work "C. I. Holyland Sc."

HOLYOKE.
A little known genre painter of some talent.

HOLZER, J. A.
Mural painter and sculptor. Born in Berne, Switzerland, in 1858. Pupil of Fournier and Bernard in Paris. His mural, "Homer," is at Princeton University, Princeton, NJ. Address in 1926, 182 East 72d Street, New York, NY.

HOLZHAUER, EMIL.
Painter and sculptor. Born Schwabisch Gmund. Germany, Jan 21, 1887. Pupil of Robert Henri, Homer Boss. Member: S. Indp. A. Address in 1929, 64 West 9th Street, New York, NY.

HOMAN, S. V.
Miniature painter, flourishing in Boston in 1844.

HOMER, WINSLOW.
This noted landscape, marine and genre painter was born in Boston, Feb. 24, 1836; died at Scarboro, ME, Sept 29, 1910. Beginning work as a lithographer when nineteen years old, he took up painting and illustrating two years later. He came to NY in 1859, and for a short time studied at the Nat'l Acad. of Design and with Frederick Rondel. He was sent by Harper & Brothers to make war paintings in 1861; he subsequently painted many pictures of black American life, and a visit to the Adirondack mountains inspired him to paint camping scenes with mountain guides. Later he traveled in England and France. He is best known by his pictures of the Maine Coast, where for many years he lived the life of a recluse at Scarboro. He was elected an Associate of the National Academy in 1864, and an Academician the following year, and was a member of the America Water Color Society and the National Institute of Arts and Letters.

HONG, ANNA HELGA.
Painter, lecturer, and teacher. Born Monona Co., IA, Feb. 21, 1894. Member: CA IC; Chicago SA. Award: Third prize for oil painting, Northwestern Painters, Seattle FAS, 1925; Tingle prize, Los Angeles Museum, 1926; second prize, Chicago Norske Club, 1926; first Eisteddfod prize, Los Angeles, 1926. Lecturer on Art appreciation, Modern Art and interior decoration. Address in 1929, Dept. of Art Northwestern University, Evanston, IL; summer, 1115 Mendocino St., Altandena, CA.

HONIG, GEORGE H.
Portrait painter, and sculptor. Born Rockport, IN, 1881. Pupil of NAD and H. A. MacNeil in New York. Member: Evansville SFA and Hist. Awards: Suydam bronze medal, NAD, 1914' Suydam silver medal, NAD, 1915. Work: Spanish-American war memorial at Salina, KS; "The Spirit of 1861" and "The Spirit of 1916," on Vanderburg County Soldiers' and Sailors' Coliseum, Evansville, IN; "The Hiker," Fairview Park, Denver, CO; portrait of Cleo Baxter Davis in Court House, Bowling Green, KY; portrait in bronze of J. B. Gresham for War Mothers of America, Evansville, IN; Service Star and Legio Memorial, Evansville, IN; Judge Thomas Towles, Sr. Memorial, Henderson, KY; Abraham Lincoln Trail markers (Portrait) Grand View, IN; Six memorials of Transylvania Company, Henderson, KY; replicas in Transylvania University, Lexington, KY, and Univ. of North Carolina, Chapel Hill, NC; Rotary Hall of Fame Memorial, Fine Arts S., Evansville; Portrait Crowder

Memorial, Evansville, Indiana and Mr. Vernon, IN, in Eagles Home at Anderson and Richmond, IN; in Masonic Temple, Evansville, IN; in Court House at Bloomington, IL, and Evansville, IN; soldier group, Shelbyville, IN; Sapello memorial, Evansville, IN; World War memorials at Evansville and Connelton, IN; bronze portrait, Rescue Mission, Evansville, IN. Address in 1929, 209 Locust Street, Evansville, IN.

HONORE, PAUL.
Painter, illustrator, writer, and lecturer. Born PA, May 30, 1885. Pupil of Brangwyn; Wicker; PAFA. Member: NAC; Wash. AC; Scarab C; Detroit ACS; GFLA; mural PS; MI. Acad. F. A.; Am. APL. Awards: Prize, Museum of Art Founders Soc., Detroit AI, 1917; Preston prize, Detroit AI, 1917; Walter Piper purchase prize, Scarab, C. Work: Murals in Dept. of Arch., Univ. of MI; County Courthouse, Midland, MI; Highland Park High School; Student Church, East Lansing; Public Library, Dearborn, MI; Player's Club, Detroit, MI; "The Loggers," State of MI; wood block prints, Detroit AI. Illustrated: "Bushranger" and "Highwaymen" (McBride & Co.); "Tales from Silverlands," "Frontier Ballads" and "The Winged Horse," (Doubleday, Doran & Co.); "Tales Worth Telling," (Century Co.); "The Winged Horse Anthology," (Doubleday, Doran & Co.); "Heroes from Hakluyt," (Henry Holt). Address in 1929, 217 Farnsworth Avenue, East, Detroit, MI; h. Royal Oak, MI.

HOOD, ETHEL P.
Sculptor. Born: Baltimore, MD, on April 9, 1908. Studied: Art Students' League; Julian Acad., Paris. Awards: gold medal, Catherine L. Wolfe Art Club, 1954; Society of Washington Artists, 1939. Collections: Radio City and French Building, Rockefeller Center, New York City; Brookgreen Gardens, SC. Address in 1980, 15 E. 61st Street, New York, NY.

HOOGLAND, WILLIAM.
Born in 1795. He was an admirable engraver in both line and stipple. He appears in NY about 1815 as the designer and engraver of vignettes. In 1826 he was working with Abel Bowen in Boston, and among his pupils there were John Cheny and Joseph Andrews. In 1841 he was again in NYC. Hoogland was one of the early American bank-note engravers.

HOOKER, MARGARET HUNTINGTON.
Painter. Born in Rochester, NY, in 1869. Studied in Art Students' League and Metropolitan Schools of NY; also studied in Paris and London. Taught art in Normal School, Cortland, NY, 1893-94; illustrated for New York Tribune, 1897; taught arts and crafts in Paris.

HOOKER, WILLIAM.
As early as 1805 Hooker was engraving in Philadelphia, and in 1810 he was one of the organizers of the Philadelphia Society of Artists. In 1816 he removed to NY and his name appears in the directories of that city until 1840. His occupation is generally given as "Engraver," but he also appears as "map-publisher" and as "instrument maker and chart-seller to the US Navy." The "New Pocket Plan of New York," of 1817, is "Drawn, engraved, published and sold" by Hooker. He engraved a few portraits in stipple, and subject plates in line, but he seems to have been chiefly employed in map engraving.

HOOKS, MITCHELL HILLARY.
Illustrator. Born in Detroit, MI, in 1923. He attended the Cass Technical High School there. His first illustration was done in 1942 for an advertising firm. A leader in the field of paperback cover illustration for many years, he has illustrated a great number of books and magazines as well. An active member of the S of I, a contributor to the USAF art program, he lives and works in New York City.

HOOPER, ANNIE BLAKESLEE.
Painter, illustrator, and craftsman. Born in California. Pupil of San Francisco Art School; ASL of NY and Charles Melville Dewey. Member: NYWCC. Address in

1929, 200 Fifth Avenue, New York, NY; h. Spuyten Duyvil, NY.

HOOPER, EDWARD.
Born in England, May 24, 1829; died in Brooklyn, Dec. 13, 1870. He was an engraver and was for many years a member of the firm of Bobbett and Hooper, wood-engravers. Mr. Hooper produced several water colors remarkable for their accuracy of drawing and harmony of color. He was one of the originators of the American Water Color Society.

HOOPER, ELIZABETH.
Painter, illustrator, craftsman, and writer. Born Baltimore, Oct. 6, 1901. Member: Balto. WCC; Balto. S. Indp. A. Address in 1929, 605 The Charles Apts., 3333 North Charles St., Baltimore, MD.

HOOPER, LAURA B.
Painter. Member: Balto. WCC. Address in 1929, Shirley and Green Spring Aves., Baltimore, MD.

HOOPER, ROSA.
Painter. Born San Francisco, CA, July 19, 1876. Pupil of San. F. Art School; San F. Art Lg. Otto Eckhardt in Dresden; Mme. de Billemont in Paris. Member: CA S. Min. P.; San F. Soc. Women P.; Alliance. Awards: Grand Prize, Alaska-Yukon Pacific Exposition, Seattle, 1909; gold and bronze medals, Panama-Pacific Exposition, San Diego, 1915; first popular vote prize, CA S. Min. P., Los Angeles CA, 1929. Address in 1929, 624 Lexington Avenue, New York, NY.

HOOPER, WILL PHILLIP.
Painter and illustrator. Born Biddeford, ME. Pupil of Benjamin Fritz and ASL of NY; MA Normal Art School, Boston, Member: NYWCC; Salma, C. Address in 1929, Villa Rosa Studios, Spuyten Duyvil, NY. Died in 1938.

HOOPLE, WILLIAM C.
Illustrator. Member: SI; GFLA. Address in 1929, 11 East 14th Street, New York, NY.

HOOVEN, HERBERT NELSON.
Painter. Born Hazelton, PA, Jan 31, 1898. Pupil of PAFA; Beaux-Arts Inst. Design; PA Museum School. IN. Art. Member: Fellowship, PAFA. Work: "Anthracite Coal Industry," Hazelton Public Library; mural decorations Church St. Louis, Waterloo, Canada; "Fleet on Narragansett Bay," Library University of Valparaiso; "End of Winter" and "Edge of the Woods," Hazleton High School Gallery; "Morning," Civic Club, Hazleton, PA. Address in 1929, Drums, PA.

HOOVER, BESSIE M.
See Mrs. H. H. Wessel.

HOOVER, CHARLES.
Illustrator. Born Washington, DC, April 8, 1897. Pupil of Hugh Breckenridge. Member: Wash. Landscape C. Address in 1929, 409 Evening Star Bldg.; h. 3024 - 45th Street, NW, Washington, DC.

HOOVER, MRS. LOUIS ROCHON.
Painter and illustrator. Born Washington, DC. Pupil of Hugh Breckenridge. Work: Portraits and advertising illustrations. Address in 1929, 3024 45th Street, NW, Washington, DC.

HOPE, THOMAS W.
Portrait and miniature painter, flourishing 1839-45 in New York.

HOPE, JAMES.
Painter. Born in England, Nov. 29, 1818, he accompanied his father to Canada; after the death of his parent he removed to Fair Haven, VT, and became interested in art. In 1853 he opened his studio in NY and was elected an Associate of the National Academy. His pictures include "The Army of the Potomac," "Rainbow Falls," "The Gem of the Forest," and the "Forest Glen," He died in 1892, in NYC.

HOPE, JOHN W.
Sculptor. Exhibited at National Academy of Design in 1925. Specialty animals. Address in 1926, 65 Gun Hill Road, NY.

HOPKIN, ROBERT.
Painter. Born Jan. 3, 1822, in Glasgow, Scotland. Went with his parents when eleven years old to Detroit, MI, where he grew up and became the head of the art interests of that city. His best

work consists of landscape and marine painting. he died on March 21, 1909 in Detroit.

HOPKINS, C. E.
Painter and etcher. Born in Cincinnati, OH, in 1886. Pupil of Newotany and Barnhorn. Member: Cincinnati Art Club. Address in 1926, 3525 Trimble Avenue, Evanston, Cincinnati, OH.

HOPKINS, CHARLES BENJAMIN.
Painter, illustrator, writer, and teacher. Born Oct. 23, 1882. Pupil of Artklan. Illustrated A Dog's Life, by Tige; author and illustrator of Comic History of our Boys in France. Instructor in Commercial Art, Maysville Business College. Address in 1929, care of S. D. Johnson Co, Marysville, CA.

HOPKINS, DANIEL.
Engraver. This man engraved the music and words for "The Rudiments of Music," etc. The book is dated in 1783, and it was published in Cheshire, CT.

HOPKINS, EDNA BOLES.
(Mrs. James R. Hopkins). Engraver. Born in Michigan in 1878. Member: Societe Internationale des Graveurs en Couleurs; Societe Internationale des Graveurs sue Bois; Societe Nationale des Beaux-Arts in Paris. Award: Silver medal, P.-P. Exp., San. F., 1915. Work in Library of Congress Washington, DC; Walker Art Gallery, Liverpool; National Museum, Stockhom; Kunst Gewerke Museum, Berlin; Bibliotheque d'Art et Archaeologie, Paris; Cincinnati Art Museum; Detroit Institute of Arts. Address in 1929, Ohio State University, Columbus, OH; 55 Rue de Dantzig, Paris, France. Died in 1935.

HOPKINS, JAMES R.
Painter. Born in Ohio, 1878. Pupil of Cincinnati Art Academy. Member: ANA; Paris AAA; Associate, Societe Nationale des Beaux Arts, Paris. Awards: Lippincott prize, PAFA, 1908; bronze medal, Buenos Aires, 1910; gold medal, P.P. Exp., San F., 1915; Harris bronze medal and prize ($300), AIC, 1916; Clarke prize, NAD, 1920. Work: "Frivolity." Cincinnati Museum; "A

Kentucky Mountaineer," Chicago Art Inst.; "Reflections," Atlanta Art Association. Address in 1929, Ohio State Univerity, Columbus, OH; 55 Rue de Dantzig, Paris, France.

HOPKINS, MARK.
Sculptor. Born Williamstown, MA, Feb. 9, 1851. Pupil of Frederick MacMonnies. Member: Societe des Artistes Francais; Union Internationale des Beaux-Arts. Address in 1929, Williamstown, MA.

HOPKINSON, CHARLES SYDNEY.
Painter. Born Cambridge, MA, July 27, 1869. Pupil of ASL of NY; Aman-Jean, Denman Ross, Carl G. Cutler. Member: ANA; Boston AG; Boston WCC; SAA, 1898; AWCS; Portrait painter,; Concord AA; Boston, SWCP. Awards: Bronze medal, Pan-Am. Exp., 1901; bronze medal, St. Louis Exp., 1904; second prize ($200), Worcester Museum, 1902 and 1905; Beck gold medal, PAFA, 1915; silver medal, P.-P. Exp., San F., 1915; silver medal, Sesqui-Centennial Exposition, Phila., 1926; Logan medal ($1,000), AIC, 1926. Represented in Rhode Island School of Design; Harvard University; collection of war portraits, National Gallery of Art, Washington; Brooklyn Museum; Brown University; Radcliffe College; Dartmouth College; University of Virginia; Cleveland Museum. Died in 1962. Address in 1929, Manchester, MA.

HOPKINSON, FRANCIS.
Painter and lawyer, signer of the Declaration of Independence, was born October 2, 1737. He drew and painted several portraits. He died May 9, 1791.

HOPPE, LESLIE F.
Designer. Born Jerseyville, IL, 1889. Pupil of Chicago AFA and AIC. Member: Palette and Chisel C. Address in 1929, 415 South Claremont Avenue, Chicago, IL.

HOPPER, EDWARD.
Painter and etcher. Born Nyack, NY, July 22, 1882. Pupil of Henri; Hayes Miller; Chase. Member: Am. Print Makers; Brooklyn SE. Awards: Bryan prize, Los Angeles Museum, 1923; Logan prize, AIC, 1923.

447

Represented in CA State Library; Pennsylvania Acad. of the Fine Arts; Brooklyn Museum; New Orleans Museum; Art Institute of Chicago; NY Public Library; Metropolitan Museum; British Museum; Fogg Museum, Cambridge; Phillips Memorial Gal., Wash., DC. Died in 1967. Address in 1929, 3 Washington Square, North, New York, NY.

HOPPIN, AUGUSTUS.
Painter and wood engraver. Born in Providence, RI, July 3, 1828. He illustrated and engraved for many publications. Died April 1, 1896 in Flushing, NY.

HOPPIN, HOWARD.
Painter. Member: Providence, AC. Address in 1929, 32 Westminster Street, Providence, RI.

HOPPIN, THOMAS FREDERICK.
Born Aug. 15, 1816 Providence, RI. Brother of Augustus Hoppin. Studied in Philadelphia and later in Paris under Delaroche. On his return to this country he opened his studio in New York. He produced statues in plaster, stained glass designs, and many etchings and illustrations of American life and history. The American Art Union in 1848 and 1850 published two of his etchings. Died Jan. 21, 1872, in Providence, RI.

HOPSON, WILLIAM FOWLER.
Etcher and engraver. Born Watertown, CT, Aug. 30, 1849. Pupil of L. Sanford in New Haven; J. D. Felter and August Will in New York. Member: Grolier C, New York; Rowfant C, Cleveland; AI Graphic A; Acorn C. and Paint and Clay C, New Haven; AFA. Award: Hon. mention for copper engraving, Pan-Am. Exp., Buffalo, 1901. Work in Chicago Art Institute; New York Public Library; Library of Congress; Metropolitan Museum; Harvard University; Yale University and other collections. Specialty, bookplates. Engraved the blocks for one edition of Webster's. Died Feb. 13, 1935. Address in 1929, 720 Whitney Avenue, New Haven, CT.

HOPWOOD.
A mixed copper-plate engraving is signed "Hopwood Sc." The title is "A Winter Piece" (snow scene with cottage in right background, tree in left; in the center of foreground is a man with a stick in his right hand standing by a horse with a pannier). This print was published in 1803 by J. Nicholdson, Halifax.

HORCHERT, JOSEPH A.
Sculptor. Born Hechingen, Germany, May 4, 1874. Studied in Staedel Art Inst., Frankfort A.M., and Royal Academie, Munich, Germany. Member: St. Louis AL; St. Louis AG. Award: Prize for Fountain, St. Louis, AL. Work: Guggenheim Memorial Fountain, St. Louis; figures on the Friedrich Bridge, Berlin; high altar, Sacrament Church, St. Louis, MO; mem. tablet, College of Pharmacy, St. Louis; pediments, High School, Jersey City, NJ, and Preparatory Seminary, St. Louis; Mem. tablet, Westminster College, Fulton, MO; portraits of Founders of Lindenwood College, St. Charles, MO. Address in 1929, 3130 South Compton Ave., St. Louis, MO.

HORD, DONAL.
Sculptor. Born Wisconsin, Feb. 26, 1902. Pupil of Santa Barbara School of the Arts. Member: NSS. Work: Bronze. "El Cacique," San Diego Fine Arts Gallery, San Diego, CA. Address in 1929, Santa Barbara School of the Arts, 914 Santa Barbara Street, Santa Barbara, CA; h. 1455 Tenth Street, San Diego, CA.

HORE, ETHEL.
See Mrs. John Townsend.

HORIUCHI, PAUL.
Artist. Born April 12, 1906 in Yamanashiken, Japan. Primarily a self-taught artist. Works in collage (rice paper); is also painter since youth. Lives in Seattle (created mural for Seattle World's Fair, 1962). Received awards from Wash. State Fair; many from Seattle Art Mus.; Ford Foundation; Seattle World's Fair; Spokane Art Board Coliseum and others. Exhibited at NY Coliseum (1959); Carnegie; Standford Univ.;

Seattle Art Mus.; PAFA; Yoseido Gallery, Tokyo; Oakland Art Mus; Reed College; Expo 74 Spokane. In collections of Wadsworth; Reed College; Harvard; University of Arizona; Denver Art Museum; Seattle Public Library; Mus. of Modern Art in Tokyo; Mead Corporation and University of Oregon.

HORN, MILTON.
Sculptor. Born Russia, Sept. 1, 1905. Pupil of Henry Hudson Kitson; Beaux- Arts Institute of Design, New York. Work: Ceiling, Hotel Savoy-Plaza, New York. Address in 1929, 128 West 23rd Street, New York, NY; h. 35 Schermerhorn Street, Brooklyn, NY.

HORNBY, LESTER GEORGE.
Illustrator, painter, and engraver. Born Lowell, MA, March 27, 1882. Pupil of RI School of Design, Providence; Pape School, Boston; ASL of NY; Laurens and others in Paris. Member: Providence AC.; Providence WCC; Chicago SE; NY SE; Salma. C.; Paris AAA (Dir. 1907-1908); Boston SWCP.; North Shore AA. Work in: Victoria and Albert Museum, London; Library of Congress, Washington, DC; New York Public Library; Art Institute of Chicago; Detroit Institute; RI School of Design, Providence; Carnegie Institute, Pittsburgh. Illustrated "Sketch-book of London," "Edinburgh," "Paris," "Boston." Series of war etchings. Address in 1929, Boston Art Club. 150 Newbury Street; 91 Pinckney Street, Boston, MA.

HORNE, LAURA TREVITTE.
Painter. Born in Dalton, GA, in 1891. Pupil of John Carlsen; Francis Jones; Van Dearing Perrine. Member: New port Artists' Association. Address in 1926, Woodstock, NY.

HORNER, T.
About 1844 Horner was living in Ossining, NY, where he engraved a large "View of New York from Brooklyn," published by W. Neale of New York.

HORNLY, LESTER GEORGE.
Painter and etcher. Born in Lowell, MA, in 1882. Student of

School of Design, Providence, RI; also studied in Paris under Jean Paul Laurens and other masters. Represented by etchings in New York and Boston Public Libraries; Congressional Library; South Kensington Museum, London. Address in 1926, 9A Park Street, Boston, MA.

HOROWITZ, BRENDA.
Painter. Born: New York City. Studied: City College of NY; Cooper Union Art School; The Hans Hofmann School of Art; City University of NY. Exhibitions: Croquis Gallery, New York City; Museum Gallery, 1971; Columbia University Gallery, 1974; Westbeth Galleries, New York City.

HORSFALL, CAROLYN SARAH.
Painter and craftsman. Born Hartford, CT, July 3, 1901. Pupil of Anna Fisher, Henry B. Snell, Geerge Pearse Ennis. Member: Springfield A. Lg.; NA Women PS; AWCS; NYWCC. Address in 1929, 150 Lexington Avenue, New York, NY.; h. 52 Huntington Street, Hartford, CT; summer, Boothbay Harbor, ME.

HORSFALL, ROBERT BRUCE.
Painter. Born in Clinton, IA, in 1869. Studied at Cincinnati Art Academy, 1886-89; gained European scholarship and studied at Art Academy, Munich, and in Paris, France. Has exhibited at Chicago, IL, since 1886; and at Midwinter Exposition, San Francisco. Made scientific illustrations for American Museum of Natural History, New York, 1898-1901; Illustrated "Land Mammals of the Eastern Hemisphere," 1912-13; also many books of birds, etc. Permanently represented by 12 backgrounds for Habitat Groups, American Museum of Natural History, New York. Address in 1926, Box 80, R. 6 Portland, OR. Died March 24, 1948.

HORTENS, WALTER HANS.
Illustrator. Born in Vienna, Austria, in 1924. He studied in Egypt and Austria and is a graduate of Pratt Inst. and the Academie Julien in Paris. His first assignment appeared in 1948 in The New York Times and since then his technical illustrations have

frequently been seen in National Geographic, Life and Time. A veteran of World War II, he is a contributor to the USAF Art Program and a member of the S of I.

HORTER, EARL.
Illustrator. Born in 1881. His etchings of large cities were of high quality. Work: "Smelters-Pittsburgh" Madison Square, NY; "Old Creole Quarters, N. Orleans." Member: SI 1910. Award: Silver medal, P.P. Exp., San. F., 1915; international watercolor, Chicago. Died in 1940.

HORTO.
This engraver is simply mentioned in Mr. Stauffer's volume as engraving portraits and views in 1830-35 for Phila. and Baltimore publishers. He probably came from Providence, RI. He engraved a business card of the Roger Williams Hotel in that city, and the card says that this house was "Formerly kept by Mr. Horton," but whether the former innkeeper was the engraver himself, or a relative, is uncertain. Horton was certainly engraving for Providence book publishers as early as 1823. In that year he engraved ten copper plates illustrating a "Complete System of Stenography," by J. Dodge.

HORTON, DOROTHY E.
Painter. Born Poplar Bluff, MO, Oct. 14, 1898. Pupil of St. Louis School of Fine Arts; PAFA; Susan Ricker Knox. Award: Second prize, Eire Art Club, 1928. Address in 1929, 3919 Sassafras Street, Erie, PA.

HORTON, ELIZABETH SUMNER.
Painter. Born Boston, June 27, 1902. Pupil of Philip Hale, Alexander and Williams James, Fred Bosley; M. Morrisset in Paris. Member: NA Women PS. Award: First prize, Junior League, Boston, 1928. Address in 1929, 97 Lee Street, Brookline, MA.

HORTON, HARRIET H.
Portrait and miniature painter. Represented by portraits in Minnesota Historical Society. She died in 1922 in St. Paul, MN.

HORTON, WILLIAM SAMUEL.
Painter and writer. Born Grand Rapids, MI, Nov. 16, 1865. Pupil of ASL and NAD in New York; Constant and Julian Academy in Paris. Member: NYWCC; ADA; Societe Moderne; Soc. Internationale, and Salon d'Automne, Paris. Awards: Gold medal, Int. Exp., Nantes, 1904; bronze medal, Orleans, 1905. Work: "Bathers Returning," Bradford Museum, England: "Good Friday in Seville" and "Soir d'Hives, Pontarlier," Luxembourg Museum: "General Pershing and the American Contingent Traversing the Place de la Concorde," July 14, 1919." National Museum, Wash., DC; and in the Musee Carnavalet, Paris, France, and in the Brooklyn Museum. Died in 1936. Address in 1929, 64 Rue de la Rochefoucauld, Paris, France.

HOSFORD, HARRY LINDLEY.
Etcher. Born Terre Haute, IN. Pupil of Chase, DuMond, Beckwith, Maynard and F. C. Jones. Member: Chicago SE. Represented in collection of the New York Public Library and the Minneapolis Institute of Arts. Address in 1929, 781 Goodrich Avenue, St. Paul, MN; summer, Lyme, CT.

HOSKIN, ROBERT.
Wood engraver. Born in Brooklyn, NY, in 1842. He studied at the Brooklyn Institute where he received the Graham medal. In 1883 he received the gold medal of the Paris Salon for engraving. He has done considerable engraving for the magazines in this country. His best known engraving is "Cromwell Visiting Milton."

HOSKINS, GAYLE PORTER.
Illustrator. Born Brazil, IN, July 20, 1887. Pupil of Vanderpoel; AIC; Howard Pyle. Award: First prize, Wilmington SFA, 1920. Work: Series of war paintings for the Ladies Home Journal; illustrated Kazan, Me, Smith, etc.; magazine cover designs; advertising work, Veedol oil, Gould Batteries, Hercules Powder Co.; "Bill and Jim" series, etc. General magazine illustration. Address in 1929, 1616 Rodney Street, Wilmington, DE.

HOSMER, FLORENCE A.
Painter. Born in Woodstock, CT.
Studied: MA School of Art; Boston
Museum of Fine Arts School; and
with Joseph DeCamp, Anson Kent
Cross, Charles Woodbury.
Collections: International Inst.
of Boston; Essex Inst., Salem, MA;
Park Street Church, Boston.

HOSMER, HARRIET.
Sculptor. Born Oct. 6, 1830 in
Watertown, MA. Studied in Lenox
and Boston. In 1852 she went to
Europe with her friend Charlotte
Cushman and studied in Rome. Her
principal statues were: "Puck,"
"Beatrice Cenci," "Zenobia,"
"Sleeping Faun," and a statue of
Thomas H. Benton cast in bronze for
Lafayette Park, St. Louis. Died
Feb. 21, 1908, in Watertown.

HOSTATER, ROBERT B.
Painter. Born in San Francisco.
He lived and studied for more than
twentey-five years in Paris.
Exhibited at the Salon.

HOTCHKISS,
A little known landscape painter
who worked much of his time in
Italy. He painted views of "Mount
Aetna" and "Colosseum by
Moonlight."

HOTCHKISS, WALES.
Painter. Born in Bethany, CT, in
1826. Pupil of George W. Flagg in
New Haven. He painted many
portraits in oils, but his forte
was in water color. He lived in
Northampton for years.

HOTTINGER, WILLIAM A.
Illustrator. Born Philadelphia,
PA, Oct. 11, 1890. Pupil of Carl
von Marr. Member: Allied AA.
Address in 1929, 127 North Dearborn
Street, Chicago, IL; h. Glen Ellyn,
IL.

HOTVEDT, CLARENCE ARNOLD.
Painter and teacher. Born Eau
Claire, WI, April 16, 1900. Pupil
of AIC. Member: Alumni, AIC;
Wichita AG. Address in 1929, 411
Avenue C, Wichita, KS.

HOTVEDT, KRIS J.
Printmaker and instructor. Born in
Wautoma, WI, in 1943. Studied:

Layton School of Art, Milwaukee,
WI; San Francisco Art Inst., CA;
Instituto Allende, San Miguel de
Allende, Gto. Mexico. Exhib.:
Pembroke State University, NC,
1968; Arizona State Univ., Tempe,
1973; Oklahoma Art Center, Oklahoma
City, 1974; Los Llanos Gal., Santa
Fe, 1980, and Ledoux Gal., Taos,
NM, 1981; many others.
Collections: Atalya School Art
Collection, Santa Fe, NM;
University of Sonora, Hermosillo,
Mexico; Huntington Art Alliance,
CA; others. Media: Woodcut and
serigraphs. Address in 1982, 125
Spruce St., Santa Fe, NM.

HOUDON, JEAN ANTOINE.
French sculptor. Born March 20,
1741. Came to this country in
1785. He was commissioned by the
State of Virginia to execute a
statue of Washington. He also made
busts of Franklin, Lafayette,
Thomas Jefferson, Robert Fulton,
Joel Barlow and John Paul Jones.
(See "Memoirs of Life and Works of
Houdon," by Biddle & Hart,
Philadelphia, 1911.) Died July 15,
1828 in Paris.

HOUGH, RICHARD.
Photographer and designer. Born in
Roanoke, VA, Mar. 1, 1945. Study:
Roanoke College; Rochester Inst. of
Technology, summer; Hotchkiss
Workshop, with Minor White, summer;
School of Design, CA Inst. of Arts.
Exhib.: VA Mus., Richmond; 23rd
Irish Int'l. Dublin; Soc. of
Photogr. Educ. Exhib., Univ. of IL,
Chicago; others. Mem.: Soc. of
Photogr. Educ. Address in 1976,
Los Angeles, CA.

HOUGH, WALTER.
Painter, writer, and lecturer.
Born Morgantown, WV, April 23,
1859. Pupil of E. F. Andrews, W. H.
Holmes. Member: Wash. WCC; AFA.
Address in 1929, National Museum;
1332 Farragut Street, Washington,
DC. Died in 1935.

HOULAHAN, KATHLEEN.
Painter. Born Winnipeg, CT, Jan.
31, 1887. Pupil of Robert Henri.
Member: NAC; S. Indp. A.; Seattle
Fine Arts Soc. Address in 1929,
2159 Shelby Street, Seattle, WA.

HOULTON, J.
A poorly designed and roughly engraved heading to a certificate of the Charitable Marine Society of Baltimore, is signed "J. Houlton Sculp't." As the certificate is filled out in 1797, it must have been engraved prior to that date. The design shows Columbus handing a book to a sailor; ship in full sail; lighthouse, etc., in the background. The plate is further signed "F. Kemelmeyer Deilin't."

HOUSE, JAMES.
Born in 1775. According to Dunlap, House painted a number of portraits in Philadelphia, but gave up art and entered the United States Army. He was known as Colonel House in 1814. Died Nov. 17, 1834.

HOUSE, JAMES JR.
Illustrator and teacher. Born Benton Harbor, MI, Jan. 19, 1902. Pupil of University of MI; PAFA. Award: John Frederick Lewis first prize for caricature, Phila. WCC, 1925. Illustrations in The New Yorker, Life, Collier's and numerous newspapers. Exhibited at PAFA in 1925. Address in 1929, 2007 Spruce Street, Philadelphia, PA.

HOUSE, T.
He was a bank-note engraver, chiefly employed in Boston. He engraved a few portraits for book publishers and he seemd to be working as early as 1836. He died about 1865. His full name may have been Timothy House.

HOUSTON, FRANCES C. LYONS.
(Mrs. William C. Houston). Painter. She was in born Jan. 14, 1867, in Hudson, MI. Studied in Paris under Lefebvre and Boulanger. Painted a portrait of Ethel Barrymore. Died in 1906 in Windsor, VT.

HOUSTON, GRACE.
Painter and teacher. Born Marysville, OH. Pupil of NY School of Applied Design; Provincetown Art Colony. Member: Pittsburgh AA; Alliance. Art Supervisor, Pittsburgh, PA. Address in 1929, Indiana State Teachers College, Art Dept., Indiana, PA; summer, PA State Collge, Art Dept., State College, PA.

HOUSTON, H. H.
He was one of the earliest good stipple-engravers of portraits who worked in the United States. He probably came here from Ireland as the Hibernian Magazine, of Dublin, contains portraits very similar in execution of his known work and signed "H. Houston." Houston appears in Philadelphia in 1796 and as his last dated work was done in 1798, his stay here was a comparatively short one. He engraved two separate plates of John Adams, and portraits of Washington; Rittenhouse; Kemble as Richard III; Kosciusko, etc. The first state of the John Adams plates published in Philadelphia in 1797 is lettered "H. H. Houston, Sculp't."

HOUSTON, NORA.
Painter, lecturer, and teacher. Pupil of Kenneth Hayes Miller, Vonnoh, Henri and Chase; Simon, Blanche, Menard and Cottet in Paris. Award: Hon. mention, Appalachian Exp., Knoxville, 1910. Address in 1929, 100 North Fourth Street, 519 East Franklin Street, Richmond, VA.

HOVENDEN, MARTHA.
Sculptor. Born Plymouth Meeting, May 8, 1884. Pupil of Charles Grafly, H. A. MacNeil. Member: Fellowship PAFA; Plastic C.; Wash. AC. Exhibited at PAFA in 1924. Died 1941. Address in 1929, Plymouth Meeting, PA.

HOVENDEN, THOMAS.
Painter. Born in 1840 in Dunmanway, County Cork, Ireland; died 1895 at Plymouth Meeting, PA. Studied at the Cork School of Design. Came to New York in 1863 and entered the school of the National Academy of Design; studied in Paris under Cabanel. He painted "Jerusalem the Golden," "Last Moments of John Brown," and "A Brittany Image Seller." Elected Member of the National Academy in 1882.

HOVEY, OTIS.
Painter. Born in 1788 in MA. Dunlap mentions him as a youthful genius. He made several copies of paintings that possessed merit. He

452

later lived in Oxford, NY. He painted a few portraits but was not successful.

HOW, KENNETH GAYOSO.
Painter and artist. Born Wantaugh, LI, NY, June 8, 1883. Pupil of Jane Peterson; Henry B. Snell. Member: NYWCC; NY. Arch Lg.; Salma C.; AWCS; AFA. Work: Buckwood Inn, Shawnee-on-Delaware, PA; additions to Hotel Gramatan, Bronxville, NY; "Oscela," Gramatan Inn, Daytona, FL. Address in 1929, 145 East 57th Street, h. 400 East 58th Street, New York, NY.

HOWARD, CECIL DE BLAQUIERE.
Sculptor. Born in Canada, April 2, 1888. At the age of thirteen he started working at the Art School, Buffalo, NY. Studied at ASL. Had done many portraits and animal studies. Worked directly in stone and marble. In collections of Albright-Knox and Whitney. Created memorials at Hautot-sur-mer and Ouville-de-Riviere, (France). Member of NA and NIAL. Died in 1956.

HOWARD, CLARA FRANCES.
Miniature painter, and teacher. Born 1866 in Poughkeepsie, NY. Pupil of NAD and ASL of NY under Brush and Chase. Member: NA Women PS; Am. S. Min. P. Address in 1929, 55 South Hamilton Street, Poughkeepsie, NY. Died before 1940.

HOWARD, DAN F.
Painter. Born in Iowa City, IA, Aug. 4, 1931. Study: Univ. of Iowa. Work: Lowe Art Museum, Miami, FL; Parthenon, Nashville, TN; Masur Museum of Art, LA; West Collection of Contemp. Art, St. Paul, MN; and others. Exhibitions: Lowe Art Mus.; Ark. Arts Ctr.; Jocelyn Art Mus., Omaha; West 79/The Law Nat'l Exhib., MN Mus. of Art, St. Paul; Nat'l Ptg. & Sculpt. Exhib., OK Art Ctr.; many more. Awards: Miami Nat'l 1st Prize; Bellinger Prize, Chautauqua Exhib. of Am. Art, NY; Purch. award, West 79/The Law; etc. Teaching: AR State Univ.; KS State Univ.; Univ. of NE, Lincoln. Mem.: Coll. Art Assn. of Am.; Am. Federation of the Arts; Nat'l Council Art Administrators; others.

HOWARD, EDITH LUCILE.
Painter and teacher. Born Bellows Falls, VT. Pupil Phila. School of Design for Women under Daingerfield, Snell. Member: NYWCC; Phila. Alliance; Plastic C.; Lyceum Club of London and Paris. Awards: Hon. mention, Plastic C, 1915; gold medal Plastic C., 1917. Instructor and lecturer, Philadelphia School of Design for Women. Address in 1929, 1206 Carnegie Hall, New York, NY; h. 1313 West 8th Street, Wilmington, DC.

HOWARD, ELOISE.
Painter. Member: NA Women PS. Exhibited "Summer" (decorative panel) at 33rd An. Exb. of NA of Women P and S. Address in 1929, 57 East 59th Street, New York, NY; care of Tiffany Foundation, Oyster Bay, LI, NY.

HOWARD, LINDA.
Sculptor. Born: Evanston, IL, Oct. 21, 1934. Studied: University of Denver, Denver, CO; Hunter College, CUNY, New York City. Awards: Creative Artists Public Service Grant, 1975; North Jersey Cultural Council, 1974; New England Artists, 1970. Exhibitions: Silvermine Guild, CT, 1971; Philadelphia Civic Center Museum, 1974; Sculpture Now Gallery, New York City, 1975. Aluminum monumental sculpture. Address in 1980, 11 Worth St., New York, NY.

HOWARD, MARION.
Landscape painter and dec. Born Roxbury, MA, 1883. Pupil of Boston Museum School under Tarbell, Benson and Hale; also of Chase and Edward H. Barnard. Address in 1929, North Conway, NH.

HOWE, ARTHUR VIRGIL.
Painter. Born in 1860. Specialty, landscape painting. Died in 1925 in Troy, NY.

HOWE, GEORGE.
Illustrator. Born in Salzburg, Austria, in 1896. He ran away to America at the age of 14. After studying in Paris for two years, he returned, making the United States his home. Before his career as a magazine illustrator began, he was

forced to work at assorted odd jobs, from chauffeuring to scenery painting for movie companies. His illustrations, most of which were done in watercolor, executed in a flat, posterlike manner, were seen in Collier's, American, Woman's Home Companion and Good Housekeeping. One of his last assignments was a series of paintings that were seen as posters for the Barnum and Bailey Circus. Died in 1941.

HOWE, WILLIAM H.
Painter. Born at Ravenna, OH, in 1846. He began the study of art in 1880 at the Royal Academy of Dusseldorf, Germany, and after working there two years went to Paris. Here he studied with Otto de Thoren and F. de Vuillefroy and had a picture accepted at the Salon of 1883. For ten years thereafter he was successful exhibitor at the Salon and other European exhibitions. Returning to the United States, he was elected a National Academician in 1897 and a Member of the Society of American Artists in 1899. At the Paris Exposition of 1889 he was awarded a medal of the second class. At London in 1890 he received a gold medal, and in the same year the Temple Gold Medal at the Pennsylvania Academy of Fine Arts, Philadelphia, PA, and a gold medal at Boston. A medal was awarded to him at the Chicago World's Fair in 1893, a gold medal at San Francisco in 1894, and a gold medal at Atlanta in 1895. He was an Officier d'Academie and a Chevalier of the Legion of Honor, both by decree of the French Government. In permanent collections of the St. Louis Museum of Fine Arts and in the Cleveland Museum. Died in Bronxville, NY, in 1929.

HOWE, ZADOC.
Born 1777 in CT. This name, as "Z. Howe Sc't," is signed to a poorly engraved figure of a man used as a frontispiece to "A New Collection of Sacred Harmony, etc." by Oliver Brownson, Simsbury, CT, 1797. The music in this collection is also doubtless engraved by Howe. Died 1852 in MA.

HOWELL, FELICIE WALDO.
Painter. Born Honolulu, Sept. 8, 1897. Pupil of Corcoran Art School, Washington, SC, under E.C. Messer; Phila. School of Design for Women; and Henry B. Snell. Member: ANA, 1922; Phila. WCC.; Concord AA; Allied AA; Barnard C.; Painter and Sculptors Gal. Assn.; NYWCC; SPNY; Wash. WCC; AWSC. Awards: Prize, NA Women Painters and Sculptors, 1916; first hon. mention, Concord Arts Assoc., 1919; silver medal, Soc. Wash. Artists, 1921; second Hallgarten prize, NAD, 1921; silver medal, Wash. WCC, 1921; Mr. and Mrs. Augustus S. Peabody prize, AIC, 1921; bronze medal, S. Wash. A., 1922; hon. mention State Fair, Aurora, IL, 1922; William H. Tuthill purchase prize, international water color exhibition; Chicago Art Institute, 1927. Work: "A New England Street." Corcoran Gallery, Washington; "The Avenue of the Allies," American Legion Building, Gloucester, MA; "Gramercy Park, New York," Herron Art Inst.; "The Flower Women," Telfair Academy, Savannah; "The Pierce-Nichol House, Salem," Metropolitan Museum of Art, New York. Instructor in painting, New York School of Fine and Applied Art; summer class, Gloucester, MA. Address in 1929, 224 East 49th Street, New York, NY.

HOWELL, JAMES.
Painter. Born in Kansas City, MO, Nov. 17, 1935. Work: Private collections. Exhibitions: Butler Art Inst. Mid-Year Annual; Northwest Watercolor Annual; Frye Museum Puget Sound Annual; Springfield Art Soc. Annual; Westchester Art Soc. Annual; and others. Address in 1970, Box 6773 Rt. 6, Bainbridge Island, WA.

HOWELLS, ALICE IMOGEN.
Painter, sculptor, and craftsman. Born Pittsburgh, PA. Pupil of ASL of NY; Robert Henri, William Chase. Member: Art Centre of the Oranges; Catherine Lorillard Wolfe AC. Award: Silver medal, Panama-Pacific Exposition, San Francisco, 1915. Died 1937. Address in 1929, 67 North Munn Avenue, 551 Commerical Street, Provincetown, MA.

HOWES, SAMUEL P.
Portrait, landscape, and miniature painter, who flourished 1829-35 in Boston. He exhibited a portait of S. Baker in 1833 at the Boston Athenaeum.

HOWITT, JOHN NEWTON.
Painter and illustrator. Born in White Plains, NY, May 7, 1885. Pupil of Art Students' League of New York. Member: Society of Illustrator; Guild of Free Lance Artists; League of New York Artists. Died 1958. Address in 1926, 147 West 23d Street, New York.

HOWLAND, ALFRED CORNELIUS.
Painter. Born in Walpole, NH, Feb. 12, 1838; died in Pasadena, CA, March 17, 1909. Studied art in Boston and New York and was a pupil of the Royal Academy and of Albert Flamm in Dusseldorf, and of Emile Lambinet in Paris. He became an Associate of the National Academy of Design in 1874 and an Academician in 1882. He was a regular exhibitor in New York and his works were frequently seen in Paris and Munich. His studio, during the winter, was in New York, while his summer home was "The Roof Tree," Williamstown, MA. He painted "Friendly Neighbors" and "The Old Windmill."

HOWLAND, EDITH.
Sculptor. Born March 29, 1863 in Auburn, NY. Studied at Vassar College. Pupil of Gustave Michel in Paris, and of Augustus Saint-Gaudens. Member: Art Students' League of New York; National Academy of Women Painters and Sculptors. Award: Honorable mention, Paris Salon, 1913. Represented in Metropolitan Museum by marble group "Between Yesterday and Tomorrow."

HOWLAND, GEORGE.
Painter. Born in New York City in 1865. Pupil of Benjamin-Constant, Laurens and Collin in Paris. Awards: Honorable mention, Paris Salon, 1914; silver medal, Paris Salon, 1921. Member: Chevalier of the Legion of Honor of France. Died 1928 in France. Address in

1926, 29 Quai Voltaire, Paris, France.

HOWLAND, MRS. ANNA GOODHART.
Painter. Born Atchison, KS, May 10, 1871. Pupil of Corcoran School of Art, Wash., DC. Member: Wash. WCC. Address in 1929, 2412 Pennsylvania Avenue, NW, Washington, DC; summer, Beltsville, MD.

HOWS, JOHN AUGUSTUS.
Painter. Born 1832 in New York City, he graduated from Columbia in 1852. He studied art and in 1862 was elected an Associate Member of the National Academy. He has been a wood engraver, landscapist, and illustrator. Among his paintings are "An Adirondack Lake," Sanctuary of St. Alban's Church, NY, and "Paul Smiths, Saint Regis." He died Sept. 27, 1874, in NYC.

HOXIE, VINNER REAM.
Sculptor. Born in Madison, WI, on Sept. 25, 1847, and died in Wash., DC. on Nov. 2, 1914. She studied under Bonnat in Paris and with Majolilin in Rome. Her statues of Abraham Lincoln, in the rotunda of the Capitol, Washington, DC, and Admiral Farragut, standing in in Farragut Square, Washington, were executed under commissions from Congress. Among her other works were many portrait busts and medallions of prominent Americans and foreigners, and a number of ideal statues.

HOYLE, ANNIE ELIZABETH.
Painter, illustrator, and teacher. Born Charlestown, WV, April 29, 1851. Pupil of Rouzee; Uhl; George H. Story in NY; Henry Mosler and Julian Academy in Paris. Member: Wash. AC; AFA. Illustrated: "Forest Trees in Pacific Slope" and "Forest Trees of Rocky Mountains," by George B. Sudworth (U.S. Gov't); "Native American Forage Plants" and "Range and Pasture Management," by Arthur W. Sampson; "Important Western Browse Plants," by Wm. A. Dayton (U.S. Gov't); "Important Southwestern Range Plants," by Dayton and N. W. Talbot (U.S. Gov't); "Forest Trees of Illinois"; "Forest Trees of Texas." Address in 1929, Atlantic Bldg., 930 F.

St.; h. 3931 Huntington Street, Chevy Chase, Washington, DC.

HOYT, ALBERT G.
Painter. Born Dec. 13, 1809 in Sandwich, NH. He studied in France and Italy and on his return to this country settled in Boston where he painted many portraits. He was the first President of the Boston Art Club. His full length portrait of Daniel Webster is owned by the Union League Club of New York. Died Dec. 19, 1856 in W. Roxbury, MA.

HOYT, EDITH.
Landscape painter. Born West Point, NY, April 10, 1890. Pupil of Charles Woodbury, E.C. Messer, Henry Moser; Corcoran School of Art. Member: S. Wash. A.; Wash. WCC. Work: Painting of XVIIth Century Manor House, Museum of Society of Historic Monuments, Quebec, Canada. Address in 1929, 1301 21st Street, NW, Washington, DC.

HOYT, HETTIE J.
Painter and sculptor. Born Harvard, IL. Pupil of Carl Marr, F.W. Heine, Fred Grant. Work: "Fleur de Lis and Lillies," D. A. R. Continental Hall, Wash., DC; "Chrysanthemums," Woman's Club, Milwaukee; "Zinnias," College Woman's Club, Milwaukee. Specialty still life and flowers. Address in 1929, care Frank M. Hoyt, 209 Wisconsin Avenue, Milwaukee, WI; summer, The Shelter, Oconomowoc, WI.

HOYT MARGARET, (HOWARD) (YEATON).
Painter and etcher. Born Baltimore, MD, July 1, 1885. Pupil of Gabrielle DeV. Clements, Theresa Bernstein, William Meyerowitz. Member: AFA; Gloucester SA; North Shore AA; Rockport AA; SSAL. Died 1943. Address in 1929, 206 Washington Street, Lexington, VA; summer, Lanesville, Gloucester, MA.

HSIAO, CHIN.
Painter and sculptor. Born in Shanghai, China, Jan. 30, 1935. Study: Taipei Normal College; with Li Chun-Sen, Taipei, Taiwan. Work: Museum of Modern Art, The Metropolitan Museum, NYC; Nat'l Gallery of Mod. Art, Rome; Phila. Mus. of Art; etc. Comn.: Mural, Mr. S. Marchetta, Messina, Sicily. Exhibitions: Carnegie; 7th Biennial Sao Paulo, 1963; 4th Salon, Galeries-Pilotes, Louisanne, Switz, and Paris; plus others. Awards: City of Capo d'Orlando Italy, prize. Media: Metal construction, acrylic, ink. Living in NYC in 1970. Address in 1982, Milano, Italy.

HUBARD, WILLIAM JAMES.
Portrait painter. Born in Warwick, England, in 1807; died in Richmond, VA, 1862. Had assistance and advice of Robert W. Weir and Thomas Sully. Exhibited at the National Academy of Design, 1834. At one time he painted portaits in Baltimore. Represented by portrait of John C. Calhoun in Corcoran Gallery, Washington, DC. Died Feb. 15, 1862.

HUBBARD, C(HARLES) D(ANIEL).
Painter, illustrator, and teacher. Born Newark, NJ, July 14, 1876. Pupil of Kenyon Cox and John H. Niemeyer. Member: New Haven PCC; Salma C. Died 1951. Address in 1929, 37 Park 57th Street, New York, NY.

HUBBARD, FRANK MCKINNEY.
Caricaturist. Born in Bellefontaine, OH, 1868. Employed as Caricaturist on Indianapolis News since 1891. Died 1930 in Indianapolis, IN. Address in 1926, Indianapolis News, Indianapolis, IN.

HUBBARD, MARY W(ILSON).
Painter. Born Springfield, MA, April, 1871. Pupil of ASL of NY; Constant in Paris. Member: NA Women PS; NYWCC. Address in 1929, 445 East 57th Street, New York, NY.

HUBBARD, PLATT.
Painter. Born in Columbus, OH, in 1889. Pupil of Robert Henri; has also studied in Paris. Died 1946. Address, Old Lyme, CT.

HUBBARD, RICHARD W.
Painter. Born Oct. 1816 in Middletown, CT. American landscape painter, Lake George and the Connecticut River are his favorite

456

scenes. In 1858 he was elected a member of the National Academy. Among his paintings are "High Peak;" "North Conway;" "Vermont Hills;" "The Adirondacks;" "Early Autumn." He died Dec. 21, 1888, in Brooklyn, NY.

HUBBARD, WHITNEY MYRON.
Painter. Born Middletown, CT, June 18, 1875. Pupil of F. V. DuMond. Member: New Haven PCC; Brooklyn WCC; CT AFA. Award: Hon. mention, CT AFA, 1924. Address in 1929, 511 First Street, Greenport, LI, NY.

HUBBELL, HENRY SALEM.
Painter. Born Paola, KS, Dec. 25, 1870. Pupil of AIC; Whistler, Collin Laurens and Constant in Paris. Member: ANA 1906; Paris SAP; Portrait P; NAC (life); Allied AA; Salma. C.; Fla. Soc. A. and S. (President); Century Assn. Awards: Hon. mention Paris Salon, 1901; third class medal, Paris Salon, 1904; third prize, Worcester (MA) Musuem, 1905; third Harris prize and bronze medal, AIC, 1910. Prof. of Painting and Dir. School of Painting and Decoration, Carnegie Institute of Technology, Pittsburgh, PA, 1918-1921. Member: Board of Regents, Univ. of Miami, FL. Work: "Child and Cat," Luxembourg, Paris; "The Samavar", Miniature, Museum of Lille, France; "Larkspurs," Government Collection, France; "The Brasses," Wilstack Collection, Phila.; "Paris Cabman," Union Lg. C., Phila.; "Women with Fan," Art Assoc., Grand Rapids. Died Jan. 9, 1949. Address in 1929, 1818 Michigan Ave, Miami Beach, FL.

HUDNUT, ALEXANDER M.
Painter. Born Princeton, NJ. Member: Salma. C.; Century Assn.; Lotos Club; NYWCC; Grolier C. Address in 1929, 50 Broadway; h. 19 West 54th Street, New York, NY; summer, Allenhurst, NJ.

HUDNUT, JOSEPH.
Painter. Member of the Salmagundi Club of New York. Address in 1926, 44 West 10th Street, New York.

HUDSON, CHALRES BRADFORD.
Painter and writer. Born Ontario, Canada, Jan. 17, 1865, of American

parents. Pupil of Brush and Chase; Bouguereau in Paris; Columbia University, NY. Awards: Silver medals for drawings and paintings, Exposition, Bergen, Norway, 1898; Paris Exposition, 1900. Represented by etchings at Boston Museum of Fine Arts; Mural Paintings at the CA Academy of Sciences, San Francisco. Author of "The Crimson Conquest," "The Royal Outlaw," and magazine and newspaper articles. Address in 1929, 317 Alder Streeet, Pacific Grove, CA. Died in 1939.

HUDSON, CHARLES WILLIAM.
Painter. Born Boston, Aug. 21, 1871. Pupil of Boston Museum School under Grundmann, Tarbell and Benson. Member: Boston WCC; NYWCC (Life). Died 1943. Address in 1929, 13 Hilton Street, Hyde Park, Boston, MA; summer, W. Thornton, NH.

HUDSON, ELMER F(ORREST).
Marine painter. Born Boston, Aug. 14, 1862. Member: Boston AC; Copley S, 1895; Salma. C. Address in 1929, Monhegan Island, ME. Died before 1940.

HUDSON, ERIE.
Marine painter. Born Boston, MA. Member: NA, ANA, 1926; North Shore AA; Salma. C.; NAC. Awards: SIlver medal, Sesqui-Centennial Expo., Phila., 1926; Marine prize, North Shore AA, 1929. Died Dec. 22, 1932. Address in 1929, 29 East 9th Street, New York, NY; summer, Monghegan Island, ME.

HUDSON, HENRIETTA.
Illustrator, writer, and teacher. Born Hudson City, NJ, May 9, 1862. Member: NAC. Illustrated: "The Blue Veil" and "Roses Red." Address in 1929, Bolton Landing-on-Lake George, NY.

HUDSON, JULIEN.
Painter of miniatures. Born in New Orleans. Studied art in Paris. Had a studio from 1837 to 1844, the year of his death, at 120 Baronne Street, New Orleans.

HUDSON, WILLIAM JR.
Born in 1787. Portrait miniature and landscape artist, flourishing in Boston, 1829-1855.

HUDSPETH, ROBERT NORMAN.
Painter, craftsman and teacher. Born Caledonia, Ontario, Canada, July 2, 1862. Pupil of Academie Julian under Bouguereau, Ferrier, Bashet and Douvet. Work: Portrait miniature owned by the late Lord Milner, England; case owned by H. R. H. Queen Mary of England. Died 1943. Address in 1929, 49 Thoreau Street, Concord, MA.

HUELSE, CARL.
Sculptor. Exhibited at Annual Exhibition of NAD, New York, 1925. Address in 1926, Philadelphia, PA.

HUENS, JEAN LEON.
Illustrator. Born in Melsbroeck, Belgium, in 1921. He trained at La Cambre Acad. prior to 1943, when his illustrations for a children's book by a Belgian publisher marked the start of his career. His illustrations have frequently been seen in America since 1962 when he began painting covers for The Saturday Evening Post and Reader's Digest. Most recently he has been a frequent contributor to National Geographic. The S of I has selected his works for several of their Annual Exhibits, and in 1973 The Securite Routiere Europeenne awarded him First Prize for his poster Against Drunkenness at the Steering Wheel.

HUESTIS, JOSEPH W.
Painter. Member of Society of Independent Artists. Address in 1926, 564 Jefferson Avenue, Brooklyn, NY.

HUEY, FLORENCE G(REENE).
(Mrs. J. Wistar Huey). Portrait painter. Born Philadelphia in 1872. Pupil of Gabrielle D. Clements, Joseph De Camp and Cecilia Beaux; PAFA. Member: PA S. Min. P; Balto. WCC. Award: Charlotte Ritchie Smith Memorial prize, Balto. WC. and Min. Exp., 1927. Address in 1929, Ruxton, Baltimore Co., MD.

HUF, KARL (PHILIP).
Painter and illustrator. Born Philadelphia, PA, Sept. 28, 1887. Pupil of PAFA; Chase; Breckenridge; Anshutz; Weir; McCarter. Illustrations for The Ladies' Home Journal; advertisements and illustrations in newspapers and magazines. Address in 1929, Asst. Art Director, F. Wallis Armstrong Co., 16th and Locust Sts.; h. 3850 North Smedley St., Philadelphia, PA. Died in 1937.

HUFF, WILLIAM GORDON.
Painter and sculptor. Born Fresno, CA, Feb. 3, 1903. Pupil of B. Bufano, Edgar Walter, Arthur Lee. Awards: Second sculpture award, Palace of FA, San Francisco, 1922; first sculpture prize, CA SFA, San Francisco, 1923. Address in 1929, 2706 Fulton Street, Berkeley, CA; summer, Rock Tavern, NY.

HUFFAKER, SANDY.
Illustrator. Born in Chattanooga, TN, in 1943. He attended the University of Alabama and studied under Daniel Schwartz at the ASL. He was a political cartoonist for The News and Observer in Raleigh, NC before coming to NY as a free-lancer. His artwork has been seen in Sports Illustrated, Business Week, Time and The New York Times, which sponsored his nomination for a Pulitzer Prize in 1977. Exhibitions of his paintings and drawings have been held at the Greengrass Gallery, Puck Gallery and Hunter Gallery of Chattanooga. A member of the S of I, he presently lives and works in NY.

HUGER, EMILY HAMILTON.
Painter, craftsman, writer, lecturer, and teacher. Born New Orleans, LA, Jan. 11, 1881. Pupil of Ellsworth Woodward, Chase, W. A. Bell and Breckenridge. Member: New Orleans AA; Western Arts Asso.; SSAL; AFA; Newcomb Art Alumnae Assoc. Head of Art Dept., Southwestern LA Inst. Lafayette, LA. Died 1946. Address in 1929, 1202 Johnston Street, Lafayette, LA.

HUGHES, DAISY MARGUERITE.
Painter and teacher. Born Los Angeles, CA; 1882. Pupil of L. E.

Garden Macleod, Ralph Johonnot, Rudolph Schaeffer, George Elmer Browne, and C. P. Townsley. Member: CA AC; Art Teachers' Assoc. of Southern CA.; NA Women PS; Allied AA; AFA. Address in 1929, care of Messrs. Munroe & Co., 4 Rue Ventadour, Paris, France; 614 South Normandie Avenue, Los Angeles, CA.

HUGHES, GEORGE.
Illustrator. Born in New York City in 1907. He studied at the NAD and ASL. For a short time he worked in Detroit as a special designer in the auto industry. He began his long-standing career with The Saturday Evening Post in the 1940's and did his first cover in 1948. Living in Arlington, VT, for many years, he was a neighbor of Norman Rockwell, John Atherton and Mead Schaeffer. He now lives in Wainscott, NY.

HUGHES, ROBERT BALL.
Sculptor. Born Jan. 19, 1806, in London, England, where he studied and received the silver medal of the Royal Academy. He came to the United States in 1829 and settled first in New York and later in Dorchester, MA. He modeled the groups, "Little Nell," "Uncle Toby and the Widow Wadman," preserved in plaster at the Boston Athenaeum. His life-size high-relief of Bishop Hobart of New York is in the vestry of Trinity Church, New York. He died March 5, 1868 in Dorchester, MA.

HUGHES, ROY V.
Painter and illustrator. Born Elmira, NY, Feb. 14, 1879. Pupil of F. V. DuMond, ASL of NY. Member: Pitts AA. Address in 1929, 1517 Park Blvd., Dormont, Pittsburgh, PA.

HUGHES-MARTIN, AGNES.
Painter and illustrator. Born Claremorris, Co. Mayo, Ireland, Dec. 11, 1898. Pupil of H. George Robertson Martin. Member: Boston S. Indp. A. Address in 1929, care of Mrs. Lyman, 111 Alexander Street, Dorchester, Boston, MA.

HULBERT, CHARLES ALLEN.
Painter. Born Mackinac Island, MI. Pupil of PAFA; Metropolitan Museum Art School, and Artists-Artisan Institute in New York. Member: Salma. C.; Brooklyn PS; Pittsfield (MA) AA. Work: "The Old Trunk," Public Library, Erie, PA; "Portrait of Secretary Edward Lazansky," in the Capitol, Albany, NY. Address in 1929, South Egremont, MA. Died in 1939.

HULBERT, KATHERINE ALLMOND.
(Mrs. Charles A. Hulbert). Painter. Born in Sacramento Valley, CA. Pupil of San Francisco School of Design' NAD and John Ward Stimson in NY. Member· NA Women PS; Brooklyn PS; Pittsfield (MA) AL. Work: "The Old Mill," Library of Girls' High School, Brooklyn. Died in 1961. Address in 1929, South Egremont, MA.

HULL, MARIE ATKINSON.
Painter. Born Summit, MI, Sept. 28, 1890. Pupil of PAFA; ASL of NY; John F. Carlson. Member: Mississippi AA; SSAL; Fellowship PAFA; New Orleans AA; New Orleans ACC; AFA. Award: Miss. AA gold medal, 1920; first prize, SSAL, 1926; second prize ($2500) Davis Wildflower Competition, San Antonio, TX, 1929. Work: "Ancient Oaks, Biloxi," owned by Mississippi Art Association. Address in 1929, 825 Belhaven Street, Jackson, MI.

HUMES, RALPH H(AMILTON).
Sculptor. Born Philadelphia, Dec. 25, 1902. Pupil of Albert Laessie. Address in 1929, PAFA, Broad and Cherry Sts, Phila.; h. Amelia Court House, VA; summer, Chester Springs, PA.

HUMPHREY, DAVID W.
Painter and illustrator. Born in Elkhorn, WI, in 1872. Pupil of Art Institute of Chicago; of Julien Academy, Paris; studied with Whistler in Paris. Address in 1926, 259 West 23d Street, New York.

HUMPHREY, ELIZABETH B.
Painter. Born in Hopedale, MA, about 1850. She was a pupil at the Cooper School of Design and of Worthington Whittredge. Her

professional life was devoted chiefly to designing illustrations. She made some excellent sketches and paintings during a trip to California. Her illustrations include landscape, still-life and figures.

HUMPHREY, WALTER B.
Illustrator. Member: New Rochelle AA. Address in 1929, 94 Mayflower Avenue, New Rochelle, NY.

HUMPHREYS, ALBERT.
Painter and sculptor. Born near Cincinnati, OH. Pupil of Gerome and Alexander Harrison in Paris. Represented by paintings in Detroit Institute of Art and Boston Public Library. Represented by sculptures in Nat'l. Gall. of Art, Wash., DC, and Children's Fountain, South Manchester, CT. Address in 1926, 96 Fifth Avenue, NY. Died in 1922.

HUMPHREYS, FRANCIS.
Born 1815 in Ireland. Capitol engraver of portraits and subject plates in both mezzotint and in line. He was employed in 1850-58 by the Methodist Book Concern, of Cincinnati, OH.

HUMPHREYS, MALCOLM.
Painter. Born Morristown, Nov. 7, 1894. Pupil of John H. Carlson, Charles W. Hawthorne, Charles Rosen, George Elmer Browne. Member: Salma C.; Allied AA; S. Indp. A; AFA; Palm Beach AL. Awards: Third Hallgarten prize, NAD, 1929; hon. mention, Allied AA, 1929; Ranger Fund purchase award, NAD, 1929. Address in 1929, 11 Franklin Place, Morristown, NJ; summer, Care of Munroe and Co., 4 Rue Ventadour, Paris, France.

HUMPHREYS, MARIE CHAMPNEY.
Miniature painter, who exhibited in Europe and America. She was born in Deerfield MA, in 1867, and was the daughter of J. Wells Champney, well known for his art works. She died in New Rochelle, NY, on Dec. 1, 1906.

HUMPHREYS, SALLIE THOMSON.
Painter, designer, lecturer, and teacher. Born Delaware, OH. Pupil of Emma Humphreys; Washington, DC,

ASL; NY School of FAA; studied at Colarossi Academy in Paris; and various places in Europe. Member: Coll. AA; Wash. WCC; Wash. AC; AFA. Designs for textiles, wall paper, cretonne, cotton and linen materials reproduced by leading firms. Author of lectures on "Design," "Design in Its Relation to the Home," "Textile Design," "Interior Decoration," and "The Value of Art Instruction to the College Student." Instructor in design, Washington Art Students' League, 1897-1904; Baltimore Water Color Club, 1902-1903. Director, School of Fine Arts, Ohio Wesleyan University. Address in 1929, School of Fine Arts, Ohio Welsleyan University; h. 162 North Sandusky Street, Delaware, OH.

HUMPHREYS, WILLIAM.
Engraver. Mr. Baker, in his "American Engravers," says that William Humphrys was born in Dublin in 1794. He adds that he learned to engrave with George Murray in Philadelphia; went to England in 1823; returned to this country in 1843 and in 1845 again went abroad to remain there for the rest of his life. Mr. Baker credits him with numerous small "Annual" plates, but says that he was principally engaged in bank-note engraving. Died Jan. 21, 1865 in Genoa, Italy.

HUMPHRIES, CHARLES H.
Sculptor. Born in England, 1867. Member: NSS, 1908; S. Indp. A. Address in 1929, 214 East 45th Street, New York, NY.

HUNT, CLYDE DU V.
Sculptor. Born in Scotland in 1861. Student of MA Institute of Technology, Boston. Represented in Metropolitan Museum of Art, New York, by marble statue, "Nirvana." Address in 1926, Weathersfield, VT.

HUNT, ESTHER.
Painter and sculptor. Born Grand Island, NE, Aug. 30, 1885. Pupil of Chase. Member: Laguna Beach AA. Award: Gold medal for sculpture, Pan-Calif. Exp., San Diego, 1916. Address in 1929, 142 East 18th Street, New York, NY.

HUNT, LEIGH HARRISON.
Etcher, teacher, writer, and lecturer. Born Galena, IL, May 19, 1858. Pupil of Henry Farrer. Member: A. Fund S.; Soc. of American Etchers; Arti et Amicitae, Holland (cor.). Address in 1929, 600 West 146th Street, New York, NY. Died in 1937.

HUNT, LYNN BOGUE.
Illustrator. Member: SI. Address in 1929, 41 Union Square, NYC.

HUNT, MABELLE ALCOTT.
Painter, craftsman, and teacher. Born New York City, Sept. 1, 1898. Pupil of Whittaker and Holland at Adelphia Institute, Brooklyn, NY.; Savannah AC. Specialty, blockprints. Address in 1929, 601-45th Street, East; h. "Chatham Crescent," Savannah, GA.

HUNT, P. C.
Painter. Member: Boston AC. Address in 1929, 26 Park Drive, Brookline, MA.

HUNT, SAMUEL VALENTINE.
Engraver. Born in Norwich, England, Feb. 14, 1803; died at Bay Ridge, NY, in 1893. Hunt was originally a taxidermist and was a self-taught artist and engraver. He came to the United States in 1834 and was then an excellent line-engraver of landscape. He worked for New York and Cincinnati publishing houses.

HUNT, THOMAS L.
Painter. Exhibited at Penna. Academy of Fine Arts Annual Exhibition of 1924. Address, Laguna Beach, CA. Died in 1938.

HUNT, UNA CLARKE.
(Mrs. Arthur P. Hunt.). Painter and illustrator. Born Cincinnati, OH, Jan. 6, 1876. Pupil of Boston Museum School and Denman W. Ross. Member: Wash. WCC. Work: Reredos in St. Michael's Church, Geneseo, NY. Address in 1929, Pasaconaway, NH.

HUNT, WILLIAM MORRIS.
Painter. Born March 31, 1824 in Brattleboro, VT; died, Isles of Shoals, NH, Sept. 8, 1879. Studied at Dusseldorf; pupil of Couture in Paris; influenced by Millet and the Barbizon School. In 1862 he settled in Boston where he spent most of his life. He painted many portraits of noted persons, was the author of many original sketches of types of Parisian life, and is well known for his mural paintings in the State Capitol at Albany, NY. Represented at the Metropolitan Museum, New York, by a "Landscape" and "Girl at a Fountain;" at Washington by "The Spouting Whale."

HUNTER, EVANGELINE D.
Miniature painter. Exhibited at the Penna. Academy of Fine Arts, Philadelphia, 1925. Address in 1926, 4205 Sansom Street, Philadelphia, PA.

HUNTER, FRANCES TIPTON.
Illustrator. Born Howard, PA, Sept. 1, 1896. Pupil of Thornton Oakley; PAFA. Member: SI; Williamsport AG; Fellowship PAFA. Specialty, illustrations of children for magazines. Died 1957. Address in 1929, 2101 Chestnut Street, Philadelphia, PA.

HUNTER, ISABEL.
Painter and teacher. Born San Francisco, CA. Pupil of Arthur Mathews, Emil Carlsen, Joullin; San F. A. Inst.; ASL of NY. Member: San F. AA.; San F. S. Women A. Address in 1929, Monterey, CA; h. 2050 Santa Clara Avenue, Alameda, CA.

HUNTER, JOHN YOUNG.
Painter. Exhibited water colors at the Penna. Academy of Fine Arts, Philadelphia, 1925. Address in 1926, 58 West 57th Street, New York.

HUNTER, LIZBETH C(LIFTON).
Painter. Born Gilroy, CA, Nov. 29, 1868. Pupil of Henry B. Snell. Member: NYWCC; Boston WCC; NA Women PS; AFA. Address in 1929, 156 East 37th Street, New York, NY.

HUNTER, ROBERT DOUGLAS.
Painter. Born in Boston, MA, March 17, 1928. Study: Cape Sch. of Art, Provincetown, MA, with Henry Hensche; Vesper George Sch. of Art, Boston; also with R. H. Ives Gammell, Boston. Work: The

Chrysler Art Museum, MA; The Maryhill Museum, WA; Northeastern Univ.; Tufts Univ.; Boston Univ. Medical Ctr.; MIT; others. Comn.: Mural, Church of St. Mary of the Harbor, Provincetown, MA; Emmanual Church, West Roxbury, MA. Exhib.: Acad. Artists Show, Springfield, MA; Am. APL Show, NYC.; New England Artists Exhib., Boston. Awards: New England Artists-Gold Medals; American Artists Professional League; many others. Teaching: Vesper George Sch. of Art, from 1955; Worcester Art Mus.; Mt. Ida Jr. College, Newton, MA. Mem.: Guild of Boston Artists; Am. APL; Acad. Artists Assn.; Grand Central Art Gallery; others. Media: Oil. Address in 1982, 250 Beacon St., Boston, MA.

HUNTINGTON, ANNA HYATT.
Sculptor. Born Cambridge, MA, March 10, 1876. Pupil of H. H. Kitson in Boston; MacNeil and Borglum in New York. Member: ANA, 1916, NA, 1923; NSS, 1905; AFA. Awards: Hon. mention, Paris Salon, 1910, silver medal P.-P. Exp., San F., 1915; purple rosette from French Gov., 1915, gold medal, Plastic C., 1916; Saltus medal, NAD, 1920, 1922; Legion of Honor, 1922. Work: "Lion," erected at Dayton, OH; "Joan of Arc," New York City; Gloucester, MA; Blois, France; Cathedral of St. John the Divine, New York. Address in 1929, 1 East 89th Street, New York, NY.

HUNTINGTON, CLARA.
Sculptor. Born Oneonta, NY, Feb. 2, 1878. Pupil of Arturo Dazzi in Rome. Member: NA Women PS. Work: Portrait bas relief of H. E. Huntington, Henry E. Huntington Library and Art Gallery, San Marino, CA. Address in 1929, Los Gatos, CA; Forti Di Marmi, (Lucca) Italy.

HUNTINGTON, D(ANIEL) R(IGGS).
Painter and artist. Born Newark, NJ, Dec. 24, 1871. Member: Seattle FAS; Wash. Chap. AIA. Work: Firlands Hospital Group, University Bridge Piers, Seattle, WA; rose garden, Woodland Park, fountain and Harding Memorial in collaboration with Alice Carr. Address in 1929, 455-456 Empire Bldg.; h. 138 East 52nd Street, Seattle, WA.

HUNTINGTON, DANIEL
Portrait and genre painter. Born in New York, Oct. 14, 1816. Died in New York, April 18, 1906. Pupil of Professor Samuel F. B. Morse, 1835, and later of Inman; also of G. P. Ferrero in Rome. Elected Associate of the National Academy, 1839; National Academy, 1840; President of National Academy, 1862-1869 and 1877-1891; Vice-President of the Metropolitan Museum of Art, New York, 1870-1903.

HUNTINGTON, ELEAZER.
Engraver. Born in 1789, he resided at Hartford, CT, and was the son of Nathaniel Gilbert and Betsy (Tucker) Huntington. In 1825 he published at Hartford "The American Penman Etc.," written and engraved by Eleazer Huntington. In 1828 he engraved, in line, maps, diagrams and a series of small American views for a school atlas, published in New York. He engraved a fairly well executed portrait of himself.

HUNTINGTON, MARGARET WENDELL.
Painter. Born 1867. Member: NA Women PS. Award: Hon. mention, NA Women PS, 1927. Died 1955. Address in 1929, 13 East 9th Street; 7 East 12th Street, 53 Washington Square, New York, NY.

HUNTLEY, SAMANTHA LITTLEFIELD.
Painter. Born Watervliet, NY. Pupil of ASL of NY under Twachtman and Mowbray; Ecole des Beaux Art, Paris, under Cuyer; Ecole Normale d'Enseignement du Dessin, Paris, under Lefebvre and Robert-Fleury. Member: NAC; AFA. Work: "Daniel S. Lamont," owned by the War Dept., Wash., DC; "William F. Vilas," owned by the State Historical Library and Court House, Madison, WI; "Archbishop John J. Glennon," Archbishop's House, St. Louis, MO; "Frank W. Higgins," Capitol, Albany, NY; "J. Townsend Lansing," "Girl in Black," and "John E. McElroy," Albany , NY. Historical and Art Society; "Wm. F. Gurley," Emma Willard School Collection, Troy, NY; "Gen. John M. Schofield," Schofield Barracks, Honolulu, Hawaii; Dr. Charles Doolittle

Walcott, and Dr. Charles Greenley Abbot, Smithsonian Institution, Washington, DC. Died June 19, 1949. Address in 1929, Wildflower Haven, Kinderhook, NY.

HUNTLEY, VICTORIA H.
Lithographer. Born: Hasbrouck Heights, NJ, in 1900. Studied: Art Students' League; also with John Sloan, Max Weber, William C. Palmer and Kenneth Hayes Miller. Awards: Art Inst. of Chicago, 1930; Philadelphia Printmakers Club, 1933; Library of Congress, 1945, 1949; Association American Artists, 1946; grant, American Academy of Arts and Letters, 1947; Guggenheim fellowship, 1948; Society of American Graphic Artists, 1950, 1951; Art Students League, 1950, 1951. Collections: Metropolitan Museum of Art; Art Inst. of Chicago; Boston Museum of Fine Arts; Philadelphia Museum of Art; Cleveland Museum of Art; Whitney Museum of American Art; International Business Machines; Library of Congress; Brooklyn Museum; University of FL; University of Michigan; Albany Printmakers Club; Rochester Memorial Museum; Art Students' League; Cincinnati Museum Association; Paris, France, 1954; also touring Italy, 1955-56, 1956-57; Museum of Fine Arts of Houston; PAFA; New York Public Library; Newark Public Library; Philadelphia Printmaker Club; University of Glasgow; Italian Government; United States Post Office, Springville, NY; Greenwich, CT.

HUNTOON, MARY.
Painter, sculptor, etcher, and teacher. Born Topeka, Nov. 29, 1896. Pupil of Joseph Pennell. Address in 1929, 11 Rue Scribe, Paris IX, France; summer, 219 Huntoon Street, Topeka, KS.

HURD, E.
A line-engraver of buildings, etc., working about 1840. His work possessed little merit.

HURD, ELEANOR HAMMOND.
Painter. Born Kalamazoo, MI. Pupil of Charles Hawthorne, Hugh Breckenridge, Charles Woodbury.

Member: Balto. WCC; Friends of Art.; Balto. IA. Address in 1929, 4407 Keswick Road, Baltimore, MD; summer, Seal Harbor, ME.

HURD, NATHANIEL.
Engraver. Born in Boston, MA, 1730; died there in 1777. Nathaniel Hurd advertised his business as follows: "Nathaniel Hurd Informed his Customers he has remov'd his shop from MacCarty's corner, on the Exchange, to the Back Part of opposite Brick Building where Mr. Ezekiel Pirce Kept his Office. Where he continues to do all sorts of Goldsmith's work. Likewise engraves in Gold, Silver, Copper, Brass and Steel, in the neatest, Manner, and at reasonable Rates." But Hurd was engraving upon copper at an earlier date than this, as a bookplate of Thomas Dering is noted as engraved by Hurd in 1749. In 1762 he engraved a rare caricature portrait of Dr. Seth Hudson, a notorious character, and in 1764, a portrait of Rev. Joseph Sewall. With these exceptions and that of a Masonic notice engraved about 1764, numerous book-plates constitute the known engravings of Nathaniel Hurd.

HURD, PETER.
Painter and illustrator. Born Rosewell, Feb. 22, 1904. Pupil of NC Wyeth; PAFA. Member: Fellowship PAFA; Wilmington SFA. Illustrated "The Last of the Mohicans" (David McKay); "American History," by T. S. Lawler (Ginn and Co.). Address in 1929, Roswell, NM.

HURLEY, EDWARD TIMOTHY.
Painter, illustrator, etcher, and craftsman. Born Cincinnati, OH, Oct. 10, 1869. Pupil of Cincinnati, Art Academy under Frank Duveneck. Member: Cincinnati AC; Chiacgo SE; Richmond Art Assn.; Crafters Company of Cincinnati. Awards: Gold medal for originality in art workmanship, St. Louis World's Fair, 1904; Logan Medal, AIC, 1921; landscape prize, Columbus, 1921. Work: "Midnight MA," Cincinnati Museum; etchings in Richmond (IN) Art Association; Art Association of Indianapolis; Detroit Institute; Toledo Museum of

Art; NY Public Library, Library of Congress, Washington, DC; Chicago Art Institute; British Museum, London, England. Illustrated with etchings and published seven books on Cincinnati. Died 1950. Address in 1929, Rookwood Pottery; h. 2112 St. James Avenue, W. H. Cincinnati, OH.

HURRY, LUCY WASHINGTON.
Painter, craftsman and dec. Born Hagerstown, MD, in 1884. Pupil of ASL of NY under Kenyon Cox; Marshall Fry; Fayette Barnum. Member: NYWCC; NA Women PS. Address in 1929, 60 Greenwich Street, Hempstead, LI, NY.

HURST, CLARA SCOTT.
Painter and teacher. Born Kirwin, Dec. 27, 1889. Pupil of Katherine L. Perkins, George M. Stone, Birger Sandzen. Awards: First prize in landscape and second in oil, State Fair, Topeka, KS, 1927; first prize in design and first prize in miniature, State Fair, Topeka, 1926; prizes, Hutchinson, KS, 1927. Address in 1929, Kirwin, KS.

HURST, EARL OLIVER.
Illustrator. Born in Buffalo, NY, in 1895. He studied at the Albright Art School, Cleveland School of Art and later at the University of Beaune in France. His work appeared on the cover of Judge as early as 1924 and very often in Collier's in the early 1930's. He was an active illustrator for magazines, working until 1956. He has had exhibits at the Silvermine Gallery, S of I and a One-Man Show at the Boothbay Harbor Gallery.

HURTT, ARTHUR R.
Painter and illustrator. Born in Wisconsin, Oct. 31, 1861. Pupil of Douglas Volk, Irving Wiles, ASL of NY. Studied in France. Member: CA AC; MN AL. Award: Bronze medal, Pan. CA Exp., San Diego, 1915. Painter of stage scenery, murals and panoramas. Work in State Bldg., Exposition Park, Los Angeles. Address in 1929, 1518 Mohawk Street, Los Angeles, CA.

HUSE, MARION.
Painter. Born in Lynn, MA. Studied: New School of Design, Boston; Carnegie Inst. of Technology; also with Charles Hawthorne. Awards: Springfield Art League, 1925, 1936, 1941; CT Acad. of Fine Arts, 1933; Albany Inst. of History and Art, 1938, 1944. Collections: Lawrence Mus. of Art, Williamstown, MA; Wood Gallery of Art, Montpelier, VT; Bennington Vermont Mus. of History and Art; Boston Mus. of Fine Arts; Alabama Polytechnic Inst.; Am. Association of Univ. Women; Univ. of Wisconsin; Library of Congress; US State Dept; Howard U.; Virginia Mus. of Fine Arts; Victoria and Albert Mus., London, England; Nelson Gallery of Art; Tel-Aviv Mus.; State Teachers College, Albany, NY; Munson-Williams-Proctor Inst.

HUTAF, AUGUST WILLIAM.
Painter and illustrator. Born Hoboken, NJ, Feb. 25, 1879. Pupil of W.D. Streetor. Member: Am. Numismatic Society; SI. Specialty posters, book covers and decorations. Created poster "The Spirit of the Fighting Tanks", 5th Liberty Loan. Died 1942. Address in 1929, 1-31st Street, Woodcliff-on-Hudson, NJ.

HUTCHENS, FRANK TOWNSEND.
Painter and lecturer. Born in 1869 in Canandaigua, NY. Pupil of ASL of NY, under Wiles, DuMond, Mowbray and George de Forest Brush; Julian Acad. under Constant and Laurens, and Colarossi Acad. in Paris. Member: NAC; Aquarelists; Allied AA; Paris AAA; Salma. C.; AWCS; AFA. Work: "Betrayal of Christ," Carnegie Library, Sioux Falls, S. Dak.; portrait of Gen. Edgar S. Dudley, Mus. at West Point, NY; "Autumn Afternoon," Art Club, Erie, PA; "A Winter Morning," Herron Art Inst., Indianapolis; "Twilight in Picardie," Toledo Museum; "Hon. James W. Wadsworth," Capitol, Albany; "Olive Garden, Capri," Sioux Falls Art Assn.; "Old Cafe in Sidi-Bou-Said," Memorial Art Gallery, Rochester; "Street Market, Tunis" and "Old Arab Quarter, Tunis," Syracuse Museum of Fine Arts; "Bab Menara at Sunset," High Museum of Art Atlanta; "Returning

Home," Buckner Collection, Milwaukee Art Institute; portrait, "Gov. Chas. M. Floyd," Capital, Concord, NH; "The Dunes," Warren AA, Warren, PA. Address in 1929, 47 Fifth Avenue, New York, NY; h. Norwalk, CT. Died in 1937.

HUTCHINS, JOHN E.
Painter. Born in Wyoming, PA, in 1891. Address in 1926, 709 Putnam Avenue, Brooklyn, NY.

HUTCHINS, MAUDE PHELPS.
Sculptor. Born New York City, Feb. 4, 1899. Pupil of Robert G. Eberhard; Yale School of Fine Arts. Member: New Haven PSS; NA Women PS. Award: Floyd Warren prize, Beaux-Arts Inst. of Design, New York, 1925. Address in 1929, Presidents House, University of Chicago, Chicago, IL.

HUTCHINS, WILL.
Painter, writer, lecturer, and teacher. Born Westchester, CT, June 11, 1878. Pupil of Yale School of Fine Arts. Laurens in Paris. Head of Art Department, American University, Wash., DC. Address in 1929, American Univ.; H. 1348 Euclid Street., Wash., DC.

HUTCHINSON, ALLEN.
Sculptor. Born Handford, Stotre on Trent, Staffordshire, England, Jan. 8, 1855. Pupil of Jules Dalou. Works: "King Kalakana," Hawaiian types and figures and busts of Hawaiian notables, etc., Bishop Museum, Honolulu; "Sir Alfred Stephen," National Art Gallery, Sydney, New South Wales; busts of Robert Louis Stevenson, Honolulu Academy of Arts and the Stevenson Society of America, Saranac Lake, NY; Auckland Art Museum, New Zealand. Address in 1929, 25 Dongan Place, New York, NY.

HUTCHINSON, ELLEN WALES.
Painter and teacher. Born East Hartford, CT, June 12, 1868. Pupil of C. E. Porter, Geo. Thomson; Guy Wiggins. Member: CT AFA; New Haven PCC; New Haven BPC. Address in 1929, 866 Elm Street, New Haven, CT. Died in 1937.

HUTCHINSON, FREDERICK W.
Painter. Born Montreal, Canada. Pupil of Jean Paul Laurens, Benjamin Constant. Member: ANA; Allied AA; Salma. C. Represented in Cleveland Museum of Art; Art Gallery, Toronto, Canada. Address in 1929, care of the Salma. C., 47 Fifth Avenue, New York, NY.

HUTSALIUK, LUBO.
Painter. Born in Lvov, Ukraine, April 2, 1923; US citizen. Study: Cooper Union Art Sch. Work: Palm Springs Desert Mus., CA; VT Art Ctr., Manchester; Bibliotheque Nat'l., Paris. Exhib.: Galerie Norval, Paris, 1959; Angle de Faubourg, Paris, 1963; Hilde Gerst Gallery, NYC, 1966; Galerie Royale, Paris; 1976; 25 yrs. retro, USOM Gallery, NYC, 1980; and others. Mem.: Audubon Artists. Media: Watercolor, oil. Address in 1982, 260 Riverside Drive, New York, NY.

HUTSON, CHARLES WOODWARD.
Painter, writer, and teacher. Born McPhersonville, SC, Sept. 23, 1840. Pupil of Ethel Hutson. Member: New Orleans ACC; Southern SAL; NOAA; Gulf Coast AA. Died in 1936. Address in 1929, 7321 Panola Street, New Orleans, LA.

HUTSON, ETHEL.
Painter, illustrator, writer and teacher. Born Baton Rouge, LA. April 19, 1872. Pupil of Mrs. J. P. McAuley, Arthur W. Dow, Ellsworth Woodward, etc. Member: NOAA; NOACC; SSAL. Address in 1929, 7321 Panola Street, New Orleans, LA.

HUTT, HENRY.
Illustrator. Born in Chicago, IL, in 1875. Pupil of Chicago Art Institute. His studio was in NYC and he illustrated for the leading magazines and periodicals.

HUTT, JOHN.
Engraver. In Rivington's New York Gazette for 1774, is following: "John Hutt, Engraver in general, from London, at Mr. Hewitt's directly opposite the Merchants' Coffee House, in Dock Street, New York. Engraves-Coats of Arms, Crest, Seals and Cyphers, Bills of Exchange, Bills of Lading,

Shop Bills, Bills of Parcels, Card Plates, etc. Architecture, Frontispieces, Doorplates, Compliment Cards, Plate Dog-Collars, Etc., Stamps, etc. Gentlemen disposed to employ him may depend on the utmost neatness and dispatch." The only examples of Hutt's work known are some book-plates and a few diagrams engraved in connection with John Norman and published in Philadelphia in 1775.

HUTTBUG, CHARLES E.
Painter. Born Sweden, May 16, 1874. Pupil of Talmadge and Oslen in England. Member: Gulf Coast AA. Award: Gold medal, Gulf Coast AA, 1927. Address in 1929, 429 Porter Ave., Biloxi, MI.

HUTTON, DOROTHY WACKERMAN.
Painter and designer. Born Cleveland, OH, Feb. 9, 1899. Pupil of MN School of Art, Mary Moulton Cheney, Richard Lahey, Anthony Angarola, Andre L'hote. Member: Alliance. Address in 1929, 3964 Packard Street, Long Island City, NY.

HUTTON, ISAAC AND GEORGE.
Engravers. This firm of jewelers and silversmiths, of Albany, NY, working about 1796, made dies for seals; one for the Union College, at Schenectady, NY. But as this firm employed engravers, among them Gideon Fairman (about 1795), the actual work was probably done by someone in their employ. Issac was born in 1767 and died Sept. 8, 1855, in NYC.

HUTTON, J.
A fairly well-engraved line plate of a battle scene is signed "J. Hutton, Sc't Alb'y." The print was apparently made about 1825-30, but no other work by Hutton is known.

HUTTY, ALFRED HEBER.
Painter and etcher. Born Grand Haven, MI, Sept. 16, 1877. Pupil of St. Louis School of Fine Arts; ASL of NY under Chase and Birge Harrison. Member: Salma. C.; Woodstock AA; S. Wash. AC; North Shore AA; Chicago SE; NAC; Brooklyn SE; British S. Graphic A. London;

Allied AA; Rockport AA; AWCS; Print S. of England. Awards: City Art and Design Committee prize, Scarab C, Detroit 1921; hon. mention, KS Cieyt AI, 1922; Scarab C. gold medal, Detroit IA 1923; first medal fot etching MI AI 1923; Logan prize and medal, Chicago SE, 1924; Shaw Prize, Salma, C., 1924; Clark prize, Detroit IA, 1925; Landscape prize, New Haven PCC, 1925; Howe Prize, Detroit IA, 1926. Represented in Gibbes Memorial Art Gallery, Charleston, SC; Art Inst. of Chicago, Detroit Inst.; Library of Congress, Washington, DC; Cleveland Museum; NY Public Library; Los Angeles Museum; Municipal Gallery, Phoenix, AZ; Governor's Mansion, Jackson, MI, United States Nat'l Museum; CA State Library; University of MI; Colorado State Library; John Herron Art Institute, Indianapolis; Bibliotheque Nationale, France. Made 1924 Associate Plates for the Printmakers of CA, and North Shore Art Asso. Address in 1929, Broadview Woodstock, NY; 46 Tradd Street, Charleston, SC.

HUYSSEN, ROGER.
Illustrator. Born in Los Angeles in 1946. He attended the University of California at Santa Barbara and the ACD. After working briefly for a design firm in California, he moved to NY in 1974 as a free-lance illustrator for advertising and editorial clients. His airbrush and watercolor work has been seen on Columbia Records covers and several movie posters. He is a member of the S of I.

HYATT, ANNA VAUGHAN.
Mrs. Archer M. Huntington. (See Huntington).

HYATT, HARRIET RANDOLPH.
See Mrs. Mayor.

HYDE, DELLA MAE.
Painter and teacher. Born Oakland, MD. Pupil of NAD, ASL of NY; Henri, Mora, Bridgeman. Member: Brooklyn S. Modern A.; Salons of America; ASL of NY; Gloucester SA. Wash. AC. Address in 1929, 1517 H Street, NW; h. "The Ritz," 163 Euclid Street, NW. Washington, DC summer, Rockaway Inn, East

Gloucester, MA.

HYDE, HALLIE CHAMPLIN.
(Mrs. Edward B. Hyde). See Mrs. Fenton.

HYDE, HELEN.
Painter and etcher. Born April 6, 1868 in Lima, NY, in 1863. Member of the Chicago, also California Society of Etchers. Represented in Library of Congress, Washington; New York Public Library; Boston Museum. She died in Pasadena, CA, on May 13, 1919.

HYDE, RUSSELL TABER.
Painter, etcher, lecturer, and teacher. Born in Waltham, MA. July 14, 1886. Pupil of Laurens Baschet, Richer. Member: Pittsburgh, AA. Asso. Prof., Fine Arts Dept., Carnegie Inst. of Tech., Pittsburgh. Address in 1929, 2 Roselawn Terrace, Waltham, MA.

HYDT, WILLIAM HENRY.
Portrait painter. Born New York, Jan. 29, 1858. Pupil of Boulanger, Lefebvre, Doucet and Alexander Harrison in Paris. Member: ANA 1900; SAA 1893; Century Assoc. Awards: Hon. Mention, Paris Exp., 1900; bronze medal, Pan Am. Exp., Buffalo, 1901; hon. mention, P.-P. Exp. San F. 1915. Died in 1943. Address in 1929, 829 Park Avenue, New York, NY.

HYETT, WILL J.
Painter. Born Cheltenham, England, Jan 10, 1876. Pupil of Sir Alfred East. Member: Pittsburgh AA; Pittsburgh Arch. C. Awards: Bronze medal, P.P. Exp. San F., 1915; third honor, Pittsburgh AA, 1917. Address in 1929, Care of Gillespie Galleries, 639 Liberty Ave., Pittsburgh, PA; h. Gibsonia, PA.

IACOVLEFF, ALEXANDRE.
Painter and illustrator. Born in St. Petersburg (Leningrad) on June 13, 1887. Studied: Imperial Academy of Fine Art in Moscow under Prof. Kardovsky. Received a traveling scholarship from the Academy in 1913 in Italy and Spain. Traveled extensively after 1917 to Mongolia and Japan. Produced numerous life-size ethnological portraits in sanquine and pastel. In 1922, published limited editions of his sketches and paintings of Far East, also a book on the Chinese and Japanese theaters. In 1925, Official Artist for the Citroen sponsored expedition to Africa, during which he produced more than 500 drawings and paintings. Published album of prints, Pictures of Asia, highly celebrated. Taught at the Boston Museum School, 1934-37 as head of the Painting Dept. Underwent radical change in style, towards free-drawn, fanciful and symbolic work. Exhibitions of his work were held in China, Europe, Australia. American Exhib.: The National Geographic Society, Wash., DC, 1934; Carnegie Inst., Pitt., PA, 1924, 1938; Knoedler's in NYC, 1936; Boston Mus. of FA, 1937; Dayton Art Inst. and MN Inst. of Art, 1938; Memorial exhibition held in his honor at the Grand Central Art Galleries, NYC, 1939; Apollo Gallery, Poughkeepsie, NY, 1979-83. He died suddenly of cancer in 1938 in Paris.

IANNELLI, ALFONSO.
Painter, sculptor, craftsman, writer, lecturer and teacher. Born Andretta, Italy, Feb. 17, 1888. Pupil of Gutzon Borglum; George B. Bridgman, William St. John Harper. Represented by sculpture in Sioux City Court House, Sioux City, IA; design and sculpture, Immaculata High School, Chicago; Midway Gardens, Chicago; St. Francis Xavier School, Wilmette, IL; Church of St. Thomas the Apostle, Chicago; "Youth," Art Institute of Chicago; sculpture and stained glass, St. Thomas Aquinas High School, Racine, WI; St. Patrick's Church, Racine, WI. Address in 1929, Park Ridge, IL; summer, Palatine, IL.

IARICCI, A(RDUINO).
Painter. Born Italy, May 2, 1888. Self-taught. Member: S. Indp. A; Salons of Am.; Bronx AG. Address in 1929, 57 West 175th St., New York City.

ICKES, PAUL A.
Painter and illustrator. Born Laclede, MO, April 2, 1895. Pupil of Bridgman, N. Fechin, Leith-Ross. Member: GFLA; SI. Address in 1929, 32 West 10th St., New York, NY; summer, Center Lovell, ME.

IDE, ALICE STEELE.
See Mrs. Foster Hannaford.

IHRIG, CLARA LOUISE.
Painter, sculptor and illustrator. Born Oakland, Pittsburgh, PA, Oct. 31, 1893. Pupil of Sparks, Zeller and Sotter. Member: Asso. Artists of Pittsburgh. Address in 1929, 12 Buffalo St., Pittsburgh, PA.

ILLAVA, KARL.
Sculptor. Member: NSS. Work: War Memorial, 66th St. and Fifth Ave., New York; War Memorial, Gloversville, NY. Address in 1929, Hartsdale Rd., Elmsford, NY.

ILLIAN, GEORGE (JOHN).
Illustrator. Born Milwaukee, WI, Nov. 29, 1894. Pupil of Milwaukee Art Inst.; AIC; ASL of NY. Member: SI; Players; GFLA; Salma. C. Address in 1929, 140 East 39th St.; 16 Gramercy Park, New York, NY.

ILLMAN, THOMAS.
Born in England. He was engraving in London in 1824, and about six years later he came to New York, and at once formed the engraving firm of Illman & Pilbrow. He worked in stipple and in mezzotint, and was a good engraver. Illman Sons, about 1845, engraved portraits for both New York and Philadelphia publishers.

ILSLEY, FREDERICK J(ULIAN).
Painter. Born Portland, Mar. 6, 1855. Self taught. Member: Portland SA; Salma. C.; Rockport AA; Am. APL; Hayloft C; AFA. Address in 1929, 15 Powsland St., Portland, ME; summer, Rockport, MA

IMBERT, ANTHONY.
Lithographer and marine painter. A French naval officer. He was the proprietor of an early lithographic establishment in New York. He was located at 79 Murray St., and in 1831 he had moved to 104 Broadway. Died before 1838.

IMLER, E(DGAR).
Painter and etcher. Born St. Clairsville, PA, Jan. 31, 1894. Pupil of AIC; PAFA. Member: ASL of NY; Louis Comfort Tiffany Foundation. Address in 1929, 131 West 23rd St., NYC; summer Osterburg, PA.

IMRIE, HERBERT DAVID.
Etcher. Born Napa, CA, Mar. 8, 1886. Pupil of Piazzoni. Member: Calif. SE. Address in 1929, 782 San Luis Rd., Berkeley, CA.

INDIANA, ROBERT.
Painter. Born Sept. 13, 1928, in New Castle, IN. Studied at Herron School of Art, Indianapolis, Munson-Williams-Proctor Inst., Utica; holds BFA (1953) from Chicago Art Inst.; was artist-in-residence at Aspen Inst. (1968). Awarded Hon. DFA from Franklin and Marshall Col. (1970), and from U. of Indiana (1977). Received Indiana State Com. on the Arts Award. Exhibited at the Stable Gallery, NYC (1962), Dartmouth, Bowdoin, Brandeis (all in 1970), Indianapolis (1978), many others of MOMA; Brandeis; Baltimore; Whitney; Art Gallery of Toronto; Honolulu Academy; U. of Penn.; U. of Texas, others.

INGELS, FRANK LEE.
Painter. Member: Chicago SA; CA AC. Address in 1929, 1500 Lowell Ave., Los Angeles, CA.

INGERLE, RUDOLPH F.
Painter. Born Vienna, Austria, April 14, 1879. Member: Cliff Dwellers; Palette and Chisel Club; Bohemian AC; Municipal AL; North Shore AA; Alumni, AIC; Chicago PS. Awards: Brower prize ($300), AIC, 1927; Hearst prize ($300), and Assn. Chicago PS, gold medal, 1928. Work: "After the Storm," City of Chicago; "Moonrise," Arche Club, Chicago; represented in Municipal A.L. Collection, Chicago. Address in 1929, 339 Laurel Ave., Highland Park, IL; 218 South Wabash Ave., Chicago, IL.

INGERSOLL, ANNA.
Painter. Exhibited at the Penna. Academy of Fine Arts in 1924. Address in 1929, 1815 Walnut St., Philadelphia.

INGERSOLL, EMMA K. HESS.
(Mrs. D. W. Ingersoll). Painter and teacher. Born Chicago, IL, Jan. 18, 1878. Pupil of AIC. Member: Designers' Alumni of AIC; Penn. S. Min. P. Award: Bronze medal for miniatures, St. Louis Exp., 1904. Address in 1929, Chestertown, MD.

INGHAM, CHARLES CROMWELL.
Painter. Born 1796 in Dublin. He studied in the Academy there and obtained a prize for "The Death of Cleopatra;" settled in New York in 1817; was one of the founders of the National Academy of Design and its Vice-President 1845-50. His best-known picture, "The White Plume," was engraved by A. B. Durand. Among his well-known portraits are those of Edwin Forrest, Lafayette, De Witt Clinton, Gulian C. Verplank and Catharine M. Sedgwick. Specialty was portraits of women and children. Died Dec. 10, 1863, in NYC.

INGHAM-SMITH, ELIZABETH.
(Mrs. E. Ingham-Smith). Painter and craftsman. Born Easton, PA. Pupil of PAFA; Henry B. Snell; Whistler in Paris; Alex Jameson in London. Member: Phila. WCC; NYWCC; Wash. WCC. Address in 1929, Old Inn, North Shirley, MA.

INGLIS, JOHN J.
Painter, illustrator, and craftsman. Born Dublin, Ireland, Aug. 26, 1867. Pupil of Gerome, Courtois, and Collin in Paris, and studied in London. Member: Royal Hibernian Academy of Arts, Dublin; Rochester AC; Genesseans. Award: Taylor Scholarship for painting, Dublin Academy; gold medal Rochester Exposition, 1925. Died in 1946. Address in 1929, 83 Reynolds Arcade; h. 320 Inglewood Dr., Rochester, NY.

INGRAHAM, GEORGE H.
Etcher. Born in New Bedford, MA, in 1870. Address in 1926, 1127 Guardian Bldg., Cleveland, OH.

INGRAHAM, KATHERINE ELY.
Etcher. Born in Minneapolis, MN, in 1900. Studied: Univ. of Wisconsin; Art Students League, and with Joseph Pennell. Awards: Madison Art Association, 1944, 1946. Collection: Library of Congress.

INMAN, HENRY.
Portrait, genre, miniature, and landscape painter. Born Oct. 28, 1801, in Utica, NY. Studied under John Wesley Jarvis in New York City. He went to Europe in 1845, remaining about a year. He painted Wordsworth, Macaulay, Dr. Thomas Chalmers and others. Among his sitters in this country were many distinguished men, whose portraits are preserved in public collections in Boston, New York, Philadelphia and elsewhere. He was, between 1831 and 1835, associated with Col. Cephas G. Childs in a lithographic printing and publishing business carried on in this city, and was a Director of the Penna. Academy of Fine Arts in 1834. His portrait of Chief Justice Marshall was lithographed by A. Newsam and engraved by A. B. Durand. He was vice-president of the National Academy from 1820 to 1830 and again from 1838 to 1844. From 1831 to 1835 he lived at Mt. Holly, NJ, and in Philadelphia. In 1843 he sailed for England; returned to US late in 1845; died Jan. 17, 1846. Tuckerman gives a long account of Inman in his "Book of Artists."

INMAN, J. O'BRIEN.
Painter. Born June 10, 1826, in NYC. Son of Henry Inman. As a young man he painted portraits in the Western States; later he moved his studio to New York. In 1866 he went to Europe and opened his studio in Rome. He was elected an associate of the National Academy of Design in 1865. He died May 28, 1896, in Fordham, NY.

INNESS, GEORGE
Landscape painter. Born in Newburg, NY, May 1, 1825. Except for some elementary instruction in his youth in Newark, NJ, and a few months' study under Regis Gignoux in NY, he received no academic art education. Through a long course of patient study from Nature, he learned to express his ideals on canvas. His work is distinctly divided into two periods, the first covering the years during which, in conscientious, analytical fashion, he painted scenes in this country, Italy and other parts of Europe; the second embracing the time from about 1878 to his death, during which he became more and more a synthesist. In this latter period his work evoked such power, individuality and beauty of color and composition as to place his work among that of the greatest artists of the nineteenth century. There are points of similarity in his development and that of two great Frenchmen, Corot and Rousseau. Both had more academic training than Inness, but both, in their landscape work, went through the analytical stages that mark the earlier pictures of Inness. The landscapes of George Inness show the same sort of grasp as those of the two masters mentioned above, the same intensity of purpose, the same general conception of nature, and they possess a great quality of tone, and an unusual depth and variety of color. His pictures are in galleries and museums, and his "Georgia Pines" is in the William T. Evans Collection. In 1868 he was elected to the National Academy and was also member of ASL. Died, while on a trip in Scotland, Aug. 3, 1894.

INNESS, GEORGE JR.
Painter. Born in Paris, France, in 1853. He was a pupil of his father in Rome, Italy; studied one year in Paris. Lived in Boston and New York, where he occupied a studio with his father (1878). He resided with his family in Montclair, NJ, after 1880, but had a studio in Paris; exhibited annually at Paris Salon; honorable mention, Paris Salon, 1896, and gold medal, 1900. Officer Academie des Beaux Arts, Paris, 1902. Elected Associate Member of the National Academy, 1895; National Academy, 1899. Art

signature always "Inness, Jr."
Author of "Life and Letters of
George Inness," 1917. His painting
"Shepherd and Sheep" is in the
Metropolitan Museum. Address in
1926, Care of Century Co., 353
Fourth Ave., New York. Died July
27, 1926, in Cragsmoor, NY.

INOUYE, CAROL.
Illustrator. Born in Los Angeles,
in 1940. She attended Chouinard
Art Institute and UCLA. She began
her career as a graphic designer
and art director for several
publishing houses. Her first
published piece, entitled Creative
Living, appeared in 1975. She
wrote and illustrated the book
Naturecraft and has done editorial
illustrations for Reader's Digest,
Gallery and Guideposts. Presently
living in New York City, she is a
member of the S of I.

INUKAI, KYOHEI.
Painter. Award: Maynard prize
($100) NAD, 1926. Exhibited
self-portrait at NA and at PAFA in
1925. Address in 1929, 200 West
57th St.; 46 Washington Sq., New
York, NY.

INVERNIZZI, PROSPER.
Painter. Exhibited at Penna.
Academy of Fine Arts in 1924.
Address in 1926, 500 West 178th
St., New York.

IORIO, ADRIAN J.
Painter, illustrator, writer and
lecturer. Born New York, NY, May
13, 1879. Illustration and
decoration; technical, biological,
microscopical designs and diagrams
for textbooks, etc. Faculty member
MA School of Art. Died in 1957.
Address in 1929, 383 Boylston St.,
Boston, MA; Laboratory, 28 Park
St., Randolph, MA.

IPPOLITO, ANGELO.
Painter and educator. Born in
Arsenio, Italy, on Nov. 9, 1922; US
citizen. Studied: Ozenfant School
of Fine Arts; Brooklyn Museum
School of Art; Instituto Meschini,
Rome, Italy. Collections: Whitney
Museum of American Art; Phillips
Collection, Wash., DC;
Munson-Williams-Proctor Institute;
Sarah Lawrence College. Exhib.:

Carnegie; Whitney; MOMA; Sao Paulo
Biennial, Brazil; others. Awards:
Fulbright Fel., Florence; Tiffany
Grant; others. Rep. by Grace
Borgenicht Gal., NYC. Address in
1982, Binghampton, NY.

IPSEN, ERNEST L.
Portrait painter. Born Malden, MA,
Sept. 5, 1869. Pupil of Boston
Museum School; Royal Academy at
Copenhagen. Member: ANA; NA,
1924; NAC (life); Allied AA; Salma.
C.; Century Asso.; AWCS; NYWCC;
AFA. Award: Proctor Prize, NAD,
1921; Isaac N. Maynard Prize, NAD
(best portrait) 1929. Represented
in Chicago Art Institute;
Massachusetts Institute of
Technology; Boston State House;
Trenton State House; New Bedford
City Hall; Johns Hopkins Univ.;
Butler Art Inst., Youngstown, OH;
"Judge John W. Hogan," Court of
Appeals, New York; "Dr. Warfield,"
Princeton Theological Seminary;
"Dr. John Bates Clark," Carnegie
Endowment for International Peace;
"A. Nathan Meyer," Barnard College,
Columbia Univ.; "Dr. John Bates
Clark," Columbia Univ.; "Hon. Elihu
Root," Century Assoc., NY; "Edwin
Howland Blashfield," National
Academy of Design, NY; "Thomas U.
Slocum," Harvard Club, NY; "Rev.
Henry Van Dyke," Princeton Club,
NY; "Dr. William F. Whitney,"
Harvard Medical School, Boston;
"Hon. Abram I. Elkus" and "Justice
Hogan," Court of Appeals, Albany,
NY; "Lee Kohns," NY Board of Trade
and Transportation; "Dr. Arthur
Cushman McGiffert," Union
Theological Seminary; "George A.
Plimpton," Amherst College, MA;
"Irene Sutliffe," Director's Room,
New York Hospital; "Hon. William
Howard Taft," Chief Justice U. S.
Supreme Court, for United States
Supreme Court, Washington; and many
others. Died in 1951. Address in
1929, 119 East 19th St., New York,
NY.

IRELAND, LEROY.
Painter. Born Philadelphia, PA,
Dec. 24, 1889. Pupil of PAFA;
William M. Chase; Daniel Garber;
Emil Carlsen in New York. Member:
Salma. C.; Fellowship, PAFA; A.
Fund S. Work: "God of the Snake
Dance," Dallas Art Association;

"Osiris," Museum, San Antonio, TX. Address in 1929, 140 West 57th St., New York, NY.

IRELAND, WILLIAM ADDISON.
Illustrator. Born Chillicothe, OH, Jan. 8, 1880. Member: Columbus PPS. Died in 1935. Address in 1929, Columbus Evening Dispatch; h. 264 Woodland Ave., Columbus, OH.

IRISH, MARGARET HOLMES.
Painter. Born Blenheim, Canada, in 1878. Pupil of St. Louis School of Fine Arts. Member: Alliance; S. Indp. A.; Twentieth Century C., St. Louis; AFA. Award: Prize, State Fair, St. Louis, 1912. Address in 1929, No. 79 South Rock Hill Rd.; h. R. 6, Box 98, Webster Groves, MO.

IRVIN, REA.
Illustrator. Born San Francisco, CA, Aug. 26, 1881. Pupil of Hopkins Art Institute, San Francisco. Member: SI 1913. Work: Illustrated "Opera Guyed," by Newman Levy. (Knopf). Died in 1972. Address in 1929, Spuyten Duyvil, NY.

IRVIN, VIRIGINIA H.
Painter. Born in Chicago, IL, in 1904. Studied: Art Institute of Chicago; and with Elsie Dodge Pattee. She is a miniature painter. Awards: American Society of Miniature Painters, 1944; Calif. Society of Miniature Painters, 1947, 1949; Penn. Society of Miniature Painters 1950, National Association of Women Artists, 1954, 1958. Collection: Philadelphia Museum of Art.

IRVINE, LOUVA ELIZABETH.
Artist and filmmaker. Studied: Hans Richter Film Institute, CCNY; School of Visual Arts; Art Students League. Films: "Sophie Newman, J. Skiles, NYC;" "Elegy for My Sister;" "Rain." Exhibitions: Festival of Women's Films, 1972; Second International Festival of Cinema, Montreal, 1972; Women's Interart Center, 1973; Whitney Museum, 1972. New Film: "Portrait of Thomas Messer" (Director of the Guggenheim Museum).

IRVINE, WILSON HENRY.
Landscape painter. Born Byron, IL, Feb. 28, 1869. Pupil of AIC. Member: ANA, 1926; Chicago SA; Chicago WCC; Cliff Dwellers; Palette and Chisel C., Chicago; Salma. C.; Allied AA. Awards: Cahn prize ($100), AIC 1912; Carr prize ($100), AIC 1915; silver medal, P.-P. Exp., San F., 1915; medal, Chicago SA 1916; Palette and Chisel C. Prize, AIC 1916; Grower prize, AIC 1917. Work: "The Road" and "Autumn," AIC, Mun. AL purchase, 1911; "Early Spring," Sears Memorial Museum, Elgin, IL. Represented in Rockford, IL, Art Assn. Died in 1936.

IRVING, JOAN.
Painter. Born in Riverside, CA, 1916. Studied: Riverside CA College; Art Center School, Los Angeles, CA; and with Barse Miller. Awards: Festival of Art, Laguna Beach, 1951; CA Watercolor Society, 1951; National Orange Show, 1951. Collections: Metropolitan Museum of Art; Newport High School Collection.

IRVING, JOHN BEAUFAIN.
Painter. Born Nov. 26, 1825, in Charleston, SC. He studied in Charleston, and, in 1851, he went to Europe and studied with Leutz. On his return he had a studio in Charleston and later in New York. Elected an Associate of the National Academy and an Academician in 1872. His portraits and historical subjects are spirited and rich in color, he also painted genre subjects. Died in NYC, April 20, 1877.

IRWIN, BENONI.
Painter. Born in 1840 at Newmarket, Canada. Pupil of the National Academy of Design in New York; Carolus Duran in Paris. Represented at the Metropolitan Museum, New York, by a life-size bust portrait of Charles H. Farnham. Represented at the Corcoran Art Gallery, Washington, DC, by a portrait of Edward C. Messer. Died in 1896 at South Coventry, CT.

ISAACS, WALTER F.
Painter, writer, lecturer and teacher. Born Gillespie, IL, July 15, 1886. Pupil of Chase, DuMond, Guerin, Friesz. Member: Western Asso. Museum Directors; Pacific Arts A. Address in 1929, Univ. of Washington, Seattle, WA.

ISHAM, RALPH.
Portrait and landscape painter. Born about 1820 in Connecticut. He was connected with the Wadsworth Athenaeum Gallery when it was first opened. He died early in life.

ISHAM, SAMUEL.
Painter. Born in NYC on May 12, 1855. Pupil of Julien Academy, Paris, under Jacquesson de la Chevreuse, Boulanger and Lefebvre. He exhibited at Paris Salons and in most of the larger American exhibitions. He was a member of the jury of the Pan-American Exposition, Buffalo, 1901, and received a silver medal at the St. Louis Exposition, 1904. He was elected an Associate of the National Academy in 1900 and an Academician in 1906, and also held membership in the New York WCC; New York Architectural League; the National Institute of Arts and Letters. He was the author of "A History of American Painting," 1905. He died in Easthampton, Long Island, NY, June 12, 1914.

ISRAEL, NATHAN.
Painter. Born in Brooklyn, NY, in 1895. Pupil of Max Weber; K. H. Miller; B. Robinson. Member: Art Students' League of New York; Society of Independent Artists. Address in 1926, 15 Kossuth Place, Brooklyn, NY.

ITALIANO, JOAN MYLEN.
Sculptor and educator. Born in Worcester, MA. Studied: Siena Heights College, Adrian, MI; Barry College, Miami, FL. Awards: Toledo Annual, 1950; Palm Beach Art League, 1955, 1956. Collections: The Navy Base Chapel, Key West, FL; The Holy Ghost Seminary, Ann Arbor, MI; St. Thomas Aquinas High School, Chicago, IL; Mary Manning Walsh Home, NYC. Media: Metal, wood, and enamel. Address in 1982, Boylston, MA.

IVERD, EUGENE.
Painter, illustrator and teacher. Born St. Paul, MN, Jan. 31, 1893. Pupil of PAFA. Cover designs for The Saturday Evening Post. Died in 1938. Address in 1929, 15 West 7th St.; h. 1318 West 30th St., Erie, PA.

IVES, CHAUNCEY BRADLEY.
Sculptor. Born Dec. 14, 1810, in Connecticut. Had a studio for years in Rome. His best known statues are "Pandora," "Rebecca," "Bacchante," and his statues of Roger Sherman and Jonathan Trumbull are in the Capitol at Washington, DC. Died Aug. 2, 1894, in Rome.

IVES, HALSEY COOLEY.
Landscape painter. Born Oct. 27, 1847, in Montour Falls, NY. He taught in St. Louis and became director of the Museum of Fine Arts. He received medals for his landscapes. He died in England May 5, 1911.

IVES, NEIL MCDOWELL.
Painter. Born St. Louis, MO, in 1890. Pupil of DuMond, Carlsen and Dasburg. Address in 1926, Woodstock, NY. Died Sept. 12, 1946.

IVES, PERCY.
Portrait painter. Born in Detroit, MI, in 1864. Studied at Penna. Academy of Fine Arts and in Paris, France. Exhibited in Paris, New York, Boston, Philadelphia, Cincinnati, Chicago, etc.; painted portrait of Grover Cleveland, Sec. of War Alger, Postmaster-General Dickinson, etc. Received honorable mention, Buffalo Exposition, 1901; member of Jury of Admission, Art Department, St. Louis Exposition, 1904. Member: Detroit Museum of Art; Society of Western Artists; Fine Arts Society, Detroit; Archaeology Institute of America. Address in 1926, 502 Cass Ave., Detroit, MI.

IVONE, ARTHUR.
Sculptor. Born Naples, Italy, May 29, 1894. Pupil of Mossuti, Naples; Ettene Ferrari, Rome; C. J. Barnhorn, Cincinnati. Member: Cincinnati AC. Work: Stephen C. Foster Memorial bronze bust, Music

Hall, Cincinnati, OH. Address in
1929, 127 East Third St., Studio
Bldg., Cincinnati, OH.

IVORY, P. V. E.
Illustrator. Pupil of Howard Pyle.
Member: Salma. C.; SI. Address in
1929, 51 West 10th St., New York,
NY; Harriman, NY.

IZOR, ESTELLE PEELE.
Painter. Pupil of Forsyth and
Steel in Indianapolis; Freer and
Vanderpoel in Chicago; Chase and
Herter in New York; H. D. Murphy in
Boston. Member: Indianapolis Art
Club. Address in 1926, "The
Wellington," West Michigan St.,
Indianapolis, IN.

JACKSON, ANNIE HURLBURT.
Painter. Born Minneapolis, MN,
Aug. 19, 1877. Pupil of Eric Pape;
Murphy; Woodbury. Member: Copley
S.; Boston GA; Pa. S. Min. P.; Am.
S. Min. P.; AFA. Award: Gold
medal, Sesqui-Centennial
Exposition. Phila., 1926.
Specialty, miniatures. Address in
1929, 329 Tappan St., Brookline,
MA.

JACKSON, EVERETT GEE.
Painter and teacher. Born Mexia,
TX, Oct. 8, 1900. Pupil of AIC.
Member: SSAL. Awards: First Anne
Bremer Prize, San Francisco Art
Assoc., San Francisco, 1929; hon.
mention, Bohemian Club, San
Francisco, 1928. Work: "Spring in
Coyoacan," Houston Museum of Fine
Arts, Houston, TX. Address in 1929,
638 South McKinney St., Mexia, TX;
summer, Sul Ross State Teachers
College, Alpine, TX.

JACKSON, HAZEL BRILL.
Sculptor. Born Philadelphia, PA,
Dec. 15, 1894. Pupil of school of
the Museum of Fine Arts, Boston;
Bela Pratt and Angelo Zanelli in
Rome. Member: Circolo Artisco of
Rome; L. C. Tiffany Foundation;
Boston Soc. Sculptors. Works:
"Memorial Tables," Andover
Theological Seminary; "The
Starling" and "The Pelican,"
Concord, Mass., Art Museum.
Address in 1929, Via Margutta 48,
Rome, Italy.

JACKSON, JOHN EDWIN.
Painter and illustrator. Born
Eagleville, Tenn., Nov. 7, 1876.
Pupil of NAD; ASL of NY. Member:
Salma. C.; SI; GFLA. Award:
Prize, Nashville Art Club, 1923.
Work: "Wall Street", National City
Bank, New York; "Broadway,"
Nashville Art Club, Nashville,
Tenn.; "Lower New York," New York
Public Library. Illustrated "Land
of Journeys Ending" (Century Co.).
Illustrations in Harper's,
Scribner's. Address in 1929, 256
West 12th St., New York, NY.

JACKSON, LESLEY.
Painter and etcher. She was born
Rochester, MN. Pupil of Wash. ASL;
Edmund C. Messer; Charles W.
Hawthorne; Henry B. Snell. Member:

S. Wash. A.; Wash. WCC; NYWCC; AFA.
Awards: Second Corcoran prize,
Wash. WCC, 1905; figure painting
prize, New Haven PCC, 1924.
Specialty watercolors and etching.
Address in 1929, "The Concord,"
Washington, DC.

JACKSON, MARTIN J(ACOB).
Painter. Born Newburgh, NY, April
12, 1871. Pupil of Cooper Union
and NAD under Edgar M. Ward in New
York; Comelli in London; also
studied in Paris, Brussels and
Antwerp. Member: S. Indp. A.;
Buffalo Indp. A.; A. Lg. of Los
Angeles. Awards: Silver medal for
oil painting and silver medal for
water colors, Alaska-Yukon Exp.,
Seattle, 1909. Designer of costumes
and illuminator. Address in 1929,
Bradbury Bldg., Los Angeles, CA.

JACKSON, MAY HOWARD.
Sculptor. Born Philadelphia, PA,
May 12, 1877. Pupil of PAFA.
Member: S. Indp. A. Award:
Harmon, sculpture, 1928. Work:
"William P. Price," St. Thomas'
Church, Phila.; "Paul Lawrence
Dunbar," Dunbar High School,
Washington, DC; William H. Lewis,
ex-Asst. Attorney General; Kelly
Miller, Howard University,
Washington, DC. Address in 1929,
1816-16th St., Washington, DC.

JACKSON, NIGEL LORING.
Painter and art administrator.
Born in Kingston, Jamaica, Jan. 23,
1940. Study: Manhattan Community
College; New Sch. for Social
Research; ASL, 3-year scholar,
1971. Work: NY Harlem Music Ctr.;
Ministerial Interfaith Assn.;
others. Comn.: NY Harlem Music
Ctr. Exhib.: Interracial Council
on Bus. Opp., NYC; NY Int'l. Art
Show; Act of Art, NYC; and others.
Awards: Silver award, NY Int'l.
Art Show. Reviews: NY Times.
Mem.: ASL. Media: Oil. Address
in 1976, 403 W. 21st St., NYC.

JACKSON, ROBERT FULLER.
Painter, illustrator, artist, and
teacher. Born Minneapolis, MN,
July 22, 1875. Member: Boston
Arch. C. Award; Special prize for
painting of Indian Hunter by Cyrus
Dallin, at Arlington, MA, Boston
Arch. C. Award: Special prize for

painting of Indian Hunter by Cyrus Dallin, at Arlington, MA, Boston Arch. Club, 1924. Represented in Brookline Public Library; Huntington Hall, MA Inst. of Tech., Boston. Address in 1929, 9 Cornhill, Boston; h. 329 Tappan St., Brookline, MA.

JACOBS, LEONEBEL.
Portrait painter, sculptor and teacher. Born Tacoma, Washington. Pupil of Brush, Hawthorne. Member: PBC; AFA. Work: Portraits of Mrs. Calvin Coolidge, Sir John Lavery, Mrs. William B. Maloney, Prince de Ligne, Lt. Lester Maitland, Dean Hubert E. Hauks, Dr. Frances Carter Wood. Address in 1929, 51 West 10th St., New York, NY.

JACOBS, MICHEL.
Portrait painter, sculptor and teacher. Born Montreal, Canada, Sept. 10, 1877. Pupil of Laurens in Paris; E. M. Ward at NAD. Member: Salma. C.; S. Indp. A.; A. Fellowship; GFLA. Work: "Portrait of Senator Underwood" and "Portrait of Champ Clark," in the Capitol, Washington; 26 portraits in Baron de Hirsch Inst., Montreal, Canada; Medal for "Military Order of World War." Author of "The Art of Color," "The Art of Composition" and "The Study of Color." Director of the Metropolitan Art School. Address in 1929, 58 West 57th St., New York, NY.

JACOBSEN, MRS. E. M. P.
See Plummer.

JACOBSON, ARTHUR ROBERT.
Painter and printmaker. Born in Chicago, IL, on Jan. 10, 1924. Husband of Ursula Jacobson, painter and sculptor. Studied at Univ. of Wis., Madrid Print Workshop, Spain; London. In collections of Dallas Mus. of Art; PAFA. Exhibitions: Corcoran Biennial of Ptg.; Library of Congress; Watercolor USA, Springfield, IL; others. Awards: Purchase award, PAFA, and Dallas Mus. of Art; others. Address in 1982, Phoenix, AZ.

JACOBSON, OSCAR B(ROUSSE).
Painter, lecturer, writer and teacher. Born Westervik, Sweden, May 16, 1882. Pupil of Birger

Sandzen, Weir, Albert Thompson and Neimeyer; Yale art School Member: College AA; Oklahoma AA; S. Indp. A; AFA. Work: "Prayer for Rain," McPherson Art Gallery, KS; "Voices of the Past," Bethany Art Gallery, Lindsborg, KS; "Portrait of Gov. Williams," State Capitol, Oklahoma City, OK; "Rio Grande," Hayes Normal School. Director, University of Oklahoma School of Art. Represented in collection of the University of Oklahoma, Norman. Address in 1929, University of Oklahoma; h. 609 Chautauqua St., Norman, OK.

JACOBSON, URSULA MERCEDES
Painter and sculptor. Born in Milawaukee, WI, on March 26, 1927. Wife of Art Jacobson who is also a painter. Studied: Milawaukee State Teachers College; Cleveland School of Art; Univ. of Wisconsin. Awards: Wisconsin Designer Craftsmen, Milwaukee, 1948; Weatherspoon Annual, NC, 1967; Phoenix Art Museum, 1974. Exhibitions: Yares Gallery, AZ, 1965; Bolles Gallery, San Francisco, 1966; Four Corners Biennial, Phoenix Art Museum, 1971-75. Address in 1982, Phoenix, AZ.

JACOVLEFF, ALEXANDER.
See Iacovleff, Alexander.

JACQUES, BERTHA E.
Etcher. Born in Covington, OH. Studied: Chicago Art Institute. Collections: NY Public Library; Congressional Library, Wash., DC.

JAEGERS, AUGUSTINE.
Sculptor. Born Barmen, Germany, Mar. 31, 1878. Brought to America in 1882. Pupil of ASL of NY; NAD; Ecole des Beaux-Arts in Paris under Mercie. Member: NSS, 1909. Awards: Collaborative and Avery prize, Arch. Lg. of NY, 1909. Work: Sculpture on arches in Court of Four Seasons, San Francisco Exposition, 1915; Frey and Lopez Memorial, New York. Address in 1929, 370 First Ave., Long Island City, NY.

JAMAR, S. CORINNE.
Miniature painter. Born Elkton, MD, 1876. Pupil AIC; Drexel Inst.,

Phila.; Maryland Inst., Baltimore. Award: 1st prize, Southern SAL., 1921-22. Address in 1929, Elkton, Cecil Co., MD.

JAMBOR, LOUIS.
Painter. Born Nagyvarad, Hungary, Aug. 1, 1884. Pupil of Academi of Art, Budapest. Awards: First prize, City of Budapest, 1919; Baron Kohner prize, Budapest, 1921. Work: Main altar painting, St. Stephen Church, New York, NY. Address in 1929, 200 West 57th St., New York, NY; summer, Southampton, LI, NY.

JAMES, ALEXANDER R.
Painter. Born Cambridge, Mass., 1890. Pupil of Museum of Fine Arts, Boston, A. H. Thayer. Member: Boston GA. Work: "Portrait of Prof. William James" and "Portrait of a Girl," Museum of Fine Arts, Boston. Died in Feb., 1941. Address in 1929, Dublin, NH.

JAMES, AUSTIN.
Sculptor. Born Philadelphia, PA, Mar. 12, 1885. Pupil of Calif. School of Fine Arts; Bufano, Stackpole, Mora. Member: Carmel AA; Los Angeles PS; Pasadena AI. Address in 1929, 2282 Pepper drive, Pasadena, CA; summer, Pebble Beach, CA.

JAMES, EVA GERTRUDE.
Painter, sculptor, craftsman, writer and teacher. Born Morgan Co., IN, July 18, 1871. Studied in Indianapolis, and with Robert E. Burke, Indiana Univ. Member: Ind. AC.; Hoosier Salon. Award: Prize, Indiana State Fair, 1924 and 1925. Address in 1929, 526 Eagle St., Terre Haute, IN; 1048 W. 28th St., Indianapolis, IN.

JAMES, EVALYN GERTRUDE.
Painter, illustrator, craftsman, writer, lecturer, and teacher. Born Chicago, IL, May 22, 1898. Pupil of Rhoda E. Selleck; William Forsyth and R. E. Burke. Member: Indiana AC.; Herron Art School Alumni; Hoosier Salon; Western Arts Assoc.; Survey Com. Ind. Fed. of A. C.; Chrm. State Com. Art Courses for Schools of Ind. Awards: Ind. State Fair 1920, 1924-25. Head of Art Dept. Indiana State Teachers College. Illustrated numerous books on scientific subjects. Represented in the Shortridge High School, Indianapolis, IN. Address in 1929, 526 Eagle St., Terre Haute, IN; 1048 W. 28th St., Indianapolis, IN.

JAMES, H(AROLD) FRANCIS.
Painter, writer, lecturer, and teacher. Born Drayton, England, Nov. 9, 1881. Pupil of Jean Paul Laurens in Paris. Member: Western AA. Author of "Color Tables for High Schools," "Grade Color Tablet." Address in 1929, Ft. Wayne Art School and Museum; h. 904 West Berry, Fort Wayne, IN; summer, Lorient, Hardin, IL.

JAMES, JOHN WELLS.
Painter. Born Brooklyn, NY, Feb. 22, 1873. Pupil of James Knox. Member: Salma. C.; AFA. Address in 1929, 1239 Dean St., Brooklyn, New York, NY.

JAMES, ROY HARRISON.
Illustrator. Born Zalma, MO, May 10, 1889. Member: St. Louis AG. Specialty, cartoons. Address in 1929, St. Louis Star Bldg., 12th and Olive St.; h. 8103 Madison St., Vinita Terrace, St. Louis, MO.

JAMES, ROY WALTER.
Painter, sculptor, writer, and teacher. Born Gardena, CA, Sept. 23, 1897. Self taught. Member: Calif. AC.; Laguna Beach AA.; Long Beach AA.; GFLA. Work: "Sentinel by the Sea," Long Beach Public Library; "Sunset," Long Beach High School; "Old Baldy," Public Library, Covina; "Light the Crown of Beauty," High School, Covina, CA. Address in 1929, Covina, CA.

JAMES, WILL.
Painter, illustrator, etcher, and writer. Born Great Falls, MT, June 6, 1892. Award: Newberry medal, Am. Library Assn. (novel) 1927. Author and illustrator of: "The Drifting Cowboy;" "Cowboys, North and South;" "Smoky;" "Cow Country;" "Sand;" (Chas. Scribner's). Died in 1942. Address in 1929, Pryor, MT.

JAMES, WILLIAM.
Painter and techer. Born Cambridge, MA, June 17, 1882.

Pupil of Benson and Tarbell. Member: Boston GA. Award: Silver medal, P.-P. Exp., San F., 1915; Beck gold medal, PAFA, 1925. Represented in Fenway Court, Boston; Rhode Island School of Design, Providence. Address in 1929, Riverway Studios, Boston, MA; h. 95 Irving St., Cambridge, MA.

JAMESON, DEMETRIUS GEORGE
Painter and printmaker. Born in St. Louis, MO, Nov. 22, 1919. Study: Corcoran School of Art, Wash., DC; Wash. Univ. School of Fine Arts; Univ. of IL School of Fine and Applied Arts, Urbana. Work: Victoria & Albert Mus., London; Denver, Portland (OR), Seattle Art Museums; Am. Embassy, Athens; others. Exhibition: Guggenheim Museum; Seattle World's Fair; Corcoran; 4th Int'l. Print Show, Italy; Butler Inst., Youngstown, OH; many others. Awards: Portland, Denver, Seattle Art Mus.; St. Louis City Art Mus.; etc. Teaching at Oregon State Univ. from 1950. Mem.: Portland (OR) Art Assn.; Artists Equity Assn.; others. Works in oils. Address in 1982, Corvallis, OR.

JAMESON, MINOR S(TORY).
Painter. Born New York, NY, Aug. 26, 1873. Pupil of Cullen Yates and John F. Carlson. Member: S. Wash. A. (pres.); Wash. Ldscp. C. Award: First Prize (silver medal), Wash. SA, 1924. Landscape painter. Address in 1929, 13 Oxford St., Chevy Chase, MD.

JAMESON, SAMILLA LOVE.
(Mrs. Heinzmann). Painter, sculptor, illustrator and craftsman. Born Indianapolis, IN, Apr. 22, 1881. Pupil of AIC; Detroit FAA; Carnegie Inst. of Tech.; De Lug, Vienna. Member: S. Indp. A. Work: Thomas Paine Memorial Tablet, New York; Henry Hudson Tablet, Amsterdam, Holland. Address in 1929, Willow Bridge Studio, cor. Amboy Rd. and Terrace Ave., Prince Bay, New York, NY.

JAMIESON, BERNICE (EVELYN).
Painter, etcher, and teacher. Born Providence, RI, Apr. 18, 1898. Pupil of RI School of Design.

Member: Prov. AC. Address in 1929, 41 North St., Meshanticut Park, Cranston, RI.

JAMIESON, MITCHELL.
Illustrator. Born in Kensington, MD, in 1915. Attended the Abbott School of Fine Arts and studied at the Corcoran School of Art. During World War II, as an official combat artist, he began reporting on naval operations in the Pacific. These illustrations were reproduced in Fortune and Life, among others.

JAMISON, CECILIA VIETS DAKIN HAMILTON
Author and artist. Born in Yarmouth, Nova Scotia, in 1837. Educated privately in Boston, NY, and Paris. She traveled to Rome to continue her studies and remained there for three years. Among her best known portraits were one of Longfellow (now at Tulane Univ.) and one of naturalist Louis Agassiz (now at the Boston Society of Natural History). During the 1880s Mrs. Jamison became well known as a writer of juvenile literature as well as of adult romances. A frequent contributor to St. Nicholas, and many of her novels were serialized in Harper's, Scribner's and Appleton's. Her books included The Story of an Enthusiast, 1888, Lady Jane, 1891, Toinette's Philip, 1894, Seraph, the Little Violiniste, 1896, Thistledown, 1903, and The Penhallow Family, 1905. She died in Roxbury (now part of Boston) on April 11, 1909.

JAMPEL, JUDITH.
Illustrator. Born in London, England, in 1944. Attended Hunter College and SVA in NY. Her first published illustration was a self-promotional booklet entitled, Sorry but we don't hire women because. She works with nylon fabric, polyester fabric, real hair, and props to create her three-dimensional figures. She received the Hamilton King Award and Award of Excellence from the S of I in 1975. Her artwork has been shown at the Greengrass Gallery in NYC.

JANOWSKY, BELA.
Sculptor and instructor. Born in Budapest, Hungary, in 1900. Studied: Ontario College of Art; PAFA; Cleveland School of Art; Beaux-Arts Institute of Design; and with Alexander Blazys and Charles Grafly. Award: Allied Artists of America, 1951. Collections: Queens Univ., Kingston, Ontario; Royal Society of Canada; US Department of Commerce Building, Wash., DC; US Post Office, Cooperstown, NY; Naval Shipyard, Brooklyn, NY. Address in 1980, 52 W. 57th St., NY, NY.

JANSSON, ALFRED.
Painter. Born in Sweden, 1863. Studied in Stockholm, Christiania, and Paris. Member: Palette and Chisel C.; Chicago SA; Chicago AC; Chicago AG; Swedish Am. A. Awards: Swedish American Artists 3d prize, 1911; second prize, 1913 and first prizes, 1915 and Rosenwald purchase prize ($200), AIC 1912; Carr landscape prize, AIC 1914. Work: "Icy Rocks," Municipal Commission purchase. Address in 1929, 1851 Byron St., Chicago, IL.

JANVIER, ALBERT WILSON.
Crayon-portrait draughtsman. He was doing portrait work in Philadelphia about 1858.

JANVIER, CATHERINE ANN (MRS.).
Painter. Born in Philadelphia. Her early life was passed in China; studied in the Penn. Academy of Fine Arts and Art Students' League, New York. Pictures: "Geoffrey Rudel and the Countess of Tripoli," "The Princess Badroulbadour," "Daniel at Prayer," "The Violinist," etc. Member: Art Students' League; Fine Arts Society of New York. Died on Dec. 12th, 1923.

JAQUES, BERTHA E.
Etcher, printer, writer, and teacher. Born Covington, OH. Pupil of AIC. Member: Chicago SA; Chicago SE; Calif. SE; Calif. P.M. Award: Bronze medal, P.-P. Exp., San F., 1915. Work in: Art Institute of Chicago; New York Public Library; Library of Congress, Smithsonian Inst., Washington, DC; St. Paul Institute

of Art. Address in 1929, 4316 Greenwood Ave., Chicago, IL.

JAQUES, F(RANCIS) L(EE).
Painter. Born Geneseo, IL, on Sept. 28, 1887. Pupil of C. C. Rosenkranz. Member: Salma. C. Work: Background of flying bird grp. (dome), murals of reptiles, groups and backgrounds, American Museum of Natural History, New York. Address in 1929, 515 Edgecombe Ave., New York, NY.

JARVIS, CHARLES WESLEY.
Portrait, miniature, and historical painter. The second son of John Wesley Jarvis, he was born in NYC, probably in 1812, and brought up by his mother's family, the Burtises of Oyster Bay, Long Island. About 1828 he was apprenticed to Henry Inman, with whom he worked in NYC and Philadelphia until 1834. Returning to NYC the younger Jarvis established himself as a portrait painter and worked there until his death, which occurred at his home in Newark, NJ, on February 13, 1868.

JARVIS, JOHN WESLEY.
Painter and engraver. Born in England in 1780. A nephew of John Wesley. He was brought to Phila. at five years old, and educated there; spent much of his time out of school with Pratt, Paul, Clark and other minor painters. He met Gilbert Stuart, who "occasionally employed Paul to letter a book" in one of his pictures; was apprenticed to Edward Savage, to learn engraving, and with him went to NY. He learned to draw and engrave from D. Edwin, who was employed by Savage on his first arrival in this country; finally engraving on his own account. He made several trips South, with Henry Inman as assistant on his first trip to New Orleans, where he finished six portraits a week, probably in 1833. It was after this that he painted his most important works, the full-length portrait of military and naval heroes for the City of NY. He died in extreme poverty Jan. 12, 1840 in NYC. While Jarvis was in NY he published the prints of other engravers, notably those of Robert

479

R. Livingston, published in 1804 and engraved by George Graham.

JARVIS, W. FREDERICK.
Painter, lecturer, and teacher. Monroe County Ohio. Pupil of Silas Martin, Charles Bullette, and Madam Schille. Member: SSAL; S. Indp. A. Award: Gold medal, Tri-State Fair, 1926. Address in 1929, 315 East Quincy St., San Antonio, TX.

JAY, CECIL (MRS.).
Miniature painter and portrait painter in oil. Member of New York Water Color Club.

JECT-KEY, ELSIE.
Painter. Born in Koege, Denmark. Studied: Art Students League, with Frank DuMond, George Bridgman, and Homer Boss; National Academy of Design, with Murphy, Olinsky, and Neilson; Beaux-Arts Institute of Design. Exhibited widely in the US and abroad. Media: Oil and watercolor. Address in 1980, 333 E. 41st St., NY, NY.

JEFFERSON, JOSEPH.
Painter and actor. Born Feb. 20, 1829 in Philadelphia. Died at Palm Beach, Florida, on April 23, 1905. He painted "The Coast of Maine" and "Massachusetts Bay."

JEFFREYS, LEE.
Painter, writer, lecturer, and teacher. Born New York City, on Jan. 24, 1901. Pupil of ASL of NY; Julian Academy in Paris. Member: NAC; Grand Central Gallery; Soc. of Amer. Artists in Paris. Address in 1929, 915 First Bank Bldg.; h. Sherman Drive Extension, Utica, NY; summer, R.F.D No. 2, Barneveld, Herkimer Co., NY.

JEFFRIES, L(ULU) R(ITA).
(Mrs. H. P. Jeffries). Painter, illustrator, writer, and teacher. Born Nova Scotia. Pupil of Paul Moschowitz and Pratt Inst. Member: Newport AA. Address in 1929, Sussex Corners, N.B., Canada.

JEMNE, ELSA LAUBACH.
Painter and illustrator. Born St. Paul Minn., in 1888. Pupil of Violet Oakley, Cecilia Beaux, Daniel Garber, Emil Carlsen, and Joseph Pearson. Member: St. Paul

AS; Fellowship PAFA; Mural P. Awards: Silver medal, St. Paul Inst., 1911; J. J. Hill gold medal, St. Paul Inst., 1915; Cresson European Scholarship, PAFA, 1914 and 1915; gold medal for painting. St. Paul Institute of Art, 1916; gold medal, painting, Minn. State Fair, 1921; first prize for painting, Minneapolis. Minn. Mural decorations in Central High School, Minneapolis; Stearns County C.H., St. Cloud, Minn.; Leamy Home, Philadelphia; Nurses Home, St. Luke's Hospital, St. Paul, Minn. Address in 1929, 212 Mt. Curve Blvd., St. Paul, Minn.

JENCKES, JOSEPH.
Born in England in 1602, he emigrated to America in 1642. He was an inventor and die-sinker. He was employed by the Lynn Iron Works to make the dies for the "pine-tree shilling." He built the first American fire-engine. He died in 1683.

JENKINS, H(ANNAH) T(EMPEST).
Painter, writer, lecturer and teacher. Born Philadelphia, PA. Pupil of Spring Garden Inst., School of Industrial Art and PAFA in Philadelphia; Robert Fleury and Constant in Paris; Tackouchi Seiho in Kyoto, Japan. Member: Plastic C.; Fellowship PAFA.; Southern Calif. AC; Laguna Beach AA. Award: Diploma, Alaska-Yukon-Pacific Expo., Seattle, 1909. Professor Emeritus of Art Dept. of Pomona College, Claremont, Calif. Died in 1927. Address in 1929, Sumner Hall, Pomona College, Claremont, Los Angeles Co., Calif.

JENKINS, MATTIE M(AUD).
Miniature painter and illustrator. Born South Abington, Mass., on July 29, 1867. Pupil of Henry Cook, Ethel B. Colver and Charles W. Reid. Member: Brockton AC. Address in 1929, 704 Washington St., Whitman, Mass.

JENKINS, PAUL.
Born July 12, 1923 in Kansas City, MO. Studied at Kansas City Art Institute, and Art Students' League of NYC. Awarded Hon. DH, Linwood College (1973), Officier des Arts Et Lettres (1980). Lived in Paris.

Exhibited at Studio Paul Fachelti, Paris (1954); Martha Jackson Gallery, NYC (multiple); A. Tooth & Sons, London; MOMA; Whitney; Carnegie; Osaka & Tokyo (1959); Guggenheim; Louvre, Paris; and Corcoran Gallery, Wash., DC. In collections of MOMA; Guggenheim; U. of CA/Berkeley; Brooklyn Mus.; Chrysler Art Mus., Provincetown; Whitney; Tate Gallery, London; Stedelijk Mus., Amsterdam. Rec. Golden Eagle Film Award (1966) for "Ivory Knife," (autobiog.).

JENKS PHOEBE, PICKERING HOYT.
(Mrs. Lewis E. Jenks). Portrait painter. Born in Portsmouth, NH, July 28, 1847. She came to Boston to live when sixteen and made it her home. Her best portraits have been of women. Among her many sitters were Mrs. Ellis L. Mott and daughter, Mrs. S. A. Bigelow, Mrs. Harrison Gardiner, Mrs. C. C. Walworth, Mrs. Edward Taylor, Mrs. Henry Landcaster, and a large portrait of the two Lovering boys. She died in New York City on Jan. 20, 1907.

JENNEWEIN, CARL PAUL.
Sculptor. Born on Dec. 2, 1890, in Stuttgart, Germany. In US since 1907. Studied at ASL. Opened his studio in 1921. Member: NSS; NY Arch. Lg.; (hon.) AIA; Amer. Academy in Rome Alumni. Awards: Collaborative prize for sculpture and Avery prize, NY Arch. Lg., 1915; Am. Acad. in Rome Fellowship in sculpture, 1916-19; hon. mention, AIC, 1921; Medal of Honor, Arch. Lg. of NY, 1927. Represented in Metropolitan Museum of Art; Corcoran Gallery, Washington; Baltimore Museum of Art; Darlington memorial fountain, Washington, DC; frieze, Eastman School of Music, Rochester, NY; Dante Tablet, Ravenna, Italy; Phila. Museum of Art; Barre, VT, war memorial; Lincoln Life Ins. Bldg., Ft. Wayne, Ind.; portrait of G. B. McClellan, Caruso Memorial, Metropolitan Opera House; Cunard Bldg. decoration and in the Woolworth Bldg., New York; Plymouth, Mass., memorial fountain; Levi tomb, Mt. Pleasant, NY; Providence War Memorial; mural decorations, Church of the Ascension, Kingston, NY. Address

in 1929, 538 Van Nest Ave., Bronx, New York, NY.

JENNEY, EDGAR WHITEFIELD.
Painter and architect. Born in New Bedford, Mass., on Dec. 11, 1869. Pupil of Major in Boston; Laurens, Emmanuel and Cavaille Coll., Paris. Member: Mural P.; NY Arch. Lg.; AFA. Work: Decorations in Wisconsin State Capitol; Union Central Life Insurance Co., Cincinnati, Ohio; Senate Chamber and House of Commons, Ottawa, Canada; Hibernia Bank, New Orleans, LA; Standard Oil Bldg., Hotel Roosevelt, and Equitable Insurance Bldg. in New York City; Palmer House, Chicago, Ill. Address in 1929, 13 Vestal St., Nantucket, Mass.

JENNINGS, DOROTHY.
Painter and sculptor. Born in St. Louis, on Nov. 19, 1894. Pupil of Nancy Hahn, Victor Holm, G. Goetsch, W. Ludwig, F. Conway, and W. Wuerpel. Member: St. Louis AL. Award: Prize for sculpture, St. Louis Artists Guild, 1928. Address in 1929, 922 Syndicate Trust Bldg.; h. 7057 West Park, St. Louis, MO.

JENNINGS, LOUISE B.
(Mrs. H. S. Jennings). Painter. Born in Tecumseh, Mich., on Nov. 6, 1870. Pupil of William M. Chase, Hugh Breckenridge, DeNeal Morgan, and Bryant. Member: Balto. WCC; Balto. S. Indp. A; AFA; Fellowship PAFA. Address in 1929, 505 Hawthorn Rd., Roland Park, Baltimore, MD; summer, Woods Hole, Mass.

JENNINGS, SAMUEL.
Painter. Native of Philadelphia. In 1792 he painted a large and imposing allegorical picture which he presented to the Philadelphia Library, called "The Genius of America Encouraging the Emancipation of the Blacks." Jennings went to London, and Dunlap says that he was there in 1794. Created portraits and miniatures in crayon and oil media.

JENNINGS, WILLIAM.
Portrait painter. One of his pictures is signed and dated 1774.

JENNYS, J. WILLIAM.
Painter. He painted portraits of
Col. and Mrs. Constant Storrs,
which are dated 1802 and owned by
John F. Lewis, Philadelphia. (May
be William Jennings, above).

JENNYS, RICHARD JR.
Engraver. A well-executed
mezzotint portrait of the Rev.
Johathan Mayhew is signed by
Richard Jennys, Jr., as engraver.
It was published in Boston about
1774 and was "Printed and Sold by
Nat. Hurd, Engraver, on ye
Exchange."

JENSEN, H(OLGER) W.
Painter. Born in Denmark, on Jan.
6, 1880. Pupil of AIC; Chicago
Academy FA. Member: Chicago PS;
Austin, Oak Park and River forest
AL; Palette and Chisel C., Chicago;
Chic. Galleries Assn. Address in
1929, Route No. 3 Grand Detour,
Dixon, Ill.

JENSEN, THOMAS M.
Portrait painter. Born in
Apenrade, Denmark in 1831. He came
to this country in 1870. He
painted many of the portraits of
the New York judges which are now
in the Kings County Court House and
the City Hall of New York City.
Among his best known portraits were
those of Roswell C. Brainard;
Michael McGoldrick; and Hamilton W.
Robinson. He died March 6, 1916 in
Bay Ridge, NY.

JEPSON, MRS. W. R.
See Wiles, Gladys.

JEROME, ELIZABETH GILBERT.
Painter. Born Dec. 18, 1824, in
New Haven, Conn. Studied in the
National Academy, New York, under
E. Leutze. Also worked in crayon.
She exhibited in the National
Academy in 1866, and excelled in
ideal figure painting. Died Apr.
22, 1910 in New Haven, Conn.

JEROME, IRENE ELIZABETH.
Painter and illustrator. Born in
New York State in 1858, and with
the exception of a few lessons was
self-taught in art. In 1882 she
exhibited eighteen sketches of
Colorado which had decided merit.
Among her work was considerable

illustrating for books and other
publications.

JERRY, SYLVESTER.
Painter. Born in Woodville, Wisc.,
on Sept. 20, 1904. Pupil of Layton
Sch. of Art; ASL of NY. Member:
Wisc. PS; ASL of NY. Address in
1929, 190 Concordia Ave.,
Milwaukee, Wisc.; summer,
Woodstock, NY.

JETTER, FRANCES.
Illustrator. Born in NY, in 1951.
Attended PSD. In 1974 her career
began with illustrations for a
psychology book by John Wiley and
Sons. She has designed bookjackets
as well as editorial illustrations
for The New York Times,
Institutional Investor, The
Independent (a United Nations
publication), and others. Her
illustrations have appeared in the
Annual Exhibitions of the S of I
and in Graphis Annual.

JEWELL, FOSTER.
Painter. Born in Grand Rapids, on
July 21, 1893. Pupil of Mathias J.
Alten. Address in 1929, 447 College
S. E., Grand Rapids, Mich.

JEWETT, CHARLES A.
Engraver. Born in Lancaster, MA,
in 1816; died in NY in 1878. This
good line-engraver of subject
plates was engraving in New York in
1838. He later removed to
Cincinnati, OH, and about 1853 he
was conducting an extensive
engraving business in that city.
In 1860 he was again located in NY.

JEWETT, FREDERICK STILES.
A marine and landscape painter.
Born Feb. 26, 1819, in Simsbury,
CT. He moved to the West Indies
when 22, and visited Europe, but
lived most of his life in his
native state CT. One of his best
paintings is in the Wadsworth
Athenaeum. Died Dec. 26, 1864, in
Cleveland, OH.

JEWETT, MAUDE SHERWOOD.
(Mrs. Edward H. Jewett).
Sculptor. Born in Englewood, NJ,
on June 6, 1873. Pupil of ASL of
NY. Member: NA Women PS;
Alliance; AFA; Am. APL. Work:
Fountain in Cleveland Museum;

Soldiers and Sailors War Memorial, East Hampton, LI, NY Specialty sun-dials. Was living in New York City in 1926. Address in 1929, Easthampton, Long Island, New York. Died April 17, 1953 in Southampton, LI.

JEWETT, WILLIAM
Portrait, genre and landscape painter. Born in East Haddam, Conn., Jan. 14, 1790. He was apprenticed to a coach maker, and when eighteen years of age he met Samuel Waldo, and going to New York with him he formed the partnership of Waldo & Jewett, with whom he collaborated in painting many excellent portraits of prominent men. He was elected an associate member of the National Academy of Design in 1847. He died Mar. 24, 1874, in Bergen, New Jersey.

JEWETT, WILLIAM S.
Painter. Born in South Dover, NY, 1812. He came to New York City as a very young man and studied at the Schools of the National Academy of Design. In 1845 he was elected an Associate Member. He sailed in 1849 from New York for San Francisco where he resided for years and painted a number of pictures, and prospected for gold. He died Dec. 3, 1873, in Springfield, MA.

JEX, GARNET W.
Painter. Member: S. Wash. A.; SSAL; AFA. Address in 1929, 631 Orleans Place, NE, Washington, DC.

JIRAK, IVAN.
Painter. Born in Allegheny, PA, on Nov. 5, 1893. Pupil of Christian Walter. Member: Pitts. AA; AFA. Awards: $100 prize, Pitts. AA, 1922. Work: "Peonies," Public Schools of Pittsburgh. Address in 1929, 408 Fairywood Ave., Pittsburgh, PA.

JIROUCH, FRANK LUIS.
Painter and sculptor. Born in Cleveland, Ohio, on March 3, 1878. Pupil of Mantzen, Ludikie, Grafly, Garber, Pearson, Landowski, Bouchard. Member: NSS; Cleveland SA; Fellowship PAFA. Work: Bronze relief in Church of Lady of Lourdes; "Diana of Ephesus," Union

National Bank; Stone pediment, United Saving and Trust Bank; Chapman Memorial, Cleveland Ball Park; Altar of Sacrifice, Cleveland; Spanish War Monument, Columbus, Ohio; "Day and Night," Wade Park, Cleveland; Maine Memorial Tables, Havana, Cuba. Address in 1929, 1445 East 47th St., Cleveland, Ohio.

JOB, ALICE E.
Painter and writer. Born Alton, Ill. Pupil of Lebvre, Constant and Puvis de Chevannes in Paris. Member: NA Women PS; Nat'l. Lg. of Am. Pen Women. Address in 1929, 70 Fifth Ave.; h. Hotel Albert, 65 University Pl., New York, NY.

JOCELYN, NATHANIEL.
Portrait painter and engraver. Born in New Haven, CT, in Jan. 31, 1796; died there Jan. 13, 1881. Nathaniel Jocelyn was the son of a watchmaker. At the age of eighteen years he was apprenticed to an engraver, and when he was twenty-one he entered into partnership with Tisdale, Danforth and Willard, in the Hartford Graphic and Bank-Note Engraving Company; he later, with Mr. Danforth, virtually founded the National Bank-Note Engraving Company. Dissatisfied with engraving, Jocelyn gave it up in 1820 and became a painter of portraits, and exhibited at the National Academy in 1826. He went abroad with S. F. B. Morse in 1829-30, and became a meritorious portrait painter. He was made an Academician of the National Academy of May 13, 1846. Brother of Simeon Jocelyn.

JOCELYN, SIMEON S.
Engraver and painter. Born in New Haven, CT, Nov. 21, 1799; died in Tarrytown, NY, Aug. 17, 1879. S. S. Jocelyn was engraving line portraits in New Haven, after drawings by N. Jocelyn, as early as 1824, and in 1827 the engraving firm of N. & S. S. Jocelyn was in business in that city. S. S. Jocelyn and S. B. Muson were also associated as engravers. He also painted miniatures and oils. The latter part of his life was passed in New Haven, CT.

JOHANSEN, ANDERS D.
Painter and illustrator. Born in
Denmark. Pupil of Anna Fisher,
Walter Beck, W. S. Taylor, Max
Herrmann and Pratt Inst. Member:
Scandinavian-American Artists;
Tiffany Foundation; AWCS (assoc.).
Award: Pratt Art Alumni European
Fellowship, 1924. Address 1929,
309 Washington Ave., Brooklyn, NY.

JOHANSEN, JOHN C(HRISTEN).
Painter. Born Copenhagen, Denmark,
Nov. 25, 1876. Pupil of AIC;
Duveneck, Julian Academy in Paris.
Member: ANA 1911; NA, 1915; Port.
P.; Players; NAC; Salma. C., 1906;
MacD. C.; AFA. Awards: Municipal
League Purchase prize and Young
Fortnightly prize, AIC, 1903; hon.
men. Art C. of Chic., 1903; silver
medal, Chic. SA, 1904; bronze
medal, St. Louis Exp., 1904; gold
medal, Buenos Aires Exp., 1910;
Saltus gold medal, NAD, 1911;
Harris silver medal ($500), AIC,
1911; hon. mention, CI Pitts.,
1912; H. S. Morris prize, Newport
AA, 1915; gold medal, P.-P. Exp.,
San F., 1915; silver medal,
Sesqui-Centennial Expo., Phila.,
1926; Wm. M. R. French memorial
gold medal, AIC, 1928. Represented
in Nat. Gallery, Santiago, Chili;
Pennsylvania Acad. of the Fine
Arts; "Piazza San Marco," Art
Institute of Chic.; "Fiesole,"
Public Gal., Richmond, Ind.;
Museum, Dallas, Tex.; Conservative
Club, Glasgow; Art Museum,
Syracuse, NY; Union League of
Chicago; Proteus Club, Des Moines,
IA; Arche Club, Chicago; University
Club, Chicago; Gallery of
Vincennes, Ind.; State Normal
School, Terre Haute, Ind.; Herron
Art Institute; Masonic Temple, New
York, NY; Wisconsin, Cornell and
Clark Universities; National and
Corcoran Galleries of Art,
Washington, DC; Wells College.
Died in 1966. Address in 1929, 12
West 9th St., New York, NY.

JOHANSEN, M. JEAN MCLANE.
(Mrs. John C. Johansen). See
McLane.

JOHANSON, PATRICIA.
Landscape-sculptor. Born in 1940.
Studied: Bennington College;
Hunter College; City College,

School of Architecture. Awards:
Guggenheim Fellowship, 1970.
Large-scale projects: Gardens,
House and Garden, 1969; Cyrus
Field, 1970-present; Con Edison
Indian Point Visitors Center, 1972;
designs for the new Yale Univ.
Colleges, 1972; projects for
Columbus East High School,
Columbus, IN, 1973.

JOHN, FRANCIS COATES.
Painter. Born in Baltimore, in
1857. Studied at Ecole des Beaux
Arts in Paris, under Yvon, Lehmann,
Boulanger and Lefebvre. He has had
a studio in New York since 1882.
Specialty, figure painting. He won
Clarke prize, National Academy of
Design. Elected member of the
National Academy in 1894. Member:
National Institute of Arts and
Letters; American Federation of
Arts. Address in 1926, 33 W. 67th
St., New York.

JOHN, GRACE SPAULDING.
Painter, writer, and lecturer.
Born in Battle Creek, Mich., on
Feb. 10, 1890. Pupil of Charles
Hawthorne, Daniel Garber, Fred
Weber. Work: Portrait of Aloysius
Larchmillar, Statehouse, Oklahoma
City, Okla.; "The Onion Cart,
France," Museum of Fine Arts,
Houston, Tex. Died in 1972.
Address in 1929, 808 Louisiana St.;
h. 1306 Barbee St., Houston, Tex.

JOHNS, CLARENCE M.
Painter. Born in Pittsburgh, PA,
in 1843. Pupil of Penn. Academy of
Fine Arts, and later studied in
Paris. He was widely known for his
animal pictures. He served for
years on the jury of awards for the
Carnegie Art Exhibitions at
Pittsburgh. He died in 1925.

JOHNSEN, MAY ANNE.
Painter. Born in Port Chester, NY,
in 1921. Studied with John
Carroll. Awards: Silvermine Art
Guild; Columbia Fair; Hamilton, OH,
Miniature Painters. Exhibitions:
Min. Ptrs., Sculpt., Gravers Soc.
of Washington, 1962-72; Catharine
Lorillard Wolfe Nat'l. Art Show,
NYC, 1964; others. Works in silver
point and oil. Lives in Brainard,
NY.

JOHNSON, ADELAIDE.
Sculptor. Born Plymouth, IL.
Pupil of Monteverde and Fabi Altini
in Rome. Work: Portrait bust of
Susan B. Anthony, Metropolitan
Museum, New York; portrait bust of
Hiram W. Thomas, Chicago Historical
Soc.; portrait monument ot Lucretia
Mott, Elizabeth Cady Stanton and
Susan B. Anthony, National Capitol,
Washington. Address in 1929, 230
Maryland Ave., NE, Washington, DC.

JOHNSON, ARTHUR A(LOYSIUS).
Illustrator, designer, lecturer,
and teacher. Born in Joliet, IL,
on June 29, 1898. Work: Posters
for Chicago Rapid Transit Co.,
Chicago North Shore Milwaukee
Railroad and Chicago South Shore
South Bend Railroad. Address in
1929, 59 East Adam St.; 410 So.
Michigan Ave., Chicago, IL; 202
Herkimer St., Joliet, IL.

JOHNSON, ARTHUR C(LARK).
Painter and teacher. Born in Hyde
Park, MA, on Sept. 5, 1897. Pupil
of Tarbell, Meryman, Hale, Bosley,
E. L. Major, and F. W. Brown.
Instructor, School of Art,
Springfield, IL. Director,
Springfield Art Association.
Address in 1929, 56 Harvard Ave.,
Hyde Park, MA; summer, Hampton, NH.

JOHNSON, BELLE.
Sculptor. Exhibited at Penn.
Academy of Fine Arts, Philadelphia,
in 1925. Address in 1926, 200
Claremont Ave., NY.

JOHNSON, BUFFIE.
Painter and lecturer. Born in NYC
on Feb. 20, 1912. Studied: Univ.
of CA at Los Angeles; Art Students
League. Collections: Boston
Museum of Fine Arts; Baltimore
Museum of Art; Newark Museum of
Art; Walker Art Center,
Minneapolis, MN; Metropolitan
Museum of Art; Cincinnati Museum
Association. Address in 1980, 102
Green St., NY, NY.

JOHNSON, BURT W.
Sculptor. Born in Flint, OH, in
1890. Pupil of Louis Saint
Gaudens; J. E. Fraser; Robert
Aitken; George Bridgman. Member:
Laguna Beach Artists' Association.
Work: "Spanish Music Fountain" and
"Greek Tablet," Pomona College,
Claremont, CA; panel, "Christ," St.
Francis Hospital, La Crosse, WI;
memorial fountain, Huntington Park,
CA; Pomona Valley memorial
monument, Pomona, CA; E. N. Dimick
statue, West Palm Beach, CA.
Address in 1926, 86 Grove St.,
Flushing, NY. Died March 27, 1927,
in Claremont, CA.

JOHNSON, C. EVERETT.
Painter, illustrator, writer and
lecturer. Born in Gilroy, CA, on
Dec. 7, 1866. Pupil of AIC;
Richard Miller in Paris. Member:
Cliff Dwellers; Chicago AC. Work:
Advertising illustration for
Washburn Crosby Co.; Quaker Oats
Co.; CA Fruit Growers Exchange.
Address in 1929, 2656 Tanoble Dr.,
Altadena, CA.

JOHNSON, CLARENCE R.
Painter. Member: Fellowship PAFA.
Awards: Hallgarten prize ($300),
NAD, 1925; bronze medal,
Sesqui-Centennial Expo., Phila.,
1926, Peabody prize ($200), AIC,
1926. Address in 1929,
Lumberville, PA; 15 Windermere
Ave., Landsdowne, PA.

JOHNSON, CONTENT.
Painter. Born Bloomington, IL.
Pupil of Julian Academy under
Constant and Laurens in Paris; NY
School of Art under Chase. Member:
SPNY; PBC. Died Nov. 9, 1949.
Address in 1929, 200 West 57th St.,
New York, NY.

JOHNSON, CORDELIA.
Painter. Born Omaha, July 11,
1871. Pupil of J. Laurie Wallace.
Member: Omaha Art Guild. Address
in 1929, 2346 South 34th St.,
Omaha, NE.

JOHNSON, DAVID.
Painter. Born May 10, 1827, in New
York. At the beginning of his
artistic career he received a few
lessons from J. F. Cropsey. He
studied the works of the great
European masters of landscape
painting, but his professional life
passed entirely in New
York, and he had never been abroad.
He was elected a National
Academician in 1861, and was one of
the founders of the Artists' Fund

485

Society. At the Centennial Exhib. at Phila. in 1876 he exhibited "Scenery on the Housatonic," "Old Man of the Mountains," and "A Brook Study, Orange County, NY," and received one of the first awards. His pictures are notable for fine color and excellent drawing. He died Jan. 30, 1908, at Walden, NY.

JOHNSON, DAVID G.
Painter and line-engraver of portraits and views of little merit, who was working in New York in 1831-35, and again in 1845.

JOHNSON, DOUGLAS.
Illustrator. Born in Toronto, CN, in 1940. Studied at the Ontario College of Art for three years. The start of his career in Toronto in 1960 led to his success as an illustrator, his distinctive style being in great demand among magazine and book publishers. His work has been exhibited at the Art Gallery of Ontario, the Brooklyn Museum, and the S of I for which he produced the Illustrators 13 exhibition poster. He was an instructor at SVA until 1974 and creative director of The Chelsea Theatre Center. He lives in NY and co-directs Performing Dogs, an advertising consultant group.

JOHNSON, EASTMAN.
Genre and portrait painter. Born Jonathan-Eastman Johnson in Lovell, ME, July 29, 1824; died in New York, April 5, 1906. He studied in Dusseldorf, Rome, Paris and The Hague, and settled in New York, becoming a member of the NAD in 1860. He was the son of Philip C. Johnson, Secretary of State for Maine. He worked in a lithographic establishment in Boston in 1840 and after a year went to Augusta, ME, where he commenced making portraits in black crayon. He also visited Newport. In 1845 the family moved to Washington, DC, and young Johnson drew many crayon portraits, working in the Senate Committee Rooms at The Capitol. In 1858 he moved to New York where he remained the rest of his life except for a period spent in Boston and in visits to Europe in 1885, 1891 and 1897.

JOHNSON, EDYTH A. B.
Miniature painter. Born Portsmouth, NH, Jan. 26, 1880. Pupil of Twachtman, Alice Beckington, Carroll Beckwith. Member: Plastic C.; Print C.; Fairmount Park AA. Address in 1929, Hamilton Court, 39th and Chestnut Sts., Philadelphia, PA.

JOHNSON, ELENA MIX.
(Mrs. Alexander L. P. Johnson). Painter. Born Nogales, AZ, Aug. 19, 1889. Pupil of Daniel Garber, Henry McCarter, Joseph T. Pearson, Charles Grafly. Member: Fellowship PAFA; AFA; Am. APL. Address in 1929, 2045 Park Rd., NW, Washington, DC. Died in 1939.

JOHNSON, F.
Painter. Member: Boston AC. Address in 1929, 22 Kensington Ave., Bradford, MA.

JOHNSON, FRANK EDWARD.
Painter, writer, and lecturer. Born Norwich, CT, July 6, 1873. Pupil of Laurens and Constant in Paris. Member: Wash. WCC. Died in 1934. Address in 1929, 31 General Lee, Marianao, Cuba; summer, Norwich, CT.

JOHNSON, FRANK TENNEY.
Painter and illustrator. Born near Big Grove, IA, June 26, 1874. Pupil of Lorenz, Heinie and Henri, ASL of NY; NY School of Art. Member: ANA; NYWCC; Allied AA; Salma. C.; AFA; SPNY; Laguna Beach AA; CA AC; Painters of the West; AWCS. Awards: Hon. mention, WI PS, 1919; Shaw purchase prize ($1,000), Salma. C., 1923; Edgar B. Davis prize ($1,250) Texas Wild Flower Competition, 1929; silver medal, Brown and Bigelow, Allied AA, 1929. Represented in National Gallery, Washington, DC; Dallas Art Assoc.; main drop curtain and murals, Carthay Circle Theatre, Los Angeles, CA. Died in 1939. Address in 1929, 48 Charles St., New York, NY; 22 Champion Pl., Alhambra, CA.

JOHNSON, G(RACE) M(OTT).
Sculptor. Born New York City, July 28, 1882. Pupil of Gutzon Borglum. Studied at ASL. Member: NA Women PS; Grand Central Gal.; NSS. Awards: McMillin Sculpture prize, NA Women PS, 1917; Joan of Arc medal, NA Women PS, 1927. Specialty, animals. In collections of Whitney and Brookgreen Gardens. Address in 1929, Elmsford, Westchester Co., NY; Santa Fe, NM.

JOHNSON, HARRY LEROY.
Min. painter. Member: PA S. Min. P.; Am. S. Min. P. Address in 1929, 3030 Park Ave, Swarthmore, PA.

JOHNSON, HELEN LESSING.
(Mrs. Frank Edgar Johnson). Painter, illustrator, and etcher. Born Poughkeepsie, NY, May 31, 1865. Pupil of Charles Melville Dewey. Member: Yonkers AA. Died in 1946. Address in 1929, 16 Amackassin Terrace, Yonkers, NY.

JOHNSON, HELEN SEWELL.
Painter, illustrator, and etcher. Born Cambridge, MD, Sept. 1, 1906. Pupil of Charles Hawthorne, Richard Meryman; NAD. Address in 1929, 806 Ambassador Apt.; h. 220 Portner Apts., Washington, DC.

JOHNSON, HERBERT.
Illustrator and cartoonist. Born Sutton, NE, Oct. 30, 1878. Member: SI 1913; Phila. AC; Phila. Sketch C; Phila. Print C; Phila. Alliance; S. Allied A; GFLA. Former connections with Denver Republican; Kansas City Journal; Phila. North American Staff Cartoonist for Saturday Evening Post since 1912. Died in 1946. Address in 1929, Morningside Farm, Huntingdon Valley, PA.

JOHNSON, HORACE C.
Portrait painter. Born in Oxford, CT, in 1824. He was a student of the National Academy, also of the English Life Schools. He settled in Waterbury, CT. Among his pictures are the "Roman Mother," "Rebecca at the Well," and "Italian Girls at the Fountain."

JOHNSON, IRENE CHARLESWORTH.
Sculptor. Born Gering, NE, Sept. 27, 1888. Pupil of Zolany.

Member: Nashville AA. Awards: second prize for sculpture, All Southern Exhibition, 1921; first prize for sculpture, Southern SAL, 1925. Address in 1929, Tereace Garden, Dickerson Rd., Nashville, TN.

JOHNSON, J. THEODORE.
Painter and teacher. Born Oregon, IL, Nov. 7, 1902. Pupil of Leopold G. Seyffert, Leon Kroll, Andre L'hote. Awards: Logan medal and prize of $500, AIC, 1928; Eisendrath prize, AIC 1928; Logan gold medal and prize of $2,500, AIC, 1928; first prize and first popularity prize, Swedish Club, Chicago, 1929; prize ($750), Chicago Galleries Association 1929. Work: "Portrait of Mary" and "The Black Mantilla," Art Institute of Chicago, Chicago, IL. Address in 1929, 147 East Ontario St., Chicago, IL; summer, care of National City Bank, 41 Boulevard Heussmann, Paris, France.

JOHNSON, JEANNE PAYNE.
(Mrs. Louis C. Johnson). Painter. Born near Danville, OH, April 14, 1887. Pupil of ASL of NY; Mme. LaForge, Richard Miller and Lucien Simon in Paris. Exhibited at PAFA in 1925. Died in 1958. Member: Brooklyn S. Min. P.; NA Women PS. Address in 1929, 39 Remsen St., Brooklyn, New York, NY; summer, Stony Brook, LI, NY.

JOHNSON, JESSAMINE INGLEE.
Painter and teacher. Born Delphi, IN, Dec. 2, 1874. Pupil of Herron Art Institute, Indianapolis. Member: Ind. AC. Award: "Friend of Art" prize ($100), Hoosier Salon, Chicago, 1929. Address in 1929, 1221 Central Ave., Connersville, IN.

JOHNSON, JOSEPH HOFFMAN.
Portrait painter. Born in 1821; died in 1890. He painted several portraits for the City of New York.

JOHNSON, MARIE RUNKLE
Painter. Born Flemington, NJ, Dec. 21, 1861. Pupil of Collin, Girardot, Courtois and Prinet, in Paris; Chase, in New York. Member: Calif. AC. Award: Medal, Pan.-Cal. Exp., San Diego, 1915.

Address in 1929, 255 South Fair Oaks Ave., Pasadena, CA.

JOHNSON, MARSHALL.
Painter. Born in Boston. Pupil of Lowell Institute. Painter of the United States Frigate, "Constitution." Died in 1915 in Boston, MA.

JOHNSON, MARY ANN.
Painter. She Excelled in still-life subjects. She died in New London, CT, where much of her best painting was done.

JOHNSON, MERLE DeVORE.
Illustrator. Born Oregon City, OR, Nov. 24, 1874. Member: GFLA. Died in 1935. Address in 1929, 243 West 34th St., New York, NY.

JOHNSON, NEOLA.
Painter, sculptor, illustrator, and teacher. Born Chicago, IL. Pupil of Anthony Angarola and Cameron Booth. Member: Gary PPC. Address in 1929, 1300 West Fifth Ave., Gary, IN; summer, Lindstrom, MN.

JOHNSON, SAMUEL FROST.
Painter. Born in New York City, Nov. 9, 1835. He studied in the life schools of the National Academy and afterwards in the Academies of Brussels and Paris. He painted for some time in London, and on his return to this country accepted a professorship in the Metropolitan Museum. His works include "Les Pommes" shown at the Salon in 1869; "Moorland Landscape;" portraits of Cardinal McCloskey and Lady Helen Blackwood.

JOHNSON, THOMAS.
Wood-engraver. He engraved a series of portraits of musicians in 1878.

JOHNSON, WILLIAM T.
Engraver and/or watercolorist. W. T. Johnson was listed by Stauffer as engraver of subject plates for Sartain's Magazine, c. 1850. This may have been the William T. Johnson of Philadelphia who exhibited a water color drawing at the American Institute in 1849.

JOHNSTON, DAVID CLAYPOOLE.
Engraver. Born in Phila. on Mar. 1799; died at Dorchester, MA, Nov. 8, 1865. In 1815, Johnston was a pupil of the Philadelphia engraver Francis Kearney, and in 1819 he was in business for himself etching caricatures of Philadelphia celebrities. The complaints of some of his victims finally became so loud that the publishers and print-sellers declined to handle his plates. Johnston engraved a few good portraits in stipple and some line illustrations for the Boston publishers, and he also drew upon stone for lithographers. He is best known, however, by his annual publication of "Scraps," first issued in 1830. This Annual was usually made up of four to six sheets, each containing from nine to twelve small etched caricatures of local, social, or political significance, all designed and etched by Johnston. The character and general excellence of these etchings gained for Johnston the name of "The American Cruikshank."

JOHNSTON, HENRIETTA.
Artist. Of her earlier life nothing is known. Emigrated to America in 1707 and settled in Charleston, SC. Untrained, she employed native talent to produce portraits of frank, unadorned directness. They were small, generally 9 by 12 inches and never larger than 14 by 16, and were done in pastels, a technique only then coming into widespread use. She was almost certainly the earliest woman artist in America. Some 40 portraits by her are known, most done between 1707 and 1720. A number of portraits done in NY as late as 1735 have been attributed to her. She died in Charleston on March 9, 1728 or 1729.

JOHNSTON, JOHN
Painter. Born in Boston in 1753; died June 29, 1818. He was the son of Thomas Johnston, who kept a shop in Brattle Street, where he sold colors, made charts, painted coats of arms, and engraved portraits, music plates, etc. John Johnson had military service in the Revolution, reaching the rank of Major, and was an original member

of the "Cincinnati." He painted many portraits of public men of Mass., and his pictures, although deficient in drawing, possessed talent. Also used pastels.

JOHNSTON, JOHN BERNARD.
Landscape painter. Born in Boston in 1847. He was a pupil of William Morris Hunt, and died in 1886. Represented in Boston Museum of Fine Arts by "Landscape with Cattle."

JOHNSTON, MARY G.
Painter and etcher. Born Evansville, IN, Nov. 16, 1872. Pupil of Chautauqua Summer Schools; Charles W. Hawthorne, Richard Miller, and James Hopkins. Member: Louisville AA; Louisville AC; Louisville Handicraft G. Address in 1929, Pewee Valley, KY.

JOHNSTON, MARY VIRGINIA DEL C(ASTILLO).
Painter. Born Puerto Principe, Cuba, Aug. 16, 1865. Pupil of E. H. Andrews, E. C. Messer, and Robert Henri. Member: S. Wash. A.; League of Am. Pen Women. Address in 1929, 563 41st Ave., San Francisco, CA.

JOHNSTON, ROBERT E.
Illustrator. Born Toronto, Canada, Sept. 14, 1885. Pupil of Harvey Dunn; Walter Sickert in London. Member: SI; Arts and Letters Club of Toronto. Address in 1929, 490 Broad Ave., Leonia, NJ.

JOHNSTON, RUTH.
Painter, illustrator, writer, lecturer, and teacher. Born Sparta, GA, April 26, 1864. Pupil of Cos, Beckwith, and Blum. Member: Balto. WCC.; ASL of NY Illustrator for magazines and children's calendars. Formerly Instructor, Maryland Institute, Baltimore. Address in 1929, Pen Lucy, Catonsville, MD.

JOHNSTON, THOMAS I
Engraver. Born in Boston, MA, in 1708; died there May 8, 1767, and was buried in King's Chapel burying ground. The Boston Evening Post (1767) says: "Last Friday Morning, died here Mr. Thomas Johnston, Japanner, Painter and Engraver, after a short illness, being seized

with an Apoplectic Fit a few days before." Johnston was a fairly good engraver of maps, buildings, book-plated, sheet music, etc., and he was also a heraldic painter. His plan of Boston, signed as "Engraven by Thos. Johnson, Boston, N.E.," is dedicated "to His Excellency William Burnet, by the publisher, William Burgis." He was also an organ builder of some reputation in his day. Among his eleven children were William and John, both portrait painters. His engravings are listed in Stauffer's and Fielding's books on American Engraving.

JOHNSTON, THOMAS MURPHY.
Portrait draughtsman in crayons and oils. Born 1834. The latter part of his life he lived in Dorchester. He was the son of David C. Johnston, and was working in Boston, Mass., in 1856-1868.

JOHNSTON, YNEZ.
Painter and printmaker. Born in Berkeley, CA, on May 12, 1920; Studied: Univ. of CA at Berkeley. Awards: Guggenheim fellowship, 1952-53; Tiffany Found. grant, 1955; Met. Mus. of Art, 1952. Collections: Santa Barbara Museum of Art; Met. Mus. of Art; City Art Museum of St. Louis; Los Angeles Mus. of Art; Philbrook Art Center; Univ. of Michigan; Univ. of Illinois; Wadsworth Atheneum; Philadelphia Museum of Art; Whitney. Address in 1980, 579 Crane Blvd., Los Angeles, CA.

JOHNSTONE, JOHN HUMPHREYS.
Painter. Born in New York in 1857. Pupil of John La Farge in New York, and of Lefebvre and Doucet in Paris. His paintings are in the Luxembourg in Paris; Wilstach Gallery, Philadelphia; Carnegie Institute, Pittsburgh. Address in 1926, Paris, France.

JOHNSTONE, WILL.
Illustrator. Member: SI. Address in 1929, care of the "Evening World," Pulitzer Bldg., New York, NY.

JOINER, HARVEY.
Painter. Born Charlestown, IN, April 8, 1852. Self-taught.

Member: Louisville Artists Lg. Specialty, Kentucky beachwoods. Address in 1929, 405 Equitable Bldg., Louisville, KY; h. Prather, IN.

JONES, A. L.
Plates so signed are really engraved by W. S. Lawrence, an apprentice to Alfred Jones, and were finished by Mr. Jones. A further notice of Lawrence will be found in its proper place.

JONES, ALBERTUS EUGENE.
Painter and teacher. Born South Windsor, CT, Oct. 31, 1882. Pupil of Charles Noel Flagg. Member: Conn. AFA; Salma. C.; PCC. Award: Dunham prize, Conn. AFA, 1912 and 1927. Instructor of drawing and painting, Hartford Art Society School. Died in 1957. Address in 1929, South Windsor, CT.

JONES, ALFRED.
Engraver and painter. Born Apr. 7, 1819, in Liverpool, England. Accidentally killed in New York, April 28, 1900. Mr. Jones came to the United States as a very young man and in 1834 he was apprenticed to the engraving firm of Rawdon, Wright, Hatch & Edson, of Albany, NY. He later studied at the National Academy of Design, in New York, and in 1839 he was awarded the first prize in drawing. Mr. Jones was made an Academician of the National Academy in 1851. About 1841 Alfred Jones began engraving over his own name, and in 1843 he engraved in line his first large plate, "The Farmers' Nooning," after the painting by W. S. Mount; this plate was executed for the American Art Union. As a line-engraver Mr. Jones had few, if any, superiors in this country, and his large plate of "The Image Breaker," published by the American Art Union in 1850, is deservedly recognized as one of the best engravings ever produced in the United States. Among other fine examples of his work published by the Art Union are "Mexican News" (1851), "The New Scholar" (1850), and "The Capture of Major Andre." Mr. Jones continued to engrave with undiminished skill up to the time of his death; his late portraits of

Washington, A. B. Durand and Thomas Carlyle being admirable examples of a combination of line work with etching.

JONES, BAYARD.
Illustrator. Born in Rome, GA, in 1869. Pupil of Laurens and Constant in Paris. Address in 1926, 40 West 28th St., New York.

JONES, BENJAMIN.
Engraver. Located in Philadelphia in 1798-1815, inclusive. He engraved in line subject-plates possessing little merit, and Dunlap says that he was living in 1833.

JONES, C(ORA) ELLIS.
Painter. Born Aurora, IL, May 14, 1875. Pupil of Roderick Mackenzie and George Elmer Browne. Member: Birmingham AC; SSAL; Gloucester SA; AFA. Works: "Mount Hood" and "The Pool," Library of Birmingham Southern College. Address in 1929, 2420 Arlington Ave., Birmingham, AL.

JONES, CARMINTA DE SOLMS.
Painter. Exhibited in Penn. Academy of Fine Arts, Philadelphia, 1925. Address in 1926, 1822 Chestnut St., Philadelphia.

JONES, DOROTHY B.
Painter. Born April 27, 1908. Member: Conn. AFA. Awards: Prize, Springfield Art League, 1926; hon. mention, Conn. AFA, 1929. Address in 1929, 34 East 11th St., New York, NY; h. South Windsor, CT.

JONES, ELIZABETH SPARHAWK.
See Sparhawk-Jones.

JONES, EUGENE ARTHUR.
Painter. Born Brooklyn, NY. Pupil of J. H. Boston, Fred'k J. Boston. Member: Brooklyn SA; Allied AA; Salma. C. Work: "Moonlight," Newark Museum, Newark, NJ; "Brooklyn Bridge Twilight," Fort Worth Art Museum, Fort Worth, Tex. Address in 1929, 61 Poplar Ave., Brooklyn, NY.

JONES, FITZGERALD.
This good engraver of subject-plates and portraits in mezzotint and in stipple was

originally a printer in Carlisle, PA. It is not known where or when he learned to engrave, but in 1854 he was in business in Cincinnati, OH, as a "practical portrait, historical and landscape engraver, and Plain and color printer," according to his business-card. He also worked for many years for the Western Methodist Book Concern, of Cincinnati.

JONES, FRANCIS C(OATES).
Painter and teacher. Born Baltimore, MD, July 25, 1857. Pupil of Boulanger and Lefebvre at Ecole des Beaux-Arts in Paris. Member: ANA 1885; NA 1894; SAA 1882; AWCS; NY Arch. Lg. 1888; Mural P; Nat. Inst. A. L.; NAC; A. Aid S.; Century Assoc.; SI; Lotos C.; Salma. C.; AFA. Awards: Clarke prize, NAD 1885; silver medal, Pan-Am. Exp., Buffalo, 1901 silver medal, St. Louis Exp., 1904; Isidor medal, NAD 1913; silver medal, P.-P. Exp., San F., 1915. Address in 1929, 33 West 67th St., New York, NY.

JONES, GRACE CHURCH.
("Jonzi"). Painter and teacher. Born West Falls, NY. Pupil of Colarossi Academy; Academie de la Grande Chaumiere in Paris; ASL of NY. Member: AFA; Denver A Museum. Address in 1929, 2295 E. Louisiana Ave., Denver, CO.

JONES, HUGH BOLTON.
Painter. He was born in Baltimore in 1848, and began his art studies in that city. He went to France in the seventies, and became a member of the artist colony at Pont Aven, in Brittany. Many good pictures from his easel date from that period. Later on he travelled in Spain and in Northern Africa, but for ten or fifteen years he found all his subjects in the United States, whether in picturesque fields and forests of New Jersey, or along the Massachusetts coast. He was elected a National Academician in 1833, and became a member of the Society of American Artists, and the American Water Color Society. Mr. Jones had a studio in New York, but, like many of our landscape painters, spent more months of the year in the country than in town. Address in 1926, 33 West 67th St., New York. Died in 1927.

JONES, JESSIE BARROWS.
Painter and craftsman. Born, Cleveland, OH, March 15, 1865. Pupil of Twachtman, Chase, Hitchcock. Member: Cleveland AA.; Alumni AAO. Cleveland School of Art. Died in 1944. Address in 1929, 11896 Carlton Road, Cleveland, OH; 432 South Beach St., Daytona, FL.

JONES, KEITH.
Illustrator. Born Cardiff, Wales, Jan. 10, 1950. Study: Kingsway-Princeton College and Camden Arts Centre, London, 1974; Livingston College, Rutgers Univ., BA 1982. Work: Jane Voorhees Zimmerli Art Museum & Old Queens Gallery; private collections in Eng., Ger., Greece, Italy, US, Wales. Exhib.: Soc. of Illustrators, NYC, 1981; Arts NW Gallery, Seattle, solo, 1981; 13th Annual Int'l. Exhib., LA WC Soc., New Orleans, 1983; others in NJ, NY. Awards: Certif. of merit, Soc. of Illustrators, 1981; hon. mention, West '82 Art and the Law; Pres. Award for graphics, Knickerbocker Artists 32nd Annual. Address in 1983, 1050 George St., New Brunswick, NJ.

JONES, LEON FOSTER.
Painter. Born Manchester, NH, Oct. 18, 1871. Pupil of Cowles Art School in Boston under Major and DeCamp. Member: Salma. C.; A. Fund S. Award: Silver medal, P.-P. Exp., San. F., 1915. Represented in the Boston Museum of Fine Arts. Died in 1940. Address in 1929, Port Jefferson, LI, NY.

JONES, LOIS MAILOU.
(Mrs. V. Pierre-Noel). Painter. Born in Boston, MA, in 1906. Studied: Boston Normal Art School; Boston Mus. of Fine Arts School; Columbia Univ.; Howard Univ.; and in Paris and Rome. Awards: Fellowship, General Education Board, 1937, 1938; Boston Museum of Fine Arts School, 1926. National Museum, Wash., DC, 1940, 1947, 1954; Corcoran Gallery of Art, 1941, 1949; Atlanta Univ., 1942,

1949, 1952, 1955; Haitian Government, 1954; Lubin award, 1958. Collections: Brooklyn Museum; International Business Machines; Palais National, Haiti; Atlanta Univ.; Howard Univ.; West Virginia State College; Rosenwald Foundation; Retreat for Foreign Missionaries, Wash., DC; Barnett Aden Gallery. Address in 1980, 4706 17th St., NW, Wash., DC.

JONES, LOUIS E(DWARD).
Painter. Born Rushville, PA, Mar. 7. 1878. Pupil of PAFA; Birge Harrison, John F. Carlson. Member: Fellowship PAFA; AFA. Address in 1929, Woodstock, NY.

JONES, MARGUERITE M(IGNON).
Painter and illustrator. Born Chicago, IL, Dec. 12, 1898. Pupil of Chicago, AFA. Member: GFLA. Illustrated: "The Brownie Twins in Pancake Town," by E. B. Neffies (Albert Whitman). Address in 1929, 1466 Pensacola Ave., Chicago, IL.

JONES, MARTHA M(ILES).
Painter, craftsman, and teacher. Born Denison, IA, April 28, 1870. Pupil of Vanderpoel; and studied in Paris. Member: Calif. AC.; San Diego AG; Laguna Beach AA; La Jolla AC; Calif. S. Min. P. Died in 1945. Address in 1929, 4380 Valle Vista, San Diego, CA.

JONES, NANCY C(HRISTINE).
Painter and teacher. Born Providence, RI, May 7, 1888. Pupil of RI School of Design, Charles Hawthorne, Harry Leith-Ross and Fontainebleau School of Fine Arts, Paris. Member: Providence AC; Providence WCC; AFA. Address in 1929, Diamond Hill, Manville, RI.

JONES, NELL CHOATE.
Painter. Born Hawkinsville, GA. Pupil of Fred J. Boston, John Carlson, Ralph Johonnot; Gorguet. Member: Brooklyn SA; NA Women PS.; SSAL; Catherine Lorillard Wolfe AC. Represented in High Museum, Atlanta, GA, and Fort Worth Art Museum, Forth Worth, TX. Address in 1929, 61 Poplar St., Brooklyn, NY; summer, Woodstock, NY.

JONES, PAUL.
Painter. Born Harrodsburg, KY, June 9, 1860. Pupil of Flameng, Courtois, Laurens, and others in Paris. Member: Cincinnati AC (pres.); Duveneck S.; Cincinnati MacD. C. Author of "Marco Polo" and librettist of Grand Opera, "Paoletta." Specialty, portraits. Address in 1929, 2611 Essex Place, Cincinnati, OH.

JONES, R. S.
A line-engraver working in Boston in 1873.

JONES, ROBERT.
Illustrator. Born in Los Angeles, CA, in 1926. Attended the Univ. of Southern CA and ACD. He had practical training as an animator at Warner Brothers Studios before coming to NY in 1952 to join Charles E. Cooper Studio with whom he was associated for 12 years. Many magazines have published his work, most notably The Saturday Evening Post, and among his many advertising clients is Exxon Corporation, for whom he developed the Exxon Tiger as their symbol. A member of the S of I for 20 years, he was awarded a Gold Medal from their 1967 Annual Exhibition.

JONES, S. K.
Born in Clinton, CT, in Feb., 1825. After 1861 he painted in New Haven, his specialty being portraits.

JONES, SETH C.
Painter, illustrator, and teacher. Born Rochester, NY, July 15, 1853. Pupil of Wm. H. Holmes and Thomas Moran. Member: Rochester AC; Picture Painters C; Municipal Art Com.; Chicago A.G. Address in 1929, Municipal Bldg.; h. 137 Frost Ave., Rochester, NY; summer, Linden, NY.

JONES, SUSAN.
Painter, illustrator, and teacher. Born Phila., PA, Dec. 12, 1897. Pupil of PAFA. Member: Fellowship, PAFA. Work: Portrait covers for "Mary," "Marge," and "Michael" by Nelia Gardner White; Still-life illus. for "Wearever Aluminums" catalogue. Address in 1929, 3845 North Park Ave., Phila. PA.

JONES, THOMAS
Painter. Exhibited at the Penn.
Academy, Philadelphia, in 1924.
Address in 1926, 5113 Chester Ave.,
Philadelphia, PA.

JONES, THOMAS DOW.
Sculptor. Born Dec. 11, 1811, in
Oneida Co., NY. Little is known of
him except from letters written by
him in October and November, 1857,
to Honorable Lewis Cass and Capt.
Meigs. The letters refer to a bust
of the Honorable Lewis Cass
executed nine years previous to
this time. He also refers to a bust
of Honorable John C. Breckenridge,
on which he was then engaged, and
to the fact that he himself was a
western sculptor. In November,
1857, he resided in Cincinnati, OH.
He was elected an Associate Member
of the National Academy in 1853.
He died Feb. 27, 1881, in Columbus,
OH.

JONES, THOMAS HUDSON.
Sculptor. Born Buffalo, NY, July
24, 1892. Award: Prix-de-Rome,
1919-22. Work: "Gen. U. S. Grant,"
Hall of Fame, New York; portrait
figure "Dr. Moore," Park in
Rochester, NY; medal, Columbia
University, NY; Skinner Memorial
Relief, Holyoke, Mass.; Munger
Relief Birmingham, Ala.; Figure,
"Christ," St. Matthews Church,
Washington, DC; Eno Memorial,
Trinity College, Hartford, Conn.;
Trowbridge Portrait, American
Academy, Rome, Italy; William
Rutherford Mead Portrait, NYC;
Meldrum Memorial Relief, Library,
Houston, Tex.; Morton Memorial,
Burlington, Wis.; Awarded sculpture
for Tomb of Unknown Soldier,
Arlington National Cemetery.
Address in 1929, 144 Bleecker St.,
New York, NY.

JONES, WILLIAM FOSTER.
Born 1815 in Penn. An American
portrait and historical painter
working in Philadelphia about 1850.
He also painted miniatures, several
being signed and dated 1847-1849,
and worked in crayon.

JONES, WILLIAM R.
Engraver of portraits in the
stipple manner. Born in the United
States. He first appears in

Philadelphia in 1810, when he was
an Associate of the Society of
Artists of the United States,
organized in Philadelphia in that
year. As an engraver his name
appears in the directories of
Philadelphia in 1811-24, inclusive.

JONGERS, ALPHONSE.
Portrait painter. Born in France,
Nov. 17, 1872. Pupil of Ecole des
Beaux-Arts under Delaunay and
Gustave Moreau; studied two years
in Spain. Came to US in 1897.
Member: SAA 1905; ANA 1906; Lotos
C. Awards: Silver medal, St.
Louis Exp., 1904; third class
medal, Paris Salon, 1909. Work:
"William T. Evans," National
Gallery, Washington, DC; "Louise"
and "Arthur H. Hearn," Metropolitan
Museum, New York, NY. Died Oct. 2,
1945.

JONNIAUX, ALFRED
Painter. Born in Brussels,
Belgium; US citizen. Study: Acad.
Beaux Arts, Brussels; Calvin
Coolidge College of Liberal Arts.
Work: de Young Mem. Mus., San
Fran.; Palais des Beaux Arts,
Brussels; Royal Soc. Portrait
Ptrs., London; US Capitol, Wash.;
Brandeis Univ.; plus others.
Exhibitions: Smithsonian Inst.
Invit.; Royal Acad., London;
Kennedy Galleries, NYC; and others.
Address in 1976, 712 Bay Street,
San Francisco, CA.

JONSON, C. RAYMOND.
See Jonson, Raymond.

JONSON, JAMES.
Illustrator. Born in St. Louis,
MO, in 1928. Attended Wash. Univ.
and the Jepson Art School of Los
Angeles. His first work appeared
in Westways in 1948 and he has
since won awards from the Los
Angeles ADC, the S of I and First
Prize at the National Art Mus. of
Sport Competition. He has
illustrated several sports books
and many magazines, including Look,
The Saturday Evening Post,
Seventeen, Playboy, Boys' Life, Ski
and Sports Illustrated. His works
are in the collections of Circle
Galleries, Ltd. Currently he is
producing lithographics at the
American Atelier.

JONSON, RAYMOND.
Painter. Born Chariton, IA, July 18, 1891. Pupil of W. J. Reynolds and B. J. O. Nordfeldt. Member; MacDowell Colony. Work: "The Bur Reed," a decoration, City of Chicago; "Irony," University of Oklahoma, Norman; "Mountain Vista," Mississippi Art Assoc., Jackson, Miss.; "The Temple," Milwaukee Art Inst.; "Earth Rhythms No. 1," Corona Mundi, New York; "Light," Museum of Mexico, Santa Fe. Address in 1929, Camino Atalaya, Sante Fe, NM.

JORDAN, DAVID W(ILSON)
Landscape painter. Born Harrisburg, PA, June 2, 1859. Pupil of PAFA under Schussele and Eakins. Member: Phila. Sketch C; Fellowship PAFA. Address in 1929, 43 West 87th St., New York, NY.

JORDAN, F(REDD) E(LMER).
Sculptor and craftsman. Born Bedford, IN, Nov. 25, 1884. Award: Prize ($200), Hoosier Salon, Chicago, 1928. Address in 1929, 559 Hendrie St., Detroit, MI.

JORDAN, HENRY.
Born in England. Came to the United States about 1836, and was for a time in the employ of Alfred Jones, in New York City. Jordan was good line-engraver of landscape, and was later a member of the engraving firm of Jordan & Halpin. He returned to England for a time, but ultimately settled in the United States.

JORDAN, MILDRED C.
Miniature painter. Born in Portland, ME. Pupil of Yale School of Fine Arts. Member: New Haven Paint and Clay Club. Address in 1926, 129 Whalley Ave., New Haven, CT.

JORGENSEN, JORGEN.
Painter, sculptor, and etcher. Born Denmark, Dec. 6, 1871. Member: S. Indp. A.; Newark Outdoor Sketch C. Etchings in the Newark Museum. Address in 1929, 10 Franklin Ave., Maplewood, NJ.

JOSEPH, ADELYN L.
Sculptor and illustrator. Born in Chicago in 1895. Pupil of Mulligan and Polasek. Member: Chicago Society of Artists; Society of Women Sculptors. Address in 1926, 4334 Drexel Blvd., Chicago, IL.

JOSEPH, JOAN A.
Sculptor. Exhibited "The Art Student" at the Academy of Fine Arts, Philadelphia, 1924. Address in 1926, 4320 Drexel Boulevard, Chicago, IL.

JOSEPHI, (ISAAC).
Miniature painter and landscape painter. Born in New York. Pupil of ASL of NY; Bonnat in Paris. Member: AS Min. P.; AWCS; Royal Soc. of Min. Painters, London; Lotos C. Awards: Hon. mention, Paris Exp., 1900; silver medal, Charleston Exp., 1902. Address in 1929, 924 West End Ave.; 2178 Broadway, New York, NY.

JOSEPHS, WALTER W.
Painter. Born Philadelphia, PA, Feb. 11, 1887. Pupil of PAFA; Daniel Garber. Member: Phila. AC. Address in 1929, 200 South 15th St., Philadelphia, PA.

JOSHI, SATISH.
Painter. Born in India on Feb. 28, 1944. He emigrated to US in 1969. Studied at New Delhi College of Art, India. In collections of Pratt Inst.; Whitney, NYC; CBS; Lalitkela Academy of India; others. Exhibited at galleries in India, 1966, 1967, 1968; Columbia Univ., NYC, 1975; Gallery One, NYC, 1975; Silvermine Guild, 1977; Bronx Museum of Arts, NY, 1981; Phoenix Gallery, NYC, 1982; Cygnus Gallery, San Diego, CA, 1983; many other group and solo shows. Received Royal Drawing Society of London special achievement award, 1963. Teaches at Riverdale (NY) Country School. Lives and works in NYC. Represented by The Phoenix Gallery, NYC; Corporate Art Source, Chicago; Cygnus Gallery, San Diego.

JOSIMOVICH, GEORGE. M
Painter. Born Mitrovica, Srem, Yugoslavia, May 3, 1894. Pupil of AIC; George Bellows, Randall Davy. Member; Chicago SA; NJSA; S. Indp. A. Address in 1929, 1460 East 57th St.; h. 5509 Everett Ave., Chicago, IL.

JOSLYN, FLORENCE BROWN.
Painter and illustrator. Pupil of John Carlson. Member: Assoc. of Okla. Artists. Address in 1929, 628½ West 9th St., Oklahoma City, OK.

JOUETT, MATTHEW HARRIS.
Portrait painter. Born in Mercer County, KY, Apr. 22, 1787., died in Lexington KY, Aug. 10, 1827. After studying with Gilbert Stuart in Boston, he returned to Lexington, KY, and there painted many portraits. He also worked in Natches, Louisville, and New Orleans. About 350 portraits have been recorded as painted by him. He is represented in the Metropolitan Museum of New York by his portrait of John Grimes.

JOULLIN, AMEDEE.
Painter. Born in San Francisco on June 13, 1862. Studied there and in France. Her specialty was Indian pictures. She is represented in many galleries in California. She died in San Francisco on Feb. 3, 1917.

JOULLIN, LUCILE.
See Benjamin, Mrs. L. J.

JOURDAIN, JEAN.
(Dorothy Jean Jordan). Painter. Born in New London, CN, May 13, 1912. Study: Art Students Lg., NYC, under Oscar Van Young, Francis de Erdley, Leonard Edmondson. Work: Represented in numerous coll. in the US, Can., Europe. One-woman shows: Pasadena Art Mus.; Occidental Col.; Palos Verdes Art Assn.; Cowie Gal., Los Angeles; Amerson Gal., Tucson, AZ; and many others. Exhib.: Nat'l Gal. of CN, Ottawa; MOMA, NYC; Metropolitan Mus. of Art, NYC; Honolulu Acad. of Arts, HI; Toronto Mus. of Art, CN; Cleveland Mus. of Art; Marion Koogler McNay Mus., San Antonio, TX; de Young Mus., San F., CA; Palace of Legion of Arts, San F.; San Diego Mus.; Santa Barbara Mus.; and many others. Awards: Pasadena Art Mus.; Los Angeles Co. Mus.; CA State Fair; Laguna Festival of Arts; CA Watercolor Society. Mem.: Pasadena Society of Artists; CA WC Soc.; board of Pasadena Art Mus.

Address in 1983, 3726 Canyon Crest Road, Altadena, CA.

JU, I-HSIUNG.
Painter and educator. Born in Kiangsu, China, Sept. 15, 1923. Study: Nat'l. Univ. of Amoy, China; Univ. of Santo Tomas, Manila. Work: Philippine Cult. Ctr., Manila; Nat'l. Mus. of Hist., Taipei, Taiwan; Int'l. Ctr., Univ. of CT; DuPont Art Gallery, Wash. & Lee Univ.; and others. Comn: Gulf States Paper Co., Tuscaloosa, AL; many more. Exhibitions: Asian Arts Festival, Univ. of Philippines; 10th Japan Nan-ga-in Exhib., Tokyo, Kyoto, and Osaka Mus.; Nat'l. Ptg. & Callig. Exhib.: Nat'l. Gallery, Taipei; etc. Awards: South-East Asia Art Exhibit; Chinese Artists' League; Art Educ. of the Year, Taiwan; Contrib. to the Arts award, Nat'l. Mus. of Hist., Taipei; etc. Teaching: U. of VA and Washington & Lee U., 1969 to pres.; plus others. Mem.: VA Mus. of Fine Arts; Coll. Art Assn. of Am. Media: Ink, acylic, watercolor. Address in 1982, Washington & Lee Univ., Lexington, VA.

JUDKINS, MISS E. M.
Portrait artist in crayons, who worked in New England about 1847.

JUDSON, ALICE.
Painter. Born Beacon, NY. Pupil of ASL of NY and J. H. Twachtman. Member; NA Women PS.; Eclectics; Pitts. AA.; North Shore AA; Gloucester SA; Plastic C; PBC; Wash. WCC; AM. APL. Award: Russell Memorial Prize, Pitts. AA. Work: Over mantle decoration, Administration Bldg., Mattewan State Hospital, Beacon, NY; "The Day's Done," Pittsburgh Friends of Art. Died April 3, 1948. Address in 1929, 58 West 57th St., New York, NY; h. 9 Leonard St., Beacon, NY.

JUDSON, ALMIRA.
Painter. Born Milwaukee, WI. Pupil of Woman's Academy, Munich; Colarossi and Garrido Studios in Paris; Henri in New York. Member: San Francisco S. Women A. Address in 1929, 123 Edgewood Ave., San

495

Francisco, CA; summer, Los Gatos, CA.

JUDSON, MINNIE LEE.
Landscape painter. Born Milford, CT, Oct. 20, 1865. Pupil of Yale School of Fine Arts. Member: Conn. AFA; New Haven PCC; AFA. Died in 1939. Address in 1929, Main St., Stratford, CT.

JUDSON, WILLIAM LEES.
Painter. Born in Manchester, England, in 1842. Came to America in 1852. Pupil of J. B. Irving in New York, and of Boulanger and Lefebvre in Paris. Address in 1926, 212 Thorne St., Los Angeles, CA. Died in 1928.

JUENGLING, FREDERICK.
Engraver and painer. Born in New York City in 1846. He studied art there and attained high rank as an engraver. He was a founder of the American Society of Wood-Engravers. He received honorable mention at the Paris Salon. Among his works are "The Professor," engraved after Duveneck, "The Voice of the Sea." His paintings include "The Intruder," "Westward Bound," and "In the Street". He died in 1889.

JUERGENS, ALFRED.
Painter. Born Chicago, Aug. 5, 1866. Pupil of Chicago AD; Munich Royal Academy, under Gysis and Diez. Member: Chicago SA; Munich Artists Assoc.; Artists Assoc. of Ger.; Soc. Inter. des Beaux-Arts. Awards: Silver medal, Madrid and Munich; Cahn prize ($100), AIC 1914; bronze medal, P.-P. Exp., San F., 1915; William Randolph Hearst $300 prize, AIC; Business Men's AC Prize ($200), AIC, 1923. Work: "John the Baptist at the River Jordan" and "Suffer Little Children to Come Unto Me," St. Paul's Church, Chicago; "November Afternoon," Cliff Dwellers Club, Chicago; "Afternoon in May," Municipal Gallery, Art Institute, Chicago, 1913; "Lilac Time," Union League Club, Chicago; "A Lilac Bush," Clark Gallery, Grand Rapids, MI; "Field Flowers," Women's City Club; "The Lilac," West End Woman's City Club, Chicago, IL; "A Ravine in Winter," Oak Park Club, IL.

Address in 1929, 213 South Grove Ave., Oak Park, IL.

JULIO, E. B. D. FABRINO.
Painter. Born on the Island of St. Helena, of an Italian father and a Scotch mother, in 1843. He died in Georgia in 1879. Specialty, portraits, genre and landscape. Julio came to the United States in 1861, and to New Orleans in the latter part of the "60's," where he resided the greater part of the time during the remainder of his life, except the year 1872, which he spent in Paris as a student of Leon Bonnat. His "Diana," "Harvest Scene," and several Louisiana landscapes were exhibited at the Centennial at Philadelphia in 1876.

JULIUS, OSCAR H.
Painter. Member: Salma. C.; AWCS; Allied AA. Address in 1929, 67 West 87th St., New York, NY.

JULIUS, VICTOR.
Painter, illustrator, and teacher. Born Boston, MA, July 26, 1882. Pupil of NAD, ASL of NY. Member: NYWCC; Salma. C.; A. Fellowship. Address in 1929, 67 West 87th St., New York, NY; Malvern, LI, NY. Died before 1940.

JUNGE, CARL S(TEPHEN).
Painter and illustrator. Born Stockton, CA, June 5, 1880. Pupil of Hopkins Art Inst., San Francisco; Chicago AI; School of Art in London; Julian Academy in Paris. Member: Chicago Allied AA; Oak Park and River Forest AG; Chicago Writers G. Awards: Prizes 1916, 1917, 1922, and 1925 from American Bookplate Society; 1926 from the Bookplate Assoc. International. Author and illustrator of "Bookplates"; author and designer "Junge Decorators". Represented in Library of Congress, Washington; Museum Fine Arts, Boston; Metropolitan Museum of Art; British Museum. Address in 1929, 143 South Harvey Ave., Oak Park, IL.

JURECKA, CYRIL.
Sculptor. Born Moravia, Czechoslovakia on July 4, 1884. Pupil of Academy of Fine Arts, Prague. Member: Calif. AC. Died

496

in 1960. Address in 1929, 1115 N.
El Centro Ave., Hollywood, CA.

JUSTICE, JOSEPH.
Engraver. In 1804 Justice was
working in New York in connection
with Scoles, and the directories of
Philadelphia locate him in that
city as an engraver from 1810 until
1833. His plates show an
ineffective combination of etchings
and stipple work, poorly done.

JUSTICE, MARTIN.
Illustrator and painter. Member:
SI 1911. Address in 1929, 945
Orange St., Los Angeles, CA; 1832
Ivar Ave., Hollywood, CA.

JUSTIS, LYLE.
Illustrator. Born in Manchester,
VA, in 1892. He was considered a
master of pen and ink despite his
lack of formal art training. His
first published works were sheet
music illustrations which led to
assignments from major magazines
and several advertising clients.
Among his best known illustrations
were those done for the Grosset and
Dunlap 1930 edition of Robert Louis
Stevenson's Treasure Island. Noted
for his historical drawings, he was
a member of the Sketch Club and Pen
and Pencil Club. Died in 1960.

JUSZKO, J(ENO).
Sculptor. Born in Hungary, Nov.
26, 1880. Member: NSS; Salma. C.;
Am. Numismatic Soc.; NY Arch. Lg.
Work: Monument of Archbishop Samy,
Santa Fe, NM. Died in 1954.
Address in 1929, 59 East 59th St.,
New York, NY.

KACERE, JOHN.
Painter. Born June 23, 1920 in Walker, Iowa. Earned B.F.A. and M.F.A. from State U. of Iowa. Taught at U. of Manitoba, U. of Fla.; Cooper Union, Parsons and U. of N. Mexico. Exhibited at Labriskie Gallery, Allan Stone Gallery (Both NYC); MOMA; Corcoran; Yale; U. of Colo.; Walker Art Center; Mus. of Contemp. Art, Chicago; Byron Gallery, NYC. In collections of Yale; Mt. Holyoke College; Wadsworth; Brandeis U.; and Stedelijk Mus., Amsterdam.

KAELIN, CHARLES SALIS.
Painter. Born in Cincinnati in 1858. Pupil of Cincinnati Art School; Art Students' League of New York; Cincinnati Museum Association. Exhibited at Paris Exposition, 1900. Member: Society Western Artists; Cincinnati Art Club. Address in 1926, Rockport, Mass.

KAESELAU, CHARLES ANTON.
Painter. Born Stockholm, Sweden, June 25, 1889. Pupil of Charles W. Hawthorne. Member: Amer. Scandinavian Foundation; Provincetown AA. Work: "Mother and Child," Zachau Gallery, Uddevalla, Sweden; "Ice Floes," Provincetown Art Museum. Address in 1929, Court St.; h. 530 Commercial St., Provincetown, Mass.

KAHILL, JOSEPH B.
Portrait painter. Born Alexandria, Egypt. May 15, 1882. Pupil of Charles L. Fox, Richard Miller, Collin and Prinet in Paris. Member: Paris AAA; PSA of Portland. Represented in Walker Art Gallery of Bowdoin College and the Sweat Memorial Museum, Portland, ME. Died in 1957. Address in 1929, 562 Congress St.; h. 2 Crescent St., Portland, ME.

KAHILL, VICTOR.
Sculptor. Exhibited "A Study," at the Penna. Academy of Fine Arts, Philadelphia, 1924. Address in 1926, 3610 Spring Garden St., Philadelphia.

KAHLE, JULIE.
Painter. Member: NA Women PS.; A.S. Min. P.; Pa. Soc. Min. P.

Address in 1929, 325 West End Ave., New York, NY. Died in 1937.

KAHLER, CARL.
Painter. Exhibited at Philadelphia, 1921, Academy of Fine Arts, Exhibition of "Paintings Showing the Later Tendencies in Art." Address in 1926, 49 West 8th St., New York City.

KAHN, ISAAC.
Painter and sculptor. Born Cincinnati, Aug. 16, 1882. Pupil of Duveneck. Member: Cin. AC; Ceramic Soc. Address in 1929, 4609 Eastern Ave.; h. 327 Kemper Lane Apts., Cincinnati, Ohio.

KAINZ, MARTIN.
Painter and etcher. Born Dachau, Bavaria, Germany, May 7, 1899. Pupil of Munich Academy. Member: New Rochelle AA. Address in 1929, 1071 Clay Ave., Pelham Manor, NY.

KAISER, AUGUST.
Painter, illustrator and etcher. Born in Germany in 1889. Address in 1926, 11 East 35th St., New York.

KAISER, CHARLES.
Illustrator. Member: SI.; GFLA. Address in 1929, 119 East 34th St., New York, NY; 175 Beachwood Ave., Mt. Vernon, NY.

KAISH, MORTON.
Born Jan. 8, 1927. In Newark, NJ. Earned B.F.A. from Syracuse; studies at Chaumiere, Paris and Institute d'Arte, Florence. Taught at Everson Mus. of Art, Syracuse; Dartmouth and Columbia Rec. H. T. Leavenworth award at Syracuse (1949). Awards from Everson (1950) and Am. Printmakers (1962). Exhibited at Staempfli Gallery (1964); MOMA; Art Inst. of Chicago (1964); U. of Nebraska; New School of Soc. Research; Whitney; and Am. Inst. of Arts & Letters (Multiple). In collections of Syracuse; Phil. Print Club, Brooklyn Mus. and private collections.

KAJIWARA, TAKUMA.
Painter. Born Japan, Nov. 15, 1876. Member: St. Louis AG.; 2x4 Soc., St. Louis; AFA. Award: First portrait prize, St. Louis AG,

498

1922; Carl Weimar prize, St. Louis AG., 1924; silver medal, Kansas City Al., 1926; Mallinckrodt portrait prize, 1926; Baldwin portrait prize, 1928. Exhibited at PAFA, 1925. Died in 1960. Address in 1929, 750 Century Bldg.; h. Jefferson Hotel, St. Louis, MO.

KALB, MARTY JOEL.
Painter. Born in Brooklyn, NY, April 13, 1941. Study: MI State Univ.; Yale Univ.; Univ. of CA, Berkeley. Work: Speed Mus., Louisville, KY.; Ohio Wesleyan; Univ. of MA. Exhib.: Columbus (OH) Gallery of Fine Art Invit.; Canton (OH) Art Inst.; others. Awards: Ohio Arts Council Grant. Teaching: Ohio Wesleyan Univ., 1967 to present. Mem.: Coll. Art Assn. of Am. Media: Acylic. Dealer: Allan Stone Gallery, NYC. Address in 1982, 165 Griswold St., Delaware, OH.

KALDENBERG, FREDERICK ROBERT.
Sculptor. Born in New York in 1855; died 1923. Self-taught in art. Took up carving in meerschaum at ten years of age, and at fourteen commenced ivory carving, being the first native American to do this work. Some of his productions were in the possession of the late Russian Emperor, the King of Belgium and the Presidents of Venezuela and Mexico, and among the relics of Gen. US Grant; also in the gallery of George W. Vanderbilt, the Smithsonian Inst., and the palace of Li Hung Chang, etc.

KALISH, MAX.
Sculptor. Born Poland, March 1, 1891. Pupil of Matzen, Adams, Calder, Injalbert. Member: AFA. Awards: First prize for sculpture. Cleveland Museum of Art, 1924 and 1925. Work: "Laborer at Rest" and "Torso," Cleveland Museum of At. Died in 1945.

KALLEM, MORRIS J.
Painter. Exhibited portraits at Annual Exhibition, 1925, of National Academy of Design, New York. Address in 1926, 1916 Grand Concourse, New York.

KALLOS, ARPAD.
Painter. Born Hungary, Sept. 9, 1882. Pupil of Edward Ballo and Julius Benczur. Member: Soc. Hungarian A.; Cleveland SA. Awards: Prize for nude, 1916 and Countess Nadanyl prize, 1917 at the Hungarian National Exhibition. Work: "Nude in Violet" and "Nude in Red," Hungarian Andrassy Museum, Budapest; "Briedermeyer," owned by the former Hapsburg Dynasty of Austria-Hungary.

KALTENBACH, LUCILE.
Painter, illustrator and writer. Born Durban, South Africa. Pupil of AIC; John Norton; Allen St. John; Andre L'hote in Paris. Member: Alumni AIC; ASL of Chicago. Award: Municipal Art League prize, ASL of Chicago, 1927; Rogers Park Woman's Club prize, AIC, 1928. Specialty, water color painting. Address in 1929, 4101 Grace St., Chicago, Ill.

KAMP, GLINTEN.
Painter. Exhibited water colors at the PAFA, 1925. Address in 1926, 19 East 16th St., New York City.

KAMPF, MELISSA Q.
Painter and teacher. Born Philadelphia, May 1, 1867. Pupil of Chase, Poore, Carolus Duran. Member: S. Indp. A.; Norfolk VA. Award: Gold medal, Norfolk VA, 1922. Address in 1929, 722 Virginia Ave., Norfolk, VA; summer, Chenango Lake, South New Berlin, NY.

KANE, JOHN.
Painter. Born in 1860 in Scotland. Emmigrated to US with parents in 1871, settling in Pittsburgh. Worked in coal mines since the age of 9 and at numerous other laboring jobs with the railroad and steel mills. Lost a leg in a train mishap in 1891. As a result, he took up his childhood passion of painting. Untrained artist. Painted pictures for pleasure, painted railroad cars, portraits on beaverboard. Did portraiture for working class people in Pittsburgh, PA. At age 67, 1927, 1st exhibit at Carnegie Institute's Pittsburgh International. His most famous

work is entitled "Self-Portrait," painted in 1929. Media: oil.

KANE, MARGARET BRASSLER.
Sculptor. Born in East Orange, NJ, in May 25, 1909. Studied: Syracuse Univ.; Art Students' League; and with John Hovannes. Awards: National Association of Women Artists, 1942, 1951; NJ State Exhibition, 1943; NY Architectural League, 1944; Brooklyn Museum, 1946, 1951; Greenwich Society of Art, 1952, 1954, 1958; Silvermine Guild Art, 1954-1956. Collections: US Maritime Commission, Fairplay, Colorado; Limited Editions Lamp Company. Address in 1980, 30 Strickland Rd., Cos Cob, CT.

KANTOR, MORRIS.
Painter. Born in Russia, April 15, 1896. Arrived in US in 1911. Studied and taught at ASL. Pupil of Homer Boss. Member: S. Indp. A. Died in 1974. Rep. at the Art Inst. of Chicago, MMA, Mus. of Modern Art, and the Detroit Institute of Art. Address in 1929, 1947 Broadway, New York, NY.

KAPPEL, PHILIP.
Painter, illustrator and etcher. Born Hartford, Conn., Feb. 10, 1901. Pupil of Pratt Inst.; Philip Little. Member: North Shore AA; Marblehead AA; Chic. SE; MacDowell C. of NY; AFA. Awards: First prize, Marblehead AA, 1925; Bijur prize, Brooklyn SE, Brooklyn Museum, 1926. Illustrated: "The Story of Man's Work," and "Lord Timothy Dexter" (Minton Balch & Co.). Represented in "Fine Prints of the Year," 1926 and 1927; and Bibliotheque Nationale, Paris. Address in 1929, 500 Fifth Ave., New York, NY; summer, care of Philip Little, Salem, Mass.

KAPPEL, R. ROSE.
(Mrs. Irving Gould). Painter. Born in Hartford, CT, in 1910. Studied: Pratt Institute Art School; NY Univ.; Harvard Univ.; Fordham Univ.; Wash. Univ. Award: NAD, 1956. Collections: Library of Congress; Gloucester Art Assoc.; Boston Museum of FA; Cleveland Museum of Art; Fogg Museum of Art; Culture & Health School, Brooklyn.

Address in 1980, 35-36 76th St., Jackson Heights, NY.

KAPPES, KARL.
Painter and teacher. Born Zanesville, Ohio, May 28, 1861. Pupil of William M. Chase in New York; Benjamin Constant in Paris; Carl Marr in Munich. Member: Scarab C; AFA. Died in 1943. Address in 1929, 410 Monroe St., Toledo, Ohio; summer, Liberty Center, Ohio.

KAPPES, WALTER.
Painter of Black American Life.

KARASZ, ILONKA.
Painter, illustrator, craftsman, and teacher. Born Budapest, July 13, 1896. Studied at Royal School of Arts and Crafts, Budapest. Member: Am. Union Dec. A. Address in 1929, 140 East 34th St., New York, NY; summer, Brewster, NY.

KARCHIN, STEVE.
Illustrator. Born in Brooklyn, NY, in 1953. Attended PI from 1971 to 1974 where he studied under Jerry Contreras and David Byrd. His first work appeared in Guideposts in 1974. Selected for every Annual Exhibition of the S of I since 1973, his editorial illustrations have been published in Redbook, American Way and Guideposts and he has done several covers from Avon.

KARFIOL, BERNARD.
Painter. Born May 6, 1886 in Brooklyn Ny. Awards: Hon. Mention, Pan- American, Los Angeles, 1925; hon. mention. International Exhib. Carnegie Inst. Pittsburgh, 1927; W. A. Clark first prize and Corcoran gold medal, 1928, Washington. Represented in Corcoran Gallery and Phillips Memorial Gallery, Washington, DC, and Newark Museum, Newark, NJ. Author of many non-fiction books, including Wilderness: A Journal of Quiet Adventure in Alaska, and Greenland Journal. Elected hon. memb. U.S.S.R. Acad. of Art. Died Aug. 16, 1952. Address in 1929, 136 West 77th St., New York, NY; summer, Ogunquit, ME.

KARFUNKLE, DAVID.
Painter, sculptor and etcher. Born in Austria. Pupil of NAD, New York. Address in 1926, 13 East 14th St., New York City.

KARLIN, EUGENE.
Illustrator. Born in Kenosha, Wisconsin in 1918. He received scholarships from The Chicago Professional School of Art, AIC and ASL. He is presently a teacher at the SVA and has won numerous awards from the ADC, AIC, S of I and AIGA. He has illustrated for all the major magazines and done extensive book illustration for such publishing houses as Macmillan, Golden Press, Random House, Houghton Mifflin, Bantam, and many others.

KARST, JOHN.
Wood engraver. Born in Germany in 1836; died in De Bruce, NY, in 1922, having lived his entire professional life in this country.

KASE, PAUL G(EORGE).
Painter and craftsman. Born Reading, PA, Nov. 4, 1896. Pupil of Breckenridge and PAFA. Member: Fellowship PAFA; AFA. Work: "Rocks, Bluff Point," Reading Museum of Art.

KASSOY, HORTENSE.
Sculptor. Born in Brooklyn, NY, on Feb. 14, 1917. Studied: Pratt Institute; Columbia Univ.; Univ. of Colorado. She was awarded a prize at Painter's Day at the NY World's Fair. Exhibitions: Toledo Museum, Ohio, 1947; A.C.A. Gallery, 1954; National Academy of Design, 1962; Brooklyn Museum, 1974; Lincoln Center, 1975. Vice President of Artists Equity Assoc. of NY, 1975. Media: Wood, marble, batik, watercolor. Address in 1980, 130 Gale Pl., Bronx, NY.

KASTEL, ROGER K.
Illustrator. Born in White Plains, NY, in 1931. Attended the ASL and Frank Reilly School of Art for six years. His first published work appeared in 1962 for Pocket Books at which time he was also free-lancing for advertising agencies. Included among the many paperback covers which he has illustrated is the much publicized Jaws, published by Bantam. His works have been exhibited at the Salmagundi Club and the Grand Central Gallery in New York.

KAT, WILLIAM.
Painter and etcher. Born Holland, April 27, 1891. Pupil of School van Kunstnyverheid, Holland. Member: AWCS (asso.); AGA. Work: "Peat Ships," Oberlin College, Oberlin, Ohio. Address in 1929, 89 Seaman Ave., New York, NY.

KATES, HERBERT S.
Illustrator and etcher. Born New York City, Jan. 12, 1894. Member: SI. Works: Illustration for Harper's Magazine, Arts and Decoration, The Sketch Book Magazine, etc. Address in 1929, 48 West 48th St., New York, NY; h. 33 Halcyon Terrace, New Rochelle, NY.

KATO, KENTARO.
Painter. Born in Japan in 1889. Won second Hallgarten prize, National Academy of Design, 1920. Address in 1926, 680 Fifth Avenue New York.

KATOAKA, GENJIRO.
Painter. Born in Japan in 1867. Came to America and studied with Twachtman in New York. Member of New York Water Color Club. Address in 1926, Tokio, Japan.

KATZ, HILDA.
(Hilda Weber). Painter. Born June 2, 1909. Studied: National Academy of Design; New School for Social Research. She is also a graphic artist. Awards: National Assoc. of Women Artists, 1945, 1947; Mississippi Art Assoc., 1947; Society of American Graphic Artists, 1950. Collections: Library of Congress; Baltimore Museum of Art; Fogg Museum of Art; Santa Barbara Museum of Art; Colorado Springs Fine Arts Center; Society of American Graphic Artists; Pennell Collection; Syracuse Univ.; Calif. State Library; NY Public Library; Addison Gallery of American Art; Newark Public Library; Penn. State Teachers College; Springfield Missouri Art Museum; Penn. State Univ.; Metropolitan Museum of Art;

Bezalel Museum, Israel. Address in 1980, 915 West End Ave., NY, NY.

KATZ, MORRIS.
Painter. Born in Poland, March 5, 1932. Study: Ulm, West Germany, and Gunsburg; with Hans Facler; ASL. Work: Evansville Mus. of Arts & Sci., Indiana; Butler Inst. of Am. Art, Youngstown, Ohio; St. Lawrence Univ. Art Ctr., Canton, NY; and many more. Exhibitions: Instant Art Shows worldwide. Mem.: Am. Guild of Variety Artists; Int'l. Platform Assn.; Artists Equity Assn.; Int'l. Arts Guild, Monaco. Technique: Instant art -- use of palette knife with tissue paper and liberally applied paint. Media: Oil, pencil. Address in 1982, 406 6th Avenue, New York, NY.

KATZEN, LILA.
Sculptor and educator. Born in NYC. Studied: The Art Students' League, NYC; Cooper Union, NY. Awards: Goodyear Fellow, Foxcroft School, Virginia; Creative Arts, The American Association of Univ. Women; Corcoran Gallery of Art, Wash., DC 1959; Fellowship, Tiffany Found., 1964. Commissions: Lannan Foundation, Palm Beach, Florida; Architectural League of NY; Chesapeake & Potomac Telephone Company, Baltimore, Maryland. Media: Plastics and steel. Address in 1980, 345 Broadway, NY, NY.

KATZIEFF, JULIUS D.
Painter and etcher. Born in 1892. Pupil of Boston Museum of Art and Penna. Academy of fine Arts. Address in 1926, 126 Dartmouth St., Boston, Mass.

KAUFFMANN, ROBERT C.
Painter and illustrator. Born Chicago, Jan. 23, 1893. Pupil fo AIC. Member: GFLA. Address in 1929, 2 West 67th St., NYC.

KAUFMAN, JOHN FRANCOIS.
Painter, sculptor and etcher. Born Uznach, Switzerland, Oct. 31, 1870. (Naturalized citizen of the United States). Pupil of Gerome, Ecole Nationale des Beaux-Arts, Paris. Award: Hon. mention, Paris Salon, 1927. Works: "Portrait Hon. Asa

Bird Gardner," War Department, Washington, DC; decorations in Monumental Church, Richmond, VA; monumental bronze bust, Poughkeepsie, NY. Address in 1929, 94 West Houston St., New York, NY.

KAUFMAN, THEODORE.
Painter. Born in Nelson, Hanover, in 1814. He studied abroad, and returning to this country fought in the National Army during the Civil War. Subsequently he resided in Boston. His works include "Genl. Sherman near the Watchfire," "On to Liberty," "Farragut in the Rigging."

KAUFMANN, FERDINAND.
Painter. Born Oberhausen, Germany, Oct. 17, 1864. Pupil of Laurens, Constant and Bouguereau in Paris. Member: Paris AAA; Pittsburgh AA; North Shore AA. Address in 1929, 9 Wood St., Pittsburgh, PA.

KAULA, LEE LUFKIN.
(Mrs. W. J. Kaula). Painter. Born Erie, PA. Pupil of C. M. Dewey in New York; Aman-Jean in Paris. Member: NA Women PS. Award: Hon. mention, Conn. AFA., 1925. Address in 1929, 311 Fenway Studios, 30 Ipswich St., Boston, Mass.; summer, New Ipswich, NH.

KAULA, WILLIAM J(URIAN).
Landscape painter. Born Boston, 1871. Pupil of Normal Art School and Cowles Art School in Boston; Collin in Paris. Member: Boston AC; NYWCC; Paris AAA; Boston WCC; Boston GA; Boston SWCP. Awards: Bronze medal, P.-P. Exp., San F., 1915; hon. mention, Buffalo SA, 1924; hon. mention, Conn. AFA, 1924. Address in 1929, 311 Fenway Studios, 30 Ipswich St., Boston, Mass.

KAVANAUGH, KATHARINE.
(Mrs. William V. Cahill). Painter. Born in Almouth, KY, in 1890. Pupil of Wm. V. Cahill. Address in 1926, 2625 Polk St., San Francisco, Calif.

KAVANAUGH, MARION.
See Mrs. Elmer Wachtel.

502

KAWACHI, J. B.
Painter. Born in Toyoaka Tajima, Japan, in 1885. Studied in Japan. Address in 1926, 170 Fifth Ave., New York, NY.

KAWAMURA, GOZO.
Sculptor. Born Japan, Aug. 15, 1886. Pupil of MacMonnies, and studied in Paris. Member: Am. Numismatic A. Member: Am. Numismatic A. Work: Memorial tablet of World War, American Jersey Cattle Club; "Portrait of Prince Katcho," Japanese Imperial Family; ideal type of cow and bull for Holstein-Friesian Asso. of America, to be placed in every college of agriculture in the United States. Address in 1929, 96 Fifth Ave.; 5 West 16th St., NYC.

KAY, GERTRUDE A(LICE).
Illustrator. Born Alliance, Ohio, July 8, 1884. Pupil of Howard Pyle. Member: GFLA; Plastic C; NAC; NA Women PS. Illustrations for Ladies' Home Journal, etc., and juvenile books. Address in 1929, 133 South Union Ave., Alliance, Ohio. Died in 1939.

KAY-SCOTT, CYRIL.
Painter and teacher. Born Westport, MO, Jan. 3, 1879. Pupil of Colarossi Academy, Paris. Director, School of Painting, El Paso and Summer School of Painting, Santa Fe. Address in 1929, 1429 East Yandell Blvd.; h. 801 Austin St., El Paso, Tex.; summer, 415 San Francisco St., Santa Fe, NM.

KAYE, ELIZABETH GUTMAN.
Painter. Born in Baltimore, MD, in 1887. Pupil of S. Edwin Whiteman, Hugh Breckenridge and H. B. Snell. Address in 1926, 856 Park Ave., Baltimore, MD.

KEANE, THEODORE J.
Painter. Born in San Franciso in 1880. Pupil of Calif. School of Design and AIC. Member: Palette and Chisel C.; Chicago SA; Cliff Dwellers; NAC; Attic C. of Minneapolis. Specialty animal etchings. Formerly director of Minneapolis Society of Fine Arts and dean of School of the Chicago Art Institute. Address in 1929, 220 South Michigan Ave., Chicago, Ill.

KEARNY, FRANCIS.
Engraver. Born in Perth Amboy, NJ, about 1780. Kearny is said to have been a nephew of Commodore James Lawrence, and Westcott, in his History of Philadelphia, says that he learned drawing with Archibald and Alexander Robertson, and engraving with Peter R. Maverick, in New York City. Kearny was in business in New York in 1798-1801, as an engraver. In 1810 he appeared in Philadelphia and remained there continuously until 1833. Kearny founded his fame as an engraver upon a faithful copy of "The Last Supper," after Raphael Morghen. He did considerable work in line, stipple, and aquatint for the magazines, "Annuals," and book publishers, and in 1820-23 he was interested in bank-note work as a member of the firm of Tanner, Vallance, Kearny & Co., of Philadelphia.

KEASBEY, HENRY T(URNER).
Painter. Born Philadelphia, Sept. 23, 1882. Pupil of Herkomer, Brangwyn, Swan, Talmage. Member: North Shore AA. Address in 1929, Hotel Chelsea, West 23rd St., New York, NY; summer, 6 Lookout Court, Marblehead, Mass.

KEAST, SUSETTE SCHULTZ.
Painter. Born in Philadelphia in 1892. Pupil of Breckenridge, Anshutz and Chase. Member of Fellowship of Penna. Academy of Fine Arts. Address in 1926, 1928 Rittenhouse Square, Philadelphia.

KEATS, EZRA JACK.
Illustrator. Born in Brooklyn, NY, in 1916. He had no formal art training, yet in 1948 his first illustration appeared in Collier's. A well-known children's book illustrator, he received the Horn Book Award from the Boston Globe and two Caldecott Awards. The five UNICEF cards he contributed in 1965 raised $500,000 for medical aid for needy children. All of his manuscripts and illustratons are owned by Harvard University.

KECK, CHARLES.
Sculptor. Born NYC, Sept. 9, 1875.
Pupil of NAD; ASL of NY; Philip
Martiny; Augustus Saint-Gaudens;
Amer. Acad. in Rome; studied in
Greece, Florence and Paris.
Member: NA; NY Arch. Lg., 1909;
Numismatic Soc.; AFA; Alumni Asso.,
Amer. Acad. in Rome. Award:
Rinehart scholarship to Rome,
1901-1905; gold medal, Arch. Lg. of
NY, 1926. Work: "Stonewall
Jackson," Charlottesville, VA;
"Booker T. Washington," Tuskegee,
AL; Geo. Washington Monument,
Palermo Park, Buenos Aires; Sloane
Tablet, Robert College,
Constantinople; Lewis and Clark
Monument, Charlottesville, VA;
Citizen Soldier, Irvington, NJ;
Mohammed Statue, Institute of Arts
and Sciences, Brooklyn, NY;
Soldiers' Memorial, Brooklyn; "Geo.
F. Johnson," Binghamton, NY; "Geo.
Rogers Clark," Springfield, Ohio;
Liberty Monument, Ticonderoga, NY;
Memorial Tablet and Friendship
Panel, Yale Univ. Club, NYC;
Soldiers' Memorial, Harrisonburg,
VA; War Memorial, Montclair, NJ;
Columbia Univ. Pylons (2) Science
and Letters, NYC; Wrenn
Tablet-Tennis Champion, Forest
Hills Stadium, LI; Mitchell
Monument, Scranton, PA; Pittsburgh
Soldiers' Monument, Pittsburgh;
Swope Memorial, Kansas City, MO;
Soldiers' Monument, Lynchburg, VA;
Souvenir Gold Dollar, San Fran.
Exposition; Souvenir Gold Dollar,
San Francisco Exposition; Souvenir
Half Dollar Sesqui-Centennial
Exposition, and US Steamship
"Maine" Memorial Tablets, for the
US Gov't.; sculpture on the NY
State Education Bldg., Albany, NY;
Manchester Bridge, Pittsburgh City
Hall; Wilmington City Hall; Oakland
City Hall. Died in 1951.

KEEFER, ELIZABETH E.
Etcher and teacher. Born Houston,
Tex., Nov. 4, 1899. Pupil of AIC;
Joseph Pennell. Member: ASL of
Chicago; ASL of NY; PBC. Address
in 1929, Avenue D; h. Avenue C,
Alpine, Tex.

KEELER, (R.) BURTON.
Painter. Born Philadelphia, April
5, 1886. Pupil of PAFA. Member:
N.Y. Arch. Lg.; GFLA. Awards:

Cresson Traveling Scholarship,
PAFA, 1911 and 1912. Address in
1929, 50 Gramatan Ave., Mt. Vernon,
NY.

KEELER, CHARLES BUTLER.
Painter and etcher. Born Cedar
Rapids, IA, April 2, 1882. Pupil
of AI Chicago; Johansen Stevens.
Member: Chicago SE.; Calif. PM;
New Haven PCC. Awards: Silver
medal for etchings, St. Paul Inst.,
1915; hon. mention, P.-P. exp., San
F., 1915. Represented in St. Paul
Inst.; Los Angeles Museum:
etching. Am. Inst. Graphic Arts
"Fifty Prints of the Year," 1927.
Address in 1929, Fin del Viaje,
Glendora, Los Angeles Co., Calif.

KEELER (LOUIS, BERTRAND) ROLSTON.
Painter. Born in New York in 1882.
Pupil of National Academy of
Design. Address in 1929, Sammis
Ave., Huntington, Suffolk County,
NY.

KEEN, LILA MOORE.
Painter. Born in Cleveland, GA, in
1903. Studied: Agnes Scott
College; and with Wayman Adams.
Noted for her portraits, and
flowers in watercolor, especially
camellias and magnolias. Awards:
National Gallery, 1945, 1946, 1947.
She exhibited widely in the
Southeastern US. Died in 1963.

KEENAN, WILLIAM.
This etcher of portraits, and
line-engraver of vignettes and
subject- plates, was working for
the magazine and book publishers of
Phila. in 1830-33. He then
apparently located himself in
business in Charleston, SC, as we
find an aquatint view of
Charleston, engraved by Keenan and
published by him at "132 King St.,
Charleston, SC," and other plates
executed for book publishers in
that city, in 1835. Some of these
latter plates are inscribed as
"Drawn, Engraved and Printed by W.
Keenan."

KEENER, ANNA E(LIZABETH).
Painter and writer. Born Flagler,
Colo., Oct. 16, 1895. Pupil of
Birger Sandzen. Member: NOACC.
Awards: Bronze Medal for wood
engraving, Kansas-Missouri-Oklahoma

Exhibition; hon. mention for linoleum cut, Kansas Missouri Oklahoma Exhibition, 1923. Work: "Barn on the Hill," San Francisco Public Library; "Oxen and Carts," Bethany College, Lindsborg, Kan.; "Wyoming Landscape," Oklahoma University, Norman, Okla.; "Bird's Mine," Sul Ross State Normal, Texas; represented in Smoky Hill AC, Lindsborg, Kansas; Pawhuskee, Okla., Schools; author of "Spontaneity in Design," 1923.

KEENEY, ANNA.
Sculptor. Born Falls City, Ore. Pupil of Avard Fairbanks, Harry P. Camden. Work: "Fallen Aviator," First National Bank, Condon, Ore.; "Eve," University of Ore. Address in 1929, University of Oregon; .h. 1380 Beech, Eugene, Ore.; summer, Olex, Ore.

KEEP, HELEN ELIZEBETH.
Painter, illustrator and craftsman. Born Troy, NY. Pupil of AIC; Detroit Art Museum School; Frederick W. Freer. Member: Detroit Women Painters; Detroit SAC; Founders Asso. of Detroit AI. Address in 1929, 2247 Jefferson Ave., East, Detroit, Mich.

KEFFER, FRANCES.
Painter and teacher. Born Des Moines, IA, Jan. 6, 1881. Pupil of Pratt Inst., Alex. Robinson, Frank Brangwyn, Ossip Linde. Member: NA Women PS; Nanuet Painters; Brooklyn SA.; Brooklyn SPS.; PBC. Award: $100 prize, Woman's Club, Des Moines, Iowa, 1912. Died in 1954.

KEHRER, F. A.
Illustrator. Member: Pen and Pencil Club, Columbus. Address in 1926, 24 W. Maynard Ave., Columbus, Ohio.

KEISTER, ROY C.
Illustrator. Born in Ohio in 1886. Pupil of Art Institute of Chicago. Address in 1926, 1906 Republic Bldg., Chicago, Ill.

KEITH, DORA WHEELER.
(Mrs. B. Keith). Painter, illustrator and craftsman. Born Jamaica, LI, NY, March 8, 1857. Pupil of ASL of NY and of Chase; studied in Paris. Member: ANA

1906; SAA 1886. Awards: Prang prize ($500), 1885; Prang prize ($2,00), 1886; hon. mention, Pan-Am. Exp., Buffalo, 1901. Died in 1940. Address in 1929, 33 West 67th St., New York, NY; and Onteora, Catskill, NY.

KEITH, WILLIAM.
Landscape and portrait painter. Born in Scotland in 1839; died in California in 1911. Pupil of Achenbach and Carl Marr. Represented in Corcoran Art Gallery by Portrait of Irving M. Scott, builder of ships for the United States Navy.

KELLEHAR, DANIEL JOSEPH.
Painter. Born in Erie, PA, Nov. 15, 1930. Study: Edinboro State College; Syracuse Univ. Work: Wash. & Jefferson College, PA; Hemingway Collection, NY; Erie Publ. Lib., PA; others. Exhibitions: Nat'l. Soc. of Painters in Casein, NY; Butler Inst. of American Art, Youngstown, Ohio; Audubon Artists, NYC; Watercolor USA, Springfield, Missouri; others. Awards: Mainstreams '69 Marietta College Award of Excellence; Washington & Jefferson College; others. Mem.: Erie Art Ctr.; Chautauqua Inst. of Art, NY; PA Art Educ. Assn. Media: Acrylic and collage. Address in 1980: 427 E. 8th Street, Erie, PA.

KELLER, ARTHUR I.
Painter and illustrator. Born in 1867; died in 1924. Pupil of National Academy of Design; also studied in Munich. Member of American Water Color Society and New York Water Color Club. He is represented by a painting "The Mass," in the Munich Academy.

KELLER, CLYDE LEON.
Painter and teacher. Born Salem, Ore., Feb. 22, 1872. Pupil of E. W. Christmas, R. B. A., in London. Member: S. Oregon A. Palette Club. Work: "After the Shower" and "California Marshes," Liberty Theatre, Portland, Ore.; "Columbia River," B.P.O.E. Club, Portland; "The Tualatin," Portland Press Club. Died in 1941. Address in 1929, 450 Washington St.; h. 512

East 55th St., North, Portland, Ore.

KELLER, DEANE.
Painter. Born New Haven, Dec. 14, 1901. Pupil of Edwin C. Taylor, Eugene F. Savage. Awards: American Academy in Rome prize, Grand Central Galleries, New York, 1926; figure composition prize, New Haven Paint and Clay Club, 1926. Address in 1929, Yale School of the Fine Arts; h. 55 Huntington St., New Haven, Conn.

KELLER, GRACE.
(Mrs. John M. Keller). Painter. Member: Balto. WCC. Address in 1929, Chadford Apts., Roland Park, Baltimore, MD.

KELLER, HENRY GEORGE.
Painter. Born Cleveland, Apr. 3, 1870. Pupil of Bergman at Dusseldorf; Balsche at Karlsruhe; Zugel at Munich. Awards: Silver Medal, Munich, 1902; special awards for maintained excellence, Cleveland Museum; also represented in the Phillips Memorial Art Gallery, Washington, DC. Instructor of composition and design, Cleveland School of Art. Died in 1949. Address in 1929, 1381 Addison Road, Cleveland, Ohio.

KELLER, MRS. BURTON.
See Southwick.

KELLEY, GARY R.
Illustrator. Born in Algona, Iowa, in 1945. Studied: Univ. of Northern Iowa and was a pupil of John Page, a print-maker. Better Homes and Gardens published his first illustration in 1970. His artwork is owned by the Artworks Gallery in Keokuk, Iowa, and the Three-Rooms-Up Gallery in Minneapolis. Private collectors in Iowa, Calif., Florida, Arizona, and Wash., DC, own his paintings, drawings, and prints.

KELLEY, MAY McCLURE.
(Mrs. William Fitch Kelley). Painter and sculpture. Pupil of Cincinnati Art School, Herbert Vos, Charles W. Hawthorne, Brenda Putnam, G. J. Zolnay, Jo Davidson, Antoine Bourdelle. Member: Wash. AC; S. Wash. A. Works:

Bas-relief portrait, Grace Coolidge, The White House; "Adoration," Woman's Universal Alliance, Washington, DC. Address in 1929, 2207 Massachusetts Ave., Washington, DC; Knole, Rockville Pike, MD.

KELLNER, CHARLES H(ARRY).
Painter. Born Kasa, Czechoslovakia, Sept. 13, 1890. Pupil of W. Reynolds, Victor Higgins, Harry Lachman, Pierre Bonnard. Member: Chicago SA; New York SA; Ill. AFA.; All-Ill. SFA; Chicago Palette and CC; Springfield AA; Am. APL. Award: 1st prize, Bellevue, France, Academy, in portrait and landscape. Work: "Sunny Morning, St. Cloud, Paris," owned by the United States Government; "Reflecting Pool, Villa D'Esti, Tivoli," Phi Sigma Sigma Sorority House, Univ. of Illinois, Champaign; "Mme. R.", Vanderpoel Art Assn., Chicago. Address in 1929, Kellner Studios, 1022 Argyle St.; h. 5059 Kenmore Ave., Chicago, Ill.

KELLOG, MINER KILBOURNE.
Painter. Born in Cincinnati, Ohio, Aug. 22, 1814. He resided abroad. He painted a portrait of General Scott, in the City Hall, New York, also a replica of the head. During a visit to this country he sold many excellent examples of his work. He has also painted miniatures. Died 1889.

KELLOGG, EDMUND P(HILO).
Painter, illustrator and teacher. Born Chicago, Sept. 11, 1879. Pupil of Freer, Duveneck, Chase and Albert Herter. Member: Designers Alumni of AIC; Chicago AC; Chicago Arch C. Represented in St. Paul Institute; "Ready for Flight," Chicago Athletic Asso.; "A French Garden," Indianapolis Athletic Club; mural paintings in Metropolitan Theatre, Boston, Mass.; mural decoration, Church of the Sacred Heart, Rochester, NY. Instructor at The Academy of Fine Arts, Chicago, Ill Address in 1929, 4332 Oakenwald Ave., Chicago, Ill.

KELLOGG, J. G.
Engraver of portraits in line, working in New Haven, Conn., about

506

1850. He was born in Tooland, Conn., in 1805, and died in Hartford, Conn., in 1873.

KELLOGG, JANET REID.
Painter and illustrator. Born Merrill, Wis., Jan. 19, 1894. Pupil of George Elmer Browne. Member: Wis. PS. Award: Medal, Milwaukee Art Institute, 1929. Address in 1929, 31 Bayley Ave., Yonkers, NY.

KELLY, ANNIE D.
Painter. Member: Wash. WCC.; S. Wash. A.; Wash. AC. Address in 1929, 1919 N. St., N.W., Washington, DC.

KELLY, EDNA.
Sculptor. Born Bolivar, NY, July 23, 1890. Pupil of Cincinnati Art Academy, Ella Buchanan. Member: Calif. AC; Long Beach AA; Lagauna Beach AC. Awards: Prize, Pomona-Los Angeles County Fair, 1927; medal and award, Panama Pacific Exposition, Long Beach, 1928.

KELLY, GRACE VERONICA.
Painter, illustrator, writer and teacher. Born Cleveland, Jan. 31, 1884. Pupil of H. G. Keller. Awards: Second prize for water color, 1924; second prize for landscape and hon. mention for water color, Cleveland Museum of Art, 1925. Work: "Sunset on the Cuyahoga River," Cleveland Heights Public Schools; "Back Yard Activities," owned by the City of Cleveland. Illustrates for papers and magazines. Art critic for "Cleveland Plain Dealer." Address in 1929, Standard Theatre Bldg., 811 Prospect Ave.; h. 1835 Wadene St., East Cleveland, Ohio.

KELLY, J. E.
This engraver in 1851 had an office at 141 Fulton St., New York City. He engraved portraits in a mixed manner.

KELLY, J. REDDING.
Portrait painter and teacher. Born in New York, Aug. 5, 1868. Pupil of NAD. Member: Salma. C. 1898. Work: Portrait Abraham Lincoln reproduced New York Sunday Times, 1929. Professor in Art Dept.,

College of the City of New York. Died in 1939. Address in 1929, 55 West 95th St., New York, NY.

KELLY, JAMES E(DWARD).
Sculptor and illustrator. Born New York, July 30, 1855. Pupil of NAD and ASL of NY; Theodore Robinson and Carl Hirschberg. Illustrated for Harper's, etc., until 1881; since exclusively sculptor. Work: "Monmouth Battle Monument"; equestrian Gen. Sherman; "Col. Roosevelt at San Juan Hill," etc. Address in 1929, 318 West 57th St., New York, NY.

KELLY, LOUISE.
(Mrs. Edward P. Kelly). Painter and lecturer. Born Waukon, IA, June 14, 1879. Pupil of AIC; PAFA; George Elmer Browne. Member: AFA; NA Women PS; Chicago Gal. A; Provincetown AA; Minneapolis SFA. Address in 1929, Apt. 902, Leamington Hotel, Minneapolis, Minn.; summer, Provincetown, Mass.

KELLY, THOMAS.
Born in Ireland about 1795; died in the Almshouse in New York City about 1841. The professional career of this very good engraver in line and in stipple is difficult to trace. He was working for Boston publishers in 1823, but was in Philadelphia in 1831-33, and in New York in 1834-35. Kelly was associated for a short time with Joseph Andrews in Boston. Besides his portraits he engraved a considerable number of good plates for the "Annuals" and magazines.

KELMAN, BENJAMIN.
Painter and illustrator. Born in 1890. Pupil of Penna. Academy of Fine Arts and National Academy of Design. Address in 1926, 1692 Park Ave., New York City, NY.

KEMBLE, E(DWARD) W(INDSOR).
Illustrator. Born Sacramento, Cal., Jan. 18, 1861. Self-taught. Specialty, Black American subjects. Illustrated: Uncle Tom's Cabin, Huckleberry Finn; author Kemble's Coons. Died in 1933.

KEMEYS, EDWARD.
Born in Savannah, GA, in 1843. He studied in New York and later in

Paris. He made a specialty of the wild animals of the American continent. His "Fight between Buffalo and Wolves" was exhibited in the Salon of 1878. Among his works: "Panther and Deer," "Coyote and Raven"; he made the colossal head of a Buffalo for the Pacific railroad station at St. Louis. A collection of some fifty of his small bronzes are at the National Gallery in Washington, DC. He died at Georgetown Heights, Washington, DC, in 1907.

KEMMELMYER, FREDERICK.
Painter. He was an active painter in Baltimore, MD about 1788 to 1803. He advertised himself as a portrait painter. An artist by that name made a sketch from life of Washington on Oct. 2nd, 1894, when the latter was reviewing the Western troops at Cumberland, MD.

KEMP, OLIVER.
Painter, illustrator and writer. Born Trenton, NJ, May 13, 1887. Pupil of Howard Pyle, Chase, Gerome. Illustrations for Scribner's, Harper's, Century, Saturday Evening Post. Director, School of Industrial Arts, Trenton, NJ. Member: Wilmington SA. Died in 1934. Address in 1929, 922 Transportation Bldg., Detroit, Mich.; summer, Bowerbank, Piscataquis Co., Maine.

KEMPER, RUBY WEBB.
Painter and craftsman. Born Cincinnati, Ohio, Dec. 8, 1883. Pupil of T. E. Noble, L. H. Meakin, W. H. Fry, Frank Duveneck, Anna Riis. Member: Cincinnati Ceramic Club; Cincinnati Woman's AC; The Crafters Soc. Address in 1929, Milford, Ohio.

KEMPSTER, RUTH.
Painter. Born in Chicago, IL, in 1904. Studied: Los Angeles County Art Institute; Art Students' League; Academie des Beaux-Arts; National Academy, Florence, Italy. Awards: Calif. State Fair, 1931, 1932, 1936; Pasadena Society of Art, 1936, 1940, 1944, 1951; Women Painters of the West, 1951; International Olympics Games, Exhibition, 1932; Collections: Pasadena Art Institute; Huntington

Memorial Hospital, Pasadena. Toured Korea as portrait artist for Armed Forces, Far East Command, 1953.

KEMPTON, ELMIRA.
Painter and craftsman. Born Richmond, Ind., Aug. 9, 1892. Pupil of James R. Hopkins, H. H. Wessel; C. J. Barnhorn. Member: Indiana Artists' Club; Richmond Palette Club. Address in 1929, 75 South 17th St., Richmond, Ind.

KENDAL, ELIZABETH
Painter, sculptor and illustrator. Born in 1896. Pupil of Yale School of Fine Arts. Address in 1926, 58 Trumbull St., New Haven, Conn.

KENDAL, H. H.
Painter. Member: Boston AC. Address in 1929, 142 Berkeley St., Boston, Mass.

KENDALL, BEATRICE.
Painter, craftsman and teacher. Born New York City, Jan. 14, 1902. Pupil of Sergeant Kendall. Member: AFA. Award: Winchester Fellowship, Yale University, 1922; Landscape prize, New Haven PCC, 1926. Work: Three portraits, Lawrenceville School, Lawrenceville, NJ. Specialty Screens and Decorations. Address in 1929, Hot Springs, VA.

KENDALL, KATE.
Painter, of Cleveland, Ohio. Exhibited water colors at the Penna. Academy of Fine Arts. Deceased 1915.

KENDALL, MARGARET (STICKNEY).
Miniature painter. Born Staten Island, NY, Nov. 29, 1871. Pupil of J. Alden Weir, and Julius Rolshoven. Member: Am. S. Min. P.; New Haven PCC. Award: Bronze medal, St. Louis Exp., 1904. Address in 1929, Simsbury, Conn.

KENDALL, MARIE B(OENING).
Painter and teacher. Born Mt. Morris, NY, Aug. 16, 1885. Pupil of William M. Chase and Jean Mannheim, Los Angeles College of Fine Arts. Member: Calif. AC; West Coast Arts; S. Indp. A.; Laguna Beach AA; N.A. Women PS. Work:

Three paintings in the Virginia Hotel, Painting in Seaside Hospital, and Polytechnic High School, Long Beach, Calif.; Teachers College, Mt. Pleasant, Mich. Magazine Covers. Address in 1929, 2306 Lime Ave., Long Beach, Calif.; Summer, Laguna Beach, Calif.

KENDALL, WILLIAM SERGEANT.
Painter and sculptor. Born Spuyten Duyvil, NY, Jan. 20, 1869. Pupil of ASL of NY; Eakins in Philadelphia; Ecole des Beaux-Arts and Merson in Paris. Member: SAA 1898; ANA 1901, NA 1905; Nat. Inst. AL; NYWCC; Conn. AFA; Century Assoc.; New Haven PCC. Dean, School of Fine Arts of Yale Univ. 1913 to 1922. Awards: Hon. mention, Paris Salon, 1891; medal, Columbian Exp., Chicago, 1893; Lippincott prize, PAFA 1894; hon. mention, Tennessee Centennial Exp., Nashiville, 1897; second prize, Worcester Museum, 1900; bronze medal, Paris Exp., 1900; bronze medal, C.I. Pittsburgh, 1900; second prize, Worcester Museum, 1901; silver medal for painting, bronze medal for drawing and hon. mention for sculpture, Pan-Am. Exp., Buffalo, 1901; Shaw prize, SAA 1901; Shaw Fund Purchase, SAA 1903; gold medal, St. Louis Exp., 1904 Isidor medal, NAD 1908; Harris prize, AIC 1908; Palmer gold medal, AIC 1910; gold medal for painting and silver medal for sculpture, P.-P. Exp., San F., 1915; Butler prize, AIC, 1918; gold medal Miss AA, 1926; Isidor medal, NAD, 1927. Work: "Beatrice," Pennsylvania Academy, Phila; "The Seer" and "Psyche," Metropolitan Museum, New York; "An Interlude," National Gallery, Washington; "Narcissa," Corcoran Gallery, Washington; "Crosslights," Detroit Institute of Arts; "Intermezzo," R.I. School of Design, Providence, and in many private collections. Died in 1938. Address in 1929, Hot Springs, VA.

KENNEDY, JAMES.
Engraver in line and stipple. In 1797 he was working for the New York publisher, John Low. He remained in that city until 1812, and then went to Philadelphia, as he was later employed by the publishers S. F. Bradford and T. W. Freeman, both of that city.

KENNEDY, LAWRENCE.
Painter. Born Pittsburgh, PA, Oct. 31, 1880. Pupil AIC. Member: Chicago SA; Cliff Dwellers. Address in 1929, 30 North Michigan Blvd., Chicago, Ill.; h. 29 N. Oak St., Hinsdale, Ill.

KENNEDY, OWEN W.
Painter. Born Washington, DC, May 26, 1891. Pupil of Worcester, Mass., Art Museum School. Member: Business Men's AC of Boston. Address in 1929, Boylston, Mass.

KENNEDY, S.
Engraver. Working in Philadelphia in 1813 with William Charles, who was best known by his series of caricatures of the War of 1812.

KENNEDY, SAMUEL J.
Painter. Born in Mt. Pleasant, Mich., in 1877. pupil of Henri Martin. Work: "Young Genius," Mt. Pleasant Public Gallery; "The Marshes," Library of Michigan Agricultural College. Address in 1926, 4 East Ohio St., Chicago, Ill.

KENNEL, LOUIS.
Painter. Born North Bergen, NJ, May 7, 1886. Pupil of George Bridgman, Wm. H. Lippincot, Charles Graham, Ernest Gros. Member: S. Indp. A. Designs stage scenery.

KENNY, THOMAS HENRY.
Painter. Born in Bridgeport, CT, Jan. 12, 1918. Study: Knox College; Ohio Christian Univ. Work: Met. Mus. of Art, NYC; Phila. Mus. of Art; Stedelijk Mus., Amsterdam; Mus. Mod. Art, Mexico City; numerous others in US and abroad. Exhib.: Boston Athenaeum; Modern Art Museum, Haifa; Stedelijk Museum; Museum Modern Art, Mexico City; Fine Arts Museums in Sao Paulo, Rio de Janeiro, Ireland, Belgium, Helsinki, Israel, France; and many others. Awards: Life Fellow, Royal Society of Arts, London; Col. Art Assn. of Am.; Am. Federation of Arts; Inst. of Contemp. Arts, London. Living in Roslyn, NY in 1970. Address in

1980, 3920 Catamarca Drive, San Diego, CA.

KENSETT, JOHN FREDERICK.
Born in Cheshire, Conn., in 1818; died in NYC in 1872. In 1840 he went to England to study art, and during his five years' stay in that country he partially supported himself by engraving. Kensett continued his studies in Rome and returned to the US in 1848. He opened a studio in NY and established a reputation as a painter of landscape. In 1850 he sent a painting to the Royal Academy for exhibition, which was highly praised. He was elected a National Academician in 1849. He is represented in the Metropolitan Museum by his painting "Lake George," also a number of landscapes painted in 1871. He is considered one of the most distinguished landscape painters of the last generation. Died in 1972.

KENSETT, THOMAS.
Engraver. In 1812 Thomas Kensett was a member of the engraving and print-publishing firm of Shelton & Kensett, located at Cheshire, Conn. As evidence that he was an engraver himself, we have a well-executed map of Upper and Lower Canada, published in 1812, and signed "Kensett Sculp. Cheshire, Conn't." Another large plate entitled "Brother Jonathan's Soliloquy on the Times" is signed "Kennsett, Painte. et Sculp." Mr. H. W. French, in his "Art and Artists in Connecticut," says that Thomas Kensett came from England to Cheshire in 1812, and had previously been an engraver at Hampton Court, in England, and Mr. James Terry says that he was born in England in 1786 and died in 1829.

KENT, ADA HOWE.
Painter. Born in Rochester, NY. Pupil of Brush, Abbott Thayer and Whistler. Member: New York Water Color Club. Address in 1926, 29 Atkinson St., Rochester, NY.

KENT, ROCKWELL.
Painter and illustrator. Born Tarrytown Heights, NY, June 21,

1882. Pupil of Chase, Henri, Hayes Miller, Thayer. Work: "Marine," in Metropolitan Museum, New York, NY; "Lone Woman," "Mother and Children," Brooklyn Museum. Author and illustrator of Voyaging (G. P. Putnam's Sons), and Wilderness. Address in 1929, Ausable Forks, NY.

KENYON, HENRY R.
Painter. Member: Providence AC; North Shore AA. Work: "Landscape, Holland," "November Twilight" and "Venice," Rhode Island School of Design, Providence. Address in 1929, Ipswich, Mass.

KEPES, GYORGY.
Painter. Born Oct. 4, 1906 in Selyp, Hungary. Earned master's from Royal Acad. Fine Arts, Budapest (1929). Resides in U.S. Taught at Inst. of Design, Chicago (1937-43); MIT as Prof. of Visual Design since 1946. Awarded Guggenheim, 1960; Fine Arts Award, Am. Inst. of Architects. Exhibited at Art Inst. of Chicago (1944); San Diego Fine Arts Gallery, NH; Everson Mus. at Syracuse; Baltimore; Dallas; Mus. FA Houston; Whitney; MOMA and others. In collections of Mus. FA, Boston; Addison; MOMA; Harvard; Whitney; Brooklyn; Albright. Knox Gallery; S.F. Mus. of Art; Brandeis; and U. of Illinois. Mural Commissions; Harvard Sheraton Hotel, others.

KEPLINGER, LENA MILLER.
Painter. Member: Wash. WCC; Wash. SA. Address in 1929, Bethesda, MD.

KEPPLER, GEORGE.
Sculptor. Born in Germany in 1856. He came to America, and lived in Providence, RI. Address in 1926, 58 Westleyan Ave., Providence, RI.

KEPPLER, JOSEPH.
Illustrator and caricaturist. Born in Vienna in 1838. He came to America about 1868. In 1873 he was in New York as a cartoonist for Frank Leslie's Weekly. He also was sucessful with lithography. He died in New York in 1894.

KER, MARIE SIGSBEE.
See Mrs. A. O. Fisher.

KERKAM, EARL.
Painter. Born 1890 in Wash., DC. Studied at Chaumiere, Paris; Inst. of Art, Montreal; ASL and PAFA. Taught at Chaumiere and privately, and at NY Studio School. Exhibited in Paris, and at Bonestell Gallery (1944); Charles Egan Gallery (many); World House Gallerie, NYC. In collection of Phil. Mus. of Art and many private collections. Died Jan., 1965.

KERMES, CONSTANTINE JOHN.
Painter and printmaker. Born in Pittsburgh, PA, Dec. 6, 1923. Study: Carnegie-Mellon Univ., with Victor Candell, Leo Manso, Frank Lloyd Wright. Work: Storm King Art Ctr., Mountainville, NY; Penn. State Univ.; Hershey Med. Ctr., PA; others. Comn.: Icon ptgs., Holy Cross Greek Orthodox Church, Pittsburgh; PA Hist. & Mus. Commission, Cornwall Mus.; Sperry Rand Corp., PA, & Brussels, Belgium; and others. Exhib.: Butler Inst. of Am. Art, Youngstown, Ohio; Smithsonian Inst., Wash. DC; Grimaldis Gallery, Baltimore; PA WC Soc.; many more. Awards: Annual Design Review Awards; Indust. Design Magazine, 4 yrs.; Am. Iron & Steel Inst., 4 yrs.; others. Media: Oil, acrylic, woodcut, lithograph. Dealer: Jacques Seligman Gal., NYC. Address in 1982, 981 Landis Valley Road, Lancaster, PA.

KERNAN, F. G.
This man was an engraver of portraits, in a mixed style, located in New York in 1870.

KERNAN, JOSEPH F.
Painter and illustrator. Born Brookline, Mass., Sept. 13, 1878. Pupil of Eric Pape. Member: GFLA; Am. APL. Specialty, national advertising and magazine covers. Address in 1929, 875 West 181st St., New York, NY.

KERNS, FANNIE M.
Painter, illustrator, designer and teacher. Born Los Angeles, Calif. Pupil of Arthur Dow, Frank Ingerson, Ralph Johonnot. Member: Boston SAC; So. Calif ACS; So. Calif. A. Teachers Asso. Awards: First Prize for landscape, Los Angeles Museum, 1924. Address in 1929, 916 Grattan St., Los Angeles, Calif.

KERR, GEORGE.
Illustrator. Member: SI 1913. Address in 1929, Art Department, N.Y. Journal; Kamac Products Co., 249 West 34th St., New York, NY.

KERR, IRENE WAITE.
Painter. Born Pauls Valley, Okla., 1873. Pupil of Walcott, Clarkson, William M. Chase, James Fraser, DuMond and F. L. Mora. Address in 1926, 144 East 14th St., Oklahoma City, Okla.

KERR, JAMES W(ILFRID).
Painter and etcher. Born New York City, Aug. 7, 1897. Pupil of Howard Giles. Member: AFA. Address in 1929, 736 West 173rd St., New York, NY.

KERR, KENNETH A.
Painter. Born in Pittsburgh, PA, February 10, 1943. Exhibitions: National Watercolor Society; others. Awards: American Inst. of Fine Arts; National Soc. of Art Directors. Media: Watercolor. Address in 1970, 1015 W. Palm St., San Diego, CA.

KERSHAW, J. M.
This engraver of buildings, etc., was working in St. Louis, MO, in 1850.

KERSWILL, J. W. ROY.
Painter. Born in Bigbury, Eng., Jan. 17, 1925; US citizen. Study: Plymouth College of Art, Eng.; Bristol College of Art. Work: Wyoming State Art Gallery; Mountain Man Museum, Wyoming; Grand Teton Natural Hist. Asn.; Dept. of Interior; others. Comn.: Alpenhof, Teton Village, Wyoming; etc. Mem.: Am. APL; Artists Equity Assn. Media: Watercolor, oil. Address in 1982, Jackson Hole, Wyoming.

KETCHAM, AUSTIN.
Painter and teacher. Born Richmond Hill, LI, Oct. 29, 1898. Pupil of AIC; Lewis Inst.; Bertha E. Perrie. Member: Alumni Chicago Art Inst.; Kansas City SA. Award: J. B. Irving portraiture prize,

Missouri Kansas Oklahoma Exhibition, 1923. Address in 1929, Kansas City Art Inst.; 2615 Troost Ave., Kansas City, MO; summer, Art Institute, Chicago, Ill.

KETCHAM, SUSAN M.
Painter. Born Indianapolis, Ind. Pupil of ASL of NY, under Chase and Bell; AIC. Member: ASL of NY; NA Women PS. Award: Elling prize, NY Woman's AC 1908. Work: "A Young Student," "Beatrix," "The Restless Sea, Oqunquit, ME," Herron Art Inst., Indianapolis. Address in 1929, 1010 Carnegie Hall, New York, NY; summer, Ogunquit, ME. Died in 1937.

KETTEN, MAURICE.
Painter, illustrator and cartoonist. Born in Florence, Mar. 2, 1875. Pupil of Cabanel, Delaunay, Moreau, Ecole des Beaux Arts, Paris. Member: SI. Work: "Can You Beat It," "Such Is Life," and "The Day of Rest" - daily cartoons in the "Evening World." Address in 1929, care the New York World, 63 Park Row; h. Hotel St. Regis, 2 East 55th St., New York, NY; summer, West Outlet, ME.

KETTERER, GUSTAV.
Painter and craftsman. Born Germany, May 20, 1870. Pupil of PAFA. Member: Phila. AC; Phil. Alliance; T. Sq. C.; Arts and Trades C., NY. Work: Interior decorator of Detroit Museum of Art; Indianapolis Library; Hartford County Court House; murals of Keneseth of Israel Temple; decoration, exterior and interior, Persian Bldg., Sesqui- Centennial.

KEUHNE, MAX.
Painter. Born in New York, 1880. Pupil of Kenneth Hayes Miller, Chase and Henri. Address in 1926, 18 Bank St., New York, NY.

KEY, F. C.
The firm of F. C. Key & Sons, of No. 123 Arch St., Philadelphia, was engaged in die-sinking and embossing, about 1850. A fairly well-executed head of Millard Fillmore was published by this firm. It is embossed on white paper, surrounded by an oval in gold, with the name and publisher also printed in gold.

KEY, JOHN ROSS.
Painter. Born July 16, 1837, in Maryland. Studied in Paris. Studio in Chicago and Boston. Principal paintings: "Marblehead Beach;" "Newport;" "Golden Gate, San Francisco." He was also sucessful in his work in black and white. He died in Baltimore, March 24, 1920.

KEY, MABEL.
Painter. Born in Paris, France, 1874, of American parents. Awards: Honorable mention for water color, St. Paul Institute, 1915; silver medal, St. Paul Institute, 1916; silver medal, Wisconsin Painters and Sculptors. Instructor in Milwaukee Art Insitute. Address in 1926, Fullerton Parkway, Chicago, Ill.

KEY, WILLIAM H.
Engraver. Born in Brooklyn, NY; was living in 1892. From 1864 until 1892 and possibly later, Key was an assistant engraver for the US Mint at Philadelphia. Key engraved the dies for the Kane Expedition medal, and a medal for Archibishop Wood.

KEYS, HARRY J.
Illustrator. Member: Pen and Pencil Club, Columbus. Address in 1926, "Columbus Citizen," Columbus, Ohio.

KEYSER, EPHRAIM.
Sculptor and teacher. Born Baltimore, Oct. 6, 1850. Pupil of Royal Academies in Munich and Berlin. Member: NSS 1907; Charcoal C. of Balto.; AFA. Awards: Silver medal, Munich Academy; first class medal, New Orleans Exp., 1885. Work: Maj. Gen. Baron de Kalb, Annapolis, MD.; memorial to Pres. Chester A. Arthur, Rural Cemetery, Albany, NY; "Psyche," life size marble, Cincinnati Art Museum; "Bust of Sidney Lanier," Johns Hopkins University. Instructor Rinehart School for Sculpture, Maryland Inst. Address in 1929, 20 Overhill Road, Roland Park, Baltimore, MD. Died in 1937.

KEYSER, ERNEST WISE.
Painter and sculptor. Born Baltimore, MD, 1875. Pupil of Maryland Inst. Art School in Baltimore; ASL of NY; Julian Academy in Paris; Augustus Saint-Gaudens. Member: NSS 1902; Paris AAA; NY Arch. Lg. 1908. Award: Gold medal, New York S. Arch., 1923. Work: "Enoch Pratt Memorial," Baltimore; Adm. Schley statue, Annapolis; "Sir Galahad" for Harper memorial, Ottawa, Canada. Died in 1959. Address in 1929, 59 West 12th St.; 249 West 74th St., New York, NY.

KIBBEY, ILAH MARIAN.
Landscape painter. Born Geneva, Ohio. Pupil of Hugh Breckenridge; Charles Wilimovsky; Henry B. Snell; Lester Stevens; Kansas City AI; AIC. Member: NA Women PS; North Shore AA; Rockport SA; Kans. City SA. Awards: J. B. Irving prize, for small oil painting, Kansas City AI, 1921; silver medal in graphic arts, bronze medal for water color, Midwestern AA, 1921; silver medal in graphic arts, bronze medal for water color, Midwestern AA, 1921; silver medal, water colors, Midwestern AA, 1923; silver medal, Midwestern AA, 1927; purchase prize, Midland Theatre, Kans. City, 1928; purchase prize, Missouri State Fair, 1928. Died in 1958. Address in 1929, 4415 Warwick Blvd., Kansas City, MO; summer, Rockport, Mass.

KIDD, STEVEN R.
Illustrator. Born in Chicago in 1911. Studied at the AIC and later at the ASL, GCSA, and PI in NY. His instructors, including Harvey Dunn, George Bridgman, and Henry Varnum Poore, were some of the best known artists of their day. He started working in 1926 in Chicago and has since illustrated many books and magazines such as Cosmopolitan, Redbook, Forbes, and Argosy. He is currently teaching at the ASL.

KIDDER, FRANK HOWARD.
Painter. Born in Litchfield, Conn., in 1886. Pupil of Kenneth Hayes Miller and Denys Wortman. Address in 1926, 210 South Main St., New Canaan, Conn.

KIDDER, HARVEY W.
Illustrator. Born in Cambridge, MA, in 1918. Graduated from the Child-Walker School of Design having studied with Lawrence Beal Smith and Arthur Lougee. His long career in editorial and book illustration began with Houghton Mifflin in 1939, and his artwork has since been used by Reader's Digest, Ford Times, True, Argosy, Lithopinion, Golf Digest, and many others. A member of the S of I, he has participated in the USAF Art Program and the National Park Service Art Program.

KIDDER, JAMES.
The "Polyanthos," Boston, June, 1813, refers editorially to an aquatint, "View on Boston Common," contained in the number, and says it is "a specimen of the talents of Master J. Kidder, a youth of Boston, and also his first essay in aquatinta," Kidder's few plates, all in aquatint, represent views in and about Boston. Kidder designed plates engraved by Abel Bowen about 1823.

KIEFER, SAM P.
Painter. Member: Pen and Pencil Club, Columbus, Ohio. Address in 1926, 147 West Maynard Ave., Columbus, Ohio.

KIENBUSCH, WILLIAM.
Painter. Born April 13, 1914 in NYC. Earned B.A. from Princeton (1936), attended Art Students' League following year studied with Henry Varnum Poor, Abraham Rattner, and Stuart Davis. Taught at Brooklyn Mus. Art School. Rec. awards from Brooklyn Mus.; MMA; NY State Fair; Boston Arts Festival; Ford Foundation. Exhibited at U. of Maine; Cornell; Princetown; Whitney; Carnegie; Albright-Knox; Walker; MOMA; MMA. In collections of Portland Mus.; Montelau (NJ) Art Mus.; Boston; Dartmouth; U. of Nebraska; Wichita Art Mus.; PAFA; Wadsworth; Carnegie; Munson-William- Proctor Inst.; MOMA, and others.

KIHN, W(ILFRED) LANGDON.
Painter. Born Brooklyn, Sept. 5, 1898. Pupil of Homer Boss; ASL of NY; F. W. Reiss. Member: Brooklyn

SA; Salma. C. Work: 2 portraits of Indians, and "Prairie, Montana," Litchfield (Conn.) Museum; 4 Indian portraits, Ohio State Univ., Columbus, O.; Indian portrait, Seattle Fine Arts Society; Indian portraits, Provincial Museum of British Columbia, Victoria; 8 Indian portraits and landscapes, Montreal Gallery of Art; Indian portrait and landscape, Natl; Gallery of Art, Ottawa, Canada; Indian portraits and landscape, Royal Ontario Museum, Toronto; Indian portraits, Museum of Winnipeg, Canada; 15 Indian portraits, David Thompson Memorial, British Columbia; Indian portraits and landscape, Art Center, Vancouver, B. C. Instructor, Kihn-Ten Eyck Art School, Stamford, Conn. Address in 1929, Ocean Drive West, Shippan Point, Stamford, CT.

KILBERT, ROBERT P.
Painter, lecturer and teacher. Born Germany, Sept. 14, 1880. Pupil of J. Francis Smith. Member: PCC. Address in 1929, 58 West Washington St.; h. 3741 North Kildare Ave., Chicago, Ill.; summer, Treasure Hill Art Academy, Bridgman, Mich.

KILBRUNN, L.
Painter. According to Dunlap. (See Kilburn).

KILBURN, (OR KILBRUNN) LAURENCE.
Painter. Born in 1720. He arrived from London in 1754, and advertised in the New York papers soliciting business. There are a number of portraits in New York by Kilburn which show him to have had some skill as a portrait painter; a bunch of flowers at the breast, or a flower held in the hand were among two of the characteristics of his style. He died June 28, 1775 in NYC. (See portrait of Mrs. Philip Schuyler, at New York Historical Society.)

KILENYI, JULIO.
Sculptor, medalist. Born in Hungary, 1885. Member: NY Arch. Lg.; NSS; Am. Numismatic Soc.; Allied AA; AFA. Designer of distinguished service medal of the US Navy Dept.; Lindbergh medal of St. Louis; Benjamin Franklin medal for 200th anniversary, Saturday Evening Post; Commander Byrd North Pole medal; Thomas A. Edison medallion for Edison Pioneers; Gen. Pershing medallion for American Legion; Judge E. H. Gary for US Steel Corp.; medal for 150th anniversary Battle of Lexington; medal for 150th anniversary Battle of Bunker Hill. Represented in the Metropolitan Museum of Art and Numismatic Museum, New York; Cleveland Museum of Art; Boston Museum of Fine Arts; Massachusetts Historical Museum. Address in 1929, 1 West 67th St., New York, NY.

KILHAM, JANE HOUSTON.
Painter. Born Modesto, Calif., Feb. 22, 1870. Pupil of Emil Carlsen, Raphael Collin, Paul Serusier. Member: North Shore AA; Gloucester SA; (pres.) Boston S. Indp. A. Award: Schneider Prize, Boston AC, 1925. Address in 1929, h. 42 West Cedar St., Boston, Mass.; summer, "The Clearing," Tamworth, NH.

KILHAM, WALTER H.
Painter and artist. Born Beverly, Mass., Aug. 30, 1868. Member: AIA. Address in 1929, 9 Park St.; h. 42 West Cedar St., Boston, Mass. Died 1948.

KILM, WILFRED LANGDON.
Painter. Born in Brooklyn, NY, in 1898. Pupil of Art Students' League, New York, Specialty, painting of American Indians. Address in 1926, 46 West 85th St., New York.

KILMER, DAVID L.
Illustrator. Born in Waterloo, Iowa, in 1950. Attended the Colorado Institute of Art in 1968 and 1969. His first published illustration was in 1970 for the Testor Corp., and he has since received awards from the Curtis Paper Co., Art Direction, and the Chicago '75 exhibit. From 1973 through 1976 his work has been selected to hang in S of I Annual Exhibitions.

KILPATIRCK, AARON (EDWARD).
Painter. Born St. Thomas, Canada,
Apr. 7, 1872. Pupil of William
Wendt. Member: Calif. AC;
Painters of the West; Laguna Beach
AA. Awards: Silver and bronze
medals, at the Panama-Calif. Exp.,
San Diego, 1915. Work: "Blue
Gums," owned by the Los Angeles
Athletic Club. Address in 1929,
5199 Ellenwood Drive, Eagle Rock,
Calif.

KILPATRICK, DeREID GALLATIN.
Painter and sculptor. Born
Uniontown, Sept. 21, 1884. Pupil
of Lucien Simon, Rene Prinex, Emil
Menard, Antoine Bourdelle, Raphael
Collin. Studied in Paris. Work:
Statue of Young George Washington,
Lincoln Highway at Waterford, PA;
statue of Colonel William Crawford,
Connellsville, PA; bas reliefs,
Methodist Episcopal Church,
Greensburg, PA; old portraits,
Court House, Uniontown, PA.
Address in 1929, care of Dr. A. G.
Morgan, 45 Prospect Pl., New York,
NY; h. care of Dr. J. J.
Kilpatrick, Bellefonte, PA; summer,
The White Swan Hotel, Uniontown,
PA.

KILVERT, B. CORY.
Illustrator. Born in 1881. A
graduate of the ASL, he was a
prolific illustrator of children's
books. His illustrations, often of
golf scenes, appeared in Life. He
devoted himself to watercolor and
seascape painting in his later
years. Died in 1946 in NYC.

KIMBALL, ALONZO MYRON.
Painter and illustrator. Born in
Green Bay, Wisc., in 1874; died in
Evanston, Ill., in 1923. He was a
pupil of the Art Students' League,
New York, and of the Julien
Academy, Paris, under Lefebvre and
Whistler. He was a member of the
Society of Illustrators, 1911.

KIMBALL, ISABEL MOORE.
Sculptor. Born Wentworth, Mitchell
Co., IA. Pupil of Herbert Adams.
Member: SPNY; N.A. Women PS;
Brooklyn SA; PS; AGA. Work:
"Wenonah" Fountain in Central Park,
Winona, Minn.; gold medal, Y.M.C.A.
swimming and life saving; Richards
memorial tablet, Vassar College;
Barrett memorial, Historical Soc.,

Des Moines, Iowa; War Memorial
Tablet for Essex, Conn.; war
memorial tablet, Burnett Hills, NY;
war memorial tablet, Mountainville,
NY; Burnett Memorial Tablet,
Central High School, Kalamazoo,
Mich. Address in 1929, 246 Fulton
St.; Brooklyn, New York, NY.

KIMBALL, KATHARINE.
Etcher and illustrator. Born in
New Hampshire. Pupil of NAD in New
York; Royal College of Art, London.
Member: Asso. Royal Soc. of
Painter-Etchers and Engravers,
London; Societaire Section de
Gravavure, Salon d'Automne, Paris;
Chicago SE; Calif. PM. Award:
Bronze medal, P.-P. Exp., San F.,
1915. Illustrated: Okey's "Story
of Paris"; Gialliat-Smith's
"Brussels;: Stirling Taylor's "
"Canterbury" and "Rochester," etc.
Work: Bibliotheque d'Art et
d'Archeologie, Paris. Work in
Victoria and Albert Museum and
British Museum, London; New York
Public Library; Boston Museum of
Fine Arts; Library of Congress,
Washington, DC.; Oakland (Calif.)
Public Museum; Public Reference
Library, Bath, Somerset, England.
Address in 1929, care of Brown,
Shipley & Co., 123 Pall Mall,
London, SW., England.

KIMBERLY, CORA DRAPER.
Painter. Born in St. Louis, MO, in
1876. Studied: Wash. Univ; Boston
Museum of Fine Arts; Art Institute
of Chicago; Chicago Academy of Art;
and with Farnsworth, Vanderpoel,
Messer, and Hawthorne. Award:
Society of Wash. Artists.
Collections: Interiors of White
House, Arlington House, Dumbarton
House, and Mt. Vernon.

KIMBERLY, DENISON.
Engraver and painter. Born in
Guilford, Conn., in 1814. Kimberly
was a fellow-student with George H.
Chushman in the engraving
establishment of Asaph Willard, and
as a line-engraver of portraits he
achieved considerable success. He
was working in 1830 for S. Walker,
the Boston publisher, and was later
connected with the Franklin Print
Company, of Boston. In 1858
Kimberly abandoned engraving for
painting; he studied in Boston, and

515

in 1862 he opened studios in Hartford and in Manchester. He was chiefly engaged in portrait work, producing good likenesses, strong and free in outline, yet remarkably soft in feature. The portrait of his friend Seth W. Cheney is one of his best works. Died in 1863.

KIMBERLY, JAMES H.
Miniature artist, flourishing 1841-43, in New York.

KIMBLE, RICHARD M.
Painter. Born NYC. Member: Allied AA; Salma. C.; NAC. Work: "The Old Antique Shop," PAFA. Address in 1929, 30 East 14th St.; h. 616 West 116th St., New York, NY, summer, Baniff, Alberta, Canada.

KIMMEL, LU.
Illustrator. Born in Brooklyn, NY, in 1908. He was a pupil of Will Taylor, Pruett Carter, George Luks, Max Hermann, and Michel Jacobs at PI. In 1933, he won an award from the National Red Cross Poster Competition while illustrating regularly for The Saturday Evening Post, Country Gentleman, Household Magazine, Field and Stream, and others. A member of the S of I, he lectured at the Queensboro Teachers' Association and was an art instructor at the Commercial Illustrations Studios in NY. Died in 1973.

KIMMEL, P. K.
Engraver of vignettes and portraits working in New York about 1850, and was later a member of the engraving firm of Capewell & Kimmel, of the same city. There was also an engraving firm of Kimmel & Foster. May be same as Christopher Kimmel, born 1830, in Germany.

KIMURA, SUEKO M.
Painter. Born in Hawaii in 1912. Studied: Univ. of Hawaii; Chouinard Art Institute, Los Angeles, CA; Columbia Univ.; Brooklyn Museum Art School. Awards: Artists of Hawaii; Easter Art School; Wichita Art Museum, Kansas. Collections: State Found. on Culture and the Arts; Contemporary Art Center; Department of Education, Artmobile. Address

in 1980, 2567B Henry St., Honolulu, HI.

KINDLER, ALICE RIDDLE.
(Mrs. Hans Kindler). Painter. Born Germantown, PA, Oct. 3, 1892. Studied PAFA. Works: "The Yellow Still Life," Pennsylvania Academy of the Fine Arts, Philadelphia; Mural, "The Canterbury Pilgrimage," West Philadelphia High School. Address in 1929, Hotel du Chateau, Chantilly, France.

KING, ALBERT F.
Painter. Born Pittsburgh, PA, Dec. 6, 1854. Self-taught. Member: Pittsburgh AA; Pittsburgh AS. Work: portrait in Homeopathic Hospital and in Duquesne Club, Pittsburgh, PA. Address in 1929, Fifth Ave. Arcade Bldg.; 815 South Braddock Ave., Pittsburgh, PA.

KING, CHARLES B.
Painter and etcher. Born in California in 1869. Pupil of Laurens in Paris, and of Brangwyn in London. Represented in New York Public Library, and Library of Congress, Washington, DC. Address in 1926, 814 Jefferson Ave., Detroit, Mich.

KING, CHARLES BIRD.
Born in Newport, RI, in 1785. He first studied with Edward Savage, and in 1805 he went to London where he continued his studies. He returned in 1812, had a studio in Philadelphia, and in 1816 moved to Washington, DC. He died in Washington March 18, 1862, leaving a number of his pictures and several thousand dollars to the Redwood Library of Newport, RI. His portrait of John C. Calhoun is in the Corcoran Art Gallery, Washington, DC. Hon. mention of NA.

KING, ELIZABETH D. (BESSIE).
Painter. Born Aug. 14, 1855. Pupil of Candler School of Art, Detroit. Member; Atlanta AA. Represented in the Detroit Museum of Art. Detroit, Mich. Address in 1929, 384 Dargan Pl., S. W., Atlanta, GA.

KING, EMMA B.
Painter. Born Indianapolis. Pupil
of Cox, Beckwith, Chase and ASL in
New York; Boulanger, Lefebvre,
Carolus-Duran and Edwin Scott in
Paris. Member: ASL of NY; Indiana
AC. Address in 1929, 2118 North
Talbot St., Indianapolis, Ind.

KING, F(REDERIC) L(EONARD).
Painter and illustrator. Born New
York, Aug. 31, 1879. Pupil of
Bridgman; Chase; Cox; Arthur W.
Dow. Member: Salma. C.; Boston
AC; North Shore AA; Rockport AA.
Address in 1929, 4 Champney Pl.,
Boston, Mass.; summer, The
Forecastle, Rockport, Mass.

KING, FRANCIS SCOTT.
Painter. Born in Auburn, ME, in
1850. Designer and engraver on
copper. Designer of "Libris" of
the printer's devil; designed the
"Sylvester" bronze tablet for Johns
Hopkins University; also seal for
The Rockefeller Institute for Med.
Research, New York; designed and
engraved copper plates for "The
Boston Port Bills," published by
Grolier Club, New York; designed
and engraved on copper numerous
important plates for the Society of
Iconophiles, New York. Member:
Society of American Wood Engravers.
Address in 1926, 106 South 7th St.,
Newark, NJ.

KING, FRANK S.
Engraver. Well known as a wood
engraver, and later turned to
copper plate engraving. He
executed a series of wood
engravings after the wood of
Burne-Jones.

KING, GEORGE B.
This line-engraver produced some
portraits and book illustrations of
lesser merit for the New York
publishers of 1830-34.

KING, GERTRUDE.
(Mrs. L. H. Colville). Painter,
craftsman and teacher. Born
Newark, NJ. Pupil of R. H.
Johonnot, I. W. Stoud. Member: NA
Women PS. Address in 1929,
Mendham, NJ.

KING, GILLIS.
Painter. Born Dewville, Tex., Feb.
8, 1904. Pupil of S. E. Gideon,

Michel Jacobs, George Bridgman.
Member: Tex. FAA; SSAL; AFA.
Work: "Sugar Maples," Austin Art
League, Austin, Tex.; "The Road,"
San Angelo Art League, San Angelo,
Tex. Address in 1929, 618 North
Second, Ft. Worth, Tex.; h. 2702
East Ave., Austin, Tex.

KING, HAMILTON.
Painter and illustrator. Born
Lewiston, ME, Dec. 21, 1871. Pupil
of Julian Academy in Paris.
Member: SI 1915; AFA. Died in
1952. Address in 1929, 200 West
57th St., New York, NY; East
Hampton, LI, NY.

KING, JAMES.
Painter, etcher and engraver. Born
in New York in 1852. Pupil of Art
Students' League, New York; also of
Ecole des Beaux Arts under Gerome.
He died at Montclair, NJ, in 1925.
He made a specialty of portraits
and marine views.

KING, JAMES S.
Engraver. The "Ladies Repository,"
published in Cincinnati in 1852,
contains some good line
subject-plates signed by James S.
King as engraver.

KING, JOHN.
Portrait painter of the Civil War
period. (See his portrait of Gen.
Henry Lee, Gov. of Virginia.)

KING, JOHN CROOKSHANKS.
Sculptor. Born in Scotland Oct.
11, 1806; died in Boston April 22,
1882. He modeled busts of many
public men and made cameo
likenesses. He resided in New
Orleans, LA, and later in Boston,
Mass. Among his best known busts
are: "Daniel Webster," "John
Quincy Adams," "Louis Agassiz" and
"Emerson."

KING, LOUIS H.
See Mrs. Kenyon Cox.

KING, MARION P(ERMELIA).
Sculptor. Born Ashtabula, Ohio,
Oct. 7, 1894. Pupil of Charles
Grafly. Member: Cleveland School
of Art Alumni; Fellowship PAFA;
Allied AA; S. Indp. A; AFA.
Awards: Cresson Traveling
Scholarship PAFA, 1923-25; Stimson

Prize, 1925. Address in 1929, 14 Sherman St., Ashtabula, Ohio.

KING, PAUL.
Painter. Born Buffalo, NY, Feb. 9, 1867. Pupil of ASL of Buffalo; ASL of NY under Mowbray. Member: ANA; Salma. C.; AC Phila.; A. Fund S.; A. Aid S.; NAC; Inter. Soc. AL; PS Gallery Assn.; Fellowship PAFA; Allied AA; AFA. Awards: Shaw prize, Salma. C; 1906; Inness Prize, Salma C., 1906; hon. mention AC Phila., 1911; gold medal, Phila. AC, 1913; silver medal, P.-P. Exp., San F., 1915; Phila. prize, PAFA, 1918; first Altman prize ($1,000), NAD, 1923; Isidor prize, Salma. C., 1928. Work: "A Cool Retreat," Engineers Club, New York; "Boulder Pass," Art Club of Philadelphia; "Sailing Boats," Reading Museum; "The Old Farm," Albright Gallery, Buffalo; "Hauling Logs," Butler Art Inst., Youngstown, Ohio; "Passing of Winter," Harrison Gallery, Los Angeles Museum; "Landscape," Art Museum, Houston, Tex.; "Autumn," "Winter," "Autumn Trees," New Pantheon, Nashville, Tenn.; "Winter Woods," Buffalo Athletic Club; "Nearing Home," Quinnipiack Club, New Haven. Represented in National Gallery, Washington. Address in 1929, Stony Brook, LI, NY; 275 Pawling Ave., Troy, NY.

KING, SAMUEL.
Portrait painter in oils and miniature. Born in Jan. 24, 1749 in Newport, RI. He painted a miniature of Rev. Ezra Stiles, President of Yale University in 1770, and a portrait in oil in 1771. In the winter of 1771-72 he was painting in Salem, Mass. In 1780 King made a copy of Peale's portrait of Washington, belonging to John Hancock, which was sent to France. King had as pupils, Stuart, Allston, Malabone and Charles B. King. He died Dec. 30, 1819, in Newport, RI.

KING, VIRGINIA M.
Sculptor. Born in Norfolk, VA, 1879. Pupil of Salon Borglum and of Harriet Frishmuth. Address in 1926, Keokuk St., Chevy Chase, Washington, DC.

KING, WILLIAM.
Sculptor. Born Feb. 25, 1925, in Jacksonville, Fla. Studied at U. of Fla (1942-4); Cooper Union; (1945-8); Academia dei Belli Arte, Rome. Taught at Brooklyn Mus., Art School, Berkeley and Art Students League (1968-9). Rec. awards from Cooper Union (1948 & 1946); Moorehead Patterson Sculpture Award(1961). Awarded Fullbright, 1949. Exhibited at Roko Gallery (1948); Phil. Mus. of Art; MOMA (1955); Guggenheim; Cooper Union; Whitney and others. In collections of Whitney; Addison; Syracuse U.; Cornell and Bankers Trust in NYC.

KING, WYNCIE.
Illustrator. He was born Covington, GA, Sept. 21, 1884. Address in 1929, College Inn, Bryn Mawr, PA.

KINGMAN, DONG M.
Painter and illustrator. Born in Oakland, CA, on Mar. 31, 1911. Studied at Lingnan School, Hong Kong, with Sze-To-Wai, 1926; Fox and Morgan Art School, Oakland. In collections of Met. Mus. of Art, MOMA, Whitney, in NYC; Boston Mus. of FA; de Young Mus., San F.; plus commissions in NYC, San F., and Hong Kong. Exhibited at Am. WC Soc.; San Fran. Art Assn.; Met. Mus. of Art WC exhib.; Whitney annual; others. Received awards: San F. Art Assn. ann., 1936; Met. Mus. of Art WC exhib., and Am. WC Soc. Ann. Taught at ASL; Columbia U., 1946-1954; Hunter College, 1948-1953; Famous Artists School, Westport CT, from 1954. Member of Am. WC Soc.; others. Media: Watercolor and lacquer. Rep. by Hammer Galleries, NYC. Address in 1982, 21 W. 58th St., NYC.

KINGSBURG, EDWARD R.
Painter. Born in Boston, Mass. Pupil of School of Boston Museum of Fine Arts; also studied in Paris. Mural painting in Charlestown, Mass., High School. Address in 1926, 24 St. Botolph St., Boston, Mass. Died in 1940.

KINGSBURY, EDNA (A.)
Painter. Born Xenia, Ohio, May 5, 1888. Pupil of J. Otis Adams, Otto Stark, William Forsythe. Member:

518

Springfield AA; S. Indp. A. Address in 1929, 1128 East Ohio St., Indianapolis, Ind.

KINGSBURY, EDWARD R(EYNOLDS).
Painter. Born Boston. Pupil of Mass. Normal Art School and Boston Museum School; studied in Paris. Member: Boston AC; Salma. C.; AFA. Work: "Time and the World," mural painting in Charlestown (Mass.) High School, etc. Died in 1940. Address in 1929, Boston Art Club, 150 Newbury St., Boston, Mass.; summer, Ogunquit, ME.

KINGSLEY, ELDRIDGE.
Wood engraver and painter. Born in 1842; died in New York in 1918. Pupil of Cooper Institute of New York. Awarded gold medal at the Paris Exposition of 1889. Many examples of his work are in the Print Department of the New York Public Library. He was a member fo the Society of American Wood Engravers.

KINNEY, BENJAMIN HARRIS.
Sculptor. Born Feb. 7, 1821, in Mass. His bust of Isaiah Thomas is owned in Worcester, Mass. Died Dec. 1888, in Worcester.

KINNEY, MARGARET WEST.
(Mrs. Troy Kinney). Illustrator. Born Peoria, Ill., June 11, 1872. Pupil of ASL of NY; Julian Academy in Paris under Robert-Fleury, Collin, Merson and Lefebvre. Member: Assoc. SI 1912. Address in 1929, R.F.D. No. 1. Falls Village, Conn.

KINNEY, TROY.
Painter, illustrator, etcher. Born Kansas City, MO, Dec. 1, 1871. Pupil of AIC. Member: Chicago SE; Brooklyn SE; NY Arch. Lg.; Phila. PC. Work in Chicago Art Institute; Cleveland and Brooklyn Museums; New York Public Library; Library of Congress, Washington, DC. Specialty, etchings. Died in 1938. Address in 1929, R.F.D. No. 1. Falls Village, Conn.

KINSELLA, JAMES.
Painter. Born in New York in 1857; died in 1923. Pupil of National Academy of Design; Ecole des Beaux Arts in Paris. Member: National

Art Club. Work: "Seven O'Clock from Manasquan," Museum of Newark, NJ, Technical School.

KINSEY, ALBERTA.
Painter. Native of West Milton, Ohio, and studied art in the Cincinnati Art Academy and in the Chicago Art School. Instructor of art in Lebanon University, Lebanon, Ohio. Member: Women's Art Club, Cincinnati; Art Association, and Arts and Crafts Club, New Orleans. Architectural work, and landscapes in oil and water colors. Represented in Cincinnati Art Museum and in the Delgado Museum.

KINSEY, HELEN F(AIRCHILD).
Painter, illustrator, writer and teacher. Born Philadelphia, Aug. 12, 1877. Pupil of Thouron; W. M. Chase; Beaux; Anshutz; Breckenridge; Grafly; Dr. James P. Haney; Arthur W. Dow. Member: Plastic C; Fellowship PAFA; Eastern AA; Phila. Art Teachers Asso.; Phila. Alliance; AFA. Address in 1929, 1301 Spring Garden St.; h. 1015 So. St. Bernard St., Philadelphia, PA.

KINSEY, NATHANIEL JR.
Engraver. Born 1829 in Delaware. In 1854-55 this good landscape engraver was employed by the Western Methodist Book Concern, of Cincinnati, Ohio.

KINSMAN-WATERS, RAY.
Painter, craftsman and teacher. Born Columbus, Ohio, July 21, 1887. Pupil of Columbus Art School; Alice Schille. Member: NYWCC; Lg. of Columbus A.; Ohio WCC. Awards: Water color prize, Lg. of Columbus A., 1923. Address in 1929, 1143 Lincoln Rd., Columbus, Ohio.

KIRALFY, VERONA A(RNOLD).
Portrait painter. Born New York City, Oct. 1, 1893. Pupil of Chase and ASL of NY. Member: Pittsburgh AA. Award: 1st honor, Pitts. AA, 1922. Address in 1929, Central Athletic Bldg., Craig and Filmore Sts., Pittsburgh, PA.

KIRBY, C. VALENTINE.
Craftsman, writer, lecturer and teacher. Born Canajoharie, NY, July 19, 1875. Pupil of ASL of NY;

Chase School of Art, NY; studied in Europe. Member: Eastern AA; Western AA; Phila. Alliance; Phila. Sketch C. Instructor of fine and industrial arts, Manual Training H.S., Denver, Colo., 1900-10; director of art instruction, Buffalo, 1911, 1912; Pitts., PA, 1912-20; State Director of Art Education for Penna. since 1920. Lecturer at Carnegie Inst. of Tech., Univ. of Pittsburgh, Penna. State College. Am. representative and speaker, International Art Congress, Dresden, 1912. Assisted in survey of art in Am. Industry, 1920; Comm. Internat'l Art Congress, Prague, 1928; Advisory Comm., Carnegie Corp.; Art Comm., Nat'l Congress of Parents and Teachers; Federated Council on Art Edu. Author: The Business of Teaching and Supervising the Arts. Address in 1929, State Dept. of Public Instruction; h. 219 State St., Harrisburg, PA.

KIRK, FRANK C.
Painter. Born Russia, May 11, 1889. Pupil of PAFA. Member: Phila. Alliance; Fellowship PAFA; S. Indp. A; Salons of Am; PAL; Grand Cent. AG; North Shore AA. Work: Five paintings owned by the Graphic Sketch Club, Philadelphia; "Tuscannian Vase," Trenton Museum, Trenton, NJ; murals, Victoria Theatre, Mahanoy City, PA; Royal Theatre, Felton Theatre, Bronson Theatre, Philadelphia; Grand Theatre, Norfolk, VA; theatres at Reading and Phoenixville, Penn. Died in 1963. Address in 1929, 407 Locust St., Philadelphia, PA.

KIRK, JOHN.
Engraver. Born 1823, in England; died in the United States about 1862. Kirk came to the United States about 1841, and was largely employed by the publishers G. P. Putnam, and by A. B. Hall and other New York engravers. He did some admirable work in line.

KIRK, MARIE LOUISE.
Painter and illustrator. Born in Philadelphia. Student of Philadelphia School of Design and of the Penna. Academy of Fine Arts. Received the Mary Smith

prize at the Penna. Academy of Fine Arts in 1894.

KIRKBRIDE, E(ARIE) R(OSSLYN).
Painter and illustrator. Born Pittsburgh, March 11, 1891. Pupil of Vanderpoel; Buehr; Clarkson. Member: Cliff Dwellers; Palette and Chisel C. Illustrated: "Sunny Sam" (Reilly and Lee Co.); "Myself and Fellow Asses," by Thos. Temple Hoyne; stories for Red Book. Died in 1968. Address in 1929, Fine Arts Bldg., 410 South Michigan Blvd.; h. 5493 Cornell Ave., Chicago, Ill.; summer, Eagles Nest Camp, Oregon, Ill.

KIRKHAM, CHARLOTTE BURT.
Painter and teacher. Born East Saginaw, Mich. Pupil of Douglas Volk, Burtis Baker, Lefebvre in Paris. Member: Wash. SA; Springfield A. Lg.; Springfield AG. Address in 1929, 66 Harrison Ave.; h. 107 Maplewood Ter., Springfield, Mass.

KIRKLAND, VANCE H.
Painter, lecturer and teacher. Born Convoy, Ohio, Nov. 3, 1904. Pupil of Henry G. Keller, Frank N. Wilcox. Member: Cleveland Art Center. Award: Hon. mention, Cleveland Museum of Art, 1927. Gives gallery talks at Denver Art Museum. Director, Chappell School of Art. Address in 1929, 1300 Logan St.; h. 970 Pearl St., Denver, Colo.

KIRKPATRICK, FRANK LE BRUN.
Painter. Exhibited water colors at the Penna. Academy of Fine Arts, Philadelphia. Died in 1917.

KIRKPATRICK, MARLON POWERS.
(Mrs. W. A. Kirkpatrick). See Powers.

KIRKPATRICK, W(ILLIAM) A(RBER-BROWN).
Painter and illustrator. Born in England, Nov. 7, 1880. Studied under Laurens in Paris; and London. Member: GFLA; St. Botolph C. Address in 1929, 30 Ipswich St., Boston, Mass.; summer, Friendship, ME.

KIRKUP, MARY A.
Painter, writer and lecturer. Born Fort Atkinson, IA. Pupil of ASL of

520

NY; Lasar in Paris. Pupil of ASL of NY; Lasar in Paris. Member: Lg. of Amer. Pen Women; New Rochelle AC; Yonkers AA. Award: Adolph Grant prize, New Rochelle AA, 1926; landscape prize, Catherine Lorillard Wolfe AA, New York, 1927.

KIRMSE, MARGUERITE.
Painter, sculptor, illustrator and etcher. Born Bournemouth, England, Dec. 14, 1885. Pupil of Frank Calderon. Member: Phila. PC; Springfield AA. Illustrated "Bob, Son of Battle," by Ollivant. Died in 1954. Address in 1929, 231 East 48th St., New York, NY; summer, Bridgewater, Conn.

KIRPAL, ELSA.
See Mrs. Tower Peterson.

KIRSCH, AGATHA (BEATRICE).
Painter, illustrator, craftsman and teacher. Born Creston, IA, May 9, 1879. Pupil of Arthur V. Frasier; Seattle Art School under Ella Shepherd Bush; Johonnot; Art Dept., University of Washington. Award: Hon. mention, Seattle FAS. Address in 1929, 503 Washington Mutual Savings Bank Bldg., cor. Second Ave. and Spring St.; h. 7582 - 45th Ave., SW, Seattle, Wash.

KIRSHNER, RAPHAEL.
Painter and illustrator. Born in Vienna in 1876; died in New York City in 1917. He painted a series of prominent American women.

KISER, VIRGINIA LEE.
Painter, etcher and craftsman. Born Virginia. Pupil of William M. Chase, F. Vincent DuMond, F. Luis Mora, Joseph Pennell. Member: Columbus AL; Pittsburgh Asso. A; AFA; Ohio WCP. Address in 1929, 81 Miami Ave., Columbus, Ohio.

KISHI, MASATOYO.
Born: Sakai, Japan, in 1924. Graduated from the Sakai Middle School in 1941 and completed his studies in the science course at the Tokyo Physical College in 1945. He organized the Tekkeikai Group in 1958. Exhibitions: Sogo Art Gallery, Osaka, 1956; Maruzen Gallery, Tokyo, 1957; Hakuho Gallery, Osaka, 1957, 1960; Takasnimaya Art Gallery, Osaka,

1958; Thibaut Gallery, New York, 1961; Museum of Art, Carnegie Institute, Pittsburgh, 1961. Bolles Gallery, San Francisco, 1961. Came to US in 1960; lives in San Francisco.

KISSACK, R. A.
Painter. Born St. Louis, March 4, 1878. Pupil of St. Louis School of Fine Arts and Studied in Paris. Member: St. Louis AG. Awards: Gold medal, St. Louis School of Fine Arts; George Warren Brown prize for figure painting, St. Louis AG. WorK: Decoration in Missouri State Capitol, portraits. Director of Art Education, New York University. Address in 1929, 15 West 11th St., New York, NY.

KISSELL, ELEONORA.
Painter and etcher. Born Morristown, Oct. 23, 1891. Member: NA Women PS. Address in 1929, 159 East 61st St., New York, NY; summer, Morristown, NJ.

KITCHELL, JOSEPH GRAY.
Painter and writer. Born in Cincinnati, Ohio, in 1862. Photographic editor of Quarterly Illustrator. In 1900 he produced the Ketchell "Composite Madonna," a merging of the most important madonnas painted by the great masters during 300 years, which attracted wide attention in America and Europe. In 1915 he invented and patented a new method of reproducing pictures known as "Sub-Chromatic Art," examples of which were accepted by the Metropolitan Museum; National Academy of Design; Congressional Library; British Museum; Bibliotheque Nationale, Paris, etc. Address in 1926, Mountain Lakes, NJ.

KITSON, H(ENRY) H(UDSON).
Sculptor. Born Huddersfield, England, April 9, 1865. Pupil of Ecole des Beaux-Arts in Paris under Bonnaissieux. Member: Coply S., 1899; Boston SAC; Boston AC; Eclectics. Awards: Three gold medals, Mass. Charitable Mechanics; Association, New York, 1886; bronze medal, Paris exp., 1889; medal, Columbian Exp., Chicago, 1893; decoration from King of Rumania;

medal Paris Exp., 1900. Work: "The Minute Man," Lexington, Mass.; Cedar Rapids, Iowa; Dyer Memorial Fountain, Providence; W. M. Hunt Memorial, Boston; "Music of the Sea," Boston Museum; "Viscount James Bryce," bronze bust, National Gallery, Washington, DC; National Gallery, London, England; Newark Museum; "Admiral Selfridge," Vicksburg, Miss.; "Roger Conant statue," Salem, Mass.; "Patrick A. Collins Monument," "Robert Burns Monument," "Henry B. Endicott Memorial," "Gov. Banks' Monument," Boston, Mass.; "Farragut Statue;" "Lt. Gen. Stephen D. Lee," "Gen. Martin L. Smith," "Iowa State Memorial," Vicksburg, Miss.; "Thomas A. Doyle statue," Providence, RI; "Walt Whitman," bust, London, England' "Elizabeth, Queen of Roumania (Carmen Sylva)," "Carol, King of Roumania," Bucharest, Roumania; "Christ," Drexel Memorial Chapel, Philadelphia, PA; "Haynes Memorial," Newark, NJ. Died in 1947. Address in 1929, 4 Harcourt St., Boston, Mass.

KITSON, SAMUEL JAMES.
Sculptor. Born in England in 1848, he came to America in 1878, having studied in Italy. He produced such work as the "Sheridan Monument" and the portrait of Gov. Greenhalge in the State House at Boston. He died in New York in 1906.

KITSON, THEO ALICE RUGGLES.
(Mrs. H. H. Kitson). Sculptor. Born Brookline, Mass., 1876. Pupil of H. H. Kitson in Boston; Dagnan-Bouveret in Paris. Member: Copley S. NSS. Awards: Hon. mention, Paris Salon, 1890; two medals, Mass. Charitable Mechanics; Assoc.; bronze medal, St. Louis Exp., 1904. Work: "Minute Man of '76," Framingham, Mass.; soldier monuments at Goshen, NY; Walden, NY; Vicksburg, Miss.; Minneapolis, Minn.; Pasadena, Calif.; Providence, RI; Little Falls, RI; Ashburnham, Mass.; North Andover, Mass.; North Attleboro, Mass.; Sharon, Mass.; Topsfield, Mass.; Spanish war monuments at Schenectady, NY, and Lynn, Mass.; World War memorials, Dorchester, Mass; Brookline, Mass.; Francestown, NH; Equestrian Statue of Victory, Hingham, Mass.; portrait statue of "Gen. Kosciuszko," Public Gardens, Boston, Mass.; Memorial statue, Mt. Auburn, Cambridge, Mass. Address in 1929, Framingham, Mass.

KITT, KATHERINE F(LORENCE).
Painter, illustrator and teacher. Born Chico, Calif., Oct. 9, 1876. Pupil of Richard Miller, Henri Morrisot. Member: Cincinnati Woman's AC; NAC; AFA. Head of art dept., University of Arizona, since 1925. Address in 1929, 319 South Fourth Ave., Tucson, Ariz.

KITTS, J(ESSIE) De L(ANCEY).
(Mrs. L. T. Kitts). Painter and craftsman. Born Knoxville, Tenn., Oct. 9, 1869. Pupil of Minn. Sch. of Fine Arts; San Francisco Sch. of Fine Arts. Member: San Francisco S. Women A. Address in 1929, 1248 25th Ave., San Francisco, Calif.

KIYOKAWA, TAIJI.
Painter. Born 1919 in Hamamatsu, Japan. Graduated from Keio Univ., Tokyo; studied in France and U.S. Taught at Tokyo Univ. of Arts; residing in San F., Calif. Received awards from Nat. Western Mus. in Tokyo. Exhibited at many Tokyo galleries; Zen Center, San F. (1964); San F. Art Center; Cal. Palace, and Triangle Gallery, San F. In collections of International theatre of Tokyo and San F. Mus. of Art.

KLAGES, FRANK H.
Painter and illustrator. Born in Philadelphia in 1892. Pupil of Penna. Academy of Fine Arts. Address in 1926, 2027 North 31st St., Philadelphia.

KLAGSTAD, AUGUST.
Painter. Born Bingen, Norway, Aug. 14, 1866. Pupil of Feudell, W. J. Reynolds, AIC, and Chicago Academy of Fine Arts. Member: Scandinavian Art Soc. of America; AFA. Award: Hon. mention Minneapolis Inst., 1915. Specialty, portraits and church paintings.

KLAR, WALTER H(UGHES).
Painter, writer, lecturer and teacher. Born Westfield, Mass.,

March 20, 1882. Pupil of Ernest L. Major, Joseph DeCamp, Richard Andrews. Member: Springfield AL. Award: First honor, Pittsburgh Associated Artists, Pittsburgh, PA, 1919. Address in 1929, 41 Dartmouth St., Springfield, Mass.

KLASSTORNER, SAMUEL.
Sculptor and teacher. Born Russia, Feb. 25, 1895. Pupil of AIC. Member: Chicago PS. Awards: Englewood Woman's Club prize, 1921, from Chicago Soc. A.; Frank G. Logan medal and $200, Chicago Soc. A.; hon. mention, Painters and Sculptors, 1923, Art Inst. of Chicago. Address in 1929, 1140 North La Salle St., h. 6252 Drexel Ave., Chicago, Ill.

KLAUBER, ALICE.
Painter. Born San Diego, May 19, 1871. Pupil of Chase; Henri. Award: Prize, Fine Arts Gallery, San Diego, 1927. Chairman of Art Dept., San Diego Exp., 1915-16. Designed and directed finish and furnishings, for the "Persimmon Room" of the Exposition, for the living rooms of the Community Center in Balboa Park, for the new Y. W. C. A. in San Diego, and for the San Diego Wednesday Club House. Address in 1929, 2429 Fifth St., San Diego, Calif.

KLAUDER, MARY.
Sculptor. Exhibited "A study" at the Penna. Academy of the Fine Art, Philadelphia, 1914. Address in 1926, Bala, Penna.

KLAW, ALONZO.
Painter. Born Louisville, KY, Apr. 15, 1885. Pupil of New York School of Art, ASL of NY. Member: Salma. C.; AWCS; NYWCC. Address in 1929, Carmel, NY.

KLEIMINGER, A. F.
Painter. Born Chicago, Ill., Dec. 4, 1865. Pupil of Henri Martin. Member: Chicago SA; S. Indp. A.; New Bedford SA. Address in 1929, 4164 Lake Park Ave., Chicago, Ill.; summer, Nonquitt, Mass.

KLEIN, BENJAMIN.
Painter, illustrator and etcher. Born Austria-Hungary, Sept. 4, 1898. Pupil of Margaret and Troy

Kinney; NAD, and Europe. Award: Hon. mention. Eberhard Faber Competition, and Van Dyke Contest for Drawing, 1927. Illustrations for many magazines. Address in 1929, 130 West 95th St., New York, NY.

KLEIN, ISIDORE.
Painter and illustrator. Born Russia, Oct. 12, 1897. Pupil of NAD. Member: S. Indp. A. Illustrations in The New Yorker, Life, Judge, New Masses. Address in 1929, 145 West 14th St., New York, NY.

KLEIN, NATHAN.
Painter. Exhibited in 1925, at Annual Exhibition of National Academy of Design, New York. Address in 1926, 1841 61st St., Brooklyn, NY.

KLEITSCH, JOSEPH.
Painter, lecturer and teacher. Born Banad, 1885. Studied in Chicago, Budapest, Munich and Paris. Member: Chicago PS; Palette and Chisel C.; Chicago SA; Laguna Beach AA. Awards: Gold medal, Palette and Chisel C.; silver medal, Painters and Sculptors Club; first prize, State Fair, Sacramento, Calif.; grand prize and figure prize, Laguna Beach AA; purchase prize, Arche Club, Chicago. Address in 1929, Laguna Beach, Calif.

KLEMPNER, ERNEST S.
Painter. Born Vienna, Austria, July 26, 1867. Pupil of L'Allemand. Member: AFA. Work: "Portrait of an Actor," City of Vienna; "Francis Burley, Esq.," Chicago Historical Society; "Dr. Otto C. Schmidt," Dr. Archibald Church Library, Chicago. Etchings of King George V, Lord Northcliffe and others. Illustrates for Punch, Illus. London News, Graphic, etc. Address in 1929, 410 South Michigan Ave., Chicago, Ill.; h. Lake Bluff, Ill.

KLEPPER, FRANK L.
Painter and teacher. Born Plano, Texas, May 3, 1890. Pupil of AIC; Harry Lachman in Paris. Member: SSAL; Dallas AA. Award: Hon. mention, Texas State Artists, 1916;

Everts gold medal, Texas State Artists, 1920; Woman's Forum medal, Texas State Artists, 1922; purchase prize, Texas Artists, 1928; hon. mention, Davis Competitive exhib., 1929. Represented in Collection of Woman's Forum, Dallas; High Schools, McKinney, and Plano, Tex. Died in 1950. Address in 1929, McKinney, Texas.

KLEPPER, MAX FRANCIS.
Painter. Born in Germany in 1861. Came to America in 1876 and settled in Toledo, Ohio. Established himself in New York, working on magazine illustration. He also specialized in animal pictures. He died in Brooklyn, NY in 1907.

KLINE, GEORGE T.
Lecturer and teacher. Born Baltimore, MD, Aug. 22, 1874. Pupil of S. E. Whiteman. Member: St. Louis AL; AFA. Illustrated scientific articles. Died in 1956. Address in 1929, St. Louis Univ. School of Medicine, 1402 South Grand Ave., St. louis, MO.

KLINE, HIBBERD VAN BUREN.
Painter, illustrator and etcher. Born Auriesville, NY, Nov. 8, 1885. Pupil of College of FA, Syracuse Univ.; and ASL of NY under Chase and Mora. Member: AFA, Professor of illustration, Dept. of Art, Syracuse Univ. Address in 1929, 523 Clarendon St., Syracuse, NY; summer, Fort Hunter, NY.

KLINE, WILLIAM F(AIR).
Mural painter, illustrator and craftsman. Born Columbia, SC, May 3, 1870. Pupil of NAD under Low and Ward, and of John La Farge in New York; Juliean Academy under Bouguereau and Constant, and Colarossi Academy in Paris. Member: ANA 1901; Mural P.; NYWCC, 1918; AWCS, 1919; AFA. Awards: Lazarus traveling scholarship 1894; silver medal, Pan-Am. Exp., Buffalo, 1901; Clarke prize, NAD 1901; second Hallgarten prize, NAD 1903; bronze medal for painting and gold for window, St. Louis Exp., 1904. Work: Crerar Memorial Window, Second Presbyterian Church, Chicago, Ill. Died July 30, 1931

in Anniston, Ala. Address in 1929, 244 West 14th St., New York, NY.

KLIROS, THEA.
Illustrator. Born in NYC in 1935. Attended Bennington College and Yale Univ. before beginning her career in 1953 with a woodcut for Seventeen. Best known for her fashion illustrations, she has had her artwork exhibited in Wash., DC, and Spain.

KLITGAARD, GEORGINA.
Painter. Born in NYC on July 3, 1893. Studied: Barnard College. Awards: Pennsylvania Academy of Fine Arts, 1930; Pan-American Exposition, 1931; Guggenheim fellowship, 1933; Carnegie Institute; Art Institute of Chicago. Collections: Metropolitan Museum of Art; Whitney Museum of American Art; Newark Museum; Dayton Art Institute; New Britain Art Institute; Brooklyn Museum; Wood Gallery of Art, Montpelier, Vermont; United States Post Office, Poughkeepsie, NY; Goshen, NY; Pelham, Georgia. Address in 1980, Bearsville, NY.

KLOPPER, ZANWILL D.
Painter and illustrator. Born in Russia, in 1870. Pupil of Julien Academy in Paris. Specialty, anatomical drawings. Represented by "Immaculate Conception," and mural decorations in "St. Mary's of the Woods." Address in 1926, 1642 West Division St., Chicago, Ill.

KLOTZ, ISIDORE E.
Painter. Exhibited "The Rose Bower" at the Penna. Academy of Fine Arts, Philadelphia, 1925. Address in 1926, East Gloucester, Mass.

KLOUS, ROSE M.
(Mrs. Isidore P. Klous). Painter and etcher. Born St. Petersburg, Petrograd, Russia, May 28, 1889. Pupil of ASL of NY; Grand Central School of Art; Julian Academy, Paris. Member: ASL of NY.; Gloucester SA; S. Indp. A. Address in 1929, 205 West 57th St., New York, NY; summer, 7 Marble Rd., East Gloucester, Mass.

KLUMBKE, ANNA ELISABETH.
Painter. Born San Francisco, Calif., in 1856. Pupil of Rosa Bonheur, Robert-Fleury, Lefebvre and Julian Academy in Paris. Member: Copley S. 1893. Awards: Hon. mention, Paris Salon, 1885; silver medal, Versailles, 1886; Temple gold medal, PAFA 1889; bronze medal, St. Louis Expo., 1904. Author of "Rosa Bonheur, sa vie son oeuvre." Work: "In the Wash House," Pennsylvania Academy of the Fine Arts, Philadelphia. Died Feb., 1942. Address in 1929, Chateau-de-By, 12 Rue Rosa Bonheur, Thomery, Seine-et-Marne, France.

KLUTH, ROBERT.
A marine and landscape painter. Born in Germany in 1854. He came to America at the age of seven years. He studied art in America, Germany and Norway. He was one of the founders of the Brooklyn Society of Artists. Many of his paintings of Norwegian fjords were purchased by Andrew Carnegie, for public libraries. He died in Brooklyn, NY, in September, 1921.

KNAP, J(OSEPH) D(AY).
Painter, illustrator and etcher. Born Scotdale, PA, June 7, 1875. Pupil of J. H. Holden. Address in 1929, Villa Charlotte Bronte, 2501 Palisades Ave., New York, NY.

KNAPP, CHARLES W.
Painter of landscapes. Born in Philadelphia in 1823; he died there May 15, 1900.

KNAPP, GRACE Le DUC.
(Mrs. C. C. Knapp). Painter and illustrator. Born in Minnesota, Jan. 28, 1874. Pupil of ASL of NY; Corcoran Art School, Wash., DC. Member: Wash. WCC. Address in 1929, 2471 Mohawk St., Pasadena, Calif.

KNATHS, (OTTO) KARL.
Painter. Born Eau Claire, Wis., Oct. 21, 1891. Pupil of AIC. Award: Harris silver medal ($500), AIC, Chicago, 1928. Represented in the Phillips Memorial Gallery, Washington, DC. Died in 1971. Address in 1929, 8 Commercial St., Provincetown, Mass.

KNAUBER, ALMA JORDAN.
Painter and lecturer. Born Cincinnati, Ohio, Aug. 24, 1893. Pupil of F. Duveneck, L. H. Meakin, C. J. Barnhorn, Hopkins, Hawthorne and studied in France and England. Member: Cincinnati Woman's AC; Am. APL; Am. Artists Prof. Lg.; Tau Sigma Delta, hon. arch. Frat.; College AA; Columbus AL; Ohio WCS; Western AA. Address in 1929, School of Household Administration, The University of Cincinnati; 3331 Arrow Ave., Cincinnati, Ohio.

KNEASS, WILLIAM.
Engraver. Born Sept. 25, 1780 in Lancaster, PA; died in Philadelphia, Aug. 27, 1840. It is not known with whom Kneass learned to engrave, but he worked continuously in Philadelphia as an engraver from 1805 to the time of his death. On Jan. 29, 1824, he was appointed engraver and die-sinker at the US Mint, succeeding Robert Scot. His work is usually in line, though he produced some good aquatint views. He was a member of the firm of Kneass & Dellaker, general engravers.

KNECHT, K(ARL) K(AE).
Cartoonist and illustrator. Born Iroquois, S. Dak., Dec. 4, 1883. Pupil of AIC. Member: Hoosier Salon; Cartoonists of America. On staff of "Evansville Courier." Address in 1929, Courier Bldg.; 111 Adams Ave., "The Jae-Kae," Evansville, Ind.

KNECHT, FERN, (ELIZABETH) EDIE.
Painter. Born Du Bois, Neb. Pupil of John Carlson, Charles Hawthorne. Award: John Beverly Robinson prize, St. Louis Artists Guild, 1925. Address in 1929, 906 A.O.U.W. Bldg.; h. Capitol Hill Apt. Hotel, Little Rock, Ark.

KNEELAND.
(Possibly Horace Kneeland who lived 1808-60.). Sculptor. His spirited basrelief of a "Trotting Horse" is owned in Washington, DC.

KNIFFIN, H(ERBERT) R(EYNOLDS).
Painter and teacher. Studied at Cooper Union; NAD; School of Design and Teachers College, Columbia University, and in Paris and

Munich. Instructor, Pope Pius Art and Industrial School, 1906-07; Greenwich Handicraft School, 1908; Assistant Director of Art Instruction, Newark, NJ; Instructor, University of Pittsburgh, 1912-17; director of art, Ethical Culture School since 1918, and Fieldstone Professional Art School. Author of "Elements of Art Appreciation," "Fine Arts and Education," etc. Address in 1929, 3902 Spuyten Duyvil Parkway, NYC.

KNIGHT, AUGUSTA.
Painter, craftsman and designer. Born Augusta, Ill. Pupil of St. Louis School of FA; ASL of NY; Pratt Inst., Brooklyn; AIC; and Charles Hawthorne. Member: Omaha AG. Award: Hon. mention for water colors, St. Paul Institute, 1916; Robert Morsman prize, Nebraska Artists. 1922; hon. mention, water colors. Midwestern Artists, Kansas City Art Inst., 1924. Director of Art University of Omaha. Address in 1929, 4216 Harney St., Omaha, Neb. Died in 1937.

KNIGHT, CHARLES.
Miniature painter, flourishing in Philadelphia 1811-16. He exhibited at Exhibition of Society of Artists, Philadelphia, 1811.

KNIGHT, CHARLES R(OBERT).
Painter and sculptor. Born Brooklyn, NY, in 1874. Pupil of Brush and DuMond. Work: Mural decorations of prehistoric animals and men, American Museum of Natural History, New York; Los Angeles Museum; Field Museum, Chicago. Specialty, animals and birds, modern and fossil. Died April, 1953 in NYC. Address in 1929, 27 West 67th St., New York, NY.

KNIGHT, CLAYTON.
Painter and illustrator. Born Rochester, NY, March 30, 1891. Pupil of Von der Lancken, Henri, and Bellows. Member: GFLA; SI Illustrates for magazines. Address in 1929, 680 Madison Ave., New York, NY; h. Roslyn, LI, NY.

KNIGHT, DANIEL RIDGWAY.
Painter. Born March 15, 1840, in Philadelphia. Died in France in

1924. Pupil of Penna. Academy of Fine Arts, and of Meissonier in Paris. Officer of the Legion of Honor of France. He is represented in the Penna. Academy of Fine Arts by "Hailing the Ferry," and in Brooklyn Institute Museum by "The Shepherdess." Died March 9, 1924.

KNIGHT, E. H.
Engraver. Born in Brooklyn, NY, in 1853. He died there in 1896. In 1867 E. H. Knight studied engraving with H. B. Hall; he was then in the employ of H. B. Hall & Sons, and was later a partner in this firm. As an engraver, his individuality was lost in the signed work of the firm, but his name appears on a fine portrait of Charles Dickens.

KNIGHT, KATHERINE STURGES.
Illustrator. Member: SI. Address in 1929, Roslyn, LI, NY.

KNIGHT, L(OUIS) ASTON.
Landscape painter. Born Paris, France, 1873, Pupil of Lefebvre, Robert-Fleury and of his father, Ridgway Knight, in Paris. Member: Rochester AC. Awards: Bronze medal, Paris Exp., 1900; hon. mention, Paris Salon, 1901; gold medal, Rheims Exp., 1903; gold medal, Lyons Exp., 1904; gold medal, Nantes Exhib., 1904; gold medal, Geneva Exh., 1904; third class medal, Paris Salon, 1905; second class medal, Paris Salon, 1906; gold medal, AAS 1907; Knight of the Legion of Honor, 1920. Work: "The Torrent," Toledo Museum of Art; "The River Wharf," "Sous le Moulin," Luxembourg Museum, Paris. Represented in Rochester Memorial Art Gallery. Died May 8, 1948, in NYC. Address in 1929, 147 Rue de la Pompe, Paris, France; Beaumont le Roger Eure, France.

KNIGHT, T.
Engraver. In 1856, and possibly earlier, Knight was a partner of George Girdler Smith, of Boston, along with W. H. Tappan, the firm name being Smith, Knight & Tappan. His name is signed to some very good portraits executed in both line and stipple.

526

KNOPFE, NELLIE A(UGUSTA).
Painter, lecturer and teacher.
Born Chicago, in 1875. Pupil of
AIC under Vanderpoel and Freer;
Charles H. Woodbury; John F.
Carlson; Birger Sandzen. Member:
AWCS; AIC Alumni; College Art
Assn.; NA Women PS; Chicago Gal. A;
Ill. AFA; S. Indp. A. Director
School of Fine Arts and Professor
of Art, Illinois Woman's College.
Represented in John H. Vanderpoel
memorial collection; permanent
collection, Lafayette, Ind., Art
Assn., and private collections.
Address in 1929, Illinois Woman's
College, Jacksonville, Ill.; h. 435
Robinson St., West Lafayette, Ind.

KNOTT, ARTHUR HAROLD.
Painter. Born Toronto, Canada, May
22, 1883. Pupil of Birge Harrison,
George Bridgman. Hermon Dudley
Murphy, Pratt Institute. Address
in 1929, Morro Bay, Calif.

KNOWLES, ELIZABETH McG.
Painter. Exhibited at 33d Annual
Exhibition of Nat. Assoc. of Women
Painters and sculptors. Address in
1926, 19 East 49th St., NYC.

KNOWLES, FARQUHAR MCGILLVRAY.
Painter, illustrator, writer,
lecturer and teacher. Born
Syracuse, NY, May 22, 1860.
Studied in the United States,
England, France and Canada.
Member: R.C.A.; Allied AA;
Brooklyn S. Min. P. Awards: Hon.
mention, Pan-Amer. Exp., Buffalo,
1901; medal, La. Purchase Exp.,
St. Louis, 1904; medal,
Panama-Pacific Exp., San Francisco,
1915. Represented in National
Galleries of Ottawa, Toronto,
Winnipeg, Edmonton, Regina and
Chicago. Died in 1932. Address in
1929, care of Babcock Art Gallery,
5 East 47th St., New York, NY.

KNOWLTON, HELEN MARY.
Born in Littleton, Mass., Aug. 16,
1832. Pupil of William M. Hunt,
she opened a studio in Boston in
1867. She has exhibited many
charcoal sketches as well as
landscapes and portraits in oil.
Some of her most effective work is
in charcoal. She has also
published "Talks on Art," of
William M. Hunt. The Boston Museum
of Fine Arts owns her "Haystacks."
She died in 1918.

KNOX, JAMES.
Painter. Born Glasgow, Scotland,
April, 1866. Member: NYWCC;
Allied AA; AFA. Work: "First
Attack of the Tanks," U.S. National
Museum, Washington, DC. Address in
1929, Hotel St. George, Brooklyn,
New York, NY.

KNOX, SUSAN RICKER.
Painter. Born Portsmouth, NH.
Studied in Philadelphia, New York
and Europe. Member: NAC; Pen and
Brush; SPNY; NA Women PS.; Conn.
AFA. Buffalo SA; Chicago Gal. A;
New Haven PCC; North Shore AA;
Springfield (Mass.) AL. Award:
Hon. mention, Conn. AFA, 1927.
Specialty, portraits. Address in
1929, 119 East 19th St., New York,
NY; summer, York Harbor, Maine.

KNUDSON, HELEN ELIZA.
Painter. Born Farmingdale, Ill.
Member: AFA; WAA; Ill. AFA;
Springfield AA. Address in 1929,
1141 Williams Blvd., Springfield,
Ill.

KNUTESON, OSCAR.
Painter. Member: Laguana Beach
AA. Address in 1929, 125 Rotdale
Trail, Laurel Canyon, Hollywood,
Calif.; Laguna Beach, Calif.

KOBBEE, MARIE O(LGA).
Painter. Born New Brighton, SI,
NY, 1870. Member; NYWCC.
Specialty pastel portraits and
portrait drawings. Address in
1929, 77 East 89th St., New York,
NY; Stockbridge, Mass.

KOBMAN, CLARA H.
Painter. Member: Cincinnati
Woman's AC. Address in 1929, 5
Marguerite Bldg., Main and Foraker
Terrace, Norwood Ohio.; 3 Eden Park
Terrace, Cincinnati, Ohio.

KOCH, HELEN C.
Painter, craftsman, teacher and
designer. Born Cincinnati, Ohio,
March 2, 1895. Pupil of L. H.
Meakin, James Hopkins, Henry B.
Snell. Member: Western AA;
Cincinnati Woman's AC; Crafters.
Address in 1299, 253 Hearne Ave.,
Cincinnati, Ohio.

KOCH, JOHN.
Painter. Born Toledo, Ohio, Aug.
18, 1910. Pupil of A. Valerio, L.
Makielski, Richard Miller. Member:
Mich. Acad. Science, Arts and
Letters. Died in 1978. Address in
1929, 2003 Day St., Ann Arbor,
Mich.; summer, 16 bis Rue Bardinet.
Studio 20, Paris, France.

KOCH, PETER.
Painter, illustrator, lecturer and
teacher. Born Saint Marys, Ohio,
Dec. 25, 1900. Pupil of Duveneck,
Hopkins, John Norton. Member: Ill.
SFA; Minn. AI. Address in 1929,
112 Locust St., Chicago, Ill.

KODA-CALLAN, ELIZABETH.
Illustrator. Born in Stamford, CT,
in 1944. Attended Siena Heights
College in Michigan, Univ. of
Dayton in Ohio, and SVA in NYC.
She studied under James McMullan
and has done extensive work for
Scholastic Magazine and New York
Magazine. Her first published
illustration was done for Arista
Records in October 1974.

KOECHL, PAUL.
Painter and teacher. Born
Brooklyn, July 27, 1880. Pupil of
Homer Boss. Member: S. Indp. A.
Address in 1929, 1947 Broadway; h.
270 Park Ave., New York, NY.

KOEHLER, P. R.
Landscape painter. Exhibited
"Early Evening" in New York.

KOEHLER, ROBERT.
Painter. Born in Hamburg, Germany,
in 1850; died in 1917. He was
brought to the US in 1854. Studied
at Milwaukee, Wis., and there
learned lithography which he
practiced in Pittsburgh, PA, and
in NY; studied drawing in night
classes at NA in 1877; organized
the American department of the art
exhibition, Munich, 1883 and 1888;
director of Minneapolis School of
FA since 1893. Principal paintings:
"Holiday Occupation;" "Her Only
Support;" "The Socialist;" "The
Strike;" "Violet;" "Judgment of
Paris;" "Love's Secret;" "The
Family Bible;" "Father and Son;"
"Salve Luna." Member: Society of
Western Artists; Minneapolis
Society of Fine Arts; Minneapolis
Art League; City Art Commission,
Minn.; State Art Society.

KOEHLER, SYLVESTER R.
Painter. Born in Germany in 1837;
died at Littleton, NH, on Sept.
10th, 1900.

KOEN, IRMA RENE.
Painter, writer, lecturer. Born
Rock Island, Ill. Pupil of C. F.
Brown, Lathrop, Snell; studied
abroad. Member: NYWCC; Chicago
PS; N.A. Women PS; Ill. AFA;
Chicago AC. Represented in Toledo
Museum; Pennsylvania Academy of the
Fine Arts; Peoria Art Association.
Address in 1929, care the Chicago
Galleries Association, Chicago,
Ill.; h. 3637 Twelfth St., Rock
Island, Ill.; Summer, Boothbay
Harbor, ME.

KOENIGER, WALTER.
Painter. Born Germany, May 6,
1881. Pupil of Duecker; von
Gebhard. Member: Salma. C. Work:
"The Silent Places," Toledo Museum;
author of "Koeniger Painter of
Snow" in "International Studio,"
June, 1925. Address in 1929, 222
West 59th St., New York, NY,
summer, Woodstock, NY.

KOERNER, HENRY.
Painter and lecturer. Born in Aug.
28, 1915, in Vienna, Austria.
Studied at the Acad. of Appl. Art,
Vienna. Also in Vienna studied
with Theodore Slama. His work has
been exhibited at Museum of Modern
Art, 1942, in the Nat. War Poster
Competition; Phil. Museum Art,
1950; Artist of the Year, Pitt.,
1963. Taught at the
Munson-Williams-Proctor Inst.,
1947-48; artist in residence,
Chatham Col., 1952-53 and Wash.
Univ., 1956, Awards include the
National War Poster Competition,
1942, Mus. of Modern Art Temple
Award, Art Inst. of Phil. and First
Prize at the National Cancer
Association, 1939. Commissioned
for 65 Time Magazine portraits.
Media: Ink, watercolor and oil.
Living in Pittsburgh, PA.

KOEVOETS, H. & C.
This firm was engraving and publishing portraits in New York about 1870.

KOHLER, ROSE.
Painter and sculptor. Born Chicago, Ill. Pupil of Cincinnati Acad. under Duveneck and Barnhorn. Member: Cincinnati Woman's AC; Am. APL. Died in 1947. Address in 1929, 2 West 88th St., NYC.

KOHLMANN, RENA TUCKER.
See Magee, Rena Tucker Kohlmann.

KOHLMEYER, IDA R.
Painter. Born on Nov. 3, 1882. Studied: Newcomb College; Newcomb Art Department, Tulane U. Awards: Southeastern Annual Exhibition, Atlanta, Georgia; Biennial Exhibition of Contemporary American Painting, Wash., DC. Address in 1980, 9811 Madison Ave., NYC.

KOHN, IRMA.
Landscape painter. Born in Rock Island, Ill. Represented in Toledo Museum and Penna. Academy of Fine Arts, Philadelphia.

KOLLER, E. LEONARD.
Sculptor, illustrator, writer, lecturer and teacher. Born Hanover, PA, Dec. 8, 1877. Studied under Pyle, Morse and Willett. Member: Eastern AA; AFA. Work: Soldiers Memorial Monument, near Gettysburg battlefield, and memorial windows in Pittsburgh and Philadelphia. Author of text books on design, illustrations and lettering. Address in 1929, 633 Jefferson Ave., Scranton, PA.

KOLLOCK, MARY.
Painter. Born in Norfolk, VA, in 1840. She studied at the Academy of Fine Arts, Philadelphia. Later she spent a year in Paris at the Julien School. She was a member of the Art Students' League, and exhibited at the National Academy of Design, NY. Among her works: "A November Day"; "Glimpse of the Catskills"; "Midsummer in the Mountains," which was exhibited in 1876 at the "Centennial," Philadelphia, PA.

KOLSKI, GAN.
Painter, illustrator and teacher. Born Poland. Award: Silver and bronze medal, NAD, 1922, 1923. Address in 1929, 23 Minetta Lane, New York, NY.

KOMINIK, GERDA.
Painter. Born in Vienna, Austria. Awards: Riverdale Outdoor Show; Reilly's School of Fine Arts; Romanofsky's gold medal; San Miguel de Allende, Mexico. Collections: In Canada, Austria, England, Mexico, and the US. Exhibitions: ASL, AAA, NA, NYC galleries.

KOMODORE, BILL.
Painter. Born Oct. 23, 1932, in Athens, Greece. Became U.S. citizen (1947). Earned BA and MFA (1957) from Tulane Univ. Studied with Hans Hofmann. Is also a photographer. Taught at Commercial Art School, Dallas; Fla. School for Deaf and Blind (St. Augustine); and at his own School in St. Aug., Fla. Awarded Carnegie Scholarship, 1956, and awards from Dallas Mus. F. Arts (1960); Texas Comm. on Arts grant (1980), others. Exhibited at Chrysler Art Mus.; 1961 Texas State Fair; Albright-Knox; Whitney, many others. In private collections, and in those of the Nat. Gal. of Art; Whitney; Walker Art Center.

KOMROFF, MRS.
See Elinor M. Barnard.

KONI, NICOLAUS.
Sculptor. Born in Hungary, May 6, 1911; US citizen. Study: Acad. of Fine Art, Vienna; Masters School, Paris; Masters Sch., Florence. Work: Okla. Art Ctr., Okla. City; Forrestal Bldg.; Metrop. Opera House; Kennedy Ctr., Wash. DC; many others. Exhib.: Whitney, NYC; Birmingham (AL) Mus. of Fine Art; Parrish Art Mus., South Hampton, NY; Milch Galleries, NYC; Int'l. Sculpture Expo, Paris; many others. Awards: First prize in Art, Parrish Art Mus. Mem.: Nat'l. Sculpture Soc.; Quilleis Art Soc. Media: Wood, marble, bronze, jade, gold. Living in NYC in 1970. Address in 1982, Palm Beach, Florida.

KONTI, ISIDORE.
Sculptor. Born Vienna, Austria, July 9, 1862. Pupil of Imperial Academy in Vienna under Helmer and Kundmann. Came to United States in 1890. Member: ANA, 1908; NA, 1909; NAC; Yonkers AA; NSS, 1897; NY Arch. Lg., 1901; Salma. C., 1904; Allied AA; AFA. Award: Gold medal, St. Louis Exp., 1904. Work: "Genius of Immortality," Metropolitan Museum, New York, and Detroit Inst.; "Illusion," owned by the Italian government; "South America," group for Bureau of American Republics Building, Washington, DC; medal "Landing of Jews in America," Minneapolis Institute; "Orpheus," Peabody Inst. Baltimore, MD; monument of Kit Carson and Lt. Beal, National Museum of Art, Washington; statues of Justinian and Alfred the Great, Court House, Cleveland; three fountains, Audubon and City Park, New Orleans; "Rev. Morgan Dix," Trinity Church, New York; memorial to Bishop Horatio Potter, St. John's Cathedral, New York; memorial to heroes of World War, Yonkers, NY; "The Despotic Age," St. Louis Museum and Corcoran Gallery, Washington, DC; "Dancer," Museum, Newark, NJ; Lincoln Memorial, and Hudson-Fulton Memorial, Yonkers, NY; executed McKinley Memorial, Philadelphia, from sketch of the late Charles Lopez and fountain figure, Plaza, NYC, from sketch of the late Carl Bitter. Died Jan. 11, 1938 in Yonkers, NY. Address in 1929, 314 Riverdale Ave., Yonkers, NY.

KOONS, DARELL J.
Painter. Born in Albion, MI, Dec. 18, 1924. Study: Bob Jones Univ.; West. Mich. Univ.; East. Mich. Univ. Work: Butler Inst. of American Art, Youngstown, Ohio; SC Collections. Teaching: Bob Jones Univ., from 1955 to present. Exhibitions: Acquavella Galleries, NY; Southeastern Exhibits, Atlanta, GA; Ohio State College Invit., Calif.; and others. Awards: Realistic Artist Ass'n., Springfield, Mass.; Society of Four Arts, Florida; Guild SC Artists; others. Mem.: Greenville Art Assn. and Guild; Guild of SC Artists. Media: Watercolor,

acrylic. Address in 1982, 6 Yancy Drive, Greenville, SC.

KOOPMAN, AUGUSTUS.
Painter and etcher. Born in Charleston, SC, in 1869. Studied at the Penna. Academy of Fine Arts and later in Paris. Represented in Philadelphia Art Club by "The Old Troubadour;" his dry-points and etchings are in the Congressional and New York Public Libraries. He died in 1914.

KOOPMAN, JOHN R.
Painter. Born Falmouth, Mich., June 5, 1881. Pupil of Chase, Henri, K. H. Miller, Wiles. Member: Salma. C.; NYWCC. Exhibited water colors at PAFA. Awards: first water color prize, annual exhibition Michigan Artists, Detroit, 1924; water color purchase prize, Michigan State Fair, 1924; Isidor prize, NYWCC, 1929. Instructor in Drawing and Painting, Brooklyn Institute of Arts and Sciences, and Grand Central School of Art. Died in Sept. 16, 1949. Address in 1929, 257 West 86th St., New York, NY.

KOPMAN, BENJAMIN D.
Painter. Born in New York. Member of the Allied Artists of America, New York. Represented in Brooklyn Institute of Arts and Sciences; Penna. Academy of Fine Arts, Philadelphia. "Portrait of a Young Man" at Penn. Academy of Fine Arts. Address in 1926, 8 East 15th St., New York. Died in 1965.

KOPMAN, KATHARINE.
Native of New Orleans. Studied under Molinary, Newcomb School of Art, and with Dodge Macknight. Instructor of drawing and design, Newcomb High School; Newcomb School of Art; supervisor of art, Alexandria Grammar Schools Alexandria, LA. Specialty landscapes.

KORAS, GEORGE.
Sculptor. Born in Florina, Greece April 1, 1925; US citizen. Study School of Fine Arts, Athens Greece; study in Paris and Rome 1955; ASL, 1957; with Jacque Lipchitz, 1955-59. Work: W. P Chrysler Collection; Provincetow

(MA) Museum; Norfolk (VA) Museum; Nat'l. Mus. of Athens, Greece. Comn: Board of Educ., Queens and Bronx, NY. Exhibitions: Panhellenios Zapeion, Athens; Brooklyn Mus.; PAFA; Silvermine Guild Artists; Consulate General of Greece. Awards: Brooklyn Mus.; PAFA; Hofstra Univ. Teaching: SUNY Stony Brook, from 1966 to present. Mem.: Audubon Artists. Media: Bronze. Address in 1982, Flushing, NY.

KORBEL, MARIO J.
Sculptor. Born Osik, Czechoslovakia, March 23, 1882. Came to U.S. at age 18, returned to Europe to study in Paris and Munich. Later est. studio in Prague. Member: Chicago SA; NSS (asso.). Award: Shaffer prize, AIC, 1910. Work: Dancing group, Cleveland Museum; "Andante," Metropolitan Museum of Art; Minerva," University of Havana, Cuba; marble bust in Chicago Art Institute; McPhee Memorial monument, Denver. Also in collections of the Vatican; Cranbrook Acad. of Art; Nat. Gal. of Canada and Whitney, and many private collections. Died in 1954. Address in 1929, 54 West 74th St., New York, NY.

KORNHAUSER, DAVID E.
Painter. Studied at Penna. Academy of Fine Arts. Represented at Penna. Academy of Fine Arts by "Along the Schuylkill River."

KORZYBSKA, MIRA EDGERLY.
(Countess Alfred de Korszybaska). Painter, writer and lecturer. Born Aurora, Ill., Jan. 16, 1879. Work: "Mrs. Lawrence Drummond with Jim," Metropolitan Museum, New York; "Alfred Skarbek de Korzybska," Chicago Art Inst. Address in 1929, care of the Fifth Aveue Bank, New York, NY; h. 66 Weleza St., Warsaw, Poland.

KOSCIUSKO, TADEUSZ ANDRZEJ BONAWENTURA.
A Polish soldier who fought in the American Revolution, was born in Lithuania in Feb. 12, 1746 and died in Switzerland Oct. 15, 1817. He drew a portrait of General Gates and several of the other Revolutionary soldiers. Worked in both crayon and oils.

KOSH, A. E.
Born in Germany in 1838; died in this country in 1897. Kosh was an engraver of landscape and subject-plates for magazines, and came to the United States in 1868.

KOSICKI, C(ATHERINE) W(ATHA).
Painter. Born May 12, 1890. Pupil of Frederick Mozitz, Riga, Latvia. Member: Detroit S. Women P; S. Indp. A; Detroit S. Indp. A. Award: First prize, Michigan State Fair, 1928. Address in 1929, 3779 Collingwood Ave., Detroit, Mich.

KOSLOW, HOWARD.
Illustrator. Born in Brooklyn, NY, in 1924. Attended PI and the Cranbrook Academy of Art in Michigan. His career began in 1946 with Hilton Hotel advertising series and went on to include book, poster, and editorial illustration. Some of his clients are Boys' Life, Popular Science, Reader's Digest, and the United States Postal Service. The Smithsonian Institution and the National Park Service own his work and his illustrations have been shown in galleries nationwide.

KOSSIN, SANFORD.
Illustrator. Born in Los Angeles, in 1924. Studied at the Jepson Art Institute before coming to NY in 1952. Early in his career he was a frequent contributor to Galaxy Magazine, illustrating science fiction stories. He has recently been painting for paperback book publishers and has had exhibits in the S of I Annual Exhibitions several times. He illustrated a series on the Bay of Pigs for Life in 1963 and his work has appeared in Argosy and The Saturday Evening Post. His works are in the USAF Museum and the Douglas MacArthur Memorial.

KOST, FREDERICK W.
Landscape painter. Born in New York, in 1861. Student of National Academy of Design, NY, and studied later in Paris and Munich. Elected National Academician in 1906. Received honorable mention at Paris

531

Exhibition, 1900. Represented at Penna. Academy of Fine Arts, Philadelphia, and in the Brooklyn Institute. He died at Brookhaven, LI, in 1923.

KOTZ, DANIEL.
Landscape painter. Born near South Bend, Ind., March 21, 1848. Pupil of Henry F. Spread. Member: Salma C.; Nanuet P. Address in 1929, 3779 Collingwood Ave., Detroit, Mich.

KOWAL, DENNIS J.
Sculptor and writer. Born in Chicago, Ill., Sept. 9, 1937. Study: Art Inst. of Chicago; Univ. of Ill., Chicago; So. Ill. Univ. Work: Gillette Corp., Boston; Brockton Art Ctr.; MBTA Sta., Prudential Auditorium, Boston; many others. Comn: Monuments, Milton Acad., Mass.; numerous corporations, banks, etc. Exhib.: 66th Chic. Artists Annual, Art Inst. of Chicago; Robert Freidus Gallery, NYC; Mead Art Mus., Amherst College, Mass.; Gilbert Gallery Ltd., Chicago; many others. Awards: Numerous, since 1970. Mem.: Boston Visual Artists Union; New Eng. Sculptors Assn., Boston; others. Author: Casting Sculpture; Artists Speak, NY Graphic Soc. Address in 1982, 602 Jerusalem Road, Cohasset, MA.

KOWNATZKI, HANS.
Painter and sculptor. Born Konigsberg, Germany, Nov. 26, 1866. Pupil of Neide, Knorr, Koner and Lefebvre. Award: First prize for sculpture, S. Wash. A., Washington, DC, 1929. Died in 1939. Address in 1929, Peconic, LI, NY.

KRAFFT, CARL R.
Painter. Born Reading, Ohio, Aug. 23, 1884. Pupil of AIC; Chicago FA Academy. Member: Chicago PS.; Painters and Sculptors Gal. A.; Cliff Dwellers; Society of Ozark Painters; Austin, Oak Park and River Forest Art Lg.; Chicago Gal. A; Ill. Acad FA; Grand Cent. AG. Awards: Englewood Womans' Club prize AIC, 1915; Municipal Art Lg. Purchase prize, 1916; hon. mention, Chicago AG, 1916; Fine Arts Bldg. prize, Artists Guild, 1917; 2nd

($200), Logan Medal, AIC, 1920; bronze medal, Illinois Artists Exposition, 1920; silver medal, Chicago SA, 1921; bronze medal, Central States exhibition, Aurora, 1922; first Logan medal and $500, AIC, 1925; Medal of Honor, Allied AA, 1925; Harry Frank prize for figure composition, AIC, 1925. Represented by "Charms of the Ozarks," Municipal Art League Collection, Chicago; collection of Peoria (Ill.) Soc. of Allied Arts; "Ozark Zephyrs," Englewood Woman's Club; "Cliff at Morning, Ozarks," Harrison Gallery, Los Angeles Museum; "The Bridge" and "The Squatter's Shack," Art League, Aurora, Ill.; "Quiet of Evening," Arche Club, Chicago; "Morning Fog," and "Mill Creek in Winter," City of Chicago; "Day after Christmas" and "Woods in Snow," in Oak Park Art League; "Tree Tapestry," South Shore Country Club, Chicago; "November Snow," Wichita; Falls, Tex.; "The Red Sleigh," Lincoln School, River Forest, Ill.; "Ozark Palisades," University of Illinois; "Morning Light" Illinois State Museum; series of murals, First National Bank, Elmhurst, Ill.; "Autumn Spirit," Richmond, Indiana Art Association; "December Day," Howe School, Austin; "Winter," Faulkner School, Chicago; "Afternoon," Holmes School, Oak Park; "Triad of Life," Y.M.C.A. Austin. Address in 1929, 416 North Harvey Ave., Oak Park, Ill. Died in 1938.

KRAMER, SCHEIRE B.
Portrait painter. His portrait of William L. Strong, Mayor of New York, is in the City Hall. It is signed and dated 1898.

KRASNER, LEE.
Painter. Born in Brooklyn, NY, in 1911. Studied: Cooper Union Art School; National Academy of Design; Hans Hofmann School of Art. Collections: Whitney Museum of American Art; Philadelphia Museum of Art. Address in 1980, The Springs, East Hampton, NY.

KRATINA, JOS(EPH) M.
Sculptor and teacher. Born Prague, Feb. 26, 1872. Pupil of L'Ecole des Beaux Arts and Julian Academy

in Paris. Member: Alliance; Brooklyn SA. Address in 1929, 109 Berkeley Pl., Brooklyn, NY; summer, Mt. Tremper, NY.

KRATOCHVIL, STEPHEN.
Painter. Born Czechoslovakia, June 8, 1876. Pupil of P. Albert Laurens; J. Pierre Laurens; H. Royer in Paris. Member: Cleveland SA. Address in 1929, 1898 East 82nd St., New York, NY.

KRAUS, ROBERT.
Sculptor. Deceased. He was the sculptor for the Crispus Attucks monument.

KRAVJANSKY, MIKULAS.
Painter, printmaker and teacher. Born in Czechoslovakia May 3, 1928. Left Europe in 1968. Study: Acad. of Arts, Bratislava, Czech., Faculty of Scenography, 1957. Design work: Scenic Artist and Technical Producer, State Theatre, Presov, Czech.; Chief Set Designer, Czechoslovak Televison, Bratislava; over 450 productions for Nat'l Theatre and Nat'l. Film Board of Czech., including opera, ballet & drama, 1957-68. Exhib.: Designs and paintings exhib. in Prague, Budapest, Vienna, Warsaw, Paris, Berlin, Cairo, Brennala of FA at Sao Paolo, FA Gallery in Toronto, & NYC. Teaching: Lecturer, Acad. of Arts, Bratislava; Assistant Professor, Univ. of Bratislava, 1965-68; Assist. Master, Humber College, Toronto, 1969-75.

KREHBIEL, ALBERT H.
Painter and teacher. Born Chicago, Ill. Pupil of AIC and Frederick Richardson; Laurens in Paris. Member: Chicago PS.; Chicago WCC; Cliff Dwellers; Mural P. Instructor AIC; Arch. Dept., Armour Inst. Work: Mural decorations for Supreme Court, Springfield, Ill. Died in 1945. Address in 1929, Park Ridge, Chicago, Ill.

KREHBIEL, DULAH EVANS.
(Mrs. Albert Krehbiel). Painter and illustrator. Pupil of AIC; W. Appleton Clark and ASL in NY. Member: Chicago AC; Cordon C.; Chicago SA. Designer and publisher of Ridge Craft cards. Address in 1929, Park Ridge, Chicago, Ill.

KREIGHOFF, W(ILLIAM) G(EORGE).
Painter. Born Philadelphia, Aug. 31, 1875. Pupil of Chase, Meakin, Sharp. Member: Phila. Alliance; Phila. Soc. AA. Work: "Portrait of Judge J. M. Patterson," Philadelphia Law Assn.; "Portrait of President Bigell," State College, Tex. Address in 1929, 10 South 18th St.; h. 1915 Rittenhouse St., Philadelphia, PA.

KREMELBERG, MARY.
(Mrs. Frederick Gibson). Painter. Member: NA Women PS; Fellowship PAFA; Balto. WCC. Address in 1929, 1007 No. Charles St., Baltimore, MD.

KRENTZIN, EARL.
Sculptor and silversmith. Born in Detroit, Michigan, Dec. 28, 1929. Graduated from Cass Technical High School, 1948; Wayne State Univ., BFA 1952; Cranbrook Academy, Michigan, MFA, 1954; Royal College of Art, London, 1957-58. In collections of Detroit Inst. of Art, MI; Cranbrook Galleries, MI; St. Paul (MI) Art Ctr.; Jewish Mus., NYC; others, including commissions. Exhibited at Mus. of Contemp. Crafts, NYC, 1963, 65; one-man shows, Kennedy Galleries, NYC, 1968-75; Detroit Inst. of Art, 1978, Oshkosh Mus., 1982. Awarded prize at Detroit Inst. of Arts, 1952; Fulbright Fellowship, 1957-58; Tiffany Grant, 1966; Wichita Arts Ctr., Kans., 1966. Works in fiber, clay, metal, silver. Represented by Kennedy Galleries, NYC. Address in 1982, Grosse Pointe, Michigan.

KRETZINGER, CLARA JOSEPHINE.
Painter. Born Chicago. Pupil of AIC and Chicago AFA; Lefebvre, Robert- Fleury, Laurens, Congdon and Richard Miller in Paris. Member: Chicago SA; Chicago AC; AFA. Award: Hon. mention, Paris Salon. Represented in Beloit Art Museum. Address in 1929, 11 Rue Schoelcher, Paris, France; h. 917 Monadnock Bldg., Chicago. Ill.

KREUTZBERG, MARGUERITE G.
Painter. Born Elgin. Ill., Sept. 14, 1880. Pupil of W. P. Henderson. Member: Chicago AC. Award: Butler Purchase Prize, AIC, 1923. Work: "A Little Venus of the Steppes," Chicago Public Schools; mural decoration in public school, Lake Bluff, Ill. Address in 1929, Graham Ave., Bethlehem, PA.

KRIMMEL, JOHN LEWIS.
Portrait and genre painter. Born in 1789 in Wurtemberg, Germany. He came to this country in 1810 to join his brother who was a merchant of Philadelphia. Disliking trade, he continued the course he had begun in Germany, and painted small portraits. In 1812, he exhibited at the Penna. Academy of Fine Arts a picture of Centre Square, Philadelphia, containing numerous small figures, and painted many other works of like character, two of which are owned by the Penna. Academy. He was President of the Society of American Artists. He drowned in Wissahickon Creek, Philadelphia, on July 15, 1821.

KRIZE, EMILIE M.
Painter. Born Luzerne, PA, in 1918. Studied: Maryland Institute; Penn. Academy of Fine Arts; Johns Hopkins Univ.; Norfolk Division of William and Mary College; and with Maroger. Award: Traveling scholarship, Maryland Institute. Collections: Planters Nut and Chocolate Company Club; Norfolk Naval Shipyard Library; State House, Annapolis, Maryland.

KROLL, LEON.
Painter and teacher. Born New York, Dec. 6, 1884. Pupil of ASL of NY and NAD; Laurens in Paris. Instructor at NAD, 1911-18. Member: NA 1927; NAC (life); S. Indp. A; New Soc. Etchers; New Soc. A.; Phila. AC.; New York Soc. of Etchers; Boston AC. Awards: Porter prize, Salma. C., 1914; bronze medal, P.-P. Exp., San F., 1915; Logan prize AIC, 1919; Purchase prize AIC, 1919; first prize, Wilmington SFA, 1921; Clarke prize, NAD, 1921; first Altman prize, NAD, 1922; Potter Palmer gold medal and $1,000 AIC, 1924; hon. mention Inter. Exhib.,

Carnegie Inst., 1925; Temple gold medal, PAFA, 1927. Work: "A Basque Landscape," Pennsylvania Academy of Fine Arts, Philadelphia; "North River Front," "Leo Ornstein at the Piano," Art Institute of Chicago; "In the Country," Detroit Institute; "Broadway and 42nd St.," Harrison Gallery, Los Angeles Museum; "Sleep," St. Louis Museum; "Study for Sleep," and "Central Park, Winter," Cleveland Museum; drawings, Metropolitan Museum, New York; four drawings, Art Inst. of Chicago. Visiting critic, Maryland Inst., 1919-23; Art Inst. of Chicago, 1924-25. Died in 1974. Address in 1929, care W. S. Budworth and Son, 424 West 52nd St., New York, NY.

KRONBERG, LOUIS.
Painter and teacher. Born Boston, Mass., Dec. 20, 1872. Pupil of Museum of Fine Arts, Boston; ASL of NY; Julian Academy under Benjamin-Constant, Laurens and Collin in Paris. Member: Boston AC; Boston GA; Copley S.; Salma. C.; Assoc. Salon Nat.; AWCS; NYWCC; Boston SWCP. Awards: Longfellow traveling scholarship, Boston Museum, 1894-97; silver medal, P.-P. Exp., San F., 1915; Shaw prize, Salmagundi Club, 1919. Work: "Pink Sash," Metropolitan Museum, New York; "Behind the Footlights." Pennsylvania Academy of the Fine Arts, Philadelphia; "Ballet Girl Preparing for the Dance," Boston Museum of Fine Arts; "Oriental Dancer," Herron Art Institute, Indianapolis; "Ballet Girl in White," "La Guitana," "At the Window," and others, Gardner collection, Boston, Mass.; "The Ballet Girl," Butler Art Inst., Youngstown, Ohio; "Spanish Dancer," Albright Art Gallery, Buffalo; "Ballet Girl," San Diego Fine Arts Gallery. Died in 1964. Address in 1929, Salmagundi Club, 47 Fifth Ave., New York, NY; care of Boston Art Club, Newbury and Dartmouth Sts., Boston, Mass.

KRUELL, GUSTAVE.
Wood engraver. Born in Germany, in 1843. He organized the American Wood Engravers' Society, of which he was president. He received many honorable mentions and medals for

his work. His engraved portraits include those of Darwin, Wm. Lloyd Garrison and Lincoln. He published "A Portfolio of National Portraits." He died in California in 1907. (See "History of Wood Engraving," by W. J. Linton.)

KRUGER, LOUISE.
Sculptor and designer. Born in Los Angeles, CA in 1924. Studied: Scripps College, CA; ASL; and with Capt. Sundquist, shipbuilder; F. Guastini, Pistoia, Italy; Chief Opoku Dwumfour, Kumasi, Ghana. Collections: MOMA; NY Lib. Print Coll.; Mod. Mus., Sao Paulo; Brooklyn Mus. Exhib.: Met. Mus.; Whitney; Moma; AIC; Kunsthaus, Zurich. Works in wood, bronze. Lives in NYC.

KRUPP, LOUIS.
Painter and designer. Born in Miesenbach, West Germany, Nov. 26, 1888; US citizen. Study: Art Inst. of Chicago; ASL; with Wellington J. Reynolds, Karl Buehr, Charles Schroeder, Elmer Forsberg, George B. Bridgman. Work: Inst. Zacatecano Bellas Artes, Mex. Exhib.: El Paso Art Mus.; Am. APL Grand Nat'l. Awards: Hon. Mention, Art Inst. of Chicago; 1st prizes, El Paso Art Assn. Mem.: Am. APL; El Paso Art Assn.; Nat'l. Soc. Arts & Letters; others. Media: Oil, watercolor, charcoal. Address in 1976, El Paso, TX.

KRYZANOVSKY, SARI.
Painter. Born Lexington, KY. Pupil of Roman Kryzanovsky. Award: First water color prize, Detroit Inst. of Art, 1925. Address in 1929, 2156 East Jefferson Ave., Detroit, Mich.

KUEMMEL, CORNELIA A.
Painter, sculptor and teacher. Born Glasgow, Howard Co., MO. Pupil of St. Louis School of Fine Arts, under John Fry and E. Wuerpel. Member: St. Louis AG. Address in 1929, Pritchett College, Glasgow, MO. Died in 1937.

KUHLMAN, G. EDWARD.
Painter, writer and lecturer. Born Woodville, Ohio, Sept 26, 1882. Pupil of PAFA; AIC. Studied abroad. Represented in Public Museum, Oshkosh, Wis. Specialty, altar paintings for churches and landscape. Address in 1929, 107 West First St., Oil City, PA.

KUHN, HARRY P(HILLIP).
Painter and craftsman. Born Zurich, Switzerland, Nov. 27, 1862. Award: Gold medal, Louisiana Purchase Exp., St. Louis, 1904. Address in 1929, Colt Bldg., Paterson, NJ; summer, Wheelerville, PA.

KUHN, ROBERT J.
Sculptor. Exhibited at National Academy of Design, 1925. Address in 1929, Richmond Hill, NY.

KUHN, WALT.
Painter. Born Oct. 27, 1880, in NYC. Exhibited in Philadelphia, 1921, at "Exhibition of Paintings Showing the Later Tendencies in Art," Penna. Academy of Fine Arts. Address in 1926, 11 East 13th St., New York City. Studied abroad and taught at ASL and NY School of Art. Died July 13, 1949 in NYC.

KUMM, MARGUERITE ELIZABETH.
Painter, engraver, and etcher. Born in Redwood Falls, MN. Studied: Minneapolis School of Art; Corcoran Art School; and with Cameron Booth, Richard Lahey, Anthony Angarola. Awards: Society of American Graphic Artists, 1943; Library of Congress, 1951; International award, in Decorator Designer, NY, 1926. Collections: Library of Congress; Boston Museum of Fine Arts; Valentine Museum; Virginia Museum of Fine Arts; Oregon State College; Society of American Graphic Artists; Wash. County Museum of Fine Arts, Hagerstown, Maryland; Witte Memorial Museum; Penn. State Univ.; Metropolitan Museum of Art; Smithsonian Institute; Mint Museum of Art; Butler Art Institute; Lowry Hill Children's Clinic, Minneapolis, MN. Address in 1980, 212 Noland St., Falls Church, VA.

KUMME, WALTER (HERMAN).
Painter and teacher. Born Philadelphia, PA, Dec. 16, 1895. Pupil of PAFA. Member: Fellowship PAFA; T. Square C.; Wilmington SFA. Award: Cresson traveling

scholarship, 1914, PAFA. Address in 1929, 130 Charles St., New York, NY.

KUNIYOSHI, KATHERINE SCHMIDT.
Painter. Born Xenia, Ohio, Aug. 15, 1898. Pupil of Kenneth Hayes Miller. Member: S. Indp. A. Address in 1929, Ardsley Studios, 110 Columbia Heights, Brooklyn, NY; summer, Ogunquit, ME.

KUNIYOSHI, YASUO.
Painter. Born Okayama, Japan, Sept. 1, 1893. Pupil of Kenneth Hayes Miller. Member: Brooklyn Modern A.; Salons of Am.; Modern A. Award Guggenheim Fellowship (1935-6). Taught at ASL. Hon. member of Nat'l. Inst. Arts and Letters. Pres. of Artists Equity. Died in 1953. Address in 1929, 106 Columbia Heights, Brooklyn, NY; summer, Ogunquit, ME.

KUNSTLER, MORT.
Illustrator. Born in Brooklyn, in 1931. Studied at Brooklyn College, UCLA, and PI. In 1949 he published his first illustration, a black and white line drawing, for Handy Football Library. He is best known for his intricate and realistic historical paintings. His works are owned by the Daytona Beach Museum of Arts and Sciences, Air Force Museum in Colorado, Favell Museum in Oregon, and others.

KUNTZE, EDWARD J.
Born in Prussia in 1826. Studied in Stockholm Sweden. He came to New York in 1852, and in 1869 was elected an Associate of the National Academy. Among his works are statuettes of Irving, Lincoln, and a statue of "Psyche" and one of "Puck." He also exhibited three etchings at the National Academy in 1868. Died in 1910.

KUPER, ROSE.
Painter. Studied: Hunter College; in France; and with Hans Hofmann, Abraham Rattner. Awards: National Assoc. of Women Artists, 1952; Brooklyn Society of Art, 1954; Village Art Center. Collections: San Diego Fine Arts Society; Philbrook Art Center; Dallas Museum of Fine Arts; Santa Barbara Museum of Art; Jewish Museum, NY; Hunter

College; Long Island Univ.; Fashion Institute of Technology; Ashlawn, Virginia (home of James Monroe); Riverside Museum; Design Center, NY.

KUPFER, R.
Engraver. Line-engravings of some merit, published in New York magazines about 1865, after drawings by Thos. Nast and other American designers, are so signed. Among other prints engraved by Kupfer is a folio plate of view of New York, published in 1867.

KUPFERMAN, MURRAY.
Painter. Born Brooklyn, NY, March 10, 1897. Pupil of Pratt Inst.; NAD; Beaux Arts Inst. of NY. Represented in National Academy of Design, New York Water Color Club, Architecture League, Corcoran Gallery, Penn. Acad. of the Fine Arts. Brooklyn Museum, also private collections abroad. Scenic decorations, "America's Answer," Military Park Building, Newark, NJ. Specialty, landscapes. Address in 1929, 2003 E. 22nd St., Brooklyn, NY.

KURTZ, BENJAMIN.
Sculptor. Member: Fellowship PAFA. Awards: Bronze medal, sesqui- Centennial Expo., Phila., 1926; Spalding prize ($1,000). AIC, 1926, 215 Woodlawn Rd., Roland Park, Baltimore, MD; 704 South Washington Square, Philadelphia, PA.

KURTZ, JULIA WILDER.
Painter and teacher. Born Harrodsburg, KY. Pupil of Art School of the Buffalo Fine Arts Academy, Richard E. Miller, Charles Hawthorne. Member: Buffalo SA; Buffalo G. Allied Arts; AFA. Address in 1929, 269 Richmond Ave., Buffalo, NY.

KURTZ, WILBUR G.
Painter and illustrator. Born Oakland, Ill., Feb. 28, 1882. Pupil of AIC. Member: Atlanta AA. Represented in Atlanta Woman's Club; Atlanta Federal Reserve Bank; five murals in National Bank of Abbeville, SC; proscenium decoration, Auditorium. Macon. GA.

Address in 1929, 907 Penn Ave., NE, Atlanta, GA.

KURTZWORTH, H(ARRY) M(UIR).
Painter, designer, lecturer, writer and teacher. Born Detroit, Mich., Aug. 12, 1887. Pupil of Detroit Museum School of Art under Paulus and Gies; Detroit Academy of Fine Arts under Wicker; Columbia University New York, under Dow; PA. School of Industrial Art; and with Julius Melchers. Member: Fourth International Art Congress, Dresden, 1912; Detroit Soc. A. and C. Award: Hon. mention. Kansas City AI, 1923. Organizer and director Grand Rapids School of Art and Industry, 1916-20. Director, Michigan Art Institute, 1918-24. Director Modern Home Bureau. Author of "Industrial Art a National Asset." 1919; "How to Use Your Talent," 1924. Editor, "Western Art Annual," 1922. Address in 1929, 832 Hinman Ave., Evanston, Ill.; h. 2136 Stanley Ave., Detroit, Mich.

KURZ, DIANA.
Painter and educator. Born in Vienna, Austria. Studied: Brandeis Univ.; Columbia Univ. Awards: Yaddo Fellowship, 1968-1969; US Government Fulbright Grant in Painting to France, 1965-1966. Exhibitions: Green Mountain Gallery, NYC, 1972-1974; Brooklyn College, 1974; Univ. of Michigan, 1965. Media: Oil and watercolor. Address in 1980, 152 Wooster, NY, NY.

KURZ, LOUIS.
Mural painter and one of the founders of the Chicago Art Institute. He was born in Austria in 1833, and came to America in 1848. He fought for the North in the Civil War, and he was a personal friend of Lincoln. His sketches of the Civil War were the first to be issued after the close of the conflict. He died in Chicago, Ill., March 21, 1921.

KUTCHIN, LOU.
Painter. Exhibited water colors at the Penna. Academy of Fine Arts, Philadelphia, 1925. Address in 1926, 2038 Spruce St., Philadelphia.

KYLE, JOSEPH.
Painter. Born in 1815, in Ohio. His work was portraiture, genre subjects and still-life. In 1849 he was elected an Associate Member of the National Academy of Design. He died in 1863 in NYC. His painting, "A Family Group," is owned by the Academy of Fine Arts, Elgin, Illinois.

LaBRUCE, FLORA M(c DONALD).
Painter, craftsman, writer, and teacher. Born New York City. Pupil of Cooper Institute; John Mc Nevins. Member: Carolina AA; Sketch C.; Southern SAL. Address in 1929, Gibbes Art Building, 176 Meeting St., Charleston, SC; summer, "Gleneden," Edneyville P.O., NC.

LACEY, BERTHA J.
Painter. Born Perrysville, IN, 1878. Pupil of Vanderpoel, Meakin and Duveneck. Member: ASL of Chicago; Indiana Artists; Cincinnati Woman's AC; NAC; The Cordon, Chicago. Award: Prize for group of miniatures, Hoosier Salon, Chicago, 1927. Died in 1943. Address in 1929, Perrysville, IN.

LaCHAISE, GASTON.
Sculptor. Born Paris, March 19, 1882. Died Oct. 19, 1935 in NYC. Pupil Bernard Palissy; Ecole des Beaux Arts under Gabriel Jules Thomas, also a sculptor. Work: "Seagull," National Coast Guard Memorial; decoration frieze, American Telephone and Telegraph Building, New York; Cleveland Museum of Art; Newark Museum; Pennsylvania Museum; Morgan Memorial Museum, Hartford, Conn.; Phillips Memorial Gallery, Washington; Smith College Art Museum, Northampton, Mass; Whitney Mus. of Art, New York; Toledo Art Museum; Wichita Art Mus.; Rockefeller Center and many private collections. Published Gaston Lachaise: sixteen reproductions in collotype, with introduction by A. E. Gallatin. Address in 1929, The Grosvenor, 35 Fifth Ave., New York, NY; summer, Georgetown, ME.

LaCHANCE, GEORGE.
Painter. Born Utica, NY, Oct. 13, 1888. Pupil of Old St. Louis Art School. Member: Hoosier Salon; S. Indp. A; AFA. Work: Historical mural, County Court House, Vincennes, Ind.; 14 industrial murals, New Toledo Scale Auditorium, Toledo; portrait, Donors Gallery, DePauw University, Greencastle, IN.

LACHER, GISELLA LOEFFLER.
Painter. Born Vienna, Austria, Sept. 24, 1900. Pupil of Mary McCall, Hugh Breckenridge. Member: St. Louis AG; Alliance; Boston SAC. Awards: First prize for water color, GFLA, 1919 and 1920, decoration prize, 1927; special prize, 1928; hon. mention, Kansas City Art Inst., 1923. Works: "The Offering," Soldan High School, St. Louis; "Wonder," Cleveland High School; painting, Community High School. Address in 1926, Rt. 12, Box 192a, Kirkwood, MO.

LACHMAN, HARRY.
Painter. Born La Salle, IL, June 29, 1886. Member: Societe Inter. des Artistes et Sculpteurs; Societe Paris Moderne; Chevalier of the Legion of Honor, France. Work: "Toledo," Delgado Museum of Art, New Orleans, La.; "St. Nicolas du Chardonnet," "Uzerche," "Antibes" and "The Valley of Les Andelys," in Musee du Luxembourg; "Printemps Parisien," Musee du Petit Palais, Paris; "Old Tower" and "Old Church," Chicago Art Institute; "Notre Dame," Memphis Women's Club. Address in 1929, Riviera Studios, St. Andre, Nice, France.

LADD, ANNA COLEMAN.
(Mrs. Maynard Ladd). Sculptor. Born Phila., PA, July 15, 1878. Studied in Paris and Rome. Member: Concord AA; NSS, 1915 (Assoc.); Boston GA; North Shore AA; AFA. Award: Hon. mention, P.-P. Exp., San F., 1915. Work: Bronzes in Boston Art Mus.; Rhode Island School of Design; Gardner Mus., Boston; Borghese Collection, Rome; Boston Public Gardens Fountain; Memorials in Hamilton, Beverly Farms, Manchester, South Bend, Brookline and Grand Rapids. Founded ARC, Studio of Portrait Masks, France, 1917-19. Died in 1939. Address in 1929, 270 Clarendon St., Boston, MA; summer, Beverly Farms, MA.

LADD, LAURA D. STROUD.
Painter. Born Phila., PA, July 1, 1863. Pupil of Phila. School of Design for Women and PAFA. Member: Fellowship PAFA; Plastic C.; Phila. WCC; Alliance; NA Women PS; North Shore AA; AFA. Died in 1943.

538

LAESSLE, ALBERT.
Sculptor. Born Philadelphia, March 28, 1877. Pupil of Spring Garden Inst., Drexel Inst., PAFA, Charles Grafly, and studied in Paris. Member: ANA; NSS, 1913; Fellowship PAFA; Phila. Alliance; New SA of NY; Societe des Amis de la Medaille d'Art, Brussels; Philadelphia Alliance. Awards: Stewardson prize, 1902, and Cresson traveling scholarship, PAFA, 1904; bronze medal, Buenos Aires, 1910; PAFA Fellowship prize ($100), 1915; gold medal, P.-P. Exp., San Francisco, 1915; first sculpture prize, Americanization through Art, Philadelphia, 1916; Widener gold medal, PAFA, 1918; hon. mention AIC, 1920; gold medal, Sesqui-Centennial Exposition, Phila., 1926; prize ($300) best outdoor decorative group, Phila. Art Alliance, 1928; James E. Mc Clees prize, 1928. Work: "Turtle and Lizards," "Blue Eyed Lizard," and "Chanticleer," Pennsylvania Academy, Philadelphia; "Heron and Fish," Carnegie Institute, Pittsburgh; 3 small bronzes, "An Outcast," "Locust and Pine Cone," "Frog and Katydid," Peabody Inst., Baltimore; "Victory" and "Turning Turtle," Metropolitan Museum, New York; "The Bronze Turkey," Philadelphia AC; "Penguins," Phila. Zoological Gardens; "Billy," Rittenhouse Square, Philadelphia; "Hunter and First Step," Concord Art Assoc., Concord, Mass.; Dancing Goat, Pan, Billy, Duck, Turtle, Frogs for Fountain, Camden, New Jersey. Instructor PAFA Country School, Chester Springs, Pennsylvania. Died in 1954. Address in 1929, 131 North 20th St., Philadelphia, Pennsylvania; h. 511 Runnymede Ave., Jenkintown, Pennsylvania.

LaFARGE, BANCEL.
Painter and craftsman. Member: Mural P.; NYWCC; Century Assoc.; Paris AAA; Nat. Inst. AL; New Haven PCC; AFA. Work: mural paintings "Crucifixion," "Madonna Enthroned," "Christ in Glory," "Christ Blessing Children," in Church of Blessed Sacrament, Providence, RI; mosaics, "Crowning of the Virgin," "The Trinity," St. Charles College, Catonsville, MD. Died in 1938.

Address in 1929, Edgehill, Mt. Carmel, CT.

LaFARGE, JEAN.
Miniature painter. Father of the artist John La Farge. He was a French refugee from Santo Domingo, and came to New York and painted miniatures in the early part of the nineteenth century.

LaFARGE, JOHN.
Landscape and figure painter, decorator, glass painter and sculptor. Born March 31, 1835 in New York; died Nov. 14, 1910 in Providence, RI. Pupil of William M. Hunt in Boston, and Couture in Paris. Elected member of National Academy, 1869. Member of ASL, NIAL, AIA and Fr. Legion of Honor. Represented in Metropolitan Museum, New York, and Boston Museum of Fine Arts. (See "American Painting and its Tradition," by John C. Van Dyke.)

LaFARGE, MABEL.
(Mrs. Bancel La Farge). Painter. Born Cambridge, MA, June 26, 1875. Pupil of John La Farge. Member: New Haven PCC. Award: Member prize, New Haven PCC, 1927. Died in 1944. Address in 1929, Mt. Carmel, CT.

LaFAVOR, WILL.
Sculptor. Exhibited "Herr Meisner," at the Penna. Academy of the Fine Arts, Philadelphia, 1914. Address in 1929, Washington Park Field House, Pittsburgh, PA.

LaFONTAINE, RACHEL ADELAIDE.
Painter and author. Born in Zonnemaine, Holland, 1845. Took course at Art Students' League, New York; afterward studied under Charles Melville Dewey, J. H. Beard, Sr., and Harry Chase, New York. Traveled in England, France and Holland, 1878. Specialty, sundowns and marines. First exhibited in National Academy of Design, 1885. Illustrated several de luxe editions. Address in 1926, Care Thomas Whittaker, Inc., New York.

LaGATTA, JOHN.
Painter and illustrator. Born Naples, Italy, May 26, 1894. Pupil

539

of Howard Giles, Kenneth Hayes Miller. Frank Parsons, NY Sch. of Fine and Applied Art. Member: SI; GFLA. Illustrated covers for most major magazines, 1920's and 30's. After many years in NYC, moved to Los Angeles, taught at Art Ctr. College of Design. Died in Pasadena, CA in 1977. Address in 1929, 12 Band St.; 80 West 40th St., New York, NY; h. Baldwin Harbor, LI, NY.

LAGUNA, MURIEL.
Painter and instructor. Born in NYC. Studied: NY Univ.; The New School; Brooklyn Museum Art School. Awards: Long Island Festival Competition, 1958; The National Assoc. of Women Artists, 1967; The Grace F. Lee Memorial Prize, 1967. Exhibitions: NY Center Gallery; Chatham College, Pittsburgh, Penn.; The Penn. Academy of Fine Arts Annual, Phil. Media: Oil and acrylic. Address in 1980, 342 Christopher St., Oceanside, NY.

LAHEY, RICHARD (FRANCIS).
Portrait painter, etcher and teacher. Born Jersey City, NJ, June 23, 1893. Pupil of Bridgman, Henri, K. H. Miller. Member: S. Indp. A; Century Assn., AFAS; ASL of NY. Award: Tuthill prize, AIC, 1925; Beck gold medal, PAFA, 1929. Work: "Down by the River," Pennsylvania Acad. of the Fine Arts; "Pont Neuf," Brooklyn Museum; "Fourteenth of July," Detroit Museum; etchings, Metropolitan Museum, Newark (NJ) Public Library, Detroit Museum. Instructor, Art Students' Lg. of NY. Died in 1979. Address in 1929, 2695 Boulevard, Jersey City, NJ.

LAIDLAW, JENNIE L.
Painter. Born Milwaukee, MN, Sept. 28, 1861. Member: NA Women PS; NAC. Address in 1929, Spuyten Duyvil, New York, NY.

LAITE, GORDON.
Illustrator. Born in NYC in 1925. Attended Beloit College in Wisconsin and the AIC. Though he has used several media throughout his career, his work is predominantly in line. His children's book illustrations have been published by Holt and Abingdon Press, for whom he illustrated Good King Wenceslas and The Story of Saint Nicholas. He has lived most of his life in Gallup, New Mexico.

LAKEMAN, NATHANIEL.
Painter. Born in 1756. He painted quite a number of portraits, many of them in Salem, MA, about 1820.

LAKEY, EMILY JANE.
Painter. Born at Quincy, NY, June 22, 1837. She studied art in Ohio and Tennessee, and exhibited at Chicago, and in the National Academy. In 1877 she studied in Paris under Emile Van Marcke. Her best known paintings are the "Leader of the Herd" and "An Anxious Mother." Died Oct. 24, 1896 in Cranford, NJ.

LALANNE, MARY E.
Miniature painter, flourishing in Boston, 1833. Exhibited several miniatures at the Boston Athenaeum in 1833.

LALIBERTE, NORMAN.
Illustrator. Born in Worcester, MA, in 1925. Studied: Montreal Museum of Fine Art, Cranbrook Academy of Art and Institute of Design in Chicago. He received a Masters in Art Education from Illinois Tech. An author and illustrator, he has had over 50 One-Man Exhibitions and has designed many banners. Among the books he has illustrated is The Rainbow Box, a book of poems by Joseph Pentauro.

LALONDE, J(OSEPH) W(ILFRID).
Painter and sculptor. Born Minneapolis, Minn., March 19, 1897. Pupil of Gustave Goetsch, F. Luis Mora, F. V. DuMond, Stanislas Stickgold. Award: First painting prize, Minn. State AS, 1923. Work: Mural of Joan d'Arc and St. Louis, St. Louis Church, St. Paul, MN; over altar, St. Adelbert's Church, St. Paul. Address in 1929, 53 Greenwich Ave., New York, NY; h. 1790 Grand Ave., St. Paul, MN.

LAMAR, JULIAN.
Painter. Born Augusta, GA, Oct. 14, 1893. Pupil of Chase in Florence; Marr in Munich; Corcoran Gallery; PAFA. Member: NAC;

Newport AA; Salma. C.; AFA. Work: "Prof. Henry Fairfield Osborn," Administration Bldg., Zoological Gardens, New York, NY; "Cornelius Dewitt Willlcox" and "Major General Fred W. Sladen," Military Academy, West Point, NY; "George M. Plimpton," Barnard College, New York City; "President John Grier Hiben," Nassau Hall, Princeton Univ.; "President C. C. Cuyler," Princeton Club, New York City; "President Franklin H. Martin," American College of Surgeons, Chicago. Address in 1929, 15 Gramercy Park, New York, NY.

LAMB, ANTHONY.
Engraver. The New York Mercury, of Dec. 1, 1760, contains the following advertisement: "Maps, Plans, Coats of Arms, Shop Bills, Monthly Returns and other Engraving neatly done on Silver, Copper, etc., with Care and Dispatch, and all sort of Copper Plate Printing done in the best manner and at Reasonable Rates, at Anthony Lamb's, at Sir Isaac Newton's Head, New York."

LAMB, CHARLES R(OLLINSON).
Painter, craftsman, and architect. Born in New York. Pupil of ASL of NY. Member: Mural P.; NSS (lay); NY Municipal AS; ASL of NY; NAC; NY Arch. Lg.; AFAS; Nat. S. Craftsman. Specialty, religious, historical and municipal art. Address in 1929, 23 Sixth Ave.; h. 360 West 22d St., New York, NY.

LAMB, ELLA CONDLE.
(Mrs. Charles R. Lamb). Painter, illustrator, and craftsman. Born New York. Pupil of Wm. M. Chase and C. Y. Turner in New York; Hubert Herkomer in England; Collins and Courtois in Paris. Member: Mural P.; NAC. Awards: Dodge prize, NAD, 1889; hon. mention, Columbian Exp., Chicago, 1893; Medal, Atlanta Exp., 1895; hon. mention, Pan-Am. Exp., Buffalo, 1901. Represented in collection of the National Arts Club. Specialty, mural decorations, stained glass and portraits. Address in 1929, 360 West 22d St., New York, NY; summer, Cresskill, NJ.

LAMB, F. MORTIMER.
Painter. Born Middleboro. MA, 1861. Pupil of MA Normal Art School; School of Boston Museum of Fine Arts; Julian Academy in Paris. Member: NYWCC; AWCS; Wash. WCC; New Haven PCC; Boston SWCP; Boston AC. Awards: Gold medal, 20th Century Exp., Boston, 1900; silver medal, P.-P. Exp., San F., 1915. Work: Mem. corridor, City Hall, Brockton, MA; "The Good Samaritan," Universalist Church, Stoughton, MA; "Spring," Chicataubut Club, Stoughton, MA; 2 landscapes and five portraits in Christian Science Students' Library, Brookline, MA; portrait of "Dean Bennett," Boston Univ. Law School; four murals, First Baptist Church, Montclair, NJ. Died in 1936. Address in 1929, Stoughton, MA.

LAMB, FREDERICK STYMETZ.
Painter. Born in New York in 1863. Brother of Charles Rollinson Lamb. Student of Art Students' League, New York; pupil of Lefebvre, Boulanger and M. Millet in Paris. Honorable mention, Chicago Exposition, 1893; gold medal, Atlanta Exposition, 1895; received gold medal from French Govt. Member: National Society of Mural Painters; National Art Club; Art Students' League. Address in 1926, 23 6th Ave., New York.

LAMB, JOHN.
A New York silversmith. In the "Mercury" of 1756, he advertises "Engraving in gold, silver, copper and other materials, by John Lamb."

LAMB, KATHERINE S(TYMETS).
Painter, illustrator, craftsman, and teacher. Born Alpine, NJ, June 3, 1895. Pupil of NAD; ASL of NY; Woman's Art School of Cooper Union. Member: NAC; Mur. PS; ASL of NY. Work: Froehlich memorial stained glass window, Newark Museum, Newark, NJ; "Adoration of the Cross," three murals in reredos, Christ Church, Hackensack, NJ; "Christ in Glory," mosaic reredos, Christ Lutheran Church, New York. Specialty, designs for stained glass and mosaic and decorative illustrations. Address in 1929, 23 Sixth Ave.; h. 346 West 22nd St.,

New York, NY; summer, Cresskill, NJ.

LAMB, THOMAS B.
Illustrator. Member: SI. Address in 1929, 156 Fifth Ave., NYC.

LAMBDEN, HERMAN.
Painter. Born New Rochelle, NY, Jan. 4, 1859. Pupil of Rondel, Hartman and Yates. Member: New Rochelle AA; AFA. Died in 1935. Address in 1929, 115 Paine Ave., New Rochelle, NY.

LAMBDIN, GEORGE COCHRAN.
Painter. Son of James R. Lambdin. He was born in Philadelphia in 1830. He painted portraits, but was better known for his flower painting, his flower pieces and roses being much sought after at the time. He was elected a National Academician of the National Academy of Design in 1868. He died in Germantown, PA, on Jan. 28, 1896.

LAMBDIN, JAMES REID.
Painter. Born in Pittsburgh, May 10, 1807. He came to Philadelphia in 1823 to study painting, working under E. Miles for six months, and afterwards under Sully for a year. Also painted in miniature. Returned to Pittsburgh, where, about 1828, he established a Museum and Gallery of the Fine Arts, the first public exhibition of works of art in the West. About four years later he removed with his collection to Louisville. He lived in Philadelphia after 1838, in which year he was made Corresponding Secretary of the Artists' Fund Society. He was Vice-President of the same Society, 1840-43; Corresponding Secretary again in 1844; President in 1845-67. He painted many portraits in Washington, including several of the Presidents, one of Webster and one of Chief Justice Marshall. He was an active officer of the Pennsylvania Academy of the Fine Arts. He died in Philadelphia, Jan. 31, 1889.

LAMBERT, GERTRUDE A.
Painter. Born So. Bethlehem, PA, Aug. 10, 1885. Pupil of Phila.

School of Design for Women and PAFA. Member: Fellowship PAFA; Plastic C.; NA Women PS. Awards: Cresson traveling scholarship, PAFA, 1912-13; Mary Smith prize, PAFA, 1915; silver medal, P.-P. Exp., San F., 1915. Work: "The Little Market, Baveno," PAFA. Instructor in water color, Philadelphia School for Women, 1910-11. Address in 1929, 12 East 15th St., New York, NY; h. 215 So. Center St., Bethlehem, PA.

LAMBERT, NORA SARONY.
Painter. Born in England, Feb. 24, 1891. Pupil of George de F. Brush, Kenneth Miller, George Breck, Francis Jones. Address in 1929, Rouses Point, Clinton Co., NY.

LAMBERT, SAUL.
Illustrator. Born in NYC in 1928. Attended Brooklyn College and studied under Ad Reinhardt. His first published work appeared in Esquire in 1960 and his paintings have since appeared in most major publications. He has illustrated many books and produced posters for ABC and Columbia records. His works have been exhibited at the Bolles Gallery and the City Center Gallery in NY.

LAMIS, LEROY.
Sculptor. Born Sept. 27, 1925, in Eddyville, Iowa. Earned B.A. from New Mexico Highlands U. (Los Vegas) 1953; MA, Columbia U. 1956. Taught at Cornell College (Iowa) 1956-60 and Indiana State U. since 1961. Awarded residency, Dartmouth, 1970, and received awards from Des Moines Art Center (1958) and NYS Council on Arts. Exhibited at Clarke College (1957 and 1961); State U. of Iowa; Albright-Knox; Denver Art Mus.; Whitney Mus.; Ball State Teachers C, Ind.; Scripps C. and others. In collections of Whitney; Albright-Knox; Staempfli Collection; Hirshhorn Collection and many private collections.

LAMONT, DANIEL G.
Historical painter and portrait painter in oils and miniatures, flourishing in New York, 1846-47.

542

LAMONT, FRANCES KENT.
Sculptor. Pupil of Solon Borglum and Mahonri Young. Represented in Cleveland Mus. of Art; memorial. to the wars of America, New Canaan, CT; Spanish-American war memorial, New Rochelle, NY. Died in 1975. Address in 1929, 1443 Marion St., Denver, CO; Perry Park Ranch, Larkspur, CO.

LAMPKIN, R(ICHARD) H(ENRY).
Painter. Born Georgetown, KY, June 11, 1866. Pupil of H. D. Fulhart; Cin. Art Acad. Address in 1929, 146 W. McMillan St., Cin., OH.

LANDAU, JACOB.
Illustrator. Born in Philadelphia in 1917. He attended the Museum Art School and the New School for Social Research and later studied in Paris. His career in magazine illustration began with the editorship of At Ease. He has worked extensively in advertising design for IBM, Steuben Glass, and others. An instructor at the Philadelphia Museum Art School, he has also served as chairman of the design department at PI.

LANDEAU, SANDOR L.
Painter. Born in Hungary, 1864. Pupil of Laurens and Constant in Paris. Member: Paris AAA. Awards: Second Wanamaker prize, Paris AAA; hon. mention, Pan-Am. Exp., Buffalo, 1901; hon. mention, Paris Salon, 1905; third class medal, Paris Salon 1907. Address in 1929, care of Paul Foinet, 21 Rue Brea, Paris, France.

LANDECK, ARMIN.
Painter and engraver. Born in Wisconsin, June 4, 1905. Trained as an architect at Columbia Univ. Studied etching with Stanley William Hayter in NY Member of the National Academy of Design, the American Institute of Arts and Letters and the International Institute of Arts and Letters. Collections: The Metropolitan Museum of Art, the Museum of Modern Art, the Swedish National Museum, and others. Works and lives in Litchfield, CT.

LANDER, LOUISA.
Sculptor. Born in Salem, MA, Sept. 1, 1826. Began her art career by modelling likenesses of members of her family; went to Rome, 1855, and studied under Thomas Crawford. Among her first notable works were figures of marble, "Today" and "Galatea." Among her later works are: a bust of Gov. Gore, of Mass.; bust of Hawthorne; statues of "Virginia Dare;" "Undine;" "Virginia;" "Evangeline;" "Elizabeth;" "The Exile of Siberia"; "Ceres Mourning for Proserpine;" "A Sylph Alighting;" "The Captive Pioneer;" also many portrait busts. Address in 1926, 1608 19th St., Washington, DC. Died Nov. 14, 1923.

LANE, CHRISTOPHER.
Painter. Born June 7, 1937, in NYC. Studied at H.S. of Music and Art, NYC; Goddard Col., VT; Sch. of Ptg. and Sculpture, Mexico City. In Mexico and Paris from 1957 to 1962. Exhibited at Beaux Arts Gal., London (1962); Osborne Gal, NYC (1958); City Center Gal., NYC; II Biennale, Paris; MOMA; Yale; U. of IL; and in many private coll.

LANE, KATHARINE W(ARD).
Sculptor. Born Boston, MA, Feb. 22, 1899. Pupil of Anna Hyatt Huntington, Charles Grafly, Brenda Putnam. Member: Guild Boston A; NA Women PS; North Shore AA; Boston SS; NSS. Awards: Bronze medal, Sesqui-Centennial Exposition, Phila., 1926; Widener Memorial gold medal, PAFA, 1927; Joan of Arc gold medal, NA Women PS, 1928; hon. mention, Paris Salon, France, 1928. Address in 1929, 53 Marlboro St., Boston, MA; summer, Manchester, MA.

LANE, MARIAN.
Painter and craftsman. Born Great Gransden, Huntingdonshire, England. Member: Wash. WCC; Wash. SAC; NY Guild of Bookworkers. Address in 1929, care Arts Club, 17th and I Streets, NW, Washington, DC.

LANE, MARION
Sculptor. Studied: Brooklyn Museum Art School; The Art Students' League, NYC; Pratt Institute. Exhibitions: Brooklyn Museum; Montclair Museum; Edward

543

Williams College, 1971. Awards: Brooklyn Museum, 1958; Montclair Museum, 1960, 1964; Atlantic City Annual, 1963.

LANE, MARY COMER.
Painter. Member: Balto. WCC; SSAL. Address in 1929, 26 Gaston St., Savannah, GA.

LANE, SUSAN MINOT.
Painter. Born in Cambridge, MA, in 1832. She was a pupil of William Morris Hunt. She is represented by a painting in the Boston Museum of Fine Arts. She died in 1893, in Cambridge, MA.

LANE, THOMAS HENRY.
Painter. Worked in portraits and miniatures. He was born Feb 14, 1815, and died Sept. 27, 1900, at Elizabeth, NJ.

LANE, WILLIE BAZE.
Painter, lecturer and teacher. Born Mason, TX, March 16, 1896. Pupil of Nordfeldt in Santa Fe. Member: Okla. AA; Chickasha AL; Okla. City AL; Okla. Traveling Exhibitors. Work: Murals in First Christian Church and First Baptist Church, Chickasha. Address in 1929, 1121 Florida Ave., Chickasha, Okla.; summer, Santa Fe, NM.

LANG, CHARLES M.
Painter, sculptor, illustrator, craftsman, and teacher. Born Albany, NY, Aug. 26, 1860. Pupil of Julius Benzur, Prof. Lofftz; studied in Venice and London. Member: Salma. C. Work: "Gov. David B. Hill," "Gov. Roswell P. Flower," City of Albany, NY; "Hugo Flagg Cook," Capitol, Albany; Judges Parker and Houghton, Court House, Albany; bust of James Ten Eyck, Masonic Temple, Albany; "Gen. Joseph B. Carr," "Cuett" and "Warren," Troy, NY; "Morgan J. O'Brien," Manhattan Club, New York City; "Bishop Rooker," "Gen. C. P. Easton," "Prof. Robinson," Albany High School, Ithaca, NY. Died in 1934. Address in 1929, Miller Bldg. Studio, 1931 Broadway; 47 Fifth Ave., New York, NY.

LANG, GEORGE S.
Engraver. Born in Chester County, PA, in 1799; living in Delaware County, PA, in 1883. Baker said that Lang was a pupil of George Murray, the Philadelphia engraver, in 1815, and that he abandoned engraving early in life. The Philadelphia directories, however, contain his name as "engraver" until 1833, and as his signed work is scarce, he was probably employed in bank-note work. He was a good line-engraver.

LANG, LOUIS.
Painter. Born in Wurtemberg, Germany, March 29, 1824. He came to America in 1838, and settled in Philadelphia. He was elected a National Academician in 1852, and was a member of the Artists' Fund Society. His work was portraits and historical scenes. Work: "Maid of Saragossa," "Blind Nydia" and "Romeo and Juliet" in the Century Club, New York. He died May 6, 1893, in NYC.

LANGERFELDT, THEODORE O.
Painter. Born in Germany in 1841. He came to Boston, Mass., in 1868. He painted chiefly in water colors, and one of his architectural paintings was awarded a prize at the Centennial Exhibition in Philadelphia in 1876.

LANGHORNE, KATHERINE.
See Adams, K. Langhorne (Mrs.).

LANGLEY, ELIZABETH.
Painter and etcher. Born Chicago, IL, May 20, 1907. Pupil of Arthur Carles, Hugh Breckenridge; ASL of NY. Address in 1929, 2038 Spruce St., Philadelphia, PA; summer, High Point, NJ.

LANGLEY, SARAH.
(Mrs. Earl Mendenhall). Painter, sculptor, illustrator, writer and teacher. Born Texas, July 12, 1885. Pupil PAFA. Member: Fellowship PAFA. Works: "Jewels," Pennsylvania Academy of the Fine Arts. Address in 1929, 329 Walnut St., Philadelphia, PA; summer, Forest Inn, Eagles Mere Park, PA.

LANGTON, BERENICE FRANCES.
(Mrs. Daniel W. Langton). Sculptor. Pupil of Augustus Saint-Gaudens in New York; Rodin in Paris. Member: NA Women PS.

544

Awards: Bronze medal, St. Louis Exp., 1904; Helen Foster Barnett prize for sculpture, NA Women PS, 1915. Died in 1959. Address in 1929, 207 East 17th St., New York, NY; care American Express Co., 11 Rue Scribe, Paris, France.

LANGTRY, MARY.
Painter. Member: NYWCC; NA Women PS. Address in 1929, Box 41, Tompkins Cove, NY; 241 Ryerson St., Brooklyn, New York, NY.

LANGZETTEL, GEORGE H(ENRY).
Painter and teacher. Born Springfield, MA, April 3, 1864. Pupil of Yale School of the Fine Arts. Member: New Haven PCC. Instructor in Drawing and Secretary, Yale School of the Fine Arts. Address in 1929, Yale School of Fine Arts; h. 725 Whitney Ave., New Haven, CT.

LANKES, J(ULIUS) J.
Painter, illustrator, etcher, artist, craftsman and writer. Born Buffalo, NY, Aug. 31, 1884. Pupil of Mary B. W. Coxe; Ernest Fosbery; Philip Hale; W. M. Paxton. Member: Calif. PM; Print Soc. of England; Am. APL. Represented in permanent print collections of the Boston, New York and Newark Public Libraries; Metropolitan and Brooklyn Museums; Carnegie Inst., Pittsburgh; Library of Congress, Washington, DC; British Museum; California State Library. Illustrations for "New Hampshire," and "Westrunning Brook," by Robert Frost; "Homes of the Freed," by Rossa B. Cooley; "Marbacka," by Selma Lagerlof; "May Days," ed. by Genevieve Taggard; "Spring Plowing," by Charles Malan. Died 1960. Address in 1929, Hilton Village, VA.

LANMAN, CHARLES.
Painter. Studied with Asher Durand. Born in Monroe, Mich., 1819. He was elected an Associate Member of the National Academy in 1847. His largest picture, "View of Filziyama," was purchased by the Japanese government. Published The Private Life of Daniel Webster. He died March 4, 1895.

LANSIL, WALTER F.
Born in Bangor, ME, in 1846. He early became familiar with ships and the sea. He studied abroad and on his return to this country set up his studio in Boston, where he became well known in his style of painting. Among his works: "Crossing the Georges" and "View of Charlestown, with Shipping."

LANSNER, FAY.
Painter and tapestry artist. Born in Phila., PA, in 1921. Study: Tyler School of Fine Arts, Temple Univ., 1945-47; Columbia Univ. with Susanne Langer; ASL, 1947-48; Hans Hoffman School 1948-50; with Fernand Leger, Andre L'hote, Paris, 1950. Work: Newsweek, NYC; Ciba-Geigy Corp., Ardsley, NY; Cite des Arts, Paris; Neuberger Mus., SUNY Purchase; Corcoran Gal., Wash. DC; Met. Mus., NYC; Phila. (PA) Mus. of Art; and many other mus., corp., and private coll. One-woman shows: Galerie 8, Paris, 1951; Hansa Gal., NYC, 1954, 56, 58; Kornblee Gal., NYC, 1964, 66; Benson Gal., Bridgehampton, LI, NY, 1970, 72, 76, 78, 80, 82; Ingber Gal., NYC, 1980; Phoenix Gal. II, Wash. DC, 1982; and many more. Exhib.: Davis Gal., NYC; Zabriskie Gal., NYC; Tibor de Nagy Gal., NYC; Contemp. Art Mus., Houston, TX; Kornblee Gal., NYC; Sch. of Visual Arts, NYC; Weatherspoon Art Gal., Greensboro; Corcoran Gal., Wash. DC; MOMA, NYC (lending svc.); 17th Brooklyn Mus. Print Annual; La Demeure Tapestry, Paris; Am. Fed. of Arts, Mus. Section, Guild Hall, East Hampton, LI, NY; U. of North Dakota; Cite des Arts, Paris; Met. Mus. Art; Denver (CO) Art Mus; and many others. Mem.: Co-founder, Women in the Arts, with Ce Roser. Bibliog.: Numerous reviews in Art News, Art in America, Craft Horizons, NY Times, etc.; books; broadcasts taped interviews. Media: Oil, pastel, charcoal, pencil, lithograph, collage, watercolor, tapestry. Rep.: Marlborough Graphics, and Arras Gal., NYC. Address in 1983, 810 Broadway, NYC.

LAPLANTE, LOUISE A.
Painter. Born in Dover, NH, in 1950. Study: Ralph Della Volpe;

545

Art Inst. of Boston, BFA 1974; College of New Rochelle, MA 1976; State Univ. of NY at Albany. Work: Private collections. One-woman shows: Univ. of VT & SUNYA, 1976; Albany (NY) Inst. of History and Art, 1979; Gallery on Paper, Lenox, MA, 1982, and others. Exhib.: 20th Annual Nat'l Exhib. of Prints & Drawings, Oklahoma Art Center, Oklahoma City, 1978; Adirondack Reg'l. Art Exhib., Hyde Collection, Glens Falls, NY, 1978; New Eng. Arts Festival & Showcase, Northampton, MA, 1981; The Main Artery, Northampton, MA, 1982; other exhibitions in MA and VT. Address in 1983, 66 Franklin St., Northhampton, MA.

LAPSLEY, ROBERT ERNEST.
Illustrator. Born in Memphis, TN, in 1942. Attended: North Texas State Univ. for three years before leaving for Los Angeles where he studied at the ACD until 1970. He has exhibited his work at the S of I Annual Exhibitions.

LARNED, MARGUERITE YOUNGLOVE.
Painter. Member: NA Women PS; PBC; Elizabeth SA. Address in 1929, 62 Washington Sq., New York, NY.

LARSEN, (CHARLES) PETER.
Painter, etcher and craftsman. Born Philadelphia, March 7, 1892. Pupil of PAFA. Member: Chicago SE. Represented in Chicago Art Institute. Address in 1929, 27 West 8th St., New York, NY; h. 662 Madison Ave., York, PA.

LARSEN, B(ENT) F(RANKLIN).
Painter and teacher. Born Monroe, UT, May 10, 1882. Pupil of Walter Sargent, Lee R. Randolph, Henri Royer, Paul Albert Laurens, Jules Pages. Member: Amer. S. Indp. A; Amer. Artists Prof. Lg.; Pacific AA; Western AA; AFA. Awards: Utah prize, Springville National Exhibition, 1926; first prize, Utah County Exhibition, 1927. Work: "The Mother Tree" and "Belgium Fields," Springville Gallery, Springville, Utah; "In Dragon Land" and "Sunlit Mountain," Alice Art Collection, State Capital, Salt Lake City; "Rock Canyon," Utah County Collection, County Gallery,

Provo; "The Joshua," Gila College, Thatcher, Ariz. Died in 1970. Address in 1929, 733 North Fifth West, Provo, UT.

LARSEN, MAY SYBIL.
Painter. Born Chicago, IL. Pupil of AIC; Sloan; Davey. Member: S. Indp. A.; Chicago NJSA. Died 1953. Address in 1929, 4437 North Francisco Ave., Chicago, IL.

LARSH, THEODORA.
(Mrs. Francis Dane Chase). Miniature painter and teacher. Born Crawfordsville, IN. Pupil of ASL of NY; AIC; Beaux; Vanderpoel; Bridgman; George Luks; Hawthorne; Johansen; Mme. La Forge in Paris. Member: NA Women PS; ASL of Chicago; Alliance; Indiana AL; ASL of NY; Hoosier Salon; Am. APL; Crawfordsville (Ind.) AL (hon.). Award: Griffith prize, miniatures, Hoosier Salon, 1926. Director NY Lg. of Business and Professional Women. Died in 1955. Address in 1929, 152 Carnegie Hall, New York, NY; summer, 4 Montrose Ave., Argyle Park, Babylon, LI, NY.

LARSON, FRED T.
Painter. Born Chicago, April 19, 1868. Pupil of AIC. Member: Palette and Chisel C. Specialty, woodcuts and color block prints. Address in 1929, 55 E. Washington St.; 2935 North Whipple St., Chicago, IL.

LARTER, JOSENIA ELIZABETH.
(Mrs. W. H. D. Cox). Painter, illustrator, etcher and teacher. Born Newark, NJ, April 6, 1898. Pupil of Gruger, Rosen, Henri, Du Mond, Bridgman, Pennell, Ida W. Stroud, Van Sloun, Charles S. Chapman. Member: AFA. Awarded $1,000, trade mark contest, 1922, Lawyers Mortgage Co. Specialty, figure composition. Address in 1929, 395 Parker St., Newark, NJ.

LASKY, BESSIE.
Painter. Born Boston, Mass., April 30, 1890. Pupil of Felicie Waldo Howell. Member: NA Women PS; North Shore AA; New Haven PCC; AFA. Work: "Interior," Newark Museum. Address in 1929, 910 Fifth Ave.; summer, 609 Palisades Beach Blvd., New York, NY.

LASSAW, IBRAM.
Sculptor. Born May 4, 1913, in
Alexandria, Egypt; became US
citizen. Studied with Dorothea H.
Denslow at Sculpture Center, NYC
(1926-30); at Beaux-Arts Inst. and
City College, NYC. Taught at Am.
U., Wash. DC; Duke U.; Berkeley C.;
Brandes U. and Mt. Holyoke C.
Founder of Am. Abstract Artists.
Exhibits include those at Kootz
Gallery (many since 1951); MIT;
Duke U.; MOMA; Carnegie; Seattle
World's Fair (1962); U. of
Illinois; Whitney Gallery of Nat.
Inst. for Arts and Letters. In
collections of Harvard U.; Wash.
U.; Newark Mus.; Wadsworth Mus.;
Baltimore Mus. Cornell U.; Whitney
Mus., MOMA; Kneses Tifereth Israel
Synagogue, Port Chester, NY, Beth
El Temples of Providence and
Springfield, and others.

LASSELL, CHARLES.
Illustrator. Member: SI. Address
in 1929, Westport, CT.

LATHROP, DOROTHY PULIS.
Painter and illustrator. Born
Albany, NY, April 16, 1891. Pupil
of A. W. Dow; Henry McCarter; F.
Luis Mora. Member: Fellowship
PAFA; NA Women PS. Illustrated,
"The Three Mulla-Mulgars,"
"Down-Adown-Derry" and "Crossings,"
by Walter de la Mare; "A Little Boy
Lost," by W. H. Hudson; "The
Grateful Elephant," translated by
E. W. Burlingame and "Silverhorn,"
by Hilda Conkling; "Made-to-Order
Stories," by Dorothy Canfield; "The
Light Princess," by George
MacDonald; "Tales from the
Enchanted Isles," by Ethel May
Gate. Illustrated for magazines.
Address in 1929, 151 South Allen
St., Albany, NY.

LATHROP, ELINOR L.
Painter and sculptor. Born in
Hartford, CT, 1899. Pupil of Hale,
Logan and Jones. Address in 1926,
96 Niles St., Hartford, CT.

LATHROP, FRANCIS.
Painter. Born at Sea, June 22,
1849. He was educated in New York
City and in Germany. He exhibited
at the Society of American Artists
in 1878, portraits of Ross R. and
Thomas Winans. He devoted himself
chiefly to mural painting, and
designing of stained glass. He
executed wall paintings at Bowdoin
College Chapel; Metropolitan Opera
House, New York; and decorations
for Trinity Church, Boston.
Elected an Associate Member of the
National Academy in 1906, three
years before his death. He was
also a member of the Society of
American Artists. He died Oct. 18,
1909, in Woodcliffe Lake, NJ.

LATHROP, GERTRUDE K.
Sculptor. Born Albany, NY, Dec.
24, 1896. Pupil of Solon Borglum
and Charles Grafly. Sister of
illustrator Dorothy Pulis Lathrop.
Mother was painter. In collections
of Brookgreen Gardens; Nat. Collec.
of Fine Arts, Wash. DC; Albany
Public Library; Houston Pub.
Library. Member: Soc. Animal PS;
NA Women PS; NSS (Assoc.). Award:
Hon. mention, AIC, 1924; Helen
Foster Barnett prize, NAD, 1928.
Address in 1929, 151 South Allen
St., Albany, NY.

LATHROP, IDA PULIS.
(Mrs. Cyrus Clard Lathrop).
Painter. Born Troy, NY, Oct. 27,
1859. Self-taught. Member: NA
Women PS. Work: "Still Life,"
Prendergast Art Gallery, Jamestown,
NY Specialty, portraits and still
life. Died in 1937. Address in
1929, 151 South Allen St., Albany,
NY.

LATHROP, W(ILLIAM) L(ANGSON).
Painter. Born Warren, IL, March
29, 1859. Member: ANA 1902. NA
1907; NYWCC; Rochester AC. Awards:
Evans prize, AWCS, 1896; gold
medal, AC Phila., 1897; Webb prize,
SAA, 1899; bronze medal, Pan-Am.
Exp., Buffalo, 1901; third prize
($500), C. I. Pittsburgh, 1903;
second prize, Worcester, 1904;
bronze medal, St. Louis Exp., 1904;
gold medal for oil painting and
silver medal for water colors,
P.-P. Exp., San F., 1915. Work:
"The Meadows," Metropolitan Museum,
New York; "Clouds and Hills,"
Minneapolis Museum; "Three Trees,"
National Museum of Art, Washington;
"Abandoned Quarry," Carnegie
Institute, Pittsburgh; "Old Covered
Bridge," Hackley Art Gallery,
Muskegon, Mich. Died in 1938.

Address in 1929, New Hope, Bucks Co., PA; care of the Ferargil Galleries, 607 Fifth Ave., New York, NY.

LATILLA, EUGENIO.
Painter. Born in 1808. He lived in Italy for years, but later moved his studio to New York. His portraits were excellent; he painted many of the most eminent American clergymen. Latilla taught for some years in the School of Design in New York. Died Oct. 30, 1861 in Chappaqua, NY.

LAUBER, JOSEPH.
Mural painter, etcher and craftsman. Born Meschede, Westphalia, Germany, Aug. 31, 1855; came to US at age of nine. Pupil of Karl Muller, Shirlaw and Chase; worked with La Farge. Member: Mural P.; NY Arch. Lg., 1889; A. Fellowship, Inc. (President); Salma. C., 1902; Faculty C. Col. Univ. Awards: Hon. mention for mosaics and glass, Columbian Exp., Chicago, 1893; gold and bronze medals for mosaic and mural designs Atlanta, 1895; medals, for etchings and mural work, Midwinter Fair, Calif. Specialty, stained glass, mosaics and murals. Work: Painting; Sixteen symbolic figures, Appellate Court, NY; portrait of ex-speaker Pennington, House of Representatives, Wash., DC; windows in Church of the Ascension, NY; Trinity Lutheran Church, Lancaster, PA; painting of Christ, Euclid Ave. Baptist Church, Cleveland, Ohio. Instructor of art at Columbia Univ., NY. Died Oct. 19, 1948. Address in 1929, 371 West 120th St., New York.

LAUDERDALE, URSULA.
(Mrs. Edward Seay Lauderdale). Painter, lecturer and teacher. Born in 1880. Pupil of Henri; Reaugh; ASL of NY; Devol; Maurice Braun. Member: Dallas AA; Fort Worth AA; Dallas Woman's Forum; Southern SAL; AFA. Work: Stained glass window, "Ruth," City Temple, Dallas, Texas. Died in 1933. Address in 1929, 3401 Princeton Ave., Dallas, TX.

LAUGHLIN, ALICE D(ENNISTON).
Painter, illustrator, and engraver. Born Pittsburgh, PA, Oct. 19, 1895. Member: ASL of NY; AFA; NAC. Represented by woodcuts in the Rochester Memorial Gallery, Rochester, NY; New York Public Library; Phillips Memorial Gallery, Washington, DC. Died 1952. Address in 1929, 133 East 64th St., New York, NY; summer, Hyannisport, MA.

LAUNE, PAUL SIDNEY.
Painter and illustrator. Born Milford, NE, May 5, 1899. Pupil of Chicago AFA. Award: Silver medal for graphic arts at Midwestern Exhibition, 1924, Kansas City, MO, AI. Represented in High School Collections, McPherson, KS.

LAUNITZ, ROBERT EBERHARD.
Sculptor. Born Nov. 4, 1806, in Latvia. In 1830 he came to America and was elected a member of the National Academy in 1833. Among his productions are the Pulaski monument in Savannah, GA; the Battle monument in Frankfort, KY; the monument to General George H. Thomas in Troy, NY. He was connected in his work with the sculptor John Franzee in New York. He died Dec. 13, 1870, in NYC.

LAURENCE, SIDNEY.
Painter. Born NY, Oct. 14, 1865. Member: Salma C. Address in 1929, Anchorage, AK.

LAURENT, ROBERT.
Sculptor. Born Concarneau, France, June 29, 1890. Pupil of Hamilton Easter Field with whom he came to US at age 12; Maurice Sterne; British Acad. in Rome. Member: Salons of Amer.; Mod. Artists of Amer.; Brooklyn Soc. Mod. A. Award: Logan medal, AIC, 1924. Represented in Art Inst. of Chicago; Newark Mus.; Brooklyn Mus., Corona Mundi; Vassar Coll.; Whitney Mus. Instructor at Ogunquit (ME) School of Art; Master Inst. of United Arts, and ASL, New York. Died 1970. Address in 1929, 106 Columbia Hghts., Brooklyn, New York, NY; summer, Ker Fravaal, Cape Neddick, ME.

LAURENT.
A little known genre painter who worked in America with some success.

LAURIE, ALEXANDER.
Same as Alexander Lawrie.

LAURIE-WALLACE, J(OHN).
Painter, sculptor, illustrator, lecturer, and teacher. Born Garvagh, Ireland, July 29, 1864. Pupil of Thomas Eakins; PAFA. Member: Omaha AG; Chicago SA. Address in 1929, 5804 Leavenworth St., Omaha, NE.

LAURITZ, PAUL.
Painter. Born Larvik, Norway, April 18, 1889. Member: CA AC; Los Angeles PS; Artland C. Awards: Second prize, 1920, first prize, 1922, first prize, 1923, second prize, 1924, hon. mention, 1925, third prize, 1926, State Fair, Sacramento, CA; hon. mention, State Fair, Arcadia, CA, 1923; first prize, State Fair, Santa Ana, CA, 1923; hon. mention, State Fair, Phoenix, AZ, 1925. Died in 1975. Address in 1929, 3955 Clayton Ave., Los Angeles, CA.

LAUTER, F(LORA).
Painter. Born in New York in 1874. Pupil of Henri, Chase and Mora in New York. Member: Women's Inter. Art Club, London; Salons of America; Buffalo S. Indp. A.; S. Indp. A.; Indp. A. of Chicago; Hoosier Salon; Indianapolis AG; Alliance; East Gloucester AC; North Shore AA. Address in 1929, 612 East 13th St., Indianapolis, IN.

LAUTZ, WILLIAM.
Sculptor. Born in Unstadt, Germany, April 20, 1838. He came to the United States in 1854 and settled in Buffalo, NY. Some of his work was in the Buffalo Historical Society NY Building. He died June 24, 1915, in Buffalo.

LAUX, AUGUST.
Painter. Born in the Rhine Pfaiz, Bavaria, in 1847; died in Brooklyn, NY, July 21, 1921. Removed with his parents to New York in 1863, and studied at the National Academy of Design. Exhibited in spring of 1870 at National Academy, and became notable for decorative work, but after 1880 gave his attention to genre and still-life pictures.

LAVALLE, JOHN.
Painter. Born Nahant, Mass., June 24, 1896. Pupil of Philip Hale and Leslie Thompson; School of Boston Museum of Fine Arts; Julian Academy in Paris. Member: Boston GA; Boston SWCP; Copley S; Grand Cen. AGA; Gloucester AA; St. Botolph C, Boston. Represented in Brooklyn Museum, Columbia University Club, New York. Address in 1929, Fenway Studios, 30 Ipswich St., Boston, MA; h. 32 Bates St., Cambridge, MA.

LaVALLEY, J(ONAS) J(OSEPH).
Painter. Born Rouses Point, NY, Aug., 1858. Member: Springfield AL; Conn. AFA. Work: "Birth of Springfield," owned by City of Springfield. Represented in Springfield Art Museum; Mass. Agricultural College. Address in 1929, 1537 Main St.; h. 101 Allen St., Springfield, MA.

LAVIGNE.,
Engraver. The few known plates signed by Lavigne are well executed in stipple, and appear in the "Polyanthos," published in Boston in 1914.

LAW, MARGARET MOFFETT.
Painter and teacher. Born Spartanburg, SC. Pupil of Chase Henri, Mora and Hawthorne; Andre L'hote. Member: Balto. WCC; Southern SAL; New Haven PCC; S. Indp. A.; NA Women PS; Wash. WCC; Kenilworth AC; Balto. Indp. S; Balto. Handicraft C; AFA. Work: "Feeding Chickens," Kennedy Library, Spartanburg, SC; "Wayside Chat," Converse College, SC; "A Short Crop," Phillips Memorial Gallery, Washington, DC; "Under the Mimosa," Art Club, Spartansburg, SC; "The Road to Town," Clifton Park High School, Baltimore, MD. Died in 1958. Address in 1929, 13 East Read St., Baltimore, MD; h. 364 Spring St., Spartanburg, SC.

LAW, PAULINE ELIZABETH.
Printer. Born in Wilmington, DE, Feb. 22, 1908. Studied: Art Students' League; Grand Central Art School; and with Carlson, Hibbard,

and Snell. Awards: Hudson Valley Art Assoc. 1955, 1957; Pen and Brush Club; Catherine L. Wolfe Art Club. Collection: Athens, Greece, Museum of Art. Address in 1980, 15 Gramercy Park, NY, NY.

LAWFORD, CHARLES.
Painter. Member: Attic C., Minneapolis; Minneapolis AL. Awards: First prize ($100), Minneapolis Inst., 1915; bronze medal, St. Paul Inst., 1917; gold medal, Minnesota State Art Commission, 1917.

LAWGOW, ROSE.
Painter, illustrator, and craftsman. Born Portland, OR, Jan. 20, 1901. Member: Seattle FAS. Address in 1929, R. 7, Box 285, Seattle, WA.

LAWLESS, CARL.
Painter. Born in IL, Feb. 20, 1896. Pupil of PAFA; Chicago AFA. Member: Phila. Sketch C.; Fellowship PAFA; Phila. Alliance; Phila. AC; Conn. AFA. Awards: Cresson Traveling Scholarship, PAFA, 1921; Fellowship prize, PAFA, 1923; Murphy memorial prize, NAD, 1923; hon. mention, Conn. AFA, 1925. Represented in National Academy of Design, New York; Springfield, Mass., Art Association; Columbus Academy of Art; Art Institute of Chicago. Address in 1929, 20 Orchard Lane, Mystic, CT.

LAWLOR, GEORGE W(ARREN).
Painter. Born Chelsea, MA, Oct. 21, 1878. Pupil of Julian and Colarossi Academies and Ecole des Beaux-Arts in Paris. Member: Boston AC. Address in 1929, Poplar Street Studios, Brooklyn, NY.

LAWMAN, JASPER HOLMAN.
Landscape and portrait painter. Born in Cleveland, OH, in 1825. Studied abroad. He painted many of the leading families in western Pennsylvania. He died April 1, 1906, in Pittsburgh, PA.

LAWRENCE, CHARLES B.
Painter. Born in Bordentown, NJ. He removed to Philadelphia about 1813. He was a pupil of Rembrandt Peale, and is said also to have

studied with Stuart. He finally abandoned art for commerce. His portrait of Jose Franciso Correa de Serra, the distinguished Portuguese botanist, is owned by the American Philosophical Society, Philadelphia. He also painted some landscapes.

LAWRENCE, EDNA W.
Painter and teacher. Born Concord, NY, Nov. 27, 1898. Pupil of RI School of Design; Aldra Hibbard. Member: Prov. AC; Prov. WCC. Address in 1929, 98 Jenkins St., Providence, RI; summer, 332 Center St., Richmond, SI, NY.

LAWRENCE, HELEN (CHRISTOPHER).
Painter and teacher. Born Red Oak, IA, July 12, 1895. Pupil of ASL of NY; Grand Central School of Art; Mafori-Savini Academy, Florence. Member: NA Women PS; AWCS; Silvermine GA. Address in 1929, "Ashlands," Darien, CT.

LAWRENCE, (OR LAURENCE) SAMUEL.
Portrait painter. Born in Surrey, England in 1812. In 1854 he was living in the United States, where he painted or drew the portraits of a number of prominent men. Died Feb. 28, 1884, in London.

LAWRENCE, W. S.
This landscape engraver was an apprentice with Alfred Jones in 1840, and in 1846 he was engraving over his own name for New York publishers. Plates signed "A. L. Jones" were executed by Lawrence when an apprentice with Jones, and were finished by the latter.

LAWRENCE, WILLIAM RODERICK.
Painter. Born March 3, 1829. His figure paintings were all of a peculiarly imaginative tendency, but most carefully drawn. There are two in the Wadsworth Gallery in Hartford, CT: "The Royal Children" and "Napoleon at Waterloo." He spent his entire live in Hartford, CT, and died there Oct. 9, 1856.

LAWRENCE-WETHERILL, MARIA.
Painter and etcher. Born Philadelphia, PA, Dec. 11, 1892. Pupil of Clinton Peters, Guillomet, Bashet and Pagess. Member: NA Women PS; NAC; Phila. Print C; Am.

APL; AFA. Address in 1929, National Arts Club, New York, NY; Palm Beach, FL.

LAWRIE, ALEXANDER.
(A.K.A.: Laurie). Portrait painter, engraver and crayon portrait draughtsman. Born in New York City Feb. 25, 1828. He exhibited a crayon portrait of Thomas Sully at the Pennsylvania Academy in 1854. He studied both at the National Academy and at the Pennsylvania Academy of Fine Arts. Later he was a pupil of Leutze in Dusseldorf, and of Picot in Paris. Appleton's "Cyclopaedia" notes that "He has made upward of a thousand crayon heads, including likenesses of Richard H. Stoddard and Thomas Buchanan Read." Among his best portraits in oil is the likeness of Judge Sutherland, painted for the New York Bar Association. He also painted landscapes. In 1866 he was elected an Associate Member of the National Academy of Design. He died Feb. 15, 1917.

LAWRIE, LEE.
Sculptor. Born Rixford, Germany, Oct. 16, 1877. Instructor in sculpture Harvard University, 1910-12; Yale University, 1908-18. Member: ANA; NSS; NAC; NY Arch. Lg.; Century C; (hon.) AIA. Award: Gold medal, AIA, 1921 and 1927; hon. award, Southern California Chapter, AIA, 1926. Work: Decorations in United States Military Academy, West Point; Church of St. Vincent Ferrer, and reredos of St. Thomas' Church, New York; Harkness Memorial Tower and Archway, Yale University; National Academy of Sciences, Washington, DC; Nebraska State Capitol; small marble head of woman, Metropolitan Museum of Art, New York; Los Angeles Public Library; Bok Carillon Tower, Florida; Goodhue Memorial, New York. Died in 1963. Address in 1929, 149 East 119th St., New York, NY.

LAWSON, ADELAIDE J.
Painter. Born New York, NY, June 9, 1890. Studied at ASL of NY. Member: S. Indp. A.; Salons of America; NY Soc. Women A. Address in 1929, 10 Vannest Pl., New York, NY.

LAWSON, ALEXANDER.
Engraver. Born in Ravenstruthers, Lanarkshire, Scotland, Dec. 18, 1773; died in Philadelphia, Aug. 22, 1846. An extended memoir of Alexander Lawson was read before the Pennsylvania Historical Society, in 1878, by the late Townsend Ward and from this paper the following brief sketch is compiled. Alexander Lawson was left an orphan at the age of fifteen years and was cared for by an elder brother residing in Liverpool. As he sympathized deeply with the Revolutionary movement in France, in 1793 Lawson determined to seek his future in that country, and as he could not obtain a direct passage from England, he sailed for the United States, expecting to return on a French vessel. He landed at Baltimore on July 14, 1794, and was so well pleased with the social and political conditions existing in this country that he changed his plans and concluded to cast in his lot with the Americans. He went to Philadelphia, and as he seemed to have some knowledge of engraving, he first found employment with the engravers "Thackara & Vallance." Some time after this he commenced business for himself, and first attracted attention by his admirable plates for an edition of Thomson's "Seasons." In 1798 Lawson met his fellow-countryman, Alexander Wilson, and a firm and lasting friendship resulted. Lawson engraved the best plates in Wilson's famous Ornithology, the first volume of which was issued in 1808, and also those in its continuation, by Charles Lucien Bonaparte.

LAWSON, ERNEST.
Landscape painter. Born in CA, 1873, Studied in KS City; ASL of NY; and in Paris. Member: ANA 1908; NA 1917; Inst. A and L; NAC; New Soc. A. Awards: Silver medal, St. Louis Exp., 1904; Sesnan medal, PAFA 1907; gold medal, AAS 1907; first Hallgarten prize, NAD 1908; gold medal, P.-P. Exp., San F., 1915; Altman prize ($500) NAD 1916; second W. A. Clark prize ($1,500), and Corcoran silver medal, 1916; Inness gold medal, NAD 1917; Temple

gold medal, PAFA, 1920; Altman prize ($1,000), NAD, 1921; first prize, Pittsburgh Intn. Exp., 1921. Work: "An Abandoned Farm," National Gallery, Washington; "The Swimming Hole," Art Museum, Montclair, NJ; "Winter," Met. Mus., NY; "Landscape" and "Winter," Brooklyn Museum; "Road at the Palisades," City Art Museum, St. Louis; "Boat House, Harlem River, Winter," Corcoran Gallery, Washington, DC; "Spring" and "Ploughed Field," Harrison Gallery, Los Angeles Museum; and in museum at Worcester, MA; Chicago, IL; San Fran., CA; Pittsburgh, PA; Youngstown, OH; Savannah, GA. Died on Dec. 18, 1939. Address in 1929, care of Ferargil Gallery, 37 East 57th St., NYC.

LAWSON, HELEN E.
Engraver. This daughter of Alexander Lawson made the drawings for her father's illustrations in the works of Prof. Haldeman and Dr. Binney, and she also engraved several plates of birds for a publication of about 1830. She showed decided talent in this work.

LAWSON, JESS M.
Sculptor. Born in Edinburgh, Scotland, 1885. Member: National Sculpture Society; National Academy of Women Painters and Sculptors. Awards: Helen Foster Barnett prize, National Academy of Design, 1918; Widener gold medal, Penna. Academy of Fine Arts, 1919. Address in 1926, 120 Lexington Ave., New York, NY.

LAWSON, KATHARINE S(TEWART).
Sculptor. Born Indianapolis, IN, May 9, 1885. Pupil of Lorado Taft, Hermon A. MacNeil. Member: NA Women PS; Ind. SS. Award: Shaw prize, NAD, 1921. Address in 1929, Box 298, Saugatuck, CT; "Lone Pine Studio," Westport, CT.

LAWSON, OSCAR A.
Engraver. Born in Philadelphia, Aug. 7, 1813; died there Sept. 6, 1854. This son of Alexander Lawson was probably a pupil of his father, and he became an accomplished line-engraver. Also painted landscapes and portraits. He furnished a number of small plates for the "Annuals;" but about 1840 he entered the service of the U. S. Coast Survey, at Washington, as a chart engraver, and he remained there until failing health compelled him to resign in 1851.

LAWSON, THOMAS BAYLEY.
Painter. Born in Newburyport, MA, Jan. 13, 1807. He drew from the Antique in the National Academy of Design, NY, for six months in 1831; returned to Newburyport, and commenced painting portraits in 1832. In 1844 he painted a portrait of Daniel Webster. Lawson died Jan. 4, 1888 in Lowell, MA.

LAWSON-PEACEY, JESS M.
Sculptor. Born Edinburgh, Scotland, Feb. 18, 1885. Member: British Institute, Assoc. Royal College of Art, London; Alliance; NSS; NA Women PS; ARBS, London. Awards: Widener gold medal, PAFA, 1919; medal, Int. Exposition, Paris, 1926; McClees prize, PAFA, 1927. Address in 1929, 757 Madison Ave., New York, NY.

LAX, DAVID.
Painter. Born in Peekskill, NY, May 16, 1910. Study: Ethical Cultural School, scholar., 1924-28, with H. R. Kniffen, Victor D'Amico, Victor Frisch; Archipenko Art School, with Alexander Archipenko. Work: Gallery Mod. Art, NYC; Clearwater Mus., FL; Pentagon War Art Collection; SUNY Collection; others. Comm.: Many for Irving Mills Collection, 1932-42; combat ptgs. for Pentagon, 1942-50; NY in the 50's, Dutchess Community College; others. Exhibitions: Corcoran; Carnegie Institute; Nat'l. Arts Club Annual, NYC; National Gallery; Philadelphia Art Alliance; many others. Awards: Mills Artists Fellow, 1932-42; bronze star, War Art, 1945; silver medal, Int'l. Inst. Arts & Letters. Teaching: Dutchess Comm. Coll., Poughkeepsie, NY; SUNY. Mem.: Assoc. of AM. Artists; Dutchess Co. Art Assoc.; Int'l. Inst. Arts & Letters; etc. Rep.: Washington Irving Gallery, NYC. Address in 1982, Box 94, Red Hook, NY.

LAY, OLIVER INGRAHAM.
Painter. Born in NYC in 1845. He died there in 1890. He studied at the Cooper Institute, and the National Acad., and was also a pupil of Thomas Hicks. Elected an Associate Member of the National Acad. in 1876. He painted many portraits, and some genre subjects. His copy of Stuart's portrait of Chief Justice John Jay was owned by the New York Historical Society.

LAYBOURNE-JENSEN, (LARS PETER).
Painter and sculptor. Born in Copenhagen, Denmark, in 1888. Pupil of Danish Academy. Member: Society of Independent Artists. Address in 1926, 211 Locust St., Roselle Park, NJ.

LAZARD, ALICE ABRAHAM.
Painter. Born in New Orleans, LA, in 1893. Pupil of Charles Sneed Williams and of the Art Institute of Chicago. Member: Springfield, Ill., Artists' Association; Art Club of Chicago; Art Institute of Chicago Alumni Association. Address in 1926, Klaubers, Louisville, KY.

LAZARUS, JACOB HART.
Portrait painter. Born in New York City in 1822; he died there in 1891. He studied portraiture with Henry Inman, whose portrait he painted; it was given by the artist's widow to the Metropolitan Museum, NY. He also painted miniatures and the one he painted of Chas. A. May was exhibited at the Centennial of the National Academy in 1925. He was elected an Associate Member of the National Academy of Design in 1849.

LAZARUS, M(INNIE) RACHEL.
Painter, craftsman and teacher. Born Baltimore, MD, Dec. 4, 1872. Pupil of Dewing Woodward; Julian Academy, Paris; Louis DesChamps. Member: Blue Dome Fellowship; Balto. WCC; Handicraft C. of Balto. Award: First prize for portrait, FL Federation of Arts, 1928. Director, Blue Dome Fellowship, Coral Gables, FL Address in 1929, 3650 S. W. 23rd St., Coral Gables, Miami, FL.

LAZZELL, BLANCHE.
Painter and etcher. Born Maidsville, Monongalia Co., W. VA. Pupil of Chase, Schumacher, Charles Guerin, Andre L'hote and Albert Gleizes. Member: S. Indp. A; Provincetown Printers; Provincetown AA; Societe Anonyme; NYSWA. Works: Wood block-prints, "The Violet Jug," Detroit Art Inst.; "Tulips," "The Monongahela," "Trees" and "Fishing Boat," W. VA University Library. Died in 1956. Address in 1929, Provincetown, MA; h. Morgantown, W. VA.

LEA , TOM.
Illustrator. Born in El Paso, TX, in 1907. Studied at the AIC and under John Norton. His work for Life during World War II brought him considerable recognition and throughout his career he has illustrated over 50 books about the American West and the war, seven of which he also wrote. His works are in the collections of the Univ. of TX and the Dallas Museum of Fine Art. He exhibited his artwork at the Whitney Museum in 1938.

LEACH, BERNARD.
Painter and etcher. Born in Hong Kong, China, 1887. Pupil of Slade Sch. of London and of F. Brangwyn. Member: Chicago SE. Address in 1926, c/o Dr. W. E. Hoyle, Crowland, Liandaff, Cardiff, Wales.

LEACH, ETHEL, P(ENNEWILL) B(ROWN).
Painter, illustrator, and etcher. Born Wilmington, Del. Pupil of Twachtman, Howard Pyle. Member: Phila. Plastic C; Phila. Alliance; Fellowship PAFA; Wilmington SFA; AFA. Work: "'Totin' Clo'es," Miss. Art Association, Jackson; portrait of "Gov. Wm. D. Denney," State House, Dover, Del.; illustrated "Catching Up with the Circus," by Gertrude Crownfield. Address in 1929, Frederica, Del.; summer, Rehoboth Beach, DE.

LEACH, SAMUEL.
Engraver. The Pennsylvania Gazette of Dec. 1741 advertises that "Samuel Leach, from London, performs all sorts of Engraving, such as Coats of Arms, Crests, Cyphers, Letters and SC, on Gold, Silver or Copper. Also engraving

of all kinds for Silversmiths. N. B. The said Leach may be heard of at Mr. Samuel Hazard's, Merchant, opposite the Baptist Meeting House, in Second Street, or at Andrew Farrels, Tanner, in Chestnut St., Philadelphia."

LEAKE, GERALD.
Painter. Born London, Eng., Nov. 26, 1885. Member: Salma. C.; Allied AA; Arch. Lg. of NY; Mural P; AWCS; NAC. Awards: Prize ($1,000), Salma. C., 1923; Plympton prize, Salma. C., 1926; Shaw prize, Salma. C., 1927; gold medal, Allied AA, 1929. Died in 1975. Address in 1929, 51 West 10th St., NYC.

LEALE, MARION.
Miniature painter. Born New York, NY. Pupil of ASL of NY; Lucia Fairchild Fuller. Member: S. Indp. A.; NYSC; Nat. L. Am. PW; Baltimore WCC. Address in 1929, 1261 Madison Ave., New York, NY.

LEAMING, CHARLOTTE.
Painter and teacher. Born Chicago, IL, Jan. 16, 1878. Pupil of Freer, Chase, Duveneck, Herter. Member: Chicago SA; Chicago ASL; Colorado Springs AS. Award: Corona Mundi Prize ($100), 1924. Address in 1929, Parkins Fine Arts Bldg., Cache le Poudre; h. 1614 Wood Ave., Colorado Springs, CO.

LEARNED, ARTHUR G(ARFIELD).
Painter and illustrator. Born Chelsea, MA, Aug. 10, 1872. Studied in Munich, Vienna and under Laurens, Steinlen and others in Paris. Member: NAC; MacD. C. Work in: New York Public Library; Brooklyn Institute Museum; Library of Congress, Washington, DC; University of PA. Specialty, portraits and decorations. Address in 1929, 36 Gramercy Park, New York, NY; summer, Brucehaven, Stamford, CT.

LEAVITT, D(AVID) F(RANKLIN).
Illustrator and decorator. Born St. Louis, Aug. 28, 1897. Studied in Paris. Award: Third prize, St. Louis AG, 1927. Address in 1929, 5603 Cabanne Ave., St. Louis, MO.

LEAVITT, W. H.
Painted portraits in New Orleans in 1904, and afterwards had a studio at 622 Commerical Place.

LeBLANC, MARIE de HOA.
Painter, illustrator and teacher. Born New Orleans, Nov. 23, 1874. Pupil of AIC; D. W. Ross; Martin Heyman in Munich. Member: NO AA; SSAL. Award: Gold medal, NO AA, 1914. Work: "Paysage d'Automne," Delgado Museum of Art, New Orleans. Address in 1929, 905 Dumaine, New Orleans, LA.

LEBRUN, RICO.
Painter, sculptor, and printmaker. Born in Naples, Italy, in 1900. Studied at Academy of Arts and National Technical Institute, Naples. After moving to US in 1924, returned frequently to Italy to study Renaissance and Baroque masters. Lived in Springfield, IL, 1924; moved to NYC in 1925, where he became a successful advertising artist, taught at ASL. Settled in California in 1938, taught there, and had many exhibitions. Style developed from his paintings of cripples, beggars, and harlequins in traditions of Velasquez, Goya, Picasso. Other work includes Crucifixion drawings begun in 1947 for Triptych, Syracuse Univ.; drawings of Buchenwald and Dachau. Highly influential artist on West Coast. Also taught in Mexico at Escuela de Bellas Artes, San Miguel de Allende; in Italy at Am. Acad., Rome. Died in 1964. Represented by Kennedy Galleries, NYC.

LeCASTRO, A.
Miniature painter. A miniature painted on ivory of a gentleman evidently of the southern states is signed "A. Le Castro."

LeCLEAR, THOMAS.
Portrait painter. Born in Owego, NY, March 11, 1818. He was elected a member of the National Academy, 1863. He is represented by a portrait of "William Page," in the Corcoran Gallery, Washington, DC. Died Nov. 26, 1882, in Rutherford Park, NJ.

LeCOUNT & HAMMOND.,
Engravers. Well-engraved landscape plates published in 1840 are thus signed. The second member of the firm was probably J. T. Hammond, who was in business as an engraver in Philadelphia in 1839.

LEDDEL, JOSEPH JR.
Engraver. The New York Weekly Post Boy, in 1752, contains the advertisement of Joseph Leddel, Jr., for the sale of all manner of pewterwork. At the end of this advertisement he says that "He also engraves on Steel, Iron, Gold, Silver, Copper, Brass, Pewter, Ivory or Turtle Shell, in a neat manner very reasonably."

LEDGERWOOD, ELLA RAY.
(Mrs. H. O. Ledgerwood). Painter and teacher. Born Dublin, TX. Pupil of Irving Wiles, Kenneth Hayes Miller. Member: Ft. Worth AA; Painters C; Ft. Worth Art Com. Address in 1929, Central High School; h. 2808 Hemphill St., Ft. Worth, TX.

LeDUC, A(RTHUR CONRAD).
Painter. Born Washington, DC, March 23, 1892. Pupil of John Sloan; Corcoran School; Academie Julian, Colarossi. Member: S. Indp. A; Salon d'Automne; Soc. Modern Arts. Address in 1929, King's Highway, Haddonfield, NJ.

LeDUC, ALICE SUMNER.
Painter, illustrator, and craftsman. Born Hastings, MN. Address in 1929, 2512 Humboldt Ave., South, Minneapolis, Minn.; summer, Hastings, MN.

LEE, AMY FREEMAN.
Painter and lecturer. Born in San Antonio, TX, in 1914. Studied: Univ. of TX; Incarnate Word College. Awards: San Antonio Artists, 1949, 1956; Smith College, 1950; Boston S. Indp. A. Charles Rosen award, 1950; TX FA Assoc., 1950, 1958; TX WCS, 1955; Neiman-Marcus award, 1953; Grumbacher award, 1953; Hall Memorial, 1954; Rosengren award, 1953; Silvermine Guild, 1957; Beaumont Mus., 1957; "Artist of the Year," San Antonio, 1958; Theta Sigma Phi Headliner award,

1958. Collections: Witte Memorial Museum; Smith College; Baylor Univ.; Baltimore Museum of Art; Dallas Republic National Bank. Address in 1980, 127 Canterbury Hill, San Antonio, TX.

LEE, ARTHUR.
Sculptor. Born Trondjhem, Norway, May 4, 1881. Studied in Paris, London and Italy. Award: Widener Mem. Gold medal at PAFA in 1924. Work: "Eureka," torso, Cooper Union, New York; "Volupte", torso, Metropolitan Museum, New York, and Valentine Museum, Richmond, VA. Died in 1961. Address in 1929, 9 MacDougal Alley, New York, NY.

LEE, BERTHA STRINGER.
Painter. Born San Francisco, Dec. 6, 1873. Pupil of Wm. Keith in San Francisco; Joseph Mathews in New York; studied abroad. Member: San Francisco Art Assoc.; California AC; Arts and Crafts C. Awards: Chicago Exp., 1893; Seattle Exp., 1909; San Francisco Art Assoc.; Sacramento State Fair. Work: "Monterey Coast," Del Monte Art Gallery; "In the Gloamings," Golden Gate Park Museum, San Francisco. Died in 1937. Address in 1929, 2744 Steiner St., San Francisco, CA.

LEE, DORIS.
Painter. Born in Aledo, IL, on Feb. 1, 1905. Studied: Rockford College; Kansas City Art Institute, and with Ernest Lawson; California School of Fine Arts, with Arnold Blanch; and with Andre L'Hote in Paris. Awards: Art Institute of Chicago, 1935, 1936; Penn. Academy of Fine Arts, 1944; Rockford College; Russell Sage College; Carnegie Institute, 1943; Library of Congress, 1947; Art Directors Club, NY, 1946, 1950, gold medal, 1957; Worcester Museum of Art, 1938. Collections: US Post Office, Wash., DC; Art Institute of Chicago; Metropolitan Museum of Art; Library of Congress; Albright Art Gallery; Univ. of Nebraska; Cranbrook Museum; Encyclopedia Britannica Collection; Penn. Academy of Fine Arts; Lowe Gallery, Miami; Honolulu Academy of Fine Arts; Rhode Island School of Design; University of Arizona; Rockford College; Mt. Holyoke

Museum; Florida Gulf Coast Art Center.

LEE, GEO(RGE) D.
Painter and teacher. Born St. Louis, MO, Dec. 1, 1859. Member: AFA; Louisville AA; SSAL. Died in 1939. Address in 1929, Kenyon Bldg., 112 South Fifth St.; h. 163 Crescent Ave., Louisville, KY.

LEE, HENRY C.
Painter, writer and lecturer. Born New York City, May 3, 1864. Pupil of Josef Israels and George Holston. Member: Lotos C.; Salma C; Paris Groupe PSA; SI. Work: "French Dunes," Bohemian Club, San Francisco, Calif. Address in 1929, Cornwall, NY.

LEE, HENRY J.
Painter and illustrator. Member: SI. Address in 1929, Harmon-on-Hudson, NY.

LEE, HOMER.
Engraver. Born May 18, 1855 in Mansfield, OH. He was the son of John Lee, an engraver, and received some instruction from his father in this art. He was later regularly apprenticed to a steel-engraver in New York City, but his master having failed before the expiration of his apprenticeship, he began business for himself as Homer Lee & Co. He was successful, and in 1881 he founded the Homer Lee Bank Note Co. of New York. Later he was vice-president and director of the Franklin-Lee Bank Note Co., of the same city. Mr. Lee studied art in Canada and in Europe, and received honorable mention for one of his paintings at the Vienna Exposition of 1873. He also received honorable mention in the Paris Exhibition of 1900, and the bronze medal at the Charleston Exposition, 1902. He died Jan. 26, 1923, in NYC.

LEE, LAURA.
Painter. Born Charlestown, MA, Mar. 17, 1867. Pupil of School of Boston Museum of Fine Arts; Julian Academy in Paris. Member: Copley S.; NA Women PS; Boston SAC; AFA. Address in 1929, 56 William St., Stoneham, MA.

LEE, M(ANNING) de V(ILLENEUVE).
Painter and illustrator. Born Summerville, SC, March 15, 1894. Pupil of PAFA under Garber, Breckenridge, Pearson and Harding. Member: Fellowship PAFA; SSAL. Award: Cresson Traveling Scholarship, PAFA, 1921; second Toppan prize, PAFA, 1923. Work: Portrait of Freas Styer, US Mint, Phila.; series of five marine paintings, US Naval Academy. Illustrated: "The Blue Fairy Book" and "The Red Fairy Book," by Lang (Macrae-Smith); "Spanish Dollars" and "The Overland Trail," Reginald Wright Kauffman (Penn Pub. Co.); "Historic Ships," "Historic Railroads," "Historic Airships," Rupert Sargent Holland (Macrae-Smith Co.) and others. Address in 1929, 5835 Wissohickon Ave., Philadelphia, PA.

LEE, ROBERT J.
Illustrator. Born in Oakland, CA, in 1921. Attended the Academy of Art College in San Fran. for four years. He served in the Air Force as a special service artist and later taught at the Academy Art College, PI, and is presently Assistant Professor of Fine Arts at Marymount College. His first work appeared in Western Advertising in 1946 and he has since had several One-Man Shows and group exhibitions in NY, Chicago, St. Louis, and San Fran. His paintings have been exhibited in the Smithsonian Institution and several university museums.

LEE, SELMA.
Painter, etcher and teacher. Born New York, Nov. 5, 1879. Pupil of Mielatz, Robert Henri, Charles Curran. Member: Brooklyn SE; Chicago SE; Broadmoor AA. Address in 1929, 271 Madison Ave, care of Louis F. Lee, New York, NY.

LEEDY, LAURA A.
Painter and teacher. Born Bloomington, IL, Oct. 26, 1881. Pupil Anthony Angarola and George Elmer Browne. Member: St. Paul ASL. Award: Hon. Mention, Minn. State Fair, 1925 and 1928. Address in 1929, 713 Fairmount Ave., St. Paul, MN.

LEEPER, DORIS MARIE.
Painter and sculptor. Born Charlotte, NC, April 4, 1929. Studied: Duke Univ., BA in Art History; self-taught as an artist. Collections: National Collection of Fine Arts, Wash., DC; 180 Beacon Collection, Boston; Chase Manhattan Bank; Reserve Insurance, Orlando, Florida; Bank of NY; Jacksonville Art Museum, Florida. Awarded an individual grant from the National Endowment of the Arts, 1972. She is represented by Bertha Schaefer Gallery, NYC. Media: Oil, fiberglass, metal concrete. Address in 1980, P.O. Box 2093, New Smyrna, FL.

LEEPER, VERA B(EATRICE).
Painter and craftsman. Born Denver, CO, March 13, 1893. Pupil of Eben S. Comins, Boston Museum School, and studied in Paris. Member: Mural P; AFA. Award: Prize, C. L. Wolfe AC, 1922; first prize, Art Center of the Oranges, 1927. Work: Murals in Roger Sherman Restaurant, New Haven, CT; Garde Theatre, New London, CT; Commodore Hull Theatre, Derby, CT; Old English Room, Morene Products Co., NYC. Specialty, murals and portraits. Address in 1929, Yorktown Heights, NY.

LEES, HARRY H.
Illustrator. Member: SI; GFLA. Died in 1959. Address in 1929, 334 West 22nd St., New York, NY.

LEFF, RITA.
Painter and printmaker. Born in NYC, in 1907. Studied: Art Students' League; Brooklyn Museum School of Art, and with George Picken, Louis Schanker, Abraham Rattner and Adja Yunkers. Awards: Audubon Art, 1955-1958; National Academy of Women Artists, 1951, 1954, 1955, 1958; Brooklyn Society of Art, 1950, 1953, 1957; Brooklyn Museum Alumni Assoc., 1955-1957; Boston Printmakers, 1954; Society of American Graphic Artists, 1954; Village Art Center, 1953-1955; Creative Graphic Exhibition, 1958. Collections: Metropolitan Museum of Art; Library of Congress; Univ. of Maine; Penn. State Univ.; Dallas Mus. of Fine Arts; Abraham Lincoln High Sch.; Contemporary Gallery,

1956. Media: Oil, collage, watercolor. Address in 1980, 1707 Consulate Pl., West Palm Beach, FL.

LEFFERTS, WINIFRED E(ARL).
Painter and illustrator. Born Newtonville, MA, Oct. 9, 1903. Member: AWCS; NYWCC; NA Women PS; Brooklyn SA. Address in 1929, 311 Washington Ave., Brooklyn, NY.

LEGGETT, R.
This good line-engraver of landscapes was working abut 1870 and signed plates from "No. 4 John St., New York."

LEHMAN, GEORGE.
Painter and engraver. Born in Lancaster County, PA; died in Philadelphia in 1870. About 1829 Lehman painted, engraved aquatint, and hand-colored a series of admirable views of Pennsylvania towns. He also aquatinted a number of smaller plates and drew for engravers. In 1835-37 he was in the lithographing business in Philadelphia, and was later a member of the print publishing firm of Lehman & Baldwin, of the same city. In 1830 he painted a number of landscapes in Philadelphia.

LEICH, CHESTER.
Painter and etcher. Born Evansville, IN, Jan. 31, 1889. Studied in Florence, Munich, Berlin, and with Siebelist in Hamburg. Member: Chicago SE; Brooklyn SE. Address in 1929, 117 Christie St., Leonia, NJ; h. 610 Riverside Ave., Evansville, IN.

LEIGH, HOWARD.
Painter, etcher, and craftsman. Born Cecelia, KY, Aug. 9, 1896. Pupil of Paul Mauron and John Albert Seaford. Award: Hon. mention, Paris Salon, 1927. Work: Lithographs of the Great War in Musee de la Guerre, Paris; New York Public Library; Boston Public Library; Henry Co. Historical Society, New Castle, Ind. Address in 1929, Hoosier Art Patrons Assn., 211 W. Wacker Dr., Chicago, IL.

LEIGH, WILLIAM R(OBINSON).
Painter, illustrator, and writer. Born Berkeley Co., W. VA, Sept. 23, 1866. A child artist, he won

Corcoran prize at age 12. Pupil of Maryland Inst., Baltimore, under Hugh Newell; Raupp, Gysis, Loefftz and Lindenschmid in Munich. Member: Allied AA; Salma. C.; AWCS. Awards: Hon. mention, Paris Salon, 1892; two silver and three bronze medals, Munich Academy; first class medal, Appalachian Exp., Knoxville, TN, 1911. Work: 3 portraits, Washington and Lee University; "Getting Acquainted," Nayasset Club, Springfield, Mass.; "The Great Spirit," "The Poisoned Pool," "The Maya Historian," "The Stampede," "Hunting with the Boomerang-Hopi Reservation," Fine Arts Museum, Huntington, LI, NY. Publ. book on drawing western ponies. Died March 11, 1955. Address in 1929, 61 Poplar St., Brooklyn, NY; 1680 Broadway, New York, NY.

LEIGHTON, CLARE.
Engraver and writer. Born in London, England, Apr. 12, 1901. Came to the United States in 1939; became a citizen in 1945. Member of the National Institute of Arts and Letters, an academician of the National Academy of Design, and a fellow of the Royal Society of Painters, Etchers, and Engravers, London. Awarded an honorary Doctor of Fine Arts by Colby College, Maine. Collections: The Museum of Modern Art, The Metropolitan Museum of Art, New York; The Library of of Congress, Washington; The Art Institute of Chicago; The Cleveland Museum of Art; The British Museum, The Victoria and Albert Museum, London; The National Gallery, Stockholm; The National Gallery, Ottawa. Major retrospective at the Boston Public Library in 1977. Living in Woodbury, CT.

LEIGHTON, KATHERINE W(OODMAN).
Painter. Born Plainfield, NH, March 17, 1876. Pupil of Boston Normal Art S. Member: Calif. AC; West Coast Arts; Artland C. Died in 1952. Address in 1929, 1633 West 46th St., Los Angeles, CA.

LEIGHTON, SCOTT.
Animal painter. Born in Auburn, ME, in 1849. His best work is as a painter of horses. Mr. Leighton's horses are always technically good

in drawing. He was a member of the "Art Club" of Boston. His death occurred in 1898.

LEISENRING, L. MORRIS.
Painter and architect. Born Lutherville, MD, Oct. 29, 1875. Pupil of Maryland Institute; Drexel Institute; PAFA; Univ. of Pennsylvania; Duquesne in Paris; American Academy in Rome. Member: Washington AC; Washington WCC; Wash. Chapter AIA. Address in 1929, 1320 New York Ave.; h. 177 Church St., Washington, DC.

LEISENRING, MATHILDE MUEDEN.
(Mrs. L. M. Leisenring). Portrait painter. Born Washington. Pupil of ASL of NY and of Washington; Laurens, Constant and Henner in Paris. Member: S. Wash. A; Wash. WCC; Wash. AC. Awards: Third Corcoran prize, S. Wash. A. 1903; second Corcoran prize, Wash. WCC 1903; second honor, Appalachian Exp., Knoxville, Tenn., 1910. Instructor, Corcoran Gallery, Wahington. Address in 1929, 1777 Church St., Washington, DC.

LEITH-ROSS, HARRY.
Painter. Born Mauritius, Jan. 27, 1886. Pupil of Birge Harrison and J. F. Carlson; Laurens in Paris. Member: ANA; Salma. C.; CT AFA; Allied AA; AFA. Awards: Porter prize, Salma. C., 1915; Charles Noel Flagg prize, CT AFA, 1921; second prize, Duxbury, MA, AA, 1921; hon. mention, CT AFA, 1922; hon. mention, S. Wash. A., 1924; landscape prize, New Haven PCC, 1924; Ranger purchase, NAD, 1927; Burton Mansfield prize, New Haven, 1928. Address in 1929, Woodstock, Ulster Co., NY.

LEITNER, L(EANDER).
Painter, illustrator, and craftsman. Born Delphos, OH, April 30, 1873. Pupil of ASL of NY; J. B. Whittaker, Henry Prellwitz, Joseph Boston and F. V. DuMond. Member: S. Indp. A.; Alliance. Address in 1929, 348 East 50th St., New York, NY; summer, Edgemoor, DE.

LELAND, CLARA WALSH.
(Mrs. D. R. Leland). Painter. Born Lockport, NY, June 2, 1869.

Pupil of PAFA; Whistler School, Paris; William Chase, Cecilia Beaux. Works: "The Garden," Lincoln Public Schools; "Copper and Gold," Prescott School, Lincoln. Address in 1929, 325 North 14th St., Lincoln, NE.

LELAND, HENRY.
Painter. Born in Walpole, MA, in 1850. His early death was the result of an accident. In 1876 he exhibited the portrait of Mlle. D'Alembert at the Paris Salon, and in 1877 "A Chevalier of the Time of Henry III" and "An Italian Girl." He died in 1877.

LELLA, CARL.
Painter. Born Bari, Italy, Feb. 4, 1899. Pupil of Barry Faulkner. Member: Mural P; Arch. Lg. of NY. Work: Four mural panels, Farmers National Bank, Reading, PA; mural, "The Arts and Sciences," Bushwick High School, Brooklyn, NY. Address in 1929, 11 West 29th St., New York, NY; h. Colonia, NJ.

LEM, RICHARD DOUGLAS.
Painter. Born in Los Angeles, CA, Nov. 24, 1933. Study: Univ. Calif., Los Angeles; Calif. State, Los Angeles; Otis Art Inst.; Calif. Inst. of Arts; with Rico Herbert Jepson. Work: San Diego Fine Arts Gallery; numerous private collections. Exhibitions: Phoenix Art Mus., 1961; San Diego Fine Arts Gallery, 1965; Palos Verdes Art Gal., 1968; Kottler Galleries, NYC, 1973; Galerie Mouffe, Paris, 1976; and others. Awards: Los Angeles Fine Arts Soc. and Art Guild Award for painting, 1965. Media: Oil, watercolor. Address in 1982, 1861 Webster Avenue, Los Angeles, CA.

LEMET, LOUIS.
Engraver. Born 1779. He was a close follower of the methods of St. Memin, producing portraits by the same means, and identical in appearance and size. Also worked in crayon. He was located in Philadelphia in 1804. Died Sept. 30, 1832.

LEMLY, BESSIE CARY.
Painter, craftsman and teacher. Born Jackson, June 4, 1871. Pupil of ASL of NY, Pedro J. Lemos, E. A.

Webster and Maud M. Mason. Member: Miss. AA; Art Study C.; (Dir.) Southern SAL; College AA; AFA. Represented by "The Meadow," collection of the Mississippi Art Association. Address in 1929, Belhaven College; h. 620 North St., Jackson, MS.

LEMOS, PEDRO J.
Painter, etcher, illustrator, craftsman, writer, and teacher. Born Austin, NV, May 25, 1882. Pupil of Mary Benton, Arthur Dow, San Francisco Inst. of Art. Member: CA SE. (dir.); Chicago SE; Bohemian C; Carmel AA (pres.). Awards: Hon. mention for etching, P.-P. Exp., San F., 1915; gold medal for prints, California State Fair, 1916. Director, Museum of Fine Arts, Leland Stanford University; editor, School Arts Magazine. Director, Amer. Art Aid. Author of "Print Methods;" "Art Simplified;" "Applied Art;" "Color Cement Handicraft;" "The Bird in Art;" "The Tree in Art;" "Principles of Beauty in Design;" "Plant Form in Design;" "Indian Decorative Designs;" "Oriental Decorative Designs." Died in 1945. Address in 1929, Museum of Fine Arts, Leland Stanford Junior University, Stanford University, CA; h. 460 Churchill Ave., Palo Alto, CA.

LENEY, WILLIAM SATCHWELL.
Engraver. Born in London, England, Jan. 16, 1769; died at Longue Pointe, near Montreal, Canda, Dec. 31, 1831. Leney was of Scotch descent. He is said to have been a pupil of the well-known English engraver Peltro W. Tompkins, and Leney's work bears evidence of a careful training in the art of stipple engraving. About 1805 Leney was induced to come to the United States; he settled in New York and seems to have had abundant employment. One of Leney's early plates executed in this country is that of "Moses in the Bulrushes," done for Collins' Bible published in 1807; for this plate he is said to have received a gold medal.

L'ENGLE, LUCY.
Painter. Born NY, Sept. 28, 1889. Member: NYSWA; Provincetown AA.

Address in 1929, 151 East 53rd St.;
h. 535 Park Ave., New York, NY;
summer, Truro, MA.

L'ENGLE, W(ILLIAM) JOHNSON, JR.
Painter. Born Jacksonville, FL,
April 22, 1884. Pupil of Richard
Miller, J. P. Laurens, Collin and
Louis Biloul. Member: S. Indp.
A.; Provincetown AA Died in 1957.
Address in 1929, 151 East 53rd St.,
New York, NY.

LENSKI, LOIS.
(Mrs. Arthur Covey). Painter and
illustrator. Born Springfield, OH,
October 14, 1893. Pupil of Kenneth
H. Miller; Walter Bayes in London.
Award: Logan medal, AIC, 1923.
Author and illustrator of "Skipping
Village," "A Little Girl of 1900"
(Stokes), "Jack Horner's Pie,"
"Alphabet People" (Harpers), "The
Wonder City" (Coward-McCawn), and
illustrator of numerous other
children's books. Work: Mural
decorations for Children's
Orthopedic Hospital, Orange, NJ;
Lord and Taylor's, New York.
Address in 1929, Harwinton, CT.

LENT, MARGARETE.
Painter and teacher. Born
Washington, DC, Oct. 6, 1896.
Pupil of Corcoran School of Art,
Wash., DC; NY School of Fine and
Applied Art; Hawthorne; Snell.
Member: AWCS; NA Women PS; Wash.
WCC; Wash. AC; NYWCC. Awards:
Helen Willoughby-Smith prize,
NYWCC, 1928; NYWCC prize, 1929.
Address in 1929, 1528 Corcoran St.,
Washington, DC.

LENTELLI, LEO.
Painter and sculptor. Born
Bologna, Italy, Oct. 29, 1879.
Came to US in 1903. Member: NSS
1907; NY Arch. Lg. 1909. Awards:
Prizes from NY Arch. Lg. (1911,
1913, 1921); purchase prize, San F.
AA 1916; gold medal for sculpture,
NY Arch. Lg., 1922. Work: Figure
of the Saviour and sixteen angels
for the reredos of the Cathedral of
St. John the Divine, NY; group over
entrance of Mission Branch Lib.,
San F.; 5 figures for facade of San
F. Pub. Lib.; decorations for St.
Louis Orpheum Theatre; Flagpole,
Rice Memorial Playfield, Pelham,
NY; panels, Straus Bank Bldg., NY;

groups for P.-P. Exp., San F.;
decorations for 16th St. Bridge,
Pittsburgh; panel for Corning Free
Academy; equestrian statue of R. E.
Lee, Charlottesville, VA; entrance,
Straus Bank Bldg. Chicago;
sculpture for facade of the
Steinway Bldg., NY. Instructor of
sculpture, Cal. Sch. of FA; former
instructor of modeling, ASL of NY.
Died in 1962. Address in 1929, 51
W. 10th St., NYC.

LENZ, ALFRED DAVID.
Sculptor. Born in Fond du Lac, WI,
in 1872. Specialty, bronze
statuettes. Member of National
Sculpture Society. Died on Feb.
16, 1926 in Havana, Cuba.

LENZ, FRANCES H.
Painter and teacher. Born Elmira,
NY, February, 1899. Pupil of
George Bridgman, Von Schlegell,
Charles Martin. Member: S. Indp.
A. Address in 1929, 120 West 12th
St., New York, NY; summer,
Provincetown, MA.

LENZ, OSCAR.
Sculptor. Born in Providence, RI,
in 1874. Studied under Saint
Gaudens in New York and under
Saulievre in Paris. After his
return to this country he executed
the Colonial Group at Charleston,
SC, and some of the groups in the
Pennsylvania Railroad Station in
New York. He died June 25, 1912.

LEONARD, B(EATRICE).
Painter. Born Marion, IN, July 11,
1889. Pupil of Chicago AFA.
Member: Hoosier Salon; Bronx AG;
S. Indp. A. Address in 1929, 57
West 175th St., New York, NY.

LEONARD, GEORGE H(ENRY).
Landscape painter and writer. Born
Boston, MA, May 3, 1869. Pupil of
Gerome, Bouguereau and Aman-Jean in
Paris. Member: Paris AAA; Boston
AC; Copley S; AFA. Address in
1929, 65 New South St.; h. 15
Dryads Green, Northampton, MA.

LEONARD, WILLIAM J.
Painter. Born in Hinsdale, NH, in
1869. Pupil of Laurens and
Constant in Paris. Address in
1926, Norwell, MA.

LEPELLETIER, MICHAEL.
Engraver. Maps and plans published
by T. C. Fay, of New York, in 1814,
are signed "Lepelletier, Sculpt.,
New York."

LEPPERT, RUDOLPH E.
Illustrator. Born New York City,
Dec. 20, 1872. Pupil of G. de F.
Brush, and Baron deGrimm. Member:
Salma. C; AFA. Address in 1929,
Art Director, Funk and Wagnalls
Co., 354 Fourth Ave., New York, NY;
2 Wagner Ave., Mamaroneck, NY.

LeROY, ANITA.
Painter. Born in Philadelphia.
She studied at the Penna. Academy
of Fine Arts. Specialized in Dutch
scenes.

LeROY, HAROLD M.
Painter. Born in NYC, Dec. 12,
1905. Study: Columbia Univ.;
Brooklyn Mus. of Art Sch.; ASL;
Hans Hoffman Art School. Work:
Butler Inst. of Am. Art,
Youngstown, OH; Chrysler Mus. at
Norfolk, VA; Slater Mem. Mus.,
Norwich, CT; Smithsonian; others.
Exhibitions: Museum of Modern Art,
Paris, guest of Soc. de L'Ecole
Francaise; Nat'l. Academy, Audubon
Artists; Am. Soc. Contemp. Artists
Annual, Lever House, NYC; Brooklyn
Museum; and others. Awards:
Heydenryk Award, Graphic Art, 1977;
Am. Vet. Award, oil ptg., 1979;
Binney & Smith award, oil ptg.,
1981. Mem.: Artists Equity Assn.;
Metrop. Ptrs. & Sculptors; Am. Vet.
Soc. Artists; Am. Soc. Contemp.
Artists; etc. Media: Oil,
serigraph. Address in 1982, 1916
Avenue K, Brooklyn, NY.

LESHER, MARIE PALMISANO.
Sculptor. Born in Reading, PA,
Sept. 20, 1919. Studied: The Art
Students' League, NYC; Berte Studio
in Phil.; Univ. of Houston, TX.
Awards: International Exhibition,
Berwick, Penn., 1970; Beaumont Art
Museum, 1971-1973; Del Mar College,
Corpus Christi, TX, 1972.
Collections: Carver Museum,
Tuskegee, AL; Art Guild,
Shreveport, Louisiana; Laguna
Gloria Art Museum, Austin, TX.
Media: Bronze, clay, and wood.
Address in 1980, 10130 Shady River
Rd., Houston, TX.

LESLIE, ANNE.
Portrait artist. Born in 1792.
Sister of the artist Charles Robert
Leslie. She showed considerable
artistic talent. In 1822 she
copied several portraits, and drew
original crayon portraits of her
friends. She also copied a number
of her brother's paintings; her
copy of the "Duchess and Sancho,"
exhibited at the Penna. Academy of
the Fine Arts in Philadelphia in
1847, was admirably executed.
Still living in 1860.

LESLIE, CHARLES ROBERT.
Born in London, England, of
American parents on Oct. 19, 1794;
brought by his parents to
Philadelphia in 1800, and
apprenticed to Bradford & Inskeep,
booksellers, but developed a taste
for art, as evinced by three early
water color sketches of noted
actors in character, later hung in
the print room of the Penna.
Academy of Fine Arts. These
drawings so interested his
employer, Mr. Bradford, that he
obtained subscriptions for sending
young Leslie to London. Mr.
Bradford was at that time a
Director of the Academy, and at a
special meeting of the Board held
in 1811 he introduced the following
resolutions, which were adopted:
"Resolved, that this Academy,
having examined the drawings
produced at the exhibition by
master Leslie, are of the opinion
that such rare talents evinced so
early in life, give promise of
great celebrity and usefulness, if
fostered by the smiles of public
patronage". Leslie arrived in
London, Dec. 1811, and studied at
the Royal Academy and with West and
Allston. He was elected to the
Royal Academy in 1826. He was
appointed in 1833 Professor of
Drawing at the U. S. Military
Academy at West Point, NY. He
returned to London and died there
on May 5, 1859. His works include
"Uncle Toby and the Widow," "Anne
Page and Master Slender," and "The
Murder of Rutland by Clifford,"
owned by the Penna. Academy of Fine
Arts, Philadelphia.

561

LESLIE, ELIZA.
Authoress and artist, and sister of
Anne Leslie and Charles Robert
Leslie. Was born in Philadelphia,
Nov. 15, 1787; died in Gloucester,
NJ, on Jan. 1, 1858. She made a
few crayon portraits.

LESNICK, STEPHEN WILLIAM.
Painter. Born in Bridgeport, CT,
March 22, 1931. Study: Silvermine
College of Art; Art Career School;
with Revington Arthur, John
McCleand, Jack Wheat, Carl Symon.
Work: Gov. Paul Laxalt, NV; Burndy
Library, Norwalk, CT; Boulder City
Hosp. Art Collection, NV.
Exhibitions: All New Eng. Art
Exhib, CT, 1955; Layout and Design
Int'l. Comp., Japan, 1963; Ann. Am.
Wc Soc. Show, 1968; and many
others. Awards: Int'l. Industrial
Design Show, Japan; Franklin Mint;
others. Mem.: Nev. State WC Soc.
Address in 1982, 1127 Westminister
Ave., Las Vegas, NV.

LESSHAFFT, FRANZ.
Painter. Born Berlin, GR, March 8,
1862. Pupil of Royal Acad. of F.A.
Berlin, under Anton V. Werner,
Thumann and Meyerheim. Member:
Phila. Sketch C.; Fellowship PAFA;
S. Indp. A.; Phil. AC; Art Teachers
Assn. Awards: Hon. mention,
Berlin; hon. mention for water
color, AAS, 1902. Address in 1929,
1020 Chestnut St., Phila., PA.

LESTER, WILLIAM H.
Illustrator and etcher. Born in
Valparaiso, Chili, SA, 1885. Pupil
of Art Institute of Chicago.
Member: Chicago Society of
Etchers; Brooklyn Society of
Etchers. Address in 1926, 121
South Hill St., Los Angeles, CA.

LESUEUR, ALEXANDER CHARLES.
(Name may be Charles Alexander
Lesueur.) Born Jan. 1, 1778 at
Havre de Grace, France; died there
Dec. 12, 1846. In 1815 he came to
Philadelphia on the invitation of
William Maclure, the geologist,
and assisted him in a study of
American Zoology. He finally
settled in Philadelphia and taught
drawing and painting, and he became
a prominent member of the American
Philosophical Society, and of the
Academy of Natural Sciences. The

Journal of the Academy of Natural
Sciences for 1818 contains a number
of plates illustrating papers upon
natural history beautifully etched
by Lesueur. He returned to France
in 1837 and was for a time curator
of the Museum of Natural History at
Havre.

LEUSCH, FRANZISKA A.
Painter. Born in Philadelphia, PA.
Pupil of Fred Wagner. Instructor
in Philadelphia Normal School.
Address in 1926, 114 Wharton Ave.,
Glenside, PA.

LEUTZE, EMANUEL.
German historical painter. He was
born in the village of Emingen,
near Reutlingen, in Wurtemburg, May
24, 1816. He went as a child to
Philadelphia, where he was
instructed by John A. Smith, a
portrait painter. In 1841 he
returned to Europe and pursued his
studies at Dusseldorf under
Lessing; but as he did not hold
with the views of that academy, he
established an atelier of his own.
In 1842 he visited Munich, Venice
and Rome, and returned to
Dusseldorf, in 1845, and there
executed a considerable number of
paintings. He obtained in 1850 the
gold medal at Berlin for his
"Washington Crossing the Delaware,"
in the Kunsthalle at Bremen.
(Replica at the Metropolitan
Museum, New York.) After having
been in America in 1851, and again
in 1859, he established himself
there in 1863, and died in
Washington, DC, July 18, 1868.

LEVEE, JOHN.
Painter. Born April 10, 1924, in
L.A., CA. Also a sculptor. Earned
B.A. from UCLA; also studied at New
School for Soc. Research and
Academie Julian, Paris. Taught as
visiting prof. at U. of Illinois;
NYU; Wash. U.; USC. Awarded grand
prize at I Biennial, Paris (1959);
Ford fellow (1969). Awards from
Salon de Deauville and Academie
Julian, Paris, and Woolmark
Foundation. Exhibited at Corcoran
Mus.; Carnegie I.; Aldrich Mus.
(Ridgefield, Conn.); MOMA; Brooklyn
Mus.; Whitney Mus.; Haifa of Art,
Israel; Walker Mus.; others. In
collections of Guggenheim; Cinn.

Art Mus.; Wash. U.; MOMA; Whitney Mus.; Wash. Gallery of Mod. Art, and others internationally.

LEVER, HAYLEY.
Painter, etcher and teacher. Born Adelaide, South Australia, Sept. 28, 1876. Studied in Paris, London, New York. Member: ANA, 1925; Royal British Artists, London; Royal Inst. Oil Painters, London; Royal West of England Academy; NAC (life); Contemporary; New Soc. A. Awards: Honorable mention, CI Pittsburgh, 1913; silver medal, NAC, 1914; Carnegie prize, NAD, 1914; gold medal, P.-P. Exposition, San F., 1915; gold medal, NAC, 1916; Sesnan gold medal, PAFA, 1917; Phila. WCC prize, 1918; fourth prize ($200), NAC, 1922; bronze medal, Sesqui-Centennial Exposition, Phila., 1926; Temple gold medal, PAFA, 1926; Temple gold medal, PAFA, 1926. Work: "Port of St. Ives," Sydney Art Gallery, Australia; "Fishing Boats," Adelaide Art Gallery, Australia; "Winter, St. Ives," Brooklyn Institute Museum; "Sunshine, St. Ives, Cornwall," Pennsylvania Academy of the Fine Arts, Philadelphia; "Dawn," Corcoran Gallery, Washington, DC; "Smeaton's Quay, St. Ives," Fort Worth (Tex.) Museum; "Boats, Gloucester," and "Changing Nets, Gloucester," Detroit Institute; "Gloucester, Mass.," and "Fishing Boats at St. Ives," Harrison Gallery, Los Angeles Museum; "Fishermen's Quarters," Dallas Art Museum; "Hudson River," National Arts Club; "Herring Boats," Phillips' Memorial Gallery, Washington; "Dancing Boats," Des Moines Art Museum, IA; "French Crabbers," Lincoln Univ., Lincoln, Neb.; "Gloucester," Telfair Museum, Savannah; "Boats," etching, Baltimore Museum, MD; Presidential Yacht "Mayflower," The White House, Wash., DC; "Tuna Boats and Sails," Metropolitan Mus., NY; three watercolors, Brooklyn Mus.; "Midday in the Harbor," City Art Mus., St. Louis; "Fishing Boats, Gloucester, Mass.," Mus. of Fine Arts, Syracuse, NY; "Bathing Beach," Art Mus., Montclair, NJ. Instructor at Art Students' League

of NY. Address in 1929, 215 West 57th St., New York, NY.

LEVI, JULIAN CLARENCE.
Painter, etcher, and architect. Born New York City, Dec. 8, 1874. Pupil of William R. Ware at Columbia University; Scellier de Gisors at the Ecole des Beaux-Arts in Paris. Member: AIA; French Inst. in Am.; Societe Architects Diplomes par le Gouvernement Francais; S. B.-A. A.; B.A.I.D.; AFA; Arch. Lg. of NY. Awards: French Government Diploma, 1904; hon. mention, Paris Salon, 1904; Chevalier, Legion of Honor, 1921, also Officier de l'Instruction Publique, 1927; gold medal, Santiago di Chili, 1923; hon. mention, Turin, Italy, 1926; silver medal, Societe des Architectes Diplomes par le Gouvernement Francais, 1927. Address in 1929, Tilden Bldg. 105 W. 40th St; h. 205 West 57th St., New York City.

LEVIN, ALEXANDER B.
Painter and illustrator. Born Russia, Feb. 19, 1906. Pupil of Daniel Garber, Pearson, George Harding. Member: Fellowship PAFA. Award: First Packard prize, PAFA, 1927. Address in 1929, Pennsylvania Academy of the Fine Arts, Chester Springs, PA.

LEVINE, JACK.
Painter. Born in Boston, MA, Jan. 3, 1915. Study: Children's classes, Boston Mus. of Fine Arts; with Denman Ross, 1929-31; with Harold Zimmerman; Colby College, hon. DFA, 1946. In collections of Met. Mus. of Art; MOMA; Whitney; Walker Art Ctr., Minneapolis; Art Inst. of Chic.; others. Exhibited at Fogg Art Mus. (during high school); Inst. Contemp. Art, Boston, 1953; Whitney, 1955; Palacio Bellas Artes, Mexico City, 1960; annually, Carnegie Inst. and Art Inst. of Chicago; Corcoran; MOMA; PAFA; many others. Won Guggenheim Fellowship, 1945, 46; Corcoran Award 1959; Altman Prize, NAD, 1975; others. Has taught at Art Inst. Chic.; PAFA; Am. Art Sch., NYC; others. Member of Nat'l. Inst. of Arts and Letters; Artists Equity Assn.; Am. Acadm. Arts and Letters; Nat'l. Acad. of

Arts and Letters; others. Represented by Kennedy Galleries. Address in 1982, 68 Morton Street, NYC.

LEVITT, JOEL J.
Painter and etcher. Born Kiev, Russia, Feb. 1, 1875. Pupil of Odessa Art School; Academy of Design, Petrograd; Ilia Repin. Member: Salma. C.; North Shore AA; Allied AA; Am. APL. Represented in the Petrograd Museum; Wilna Museum, Russia; National Gallery of Canada, Ottawa; Museum of Broadmoor Art Academy, Colorado Springs, Colo. Died in 1937. Address in 1929, 39 West 67th St., New York, NY.

LEVITZ, EBBITT A.
Painter. Born New Haven, CT, Sept. 17, 1897. Pupil of Sargeant Kendall; Yale Art School. Member: Queensboro AA; S. Indp. A. Address in 1929, 20 Canal St., Jamaica, NY; h. 120-86 Lincoln Ave., South Ozone, NY; summer, 10 Scranton St., New Haven, CT.

LEVONE, ALBERT JEAN.
Illustrator. Born Russia, Oct. 25, 1895. Pupil of Thornton Oakley and J. R. Sinnock. Illustrated for "The Designer," "Century," etc. Address in 1929, 2461 North 30th St., Philadelphia, PA.

LEVY, ALEX(ANDER) O(SCAR).
Painter and illustrator. Born Bonn, Germany, May 26, 1881. Pupil of Duveneck, Chase, Linde and Henri. Member: Buffalo SA; Buffalo AC; S. Indp. A.; Salons of America; Art Directors. Awards: First hon. mention, Buffalo SA, 1922; hon. mention, Buffalo SA, 1923; Fellowship prize, Buffalo SA, 1924. Address in 1929, 41 Berkeley Place, Buffalo, NY.

LEVY, BEATRICE S.
Painter and etcher. Born Chicago, April 3, 1892. Pupil of AIC; Voyt Preissig and Charles Hawthorne. Member: Chicago SE; Chicago AC; Chicago SA. Awards: Hon. mention for etching, P.-P. Exp., San. F., 1915; Jenkins prize, AIC, 1923; gold medal, Chicago SA, 1928; prize, Illinois Academy, Springfield, 1928. Work in: Chicago Art Institute; Los Angeles

Museum; Smithsonian Institution, Washington, DC; Corona Mundi Collection, New York; Bibliotheque Nationale, Paris. Died in 1974. Address in 1929, 1504 East 57th St., h. 5724 Blackstone Ave., Chicago, IL.

LEVY, WILLIAM AUERBACH.
Painter and etcher. Born in Brest-Letovsk, Russia, in 1889. Studied at National Academy of Design, and Academie Julien, Paris. Represented in permanent collection of Carnegie Institute, Pittsburgh; Art Institute, Chicago; Art Museum, Boston; Public Library, New York, and in important private collections. Awarded Mooney traveling scholarship, 1911; 1st prize, Chicago Society of etchers, 1914; bronze medal, San Francisco Exposition, 1915. Instructor of etching, National Academy of Design, and in the Educational Alliance, New York. Member: Painters-Gravers of America; Chicago Society of Etchers. Address in 1926, 230 East 15th St., New York, NY.

LEWICKI, JAMES.
Illustrator. Born in Buffalo in 1917. Attended PI and the Art School of the Detroit Society of Arts and Crafts. While attending PI he illustrated his first book, New York: From Village to Metropolis by Robert Swan. Winner of first prizes from Hallmark Cards and the Audubon Artists, in 1969 he illustrated The Golden Bough by Fraser for Limited Editions. He taught art for 15 years at CW Post College and later was department chairman and director of their graduate art program.

LEWIS, ALICE L.
Painter and teacher. Born Providence, RI, Dec. 6, 1872. Pupil of Collin in Paris; J. L. Tadd in Philadelphia; RI School of Design; Douglas Donaldson, Hollywood, CA. Member: Boston SAC; Pittsfield AL. Art Instructor, Berkshire School for Crippled Children. Address in 1929, 472 West St., Pittsfield, MA; h. 62 Benevolent St., Providence, RI.

564

LEWIS, (ARTHUR) ALLEN.
Painter, etcher, illustrator and teacher. Born Mobile, AL, April 7, 1873. Pupil of George Bridgman in Buffalo; Gerome in Paris. Member: ANA; Chic. SE; AI Graphic A; Stowaways; Calif. PM. Awards: Bronze medal, St. Louis Exp., 1904; Logan prize, Chicago SE, 1915; gold medal, P.-P. Exp., San F., 1915; Barnett prize, Brooklyn SE, 1917; silver medal, Sesqui-Centennial Exposition, Phila., 1926; Nathan I. Bijur prize, Brooklyn SE, 1928; John J. Agar prize, NAC, 1928. Work in: New York Public Library; Brooklyn Institute Museum; Herron Art Institute, Indianapolis; Chicago Art Institute; Oakland (Calif.) Public Museum; Newark Public Library; Detroit Institute of Arts; Metropolitan Museum of Art; Cleveland Museum; Columbia University Library, New York; British Museum. Teacher of wood engraving, color printing, etching and illustration, Art Students' League of New York. Illustrated "Short Stories," by Walt Whitman (Columbia University Press); "Journies to Bagdad," by Charles Brooks (Yale Univ. Press); "Paul Bunyon," by James Stevens (Alfred A. Knopf); "Jesus Christ in Flanders," by Honore de Balzac; "Divers Proverbs," by Nathan Bailey (Yale Univ. Press). Died in 1957. Address in 1929, 41 Union Sq., New York, NY; h. 211 Lafayette Ave., Brooklyn, NY.

LEWIS, DAVID.
Portrait painter. In 1805 he had his studio at 2 Tremont St., Boston, MA.

LEWIS, EDMOND DARCH.
Landscape painter. Also painted marine views. Born Oct. 17, 1835, and lived in Phila. Tuckerman mentions his paintings as having decided merit. Among his works are "Queen of the Antilles," "Fairmount Park," "Bass Rocks, after a Storm" and "Casino at Narragansett Pier." He died Aug. 12, 1910, in Phila.

LEWIS, EDMONIA.
Sculptor. Born near Albany, NY, July 4th, 1845. She was part Indian by birth. Her work shows considerable ideality and talent, and her chief patronage was from abroad. She also executed portrait busts of Henry W. Longfellow, Charles Summer, John Brown and Abraham Lincoln.

LEWIS, H(ERBERT) T(AYLOR).
Painter and teacher. Born Chicago, Dec. 30, 1893. Pupil of AIC; Julian and Delecluse in Paris. Member: Chicago NJ SA. Instructor, Rockford College. Address in 1929, Rockford College, Rockford, IL.

LEWIS, HELEN V(AUGHAN).
Painter. Born New York City, March, 1879. Pupil of Cox, Du Mond and Beckington. Member: PA S. Min. P. Address in 1929, Irvington-on- Hudson, NY.

LEWIS, J.
This engraver signs his name "J. Lewis Sculpt." to several maps illustrating a bible published by S. Etheridge, of Charlestown, Mass., 1813. The same man probably engraved the book-plate of Dr. Peter Middletown, who died in New York in 1781. This plate bears evidence of American origin and would thus locate Lewis in New York at a considerably earlier date than that above mentioned.

LEWIS, J(EANNETTE) MAXFIELD.
Painter. Born Oakland, CA, April 19, 1894. Pupil of Gottardo Piazzoni, Winold Reiss, Armin Hansen. Member: San Francisco S. Women A; Oakland AL. Address in 1929, 3136 Huntington Blvd., Fresno, CA; summer, General Delivery, Monterey, CA.

LEWIS, JAMES OTTO.
Born Feb. 3, 1799 in Phila. This engraver in the stipple manner first appears in books published in Philadelphia in 1815. Engraved the portrait of Lewis Cass, secretary of war under President Jackson, in 1831. There is no record of such an engraver in the Philadelphia directories, and in the New York directory the nearest approach to this name is "Joseph Lewis, engraver and sealcutter" in 1816-23. Lewis probably spent some time in the western country, as he

published in Philadelphia, in 1835, "The North American Aboriginal Portfolio," a collection of lithographic portraits of Indians; some of these are inscribed as "Painted from life by J. O. Lewis, at Detroit, 1833." His engraving of Commodore Decatur full-length, standing on deck of ship, after G. Strickland, is a creditable piece of stipple engraving. Died in 1858, in NYC.

LEWIS, JOSEPHINE M(ILES).
Painter. Born New Haven, CT. Pupil of John F. Weir and John H. Niemeyer at Yale School of Art; Frederick MacMonnies and Aman-Jean in Paris. Member: NA Women PS; New Haven PCC; NYSP; Allied AA. Awards: Shaw memorial prize, NAD, 1916; 1st prize, New Haven PCC, 1923. Address in 1929, Carnegie Studios, 154 West 57th St., New York, NY.

LEWIS, MRS. LAURA C.
Painter. Born Philadelphia, PA, Aug. 21, 1874. Pupil of Phila. School of Design for Women; PAFA; Elliott Daingerfield; W. L. Lathrop and William M. Chase. Member: Plastic C. Address in 1929, 2004 Ontario St., Philadelphia, PA.

LEWIS, PHILLIPS F(RISBLE).
Painter. Born Oakland, CA, Aug. 26, 1892. Pupil of Calif. School of Arts and Crafts and Armin C. Hansen. Member; San F. AA; Oakland AL; San F. Galerie Beaux Arts; AFA. Awards: Hon. mention, Palace of Fine Arts, San Francisco, 1922; hon. mention, Berkeley Lg. FA, 1924; hon. award, Springville, Utah, 1926; second prize, State Fair, Phoenix, Ariz., 1927. Represented in Oakland Public Art Gallery. Died in 1930. Address in 1929, 5233 Broadway Terrace, Oakland, CA.

LEWIS, WILLIAM.
Born 1788 in Salem, MA. He was painting portraits there in 1812. His work appeared frequently in the early exhibitions at the Boston Athenaeum. Also a miniaturist.

LEWIS, YARDLEY.
The following appeared in the Boston Weekly Journal of Dec. 13,

1737: "Yardley Lewis of London, late from Ireland, dwelt lately in widow Howard's house near the north market place. Draws family pictures by the Life, also surveys and draws maps."

LEYENDECKER, FRANK X.
Painter and illustrator. Born in Montabour, Germany in 1877. He came to America in 1883. Studied at Chicago Art Institute and Julien Academy; pupil of Laurens and Constant. He was also a designer and painter of stained glass windows. He died Apr. 19, 1924, in New Rochelle, NY.

LEYENDECKER, JOSEPH CHRISTIAN.
Painter and illustrator. Born Montabour, Germany, March 23, 1874. Pupil of AIC; Julian Academy in Paris, 1896. Member: Salma. C. Opened Chicago studio with brother, Francis, in 1897. Illustrated "Saturday Evening Post" cover, May 1899; many other paintings for the "Post." Worked for Cluett, Peabody & Co., originated Arrow Shirt Collar Man. Advertised apparel of B. Kuppenheimer, Hart Schaffner & Marx. Member: Salma. C. Died July 26, 1951. Address in 1929, Mt. Tom Road, New Rochelle, NY.

LIBERMAN, ALEXANDER.
Painter. Born 1912 in Kiev, Russia. Studied with Andre L'hote (in Paris) 1929-31, and arch. with August Perret at Ecole des Beaux Arts, Paris 1930-2. U.S. citizen. Art Director of "Vogue" magazine from 1943. Exhibited at MOMA; Bennington College,; Guggenheim and Whitney Museums, NYC; L.A. County Museum; Corcoran Gallery of Art, Wash. DC; Tokyo Biennale (1962); Milwaukee Art Center and NY World's Fair (1964). In collections of Art Inst. of Chicago; Smith College; Whitney Mus.; Addison Gallery; Chase Manhattan Bank; Albright-Knox; Yale U.; Wash. Gal. of Mod. Art; MOMA; Tate Gallery, London.

LICHTEN, FRANCES M.
Painter, illustrator and etcher. Born in 1889, in Bellefonte, PA. Member: Phila. WCC; Phila. Print C. Died in 1961. Address in 1929,

1709 Sansom St., h. 633 North 17th St., Philadelphia, PA.

LICHTENAUER, J(OSEPH) MORTIMER.
Painter. Born New York, May 11, 1876. Pupil of Mowbray in New York; Merson and Laurens in Paris; and in Italy. Member: NY Arch Lg., 1902; Mural P.; ASL of NY; Salma. C.; Silvermine GA; AFA; Wash. AC Awards: President's prize, NY Arch. Lg., 1903 and 1907. Work: Proscenium Arch, Wallach Theatre, New York; 35 panels in Shubert Theatre, New York; "Portrait of Gen. Julius Stahel"; "Portrait of Gen. Palmer Pierce," National Museum of Art, Washington; represented in Metropolitan Museum of Art, Brooklyn Museum of Art. Specialty, murals. Address in 1929, Mortimer, care Simpson, 115 East 40th St., New York, NY; Westport, CT.

LICHTENSTEIN, ROY.
Painter. Born Oct. 27, 1923, in NYC. Earned B.F.A. and M.A. at OH State U. Taught there and at St. U. of NY (Oswego); Rutgers U., NJ. Awarded Hon. DFA, Cal. Institute (1977) and Skowhegan graphics award (1977). Created mural for NYS at World's Fair (1964), and Expo Montreal billboard (1967). Exhibited at Carlebach Gal., NYC (1951); Heller Gal. and Castelli Gal., NYC; Wadsworth Atheneum; Dallas Mus. of Contemp. Arts; Dwan Gal., LA; Guggenheim Mus. NYC; Cal. State U.; School of Visual Arts, NYC (1976); U. of Miami (1979). In collections of Brooklyn Mus.; Butler Inst. of Am. Art, Youngstown; Guggenheim Mus., NYC; MOMA, NYC; Whitney Mus., NYC; Stedelijk of Amsterdam, and Dusseldorf.

LICHTIN, ROSA.
(Mrs. Aaron Lichtin). Painter. Born Russia, Dec. 31, 1898. Pupil of PAFA. Member: Fellowship PAFA; Graphic Sketch C. Work: "Portrait of Dr. Theodor Herzl," Headquarters of North Philadelphia Zionist District. Address in 1929, 1545 South 7th St., Philadelphia, PA; summer, Wildwood Crest, Wildwood, NJ.

LICHTNER, (F) SCHOMER.
Painter and illustrator. Born Peoria, Ill., Mar. 18, 1905. Pupil of Gustave Moeller, Boardman Robinson. Member: Wisc. PS. Address in 1929, 1104 - 49th St., Milwaukee, WI.

LIDDELL, KATHARINE (FORBES).
Painter. Born Montgomery, AL. Pupil of E. Ambrose Webster. Member: Provincetown AA; NYS, Women A. Address in 1929, 259 Bradford St., Provincetown, MA.

LIE, JONAS.
Landscape painter. Born Norway, April 29, 1880. Pupil of NAD and ASL of NY. Member: ANA, 1912; NA, 1925; Salma. C.; New Soc. A.; NAC; Century C; AFA; (hon.) Boston AC; (hon.) Three AC. Awards: Silver medal, St. Louis Exp., 1904; first Hallgarten prize ($300), NAD, 1914; silver medal, P.-P. Exp., San F., 1915; Greenough memorial prize, Newport, RI, 1916; gold medal, Art Week, Phila., 1925; first prize, Chicago Norske Klub, 1925 and 1927; first prize, High School AA, Springville, UT, 1927; Carnegie prize, NAD, 1927; Maida Gregg memorial prize, NAC, 1929. Work: "Fishing Boats at Sunrise," Carnegie Institute, Pittsburgh; "The Conquerors," Metropolitan Mus., NY; "Culebra Cut," Detroit Mus.; "Afterglow," Art Inst. of Chicago; "Ice Harvest," Luxembourg Museum, Paris; also represented in Peabody Institute, Baltimore, MD; Memorial Art Gallery, Rochester, NY; Museum of Art, Syracuse, NY; art Association of Dallas, TX; Art Assn. of Lafayette, Ind.; Boston Mus. of Fine Arts; Cleveland Mus.; Brooklyn Inst. of Art and Science; Albright Art Gallery, Buffalo; Telfair Academy, Savannah, GA; Corcoran Gallery, Wash., DC; Cedar Rapids Art Assoc., Cedar Rapids, IA; Elmira Art Assoc., Elmira, NY; RI School of Design, Providence. Series of paintings of Panama Canal was presented as memorial to Gen. Goethals, 1929, to US Military Academy, West Point, NY. Died in 1940. Address in 1929, 40 West 59th St., NYC.

LIGGET, JANE STEWART.
Painter. Born Atlantic City, NJ, Sept. 4, 1893. Pupil of PAFA. Member: Fellowship PAFA; Phila. Alliance; Plastic C; AFA. Award: Cresson Traveling Scholarship, PAFA. Address in 1929, 157 North 21st St., Philadelphia, PA; Merion Manor, Merion, PA.

LILLIE, ELLA FILLMORE.
Lithographer. Born in Minneapolis, MN. Studied: Minn. School of Fine Arts; Art Institute of Chicago; NY School of Fine Arts; Cin. Art School. Awards: Southern Printmakers, 1938; Hoosier Salon, 1945, 1950, 1956, 1958; John Herron Art Institute, 1956; Northwest Printmakers, 1940; Springfield MO, 1941, 1942; Library of Congress, 1945; Indiana Printmakers, 1947; Boston Printmakers, 1948; Society of American Graphic Artists, 1951. Collections: Seattle Art Mus.; Library of Congress; Dayton Art Institute; CA State Library; Fleming Mus.; Boston Mus. of Fine Arts; Wesleyan College, Macon, GA; Met. Mus. of Art; Penn. State Univ.; Colt, Avery, Morgan Mem.; Carnegie Institute; Art Institute of Chicago; Toledo Mus. of Art; Telfair Academy; High Mus. of Art; Brooks Memorial Art Gal. Honolulu Institute of Art; Minn. Art Institute.

LIMBACH, RUSSELL T.
Painter, illustrator, etcher and teacher. Born Massillon, OH, Nov. 9, 1904. Awards: First prizes in lithography and illustration, 1926, 2nd prizes, 1927; 1st prize in lithography, 2nd prize for water color, 3rd prize for illustration, 1928, Cleveland Museum of Art. Work: "Spring Night," Los Angeles Museum of Art, Los Angeles, Cal.; "The Bathers," "Fraternity House" and "The Iron Fence," Cleveland Museum of Art. Address in 1929, 305 Union Trust Co.; h. 10115 Superior Ave., Cleveland OH.

LIMERICK, J(AMES) ARTHUR.
Painter, craftsman, lecturer and teacher. Born Philadelphia, PA, July 19, 1870. Pupil of Boyle, Grafly, Anshutz, Thouron. Member: Balto. Friends of Art; Balto. WCC.

Awards: Medal awarded by City of Baltimore for execution of bronzes supplied the city; gold medal of honor, Maryland Inst., Baltimore, 1921. Founded statues of "Benjamin Franklin," Waterbury, Conn., "Alexander Agassiz," Calumet, Mich., and "Robert Morris," Philadelphia, all by Paul W. Bartlett. Address in 1929, 960 North Howard St., Baltimore, MD; h. 102 Longwood Road, Roland Park, MD.

LINCOLN, AGNES HARRISON.
Painter. Born Minneapolis, MN. Pupil of Alden Weir and Edmund Tarbell. Award: Fawsett prize ($100), Milwaukee AI. Died in 1950. Address in 1929, 2509 Irving Ave., South, Minneapolis, MN.

LINCOLN, F. FOSTER.
Illustrator. Member: SI 1910. Address in 1929, Union Village, RFD, Woonsocket, RI.

LINCOLN, JAMES SULLIVAN.
Born in Taunton, MA, May 13, 1811. He came to Providence, RI, at the age of ten and was apprenticed to an engraver. At 17 he chose the profession of portrait painting and established his studio at Providence. He became the first president of the Providence Art Club, and died Jan. 18, 1888.

LINDBERG, ARTHUR H.
Painter and illustrator. Born Worcester, MA, Sept. 29, 1895. Pupil of Walter Beck; Pratt Inst.; Frank Du Mond; George Bridgman; ASL of NY. Member: Scandinavian American Artists.

LINDBERG, T(HORSTEN) (HARALD) (FRED).
Painter, illustrator and craftsman. Born Stockholm, Sweden, Jan. 13, 1878. Pupil of Higher Art Industrial School, Stockholm, Sweden. Member: Wis. PS; Scandinavian-American A; AFA. Address in 1929, 2701 Camden Ave., Omaha, NE.

LINDE, OSSIP L.
Painter. Born Chicago. Pupil of AIC; Laurens in Paris. Member: Allied AA; Salma. C.; SPNY. Awards: Hon. mention, Paris Salon, 1907; third class medal, Paris Salon, 1910. Represented in

568

Oakland Museum. Died in 1940. Address in 1929, care of Guaranty Trust Co., 1 Rue des Italiens, Paris, France; Westport, CT.

LINDENMUTH, MRS. TOD.
See Warren, E. B.

LINDENMUTH, TOD.
Painter. Born Allentown, PA, May 4, 1885. Pupil of Henri, Webster and Browne. Member: Salma. C.; Provincetown AA. Work: "Mending Nets" and "Provincetown Wharf," Toledo Museum; "Garden Near the Dunes," Pennsylvania State College Museum; "The Runway," Rochester Memorial Art Gallery; "The Red Sail," Pennsylvania Academy of the Fine Arts; and represented in the New York Public Library. Address in 1929, 159 Commercial St.; h. 56 Commercial St., Provincetown, MA.

LINDER, C. BENNETT.
Painter. Born Helsingfors, Finland, April 6, 1886. Member: Salma. C. Address in 1929, Carnegie Hall; h. 143 West 57th St., New York, NY.

LINDER, HENRY.
Sculptor. Born Sept. 26, 1854, in Brooklyn, NY. Exhibitor at the National Sculpture Society, of busts, and the sitting figures "Music" and "Spring." Died Jan. 7, 1910, in Brooklyn.

LINDER, JEAN.
Sculptor. Born in Berkeley, CA, in 1939. Studied: Univ. of CA at Berkeley; San Fran. Art Institute. Exhibitions: Oakland Museum, 1962; Richmond Museum, 1963; Whitney Museum of American Art, 1966, 1970; 55 Mercer, NYC, 1972. Collections: San Fran. Museum, CA; Rose Art Museum of Brandeis Univ.; Trenton State Museum, NJ.

LINDIN, CARL (OLOF) (ERIC).
Painter. Born Sweden, 1869. Pupil of Laurens, Constant and Aman-Jean in Paris. Member: Woodstock AA. Awards: First, 1919, and second prize, 1925-28, Swedish Club, Chicago. Decorations in Hull House, Chicago, Ill. Died in 1942. Address in 1929, Woodstock, Ulster Co., NY.

LINDING, HERMAN M.
Painter and sculptor. Born in Sweden in 1880. Pupil of Callmander, Carl Wilhelmson, and of Colarossi. Member: Society of Independent Artists; Whitney Studio Club; Alliance. Address in 1926, 154 East 64th St., New York, NY.

LINDNEUX, ROBERT O(TTAKAR).
Painter. Born New York, NY, Dec. 11, 1871. Studied in Dusseldorf, Germany, with Benjamin Vautier. Specialty, the Indian; animals and scenes of western outdoor life. Died in 1970. Address in 1929, 3039 East Colfax Ave., Denver, CO; summer, Pahaska Tepee, Lookout Mountain, CO.

LINDSLEY, E(MILY) E(ARLE).
Painter, illustrator and teacher. Born New Rochelle, NY, Feb. 25, 1858. Pupil of W. Chase, John Weir, C. Ferrari. Member: NA Women PS. Died in 1944. Address in 1929, 23 Chatsworth Ave., Larchmont, NY; winter, "Amber Beach," St. Cloud, FL.

LINEN, GEORGE.
Painter. Born in Greenlaw, Scotland in 1802. He was a student of the Royal Scottish Academy in Edinburgh. In 1843 he settled in New York, and painted portraits in oil, of a small size. He died in New York, in 1888.

LINES, C(HARLES) M(ORSE).
Painter and artist. Born Angola, IN, Dec. 15, 1862. Member: Cleveland SA; Cleveland Print C; AFA. Address in 1929, 1827 Cadwell Ave., Cleveland Heights, Ohio; summer, Rockport, MA.

LINFORD, CHARLES.
Landscape painter. Born in Pittsburgh, PA, in 1846, he died in 1897. His painting "Lowland Woods" was owned by the Penn. Academy of Fine Arts, Philadelphia.

LINK, B. LILLIAN.
Sculptor. Born New York. Pupil of Mrs. Charles Sprague-Smith, George Grey Barnard and Herbert Adams. Member: MacD. C.; Alliance; NA Women PS. Awards: Avery prize, NY Arch. Lg., 1907; sculpture prize, NY Woman's AC, 1912.

Address in 1929, 88 Chestnut St., Boston, Mass.; 260 West 76th St., New York, NY.

LINN, WARREN.
Illustrator. Born in Chicago in 1946. Received his BFA from the AIC in 1968. His editorial illustrations have appeared often in Playboy since 1967. Rolling Stone and The New York Times, among others, have used his work. As a book illustrator he has painted covers for St. Martin's Press and Scott, Foresman and Co. The Chicago AG awarded him prizes in 1972 and 1973.

LINQUIST, MARLENE.
Painter. Studied: Univ. of Rochester; Ohio Univ., Athens; NY Univ. She was awarded a prize for painting at the Miami Museum of Modern Art. Exhibitions: Rockefeller Art Gallery, State Univ. College, Fredonia, NY; Joe and Emily Lowe Art Gallery; Design Center, Miami, FL.

LINSON, CORWIN KNAPP.
Painter, illustrator, craftsman, and writer. Born Brooklyn, NY, Feb. 25, 1864. Pupil of Ecole des Beaux Arts; Academie Julian; Gerome and Laurens in Paris. Member: NYWCC; Salma. C.; Allied AA. Work: Portrait of "Hon. Edmund Wilson," Mon. Co. Court House, Freehold, NJ; "Mark Hopkins," Williams College; "Col. C. J. Wright," New York Military Academy; "Dr. Hunter McGuire," St. Luke's Hospital, Richmond, VA; "A Summer Chautauqua," Swathmore Chautauqua Assn.; five memorial windows, Baptist Temple, Brooklyn, NY. Illustrated: "I.N.R.I.," by Rosegger; "The Lost Word," by Dr. H. Van Dyke; "Life of the Master," by Dr. Watson; "Modern Athens," by George Horton; own articles in "Scribner's," "Century," "Cosmopolitan," "The House Beautiful," etc., including "Pont Aven Vignettes," "Color at Vesuvius," "Sunset at Jerusalem." Died in 1934. Address in 1929, Atlantic Highlands, NJ.

LINTON, FRANK BENTON ASHLEY.
Painter. Born Philadelphia, Feb. 26, 1871. Pupil of Thomas Eakins in Philadelphia; Gerome, Benjamin-Constant, Bouguereau, Bonnat and Laurens in Paris. Member: Internationale Union des Beaux-Arts et des Lettres, Paris; Phila. AC. Award: Medaille de Bronze, Paris Salons, 1927; "Officier d'Academie," French Govt. 1928. Represented in Johns Hopkins University, Baltimore, MD; Girard College, Hahneman College, College of Physicians and the Baldwin Locomotive Works, all in Philadelphia; "La derniere retouche," owned by the French Government, Died in 1944. Address in 1929, 2037 Delancey St., Philadelphia, PA.

LINTON, WILLIAM JAMES.
Wood engraver, designer, and water color painter. Born in London, England in 1812. He came to the United States in 1866. He was elected a member of the National Academy of Design in 1882; was also author of "History of Wood Engraving in America." Member of Society of Painters in Water Colors. Died Dec. 29, 1897 at "Appledore", New Haven, CT.

LION, JULES.
Lithographer. Born 1816 in France. He opened a studio in New Orleans in 1839, bringing with him the first daguerreotype outfit used in that city. He had exhibited in the Salon, Paris , 1831 and 1836. He remained in New Orleans making lithograph portraits of the leading statesmen of the South until 1865, after which no record of him is found. Also painted miniatures and portraits.

LIPCHITZ, JACQUES.
Sculptor. Born in Druskieniki, Lithnuania, Aug. 22, 1891. Study: Ecole Beaux-Arts, Paris, 1909-11, with Jean Antonine Ingalbert & Dr. Richet; Academy Julian, Paris, with Raoul Verlet; Acad. Colarossi, Paris; Columbia Univ., Lion. LHD, 1968. Work: Mus. Arte Mod. Paris; Mus. Grenoble, France; MOMA and Met. Mus. Art, NYC; Albright-Knox Art Gallery, Buffalo, NY; Phila. Mus. of Art; and many others. Comn.: Prometheus, Paris World's Fair, 1937; sculpture, Fairmount Park Assn., Phila., 1964;

Presidential Scholars Medallion, 1964; others. Exhib.: Met. Mus. of Art, retrospective, 1972; many others in US. & abroad. Awards: Gold Medal, sculpture, Am. Acad. Arts and Letters and Nat'l. Inst. Arts & Letters, 1966. Bibliog.: Maurice Raynal, Jeanne Bucher, Paris, 1947; Henry R. Hope, MOMA, 1954; Bert Van Bork, Crown, 1966. Mem.: Am. Acad. Arts & Letters; Nat'l. Acad. Arts & Letters. Died in 1973.

LIPPERT, LEON.
Painter. Born in Bavaria, March 15, 1863. Pupil of Cincinnati Art Academy, under Nowottny and Duveneck, and studied abroad. Member: Cincinnati AC. Died in 1950. Address in 1929, 119 E. Fifth St., Government Sq., Cincinnati, Ohio; h. 658 Nelson P., Newport, KY.

LIPPINCOTT, MARGARETTE.
Painter. Born in Philadelphia in 1862. Student of the Penna. Academy of Fine Arts, Philadelphia. Her specialty was flower painting. Died Sept. 1910.

LIPPINCOTT, WILLIAM HENRY.
Painter. Born in Philadelphia on Dec. 6, 1849. Began study of art in Penna. Academy of Fine Arts; became designer of illustrations, later, scenic artist; was a pupil of Leon Bonnat, 1874, remaining in Paris 8 years, and regularly exhibiting at Paris Salons. He returned to the U.S., 1882; established a studio in New York. He was a professor of painting, National Academy of Design. Painted portraits, figure compositions and landscapes; was a regular contributor to American art exhibitions. "The Duck's Breakfast," "Love's Ambush," and "Pleasant Reflections" are his most important pictures. Elected Associate Member of the National Academy, 1884; National Academy, 1896. Member: American Water Color Society; Society of American Etchers; Century Association. Died March 16, 1920 in NYC.

LITLE, ARTHUR.
Illustrator. Member: SI 1912; AI Graphic A; Salma. C. Address in 1929, 27 West 67th St.; care Salmagundi Club, 47 Fifth Ave.; 15 West 29th St., New York, NY.

LITTLE, EDITH TADD.
Painter, sculptor, illustrator, artist, craftsman, writer, lecturer and teacher. Born Philadelphia, June 27, 1882. Pupil of PAFA; Chase; Beaux; Grafly. Member: Fellowship PAFA; Florida Assn. Architects. Chairman of art, Florida Federation of Women's Clubs. Chairman of Fine Arts, Puiellas Co. Federation of Women's Clubs. Address in 1929, Florida Art School; h. 2739 Second Ave., North, St. Petersburg, FL.

LITTLE, GERTRUDE L.
Painter. Born Minneapolis, MN. Pupil of Seattle AS; ASL of NY; School of Am. S. Min. P. of NY; William M. Chase. Member: Calif. S. Min. P.; West Coast Arts; Penn. S. Min. P. Awards: 1st prize, for miniature, Seattle FAS, 1921; 1st prize, Calif. S. Min. P., 1923; hon. mention, 1924 first prize and popular vote prize, 1925, second prize and popular prize, 1928, Calif. S. Min. P.; hon. mention, Los Angeles Museum, 1925; second special prize, San Diego FAS, 1926; silver medal, Pac. Southwest Expos., 1928; first prize, Los Angeles County Fair, 1928. Address in 1929, 4417 Prospect St., Los Angeles, CA.

LITTLE, JOHN WESLEY.
Landscape painter. Born in Forksville, PA, in 1867. Studied at National Academy of Design, New York, 1888-94, and with Leonard Ochtman; went abroad for travel and study 1899-1900 and 1905. He exhibited at the St. Louis Exposition; PAFA; Phila. AC; AWCS; NY WCC; Chicago AI; Washington WCC; International Exhibition, Montevideo, 1911; Panama, P.I., Exposition, etc. Awards: Silver medal, American Art Society, 1901. Member: Philadelphia, Washington and Chicago water color clubs; Philadelphia Sketch Club. Died in 1923 in Williamsport, PA.

LITTLE, NAT(HANIEL) (STANTON).
Illustrator. Born Helena, MT, Feb. 18, 1893. Pupil of ASL of NY;

PAFA. Member: Fellowship PAFA; Phila. Sketch C. Awards: Beck prize, Phila. WCC, 1923; gold medal, Fellowship PAFA, 1925. Address in 1929, 1010 Clinton St., Philadelphia, PA.

LITTLE, PHILIP.
Painter and etcher. Born Swampscott, MA, Sept. 6, 1857. Pupil of Boston Museum School. Member: Boston GA; Chicago SE; Portland (ME) AA (life); Brooklyn SE; NAC (life); Boston SWCP; AFA. Awards: Hon. mention AIC, 1912, for "The Brook"; silver medal P.-P. Exp., San F., 1915. Work: "In the Wake of the Moon," Pennsylvania Academy, Philadelphia; "Where Hawthorne Wrote and Derby Traded," City Art Museum, St. Louis, MO; "The Upper Ipswich River," Minneapolis Society of Fine Arts; "Seining at Dawn," Bowdoin College Art Gallery, Brunswick, ME; "Gulls in Fog," Portland (ME) Society of Art; "Surf at Sunset," Nashville Art Association; "Awakening of the Day," Milwaukee Art Association; "The Old Wharf," Dubuque Art Association; "A Relic of History," Essex Inst., Salem; "Transport Going East off Marblehead, 1917," RI School of Design; "February Thaw," Boston Museum; etchings in Congressional Library, Washington; New York Public Library; "Salem's Old Wharves," Bibliotheque Nationale, Paris, and other places. Curator Art, Essex Institute, Salem, Mass. Died in 1942. Address in 1929, Daniel's Street Court; h. 10 Chestnut St., Salem, MA; summer, MacMahan Island, ME.

LITTLE, TRACEY M(AY) (BATES).
Etcher. Born Whitehall, IL, May 24, 1879. Pupil of Frank DuMond. Member: Provincetown AA; Art Centre of the Oranges. Address in 1929, 3 Brookside Rd., South Orange, NJ; summer, 349-A Commercial St., Provincetown, MA.

LITTLEJOHN, C(YNTHIA) (PUGH).
Painter. Born Assumption Parish, LA. Pupil of Ellsworth Woodward and A. A. Dow. Member: NAC; Newcomb Art Alumnae; SSAL; Amer. Soc. Bookplate Collectors and Designers. Address in 1929, 1221 Leontine, New Orleans, LA.

LITZINGER, DOROTHEA M.
Painter and etcher. Born in Cambria County, PA, Jan. 20, 1889. Pupil of National Academy of Design. Illustrated for "County Life in America"; well known for her flower painting. Died Jan. 4, 1925 in NYC.

LIVERMORE, MARY SPEAR MASON.
Miniature painter. Born in 1806. Flourished 1847 to 1848 in Boston, MA.

LIVINGSTON, CHARLOTTE.
Painter. Born New York City. Pupil of George Maynard; Ivan Olinsky. Member: Bronx AG; Am. APL; Bronx Inst. A; Ixia S; AFA. Address in 1929, 2870 Heath Ave., Kingsbridge, Bronx, New York, NY.

LIVINGSTON, HARRIET.
Amateur miniature painter. She became the wife of Robert Fulton, 1808, and painted a miniature of her father, Walter Livingston, reproduced in C. W. Bowen's "Centennial of the Inauguration of Washington." Died in 1824.

LLERENA, CARLOS ANTONIO.
Illustrator. Born in Peru in 1952. Worked as an illustrator in South America before coming to the US in 1971. He studied at the Ringling School of Art and SVA, where he is presently an instructor. In addition to editorial art for magazines and children's books which he has illustrated, his works have also appeared on the Op-Ed page of The New York Times. While working in pen and ink for the most part, he has recently been doing woodcuts.

LLOYD, LUCILE.
Mural painter. Born Cincinnati, Aug. 20, 1894. Pupil of Frank Fairbanks, and Eugene Savage. Member: American Bookplate Soc. Work: "The Madonna of the Covered Wagon," So. Pasadena Jr. H.S., CA. Address in 1929, 1125 East Raleigh St., Glendale, CA.

LLOYD, SARA A. W.
Painter. Pupil of Swain Gifford, Volk and Chase in New York. Among her paintings are "Sunshine and Shadow" and portraits of W. J.

Morehead, John Jones, and Miss Slade. Address in 1926, Hamilton, NY.

LOBER, GEORG JOHN.
Sculptor. Born Chicago, IL, Nov. 7, 1892. Pupil of Calder, Borglum and Longman, NAD and Beaux Arts Inst. Member: NY Arch. Lg.; NSS; Conn. AFA; Salma. C.; Allied AA. Awards: Avery collaborative prize, NY Arch Lg., 1911; hon. mention, AIC, 1918, 1920; first prize, Conn. AFA, 1924; prize, Art Centre of the Oranges, 1926. Represented in Corcoran Gallery, Washington, DC, and Montclair Museum, Montclair, NJ. Work: Permanent Exhibition Medals, Numismatic Museum, NY; Bronze statue "Eve," Metropolitan Mus., NY; Byzantine Madonna in Silver, Brooklyn Museum, Brooklyn, NY; Eleanor T. Woods, "Peace Memorial," Norfolk, VA; Nineteen Lincoln Memorial Tablets, State of Illinois; John Wells James Memorial, MA; "Mother's Memorial," 71 Regiment Armory, New York City; Caleb Thomas Winchester Memorial, Wesleyan College, Middletown, CT; marble Baptistry, First Baptist Church, Plainfield, NJ; St. Peter and St. Paul, Church of Our Lady of Consolation, Pawtucket, RI; Memorial Central Park, NYC to honor NYC Employees; bronze portrait, Frank Bacon, Golden Gate Museum, San F., CA; also important portraits. Died in 1961. Address in 1929, 6 East 15th St., New York, NY; h. Montclair, NJ.

LOCKE, ALEXANDER S.
Mural painter. Born New York, Feb. 14, 1860. Pupil of John La Farge. Member: NY Arch. Lg., 1894; Mural P.; NAC. Address in 1929, 103 Pineapple St.; h. 87 Winthrop St., Brooklyn, New York, NY.

LOCKE, ALICE G.
Painter and teacher. Born Lexington, MA, Sept. 18, 1883. Pupil of Henry B. Snell. Member: NA Women PS; Gloucester AA; Brooklyn SA; North Shore AA. Address in 1929, 183 Union St., Flushing, NY; summer, Rocky Neck Road, East Gloucester, MA.

LOCKE, CHARLES (WHEELER).
Painter, illustrator, etcher, and teacher. Born Cincinnati, OH, Aug. 31, 1899. Pupil of Joseph Pennell, H. H. Wessel, John E. Weis, etc. Member: Duveneck S. Represented in Met. Mus., NY; British Museum, London; Cincinnati Museum. Address in 1929, 78 Columbia Heights, Brooklyn, NY; summer, 3906 Hazel Ave., Norwood, OH.

LOCKE, LUCIE H.
Painter. Born Valdosta, GA, in 1904. Studied: Newcomb College, Tulane Univ.; San Antonio School of Art; and with Charles Rosen, Xavier Gonzales, Increase Robinson, Frederic Taubes, and others. Awards: Corpus Christi Art Found., 1946, 1949, 1954, 1955. Collections: Montgomery Museum of Fine Arts; Del Mar College; Corpus Christi Art Found.; Corpus Christi Civic Center.

LOCKMAN, DeWITT McCLELLAN
Born: July 30, 1870 in NY. Pupil of James H. Beard, Nelson N. Bickford and William Sartain. Studied in Europe 1891-1892; 1901-1902. Represented in the permanent collections of The Met. Mus. of Art, NY; The Nat. Acad. of Design, NY; The Numismatic Soc., NY; Yale Univ., New Haven, CT, and numerous others. Notable portraits include Gen. John Pershing and F. D. Roosevelt. Member: ANA 1917; NA 1921; Port. P.; Salma. C.; Allied AA; AFA. Award: Silver medal, P.-P. Exp., San F., 1915; Lippincott prize, PAFA, 1918. Died July 1, 1957. Address in 1929, 58 West 57th St., New York, NY.

LOCKPEZ, INVERNE.
Sculptor. Born in Havana, Cuba, in 1941. Studied: The National Academy of San Alejandro, Havana: Atelier of Lolo Soldeville, Paris. Living and working in NYC since 1966. Grants: Cintas Found., NY, 1970-1971; CAPS, NYS Council on the Arts, 1973. Commissions: Latin-American Theater, NY, 1969; Sculpture, NYC Public Arts Council, McKenna Square, 1972.

LOCKSPEISER, (ELEANORE).
Painter. Born in NYC June 16, 1900. Study: With Max Weber;

573

Louvre Print Room; Slade School, London. Work: Smithsonian Archives; Museum of the City of NY; Franklin Marshall College Art Center; Sperry Modern Art; private collections in Paris, London, NY, Philadelphia, Los Angeles, Chicago. Exh.: Whitney Museum Annual; Los Angeles Fine Arts Museum; Jewish Museum First International Show; London Group and Redfern Gallery, London; solo shows at Feigl Gallery; Phoenix Gallery; Whittenberg Etching Show; Woodstock Hist. Soc.; Hudson Art Consortium Retrospective, 1951-83; wall in New Paltz (NY) Gallery - CETA project; panels in Legislative Office Bldg., Albany, NY. etc. Address in 1983, 120 W. 86th St., NYC.

LOCKWOOD, J. W(ARD).
Painter. Born Atchison, KS, Sept. 22, 1894. Pupil of Dept. of Fine Arts, Univ. of Kansas; PAFA; Ransom Academy in Paris. Member: Fellowship PAFA. Died in 1963.

LOCKWOOD, WILTON (ROBT.).
Portrait painter. Born Sept. 12, 1862, in Wilton, CT. He was also known for his flower painting. Pupil of John LaFarge; also studied for ten years in Paris. Elected Associate Member of the National Academy in 1906 and Academician, 1912. He died in Brookline, MA, on March 20, 1914. His portrait of John LaFarge was placed in the Boston Museum of Fine Arts; his flower piece "Peonies" was purchased by the Corcoran Art Gallery of Washington, DC.

LODIGENSKY, THEODORE.
Illustrator. Born in Paris, FR, in 1930. Attended the Society of Arts and Crafts School in Detroit for four years, studying under Guy Palazzola. He began his career in Michigan in 1953 and has since illustrated for such magazines as Automobile Quarterly, Car Classic, Playboy, Rod and Gun and Mechanics Illustrated. An industrial designer as well as an artist, his works have been shown at the Detroit Museum of Art and the S of I Annual Exhibitions.

LODWICK, AGNES.
Painter and teacher. Born Bergen Point, NJ. Pupil of St. Louis School FA, Frank Swift Chase. Member: Western AA; St. Louis AG; St. Louis Alliance; Players. Address in 1929, 4 rue de Chevreuse, Paris, France; summer, Nantucket, MA.

LOEB, DOROTHY.
Painter and etcher. Born in Bavaria in 1887 of American parents. Pupil of AIC; studied in Paris and Munich. Member: Provincetown AA. Address in 1929, Litchfield, CT; summer, Provincetown, MA.

LOEB, LOUIS.
Painter. Born Nov. 7, 1866, in Cleveland, OH. He studied in Paris under Gerome. Elected a member of the National Academy in 1906. Specialty, figure painting. He was a member of the Society of American Artists. He died July 12, 1909 in Canterbury, NH.

LOEBL, FLORENCE WEINBERG.
Painter. Born in New York in 1894. Pupil of Kenneth Hayes Miller. Member: S. Indp. A.; League of New York Artists. Address in 1926, 135 West 79th St., NYC.

LOEFFLER, GISELLA.
See Lacher, Gisella Loeffler.

LOEWENGUTH, FREDERICK M.
Painter and craftsman. Born Rochester, NY, April 18, 1887. Studied in London and Paris. Member: Rochester Art Club. Address in 1929, 401 Powers Bldg., Rochester, NY.

LOFTING, HUGH.
Illustrator, writer and lecturer. Born Maidenhead, EN, Jan. 14, 1886. Illustrated "Story of Doctor Doolittle;" "Voyages of Doctor Doolittle;" "Doctor Doolittle's Post Office;" "Doctor Doolittle's Circus;" "Doctor Doolittle's Zoo;" "Doctor Doolittle's Caravan;" Doctor Doolittle's Garden;" "Dr. Doolittle in the Moon;" "The Story of Mrs. Tubbs;" "Porridge Poetry;" "Noisy Norah," etc. Address in 1929, c/o F.A. Stokes Co., 443 4th Ave., NYC.

LOGAN, HERSCHEL C.
Engraver, etcher, and block printer. Born Magnolia, MO, April 19, 1901. Pupil of Chicago Acad. FA; Federal Schools, Inc. Member: Wichita AG. Awards: Bronze medal, Kansas City AI., 1926 and 1927. Work: Three woodcuts owned by The Century Co. Address in 1929, 440 North Madison Ave., Wichita, KS.

LOGAN, ROBERT FULTON.
Painter, etcher, and teacher. Born Lauder, Manitoba, Canada, March 25, 1889. Pupil of Boston School of the Museum of Fine Arts; AIC; Philip L. Hale. Member: NAC; CT AFA; Chicago SE; Soc. Int. Gravure Originale en Noir; Paris AAA; Salma. C. Award: Logan medal, Chicago SE, 1922. Work: "Spanish Iris," Art Society of Hartford; "Les Molineaux-Billancourt," Luxembourg Museum, Paris. Etchings in Chicago Art Institute; Library of Congress, Washington, DC; Metropolitan Museum of Art; New York Public Library; Morgan Memorial Art Museum, Hartford; CT State Library; Ann Arbor Art Museum; British Museum, London; Fitzwilliam Memorial Art Museum, Cambridge, Eng.; Luxembourg Museum; Bibliotheque Nationale, Paris. Assistant Director, Atalier of Painting, Bellevue Art Training Centre, A.E.F., 1919. Died in 1959. Address in 1929, Villa Adrien, 33 Route des Gardes, Bellevue, Seine et Oise, France.

LOGGIE, HELEN A.
Etcher. Born in Bellingham, WA. Studied: Smith College; Art Students League; and with John Taylor Arms, Mahonri Young. Awards: Albany Printmakers Club, 1953; Florida Southern College, 1952; National Academy of Design, 1955; Northwest Printmakers, 1939; Library of Congress, 1943; Pacific Northwest Arts and Crafts Assoc., 1950. Collections: Univ. of Nebraska; Library of Congress; Museum of Fine Arts of Houston; Seattle Art Museum; Western Washington College of Education; Springfield Museum of Art; Library of Congress; Metropolitan Museum of Art; Penn. State Univ.; National Museum, Stockholm; Glasgow Univ., Scotland; British Museum, England;

Lyman Allyn Museum; International Business Machines; Albany Institute of History and Art; Philadelphia Museum of Art.

LOMBARD, WARREN P(LIMPTON).
Etcher. Born West Newton, MA, May 29, 1855. Member: Ann Arbor AA; AFA. Died in 1939. Address in 1929, 805 Oxford Rd., Ann Arbor, MI; summer, Monhegan, ME.

LONDON, FRANK (MARSDEN).
Painter. Born Pittsboro, NC, May 9, 1876. Pupil of Arthur Dow, William Chase, Kenyon Cox. Award: Hon. mention, International Exhibition, Bordeaux, France, 1927. Died in 1945. Address in 1929, 317 East 51st St.; h. 215 East 48th St., New York, NY.

LONDONER, AMY.
Painter. Born in Lexington, MO, in 1878. Pupil of Robert Henri and of John Sloan. Member: Art Students' League of NY; Society of Independent Artists; League of NY Artists. Address in 1926, 1947 Broadway, NY. Died in 1953.

LONG, ADELAIDE HUSTED.
(Mrs. George T. Long). Painter, teacher, and writer. Born New York. Pupil of ASL of NY, John Twachtman, Ernest Knaufft and George T. Collins; Anglade in Paris. Member: NAC; AFA. Address in 1929, 57 North Broadway, White Plains, NY.

LONG, DANIEL A.
Illustrator. Born in Columbus, OH in 1946. Attended Southwestern College and the ACD. He now works for the US Navy, Xerox, American Express, Panasonic, Merrill Lynch, the New York Daily News and London Records. His first illustration was done for Columbia Records in 1975. He illustrated the book Human Sexuality, published by McGraw-Hill in 1976.

LONG, ELLIS B.
Painter and sculptor. Born in Baltimore, MD, in 1874. Pupil of Andre Castaigne and of E. S. Whiteman in Baltimore; of Cox, Mowbray, Saint Gaudens and D. C. French in New York. Address in

1926, 127 Richmond St., Baltimore, MD.

LONGACRE, JAMES BARTON.
Engraver. Born in Delaware County, PA, Aug. 11, 1794; died in Phila., Jan. 1, 1869. Longacre was taught to engrave by George Murray, in Phila. His earliest work was done for S. F. Bradford's Encyclopedia, but he first attracted attention by his admirable large plate of Andrew Jackson, after the portrait by Thomas Sully, published in Phila. in 1820. He soon found abundant employment in engraving portraits in the stipple manner, many of them done after his own drawings from life. About 1830 in connection with James Herring, Longacre conceived the idea of publishing "The American Portrait Gallery," a series of biographical sketches of statesmen, military and naval heroes. These were to be illustrated by portraits, and Longacre engraved a number of these himself and drew the originals for other engravers; taken as a whole it was the best series of portraits engraved in the US up to that time. The large plates of Longacre are remarkable for their faithfulness as portraits, and for the beauty of their execution. The majority of them are done in the stipple manner; but his large plate of Charles Carroll, after the painting by Chester Harding, proves him to have been an accomplished line-engraver. In 1844 Mr. Longacre was appointed engraver to the US. Mint, succeeding C. Gobracht, and he held the position until his death. Longacre painted, in oil, many of the originals of the engraved portraits; they are cabinet size and carefully painted.

LONGACRE, LYDIA E(ASTWICK).
Miniature painter. Born New York, Sept. 1, 1870. Pupil of ASL of NY, under Chase and Mowbray; Whistler in Paris. Member: Am. S. Min. P.; Pa. Soc. Min. P.; NA Women PS. Died in 1951. Address in 1929, 27 West 67th St., New York, NY.

LONGFELLOW, ERNEST WADSWORTH.
Painter. Born in Cambridge, MA, in 1845. Studied art in Paris under Hebert Bonnat and Couture. His best known landscapes and compositions are: "Misty Morning;" "The Choice of Youth;" "Italian Pifferari;" "Morning on the Aegean;" "The Matterhorn;" "Evening on the Nile;" "First Love;" Portrait of H. W. Longfellow, etc. "Marine" (signed "Ernest Longfellow 1875") is owned by the Boston Museum of Fine Arts. Died Nov. 23, 1921 in Boston, MA.

LONGFELLOW, MARY KING.
Painter. Member: Boston WCC. Address in 1929, 116 State St., Portland, ME.

LONGLEY, BERNIQUE.
Painter and sculptor. Born in Moline, IL, in 1923. Studied: Art Institute of Chicago; and with Francis Chapin and Edouard Chassaing. Award: Lathrop traveling scholarship, Art Institute of Chicago, 1945; Museum of New Mexico; Mexico State Fair. Collections: Museum of New Mexico; Dallas Art Museum; mural, LaFonda Del Sol Restaurant, NY; mural, Alexander Girard Home, Santa Fe. Exhib.: AIC; NM Mus. of Fine Arts; Santa Fe Festival of Arts; etc. Media: Oil and acrylic. Address in 1980, 427 Camino del Monte Sol, Santa Fe, NM.

LONGMAN, (MARY) EVELYN B(EATRICE).
(Mrs. N. H. Batehelder). Sculptor. Born Winchester, OH, Nov. 21, 1874. Pupil of AIC under Taft; French in NY. Member: NSS 1906; ANA 1909; NA, 1919; Am. Numismatic Soc.; NY Municipal AS; Concord AA; Conn. AFA; AFA. Awards: Silver medal, St. Louis Exp., 1904; silver medal, P.-P. Exp., San F., 1915; Shaw memorial prize, NAD, 1918 and 1926; W.M.R. French gold medal, AIC, 1920; Widener gold medal, PAFA, 1921; Watrous gold medal, NAD, 1924; Flagg prize, Conn. AFA, 1926. Work: Bronze doors of Chapel, US Naval Academy, Annapolis; bronze door of Library, Wellesley College, Wellesley, Mass.; Ryle memorial, Public Library, Paterson, NJ; "Torso," bust of Henry Bacon, and "Victory," Metropolitan Museum, New York; "Victory," and "Electricity," Toledo Museum; Allison monument, Des Moines, IA; "Electricity," American Telephone and Telegraph

Bldg., New York; centennial monument, Chicago; Naugatuck War Memorial, Naugatuck, Conn.; Theodore C. Williams Memorial, All Souls' Church, New York; Spanish War Memorial, Hartford, Conn.; also represented in Chicago Art Institute; City Art Museum, St. Louis; Cincinnati Museum of Art; Cleveland Museum; Herron Art Inst., Indianapolis. Died in 1954. Address in 1929, Windsor, CT.

LONGPRE, PAUL De.
Painter. Born in France in 1855, he came to the United States in 1890 and died in Hollywood, Los Angeles, CA, in 1911. His specialty was floral painting, and his first exhibition in New York in 1896 was composed entirely of floral subjects.

LONGYEAR, WILLIAM LLONYN.
Illustrator, writer and teacher. Born Shokan, NY, June 17, 1899. Pupil of Frank DuMond; ASL of NY. Member: College AA; Eastern AA. Author of "Practical Folio of Lettering;" illustrated "Industrial and Applied Arts Drawing Books" and "Practical Drawing Books". Address in 1929, 253 Washington Ave., Brooklyn, NY; summer, Berkshire Summer School of Art, Monterey, MA.

LOOMIS, CHESTER.
Painter. Born Oct. 18, 1852 near Syracuse, NY; died in Englewood, NJ, in Nov. 1924. Portrait and landscape painter. Pupil of Harry Thompson and Bonnat in Paris. He was elected an Associate Member of the National Academy in 1906. He also executed several mural paintings.

LOOMIS, MANCHUS C.
Painter. Born at Fairview, PA. Studied at San Francisco School of Design under Virgil Williams, and at the Chicago Art Institute under Vanderpoel, Grover and Boutwood. Member: Palette and Chisel C.; AIC Alumni. Address in 1929, 30 East Randolph St.; 3919 North Kenneth Ave., Chicago, IL.

LOOMIS, WILLIAM ANDREW.
Illustrator. Born Syracuse, NY, June 15, 1892. Pupil of Frank DuMond, George Bridgman, Leopold

Seyffert, John Carlson, NY ASL. Member: GFLA; Assn. Arts and Industries, Chicago; AIC; Palette and Chisel C. Awards: $1,000, Harvard Awards for advertising; first prize for poster from the U.S. Shipping Board. Specialty, advertising illustrations. Taught at Am. Acad. of Art in Chicago. Died in 1959. Address in 1929, 737 N. Michigan Ave.; h. 6926 Oleander Parkway, Chicago, IL; summer, Williams Bay, WI.

LOOP, HENRY A. (MRS.).
See Loop, Jeanette Shepperd Harrison.

LOOP, HENRY AUGUSTUS.
Distinguished portrait and figure painter. He was born in Hillsdale, NY, Sept. 9, 1831. He studied with Henry Peters Gray; also with Couture in Paris. One of his best portraits was that of Judge Skinner of Buffalo. In 1861 he was elected to the National Academy, and in 1863 to the Century Club. He died Oct. 20, 1895, at Lake George, NY.

LOOP, JEANETTE SHEPPERD H.
(Mrs. Henry A. Loop). Painter. Born March 5, 1840 in New Haven, CT. A portrait and figure painter, she was a pupil of Henry Loop, whom she married c. 1865. She was a sister of Judge Lynde Harrison. Specialized in children's portraits. Had studio in NYC. Elected Assoc. Member of NA in 1875. Died April 17, 1909 in Saratoga, NY.

LOOP, LEOTA WILLIAMS.
Painter and teacher. Born Fountain City, IN, Oct. 26, 1893. Pupil of Olive Rush; William Forsyth, R. L. Coats. Member: Indiana AC; Hoosier Salon; Kokomo ASI; Kokomo AA; AFA; AL of No. Ind.; Soc. IA; Salons of Am. Represented in Elwood High School; Tipton Library, Milwaukee Children's Home; High School and Woman's Department Club, Kokomo, Ind. Address in 1929, 1423 West Sycamore, Kokomo, Indiana; summer R.R. No. 2, Martinsville, IN.

LOPEZ, CHARLES A.
Sculptor. Born in Mexico in 1869. He came to New York when a youth

and studied with Ward of New York, and afterwards at the Ecole des Beaux Arts in Paris. Awarded first prize for McKinley Monument, Philadelphia. He was elected in 1906 an Associate of the National Academy, but died in the same year.

LORAN, ERLE.
Painter. Born Oct. 3, 1905 in Minneapolis, MN. Studied at U. of Minn.; at Minn. School of Art; and with Hans Hofmann. Taught at Berkeley from 1936. Awarded Paris Prize from Chaloner Foundation, NYC (1926); S.F. Mus. of Art award; Cal. Palace, S.F. awards (1956 & 1963); Purchase Prize. Exhibited at Kraushaar Gallery, NYC (1931); S.F. Mus. of Art (many since 1939); Santa Barbara Mus.; Stanford; MOMA; Carnegie; Cranbrook Acad. of Art (Mich.); and MMA. In collections of Brigham Young U.; US State Dept.; Denver Art Mus.; Fine Arts Gallery, San Diego; U. of Minn.; IBM and many private collections.

LORD, CAROLINE A.
Painter and teacher. Born Cin., OH, March 10, 1860. Pupil of Cin. Art Acad.; ASL of NY; Julian Academy in Paris. Member: Cin. Woman's AC (hon.). Instructor in Cin. Art Acad. Awards: Bronze medal, Columbian Exp., Chicago, 1893; Fellowship Prize, Buffalo FAS, 1925. Work: "First Communion" and "Old Woman," Cin. Mus. Address in 1929, 975 E. McMillan St., Cin., OH.

LORD, EVELYN RUMSEY.
Painter. Born in Buffalo, NY. Pupil of Buffalo Art School, C. W. Hawthorne, Charles Woodbury. Member: Buffalo SA. Award: Fellowship prize, Buffalo, 1916 and 1925. Address in 1929, 18 Tracy St., Buffalo, NY.

LORD, HARRIET.
Painter, etcher, craftsman and teacher. Born Orange, NJ, March 7, 1879. Pupil of Edmund Tarbell, F. W. Benson, Joseph de Camp, W. L. Lathrop. Member: NAC; NA Women PS; AFA. Died in 1958. Address in 1929, 25 East End Ave., New York, NY; summer, Nantucket, MA.

LORD, JAMES BROWN.
Painter. Born in 1859. He died in 1902.

LORD, PHOEBE GRIFFIN.
(Mrs. P. G. L. Noyes) Born in 1831. Died in 1875. Miniature painter in water color.

LORENZ, RICHARD.
Painter. Born in Germany in 1858. He came to this country as a young man. In 1905 he was awarded the "Osborne prize." He was a member of the Society of Western Artists. Among his works were "A Critical Moment;" "Burial on the Plains;" "Plowing in Saxony." He died in Milwaukee, Wisc., in 1915.

LORENZANI, ARTHUR EMANUEL.
Sculptor and teacher. Born Carrara, Italy, Feb. 12, 1885. Pupil of Reale Academia di Belle Arti, Carrara and Rome. Member: NSS; NY Arch. Lg. Award: $200 prize at International Exp., Parma, Italy. Came to US in 1913. Address in 1929, 232 West 14th St., New York, NY.

LORING, CHARLES GREELEY.
Painter. Born in 1828. He died in 1902.

LORING, FRANCIS WILLIAM.
Painter. Born in Boston, MA, in 1838. He studied in Europe and died in Meran, Austria, in 1905. His painting "The Bridge of Chioggia" is dated 1886, and is owned by the Boston Museum of Fine Arts.

LORING, WILLIAM CUSHING.
Painter and teacher. Born Newton Center, MA, Aug. 10, 1879. Studied in New York, Boston, London and Paris. Member: Boston AC; AFA; Prov. AC. Represented in Brown University; Rhode Island State House; Rhode Island School of Design; Harvard University; and numerous institutions in New York City. Contributor of articles to magazines on subjects related to American Art. Address in 1929, Kirkside, Wayland, Mass.; 687 Boylston St., Boston, MA.

LORNE, NAOMI.
Painter. Born in NYC. Studied: City College of NY; Hunter College and with A.T. Hibbard, George Bridgmann and Frederick J. Waugh. Awards: Audubon Artists, 1944, 1947; Silvermine Guild Artists, 1956; National Assoc. of Women Artists, 1956. Collection: Staten Island Hospital; General Steel Corporation; American Cyanamid Company; Ain-Harod Museum, Israel; Maryknoll Teacher College.

LORRAINE, ALMA ROYER.
Painter and teacher. Born Randolph, OH. Pupil of AIC; Alexandra Harrison; Bouguereau in Paris; Molinari in Rome. Award: Silver medal, Alaska-Yukon-Pacific Exp., Seattle, 1909. Work: "Aqueducts of Claudius," West Chester Seminary. Specialty, oil portraits and studies of animals. Address in 1929, 1617 California Ave., Seattle, Wash.

LORRAINE, HELEN.
Medical illustrator. Born Webster Grove, MO, June 23, 1892. Pupil of Nora Houston, Adele Clark and Max Brodel. Member: Va. Lg. of Fine A and H. Address in 1929, St. Elizabeth's Hospital; h. 3414 Monument Ave., Richmond, VA.

LOS, NAUM MICHEL.
Sculptor and teacher. Born Ukraine, Oct. 19, 1882. Pupil of Paul DuBois, Victor Rousseau. Work: Bust of Oscar Browning, Kings College, Cambridge, MA. Address 1929, 1947 Broadway, NYC.

LOSSING, BENSON JOHN.
Illustrator. Born Feb. 12, 1813 in Beekman, NY. He made numerous drawings for illustrating his "Field Book of the Revolution." He died in Dover Plains, NY, June 3, 1891. Was editor of "Poughkeepsie Casket," and was taught wood engraving by his engraver, J. A. Adams. (See "Biographical Notice" of Lossing, prepared for the Worcester Society of Antiquity in 1892.)

LOTARE, CARL.
Painter. Died in 1924. Painter of American Indian subjects; he also did some mural painting.

LOTHROP, KRISTIN CURTIS.
Sculptor. Born in Tucson, AZ, Feb. 8, 1930. Study: Bennington College; sculpture with George Demetrois, 4 years. Exhibitions: Nat'l. Sculpture Soc., 1967-71; Hudson Valley Art Assn., 1968; Nat'l. Academy of Design, 1968-71; Allied Artists of America, 1969. Awards: Mrs. Louis Bennett Award, Nat'l. Sculpture Soc., 1967; Thomas R. Proctor Award, Nat'l. Academy of Design, 1968; Daniel Chester French Award, 1970. Mem.: New England Sculptors Assn.; Nat'l. Sculpture Soc. Media: Bronze, Wood, Stone. Address in 1982, Manchester, MA.

LOUD, H. C.
Crayon portrait draughtsman who was working in Philadelphia about 1850.

LOUD, MARION V.
Painter, writer, lecturer and teacher. Born Medford, MA, Oct. 6, 1880. Pupil of Denman Ross; Eben Comins; John Wicker; H. H. Clarke; Deborah Kallen; Lawrence Grant. Member: Detroit S. Women P.; SAC. Award: Hon. mention, Detroit Fed. of Women's Clubs, Indp. Show, 1924. Illustrated "A Picnic On a Pyramid," by M. V. Loud. Address in 1929, 2555 Burns Ave.; h. 46 Davenport St., Detroit, MI.

LOUDERBACK, WALT.
Illustrator. Born Valparaiso, IN, in 1887. Pupil of AIC. Member: Salma. C.; NAC; GFLA. Died in 1941. Address in 1929, care of Will Perrin, Hearst's International Magazine, 119 West 40th St.; 266 West 12th St., New York, NY.

LOVE, G.
Engraver. This name as engraver is appended to a frontispiece to Watts' "Divine Songs," published in Philadelphia in 1807 by L. Johnson.

LOVE, G(EORGE) PATERSON.
Painter, illustrator, and etcher. Born Providence, RI, March 28, 1887. Pupil of Edmund C. Tarbell and Frank W. Benson. Member: Boston AC; Copley S.; Providence AC; Providence WCC; AFA. Address in 1929, 270 Boylston St., Boston, Mass.; h. 29 Waterman St., Providence, RI.

LOVEGROVE, STANLEY D.
Painter, illustrator, and etcher. Born East Orange, NJ, Feb. 19, 1881. Pupil of Thomas Anshutz at PAFA. Member: Phila. Sketch C.; Phila. Alliance; Phila. WCC; Phila. Print. C. Address in 1929, Evening Bulletin, City Hall Sq.; h. Phila. Sketch Club, 235 S. Camac St., Philadelphia, PA.

LOVELAND, JOHN W(INTHROP).
Painter and sculptor. Born West Pittston, PA, Oct. 1, 1866. Pupil of Swain Art School, New Bedford, Mass., under Harry Neyland. Member: Wash. SA. Address in 1929, Wardman Park Hotel, Washington, DC; summer, Nantucket, MA.

LOVELL, KATHARINE ADAMS.
Painter. Born New York City. Pupil of Pratt Inst.; W. M. Chase, C. W. Hawthorne, John Carlson. Member: NA Women PS; PBC; Brooklyn SA; Brooklyn PS. Address in 1929, 32 St. Paul's Pl., Brooklyn, NY.

LOVELL, TOM.
Illustrator. Born in NYC in 1909. Received his BFA in 1931 from Syracuse Univ. In 1930 his first illustrations were published in a book entitled Gangster Stories. He has illustrated for all the major magazines and has won two Gold Medals from the S of I, two from the National Cowboy Hall of Fame and the Syracuse Centennial Gold Medal in 1970. His works are owned by the New Britain Museum of American Art, USMC Headquarters and the National Cowboy Hall of Fame in Oklahoma City.

LOVEN, FRANK W.
Painter and illustrator. Born Jersey City, NJ, Oct. 2, 1868. Pupil of Birge Harrison, F. V. Du Mond and John Carlson. Member: Salma. C. Represented in Hoboken Public Library. Address in 1929, 3435 Boulevard, Jersey City, NJ.

LOVETT, ROBERT.
Born 1796 in NYC. According to Poulson's Advertiser, Lovett was an engraver upon metal and stone, located in Philadelphia in 1816-22, inclusive. He was principally engaged in engraving seals and dies. He moved to New York about 1825, but later returned to Philadelphia.

LOVETT, WILLIAM.
Portrait and miniature painter of Boston, MA. Born in 1773. His work was excellent, as shown by his miniature of Rev. John Clarke, at one time owned by the Essex Institute of Salem, MA. He died in 1801.

LOVETT-LORSKI, BORIS.
Sculptor. Born in Russia in 1891. Address in 1926, Layton Art School, Milwaukee.

LOVINS, HENRY.
Painter, craftsman, writer, lecturer and teacher. Born New York City, March 12, 1883. Pupil of Jean Mannheim, William M. Chase, Robert Henri, Edgar L. Hewett. Member: Los Angeles PS; International Artists C. and Artland C., Los Angeles. Work: Maya Indian murals and windows, San Diego Museum, San Diego, CA; "City of the Sun" also Maya Priests and figure glyphs, Santa Fe Museum, Santa Fe, NM; "The Miracle Man," Southwest Museum, Los Angeles; Aztec, Mayan, American Indian, Chinese, Egyptian, Persian murals and decorations, Whitley Park Country Club, Hollywood; marine decorations and windows, Sea Breeze Beach Club, Santa Monica, CA. Address in 1929, Hollywood, CA; h. 1752 South Wooster St., Los Angeles, CA; summer, Carmel-by-the-Sea, CA.

LOW, MARY FAIRCHILD.
(Mrs. Will H. Low). Painter. Born New Haven, CT, Aug. 11, 1858. Pupil of St. Louis School of Fine Arts; Carolus-Duran and Julian Academy in Paris. Member: SAA 1896; ANA, 1906; International Woman's AC, London; Assoc. Soc. Nat. des Beaux Arts. Awards: Paris, three years' scholarship from St. Louis School of Fine Arts; medal, Columbian Exp., Chicago, 1893; bronze medal, Paris Exp., 1900; bronze medal, Pan-Am. Exp., Buffalo, 1901; gold medal, Dresden, 1902; Julia Shaw prize, SAA, 1902; gold medal, Normandy Exp., Rouen, 1903; gold medal, Marseilles, 1905.

Represented in Museum at Rouen, France; Union League Club, Chicago; City Art Museum, St. Louis; Museum of Vernon, France; Art Inst. of Chicago. Died May 23, 1946. Address in 1929, Lawrence Park, Bronxville, NY.

LOW, WILL H(ICOK).
Painter, illustrator, teacher, writer, and lecturer. Born Albany, NY, May 31, 1853. Pupil of Ecole des Beaux-Arts, under Gerome, and of Carolus-Duran in Paris. Member: ANA 1888, NA 1890; SAA 1878; Mural P.; NY Arch. Lg. 1889; Century Assoc.; Lotos C.; Nat. Inst. AL. Member: International Jury of Awards, St. Louis Exp., 1904. Awards: Silver medal for drawing, Paris Exp., 1889; medal, Columbian Exp., Chicago, 1893; Lotos Club Fund, NAD 1895; silver medal, Pan-Am. Exp., Buffalo, 1901. Work: "The Orange Vender" and 60 drawings, Art Inst., Chicago; "Christmas Morn," National Gallery, Washington; "Aurora," Metropolitan Museum, New York, NY; mural decorations, ceiling of reception room and ballroom, Waldorf-Astoria Hotel, New York; panels in Essex Co. Court House, Newark, NJ; Luzerne Co. Court House, Wilkes-Barre, PA; Federal Bldg., Cleveland; St. Paul's P.E. Church, Albany, NY; "The Sylvan Year," Art Museum, Montclair, NJ; 32 panels in State Education Bldg., Albany, NY; Frieze in Legislative Library, NY State Capitol; decorative painting, "Victory 1918," Columbia Univ. Author: "A Chronicle of Friendship," "A Painter's Progress." Delivered Scammon course of lectures, AIC 1910. Died in 1932. Address in 1929, Lawrence Park, Bronxville, NY.

LOWDON, ESLIE MOTZ.
Miniature painter. Born Waco, TX. Pupil of ASL of NY; Am. School of Min. P. Member: NA Women PS; SSAL. Award: Balch prize ($200) and popular vote award, Los Angeles Museum, 1927. Address in 1929, 424 East 57th St., New York, NY.

LOWE, ALICE LESZINSKA.
See Mrs. H. G. Ferguson.

LOWE, R.
This man was working as a commercial engraver on copper in 1851, his office being at 104 Broadway, NY. He engraved diplomas, etc.

LOWELL, NAT.
Etcher, lecturer and teacher. Born in Riga, Latvia, Nov. 3, 1880. Pupil of Carrol Beckwith, Siddons Mowbray. Represented by etchings in the Metropolitan Museum of Art, New York; New York Public Library. Address in 1929, Monsey, NY.

LOWELL, ORSON BYRON.
Illustrator and cartoonist. Born Wyoming, IA, Dec. 22, 1871. Pupil of Vanderpoel and Grover at AIC, 1887-1893 Member: SI, 1901; GFLA; New Rochelle AA. Work: Illustrations in a number of American periodicals; original drawings in Cincinnati Museum; La Crosse (Wis.) AA; Maryland Institute, Baltimore; Mechanics' Institute, Rochester. Best known for his social cartoons, drawings, paintings and posters. Illustrated The Court of Boyville, W.A. White (Doubleday, 1899), and Love in Old Clothes, H. C. Brunner (Scribner's, 1896). Died in 1956. Address in 1929, Astor Trust Bldg., 5th Ave. and 42nd St., New York; h. Rochelle Park, New Rochelle, NY; summer, Stockbridge, MA.

LOWELL, SHELLEY.
Painter and sculptor. Born in 1946. Studied: Pratt Institute, Brooklyn, NY. Exhibitions: The Erotic Art Gal., NYC; International Mus. of Erotic Art, San Fran., CA; The Bronx Museum of Art, Bronx, NY 1975. In the collection of Mem. Sloan-Kettering Cancer Center, NYC.

LOWENGRUND, MARGARET.
Painter and etcher. Born Philadelphia, PA. Pupil of Joseph Pennell. Member: ASL of NY. Died in 1957. Address in 1929, 19 East 59th St., New York, NY.

LOWENHEIM, F(REDERICK).
Illustrator. Born Berlin, Germany. Pupil of Kunst-Schule, Berlin; AIC. Member: SI, 1911; Salma. C., 1911; GFLA; New Rochelle AA; AFA.

Address in 1929, 38 Premium River Road, Hazelhurst, New Rochelle, NY.

LOWERY, ROBERT S.
Illustrator. Born in Birmingham, AL, in 1950. Received a scholarship to the ASL to study under Steven Kidd and Leslie Willett. He began his career as a sports artist with a pen and ink drawing of Muhammand Ali for The New York Times. Madison Square Garden has subsequently commissioned him to produce fight posters and his works have appeared in Ring Magazine as well as in NFL and NBA stories for The New York Times. His work is in the collections at the NY Jazz Museum, Madison Square Garden and ASL.

LOWNES, CALEB.
Engraver. The Pennsylvania Magazine, Philadelphia, 1775, contains a fairly well-engraved line plate of a "New Plan of Boston Harbour," signed C. Lownes, Sculp. This Caleb Lownes was a die-sinker and sealcutter in business in Philadelphia, and was a prominent citizen of that city. In 1779, according to the Minutes of the Supreme Executive Council, he cut a seal for the Pennsylvania Board of Admiralty.

LOWREY, ROSALIE.
Painter and illustrator. Born Dayton, February 27, 1893. Pupil of ASL of NY; Dayton AI; PAFA. Member: Ohio WCS. Work: "Portrait of Leola Clark," Patterson School, Dayton; "Portrait of Grace Greene," Dayton Junior Teachers' College, Dayton. Illustrated "Our Little Folks" (U. B. Publishing House). Address in 1929, 1035 Harvard Blvd., Dayton, OH.

LOZOWICK, LOUIS.
Painter, illustrator, etcher, writer, and lecturer. Born Russia, January, 1892. Pupil of NAD. Author of "Modern Russian Art." Illustrations in "Nation," "Theatre Arts Monthly," "Herald-Tribune." Died in 1973. Address in 1929, 792 Lexington Ave., New York, NY.

LUCAS, ALBERT P(IKE).
Painter and sculptor. Born Jersey City, NJ, in 1862. Pupil of Hebert, Boulanger, Dagnan-Bouveret and Courtois in Paris. Member: NA, 1927; Soc. Nat. des Beaux-Arts, Paris; NAC; Lotos C.; Allied AA; Salma. C.; NSS; Fine Arts Fed. of NY; SPNY. Awards: Hon. mention, Paris Exp., 1900; bronze medal, Pan-Am. Exp., Buffalo, 1901. Work: "October Breezes," National Gal., Wash.; "Ecstasy," marble bust, Met. Mus. NY. Died in 1945. Address in 1929, 1947 Broadway, NYC.

LUCAS, JEAN W(ILLIAMS).
Painter and teacher. Born Hagerstown, MD, Aug. 5, 1873. Pupil of Henri, Daingerfield and Whittemore. Member: NA Women PS; Pa. S. Min. P. Award: Honorable mention for miniature, P.-P. Exp., San Francisco, 1915. Address in 1929, Penn Hall School, Chambersburg, PA; 20 Broadway, Hagerstown, MD.

LUCE, LAURA H.
Landscape painter, teacher, and lecturer. Born Salem, NY, June 19, 1845. Pupil of A. H. Wyant, C. B. Coman and H. B. Snell in New York. Member: NA Women PS. Address in 1929, 120 East Main St., Titusville, PA.

LUCE, LEONARD E.
Painter and illustrator. Born Ashtabula, OH, Sept. 27, 1893. Pupil of Gottwald, Keller and DuMond. Member: Cleveland SA. Address in 1929, Keith Bldg., Euclid at 17th St.; h. 3291 Yorkshire Road, Cleveland, OH.

LUCE, MARIE HUXFORD (Mrs).
Painter. Born Skaneateles, NY. Pupil of J. S. H. Keever in Holland; Mr. and Mrs. Charles H. Woodbury in Boston. Member: NYWCC; AFA. Address in 1929, Viale Duca di Genova, 36, Florence, Italy; Skaneateles, NY.

LUCE, MOLLY.
(Mrs. Alan Burroughs). Painter. Born Pittsburgh, PA, Dec. 18, 1896. Pupil of Kenneth Hayes Miller. Member: NYS Women A; ASL of NY. Died before 1940. Address in 1929, 27 Wellington Lane, Belmont, MA.

LUCHTEMEYER, EDWARD A.
Painter and illustrator. Born St. Louis, MO, Nov. 19, 1887. Self-taught. Member: St. Louis AL; St. Louis AG; Oakland AL. Represented in all branch libraries in St. Louis; also St. Louis Art League. Address in 1929, 817 Newport Ave., Webster Groves, MO.

LUCIONI, LUIGI.
Painter and etcher. Born Malnate, Italy, Nov. 4, 1900. Pupil of William Starkweather. Member: Allied AA; Brooklyn SE. Awards: Bronze medal, L. C. Tiffany Foundation, New York, 1928; medal of honor, Allied Artists of America, New York, 1929. Work: "Interior," High Museum, Atlanta, GA. Address in 1929, 64 Washington Sq., South, New York, NY; h. 403 New York Ave., Union City, NJ.

LUDEKENS, FRED.
Illustrator. Born in Huoneme, CA, in 1900. Grew up in Canada and studied art briefly in Calif. He began as an artist for a San Fran. ad agency and went on to become an art director for Lord and Thomas. In 1931 he came to NY and launched a second career as an editorial illustrator for the major magazines, among them The Saturday Evening Post. His illustrations of Western towns were particularly popular, as well as his more recent science fiction work. He headed the FAS in the 1960's while holding a creative position at Foote, Cone and Belding.

LUDOVICI, ALICE E.
Painter. Born Dresden, Germany, Nov. 7, 1872. Pupil of Julius Ludovici in NY; studied in Europe. Member: CA S. Min. P.; AFA. Awards: Silver medal for miniatures, Alaska-Yukon-Pacific Exp., Seattle, 1909; gold medal for miniatures, Calif. S. Min. P., 1914; gold medal, Pan-Calif. Exp., San Diego, 1915, for miniatures. Specialty, pastel portraits and miniatures on ivory. Address in 1929, 167 North Orange Grove Ave., Pasadena, Calif.

LUFKIN, LEE.
See Mrs. Wm. J. Kaula.

LUGANO, INES SOMENZINI.
Painter. Born in Verretto, Pavia, Italy. Studied: Academy of Fine Arts, Pavia, Italy; and with Romeo Borgognoni. Known as a miniature and portrait painter. Awards: National Exhibition, Milano, Italy; CA Society of Miniature Painters, 1935; New Orleans Art Assoc., 1939. Collections: Tulane Univ.; Delgado Museum of Art.

LUINI, COSTANZO.
Sculptor and craftsman. Born Milan, Italy, Aug. 31, 1886. Pupil of Aitken and MacCartan. Member: NY Arch. Lg.; AFA; Boston SAC; AL of Nassau Co. Works: Medals, Walter Scott, T. Edison, T. Vail, Soc. des Femmes de France a NY; Gen. Pershing; Wall Tablet for US Naval Academy. Address in 1929, 4218-78th St., Elmhurst, LI, NY.

LUKEMAN, (HENRY) AUGUSTUS.
Sculptor. Born Richmond, VA, Jan. 28, 1872. Pupil of Launt Thompson and D. C. French in NY; Ecole des Beaux-Arts in Paris, under Falguiere. Member: ANA 1909; NY Arch. Lg. 1898; NSS 1898. Award: Bronze medal, St. Louis Exp., 1904. Work: "McKinley," Adams, MA, and Dayton, OH; "Manu," Appellate Court, NY; four figures for Royal Bank Bldg., Montreal; four figures. Brooklyn Institute Museum; Columbus Customs House; "Prof. Joseph Henry," Princeton Univ.; "Kit Carson," Trinidad, CO; Straus Mem., NY, 1915; US Grant mem., San Diego, CA; Soldiers' monument, Somerville, MA; statue, "Franklin Pierce," Concord, NH; "Women of the Confederacy," monument, Raleigh, NC; "Gen. Wm. Shepard," Westfield, MA; "Honor Roll," Prospect Park, Brooklyn, NY; "Soldiers' Memorial," Red Hook Park, Brooklyn, NY; Equestrian Statue, Francis Asbury, WA; Francis Asbury, Drew Seminary, Madison, NJ; General Gregg, Reading, PA; War Memorial, Pittsfield, MA; Masonic War Memorial, Elizabeth, PA; War Memorial, Wilmington, DE; Statues of Sen. James George and Jefferson Davis for Statuary Hall, Capitol, Washington; Stone Mountain Confederate Memorial, GA. Address in 1929, 160 West 86th St., New York, NY; summer, Stockbridge, MA.

LUKIN, SVEN.
Painter. Born Feb. 14, 1934 in Riga, Latvia. Studied architecture at U. of Penn. Living in NYC. Awarded Guggenheim (1966). Exhibited at Nexus Gallery (Boston), 1959; Betty Parsons Gal., Martha Jackson Gal., Whitney Mus., Guggenheim Mus. (all in NYC); Dwan Gal. (LA). In collections of LA County Mus.; Albright-Knox Gallery, Buffalo, NY; U. of Texas; Allentown (PA) Art Mus.; and Larry Aldrich Mus. (Ridgefield, CT).

LUKITS, THEO(DORE) N(IKOLAI).
Painter and sculptor. Member; Inter. AC, Los Angeles; Am. APL. Awards: Brand Memorial Prize, 1918, and Bryan Lathrop scholarship, 1919, K. A. Buehr prize, 1917, H. Walcott prize, 1917, G. W. Eggers prize, and hon. mention, 1919, AIC. Restored masterpiece, (El Greco) 1925 at the Santa Barbara, CA, Mission. Address in 1929, 121 S. Normandie Ave., Los Angeles, CA.

LUKS, GEORGE (BENJAMIN).
Painter. Born Williamsport, PA, August 13, 1867. Pupil of PAFA and Dusseldorf Academy; studied in Paris and London. Member: Port. P.; Am. PS; NYWCC; Boston AC. Awards: Fourth W. A. Clark prize ($500), and Corcoran hon. mention, 1916; Hudnut prize, NYWCC, 1916; Temple gold medal, PAFA, 1918; Logan Medal, AIC, 1920 and 1926; Locust Club gold medal, Phila., 1927. Represented in Metropolitan Museum, NY; Delgado Museum, New Orleans; Milwaukee Art Institute; Detroit Art Institute; Cleveland Museum; Harrison Gallery, Los Angeles; Phillips Memorial Gallery, Washington, DC; New York Public Library; Barnes Museum, Philadelphia; Library, and murals for Neco Allen Hotel, Pottsville, PA. War Correspondent in Cuba, 1895-96. Died October 30, 1933 in NYC. Address in 1929, 141 East 57th St.; 693 Fifth Ave., NYC.

LUM, BERTHA.
Painter and etcher. Born in Iowa. Pupil of AIC; Frank Holme and Anna Weston. Member: Boston SAC; Calif. SE; Asiatic Soc. of Japan;

Alumni AIC; CA PM. Award: Silver medal, P.-P. Exp., San. F., 1915. Specialty, wood block prints. Address in 1929, 136 St. Anne Alley, Chinatown; h. 3665 Washington St., San Francisco, CA; 44 Chiang Tsa, Hu Tang, Peking, China.

LUMIS, HARRIET R(ANDALL).
(Mrs. Fred W. Lumis). Painter. Born Salem, CT, May 29, 1870. Pupil of Willis S. Adams; Leonard Ochtman; NY Summer School of Art; Hugh Breckenridge; E. P. Hayden. Member: CT AFA; Springfield Art Lg.; Phila. Alliance; NA Women PS; Gloucester SA. Award: Hon. mention, CT AFA, 1925. Work: "Autumn Woodland," Springfield Art Museum, Springfield, MA; "Spring in New England," Paseo High School, Kansas City, MO. Died in 1953. Address in 1929, 28 Bedford Road, Springfield, MA.

LUMSDON, CHRISTINE MARIE VOSS.
Painter, writer, lecturer, and teacher. Born Brooklyn, NY. Pupil of Carolus-Duran, Henry Mosler, Childe Hassam and George de Forest Brush. Member: NA Women PS; NAD (life); S. Indp. A.; Brooklyn Inst. Art and Science. Award: Salon, Paris, 1904. Work: "Ideal Head of Our Lord," exhibited and reproduced AAA, over 1700 copies sold. Author, "La Belle Feroniere," copyright drama. Lecturer on art subjects. Died in 1937. Address in 1929, Carnegie Studios, 154 West 57th St., New York, NY.

LUND, BELLE JENKS.
Painter. Born Alexandria, SD, Aug. 22, 1879. Pupil of F. F. Fursman, E. A. Rupprecht, E. Cameron and AIC. Member: Indiana AC; Hoosier Salon; Alumni, AIC. Work: "Dune Country," Kappa Sigma House, LaFayette, IN; "Lily Pond," Elk's Club, Hammond, IN; "Norwegian Landscape," Lake-Hills Country Club, Lake Co., IN. Address in 1929, 160 Waltham St., Hammond, IN.

LUND, THEODORE F.
Miniature painter. Flourished in NY, 1841-44. Exhibited 1836-7 under names H. Lund and F. Lund.

LUNDBERG, A. F.
Painter. Exhibited "Lawn Party" at the PAFA, Philadelphia, 1914. Address in 1926, 48 North Grant Ave., Columbus, OH.

LUNDBORG, FLORENCE.
Painter and illustrator. Born San Francisco, CA. Studied at Mark Hopkins Inst. of Art, and in Paris and Italy. Member: NA Women PS; San F. AA; Gamut C. Awards: Gold medal, San F., AA; bronze medal, P.-P. Exp., San F. 1915. Work: Mural decorations for CA bldg. at Panama-Pacific Exposition; "Queen of Hearts," at Henriettes, Paris; Wadleigh High School, NYC. Illustrated "Rubaiyat," "Yosemite Legends," "Honey Bee," "Odes and Sonnets," etc. Died in 1949. Address in 1929, 12 East Eighth St., New York, NY.

LUNDEBERG, HELEN.
Painter. Born June 24, 1908 in Chicago. Studied with Lorser Feitelson, whom she married. Exhibited at Pasadena Art Mus. (1953); Long Beach Mus. of Art; Scripps College; MOMA; Carnegie I.; Brooklyn Mus.; Denver Art Mus.; U. of Illinois; Seattle Art Mus.; S.F. Mus. of Fine Art; Mus. of Art in Sao Paulo, Brazil. In collections of L.A. County Mus., Santa Barbara Mus. and Chaffer C. (all in CA); Hershhorn Mus. and Nat. C. of Fine Arts (both in Wash., DC); S. F. Mus. of Art.

LUNDGREN, MARTIN.
Mural painter. Born in Sweden in 1871. Pupil of AIC, and Louis Betts. Member: Palette and Chisel C.; Chicago NJSA. Address in 1929, 5242 Bernard St., Chicago, IL.

LUNDIN, EMELIA A.
Painter. Born Stockholm, Sweden, Jan. 16, 1884. Pupil of Paul Gustin, F. Tadema. Member: Seattle Fine Arts Soc. Address in 1929, 8741 Dayton Ave., Seattle, WA.

LUNDQUIST, EINAR.
Painter. Born Shovde, Sweden, Aug. 4, 1901. Pupil of Daniel Garber; AIC. Member: Amer. Artists Prof. Lg.; Swedish-American AA. Awards: First prize for water color,

Swedish-American AA, Chicago, 1929; 1st prize for water color, Swedish Club, Chicago, 1929. Address in 1929, 1512 Sixth St., Rockford, IL.

LUNGREN, FERDINAND HARVEY.
Painter. Born in Toledo, OH, in 1857. He came to NY to study art at an early age. His best known painting was "Shadows on the Snow." He also did many illustrations for magazines. Died in 1932.

LUNGREN, FERNAND.
Painter and illustrator. Born Maryland, Nov. 13, 1859. Member: Santa Barbara AL; Community AA, (director); AFA. Specialty, the desert. Address in 1929, Mission Canyon Road, Santa Barbara, CA.

LUPTON, FRANCES PLATT TOWNSEND.
According to Dunlap, in his "History of the Arts," a Mrs. Lupton modelled and presented a bust of Governor Throop to the National Academy of Design, and was a member of the NA.

LUQUIENS, ELIZABETH KOLL.
Painter. Born Salem, Ohio, Jan. 19, 1878. Pupil of Albert G. Thompson; Delecluse and Mucha in Paris. Member: New Haven Paint and Clay C.; CT AFA. Address in 1929, 189 East Rock Road, New Haven, CT; summer, Waterville, NH.

LUQUIENS, HUC MAZELET.
Painter and etcher. Born Auburndale, MA, June 30, 1881. Pupil of Bonnat and Merson in Paris. Member: Chicago SE; CT AFA; New Haven PCC; CA SE; Honolulu AA. Award: Winchester fellowship, Yale Art School, 1904; first prize, New Haven PCC, 1925. Represented by etchings in the New York Public Library; National Museum, Washington, DC; Yale School of the Fine Arts Museum, New Haven, CT; Academy of Arts, Honolulu. Instructor of art, University of HI. Died in 1961. Address in 1929, 1646 Bingham St., Honolulu, HI.

LUSH, VIVIAN.
Sculptor. Born in NYC in 1911. Studied: Leonardo da Vinci Art School; National Academy of Design; Art Students League; also with Attilio Piccirilli, Charles Keck,

and Robert Aitken. Award: National Assoc. of Women Artists. Collections: Riverside Church, NY; Rockefeller Center, NY; Port Richmond High School; Unity Hospital, Brooklyn, NY; Roosevelt High School; Bronx, NY; Children's Wing, Public Library, Trinidad, British West Indies.

LUTHER, JESSIE.
Painter, sculptor, craftsman, writer, lecturer, and teacher. Born Providence, RI, Nov. 3, 1860. Pupil of S. R. Burleigh; Paul Bartlett and Raphael Collin in Paris. Member: Providence AC and Boston SAC; Providence HC; Phila. ACG; Boston Weavers Guild. Address in 1929, 2098 Pawtucket Ave., East Providence, RI; h. Box 546, Providence, RI.

LUX, GWEN.
(Gwen Lux Creighton). Sculptor. Born in Chicago, IL. Studied: MD Institute of Art; Boston Museum of Fine Arts School, in Paris; and with Ivan Mestrovic, Yugoslavia. Awards: Guggenheim fellowship, 1933; Detroit Institute of Art, 1945, 1956; National Lithograph prize, 1947; National Assoc. of Women Artists, 1947; Audubon Artists, 1954. Collections: Assoc. of American Artists; Radio City, NY; McGraw-Hill Bldg., Chicago; Trustees Sys. Svc., Chicago; Univ. of AR; Victoria Theatre, NY; Bristol Tenn. Hospital; Steamship "United States;" Texas Petroleum Club, Dallas; Northland Shopping Center, Detroit; General Wingate School, Brooklyn; General Motors Research Center, Detroit; Socony Building, NYC; R. H. Macy-Roosevelt Field, NY; Public School 19, NYC; Aviation Trades High School, Long Island, NY; Country Day School, Lake Placid, NY. Address in 1980, 4340 Pahoa Ave., Honolulu, HI.

LUZAK, DENNIS.
Illustrator. Born in Chicago in 1939. Received his BFA from the Univ. of Notre Dame in 1961. He began his career as a designer for Chrysler and Ford Motor Co., but in 1969 joined the staff of Jack O'Grady Studios in Chicago. Later he moved to NY where his illustrations have appeared in major magazines and books as well as in the S of I Annual Exhibition.

LYBRAND, JACOB.
Engraver. About 1820, J. Lybrand neatly engraved in line a view of the Gilpin paper-mill, on Brandywine Creek, PA, after a drawing by B. K. Fox. Possibly a little earlier than this he was engraving in connection with R. Campbell, of Philadelphia; these latter plates were also in line, but very simple in character.

LYMAN, JOSEPH.
Painter. Born in Ravenna, OH, on July 17, 1843. He visited Europe for study, and on his return to New York was elected an Associate Member of the National Academy of Design (1866). His most important paintings are "Summer Night," "Moonlight," "Sunset on the Maine Coast," and "Waiting for the Tide." He died Mar. 5, 1913 in Wallingford CT.

LYMAN, MARY ELIZABETH.
Painter. Born Middlefield, CT, Dec. 2, 1850. Pupil of Bail, Yale School of Fine Arts, and John H. Niemeyer. Member: New Haven PCC. Address in 1929, Middlefield, CT.

LYMAN, SYLVESTER S.
Born in Easthampton, MA, Sept. 24, 1813. He first painted portraits, and later landscapes. He worked largely in Hartford, CT.

LYNCH, ANNA.
Miniature painter. Born Elgin, IL. Pupil of AIC; Bouguereau, Simon, Cottet and Mme. Debillemont in Paris. Member: Alumni AIC; Chicago PS; PA S. Min. P.; Chicago City Commission for Public Art; Paris A. Woman's AA; Chicago AC; Chicago S. Min. P.; Cordon C; Chicago Gal. A. Awards: Miniature prize, Chicago AC; bronze medal, P.-P. Exp., San F., 1915; hon. men., AIC; award of merit, Chicago Art Inst. Alumni; purchase prize, Arche Club; three purchase prizes, Chicago Gallery A., 1927. Work: Portrait of Judge Joseph E. Gary, Chicago Court House; portrait of Judge Arba E. Waterman, Memorial Hall, Chicago; two paintings, City

Commission, Chicago. Address in
1929, 9 Tree Studio Bldg., Chicago,
IL; h. 54 South Crystal St., Elgin,
IL.

LYNCH, MARY BRITTEN.
Painter. Born in Pruden, KY, on
Sept. 30, 1933. Studied: Univ. of
Tenn. at Chattanooga. Awards:
N.A.W.A. Annual, National Academy
Galleries, NYC; Tenn. All-State,
Nashville, TN; 4th Annual Print and
Drawing Exhibitions, AR Art Center,
Little Rock. She has exhibited
widely in the Southeastern US and
has been very active in the TN
Watercolor Society. Media:
Acrylic and watercolor. Address in
1980, 1505 Woodnymph Trail, Lookout
Mountain, TN.

LYNCH, VIRGINIA.
Painter, writer, lecturer, and
teacher. Born New York City.
Pupil of Julius Schledorn; ASL of
NY; studied in China and Japan.
Member: NAC; NA Women PS; C. L.
Wolfe AC. Award: Watercolor
prize, C. L. Wolfe AC, 1922.
Instructor, Columbia University.
Address in 1929, 270 East 142nd
St., New York, NY.

LYND, J. NORMAN.
Illustrator. Born Northwood, Logan
Co., OH, Nov. 15, 1878. Member:
SI, 1913; GFLA. Address in 1929,
300 Denton Ave., Lynbrook, LI, NY.

LYNN, MRS. KATHARINE N.
Painter. Born Philadelphia, May
13, 1875. Pupil of Penn. School of
Indus. Art; ASL of NY; Colarossi
School; Constant and Mme. Richard
in Paris. Member: NA Women PS;
Phila. Alliance; PA School of
Indus. Art Alumni; Wash. WCC; Wash.
AC. Address in 1929, Nantucket,
MA.

LYON, JEANNETTE AGNEW.
(Mrs. William T. Lyon). Landscape
painter. Born Pittsburgh, PA, Dec.
3, 1862. Pupil of Robert C. Minor
of New York; Mesdag at the Hague;
Constant in Paris. Member:
Cleveland Woman's AC; North Shore
AA. Address in 1929, 2330 Euclid
Blvd., Cleveland, OH.

M. (J.) AE.
14 Sculp. 1758. This early American engraver can not be identified by the compiler. The only evidence of his existence is a small quarto portrait of Frederick III of Prussia, "folded and inserted" in the NY Almanac for 1759; NY: Printed and Sold by Hugh Gaine at the Bible and Crown in Hanover Square. This print may be described as follows: Exceedingly rude line work with an attempt at stipple in the face. Vignette; half length in uniform, standing to right, face front, right hand on hip, left hand on hilt of sword resting on point; muzzle of cannon in right base. Inscription: "J.M. AE 14 Sculpt 1758 Frederick the Third The Great King of Prussia, Sold by J. Turner in Arch Street, Philadelphia."

MA-PE-WE, (VALINO FHIJI).
Painter. Pueblo Indian of the Pueblo Zia, Jenez Valley, NM. Born 1900. Represented in the Santa Fe Museum, Santa Fe, NM. Address in 1929, care of Mrs. Van Stone, Santa FE, NM.

MAAS, JACOB.
Engraver. Born 1800 in PA. The only mention found of Jacob Maas is in connection with the engraving and sale of "Lafayette and Washington Badges" in 1824. The Philadelphia newspapers of that year contain conditions of sale of "their plates"; and this notice is signed jointly by "J. L. Frederick and Jacob Maas, Engravers."

MACARAY, LAWRENCE RICHARD.
Painter. Born in Elsinore, CA, May 8, 1921. Study: Whittier College; Calif. State Univ., Long Beach. Work: Bowers Museum, Santa Clara, CA; Thompson Industries, Los Angeles; Bertiand Russell Peace Foundation, Nottingham, Eng.; others. Exhibitions: Annual Palos Verdes; Mus of Art; All Calif. Art Exhib., San Bernadino; Bertand Russell Cent., Nottingham, Eng.; etc. Awards: So. Calif. Expo. Prize, Del Mar; others. Media: Oil. Address in 1982, 628 N. Buttonwood St., Anaheim, CA.

MaCARTNEY, CATHERINE (NAOMI).
Painter and teacher. Born Des Moines, IA. Pupil of Charles A. Cumming, Richard Miller, Henry Hunt Clark; Colarossi Academy, Paris. Member: IA AG (Pres.); NA Women PS; College AA; L.C. Tiffany Foundation. Awards: Second, prize, Des Moines Women's Club, 1912; first prize, Des Moines Women's Club, 1914; gold medal for design, Iowa State Fair, 1916; gold medal for painting, Iowa State Fair, 1921. Work: "Late Summer," F. L. Owen Collection Des Moines, IA. Address in 1929, 318 Physics Hall; H. Burkley Place, Iowa City, Iowa.

MACAULAY, DAVID ALEXANDER.
Illustrator and designer. Born in Burton on Trent, Eng., Dec. 2, 1946. Study: RI Sch. of Design, B. Archit. Work: Cooper Hewitt Mus., NYC. Exhib.: Children's Book Illus., Mus. of Contemp. Art, Houston, TX, 1975; SPACE Gallery of Architecture, NYC, 1976; Annual Int'l. Exhib. of Children's Book Illus., Bologna, Italy, 1976 & 1977; 200 years of Am. Illus., Mus. of Hist. Soc. of NY, 1977; Children's Book Art, Monterey (CA) Penninsula Mus. of Art, & Triton Mus. of Art, Santa Clara, 1978-79. Awards: First runner-up, Caldecott Medal, Am. Library Assn., 1974-78; Deutscher Jugendbuchpreis, Germany, 1975; Medal, Am. Inst. of Archit., 1978. Media: Pen and ink. Publ.: Numerous. Address in 1982, 27 Rhode Island Ave., Providence, RI.

MaCAULEY, CHARLES RAYMOND.
Illustrator. Born in Canton, Ohio, in 1871. Executed cartoons and illustrations in the leading publications. Address in 1926, 82 West 12th Street, NY. Died in 1934.

MacCAMERON, ROBERT LEE.
Painter. Born in Chicago, Jan. 14, 1866; died in N.Y., Dec. 29, 1912. Figure and portrait painter. Pupil of Gerome and Collin in Paris. Awards: Hon. mention, Paris Salon, 1904; Third Class medal, Paris Salon, 1908; Legion of Honor, 1912. Elected Associate of the NA, 1910. Member: Paris Soc. of Amer. Ptrs.; International Society of Painters, Sculptors and Gravers, London;

National Society of Portrait Painters, NY Represented by "Groupe D'Amis," painted 1907, and "The Daughter's Return," at the Metropolitan Museum in NY.

MacCHESNEY, CLARA TAGGART.
Painter. Born in Brownsville, CA. Pupil of Virgil Williams, San Francisco; H. S. Mowbray and J. C. Beckwith of NY; also of Courtois and Girardot at Colarossi School, Paris, France. Exhibited, Paris Salon, 1896, 1898; Paris Exposition, 1900; bronze medal, Buffalo Exposition, 1901; St. Louis Exposition, 1904. Member: NY Water Color Club. Died in 1938. Address in 1926, 15 W. 67th Street, New York.

MacCORD, CHARLES WILLIAM.
Painter. Born in Allegheny City, PA, Feb. 3, 1852. Self taught. Work: "Light on the Hills," Bridgeport Public Library; "The Last Ray," Sea Side Club, Bridgeport. He died Jan. 7, 1923, in Bridgeport, CT.

MacCORD, MARY NICHOLENA.
Painter. Born Bridgeport, CT. Member: NAC; NA Women PS; AWCS; CT. AFA; NYWCC; New Haven PCC; NY Soc. Painters; Wash. WCC; Allied AA; AFA. Award: Harriet Brooks Jones prize, Balto. WCC, 1923. Exhibited at PAFA in 1925. Address in 1929, 839 West End Ave., New York, NY.

MacDERMOTT, STEWART SINCLAIR.
Painter and etcher. Born New York, July 14, 1889. Pupil of ASL of NY; Beaux Arts Inst. of Design, NY; Ecole des Beaux Arts, Fontainebleau, France. Member: Alliance. Represented in print collection of the Metropolitan Museum of Art. Address in 1929, 51 West 10th Street, h. 323 West 84th Street, New York, NY.

MacDONALD, FRANK E.
Painter and illustrator. Born Kansas City, Feb. 8, 1896. Pupil of Roland Thomas, G. V. Millett, J. D. Patrick. Member: Kansas City AG. Address in 1929, 4420 Norledge Place, Kansas City, MO.

MacDONALD, HAROLD L.
Born in Manitowoc, WI, in 1861. He was a pupil of Boulanger and of Lefebvre in Paris. For many years he resided in Washington, D.C., where he maintained a high standard as a portrait painter; Work: Portrait of William Griffith, Capitol, Washington, D.C.

MacDONALD, JAMES WILSON ALEXANDER.
Sculptor. Born Aug. 25, 1824 in Steubenville, OH. He started his art studies in 1840, and in 1849 went to NY. Among his busts are those of John Van Buren and Charles O'Connor. He was the possessor of Houdon's original model of Washington from which he made several bronze busts. He also painted a few portraits and landscapes. Died Aug. 14, 1908 in Yonkers, NY.

MacDONALL, ANGUS.
Painter and illustrator. Born in St. Louis in 1876. Illustrator and cartoonist for: Life; Scribner's; American; Red Cross Magazine; Ladies' Home Journal; Harper's. Address in 1926, Westport, CT.

MacDOWELL, SUSAN HANNAH.
Painter. Born in Philadelphia in 1851. Student at PAFA. Pupil of Prof. C. Schussele and of Thomas Eakins. Her paintings are largely portraits, and are generally owned in Philadelphia where her professional life was spent.

MacEWEN, WALTER.
Painter. Born in Chicago in 1860. Genre painter. Pupil of Cormon and of Robert-Fleury in Paris. Awards: Honorable mention, Paris Salon, 1886; silver medal, Paris Expo, 1889; first class gold medal, Berlin, 1891; Lippincott prize, Penna. Academy of The Fine Arts, 1902; Harris prize, Chicago, 1902; gold medal, St. Louis Expo., 1904; first medal, Liege Expo., 1905. Elected Associate of Nat. Acad., 1903. Member: Paris Society of American Painters; National Inst. of Arts and Letters. Represented by "An Ancestor" at the Corcoran Art Gallery, Washington, D.C. Address in 1926, Care of Century Association, 7 West 43 Street, New York City. Died in 1943.

MacFARLAN, CHRISTINA.
Painter. Born in Philadelphia. Pupil of Chase and Breckenridge at Penna. Academy of Fine Arts. Address in 1926, Studio, 1805 Chestnut Street, Philadelphia, PA.

MacFARLANE, MRS. SCOTT B.
Illustrator. Born Santa Barbara, CA, Sept. 23, 1895. Pupil of Dante Ricci in Rome; Arthur Musgrave. Address in 1929, 3255 N. Street, Washington, D.C.

MacGILVARY, NORWOOD HODGE.
Painter. Born in Bangkok, Thailand, Nov. 14, 1874. Pupil of Davidson College; Mark Hopkins Inst., San Francisco; Myron Barlow; Laurens in Paris. Member: NYWCC; AWCS; Allied AA; Providence AC; NY Arch. Lg.; Salma. C.; Pitts. Arch Lg. Awards: Silver medals, Panama-Pacific Exp., San Francisco, 1915. Work: "Twilight After Rain," National Gallery of Art, Washington, D.C. Died in 1950. Address in 1929, Carnegie Inst. of Technology; h. 8 Roselawn Terr., Pittsburgh, PA.

MacGINNIS, HENRY R.
Painter and teacher. Born Martinsville, IN, Sept. 25, 1875. Pupil of J. O. Adams and T. C. Steele, Indiana; Collin and Courtois in Paris; Royal Academy, Munich. Member: S. Ind. A.; Beachcombers. Award: Hon. mention, Royal Acad., Munich. Work: Mural painting, Mem. Room, Gregory School, Trenton, NJ; portraits in Customs House, NY and Masonic Temple, Trenton; faience tile mural, St. Thomas' Church, Woodhaven, LI, NY. Address in 1929, School of Industrial Arts, State and Willow Streets, h. 38 West State Street, Trenton, NJ; summer, Wentworth, N.H.

MacGREGOR, SARA NEWLIN.
(Mrs. Donald MacGregor). Miniature painter and illustrator. Born in Pennsylvania. Pupil of William M. Chase, Ben Gilman, Cecilia Beaux and Henry Thouron. Member: Fellowship PAFA; Plastic C. Award: Bronze medal, AAS, 1902. Address in 1929, Pine Crest, Princeton, NJ.

MACHETANZ, FRED.
Painter and lithographer. Born in Kenton, Ohio, 1908. Study: Ohio State Univ. BA 1930, MA 1935; Chicago AI. 1930-32; Am. Acad., Chicago, 1930-32; ASL, 1945; Univ. of Alaska, Hon. DFA, 1973. Work: Univ. of Alaska Mus.; Alberta (Can.) Mus., Calgary; Anchorage Hist. & FA Mus.; Frye Art Mus., Seattle; and others. Comn.: Scripps Inst. Research Ship, 1963; Dept. of Interior, 1969; The Tender Arctic, Frye Mus., Seattle, 1973; North Slope Borough, Fairbanks, 1981; and others. Exhib.: (One man shows). Univ. of Alaska, 1964 & 72; Anchorage Hist. & FA Mus., 1968, 74, 80; Frye Mus. Seattle, 1972; Tryon Gallery Ltd., London, 1979. Awards: Silver Medal, North Am. Wild Animals Art Exhib., 1979; Artist of the Year, Am. Artist Mag., 1981. Teaching: Univ. of Alaska, 1964-present. Mem.: Soc. of Animal Artists; Explorers Club. Media: Oil, lithograph.

MacINTOSH, MARIAN T.
Painter. Born Belfast, Ireland. Pupil of Heinrich Knirr and Henry B. Snell. Member: Phila. Alliance; Plastic C.; NA Women PS; AFA. Address in 1929, 291 Nassau Street, Princeton, NJ.

MACK, STANLEY.
Illustrator. Born in Brooklyn, New York in 1936. He attended RISD. His drawings have appeared on the Op-Ed page of The New York Times where he was Art Director of their Sunday Magazine section. His pen and ink work also appears in Stan Mack's Real Life Funnies in the Village Voice.

MacKALL, R. McGILL.
Painter, etcher, and craftsman. Born Baltimore, April 15, 1889. Pupil of Laurens and Richard Miller in Paris; ASL of NY.; Royal Academy in Munich. Member: Salon d'Automne, Paris; Charcoal C; Washington AC: Mural P; NY. Arch Lg. Work: Mural decorations in First English Lutheran Church; St. Lukes' Church, Baltimore; stained glass window, Christ P. E. Church, Luray, VA; murals, State of MD; City of Baltimore; War Memorial Building, Baltimore; Lobby

Decorations, Woodrow Wilson Hotel, New Brunswick, NJ. Address in 1929, Hampden Hall, 3553 Roland Ave., h. Cecil Apts., 1117 North Eutaw Street, Baltimore, MD.

MacKAY, EDWIN MURRAY.
Painter. Born in Detroit, MI. Pupil of Laurens, Blanche and Kenyon Cox. Member: CT. Society of Artists. Work: Portaits of "Ex-Gov. Sleeper", Mich. State Capitol Bldg.; "Justice Ostrander", Mich. Supreme Court, Lansing, MI. Drawings in NY Public Library. Address in 1926, 241 East Euclid Ave., Detroit, MI. Died Feb. 28, 1926.

MacKAY, WILLIAM ANDREW.
Mural Painter, and illustrator. Born Philadelphia, PA, July 10, 1878. Pupil of Constant and Laurens in Paris; Acad. in Rome; Robert Reid in NY. Member: SI 1910; Mural P; NY Arch. Lg. 1911; Players C; Paris AAA. Work: Mural paintings in: Senate Reading Room, Congressional Lib., Washington, DC; House of Representatives, St. Paul, MN; Supreme Court Room, Essex County Court House, Newark, NJ; Castlegould, Port Washington, LI, NY; decoration and painting, Knickerbocker 42nd St. Bldg., New York, NY; Illinois Merchants Trust Co., Chicago, IL; St. Georges Church, Stuyvesant Square, New York. Died in 1939. Address in 1929, 345 East 33rd Street, "The Players," 16 Gramercy Park, New York, NY; summer, Coytesville, Fort Lee, NJ.

MacKENSIE, E.
This accomplished engraver of portraits in the stipple manner came from England in 1833-34 to engrave for the "National Portrait Gallery". He remained in the United States, and was later employed doing portrait work for the Methodist Book Concern, of NY.

MacKENZIE, RODERICK D.
Painter, sculptor, illustrator, etcher, writer, lecturer, and teacher. Born London, England, April 30, 1865. Pupil of the School of the Museum of Fine Arts, Boston; Constant, Laurens, Jules Lefebvre, Chapu and the Ecole Nationale des Beaux-Arts in Paris. Member: Royal Society of Arts, London; AFA. Award: Curzon gold medal, India. Work: "State Entry Delhi, Durbar, 1903," Museum at Calcutta; "The Chitor Elephants," gate of Fort, Delhi, India; "Afghans" and "Beluchis"; series of night pictures of steel works, Birmingham, AL.; eight murals and bas-relief panels, Rontunda and Dome, State Capitol, Montgomery, AL.

MacKILLOP, WILLIAM.
Painter. Born Philadelphia, PA. Pupil of St. Louis School of Fine Arts; Jean Paul Laurens and Ernest Laurent in Paris. Member: Allied AA; Salma. C. Award: Silver medal, P.P. Exp., San F., 1915. Address in 1929, Van Dyck Studios, 939 Eighth Avenue, New York, NY.

MacKINNON, MRS. MARY.
Painter and illustrator. Born New York City, March 23, 1890. Member: SI; GFLA. Represented by portrait and fashion work in Harper's Bazaar; advertising work for Lux, MacCallum Hosiery. Address in 1929, 25 West 11th Street, New York, NY; summer, Easthampton, L.I., NY.

MacKLOW, J.
A well-engraved portrait of Martha Washington, after the painting by Woolaston, is signed by this man about 1835; it is further inscribed as "Engraved expressly for the Christian Family Annual."

MacKNIGHT, DODGE.
Painter. Born Providence, R.I., Oct. 1, 1860. Pupil of Cormon in Paris. Member: New Soc. A. Work: Thirty water colors, Museum of Fine Arts, Boston; "The Almond Tree", Institute of Arts, Detroit; "The Bed of the Brook", R.I. School of Design, Providence; ten water colors, Fogg Museum, Cambridge, MA; collection of pastels and water colors in "Macknight Room," Gardner Museum, Boston; water colors in Brooklyn Museum and Worcester Museum. Address in 1929, East Sandwich, MA.

MacKUBIN, FLORENCE.
Portrait and miniature painter. Born in 1866 in Florence, Italy. She studied in France and Italy. Her portraits include "Gov. Lloyd Lowndes", Prof. Basil Gildersleeve and Prof. Marshall Elliot. Her miniatures are in the Walters Art Gallery, Baltimore. She died in Baltimore, MD. Feb. 1, 1918.

MacLANE, JEAN.
(Mrs. John C. Johansen), Portrait painter. Born Chicago, IL, Sept 14, 1878. Pupil of AIC; Duveneck. Member: ANA, 1912; NA, 1926; Port. P.; NAC. Awards: Bronze medal, St. Louis Exp., 1904; first prize, Inter. Lg., Paris, 1907 and 1908; Elling prize, NY Woman's AC, 1907; Burgess prize, NY Woman's AC, 1908; Julia A. Shaw prize, NAD, 1912; third Hallgarten prize, NAD, 1913; Lippincott prize, PAFA, 1914; silver medal, Panama- Pacific Exp., San Francisco, 1915; Harris silver medal and prize, AIC, 1924. Work: Portrait of "Hon. Brant Whitlock" and "Along the Beach-Devonshire," Museum of Art, Toledo, Ohio.; "Virginia and Stanton," Art Institute of Chicago; "Girl in Green," Syracuse Art Museum; "Portrait of a Boy," San Antonio(Texas) Museum; "Queen Elizabeth of the Belgians," war collection of portraits, National Gallery of Art, Wash., D.C. Address in 1929, 12 West 9th St., NYC.

MacLAUGHLIN, DONALD SHAW.
Etcher and painter. Born in Boston in 1876. Awarded medals for etching. Address in 1926, 569 Fifth Avenue, New York. Died in 1938.

MacLEARY, BONNIE.
Sculptor. Born San Antonio, Texas. Pupil of Julian Academy, Paris; James E. Fraser; ASL of NY. Member: NA Women PS; NAC; Allied AA; Am. APL. Work: "Aspiration," Metropolitan Museum of Art, New York; "Ouch!", Children's Museum, Brooklyn, NY; Munos Rivera Monument, Rio Piedras, Puerto Rico; World's War Memorial Monument, San Juan, Puerto Rico. Address in 1929, 22 Charles St., New York, NY; summer, San Juan, Puerto Rico.

MacLELLAN, CHARLES A.
Painter and illustrator. Born Trenton, Ontario, Canada. June 22, 1885. Pupil of AIC; Howard Pyle. Member: Wilmington SFA. Address in 1926, 1305 Franklin Street, Wilmington, DE; summer, Trenton, Ontario, Canada.

MacLEOD, ALEXANDER S.
Painter and etcher. Born Orwell, Prince Edward Island, Canada, April 12, 1888. Pupil of Van Sloun. Member: Calif. SE. Address in 1929, 5974 Vine Street, Kerrisdale P.O., B. C., Canada.

MacMONNIES, FREDERICK WILLIAM.
Painter and sculptor. Born Brooklyn, NY, Sept. 28, 1863. Pupil of NAD; ASL of NY; Augustus Saint-Gaudens; Falguiere, Ecole des Beaux Arts and Mercie in Paris. Member: SAA 1891; ANA 1901; NA 1906; NY Arch. Lg. 1892; Nat. Inst. AL; NAC. Awards: Hon. mention, Paris Salon, 1891; medal, Columbia Exp., Chicago, 1893; first class gold medal, Antwerp, 1894; medal, Phila. AC, 1895; medal, Atlanta Exp., 1895; grand prize of honor, Paris Exp., 1900; medal, Munich; first prize, Boston AC; hon. mention for painting, Paris Salon, 1901; third medal for painting, Paris Salon, 1904. Chevalier of the Legion of Honor, 1896; Chevalier Order of St. Michael of Bavaria. Work: "Army" and "Navy" and "Horse Tamers," "J. S. T. Stranahan," "General Slocum," Brooklyn, NY; "Bacchante," Metropolitan Museum of Art, New York, and Luxembourg, Paris; "Victory," West Point, NY; "Sir Henry Vane," Boston Public Library; central bronze door and statue of "Shakespeare," Library of Congress, "Gen. McClellan," Washington, DC; "Pioneer Monument," Denver; "Pan of Rohalion," Fine Arts Academy, Buffalo, NY; "Nathan Hale," Civic Virtue," fountain, New York; "Washington at Princeton," Princeton, NJ. Address in 1929, 20 West 10th Street, New York, NY; Giverny-par-Vernon, Eure, France.

MacMONNIES, MARY FAIRCHILD.
See Mrs. Will H. Low.

MacMORRIS, LEROY DANIEL.
Painter, illustrator, and etcher.
Born Sedalia, MO, April 1, 1893.
Pupil of Pennell; Leon Gaspard;
Gorguet and Despujols. Member: L.
C. Tiffany Foundation AG; ASL of
NY; Kansas City AA. Address in
1929, 906 Carnegie Hall, NYC; care
of Hastings and Sells, 43 Rue La
Chaussee D'Antin, Paris, France.

MacNEIL, CAROL BROOKS.
Sculptor. Born Chicago, IL, Jan
15, 1871. Pupil of AIC under
Lorado Taft; MacMonnies and
Injalbert in Paris. Member: NSS,
1907; NA Women PS. Awards: Hon.
mention, Paris Exp., 1900; bronze
medal, St. Louis Exp., 1904.
Address in 1929, 679 Northern
Blvd., College Point, LI, NY.

MacNEIL, HERMON ATKINS.
Sculptor. Born Everett, MA, Feb.
27, 1866. Pupil of MA. Normal Art
School in Boston; Chapu at Julian
Acad. and Falguiere at Ecole des
Beaux-Arts in Paris. Member: NSS,
1897; ANA, 1905; NA, 1906; SAA,
1901; NY Arch. Lg. 1902; Century
Assoc.; NY Municipal AS; National
Inst. AL; AFA. Awards from:
Columbian Expo., Chicago, 1893;
Atlanta Expo., 1895; Paris Expo.,
1900; American Expo., Buffalo,
1901; Charleston Expo., 1902; St.
Louis Expo., 1904; Jewish
Settlement in America; Panama-
Pacific Expo., San Francisco, 1915;
medal of honor for sculpture, NY
Arch. Lg., 1917. Designer of
Pan-American medal of award, NY
Arch. Lg. medal of honor; US
Government quarter dollar.
Sculptures at City Park, Portland,
Oregon; Albany, NY; State Capitol
at Hartford, CT. In collections of:
MMA; Corcoran; AIC; Montclair (NJ)
Art Museum; Northwestern Univ.;
Cornell, and Hall of Fame, NYU.
Address in 1929, 679 Northern
Blvd., College Point, LI, NY.

MacNUTT, J. SCOTT.
Painter. Born Fort D. A. Russell,
WY, Jan., 11, 1885. Pupil of
Woodbury; School of the Boston
Museum. Member: St. Louis AG;
AFA. Instructor, St. Louis School
of Fine Arts, 1927-28. Address in
1929, 72 Vanderventer Place, St.
Louis, MO; summer, Ogunquit, ME.

MACOMBER, MARY L.
Painter. Born in Fall River, MA,
Aug. 21, 1861. Student of Boston
Museum Art School, and pupil of
Duveneck. Member of the Boston
Guild of Artists. She died in
Boston on Feb. 6, 1916.

MACOMBER, STEPHEN.
Painter. Member: Prov. WCC;
Mystic SA. Address in 1929, 187
High Street, Westerly, RI.

MacRAE, ELMER LIVINGSTON
Painter. Born New York, July 16,
1875. Pupil of ASL of NY under
Twachtman, Beckwith, Blum and
Mowbray. Member: NYWCC; Am. PS;
Pastelists; Greenwich SA. Award:
Second hon. mention for "Calla
Lilies," Greenwich Society of
Artists, 1929. Address in 1929, 12
West 69th Street; care Montross
Gallery, 26 East 56th Street, New
York, NY; Cos Cob, CT.

MacRAE, EMMA FORDYCE.
Painter. Born Vienna, Austria,
April 27, 1887. Pupil of Luis
Mora, Robert Reid, Kenneth Hayes
Miller. Member: MacD.C.; NA Women
PS; North Shore AA; Allied AA; NAC;
Am. WA; AFA; NYSP; Grand Cent. GA;
Mural Painters. Awards: Hon.
mention, NA Women PS, 1927; Gould
prize, NA Women PS, 1928. Address
in 1929, 12 West 69th Street, New
York, NY; summer, Atlantic
Highlands, Gloucester, MA.

MacRUM, GEORGE H.
Painter and teacher. Pupil of ASL
of NY. Member: Allied AA; Salma.
C.; Phila. AC. Awards: Gold
medal, Appalachian Exp., Knoxville,
TN, 1911; Turnbull prize, Salma.
C., 1914; silver medal,
Panama-Pacific Exp., San Fran.,
1915. Work: "The Pile Driver,"
PA. Academy of the Fine Arts; "The
Pardon on the Mountain," Canadian
National Gallery, Toronto, Canada.
Address in 1929, 1320 Pacific St.,
Brooklyn, NY.

MacSOUD, NICOLAS S.
Painter. Born Zahle, Mt. Lebanon,
Syria, March 7, 1884. Pupil of
NAD. Member: Brooklyn S. Min. P.;
Brooklyn SA; Salma. C.; Wash. WCC;
PS (Pres.). Work: "The Holy
Sepulchre," Brooklyn Museum,

Brooklyn, NY. Address; in 1929, 320 Fifth Ave., NYC; h. 566 Fifth St., Brooklyn, NY; summer, New Monterey Hotel, Asbury Park, NJ.

MACY, HARRIET.
Painter. Born Des Moines, IA, in 1883. Pupil of Cumming School of Art, Des Moines; ASL of NY. Member: Iowa AG. Awards: Des Moines Women's C., 1915; gold medal, Des Moines Women's C., 1923; purchase prize Des Moines Women's C., 1924; gold medal, Des Moines Women's C., 1927. Address in 1929, 1321-28th St., Des Moines, IA.

MACY, WILLIAM STARBUCK.
Born in New Bedford, MA, in 1853. He studied art at the Nat. Acad. NY, and at Munich. His best work represents familiar New England effects. He had studios in New York and New Bedford. Among his works are "Edge of the Forest", "Winter Sunset", and "The Old Mill." He died in 1916.

MADEIRA, CLARA N.
Painter. Exhibited water colors at the Penna. Academy of Fine Arts, Phila., 1925. Address in 1926, 2300 Pine Street, Philadelphia, PA.

MADSEN, OTTO.
Painter and illustrator. Born in Germany, April 30, 1882 of Danish parents. Pupil of Wilimovsky, Berninghaus, Tolson and Ivan Summers. Member: St. Louis PBC; Kansas City SA. Work: "Baptism of Christ in the Jordan", First Baptist Church, St. Louis; decorative panels in the CA. State Bldg., and Transportation Bldg. Panama-Pacific Exp., San Francisco, 1915. Address in 1929, 922 Broadway; h. 825 E. 42nd St., Kansas City, MO.

MADSEN, VIGGO HOLM.
Printmaker and craftsman. Born in Kaas, Denmark, Apr. 21, 1925, US citizen. Study: Anderson College, Syracuse Univ.; NYU; Columbia Univ. Teachers College; Adelphi Univ.; Inst. Allende, San Miguel, Mex.; Det Danske Selskab, Den. Work: Phila. Ctr. for Older People, PA; C. W. Post College, Brookville, NY; and others. Exhib.: NAD Show, NYC; Drawing USA II, Smithsonian;

Ore. State Univ.; Silvermine Guild Artists Print Show; and others. Awards: Award of Excellence, C. W. Post College; Cover Design Award, NYS Teachers Assn.; and others. Teaching: Roslyn High School, NY, 1960-82; Nassau Comm. College, 1966- present; etc. Mem.: LI Craftsmen's Guild; NYS Art Teachers Assn.; Am. Crafts Council; and others. Address in 1982, 5 Meldon Avenue, Albertson, NY 11507.

MAESCH, FERDINAND.
Painter. Born Muhlhausen, Germany, June 21, 1865. Studied in Germany and France. Work: Portrait of Hon. Herbert T. Ketcham, Surrogate Court, Kings Co., NY. Died in 1925, in Yonkers, NY.

MAFFIA, DANIEL J.
Illustrator. Born in Nevers, France in 1937. He attended the School of Industrial Art where he was a pupil of Vogel. Among his clients are Esquire, Limited Editions Club and the National Park Service. His evocative paintings have been featured in Idea magazine's edition of New York illustrators and selected for inclusion in S of I Annual Exhibitions.

MAGAFAN, ETHEL.
Painter. Born: Chicago, Illinois in 1916. Studied: Colorado Springs Fine Arts Center; and with Frank Mechau, Boardman Robinson and Peppino Mangravite. Awards: Fulbright fellowship, 1951; Tiffany scholarship, 1949; Stacy scholarship, 1947; National Academy of Design, 1951, 1956; Hallmark award, 1952; American Watercolor Society, Pomona, California, 1956; Norfolk Museum of Art, 1957; Ball State Teachers College, 1958. Collections: Metropolitan Museum of Art; Denver Art Museum; World's Fair, New York, 1939; Wilmington Society of Fine Arts; Norfolk Museum of Art; Des Moines Art Center; Senate Chamber, Recorder of Deeds Building, Social Security Building, Washington, DC, United States Post Office, Auburn, Nebraska; Wynne Arkansas; Madill, Oklahoma; South Denver Branch, Colorado.

MAGAGNA, ANNA MARIE.
Illustrator. Born in Wilkes-Barre, Pennsylvania in 1938. She attended Marywood College in Scranton, ASL and SVA in NY. She has been on the faculty of PI since 1971. Her free-lance art career began in 1958 with the children's book Christmas Miniature by Pearl S. Buck which she illustrated for John Day Co. She has since worked for magazines such as Vogue and Harper's Bazaar. A member of the S of I since 1971, she lives in New York City.

MAGEE, ALAN.
Illustrator. Born in Newtown, PA, in 1947. He attended the Tyler School of Art and Philadelphia College of Art. His first published illustration was seen on the cover of Scholastic Magazine in 1969. Since then his work has appeared in McCall's, Good Housekeeping, Penthouse, Viva, New York Magazine and The New York Times. He has illustrated several book covers for Ballantine, Fawcett, Bantam, Pocket Books and Random House, and won a New York Book Publishers Award in 1976.

MAGEE, JAMES C.
Landscape painter. Born in Brooklyn in 1846. Pupil of Penna. Academy of Fine Arts and of Chase in New York and of Robert Henri in Paris. He died Jan. 15, 1924. Represented in the Johnson collection in Philadelphia and the Lord Richmond collection, London.

MAGEE, RENA TUCKER KOHLMAN.
(Mrs. Franklin Magee). Painter, sculptor, and writer. Born Indianapolis, Nov. 29, 1880. Pupil of Joseph DeCamp, Charles H. Woodbury and George Gray Barnard. Member: NSS. Director of Exhibitions, Milch Galleries. Address in 1929, 108 West 57th Street, New York, NY.

MAGENIS, H.
Portrait painter. He worked in Philadelphia in 1818.

MAGER, (CHARLES A.) GUS.
Painter, writer, and cartoonist. Born Newark, NJ, Oct. 21, 1878. Member: Modern AA; Salons of America; Modern A. Address in 1929, 204 Prospect Street, South Orange, NJ.

MAGIE, GERTRUDE.
Painter. Born Trenton, NJ, Oct. 1, 1862. Pupil of Chase, Hawthorne, Martin, Morriset Guerin, Bridgman. Member: NA Women PS.; Washington AC; AFA. Address in 1929, 321 Nassau Street, Princeton, NJ; summer, 21 Rue le Verrier, Paris, 6me, France.

MAGNUSSON, KRISTJAN H.
Painter. Born Isafjord, Iceland, March 6, 1903. Pupil of John Sharman. Address in 1929, 46 Meddow Croft Road, Winchester, MA.

MAGONIGLE, EDITH M.
Mural painter. Born Brooklyn, NY, May 11, 1877. Member: NA Women PS. (pres.; hon. vice-pres.); Mural P; AFA. Work: Frieze on Administration Bldg., Essex County Park Commission, Newark, NJ; "Tragedy" and "Comedy," The Playhouse, Wilmington, DE. Address in 1929, 829 Park Avenue, New York, NY.

MAGONIGLE, H. VAN BUREN.
Architect, painter, sculptor, and writer. Born Bergen Heights, NJ, Oct. 17, 1867. Offices of Vaux & Radford; Charles C. Haight; McKim, Mead & White. Member: ANA; Fellow AIA; NY Arch. Lg. (pres.); Alumni American Academy in Rome (past Pres.); NSS (vice-pres.); Salma. C.; AFA; Soc. Beaux-Arts; NY Chapter AIA (Pres.). Awards: Gold medal, NY Arch. Lg., 1889; Rotch Traveling Scholarship, 1894. Work: McKinley National Memorial, Canton, OH; National Maine monument, and Firemen's Memorial, both in New York City; Liberty Memorial, Kansas City, MO; Arsenal Technical Schools, Indianapolis. Author of "The Nature, Practice and History of Art"; "The Renaissance," etc. Address in 1929, 101 Park Avenue; h. 829 Park Avenue, New York, NY.

MAGRATH, WILLIAM.
Born in Ireland, on March 20, 1838. He came to America in his youth. Member of Nat. Acad. of Design. His first studio was in NYC, and later he established his studio in Washington, D.C. Among his works

are "Irish Peasantry", "Courtyard with Donkey", and the "Irish Interior," He died in 1918, in Brighton, NY.

MAHIER, EDITH.
Painter. Born in Baton Rouge, LA. Pupil of NY School of Fine Arts. Taught in Department of Art, University of Oklahoma, Norman, Ok.

MAHLER, REBECCA.
Painter and teacher. Born New York City. Pupil of William M. Chase. Address in 1929, 320 West 83rd Street, New York, NY.

MAHON, JOSEPHINE.
Painter, sculptor, craftsman, writer, and teacher. Born Caldwell, NJ, Oct. 31, 1881. Pupil of Charles W. Hawthorne, Richard Hayley Lever. Address in 1929, Bloomfield Avenue, West, Caldwell, NJ; summer, "Wateredge," Nantucket, MA.

MAHONY, FELIX.
Painter, illustrator, lecturer, and teacher. Born New York, NY. Pupil of Steinlen in Paris; Corcoran School of Art, Wash., DC.; New York School of Fine and Applied Arts in NY, and Paris. Member: Wash. AC; Beachcombers; Provincetown AA; S. Wash. A. Director, National School of Fine and Applied Art, Washington, D.C. Address in 1929, Conn. Ave. and M. St.; h. The Champlain, 1424 K Street, Washington, D.C.

MAILMAN, CYNTHIA.
Painter. Born Dec. 31, 1942, in Bronx, NY. Studied: Pratt Institute, Brooklyn, New York, Dec. 31, 1942; The Art Students League; Brooklyn Museum Art School. Exhibitions: Sequoia Gallery, Los Altos, Calif., 1971; SOHO 20, NYC, 1974; Queens Museum, Flushing Meadow, NY, 1975. Some of her work is in the collection of The Prudential Life Insurance Company. Media: Acrylic on canvas. Address in 1980, Staten Island, NY.

MAIN, WILLIAM.
Engraver. Born in 1796 in New York City. He practiced engraving there between 1821 and 1833. According to Wm. Dunlap, Main, as a young man, was taken to Italy by Mauro Gandolfi, who came to this country, in 1817, under contract to engrave Col. Trumbull's "Declaration of Independence". Gandolfi broke his contract and returned home the same year, and took Main with him under promise of teaching him engraving. For some reason not stated, Main was abandoned in Florence, and he then applied to Morghen and was admitted, and spent three years in the studio of that great master. This statement of Dunlap is supported by the fact that the peculiar engraving table brought by Main from Florence was for many years in the possession of James Smillie, in NY, and was always known among engravers as the "Morghen table". In 1820 William Main returned to NY full of enthusiasm for his art. He eventually found employment and engraved a few portraits and book illustrations. William Main was one of the founders of the National Academy of Design in 1826; member of the class of engravers which included Durand, Danforth, Peter Maverick and C. C. Wright. He seems to have left NY in 1833, but returned and died there in 1876.

MAININI, TROVATORE.
Painter and craftsman. Born Barre, VT. Pupil of Carlo Abate, Leslie Thompson and C. J. Connick. Member: Boston SAC and Boston AC. Address in 1929, 9 Harcourt Street, Boston, MA; h. 56 Liberty Square, Quincy, MA.

MAJOR, ERNEST L.
Painter and teacher. Born Washington, D.C., 1864. Pupil of ASL of NY, and Boulanger and Lefebvre in Paris. Member: Boston AC; Boston GA. Awards: Silver medal, P. P. Exp., San F., 1915; Bok prize, PAFA, 1917. Instructor in Massachusetts School of Art, Boston. Address in 1929, Fenway Studios, Boston, MA.

MAJOR, JAMES PARSONS.
Engraver. Born at Frome, Somersetshire, England, in 1818. Mr. Major came to the U.S. as a bank-note engraver in 1830. He resided in Brooklyn until 1872, and for over fifty-five years was in

596

charge of the engraving and modeling department of what is now the American Bank-Note Co., of NY. He died at Somerville, NJ, Oct. 17, 1900.

MAKARENKO, ZACHARY PHILIPP.
Painter and sculptor. Born in North Caucacus, Russia, Feb. 20, 1900; US citizen. Study: State Univ. Acad. of Fine Arts, Kiev; Study in Germany and Italy. Work: Public & Private Collection, Worldwide. Exhib.: Angelicum, Regional Ital. IV Relig. Exhib., Milan, 1947; USA Relig. Exhib. Burr Gallery, NYC, 1958; Am. APL Grand Mat'l., NYC, 1966; NAD Galleries, NYC, 1971; others. Awards: Am. APL, 1966; Medal of Honor, Ptr. & Sculpt. Soc. Exhib., Jersey City (NJ) Mus., 1971; AAA Gold Medal of Honor, Sculpt., NAD Galleries, 1971; others. Mem.: Fellow Am. APL. Address in 1980, 7332 Kennedy Blvd., North Bergen, NJ.

MAKIELSKI, BRONISLAV A.
Painter and teacher. Born South Bend, IN, Aug. 13, 1901. Pupil of AIC; Leon A. Makielski. Member: Alumni AIC; Delta Phi Delta; Scarab C. Work: Altar piece, Church of the Holy Comforter, Charlottesville, VA. Address in 1929, 3408 Woodward; h. 1122 West Harvey Street, South Bend IN; summer, University, VA.

MAKIELSKI, LEON A.
Painter. Born Morris Run, PA, May 17, 1885. Pupil of AIC; Julian Academy and Grande Chaumiere Academy in Paris. Member: Scarab C; AFA. Awards: John Quincy Adams Traveling Scholarship, AIC, 1908; 2nd prize, 1918; 3rd prize, 1919; 1st prize, 1920, Detroit Inst. of Arts; Frank C. Herker prize, Detroit, 1923 and 1925. Instructor in Arch., U. of Mich.; Instructor in portrait painting, Detroit School of Applied Arts. Address in 1929, 3408 Woodward Avenue, Detroit, MI; R.F.D. 5, Geddes Avenue, Ann Arbor, MI.

MALBONE, EDWARD G.
Minature painter. Born in Newport, RI, in Aug. 1777. Received some instruction from a local scene painter. Established himself in Boston as a miniature painter when about nineteen, and formed a close friendship with Washington Allston; afterward opened studios successively in NY and Phila. Removed with Allston, in the winter of 1800, to Charleston, SC, where some of his best works were produced. Accompanied Allston to London in May 1801, and while there painted his largest and most celebrated miniature, "The Hours," in the Providence Athenaeum - a group of three beautiful young girls representing the Past, the Present, and the Future. On returning to US, he chose Charleston for his permanent residence, visiting the North periodically. In 1806, travelled to Jamaica for his health. Died in Savannah, GA, May 7, 1807, on his way to Newport, RI. Malbone was the foremost American miniature painter. He also occasionally painted in oils and drew pastel portraits. One hundred and fifty-seven miniatures by him are listed in "Early American Portrait Painters in Miniature," by Theodore Bolton, NY, 1921.

MALCOM, JAMES PELLER.
Engraver and draftsman. Born in Philadelphia in Aug., 1767. Malcom began to engrave in Philadelphia prior to 1786, as he designed and engraved the frontispiece of the "Lyric Works of Horace" by John Parke, Philadelphia, 1786. Attended the Royal Academy, England. Worked for the Gentleman's Magazine and other English periodicals. As an engraver and upon his earlier prints he signed but as an author and upon his later prints he signed his name Malcom; "James Peller Malcolm F.A.S." Died in London, England, April 5, 1815.

MALCOM, THALIA WESTCOTT.
(Mrs. Donald Malcom). Painter. Born in New York City, Sept. 10, 1885. Pupil of Randall Davey and Albert Andre. Member: NYWCC; S. Indp. A; Alliance; French Inst. in U.S. (life); Met. Mus. of Art (Life); Am. Assn. Mus.; Am. APL; AFA. Address in 1929, 104 Rue de L'Universite, Paris, France.

MALCYNSKI, ELIZABETH P.
Illustrator. Born in Brooklyn, New York in 1955. She studied art for four years at the PSD. She illustrated the cover for Day Care Magazine in 1976 and has since illustrated for Bantam and Columbia Records. She is a descendant of George Luks of the Ashcan School.

MALHAUPT, FREDERICK J.
Painter. Exhibited at Nat. Acad. of Design, New York, 1925. Address in 1926, Gloucester, MA.

MALLARY, ROBERT.
Sculptor. Born Dec. 2, 1917 in Toledo, OH. Studied with John Emmett Garrity and at Escuela Arts Library, Mexico City. Taught at Univ. of New Mexico, Pratt, and Amherst. Exhibited at Allan Stone Gallery (1961-2); MOMA; Seattle World's Fair (1962); Mus. of Arte Moderna, Sao Paulo, and Inst. of Contemp. Art, London. In collections of MOMA; Albright-Knox; Houston's Mus. of Fine Arts; Smith College; Brandeis; Whitney; LA County Mus. and Berkeley.

MALLISON, EUPHAME CLASON.
Painter, craftsman, and teacher. Born in Baltimore, MD, April 30, 1895. Pupil of Gamba de Preydour. Member: Southern SAL; Baltimore WCC. Represented at Pennsylvania State College. Address in 1929, Box 512, University, Virginia.

MALLONEE, MISS JO.
Painter. Born in Stockton, NY, in 1892. Pupil of G. Bridgeman. Member: Art Students' League of New York; League of New York Artists. Address in 1926, 39 West 39th Street, New York, NY.

MALM, GUSTAV N.
Painter, illustrator, craftsman and writer. Born Svarttorp, Sweden, Jan. 20, 1869. Studied in Sweden. Member: Smoky Hill Art Club. Author and illustrator of "Charlie Johnson," a study of the Swedish Emigrant. Address in 1929, Malm Studio, Lindsborg, KS.

MALONE, BLONDELLE.
Painter. Member: NA Women PS; AFA. Address in 1929, 1741 Rhode Island Avenue, Washington, D.C.

MALONE, LAETITIA HERR.
(Mrs. John E.) Painter and illustrator. Born in Lancaster, PA, in 1881. Pupil of Chase, Mora, Beaux, Anshutz, and McCarter at Penna. Acad. of Fine Arts. Member: Penna. Acad. of Fine Arts; Philadelphia Art Alliance. Address in 1926, Lancaster, PA.

MALONE, ROBERT JAMES.
Etcher, caricaturist. Born Birmingham, AL, March 14, 1892. Work published in "New York Times," "Cosmopolitan," "International Book Review," "Review of Reviews," "The London Graphic." Address in 1929, St. James, LI, NY.

MALONE, ROBERT R.
Painter and printmaker. Born in McColl, SC, Aug. 8, 1933. Study: Furman Univ.; Univ. of NC; Univ. of Chicago; State Univ. of Iowa. Work: Smithsonian Institution; Libr. of Congress; NY Public Libr.; Phila. Mus. of Art; Calif. (San Fran.) Palace of Legion of Honor; others. Comn: Int'l Graphic Arts Soc. NYC; Ferdinand Roten Galleries, Baltimore; Lakeside (Mich.) Studio; many more. Exhib.: 15th Nat'l. Print Exhtn., Brooklyn Museum; New Talent in Printmaking 1968, AAA, NYC; Biennale Internationale De L'Estampe/Paris. Awards: Purchase Award, Colorprint USA, Tex. Tech. Univ.; Recent Am. Graphics Purchase Award, Univ. of Wis., Madison; So. IL Univ. Sr. Resident Scholar Award. Teaching: So. IL Univ., 1970-present; others. Mem.: Col. Art Assn. of Am. Media: Oil, lithography, etching.

MANBERT, BARTON.
Painter and etcher. Born Jamestown, NY. Pupil of George Bridgman, Lucian Hitchcock and Reynolds. Member: Calif. AC.; Glendale AA. Award: Bronze medal, San Diego Exp., 1915. Address in 1929, 621 South Columbus Avenue, Glendale, CA; summer, Balboa Island, CA.

MANCHESTER, MRS. ARTHUR WILLIAMS.
See Waite, Emily Burling).

MANDELMAN, BEATRICE M.
Painter. Born: Newark, New Jersey in Dec. 31, 1912. Studied: Art

Students League; Newark School of Fine and Industrial Arts. Collections: Metropolitan Museum of Art; Museum of New Mexico; University of Omaha. Media: Acrylic and collage. Address in 1980, Box 891, Tao, NM.

MANDL, A.
Painter. Born in Munich in 1894. Pupil of Daniel Garber and LeRoy Ireland. Member: Fellowship, Penna. Academy of Fine Arts.

MANDZIUK, MICHAEL DENNIS.
Painter and serigrapher. Born in Detroit, MI, January 14, 1942. Work: Minn. Mus. of Art, St. Paul; Borg Warner Corp., Chicago; Art Ctr. Collection, Park Forest, IL. Exhib.: Minn. Mus. Art Drawing Biennial, St. Paul, 1973; Bulter Inst. Am. Art, Youngstown, Ohio, 1973-74; Ukranian Inst. of Mod. Art, Chicago, 1975; Battle Creek Art Ctr., Mich.; others. Media: Silk screen. Address in 1982, Allen Park, MI.

MANGRAVITE, PEPPINO.
Painter. Born Lipari, Italy, June 28, 1896. Pupil of E. Guastini. Member: S. Indp. A.; Salons of America; Brooklyn S. Modern A. Award: Gold medal, Sesqui-Centennial Expo., Phila., PA, 1926. Represented in the Phillips Memorial Gallery, Washington, DC. Art director, Avon College, Avon, CT; Birch-Walthen Schools, NY. Address in 1929, 7 Oakland Street, Rye, NY.

MANGUM, WILLIAM.
(Goodson). Painter and sculptor. Born in Kinston, NC. Study: Corcoran Sch. of Art, Wash. DC; ASL; Univ. of NC, Chapel Hill. Work: Carl Sandburg Memorial, Flat Rock, NC; "Lamp of Learning" Monument, Greensboro, NC; NC Museums; private collections, including R. Phillip Hanes. Exhibitions: Isaac Delgado Museum; Galerie Paula Insel Exhib. and Brodley Gallery Nat'l., NYC; N.C. Museum of Art; Museum of Art, Springfield, Mass.; Virginia Museum of Fine Art; Southeast, Ctr. of Contemp. Art, Winston-Salem, NC. Awards: VA Mus. of Fine Art; Delgado Mus. Award, NC Mus. of Art.

Mem.: So. Assn. of Sculptors. Address in 1980, Salem College, Winston-Salem, NC.

MANIATTY, STEPHEN GEORGE.
Painter. Born in Norwich, CT, Sept. 5, 1980. Study: Mass. School of Art. Work: Holyoke Mus., Mass.; Historical Murals, Franklin Trust Co., Greenfeld, Mass. Exhib.: Hudson Valley Art Assn., White Plains, NY, 1972; Am. APL, NYC, 1972; Guild of Boston Artists, 1975; others. Awards: Hudson Valley Art Assoc., NY; Rockport Art Assoc., Mass., Gold Medal of Honor 1968; American Artists Professional League, NY, Gold Medal 1970; and many others. Mem.: Salmagundi Club; Guild of Boston Artists; Hudson Valley Art Assn.; Am. APL; So. VT Art Assn.

MANIEVICH, ABRAHAM.
Painter. Born in Russia, Nov. 25, 1882. Pupil at Gov't Art School, Kiev; Art Academy, Munich. Work: "Through the Branches," Luxembourg Mus. Paris, "Rome, Italy," and "Spring, Capri, Italy," Horvatt Gallery, Geneva; "Paris, Parc de Montsouris," Imperial Academy of Art, Petrograd; "Autumn Symphony," Fund Mus., Moscow; "Miestetchks" and "My Birthplace," Museum of Art, Kiev; landscape and "Birch," Brooklyn Museum of Art. Address in 1929, 3751 Giles Place, Bronx, NY.

MANIGAULT, EDWARD MIDDLETON.
Painter. Born in London, Ontario, CN, June 14, 1887. Pupil of Kenneth Hayes Miller. Address in 1926, 130 West 57th Street, New York, NY. Died Sept. 4, 1922, in San Francisco, CA.

MANLEY, THOMAS R.
Painter and etcher. Born Buffalo, NY, Nov. 29, 1853. Pupil of PAFA. Member: NAC; NYWCC. Award: Bronze medal for etchings, St. Louis Exp., 1904. Work in: Montclair Art Association, and the Yale Club, New York, NY. Address in 1929, 38 St. Luke's Place, Montclair, NJ.

MANLY, JOHN.
The only evidence of this man as an engraver is found in an etched portrait of Washington, executed

after 1789. Manly is said to have been a die-sinker, and apparently flourished about 1800. In an advertisement in the Freeman's Journal, Phila., 1790, "an Artist" proposes "a subscription for a medal of George Washington." Subscriptions were received at Wilmington by Peter Rynberg, and in Philadelphia by J. Manly, "in the care of Robert Patton, Postmaster." This would indicate that Manly was then in Philadelphia - if he were not the "artist" referred to. In 1772 he was painting portraits in Virginia.

MANN, JACK.
Painter. Exhibited at National Academy of Design, New York, in 1925. Address in 1926, 15 East 14th Street, New York.

MANN, PARKER.
Painter. Born in Rochester, NY, July 6, 1852. Studied at Ecole des Beaux Arts, Paris. Engaged as landscape painter in Washington most of the time from 1887-98; in NY, 1899-1906. Spent several years painting in England, France, Holland, Switzerland, Italy, and Spain. He died on Dec. 15th, 1918 in Princeton, NJ.

MANNHEIM, JEAN.
Painter. Born Krevznach, Germany, Nov. 18, 1863. Pupil of Ecole Delecluse, Colarossi, London School of Art. Member: CA A.C.; Laguna Beach AA. Awards: Gold medal, Seattle Exp., 1909; gold and silver medals, San Diego Exp., 1915. Represented in Denver (CO) Museum. Address in 1929, 500 Arroyo Drive, Pasadena, CA.

MANOIR, IRVING K.
Painter, illustrator, and teacher. Born Chicago, IL, April 28, 1891. Pupil of Wellington Reynolds, H. M. Walcott; Chicago AFA; AIC. Member: Chicago PS; AIC Alumni; Chicago AC; Chicago Gal. A.; St. Petersburg AC; Laguna Beach AA; Artland C. Awards: Goodman prize, Chicago AIC, 1915; first landscape prize, Laguna Beach AA, 1925. Work: "Blue Hills," in Joliet (IL) Public Lib.; mural decoration in Vincennes (IN) High School. Represented in Milwaukee Art Inst.;

Chicago Municipal Collection. Address in 1929, h. 821 North Trumbull Avenue, Chicago, IL.

MANON, ESTELLE REAM.
Painter. Born in Lincoln, IL, in 1884. Pupil of William M. Chase and Charles W. Hawthorne. Member: St. Joseph Art League; Oklahoma Art League. Head of art department, Oklahoma City High School. Address in 1926, 716½ Tely Street, St. Joseph, MO.

MANSFIELD, BLANCHE McMANUS.
(Mrs. Francis Miltoun Mansfield) Illustrator and Painter. Born East Feliciana, LA, Feb. 2, 1870. Studied in Paris. Specialty, book and periodical illustration. Author"The American Woman Abroad," "Our French Cousins," etc. Address in 1929, 9 Rue Falguiere, Paris, France.

MANSFIELD, LOUISE BUCKINGHAM.
Painter and illustrator. Born Le Roy, NY. Pupil of ASL of NY. Member: N.A. Women PS; Brooklyn SA; Brooklyn WCC; ASL of NY; AFA. Address in 1929, 368 Hancock Street, Brooklyn, NY.

MANSHIP, PAUL.
Sculptor. Born St. Paul, MN, Dec. 25, 1885. Member: ANA, 1914; NA, 1916; NSS, 1912; Amer. Inst. of Arts and Letters, 1918; Chevalier, Legion d'Honneur, 1929; Century Assoc. Awards: American Academy in Rome scholarship, 1909-12; Barnett prize, NAD, 1913; Widener gold medal, PAFA, 1914; gold medal, P. P. Exp., San F., 1915; Helen Foster Barnett prize, NAD, 1917; gold medal, AIA., 1921; medal, Amer. Numismatic Soc., 1924; gold medal, Phila. AA., 1925; Gold medal, Sesqui-Centennial Expo., Phila., 1926. Work: "Centaur and Nymph," Metropolitan Museum, New York; "The Duck Girl," bronze fountain, Fairmount Park, Philadelphia; "Centaur and Dryad" and "Flight of Night," Detroit Inst. of Arts; "Indian and Pronghorn Antelope" and "Dancing Girl and Fawns," Art Inst. of Chicago; City Art Museum, St. Louis; Pratt Inst., Brooklyn; "Playfulness," MN Institute of Art; "Dancer and Gazelles," Cleveland

600

Museum; Toledo Museum of Art; Luxembourg, Paris, also Corcoran Gallery of Art, Washington, D.C.; designer of Civic Forum medal; J. P. Morgan Memorial, Metropolitan Museum of Art; Portrait of John D. Rockefeller; War Memorial, American Academy in Rome, Italy; War Memorial, Detroit Athletic Club; "Indian Hunter," fountain group, Cochran Memorial Park, St. Paul, MN. Address in 1929, 319 East 72nd Street, New York, NY.

MANSO, LEO.
Painter. Born April 15, 1914 in NYC. Studied at Nat. Acad. of Design, and New School for Soc. Research. Taught at Columbia (1951-6); Smith; Univ. of Mich.; Cooper Union, NYU, ASL, Am. Acad. in Rome. Co-founder of the Provincetown Workshop (1959). Rec. awards from Audubon Artists (1952 1957); Am. Acad. of Arts & Letters; PAFA; Univ. of Illinois, Wesleyan and Ford Foundation. Exhibited at Norlyst Gallery, NYC (1947); Grand Central Moderns (many, 1957-64); Babcock Galleries, NYC; Whitney; Univ. of Nebraska; Walker; MOMA; PAFA and Brooklyn. In collections of Boston MFA; Univ. of Illinois; Whitney; PAFA; Brandeis; Nebraska Art Assoc.; Brooklyn Mus.; MOMA; Worcester (MA) Museum, and many private collections.

MANUEL, BOCCINI.
Painter and sculptor. Born Pieve di Teco, Italy, Sept. 10, 1890. Pupil of Andri Favori, Andre Derain. Member: ASL of NY; S. Indp. A.; Salons of Am. Address in 1929, 415 Madison Avenue; h. 29 East 48th Street, New York, NY; summer, 32 Midland Avenue, Rye, NY.

MANUEL, MARGARET.
Etcher. Born Hawick, Scotland. Pupil of Ernest Haskell and NY School of Applied Design for Women. Member: Brooklyn SE; NA Women PS; AFA. Work: "On the Edge of the Cumberlands-Tenesee," Chicago Art Institute; "Logan-Lee,Pentland Hills"; National Museum, Washington, D.C.; "On The Edge of the Cumberlands-Tennessee" and "Maine Seascape," Corona Mundi, International Art Center, New York City; "In the Heart of the Cumberlands-Tennessee," Bibliotheque Nationale, Paris, France (permanent collection). Address in 1929, Harperley Hall, 1 West 64th Street, New York, NY.

MANY, ALEXIS B.
Painter. Born Indianapolis, IN, Aug. 10, 1879. Member: Salma. C.; Wash. SA; Wash. AC. Awards: Bronze medal, S. Wash. A., 1921; Corcoran prize, S. Wash. A., 1921; 1st prize, CA AC., 1921. Address in 1929, 1710 Third Street, N.E., Washington, D.C.

MAPES, JAMES JAY.
Amateur miniature painter. Born in Maspeth, L.I. 1806. He is noted by William Dunlap in his "History of the Arts of Design." From 1835 to 1838 he was "Professor of Chemistry and Natural Philosophy of Colors," at the National Academy and was hon. member of the NA. He died Jan. 19, 1866, in NYC.

MAPLESDEN, GWENDOLINE ELVA.
Painter, sculptor, illustrator, writer, lecturer, and teacher. Born Secunderabad, India, Sept. 3, 1890. Pupil of Daniel Garber, Geo. Bridgman, Vincent DuMond. Member: NA Women PS; Fellowship PAFA; Alliance; NYSC; ASL of NY; Amer. Artists Prof. Lg. Author of "A Comparison Between Eastern and Western Ideals of Art." Address in 1929, 523 West 121st Street; h. 435 West 119th Street, New York, NY; summer, Suffield, CT.

MARAFFI, LUIGI.
Sculptor and craftman. Born Aversan, Italy, Dec. 4, 1891. Pupil of Grafly. Member: Graphic Sketch C., Phila.; Fellowship PAFA. Award Stewardson prize and two Cresson Scholarships PAFA. Work: Bronze portrait of Edward T. Stotesbury, Drexel Bank, Phila. Address in 1929, 6th and Section Street, Mount Vernon, WA.

MARAS, M.
French miniature artist who flourished in NY from 1800 to 1802; he later went to Constantinople and became painter to the Sultan.

MARBLE, JOHN NELSON.
Painter. Born in 1855. He studied in France and Italy. He painted portraits of Bishop Phillips Brooks, Judge Henry E. Howland and Mary Baker Eddy. He died in Woodstock, VT, April 1, 1918.

MARCHANT, B.
The only engravings known by Marchant are line illustrations in "The Narrative of Capt. James Riley," published in NY in 1816.

MARCHANT, EDWARD DALTON.
Born in Edgartown, MA, Dec. 16, 1806. He painted portraits in Phila. and NY for many years. He also resided in Nashville, TN. He settled in Phila. in 1845. He first exhibited in 1829 at the National Academy of Design. He was a member of the Union League Club of Phila. where several of his portraits are owned. He died in Asbury Park, NJ, Aug. 15, 1887. In 1833 he was elected an Associate Member of the National Academy.

MARCHANT, G. W.
Actually Merchant, G. W. (See entry).

MARCUS, MARCIA.
Painter. Born: New York in Jan. 11, 1928. Studied: NY University; Cooper Union Art School; Art Students League; and with Edwin Dickinson. Collections: Whitney Museum of American Art; Newark Museum. Address in 1980, New York City.

MARCUS, PETER.
Painter, etcher, and writer. Born in New York City, Dec. 23, 1889. Pupil of Ecole des Beaux Arts, Ecole des Beaux Arts Decoratifs in Paris; Charles H. Davis; Henry W. Ranger. Member: NY Arch. Lg.; CT AFA.; Lotos C.; Salma. C.; New Haven PCC; Brooklyn SE; Mystic SA. Award: Hon. Mention, CT AFA, 1918. Author and illustrator of "New York, the Nation's Metropolis." Address in 1929, 155 West 58th Street, 30 West 59th Street, NYC; Water Street, Stonington, CT.

MARDON, ALLAN.
Illustrator. Born in Welland, Ontario in 1931. He graduated from the Ontario College of Art and studied at the Edinburgh School of Art and Slade School of Fine Art. His editorial illustrations are in great demand and are seen regularly in Time and Sports Illustrated. His Time covers have been exhibited overseas and he has shown work in the S of I Annual Exhibitions, the General Electric Gallery and Circle Gallery, which has issued his NBA lithographs as part of its 1977 Official Fine Art Sports Collection.

MARE, JOHN.
Portrait painter. Born 1739 in NYC. He is recorded in the city of New York as a "Limner." He painted the portrait of Robert Monckton, Governor of NY in 1761; he signed his portrait of John Ketelas "Jno. Mare Pinxt, 1767." Three other portraits painted by him in 1766, 1767 and 1768 have been identified. Died in 1795.

MARE, JOHN De.
Engraver. Born in Belgium, he belonged to a noble and ancient family, and was himself a highly cultivated man. It is not known where he learned to engrave; but he appeared in NY about 1850, and engraved in line a few admirable book illustrations. He is said to have returned to Europe about 1861.

MARGOULIES, BERTA.
Painter. Born: Milwaukee, Wisconsin in 1907. Studied: Smith College; Silvermine Guild School of Art; and with Revington Arthur, Gail Bymon, Umberto Romano and Robert Rocher. Awards: Burndy Enginering award, Silvermine Guild, 1957; Electric Regulator Corporation, 1954; New Haven Paint and Clay Club, 1955; Springfield Art Legue, 1957; Chautauqua Art Assoc., 1958. Collections: Burndy Library, Norwalk, CT; Springfield Museum of Art; New Haven Paint and Clay Club.

MARGULIES, JOSEPH.
Painter and etcher. Born in Austria, July 7, 1896. Pupil of Joseph Pennell; NAD; ASL of NY; Ecole des Beaux Arts, Paris. Member: ASL of NY; Louis Comfort Tiffany Guild; Alliance. Work:

Portrait of Judge Garvin, Federal Court, Brooklyn; Portrait, Morris Raphael Cohen, College of City of New York; Portrait, Dr. Frederick Paul, De Witt Clinton High School; Portrait, Attorney General Albert Ottinger of New York, State Capitol, Albany, NY. Address in 1929, 310 West 75th Street, New York, NY.

MARGULIES, PAULINE.
Sculptor. Born in NY in 1895. Pupil of Eberle, Brewster and Fraser. Address in 1926, Cooper Hall, 20 East 7th Street, New York City.

MARIE-TERESA, (SISTER).
Painter and teacher. Born Stillwater, MN, April 27, 1877. Pupil of New York School of Art; ASL of NY; PAFA; Robert Henri. Studied in Florence and Munich. Awards: Hon. mention for painting, St. Paul Inst., 1916; bronze medal for oil, St. Paul Inst., 1918; hon. mention, MN State Art, 1919; silver medal and prize, MN AA, 1920; hon. mention, MN State Fair, 1922; special mention, MN State Art S., 1923. Member: St. Paul AS. Address in 1929, The College of St. Catherine, St. Paul, MN.

MARIL, HERMAN.
Painter and printmaker. Born in Baltimore, MD, Oct. 13, 1908. Study: MD Inst. of Fine Arts. Whitney Mus., and Met. Mus. of Art, NYC; Baltimore Mus.; Nat'l. Collection of Fine Arts, Smithsonian Inst.; Scranton, PA, Post Office Murals; and others. Exhib.: San Fran. Golden Gate Expos.; Carnegie Inst. Ann., 1940-45; retrospective, Baltimore Mus., 1967; PAFA; Corcoran Gallery, Wash. EC, Biennnials; and many others. Awards: Stefan Hirsch Mem. Award, Audubon Artists, 1972; Inst. Arts & Letters, Acad. Arts & Letters, NYC, 1978. Teaching: Univ. of MD, 1947-present. Mem.: Baltimore Mus. of Art; Col. Art Assn.; Artists Equity Assn.; Assoc., NAD. Media: Oil, acylic, casein. Rep.: Forum Gallery, NYC.

MARIN, JOHN.
Painter and etcher. Born Rutherford, NJ, 1870. Pupil of ASL

of NY; PAFA. One of the "291" group of the "Seven Americans" at the Intimate Gallery, New York. Represented in the Metropolitan Museum of Art, New York; Brooklyn Museum of Art; San Francisco Museum of Art, San Franciso, CA; Phillips Memorial Gallery, Washington, DC. Address in 1929, 253 Clark Terrace, Cliffside, NJ.

MARK, LOUIS.
Painter. Born Hungary, Aug. 25, 1867. Pupil of Bouguereau in Paris. Member: NAC. Work: "Trinquets," Royal Museum, Budapest; "Explorer Robert Peary," Brooklyn Museum, Brooklyn, NY; "Tvyll," Albright Art Gallery, Buffalo, NY. Address in 1929, 200 West 57th Street, New York, NY; h. Benczur-Ucca- 7, Budapest, Hungary.

MARK, PHYLLIS.
Sculptor. Born in NYC. Studied: Ohio State Univ.; with Seymour Lipton. Exhibitions: Drew Univ., 1969; Morris Museum, NJ, 1970; The Hudson River Museum, 1971-1972. Collections: Dickerson-White Museum; Cornell Univ.; The RCA Corporate Collection; Syracuse Univ.

MARKELL, ISABELLA BANKS.
Graphic Artist. Born: Superior, Wisconsin. Studied: Maryland Inst.; PAFA; Ecole des Beaux-Arts, Paris and with O'Hara, Brackman and Farnsworth. Awards: Boston Printmakers; Pen and Brush Club, 1953; Providence, Rhode Island, 1953, 1955; National Association of Women Artists, 1958; Wilmington Society of Fine Art, 1958. Collections: NY Public Library; New York Historical Society; Museum, City of NY; Northwest Printmakers; Metropolitan Museum of Art; State College; Philadelphia Free Library; Philadelphia Printmakers Club; New York Hospital; Providence Museum of Art; Grinnell Public Library; Wilmington Society of Fine Arts.

MARKHAM, CHARLOTTE H.
Painter. Born in Wisconsin in 1892. Pupil of Art Institute of Chicago. Address in 1926, 704 Marshall Street, Milwaukee, WI.

603

MARKHAM, MARION E.
Painter. Born in Syracuse, NY, in 1875. Pupil of Chase. Represented by "Girl in Red" and "Portrait of a Child," at Syracuse Museum of Fine Arts. Address in 1926, 430 La Fayette Street, New York.

MARKLE, ALVAN, JR.
Painter. Born Hazleton, July 28, 1889. Pupil of H. N. Hooven. Member: Phila. AC; Grand Central GA. Address in 1929, 333 West Green Street, Hazleton, PA.

MARKOE, FRANCIS HARTMAN.
Painter, writer, lecturer, and teacher. Born New York City, June 11, 1884. Pupil of Alden Weir. Member: Mural P; Arch. Lg. Address in 1929, 535 Park Avenue, New York, NY.

MARKS, STELLA LEWIS.
Painter. Born Melbourne, Australia, Nov. 27, 1892. Member: R.M.S., London; N.A. Women PS.; Am. S., Min. P. Work: "H. R. H. The Princess Patricia of Connaught," owned by the English Royal Family; miniature of "Maud Allen," National Gallery of Victoria, Melbourne, Australia. Address in 1929, Larchmont Hills Apts., Larchmont, NY.

MARKS, WILLIAM.
Illustrator, of Calumet, MI, died Sept 7, 1906.

MARR, CARL.
Painter, illustrator, and teacher. Born Milwaukee, WI, Feb. 14, 1858. Pupil of Weimar Academy under Schaus; Berlin Academy under Gussow; Munich under Seitz and Lindenschmit. Member: Academies of Munich, Berlin, Athens, etc.; Nat. Inst. A. L. Awards: Gold medal, Prize Fund Exhibition, New York, 1886; medals, Vienna, Berlin, Munich, Dresden, Madrid, Salzburg, Barcelona, Antwerp, Budapest; first medal, Liege, 1905. Work: "Dusk," Museum of Art, Toledo; "Gossip" and "The Mystery of Life," Metropolitan Museum, New York. Address in 1929, Solln II, C., Munich, Germany.

MARS, ETHEL.
Painter, engraver and craftsman. Born Springfield, IL. Member:

Salon d'Automne, Paris; Societe Nationale des Beaux Arts, Paris. Represented in collection of the French Government. Specialty, colored woodblock prints. Address in 1929, Vence, Alp. Mar., France.

MARSAC, HARVEY.
This name appears as an "engraver" in the New York Directory for 1834. As no work signed by him has been found by the compiler, it can not be positively stated that he engraved on copper.

MARSCHNER, ARTHUR A.
Painter, illustrator, and etcher. Born Detroit, MI, April 11, 1884. Pupil of J. P. Wicker. Member: Scarab C. Award: Prize, Scarab C. 1926. Address in 1929, 1479 Seyburn Avenue, Detroit, MI.

MARSDEN, EDITH FRANCES.
Painter, craftswoman, and teacher. Born Utica, NY, Sept. 22, 1880. Pupil of Birge Harrison, Arthur Freedlander, Henry R. Poore, Harry Leith-Ross, George Pearse Ennis; NY School of Fine and Applied Art. Member: Springfield AL; Springfield AG; Alliance; EAA. Address in 1929, High School of Commerce; h. 8 Buckingham Street, Springfield, MA.

MARSDEN, RUTH GLADYS.
Painter and teacher. Born Pittsfield, MA, March 11, 1898. Pupil of NY School of Fine and Applied Art; Grand Central School of Art. Member: Springfield AL; Springfield AG; EAA. Address in 1929, Artists Guild, Harrison Avenue; h. 8 Buckingham Street, Springfield, MA.

MARSH, ALICE RANDALL (MRS).
Miniature painter. Born in Coldwater, MI. Pupil of Art Institute of Chicago; also of Merson, Colin, Whistler and MacMonnies in Paris. Member: American Society of Miniature Painters. Address in 1926, Nutley, New Rochelle, NY.

MARSH, ANNE STEELE.
Painter and printmaker. Born: Nutley, New Jersey in Sept. 7, 1901. Studied: Cooper Union Art School. Award: Philadelphia

Printmakers Club, 1952. Collections: Museum of Modern Art; Library of Congress; Montclair Art Museum; Newark Public Library; Metropolitan Museum of Art; Collectors of American Art; Philadelphia Museum of Art.

MARSH, CHARLES HOWARD.
Painter, etcher, and teacher. Born Magnolia, IA, April 8, 1885. Pupil of W. V. Cahill, Guy Rose, Clarence Hickle, Gorguet and Despujol in Paris, and Stickney Memorial School of Pasadena. Member: Calif. AC: Laguna Beach AA; Calif. WCS. Award: First prize, Southern California Fair Exhibition, Riverside, Calif., 1920. Address in 1929, Director European School, Fort Wayne, IN.

MARSH, FRED DANA.
Painter. Born Chicago, IL, April 6, 1872. Pupil of AIC. Member: SAA 1902; ANA 1906; NY Arch. Lg. 1902; Mural painter. 1904; New Rochelle AA; AFA. Awards: Bronze medal, Paris Exp., 1900; Silver medal, Pan-Am. Exp., Buffalo, 1901; bronze medal, St. Louis Exp., 1904. Work: Steamer "Berkshire," Rochester Art Gallery; decorations in Hotel McAlpin, NY; United Engineering Societies Bldg.; Museum of Safety, New York, NY; Automobile Club of America; Detroit Country Club. Pictorial Maps in SS. Malolo and many privately owned. Address in 1929, Wykagyl Park, New Rochelle, NY; Sakonnet Point, RI.

MARSH, HENRY.
Wood engraver. His work appeared in "The Riverside Magazine" published by Hurd & Houghton. He also executed the splendidly engraved wood-cuts of insects in Harris' "Insects Injurious to Vegetation." This work of patience, and requiring remarkable eyesight, shows also true artistic skill, and evidences the great talent of the engraver.

MARSH, LUCILE PATTERSON.
Illustrator. Born Rapid City, SD, Oct. 21, 1890. Pupil of AIC. Work: Advertising for Lux, Pet Milk, Post Toasties, Val Spar Paints, Ivory Soap, Jello, etc.; illustrations for "Woman's Home Companion"; "Saturday Evening Post"; "Good Housekeeping." Address in 1929, 412 West 20th Street, New York, NY; summer, "The Sycamores," Torresdale, PA.

MARSH, MARY E.
(Mrs. Conrad Buff) Painter and writer. Born Cincinnati, OH. Pupil of Birger Sandzen, Chicago AFA, Cincinnati Art Academy. Member: Calif. AC; Laguna Beach Art Assoc. Address in 1929, 1428 Holbrook Street, Eagle Rock, CA.

MARSH, REGINALD.
Illustrator. Born in Paris in 1898. He attended Yale University where he began his career illustrating for the Yale Record. He came to NY in 1920 and served as a staff artist for the Daily News and as a cartoonist at The New Yorker. Best known for his painting of NY scenes, he was in demand for his magazine work and, later in his career, for book illustration. He illustrated Anatomy for Artists in 1945. Painter and illustrator. Born in 1898, in NYC. Studied at Yale, graduating in 1920. Made numerous illustrations for the Yale Record, drew cartoons for Vanity Fair, Harper's Bazaar and the Daily News, approx. 4,000 drawing in three years. Studied with John Sloan and George Luks. Studied in Europe. Some notable paintings in oil include "Why Not Use The L?", 1930 and "Negroes on Rockaway Beach", 1934. Died in 1954.

MARSH, WILLIAM R.
Was engraving vignettes, advertising cards, etc., in New York, from 1833-43.

MARSHALL.
In Judge Marshall's "Life of George Washington," published by C.P. Wayne, Phila., 1804-07, one of the illustrative maps is signed "Marshall Sct." This map represents the relative positions of the American and British forces prior to the Battle of White Plains, Oct. 28, 1776.

MARSHALL, FRANK HOWARD.
Painter. Born in England, 1866. Pupil of ASL of NY; Chase School,

New York; Julian Academy in Paris under Laurens; studied in Madrid and London. Member: Salma C., 1910; AFA. Address in 1929, Palo Alto, CA.

MARSHALL, FRANK WARREN.
Landscape painter, craftsman, and teacher. Born Providence, RI, Sept. 24, 1866. Pupil of RI School of Design; Julian Academy, Paris. Member: Providence AC; Providence WCC. Address in 1929, 652 Angell Street, Providence, RI.

MARSHALL, MARGARET J.
Illustrator. Born Philadelphia, PA, July 29, 1895. Pupil of PAFA. Member: Plastic C.; Fellowship PAFA. Awards: Cresson Traveling Scholarship, PAFA, 1918. Illustrated "Children of the Alps," published by Lippincott & Co. Address in 1929, 223 S. Sixth Street, Torresdale, Philadelphia, PA.

MARSHALL, MARY E. (MRS.).
Painter. Born Plainfield, PA. Pupil of Dow; Walter Sargent; Breckenridge. Member: Alumni PMSIA; Fellowship PAFA; Phila. Art Alliance; Plastic C; N.A. Women PS; Eastern AA; North Shore AA; AFA. Special assistant in the dept. of art education, Phila. Public Schools, and director, School Art Lg., Philadelphia. Address in 1929, 111 South 21st Street, Philadelphia, PA; summer, Wonson's Dock, East Gloucester, MA.

MARSHALL, MAY CHISWELL.
Painter. Born Markham, VA. Pupil of Chase, Webster, Critcher, Corcoran School of Art. Member: S. Wash. A.; SSAL; Wash. AC; Provincetown AA. Address in 1929, 1701 K Street, N. W., Washington, D.C.; summer, 6 Priscilla Alden Road, Provincetown, MA.

MARSHALL, RACHEL.
See Mrs. Arthur L. Hawks.

MARSHALL, THOMAS W.
Landscape and genre painter. Born in 1850, he died in 1874. Exhibited at National Academy , 1871, "Near Bellows Falls." His work showed much promise.

MARSHALL, WILLIAM EDGAR.
Painter and engraver. Born in New York, June 30, 1837. Employed by the American Bank Note Company in 1858, but subsequently painted portraits in oil and engraved large portraits in line. He settled in Boston, but in 1864-66 traveled in Europe, residing chiefly in Paris, where he exhibited in the Salons of 1865 and 1866. Among his more noteworthy achievements were engravings after Stuart's "Washington" and Da Vinci's portrait of Christ; his heroic ideal painting of Christ, which he also engraved; and also engravings of many distinguished persons, including Lincoln, Longfellow, Cooper, Garfield, Beecher, Grant, Sherman, Blaine, Hancock, Harrison, McKinley, and Roosevelt, most of which were reproduced from oil paintings by himself. Represented at the National Gallery, in Washington, D.C., by his portrait of Longfellow, and self-portrait at the age of 23.

MARSHBURN, THERESA.
Watercolorist. Studied: New York Univ.; Fairleigh Dickinson Univ., NJ; The Art Students' League, NY. Awards: Marquette Univ., Milwaukee, Wisconsin, 1973; Flint Art Museum, Michigan, 1973; Wisconsin Festival of Arts, 1974. Exhibitions: Columbia University, NY, 1966; Artesaneos Festival, Albuquerque, NM, 1973; El Paso Museum of Art, TX, 1974.

MARSIGLIA, GERLANDO.
Portrait painter. Born in Italy in 1792, he arrived in New York about 1817. In 1826 he was elected a member of the National Academy of Design. His copy of the portrait of General Von Steuben after Ralph Earl is owned by the City of New York. He died Sept 4, 1850, in NYC.

MARSTON, J. B.
Portrait painter, who worked in Boston in 1807. His portrait of Gov. Caleb Strong is in the MA Historical Society.

MARTIN.
Portrait draftsman in crayons. Martin was an Englishman who came

from Sheffield to NY about 1797. His work was in steady demand, and he worked there until 1808.

MARTIN, AGNES.
Painter. Born: Macklin, Can. March 22, 1911. Studied: Columbia University. Collections: Union Carbide Co., Wadsworth Atheneum; Whitney Museum of American Art and The Solomon R. Guggenheim Museum. She has exhibited widely throughout the United States. Address in 1980, Galuteo, New Mexico.

MARTIN, CHARLES.
Portrait painter. Born in 1820. He flourished about 1850, in Bristol, Rhode Island. In 1851 he exhibited at the NA in NY. Died April 5, 1906 in London, England.

MARTIN, D.
He engraved at least one portrait, and also some of the maps found in The Monthly Military Repository, published by G. Smith, New York, 1796. These are maps of military operations during the Revolution.

MARTIN, E.
In 1826 this man was engraving buildings, etc., for Cincinnati publishers.

MARTIN, EDNA M.
Painter and teacher. Born Seekonk, MA, March 1, 1896. Pupil of RI School of Design. Member: Providence WCC; Providence Handicraft C.; Providence AC. Represented in RI School of Design Gallery. Address in 1929, 227 Fall River Avenue, Seekonk, MA.

MARTIN, GAIL W.
Painter and educator. Born: Tacoma, Washington in 1913. Studied: John Herron Art School; State University, Iowa; and with Philip Guston, Fletcher Martin and Emil Ganso; Boston Museum Art School with Karl Zerbe. Awards: Art Guild of St. Louis, 1943; Norwich CT, 1955; New England Drawing Exhibition, 1958; Mary Millikan European traveling scholarship, John Herron Art School, 1937. Collections: Lib. of Congress; Wadsworth Atheneum,

Hartford, CT; United States Post Office, Danville, Indiana.

MARTIN, HOMER DODGE.
Painter and illustrator. Born in Albany, NY, on Oct. 28, 1836. He studied painting with William Hart, at the National Academy, and in 1878 was one of the founders of the Society of American Artists. In 1875 he was elected a National Academician. His early work followed the conventional lines of the Hudson River School, and he was, in a sense, the first American impressionist. His noted works, such as "Normandy Trees," "Adirondack Scenery," "River Scene" (Metropolitan Museum, New York), and "Old Church in Normandy," are among the most individual productions of American Art, and his work as a whole occupies a place by itself owing to its intrinsic beauty and admirable personal quality. He died Feb. 12, 1897, in St. Paul, MN.

MARTIN, JEROME.
Illustrator. Born in New York City in 1926. He studied at Cooper Union and NYU. His first piece appeared in Fortune in 1959, which led to assignments for Sports Illustrated, Playboy, Life and The Saturday Evening Post. Numerous awards from the AIGA, ADC, and a Gold Medal from the S of I are the result of his efforts in the profession. His artwork has been shown at the Museum of Modern Art, Whitney Museum, Metropolitan Museum of Art and in the LC.

MARTIN, JOHN BLENNERHASSET.
Engraver. Born Sept. 5, 1797 in Ireland. Several stipple portraits, fairly well engraved, and published in Richmond, VA, in 1822, are signed "Engraved by J. B. Martin, Richmond." He drew upon stone a good quarto portrait of John Randolph, of Roanoke. This lithograph was printed by Cephas G. Childs, but is signed as "Drawn on Stone & Published by J. B. Martin, Richmond." Also painted portraits and miniatures. Died Oct. 22, 1857 in Richmond, VA.

MARTIN, JOHN.
Illustrator. Born in Camden, NJ in 1946. He graduated in 1968 from the Phila. College of Art. Among his instructors were Albert Gold, Jack Freas and Ben Eisenstat. After military service as an art director for the psychological operations group in Vietnam, he returned to NJ, whereupon he began free-lancing. Among his clients are Reader's Digest, Seventeen, Nonesuch Records, Elektra Records and Bell Telephone Company as well as book publishers. His wife, Nancy, is also an illustrator.

MARTIN, MARIA.
(Mrs. Maria Bachman). Painter. Born in Charleston, South Carolina, on July 3, 1796. In 1831 she met the naturalist and artist John James Audubon. With instruction from Audubon she began developing her artistic talent, and before long she was actively assisting him in his work by painting in backgrounds for his watercolor portraits of birds. A great many of the color plates in Birds of America and of those plates later issued separately in America featured her work, and it is possible that some of her watercolors of birds may have been touched up and used by Audubon as well. In this work she was one of his three principal assistants and the only woman. She also contributed a number of drawings to John Edwards Holbrook's North American Herpetology, 1836-1842. Audubon named the Maria's woodpecker - Picus martinae - a subspecies of hairy woodpecker, for her. Died in Columbia, South Carolina, on December 27, 1863.

MARTIN, MRS. MARSHALL B.
Painter. Member: Providence WCC. Address in 1929, 1113 Turks' Head Bldg.; 336 Doyle Avenue, Providence, RI.

MARTIN, NANCY YARNALL.
Illustrator. Born in Camden, New Jersey in 1949. She studied at the Corcoran School of Art and Philadelphia College of Art under Ben Isenstat and Albert Gold. Her work appeared in the Illustrators 18th Annual Exhibition at the S of

I. She and her husband, illustrator John W. Martin, presently live in Pennsauken, New Jersey.

MARTIN, ROBERT.
Born in Scotland. In 1860 this man produced some excellent line illustrations for Cooper's works, published in NY.

MARTIN, STEFAN.
Illustrator. Born in Elgin, Illinois, he studied for four years at the AIC under Ben Shahn. His work appeared in Natural History magazine in 1960 and he has had assignments from book companies including E. P. Dutton, Coward-McCann, Scribner's and Grosset and Dunlap. Best known for his paintings and woodcuts, he has twice won awards from the AIGA. He is represented in the collections of the Philadelphia Museum, LC, Metropolitan Museum of Art and AIC.

MARTIN, WILLIAM A. K.
Marine, landscape, and historical painter. Born in Philadelphia in 1817. He studied painting abroad, and portraiture under John Neagle, in Philadelphia. The Wilstach Collection in Fairmount Park owns his picture "Bruce Defending the Path At Delrey." He painted many of the old "men-of-war" of the U.S. Navy. He died in Philadelphia in 1867.

MARTINET, MARJORIE DORSEY.
Painter and teacher. Born Baltimore, MD, Nov. 3, 1886. Pupil of MD Inst., PAFA, Chase, Cecilia Beaux. Member: MD Inst. Alumni; Fellowship PAFA; Phila. Alliance; Balto. Mus. of Art. Awards: Cresson European Scholarship, PAFA; Thouron prize for composition, PAFA. Director, Martinet School of Art, Baltimore. Address in 1929, 10 East Franklin Street; h. 4102 Ridgewood Avenue, West Arlington, Baltimore, MD.

MARTINEZ, XAVIER.
(Timoeteo Martinez y Orozco). Painter, etcher, and teacher. Born Guadalajara, Mexico, Feb. 7, 1874. Pupil of Mark Hopkins Inst., San Francisco; Ecole des Beaux-Arts under Gerome and Carriere. Member:

San F. Sketch C.; Bohemian C. Awards: Gold medal, San F. Art Assoc. 1895; hon. mention, Paris Exp., 1900; gold medal, as collaborator in exhib. of CA School AC, and hon. mention for etching, P. P. Exp., San Francisco, 1915. Address in 1929, 816 Scenic Avenue, Piedmont, CA.

MARTINI, HERBERT E.
Painter, illustrator, etcher, writer, and lecturer. Born Brooklyn, NY, Jan. 8, 1888. Pupil of F. V. DuMond and Munich Royal Academy under Angelo Jank. Member: Stowaways. Work: Illustrated, "Golden Treasury Readers" and "French Reader"; author, "Color." Address in 1929, 97 Harris Avenue, Long Island City, NY.

MARTINO, ANTONIO PIETRO.
Painter. Born Philadelphia, PA, April 13, 1902. Member: Phila. Sketch C; Phila. Alliance. Awards: Hon. mention, Phila. Sketch C, 1925; hon. mention, Phila. AC, 1925; Murphy Memorial prize, NAD, 1926; medal, Phila. Sketch C, 1926; bronze medal, Sesqui-Centennial Expo., Phila., 1926; first Hallgarten prize, NAD, 1927. Work: "Sunlight and Shadow," Reading Museum, Reading, PA. Address in 1929, 34 South 17th Street, h. 127 N. Gross Street, Philadelphia, PA.

MARTINO, MICHEL.
Sculptor. Born Alvignano, Casserta, Italy, Feb. 22, 1889. Pupil of Lee Lawrie and H. Kitson. Award: English Fellowship prize of Yale University for study abroad. Work: "Landing of Pilgrims," "Battle of Lexington," Strong School, New Haven; White Plains High School Memorial Tablet; Commemorative medal, American Public Health Society; Memorial Flag Staff, Brooklyn, NY; Spanish War memorial, New Haven; pediment for St. Anne Church, Hartford, CT. Address in 1929, 211 Clay Street, New Haven, CT; h. 14 Myron Street, Norris Cove, CT.

MARTINY, PHILIP.
Sculptor. Born in Alsace France, in 1858. He came to America in the early eighties. Pupil of Eugene

Dock in France; Augustus Saint Gaudens in United States. Elected Associate Member of National Academy 1902. Member: NY Architectural League. Work: Doors for St. Bartholomew's Church, NY; McKinley Monument, Springfield, MA; Soldiers and Sailors Monument, Jersey City, NJ; portrait statue of ex-Vice-President G. A. Hobart, Paterson, NJ; sculpture in Hall of Records, NY; two groups in Chamber of Commerce, NY. Address in 1926, 400 West 23d Street, New York, NY. Died June 26, 1927 in NYC.

MARTMER, WILLIAM P.
Painter. Born in Detroit, Mich., Sept. 25, 1939. Study: Art School of Society of Arts & Crafts; Cranbrook Academy of Art; Wayne State Univ.; Univ. of Mich. Work: Cranbrook Academy Museum; General Motors Corporation. Exhibitions: Cranbrook Art Academy Gallery; Northern Illinois University Art Dept.; Brooklyn Museum, Print Show; Wayne State Univ. Alumni, Invitational; The Raven Gallery, Detroit, Michigan. Awards: Lewis Art Prize, Huntington Woods Ann. Popular Prize, Kalamazoo Art Center; Popular Prize, Scarab Club of Detroit; and others. Teaching: Instructor, Detroit Inst. of Arts; Instructor Wayne State University. Mem.: Scarab Club, Detroit. Media: Oil. Address in 1982, Coloma, Mich.

MARULIS, ATHAN.
Painter. Born in Athens, Greece, in 1889. Pupil of Manos; Paul M. Gustin; Yasushi Tanaka. Member: Seattle Fine Arts Society. Address in 1926, 211 Fourth Avenue, North Seattle, WA.

MARWEDE, RICHARD L.
Painter. Born New York, NY, Feb. 5, 1884. Pupil of ASL of NY. Member: ASL of NY; Alliance. Address in 1929, 976 Anderson Avenue, New York, NY.

MASE, CAROLYN CAMPBELL.
Landscape Painter. Born Matteawan, NY. Pupil of J. H. Twachtman. Member: CT AFA; NA Women PS: Wash. AC. Address in 1929, 1600 Genesee Street, Utica, NY.

MASON, ABRAHAM JOHN.
English engraver. Born April 4, 1794 in London. He was best known for his wood engraving. Studied Robert Branston. He came to this country in 1829, and settled in NY, and the following year he was elected an Associate of the National Academy of Design, and professor of wood engraving; he also lectured on this subject in Boston. Mason, finding his occupation unprofitable, returned to London in 1839. He died in England.

MASON, ALICE TRUMBULL.
Painter. Born: Litchfield, CT in 1904. Awards: Philadelphia Printmakers Club, 1946; Society of American Grpahic Artists, 1947; Silvermine Guild, 1952. Collections: Museum of Modern Art; New York Public Library; Berkshire Museum of Art; Library of Congress; Brooklyn Museum; Solomon Guggenheim Museum of Art; Philadelphia Museum of Art.

MASON, ALVA.
Engraver. About 1819 the firm of W. and A. Mason advertised as "Engravers of brass ornaments for book-binding etc.; charter and Patent Medicine Seals, Embossing plates and Brass Engraving for Typographical Printing." Their establishment was located at No. 15 South 4th Street, Philadelphia.

MASON, C. D.
Sculptor. Born in France in 1830; came to New York in 1860. He worked in NY, Philadelphia, and in Chicago. He died in July, 1915, in Mineola, L.I.

MASON, D. H.
The Philadelphia directories of 1805-18 contain the name of D. H. Mason, "music-engraver." In 1816 he executed vignettes for the bank-note engraving firm of Murray, Draper, Fairman Co., Phila., and in 1830 Mason signed a certificate as "Architect and Engraver."

MASON, ELEANOR.
Miniature painter. Exhibited at the Penna. Academy of Fine Arts, Philadelphia, 1925. Address in 1926, 871 Beacon Street, Boston, MA.

MASON, FRANK HERBERT.
Painter. Born in Cleveland, Ohio, Feb. 20, 1921. Study: Nat'l. Acad. of Design, NYC, with George Nelson, 1937-38; ASL, with Frank Vincent DuMond, 1937-51. Work: Butler Inst. of Amer. Arts, Young, Ohio; Am. Embassy, London; US War Dept.; others. Paintings: St. Anthony of Padua, 11th Cert. Church of San Gioranni di Malta, Venice; Resurrection, Old St. Patrick's Cathedral, NYC; San Rocco, Church of Santa Vittoria, Italy; Murals, King Faisel Naval Acad., Saudi Arabia. Exhib.: Palais des Congres, Monaco, 1968; Nat'l. Arts Club, NYC, 1973; Mood Gallery, San Fran., 1977 & 79; Met. Mus., NYC, 1979. Awards: Nat'l. Academy of Design; Popular Prize, Assoc. Artists of Pittsburgh, Carnegie Inst.; Penn-National Legionier; Prix du Nord, Expos Intercontinentale, Monaco; etc. Teaching: Art Students League, NYC, 1950-present. Mem.: ASL; Nat'l. Soc. Mural Painters; Int'l. Inst. Conserv. of Hist. & Artistic Works; Academician, NAD. Media: Graphics, watercolor. Address in 1982, 385 Boroome Street, New York, NY 10013.

MASON, GEORGE.
Limner and crayon portrait draftsman. He inserted an advertisement in the Boston Chronicle for June, 1768, stating that he drew "portraits in crayon for two guineas each." Died in 1773 in Boston.

MASON, JOHN.
Painter and designer. Born New York, NY, 1868. Pupil of Julian Academy in Paris under Laurens and Constant. Member: Alliance. Award: Bronze medal, Paris Exp., 1889. Work: Decoration of dining room of Harmonic Club, New York; "Portrait of Admiral Dewey" and "Portrait of Major S. Ellis Briggs," in Armory, New York City; decorations, Wanamaker's; Gueting's Shoe Store; Louis Mark Shoe Store, Inc.; Blum Store and Dalsimer Shoe Store in Philadelphia. Address in

1929, 1506 Sansom Street; h. 1608 Pine Street, Philadelphia, PA.

MASON, JONATHAN (JR.).
Portrait painter. Born in 1795. Lived on Mt. Vernon Street, Boston. Exhibited portraits and figure subjects 1828-34 at the Boston Athenaeum, among them his Self-portrait. Died in 1884.

MASON, MARY STODDERT.
Sculptor. Born in Jackson, TN. Principal works, "Pilgrim Mother," "The Spirit of the New Era," and "Woman Triumphant." Address in 1926, Elmsford, Westchester County, NY. Died in 1934.

MASON, MARY TOWNSEND (MRS.).
(Mrs. Wm. Clarke Mason). Painter. Born Zanesville, OH, March 21, 1886. Pupil of Chase and Breckenridge at PAFA; Maryland Inst., Baltimore. Member: Fellowship PAFA; Phila. Alliance; Plastic C., 1917; NA Women PS; AFA; SSAL. Awards: Cresson traveling scholarship, PAFA, 1909; Gold medal, Plastic C., 1921 and 1924; Mary Smith prize, PAFA, 1922. Work: "Blue and Gold," Fellowship PA Acad. of the Fine Arts; "Still Life with Fruit," PA Acad. of the Fine Arts. Address in 1929, 8233 Seminole Avenue, Chestnut Hill, Philadelphia, PA.

MASON, MAUD M.
Painter, craftswoman, and teacher. Born Russellville, KY, March 18, 1867. Pupil of Chase, Dow and Snell in New York; Brangwyn in London. Member: NY Soc. Ceramic A; Boston SAC; NA Women PS; NAC; Pen and Brush C.; SPNY; Allied AA.; AWCS; NY WCC; AFA. Awards: Gold medal, P. P. Exp., San F., 1915; bronze medal, NAC, 1920; 1st prize, N.A. Women PS, 1922. Address in 1929, 36 Gramercy Park, New York, NY; summer, New Canaan, CT.

MASON, ROBERT LINDSAY.
Illustrator, painter, and writer. Born Knoxville, TN, June 5, 1874. Pupil of Howard Pyle. Member: East Tennessee FAS; Wilmington FAS. Award: Rush Strong medal, Southern Appalachian Expo. Work: Illustrations for books and magazines, "Harper's," etc.; author

of "The Lure of the Great Smokies" (Houghton Mifflin Co., Boston); author of short stories and articles on out-of-door life in the Great Smoky Mts., with illustrations. Address in 1929, 230 East Church Avenue, Knoxville, TN.

MASON, ROY M.
Painter. Born Gilbert Mills, NY, March 15, 1886. Self-taught. Member: Buffalo SA; Salma. C.; AFA. Awards: First prize, Buffalo SA, 1928; hon. mention, Rochester, 1928. Address in 1929, Turner Building; h. 1 Richmond Avenue, Batavia, NY.

MASON, W. SANFORD.
Painter, engraver, and copyist. He was working in Philadelphia about 1865. He made several copies of "The Washington Family, at Mount Vernon" after the painting by Savage.

MASON, WILLIAM ALBERT.
Painter and instructor. Born in Cambridge, MA, in 1885. Director of art education in the public schools of Philadelphia. Died Dec. 23, 1920 in Philadelphia.

MASON, WILLIAM G.
This line-engraver of buildings, etc., was located in Philadelphia in 1822-45, except during the years 1823-29. He made the illustrations for Joshua Shaw's "U. S. Architecture," and for other publications by the same author. Also painted landscapes.

MASSEY, ROBERT JOSEPH.
Painter and Educator. Born in Ft. Worth, Texas, May 14, 1921. Study: Okla. State Univ.; with Doel Reed; Univ. of Havana; Univ. of Mich.; Syracuse Univ.; Univ. of Tex., Austin. Work: Dallas Museum of Fine Art; Syracuse Museum of Art; Society of American Graphic Artists; El Paso Mus. of Art; Univ. of New Mexico; and others, plus several commissions. Exhib.: Nat'l. Sm. Ptg. Exhib., Univ. of the Pacific, Stockton, Calif.; Ann. Gulf Coast Exhib., Mobile, Ala.; Sm. Ptg. Show, Albuquerque, NM; State Art Exhib., Port Arthur, Texas; and others. Awards:

Honorable Mention, El Paso Art Annual; Honorable Mention, Graphics, El Paso; John Chapman Purchase Award for Painting, Syracuse; Carnegie Institute Sel. from Lib. of Congress; and others. Teaching: The Univ. of Texas at El Paso; and others. Media: Egg Tempera. Address in 1982, 708 McKelligon, El Paso, TX.

MASSON, EMILE.
Crayon portrait draftsman who was working in Boston, MA, 1852-1856.

MAST, JOSEPHINE.
Painter and teacher. Born New York City. Pupil of George Elmer Browne, Henry B. Snell, Hayley Lever. Member: NYWCC (assoc.); Provincetown AA; NA Women PS; NAC. Address in 1929, 140 Halsey Street, Brooklyn, NY; summer, Provincetown, MA.

MASTERS, FRANK B.
Illustrator. Born Watertown, MA, Sept. 25, 1873. Pupil of C. H. Woodbury and Howard Pyle. Member: SI, 1907; Salma. C. Address in 1929, 1 Morris Crescent, Yonkers, NY.

MATHEWS, ARTHUR FRANK.
Painter and teacher. Born Wisconsin, Oct. 1, 1860. Pupil of Boulanger in Paris; also studied architecture. Member: Phila. AC. Award: Gold medal, murals AIA, 1925. Work: Mural decoration (6 Panels), Oakland (CA) Library; mural paintings, California State Capitol Bldg; 4 triptych panels, Univeristy of CA Library; Library of Stanford University; decorations wall and dome of Commanding Hall, Masonic Temple, San Francisco; "California Landscape," Metropolitan Museum, New York. Director California School of Design 1890-1906. Address in 1929, 670 Fell Street, San Francisco, CA.

MATHEWS, FERDINAND SCHUYLER.
Painter, craftsman, illustrator, and writer. Born New Brighton, SI. NY, May 30, 1854. Pupil of Cooper Union in NY; traveled in Italy. Author and illustrator: "Familiar Trees," "Fieldbook of American Wild Flowers," "Fieldbook of Wild Birds and Their Music," "Fieldbook of American Shrubs and Trees," "Book of Birds for Young People," "Book of Wild Flowers for Young People." Botanical artist on staff of Gray Herbarium, Harvard University. Specialty, landscape in water color and illumination. Address in 1929, 17 Frost Street, Cambridge, MA.

MATHEWS, LUCIA KLEINHANS.
(Mrs. Arthur F. Mathews). Painter, illustrator, and craftsman. Born San Francisco, CA. Aug. 29, 1882. Pupil of A. F. Mathews, Whistler. Award: Silver medal, P. P. Exp., San F., 1915. Specialty, theatre decorations and furniture. Address in 1929, 670 Fell Street, San Francisco, CA.

MATHEWSON, FRANK CONVERS.
Painter. Born Barrington, RI, May 12, 1862. Pupil of Laurens and National School of Decorative Art in Paris. Member: NYWCC; Providence AC; Providence WCC; Alliance; North Shore AA. Award: Sullivan prize, Providence, 1903. Work: "Ogunquit Pasture," Rhode Island School of Design, Providence; "The Weisser Thurm," Boston Art Club. Address in 1929, 29 Waterman Street., Providence, RI; summer, Matunuck, South Kingston, RI.

MATHIEU, HUBERT.
Illustrator and etcher. Born Brookings, SD, Jan. 4, 1897. Pupil of Harvey Dunn and Henry Raleigh. Member: SI; GFLA; Am. APL. Illustrator for magazines, newspapers, and advertising; pastels and watercolors; portraits. Address in 1929, 1931 Broadway, New York, NY; summer, Westport, CT.

MATHUS, HENRY.
Painter and craftsman. Born Boston, MA, April 19, 1870. Pupil of RI School of Design. Member: Providence AC; Providence WCC. Address in 1929, 39 Henry Street, Edgewood, Cranston, RI.

MATSON, GRETA.
Painter. Born: Claremont, VA in 1915. Studied: Grand Central Sch. of Art; and with Jerry Farnsworth. Awards: NAD, 1943, 1945; Southern States Art Lg., 1945, 1946; Virginia Art, 1943, 1945, 1955;

Nat'l Assn. of Women Artists, 1943, 1952, 1953, 1955-1958; State Teachers Col., Indiana, PA, 1945, 1949, 1950; Norfolk Mus. of Art, 1943, 1948, 1954; Alabama Watercolor Soc., 1950, 1951; Mississippi Art Assn., 1951; Pen and Brush Club, 1948, 1951, 1952, 1954, 1956, 1958; CT Acad. of FA, 1952, 1953; New Orleans Art Assn., 1949, 1952; Butler Art Inst., 1948; NJ Artists, 1948, 1951; VA Mus. of Fine Arts, 1957; NJ Soc. of Painters and Sculptors, 1957. Collections: VA Mus. of Fine Arts; Norfolk Mus. of Art, State Teachers Col., Indiana, PA; New Britain Art Inst.; Texas Technical College; William and Mary College,; TX College of Art and Industry; Mary Calcott School, Norfolk, VA; Florida Southern College; Longwood College, Farmville, VA; Little Rock Museum of Fine Arts; Seton Hall University. Media: Oil and watercolor. Address in 1980, 8750 Old Ocean View Road, Norfolk, VA.

MATTEI, VIRGILIO P.
Painter and illustrator. Born Puerto Rico, June 30, 1897. Member: S. Indp. A. Award: First prize, Exhibition, Ponce, 1919. Address in 1929, Box 102; h. 49 Campos Street, Ponce, Puerto Rico.

MATTERSON, TOMKINS HARRISON.
Born in New York in 1813. (See Matteson, Tomkins Harrison).

MATTESON, BARTOW VAN VOORHIS.
Painter and illustrator. Born Buffalo, NY, Dec. 3, 1894. Pupil of School of Fine Arts of the Albright Art Gallery, Buffalo, NY; ASL of NY; Pratt Inst. Illustrator for "The Saturday Evening Post" and "The Country Gentleman." Address in 1929, Van Dyck Studio Bldg., 939 Eight Avenue, New York, NY; summer, Sturgeon Point, Derby, NY.

MATTESON, M. TOMKINS.
Born in New York, in 1813. Signature of Tomkins Harrison Matteson. (See entry).

MATTESON, TOMKINS HARRISON.
Born in Peterborough, NY, May 2, 1813. In 1839 he began to paint portraits of merit, and was brought

into notice by his "Spirit of '76" purchased by the American Art Union. His work was chiefly portraiture and historical painting. He became an Associate Member of the National Academy of Design in 1847. He died Feb. 2, 1884 in Sherburne, NY.

MATTHEWS, ANNA LOU.
Sculptor, painter, and illustrator. Born Chicago, IL. Pupil of Taft and Vanderpoel at AIC; Chicago Art Academy; Ecole des Beaux-Arts and under Simon, Max Bohm and Garrido in Paris; Brangwyn in London. Member: Assoc. Chic. PS. Awards: Hon. mention, MN. State Art. Com., 1913; second sculpture prize, MN. State Art Com., 1914; Rosenwald prize, AIC, 1921; Harry A. Frank Prize, AIC, 1929. Represented in St. Paul Institute of Art; Juvenile Court Room; murals, Walter Scott School, Rosenwald collection, and city of Chicago Collection, Chicago, IL. Address in 1929, 6016 Ellis Avenue, Chicago, IL.

MATTHEWS, GEORGE BAGBY.
Painter. Born in Tappahannock, VA, in 1857. Studied art abroad, 1880-83; pupil of Carolus Duran, Paris. Among his historical paintings are "Lee and His Generals," "The Crucifixion," "Jefferson Davis," "John Paul Jones," "Stonewall Jackson," "Lee," "Daughter of the Confederacy," "Gen. Tyler," "Patrick Henry," "General Joe Wheeler," "Colonel John S. Mosby," "Battle of the Merrimac with the Monitor," "Last of the Wooden Navy." Address in 1926, Washington, D.C.

MATTHEWS, WILLIAM.
Portrait painter. Born in Bristol, England, in 1821, he died in Washington, D.C., in 1905.

MATTHEWS, WILLIAM F.
Painter. Born St. Louis, MO, 1878. Pupil of St. Louis School of Fine Arts. Member: St. Louis AG; 2 x 4 Soc.; Soc. of Ancients; Brooklyn SA; Kit-Kat C; PS; Arch. Lg. of NY. Awards: Ives landscape prize, St. Louis AG, 1914 and 1915. Address in 1929, 103 Pierrepont Street, Brooklyn, NY.

MATTOCKS, MURIEL.
See Cleaves, Muriel Mattocks.

MATTSON, HENRY ELIS.
Painter. Born Sweden, Aug. 7, 1887. Pupil of Worcester Art Museum. Member: Woodstock AA. Work: "Wild Flowers," Phillips Memorial Gallery, Washington, D.C.; "Self Portrait," Municipal Art Gallery, Davenport, IA. Address in 1929, Woodstock, NY.

MATULKA, JAN.
Painter. Born in Czechoslovakia, 1890. Pupil of NAD. Studio in Paris. Collections in: Whitney, NY Public Library; Penn. Acad. of Fine Arts; San. F. Museum of Art; Detroit Inst. of Art; Yale Univ. Art Gallery. Address in 1929, 18 East 88th Street, New York, NY.

MATZAL, LEOPOLD CHARLES.
Painter and teacher. Born Vienna, Austria, Aug. 13, 1890. Studied in Austria. Award: Murray prize, Art Center, Orange, NJ, 1927. Work: "Portrait of Judge James F. Minturn" and "Portrait of Vice-Chancellor John T. Fallon," State House, Trenton, NJ; "Mayor P. R. Griffin," City Hall, Hoboken; "Librarian T. F. Hatfield," Public Library, Hoboken; "Mayor Frank Hague," City Hall, Jersey City. Address in 1929, 660 Mt. Prospect Street, Newark, NJ.

MATZEN, HERMAN N.
Sculptor and teacher. Born in Denmark, July 15, 1861. Pupil of Munich and Berlin Academies of Fine Art. Member: NSS; NAC; Cleveland SA. Awards: Second medal, Berlin, 1895; first medal, Berlin Exp., 1896. Work: "War" and "Peace," Indianapolis Soldiers and Sailors Monument; "Schiller Monument," Detroit; "Law" and "Justice," Akron (OH) County Court House; "Wagner Monument," Cleveland; Burke Mausoleum; "Moses" and "Gregory," Cleveland Court House; "Cain and Abel," Lake County Court House; Tom L. Johnson monument, Cleveland Public Square; Holden Mausoluem; Thomas White Memorial, Cleveland; Holden Memorial Tablet, Harvard University, Cambridge; Haserot Monument, Cleveland; Hatch Memorial, Western Reserve

University, Cleveland. Address in 1929, 5005 Euclid Avenue, h. 2423 Woodmere Drive, Cleveland, OH. Died in 1938.

MATZINGER, PHILIP FREDERICK.
Painter, lecturer, and teacher. Born Tiffin, OH in 1860. Pupil of John H. Vanderpoel, AIC. Member; Fresno AA; Laguna Beach AA; Pasadena SA; AFA. Address in 1929, 211 Patterson Building, Fresno, CA. Died in 1942.

MATZKE, ALBERT.
Painter and illustrator. Born in Indianapolis, IN, in 1882. Pupil of Art Students' League of NY under Du Mond and George Bridgman. Address in 1926, 244 West 14th Street, New York, NY.

MAUCH, MAX.
Sculptor. Born Feb. 6, 1864 in Vienna, Austria. He has exhibited at the National Sculpture Society, New York. He died in Chicago, IL, on Feb. 13, 1905.

MAULL, MARGARET HOWELL.
Illustrator. Born Whitford, PA, June 22, 1897. Pupil of Henry McCarter. Member: Fellowship PAFA; Phila. AG. Address in 1929, 340 West 55th Street, New York, NY; h. 2227 DeLancey Place, Philadelphia, PA.

MAUNSBACH, HANS ERIC GEORGE CHRISTIAN
Portrait painter. Born Sweden, Jan. 5, 1890. Studied in Sweden, France, England, and America. Member: Alliance; S. Indp. A.; Scandinavian Amer. Artists; Amer. APL; Salons of Amer. Work: "Portrait of Judge C. H. Duell," Court of Appeals, District of Columbia; "Portrait of Ossip Gabrilowitsch," Orchestra Hall, Detroit; "Portrait of Clara Clemens," for Detroit; "Portrait of Mr. and Mrs. P. A. Peterson," Swedish-American Hospital, Rockford, IL. Address in 1929, Care of the Ainslie Galleries, 677 Fifth Avenue; h. Sherwood Studios, 58 West 57th Street, New York, NY. Died in 1969.

MAURER, ALFRED HENRY.
Painter. Born New York, April 21, 1868. Pupil of NAD under Ward;

studied in Paris. Member: Paris AAA; Paris SAP. Awards: Inness prize, Salma. C., 1900; first prize ($1,500), C. I. Pittsburgh, 1901; first prize, Worcester, 1901; bronze medal, Pan-Am. Exp., Buffalo, 1901; silver medal, St. Louis, 1904; third medal, Liege Exp., 1905; gold medal Int. Exp., Munich, 1905. Represented in Memorial Hall Museum, Philadelphia, PA; Phillips Memorial Gallery, Washington, D.C.; Barnes Collection, Philadelphia, PA. Address in 1929, 404 West 43rd Street, New York, NY.

MAURER, LOUIS.
Painter. Born Feb. 21, 1832 in Biebrich, Germany. Lived in New York and worked for Currier & Ives. His specialty was sporting and racing prints. Died July 19, 1932 in New York City.

MAURONER, FABIO.
Etcher. Born Tisano, Italy, July 22, 1884. Pupil of E. M. Lynge. Member: Chicago SE; Calif. PA. Work: "La Tiarretta," Public Library, New York, NY; "Cypress of Michelangelo," Art Institute of Chicago. Address in 1929, 1111 San Trovaso, Venice, Italy.

MAURY, CORNELIA FIELD.
Painter. Born New Orleans, LA. Pupil of St. Louis School of Fine Arts; Julian Academy in Paris. Member: St. Louis AG. Awards: Bronze medal, Portland Exp., 1905; hon. mention, Kansas City, AI, 1923; second prize, St. Louis AL, 1926; hon. mention, St. Louis AG., 1927. Represented in City Art Museum, and Public Library, St. Louis. Address in 1929, 5815 Pennsylvania Avenue, St. Louis, MO.

MAUVAIS, A.
Portrait painter in oil and miniatures, flourishing in 1776 in Savannah, Georgia. An excellent example of his work is the miniature of Maj. John Gedney Clark (1737-1784), a British Army officer, which is in the collection of the Essex Institute, Salem, MA.

MAVERICK, ANN.
This daughter of Dr. Alexander Anderson and the wife of Andrew Maverick was a capital wood-engraver, somewhat later than 1830. Two other members of the Maverick family, Octavia and Catherine, were engaged in art work; the first named was a teacher of drawing in the Packard Institute, of Brooklyn; the other held a similar position in Madame Willard's School, in Troy, NY.

MAVERICK, EMILY.
Engraver. Born April 3, 1803 in NYC. Daughter of Peter Maverick. Engraved Stipple illustrations for an edition of Shakespeare published about 1830. (See Maverick, Maria). Member of the NA, and also a lithographer. Died in 1850.

MAVERICK, MARIA ANN.
Engraver. Born May 15, 1805 in NYC. Daughter of Peter Maverick. She engraved several admirable stipple illustrations for an edition of Shakespeare, published about 1830, as did her sister Emily. Maria died Jan. 12, 1832 in NYC.

MAVERICK, PETER.
Engraver. Born in NYC, Oct. 22, 1780; died there June 7, 1831. Peter Maverick was the son and pupil of Peter Rushton Maverick, one of the early engravers of New York. In 1802 Peter Maverick was in business in New York as an engraver; but at a later period he removed to Newark, NJ, where he was the preceptor, and in 1817 the partner, of A. B. Durand. Maverick returned to New York and there conducted an extensive establishment as a general engraver and copperplate printer, and to this business he finally added lithography. Peter Maverick was one of the founders of the National Academy of Design in 1826, and the "Historic Annals of the Academy" refer to him as excelling in "letter engraving and bank-note work." A portrait of Peter Maverick is in existence painted by John Neagle. He was a brother of Samuel Maverick.

MAVERICK, PETER (JR.).
All that is known of this man is that he was a son of Peter Maverick, and the NY directories

for 1832-45 give his occupation as "engraver and lithographer."

MAVERICK, PETER RUSHTON.
Engraver. Born in NY, April 11, 1755. Peter Rushton Maverick was probably originally a silversmith, and he advertised in the NY papers of the day that he was in the engraving, seal sinking, and copperplate printing business, and also engraved the tea table ware. In 1788 he represented the engravers of his city in the Federal Procession of that year. Peter R. Maverick had three sons- Samuel, Andrew and Peter. Samuel and Peter were also engravers and plate printers, and Andrew published prints in connection with Cornelius Tiebout. Died Dec. 12, 1811 in NYC.

MAVERICK, SAMUEL.
Born June 5, 1789 in NYC. This name is signed as engraver to book illustrations published in NY in 1824. The NY directories call Samuel Maverick a "copperplate printer," in 1805, and in 1819-37 the occupation becomes "Engraver and Copperplate printer." The name appears in these directories until 1847, although he died Dec. 4, 1845 in NYC.

MAWICKE, TRAN J.
Illustrator. Born in Chicago, IL in 1911. He studied at the American Academy and AIC. His career began in advertising in 1929 and later he had assignments from major magazines of the 1930's and 1940's. Among his clients were Pepsi-Cola, Phillips 66 and Camel Cigarettes. He began illustrating for book publishers in the late 1950's and has since worked for W. W. Norton, Putnam's and Grosset and Dunlap. A past present of the S of I (1960-1961), he has participated in the USAF Art Program and traveled overseas to record the Air Force Story. He has had many One-Man Shows and group exhibits across the United States.

MAX, PETER.
Painter and printmaker. Born in Berlin, Germany, Oct. 19, 1937; US citizen. Study: ASL; Pratt Inst.; Sch. of Visual Arts. Comn.:

World's Fair US Postage Stamp, Spokane, Wash., 1974; Border Sta. Welcoming Billboards, GSA, Can. and Mex. Borders, 1976; UNICEF Int'l. Flags Stamp Program, 1981; others. Exhib.: de Young Mem. Mus., San Fran., 1970; London Arts Gallery Peter Max. Exhib., travelling, 1970; Smithsonian, 1972-74; Corcoran Gallery, Wash., DC, 1981; others. Awards: Am. Inst. of Graphic Arts; Soc. of Illustrators; Int'l. Poster Comp., Poland; others. Pos.: Daly-Max Design Studio; Gen. Foods; Elgin Nat'l. Industries Takashimaya Ltd., Japan,; Van Heusen; UN; others. Address in 1982, Peter Max Enterprises, NYC.

MAXON, CHARLES.
The NY directory for 1833 contains this name as "engraver." No copperplate is known so signed.

MAXWELL, CORALEE DeLONG
Sculptor. Born in Ohio, Sept. 13, 1878. Pupil of Herman Matzen. Member: Cleveland Woman's AC; Cleveland Art Center; AFA. Award: Hon. mention, Cleveland Museum of Art, 1926; first prize, Bernards Gallery, NY, 1928. Address in 1929, 1935 East 93rd Street, Cleveland, OH.

MAXWELL, GUIDA B.
Painter. Born Philadelphia, PA. Pupil of Fred Wagner, Martha Walter. Member: Phila. Alliance; Lyceum C., London. Address in 1929, 180 Manheim Street, Germantown, Philadelphia, PA.

MAXWELL, JOHN ALAN.
Illustrator. Born Roanoke, VA, March 7, 1904. Pupil of Frank V. DuMond, George Luks, George B. Bridgman, Joseph Pennell. Illustrations in "The Cripple Lady of Peribonka," "Off the Deep End," and "The Seacoast of Bohemia" (Doubelday, Doran). Address in 1929, 841 West 177th Street, New York, NY.

MAY, BEULAH.
Sculptor. Born Hiawatha, KS, June 26, 1883. Pupil of Lorado Taft, Wm. Chase, Charles Grafly. Member: Calif. AC.; West Coast Arts, Inc., Calif. S. Gd. Address in 1929,

Fruit and Mabury Streets.; h. R.F.D. No. 1, Santa Ana, CA.

MAY, EDWARD HARRISON.
Painter. Born in Croydon, England in 1824. He came to America as a boy of ten. He studied under Daniel Huntington, and his early work met with fair success in NY in the days of the Art Union. He painted portraits and historical scenes. Member of the NA. He studied abroad, and came back to America for visits. The Union League Club of NY owns several of his portraits. He died May 17, 1887 in Paris.

MAY, PHIL.
Painter and illustrator. He was born in 1864, and died in 1903. He illustrated many books, magazines and other publications in NY.

MAYER, BELA.
Painter. Born Hungary, Aug. 5, 1888. Pupil of C. Y. Turner, Olinsky and Ward. Member: Salma. C.; Gd. of Am. P.; Allied AA. Address in 1929, 320 Fifth Avenue, New York, NY; summer, Beacon Hill, Port Washington, L.I., NY.

MAYER, CASPER.
Sculptor. Born in Bavaria, Dec. 24, 1871. Pupil of J. Q. A. Ward, schools of Cooper Union and NAD in NY. Award: Silver medal, St. Louis Exp., 1904. Maker of anthropological groups for American Museum of Natural History and State Museum, Albany. Address in 1929, American Museum of Natural History, New York, NY; h. 24 Carver Street, Astoria, L.I., NY.

MAYER, CONSTANT.
Painter. Born Oct. 3, 1832 in France. He studied under Cogniet, and came to NY in 1857. He was elected an Associate of the National Academy in 1866; he was also a member of the American Art Union. Mr. Mayer was best known for his genre pictures but he painted portraits of Gen'l Grant, Gen'l Sherman and many other prominent men. He died May 12, 1911 in Paris.

MAYER, FRANK BLACKWELL.
Painter. Born Dec. 27, 1827 in Baltimore, Maryland. Portrait and genre painter. Pupil of Alfred Miller in Baltimore, and of Gleyre and Brion in Paris. Painted in Paris, 1864-69. Medal and Diploma, Philadelphia, 1876; Medal of Maryland Institute. Represented by "Leisure and Labor," at the Corcoran Gallery. Died July 28, 1899 in Annapolis, Maryland.

MAYER, HENRY (HY).
Caricaturist, illustrator, etcher and author. Born at Worms-on-Rhine, Germany, July 18, 1868. He was the son of a London merchant, and came to the US in 1886. Work: "Impresssions of the Passing Show," New York Times; editor in cheif of Puck. Contributor to many weeklies in the United States and Europe; originator of "Travelaughs" for moving pictures. "Autobiography of a Monkey"; "Fantasies in Ha-ha"; "A Trip to Toyland"; "Adventures of a Japanese Doll"; "Hy Mayer Puck Album"; "In Laughland." Address in 1929, 300 Flax Hill Road, Norwalk, CT.

MAYER, LOUIS.
Painter and sculptor. Born Milwaukee, WI, Nov. 26, 1869. Pupil of Max Thedy in Weimar; Paul Hoecker in Munich; Constant and Laurens in Paris. Member: Salma. C.; Wisconsin PS. Awards: Bronze medal for sculpture, St. Paul Art Institute, 1915; Silver medal, Panama-Pacific Exposition, San Francisco, 1915; hon. mention, sculpture, Art Institute of Chicago, 1919; special mention, Milwaukee Art Institute, 1922. Work in: State Historical collections at Des Moines, Iowa and Madison, Wisconsin; Public Library, Burlington, Iowa; Springer Collection, National Museum, Washington, D.C.; Milwaukee Art Institute; busts of Lincoln, Emerson and Whitman, Community Church, New York City; bust of George F. Greer, and relief tablet to American Labor, National McKinley Birthplace Memorial, Niles, Ohio. Address in 1929, Salmagundi Club, New York,

NY; summer, R.F.D. No. 2, Hopewell Junction, NY.

MAYER, MERCER.
Illustrator. Born in Little Rock, Arkansas in 1943. She attended the Honolulu Academy of Arts and ASL. She illustrated A Boy, a Dog and a Frog for The Dial Press in 1967 and has worked for magazines and book publishers.

MAYFIELD, ROBERT BLEDSOE.
Painter and etcher. Born Carlinville, IL, Jan. 1, 1869. Pupil of St. Louis School of Fine Arts; Julian Academy in Paris under Lefebvre and Constant. Award: First gold medal of New Orleans Art Assoc. Work: "In the Studio," "The Giant Oak," Delgado Museum of Art, New Orleans, LA. Associate editor of the "New Orleans Times-Picayune." Address in 1929, 8327 Sycamore Street, New Orleans, LA.

MAYHEW, NELL BROOKER.
Landscape painter, etcher and lecturer. Born Astoria, IL. Pupil of University of IL under Newton A. Wells; AI Chicago under Johansen. Member: West Coast AC; Laguna Beach AA; Southern CA SAC. Award: Medal for color etching, Alaska-Yukon Exp., Seattle, 1909. Represented by "Adobe," color etching in State Library, Sacramento, CA; "Santa Inez Mission," color etching in Oregon State Museum, Salem; color etchings in Ambassador Hotels at Los Angeles, CA and Atlantic City, NJ. Address in 1929, 5016 Aldama Street, Los Angeles, CA.

MAYNARD, GEORGE WILLOUGHBY.
Painter. Born March 5, 1843, in Wash., DC. Studied at Royal Acad. of FA, Antwerp. Had a studio in Paris in 1878, but later located in NY. Member: National Academy, in 1885; American Water Color Society; Society of American Artists. Died April 5, 1923 in NYC.

MAYNARD, RICHARD FIELD.
Portrait painter. Born Chicago, IL, April 23, 1875. Pupil of Chase, Irving R. Wiles and Blum in New York. Member: NYWCC; MacD.

C.; Allied AA; SPNY; GFLA. Address in 1929, 33 West 67th Street, New York, NY; summer, White Sand Beach, Black Hall, CT.

MAYOR, MRS. HARRIET HYATT.
Painter, sculptor, and teacher. Born Salem, MA, April 25, 1868. Pupil of Henry H. Kitson and Dennis Bunker in Boston. Member: AFA. Award: Silver medal, Atlanta Exp., 1895. Work: Memorial tablet, Princeton University; tablet, Carnegie Inst., Washington, D.C.; tablet to Alpheus Hyatt, Woods Hole, MA.; historical tablet, Gloucester, MA; bust of Rear Admiral Goldsboro, Annapolis. Address in 1929, Annisquam, MA, winter, Princeton, NJ.

MAYORGA, GABRIEL HUMBERTO.
Painter and sculptor. Born in Colombia, S. Am., March 24, 1911; US citizen. Study: NAD, painting with Leon Kroll, Ivan Olinsky, etching with Aerobach-Levi, sculpture with Robert Aikin; ASL, with Brackman; Grand Central Art School, NYC, with Harvey Dunn. Work: West Point Museum; Inst. Ingenieros, Bogota, Colombia; Art Gallery of Barbizon-Plaza, NYC; plus many painting and portrait commissions from 1955. Exhib.: Inst. Ingenieros, Bogota, Colombia; Art Gallery of Barbizon-Plaza, NYC; Mayorga Art Gallery; Int'l. Expos, Paris; Int'l. Art Show, NYC. Art Positions: Instructor, Pan-America Art School, NYC; Art Director, Mannequins by Mayorga Inc., NYC; others. Media: Oil, watercolor; epoxy plastic, polyester plastic. Address in 1982, 331 W. 11 Street, New York, NY.

MAYR, CHRISTIAN.
Painter. Born 1805 in Germany. He was painting portraits and figure pieces in NY in 1840. Also designer and daguerreotypist. He was elected a member of the National Academy of Design in 1849. His painting "Reading the News" is in the permanent collection of the National Academy, and was exhibited in their Centennial Exhibition of 1925. Died Oct. 19, 1851 in NYC.

MAZUR, WLADYSLAW.
Sculptor. Born in Poland in 1874. Pupil of Academy of Fine Arts at Vienna. Address in 1926, 1070 Central Avenue, Cincinnati, OH.

MAZZANOVICH, LAWRENCE.
Landscape painter. Born California, Dec. 19, 1872. Pupil of AIC and ASL of NY. Member: Salma. C., 1905; NAC (life), 1913; AFA. Represented in Hackley Gallery, Muskegon, MI, and Chicago Art Institute. Address in 1929, Tryon, NC.

MAZZONE, DOMENICO M. Z.
Sculptor and painter. Born in Rutigliano, Italy, May 16, 1927. Work: Museum of Foggia, Italy; Monument in Rutigliano, Italy; Monument in Barletta, Italy; S. Fara Temple, Bari, Italy; UN Bldg, NYC. Exhib.: Nat'l. Exhib. Marble, Carrara, Italy; Nat'l. Exhib., San Remo, Italy; Gubbio, Italy; Silvermine, CT; Italian Club Exhib.; UN Bldg., NYC. Awards: Silver Medal, Carrara Exhib.; Gold Medal, Exhib. in Ft. Viareggio; Bronze Medal of Copernicus. Address in 1983, Jersey City, NJ.

McAULIFFE, JAMES J.
Painter. Born in St. Johns, New Foundland, Canada in 1848. He studied in the Boston Art School, and made a specialty of religious and marine subjects. His "Ecce Homo" and seventy-five life-size figures are in the Roman Catholic Cathedral in St. John, New Brunswick. He is also represented by "The Constitution" in the Parlin Library, Everett. He died at Medford, MA, Aug. 22, 1921.

McBRIDE, EDWARD J.
Cartoonist. Born St. Louis, MO, March 10, 1889. Pupil of Berdanier; St. Louis SFA. Member: Amer. A. Cartoonists and Caricaturists; St. Louis Sketch C. Award: First prize for book cover, World's Fair, St. Louis, 1904. Work "The Night Rider," Congressional Gallery, Wash., D.C. Art Manager, New York Tribune Syndicate. Address in 1929, NY Tribune Syndicate, 225 West 40th Street,; h. 139 West 103rd Street, NYC; summer, Great Neck, L.I., NY.

McBRIDE, EVA ACKELY.
(Mrs. James H. McBride). Painter and etcher. Born Wisconsin, Dec. 27, 1861. Pupil of H. J. Breuer and W. M. Chase. Member: Calif. AC; Pasadena SA; La Jolla AC. Address in 1929, 489 Bellefontaine Street, Pasadena, CA.

MCBRIDE, JAMES JOSEPH.
Painter. Born in Ft. Wayne, Ind., May 19, 1923. Study: Ft. Wayne Art Inst.; Cape Cod Sch. of Art, Provincetown, MA; PAFA; Barnes Foundation of Mod. Art, Merion, PA. Work: Regional collections. Exhibitions: Water Color U.S.A. 1962-70; American Society of Casein Painters, 1970- 74; Am. WC Soc., NYC, 1972, 75. Midwest WC Show, 1977; others. Awards: Best of Show, Ind. Artist Ann., 1978-79; Midwest WC Soc., 1979. Teaching: Ind. Univ. Purdue Univ., Ft. Wayne, 1971 to present; others. Mem.: Hoosier Solon Assn; Ind. Artists Club; Nat'l. Soc. Painters in casein and acrylic; others. Media: Watercolors. Address in 1980, Fort Wayne, Ind.

McBURNEY, JAMES E.
Painter, illustrator, lecturer, and teacher. Born Lore City, OH, Nov. 22, 1868. Studied with Arthur W. Dow, Howard Pyle, Charles H. Davis, and in Paris. Member: Calif. AC; Cliff Dwellers, Chicago; Chicago PS; All-Ill. SFA. Award: Silver medal, Pan. Calif. Exp., San Diego, CA, 1915. Work: "The Mission Period" and "The Spanish Period," Southern Calif. Counties' Commission, San Diego; eight panels, Nat. Bank of Woodlawn, Chicago; five historical panels, Federal Bank and Trust Co., Dubuque, IA, Madison, WI, twenty panels, D.C. Wentworth School, Chicago; twelve industrial panels, State Agricultural Expo., Los Angeles; three panels, "Life of George Rogers Clark," Parkside School, Chicago; twelve panels, "Women Through the Ages," Women's League Building, University of Michigan, Ann Arbor, MI. Instructor, College of Fine and Applied Arts, A.E.F. University, Cote d'Or, France, 1919. Lecturer on History of Art, AIC, 1920. Director, School Department, Art

Inst. of Peoria, 1925-1926. Address in 1929, 1521 East 61st Street, Chicago, IL.

McCABE, E.
This engraver of vignettes was seemingly working in NY about 1855.

McCAIG, MRS. FLORA T.
Painter. Born Royalton, NY in 1856. Pupil of PAFA, B. F. Ferris, G. W. Waters and Carroll Beckwith. Work: "A Mothers' Meeting," Women's Union, Buffalo, NY; "First Lessons," Kindergarten Training School, Buffalo, NY. Address in 1929, R. 1, Box 415, La Canada, CA; 713 Michigan Ave., Flintridge, CA.

McCALL, ROBERT T.
Illustrator. Born in Columbus, Ohio in 1919. He studied at the Columbus Fine Art School. After serving as a bombardier in World War II, he returned to his career, at first Chicago, then NY, frequently illustrating for Reader's Digest, Popular Science, Life and Collier's. His first love, science fiction, led him to many interesting projects, most notable of which was an assignment to paint a mural at the National Air and Space Museum. He has designed postage stamps for the space program and has been invited to record several space shots including the recent Apollo-Soyuz mission.

McCALLUM, ROBERT HEATHER.
Painter and illustrator. Born Rochester, NY, Aug. 28, 1902. Pupil of Lamorna Birch. Member: Scarab C. Address in 1929, 1404 Maccabees Bldg.; h. 303 East Forest Avenue, Detroit, MI.

McCARTAN, EDWARD.
Sculptor. Born Albany, NY, Aug., 1879. Pupil of ASL of NY; Ecole des Beaux Arts in Paris; Pratt Inst. Member: ANA; NA, 1925; NSS, 1912; NY Arch. Lg.; Beaux Arts Inst. Des.; AFA; Nat. Inst. AL; Concord AA (Pres.); Art Comm. City of NY. Awards: Barnett prize for sculpture, NAD, 1912; Widener gold medal, PAFA, 1916; medal of honor for sculpture, NY Arch Lg., 1923; gold medal of honor, Concord AA.

Represented in Fine Arts Academy, Buffalo; Metropolitan Museum, New York; City Art Museum, New York, NY.

McCARTER, HENRY.
Illustrator and teacher. Born Norristown, PA, July 5, 1886. Pupil of Eakins in Philadelphia; Puvis de Chavannes, Bonnat and Alexander Harrison, Toulouse Lautrec, M. Roll, M. Rixens, in Paris. Member: Fellowship PAFA. Awards: Bronze medal, Pan-Am. Exp., Buffalo, 1901; silver medal, St. Louis Exp., 1904; Beck prize, Phila. WCC 1906; gold medal for illustrations, second gold medal for decoration and color, P.- P. Exp., San F. 1915. Address in 1929, Pennsylvania Academy and Fine Arts Country School, Chester Springs, PA. Died in 1942.

McCARTHY.
A line-engraver of portraits, in the employ of J. C. Buttre, NY, from 1860-65.

McCARTHY, C. J.
Illustrator. Born Rochester, NY, May 21, 1887. Pupil of F. Luis Mora and F. R. Gruger. Member: GFLA; SI. Address in 1929, 40 Gramercy Park; 143 East 21st Street, New York, NY; summer, Woodstock, NY. Died 1953.

McCARTHY, ELIZABETH WHITE.
Painter. Born Lansdowne, PA, June 3, 1891. Pupil of Archambault; E. D. Taylor; H. L. Johnson. Member: PA S. Min. P; AFA. Address in 1929, 1912 South Rittenhouse Square, Philadelphia, PA.

McCARTHY, HELEN K.
Painter. Born in Poland, OH, in 1884. Pupil of Phila. School of Design. Member: Plastic Club; Alumni of Penna. School of Design; International Society Art league; Nat. Assoc. of Women Painters and Sculptors. Address in 1926, 1716 Chestnut Street, Philadelphia, PA.

McCARTNEY, EDITH.
Painter. Member: Wash. WCC. Address in 1929, 14 Christopher Street, New York, NY.

McCLAIN, HELEN CHARLETON.
Painter. Born Toronto, Ont., CN,
May 25, 1887. Member: NA Women
PS. Award: National Arts Club
prize, NA Women PS, 1918. Address
in 1929, Care of Miss MacDonald, 92
Will's Hill Avenue, Toronto, CN.

McCLELLAND, D.
In 1850 this name appears on a map
of the City of Washington, signed
as "Eng. and pub. by D. McClelland,
Washington, 1850."

McCLUNG, FLORENCE.
Painter. Born: St. Louis,
Missouri in 1896. Studied:
Southern Methodist University;
Texas State College for Women;
Colorado College; Toas, New Mexico;
and with Adolph Dehn, Alexandre
Hogue, Frank Reaugh, Richard Howard
and Frank Klepper. Awards: Dallas
Allied Artists, 1942, 1943, 1944,
1946; National Association of Women
Artists, 1945; Pepsi-Cola, 1942.
Collections: Metropolitan Museum
of Art; Dallas Museum of Fine Arts;
Library of Congress; Mint Museum of
Art; High Museum of Art; Delgado
Museum; Birmingham Alabama Library;
Univ. of Kansas; Univ. of Texas.

McCLURE, CAROLINE SUMNER.
(Mrs. G. G. McClure). Sculptor and
writer. Born St. Louis, MO. Pupil
of Lorado Taft, Hermon MacNeil.
Member: NAC. Work: Figure of
Victory for dome of the Missouri
Building, World's Fair, Chicago,
1904. Address in 1929, 640
Riverside Drive, New York, NY.

McCLUSKEY, WILLIAM.
Some very well executed subject
plates, signed by "Wm. McCluskey"
as engraver, were published in
The New Mirror, New York, about
1845.

McCOLL, MARY A.
Painter, craftwoman, writer, and
teacher. Born Forrest, Ontario,
Canada. Pupil of Cornoyer,
Courtois, John Carlson, Hugh
Breckenridge; Hans Hofmann in
Munich. Member: St. Louis AG; St.
Louis AL; Western AA. Awards:
First prize for figure painting,
St. Louis Artists Guild, 1916,
1917, 1918; hon. mention for
landscape, Black and White

Competition, Chicago, 1929. Work:
"Reflections" and "Still Life,"
Town Club, St. Louis, MO. Address
in 1929, 3608 Castleman Avenue, St.
Louis, MO; summer, Kimmswick, MO.

McCOMAS, FRANCIS.
Painter. Born Fingal, Tasmania,
Australia, Oct. 1, 1874. Member of
the jury, Panama-Pacific
International Exp., 1915. Member:
Phila. WCC; AWSC. Awards: Dana
gold medal, Phila. WCC, 1918;
Hudnut prize, AWCS, 1921; Phila.
WCC prize, 1921. Work: Two mural
decorations on the Del Monte Lodge,
Pebble Beach, CA; mural
decorations, Del Monte Hotel, Del
Monte, CA; and represented in the
Metropolitan Museum of Art, NY,
Park Museum of San Francisco and
Portland Art Society. Address in
1929, Pebble Beach, CA.

McCOMB, MARIE LOUISE.
Illustrator and painter. Born
Louisville, KY. Pupil of PAFA.
Member: Fellowship PAFA. Award:
Traveling Scholarship PAFA, 1912.
Address in 1929, 41 East 59th
Street, New York, NY.

McCONAHA, LAWRENCE.
Painter. Born Centerville, IN,
Aug. 8, 1894. Pupil of George H.
Baker, Guy Wiggins. Member:
Springfield AA; Palette C. of
Richmond. Awards: Earlham College
prize, Hoosier Salon, Chicago 1927;
Edward Rector Memorial prize,
Hoosier Salon, Chicago, 1929.
Address in 1929, 405 Pearl Street,
Richmond, IN.

McCONNELL, GENEVIEVE KNAPP.
(Mrs. Guthrie McConnell). Painter,
illustrator, and writer. Born St.
Louis, MO, March 18, 1876. Pupil of
St. Louis School of Fine Arts.
Member: Plastic C; St. Louis AG.
Author and illustrator of "The
Seeing Eye" (Cornhill Pub. Co.).
Author of children's stories in
juvenile magazines. Address in
1929, 4915 Argyle Place, St. Louis,
MO; summer, Easton MD.

McCONNELL, GERALD.
Illustrator. Born in East Orange,
NJ in 1931. He studied at the ASL
under Frank Reilly, after which he
apprenticed with Dean Cornwell. He

began free-lancing in the mid-1950's, working for advertising agencies and publishers. He has served on the Board of Directors of the S of I since 1963 and its Executive Committee since 1967. A founding member of GAG in NYC, he has been on its Executive Committee since 1969. His works are in the collections of the S of I, USAF and National Park Service and have been shown in the galleries of Master Eagle, Fairtree, Greengrass and the S of I. He is best known for his three-dimensional art; his book on the subject, Assemblage, was published in 1976.

McCORD, GEORGE HERBERT
Painter. Born Aug. 1, 1848 in NYC. He first exhibited at the National Academy in 1870. Among his most important works are "Sunnyside" (home of Washington Irving); "Cave of the Winds, Niagara" and "The Genesee Valley." Elected as Associate of the NA in 1880. He died in NYC on April 6, 1909.

McCORKLE, LOUIS W. (REVEREND).
Painter. Born in St. Louis, MO, in 1921. Study: Largely self-taught; drawing lessons at School of Fine Arts, Washington Univ., St. Louis; art studies with Helen Mederos, Virginia McCloud. Ordained a Catholic priest, 1953. Work: Private collections; MO public collections of City of Hannibal, Diocese of Jefferson City, Order of Sisters of St. Francis of Maryville. Exhib.: Artist in Residence Exhib., London, 1976; Grand Nat'l Exhib., NYC, 1976. Teaching: Art Instr., St. Thomas Seminary, Hannibal, MO, from 1970. Mem.: Am. Artists Professional Lg. (life). Style & Technique: Florals executed in heavy impasto, brilliant color. Media: Oils. Address in 1983, P.O. Box 551, Hannibal, MO.

McCORMACK, NANCY.
Sculptor. (See Cox-McCormack.)

McCORMICK, HOWARD.
Painter, illustrator, and engraver. Born in Indiana, Aug. 19, 1875. Pupil of Forsyth and Chase; Laurens in Paris. Member: Salma. C.,

1907; GFLA. Work: Hopi, Apache and Navajo habitat group, American Museum of Natural History, New York; "Hopi World" (gesso), John Herron Art Inst.; Wood engravings in numerous magazines. Address in 1929, Leonia, NJ.

McCORMICK, KATHERINE HOOD.
Painter and illustrator. Born Philadelphia, PA, Sept 17, 1882. Pupil of PAFA; Drexel Inst. and Fred Wagner. Member: Fellowship PAFA; Philadelphia Alliance. Award: First hon. mention, Philadelphia, Sketch Club, 1923. Address in 1929, 3416 Race Street, Philadelphia, PA; summer, Pocono Lake Preserve, Monroe, Co., PA.

McCOSH, DAVID JOHN.
Painter, illustrator, etcher and teacher. Born Cedar Rapids, July 11, 1903. Pupil of George Oberteuffer, G. DeForest Shook. Member: Theta Chi Phi. Work: "The Prodigal Son," Cedar Rapids Art Association. Address in 1929, 1705 Mt. Vernon Avenue, Cedar Rapids, IA.

McCOUCH, D. W.
Painter. Exhibited at Penna. Academy of Fine Arts, Philadelphia, 1921; represented in "Exhibition of Paintings Showing the Later Tendencies in Art." Address in 1926, St. Martin's Lane, Chestnut Hill, Philadelphia.

McCOUCH, GORDON MALLET.
Painter and etcher. Born Philadelphia, PA, Sept. 24, 1885. Pupil of Howard Pyle in Wilmington; George Bridgman in NY; Heinrich von Zugel in Munich. Member: Zurcher Kunstgesellschaft; Gesellschaft Schweizerischer Maler, Bildhauer und Architekten. Address in 1929, Porto di Ronco, Switzerland. Died 1959.

McCREA, SAMUEL HARKNESS.
Landscape painter. Born Palatine, Cook Co., IL, March 15, 1867. Studied in San Francisco, Chicago, New York, Paris and Munich. Member: Salma. C. Address in 1929, Scraggycrag, Darien, CT.

McCREERY, FRANC ROOT.
(Mrs. Earl A. McCreery). Portrait painter, draftsman, and illustrator. Born Dodge City, Kansas. Pupil of Buffalo School of Fine Arts; Students School of Art, Denver; AIC. Member: Buffalo SA; Lg. Am. Penwomen; G. Allied A. Member of faculty of Buffalo School of Fine Arts. Address in 1929, 1110 Elmwood Avenue; h. 15 Elmview Place, Buffalo, NY. Died in 1957.

McCULLOUGH, LUCERNE.
Painter. Born: Abilene, Texas in 1916. Studied: Tulane University; ASL. Awards: Art Students League; Art Directors Club, 1944; Direct Mail Advertising Association, 1944, 1945; Silvermine Guild of Artists, 1954, 1956. Collections: Museum of Modern Art; San Angelo Museum of Art; NAD; United States Post Office, Booneville, NY; United States Post Office, Thomaston, CT.

McCULLOUGH, MAX.
(Mrs. Marshall McCullough). Painter and teacher. Born Elmwood Plantation, Lee Co., AK, Nov. 9, 1874. Pupil of Vincent Nowottney, L. H. Meakin, Emile Renard, LeFarge, Debillemont-Chardon. Member: Miss. AA; Highland Park SFA, Dallas; SSAL. Address in 1929, Corner Dixie and Plummer Streets, h. 308 South Dixie Street, Eastland, Texas.

McCUTCHEON, JOHN TINNEY.
Caricaturist. Born near South Raub, Tippecanoe Co., IN, May 6, 1870. Pupil of Ernest Knaufft at Purdue University. Member: SI 1911. On staff Chicago "Tribune", 1903; correspondent during Spanish War and World War I. Author: "Stories of Filipino Warfare," "Bird Center Cartoons," "In Africa," etc. Address in 1929, Care the Chicago Tribune, Tribune Tower, 31st Floor; h. 2450 Lakeview Avenue, Chicago, IL.

McDONALD, MRS. ANN HEEBNER.
Painter. Born Philadelphia, PA. Pupil of PAFA; Hugh H. Breckenridge; Whistler School in Paris. Member: Fellowship PAFA; Phila. Alliance. Represented in the John Lambert Fund and Fellowship collections of the Pennsylvania Academy of the Fine Arts. Address in 1929, 8305 Seminole Avenue, Chestnut Hill, Philadelphia, PA.

McDONALD, WILLIAM PURCELL.
Painter. Born Cincinnati, OH, Sept 18, 1863. Pupil of Cincinnati Art Academy under Duveneck. Member: Cincinnati AC; Duveneck Soc. PS. On Rookwood Pottery staff from 1882. Address in 1929, Rookwood Pottery, Cincinnati, OH.

McDOUGAL, JOHN A.
Miniature painter, flourishing 1836-81 in NY and Newark.

McDUFFIE, JANE.
See Thurston, Jane McDuffie.

McENTEE, JERVIS.
Painter. Born July 14, 1828 in Rondout, NY. Specialty, landscapes. Studied with F. E. Church. Elected Associate Member of the National Academy, 1860; National Academy, 1861. Represented by "Eastern Sky at Sunset," at Corcoran Art Gallery Washington, D.C. Was also draftsman for wood engravers. Died Jan. 27, 1891 in Rondout, N.Y.

McEWEN, KATHERINE.
Painter. Born Nottingham, England, July 19, 1875. Pupil of Chase, Miller, Wicker and Woodbury. Member: Detroit SAC; Detroit S. Women P. Work: Water colors in Detroit Institute of Arts; frescos in Christ Church, and ceilings in Arts and Crafts Building, Cranbrook, MI. Address in 1929, Seven Dash Ranch, Johnson AZ.

McEWEN, WALTER.
Painter. Born Chicago, IL, Feb. 13, 1860. Pupil of Cormon and Robert- Fleury in Paris. Member: ANA 1903; Paris SAP; Nat. Inst. A.L. Counselor Cresson Scholarship, PAFA Students. Awards: Hon. Mention, Paris Salon, 1886; Silver medal, Paris Exp., 1889; first class gold medal, Berlin, 1891; medal Columbian Exp., Chicago, 1893; medal of honor, Antwerp, 1894; second class medal, Munich, 1897; silver medal, Paris Exp., 1900; first gold medal, Munich, 1901; first class medal, Vienna, 1902; Lippincott prize, PAFA 1902;

Harris prize, AIC 1902; gold medal, St. Louis Exp., 1904; First medal Liege, 1905; hors concours (jury of awards), P.- P. Exp., San F., 1915; Chevalier Legion of Honor 1896, Officer 1908; Order of St. Michael, Bavaria; Order of Leopold II Belgium, 1909; Proctor prize, NAD, 1919. Work: "Sunday in Holland," Luxembourg Museum, Paris; decorations in Library of Congress, Washington; "An Ancestor," Corcoran Gallery, Washington; "The Letter," Art Association, Indianapolis; "Lady in a White Satin Gown" and "The Judgement of Paris," Art Institute of Chicago; "Phyllis," Pennsylvania Academy, Philadelphia; "Lady of 1810," Telfair Museum, Savannah; "Waiting," Honolulu Museum; "L'Absente," Musee, Liege, Belgium; "Enfant Hollandais," Musee, Budapest; "Famille Hollandais, Musee, Ghent, Belgium; "The Interlude," Los Angeles Museum; "The Ghost Story," Cleveland Museum of Art. Address in 1929, 11 Rue Georges Berger; h. 59 Rue Galilee, Paris, France; Century Assoc., 7 West 43d Street, New York, NY. Died 1943.

McEWEN, WILLIAM.
A little known landscape painter, a friend and pupil of George Inness.

McFADDEN, SARAH YOCUM.
See Mrs. Frederick A. Boyle.

McFEE, HENRY LEE.
Painter and teacher. Born St. Louis, MO., April 14, 1886. Member: New Soc. A.; Modern AA. Represented in Phillips Memorial Gallery, Washington, D.C. Address in 1929, Woodstock, Ulster County, NY. Died in 1953.

McGIBBON, JAMES.
He was a miniaturist and portrait painter who worked in Boston, MA, in 1801.

McGILLIVRAY, FLORENCE HELENA.
Painter. Born Whitby, Ontario, CN, 1864. Pupil of Simon and Menard in Paris. Member: Inter. Art Union, Paris; N.A. Women PS; Ontario SA. Work: "Afterglow," and "Stack in Winter," owned by the Canadian Government. Address in 1929, 292 Frank Street, Ottawa, Ont., CN; summer, Whitby, Ontario, CN.

McGINNIS, ROBERT E.
Illustrator. Born in Cincinnati, Ohio in 1926. He attended Ohio State University for four years and the Central Acad. of Commercial Art. He began his career with The Saturday Evening Post in 1960 and has worked extensively for Good Housekeeping since then. As well as illustrating for paperback book publishers he has also produced over 50 movie posters, most notably those for the James Bond movies in the 1960's. A member of the S of I, he lived in Old Greenwich, CT.

McGOFFIN, JOHN.
Engraver. Born in Philadelphia, PA, in 1813. McGoffin was an excellent line-engraver of landscape and subject plates. He was a pupil of James W. Steel, of Philadelphia, and was in the employ of that engraver in 1834. He painted miniatures for some years, but he evidently continued to engrave, and was working at least as late as 1876.

McGRATH, JOHN.
Etcher. Born Ireland, Nov. 4, 1880. Self taught. Member: Balto. WCC; Charcoal C. Address in 1929, 209 West Saratoga Street; 812 Cator Avenue, Baltimore, MD; summer, Pine Cove, Earleigh Heights, MD.

McGRATH, SALLIE TOMLIN.
Painter. Born Galena, IL. Pupil of Christine Lumsdon. Member: Salons of America. Address in 1929, 1111 Carnegie Studio; h. 1065 Lexington Avenue, New York, NY.

McHUGH, ARLINE B.
Painter and illustrator. Born Owensboro, KY, March 9, 1891. Pupil of H. R. Ballinger; Alta W. Salisbury; Gerome De Witt. Member: New Rochelle AA; C. L. Wolfe AC. Address in 1929, 66 North Chatsworth, Larchmont, NY.

McILHENNEY, CHARLES M.
Painter. Born in Philadelphia in 1858. Studied at the Penna. Academy of Fine Arts in 1877. He established his studio in New York

City. Among his pictures are "A Gray Summer Noon," "The Old Old Story," and "The Passing Storm." Elected an Associate Member of the National Academy in 1892. He died in 1904.

McINTIRE, KATHERINE ANGELA.
Painter and etcher. Born near Richmond, VA, in 1880. Pupil of Chase, Alice Beckington, George Bridgman in NY; also of Mme. La Forge in Paris. Address in 1926, 160 Waverly Place, New York, NY.

McINTOSH, PLEASANT R.
Painter. Born New Salisbury, IN, Oct. 4, 1897. Pupil of AIC. Member: Hoosier Salon. Award: Second Huntington prize, Columbus Gallery of Fine Arts, 1925; Erskine prize, Hoosier Salon, 1927; Chamber of Commerce medal, Peoria, IL, 1929. Director, School of the Art Institute of Peoria and head of Art Dept., Bradley Polytechnic Inst., Peoria, from 1926. Address in 1929, Art Inst. of Peoria, Hamilton Boulevard and Randolph Street, Peoria, IL; New Salisbury, IN.

McKAY.
Painter. No work is known of this portrait painter but his painting of John Bush (1755-1816) and that of Abigail Bush (1765-1810) which are signed "McKay," and belong to the American Antiquarian Society of Worcester, MA.

McKEE, DONALD.
Illustrator and etcher. Born Indianapolis, IN, March 1, 1883. Pupil of NY School of Art. Illustrations in Life, Judge, Saturday Evening Post and Collier's. Address in 1929, 66 King Street, Westport, CT.

McKEE, JOHN DUKES.
Illustrator. Born Kokomo, IN, Dec. 4, 1899. Pupil of E. Forsberg. Awards: Third prize, Hoosier Salon, 1925; first prize, Hoosier Salon, 1926. Address in 1929, 185 N. Wabash Avenue., h. 6951 Ogleby Avenue, Chicago, IL.

McKEE, S. ALICE.
(Mrs. Charles Atherton Cumming). Painter and teacher. Born Stuart, IA, March 6, 1890. Pupil of Charles A. Cumming. Member: Iowa AG; AM. APL. Awards: Gold medal, Iowa State Fair, 1923, 1924; purchase prize, Des Moines Women's Club, 1925. Work in Des Moines Women's Club, and Iowa State Historical Gallery. Address in 1929, Cumming School of Art, Des Moines, IA; San Diego, CA.

McKENZIE, ROBERT TAIT.
Sculptor, writer and lecturer. Born Almonte, Ont., Canada, May 26, 1867. Member: Phila. Sketch C.; Fellowship PAFA (assoc.); Century Assoc.; Phila. AC; AFA. Awards: Silver medal, St. Louis Exp., 1904; King's medal, Sweden, 1912; hon. mention, P.-P. Exp., San F., 1915. Work: "Sprinter," Fitz William Museum, Cambridge, England; "College Athlete," Ashmolean Museum, Oxford, England; "Juggler" and "Competitor," Metropolitan Museum, NY; "Competitor," Canadian National Gallery, Ottawa, CN "Onslaught", a group and "Relay," statuette, Art Gallery, Montreal, CN; "The Plunger and the Ice Bird"; statuettes "Boy Scout" and "Blighty" and "Capt. Guy Drummond," memorial statue, Canadian War Museum, Ottawa, Canada; portraits in low relief of F. K. Huger and Crawford W. Long, Univ. of GA; Dr. W. W. Keen, Brown Univ., Providence; "The Youthful Benjamin Franklin," bronze statue, Univ. of PA campus and Newark Museum; "Portrait of Weir Mitchell," and medals for Franklin Inst. Phila., University of Buffalo, Achilles Club, London and ICAA; "Baron Tweedmouth" and "Lady Tweedmouth," Guisachan, Scotl'd; fountain with panel in high relief, "Laughing Children," Athletic Park Playground, Philadelphia; statues, "Provost Edgar F. Smith" and "Rev. George Whitfield," Triangle of the University of PA dormitories, 1919; "Norton Downs, Aviator," St. Paul's School; Victory Memorial, Cambridge, England; memorial statue, Col. George Harold Baker, Parliament Bldgs., Ottawa, CN; "William Cooper Proctor," and "Dean West," Princeton, NJ; "Flying Sphere," St. Louis Art Museum; Scottish-American War Memorial, Edinburgh, Scotland; General Wolfe, Greenwich, England. Professor and

director of department in Physical education, University of PA. Address in 1929, University of Pennsylvania; h. 2014 Pine Street, Philadelphia, PA. Died in 1938.

McKEOWN, WESLEY BARCLAY.
Illustrator. Born in Jersey City, in 1927. He graduated in 1950 from the Newark School of Fine and Industrial Arts. Shortly thereafter, his illustrations appeared in advertisements, magazines and books as well as in technical and trade publications. A member of the S of I, he contributed to the USAF Art Program and was active on many committees before becoming President from 1968 to 1970. He was commissioned to produce a series of postage stamps on the metric system in 1974. Died in 1975.

McKERNAN, FRANK.
Painter and illustrator. Born Philadelphia, PA, Sept. 19, 1861. Pupil of PAFA and of Howard Pyle. Member: Phila. Sketch C.; Fellowship PAFA. Address in 1929, Ridley Park, PA.

McKINNEY, GERALD T.
Painter and illustrator. Born Garland, PA, Feb. 26, 1900. Pupil of E. M. Ashe; C. J. Taylor; H. S. Hubbell; Norwood MacGilvary. Member: Pittsburgh AA. Address in 1929, Youngsville, PA.

McKINNEY, ROLAND JOSEPH.
Painter, lecturer, and teacher. Born Niagara Falls, NY, Nov. 4, 1898. Pupil of Leopold Seyffert and Wellington Reynolds. Member Chicago ASL. Work: "The Ascension," mural painting, First Presbyterian Church, Davenport, IA. Address in 1929, care of Municipal Art Gallery; h. 2016 Main Street, Davenport, IA.

McKINSTRY, GRACE E.
Portrait painter, sculptor, and teacher. Born Fredonia, NY. Pupil of ASL of NY; AIC; Julian and Colarossi Academies and Raphael Collin in Paris. Member: Am. APL; AFA; NAC; Lg. APW (hon.). Work: Portraits in the Capitol, St. Paul, MN, Minneapolis; Lake Erie College, Painesville, OH; Charleston College, Northfield., MN; Shattuck School, Faribault. MN; Army and Navy Club, Washington, DC; Woman's Club, Minneapolis; Beloit (WI) College; Pomona College, CA, etc. Address in 1929, Pen and Brush Club, New York, NY.

McLAIN, MARY.
Miniature painter. Exhibited at the Penna. Academy of Fine Arts, Philadelphia, 1925. Address in 1926, 111 East 56th Street, New York.

McLAINE, M. JEAN.
(Mrs. John C. Johansen). Portrait painter. Born in Chicago, IL in 1878. Graduated from Art Institute of Chicago in 1897, with honors and prizes. Awards: Hallgarten prize, 1913, National Academy of Design; Walter Lippincott prize, Penna. Academy of Fine Arts, 1913; silver medal, Panama P.I. Exp., 1915. Represented in private galleries throughout U.S.; in Museum of Art, Syracuse, NY; Art Institute, Chicago; San Antonio Art Museum; Toledo Museum of Art; etc. Elected Associate Member of the National Academy; also member of the International Art League, Paris; MacDowell Club, New York; National Association of Portrait Painters. Address in 1926, 12 West 9th Street, New York, NY.

McLAUGHLIN, CHARLES J.
Painter, draftsman and decorator. Born Covington, KY, June 6, 1888. Pupil of Cincinnati Art Academy; Ecole des Beaux Arts, Fontainebleau and Duveneck; studied architecture in France, Belgium, Italy and Greece. Member: Cincinnati AC; MacD. C. of Cincinnati; Cincinnati Arch. Lg. Designer at Rookwood Potteries, 1913-1920; teacher of architectural design, Dept. of Architecture, A. and M. College of Texas, College Station, 1926-1927. Address in 1929, Ferro Concrete Construction Co., Cincinnati, OH, 321 Front Street, Covington, KY.

McLAUGHLIN, MARY LOUISE.
Painter and etcher. Born in Cincinnati, OH, in 1847. She began making porcelain called Losanti ware in 1898; exhibited first in Paris Exp., 1900; silver medal for

decorative metal work, Paris Exp., 1899; hon. mention for china painting, Chicago Exp. Honorable member of Cincinnati Woman's Club. Member: Woman's Art Club; National League of Mural Painters. Address in 1926, 4011 Sherwood Avenue, Annsby Place, Cincinnati, OH. Died in 1939.

McLAWS, VIRGINIA RANDALL.
Painter and teacher. Born Augusta, GA, Aug. 29, 1872. Pupil of Charcoal C. School, Balto.; NY School of Fine and Applied Arts; Caro-Delvaille, Paris; summer schools of PAFA, ASL of NY. Member: Southern SAL; College AA; AFA. Address in 1929, Sweet Briar College, Sweet Briar, VA.

McLEAN, JAMES AUGUSTUS.
Painter and etcher. Born Lincolnton, NC, May 2, 1904. Pupil of Daniel Garber, Joseph Pearson, Charles Garner. Member: Fellowship PAFA; SSAL. Address in 1929, 406 East Main Street, Lincolnton, NC.

McLEAN, WILSON L.
Illustrator. Born in Glasgow, Scotland in 1937. He had no formal art training. In 1969 his first illustration was published by Woman's Own magazine and he has since worked for Sports Illustrated, Esquire, Oui, Playboy, Penthouse, McCall's, and Quest. He has won a Gold Medal from the ADC Show, Awards of Excellence from the S of I, a Silver Medal from the One Show and a Clio for a TV commercial. The Greengrass Gallery has exhibited his work.

McLELLAN, H. B.
About 1860 this stipple-engraver of portraits was located in Boston, MA.

McLELLAN, RALPH.
Painter, etcher, and teacher. Born San Marcos, Texas, Aug. 27, 1884. Pupil of Philip Hale, Edmund Tarbell and Frank Benson in Boston. Member: Boston Museum AA; Texas FAA; Phila. Alliance; SSAL; North Shore AA. Awards: Dunham prize, CT AFA, 1917; Isidor medal, NAD, 1919; hon. mention, SSAL, Houston, Texas, 1928. Represented in Southwest Texas Teachers College Museum. Instructor in Pennsylvania School of Industrial Art. Address in 1929, 7906 Lincoln Drive St. Martins; Pennsylvania Museum of Art, Pine and Broad Steets, Philadelphia, PA.

McLENEGAN, HARRY RICHARDSON.
Painter, craftsman, and teacher. Born Milwaukee, WI, July 11, 1899. Pupil of Emma M. Church; Maybelle Key; Dudley Crafts Watson; Gerrit Sinclair; Charlotte Partridge. Member: Wis. PS. Address in 1929, The Westlake, 394 Summit Avenue, South, Milwaukee, WI.

McMAHON, FRANKLIN.
Illustrator. Born in Chicago, IL in 1921. He attended the AIC, Institute of Design, American Academy of Art and the Chicago Acad. of Art from 1939-1950. He studied under E. W. Ball, Francis Chapin and Paul Weighardt. In 1939 he published his first illustration for Collier's. Aside from being an illustrator who has worked for all major magazines, he has done eight 16 mm documentaries on art, and in election years from 1964 to 1976 he made films for television on art and politics called The Artist as a Reporter. He has worked extensively for the American space program covering the launching of Gemini III, Apollo X, and Apollo XI, the first man on the moon.

McMAHON, MARK ANDREW.
Illustrator. Born in Chicago, IL in 1950. He attended the North Shore Art League, Deerpath Art League and Adam State College. He has worked for many magazines, including Chicago, US Catholic, The Uptowner and Chicago Tribune. His on-the-spot illustrations have led to assignments covering tennis, skiing and rodeo events for TV and magazines. His work has been shown in many exhibits in Kentucky, Colorado and the Chicago area.

McMANUS, BLANCHE.
See Mrs. F. M. Mansfield.

McMANUS, GEORGE.
Illustrator. Member: SI. Address in 1929, International Features

Service, 246 West 59th Street, New York, NY.

McMANUS, JAMES GOODWIN.
Painter and teacher. Born Hartford, CT, Feb. 5, 1882. Pupil of C. N. Flagg, Robert B. Brandegee, W. G. Bunce, Montague Flagg and Walter Griffin. Member: CT. AFA; Hartford Municipal Art Soc.; Salma. C.; Springfield, A. Lg; Lyme AA; New Haven PCC. Awards: Hon. mention, CT AFA, 1922; Alice C. Dunham prize and popular prize, 1923; hon. mention 1928, and Cooper prize, 1929; hon. mention, New Haven PCC, 1928. Work: "Portrait of Alfred E. Burr," Burr Grammar School, Hartford; "Dr. George C. Bailey," Brown School, and St. Francis' Hospital, Hartford; "Thomas Snell Weaver," Weaver High School, Hartford. Instructor at Hartford Public High School and the CT League of Art Students. Address in 1929, 86 Pratt Street; P.O. Box 298; h. 843 New Britain Avenue, Hartford, CT.

McMEIN, NEYSA MORAN.
(Mrs. John G. Baragwanath). Painter and illustrator. Born Quincy, IL, Jan. 25, 1890. Pupil AIC. Member: SI; GFLA. Work: Covers for "McCall's" "Saturday Evening Post," "Woman's Home Companion." Address in 1929, 1 West 67th Street, New York, NY.

McMILLAN, LAURA BROWN (MRS.).
Painter, writer, and teacher. Born Malone, NY, April 23, 1859. Pupil of John Herron Art Inst.; De Pauw University; Emma King; Edward Sitsman; George Innis, Jr. Member: Indiana AC; Art Department Kokomo Woman's C; Kokomo AA; Hoosier Salon. Work: "Autumn Time," Tipton Public Library; "Along the Stream," High School, Howard, IN; "Late Winter," Kokomo Women's Club House; "Morgan County Hills," Howard Co. Hospital; "Autumn Time," Y.W.C.H. Building. Address in 1929, 221 East Taylor Street, Kokomo, IN.

McMILLAN, MARY.
Painter. Born Ilion, NY, March 29, 1895. Pupil of Mabel Welch. Member: Brooklyn S. Min. P.; N.A. Women PS; A. Soc. Min. P.; Penna.

S. Min. P.; Nat. Lg. APW; AFA. Address in 1929, 941 James Street, Syracuse, NY. Died 1958.

MCMILLEN, MILDRED.
Wood engraver. Born in Chicago, IL, in 1884. Studied in Chicago, New York, and Paris. Represented in the National Museum of Canada; Ottawa and New York Public Libraries. Address in 1926, 3 Central Street, Provincetown, MA.

McMURTRIE, EDITH.
Painter and teacher. Born Philadelphia, PA. Pupil of PAFA. Member: Fellowship PAFA; S. Indp. A.; Phila. Alliance; Plastic C; Eastern AA; Phila. Art Teachers A. Award: Cresson traveling scholarship, PAFA; Mary Smith prize, PAFA, 1929. Work: "The Circus," Pennsylvania Academy of Fine Arts. Instructor, William Penn High School. Address in 1929, 1430 South Penn Square; h. 5302 Knox Street, Philadelphia, PA; summer, Orr's Island, ME. Died 1950.

McNAIR, WILLIAM.
Painter. Born Oil City, PA, Sept. 24, 1867. Pupil of George deF. Brush at ASL of New York. Member: AFA. Address in 1929, 5 East 79th Street, New York, NY; summer, Bar Harbor, ME.

McNAMARA, MARY E.
Painter. Member: S. Wash. A. Address in 1929, 1711 Que Street, Washington, D.C.

McNEELY, JUANITA.
Painter. Born in St. Louis, MO in 1936. Studied: Wash., Univ., St. Louis; Southern Illinois Univ., Carbondale; also studied in Mexico. Exhibitions: Prince Street Gallery, NYC; Westbeth Galleries, NYC; Philadelphia Museum of Art. Collections: National Museum of Art, China; Palacio De Las Bella Artes, Mexico; St. Louis Art Museum.

McNULTY, WILLIAM CHARLES.
Etcher. Born Ogden, Utah, March 28, 1889. Member: Salma. C. Address in 1929, 404 West 20th Street, New York, NY; summer, Rockport, MA. Died 1963.

McPHERSON, W. J.
Flourished in Boston, 1846-47, as a miniature painter.

McQUAID, MARY CAMERON.
Etcher, and Mural painter. Born Jacksonville, FL, Nov. 21, 1886. Pupil of NAD; ASL; Cooper Union; Atelier of Ettore Cadorin. Member: Alliance. Address in 1929, 440 Riverside Drive, New York, NY.

McRAE, JOHN C.
This artist engraved portraits and subject plates, in both line and stipple, for New York publishers in 1855. He executed several large and excellent subject plates for framing, and was working in 1880. A portrait of John Wesley, in mezzotint, and published by Harper & Brother, New York, is signed Mc Rae sc." While inferior in execution to his other work, this may have been engraved by John C. McRae.

McRICKARD, JAMES P.
Painter. Born Nov. 7, 1872. Pupil of ASL of NY; Douglas Volk, and George de Forest Brush. Member: Salma. C. Address in 1929, 39-15-215th Place, Bayside, L.I., NY.

McVEIGH, BLANCHE.
Etcher. Born: St. Charles, Missouri. Studied: St. Louis School of Fine Arts; Art Institute of Chicago; PAFA; Art Students' League; with Daniel Garber, Doel Reed. Awards: Dallas Printmakers Club, 1942, 1944, 1947, 1948, 1950; CT Acad. of Fine Arts, 1941; Southern States Art League, 1945; Texas General Exhibition, 1944, 1945; Texas Fine Arts Assoc., 1946; 100 Prints, Chicago, 1936, 1938; Ft. Worth Art Assoc., 1948, 1950, 1952; Library of Congress, 1947. Collections: Museum of Fine Arts of Houston; Ft. Worth Art Association; Oklahoma Agricultural and Mechanical College; Dallas Museum of Fine Arts; Cincinnati Museum Association; Carnegie Inst.; Library of Congress; University of Texas.

McVICKER, CHARLES T.
Illustrator. Born in Canonsburg, PA in 1930. He studied under John LaGatta at the ACD for four years. His career began in 1957 with an assignment for Good Housekeeping and he has since worked for Popular Mechanics, Family Circle and the American Journal of Nursing. His illustrations are part of the collections of the National Historical Society and the United States Capitol. A member of the AWS, he was elected President of the S of I in 1976.

MEADE, LARKIN GOLDSMITH (or MEAD).
Sculptor. Born in Chesterfield, New Hampshire, on Jan. 3, 1835. He studied under Henry Kirke Brown. His statue of Ethan Allen is in Washington, D.C., and his statue of Abraham Lincoln is in Springfield, IL. In 1878 he resided in Washington, D.C., and assisted the commission in the completion of the Washington Monument. He died in Florence, Italy, on Oct. 15, 1910.

MEADOWS, CHRISTIAN.
Engraver. Born in 1814 in England. Engraver of portraits and buildings, signed himself thus 'at Windsor, VT. He was working about 1850 - 55.

MEADOWS, ROBERT MITCHELL.
A very well-executed stipple portrait of Edward Jenner, M.D., was engraved by R. M. Meadows and published in the Analectic Magazine for 1817. Meadows also engraved a portrait of F. Asbury for an American publication, but it is not certain that either of these plates was necessarily engraved in the US. Nagler, in his Kunstler-Lexicon, refers to a Robert Meadows who flourished in the first quarter of the 19th and engraved for the Shakespeare Gallery, of London.

MEAGHER, MARION T.
Painter, sculptor and teacher. Born in New York City. Pupil of National Academy of Design, and of Chase, Beckwith, and R. Swain Gifford in New York; he also studied in Paris and Antwerp. Artist of the Dept. of Anthropology, American Museum of Natural History, and New York Ophthalmic College. Address in 1929, 939 Eighth Avenue, New York, NY; summer, Fisher's Island, NY.

MEAKIN, LEWIS HENRY.
Landscape painter and etcher. Born in Newcastle, England. He came to this country as a child; studied art in Europe, and taught in Cincinnati. He is represented at the Cincinnati Museum. He was elected an Associate Member of the Nat. Acad. of Design in 1913. Died Aug. 14, 1917 in Boston, MA.

MEANCE.
French miniature painter, flourishing in New York, 1795. Portrait of N. G. Dufief, engraved by Edwin. (See Fielding, Edwin Catalogue, No. 60).

MEARS, HELEN FARNSWORTH.
Sculptor. Born in Oshkosh, WI, in 1878. Studied in New York and Paris. First success "Genius of Wisconsin," exhibited at Chicago Exp., 1893; executed "The Fountain of Life," 1904; marble statue of Frances E. Willard, 1905, placed in the Capitol, Washington; portrait bust of George Rogers Clark; also bust of William L. G. Morton, M.D., placed in Smithsonian Institution; portrait reliefs of Augustus St. Gaudens, Louis Collier Wilcox and Edward A. McDowell. She died in NY, on Feb. 17, 1916.

MEARS, HENRIETTA DUNN.
Painter and etcher. Born Milwaukee, WI, Feb 28, 1877. Pupil of ASL of NY, Hawthorne and Pape. Member: Copley S.; Provincetown AA; West Coast Arts; Berkeley Lg. FA. Award: First prize, MN State Fair, 1927. Address in 1929, Dodd Road, St. Paul, MN; summer, Provincetown, MA.

MEDAIRY & BANNERMAN.
This firm was engraving portraits and book-plates in Baltimore, MD, in 1828-29. The second member of the firm was doubtless W. W. Bannerman, already referred to.

MEDARY, AMIE HAMPTON.
Miniature painter. Born Eastern Point, Groton, CT, July 24, 1903. Pupil of PAFA, School of Boston Museum of Fine Arts, and A. Margaretta Archambault. Address in 1929, 115 High Street, Taunton, MA; 383 Boylston Street, Boston, MA.

MEEDER, PHILIP.
Wood engraver. Born in Alsace, France. He came to the U.S. as a boy. He was associated with the wood-engraver Frederick Y. Chubb, under the firm name of Meeder and Chubb. He died in New York City, June 27, 1913.

MEEKER, JOSEPH RUSLING.
Landscape painter. Born in Newark, NJ, in 1827. He showed a special interest in southern scenery. Among his paintings are "The Indian Chief"; "Louisiana Bayou", and "The Lotos Eaters."

MEEKS, EUGENE.
Born in New York in 1843. He spent much of his time abroad. Among his works are: "Gondola Party, Venice" and the "Halt at the Golden Lion."

MEER, JOHN.
He is included in Dunlap's list of artists and is described as an enamel painter. He was also a bank-note engraver, japanner and glass painter.

MEESER, LILLIAN B.
(Mrs. Spenser B. Meeser). Painter. Born Ridley Park, PA. Pupil of PAFA: ASL of NY; Worcester Art Museum. Member: Fellowship PAFA; Plastic C.; Phila. Alliance; North Shore AA; Provincetown AA; AFA. Awards: Hon. mention, 1921, and silver medal, 1922, Plastic C.; Mary Smith prize, PAFA, 1923; gold medal in decoration, Arch. Lg. of NY, 1928. Represented in the Reading Museum, Penn. State College Art Gallery, Fellowship Pennsylvania Academy of the Fine Arts. Work: Hotchkiss Memorial, St. Pauls Church, New Haven, CT; Altarpiece, Christ Church, Cranbrook, MI, Apse Dome, St. Bartholomew's Church, New York; three altars, Convent of the Sacred Heart, Overbrook, Penn.; floor, Baltimore Trust Co., Baltimore, MD. Address in 1929, Crozer Campus, Chester, PA; summer, South Wellfleet, Cape Cod, MA.

MEGE, VIOLETTE.
Painter and sculptor. Born in Alger, French Algiers, in 1889. Pupil of George Rochegrosse, Ecole Nationale des Beaux Arts, Academie

Julien, J. P. Laurens and Humbert, in Paris. Address in 1926, 119 West 87th Street, New York, NY.

MEIERE, HILDRETH.
Mural painter. Born New York City. Pupil of F. V. DuMond; Kenneth H. Miller; Frank Van Sloan. Member: ASL of NY; Mural P. Work: Rotunda dome, Nat'l Acad. of Sciences Wash., D.C.; domes, ceilings and floors, Neb. State Capitol, Lincoln; Cowdin Memorial, St. Mark's Church. Mt. Kisco, NY; Cornell Memorial, St. Martin's Church, Providence, RI; Winthrop Memorial, St. John's Church, Beverly Farms, MA, Bennett Memorial, Christ Church Cathedral, Lexington, KY. Address in 1929, Rodin Studios, 200 West 57th Street; h. 620 Park Avenue, New York, NY. Died in 1961.

MEIERHANS, JOSEPH.
Painter. Born in Ober-Lunkhofen -Aargan, Switzerland, Feb. 22, 1890. Pupil of A.N. Lindenmuth, John Sloan. Member: S. Indp. A.; ASL of NY. Address in 1929, 284 Garden Avenue, Mt. Vernon, NY.

MEINSHAUSEN, GEORGE F. E.
Painter, illustrator, and wood engraver. Born Achim, Hanover, Germany, Jan. 6, 1855. Pupil of Cincinnati Art Academy. Award: Silver medal, St. Louis Exp., 1904. Work: Water colors, "The Phantom Ship" and "The Life Boat," and wood-engraving of same, Art Museum, Cincinnati; prints in Carnegie Institute, Pittsburgh; Library of Congress, Washington, D.C.; New York Lenox Public Library. Address in 1929, 4615 Station Avenue, Norwood, OH.

MEISSNER, ALFRED.
Portrait painter and illustrator. Born in Chicago in 1877. Pupil of Art Institute of Chicago. Address, 3057 North Christiana Avenue, Chicago, IL.

MEISSNER, LEO JOHN.
Painter. Born Detroit, MI, June 28, 1895. Pupil of John Wicker; Detroit School of Fine Arts. Member: Print C; Boston S. Indp. A; Springfield AA. Address in

1929, 96 Wadsworth Terrace, New York, NY; summer, Monhegan, ME.

MELCHER, MRS. BERTHA CORBETT.
Illustrator and painter. Born in Denver, CO, in 1872. Pupil of Volk in Minneapolis; Pyle at Drexel Institute, Philadelphia. Specialty, miniatures and illustrations for children's books. Address in 1926, Topanga, CA.

MELCHERS, J. GARI.
Painter. Born Detroit, MI, Aug. 11, 1860. Pupil of Dusseldorf Academy, 1877-80; Lefebvre and Boulanger in Paris. Member: ANA 1904, NA 1906; Paris SAP; Soc. Nat. des Beaux-Arts, Paris; Inter. Society of Artists, London; Munich Secession (cor.); Berlin R. Acad.; Nat. Inst. A.L.; New Soc. A; NAC; AFA. Awards: Hon. mention, Paris Salon, 1886; first class medal, Amsterdam, 1887; 3rd class medal, Paris Salon, 1888; 1st class medal, Munich, 1888; grand prize, Paris Exp., 1889; first prize, AIC 1891; medal of honor, Berlin, 1891; gold medal, AC Phila., 1892; medal of honor, Antwerp, 1894; Temple gold medal, PAFA, 1896; 1st class medal, Vienna, 1898; gold medal, Pan-Am. Exp., Buffalo, 1901; gold medal, St. Louis Exp., 1904; second W. A. Clark prize, Corcoran Gallery, 1910; gold medal, Sesqui-Centennial Exp., Phila., 1926; popular prize, Carnegie Inst. Exh., 1927; popular prize, Corcoran Gallery, 1928. Knight of the Order of St. Michael of Bavaria; Chevalier of the Legion of Honor of France, 1895; Officer, 1904; Officer R. Prussian Order of Red Eagle, 1907. Work: Luxembourg Museum, Paris, France; Corcoran; Carnegie Institute; National Gallery; Institute of Arts, Detroit; AIC; MMA; Minn. Inst.; R.I.S.D.; L.A. Museum; St. Louis; Providence and Toronto Museum. Address in 1929, 80 W. 40th Street, New York, NY; Fredericksburg, VA.

MELIODON, JULES ANDRE.
Sculptor and teacher. Born Paris, France, June 1, 1867. Pupil of Falguiere, Fremiet, Barrau and Message in Paris. Member: NY Arch. Lg.; Soc. des Artistes Francais; Soc. Des Professeurs Francais en Amerique; Alliance.

631

Awards: Hon. mention, Paris Salon, 1902; Diploma of Officer of Academy, 1898; Diploma of Officer of Public Instruction, 1904. Work: "The Explorer Lesueur, " Museum of Natural History , Paris; decorative sculpture on the reconstructed Sorbonne, Paris; Bahai's Vase (with Tiffany and L. Bourgeois, architect); soldiers monument, Bloomingdale, NJ; Roxy theatre, (in cooperation) New York City. Instructor at University of Pennsylvania. Address in 1929, Lincoln Park, NJ.

MELLON, ELEANOR M.
Sculptor. Born Narbeth, PA, Aug. 18, 1894. Pupil of V. D. Salvatore, Edward McCartan, A. A. Weinman, Robert Aitken, Charles Grafly, Harriet Frishmuth. Member: NSS; AFA. Address in 1929, 155 East 72nd Street, New York, NY; summer, Morristown, NJ.

MELLOR, MARGARET W.
Painter. Exhibited water colors at the Penna. Academy of Fine Arts, Phila., 1925. Address in 1926, 5203 McKean Avenue, Germantown, Phila., PA.

MÉLOSH, MRS. MILDRED E.
Painter, writer, lecturer, and teacher. Born Jersey City, NJ, Aug. 8, 1901. Pupil of Christine Lumsdon. Member: Salons of America; Jersey City WCC; S. Indp. A. Address in 1929, Carnegie Hall, New York, NY; h. 145 Belmont Avenue, Jersey City, NJ; summer, Harrison, ME.

MELTON, CATHARINE PARKER.
Painter. Born Nashville, TN. Pupil of Corcoran School of Art; Henry B. Snell. Member: Wash. AC; C. L. Wolfe AC. Address in 1929, 1831 G. Street, N. W. Washington, D.C.

MELTZER, ARTHUR.
Painter. Born Minneapolis, MN, July 31, 1893. Pupil of Robert Koehler; PAFA. Member: Fellowship PAFA; Phila. Sketch C; Phila. Alliance; Mystic SA. Awards: Cresson traveling scholarship, PAFA, 1921; first hon. mention, Phila. Sketch C., 1924; hon. mention, MN State Fair, 1923;

Fellowship prize, PAFA, 1925; hon. mention, Phila. AC, 1926; hon. mention, Phila. Sketch Club, 1927. Represented in Carlisle Art Museum; Columbus Gallery of Fine Arts. Instructor, School of Design, Philadelphia. Address in 1929, Sterner Mill Road, Langhorne, PA; summer, Mystic, CT.

MELTZOFF, STANLEY.
Illustrator. Born in New York City, in 1917. He studied at the Institute of Fine Arts of NYC, ASL of NAD. His first works appeared in Stars and Stripes prior to 1945 and in Who in 1946. In addition to his various poster and book illustrations, his pieces appeared in Life, McCall's, The Saturday Evening Post, National Geographic and Sports Illustrated. The ADC and the S of I in NY have awarded him many prizes for his paintings. His specialty as an art historian is Florentine Quattrocento painting.

MELVILL, MRS. ANTONIA.
Portrait painter. Born Berlin, Germany, Nov. 28, 1875. Came to America in 1894. Studied in London under W. P. Frith and at the Heatherley School of Art. Member: S. Indp. A. of New York; AFA; Am. APL. Award: Prize, State Fair, Sacramento, CA., 1926. Work: "Portrait of Bishop J. H. Johnson," Good Samaritan Hospital, Los Angeles; "Portrait of Mrs. Dollard," Capitol at Pierre, SD; Public Library, Sacramento, CA; Portrait of Prof. Emery Harvard Military School, Los Angeles; "Pierrot." Alhambra Theatre, Sacramento, CA. Address in 1929, 717 South Alvarado Street, Los Angeles, CA.

MENDENHALL, EARL (MRS.).
See Langley, Sarah.

MENDENHALL, EMMA.
Painter. Born Cincinnati, OH. Pupil of Cincinnati Art Academy under Nowottny and Duveneck; Julian Academy in Paris; summer school under Mrs. Rhoda Holmes Nicholls, Woodbury and Snell. Member: Cincinnati Woman's AC; AWCS; N. A. Women PS; Cincinnati MacDowell C.; NYWCC; Wash. WCC. Address in 1929,

2629 Moorman Avenue, Walnut Hills, Cincinnati, Ohio.

MENG, JOHN.
American portrait painter. Born about 1734 in Germantown, Philadelphia. He died in the West Indies in 1854. A few of his paintings are preserved in the old Germantown families and in the Penna. Historical Society of Philadelphia.

MENNIE, FLORENCE.
Painter. Born New York City. Pupil of George Bellows, Luis Mora. Member: S. Indp. A; Silvermine GA; Salons of Am. Address in 1929, R. F. D. 36, Wilton, CT.

MENTE, CHARLES.
Painter and illustrator. Born in NY. Pupil of Gabi and Loefftz in Munich. Member: AWCS; Chicago WCC. Awards: First prize, Chicago SA, 1893; gold medal, AC Phila., 1895; silver medal and hon. mention, Atlanta Exp., 1895; Evans prize, AWCS, 1904. Address in 1929, Congers, NY.

MENTEL, LILLIAN A.
Painter, illustrator, and teacher. Born Cincinnati, OH, Nov. 2, 1882. Pupil of Cincinnati Art Academy and Pratt Inst. Member: Cincinnati Woman's AC. Address in 1929, Priscilla Apt. 9, Michigan Avenue, Hyde Park, Cincinnati, OH.

MENZEL, HERMAN E.
Painter. Born Chicago, IL, Oct. 19, 1904. Pupil of William B. Owen, Jr. Address in 1929, 8332 South Green Street, Chicago, IL.

MENZLER-PEYTON, BERTHA S.
Landscape painter. Born Chicago, IL. Pupil of AI Chicago; Merson, Collin and Aman-Jean in Paris. Member: Chicago SA; Chicago WCC; N.A. Women PS; NYWCC; AWCS; Allied AA; SPNY; North Shore AA. Awards: Special prize, AIC, 1903; Young Fortnightly prize, AIC, 1909; Grower prize, AIC, 1910; landscape prize, NA Women PS.,1926. Work in: Union League Club, Chicago; Nike and Klio Clubs and West End Woman's Club, Chicago; Evanston (IL) Woman's Club; Mural decorations in Fine Arts Bldg., Chicago. Address in 1929, care Budworth and Son, 424 West 52nd Street, New York, NY; summer, Reed Studio Bldg., East Gloucester, MA.

MERCER, GENEVA.
Sculptor. Born Jefferson, Marengo Co., AL, Jan. 27, 1889. Pupil of G. Moretti. Member: Pitts. AA. Work: "Rev. James L. Robertson," "Soldiers Memorial," Bronxville (NY) Reformed Church; memorial to Florence McComb, Osceola School, Pittsburgh, PA. Address in 1929, Demopolis, Marengo Co., AL.

MERCER, WILLIAM.
Portrait painter. Born 1773. Worked in oils and miniatures and painted historical scenes. Flourished in Philadelphia. Pupil of Charles Wilson Peale, he became an excellent portrait painter. Died in 1850.

MERCHANT, G. W.
A well-engraved plan of the floor of the Senate chamber, at Albany, NY, is signed "G. W. Merchant Engr. & Pub." The plan is used as a frontispiece to the "Legislative Manual of the State of New York, 1834," and it was published at Albany in that year.

MERFELD, GERALD LYDON.
Painter. Born in Des Moines, Iowa, Feb. 19, 1936. Study: Am. Acad. of Art, with William Mosby, 1954-57. Work: McDonough Collection of Am. Art; US Navy Arch. Exhib.: Hope Show, Butler Inst. Am. Art, 1972, 74, 76, 78, 80; Allied Artists of Am. Annual, NYC, 1975-77; Knickerbocker Artists, NYC; Nat'l. Acad. of Western Art, 1979; and others. Awards: Seley Gold Medal, Salmagundi Club; Okla. Mus. of Art Award; 1st Prize Butler Inst. of Am. Art; others. Combat Artist, US Navy, Vietnam & Mediterranean; Art Instructor. Media: Oil, pastel, conte crayon. Address in 1982, 104 Oak St., New Lenox, IL.

MERINGTON, RUTH.
Painter and teacher. Born London, England. Pupil of NAD and ASL in NY, under Edgar M. Ward; Bruce Crane and Birge Harrison; Julian Academy in Paris under Constant.

Address in 1929, 1 Wallace Street, Newark, NJ.

MERKL, ELISSA F.
Painter. Born in Colo. Springs, July 2, 1949. Study: Marymount Col., Tarrytown, NY. Work: Coll. of private individuals in US, Eng., Ger., Venezuela; SONY Corp., NJ; and more. One-person shows: Douglass Col. Ctr., NJ; Arnot Art Mus., Elmira, NY; Summit Art Ctr. Members Gal., NJ; and more. Exhib.: Int'l Miniature Print Biennial, Space Grp. Art Gal., Seoul, Korea; Garden State Arts Ctr., Holmdel, NJ; Int'l Soc. of Artists, Nat'l Arts Club, NYC, and Foothills Art Ctr., Golden, Colo.; "Am. Artist" Nat'l Comp., Circle Gal., NYC; Arts Club, Wash. DC; Zaner Gal., Rochester, NY; Pratt Graphics Ctr. Awards: Grumbacher bronze medallion; purchase award, Nat'l Western Painting Exhib., Bosque Art Gal., NM; many others. Mem.: Pratt Graphics Ctr.; Printmaking Council of NJ; other NJ associations. Media: Acrylic, serigraph. Address in 1983, 22 Fairview Rd., Millburn, NJ.

MERO, LEE.
Illustrator. Born Ortonville, MN, May 30, 1885. Pupil of Robert Koehler in Minneapolis; Robert Henri in NY. Member: Minneapolis SFA. Specialty, design and decorative illustration, mottoes and greeting cards. Address in 1929, Care of The Buzza Co., Minneapolis, MN.

MERRELS, MRS. GRAY PRICE.
Miniature painter. Born Topeka, KN, 1884. Pupil of ASL of NY under Shirley Turner. Member: Brooklyn Soc. Min. P. Address in 1929, 248 Oxford Street, Hartford, CT.

MERRILL, FRANK T.
Painter. Born in Boston in 1848. He studied art at the Lowell Institute, and at the Boston Museum of Fine Arts; he also studied in France and England. His water colors are free in wash and color, and he also was very successful with his etchings. Merrill's work has been used extensively for illustrating and may be found in

Thackeray's "Mahogany Tree" and in Irving's "Rip Van Winkle."

MERRILL, HIRAM CAMPBELL.
Painter, and wood engraver. Born Boston, MA, Oct. 25, 1866. Pupil of Douglas Volk; ASL of NY. Member: NYWCC, 1914. Awards: Bronze medal, Pan Am. Exp., Buffalo, 1901, and at St. Louis Exp., 1904, for wood engraving. Work in: Carnegie Institute, Pittsburgh. Address in 1929, 1800 Mass. Avenue, Cambridge, MA.

MERRILL, KATHERINE.
Painter and etcher. Born Milwaukee, WI. Pupil AI Chicago; Brangwyn in London. Member: Chicago SE; Brooklyn SE; CA SE; N.A. Women PS. Represented in print collections of Library of Congress, Washington, D.C.; Corcoran Gallery of Art, Washington, DC; New York Public Library; Art Institute of Chicago; Milwaukee Art Institute; Newark Public Library; Springfield Public Library; art dept. of Beloit College, Beloit, WI; Hackley Gallery of Art, Muskegon, MI.; Bibliotheque Nationale, Paris, France; collections of ex libris in bookplate collection of Metropolitan Museum of Art, New York; Widener Memorial Library, Harvard University and the University of Chicago. Address in 1929, 107 East 73rd Street, New York, NY.

MERRIMAN, HELEN BIGELOW.
(Mrs. Daniel Merriman). Painter and writer. Born Boston, MA. July 14, 1844. Pupil of Wm. Hunt. Member: Boston WCC; AFA. Address in 1929, 73 Bay State Road, Boston, MA; summer, Intervale, N.H.

MERRITT, ANNA LEA.
(Mrs. Henry Merritt). Painter and writer. Born Philadelphia, PA, Sept. 13, 1844. Pupil of Henry Merritt in London. Awards: Centennial Exp., Philadelphia, 1876; hon. mention, Paris Exp., 1889; two medals (oil painting and mural decoration), Columbian Exp., Chicago, 1893; medal, Atlanta Exp., 1895; medal, Pan-Am. Exp., Buffalo, 1901. Work: "Love Locked Out," National Gallery of British Art, London; "Piping Shepherd,"

Pennsylvania Academy, Philadelphia; numerous portraits, including "James Russell Lowell," Memorial Hall, Harvard University, Cambridge, and "Mrs. Arnold Toynbee," Lady Margaret Hall, Oxford; eight mural paintings in St. Martin's Church, Wanersh, Guildford, England. Author "Memoir of Henry Merritt," "A Hamlet in Old Hampshire," "An Artist's Garden." Address in 1929, The Limes, Hurstbourne-Tarrant, Andover, Hampshire, England.

MERTON, OWEN.
Painter. Born Christchurch, New Zealand, May 14, 1887. Pupil of Tudor-Hart in Paris. Represented in the National Gallery of New Zealand. Designs and color schemes for flower gardens. Address in 1929, 50 Virginia Road, Douglaston, Long Island, NY.

MERWIN, ANTOINETTE de FOREST (MRS.).
Painter and teacher. Born Cleveland, OH, July 27, 1861. Pupil of ASL of NY; St. Paul School of Fine Arts under Burt Harwood; Merson; Courtois; Collin and James McNeill Whistler. Member: Calif. AC; Pasadena SA; Pasadena FAS; San Diego AG. Award: Honorable mention, Paris Salon, 1900. Works: "Fisherfolk, Volendam Noord, Holland, " owned by the Boston Art Club; "California Fruit and Flowers," Cuyamaca Club, San Diego, CA. Address in 1929, 1064 Armada Drive, Pasadena, CA.

MERWIN, HESTER.
(Mrs. Edward Lindsley Ayers.) Painter. She is also known for her drawings. Born in Bloomington, IL. Studied: In Italy before attending The Chicago Art Institute; Pasadena Art Institute and with Howard Giles, Andrew Dasburg, and Ward Lockwood. She has shown in leading NY galleries and in more than sixty one-man shows throughout the United States. She has made many drawing safaris in Africa, and has travelled also to Afghanistan, Mexico, South Pacific, and the British West Indies. Her drawings of the last few surviving Island Caribs on the island of Cominica in the permanent collection of the Smithsonian Institution in Washington, D.C.

MESS, EVELYNNE B.
Etcher. Born: Indianpolis, Indiana in 1903. Studied: John Herron Art Inst.: Butler University; Art Inst. of Chicago; Ecole des Beaux-Arts, Fontainebleau, France; and with Andre Strauss and Despujols. Awards: Indiana State Fair, 1930, 1950, 1951, 1958; National Society of Arts and Letters, 1948; Indiana Art, 1949, 1955; California Society of Etchers; Holcomb prize, John Herron Art institute, 1958; Hoosier Salon, 1947, 48, 50, 53, 58; others. Collections: John Herron Art Institute; Library of Congress

METCALF, ELIAR.
Painter. Born in Franklin, MA, Feb. 5, 1785. He studied under Samuel Waldo. Metcalf resided and painted portraits in New Orleans, 1818- 1823; they were considered excellent. He appears in the 1822 New Orleans directory as "portrait and miniature painter, 25 Magazine Street, above Common." In Sept. 1817 The New York Commercial Advertiser notes as follows: "E. Metcalf, Portrait and Miniature Painter having recovered his health has returned to the city and resumed the exercise of his profession at No. 152, Broadway." He painted an excellent portrait of the artist Asher B. Durand, now in the New York Historical Society. Died Jan. 15, 1834, in NYC.

METCALF, WILLARD LEROY.
Painter. Born in Lowell, MA, in 1858; died in New York, March 9, 1925. Pupil of George L. Brown in Boston, and of Boulanger and Lefebvre in Paris. Honorable mention, Paris Salon, 1888; medal, Columbian Exp., Chicago, 1893; Temple gold medal, Penna. Academy of Fine Arts, 1904; gold medal and first prize, Corcoran Gallery of Art, Washington, 1907; Harris medal and prize, Art Institute of Chicago, 1910. Represented by "The Birches" and "My Pastoral," Boston Museum of Fine Arts, Boston MA; also "May Night" at the Corcoran Art Gallery. Taught, ASL. Member

of NIAL and Am. WC Society.

METEYARD, THOMAS BUFORD.
Painter. Born at Rock Island, IL, Nov. 17, 1865. Studied in Europe, and exhibited pictures at Paris Salon, Chicago Exposition, Society of American Artists, New York, Penna. Academy of Phila., St. Louis Exp., 1904, and other exhibitions in US. Decorator for "Songs from Vagabondia" (by Bliss Carman and Richard Hovey) and numerous other books. Address in 1926, Moses Hill farm, Fernhurst, Sussex, England. Died in Vaud, Switzerland on March 17, 1928.

METHVEN, H. WALLACE.
Painter and etcher. Born Philadelphia, PA. Pupil of Henry F. Spread, Kenyon Cox, Beckwith and Laurens. Member: Paris AAA. Address in 1929, 3 Rue Campagne Premiere, Paris, France.

MEURER, CHARLES A.
Painter. Born Germany, March 15, 1865. Pupil of Julian Academy, Bouguereau, Doucet and Ferrier in Paris. Member: Cincinnati AC. Specialty, still life; also sheep and cattle. Address in 1929, Terrace Park, OH.

MEUX, GWENDOLYN D.
Painter. Member: Boulder AA; OK AA. Award: Silver medal for painting, Kansas City AI, 1923; hon. mention, Denver Museum Exhib., 1928; Silver medal, drawing, Kansas City, AI, 1929. Address in 1929, care University of Colorado, Boulder, CO.

MEWHINNEY, MRS. ELLA K.
Painter. Born Nelsonville, TX, June 21, 1891. Pupil of George Bridgman; Robert Reid; Randall Davey. Member: SSAL; Texas FAA. Award: Hon. mention, Dallas Women's Forum, 1925; first prize, flower painting, SSAL, ($50); hon. mention, Davis competition ($100), 1928; third prize, Davis competition, Texas, ($500), 1929. Address in 1929, Holland, Texas.

MEYENBERG, JOHN C.
Sculptor and craftsman. Born Tell City, IN, Feb. 4, 1860. Pupil of

Cincinnati Art Academy under Thomas S. Noble; Beaux-Arts in Paris under Jules Thomas. Member: Cincinnati AC. Work: "Egbert Memorial," Fort Thomas, KY; "Pediment," Covington(KY) Carnegie Library; "Aunt Lou Memorial," Linden Grove Cemetery; Theodore F. Hallam, bust, Court House, Covington, KY; "Nancy Hanks," Lincoln Park entrance, State of Indiana; "Benn Pitman Memorial," Cincinnati Public Library. Address in 1929, Tell City, IN.

MEYER, ALVIN WILLIAM.
Sculptor. Born Bartlett, IL, Dec. 31, 1892. Pupil of MD Inst., PAFA under Charles Grafly. Member: Char. C. Award: Cresson Traveling Scholarship and Rinehart Traveling Scholarship of the Peabody Inst.; Prize of Rome, Amer. Academy in Rome, 1923. Address in 1929, 1193 Broadway, New York, NY; 333 N. Michigan Avenue, Chicago, IL; h. Cambridge, MD.

MEYER, CHRISTIAN.
Landscape painter. Born in Germany in 1838, he came to this country as a young man. His paintings were shown at exhibitions of the Society of American Artists and at the National Academy of Design. He died in Brooklyn, NY., April 15, 1907.

MEYER, ENNO.
Painter, sculptor, illustrator, and etcher. Born Cincinnati, OH, Aug. 16, 1874. Pupil of Duveneck. Member: Cincinnati AC. Specialty, animals. Address in 1929, Milford, OH.

MEYER, ERNEST.
Painter. Born at Rothenburg, Germany, Dec. 24, 1863. Pupil of Chase, Twachtman, Ward, Beckwith, DuMond, Turner. Member: CT AFA; Salma. C. Address in 1929, Tylerville, CT. Died in 1861.

MEYER, GEORGE BERNHARD.
Miniature painter. Member: Charcoal C. Address in 1929, 1230 St. Paul Street; East Pleasant Street, Baltimore, MD.

MEYER, HENRY HOPPNER.
Stipple engraver and portrait painter in oils and miniatures. Born in England in 1783. In 1830 he came to New York and engraved portraits and painted miniatures. Among his miniatures he painted one of President Jackson in 1833. He also engraved several plates for Longacre & Herring's "National Portrait Gallery," 1834. He died May 28, 1847, in London.

MEYER, HERBERT.
Painter and illustrator. Born New York, NY, March 6, 1882. Pupil of ASL of NY, Twachtman and DuMond. Member: Salma. C.; NY Arch. Lg.; Allied AA; NYWCC; AWCS. Address in 1929, 108 East 82nd Street, New York, NY; Dorset, VT. Died 1960.

MEYERCORD, GRACE E.
Miniature painter. Exhibited at the Penna. Academy of Fine Arts, Philadelphia, 1925. Address in 1926, 329 West 84th Street, New York.

MEYEROWITZ, WILLIAM.
Painter and etcher. Born in Russia, July 15, 1889. Pupil of NAD. Member: S. Indp. A.; Gloucester S A; Brooklyn SE; North Shore AA; CT AFA; Salons of Am. Award: Hon. mention, CT AFA, 1923. Etchings in Public Library, Concord, MA, and Ralph Cross Johnson Collection, Washington, D.C.; painting in the Phillips Memorial Gallery, Washington, D.C.; "Fruit and Drapery," Albright Art Gallery, Buffalo, NY; "The Musician," Brooklyn Museum of Art. Address in 1929, 39 West 67th Street, New York, summer, 44 Mt. Pleasant Ave., East Gloucester, MA.

MEYERSAHM, MRS. EXENE REED.
Painter. Born Northville, MI. Pupil of RI School of Design; Boston Museum of Fine Arts; Charles Hawthorne. Member: Prov. AC; NAC. Address in 1929, 508 Slade Bldg., 44 Washington Street; h. 111 Congress Avenue, Providence, RI.

MEYLAN, PAUL JULIEN.
Illustrator and painter. Born Canton of Vaud, Switzerland, May 17, 1882. Pupil of NAD in New York. Member: SI, 1907; AAS;

GFLA. Illustrated: "Two Faces," by Marie Van Vorst; "The Poor Lady," by Mary E. Wilkins Freeman; "Sarolta," by Agnes and Egerton Castle; "Come Out of the Kitchen" and "Ladies Must Live," by Alice Duer Miller; "The Unexpected, by Elizabeth Jordan, etc. Address in 1929, R.F.D. 3, Bethel, CT; 140 Wadsworth Avenue, New York, NY.

MEYNER, WALTER.
Painter and illustrator. Born Philadelphia, PA, Feb. 12, 1867. Pupil of PAFA. Member: Salma. C.; Fellowship PAFA; S. Indp. A.; Allied AA. Address in 1929, 150 Nassau Street, New York, NY.

MEYRICK, RICHARD.
The *American Weekly Mercury*, Philadelphia, No. 516, 1729, contains the following advertisement: "Richard Meyrick, Engraver, removed from the Lock and Key in Chesnut Street to the Widow Walker's, in Front-Street Phila." Meyrick was probably an engraver for silversmiths.

MEYROWITZ, JENNY DELONY RICE.
Painter of portraits and miniatures. Born in Washington, Hemstead County, Ark. Studied at Cincinnati Art Academy, and took Med. School course in "Artistic Anatomy," St. Louis School of Fine Arts; pupil of Julien, Delaunee and Delecluse studios, Paris. Studio in New York, 1900. Art Instructor, VA Female Institute, Roanoke, VA, 1893-94; Norfolk, VA College; Director of Art, State University of AK, 1907-09. Exhibited at National Academy of Design, New York Water Color Club, National Arts Club, Woman's Art Club, Miniature societies of New York, Boston and Phila., etc. Painted portraits of Jefferson Davis; Mrs. Jefferson Davis; George G. William, Pres., Chemical National Bank, New York; Mrs. Hetty Green; Dr. George Taylor Stewart, etc. Member: Society of Women Painters and Sculptors. Address in 1926, 140 West 57th Street, New York.

MEYVIS, ALME LEON.
Painter. Born St. Gilles - Waes, Belgium, May 17, 1877. Pupil of Mechanics' Inst., Rochester; Royal

Academy, The Hague. Member: Rochester AC; Arti et Amici, Amsterdam. Awards: Hon. mention, Buffalo Soc. of Artists, 1903; silver medal, Ville de Paris, 1904; silver medal, Enghien-les-Bains, 1904; bronze medal, Inter.Exp., Utrecht, Holland, 1909. Work in: Modern Museum, The Hague, Holland; Sibley Hall Library, Rochester. Address in 1929, 22 Centennial Bldg.; h. 360 Main Street, East Rochester, NY.

MICHAEL, MRS. D. D.
See Wolfe, Natalie.

MICHOD, SUSAN ALEXANDER
Painter. Born on Jan. 3, 1945. Studied: Smith College, Northampton, Mass.; Univ. of Michigan; Pratt Institute, Brooklyn. Awards: Artists Guild of Chicago, 1973; North Shore Art League, Chicago 1971; Illinois State Museum, 1974. Collections: Illinois State Museum; Hastings College, Nebraska. Media: Acrylic, watercolor.

MICKS, JAY RUMSEY.
Illustrator. Born Baltimore, MD, Feb. 22, 1886. Pupil of Henry McCarter. Illustrations for Everybodys, Scribner's, Harper's, Red Book. Address in 1929, 53 Washington Sq., South, New York, NY; summer, 66 Cayuga Street, Seneca Falls, NY.

MIDDAUGH, ROBERT.
Painter. Born May 12, 1935 in Chicago. Earned BFA from Art. Inst. of Chicago (1964). Also studied at Univ. of Chicago. Curator of art collection, first Nat. Bank of Chicago. Taught at Chicago Acad. of Fine Arts. Rec. Scholarships from Univ. Club of Chic. Exhibited at Art Inst. of Chicago; Covenent Club, Chicago; Illinois State Fair, PAFA, and VA Museum of Fine Arts. In collections of Art Inst. of Chicago; Phoenix Art Museum; Boston; Worcester Art Museum.

MIDDLETON, STANLEY GRANT.
Painter. Born Brooklyn, NY. Pupil of Jacquerson de la Chevreuse, Harpignies, Constant, Dagnan-Bouveret and Julian Academy

in Paris. Member: A. Fund S.; Lotos C; Salma. C.; Awards: Hon. mention, Pan-Am. Exposition, Buffalo, 1901; hon. mention, Charleston Exp., 1902. Work: "Normandy Fish Wife," Hamilton Club, Brooklyn; "En Costume de Bal," Lotos Club, New York; "Hon. Lynn Boyd," Capitol, Washington; "Hon. Andre D. White," National Gallery, Washington; "Col. William S. Gordon," West Point Library; "Theodore Connoly," City Hall, New York; "Albert S. Bickmore," Museum of Natural History, New York; "Hon. Carter Glass," Harvard University; "Woodrow Wilson," Princeton Library; "Hon. James J. Walker," Mayor of New York City; Gen. Robert Bullard, Gen. John F. O'Ryan, 27th Division, Gen. Robert Alexander, 77th Division, Gen. Farrington Austin, Bronx Armory, New York. Address in 1929, 1 West 67th Street, New York, NY.

MIDDLETON, THOMAS.
Engraver. Born on the family estate of Fanclure, Scotland, 1797; died in Charleston, S.C., Sept. 27, 1863. He was the third son of the Honorable Thos. Middleton of Charleston, S.C. In the Middleton Records he is referred to as an amateur painter of considerable talent.

MIELATZ, CHARLES F. W.
Etcher and painter. Born in Bredding, Germany, in 1864. Pupil of Chicago School of Design. Elected an Associate Member of the National Academy in 1906. Died on June 2, 1919 in NYC.

MIELZINER, JO.
Painter and draftsman. Born Paris, France, March 19, 1901. Pupil of Leo Mielziner, NAD, ASL of NY., PAFA, Joseph Urban, Robert Edmond Jones. Member: Salma. C. Specialty, Stage Designs. Address in 1929, 148 East 53rd Street, New York, NY.

MIELZINER, LEO.
Painter, sculptor, illustrator, etcher, and lecturer. Born New York City, Dec. 8, 1869. Pupil of Cincinnati Art Academy; Ecole des Beaux-Arts, Julian Academy, Colarossi Academy, Paris; Kroyer in

Denmark. Member: Boston AC; Cincinnati AC; Salma. C. Work: "Portrait of John Bassett Moore," Kent Hall, Columbia University, New York, University of Delaware and State Dept., Washington, D.C.; "Portrait of Nathan Abbot," "Portrait of Harlan Fiske Stone," Kent Hall, Columbia Univ., NY; "Portrait of Solomon Schechter," Jewish Theological Seminary, New York; "Portrait of Moses Mielziner," Hebrew Union College, Cincinnati; "Portrait of Woodrow Wilson," Democratic Club, New York; "Portrait of Elizabeth Milbank Anderson," Barnard College, NY; miniature, "Mother and Child." Boston Art Museum; lithograph, "Boy in Fur Cap," Brooklyn Art Museum; silverpoint, "Arabesque," Worcester Art Museum, Worcester, MA; "Portrait of Louis Loeb," Metropolitan Museum of Art, NY; "Portrait of Isaac M. Wise," Cincinnati Art Museum; portraits of General Pershing, Woodrow Wilson, Theodore Roosevelt, New York Public Library. Address in 1929, 47 Washington Square, New York, NY; summer, Head O'Pamet North, Truro, MA. Died in 1935.

MIFFLIN, JOHN HOUSTON.
Born in 1807 in PA. Miniature painter, who flourished in New York, 1840-42. He is said to have painted portraits in Philadelphia in 1832. Died in 1888 in Columbia, PA.

MIGNOT, LOUIS REMY.
Painter. Born in Charleston, S.C., in 1831. He studied in Holland and opened his studio in NY about 1855, as a landscape painter. He went to South America with Frederick E. Church and painted tropical scenes. Elected National Academician in 1859. He died in Brighton, England, Sept 22, 1870; after his death a collection of his paintings was exhibited there.

MIHALIK, JULIUS C.
Painter, craftsman, writer, lecturer, and teacher. Born Budapest, Hungary, March 26, 1874. Pupil of Academy of Fine Arts, Budapest. Member: Art Teachers G., London (hon.); Etchers-Painters Soc., Budapest (hon.); Boston Soc.

AC; AFA. Address in 1929, 11480 Hessler Road, Cleveland, OH. Died 1943.

MIKELL, MINNIE.
(Mrs. Alexander B. Mikell). Painter and etcher. Born Charleston, SC, Dec. 18, 1891. Pupil of Alfred Hutty; Joseph Pennell. Member: SSAL; Charleston EC; Carolina AA. Address in 1929, R.F.D. No. 1, Charleston, SC.

MILAM, MRS. ANNIE NELSON.
Painter. Born Homer, LA, Nov. 20, 1870. Pupil of John Carlson. Member: El Paso AC; AFA. Award: Second prize, Southwestern Exp., El Paso, 1924. Address in 1929, Canntillo, Texas. Died 1934.

MILBANK, MARJORIE R.
(Mrs. Albert G. Milbank). Painter. Born Lynn, MA, June 15, 1875. Member: NA Women PS. Address in 1929, 480 Park Avenue, NY; summer, Lloyd Harbour, Huntington, L.I., NY.

MILBOURNE, C.
English scene-painter, who was brought from London in 1793 by Wignell for the Chestnut Street Theatre. He painted some scenes of Phila. "View of Arch Street Wharf With Boats Sailing on the Delaware;" also a view, "Third and Market Sts., Phila.," both remarkable for their excellence. (First name may be Cotton).

MILBURN, OLIVER.
Painter and etcher. Born Toronto, Can., Sept. 17, 1883. Pupil of Los Angeles AI; Chouinard School of Art. Member: CA AC. Address in 1929, 536 North Las Palmas, Los Angeles, CA.

MILES, CYRIL.
Painter. Born in Boston, Mass., June 13, 1918. Study: Wayne State Univ. Work: Instituto Mexicano Northamericano de Relationes Culturales, Mexico; IBM, Southfield, Mich.; Michigan Academy of Arts & Sciences; plus commissions. Exhibitions: Chicago Art Institute, Int'l. Watercolor Exhib.; Drawing U.S.A., St. Paul, Minn.; Northamerican Mex. Cult. Inst.; Premier Invenaire Int'l.

Poesie Elementaire, Paris. Awards: Citation, Mex. Gov't.; Gold Medal, Acad. Italia delle Arti; Mich. Art Educ. Assn. Award; and others. Teaching: Detroit Inst. of Art; Highland Park Community College. Mem.: Mich. Acad. Arts & Letters; Mich. WC Society; Nat'l. Art Educ. Assn.; Detroit Inst. of Art Founders Soc.; others. Media: Acrylic, Collage.

MILES, EDWARD.
Miniature painter and portrait artist in crayons. Born Oct. 14, 1752 in Yarmouth, England. He was employed by Sir Joshua Reynolds to make miniature copies of his portraits. He exhibited in the Royal Academy in 1775-79. In 1807 he settled in Philadelphia, where he died March 7, 1828. The directory entries list him both as a portrait painter and drawing teacher.

MILES, HAROLD W.
Painter and teacher. Born Des Moines, IA, Sept. 2, 1887. Pupil of C.S. Cumming and J. F. Smith; Colarossi Academy in Paris. Member: Calif. AC; Calif. WCC; Hollywood Lg. Arch. Work: Mural decorations in West Des Moines High School; illustrated "Girls of High Sierras." Art Director for "Dorothy Vernon of Haddon Hall"; "What Price Glory"' "King of Kings," etc. Instructor in art, Univ. of Iowa; head of art dept., Hollywood High School for five years; instructor, Otis Art Inst., Los Angeles, for one year. Address in 1929, 6154 Glen Holly, Hollywood, CA.

MILES, JEANNE PATTERSON.
Painter. Born: Baltimore, Maryland. Studied: George Washington University; Phillips Memorial Gallery, Washington, DC.; Grande Chaumiere, Paris; Atelier Marcel Gromaire, Paris; NY University. Awards traveling scholarship, 1937-1939. Collections: mural (100 portraits) Ramon's, Washington, DC; Kentile Company, NY and Philadelphia, PA; Santa Barbara Museum of Art. Address in 1980, 463 West Street, New York, New York.

MILIONE, LOUIS.
Sculptor and teacher. Born Padua, Italy, Feb. 22, 1884. Pupil of Charles Grafly; Herman Deigendesch; Porter. Member: Fellowship PAFA. Awards: Cresson Scholarship, PAFA, 1907. Work: "Brig. Gen. Kirby Smith," Vicksburg, MI; and in Church of the Redeemer, Bryn Mawr; Germantown High School, Philadelphia. Address in 1929, 121 South 24th Street; h. 1426 South 9th Street, Philadelphia, PA.

MILLAR, ADDISON THOMAS.
Painter and etcher. Born in Warren, Ohio on Oct. 4, 1860. Pupil of Chase in New York and of Constant in Paris. He is represented by paintings in Rhode Island School of Design, and in the Detroit Museum of Art. His etchings are in the New York Public Library and Congressional Library, Washington, D.C. He was killed in an automobile accident, Dec. 8, 1913.

MILLARD, C. E.
Painter and illustrator. Member: GFLA. Work: Illustrated "The Prince of Wails," by Pauline F. Geffen (Simon and Schuster). Address in 1929, Greenley Arcade, 132 West 31st Street, New York, NY.

MILLBOURN, M. VAUGHN.
Painter, craftsman, and teacher. Born Charlotte, MI, Sept. 8, 1893. Pupil of AIC. Member: GFLA; Soc. Typographic Arts. Address in 1929, Pittsfield Bldg., 55 E. Washington Street; h. 5311 Glenwood Avenue, Chicago, IL.

MILLER, ALFRED JACOB.
Painter. Born Jan 2, 1810, in Baltimore. Studied first under Sully; visited Europe in 1833, studying in Paris, Rome and Florence. He accompanied Sir William Drummond Stewart, a Scotch Baronet, to the Rocky Mountains in 1837, making a series of sketches which were the groundwork of the very interesting gallery of pictures now in Murthely Castle. These pictures were reproduced in water colors for W. T. Walters, of Baltimore. Miller died June 26, 1874, in Baltimore, MD.

MILLER, ANNA HAZZARD.
(Mrs. Edward J. Miller). Painter and teacher. Born Minnesota, June 4, 1863. Pupil of Maurice Braun; Randall Davey, Ernest Lawson. Member: Oklahoma Art League; Oklahoma State Artists Assoc.; MacD. C. of Allied Arts. Work: "Mission Valley," University of Oklahoma. Address in 1929, 828 West 15th Street, Oklahoma City, Oklahoma.

MILLER, BARSE.
Painter. Born New York City, Jan. 24, 1904. Pupil of NAD; Snell; PAFA; Breckenridge. Member: North Shore AA; Fellowship PAFA; Calif. A.C.; Gloucester AA; Calif. WCS; Laguna AA. Awards: First Cresson Travelling Scholarship, PAFA, 1922; Second Cresson Travelling Scholarship to Europe, 1923; hon. mention, Arizona State Fair, 1925; second award for water color, Los Angeles, C. Fair, 1925; first landscape prize, Arizona State Fair, 1927; spec. award of honor, Springville Nat. Art Exhib., Utah, 1928; second Purchase prize, Rocky Mt. Exhib. Modern Art, Logan, Utah, 1929. Represented in Fine Arts Gallery, San Diego, CA; Purchase Fund Fellowship PAFA; Muncipal Collection, Phoenix, AZ; Bentley Collection, Boston; Logan Sr. H.S., Logan, Utah. Address in 1929, 828 So. Lucerne Boulevard, Los Angeles, CA; summer, care of Warren Hastings Miller, Grapevine Road, East Gloucester, MA.

MILLER, BENJAMIN.
Painter and Wood-engraver. Born Cincinnati, OH 1877. Pupil of Duveneck. Awards: First hon. mention, Print Club of Phila., 1929. Represented in Bibliotheque Nationale, Paris; permanent collections, Cincinnati Art Museum, and Minneapolis Institute of Fine Arts. Address in 1929, 131 East 3rd Street, Cincinnati, OH.

MILLER, CHARLES HENRY.
Landscape painter. Born in New York, March 20, 1842. He first exhibited at the National Academy of Design in 1860; was elected an Associate in 1873, and an Academician, in 1875. Gold medal at Philadelphia, 1876; also

exhibited in Boston and New Orleans exhibitions. Represented in Metropolitan Museum by "Sunset, East Hampton"; also by paintings in the Brooklyn Museum and the Rhode Island School of Design. Died Jan. 23, 1922 in NYC.

MILLER, CORA E.
Painter. Born Jenkintown, PA. Pupil of PAFA; Hugh Breckenridge; Fred Wagner. Member: Fellowship PAFA, Plastic C. Address in 1929, 4524 Springfield Avenue, Philadelphia, PA.

MILLER, D. ROY.
Painter. Born Mechanicsburg, PA, Feb. 8, 1891. Pupil of Garber, Breckenridge, Pearson. Award: European Traveling Scholarship, PAFA, 1916. Resident Manager, Penna. Academy of the Fine Arts, Chester Springs. Address in 1929, Pennsylvania Academy of the Fine Arts, Chester Springs, Chester Co PA.

MILLER, DELLE.
Painter, craftswoman, and teacher. Born Independence, KN. Pupil of Kansas City Art Inst.; Arthur W. Dow; Hugh Breckenridge, ASL of NY. Member: North Shore AA; NA Women PS; Western AA; Kansas City SA. Awards: Purchase prize, Kansas City Art Institute, 1922; hon. mention, Missouri-Kansas and Oklahoma Artists Exposition, 1923; prize, KCS of A, 1928. Work: "Morning Light of the Harbor," Kansas City Art Inst.; "The Doorstep Garden." Greenwood School; "A New England Lane," Kansas City Public Library; "The Willows," Pittsburg, Kansas State Normal School; "Unconquered," N.W. Missouri State Teachers College. Address in 1929, 3448 East 62nd Street, Kanasas City, MO.

MILLER, ELEAZER HUTCHINSON.
Painter. Born in Shepherdstown, WV, in 1831. Painter in oils and water colors; also portraitist etcher and illustrator. Visited Europe in 1875. Lived and worked in Washington after 1848. He was one of the organizers of the old Washington Art Club, and also aided in the organization of the Society of Washington Artists, of which he

was three times the president. He was an etcher of prominence. Represented at Corcoran Art Gallery by "Moonrise and Twilight" (water color), painted in 1907. Died April 4, 1921, in Wash., D.C.

MILLER, ELIZABETH S.
Painter. Born: Lincoln, Nebraska in 1929. Studied: University of Nebraska, with Rudy Pozzatti, Walter Meigs, Kady Faulkner; Des Moines Art Center, with Louis Bouche; University of Colorado, with Carl Morris. Awards: Lincoln Art Guild, 1951; Iowa State Fair, 1956; Des Moines Art Center, 1956; 1958; Mulvane Art Museum, Topeka, 1958. Collections: Lincoln Art Guild; Lutheran Life of Christ collection, Des Moines Art Center; Mulvane Art Museum.

MILLER, EVYLENA NUNN.
Painter. Born in Mayfield, Kansas July 4, 1888. Studied: Pomona College; University of California; Art Students League; also studied abroad. Awards: Women's Club, Hollywood, California, 1930; California State Fair, 1925; Festival Allied Artists, 1934; Los Angeles Art Museum, 1937; Laguna Beach Art Association, 1953; Death Valley Exhibition, 1954. Collections: Smithsonian Inst.; Pomona College; Women's Christian College, Tokyo and Kobe, Japan; Chinese Young Mens Christian Assn., California; Bowers Memorial Museum, Santa Anna, CA.

MILLER, GEORGE M. (or MILER).
A Scottish sculptor and modeller, who came to this country towards the latter part of the eighteenth century. He made busts of C. W. Peale, Bishop White, Commodore Bainbridge, Mrs. Madison, Mrs. Jerome Bonaparte, and in 1798, of Washington. He was a member of the Penna. Academy of Fine Arts and the Columbian Society of Arts. He died in 1819.

MILLER, GODFREY.
Miniature painter, who flourished in New York, 1841-87.

MILLER, HARRIETTE G.
Sculptor. Born Cleveland, OH. Member: Am. Woman's Assn.; NA

Women PS; Alliance. Address in 1929, Whimsy Farm, Arlington, VT; 17 rue de la Tour, Paris, France.

MILLER, IRIS MARIE ANDREWS.
(Mrs. Wm. N. Miller). Painter. Born Ada, OH, March 28, 1881. Pupil of Chase, Henri, Breckenridge, Mora. Member: Detroit S. Women P.; NA Women PS; NAC; AFA. Awards: Portrait prize, exhibition by MI. Artists, 1923; Founders prize, MI Artists Exh. 1924; Scarab gold medal, MI Artists Exh., 1929. Address in 1929, 1135 Chicago Blvd., Detroit, MI.

MILLER, J. PINDYCK.
Sculptor. Born in NYC in 1938. Study: Student apprentice to Alexander Archipenko, Woodstock, NY; Middlebury College, VT, BA 1960; Brooklyn Mus. School of Art, NY, 1960-61; Silvermine Guild Sch. of Art, New Canaan, CT, 1960-61. US Army Illustrator, 1961- 63. One-man shows: Katonah (NY) Gal., 1967; Sculpture 1972-1978, SUNY Albany, 1978; Recent Steel Sculpture and Selected Work of the 70's, Bethel (CT) Gal., 1979; Recent Sculpture & Wall Reliefs & Selected Work of 70's, Vassar College, Poughkeepsie, NY, 1981. Exhib.: Katonah (NY) Gal., 1966-78; Rose Fried Gal., NYC, 1968; Phoenix Gal., NYC, 1971; Gruenebaum Gallery, NYC, 1975; 28th Annual New England Exhib., Silvermine Guild, CT, 1977; others. Address in 1983, Brewster, NY.

MILLER, JOAN I.
Painter and printmaker. Born in Brooklyn, NY, Nov. 9, 1930. Study: Tyler Sch. of Art, Temple Univ., BFA; Brooklyn Mus.; Parsons Sch.; Ruth Leaf Studio (Etching). Work: Butler Inst., Younstown, OH; Slater Mem. Mus., Norwich, CT; Phila. Mus. of Art Lending Lib. One-woman shows: Ocean Colony, Amagansett, NY; Phoenix Gal., NYC, 1978,81,83; Artists Proof Gal., East Hampton, LI, NY. Exhib.: Palazzo Vecchio, Florence; Phila. Print Club; Corcoran Gal., Wash. DC; Brooklyn Mus.; Nat'l Arts Club; Nat'l Acad.; Lever House; Arch. Lg.; Guild Hall, East Hampton, LI, NY; and many others. Awards: Nat'l Arts Club award for painting, Soc. of

642

Painters in Casein; Nat'l Acad. award, Nat'l Assn. of Women Artists. Mem.: Phoenix Gal., NYC; Nat'l Assn. of Women Artists. Address in 1983, 1192 Park Ave., NYC.

MILLER, JOSEPH MAXWELL.
Sculptor. Born Baltimore, MD. Dec. 23, 1877. Pupil of Maryland Inst. School of Art and Design, Rinehart School of Sculpture and Charcoal C. in Baltimore; Julian Acad. in Paris under Verlet. Awards: Gold medal of honor, Maryland Inst. School of Art and Design, 1897; Rinehart scholarship to Paris, 1901 - 1905; hon. mention, Paris Salon, 1902; silver medal, St. Louis Exp., 1904; Officier d'Academie, 1912; hon. mention for medals, P.- P. Exp., San F., 1915. Work: "Cardinal Gibbons," PA. Academy of the Fine Arts, and Metropolitan Museum, New York; "Ishmael," St. Louis Museum; "Separation of Orpheus and Eurydice," Peabody Institute, Baltimore; "Bust of Lady," Walters Gallery, Baltimore; monuments to French soldiers, Annapolis, MD; "School Children," Baltimore, MD; "Daniel Coit Gilmore Memorial," Johns Hopkins University, Baltimore. Address in 1929, 1335 Greenmount Avenue; h. 171 Bolton Street, Baltimore, MD.

MILLER, JULIET SCOTT.
Painter, illustrator, and teacher. Born Alexandria, VA, Dec. 12, 1898. Pupil of Boardman Robinson; G. P. du Bois; Minneapolis School of Art. Member: ASL of NY. Address in 1929, 51 East 9th Street, New York, NY.

MILLER, KATE RENO.
Painter. Born in Illinois. Pupil of Cincinnati Art Academy; Duveneck; Hawthorne. Member: Cincinnati Woman's AC. Instructor, Cincinnati Art Academy. Address in 1929, Art Academy; h. and studio, 4919 Ash Street, Norwood, Cincinnati, OH.

MILLER, KENNETH HAYES.
Painter, teacher, and etcher. Born Kenwood, NY, March 11, 1876. Pupil of ASL of NY under Mowbray and Cox; New York School of Art under Chase. Work: "Interior" and "Woman in a Sculpture Gallery," Harrison Gallery, Los Angeles Museum; portrait of "Albert P. Ryder," "Apparition," "Consulting the Cards" and "White Kimono," Phillips Memorial Gallery, Washington, D.C.; Figures with landscape, Metropolitan Museum; Etchings, Print Collections, Public Library and Metropolitan Museum, New York. Instructor of painting and composition, Art Students' League of NY. Address in 1929, care F. K. M. Rehn Gallery, 693 Fifth Avenue; 30 East 14th Street, New York, NY.

MILLER, LESLIE W(ILLIAM).
Painter, teacher, writer, and lecturer. Born Brattleboro, VT, Aug. 5, 1848. Pupil of MA Normal Art School and School of Boston Museum. Member: AC Phila.; Eastern Art Teachers' Assoc.; T. Sq. C. (hon.); Boston AC; Fairmount Park AA; AIA (hon.). Principal Emeritus, School of Industrial Art of the Pennsylvania Museum. Address in 1929, Oak Bluffs, MA.

MILLER, MARGUERITE C(UTTINO).
Painter and teacher. Born Charleston, June 11, 1895. Pupil of PAFA. Member: Fellowship PAFA; SSAL; Sketch C. of Carolina AA. Address in 1929, Studio 3, Gibbes Art Gallery; h. 138 Wentworth Street, Charleston, SC; summer, 807 Flemming Street, Hendersonville, NC.

MILLER, MAUDE ALVERA.
Painter, craftsman, and teacher. Born Skylands, CA, July 31, 1883. Pupil of George Leykauf. Member: San Francisco S. Women A. Award: Bronze medal, Panama-Pacific Exp., San Francisco, 1915. Address in 1929, 3412 Holly Avenue, Oakland, CA; h. 235 North Hancock Street, Los Angeles, CA.

MILLER, MILDRED BUNTING.
Painter and teacher. Born Philadelphia, PA, June 21, 1892. Pupil of Anshutz, Vonnoh, Garber, Breckenridge and Violet Oakley. Member: Fellowship PAFA; Phila. Alliance; Plastic C., Phila. Awards: Two Cresson Scholarships, PAFA; Mary Smith prize, PAFA, 1920. Work: Reflections," and "Paddock," Fellowship Pennsylvania Academy of

the Fine Arts, Phila.; "Belgian Refugees," Mississippi Art Assoc., Jackson, MS; "Descending Night," Pennsylvania Academy of the Fine Arts. Address in 1929, Pennsylvania Academy of the Fine Arts, Chester Springs, Chester Co., PA.

MILLER, MINNIE M.
Painter. Member: Plastic C.; Fellowship PAFA; AFA; Phil. Alliance; Alumnae Phil. School of Des. Represented in Reading PA Museum. Address in 1929, 3025 Queen Lane, Germantown, PA.

MILLER, OSCAR.
Painter. Born New York, 1867. Pupil of Constant and Laurens in Paris. Member: New York Watercolor Club. Address in 1929, Bristol Ferry, RI.

MILLER, REEVA A.
Painter. Born: Hollywood, CA in 1912. Studied: Santa Monica City College; University of California at Los Angeles. Awards: Santa Monica Art Assn., 1945, 1956. Collections: Dome, Al Jolson Memorial, Los Angeles; Beth Sholom Temple, Santa Monica (stained glass windows); Maarev Temple, Encino, California; Temple Sinai, Oakland, California; Temples in Santa Monica, Inglewood, Long Beach and Burbank, California; Camp Shrader, Colorado.

MILLER, RICHARD E.
Painter and illustrator. Born St. Louis, MO, March 22, 1875. Pupil of St. Louis School of Fine Arts; Constant and Laurens in Paris. Member: ANA 1913; NA 1915; Port. P.; St. L. AG; Salma. C.; Inter. Soc. of Painters, Sculptors and Gravers; Paris AAA; Paris SAP; Port. P.; North Shore AA. Awards: Third medal, Paris salon, 1900; bronze medal, Pan-Am. Exp., Buffalo, 1901; silver medal, St. Louis Exp., 1904; second medal, Paris Salon, 1904; second medal, Liege Exp., 1905; Knight of the Legion of Honor, France, 1908; Temple gold medal, PAFA, 1911; Palmer gold medal, AIC, 1914; Clark prize, NAD, 1915; medal of honor, P.- P. Exp., San F., 1915. In collections of Luxembourg Gal.,

Paris; MMA; Gallery of M.A. (Rome,Italy); Corcoran; St. Louis; Albright; PAFA; AIC; Detroit; Cincinnati; Queen City AC, Cin.; Carnegie; State Capitol, Jefferson City, MO; Royal Museum of Christiania; King of Italy's private collection; Museum of Fine Arts, Antwerp; Modern Gallery of the City of Venice; Musee du Petit Palais, Paris. Address in 1929, Care Grand Central Galleries, 15 Vanderbilt Avenue, New York, NY; Provincetown, MA.

MILLER, SUSAN BARSE (MRS.).
Painter. Born Adrian, MI. Pupil of Colarossi Academie de la Grand Chaumiere, Paris; Hugh Breckenridge, William M. Chase. Member: North Shore AA; Fellowship PAFA. Work: "The Tuareg Girl," Los Angeles Museum; "Zobieda," Pasadena Museum, Pasadena, CA. Address in 1929, Grapevine Road, East Gloucester, MA.

MILLER, WILLIAM.
Engraver. Born in New York, Dec. 3, 1850, of German parents; died Jan. 10, 1923. Started engraving on wood at Frank Leslie's publishing house, 1868; studied drawing, etc., in Germany, 1871-73; associated with Frederick Juengling, 1877-89. Exhibited in New York; Munich Salon; Paris Exposition, 1900. Medal, Chicago Exp., 1893; Buffalo Exp., 1901.

MILLER, WILLIAM.
Sculptor, of Providence, RI. He executed a series of large medallions of distinguished native citizens, civil and military.

MILLER, WILLIAM H.
Born 1820 in England. Miniature painter, who flourished about 1846-47, New York.

MILLER, WILLIAM HENRY.
Portrait painter. Born in Phila., PA, in 1854. Pupil of PAFA under Eakins. Member: Fellowship of PAFA; Phila. Sketch Club. Instructor of drawing, Episcopal Academy, Philadelphia. Address in 1926, 102 West Montgomery Avenue, Ardmore, PA.

MILLESON, ROYAL HILL.
Landscape painter. Born in Batavia, Ohio, in 1849. Member: Chicago Society of Artists; Boston Art Club. Work: "Mt. Hood, Oregon," Herron Art Institute, Indianapolis. Author, "The Artist's Point of View." Address in 1926, 2336 Osgood Street, Chicago, IL.

MILLET, CLARENCE.
Painter and teacher. Born Hahnville, LA, March 25, 1897. Pupil of George Bridgman; ASL of NY. Member: New Orleans AA; New Orleans ACC; AFA; SSAL; Miss. AA. Award: Silver and gold ribbons, Miss. AA, 1925-1926, and gold medal, 1927; purchase prize, Miss. Fair Assn., 1928; Wm. P. Silva prize ($100), SSAL, 1929. Represented in LA Polytechnic Institute, Ruston, LA; Municipal Art Gallery, Jackson, MS; Warren Easton High School, New Orleans. Address in 1929, 628 Toulouse Street; h. 1240 North Galvez Street, New Orleans, LA.

MILLET, FRANCIS DAVIS.
Painter. Born in 1846 in Mattapoisett, MA. Graduated at Howard University, 1869. Awarded medal at Royal Academy of Antwerp. He was elected a National Academician in 1885, and served one or two terms as vice-president. His painting "At the Inn" was exhibited at the Centennial Exhibition of the National Academy of Design in 1925. Died April 15, 1912 on the S. S. Titanic.

MILLET, GERALDINE R.
(Mme. Francois Millet). Painter. Born in America. Pupil of Alfred Stevens in Paris, and Maurice Denis. Studied fresco painting with Baudoin at Fontainebleau. Address in 1929, Barbizon, S. et M., France.

MILLET, THALIA W.
See Malcom, Thalia Westcott.

MILLETT, G. VAN.
Painter. Born Kansas City, MO, April 5, 1864. Pupil of Royal Academy of Fine Arts in Munich, under Gysis and Loefftz. Award: Silver medal, Munich Academy.

Represented in Kansas City Art Institute; Public Library and City Hall, Kansas City. Address in 1929, 520 Studio Bldg.; h. 421 West 61st Street Terrace, Kansas City, MO.

MILLIER, ARTHUR.
Etcher. Born Weston Super Mare, Somerset, England, Oct. 19, 1893. Pupil of Calif. School of FA. Member: Chicago SE; Calif. SE; Calif. PM; Calif. AC. Award: Prize, Calif. SE, 1922 and 1928. Represented by etchings in the Art Inst. of Chic. and the Los Angeles Museum. Editor of "Art and Artists" page, Los Angeles Times. Address in 1929, "Los Angeles Times," 100 North Broadway, Los Angeles, CA.

MILLIGAN, GLADYS.
Painter. Studied: Western College for Women, Oxford, Ohio; Westminster College, New Wilmington, PA; Pratt Inst. of Art School; Fontainbleau, France; and with George Luks, and Andre L'Hote, in Paris. Collection: Phillips collection, Washington, DC.

MILLMORE, JOSEPH.
Sculptor. Born in Ireland in 1842. Brother of Martin Millmore. He worked with his brother on the memorial to the Union dead in Mount Auburn Cemetery, Cambridge, MA. He died in 1886.

MILLMORE, MARTIN.
Sculptor. Born in 1845. He entered the studio of Thomas Ball in Charlestown in 1860. He soon took a studio and modeled busts of Longfellow and Sumner, and also executed marble statues for Horticultural Hall, Boston. Millmore executed a bust of George Ticknor for the Public Library, Boston; also busts of C.O. Whitmore, General Thayer, and an ideal bust of "Miranda." He died in 1883.

MILLS, CLARK.
Sculptor. Born Dec. 18, 1810. He lived in Charleston, SC, where he discovered a method of taking casts from the living face. He executed busts of a number of eminent South Carolinians. He designed the

Jackson monuments in Washington and New Orleans; also designed a scene in the battle of Princeton with a statue of Washington. This was dedicated in Washington, D.C., on Feb. 22, 1860. He died Jan. 12, 1883, in Wash., DC.

MILLS, THEODORE AUGUSTUS.
Sculptor. Born in Charleston, SC, in 1839. Eldest son of Clark and Eliza S. Mills. During his boyhood he pursued modeling as an amusement, without regular instruction, until 1860, when he entered the Royal Art Academy of Munich as a pupil, receiving a prize for his composition, "Penelope Presenting the Bow of Ulysses to the Suitors"; this is said to be the only instance where a prize was conferred by this academy upon an American. Returned to United States and commenced work in the studio of his father Clark Mills, then engaged in making a model for a proposed memorial in Washington to President Lincoln; was afterwards employed by the National Museum, Washington, and later at the Carnegie Institute, Pittsburgh. He died Dec., 1916, in Pittsburgh, PA.

MILLS, THOMAS HENRY.
Painter, illustrator, etcher, and writer. Born Hartford, CT. Pupil of Kenyon Cox and W. M. Chase. Member: North Shore AA; AFA. Address in 1929, Bass Rocks, Gloucester, MA.

MILNE, DAVID B.
Painter and illlustrator. Born Paisley, Ontario, CN, Jan. 8, 1882. Pupil of ASL of NY, under Du Mond, Reuterdahl and Bridgman. Member: NYWCC; Phila. WCC. Award: Silver medal, P.- P. Exp., San F., 1915. Represented in Canadian War Memorials Collection, Ottawa. Address in 1929, care of Rene Clarke, 247 Park Avenue, New York, NY.

MILNE, MAY FRANCES.
Painter. Born in Brooklyn NY, in 1894. Address in 1926, Boston Corners, Columbia County, NY.

MILSOM, EVA GRACE.
Painter, craftswoman, writer and teacher. Born Buffalo, NY, Dec. 8, 1868. Studied with Bischoff, Rose Clark and J. H. Mills, and in Europe. Member: Buffalo SA; Buffalo GA; Buffalo S. Min. P.; Buffalo AC. Chairman of Art, Western NY. Fed. of Women's Clubs. Represented in Albright Art Gallery, Buffalo. Died in 1944. Address in 1929, Milsom Manor, Lake Shore, Angola, NY.

MINAZZOLI, EDWARD A.
Sculptor. Born Momo, Italy, Aug. 16, 1887. Pupil of ASL of NY; Niehaus, Fraser, Bartlett; Antonin-Mercie at Ecole des Beaux Arts in Paris. Member: Paris AAA; AFA. Awards: Chevalier order of Donilo, 1918; Chevalier of the Crown of Italy, 1922; hon. mention, Paris Salon, 1929. Works: Groups, "Apparition N.D. de Lourdes" and "St. Theresa of Lisieux," at Cathedral of Chatillon, Loire, France; group, Fountain garden, Poughkeepsie and Statue, West NY. Address in 1929, 18 Bld. Edgar Quinet; h. 17 bis Rue Campagne Premiere, Paris XIV, France, 60 - 19th Street, West New York, NJ.

MINER, EDWARD HERBERT.
Painter and illustrator. Born Sheridan, NY, Jan. 23, 1882. Member: Salma. C.; SI. Work: Series of paintings of horses and of cattle owned by the National Geographic Society. Address in 1929, Westbury, L.I., NY.

MINER, FRED R.
Painter and writer. Born New London, CT, Oct. 28, 1876. Pupil of ASL of NY; William Wendt, John Carlson. Member: Calif. AC; Laguna Beach AA; S. Indp. A. Award: Bronze medal, Exp., San Diego, 1915. Work: "The Old Oak," Union Lg. Club, Los Angeles; "Late Afternoon, Garapatos Canon," Glendale Sanitarium, CA. Address in 1929, 1045 Stevenson Avenue, Pasadena, CA.

MINER, GEORGIA WATSON.
(Mrs. Lewis H. Miner). Painter, craftswoman, writer, lecturer, and teacher. Born Springfield, IL, April 4, 1876. Pupil of C. A.

Herbert and Dawson-Watson, Mabel Dibble, Matilda Middleton. Member: Chicago AG; Springfield AA. Awards: IL State Centennial medals, 1918, for best painting and work in ceramics. Represented in Springfield Art Assoc. Address in 1929, 1717 South 6th Street, Springfield, IL; summer, Old Mission, MI.

MINGO, NORMAN THEODORE.
Painter and illustrator. Born Chicago, IL, Jan. 20, 1896. Pupil of Chicago AFA; AIC; ASL. Address in 1929, Lake Michigan Bldg., Chicago, IL; h. 740 Hinman Avenue, Evanston, IL.

MINKER, GUSTAVE (SR.).
Painter. Born Germany, May 18, 1866. Pupil of Westheld in Germany, F. Ballard Williams and Gustave Cimiotte. Member: Newark AC; Art Centre of the Oranges; Montclair AA; AFA. Address in 1929, 187 Garden Avenue, Belleville, NJ.

MINOR, ANNE ROGERS.
(Mrs. George Maynard Minor). Painter. Born East Lyme, CT, April 7, 1864. Pupil of Robert C. Minor. Member: AFA; New Haven PCC; CT AFA. Address in 1929, Waterford, CT.

MINOR, ROBERT CRANNELL.
Painter. Born April 30, 1839 in New York. Died in Waterford, CT, Aug. 3, 1904. Landscape painter. Pupil of Van Luppen in Antwerp; and of Diaz and Boulanger in Paris. Awards: Hon. mention, Paris Exp, 1900; silver medal, Pan-American Exp., Buffalo, 1901. Elected to National Academy, 1897; Society of Landscape Painters. Represented at Corcoran Art Gallery, Washington, D.C., by "Eventide."

MINOR, WENDELL GORDON.
Illustrator. Born in Aurora, Illinois in 1944. He studied at the Ringling School of Art from 1963 to 1966. He worked as a designer for Hallmark Cards and his first works appeared in their Cards Magazine. He was an art director and designer, both in Chicago and NY, before beginning a free-lance illustration career in 1970. His clients include Bantam, Random House, Avon, Dell and other book publishers. He has had exhibitions in NY at the Greengrass and Chisholm Galleries and in New Mexico at the Brandywine Gallery. He is a member of the faculty at SVA.

MIRANDA, FERNANDO.
Sculptor. Exhibited at National Sculpture Society, New York.

MIRKO, BASALDELLA.
Sculptor. Born 1910 in Undine, Italy. Studied in Venice, Florence and Rome. Director of Design Workshop at Harvard Univ. since 1957. Rec. awards from Sao Paulo Museum; the Carrara sculpture prize, and Gold medal from Republic of Italy. Exhibited at Galleria La Cometa (Rome) 1935; Comet Gallery NYC (1947; 1949); RI School of Design; Inst. of Contemp Art (Boston); Univ. of Illinois; many other international galleries.

MISH, CHARLOTTE (ROBERTA).
Painter, sculptor, illustrator, craftswoman, writer and teacher. Born Lebanon, PA, Aug. 17, 1903. Pupil of W. L. Judson, F. Tadema, F. Vincent DuMond, ASL of NY; College of F.A., Univ. So. Calif. Member: Portland AA; Oregon SA. Work: Music Box Theatre, Seattle. Address in 1929, 962 Mount Adams Drive, Portland, OR; 1528 E. Madison Street, Seattle, WA.

MITCHELL, ALFRED R.
Painter and teacher. Born York, PA, June 18, 1888. Pupil of Daniel Garber, Joseph T. Pearson, and Maurice Braun. Member: Fellowship PAFA; San Diego FAS; Calif. AC. Awards: Silver medal, Panama-California Exposition, San Diego, 1915; Cresson Traveling Scholarship, PAFA, 1920; Philadelphia prize, PAFA, 1920; Art Guild prize, San Diego FAS, 1926. Work: "In Mission Valley, San Diego," Reading Museum, Reading, PA. Address in 1929, 1527 Granada Avenue, San Diego, CA.

MITCHELL, ARTHUR.
Painter. Born Gillespie, IL, Feb. 5, 1864. Pupil of St. Louis School of Fine Arts. Member: 2 x 4 Soc.;

St. Louis AG. Address in 1929, 4211 Castleman Avenue, St. Louis, MO.

MITCHELL, CHARLES DAVIS.
Illustrator. Born in Wilmington, Delaware in 1887. He maintained a studio in Philadelphia throughout his career. His charcoal and pencil drawings, often of beautiful women, appeared for many years in Redbook, McCall's, Delineator, Cosmopolitan, and others. He was a member of the AG and Art Club of Philadelphia.

MITCHELL, E.
Engraver. Fenshaw, in his work on book-plates, says that this English book-plate engraver was working in the U.S. in 1790. American book-plates so signed are found.

MITCHELL, G. BERTRAND.
Illustrator. Member: Salma. C. Address in 1929, Rutherford, NJ.

MITCHELL, GLEN.
Painter and illustrator. Born New Richmond, IN, June 9, 1894. Pupil of Chicago AFA; AIC; AGC, Paris; additional studies in Spain, Italy, Egypt and Palestine. Awards: First Alumni AIC prize, AIC, 1919, 1920, 1921; fellow, Guggenheim Memorial Foundation, 1926-1927. Work: "Sacrifice," First M. E. Church, New Richmond, IN; "Emigrants," Rotary C., Chicago. Illustrated "The Heritage" (Scribner's); illustrations for "Liberty Weekly," "Ladies Home Journal," "Woman's Home Companion," "Colliers Weekly." Address in 1929, 2 East 12th Street, New York, NY.

MITCHELL, GURNSEY.
Sculptor, who died in Rochester, NY, Aug. 1, 1921. He was a graduate of the Ecole des Beaux Arts in Paris. Among his best known works are the statue of Martin B. Anderson, former president of the Univ. of Rochester; "Aurora"; "The Young Botanist"; "David and Goliath."

MITCHELL, HARVEY.
Portrait painter. Born c. 1801 in VA. He was painting in 1830 at Charleston, SC.

MITCHELL, JAMES MURRAY.
Painter, illustrator, and etcher. Born Edisto Island, SC., Nov. 9, 1892. Member: SI. Address in 1929, 116 West 39th Street, New York, NY; h. 9429 210th Street., Queens Village, NY.

MITCHELL, JOHN.
Painter. Born in Hartford, CT, in 1811. Died in 1866 in NYC. His work was largely done in Hartford and in New London.

MITCHELL, JOHN BLAIR.
Painter. Born in Brooklyn, NY, Jan. 30, 1921. Study: Pratt Inst., Cert. 1939-43; Pratt Inst. Sch. of Educ., 1946-47; Columbia Univ. Teachers College; Pratt Graphics Arts Ctr., with Edmondson, Rogalski, and Ponce de Leon; NYU Sch. of Educ. PhD, 1963. Work: Metropolitan Museum of Art; Baltimore Museum of Art; Lib. of Congress; Silvermine Guild Artists, Conn.; others. Exhibitions: Corcoran Gallery, Wash. DC; Lib. of Congr. Nat'l. Print Exhib.; Silvermine Guild; Baltimore Museum of Art; Johns Hopkins; and others. Awards: Silvermine Guild of Artists; Library of Congress; Corcoran Gallery of Art; MD State Arts Council; Works in Progress Grant. Teaching: Columbia Univ. Teachers College, 1949-80; and others. Mem.: Artists Equity Assn.; Baltimore Print Club. Address in 1982, 9918 Finney Drive, Baltimore, Maryland.

MITCHELL, LAURA M.D.
Miniature painter. Born Halifax, Nova Scotia, Canada. Pupil of George Bridgman, Kenyon Cox, Alice Beckington at ASL of NY, Lucia Fairchild Fuller. Member: Calif. S. Min. P. (pres. and founder); Calif. AC; Pasadena Soc. Women PS. Awards: First prize, C.L. Wolfe Art Club, New York, 1908; gold medal, Panama-Calif. Exp., San Diego, 1915; gold medal, Panama-Calif. Intn'l. Expo., San Diego, 1916; popular prize, CA. S. Min. P.; 1923; hon. mention, Calif. S. Min. P., 1924, and 1925; special gold medal, Pac. Southwest Exp., 1928; Mrs. Oliver P. Clark Prize, Calif. S. Min. P., and Popular vote prize, 1929. Address in 1929, 307

South 4th St., Alhambra, California.

MITCHELL, THOMAS JOHN.
Painter. Born Rochester, NY, Feb. 22, 1875. Pupil of Rochester Art School. Member: Rochester AC; Buffalo SA; Geneseeans; Salma. C. Address in 1929, 41 Heidelburg Street; 70 Reynolds Arcade, Rochester, NY.

MITTELL, SYBILLA.
See Weber.

MITTLEMAN, ANN.
Painter. Born: New York City. Studied: New York University; and with Philip Evergood, Robert Laurent and Tschacbasov. Collections: Everhart Museum of Art; Seattle Art Museum; Zanesville, Ohio; Smith College; Jewish Museum; Hickory, North Carolina; New York University Museum; Richmond Indiana Art Association; Evansville Indiana; Florence South Carolina Museum of Art; Delgado Museum of Art; Lowe Gallery of Art, Coral Gables; Birmingham Museum of Art.

MIX, FLORENCE.
Painter of portraits and landscapes. She was born in Hartford, CT, in 1881. Died in Oct. 1922, in Glenwood, L.I., NY.

MOCK, GEORGE ANDREW.
Painter. Born Muncie, IN, May 18, 1886. Pupil of AIC. Member: Indiana AC; Brown Co. Group of P; Hoosier Salon. Address in 1929, R. F. D. No. 4, Muncie, IN.

MOCK, GLADYS AMY.
Painter. Born: New York City. Studied: Art Students' League, and with Kenneth Hayes Miller. Awards: National Association of Women Artists, 1946, 1954; Pen and Brush Club, 1946, 1955; Champlain Valley Exhibition, 1951. Collections: PAFA; Todd Museum, Kalamazoo, Michigan; Library of Congress; Kansas State College; Hays, Kansas; Metropolitan Museum of Art; Smithsonian Inst. Living in NYC in 1929.

MODRA, THEODORE.
Painter. Born in Poland, May 13, 1873. Pupil of Henri; Colarossi Academy, Paris; Groeber in Munich. Member: NAC; MacD. C.: Calif. AC: Allied AA; S. Indp. A; Calif. WCS; Los Angeles PSC, Artland C; Laguna Beach AA. Address in 1929, 2003 Canyon Drive, Hollywood, CA.

MOELLER, GUSTAVE.
Painter and teacher. Born Wisconsin, April 22, 1881. Studied in Milwaukee, New York, Paris and Munich. Member: WI PS. Awards: Hon. mention, Milwaukee, AI, 1917; hon. mention, PS, 1922; silver medal, Milwaukee AI, 1923; Milwaukee Journal Purchase prize, 1926. Director, Dept. of Art, State Teacher's College, Milwaukee. Address in 1929, 1039 Third Street, h. 1079 39th Street; Milwaukee, WI.

MOELLER, HENRY NICHOLAS.
Painter and sculptor. Born New York City, Jan. 5, 1883. Pupil of Hinton, Curran, MacNeil, Aitken. Work: Memorial tablet to Elisha Kent Kane in the Grand Lodge of Masons of Cuba. Address in 1929, 140 West 88th Street, New York, NY.

MOELLER, LOUIS CHARLES.
Painter. Born New York, Aug. 5, 1855. Pupil of NAD in New York; Diez and Duveneck in Munich. Member: ANA 1884, NA 1894. Work: "Disagreement," Corcoran Gallery, Washington. Address in 1929, 714 Park Avenue, Weehawken, NJ.

MOELLER, SELMA M. D.
Miniature painter. Born New York, Aug. 3, 1880. Pupil of ASL of NY under Cox, Chase, Birge Harrison, F. V. Du Mond; Lucia Fairchild Fuller and Alice Beckington for miniature painting. Member: NA Women PS; Brooklyn S. Min. P. Award: Silver medal, P.- P. Exp., San F., 1915. Address in 1929, 450 Riverside Drive, New York, NY; summer, Hickory Bluff, South Norwalk, CT.

MOEN, ELLA CHARLOTTE.
Painter and teacher. Born Bottineau, ND, March 18, 1901. Address in 1929, 1439 Poplar Avenue, Fresno, CA.

MOERSCHEL, CHIARA.
Painter. Born in Trieste, Italy, Nov. 15, 1926. Exhibitions: Several one-man shows; numerous group shows including Spanish Int'l. Pavillion; Watercolor, U.S.A. 1970; Springfield Art Museum. Awards: Gustave Goetsch Memorial Prize; Lone Vasen Award; and many others. Collections: Several private and institutional collections here and abroad.

MOFFAT, J.
A fairly well-engraved line portrait of Robert Burns is signed as "Eng'd on Steel by J. Moffat." This print was published by Wm. Pearson, New York, 1830-35; but it is possibly the work of a Scotch engraver and the plate was brought over to America for publication.

MOFFETT, ANITA.
Painter. Member: GFLA; Wash. AC. Address in 1929, 435 West 119th Street, New York, NY.

MOFFETT, ROSS E.
Painter. Born Iowa, Feb. 18, 1888. Pupil ASL of NY; AIC; Charles W. Hawthorne. Member: Chicago Gal. A. Awards: Silver medal, AIC, 1918; first Hallgarten prize, NAD, 1921; hon. mention, Carnegie Inst., 1921; French Memorial gold medal, AIC, 1927. Work: "A Street in Provincetown," Pennsylvannia Academy of the Fine Arts, Philadelphia; "Dunes in Winter," Speed Memorial Museum, Louisville, KY; "Winter in Provincetown," Albright Art Gallery, Buffalo, NY; "The Red Dory," University Club Gallery, Lincoln, Neb. Address in 1929, Provincetown, MA.

MOFFITT, JOHN M.
Sculptor. Born in England in 1837. He came to the US as a youth. He designed the figures that represent the four ages of man at the entrance to Greenwood Cemetery, the reredos in the Packer Mem. Church, and many altars in the principal churches of NY. He died in 1887.

MOHN, CHERI.
Painter. Awards: Mademoiselle's one of ten Top Women Artists in the United States. Work: Butler Inst.; Phoenix Gal., Phila.; others

Media: Watercolor and oil. Living in North Lima, Ohio, in 1982.

MOILAN, OTTO E.
Painter. Born Finland. Pupil of MN School of Art. Address in 1929, 422 Kasota Bldg.; 2621 Clinton Avenue, Minneapolis, MN.

MOISE, THEODORE SYDNEY.
Portrait painter. Born in Charleston, SC, in 1806. He died in 1883 in Natchitoches, LA. In 1850 his studio was at 51 Canal Street, New Orleans, and he painted many portraits in Louisiana. He painted a standing portrait of Henry Clay now owned by the Metropolitan Gallery of New York.

MOLAND.
In 1839 this name "Moland Sc." is signed to fairly well-engraved script and sheet music, published in Philadelphia by George Willing.

MOLARSKY, ABRAHAM.
Painter. Born in Russia in 1879. Pupil of Chase in Philadelphia and of the Penna. Academy of Fine Arts. Address in 1926, 62 High Street, Nutley, NJ.

MOLARSKY, MAURICE.
Painter. Born Kiev, Russia, May 25, 1885; American citizen. Studied at School of Industrial Art and PAFA, Philadelphia; and in France and England. Member: Allied AA; Am. APL; Phila. Alliance; Fellowship PAFA. Awards: Henry Thouron prize in comp. and Cresson Scholarship PAFA; hon. men., Phila. AC; Fellowship prize PAFA; silver medal, P.- P. Exp., San. F., 1915; gold medal, Art Club of Philadelphia, 1919; silver medal, Sesqui-Centennial Exp., Phila., 1926. Represented in Phila. Art Club collection; Jefferson College, Philadelphia; "Still Life," Butler Art Inst., Youngstown, OH; mural decorations in the Elks' Home, and in other public buildings, Philadelphia, PA. Address in 1929, 10 South 18th Street; h. 242 South 49th Street, Philadelphia, PA.

MOLIN, C. GUNNAR.
Painter. Born in Stockholm, Sweden. Pupil of ASL of NY.

Member: Scandinavian-American A; Am. APL. Address in 1929, 180 State Street, Brooklyn, NY.

MOLINARY, MARIE SEEBOLD.
(Mrs. Andres Molinary). Painter. Born New Orleans, LA, 1876. Pupil of William Chase and A. Molinary. Member: N.O. AA; N.O. ACC. Work in Delgado Museum, New Orleans. Address in 1929, 2619 St. Charles Avenue, New Orleans, LA.

MOLINEUX.
Engraver. In 1831 there was published by Luke Loomis & Co., of Pittsburgh, PA, a German work entitled "The Life and Works of Johann Friedrich Oberlin," with an introduction by prof. S. S. Schmucker, of the Theological Seminary at Gettysburg, PA. The frontispiece to this book is an engraved silhouette of Oberlin, signed "Molineux Sc. Pitt." The same Molineux engraved upon copper for this work a fairly well-executed portrait of Louis Schepler, and views of the residences of Oberlin and some of his fellow workers. No other examples of the engraved work of Molineux are known to Fielding in 1926.

MOLL, AAGE (PETER) (MARINUS).
Painter. Born Ribe, Denmark, Feb. 9, 1877. Pupil of Charles Noel Flagg, James G. McManus. Member: CT. AFA; Scandinavian Am. A; Gloucester SA. Address in 1929, 142 Freeman Street, Hartford, CT.

MOLYNEUX, EDWARD F(RANK).
Illustrator. Born London, England, Feb. 29, 1896. Pupil of Pratt Inst., Brooklyn, NY. Member: SI; Art Directors C. Address in 1929, 16th Floor, 40 East 34th Street; h. 25 Fifth Avenue, New York, NY.

MOMBERGER, WILLIAM.
Painter. Born in Frankfurt, Germany, June 7, 1829. He came to the United States in 1848. He painted several landscapes, but gave much of his time to illustrating. Worked in NYC for many years.

MONACHISE, NICOLA.
Painter. Born 1795 in Italy. Nothing is known of his work except that he painted historical pieces and portraits, and that his studio was at 98 Locust Street, Phila. Died in 1851 in Phila., PA.

MONAGHAN, GERTRUDE.
Painter. Born West Chester, PA. Pupil of Phila. School of Design; PAFA. Member: Fellowship PAFA; Plastic C; Print C. Specialty, mural decorations and lunettes. Address in 1929, 3309 Baring Street, Philadelphia, PA.

MONKS, EDWARD E.
Illustrator. Member: SI; GFLA. Address in 1929, 40 Gramercy Park, New York, NY.

MONKS, JOHN AUSTIN SANDS.
Painter. Born in Cold Spring-on-Hudson, NY, on Nov. 7, 1850. Studied wood engraving and etching in 1869. Pupil in painting of George Inness, 1875. Engaged in art work after 1874. His specialty was painting sheep. Member: Copley Society, Salma. C.; New York Etching, Boston Art. Died March, 1917 in Chicago, IL.

MONRAD, EMILY.
Painter, lecturer, and teacher. Born Sweden, Jan. 30, 1877. Pupil of Viggo Johansen, Copenhagen. Member: New Haven PCC; Plainfield AA; New Educ. F. Address in 1929, Knox School, Cooperstown, NY; h. 166 Putnam Avenue, New Haven, CT.

MONRAD, MARGARET.
Sculptor and teacher. Born New Zealand, June 10, 1879. Pupil of Royal AFA, Copenhagen. Member: NA Women PS; New Haven PCC; Plainfield AA; New Haven PBC. Address in 1929, 166 Putnam Avenue, Whitneyville, New Haven, CT.

MONTAGUE, HARRIOTTE LEE TALIAFERRO.
Painter. Pupil of George de Forest Brush and Twachtman in NY; Angelo Yank, Fehr, Hummel and Knurr in Munich; Simon in Paris. Member: Richmond Art Club. Work: "Portrait of Capt. Sallie Tompkins," Richmond Art Club; portrait in D.A.R. Hall, Washington, DC. Represented in

651

Confederate Museum and the State Library in Richmond; also in Westmoreland (VA) Court House. Address in 1926, 1609 Hanover Avenue, Richmond, VA.

MONTANA, PIETRO.
Sculptor. Born Alcamo, Italy, June 29, 1890. Pupil of Bruwester. Member: NSS; Arch. Lg. of NY. Work: "Doughboy Monument," New York, NY; War Monument, Heisser Square, Brooklyn, NY; "The Victory," Freedom Square, Brooklyn; "The Dawn of Glory," Highland Park, Brooklyn; "Mark Twain and Washington Twing," memorial tablet, Ninth Street and Fifth Avenue, New York, "The Minute Man," East Providence, RI; "Mother Davison," Governor's Island, NY; War Memorial, Sicily, Italy; "Weisserberger Memorial," City Cemetery, Alliance, Ohio. Address in 1929, 28 East 14th Street, New York, NY.

MONTGOMERY, ALFRED.
Painter. His specialty was depicting farm life. He was born in 1857 and died in Los Angeles, CA, on April 20, 1922.

MONTGOMERY, R.
Engraver. The only example of the work of this engraver seen by Fielding is a book-plate of James Giles, signed "R. Montgomery, Sculp." The plate is armorial, with a cannon and American flag introduced into the decoration, and it is crude enough in execution to have been the work of some apprentice or local engraver. Some collectors of "ex libris" asserted that the engraver of the plate was Gen. Richard Montgomery, who was killed at Quebec in 1775. This book-plate was probably engraved by Robert Montgomery, who advertised in the New York Packet in 1783, as "Watch-Maker, Clock Maker and Engraver."

MOONEY, EDWARD L.
Painter. Born March 25, 1813 in NYC. He began his art studies at the Academy of Design. He became a pupil of Henry Inman, and copied much of his work; later he studied with William Page. He painted many excellent portraits of prominent men; his picture of Gov. Wm. H. Seward was placed in the State House in Albany, and he painted several portraits of the Mayors of New York, for City Hall. He died in June, 1887, in NYC.

MOORE, BENSON BOND.
Painter, etcher, and illustrator. Born Washington, D.C., Aug. 13, 1882. Pupil of Corcoran School of Art, Washington. Member: Wash. SA; Wash. WCC; Wash. Landscape C; SSAL; Miss. AA; New Haven PCC; CT; AFA; New Orleans AA; Springfield AL; AFA. Represented by five etchings in Library of Congress; four drypoints in White House; drypoint in NY Public Library; two drypoints, Houston Museum of Fine Arts; drypoint, Bibliotheque Nationale, Paris; three drypoints, Philadelphia Art Alliance; three drypoints, Smithsonian Inst.; drypoint, Washington Arts Club. Address in 1929, 105 R. Street, N.E., Washington, D.C.

MOORE, BETHUEL C.
Painter and teacher. Born Barbourville, KY, June 15, 1902. Pupil of Charles Hawthorne, Olinsky, E. A. Jones. Member: Tiffany Foundation; Louisville AA; Louisville AC. Award: First prize, Louisville AA, 1928. Address in 1929, 1116 Starks Bldg.; h. Weissinger Gaulbert, Louisville, KY.

MOORE, BRUCE.
Sculptor. Born Bern, Kansas, Aug. 5, 1905. Pupil of Charles Grafly, Albert Laessle. Member: Fellowship PAFA; Wichita AG. Award: Widener gold medal, PAFA, 1929. Work: Portrait busts of Col. Thomas Fitch and Henry Wallenstein, Wichita Consistory; portrait bust of Dr. A. H. Fabrique, Wichita Medical Society; "Feline," High School, Wichita; "Black Panther," Friends of Art, Wichita; sculptural designs and terra cotta decorations on the High School, Wichita. Address in 1929, Butts Bldg., Wichita, Kansas.

MOORE, CECIL GRESHAM.
Painter, illustrator, craftsman, writer and teacher. Born Kingston, Ontario, Canada, June 12, 1880.

Pupil of Rochester Athenaeum and Mechanics Inst. Member: Rochester AC. Specialty, decorations and color. Address in 1929, 86 State Street, Rochester, NY; summer, Rideau River, Kingston, Ontario, Canada.

MOORE, CLAIRE.
Printmaker. Studied: Siqueiros Workshop; The Art Students League, NYC; with Werner Drewes and Fernand Leger. Exhibitions: Museum of Modern Art; The Metropolitan Museum of Art; The Green Mountain Gallery, NYC. Collections: The Newark Public Library, NJ; The Univ. Museum, Minneapolis, Minnesota. Publishes The Children's Underground Press. Noted for her experimentation with mimeograph-machine printing techniques.

MOORE, EDWIN A.
Painter. Born in Hartford, CT, in 1858. He was a son of Nelson A. Moore, and followed his father's profession of painting. Address in 1926, 901 West Lane, Kensington, CT. Died in 1925.

MOORE, ELLEN MARIA.
Miniature painter. Born in Kensington, CT. Pupil of Art Students' League of New York; also of Mary Elmer and I. A. Josephi. Address, Kensington, CT.

MOORE, FRANK M(ONTAGUE).
Painter. Born Taunton, Somersetshire, England, Nov. 24, 1877. Pupil of H. W. Ranger. Member: NYWCC; Salma. C; CA WCS; AFA. Work: "Old Quarry in Moonlight," Honolulu Academy of Arts. Address in 1929, care Boardman Bros. Co., 32 Montgomery Street, San Francisco, CA.

MOORE, H. W.
Painter. Member: Boston AC. Address in 1929, Main Street, Hingham, MA.

MOORE, H(ARRY) HUMPHREY
Painter. Born in NYC, in 1844. Pupil of Bail in New Haven; S. Waugh in Phila.; Ecole des Beaux Arts in Paris, under Gerome, Boulanger and Yvon. Member: Rochester Art Club. His work is principally concerned with Moorish,

Spanish, and Japanese subjects. Address in 1926, 75 Rue de Courcelles, Paris, France. Died Jan. 2, 1926 in Paris, France.

MOORE, ISAAC W.
Engraver, who was engraving good line portraits and historical plates in 1831-33, for Philadelphia periodicals.

MOORE, LOU WALL (MRS.).
Sculptor. Member: Chicago Society of Artists. Award: Bronze medal, St. Louis Exposition, 1904. Address in 1926, 5476 Ridgewood Court, Chicago, IL.

MOORE, MARTHA.
(Mrs. Charles H. Rathbone, Jr.). Sculptor. Born New Britain, CT, Dec. 30, 1902. Pupil of Archipenko. Member: NAC; S. Indp. A. Address in 1929, 75 Central Park West, New York, NY; summer, Concarneau, Finistere, France.

MOORE, MARY VIRGINIA.
Painter and teacher. Born Brownsville, TN. Pupil of Chase, Henri, Timmons, Miller, NY School of Art, AIC. Member: Western AA. Director of Art, Memphis Schools. Address in 1929, Board of Education Office, Goodwyn Inst.; h. 1782 Peabody Avenue, Memphis, TN; summer, Brownsville, TN.

MOORE, NELSON AUGUSTUS.
Born in CT, Aug. 2, 1824. He studied with Cummings, and later with Daniel Huntington. His pastoral scenes show great merit; "The Genius of Liberty" was also considered a great success.

MOORE, T.
This stippler-engraver of portraits signs himself on one of his plates "T. Moore (successor to Pendleton) Boston."

MORA, DOMINGO.
Sculptor, who exhibited at National Sculpture Society, New York.

MORA, FRANCIS LUIS.
Painter, illustrator, and teacher. Born Montevideo, Uruguay, July 27, 1874. Pupil of School of Boston Museum, under Benson and Tarbell; ASL of NY under Mowbray. Member:

ANA 1904; NA 1906; ASL of NY; Salma. C., 1899; SI 1901; SAA 1905; NY Arch. Lg. 1903; AWCS; NYWCC; Allied AA; NAC; Port. P; AFA. Awards: Gold medal, AC Phila., 1901; gold medal, AAS, 1902; 2 bronze medals, St. Louis Exposition, 1904; first Hallgarten prize, NAD, 1905; Beal prize, NYWCC, 1907; Evans prize, Salma. C., 1908; Shaw prize, Salma. C., 1910; gold medal for oil painting and gold medal for water color painting, P.- P. Exposition, San F., 1915. Work: Decoration for Lynn (MA) Public Library; "Spanish Merrymakers," Museum of Art, Oakland, CA; "Jeanne Cartier," Toledo Museum; "Color Harmony," Newark Museum Association; "The Fortune Teller," " Butler Art Institute, Youngstown, OH. Address in 1929, Cedar Hill, Gaylordsville, CT. Died in 1940.

MORA, JO(SEPH) (J).
Sculptor. Born Montevideo, Uraguay, SA., Oct. 22, 1876. Pupil of Domingo Mora; J. DeCamp; J. C. Beckwith. Member: NSS (assoc.). Work: "Cervantes Monument," San Francisco, CA; "Doughboy," San Raphael, CA; "Bret Harte Memorial," Bohemian Club, San Francisco, CA; "Junipero Serro Sarcophagus," Mission, San Carlos, Carmel, CA.; heroic pediments, Don Lee Building and Stock Exchange, San Francisco, CA and Pacific Mutual Building, Los Angeles; heroic figures, Scottish Rite Temple, San Jose, CA. Address in 1929, Pebble Beach, CA; h. Carmel, CA.

MORAHAN, EUGENE.
Sculptor. Born Brooklyn, NY, Aug. 29, 1869. Pupil of Augustus Saint-Gaudens. Member: NSS. Work: Alfred Gwynne Vanderbilt memorial fountain, Newport, RI; Elks Memorial, Buffalo; Soldiers and Sailors Memorial, Carroll Park, Brooklyn, NY; Cuddy Memorial, St. Barnabas' Church, Bexhill, England; Gen. Samuel Welch Monument Buffalo, NY. Address in 1929, 1931 Broadway, NYC; h. 305a President Street, Brooklyn, New York, NY.

MORALES, ARMANDO.
Painter. Born Jan. 15, 1927 in Granada, Nicaragua. Also a printmaker. Studied at School of Fine Arts, Managua. Awarded Travelling Grant from Am. Council on Educ., Wash. DC; Guggenheim, 1958; Org. of Am. States fellow, 1962-4; award from Houston Museum of Fine Arts. Exhibited at Angellski Gallery, NYC 1962; Pan Am. Union, Wash. DC; Sao Paulo, Brazil; Houston; MOMA; Carnegie; Guggenheim; Univ. of MI; Phillips Exeter Acad.; Time Life Bldg.; Duke Univ.; Mt. Holyoke; NY World's Fair, 1964; Cornell Univ. and many others. In collections of Houston; Guggenheim; Pan-Am. Union; Wash., DC; MOMA; Caracas; Inst. of Art, Detroit, and Phila. Museum of Art.

MORAN, EDWARD.
Painter. Born in England, Aug. 19, 1829. Came to the U.S. in 1844. Lived in New York and Philadelphia. Member: Penna. AFA. Exhibited in Philadelphia in 1853. Painted fishermen at their toil, and water scenes and vessels. Represented in Wilstach collection, Fairmount Park, Philadelphia. He died June 9, 1901 in NYC.

MORAN, EDWARD PERCY.
See Moran, Percy.

MORAN, JOHN LEON.
Painter. Born in Philadelphia, PA, Oct. 4, 1864. Studied art under his father, Edward Moran; at the National Academy of Design, NY; also in London and Paris. Returned to the U.S. in 1879 and established a studio in NY in 1883. He was a frequent exhibitor at the NAD, NY, and elsewhere; Gold medal, AC Phila., 1893; gold medal, AAS, 1902. Principal paintings: "Waylaid," 1885; "An Interrupted Conspiracy," 1886; "An Amateur," 1887; "The Duel," 1887; "An Idyll," 1888; "Eel Fishing," 1888; "Intercepted Dispatches," "Madonna and Child;" "Between Two Fires." Address in 1929, 97 Mercer Avenue, Plainfield, NJ. Died in 1941 in Watchung, NJ.

MORAN, MARY NIMMO
(Mrs. Thomas). Etcher. Born in 1842. Her plates as a rule are bold and direct and are marked by energetic emphasis. Her work stands high among the women etchers

in this country. Died Sept. 24, 1889.

MORAN, PERCY.
Painter and etcher. Born Philadelphia, PA, July 29, 1862. Pupil of his father, Edward Moran; PAFA under S. J. Ferris; NAD, in New York: studied four years in Paris and London. Member: AWCS. Awards: First Hallgarten prize, NAD, 1886; first gold medal, AM. Art Assoc., NY, 1888. Work: "Castle Garden, NY," Wilstach Gallery, Philadelphia, PA; "Washington and Betsy Ross," Masonic Hall, Chicago; "Signing the Compact on Mayflower," Plymouth Museum; "The Woodcutter's Daughter," Hamilton Club, Brooklyn. Address in 1929, Easthampton, Long Island, NY.

MORAN, PETER.
Painter and etcher. Born March 4, 1841 in Bolton, Lanscashire, England. Studied with his brothers Thomas and Edward Moran; also in England, in 1863. Member: Phila. AC. Pres. of the Society of Etchers. His paintings are principally of landscapes and animal subjects. Died Nov. 9, 1914 in Phila., PA.

MORAN, THOMAS.
Painter and etcher. Born in Lancashire, England, Jan. 12, 1837, but was brought to the United States when a boy of seven. He began his art career as a wood engraver in Philadelphia and in his hours of leisure taught himself to paint in water color and afterwards in oils. His brother, Edward Moran, gave him the benefits of the instruction he had himself received. In 1862, he went to England and made a study of the masters in the Nat. Gallery, receiving a strong impression from the work of J. Turner. In 1872, Mr. Moran established himself permanently in NY. He spent his summers at his country home at Easthampton, L.I. He was elected a National Academician in 1884, and was a member of PAFA, AFS, AWCS; the New York Etching Club; SAE. The subjects of his pictures were taken from one or another of the places he visited and studied such

as Venice, Yellowstone Park, Niagara, the luxuriant meadows of Kent and Sussex, and the quiet villages and pastures of Long Island. As a water color painter and as an etcher his skill and fertility of invention were equally notable. Died Aug. 26, 1926 in Santa Barbara, CA.

MORANGES.
Miniature painter, who flourished in Baltimore, 1795.

MORAS, FERDINAND.
Engraver. Born in Germany in 1821, he studied lithography at Elberfeld. He established one of the first lithographic plants in this country, and was the first lithographer to attempt color printing with this process of engraving. In 1844 Thomas Moran became apprenticed to Moras in Philadelphia. In 1882 he published a book of poems of which he was the author, illustrator and engraver. He died in 1908.

MOREIN, J. AUGUSTUS.
Born c. 1810 in West Indies. Portrait painter in oils and miniatures, who flourished in NY in 1841-42.

MORETTI, GIUSEPPE.
Born in 1859. Italian sculptor, who came to New York and exhibited at the National Sculpture Society. Died in 1935.

MOREY, BERTHA GRAVES.
Painter, etcher, craftswoman, illustrator, writer, and teacher. Born Ottumwa, IA, July 22, 1881. Pupil of AIC. Award: Prize ($100) for Silk design, Art Alliance of America, 1918. Address in 1929, 327 West Fourth Street, Ottumwa, Iowa.

MORGAN, ALEXANDER CONVERSE.
Painter. Born Sandusky, OH, July 1, 1849. Member: Artists' Fund S. (pres.); Century Assoc.; Salma. C. Address in 1929, 134 West 73rd Street, New York, NY.

MORGAN, EMMYLOU.
(Mrs. Ralph Depew Morgan). Painter. Born Albany, NY, Sept. 10, 1891. Pupil of Urquhart Wilcox.

Member: Buffalo SA; Guild of Allied A; NAC; Am. APL. Awards: First hon. mention, Albright Art Gallery, Buffalo, 1927, and Cary cash prize, 1928. Address in 1929, 27 Vernon Place, Buffalo, NY.

MORGAN, FRANKLIN TOWNSEND.
Painter, illustrator, etcher and craftsman. Born Brooklyn, NY, Dec. 27, 1883. Pupil of Bridgman, Carlsen. Member: Phila. Sketch C; Phila. PC. Address in 1929, Moylan, Rose Valley, PA.

MORGAN, GEORGE T.
Engraver. Born in Birmingham, England, in 1845, was living in Philadelphia in 1892. Morgan studied at the art school in Birmingham and won a national scholarship in the South Kensington Art School, where he was a student for two years. He came to the U.S., and in 1875 he was made an assistant engraver in the U.S. Mint in Philadelphia, and remained there a number of years. He designed and executed the dies for the once famous "Bland Dollar."

MORGAN, GEORGIA WESTON.
Painter. Born Virginia. Pupil of John Carlson; Daniel Garber; Joseph Pearson; Fred Wagner; Hugh Breckenridge; ASL. of NY; Julian Academy, Beaux Arts and Mme. La Forge in Paris. Member: Southern SAL; Gloucester North Shore AA; Lynchburg AC (President); Fellowship PAFA. Work: Mural decorations in Euclid Avenue Christian Church, John Wyatt Public School, Garland-Rhodes Public School, R. E. Lee High School, Lynchburg, VA, and Lynchburg College. Head of Art Dept., Lynchburg College. Address in 1929, Lynchburg College, Lynchburg, VA.

MORGAN, LOUIS.
American landscape painter. Born Nov. 21, 1814, in PA. Died in 1852 in TN.

MORGAN, LYNN THOMAS.
Painter and illustrator. Born Richmond, IN, April 24, 1889. Pupil of William Forsyth, Meakin, James Hopkins, George Bridgman. Member: SI; Alliance. Address in 1929, 49 West 45th Street, New York, NY; h. 156 23rd Street, Jackson Heights, L.I., NY.

MORGAN, M. De NEALE.
Painter and etcher. Born San Francisco, CA. Pupil of San Francisco Art Institute, and Chase. Member: San Francisco Art Assoc.; Carmel Club Arts and Crafts; N.A. Women PS; Calif. WCS; West Coast Arts. Work: Memorial Museum, Los Angeles, Del Monte Gallery; San Francisco Art Assoc.; "Cypress and Cliffs," University of Texas; Stanford Univ.; Univ of Southern CA; "Tall Cypress," Lindsay High School; "Spring- Clouds," Salinas High School. Address in 1929, Box M, Carmel By the Sea, CA.

MORGAN, MATTHEW SOMERVILLE.
Painter. Born in London in 1839. He came to the United States in 1870 and worked in New York in 1880. He went to Cincinnati, and in 1883 founded there the Morgan Art Pottery Co. and Art Students' League. He painted a series of large panoramic pictures of the battles in the Civil War, which were exhibited in Cincinnati in 1886. He died in NYC in 1890.

MORGAN, THEODORE J.
Painter. Born Cincinnati, OH, Nov. 1, 1872. Member: Wash. SA; Wash. AC; NAC; NYWCC; Beachcombers; Wash. WCC; San Diego AA; San Antonio AL; San Antonio Palette Assn. Awards: First prize ($1,500) Texas Wild Flower Competition, 1928; gold medal, most meritorious painting, Davis Wild Flower Competition, also hon. mention, 1929. Represented at Univ. of Indiana, Bloomington, IN; Aurora, (IL.) Art Assoc.; Women's Hospital, Cleveland, OH; Museum of Fine Arts, Houston, TX; Delgado Museum of Art, New Orleans, LA; Witte Memorial Museum, San Antonio, TX; Women's Building, Harlingen, Texas. Address in 1929, 456 N. Street, S. W., Washington, D.C.; Provincetown, MA.

MORGAN, WALLACE.
Illustrator. Born in NYC in 1873. Studied at NAD. Member: SI; GFLA; NAD; ASL. Official artist with American Expeditionary Forces in France during World War I. Worked with NYC newspapers, "The Sun."

Taught at ASL. Died in 1948. Address in 1929, 33 West 67th Street, New York, NY.

MORGAN, WILLIAM.
Born in London, England, in 1826. He came to this country in his early life. He received his training in the schools of the National Academy of which he became an Associate in 1865. His works include "Emancipation;" "The Legend;" "Song without Words;" "Motherhood;" "Summer;" "Blowing Bubbles." He died in 1900.

MORIN, HAROLD N.
Painter. Born Helsingborg, Sweden, Jan. 10, 1900. Pupil of MN School of Art. Address in 1929, 3241-37th Avenue, South, Minneapolis, MN.

MORIN, JOHN F.
Engraver of maps, business cards, etc., who was working in NY in 1825- 31, as shown by dates of publication on his few signed plates. In 1825 he engraved in connection with S. Maverick, and was then apparently in the employ of that engraver and copperplate printer. In 1831 Morin engraved a good map of New York City for "The Traveller's Guide through the State of New York," published in New York in that year.

MORLEY, HUBERT.
Painter and etcher. Born La Crosse, WI. Pupil of AIC: Chicago AFA. Member: Chicago SE. Address in 1929, 162 East Superior Street, Chicago, IL.

MORLEY, RUTH KILLICK.
Sculptor, craftswoman, and teacher. Born London, England, June 8, 1888. Pupil of Jean Dampt; Bourdelle. Member: Alliance. Address in 1929, 234 West 15th Street, New York, NY.

MORO, PAOLO.
Painter. Exhibited at National Academy of Design, New York, 1925. Address in 1926, 2104 Vyse Avenue.

MOROSOFF, VADIM VLADIMIROVICH.
Painter. Born Russia, April 9, 1874. Member: S. Indp. A. Address in 1929 care of Dr. R.

Lerner, 1148 Eastern Parkway, Brooklyn, NY.

MORPURGO, VILNA JORGEN.
Painter. Born: Oslo, Norway in 1900. Studied: Maison Wateau, Paris; sculpture with Karl Eldh in Sweden. Collections: Gallery of Modern Art, Stockholm; in Royal collections in Sweden, Belgium and Italy.

MORRELL, IMOGENE ROBINSON.
Painter. Born in Attleboro, MA; died in Washington, D.C., in 1908. Studied art under Gamphausen, and in Paris Couture. Resided in Paris for several years and enjoyed the friendship of Meissonier, Bouguereau and other prominent artists of France. On her second visit to Paris she was accompanied by Elizabeth Jane Gardner, who became a pupil and later the wife of W. A. Bouguereau. Mrs. Morrell's work was recognized by medals at the Mechanics' Institute in Boston and at the Centennial Exposition in Philadelphia. Among her important pictures are: "First Battle between the Puritans and the Indians," "Washington and his Staff Welcoming a Provision Train," and "David before Saul."

MORRIS, ADELAIDE.
Painter. Born Brooklyn, NY, Jan. 11, 1898. Pupil of NY School of Fine and Appied Art; ASL of NY. Member: S. Indp. A. Address in 1929, Ardsley Studio, 110 Columbia Heights, Brooklyn, NY; summer, Scotland Hill Road, Spring Valley, NY.

MORRIS, CATHERINE WHARTON.
See Wright, Mrs. Catherine Morris.

MORRIS, ELLWOOD.
Painter. Born Richmond, IN, June 5, 1848. Member: Richmond AA; Richmond Palette C. Work: "Autumn Tints and Shadows," Richmond Art Association. Address in 1929, Masonic Temple, 9th Street, h. 43½ South 19th Street, Richmond, IN. Died in 1940.

MORRIS, FLORANCE.
Painter. Born Nevada, MO, March 5, 1876. Pupil of W. E. Rollins; A. J. Hammond; L. Brezoli. Member:

657

N. M. Archeological Soc.; AFA; S. Indp. A. Award: First prize, Tri-State Fair, NM Texas, and OK, 1925. Work: "The Papose," Museum of Art and Archeology, Santa Fe, NM; Portrait of Mrs. Virginia A. Stockard, Supreme National Board of P. E. O., Wesleyan College, Mt. Pleasant, IA. Address in 1929, Old Church Studio, 4th and Penn, Roswell, NM.

MORRIS, GEORGE L. K.
Painter. Born Nov. 14, 1905 in NYC. Earned B.A. from Yale; studied at ASL, 1928-30. Taught at St. John's College, Annapolis. Received Temple Gold Medal from PAFA, 1967, and awards from Butler Inst. of Am. Art, Youngstown, and Berkshire Museum. European lecture tour, 1952. Exhibited at Valentine Gallery, NYC; Berkshire; Yale; Downtown Gallery (many, 1944-51); Whitney; Carnegie, and others. In collections of Univ. of Illinois; Yale Univ.; Phil. Museum of Art; Brandeis; Phillips Gallery, Wash. D.C.; PAFA; Whitney; MMA; Univ. of Georgia, and Munson-Williams-Proctor Inst.

MORRIS, PAUL WINTERS.
Sculptor. Born in Du Quoin, IL, Nov. 12, 1865. He studied with Saint Gaudens, and under D.C. French in New York. He died in New York City, Nov. 16, 1916.

MORRIS, ROBERT. C.
Painter. Born Anderson, Jan. 6, 1896. Member: Anderson SA. Address in 1929, 2609 Jackson Street, Anderson, IN.

MORRIS, VIRGINIA LEIGH.
Sculptor. Born Norfolk, VA Oct. 16, 1899. Pupil of Solon Borglum, Harriet Frishmuth, Yale School of Fine Arts. Member: Norfolk SA; S. Wash. A.; Wash. AC; SSAL. Awards: Florence K. Sloane prize, 1921 and 1926, and Elsie Stegman prize, 1921, Norfolk SA. Address in 1929, 596 Mowbray Arch, Norfolk, VA.

MORRISON, DAVID HERRON.
Painter. Born Rawalpindi, Punjab, India, Nov. 15, 1885. Pupil of Kenneth Hayes Miller and Geo. B. Bridgman. Member: NY ASL.; Salons of Am. (Director and Treas.).

Instructor drawing and painting, Allen Stevenson School, New York. Address in 1929, 28 Greenwich Avenue, New York, NY. Died in 1934.

MORRISON, ZAIDEE LINCOLN.
Portrait painter. Born Skowhegan, ME, Nov. 12, 1872. Pupil of J. H. Twachtman, F. V. DuMond, Chase, R. H. Nicholls. Member: ASL of NY; Alliance; NYWCC (Assoc.); NA Women PS; North Shore AA. Work in Mary Lyon Room, Mount Holyoke College, MA; Colby Univ., Waterville, ME; Smithsonian Inst., Washington, D.C. Address in 1929, 58 West 57th Street, New York, NY; summer, East Gloucester, MA.

MORROW, JULIE.
(Mrs. Cornelius Wortendyke De Forest). Painter, writer, and teacher. Born New York, NY. Pupil of Lie, Carlson and Hawthorne. Member: NA Women PS; Provincetown AA; Marblehead AA; Cincinnati AC; American APL; Laguna Beach AA; AFA. Represented in Wadleigh Library, New York City. Address in 1929, Riverview Apartments, Cincinnati, OH.

MORSE, ANNA G.
Painter, craftswoman, and teacher. Born Leominster, MA. Pupil of Jules Lefebvre and T. Robert-Fleury in Paris. Member: PBC; Alliance; C. L. Wolfe AC. Awards: Water color prize, Wanamaker's, Phila., 1910; water color prize, C. L. Wolfe AC, New York, 1920. Address in 1929, 77 Irving Place, New York, NY. Died 1954.

MORSE, ANNE GODDARD.
Painter and illustrator. Born in Providence, RI, Jan. 17, 1855. Pupil of MA Normal Art School; NY ASL; Wyatt Eaton in NY; John La Farge for stained glass. Member: Providence WCC. Address in 1929, Hope Hospital, 1 Young Orchard Avenue, Providence, RI.

MORSE, EDWARD LIND.
Painter and writer. Born in Poughkeepsie, NY, March 29, 1857. Studied at Royal Academy Art, Berlin, 1884-88; Grand Ducal Academy of Art, Weimar, Germany, 1888-91; Julien Academy, Paris,

1891-92. Exhibited in Paris Salon, 1893; held exhibitions at Nat. Acad. of Design; etc. Special exhibitions of work in Washington, New York, Chicago, St. Louis, Etc. Member: AFA. Died June 9, 1923, in Pittsfield, MA.

MORSE, HAZEN.
Engraver. In the New England Palladium of July 20, 1824, "Hazen Morse, Engraver," announced that he has removed from No. 6 Congress Street to Congress Square," A few doors south of the Exchange Coffee House," and he there "continues the business of Copper Plate engraving, in its various branches." Copperplate printing was also done at the same place. For a time Hazen was in the employ of the Boston engraving firm of Annin & Smith. According to the advertisement quoted above he seems to have been chiefly engaged in engraving doorplates, brass numbers for doors, coffin-plates, stencil-plates, etc. The only signed copperplate known to Fielding in 1926 is the "Carey" book-plate inscribed "H. Morse Sc."

MORSE, HENRY DUTTON.
Painter. Born in Boston, MA. April 20, 1826, where he continued to reside. He had no regular instruction in art and was not considered a professional artist; still, in his leisure hours, for many years, he painted pictures, generally of animals, that met with a ready sale in Boston. He was a member of the Boston Art Club, and the son of Hazen Morse. Died Jan. 12, 1888 in Jamaica Plains, MA.

MORSE, IRENE MILNER.
(Mrs. Norman K. Morse). Painter. Born Philadelphia, PA March 16, 1894. Pupil of PAFA. Member: Fellowship PAFA. Address in 1929, 6907 Henley Street, Mt. Airy, Philadelphia, PA; summer, Avalon, NJ.

MORSE, JEAN H.
Painter. Born Derby, CT, Sept. 7, 1876. Pupil of Yale Art School, Chase, Woodbury. Member: New Haven PCC; Northern Valley (NJ) AA; AFA. Address in 1929, Spring Lane, Englewood, NJ; summer, Cotuit, MA.

MORSE, MARY MINNS.
Painter. Born in Dorchester, MA, in 1859. Pupil of Ross Turner and Louis Ritter in Boston; of George Hitchcock in Holland. Member: Boston WCC; Copley Society. Specialty, landscape and marines in water colors. Address in 1926, 211 Savin Hill Avenue, Boston, MA.

MORSE, NATHANIEL.
Engraver.
The only engraving by Nathaniel Morse found by Fielding is a portrait of Rev. Matthew Henry, engraved in line after a print by George Vertue. This portrait is the frontispiece to "The Communicant's Companion, etc.," by Matthew Henry, published in "Boston in New England, re-printed for T. Phillips at the Stationer's Arms, next to Mr. Dolbear, the Braziers, 1731." The MA Archives contain a copy of a bill of 1735, showing that Morse was paid for engraving and printing a plate for Massachusetts paper money. This bill is signed "Nat. Mors," as is the engraving of Matthew Henry referred to above. Died in Boston, June 1748.

MORSE, PAULINE HESTIA.
Painter. Born Marlbourough, MA. Pupil of Dante Ricci, Humann, Rice, Snell. Member: S. Indp. A; AFA. Address in 1929, 15 Irving Street, Worcester, MA.

MORSE, SADIE MAY.
Painter, craftswoman and teacher. Born in Lexington, MA, May 5, 1873. Pupil of MA Normal Art School, Boston; also studied one year in Italy. Member: Hingham Arts and Crafts Society; Boston SAC; AFA; Boston PWC. Educational director under Federal Board for Vocational Education. Address in 1926, 11 Hancock Avenue, Lexington, MA.

MORSE, SAMUEL FINLEY BREESE.
Inventor, figure and portrait painter and sculptor. Born in Charlestown, MA, April 27, 1791. He became graduated from Yale in 1810; became a pupil of Washington Allston whom he accompanied the following year to London, where he studied under Benj. West. Returned to America in 1815 and painted

portraits in Boston, MA; Concord, NH; in Charleston, SC. Settled in NY in 1823, where, in 1826 he became one of the original founders of the NAD and its first President, serving from 1827-45 and again, 1861-62. Among his most important paintings is the full-length portrait of Lafayette in the NYC Hall, and the large picture of the old "House of Representatives by Candle Light," now in the Corcoran Gallery of Art, in Washington, D.C. His model of a "Dying Hercules," made to assist him in painting a picture of this subject which was exhibited in 1813 at the Royal Acad., was awarded gold medal. Died NYC, April 2, 1872.

MORSE & TUTTLE.
(Hazen Morse and Joseph Tuttle). In 1840 this firm was engraving maps in Boston, MA.

MORTON, CHRISTINA.
(Mrs. Benjamin A. Morton). Painter. Born in Dardanelle, Ark. Member: AAA; AFA; NA Women Painters and Sculptors; MacD. C. Work: Paintings of Martinique reproduced in "The Veiled Empress," by B. A. Morton Address in 1929, 27 West 67th Street, New York, NY.

MORTON, JOHN LUDLOW.
Painter. Born in 1792. He was a native of New York, and a son of General Morton. His best known painting was a historical scene from Scott's "Ivanhoe." He was elected an Academician in 1831. He died in New York on Aug. 1, 1871, having been active all his life from his student days in the National Academy of Design.

MORTON, JOSEPHINE A.
Painter. Born in Boston, MA, in 1854. Pupil of Eakins; of Laurens and Constant in Paris. Member: Newport Artists' Association; Society of Independent Artists. Address in 1926, 144 Main Street, Williamstown, MA.

MOSCHCOWITZ, PAUL.
Portrait painter and teacher. Born Giralt, Hungary, March 4, 1876. Pupil of ASL in New York; Julian Academy in Paris. Member: SAA 1901; ANA 1906. Awards: Silver

medal, St. Louis Exp., 1904. Instructor, Pratt Inst. Brooklyn, NY. Address in 1929, 104 West 40th Street, h. 477 West 140th Street, New York, NY.

MOSE, CARL C.
Sculptor and teacher. Born Copenhagen, Denmark, Feb. 17, 1903. Pupil of Lorado Taft, Albin Polasek, Leo Lentelli. Member: S. Wash. A; AFA. Work: Figures of Apostles for the Washington Cathedral, Mt. St. Albans, Washington, D.C.; medal for the American Medical Association; decorations on Y.M.C.A., Chicago, IL. Address in 1929, 217 Randolph Place, N. E.; h. 1708 Third Street, N. E., Washington, D.C.

MOSELEY, HELEN E.
Painter. Born Sept. 21, 1883, in Grand Rapids, MI. Exhibited at 33d Annual Exhibition of National Association of Women Painters and Sculptors, "Gloucester Moors." Studied at AIC and with Robert Henri, Hugh Breckenridge & Chas. Hawthorne. Member of Nat. Assoc. of Women Painters and Sculptors. Died April 22, 1928, in Boston, MA. Address in 1926, Grand Rapids, MI.

MOSER, JAMES HENRY.
Painter. Born in Whitby, Ontario, Canada, in 1854. Landscape painter in oils and water colors. Pupil of John H. Witt and Charles H. Davis. Awards: medal, Atlanta Exp., 1895; first Corcoran prize, Washington Water Color Club, 1900; bronze medal, Charleston Exp., 1902, etc. Represented at the Corcoran Art Gallery, Washington, D.C., by "Winter Sunshine" (water color), painted in 1895; "The Mountain Road" (water color), painted in 1904. Died Nov. 10, 1913 in Wash. DC.

MOSER, JULON.
Painter. Born: Schenectady, New York in 1900. Studied: Chouinard Art Institute; University of California; Scripps College; and with Millard Sheets, Glen Wessels Frank Taylor Bowers. Awards Greek Theatre, Los Angeles, 1951 1955; Pasadena Art Institute, 1951 Women Painters of the West, 1938 1940, 1942, 1944; Laguna Beach

660

1953; Wilshire Ebell Club. Collection: Clearwater Museum of Art. Adddress in 1980, Dean Drive, Ventura, CA.

MOSES, ANNA MARY ROBERTSON.
"Grandma Moses". Painter. Born on September 7, 1860, in Greenwich, NY. In 1887 she married and in 1905, moved to a farm near Eagle Bridge, Rensselaer County, NY, where she lived the rest of her life. In 1918 she tried painting a scene on the fireboard of her fireplace, but it was not until her late seventies, when arthritis forced her to give up making worsted embroidery pictures, that she turned to oil paints to occupy her time. In October 1939 three paintings were exhibited at the Museum of Modern Art in NYC in "Contemporary Unknown Painters." In October 1940 a one-man show of 35 paintings was held at Galerie St. Etienne in NYC. In November 1940 of that year Gimbel's department store brought "Grandma" Moses to NYC on the opening day of a Thanksgiving exhibition of her works. Her paintings were shown throughout the US and in Europe in some 150 one-man shows and 100 more group exhibits. Grandma Moses produced some 2000 paintings in all, mainly on masonite board. She died on December 13, 1961, at the age of a hundred and one, in Hoosick Falls, New York.

MOSES, THOMAS G.
Landscape painter. Born Liverpool, England, in 1856. Pupil of AIC, and of R. M. Shurtleff. Member: Palette and Chisel C.; Calif. AC; Laguna Beach AA; Salma. C. Address in 1929, 417 South Clinton Street, Chicago, IL; h. 233 South Euclid Avenue, Oak Park, IL.

MOSKOWITZ, ROBERT.
Painter. Born June 20, 1935, in Brooklyn, NY. Studied at Pratt, 1955-7. Awarded Guggenheim, 1967 and NYS Council on Arts, 1973. Exhibited at Leo Castelli Gallery, NYC, 1962; MOMA; Albright-Knox; Brandeis and Wadsworth. In collections of Whitney; Brandeis; MOMA; Albright-Knox and many private collections.

MOSLER, HENRY.
Born June 6, 1841, in New York. Figure and genre painter. Pupil of James H. Beard in Cincinnati; Mucke and Kindler in Dusseldorf; Hebert in Paris; Wagner in Munich. Awards: medal, Royal Academy, Munich, 1874; honorable mention, Paris Salon, 1879. Represented at the Corcoran Art Gallery by "Saying Grace," painted in 1897. Died April 21, 1920 in NYC.

MOSS, DONALD.
Illustrator. Born in Somerville, MA in 1920. He studied at PI and ASL with such eminent instructors as Paul Rand, Will Burton and Howard Trafton. His first illustration was done for Collier's in 1948. He has specialized in sports art for many years and has worked for Sports Illustrated for over 20 years. In 1976 he designed the United States Olympic stamps.

MOSS, ELLA A.
Painter. Born in New Orleans in 1844. Studied in Europe, and opened her studio in NY. She painted many portraits of prominent people and exhibited in the National Academy in 1878.

MOSS, IRENE.
Painer. Born in Eperjes, Czech. Exhibitions: Peter Rose Gallery NYC; Bacardi Art Gallery, Miami, Florida, 1974; Suffolk Museum, Long Island, NY, 1971. Collections: Akron Art Institute, Akron, Ohio; Norfolk Museum, Norfolk, Virginia; The New Britain Museum of American Art, New Britain, Conn.

MOTE, ALDEN.
Portrait and landscape painter. He was born in West Milton, OH, on Aug. 27, 1840, and after 1880 lived in Richmond, IN. Represented by a portrait of Daniel G. Reid in the Reid Memorial Hospital, Richmond, IN. Died Jan. 13, 1917, in Richmond, IN.

MOTE, W. H.
This English portrait-engraver did a large amount of work in London in the first half of the 19th century. He engraved portraits of Charles Carroll, of Carrollton, Epes Sargent, and other Americans, and

subject plates engraved by him were used in American publications; but no evidence was found by Fielding that Mote ever actually engraved in this country. The plates mentioned were probably brought over here for publication.

MOTHERWELL, ROBERT.
Painter. Born Jan. 24, 1915, Aberdeen, WA. A.B., Stanford, 1936; Harvard Grad. School, 1937, and Columbia, 1940. Taught at Univ. of Penn. and Columbia. Awards: Guggenheim Museum, 1964; Belgian, 1966, and French, 1977. PA Academy Fine Arts, 1979. Exhibited at MOMA, MMA, Phillips Gallery, (Wash. D.C.); Tate; Guggenheim. Paintings hang internationally, incl. Addison at Andover, MA, Baltimore Mus. of Art, Harvard, Cleveland, Yale, MOMA, Met. Mus. of Art, Whitney, Museu de Arte Moderna in Rio, Tel Aviv, Art Gallery of Toronto. Murals in Kennedy Fed. Bldg, Boston; Univ. of Iowa Art Mus.; Nat. Gallery, Wash. D.C.

MOTLEY, ARCHIBALD JOHN JR.
Painter. Born New Orleans, LA, Oct. 7, 1891. Pupil of Karl Buehr. Member: Chicago SA; IL AFA. Awards: Frank G. Logan medal and prize, AIC, 1925; Joseph N. Eisendrath prize, AIC, 1925; first Harmon Foundation award, gold medal and prize, New York, 1928. Address in 1929, 350 West 60th Street, Chicago, IL.

MOTLEY, ELEANOR W.
(Mrs. Thomas Motley). Painter. Member: Museum School AA; Boston GA; Boston SWCP. Represented in Boston Museum of Fine Arts. Address in 1929, 22 Commonwealth Avenue, Boston, MA.

MOTT-SMITH, MAY.
(Mrs. Small). Miniature Painter, sculptor, and craftswoman. Born Honolulu, HI, March, 17, 1879. Pupil of Colarossi Academy; Van Der Weyden; Spicer Simson. Member: Calif. AC; S. Indp. A.; Calif. Soc. Min. P.; Calif. Sculptors S.; NA Women PS; AM. Numis. Soc.; AFA. Awards: Bronze medal for small relief, Panama-Calif. Exp., San Diego, 1915; silver medal for jewelry, P.- P. Exp., San F., 1915. Address in 1929, 17 West 47th Street, New York, NY.

MOTTET, JEANIE GALLUP.
(Mrs. Henry Mottet). Painter. Born Providence, RI, in 1884. Pupil of ASL of NY, Chase, Richard E. Miller, E. Ambrose Webster. Member: NA Women PS; Provincetown AA; NAC; AFA. Chairman of exhibition committee and Curator of painting, Museum of French Art, New York, NY. Decorated Officier d'Academie by Minister of Beaux Arts, Paris, 1918, and Officier d'Instruction Publique, 1929. Represented in Musee du Luxembourg, Paris. Address in 1929, 47 West 20th Street, New York, NY.

MOTTO, JOSEPH C.
Sculptor. Born Cleveland, OH, March 6, 1892. Pupil of Matzen, MacNeal and Heber. Member: Cleveland SA; Cleveland SS. Award: First prize, Cleveland Museum of Art, 1922. Work: Shakespeare bust, City of Cleveland; bust of "Prof. Wilson," Western Reserve Univ., Cleveland; "Matzen" bust, Cleveland School of Art; "Lincoln" bust, Hawken School, South Euclid. Address in 1929, Hawken School, South Euclid, OH; h. 1536 East 41st, Cleveland, OH.

MOTTRAM, C.
Engraver. Born 1817. A fine line-engraving, signed by C. Mottram as engraver, represents a view of the city of New York from the Brooklyn shore. It is made from a drawing executed by J. W. Hill, New York, 1855, and was published there that same year. John William Hill was the son of John Hill, the aquatint-engraver, who came to the United States in 1816 and died here in 1850.

MOTZ, MRS. RAY ESTEP.
Painter, etcher, and teacher. Born Whitsett, PA, May 27, 1875. Pupil of Carnegie Inst. of Technology; AIC; NY. School of Fine and Applied Arts. Member: Asso. A. of Pittsburgh. Award: First prize for oil, Assoc. A. of Pittsburgh, 1929. Address in 1929, 338 Oneida Street, Monessen, PA; summer, Shelburne Falls, MA.

MOTZ-LOWDON, ELSIE.
  See Lowdon Elsie.

MOULD, J. B.
  This name is signed as engraver to
  good stipple portraits published in
  New York about 1830, but as the
  portraits are those of foreigners
  it is possible that these plates
  were imported.

MOULTHROP, REUBEN.
  Portrait and miniature painter.
  Born in 1763. He also modelled in
  Wax. He died in East Haven, CT, in
  1814. His portraits of Ezra Stiles
  and Jonathan Edwards are good
  examples of his work. Died July
  29, 1814.

MOULTON, CLAXTON B.
  Painter. Exhibited "Portrait of a
  Boy" at Penna. Academy of Fine
  Arts, Philadelphia, 1921. Address
  in 1926, 172 Townsend Street,
  Boston, MA.

MOULTON, MRS. SUE BUCKINGHAM.
  Painter. Born Hartford, CT, Jan.
  20, 1873. Pupil of Andrews, Moser,
  Frisbie. Member: Alliance;
  Ceramic Lg.; AFA. Award:
  Micherson memorial prize. Work:
  Mural painting in the Philomusian
  Club, Philadelphia. Specialty,
  miniature painting. Address in
  1929, 901 South 47th Street,
  Philadelphia, PA.

MOUNT, HENRY SMITH.
  Painter. Born Oct. 9, 1802. in
  Stony Brook, LI, NY. He was a
  brother of Wm. S. and Shephard
  Alonzo. He was elected an
  Associate Member of the National
  Academy in 1832 and exhibited
  frequently. He died Jan. 20, 1841,
  in Setauket, LI, NY.

MOUNT, SHEPARD ALONZO.
  Painter, brother of W. S. Mount.
  Born July 17, 1804. He was a
  distinguished portrait painter.
  Became an Associate of the National
  Academy, 1831, and Academician in
  1842. He painted portraits of
  Martin Van Buren and other
  distinguished statesmen. Died
  Sept. 18, 1868, in Setauket, L.I,
  NY.

MOUNT, WILLIAM SIDNEY.
  Painter. Born in Setauket, L.I,
  Nov. 26, 1807. Pupil of the
  National Academy of Design; he had
  a studio in New York for many
  years. Exhibited often at the
  Academy. He was elected a Member
  of the National Academy of Design.
  Represented in Metropolitan Museum
  of Art, and in the National
  Gallery, Washington, D.C. Died
  Nov. 19, 1868 in Setauket, L.I, NY.

MOUNTFORT, ARNOLD.
  Painter. Born in Eggbaston,
  England, in 1873. Pupil of
  Birmingham Municipal School of Art,
  England. Address in 1926, Sherwood
  Studios, 58 West 57th Street, New
  York, NY. Died Aug. 13, 1942.

MOUNTFORT, JULIA ANN.
  Painter, illustrator, and writer.
  Born Coaticooke, Canada, Jan. 14,
  1892. Pupil of Fox Art School; AIC;
  Chicago AFA; Sargent; Townsley,
  etc. Member: Chicago NJSA; Chicago
  SA; Southern SAL; South Shore
  Artists; All-Ill. SA. Address in
  1929, Azalea Courts, Mobile, AL;
  summer, "House With Red Blinds,"
  Bristol Road, Damariscotta, ME.

MOWAT, H. J.
  Illustrator. Member: SI 1912;
  Salma. C. Address in 1929,
  Westport, CT; 563 Victoria Avenue,
  Westmount, Quebec, CN; 315 Tote
  Road W., Montreal, Quebec, CN.

MOWBRAY, HENRY SIDDONS.
  Painter. Born in Alexandria,
  Egypt, Aug. 5, 1858; brought to
  United States in 1859. Studied
  painting under Bonnat, Paris, 1878;
  in NY after 1878. Principal works;
  "A Lady in Black"; "Evening
  Breeze"; "Le Destin"; mural
  decorations in residences of F. W.
  Vanderbilt, C. P. Huntington, J.
  Pierpont Morgan; Appellate Ct.
  House, and Univeristy Club Library,
  New York; residence of Larz
  Anderson, Washington; Federal Court
  Room, Cleveland. Elected member of
  the National Academy, 1891. Also
  member of CT. AFA, NIA, and
  director of Am. Academy in Rome,
  1903-4. Address in 1926,
  Washington, CT. Died Jan 13, 1928
  in Wash., D.C.

MOWBRAY-CLARKE, JOHN FREDERICK.
Sculptor. Born Jamaica, West
Indies, Aug. 4, 1869. Pupil of
Lambeth School, London. Member:
AM. PS. Represented in
Metropolitan Museum, NY; Newark,
(NJ.), Museum; British Museum,
London. Address in 1929, "The
Brocken," Pomona, Rockland Co., NY.

MOYNIHAN, FREDERICK.
Sculptor. Born in 1843 on Island
of Guernsey. Made a specialty of
military figures of the Civil War
period. Died Jan. 9, 1910 in NYC.

MOZIER, JOSEPH.
Sculptor. Born in Burlington, VT,
Aug. 12, 1812. He studied sculpture
for several years in Florence, and
then went to Rome, where he spent
the greater part of his
professional career. Among his
best works are "Esther," the "Wept
of Wish-ton-Wish," "Tacite,"
"Truth," the "White Lady of
Avenel," "The Peri," "Pocahontas,"
"Prodigal Son," "Rizpah," and "Il
Penseroso" in marble; the last was
transferred from the Capitol in
1888 to the National Gallery,
Washington, D.C. Died in Faide,
Switzerland on Oct. 3, 1870.

MUEDEN, MATHILDE.
See Mrs. L. M. Leisenring.

MUELLER, ALEXANDER.
Painter, lecturer, and teacher.
Born Milwaukee, WI, Feb. 29, 1872.
Pupil of Richard Lorenz in
Milwaukee; Max Thedy in Weimar;
Carl Marr in Munich. Member:
Wisconsin PS. Address in 1929,
2955 Monterey Road, San Marino, Los
Angeles Co., CA. Died in 1935.

MUELLER, CARL.
Illustrator. Member: SI. Address
in 1929, Westport, CT.

MUELLER, HENRIETTE WATERS.
Painter and sculptor. Born:
Pittsburgh, PA on April 13, 1915.
Studied: Northwestern University;
Art Inst. of Chicago; Art Students'
League; Univ. Of Wyoming; and with
Will Barnet, Ilya Bolotowsky, John
Opper and George McNeal. Awards:
Mary Griffiths Marshall Memorial
fellowship, Alpha Chi Omega, 1952;
Tri-State Exhib., 1958; Cummington

fellowship, 1954. Collections:
New York Public Library; Joslyn Art
Museum; Henry Gallery, University
of Washington; Nelson Gallery of
Art; Woman's College, University of
North Carolina. Media: Oil,
watercolor, acrylic, steel and
aluminium. Address in 1980, 1309
Steele Street, Laramie, Wyoming.

MUELLER, JOHN CHARLES.
Illustrator, craftman, draftsman,
and writer. Born Cincinnati, OH,
Nov. 3, 1889. Pupil of Nowottny,
Duveneck, Meakin, Miller,
Cincinnati Art Academy. Member:
Cincinnati AC. Awards: Hon.
mention for book cover, Advertisers
Club of the World; first prize for
emblem design, Nat. Asso.
Advertising Specialty
Manufacturers. Designer of the
official flag for the City of
Norwood, OH. Address in 1929, 2042
Weyer Avenue, Norwood, OH.

MUELLER, LOUIS F.
Painter. Born Indianapolis, IN,
April 29, 1886. Pupil of Zugel,
Habermann, and Marr in Munich.
Member: Royal Bavarian Akademie,
Munich. Address in 1929, 2209
Ashland Avenue, Indianapolis, IN.

MUELLER, MICHAEL J.
Painter, craftsman, and teacher.
Born Durand, WI, Dec. 3, 1893.
Pupil of Sargeant Kendall, Winter,
Savage, E. C. Taylor, Rittenberg,
Bridgman, DuBois. Address in 1929,
Van Dyck Bldg., 939 Eighth Avenue,
New York, NY; h. Cable, WI.

MUENDEL, GEORGE F.
Painter. Born West Hoboken, NJ,
1871. Pupil of Ochtman and ASL of
NY. Member: CT AFA; Silvermine
GA; AFA. Awards: Prize ($100), CT
AFA, 1914. Address in 1929,
Rowayton, CT.

MUGFORD, WILLIAM.
Portrait painter. The Peabody
Museum of Salem, MA, owns a crayon
portrait by William Mugford.

MUHLHOFER, ELIZABETH.
Painter. Born Maryland. Pupil of
Corcoran School under Moser,
Brooke, and Messer. Member: Wash.
WCC; S. Wash. A.; Chicago WCC.

664

Address in 1929, 130 Eleventh Street, S. E., Washington, D.C.

MUIR, EMILY.
Painter. Born: Chicago, IL in 1904. Studied: Vassar College; Art Students League with Richard Lahey, John Carroll, George Bridgman and Leo Lentelli. Collections: Brooklyn Museum; University of Maine; United States Government; Moore-McCormack Lines; American Caribbean Lines; American Scantic Lines; French Line; Pan-American Airways; Finnish Travel Bureau; Swedish Travel Bureau; Aluminum Corporation of America.

MULHAUPT, FREDERICK JOHN.
Painter. Born Rockport, MO, March 28, 1871. Pupil of Art Academy in Kansas City; AIC; Paris schools. Member: ANA; Palette and Chisel C., Chicago; Salma. C.; Paris AAA; NAC (life); Allied AA; North Shore AA. Awards: Evans prize, Salma. C.; Proctor prize, Salma. C., 1921; bronze medal for landscape, Philadelphia Art Week, 1925; popular vote, Allied Artists of America, 1925; Gedney Bunce prize, CT. AFA, 1927. Represented in the John Herron Art Inst., Indianapolis; Reading (PA) Museum of Fine Arts. Address in 1929, 209 Bradford Bldg., Gloucester, MA; h. 9 Highland Ct., East Gloucester, MA.

MULLEN, BUELL.
Painter. Born: Chicago, IL. in 1901. Studied: Tyler Sch. of Art; British Acad. of Art, London; Rome, Italy with Petrucci, and Lipinsky; and in Belgium with Cucquier. Collections: Lib. of Congress (1st mural to be made of stainless steel); US Naval Research Laboratory, Ministry of Public Works, Rio de Janeiro; Ministry of War, Buenos Aires; Great Lakes Naval Station; Dun & Bradstreet; Metal Research Laboratory, Niagara; Electronic Tower, Internat'l Telephone and Telegraph Company; General Motors Styling Admin., Detroit; US Steel panels for private car; Nat'l Carbon Laboratory; Searle Laboratory; Inland Steel, Indiana Harbor; stainless steel mural, ceiling North Adams MA Hospital; Sorg Paper Middletown, Ohio; Gardner Board and Carton Co., Middletown; Allegheny Ludlum Steel Laboratory; John Woodman Higgins Armory, Worcester, MA; Republic Steel Co.; Physics Auditorium, Case Inst. of Tech.; Am. Soc. of Chemists, Washington, DC.

MULLEN, RICHARD.
Wood engraver. Born in Germany in 1849. He came to this country when a boy and was educated at the Cooper Union, and at the National Academy of Design. He illustrated many of the early New York magazines with wood cuts until his work was replaced by the photo-engraving process. He died in Brooklyn on Nov. 17, 1915.

MULLER, HECTOR.
Dunlap noted him as a landscape painter, working in New York, 1828 - 53. Also painted portraits and miniatures.

MULLER, OLGA POPOFF (MRS.).
Sculptor. Born New York City, Dec. 1, 1883. Member: NA Women PS. Awards: Cahn hon. mention, AIC, 1911; McMillin prize, N.A. Women PS, 1914; medal of honor, Paris exhibition of women's works; bronze medals, P.- P. Exp., San F., 1915; hon. mention, NA Women PS, 1925. Address in 1929, 121 Jamaica Avenue, Flushing, NY.

MULLER-URY, ADOLPH.
Portrait painter. Born Airolo Ct., Ticino, Switzerland, March 28, 1868. Came to US in 1888. Pupil of Royal Academy in Munich; Ecole des Beaux- Arts in Paris under Cabanel. Member: Lotos C. Work: Portraits of President McKinley; General Grant; Senator & Mrs. Depew; Senator Hanna, and others. Address in 1929, 33 West 67th Street, New York, NY.

MULLIGAN, CHARLES J.
Sculptor. Born in Riverdale Ireland, Sept 28, 1866. He came to America as a boy and worked with a stone cutter near Chicago. Studied at Chicago Art Institute, and later under Falguiere, in Paris. Among his statues are "The Three Sisters," at Springfield, Illinois;

Lincoln, known as "The Rail Splitter," and a statue of Col. Finnerty. He died March 25, 1916 in Chicago, IL.

MULLIKEN, JONATHAN.
Engraver. Born in Newburyport, MA, in 1746; died there June 1782. The only known copper-plate engraving by Mulliken is a very close copy of Paul Revere's "Massacre" plate, though there is no indication of the date of production. He was probably a self-taught engraver, producing some of his own metal clock faces, an accomplishment not rare among the early clockmakers. Died June 19, 1782.

MULLIKIN, MARY AUGUSTA.
Painter and lecturer. Born in Ohio. Pupil of Walter Beck in Cincinnati; Birge Harrison at Woodstock; Whistler in Paris. Member: China Soc. of Science and Arts; Work: Lasell Seminary, Auburndale, MA; Peking Inst. of Fine Arts; in collection of Ex-Pres. Hsu Shih Chang of China. Address in 1929, 397 Elfin Terrace, Tientsin, China.

MULLIN, CHARLES EDWARD.
Painter, etcher, and teacher. Born Chicago, IL, July 6, 1885. Pupil of AIC. Member: Chicago SA; Chicago NJSA. Award: Edward B. Butler purchase prize ($200), AIC, 1929. Address in 1929, Highland Avenue, at 143rd Street, Orland Park, IL.

MULLINS, FRANK.
Illustrator. Born in Springfield, MA in 1924. He received his BFA from PI in 1959 and his MA from Columbia University in 1966. His first illustration was a portrait of Murray Rose done as a cover for Sports Illustrated in 1961.

MULRONEY, REGINA W.
Sculptor, illustrator, writer, and teacher. Born New York, NY, Dec. 4, 1895. Pupil of ASL of NY, and San Francisco Art School. Member: Lorillard Wolfe C.; Louis Comfort Tiffany Foundation; Phila. Alliance; Phila. SA; NA Women PS. Award: Lorillard Wolfe prize for sculpture, 1929. Address in 1929, 694 Madison Avenue, New York, NY;

summer, 2476 Broadway, San Francisco, CA.

MULVANEY, JOHN.
Painter. Born in 1844, he came to this country when he was twenty. He specialized in painting Western, Indian, and army life; he was best known for his "Custer's Last Rally." He also painted many portraits, one of his last being that of Bishop Mc Donnell of Brooklyn. He died in New York in May, 1906.

MUMFORD, ALICE TURNER.
See Mrs. Roberts.

MUMFORD, EDWARD WILLIAM.
Engraver. Born in 1812. From 1835-40 Mumford was engraving landscapes and subject plates for Philadelphia publishers. Died in 1858.

MUMMERT, SALLIE BLYTH.
Painter. Born Cisco, Texas. Pupil of Aunspaugh Art School, Dallas. Member: S. Indp. A.; Fort Worth AA. Award: Linz medal for best figure, Woman's Forum Annual Art Exhibit, Texas. Address in 1929, 1308 South Adams Street, Fort Worth, Texas.

MUNDAY, ROSEMARY.
Painter. Exhibited at the Penna. Academy of Fine Arts, Philadelphia, 1914. Address in 1926, Norway, ME.

MUNDY, ETHEL FRANCES.
Sculptor. Born: Syracuse, New York. Studied: Art Students League; Fontainebleau School of Art, France; also with Rochester Mechanics Inst.; and Amy M. Sacker, Boston. Work: Syracuse Museum of Fine Arts; Frick Gallery, NY; J. B. Speed Memorial Museum; Louisville Kentucky Museum of Art. She discovered a new composition for use in wax portraiture and revived the art of wax portraiture which was known in Europe for 500 years before being lost in the 18th century. Address in 1929, Syracuse, NY.

MUNDY, LOUISE EASTERDAY.
Painter and teacher. Born Nokomis, IL. Pupil of Univ. of Neb.; AIC; Stout Inst.; Chicago Academy of

Fine Arts. Member: Neb. AA; Lincoln AG. Address in 1929 University of Nebraska; h. 1507 R Street; Lincoln, Neb.

MUNGER, ANNE WELLS.
(Mrs. W. L. C. Munger). Landscape painter. Born Springfield, MA, July 17, 1862. Pupil of Philip Hale, Woodbury and De Camp in Boston; Brush in New York. Member: Boston SAC; Provincetown AS; New Orleans AA; SSAL; Gulf Coast AA; AFA; Southern AA; Miss. AA. Address in 1929, Pass Christian, MS.; summer, South Wellfleet, MA. Died in 1945.

MUNGER, CAROLINE.
Miniature painter. Born May 15, 1808 in E. Guilford, CT. She was the daughter of George Munger. In 1831 she married Horace Wasburn, and exhibited miniatures at the National Academy of New York in 1841. She died Jan. 4, 1892 in Madison, CT.

MUNGER, GEORGE.
Engraver. Born Feb. 17, 1781, in Guilford, CT. Munger was a miniature painter of some merit, and the firm of N. & S. S. Jocelyn engraved plates after portraits painted by him. In 1816, N. Jocelyn and G. Munger, of New Haven, CT, published a large aquatint view of the Island of St. Helena. This plate is signed "G. Munger, Sculp.;" but it is the only example of his engraved work found. Munger was some relation of Anson Dickinson, the miniature painter, Also born in CT. Two of Munger's daughters became artists. He died July 2, 1825.

MUNN, GEORGE FREDERICK.
Artist. Born in Utica, NY, in 1852. Studied in the National Academy, NY, and later in England in the studio of George F. Watts. He exhibited in many of the galleries. Died Feb. 10, 1907 in NYC.

MUNN, MARGUERITE CAMPBELL.
Painter. Born Washington, D.C. Pupil of Henry B. Snell. Member: S. Wash. A.; Wash. WCC; Wash. AC; NA Women PS.; NAC. Address in 1929, McLean Bldg., 1517 H Street;

h. 1842 16th Street, N. W., Washington, D.C.

MUNRO, ALBERT A.
Painter and etcher. Born in Hoboken, NJ, in 1868. Address in 1926, Springfield, L.I., NY.

MUNROE, MARJORY.
Painter. Born in New York, NY, in 1891. Pupil of Frank Du Mond, E. Percy Moran, and of George Elmer Browne. Address in 1926, 12 East 30th Street, New York, NY.

MUNROE, SALLY C.
(Mrs. Vernon Munroe). Painter. Born New York, Jan. 24, 1881. Pupil of Cox, Woodbury. Member: NA Women PS; AFA. Specialty, landscape and figures. Address in 1929, 1172 Park Avenue, New York, NY; summer, Litchfield, CT.

MUNROE, SARAH SEWELL.
Painter. Born: Brooklyn, New York. Pupil of Hassam, Miller, Hawthorne. Awards: Corcoran prize, Washington Water Color Club; Society of Washington Artists, 1921, 1923. Member of Wash. SA; NA Women PS; Wash. WCC; AFA. Address in 1929, 1905 N. St. Wash., DC; summer, "Windover," Provincetown, MA.

MUNSELL, ALBERT HENRY.
Portrait painter. Born in Boston in 1858. Student of Ecole des Beaux Arts in Paris. Exhibited at Paris Salon, 1886-87-88; also in Boston, New York, Chicago, and Pittsburgh. Instructor in MA Normal Art School after 1881; lecturer on artistic anatomy and color composition. He patented new instruments for color measurement, and invented a system of pigment colors, which was introduced in schools of Boston, NY, Baltimore, Mexico City, etc. Author: Color Notation, 1905; Atlas of the Color System, 1910. Address in 1926, 221 Columbus Avenue, Boston, MA.

MUNSELL, WILLIAM A. O.
Painter and architect. Born Cold Water, OH, March 2, 1866. Member: AIA; S. Indp. A.; Laguna Beach AA; Allied Arch. Assoc. Represented in Los Angeles Museum; Scottish Rite

Cathedral, Los Angeles; San Marino City Hall; hospital for tubercular soldiers, Soldiers' Home, CA. Address in 1929, Suite 631, 714 West 10th Street, Los Angeles, CA; h. 2405 Ridgeway Road, San Marino, CA.

MUNSON, LUCIUS.
Painter. Born in New Haven, CT, in 1796. In 1820 he visited South Carolina and painted many portraits, and had hopes of being able to study in Europe, but sickness prevented and he died in Turks Island, in 1823.

MUNSON, SAMUEL B.
Engraver. Born May 29, 1806, in CT. From 1830-35 Munson was engraving in New Haven in conjunction with S. S. Jocelyn of that town, but about 1836 he removed to Cincinnati, OH, and was a member of the banknote engraving firm of Doolittle & Munson. For a time he was associated with G. K. Stillman in engraving and publishing prints. Died April 6, 1880 in Cincinnati, Ohio.

MUNZIG, GEORGE CHICKERING.
Portrait painter. Born in Boston in 1859. His specialty was portraits in crayon. Member of the Boston Art Club. He exhibited in Philadelphia, New York, Cleveland, and Boston. Died March 5, 1908 in NYC.

MURANYI, GUSTAVE.
Painter. Born Temesvar, Hungary, Aug. 1, 1881. Studied in England. Specialty, portraits. Address in 1929, Room 1209, Carnegie Hall, New York, NY.

MURCH, WALTER TANDY.
Painter. Born in Toronto, Ontario, Canada, in 1907. Learned woodworking, architectural drafting at Toronto Technical High School; entered Ontario College of Art in 1925; formal art training, NYC with Kenneth Hayes Miller; Arshile Gorky at Grand Central School. Worked as assistant stained-glass designer for NY company, and other jobs. Used a variety of discarded objects such as machine parts, broken dolls, light bulbs, car parts as subjects for the compositions for

which he became well known. Died in 1967. Represented by Kennedy Galleries, NYC.

MURDOCH, DORA LOUISE.
Painter and craftswoman. Born New Haven, CT, Sept. 14, 1857. Pupil of Lucien Symon, Courtois, Rixen and Boutet de Monvel in Paris. Member: NYWCC; AWCS; Baltimore WCC; AFA; Wash. WCC. Awards: Purnell prize, Baltimore WCC, 1903; Balto. water color prize, Peabody Inst., 1922. Address in 1929, 245 West Biddle Street, Baltimore, MD.

MURDOCH, FLORENCE.
Painter, craftswoman, and teacher. Born Lakewood, NY, June 14, 1887. Pupil of Nowottny, Meakin, Ensign, and Carlson. Member: Cincinnati Women's AC; Alliance; Boston SAC; Ohio WCS. Address in 1929, 2448 Maplewood Avenue, Cincinnati, OH.

MURDOCH, FRANK C.
Painter. Member: Pittsburgh Artists' Association. Address in 1926, 5709 Woodmont Street, Pittsburgh, PA.

MURPHY.
A crudely engraved line frontispiece, representing "Wisdom," is signed "Murphy Sculp." This plate was published in New York in 1807. The design shows Minerva armed with spear and shield standing in center, with a flying Cupid and palm tree to left and a lamb at her feet. No other example of Murphy's work has been seen.

MURPHY, ADA CLIFFORD.
(Mrs. J. Francis Murphy). Painter and illustrator. Pupil of Cooper Union and Douglas Volk in New York. Member: NA Women PS; NAC. Awards: Hallgarten prize, NAD, 1894; hon. mention. Pan-Am. Exp., Buffalo, 1901. Address in 1929, Arkville, NY.

MURPHY, CHRISTOPHER (JR.).
Painter, etcher, and teacher. Born Savannah, GA, Dec., 1902. Pupil of Du Mond, Bridgman, Clark, Chadwick and Pennell; ASL of NY. Member: Savannah AA; SSAL; Georgia Assn. Artists (treas.). Award: Etching prize, SSAL Exhib., 1927. Address

in 1929, 11 East Perry Street, Savannah, GA.

MURPHY, H. DUDLEY.
Painter, illustrator, etcher, craftsman, and teacher. Born Marlboro, MA, Aug. 25, 1867. Pupil of Boston Museum Sch.; Laurens in Paris. Member: Copley S., 1886; Boston WCC; Salma. C.; Boston SAC; Boston GA; NAC; Boston AC; Boston SWCP; MA State Art Com.; PS Gallery Assoc. Awards: Bronze medal, Pan-Am. Exp., Buffalo, 1901; silver medal for portrait and bronze medal for water color, St. Louis Exp., 1904; silver medal for oil painting and silver medal for water colors, P.- P. Exp., San F., 1915; Peterson prize, AIC, 1922. Work: "Mt. Monadnock," "Charles H. Woodbury," and portrait of H. O. Tanner, Art Inst. of Chicago; "The Opal Sunset," Art Assoc., Nashville, TN; "Murano" and "Still Life," Albright Art Gallery, Buffalo, NY; "Moro Castle, San Juan," Dallas (TX) Museum of FA; "Tropic Castles," Cleveland Art Museum. Instructor in drawing and member of Faculty of Architecture, Harvard Univ. Address in 1929, Lexington, MA.

MURPHY, HENRY CRUSE (JR.).
Painter, illustrator, and teacher. Born Brooklyn, NY, Feb. 26, 1886. Self taught. Member: Salma. C.; Greenwich SA; AFA. Work: "27th Division Breaking the Hindenburg Line," National Museum, Washington. Specialty, Marine paintings and illustrations in color for reproduction purposes. Address in 1929, Cat Rock Road, Cos Cob, CT.

MURPHY, JOHN FRANCIS.
Landscape painter. Born in Oswego, NY, in 1853. He was largely self-taught. He first exhibited at the National Academy of Design in New York in 1876. He won many prizes, medals, and honors for his work in landscapes and his paintings are said to rank with Inness, Wyant and Homer Martin, and are included in most of the prominent collections in America. He was elected a member of the National Academy in 1887. His studio was (for years) in New York. He died Jan. 29, 1921, in NYC.

MURPHY, JOHN J. A.
Painter. Member: Guild of Free Lance Association. Address in 1926, 21 Greenwich Avenue, New York, NY.

MURPHY, L. M.
Painter. Member: California Art Club. Address in 1926, 115½ North Main Street, Los Angeles, CA.

MURPHY, MICHAEL THOMAS.
Sculptor. Born in Bantry, County Cork, Ireland, in 1867. Apprenticed as marble carver in Cork; studied in School of Art, Cork, and later at Royal College of Art, London; also in Paris and Italy. Came to United States in 1912. Specialized in portraits and figure subjects in relief. Exhibited at Art Institute Chicago, 1918. Principal works: Busts of Most Rev. George W. Mundelein and of Dr. John B. Murphy, of Chicago; "Aaron Blessing the Israelites," 4th Presbyterian Church, Lincoln Parkway, Chicago; heroic size figures representing an athlete and a student, University of Michigan, Ann Arbor; etc. Member Art Workers' Guild, Artists' Annuity Fund, London; Chicago Society of Artists. Address in 1926, 4 E. Ohio Street, Chicago, IL.

MURPHY, MINNIE B. HALL.
(Mrs. Edward Roberts Murphy). Painter, sculptor, writer, lecturer, and teacher. Born Denver, CO, May 2, 1863. Pupil ASL of NY; AIC; Henry Read in Denver. Member: NAC; Denver AC. Address in 1929, 805 Gaylord Street, Denver, CO.

MURPHY, NELLY LITTLEHALE.
(Mrs. H. Dudley Murphy). Painter, illustrator and etcher. Born Stockton, CA, May 7, 1867. Pupil of Joseph De Camp and C. Howard Walker. Member: Copley S.; Boston SWCP; Boston GA. Award: Purchase prize for water color, Boston AC, 1929. Represented, permanent collection, Boston Museum of Fine Arts. Address in 1929, Lexington, MA.

MURPHY, WILLIAM D.
Painter. Born in Madison County, AL, on March 11, 1834. In 1863 he

669

received his first art education from William Cooper, a portrait painter, of Nashville, TN. Married Harriet Anderson, a pupil of Lorenz and William Morgan, in 1887. Since that time Mr. and Mrs. Murphy continuously engaged in portrait painting, their work being conducted jointly. The list of works from their studio contains the portraits of eminent public men, including those of President Lincoln, President McKineley. President Roosevelt, Admiral Dewey, Admiral Schley, and others.

MURRAY, GEORGE.
Born in Scotland. Dunlap said that Murray was a pupil of the well-known English engraver Anker Smith, and he was certainly engraving portraits, etc., in London in 1796. Murray appeared in Philadelphia in 1800, coming to that city from one of the Southern States. He was prominent in the Philadelphia Society of Artists in 1810, and in 1810-11 he organized the banknote and general engraving firm of Murray, Draper, Fairman & Co. Died July 2, 1822 in Philadelphia, PA.

MURRAY, GRACE H.
(Mrs. A. Gordon Murray). Painter. Born New York, Nov. 9, 1872. Pupil of Bouguereau and Gabriel Ferrier. Member: NA Women PS; Amer. Soc. Min. P. (Sec.); PA Soc. Min. P. (hon. life mem.). Address in 1929, 152 West 58th Street, New York, NY; summer, Pine Tree Farm, North Hampton, NH.

MURRAY, JOHN.
In Rivington's Royal Gazette, in 1776, we find the following: "John Murray, in the 57th Regiment from Edinburgh, engraves all manner of silver-plate, seals, coats of arms, etc."

MURRAY, RICHARD DEIBEL.
Painter and sculptor. Study: Univ. of Notre Dame; Georgetown Univ., DC; Univ. of PA. Work: American College of Surgeons; Vienna Statsoper; Mill Creek Park; Rose Garden and Youngstown Symphony Center. Exhibitions: Butler Art Institue, Youngstown; Arkep Gallery, NY; Kottler Galleries, NY; Canton Art Institute, Canton, OH; and others. Awards: Citation, City of Youngstown, OH; others. Address in 1982, Youngstown, OH.

MURRAY, SAMUEL.
Sculptor and teacher. Born Philadelphia, PA, June 12, 1870. Pupil of Thomas Eakins. Awards: Diploma, Columbian Exp., Chicago, 1893; gold medal, AC Phila., 1894; hon. mention, Pan-Am. Exp., Buffalo, 1901; silver medal, St. Louis Exp., 1904. Work: "Prophets," Witherspoon Bldg., Philadelphia; "Com. Barry" and "Joseph Leidy" and J. H. Windrim portrait, Smith Memorial, Fairmount Park, Philadelphia; Pennsylvania State Monument, Gettysburg, PA; Corby statue, Notre Dame Univ., Notre Dame, IN; portrait, Dr. J. C. Wilson, Jefferson Medical College, Philadelphia. Address in 1929, 3326 Lancaster Avenue; h. 3324 Lancaster Avenue, Philadelphia, PA.

MUSGRAVE, ARTHUR FRANKLYN.
Painter. Born Brighton, England, July 24, 1880. Pupil of Stanhope Forbes, Newlyn School of Art, Cornwall; Munich. Member: Provincetown AA; Wash. WCC; S. Wash. A.; NYWCC. Address in 1929, 15 Raymond Street, Cambridge, MA.

MUSGRAVE, EDITH.
Painter and writer. Born New York City, Dec. 25, 1887. Pupil of E. M. Ashe, G. B. Bridgman, J. C. Johansen, Alon Bement; ASL of NY. Address in 1929, 534 East Third Street, Mt. Vernon, NY.

MUSGRAVE, HELEN GREENE.
Painter and teacher. Born Cincinnati, OH., March 6, 1890. Pupil of Cincinnati Art Acad.; Julian Academy in Paris; NY School of Fine and Applied Art. Member: Provincetown AA. Address in 1929, Truro, MA.

MYERS, LOUIS.
Illustrator. Born in Paris, France in 1915. He studied for many years at the New School for Social Research and the ASL. His first work, a children's book entitled Clementina, was published by Western Publishing. He has since illustrated many magazines and

books in his unique cartoon style. He presently lives in Peekskill, NY.

MYERS, O. IRWIN.
Painter and illustrator. Born in Bananza, NE, in 1888. Pupil of Art Institute of Chicago and of Chicago Academy of Fine Arts. Member: Chicago Society of Artists; Chicago AC; Chicago Society of Independent Artists; Alumni Art Institute of Chicago. Address in 1926, Studio Bldg., 4 East Ohio Street, Chicago, IL.

MYRHL, SARAH.
Painter. Born in New York City in 1912. Studied: Hunter College; New School for Social Research; Columbia Univ.; Art Students' League; and with Brook, Zorach, and Kuniyoshi. Award: Metropolitan scholarship from Art Students' League. Collections: Mural, La Guardia Sea Plane Base, New York; also in private collections in United States and Japan.

NADELMAN, ELIE.
Sculptor and etcher. Born Warsaw, Poland, Feb. 23, 1882. Studied in Munich and Warsaw, then went to Paris for 12 years, c. 1905. Member: NSS; NY Arch. Lg.; Modern AA; Salons of America; S. Indp. A.; New Soc. A; Beaux Arts Inst. of Design; Mun. AS; AFA. Died in 1946. Address in 1929, 6 East 93rd St., New York, NY; summer, Riverdale-on- Hudson, NY.

NAEGELE, CHARLES FREDERICK.
Portrait painter. Born Knoxville, Tenn., May 8, 1857. Pupil of William Sartain, Chase and C. Myles Collier. Member: A. Fund S.; Salma. C. 1893; Lotos C.; Atlanta Art Assn.; NAC; GFLA. Awards: Gold medal, Mechanics Fair, Boston, 1900; silver medal, Charleston Exp., 1902. Work: "Mother Love," National Gallery, Washington. Originated method of holding exhibitions by which system public collection of art works may be established. Died in 1944. Address in 1929, R. F. D. Marietta, GA.

NAGAOKA, SHUSEI S.
Illustrator. Born in Nagasaki, Japan in 1936. Studied: Musashino Art Univ. for three years. In the 1960's he had his first illustration published in Boys Magazine in Tokyo and has since received awards from the AIGA and the S of I in NY. His works are in Yokohama Marine Museum in Japan.

NAGEL, ELIZABETH and EDWARD.
Painters. Exhibited in Phila., 1921, at "Exhibition of Paintings Showing the Later Tendencies in Art," Penna. Academy of Fine Arts. Address in 1926, 77 Washington Place, New York City.

NAGEL, HERMAN F.
Painter. Born in Newark, NJ, in 1876. Pupil of NAD. Member: Society of Independent Artists. Address in 1926, 23 Pennington Street, Newark, NJ.

NAGLER, EDITH KROGER.
Painter, illustrator, etcher and writer. Born New York City, June 18, 1895. Pupil of ASL of NY; NAD Schools. Member: AWCS; Springfield AL; Bronx AG; Salons of Am. Address in 1929, Spuyten Duyvil, NY; summer, Stone House, Huntington, MA.

NAGLER, FRED.
Painter, etcher and writer. Born West Springfield, MA, Feb. 27, 1891. Pupil of ASL of NY. Award: Hallgarten prize, NAD, 1923; hon. mention, New Haven PCC, 1928. Address in 1929, Spuyten Duyvil, NY; summer, Huntington, MA.

NAHL, PERHAM W.
Painter and teacher. Born San Francisco, CA, Jan. 11, 1869. Studied in San Francisco, Paris, and Munich. Member: Calif. SE; FAA of the Univ. of CA; San F. AA. Represented in the Palace of Fine Arts, San Francisco; Municipal Art Gallery, Oakland; University of California. Associate Professor of Art, University of California. Died in 1935. Address in 1929, 6043 Harwood Avenue, Oakland, CA; Univ. of California, Berkeley, CA.

NAKAMIZO, FUJI.
Painter and etcher. Born Japan, Jan. 17, 1895. Pupil of Joseph Pennell, W. De Leftwich Dodge, Frank DuMond. Award: Hon. mention, Annual Arizona Art Exh., Ariz. State Fair, 1927. Died in 1950. Address in 1929, Studio No. 1, 1270 Sixth Ave., New York, NY; summer, Branchville, CT.

NANKIVELL, FRANK ARTHUR.
Painter. Born in Maldon, Victoria, Australia, 1869. Studied art in Japan, 1891-94; in San Francisco, 1894-96. Published and illustrated fortnightly magazine Chic, and made drawings for San Francisco Call, Examiner, and Chronicle; moved to New York in 1896, and illustrated daily papers; joined staff of Puck, May, 1896, as cartoonist and caricaturist. He also studied portrait painting in New York and London; later occupied as painter, illustrator and etcher for Ladies' Home Journal. Member of Association of American Painters and Sculptors. Died in 1959. Address in 1926, 33 West 14th St., New York.

NASH, FLORA.
Illustrator. Member: SI; GFLA. Address in 1929, 19 Park Ave.; 73 Riverside Dr., New York, NY.

NASH, KATHERINE E.
Sculptor and educator. Born in Minneapolis, Minn., in 1910. Studied: Univ. of Minn.; Minneapolis School of Art; Walker Art Center. Awards: National Delta Phi Delta Competition, 1932; Minnesota State Fair, 1941, 1942, 1944; Minneapolis Institute of Art, 1944; Swedish-American Exhibition, 1948; Lincoln Art Guild, 1950; Nebraska State Fair, 1951, 1952; Joslyn Art Museum, 1954; Nebraska Art Assoc., 1955; Walker Art Center, 1951; Sioux City, 1952. Collections: Univ. Medical Building, Omaha; Buffalo Minnesota Court House; Walker Art Center; Lincoln Art Guild; Nebraska Art Assoc.; Kansas State College; Concordia College; Minneapolis Public Library; Joslyn Art Museum; Omaha Assoc. of Art. Address in 1980, 21450 Excelsior Blvd., Excelsior, MN.

NASH, MARY HARRIET.
Painter and photographer. Born in Wash., DC, in 1951. Study: George Wash. U., BA Painting, 1973; Wash. State U., MFA Painting, 1976, with G. Hansen, P. W. Siler, Rbt. Helm, Francis Ho. Work: Wash. State U.; The 2nd Str. Gal., Charlottesville, VA; MacDowell Colony, Peterborough, NH; Geo. Wash. U. Permanent Coll.; Erie (PA) Art Center; Cleveland State U. One-person shows: MFA thesis, Wash. State U., 1976; 2nd St. Gal. Charlottesville, VA, 1978. Exhib: Pyramid Gal. Ltd., Wash. DC, 1978; Janet Fleisher Gal., Phila., PA, 1979; Osuna Gal., Wash. DC, 1979; Image Gal., Stockbridge, MA, 1979; Geo. Wash. U., 1980; So. OH Mus. and Cultural Ctr., Portsmouth, OH, 1981; and others. Awards: MacDowell Colony Fellowship, Peterborough, NH, 1977; hon. men., Southeastern Ctr. for Contemporary Art, Winston-Salem, NC, 1979. Bibliog.: Numerous reviews, articles. Mem.: Col. Art Assn.; MacDowell Colony Fellows; Women's Caucus for Art. Style: Folk art. Media: Oils, acrylic on canvas;

ink on paper. Address in 1983, Vienna, VA.

NASH, WILLARD AYER.
Painter and etcher. Born Philadelphia, PA, March 29, 1898. Pupil of John P. Wicker. Member: The Six Men; Scarab C. of Detroit. Died in 1943. Address in 1929, 566 Camino del Monte Sol, Sante Fe, NM.

NASON, GERTRUDE.
Painter and teacher. Born Boston, MA, Jan. 7, 1890. Pupil of Joseph De Camp, Edmund Tarbell. Member: Copley S; PBC; North Shore AA; Conn. AFA. Died in 1969. Address in 1929, 405 Bleecker St., New York, NY; summer, Lyme, CT.

NASON, THOMAS W(ILLOUGHBY).
Illustrator. Born Lowell, Mass., Jan. 7, 1889. Award: Prize for best print, Philadelphia Print Club, 1929. Address in 1929, 34 Spring St., Reading, Mass.

NAST, THOMAS.
Painter and illustrator. Born Sept. 27, 1840, at Landau, Bavaria, Germany. Studied at NAD. Lived chiefly in New York, and was famous as a caricaturist. Assignments in London and Sicily in 1860; reported for "Harper's" during Civil War and until 1886. His political cartoons were very influential. Credited with initiating the donkey and elephant as political symbols. His head of Christ painted in 1900 is in the Metropolitan Museum of New York. Died Dec. 7, 1902, at Guayaquil, Ecuador, where he was the American Consul-General.

NATHUKA, KURUMI.
Born Tokyo, Japan in 1940. Studied: Tokyo Art University, University of Delaware, Vassar College. Exhibited: Silver Mine Art Guild New England Exhibition, West Chester Art Association, Boston Philharmony Hall, Vassar College Art Gallery. Collection: Tokyo Art University. Many private collections in East Coast.

NAUMAN, F(RED) R(OBERT).
Painter, etcher and architect. Born St. Louis, Jan. 7, 1892. Award: Landscape prize, St. Louis AG, 1919. Address in 1929, 3832

West Pine Blvd.; 107 Austin Place, Glendale, MO.

NAVE, ROYSTON.
Painter. Born La Grange, Texas, Nov. 5, 1876. Pupil of Robert Henri Member: Salma. C. Exhibited "Norma" at the Penna. Academy of Fine Arts, Philadelphia, 1921. Address in 1926, 146 West 59th St., New York.

NAVIGATO, ROCCO D.
Painter. Member: GFLA; Palette and Chisel C. Address in 1929, 2321 East 70th Pl., Chicago, Ill.

NAYLOR, ALICE STEPHENSON.
Painter. Born in Columbus, TX. Studied: Witte Memorial Museum School of Art, San Antonio Art Institute, and with Charles Rosen, Etienne Ret, Andrew Dasburg, Xavier Gonzalez and Dan Lutz. Awards: River Art Group, 1953-1956; Texas Watercolor Society, 1953, 1958; Texas Art Mart, Austin, 1955; "Woman of the Year, " 1953, San Antonio; Texas Fine Arts Association, 1957; Columbus Texas Art Fair, 1957-1958; Beaumont Art Museum, 1958. Address in 1980, 125 Magnolia Dr., San Antonio, TX.

NEAGLE, JAMES.
Engraver, who died in Philadelphia, in 1822, "aged 53 years." The directories of Philadelphia contain his name for 1820-22, inclusive, as an "engraver." In 1819 he was engraving in Philadelphia, and a few well-executed portraits bear his name. His signed work is very scarce and he was possibly chiefly engaged in banknote work. Died June 24, 1922.

NEAGLE, JOHN.
Portrait painter. Born in Boston, Nov. 4, 1796; died in Phila., Sept. 17, 1865. Born of Phila. parents during their residence in Boston; educated in Phila., including some instruction with Pietro Ancora, a drawing-teacher. Also studied with Bass Otis, for two months. In 1818 he set up as a portrait painter, moving to Lexington, KY. But after two years spent there and at other points in the Mississippi Valley, he returned to Phila. and married a daughter of Thomas Sully, the

artist. His first success was a portrait of the Rev. Dr. Joseph Pilmore, one of the pioneers of Phila. Methodism. His masterpiece, however, is a full-length of Patrick Lyon, the noted blacksmith, at his forge, which long hung in the galleries of the Academy of the Fine Arts. Other portraits may be seen at the Union League, the Univ. of Penn., the Phila. Library and the rooms of the Phila. Law Association. He was one of the founders, and for eight years the president, of the Artist's Fund Society. An exhibition of his work was held at the Penna. Academy of Fine Arts in 1925. The Catalogue included a Memoir of the artist and a description of about 200 of his paintings, written by Mantle Fielding. John Neagle was elected an Honorary Member of the National Academy of Design in 1828.

NEAGLE, JOHN B.
Engraver. Born in England about 1796; died in Philadelphia in 1866. J. B. Neagle is said to have been the son of the English engraver John Neagle, born in 1760, and he was probably a pupil of his father. He came to Philadelphia when quite young, as he engraved, in 1815-18, a portrait of Dr. Caspar Wistar for "Delaplaine's Gallery."

NEAL, DAVID.
Painter. Born in Lowell, Mass., Oct. 20, 1838. He went to Europe in 1862; studied in Paris and Munich. He painted numerous historical romantic works, including "Mary Stuart and Riccio," "Oliver Cromwell Visits John Milton," "Nuns at Prayer," "James Watt in the Crypt," "Retour de Chasse," etc. His later work was portraiture, including portraits of Adolph Sutro; Rev. Mark Hopkins; Judge Hoffman of Calif.; D. O. Mills; Teackle Wallis; Misses Gladys and Beatrice Mills (daughters of Ogden Mills); Prof. Henry Green; Whitelaw Reid, etc. Died May 2, 1915 in Munich, Germany.

NEAL, GRACE PRUDEN.
Sculptor. Born St. Paul, MN, May 11, 1876. Studied in Chicago and Paris. Awards: First prize,

Minnesota Art Soc., 1906; hon. mention, AIC, 1917.
Work: Statue presented to London by the Associated Advertising Clubs of the World; Memorial, Cochran Park, St. Paul, MN; bust, Gov. A. O. Eberhard, Minnesota. Address in 1929, 38 West 76th St., New York, NY.

NEALE, MARGUERITE B.
Painter. Member: Wash. WCC. Address in 1929, La Salle Apartments, Washington, DC.

NEANDROSS, LIEF.
Painter. Member: NYWCC; NSS (assoc.). Address in 1929, Ridgefield, NJ.

NEANDROSS, SIGURD.
Sculptor. Born Stavanger, Norway, Sept. 16, 1871; came to America at age of 10; US citizen, 1894. Pupil of Cooper Union evening classes in New York; P. S. Kroyer and Stefan Sinding in Copenhagen. Member: NSS. Award: Mention, collaborative competition, NY Arch. Lg., 1915. Died in 1958. Address in 1929, Ridgefield, NJ.

NEBEL, BERTHOLD.
Sculptor. Member: NSS (assoc.). Award: Fellowship American Academy at Rome, 1914-17. Died in 1964. Address in 1929, Bible House, New York, NY; American Academy in Rome, Porta San Pancrazio, Rome, Italy.

NEEBE, MINNIE HARMS.
Painter. Born in Chicago, Ill., in 1873. Pupil of Hawthorne, Browne, Webster, Reynolds, Ufer. Member of Chicago Society of Artists. Address in 1926, 1320 Clybourn Ave., Chicago, Ill.

NEEDHAM, A(LFRED) C(ARTER).
Painter. Born Beechville, Canada, Jan. 28, 1872. Member: Copley S.; Rockport AA; Gloucester North Shore AA. Address in 1929, 10 High St., Boston, Mass.; h. Manchester, Mass.

NEEDHAM, CHARLES AUSTIN.
Landscape painter. Born in Buffalo, NY, on Oct. 30, 1844; died Nov. 24, 1923. Pupil of Art Students' League, and of August Will of New York. Honorable mention and medal, Atlanta

International Exposition, 1895; honorable mention, New York State Agricultural Exposition, Syracuse, 1898. Represented in St. Louis Museum of Fine Arts, and in Annual Exhibition of American Water Color Society, 1906-7-8. Member: American Water Color Society; New York Water Color Club.

NEELD, C(LARENCE) E(LLSWORTH).
Painter. Born New Albany, Ind., May 7, 1895. Pupil of Menoir, Claude Buck, James Topping. Member: Hoosier Art Patrons A; All-Illinois, SFA. Address in 1929, 270 Bryant Ave., Glen Ellyn, Ill.

NEGRON, WILLIAM.
Illustrator. Born in Bayonne, NJ, in 1925. Studied: Cooper Union, SVA and the Pratt Graphics Workshop. For several years he held the position of art director for Clairol. His editorial illustrations have appeared in The New York Times, Exxon's magazine The Lamp and in several travel books. In addition to his editorial work, he is active in advertising design and book illustration for such clients as Houghton Mifflin.

NEGUS, CAROLINE.
Painter. Born in 1814. Portrait painter in crayon and miniatures, working in Boston, Mass., 1844-56. She shared a studio with her cousin, the artist George Fuller. Died in 1867.

NEHLIG, VICTOR.
Painter. Born in Paris in 1830. Pupil of Cogniet. He came to the United States in 1856, having resided for some time in Cuba. He settled in New York where he was elected an Associate Member of the National Academy in 1863, and an Academician in 1870. Many of his works are historical subjects; his "The Cavalry Charge" was in the New York Historical Society. Among his best known paintings are "Battle of Antietam," "Waiting for the Enemy," "Gertrude of Wyoming," and "The Artist's Dream." Died in 1909.

NEIBART, WALLY.
Illustrator. Born in Camden, NJ, in 1925. Studied for four years

under Henry Pitz at the Philadelphia College of Art, where he later returned to teach drawing. Since 1952, the year of his first illustration for the Philadelphia Inquirer, he has worked for many major magazines including Esquire, Playboy, Good Housekeeping and The New Republic. His works are in several private collections and have been shown in exhibitions at the Philadelphia Art Alliance, Widmeir and Chelterham Art Center.

NEILL, FRANCIS ISABEL.
Painter, etcher and teacher. Born Warren, PA, July 24, 1871. Studied in New York, Boston and Paris. Member: NA Women PS; Buffalo AA; MacD. C. Address in 1929, Harperley Hall, 1 West 64th St., New York, NY.

NEILL, JOHN R.
Illustrator. Member: Salma. C.; Fellowship PAFA. Address in 1929, 36 East 28th St.; 593 Riverside Drive, New York, NY.

NEILSON, RAYMOND P(ERRY) RODGERS.
Painter. Born New York, 1881. Pupil of ASL of NY and Chase in New York; Laurens and Lucien Simon and of Richard Miller in Paris. Member: ANA, 1925; Salma. C. Awards: Silver medal, Paris Salon, 1914; silver medal, P.-P. Exp., San F., 1915. Work: "Le Chapeau Noir," owned by French Government. Died in 1964. Address in 1929, 114 East 66th St., New York, NY.

NEIMAN, LEROY.
Painter and printmaker. Born in St. Paul, MN, June 8, 1926. Study: Art Inst. of Chicago; Univ. of Chicago; Univ. of Chicago; Univ. of IL. Collections: Illinois State Museum; Joslyn Museum, Omaha; Wodham College, Oxford, England; National Museum of Sport, NY; Hermitage, Leningrad, USSR; and others. Comn.: Murals, Continental Hotel, Chicago, 1963. Swedish Lloyd Ship, Stockholm, 1966; Sportsmen's Park, Cicero, IL, 1976; others. Exhibitions: O'Hana Gallery, London; Galerie O. Bosc, Paris; Group shows: Carnegie Internat'l, Pittsburgh; Corcoran American, Washington, DC, 1957; Art Inst. of Chicago, 1960; Hammer Galleries, NYC, 1979; Neiman-Warhol, Los Angeles Inst. Contemp. Art, 1981; others. Awards: Salon d'Art Moderne, Paris; outstanding sports artist awards, Amateur Athletic Union; others. Positions: Sports Artist, NY Jets; ABC-TV; Major League Baseball Promotions; 1972 & 76; Teacher of Art Inst. of Chicago, 1960-70; others. Media: Oil, enamel, serigraph, etching. Rep's.: Hammer Galleries, NYC. Address in 1983, 1 W. 67th, New York, NY.

NELL, (MISS) TONY.
Painter, illustrator and teacher. Born Washington, DC. Pupil of Chase; DuMond; Denver Students' School of Art. Member: NYWCC; Chicago WCC. Awards: Beal prize, NYWCC, 1910; Harriet Brooks Jones prize, Baltimore WCC, 1921. Address in 1929, 2 Riverview Terrace, New York, NY.

NELL, WILLIAM.
Painter. Exhibited a landscape at the Penna. Academy of Fine Arts, Philadelphia, 1921. Address in 1926, 106 South Troy Ave., Ventnor, NJ.

NELSON, G. PATRICK.
Illustrator. Member: SI; GFLA; Salma. C. Address in 1929, 1947 Broadway, Rm. 622, New York, NY.

NELSON, GEORGE LAURENCE.
Painter and teacher. Born New Rochelle, NY, Sept. 26, 1887. Pupil of NAD; Laurens in Paris. Member: ANA, 1929; Allied AA; Salma. C.; AWCS; Conn. AFA; NYWCC; NY Arch. Lg. (assoc.); Kent AA. Awards: Dunham portrait prize, Conn. AFA, 1918 and 1928; Isidor gold medal, NAD, 1921. Work: Portraits in New York Hospital and Mt. Sinai Hospital, New York; Reed Memorial Library, Carmel, NY; murals, "The Ideal School," School 55, the Bronx; "The Graduate," State Normal School, Plattsburgh, NY; portrait of Admiral Sims, Peace Palace, Geneva, Switzerland; "The Winged Book," mural, School 40, New York, NY. Instructor, National Academy of Design. Address in 1929, 15 West 67th St., New York, NY.

NELSON.
Dunlap records in his sketch of Chester Harding a portrait painter of that name who painted signs. Nelson had painted on his own sign a copy of Sir Joshua Reynolds' "Infant Artists." He painted portraits of Harding and his wife for $10 each, but refused to give the former any information about his method of working.

NEMOEDE, EDA.
See Mrs. Casterton.

NESBIT, ROBERT H.
Landscape painter. Elected an Associate Member of the National Academy of Design. His painting "The Hurrying River," at one time owned by the Telfair Academy of Savannah, GA, was exhibited at the Centennial Exhibition of the National Academy, 1925. Address in 1926, South Kent, Conn.

NESBITT, LOWELL.
Painter and printmaker. Born in Baltimore, MD, Oct. 4, 1933. Study: Tyler Sch. Fine Arts, Temple U., Phila., BFA; Royal College of Art, London. Work: Corcoran Gallery, Wash., DC; Detroit Art Institute; Library of Congress, Wash., DC; MOMA, NYC; Art Inst. Chicago; Nat'l. Aeronautic and Space Admin. (NASA); Yale Univ. Art Gallery; Environmental Protection Agency Wash., DC; Nat'l Gal. of Art, Wash., DC; many others in US; Aachen, Ger.; Wellington, New Zealand; Paris; Goteborg, Sweden; Monrovia; Tanzania; Tel Aviv. One-man shows: Baltimore Mus. of Art 1958, 69; Corcoran Gallery, Wash., DC, 1964, 75; Rolf Nelson Gallery, Los Angeles, 1965, 66; Gertrude Kasle Gallery, Detroit, 1966, 67, 69, 70, 71, 73; Gallerie M.E. Thelen, Cologne, Ger., 1969, 70, 72; Andrew Crispo Gallery, NYC, 1975, 77; and many others in US, London, Zurich, Copenhagen, Brussels, Toronto, Caracas, Sweden (Goteborg and Malmo).

NESEMAN, ENNO.
Painter. Born in Maysville, Calif., April 25, 1861. Pupil of Alfred Hart. Member: Society of Independent Artists. Work: "The First Discovery of Gold in California at Sutter's Mill," De Young Memorial Museum, San Francisco, California. Address in 1926, 1635 Euclid Ave., Berkeley, Calif. Died in 1949. (Also spelled Eno Nesemann).

NESMITH, J. H.
Engraver. In 1805-18 this line-engraver was making illustrations for the encyclopedia published by S. F. Bradford, of Philadelphia. In 1824 his name as engraver is associated with that of J. B. Longacre, and in 1828 Nesmith was working for New Haven publishers.

NESSIM, BARBARA.
Illustrator. Born in NYC in 1939. Received a BFA from PI and taught at SVA from 1967 to 1975. Her works have been shown in the Louvre, Mead Gallery, Whitney Museum, AIGA and the Erotic Art Gallery and have received awards from the S of I, AIGA and ADC. Her poster works were commissioned by Lincoln Centre and WBAI.

NETTLETON, WALTER.
Landscape painter. Born New Haven, Conn., June 19, 1861. Pupil of Boulanger and Lefebvre in Paris. Member: ANA, 1905; SAA, 1901. Awards: Hon. mention, Paris Salon, 1892; silver medal, St. Louis Exp., 1904; gold medal, AAS, 1907; bronze medal, Buenos Aires and Santiago Exp., 1910. Work: "December Sunshine," Yale Art Museum, New Haven; "A January Morning," Museum of Art, New Britain, Conn.; "The Beloved Physician," Jackson Library, Stockbridge, Mass.; "Waldesdammerung," Vassar College Art Gallery. Address in 1929, Stockbridge, Mass.

NEUBAUER, FREDERICK AUGUST.
Landscape painter and illustrator. Born in Cincinnati, 1855. Pupil of Cincinnati Art Academy. Member: Cincinnati Art Club. Address in 1929, 22 Hulbert Block, Sixth and Vine Sts., Cincinnati, Ohio.

NEUFELD, PAULA.
Painter. Born in Berlin, Germany. Studied: Art Institute, Berlin; Berlin Academy of Art; and with von Koenig, Eugene Spiro, and Willy

Jaekel; Colorado Springs Fine Arts Center. Award: Fellowship, Huntington Hartford Foundation, 1957. Collections: Bernheimer Memorial, Kansas City, Missouri; Temple B'nai Jehudah, Kansas City; Mannheim Museum, Germany; Jewish Museum, Berlin; Jackson County Circuit Court.

NEUHAUS, EUGEN.
Painter, writer, lecturer and teacher. Born Barmen, Germany, Aug. 18, 1879. Pupil of Royal Art School, Kassel; Institute of Applied Art, Berlin. Member: San Francisco AA. Chairman of Western Advisory Committee and member of Int. Jury of Awards, Panama-Pacific Exp., San Francisco, 1915. Professor of Art, University of California. Died in 1963. Address in 1929, 2922 Derby Street, Berkeley, Calif.

NEUHAUSER, MARGUERITE PHILLIPS.
(Mrs. Roy L. Neuhauser). Painter. Born in North Arlington, VA, in 1888. Pupil of Bertha Perrie, George Noyes, Corcoran School of Art. Member: S. Wash. A.; Wash. AC; SSAL; North Shore AA. Address in 1929, 1847 Kalorama Rd., Washington, DC.

NEUMAN, ROBERT S.
Painter. Born Sept. 9, 1926 in Kellogg, Idaho. Studied at S.F. Art Inst.; Cal. Col. of Arts and Crafts; Mills College; and at Kunste in Karlsruhe, Germany. Taught at Brown, Harvard, and Keene State Col., NH. Awarded Fullbright (1953); Guggenheim (1958) and award from Boston Arts Festival. Exhibited at Gump's Gallery, S.F. (1952); Felix Landau Gallery, L.A. (1954); Swetzoff Gallery, Boston; Allan Stone Gallery, NYC; Denver; Carnegie; and Seattle World's Fair (1962). In collections of Yale; Worcester Art Mus.; MOMA; Inst. of Contemp. Art; S.F. Mus. of Art; Boston, and Addison Gallery.

NEVELSON, LOUISE.
Sculptor and printmaker. Born in Kiev, Russia, Sept. 23, 1900. Studied in US, Europe and Central America; ASL, 1928-30; with Hans Hofmann, Munich, 1931; assistant to Diego Rivera, 1932-33.

Collections: Museum of Fine Arts, Houston; Farnsworth Museum, Rockland, Maine; Brandeis Univ.; Birmingham Museum of Art; Whitney Museum of American Art; Museum of Modern Art; St. Peter's Church, NYC; NY Univ.; Queens College; Carnegie Institute; Riverside Museum, NYC; Univ. of Nebraska; Brooklyn Museum. Exhib. at Brooklyn Mus.; Nierendorf Gal.; Grand Central Moderns Gal.; Whitney; MOMA; many others. She has been called "the most distinguished woman sculptor in America and one of the great sculptors of the world." Her wooden assemblage sculpture is usually painted black. Other media include stone, plaster, terra cotta, metals; other colors are white and gold. Address in 1982, 29 Spring St., NY, NY.

NEVIN, BLANCHE.
Sculptor. Born in 1838 in Mercersburg, Penna. She studied art in Philadelphia, and later in Italy. She executed many portrait busts, and her statue of Peter Muhlenberg was erected in the Capitol in Washington, DC. She died April 21, 1925 in Lancaster, PA.

NEWBY, MRS. RUBY WARREN.
Painter, craftswoman and teacher. Born Goff, Kans., July 28, 1886. Pupil of Everett Warner; Kathryn Cherry; R. P. Ensign; Ernest Watson; Will Taylor; Gustave Cimiotti; Merlin Pease. Member: Orlando AA; SSAL; AFA. Awards: First and second prize, South Florida Fair, 1927; Carnegie Scholarship, Harvard S. S., 1928-29; Orange Co. C of C prize, 1928 (landscape), Gainesville, Fla. Work: "Woods Interior," Orlando Public Library. Director of Art, Rollins College, Winter Park, Fla. Address in 1929, Rollins College, Winter Park, Fla.; h. 1358 Richmond Rd., Winter Park, Fla.

NEWCOMB, D.
This name as engraver appears upon vignettes on the title-page of books published in Boston, in 1820. Judging from his work, Newcomb was probably one of the banknote

engravers then in business in Boston.

NEWCOMBE, GEO. W.
Painter. Born Sept. 22, 1799 in England. He came to New York in 1829 and became a successful painter of portraits in oils and miniatures. He was elected an Associate Member of the National Academy in 1832. He died in New York, Feb. 10, 1845.

NEWELL, G(EORGE) GLENN.
Painter. Born Berrian Co., MI, 1870. Pupil of NAD under F. C. Jones and Ward; Teachers College, New York, under Will S. Robinson, and W. H. Howe. Member: ANA; Salma. C., 1898; AWCS; NAC; Allied AA; Am. Soc. Animal PS; NYWCC; Am. PS; Lotos C.; Aquarellists; SPNY. Awards: Prize ($500) Salma. C., 1906; Speyer prize, NAD, 1923. Work: "Mists of the Morning," National Gallery, Washington; "Twilight," Detroit Institute; "My Pets" and "The Old Red Mill," Art Assn., Dallas, TX; "The Unconquered" and "Monarch of All He Surveys," "The Drovers' Inn," Butler Museum, Youngstown, Ohio. Represented in National Arts Club; Lotos Club; Salmagundi Club. Specialty, cattle and sheep. Died in 1947. Address in 1929, 57th St. and Seventh Ave., New York, NY.

NEWELL, HUGH.
Born in Belfast, Ireland, Oct. 4, 1830. He came to this country as a youth and resided for eight years in Pittsburgh, Penna., moving to Baltimore when he became connected with the Maryland Institute and the Johns Hopkins University. He was a member of the American Water Color Society. Among his pictures are "The Country Musician," "The Cottage Window," "In the Sugar Camp" and "Woods in Winter." Died in Bloomfield, NJ.

NEWELL, PETER SHEAD HERSEY.
Illustrator. Born March 5, 1862 in McDonough County, Illinois. Pupil of ASL of New York. He died in Little Neck, LI, Jan. 15, 1924. Most of his work was done for the Harpers publishing firm.

NEWER, THESIS.
Painter. 876 Adams Ave., Franklin Square, NY. Born: NY, January 6, 1918. Study: Acad. Delle Belle Arte, Florence, 4 yrs.; Pratt Inst. Interior Design, Grad. Work: Private Collections only. Exhibitions: Allied Artists of America; American APL; Knickerbocker Artists; Hudson Valley Art Assn.; others. Awards: National Art League, gold medal, Nat'l Arts Chile; Am. APL; C. Lorillard Wolfe Art Club; and others. Mem.: Am. APL; Catharine Lorillard Wolfe Art Club; Nat'l. Art League; AAA; others. Rep.: Thomson Gallery, NYC.

NEWHALL, DONALD V.
Painter and illustrator. Born in England in 1890. Pupil of Penna. Academy of Fine Arts. Address in 1926, 140 West 57th St., New York.

NEWHALL, HARRIOT B.
Painter, etcher and teacher. Born Topeka, Kansas, June 23, 1874. Pupil of Benson, Tarbell, and Hawthorne. Member: Copley S.; Provincetown AA. Address in 1929, 157 Commercial St., Provincetown, Mass.

NEWLIN, SARA JULIA.
See Mrs. Donald MacGregor.

NEWMAN, ALLEN GEORGE.
Sculptor. Born New York, Aug. 28, 1875. Pupil of J. Q. A. Ward. Member: ANA, 1926; NSS, 1907; Beaux-Arts Inst.; NAC; Numismatic Soc.; AFA. Award: NAC prize ($500) for design for "Valor Medal." Work: Marble figures; "Day and Night," Harriman Bank, New York; Henry Hudson Monument, New York; "The Hiker," Providence, RI; "Gate City Guard Peace Monument" and portrait of "Joel Chandler Harris Monument," Atlanta, GA; statue of "Governor Oates," Montgomery, AL; "Gen. Philip Sheridan Monument," Scranton, PA; "Doughboy Monument," Pittsburgh, PA. Died in 1940. Address in 1929, 1947 Broadway; h. 263 West 71st St., New York, NY; summer, Marbletown, NY.

NEWMAN, ANNA MARY.
Painter, illustrator and teacher. Born Richmond, IN. Pupil of AIC; School of Applied and Normal Art, Chicago; Overbeck School of Design and Pottery, Cambridge City, IN. Member: Alumni AIC; Chicago ASL; Richmond AA; Ind. AC; Richmond Palette C; AFA. Awards: Richmond AA prize, 1908; Indiana State Fair prize, 1914. Work: "Old Irish Chain Quilt," Vanderpoel Memorial, Chic.; "William Mossman," Y.M.C.A., Fort Wayne, IN; "Chester T. Lane," High School, Fort Wayne, IN; "Judge Erwin," Supreme Court, Indianapolis. Instructor in Art at Fort Wayne High School. Address in 1929, 25 North 16th St., Richmond, Ind.

NEWMAN, B. P.
Newman was a very good engraver of landscape, working in New York in 1860.

NEWMAN, BLOSSOM.
Sculptor. Studied: Pratt Institute, Brooklyn, New York; University of Hartford Art School, Connecticut; Museum School, Boston, Massachusetts; Karlsruhe, Germany. Awards: Lowell Art, 1967; Sudbury Art, 1965. Exhibitions: Boston Center for Adult Education, 1974; Copley Society, Boston, 1974; Manchester Art Association, Massachusetts, 1974.

NEWMAN, CARL.
Painter. Born in 1858. Exhibited in Philadelphia in 1921, in "Exhibition of Paintings Showing the Later Tendencies in Art," PAFA. Address in 1926, Beth Ayres, Penna. Died in 1932.

NEWMAN, CLARA G.
Painter and teacher. Born Brownsville, Neb., Sept. 10, 1870. Pupil of J. E. Forkner, Felix Mahony, Elizabeth Overbeck Potter, Randolph La Salle Coates. Member: Hoosier Salon; Richmond AA; Richmond PC. Address in 1929, 59 South 17th St., Richmond, Ind.

NEWMAN, ELIAS.
Painter, writer and teacher. Born Poland, Feb. 12, 1903. Pupil of NAD; Educational Alliance Art School, New York. Member: S.

Indp. A; Soc. Palestine Artists. Work: "Vade Muserarah," Baltimore Museum of Art, Baltimore, MD. Address in 1929, 1604 49th St., Brooklyn, NY.

NEWMAN, HARRY W.
Painter and teacher. Born London, England, June 26, 1873. Pupil of Bridgman, Henri. Member: Bronx AG; Salma. C. Address in 1929, 3016 Bronx Blvd., Williamsbridge, New York, NY.

NEWMAN, HENRY RODERICK.
Painter. Born in New York City about 1833. He had his studio in New York State in 1861-69, and after that in Florence, Italy. He is noted for his water color painting of architectural subjects, landscapes and flower pieces. He was a friend of John Ruskin. Died in 1917 in Florence.

NEWMAN, HENRY.
Portrait painter. Born in 1843. Dealer in artists' supplies. He lived in Philadelphia for over fifty years. He died in 1921.

NEWMAN, ISIDORA.
Painter, sculptor, illustrator, craftswoman, writer and lecturer. Born New Orleans, LA, April 23, 1878. Author of "Fairy Flowers." Address in 1929, 2 West 89th St.; h. 285 Central Park West, New York, NY.

NEWMAN, JOSEPH.
Painter. Born New York City, Sept. 4, 1890. Pupil of Pratt Inst.; Whittaker. Member: Allied AA; Salons of Am.; Painters and Sculptors; Brooklyn SA; Tiffany Foundation Alumni; NYWCC. Represented in Newark Museum, Newark, NJ. Address in 1929, 609 Rutland Rd., Brooklyn, NY.

NEWMAN, ROBERT LOFTIN.
Painter. Born 1827. Born in Richmond, VA. As a youth he read much about art, and in 1850 went to Europe with the intention of studying at Dusseldorf, but having stopped in Paris, he entered the atelier of Thomas Couture. Upon returning to Tennessee he made a second trip to Paris in 1854, and formed the acquaintance of William

M. Hunt, who introduced him to Jean Francois Millet. In 1882 and subsequently he made several trips to Barbizon, and his work shows the influence of the group of masters who made that modest village a household word. He has been called the American Diaz on account of his poetic coloring. Died March 31, 1912 in NYC.

NEWMAN, WILLIE BETTY.
(Mrs. J. W. Newman). Painter. Born Murfreesboro, Tenn. Pupil of Cincinnati Art School under T. S. Noble; Constant, Bouguereau, Bachet, Robert Fleury and Laurens in Paris, and in Holland and Italy. Awards: Hon. mention, Paris Salon, 1900; gold medal, Nashville AA; first prize, Tenn. State Fair, 1914-15-16-17. Work: "Fisherman's Daughter," Cincinnati Museum; "En Penitence," Nashville Art Association; "Le Pain Benite," Centennial Club, Nashville; "Reverie," Philadelphia Art Club; "Mrs. E. W. Cole," and "Bishop Galloway," Vanderbilt University; "Bishop Galloway," University of Mississippi; "Hon. John Bell," U. S. Capitol, Washington. Address in 1929, Hotel Tulane, Nashville, Tenn.

NEWPORT, JAMES W.
Miniature painter, who flourished in Philadelphia, 1846-47, and exhibited at the Penna. Academy in 1847.

NEWSAM, ALBERT.
Lithographer. Born, deaf and dumb, May 20, 1809, at Steubenville, Ohio; died near Wilmington, Del., Nov. 20, 1864. His natural artistic bent was cultivated by placing him under the tuition of the artists George Catlin and Hugh Bridport. In 1927 Newsam was apprenticed to Cephas G. Childs to be taught engraving, and two examples of copperplate engraving are known to Fielding signed "A. Newsam, sc. Deaf & Dumb, Childs dir." These are two good stipple-engravings of "Anna" and "Queen Dido," published in the Casket of Philadelphia. A catalogue of the "Lithograph Portraits of Albert Newsam" was written by Danl. Stauffer and

published in the Pennsylvania Magazine of History and Biography, Oct. 1900-Jan. 1901, and April 1901.

NEWTON, EDITH WHITTLESEY.
Painter. Born in 1878. Exhibited at the 33d Annual Exhibition of the National Association of Women Painters and Sculptors. Address in 1926, New Milford, Conn.

NEWTON, FRANCIS.
Painter. Born in Lake George, NY, in 1873. Pupil of Howard Pyle in Wilmington, Del.; Art Students' League and Chase School, New York; Drexel Institute, Philadelphia; Colarossi Academy in Paris. Member: New York Architectural League, 1911; Wilmington SFA; Am. APL; Mural Painters; New York Municipal Artists' Society; League of New York Artists. Died in 1944. Address in 1929, Easthampton, LI, NY.

NEWTON, GILBERT STUART.
Portrait painter. Born Sept. 20, 1794 in Halifax, Nova Scotia, Canada; died Aug. 5, 1835 in Chelsea, England. He was the nephew of Gilbert Stuart and studied for a while under his uncle. He went to France and England and arrived in London in company with C. R. Lelie in 1817. Dunlap in his "History of the Arts of Design" gives an extended account of Newton, and quotes Washington Irving's recollections of the artist.

NEWTON, JOSEPHINE PITKIN.
(Mrs. R. C. Newton). Painter. Member: NA Women PS. Address in 1929, Scarsdale, NY.

NEWTON, MARION C.
Painter. Born in Boston, MA, in 1902. Studied: Radcliffe College; Parsons School of Design; and with Ivan Olinsky, Lydia Field Emmet, and George Bridgman; also studied in Paris. Collections: Metropolitan Museum of Art; Museum of City of NY; Detroit Institute of Art; US Lines; Baseball Hall of Fame, Cooperstown, NY; Ladies Home Journal, Good Housekeeping, and McCalls.

NEY, ELIZABETH.
Sculptor. Born in 1833 in Westphalia, Ger., and patronized by the "mad king" Ludwig II of Bavaria. She left her home for political reasons, and settled in Texas in 1873. Her memorial to Genl. Albert Sidney Johnson for the cemetery at Austin, Texas, is very fine. Died June 30, 1907, in Austin, TX.

NEYLAND, HARRY.
Painter and sculptor. Born McKean, Erie Co., Penn. in 1877. Pupil of NY ASL, Paris. Works: Memorial tablets, Whaling Enshrined, Inc.; "Surf and Sunlight," Hudson Motor Car Co. Illustrations for "Cap'n George Fred," pub. by Doubleday, Doran and Co. Address in 1929, Cor. Orchard and Hawthorn Sts., New Bedford, Mass.; h. So. Dartmouth, Mass.

NICHOLDSON, J. D.
Engraver. As "J. D. Nicholdson sc" this name is signed to line work done for an encyclopedia published by E. Lucas, Jr., Baltimore, MD. The date is about 1830.

NICHOLLS, BURR H.
Painter. Born Dec., 1848, in Lockport, NY. He studied with Sellstedt in Buffalo, and with Carolus-Duran in Paris. Represented at Penna. Academy of Fine Arts by "Effect of Sunlight"; at Peabody Institute, Baltimore, by "Hunting Up a Quotation"; in Fine Arts Academy, Buffalo, by "A Group of Fowls." He died May 12, 1915, in Stamford, Conn.

NICHOLLS, JOSEPHINE (LEWIS).
(Mrs. Burr H. Nicholls). Painter, writer and lecturer. Born Hamilton, Ontario, Canada, Sept. 26, 1865. Pupil of Siddons Mowbray, George Bridgman, Lucius Hitchcock. Member: Alliance; Prof. AL; Guild of Allied Arts; Buffalo SA; Lg. Am. Pen Women. Award: Hon. mention, Pan-Am. Exp., Buffalo, 1901. Address in 1929, 188 Franklin St., Buffalo, NY.

NICHOLLS, MRS. RHODA HOLMES.
Painter, illustrator, writer and teacher. Born Coventry, England, March 28, 1854; came to America in 1884. Pupil of Bloomsbury School of Art in London; Cammerano and Vertunni in Rome. Member: ASL of NY; AWCS; NYWCC; ASMP; MacD. C.; Woman's Art Assoc., Canada (hon.); SPNY; NA Women PS. Awards: gold medal, Competitive Prize Fund Exh., New York; medal, Columbian Exp., Chicago, 1893; medal, Atlanta Exp., 1895; medal, Nashville Exp., 1897; medal, Boston; medal, Charlotte, NC; bronze medal, Pan-Am. Exp., Buffalo, 1901; bronze medal, Charleston Exp., 1902; bronze medal, St. Louis Exp., 1904. Work: "The Scarlet Letter," "Those Evening Bells," "Indian After the Chase," and "Searching the Scriptures," Boston Art Club; "Prima Vera, Venezia," and "Water Lilies," Boston Museum of Fine Arts. Living in New York in 1926. Address in 1929, Stamford, CT.

NICHOLS, EDWARD W.
Painter. Born April 23, 1819 in Orford, NH. He was elected an Associate Member of the National Academy in 1861. He died Sept. 21, 1871 in Peekskill, NY.

NICHOLS, FREDERICK B.
Engraver. Born in Bridgeport, Conn., in 1824. Mr. Nichols learned to engrave with the New York firm of Rawdon, Wright, Hatch & Smillie, the last being his chief instructor. He then went into business for himself, and about 1846 he published "Nichols Illustrated New York," with views engraved by himself. In 1848 he invented a process for relief-engraving. Mr. Nichols was a good landscape engraver and did considerable work for the New York publishers, but in 1858 he abandoned engraving with the intention of promoting certain inventions of his own. Died in 1906 in Bridgeport.

NICHOLS, H(ARLEY) D(eWITT).
Landscape painter and illustrator. Born Barton, Washington Co., WI, Feb. 3, 1859. Pupil of Hakel in Munich. Member: NYWCC; Salma. C.; GFLA. Illustrated "French and English Furniture" and "Loves of Great Poets," Did architectural illustrations for books and magazines, chiefly for "Harper's"

and "Century." Address in 1929, 189 Montague St.; h. 1208 Pacific St., Brooklyn, NY.

NICHOLS, HENRY HOBART.
Landscape painter and illustrator. Born Washington, DC, May 1, 1869. Pupil of Howard Helmick and ASL in Washington; Julian Academy and Castellucho in Paris. Member: ANA 1912; NA 1920; S. Wash. A.; Fellowship PAFA; Wash. WCC; NYWCC; Salma. C.; NAC; Allied AA; Lotos C; Cosmos C; Cent. C; Conn. AFA; North Shore AA. Awards: Second Corcoran prize, Wash. WCC, 1901; Parsons prize, S. Wash. A., 1902; Parsons prize, Wash. WCC, 1904; first Corcoran prize, Wash. WCC, 1906; Turnbull prize ($100), Salma. C., 1913; Evans prize ($100), Salma C., 1915; bronze medal, NAC, 1915; silver medal ($300), NAC, 1920; 2nd Altman prize, NAD, 1923; Vezin prize, Salma. C., 1924; first Altman prize, NAD, 1925; Salma. C. prize ($1,000), 1927; NAD Club prize ($1,000), 1928. Assistant to Director of Fine Arts, U.S. Commission, Paris Exp., 1900. Work: "Moonrise at Ogunquit," National Gallery, Washington; Museum of Natural History, New York; Corcoran Gallery of Art, Washington, DC; Metropolitan Museum, New York. Died in 1962. Address in 1929, Lawrence Park, West, Bronxville, NY.

NICHOLS, JOHN W.
Etcher. Born Keokuk, Iowa, Aug. 1, 1881. Pupil of Charles A. Cumming; Scott Clifton Carbee; Ernest Haskell. Address in 1929, 520 Steinway Hall, New York, NY; h. 105-14 29th Ave., E. Elmhurst, NY; summer, Commonwealth Art Colony, Boothbay Harbor, ME.

NICHOLS, PEGGY (MARTIN).
Painter and sculptor. Born in Atchison, Kans., in 1884. Pupil of Cecilia Beaux and Chase. Member: California Art Club. Address in 1926, 517 South Coronado St., Los Angeles, Calif.

NICHOLS, SPENCER B(AIRD).
Painter and teacher. Born Washington, DC, Feb. 13, 1875. Pupil of ASL in Washington under Howard Helmick; Corcoran Art School. Member: ANA; Allied AA; NY Arch. Lg.; Wash. WCC; S. Wash. A.; Salma. C.; NYWCC; AWCS; Grand Central AG; NAD (assoc.). Award: Third Corcoran prize, S. Wash. A., 1901. Work: "Andrew Stephenson" and "John Marshall," House of Representatives, US Capitol; "Holy City," mural in Fifth Avenue Presbyterian Church, New York; Ranger Fund Purchase, "The Bathers," Beloit, WI, Art Gallery. Died in 1950. Address in 1929, Kent, CT.

NICHOLS, WARD H.
Painter. Address in 1982, Wilkesboro, NC. Born in Welch, WV, July 5, 1930. Work: Springfield Mus. of Art, MA; Huntington Gallery of Art, WV; others. Exhibitions: National Academy Galleries, NY; Museum of Fine Arts, Spgfld, MA; Miss. Mus. of Art, Jackson; others. Awards: Grumbacher Award of Merit, El Paso Mus. of Art, TX; Merit award, Miss. Mus. of Art, Jackson; others. Media: Oil.

NICHOLSON, DELOS CHARLES.
Illustrator, lecturer and teacher. Born Edgerton, WI. Member: 2 x 4 Soc.; Faculty of St. Louis School of Fine Arts. Address in 1929, 864 Providence Ave., Webster Groves, MO.

NICHOLSON, ISABEL L(EDCREIGH).
Painter and sculptor. Born St. Louis, March 28, 1890. Pupil of Tarbell; Richard Brooks; Lee Randolph; Ruth Ball; Bohnen and Loup in Lausanne. Member: NA Women PS; San Diego SFA; Carmel SAC; AFA. Address in 1929, Studio Bldg.; h. La Playa Hotel, Carmel, CA.

NICHT, EDWARD W(ILLIAM).
Painter. Born Auburn, NY, March 7, 1872. Pupil of H. R. Poore; Leith-Ross. Award: First prize for group of water colors, NY State Fair, Syracuse, 1912. Address in 1929, 135 Minerva St., Syracuse, NY.

NICOLL, JAMES CRAIG.
Marine painter and etcher. Born Nov. 22, 1847 in NYC. Elected an Associate of the National Academy of Design, 1880, and an

Academician, 1885. He worked with M. F. H. de Haas. Represented by "Squally Weather" in the Metropolitan Museum of New York. He was awarded many mentions and medals for his marine painting and etchings, and his water colors were well known; among those exhibited were "On the Gulf of St. Lawrence," "Off Portland Harbor" and "Stormy Day at Block Island." Died July 25, 1918 in Norwalk, Conn.

NICOLOSI, JOSEPH.
Painter, sculptor, etcher, architect, writer, lecturer and teacher. Born Sicily, Aug. 4, 1893. Came to U.S. in 1912. Pupil of Beaux Arts Inst., Solon Borglum, Edward McCarten. Member: NSS; NY Arch. Lg. Awards: Two bronze medals, 1917, 1919; five second-place medals, Beaux Arts Institute. Work: Dr. M. B. Heyman, Manhattan State Hospital; New Brighton, Penn., War Memorial; World War Memorial, Morristown, NJ. Died in 1961. Address in 1929, 3 East 14th St., New York, NY.

NICOLSON, EDITH REYNAUD.
(Mrs. H. W. Nicolson). Illustrator. Born in Mount Vernon, NY, in 1896. Pupil of New York School of Applied Design for Women. Address in 1926, 4 Parmley Place, Summit, NJ.

NIEDECKEN, GEORGE MANN.
Mural painter, architect and decorator. Born Milwaukee, Wis., Aug. 16, 1878. Pupil of AIC, Mucha, Robert-Fleury, Lefebvre and Laurens in Paris. Address in 1929, 449 Jefferson St.; h. 851 Marietta Ave., Milwaukee, Wis.

NIEHAUS, CHARLES H(ENRY).
Sculptor. Born Cincinnati, Ohio, Jan. 24, 1855. Pupil of McMicken School in Cincinnati; Royal Academy in Munich. Member: ANA, 1902; NA, 1906; NY Arch. Lg. 1895; NSS 1893; Salma. C., 1908; Nat. Inst. AL. Awards: Gold medal, Pan-Am. Exp., Buffalo, 1901; gold medal, Charleston Exp., 1902; gold medal, St. Louis Exp., 1904. Work: "Dr. Hahnemann" and "John Paul Jones," Washington, DC; "Garfield," Cincinnati, Ohio; Astor Memorial doors, Trinity Church, New York;

"Caestus" and "The Scraper," Metropolitan Museum, New York; "Francis Scott Key," Baltimore; Soldiers and Sailors monuments, Hoboken, Newark and Hackensack, NJ; statues of Clay and McDowell, Statuary Hall, Capitol, Washington. Died June 19, 1935. Address in 1929, Eagle Crest Studio, Grantwood, NJ.

NIELSON, HARRY A.
Painter. Born in Slagelse, Denmark, in 1881. Pupil of Art Institute of Chicago; Jean Manheim. Member: California Art Club. Address in 1926, 701 California Terrace, Pasadena, Calif.

NIEMEYER, JOHN H(ENRY).
Painter, teacher and lecturer. Born Bremen, Germany, June 25, 1839; came to U.S. in 1843. Pupil of Gerome and Yvon at Ecole des Beaux-Arts, and of Jacquesson de la Chevreuse and Cornu in Paris. Member: SAA, 1882; ANA, 1906; Paris AAA; Conn. AFA; New Haven PCC. Award: Hon. mention, Pan-Am. Exp., Buffalo, 1901. Prof., Yale School of Fine Arts, 1871-1908; emeritus after 1908. Represented in Smith College Art Gallery; Yale School of Fine Arts. Address in 1929, 251 Lawrence St., New Haven, Conn.

NIEPOLD, FRANK.
Painter and craftsman. Born Frederick, MD, Jan. 1, 1890. Pupil of Corcoran School of Art, Washington. Member: Wash. AC; S. Wash. A. Address in 1929, 307 Seventh St., S.W.; h. 3321 Garfield St., N.W., Washington, DC.

NIGHT, EDWARD W.
Painter. Born in Auburn, NY, in 1872. Address in 1926, 105 Cook St., East Onondaga, Syracuse, NY.

NILES, ROSAMOND.
Painter and etcher. Born Portsmouth, NH, Nov. 5, 1881. Pupil of DuMond; Pennell; Andre L'hote; Edouard Leon. Member: NA Women PS; NAC; SSAL. Address in 1929, 9 Gramercy Park; h. 15 Gramercy Park, New York, NY.

NISBET, ROBERT H.
Painter and etcher. Born Providence, RI, Aug. 25, 1879.

Pupil of RI School of Design; ASL of NY. Member: ANA, 1920; NA, 1928; NY Arch. Lg., 1912; Providence AC; Conn. AFA; NAC (life); Salma. C.; Allied AA; Lotos C. (artist life); ASL of NY; AFA; A Fund S; Kent AA (pres.). Awards: Dunham prize, Conn. AFA, 1913; third Hallgarten prize, NAD, 1915; silver medal, P.-P. Exp., San Francisco, 1915; prize, Conn. SA, 1915; Ranger Fund Purchase, NAD, 1923; Bryan prize, Los Angeles Museum, 1925; prize and medal, NAC, 1927; hon. mention, Exhib. Living Am. Etchers, 1927-28. Work: "Eve of St. John," Nat'l Arts C., New York; "Earliest Spring," RI School of Design, Providence; "The Emerald Robe," Butler Art Institute, Youngstown, Ohio; "Falls at Bulls Bridge," Lotos Club; "Winter," Plantations Club, Providence, RI; "The Hurrying River," Telfair Academy, Savannah; "Promise of Spring," Rhode Island Hospital, Providence; "The Trout Stream," Connecticut Agricultural College; etchings, Milwaukee Art Inst.; Detroit Museum; Brooklyn Museum; University of Nebraska, Lincoln; etchings, New York Public Library; Bibliotheque National, Paris, France. Died April 19, 1961. Address in 1929, South Kent, CT.

NITZSCHE, ELSA KOENIG.
Painter, illustrator and lecturer. Born Philadelphia, PA, in 1880. Pupil of Elliot Daingerfield, Dagnan Bouveret. Work: "Boy Blowing Bubbles," Art Club, Philadelphia; portrait in National Museum, Washington, DC. Author and illustrator of "Dickel and the Penguin." Died in 1952. Address in 1929, 1024 Westview Ave., Germantown, Philadelphia, PA.

NIVEN, FRANK R.
Painter and illustrator. Born in Rochester, NY, in 1888. Pupil of S. C. Jones. Member: Rochester Art Club. Address in 1926, 402 Municipal Bldg., Rochester, NY.

NOBLE.
Painter. His picture of John Brown on his way from prison to the gallows, embracing the negro children, is well known. His painting of the "Slave Mart" attracted much attention in the days of the Civil War and was exhibited in Boston and at the Capitol in Washington, DC.

NOBLE, JOHN.
Painter. Born Wichita, Kan., March 15, 1874. Pupil of Cincinnati Academy of Fine Arts; Laurens and Julian Academy in Paris; Academy des Beaux Arts, Brussels. Member: ANA, 1924; NA; Paris American Art Association; Society of Artists of Picardy; Independents of Paris; Allied Artists, London; Conn. AFA; Provincetown AA. Award: Salmagundi purchase prize ($1,000), 1922; W. A. Clark prize ($500) and hon. mention, Corcoran Gallery, Washington, DC., 1924; Athenaeum prize, Hartford, Conn.; Carnegie prize, NAD. Represented in Delgado Museum, New Orleans; Academy of Design, Rhode Island; Dallas Museum, Dallas, Texas; Wichita Museum, Wichita, Kan. Died in 1934. Address in 1929, care of Milch Galleries, 108 West 57th St., New York, NY.

NOBLE, WILLIAM CLARK.
Painter and sculptor. Born Gardiner, ME, Feb. 10, 1858. Pupil of Pierce and Greenough, and Taft in London. Member: NSS; NAC. Work: Walters' Memorial, W. E. Channing and Soldiers and Sailors Monument, Newport, RI; memorial to Bishop Phillips Brooks in Church of the Incarnation, New York; portrait bust of Gen. Potter, Chamber of Commerce, New York; Challenge statue and Gen. Christ statue, Antietam, MD; Gov. Curtin, Bellefonte, PA; jewelled crucifix in Church of St. Mary the Virgin; "Mother's Memorial," and "Major Pierre Charles L'Enfant Memorial," Washington, DC. Died in 1938. Address in 1929. 1630 16th St., Washington, DC.

NOCI, ARTURO.
Painter, illustrator and teacher. Born Rome, Italy. Pupil of Institute of Fine Arts, Rome. Work: "Venetian Interior," Rochester Museum, Rochester, NY; "Riflesso d'oro" and "Nella Cabina," Galleria d'Arte Moderna, Rome, Italy.

685

NOCOUET, PAUL ANGE.
Belgian sculptor. Born in Brussels in 1877. He came to America in 1903. His bronze "American Football" brought him recognition; it was presented to Columbia University. He received many awards. He died in 1906 in a balloon accident. The Belgian and French governments ordered casts made of his work here.

NOGUCHI, ISAMU.
Sculptor. Born in 1904. Exhibited at Penna. Academy of Fine Arts, Philadelphia, 1926. Address in 1926, 127 University Place, NY.

NOLAND, KENNETH.
Painter. Born April 10, 1924 in Asheville, NC. Studied 4 years at Black Mt. College, and with the late sculptor, Ossip Zadkine, in Paris. Taught at Inst. of Comtemp. Arts, Catholic Univ. in Wash., DC, and Bennington College. Received Inst. Torcuato DiTella (Buenos Aires) award (1964) and Corcoran award. Exhibited at Tibor de Nagy, NYC (1956-8); Fogg Art Mus.; MMA (1970); Guggenheim; Kootz Gallery, NYC; Whitney; Seattle World's Fair(1962); Art Inst. of Chicago. In the collections of Detroit Inst. of Arts; Whitney; Brandeis; Harvard; Albright-Knox Art Gallery, Buffalo; MOMA; City Mus. of St. Louis; Tate Gallery, London.

NOLF, JOHN T(HOMAS).
Painter and illustrator. Born Allentown, PA, July 23, 1871. Pupil of AIC; Wellington Reynolds; Francis Smith; John Vanderpoel. Member: Chicago Gal. A; Oak Park AL; Chic. Assn. PS; Ill. Acad. of FA. Award: Rosenwald Prize, AIC, 1924; gold medal, Oak Park AL, 1928; Wm. Ormond Thompson prize, 1929; purchase prize, Chicago Municipal AL, 1929. Work: "Thunder Cloud," Chicago Public School Art Society; "Myrtle" and "Wizzard," Oak Park Public Schools; "The Wanderer," Northwestern University Fraternity, Chicago; "Little Joe," Kennilworth High School, Chicago; "Boys Plowing," Municipal Art League, Chicago. Died in 1954. Address in 1929, care of Oak Park Art League, Oak Park, Ill.; summer, Grand Detour, Dixon P.O., Ill.

NOLL, ARTHUR HOWARD.
Engraver. Born in Caldwell, NJ, in 1855. Specialty, bookplate engraving. Address in 1926, 608 Woodlaun St., Memphis, Tenn.

NORCROSS, ELEANOR.
Painter. Born in Massachusetts. Pupil of William M. Chase in New York; Alfred Stevens in Paris. She died in Paris in 1923, and a memorial exhibition of her painting was held in the Louvre by the French Government. Her studio had been in Paris for more than thirty years.

NORDBERG, C. A(LBERT).
Painter and teacher. Born Chicago, Ill., Oct. 19, 1895. Pupil of Robert Reid, John F. Carlson, Birger Sandzen, Everett Warner. Member: Broadmoor Art Academy and Colorado Springs SP; Chicago SP; Denver SP; Soc. Amer. P. Work: Mural, "Indians of Pike's Peak Region," and "Towering Pine," Cheyenne School, Colorado Springs, Colo.; mural, "The Messa," Richmond, Ind.; "The Peak," Vanderpoel Memorial Collection, Chicago. Address in 1929, 2700 Payne St., Evanston, Ill.; Broadmoor Art Academy, Colorado Springs, Colo.; Art Institute, Chicago, Ill.

NORDELL, CARL JOHN.
Painter. Born Copenhagen, Denmark in 1885. Pupil of Boston Museum School under Tarbell; ASL of NY under Bridgman and Du Mond; Julian Academy in Paris under Laurens; RI School of Design. Member: ASL of NY; Boston AC; Boston WCC; Providence AC; North Shore AA; Salma. C.; Calif. P.M.; Brooklyn S.E.; Allied AA. Awards: Fourth W. A. Clark prize ($500) and hon. mention, Corcoran Gallery, Washington, 1912; silver medal, P.-P. Exp., San F., 1915; first prize, Swedish-American Exhibition, Chicago, 1917. Address in 1929, Fenway Studios, 30 Ipswich St., Boston, Mass.

NORDELL, EMMA PARKER.
(Mrs. Carl J. Nordell - "Polly Nordell"). Painter. Born Gardner, Mass. Pupil of S.R. Burleigh, Stacy Tolman, Du Mond, Henri. Member: Providence WCC; North Shore AA; NYWCC. Address in 1929, Fenway Studios, 30 Ipswich St., Boston, Mass.; summer, Reed Studios, East Gloucester, Mass.

NORDFELDT, B(ROR) J(ULIUS) (OLSSON). Painter, etcher, engraver and teacher. Born Tulstorg, Scania, Sweden, April 13, 1878. Pupil of AIC; Albert Herter in New York; Laurens in Paris; Frank M. Fletcher in Reading, England. Member: Taos SP; New Mexico SP; Chicago SE; Brooklyn SE. Awards: Silver medal, Milan, Italy, 1906, for wood block prints; silver medal for etching, P.-P. Exp., San F., 1915; Logan medal, AIC, 1926; bronze medal, Sesqui-Centennial Exposition, Phila., 1926. Work in Sidney (Australia) Museum of Fine Arts; Chicago Art Ins.; NY Public Lib.; Toledo Art Mus.; Bibliotheque des Arts et Archeologie, Paris; National Museum, Christiania, Norway; Detroit Inst. of Arts; Toronto Art Museum; Museum of New Mexico. Died in 1955. Address in 1929, Santa Fe, NM.

NORLING, ERNEST (RALPH).
Painter, illustrator and etcher. Born Pasco, Wash., Sept. 26, 1892. Pupil of F. Tadema, E. P. Ziegler. Member: Seattle AI; L. C. Tiffany Foundation. Address in 1929, 516 White Bldg.; h. 2453 22nd Ave., North, Seattle, Wash.

NORMAN, DaLORIA.
Painter and craftswoman. Born Leavenworth, Kan., Nov. 18, 1872. Studied abroad. Work: "Ecclesiastes," "Song of Solomon," (illuminations), New York Public Library; "Passing of the Seasons" (mural fresco), Public Library, Teaneck, NJ. Specialties, oil fresco, water color portraits, illuminations. Died in 1935. Address in 1929, Crossway Studio, Lyme, Conn.

NORMAN, EMILE.
Painter and Sculptor. Address in 1982, Carmel, CA. Born in El Monte, CA, April 22, 1918. Work: San Francisco Museum of Art; Oakland Art Museum. Comn.: Mosaic Window & Marble relief, Masonic Mem. Temple, San Francisco; horse in wood, Crown Zellerbach Bldg., San Fran.; bronze of "St. Francis and Wood Inlay Mural," Bank of CA, San Fran. Exhib.: Relig. Art Show, de Young Mus., San Fran., 1953; Soc. Contemp. Art Annual, Art Inst. of Chicago, 1960; design & aesthetics in wood, Lowe Art Ctr., Syracuse Univ., 1967; and others. Mem.: Carmel Art Assn.; Nat'l. Soc. of Mural Painters. Media: Oil, acrylic, wood, precious metals.

NORMAN, GEOFFREY R(ICH).
Painter and illustrator. Born London, England, Feb. 21, 1899. Address in 1929, 400 East 59th St., New York, NY; summer, Crossway Cottage, Lyme, Conn.

NORMAN, JOHN.
Engraver. Born c. 1748. According to the New England Palladium and Commercial Advertiser, in 1817, John Norman died in Boston "aged 69 years." That he was an Englishman is shown by his advertisement in the Pennsylvania Journal of May 11, 1774, which probably notes his first appearance in this country. A number of his plates are more or less modified copies of English orginals. His chief claim to fame is the fact that he was probably the first engraver in America to attempt a portrait of Washington, about 1779.

NORRIS, S. WALTER.
Landscape painter and writer. Born Philadelphia, PA, Jan. 12, 1868. Pupil of PAFA; Legros in Paris. Member: Phila. Sketch C.; Fellowship PAFA; Phila. Alliance; Phila. AC; AFA. Address in 1929, 1716 Chestnut St.; h. 135 South 18th St., Philadelphia, PA; summer, Ogunquit, ME.

NORRIS, W. J.
Illustrator and commercial designer. Born Chicago, Ill., Aug. 20, 1869. Member: Pen and Pencil C., Columbus; Art Lg. Address in 1929, 35 West Gay St.; h. 56 East 8th Ave., Columbus, Ohio.

NORSTAD, MAGNUS.
Painter. Born Norway, June 24, 1884. Pupil of NAD. Member: GFLA. Awards: Hon. mention, Minnesota State Art Exh., 1914; silver medal, St. Paul Inst., 1917; prize for group of four pictures at Minnesota State Art Exh., 1917. Work: "The City on the Hill," St. Paul Institute. Address in 1929, 303 Fifth Ave., New York, NY.; Valhalla, NY.

NORTHCOTE, STAFFORD M(ANTLE).
Wood engraver. Born Brooklyn, NY, July 7, 1869. Studied engraving with E. Heineman; drawing and painting at Art Inst., Brooklyn, under Boyle. Awards: Hon. mention, Pan-Am. Exp., Buffalo, 1901; bronze medal, St. Louis Exp., 1904. Died Nov. 15, 1949. Address in 1929, 288 Carlton Ave., Brooklyn, New York, NY.

NORTON, CLARA MAMRE.
Painter. Exhibited water colors at the Penna. Academy of the Fine Arts, Philadelphia, 1925. Address in 1926, 49 Woodland St., Bristol. Conn.

NORTON, ELIZABETH.
Painter, sculptor and block printer. Born Chicago, Ill., Dec 16, 1887. Pupil of AIC; ASL of NY; NAD. Member: Alliance; Calif. PM; Palo Alto AC; San Fran. S. Women A; AFA. Work: Wall fountain in Detroit Athletic C.; Library of Congress and Smithsonian Institute, Washington, DC; Public Library, Springfield, Mass. Address in 1929, 353 Lowell Ave., Palo Alto, Calif.

NORTON, HELEN G(AYLORD).
Painter. Born Portsmouth, Ohio, April 12, 1882. Pupil of Mills College; Jean Manheim. Member: Laguna Beach AA; Calif. AC. Awards; Second prize, Riverside Co. Fair, 1914; First prize, Southern Calif. Fair, 1920; 2nd prize, 1921; 1st prize, Southern California Fair, 1922 and 1923. Specialty, Landscapes and marines. Address in 1929, Laguna Beach, Calif.; h. 189 Magnolia Ave., Riverside, Calif.

NORTON, JOHN WARNER.
Painter. Born Lockport, IL, 1876. Pupil of AIC. Member: Chicago SA. Award: Harris bronze medal ($300), AIC, 1926. Instructor, Chicago Academy of Fine Arts. Work: Series of mural paintings in the Frank G. Logan Archaeological Museum, Beloit, Wis. Died in 1934. Address in 1929, 10 East Ohio St., Chicago, Ill.; Lockport, Ill.

NORTON, WILLIAM EDWARD.
Painter. Born June 28, 1843 in Boston. Pupil of Lowell Institute, Boston; George Inness; Jacquesson, de la Chevreuse, and A. Vollon, Paris. Awarded 3 gold medals in America; honorable mention, Paris Salon, 1895. Exhibited at Paris Exposition, 1900; regular exhibitor at the Royal Academy, London. Also exhibited in Philadelphia, Chicago, and St. Louis expositions. Awarded Osborne prize for marine painting, 1905, and again in 1906. Died Feb. 25, 1916 in NYC.

NOTARO, ANTHONY.
Sculptor. 19 Lafayette Pl., Irvington, NJ 07111. Born: Italy, January 10, 1915; US citizen. Study: Rinehart School of Sculpture, MD Inst., Baltimore, 1935-39 with Wm. Simpson, Herbert Adams; also with Melvina Hoffman. Collections: The Hall of Fame for Great Americans; Student Center, Seton Hall Univ.; National Commemorative Society; and many others. Comn.: Wrestling group. Council Am. Artists Soc.; Figure of "Winter", Nat'l. Sculpture Soc; portrait, Jimmy Carter; Football players, AAA; others. Exhib.: NAD; Nat'l Sculpture Soc.; Lever House; Allied Artists of America; Italian Cult. Ctr., Chicago; and many others. Awards: Bicentennial Exhib., Nat'l Sculpture Soc.; Hudson Valley Art Assn.; plus many others. Mem.: Fellow, Nat'l Sculpture Soc.; Am. APL; AAA. Address in 1982, Mendham, NJ.

NOTHERMAN, G.
Engraver. A Harrison campaign badge issued in Baltimore in 1840 is signed as "Drawn & Eng. by G. Notherman, Jr." The work is well done in line. The Badge was done by "Notherman & Mettee, Balt."

NOTMAN, HOWARD.
Painter. Born Brooklyn, NY, April
20, 1881. Pupil of Constantin
Herzberg, Brooklyn Polytechnic
Institute. Member: Brooklyn SA;
S. Indp. A.; Brooklyn S. Modern A.;
AFA. Address in 1929, 136
Joralemon St., Brooklyn, New York,
NY; summer, Keene Valley, Essex
Co., NY.

NOURSE, ELIZABETH.
Painter. Born Cincinnati, Ohio,
1860. Pupil of Art Academy in
Cincinnati; Lefebvre, Henner and
Carolus-Duran in Paris. Member:
Soc. Nat. des Beaux-Arts, 1901;
Paris Woman's AAA; NA Women PS
(hon.). Awards: Medal, Columbian
Exp., Chicago, 1893; third class
medal, Inst. de Carthage, Tunis,
1897; first class gold medal,
Nashville Exp., 1897; silver medal,
Paris Exp., 1900; silver medal, St.
Louis Exp., 1904; gold medal, P.-P.
Exp., San F., 1915; Laetare medal,
Univ. of Notre Dame, So. Bend,
Ind., 1921. Work: "Closed
Shutters," Luxembourg Mus., Paris;
"Peasant Woman of Borst" and "First
Communion," Cincinnati Mus.;
"Twilight," Toledo Museum; "Happy
Days," Detroit Inst.; "Mother and
Children," Art Inst., Chicago;
"Fisher Girl of Picardy," Nat'l
Gallery,WA; "Under the Trees,"
Nebraska Mus.; "Summer," Mus.,
Adelaide, Australia; "Summer
Hours," Museum, Newark, NJ. Died
in 1938. Address in 1929, 80 Rue
d'Assas, Paris, France.

NOVANI, GUILLO.
Sculptor. Born Massa-Carrara,
Italy, June 11, 1889. Pupil of
Academy of Massa-Carrara and
Beaux-Arts Institute in New York.
Address in 1929, 1347 Intervale
Ave.; 126 East 75th St., New York,
NY.

NOVELLI, JAMES.
Sculptor. Born in Italy in 1885.
He came to New York in 1890.
Studied abroad in 1908. Work:
"Rock of Ages," Durham, NC; bronze
busts of Thos. Stewart, Julius
Berger and Irving Green; also
numerous busts in terra-cotta.

NOVELLI, R(UDOLFO).
Painter. Born Italy, Dec. 28,
1879. Pupil of Peters. Work:
"Poppy," "Zinnias" and
"Carnations," Funk and Wagnalls
Co., New York. Address in 1929,
670 St. Ann's Ave., Bronx, NY.

NOXON, GRACE P.
Painter, writer, lecturer and
teacher. Born Ossining, NY. Pupil
of Laurens; Ecole des Beaux-Arts;
Chase at ASL of NY; NY School of
Applied Design. Member: S. Indp.
A. Address in 1929, 710 Carnegie
Hall, 56th St. and 7th Ave., NYC.

NOYES, BERTHA.
Painter. Member: S. Wash. A.;
Wash. WCC; Wash. AC; NA Women PS;
AFA. Address in 1929, 614 19th
St., N.W., Washington, DC.

NOYES, GEORGE L.
Painter. Born in Canada. Pupil of
Courtois, Rixen, Le Blanc and
Delance in Paris. Member: Boston
AC; Boston SWCP; Boston GA. Award:
Silver medal, P.-P. Exp., San F.,
1915. Work: "Gloucester Wharves,"
Museum of Fine Arts, Boston; "New
Hampshire Hills," Des Moines Art
Museum; "Road to Lisbon," Utah
State Museum. Died in 1951.
Address in 1929, 81 Chestnut St.,
Boston, Mass.

NOYES, JOSIAH.
Engraver. Was working in 1799. He
engraved a copper plate for the
Social Friends' Library of
Dartmouth College.

NUDERSCHER, FRANK.
Painter, illustrator, etcher and
teacher. Born St. Louis, MO, July
19, 1880. Self-taught. Member:
St. Louis AG; 2x4 Soc. Awards:
1st thumb-box prize, 1917; 1st
prize, St. Louis Salon, 1916, 1921;
1st prize, Chamber of Commerce
($350) prize, 1919, 1921, 1926.
Work: Mississippi River scenes, in
Chamber of Commerce, St. Louis, MO;
Monday Club, Webster Groves, MO;
"The Great Crossing," State
Capitol, Jefferson City, MO; "The
Eads Bridge," City Art Museum, St.
Louis; decorations, St. Louis
Zoological Gardens; decorations,
Hamburg-American Liner St. Louis.

Died in 1959. Address in 1929, St. Louis and Arcadia, MO.

NUNAMAKER, K. R.
Landscape painter. Exhibited at National Academy of Design, New York, 1925. Address in 1926, Center Bridge, Penna.

NUNN, EVYLENA.
Painter. Born in Mayfield, Kans., in 1888. Pupil of Art Students' League of New York; Berkshire Summer School of Art; A. A. Hills; School of Art and Design of Pomona College. Also studied in Japan. Member: California Art Club; Laguna Artists' Association. Address in 1926, 802 North Ross St., Santa Ana, Calif.

NUNN, FREDERIC.
Painter. Born Philadelphia, PA, Aug. 18, 1879. Pupil of PAFA under Anshutz, Breckenridge, Chase and Cecilia Beaux. Member: Fellowship PAFA; Atlantic City AA; Phila. Alliance; Phila. WCC; S. Indp. A. Represented in the collection of the Fellowship of the Pennsylvania Academy of the Fine Arts, Philadelphia; Reading (PA) Museum; Los Angeles Museum. Specialty, marines and landscapes. Died in 1959. Address in 1929, R. F. D., Cape May Court House, NJ.

NURICK, IRVING.
Illustrator. Born in Brooklyn, NY, in 1894. He was trained at PI, the ASL and in Paris. His illustrations in Ladies' Home Journal for Elizabeth Woodward's Sub Deb articles were published for 15 years. The acclaim from this series and other magazine work led to assignments from such advertisers as Wesson Oil, Adams Hats, Sloane's Furniture and Kimberly Clark Products. A member of the AWS, Artists and Writers and a Life Member of the S of I, he had One-Man Exhibitions in the U.S. and in Paris, where he lived for many years. The NAD awarded him the Ranger Prize in 1957 and the Samuel Finley Breeze Award in 1960. Died in 1963.

NUSE, R(OY) C(LEVELAND).
Painter and teacher. Born Springfield, Ohio, Feb. 23, 1885.

Pupil of Duveneck, Cincinnati Art Academy, PAFA. Awards: Cresson European Scholarship, PAFA, 1918; second Cresson, first Toppan and first Thouron prizes, PAFA, 1918; medal, Phila. Sketch C., 1921. Represented in collection of Beaver College, Penn. Director of Beechwood School of Fine Arts, Jenkintown, PA. Address in 1929, Rushland, PA.

NUYTTENS, J(OSEF) P(IERRE).
Painter and etcher. Born Antwerp, Aug. 7, 1885. Studied at Antwerp Royal Academy, Ecole des Beaux-Arts in Paris and in Brussels. Awards: Bronze medal from Queen of Belgium, 1918; Chevalier of the Order of Leopold II. Member: Cliff Dwellers, Chicago; Alumni AIC. Work in Chicago Art Institute; White House, Washington; Royal Palace, Brussels, Belgium; State House, Springfield, Ill. Represented in Vanderpoel AA collection, Chicago. Address in 1929, Hotel des Artistes, 1 West 67th St., New York, NY.

NYE, E.
Portrait painter. Advertised as a "Portrait Painter," in the Rural Visitor, Burlington, NJ, March 25th, 1811.

NYE, EDGAR.
Painter. Born Richmond, VA, April 30, 1879. Pupil of Corcoran School of Art, Washington, and John Noble Barlow, England. Member: Wash. SA; Wash. WCC; Wash. Landscape C. Awards: Hon. mention, 1926; bronze medal, 1927, Wash. SA. Work: Picture in Plymouth Gallery, England. Specialty, landscape. Died in 1943. Address in 1929, 1008 Taylor St., N.E., Washington, DC.

NYE, ELMER L.
Etcher. Born in St. Paul, Minn., in 1888. Member: Minneapolis Attic Club. Award: First prize, poster, Minn. Society of Artists. Address in 1926, Grand Fords, Santa Fe, NM.

NYHOLM, ARVID FREDERICK.
Painter. Born in 1866 in Stockholm, Sweden. Pupil of Anders Zorn, and of Colarossi Academy in

Paris. Represented by "Captain
John Ericson," National Gallery,
Washington, DC, and "General
Whipple," West Point Academy. Died
Nov. 14, 1927 in Chicago, Ill.

OAKES, W(ILBUR) L.
Painter. Born Cleveland, Dec. 1, 1876. Pupil of F. C. Gottwald; A. T. Hibbard at Rockport MA; Cleveland SA. Address in 1929, 1464 Lincoln Avenue, Lakewood, Cleveland, OH. Died in 1934.

OAKEY, MARIA R.
See Mrs. T. W. Dewing.

OAKLEY, FRANK F.
Engraver and lithographer. About 1860 Oakley was engraving vignettes in line, and probably banknote work, at 204 Washington St., Boston. His work is very good, though very few signed pieces have been seen.

OAKLEY, GEORGE.
Painter. Born in 1793. He was elected an Associate Member of the National Academy in 1827. He died in 1869.

OAKLEY, THORNTON.
Illustrator, painter, writer, arch., Lecturer and and teacher. Born Pittsburgh, PA, 1881. Studied architecture at Univ. of PA. (B.S., 1901, and M.S., 1902); pupil of Howard Pyle at Wilmington. Member: Phila. WCC, SI, 1913; Fellowship PAFA; Phila. Alliance (Dir.); Wilmington Society Fine Arts. Awards: Brooke Memorial prize, Univ. of PA., 1902; Beck prize, Phila. WCC, 1914; P.- P. Exp., San. F., 1915. Instructor in drawing, Univ. of PA., 1914-15; In charge, Dept. of Illustration, School of Industrial Art of the PA Museum, 1914-1919, 1921. Drawings of Hog Island adopted 1918 by US for Foreign News Service; Lithographs, painting and drawings in Library of Congress; Boston Public Library; NY Public Library; Phila. Free Library; Newark Free Library; State Library of CA Seattle Public Library; St. Louis Public Library; Musee de la Guerre, Paris; British Mus., London; Library, Historical Soc. of PA; Musee de Lourdes, France; Nat'l Library of Brazil; Milwaukee Art. Inst.; Luxembourg Museum, Paris. Books with Amy Oakley, "Hill Towns of the Pyrenees," 1923, "Cloud-lands of France," 1927, and "Enchanted Brittany," 1930 (The

Centruy Co.); with H. M. Lippincott, "Philadelphia," 1926; illustrator, "Westward Ho!" 1920; "Autobiography of Benjamin Franklin," 1927; Folk Tales of Brittany, 1929. Work appeared in Harper's, Scribner's and Century. Died April 1953, in Byrn Mawr, PA. Address in 1929, Villa Nova, PA.

OAKLEY, VIOLET.
Mural painter, illustrator, and craftsman. Born in 1874 in New York. Pupil of ASL of NY.; Drexel Inst. under Howard Pyle; PAFA under Joseph De Camp and Cecilia Beaux; Aman-Jean, Collin and Lazar in Paris. Member: ANA; Phila. WCC; Fellowship PAFA; NYWCC; Circulo de Bellas Artes Madrid, Spain; Mural P.; AIA (hon.); Phila Alliance. Awards: St. Louis Exposition, 1904; PAFA 1905; P.- P. Exposition, San Francisco, 1915; NY Arch. Lg. 1916; Phila. prize, PAFA, 1922. Work: Decorations in All Angels Church, NY; frieze,"Founding of the State of Liberty Spirtitual," 18 panels, State Capitol, Harrisburg; panel, "The Constitutional Convention," Cuyahoga Co., C. H. Cleveland; 9 panels, "The Creation and Preservation of the Union," Senate Chamber, Harrisburg; "The Building of the House of Wisdom," 13 panels and glass dome, Hannah PA House, two portraits, PAFA; triple panel, "The Great Wonder," Alumnae House, Vassar College; medal of the Philadelphia Award: "The Opening of the Book of the Law," Supreme and Superior Court Room, State Capitol, Harrisburg. Died in 1961. Address in 1929, Lower Cogslea, St. George's Road, Mt. Airy P. O. , Philadelphia, PA.

OBERHARDT, WILLIAM.
Painter, illustrator, and etcher. Born Guttenburg, NJ., Sept. 22, 1882. Pupil of NAD; Carl V. Marr and Ludwig V. Herterich, Munich Academy of Fine Arts. Member: SI; AG: Art Directors' Club. Work: Portrayed President Harding, Thomas A. Edison, Henry Cabot Lodge, J. G. Cannon, Chief Justice Taft, Mrs. Fisk, Rachmaninoff, Luther Burbank, Hudson Maxim, C. D. Gibbson, Joseph Pennell, Maj. Gen. James G. Harboard, Portrayed for Government 1919, twenty-five members Division

of Pictorial Publicity for records of archives, Washington, D.C. Illustrator for leading magazines. Address in 1929, 41 Union Square, New York, NY; h. 538-2nd Ave., Pelham, NY; summer, Quonocontang Beach, RI. Died in 1958.

OBERTEUFFER, GEORGE.
Painter. Born Philadelphia, PA, 1878. Pupil of Chase, Anchutz. Member: Salon d'Automne; Salon des Independents; Chicago Gal. A.; Chicago PS. Awards: Gold medal, Wisconsin PS, 1922; Sesnan medal, PAFA, 1922; Logan medal ($750), AIC, 1926; third prize ($500), Chicago Gal. A., 1927. Works: "Stevenson's Moret," and "Eglise St. Roch." Brooklyn Museum; "Springtime, Paris," National Gallery of New South Wales; "Winter," owned by French Government. Represented in Phillips Gallery, Washington; Grand Rapids Museum; Milwaukee Art Inst.; Columbus, OH, Art Museum. Instructor, Pennsylvania Academy of the Fine Arts and Chicago Art Institute, 1924-25. Address in 1929, Tree Bldg., 9 E. Ontario Street, Chicago, IL.

OBERTEUFFER, HENRIETTE AMIARD.
Painter. Born Havre, France, 1878. Pupil of Laurens, Constant. Member: Salon d'Automne, Salon des Independents; Chicago Gal. A. Work: Still life owned by Franch Government; represented in Duncan Phillips Gallery, Washington, D.C. Awards: Medal of honor, Milwaukee AI; Brower prize ($300), AIC, 1926; Logan medal ($750), AIC, 1927. Died in 1962. Address in 1929, 9 E. Ontario Street, Chicago, IL.

O'BRIEN, CATHERINE C.
Painter. Born New York. Pupil of Granbury, Walter Chirlaw, Arthur W. Dow. Member: S. Indp. A. Address in 1929, Butler Hall, 400 West 119th Street, New York, NY; summer, Southampton, LI, NY.

O'BRIEN, JOHN.
Sculptor. Born in Ireland in 1834, he died at Galveston, TX, on Dec. 20, 1904.

O'BRIEN, R.
Portrait engraver. Worked for many years for the NY engraver, A. H. Ritchie.

O'BRIEN, SEUMAS.
Sculptor and writer. Born in Glenbrook, Co. Cork, Ireland, in 1880. Instructor in art, Cork School of Art, Mt. St. Joseph's Monastery (Cork); Queenstown Tech. School; Metropolitan School of Art (Dublin) until 1912; Abbey Theatre dramatist and lecturer, 1913-17; exhibited at Royal Hibernian Academy. Awarded silver medal (sculpture) by Bd. of Edn., London, 1912. Came to US in 1913. Address in 1926, 117 W. 90th St., NYC.

O'BRIEN, SMITH.
Painter, etcher and arch. Born Cork, Ireland. Pupil of Calif. School FA; Andre L'hote Acad., Paris. Member: Calif. SE (pres.); San Francisco AA; San Francisco. Beaux Art C. Award: Hon. mention-picture, San Diego, 1927. Address in 1929, 110 Sutter St., h. 2032 Baker St., San Francisco, CA.

O'CALLAHAN, C(LINTON) C(LEMENT).
Painter. Born Hartford, CT, Feb. 19, 1890. Pupil of C. Noel Flagg, Charles Guerin. Member: Paris AAA. Address in 1929, Amer. Art Asso., 4 Rue Joseph Bara, Paris, France.

OCHTMAN, DOROTHY.
Painter. Born Riverside, CT, May 8, 1892. Pupil of NAD and Ochtman. Member: ANA 1929; Allied AA; Greenwich SA; NA Women PS; SPNY; PS Gallery Assoc. Awards: Shaw prize, NAD, 1921; third Hallgarten prize, NAD, 1924; hon. mention, Exposition of Women's Arts and Industries, 1926, and first prize, 1927; Guggenheim European Scholarship, 1927; first hon. mention, Greenwich Society of Artists, 1928-1929. Died in 1971. Address in 1929, Cos Cob, CT.

OCHTMAN, LEONARD.
Landscape painter. Born Zonnemaire, Holland, Oct. 21, 1854; came to Albany, NY, 1866. Self-taught. Member: SAA 1891; ANA 1898; NA 1904; AWCS; NY WCC; Brooklyn AC; A. Fund S.; A. Aid S.; Salma. C. 1901; Lotos C.; NAC; Nat.

Inst. A. L.; Greenwich Society of Artists; AFA. Awards: Columbian Exp., Chic. 1893; AC Phila. 1894; Pan-Am Exp., Buffalo, 1901; Charleston Exp., 1902; Morgan prize, Salma. C. 1902; Shaw Fund prize, SAA 1902; NAD1903; Evans prize, Salma. C. 1903; Webb prize, SAA 1904; 2 gold medals, St. Louis Exp., 1904; Inness prize, Salma. C. 1906; Evans prize, Salma C. 1907; Knoxville Exp., 1911; P.- P. Exp., San F., 1915; 1st People's Prize, Greenwich Soc. of Artists, 1929. In collections of Met. Mus. Art, Brooklyn Inst. Mus.; City Art Mus., St. Louis; Columbus Gal. Art; Corcoran Gal. and Nat'l. Gal. (both in Wash; D.C.; Mus. Art, Fort Worth, TX; Dallas AA; Hackley Art Gal., MI, Butler Art Inst, OH, Albant Inst. Died in 1934.

OCHTMAN, MINA FUNDA.
(Mrs. Leonard). Painter. Born in Laconia, NH, in 1862; died in 1924. She was a member of the American Water Color Society and the National Association of Women Painters and Sculptors. Her pictures have been shown in exhibitions throughout the country.

O'CONNOR, ANDREW.
Sculptor. Born Worcester, MA, June 7, 1874. Pupil of his father. Member: ANA, 1919; Nat. Inst. AL. Awards: Bronze medal, Pan-AM. Exp., Buffalo, 1901; gold medal, Paris Salon, 1906; silver medal, Barcelona, Spain, 1907. Work: Central Porch, St. Bartholomew's Church, NY; Liscurn Memorial, Arlington; Thomas Memorial, Tarrytown; "Inspiration," St. Louis; "Justice," Newark; "Lawton," Indianpolis; "Wallace," Washington; "1898," Worcester; "Lincoln," Springfield; "Roosevelt Memorial," Glen View, IL; "Lafayette," Baltimore; "Justice," The Hague; "1917," Boston; statues in the Luxembourg; Musee des Arts Decoratif, Paris. Died June 9, 1941. Address in 1929, Paxton, MA.

O'CONNOR, HENRY M.
Painter and etcher. Born Brookline, MA, March 5, 1891. Pupil of MA. Normal Art School and Boston Museum School. Member: Boston SE; Copley S.; Chicago SE.

Address in 1929, 58 Putnam Avenue, Cambridge, MA.

ODDIE, WALTER M.
Landscape painter. Born in 1808. He was elected an Associate Member of the National Academy of Design in 1833. He died in 1865.

O'DONOVAN, WILLIAM RUDOLPH.
Sculptor. Born in Preston County, VA, in 1844. Self-taught in art. He established a studio in New York and has executed many important portrait busts and bas-reliefs, including: Wm. Page, National Academy, which was presented to the National Academy of Design; Arthur Quartly, National Academy; Thomas Eakins, National Academy; Edmund Clarence Stedman; busts of Walt Whitman and Gen. Joseph Wheeler; equestrian statues of Lincoln and Grant for Soldiers' and Sailors' Arch, Prospect Park, Brooklyn; reliefs for Oriskany battle monument; statue of Archbishop Hughes, St. John's College, Fordham; memorial tablet to Bayard Taylor, Cornell U.; a statue to the captors of Major Andre, Tarrytown, NY. He was one of the four founders of the famous Title Club; also a member of the Hudson-Fulton Commission. Elected Associate Member of the National Academy, 1878. Member: Society of Amer. Sculptors; Architectural League. Died in 1920.

OEHLER, BERNICE (OLIVIA).
Painter, illustrator, writer, lecturer, and teacher. Born Lake Mills, WI. Member: AIC Alumni A. Formerly instructor of drawing, High School, Madison, WI; formerly instrutor in art, University of Wisconsin. Illustrated series of Lincoln School Readers; "General Language," by S. A. Leonard; "The Dance," by Margaret H. Doubler; "Educational Story Plays and School Room Games," by Emily Elmore and Marie Carus; "Tales of Leather Stocking," by Annie Marble; "The Juniors' Own Composition Book," by Leonard and McFadden; "Chico, the Circus Cherub," by Stella Burke May; Books VII and VIII of "Real Life Readers," Leonard-Theisen; author and illustrator of "A Series of Decorative Figures from the

Dance" and "Figure Sketching." Permanent artist for Ruth St. Denis. Address in 1929, Lake Mills, WI; 125 E. 30th Street, New York, NY.

OERTEL, JOHANNES ADAM.
Engraver and portrait painter. Born in Furth, near Nuremberg, Germany, Nov. 3, 1823. Oertel was apprenticed to J. M. E. Muller, a well-known engraver of Nuremberg; but as a result of the German revolution of 1848 he came to America and settled in Newark, NJ. He at first tried painting and then resorted to engraving, doing much work for the banknote companies. He finally attained success with his pictures of army life done from studies made in Virginia during the Civil War. He was rector of a number of churches at various times and was professor in an art school in St. Louis for two years. All of this time he was busy painting especially in the line of Christian art, and at carving church decorations. About 1857 he assisted in decorating the Capitol at Washington. Died Dec. 9, 1909, in Vienna, VA.

OESTERMANN, MILDRED (CAROLINE).
Painter, etcher, and craftsman. Born San Francisco, CA, Aug. 23, 1899. Pupil of Gertrude Partington Albright; Lee F. Randolph; Constance L. Macky; E. Spencer Macky. Member: Calif. SE; San Francisco Soc. of Women A; Am. APL. Address in 1929, 1462 7th Avenue, San Francisco, CA.

OF, GEORGE FERDINAND.
Painter. Born New York, NY, Oct. 16, 1876. Pupil of ASL of NY; Weinhold in Munich; Delecluse Academy in Paris. Address in 1929, 1030 Lydig Ave., New York, NY.

OFFICER, THOS. S.
Miniature painter. Born in Carlisle, PA, in 1820. He had his studio in New Orleans, Philadelphia and New York, but passed the last years of his life in California. His work is remarkable for crisp, fresh color and artistic delicacy. He died in 1860.

OGDEN, HELEN EASTMAN.
See Mrs. Campbell.

OGDEN, HENRY ALEXANDER.
Illustrator. Born Philadelphia, PA, July 17, 1856. Pupil of NAD; ASL of NY. Member: SI, 1911; AFA. Work: Collection of uniforms of the US Army, 1775-1906, made by order of Quarter-Master General's Dept. Author and illustrator of "The Boy's Book of Famous Regiments," etc. Specialty, military and historical subjects. Died June 13, 1936. Address in 1929, 200 Fifth Avenue, New York, NY; Englewood Club, Englewood, NJ.

OGDEN, LYMAN GARFIELD.
Painter and illustrator. Born in Walton, NY, in 1882. Pupil of Thomas Anshutz; Robert Henri. Address in 1926, East St., Walton, NY.

OGILVIE, CLINTON.
Painter. Born in NYC, 1838. He studied painting under James Hart. He went abroad for four years and on his return was elected an Associate Member of the National Academy. He has since exhibited "Among the Adirondacks," "The Mountain Brook," "Lake Como." He died Nov. 29, 1900, in NYC.

O'HARA, DOROTHEA WARREN.
Sculptor. Born Malta Bend, MO. Pupil of Royal College of Art, College of Art, London; School of Design, Munich. Member: NAC; PBC; Silvermine GA; Darien GA. Work: Large carved white bowl, Metropolitan Museum of Art, NYC. Address in 1929, Darien, CT.

O'HARA, ELIOT.
Painter. Born Waltham, MA, June 14, 1890. Pupil of Russell T. Hyde; Charles Hopkinson; Andre L'hote. Member: Am. WCS; AFA. Award: Fellow Guggenheim Mem. Foundation, 1928. Address in 1929, 44 Greenwood Lane, Waltham, MA.

O'HARA, SUSAN.
Miniature painter, who flourished in 1834, in NY.

O'KEEFFE, GEORGIA.
Painter. Born in Sun Prairie, Wisconsin, Nov. 15, 1887. Study:

Art Institute of Chicago, with John Vanderpoel, 1905-06; ASL, with William M. Chase, 1907-08; University of Virginia, with Alon Bement, summer 1912; Columbia University, with Arthur Dow, Alon Bement, 1914-16; Mills College, 1952; Randolph-Macon Women's College, 1966; Hon. DFA, William & Mary College, 1938, University of New Mexico, 1964, Brown University, 1971, and Minneapolis College of Art and Design, 1972; Honorary Litt. D, University of Wisconsin, 1942, and Mt. Holyoke College, 1971; Honorary LHD, Columbia University, 1971. Work: Metropolitan Museum of Art, Museum of Modern Art, Whitney Museum, all New York City; Brooklyn Museum, New York; Art Institute of Chicago; others. Exhibitions: Retrospectives Art Institute of Chicago, 1943, Museum of Modern Art, 1946, Worcester Museum of Art, 1960, Museum of Fine Arts Houston, 1966, Whitney Museum, 1970; Guggenheim Museum, New York City; plus many others. Awards: Gold medal, painting, National Institute of Arts & Letters, 1970; M. Carey Thomas Award, Bryn Mawr College, 1971; Edward MacDowell Medal, Bryn Mawr College, 1972; and others. Member: National Institute of Arts & Letters; American Academy of Arts & Letters; American Academy of Arts & Sciences. Address in 1982, Abiquiu, New Mexico.

O'KELLEY, ALOYSIUS.
Painter. Born in Dublin, Ireland, in 1853. Pupil of Bonnat and Gerome at the Ecole des Beaux Arts in Paris. Member: New York Water Color Club. Address in 1926: 402 Clermont Avenue, Brooklyn, New York.

OKEY, SAMUEL.
Engraver. Born 1765. John Chaloner Smith, in his "British Mezzotints," says that Samuel Okey, an engraver in mezzotint, was awarded premiums in 1765 and 1767, by the London Society of Arts, presumedly for his engravings. Soon after the date mentioned Samuel Okey must have sailed for America. In 1773, '74 and '75 he was engraving and publishing portraits in mezzotint in Newport, Rhode Island, his business partner being Charles Reak.

OKON, MEJO.
Ilustrator. Born in Indianapolis, in 1953. Studied: Rochester Institute, Syracuse University, and Herron School of Art until 1975. She began her career in Indianapolis with Young World Magazine in 1976. She has won a Gold Medal from the Indianapolis ADC and her work was accepted for the Society of Illustrators Annual Exhibition in 1976.

OLDENBURG, CLAES THURE.
Sculptor. Born in Stockholm, Sweden, January 28, 1929. Study: Yale University; Art Institute of Chicago. Work: Albright-Knox Gal., Buffalo; MOMA; Art Institute of Chicago; many others. Comn.: Oberlin College, Ohio; City of St. Louis, Missouri; Yale University; Walker Art Center, Minneapolis; Hirshhorn Museum, Washington, DC; others. Exhibitions: Metropolitan Museum of Art, New York City; Museum of Modern Art, New York City; Pasadena Art Museum, California; Kunsthalle, Tubingen, Germany; Expo '70, Osaka, Japan; "Seattle Art Museum; Whitney Museum, and many others in United States, Amsterdam, Baden-Baden, London, Stockholm, Denmark, Paris, New Delhi, etc. Address in 1982, 556 Broome Street, New York City.

OLDS, ELIZABETH.
Painter and printmaker. 2221 Alvarado Ln, Sarasota, FL 33581. Born December 10, 1895 in Minneapolis, Minnesota. Studied arch. at University of Minnesota 1916-18; Art Students' League with George Luks and George Bridgman, 1920-23; First woman to receive a Guggenheim Fellowship for the study of painting abroad. Employed on WPA Fed. Art Project, 1935-40. Member of Amer. Artists' Congress. Exhibitions: Artists for Victory, Metropolitan Museum of Art, 1942; Museum of Modern Art 1940's; Whitney Museum of American Art.

OLINSKY, IVAN GREGOROVITCH.
Painter. Born in Russia 1878. Studied at NAD and in France and Italy. Member: ANA, 1914; NA,

1919; Mural P.; NY Arch. Lg., 1912; Salma. C.; AAS; allied AA; Lotus C.; AFA. Awards: Clarke prize ($300), NAD, 1914; Shaw purchase prize, Salma C., 1919; purchase prize, Lyme AA, 1922; Eaton purchase prize, Lyme AA, 1926. Work: "Ada," Omaha Society of Fine Arts; "Young Girl, "Detroit AC; "Gossip," Dallas (TX) Art Assn.; "Old Fashioned Gown" and "Two Girls," Detroit Inst.; portraits of Mr. Stambaugh and Mr. J. G. Butler; "Springtime," "Fairy Tales," Butler Art Inst. Youngstown, OH; "Adoration," Art Association, Norfolk, VA. Address in 1929, 27 West 67th Street, New York, NY.

OLIVER, FREDERICK W.
Painter. Born New York, Sept 4, 1876. Pupil of DeCamp, Major, S. C. Carbee. Member: Boston AC.; Copley S. Address in 1929, Fenway Studios, 30 Ipswich Street, Boston, MA; h. 27 Mountford Road, Newton Highlands, MA.

OLIVER, JEAN NUTTING.
Painter, teacher, and writer. Born Lynn, MA. Pupil of Boston Museum School, C. H. Woodbury, Philip Hale. Member: Copley S., 1883; NA Women PS; Boston GA; CT AFA; Concord AA; Provincetown AA; North Shore AA. Awards: Hudson prize, PAFA, 1916; "People's Prize," Boston Women Painters Exhibition, 1917. Address in 1929, Studios, 30 Ipswich St., Boston, MA; summer, East Gloucester, MA.

OLIVER, MYRON ANGELO.
Painter and craftsman. Born Fulton, Kansas, June 16, 1891. Pupil of Chase, Du Mond, Poor. Member: Salma. C.; Laguna Beach AA. Address in 1929, 110 Main Street; h. 502 Peirce Street, Monterey, CA.

OLSEN, HARRY EMIL.
Painter. Born in 1887. Exhibited water colors at the Penna. Academy of the Fine Arts, Philadelphia, 1925. Address in 1926, 2 Glenada Place, New York.

OLSON, ALBERT BYRON.
Painter and craftsman. Born Montrose, Colo., May 3, 1885. Pupil of PAFA under Chase, Anshutz

and McCarter. Member: Denver AC. Represented in collection of Denver Art Museum, St. Mark's Church, murals in St. Martin's Chapel and Ilyria Branch Library, Denver. Died in 1940. Address in 1929, 817 Pearl Street, Denver, CO.

OLSON, CARL G(USTAF) T(HEODORE).
Painter, sculptor, craftsman, and teacher. Born Sweden, June 7, 1875. Pupil of Peter Roos. Member: Copley S. Address in 1929, 60 Pine Street, Belmont, MA.

OLSON, JOSEPH OLAF.
Painter, sculptor, etcher, artist, craftsman, writer, and lecturer. Born Buffalo, Minn., Jan 28, 1894. Pupil of F. Tadema, George Bellows. Member: Salma. C.; Painters and Sculptors Gal. Asso.; NYWCC. Work: "Pyrenees Mountains," Baltimore Museum. Address in 1929, 144 Bleecker Street, New York, NY.

OLSON-MANDLER, SUE POSPESCHIL.
Painter and printmaker. Born in Janesville, WI, June 17, 1941. Study: U. of WI at Whitewater, 1961-62; with Prof. Rbt. Raushenberger, U. of Ill.; with Maryalice Wells, T. Palmerton, Rbt. A. Nelson at U. of Neb., Omaha, & Creighton workshops; S. Buchanan, U. of Neb., Omaha; workshops with H. Walkinshaw, 1980, D. Kingman & C. Croney, 1981; Bellevue (Neb.) Col., 1982. Work: Collections of Bob Hope, Gerald Ford, many Neb. corp. and insts. Exhib.: Numerous shows at univs., museums in Neb. Comn.: Record album and magazine covers, book illustr., arch. renderings; silhouettes, portraits in ink, pen and ink note cards. Awards: 1976-1983, many awards in local and state exhib. and competitions. Mem.: U. Neb., Omaha, Fine Arts Advisory Comm., 1975-83; Nat'l WC. Media: Ink/wash arch. drawings & portraits; oils, acrylic, watercolor, pastel; cut silhouettes. Address in 1983, Bellevue, Neb.

OLSTOWSKI, FRANCISZEK.
Painter, sculptor, illustrator, and teacher. Born Zaborowo, Poland, March 25, 1901. Pupil of his father. Member: New York P. and

697

S.; Buffalo SA; Chicago NJSA: S. Indp. A.; Salons of Amer.; Alliance. Work: "Abraham Lincoln," Newspaper Men's Club, New York City; "Don Basco Group," Salesian School, New Rochelle, NY; "Madonna Christiana," St. Mary's Church, New York City; "The Great America," Foreign Affairs Bldg., Warsaw, Poland; "John E. Kellerd as Mephisto," Theatre League, Buffalo; Marguertie Olstowski," Gardner Dancing School, Toledo, OH. Address in 1929, 322 West 101st Street, New York, NY; h. 50 Titus Avenue, Buffalo, NY.

O'MALLERY, POWER.
Painter, illustrator, etcher, and lecturer. Born County Waterford, Ireland. Pupil of Shirlaw, Henri, NAD. Award: First prize, Cronach Sailteen, Dublin, 1924. Represented in Phillips Memorial Gallery, Washington, D.C. Address in 1929, *See Vol. XXIV.

O'MEALLIE, KITTY.
Painter. Born in Bennettsville, South Carolina, in 1916. Studied: Newcomb Art School with Xavier Gonzales and Will Stevens. Primarily a nature painter but also executed group paintings of human face and figure, semi-abstract compositions in oil, acrylic, charcoal and mixed media. Awards: Gulf Coast Annual Exhibition, Pass Christian, Mississippi; Masur Museum of Art's 5th Monroe Annual, Monroe, Louisiana; Edgewater Plaza 5th Art Exhibit, Gulfport-Biloxi, Mississippi; Biloxi Art Associations Annual Tri-State Show; 2nd Greater New Orleans National Exhibition. Collections: Wake Forest Univ.; Winston-Salem, North Carolina; St. Martin's Protestant Episcopal School, Metairie, Louisiana; Madewood Plantation, Assumption Parish, Louisiana; Downtown Gallery, New Orleans; Sellers and Sanders Clinic, New Orleans.

ONDERDONK, ELEANOR.
Painter and teacher. Born San Antonio, Texas, Oct. 25, 1886. Pupil of Du Mond; Johansen; Lucia Fuller; Alice Beckington; George Bridgman; John F. Carlson. Address in 1929, 128 West French Place, San Antonio, Texas.

ONDERDONK, JULIAN.
Painter. Born in 1882 in San Antonio, TX. Pupil of Chase, Henri, and of his father R. J. Onderdonk. Represented by "Springtime," Dallas Art Association, and "Morning Sunlight" in the San Antonio Art League. Died Oct. 27, 1922 in San Antonio.

ONDERDONK, ROBT. JENKINS.
Painter. Born in Baltimore, MD, on Jan. 16, 1853. He studied under Chase and Wyant in NY. Specialty, flower painting. He died in San Antonio, TX, July 2, 1917.

O'NEILL, JOHN A.
Engraver. Born in NJ. He worked chiefly in the city of New York, engraving portraits and historical subjects. During the Cleveland administration, O'Neill was chief engraver to the Treasury Department at Washington, D. C. In 1876 he was mayor of Hoboken, NJ.

O'NEILL, R. E.
Painter. Born in Trenton, NJ, in 1893. Pupil of A. W. Dow; Lachman; Angel Zarrago, and of C. H. Martin. Member: Society of Independent Artists. Address in 1926: 331 Johnston Ave., Trenton, NJ.

O'NEILL, ROSE CECIL.
Illustrator. Born in Nebraska, in 1875. A self-taught artist, she wrote and illustrated the unpublished novel Calesta at age 19. Shortly thereafter she came to NY where she worked for Truth, Life, Collier's and Harper's publications. She married in 1896 and became a staff artist for Puck. Five years later she was divorced, left Puck, and was soon married to its editor, Leon Wilson. In 1904 she wrote The Loves of Edwy for Harper's and illustrated her husband's novels. Early in 1908 she divorced Wilson and moved to Bonniebrook in Missouri, where she originated the Kewpies, the cherubic creatures that made her famous. The Kewpies first appeared in Ladies' Home Journal in 1909 and were later seen in Woman's Home Companion, Good Housekeeping and as

a comic strip in The New York Journal in the 1930's. The ubiquitous use of her characters culminated in the creation of the Kewpie Doll in 1912. Died in 1944.

ONTHANK, NATHAN B.
Portrait painter, who flourished in Boston from 1850 to 1879. The Gallery in Independence Hall, Philadelphia, has a copy of the portrait of Samuel Adams by Copley that was painted by Onthank.

OPERTI, ALBERT.
(Jasper Ludwig Roccabigliera). Painter. Born in Turin, Italy, in 1852. He became artist, caricaturist, and scenic artist in New York theatres. Studied Arctic history; made 2 voyages to Arctic regions with Comdr. R. E. Peary, U. S. N.; painted historical pictures, "Rescue of the Greeley Party" and "Farthest North," for army and navy depts., Wash.; also "The Schwatka Search," "Finding De Long in the Lena Delta (Jeanette)"; "Dr. Kane"; portrait of Comdr. Peary; mural paintings in Amer. Mus. of Natural His., NY, and in the Pittsfield, MA, Mus. Address in 1926, Amer. Mus. of Natural History, NYC.

OPPER, FREDERICK BURR.
Cartoonist. Born Madison, Lake Co., OH, Jan. 2, 1857. Member: SI 1910. On staff of "Journal" since 1899. Illustrated "Mark Twain," "Mr. Dooley." Address in 1929, 62 Circuit Road, New Rochelle, NY.

OPPER, LAURA.
Portrait painter. Studied at National Academy of Design under Chase and Beckwith; also studied abroad. Member of Art Students' League, New York. She died in New York City on Sept. 18, 1924.

ORD, JOSEPH BIAYS.
Portrait painter. Born in 1805 in Phila.; also well known in Philadelphia as a still-life and religious painter. He was a member of the first Council of the Artists' Fund Society in 1835. His portrait of his father, the ornithologist, is owned by the Academy of Natural Sciences. He died in Philadelphia in 1865.

ORDWAY, ALFRED.
Painter. Portraitist and landscapist. Born in 1819. Resident of Boston and founder of the Boston Art Club in 1854. His specialty was landscape painting. Among his best known works were "On the Charles River," "Newton Lower Falls," and "Arline." He died on Nov. 17, 1897, in Boston.

OREN, MAURY.
315 East 56th, New York, NY. Born in Pasadena, CA, Aug. 6, 1930. Work: Stanley Marcus, Dallas; Mrs. Harcourt Amory, Jr., NYC. Exhib.: York Gallery, NY; Litchfield Gallery, CT; Bramante Gallery, London; Oliva Gallery, NYC; Norma Clark Gallery, London; Fairmount Galley, Dallas, TX.

ORENTLICHERMAN, ISAAC HENRY.
Painter. Born Russia, Nov. 3, 1895. Pupil of Sergeant Kendall; Laurens and Lapparra in Paris. Member: Meriden SAC.; S. Indp. A. Address in 1929, 545 Miller Avenue, Brooklyn, NY.

ORFUSS, ELSIE.
Painter. Born in Harrisburg, PA, in 1913. Studied: Grand Central School of Art; Hans Hofmann School of Fine Arts; Art Students League; also in Europe. Award: National Association of Women Artists, 1956. Collection: Chrysler Collection.

ORGAN, MARJORIE.
(Mrs. Robert Henri). Caricaturist. Born New York, NY., Dec. 3, 1886. Pupil of Dan McCarthy and Robert Henri. Member: S. Indp. A.; NYS Women A. Work: "Reggie and the Heavenly Twins," "The Man Haters' Club," "Strange What a Difference a Mere Man Makes," in New York "Journal"; caricatures of stage, etc., for New York World. Died in 1931. Address in 1929, 10 Gramercy Park, New York, NY.

ORLOFF, GREGORY.
Painter. Born Russia, March 17, 1890. Pupil of Ivan Olinsky, K. Buer; Kokenev in Russia. Member: Chicago SA; Chicago NJSA; South Side AA. Address in 1929, 59 East Van Buren Street, Chicago, IL

ORMSBY, WATERMAN LILLY.
Engraver. Born in Hampton, Windham County, Conn, in 1809; died in Brooklyn, NY, in 1883. Ormsby was a student in the NAD, in 1829, and though his preceptor in engraving is unknown, he was engraving over his own name in Albany, NY, at an early date; he was also engraving for Carter, Andrew & Co., of Lancaster, Mass. Being of a decided mechanical turn of mind he invented a ruling-machine, a transferpress, and a "grammagraph," a device for engraving on steel, directly from medals and medallions. Died Nov. 1, 1883.

ORR, ALFRED EVERITT.
Painter and illustrator. Born in New York in 1886. Pupil of NY Art Students' League; W. M. Chase; the Royal Academy, London. Author of poster "For Home and Country" (5th Liberty Loan). Address in 1926, 14 West 72d St., New York.

ORR, ELEANOR MASON.
Painter. Born Newton Centre, MA, Aug. 15, 1902. Pupil of Boston Museum School of Fine Arts. Member: Copley S. Address in 1929, 66 Pleasant Street, Newton Centre, MA.

ORR, FRANCES MORRIS.
Painter. Born in Springfield, Mo., in 1880. Pupil of G. A. Thompson. Address in 1926: Woodland Road, Sewickley, PA.

ORR, JOHN WILLIAM
Wood engraver, who was born in Ireland, March 31, 1815. He was brought to this country as a child. He studied engraving on wood in New York, and later established there the most important engraving business in that section of the country. He produced the frontispieces for Harper's Illustrated Shakespeare. He died on Mar. 4, 1887, in Jersey City, NJ.

ORR, LOUIS.
Painter and etcher. Born Hartford, CT, May 19, 1879. Pupil of Laurens in Paris; Knight of the Legion of Honor. Work: Mural decorations in State Bank, Hartford, CT; 22 original Pencil drawings "Rheims Cathedral, 1917," and 11 etchings in the Luxembourg, Paris; one etched copper plate in the Louvre, Paris; one plate in New York Public Library; two etchings in Oakland (CA.) Museum; etching in Strasbourg Mus; 3 etchings Rheims of Cathedral, National American Red Cross; 2 plates in French Goverment collection. Address in 1929, 5 Rue Mazarine Paris, France.

ORTLIP, AIMEE E.
(Mrs. H. W. Ortlip). Painter. Born Philadelphia, PA., April 21, 1888. Pupil of William M. Chase, Sargeant Kendall, Henry McCarter. Address in 1929, Old Palisade Road, Fort Lee, NJ.

ORTLIP, H. WILLARD.
Painter. Born Norristown, PA, March 28, 1886. Pupil of William M. Chase, Sargeant Kendall, Henry McCarter. Award: Popular vote prize ($100), Woman's Club, Patterson, NJ, 1928. Work: Decorations featuring historic incidents, Hotel Huntington, LI, NY. Address in 1929, Old Palisade Road, Fort Lee, N.J.

ORTMAN, GEORGE.
Painter. Born Oct. 17, 1926 in Oakland, CA. Studied at Berkeley (1947-8); Hans Hofmann School (1950-1); and W. Andre L'Hote in Paris (1950). Taught at School of Visual Arts (NYC); NYU; Princeton and now at Cranbrook Acad. of Art. Awarded Guggenheim (1965); Birmingham Museum of Art Religion in Art prize; NJ State Museum prize (1967). Exhibited at Tanger Gallery (NYC) 1954; Wittenborn Gal. (NYC), 1956; Fairleigh Stable Gal. (NYC), 1953 - 1961; Dickson U (1962); S. F. Museum of Art (1952 & 1963) Seattle World's Fair (1962); Jewish Museum (NYC); Wash. Gallery of Mod. Art; MOMA, NYC; Carnegie Inst. In collections of Whitney Mus. and MOMA (both in NYC); De Cordova Art Mus., Lincoln, Mass; Albright-Knox Art Gal., Buffalo, NY; New York U.; Walker Art Center; Michener Foundations; private collections.

ORTMAYER, CONSTANCE.
Sculptor and educator. Born in NYC on July 19, 1902. Studied: Royal

Academy of Fine Arts, Vienna, Austria. Awards: National Academy of Design, 1935; Whitney Museum of American Art, 1940; Florida Federation of Art, 1948; Rollins College, 1947. Exhib.: Brooklyn Mus.; Whitney; PAFA; others. Collections: Brookgreen Gardens, South Carolina; American Numismatic Society, NY; US Post Office, Arcadia, Florida; US Post Office, Scottsboro, Alabama. Teaching: Prof. of sculpt., Rollins College, from 1937 (also chairman of art dept.). Address in 1980, 617 W. Second N. St., Morristown, TN.

ORWIG, LOUISE.
Painter. Born Miffinburg, PA. Pupil of William M. Chase, Henry McCarter and Daniel Garber. Member: Fellowship PAFA; Des Moines AFA. (Sec.); Des Moines Sketch C; Iowa AC. Awards: Cresson scholarship, PAFA, 1911; prize ($100), 1911; first prize, 1919 and 1920, gold medal and $100 purchase prize, 1921; $100 purchase prize, 1923; hon. mention, 1927, all from the Women's Club of Des Moines. Address in 1929, Public Library, Des Moines, Iowa.

OSBORN, FRANK C.
Painter and craftsman. Born Altamont, NY, June 13, 1888. Member: S. Indp. A.; Salons of Am. Alliance. Address in 1929, 20 West 22nd Street, h. 1 Fifth Ave., New York, NY.; summer, West Georgetown, ME.

OSBORN, M.
This stipple-engraver of portraits was working in Baltimore, MD, in 1812. In 1820 Osborn was located in Philadelphia.

OSBORN, MILO.
Born c. 1810 in Mass. In 1836 this very clever line-engraver of portraits and landscape was employed in New York. He was later working for Philadelphia magazines. One of his contemporaries says that he became dissipated and disappeared.

OSBORNE, LILLIE.
(Mrs. Lithgow Osborne). Sculptor. Born Aalholm, Denmark, March 8, 1887. Studied in Copenhagen, Rome,

Paris. Specialty, portrait-statuettes of children and animals. Address in 1929, 99 South Street, Auburn, NY.

OSGOOD, CHARLES.
Portrait painter. Born Feb. 25, 1809, in Salem, MA. In 1827 he opened his studio in Boston, and in 1828 he returned to Salem where he lived until his death. His portraits hang in the historical societies in Boston, Worcester and the Peabody Museum of Salem. Died in 1890.

OSGOOD, HARRY H.
Painter and etcher. Born in Illinois, 1875. Pupil of Julien and Colarossi Academies in Paris. Address in 1926, 1538 East 57th St., New York.

OSGOOD, SAMUEL TILLMAN.
Portrait painter. Born June 9, 1808, in New Haven, CT. Studied art in Europe, and settled in New York. The New York Historical Society owns a number of his portraits. He is said to have died in California in 1885.

OSNIS, BENEDICT A.
Portrait painter. Born in Russia in 1872. Pupil of Penna. Academy of Fine Arts. Address in 1926, The Art Club, Philadelphia.

OSSORIO, ALFONSO.
Sculptor and painter. Born Aug. 2, 1916 in Manila, Phillipines. Studied at Harvard (1938); and R.I. School of Design (1938-9). Lives in U.S. Exhibited at Wakefield Gallery (NYC), (1941-61); Galerie Paul Facchetti, Paris (1951); Betty Parsons Gal., Cordier and Warren, MOMA, and Whitney Mus. (all in NYC). In private collections, and in those of the Guggenheim; Phil. Museum of Art; NYU; Whitney and MOMA.

OSTER, JOHN.
Painter, craftsman, and teacher. Born Heidelberg, Germany, Sept. 14, 1873. Pupil of Douglas Volk; NAD. Work: Stained glass windows, Harvard University Museum, Cambridge, MA; John Singer Sargent stained glass window, Boston, MA.

Address in 1929, 279 Columbia Avenue, Jersey City, NJ.

OSTHAUS, EDMUND.
Painter. Born at Hildesheim, Germany, in 1858. Pupil of Andreas Muller, Peter Jansen, E. V. Gebhardt, E. Deger and C. Kroner. He came to the United States in 1883; called to Toledo, Ohio, as principal of the Toledo Academy of Fine Arts, 1886; this school was later abandoned; he devotes his entire time to pictures; paints principally pictures of shooting and fishing, hunters and dogs being the general subjects. Address in 1926, 27 Bedford Road, Summit, NJ. Died Jan. 30, 1928 in Jackson County, FL.

OSTRANDER, PHILLIP.
Landscape engraver. Worked in New York, and later in Cincinnati, OH, from 1850-55.

OSTRANDER, WILLIAM CHEESEBROUGH.
Painter. Born New York, NY, March 5, 1858. Pupil of Carl Hecker, Murphy, Scott and Venino. Member: Salma. C., 1897; A. Fund S; NYSC; Amer. Inst. Graphic A; AFA. Address in 1929, c/o J. Ross Mackenzie, 3472 E. Hill Street, Huntington Park, CA.

OSTROM, CORA CHAMBERS.
Painter. Born Harrison, Ark., Sept. 2, 1871. Pupil of Maria Brown; Wells; Arpa. Member: San Antonio AL; SSAL. Address in 1929, 305 Ceylon Street, Eagle Pass, Texas.

OSTROWSKY, ABBO.
Painter, etcher, and teacher. Born Russia, Oct. 23, 1889. Studied in Russia; pupil of NAD; Turner; Maynard. Member: S. Indp. A.; Am. APL; Salons of Am.; Paris S. Indp. A. Work: Bibliotheque Nationale, Paris; Gregg Collection, Univ. of Nebraska. Founder and Director, Educational Alliance Art School, New York. Address in 1929, Alliance, 197 East Broadway; h. 31 Gramercy Park, New York, NY.

OSTROWSKY, SAM.
Painter, lecturer, and teacher. Born Russia, May 5, 1885. Pupil of Harry Wolcott and AIC, Laurens and Academie Julian in Paris. Member: S. Indp. A. Award: Hon. mention, AIC. Address in 1929, 1868 South Central Park Avenue, Chicago, IL.

OTIS, AMY.
Miniature painter and teacher. Born Sherwood, NY. Pupil of Philadelphia School of Design and PAFA; Colarossi Academy, Courois and Garrido in Paris. Member: Plastic C.; Phila. WCC; PA S. Min. P., Fellowship PAFA. In charge, Art Dept. Wheaton College. Address in 1929, Wheaton College, Norton, MA.

OTIS, BASS.
Painter and engraver. Born July 17, 1784 in Bridgewater, MA. Made the first lithograph in the United States. Apprenticed as a youth to a scythemaker, it is not known from whom he gleaned instruction in art, but in 1808 he was painting portraits in New York and four years later settled in Philadelphia. His well-known portrait of President Jefferson was engraved for Delaplaine's "Portrait Gallery" and many other celebrities sat for him. One of his best works is a portrait of himself, painted shortly before his death. In 1815 he invented the perspective protractor, which was well-received by his co-workers in art, and in 1819, for the July issue of the Analectic Magazine, he produced the first lithograph in this country. The design was made on a stone brought from Munich and he did the printing himself. Only one composition from his brush is known -- a large interior of a smithy, possibly the one in which he served his apprenticeship. This was first exhibited at the Pennsylvania Academy of the Fine Arts in 1819, and was afterwards presented to that institution. In 1815 he painted a delightful portrait of John Neagle, at the age of nineteen, who worked in his atelier. Died Nov. 3, 1861 in Philadelphia.

OTIS, GEO(RGE) DE(MONT).
Painter. Born Sept. 21, 1877. Pupil of John Carlson, R. Schmidt, Reynolds, Poole, Vanderpoel, Robert Henri. Member: Calif. AC; Los Angeles PS; Palette and Chisel C.

of Chicago; Laguna Beach AA; Cliff Dwellers. Award: State prize, Sacramento, Calif., 1925. Work: "Little Blue House," Art Inst. of Chicago; "Pigeon Hill," Hackley Gallery of Fine Arts, Muskegon, MI. Address in 1929, 304 Avon Street, Burbank, CA.

OTIS, SAMUEL DAVIS.
Painter, illustrator, and teacher. Born Sherwood, NY, July 4, 1889. Pupil of Henry McCarter. Member: Silvermine GA; GFLA. Illustrated "Cyrano de Bergerac" and "Francesca da Rimini"; illustrations for Harpers Bazaar. Address in 1929, Norwalk, CT.

OTNES, FRED.
Illustrator. Born in Junction City, Kansas, in 1926. He attended the AIC and the American Academy. Since 1946 his illustrations, exhibiting his fine draftsmanship, have appeared in publications including True, The Saturday Evening Post and Reader's Digest. Recently he has concentrated on intricate and superbly crafted assemblages and elegant illustrations utilizing new photographic and printing techniques. He has received over 100 honors, including the Hamilton King Award from the S of I, and is a founding member of the Illustrators Workshop.

OTT, RALPH C.
Painter. Born Springfield, MO. Pupil of Constant and Laurens. Member: Phila. AC. Represented State Capitol, Jefferson City, MO; Public Library, Springfield, MO; City Art Museum and Masonic Lodge, St. Louis, MO. Address in 1929, 809 East Grand Avenue, Springfield, MO.

OTTER, THOMAS.
Painter. Resided in Philadelphia. Represented by his picture "Moonlight," painted in 1860, in the Wilstach Collection, Fairmount Park, Philadelphia. Also an engraver.

OTTIANO, JOHN WILLIAM.
Sculptor and Jeweler. 1115 Glen Lake Blvd., Pitman, NJ 08071. Born in Medford, MA, July 23, 1926.

Study: Mass. College of Art; Boston Univ.; Penn. State Univ. Work: University of Western Illinois, IL; The Pennsylvania State Univ.; Glassboro State College, NJ; private collections. Commissions for Glassboro State College and NJ Art Educ. Assn. Exhib.: The Penn. Academy of Fine Arts, PA; The Speed Art Museum, KY; Nat'l. Acad. Galleries, NYC; and others. Teaching: Glassboro State Col., NJ; and others. Mem.: Am. Assn. of Univ. Professors; NJ Art Educ. Assn.; NJ Designer-Craftsmen Assn.; Artists Equity Assn.; Nat'l. Art Educ. Assn. Media: Bronze, gold, silver.

OURDAN, JOSEPH PROSPER.
Engraver. Born in New York City, Feb. 16, 1828; died in Washington, DC, May 10, 1881. Joseph P. Ourdan was the son of Joseph James Prosper Ourdan, and served his apprenticeship as an engraver with W. L. Ormsby, of NY. Over his own name he engraved in line some good portraits and illustrative works for the book publishers, and the firm of Packard & Ourdan produced portraits in mezzotint; but he early became interested in banknote work and was in the employ of the Continental and the National banknote companies, of New York, and of the American Bank Note Company, of Philadelphia.

OURDAN, JOSEPH JAMES PROSPER.
Engraver. Born in Marseilles, France, in March, 1803; died in Washington, DC, Oct. 25, 1874. Jos. J. P. Ourdan came to New York in 1821; moved later to Philadelphia, and having learned to engrave through instruction by his son, Joseph P. Ourdan, he became an expert letter engraver. In this capacity he was employed by the United States Treasury Department, at Washington, from 1866 until his death.

OURDAN, VINCENT LE COMTE.
Engraver. Born in Brooklyn, NY, in 1855. He served his apprenticeship as an engraver with the Columbian Bank-Note Company, of Washington, DC, from 1875 to 1878; for some time he was employed in the Bureau

of Engraving and Printing, and then returned to the Columbian Company and was with the latter until it went out of business. In 1882 Mr. Ourdan went to the United States Hydrographic Office, in Washington, and there created the Mechanical Engraving Department.

OUREN, KARL.
Painter. Born Fredrikshald, Norway, Feb. 5, 1882. Studied in Copenhagen and at AIC; Hans Larvin at Palette and Chisel C., Chicago. Member: Palette and Chisel C.; AIC Alumni; Scandinacian American A.; Chicago Gal. A. Award: Gold medal, Palette and Chisel C., 1919. Represented, Milwaukee Art Institute. Died in 1943. Address in 1929, 2334 North Sawyer Ave., Chicago, IL

OURLAC, JEAN NICOLAS.
Painter. Born in New Orleans, LA, in 1789; died in 1821 in Paris. The subjects of his paintings are mostly taken from American scenery.

OUTBANK, NAHUM BALL.
Painter. Born 1823. Lived in Boston from 1856-79. He painted portraits of John Brown, Wendell Phillips, and others of his friends. Died in 1888.

OUTCAULT, RICHARD F.
Comic illustrator. Born Jan. 4, 1863 in Lancaster, OH. Studied at McMicken U., Cincinnati, OH. Created 1st full page color comic ever published, "Hogan's Alley" (N.Y. Sun. World). Syndicated work. Also created "The Yellow Kid" and the very popular "Buster Brown," based on his son Richard, Jr. On staff of the New York Journal since 1905. Member: Salmagundi Club. Painted last 10 yr. of life. Died Sept. 25, 1928 in Flushing, L.I., NY.

OVERBECK, MARY FRANCIS.
Painter and craftsman. Born Cambridge City, Indp, Jan. 28, 1878. Pupil of Arthur Dow at Columbia Unviersity, New York. Member: Cincinnati Woman's AC; Indiana Artists' Club. Specialty, Overbeck Pottery. Represented by Overbeck Pottery at John Herron Art Institute, Indianapolis, IN; and

Gen. Fed. of Woman's Clubs, Washington, D.C. Address in 1929, Cambridge City, IN.

OVRYN, BENJAMIN S.
Painter. Born Russia, Oct. 3, 1892. Pupil of Ladisenski. Member: S. Indp. A; Alliance; Salons of Am. Address in 1929, 17 Cook Street, h. 890 Flushing Ave., Brooklyn, NY; summer, Piermont, NY.

OWEN, MRS. ESTHER S. D.
(Mrs. Charles H. Owen) Painter. Born Sept. 19, 1843 in Boston, MA. Pupil of Votin, Geary and Tuckerman. Member: Conn. Academy of Fine Arts. Represented in Worcester Art Museum. Died Sept. 20, 1927 in Hartford, CT.

OWINGS, THOMAS BOND.
Painter. Member: Balto. WCC. Address in 1929, 1215 John Street, Baltimore, MD.

PACH, WALTER.
Painter. Born in New York, July 11, 1883. Pupil of Leigh Hunt, Chase and Henri in New York. Member: Societe des Artistes Independants, Paris; S. Indp. A. Represented in Metropolitan Museum of Art; Cleveland Museum of Art; Newark Museum. Articles in Scribner's, Century, Harper's, La Gazette des Beaux Arts. Author of The Masters of Modern Art, Georges Seurat, Modern Art in America and Ananias or the False Artist. Died in 1958. Address in 1929, 48 West 56th St., New York.

PACKARD, MABEL.
Miniature painter. Born in Iowa. Pupil of AIC; Colarossi Academy and Mme. La Forge in Paris. Member: Chicago SA. Award: Bronze medal, St. Louis Exp., 1904. Address in 1929, 2031 Berkshire Ave., South Pasadena, Calif.

PACKER, FRANCIS H(ERMAN).
Sculptor. Born in 1873. Member: NSS 1905. Died in 1957. Address in 1929, Rockville Center, LI, NY.

PACKMAN, FRANK G.
Painter, illustrator and etcher. Born England, June 5, 1896. Pupil of John P. Wicker, Paul Honore. Member: Scarab C; Mich. Academy Science, Arts and Letters. Address in 1929, 1512 Book Tower, Detroit, Mich.; h. 2822 Benjamin Ave., Royal Oak, Mich.; summer; Petoskey. Mich.

PADDOCK, ETHEL LOUISE.
Painter. Born New York City, April 19, 1887. Pupil of New York School of Art, and Henri. Member: S. Indp. A.; NA Women PS; PBC; NY Soc. Women A; Salons of Am.

PADDOCK, JOSEPHINE.
Painter. Exhibited at the Penna. Academy of Fine Arts, Philadelphia, 1914. Portraits, "Miss Trelawney" and "The Sealskin Muffs." Address in 1926, 130 West 57th St., New York City.

PADDOCK, WILLARD D(RYDEN).
Painter and sculptor. Born Brooklyn, NY, Oct. 23, 1873. Pupil of Herbert Adams in New York; Pratt Inst. in Brooklyn; Courtois and Girardot in Paris. Member: ANA;

NY Arch. Lg.; Salma. C., 1904; MacD. C.; NSS, 1915; A. Aid S.; Allied AA; Wash. AC; century Asso. Died in 1956. Address in 1929, South Kent, Conn.

PAEFF, BASHKA (WAXMAN).
Sculptor and teacher. Born Misk, Russia, Aug. 12, 1893. Pupil of Bela Pratt. Member: Boston GA; Detroit SAC; BSAC; Boston SA; MacDowell Colony. Work: Mass. Chaplains' War Memorial Hall of Fame, State House, Boston; World War Memorial, State of Maine, Kittery, ME; bronze bas-relief of "Dr. Elmer E. Southard," Boston Psychopathic Hospital; John E. Warren Memorial bronze fountain, Westbrook, ME; Julius Rosenwald fountain, Ravina, Ill.; bronze bas-relief for "Dr. E. Fernald," Fernald State School, Waverly, Mass.; "Boy and Bird" fountain, Stoughton, Mass.; "Judge Manly B. Allen" for City of Birmingham, Ala.; bronse bas-relief, "Ellen H. Richards," Mass. Institute of Technology; bronze bas-relief, C. H. Hovey Co., Boston, Mass. Died in 1979. Address in 1929, 38 Joy St., Boston, Mass.

PAGE, GROVER.
Illustrator and cartoonist. Born Eastonia, NC, Nov. 10, 1892. Pupil of AIC; Chicago AFA. Member: Louisville AA. Specialty, cartoons. Died in 1958. Address in 1929, Louisville Courier-Journal; Louisville, KY; h. 1703 DePauw Pl., New Albany, Ind.

PAGE, KATHERINE S(TUART).
Painter. Born Cambridge, MD. Pupil of Phila. Sch. of design for Women; Margaretta Archambault. Member: Phila. PC. Specialty, miniatures. Address in 1929, 1524 - 28th St., NW, Washington, DC; summer, South Boston, VA.

PAGE, MARIE D(ANFORTH).
(Mrs. Calvin G. Page). Portrait painter. Born Boston. Pupil of School of the Boston Museum of Fine Arts. Member: ANA; Copley S; Concord AA; Boston GA; AFA. Awards: Bronze medal, P.-P. Exp., San F., 1915; Bok prize, PAFA, 1916; first prize and hon. men., Duxbury AA, 1920; Greenough prize,

Newport AA, 1921; Isidor prize, NAD, 1923; bronze medal, Sesqui-Centennial Exposition, Phila., 1926; Thomas R. Proctor prize, NAD, 1928; Harold H. Swift prize, Grand Cent. Gallery, 1928. Died in 1940. Address in 1929, 128 Marlborough St., Boston, Mass.

PAGE, WALTER GILMAN.
Painter and writer. Born Boston in 1863. Pupil of Boston Museum School; Boulanger and Lefebvre in Paris. Member: Boston Museum School Alumni Asso.; Portland SA (life); Springfield AS; AFA; Mass. State Art Commission. Work: "A Head," Toledo Museum of Art; "Lillian," Art Museum, Portland, ME; portraits in Massachusetts State House; Portland (ME) City Hall; Bowdoin College; Maine Historical Society; Colby College, Maine; Vermont State House; Worcester Public Library; Fall River Public Library; Fall River Public Library; Lowell City Hall; Dracut Public Library; Tufts College, Mass. Died in 1934. Address in 1929, Nantucket, Mass.

PAGE, WILLIAM.
Painter. Born Jan. 23, 1911 in Albany, NY. He moved with his family to New York City in 1820 and entered the law office of Frederick De Peyster when quite a young man, but soon devoted himself entirely to art, studying under Professor Morse, and in the Schools of the National Academy. He painted portraits in Albany, 1828-29, returned to New York, and, later, opened a studio in Boston, where he remained until he went to Europe. He was for many years considered the leading American portrait painter in Rome. Elected a member of the National Academy in 1836, and delivered lectures to the Academy students which were highly esteemed. Among his earlier works are a "Holy Family," belonging to the Boston Athenaeum, a portrait of Governor Marcy, in the City Hall, New York, and "The Infancy of Henry IV." His exhibits in the National Academy include "Antique Timbrel Player," 1871; "Farragut's Triumphant Entry into Mobile Bay," 1872; "Shakespeare," 1874; "Shakespeare, from the German Death Mask," 1876. He was much impressed with the death mask of Shakespeare and wrote several articles in support of its authenticity. He painted a head of "Christ" which attracted much attention, because of the deep religious sentiment it expressed. A number of Page's pictures were on exhibition in New York in the winter of 1877, including his "Shakespeares" and his celebrated "Venus," painted in Rome, 1859, and exhibited in London and other cities including Philadelphia. The Penna. Academy has an interesting genre painting by Page, of excellent qualities, but in curious condition as to color--it being possibly one of the experiments in color which the artist was reputed to be fond of trying. He died at his home on Staten Island, Oct. 1, 1885.

PAGES, JULES.
Painter and teacher. Born San Francisco, Calif., 1867. Pupil of Constant, Lefebvre and Robert-Fleury in Paris. Awards: Hon. mention, Paris Salon, 1895; third medal, Paris Salon, 1899; second medal, Paris Salon, 1905. Knight of the Legion of Honor, 1910. Instructior at the Julian Academy night class since 1902; life class since 1907. Member: Int. Soc. Paris SP. Represented in Museum of Pau, France; Museum of Toulouse, France; the Luxembourg, Paris; Golden Gate Park Museum and Art Inst., San Francisco; Municipal Art Gallery, Oakland, Calif. Died May 22, 1946. Address in 1929, 42 Rue Fontaine, Paris, France.

PAGET-FREDERICKS, J(OSEPH) (ROUS).
Painter, illustrator, writer and lecturer. Born San Francisco, Calif., Dec. 22, 1903. Pupil of Leon Bakst, John Singer Sargent. Member: Los Angeles Museum Patrons Assoc. Represented in the collection of Mills College, Calif. Author and illustrator of "Green Peas", "Miss Pert's Christmas Tree" (Macmillan); "Pavlowa Impressions," "Atlantis," "These Younger Years" and "Red Roofs and Flowerpots". Illustrator of "The Collected Poems of Edna St. Vincent Millay" (Harper). Lecturers on "Creative Imagination in the Arts." Died in

1963. Address in 1929, 2503 Hilgard Ave., Berkeley, Calif.; summer, Iona Island, NY; Chardstock House, Sommerset, England.

PAGON, KATHERINE DUNN.
(Mrs. William Watters Pagon). Painter. Born Chestnut Hill, Philadelphia, Dec. 25, 1892. Pupil of PAFA; Hugh Breckenridge. Member: Fellowship PAFA; MD Inst. Alumni A. (asso.); Friends of Art; alto. S. Indp. A; AFA. Address in 1929, 114 St. John's Road, Roland Park, Batimore, MD.

PAINE, MAY.
Painter. Born Charleston, SC, May 7, 1873. Pupil of Leith-Ross; Frank Chase; Gruppe; Alfred Hutty; Ivan Summers. Member: SSAL. Award: First prize, SSAL. Address in 1929, 47 Meeting St., Charleston, SC.

PAINE, RICHARD G.
Sculptor. Born in Charleston, SC, in 1875. Pupil of Amateis and Kemeys. Address in 1926, East Falls Church, VA.

PALL, AUGUSTIN G.
Painter. Member: Chicago Society of Artists. Address in 1926, 19 East Pearson St., Chicago, Ill.

PALLADINI, DAVID.
Illustrator. Born in Roteglia, Italy, in 1946. Studied art from 1964 to 1968 at PI under Jacob Landau and Gabriel Laderman. He produced a poster for Lincoln Center's Vivian Beaumont Theatre in 1965 and has worked for many major magazines and book companies. He has exhibited illustrations at the AIGA, S of I and Saks Fifth Avenue Galleries; his works are also in the collection of the Museum of Warsaw, Poland.

PALLISON.
A landscape painter, noted in Tuckerman's "American Artist Life."

PALMER, (JESSIE) (A.).
Painter. She was born Lawrence, Tex., Oct. 19, 1882. Pupil of Frank Reaught, Martha Simkins, John Carlson. Member: Tex. FAA; SSAL; Reaugh AC; Amarillo AA. Awards: Evert's medal, Dallas Forum,

Dallas, Tex., 1924; 1st prize, Tex.-Okla. Fair, 1926, 1927; hon. mention, Tex. FAA, Nashville, Tenn., 1927. Work: "Bluebonnets," Travis School, Dallas; "In Colorado," Dallas Woman's Forum, Dallas, Tex. Address in 1929, 905 Polk St.; h. 806 Palo Duro St., Amarillo, Tex.

PALMER, ADELAIDE.
Painter. Born Orford, NH. Pupil of John J. Enneking. Member: Copley S. 1893. Address in 1929, 739 Boylston St., Boston, Mass.; summer, Piermont, NH.

PALMER, E. V.
See Elizabeth Palmer Bradfield.

PALMER, ERASTUS DOW.
Sculptor. Born April 2, 1817 in Pompey, Onondaga County, NY. He first executed cameo portraits and finally undertook real sculpture. All his knowledge was acquired in America, and it was not until he had become famous that he visited Europe. Among his best known works are "The Indian Girl;" "White Captive;" "Morning and Evening." He died in Albany, NY, March 9, 1904.

PALMER, FRANCES FLORABOND.
Painter. Born in Leicester, Eng., in 1812. Came to NYC in early 1840's; worked for Currier & Ives from 1849 for many years. Her specialty was sporting scenes; well known for land and townscapes. Her lithographs were also published by Nathaniel Currier. She was the only woman in her field and was considered one of the best Am. lithographers. Died Aug. 20, 1876.

PALMER, FREDRIKKE S(CHJOETH).
Painter. She was born Drammen, Norway, May 26, 1860. Pupil of Knut Bergslien in Christiania; Carl Gussow in Berlin. Member: New Haven Paint and Clay C. Staff artist for Woman's Journal. Address in 1929, 1450 Kewalo St., Honolulu, T.H.

PALMER, HATTIE VIRGINIA YOUNG.
(Mrs. C. F. Palmer). Painter and teacher. Born Ripley, Ohio. Pupil of the Cincinnati Art Academy.

Member: Houston AL; Ind. AA; Ind. State Keramic C; Tex. FAA; Am. APL; SSAL. Address in 1929, 2616 Albany St., Houston, Tex.

PALMER, HERMAN.
Painter, sculptor, illustrator and etcher. Born Farmingham, Utah, March 17, 1894. Pupil of Mahonri Young. Member: NYWCC. Illustrated "Hidden Heroes of the Rockies." Address in 1929, 961 Madison Ave., New York, NY.

PALMER, J.
A number of large and fairly well-executed Bible illustrations, published in New York in 1826, are signed "J. Palmer, Sc."

PALMER, LEMUEL.
Illustrator, draughtsman and lecturer. Born Portland, ME, Nov. 1, 1893. Pupil of Richard Andrews; Mass. Sch. of Art. Awards: Strathmore award, Springfield AG, 1927; Milton Bradley award, Springfield AG, 1928. Address in 1929, Studio Bldg., 215 Dwight St.; h. 11 Priscilla St., Springfield, Mass.

PALMER, LUCIA A.
Painter. Born in Dryden, NY. Prize winner in Paris Exposition, 1900. Member: Woman's National Press Association, Washington. Address in 1926, Park Hill-on-Hudson, New York.

PALMER, MARGARET LONGYEAR.
Sculptor, craftsman and teacher. Born Detroit, Aug. 19, 1897. Pupil of John Wilson. Member: Detroit SAC; Detroit S. Women P. Award: First prize, Mich. State Fair, 1921. Address in 1929, 2 McKinley Pl., Grosse Pointe Farm, Mich.; 8103 Agnes Ave., Detroit, Mich.; summer, Huron Mountain Club, Huron Mountain, Mich.

PALMER, PAULINE.
(Mrs. Albert E. Palmer). Painter. Born McHenry, Ill. Pupil of AIC, Chase, Miller and Hawthorne; Collin, Prinet, Courtois and Simon in Paris. Member: Chicago PS (pres.); Rockford AA; Chicago WCC; Chicago Municipal AL; Chicago Art Guild; Chicago AC; Cordon C.; Chicago Alliance; Alumnae AIC;

Painters and Sculptors Gallery Asso.; Chicago SA; Ill. AFA; Grand Cent. Gal. Awards: Bronze medal, St. Louis Exp., 1904; Young Fortnightly prize, AIC, 1907; Marshall Field prize, AIC, 1907; Thompson portraiture prize, AIC, 1914; participant in Fine Arts prize, SWA, 1915; hon. mention, Chicago AG, 1915; Cahn hon mention, AIC, 1916; Rosenwald purchase prize, AIC, 1916; Carr prize, AIC, 1917; Butler Purchase Prize, AIC, 1920; silver medal, Chicago SA, 1920; silver medal, Peoria, 1921; Fine Arts Bldg. prize ($500), AIC, 1924; Rosenwald prize, AIC, 1916 hon. mention AIC, 1916; Carr prize, AIC, 1917; Butler Purchase Prize, AIC, 1920; silver medal, Chicago SA, 1920; silver medal, Peoria, 1921; Fine Arts Bldg. prize ($500), AIC 1924; hon. mention, N.A. Women PS, 1924; Rosenwald prize ($300), AIC, 1926; purchase prize ($500), Chicago Galleries Assn., 1928, and prize ($400), 1929. Represented in permanent collections of West End Woman's Club; Municipal Art League collection at Art Institute of Chicago; Nike Club; Klio Association and Arche Club, all of Chicago; public school collection of Decatur, Ill.; Muncie (Ind.) Art Association; "Village by the Sea" and "The Gingham Girl," Chicago Municipal Commission; Aurora, Ill., art Association; Rockford, Ill., Art Association; Rogers Park Woman's Club; Springfield, Ill., Art Association; Delgado Museum of Art, New Orleans; Aurora, Ill., Art League; San Diego Museum; Acad. of Fine Arts, Elgin, Ill. Died in 1938. Address in 1929, 4 East Ohio St., Chicago, Ill.; summer, 5 Webster Pl., Provincetown, Mass.

PALMER, WALTER L(AUNT).
Landscape painter. Born Albany, Aug. 1, 1854; son of the sculptor, Erastus Dow Palmer. Pupil of F. E. Church at Hudson, NY; Carolus-Duran in Paris. Member: ANA 1887; NA 1897; NA 1897; SAA 1881; NYWCC; AWCS; Salma. C. 1901; Pastel; Century Assoc.; AFA; Union Inter. des Beaux-Arts et des Lettres; NY State Fine Arts Commission. Awards: Second Hallgarten prize, NAD, 1887; medal, Columbian Exp., Chicago, 1893; gold medal, AC

Philadelphia, 1894; Evans prize, AWCS, 1895; second prize, Tennessee Centennial Exp., Nashville, 1897; hon. mention, Paris Exp., 1900; silver medal for water color, Pan.-Am. Exp., Buffalo, 1901; silver medal for water color, Charleston Exp., 1902; silver medal for water color and bronze medal for oil, St. Louis Exp., 1904; silver medal, Philadelphia, 1907; bronze medal, Buenos Aires Exp., 1910; Butler prize, AIC, 1919; Du Pont prize, Wilmington, 1926 and 1928. Specialty, winter landscapes. Work: "Sundown At Walpole, NH," Buffalo Fine Arts Academy, Buffalo, NY; "The Pasture Fence," Public Gallery, Richmond, Ind.; "Lingering Oak Leaves," Omaha (Neb.) Art Society; "Under the Pines," Memorial Art Gallery, Rochester, NY; "Silent Dawn," and "La Salute at Noon," Metropolitan Museum of Art; "The Dell," art Museum, Youngstown, O." "An Upland Stream," Museum of Fine Arts, Boston, Mass. Died April 16, 1932 in Albany, NY.

PALULIAN, DICKRAN P.
Illustrator. Born in Pontiac, Michigan, in 1938. Studied for two years at the Society of Arts and Crafts in Detroit and began his career there in 1958. The recipient of awards from the Michigan Watercolor Show, Detroit ADC and GAG of Detroit, he has illustrated for many magazines and has often exhibited his work in the Detroit area.

PANCOAST, HENRY B., JR.
Painter. Exhibited "Landscape" at the Penna. Academy of Fine Arts, Philadelphia, 1924. Address in 1926, 2201 Chestnut St., Philadelphia.

PANCOAST, MORRIS HALL.
Painter and illustrator. Born Salem, NJ, April 27, 1877. Pupil of PAFA under Anshutz; Julian Academy under Laurens in Paris. Member: Fellowship PAFA; Salma. C.; Phila. Alliance; North Shore AA; Conn. AFA. Award: Gold medal, Fellowship PAFA, 1924. Work: "Pennsy Train Shed," Pennsylvania Academy of the Fine Arts, Philadelphia; "Easter Snow Storm,"

Municipal Art League, Williamsport, PA; "The Art League, Williamsport, PA; "The Edge of a New England Village," Houston Art Museum; "Portugese Hill," Museum of Fine Arts, Reading, PA; drawings in Milwaukee Art Institute. Address in 1929, 47 Fifth Ave., New York, NY; summer, Rockport, Mass.

PANDICK, JOHN.
Painter. Exhibited at Philadelphia, 1921, in "Exhibition of Paintings Showing Later Tendencies in Art." Address in 1926, Fanwood, NJ.

PAOLO, CARTAINO S.
Sculptor. Born in Italy in 1882. Pupil of American Academy in Rome. Work: Bust of Ex-Gov. MacCall in Boston State House; Cardinal O'Connell in Boston Cathedral; marble memorial in Cathedral of St. John the Divine, New York. Address in 1926, 80 Washington Square, New York City.

PAPE, ALICE MONROE.
(Mrs. Eric Pape). Painter. Born Boston, Mass. Died May 17, 1911 in Manchester, Mass.

PAPE, ERIC.
Painter and illustrator. Born San F, CA, Oct. 17, 1870. Pupil of Emil Carlsen in NY; Ecole des Beaux-Arts in Paris under Gerome, Constant, Lefebvre, Doucet and Delance. Member: United Arts C., London; Royal Soc. of Arts, London; Atlantic Union, London; North British Academy; Players C., NY. Director, Eric Pape School of Art 1898 to 1913. Awards: Five medals and diplomas at various exhibitions. Illustrations for The Fair God, The Scarlet Letter, The Life of Napoleon Bonaparte; Life of Mahomet; Poetical Works of Madison Cawein; portraits for The Memoirs of Ellen Terry. Monument at Stage Fort Park, Gloucester, commemorating founding of Massachusetts Bay Colony, 1623. Director of pageants, "The Canterbury Pilgrims," Gloucester, MA, 1908 and "The Flowers of the Sea," Lookout Hill, MA, 1912. Died in 1938. Address in 1929, "The Plains," Manchester by-the-Sea, MA; and the Players, Gramercy Park, NY.

PAPPRILL, HENRY.
This engraver in aquatint produced at least two very large plates. One shows New York as seen from Governor's Island; the other is a most interesting and detailed view over the city from the steeple of St. Paul's Church. The first was engraved from a sketch made by F. Catherwood, and the other from a drawing by J. W. Hill. These plates were published in New York in 1849, and the view from St. Paul's steeple was reissued in 1855 with many changes in the buildings shown. There were also several editions of the other plate.

PAQUET, ANTHONY C.
Engraver. Born in Hamburg, Germany, in 1814; died in 1882 in Philadelphia. Paquet came to the United States in 1848 and found employment here as a die-sinker. From 1857 until 1864 he was assistant engraver of the U.S. Mint in Philadelphia. Among others he engraved the dies for medals of Buchanan, Everett, Grant, and Johnson.

PARADISE, JOHN.
Painter. Born Oct. 24, 1783 in New Jersey. He became a member of the National Academy of Design upon its formation in 1826. He painted many portraits of Methodist divines, his drawings being correct, but his ability as an artist not very high. His son John W. Paradise was an admirable engraver of portraits. Died Nov. 26, 1833 in NYC.

PARADISE, JOHN WESLEY.
Engraver. Born in New Jersey in 1809. John W. Paradise was the son of John Paradise was the son of John Paradise, an American portrait-painter who was born in 1783 and died in 1834. The son was a pupil of A. B. Durand and in time became an admirable line-engraver of portraits. He was one of the founders of the National Academy in 1826. Later in life John W. Paradise was chiefly employed as a banknote engraver, and he was working in this branch of his profession up to the time of his death. Died Aug. 17, 1862, in NYC.

PARAMINO, JOHN F.
Sculptor and teacher. Born Boston, 1889. Pupil of Augustus Saint-Gaudens and Bela L. Pratt. Member; Boston GA. Address in 1929, 295 Huntington Ave., Boston, Mass.; 28 Everett St., Arlington, Mass.

PARCELL, L. EVANS.
Illustrator. Member: SI. Address in 1929, 116 Duncan Ave., Washington, PA.

PARCELL, MALCOLM (STEPHENS).
Painter and etcher. Born Jan. 1, 1896. Pupil of Carnegie School of Fine Arts. Member: Pitts AA. Awards: Saltus gold medal, NAD, 1920. Work: "In a Pensive Mood," "Old Gate, Trinity Hall," Butler Art Institute, Youngstown, Ohio. Address in 1929, care of the Macbeth Galleries, 450 Fifth Ave., New York, NY; Casino Bldg., Main St., Washington, PA.

PARIS, W(ILLIAM) FRANCKLYN.
Mural painter, architect, writer and lecturer. Born in New York. Pupil of ASL of NY; Julian Academy in Paris; Salvi in Rome. Member: NY Arch. Lg. 1898; NSS (lay); Century Assn.; Museum of French Art (bd. trustees); A. Aid S.; Alliance; Societe Histoire d'Art Francaise; Societe Gens de Lettres de France; hon. fellow for life, Met. Museum of Art, NY; Awards: Legion of Honor of France; Knight of the Crown of Belgium; made "Knight of the Crown of Italy," 1924. Author: Rodin as a Symbolist; Biography of Albert Besnard; The French Institute and American Art; Modern Gobelin Tapestries; Decorative Elements in Architecture, The House that Love Buildt, etc. Lecturer, Univ. of PA, Vassar College, St. John's College, Univ. of MD, Cornell Univ. US Commissioner of Decorative Art, Paris Exp., 1900. Address in 1929, 7 East 48th St.; h. 11 East 68th St., New York, NY.

PARIS, WALTER.
Painter. Born Feb. 28, 1842 in London, England. Specialty, water color painting. He died in Washington, DC, on Nov. 26, 1906.

PARISSEN, OTTO.
Engraver. Born 1723. A silversmith and engraver on silver, he also designed the ornaments on the silverware he made. He was a native of Prussia and resided in New York City. His son painted miniatures. Died Jan. 17, 1811 in New Rochelle, NY.

PARISSEN, PHILIP.
Miniature painter, who flourished in 1798-1812 in New York. He was the son of a silversmith who came from Prussia. Died in 1882. Also listed as Parisen and Parisien.

PARISSEN, WILLIAM D.
Miniature painter. Born in 1800 in NYC. Flourished in 1819-32 in New York. Son of Philip Parissen. Died April 9, 1832.

PARK, ASA.
Portrait painter, who flourished about 1800, and died in 1827, in Lexington, Kentucky. Also painted still life.

PARKE, JESSIE BURNS.
Painter, illustrator, etcher. Born Paterson, NJ, Dec. 2, 1889. Pupil of Mary Morgan in Paterson; School of Applied Design for Women, New York; School of the Boston Museum of Fine Arts. Member: Alliance; AFA. Work: Portrait of Dean Roscoe Pound of Harvard Law School, Northwestern Univ., Evanston, Ill. Address in 1929, 121 Newbury St., Boston, Mass.; h. Robbins Road, Arlington Heights, Mass.

PARKER, A(NNA) B(ENEDICT).
(Mrs. Neilson T. Parker). Painter. Member: NA Women PS; NAC. Address in 1929, Woodstock, NY.

PARKER, ALFRED CHARLES.
Illustrator. Born in St. Louis, MO, in 1906. Studied at the St. Louis School of Fine Arts of Wash. Univ. and came to NY in the mid-1930's. His illustrations depicting mothers and daughters for Cosmopolitan and Ladies' Home Journal were trendsetters of the era. Since his first assignment in 1933 for Woman's Home Companion, his illustrations have appeared in women's magazines and have earned him a number of awards, including

election to the S of I Hall of Fame in 1965. He has served as President of the Westport Artists and as a founding faculty member of the FAS. His artwork has been exhibited in the US and Canada and is in many major collections. A long-time resident of NY and Westport, he now resides in Carmel Valley, Calif.

PARKER, CHARLES H.
Engraver. Born in Salem, Mass., about 1795; died in Philadelphia in 1819. Parker was a pupil of Gideon Fairman. He worked in Europe for a time, and about 1812 he was in business as an engraver in Philadelphia. He is referred to as the "best engraver of script, maps and ornament of his time." He was the engraver of the beautiful script on the title-page of the Analectic Magazine, of Philadelphia, and did considerable work of this character.

PARKER, CORA.
Painter and illustrator. Born in Kentucky. Pupil of Cincinnati Art School; Julian Academy in Paris. Member: Greenwich SA. Work: "Blue Waters of Gloucester," Kansas City (MO.) Art Club; "Prune Orchard, California," Nebraska Art Association, Lincoln. Custodian Art Gallery, Bruce Museum, Greenwich, Conn. Address in 1929, Greenwich, Conn.

PARKER, CUSHMAN.
Illustrator. Born Boston, Mass., April 28, 1881. Pupil of Laurens and Carl Marr. Member: SI; GFLA. Designer of covers for Saturday Evening Post, McCall's, Collier's, etc. Address in 1929, Woodstock, Ulster Co., NY; Onset, Mass.

PARKER, EDGAR.
Painter. Born in Mass. in 1840. He spent his professional life in Boston. Three of his portraits are in Faneuil Hall (Sumner-Wilson & Winslow); Whittier gave him sittings in 1875. He painted "Embarkation of the Pilgrims," after Weir.

PARKER, EMMA ALICE.
Painter and illustrator. Born in Gardner, Mass., in 1876. Pupil of

Sydney R. Burleigh, Robert Henri, F. V. Du Mond and of H. R. Poore. Member: Providence Water Color Club. Address in 1926, 42 College St., Providence, RI.

PARKER, GEORGE.
Engraver. Born in England, he was engraving excellent stipple portraits in London in 1832. He came to the United States about 1834, to work for Longacre & Herring on "The National Portrait Gallery" plates, and he seems to have remained continuously in this country until his death, which occurred about 1868. Parker engraved a considerable number of good portraits.

PARKER, GEORGE WALLER.
Painter. Born New York, NY, Sept. 17, 1888. Pupil of ASL of NY. Member: Salma. C.; Portland AS; Societe Colonial des Artists Francais; AAA. Award: Plaquette de grand prix, Expostion Coloniale, Strasbourg, 1924. Work: "Villiage Indigene, Touggourt," Memorial Art Gallery, Rochester; "Moonlight in Andulusia," Newark Museum, Newark, NJ; "Three Birches," Portland Museum, Portland, ME. Died in 1957. Address in 1929, 13 rue Boissonade, Paris XIV; h. 246; Boulevard Raspail, Paris, France.

PARKER, HARRY HANLEY.
Mural painter and sculptor. Born in Philadelphia on Nov. 29, 1869. Studied at Penna. Academy of Fine Arts. Died March 16, 1917, in Philadelphia.

PARKER, JOHN ADAMS.
Painter. Born Nov. 29, 1829 in New York City. He was elected an Associate Member of the National Academy in 1869. Mountain scenery has claimed his attention, and the Adirondacks, Catskills, and White Mountains Have furnished him subjects for most of his pictures. Died c. 1905.

PARKER, JOHN F.
Painter and sculptor. Born in New York City in 1884. Pupil of Henri in New York; also studied in England and with Laurens and Steinlen in Paris. Member: Alliance. Award: Whitney prize,

Labor Competition. He directed a pageant for the City History Club, New York, 1916; also the Westfield 200th Anniversary Pageant, etc. Represented in National Gallery, Wash., DC. Address in 1926, 401 Convent Ave., New York, NY.

PARKER, LAWTON S.
Portrait painter and teacher. Born Fairfield, Mich, Aug. 7, 1868. Pupil of Gerome, Laurens, Constant, Besnard and Whistler in Paris; Chase in NY. Instructor, St. Louis School of Fine Arts, 1892; director of fine arts, Beloit College, 1893; pres., NY School of Art, 1898-9; director of Parker Academy, Paris, 1900; non-resident professor, Art Inst. of Chicago, 1902; pres., Chicago Academy of Fine Arts, 1902. Member: ANA 1916; Chicago SA; Paris AAA; NAC. Awards: John Armstrong Chandler five-year European Scholarship, 1896; hon. mention, Paris Salon, 1900; third medal, Paris Salon, 1902; silver medal, St. Louis Exp., 1904; gold medal, Inter. Exp., Munich, 1905; hon. mention, CI Pittsburgh, 1907; first medal, Chicago SA, 1908; Cahn prize, AIC 1909; gold medal, Paris Salon 1913; medal of honor, P.-P. Exp., San F., 1915; Altman prize, NAD, 1916. Work: President Harry Pratt Judson and Martin A. Ryerson, Chicago Univ.; Judge Peter S. Grosscup and Judge James G. Jenkins, US Court of Appeals, Washington; "Portrait of the Lady," Art Insitute of Chicago; "The Masquerader," "Sous Bois," Harrison Gallery, Los Angeles Museum. Address in 1929, care of The National Academy of Design, 215 West 57th St., New York, NY.

PARKER, MRS. NEILSON R.
See Steele, Zulma.

PARKER, ROBERT ANDREW.
Illustrator. Born in Norfolk, VA, in 1927. Attended the AIC and Atelier 17 in NY before beginning his career in 1954. His watercolors and etchings have since appeared in Fortune, Sports Illustrated, Travel and Leisure, and The Lamp. In 1976 he produced a poster, entitled Third Century, for Mobil Oil. His paintings have been part of exhibitions at the

Whitney Museum, Museum of Modern Art and Los Angeles County Museum.

PARKER, STEPHEN HILLIS.
Portrait painter. Born in 1852. He was a friend of John Sargent and a fellow-pupil in Paris. He made his home for years in New York City, but lived in Italy and France for the last thirteen years of his life, and did little or no painting. He died in Florence, Italy on May 17, 1925.

PARKER, THOMAS H.
Miniature painter. Born in Sag Harbor, Long Island, in 1801. He studied under Rogers in New York, and later removed to Hartford, Conn., where he became most popular in his profession; he was painting there in 1829. He died after 1851.

PARKER, WENTWORTH.
Painter and etcher. Born Terre Haute, Ind., Oct. 11, 1890. Pupil of William Forsyth. Address in 1929, 815 South 6th St.; Terre Haute, Ind.

PARKHURST, ANITA.
(Mrs. Willcox). Painter and illustrator. Born Chicago, Nov. 11, 1892. Pupil of AIC. Member: GFLA; SI Covers for Saturday Evening Post, Collier's, etc. Address in 1929, Box 44, Tompkinsville, SI, NY; Ocean Terrace, Dongan Hills, SI, NY.

PARKHURST, C. E.
Illustrator. Born in Toledo, Ohio, in 1885. Pupil of Vanderpoel, Freer and Armstrong. Member: New York Architectural League. Award: Three honorable mentions, Art Institute of Chicago, 1906. Address in 1926, 63 East 59th St., New York, NY.

PARKHURST, THOMAS SHREWSBURY.
Landscape painter and illustrator. Born Aug. 1, 1853 in Manchester, England. Self-taught. Member: Toledo Tile Club; National Art Club. Work: "October Skies" and "The Spirit of the Maumee," Toledo Museum of Art; "Landscape," Grand Rapids Art Association; "Chariot of the Sky," Oakland, California, Art Museum; represented in Lima, Ohio, Art League; Des Moines, IA, Art

Club; Oklahoma Art League. Died in Carmel, California in 1923.

PARKMAN.
A landscape painter noted in Tuckerman's "American Artist Life."

PARKS, CHARLES CRUPPER
Sculptor. Address in 1982, Wilmington, DE. Born: Onancock, VA, June 27, 1922. Study: PAFA. Work: Commissions for H. B. du Pont, Wilmington, DE; Byrnes Foundation, Columbia, SC; Brandywine River Mus; Mystic Seaport Mus.; Equitable Bldg., NYC. Exhib.: Nat'l Sculpture Soc. Annual, 1962-77; NAD, 1965-77; and others. Awards: Wemys Foundation Travel Grant, Greece, 1965; Am. APL, gold medal, 1970; Nat'l Sculp't. Soc., Gold Medal, 1971; others. Mem. of Advisory Committee John F. Kennedy Ctr., 1968-present. Mem.: Fellow NSS; AAA; NAD; Del. State Arts Council.

PARKYNS, GEORGE ISHAM.
Born c. 1750. This English artist and designer for engravers came to Philadelphia about 1795. His only known print is a large and good aquatint view of Mount Vernon. He is said to have been employed by T. B. Freeman, the Philadelphia publisher of books and prints. Died c. 1820.

PARRISH, CLARA WEAVER.
(Mrs. Wm. P.). Painter and etcher. Born in Selma, Ala. Pupil of Art Students' League of New York, under Chase, Mowbray, Cox and J. Alden Weir; under Collin in Paris. Member: New York Water Color Club; National Academy of Women Painters and Sculptors; National Art Club. Awards: Watrous prize, NY Women's Art Club, 1902 and 1913; silver medal, Appalachian Exposition, Knoxville, 1910; silver medal, Panama-Pacific Exposition, San Francisco, 1915. Died Nov. 13, 1925 in NYC.

PARRISH, MAXFIELD FREDERICK.
Painter and illustrator. Born Philadelphia, PA, July 25, 1870; son of Stephen Parrish. Pupil of PAFA; Howard Pyle, Drexel Inst. Had studio in Phila. for many years. Member: SAA 1897; ANA

1905, NA 1906; Fellowship PAFA. Awards: Hon. mention, Paris Exp., 1900; silver medal for drawings, Pan-Am. Exp., Buffalo, 1901; Beck prize, Phila. WCC, 1908; gold medal, NY Arch Lg., 1917. Illustrated for magazines; did advertisements; illustrated Arizona desert life for The Century; later worked on landscape murals. Designed own home in Windsor, VT. Died in 1966. Address in 1929, Windsor, VT.

PARRISH, STEPHEN WINDSOR.
Painter and etcher. Born in Phila., PA, July 9, 1846. Member: R. Soc. Painter-Etchers, London; NY Etching C. Work: "The Break-up of Winter, Cornish, NH," painting, Toledo Museum of Art; "Winter at Trenton, NJ," Carnegie Institute, Pittsburgh. Died in 1938. Address in 1929, Windsor, VT.

PARROTT, WILLIAM SAMUEL.
Painter of Western scenery. Born in 1844 in Missouri. He went West in 1847, and died at Goldendale, Washington, in May, 1915.

PARSELL, ABRAHAM.
Miniature painter, who flourished in 1825-47 in New York. Born c. 1792 in New Jersey.

PARSELL, JOHN H.
Miniature painter, who flourished in 1846-47 in New York.

PARSHALL, DeWITT.
Landscape painter. Born Buffalo, NY, Aug. 2, 1864. Pupil of Cormon and Alexander Harrison and Julian Academy in Paris. Member: ANA 1910; NA 1917; Allied AA; SMPF West; Inter. Soc. AL; Lotos C. (life); Century Assoc.; NAC (hon.); MacD. C.; Calif. AC; S. Indp. A.; Painters of the West; AFA. Award: Gold medal, Painters of the West, 1928. Work: "Catskills" and "Great Abyss," Metropolitan Museum, New York; "Granite Gorge," Toledo (O.) Museum of Art; "Isis Peak," Syracuse (NY) Museum of Art; "Hermit Creek Canyon," Worcester Art Museum; "Grand Canyon," Detroit Institute of Arts; "Platform Rock," Hackley Gallery of Fine Arts, Muskegon, Mich.; "Night-Grand Canyon" Fine Arts Gallery," San Diego, Calif. Died in 1956. Address in 1929, Hot Springs Rd., Santa Barbara, Calif.

PARSHALL, DOUGLASS EWELL.
Painter. Born New York, NY, Nov. 19, 1899. Pupil of DeWitt Parshall. Member: ANA, 1927; Calif. AC; Painters of the West. Awards: Silver medal, Painters of the West; second Hallgarten prize, NAD, 1924 and 1927; gold medal, Painters of the West, Los Angeles, 1926; first hon. mention, Painters and Sculptors, Los Angeles Museum, 1927. Represented by "Marine," Syracuse Museum; "Troops Entering Arras," National Gallery, Washington, DC; "Great Surge," Reading, PA. Museum; "Negress," Kansas City Museum; "Freight Yards," San Diego Museum; Sycamore and River," Detroit Museum. Address in 1929, Santa Barbara, Calif.

PARSONS, CHARLES.
Born in Hampshire, England on May 8, 1821. He came to this country at an early age. Studied with George Endicott in NYC. He painted in oil and water color, besides having learned the art of lithograpy. He was elected an Associate Member of the National Academy of Design, and of the New York Water Color Society. Died Nov. 9, 1910 in Brooklyn, NY.

PARSONS, EDITH BARRETTO STEVENS.
Sculptor. Born Houston, VA, July 4, 1878. Pupil of ASL of NY under French and Barnard. Member: NA Women PS; NSS. Work: Memorial fountain to John Galloway, Public Park, Memphis; figures for Liberal Arts Bldg., St. Louis; memorial monument, St. Paul; "Duck Girl," Metropolitan Museum; Monument to Soldiers of World War, Summit, NJ. Died in 1956. Address in 1929, 13 Van Dam St., New York, NY; summer, Quogue, LI, NY.

PARSONS, ETHEL M.
Painter. Member: Mural P. Address in 1929, 2 East 81st St., New York, NY.

PARSONS, THEOPHILUS.
Painter and writer. Born New York, NY, June 20, 1876. Pupil of John Carlson. Member: Wash. SA; Wash. AC. Address in 1929, 1620 P St., N.W., Washington, DC; summer, Nonquit, Mass.

PARTEE, McCULLOUGH.
Illustrator. Born Nashville, Tenn., Feb. 19, 1900. Pupil of Pruett Carter; Cunn; Reynolds. Illustrates for Liberty; Colliers; Country Gentlemen; People's Home Journal. Address in 1929, 1916 Hayes St., Nashville, Tenn.

PARTINGTON, RICHARD L.
Painter. Born in England in 1868. Member of San Francisco Art Association. Address in 1926, 1713 Sansom St., Philadelphia.

PARTON, ARTHUR.
Landscape painter. He was born at Hudson, NY, March 26, 1842, and studied in Philadelphia under William T. Richards. In 1869 he visited Europe and obtained some effective studies of Scotch and English scenery. He was elected a Naitonal Academician in 1884, and is a member of the American Water Color Society. Represented in the Metropolitan Museum; also exhibited in Paris, in 1889. He died March 7, 1914, in Yonkers, NY.

PARTON, ERNEST.
Landscape painter. Born Hudson, NY, March 17, 1845. Member: A Fund S; Royal Inst. of Painters, London. Awards: Hon. mention, Paris Exp., 1889; hon. mention, Paris Exp., 1889; hon. mention, Paris Exp., 1900. Has resided in England since 1873. Died Sept. 16, 1933. Address in 1929, 86 Goldhurst Terrace, London, NW, England.

PARTON, HENRY WOODBRIDGE.
Painter. Born Hudson, NY, in 1858. Member: NA; Painters and Sculptors Gallery Assn.; Salma. C., 1889; Century Assn.; AFA; NAC. Awards: Small picture prize, NAC, 1928; William C. Gregg purchase prize, NAC, 1929. Represented in Univ. of Nebraska, Lincoln, Neb.; Reading Mus., Reading, PA. Address in 1929, 119 East 19th St., NYC.

PARTRIDGE, CHARLOTTE RUSSELL.
Painter, lecturer and teacher. Born Minneapolis. Pupil of Emma M. Church, John Carlson, AIC. Member: AFA. Director, Layton Art Gallery. Founder and director, Layton School of Art. Address in 1929, Layton Art Gallery, 438 Jefferson St.; h. 802 Frederick Ave., Milwaukee, Wis.

PARTRIDGE, JOSEPH.
Painter. He painted a portrait of Rev. Stephen Gano of Providence, RI, which was engraved and published by Pekenino in 1822.

PARTRIDGE, ROI.
Etcher. Born Centralia, Wash., Oct. 14, 1888. Pupil of NAD in NY. Member: Calif. P.M.; Chicago SE; Brooklyn SE; Calif. SE. Awards: Two silver medals, Alaska-Yukon-Pacific Exp., Seattle, 1909; Logan medal, AIC, 1921; H. W. O'Melveney prize, Calif. PM, 1922; Nahl prize, San F., 1922; Buma Prize, Calif. PM, 1925. Work in New York Public Library, Newark, (NJ) Public Library; Library of Congress, Washington, DC; Palace of Legion of Honor, San Francisco, Calif.; Worcester (Mass.) Art Museum; Art Institute of Chicago; Walker Art Gallery, Liverpool, England; Toledo Museum of Art; Carnegie Institute, Pittsburgh; Calif. State Library, Sacramento; Los Angles Museum; Toronto Art Gallery; Academy of Arts, Honolulu. Address in 1929, Mills College P.O., Calif.

PARTRIDGE, W(ILLIAM) H.
Painter. Born Whelling, W. VA, Sept. 21, 1858. Pupil of Mass. School of Art; Boston Museum of Art. Member: Boston AC; Springfield AL; Gloucester SA; Business Men's AC of Boston. Work: "Old House, France," Library, Wellesley, Mass. Address in 1929, 39 Pine St., Wellesley Hills, Mass.

PARTRIDGE, WILLIAM ORDWAY.
Sculptor and writer. Born Paris, France, April 11, 1861. Studied in New York, Paris, Florence and Rome. Member: Lotos C.; NY Arch. Lg. Work: Equestrian statue of Gen. Grant, Union Lg. Club, Brooklyn; statue of Alexander Hamilton, Brooklyn; "Shakespeare" Lincoln

Park, Chicago; "Pocahontas", Jamestown, VA; "Nathan Hale," St. Paul, Minn. font, Catherdral of St. Peter and St. Paul, Washington, DC; Schermerhorn Memorial, Columbia Univ., New York. Author: "Art for America", "The Song of Life of a Sculptor", "The Technique of Sculpture". Died in 1930. Address in 1929, Cosmos Club, Wash., DC.

PASCHKE, EDWARD.
Illustrator. Born in Chicago, IL, in 1939. Studied at the AIC, where he received both his BFA and MFA. He has exhibited his work at the Whitney Museum, Museum of Contemporary Art in Chicago, Washington, and Mexico City and the Darthea Speyer Gallery in Paris. The AIC, Brooklyn Museum, the Museum of Modern Art in Vienna, Austria, and the Museum Boymans in Rotterdam own his work. He has taught painting, drawing, and design at the School of the AIC, Barat College in Illinois and Columbia College in Chicago.

PASCIN, JULES.
Painter. Born in Bulgaria, 1885. Studied in Vienna. Died in 1930. Address in 1929, care of Bernheim Jeune and Co., Paris, France.

PASZTHORY, ARPAD.
Painter of "A Negro Newsboy;" standing, three-quarter length; wall background. Sold in New York Auction.

PATIGIAN, HAIG.
Sculptor. Born in Armenia, Jan. 22, 1876. Pupil of Marquet in Paris. Member: NSS; Societe des Artistes Francais; National Inst. Arts and letters. Member: Jury of Awards, Panama-Pacific International Exp., San Francisco, 1915. Work: "Ancient History," Bohemian C., and "Gen. Funston," City Hall, San Francisco; monument to Dr. Rowell, Fresno, Calif.; marbel bust, Helen Wills, Palace of Legion of Honor; bust of John Keith, Memorial Museum, San Francisco; pediment for Metropol'n Life Bldg., San Francisco; allegoric figures and tympanum for Memorial Museum, "Gen. Pershing" monument, and "Lincoln" monument,

San Francisco, etc. Address in 1929, 3055 Webster St.; h. 898 Francisco St., San Francisco, Calif.; and Bohemian Club, San Francisco.

PATTEE, ELSIE DODGE.
Painter, illustrator, lecturer and teacher. Born Chelsea, Mass., Sept. 4, 1876. Pupil of Julian Academy in Paris. Member: AS Min. P.; NA Women PS. Awards: Silver medal, Panam-Pacific Exp., San F., 1915; hon. mention, Concord AA, 1921; hon. mention, NA Women PS, 1921; first Balch prize, Calif. S. Min. P., 1927. Address in 1929, 1186 Lexington Ave., New York.

PATTERSON, AMBROSE.
Painter and teacher. Born Daylesford, Victoria, Australia. Member: Calif. PM; Salon d'Automne, Paris. Works: "Boulevard Waterloo, Brussels," Naitonal Gallery, Adelaide, Australia, and "Collins St., Melbourne," National Gallery, Sydney, Australia; portrait C. C. Kingston, Australian Commonwealth Government. Address in 1929, Dept. of Painting, University of Washington, Seattle, Wash.

PATTERSON, C(HARLES) R(OBERT).
Marine painter. Born in England, July 18, 1878. Member: NAC; Salma. C.; Allied AA; AWCS; NY Soc. P. Work: "Journeys' End," Royal Victoria Museum, Halifax; "Rounding the Buoy," Butler Art Institute, Youngstown, Ohio; "Old Ironsides," Museum of Fine Arts, Boston, Mass.; "Slipping Away from the Land," Museum, Trenton, NJ. Address in 1929, 344 West 72nd St., New York, NY.

PATTERSON, CHARLES WESLEY.
Painter and teacher. Born Belle Vernon, PA, Aug. 5, 1870. Pupil of PAFA. Member: Pitts. AA. Awards: Second honor, Pitts. AA, 1914; prize, Friends of Pittsburgh Art, 1921; prize, Pittsburgh AS, 1924. Represented, 100 Friends of Art, Pittsburgh, PA. Died in 1938. Address in 1929, Woodbine and Stanton Ave., Pittsburgh, PA.

PATTERSON, CHATHERINE NORRIS.
Miniature painter. Born in Philadelphia. Studied at the PAFA, Phila. She has exhibited at the PAFA Exhibitions and in other places. Address in 1926, 2200 St. James Place, Philadelphia, PA.

PATTERSON, HOWARD A(SHMAN).
Painter. Born Philadelphia, PA, Sept. 13, 1891. Pupil of Phila. Ind. Art School; PAFA; ASL of NY. Member: Fellowship PAFA; Phila. Sketch C.; New Mex. Painters. Work: "Lines and Patches," Fellowship of the Pennsylvania Academy of the Fine Arts, Philadelphia, "Flox," Luxembourg Museum, Paris. Address in 1929, 542 Camino del Monte Sol, Santa Fe, New Mexico.

PATTERSON, MARGARET (JORDAN).
Painter and illustrator. Born Soerabaija, Java. Pupil of Pratt Inst. under Arthur Dow in Brooklyn; Charles H. Woodbury in Boston; Castellucho in Paris. Member: Boston SWCP; AFA; Copley S; 1900; Phila. WCC; NA Women PS; Calif. PM; Print Soc. of Eng.; Providence WCC. Award: Hon. mention for etching, P.-P. Exp., San F., 1915. Work: "Basque Fishing Boats," Museum of Fine Arts, Boston; represented in Oakland (Calif.) Art Museum; Metropolitan Museum; Univ. of Calif.; Smith College; Cleveland Art Museum; Springfield, Mass., Public Library; Victoria and Albert Museum, Kensington, Eng.; Print collection, Museum, Genoa, Italy, Director, art department, Dana Hall School, Wellesley, Mass. Address in 1929, Trinity Court, Boston, Mass.

PATTERSON, REBECCA BURD PEALE.
Painter. Born Philadelphia, PA. Pupil of PA. Museum and School of Ind. Art, Phila.; Rebecca Van Trump and W. J. Whittemore, New York; A. Margaretta Archambault. Member: PA. Soc. Min. P. Died in Sept., 1952. Address in 1929, 5522 Morris St., Germantown, Philadelphia, PA.

PATTERSON, ROBERT.
Illustrator. Born in Chicago, Ill., in 1898. Pupil of Harvey Dunn, Walt Louderback, Carl

Erickson. Had studio in Chicago. Moved to NYC in 1922; received fashion illustration assignments. Assignment in Paris in 1924 for "Judge." Began work for Vogue in Paris in 1927. Returned to US in 1934; worked for McCall's, Good Housekeeping, Ladies' Home Journal, etc. Instructor, Famous Artist Sch. Member: SI; GFLA. Address in 1929, 44 West 10th St., New York, NY.

PATTERSON, RUSSELL.
Painter and illustrator. Born Omaha, Neb., Dec. 26, 1896. Pupil of Monet. Studed at McGill Univ., Canada; Art Inst. of Chic.; Acad. of Fine Arts. Worked in Hollywood and on Broadway in 1930's; designed costumes for Ziegfield, windows for Macy's, hotel lobbies, restaurants; illustrated for advertisements and magazines. Member: Chicago AC and Chicago AG. Died in 1977. Address in 1929, Belmont Hotel, Chicago, Ill.; summer, Lake Forest, Ill.

PATTERSON, VIOLA.
(Mrs. Ambrose Patterson). Painter, illustrator, craftsman and teacher. Born Seattle, May 20, 1898. Member: Seattle AI; North West PM. Awards: First prize, Black and White Exh., Phoenix, Ariz., 1928; Katherine B. Baker memorial prize, Seattle Art Institute, 1928. Address in 1929, 4725 Fifteenth St., NE Seattle, Wash.

PATTISON, JAMES WILLIAM.
Painter. Born in Boston on July 14, 1844. Painter of figures, domestic animals, landscapes, marines, etc.; exhibitor at Paris Salon, 1879-81; at National Academy, New York, for many years; at American Water Color Society, New York, 15 years; Penna. Academy of Fine Arts; at Art Insitute of Chicago, many times; Chicago Exposition, 1893; St. Louis Exposition, 1904; also medal at Boston, 1882; was a constant exhibitor at art galleries all over the country. Director of School of Fine Arts, Jacksonville, Ill., 1884-96; faculty lecturer on the collections, Art Institute of Chicago after 1896; editor, Fine Arts Journal, Chicago, in 1910. Ex-pres., Chicago Society of

artists; member of the Municipal Art League of Chicago; also of Society of Western Artists. Died on May 29, 1915 in Asheville, NC.

PATTISON, MRS. SIDNEY.
See Marylka Modjeska.

PATTON, ELIZABETH.
Painter. Exhibited "Landscape" at the Penna. Academy of the Fine Arts, 1926. Address in 1926, 1522 Chestnut St., Philadelphia, PA.

PATTON, KATHARINE.
Painter. Born Philadelphia. Pupil of Cox, Hawthorne and Snell in New York; Frank Brangwyn in London. Member: NA Women PS; Phila. WCC; Fellowship PAFA; Plastic C.; Phila. Alliance; AFA. Awards: Silver medal for water color, Knoxville, Tenn. Exp., 1913; prize for landscape, NA Women PS, 1918; Mary Smith prize, PAFA, 1921; special award of honor, National Art Exhibition, Springville, Utah, 1926. Work: "The Maple Woods," Pennsylvania Academy of the Fine Arts; "Wood Interior," Fellowship, Pennsylvania Academy of the Fine Arts, Philadelphia; "Through the Old Window Screen," South High School, Philadelphia, PA; "The Wooded Path, September," Municipal Collection, Trenton, NJ. Address in 1929, 1522 Chestnut St., Philadelphia, PA.

PATTON, KATHERINE MAXEY.
Painter. Award: Mary Smith prize, Penna. Academy of Fine Arts, 1921. Address in 1926, 718 Southwest St., Wheaton, Ill.

PATTON, ROY EDWIN.
Painter, etcher, lecturer and teacher. Born Springfield, Ohio, April 7, 1878. Pupil of Catlin, Erickson, Cross. Member: Erie AC; Fine Art Palette C. Address in 1929, 131 West 18th St., Erie, PA.

PATTY, W(ILLIAM) A(RTHUR).
Painter. Born New Hartford, Conn., March 17, 1889. Pupil of Charles Noel Flagg, Robt. B. Brandegee, Edgar M. Ward. Member: Brooklyn SA; S. Indp. A; Brooklyn WCC; PS; Conn. AFA; Allied AA; Fifteen Gallery NY. Died in 1961. Address

in 1929, 7501 Ridge Blvd., Brooklyn, NY.

PAUL, CHARLES R.
Illustrator. Born in Indiana, PA, in 1888. Pupil of Anshutz, Chase and McCarter. Member: Philadelphia Sketch Club. Address in 1926, 17th St. and the Parkway, Philadelphia, PA. Died in 1942.

PAUL, EUGENE.
Engraver. Born c. 1830 in France. The only known print engraved by this man is a large and excellent mezzotint portrait of Henry Clay, published by R. A. Bachia, New York, 1855. This print is signed "Eng'd by E. Paul."

PAUL, HORACE A.
Painter. Exhibited at the penna. Academy of Fine Arts, Philadelphia, 1924. Address in 1926, 2160 North Van Pelt St., Philadelphia.

PAUL, JEREMIAH.
Painter. Painted portraits from 1791 to about 1820. Died July 13, 1830 in St. Louis, Missouri. His studio was No. 35 South Fourth St., Philadelphia. Work: Portrait of Mrs. Rachel West Clarkson; bust, wears cap tied under chin, arms crossed in lap. Owned by Worcester Art Museum. Portrait of Tench Coxe; bust to left. Owned by Brinton Coxe, Philadelphia. Also executed other types of paintings.

PAULDING, JOHN.
Sculptor. Born Dark County, Ohio, April 5, 1883. Pupil of AIC. Member: Alumni AIC; Chicago Gal. A; Cliff Dwellers; Chicago PS. Died in 1935. Address in 1929, 1600 Monroe Bldg., 104 South Michigan Ave., Chicago, Ill.; h. Park Ridge, Ill.

PAULIN, TELFORD.
Painter. Member: Mural P. Address in 1929, 111 East 10th St., New York, NY.

PAULUS, FRANCIS PETRUS.
Painter and etcher. Born Detroit, Mich., March 13, 1862. Pupil of PAFA; Royal Academy in Munich under Loefftz; Ecole des Beaux-Arts in Paris under Bonnat. Member: Chicago SE; NAC; La Gravure

Originale en Noir; Societe Inter. des Beaux-Arts et des Lettres. Work: "Alley in Bruges," Herron Art Institute, Indianapolis; "Low Tide," "Fish Market," "Shimmering Sea," "Old Bridge, Bruges," and set of etchings Detroit Institute; "Old Canal," Bruges, McGregor Library, Highland Park, Mich. Etchings in: New York Public Library; Library of Congress, Washington, DC; Oakland (Calif.) Mus'm; Musee Moderne, Bruges; Royal Academy of Fine Arts, Munich. Died in 1933. Address in 1929, 917 E. Jefferson Ave., Detroit, Mich.

PAUS, HERBERT ANDREW.
Illustrator. Born in Minneapolis, MN, in 1880. Studied at the ASL under George Bridgman. After his first illustration, an editorial cartoon, appeared in 1896, he did many covers for The Saturday Evening Post, Woman's Home Companion, Collier's, Popular Science, and Redbook. In World War I he did the poster Over the Top and later worked on many book illustrations such as The Children's Blue Bird by Madame Maurice Maeterlinck. In 1913 he designed the stage set for The Betrothal by Maeterlinck. Died in 1946.

PAXON, EDGAR SAMUEL.
Illustrator and painter. Born in East Hamburg, NY, in 1852. Specialty, Indians and American pioneers. Work: Eight murals in Missoula County court House; six murals in Montana Capitol; "Custer's Last Fight," exhibited in many cities. Address in 1926, 611 Stephens Ave., Missoula, Montana.

PAXSON, ETHEL.
(Mrs. Clement Esmond). Painter and illustrator. Born in Meriden, Conn., in 1885. Pupil of Chase, Poore, and Penna. Academy of Fine Arts. Address in 1926, Kew Gardens, Long Island, New York.

PAXTON, MRS. ELIZABETH OKIE.
Painter. Born Providence, RI. Pupil of W. M. Paxton. Member: Boston GA; North Shore AA. Award: Silver medal, Panama-Pacific Exp., San F., 1915; Alice Worthington Ball Prize, North Shore, AA, 1927.

Address in 1929, 19 Montvale Rd., Newton Centre, Mass.

PAXTON, W. A.
Painter. Member: California Art Club. Address in 1926, 955 Edgeware Road, Los Angeles, Calif.

PAXTON, WILLIAM M(cGREGOR).
Painter and teacher. Born Baltimore, MD, June 22, 1896. Pupil of Ecole des Beaux-Arts in Paris under Gerome; Dennis M. Bunker in Boston. Member: ANA 1917; Copley S. 1894; Boston GA; St. Botolph C., Boston; Phila. AC; Allied AA; AFA. Awards: Hon. mention, Pan-Am. Exp., Buffalo, 1901; bronze medal, St. Louis Exp. 1904; Lippincott prize, PAFA 1915; hors concours (jury of awards), P.-P. Exp., San F., 1915; Popular prize, Corcoran Gallery, Wash., 1919; Phila. prize and Stotesbury prize, PAFA, 1921; Carroll Beck portrait prize, PAFA, 1928. In collections of PA; MMA; Corcoran's Boston; Detroit; Wadsworth and Butler. Mural: Army and Navy Club. Died May 13, 1941 in Boston. Address in 1929, 19 Montvale Road, Newton Centre, Mass.; Riverway Studios, 120 Riverway, Boston, Mass.

PAYNE, EDGAR ALWIN.
Painter. Born Washburn, MO, March 1, 1882. Pupil of AIC; chiefly self-taught. Member: Salma. C.; Allied AA; International Society AL; Calif. AC; 10 Painters of Los A.; Laguna Beach AA; Alumni AIC; Chisel Club, 1913. Awards: Gold medal, Sacramento State Fair, 1918; silver medal, Sacramento, 1919; Cahn prize, AIC, 1920; first prize ($250) Southwest Museum, 1921; hon. mention, Paris Salon, 1923; gold and bronze medals, Los Angeles Museum, 1926. Works: Mural decorations, American and Empress Theatres, Chicago; Northern Hotel, Billings, Mont.; Clay County Court House, Brazil, Ind.; Hendricks County Court House, Danville, Ind.; Hendricks County Court House, Danville, Ind.; Queen theatre, Houseon, Tex.; "Hills of el Toro," Nebraska Art Asso., Lincoln; "The Hills of Marin," Peoria (Ill.) Society of Allied Arts; "Pleasant Valley," Chicago Municipal Art

Commission purchase; "The Restless Sea," Herron Art Institute, Indianapolis; "Topmost Peaks," Janesville (Wis.) Art Assn.; "High Sierras," Southwest Museum, Los Angeles; "Fifth Lake," National Academy of Design, New York. Died in 1947. Address in 1929, 1931 Broadway, New York, NY.

PAYNE, ELSIE PALMER.
(Mrs. Edgar A. Payne). Painter, lecturer and teacher. Born San Antonio, Tex., Sept. 9, 1884. Pupil of A. W. Best in San Francisco and of Chicago Fine Arts School. Member: Laguna Beach AA; West Coast Arts, Inc.; Los Angeles WCS. Address in 1929, Netherlands Ave., New York, NY; Stendahl Gallaries, Ambassador Hotel, Los Angeles, Calif.; summer, Laguna Beach, Calif.

PAYNE, EMMA LANE.
Painter, illustrator and teacher. Born Canada, May 5, 1874. Pupil of F. C. Gottwald; Leonard Ochtman. Member: Cleveland Woman's AC; Cleveland SA. Address in 1929, Studio Stop, 14 RFD, Euclid, Ohio.

PAYNE, JEANNE.
See Mrs. Louis C. Johnson.

PEABODY, AMELIA.
Sculptor. Born Marblehead Neck, July 3, 1890. Pupil of Boston Museum of Fine Arts School and Charles Grafly. Member: Copley S; Boston SS; Marblehead AA; AFA. Work: "End of an Era," marble, Museum of Fine Arts, Boston, Mass. Address in 1929, Fenway Studios, 30 Ipswich St.; h. 120 Commonwealth Ave., Boston, Mass.; summer, Dublin, NH.

PEABODY, EVELYN.
Sculptor, who exhibited at the Penna. Academy of the Fine Arts, Philadelphia, 1924. Address in 1926, 1620 Summer St., Philadelphia.

PEABODY, M. M.
Engraver. The earliest plate by this engraver is a very large and crudely executed engraving of "The Unjust Sentence of the Jews against Jesus Christ the Saviour of the World." This print was engraved and published in 1823. Place of publication unknown but in 1835 M. M. Peabody was located in Utica, NY, where he engraved maps in line, and general book illustrations in stipple. A few portraits, signed "M. Peabody," were probably the work of the above.

PEACEY, JESS.
See Lawson.

PEACOCK.
An early New England portrait painter, of whom little is known. The American Antiquarian Society of Worcester, Mass., have two portraits of John and Mrs. Charles Bush which are attributed to "Peacock."

PEAK, ROBERT.
Illustrator. Born in Colorado, in 1928. Received his art training at the ACD. After his arrival in NY, he was given assignments from advertising clients and periodicals such as Cosmopolitan and Newsweek. His deceptively simple style and innovative techniques have placed him in great demand among major magazines. A regular contributor to TV Guide and Sports Illustrated, he has also illustrated posters for movies such as "Rollerball," "Mame," and "The Missouri Breaks." Among his many citations are Artist of the Year in 1961 from the AG of NY and from the S of I, and the Hamilton King Award in 1968, in addition to several Awards of Excellence and Gold Medals from the Annual Exhibitions.

PEALE, ANNA CLAYPOOLE.
Painter. Daughter of James Peale, and grandchild of James Claypoole. She was born 1791. She painted still-life subjects, and later took to miniature painting. She painted Gen. Lallemand, President James Monroe, Maj.-Gen. Jackson, and Commodore Bainbridge. Died Dec. 25, 1878 in Phila.

PEALE, CHARLES W
Painter and engraver. Born in Charlestown, MD, on April 15, 1741 died in Phila., on Feb. 22, 1827. Peale is said to have been apprenticed to a saddler in Annapolis, MD, but he went to

Boston to Study art, possibly with J. S. Copley. Went to London where he studied painting miniatures, engraving mold in wax, and plaster work. Was in Phila. in 1775 and took part in the Revolution and politics. Painted portraits of many prominent men, George Washington. Established in Phila. the Museum and Art Gallery, opened in 1802. In 1794, Peale est. a short-lived assoc. of fine arts, the Columbianum. In 1806 helped PAFA, and lived to exhibit first 17 years. Father of Rembrandt Peale. Died in 1827 in in Phila.

PEALE, JAMES JR.
Marine painter. Born March 6, 1789, in Philadelphia. He was the son of James Peale, who was born in 1749 and died, 1831. He exhibited paintings of the sea in the early Philadelphia exhibitions. His sisters were also painters. Died Oct. 27, 1876 in Philadelphia.

PEALE, JAMES.
Younger brother of Charles Willson Peale, was bron at Chestertown, MD, in 1749. As a youth he lived with his brother and learned the trade of chaisemaker. At about the time Charles Willson Peale returned from London and chiefly due to his instruction and influence, James Peale gave up his trade to become a painter. He devoted some attention to portraiture, executed some landscapes, and even attempted some historical composition, but it is as a miniature painter that he is best known. During the Revolutionary War, James Peale, like his brother Charles, served as an officer in the Continental Army under Washington, first as an Ensign in the Maryland Battalion, Colonel Smallwood commanding, in 1776; then as a First Lieutenant of the First Battalion of Maryland Regulars, Colonel John H. Staul commanding, in 1777, being later (1778) promoted to a captaincy in the First Maryland Regiment of the Continental Line. He was a good soldier and bore an enviable military record. James Peale painted two portraits of Washington, one of which is owned by the City of Philadelphia and hangs in the Naitonal Portrait

Gallery at Independence Hall; the other is owned by the New York Historical Society. Most of his lifetime was spent in Philadelphia, though he worked and resided for a time in the Southern States. He was married and had six children, all but one of whom were girls. Of these children James, Jr., Anna and Sarah were painters. He was a member of the Maryland Society of the Cincinnati. James Peale died in Philadelphia on May 24, 1831.

PEALE, MARIA.
Daughter of James Peale. Born in 1787. She commenced painting still-life subjects about 1810. Died March 27, 1866 in Philadelphia.

PEALE, MARY J.
Painter. Born Feb. 16, 1827. She was the daughter of Rubens Peale and a granddaughter of Charles Willson Peale. She died in Pottsville, PA, in Nov., 1902.

PEALE, RAPHAELLE.
Portrait, miniature and still-life painter. He was a son of Charles Willson Peale and was born Feb. 17, 1774 in Annapolis, MD. In 1801 he advertised as a portrait painter with his studio at No. 28 Powel St., Philadelphia. He died March 5, 1825, in Phila.

PEALE, REMBRANDT.
Son of Charles Willson Peale, was born in Bucks County, Penna., Feb. 22, 1778. His father instructed him from an early age. At 17 he obtained a sitting from George Washington. This portrait painted in 1823, is not the familiar Rembrandt Peale portrait, a composite head known as the Porthold portrait, of which he made many copies. About 1795, Charles Willson Peale retired and recommended his son. The younger Peale, did not meet with great success and left Phila. for Charleston, SC. In 1801 he went to England to study Benjamin West. Painted a few portraits, and because of ill health decided to abandon art for agriculture. Returned to US, was in demand as a painter, and in 1804 established a studio in Philadelphia. In 1807

went to Paris, where he painted eminent Frenchmen, including Jacques Louis David, Dominique Vivant Denou, and Jean Antoine Houdon, now owned by PAFA. Returned to Phila. Painted most important work, "The Court of Death." Established Museum and Gallery of Paintings in Baltimore. Remained there 9 years. In 1829, made last trip to France and Italy. One of first in US to make lithographic drawings. In 1834, moved to NY returning later to Phila., for the remainder of his life. One of founders of PAFA, and one of original members of NAD. Died October 3, 1860. In 1923 a Memorial Exhibition of Peale's work was held at PAFA.

PEALE, RUBENS.
Born May 4, 1784 in Phila. Son of Charles Willson Peale. He painted in an indifferent manner, usually animals of still life. Died July 17, 1865.

PEALE, SARAH MIRIAM.
Painter. Born in Phila., PA, on May 19, 1800. Sister of Anna Claypoole Peale. Exhibited "Portrait of a Lady" at PAFA, 1818; portraits and still lifes at PAFA, 1819. At Charles W. Peale's studio in Wash., DC, briefly; then launched independent career as portraitist, working in Phila. and Baltimore. Elected to PAFA in 1824, exhibited there annually until 1831. Often shared studio with her sister. Portraits distinctive for detailed furs, laces, fabrics. Subjects included Thos. Hart Benton, Caleb Cushing, Daniel Webster, Marquis de Lafayette (1825), and others. Moved to St. Louis, MO, in 1846; leading portraitist there for 32 yrs. Also painted still lifes. Returned to Phila. in 1878, to live with her sister; died there on Feb. 4, 1885.

PEALE, TITIAN.
Born Nov. 17, 1799. Best known as a student of natural history, and in his artistic labors devoted himself to animal life. Executed most of the plates for Charles L. Bonaparte's work on "American Ornithology." Also exhibited water color drawings of animals in the

PAFA. Son of the artist Charles Willson Peale. Died March 13, 1885 in Phila.

PEARCE, CHARLES SPRAGUE.
Painter. Born in Boston on Oct. 13, 1851. Studied under Bonnat, Paris. Awards: Silver medals, Boston, 1878, 1881; gold medal, 1884, for best figure picture, PAFA, 1881; Temple gold medal, 1885; honorable mention, Paris Salon, 1881. Elected Associate Member of the National Acadmey of Design. Represented in AIC by "The Beheading of John the Baptist." Died May 18, 1914, in Paris, France.

PEARCE, EDGAR LEWIS.
Painter and etcher. Born in 1885. Pupil of Chase and Weir. Represented in Penn. Academy of Fine Arts; National Academy of Design, New York; Carnegie Institute of Pittsburgh. Address in 1926, 3620 Washington Blvd., St. Louis, MO.

PEARLMAN, CHARLOTTE FRANK.
Painter. Born in Washington, DC, Aug. 12, 1925. Studied at University of MD; de Burgos School of Art; American University, Washington, DC. Exhibited at 5th Annual Area Exhibition, Corcoran; Memorial Show, Gallery of Northern Virginia Art League; Washington, Women's Art Center; Maryland Park and Planning Commission; others. Received awards from VA Art League; Montgomery Co. Art Assn.; MD Federation of Arts; etc. Member of Artists Equity Assn.; others. Living in Bethesda, MD, in 1982.

PEARLSTEIN, PHILIP.
Painter. Born May 24, 1924 in Pittsburgh, PA. Educated at Carnegie Institute of Tech. (BFA, 1949) and NYU (MA). Taught at Pratt, Yale, and at Brooklyn College since 1963. Awarded Fullbright (1958), Nat. Council of Arts grant, and Guggenheim Exhibited at Tanager Gallery, NY (1955); A. Frumkin Galleries in NY and Chicago (many since 1960); Reed College; SUNY/Purchase; Carnegie PAFA; MIT; Smithsonian; Yale; De Moines Ar

Center; Helsinki and Japan. In collections of Corcoran gallery, Wash. DC; Univ. of Neb./Lincoln; Syracuse Univ.; Whitney; MOMA; Vassar College; Whitney and R.P.I.

PEARSON, EDWIN.
Sculptor. Born near Yuma, Colo., Dec. 20, 1889. Pupil of AIC; Munich Royal Academy; Hermann Hahn. Work: Bust of William Shakespeare, Munich Theater Museum and State Library, Weimar, loaned by Shakespeare Society; portrait of Prof. Franz Jacobi, Clara Zeigler Museum, Munich. Address in 1929, 545 Fifth Ave., New York, NY; h. Crystall Lake, Ill.

PEARSON, JOSEPH O.
Painter and engraver. He served in the Civil War, and lived in Brooklyn for twenty years, and died in Little Falls, NJ, July 12, 1917. Specialty, title pages and covers for music.

PEARSON, JOSEPH T. JR.,
Painter and teacher. Born Germantown, Feb. 6, 1876. Pupil of J. Alden Weir and Wm. M. Chase. Member: ANA; NA 1919; Fellowship PAFA. Award: Second Hallgarten prize, NAD, 1911; hon. mention, C.I. Pittsburgh, 1911; Sesnan medal, PAFA, 1911; Inness medal, NAD, 1915; gold medal, P.-P. Exp., San F., 1915; Harris silver medal and prize ($500), AIC 1915; Temple gold medal, PAFA 1916; Stotesbury prize, PAFA 1916; Stotesbury prize, PAFA 1916; Beck gold medal, PAFA 1917; Saltus gold medal, NAD, 1918; Potter Palmer gold medal ($1,000), AIC, 1918; gold medal, Sesqui-Centennial Expo., Phila., 1926. Instructor, Pennsylvania Academy of the Fine Arts. Died in 1951. Address in 1929, Huntington Valley, Montgomery Co., PA.

PEARSON, MARGUERITE S(TUBER).
Painter. Born Philadelphia, PA. Pupil of Boston Art Museum School, under William James and Frederic Bosley; Rockport Summer Shcool, under H. Leith-Ross and A. T. Hibbard. Member: North Shore AA; Allied AA; Conn. AFA; Rockport AA; Am. APL; AFA. Address in 1929, 401 Feway Studios, 30 Ipswich St., Boston, Mass.; 369 Broadway, Somerville, Mass. summer, Rockport, Mass.

PEARSON, RALPH M.
Etcher. Born Angus, IA, May 27, 1883. Pupil of AIC under C. F. Browne and Vanderpoel. Member: ASL of Chicago; Chicago SE; NY SE; Calif. AC; Calif. PM; Calif. SE; Brooklyn SE. Awards: Prize, Chicago SE, 1914; silver medal for etching, P.-P. Exp., San F., 1915; first prize for bookplate, Amer. Bookplate Soc., 1917; Calif. PM, 1922. Work in: NY Public Library; Library of Congress, Wash., DC; Mechanics' Inst., Rochester, NY; Art Inst. of Chicago; Museum of Fine Arts, Los Angeles; Avery Library, Columbia Univ. NY; Portfolio of twelve original etched book plates published by Amer. Bookplate Society. Author of "How to See Modern Pictures," Dial Press, 1925; "Fifty Prints of the Year" (John Day Co.), for the Amer. Inst. of Graphic Arts, 1927; Woodcuts," Encyclopaedia Brittanica 1929; "Seeing Pictures," series in Forum Magazazine. Died in 1958. Address in 1929, 10 East 53rd St., New York, NY.

PEASE, C. W.
Miniature painter, who flourished in Providence, RI, in 1844.

PEASE, ERNEST SHERMAN.
Painter in water colors. A son of the engraver J. I. Pease. Born in Philadelphia in 1846. His specialty is painting birds and animals.

PEASE, JOSEPH IVES.
Engraver. Born Aug. 9, 1809 in Norfolk, Conn. In his early youth Pease showed very considerable mechanical ability, and among other things he designed and built a power-loom and also invented a propeller for boats. He finally became an apprentice with the Hartford engraver Oliver Pelton, and remained with him until 1830. In 1835 Pease located himself in Philadelphia and engraved portraits for the National Portrait Gallery and did a considerable amount of work for the "Annuals"; these small plates are the best examples of his skill as an engraver in line. In

723

1848 he went to Stockbridge, Mass., and finally settled on the farm where he died. He practically devoted the later portion of his life to banknote engraving and crayon portraits. Died at Twin Lakes (near Salisbury) CT, on July 2, 1883.

PEASE, RICHARD H.
Engraver. Born Feb. 19, 1813, Norfolk, Conn., he was living in 1869. He was a brother of Joseph Ives Pease, engraver. R. H. Pease apparently began business as a wood engraver in Albany, NY, though he also engraved in a rather labored manner upon copper. He furnished many illustrations for publications of the state of New York.

PEASLEY, A. M.
A map engraver working at Newburyport, Mass., in 1804. Examples of his work are to be found in "The American Coast Pilot," by Capt. Lawrence Furlong, printed for Ed. M. Blount, Boston. He also engraved at least one portrait that of Sauvin executed in line combined with roulette work.

PEBBLES, FRANK M.
Painter. Born Oct. 16, 1839 in Wyoming Co., NY. Pupil of National Academy of Design, and of G. A. P. Healy in Chicago. Address in 1926, 1160 Bay St., Alameda, Calif.

PECK, ANNE MERRIMAN.
(Mrs. Frank E. Fite). Painter, illustrator and writer. Born Piermont, NY, July 21, 1884. Pupil of Robert Henri and Irving R. Wiles. Specialty, children's portraits and woodcuts. Author and illustrator "Storybook Europe," Harper Bros.; "A Vagabond's Provence," Dodd Mead & Co. Illustrates for Harper Bros., MacMillian Co., and Minton Balch Co. Address in 1929, Croton-on-Hudson, NY.

PECK, CLARA ELSENE.
Painter and illustrator. Member: SI, 1912 NYWCC; NA Women PS; Fellowship PAFA; GFLA; Am. APL. Award: Watrous prize, NY Women's PS, 1921, and poster prize, 1922.

Address in 1929, 531 West 122nd St., New York, NY.

PECK, HENRY J(ARVIS).
Painter, illustrator, etcher and writer. Born Galesburg, Ill., June 10, 1880. Pupul of Eric Pape and Howard Pyle; Rhode Island School of Design. Member: Prov. AC; North Shore AA. Address in 1929, 5 East 14th St., New York, NY; h. 259 Benefit St., Providence, RI.

PECK, NATALIE.
Painter. Born Jersey City, NJ, Feb. 27, 1886. Pupil of Kenneth Hayes Miller. Member: Salons of A; Springfield AA. Work: "Storm Clouds," in Pennsylvania Academy of the Fine Arts. Address in 1929, 12 West 92nd St., New York, NY.

PECK, ORIN.
Painter. Born in Delaware County, NY, in 1860. He was in charge of the artistic work planned for the ranch of W. R. Hearst in northern California, and had painted several portraits of the Hearst family. He was awarded a gold medal at the Columbian Exposition, Chicago, 1893, for his "Scene in the Garden of the Santa Barbara Mission." He died in Los Angeles, Calif., January 20, 1921.

PECKHAM.
A landscape painter noted in Tuckerman's "American Artist Life."

PECKHAM, MARY C.
(Mrs. F. H. Peckham). Painter. Born Providence, Oct. 26, 1861. Pupil of Mary C. Wheller, Raphael Collin, Abbott Thayer. Member: Prov. AC; Prov. WCC; AFA. Address in 1929, Handicraft Club, 42 College St.; h. 96 Lloyd Ave., Providence, RI.

PECKHAM, ROBERT.
Portrait painter. Born in Mass., Sept. 10, 1785. He traveled mostly in the country districts of New England, but established himself for a while in Boston. Most of his portraits are flat, hard and stiff. Peckham painted John Greenleaf Whittier in 1833. Died June 29, 1877 at Westminster, Mass.

PECKHAM, ROSA F.
Nothing is known of this artist except that in the Phillips Academy, Exeter, NH, there is a portrait of Rev. Aug. Woodbury, which is signed "Rosa F. Peckham."

PECORINI, (COMTESSA) MARGARET B.
Painter. Born Philadelphia, PA, Aug. 18, 1879. Pupil of Julian Academy, Paris. Specialty, children's portraits. Address in 1929, 70 bis rue Notre Dames des Champs, Paris, France; h. 114 East 84th St., New York, NY; summer, Morgan & Co., 14 Place Vendome, Paris, France.

PEDDLE, CAROLLINE.
See Mrs. Ball.

PEDRETTI, HUMBERTS.
Sculptor. Exhibited at PAFA, Philadelphia, 1926. Address in 1926, Hollywood, Calif.

PEEBLES, ROY B.
Painter. Aug. 9, 1899. Pupil of Gustave Cimoitti, ernest W. Watson, Clinton Balmer, Will Taylor, Norwood MacGillverary, Member: S. Indp. A; Salons of Amer. Died in 1957. Address in 1929, 34 Main St., North Adams, Mass.; h. 13 Morningside Ave., Adams, Mass.

PEELE, JOHN THOMAS.
Painter. Born April 11, 1822 in England, he came to this country as a child. He settled in New York, and in 1846 was elected an Associate Member of the National Academy. He painted portraits and genre subjects. Among his works are "Children of the Woods" (147), "Highland Supper," "The Village School" and "The Birds' Nest." Died May 19, 1897 in London, England.

PEETS, ORVILLE HOUGHTON.
Painter and etcher. Born Cleveland, Ohio, Aug. 13, 1884. Pupil of Baschet and Laurens in Paris. Member: Salma. C. Award: Hon. mention, Paris Salon, 1914. Painting owned by French Government in the Luxembourg, Paris; represented in the Hispanic Museum, New York; and by etchings and woodcuts in Museum of Art, Cleveland, Ohio. Died in 1968.

Address in 1929, 683 Lake View Road, Cleveland, Ohio; Woodstock, NY.

PEIRCE, H. WINTHROP.
Painter and illustrator. Born Boston, Nov. 25, 1850. Pupil of Boston School under Grandmann and Rimmer; Bouguereau and Robert-Fleury in Paris. Member: Copley S. 1879; Boston SWCP; North Shore AA; Springfield AA. Work in: John-Esther Gallery, Andover; Phillips Academy, Andover, Mass.; Bowdoin College, Brunswick, ME; Public Library, Malden, Mass. Died in 1935. Address in 1929, West Newbury, Mass.

PEIRCE, THOMAS MITCHELL.
Painter. Born in Grand Rapids, Mich., in 1864. Address in 1926, Bartholdi Building, Madison Square, New York.

PEIRCE, WALDO.
Painter. Born in 1884. He exhibited "La Sevilliana" at the Penna. Academy of Fine Arts in Philadelphia, 1915. Address in 1926, Hotel Ansonia, New York City. Died in 1970.

PEIRSON, ALDEN.
Painter. Born in Baltimore in 1873. Began his work in Baltimore, 1894; art manager of the American Magazine since 1912; manager of the Caxton Advertising Co. Address in 1926, 64 East 34th St., New York, NY.

PEIXOTTO, ERNEST (MRS.).
Painter. Born in San Francisco. Pupil of San Francisco Artists' Association, and of Delecluse. Member: National Academy of Women Painters and Sculptors. Address in 1926, 137 East 66th St., New York, NY.

PEIXOTTO, ERNEST C(LIFFORD).
Painter, illustrator and writer. Born San Francisco, CA, Oct. 15, 1869. Pupil of Constant, Lefebvre and Doucet in Paris. Member: ANA 1909; Mural P. (pres.); NY Arch. Lg. 1911; SI 1906; Salma. C.; MacD. C.; Allied AA; AFA; Societe des Artistes Francais. Awards: Hon. mention Paris Salon, chevalier of the Legion of Honor, 1921; Officer,

1924. Work: Scenes from "Le Morte d'Arthur" in Library of Henry A. Everett, near Cleveland, Ohio.; represented in Nat'l Gallery, Washington, DC; Hispanic Museum, New York, NY; murals in Seaman's Bank, Bank of NY, and Embassy Club, NYC; illustrations for Roosevelt's Life of Cromwell; Wanderings by Clayton Hamilton (Doubleday Doran & Co.). Author: By Italian Seas, Romantic California, Our Hispanic Southwest, The American Front etc. Official artist, American Expeditionary Forces, 1918. Director, Atelier of Painting, A.E.F. Art Training Center, Bellevue, France, 1919, Director, Dept. of Mural Painting, Beaux Arts Inst., New York, Chairman, American Committee, Fontainebleau School of Fine Arts. Died in 1940. Address in 1929, 137 East 66th St., New York, NY; and Credit Lyonnais, Paris, France.

PEIXOTTO, GEORGE.
Painter. Born Cleveland, Ohio. Pupil of Meissonier and Munkacsy. Member: Societe des Artistes Francais. Award: Silver medal, Royal Academy, Dresden. Represented in Eastnor Castle, England; Corcorcan Gallery, Washington, DC; Widener Memorial Library, Harvard University; murals in New Amsterdam Theater, and Park National Bank, NY. Address in 1929, "The Chalet," Crestwood, Westchester Co., NY; summer, Martha's Vineyard, Mass.

PEIXOTTO, MARY H.
(Mrs. Ernest Peixotto). Painter. Born in San Francisco. Pupil of Emil Carlsen; Atelier Delecluse, Paris. Member: NA Women PS; MacD. C.; NY School of Design. Address in 1929, 137 East 66th St., New York, NY.

PEKENINO, MICHELE.
Engraver, who appears to have been in New York in 1820, and his latest prints are dated in 1822, so that his stay here was a comparatively short one; though he engraved about thirty plates while in the United States. He was located in Philadelphia in 1821-22. That he was an intimate friend of A. B. Durand is shown by each having engraved the other's portrait and adding very friendly inscriptions, but Dunlap's story that Durand taught Pekenino to engrave is very dubious, to say the least. Durand was a line-engraver; and Pekenino's portrait of Durand, done evidently soon after his arrival in New York, is executed in stipple and is a most excellent piece of work, showing the touch of a master rather than that of an apprentice.

PELHAM, HENRY.
Engraver. Born Feb. 14, 1749 in Boston; accidentally drowned in Ireland in 1806. Henry Pelham was the son of Peter Pelham and of his second wife, Mary Singleton Copley; he was thus the half-brother of John Singleton Copley. The late Wm. H. Whitmore says that Henry Pelham certainly engraved a picture of "The Finding of Moses," but he neither describes the print nor does he give his authority. The late Paul Leicester Ford also prints a letter of March 29, 1770, from H. Pelham to "Mr. Paul Revere," in which he says; "When I heard that you was cutting a plate of the late Murder, I thought it impossible as I knew you was not capable of doing it unless you copied it from mine, etc." In another letter to Charles Pelham written May 1, 1770, Henry Pelham says: "Inclosed I send you two of my prints of the late Massacre." No such prints by Pelham are known. But several water color copies of the Massacre picture have been preserved which are exactly the same in design as the Revere plate, but much superior to it as to details and in the expression of the faces. Some claim that these water colors are the work of Henry Pelham, and are the "prints" referred to, and that Revere used one of these as the original of his plate, and hence the complaint o Pelham to Revere.

PELHAM, PETER.
Portrait painter and engraver Born in 1697 in England, he came to Boston with his wife and family i 1726. In 1734, he married hi second wife, and a child was bor in Newport. In 1748, he marrie again, the widow of Richard Copley

whose son John Singleton Copley, then eleven years of age, was destined to become celebrated as a portrait painter, and must have acquired the rudiments of art from his step-father. In the Antiquarian Society at Worcester is the portrait painted by Peter Pelham of the Rev. Increase Mather, who died in 1728. He painted other portraits that are known, and was the earliest engraver in America. His works in Mezzotint are highly esteemed, a number of which are engraved from portraits by Smibert. He died in Boston in Dec. 1751.

PELIKAN, A(LFRED) G(EORGE).
Painter, writer, lecturer and teacher. Born Breslau-Silesia, March 5, 1893. Pupil of H. S. Hubbell, Hawthorne, Bicknell, E. Savage. Member: Am. APL; Wis. SAC; Am. Inter-Prof. Inst. Represented: The Kent Scientific Museum, South Sea Islands. Author: "The Graphic Aids" series. Member: Educational Staff Bureau of University Travel; Supt. FA Galleries, Wis. State Fair; Director, Milwaukee Art Inst.; Director of Art Education, Milwaukee Public Schools. Address in 1929, 624 - 57th St., Milwaukee, Wis.

PELL, ELLA FERRIS.
Painter, sculptor and illustrator. Born St. Louis, MO, Jan. 18, 1846. Pupil of Cooper Union in New York under Rimmer; Laurens, Ferdinand Humbert and Gaston St. Pierre in Paris. Work: "Salome" painting owned by Boston Art Club; "Andromeda" heroic statue. Address in 1929, Beacon, NY.

PELLEGRINI, ERNEST (G.).
Sculptor. Born S. Ambrogio di Verona, Italy, August 18, 1889. Pupil of Academy of Verona. Member: Boston SS; Copley S; North Shore AA. Work: Reredos, St. Luke's Cathedral, Portland, ME; Triptych, St. Chrysostom's Church, Chicago, Ill. Died in 1955. Address in 1929, 168 Dartmouth St., Boston, Mass.

PELTON, AGNES.
Painter. Born Stuttgart, Germany, of American parents, Aug. 22, 1881.

Pupil of Pratt Inst. under Dow; W. L. Lathrop, Hamilton E. Field; and in Rome. Member: NA Women PS; Assn. A of LI; AFA. Work: Portraits of Henry Leslie Perry, Henry Leslie Perry Memorial Library; and of William Wright Abbot, First Nat'l. Bank, Louisville, GA. Died in 1961. Address in 1929, Hay Ground Windmill, Water Mill, LI, NY.

PELTON, OLIVER.
Engraver. Born Aug. 31, 1798 in Portland, Conn. He was first a pupil and then a partner of Abner Reed, in Hartford. In 1827 he was established in business as an engraver in Boston, and in 1836 the firm of Pelton & Terry was engraving banknotes in the same city. His son, Edward B. Pelton, was born in Boston in 1840, and was later a publisher in New York. Oliver Pelton was a fairly good line engraver of portraits and worked at his profession up to within a few years of his death. he also engraved a number of small subject-plates for the "Annuals." Died Sug. 15, 1882 in E. Hartford, Conn.

PEMBER, ADA HUMPHREY.
Painter. Born in Shopiere, Wisc., in 1859. Pupil of W. M. Clute and F. Fursman. Member: Janesville Art League; Wisconsin Painters and Sculptors. Address in 1926, 103 Jackson St., Janesville, Wisconsin.

PEMBROOKE, THEODORE KENYON.
Landscape painter. Born in Elizabeth, NJ, in 1865; died Sept. 22, 1917 in New York City.

PENDLETON, JOHN.
Lithographer. Born in 1798 in New York State. While traveling in France he became interested in lithographs and studied the art under the best masters in Paris. On returning to America, he settled in Boston with his brother, a copperplate printer, and there they established a lithographing establishment about 1825. Died March 10, 1866.

PENDLETON W(ILLIAM), L(ARNED) MARCY.
Painter. Born Paris of American parents, Feb. 19, 1865. Pupil of

Carolus Duran. Member: S. Indp. A.; Salons of America. Award: Honorable mention, Paris Salon, 1888.

PENFIELD, EDWARD.
Painter and illustrator. Born in Brooklyn, NY, in 1866. Pupil of Art Students' League of New York. Member: Society of Illustrators, 1901. Specialty, posters and cover designs. Author and illustrator of "Holland Sketches" and "Spanish Sketches;" decorations for Rochester Country Club; editor for Harper's, 1890-1901; instructor, ASL. Had profound impact on Am. illustration. He died Feb. 8, 1925, in Beacon, NY.

PENFOLD, FRANK C.
Born in Buffalo, NY. Received honorable mention in Paris Salon, 1889, for his painting, "Stormy Weather, North Sea."

PENMAN, EDITH.
Painter. Member of National Association of Women Painters and Sculptors. Exhibited in Annual Exhibition, 1923-24. Address in 1926, 939 Eighth Ave., New York.

PENNELL, JOSEPH.
Etcher, lithographer, illustrator and author. Born in Philadelphia, Penna., July 4, 1860. Pupil of Penna. Academy of Fine Arts, and Penna. School of Industrial Art. Taught at ASL. Awards: 1st class gold medal, Paris Exposition, 1900; Dresden, 1902; Grand Prize, St. Louis Exposition, 1904; gold medal, Liege, 1905; Grand Prix, Milan, 1906; Barcelona, 1907; Brussels, 1910; Diplome d'Honneur, Amsterdam, 1912; 2 medals, London, 1913; Florence, 1914; commemorative medal same, 1915. Represented in the Luxembourg, and in the collection of the city of Paris; also in Cabinet des Estamps (France); Uffizi Gallery (Florence); British Museum; S. Kensington Museum; Guildhall Gallery, London, and in many state and municipal collections in Europe and the United States; Library of Congress, Washington; Penna. Academy, Phila.; Carnegie Institute, Pittsburgh. Elected Associate Member of the National Academy in 1907, and an Academician in 1909. Author of Lithography and Lithographers, 1900; The Authorized Life of J. McN. Whistler (with Mrs. Pennell), 1910. Pictures of War Work in America, 1918; he has also illustrated a great number of books; contributor to the leading magazines. Address in 1926, Century Club, New York, NY. Died April 23, 1926, in Brooklyn, NY.

PENNEY, L. P.
Miniature painter, who flourished in Boston, 1845.

PENNIMAN, H. A. F.
Painter. Born in New York, NY, in 1882. Pupil of Twachtman, Beckwith, S. E. Whiteman, Everett L. Bryant and Anshutz; also studied in Germany. Member: Society of Independent Artists. Address in 1926, 609 Cathedral St., Baltimore, MD.

PENNIMAN, JOHN RITTO.
Painter. Born Jan. 30, 1783 in Milford, Mass. Lived and worked for many years in Roxbury, Mass. He was married in Boston in 1805. He painted a well-executed picture of the Boston Common and other views in and about Boston. Died in 1830.

PENNIMAN, LEONORA NAYLOR.
Painter. Born Minneapolis, Minn., April 2, 1884. Pupil of Emma Siboni. Member: Santa Cruz; San F. SWA. Address in 1929, 317 Water St., Santa Cruz, Calif.; summer, Brookdale, Calif.

PENNINGTON, HARPER.
Painter. Born in Newport, RI, in 1854. Pupil of Gerome at the Ecole des Beaux Arts, and of Carolus-Duran and Whistler, 1874-86, during which period he also spent some time in Italy. Died March 15, 1920 in Baltimore, MD.

PENNOYER, A(LBERT) SHELDON.
Painter. Born Oakland, Calif., April 5, 1888. Pupil of Ecole des Beaux-Arts, Academies Julian and Grande Chaumiere. Rene Menard and Lucien Simon in Paris; Naum Los in Rome, Giuseppe Casciaro and Carlandi in Italy; Harold Speed in

London; PAFA. Member: Am. WCS; AFA. Work: "Church of the Spirito Santo, Ronda," Metropolitan Museum of Art. Died in 1957. Address in 1929, 116 East 66th St., New York, NY; P.O. Box 373, Litchfield, Conn.

PEPPER, CHARLES HOVEY.
Painter. Born Waterville, ME, Aug. 27, 1864. Pupil of Chase in NY; Constant, Laurens and Aman-Jean in Paris. Member: NYWCC; Boston WCC; Copley S. 1900; Boston AC; New Haven PCC; Concord AA; Boston SWCP. Died in 1950. Address in 1929, Fenway Studios, 30 Ipswich St., Boston, Mass.; h. Concord, Mass.

PEPPER, ROBERT RONALD.
Illustrator. Born in Portsmouth, New Hampshire, in 1938. Attended Los Angeles City College and received a BA in advertising illustration from ACD. Since his first published work for The Saturday Evening Post in 1964, he has won awards from the Society of Publication Designers, Mead Library of Ideas and the S of I. His covers for Ace, Ballatine, Avon, Dell, and the New American Library won him an award from Fantasy/Science Fiction Readers. He has also produced several posters and illustrated for major magazines.

PERARD, VICTOR S(EMON).
Illustrator and etcher. Born Paris, France, Jan. 16, 1870. Pupil of NAD and ASL of New York; Ecole des Beaux-Arts in Paris, under Gerome. Member: SI. Instructor at Cooper Union. Specialty, character sketches. Died July 9, 1959 in Bellport, LI, NY. Address in 1929, 55 Charles St., New York, NY.

PERCIVAL, EDWIN.
Painter. Born in Kensington, Conn., in 1793. In 1830 he went to Hartford, to study art. He was gifted but very eccentric. His drawing was good and the coloring of his pictures pleasing. He excelled in ideal sketches; the "Three Daughters of Job" was his best known work. He spent some years in Albany, and died of depressing melancholy, starving to death.

PERCY, ISABELLE CLARK.
(Mrs. George Parsons West). Illustrator. Born Alameda, Calif. Pupil of Mark Hopkins Inst., San Francisco; Dow and Snell in New York and Europe; Brangwyn in England. Member: Women's AA; San F. AA. Awards: Hon. mention, Paris Salon, 1911; hon. mention, California bookplate and poster competitions; bronze medal for lithography, P.-P. Exp., San F., 1915. Professor of design and composition, Calif. School of Arts and Crafts, Oakland. Address in 1929, 220 Spencer St., Sausalito, Calif.

PERDUE, W. K.
Painter, craftsman and writer. Born Minerva, Ohio, May 17, 1884. Pupil of Dr. Esenwein. Address in 1929, 2915 Tenth St., N.W., Canton, Ohio.

PERERA, GINO.
Painter and sculptor. Born Siena, Italy, Aug. 2, 1872. Pupil of Royal Academy, Rome; School of Boston Museum; H. D. Murphy, Birge Harrison and Ochtman. Member: Boston AC; St. Botolph C; Copley S; Salma. C. Address in 1929, 382 Commonwealth Ave., Boston, Mass.

PEREZ, FRANCISCO.
Sculptor. 285 Oak Street, Patchogue, NY 11772, Born: New York City, Aug. 24, 1934. Gallery: Elicofon Gallery, 396 Broadway, New York, NY. Work: Private collections, including H. F. Guggenheim, J. P. Morgan; many public collections. Exhibitions: Loeb Student Center, NYU, NY; Brooklyn Museum, NY; Museum of Fine Arts, MA; and others.

PERFILIEFF, VLADIMIR.
Painter. Born Russia, Dec. 20, 1895. Pupil of Snell. Garber, Breckenridge, McCartan, Carrois, Jos. Pearson, Schouhaieff, Andre L'hote. Member: Fellowship PAFA; Phila. Alliance; Phila. Sketch C. Address in 1929, 2116 Chancellor St., Philadelphia, PA.

PERINE, GEORGE EDWARD.
Engraver. Born in South Orange, Essex County, NJ, on July 9, 1837. Mr. Perine was of Huguenot and Dutch descent, his ancestors having settled on Staten Island and in Ulster County prior to the Revolution. On May 25, 1852, he commenced engraving under Thomas Doney, of New York, and in 1856-58 he was with W. W. Rice, an excellent line and bank-note engraver of Scotch Plains. During this time and before he was nineteen years old, he engraved in mezzotint his large plate of "The Signing of the Compact in the Cabin of the Mayflower." In 1858-60 Mr. Perine was in the employ of New York engravers, and in the latter year he began engraving on his own account and established, in time, an extensive and very successful business in NYC. Portrait engraving formed the chief part of his work; and while he employed many engravers in his establishment he is said to have finished every plate himself. Died Feb. 3, 1885 in Brooklyn, NY.

PERKES, LINNETTE MOENCH
Painter, graphic artist, and illustrator. Born Chicago, IL. Studied at the Univ. of Utah. Studied privately with Alvin Gittenes, Howard Sanden and Daniel Green. Awards include 1st and 2nd prize in All-Utah Commercial Art Exhib.; 2nd and 3rd Prizes in Southern Calif. Exhibition. Media: oils, charcoal, pastels, pen and ink. Address in 1983, 1583 Lime Grove Rd., Poway, Calif.

PERKINS, CHARLES CALLAHAN.
Born in Boston in 1823. President of the Boston Art Club, 1871. Honorary life member of the Metropolitan Art Museum of NY. Though not a professional artist he drew and etched the plates to illustrate a number of the books on art and artists of which he was the author. Died in 1886.

PERKINS, E. G.
A line portrait of no particular merit, published by Samuel W. Wheeler, of Providence, RI, in 1831, is signed "E. G. Perkins, Sc."

PERKINS, GRANVILLE.
Born Oct. 16, 1830 in Baltimore, MD. He studied in Philadelphia under James Hamilton. He devoted himself to scene painting and illustrating. He was a member of the Water Color Society, and exhibited frequently at the National Academy of Design. Died April 17, 1895 in New York City.

PERKINS, HARLEY.
Portrait painter. Pupil of DeCamp. Tarbell, Benson, Mass. Normal Art School, Boston Museum School. Member: Boston AC. Art editor and critic for Boston "Evening Transcript." Address in 1929, Fenway Studios, 30 Ipswich St., Boston, Mass.

PERKINS, JACOB.
Born in Newburyport, Mass., in 1776; died in London, England, in 1849. Perkins was not known to have been an engraver on copperplate, but his influence upon the development of bank-note engraving was so marked that he deserves mention among engravers. As a silversmith in his native town he made the dies for the Massachusetts copper coinage of 1787, and he was early prominent as an inventor of machines for various purposes. In 1810 he found means for the important substitution of steel for copper plates in engraving bank-notes, thus greatly prolonging the life of the plate.

PERKINS, JOHN U.
Painter. Born in Washington, DC, in 1875. Pupil of Chase. Member of Society of Washington Artists. Address in 1926, 815 A St., N.E., Washington, DC.

PERKINS, JOSEPH.
Engraver. Born Aug. 19, 1788 in Unity, NH. Joseph Perkins graduated from Williams College in 1814; in 1818 he went to Philadelphia and there learned script engraving. He established himself in business in that city, but in 1825 he removed to New York and with A. B. Durand he became a member of the bank-note engraving firm of Durand, Perkins & Co. Died April 27, 1842 in New York City.

PERKINS, LUCY FITCH.
(Mrs. Dwight H. Perkins). Illustrator and teacher. Born Maples, Ind., July 12, 1865. Pupil of Boston Museum School. Author and illustrator of "A Book of Joys," "The Goose Girl," "The Dutch Twins," "The Scotch Twins," "Dandelion Classics," "Cornelia," and other books for childrens. Died in 1937. Address in 1929, 2319 Lincoln St., Evanston, Ill.

PERKINS, MARY SMYTH.
(Mrs. William F. Taylor). Painter. Born Philadelphia. Pupil of PAFA; Robert Henri; Philadelphia School of Design under William Sartain; Lawton Parker School, Cottet and Simon in Paris. Member: NS Women PS. Award: Mary Smith prize, PAFA, 1907. Work: "Portrait of James L. Miles," City Hall, Philadelphia, PA. Address in 1929, Lumberville, PA.

PERKINS, MISS.
Portrait draughtsman in pastel. She was a sister of Dr. Perkins. Portraits in pastel (probably by Miss Perkins) of Caleb Perkins, Lucy Perkins, and Sarah Perkins are owned by the Connecticut Historical Society. She was working in Connecticut about 1790.

PERKINS, WILLARD.
Painter, who exhibited water colors at the Penna. Academy of the Fine Arts, Philadelphia, 1925. Address in 1926, Fort Washington, Pennsylvania.

PEROT, JAMES.
Engraver. He was one of the Huguenot settlers of New Rochelle, NY, and was a silversmith of that place, and later of Bermuda and Philadelphia. He was a brother-in-law of Robert Elliston of New York. He was probably the founder of the Perot family in Philadelphia, and the father of Elliston Perot, a prominent merchant of Philadelphia, about 1790. A Chippendale bookplate of James Perot with a wide engraved border is said to have been engraved by Perot himself.

PERRETT, A. LOUISE.
Painter, illustrator and teacher. Born Chicago, Ill. Pupil of AIC; Howard Pyle; John Carlson. Member: Chicago SA; Oak Park, River Forest and Austin AL. Instructor, Art Institute of Chicago. Address in 1929, 150 North Scoville Ave., Oak Park, Ill.

PERRETT, GALEN JOSEPH.
Painter and illustrator. Born Chicago, IL, Sept. 14, 1875. Pupil of AIC; Munich Art Academy, Germany; Colarossi and Julian Academy in Paris. Member: Salma. C.; NYWCC; AFA. Represented in Newark, NJ, Museum. Address in 1929, 51 West 10th St., New York, NY; h. 492 Mt. Pleasant Ave., Newark, NJ; Rockport, Mass.

PERRINE, VAN DEARING.
Painter. Born Garnett, KS, Sept. 10, 1869. Self-taught. Member ANA; New Soc. A. Awards: Silver medal, Charleston Exp., 1902; hon. mention, CI Pittsburgh, 1903; silver medal, P.-P. Exp., San F., 1915. Experiments with color music. Represented in Phillips Memorial Gallery, Washington, DC. Died Dec. 10, 1955 in Stamford, CT. Address in 1929, 42 Prospect Ave., Maplewood, NJ.

PERRY, CLARA FAIRFIELD.
Painter and lecturer. Born Brooklyn, NY. Pupil of Walter Scott Perry, Henry B. Snell, Ettore Caser. Member: Meridien C; Brooklyn SA; Brooklyn SA; Brooklyn PS. Died in 1941. Address in 1929, 56 Cambridge Pl., Brooklyn, New York, NY; summer, Elmcroft, Stoneham, Mass.

PERRY, CLARA G(REENLEAF).
Painter, sculptor and lecturer. Born Long Branch, NJ, Aug. 22, 1871. Pupil of Robert Henri. Member: Copley S.; NA. Women PS.; Wash. AC. Address in 1929, care of Mrs. David Perry, The Wyoming, Wash., DC; summer, Chavaniac Lafayette, Haute Loire, France.

PERRY, EDITH DEAN WEIR.
(Mrs. James DeWolf Perry). Miniature painter. Born New Haven, CT, Aug. 17, 1875. Pupil of Yale School of Fine Arts under her

father, John F. Weir; of Lucia Fairchild Fuller and of Adele Herter. Member: Providence AC. Award: Hon. mention, Pan-Am. Exp., Buffalo, 1901. Work: "Virgin and Child," St. Paul's Church, New Haven, CT; Tabernacle door, Christ Church, West Haven, CT. Specialty, portrait miniatures. Address in 1929, Bishops House, Providence, RI.

PERRY, EMILIE S.
Sculptor, Medical Illustrator. Born New Ipswich, NH, Dec. 18, 1873. Pupil of School of the Boston Museum; Mass. Norma. Art School; Max Broedel. Member: Ann Arbor AA. Work: Panel in bas relief, The Women's Club, Hollywood; panel, Hollywood Library; bust of Prof. Gordon, College of Garvanza, Los Angeles. Died in 1929.

PERRY, ENOCH WOOD.
Painter. Born July 31, 1831 in Boston, Mass. Came to New Orleans in 1848; went to Europe and studied in Dusseldorf and Paris, 1852 and 1853; then to Rome and Venice, 1856 to 1858, returning to the U.S. in the latter year. In 1860 he had a studio at 108 St. Charles Street, New Orleans. He painted the splendid lifesize portrait of U.S. Senator John Slidell, now in the Louisiana State Mus. In 1861 he painted Jefferson Davis, using the map of the Confederate States as a background. He traveled extensively and was a famous international portrait painter, having painted many of the great men of his time. Among his important figure compositions is "Signing the Ordinance of the Secession of Louisiana," painted in 1861. In 1865 he settled in NY and died there in 1915. He was elected an Associate Member of the NAD in 1868, and full Academician in 1869; he was a member of the American Water Color Society. Died Dec. 14, 1915 in NY.

PERRY, IONE.
Painter. Born in New York City in 1839. Student of the Cooper Institute, and pupil of Henry Loop. Among her best known paintings are "Hypatia," "Romola," "Consuelo" and

"Elsa, at the Coming of Lohengrin." Mother of Roland Hinton Perry.

PERRY, J(AMES) R(AYMOND).
Painter. Born Northfield, Mass., April 20, 1863. Self taught. Member: Chicago SA; Business Men's AC.; South Side AA; Chicago Municipal A. Lg.; All-Ill. SFA; Ill. AFA; AFA. Represented in Chicago Public Schools. Address in 1929, 5221 Cornell Ave., Chicago, Ill.

PERRY, JOHN D.
Sculptor. Born in Swanton, Va., in 1845. He lived in New York, 1869-70, but passed the rest of his professional life in Italy and Boston. He made many portrait busts, and his statuette of Sumner was highly praised.

PERRY, LILLA CABOT.
Painter and writer. Born c. 1848 in Boston, Mass. Pupil of Cowles Art School under D. M. Bunker and R. W. Vonnoh in Boston; Julian and Colarossi academies and at Alfred Stevens' studio in Paris. Member: AFA; Boston GA; Societe des Artistes Independants, Paris; Inter. Soc. AL; Women's Inter. AC Paris and London; Nippon Bijitsu-in, Tokyo; Concord AA; Conn. AFA. Awards: Silver medal, Boston, 1892; bronze medal, St. Louis Exp., 1904; bronze medal, P.-P. Exp., San F., 1915. Work: "The Young 'Cellist," Boston Museum of Fine Arts; "Portrait fo Worthington Ford," NY Public Library; "Pair of Blue Eyes." American Federation of Women's Clubs, Wash., DC; "After the First Snow," Carolina Art Assn., Charleston. Author of "The Heart of the Weed"; "From the Garden of Hellas"; "Impressions"; "The Jar of Dreams." Died in 1933. Address in 1929, Fenway Studios, 30 Ipswich St.; h. 312 Marlborough St., Boston, MA.

PERRY, OSWALD.
Sculptor. He has exhibited in Chicago and Cincinnati.

PERRY, RAYMOND.
Painter and illustrator. Born Sterling, Ill., 1886. Pupil of AIC. Member: Salma. C., 1908;

AWCS. Windows in St. Andrews Church, Pittsburgh; Memorial Library, Hanover, PA. Died in 1960. Address in 1929, 149 East 34th St., New York, NY.

PERRY, RAYMOND W.
Painter. Born Natick, Mass., July 28, 1883. Pupil of A. K. Cross, W. D. Hamilton, Munsell, Vojteck Preissig. Member: Prov. AC; Prov. WCC; Mass. Normal AA. Address in 1929, 175 Evergreen St., Providence, RI; summer, Port Elgin, Ontario, Canada.

PERRY, ROLAND HINTON.
Portrait painter and sculptor. Born in New York, Jan. 25, 1870. Pupil of Gerome, Delance, Callot, Chapu and Puech in Paris. Member: NSS; AFA. Work: "Fountain of Neptune," Library of Congress, Washington; Langdon doors, Buffalo Historical Society; frieze, New Amsterdam Theatre, New York; "Pennsylvania; on dome of Capitol, Harrisburg; "Gen. Greene" and "Gen. Wadsworth" at Gettysburg; "New York State Memorial," Andersonville; "Gen. Curtis," Ogdensburg; "Gen. Castleman," Louisville; "New York Monument," Chattanooga; "Benjamin Rush Monument," and Lions, Connecticut Ave. Bridge, Washington; monument to 38th Infantry, Syracuse, NY. died Oct. 27, 1941. Address in 1929, 51 West 10th St., New York, NY.

PERRY, W. A.
Painter. Born in Wasepi, Mich. Pupil of San Francisco School of Art and of W. V. Cahill and John Rich. Address in 1926, 6172 Chabot Road, Oakland, Calif.

PERRY, WALTER SCOTT.
Painter, sculptor, teacher, writer and lecturer. Born Stoneham, Mass. Pupil of Langerfeldt, Higgins and Pierre Millet; Mass. Normal Art School; studied abroad. Member: NAC; Alliance; Eastern AA; Western AA; Rembrandt C. Supervisor of drawing and art education, public schools, Fall River, Mass., 1875-79; and worcester, Mass., 1879-87. Director, School of Fine and Applied Arts, Pratt Institute, since its organization, from 1887 to 1928. Author of Egypt, the Land

of the Temple Builders; With Azir Girges in Egypt; textbooks on art education; lecturer on architecture, sculpture, painting and decoration. Address in 1929, 56 Cambridge Pl., Brooklyn, New York, NY; summer, Elmcroft, Stoneham, Mass.

PERSICO, GENNARINO.
Miniature painter. He was the brother of Lugi Persico, the sculptor. He came from Naples. See "Lancaster Historical Society Papers." Exhibited at the Penna. Academy, 1827. Died c. 1859.

PESCHERET, LEON R(ENE).
Painter, illustrator, architect, draughtsman and teacher. Born London, England, March 15, 1892. Pupil of Fleury, Millet; AIC. Member: Palette and Chisel C; Arch. C. of Chicago. Decoration in Drake Hotel, Chicago; Peoria Country Club; interior of Memorial Union Bldg., University of Wisconsin. Died in 1961. Address in 1929, 5257 Magnolia Ave., Chicago, Ill.

PETERDI, GABOR.
Painter. He was born Sept. 17, 1915 in Budapest, Hungary. Citizen of US. Studied at Hungarian Acad., Budapest; and Academie Julian, and Academie Scandinavian (Paris). Awarded Prix de Rome (1930). Taught at Brooklyn Mus. Art School; Yale (prof. of art since 1960). Guggenheim fellow (1964); awards from PAFA; Boston Printmakers; Seattle Art Mus. and others. Exhibited at Levy Gal., NYC (1939); Phila. Art Alliance; Smithsonian; Brooks Mem. Art Gal.; Brooklyn; Cleveland; Oakland; Salt Lake City Art Centeri NY Public Library' Yale; Kanegis Gallery, Boston; Wesleyan; Berkeley; Univ. of Kentucky, many others. In collections of Univ. of Georgia (Athens); Wesleyan; Harvard; Addison; Univ. of Michigan; Albright-Knox; Art Inst. of Chicago; Cleveland; Vassar College; Brown U.; Syracuse; Smithsonian; Clarkson College; MOMA; Yale; Wadsworth; Univ. of N. Carolina; Rijks Mus., Amsterdam Mus. of Prague, Czech. and many others internationally.

PETERS, CARL W(ILLIAM).
Painter. Born Rochester, NY, Nov. 14, 1897. Pupil of Rosen, Ross and Carlson. Member: Rochester AC; Buffalo SA; Springfield AA; AFA. Award: Fairchild Gift of 1924 from the University of Rochester; silver medal, Rochester AC, 1925, first prize, 1927-28; third Hallgarten prize, NAD, 1926, and second Hallgarten prize, 1928; hon. mention, Buffalo SA, 1927. Address in 1929, Jefferson Ave., Fairport, NY.

PETERS, CHARLES F.
Illustrator and etcher. Born in Kristiania, Norway, in 1882. Work: Cartoons in Life; illustrations in Scribner's, Harper's and Century. Address in 1926, 412 East 50th St. New York, NY. Died June 21, 1948.

PETERS, CHARLES ROLLO.
Painter. Born in California in 1862. Pupil of Virgil Williams in San Francisco; Ecole des Beaux Arts under Gerome, and of Boulanger and Lefebvre in Paris. Member: Lotos Club; Salmagundi Club, 1901. Awards: Bronze medal, Pan-American Exposition, Buffalo, 1901; silver medal, St. Louis Exposition, 1904. Address in 1926, Monterey, Calif. Died c. 1928.

PETERS, DEWITT CLINTON.
Painter, illustrator and teacher. Born Baltimore, June 11, 1865. Pupil of Ecole des Beaux-Arts under Gerome, and of Lefebvre, Boulanger and Collin in Paris. Award: Bronze medal, Paris Exp., 1889. Specialty, portraits. Founder and principal instructor, Clinton Peters Art Classes, New York. Address in 1929, Class Studio 606, 1947 Broadway; h. Apt. 7D, 145 West 55th St., New York, NY.

PETERSEN, EUGEN H.
Painter, lecturer and teacher. Born Bluefields, Nicaragua, CA, Feb. 16, 1894. Pupil of John F. Carlson. Member: Brooklyn SA; Swedish-American Artists. Address in 1929, Summer, Monhegan Island, ME.

PETERSEN, JOHN ERIK CHRISTIAN.
Painter. Born in Denmark in 1839; died in Boston, Mass., in 1874. In 1864 he settled in this country and opened his studio in Boston, and devoted himself mainly to marine painting. His work is strong and effective. Among his paintings are "After the Collision," "Making Sail after the Gale," and "The Phantom Ship."

PETERSEN, MARTIN.
Painter. Born in Denmark, Nov. 23, 1870. Pupil of NAD. Member: NYWCC; Salma. C. 1906. Awards: Third Hallgarten prize, NAD 1905; Beal prize, NYWCC 1906; Inness prize, Salma. C. 1907. Address in 1929, 437 West 59th St., New York, NY; h. 325 Hillside Ave., West Nutley, NJ.

PETERSON, C.
American marine painter.

PETERSON, ELSA KIRPAL.
(Mrs. R. M. Tower Peterson). Sculptor. Born in New York, NY, June 16, 1891. Pupil of Edith Woodman Burroughs and J. E. Fraser. Member: Alliance; ASL of NY. Address in 1929, 67 Hillside Ave.; h. 140 Barclay St., Flushing, NY.

PETERSON, JANE.
(Mrs. M. Bernard Philipp). Painter. Born Elgin, Ill. Pupil of Brangwyn, Blanche and Sorolla. Member: Fellow, NAD; NYWCC; AWCS; NA Women PS; SPNY; Wash. WCC; Conn. AFA; Pen and Brush C; NAC; Circulo Artitico, Venice; Alliance; Hartford AA; Gloucester SA; North Shore AA; Federation Francaise des Artistes, Paris; Turkish Amer. Painters A., Constantinople. Awards: Water color prize, Girls' Art Club, Paris; hon. mention, Conn. AFA 1916; Flagg prize ($100). Conn AFA, 1917; hon. mention, NA Women PS, 1927. Work: "Glimpse of the Grand Canal," Art Association, Grand Rapids, Mich.; Girls' Art Club, Paris; Brooklyn Athletic Club; Public Schools, Evanston, Ill.; Country Club, Torrington, Conn.; Y.M.C.A., Elgin, Ill.; Boise (Idaho) Public Library; Brooklyn Museum; Syracuse Art Museum. Instructor at Art Students' League, 1914-19. Died in 1968. Address in 1929, 1007 Fifth Ave., New York, NY; and Elgin, Ill.

PETERSON, LARRY D.
Painter. Born in Holdrege, Nebraska, Jan. 1, 1935. Study: Kearney State College, 1958; Northern Colorado Univ., 1962; Univ. of Kansas; 1975. Work and Commissions: Univ. of Minn.; private collections; First Methodist Church, Kearney, Neb.; others. Exhib.: Joslyn Art Mus., Omaha, Neb., 1974, 75; Ann. Am. Nat'l. Miniature Exhib., Laramie, Wys., 1977, 80, 81; Augustana College, Sioux Falls, South Dakota, 1980; 10th Ann. Nat'l. Fall Art Fete, Scottsbluff, Neb., 1980-81; others. Awards: America's Outstanding Names and Faces, Scholastics, 1978; Gov's. Art Award, State of Neb., 1981. Teaching: Kearney (Neb.) State College, 1967 to present. Mem.: Nat'l. Art Educ. Assn.; Neb. Art Teachers Assn.; Assn. of Neb. Art Clubs; Nat'l. Art Fraternity. Media: Watercolor, acrylic. Address in 1982, 4 Seminole Lane, Kearney, NE.

PETERSON, PERRY.
Illustrator. Born in Minneapolis, MN, in 1908. Received his art training through the Federal Schools Course and later at the AIC. His career began with advertising assignments in Chicago and Detroit, but he soon moved to NY, where he worked at the Byron Musser Studio. His free-lance career began in 1942, and he illustrated for The Saturday Evening Post, Liberty, Good Housekeeping and others. Died in 1958.

PETHEO, BELA FRANCIS.
Painter and printmaker. Saint John's University, Department of Art, Collegeville, MN, address in 1982. Born in Budapest, Hungary, May 14, 1934; US citizen. Study: University of Budapest, MA 1956; Acad. Fine Arts, Vienna, 1957-59, with A. P. Guelersloh; Univ. of Vienna; Univ. of Chicago, MFA 1963. Work: Hungarian State Mus. of Fine Arts, Budapest; Kunstmus., Bern, Switz.; Univ. of MN. Perm. Collection; others. Comn.: Assn. Austrian Boy Scouts; Hall of Educ., NY World's Fair, 1964, others. Exhibitions: Hamline Univ.;

University of Chicago; Coffman Gallery, U. of MN; Biennale Wis. Printmakers; Tweed Museum of Art, MN; and others. Awards: Academy of Fine Arts, Vienna; Festival of Arts, U. of Chicago, Graphic Prize; Rockefeller Foundation Scholarship; Purchase award, Pillsbury Invit. and others. Art Positions: Artist in Residence at St. John's Univ.; lecturer at Museum of Fine Arts, Budapest; Illustrator and author of many articles on art. Mem.: Col. Art Assn. of Am.; Los Angeles Printmaking Soc. Media: Lithograph, oil, acrylic.

PETO, JOHN FREDERICK.
Painter. Born in Philadelphia, PA, in 1854. Self-taught, with one year at PAFA, 1878. Moved to Island Heights, NJ, 1889; visited the West twice; never traveled to Europe. With the exception of one exhibit at Pennsylvania Academy, no major shows until the 1950's. Painted "Trompe l'oeil" still lifes characterized by asymetrical arrangement of banal subjects such as string, tin cups, tattered books, umbrellas, torn postcards. His use of light and color are said to be reminiscent of Vermeer. Died in 1907. Represented by Kennedy Galleries, NYC.

PETREMONT, CLARICE MARIE.
Painter, illustrator, craftsman and teacher. Born Brookly, New York. Pupil of Marshall Fry and Paul Cornoyer. Member: New Haven PCC; Bridgeport AL; Boston SAC; Am. APL. Died in 1949. Address in 1929, Shelton, Conn.

PETROVITS, MILAN.
Painter. Born Vienna, Austria, Jan. 17, 1892. Pupil of Arthur C. Sparks. Member: Pitts. AA. Award: Third prize, 1922, first prize for group paintings, 1923, first prize, 1924, Pitts. AA. Work: "Portrait of An Old Man," "Girl with Guitar," and "Evening," Public School Collection, Pittsburgh. Address in 1929, 723 Liberty Ave., Pittsburgh, PA; h. Verona Road, Verona, PA.

PETRUCCELLI, ANTONIO.
Illustrator. Born in Fort Lee, NJ, in 1907. Attended the Master

School of United Arts in NY in the early 1920's. He began his career in 1929 with a House Beautiful cover and has since illustrated many books for Time-Life, as well as many magazines, over a 40-year period. His posters have won awards from House Beautiful, the American Society for Cancer Control and International Press Exhibition in Cologne, 1928. He designed the postage stamp for the Steel Centenary in 1957 and an award winning medal for the Franklin Mint in 1973.

PETRY, VICTOR.
Painter, illustrator, etcher and teacher. Born Philadelphia, PA, Oct. 9, 1903. Pupil of Frederick Waugh. Work: "White-Tailed Deer," Brooklyn Museum, Brooklyn, NY. Died July 11, 1924 in NYC. Address in 1929, 29 Cedar Lane, Douglaston, LI, NY; summer, Ogunquit, ME.

PETTICOLAS, EDWARD F.
Portrait painter in oils and miniatures. Born in 1793 in Pennsylvania, the son of Philip Petticolas. He practiced in Richmond, VA, in 1805-34, after studying with Thomas Sully in Phila. His portrait of John Buchanan is owned by the Virginia State Library, Richmond, VA. A miniature of Elihu Etting, signed on front "E. F. Petticolas 1799," was presented in 1886 by Mr. Etting to the Penna. Academy of Fine Arts. Died c. 1853.

PETTICOLAS, PHILIP A.
Miniature painter, who was born in 1760 in France. He painted for years in Richmond, VA, and died in VA Aug., 1841. It is claimed that Washington gave him sittings for a miniature in Philadelphia in 1796. He also made several miniatures of Washington from Gilbert Stuart's first portrait.

PETTINGILL, LILLIAN ANNIN.
(Mrs. C. K. Pettingill). Painter and teacher. Born Le Roy, NY, Feb. 4, 1871. Pupil of Irving R. Wiles; L. M. Wiles; Rhoda Holmes Nicholls, Chase School; ASL of NY. Address in 1929, 319 South 8th St., La Crosse, Wis.

PETTY, MARY.
Illustrator. Born in Hampton, NJ, in 1899. Her works appeared in The New Yorker from 1927 until 1966, during which time she illustrated 38 covers, her last on Mother's Day in 1966. Her artwork was often satirical, preying on rich dowagers. In 1927 she married a NY cartoonist, Alan Dunn. Died in 1976.

PEUGEOT, GEORGE I(RA).
Painter and craftsman. Born Buffalo, NY, Nov. 26, 1869. Pupil of Peter Gowans. Member: Buffalo SA. Address in 1929, 120 Highland Ave., Buffalo, NY.

PEW, GERTRUDE L.
Miniature painter, who exhibited at the Penna. Academy of Fine Arts, Philadelphia, 1925. Address in 1926, 48 East 49th St., New York.

PEYRAUD, ELIZABETH K.
(Mrs. F. C. Peyraud). Painter. Illustrator. Born Carbondale, Ill. Pupil of AIC, F. C. Peyraud. Member: Chicago PS; Chicago WCC; Cordon C; Alumni AIC; Chicago Galleries Assn. Address in 1929, 1230 Judson Ave., Highland Park, Ill.

PEYRAUD, FRANK C.
Painter. Born Bulle, Switzerland, 1858. Pupil of AIC; Ecole des Beaux-Arts, Bonnet, Friburg, Paris. Member: Chicago PS; Chicago WCC; NAC; AFA. Awards: Fortnightly prize, AIC, 1899; Butler prize, AIC, 1912; Chicago SA medal, AIC, 1912; Carr prize, AIC, 1913; Grower prize, AIC, 1915; bronze medal, P.-P. Exp., San F., 1915; silver medal, Hamilton Club, Chicago, 1920; Martin B. Cahn prize, AIC, 1921. Work in: Union League Club, Chicago; Art Institute of Chicago (Municipal AL collection); fresco in Peoria Public Library; "After Rain, Chicago," Friends of American Art, Chicago, Ill.; "Late Afternoon," Museum at Bulle, Switzerland. Died May 31, 1948. Address in 1929, 1608 Monroe Bldg.; 1230 Juson Ave., Highland Park, Ill.; Ravinia, Ill.

PEYTON, ALFRED CONWAY.
Painter and illustrator. Born Dera Doon, British India, Nov. 9, 1875. Pupil of South Kensington Schools, London, Eng. Member: AWCS; NYWCC; North Shore AA. Awards: Silver medals at Bombay and Madras, BI. Died in 1936. Address in 1929, Budworth and Son, 424 West 52nd St., New York, NY; summer, Reed studio Bldg., East Gloucester, Mass.

PEYTON, ANN MOON.
(Mrs. Philip B.). Painter and illustrator. Born in Charlottesville, VA, in 1891. Pupil of George Bellows. Address in 1926, 3804 Locust St., Philadelphia, PA.

PEYTON, MRS. ALFRED CONWAY.
See Menzler-Peyton, Bertha S.

PFEIFER, HERMAN.
Painter and illustrator. Born Milwaukee, Wis., Nov. 24, 1879. Pupil of Howard Pyle. Member: SI. Illustrations for Harper's, Certury, McClure's, Ladies' Home Journal, Good Housekeeping, etc. Address in 1929, 424 East 57th St., New York, NY; summer, Arrochar, SI, NY.

PFEIFFER, FRITZ (WILHELM).
Painter, illustrator, craftsman and writer. Born Adams County, PA, June 3, 1889. Pupil of Henri, Chase Anschutz and Breckenridge. Died in 1960. Address in 1929, 151 Richmond Hill Ave., Kew Gardens, LI, NY.

PFEIFFER, HARRY R.
Painter. Born in Hanover, PA, in 1875. Pupil of ASL, New York; Penna. Academy of the Fine Arts, Philadelphia, PA. Address in 1929, 539 West King St., York, PA.

PFEIFFER, HEINRICH.
Painter and teacher. Born Hanover, PA, Oct. 19, 1874. Pupil of PAFA; ASL of NY. Died in 1960. Address in 1929, Pfeiffers Wharf; h. 244 Commercial St., Provincetown, Mass.

PFEIFFER, JUSTUS.
Painter, who exhibited in Philadelphia, 1921, in "Exhibition of Paintings Showing the Later Tendencies of Art." Address in 1926, Care of Preston Dickinson, Long Island, New York.

PFISTER, JEAN JACQUES.
Painter and teacher. Born Switzerland. Studied at Hopkins School of FA, San Francisco, Wayman Adams and at Art School of Bremen, Germany. Member: NAC; Yonkers AA; Westfield AA; New Rochelle AA. Died in 1949. Address in 1929, care of the Holt Gallery, 630 Lexington Ave., New York, NY.

PFLAUMER, PAUL GOTTLIEB.
Painter, illustrator and craftsman. Born Philadelphia, Aug. 9, 1907. Pupil of Thornton Oakley, Luigi Spizziri, John Dull. Member: Phila. Alliance. Address in 1929, 2nd, 6965 Ogontz Ave., Philadelphia, PA.

PHELAN, HAROLD L.
Painter. Born in New York in 1881. Address in 1926, 67 West 67th St., New York City.

PHELIPS, MRS. EMILY BANCROFT.
Painter. Born England, July 1, 1869. Pupil of St. Louis School of Fine Arts and Hugh Breckenridge. Member: GFLA. Awards: Hon. mention, Portland Exp., 1905; gold medal, Sedalia, 1913 and 1918. Address in 1929, Kimmswick, MO.

PHELPS, EDITH CATLIN.
(Mrs. Stowe). Painter and etcher. Born New York City, April 16, 1879. Pupil of Hawthorne; Julian in Paris. Member: Conn. AFA; NA Women PS; Springfield AA; AFA. Awards: Hon. mention, Con. AFA, 1920, 1922. Died in 1961. Address in 1929, 161 East 74th St., New York, NY; summer, Provcincetown, Mass.

PHELPS, HELEN WATSON.
Painter. Born Attleboro, Mass. Pupil of Julian Academy and Collin in Paris. Member: NA Women PS; Providence AC; SPNY; Yonkers AA; Newport AA; PBC; NAC. Awards: Hon. mention, Pan-Am. Exp., Buffalo, 1901; NY Woman's AC prize, 1907; Elling prize, NY Woman's AC, 1909; Watrous figure prize, NA Women PS, 1914; prize, NA Women PS, 1915. Died in 1944. Address in

1929, 1 West 64th St.; 58 West 57th St., New York, NY.

PHELPS, W. P.
Painter. Born in New Hampshire, he began life as a sign painter in Lowell, Mass. He was sent abroad for study and on his return he exhibited his paintings "Morning," "Evening," and "Forest Scene near Munich" at the National Academy in New York in 1878.

PHILBRICK, ALLEN E.
Painter, etcher, lecturer and teacher. Born Utica, NY, Nov. 19, 1879. Pupil of AIC.; Laurens in Paris. Member: Chicago PS; Chicago SE. Award: Butler prize, AIC, 1923. Work: mural decoration, "Morning, Noon and Night," People's Trust and Savings Bk., Cedar Rapids, IA; Brown Memorial Window, Lake View High School, Chicago. Address in 1929, care of the Art Institute, Chicago, Ill.; h. 982 Elm St., Winnetka, Ill.; summer, R.F.D. No. 2, Montague, Mich.

PHILBRICK, OTIS.
Painter. Born Mattapan, Mass., Oct. 21, 1888. Pupil of Major and De Camp. Member: Boston SWCP. Instructor, life drawing, Mass. School of Art. Died in 1973. Address in 1929, 10 Hillcrest Parkway, Winchester, Mass.

PHILIPP, MRS. M. BERNARD.
See Jane Peterson.

PHILIPP, ROBERT.
Painter and etcher. Born New York, Feb. 2, 1895. Pupil of ASL of NY under Du Mond, and Bridgman, and NAD under Volk and George Maynard. Awards: third Hallgarten prize, NAD, 1917; second Hallgarten prize, NAD, 1922. Address in 1929, 211 West 106th St., New York, NY; 4 Square Desnouettes, Paris, France.

PHILLIBROWNE, THOMAS.
Engraver. Born in London and who was said to have been a pupil of the Findens in that city. He was engraving admirable portraits in pure line in London in 1834, and came to the United States prior to 1851, as in that year he engraved a full-length portrait of Louis

Kossuth for Boston publishers. Mr. Alfred Jones says that Phillibrowne was a very eccentric character, peculiar in appearance, and he claimed that his personal friend Hablot Knight Brown, or "Phiz," had used him as a model for the familiar "Mr. Pickwick" in his original illustrations to that story of Dickens.

PHILLIPS, AMMI.
Portrait painter, limner. Born in Coalbrook, Conn., on Aug. 24, 1788. Had begun his career by 1811, working chiefly in western parts of Conn. and Mass. and in neighboring counties of upstate NY. Latest known commission, 1862. In collections of Albany (NY) Institute; Fogg Art Mus., Boston; Met. Mus. of Art, Am. Wing; Abby Aldrich Rockefeller Folk Art Ctr., Williamsburg, VA; others, including private collectors. Bibliography: Ammi Phillips: Portrait Painter 1788-1865, by Holdridge and Black (NY, 1969); American Folk Portraits (Rockefeller Folk Art Ctr., Williamsburg) (1981); Columbia Co., NY, exhibition catalogue, Ruth Piwonka and R. H. Blackburn. Died in Curtisville, Berkshire Co., MA, July 11, 1865.

PHILLIPS, BERT GREER.
Painter, illustrator and teacher. Born Hudson, NY, July 15, 1868. Pupil of NAD and ASL in New York; Constant and Luarens in Paris. Member: Taos Soc. of Artists; Salma. C.; Chicago Gal. A. Specialty, Indian subjects. Work: Mural decorations, Pokl County Court House, Des Moines, Iowa; mural decoration, San Marcos Hotel, Chandler, Aris.; three panels State Capitol, Jefferson City, MO. Died in 1956. Address in 1929, Taos Co., New Mexico.

PHILLIPS, C. HOLMEAD.
Painter, who exhibited at the Penna. Academy of Fine Arts, Philadelphia, 1926. Address in 1926, 58 West 57th St., New York, NY.

PHILLIPS, CHARLES.
This excellent engraver of portraits in stipple was located in New York, in 1842, and was an

Englishman by birth. Very little work is signed by him, and it is said that he went into the employ of the Government at Washington, DC.

PHILLIPS, J. CAMPBELL.
Painter. Born in New York, Feb. 27, 1873. Pupil of ASL of NY under Clinedinst and Mowbray; Chase. Member: Salma. C. 1905; Lotos C. Awards: Isidor portrait prize, Salma. C, 1914. Work: "The First Born," Corcoran Gallery, Washington, DC; "The Age of Wonder," Albright Gallery, Buffalo, NY; "Paradise Bay, Lake George," Cleveland Museum; "Hon. Wm. J. Gaynor," City Hall, New York; "Hon. William G. McAdoo," "Sen. Carter Glass," US Tresury Bldg.; "Mrs. Cumming Story," Daughters of American Revolution, Washington, DC; "Dr. John A. Wyeth," Academy of Medicine, New York; "Judge John J. Brady," Bronx Co. Court House, New York City; also represented in State Capitol, Trenton; Real Estate Board of New York; Cornell University, Ithaca, NY; "Dr. Nicholas Murray Butler," Lotos Club, New York; "Dr. Stephen Smith," Metropolitan Museum of Art. Died in 1949. Address in 1929, 1108 Carnegie Hall; h. 480 Park Ave., New York, NY.

PHILLIPS, JOHN HENRY.
Etcher. Born in Wisconsin in 1876. He has Executed mural decorations in theatres. Address in 1926, 681 Fifth Ave., New York.

PHILLIPS, MARJORIE.
(Mrs. Duncan Phillips). Painter and teacher. Born Bourborn, Ind., Oct. 25, 1895. Pupil of K. H. Miller, Boardman Robinson, Gifford Beal. Member: S. Wash. A. Represented in Phillips Memorial Gallery, Washington, DC. Address in 1929, 1600 21st Street, Washington, DC; summer, Ebensburg, PA.

PHILLIPS, S. G.
Painter, who exhibited the "Little Nude" at the Penna. Academy of the Fine Arts, Philadelphia, 1921. Address in 1926, 1520 Chestnut St., Philadelphia.

PHILLIPS, W(ALTER) J(OSEPH).
Painter, etcher, craftsman, lecturer and teacher. Born Barton-on-Humber, Eng., Oct. 2, 1884. Pupil of E. R. Taylor. Member: Calif. PM; Boston SAC. Awards: Storrow prize, Los Angeles, 1926; medal, Graphic Arts C, Toronto, 1926. Work: "Water Baby," National Gallery of Canada; "Lake of the Woods," Toronto Gallery; 13 color woodcuts, British Museum; 12 color woodcuts, Victoria and Albert Museum; color woodcuts in Calif. State Library and Los Angeles Museum. Died in 1963. Address in 1929, 104 Wellington Crescent, Winnipeg, Canada.

PHILLIPS, WINIFRED E.
Painter, etcher, craftsman and teacher. Born Claybanks, Wis., Nov. 1, 1881. Pupil of Alex Mueller, Gustave Moeller, George Oberteuffer, Henry B. Snell. Member: Wis. PS; NA Women PS. Address in 1929, Art Department, State Normal School, Milwaukee, Wis., h. 265 Alice St., Wauwatosa, Wis.

PHOENIX, LAUROS M(ONROE).
Mural painters. Born Chicago, Ill., Feb 23, 1885. Pupil of AIC; Woodstock Summer School, John F. Carlson. Member: Mural P.; ASL of Chicago. Work: "Rip Van Winkle," Grill Room, St. Paul Hotel; "Aesculapius," "The Fountain of Youth" and "Old Herb Woman," Lobby of Lowry Doctors' bldg., St. Paul, Minn.; "Minnehaha," L. S. Donaldson Bldg.; "Nine Fairy Stories," New Grand Theatre; "Robin Hood," Elks Club, Minneapolis, Minn. President and managing director, The Phoenix Art Institute, Inc., New York, NY. Address in 1929, 350 Madison Ave., New York, NY; h. 20 Schudy Place, New Rochelle, NY.

PIAZZONI, GOTTARDO F. P.
Painter, etcher and sculptor. Born Intragna, Switzerland, April 14, 1872. Pupil of San Francisco Art Assn. School of FA; Julian Academy and Ecole des Beaux-Arts, Paris. Member: San F. AA; Calif. SE; Bohemian C; Club Beaux Arts San F.; AFA. Represented in the Walter Collection, San Francisco Art Association; California Palace of

the Legion of Honor; Golden Gate Park Museum, San Francisco; Oakland (Calif.) Art Gallery; Municipal Gallery, Phoenix, Ariz.; Mills College Art Gallery, Oakland, Calif. Died in 1945. Address in 1929, 712 Montgomery St.; h. 446 Lake St., San Francisco, Calif.

PICART, B.
This apparently fictitious signature, either as designer or engraver, is signed to a large and poorly engraved plate published by H. D. Robinson, New York, seemingly about 1800. The print is entitled "Church and State," and is a caricature dealing with the doctrines of Thomas Paine.

PICCIRILLI, ATTILIO.
Sculptor. Born Massa, Italy, May 16, 1866. Pupil of Accademia San Luca, Rome. Came to US 1888. Member: ANA 1909; NY Arch. Lg., 1902; Allied AA. Awards: Bronze medal, Pan-Am. Exp., Buffalo, 1901; silver medal, St. Louis Exp., 1904; hon. mention, Paris Salon, 1912; Gold medal, P.-P. Exp. San. F., 1915; Widener gold medal PAFA, 1917; Saltus gold medal, NAD, 1926. Work: "Main Memorial," New York; "MacDonough Monument," New Orleans, "Dancing Faun" and "Head of a Boy," Fine Arts Academy, Buffalo. Address in 1929, 467 East 142d St., New York, NY.

PICCIRILLI, FURIO.
Sculptor. Born Massa, Italy, March 14, 1868. Pupil of Accademia San Luca, Rome. Came to US 1888. Member: ANA; NY Arch. League., 1914 (assoc.) Awards: Hon. mention, Pan Am. Exp., Buffalo, 1901; silver medal, St. Louis Exp., 1904; silver medal, P.-P. Exp., San F., 1915. Died in 1949. Address in 1929, 467 East 142d St.; h. 1 Beach Terrace, Borough of the Bronx, New York, NY.

PICCIRILLI, HORACE.
Sculptor. Award: Speyer Memorial prize ($300), NAD, 1926. Address in 1929, 467 East 142nd St., New York, NY.

PICCIRILLI, MASO.
Sculptor. Address in 1929, 467 East 142nd St., New York, NY.

PICCIRILLI, ORAZIO.
Sculptor. Address in 1929, 467 East 142nd St., New York, NY.

PICCOLI, GIROLAMO.
Sculptor. Born Palermo, Sicily, May 9, 1902. Pupil of Wis. School of Art, Frank Vittor, Lorado Taft. Awards: Milwaukee Art Institute medal, 1922; hon. mention, Wis. PS, 1924. Work: Sculpture on the Eagles Club Bldg., Milwaukee. Instructor of Sculpture, Layton School of Art, Milwaukee. Address in 1929, 933-41 North Water St.; h. 901 Bartlett Ave., Milwaukee, Wis.

PICKENS, ALTON.
Painter, sculptor and instructor. Born in Seattle, WA, in 1917. Study: Reed College, Portland, OR, 1936-38, influenced there by calligrapher and printer Lloyd J. Reynolds; Portland Art Museum, one semester; New School for Social Research, NYC, 1939, with Seymour Lipton, sculpture; solitary study at MOMA and Met. Mus. of Art. Work: MOMA; Hirshhorn Mus. & Sculpture Garden, Wash. DC; numerous private collections. One-man exhib.: ACA Gallery, NY, 1956, 60; Indiana Univ. Art Mus., 1956; Vassar College Art Gallery, 1956, 61, 77. Exhib.: Met. Mus. Art, NYC, 1942; MOMA, 1943, 46; Art Inst. Chic., 1945, 46, 51, 54; Carnegie Inst., 1945, 46, 47; Whitney Mus., 1946, 48, 49, 50, 55; John Herron Art Mus., Indianapolis, 1947, 49; Inst. of Contemp. Arts, London, 1950; Corcoran Gal., Wash. DC, 1951; Bienal du Museu de Arte Moderna, Sao Paulo, 1951, 53; Galerie "Kunst der Gegenwart," Salzburg, 1952; ACA Gallery, NY, 1964; Rutgers Univ. Art Gal., 1977; Phila. Art Mus.; PAFA; Nat'l Inst. Arts and Letters; and many more. Teaching: Prof. art, Vassar College, from 1956. Bibliog.: Books, reviews, exhibition catalogues. Media: Oils, pen and ink, woodcut, lithograph, etching, aquatint, charcoal, pastel, watercolor; bronze. Address in 1982, Art Dept., Vassar College, Poughkeepsie, NY.

PICKERING, SIMEON HORACE.
Painter. Born Salt Lake City, Utah, Oct. 18, 1894. Pupil of AIC;

Grand Central Art Sch.; Wayman Adams, J. Wellington Reynolds. Member: S. Indp. A; Salons of Am. Address in 1929, 21 Minetta Lane, New York, NY; h. Centerville, Utah.

PICKNELL, GEORGE W.
Painter. Born Springfield, VT, June 26, 1864. Pupil of Lefebvre and Constant. Member: Salma C.; AFA. Work: "Stock Yard in Winter," Detroit Institute of Arts. Died in 1943. Address in 1929, Norwalk, Conn.

PICKNELL, WILLIAM LAMB.
Painter. Born in Massachusetts in 1853; died in Marblehead, Massachusetts, in 1897. Landscape painter. Pupil of George Inness in Rome, and of Gerome in Paris; painted in Brittany for several years under Robert Wylie. Awarded honorable mention, Paris Salon, 1880. Member Society of American Artists; Elected Associate Member of National Academy of Design; Society of British Artists. Represented by "The Road to Concarneau," painted 1880, in the Corcoran Art Gallery, Washington.

PIERCE, ANNA HARRIET.
Painter and illustrator. Born in South Britain, Conn., May 17, 1880. Pupil of F. C. Jones, George Maynard, Mora, K. H. Miller, John F. Weir, Niemeyer, E. C. Taylor; Yale School of Fine Arts; NAD; NY School of Art; Commonwealth Colony, Boothbay Harbor, ME. Member: New Haven BPC (assn.); New Haven PCC. Address in 1929, 344 Edgewood Ave., New Haven, Conn.; summer, South Britain, Conn.

PIERCE, CHARLES FRANKLIN.
Paitner. Born in New Hampshire on April 26, 1844. Specialty, landscapes. Member of Boston Art Club and Boston Water Color Society. Died March 5, 1920 in Brookline, Mass.

PIERCE, GLENN M.
Illustrator. Member: SI. Address in 1929, 2326 Grove St., Brooklyn, NY.

PIERCE, WILLIAM H. C.
Painter. Born Hamilton Co., NY. Pupil of Lowell School of design;

Mass. Inst. of Tech.; studied in Paris. Member: San Diego AG. Award: Bronze medal, P.-P. Exp., San F., 1915. Address in 1929, 124 Brooks Ave., San Diego, Calif.

PIERPONT, BENJAMIN, JR.
Pierpont engraved upon copper the music and words of "The Singing Master's Assistant; or Key to Practical Music. By William Billings, Author of the New England Psalm-Singer, etc. Boston, (New England), Printed by Draper and Folsom, 1778." This singing-book is an oblong quarto, and on the last page of music the engraver signs himself thus: "Engrav'd by Benj. Pierpont Junr. Roxbury, 1778."

PIETERSZ, BERTUS.
Painter, writer and teacher. Born Amsterdam, Holland, Sept. 13, 1869. Studied in Rotterdam, and under Harry W. Ranger. Member: AFA. Work: "Campanilo," Springfield, Mass., art Museum. Died in 1938. Address in 1929, Hancock, NH.

PIETZ, ADAM.
Sculptor and Medalist. Born Offenbach, Germany, July 19, 1873. Studied at PAFA; AIC; and in Germany. Member: Phila. Sketch C.; Fellowship PAFA; American Numismatic Soc.; NY Numismatic Soc. Work in Chicago Art Inst.; Memorial Hall, Philadelphia, and American Numismatic soc.; Navy Yard, Phila., Administration Bldg.; Huston Club, University of PA; Phila. Sketch Club; National Museum, Washington; Vanderpoel Memorial Collection, Chicago; British Museum. Assistant Engraver US Mint. Philadelphia. Address in 1929, 7025 Lincoln Drive, Germantown, PA.

PIGALLE.
Rough line engravings signed "Pigalle" are found with other plates evidently engraved by Scoles for the same work. The date is about 1800.

PIGOTT, FRANK E.
Painter. Member: Rochester Art Club. Address in 1926, Care of Steck and Spelrein Lithographic Company, 65 West Houston St., New York, NY.

PILLARS, CHARLES ADRIAN.
Sculptor. Born Rantoul, Ill., July 4, 1870. Pupil of Taft, French and Potter; AIC. Work: Memorial group to Florida's dead in the World War, Jacksonville; Bryan Memorial, Battleship Florida; Memorial Flag Staff Standard, St. Augustine; Statue of Gen. Kirby Smith and Statue of Dr. John Gorrie, United States Capitol, Washington, DC.; Statue, W. B. Barnett, Barnett National Bank, Jacksonville, Fla. Died in 1937. Address in 1929, 16 May St.; h. "Homwold," Nelmar Terrace, St. Augustine, Fla.

PIMSLER, ALVIN J.
Illustrator. Born in NYC in 1918. Attended PI and the ASL, where he studied under Howard Trafton. His first published illustration in 1940, for L. Bamberger Company, led to his successful career as a fashion artist, his work appearing in ads for Saks Fifth Avenue for 25 years. Represented in the USAF Museum, Smithsonian Institution, Portraits, Inc., and Gallery of Sports, he has taught at SVA, PSD, FIT and served for two years as President of S of I.

PINE, ROBERT EDGE.
Painter. Born in 1730 in London, son of John Pine, the engraver. He gained the premium of the Society for the Encouragement of Arts, etc., for the best historical design in 1760, and again 1762. Established himself as a portrait painter and went to Bath in 1772, and remained there until 1779. Made an exhibition in London, 1782, of a collection of pictures painted by himself in illustration of scenes in Shakespeare. He came to this country in 1783, bringing his family, and taking up his residence in Phila. He painted Washington at Mt. Vernon in 1785, belonging now to J. Carson Brevoort, Esq., of New York. The Honorable Joseph Hopkinson, second President of the Academy, writing to Mr. Dunlap in 1833, says: "I remember his arrival in this country. He brought letters of introduction to my father, whose portrait was the first he painted in America. It is now in my possession...it bears the date of 1785, and is now as fresh in color as it was on the day it was painted...Robert Morris, who patronized him, built a house in Eighth Street suitable to his objects. I remember a large picture in his gallery, of Medea murdering her children, and several others, some from Shakespeare - Prospero and Miranda, in The Tempest, I particularly recollect. Many of his pictures are scattered about in Virginia, where he went occasionally to paint portraits...P.S. He brought with him a plaster cast of the Venus, which was kept shut up in a case, and only shown to persons who particularly wished to see it, as the manners of our country at that time would not tolerate the public exhibition of such a figure." Rembrandt Peale in his "Reminiscenes" mentions seeing him in London. In Phila. he painted the "Congress voting Independence," to which Edward Savage later added. Died Nov. 19, 1788 in Philadelphia.

PINELES, MISS CIPE.
Painter and illustrator. Born Vienna, Austria, June 23, 1908. Pupil of Anna Fisher. Address in 1929, 934 Carroll St., Brooklyn, NY.

PINKNEY, ELLIOTT.
Painter, printmaker and sculptor. Born in Brunswick, GA, Jan. 9, 1934. Study: Woodbury Univ., Los Angeles, BA; Art Instruction Inc., Minneapolis. Work: Murals in Watts Towers Arts Center, Los Angeles; Church of God in Christ, Los Angeles; other work in private and institutional collections. Comn.: Watts Community Housing Corp.; Los Angeles Dept. of Parks & Recreation; Watts Alcoholic Rehabilitation Center; etc. Exhib.: Black Artists Invitational, LA Co. Mus. of Art, 1972; Environmental Billboard Art, LA, 1973; Merabash Mus., NJ, 1975; Watts Towers Arts Center Gallery, LA, 1977; Compton (CA) College Gallery, 1981; Calif. Black Printmakers 1983; many more. Mem.: Int'l. Soc. of Artists; Bunker Hill Art League. Award: Latham Found. Int'l. Poster Award; Theatre Guild Amer. Theatre Soc. & Council of Living Theatre Award;

Calif. Arts Council Grant. Address in 1983, Compton, CA.

PINKNEY, JERRY.
Illustrator. Born in Philadelphia, PA, in 1939. Studied at the Philadelphia Museum College of Art and went to school with Roger Hane. His first illustration was done in Boston for Little, Brown in 1963. He has since won many awards and illustrated for Seventeen, Post, Boys' Life, and Essence Magazine. His work has been shown at the Brooklyn Museum, S of I, Brandeis Univ. in Massachusetts and the Studio Museum in Harlem.

PINKOVITZ, H. A.
Painter, who exhibited "Anna Perry" at the Penna. Academy of Fine Arts, Philadelphia, 1921. Address in 1926, 721 Walnut St., Philadelphia.

PINTNER, DORA.
Painter. Born Hooley Hill, England. Studied in England, Scotland and in the US. Member: Alliance. Address in 1929, 45 Coolidge Hill Road, Cambridge, MA.

PIPPIN, HORACE.
Painter. Born 1888, in PA. Left school at 14, became a farm laborer, and entered the Army during WWI. He returned from the war partially paralyzed in his right arm and embittered by his war experiences. Untrained in drawing, Pippin drew since childhood but took it up seriously after the war using the right hand with the aid of the left. His first major painting is a primitive oil called "End of the War: Starting Home." Many of his pictures depict Bible scenes and of Negro family life. He began to be taken seriously at 50. He was acclaimed as the best Negro painter. One of his better known paintings is "John Brown Going to His Hanging," 1942. Died in 1946.

PITKIN, CAROLINE W.
Painter, craftsman, teacher and sculptor. Born New York City, June 12, 1858. Pupil of Chase, DuMond, Harrison, Woodbury, Brenner. Member: PBC.; Alliance; N.A. Women

PS. Address in 1929, 550 West 157th St., New York, NY.

PITMAN, HARRIETTE RICE.
(Mrs. Stephen Minot Pitman). Painter. Born Stetson, ME. Pupil of Pratt Inst. in Brooklyn. Circuit Supervisor of Art Instruction, Corning, Ithaca and Jamestown, NY, 1891-92; director of art instruction, Providence Public School, 1894- 1904; museum instructor at Museum of the RI School of Design during 1926. Member: Providence WCC. Prov. AC. Address in 1929, 1 Congdon St., Providence, RI.

PITMAN, SOPHIA L.
Painter and teacher. Born Providence, RI. Member: Providence AC; Providence WCC; Copley S. Address in 1929, 227 Benefit St.; Moses Brown School, 156 Pitman St., Providence, RI.

PITTMAN, HOBSON.
Painter, etcher and teacher. Born Tarboro, NC, Jan. 14, 1898. Pupil of Albert W. Heckman, Doris Rosenthal, Emile Walters. Member: S. Indp. A; Salons of Amer. Address in 1929, 4107 Locust St., Philadelphia, PA; summer, Woodstock, NY.

PITZ, HENRY CLARENCE.
Painter, illustrator and teacher. Born Philadelphia, PA, June 16, 1895. Pupil of Maurice Bower, Walter Hunt Everitt. Member: Phila. Sketch C.; Phila. Alliance; SI; AG; AFA; Alumni Assn. PA. Museum and School of Industrial Art; Phila. WCC. Illustrated: Master Skylark, A Connecticut Yankee in King Arthur's Court, Red Cross Knight, Story of Rolf, La Salle, Prester John, Drakes, Indian History. Work: "Apple Gathering" and "The Edge of the Meadow," West Phila. High school. Co-Author with Edward Warwick, Early American Costume. Instructor, PA Museum and School of Industrial Art, 1917-18, and summer school, 1919, 1922 and 1923. Died in 1976. Address in 1929, 3712 Woodland Ave., Drexel Hill, PA.

743

PIZZUTI, MICHELE.
Painter. Born Naples, Italy, Nov. 29, 1882. Pupil of Domenico Morelli. Address in 1929, 165 East 60th St., New York, NY.

PLACE, VERA CLARK.
Painter. Born Minneapolis, Minn., Feb. 5, 1890. Pupil of Chase, Dufner, Richard Miller, Antonio de la Gandere. Member: Attic C., Minneapolis; Alumni Minneapolis School of Art; Minneapolis SFA. Awards: First and second prizes, Minnesota State Art Exhibit. Address in 1929, 741 Kenwood Parkway, Minneapolis, Minn.

PLACKETT, EBENEZER.
Portrait and figure painter. Born in Wisconsin, 1844, he settled in New Milford in 1871.

PLANTOU, MRS. ANTHONY.
Portrait painter in oils and miniatures; also historical painter. She painted portraits in Wash., DC, about 1820. In 1821 she moved to Phila. Her portrait of Bishop Conwell, painted in 1825, is well known from the engraving.

PLASCHKE, PAUL A.
Painter and illustrator. Born Berlin, Germany, Feb. 2, 1880. Pupil of Cooper Union and ASL of NY. Member: Soc. Ind. A.; Louisville AA; Louisville AC; Ind. AA; SSAL; AFA. Award: Hon. mention, Richmond, Ind. AA, 1917; landscape prize, Nashville AA, 1925; Joseph H. Defrees prize, Hoosier Salon, 1929. Represented in Attica, Ind., Library; Lexington, KY, Library; J. B. Speed Memorial Mus., and Children's Free Hospital, Louisville, KY. Cartoonist for Louisville "Times;" Caricaturist for Louisville "Times;" caricaturist for Sunday Courier-Journal since 1913; humorous drawings in "Life," "Puck," "Judge" and other periodicals. Address in 1929, care Louisville "Times," Louisville, KY; h. 326 Beharrel Ave., New Albany, Ind.

PLASSMAN, ERNST.
Sculptor. Born June 14, 1823 in Westphalia, Germany. He came to New York in 1853 where the following year he opened "Plassman's School of Art," which he carried on until his death. He executed many models, carvings and sculptures; his statue of Franklin is in Printing-House Square, NY, and his figure of "Tammany" is on Tammany Hall, NY. Also a woodcarver. He died in New York City, on Nov. 28, 1877.

PLATT, ALETHEA HILL.
Painter. Born Scarsdale, NY. Pupil of Henry B. Snell, Ben Foster and ASL of NY; Delecluse Academy in Paris. Member: AFA; NYWCC; AWCS; NA Women PS; NAC; Pen and Brush C; SPNY; Yonkers AA; Allied AA; Conn. AFA. Awards: First prize for water color, NY Women's AC, 1903; first prize Minnesota Art Assn., Faribault, 1909; first prize Nat. Lg. of Art Chap. Am. Pen Women, 1928. Work: "Old World Work Shop," Public Library, Faribault, Minn.; "An Old Garden," Anderson (Ind.) Art Gallery; portrait of Judge Lewis C. Platt, Court House, White Plains, NY; "A Devonshire Cottage," Museum, St. Joseph, MO. Address in 1929, 939 Eighth Ave., New York, NY; h. Sharon, Conn.

PLATT, CHARLES ADAMS.
Painter, architect, landscape architect and writer. Born New York, Oct. 16, 1861. Pupil NAD and ASL in New York; Boulanger and Lefebvre in Paris. Member: SAA 1888; ANA 1897; NA 1911; Am. Acad. AL; AWCS; NY Etching C; London Soc. of Painter-Etchers; Fellow, AIA; Century Association; AFA. Awards: Webb prize, SAA, 1894; bronze medal, Paris Exp., 1900; silver medal, Pan-Am. Exp., Buffalo, 1901; medal of honor, Arch. Lg. of NY, 1913. Author; "Italian Gardens." Died in 1933. Address in 1929, 131 East 66th St., New York, NY.

PLATT, H.
Engraver. A well-executed stipple portrait of Samuel Thomson, botanist, is prefixed to his "New Guide to Health, Boston, 1832." This plate is simply signed "H. Platt," and while this signature is assumed to be that of the engraver, it may also indicate the painter. No other engraved work of Platt is known.

744

PLEADWELL, AMY M(ARGARET).
Painter and teacher. Born Taunton, Mass., Sept. 15, 1875. Pupil of Mass. Normal Art School, Boston; Grand Chaumiere and Colarossi Academies in Paris. Member: AFA; Copley S; NA Women PS.; Lyceum Club of Paris. Address in 1929, 82 Chestnut St., Boston, Mass.; summer, American Woman's Club, Paris, France.

PLEISSNER, OGDEN MINTON.
Painter. Born Brooklyn, April 29, 1905. Pupil of F. J. Boston, George Bridgman, Frank V. DuMond. Member: ASL of NY; Salma. C.; NAC; Brooklyn SA; Brooklyn A. and S. Awards: Second prize, NAC, New York, 1928; 1st prize, NAC, New York, 1929. Work: "Morning Mass," University of Nebraska, Lincoln. Address in 1929, Ovington Bldg., 246 Fulton St.; h. 186 Washington Park, Brooklyn, NY; summer, care of C. C. Moore, Dubois, Wyo.

PLEUTHNER, WALTER C.
Painter, architect and writer. Born Buffalo, NY, Jan. 24, 1885. Pupil of DuMond and Mora. Member: S. Indp. A.; American Camouflage; art in Trades C.; NY Arch. Lg. Designed Emerson Phonograph Galleries, New York. Address in 1929, 137 East 45th St., New York, NY; Scarsdale, NY.

PLOCHER, JACOB J.
Engraver. A landscape engraver, Plocher had an engraving establishment from 1815-8 in Philadelphia, (in the Shakespeare Bldg.) but before this date he did considerable work for the encyclopedia published by S. F. Bradford, Philadelphia, 1808-11. He engraved at least one meritorious large plate, a view of the "Upper Ferry Bridge Over the Schuylkill River, Philadelphia." Died Dec. 27, 1820 in Philadelphia.

PLOCHMANN, CAROLYN GASSAN.
Painter and printmaker. Born in Toledo, Ohio, May 4, 1926. Studied at Toledo Mus. Art Sch. of Design, 1943-47; Univ. of Toledo, BA 1947; State Univ. of Iowa, MFA 1949; with Alfeo Faggi, 1950; So. IU Univ., 1951-52. Works in Rudman Collection, Oakland, NJ; Butler Inst. of Am. Art, Youngstown, Ohio; and others. Exhibited at Toledo Mus. of Art, 1941 (first show, age 15); Witte Mus., San Antonio, Texas, 1968; print and drawing annual, PAFA, 1969; Phila. WC Club, 1969; and many others. Awards: G. W. Stevens Fellow, Toledo Mus., 1947-49; Tupperware Art Fund First Award, 1953; Lowe Found. Compet. Award, 1958. Member of Silvermine Guild Artists; Woodstock Art Assn.; Phila. WC Club; Toledo Fedn. of Art Societies. Represented by Kennedy Galleries, NYC. Address in 1982, Carbondale, IL.

PLOWMAN, GEORGE T(AYLOR).
Illustrator and etcher. Born Le Sueur, Minn., Oct. 19, 1869. Pupil of Douglas Volk in Minneapolis; Eric Pape in Boston; studied at Royal College of Art, South Kensington, London and in Paris. Member: Chicago SE; NY SE; Salma. C.; Boston SE; Calif. SE; NAC; Calif. PM; Brooklyn SE. Award: Bronze medal for etching, P.-P. Exp., San F., 1915. Work: Etchings in Boston Museum of Fine Arts; New York Public Library; Library of Congress, Washington; British Museum; South Kensington Museum; National Museum, Wash., DC; Luxembourg Museum; Newark Public Library; Sacramento State Museum; Albany Art Museum; Southport Museum, England; Metropolitan Museum of Art. Author: "Etchings and Other Graphic Art," 1914; "Manual of Etching," 1924 (Dodd Mead & Co.). Address in 1929, 9½ Madison St., Cambridge, Mass.

PLUMB, H(ENRY) G(RANT).
Painter and teacher. Born Sherburne, April 15, 1847. Pupil of NAD in New York; Ecole des Beaux-Arts in Paris, under Gerome. Member: Salma. C.; A. Fund S; AFA. Award: Hon. mention, Paris Exp., 1889. Died in 1936. Address in 1929, 195 Claremont Ave., New York City; summer, Sherburne, NY.

PLUMMER, ETHEL M'CLELLAN.
(Mrs. Jacobsen). Painter and illustrator. Born Brooklyn, NY, March 30, 1888. Pupil of Henri and Mora. Member: SI. Illustrated for Vanity Fair, Vogue, Life, Shadowland, New York Tribune;

745

painted portrait sketches. Died in 1936. Address in 1929, 21 East 10th St., New York, NY.

PODOLSKY, HENRY.
Sculptor. Exhibited "The Old Rabbi" at the Penna. Academy of Fine Arts, Philadelphia, 1921. Address in 1926, 1335 Greenmount Ave., Baltimore, MD.

PODWIL, JEROME.
Illustrator. Born in NY in 1938. Attended PI and the ASL from 1955 to 1960. He has illustrated for many major magazines, especially Playboy, and has received several awards, including a Gold Medal from the S of I Annual Exhibition, Awards of Excellence from Chicago 1974 and 1976, and a medal from the Communication Arts Annual.

POE, HUGH M.
Painter. Born Dallas, Tex., Dec. 14, 1902. Pupil of R. L. Mason; Forsyth; Charles Hawthorne. Member: Knoxville Sketch C.; Ind. AC; East Tennessee SFA; Hoosier Salon. Awards: Art Assoc. prize, Herron Art Inst., 1924; Cunningham prize, Hoosier Salon, Marshall Field's, Chicago, 1925. Represented at Herron art Inst., Indianapolis, and Knoxville, Tenn., Sketch Club. Address in 1929, 25½ West Washington St., Indianapolis, Ind.

POGANY (WILLIAM ANDREW) "WILLY".
Painter, sculptor, illustrator, etcher, craftsman and lecturer. Born Hungary, Aug. 24, 1882. Member: Salma. C.; Arch. Lg. of NY. Awards: Gold medals, Leipzig, and Budapest Expositions; gold medal, Panama-Pacific Exp., San Francisco, 1915; prize, NY Soc. Architects, 1922. Work: Twelve paintings, Hungarian National Gallery, Budapest. Mural Paintings for Heckscher Foundation and Peoples House, NY; ceiling murals for Italian Renaissance Room, Park Central Hotel, NY; ceiling painting for Ritz Towers, New York; mural for Niagara Falls Power Co., Buffalo. Died in 1955. Address in 1929, 200 West 57th St., h. 256 Seaman Ave., New York, NY.

POHL, DENNIS.
Illustrator. Born in Milwaukee, Wisconsin, in 1941. Received his BA from the Univ. of Wisconsin and his MFA from PI in Brooklyn. He studied under Dore Ashton and Arthur Okamura and his first published illustration, entitled Vatican Library, was done for ESP Disk in 1972. He has designed numerous album covers for RCA, Columbia, London, Arista, and Savoy.

POHL, HUGO DAVID.
Painter, illustrator, etcher, and teacher. Born Detroit, Mich., March 11, 1878. Pupil of Jean Paul Laurens. Work: "Founding of San Antonio" and "Mayor Callaghan," City of San Antonio, Tex.; "Pleading for World Peace" and "The Problem of Time," Atelier art Gallery, San Antonio, Died in 1960. Address in 1929, Brackenridge Park; h. 622 Avenue E, San Antonio, Tex.

POINCY, PAUL.
Painter. Born March 11, 1833 in New Orleans, died there in 1909. Poincy studied at the Ecole des Beaux Arts, Paris, and at Julien's Academy, Paris. He was a portrait, religious, and genre painter of merit, and his street scenes are well executed, full of poetry and charm. As a teacher and painter he had much to do with furthering interest in local art.

POINTER, AUGUSTUSA L.
Sculptor. Born Durango, Colo., May 10, 1898. Pupil of Henry Hering. Award: Avery prize, Architectural League of NY, 1928. Address in 1929, care of Henry Hering, 10 West 33rd St., NYC; h. Lincoln Park, NJ.

POLASEK, ALBIN.
Sculptor and teacher. Born Frenstat, Czechoslovakia. Pupil of Charles Grafly at PAFA; American Academy in Rome. Member: ANA; NSS, 1914 (assn.); NY Arch. Lg.; SW SC.; Chicago SA; Cliff Dellers; AFA; Alumni Assn. of the Fellowship of the Am. Acad. in Rome. Awards: Prix de Rome, Amer. Academy in Rome, 1910; hon. mention, Paris Salon, 1913; Widener gold medal, PAFA, 1914; silver medal, P.-P. Exp., San Francisco, 1915; Logan

746

medal ($1,500), AIC, 1917; Hearst prize, AIC, 1917; medal, Milwaukee Art Inst., 1917; Shaffer prize, AIC, 1917; Logan medal ($500), AIC, 1922; silver medal, Chicago SA, 1922; Fairmount Park AA prize ($500) at PAFA, 1925. Work: "Fantasy," Metropolitan Museum, New York; "F. D. Millet" bust, Pennsylvania Academy of Fine Arts, Philadelphia; "Sower," "Unfettered," busts of charles Hawthorne, Charles L. Hutchinson, Frank G. Logan, Chicago Art Institute; "Aspiration," Detroit Institute of Art; Richard Yates Memorial, Springfield, Ill.; J. G. Batterson Memorial, Hartford, Conn.; Theodore Thomas Memorial, Chicago; Woodrow Wilson Memorial, Prague, Czechoslovakia, 1928, for which artist received order of the White Lion, awarded by the Government. Head of Sculpture Department, Chicago Art Institute. Address in 1929, Tree Studio Bldg., 4 East Ohio St., Chicago, Ill.

POLK, CHARLES PEALE.
Painter. Born March 17, 1767 in MD. He was the son of Charles Willson Peale's sister Elizabeth Digby Peale who married Capt. Robt. Polk of Virginia. At the age of 18 young Polk went to live with his artist uncle in Philadlephia. He painted portraits of General Washington, Rochambeau, and other noted men of the American Revolution, and at one time held office under the Government. He died in 1822.

POLK, GEORGE.
Portrait painter. The collection of paintings at Independence Hall in Philadelphia has a portrait of Rev. George Duffield painted by George Polk.

POLK, MARY ALYS.
Painter, illustrator and teacher. Born Greenwood, Ind., Aug. 29, 1902. Pupil of William Forsyth. Award: Earlham Alumni prize, Hoosier Salon, 1927. Member: Ind. AC. Address in 1929, 3029 Blvd. Pl., Indianapolis, IN.

POLLACK, REGINALD.
Painter. Born July 29, 1924 in Middle Village, Long Island, NY.

Studied With Soyer; Wallace Harrison and at the Chaumiere, Paris. Taught at Yale; Cooper Union; UCLA; PA. State Univ. Awarded prix Neumann, 1952; Prix Othon Friesz; I. Merrill Foundation prize (1964, 1970-1). Exhibited at Peridot Gallery, NYC (May 1949-62); Dwan Gal., LA; Felix Landau Gal., LA; MOMA; Carnegie; Whitney; Art Inst. of Chicago; PAFA; Univ. of Illinois; Rasmussen Gallery, Wash. DC. In collections of Whitney; Univ. of Glasgow; Brooklyn; Worchester Art Mus.; Newark; MOMA; Tel-Ariv Mus.; and others, including private collections.

POLLEY, FREDERICK.
Painter and etcher. Born Union City, Ind., Aug. 15, 1875. Pupil of Corcoran Art School, Washington; Herron Art Inst., Indianapolis, under William Forsyth. Member: Ind. AC; Indianapolis AA; Brown Co. AA; Salma. C; Chicago Gallery A. Instructor of art at Technicial High School, Indianapolis, Ind. Died in 1958. Address in 1929, 371 South Emerson Avenue, Indianapolis, Ind.

POLLIA, JOSEPH P.
Painter and sculptor. Born in 1893. Member: Conn. AFA; NSS. Died in 1954. Address in 1929, 100 West 54th St., New York, NY.

POLLOCK, COURTENAY.
Sculptor, who exhibited at the Penna. Academy of the Fine Arts, Philadelphia, 1915. Address in 1926, "The Schuyler," 57 West 45th St., New York City.

POLLOCK, THOMAS.
Engraver. In 1839 Pollock was engraving portraits in line in Providence, RI. He was later apparently a member of the New York engraving firm of Pollock & Doty.

POMAREDE, LEON.
Portrait painter. Born c. 1807 in Tarbes, France. He opened a studio in New Orleans in 1837. Died in 1892 in St. Louis, MO.

POMEROY, FLORENCE W.
(Mrs. Ralph B. Pomeroy). Painter. Born East Orange, NJ, July 9, 1889. Pupil of Bellows; Johansen;

Nordfeldt; Homer Boss. Member: NYSC; G. of Book Workers. Address in 1929, Llewellyn Park, West Orange, NJ.

POND, EMMA McHENRY.
Painter and teacher. Born San Francisco, Calif. Pupil of William Keith. Member: San Francisco S. Women A. Address in 1929, 2621 Ridge Rd., Berkeley, Calif.

POND, THEODORE HANFORD.
Painter, craftsman, writer, lecturer and teacher. Born Beirut, Syria, Sept. 27, 1873. Graduate of Pratt Institute. Member: Boston SAC; Alliance; Am. Assn. of Museums; Assn. of Art Museum Directors; AFA; College AA. Director, Akron Art Institute. Address in 1929, Akron Art Institute, Akron, Ohio.

POOKE, MARION LOUISE.
(Mme. Bernard S. Duits). Painter, illustrator and teacher. Born Natick, Mass. Pupil of Mass. Normal Art School, Boston; School of the Museum of Fine Arts, Boston; De Camp, Tarbell, Benson, Woodbury. Member: Conn. AFA. Awards: Silver medal, P.-P. Exp., San F., 1915; Hudson prize, Conn. AFA, 1917; hon. men., NA Women PS, 1921. Instructor at, Abbot Academy, Andover, Mass.; and Walnut Hill School, Natick, Mass, 1915-23. Address in 1929, rue Chateaubriand; h. 5 rue Lyautey, Paris, France.

POOLE, ABRAM.
Painter. Born Chicago, January, 1883. Pupil of Carl Marr, Simon. Member: Chicago SA. Awards: Silver medal, Royal Academy, Munich; Hon. mention, Chicago AI, 1922; fourth Clark prize and Corcoran hon. mention, Corcoran Gallery of Art, Wash., DC, 1926; Medal of Honor, Concord, Mass., 1926; Holmes prize, AIC, 1926. Work: "Portrait," Chicago Art Institute. Died May 25, 1961. Address in 1929, 134 East 47th St., New York, NY.

POOLE, BERT.
Painter, illustrator and writer. Born North Bridgewater (now Brockton), Mass., Dec. 28, 1853. Pupil of Tommaso Juglaris and

evening art schools in Boston. Member: Copley S; Am. APL. Work: "Twentieth Century Boston," Boston Public Library; "Intermediate Thoroughfare," City Hall, Boston; "City of Cambridge, Mass," City Hall. Specialty, panoramic paintings and landscapes. Died before 1940. Address in 1929, 306 Edgehill Road, East Milton, Mass.

POOLE, EARL LINCOLN.
Painter, illustrator, writer, lecturer and teacher. Born Haddonfield, NJ, Oct. 30, 1891. Pupil of PAFA. Member: Fellowship PAFA. Work: "Eagle and Gulls," and geographic groups, Reading Public Museum. Illustrated "Birds of Virginia," etc. Director of art education, Reading School district; assistant director, Reading Public Museum. Address in 1929, Reading Public Museum and Art Gallery; h. 220 South 5th St., Reading, PA.

POOLE, FREDERIC VICTOR.
Painter, illustrator, craftsman and teacher. Born Southampton, Hants, England. Pupil of Frederick Brown in London. Member: Chicago SA; Chicago PS; Chicago Gal. A. Award: Brower prize, AIC, 1928. Work: "Portrait of President Lowden," Toronto University. Illustrated for magazines. Died in 1936. Address in 1929, 469 Deming Pl.; 65 East Elm St., Chicago, Ill.

POOLE, H(ORATIO) NELSON.
Painter, illustrator and etcher. Born Haddonfield, NJ, Jan. 16, 1885. Pupil of PAFA. Member: Calif. SE; Chicago SE; Calif. Book Plate Soc.; San F. AA. Award: First prize, Graphic Section, San F. AA, 1922; prize, Calif. SE, 1926; special medal of first award, San F. AA, 1927. Address in 1929, 728 Montgomery St., San Francisco, Calif.

POOR, HENRY V(ARNUM).
Painter and teacher. Born in Kansas, Sept. 30, 1888. Pupil of Slade School and of Walter Sickert in London; Julian Academy in Paris. Member: San Francisco SA; Calif. AC; San F. AA. Award: Walter purchase prize ($300), San F. AA, 1918. Represented in Metropolitan Museum. Died in 1970. Address in

1929, care the Montross Gallery, 26 East 56th St., New York.

POOR, HENRY WARREN.
Painter. Born in Boston, Mass., in 1863. Pupil of Mass. Normal Art School; also studied in Paris. Member: Boston Art Club. Address in 1926, Boston Normal School, Mass.

POORE, HENRY R(ANKIN).
Painter, illustrator, writer and teacher. Born Newark, NJ, March 21, 1859. Pupil of Peter Moran and PAFA in Philadelphia; NAD in New York; Luminais and Bouguereau in Paris. Member: ANA 1888; Phila. Sketch C.; AC Phila.; Salma. C.; Lotos C.; Union Inter. des Beaux-Arts et des Lettres; Fellowship PAFA, 1916; MacD. C.; NAC; Conn. AFA.; Am. Soc. Animal P. and S; AFA. Awards: 1st prize ($2,000), American Art Association; second Hallgarten prize, NAD, 1888; bronze medal, Pan-American Exp., Buffalo, 1901; silver medal, St. Louis Exp., 1904; gold medal, American Art Soc., Phila., 1906; gold medal, Buenos Aires, 1910; silver medal, P.-P. Exp., San F., 1915. Work: "Night of the Nativity," Fine Arts Academy, Buffalo; "The Shore," City Museum, St. Louis; "In the Meadow," "Hounds in Sunlight," Art Assoc., Indianapolis; "Old English Stage Hound," Worcester Museum; "Royal Buck Hounds," Philadelphia Art Club; "Grace Before Meat," Rittenhouse Club; "The Favorite," Madison Art Assn.; "Marshland Harvest," Tacoma Art Club; "The Far Hills," Government purchase, Brazil; "New England Wastes," National Museum, New Zealand. Author: "Pictorial Composition;" "The Pictorial Figure;" "The Conception of Art;" "Art Principles in Practice." Died in 1940. Address in 1929, 61 Ridge St., Orange, NJ; summer, Lyme, Conn.

POPE, ALEXANDER.
Painter and sculptor. Born in Boston in 1849. Member: Copley Society, 1893; Boston Art Club. Published "Upland Game Birds and Water Fowl of the United States." At the beginning of his career he painted and modeled animals; after

1912 he was chiefly a portrait painter. He died in Sept. 1924, in Hingham, Mass.

POPE, MRS. MARION HOLDEN.
Painter and etcher. Born San Francisco, Calif. Pupil of A Mathews; Whistler; Colarossi Academy. Member: San F. AA; Calif. SE; Kingsley C; Croker Mus. C; AFA. Work: Three mural decorations in the Carnegie Library, Oakland, Calif. Died c. 1957. Address in 1929, 3948 J. St., Sacramento, Calif.

POPE, WILLIAM FREDERICK.
Sculptor. Born in Fitchburg, Mass. in 1865. He lived for a time in Boston, Mass. He died in Boston, Mass. Oct. 22, 1906.

PORTER, BENJAMIN CURTIS.
Portrait painter. Born in Melrose, Mass., Aug. 29, 1845. Pupil of Dr. Rimmer and of A. H. Bicknell, in Boston; also studied in Europe. Awards: Bronze medal, Paris Exposition, 1900; silver medal, Pan-American Exposition, Buffalo, 1901; silver medal, St. Louis Exposition, 1904. Elected Associate Member of National Academy, 1878; National Academy in 1880; Society of American Artists; National Sculpture Society; National Institute of Arts and Letters. Died April 2, 1908 in NYC.

PORTER, BRUCE.
Mural painter, sculptor and writer. Born San Francisco, Feb. 23, 1865. Studied in England and France. Member: Am. PS. Award: Chevalier Legion of Honor of France. Work: Designed "Stevenson Memorial," San Francisco; stained glass and mural paintings in churches and public buildings of California; gardens--"Filoli" and "New Place." Author: "The Arts in California," etc. Address in 1929, Santa Barbara, Calif.

PORTER, DORIS L(UCILE).
Painter, lecturer and teacher. Born Portmouth, Feb. 7, 1898. Pupil of Hugh Breckenridge, Hans Hofmann in Munich. Member: North Shore AA; SSAL; Art Corner, Norfolk. Awards: Prize for landscape, Norfolk Society of Art,

749

1925-26-27-28-29; prize for portrait, Norfolk Society of Art, 1929. Work: "Portrait of John Marshall," Wythe House, Williamsburg, VA. Address in 1929, Brooke and Granby St., Norfolk, VA; h. 124 Dinwiddie St., Portsmouth, VA.

PORTER, ELMER J(OHNSON).
Painter, etcher and teacher. Born Richmond, May 5, 1907. Pupil of AIC. Member: Western AA; Alumni AIC. Award: M.T.R. Address in 1929, 108 South 9th St., Richmond, Ind.

PORTER, J. T.
In 1815 this line-engraver of historical plates signed himself as of Middletown, Conn. The only plates to be found are in the "Narrative of John R. Jewett," etc., published by Loomis & Richards, Middletown, Conn., in 1815.

PORTER, JAMES T(ANK).
Sculptor. Born Tientsin, China, Oct. 17, 1883. Pupil of Robert Aitken. Member: ASL of NY; San Diego Friends of Art. Work: "Portrait bust of James W. Porter," "Portrait relief of my Mother," owned by Beloit College, Wis.; portrait of Prof. Chester Lyman, Yale University; Ellen B. Scripps testimonial, La Jolla; "Portrait bust of Pres. James A. Blaisdell," Pomona College, Calif.; "Portrait of a Young Man," San Diego Fine arts Gallery, "Portrait bust of the late Bishop Bashfold," M.E. Church of North China, Peking. Address in 1929, La Mesa, Calif.; 412 East 37th St., New York, NY.

PORTER, JOHN S.
Miniature painter in Boston, Mass., in 1832-33.

PORTER, M(ARY) K(ING).
Miniature painter. Born Batavia, Ill., June 9, 1865. Pupil of Volk; ASL of Washington, DC, Bertha Perrie, Snell. Member: Wash. WCC; Wash. AC; AFA. Died in 1938. Address in 1929, 1761 Q St., Washington, DC.

PORTER, MRS. S. C.
Painter. Born in Hartford, Conn. Studied in art schools in New York and Paris. She exhibited in the Paris Salon of 1875 her "Head of a Girl;" it was also exhibited at the Centennial exhibition in Phila.

PORTER, RAYMOND A(VERILL).
Sculptor. Born Hermon, NY, Feb. 18, 1883. Member: Boston SAC; Copley S. Work: Memorial to President Tyler, Richmond, VA; statue, "The Green Mountain Boy," Rutland, VT; Victory Memorial, Salem, Mass.; World War Memorial, Commonwealth Armory, Boston, Mass. Died April 2, 1949. Address in 1929, Massachusetts Normal Art School, Boston; h. Dana Hill Apts., 331 Harvard St., Cambridge, Mass.

PORTNOFF, ALEXANDER.
Painter, sculptor and teacher. Born in Russia in 1887. Pupil of Charles Grafly; PAFA. Member: Fellowship PAFA; AFA; Phila. Alliance. Awards: Cresson European Scholarship, PAFA, 1912-13; hon. mention, P.-P. Exp., San Francisco, 1915. Represented in Milwaukee Art Inst.; Brooklyn Museum, etc. Instructor in modeling, Graphic Sketch Club. Died in 1949. Address in 1929, 718 Locust St., Philadelphia, PA; High Point, Long Beach Island, NJ.

POSSELWHITE, GEORGE W.
Engraver. Born in England about 1822. He was living in New York in 1899. Posselwhite was an admirable engraver of landscape and subject plates. He came to the United States about 1850 and was largely employed in New York and Philadelphia.

POST, CHARLES JOHNSON.
Painter and journalist. Born in New York in 1873. Since 1893 engaged as artist-journalist and editorial writer with the Associated Press, New York Daily News, Recorder, World, Journal, Herald and Globe. Illustrated for American, New York Times, Philadelphia Inquirer, the Century Magazine, Pearson's, Cosmopolitan, Harper's Weekly, Harper's Magazine, Everybody's and Outing.

750

POST, MAY AUDUBON.
Painter and illustrator. Born in New York City. Pupil of Penna. Academy of Fine Arts under Chase, Beaux, Grafly and Breckenridge; of Drexel Institute under Howard Pyle; of Lucien Simon in Paris. Member: Fellowship, Penna. Academy of Fine Arts. Award: Traveling scholarships, Penna. Academy of Fine Arts; gold medal, Art Club of Philadelphia, 1903. Address in 1926, 4446 Sansom St., Philadelphia, PA.

POST, W(ILLIAM) MERRITT.
Landscape painter. Born Brooklyn, NY, Dec. 11, 1856. Pupil of Frost Johnson; ASL of NY under Beckwith. Member: ANA 1910; AWCS; NYWCC; A. Fund S; Salma. C. 1900; Conn. AFA; NYSP. Award: Hon. mention, Pan-Am. Exp., Buffalo, 1901. Work: "Landscape," Newark Museum Association. Died in 1935. Address in 1929, Bantam, Conn.

POSTGATE, MARGARET J.
Painter and sculptor. Born Chicago, Ill. Pupil of AIC; Robert Ryland, Mahonri Young. Awards: Second prize, 1924, 3rd, prize, 1927, 1st prize, 1928, National Small Sculpture Competition, New York. Address in 1929, 281 Park Pl., Brooklyn, NY.

POTTER, AGNES SQUIRE.
Painter and teacher. Born London, Oct. 31, 1892. Pupil of NY School of Fine and Applied Art, Minneapolis AI, Hawthorne, Breckenridge. Member: Chicago AC; Cordon C.; Chicago SA; Cor Ardens. Award: Hinsdale Woman's Club prize, AIC, 1922. Work: "Coronado Beach," owned by the City of Chicago Schools. Address in 1929, 1542 East 57th St.; h. 5515 Woodlawn Ave., Chicago, Ill.

POTTER, BERTHA HERBERT.
(Mrs. Edward Potter, Jr.). Painter. Born Nashville, Tenn., March 12, 1895. Pupil of L. Pearl Saunders, E. Ambrose Webster, Hugh Breckenridge, Van D. Perrine, Edmund Greacen, Sidney Dickinson. Member: Southern SAL; North Shore AA; AFA. Address in 1929, 1709 West End Ave.; h. 3828 Whitland Ave., Nashville, Tenn.

POTTER, BESSIE.
See Mrs. Robert Vonnoh.

POTTER, EDWARD CLARK.
Sculptor. Born in New London, Conn., on Nov. 26, 1857. Studied sculpture under Mercei and Fremo, Paris. Collaborated with D. C. French in sculpture for Chicago Exposition, 1892-93; executed equestrian statues of Grant at Philadelphia, 1894; one of Washington, at Paris, 1898; Hooker, at Boston, 1904; Derens, at Worcester, Mass., 1905; Slocum, at Gettysburg; De Soto, at St. Louis Exposition, 1904; also statues in Fulton Library, Washington. Elected to National Academy of Design, 1906. Member: National Institute of Arts and Letters; National Sculpture Society; Architectural League. Died in 1923 in New London.

POTTER, H(ARRY) S(PAFFORD).
Illustrator. Born Detroit, Mich., 1870. Pupil of Constant, Laurens and Jules Simon in Paris. Member: SI 1910. Address in 1929, 539 West 112th St., New York, NY.

POTTER, LEWIS.
Sculptor and etcher. Born in 1873. "The Snake Charmer" attracted favorable comment at the Pan-American Exposition, while his busts "A Tunisian Jewess" and "A Young Bedouin" are highly praised. Died in 1912.

POTTER, MARTHA J(ULIA).
Painter and teacher. Born Essex, Conn., Jan. 14, 1864. Pupil of J. H. Niemeyer, John F. Weir, A. W. Dow, Marshall Fry. Member: N. H. Paint and Clay C.; Conn. AFA; AFA. Address in 1929, 224 Park St., New Haven, Conn.

POTTER, MARY K.
Painter and writer on art. Pupil of Metropolitan Museum and of the Art Students' League of New York; also of the Julien Academy, Paris. Address in 1926, 184 Boylston St., Boston.

POTTER, NATHAN D(UMONT).
Painter and sculptor. Born Enfield, Mass., April 30, 1893. Pupil of D. C. French and E. C.

Potter. Work: World War Memorial Column, Westfield, NJ; Equestrian Statue, William Jackson Palmer, Colorado Springs, Colo. Died in 1934. Address in 1929, 5 E. Ninth St., New York, NY; summer. Enfield, Mass.

POTTER, WILLIAM J.
Painter and teacher. Born Bellefonte, PA, July 14, 1883. Pupil of PAFA, and of Walter Sickert in London. Work: "Balearic Isles," Brooklyn Museum; "Villa Rosa and Pasquaia Harbor," Hispanic Museum, New York; Memorial Art Gallery, Rochester NY; "Porto Pi Balearics," Herron Art Institute, Indianapolis; "Cornwall Coast," Sidney Australia Museum; also represented in Cincinnati Museum of Art; Exposition Park Museum, Los Angeles. Died in 1964. Address in 1929, 51 West Tenth St., New York, NY.

POTTHAST, EDWARD HENRY.
Painter. Born in Cincinnati, Ohio, in 1857. Student in Cincinnati, Munich and Paris. Elected member of National Academy of New York in 1906. Represented in Art Museums in Cincinnati, Chicago, Brooklyn, and Buffalo, NY. Died March 10, 1927 in NYC.

POTTS, SHERMAN.
Portrait painter and miniature painter. Born Milburn, NJ, July 29, 1876. Pupil of C. N. Flagg in Hartford; PAFA; Laurens and Constant in Paris. Member: Conn. AFA; AS Min. P; Mystic SA. Award: Dunham portrait prize, Conn. Acad. FA, 1929. Address in 1929, 45 East 59th St., New York, NY; summer, Noank, Conn.

POTTS, WILLIAM S.
Engraver. Born in New Jersey; died in St. Louis in 1852. In 1824 Potts was an engraver in a New York office, working with William Chapin, but he later studied for the ministry and became a prominent Presbyterian clergyman, and in 1837 was president of the Marion College.

POUPARD, JAMES.
Engraver. Born in Martinique. Advertised in the Pennsylvania Gazette, Philadelphia, in 1772. The earliest engraving by Poupard of which we have any note is mentioned in the Gazette of June 29, 1774. James Humphreys, Jr., announces the publication of "The Search after Happiness, a Pastoral Drama, by Miss More (embellished with an elegant Copperplate Frontispiece, engraved by James Poupard, of this City)." In 1775 Poupard engraved the portrait of Dr. Goldsmith for the Pennsylvania Magazine; in 1788-89 he was engraving diagrams, etc., for the Transactions of the American Philosophical Society; and as a "seal and die engraver" his name appears continously in the Phila. directories for 1793-1807, inclusive. Poupard then moved to NY, and was engraving on wood for New York publishers in 1814. A fairly well executed portrait of John Wesley may be ascribed to this latter period.

POUSETTE-DART, NATHANIEL J.
Painter and etcher. Born St. Paul, Minn., Sept. 7, 1886. Pupil of St. Paul Art School; Henri and MacNeil in New York; PAFA. Member: NY Arch. Lg.; Mural P.; Graphic A.; Salons of America; Artists' Soc., St. Paul Inst.; Gargoyle C; Fellowship PAFA; S. Indp. A.; Art Directors C. Awards: Cresson Scholarships, 1909-10; Toppan prize, 1910, all at PAFA; hon. mention for painting and second prize for etching, 1913; third prize for painting and first prize for etching, 1914, all from Minnesota State Art Society; hon. mention for painting, St. Paul Inst., 1915, first prize for painting, Minnesota State Art Society, 1916. Died in 1965. Address in 1929, Valhalla, NY.

POWELL, ARTHUR JAMES EMERY.
Painter. Born Vanwert, Ohio, Dec. 11, 1864. Pupil of San Francisco School of Design; St. Louis School of Fine Arts; Julian Academy, Toulouse and Ferrier in Paris. Member: ANA, 1921; Salma. C. 1904; Paris AAA; A. Fund S.; Allied AA; NAC (life); NYWCC. Awards: Vezin prize ($100), Salma. C., 1913; Ranger Purchase prize, NAD, 1921.

Died in 1956. Address in 1929, 59 East 59th St., New York, NY.

POWELL, CAROLINE A(MELIA).
Wood engraver. Born Dublin, Ireland. Pupil of W. J. Linton and Tomothy Cole; studied drawing at Cooper Union and NAD in New York. Member: Soc. of American Wood Engravers. Awards: Bronze medal, Columbian Exp., Chicago, 1893; silver medal, Pan-Am. Exp., Buffalo, 1901. Work in: Boston Museum of Fine Arts; New York Public Library; Springfield (Mass.) Public Library; Carnegie Institute, Pittsburgh. Died in 1935. Address in 1929, 1034 Third St., Santa Monica, Calif.

POWELL, JENNETTE M.
Painter, etcher, craftsman and teacher. Born Kingston, Canada. Studied with Chase, Henri, Hawthorne, Parsons, Sandzen and in Paris. Address in 1929, 202 N 23rd St., Camp Hill, Penna.; winter, "House in the Pines," Norton, Mass.

POWELL, LUCIEN WHITING.
Painter. Born in Virginia, Dec. 13, 1846. Pupil of PAFA; London School of Art; studied in Rome, Venice and Paris. Member: S. Wash. A.; Wash. WCC. Award: Parsons prize, S. Wash. A. 1903. Work: "The Afterglow," and "Grand Canyon, Arizona," Corcoran Gall., Wash.; "Grand Canyon of the Yellowstone River," National Gall., Wash. Died Sept. 27, 1930. Address in 1929, Round Hill, VA.

POWELL, WILLIAM HENRY.
Portrait and historical painter. Born Feb. 14, 1823 in NYC. Represented in the Capitol, Washington, DC, by "De Soto Discovering the Mississippi River" and by the "Battle of Lake Erie." A replica of this picture is in the State Capitol of Ohio. In the painting of his "Battle of Lake Erie" persons then employed about the Capitol were used as models. For many years he occupied a studio in New York. His "Landing of the Pilgrims" was purchased by Marshall O. Roberts, and his portraits of Gen. McClellan and Maj. Anderson

are in the City Hall, New York. Died Oct. 6, 1879 in New York City.

POWERS, HIRAM.
Sculptor. Born in Vermont on a farm, July 29, 1805. He early acquired knowledge of modelling. In 1835 he went to Washington, and two years later he established himself in Florence, Italy. His work consists of busts of prominent men, statues of Adams, Jackson, Webster, Calhoun, Longfellow, Gen. Sheridan, Etc., and his best known achievement "The Greek Slave." He died June 27, 1873 in Florence, Italy.

POWERS, JOHN M.
Illustrator. Member: SI. Address in 1929, 154 Nassau St., New York, NY.

POWERS, LONGWORTH.
Sculptor. Son of Hiram Powers, who resided in Florence, Italy, for many years and died there in 1904.

POWERS, MARION.
(Mrs. W. A. B. Kirkpatrick). Painter. Born London, England, of American parents. Pupil of Garrido in Paris. Member: NA Women PS; Copley S.; GFLA. Awards: Lippincott prize, PAFA, 1907; silver medal, Buenos Aires Exp., 1910; gold medal, P.-P. Exp., San F., 1915. Work: "Tresors," in Luxembourg, Paris, bought from Salon, 1904; mural decoration for Canadian Pacific Railway, Hotel Vancouver, BC; "Little Housewife," Rhode Island School of Design. Address in 1929, Fenway Studios, 30 Ipswich St., Boston, Mass.; summer, Friendship, ME.

POWERS, PRESTON.
Portrait painter and sculptor. Son of Hiram Powers. Born in Florence in 1843. He practiced his profession in Boston, Mass., Washington, DC, and in Portland, ME. His life-bust of Whittier is in the Library at Haverhill, Mass.

PRADOS, MADAME.
Miniature portrait painter, working in New Orleans about 1800.

PRAHAR, RENEE.
Sculptor. Born in New York.
Member: NA Women PS. Died in
1962. Address in 1929, 309 West 4th
St.; 45 Christopher St., NYC.

PRASUHN, JOHN G.
Sculptor. Born near Versailles,
Ohio, Dec. 25, 1877. Pupil of
Mulligan, Taft, AIC. Member: Ind
AC; Indianapolis AA. Award:
Mildred Veronese Beatty prize,
1927. Work: Bronze tablet,
Nothern Ill, State Normal School,
De Kalb; bronze bust of "Dr. F. W.
Gunsaulus," Field Museum of Nat.
History; marble music group,
Lincoln Park Band Stand, Chicago;
two lions on Columbus Memorial
Fountain, Wash., DC; author of
article "Cement," in Scientific
American, 1912. Address in 1929,
1310 Hiatt St., Field Museum of
Nat. History, Dept. of
Anthropology, Indianapolis, Ind.

PRATHER, RALPH CARLYLE.
Illustrator and writer. Born
Franklin, PA, Nov. 4, 1889.
Specialty, animals and nature for
advertising, illustration and
design. Author, in collaboration
with Claire McCullough Prather,
articles in "Nature Magazine," etc.
Address in 1929, P.O. Box 71,
Drexel Hill, PA.

PRATT, BELA LYON.
Sculptor. Born in Norwich, Conn.,
on Dec. 11, 1867. Studied with
Saint Gaudens, Chase and Cox in New
York, and in Paris with Falguiere.
He died in Boston on May 18, 1917.
Represented by statue of Nathan
Hale at Yale University; "The
Seasons" in the Congressional
Library, Washington, and many war
monuments and memorials.

PRATT, HARRY E(DWARD).
Painter, illustrator and teacher.
Born North Adams, May 21, 1885.
Address in 1929, 125 Hall St.,
North Adams, Mass.; summer,
Jacksonville, VT.

PRATT, HENRY CHEEVES.
Landscape painter. Born June 13,
1803 in Orford, NH. He also
painted a bust-portrait of
Longfellow. Died Nov. 27, 1880 in
Wakefield, Mass.

PRATT, JULIA D.
Painter and lecturer. Born North
Collins, NY. Pupil of Otto
Schneider, Buffalo FA Acad.; Cooper
Union; NY Ind. Art School. Member:
Buffalo Indp. A.; Buffalo Allied
AA; Chicago NSA; S. Ind. A.;
Buffalo SFA. Formerly art
supervisor in Buffalo public
schools. Address in 1929, 94
Glenwood Ave., Buffalo, NY, summer,
North Collins, NY.

PRATT, MATTHEW.
Painter. Born in Phila. Sept. 23,
1734. He was the son of Henry
Pratt (goldsmith), a friend of
Doctor Franklin and one of his
famous Junto. His mother's
brother, James Claypole, "limner
and painter in general," had the
distinction, until recently, of
being the earliest native-born
American artist (1720) recorded,
and it was he who gave his nephew
the first instruction he received
in art, "from whom," to use Pratt's
language, "I learned all the
different branches of painting from
ten years of age." The earliest
work of his apparently is the
portrait of his father's friend,
Franklin, painted circa 1756, now
in the Manor House collection at
Yonkers, NY, which is also the
earliest known portrait of the
philosopher. In the summer of
1764, Pratt sailed for London,
having under his protection his
kinswoman, the fiancee of Benjamin
West, who a few months later Pratt
gave in marriage to the future
President of the Royal Academy of
Arts in London. For two and a half
years Pratt lived in the household
of West and was West's first
student. It was during this period
that he painted the picture of "The
American School"--West's
painting-room, now in the MOMA, NY,
and portraits of West and Mrs. West
in the PAFA, Phila. Matthew Pratt
died Jan. 9, 1805, and was buried
in Christ Church burying ground at
5th and Arch Streets, Phila. He
was the father of Henry Pratt, who
built the famous "yellow mansion"
which stood at Broad and Walnut
Streets, Phila., for so many years,
and he was the progenitor of many
families of prominence in that
city. He also painted a full-length

portrait of Cadwalader Colden belonging to the NY Chamber of Commerce, for that body in 1772, at a cost of thirty-seven pounds. The Spring Garden Inst. of Phila. owned at one time a full-length portrait of Gov. James Hamilton, painted by Pratt, but it has been lost for years.

PRATT, PHILIP H(ENRY).
Painter, illustrator and teacher. Born Kansas City, MO, Aug. 10, 1888. Pupil of St. Louis School FA; Phila. Industrial Art School; South Kensington, London. Member: 2x4 Soc.; St. L. AG; Camera C. Work: Mural panels for Wisconsin State Capitol.

PRATT, ROBERT M.
Portrait and genre painter. Born in 1811 in Binghamton, NY. He was a pupil of Morse and Ingham. Member of the NA. He also painted a number of miniatures. The New York Historical Society owns his portraits of Richard Hildreth and Nicholas Triest. He died Aug. 31, 1880 in New York City.

PRELLWITZ, EDITH MITCHILL.
Painter. Born in 1865 in South Orange, NJ. Pupil of ASL under Brush and Cox; Julian Academy in Paris. Member: SAA, 1898; ANA, 1906; NY Woman's AC. Awards: Second Hallgarten prize, NAD, 1894; Dodge prize; NAD, 1895; medal, Atlanta Exp., 1895; bronze medal, Pan-Am. exp., Buffalo, 1901. Died in 1944. Address in 1929, Peconic, LI, NY; 333 East 41 St., New York, NY.

PRELLWITZ, HENRY.
Painter and teacher. Born New York, Nov. 13, 1865. Pupil of T. W. Dewing and ASL in New York; Julian Academy in Paris. Member: SAA 1897; ANA 1906, NA 1912; Salma. C. 1903; Century Assn.; AFA. Awards: Third Hallgarten prize, NAD 1893; bronze medal, Pan-Am. Exp., Buffalo, 1901; silver medal, St. Louis Exp., 1904; Clarke prize, NAD 1907. Died in 1940. Address in 1929, Peconic, LI, NY; 333 East 41st St., New York, NY.

PRENDERGAST, CHARLES E.
Sculptor, etcher and craftsman. Born Boston, Mass., May 27, 1868. Member: Copley S.; S. Indp. A.; Mural P.; New Soc. A. Died in 1948. Address in 1929, 219 West 14th St.; 50 Washington Sq., New York, NY.

PRENDERGAST, MAURICE BRAZIL.
Painter. Born in Boston in 1861; died in New York Feb. 1, 1924. Pupil of Julien, Laurens and Blanc in Paris. Awarded medal at Buffalo Exposition in 1901, and at Corcoran Art Gallery, Wash., DC, in 1923, for his "Landscape with Figures."

PRENTISS, TINA.
Painter. Studied: Harvard Univ.'s Carpenter Center for the Visual Arts; Mass. College of Art. Awards: CAA, 1967; SPCA Bronze Medal Boston Tea Party Poster Award, 1973. Exhibitions: Concord Art Association, 1973; Cambridge Art Association, 1973. US Department of Labor, Women's Bureau, Wash., DC, 1974. She is represented in the collection of Paramount Pictures.

PRESCOTT, KATHARINE T.
Sculptor. Born at Biddeford, ME. Pupil of E. Boyd, Boston, and of F. E. Elwill, New York. Member: Boston Art Students' Association; Copley Society, Boston. Has exhibited at Art Institute, Chicago; National Sculpture Society; National Academy of Design, New York; Penna. Academy of Fine Arts, Philadelphia; Boston Art Club. Address in 1926, 59 5th Ave., New York.

PRESSOIR, ESTHER (ESTELLE).
Painter, illustrator, etcher, craftsman and teacher. Born Philadelphia, Oct. 4, 1905. Pupil of Hawthorne; K. Miller; Kuhn; B. Robinson; Kunstgewerbeschule in Munich. Member: NA Women PS; Providence WCC. Work: "Still Life," PAFA. Address in 1929, 8 E. 15th St., New York, NY.

PRESTON, ALICE BOLAM.
Illustrator and draughtsman. Born Malden, Mass., March 6, 1888. Pupil of Vesper L. George; Albert A. Munsell; Anson K. Cross; Felicie

Waldo Howell. Member: North Shore AA; Rockport AA; PBC. Awards: Hon. mention, 1924, first prize ($500), 1925 and 1926, special prize ($250), 1927, House Beautiful Competition cover designs. Illustrated: "The Valley of Color Days," "The Little Man with One Shoe," "Seven Peas in the Pod," "Adventures in Mother Gooseland" (Little Brown and Co.); "Peggy in Her Blue Frock" and "Humpty Dumpty House" (Houghton Mifflin Co.). Died in 1958. Address in 1929, 807 Hale St., Beverly Farms, Mass.

PRESTON, JAMES.
Landscape painter. Born in 1873. He exhibited at the Penna. Academy of Fine Arts in Philadelphia, 1915. Address in 1926, 22 West 9th St., New York. Died in 1962.

PRESTON, JESSIE GOODWIN.
Painter. Born East Hartford, Conn., Sept. 9, 1880. Pupil of William M. Chase; Robert Henri. Member: Conn. AFA; Springfield A. Lg.; Gloucester AS; New Haven PCC; AFA. Award: Hon. mention, Conn. AFA, 1924. Address in 1929, 984 Main St., East Hartford, Conn.

PRESTON, MAY WILSON.
(Mrs. James M.). Illustrator. Born in New York in 1873. Pupil of Art Students' League of New York, and of the National Academy of Design; also of Whistler School in Paris. Member: Society of Illustrators, 1904. Award: Bronze medal, Panama-Pacific Exposition, San Francisco, 1915. Died in 1949. Address in 1926, 22 West 9th St., New York, NY.

PRICE, ANNA G.
Painter and teacher. Born in New York. Pupil of ASL of NY; NY School of Art. Member: NA Women PS; PBC. Address in 1929, 145 Greenway South, Forest Hills, NY.

PRICE, CHESTER B.
Illustrator and artist. Born Kansas City, MO, June 11, 1885. Pupil of Umbdenstock in Paris; Donn Barber in New York. Member: AIA; Arch. Lg. of NY; NYAG. Specializing in architectural illustration for magazines. Co-author (illustrator) of

"Portraits of ten Country Houses designed by Delano and Aldrich." Died in 1962. Address in 1929, 201 East 40th St., New York, NY; h. 69 Kensington Rd., Bronxville, NY.

PRICE, EDITH BALLINGER.
Painter, illustrator and writer. Born New Brunswick, NJ, April 26, 1897. Pupil of P. L. Hale, A. R. James, Helena Sturtevant, Geo. Maynard and Thos. Fogarty. Member: Newport AA. Work: Author and illustrator of "Blue Magic;" "Silver Shoal Light;" "Us and the Bottleman;" "The Happy Venture;" "The Fortune of the Indies;" "Garth, Able Seaman;" "John and Susanne;" "My Lady Lee;" "Ship of Dreams;" "The Four Winds;" "Gervaise of the Garden." Address in 1929, 7 Arnold Ave., Newport; summer, "The Acorn", Wakefield, RI.

PRICE, EUGENIA.
Painter. Born in Beaumont, Tex., in 1865. Pupil of St. Louis School of Fine Arts; Art Institute of Chicago; Julien Academy in Paris. Member: Alumni, Art Institute of Chicago; Chicago Art Club; Texas Fine Arts Society; Chicago Society of Miniature Painters. Died in 1923 in Los Angeles, Calif.

PRICE, GENL. SAMUEL W.
Portrait painter. Born Aug 5, 1828 in Nicholasville, KY. Died Jan. 22, 1918 in St Louis, MO.

PRICE, GEORGE.
Born in England in 1826. This landscape engraver was a pupil of the Findens in London. Price came to the United States in 1853, did considerable work here, and returned to England in 1864.

PRICE, LLEWELLYN.
Painter, who exhibited water colors at the Penna. Academy of the Fine Arts, Philadelphia, 1925. Address in 1926, Bryn Athyn, Penna.

PRICE, M. ELIZABETH.
Painter and teacher. Born Martinsburg, West VA. Pupil Pennsylvania Museum and School of Industrial Art, PAFA. Member: Fellowship PAFA; PS; Am. Woman's Assn. Address in 1929, 140 West

57th St., New York, NY.; h. New Hope, PA.

PRICE, MARGARET EVANS.
Painter and illustrator. Born Chicago, Ill., March 20, 1888. Pupil of Mass. Normal Art School, DeCamp and Major. Work: Murals in Aurora Theatre; illustrated "Once Upon a Time;" author and illustrator of "Enchantment Tales for Children" and "A Child's Book of Myths". Address in 1929, 201 Main St., East Aurora, NY.

PRICE, NORMAN (MILLS).
Illustrator. Born Brampton, Canada, April 16, 1877. Pupil of Cruickshank, Jean Paul Laurens, Richard Miller. Member: SI; GFLA. Illustrated: "Lambs Tales from Shakespeare" (T. C. and E. C. Jack, Edinburgh); "The Children's Tennyson" (Froude, Hodder and Stoughton, London); "Chopin," "Wagner," "Mendelsohn," "Scott," "Kingsley," "E. B. Browning," "Xmas Bells," "A Legend of Jerusalem," "The Joy of the Lord" (Hodder and Stoughton, London); "The Derelict," "A Servant of Reality," "The Boomerang," "The Return of the Soldier" (Century Co.); "The Greater Glory" and "The Wall Between" (Little Brown and Co.). Died in 1951. Address in 1929, 370 Riverside Drive, New York, NY.

PRICHARD, SIDNEY.
Painter, who exhibited water colors at the Penna. Academy of Fine Arts, Philadelphia, 1925. Address in 1926, Stockton Springs, ME.

PRIEST, T.
(Theresa Khoury Struckus). Painter and printmaker. Born in Worcester, MA, Jan. 20, 1928. Studied: Worcester Art Museum School; Univ. of Mass. Exhibitions: Assumption College, Worcester, Mass.; DeCordova Museum, Lincoln, Mass.; Young American Up-coming Artists, Nashua, New Hampshire. Collections: Aldrich Museum of Contemporary Art, Ridgefield, Conn.; Honeywell Corporation, Boston, Mass.; Bundy Art Center, Waitsfield, Vermont. Media: Acrylic and oil on canvas. Address in 1982, 5 Pratt St., Worcester, MA.

PRIME, WILLIAM COWPER.
Painter. Born in 1825. He died in New York City in 1905.

PRINCE, WILLIAM MEADE.
Illustrator. Born Roanoke, VA, July 9, 1893. Pupil of NY School of Fine and Applied Art. Worked in advertising art in Chicago; moved to Conn. and illustrated for major NYC magazines. Noted for Roark Bradford's Negro stories, Collier's. Head, Art dept., Univ. of NC. Member: GFLA; Salma. C. Died in 1951. Address in 1929, Box 159, Westport, Conn.

PRIOR, CHARLES M.
Painter, etcher and teacher. Born New York, Dec. 15, 1865. Pupil of E. M. Ward and NAD. Member: S. Indp. A.; Alliance; Eastern AA; Am. APL; AFA. Address in 1929, 571 W. 139th St., New York, NY.

PRITCHARD, J. AMBROSE.
Painter. Born April 11, 1858 in Boston. Died Feb. 5, 1905 in Boston.

PROBST, THORWALD (A.).
Painter, illustrator and teacher. Born Warrensburg, MO, July 18, 1886. Pupil of Iner Olsen, Viggo Langer. Member: Calif. AC; Laguna Beach AA; Artland C. Works: Illustrations for "Poems of California Missions." Address in 1929, 1555 Altivo Way, Los Angeles, Calif.

PROCTOR, A(LEXANDER) PHIMISTER.
Painter and sculptor. Born Bozanquit, Ont., Canada, Sept. 27, 1862. Pupil of NAD and ASL in New York; Puech and Injalbert in Paris. Member: ANA 1901, NA 1904; SAA 1895; AWCS; NY Arch. Lg. 1899; NSS 1893; Nat. Inst. AL; A. Aid S.; Century Assoc.; NAC; Am. Soc. Animal P. and S. Awards: Medal, Columbian Exp., Chicago, 1893; Rinehart scholarship to Paris, 1896-1900; gold medal, Paris Exp., 1900; gold medal for sculpture and bronze medal for painting, St. Louis Exp., 1904; NY Arch. Lg. medal, 1911; gold medal, P.-P. Exp., San F., 1915. Specialty, Western subjects. Work: "Panthers," Prospect Park Brooklyn, NY; "Puma," "Fawn," "Dog with Bone"

and "Fate," Metropolitan Museum, New York; "Indian Warrior," Brooklyn Museum; "Tigers," Princeton Univ.; Buffalos and Tigers on bridges, Washington, DC; "Moose," Carnegie Inst., Pittsburgh; "Pioneer," University of Oregon, Eugene; Lions, McKinley monument, Buffalo; "Circuit Rider," State House, Salem, Ore.; equestrian statue of Col. Roosevelt, Portland, Ore., and Minot, NH; "Bronco Buster" and "On War Trail," Civic Center, Denver, Colo.; heroic Indian fountain, Lake George, NY; "Pioneer Mother," Kansas City, KS. Died in 1950. Address in 1929, American Academy in Rome, Rome (29), Italy.

PROHASKA, RAY.
Illustrator. Born in Muo Dalmatia, Yugoslavia, in 1901. Attended the Calif. School of Fine Art in San Fran. for four years. His first published illustration was a watercolor done for the Delineator in 1930 and later he illustrated the books Eddie No Name (Pantheon, 1963) and Who's Afraid (Crowell Collier, 1963). He was an artist-in-residence at Wash. and Lee Univ. from 1964 to 1969 and at Wake Forest Univ. from 1969 to 1975. His works are owned by the New Britain Museum of American Art and the Guild Hall in East Hampton, NY.

PROW, HALLIE P(ACE) (MRS.).
Painter. Born Salem, Ind., April 25, 1868. Pupil of John Herron AI, L. O. Griffith. Member: Ind. AA; Fed. of Ind. AC. Work: "A Salem Bouquet," Public Library, Salem, Ind. Died in 1945. Address in 1929, 1015 North College Ave., Bloomington, Ind.

PRUD'HOMME, JOHN FRANCIS EUGENE.
Engraver. Born on the Island of St. Thomas, West Indies Oct. 4, 1800; died in Georgetown, DC, June 22, 1892. His parents came to the United States in 1807 and settled in New York in 1809. About 1814 Prud'Homme was apprenticed to his brother-in-law Thomas Gimbrede to learn engraving, and was engraving over his own name in New York in 1821. He became a reputable engraver of portraits in stipple,

though his best work is represented by his small plates executed for the "Annuals," about 1839. Among these "The Velvet Hat" and "Friar Puck" are to be especially admired. In 1852 Prud'Homme became interested in bank-note work, and from 1869 to 1885 he was employed by the Treasury Department at Washington, DC. Prud'Homme was made an Academicain of the National Academy of Design in 1846, and in 1834-53 he was the curator of the Academy.

PUCCIARELLI, MARIO.
Born: Buenos Aires, Argentina, in 1928. Traveled and studied in England, France, and Italy. Exhibitions: Teatro Candilejas, Buenos Aires, 1957; Galeria Balatea, Buenos Aires, 1958; Galeria Pizarro, Buenos Aires, 1960. Group exhibitions: Museo Sivori, Pizarro Gallery, Van Riel Gallery, Buenos Aires, 1959; Isaac Delgado Museum of Art, New Orleans, 1960; The Solomon R. Guggenheim Museum, New York, 1960; and many others.

PUGH, MABEL.
Painter, illustrator and etcher. Born Morrisville, NC, Nov. 1, 1891. Pupil of ASL of NY; PAFA. Member: Fellowship PAFA; Plastic C; SSAL; ASL of NY. Award: Cresson Traveling Scholarship, PAFA, 1919; gold medal, Plastic C. Phila., 1926. Illustrated "In Ancient Albemarie," by Catherine Albertson; "The Adventures of Paul Bunyan" (Century Co., 1927); "Blackbeard's Treasure" (Crowell Co., 1927); "Twelve Bad Men" (Crowell Co., 1929). Address in 1929, 106 W. 57th St., New York, NY.

PULFREY, DOROTHY LING.
Painter. Born Providence, RI, April 16, 1901. Pupil of John Sharman, Arthur Heintzelman. Member: Prov. WCC. Address in 1929, 19 Greystones Ave., Sheffield, England.

PULLINGER, HERBERT.
Painter and illustrator. Born Philadelphia, Aug. 5, 1878. Pupil of PAFA under McCarter and Anshutz. Member: Fellowship PAFA; Phila. Sketch C.; Phila. WCC; AFA.

Address in 1929, 1430 South Penn Square, Philadelphia.

PULSIFER, J(ANET) D.
Painter. Born Auburn, Maine. Pupil of ASL of NY; Delance, Courtois, Aman Jean in Paris. Address in 1929, 32 Argyle Park, Buffalo, NY; summer, Scituate, Mass.

PUNCHATZ, DON IVAN.
Illustrator. Born in Hillside, NJ, in 1936. Attended SVA and Cooper Union. He worked as an art director for several years before beginning free-lance illustration in 1966. His studio, The Sketch Pad, was organized in 1970. His work for magazines such as Playboy, Oui, Penthouse, Esquire, True, and Time has earned him awards from the S of I and from many ADCs.

PUNDERSON, LEMUEL S.
This excellent engraver of portraits in stipple was working in New York in 1850-55.

PURDIE, EVELYN.
Miniature painter. Born Smyrna, Asia Minor, 1859. Pupil of Boston Museum School under Grundmann; Carolus-Duran, Henner and Mme. Debillemont- Chardon in Paris. Member: Woman's Inter. Art Society, London and Paris; Copley S. Min. P.; Boston GA. Died in 1943. Address in 1929, 383 Harvard St., Cambridge, Mass.

PURDY, MAUD H.
Painter and illustrator. Born Philadelphia, Nov. 29, 1874. Pupil of Amy Cogswell, Whitaker, etc. Member: Brooklyn AS. Illustrated, "Fundamentals of Botany," etc., by Dr. Gager. Specialty, miniatures. Address in 1929, 151 Linden Blvd., Brooklyn, NY; summer, Pomona, Rockland Co., NY.

PUREFOY, HESLOPE.
Miniature painter. Born Chapel Hill, NC, June 17, 1884. Pupil of Alice Beckington and Lucia Fairchild Fuller. Member: Pa. S. Min. P. Address in 1929, 27 Charlotte St., Asheville, NC.

PURINTON, J.
Miniature painter, who flourished in 1802, Salem, Mass.

PURSELL, HENRY.
Engraver. In the New York Mercury, in 1775, Henry Pursell advertises that he has removed "from Broadway to Dock Street, near the Old Coffee House, where he carries on the Engraving business in its different branches, viz., Copperplates of all kinds, Arms, crests, cyphers, etc., on plate. Ditto on watches. Ditto on seals of any metals. Types, Free Mason Medals. Gun furniture, Harness ditto, Cyphers, etc., on whips. Morning rings, Door plates, Dog Collars, etc."

PURVES, AUSTIN JR.
Painter, craftsman and teacher. Born Chestnut Hills, Phila., Dec. 31, 1900. Pupil of Daniel Garber; Baudouin in Paris. Member: Arch. Lg. of NY; Mural P.; Fellowship PAFA; Audac, NY. Award: Hon mention, Arch. Lg. of NY, 1926. Represented by mural, "Triptych," St. Paul's Church, Duluth, Minn. Director, Studio of Design, R. H. Macy & Co. Address in 1929, 207 East 17th St., c/o R. H. Macy & Co., 34th St. and Broadway, NYC.

PUSHMAN, HOVSEP.
Painter. Pupil of Lefebvre, Robert-Fleury and Dechenaud in Paris. Member: Calif. AC; Paris AAA; Salma. C. Awards: Bronze medal, Paris Salon, 1914; Ackerman prize, Calif. AC, 1918; silver medal, Paris Salon, 1921. Represented in Milwaukee Art Institute; Layton Art Gallery, Milwaukee; Minneapolis Art Museum; Rockford (Ill.) Art Guild; Norfolk Art Assn., Norfolk, VA. Died in 1966. Address in 1929, 154 West 57th St., New York, NY.

PUTHUFF, HANSON (DUVALL).
Painter. Born Waverly, MO. Pupil of University Art School; Denver, Col. Member: Calif. AC; Laguna Beach AA (life); Los Angeles WCS; Berkeley LFA (hon.). Awards: Two silver medals, Pan-Calif. Exp., San Diego, 1916; first prize, Calif. AC, 1916; gold medal, State Fair. Sacramento, 1918; silver medal, State Fair, Sacramento, 1919; 1st

prize, Laguna Beach AA, 1920-21; 2nd prize, Southwest Museum, Los Angeles, 1921; first prize, Springville, Utah, 1924; silver medal, Painters of the West, 1927, and silver medal, 1929. Represented in the Municipal Collection of Paintings, Denver; Los Angeles County Collection, Los Angeles Museum. Died in 1972. Address in 1929, 2744 Altura Ave., La Crescenta, Calif.

PUTNAM, ARTHUR.
Sculptor. Born Waveland, Miss., Sept. 6, 1873. Member: NSS 1913. Award: Gold medal, P.-P. Exp., San F., 1915. Work: "Snarling Jaguar," Metropolitan Museum, New York. Died in 1930. Address in 1929, care of Bohemian Club, San Francisco, Calif.; care of American Express Co., Paris, France.

PUTNAM, BRENDA.
Sculptor and teacher. Born Minneapolis, Minn., June 3, 1890. Pupil of Bela Pratt, J. E. Fraser and Charles Grafly. Member: NSS; NA Women PS; AFA. Award: Hon. mention, Chicago Art Institute, 1917; Helen Foster Barnet prize, NAD, 1922; Widener medal, PAFA, 1923; Avery prize, NY Arch. Lg., 1924. Represented in Dallas Museum, Dallas, Tex.; Hispanic Museum, New York. Address in 1929, 356 West 22nd St., New York, NY.

PUTNAM, STEPHEN G(REELEY).
Wood engraver. Born Nashua, NH, Oct. 17, 1852. Studied drawing at Brooklyn Art Assoc. and ASL of NY; pupil of H. W. Herrick, Frank French and E. J. Whitney. Awards: Bronze medal, Paris Exp., 1889; medal, Columbian Exp., Chicago, 1893; bronze medal, Paris Exp., 1900; silver medal, Pan-Am. Exp., Buffalo, 1901. Address in 1929, College Point, Queens, New York, NY.

PYE, FRED.
Painter and illustrator. Born Hebden Bridge, Yorkshire, England, Dec. 1, 1882. Pupil of Julian Academy, Colarossi Academy, Paris. Member: Nassau County AL; Salma. C.; AAA, Paris. Work: "Mer Agiteo," Luxembourg Museum, Paris, France. Address in 1929, 30 East 14th St., New York, NY; h. 30-54 - 33rd St., Astoria, NY; summer, Coleman P.O., Alberta, Canada.

PYLE, CLIFFORD C(OLTON).
Painter and illustrator. Born in Missouri, Oct. 24, 1894. Pupil of Pedro Lemos; Lee Randolph; Spencer Mackey; Gertrude Albright; Rudolph Schaeffer. Illustrator and Designer of books and textiles. Represented in Metropolitan Museum of Art. Address in 1929, John-Martin Bldg., 33 West 49th St., New York, NY.

PYLE, HOWARD.
Painter and illustrator. Born in Wilmington, Del., March 5, 1853. Began art studies at age 16 under Belgian Professor Van der Weilen in Phila.; went to NYC in 1876, studied at ASL. Stories and illustrations appeared in Scribner's and St. Nicholas magazine and established his reputation. Returned to Wilmington in 1879. His work in color reproduction techniques led to a new era in illustration. Major contribution as teacher, at Drexel Inst. from 1894; summer classes at Chadds Ford, PA; opened own studio in Wilmington, where he taught many major illustrators from 1901 to 1910. He was the author of the text and illustrations for The Merry Adventures of Robin Hood, The Wonder Clock; also illustrated many books of juvenile fiction. He was elected a member of the National Academy of Design in 1911. Died Nov. 9, 1911, in Florence, Italy, while travelling in Europe.

QUANCHI, LEON WILLIAM.
Painter. Born New York City, Sept. 23, 1892. Pupil of G. deF. Brush; F. C. Jones; Douglas Volk. Member: S. Indp. A. Address in 1929, 1560 Broadway, New York, NY; h. 406 Palmer Ave., Maywood NJ.

QUARRE, F.
Engraver. He was also a lamp-shade manufacturer located in Philadelphia in 1850, and possibly earlier. Executed an oval-shaped engraving of lace, printed in white on a brown ground. Centered in the oval is an embossed view of New York, seemingly taken from Hoboken. Below is "New York," in white on the brown ground. This view was used as a magazine illustration.

QUARTLEY, ARTHUR.
Painter. Born in France in 1839; son of Frederick William Quartley. He settled in New York in 1851. He painted signs, and later devoted his time to marine painting. He was elected an Associate of the National Academy in 1879 and an Academician in 1886. His most important pictures are "View of North River," "Trinity from the River," "Lofty and Lowly," and "Morning in New York Harbor." He died in New York in 1886.

QUARTLEY, FREDERICK WILLIAM.
Engraver and painter. Born July 5, 1808, in Bath, England. He became a wood engraver in 1852; then came to New York, where he lived his professional life. His best known work is "Picturesque America" and "Picturesque Europe." His paintings include "Niagara Falls," "Catskill Falls," and "Butter-Milk Falls." Died May 19, 1866, in NYC.

QUASTLER, GERTRUDE.
Printmaker. Born in Vienna, Austria, in 1909. Studied: Columbia Univ.; Univ. of Illinois; Chicago Institute of Design. Collections: Museum of Modern Art; Farnsworth Museum of Art; Art Institute of Chicago; Boston Museum of Fine Arts; Fogg Museum of Art; Boston Public Library; Phila. Free Library; Rhode Island School of Design; Univ. of Delaware; Univ. of Nebraska; Univ. of Maryland.

QUESNAY, ALEXANDER MARIE.
Portrait painter in miniature and portrait draughtsman in crayon. Born Nov. 23, 1755, in France. Numerous extended advertisements inserted in the New York newspapers during 1784, concerning his Academy for Dancing and Drawing, are reprinted in W. Kelby's "Notes on American Artists." He was active in New York City about 1784. Died Feb. 8, 1820, in Seine, France.

QUEST, CHARLES FRANCIS.
Painter, sculptor, illustrator and teacher. Born Troy, NY, June 6, 1904. Pupil of Fred Carpenter, Edmund Wuerpel. Member: St. Louis AG; St. Louis AL. Awards: Edward Mallinckrodt watercolor prize, St. Louis AG, 1924; Letticia Parker Williams prize, St. Louis AG, 1926, 1929; George Warren Brown prize, St. Louis AG, 1928; Black and White prize, St. Louis AL, 1928. Work: Mural decoration, Hotel Chase, St. Louis. Address in 1929, 925 Maryville Ave., St. Louis, MO.

QUIDOR, JOHN.
Painter. Born Jan. 26, 1801, in Tappan, NY. He studied with Inman, and was a pupil of John Wesley Jarvis in his New York studio. Chas. Loring Elliott studied with Quidor. Quidor painted imaginative subjects, often inspired by Washington Irving's tales. He painted "Rip Van Winkle" and "Ichabod Crane." He died Dec. 13, 1881, in Jersey City, NJ.

QUINAN, HENRY B(REWERTON).
Artist and designer. Born Sitka, Alaska, Nov. 10, 1876. Pupil of Laurens in Paris. Member: Salma C.; SI; Art Directors; AFA. Art editor of "Woman's Home Companion." Address in 1929, 250 Park Ave.; h. 321 East 43rd St., New York, NY.

QUINCY, EDMUND.
Painter and teacher. Born Biarritz, France, May 15, 1903. Pupil of George Noyes, Albert Herter, Fred Whiting, Georges Degora. Member: Springfield AL; Boston AC; Salons of Amer.; Alliance; Provincetown AA. Award: Hon. mention, Springfield AL, 1929. Address in 1929, 4 Charles River

Sq., Boston, Mass.; summer, 5 rue de Bagneaux, Paris, France.

QUINLAN, WILL J.
Painter and etcher. Born Brooklyn, NY, June 29, 1877. Pupil of J. B. Whittaker at Adelphi College; NAD in New York under Maynard and Ward. Member: Salma. C.; Brooklyn SE; Brooklyn SA; PS; Yonkers AA. Awards: Shaw black and white prize, Salma. C., 1913; Shaw etching prize, Salma. C., 1913 and 1914. Work in: New York Public Library; Oakland (Calif.) Public Museum. Address in 1929, 333 Warburton Ave., Yonkers, NY.

QUINN, EDMOND T.
Sculptor and painter. Born in Philadelphia, PA. Pupil of Eakins in Philadelphia; Injalbert in Paris. Elected Associate Member of the National Academy; National Sculpture Society, 1907. Award: Silver medal, Panama-Pacific Exposition, San Francisco, 1915. Work: Statue, "John Howard," Williamsport, PA; statue, "Zoroaster," Brooklyn Institute of Arts and Sciences; reliefs on "Kings' Mountain (SC) Battle Monument;" bust of Edgar Allan Poe, Fordham Univ., NYC; "Nymph," statuette, Metropolitan Museum, NYC; statue of Maj. Gen. John E. Pemberton, Vicksburg (Miss.) National Military Park; statue of Edwin Booth as "Hamlet," Gramercy Park, New York; bust of Prof. Hooper, Brooklyn Museum. Died in 1929. Address in 1926, 207 East 61st St., New York, NY.

QUINTON, MRS. W. W.
See Sage, Cornelia.

QUIRT, WALTER W.
Painter and teacher. Born Iron River, Mich., Nov. 24, 1902. Pupil of Layton Sch. of Art. Member: Wisc. PS. Adderss in 1929, 453 Jefferson St., Milwaukee, Wisc.

QUISTGAARD, J(OHANN) W(ALDEMAR).
Portrait painter. Born in Denmark, Feb. 9, 1877. Member: Salma. C. Work: Portraits of Joseph Choate, Chauncey M. Depew, in New York Genealogical Society; Hon. David F. Houston, US Treasury Dept.; Hon. David Meredith, US Agricultural

Dept. Died in 1962. Address in 1929, 130 West 57th St., New York, NY; summer, Bankers' Trust Co., Place Vendome, Paris, France.

RAAB, GEORGE.
Painter, sculptor, and teacher.
Born Sheboygan, WI, Feb. 26, 1866.
Pupil of Richard Lorenz in
Milwaukee; C. Smith in Weimar;
Courtois in Paris. Member:
Milwaukee AS; WI. PS. Award:
Medal, Milwaukee Art Inst., 1917.
Work: "The Lone Pine," St. Paul
Institute; "The Veil of Snow" and
"Mother," Milwaukee Art Inst.
Educational Director of Decatur
Institute of Art.

RAB, SHIRLEE.
Sculptor and jeweler. Study:
Traphagen School of Design, NYC;
New School for Social Research,
NYC; Phila. Mus. of Art; Moore
College of Art - Jewelry Major;
Phila. College of Art; Fleisher Art
Memorial; Cheltenham Township Art
Center; Rutgers Univ. (spec. prog.
for selected artists); Princeton
Atelier - masters course, bronze
casting, summer study, Florence,
Italy. Work: In private
collection. Exhib: Throughout US
since 1962; Trenton, (NJ) State
Mus.; NAD, NYC; Phila. Art
Alliance; Squibb Gallery,
Princeton, NJ. Awards: NAD, NYC;
New School, NYC; Chestnut Hill
Academy; Atlantic City Inauguration
Exhib.; Fleisher Art Memorial;
others. Currently designing
jewelry; teaching sculpture Cherry
Hill, Moorestown, Phila.

RABUT, PAUL L.
Illustrator. Born in NYC in 1914.
Attended CCNY, ASL, and GCSA. In
1935 his first illustration was
published for Ainslee's Magazine.
His work has been shown at the
Metropolitan Museum of Art, NAD in
NY, International Watercolor Show
in Chicago and Penn. Academy of
Fine Arts in Phila. Not only an
advertising illustrator for General
Motors, Ford, Western Electric,
General Electric, Shell Oil, and US
Steel, he is also an expert on
primitive art and has lectured at
PI, Newark School of Art, and the S
of I.

RACHMIEL, JEAN.
Painter. Born in
Haverstraw-on-Hudson, NY, in 1871.
Art pupil under his father; later
under George de Forest Brush, NY;
went to Paris, 1890; studied under
Jules Lefebvre; entered Ecole des
Beaux Arts and studied with Leon
Bonnat. Exhibitor in Paris Salon
annually since 1898.

RACKLEY, MILDRED.
Serigrapher. Born in Carlsbad,
New Mexico in 1906. Studied:
Univ. of Texas; New Mexico Normal
Univ.; Kunstgewerbe Schule,
Hamburg, Germany; and with Walter
Ufer and George Grosz. Awards:
Diablo Art Festival, 1958; Concord,
Calif., 1958. Collections:
Metropolitan Museum of Art Phila.
Museum of Art, Springfield Art
Museum, Princeton Printmakers Club.

RACKOW, LEO.
Illustrator. Born in Spring
Valley, NY in 1901. Attended PSD,
then GCSA as a student of Harvey
Dunn, and studied in Paris under
Leger. Over the years he has
received a number of NY ADC awards
and several of his posters are in
the LC collection. His
illustrations have appeared in The
New Yorker, Liberty, Collier's, and
True. The Museum of Modern Art,
Dudensing Gallery and Harlow
Gallery have all exhibited his
work.

RADCLIFFE, C.
Was a stipple-engraver of portraits
and vignettes located in
Philadelphia as early as 1805.

RADER, ISAAC.
Painter. Born Brooklyn, NY, Oct.
5, 1906. Pupil of Abramovsky,
Kappes, Niles, Wicker, Jean
Marchand, Andre L'hote. Member:
Detroit AC. Awards: Libbey first
prize, Toledo Painter, 1921; Hecker
prize, Detroit Inst. of Art, 1926;
Whitcomb Traveling Scholarship,
Detroit, 1927.

RADITZ, LAZAR.
Painter. Born Dvinsk, Russia,
APril 15, 1887. Pupil of Chase and
Tarbell. Member: Fellowship PAFA;
Phila. AC; Phila. Alliance; AFA.
Awards: Bronze medal, P.-P. Exp.,
San. F., 1915; second Hallgarten
prize, NAD, 1918. Work: Self
portrait, PA Academy of the Fine
Arts, Phila.; "Dr. I. M. Hays,"
American Philosophical Society,

Phila.; "Mrs. R." Reading (PA) Museum; "Judge Mayer Sulzberger" Dropsie College, Phila.; "Dr. Hobert M. Hare", University of PA, Phila.; "Daniel Baugh", Baugh Inst. of Anatomy Phila.; "Dr. S. G. Dixon", Academy of Natural Science, Phila.; "Dr. Walton Clark," Franklin Inst., Phila.; "John C. Woods," Brown Univ., Providence; "Mr. Sterling," Yale Univ., New Haven; "Dr. William J. Taylor," College of Physicians, Phila., PA. Instructor, Graphc Sketch Club.

RADITZ, VIOLETTA C.
Painter, who exhibited water colors at the PAFA, Philadelphia, 1925. Address in 1929, 143 North 20th Street, Philadelphia.

RAE, JOHN.
Illustrator, painter, and writer. Born Jersey City, NJ, July 4, 1882. Pupil of Howard Pyle and F. V. Du Mond. Member: SI, 1912; GFLA; AFA. Illustrated "The Girl I Left Behind Me," "Historic Houses of New Jersey," "The Big Family," "Pies and Pirates," "Why," "Fables in Rhyme," "American Indian Fairy Tales," "Fairy Rales From France." Author and illustrator of "New Adventures of Alice," "Grasshopper Green and the Meadow Mice"; "Granny Goose"; "Lucy Locket." Represented in Library of Congress, Washington.

RAHMING, NORRIS.
Painter and etcher. Born New York City, May 1, 1886. Pupil of H. G. Keller, Emil Garlsen, William M. Chase. Member: Cleveland SA. Awards: Second prize for landscape, 1926; hon. mention, 1928; hon. mention, 1929, Cleveland. Work: "Mt. Chocorua, NH," Newark Museum of Art, Newark, NJ; "The Bridge, Avignon," Cleveland Museum of Art, Cleveland, OH; "Carcassone," Mary Warner Fund, City of Cleveland. Died in 1959.

RAKEMANN, CARL.
Mural painter and illustrator. Born Washington, April 27, 1878. Pupil of academies in Munich, Dusseldorf and Paris. Member: X Painters of Washington. Award: Gold medal, Sesqui-Cen. Exp., Phila., 1926. Work: Four lunettes in room of Senate Committee on Military Affairs and four paintings in lobby of House of Representatives, U.S. Capitol, Washington; portrait of ex-Speaker Henderson, U.S. Soldiers Home, Tennessee; portraits for the State House, Columbus, OH; Ohio State Archaeological and Historical Society, Kenyon College, OH.

RALEIGH, HENRY.
Illustrator, etcher, lith.,and portrait painter. Born Portland, OR, Nov. 23, 1880. Pupil of Hopkins Academy, San Fran. Member: Alliance; GFLA; Salma C.; SI; Coffee House C. Award: Shaw prize for illustration, Salma. C., 1916; gold medal for advertising Art in America 1927. Worked for all major magazines. Died June 8, 1945.

RALPH, W.
Line-engraver of views, etc. He was working in Philldelphia in 1794-1808, and engraved at least one plate for the New York Magazine.

RAMAGE, JOHN.
English miniature painter. Born in 1748 in Ireland. He was living in Boston, MA, 1775, and in NY in 1777. He painted a miniature of George Washington. He became involved in debt and fled to Canada in 1794. He was buried in the Protestant Cemetery in Montreal. (See Strickland's Dictionary of Irish Artists.) Died in Montreal on Oct. 24, 1802.

RAMSDELL, FRED W.
Painter of landscapes and portraits. Born in 1865. Studied at Art Students' League, NY, and with Collin in Paris. He had a studio at Lyme, Ct. He died in 1915.

RAMSEY, L. A.
Painter, illustrator, and teacher. Born Bridgeport, IL., March 24, 1873. Pupil of Laurens and Julian Academy in Paris. Member: Soc. Utah Artists. Address in 1929, 128 South 10th Street, East, Salt Lake City, Utah.

RAMUS, MICHAEL.
Illustrator. Born in Naples, Italy, in 1917. Attended Exeter Academy at Yale Univ. and the ASL, with additional training under Harry Sternberg, Howard Trafton, and Elliot O'Hara. He has worked for Life, Sports Illustrated, Smithsonian, American Heritage, among others, and received the Award for Distinctive Merit in the 29th Annual Exhibition of the ADC.

RAND, ELLEN G. EMMET.
(Mrs. William Blanchard Rand.) Painter. Born San Francisco, CA., March 4, 1876. Studied in NY and Paris. Member: ANA, 1926; NA Women PS; Port. Painter; AFA. Awards: Silver medal, St. Louis Exp., 1904; gold medal, P.-P. Exp., San F., 1915; bronze medal, Buenos Aires Exp., 1910; Beck gold medal, PAFA, 1922; Gould prize ($250), Women PS, 1927. Work: "Portrait of Augustus Saint-Gaudens" and of "Benjamin Altman," Metropolitan Museum, New York. Died Dec. 18, 1941 in Salisbury, CT.

RAND, HENRY ASBURY.
Painter. Born Philadelphia, PA., April 1, 1886. Pupil of PAFA under Chase, Anshutz and Breckenridge. Member: Phila. Sketch C.; Fellowship PAFA. Work: "Snow Shadows," PAFA, Philadelphia.

RAND, MARGARET ARNOLD.
Painter and teacher. Born Dedham, MA, Oct. 21, 1868. Pupil of Emily D. Norcross, Clara Goodyear, Geo. H. Smillie and Henry W. Rice. Member: Copley S. 1894. Work: "Pansies," Boston Art Club. Address in 1929, 49 Kirkland Street, Cambridge, MA.

RAND, PAUL.
Painter and designer. Born in Aug. 15, 1914 in Brooklyn, NY. Studied at Pratt Inst.; Art Students' League with George Grorz; Parsons Sch. of Design. At 23 he became art director of Esquire and Apparel Arts magazines. Has written two books Thoughts on Design and The Trademark of Paul Rand. Living in Weston, Conn.

RANDALL, ASA GRANT.
Painter and teacher. Born Waterboro, ME, 1869. Pupil of Howard Helmick, Arthur Dow, A. H. Munsell, and Pratt Inst. Member: Providence WCC. Founder, Commonwealth Art Colony, Boothbay Harbor, ME. Specialty, landscape painting and block printing. Address in 1929, 32 Summer Street, Providence, RI; summer, Boothbay Harbor, ME.

RANDALL, D. ERNEST.
Painter and illustrator. Born in Rush County, IN. Pupil of Art Inst. of Chicago. Address in 1926, 1736 Union Street, San Fran., CA.

RANDALL, MRS. DARLEY.
See Talbot, Grace Helen.

RANDALL, PAUL A.
Landscape painter. Born Warsaw, IN, Sept. 29, 1879. Pupil of William Forsyth and C. A. Wheeler. Member: Indiana AC.

RANDOLPH, GLADYS C.
Painter. Born in Whitestone, Long Island, NY. Studied: NY School of Fine and Applied Arts; Terry Art Institute; Portland Oregon Art Museum; Univ. of Penn.; NY Univ.; also studied with Hobson Pittman and Revington Arthur. Awards: Miami Art League; Blue Dome; Florida Federation of Art; Terry Art Institute; National League of American Pen Women; American Artists Professional League.

RANDOLPH, LEE F.
Painter, etcher, and landscape architect. Born Revenna, OH, June 3, 1880. Pupil of Cincinnati Art Academy; ASL of NY under Cox; Ecole des Beaux-Arts and Julian Academy in Paris. Member: Chicago SE; Calif. SE; San F. AA. Awards: Bronze medal for painting, P.-P. Exp., San F., 1915; silver medal for painting, San F. AA, 1919. Work in Luxembourg, Paris. Director California School of Fine Arts. Address in 1929, care Calif. School of Fine Arts, San Francisco, CA.

RANGER, HENRY WARD.
Landscape painter. Born Jan, 1859 in Syracuse, NY, he died in New York City Nov. 7, 1916. He studied

in this country; also in France, England and Holland. He was elected an Associate of the National Academy, 1901, and Academician in 1906. Represented in Corcoran Art Gallery by the "Top of the Hill," and in the Metropolitan Museum of Art by "High Bridge" and "Spring Woods."

RANNELLS, WILL.
Painter, illustrator, and teacher. Born Caldwell, OH, July 21, 1892. Pupil of Cincinnati Art Acad. Member: GFLA. Work: Cover designs and illustrations for Life, Judge, Country Gentleman, Farm and Fireside, McClures, Outing, Sportsmen's Digest, and The People's Home Jouranl; calendar designs and backs for Congress playing cards. Illustrated Dog Stars. Specializes in portraits of dogs. Instructor, Dept. of Fine Arts, Ohio State University.

RANNEY, WILLIAM.
Painter. Born May 9, 1813, in Middletown, CT. Represented by "Duck- Shooting" in Corcoran Art Gallery, Washington, DC. Elected Associate Member of the National Academy in 1850. His work is mainly connected with the life of hunters and trappers in the West. Died Nov. 18, 1857, in W. Hoboken, NJ.

RANSOM, ALEXANDER.
Painter. Noted in Tuckerman's "American Artist Life." A portraitist.

RANSOM, CAROLINE L. ORMES.
Born in Newark, OH in 1838. She was taught by her mother in drawing and painting in water colors, and received some help from an itinerant portrait painter, who visited her father's home and painted portraits of the family. She afterwards went to NY, and studied landscape painting under A. B. Durand, and portrait painting under Thomas Hicks and Daniel Huntington. Visited Europe later, where she was for some time a pupil of Kaulbach, at Munich. Her first work of note was painted in her studio in Cleveland, OH; she afterwards worked in NY, prior to her coming to Washington, DC.,

where she maintained a studio at 915 F. Street, N.W., for many years. Among her works are: Portraits of Maj. Gen. McPherson, Salmon P. Chase, Senator Benjamin F. Wade, Joshua R. Giddings, Alexander Hamilton, John A. Dix, John W. Taylor, James A. Garfield, and Thomas Jefferson. Died Feb. 12, 1910, in Washington, DC.

RANSON, NANCY SUSSMAN.
Painter and serigrapher. Born in NYC on Sept. 13, 1905. Studied: Pratt Institute Art School; Art Students League; and with Laurent, Charlot, and Brackman. Awards: Critic's Choice Exhibition, 1947; National Association of Women Artists, 1952, 1953, 1956, 1958; National Serigraphic Society, 1953; Grumbacher award in Casein, 1954; American Color Printmakers Society, 1955; Brooklyn Society of Art, 1955; Audubon Art, 1958. Collections: Brandeis Univ.; Mexican Government Tourist Commission; Key West Art and Historical Society; Reading Public Museum; Free Library, Phila.; Museum of the City of NY; National Art Gallery, Sydney, Australia. Media: Oil, acrylic, serigraphy.

RAPHAEL, JOSEPH.
Painter. Born Jackson, Amador Co., Calif., in 1872. Pupil of San. F. AA; Beaux-Arts, Julian Academy, and Laurens in Paris. Awards: Hon. mention, Paris Salon, 1915; silver medal, P. P. Exp., San F., 1915; first purchase prize, San F. AA; gold medal, San F. AA, 1918. Work in Golden Gate Park Museum, San Francisco, and San Francisco Art Association. Died in 1950. Address in 1929, Care of Museum of Fine Arts, San Francisco, Calif; 41 Rue Engeland, Uccle, Belgium.

RASARIO, ADA.
See Cecere.

RASCHEN, CARL MARTIN.
Painter and illustrator. Born Dec. 17, 1882. Pupil of Rochester Athenaem and Mechanics Inst. and Gilbert Gaul. Member: Rochester AC; Rochester Picture Painters' C.; St. Louis Brush and Pencil C.; Geneseeans. Died in June, 1962.

RASKIN, SAUL.
Painter, illustrator, etcher, craftsman, writer, and lecturer. Born Russia, Aug. 15, 1878. Member: NYWCC; Am. WCS (asso.). Author of "Palestine in Word and Pictures." Address in 1929, 96 Fifth Ave.; 1475 Grand Concourse, New York, NY.

RASMUSSEN, BERTRAND.
Painter. Born Arendal, Norway, in 1890. Pupil of Laurens in Paris. Member: Society of Independent Artists; Brooklyn Water Color Club; League of New York Artists. Address in 1926, 468 60th Street, Brooklyn, New York, NY.

RATH, HILDEGARD.
Painter and lecturer. Born in Freudenstadt, Germany in 1909. Awards: Stuttgart, Germany; Salon of the 50 States, NY; Prix de Paris, France. Collections: Library of Congress, Wash., DC Metropolitan Museum of Art; NY Public Library. Address in 1980, P.O. Box 298, Manchester Center, VT.

RATHBONE, MRS. CHARLES H. JR.
See Martha Moore.

RATHBONE JR, CHARLES H.
Painter and etcher. Born New York, Nov. 25, 1902. Pupil of ASL of NY; Hayley Lever. Member: NAC; "The Fifteen"; S. Indp. A. Died in 1936. Address in 1929, 75 Central Park, West, New York, NY; summer, Concarneau, Finistere, France.

RATLIFF, BLANCHE COOLEY.
(Mrs. Walter B. Ratliff). Painter. Born Smithville, Texas, May 26, 1896. Pupil of O. B. Jacobson; Dura B. Cockrell. Member: Les Beaux-Arts, Norman, Okla.; Fort Worth Painters. Work in University of Oklahoma.

RATTERMAN, W. G.
Painter. Member: GFLA. Address in 1929, 67 West 67th Street, New York, NY.

RATTNER, ABRAHAM.
Painter. Born July 8, 1895 in Poughkeepsie, NY. Studied at George Washington Univ., PA Acad. of Fine Arts, and in Paris. Taught at New School for Social Research (1947-55); Brooklyn Mus. Art School; Yale (1951-3); Columbia, and Skowhegan School, ME. Lived in Paris and NYC. Awarded Cresson Fellowship from Penn. Acad. of Fine Arts (1945); hon. Mention Carnegie (1949). Exhibited at Bonjean Galleries, Paris (1935); Renaissance Soc., Univ. of Chicago (1957); Downtown Gallery, NYC (Multiple); Stendahl Gal, LA.; Kennedy Gal. (7 exb. 1969-79); Vassar (1948), others. In the collections of Yale; Vassar; Washington Univ.; New School for Soc. Research; Arizona State; Baltimore; Art Inst/Chicago; Newark Mus.; Musee du Jeu de Paume, Paris. He died Feb. 14, 1978.

RAU, WILLIAM.
Painter and illustrator. Born New York, NY, 1874. Pupil of Chase and Edgar M. Ward; NAD. Member: Inter. Soc. AL. Work: Eight mural paintings, Douglas Co. C. H. Omaha, Neb.; lunette in St. Matthews' Church, Hoboken, NJ; panels in Melrose Public Library and High Bridge Public Library, New York, NY; Patio Theatre, Brooklyn, NY; Keith Theatre, Richmond Hill, NY; Pt. Washington Theatre, Pt. Washington, NY. Address in 1929, 42d St., New York, NY; h. 8636 107th St., Richmond Hill, LI, NY.

RAUGHT, JOHN WILLARD.
Painter. Born Dunmore, PA. Pupil of NAD; Julian Academy in Paris. Member: Salma. C., 1902; AFA. Address in 1929, Dunmore, PA.

RAUL, HARRY LEWIS.
Sculptor, draftsman, lecturer, and writer. Born Easton, PA. Pupil of NY School of Art; F. E. Elwell; ASL of NY under F. V. Du Mond; PAFA under Grafly. Member: Art Centre of the Oranges (pres.); Mystic SA; AFA. Work: "Green Memorial Statue," Easton, PA; "Monument to Martyrs of the Maine" (Hail, Martyrs' statue), Northampton Co., PA.; "Soldiers' Monument" (Old Glory Statue), West Chester, PA; "Portrait, Ex Mayor Rudolph Blankenburg," Philadelphia.; Englewood, NJ, World War Memorial ("America, 1917-1918" statue); Manton B. Metcalf memorial,

Rosedale Cemetery, Orange, NJ; ("Faith, Hope and Charity," bronze group); Wilson Borough Pennsylvania World War monument; "The Face of Lincoln," Lincoln Trust Co. Bldg., Scranton, PA; Julia-Dykman Andrus memorial group, Yonkers, NY; Herbermann memorial, Sea Girt, NJ; Williams-Coolidge Memorial, Easton, PA; Herbermann Memorial, Jersey City, NJ; War Mothers Memorial, Phila., PA. Author, "The Celtic Cross for Modern Usage." Address in 1929, 312 Highland Ave., Orange, NJ; 1809 Wash. Bldv., Easton, PA.

RAUL, JOSEPHINE GESNER.
(Mrs. Harry Lewis Raul). Painter. Born Linden, NJ. Pupil of NAD; ASL of NY; GA Thompson. Member: Mystic SA; AFA; Plainfield AA; A Cen. of Oranges; NL Am. Pen W. Address in 1929, 312 Highland Ave., Orange, NJ; summer, Groton Long Point, CT.

RAVENSCROFT, ELLEN.
Painter, craftsman, and teacher. Born Jackson, MI. Pupil of Chase, Henri; Castellucho in Paris. Member: NA Women PS; NY. Soc. Women A; Provincetown AA. Awards: Portrait prize, C. L. Wolfe Art Club, 1908; landscape prize, and hon. mention, Kansas City Art Inst., 1923. Died in 1950. Address in 1929, 17 East 59th Street, New York, NY; summer, Provincetown, MA.

RAVLIN, GRACE.
Painter. Born Kaneville, IL. Pupil of AIC; PAFA under Chase; Simon, Menard in Paris. Member: Associee Societe Nationale des Beaux-Arts, Paris, 1912, and Peintres Orientalists Francais; Societaire Salon d'Automne. Awards: Third medal, Amis des Arts, Toulon, 1911; silver medal, P.-P. Exp., San F., 1915; Field and Butler prizes, AIC, 1918; Peterson prize, AIC, 1922. Work: "Procession of the Redentore, Venice," Art Institute of Chicago; "Arab Women in the Cemetery Tangier," Luxembourg, Paris; four paintings owned by French Government and two by City of Chicago; "Blue Doors," Arche Club, Chicago; "The Plaza," Newark Museum; "Market Day, Grand Socco,"

Harrison Gallery, Los Angeles Museum; Vanderpoel AA, Collection, Chicago. Address in 1929, 134 Lexington Avenue, New York, NY.

RAWDON, FREEMAN.
Engraver. Born C. 1801 in Tolland, CT. He was a pupil of his brother Ralph Rawdon, an engraver, then of Albany, NY. In 1828 he was the Rawdon of the NY engraving firm of Rawdon, Wright, & Co., and Rawdon, Wright, Hatch, and of other combinations of a later date. These firms conducted an extensive business in general and bank-note engraving, and employed many engravers. Freeman Rawdon signed very little work. Died Sept. 21, 1859 in NYC.

RAWDON, RALPH.
Engraver. In 1813 Ralph Rawdon was engraving in a very crude manner in Cheshire, CT. He was associated in this work with Thomas Kensett, the father of the American Artist. About 1816 Rawdon removed to Albany, NY, where he engraved stipple portraits over his own name, and with his brother and A. Willard he was in the bank note and general engraving business in that city.

RAWSON, CARL WENDELL.
Painter. Born Des Moines, IA, Jan. 28, 1884. Pupil of Cumming Art School; NAD; Minneapolis School of Art. Member: Attic C.; Minneapolis AS; Minnesota State AS; Palette and Chisel, Chicago. Represented by portrait in Minneapolis Institute of Arts; landscapes in Minekahda Club, Minneapolis Golf Club Galleries and Winona Country Club, Minneapolis. Address in 1929, 637 Kenwood Parkway, Minneapolis, MN.

RAYMOND, FRANK WILLOUGHBY.
Etcher and engraver. Born Dubuque, IA, 1881. Pupil of AI Chicago. Member: Cal. SW; Chicago SW; Palette and Chisel C.; GFLA. Work in: Art Institute of Chicago; Toledo Museum of Art. Address in 1929, 63 E. Adams Street, Chicago, IL.

RAYMOND, GRACE RUSSELL.
Painter and teacher. Born Mt. Vernon, OH, May 1, 1877. Pupil of AIC; School of Applied Design, NY; Corcoran School, Wash.; studied in Paris and Rome. Member: Wash. WCC; AFA. Instructor drawing and painting, Southwestern College, Winfield, KS.

RAYNAUD, LOUIS.
Painter and teacher. Born New Orleans, LA, June 18, 1905. Member: N. O. AA; SSAL; N.O. ACC. Award: Prize, San Antonio AL, San Antonio, Texas, 1929. Address in 1929, 823 Royal; h. 2329 Ursuline Avenue, New Orleans, LA.

RAYNOR, GRACE HORTON.
Sculptor. Born New York, NY, Sept. 20, 1884. Member: Art Workers C. Work: Fountain, Cherry Valley Club, Long Island, etc. Specialty, portrait statuettes and heads.

REA, GARDENER.
Illustrator. Born in Ironton, OH, in 1892. Attended Ohio Univ. in 1914, and later, the Columbus Art School. A free-lance cartoonist and writer, he worked for Judge, Life, and The New Yorker. His cartoons were exhibited in museums all over the world and he was author and illus. of the books The Gentleman Says It's Pixies, 1944, and Gardener Rea's Sideshow, 1945. He lived in Brookhaven, Long Island for many years. Died in 1966.

REA, JOHN LOWRA.
Sculptor, writer, and teacher. Born Beekmantown, NY, Jan. 29, 1882. Pupil of H. A. MacNeil; J. E. Fraser, F. V. Du Mond. Address in 1929, R. F. D. 1, Plattsburg, Clinton Co., NY.

READ, ADELE VON HELMOLD.
Painter. Born in Philadelphia. Pupil of Chase, Anshutz, PAFA. Member: Fellowship PAFA; Phila. Alliance; Plastic C; Penn. Mus. and School. Ind. A; AFA. Address in 1929, Presser Bldg., 1714 Ludlow St., Philadelphia, PA; h. 74 Lincoln Ave., Lansdowne, PA.

READ, ELMER JOSEPH.
Painter. Born Howard, Steuben Co., NY, June 19, 1862. Pupil of College of Fine Arts, Syracuse Univ.; Fremiert in Paris. During winter, painted in West Indies. Works in many private collections. Address in 1929, 11 Washington Street, Palmyra, NY.

READ, FRANK E.
Painter, etcher, and architect. Born Austinburg in 1862. Pupil of W. M. Hunt. Member: Seattle Fine Arts Society. Address in 1926, 232 Harvard, North, Seattle, Washington.

READ, HENRY.
Painter, writer, teacher, lecturer, and draftsman. Born Twickenham, England, Nov. 16, 1851. Member: Nat. Acad. A. (regent); Col. Chapter AIA (hon.); AFA. Director, Denver Students' School of Art. Work in Denver Art Museum. Died in 1935. Address in 1929, 1311 Pearl Street, h. 1360 Corona Street, Denver, CO.

READ, THOMAS BUCHANAN.
Painter. Born March 12, 1822 in Chester County, PA. He entered the studio of a sculptor in Cincinnati in 1839, but painting soon proved more attractive to him. He opened a studio in NY in 1841 and in Phila. in 1846. In 1850, however, he went to Europe, working and studying in Florence and Rome, finally making the latter city his home, with occasional visits to the US. He painted both fancy pictures and portraits, and also executed a few works in sculpture, as, for instance, a bust of General Sheridan. A portrait of himself is owned by the National Gallery of Washington, DC. Died May 11, 1872 in NYC.

READ, WILLIAM.
Portrait painter. Born in 1607 in Batcombe, England. He came over in 1635 and settled in Weymouth, MA. He lived in Boston till 1674, and died at Norwich, CT, in 1679. In 1641 he painted the portrait of Richard Bellingham, Governor of Massachusetts. The picture is inscribed "Govr. R. Bellingham, Effiegies Delin, Boston Anno Dom, 1641. Aetatis 49, W. R." This is supposed to be the earliest known portrait painted in this country.

READIO, WILFRED A.
Painter and teacher. Born
Florence, MA, Nov. 27, 1895. Pupil
of Alfred Vance Churchill, Carnegie
Inst. Tech. Member: Pitts. AA; L.
C. Tiffany AG. Award: First
honors Pitts. AA, 1921. Work:
"Curtainted Window," Public Schools
of Pittsburgh. Died in 1961.
Address in 1929, Carnegie Institute
of Technology, Pittsburgh, PA;
summer, Williamsburg, MA.

REAM, CARDUCIUS P.
Painter. Born Lancaster, OH, in
1837. He is represented in the
Chicago Art Inst. Died June 20,
1917 in Chicago, IL

REAM, VINNIE.
Sculptor. Born in Madison, WI, on
Sept. 25, 1847. Studied sculpture
under Clark Mills and Luigi Majoli.
Work: several busts of
congressmen, including bust of
Pres. Abraham Lincoln from life.
$10,000 Comm. from Congress in Aug.
1866 to make a full-size marble
statue of Lincoln for Capitol
Rotunda. Other busts included
Gustave Dore and Pere Hyacinthe.
Died in Wash., DC on Nov. 20, 1914.

REARDON, MARY A.
Painter, etcher, and muralist.
Born in Quincy, MA, 1912. Studied:
Radcliffe College; Yale Univ.
School of Fine Arts; and in Mexico.
Collections: St. Theresa's,
Watertown, Mass.; Good Shepherd
Convent, NY; Radcliffe College;
Cardinal Spellman High School,
Brockton, Mass.; Boston College;
St. Francis Xavier Chapel, Boston;
St. Peter and St. Paul Church,
Boston, Mass.; St. John's Seminary,
Boston; Maryknoll and Brookline
Chapel, Boston; Children's Medical
Center, Boston; Boston State
Teachers College; triptych, US
Ship Wasp. Address in 1980, 12
Martin's Lane, Hingham, MA.

REASER, WILBUR AARON.
Painter and lecturer. Born
Hickville, OH, Dec. 25, 1860.
Pupil of Mark Hopkins Inst. in San
Francisco; Constant and Lefebvre in
Paris. Member: San Francisco Art
Assoc. Awards: Gold and silver
medals, California Exp., 1894;
first Hallgarten prize, NAD 1897.

Specialty, portraits. Work:
"Mother and Daughter," Carnegie
Gallery, Pittsburgh; "Old Man and
Sleeping Child," Art Gallery, Des
Moines, IA; portrait of "Senator W.
B. Allison," U.S. Senate Lobby,
Washington; "Senator C. S. Page,"
The Capitol, Charleston, W. VA;
"Bishop Lewis," State Historical
Society, Des Moines, IA. Died in
1942. Address in 1929, 15 Arden
Place, Yonkers, NY.

REASON, P. H.
Engraver. This very clever Black
engraver of portraits in stipple
was educated and apprenticed to an
engraver by certain members of the
antislavery party in New York City.
He engraved a few good portraits,
but early in the 1850's, racial
prejudice compelled him to abandon
engraving for other employment.

REAUGH, FRANK M.
Painter. Born near Jacksonville,
IL, Dec. 29, 1860. Pupil of St.
Louis School of Fine Arts; Julien
Academy in Paris under Doucet.
Member: Dallas Art Association
(hon.); AFA. Work: "Driving the
Herd," Dallas (TX) Art Association;
"The Road to the Brazog," Dallas
Public Library. Specialty, Texas
cattle and western landscape.
Addresss in 1929, Oak Cliff, TX.

REBECK, STEVEN AGUSTUS.
Sculptor. Born Cleveland, OH, May
25, 1891. Pupil of Karl Bitter,
Carl Heber, Cleveland School of
Art. Member: Cleveland Sculpture
Soc.; Clev. SA; NSS (asso.).
Awards: Medal for portrait bust,
Cleveland Museum of Art, 1922;
award for sculpture, Cleveland
Museum, 1923. Work:
"Shakespeare," Cleveland, OH;
Soldiers' Memorial, Alliance, OH;
heroic statue, Sphinx, Civil Court
House, St. Louis, MO. Address in
1929, 1028 Roanoke Road, Cleveland
Heights, OH.

REBISSO, LOUIS T.
Sculptor. Born 1837 in Genoa,
Italy. He taught modelling for
years in the Art Academy of
Cincinnati. His equestrian statue
of Genl. McPherson is in Washington

and his Genl. Grant is in Chicago. Died May 3, 1899 in Cincinnati, OH.

RECCHIA, RICHARD HENRY.
Sculptor. Born Quincy, MA, Nov. 20, 1885. Studied at Boston Museum of Fine Arts School; and in Paris and Italy. Member: NSS; Boston GA; Copley S.; Boston SS (Founder); Boston AC; North Shore AA; Gloucester SA; Rockport AA. Award: Bronze medal, P. P. Exp., San F. 1915. Work: Bas-relief portrait of Gov. Curtis Guild, Boston State House; "Architecture," figure panel on Boston Museum; Red Cross panel in Musee de l'Armee, Gallery Foch, Paris; Memorial to Gov. Oliver Ames, North Easton, MA.; Sam Walter Foss Memorial panel, John Hay Library, Brown Univ., RI; Phi-Beta-Kappa tablet, Harvard University; "Disaster Relief" Model, American Red Cross Museum, Wash., DC; George E. Davenport portrait tablet, and William Hoffman, portrait tablet, Brown Univ, Providence, RI; "Youth," J. B. Speed Memorial Musem, Louisville, KY. Address in 1929, 5 St. Botolph Studios, Boston, MA.

RECKLESS, STANLEY LAWRENCE.
Painter. Born Philadelphia, PA, Aug. 22, 1892. Pupil of PAFA; and Julian in Paris. Member: Graphic Sketch Club, Philadelphia; Fellowship PAFA; Paris AAA. Awards: Cresson Traveling Scholarship, PAFA, 1915-1916; First Toppan prize, PAFA, 1916. Address in 1929, New Hope, Bucks Co., PA.

REDERUS, S. F.
Painter. Born in the Netherlands in 1854. Pupil of R. Wynkoop, Bridgeport, CT. Member: Milwaukee Art Inst.; Dubuque Artists' Society. Work represented in Presbyterian Church, Nortonville, Kansas. Address in 1926, 18 South Glen Oak Avenue, Dubuque, IA.

REDFIELD, EDWARD WILLIS.
Landscape painter. Born Bridgeville, DE, Dec. 19, 1869. Pupil of PAFA; Bouguereau and Robert-Fleury in Paris. Member: SAA 1903; Nat. Inst. AL; AC Phila.; Fellowship PAFA; Salma. C.; AFA. Awards: AC Phila. 1896; Paris Exp., 1900; Pan-Am. Exp., Buffalo,

1901; Temple medal, PAFA; St. Louis Exp., 1904; Sesnan gold medal, PAFA 1905; CI Pittsburgh; gold medal of honor, PAFA 1907; Corcoran AG 1907; Paris Salon, 1907; AIC 1909; Buenos Aires Exp., 1910; Lippincott prize, PAFA 1912; Wilmington Soc. FA; Carnegie prize, NAD, 1918, 22; Altman prize NAD, 1919; Sotesbury prize, PAFA, 1920; Saltus medal, NAD, 1927. In collections of Luxembourg, Mus. Paris; Corcoran; Cincinnati; Carnegie; Boston Mus.; PAFA; Brooklyn; Herron Art Inst., Indianpolis; AIC; Minneapolis Inst. of Art; RI Sch. of Design; MMA; Nat. Gal.; Butler; LA Mus. and Delgado Mus, N. Orleans. Died in 1965. Address in 1929, Centre Bridge Bucks Co., PA.

REDFIELD, HELOISE GUILLOU.
Miniature painter. Born Philadelphia, PA, 1883. Pupil of PAFA under Chase and Cecilia Beaux; Mme. La Forge and Delecluse in Paris. Member: Am. S. Min. P.; PA S. Min. P. Awards: Hon. mention, Buffalo SA; silver medal, P.-P. Exp., San F., 1915. Address in 1929, Barnstable, MA; Wayne. PA.

REDMAN, HENRY N.
Painter. Exhibited a landscape at the Penna. Academy of Fine Arts, 1926. Address in 1926, Boston, MA.

REDMOND, GRANVILLE.
Painter. Born Philadelphia, PA. March 9, 1871. Pupil of Mathews and Joullin; Constant and Laurens in Paris. Member: San F. AA; Calif. AC. Awards: Hon. mention and W. E. Brown gold medal at San Francisco Art Assoc.; silver medal, Alaska-Yukon-Pacific Expo., Seattle, 1909. Represented in the Washington State Capitol, Olympia; "A California Landscape," Jonathan Club, Los Angeles. Died in 1935. Address in 1929, Care of the Charlie Chaplin Film Co., 1416 North La Brea Ave., Los Angeles, CA.

REDMOND, MARGARET.
Painter and craftsman. Born Philadelphia, PA. Pupil of PAFA; Twachtman in NY; Simon and Menard in Paris. Member: Fellowship PAFA; Phila. WCC; Copley S.; Boston SAC; S. Indp. A.; Phila. Alliance;

771

AFA. Specialty, stained glass. Address in 1929, 45 Newbury Street, Boston, MA; h. Cheshan, NH.

REECE, DORA.
Painter. Born Philipsburg, PA. Pupil of Daingerfield, Snell, Seyffert, Breckenridge, Hale, Pearson, Garber, etc. Member: Fellowship PAFA: Plastic C.; Phila. Alliance; Phila. Soc. AL; AFA; PA Soc. Min. P. Address in 1929, 1540 North 55th Street, Philadelphia, PA.

REED, ABNER.
Engraver. Born in East Windsor, CT., in 1771; died in Toledo, OH. Abner Reed was apprenticed to a saddler and commenced engraving by working upon the engraved metal nameplates then used on saddles. In 1803 he settled in Hartford, CT, and regularly engaged in the business of engraving, plate printing, and sign painting. In 1811 he returned to East Windsor, and became largely interested in banknote engraving for US and Canadian Banks. He was one of the earliest banknote engravers in this country, having engraved the plates for the Hartford Bank of 1792. Among the apprentices in his employ at East Windsor were William Mason, later a well-known wood engraver of Philadelphia, Asaph Willard, later of NY, Oliver Pelton, Alfred Daggett, Vistus Balch, Fred Bissell, Ebenezer F. Reed and Lewis Fairchild, wood engravers, and William Phelps, a plate printer. Died Feb. 25, 1866 in Toledo, OH.

REED, DOEL.
Painter and etcher. Born Logansport, IN, May 21, 1895. Pupil of Meakin, Hopkins, Wessel. Member: Cincinnati MacDowell S.; Cincinnati AC; Indiana AC; Brown Co. Group of A.; Hoosier Salon; Buffalo Indp. S.; S. Indp. A.; Okla. AA. Work: "Along the Ohio," Cincinnati Art Club, "Muted Strings," A. and M. College Library, Stillwater, Okla.; "On the Banks of the Loing" and "Along the Cimerron," Okla. Art League. Address in 1929, Art Dep. A. and M. College; h. 324 Washington Street, Stillwater, Okla.; summer, Locust Hill Cabin, Nashville, IN, and Art Colony, Gypsy Camp, Siloam Springs, Ark.

REED, EARL H.
Etcher. Born Geneva, IL, July 5, 1863. Self-taught. Member: Chicago SA. Work in: Toledo Museum of Art; Library of Congress, Washington, D.C.; Chicago Art Institute; NY Public Library; St. Louis Art Museum; Milwaukee Art Inst. Author: "Etcher: A Practical Treatise;" "The Voices of the Dunes and Other Etchings;" "The Dune Country;" "Sketches in Jacobia;" "Sketches in Duneland;" "Tales of a Vanishing River" and "The Silver Arrow." Address in 1929, 4758 Lake Park Avenue, Chicago, IL.

REED, GRACE ADELAIDE.
Painter and teacher. Born Boston, MA, July 14, 1874. Pupil of Woodbury, Denman Ross, Francis Hodgkins; Delecluse and Menard in Paris; MA. Normal Art School. Member: Copley S. Address in 1929, 91 Pinckney Street, Boston, MA.

REED, HELEN.
Boston painter, who began her professional career in that city by drawing portraits in crayon. Later she went to Florence where she studied sculpture under Preston Powers, sending to America bas-reliefs in marble which have been exhibited at the Boston Art Club and in NY.

REED, LILLIAN R.
Painter and teacher. Born Philadelphia, PA. Pupil Lathrop and Daingerfield. Member: Plastic C.; Fellowship PAFA; Phila. Art Teachers' Assn.; Phila. Alliance; College AA; AFA. Award: Georgine Shillard gold medal, Plastic Club. Address in 1929, Presser Bldg., 1714 Chestnut St., Philadelphia, PA.

REEVS, GEORGE M.
Portrait painter. Born Yonkers, NY, 1864. Pupil of Constant, Laurens, Gerome. Member: Salma. C.; A. Fund S. Award: portrait prize, Salma. C., 1906. Address in 1929, 35 West 14th Street, New York, NY.

REGESTER, CHARLOTTE.
Painter, craftsman, and teacher.
Born in 1883 in Baltimore, MD.
Pupil of Rose Clark; Urquhart
Wilcox; W. M. Chase; Robert Henri;
Buffalo ASL; NY ASL. Member: NA
Women PS; Buffalo SA; PBC;
Catherine L. Wolfe AS; NY Ceramic
Soc. Award: Portrait prize,
Catherine L. Wolfe Club, 1929.
Died in 1964. Address in 1929, 150
East 34th St., New York, NY; 37
Berkeley Place., Buffalo, NY.

REHBERGER, GUSTAV.
Illustrator. Born in
Riedlingsdorf, Austria, in 1910.
He came to the US at age 13 and
attended the AIC and Art
Instruction School in Minneapolis,
as a scholarship student. In 1949
he was awarded the Most Creative
Painting from the Audubon Artists,
and in 1966 he received the Stern
Award. He has done a number of
movie posters, such as The Command,
Moby Dick, Defiant Ones, and Animal
World. He currently teaches and
lectures at the ASL in figure
drawing, composition, and painting.

REICH, JACQUES.
Painter and etcher. Born in
Hungary, Aug. 10, 1852. Studied
art in Budapest; came to US, 1873;
continued studies at Nat. Acad. of
Design, NY, Penna. Acad. of Fine
Arts, Phila. and in Paris. Located
in NY in 1885. Made most of pen
portraits for Scribner's
Cyclopaedia of Painters and
Paintings, and for Appelton's
Cyclopaedia of American Biography;
etched on copper a series of
portraits of American and English
authors; engaged in etching and
publishing a series of etched
portraits of famous Americans,
including Washington, Jefferson,
Alexander Hamilton, Benjamin
Franklin, Daniel Webster, Abraham
Lincoln, Roosevelt, Cleveland,
McKinley, Paul Jones, Andrew
Carnegie, George William Curtis,
Andrew Jackson, U.S. Grant, James
Madison, John Marshall, President
Taft, Gen. Robert E. Lee, Dr.
Andrew D. White, James Abbott
McNeill Whistler, Woodrow Wilson,
etc.; among many private plates
etched are portraits of Whitelaw
Reid, E. H. Harriman, H. H. Rogers,

John W. Mackay, Gov. Winthrop, Mark
Hanna, Charles B. Alexander, Nelson
Wilmarth Aldrich and Gen. Thomas
Hamlin Hubbard. Died July 8, 1923
in Dumraven, NY.

REICH, JOHN.
Engraver. Born in 1768 in Bavaria,
Germany. In 1806 John Reich was a
die-sinker of considerable merit,
and he was frequently employed by
Robert Scot, engraver of the United
States Mint in Philadelphia, to
prepare the dies for National coin.
He engraved the dies for several
fine medals, including Washington,
after Stuart; Franklin, from the
Houdon bust; a Peace medal of 1783,
and a Tripoli medal presented to
Com. Edward Preble in 1806. John
Reich was one of the founders of
the Society of Artists, organized
in Philadelphia in 1810, and is
entered on the list of Fellows of
the Society as "die-sinker at the
United States Mint." Died in 1833
in Albany, NY

REICHE, F.
This German engraver was executing
crude line work in Philadelphia in
1795. He was engraving portraits
on wood in 1800.

REICHMANN, MRS. JOSEPHINE.
Painter. Born Louisville, KY,
March 24, 1864. Pupil of AIC; ASL
of NY. Member: Chicago SA;
Chicago AC; Cordon C.; North Shore
AA; NA Women PS; SSAL. Died in
1939. Address in 1929, 7136
Crandon Avenue, Chicago, IL

REID, ALBERT TURNER.
Illustrator. Born Concordia, KS,
Aug. 12, 1873. Pupil of NY School
of Art and ASL of NY. Member:
GFLA; SI. Work in newspapers,
magazines and books. Owner The
Albert T. Reid Syndicate. Died in
1955. Address in 1929, Forest
Hills, LI, NY.

REID, AURELIA WHEELER.
Painter and writer. Born Beekman,
Dutchess Co., NY. Pupil of
Delecluse Academy in Paris; Cooper
Union, NY School of Art; Otis Art
Inst. of Los Angeles. Member:
Calif. Min. Soc. Address in 1929,
252 West 11th Street, San Pedro,
CA.

773

REID, JEAN ARNOT.
Miniature painter. Born Brooklyn, NY, July 22, 1882. Pupil of Robert Brandegee; Am. School of Min. Painting; ASL of NY. Member: NA Women PS; AS Min. P.; Yonkers AA. Address in 1929, care of Bankers' Trust Co., 57th Street and Madison Ave., New York, NY; summer, Struan Farms, Monterey, MA.

REID, MARIE CHRISTINE WESTFELDT.
Painter and teacher. Born New York City. Pupil of J. Alden Weir, Douglas Volk, G. Wharton Edwards and F. Edwin Elwell. Member: NA Women PS; College AA; Salons of America. Address in 1929, Box 7, South Bristol, Maine.

REID, OLIVER RICHARD.
Painter and teacher. Born Eaton, GA, Feb. 27, 1898. Pupil of Daniel Garber. Member: Salons of Amer. Award: Hon. mention, Harmon Foundation, NY, 1928. Work: "Portrait of Dr. Henry Goddard Leach," New York Public Library. Address in 1929, 169 St. Nicholas Avenue, New York, NY.

REID, ROBERT.
Painter. Born in Stockbridge, MA, in 1862. Studied at Museum of FA, Boston, 1880 (for 3 yrs. assistant instructor in same); ASL, NY, 1885-89; Academie Julian, under Boulanger and Lefebvre. Exhibited annually in the Salon, and in the Paris Exposition, 1889; returned to NY, 1889; he was one of the NY artists who painted frescoes of the domes of the Liberal Arts Bldg., Chicago Exposition; formerly instructor in painting, ASL and Cooper Institute. Awarded Clarke prize, 1897; 1st Hallgarten prize, 1898, National Academy of Design; gold and silver medals, Paris Exposition, 1900. He painted mural decorations for many public and private buildings including the Library of Congress, Washington, DC; Appellate Court House, NY; MA State House, Boston; Paulist Fathers Church, NY; Fine Arts Palace, San Francisco. Represented in Metropolitan Museum of Art; Corcoran Gallery; and National Gallery of Washington, DC; museums of MN, Omaha, Cincinnati, Indianapolis, Brooklyn; Albright Gallery, Buffalo; Nebraska Art Association, Lincoln, Nebr.; Art Associaton, Richmond, IN; etc. Elected to National Academy, 1906; member of National Inst. of Arts and Letters, and "Ten American Painters." Address in 1926, Colorado Springs, CO. Died in 1929.

REIFFEL, CHARLES.
Lanscape painter. Born in 1862 in Indianapolis, IN. Self - taught. Member: Allied AA; Contemporary; Int. Soc. A. L.; CT SA; Salma. C.; CT AFA; Buffalo SA; Silvermine GA; Wash. AC; North Shore AA; Hoosier Salon; Chicago Gal. A; San Diego AG; Calif. AC; Laguna Beach AA. Awards: Fellowship prize, Buffalo SA, 1908; Harris silver medal, AIC, 1917; hon. mention, CT. AFA, 1920; hon. mention, International Exp., Pittsburgh, 1922; Hanna prize, Indiana Hoosier Salon, Chicago, 1925; Butler prize, Hoosier Salon, Chicago, 1926; Harrison prize, Los Angeles Museum, 1926; Art Guild prize, San Diego Fine Art Gallery, 1926; Tri Kappa Sorority prize, Hoosier Salon, 1927; Fine Arts Gallery purchase prize, San Diego, 1927; John C. Shaffer grand prize, Hoosier Salon, Chicago, 1928; Hatfield gold medal, CA AC, 1928; third prize Sacramento, CA, 1928; second landscape prize Phoenix, AR, 1928; Mrs. Kieth-Spalding prize, Los Anageles Museum, 1929; grand prize, State Exhib. Santa Cruz, Calif., 1929. Work: "Railway Yards - Winter Evening," Corcoran Gallery, Washington; "In the San Filepe Vallery," San Diego Fine Arts Gallery; "In Banner Vallery," Santa Cruz, CA, Art League. Died in 1942. Address in 1929, PO Box 412, East San Diego, CA.

REINA, SALVATORE.
Sculptor. Born Santo Stefano, Girgenti, Italy, April 8, 1896. Pupil of Beaux-Arts Inst. of Design, NY. Member: Salons of Am. Address in 1929, 128 East 23rd Street, New York, NY; h. 51 Old Town Road, South Beach, SI, NY.

REINAGLE, HUGH.
Landscape, genre and scene-painter. He was the son of Frank Reinagle, the lessee of the Chestnut St. Theater, Phila. He was born in Phila. before 1790. Reinagle studied scene-painting with John J. Holland; he also painted landscapes, among which are "A View of the City of NY," "Niagara Falls," and several views on the Hudson River, NY. He worked in both water colors and oils. Died May 23, 1834 in New Orleans, LA.

REINDEL, EDNA.
Sculptor. Born in Detroit, MI, in 1900. Studied: Pratt Institute Art School. Awards: Art Directors Club, 1935; fellowship, Tiffany Found., 1926, 1932; Beverly Hills Art Festival, 1939. Collections: Metropolitan Museum of Art, Dallas Museum of Fine Arts; Whitney Museum of American Arts; Ball State Teachers College; Canajoharie Art Gallery; Life Magazine Collection; New Britain Art Inst.; Labor Bldg., Wash., DC; Fairfield Court, Stamford, Conn.; Governor's House, St. Croix, Virgin Islands; US Post Office, Swainsboro, Georgia.

REINDEL, WILLIAM GEORGE.
Painter and etcher. Born Fraser, Macomb Co., MI, June 25, 1871. Studied in America and Europe; largely self-taught. Member: Cleveland SA; Chicago SI. Represented in NY Public Library; British Museum; Victoria and Albert Museum; Metropolitan Museum; Cleveland Museum; Butler Art Institute, Youngstown, OH. Died in 1948. Address in 1929, Brushwood, R.F.D., Euclid, OH.

REINHARD, SIEGBERT.
Illustrator. Born in Germany in 1941. Began his career in 1959 and two years later came to the US. He has had his illustrations published in Oui magazine as well as accepted in several S of I Annual Exhibitions. Known for his incredibly intricate paper sculptures, he has utilized this skill in the design of many sets for television productions. He is presently working in Los Angles, Calif.

REINHART, BENJAMIN FRANKLIN.
Painter. Born in Penna. Aug. 29, 1829. He studied in the National Academy, NY. He was elected an Associate Member in 1871. Among his works, many of which have been engraved, are "Cleopatra," "Evangeline," "Young Franklin and Sir William Keith," and "Washington Receiving the News of Arnold's Treason." He died May 3, 1885 in Philadelphia.

REINHART, CHARLES STANLEY.
Painter. Born in Pittsburgh, Penna., in 1844; died in 1896. Genre painter and illustrator. Employed by Harper and Brothers. Studied in Paris, and at the Royal Academy, Munich, under Professors Streyhuber and Otto. Awards: Second medal, Paris Exposition, 1889; Temple gold medal, Pennsylvania Academy of Fine Arts, 1888. Member: of Art Clubs in Munich, Pittsburgh and NY. Represented at Corcoran Art Gallery, Washington, D.C.

REINHART, STEWART.
Painter, sculptor and etcher. Born in Baltimore in 1897. Pupil of Edward Berge and Maxwell Miller. Address in 1926, 45 Washington Square, New York, NY.

REINHART, WILLIAM HENRY.
(See Rinehart, William Henry). Born Frederick, MD. on Sept 13, 1825. Died Oct. 28, 1874.

REISNER, IRMA VICTORIA.
(Mrs. Ferdinand Betzlmann). Portrait painter. Born Budapest, Hungary, Dec. 24, 1889. Pupil of Max Klinger, Audubon Tyler. Member: North Shore A. Lg.; Chicago NJSA; All-Ill. SFA; Am. APL; AFA. Address in 1929, "Casa del Sol," Hibbard Road, N. of Lake Avenue, Wilmette, IL.

REISS, FRITZ WINOLD.
Painter, Int. Arch., and teacher. Born in Germany. Pupil of Franz Von Stuck; Royal Academy, Munich. Member: Am. Des. Gal.; Arch. Lg. Work: Appoll's Theatre, South Sea Island Ballroom of Hotel Sherman, Chicago; Restaurant Crillon, Restaurant Elysee, New York City; Tavern Club, Chicago; Hotel St.

George, Brooklyn. Special work, collection portraits of eighty-one Indians for Great Northern R. R., exhibited in principal Art Institutes and Museums in US. Address in 1929, 108 W. 16th Street, New York, NY.

REISS, LIONEL S.
Painter, illustrator, etcher, writer, and lecturer. Born Austria, Jan. 29, 1894. Studied in NY, Paris and Berlin. Member: S. Indp. A. Illustrated "Ethnic Studies of Jewish Types," "The Forum." Lecturer on "The Jew in Art." Address in 1929, 55th Street, New York, NY; summer, Provincetown, MA.

REITER, FREDA L.
Painter and graphic artist. Born in Phila., PA, in 1919. Studied: Moore Institute of Design; Penn. Academy of Fine Arts; Barnes Found.; San Carlos Academy, Mexico. Award: Graphic Sketch Club, 1938, 1940. Collections: Library of Congress; Carnegie Institute; Phila. Inquirer.

REITZEL, MARQUES E.
Painter, etcher, and lecturer, and teacher. Born Fulton, IN, March 13, 1896. Pupil of Seyffert, J. A. St. John, Kroll, Norton, Carl Buehr, Foster. Member: Chicago SA; Chicago PS; Chicago Gal. A; Hoosier Salon; Am. Coll. AS; Am. APL. Awards: Butler purchase prize , AIC, 1927 and 1928; Logan prize and medal, AIC, 1927; Muncie Star prize, Hoosier Salon, 1929. Work: "Queen Ann's Lace," Chicago Municipal Collection for public schools; "Morning Route," "His First Circus," Chicago Public Schools Art Society; "Six O'clock," Hobart (IN) High School, Rockford, IL; "July Afternoon," Rockford College; "The Last Cover," Dakota Boys School, Dakota, IL; "Swimmers," Rockford Public Schools Collection. Professor of Fine Arts, Rockford College. Director, Rockford Art Museum. Address in 1929, Rockford College, Rockford, IL; summer, "The Whipporwill," Oregon, IL.

RELYEA, CHARLES M.
Illustrator and painter. Born Albany, NY, April 23, 1863. Pupil of PAFA under Thomas Eakins; F. V. Du Mond in NY and Paris. Member: Salma. C.; Allied AA; Alliance; Players' C.; GFLA; Fellowship PAFA. Address in 1929, 15708 Quince Avenue, Flushing, LI, NY.

REMBSKI, STANISLAV.
Painter. Born Sochaczen, Poland, Oct. 8, 1896. Member: Brooklyn SA. Work: "Nude," Newark Museum, Newark, NJ; "Portrait of Father James O. S. Huntington," Kent School, Kent, CT; "Portrait of Emanuel Swedenborg," Church of the Neighbor, Brooklyn, NY. Address in 1929, 280 Hicks Street, Brooklyn, NY.

REMICK, CHRISTIAN.
Painter. Born April 8, 1726 in Eastham, MA. An early Boston artist, who painted views of Boston Harbor, and of the Boston Commons at the time of the Revolution.

REMINGTON, FREDERIC.
Sculptor, painter, etcher and illustrator. Born in Canton, NY, Oct. 4, 1861. Studied one year at Yale Art School, but otherwise was self-taught. Due to ill health he went West, after clerking in a general store, became a cowboy and later stockman on a ranch. It was from the knowledge gained in these connections and from his own experiences that sprang the inspiration for his remarkably vivid and faithful portrayal of the life on the western plains and in the mining camps, for which he became so justly renowned. His first commission, executed in the early eighties, was an Indian picture based on "Geronimo's Campaign." He produced a large number of oil paintings and about fifteen bronzes, and was the author of several books. In 1888 "The Century" published his illustrated edition of Teddy Roosevelt's Ranch Life and the Hunting Trail. Travelled with Roosevelt's Roughriders to Cuba in 1898 as artist correspondent. He received a silver medal for sculpture at the Paris Exp. in 1889; he was an Associate Member of the NAD, and a

member of the National Inst. of
Arts and Letters. In collections
of Amon Carter Mus., Tex.; Whitney
Gal. of West. Art; Remington Art
Mem., Ogdensburg, NY. Died Dec.
26, 1909, in Ridgefield, CT.

REMSEN, HELEN Q.
Sculptor. Born in Algona, Iowa, in
1897. Studied: U. of Iowa;
Northwestern U.; Grand Central
School of Art; also studied with
Georg Lober and John Hovannes.
Awards: Society of Four Arts, Palm
Beach, Florida, 1942; Norton
Gallery of Art, 1944; Dallas Museum
of FA, 1944; Florida Federation of
Art, 1941, 1942, 1944; National
Sculpture Exhib., Sarasota, 1953;
Smithsonian Inst., 1954; New Orleans
Art Assoc., 1955, 1957. Coll.:
Jungle Gardens, Sarasota; St.
Boniface Church, Sarasota.

RENAUD, PHIL.
Illustrator. Born in Edmonton,
Canada, in 1934. He studied at
Chic. AFA and then, after a brief
stay in a Chic. studio, attended
ACD, studying under J. LaGatta and
E. Edwards. Returning to Chicago,
he received many assignments from
book publishers such as Scott,
Foresman Co., Harper & Row, and
Rand McNally. Playboy, Atlanta,
and Chicago have featured his
editorial work. Lately he has been
concentrating on fine art painting.

RENAULT, JOHN FRANCIS.
Painter. The "Surrender of
Cornwallis," engraved by Tanner,
Vallance, Kearny & Co., after a
drawing by J. F. Renault, published
in 1824 was sold to subscribers.
It might be interesting to note
that the original painting of the
"Surrender of Cornwallis" by J. F.
Renault was exhibited by him
throughout the US previous to 1824.
In a prospectus published by
Benjamin Tanner in the New England
Palladium & Commercial Advertiser
for Feb. 10, 1824, we are told that
"The Engraving is executed by
Tanner, Vallance, Kearney & Co.
from an Original Drawing by J. F.
Renault."

RENCH, POLLY MARY.
Miniature painter. Working in
Phila. before the Revolution,

according to Charles Willson Peale,
who instructed her in painting.
Also mentioned in a letter from C.
W. Peale to his son Rembrant in
1812 (publ. in Sartain's
Reminiscences). She married
William Rush, modeler and carver.

RENEZETTI, AURELIUS.
Sculptor. Executed a portrait bust
of the late N. W. Ayer. Address in
1926, 226 Ionic Street,
Philadelphia, PA.

RENIER, JOSEPH.
Sculptor. Born in 1887. Member:
NSS. Award: Prize, Garden C. of
Am., 1929. Died in 1966. Address
in 1929, 402 Second Street, Union
Hill, NJ.

RENWICK, HOWARD CROSBY.
Painter. Member: Allied AA.
Address in 1929, 33 West 67th
Street, New York, NY.

RESLER, GEORGE EARL.
Etcher. Born Waseca, MN, Nov. 12,
1882. Member: Chicago SE.
Awards: First prizes, 1913 and
1923, and second prize, 1914,
Minnesota Art Commission; bronze
medal for etching, St. Paul Inst.
1918. Represented in the print
collections of the Chicago Art
Inst.; Smithsonian Inst.,
Washington; Municipal Art Gallery,
Tampa; St. Paul Institute. Address
in 1929, 45 W. 4th Street, h. 2136
Lincoln Avenue, St. Paul, MN.

RETTIG, JOHN.
Painter. Born in 1860 in
Cincinnati, OH. Pupil of
Cincinnati Art School, Duveneck and
Potthast; Collin, Courtois and
Prinet in Paris. Member: Salma.
C.; Cincinnati AC (hon.); AFA.
Died in 1932. Address in 1929,
2227 Kemper Lane, Walnut Hills,
Cincinnati, OH.

RETTIG, MARTIN.
Painter. Born Cincinnati. Pupil
of Frank Duveneck. Member:
Cincinnati AC. Address in 1929,
127 East 3rd Street.; h. 110
Findlay Street, Cincinnati, OH.

REUTERDAHL, HENRY.
Naval painter. Born Malmo, Sweden,
in 1871. Served as correspondent

during Spanish-American War; also during the first part of the European War, 1914. Contributor to leading magazines. He was attached to the Battleship Minnesota during the fleet's cruise around South America, and during the cruise to the Mediterranean, 1913. He was present during the Vera Cruz campaign, 1914. Represented in permanent collection at the United States Naval Academy, by paintings of this cruise, presented to the Navy by George Von L. Meyer, Sec. of Navy; also in the National Museum, Washington; Naval War Collection, Newport; Toledo Museum. Silver medal for painting, Panama-Pacific Exp., 1915. Painted panels for steam yachts "Noma," Vincent Astor, owner; "Viking," G. F. Baker, Jr.; for schooner "Vagrant," Harold S. Vanderbilt, owner. Formerly instructor of Art Students League. Member: Architectural League; Artists' Fund Society of NY; Associate Member of US Naval Inst.; Society of Naval Architects and Marine Engravers. Club: New York Yacht. Address in 1925, 800 Boulevard, Weehawken, NJ. Died Dec. 20, 1925 in Washington, D.C.

REVERE, PAUL.
Engraver. Born Jan. 1, 1735 in Boston, MA. The father of Paul Revere came from the Island of Guernsey and established himself in Boston as a goldsmith. In this business the son was trained in Boston, and he there learned to engrave upon silver-plate. Aside from some possible book-plates, his best known engraved plates may be noted as follows: a "Portrait of Jonathan Mahew"; "The Repeal of the Stamp Act (1766)"; the caricature of the seventeen Rescinders, and "The Landing of the British Troops" (1768); also his famous "Boston Massacre" of 1770. For the Royal American Magazine of 1774-75, Revere engraved a number of plates. His work is exceedingly crude in execution and is only valuable for its historical interest. See "Paul Revere and His Engraving," by William Loring Andrews. Died May 10, 1818 in Boston.

REYNARD, CAROLYN COLE.
Painter and instructor. Born in Wichita, KS on Aug. 6, 1934. Award: Nine awards in State, Local, and Regional Exhibs. Collections: Wichita State Univ. Gal. Address in 1980, 110 College Ave., Poughkeepsie, NY.

REYNARD, GRANT TYSON.
Painter, illustrator, and etcher. Born Grand Island, NE, Oct. 20, 1887. Pupil of AIC; Chicago AFA; C. S. Chapman and Harvey Dunn. Member: Salma. C.; SI. Died in 1967. Address in 1929, 312 Christie Hgts., Leonia, NJ.

REYNOLDS, FREDERICK THOMAS.
Etcher and mezzotint engraver. Born London, Feb. 19, 1882. Studied in London. Settled in NYC. Member: Brooklyn SE; Salma. C. Address in 1929, 17 East 14th Street; h. 602 West 157th Street, New York, NY. (Biblio.: Frederick Reynolds, An American Master of Mezzotint, by W. H. Nelson; Vol. I, The Print Connoisseur.)

REYNOLDS, HARRY REUBEN.
Painter, craftsman, lecturer, and teacher. Born Centerburg, OH, Jan. 29, 1898. Pupil of AIC; Lee Randolph, Birger Sandzen. Member: Oakland AL; Alumni AIC; Delta Phi. Delta. Award: Harper Brothers gold medal, AIC, 1923. Address in 1929, Utah Agricultural College, Logan, Utah.

REYNOLDS, THOMAS.
In the New York Daily Advertiser, 1786, Thomas Reynolds advertises that he has established a "seal manufactory in Phila.; where he engraves on stone arms, descents; and he likewise cuts on brass all sorts of state and public seals."

REYNOLDS, WELLINGTON JARARD.
Portrait painter and teacher. Born Chicago, April 9, 1866. Pupil of Laurens and Constant in Paris; Royal Academy in Munich. Member: Chicago SA; Cliff Dwellers; Chicago gal. A. Awards: Medal, Marshall Field ex., 1908; medal of honor, Chicago SA, 1910; composition prize, AIC, 1920; and Norman W. Harris medal, 1921; second prize, Paris Salon, 1925; bronze medal,

Sesqui-Centennial Expo., Phila., 1926. Work: Portrait of Mr. Hitchcock, Univeristy of Chicago; "The Coquette," Golden Gate Park Museum, San Francisco; "A Votre Sante," Piedmont Gallery, Oakland, CA; "Les Miserables," Springfield, IL, State Museum; "Portrait Decorative," City Museum, Laurel, MI. Address in 1929, 3 E. Ontario Street, Chicago, IL.

RHEAD, LOIS WHITCOMB.
Sculptor, and craftsman. Born Chicago, IL, Jan. 16, 1897. Pupil of F. H. Rhead; L. V. Solon. Member: NA Women PS; Amer. Ceramic S. Address in 1929, 504 College Street, E. Liverpool, OH; summer, Santa Barbara, CA.

RHEAD, LOUIS JOHN.
Painter. Born in Etruria, England, in 1857. Came to United States in 1883. Painter in oil and water colors, exhibiting in America and European galleries. Gold medal, Boston, 1895, for artistic posters; gold medal, St. Louis Exposition, 1904. Address in 1926, 217 Ocean Avenue, Brooklyn, NY. Died July 29, 1926 in Amityville, NY.

RHETT, ANTOINETTE FRANCESCA.
Painter and etcher. Born Baltimore, MD, Oct. 7, 1884. Pupil of Alfred Hutty. Member: Charleston EC; Artists of Charlston (assoc.); SSAL. Address in 1929, 9 Logan Street, Charleston, S.C.

RHETT, HANNAH McCORD.
Painter and teacher. Born Columbia, S.C., Feb. 28, 1871. Pupil of ASL in NY; Collin and Laurens in Paris. Member: ASL of NY; Carolina Art Assoc. (Assoc.); S. Indp. A. Awards: Bronze and silver medals, AAS. Address in 1929, Brevard, N.C.

RHIND, JOHN MASSEY.
Sculptor. Born Edinburgh, Scotland, July 9, 1860. Pupil of his father, John Rhind, R.S.A.; Dalou in Paris; came to US in 1889. Member: NSS 1893; NY. Arch. Lg. 1894; NY Municipal AS; NAC; Salma. C.; Allied AA; Brooklyn SA. Awards: National scholarship, South Kensington, London; gold medal, St. Louis Exp., 1904. Work:

Astor door, Trinity Church, NY; equestrian, "George Washington," Newark, NJ.; "Stephen Girard," Philadelphia; "Peter Stuyvesant," Jersey City; "Tobert Burns," Pittsburgh; McKinley Memorial, Niles, OH; "Apollo," "Minerva," "J. G. Butler, Jr." "Wisdom," "Authority," Butler Art Institute, Youngstown, OH.; numerous decorations for federal and municipal buildings. Died in 1936. Address in 1929, 208 East 20th Street, h. 34 Gramercy Park, New York, NY.

RHODES, HELEN NEILSON.
Painter and teacher. Born Milwaukee, WI. Pupil of Arthur W. Dow. Member: Seattle FAS; Northwest Print Makers (pres.). Awards: First prizes, 1923 and 1925, and second prize, 1924, Seattle PAS; first prize and gold medal, International Salon of Water Colors, Provincial Exhib., New Westminster, B.C., 1928. Author of articles on university problems in design. Illustrated "Paul Bunyan Comes West" (Houghton Mifflin Co.), 1928. Died in 1938. Address in 1929, Art Dept., Univ. of Washington; h. University Apts., Seattle, Wash.

RIBCOWSKY, DEY DE.
Marine painter. Born in Bulgaria in 1880. Studied in Paris. Address in 1926, 233 South Broadway, Los Angeles, CA.

RICCI, ULYSSES ANTHONY.
Sculptor. Born in 1888. Member: NSS, 1914. Died in 1960. Address in 1929, 206 East 33rd Street, New York, NY.

RICCIARDI, CAESARE.
Painter. Born in Italy in 1892. Pupil of Academy of Fine Arts, Philadelphia. Address in 1926, Art Alliance, 1823 Walnut Street, Philadelphia.

RICE, E. A.
This portrait engraver in mezzotint was working for Baltimore engravers about 1845.

RICE, JAMES R.
Engraver. Born in Syracuse, NY, in 1824. He studied engraving under

his brother W. W. Rice, of Rawdon, Wright, Hatch, & Co., of NY. He moved to Philadelphia in 1851, and as late as 1876 was engraving portraits there in connection with J. Earle.

RICE, MARGHUERITE SMITH.
(Mrs. Fred Jonas Rice). Sculptor. Born St. Paul, MN, June 11, 1898. Pupil of Edward Pausch. Member: Buffalo SA; Guild Allied A. Address in 1929, The West Brook Apts., 675 Delaware Ave., Buffalo, NY.

RICE, W. W.
Engraver of portraits and subject plates, who was a member of the firm of Rawdon, Wright, Hatch & Co., of NY in 1846. He was engraving over his own name as late as 1860.

RICE, WILLIAM CLARKE.
Painter and sculptor. Born in Brooklyn, NY, April 19, 1875. Pupil of George de F. Brush. Grad. of NY City College, 1897. Also painted mural decorations, incl. those at Park Central Hotel, NYC. Taught art and design in NYC Schools. Member of Arch. League & Nat. Soc. Mural painters. Died Feb. 13, 1928 in NYC. Address in 1926, 145 East 23d Street, New York.

RICE, WILLIAM MORTON JACKSON
Portrait painter. Born in Brooklyn in 1854. Studied painting in Paris under Carolus-Duran, in 1881-84. Elected as Associate Member of the National Academy in 1900. He died Oct. 13, 1922.

RICE, WILLIAM SELTZER.
Painter, illustrator, craftsman, writer, and teacher. Born Manheim, PA, June 23, 1873. Pupil of Phila. School of Industrial Art and of Howard Pyle at Drexel Inst., Phila. Member: Calif. SE; Calif. P.M.; San F. AA; Oakland AA; Pacific AA. Work: "The Salmon Fleet - Oakland Estuary," Calif. State Library; "Windswept Cypress" and "Old Adobe - Monterey," Calif. School of Arts and Crafts, Oakland; "Glacier High Sierras," Golden Gate Park Museum, San Francisco. Illustrator for "Phila. Times," 1885-1889; teacher

of art and drawing, Calif. Pub. Schools, 1900-1928; head of art dept., Fremont High School, Oakland, 1914-1929. Address in 1929, 2083 Rosedale Avenue, Oakland, CA.

RICE-MEYEROWITZ, JENNY DELONY.
Painter, illustrator, writer, lecturer, and teacher. Born Washington, AR. Pupil of Cincinnati Art Academy; St. Louis School of Fine Arts; William M. Chase; Julian, De Launce and Delecluse Academies in Paris. Member: NAC; NA Women PS; FAC of AR (hon). Work: Portraits of "Jefferson Davis," "Gov. George W. Donaghey" and "Gov. Thomas C. McRae," Arkansas State Capitol; "Mrs. Jefferson Davis," Confederate Museum, Richmond, VA.; "George G. Williams," NY Clearing House, New York City; "Dr. George T. Stewart," Metropolitan Hospital, New York City; "Rt. Rev. Bishop H. N. Pierce," Trinity Cathedral, Little Rock, AR.; and other public portraits. Address in 1929, 140 West 57th Street, New York, NY.

RICH, FRANCES L.
Sculptor and draftsman. Born in Spokane, WA, on Jan. 8, 1910. Studied: Smith College; Cranbrook Academy of Art; Claremont College; Columbia Univ.; with Malvina Hoffman, Carl Miles, and Alexander Jacovleff. Collections: Army and Navy Nurse Memorial, Arlington National Cemetery; Purdue Univ.; Wayside Chapel of St. Francis, Grace Cathedral, San Fran.; Mt. Angel Abbey, St. Benedict, Oregon; Hall of Fame, Ponca City, Oklahoma; Smith College; St. Peters Church, Redwood City, Calif.; Univ. of Calif., Berkeley; Madonna House, Combermere, Ontario, Canada; Carl Milles Museum Garden, Stockholm; Univ. of Oklahoma; science medal, Dr. Jonas Salk. Media: Bronze. Address in 1980, P.O. Box 213, Palm Desert, CA.

RICH, JOHN HUBBARD.
Painter. Born Boston, MA, March 5, 1876. Pupil of ASL of NY; School of Boston Museum of Fine Arts. Member: Cal. AC; Salma. C. Awards: Paige traveling scholarship from School of Boston Museum of Fine

Arts, 1905-07; silver medal San Diego Exp., 1915; Black prize, CA AC, 1917; second prize, Calif. AC, 1916; Ackerman prize, Calif. AC, 1919; silver medal, Panama-CA. Exp., San Diego, 1916; Harrison prize, Los Angeles Museum, 1922; Phoenix, Ariz., 1928; Sacramento, CA., 1928. Represented Los Angeles Museum; Utah Art Institute; University; Scripps College; University of Southern Calif.; Calif. State Fed. of Women's Clubs. Address in 1929, 2262 San Marco Drive, Hollywood, CA.

RICHARD, BETTI.
Sculptor. Born in NYC on Mar. 16, 1916. Studied: Art Students League with Mahonri Young, Paul Manship. Awards: National Academy of Design, 1947; Pen and Brush Club, 1951; gold medal, Allied Artists of America, 1956. Collections: Doors, Oscar Smith Mausoleum; Church of the Immaculate Conception, NY; Pieta Skouras Memorial, NY; Bellingrath Gardens, Mobile, Alabama; monument to race horse "Omaha" at Ak-Sar-Ben Track, Omaha; figure, Austrian Legation, Tokyo; figure, Sacred Heart Rectory, Roslindale, Mass.; House of Theology, Centerville, Ohio; statue, St. Francis of Assisi Church, NY. Address in 1980, 131 E 66th St., NY, NY.

RICHARDS, ELLA E.
Painter. Born in Virginia. Pupil of Lefebvre, Collin and Robert Fleury in Paris. Member: PBC. Specialty, portrait and genre painting. Address in 1929, 1009 Carnegie Hall, New York, NY.

RICHARDS, FREDERICK DE BERG.
Painter and etcher. Born in 1822. Lived for years in Philadelphia. He died there in 1903.

RICHARDS, FREDERICK THOMPSON.
Painter. Born in Phila., May 27, 1864. Pupil of the PAFA, Thomas Eakins, Edmund B. Bensell, and of the ASL, NY. Exhibited at the Paris Expo., 1900. On staff of Life since 1889, also Collier's Weekly; cartoonist for New York Herald, 1901-02; also for New York Times, New York Evening Mail;

Philadelphia Press and the Phila. North American. Author: "The Royal Game of Gold" (series of color prints); "Color Prints from Dickens" (portfolio); and "The Blot Book." Address in 1926, 110 West 48th Street, New York, NY. Died July 8, 1921 in Phila.

RICHARDS, GEORGE MATHER.
Painter and illustrator. Born Darien, CT, Sept. 3, 1880. Pupil of Douglas John Connah, Robert Henri, Edward Penfield. Member: Salma. C.; Silvermine G.; NY Arch. Lg. Illustrator for "The Golden Book," McMillan Co. Address in 1929, New Canaan, CT.

RICHARDS, GLENORA.
Painter. Born in New London, Ohio in 1909. Studied: Cleveland School of Art. Awards: American Society of Miniature Painters, 1947; Penn. Society of Miniature Painters, 1947; National Association of Women Artists, 1953; Washington Miniature Painters and Sculptors Society, 1956, 1957. She is a miniaturist. Collections: Phila. Museum of Art.

RICHARDS, HARRIET ROOSEVELT.
Painter and illustrator. Born Hartford, CT. Pupil of Yale School of Fine Arts; Frank Benson in Boston; Howard Pyle in Wilmington, DE. Member: Paint and Clay C. of New Haven. Illustrated Holiday edition of books by Louisa Alcott and W. D. Howells, etc. Died in 1932. Address in 1929, 422 Whitney Ave., New Haven, CT.

RICHARDS, JEANNE HENON.
Painter and etcher. Born in Aurora, IL, in 1923. Studied: Univ. of Illinois; Colorado Springs Fine Arts Center; Iowa State Univ.; also studied with William S. Hayter, Mauricio Lasansky. Awards: Fulbright fellowship, 1954-1955; Des Moines Art Center, 1953; Univ. of Southern Calif., 1954; Bradley Univ, 1954; Nelson Gallery of Art, 1954. Collections: Society of American Graphic Artists; Des Moines Art Center. Address in 1980, 9526 Liptonshire, Dallas, TX.

RICHARDS, LEE GREENE.
Painter, sculptor, and illustrator.

Born Salt Lake City, July 27, 1878.
Pupil of J. T. Harwood, Laurens and
Bonnat. Member: Salon d'Automne;
Paris AAA; Utah SA; NAC. Award:
Hon. mention, Paris Salon, 1904.
Died in 1950. Address in 1929, 125
So. 2d East, Salt Lake City, Utah.

RICHARDS, LUCY CURRIER.
(Mrs. F. P. Wilson). Sculptor.
Born Lawrence, MA. Pupil of Boston
Museum School; Kops in Dresden;
Eustritz in Berlin; Julian Academy
in Paris. Member: Copley S.;
Boston GA; NA Women PS; MacD.C.
Address in 1929, Silvermine,
Norwalk, CT.

RICHARDS, MYRA REYNOLDS.
Sculptor and painter. Born
Indianapolis, Jan 31, 1882. Pupil
of Herron Art Institute under Otis
Adams, Rudolf Schwartz and Geo.
Julian Zolnay. Member: Hoosier
Salon. Died in 1934. Address in
1929, 446 North Alabama Street,
Indianapolis, IN.

RICHARDS, OREN C.
Painter. Born in South Boston in
1842. In 1860 he studied under
George Innes at Medford, MA. He
painted scenery at nearly all the
Boston theaters, and easel-pictures
of still-life in oils.

RICHARDS, THOMAS ADDISON.
Painter. Born Dec. 3, 1820 in
London England. He came to America
in 1831, his early years being
passed in Gerogia and the
Carolinas. He painted landscapes
and views of Lake George and the
White Mountains. He became
Secretary of the National Academy
of Design and had his studio in NY.
He also was well known as an author
and illustrator of books on art and
travel. He died at Annapolis, MD,
June 29, 1900.

RICHARDS, WALTER DuBOIS.
Illustrator. Born in Penfield, OH,
in 1907. Studied at the Cleveland
Institute of Art under Henry G.
Keller, Frank Wilcox, and Carl
Gaertner. In 1930 his first
published illustration was done in
dry brush for Child Life magazine.
He won the highest award in
lithography from the Cleveland
Museum, the Lily Saportas Award

from the AWS in 1962 and a Special
Award from the USAF in 1964. He
has done extensive book, magazine,
and poster illustrations since 1940
and his work appeared in the 200
Years of Watercolor Painting
exhibition in 1966 at the
Metropolitan Museum of Art.

RICHARDS, WILLIAM TROST.
Marine painter. Born Philadelphia,
PA, Nov. 14, 1833. Pupil of Paul
Weber; later studied in Florence,
Rome and Paris. Awards: Medal,
Centennial Expo., Phila, 1876;
Temple medal, Pennsylvania Academy
of the Fine Arts, 1885; bronze
medal, Paris Exp., 1889. Member:
American Water Color Society;
honorary member, National Academy
of Design. Represented by "On the
Coast of NJ," painted to order for
the Corcoran Art Gallery, 1883;
also "On the Coast of New England,"
painted in 1894. See "Life of
William T. Richards," by Harrison
S. Morris, Philadelphia, 1912.
Died Nov. 8, 1905 in Newport, RI.

RICHARDSON, ANDREW.
Born 1799 in Scotland. This man is
noted in Tuckerman's "Artists Life"
as painting landscapes about 1860.
The National Academy of Design
elected Andrew Richardson a member
in 1833. He died in 1876, in NYC.

RICHARDSON, CATHERINE PRIESTLY.
Painter. Born New York City, Nov.
22, 1900. Pupil of Philip L. Hale.
Member: NA Women PS. Award:
First prize in open competition of
life drawings, Boston, 1921.
Address in 1929, 11 Welch Road,
Brookline, MA.

RICHARDSON, CLARA VIRGINIA.
Painter, etcher, and teacher. Born
at Philadelphia, April 24, 1855.
Pupil of Ferris, Moran,
Daingerfield and Snell. Member:
Plastic C.; Phila. Alliance;
Alumnae of the Phila. School of
Design for Women. Address in 1929,
"The Sherwood," Portland, ME.

RICHARDSON, CONSTANCE COLEMAN.
Painter. Born in Indianapolis, IN,
on Jan. 18, 1905. Studied: Vassar
College; Penn. Academy of Fine
Arts. Collections: John Herron
Art Institute; Detroit Institute of

782

Art; Penn. Academy of Fine Arts; Saginaw Museum of Art; Grand Rapids Art Museum; New Britain Institute. Address in 1980, 285 Locust St., Phila., PA.

RICHARDSON, FRANCIS HENRY.
(See Richardson, Frank Henry). Artist. Born Boston, MA. on July 4, 1859. Died in 1934.

RICHARDSON, FRANK HENRY.
Painter. Born Boston, MA, July 4, 1859. Pupil of Julian Academy in Paris under Boulanger and Lefebvre. Member: Salma. C., 1901; Gloucester SA; North Shore AA. Awards: Hon. mention, Paris Salon, 1899; bronze medal, AAS, 1902. Work: "Hauling Seaweed," Boston Art Club; "Breton Widow at Prayer," Lasell Seminary, Auburndale, MA; "Portrait of Rear Admiral George F. F. Wilde," Town Hall, Braintree, MA.; "Dr. William C. Collar," Roxbury Latin School, Boston, MA. Died in 1934. Address in 1929, County Road, Ipswich, MA.

RICHARDSON, FREDERICK.
Illustrator, painter, and teacher. Born Chicago, IL, Oct. 26, 1862. Pupil of St. Louis School of Fine Arts; Doucet and Lefebvre in Paris. Member: Century Assoc.; SI, 1905; AFA. Died in 1937. Address in 1929, Century Assoc., 7 West 43d Street, New York, NY; Cliff Dwellers, Chicago, IL.

RICHARDSON, GRETCHEN.
Sculptor. Born in Detroit, MI, in 1910. Studied: Wellesley College; Art Students League with William Zorach; Academy Julian, Paris. Awards: National Association of Women Artists, 1952, 1955.

RICHARDSON, HELEN ELY.
Sculptor, who exhibited at the Penna. Academy of the Fine Arts, Philadelphia, 1924. Address in 1926, 213 Alexandrine Street, Detroit, MI.

RICHARDSON, MARGARET F.
Painter. Born Winnetka, IL, Dec. 19, 1881. Pupil of DeCamp; Ernest L. Major, Tarbell. Member: AFA. Awards: Harris bronze medal and prize ($300). AIC, 1911; Maynard portrait prize ($100), NAD, 1913;

second prize, Duxbury AA, 1920. Work: Self portrait, PAFA. Address in 1929, 274 Commonwealth Ave., Boston, MA.

RICHARDSON, MARION.
Painter, and etcher. Born Brooklyn, NY, Jan. 24, 1877. Pupil of Chase, Du Mond, Senseney and others. Member: Calif. PM.; NA Women PS; AFA. Died Dec., 1952. Address in 1929, 19 East 71st Street, New York, NY.

RICHARDSON, MRS. MARY CURTIS.
Painter. Born NY, April 9, 1848. Pupil of Benoni Irwin, Virgil Williams and William Sartain. Member: AFA. Awards: Norman Dodge prize, NAD, 1887; medals for figure painting, CA. State Fair, 1887, and Industrial Exp., San. F., 1915; medals for figure painting, CA State Fair, 1916, 1917, 1919. Work in: Golden Gate Park Museum, San Francisco; Music and Art Association, Pasadena, Calif., Calif. Palace of the Legion of Honor, San Francisco. Address in 1929, 1032 Vallejo Street, San Francisco, CA.

RICHARDSON, MARY NEAL.
Portrait painter. Born Mt. Vernon, ME, Feb. 17, 1859. Pupil of Boston Museum School; Colarossi Academy and A. Koopman in Paris. Member: Copley S. 1897. Work: "Prof. Charles C. Hutchins," Walker Art Gallery, Bowdoin College, Brunswick, ME. Address in 1929, 309 Fenway Studios, 30 Ipswich Street, Boston, MA; summer, Canton, ME.

RICHARDSON, S.
This man was a bookplate engraver apparently working about 1795, but with no indication of locality. The one known example of his work represents a woman with left hand on an anchor, with ships in the distance. In the base is a blank tablet surmounted by an urn. On the tablet is written in ink "I. H. Swale, 1795." The plate is signed "S. Richardson Sculpsit."

RICHARDSON, THEODORE.
Landscape painter. Born Readfield, ME, in 1855. For years he made a

specialty of Alaskan scenery. He died Nov. 1914, in Minneapolis, MN.

RICHERT, CHARLES HENRY.
Painter. Born Boston, MA July 7, 1880. Pupil of De Camp, Andrew and Major in Boston. Member: Boston SW CP; CT AFA; Boston AC; AM WCS. Address in 1929, 10 Linden Street, Arlington Heights, MA; summer, Ellsworth, ME.

RICHEY, OAKLEY E.
Painter, craftsman, writer, lecturer, and teacher. Born Hancock Co., In., March 24, 1902. Pupil of Forsyth, Hadley, Pogany, Stuart Walker, Kimball, G. Bridgman. Member: IN AA. Art Director, Stuart Walker Repertory Co., 1921-1923; instructor in decorative arts, John Herron Art School, 1924-1927. Writer and director of numerous pageants and masques "Ages of Beauty," "Masque of Legends," "Feast of Trimont," "Masque of the Hours," Pageant of the Palette," etc. Address in 1929, care of the John Herron Art School; h. 1433 North Pennsylvania Street, Indianapolis, IN.

RICHMOND, AGNES M.
Painter. Born Alton, IL. Pupil of ASL of NY; St. Louis School of Fine Arts. Member: NA Women PS; Allied AA.; Brooklyn SA; Brooklyn Modern A; Goucester SA.; CT. AFA. Awards: Watrous figure prize, NA Women PS., 1911; water color prize, NA Women PS., 1922. Address in 1929, 211 Greene Ave., Brooklyn, NY.

RICHTER, WILMER SIEGFRIED.
Illustrator. Born Philadelphia, Penn., Jan. 20, 1891. Pupil of School of Industrial Art, Philadelphia. Member: Phila. Sketch C. Address in 1929, 1214 Walnut Street, Philadelphia, Penn.; h. 39 Penn. Ave., Brookline Manor, Del. Co., Penn.

RICKETSON, WALTON.
Sculptor. Born May 27, 1839 in New Bedford, MA. Engaged as sculptor since 1870. Among his notable works are: Portrait busts of A. B. Alcott, Louisa May Alcott, Henry D. Thoreau, George William Curtis, R. W. Emerson; also intaglios, bas-releifs; he was the designer of the Gesnold memorial tower on the Island of Cuttyhunk, MA, in 1902. Address in 1926, 10 Anthony Street, New Bedford, MA.

RIDDELL, MRS. ANNETTE IRWIN.
Painter. Born Oswego, NY. Pupil of Vanderpoel; Freer; AIC; Collin; Courtois; Girardot; Royer and Prinet at Julian Academy in Paris. Member: Laguna Beach AA; Alumni AIC. Address in 1929, Riddell Studio, Coast Blvd. at Diamond St., Laguna Beach, CA.

RIDDELL, WILLIAM WALLACE.
Painter. Born Chicago, IL, March 21, 1877. Pupil of AIC; Constant and Laurens in Paris. Member: Palette and Chisel C.; Laguna Beach AA; AFA. Address in 1929, Riddell Studio, Laguna Beach, CA.

RIDDLE, ALICE L.
See Mrs. Hans Kindler.

RIDER, ALEXANDER.
Historical and miniature painter, who flouished 1810-25 in Philadelphia. Rider came to the United States with his countryman Krimmel from Germany, and in 1811 he is listed as a "Fancy Painter," and in 1812 as a "Miniature Painter." There was a Rider in Charleston, S.C. in 1819 but it is not certain that he was the same man.

RIDER, CHARLES JOSEPH.
Painter, draftsman, lecturer, and teacher. Born Trenton, NJ, Jan 21, 1880. Pupil of William M Chase, S. Macdonald-Wright Member: Amer. Soc. of Bookplate Collectors and Designers. Address in 1929, 611 - 36th Street, San Pedro, CA.

RIDGWAY, W.
This excellent engraver of historical subjects in line was working in New York in connection with Wm. Wellstood, and was engraving for New York publishers at a much later date.

RIEKER, ALBERT GEORGE.
Sculptor. Born Stuttgart, Germany Oct. 18, 1890. Pupil of Academy of Fine Arts, Munich; Acad. of Fine Art, Stuttgart. Member: N.O. ACC

N.O. AA; SSAL. Work: E. V. Mente Monument, Mente Park, New Orleans; Joseph Sinai memorial, Masonic Temple, New Orleans; Colonel William Temple Withers monument, Vicksburg National Military Park, Vicksburg, MI; Rabbi Max Heller memorial, Temple Sinai, New Orleans; bas-reliefs, "Life and Death," Vaccaro Mausoleum, Metairie Cemetary, New Orleans. Died in 1959. Address in 1929, 628 Toulouse Street, h. 4714 St. Peter Street, New Orleans, LA.

RIES, GERTA.
Sculptor, who exhibited a portrait of John Cotton Dana at the Annual Exhibition of the National Academy of Design, 1925. Address in 1926, 130 Henry Street, Brooklyn, NY.

RIESENBERG, SIDNEY.
Painter and illustrator. Born Chicago, IL, Dec. 12, 1885. Pupil of AIC. Address in 1929, 739 Palisade Ave., Yonkers, NY.

RIGBY, MRS. F. G.
Portrait painter, who died in New York. Her husband, also a portrait painter, is deceased.

RIGGS, ROBERT.
Painter. Born in 1896. Exhibited water colors at the Penna. Academy of Fine Arts, Philadelphia, 1925. Address in 1926, 218 Walnut Street, Philadelphia, PA.

RIGNEY, FRANCIS JOSEPH.
Painter, illustrator, and writer. Born Waterford, Ireland, Jan. 20, 1882. Pupil of Metropolitan School of Art, Dublin. Member: NAC. Illustrated: "The Clipper Ship" and "Ships of the Seven Seas," by Daniel Hawthorne. Art Editor, "Boy's Life Magazine." Address in 1929, 62 East 90th Street, New York, NY.

RIIS, ANNA M.
Draftsman, craftsman, and teacher. Born in Norway. Pupil of Royal and Imperial School for Art and Industry, Vienna; Royal Art School of Christiania. Member: Cincinnati Woman's AC; Crafters; Cincinnati Ceramic C. Address in 1929, care of Art Academy; h. 3325 Burnet Ave., Cincinnati, OH.

RILEY.
This name, as "Riley, Engraver," is signed to poorly engraved music and words published by J. & M. Paff, City Hotel, Broadway, New York. The date is apparently about 1800.

RILEY, KENNETH.
Illustrator. Born in Waverly, MO, 1919. Studied at KCAI and the ASL, where he was taught by Harvey Dunn, DuMond, Benton, and George Bridgman. He illustrated The Greatest Story Ever Told by Anthony Trollope and he has done work for The Saturday Evening Post, Life, National Geographic, Reader's Digest, and McCall's. His work is owned by the Custer Museum, West Point Museum and the White House Collection.

RILEY, MARY G.
Painter. Born Washington, D.C. in 1883. Pupil of Birge Harrison and Henry B. Snell. Member: S. Wash. A.; NA Women PS.; Wash. AC.; NAC; AFA. Award: Bronze medal, S. Wash. A., 1923; purchase prize, NAC, 1928. Died in 1939. Address in 1929, 2141 Le Roy Place, Washinton, D.C.

RILEY, NICHOLAS F.
Illustrator. Born in Brooklyn, NY, in 1900. Attended PI and Mr. Scott School in Paris. His first illustration was a full color oil done for the West Point Year Book in 1928. Good Housekeeping, The Saturday Evening Post, Woman's Home Companion, and Field and Stream are some of the magazines for which he illustrated. His portrait work was selected and hung at the Paris Grand Salon in 1925. Died in 1944.

RIMMER, WILLIAM HENRY.
Sculptor and painter. Born Feb. 20, 1816 in Liverpool, England. He died in South Milford, MA, Aug. 20, 1879. He came to this country in 1818, and in 1860 modelled the "Falling Gladiator" now in the Boston Museum of Fine Arts. He painted a number of other pictures besides producing numerous works of sculpture. It is however as a teacher that Dr. Rimmer is best known.

RINEHART, WILLIAM HENRY.
Sculptor. Born in Frederick, MD,
Sept. 13, 1825. He worked with a
stone cutter and studied drawing in
Baltimore. In 1855 he went to Italy
to study and while there executed
the bas-reliefs of "Night" and
"Morning." In 1857 he opened his
studio in Baltimore. His best known
statues are "Clytie" owned by the
Peabody Inst. and "Rebecca" in the
Corcoran Art Gallery. He executed
many portrait busts. His statue of
Chief Justice Taney ordered by the
State of MD was unveiled at
Annapolis in 1872. Died Oct. 28,
1874 in Rome, Italy.

RING, ALICE BLAIR.
Painter. Born Knightville, MA.
Pupil of Laurens, Julian Dupre,
Hitchcock, Mme. La Forge and
Meichers in Paris; ASL of NY and in
Washington. Member: Cleveland
Woman's AA; Laguna Beach AA; Calif.
S. Min. P.; AFA. Award: First
prize for oil painting, Pomona,
1922; hon. mention, miniature, Long
Beach, CA., 1928. Address in 1929,
225 East Pasadena Street, Pomona,
CA.

RINGIUS, CARL.
Painter, craftsman, and writer.
Born Bastad, Sweden, Dec. 3, 1879.
Pupil of Charles Noel Flagg and
Robert B. Brandegee at Hartford.
Member: CT AFA; Soc. of Graphic
Art, Stockholm; Chicago AG;
Gloucester SA; Provincetown AA;
Scandinavian Am. A.; Springfield A.
Lg.; Salma. Club; Springfield (IL)
AA; Alliance; North Shore AA; IL.
Acad. FA; Swedish-AM. AA; Am. APL.
Represented Vanderpoel Art Assn.,
Chicago; "Sweden in Foreign Lands,"
Museum, Gothenburg; "Evening Gold,"
State Museum, Springfield, IL.
Address in 1929, 62 Vernon Street,
Hartford, CT; summer, East
Gloucester, MA.

RIOPELLE, JEAN PAUL.
Born in Montreal, Canada, in 1923.
Largely self-taught. Since 1947 he
has lived in Paris France.
Exhibitions: Galerie Greuse,
Paris, 1950; Galerie Springer,
Berlin, 1951; Galerie Fachetti,
Paris, 1952; Galerie Henriette
Niepoe, Paris, 1952; Galerie Pierre

Loeb, Paris, 1953; Galerie Evrard,
Lille, France, 1954; Pierre Matisse
Gallery, New York, 1954; Galerie
Rive Droite, Paris, 1954; Gimpel
Fils Gallery, London, 1956; Galerie
Jacques Dubourg, Paris, 1956, 1960;
Galerie Kolnischer Kunstverein,
Cologne, 1958; Galerie Kestner
Gesellschaft, Hannover, 1958;
Galerie Kunst und Museumsverein,
Wuppertal, Germany, 1958;
Kunsthalle, Galerie Richentor,
Basel, 1959; Galerie Ann Abels,
Cologne, 1959. Group Exhibitions
at the Venice Biennale d'arte,
1954; Museu de Arte Moderna de Sao
Paulo, Brazil, 1955, 1961;
Leverkusen, Holland, 1956; the
Galerie Charpentier, Paris,
1956-1958; Bonn, Germany, 1957;
Arthur Tooth & Sons, London, 1957;
The National Gallery of Canada,
Ottawa, 1957, 1963; Galerie Kleber,
Paris, 1957; Palais des Beaux Arts,
Brussels, 1958; Kassel, Germany,
1959; Krakow, Poland, 1959; Walker
Art Center, Minneapolis, 1959;
Warsaw, Poland, 1959; Goteborg,
Sweden, 1960; Kyoto, Japan, 1960;
the Salon de Mai, Grand Palais,
Paris, 1960; Tokyo, Japan, 1960;
Kolnischer Kunstverein, Cologne,
1962.

RIPLEY, AIDEN LASSELL.
Painter. Born Wakefield, MA, Dec.
31, 1896. Pupil of the School of
the Museum of Fine Arts, Boston.
Member: Boston GA; Boston WCS;
Copley S. Awards: Logan purchase
prize and medal, AIC, Chicago, IL,
1928; co winner, first Dacre Bush
prize, Boston WCS, 1929. Work:
"Swedish Peasant Girls," Art
Institute of Chicago, Chicago, IL.
Died in 1969. Address in 1929, 98
Chestnut Street, Boston, MA.

RIPLEY, LUCY PERKINS.
Sculptor. Born in Minnesota.
Pupil of Saint Gaudens. Member:
NA Women PS; NSS. Awards: Barnett
prize, NA Women PS, 1919; bronze
medal, St. Louis Exp., 1904. Died
Sept 5, 1949. Address in 1929,
East 17th Street, 12 West 10th
Street, New York, NY.

RISQUE, CAROLINE EVERETT.
Sculptor. Born St. Louis, MO,
1886. Pupil of St. Louis School of
Fine Arts under Zolnay and

Colarossi Academy in Paris under Injalbert and Paul Barlett. Member: St. Louis AG. Awards: Western prize ($50), St. Louis AG., 1914; Halsey C. Ives prize, St. Louis AG., 1922; thumbbox prize, St. Louis A. Lg., 1924; small sculpture prize, St. Louis AG., 1924. Represented in Museum of New Orleans; St. Louis Artists' Guild. Address in 1929, 7263 Henderson Avenue, Clayton, MO.

ISWOLD, GILBERT P.
Sculptor. Born in Sioux Falls, S.D., in 1881. Pupil of Lorado Taft and of Charles Milligan. Work: "Statue of Stephen A. Douglass," Springfield, IL; "Mormon Pioneer Monument," Salt Lake City, Utah. Address in 1926, 1038 Fine Arts Building, 410 South Michigan Avenue, Chicago, IL.

ITCHIE, ALEXANDER.
Painter. Born Scotland, Feb. 19, 1863. Pupil of RI School of Design. Member: S. Indp. A.; Brooklyn SA. Address in 1929, Harrison Ave., Hicksville, LI, NY.

ITCHIE, ALEXANDER HAY.
Born Jan. 14, 1822 in Glasgow, Scotland. Ritchie studied drawing in Edinburgh under Sir Wm. Allan, and came to NY in 1841. He apparently learned to engrave after he reached this country; but he ultimately established an extensive general engraving business in NY, his earlier prints being issued about 1847. Ritchie himself was a very clever engraver of portriats in mezzotint, and it is claimed that he finished every plate that went out of his establishment. He also painted in oils, and began exhibiting at the Academy in 1848, and was an Associate Member in 1863, and in 1863, and an Academician of the National Academy of Design in 1871. Died Sept. 19, 1895 in New Haven, CT.

ITMAN, LOUIS.
Painter. Born in Russia, Jan. 6, 1889. Pupil of William Chase, John Vanderpoel, W. J. Reynolds. Awards: Silver medal, Panama-Pacific Int. Expo., San Francisco, 1915; first prize, Chicago AG, 1915. Work: "Early

Morning," Chicago Municipal Art League; "Sun Spots" and "Spring Morn," Des Moines Gallery, Des Mones, Iowa. Died in 1963. Address in 1929, 1826 Millard Ave., Chicago, IL; summer, Giverny, Eure, France.

RITSCHEL, WILLIAM.
Marine painter. Born Nuremberg, Germany, July 11, 1864. Pupil of F. Kaulback and C. Raupp in Munich; came to U.S. in 1895. Member: ANA 1910, NA 1914; NYWCC; AWSC; Salma. C. 1901; A. Fund S.; NAC; Kunstverein, Munich; Allied AA; Calif. WCS. Awards: Hon. mention, Salma C.; hon mention, CI Pittsburgh, 1912; Carnegie prize, NAD, 1913; gold medal, $1,000, NAC, 1914; gold medal, P.-P. Exp., San F., 1915; gold medal, State Fair, Sacramento, CA, 1916; gold medal, Phila. AC, 1918; Ranger purchase prize, NAD, 1921; Isidor medal, Salma. C., 1923; Harris prize, AIC, 1923; R. F. prize, 1923-1926. Work: "Rocks and Breakers," PA Acad. of the Fine Arts; "Across the Plains, AR," Ft. Worth (TX) Mus.; "Desert Wanderers," Chicago Art Inst.; "Fog and Breakers," Detroit Art Club; "Rockbound Coast," City Art Mus.; St. Louis; "Evening Tide, CA," Smithsonian Inst, Wash. DC; "Carmel-by-the-Sea and Point Lobos," LA Mus.; "Inrush of the Tide," Albright Art Gallery, Buffalo. Died in 1949. Address in 1929, care of the Milch Galleries, 108 West 57th Street, New York, NY.

RITTENBERG, HENRY R.
Painter and teacher. Born Libau, Russia, Oct. 2, 1879. Pupil of W. M. Chase at PAFA; Bavarian Academy; Ludwig Heterich in Munich. Member: NA; Fellowship PAFA; Phila. AC; Salma. C.; NAC; Allied AA.; Wash. AC; McD. Club of NY; Painters and Sculptors Gallery Assoc; Beaux Arts Inst. of Design; Alliance; A. Fund Soc.; A. Fellowship. Awards: Cresson Traveling Scholarship, PAFA, 1904; Hon. mention, AC Phila, 1906; Maynard portrait prize, NAD, 1920; Harris prize, AIC, 1925; Proctor portrait prize, NAD, 1926. Work: "Caroline Augusta," "Still Life Fish," Butler Art Inst., Youngstown, OH. Instructor, ASL of NY; Beaux Arts Inst. of Design.

Address in 1929, 222 W. 59th Street, New York, NY.

RITTER, ALONZO W.
Painter. Born Hagerstown, MD, Jan. 7, 1898. Pupil of D. M. Hyde. Member: Balto. SIA1; NYSIA; Am. APL. Address in 1929, 863 Dewey Ave., Hagerstown, MD.

RITTER, ANNE GREGORY.
Painter and cratfsman. Born Plattsburg, NY, July 11, 1868. Pupil of Charles Melville Dewey and Robert Reid. Member: Boston SAC; AFA. Awards: Bronze medal for pottery, St. Louis Exp., 1904; first prize, Boston SAC, 1907. Work: "Anne in the Garden," Broadmoor Art Academy; "March Landscape," Denver Art Museum. Died in 1929. Address in 1929, 1152 York Street, Denver, CO.

RIVERA, SOPHIE.
Photographer. Studied: Educational Alliance, NYC; Apeiron Workships, Inc., Millerton, NY; New School for Social Research, NYC. Exhibitions: Crossroads Gallery, NYC, 1974; Third Eye Gallery, NYC, 1973; Women's Interart Center, NYC, 1973, 1974, 1975. Collections: Apeiron Workshops, Inc.; Women's Interart Center, NYC.

RIX, JULIAN.
Painter. Born in Peacham, VT, in 1850; died in NY in 1903. Landscape painter. Self-taught. Commenced painting at the age of twenty-two, as a sign and decorative painter in San Francisco; afterward came East and settled in NY. Represented by "Pompton Plains, New Jersey," painted in 1898, at the Corcoran Gallery.

ROBB, ELIZABETH B.
Painter. Member: Pitssburgh AA; AFA. Awards: Third prize, AA Pittsburgh, 1914; first prize, AA Pittsburgh, 1915. Address in 1929, 24 Herron Ave., Emsworth, PA.

ROBBINS, ELLEN.
Painter in water colors, and pupil of the New Enlgand School of Design. Was born in 1828 and died in 1905. She is spoken of by Tuckerman in his "American Artists Life" as receiving many orders for exquisite water color painting of flowers and autumn leaves.

ROBBINS, FREDERICK (GOODRICH).
Painter, etcher, lecturer, and teacher. Born Oak Park, IL, May 8, 1893. Pupil of Carl N. Werntz Spencer Mackey, Lee Randolph Breckenridge, Meryman, Constance Mackey, Hendrick de Rooy. Address in 1929, 1923 Callowhill Street Philadelphia, PA.

ROBBINS, HORACE WOLCOTT.
Born Oct. 21, 1842 in Mobile, AL. He was elected an Associate Member of the National Academy in 1864 and an Academician in 1878, and in 1882 became recording secretary. He has worked both in oil and water colors, his pictures being chiefly landscapes of mountain and lake scenery. Among his works are "New England Elms," "Lake Katahdin, Maine," and Views of Jamaica. In 1865 he visited the West Indies with Frederick E. Church. He died Dec. 14, 1904, in NYC.

ROBBINS, JOHN WILLIAMS.
Painter and etcher. Born Windam, CT, Feb. 16, 1856. Studied in Boston and at New York art schools. Member: CT. AFA. Inventor of "The Bruleprint" and "Brulechrome." Died in 1939. Address in 1929, 2 Rockland Ave., Dorchester, Boston, MA.

ROBBINS, THERESA REYNOLDS.
Painter. Born Boston, May 8, 1893. Pupil of Philip L. Hale, Rosamon Smith. Member: Gloucester SA. Address in 1929, 22 Carlton Street, Brookline, MA; summer, Cottage Inn, Pearl Street, Nantucket, MA.

ROBERTS.
Engraver. Some rather poor line book illustrations published in N in 1841 are thus signed.

ROBERTS, ALICE MUMFORD.
See Culin.

ROBERTS, BISHOP.
Portrait painter and engraver, who was working in Charleston, S.C., in 1735. His advertisement appears in the South Carolina Gazette of May 1735. Died in Oct., 1739.

ROBERTS, BLANCHE G.
Sculptor, who exhibited "Beatrice" at Penna. Academy of Fine Arts in Philadelphia, 1915. Address in 1926, 284 Reservoir Place, Bronx, NY.

ROBERTS, EDITH ADELINE.
Painter and craftsman. Born Germantown, PA, June 8, 1887. Pupil of NY School of Fine and Appied A.; PAFA; Cecil Chichester, John Carlson, Chas. Rosen, Henry McFee, Andrew Dasburg. Member: Alliance; Woodstock AA. Address in 1929, Woodstock, NY.

ROBERTS, ELIZABETH WENTWORTH.
Painter. Born in Philadelphia, PA, in 1871. Pupil of Elizabeth Bonsall and of H. R. Poore in Philadelphia; of Bouguereau, Robert-Fleury, Lefebvre and Merson in Paris. Member: Penna. Academy of Fine Arts. Awards: Mary Smith prize, Penna. Academy of Fine Arts, 1889; honorable mention, Paris Salon, 1892. Work: "The Boy with the Violin," Pennsylvania Academy, Philadelphia; "The Madonnas of Marks," Asilo Giovanni in Bragora, Venice, Italy; "Reflections," Public Library, Concord, MA; "Concord March," Fenway Court, Boston. Address in 1926, Concord, MA Died March 12, 1927 in Concord, MA.

ROBERTS, HOWARD.
Sculptor. Born in Phialdelphia, April 1843. He studied art at the Penna. Academy of the Fine Arts. Modelled statuettes of Hawthorne's "Scarlet Letter," "Hypathia" and "Lucille," and numerous portrait busts. His statue of Robert Fulton is in the Capitol in Washington, D.C. He died in Paris in April, 1900.

ROBERTS, JOHN.
Painter and engraver. Born in Scotland in 1768; died in NY in 1803. He came to NY in 1793, says Wm. Dunlap. Roberts was engraving views, script, etc., in NY in 1796, and his name as an engraver appears in the directories of 1802-03. Dunlap describes him as a sort of universal genuis, ready to do anything, but erratic and incapable of turning his advantages to personal account. A small mezzotint portrait by him, of Washington, exists, which is extremely rich in effect and shows fine execution. Dunlap says this was engraved by Roberts in NY, in 1799, from a miniature portrait by Benjamin Trott. Owing to some misunderstanding between the painter and the engraver Roberts deliberately destroyed the copperplate and a few proof impressions alone remain. He painted miniatures, drew portraits in crayon, and was a musician, of no mean skill; but he abused his gifts, and died.

ROBERTS, MORTON.
Illustrator. Born in Worcester, MA, in 1927. Graduated from Yale Univ. School of Fine Arts. He illustrated for many major magazines, most notably Life, for which he painted a series on The History of Russia and The Story of Jazz. Among his many awards was the Edward Austin Abbey Fellowship from the NAD. He was an instructor of life drawing at PI. Died in 1964.

ROBERTS, NORMAN L.
Painter. Born Ironia, NJ, Aug. 8, 1896. Pupil of Henry G. Keller. Work: "Forgotten Days," Junior League Club, Cleveland, OH; "The Golden Fleece," Public Library, Cleveland, OH. Address in 1929, 3 West 108th Street, New York, NY.

ROBERTS, MRS. VIOLET KENT.
Painter, illustrator, and writer. Born The Dalles, OR, Nov. 22, 1880. Pupil of Benson, Beck, Moschcowitz, Prellwitz. Member: Alumni Pratt Inst. Died in 1958. Address in 1929, 3037 Dent Palce, N. W. Washington, D.C.

ROBERTSON.
Engraver. A large and well engraved front piece, apparently intended for an edition of Cook's Voyages, of about 1815, is signed "Robertson Sc." While this plate bears some indication of American origin, it may be English.

ROBERTSON, ALEXANDER.
Miniature painter. Born May 13, 1768. He also worked in water colors, chiefly in landscape. Like

his brother Archibald he was well known as a teacher. He died in 1841, in NYC.

ROBERTSON, ARCHIBALD.
Painter, designer and etcher. Born May 8, 1765 in Monymusk, near Aberdeen, Scotland. He studied art in Edinburgh and London from 1782 to 1791. In the latter year he came to the U.S., bringing with him from his patron, the Earl of Buchan, and for presentation to General Washington, a box made of the oak that sheltered Sir William Wallace after the battle of Falkirk. At the request of the Earl of Buchan, Washington sat for his portrait to Robertson. From 1792 to 1821 he followed his profession in NY as a painter, largely in water colors, and was a teacher of drawing. He designed for engravers and the early lithographers of NY, and drew a number large views of NY, which were engraved. A Robertson was one of the founders and a director of the American Academy of Art. Died Dec. 6, 1835 in NYC.

ROBERTSON, W.
Engraver. This man was a script engraver employed in New York in 1831.

ROBERTSON, WALTER.
Born in Dublin, in 1793, he sailed with Gilbert Stuart for the United States. He worked in Phila. and New York, copying some of Stuart's portraits in miniature, and painting a number of miniatures of his own composition. Died in 1802 in India.

ROBESON, EDNA AMELIA.
Miniature painter. Born in Davenport, IA, in 1887. Pupil of Frank Phoenix and of the Art Student's League of New York. Member: Penna. Society of Miniature Painters. Address in 1926, Bettendorf, IA.

ROBIN, AUGUSTUS.
Engraver. Born in New York of French parentage. This good engraver of portraits and subject plates was in the employ of J. C. Buttre, of New York, for nearly forty years.

ROBINS, SUSAN P.B.
Painter. Born in Boston, 1849. Pupil of John Johnston, Ross Turner and F. Crowninshield; also of the Boston Museum School of under Philip Hale. Member: Copley Society, 1894. Address in 1926, 95 Mt. Vernon St., Boston, MA.

ROBINSON.
Engraver. This name is signed to a number of small, wonderfully designed, but poorly engraved plates illustrating an edition of Weems' "Life of Washington," published in 1815 by Matthew Carey, of Philadelphia.

ROBINSON, ADAH MATILDA.
Painter, artist, writer, lecturer, and teacher. Born Richmond, IN, July 13, 1882. Pupil of John F. Carlson, George Elmer Browne and AIC. Member: Okla. AA; Tulsa AA; AFA. Address in 1929, 1119 South Owasso, Tulsa, Okla.

ROBINSON, ALEXANDER.
Painter and teacher. Born Portsmouth, NH, May 11, 1867. Pupil of Lowell School of Design (Boston Museum of Art); Academie Julian, Paris, under Doucet and Constant. Member: NYWCC; Phila. WCC; Chicago WCC; AWSC; Salma. C.; Societe Nationale des Aquarellistes; Societe des Artistes Independents and Societe des Artistes Coloniale in Paris; Cercle d'Art, Tournai and Bruges, Belgium; United Arts Club, London. Award: Silver medal, P. P. Exp., San F., 1915. Work: "Church Interior" and group of 11 pastels, Toledo Art Museum; "Falling Leaves," Rockford (IL) Art Assoc; "Canal Venice," Mississippi Art Assoc, Jackson; "Jehaun-Ara," Pennsylvania Academy of the Fine Arts; ten painting and nine aquarelles, Delgado Museum, New Orleans; "Dordrecht" and "Spanish Coast," five aquarelles and twelve drawings, Newcomb Art Gallery, Tulane Univ., New Orleans; twenty-seven Italian water colors, Desmond Fitzgerald Art Gallery, Brookline, MA; "La Dame aux Tulipes" and "Summer," Museum d'Ixelles; "Autumn, England," Moscow (Russia); and in collection at Glasgow, Dundee, London, and Manchester (England). Address in

1929, 235 Faubourg Street, Honore, Paris, France; 18 Aldworth Street, Jamaica Plain, Boston, MA.

ROBINSON, ALONZO CLARK.
Sculptor and writer. Born Darien, CT, Sept. 3, 1876. Member: Soc. Inter. des Beaux-Arts et des Lettres. Address in 1929, 6 Rue Aumont- Therville; h. 17 Rue Cardinet, Paris, France.

ROBINSON, BOARDMAN.
Illustrator. Born in Nova Scotia, Canada, in 1876. Studied at the Mass. Normal Art School and in Paris. He worked as an art editor and illustrator for several magazines and also painted murals for Rockefeller Center in NY and the Department of Justice building in Washington. He illustrated Dostoievsky's The Brothers Karamazov in 1933 and The Idiot in 1916, both published by Random House. Since 1930 he has been a teacher and art director at the Colorado Springs Fine Arts Center. Died in 1952.

ROBINSON, CHARLES DORMAN.
Landscape and marine painter. Born in Vermont in 1847. Pupil of William Bradford, 1862; of Geo. Inness and M. F. H. DeHaas, 1863; of Gignoux and Cropsey, Newport, VT, 1866-67; studied under Boudin; also studied methods of Segantini, 1900, Paris. Resided in VT, 1861-73; in Clinton, IA; San Francisco since 1874 (except in Paris, France, 1899-1901). Dean of Pacific Coast artists. First diploma, Mechanics' Fair, San Francisco, 1860; money award, Sacramento State Agricultural Society, 1878; gold medal, same, 1903. Spent 19 seasons in the Yosemite and the high Sierras; has 84 paintings, mostly of the Yosemite Valley, in Great Britain. Member: San Fran. Art Association.

ROBINSON, DAVID.
Painter and illustrator. Born Warsaw, Poland, July 31, 1886. Studied in America, France and Germany. Member: SI, 1910; Salam. C.; S. Indp. A.; GFLA; Silvermine GA; AFA. Address in 1929, Silvermine, CT.

ROBINSON, FLORENCE VINCENT.
Painter. Born Boston, MA, Nov. 18, 1874. Pupil of Vignal in Paris. Member: Societe des Aquarellists, Paris; AWCS. Work: In Harvard Univ., Cambridge; Cleveland School of Art; Government collection of France; "Chateau de Versailles," Boston Museum of Fine Arts; 12 water colors of Spain, Hispanic Museum, New York; Brooklyn Museum of Fine Arts. Died in 1937. Address in 1929, 139 East 66th Street, New York, NY.

ROBINSON, HELEN AVERY.
Sculptor. Born in Louisville, Kentucky. She studied under Solon H. Borglum. Address in 1926, 200 West 58th Street, New York.

ROBINSON, IRENE BOWEN.
(Mrs. W. W. Robinson). Painter. Born South Bend, Wash., Nov. 27, 1891. Pupil of John F. Carlson; Otis AI. Member: Calif. AC; Laguna Beach AA; Calif. WCS; West Coast Arts, Inc.; "Younger Painters." Address in 1929, 2310 Palm Grove Ave., Los Angeles, CA.

ROBINSON, JOHN.
Miniature painter. Born C. 1774. He was an English artists who settled in Philadelphia., in 1817, where he died about 1829. He showed a miniature of West, with picture of "Christ Rejected" in the background, and said that Benj. West had sat for it. A miniature of Saml. Milligan is signed "J. R. 1819."

ROBINSON, L. S. MONA.
Painter, who exhibited in the Annual Exhibition of the Penna. Academy of Fine Arts, Philadelphia, 1924. Address in 1926, Paoli, Penna.

ROBINSON, NANCY BELL.
Painter and teacher. Born Big Cove, PA. Pupil of Deigendeisch and School of Industrial Art, Philadelphia. Member: Phila. Alliance; Plastic C. Address in 1929, Presser Bldg., 1714 Chestnut Street.; h. 2012 Mt. Vernon Street, Philadelphia, PA.

ROBINSON, NORA B.
Miniature painter, who exhibited at the PAFA, Philadelphia, 1925. Address in 1926, 9 Cedar Ave., Rockville Centre, Long Island, NY.

ROBINSON, THEODORE.
Painter of landscapes and figures subjects. Born in Irasburg, Vermont, 1852; died in New York in 1896. Pupil of Carolus-Duran and of Gerome. Awarded the Webb prize, 1890; Shaw prize, 1892. Represented by "Valley of the Seine from Giverny Heights," in the Corcoran Art Gallery. See Scribner's Magazine, "Field of Art" by Eliot Clark.

ROBINSON, THOMAS.
Painter. Born in Nova Scotia, Aug. 23, 1834. The Worcester Art Museum owns his painting "Fowls in Yard." He also painted a portrait group of five dogs that attracted much attention. Died March 1, 1888 in Providence, RI.

ROBINSON, VIRGINIA C.
Painter. Born in Maryville, MO. Studied: William Woods College; Northwest Missouri State College; Columbia Univ. Awards: Kappa Pi, 1955; Collections: Mississippi Department of Archives and History, Jackson, Mississippi State College for Women; Blue Ridge Assembly, Black Mountain, North Carolina.

ROBINSON, W.
Engraver. Born 1825-30 this W. Robinson etched in a fairly good style a Masonic certificate published by R. D. Desilver, of Philadelphia. This may be the "Robinson" noted above.

ROBINSON, WILLIAM S.
Painter. Born East Gloucester, MA, Sept. 15, 1861. Pupil of MA. Normal Art School in Boston; Julian Academy in Paris. Member: ANA 1901, NA 1911; AWCS 1897; NYWCC 1891; Salma. C., 1896 (life); Lotos C., 1900 (life); A. Fund S., 1889; NAC, 1917 (life); Allied AA, 1919. Awards: Hon. mention, Paris Exp., 1900; hon. mention, Pan-Am. Exp., 1900; hon. mention, Pan-Am. Exp., Buffalo, 1901; Newhouse prize ($500), Salma C., 1901; bronze medal, St. Louis Exp., 1904;

Carnegie prize ($500), NAD, 1910; silver medal, Buenos Aires Exp., 1910; silver medal, P. P. Exp., San. F., 1915; bronze medal, Dallas, TX, Exh., 1915; Turnbull prize, Salma. C., 1917; fourth W. A. Clark prize ($500), and hon. mention, Corcoran Gallery, Washington, 1919; James W. Porter prize, Salma. C., 1922; Museum purchase prize ($500), 1925; Woodhull Adams Mem. sketch prize 1927; prize ($300), 1928 Lyme Art Assn.; 1st Altman prize (best landscape) ($1,000), NAD, 1929. Work: "The Golden Bough," Carnegie Institute, Pittsburgh; "Golden Days," Art Museum, Dallas, Texas; "Monhegan Headland," National Gallery, Washington, D.C. Museum o: Art, Cleveland, OH. Instructor NAD schools, 1920- 1928; CT College New London, CT, 1928. Died in 1945. Address in 1929, Old Lyme CT.

ROBINSON, WILLIAM T.
Painter. Born Somerville, MA Sept. 17, 1852. Pupil of George N Cass in Boston; Ecole des Beaux-Arts, Ecole de Medecine Gobelin Tapestry Schools Bouguereau and Diogene Maillart in Paris. Member: NAC (life) Represented in the Henry Gallery Seattle, Wash. Address in 1929 Dowling Bldg., Malden, MA.

ROBUS, HUGO.
Painter. Born in 1885. Exhibited in Philadelphia, 1921, i "Exhibtion of paintings Showing the Later Tendencies in Art." Address in 1926, 9 East 14th Street, New York City. Died in 1964.

ROCHE.
Engraver. Several of the plates o the American edition of Maynard' "Josephus," published in New York in 1791, are signed "Roche sc." N other plates are known.

ROCHE, M PAUL.
Etcher, painter, and teacher. Born Cork, Ireland, Jan. 22, 1885 Member: Brooklyn SW; Salma. C. AFA. Represented in Brooklyn Museum; Chicago Art Inst.; Detroit Institute; Library of Congress, Washinton, D.C. Address in 1929 723 Evesham Ave, Baltimore, MD.

ROCKEY, A. B.
Nothing is known about this painter except that he was born in Miffinsburg, Penna., in 1799. He moved to Philadelphia where he began painting about 1825. He worked in that city for many years painting portraits and copying pictures. The Penna. Historical Soc. owns several of his portraits.

ROCKWELL, EVELYN ENOLA.
Painter. Born Chicago, 1887. Pupil of PAFA; ASL of NY; Woodbury, and Chase. Member: NA Women PS; C. L. Wolfe AC. Specialty, portraits of children in pastel. Address in 1929, 40 Deepdene Road, Forest Hills, LI, NY.

ROCKWELL, NORMAN.
Illustrator. Born New York City, Feb. 3, 1894. Pupil of George Bridgman and Thomas Fogarty. Member: Salma. C.; New Rochelle AA; GFLA; SI. Famous for his illustrations for Saturday Evening Post; other magazines including American Magazine; Ladies Home Journal. Captured F. D. Roosevelt's war aims in Four Freedoms posters; Freedom of Speech poster is in collection of Met. Mus. of Art. Collections at Rockwell Mus., Stockbridge, Mass. Living in New Rochelle, NY, in 1929. Died in 1978, in Stockbridge, Mass.

ROCKWELL, ROBERT H.
Sculptor. Born Laurens, NY, Oct. 25, 1885. Represented in the Brooklyn Museum by small bronzes of animals.

ROCLE, MARGARET K.
Painter. Born Watkins, NY, March 6, 1897. Pupil of Robert Henri, Bredin, Wiles. Member: San Diego AG; S. Indp. A; Salons of Am. Address in 1929 899 Fourth Ave., Chula Vista, CA; summer, 107 Boulevard Street, Michel, Paris V. France.

ROCLE, MARIUS ROMAIN.
Painter. Born Brussels, Belgium, June 6, 1897. Member: San Diego AG; S. Indp. A; Salons of Am. Address in 1929, 899 Fourth Ave., Chula Vista, CA; summer, 107 Boulevard St. Michel, Paris V. France.

RODDY, EDITH J.
Painter. Born in Meadville, PA. Studied: Boston Museum of Fine Arts School; with Charles Hawthorne, George Pearse Ennis; and in Europe. Awards: Florida Federation of Art, 1938; Clearwater Art Association, 1946; Sarasota Federation of Art. Collections: Syracuse Museum of Fine Arts.

RODEWIG, DORIS.
Illustrator. Born in Westfield, NJ, in 1927. Attended PI and began her career as an illustrator in 1949. Since then she has shown her work in the National Arts Club, S of I, where she is a member, and the Salmagundi Club, which gave her the Best in Show Award in 1975. Her work hangs in the Pentagon and the Smithsonian Institution. Currently living in NYC, she is active in book illustration.

RODINA, K. MICHALOFF.
Sculptor. Exhibited at Penna. Academy of Fine Arts, Philadelphia, in 1915. Address in 1926, 439 Sixteenth Street, Brooklyn, NY.

ROE, MRS. ROBERT.
See Julie Stohr.

ROECKER, HENRY LEON.
Painter. Born Burlington, IA. Pupil of Academy of Design in Chicago; Gysis at Royal Academy in Munich. Member: Chicago SA; Chicago WCC; "The Cliff Dwellers"; "Cor Ardens." Awards: Hon. mention, Munich, 1889; Yerkes prize, AIC 1894; Arche C. prize, AIC 1897; Chicago SA medal, 1909; Carr prize, AIC 1911. Address in 1929, 444 East 42d Place, Hyde Park, Chicago, IL.

ROEHLK, ERNST.
Painter. Member: Chicago SA. Address in 1929, 115 East 30th Street, New York, NY.

ROERICH, NICHOLAS KONSTANTIN.
Painter. Born in 1874 in Russia. He came to America about 1920. Has painted Western scenes, also coast and lake vies in Maine. In 1921 he organized the "Master Institute of

United Arts" in New York City. Address in 1926, 310 Riverside Drive, New York City. He died in 1947.

ROGALL, WILHELMINE.
Painter. Member: NA Women PS. Address in 1929, 115 East 30th Street, New York, NY.

ROGERS, ADELE (MRS.).
Painter. Born Mount Vernon, NY, July 7, 1861. Pupil of Cooper Union, William M. Chase, Charles Hawthorne. Member: Provincetown AA; Fellowship PAFA; SSAL; Penn. Acad. FA. Address in 1929, East Palatka, Fla.; summer, Provincetown, MA.

ROGERS, BARKSDALE.
Illustrator and painter. Born Macon, GA. Pupil of Steinlen in Paris; also studied in Munich. Member: Greenwich SA; SI. Work: Illustrations for "Judge," "The New York Sunday World," "Scribners' Magazine" and "Puck." Address in 1929, Greenwich, CT.

ROGERS, CHARLES.
Miniauture painter, who flourished in Boston about 1846.

ROGERS, FRANCES.
Painter and illustrator. Born Grand Rapids, MI. Pupil of Howard Pyle. Member: GFLA. Illustrations for current magazines. Address in 1929, 350½ West 24th Street, New York, NY; summer, Bearsville, NY.

ROGERS, FRANKLIN WHITING.
Born in Cambridge, MA, in 1854. Pupil of J. Foxcroft Cole in 1874. He has devoted himself especially to the painting of dogs. Among his works are "The Two Friends," "Steady" and "Resignation."

ROGERS, GRETCHEN W.
Painter. Member: Boston GA; AFA. Award: Silver medal, P.-P. Exp., San. F., 1915. Exhibited portrait entitled "Young Girl" at PAFA (1914). Address in 1929, 210 Fenway Studios, Boston, MA.

ROGERS, HENRY W.
Miniature portrait painter, who flourished in Salem about 1782.

ROGERS, HOWARD.
Illustrator. Born in Medford, Oregon, in 1932. Studied at the ACD, where he graduated with honors in Advertising Illustration. Before becoming a free-lance illustrator, he worked for McNamara Studio, Graphic House and New Center Studio in Detroit. He has won several awards including an Award of Excellence from the S of I.

ROGERS, JANE.
Painter. Born New York, Aug. 1, 1890. Member: S. Indp. A; Salons of Am. Address in 1929, 28 West 63rd Street,; h. 210 West 70th Street, New York, NY; summer, Woodstock, NY.

ROGERS, JOHN.
Engraver. Born in England about 1808; died in New York about 1888, says Mr. Samuel Hollyer. Rogers came to NY in 1850-51, and he engraved for the book publishers a large number of portraits and some subjects plates. He generally worked in line and was a very good engraver.

ROGERS, JOHN.
Sculptor and modeller, who was born in Salem, MA, Oct. 30, 1829. His well-knonwn "Rogers Groups" were familiar subjects connected with the Civil War. His best known group of the "Slave Auction" was done in 1859. Mr. Rogers also executed the equestrian statue of General Reynolds which stands before the City Hall in Philadelphia. He was elected a member of the National Academy of Design in 1863, and belonged to the National Sculpture Society. He died July 26, 1904 in New Canann CT.

ROGERS, JOHN ARTHUR.
Etcher and Arch. Born Louisville KY, April 12, 1870. Pupil of AIC MA Inst. Tech. Ralph Seymour Member: SSAL. Died in 1934 Address in 1929, 508 Bellevue Ave. Daytona Beach, FL.

ROGERS, LOUISE DE GIGNILLIET.
Painter and etcher. Born Macon GA. Pupil of Steinlen, Paris Robert Henri, and also studied in

Munich. Member: Brooklyn SE; CT. SA. Painted portraits of Ex-Vice-Pres. Marshall, William Jennings Bryan, Senator Tillman and others. Address in 1929, Greenwich, CT.

ROGERS, MARGARET ESTER.
Painter. Born Birmingham, England, May 1, 1872. Pupil of F. L. Heath, L. P. Latimer and A. L. Bower. Member: West Coast Arts; Santa Cruz AL; Berkeley Lg. FE; San F. SWA; Oakland AL. Award: Hon. mention Statewide Exh., Santa Cruz, 1928. Died in 1961. Address in 1929, 99 Pilkington Ave., Santa Cruz, CA.

ROGERS, NATHANIEL.
Painter. Born in Bridgehampton, Long Island, 1788. He went to NY in 1811 and became a pupil of Joseph Wood, and soon took high rank as a painter of miniatures, among which were those of Fitz-Greene Halleck and Joseph Rodman Drake. He was one of the founders of the National Academy of Design in New York. Died Dec. 6, 1844 in Bridgehampton.

ROGERS, RANDOLPH.
Sculptor. Born in Waterloo, New York on July 26, 1825. About 1850 he went to Italy to study, and on his return he opened his studio in NY. In 1858 he designed the bronze doors for the Capitol in Washington. He also executed portrait statues of Abraham Lincoln for Philadelphia and of William H. Seward for NY. He resided in Italy from 1860. Died Jan. 15, 1892, in Rome.

ROGERS, MRS. RICHARD.
See Bean, Mary.

ROGERS, WILLIAM ALLEN.
Illustrator and writer. Born Springfield, OH, May 23, 1854. Member: SI (hon.); GFLA (hon.). Chevalier of the Legion of Honor, 1921. Work: Poster "Paid for in Full," Smithsonian Inst, Washington, D.C.; cartoons of war in "New York Herald." Author of "A World Worth While." Died in 1931. Address in 1929, 1404 29th Street, N. W. Washington, D.C.

ROHN, RAY.
Illustrator. Member: SI. Address in 1929, 218 Walnut Street, Philadelphia, PA.

ROLLE, A. H. O.
Painter. Born Minnesota, March 30, 1875. Pupil of Corcoran School of Art, Washinton, D.C. Member: S. Wash. A.; Wash. landscape C.; Wash. WCC; AFA. Address in 1929, 1422 Buchanan Street, N. W. Washington, D.C.

ROLLINSON, CHARLES.
Egnraver. Born c. 1793. Also a copperplate printer, living in New York in 1808-1832. He was probably a son, or other near relative, of William Rollinson, as his address for a considerable time was No. 28 John St., the same as that of Wm. Rollinson. The only plates found by the compiler, and signed by C. Rollinson as engraver, consist of architectural subjects, diagrams, etc. Died Jan. 19, 1833.

ROLLINSON, WILLIAM.
Engraver. Born in Dudley, Staffordshire, England, April 15, 1762; died in NY on Sept. 21, 1842. Rollinson was probably a silversmith and learned to engrave upon plate. He came to the United States prior to 1789, as he is credited with having ornamented the silver button on the coat worn by Washington at his inauguration as President. His earliest work upon copperplate appears in the American edition of Brown's family Bible, published in NY in 1792. This work is crude, though his small profile of Washington-executed in 1791, according to Wm. Dunlap-is a much better piece of work. Rollinson rapidly progressed in the art of engaving, and about 1796 he changed his style to stipple and furnished some very good portrait plates for the Analectic and other magazines. His large plate of Alexander Hamilton is said to have been commenced in 1800 and published by Rollinson, and the painter Archibald Robertson, in 1805.

ROLPH, JOHN A.
Engraver. Born 1799 in Essex, England. This reputable landscape engraver was working in NY,

1834-46., and probably later. Also a painter. Died in 1862.

ROLSHOVEN, JULIUS.
Painter and teacher. Born Detroit, Oct. 28, 1858. Pupil of Cooper Union, New York; Hugo Crola at Dusseldorf; Loefftz in Munich; Frank Duveneck in Florence; Robert-Fleury in Paris. Member: ANA; Soc. Nat. des Beaux-Arts, Paris; Secession, Munich; Detroit Fine Arts Soc. (hon.); International Art Congress; Paris Soc. A. and L.; Scarab Club, Detroit; Foreign Arts Club, Florence; Bene Merensa Societa di Belle Arts, Florence, Taos SA; NAC. Awards: Second medal, Paris Exp., 1889; hon. mention, Paris Exp., 1900; bronze medal, Pan-Am. Exp., Buffalo, 1901; medals, Munich, Berlin, Brussels and Chicago; silver medal, St. Louis Exp., 1904; Hors Concours, Societe Exp., 1904; Hors Concours, Societe Francaise, Paris. Work: "Chioggia Fishing Girl," and two etchings, Cincinnati Museum; "The Refectory of San Damaino, Assisi, "Detroit Inst.; represented in MN Museum, Brooklyn Museum, Detroit Athlectic Club, San Francisco Bohemian Club, Union Leauge Club of Chicago, Baltimore Museum Montclair Museum, Santa Fe Museum. Died Dec. 7, 1930 in NYC. Address in 1929, 140 West 57th Street, New York, NY.; 21 Viale Michelangelo, Florence, Italy.

ROMANO, CLARE CAMILLE.
Painter, lithographer, and printmaker. Born in Palisade, NJ, in 1922. Studied: Cooper Union Art School; Ecole des Beaux-Arts, Fontainebleau, France; Instituto Statale d'Arte, Florence Italy. Awards: Fulbright fellowship, 1958-1959; Tiffany Found., 1952; Brooklyn Museum; Metropolitan Museum of Art; NY Public Library; Library of Congress; Rochester Memorial Art Gallery; Penn. State Univ. Address in 1980, Sch. Art and Design, Pratt Inst., NY, NY.

ROMANO, NICHOLAS.
Painter, sculptor, craftsman, and writer. Born Montoro, Italy, Dec. 6, 1889. Pupil of Albert Laessle. Award: Hon. mention, AIC, 1928. Represented in Pennsylvania Academy

of the Fine Arts; Philadelphia Ar Alliance; Graphic Sketch Club o Philadelphia; Albright Gallery Buffalo; Memorial Gallery Rochester. Address in 1929, 31 Race Street, h. 826 Reed Street Philadelphia, PA.

ROMANS, BERNARD.
Engraver. Born in Holland abou 1720; died at sea in 1784. Roman was educated in England, and abou 1755 he came to the America Colonies. At the outbreak of th Revolution he entered the servic of the American Colonies, and wa present at Lexington and Bunke Hill, according to the statemen made in connection with hi published proposals for issuing hi view of the Battle of Bunker Hil and his map of Boston. Romans i referred to in the New York Mercur of 1775 as "The most skillfu draughtsman in all America," thoug his view of the battle of Bunke Hill is anything but artistic i its composition. He engraved thi view on a large scale, and it wa published by Nicholas Brooks, o Philadelphia, in September an October, 1775; "An Exact View o the Late Battle of Charlestown June 17, 1775" to give the plat its full title. It was re-engrave by Robert Aitken on a small scal and published PA Magazine for 1775

RONDONI, ROMOLO.
Sculptor, who exhibited at th Penna. Academy of the Fine Arts Philadelphia, 1914. Address i 1926, 35 East 30th Street, New Yor City.

RONINSON, RUTH C.
See Treganza.

RONNEBECK, ARNOLD.
Sculptor, writer, and lecturer Born Nassau, Germany, May 8, 1885 Pupil of Aristide Maillol and Emil Bourdelle in Paris. Awards Silver medal, Kansas City MO, 1928 Fine A. medal, City Club, Denver 1928. Work: Sixteen panels "Th History of Money," Denver Nationa Bank; "Madonna and Angels," St John's Cathedral, Denver Director, Denver Art Museum Address in 1929, 1300 Logan Street h. 2565 Albion Street, Denver, CO.

RONNEBECK, LOUISE E.
Painter. Born in Phila. PA, in
1901. Studied: Barnard College;
Art Students' League; American
School, Fontainebleau, France; also
studied with George Bridgman and
Kenneth Hayes Miller. Collections:
County Hospital, Greeley, Colorado;
Morrey Junior High School, Denver,
Colorado; Children's Hospital,
Denver, Colorado; Sloanes Lake Club
House, Denver, Colorado; Bermuda
High School for girls; Bermuda
Department of Agriculture; US Post
Office, Worland, Wyoming; Grand
Junction Colorado.

ROOK, EDWARD FRANCIS.
Painter. Born New York, NY, 1870.
Pupil of Constant and Laurens in
Paris. Member: ANA 1908; NA 1924;
Lotos C.; Lyme AA. Awards: Temple
gold medal, PAFA 1898; bronze
medal, Pan-Am. Exp. Buffalo, 1901;
two silver medals, St. Louis Exp.,
1904; bronze medal, CI. Pittsburgh,
1910; silver medal, Buenos Aires
Exp., 1910; gold medal, P. P. Exp.,
San. F., 1915; third W. A. Clark
prize ($1,000), and bronze medal,
Corcoran Gallery, Washington, 1919.
Work: "Deserted Street-Moonlight,"
PA. Acad., Philadelphia; "Pearl
Clouds-Moonlight" and "Wisteria,"
Cincinnati Museum; represented in
Boston Art Club and in Lotos Club,
New York, and Portland Art Museum.
Died in 1960. Address in 1929,Old
Lyme, CT.

ROOS, PETER.
Painter and teacher. Born Sweden,
Feb. 22, 1850. Member: Boston AC.
Award: Medal, Boston, 1874.
Specialty, landscape. Address in
1929, 24 Sacramento Street,
Cambridge, MA.

ROOSEVELT, SAMUEL MONTGOMERY.
Portrait painter. Born July 20,
1863 in New York City. Pupil of
Art Students' League of New York;
Academie Julian, Paris. Painted
portraits of Theodore Roosevelt,
Bishop James H. Darlington, Oliver
Belmont, Hudson Maxim, Henry F.
Shoemaker, Earl of Kintare, etc.
Member: National Association of
Portrait Painters; Artists' Fund
Society; Chevalier Legion of Honor,
France; Died Aug. 19, 1920 in NYC.

ROOT, ORVILLE HOYT.
Painter, who exhibited at the
Penna. Academy of Fine Arts,
Philadelphia, 1914. Address in
1926, Paris, France.

ROOT, ROBERT MARSHALL.
Painter and illustrator. Born
Shelbyville, IL, March 20, 1863.
Pupil of Constant, Laurens and
Lefebvre. Member: Brown Co.
Lefebvre. Member: Brown Co. (IN)
AA; Springfield (IL) AA; All-Ill.
SFA. Award: State Centennial
Medal, Springfield, 1918. WOrk:
Historical painting "Lincoln and
Douglass Debate, 1858" Springfield;
"Portrait Lt. Gov. Barat O'Harra",
Lt. Governor's office, Springfield;
"The Power, The Wisdom, The Justice
of the Law" in Atty. General's
office, Springfield. Address in
1929 Syndicate Bldg., Shelbyville,
IL.

ROPES, JOSEPH.
Painter. Born in Salem, MA, in
1812. He studied at the National
Academy of Design in NY in 1847.
He was in Italy from 1865 to 1876,
and exhibited landscapes in the
Centennial Exposition in
Philadelphia in 1876. His studio
was in Germantown for ten years.
He died in New York in 1885.

RORIMER, LOUIS.
Sculptor, Int. Arch. Craftsman,
lecturer, and teacher. Born
Cleveland, Sept. 12, 1872. Pupil
of Puech, Widaman, Le Blanc.
Member: Cleveland SA; Salma. C.;
Arts in Trade C. Died in 1939.
Address in 1929, Rorimer Brooks
Studios, 2232 Euclid Ave., h. Wade
Park Manor, Cleveland, OH.

ROSA, GUIDO.
Illustrator and draftsman. Born
New Jersey, Aug. 8, 1888. Pupil of
Edoardo Berta. Member: Salma. C.;
GFLA; AI Graphic A; AFA. Award:
Bronze medal, AI Graphic A, 1920.
Specialty, illustration and
decoration for magazines. Address
in 1929, 178 Eighteenth Street,
Union City, NJ.

ROSA, LAWRENCE.
Illustrator, and draftsman. Born
New Jersey, Aug. 10, 1892. Pupil
of Edoardo Berta. Member: Salma.

C.; GFLA; AI Graphic A. Award:
Bronze medal, AI Graphic A, 1920.
Specialty, magazine illustrations
and decoration. Address in 1929,
178 Eighteenth Street, Union City,
NJ.

ROSE, GEORGE L.
Painter. Born Newport, Rhode
Island, Oct. 8, 1861. Pupil of
John La Farge. Member: Mural
Painters. Address in 1929, 93
Valley Road, 6 Laural, Upper
Montclair, New Jersey.

ROSE, GUY.
Painter. Born in San Ganriel, CA,
in 1867. Pupil of Emil Carlsen in
San Francisco; Lefebvre, Constant
and Doucet in Paris. Member:
California Art Club. Awarded
honorable mention, Paris Salon,
1894; gold medal, Panama-California
Expo., San Diego, 1915; prize,
California Art Club, 1916. Died
Nov. 17, 1925.

ROSE,, RUTH STARR.
Painter and sculptor. Born in Eau
Claire, WI, July 12, 1887.
Studied: Vassar College; Art
Students' League of New York; and
with Hayley Lever. Member of
Southern States Art League;
Montclair Art Association; National
Arts Club, New York. Awards:
National Association of Women
Artists, 1937, 1944; State of New
Jersey, 1944; Washington
Printmakers, 1951; Norfolk Museum
of Art and Science, 1950; Corcoran
Gallery of Art, 1951; Virginia
Printmakers, 1957; Washington Area
Printmakers, 1957; Art Fair,
Alexandria and Washington, 1957;
Religious Art Fair, 1958.
Collections: Library of Congress;
Metropolitan Museum of Art; Vassar
College; Phila. Museum of Art;
Wells College; Williams College;
Milliken College; Norfolk Museum of
Arts and Science. Address in 1929,
Pickboune, Euston, MD; h. 71
Mountain Ave., Caldwell, NJ.

ROSELAND, HARRY.
Painter. Born Brooklyn, May 12,
1868. Pupil of J. B. Whittaker in
Brooklyn; Beckwith in NY. Member:
Brooklyn AC; Salma. C. 1896;
Brooklyn PS; Brooklyn SA. Awards:

Gold medal, Brooklyn AC 1888;
second Hallgarten prize, NAD 1898;
silver medal, Boston, 1900; bronze
medal Charleston Exp. 1902; silver
medal, AAS 1902; gold medal,
Boston, 1904; gold medal, AAS,
1907. Work: "The Blessing,"
"Toilers of the Field," Brooklyn
Inst. of Arts and Sciences;
Charleston Art Museum; Huntington
Art Museum. Specialty, negro
subjects. Address in 1929,
Ovington Studios, 246 Fulton
Street; h. 389 Bergen Street,
Brooklyn, NY.

ROSEN, CHARLES.
Painter. Born Westmoreland Co.,
PA, April 28, 1878. Pupil of NAD
and NY School of Art under Chase,
Du Mond and F. C. Jones. Member:
ANA 1912, NA 1917; NAC. Awards:
Third Hallgarten prize, NAD, 1910;
first Hallgarten prize, NAD, 1912;
Shaw purchase prize ($500), Salma.
C., 1914; hon. mention, CI
Pittsburgh, 1914; silvermedal,
P.-P. Exp., San F., 1915; Inness
gold medal, NAD, 1916; Altman prize
($1,000), NAD, 1916; first prize,
Columbus AL, 1925; Sesnan gold
medal, PAFA, 1926. Work: "Washed
Out Bottomlands," Minneapolis
Society of Fine Arts; "Late
Sunlight," Duluth Fine Arts Assoc.;
"Frozen River," Delgado Museum, New
Orleans, LA; "Winter Sunlight,"
Butler Art Inst., Youngstown, OH;
"North Haven," City Coast,"
University of Michigan, Ann Arbor.
Died in 1950. Address in 1929,
Woodstock, NY.

ROSEN, KAY.
Sculptor. Born in Corpus Christi,
TX, in 1943. Studied: Newcomb
College, New Orleans; Northwestern
Univ.; The Art Institute of
Chicago. Exhibitions: Del Mar
College, Texas; Univ. of Chicago;
ARC Gallery, Chicago, 1975.

ROSENBAUER, WILLIAM WALLACE.
Sculptor, craftsman, and teacher.
Born Chambersburg, PA, June 12,
1900. Pupil of St. Louis School of
Fine Arts; Alexandre Archipenko.
Member: Kansas City SA. Award:
Silver medal, Kansas City Art
Inst., 1925, 1926, and 1929; gold
medal, Kansas City AI, 1927; first
sculpture award, Second Missouri

Art Exhib. St. Louis, 1929. Address in 1929, care of the Kansas City Art Inst.; h. 3500 Crillham Road, Kansas City, MO.

ROSENBERG, HENRY MORTIKAR.
Painter. Born New Brunswick, NJ, Feb. 28, 1858. Pupil of Royal Academy in Munich; studied in Florence and Venice. Member: Salma. C., Vice-Pres. Nova Scotia College of Art, Halifax. Died in 1947. Address in 1929, Hotel Sitronelle, Citronell, AL; Halifax, N.S.; h. Dartmouth, N.S.

ROSENBERG, JAMES N.
Painter. Born Allegheny City, PA, Nov. 20, 1874. Member: NAC; S. Indp. A.; Wash. AC; AFA. Died in 1970. Address in 1929, 165 Broadway; 27 West 67th Street, New York, NY.

ROSENBERG, LOUIS C.
Illustrator and etcher. Born Portland, OR, May 6, 1890. Pupil of MA Inst. of Tech.; American Academy in Rome; Royal College of Art, London. Member: Phila. SE; Brooklyn SE; Chicago SE; Royal Soc. Painters, Etchers and Engravers. Awards: Silver medal, Calif. PM, 1924; Logan medal, Chicago SE, 1925 and 1927. Prints in Smithsonian Institution and Congressional Library, Washington, DC; Victoria and Albert Museum, London; British Museum, London, New York Public Library. Address in 1929, Greenfield Hill, Fairfield, CT.

ROSENBERG, MANUEL.
Illustrator, caroonist, writer, lecturer, and teacher. Born New Orleans, Jan. 29, 1897. Pupil of Duveneck; Meakin; Carl Werntz; John Maynard. Member: Commercial AC of Cincinnati; Western AA. Author of "Newspaper Art," "Practical Art," "Cartooning and Drawing," "Art in Advertising" (Harper Bros., 1929). Art Editor "The Cincinnati Post." Chief artists, The Scripps-Howard League of Newspapers. Address in 1929, The Cincinnati Post; Artists' Bldg., 35 East Third Street, h. 3592 Bogart Ave., Avondale, Cincinnati, OH.

ROSENBERG, SAMUEL.
Portrait painter. Born Philadelphia, PA, June 28, 1896. Pupil of Collens, Sparks and Volk. Member: Pittsburgh AA. Award: 1st prize, Pitts. AA, 1920. Represented in Pittsburgh public schools. Address in 1929, Carnegie Inst. of Technology; h. 340 Coltart Ave., Pittsburgh, PA.

ROSENBERG, SAMUEL MARTIN.
Painter and teacher. Born Washington, DC, Dec. 1893. Member: Springfield AL; Springfield, AG. Address in 1929, 2690 Main Street, Springfield, MA.; summer, Congmond Lake, Southwick, MA.

ROSENBLUM, REGINA.
Painter. Born in Poland in 1948. Studied: School of the Art Institute of Chicago; Northwestern Univ. Awarded a Ford Found. Fellowship in 1970-1972. Exhibitions: Lever House, NYC, 1968; Women Choose Women Show, Wabash Transit Gallery, Chicago, 1973; ARC Gallery, Chicago, 1974.

ROSENFELD, MORT.
Illustrator. Born in Brooklyn, NY, in 1928. Attended the School of Industrial Art and the ASL. His first published illustration, an advertisement for US Rubber, appeared in Life magazine in 1948. Though primarily concentrating on editorial work, he has also illustrated books, including Eight Bailed Out (1952) and Where Love Has Gone (1960). The Silvermine Guild and New Haven Paint and Clay Gallery have exhibited his work.

ROSENKRANZ, CLARENCE C.
Painter. Born Hammondsport, NY. Pupil of John Ward Stimson, W. M. Chase and Walter Shirlaw. Member: Buffalo Fine Arts Academy; first prize, 1911, second hon. mention, 1912, Buffalo Fine Arts Academy; first prize, MN Ar Co., 1913. Work: "New England Winter," Min. Art Society, and in Hibbing and Buhl, MN, Public Libraries. Instructor, Minnesota Art School, St. Paul. Address in 1929, 48 East 4th Street, St. Paul. MN.

ROSENMEYER, BERNARD JACOB.
Painter and illustrator. Born NY
in 1870. Pupil of ASL of NY under
Mowbray; Constant and Laurens in
Paris. Member: SI, 1902. Work
in: Carnegie Inst., Pittsburgh;
Print Dept. of NY. Public Library.
Address in 1929, 140 Wadsworth
Ave., New York, NY.

ROSENTHAL, ALBERT.
Portrait painter, and etcher. Born
Philadelphia, Jan. 30, 1863. Pupil
of his father, Max Rosenthal and of
PAFA; Ecole des Beaux-Arts in Paris
under Gerome; studied in Munich.
Member: Fellowship PAFA; Charcoal
C., Balto.; Wash. AC; Salma. C.;
Locust C., Philadelphia; AFA.
Awards: Bronze medal, St. Louis
Exp., 1904; bronze medal, P.-P.
Exp., San F., 1915. Represented in
Brooklyn Museum; Butler Art Inst.,
Youngstown, OH; Los Angeles Museum;
Kansas City Art Inst.; Detroit
Inst.; St. Louis Museum; Dallas,
TX, AA; Providence School of
Design. Died in 1939. Address in
1929, 10 South 18th Street,
Philadelphia, PA.

ROSENTHAL, DAVID.
Painter and illustrator. Born in
Cincinnati, OH, in 1876. Studied
in Italy. Address in 1926, 30
Hurbert Block, Cincinnati, OH.
Died in 1949.

ROSENTHAL, DORIS.
Painter. Born in Riverside, CA.
Studied: Teachers College, Los
Angeles, Calif.; Columbia Univ.;
Art Students League with George
Bellows and John Sloan. Awards:
Guggenheim fellowship, 1932, 1936;
Northwest Printmakers; National
Academy of Design, 1952; American
Academy of Arts and Letters grant,
1952. Collections: Metropolitan
Museum of Art; Addison Gallery of
American Art; Museum of Modern Art;
Colorado Springs Fine Arts Center;
Rochester Memorial Art Gallery;
Toledo Museum of Art; Univ. of
Arizona; Library of Congress; San
Diego Fine Arts Gallery; Davenport
Municipal Art Gallery; Cranbrook
Academy of Art. As a lithographer
also she was a compiler on the
Encyclopedia Britannica.

ROSENTHAL, LOUIS.
Sculptor. Born Lithuania, Feb. 5
1887. Came to US in 1907. Afte
studying with Keyser in Baltimore
he won scholarship to study abroad
Pupil of Ephraim Keyser. Member
Royal Soc. Min. PS, England; NSS
College AA. Address in 1929, 7
Sixth Ave., San Francisco, CA.

ROSENTHAL, MAX.
Etcher and lithographer. Born i
Turek, Russian Poland, Nov. 23
1833. Mr. Rosenthal studied drawin
and painting in Paris. He came t
Phila. in 1849 and there continue
his studies at the Pennsylvani.
Academy of Fine Arts. Having bee
a pupil of the famous Thurwanger i
Paris and in Phila., in connectio
with his brother, Mr. Rosentha
established himself in th
lithographic business in the latte
city, and he made notable progres
in developing the then new art o
Chromo-lithography in this country
In 1884, Mr. Rosenthal turned hi
attention to etching, and i
connection with his son, Alber
Rosenthal, issued a series o
portraits of men prominent i
American history. In 1890 he too
up the work of engraving i
mezzontint, and as he was already
reputable painter of portraits an
historical subjects, his artisti
training led him to produc
mezzotinto portraits of merit
Died Aug. 8, 1918, in Phila.

ROSENTHAL, MICHAEL.
painter. Born in Russia, 1885
Pupil of Robert Henri. Address i
1926, 1947 Broadway, NYC. Died i
1941.

ROSENTHAL, MILDRED.
(Mrs. Hyman Rosenthal). Painter
Born Panama. Pupil of Calif
School of FA. Member: Sa
Fran., S. Women A. Address i
1929, 76 Sisth Ave., San Fran., CA

ROSENTHAL, TOBY EDWARD.
Painter. Born in New Haven, CT, i
1848. Studied drawing under Henr.
Bacon, and painting under Fortunat
Arriola, San Francisco; student a
Royal Academy, Munich, unde
Straehuber, Carl Raupp and Carl co
Piloty, 1865-72. Professionall
engaged as a painter since leavin

the academy, having classes in painting and composition. He painted chiefly figural compositions and genre work; also painted many portraits in CA, England and Germany. Medals at Centennial Expo., Phila., 1876; Royal Academy, Munich; International exposition, Munich. Died in 1917, in Berlin.

ROSENZWEIG, LIPPA.
Sculptor. Exhibited at Penna. Academy of the Fine Arts, Phila., 1926. Address in 1926, 1030 N. 13th Street, Philadelphia, PA.

ROSS, ALEX.
Illustrator. Born in Dunfermline, Scotland, in 1908. He came with his family to America and settled in the Pittsburgh area. He attended Carnegie Institute of Technology and later received an honorary degree from Bsoton College. His art career began in Penn., but he soon came to NY and worked in advertising. In 1942 he painted the first of 130 covers for Good Housekeeping. He has contributed to the USAF Art Program and his works are in the collections of the New Britain Museum of American Art, the Mormon Church, (six murals exhibited at the NY World's Fair) and Fairfield Univ. where he is on the board of trustees.

ROSS, DENMAN WALDO.
Painter, writer, lecturer, and teacher. Born Cincinnati, OH, Jan. 10, 1853. Member: Copley S. 1892; Boston SAC (life); AFA: Boston S. Arch.; Arch. C.; Fellow Am. Acad. Art and Letters. Trustee Museum of Fine Arts, Boston. Lecturer on "Theory of Design" at Harvard Univ. Died in 1935. Address in 1929, 24 Craigie Street, Cambridge, MA.

ROSS, LAUREL BERGER.
Painter. Born in Youngstown, OH, on Dec. 12, 1947. Studied: Carnegie-Mellon Univ.; The AIC. Exhibitions: Univ. of Illinois, Medical Center; ARC Gallery, Chicago. Address in 1980, 1841 Halekoa Dr. Honolulu, HI.

ROSS, RAYMOND L.
Painter. Born Cattaraugus, NY, April 6, 1880. Member: Wash. WCC.

Address in 1929, 3212 17th Street, N. E. Washington, D.C.

ROSSE, HERMANN.
Painter, illustrator, Arch., Craftsman, lecturer, and teacher. Born The Hague, Holland, Jan. 1, 1887. Studied in Holland. Member: Kunstkring of The Hague; Cliff Dwellers, Chicago. Award: Medal of honor, P.-P. Exp., San F., 1915. Work: Painting in dome of the Peace Palace, The Hague; mural decorations in Salt Lake City Orpheum Theatre. Illustrated "Wonder Tales from Windmill Lands," by F. J. Olcott (Longmans, Green and Co.). Address in 1929, Pomona, NY; summer, 20 Niewe Uitleg, The Hague, Holland.

ROSSEAU, PERCIVAL LEONARD.
Painter. Born Point Coupee parish, LA, Sept. 21, 1859. Pupil of Lefebvre, Herman Leon, and Robert-Fleury in Paris. Member: Lyme AA; Lotos C. Awards: Hon. mention, Paris Salon, 1900; third class medal, Paris Salon, 1906. Died in 1937. Address in 1929, Grassy Hill, Lyme, CT.

ROSSITER, THOMAS P.
Portrait and historical painter. Born Sept. 29, 1818, in New Haven, CT. Pupil of Nathaniel Jocelyn; also studied in London and Paris. In 1846 he opened his studio in New York. He was elected an Associate Member of the National Academy in 1840, and an Academician in 1849. He painted "Washington's Entry into Trenton," and a series of pictures on the "Life of Christ." He died at Cold Spring, NY, on May 17, 1871.

ROST, CHRISTIAN.
Engraver. Born in Germany. He studied in Paris and in London, and in the latter city he made the drawings and engraved on wood for a work describing the exhibites at the London World's Fair of 1850. It is not known when Mr. Rost came to the US, but he was engraving very good portraits and subject plates in line in New York in 1860. In 1865, he was in the employ of George E. Perrine, and at a later date he was employed by the American Bank Note Co. He died at Mount Vernon, NY.

801

ROTH, ERNEST DAVID.
Painter and etcher. Born Stuttgart, Germany, Jan. 17, 1879. Pupil of NAD in NY; etching under James D. Smillie. Member: ANA; NYWCC; Salma. C.; Chicago SE; NY SE; Calif. SE; AWCS; Wash. WCC; Allied AA; Calif. PM. Awards: Third Shaw prize for black and white, Salma. C., 1911; first Shaw prize for black and white, Salma. C., 1912; first prize for architectural subject, Chicago SE, 1914; Vezin thumb-box prize, Salma. C., 1915; bronze medal for painting and silver medal for etching, P.-P. Exp. San F. 1915; J. Sanford Saltus prize, Salma. C., 1917; first hon. mention, Chicago Art Inst., 1917; Shaw prize, Salma. C., 1918; Bryan prize, Calif. PS, 1922. Prints in: New York Public Library; Boston Museum of Art; Library of Congress, Washington, DC; Public Library, Newark NY; Chicago Art Inst.; Minneapolis Inst. of Art; Uffizi Gallery. Florence, Italy. Address in 1929, 5 East 14th Street, 5 Bank Street, 222 East 71st Street, NY.

ROTH, FRANK.
Painter. Born Feb. 22, 1936, in Boston, MA. Studied at Cooper Union (1954) and Hans Hofmann School (1955). Awarded Chaloner and Guggenheim (1964) fellowships. Taught at Iowa, and at School of Visual Arts (NYC) since 1963. Rec. Nat. Endowment for Arts (1977). Exhibited at Artists Gal. (NYC) 1958; Whitney; Univ. of Nebraska; Univ. of Colorado; Toledo Museum of Art; Amherst; Lehigh Univ.; Ulster Mus. in Belfast; and Phil. Art Alliance. In collections of Albright-Know; the Tate; Santa Barbara Museum of Art; Baltimore; Mich. Sate Univ.; Walker Art Center; Chase Manhattan Bank; Whitney and Manuf. Hanover Trust.

ROTH, FREDERICK GEORGE RICHARD.
Sculptor. Born Brooklyn, NY, April 28, 1872. Pupil of Hellmer and Meyerheim in Vienna. Member: ANA 1906, NA 1906; NY Arch. Lg., 1902; Nat. Inst. AL; SAA 1903; NSS, 1910; New Soc. of A.; Soc. Animal P & S. Awards: Silver medal, St. Louis Exp., 1904; silver medal, Buenos Aires Exp., 1910; gold medal, P. P. Exp., San F., 1915; Ellen Speyer

memorial prize, NAD, 1924; NAC prize, 1924; William O. Goodman prize, 1928. Represented in Metropolitan Museum, New York; Detroit Inst. of Arts; Cincinnati Museum; Children's Museum, Boston; San Francisco Museum; Museum, Newark, NJ; Equestrian Washington, Morristown, NJ. Died in 1944. Address in 1929, Sherwood Place, Englewood, NJ.

ROTH, HERBERT.
Illustrator. Member: SI 1912. Address in 1929, care of NY World," New York, NY.

ROTHBORT, SAMUEL.
Painter. Member: S. Indp. A.; Brooklyn SA. Address in 1929, President Street, Rosedale, SI, NY.

ROTHERMEL, PETER FREDERICK.
Born in Luzerne County, PA, July 8, 1817. He was an eminent American historical painter, and one of the greatest colorists this country has produced, and a master of composition involving the management of large masses of figures. He began the active practice of his profession in 1840, by painting portraits in Philadelphia, having received instructions from Bass Otis; he went to Europe in 1856, spending some time in the art centers of the Continent, and painting his first Historical picture. He was an active member of the Artists' Fund Society of Phila., of which he was elected Vice-President in 1844, and was made a Director of Penna. Academy of Fine Arts in 1847-55. Among his best known works are "St. Agnes," painted in 1858, and now in Russia; "Patrick Henry before the Virginia House of Burgesses," engraved by Alfred Jones for the American Art Union of Philadelphia, 1852; "St. Paul, on Mars Hill"; "Amy Robsart interceding for Leicester," property of Mrs. Blanchard; also the colossal picture of the Battle of Gettysurg, ordered by the Legislature of Pennsylvainia, and finished in 1871. The last-named picture, which has been engraved by John Sartain, is preserved in Memorial Hall, Fairmount Park, Philadelphia.

He died in Penna., on Aug. 15, 1895.

ROTHKO, MARK.
Painter. Born: Sept. 25, 1903 in Dvintka, Russia. Studied at Yale Univ. 1921-23; ASL, 1925 with Max Weber. He taught at the center Academy in Brooklyn from 1929 to 1952; Brooklyn College 1951-54; Tulane Univ., 1956. Co-founder of The Group in 1935, a group of expressionists. Worked on the Federal Arts Proj. from 1936-1937. Exhibitions: His first was in 1933 at the Contemporary Arts Gallery in NYC. XXIX Venice Biennial, 1958; MOMA, 1961; Whitechapel Art Gallery, London, 1961; Caregie, 1958, '61; among many others. Collections are held at the Brooklyn Mus.; Chicago Art Inst., Dusseldorff KN-W; Vassar College. Died by suicide February 25, 1970 in NYC.

ROTHWELL, ELIZABETH L.
Painter. Member: Pittsburgh Art Assoc. Award: Third prize, Pittsburgh AA, 1915. Address in 1929, 6432 Darlington Road; 435 Atwood Street, Pittsburgh, PA.

ROTHWELL, J.
Engraver. This man was engraving book illustrations, in a crude line manner, in New York in 1841.

ROTHWELL, MRS. VIOLET HAMILTON.
Painter. Born NYC, March 27, 1890. Pupil of Christine Lumsdon; Academie de Passy in Paris. Address in 1929, Carnegie Hall; h. 311 West 95th Street, NYC; summer, "Woods Holow," Remsenburg, LI, NY.

ROUDEBUSH, JOHN H.
Sculptor. He was awarded a medal at the Paris Exposition of 1900, and at Buffalo in 1901, for his group, "The Wrestlers."

ROUGERON, MARCEL JULES.
Landscape painter. Born Paris, France, Oct. 6, 1875; son of the artist, Jules James Rougeron. Pupil of Julian Academy, Ecole des Beaux-Arts, Gerome, J. G., Vibert, L. Van den Bergh. Member: NAC; Lotos C; Wash. AC; AFA; Montreal AC; Societe des Artistses Francais; Societe Royale Artistes Belges. Awards: Mention, Paris, 1902; Officer of Public Instruction, France, 1900. Specialty, Restoration of Paintings. Address in 1929, 101 Park Ave., New York, NY.

ROULAND, ORLANDO.
Painter and teacher. Born Pleasant Ridge, IL, Dec. 21, 1871. Pupil of Mac Thedy in Germany; Julian Academy in Paris under Laurens and Constant. Member: Salma. C., 1901; Paris AAA; Lotos C.; Allied AA; Mac D. C.; Alliance; North Shore AA; Springfield AA; AFA. Award: popular prize ($50), Duxbury AA, 1921. Work in: Yale Univ., New Haven, CT; Trinity College, Cambridge Univ., England; University of Texas; Historical Society, St. Paul, MN; Wheaton Seminary, Norton, MA; Carnegie Inst, Washington, D.E.; Engineers Club and Society of Mining Engineers, New York, NY; City Club, Boston; Art Museum, Montclair, NJ; National Gallery, Washington, DC; Public Library, Lexington, KY; Amherst College; Art Club, Erie, PA; Columbia University and Lotos Club, NY; Rollins College, Winter Park, FL. Died June 26, 1945. Address in 1929, 130 West 57th Street, New York, NY; summer, 5 Lookout Court, Marblehead, MA.

ROWE, CLARENCE HERBERT.
Illustrator and etcher. Born Philadelphia, PA, May 11, 1878. Pupil of Max Bohm, PAFA, Bouguereau and Ferrier in Paris. Member: Salma. C.; SI; Calif. PM; GFLA. Died in 1930. Address in 1929, Cos Cob, CT.

ROWE, CORINNE FINSTERWALD.
Painter. Born Marion, WI, Nov. 5, 1894. Pupil of John P. Wicker. Died in 1965. Address in 1929, 229 East 68th Street, New York, NY.

ROWE, J. STAPLES.
Portrait painter. Born in 1856. He studied in Boston and New York, and painted life size portraits and miniatures. He died in New York.

ROWELL, FANNY.
(Mrs. Horace C. Wait Taylor). Painter. Born in Princeton, NJ; May 11, 1865. Pupil of J. B. Whittaker in Brooklyn; Colarossi Academy in Paris; Trager at Sevres. Taught arts and crafts to mountain children near her summer home, Tamasee, NC. Member: National Art Club; New York Municipal Artists' Society. Address in 1926, National Arts Club, 14 Gramercy Park, New York, NY. Died on April 22, 1928.

ROWLAND, W. E.
Painter and illustrator. Born Trinidad, CO. Pupil of AIC. Member: Calif. AC; Laguna Beach AA. Award: Second prize, Woman's Club, Phoenix, Ariz, 1923. Address in 1929, 3448 Gardenside Lane, Los Angeles, CA.

ROWLAND, WILLIAM.
Miniature painter, who flourished about 1777 in NY. He came from Glasgow, Scotland and settled in New York.

ROWSE, SAMUEL WORCESTER.
Painter. Born Jan 29, 1822 at Bath, ME. He died May 26, 1901, at Morristown, NJ. After a brief period in Augusta, Maine, as an engraver, Samuel W. Rowse came to Boston in 1852 and worked for a lithographic firm. He soon after established himself as an excellent crayon portrait draughtsman. At the Studio Building where he lived in1861, and worked for a number of years, he had as a friend Eastman Johnson. In 1872, with his friend Chauncey Wright, he visited London and was frequently the guest of Charles Eliot Norton; also met Ruskin there. About 1880 he moved to NY. With his friend Eastman Johnson he again visited London in 1891. He is represented in the large portrait by Eastman Johnson, called "Two Men," now at the Metropolitan Museum and reproduced in the World's Work, in 1906. He finally settled in Morristown, NJ, where he died, leaving a considerable estate. His work was regularly in demand and in later years he was well paid. His portraits are in black crayon and are quite large.

ROYCE, ELIZABETH R.
Sculptor. Member of National Association of Women Painters and Sculptors. Address in 1926, 11 Greycourt, Ithaca, NY.

ROYER, JACOB S.
Painter and craftsman. Born Waynesboro, PA, Nov. 9, 1883. Pupil of Dayton AI; Robert Oliver, T. C. Steele. Member: Dayton AG; Am. APL. Work: "September Evening," Dayton Art Institute. Address in 1929, 917 Manhattan Ave., Dayton, OH.

RUBENSTEIN, LEWIS.
Painter and printmaker. Born in Buffalo, NY, Dec. 15, 1908. Study: Harvard U., AB 1930; Bacon traveling fellow 1931-33; painting with Leger and Ozenfant, Paris; fresco with Rico Lebrun, Lithography with Emil Ganso, NY; Sumi with Keigetsu, Tokyo. Work: Fogg Art Mus., Boston; Mus., RI Sch. of Design; Vassar Col. Art Gal.; Ford Found.; Butler Inst. Am. Art, Youngstown, OH; Tokyo Univ. of Arts. Comm.: Frescoes, Busch Reisinger Mus., Harv. U.; murals, US Post Office, Wareham, MA; Jewish Ctr., Buffalo; etc. Exhib: Whitney, 1938; NAD, 1946, 52, 56 & 63; Libr. Congress, 1952-60; Soc. Am. Graphic Artists, NYC, 1952-81; Am. Watercolor Soc., NYC, 1955, 64; Barrett House, Poughkeepsie, NY, 1979; many others. Awards: Fulbright Grant, Japan, 1957-58; State Dept. Grant, So. Am.; Soc. Am. Graphic Artists, 1952, 54; Silvermine Guild of Artists, 1959; Empire State Architects Award - Mural Ptg. Prof. of ptg., Vassar Col., 1939-74.

RUBINS, HARRY W.
Painter and etcher, Dec. Born Buffalo, NY, Nov. 25, 1865. Pupil of AI Chicago. Member: Chicago SE; Minneapolis SFA. Work: NY Public Library; painted decorations in Lake School Library, Minneapolis; Chapel, St. Marks Church, Minneapolis; Nazareth Hall, St. Paul, MN; Northwestern Nat'l. Life Bldg., Minneapolis; Children's Hospital, Cincinnati. Died in 1934. Address in 1929, 1200 2nd Ave., South Minneapolis, MN.

RUCKSTULL, FREDERIC WELLINGTON.
Sculptor, lecturer and writer.
Born Breitenbach, Alsace, May 22,
1853. Pupil of Boulanger and
Lefebvre, Julian Acad., Paris; and
of Merice, Rollins Acad. Member:
NSS 1893; NY Arch. Lg. 1894; NAC;
Nat. Inst. AL; NY. Municipal AS;
Brooklyn SA. Awards: Hon.
mention, Paris Salon, 1888; medal,
Columbian Exp., Chicago, 1893.
Sect., Comm. for erection of Dewey
Arch, 1898; of sculpture, St. Louis
Exp., 1904. Work: "Evening,"
life-size marble, Metropolitan
Museum, NY, equestrian statues of
"Gen J. F. Hartranft," Harrisburgh,
PA. "Gen. Wade Hampton," Columbia,
S.C.; "Confederate Monument,"
Baltimore; "Defense of the Flag,"
Little Rock, Ark.; "Women's
Monument," Columbia, SC. "John C.
Calhoun," "Wade Hampton," and "U.
M. Rose," the Capitol, Wash.;
"Solon," "Goethe," "Franklin,"
Macaulay," Library of Congress,
Wash.; "Wisdom" and "Force,"
Appellate Court, NY; "3 Partisan
Generals Monument," Columbia, SC.;
"Confederate Monument," Salisbury,
NC; "Soldiers' Monument," Jamaica,
NYC; "Mercury Teasing Eagle of
Jupiter," St. Louis; Penn. Soldier
Monument, Petersburg, VA;
"Phoenicia," NY Customs House;
"Minerva," Liberty Monument,
Battlefield of Long Island;
"America Remembers," Civil War
Monument, Stafford Springs, CT.
Died in 1942. Address in 1929,
National Arts Club, 15 Gramercy
Pk., New York, NY.

RUDD, EMMA R.
Painter, who exhibited at the 33d
Annual Exhib. of Nat. Assoc. of
Women Painters and Sculptors, New
York. Address in 1926, Lyons, NY.

RUDDER, STEPHEN CHURCHILL DOUGLAS.
Painter, illustrator, etcher,
craftsman, writer, and lecturer.
Born Salem, May 12, 1906. Pupil of
AIC. Member: ASL of Chicago;
Alumni AIC; Hoosier Salon, IN AA.
Address in 1929, The Judas Tree,
403 Charlestown Road, Salem, IN.

RUDERSDORF, LILLIAN.
Painter. Born in Clarkson, Neb.,
in 1882. Pupil of University of
Neb.; Art Institute of Chicago.

Address in 1926, 21 East Van Buren
Street, Chicago, IL.

RUDOLPH, MRS. PAULINE DOHN.
Painter. Born Chicago. Pupil of
PAFA; Boulanger, Lefebvre, Lasar
and Couture in Paris. Member:
Palette Club; Cosmopolitan C.,
Chicago; Chicago, SA' AFA/ Award"
first Yerkes prize, Chicago SA.
Address in 1929, Winnetka, IL.

RUDY, MARY E.
Painter. Born in Burlington, IA.,
in 1861. Pupil of Art Institute of
Chicago. Address in 1926, 4516
Lake Park Avenue, Chicago, IL.

RUFFINS, REYNOLD.
Illustrator. Born in NYC in 1930.
Graduated from Cooper Union in
1951, the year his first
illustration was published. An
early member of Push Pin Studios,
he has worked in advertising
agencies and been a partner in his
own studio. A regular contributor
to Family Circle, he designed and
illustrated several children's
books for Charles Scribner's Sons.
The AIGA, ADC, S of I and The New
York Times Book Review have all
presented him with awards.

RUGGLES, E. JUN'R.
This man was a book-plate engraver,
apparently working between 1790 and
1800, somewhere in New England.
The only plate seen is that for
Walker Lyon; in reality a label
with peculiarly conventionalized
peacock feathers used as borders.

RUGGLES, DR. EDWARD.
Painter of small landscapes and
miniature views. He painted many
studies in the White Mountains.
His views and landscapes met a
ready sale, where the socalled
"Ruggles Gems" were in much demand.

RUGGLES, THEO ALICE.
See Mrs. H. H. Kitson.

RUHNKA, ROY.
Painter, who exhibited water colors
at the Penna. Academy of Fine Arts
Philadelphia, 1925. Address in
1925, 3616 Walnut Street,
Philadelphia.

RULE, MRS. FAY SHELLEY.
Miniature painter. Born Chattanooga, Nov. 30, 1889. Pupil of Lucia F. Fuller, Madel Welch, Alice Beckington and F. V. Du Mond. Member: Chattanooga AA. Address in 1929, 1026 East 10th Street, Chattanooga, TN.

RUMBOLD-KOHN, ESTELLE.
Painter. Award: Spalding prize ($1,000), AIC, 1925. Address in 1929, 40 West 59th Street, New York, NY.

RUMMELL, JOHN.
Painter, writer, lecturer, and teacher. Born Springville, NY, Aug. 24, 1861. Pupil of L. B. C. Josephs, John F. Carlson, F. V. Du Mond and George Bridgeman. Awards: First hon. mention, Buffalo SA, 1917; second hon. mention, Buffalo, SA, 1918 and 1919; Fellowship prize ($50), Buffalo SA, 1921. Address in 1929, 68 Greenfield Street, Buffalo, NY.

RUMMLER, ALEX J.
Painter and illustrator. Born Dubuque, IA, July 25, 1867. Pupil of Laurens in Paris. Member: Salma. C., 1900; AFA. Address in 1929, 25 Bettswood Road, Norwalk, CT.

RUMSEY, CHARLES CARY.
Sculptor. Born in Buffalo, NY in 1879; killed in automobile accident in LI, NY, Sept. 21, 1922. Studied in Boston Art School and later in Paris. He worked principally in bronze, and modelled many statues of race horses. Nephew of Seward Cary, the sculptor. In collections of Whiney; Brooklyn; Cleveland; Iriezes at approach to Manhattan Bridge & Pelham Bay PK, NYC; Victory Statue, Brooklyn, NY.

RUNGIUS, CARL (CLEMENS MORITZ).
Painter. Born in Germany in 1869. Studied painting at Berlin Art School; School of Applied Arts; Academy of Fine Arts. Began paintng in Berlin, 1889, came to the U.S. in 1894, and has since been engaged in his profession, making a specialty of painting American big game. He has exhibited at the Society of American Artists; NAD; PAFA

Elected Member of the National Academy of Design, 1920. Address in 1926, 96 Fifth Ave., NY. Died in 1959.

RUSH, OLIVE.
Painter. Born Fairmount, IN. Studied in NY, Paris, etc. Member: NYWCC; Wilmington SFA. Awards: Hon. mention, Richmond AA, 1919; first prize, Herron Art inst., 1919. Work: "The Gospel," altar panels, St. Andrew's Church, Wilmington, DE; "Fairyland in Books and in Nature," Nathaniel Hawthorne School, Indianapolis; murals, La Fonda Hotel, Santa Fe., NM. represented in Phillips Memorial Gallery, Washington; Herron Art Inst., Indianapolis; Art Museum, Worcester, MA. Address in 1929, 630 Canon Road, Santa Fe, NM.

RUSH, WILLIAM.
Sculptor. Born in Philadelphia July 4, 1756; died in that city, 1833. Apprenticed as a maker of figure-heads for ships. Notable among these were the figures "Genius of the U.S." and "Nature" for the frigates "U.S." and "Constellation," and of celebrities such as Rousseau, Franklin and Penn for other vessels. The figure of the "Indian Trader" for the Ship "William Penn" excited great admiration in London, where carvers sketched it and made casts of the head, while the figure of a river-god, carved for the ship "Ganges," is said to have been worshipped by the Hindus on her calls to Indian ports. His "Tragedy" and "Comedy," done for the first Chestnut Street Theater, may now be seen at the Forrest Home at Phila.; his "Leda and the Swan," originally placed before the first water-works on the site of the City Hall, was later moved to Fairmount, where a bronze replica - he himself worked in nothing but wood and clay-has since replaced it. For the first Custom House he designed the much admired figure of "Commerce"; for the permanent bridge at Market Street those of "Commerce" and "Agriculture"; for St. Augustine's Church a representation of the Crucifixtion. Among a large number of statues executed by him the most notable

was that of Washington, purchased by the city in 1814 and still on exhibition in Independence Hall, Philadelphia. He served in the Revolutionary Army.

RUSHTON, ROBERT.
Painter, who exhibited water colors at the Penna. Academy of Fine Arts, Philadelphia, 1925. Address in 1926, 5238 Carlisle Street, Philadephia.

RUSS, HORACE ALEXANDER.
Painter, sculptor, artists, craftsman, and teacher. Born Logtown, MI, Jan. 25, 1889. Pupil of PAFA. Member: SSAL; N. O. AA; N. O. AL; N. O. ACC; Gulf Coast AA. Address in 1929, 607 Royal Street, New Orleans, LA.; summer, Lake Shore, MI.

RUSSELL, CHARLES MARION.
Painter. Also sculptor and illustrator. Born March 19, 1864 in St. Louis, MO. Moved to Montana in 1880. Self taught. An experienced cowboy, he created many thousands of paintings, and over 100 bronzes. Had 28 one-man shows in NYC; Chi.; London. In collections of Amon. Carter Museum of West. Art, Fort Worth, TX; Buffalo Bill Cody Cntr. Wyoming; Montana Hist. Soc.; The Trigg C. M. Russell Gal., Great Falls; Norton Gal. Shreveport; Woolaroc Mus., Bartlesville. Created mural, State Capitol Helena, Mont. Wrote books, incl. Trails Plowed Under. Died Oct. 24, 1926 in Great Falls, Mont

RUSSELL, H. B.
Painter. Member: Boston AC. Address in 1929, 9 Park Street, Boston, MA.

RUSSELL, JAMES.
Painter. Born in New Albany, IN, 1873. Member painter. Born C. 1810 in N. Eng. Flourishing in Boston in 1834. Also painted portraits. Died in 1884.

RUSSELL, W. C.
Miniature painter, who flourished in New York about 1837.

RUSSELL, WALTER.
Painter, sculptor. Born Boston, May 19, 1871. Pupil of Albert Munsell and Ernest Major in Boston; Howard Pyle at Wilmington; Laurens in Paris. Member: Spanish Acad. of Arts and Letters. Award: Special mention, Turin Exposition, Italy, 1900. Specialty, portraits of children. Work: "The Might of Ages," an allegory, "A Southern Rose," Dallas Museum of Art. Art editor, "Collier's Weekly," 1897. War correspondent and illustrator for "Colliers" and "Century." Author and illustrator of "The Sea Children;" "The Bending of the Twig;" "The Age of Innocence;" "The Universal One;" "Salutation to the Day;" "The New Electric Theory." Died May 19, 1963. Address in 1929, 1 West 67th Street, New York, NY; Wash., CT.

RUSSMANN, FELIX.
Painter. Born New York City, Aug. 2, 1888. Pupil NAD; Munich Royal Academy. Member: Chicago SA; No-Jury Soc., Chic. Award: Third Hallgarten prize, NAD, 1918. Address in 1929, 3538 Lake Park, Ave., Chicago, IL.

RUTHERFORD, ALEXANDER W.
Born in 1826 in VT. He is spoken of by Tuckerman in his "American Artist Life" as a "genre painter of promise who died young." Died in 1851 in London.

RUTHRAUFF, FREDERICK G.
Painter and writer. Born Findlay, OH, Aug. 6, 1878. Pupil of William V. Cahill, William H. Claff, Henri Morrisett in Paris. Member: Berkely LFA; Calif. AC; Ogden AS. Address in 1929, 2586 Polk Ave., Ogden, Utah.

RUYL, LOUIS H.
Illustrator and etcher. Born Brooklyn, NY, Nov. 13, 1870. Member: GFLA; Stowaway Club. Illustrations for "Cape Cod, Old and New," "Old Post Road, from Boston to Plymouth," "From Provincetown to Portsmouth," Address in 1929, 45 Prospect Place, New York, NY; summer, Hingham, MA.

RUZICKA, RUDOLPH.
Illustrator, etcher, draftsman, and wood engraver. Born in Bohemia, June 29, 1883. Pupil: AIC; NY School of Art. Work: Illustrated "Fountains of Papal Rome"; "NY;" "Newark"; "Notes of Travel in Europe," by Washington Irving; examples in Art inst. of Chicago Carnegie Inst., Pittsburgh; Metropolitan Museum, NY; Library of Congress, Washington; Brooklyn Inst. of Art and Sciences; Cleveland Museum of Art. Address in 1929, Dobbs Ferry, NY.

RYDEN, HENNING.
Sculptor, draftsman, and painter. Born Sweden, Jan. 21, 1869. Pupil of AIC; studied in Berlin and London. Member: Salma. C., 1908; AFA. Award: Hon. mention, P. P. exp., San. F., 1915. Work in: American Numismatic Society. Died in 1939. Address in 1929, 47 Fifth Ave., New York, NY; 93 West Duncan Street, Columbus, OH.

RYDER, ALBERT PINKHAM.
Painter. Born March 19, 1847 in New Bedford, MA. Pupil of William E. Marshal the engraver, and of the NAD, NY. Among his works, "Death on a Pale Horse," "The Pasture," "The Curfew Hour," "Pegasus," "The flying Dutchman," "Launcelot and Elaine," and "Jonah and the Whale." He was eleced a Member of the National Academy in 1906. (See Interational Studio for July, 1925.) Died in Almhurst, NY. on March 28, 1912.

RYDER, CHAUNCEY FOSTER.
Painter. Born Danbury, CT, Feb. 29, 1868. Pupil of AIC; Julian Academy, Collin and Laurens in Paris. Member: ANA 1914; NA 1920; AWCS; Allied AA; Salma. C.; NYWCC; Lotos C; NAC; Brooklyn SE; Chicago SE; AFA. Awards: Hon. mention, Paris salon, 1907; silver medal, P.-P. Exp., San F., 1915; Baltimore WCC prize, 1920; first prize, Central State Fair, Aurora, 1922; first prize, Salma C.; Members prize, Brooklyn SE. Work in: Art Inst. of Chicago; Delgado Mus., New Orleans, LA; Wash. State Art Assoc., Seattle, Wash.; Corcoran Gal., Wash., DC; Hackely Art Gallery, Muskegon, MI; National

Exhibition Assoc., Toronto, CN; Artists Club, Denver, CO; Engineers Club, New York, NY; Societe des Amis des Arts, Douai, France; City Art Mus., St. Louis; Butler Art Inst., Youngstown, OH; Minneapolis Inst. of Arts; National Gal. Washington, DC; Wilmington SFA; Randolph Macon Woman's College, Lynchburg, VA; Quinnipiac Club, New Haven; Dayton Museum of Arts; Macon, GA, Art Assoc.; Metropolitan Museum; Rochester (NY) Memorial Art Gal.; Springfield (IL) Art Assoc.; Brooks Memorial Art Gal., Memphis, TN; NY Public Library; Art Inst. of Chicago; Dept. of Prints and Drawing, British Museum, London; Dept. of Engraving, Victoria and Albert Museum, South Kensington; Graphic Arts Dept., Smithsonian Inst., Wash., D.C.; Print Dept., Brooklyn Museum; Art Assoc. Of Indianpolis, John Herron Art Inst.; Hartford (CT) Athnaeum; Art Assoc, New Britain, CT; Unic. of Illinois, Urbana, IL; Cabinet des Estampes, Bibliotheque Nationale, Paris. Died in 1949. Address in 1929, 171 West 12th Street, New York, NY; summer, Wilton, NH.

RYDER, MARILLA.
Painter, who exhibited at Penna. Academy of Fine Arts, Philadelphia, 1924. Address in 1926, 2940 Washington Street, Roxbury, MA.

RYDER, PLATT P.
Portrait and genre painter. Born in 1821 at Brooklyn, NY, died in 1896. Pupil of Bonnat in Paris, also studied in London. Elected in 1868 an Associate of the National Academy. His portrait of Geo. P. Putnam painted in 1872, is in the Metropolitan Museum; he also painted "Clean Shave," "Reading the Cup," "Spinning Wheel" and "Watching and Waiting."

RYDER, WORTH.
Painter, etcher, writer, lecturer, and teacher. Born Kirkwood, IL, Nov. 10, 1884. Pupil of Univ. of CA; Royal Acad. Munich; Hofman Schule, Munich. Member: Beaux Arts Group, San Fran. Award: Silver medal for etching, P.-P. Exp., San F., 1915. Landscape, figure and fresco painter. Assoc. Prof. of Art, Univ. of CA. Died in

1960. Address in 1929, 2772
Hilgard Ave., Berkeley, CA.

RYDERSON, MARY MCLIVAINE.
Sculptor. Born Philadelphia, PA.
Pupil of Saint-Gaudens, Solon
Borglum and Fraser. Died in 1936.
Address in 1929, Sherwood Studios,
58 West 57th Street, New York, NY.

RYERSON, MARGERY AUSTEN.
Painter and etcher. Born
Morristown, NJ, Sept. 15, 1886.
Pupil of Robert Henri and Charles
W. Hawthorne. Member: Wash. WCC;
Brooklyn SE; Calif. PM; Grand Cent.
A. Gal.; Allied AA; Provincetown
AA. Award: Emil Fuchs prize,
Boroklyn SE, 1924. Etchings in
permanent collections of
Smithsonian Inst. Washington, DC;
Cleveland Museum of Art. Address
in 1929, Sherwood Studios, 58 West
57th Street, New York, NY.

RYLAND, MRS. L. H.
See Hamilton, Hildegarde.

RYLAND, ROBERT KNIGHT.
Mural painter and illustrator.
Born Grenada MI, Feb. 10, 1873.
Pupil of ASL and NAD in NY.
Member: Mural P.; Salma. C.; GFLA;
Alumni Am. Acad. in Rome. Awards:
Lazarus European Scholarship,
1903-1905; Altman prize, NAD, 1924;
hon. mention, AIC, 1926. Died in
1951. Address in 1929, 61 Poplar
Street, Brooklyn, NY and
Russellville, KY.

SAALBURG, LESLIE.
Illustrator. Born in 1902. Having studied briefly at the ASL, he continued his self-education at various studios. His style, often color washes over line drawings, portrayed the old, genteel manners of the elegant and was much in demand for editorial and advertising clients. His work appeared in Collier's, Vogue, Town and Country and in several portfolios for Esquire. Ford Motor Co., Cannon Mills and Hiram Walker Distillers were among his many advertising clients, earning him two awards from the NY ADC. Died in 1975.

SABATINI, RAPHAEL.
Painter. Born 1898. Exhibited "Lizza" at the Penna. Acad. of Fine arts, Philadelphia, 1924. Address in 1926, 1515 Arch. St., Philadelphia, PA.

SABIN, JOSEPH F.
Etcher and illustrator. Born in 1846, he has long been a resident of NY. Member of the NY Etchers Society. He made the illustrations for "Shakespeare's House." His "John Falstaff," after George Cruikshank, is well known. Address in 1929, Nassau St., New York City. Died in 1927.

SACHEVERELL, JOHN.
Engraver. The Pennsylvania Gazette, Philadelphia, March 15, 22, 1732-33, contains an advertisement for the sale of "A quanity of white metal, or pewter, teapots, teaspoons, etc. These are of the newest Fashion, and so very neat, as not easily to be distinguished from Silver." The importer, John Scheverell, adds to his notice that he "performs all Sorts of Engraving of Carving in Gold, Silver, Brass, Copper, or Steel, after the newest and neatest manner."

SACKER, AMY M.
Illustrator, craftsman, lecturer, and teacher. Born Boston, July 17, 1876. Pupil of DeCamp, Joseph Lindon Smith, and C. Howard Walker; studied in Rome and Athens. Member: Boston SAC; Copley S; AFA. Award: Bronze medal for book

covers. P. Am. Exp., Buffalo, 1901. Art Director in Motion Pictures. Principal of School of Design and Interior Decoration. Address in 1929 739 Boylston St.; h. 64 Charlesgate East, Boston, MA.

SACKETT, CLARA E(LISABETH).
Portrait painter and teacher. Born Westfield, NY. Pupil of ASL of NY; Aman-Jean and Delecluse and Vitti Academies in Paris. Member: Buffalo SA; Buffalo Guild of AA; Copley S.; Boston GA; ASL of NY. Award: Prize, Buffalo SA. Represented in Buffalo Historical Soc. Address in 1929, Studio 104 East 30th St., New York, NY; summer, McLean Farm, S. Cortland, NY.

SACKS, CAL O.
Illustrator. Born in Brookline, MA, in 1914. Studied with Kimon Nicoliades. Beginning his career in 1933, he has worked for the American Heritage Publishing Co., illustrated many books and had shows with General Electric, the USAF, and S of I, of which he is a member. He has two married children and resided with his wife, who is also a illustrator, in Westport, CT.

SACKS, JOSEPH.
Painter. Born in Shavli, Russia, in 1887. Pupil of the Penna. Acad. of the Fine Arts, under Anshutz, Chase and Kendall. Member: Fellowship, Penna. Acad. of the Fine Arts; Philadelphia Sketch Club; Phila. Art Alliance. Exhibited a portrait, "The Red Headed Boy," at the Penna. Acad. of the Fine Arts, Philadelphia, 1924.

SADD, HENRY S.
Born in England. He was engraving good portraits in mezzotint in NY in 1840. He produced a number of plates in this country, but Mr. Alfred Jones says that he went to Australia after a comparatively short stay in the United States.

SAECKER, AUSTIN.
Painter. Born Appleton, WI, Feb. 13, 1896. Member: Wis. PS; Fellowship PAFA. Award: Medal, Milwaukee Art Inst., 1924; Business Men's AC prize, Wis. PS. Milwaukee,

1927. Address in 1929, 110 East College Ave.; h. 414 North Union St., Appleton, WI.

SAGE, CORNELIA BENTLEY.
Painter and writer. Born Buffalo, Oct. 3, 1876. Pupil of Buffalo ASL; ASL of NY. under Twachtman, Beckwith, Wiles and Reid. Member: Buffalo SA, ASL; Am. Assoc. of Mus.; Buffalo Guild of Allied Arts; Archaeological Soc. of Am.; School Art Assoc.; Cor. member Hispanic SA; Western Assoc. Art Musum Directors. Awards: Decoration of L'Officier de l'Instruction Publique, Paris, 1917; Decoration Palme d'Academique, 1917; Cross of the Legion of Honor, 1921; Sorolla medal, 1925. Director, Albright Art Gallery, 1910-1924, and of the School of the Albright Art Gal., 1910- 1916; member of the Nat'l Advisory Committee. Sesqui Centennial Expo., Phila., 1926; elected honorary advisor, Roerich Museum, NY, 1926; Archaeological Inst. of Am., 1927. Appointed "Patron of Am. Group of Painters and Sculptors in Paris," 1927. Director, Calif. Palace of the Legion of Honor. Address in 1929, 495 44th Ave., San Francisco, CA.

SAGE, KAY.
Painter. Born in Albany, NY in 1898. Awards: Art Institute of Chicago, 1945; Corcoran Gallery of Art, 1951; Conn. Development Commission, 1951. Collections: Art Institute of Chicago; Calif. Playhouse; Whitney Museum of American Art; Wesleyan Univ., Conn.; Met. Mus. of Art; Museum of Modern Art; Walker Art Center.

SAHLER, HELEN GERTRUDE.
Sculptor. Born Carmel, NY. Pupil of ASL of NY; Enid Yandell and H. A. MacNeil. Member: NA Women PS; MacD. C.; NY. Mun. AS.; CT. AFA; Art Workers C.; Alliance; AFA. Died in 1950. Address in 1929, 1088 Park Ave., New York, NY.

SAINT, LAWRENCE.
Etcher, craftsman, writer, and lecturer. Born Sharpsburg, PA, Jan. 29, 1885. Pupil of PAFA. Chase, Beaux, Poore, Sergeant Kendall and in Europe. Member:

Fellowship PAFA. Work in Victoria and Albert Museum, London; Carnegie Inst., Pittsburgh; Bryn Athyn Church, Bryn Athyn, PA. Illustrator of "Stained Glass of the Middle Ages in England and France"; author and illustrator of "A Knight of the Cross." Director, Stained Glass Dept., Washington Cathedral, Washington, D.C. Died in 1961. Address in 1929, Huntingdon Valley, PA.

SAINT GAUDENS, ANNETTA JOHNSON.
(Mrs. Louis Saint Gaudens). Sculptor. Born Flint, OH, Sept. 11, 1869. Pupil of Columbus Art School, ASL of NY under Twachtman and Saint Gaudens. Member: NA Women PS. Awards: McMillin prize, NA Women PS, 1913; hon. mention and silver medal, Pan Calif. Exp., San Diego, 1915. Work in Boston Museum of Art. Died in 1943. Address in 1929, Windsor, VT.

SAINT GAUDENS, AUGUSTUS.
Sculptor. Born in Dublin, March 1, 1848. Family moved to US same year. At age 13 apprenticed to stone cameo cutter and studied drawing at Cooper Inst. In 1864 changed employment to Jules LeBrethon and changed art school to NAD, where he began to model from life. In 1867 went to Paris to study at Petite Ecole, and later Ecole des Beaux Arts under Jouffroy; cut cameos to earn living. Spent about 4 yrs. studying in Rome. Located in NYC in 1873 anxious to complete the Farragut Statue. In 1876 he was engaged on his portrait bust of Chief Justice Taney for the Supr. Ct. Room. By 1885 Saint Gaudens had tested his abilities and had tasted success, after earlier years of poverty. Prominent works include the Shaw Mem., Boston; the Lincoln Statue, Chicago; the Adams Mem. and many other important works. Represented in permanent collections of Met. Mus of Art; PAFA; Corcoran Art Gal., etc. Mem. collection of casts of his works in Cornish, NH, presented by Mrs. Saint Gaudens to State of NH and open to the public. Died in Cornish, Aug. 3, 1907.

SAINT GAUDENS, CARLOTTA.
(Mrs. Homer). Miniature and water color painter. Born in Rochester, NY, in 1884. Pupil of Penna. Acad. of Fine Arts and Art Students' League of NY. Address in 1926, Windsor, VT. Died in 1927.

SAINT GAUDENS, LOUIS.
Sculptor. Brother of Augustus. Born in NY, on Jan. 1, 1853. He studied in Paris, and modeled a "Faun" and "St. John" for the church of the "Incarnation," NY, and other statues. Incl. lions at Boston Public Library; facade (6 statues), Union Station, Wash., DC; Homer, Lib. of Congress; Pipes of Pan. MMA. He worked in his brother's studio and assisted him with most of his work. Died March 8, 1913.

SAINT GAUDENS, PAUL.
Sculptor and craftsman. Born Flint, OH, June 15, 1900. Pupil of Frank Applegate, O. L. Bachelor, Arnold Ronnebeck, Archipenko. Member: Boston SAC; NYSC; Chicago AG; AFA. Address in 1929, Cornish, NH; h. Windsor, VT.

SAINT LANNE, LOUIS.
Sculptor. Member: NSS 1907. Born in 1871. Address in 1929, 432 West 22nd St., New York, NY.

SAKAOKA, YASUE.
Sculptor. Born in Himeji-City, Japan in 1933 and is now a permanent resident of the US. Studied: Aoyama Gakuin Univ., Japan; Reed College; Univ. of Oregon. Awards: Playground sculpture, Albany, Oregon; Int'l Alutrusan Award: Fellowship to Rinehart Institute of Sculpture, Baltimore, MD. Collections: Hollygrove Camp on Lake Gaston, Virginia; South Hill Park, South Hill, Virginia; Parkside Gardens, Baltimore, MD.

SALA, RAFAEL.
Painter, who exhibited in Philadelphia, 1921, in "Exhibition of Paintings Showing the Later Tendencies in Art." Address in 1926, 216 West 50th St., NYC.

SALAZAR, JOSEPH D.
Portrait painter, who had his studio in New Orleans about 1792. He painted a portrait of Danl. W. Coxe, which was exhibited at the Loan Exhibition of Historic Portraits at the PAFA in 1887.

SALDUTTI, DENISE.
Illustrator. Born in Newark, NJ. Attended PSD, where she studied under Maurice Sendak. In 1974 she began illustrating and was selected to appear in the S of I Annual Show in 1975 and 1976.

SALEMME, ANTONIO.
Sculptor. Born in Italy, in 1892. Student at Boston Museum of Fine Arts and afterwards abroad. Member of National Sculpture Society. Works: Bronze statue, "Prayer," Newark Public Library; Portrait, Mr. W. A. Read, Robert Stein and Stanley Kimmel. Address in 1929, 53 Washington Square, New York. Address in 1926, 53 Washington Square, New York.

SALERNO, VINCENT.
Illustrator. Born Sicily, Italy. Feb. 10, 1893. Pupil of A. Stirling Calder, Francis C. Jones; NAD; Beaux Arts Institute. Address in 1929, 50 East 34th Street, h. 1919 Seventh Ave., New York, NY.

SALING, HENRY (FREDERICK).
Painter. Born Hartford, March 3, 1901. Pupil of Paul E. Saling; Michel Jacobs. Member: CT. AFA; Springfield AL. Address in 1929, 147 Fairfield Ave.; h. 248 Fairfield Ave., Hartford, CT.

SALING, PAUL E.
Painter. Born Germany, July 19, 1876. Studied in Germany and with Charles Noel Flagg, A. Bunce and CT. Lg. Art Students; Springfield AL. AFA. Award: Hon. mention, CT. AFA, 1915. Represented in Gallery of Storrs College, Storrs, CT; East Hartford Trust Co.; Odd Fellows Temple, Hartford, CT; Elks Temple, New London, CT. Died in 1936. Address in 1929, 147 Fairfield Ave., Hartford, CT; summer, Lyme, CT.

SALISBURY, A(LTA) W(EST) (MRS.).
Painter. Born Darnestown, MD. Pupil of Corcoran School of Art, Cullen Yates and Leon Dabo, and in Dresden. Member: NA. Women PS; Brooklyn SA.; Wolfe C.; New Rochelle AA.; CT. AFA. Address in 1929, 75 Ellenton Ave., New Rochelle, NY.

SALMON, ROBERT W.
Born C. 1775. An English marine painter, who came to this country in 1828. He was painting in Boston as late as 1840. His painting "The Wharves of Boston" hangs in the old Boston State House. "Rocks at Nahant," and a list of his paintings are preserved at the Boston Mus. of FA. Died c. 1842.

SALTONSTALL, ELIZABETH.
Lithographer. Born in Chestnut Hill, MA, on July 26, 1900. Studied: Boston Museum of Fine Arts School; and with Andre L'Hote in Paris; also with Stow Wengenroth and Frank Swift Chase. Collections: Boston Museum of Fine Arts; Boston Public Library; Library of Congress, Yale Univ. Address in 1980, 231 Chestnut Hill Rd., Chestnut Hill, MA.

SALVATORE, VICTOR D.
Sculptor, painter and teacher. Born Italy, July 7, 1885. Pupil of Charles Niehaus and A. Phimister Proctor. Member: NSS 1913; A. Aid S; Arch. Lg. of NY; Century A. Awards: Bronze medal, St. Louis Exp., 1904; silver medal, P.-P. Exp., San F., 1915; Barnett prize, NAD, 1919; hon. mention, AIC, 1919; hon mention, Concord AA, 1920. Work: Head of a Child, Met. Mus. of Art; Head of a Child, Brooklyn Mus. of Art; Head of a Girl, Mus. of Art, Portland, OR. Died in 1965. Address in 1929, 8 Macdougal Alley; h. 25 Washington Square, North, New York, NY; h. "Swanswick," Springfield Centre, Otsego Co., NY.

SAMMONS, FREDERICK HARRINGTON C.
Painter. Born in Bath, EN, in 1838. He lived in America for many years, and was connected with the AIC. He was also a skillful restorer of paintings. Died in Chicago, 1917.

SAMPLE, PAUL.
Illustrator. Born in Kentucky in Sept. 14, 1896. Received his art training from Jonas Lie. During his long career as an editorial and advertising illustrator he earned a reputation for painting country landscapes. Among his clients were Maxwell House Coffee and Ford Motor Company. His works were exhibited at the 1940 NY World's Fair and at the Golden Gate International Exposition. A long-time resident of New Hampshire, he was artist-in-residence at Dartmouth College and a member of the NAD. Died in 1974.

SAMPSON, ALDEN.
Painter. Born in Manchester, ME, in 1853. Address in 1926, 168 East 51st Street, New York, NY.

SANBORN, EARL EDWARD.
Painter and teacher. Born Lyme, NH. May 21, 1890. Pupil of Burbank, Tarbell, Benson and Paxton. Member: Boston AC. Awards: Paige European Traveling Scholarship from the Boston Museum of Fine Arts, 1914-16. Died in 1937. Address in 1929, 162 Washington St., Wellesley Hills, MA; summer, Box 33, York Beach, Maine.

SANDEFUR, JOHN COURTNEY.
Etcher. Born Indiana, May 26, 1893. Pupil of Allen E. Philbrick. Member: Chicago SE; Il. AFA. Award: Frank Cunningham prize, Hoosier Salon, Chicago, 1928. Address in 1929, 524 West 72nd Street, Chicago, IL.

SANDERS, ADAM ACHOD.
Sculptor and teacher. Born Sweden, June, 1889. Pupil of Beaux Arts Inst. of Design, New York. Member: Brooklyn SA; Bronx AF; S. Indp. A.; Brooklyn PSS; AFA. Work: "Abraham Lincoln," Lincoln Memorial Collection, Washington, D.C.; "Beethoven," Library of the Friends of Music,NY; Schubert medal, commemoration Schubert Centenary, presented to Artur Brodanzky, Conductor Metropolitan Opera House, NY. Address in 1929, 1013 Kelly Street, New York, NY.

SANDERSON, CHARLES WESLEY.
Painter. Born in Brandon, VT, in
1838. He studied in VT, later went
to Paris and studied at Julien's.
On his return to this country he
painted landscapes in water colors.
His studio was in Boston, and he
died there on March 8, 1905.

SANDHAM, HENRY.
Painter. Born in Montreal in 1842.
He worked in Canada until 1880 when
he went to England, and on his
return from abroad he established
his studio in Boston. His best
work is done in historical painting
and portraiture, and he has success
with marine painting. His
portraits of Dr. Duryea and Robert
Swan are in Boston. He was a
member of the Boston Art Club.
Died Jan. 6, 1912, in London,
England.

SANDMAN, JO.
Painter. Born in Boston, Mass. in
1931. Studied: Hans Hofmann
School of Fine Arts, Provincetown,
Mass.; Univ. of Calif. at Berkeley;
Radcliffe College, Cambridge, Mass.
Exhibitions: DeCordova Museum,
Lincoln, Mass., 1952; Nexus
Gallery, Boston, 1958, 1961; O. K.
Harris Works of Art, NYC, 1975.
Collections: Mass. Institute of
Technology, Cambridge; Addison
Gallery of American Art, Andover,
Mass.; Brockton Art Center,
Lincoln, MA.

SANDONA, MATTEO.
Painter. Born Schio, Italy, April
15, 1881. Pupil of Nani and
Bianchi. Member: San. F. AA.;
Bohemian C., San Francisco; AFA.
Awards: Silver medal, Lewis and
Clark Expo., Portland, 1905; silver
medal, Sacramento, 1917; first
prize, Sacramento State Fair, 1926;
second prize, Chicago Gal. A.,
1926. Member: International Jury
of Awards for Paintings, Panama
Pacific Expo., San Francsico, 1915.
Work: "Portrait of Mary Pickford,"
National Gallery, Washington, DC;
"Chrysanthemums," Golden Gate Park
Memorial Museum, San Francisco;
"Portrait of Hon. Sanford B. Dole,"
Punahou College, Honolulu, Hawaii;
several etchings and dry points,
Palace of the Legion of Honor, San
Francisco; "Amber Beads," Mills

College, Calif.; "Reflections,"
High School, Salt Lake City, Utah.
Address in 1929, 471 Buena Vista
Ave., San Francisco, CA.

SANDOR, MATHIAS.
Painter. Born in Hungary in 1857;
died in NYC on Nov. 3, 1920.
Educated at Art Students' League of
NY, 1885-86; Academie Julien,
Paris, 1889-90, under Francois
Flameng and Gabriel Ferrier. Came
to the US in 1881, and began making
designs for commericial purposes
and painting portraits. He became
a portrait, miniature and landscape
painter. Member of Artists Fund
Society, and of the American
Federation of Arts. He exhibits in
all important exhibitions.

SANDS, J.
An engraver of music on copper,
working in Baltimore about 1824. He
signed his name "J. Sands Sc.".

SANDZEN, SVEN BIRGER.
Painter, etcher, teacher, writer,
and lecturer. Born Bildsberg,
Sweden, Feb. 5, 1871. Pupil of
Stockholm Artists League under Zorn
and Bergh; Aman Jean in Paris; came
to US in 1894. Professor of
aesthetics and painting, Bethany
College, since 1894. Member:
NYWCC; Calif. WCS; Phila. WCC.
Awards: First Moore prize ($100),
Artists of Kansas City and
vicinity, 1917; Phila. WCC prize,
1922. Work in: National Mus.,
Stockholm; Lund Museum, Sweden;
Library of Congress, Washington;
Chicago Art Inst.; Brooklyn Museum;
Yale Art Museum; Art Museum of
Gottenburg, Sweden; Art Museum of
Santa Fe, N.M.; Graphic Coll.
Bibliotheque Nationale, Paris.
Died in 1954. Address in 1929,
Bethany College, Lindsborg, Kansas.

SANFORD, EDWARD FIELD JR.
Sculptor. Born New York, April 6,
1886. Studied: ASL of NY; NAD;
Julian Academy in Paris; Royal
Academy in Munich. Member: NSS;
Beaux Arts Inst.; NAC. Work:
"Pegasus," bronze statuette, RI.
Schl. of Design, Providence;
Charles Francis Adams Memorial,
Washington and Lee University,
Lexington, VA; Commemorative
Tablet, Columbia Univ.; Core

Memorial Norfolk, CA; 2 pediments, 4 colossal figures and 20 bas relief panels, State Capitol, Sacramento, CA.; Finial figure and 3 colossal Gothic figures for the Alabama Power Co. Bldg. Director, Dept. of Sculpture, Beaux Arts Inst. of Design, 1912-25. Address in 1929, 185 Sixth Ave., New York, NY.

SANFORD, ISAAC.
Engraver. As early as 1783 Isaac Sanford engraved a music book entitled "Select Harmony, containing the Necessary Rules of Psalmody, together with a Collection of Approved Psalm Tunes, Hymns and Anthems." By Oliver Brownson. Mr. James Terry, in referring to this book, in his "Ex Libris Leaflet, No. 4," describes the title as contained in a circle of music, and the whole within an engraving signed by I. Sanford, 1783. He published fairly well executed stipple portraits and book illustrations in Hartford, CT, as late as 1822. Died c. 1842, in Philadelphia.

SANFORD, MARION.
Sculptor. Born in Guelph, Ontario, Canada in 1904. Studied: Pratt Institute Art School; Art Students' League; and with Brenda Putnam. Awards: Guggenheim fellowship, 1941-1943; National Academy of Design, 1943; Allied Artists of America, 1945; National Academy of Design, 1947; Meriden, Conn., 1949; American Artists Professional League, 1945; Springfield Mass. Museum of Art, 1957. Collections: Penn. Academy of Fine Arts; Corcoran Gallery of Art; Brookgreen Gardens, South Carolina; Warren Penn. Public Library; Haynes Collection, Boston; Norton Hall, Chautauqua, NY; Warren General Hospital, Penn.; Cosmopolitan Club, NY; Trinity Memorial Church, Warren, Penn.; St. Marys Chapel, Faribault, Minn.; US Post Office, Winder, Georgia.

SANGER, GRACE H. H.
Painter and illustrator. Born Newark, NJ, June 15, 1881. Pupil of Howard Pyle, W. M. Chase, Hugh Breckenridge. Member: North Shore AA; Baltimore WCC. Illustrator of

"Eve Dorre" (Dorran & Co.). Address in 1929, Ruxton, MD.

SANGER, I. J.
Painter, illustrator, draftsman, and lithographer. Born Port Republic, VA, Jan. 8, 1899. Pupil of Arthur W. Dow; Columbia University. Award: Joint prize for best print, The Print Club, Philadelphia, 1929. Address in 1929, 408 West 130th Street, New York, NY.

SANGER, WILLIAM.
Painter and etcher. Born Berlin, Germany, of American parents, Nov. 12, 1875. Pupil of ASL of NY. Artists and Artisans Inst. of NY. Represented by "City of Vigo," Hispanic Society of America, New York; entire cycle of figures of the Gate of Glory, Santiago Cathedral, Spain; "Seal Cove, Grand Manan," Newark Museum; "South Bridge, Eastport" and "Surf," Brooklyn Museum. Address in 1929, 285 W. 11th Street, New York, NY; summer, Fire Island, P. Q.

SANGERNEBO, A(LEXANDER).
Sculptor. Born Estonia, Russia, May 1, 1856. Member: IN. AC. Work in: Murat Temple, Lincoln Hotel, Union Station, Guaranty Building, Blind Institution, S. Joan of Arc Church, Ayres Bldg., IN. Nat'l Guard Armory, and Indiana Theatre, Indianapolis; County Court House, Lebanon, IN. Address in 1929, 324 East 12th Street, Indianapolis, IN.

SANGERNEBO, EMMA EYLES.
(Mrs. Alexander Sangernebo). Sculptor and painter. Born Pittsburgh, PA, Jan. 23, 1877. Pupil of William Forsyth. Member: In. AC: Hoosier Salon. Work: Figure panels, Loew's Theatre, Historic panel, Washington High School, Indianapolis; Elizabeth Bartnett Hitt memorial portrait tablet, Indianapolis (IN), Woman's Department Club. Address in 1929, Market Street, h. 324 E. 12th Street, Indianapolis, IN.

SANIN, FANNY.
Painter. Born in Bogota, Colombia. Now living and working in NYC. Studied: Univ. of the Andes,

Bogota; Univ. of Illinois, Urbana, IL; Chelsea School of Art, London. Awards: I Edinburgh Open 100, Edinburgh, Scotland, 1967; II Coltejer Art Biennale, Medellin, 1970. Exhibitions: Modern Art Gallery, Monterey, Mexico, 1964; Pan- American Union Gallery, Wash., DC, 1969; Union Carbide Building, NYC, 1975. Collections: Museum of Modern Art of Bogota, Colombia; Museum of Contemporary Art, Bogota; Museum of Fine Arts of Caracas, Venezuela.

SANSAM, MISS EDITH.
Painter. Born in Evanston, IL. Studied in School of New Orleans Artists Assoc. President of the "Black and White Club." Won Pinckney Smith medal for sketches, and Artists Assoc. medal for landscape in oil.

SANTORE, CHARLES.
Illustrator. Born in Phila., in 1935. Attended the Phila. College of Art. He began his career in 1959 with an illustration for The Saturday Evening Post after studying with Henry Pitz and Albert Gold. He has illustrated for most major magazines and was awarded Gold Medals from the Phila. ADC. In 1972, he received an Award of Excellence from the S of I and the Hamilton King Award.

SARDEAU, HELENE.
Sculptor. Born in Antwerp, Belgium, in 1899. Studied: Art Students' League; NY School of American Sculpture. Award: Architectural League, 1934. Collections: Croton-on-Hudson High School; US Post Office, Greenfield, Mass.; Fairmount Park, Phila., Penn.; National Library, Rio de Janeiro; Supreme Court, Mexico City; Whitney Museum of American Art; Tel-Aviv Museum, Israel.

SARG, TONY.
Painter, illustrator, craftsman, writer, and lecturer. Born Guatemala, Central America, April 24, 1880. Member: Salma. C.; SI.; GFLA. Illustrated "Speaking of Operations" and "Fiddle D. D.," by Irvin S. Cobb. Creator of Tony Sarg's Marionettes and of motion picture shadowgraph productions;

Tony Sarg's Almanac. Died in 1942. Address in 1929, 54 West 9th Street, New York, NY; h. 24 Ivanhoe Terrace, East Orange, NJ.

SARGEANT, CLARA McMCLEAN.
Painter. Born Washington, IA, June 24, 1889. Pupil of Cleveland School of Art; ASL of NY; Corcoran School, Washington, D.C. Member: Woman's AC, Cleveland. Awards: Third portrait prize, 1922, and hon. mention, 1924-1928, Cleveland Museum of Art. Address in 1929, 2258 Euclid Ave., Cleveland, Ohio, 15706 Grovewood Ave., Northeast, Cleveland, OH.

SARGEANT, GENEVE RIXFORD.
Painter. Born San Francisco in 1868. Pupil of Emil Carlsen; Andre L'hote. Member: San. F. AA; Chicago SA. Award: Cahn prize, AIC, 1903. Address in 1929, 115 rue Notre Dame des Champs, Paris VI, France.

SARGENT, HENRY.
Painter. Born in Gloucester, MA, in 1770. He copied the work of Copley and other early American Artists. In 1790 Trumbull commended his work and in 1793 he went to London with letters to West, but returned to Boston in 1797. He received several military commissions. He studied in Gilbert Stuart's studio in Boston about 1806, with whom he was very friendly. Many of his paintings will be found in Boston. Colonel Sargent died in that city Feb. 21, 1845.

SARGENT, JOHN SINGER.
Painter. Born of American parents in Florence, Italy, in 1856. Educated in Florence, Rome, and Nice; went to Paris in 1874, where he entered studio of Carolus Duran, then the most popular portrait painter. Spent five years there at studio, assisted master with murals, and traveled to Italy and Spain, where he studied work of Velazquez. Painted portraits of Carolus Duran, considered one of his greatest pictures. Moved to London in 1884; spent much time in US painting many fine portraits in NY and Boston. Received commissions from Public Library of

816

Boston and Boston Mus. of Fine Arts to paint mural decorations for their buildings. Works include portraits of Henry G. Marquand and Wm. M. Chase, Met. Mus. of Art; "Daughters of Edward Boit," Boston Mus. of Fine Arts; "Mr. and Mrs. Field," PAFA; Edwin Booth and Joseph Jefferson as "Dr. Pangloss," the Players Club of NY; "President Lowell," of Harvard at Harvard U. Retro. of important works held Feb. - March 1924 at Grand Central art galleries, NY. Mem. Exhib held Jan - Feb. 1926 at Met. Mus. of Art, 59 oil paintings and 62 watercolors. Biographies include "Sargent," T. Martin Wood; "John S. Sargent, His Life and Work," William Howe Downes (1925). Died in London, April 15, 1925.

SARGENT, M(ARGARET) (W.).
Sculptor. Born Wellesley, MA, Aug. 31, 1892. Pupil of Woodbury and Borglum. Member: NA Women PS. Address in 1929, care of Mrs. L. A. S. McKean, Prides Crossing, MA; Wellesley, MA; summer, care Mrs. Moon, Dorset, VT.

SARGENT, MARY F.
Etcher. Born in Somerset, PA, in 1875. Studied: Penn. College for Women; Art Students' League; Columbia Univ.; and in Paris and London; also studied with William P. Robbins, Paul Bornet and St. Gaudens. Award: Penn. College for Women. Collections: Metropolitan Museum of Art; Library of Congress; Brooklyn Museum; Brooks Memorial Art Gallery; G.W.V. Smith Art Museum.

SARGENT, PAUL T(URNER).
Painter. Born Hutton, IL, July 23, 1880. Member: Brown Co. AA of IN; Hoosier Salon. Address in 1929, Carleston, IL.

SARGENT, WALTER.
Painter. Born in Worcester, MA, in 1868. Pupil of Colarossi and Delecluse Academies in Paris. Address in 1929, University of Chicago, Chicago, IL. Died Sept. 19, 1927 in North Scituate, MA.

SARKA, CHARLES NICOLAS.
Mural painter and illustrator. Born Chicago, IL, Dec. 6, 1879.

Member: Aquarellists. Awards: Collaborative prize, NY Arch. Lg., 1913; first prize for poster cover, St. Louis Pageant, 1914. Address in 1929, 692 Madison Ave, New York, NY; summer, Green Lake, Fulton Co., NY.

SARKADI, LEO (SCHULLER).
Painter, writer, and illustrator. Born Budapest, Hungary, May 24, 1879. Member: Green Room C; S. Indp. A; AFA. Address in 1929, 200 West 57th Street, h. 256 Seaman Ave., New York, NY.

SARNOFF, LOLO.
(Ms.) Sculptor and collector. Born in Frankfurt, Ger., Jan. 9, 1916; US cit. 1943. Study: Reimann Art Sch., Berlin, Ger., grad. 1936; art history at Univs. of Berlin & Florence, 1934-37. Work: Corning (NY) Mus. of Glass; Nat'l. Acad. of Sci., Wash. DC; The David Kreeger Coll., Wash. DC; Joseph H. Hirshhorn, Wash. DC; many other publ. and priv. colls. in US and abroad. Comn: "The Flame," J. F. Kennedy Center; "The Spiral Galaxy," Nat'l. Air & Space Mus.; "Today & Tomorrow," Fed. Nat'l. Mortgage Assn., all in Wash. DC. Exhib.: Agra Gal., Wash. DC, solo, 1968; Corning (NY) Mus., solo, 1970; Int'l. Kunstmesse, Basel, Switz., 1972; Nat'l. Lg. Am. Pen Women, Wash. DC, 1977; Gallery Two, Woodstock, VT, 1977; Alwin Gal., London, solo, 1981; Gal. von Bartha, Basel, Switz., solo, 1982; many other group and solo shows in US and abroad 1968 to present. Awards: "Medaglia d'Oro," Accademia Italia delle Arti e del Lavoro; Am. Artists of Renown; many other honors. Mem.: Artists Equity Assn.; Am. Pen Women; Wash. Women's Art Ctr.; Trustee, Corcoran Gal., Wash. DC. Collection: 20th cent. drawing, painting, sculpture; 18th cent. Faience; 18th cent. porcelain. 1948-61, cardiovascular physiology and research, various capacities incldg. research assist., inventor, corp. VP, Pres.; author of many scientific articles. Media: Light sculpture, plexiglass, fiberoptics, acrylic. Dealer: Gallery K, Wash. DC; Gallery Two, Woodstock, VT; Gallery von Bartha, Basel, Switz. Address

in 1983, 7507 Hampden Lane, Bethesda, MD.

SARONY, NAPOLEON.
Artist. Born March 9, 1821 in Quebec. Identified with lithographic printing houses since his thirteenth year. Also drew portraits in charcoal. He signed some pieces himself, executed in a graceful and smooth manner. Died Nov. 9, 1896, in NYC.

SARTAIN, EMILY.
Engraver. Born in Philadelphia in 1841. The daughter of John Sartain, she learned to engrave under the tuition of her father; she also studied art under Scheussele, in Phila. and under Luminais, in Paris, in 1871-75. She engraved and signed a few mezzotint portraits. In 1881-83, Emily Sartain was the art editor of Our Continent, and in 1886 she became principal of the Philadelphia School of Design for Women. Miss Sartain is also a painter of portraits and genre subjects, and exhibited at the Paris Salon in 1875 and 1883. Address in 1926, 1346 N. Broad Street, Phialdelphia. Died June 18, 1927 in Philadelphia.

SARTAIN, HARRIET.
Landscape painter. Born in Philadelphia. Pupil of Philadelphia School of Design for Women, and of Teachers College, NY. Member of Plastic Club; National Association of Women Painters and Sculptors; Philadelphia Art Alliance, and Dean of Phila. School of Design for Women. Address in 1926, 1346 North Broad St., Philadelphia, PA.

SARTAIN, JOHN.
Engraver. Born in London in 1808. Apprenticed in Feb. 1823, to John Swain, a London engraver. First significant plates were line illustrations for "The Early Florentine School," by Wm. Young Ottley, London, 1826. 1827-28 apprenticed to Henry Richter of London; engraved his first mezzotint plate, "Omphale,." Engraved "The Tight Shoe," which he brought to US and sold in 1830 to Mr. Littell, Phila. publisher. At termination of apprenticeship,

commenced own business in London, engraved portrait of Sir Charles Wilkins and Annual plates for the Ackermans. Moved to Phila., 1830; executed mezzotint plate after "Old Age," a painting by John Neagle; and line plate "Deer," in a landscape, after a painting by Thomas Doughty. In 1843 became proprietor of "Campbell's Foreign Semi-Monthly Magazine." 1841-48 was engraving for "Graham's Magazine." 1848 became part journal owner of "Sartain's Union Magazine," discontinued in 1852. Sartain was art manager and engraver for all these magazines. After 1852, devoted himself to general engraving. Total output of engraved plates approx. 1,500. Executed large portrait mezzotint plates and also painted miniatures. For life of Sartain see "The Reminiscences of a Very Old Man," by John Sartain. Died in Phila., Oct. 25, 1897.

SARTAIN, SAMUEL.
Engraver. Born Oct. 8, 1830 in Philadelphia. Samuel Sartain studied engraving under his father, John Sartain, and became an admirable engraver of mezzotint portraits. About 1851 he commenced business on his own acount in Phila., and did much work for the publishers of that period. His best plates were after the paintings of Peale, Sully and Neagle. Died Dec. 20, 1906 in Phila.

SARTAIN, WILLIAM.
Engraver. Born in Philadelphia in 1843. William Sartain, the son of John Sartain, studied mezzotint engraving with his father and issued and signed a few portrait plates. He then studied art in Paris, under Bonnat and at the Ecole des Beaux Arts, and became a reputable painter of landscape. Died in Oct. 1924, in NYC. Mr. Sartain was one of the founders of the Society of American Artists, and became an Assoc. Member of the Nat. Acad. of Design. He was president of the NY Art Club, and was later a teacher in the life class of the Art Students' League of NY. He died in 1924. He is represented in the Metropolitan

Museum of NY, and in the Corcoran Art Gallery of Washington, DC.

BARTELLE, MILDRED E.
Sculptor, who exhibited at the Penna. Acad. of Fine Arts, Philadelphia, 1924. Address in 1926, 15 Leighton Road, Wellesley, MA.

BATRE, AUGUST.
Painter. Born Norway, Feb. 19, 1876. Member: Providence WCC. Address in 1929, 22 Pullis Ave., Middle Village, LI, NY.

BATTERLEE, WALTER.
Born in Brooklyn, NY, in 1844. He was a pupil of the National Acad., also of Edwin White and Leon Bonnat. He was elected an Associate Member of the Acad. in 1879, and in 1886 he gained the Clarke prize. Among his works are "Contemplation" owned by Smith College,"Autumn," "The Cronies," and "The Fortune Teller." He died May 28, 1908, in NY.

BAUER, LEROY D.
Etcher, craftsman, and teacher. Born Dayton, Ohio, Feb. 17, 1894. Pupil of Peixotto, Hopkins, Meakin, Wessel, Keller, Orr, Lachman. Member: Bayton SE; Dayton GFA. Address in 1929, Mutual Home Bldg.; h. 506 Volusia Ave, Dayton, Ohio.

BAULNIER, H. E.
A scipt and letter engraver working in Philadelphia in 1830-40. He engraved one of the early certificated of membership of the Franklin Institute, of that city.

BAUNDER, KENDALL.
Painter. Born at Templeton, MA, in 1886. Pupil of Julien Acad. under Laurens, in Paris. Address in 1929, 47 Fifth Ave., New York, NY, or Westport, CT.

BAUNDERS, CLARA R(OSSMAN).
Painter. Member: Wash. WCC; Wash. SA; Wash. AC. Died in 1951. Address in 1929, 808 17th Street, N. W.; 2900 O St., Washington, D.C.

BAUNDERS, L. PEARL.
Painter, illustrator, and teacher. Born Tennessee. Pupil of Chase in Italy, Hawthorne, ASL of NY.

Member: Southern SAL; Nashville AA; Chicago AG; S. Indp. A.; Alliance; NA Women PS. Awards: First prize, war poster, New Orleans, 1916; first prize, Southeastern Fari Asso.; first prize, TN State Fair; first prize, NC State Fair; Chase prize, Italy; second prize, Nashville Mus. of Art, 1928; first prize, NC State Fair, 1928. Represented in collections of Art Association and Centennial Club. Nashville; Murfreesboro Women's Club; Continental Hall. D. A. R., Washington, DC; Jackson Woman's Club. Author of "Make Your Own Posters." Address in 1929, 322 North Royal St., Jackson, TN; summer, Lake Junaluska, NC.

SAUNDERS, SOPHIA.
Miniature painter, who flourished in 1851-52 in New York.

SAUTER, GEORGE.
Painter. Born in 1866. Exhibited at the Penna. Acad. of Fine Arts, Philadelphia, 1915. Address in 1929, 1 Holland Park Ave., London, England. Died in 1937.

SAVAGE, DOROTHY L.
Painter, who exhibited water colors at the Penna. Acad. of Fine Arts, Philadelphia, 1925. Address in 1926, 300 Goodwood Road, Baltimore, MD.

SAVAGE, EDWARD.
Painter. Born Nov. 26, 1761, Worcester, MA. Father of Edward, Abraham Savage, had been driven from France, by revocation of Edict of Nantes. Originally a goldsmith. He was portrait painter at 28 when he left MA. As first commissions he painted a portrait of Pres. Willard of Harvard College. His engraved portraits of General Knox and of Washington were issued in London, 1791-92-93. In 1794, Savage returned to US, living in Phila. In 1795 he exhibited the first panorama ever shown of that city, of London and Westminster, and a newspaper states that it was painted "in a circle and looks like reality." Savage apparently remained in Phila. until 1801. Then went to NY, Boston, and

Princeton. In NY Savage joined forces with Daniel Bowen, in the NY Museum. Dunlap in his "History of the Arts of Design" calls it "A mingled establishment, half painting gallery, half museum." In 1795 these collections were transferred to Boston, and presented at "The Head of the Mall" as the Columbia Mus. The engraving of the Washington Family was published by Savage in 1798. David Edwin the engraver was assisting Savage at this time. John Sartain the engraver said "Savage drew the outlines on copper, but Edwin did a large part of the engraving." This is corroborated in part by the painter, James R. Lambdin, in 1798." Besides his portraits of Washington, Savage painted portraits of Generals Wayne and Knox; also of Robert Morris, Dr. William Handy, Benjamin Rush, and John Langdon, and many others prominent at that time. Died July 6, 1817 in Princeton, MA.

SAVAGE, EUGENE F(RANCIS).
Painter. Born Covington, IN, 1883. Pupil of Corcoran Art Gallery, AIC. Member: ANA, 1924; NA, 1926; Century C.; Painter and Sculptors Gallery Assoc. Alumni Am. Acad. in Rome. Awards: American Acad. in Rome Fellowship, 1912-15; gold medal, NY Arch. Lg., 1921; Clarke prize ($300) and Saltus medal, NAD, 1922; French Memorial gold medal, AIC, 1922; Harris silver medal, AIC, 1923; second Altman prize ($500), 1923; Isidor gold medal, NAD, 1924; Schaffer prie ($500), 1925. Work: "Arbor Day," Art Inst. of Chicago; "Expulsion," St. Louis Museum of Fine Arts. Professor of painting, Yale Univ. School of Fine Arts. Address in 1929, 200 West 57th Street, New York, NY; Ossining, NY.

SAVAGE, MARGUERITE DOWNING (MRS.).
Painter and illustrator. Born Bay Ridge, LI, Sept. 6, 1879. Pupil of E. C. Messer, E. L. Morse, Richard Miller. Member: Worcester GAC. Work: Portrait of Bishop Arthur C. Coxe, Coxe Hall, Hobart College, Geneva, NY; portrait of Alfred Eels, Alpha Delta Phi Fraternity House, Cornell University, Ithaca and Leland Stanford University, CA.

Address in 1929, 41 Lancaste: Street, Worcester, MA.; summer Prouts Neck, ME.

SAVIER, HELEN.
See Mrs. F. V. DuMond.

SAVILLE, BRUCE WILDER.
Sculptor and teacher. Born Quincy MA, March 16, 1893. Pupil o Boston Normal Art School unde: Dallin, and of Mr. and mrs. Kitson Member: Copley S.; Boston AL Boston AC; NSS; NY Arch. Lg.; NAC AFA. Work: "John Hancock Statue, Quincy, MA; 3 memorials to civi war veterans, Vicksburg, (Miss Nat'l Park; Collingwood Memorial Kansas City, MO; Potter Memorial Annapolis; Memorial Angel Quinc: High School; Memorial Tablet t: Unknown Dead of World War, Quincy Canadian Infantryman, St. John': Victory figure in collaboratio: with Mossman at Chicopee, MA Forrester Memorial, Worcester, MA Memorial of 3 wars at Palmyra, ME Memorial to 104th Infantry 16tl Div., Westfield, MA; World Wa: Memorial, Upton, MA; Worl: Memorial, Ravenna, O.; Peac: memorial, Civil War, State Hous: grounds, Columbus, Ohio; Macl Memorial, Ohio State Univ.; panels, Jeffery Manufacturing Co Office Bldg. and Ohio State Worl: War Memorial, Columbus, OH; Worl: War Memorials at Glens Falls, N' and Quincy, MA; John and Joh: Quincy Adams Memorial, Wollaston MA; Anthony Wayne Memorial, Toledo Ohio; memorial group, "Until th: Dawn," White Chapel, Memorial Park Detroit, MI. Died in 1938 Address in 1929, 185 Sixth Ave., h 53 West 12th Street, New York, NY.

SAVORY.
This name is appended as engrave: to a somewhat crudely executed lin: engraving of the "Trinity Church Pittsburgh, Founded A. D. 1824." The Plate is signed "Savory Sc Pitt." There is no date, bu: appearances would indicate that th: work was done about 1830-40.

SAWRIE, MARY B (MRS.).
Miniature painter. Born i: Nashville, TN, 1879. Pupil o: Chase, Vanderpoel, Dow, and Julie:

in Paris. Address in 1926, 710 Russell St., Nashville, TN.

AWTELLE, A. ELIZABETH.
Painter. Pupil of School of Design for Women and Drexel Inst., Phila.; Corcoran Art School, Washington; Ingram Summer School, Cornwall, England.; Woodbury. Member: Wash. WCC; Wash. SA; Providence WCC; Wash. AC. Address in 1929, 2102 O St., Washington, DC; summer, Ogunquit, ME.

AWTELLE, MARY BERKELEY.
(Mrs. Charles G. Sawtelle). Painter. Born Washington, Aug. 24, 1872. Pupil of Corcoran School of Art in Washington; Delecluse and Colarossi Academies in Paris; Edwin Scott in Paris; Irving Wiles and Charles Hawthorne in NY. Member: Wash. WCC; Wash. SA; SSAL. Work: "Alice by the Sea," Isaac Delgado Museum, New Orleans, LA. Director, Asheville School of Art. Address in 1929, 147 East 37th Street, NYC; summer, care of the Asheville School of Art, Asheville, NC.

SAWYER, EDITH.
Painter. Born South Coventry, CT. Pupil of Adelphi School, ASL of NY. Member: PA. S. Min. P. Brooklyn S. Min. P.; Brooklyn AG; NA Women PS; New Haven PCC. Specialty, miniatures. Address in 1929, Ovington Bldg., 246 Fulton St., Brooklyn, New York, NY; summer, Columbia, CT.

SAWYER, EDWARD WARREN.
Sculptor. Born Chicago, IL, March 17, 1876. Pupil of J. P. Laurens, Injalbert, R. Verlet, Fremiet, A. Rodin. Awards: Bronze medal, St. Louis, 1904; prize Pan Pacific, 1914; silver medal, Ghent, 1913; hon. mention, Paris Salon, 1914. Work: Medallions, "American Indians," American Numismatic Society, New York; Art Institute of Chicago; MA Historical Society, Boston; US Mint, Philadelphia; Musee Luxembourg, Paris. Died in 1932. Address in 1929, Clos Vert La Palasse, Toulon, Var., France.

SAWYER, HELEN ALTON.
(Helen Sawyer Farnsworth). Painter. Born in Wash., DC in 1900. Studied: National Academy of Design; and with Charles Hawthrone. Awards: Hudson Valley Art Institute, 1935, 1936; Fine Prints of the Year, 1937; Ringling Museum of Art Circus Exhibition, 1950, 1951; Florida Federation of Art, 1956, 1957. Collections: Library of Congress; Toledo Museum of Art; Whitney Museum of American Art; John Herron Art Institute; Penn. Academy of Fine Arts; Vanderpoel Collection; Miami Univ., Oxford, Ohio; International Business Machines; Chesapeake and Ohio Collection; National City Bank, NY; High Museum of Art, Atlanta. Address in 1980, 3842 Flamingo, Sarasota, FL, living in MA in 1929.

SAWYER, PHIL(IP) (AYER).
Painter and lecturer. Born Chicago, IL. Pupil of Leon Bonnat in Paris. Member: Detroit S. Indp. A.; Scarab C. Work: Mural, "Progress," Gary School, Chicago; etching "L Bridge," Library of Congress, Washington, DC and NY Public Library. Died in 1949. Address in 1929, 253 East Forest St.; care of the Scarab Club, Detroit, MI.

SAWYER, WELLS M.
Painter and illustrator. Born Iowa, Jan. 31, 1863. Pupil of AIC.; Wash. ASL; Corcoran Art School; J. O. Anderson and Howard Helmick. Member: Wash. SA.; Yonkers AA; Salma. C. Represented in Museum of the City of NY. Commissioner Museum of Science and Arts, Yonkers. Died in 1961. Address in 1929, 47 Fifth Ave, NYC.

SAXON, CHARLES DAVID.
Illustrator and cartoonist. Born NYC, Nov. 13, 1920. Studied at Columbia U.; Hamilton College. In collections of Lib. of Congress; Columbia U. Received gold medal ADC NY; Venice Film Festival special award; Nat'l. Cartoonist Soc. award. Lives in New Canaan, CT.

SAXTON, JOHN G(ORDON).
Lanscape painter. Born Troy, NY, 1860. Pupil of Lefebvre, Merson and Robert Fleury in Paris. Member: Lotos C. Awards: Hon. mention, Paris Exp., 1900; hon. mention, Pan Am. Exp., Buffalo, 1901; bronze medal, St. Louis Exp.,

1904. Address in 1929, Seaford, Long Island, NY.

SAXTON, JOSEPH.
Born in Huntington, PA, in 1790; died in Washington, D.C., in 1873. Saxton was not an engraver, though he devised a medal ruling machine, among his other many inventions. While he was the constructor and curator of the standard weighing apparatus in the US Mint, in Phila. in 1842, he produced two beautifully executed portraits by means of this machine. These are portraits of Franklin Peale and of Dr. R. M. Patterson. They are inscribed "Modelled by J. G. Chapman; electrotyped by Franklin Peale; engraved with the medal ruling machine by Jos. Saxton, Mint of the United Sates, 1842." They are admirable pieces of work of this type. Previous to this date, medal ruling had been done directly from the original medal, with the disadvantage of copying all its dents, scratches, or other imperfections, and there was the possibility of injuring a valuable medal by scratching it with the tracer; then a shellac cast of the orginal was copied by the machine; but this device failed, owing to the shellac model being liable to puncture by the tracing point, thus producing false lines upon the plate being engraved. To avoid these difficulties, inherent in the older methods, Saxton made an electrotype copy of the original and used that as a model in the machine. As this model was copper, it could not be punctured, and any imperfections in the original could be corrected in the model; it provided a smooth, hard and true surface for the tracing point, and produced a perfect copy.

SAYEN, HENRY LYMAN.
Painter. Born in Chicago, IL. Exhb. in Phila., in 1921, in the "Exhibition of Paintings Showing the Later Tendencies in Art." He died April 28, 1918 in Phila.

SAZEGAR, MORTEZA.
Painter. Born in Teheran, Iran, Nov. 11, 1933; US citizen. Studied at Univ. of Tex., El Paso.; Baylor U. Med. Col.; Cornell. In

collections of Whitney; S. Fran. Mus. of Art; Corcoran; others. Exhib. at Poindexter Gal., NYC; AIC; Whitney; Corcoran. Lives in PA.

SCACKI, FRANCISCO.
Engraver. This name is signed to a large but very crudely drawn and etched view of the Battle of New Orleans. It apparently was comtemporaneous with the battle in date, and the only impression known has the second state of the plate printed on the back of the first impression. It is difficult to determine, however, whether Scacki is the engraver or the publisher of the plate, or both. The form of the signature is as follows: "Francisco Scacki Copy Right Secured."

SCALELLA, JULES.
Painter and etcher. Born Philadelphia, March 31, 1895. Pupil of Albert Jean Adolphe. Member: North Shore AA. Address in 1929, 21 East Turnbull Ave., South Ardmore, PA.

CARAVAGLIONE, CONCETTA.
Sculptor. Born New York City, July 9, 1900. Pupil of Boardman Robinson, Robert Laurent. Member: NA Women PS; Salons of Am. Address in 1929, 3 Washington Sq.; h. 1982 Lexington Ave., New York, NY.

SCARBOROUGH, JOHN.
Painter, who flouished about 1830.

SCARPITTA, G. S. CARTAINO.
Sculptor. Born Palermo, Italy, Feb. 28, 1887; settled in NY in 1910. Studied at Instituto di Belli Arti, Palermo, and in Rome. Member: NSS; Allied AA; NY Arch. Lg.; NY Numismatic Society; decorated by Japanese and Cuban governments. Awards: Barnett prize, NAD, 1914; second mention, collaborative competition, NY. Arch. Lg., 1913; hon. mention, AIC, 1923. Work: Sculpture in Church of St. John the Evangelist, Los Angeles, CA. Address in 1929, 4351 Willowbrook Ave., Los Angeles, CA.

SCARPITTA, SALVATORE.
Painter. Born 1919, in NYC. Studied in Rome from 1936 - 1959.

Returned to NYC. Taught at Maryland Inst. since 1965. Exhibited in Rome at Galleria Gartano Chiurazzi, (1949); Galleria La Tartaruga; Leo Castelli Gal., NYC (1959 - 1963); Columbus Gal. of Fine Art (Ohio); Corcoran; Art Inst. of Chicago; L'umo e l'arte (Milan 1974); Portland Center for Vis. Arts (1978). In collections of Albright Knox; LA County Mus.; Gal. of Mod. Art, Tel Aviv; Stedelylc Mus., Amsterdam; MOMA and private collections.

SCHAAF, ANTON.
Sculptor. Born in Wisconsin, Feb. 22, 1869. Pupil of Shirlaw, Cox, Beckwith, Saint Gaudens; Dewing; Cooper Union; NAD under Ward. Member: NSS; Arch. Lg. of NY; AFA. Work: Statue of General Ord, Vicksburg Nat'l Military Park; Glendale Monument and Ridgewood Monument, Brooklyn, NY.; Shaw Memorial, Woodlawn Cemetery, NY; Meredith portrait tablet, Tompkins Avenue Church, Central Congregational Church War Memorial, 14th Inf. soldiers monument and Ridgewood monument, all in Brooklyn, NY; Glendale Brooklyn War Memorial; Ericson Memorial, NY. Address in 1929, 1931 Broadway, New York, NY; h. 397 East 17th St., Brooklyn, NY. Address in 1926, 1931 Broadway, NY.

SCHAARE, HARRY J.
Illustrator. Born in NYC in 1922. Attended NYU School of Architecture and PI. His career began in 1949 with cover art for Bantam Books and he has since worked for most major book publishers and magazines, including The Saturday Evening Post, True, Reader's Digest, and Rolling Stone. He has done many posters for movies and advertising and has exhibited in the Smithsonian Institution, the Pentagon, Grand Central Gallery, S of I, of which he is a member, and in numerous other galleries. The USAF has given him assignments in America, Europe, and Asia.

SCHABACKER, BETTY BARCHET.
Painter and lecturer. Born in Baltimore, MD, on Aug. 14, 1925. Studied: Dominican College, Calif.; Conn. College for Women; Univ. of Rhode Island, Newport. Exhibitions: Erie Art Center, Erie, Penn., 1966; Chautauqua Art Assoc. Gallery, NY, 1969; Calif. National Watercolor Society Membership Show, 1975. Collections: Western Union, NY; Midland Capital Corporation, NY; McGraw-Edison, Elgin, Illinois. Media: Watercolor and cloth collage. Address in 1980, 540 Wilkins Rd., Erie, PA.

SCHABELITZ, R(UDOLPH) F(REDERICK).
Illustrator. Born Stapleton, SI, NY, June 10, 1884. Pupil of Carl Marr in Munich, and others. Member: SI; Salma. C.; GFLA. Address in 1929, 123 West 74th Street, New York, NY.

SCHAEFER, HANS.
Sculptor. Born Sternberg, Czechoslovakia, Feb. 13, 1875. Pupil of Kunstgewerbeschule, Vienna, Austria. Member: Chicago Modelers and Sculptors Lg. Address in 1929, 2417 Aubert Ave., Chicago, IL.

SCHAEFFER, MEAD.
Illustrator. Born Freedom Plains, NY, July 15, 1898. Pupil of Dean Cornwell. Member: SI. Illustrated Moby Dick, Typee, and Omoo, by Herman Melville; Les Miserables, by Victor Hugo; Wings of the Morning, by Louis Tracy; Sans Famille, by Hector Malot; King Arthur and His Nights, published by Rand, McNally & Co.; "Jim Davis," by John Masefield; "The Wreck of the Grosvenor," by W. Clark Russel. Address in 1929, Bellerose, LI, NY.

SCHAEFFER, WILLIAM G.
Painter. Member of the Washington Water Color Club. Address in 1926, 95 Madison Ave., New York.

SCHAETTLE, LOUIS.
Mural painter. Born in Chicago, he died in New York City on June 21, 1917. He painted mural decorations in Georgian Court, Lakewood, NJ.

SCHAFER, GEORGE L(ESLIE).
Illustrator and draftsman. Born Wilmington, DE, Jan. 26, 1895. Pupil of PAFA nad Bellevue Art Training Center in Paris. Member: Fellowship PAFA; Wilmington SFA.

Address in 1929, 404 South Broome St., Wilmington, DE.

SCHAMBERG, MORTON L.
Painter. Born in Philadelphia in 1881. Pupil of Wm. M. Chase. Member: Society of Independent Artists. Address in 1926, Care of W. Pach, 13 East 14th St., New York City. Died in 1918.

SCHANZENBACHER, NELLIE.
Painter. Born Louisville. Pupil of William M. Chase, Robert Henri, Luis Mora. Member: Louisville AA; ASL of NY. Work: Mural, "Christ Blessing the Multitude," St. Paul's Evangelical Church, Louisville. Address in 1929, 1016 South Jackson, Louisville, KY.

SCHAPIRO, MIRIAM.
Painter. Born Nov. 15, 1923 in Toronto, Canada. US citizen. BA, MA, MFA (1949); Univ. of Iowa. Taught at Col. Inst of Arts (1973-5), Bryn Maur (1977), Amherst (1978). Awarded Tamarind Fellowship (1963) and grant from Nat. Ed. of the Arts (1976). Exhibited at New School for Soc. Reseach; Brooklyn Mus.; Univ. of Missouri (1950), Emmerich gal., NYC (8 one person shows, 1958-73); MOMA and others. In collections of Wesleyan Univ.; St. Louis City Art Mus; Albion Col; IBM; U. of Iowa; NYC; MOMA, Stanford; United Nations; Williams Col; Whitney, Carnegie and others.

SCHAR, A(XEL) E(UGENE).
Painter and teacher. Born Oslo, Norway, April 12, 1887. Pupil of Fritz Taulow. Member: Duluth AA. Address in 1929, 2024 West Superior St.; h. 728 West Third St., Duluth, MN.

SCHARBACH, B. K.
Sculptor and watercolorist. Born in Louisville, KY, in 1936. Studied at Univ. of Louisville; Univ. of KY; Parsons Sch. of Design; Art Students' League; Silvermine Guild; Univ. of Hartford, (CT) Art School. Exhibitions: NY Council for the Arts Sponsored Show, 1971; Webb and Parsons Gallery, New Canaan, CT, 1979, 80, 82; New England Annual, Silvermine Guild, 1981; SOHO 20

Gallery, NYC, 1981, 82, 83; Lever House, NYC, 1982; others. Received Amidar Mem. Award, Silvermine Guild. Address in 1983, Darien, CT.

SCHATTENSTEIN, NIKOL.
Portrait painter. Born Poniemon, Russia, Aug. 10, 1877. Studied at Vienna, Akademie. Member: Kunstlerhaus, Vienna; Allied AA. Awards: Two gold medals, International Exp., Vienna; hon. mention, Paris; Knight Cross of the Francis Josef Order. Work: "Prisoners," National Museum, Krakow; "Portrait of Ina. Claire," Empire Theater, New York ; also represented in the Artillerie Museum, Vienna. Address in 1929, Atelier Bldg., 33 West 67th St., New York, NY.

SCHAUER, MARTHA K.
Painter, writer, lecturer, and teacher. Born Troy, Ohio, Feb. 13, 1889. Pupil of Pratt Inst. Member: Ohio WCS; Ohio Born Women A. Specialty, flower studies and still life in water color. Address in 1929, 356 Kenilworth Ave., Dayton, Ohio.

SCHEFFLER, RUDOLF.
Painter. Born Zwickau, Saxony, Dec. 5, 1884. Pupil of the Dresden Akademie, Prof. Otto Gussman, and Prof. Hermann Prell. Member: Brooklyn Soc. Modern Artists. Awards: Grand Prix de Rome; gold and silver medals of the government and Royal Acad., Dresden. Work owned by German Government and Museums; mural and mosaics in Cathedral of St. Louis and Churches in Detroit, Chicago, Los Angeles, New Orleans, etc. Address in 1929, 106 Columbia Heights, Brooklyn, NY.

SCHEIBNER, VIRA MCLIRATH.
Painter. Born Cleveland, OH, Aug. 12, 1889. Pupil of Robert Spencer, Charles Rosen; Edouard Van Waeyenberge in England. Member: Fellowship PAFA; NA Women PS. Address in 1929, 20 Aviles St., St. Augustine, FL.

SCHELL, DOROTHY ROOT.
Painter. Member: Plastic Club. Address in 1926, Middle City

Building, Phila., or 5027 Newhall St., Germantown, Phialdelphia, PA.

SCHELL, F. CRESSON.
Illustrator. Born in Philadelphia in 1857. Pupil of Thomas Eakins and Thomas P. Anshutz. Member: Artists Aid Society; Fellowship, PAFA; Phila. Art Alliance; Phila. Sketch Club. Address in 1926, 5215 Archer St., Germantown, Phila., PA.

SCHENCK, FRANKLIN LEWIS.
Painter. Born in 1855. Pupil of Thomas Eakins, who founded the Phila. Art Students' League and appointed Schenck as curator. Represented by paintings in Brooklyn Chamber of Commerce and in the Pratt Library. Address in 1926, East Northport, Long Island.

SCHETKY, CAROLINE.
Born March 3, 1790, in Edinburgh, Scotland. Miniature painter and water color artist , formerly flourished in Philadelphia and Boston. She married Samuel Richardson and exhibited at the Boston Athenaeum under that name; she also painted landscapes and flowers. Died March 14, 1852, in Boston, MA.

SCHEVILL, W(ILLIAM) V.
Portrait painter. Born Cincinnati, Ohio, March 2, 1864. Pupil of Loefftz, Lindenschmitt and Gysis in Munich. Member: Century Assoc.; Salma. C.; Kuenstler Genossenschaft; St. Louis GA; AFA. Award: Bronze medal, St. Louis Exp., 1904. Work: "In Love," Cincinnati Museum, Cincinnati; portrait sketch, Prince Henry of Prussia, Herron Art Inst., Indianapolis; Leipsic Art Museum; portrait of Chancelor Hall, and Judge Hitchcock, Washington University, St. Louis; portrait of President Taft, War Dept., Washington, DC and St. Louis Art Museum. Address in 1929, 319 East 57th Street, New York, NY.

SCHICK, FRED G.
Painter and illustrator. Born in 1893. Pupil of Wilcox and M. B. Cox. Member of the Buffalo Art Club, Buffalo, NY. Address in 1926, 546 Main St., Buffalo, NY.

SCHIFFER, ETHEL BENNETT.
(Mrs. W. B. Schiffer). Illustrator, etcher, and engraver. Born Brooklyn, New York , March 10, 1879. Pupil of Yale School of Fine Arts; ASL of NY. Member: New Haven PCC; S. Indp. A.; NA Women PS; New Haven BPC (pres); Springfield AL; Am. APL; AFA. Address in 1929, 357 Elm Street, New Haven, CT.

SCHILDKNECHT, E(DMUND) G(USTAV).
Painter and teacher. Born Chicago, IL. July 9, 1899. Pupil of Wisconsin School of Arts; PAFA; Academie Julian; Acadamie de la Grande Chaumiere and George Oberteuffer. Address in 1929, Arsenal Technical Schools, Indianapolis, IN; h. 4709 Lloyd St., Milwaukee, WI.

SCHILLE, ALICE.
Painter. Born Columbus. Pupil of Columbus Art School under Chase and Cox; Prinet, Collin, Courtois and Colarossi Acad. in Paris. Member: AWCS (assoc.); NYWCC; Boston WCC; NA Women PS; Chicago WCC; Phila. WCC. Awards: Corcoran prize, Washington WCC 1908; NY. Women's AC prize, 1908 and 1909; participant Fine Art Bldg. prize, SWA 1913; gold medal for water colors, P. P. Exp., San F., 1915; Phila. water color prize, PAFA 1915; first prize ($200) Columbus AL, 1919; Stevens prize, Columbus Art Lg., 1920; Fine Arts prize, NA Women PS, 1929. Work: "The Melon Market," Herron Art Institute, Indianapolis; "Mother and Child," Art Club, Phila.; "The Market Place," Columbus (OH) Gallery of Fine Arts. Address in 1929, 1166 Bryden Road, Columbus, OH.

SCHILLING, A(RTHUR) O(SCAR).
Painter, illustrator, and writer. Born in Germany, May 14, 1882. Studied in Chicago, Buffalo, Rochester, and Germany. Member: Buffalo SA; Rochester AC. Address in 1929, 1057 Main St., E; h. 285 Laurelton Road, Rochester, NY.

SCHLADERMUNDT, HERMAN T.
Mural painter. Born Milwaukee, WI,
Oct. 4, 1863. Member: NY Arch.
Lg., 1893; Mural P; Cent. Assn.
Awards: Allied Arts prize, Arch
Lg.; medal Columbian Exp., Chicago,
1893. Work: Stained glass windows
in Flagler Memorial Church, St.
Augustine, FL stained glass dome
lights, Emigrants Industrial Bank,
NY; Mosaic vaults, Congressional
Library, Washington; decorations,
Grand Jury Room, Court House,
Newark, NJ; Directors Room, General
Motors Co., NY; Museum of Thomas F.
Ryan, New York; mosaic glass
windows, House of Representatives,
Missouri Capitol, Jefferson City,
MO; US Post Office, Denver, CO.
Died in 1937. Address in 1929,
Lawrence Park, Bronxville, NY.

SCHLAFF, HERMAN.
Painter and sculptor. Born Odessa,
Russia, Dec. 19, 1884. Pupil of
School of Fine Arts, Odessa,
Russia. Member: AFA. Address in
1929, 703 Walnut St.; h. 4404
Germantown Ave., Philadelphia, PA.

SCHLAIKJER, J(ES) W(ILLIAM).
Painter and illustrator. Born
Sept. 22, 1897. Pupil of E.
Forsberg, H. Dunn, and D. Cornwell.
Member: SI; Salma. C.;
Scandinavian Am. A; Grand Cent.
Gal.; AFA. Award: First Hallgarten
prize, NAD, 1926; first Altman
prize, 1928. Address in 1929, 3201
Oxford Ave., Riverdale, NYC.

SCHLECHT, CHARLES.
Engraver. Born in Stuttgart,
Germany, in 1843; living in NY in
1905. Charles Schlecht was brought
to the US by his parents in 1852,
and was apprenticed to the American
Bank Note Company in 1859; he also
received instruction in his
profession from Charles Bush and
Alfred Jones. Mr. Schlecht made
bank note engraving his principal
occupation, working in NY City and
at the Bureau of Engraving and
Printing in Washington, DC. But he
also produced some admirable
portrait and subject plates for the
publishers. Two of his large
plates, executed in pure line, are
especially worthy of note. These
are "Eyes to the Blind," after a

painting by A. F. Bellows, and "The
Wish," after a painting by Percy
Moran.

SCHLEGELL, GUSTAV VON.
Painter and teacher. Born St.
Louis, Sept. 16, 1877. Pupil of
Robert Koehler in Minneapolis; Carl
Marr in Munich; Laurent and Laurens
in Paris. Member: 2 x 4 Soc. Work
in: St. Louis Artists Guild.
Address in 1929, 1921 Carrol
Street, St. Paul, MN.

SCHLEIN, CHARLES.
Painter, etcher, and teacher. Born
Russia, April 5, 1900. Pupil of
Leon Kroll. Member: Alliance.
Address in 1929, 101 Second Ave.,
New York, NY.

SCHLEINKOFER, DAVID J.
Illustrator. Born in Phila., in
1951. Attended Bucks County
Community College and the Phila.
College of Art. His first
published illustration appeared in
1974 and he has since been
illustrating paperback books and
doing editorial work for Cue and
Cosmopolitan. His artwork was
selected for S of I Annual Shows in
1975 and 1976.

SCHLEMMER, F(ERDINAND) LOUIS.
Painter and teacher. Born
Crawfordsville, IN, Sept. 26, 1893.
Pupil of Hawthorne, H.M. Walcott;
AIC. Member: IN A.S.; Hoosier
Salon. Work: "Sacred Vase," Miami
Conservatory of Art, Miami,
Florida. Address in 1929, 319
South Green St., Crawfordsville,
IN, summer, Provincetown, MA.

SCHLESINGER, LOUIS.
Sculptor. Born in Bohemia in 1874.
Member of NY Architectural League.
Address in 1926, 51 West 10th
Street, New York.

SCHLEY, M(ATHILDE) G.
Painter, illustrator, teacher, and
writer. Born Horicon, WI, May 14,
1874. Pupil of Richard Lorenz.
Member: S. Indp. A.; Chic. A.
Address in 1929, Schley Apts.; h.
322 - 15th St., Milwaukee, WI;
summer, Beaver Dam, WI.

SCHMAND, J. PHILLIP.
Portrait painter. Born Germania, PA, Feb. 24, 1871. Pupil of Mary Cox, Lucius Hitchcock, H. S. Mowbray, Vonnoh, A. P. Lucas. Member: NAC; Wash. AC.; Salma. C.; NA Women PS (assoc); AFA. Award: Albright Scholarship Buffalo, 1896. Work: Portraits of Blackstone, Pitt, Mansfield and John Marshall in Lawyer's Club, NY; "Portrait of Charles S. Green," Green Free Library, Wellsboro, PA; "Portrait of John R. Patterson," owned by the National Cash Register Co., Dayton, Ohio; "Portrait of Warren C. Hubbard," Rochester (NY) Consistory. Address in 1929, Hotel des Artistes, 1 West 67th St., New York, NY; summer, Lyme, CT.

SCHMEDTGEN, WILLIAM HERMAN.
Painter. Born in Chicago in 1862. Studied at the AIC. Pioneer in newspaper illustrating in Chicago; commercial art work, Chicago Mail, 1883; and also in St. Louis and the South; head of art department, Chicago Record, 1886-1901; now on staff of Chicago Record Herald. Illustrator for many art books and magazine articles on outdoor sports; field artist for Record, in Spanish-American war, in camp before Santiago; traveled and sketched for newspaper articles in Mexico and Cuba; traveled in Spain, Italy and N. Africa for the Record, 1900. Address in 1926, Record Herald, Chicago, IL. Died in 1936.

SCHMIDT, JULIUS.
Sculptor. Born June 2, 1923 in Stamford, CT. Earned B.F.A. (1952) and M.F.A. (1955) from Cranbrook Acad. of Art (MI); studied W. Ossip Zadkine (1953) and Acad. Fine Arts (Florence 1954). Taught at Cranbrook; KS. City Art Inst.; RI School of Design; Berkeley; now at U. of Iowa. Awarded Guggenheim (1963). Exhibited at Silvermine Guild, New Canaan, CT (1953); Santa Barbara Mus. Art; PAFA; Art Inst. of Chi.; Walker; MOMA; RI School; Carnegie; New School for Soc. Research; Swope. In collections of Art Inst. of Chi.; Whitney; U. of IL; Wash. U.; MOMA; Chase Manhattan Bank; SUNY/Oswego and Buffalo; and Albright Knox.

SCHMIDT, KARL.
Painter and teacher. Born Worcester, MA, Jan. 11, 1890. Self taught. Member: Salma. C.; Mural P. Address in 1929, Silvermine CT; care of Rockwood Pottery, Cincinnati, Ohio, 1 Melville St., Worcester, MA.

SCHMIDT, KATHERINE.
Painter. Born Xenia, Ohio, Aug. 15, 1898. Pupil of K. H. Miller. Member: Salons of America; Brooklyn Soc. Modern A. Died in 1978. Address in 1929, 106 Columbia Heights, Brooklyn, NY; summer, Ogunquit, ME.

SCHMIDT, OSCAR F.
Painter, who exhibited at the National Academy of Design, New York, 1925. Address in 1926, 301 West 24th Street, New York.

SCHMIDT, OTTO.
Painter, illustrator, and craftsman. Born Philadelphia. Pupil of PAFA under Anshutz, Touron and Chase, NAD under Emil Carlsen and Henry Ward. Member: Fellowship PAFA. Work: Mural Northeast High School, Philadelphia; decorations and illustrations for Judge, Farm Journal, Saturday Evening Post, etc. Died in 1940. Address in 1929, 3139 Belgrade St., Philadelphia, PA; summer, Lindenwold, NJ.

SCHMITT, ALBERT F(ELIX).
Painter. Born Boston, 1873. Pupil of MA Normal Art School; Cowies Art School; Boston Museum School; studied abroad. Member Copley S.; AWCS; Boston GA; Salma. C.; Boston AC.; Boston SWCP.: Wash. AC; Societe Academique d'Historie Internationale, Paris. Award: Silver medal, P. P. Exp., San F., 1915. Work in: City Art Museum, St. Louis; RI School of Design, Providence; Museum of Fine Arts, Boston; Musee du Luxembourg, Paris; Musee de Pan B. P. France; Musee de Lisbon, Portugal. Address in 1929, Hotel Grassion Pan B. P. France.

SCHMITT, CARL.
Painter. Born Warren, OH, May 6, 1889. Pupil of NAD under Carlsen; and in Florence, Italy.

827

Work: "The Mill" Butler Art Inst., Youngstown, Ohio. His mural painting of "the Nativity" was exhibited at Brooklyn Exv. of mural painters. Address in 1929, Silvermine, Norwalk, CT.

SCHMITZ, ELIZABETH T.
Painter. Born in Philadelphia. Pupil of Penna. Acad. of Fine Arts. Address in 1926, 1710 Chestnut St., Philadelphia.

SCHNACKENBERG, ROY.
Painter. Born Jan. 14, 1934 in Chicago. Earned B.F.A. from Miami U. (Oxford, Ohio). Award from Copley Foundation (1967), and Art Inst. of Chicago (1964). Exhibited at Main St. Gal. Chicago; Art Inst. of Chicago, and Corcoran. In collections of Art Inst. of Chicago and the Whitney.

SCHNAKENBERG, HENRY ERNEST.
Painter and etcher. Born New Brighton, NY, Sept. 14, 1892. Pupil of Kenneth Hayes Miller. Member: ASL of NY; S. Indp. A. Work: Still life, owned by the PA Acad. of the Fine Arts; "Mullen Plant," San Francisco Museum. Taught at ASL (1923-5). Became Pres. of ASL in 1932. Died in 1970. Address in 1929, 33 West 8th St., h. 601 West End Ave., New York, NY; summer, Manchester, VT.

SCHNEIDER, ARTHUR.
Painter and illustrator. Address in 1926, 939 Eighth Ave., New York.

SCHNEIDER, FREDERICK.
Illustrator. Born in Los Angeles in 1946. Studied at PI, SVA, and PSD in NY with Jacob Lawrence and Seymour Chwast. His first job appeared in Crawdaddy magazine in 1974 and he has since illustrated book covers, film strips, theater posters, and editorial pieces for Cue, Psychology Today, and The New York Times. He received an Award of Excellence from S of I in 1976 and has had his artwork exhibited in Battle Creek, MI.

SCHNEIDER, OTTO J.
Painter, illustrator, and etcher. Born Atlanta, IL, 1875. Member: Chicago SA; Chicago SE. Work: Etching in Art Inst., of Chicago;

Toledo Museum of Art. Died in 1946. Address in 1929, 1259 Thorndale Ave., Chicago, IL.

SCHNEIDER, ROSALIND.
Artist/film-maker. Studied: Syracuse Univ. School of Fine Arts, The Art Students League, NYC. Exhibitions: Corcoran Gallery, Wash., DC; Butler Institute of American Art, Ohio; Brooklyn Museum, NY. Film Festivals: Womens' International Film Festival, NYC; Museum of Modern Art, Paris; Museum of Graz, Austria; Artists' Space, NYC. Awarded a film retrospective at the Whitney Museum of American Art, 1973. She is a founder-member of "Women/Artist/Film-makers" and a charter member of the "Association of Independent Film-makers".

SCHNEIDER, SUSAN HAYWARD.
(Mrs. Karl Scheider). Painter. Born Pana, IL. Pupil of School of Ind. Art, Phila.; Henry Rittenberg; Fred Wagner; Carl Leopold Voss in Munich. Member: Phila. Alliance; Plastic C; AFA. Address in 1929, 1301 Spruce Street, Philadelphia, PA; summer, Glenlake Farms, Langhorne, PA.

SCHNEIDER, THEOPHILE.
Painter. Born Freiburg, Baden, Germany, Oct. 5, 1872. Pupil of Monks, Noyes, Davol. Member: Boston AC; Salma C. NAC. Award: Prize, Boston AC, 1924. Address in 1929, 380 Fulton St.; h. 134 Columbia Hgts., Brooklyn, NY; summer, Monhegan, ME.

SCHNELLE, WILLIAM G.
Painter and teacher. Born Brooklyn, NY, Jan 29, 1897. Pupil of Pratt Inst.; ASL of NY; Walter Beck and Henry B. Snell. Member: Society of the Five; NAC. Address in 1929, 8502 89th Street, Woodhaven, LI, NY.

SCHNIER, JACQUES.
Sculptor. Born Roumania, Dec. 25, 1898. Awards: First Sculpture award, San Francisco AA, 1928; first sculpture prize, North Western Art Exh., Seattle, Wash., 1928. Work: Fountain, San Francisco Playground Commission. Address in 1929, 20 Jessop Place.;

h. 628 Montgomery St., San Francisco, CA.

SCHNITTMAN, SACHA S.
Sculptor. Born in NYC on Sept. 1, 1913. Studied: Cooper Union Art School; National Academy of Design; Beaux-Arts Institute of Design; Columbia Univ.; and with Attilio Piccirilli, Robert Aitken, and Olympio Brindesi. Awards: Society of Independent Artists, 1942; City Art Museum of St. Louis, 1942; Junior League Missouri Exhibition, 1942; Kansas City Art Institute, 1942; Pan-American Architect Society, 1933; Fraser medal, 1937. Collections: Pan-American Society; American Museum of Natural History; Dayton Art Institute; Moscow State Univ., Russia; Memorial Plaza, St. Louis, Missouri; Dorsa Building, St. Louis, Missouri. Media: Marble and bronze. Address in 1980, 915 Commercial St., San Jose, CA.

SCHOENER, J.
Portrait painter in oils and miniature. He exhibited at the Pennsylvania Acad., in 1817, and was working in Philadelphia till 1827.

SCHOENFELD, FLORA.
Painter, who exhibited in Philadelphia, 1921, in "Exhibition of Paintings Showing the Later Tendencies in Art." Address in 1926, 5024 Ellis Ave., Chicago, IL.

SCHOFF, P. R.
Engraver. An excellent portrait in pure line, of Robert Baird, after a ptg. by Healy, is thus signed. No other work has been found signed by this man; it is possible that the signature is a letter engraver's error for the name below.

SCHOFF, STEPHEN ALONZO.
Engraver. Born Jan. 16, 1818 in Danville, VT. When Mr. Schoff was about eight years of age his parents moved first to Bradford, on the Merrimac, and later to Newburyport, MA. Stephen Alonzo Schoff was one of a family of six children and when he was sixteen years old he was sent to Boston and there indentured for 5 years to Oliver Pelton, an engraver of that city. Dissatisfied with the progress he was making, at the end of about 3 years, and with the consent of Mr. Pelton, Mr. Schoff became a pupil of Joseph Andrews and to this admirable line engraver says Mr.Schoff in a personal letter, "I owe more than can ever be repaid." With Mr. Andrews he went to Paris in 1840, and both young men there worked for a time in the studio of Paul Delarocher, drawing from the nude. Mr. Schoff returned to the US in 1842, and was at once employed by a bank note engraving company in NY. Died May 6, 1904 in Norfolk, CT.

SCHOFIELD, FLORA I.
Painter. Born Lanark, IL. Pupil of AIC; Friez, Gleizes, Andre L'hote in Paris. Member: Chicago AC; NA Women PS; Arts Cordon; NYS Women A. Represented in Detroit Art Institute. Address in 1929, 360 Barry Ave, Chicago, IL; 31 bis rue Campagne Iere, Paris, France.

SCHOFIELD, LOUIS SARTAIN.
Engraver. Born in 1868; a grandson of John Sartain. He is an expert line engraver and a designer of great ability, and for some years has been in the employ of the Bureau of Engraving and Printing, at Washington, DC.

SCHOFIELD, W(ALTER) ELMER.
Landscape painter. Born Philadelphia, Sept. 9, 1867. Pupil of PAFA; Bouguereau, Ferrier, Doucet and Aman Jean in Paris. Member: SAA 1904; ANA 1902; NA 1907; Nat. Inst. AL; AC Phila.; Fellowship PAFA: Century Assoc.; NAC; Salma. C.; R. S. British Artists; Chelsea Arts Club, London. Awards: Hon. mention, AC Phila. 1898; Webb Prize, SAA, 1900; hon mention, Paris Exp., 1900; hon mention, CI Pittsburgh, 1900; first Hallgarten prize, NAD 1901; silver medal; Pan Am Exp., Buffalo, 1901; Sesnan gold medal, St. Louis Exp., 1904; Inness gold medal, NAD 1911; gold medal and $1,000, NAC 1913; Temple gold medal, PAFA 1914; medal of honor, P.-P. Exp. San Fran., 1915; Altman prize ($1,000), NAD, 1920; Mrs. Keith Spalding prize, AIC ($1,000), 1921; silver medal, Sesqui Centennial Expo., Phila.,

829

1926. Work: "Sand Dunes near Lelant." Metropolitan Museum, NY; "Morning After Snow," "Cliff Shadows," Corcoran Gallery, Washington, "Midwinter Thaw, Morning," and "Landing Stage Boulogne," Cincinnati Museum; "Across the River," Carnegie Inst., Pittsburgh; "Autumn in Brittany." "The Crossroads," Albright Art Gallery, Buffalo; "Winter" PA Acad., Phila.; "Old Mills on the Somme," Herron Art Inst., Indianapolis: "The White Frost," Memorial Gallery, Rochester, NY; "The Coffer Dam." Art Institute of Chicago; "The Spring Thaw," National Arts Club. New York: "The Rapids," Brooklyn Museum; "June Morning," Des Moines City Library; "Autumn in Cornwall." Harrison Gallery, Los Angeles Museum, Museum of Art. Norfolk, VA. Died in 1944. Address in 1929, 119 East 19th St.; care of the Grand Central Art Galleries, 15 Vanderbilt Ave., New York, NY; 6816 Quincy St., Mt. Airy, Philadelphia, PA.

SCHONGUT, EMANUEL.
Illustrator. Born in Monticello, NY, in 1936. Received his BFA and MFA from PI where he was a classmate of James McMullan. This start in the illustration field was in 1963 with book covers for Macmillan. Doubleday, Dodd, Mead, New York Magazine, Sesame Street and Electric Company Magazine have all utilized his illustrating skills. He has several posters to his credit as well.

SCHONHARDT, HENRI.
Painter, sculptor, and teacher. Born Providence, April 24, 1877. Pupil of Julian Acad. under Puech, Dubois and Verlet; Ecole des Arts Decoratifs under David and Chevinard. Member: Providence AC. Award: Hon. mention, Paris, Salon, 1908. Work: "Elisha Dyer Memorial," St. Stevens Church, Providence; "Henry Harrison Young Memorial," City Hall Park, Providence; "Clytie" and "Cadmus," RI School of Design Museum, Providence; "Soldier's and Sailors' Monument," Bristol, RI; "Col. Sissons Monument," Little Compton,

RI. Address in 1929, 21 Audubon Ave., Providence, RI.

SCHONLU, W. A.
Painter, who exhibited "Snow Mountain" at the Penna. Acad. of the Fine Arts, Philadelphia, 1924. Address in 1926, 173 Pleasant St., Arlington, MA.

SCHOOK, F. DE FOREST.
Painter and teacher. Born in Michigan, 1872. Pupil of AI Chicago; H. O. Tanner, Menard and Simon in Paris. Member: Chicago SA; Chicago WCC; Chicago AG. Instructor of painting and composition, Chicago Art Institute. Died in 1942. Address in 1929, Lombard, IL; care of the Art Institute, Chicago, IL.

SCHOONMAKER, W(ILLIAM) P(OWELL).
Etcher. Born New York City, Nov. 14, 1891. Pupil of George B. Bridgman. Member: Phila. Sketch C.; Print C.; AI Graphic A.; GFLA; Art Director C; Phila. AG. Address in 1929, 1211 Walnut St.; Hotel Gladstone, Philadelphia, PA.

SCHOONOVER, FRANK E(ARLE).
Painter and illustrator. Born Oxford, NJ, Aug. 19, 1877. Pupil of Drexel, Inst., Philadelphia, under Howard Pyle. Member: SI 1905; Fellowship PAFA (assoc); Wilmington SFA. Specialty, American Indians and Canadian trappers. Illustrated and writer of books (1912-8) and Illus. of children's classics, (1920-30) Des. stained glass windows. Landscapist since 1937. Died in 1972. Address in 1929, 1616 Rodney St.; h. 2003 Bayard Ave., Willington, DE; summer, Bushkill, PA.

SCHOTTLAND, MIRIAM.
Illustrator. Born in Brooklyn, NY, in 1935. Attended PI, the New School and ASL. Her free-lance work includes children's books, trade publications, corporate and editorial illustration, as well as the 1975 International Women's Year stamp and courtroom drawings for the ABC coverage of the Ellsberg hearings. The recipient of many awards, she was given the S of I Hamilton King Award in 1970.

SCHOULER, WILLARD C.
Painter. Born Arlington, Nov. 6, 1852. Pupil of Henry Day and William Rimmer. Specialty, Western and Arabian scenes. Address in 1929, 173 Pleasant Street, Arlington, MA.

SCHOYER, RAPHAEL.
A copperplate printer living in Baltimore, MD, in 1824; in 1826 he was engraving some indifferently executed portraits in NY. His album of wood engravings is at MMA.

SCHRAM, A(BRAHAM) J(OHN).
Painter. Born Grand Rapids, MI, July 27, 1891. Pupil of Corcoran School of Art, Washington, D.C.; PAFA Summer School. Member: Wash. Landscape C.; S. Wash. A.; New Haven PCC; CT. Acad. FA. Address in 1929, 937 M St., N. W., Washington, DC.

SCHREYVOGEL, CHARLES.
Painter. Born in New York City in Jan. 4, 1861; died in Hoboken, NJ, Jan. 27, 1912. He studied in Newark, NJ, and later in Munich. In 1901 he was elected an Associate Member of the National Acad. of Design.

SCHRIER, JEFFREY A.
Illustrator. Born in Cleveland, OH, in 1943. Educated at the Cleveland Institute of Art, Calif. Institute of the Arts and the New School for Social Research in NY. Although he began his career doing fashion illustrations in Calif. in 1967, his range of work includes album covers for Warner Brothers, book covers for Ballantine and Bantam, editorial art for major magazines and several posters. Galleries in Los Angeles and NY, including the S of I Annual Exhibition in 1976, have exhibited his artwork.

SCHROFF, ALFRED HERMANN.
Painter, craftman, and teacher. Born Springfield, MA, Dec. 26, 1863. Pupil of De Camp, Major, Chominski, Cowles Art School. Member: Boston AC; Boston Arch. C.; Laguna Beach AA; Pac. AA; Oakland AL; Soc. Ore. A.; Carmel AA; Copley S. Awards: Medal for stained glass, Columbian Expo.,

Chicago, 1893; 1st prize, Seattle, 1923; 1st prize, Springville, Utah, 1923. Instructor of Fine Arts, University of Oregon; Summer School University of California. Died in 1939. Address in 1929, 969 11th Ave. 1043 Alden St., Eugene, OR; and Carmel, CA.

SCHROTH, DOROTHY L.
Painter and craftsman. Born San Francisco, May 9, 1906. Pupil of Amrian Hartwell, Rudolph Schaeffer, Lucien Lebaudt. Member: San Francisco S. Women A. Address in 1929, 325 Laguna Honda Blvd., San Francisco, CA.

SCHULENBERG, ADELE.
(Mrs. Charles K. Gleeson). Sculptor. Born St. Louis, MO, Jan. 18, 1883. Pupil of George J. Zolnay; St. Louis School of Fine Arts; Grafly; studied in Berlin. Member: St. Louis AG. Address in 1929, 115 Edwin Ave., Kirkwood, MO.

SCHULER, HANS.
Sculptor. Born May 25, 1874 Alsace-Lorraine, Germany, May 5, 1874. Pupil of Verlet in Paris. Member: NS 1908; Charcoal C. Awards: Rinehart scholarships in sculpture, Paris, 1901-1905; third class medal, Paris Salon, 1901; silver medal, St. Louis Exp., 1904; Avery prize, NY Arch. Lg., 1915. Work: "Ariadne," Walters Gallery, Baltimore; "John Hopkins Monument," Baltimore. Director, Maryland Inst. Address in 1929, Care of Maryland Institute, Mt. Royal Ave.; h. 5 East Lafayette Ave., Baltimore, MD.

SCHULMAN, A. G.
Painter. Born in Koenigsberg, Germany, in 1881. Pupil of S. J. Woolf and of the National Academy of Design, NY. Instructor, College of the City of NY. Address in 1926, 24 East 59th St., New York, NY.

SCHULTE, ANTOINETTE.
Painter. Born in NYC. Studied: Art Students' League with George Bridgman, Homer Boss; Fontainebleau School of Fine Arts, Paris; and with Lopez Mezquita. Awards: Salons of America, 1931. Collections: Benjamin West Museum;

Brooklyn Museum; Corcoran Gallery of Art; Newark Museum; Montclair Art Museum; Cincinnati Museum of Art; Metropolitan Museum of Art; French Government Collection: Aix-en-Provence, France.

SCHULTZ, GEORGE F.
Painter. Born Chicago, April 17, 1869. Award: Tuthill prize, AIC, 1918. Work: "By the Sea," Union Lg. Club, Chicago; "Among the Birches," Cliff Dwellers, Chi.; "Twilight Shadows," Arche Club, Chicago; "Autumn Weather," City of Chicago Collection; "Rocky Cove," Mt. St. Claire College, Clinton, IA; "Elephant Rock," Muscatine (IA) Art Assoc.; "After the Rain," "Autumn Gold," Muskogee (Okla.) Public Library. Specialty, landscape and marines. Address in 1929, 1900 Newport, Ave., Chicago, IL.

SCHULTZ, HARRY.
Painter. Born Sebastopol, Russia, Jan. 1, 1900. Pupil of John Sloan, Kenneth Miller. Member: S. Indp. A.; Museum of Art Culture in Russia, Leningrad. Address in 1929, 2607 Jerome Ave., New York, NY.

SCHULTZ, ISABELLE.
Sculptor, lecturer and teacher. Born Baltimore, April 20, 1896. Pupil of Ephraim Keyser and J. Maxwell Miller. Member: Balto Handicraft C. Work: Memorial tablet to W. E. Kelliot, Goucher College, Balto.; memorial tablet to John T. King, Medical and Chirurgical Bldg., Balto. testimonal tablet, Buckingham School, Frederick, MD.

SCHULTZ, SUSETTE.
See Keast, Mrs. Susette Schultz.

SCHUMACHER, WILLIAM E.
Painter. Born in Boston in 1870. Studied in Paris. Exhibited in the "Autumn Salon," Paris, until the exhibitions were discontinued; retrospective, Ferargil Gallery, NYC, 1931; other exhibitions. One of the earliest painters of the Woodstock School, he was also a gifted teacher. Held classes in NYC, and from 1913 until his death he taught at Byrdcliffe, Woodstock,

NY. Died August 30, 1931, in Kingston, NY.

SCHUSSELE, CHRISTIAN.
Painter. Born Aug. 16, 1824 in Alsace. He studied in Paris, and came to Philadelphia about 1848. He exhibited his work at the Penna. Acad. of Fine Arts, and was elected Prof. of Drawing and Painting at the Acad. where he served till his death in 1879. Many of his paintings were engraved by John Sartain. He painted "Benjamin Franklin before the Council, London, 1773," and other American Historical Scenes; painted a number of portraits of prominent Americans. Died Aug. 21, 1879 in Merchantville, NJ.

SCHUSTER, DONNA N.
Painter. Pupil of AIC, Tarbell, and Chase. Member: Calif. AC; S. Indp. A., West Coast Arts; Calif. WCS. Awards: Gold medal, MN State Art Ex., 1913; prize for painting ($100), MN State Art Ex., 1914; silver medal for water colors, P. P. Exp., San F. 1915; silver medal, Pan Calif. Exp., San Diego, 1915; first prize for water colors, Phoenix Arizona, 1918 and 1919; hon. mention, WI, PS., 1919; first prize for oil paintng, Phoenix Arizona, 1920; Ackerman prize ($100). Calif. AC., 1921; first prize, Calif. WCS, 1926; first prize, West Coast Arts, Inc., 1926. Address in 1929, 2672 Glendower Ave, Los Angeles, CA.

SCHUTZ ANTON, (JOSEPH) (FRIEDRICH).
Etcher. Born Berndorf, Rhineland, April 19, 1894. Pupil of Academie of Fine Arts, Munich, under Groeber and Peter von Halm; ASL of NY with Joseph Pennell; studied architecture at Technical Univ., Munich. Member: Brooklyn SE; Chicago SE; AFA. Represented by etchings in Brooklyn Museum; NY Public Library of Congress, Washington; Cleveland Museum of Art; St. Louis Public Library; Bibliotheque Nationale, Paris. Died in 1977. Address in 1929, 340 West 86th St., New York, NY.

SCHUYLER, REMINGTON.
Painter, lecturer, and writer. Born Buffalo, NY, July 8, 1887.

832

Pupil of George B. Bridgman, Howard Pyle, Jean Paul Laurens and Edmund Bashet. Member: SI. Works: "George Washington, the Surveyor," Washington School, New Rochelle, NY; "Siwanoy Indians," New Rochelle High School; "Approach Sign (Siwanoy Indians)," owned by the City of New Rochelle; six Indian panels Clyde Line Steamship Co. Died in 1955. Address in 1929, Lane off Wright St., Westport, CT, P. O. Box 308.

SCHWAB, EDITH FISHER. (MRS. C.).
Painter. Born in Cincinnati, OH, in 1862. Member of Nat. Association of Women Painters and Sculptors. Address in 1926, 310 Prospect St., New Haven, CT.

SCHWAB, ELOISA.
Painter. Born Havana, Cuba, July 4, 1894. Pupil of Kenneth Hayes Miller at ASL of NY; Julian Acad. in Paris. Member: Salons of Am.; ASL of NY; S. Indp. A. Address in 1929, Charmont Ct, 817 West End Ave, New York, NY.

SCHWABE, HENRY AUGUST.
Painter. Born in Oberweisbach, Germany, in 1843. Learned drawing and china decorating and at 18 worked as painter and designer of stained glass in Stuttgart; studied in Polytechnic School, Royal Acad. of Fine Arts, Munich; also in Cologne. He came to the United States in 1871, and later studied at the old Acad. of Design, NY, and under William Chase; also at Munich, Paris and in the Julien Acad. He has designed and painted church windows in NY, Pittsburgh, Chicago, etc. Awarded gold medal for stained glass design and execution, St. Louis Exposition, 1904; exhibited at NY Acd. of Design; Art Assoc. He was also a portrait figure painter. Was president of the Newark Art League, and a member of the Newark Museum Association. Address in 1926, 917 Broad St., Newark, NJ. Died Feb. 8, 1916, in South Orange, NJ.

SCHWANKOVSKY, FRED JOHN DE ST VRAIN.
Painter, writer, lecturer, and teacher. Born Detroit, MI, Jan. 21, 1885. Pupil of PAFA and ASL of NY. Member: Calif. AC; Laguna Beach AA; Pacific AA; PS. Head of Art Dept., Manual Arts High School, Los Angeles. Address in 1929, 1231 West 76th Street, Los Angeles; Laguna Beach, CA.

SCHWARCZ, D. R.
Painter. Born in Brooklyn in 1893. Pupil of Kenneth Hayes Miller, C. W. Hawthorne, Jonas Lie and R. S. Bredin. Member: National Association of Women Painters and Sculptors and League of NY Artists. Address in 1926, 272 West 90th St., New York, NY.

SCHWARM, WESLEY A.
Painter. Born in Lafayette, IN, in 1883. Pupil of Pratt Inst. and of Henri. Member of Society of Independent Artists. Address in 1926, 130 East 19th St., Brooklyn, NY.

SCHWARTKOFF, EARL C.
Painter and illustrator. Born in Ohio, in 1888. Member of Toledo Tile Club. Address in 1926, Care of Willys Overland Co., Toledo, OH.

SCHWARTZ, ANDREW (THOMAS).
Mural painter. Born Louisville, KY, Jan. 20, 1867. Pupil of Duveneck in Cincinnati; ASL of NY under Mowbray. Member: Mural Painter; NY Arch. Lg. 1904; AWCS; Circolo Artistica of Rome; Union Inter. des Beaux Arts et des Lettres, Paris; Allied AA; Salma. C.; AFA. Award: Lazarus scholarship to Italy, 1899-1902. Decorations; Kansas City Life Ins. Co., Kansas City, MO; "Christ the Good Shepherd," Baptist Church, South Londonderry, VT; represented in Cincinnati Art Museum and Utica Public Library. Died in 1942. Address in 1929, 246 Fulton Street, Brooklyn, NY.

SCHWARTZ, C.
In 1814 this stipple engraver of portraits was working in Baltimore, MD. His signed work is rare, but his large plate of Bishop James Kemp, published in Baltimore, is a capital piece of work.

SCHWARTZ, DANIEL.
Illustrator. Born in NYC in 1929. Went to RISD and ASL under scholarship. He studied with Yasuo

Kuniyoshi and John Frazier and in 1953 he published his first illustration for Theatre Arts. He has won seven Gold Medals from the S of I and the Purchase Prize from the Childe Hassam Fund of the American Academy of Arts and Letters. He has had numerous One-Man Shows and illustrates for all national magazines.

SCHWARTZ, ELIZABETH.
(Mrs. Chas. Neyland). Painter. Member of National Association of Women Painters and Sculptors. Address in 1926, 3337 North 17th St., Philadelphia, PA.

SCHWARTZ, MANFRED.
Painter, illustrator, and teacher. Born Germany, Nov. 11, 1908. Pupil of John Sloan, George Bridgman. Member: ASL of NY. Died in 1970. Address in 1929, 555 Crown St., Brooklyn, NY; summer, 64 Avenue du Maine, Paris, France.

SCHWARTZ, WILLIAM S.
Painter. Born Russia, Feb. 23, 1895. Pupil of Vilna Art School, Russia; AIC. Awards: First Kahn prize, Detroit, 1925; first Temple Beth El Sisterhood prize, Detroit, 1926; Holmes prize, IC, 1927; M. V. Kohnstamm prize, AIC, 1928. Work: "Friendly Enemies," Chicago Public Schools Coll. Represented in Univ. of Nebraska, Lincoln; Univ. of Missouri, Columbia; Univ. of Wisconsin, Madison. Address in 1929, 29 E. Ohio St., Chicago, IL.

SCHWARZ, FRANK HENRY.
Painter. Born New York City, June 21, 1894. Pupil of H. M. Walcott and C. W. Hawthorne. Member: Salma C.; Arch Lg. of NY; Mural P. Award: Fellowship American Acad. in Rome, 1921-24; Fellowship Guggenheim Memorial Foundation research in painting; Isidor prize (drawing) Salma. C. Drawing in permanent collection, Brooklyn Museum of Fine Arts. Died in 1951. Address in 1929, 114 East 28th Street, New York, NY; h. Norwalk, CT.

SCHWARZ, RUDOLF.
Sculptor. Born in Germany, he settled in Indianapolis. In 1902

he won the competition for a statue of Governor Pingree, of Michigan.

SCHWARZ, WILLIAM T(EFFT).
Painter and illustrator. Born Syracuse, NY, July 27, 1889. Pupil of Charles Hawthorne; studied in France and Spain. Work: Murals for the Onondaga Hotel, Syracuse; Utica Hotel, Utica, NY; Pontiac Hotel, Oswego, NY; Fulton National Bank, Lancaster, PA. Illustrations in The Saturday Evening Post, The Spur, World's Work, etc. In charge of the Art Unit for the History of Surgery during the World War. Address in 1929, 343 Sycamore Ave., Merion, PA; summer, care of Brown and Co., bankers, Paris, France.

SCHWARZBURGER, CARL.
Engraver. Born in Leipzig, Germany, in 1850. Studied in Leipzig and Berlin; came to America in 1874. Went to Australia, 1886-89, to illustrate the books "Picturesque Australia"; exhibited at Chicago; also Paris Exposition, 1900; medal, Buffalo Exposition, 1901. Address in 1926, 595 McDonough St., Brooklyn, NY.

SCHWARZOTT, MAXIMILIAN.
Sculptor. He has exhibited at the National Sculpture Society.

SCHWEITZER, GERTRUDE.
Painter and sculptor. Born in NYC, in 1911. Studied: Pratt Institute Art School; National Academy of Design; Julian Academy, Paris. Awards: Phila. Watercolor Club, 1936; Norton Art Gallery, 1946, 1947; Montclair Art Museum, 1947, 1952; Society of Four Arts, 1947, 1948, 1950, 1951; Miami, Florida, 1951; American Artists Professional League, 1934, 1953, 1956, 1957; American Watercolor Society, 1933. Collections: Brooklyn Museum; Canajoharie Gallery of Art; Toledo Museum of Art; Atlanta Art Assoc.; Norton Gallery of Art; Hackley Art Gallery; Davenport Municipal Art Museum; High Museum of Art; Witte Memorial Museum; Musuem of Modern Art, Paris; Museum of Albi, France; Montclair Art Museum. Address in 1980, Stone Hill Farm, Colts Neck, NJ.

SCHWEIZER, J. OTTO.
Sculptor. Born in Zurich, Switzerland, March 27, 1863. Pupil of Tuiller in Paris; Royal Aademy, Dresden; Acad. of Fine Arts, and Schilling in Dresden; Art School, Zurich; and in Italy. Member: NSS. Works: "Gen. Muhlenberg," and "James B. Nicholson," Phila.; "Gen. von Steuben," Utica, NY, and Valley Forge, PA; Abraham Lincoln and Generals Humphrey, Geary, Hays, Pleasanton, Gregg, PA. State Memorial, Gettysburg; Gen. Wells Monument for State of Vermont; Molly Pitcher Monument for State of PA at Carlisle, PA; statue and relief work, "Lincoln," and portraits of Grant, Mead, Sherman, Sheridan, Gregg, Faragut, Hancock, L. Memorial Room, Union League of Phila.; "Senator Clay," Marietta, GA; Melchior Muhlenberg with heroic size relief groups, Germantown, PA; Adj. Gen. Stewart, and "Senator George Oliver," Capitol, Harrisburg, PA; equestrian statue of Major Gen. F. W. von Steuben, Milwaukee, WI; portrait bust and symbolic group, "James J. Davis," Moosehart, IL; East Germantown War Memorial; Central High School War Memorial; Schell Memorial, Preston Retreat; Stein Memorial; busts of James J. Davis and G. P. Morgan, all at Phila., medals of Gov. Brumbaugh and Gov. Sproul of PA; Mexican War medal and World War medal, both for the State of Penna. Died in 1955. Address in 1929, 2215 West Venango St., Philadelphia, PA.

SCHWIEDER, ARTHUR I.
Painter and illustrator. Born Bolivar, MO, Dec. 2, 1884. Pupil of AIC. Illustrated: "Grey Face," "Bat Wing," "Yellow Shadows," "The Dream Detective," "The Winning Game," "The Mansion of Unrest" (Doubleday Doran & Co.). Address in 1929, 44 West 37th Street, NYC.

SCOFIELD, WILLIAM BACON.
Sculptor. Born Hartford, CT, Feb. 8, 1864. Pupil of Gutzon Borglum. Member: AFA. Work: "Good and Bad Sprit," bronze, Worcester Art Museum. Author of "Verses," and "Poems of the War"; "A Forgotten Idyl"; "Sketches in Verse and

Clay." Address in 1929, 125 Front St.; h. 46 Elm St., Worcester, MA.

SCOLES, JOHN.
This engraver of portraits and subject plates was located continuously in NY from 1793 until 1844. He probably died in the latter year, as he is then registered "John Scoles, late engraver." Scoles worked in both line and stipple, but with indifferent success. He engraved many of the views appearing in the New York Magazine, in 1793-96.

SCOMA, MARIO.
Sculptor, who exhibited "The Birthday" in Annual Exhibition, 1915, of the Penna. Academy of the Fine Arts, Philadelphia. Address in 1926, 24 Hamburg Ave., Brooklyn, NY.

SCOT,
Painter. Nothing is known of this artist, except the mention in the diary of Rev. Wm. Bentley, Oct. 3, 1803. "At Mr. Scot's saw several full lengths of Washington which pleased me, excepting the faces so different from those I saw. Several paintings did honor to this young painter; the head of Dr. Lathrop was complete, Mr. Adams I readily knew, Mr. Murry, the Universalist not so much, Gov. Strong too full faced."

SCOT, ROBERT.
Engraver. Born in England. He was originally a watchmaker. He appears in Philadelphia about 1783, and in that year he engraved a frontispiece for a Masonic sermon preached by Wm. Smith, D. D., and published by Hall & Sellars. He advertised himself as "Late Engraver to the State of Virginia," and in 1785 he was paid 16 Pounds for engraving done for the State of Pennsylvania. Scot engraved a few fairly well executed line portraits, including one of Washington, over his own name. In 1793, Robert Scot was appointed engraver to the newly established United States Mint in Philadelphia, and he is credited with having made the dies for the copper cent of 1793.

SCOTT, ANNA PAGE.
Painter. Born in Dubuque, Iowa. Pupil of Anshutz, Arthur Dow, and of the Colarossi Academy, Paris. Represented by the "Shores of the Pacific," Carnegie Library, Dubuque. Address in 1926, 1212 Locust St., Dubuque. Died Oct. 13, 1925 in Dubuque.

SCOTT, BERTHA.
Painter, writer, and teacher. Born Frankfort, March 25, 1884. Pupil of Anson K. Cross, Andrene Kauffman. Member: Louisville AC; Louisville AA. Author and Illustrator of garden articles for "House Beautiful," Died in 1965. Address in 1929, "The Attic Studio," 402 Shelby St., Frankfort, KY; summer, Care of the Cross Art School, Boothbay Harbor, ME.

SCOTT, CHARLES T.
Painter and sculptor. Born in Chester County, PA, in 1876. Pupil of Penna. Museum School of Industrial Art, Philadelphia. Address in 1926, 320 South Broad Street, Philadelphia.

SCOTT, COLIN A.
Painter. Born in Ottawa, CN, 1861. Member of Providence Art Association. Address in 1926, College St., South Hadley, MA.

SCOTT, EMILY MARIA SPAFORD.
Flower painter. Born in Springwater, NY, on Aug. 27, 1832. She studied at the Art Students' League of NY, and in Paris. She is represented by paintings in the Metropolitan Museum and in the Brooklyn Inst. Museum. She died on April 9, 1915, in NYC.

SCOTT, ERIC G(LIDDEN).
Painter, etcher, and teacher. Born Bega, Australia, July 5, 1893. Pupil of Julian Ashton, Henri Royer, Jules Pages. Member: Chicago SE; Australian Painter Etchers; Calif. SE. Represented by etching in Art institute of Chicago. Address in 1929, 37 rue Friodevaux, Paris XIV, France.

SCOTT, GERALDINE ARMSTRONG.
Painter. Born Elkhart, IN, Oct. 1, 1900. Pupil of Edward R. Sitzman; NY. School of Fine and Applied Arts

both in NY and Paris. Member: IN. AC.; Three Arts C.; Ind. AL. Award: Erskine prize, South Bend, IN, 1928. Work: "December Symphony," Butler Univ., Indianapolis, IN; "Glorious Autumn," Carnegie Library, Kokomo, IN. Address in 1929, 606 West Walnut St., Kokomo, IN.

SCOTT, JAMES.
Painter. Born Racine, WI, Sept. 3, 1889. Pupil of ASL of NY; Julian Acad., Colarossi and Grande Chaumiere in Paris. Member: Salma. C. Award: Silver Medal, Panama, Pacific Exp., San Francisco, 1915. Work: Mural, American Expeditionary Forces Unversity, France. Address in 1929, Milton, NY.

SCOTT, JEANNETTE.
Painter and teacher. Born Kincardine, Ont., CN, Sept 26, 1864. Pupil of PAFA and Phila. School of Design for Women, and studied in Paris. Member: AFA. Work in Syracuse Museum of Fine Arts. Professor of painting, Syracuse Unversity since 1895; Professor emertus, A.F.D., 1927. Died in 1937. Address in 1929, Skaneateles, NJ.

SCOTT, JOHN WHITE ALLEN.
Landscape painter. Born in Roxbury, MA, in 1815. His best known paintings are scenes in the Catskills and White Mountains. He died March 4, 1907, in Cambridge, MA.

SCOTT, JOSEPH T.
Engraver (an especially good map engraver) working in Philadelphia as early as 1795. He published an atlas of the United States, printed in Philadelphia in 1796 by Francis and Robert Bailey. Scott drew and engraved the maps.

SCOTT, JULIAN.
Painter. Born in VT, Feb. 15, 1846. He entered the army at the breaking out of the Civil War. He afterwards became a pupil of the National Acad. and studied under Leutze until 1868. His work consists chiefly of pictures of Army life; "Battle of Cedar Creek," "Charge at Antietam," "The Recall"

and the "Blue and the Gray." He died July 4, 1901, in Plainfield, NJ.

SCOTT, KATHERINE H(ALL).
Portrait and miniature painter. Born Burlington, IA. Pupil of AIC, Vanderpoel and Chase, Snow Froelich School of Industrial Art. Member: Alumni AIC; Chicago AG; Eastern Arts Asso.; AFA. Work: Portraits in Des Moines County Court House; Public Library and Merchants National Bank, Burlington, IA. Art Supervisor, State Teachers College, West Chester, PA. Address in 1929, 313 South High St., West Chester, PA.

SCOTT, MONA DUGAS.
Painter. Born Augusta, GA. Pupil of Leon Foster Jones. Member: NA Women PS. Address in 1929, 106 Morris St., Yonkers, NY.

SCOTT, R(ALPH) C.
Painter, illustrator, and teacher. Born Elliston, Newfoundland, Oct. 6, 1896. Pupil of Josph De Camp, Ernest L. Major, Aldro T. Hibbard. Member: Prov. AC; Prov. WCC; Rockport AA. Work: "South Court Street," Plantation Club, Providence. Address in 1929, "The Arlington," 41 Angell Street, Providence, RI; summer, Rockport, MA.

SCOTT, WILLIAM EDOUARD.
Painter. Born Indianapolis, 1884. Pupil of AIC; Julian and Colarossi Acad., Paris; H. O. Tanner in France. Member: Hoosier Salon; Almni, AIC; SWA; Chicago AL. Award: Municipal Art. Lg. Traveling Scholarship; Frederick Magnus Brandt prize; special gold medal and Harmon award, Harmon Foundation; Jesse Binga prize, and Eames MacVeagh prize, Chic. AL. Represented by mural decorations in Evanston, IL; Herron Art Inst., Indianapolis; Fort Wayne (IN) Court House; Lafayette (IN) Court House; Springfield, IL; State House; Schools in Inst., W. VA, and Charleston, W. VA; First Presbyterian Church, Chicago; Chicago Defender Newspaper Lobby; Binga State Bank, Chicago, Anthony Hotel, Fort Wayne, IN; Edwardsville (IL) National Bank; South Park M.

E. Church, Chicago; Paris Salon; Royal Acad., London, England; First Nat'l Bank and High School, Michigan City, IN; Peoples Finance Corp. Bank, St. Louis, MO; mural, "Jean Baptiste De Saible," John Shoop School, Chicago; one painting owned by the Argentine Government. Address in 1929, 5134 Michigan Blvd., Chicago, IL.

SCOTT, WILLIAM J.
Painter, who exhibited water colors at the Penna. Acad. of Fine arts, Philadelphia, 1925. Address in 1926, Compo Road, Westport, CT.

SCOTT, WILLIAM WALLACE.
Painter in water colors. Born in 1819. Died Oct. 6, 1905, in New Rochelle, NY.

SCRUGGS, MARGARET ANN.
(Mrs. Carruth). Etcher. Born Dallas, Feb. 18, 1892. Member: Texas FAA; Highland Park AA; Dallas AA; Reaugh AC; SSAL; AFA; Am. APL; Soc. Medalists. Address in 1929, 3715 Turtle Creek Blvd., Dallas, Texas; summer, Indian River, MI.

SCRYMSER, CHRISTABEL.
Painter. Born Brooklyn, NY, May 12, 1885. Pupil of Whittaker, Twachtman, Metcalf, Beck, Fisher; Cooper Union; Pratt Inst. Member: Brooklyn S. Min. P. Specialty, miniature painting. Address in 1929, 34 Lewis Place, Rockville Center, NY.

SCUDDER, (ALICE) RAYMOND.
Painter and craftsman. Born New Orleans, LA. Pupil of Newcomb Art School; NY School of Applied Design; Chase and Mora. Member: New Orleans A.; AFA. Address in 1929, 478 South Grand Ave., Pasadena, CA.

SCUDDER, JANET.
Sculptor. Born Terre Haute, IN, Oct. 27, 1875. Pupil of Cincinnati Art Acad. under Rebisso; Taft in Chicago; Macmonnies in Paris. Member: ANA.; NSS, 1904; NA Women PS; NAC; AFA. Awards: Medal, Columbian Exp., Chicago, 1893; hon. mention, Sun Dial Competition, NY, 1898; medal, St. Louis Expo., 1904; hon. mention, Paris Salon, 1911; Sculpture prize, NA Women PS, 1914;

silver medal, P. P. Exp., San F., 1915; Chevalier de la Legion d'Honneur, 1925. First American Woman to have sculpture bought for the Luxembourg, Paris. Work: Seal for the Associaton of the bar of the City of NY; "Japanese Art," facade of Brooklyn Institute Museum; "Frog Fountain," Metropolitan Museum, NY; "Fighting Boy Fountain," Art Inst. of Chicago, IL; 3 medallions in gold and 3 in silver, Art Assoc. Indianapolis, IN; portrait medallions in Congressional Library, Washington; Metropolitan Museum, NY; Musee du Luxembourg, Paris; medal of Indiana Centennial, Minneapolis Institute; "Medal," RI School of Design, Providence; "Tortoise Fountain," Peabody Inst., Balitmore; "Seated Fawn," Brooklyn Museum; fountain, Public School, Richmond, IN. Fountains in many private estates. Died June 9, 1940, in Rockport, MA. Address in 1929, Square de Vergennes 279 rue de Vaugirard, Pris, France; care The Colony Club, New York, NY.

SCUDDER, RAYMOND.
Painter. Born in New Orleans, LA. Pupil of Newcomb Art School; New York School of Applied Design; also Chase and Mora. Member: New Orleans Artists Association. Address in 1926, 1631 Octavia St., New Orleans, LA.

SEABURY, ROXOLI (MRS.).
Painter. Born in 1874. Pupil of D. W. Ross, Robt. Reid and of Knirr in Munich. Student of School of Boston Museum of Fine Arts. Address in 1926, Broadwater Art Acad., Colorado Springs, CO.

SEAGER, (SARA) (MRS. AND MISS).
Miniature and portrait painter, who flouished in NY, in 1834.

SEALEY, ALFRED.
Engraver. Born C. 1815 NYS. He is said to have died in 1868. Sealey was an admirable line engraver and devoted himself to bank note work in his later life. In 1856 he was apparently working in Philadelphia, but some of his signed work is dated as early as 1845. In 1860 some very good line illustrations to Coopers novels are signed

"Sealey & Smith Sculpt." This work was done in NY and may be ascribed to Alfred Sealey.

SEAMAN, CHARLES.
Portrait painter in oils and miniatures, who flourished in NY about 1834.

SEAMAN, ELAYNE.
Printmaker. Born in October 27, 1929. Work: Private collections, US and Europe. Comn: 12 drawings, Scafa-Tornabene Art Publishing Co.; Lithograph, Book-of-the-Month Club's Fine Arts 260 Series. One-man shows: Cary Arboretum, NY Botanical Garden, Millbrook, NY; Bloomingdale's Gal., Stamford, CT; Hansen Galleries, NYC; Lewis Gal., Woodstock, NY; Eisenhower Hall, US Mil. Acad., West Point, NY; Bardavon 1869 Opera House, Poughkeepsie, NY. Exhib.: Rainbow Graphics Gal., Woodstock, NY; Gal. East, Amagansett, NY; Hansen Galleries, NYC; Uptown Gal., NYC; Henri Bendel Gal., NYC; Galerie Mouffe, Paris & Biarritz, France; Salon des Artistes Francais, Grand Palais, Paris; Vassar College, Poughkeepsie, NY; Faber Birren Award Exhib., Stamford, CT; Berkshire Art Assn., Pittsfield, MA; Summergroup Gallery, Mid-Hudson Arts & Sci. Ctr., Poughkeepsie, NY, and many more. Address in 1983, Poughkeepsie, NY.

SEARCY, ELISABETH.
Landscape painter and etcher. Born Memphis, TN. Member: PBC; SSAL; AFA. Work: Etchings in the Library of Congress, Washington, D.C. Address in 1929, 353 Orleans St., Memphis, TN.

SEARLE, ALICE T.
Miniature painter. Born in Troy, NY, in 1869. Pupil of Art Students' League of NY and of the Colarossi Acad., Paris. Member of Brooklyn Artists Guild. Address in 1926, 241 Fenimore St., Brooklyn, NY.

SEARS, ELINOR LATHROP.
Painter and sculptor. Born Hartford, CT, Sept. 26, 1899. Pupil of Hale, Logan, Mora and Calder. Member: Hartford AS. Address in 1929, 86 Bretton Road,

West Hartford, CT; summer; Old Lyme, CT.

SEARS, PHILIP SHELTON.
Sculptor. Born Boston, MA, Nov. 12, 1867. Pupil of Daniel C. French and Boston Museum of Fine Arts School. Member: Boston GA; North Shore AA; Boston SS; AFA; City Art. Com., Boston. Died March, 1953, in Brookline, MA. Address in 1929, 260 Heath Street, Brookline, MA; summer, Pride's Crossing, MA.

SEARS, SARAH C(HOATE).
(Mrs. J. Montgomery Sears). Painter. Born Cambridge, MA, May 5, 1858. Pupil of Ross Turner, Joseph De Camp, Dennis M. Bunker, Edmund C. Tarbell and George de Forest Brush. Member: NYWCC; Copley S. 1891; NAC; Phila. WCC; Boston WCC; Boston SAC (life). Awards: Evans prize, AWCS, 1893; medal Columbian Exp., Chicago, 1893; hon. mention, Paris Exp., 1900; bronze medal for water color, Pan Am. Exp., Buffalo, 1901; silver medal for water color, Charleston, Exp., 1902; silver medal, St. Louis Exp., 1904. Died in 1935. Address in 1929, 12 Arlington St., Boston, MA.

SEARS, TABER.
Mural painter. Born Boston, MA, 1870. Pupil of Boston Museum School; Julian Acad. in Paris under Constant, Laurens, and Merson. Member: NY Arch. Lg., 1899; NYWCC; AWCS; Mural P.; A. Aid S.; NY Municipal AS; Century Assoc.; MacD.C. Award: Bronze medal, St. Louis Exp., 1904; Delano prize, AWCS, 1926. Work: Altar paintings, Chapel of the Intercession, St. Thomas's Church, St. James Church, First Presbyterian Church, New York City; and in Trinity Church, Buffalo, NY. Mural paintings, Grace Church Choir School, NY and City Hall, New York; Church of the Nativity and Church of the Holy Innocents, Brooklyn, NY. Died Oct. 18, 1950, in NYC. Address in 1929, 96 Fifth Ave.; h. 1060 Park Ave., New York, NY.

EATON, C. H.
Painter. Born in Monson, MA, in 1865. Self taught. Member:

Washington Society of Artists; Washington Landscape Club. Address in 1926, Glencarlyn, VA.

SEAWELL, H(ENRY) W(ASHINTON).
Painter, illustrator, and teacher. Born San Francisco. Pupil of Laurens and Constant in Paris. Member: Paris AAA; Bohemian C., San Francisco; Pac. AA of Calif. Address in 1929, 1617 California St., San Francisco, CA.

SEEBOLD, MARIE M.
See Mrs. A. Molinary.

SEIBEL, FRED O.
Cartoonist. Born Durhamville, NY, Oct. 8, 1886. Pupil of Kenyon Cox, Albert Sterner, Frank V. DuMond. Died in 1968. Address in 1929, Times Dispatch, 107 South 7th Street; h. 414 North Sheppard St., Richmond, VA.

SEIDEL, EMORY P.
Sculptor. Member: IL Acad. FA; Oak Park A Lg.; Chicago PS; Chicago Gal. A; Palette and Chisel C. Award: John C. Shafer prize, AIC, 1925; Charles Worcester prize, Palette and Chisel C., 1926; Gold medal, Palette and Chisel C, 1927; gold medal, Oak Park Art Lg., 1929. Address in 1929, 111 W. Jackson Blvd., F. C. Austin Bldg., Chicago, IL; h. 535 Franklin Ave., River Forest, IL.

SEIDEN, ART.
Illustrator. Born in Brooklyn, NY, in 1923. Received his BA degree from Queens College. His first published illustration was for a children's book, Three Mice and a Cat, which was published in 1957 by Grosset and Dunlap. His work has been on display at the Lotus Club in NYC, Univ. of Minn. (Kerlan Collection) and the Watercolor Society at the NAD, where he is a member.

SEIDENECK, GEORGE J.
Painter. Born in Chicago, IL, in 1885. Pupil of Walter Thor and von Marr. Member: Chicago Art Club; Chicago Society of Artists; Chicago Palette and Chisel Club. Work: "Portrait of Judge Seaman," Federal Building, Chicago. Address in

1926, Tree Studio Building, 4 East Ohio St., Chicago, IL.

SEIDLER, DORIS.
Painter, etcher, and engraver. Born in London, England, in 1912. Studied: with Stanley W. Hayter. Awards: National Assoc. of Women Artists; Wash. Watercolor Club; Chicago Society of Etchers. Collections: Seattle Art Museum; Library of Congress; Hofstra College, NY; Phila. Museum of Art.

SEIPP, ALICE.
Painter and illustrator. Born in 1889, in New York, NY. Pupil of ASL of NY, Ossip Linde, Douglas Volk, B. W. Clinedinst and Jane Peterson. Member: NA Women PS; NYWCC; PBC; AFA. Art editor and artist of the Woman's Inst. Address in 1929, care of The Woman's Inst., Scranton, PA.

SEISSER, MARTIN B.
Painter. Born in Pittsburgh, Penna., in 1845. He went to Europe in 1868 and studied in Munich. On his return he opened his studio in Pittsburgh, and painted many portraits. His picture "The Crusaders," painted in 1875, was stolen in 1878 at an auction sale in Philadelphia.

SEKULA, SONIA.
Painter. Born in Lucerne, Switzerland in 1918. Studied: Art Students' League; and with Morris Kantor and Kurt Roesch; also in Italy. Collections: San Fran. Museum of Art; Brooklyn Museum.

SEL, JEAN B.
Portrait painter in oils and miniatures, who flourished in 1820-1830, New Orleans. A portrait in oil by Sel of Gov. A. B. Romans is in the Louisiana State Museum. Died Jan. 28, 1832.

SELDEN, DIXIE.
Portrait and landscape painter and illustrator. Born Cincinnati, Ohio. Pupil of Cincinnati Art Acad. under Duveneck; W. M. Chase; H. B. Snell. Member: Cincinnati Woman's AC; NA Women PS; Cincinnati MacD. S. Died in 1936. Address in 1929, No. 5, The Deventer Bldg.; 1203

East McMillan St., Walnut Hills, Cincinnati, OH.

SELDEN, HENRY BILL.
Painter, etcher, and teacher. Born Erie, PA, Jan. 24, 1886. Pupil of ASL of NY; Charles Woodbury, Birge Harrison. Member: Lyme AA; AWCS; NYWCC; Allied AA; A. Fund S; CT. Acad. FA; NAC; St. Botolph; Salma. C. Award: Flagg prize, CT Acad., 1929. Asso. Prof. of Fine Arts, CT College. Died in 1934. Address in 1929, 17 Chapel St., New London, CT.

SELIGER, CHARLES.
Painter. Born June 3, 1926, in NYC. Studied at Works Progess Adm. Art School, Jersey City. Taught at Mt. Vernon Art Center (1951). Exhibited at Art of this Century Gallery, NYC (1945); Jersey City Mus.; Virg. Mus. Fine Art (Richmond); Art Inst. Chicago; Newark; Brooklyn; Munson Williams Proctor Inst.; Cornell; Whitney; Nassau Com. College; Crispo Gal., NYC, and Makler Gal. (Phila). In collections in Seattle; Whitney; Munson Williams Proctor; Baltimore; MOMA; Vassar College; the Hague; MMA and private collections.

SELINGER, JEAN PAUL.
Painter. Born in 1850. His painting "The Water Seller" is in the Boston Museum of Fine Arts. He died in Sept. 11, 1909, in Boston, MA.

SELLERS, MARY (OR MINNIE).
Painter. Born Pittsburgh, Nov. 23, 1869. Pupil of Alexander Robinson and August Hennicott in Holland. Member: Assoc. Artists of Pittsburgh; NA Women PS. Address in 1929, 6216 Howe St., Pittsburgh, PA.

SELLSTEDT, LARS GUSTAF.
Painter. Born April 30, 1819, at Sundsvali, Sweden. He came to the US in 1834 and settled in Buffalo, NY, in 1842. He devoted himself chiefly to portraiture, and his works include portraits of G. W. Clinton, M. Fillmore, B. Fitch, and G. Cleveland. He was elected an associate member in 1871 of the National Academy and an Academician in 1874, and died in 1911. For his

life see "From Forecastle to Academy," published in Buffalo, NY, in 1904. Died June 4, 1911 in Buffalo, NY.

SELTZER, ISADORE.
Illustrator. Born in St. Louis, MO, in 1930. Attended the ACD and Chouinard Art Institute. He illustrates for McCall's, Playboy, Redbook, Cosmopolitan, Seventeen, Leisure, and others. His works have been exhibited at the Louvre, the Whitney Museum and Benson Museum in Bridgehampton, NY.

SENAT, PROSPER L.
Painter. Born in Germantown, Philadelphia in 1852. Studied in Philadelphia, NY, London and Paris. Specialty, landscapes in water colors. For years he painted on the Brittany coast and at Cornwall, England. Died in Sept. 1925, in Germantown.

SENECAL, RALPH L.
Painter and illustrator. Born Bolton, Canada, Aug. 3, 1883. Pupil of NAD. Member: Springfield AC; CT SA; Springfield AC; CT SA; Springfield AL.; CT. AFA. Address in 1929, 35 Squier St., Palmer, MA.

SENSENEY, GEORGE.
Painter and etcher. Born Wheeling, W. Va, Oct. 11, 1874. Pupil of Corcoran Art School in Washington under Howard Helmick; Laurens and Constant in Paris. Member: Chicago SE; Salma. C.; Soc. des Graveurs en Couleurs.; Brooklyn SE. Award: Silver medal, P. P. Exp., San F., 1915. Work in: Library of Congress, Washington, D.C.; South Kensington Museum, London. Died in 1943. Address in 1929, The Marvellum Co., Holyoke, MA; 65 New South St., Northampton, MA.

SENYARD, GEORGE.
Painter, who died Jan. 18, 1924, in Olmstead Falls, OH. He toured the country with Lincoln, and made many sketches and drawings of him during his political debates.

SEPESHY, ZOLTAN L.
Painter and teacher. Born Kassa, Hungary, Feb. 24, 1898. Studied in Royal Acad. of Fine Arts, Budapest, Paris, Prague, Royal Acad., Vienna.

Member: Scarab C; Royal A. of Budapest. Represented by 2 murals, General Motors Bldg., Detroit, six murals, High School, Fordson, MI; paintings, Art Inst. of Detroit; San Diego, CA. Address in 1929, 2721 Gladstone Ave., Detroit, MI.

SERGEANT, EDGAR.
Painter. Born New York City, Nov. 25, 1877. Pupil of Du Mond, George Pearse Ennis and Gifford Beal. Member: Salma. C.; AFA. Address in 1929, 160 Satterthwaite Ave., Nutley, NJ; summer, North Hatley, P. Q. Canada.

SERPELL, SUSAN WATKINS.
(Mrs. Goldsborough Serpell). Painter. Born in CA, in 1875. In 1912 she was elected an Associate Member of the National Academy of Design, and received many medals and awards. Died June 18, 1913.

SERRAO, LUELLA VARNEY (MRS.).
Sculptor. Born Angola, NY, 1865. Work: "An Archbishop of Odessa," in Roman Catholic Cathedral, Odessa, Russia; "Bust of Senator Rice," State Capital of Minnesota; "Bust of Archbishop Wigger," Seaton Hall, Newark, NJ; busts of Mark Twain and Mr. Brett, Cleveland Public Library; "Monument of Archbishop Rappe," Catholic Cathedral, Cleveland, Ohio. Address in 1926, 1875 East 81st St., Cleveland, OH.

SERRON HYPPOLITE, VICTOR VALINTIN.
Painter. Born Aug. 21, 1801, in Camdebec, Florence. Painted landscapes and river views in and about New Orleans. Died Sept. 1, 1897, in Paris, France.

SERVER, J. WILLIAM.
Painter. Born in Philadelphia, PA, in 1882. Pupil of Deigendesch, Chase, and Colarossi. Member: Art Students League, Philadelphia. Address in 1926, 43 South 18th Street, Philadelphia, PA.

SERZ, JOHN.
Born C. 1810 in Bavaria. Died in Philadelphia about 1878, as the result of a fall. Serz came to Philadelphia about 1850; he engraved several large historical plates and furnished a number of

subject plates for Sartain's Magazine and other publications of that city.

SETON, ERNEST THOMPSON.
Illustrator, writer, and lecturer. Born South Shields, England, Aug. 14, 1860. Pupil of Gerome, Bouguereau, Ferrier and Mosler in Paris. Specialty, animals. Author and illustrator: "Art Anatomy of Animals," "Wild Animals I Have Known," "The Biography of a Grizzly," "Animal Heroes," "The Book of Woodcraft," "Lives of Game Animals," etc. Head of Boy Scout movement in American until 1915; Chief of Woodcraft League of America. Died in 1946. Address in 1929, Greenwich, CT.

SEVERANCE, JULIA G(RIDLEY).
Sculptor, etcher, and teacher. Born Oberlin, Ohio, Jan. 11, 1877. Pupil of ASL of NY. Member: Cleveland Woman's AC; Florida Soc. A. and Sciences. Work: "Rice Memorial Tablet," Oberlin Conservatory of Music, Oberlin College, OH; etching in Print Dept., Library of Congress, Washington, DC; Cobb Memorial Tablet, Warner Hall, Oberlin, OH; Leffingwell Tablet, St. Mary's School, Knoxville, IL; portrait of "Prof. G. F. Wright," Allen Memorial Museum, Oberlin, Ohio. Address in 1929, 68 South Professor St., Oberlin, OH.

SEWALL, BLANCHE HARDING.
(Mrs. Cleveland Sewall). Painter. Born Ft. Worth, May 12, 1889. Pupil of J. C. Tidden and Fred Wagner. Member: Southern SAL. Address in 1929, 7B The Beaconfield, Houston, TX.

SEWARD, C. A.
Painter, etcher, lecturer, and lithographer. Born in Chase, KS, March 4, 1884. Pupil of Reid, Stone, Sandzen; mostly self-taught. Member: Wichita AA; Wichita AG; Calif. PM. Award: First prize, Kansas City AI, 1924; silver medal, Mid West Artists, 1927; gold medal of Mid West Artists, 1928. Work: "The Acropolis," Kansas Masonic Grand Lodge; "Wichita in 1869," Sedgwick Co. Historical Society; lithographs in Los Angeles Museum

of History and Art; Springfield, MA, Public Library; Smoky Valley Art Club, Lindsborg, Kansas; High School Art Club, Twentieth Century Club, Wichita; California State Library; Kansas Fed. of Women's Clubs; New Mexico Fed. of Women's Clubs; Vanderpoel Memorial High School, Chicago; Mulvane Art Museum, Topeka, Kansas; Bibliotheque Nationale, Paris. Died in 1939. Address in 1929, 1534 North Holyoke Ave., Wichita, KS.

SEWELL, AMANDA BREWSTER.
Painter. Born in Essex County, NY. Studied at Art Students' League of New York, and under Julien and Carolus Duran, Paris. Began painting in Paris in 1886; exhibited at Paris Salon, 1886, 1887, 1888; awarded Dodge prize, National Acad. of Design, 1888; Clarke prize, same, 1903; bronze medal, Chicago Exposition. Principal works: Portraiture in the style and spirit of the early English masters. Elected an Associate Member of the National Academy of Design. Address in 1926, 33 West 67th St., New York City.

SEWELL, AMOS.
Illustrator. Born in San Fran., in 1901. Went to the Calif. School of Fine Arts before moving East to attend the ASL and GCSA, where he studied under Harvey Dunn. His career began in 1936 with an illustration for Country Gentleman. He contributed for over 20 years to The Saturday Evening Post; his work was very popular in the 1940's and 1950's, earning him several awards from the S of I and ADCs. His painting entitled "What It Is Like to Die" won a Special Art Award in 1944.

SEWELL, HELEN MORRIE.
Painter, etcher, and illustrator. Born Mare Island, Calif., June 27, 1896. Pupil of Frederick Baker, Otto Beck, Mac Herrmann, C. W. Hawthorne and A. Archipenko. Member: New Haven PCC; NYWCC. Died in 1957. Address in 1929, 5 Heights Road Ridgewood, NJ; summer, Burnt Hill, NY.

SEWELL, ROBERT VAN VORST.
Painter. Born in New York in 1860. Studied under Lefebvre and Boulanger, Paris, 1883-87. Won 1st Hallgarten prize, National Academy of Design, 1888; silver medal, Buffalo Exposition, for exhibit of designs of mural paintings, etc. His mural painting, "The Canterbury Pilgrims," in the great hall of Georgian Court, Lakewood, and several others are widely known; he painted "The Story of Psyche," a series of lunette decorations in the Palm Room of the St. Regis Hotel, NY. Elected Associate Member of the National Academy in 1902. Member of Society of Mural Painters; Architectural League of NY. Died Nov. 18, 1924, in Florence, Italy.

SEXTON, FREDERICK LESTER.
Painter, sculptor, illustrator, etcher, artist, lecturer, and teacher. Born Cheshire, CT, Sept. 13, 1889. Pupil of Sergeant Kendall. Member: New Haven PCC. Award: Second prize, New Haven PCC., 1923. Address in 1929, 977 Whalley Ave., New Haven, CT.

SEYFFERT, HELEN F. (MRS. L).
Painter. Member of Fellowship of the Penna. Academy of Fine Arts. Address in 1926, Care of Chicago Art Inst., Chicago, IL.

SEYFFERT, LEOPOLD (GOULD).
Painter. Born California, MO, Jan. 6, 1887. Pupil of William M. Chase. Member: ANA, 1916; NA, 1925; Portrait P.; AFA. Awards: Fellowship prize ($100), PAFA, 1913; hon. mention, CI Pittsburgh, 1913; gold medal, Phila. AC, 1915; silver medal, P. P. Exp., San F., 1915; Beck gold medal, PAFA, 1918; Altman prize ($500), NAD, 1918; first Hallgarten prize, NAD, 1918; Temple gold medal, PAFA, 1921; Proctor prize, NAD, 1921; Palmer gold medal, 1923; Logan gold medal, 1924; Hearst prize, 1924; all at AIC; silver medal Municipal AL of Chicago; Stotesbury gold medal, PAFA, 1926; gold medal, Sesqui Centennial Expo., Phila., 1926; Lippincot prize, PAFA, 1929. Work: "Model Resting," Art Inst. of Chicago; "Portrait of John c. Johnson" and "Myself," Corcoran Gallery, Washington, DC; "An Old Spanish Woman," Metropolitan Museum of Art; "Dr. Holland," Carnegie Inst., Pittsburgh; "Lacquer Screen," Penna. Acad. of the Fine Arts; "Myself," Detroit; "Myself," Chicago; "Nude with Oriental Background," Harrison Gallery, Los Angeles Museum. Died in 1956. Address in 1929, 147 East Ontario St., Chicago, IL; summer, care Morgan Harjes Co., 14 Place Vendome, Paris, France.

SEYMOUR, JOSEPH H.
Engraver. Joseph H. Seymour was in the employ of Isaiah Thomas, at Worcester, MA, as early as 1791. The Bible published by Thomas in that year contains thirty-two plates by Seymour, variously signed J. H., Jos. and J. Seymour, and in the printer's advertisement Thomas writes: "These plates were engraved in his Office (Thomas's) in this town in 1791. . . and the Editor doubts not but a proper allowance will be made for work engraved by an artist who obtained his knowledge in this country, compared with that done by European Engraver who has settled in the United State." Seymour was thus evidently trained to his art in the United States and must have been really at work in Worcester previous to 1791.

SEYMOUR, RALPH FLETCHER.
Illustrator, etcher, and teacher. Born Milan, IL, March 18, 1876. Pupil of Nowottny and Meakin in Cincinnati. Studied in Paris. Member: Chicago SI; Cliff Dwellers; NAC. Award: Cunningham prize for best group of etchings. Etchings in various art museums. Represented in Bibliotheque Nationale, Paris. Instructor, decorative illustration, Chicago Art Institute, 1909-1918. Address in 1929, 410 Michigan Blvd., Chicago, IL; h. Ravinia Lake County, IL.

SGOUROS, THOMAS.
Illustrator. Born in Chicago in 1927. Went to the Mass. College of Art for a year and completed his studies at RISD under Joseph J. C. Santoro, John Frazier, and Harvey Stein. His first piece was published in 1949 while he was

843

still a student. Since that time his artwork has earned him many awards and been shown in major museums nationwide. The Museum of Fine Arts in Jacksonville, Florida and the RISD Museum of Fine Arts have his work in their permanent collections. A participant in the Lecture Series at the S of I, he is currently the Chairman of the Design Division at RISD.

SHACKLEFORD, SHELBY.
Painter. Born Halifax, VA, Sept. 27, 1899. Pupil of Ross Moffett and Othon Friesz. Member: S. Indp. A.; Provincetown AA. Awards: Two scholarships, Maryland Institute, Baltimore. Address in 1929, 2268 Sedgwick Ave., New York, NY; summer, Provincetown, MA.

SHAFER, L. A.
Painter, etcher, and illustrator. Born Geneseo, IL, Nov. 17, 1866. Pupil of AI Chicago. Member: SI 1911; AFA. Illustrator of "The Shock of Battle," by Vaux; "The Road to Glory," by Powell; "Heading North," by Barbour; posters of the Great War. Address in 1929, 232 Liberty Ave., New Rochelle, NY.

SHAFTENBENG, LEWIS.
Miniature painter, who flourished in 1783, in Baltimore, MD.

SHAHN, BEN.
Illustrator. Born in Kovno, Lithuania, in 1898. Came to America in 1906. He worked as a lithographer's apprentice until 1930 when he completed his formal education at NYU, CCNY, and the NAD. One of America's most renowned artists, a traveler of Africa and Europe, his work is in private collections and museums around the world. He has earned innumerable prizes, including many Gold Medals from the Art Dir. Club. His illustrations have appeared in Fortune, Time, Seventeen, Esquire, Harper's, on posters for the Office of War Information and at Syracuse Univ., where his famous interpretation of the Sacco-Vanzetti trial has been translated into a wall-sized mosaic. Died in 1969.

SHALER, FREDERICK.
Painter. Born at Findlay, Ohio, on Dec. 15, 1880. Studied with Chase in NY and had a studio for years in that city. He died Dec. 27, 1916, in Taormino, Italy.

SHALLUS, FRANCIS.
Engraver. Born in Philadelphia, in 1773. He was the son of Jacob Shallus, and officer in the Revolutionary War. As a young man Francis Shallus was prominent in local politics; and in 1805 he was captain of the First Light Infantry, of Philadelphia. His profession is given as engraver from 1797 to 1821. He died in Philadelphia in 1821.

SHANE, FREDERICK.
Painter. Born Kansas City, Feb. 2, 1906. Pupil of Randall Davey. Member: Kansas City SA; S. Indp. A. Salons of Amer. Award: Bronze medal, Mid Western Exh., Kansas City, 1927; Post Dispatch prize, St. Louis, 1929. Address in 1929, 11 Charles St., NYC; summer, 3728 Tracy Ave., Kansas City, MO.

SHANNON, HOWARD J(OHNSON).
Painter and illustrator. Born Jamaica, NY, May 30, 1876. Pupil of Pratt Inst. under Herbert Adams and F. V. Du Mond. Illustrated nature and science sections, Century Dictionary; Zoological Soc. Bulletins; writer and illustrator of science articles in St. Nicholas, Harper's Magazine, Scientific Monthly, and Journal of the American Museum of Natural History. Address in 1929, 88-60 162nd St., Jamaica, Queens Borough, New York, NY.

SHANNON, JAMES JEBUSA.
Painter. Born in Auburn, NY, in 1862. He resided for many years in England. Studied at South Kensington Schools, London, under Edward Poynter. Awards: Gold medal, Paris Exposition, 1889; first class medal, Berlin; first medal, Carnegie Inst., Pittsburgh, 1897; Lippincott prize, Pennsylvania Acd of the Fine Arts, 1899; silver medal, Paris Expo., 1900; gold medal, Pan Am Expo., Buffalo, 1901. Elected an Associate Member of the Royal

Acad., 1897; Royal Acad, 1909; Associate, National Acad., 1908. His painting "Girl in Brown" is in the Corcoran Art Gallery, Washington. Died March 6, 1923, in London, England.

SHAPLEIGH, FRANK HENRY.
Born in Boston, MA, in 1842. He studied under Emile Lamton in Paris, and spent his professional life in Boston. his paintings include "Yosemite Valley," "Mount Washington," the "White Mountains" and the "Old Mill in Seabrook." Died in 1906.

SHARADIN, HENRY W(ILLIAM).
Painter, craftsman, lecturer and teacher. Born Kutztown, PA, Dec. 22, 1872. Pupil of Carrol Beckwith; School of Industrial Arts, Phila.; Metropolitan Art School, NY; Tudor Hart in Paris; Nordi in Rome. Member: NAC; AFA; EAA. Work: "Education," Chapel of State Teachers College Kutztown. Address in 1929, State Teachers College; h. College Hill, Kutztown, PA.

SHARMAN, JOHN.
Painter. Member: Phila. AC.; Boston GA.; CT. AFA. Award: Flagg prize ($100), CT. AFA, 1922. Instructor, MA School of Art. Address in 1929, 80 Somerset St., Belmont, MA.

SHARP, EVERET H(ILL).
Painter and illustrator. Born Foster, KY, Feb. 22, 1907. Pupil of Wayman Adams, George Pearse Ennis, George Luks. Awards: Culver Military Acad. prize, Hoosier Salon, Chicago, IL, 1928; Kiwanis Club Prize, Hoosier Salon, 1929. Specialty, portraits. Address in 1929, 146 McDougal St., New York; h. 523 South Council St. Muncie, IN; summer, Eastport, ME.

SHARP, J(OSEPH) H(ENRY).
Painter, illustrator, and teacher. Born Bridgeport, OH, Sept. 27, 1859. Pupil of Royal Acad. in Munich and under Marr; Julian Acad. in Paris under Laurens and Benjamin Constant; Verlat in Antwerp; Duveneck in Spain. Member: Cincinnati AC; Calif. AC; Salma. C.; Taos Soc. of Artists; Calif.

PM; AFA. Ten years on faculty, Cincinnati Art Acad. Awards: Silver medal, Dept of Ethnology, Pan Am. Exp., Buffalo, 1901; first portrait prize, Cincinnati AC, 1901; gold medal, Pan Cal. Exp., San Diego, 1915 and 1916. Specialty, types of Indians. Work: "Harvest Dance---Pueblo Indians," "Old Dog Crow Indian Chief," and "Strikes His Enemy Pretty," Cincinnati Museum; "Chief Flat Iron," Herron Art Inst., Indianapolis; "The Great Sleep," and nearly 100 portraits of Indians and Indian pictures, Univ. of CA; 11 Indian portraits, Smithsonian Inst., Washington; "1920 Ration Day on the Reservation," "A Young Chief's Mission," Butler Museum, Youngstown, Ohio; "Voice of the Great Spirit," and 15 Indian genre pictures, Smithsonian Inst., Washington; two Indian portraits, Museum of Santa Fe., N. M. Address in 1929, winter, Crow Agency, Montana; summer, Taos, N. M.; permanent, 1481 Corson St., Pasadena, CA.

SHARPE, C. W.
This line engraver of portraits and book illustrations was working in Philadelphia in 1850. There are some indications that he originally came from Boston to that city.

SHARPE, JAMES C.
Illustrator. Born in Vernon, TX, in 1936. Attended Texas Tech Univ. and graduated from ACD where he was taught by John LaGatta. An illustration published in Ford Times in 1966 was his first, and he has since worked for Bantam, Dell, Fawcett, Warner, and Berkley doing cover art. As well as illustrating books for the Franklin Library and numerous Reader's Digest Condensed Books, his work has appeared editorially in major magazines, including many Time and TV Guide covers. He is a member of the S of I, and his illustrations have been selected for their Annual Exhibitions.

SHARPE, JULIA GRAYDON.
Painter and draughtsman. Born Indianapolis, IN. Pupil of ASL of NY; W. M. Chase, Indiana School of Art; J. Ottis Adams; William

845

Forsyth; H. Siddons Mowbray; Saint Gaudens. Member: ASL of NY; Indiana SA. Represented in the Indianapolis (IN) University Club and Herron Art Inst.; MacDowell Club, New York; Richmond (IN) Art Club; memorials in the Second Presbyterian Church and the Caroline Scott Harrison Chapter House, D.A.R., Indianapolis. Specialty, portrait and landscapes, also bookplates and designing. Died in 1937. Address in 1929, 1704 North Pennsylvania St., Indianapolis, IN; summer, Idylwilde, Harbor Springs, MI.

SHARPLES, FELIX THOMAS.
Pastel artists. Son of James Sharples. Born in England C. 1786; he died in North Carolina after 1824. The pastel portrait of Alexander Hamilton owned by the NY Historical Society is done by Felix T. Sharples after the original by his father.

SHARPLES, JAMES.
Portrait painter in pastels. Born in England, in 1752. He came to America in 1796, and traveled through the country painting portraits chiefly in pastels on thick gray paper. A large collection of his work is in Independence Hall, Philadelphia, and in Bristol, England. In 1796 he drew his pastel portrait of Washington, which was frequently copied by his wife and sons. Died Feb. 26, 1811, in NYC.

SHARPLES, JAMES (ELLEN) (MRS.).
Portrait draughtsman in pastel. Born in 1769, Birmingham, England; died in 1849, in Bristol, England. Mrs. Sharples frequently copied her husband's portraits very faithfully in the exact size. After her husband's death she returned to England and settled in Bristol. In 1845 she gave two thousand pounds for the founding of the Bristol Fine Arts Acad. In her will she left, in 1849, 3,465 pounds more. At this institution there is today the "Sharples Collection" of ninety seven pictures by her husband, herself, James Junior and Rolina. Her daughter Rolinda (1794-1838) was born in NY but none of her paintings were made in this

country. (See Century Magazine, Feb., 1894. Also Magazine of American History.)

SHARPLES, JAMES. JR.
Portrait draughtsman in pastel. Born in 1789, England. The younger son of James Sharples. He frequently copied his father's work. He returned to England with his mother and sister after his father's death. Died Aug. 10, 1839, in Bristol, England.

SHATTUCK, AARON DRAPER.
Painter. Born in Francestown, NH, on March 9, 1832. In 1850 he became a pupil of Alexander Ransom in Boston. In 1852 he entered the school of the Acad. of Design in NY and in 1861 was elected an Academician. Among his works are "White Mountains in October," "Cattle," "Peaceful Days," and "Granby Pastures." Inventor of Shattuck Stretcher key for canvasses. Died July 30, 1928, in Granby, CT.

SHAVER, JAMES ROBERT.
Painter and illustrator. Born Evening Shade, Ark., March 27, 1867. Pupil St. Louis School of Fine Arts. Member: Salma. C. Author of "Little Shavers." Specialty, drawings of children. Died in 1949. Address in 1929, 13 West 23rd St., New York, NY.

SHAW, ANNIE CORNELIA.
Landscape painter. Born in West Troy, NY, in 1852. She studied in Chicago, and was elected an Associate Member of the Chicago Acad. of Design in 1873. Her principal works are "On the Calumet," "In the Clearing," "Fall Ploughing," and "The Russet Year." Died in 1887.

SHAW, H(ARRIETT) M(cCREARY) (MRS.).
Painter, writer, lecturer, and teacher. Born Fayetteville, Ark., March 17, 1865. Pupil of Denver School of Fine Arts; AIC; Magda Heurman; Samuel Richards in Munich; Charles P. Adams in Denver, CO. Awards: Silver medal for ivory miniatures, St. Louis Exp., 1904; gold and silver medals for life portraits, Seattle FAS. Author of "Outlines of American Painting."

Specialty, portraits. Died in 1934. Address in 1929, 1528 Fifth Ave., West, Seattle, Washington.

SHAW, HARRY H.
Painter. Exhibited at the Penna. Acad., of the Fine Arts, Philadelphia, 1926. Address in 1926, 1809 Callowhill St., Philadelphia.

SHAW, JOSHUA.
English landscape painter. Born in 1776, in Bellingborough, Lincolnshire, England. He practiced his profession in Phila. for many years. He came to this country in 1817, bringing with him West's picture of "Christ Healing the Sick." He died Sept. 8, 1860. in Burlington, NJ.

SHAW, STEPHEN WILLIAM.
Director and instructor of art at the Boston Athenaeum. He was born Dec. 15, 1817, in Windsor, VT and died Feb. 12, 1900, in San Francisco, CA.

SHAW, SYDNEY DALE.
Painter and craftsman. Born Walkley, England, Aug. 16, 1879. Pupil of ASL of NY; Academie Colarossi and Ecole des Beaux Arts in Paris. Member: Calif. AC; AWCS; Salma. C. Awards: Silver medal, Pan Calif. Exp., San Diego, 1915; hon. mention, Los Angeles, 1916; Hudnut prize. AWCS, NY, 1917; Auction Prize, Salma. C., 1929. Died in 1946. Address in 1929, 295 Bainbridge Ave., New York, NY.

SHEAFER, FRANCES B(URWELL).
(Mrs. Samuel Waxman). Painter, craftsman, and writer. Born in PA. Pupil of PAFA; Phila. School of Design for Women and William Sartain. Member: Plastic C.; Copley S. Award: Special silver medal, St. Louis, Exp., 1904. Address in 1929, Greenbush, Plymouth Co., MA; 21 Foster St., Cambridge, MA.

SHEAFER, FRANK W.
Painter. Born in Pottsville, PA, in 1867. Pupil of Penna. Acad. of the Fine Arts. Exhibited "Harbor Lights" at Penna. Acad. of the Fine Arts, 1915. Address in 1926, 908 Pine St., Philadelphia.

SHEAN, CHARLES M.
Portrait and mural painter. Born in Brooklyn. Studied at Art Students' League of NY and in Paris. Member of Nat. Society of Mural Painters, and Architectural League of NY. Medal for mural painting, St. Louis Exp., 1904. Author of "A Plea for Americanism in the Decoration of Public Bldgs," 1901; "Mural Painting from the American Point of View." He died on Oct. 1925, in Brooklyn.

SHECTMAN, ADELE.
Painter. Born in Cambridge, MA, in 1927. Studied: Vesper George School of Art; Boston Univ.; Boston Museum School. Exhibitions: Childrens' Art Center, Boston, 1967; Psychoanalytic Society and Institute, Boston, 1974; Goethe Institute, 1975. Collections: Leonard Morse Hospital, Natick, Mass.; Boston Univ.

SHEELER, CHARLES R. JR.
Painter. Born in Philadelphia in 1883. Pupil of Penna. Acad. of the Fine Arts under Chase. Address in 1926, 33 West 67th Street, New York, NY. Died in 1965.

SHEERER, MARY G.
Painter, craftsman, and teacher. Born Covington, KY. Pupil of Cincinnati Art Acad.; PAFA; ASL of NY. Member: N. O. AA; La. Art Teachers A; New Orleans Arts and Crafts C.; Amer. Ceramic S; AFA. Instructor, School of Art, Newcomb College, New Orleans. Assistant Director, Newcomb Pottery. Address in 1929, 1404 Audubon St.; Newcomb School of Art, New Orleans, LA; summer, Ogunquit, ME.

SHEETS, MILLARD.
Painter. Born Pomona, CA, June 24, 1907. Pupil of Chouinard School of Art, Los Angeles. Awards: Second prize, Calif. Water Color Show, 1927; third prize, Riverside County Fair, Riverside, Calif., 1928; first prize, Los Angeles County Fair, 1928; first landscape prize, Arizona State Fair, 1928; prize ($1,750), Texas National Competition, San Antonio, 1929. Address in 1929, 2509 West Seventh St., Los Angeles, CA.

SHEETS, NAN.
(Mrs. Fred C. Sheets). Painter and teacher. Born Albany, IL. Pupil of John Carlson; Robert Reid, E. L. Warner, Birger Sandzen, Nellie Knopf; Kathryn E. Cherry; Hugh Breckenridge. Member: Okla. AA; Art Lg. of Okla. City; MacDowell C; North Shore AA; NA Women PS; SSAL; AFA. Awards: Birger Sandzen prize, Broadmoor Art Acad., 1924; purchase prize, Kansas City A. I., 1924; landscape prize, Southern States Art Lg., 1929. Represented in permanent collection of the Kansas City Art Institute. Address in 1929, "The Elms," 2810 North Walker, Oklahoma City, OK.

SHEFFER, GLEN C.
Painter. Born Angola, IN, in 1881. Pupil of AIC and Chicago Acad. of Fine Arts. Member: Palette and Chisel C; Chicago Gal. A. Specialty, painting figure and decorative composition. Died in 1948. Address in 1929, 4 East Ohio Street, Chicago, IL.

SHEFFIELD, ISAAC.
Painter. Born in Guilford, CT, in 1798. He painted portraits and figure pieces in and about New London, CT. Most of his portraits are of sea captains, very red faced, with telescope in hand, standing before a red curtain. He died in 1845.

SHEGOGUE, JAMES HAMILTON.
Painter. Born Feb. 22, 1806, in Charleston, NC. Devoted himself principally to portraiture, but he did produce some landscapes and genre pieces. He first exhibited at the Nat. Acad. of Design, NY, in 1835 and became an Associate Member in 1841, and an Academician in 1843. He painted a number of prominent men and several of his portraits are owned by the city of NY. He died April 7, 1872, in Warrenville, CT.

SHEIRR, OLGA.
Painter, printmaker, and teacher. Study: Brooklyn College, BA 1953, with Rothko, Reinhardt, and Still; NY Inst. of Fine Arts, Grad. Studies, 1954; NYU Intaglio Workshop, 1961-64, with Callapai; Pratt Graphic Ctr., 1964-72, with

Michael Ponce de Leon; Bd. of Ed., NYC, lic. teacher of Fine Arts, 1970. Work: NYU Hospital; Greeville (SC) Co. Mus.; private collections. Exhib.: Noho Gallery, NYC, solo, 1975, 76, 78, 79, 80; Int'l. Art Exch., NYC, solo, 1962, 63; Int'l. Art Exch., Paris & Trouville, France, 1963; 46th Annl. Print Exhib., AAA Gal., NYC, 1965; 4th Int'l. Miniature Print Exhib., AAA Gal., NYC, 1971-74; Silvermine Guild, 1966, 1976; NY Artists Equity Assn., NYC, 1981; many other invitational, juried shows in NYC 1963 to present. Mem.: Noho Gallery, NYC; NY Artists Equity; etc. Bibliog.: Numerous articles and interviews. Address in 1983, 360 First Ave., NYC.

SHELDON, CHARLES MILLS.
Painter. Born at Lawrenceburg, IN, in 1866. Studied in Paris under Constant and Lefebvre, and at the Academie Julien, 1890-91. Traveled through the Southern States, illustrating articles for the Associated Press, 1889; illustrator on Pall Mall Budget, 1892-95; artist and correspondent for Black and White, London, in South Africa during time of Jamieson raid; thorugh Dongola Expedition, Soudan, 1896; artist correspondent of Frank Leslie's and Black and White in Cuba, 1898. Died March 15, 1928 in London.

SHELLHASE, GEORGE.
Painter, who exhibited water colors at the Penna. Acad. of the Fine Arts, Philadelphia, 1925. Address in 1926, 720 Locust St., Philadelphia.

SHEPHARD, CLARENCE.
Painter and architect. Born Cortland, NY, Oct. 27, 1869. Pupil of Keith and Griffin. Member: Kansas City SA; Mid Western A; AIA; Arch. Lg. of NY. Address in 1929, 412-15 Huntzinger Bldg., Kansas City, MO; summer, Fryeburg, ME; Bemis Pt., NY.

SHEPHERD, CHESTER GEORGE.
Painter and illustrator. Born Lathrop, MI, April 28, 1894. Pupil of AIC. Member: Palette and Chisel C.; Alumni Asso. of AIC.;

Association of Arts and Industries. Address in 1929, 1258 Columbia Ave., Chicago, IL.

SHEPHERD, J. CLINTON.
Painter and sculptor. Born Des Moines, IA, Sept. 11, 1888. Pupil of Kansas City School of FA; Art Institute of Chicago; Beaux-Arts Institute of Design, NY. Member: Arch. League. NY; Am. APL; Silvermine AG; AG of Authors League; SI. Address in 1929, R. F. D. 11, Westport, CT.

SHEPHERD, THOMAS S.
Miniature painter, who flourished 1845-46 in NY.

SHEPPARD, WARREN.
Painter, illustrator, and writer. Born Greenwich, NJ, April 10, 1858. Pupil of Hertzberg; de Haas. Work: "The Restless Sea," Albright Art Gallery, Buffalo; "The Trackless Ocean," Toledo Museum; "The Sea," Public Library, Springfield, MA; Author of "Practical Navigation." Died in 1937. Address in 1929, 55 Herkimer St., Brooklyn, NY; summer, Lincoln Park, NJ.

SHERIDAN, FRANK J. JR.
Illustrator. Member: SI. Address in 1929, care of Sheridan, Shawhan and Sheridan, 30 East 34th Street, New York, NY.

SHERIDAN, JOHN E.
Painter and illustrator. Born Tomah, WI. Member: SI 1912. Address in 1929, 35 East 49th Street, New York, NY; h. Port Washington, LI, NY.

SHERINYAN, ELIZABETH.
Painter, craftsman, and teacher. Born Armenia. Pupil of Hale, H. D. Murphy, Major, Greenwood, Cornoyer. Studied in Europe, Asia and Africa; Worcester Museum School and MA. Normal Art School. Member: CT American Federation of Arts; Springfield AL; AFA. Died in 1947. Address in 1929, 11 St. Elmo Road, Worcester, MA.

SHERMAN, ELLA BENNETT (MRS. JOHN).
Painter. Born in New York, NY. Pupil of Douglas Volk, W. M. Chase and Robert Henri. Member of Washington Water Color Club;

Washington Society of Artists. Address in 1926, 500 Powers Bldg., Rochester, NY.

SHERMAN, GAIL.
See Mrs. H. W. Corbett.

SHERMAN, STOWELL B(RADFORD).
Painter and etcher. Born Providence, Jan. 22, 1886. Pupil of RI School of Design. Member: Providence AC; Providence WCC. Address in 1929, 147 Lorimer Ave., Providence, RI; summer, Rockport, MA.

SHERMAN & SMITH.,
(George Sherman & John Calvin Smith). Engravers. This firm was designing and engraving plates for the NY New Mirror in 1841. In 1838-39 the firm of Stiles, Sherman & Smith was engraving in the same city. In both of these cases the Smith of the firm was probably Wm. D. Smith, according to Fielding.

SHERRATT, THOMAS.
About 1870 a portrait engraver of this name was working for Detroit publishers.

SHERWOOD, MARY CLARE.
Painter and teacher. Born Lyons, May 18, 1868. Pupil of ASL of NY under Weir, Chase and Cox; Conrad Fehr and Curt Hermanns in Berlin; F. Edwin Scott in Paris. Member: NA Women PS; Miss. A. Lg. SSAL; AFA. Died in 1943. Address in 1929, All Saints College, Vicksburg, MI; summer, Lyons, NY.

SHERWOOD, ROSINA EMMET.
(Mrs. Arthur M. Sherwood). Painter. Born NY, Dec. 13, 1854. Pupil of Chase in NY; Julian Acad. in Paris. Member: SAA 1886; ANA 1906; NYWCC; AWCS. Awards: Silver medal for painting, Paris Exp., 1889; medal, Columbian Exp., Chicago, 1893; bronze medals for water color and for drawing, Pan. Am. Exp., Buffalo, 1901; silver medal, St. Louis Exp., 1904. Died Jan. 19, 1948. Address in 1929, Stockbridge, MA.

SHERWOOD, RUTH.
Sculptor and teacher. Born Chicago. Pupil of Albin Polasek; AIC. Member: Alumni, AIC. Awards:

849

Bryan Lathrop foreign scholarship, 1921; John Quincy Adams prize, AIC, 1921; hon. men., AIC, 1922; Chicago Woman's Aid prize, AIC; Mrs. E. Mansfield Jones prize, Chicago Gal., 1928; Mrs. John C. Shaffer prize, AIC, 1929. Work: Memorial tablet, River Forest Women's Club; memorial tablet to James V. Clake, Evanston, IL; Safety trophy, Portland Cement Asso.; Lake Shore Bank medal for architecture. Died in 1953. Address in 1929, 3146 Lake Park Ave., Chicago, IL; summer, Chautauqua, NY.

SHERWOOD, WILLIAM (ANDERSON).
Painter and etcher. Born Baltimore, MD, Feb. 13, 1875. Member: Societe Royale des Beaux Arts Belge; Societe Royale des Aqua Fortists de Belgique; Chicago SE; Calif. PM.; AFA; Chevalier de l'Ordre de la Couronne, (Belgique). Work; Etchings owned by Queen of Belgium; etchings in Royal Library at Brussels, Musee Plantin-Moretus, Antwerp, and Library of Congress at Washington; Cleveland Public Library; Detroit Public Library; Worcester Free Library; Chicago Art Inst.; California State Library; City Library Sacramento. Died in 1951. Address in 1929, 41 Avenue Quinten Matsys, Anterp, Belgium.

SHIELDS, CHARLES.
Illustrator. Born in Kansas City, KS, in 1944. Received his BFA from the Univ. of Southern Calif., his MFA from ADC and later taught painting at Colorado Mountain College. His first illustration was done for the Saturday Review of the Arts in 1972 and he has since illustrated for Rolling Stone, Sesame Street, Genesis, City of San Francisco, Human Behavior, and others. He has received awards from the S of I.

SHIELDS & HAMMOND.
Engravers. This first name is signed to some good landscape plates published in New Orleans, in 1845. Hammond is noticed elsewhere.

SHIFF, E. MADELINE.
Painter. Born in Denver, CO. Studied: Adelphi College; Art Students League. Award: Charlotte

R. Smith memorial award, Baltimore, Maryland, 1923. Collection: Whitney Museum of American Art. See additional biographical information under Wiltz, E. Madeline Shiff.

SHILLING, ALEXANDER.
Landscape painter and etcher. Born Chicago, IL in 1859. Pupil of G. S. Collis. Member: AWCS; NY Etching C; Salma C; Century A. Awards: Gold medal, Phila. AC, 1901; silver medal, St. Louis Expo., 1904; Shaw etchings prize, Salma. C., 1913. Represented by painting in Metropolitan Museum of Art. Died in 1937. Address in 1929, 939 Eighth Ave., New York, NY.

SHINDLER, A. ZENO.
Portrait draughtsman in crayons. Born c. 1813 in Germany. He was working in Philadelphia about 1855-60.

SHINN, EVERETT.
Mural painter and illustrator. Born Nov. 6, 1873 (1876?) in Woodstown, NJ. Studied art at Penna. Academy of Fine Arts, Philadelphia. Moved to NYC in 1900; worked for The Herald and The World. City life illustrations appeared in Harper's, McClure's, Scribner's. Painted the mural decorations for The Stuyvesant Theater, New York, NY. Known as one of The Eight or Ashcan Sch. Represented in Met. Mus. of Art; Whitney; Phillips Mem. Gal., Wash., DC. Died in 1953. Address in 1926, 19 East St., New York City.

SHINN, FLORENCE SCOVEL.
Illustrator. Born in Camden, NJ, in 1869. Studied at PAFA. She became well known for her book illustrations in line and watercolor such as those done for the series Mrs. Wiggs of the Cabbage Patch and Lovely Mary by Hegan Rice in 1903. She died in her home in NYC in 1940.

SHIPMAN, CHARLES.
Engraver. In the New York Mercury in 1768 is the following; "Charles Shipman, Ivory and Hard Wood Turner,. . . engraves Copper Plate, Seals. etc."

SHIPPEN, ZOE.
Painter. Born Boston, Nov. 12, 1902. Pupil of Leslie P. Thompson, Phillip Hale, William Hazelton, John P. Wicker. Member: North Shore AA; Gloucester SA; Copley S; Boston S. Indp. A. Specialty, portraits. Address in 1929, 6 Arlington St., Annisquam, MA; h. 39 Pilgrim Road, Boston, MA.

SHIRK, JEANNETTE C(AMPBELL).
Painter and illustrator. Born Middletown, PA, April 16, 1898. Pupil of Eugene F. Savage, Charles J. Taylor, George Sotter. Member: Pittsburgh AA; Buffalo SA. Award: Third Anonymous Graph. Art prize, Pittsburgh AA, 1927. Address in 1929, Glenshaw, PA.

SHIRLAW, WALTER.
Painter and engraver. Born in Paisley, Scotland on Aug. 6, 1838. He was brought to the United States when two years old. He studied art at the National Academy and worked at bank note engraving for some time, but had a decided talent for painting. His "Sheep Shearing in the Bavarian Highland," received honorable mention at the Paris Exhibition of 1878, and his "Susannah and the Elder" (a study) is owned by the Boston Museum of Fine Arts. He was elected a member of the Nat. Acad. of Design in 1888. He died Dec. 26, 1909, in Madrid, Spain.

SHISLER, CLARE SHEPARD.
Miniature painter. Pupil of Carlotta Vanatta and Lillian Pettingill. Member: Calif. S. Min. P.; PA. Soc. Min. P.; West Coast Arts, Inc. Awards: Medal, Yukon Pacific Exp., 1909; silver medal, P.-P. Exp., San Francisco, 1915; prize Seattle FAS, 1913; prize, West Coast Arts, Inc., 1923; fourth Balch prize, Calif. S. Min. P., 1929.

SHIVA, R(AMON).
Painter. Born Spain, Oct. 17, 1893. Member: Cor Ardens; AIC Alumni; Chicago SA; Palette and Chisel C. Awards: Eisendrath prize, AIC, 1921; hon. mention, AIC, 1923. Address in 1929, 1311 North Dearborn St., Chicago, IL.

SHOEMAKER, EDNA COOKE.
(Mrs. Orlando Shoemaker). Illustrator. Born Philadelphia, June 19, 1891. Pupil of Hugh Breckenridge and Henry McCarter. Member: Phila. Alliance; Fellowship PAFA; Plastic C. Illustrated stories by Mrs. J. H. Ewing; Mrs. Milsworth Duffield; "East o' the Sun and West o' the Moon," "Mother Goose and other Nursery Rhymes," "Rip Van Winkle," "Hans Brinker or the Silver Skates," "Heidi," "The Legend of Sleepy Hollow," and stories for many magazines. Address in 1929, 4049 Locust St., Phila., PA.

SHOKLER, HARRY.
Painter. Born Cincinnati, Ohio, April 27, 1896. Pupil of Herman Wessel, Daniel Garber, Howard Giles. Address in 1929, 99½ W. 3rd Street, New York, NY.

SHONNARD, EUGENIE F(REDERICA).
Sculptor, painter, and teacher. Born Yonkers, NY, April 29, 1886. Pupil of Bourdelle and Rodin. Member: Alliance; NSS (assoc); NA Women PS. Exh. many times in Paris to 1923; moved to Santa Fe, NM, in 1928. In collections of MMA; Brookgreen Gardens, SC; NY Zoological Soc.; and private collections. Address in 1929, care of Frank W. Purdy, 37 East 57th St., New York, NY; rue Notre Dames des Champs, Paris, France.

SHOPE, HENRY B.
Etcher. Born in Baltimore in 1862. Member of Brooklyn Society of Etchers. Represented by etchings in NY Public Library. Address in 1926, 28 East 21st St., New York.

SHORE, HENRIETTA M.
Painter and teacher. Born Toronto, Canada. Pupil of Henri, Chase, Hayes Miller in NY; studied in London. Member: S. Indp. A.; NA Women PS. Awards: Silver medal, Pan Cal. Exp., San Diego, 1915; silver medal, Panama Cal. Exp., San Diego, 1916. Work: "Negro Woman and Children," National Gallery of Canada, Ottawa. Address in 1929, 152 West 57th St., New York, NY; summer, 1901 Vista St., Hollywood, CA.

851

SHORE, ROBERT.
Illustrator. Born in NYC in 1924.
Attended Cranbrook Academy in
Michigan and PI. In 1952 he was
awarded a Fulbright Fellowship in
painting. His clients have
included Esquire, Collier's,
Seventeen, Woman's Day, CBS, NBC,
and The New York Times as well as
many book publishers and
advertisers. The Detroit Institute
of Fine Arts, Smithsonian
Institution and National Gallery in
Wash., DC have all exhibited his
artwork. In 1967 he was awarded a
Gold Medal from the S of I for book
illustration.

SHOREY, GEORGE H.
Painter, illustrator, and teacher.
Born Hoosick Falls, NY, Sept. 9,
1870. Pupil of Walter Shirlaw.
Director, Artist-Artisan Institute,
1898-1903. Work: Illustrations:
"Cathedral of St. John the Divine";
"New York Parks"; "Old Kingston,"
etc.; "The Ascension," Soldiers
bronze memorial tablet, Trinity
Episcopal Church, Grantwood, NJ.
Director, Art Department Browning
School, New York, NY. Died in
1944. Address in 1929, 52 East
62nd St., New York, NY; h.
Grantwood, NJ; summer, Burnt Hills,
NY.

SHORTER, EDWARD S(WIFT).
Painter, etcher, and writer. Born
Columbus, GA, July 2, 1900. Pupil
of Corcoran School of Art;
Breckenridge School; W. L. Stevens
at Rockport, MA; M. F. Browne;
Emile Renard, Paris. Member:
North Shore AA; Wash. SA; Wash.
SWCP; SSAL; S. Indp. A; Wash. AC;
Atlanta AA: Am. APL; Chic. AL;
Macon AAA; AFA. Award: Blue
ribbon for drawing, Southern Art
Exhib., Nashville, TN, 1926; hon.
mention, Georgia Artists Exh.,
1928. Author of Bi-Weekly column
on the arts in "Macon News,"
entitled "Palette Scrapings";
Contributor to Macon Telegraph and
magazines. Address in 1929, 130
Georgia Ave., Macon, GA.

SHOTWELL, FREDERIC VALPEY.
Painter, illustrator, etcher,
lecturer, and teacher. Born
Detroit, Sept. 22, 1907. Pupil of
Berninghaus, Carpenter, Pennell,

Dodge, Bridgman, Sepeschy. Member
Detroit SE; Scarab S. Work
Assisted execution of murals fo
the Library of Fordson School
Fordson, MI; General Motors Bldg.
Detroit. Address in 1929, 23
Holybrook, Detroit, MI; summer, Ba
View, MI.

SHOTWELL, H. C.
In 1853 this landscape engraver wa
working for publishers i
Cinncinati, OH.

SHOTWELL, HELEN HARVEY.
Painter and photographer. Born i
NYC in 1908. Studied sculptur
with Bruno Zimm; oils with Edwi
Scott, a student of Whistler
Paris; watercolor with Poveda
Rome; pictorial photography wit
Flora Pitt-Conrey; still life wit
Henry Lee McFee and Judson Smith
both noted Woodstock artists
portrait with Alexander Brook a
ASL. Also worked with her mother
painter Margaret Harvey Shotwell
in their Woodstock and NYC studios
Traveled widely in Europe, Orient
and Latin America, using he
camera. In collections o
Corcoran; ASL; IBM; Arthur M
Watson; others. Exhibited at Argen
Gal., NYC; High Mus. SC; Fitchbur
(MA) Art Mus.; Carnegie; Corcoran
PAFA; Apollo Gal., Poughkeepsie
NY; Int'l. salons in US and abroad
others. Known for work with th
aging at Goddard Riverside Comm
Ctr.; other interests include musi
and writing. Member, Woodstock A
(life); Nat'l. Women Artists
Int'l. Soc. of Arts and Letter
(life); Woodstock Guild o
Craftsmen; others. Represented b
the Shuster Gallery, NYC.

SHOTWELL, MARGARET HARVEY
Painter. Born in Wyoming, Ontario
CN, in 1873. Studied at Universit
of Toronto; Sorbonne, Paris
Universities of Geneva and Rome
with Edwin Scott, a pupil o
Whistler, and with Leon Dabo, i
France. Travelled widely with he
husband, James T. Shotwell, author
historian of international stature
Exhibited in U.S. and abroa
including Paris Salon d'Automne
1911, 13; Shuster and Argen
Galleries, Cosmopolitan Club

852

Columbia Univ. all in NYC; Woodstock, NY; Apollo Gallery, Poughkeepsie, NY. One of the earliest settlers in the Woodstock art colony founded in 1902, she painted and taught there and in NYC. Awards include honorable mention in the Paris Salon d'Automne, 1911, at which Mary Cassatt also had worked. Life member of the Woodstock Artists Assn. Died in 1965.

SHOVER, EDNA M(ANN).
Illustrator, writer, and teacher. Born Indianapolis, IN. Pupil of Faber, Deigendesch, Thomas Scott, Philip Muhr; J. F. Copeland. Member: Alumni Asso. PA. Museum and School of Indp. A.; IN. AC; AFA. Author of "Art in Costume Design," published by Milton Bradley Co. Principal, Art School of the Herron Art Inst. Address in 1929, Art School of the Herron Art Inst.; h. 1468 North New Jersey St., Indianapolis, IN.

SHOWE, LOU ELLEN (MRS.).
See Chattin, Lou Ellen.

SHRADER, E(DWIN) ROSCOE.
Painter, illustrator, lecturer, and teacher. Born Quincy, IL, Dec. 14, 1879. Pupil of AIC and Howard Pyle. Member: Calif., AC.; Wilmington Soc. FA. Died in 1960. Address in 1929, Otis Art Inst., 2401 Wilshire Blvd., Los Angeles, Calif.; h. 1927 Highland Ave., Hollywood, CA.

SHRADY, HENRY MERWIN.
Sculptor. Born in New York City in 1871. Elected Associate Member of the National Academy of Design in 1909. Among his works are "Grant Memorial," "Washington," and "General Lee," at Charlottesville, VA. Died April 12, 1922, in NYC.

SHRAMM, PAUL H.
Sculptor and illustrator. Born in Heidenheim, Germany, in 1867. Pupil of Claudinso, Schrandolph and Jacob Grunenwald in Stuttgart; of MacNeil at Pratt Inst., Brooklyn. Member of NY Society of Cartoonists. Address in 1926, 671 Auburn Ave., Buffalo, NY

SHUFF, LILY.
(Lillian Shir). Painter and engraver. Born in NYC. Studied: Hunter College; Art Students' League; Brooklyn Academy of Fine Arts; Farnsworth School of Art; and with Jon Corbino. Awards: Brooklyn Society of Art, 1953, 1957; NJ Society of Painters and Sculptors, 1956; Caravan Gallery, 1958; Conn. Academy of Fine Arts, 1956. Collections: Pakistan Consulate, NY; Lane College, NY; James Fennimore Cooper High School; Georgia Museum of Fine Arts; Yale Univ.; Mueller Collection, Paris, France. Address in 1980, 155 W. 68th St., NY, NY.

SHULGOLD, WILLIAM (ROBERT).
Painter, etcher, and teacher. Born Russia. Pupil of Sparks, Sotter, Levy, Hawthorne. Member: Pittsburgh AA; Pittsburgh Palette C.; Tiffany Foundation. Work: "Sketching" and "Self Portrait," gift of Hundred Friends of Art to Pittsburgh Public Schools. Address in 1929, 19 West 8th St., NYC.

SHULL, DELLA.
Portrait painter, who exhibited portrait of Mrs. Robert Henri at Annual Exhibition, 1923, of Penna. Acad. of Fine Arts. Address in 1926, 39 West 67th St., New York.

SHULL, J(AMES) MARION.
Painter, illustrator, and writer. Born Clark County, Ohio, Jan. 23, 1872. Pupil of ASL. of NY. Member: Wash. AC. Work: 1,350 color drawings, US Dept. of Agriculture; illustrations for Country Life and Ladies Home Journal. Died in 1950. Address in 1929, Agricultural Dept., 14th and B. Sts., Washington DC; h. 207 Raymond St., Chevy Chase, MD.

SHULZ, ADA WALTER.
(Mrs. Adolph R). Painter. Born in Terre Haute, IN on Oct. 21, 1870. Pupil of Art Inst. of Chicago; Vitti Academy in Paris. Member of Chicago Society of Artists and Wisconsin Painters and Sculptors. A founder of Brown Colony of Artists, IN. Work: "Motherhood," Milwaukee Art Inst.; "Mother and Child," Art Inst. of Chicago. Specialty, children. Address in

1926, Nashville, Brown Country, IN.
Died May 4, 1928 near Nashville,
IN.

SHULZ, ADOLPH R(OBERT).
Landscape painter, and teacher.
Born Delavan, WI, June 12, 1869.
Pupil of Art Inst. of Chicago; Art
Students' League of NY; Julian
Academy in Paris under Lefebvre,
Constant and Laurens. Member:
Indiana Art Club; Chicago Society
of Artists. Awards: Young
Fortnightly prize, Art Inst. of
Chicago, 1900; Grower prize, Art
Inst. of Chicago, 1908; Municipal
Art League purchase, Art Inst. of
Chicago, 1904; Milwaukee Art
Institute medal, 1918. Work:
"Frost and Fog," Art Inst. of
Chicago. Address in 1929,
Nashville, Brown Co., IN.

SHUMACKER, ELIZABETH WIGHT.
Painter and instructor. Born in
Chattanooga, TN, on Sept. 25, 1912.
Studied: University of Chattanooga
with Frank Baisden; also with
Stuart Purser, Wiemer Purcell,
George Cress, and Joe Robertson;
studied graphics with Carolyn
Hilton; also studied at the Hunter
Gallery of Art with Gray Phillips,
James Watson, and Alan Kuzmickie.
Collections: High Museum, Atlanta;
Brooks Memorial Gallery, Memphis;
First National Bank of Little Rock;
NY Times; South Central Bell,
Birmingham. Exhibitions at High
Museum; Butler Institute,
Youngstown, OH; Brooks Memorial
Gallery; Smithsonian Institute,
Washington, DC; Heal's Art Gallery,
London, England. Media: Polymer
and collage. Address in 1980,
1400 Riverview Rd., Chattanooga,
TN.

SHUMWAY, HENRY COLTON.
Miniature painter. Born July 4,
1807, in Middletown, CT. He came
to NY in 1827 and entered as a
student in the National Academy of
Design. He began painting
professionally in 1829. Among the
prominent men who sat to him were
Henry Clay, Daniel Webster, and
Prince Napoleon (afterwards
Napoleon, III). Died May 6, 1889,
in NYC.

SHURTLEFF, ELIZABETH.
Painter. Born Concord, NH, Sept.
3, 1890. Pupil of Phillip Hale and
Frank Benson. Work: Series of
mural decorations showing seven
countries, Raymond Whitcomb Co.
Boston. Address in 1929, 86 Mt.
Vernon St., Boston, MA.

SHURTLEFF, ROSWELL MORSE.
Painter. Born June 14, 1838, at
Rindge, NH, died in 1915. Graduate
of Dartmouth Coll., 1857. He took
charge of architect's office
Manchester, NH, in 1857; worked at
lithography, in Boston, drawing on
wood and attending evening classes
Lowell Inst., in 1859; worked as
illustrator and attended Acad. of
Design, NY. He was illustrator for
magazines and books in NY for
several years. He began to paint
in oils, 1870, at first animal
pictures, later landscapes, in both
oils and water colors. Elected
Assoc. Member of the Nat. Acad. of
Design in 1881; Nat. Acad., 1890
was also a member of the AWCS
Among his works are "The Wolf at
the Door," "A Race for Life" and
"Views among the Adirondacks."
Died Jan. 6, 1915, in NYC.

SHUSTER, WILLIAM HOWARD.
Painter, etcher, and craftsman
Born Philadelphia, PA, Nov. 26
1893. Pupil of J. William Server
John Sloan. Member: S. Indp. A.
Los Cinco Pintores; Santa Fe Art
Club. Work: "The Rain Prayer,"
Newark Museum; "Carlsbad Cavern,"
Brooklyn Museum. Died in 1969
Address in 1929, Camino del Monte
Sol, Santa Fe, NM.

SHUTTLEWORTH, CLAIRE.
Painter and teacher. Born Buffalo
Pupil of Buffalo ASL; DuMond an
Bridgman; Merson, Collin and Lero
in Paris. Member: Buffalo SA; N
Women PS.; Rockport AA.; Buffal
GAA; AFA. Award: Fellowshi
prize, Buffalo SA, 1910 and 1929
special award of honor, Springvill
(Utah) High School Art Assn., 1927
Work: "The Horse Shoe Falls fro
Table Rock," Arnot Art Gallery
Elmira, NY; "Flags A Flying,
Buffalo Historical Society
Address in 1929, 508 Franklin St.
Buffalo, NY; summer

"Minglestreams," Chippawa, Ontario, Canada.

SIBBEL, JOSEPH.
Sculptor. Born in Germany. Sculpted ecclesiastical statuary. Died July 10, 1907, in NYC.

SIBONI, EMMA DENEDIKTA.
Miniature painter. Born in 1877. Exhibited at the Penna. Acad. of Fine Arts, Philadelphia, 1925. Address in 1926, 1115 Maples St., South Pasadena, CA.

SICKLES, NOEL.
Illustrator. Born in 1911. His early career as a newspaper artist and cartoonist was the basis for his predisposition for clean, expressive line drawing. Having created his adventure strip, "Scorchy Smith," he produced editorial and advertising illustrations. After instructional assignments from the Army and Navy Departments he produced a series of drawings of World War II for Life. American history illustration, his specialty, appeared in The Saturday Evening Post, This Week, Life, and the Reader's Digest.

SIEBER, EDWARD E.
Painter. Born in Brooklyn, NY, in 1862. Pupil of National Academy of Design; also studied in Paris. Specialty, landscape and cattle. Address in 1926, 9 West 14th St., New York.

SIEBERN, E.
Sculptor, who exhibited at the Annual Exhibition, 1923, Penna. Acad. of Fine Arts, Philadelphia. Address in 1926, 99 Sixth Ave., New York. Died June 14, 1942, in NYC.

SIEBERT, EDWARD S(ELMAR).
Painter, etcher, and teacher. Born Washington, D.C., July 1, 1856. Pupil of Baur in Weimar, Carl Hoff in Karlsruhe, Willian von Diez in Munich. Award: Hon. mention and one prize, Rochester, NY. Work: "Flute Player," Corcoran Gallery of Art, Washington, D.C. Address in 1929, 37 East Ave, Rochester, NY.

SIEGEL, DINK.
Illustrator. Born in Birmingham, AL, in 1915. Attended the NAD,

ASL, and American Academy of Art. His editorial work was first seen in Good Housekeeping, and this led to many years of assignments from other magazines and the subsequent appearance of his illustrations in Playboy and Field and Stream. Arrow Shirts, Ford Motor Company, and film studios have used his advertising art. He is a life member of the S of I and presently lives in NY.

SIEGLER, MAURICE.
Painter. Born in 1896. Exhibited water colors at the Penna. Acad. of Fine Arts, Philadelphia, 1925. Address in 1926, Care of Penna. Acad. of Fine Arts, Philadelphia.

SIEVERS, F(REDERICK) WILLIAM.
Sculptor. Born Fort Wayne, IN, Oct. 26, 1872. Studied in Richmond, VA; Royal Acad. of Fine Arts in Rome under Ferrari; and Julian Acad. in Paris. Work: Equestrian statue of Gen. Lee and group at Gettysburg, PA; equestrian statue of Stonewall Jackson, Richmond, VA; equestrian statue, Gen. Lloyd Tighman, Vicksburg, MI; Confederate Monuments at Abingdon and Leesburg, VA; Matthew Fontaine Maury monument, Richmond, VA. Address in 1929, Forest Hill, Richmond, VA.

SILEIKA, JONAS.
Painter and teacher. Born Lithuania, July 2, 1883. Studied at AIC and Royal Acad., Munich. Member: Amer. Fed. of Arts (Active); Art Society of Lithuania. Award: Joseph N. Eisendrath prize, AIC 1920. Work: Portrait of "Prf. J. Naujalis," "Winter in Lithuania" and "An Old Man and His Cottage," Gallery of (Tchur Lionis) Cuir Lionis, Kaunas, Lithuania. Address in 1929, Art Inst., Meno Mokykla, Lithuania; h. Jedagoniu K., P. ag. Lekeciai, Lithuania.

SILSBEE, MARTHA.
Painter. Born in Salem, MA, in 1858. Member: Boston Water Color Club. Address in 1926, 82 Chestnut Street, Boston, MA.

SILSBY, CLIFFORD.
Painter, and etcher. Born New Haven, CT, Aug. 15, 1896. Pupil of

855

Duchenaud, Royer, Laurens, Pages. Address in 1929, 1411 West Calumet Ave., Los Angeles, CA.

SILVA, FRANCIS AUGUSTUS.
Painter. Born in 1835. He worked as a sign painter until the opening of the Civil War when he entered the National Army, at the close of the war he settled in NY and devoted himself to painting marine subjects. Among his works are "Gray Day at Cape Ann," "Sunrise in Boston Harbor," and "Near Atlantic City." Member of the Hudson River School and Watercolor Society. His most important and highly valued works were his last few marine views. He died in 1886.

SILVA, WILLIAM PASEY.
Painter. Born in 1859 in, GA. Pupil of Julian Acad., in Paris under Laurens and Royer; Chauncey Ryder at Etaples, FR. Member: S. Wash. A.; Miss. AA.; Paris AAA; Southern SAL; New Orleans AA; AFA. Awards: Silver medal, Appalachian Exp., Knoxville, 1910; silver medal, Pan Cal. Expo., San Diego, 1915; gold medal, MI. Art Assoc., 1916; hon. men., Salon Artists Francais, Paris, 1922; Southern SAL prize, 1925; grand prize, Ga Ala. Exh., Nashville, 1926; popular prize, SSAL 1927; special men. of hon., UT, 1927; Davis Nat'l prize, San Antonio, TX, 1928; popular prize, State wide exhib., Santa Cruz, 1929; hon. men., Davis Nat'l Comp., San Antonio, 1929; purchase prize, Springville, UT, High Sch. AA. 1929. Work: "Pines of Picardy" Carnegie Public Lib., Chatanooga, TN; "Pine and Its Shadow," "Fog Isle of Palms," Bigges Gal., SC; "Fog Coming In Ogunquit," and 10 sketches around Forth Worth, TX, Art Assoc.;"Poplars at Twilight," 19th Century C., TN; "Foggy Day, Ogunquit," and "The Harvest Moon," Delgado Mus., LA; "A Str. in Carmel," Public Lib., CA; "Afternoon, Venice," Huntington Club, GA; "Into the Mist," Janesville (WI) Art League; "Springtime in the South," MI Art Gal., MI; "The Swelling Tide," Milwaukee Art Inst.; "Breezy Day, Gloucester," Centennial C., TN; "GA Pines," "The Magic Pool," "Mists of

Morning," TN Art Asso.; "Wind Swept Cypress," KS State Teachers Col., KS; "The Nation's Landmark," Union High School, CA; "Morning, Wash. DC," Union High Sch., Calinas, CA; "Dusk, Point Lobos," "Wisteria and Azaleas," purchased by French Govn't for State Collecton, 1926 "Springtime in the Low Country," Carey Art C., MI; "The Palmetto Shore," "Sea Island Marshes," "The Little Bridge, Magnolia," Columbia Col., Art Dept., SC; "Twilight Glow in the Garden of Dreams," High Sch Art Assoc., Springville, UT. Died 1948. Address 1929, Carmel by the Sea, CA.

SILVER, ROSE.
Painter and illustrator. Born New York City, May 8, 1902. Pupil o the Univ. of Washinton; Rudol Schaeffer. Member: Art Club Univ. of Wash. Award: Silver cup from "Judge" for cover, 1922 Address in 1929, 2014 East Cherry St., Seattle, Wash.

SILVERBERG, E. MYER.
Portrait painter. Born in Russia in 1876. Studied in Royal Academy of Fine Arts, Munich. Member of Pittsburgh Artists Association Work in High Schools and other public institutions, Pittsburgh Address in 1926, 58 West 57th Street, New York, NY.

SILVERMAN, BURTON PHILIP.
Illustrator. Born in Brooklyn, NY in 1928. Trained at Columbia Univ and intermittently attended th ASL. Among his teachers were Reginald Marsh and Julian Levi. I 1955 he began working for The New York Post and since that time hi illustrations have appeared in most national and internationa publications. A Gold Medal from the ADC One-Show was awarded to hi in 1973; he also won six prize from the NAD Annual Exhibition His work has been shown in man galleries as well as bein presented in 14 One-Man Shows. Th Phila. Museum, the Brooklyn Museum and the New Britain Museum o American Art all own his artwork.

SILVERMAN, MEL. (MELVIN FRANK)
Painter. Born 1931, in Denver, CO Earned BFA from Art Inst. o

Chicago, on Nat. Scholastic Scholarship. Studied at ASL. Awarded Lathrop Traveling Award, Feb. (1955) and Israeli Am. Culture Found., Fellowship Silvermine Guild; Boston MFA; Balter Inst. (Youngstown); U. Of Maine and others. Exhibited at Brooklyn; Buchnell U. (Penna.); Art Inst. of Chicago; Wash., D.C. Public Library; Ohio Univ.; others. In collections of Butler; U. of Maine; Phila. Mus. of Art.; Allentown Art Mus.; US Information Agency (Wash., D.C.) and others, incl. Am. Embassies. Died in 1966.

SIMEON, NICHOLAS.
Painter. Born in Switzerland in 1867. Address in 1926, 109 West 54th Street, New York City.

SIMES, MARY JANE.
Minaiture painter. Born April 1, 1807, in Baltimore, MD. He flourished 1826-31. Died May 16, 1872.

SIMKHOVITCH, SIMKHA.
Painter. Born Petrograd, Russia, May 21, 1893. Pupil of Royal Academy of Russia, Petrograd. Member: Brooklyn SA; PS. Award: First prize given by First Soviet Government in 1918 for "Russian Revolution." Works: "Victory in Death," Museum of the Winter Palace, Petrograd; "Sawing Wood" and "Under the Apple Tree," Museum of Art, Petrograd; "Head of a Woman," Krakow Musuem, Poland. Address in 1929, care of Sterner Gallery, 9 East 57th St., New York, NY.

SIMKINS, MARTHA.
Painter. Born Texas. Pupil of ASL of NY and Chase. Member: NA Women PS; PBC. Address in 1929, 939 Eighth Ave., New York, NY; summer, Woodstock, Ulster Co., NY.

SIMMANG, CHARLES JR.
Sculptor, engraver, and craftsman. Born Serbin, TX, Feb. 7, 1874. Pupil of Charles Stubenrauch. Member: AFA; San Antonio AL. Specialty, steel relief engraver. Address in 1929, 1022 E. Elmira St.; h. 218 East Josephine St., San Antonio, TX.

SIMMONS, EDWARD E.
Mural painter, and craftsman. Born Concord, MA, Oct. 27, 1852. Pupil of Boulanger and Lefebvre in Paris. Member: Tn Am. P.; Nat. Inst. AL. Awards: Hon. mention, Paris Salon, 1882; bronze medal, Paris Exp., 1889; gold medal, Pan Am Exp., Buffalo, 1901; collaborative prize, NY. Arch. Lg. 1912. Work: "The Battle of Concord" and "Restoration of Battle Flags," MA State House, Boston; "The Muses," nine panels, Library of Congress, Washington; "Justice," "The Fates" and "Liberty Equality, Fraternity," Criminal Court, NY; four pendentives, dome, Minnesota State Capitol Pierre, SD; and in Court House, Mercer, PA; Astor Gallery, Astoira, NY; Court House, Des Moines, IA; Appellate Court, NY; Memorial Hall, Harvard College. Address in 1929, Gramercy Park, New York, NY.

SIMMONS, FRANKLIN.
Sculptor, of Providence, RI. Born Jan. 11, 1842, in Lisbon, ME. He executed a bust of President Lincoln, which has been put in bronze; also statues of Roger Williams and William King, for the state of Maine. He died Dec. 6, 1913, in Rome.

SIMMONS, JOSEPH.
Engraver. The Pennsylvania Gazette for Jan. 3, 1765, contains the following advertisement: "Joseph Simmons, Engraver, from London, Cuts Coats of Arms and Cyphers in Stone, Silver or Steel, for Watches. He is to be spoke with at Mr. Robert Porter's Saddler, in Market street, Opposite the Prison. N. B. As there is no other Person of the same business on the Continent, he hopes to meet with Encouragement." Simmons was evidently a seal cutter; and special interest lies in his claim to be the only one then in business in the country.

SIMMONS, WILL.
Painter, writer, etcher, and sculptor. Born Elche, Spain, June 4, 1884. Pupil of Julian Academy, Lefebvre and Alexander Harrison in Paris; Edward Simmons in America. Member: Chicago SE; Brooklyn SE; Calif. PM. Represented in NY

Public Library; Smithsonian Inst., Washington, D.C. Specialty, Natural History. Died in 1949. Address in 1929, New Milford, 3, CT.

SIMON, EUGENE J.
Painter. Born in Hungary, May 8, 1889. Pupil of Kenneth Hayes Miller. Member: S. Indp. A; Woodstock AA.; Bronx AG. Address in 1929, 665 East 242nd St., New York, NY; summer, Woodstock, NY.

SIMON, HOWARD.
Painter and illustrator. Born New York, July 22, 1902. Member: Calif. SE. Work: "Mother Earth," Museum of the Legion of Honor, San Francisco, CA; wood engraving, "Rabelais" and "Mme. du Maupin," Baltimore Mus. of Art, Baltimore, MD. Illustrated "History of California Pathfinders" (Powell Pub. Co.). Died in 1979. Address in 1929, 246 Sullivan St., New York, NY.

SIMOND, L.
Designer of book plates. The engraving "Christ Blessing Children," done for an orphan asylum after his design, was engraved by Leney.

SIMONET, SEBASTIAN.
Painter and illustrator. Born Stillwater, MN, Oct. 19, 1898. Pupil of Univ. of MN, School of Art; NAD; ASL of NY. Award: First prize, MN State Fair, 1921; First prize for painting, NY State Fair, 1922. Died in 1948. Address in 1929, 450 Geary St., San Francisco, CA; h. 612 South 4th Street, Stillwater, MN.

SIMONNE, T.
Engraver. In 1814-16 Simone was engraving a very few, but good plates for the NY publishers, David Longworth and T. C. Fay.

SIMONS, AMORY C(OFFIN).
Sculptor. Born Charleston, SC. April 5, 1869. Pupil of PAFA; Dampt and Puech in Paris. Member: AFA; Paris AAA; NSS. Awards: Hon. mention, Paris Exp., 1900; hon. mention, Pan. Am. Exp., Buffalo, 1901; silver medal, St. Louis Exp., 1904; hon. mention, Pairs Salon,

1906; hon. mention, P. P. Exp., San G., 1915; Speyer memorial prize, NAD, 1922. In collections of Mus. of Nat. History; MMA; Buffalo Bill Mus. Cody, Wyoming Baltimore; High Mus. of Art, Atlanta; and Musee de l'Armee, Paris. Known for Sculptures of horses. Address in 1929, 2238 Canyon Dr., Hollywood, CA.

SIMONT, JOSEPH.
Illustrator. Member: SI; GFLA. Address in 1929, 20 West 10th Street; 39 West 67th St., New York, NY.

SIMPSON, C. HELEN.
See Whittemore.

SIMPSON, CLARA D(AVIDSON) (MRS.).
See Davidson.

SIMPSON, EDNA HUESTIS (MRS.).
Miniature painter. Born Troy, NY, Nov. 26, 1882. Pupil of Emma Willard Art School; Cornell Univ.; ASL of NY. Member: PA Soc. Min. P.; AFA. Address in 1929, 333 East 68th St., New York, NY.

SIMPSON, M.
This stipple-engraver designed and engraved a portrait of Washington in the center of an elaborate script memorial. This print was published in 1855 and is signed as "Designed and Engraved by S. Simpson, NY."

SIMPSON, MARIAN.
(Mrs. Lesley Simpson). Painter. Born Kansas City, MO, July 12, 1899. Pupil of H. G. Keller. Member: Club Beaux Arts, San Francisco. Awards: Hon. mention for water color, 1923 and 1924; first prize for pastel and second prize for oil, 1924, Cleveland Artists; hon. mention., San Francisco, 1927. Work "Luisita," owned by the Ward Fund, Cleveland; "Hills," Mills College Gallery, Oakland, CA; wall decoration, YWCA, San Francisco. Address in 1929, 976 Miller Ave., Berkeley, CA.

SIMPSON, MAXWELL STEWART.
Painter, etcher, and lithographer. Born Elizabeth, NJ, Sept. 11, 1896. Pupil of NAD. Member: Chicago SE; S. Indp. A. Works: "Etelka," "New

Jersey Landscape," and "Self Portrait." New York Public Library; two watercolors, Newark Museum, NJ. Address in 1929, 109 Broad St.; h. 431 Madison Ave., Elizabeth, NJ; summer, Buzzards Bay, MA.

SIMPSON, ROSLYNN MIDDLEMAN.
Painter. Born in Phila., PA, in 1929. Studied: NJ College for Women; Newark School of Fine and Industrial Arts; and with W. Benda; also studied with R. Nakian and B. Gussow. Collections: Metropolitan Museum of Art; Whitney Museum of America Art; Newark Museum of Art.

SIMPSON, WILLIAM MARK JR.
Sculptor. Born Norfolk, VA, Aug. 24, 1903. Pupil of J. Maxwell Miller; Rinehart School of Sculpture; MD Inst. Member: Norfolk SA. Awards: Sloane prizes, 1920-21-23-24 and Ferguson prize, 1923, Norfolk Society of Arts. Work: Portrait bust of Patrick Henry in Patrick Henry School, Norfolk; Athletic sketches, V. M. I., Lexington. Address in 1929, 1109 Graydon Ave., Norfolk, VA.

SIMS, AGNES.
Painter. Born in Rosemont, PA, in 1910. Studied: Phila. School of Design for Women; Philosophical Society grant, 1949; Neosho grant, 1952. Collections: Museum of New Mexico; Colorado Springs Fine Arts Center; Denver Art Museum; Brooklyn Museum; Musee de L'Homme, Paris.

SINCLAIR, ARCHIE.
Painter. Born Pitlochry, Perthshire, Scotland, Feb. 19, 1895. Pupil of John H. Dixon and Clyde Leon Keller. Member: S. Indp. A.; Chicago NJSA; Salons of America. Represented by 2 landscapes, Normal School, North Adams, MA. Address in 1929, 88 Charles St., New York, NY; h. 969 Multnomah St., Portland, Oregon.

SINCLAIR, GERRIT V.
Painter and teacher. Born Grand Haven, MI, May 1, 1890. Pupil of Chicago Art Inst. Member: WI PS (pres); Chic. Gal. Assn; Chic. SA. Awards: Medal, 1921-1928. Landscape prize, 1924, Figure prize, 1926, Milwaukee Journal

purchase prize, 1929. WI PS. Work: Murals "Christ Before Temple," St. James Church, Milwaukee; "La Salle and Tonty," Sherman Park, Chicago. Died in 1955. Address in 1929, Layton School of Art; h. 902 Newhall St., Milwaukee, WI.

SINDELAR, THOMAS A.
Illustrator. Born in Cleveland, Ohio, in 1867. Pupil of Mucha in Paris. Address in 1926, 15 Maiden Lane, New York.

SINGER, BURR.
Painter and lithographer. Born in St. Louis, MO. Studied: St. Louis School of Fine Arts; Art Institute of Chicago; Art Students' League and Waltar Ufer. Awards: Marineland Exhibition, 1955; Los Angeles County Fair, 1951, 1953. Collection: Warren Flynn School, Clayton, Missouri; Library of Congress; Beverly-Fairfax Jewish Community Center, Los Angeles; Child Guidance Clinic, Los Angeles.

SINGER, WILLIAM H. JR.
Painter. Born Pittsburgh, PA, July 5, 1868. Studied at Julian Acad., Paris. Member: ANA 1916; Pittsburgh AS; AFA; Allied AA; St. Lucas Soc. of Art, Amsterdam, Holland. Awards: Silver medal, P. P. Exp., San F., 1915; Cahn hon. mention, AIC, 1916. Royal Order of St. Olaf, conferred by King of Norway, 1929. Represented in the Portland Museum; Stedelyk, Amsterdam; Royal Museum, Antwerp; Musee de Luxembourg; Milwaukee AI; Carnegie Public Library, Fort Worth; Delgado Museum, New Orleans. Died in 1943. Address in 1929, 58 West 57th Street, New York, NY.

SINNOCK, J(OHN) R(AY).
Painter, medalist, and teacher. Born Raton, NM, July 8, 1888. Pupil of Penna. Museum and Sch. of Ind. Art for 10 years. Member: Boston AC; Phila. Sketch C.; Phila. Alliance; NSS (assoc.); AFA. Work: Mural decorations in Rosemont School, Rosemont, PA, and Frankfort High School and modeled the special commemorative coins for the Sesqui Centennial Exp., Phila., 1926; special Congressional Medal of Honor, to Thomas A. Edison, 1928.

859

Died in 1947. Address in 1929, Mint of the US; h. and studio, 2022 Spring Garden St., Philadelphia, PA.

SINZ, WALTER A.
Sculptor and teacher. Born Cleveland, Ohio, July 13, 1881. Pupil of Herman N. Matzen; Landowski in Paris. Member: Cleveland SA; Cleveland SS. Awards: Certificate of Merit, Cleveland Museum, 1922 and 1923. Work: Cleveland 125th Anniversary Medal: Fountain. Y.M.C.A., Cleveland; Cleveland Flower Show medal; sculpture group, St. Lukes Hospital, Cleveland, Ohio. Instructor in sculpture, Cleveland School of Art. Address in 1929, care of The Cleveland School of Art; h. 6013 Olive Court, Cleveland, OH.

SISSON, FREDERICK R.
Painter, etcher, and teacher. Born Providence, RI, Sept. 5, 1893. Pupil of Rhode Island School of Design, Boston Museum of Fine Arts, Abbott H. Thayer. Member: Providence AC; Providence WCC. Address in 1929, 128 North Main St.; h. 24 Thayer St., Providence, RI.

SITZMAN, EDWARD R.
Painter, lecturer, and teacher. Born Cincinnati, OH, March 31, 1874. Pupil of Duveneck; H. Farney; Cincinnati Art Academy. Member: Indiana AC; Indianapolis AA; Chic. Gal. Assn. Address in 1929, Columbia Securities Bldg., Rm. 310; h. 1422 North Dearborn St., Indianapolis, IN; summer, R. R. No. 2 Martinsville, IN.

SKELTON, LESLIE JAMES.
Painter. Born in Montreal, Can., in 1848. Studied in Paris several years. Pupil of Iwill. Landscapes in oils and pastel exhibited; Salon, Paris, 1901; Liverpool Autumn Exhibition, 1902; British and Colonial exhibition, at time of King Edward's coronation, 1902; Royal Acad., London, 1904; National Academy of Design; Denver Artists Club; Montreal Art Association; Colorado Springs; in Nat'l Gallery, Ottawa, Canada. One of his most noted productions entitled

"Gathering Storm in Ester Park" was reproduced in colors in Brush and Pencil in 1903. President of Coburn Library Book Club, Colorado Springs; Winter Night Club, 1911; Colorado Springs Art Society, 1913. Address in 1926, 1225 N. Tejon St., Colorado Springs, CO.

SKELTON, RALPH FISHER.
Painter and etcher. Born Port Byron, IL, Feb. 4, 1899. Pupil of Henry Tonks, W. W. Russell , Sir William Orpen. Address in 1929, Italian Court, 145 East Ontario St., Chicago, IL; summer, 40 Dover St., Longon, England.

SKEU, SIGURD.
Painter, who exhibited water colors at the Penna. Acad. of Fine Arts, Philadelphia, 1925. Address in 1926, 51 Popular St., Brooklyn, NY.

SKIDMORE, LEWIS PALMER.
Painter, etcher, and teacher. Born Bridgeport, CT, Sept. 3, 1877. Pupil of J. H. Niemeyer; Laurens and Bonnat in Paris. Member: Brooklyn SA; Brooklyn WCC; New Haven PCC. Died in 1955. Address in 1929, 214 Clermont Ave., Brooklyn, NY; summer, Port Jefferson, LI, NY.

SKIDMORE, THORNTON D.
Painter and illustrator. Born Brooklyn, NY, June 2, 1884. Pupil of Howard Pyle, Eric Pape. Member: SI; GFLA. Address in 1929, 1947 Broadway, New York, NY; h. 95 28th St., Jackson Heights, Elmhurst, LI, NY.

SKILES, JACQUELINE.
Sculpture, printmaker, and videotape. Born in St. Louis, MO, in 1937. Studied: Wash. Univ., St. Louis; Univ. of Wisconsin, Madison; New School for Social Research, NYC. Exhibitions: Vis-a-Vis Gallery, NYC; Univ. of Bridgeport, Conn.; Ramapo College of NJ; Women's Interart Center, NYC. Publications: Documentary History of Women Artists in Revolution; Columbus Started Something. Posters: Threat to the Peace; For Life on Earth; Liberation: Rise Up Sisters; Arising. She has been

very active in the women artists movement.

SKINNER, C(HARLOTTE) B.
(Mrs. William Lyle Skinner). Painter and etcher. Born San Francisco, June 17, 1879. Pupil of CA School of Art. Member: San Francisco S. Women A. Address in 1929, Lone Pine, Inyo Co., CA.

SKINNER, CHARLES.
This excellent bank note engraver, in the employ of The American Bank Note Company, was working in NY at least as early as 1867. He engraved in line a few portraits for the book publishers.

SKINNER, ORIN E(NSIGN).
Painter, craftsman, writer, and lecturer. Born Sweden Valley, PA, Nov. 5, 1892. Pupil of Herman J. Butler; Frank Von der Lancken. Member: Boston AC; Boston SAC; Boston Arch. C. Address in 1929, 9 Harcourt St., Boston, MA; h 37 Walden St., Newtonville, MA.

SKODIK, ANTONIN.
Sculptor. Pupil of Art Students' League and sculptor of "Montana."

SKOOG, KARL F(REDERICK).
Painter and sculptor. Born Sweden, Nov. 3, 1878. Pupil of Bela L. Pratt. Member: CT AFA; Boston SS; Boston AC. Awards: Prize, Rochester, NY, 1908; hon. mention, S.A.A., 1912; hon. mention, CT AFA, 1915, 1918; first prize S.A.A., 1918; first prize Swedish American A. 1918, 1921; hon. mention, Swedish American C., 1912, 1920; hon. mention Chicago S.A.A., 1920. Work: Bust of John Ericsson in K. of P. Bldg., Brockton MA; bronze tablet in Home for Aged Swedish People, West Newton, MA; Perry Monument, Forest Dale Cemetery; relief, J. A. Powers, Elks Bldg., Malden, MA; medallion, R. W. Emerson, Museum of Numismatic Society, NY; Soldiers Monument, Cambridge MA; Soldiers World War Monument, Cromwell, CT; "On Guard," Angell Memorial Hospital, Boston; memorial relief to A. N. Pierson, Cromwell Gardens, Cromwell, CT; "Light" and "Charity," bronze doors, Masonic Temple, Goshen, IN; memorial relief to A. P. Peterson,

John Morton Memorial Museum, Philadelphia, PA. Died in 1934. Address in 1929, 384 Boylston St., Boston, MA.

SKORA, MARIE.
Printmaker. Born in Arkansas City, KS. Studied: New Mexico Highlands Univ.; private studio in Caracas, Venezuela. Exhibitions: Chula Vista, Calif., 1954; Center of Fine Arts, Maracaibo, Venezuela, 1964; NLAPW, Wash., DC, 1973. Collections: Smithsonian Institution, Wash., DC; Museum of Fine Arts, Caracas, Venezuela; Rockville Civic Center Gallery, Maryland.

SKOU, SIGURD.
Painter, who exhibited at the National Academy of Design, NY, 1925. Address in 1926, 19 West 50th Street, New York.

SLACKMAN, CHARLES B.
Illustrator. Born in NYC, in 1934. Began his career in 1959 for Esquire and has worked for almost every national magazine, some of which are New York Magazine, The New York Times, Playboy, Audience, Evergreen Review, National Lampoon, and Time. His work has appeared in numerous shows and galleries and was the subject of a feature article in Communication Arts. He has been an instructor with R. O. Blechman at SVA since 1963. He and his wife, a ballerina, live in NYC.

SLADE, C. ARNOLD.
Painter. Born Acushnet, MA, Aug. 2, 1882. Pupil of F. V. DuMond, Laurens, Schomer and Bachet. Member: Phila. AC; Paris AA; Allied A. of London; Grand Rapids AC; Springfield (IL) AC; New Bedford AA; Phila. Sketch C. Work: "Sardine Boats, Brittany," Springfield (IL) Art Club; "Venice," Philadelphia Art Club; "The Reapers," Attleboro (MA) Public Collection; 3 paintings, Isabella Stewart Gardner Musuem, Boston; "Sea Waifs," New Bedford (MA) Public Library; "Vender of Cocoa Water," Milwaukee Art Inst.; "Christ on the Mountain," Bethany Church, Phila., PA; "Nubian Card Players," Fitzgerald Gallery, Brookline, MA. Represented in

Paramount Theatre, New York, John Wanamaker, and Elkins Collections, Philadelphia, and portraits of Hon. Charles A. Dawes, Att. Gen. Sargent, Senator Borah, etc. Address in 1929, Truro, MA.

SLADE, CORA L.
(Mrs. Abbott E. Slade). Painter. Pupil of Robert S. Dunning. Member: Providence AC., Newport AA.; Fall River AC; AFA. Died in 1937. Address in 1929, 863 High St., Fall River, MA.

SLATER, EDWIN CROWEN.
Painter, illustrator, and craftsman. Born NJ, Dec. 22, 1884. Pupil of William Chase, Cecilia Beaux, Thomas P. Anshutz, Hugh Breckenridge, Birge Harrison, Charles Grafly, Herman D. Murphy, Henry R. Poore, George Bridgeman, Walter Priggs. Member: Salma. C.; Copley S.; Fellowship PAFA. Address in 1929, 67 West 67th Street, New York, NY; h. Rockledge Drive., Pelham Manor, NY.

SLAVET, RUTH.
Sculptor. Studied: Bennington College, Bennington, Vermont; Boston Univ., School of Fine Arts; Impression Workshop, Boston. Exhibitions: Boston Summerthing Traveling Art Exhibit, Boston, 1968; Brockton Art Center, Brockton, Mass., 1972, 1973; Hayden Gallery, Mass. Institute of Technology, 1973.

SLEETH, L MacD.
(Mrs. Francis V. Sleeth). Painter, Sculptor, and teacher. Born Croton, Iowa, Oct. 24, 1864. Pupil of Whistler, MacMonnies and Emil Carlsen. Member: San F. AA; Wash. WCC; S. Wash. A.; Wash. AC; Laguna Beach AA. Work: Portrait busts in marble of "Brig. Gen'l John M. Wilson," Corcoran Gallery of Art; "Martha Washington," Memorial Continental Hall, and "Rt. Rev. Bishop Henry T. Satterlee," Cathedral Foundation, all in Wash., DC. Address in 1929, Cathedral School for Girls, Washington, DC.

SLOAN, J(AMES) BLANDING.
Painter, illustrator, etcher, craftsman, writer, and teacher. Born Corsicana, Sept. 19, 1886.

Pupil of Chicago Academy of Fine Arts; B. J. O. Nordfeldt; George Senseney. Member: Chicago SE. Address in 1929, 120 North 15th Street, Corsicana, TX.

SLOAN, JOHN.
Painter, illustrator, and etcher. Born Lock Haven, PA, Aug. 2, 1871. Member: S. Indp. A.; New SA. Awards: Hon. mention, CI Pittsburgh, 1905; bronze medal for etching, P. P. Exp., San F., 1915; gold medal, Sesqui Centennial Expo., Phila., 1926. Work in : NY Public Library; Newark (NJ) Public Library; Cincinnati Museum of Art; Carnegie Institute, Pittsburgh; Metropolitan Museum of Art; Brooklyn Museum; Museum of New Mexico; Phillips Memorial Gallery, Washington; PA State College; Barnes Foundation; Newark, NJ, Museum of Art; Detroit Inst. of Arts; Harrison Gallery, San Diego; Art Inst. of Chicago. Died in 1951. Address in 1929, 53 Washington Square, New York, NY.

SLOAN, MARIANNA.
Landscape painter, mural painter. Born Lock Haven, PA. Pupil of Robert Henri and Elliot Daingerfield in Phila. Member: Fellowship PAFA, 1916; AFA. Award: Bronze medal, St. Louis Expo., 1904. Work: "Landscape," St. Louis Club; "Rocky Beach," PA Acad. of the Fine Arts, Philadelphia; mural decorations in Church of the Annunciation, Philadelphia; and chancel, St. Thomas Church, Whitemarsh, PA. Died in 1954. Address in 1929, Moreland Ave., Chestnut Hill, PA; 44 Queen Lane, Germantown, PA.

SLOANE, MARIAN PARKHURST.
(Mrs. George Sloane). Painter. Born Salem, MA. Pupil of Boston Museum School. Member: NA Women PS.; Copley S; CT AFA. Died in 1955. Address in 1929, Fenway Studios, 30 Ipswich St., Boston, MA.

SLOCUM, ANNETTE M.
Sculptor. Born in Cleveland, OH. Studied at Penna. Acad. of the Fine Arts. Her specialty is portraiture. Address in 1926, 250 West 154th St., NY.

SLOCUM, VICTOR VAUGHAN.
Sculptor, who exhibited portraits in the Penn. Academy of the Fine Arts, 1924, Philadelphia, PA. Address in 1926, 1523 Chestnut St., Philadephia, PA.

SLOMAN, JOSEPH.
Painter, illustrator, and craftsman. Born Philadelphia, PA, Dec. 30, 1883. Pupil of Howard Pyle, B. W. Clinedinst and Clifford Grayson. Works: Art Dome, Town Hall, West New York, NJ; "Martin Luther," Church of St. John, West New York, NJ; 14 memorial windows in Hoboken, NJ; mural "Sir Philip Carteret Entering the Province of NJ, 1650," Elizabeth Carteret Hotel, Elizabeth, NJ. Illustrated "In Many Islands," "A Declaration of Dependence," "Billy Glen of the Broken Shutter," "Deer Jane," "The Escape of the Magruder," and "Alias Kitty Kasey." Address in 1929, 423 South New York Ave., Union City, NJ.

SLOPER, NORMA (WRIGHT).
Painter. Born New Haven, CT, Jan. 12, 1892. Pupil of A. E. Jones; Lucien Simon and Rene Menard in Paris. Member: Soc. CT P.; CT AFA. Award: Dunham prize, CT AFA., 1922. Address in 1929, 301 West Main St., New Britain, CT.

SLUSSER, JEAN PAUL.
Painter, craftsman, writer, and teacher. Born Wauseon, OH, Dec. 15, 1886. Pupil of John F. Carlson, Wm. M. Paxton, Philip Hate, Henry L. McFee. Member: Detroit SAC. Address in 1929, 1324 Pontiac St., Ann Arbor, MI.

SLUTZ, HELEN BEATRICE.
Painter. Born Cleveland, OH, April 15, 1886. Pupil of Cleveland School of Art. Member: Calif. S. Min. P.; Artland C. of Los Angeles; AFA. Address in 1929, 7320 Paxton Ave., Chicago, IL; 1546 North Serrano Ave., Hollywood, CA.

SMALL, MAY MOTT SMITH.
See Mott-Smith.

SMALLEY, JANET LIVINGSTON.
(Mrs. Alfred Smalley). Illustrator. Born Philadelphia, May 16, 1893.

Pupil of PAFA. Award: Cresson traveling scholarship, PAFA, 1915. Member: Fellowship PAFA. Illustrated for children's publications. Died in 1965. Address in 1929, 223 East Washington Square, Philadelphia, PA; 309 Yale Ave., Swarthmore, PA.

SMART, MISS ANNA M.
Painter. Born in 1847; died in 1914, in New York City. Specialty, water colors.

SMEDLEY, WILL LARYMORE.
Painter, illustrator, writer, and lecturer. Born Sandyville, OH, Nov. 10, 1871. Self-taught. Member of Cleveland W. C. Soc. Died in 1958. Address in 1929, Chautauqua on the Lake, NY.

SMEDLEY, WILLIAM THOMAS.
Painter. Born in Chester County, PA, on March 26, 1858. Studied engraving in Phila. and art in the Penn. Acad. of the Fine Arts; went to New York, 1878, and later to Paris; studied under Jean Paul Laurens; opened studio, New York, 1880; then became actively engaged as illustrator for Harper's and other standard periodicals. In 1882 he was engaged by publishers of Picturesque Canada to travel with Marquis of Lorne through West and Northwest Canada and to illustrate the work; he made several sketchings around the world. He exhibited at the Paris Salon, 1888. Several of his principal productions are: "An Indiscreet Question;" "A Thanksgiving Dinner;" "A Summer Occupation." Elected member of National Academy, 1905. Died March 26, 1920 in Bronxville, NY.

SMIBERT, JOHN.
Painter. Born March 24, 1688 in Edinburgh, SC. One of the earliest of the Am. portrait painters. His influence may be seen in the work of many of those who immediately followed him, and it is thought that Copley may have received instruction in his studio. Born in SC in 1688, Smilbert was first a common house painter. Later he worked for coach painters in London and afterward copied painters for dealers until he succeeded in

gaining admittance to an art academy. Leaving London he spent 3 yrs. in Italy copying Raphael and other "Old Masters," and in 1728 came to Am. with the Rev. George Berkely. A portrait of this Rev. George Berkely with his family, by Smibert, signed and dated 1729, is preserved at Yale U. Smibert married and left 2 children, one a son, Nathaniel, who became a portrait painter, and a portrait of John Lovell, a product of his brush, is now at Harvard University, Cambridge, MA. John Smibert worked mostly in Providence;died in MA, in 1751.

SMIBERT, NATHANIEL.
Painter. Born Jan. 20, 1735. Son of the artist John Smibert. He died in his 22nd year having showed a great talent for portraiture, and, had his life been spared, he would doubtless have achieved much success. His portrait of John Lowell is owned by Harvard. He died Nov. 3, 1756, in Boston, MA.

SMILLIE, GEORGE F(REDERICK) CUMMING.
Engraver. Born New York, NY, Nov. 23, 1854. Pupil of NAD and of his uncle, James D. Smillie, in Am. Bank Note Co. Principal engraver, US Bureau of Engraving, 1894 to 1922; chief work, the so called "picture notes" ($2 and $5 silver certificates of 1895); back of $100 Federal Reserve notes; large portraits or Presidents Grant, McKinley, Roosevelt, Taft, and Wilson. Address in 1929, 2631 Connecticut Ave., N. W. Washington, DC.

SMILLIE, GEORGE HENRY.
Painter. Born Dec. 29, 1840. A son of James Smillie, the celebrated line engraver, and brother of James D. Smillie, National Academy, George H. Smillie was born in that city of NY in 1840. He is one of the most widely known of American landscape painters, and his pictures are characterized by poetic sentiment and technical skill of a high order. He is a pupil of James M. Hart, National Academy. He made a sketching trip in the Rocky Mountains, the Yosemite Valley, and Florida, but the most popular of his subjects are those he found in picturesque spots in the interior and along the shores of LI. He was elected a member of the Am. Water Color Soc. in 1868, and a Nat. Academician in 1882. He is represented in the Metropolitan Museum, NY; the Corcoran Art Gal., Wash., DC; the Rhode Island School of Design; the Union League Club, of Phila. Died Nov. 10, 1921 in Bronxville, NY.

SMILLIE, HELEN SHELDON JACOBS.
(Mrs. George H.). Painter. Born in New York in 1854. Studied under Joseph O. Eaton and James D. Smillie. Painter of genre pictures in oils and water colors. Member of American Water Color Society. Address in 1926, 136 East 36th St., New York. Died July 30, 1926, in NYC.

SMILLIE, JAMES.
Engraver. Born Nov. 23, 1807, in Edinburgh, Scotland. Died Dec. 4, 1885, in Poughkeepsie, NY. He was the son of a silversmith and he was first apprenticed to James Johnston, a silver engraver of his native city, and he also received some instruction from Edward Mitchell, a portrait engraver. In 1821 he came with his family to Quebec, Canada, where his father and elder brother established themselves in business as jewelers, and James worked with them for some time as a general engraver. In 1827, under the patronage of Lord Dalhousie, he was sent to London and to Edinburgh for instruction in engraving, but he returned to Quebec after a short time, and in 1829 he went to NY. His first plate to attract attention was done after Robert W. Weir's painting of the "Convent Gate;" and in 1832-36 he engraved a series of plates for the NY Mirror after paintings by Weir. In 1832 he was made an Associate of the National Acad., and in 1851 he became an Academician.

SMILLIE, JAMES DAVID.
Painter and engraver. Born on Jan. 16, 1833, in NY. James David Smillie was a son of James Smillie, and was trained by his father as an engraver on steel. While his

864

principal work was bank note engraving he produced some excellent general work, including a series of illustrations for Cooper's novels, after designs by F.O.C. Darby. He was an excellent etcher and a founder of the NY Etching Club, and later its president. In 1864, after a visit to Europe, James D. Smillie turned his attention to painting, and in the same year he exhibited at the Acad. of Design, in NY, and was made an Associate Member of the National Acad. in 1865; he was made an Academician in 1876. As a painter in oils and water colors he obtained reputation. He was one of the founders and the president (1873-79) of the American Water Color Society; he was also president of the NY Etching Club. Died Sept 14, 1909 in NYC.

SMILLIE, WILLIAM CUMMING.
Engraver. Born in Edinburgh, Scotland on Sept. 23, 1813. Wm. C. Smillie was a brother of James Smillie and came to Canada with his father's family in 1821. After working at silver engraving for a time in Quebec, he came to NY in 1830. He early turned his attention to bank note engraving and was connected with several bank note companies, the last of which, "Edmonds, Jones & Smillie," was later absorbed by the Am. Bank Note Co. In 1866 he secured a contract to engrave the paper currency of the Canadian government, and for this purpose he established a bank note engraving company in Ottawa. In 1874 he retired from his business, but in 1882 he again established an engraving company in Canada, and he was still at the head of that company in 1889. Died in 1899.

SMILLIE, WILLIAM MAIN.
Engraver. Born in NY in 1835; died there in 1888. Wm. M. Smillie was a son of James Smillie, and was early known as an expert letter engraver. He was long employed by one of the firms that in 1857 was merged into the old American Bank Note Co.; and he was connected with the old and present American company until his death, having

been general manager of the present organization for some years.

SMITH, A.
Dunlap notes an artist of this name as having painted in NY in 1834.

SMITH, ALBERT D(ELMONT).
Painter. Born New York, NY, Feb. 14, 1886. Pupil of ASL under DuMond and Chase. Member: Chelsea AC., London; Salma. C.; Century Assoc. Work: "Portrait of Childe Hassam," Toledo Museum of Art; "Self portrait," Detroit Inst. of Arts; "Portrait of John Drew," owned by the Village of East Hampton; portrait of "Lionel Atwill as Deburau," City Art Museum, St. Louis. Died in 1962. Address in 1929, 58 West 57th St., New York, NY; summer, East Hampton, LI, NY.

SMITH, ALBERT E.
Painter, and illustrator. Born Waterbury, CT. Pupil of Yale School of Fine Arts. Member: Salma. C. Address in 1929, "Cherryledge," Cos Cob, CT.

SMITH, ALFRED EVERETT.
Portrait painter. Born Lynn, MA, in 1863. Pupil of School of Boston Museum of Fine Arts and of the Julien Academy in Paris, under Boulanger, Lefebvre, and Constant. Member of the Copley Society, Boston. Address in 1926, Boylston Street, Boston, MA. Died in 1955.

SMITH, ALICE R(AVENEL) HUGER.
Painter and teacher. Born Charleston, SC, July 14, 1876. Member: SSAL; Carolina AA; AFA. Work: "Solitude," Delgado Art Mus.; "The Coming of Night at Kecklico," Carolina Art Assoc.; "The Ashepoo Swamp," Atlanta Art Assoc. Illustrator and joint author of "The Dwelling Houses of Charleston," "The Life of Charles Fraser" and "The Pringle House." Work: "The White Heron," Brooklyn, Inst. of Arts and Sciences; "A Snowy Heron Amid the Lotus," Albany Inst. of History and Art. Address in 1929, 8 Atlantic St.; h. 69 Church St., Charleston, SC.

SMITH, ALLEN.
Portrait and landscape painter. Born in 1810, in RI. He lived in

Cleveland from 1841 to 1883, painting many excellent portraits of prominent citizens. In his later years he painted landscapes. His work compares with that of Healy, Huntington, and Elliott, who lived during the same period. He died in 1890, in Cleveland, OH.

SMITH, ANITA M(ILLER).
Painter and craftsman. Born Torresdale, PA, Oct. 20, 1893. Pupil of Carlson and NY ASL. Member: NA Women PS; Alliance; ASL of NY; Woodstock AA. Work: "Houses in the Dunes," PAFA. Address in 1929, Lake Hill, Ulster Co., NY; h. 123 East 53rd St., New York, NY; Woodstock, NY.

SMITH, ANNE FRY.
Painter. Born Philadelphia, PA, Jan. 25, 1890. Pupil of Fred Wagner, PAFA. Member: Plastic C.; Phila. Alliance. Work: "The Covered Bridge," PA. State College. Address in 1929, Bridge St., Oreland, PA.

SMITH, ARCHIBALD CARY.
Marine painter. Born in NY, in 1837, and lived his professional life in that city. Pupil of M.F.H. DeHaas. He exhibited frequently at the National Academy, New York, and painted many pictures of private yachts.

SMITH, BELLE PATTERSON.
(Mrs. Myron O. Smith). Painter. Member: Wash. WCC. Address in 1929, 2121 F. St.; 720 21st St., N. W., Washington, DC.

SMITH, C. H.
In 1855-60 this capital line engraver of portraits and book illustrations was working in Philadelphia and in NY.

SMITH, CARL ROHL.
Sculptor. Born in Copenhagen, Denmark. His studio was for years in Washington, DC, where he designed the Sherman Monument in front of the Treasury Building. He died in Copenhagen, on Aug. 22, 1900.

SMITH, CHARLES L. A.
Painter. Born NY, Jan. 11, 1871. Self-taught. Member: Boston AC; Calif. AC; Calif. WCC; Chicago SA; Soc. Western Artists. Represented in Lawrence (MA) Art Musuem. Address in 1929, 1129 North El Centro Ave., Hollywood, CA.

SMITH, CHARLES W(ILLIAM).
Illustrator, craftsman, and writer. Born Lofton, VA, June 22, 1893. Pupil of Richard N. Brooke, Sergeant Kendall; M. Ligeron in Paris. Member: GFLA; AI Graphic Arts Leaders Exh., 1926. Author of book on block printing. Address in 1929, 1207 West Franklin St., Richmond, VA, summer, Waynesboro, VA.

SMITH, DAN.
Illustrator. Born in 1864. Member: SI 1912. Died in 1934. Address in 1929, "NY World," New York, NY.

SMITH, DE COST.
Painter. Member Salma. C. 1891. Died in 1939. Address in 1929, 146 West 55th St.; h. 144 West 73d St., New York, NY.

SMITH, DUNCAN.
Mural painter and illustrator. Born in Virginia, 1877. Pupil of Cox, Twachtman, and DeCamp. Member of National Society of Mural Painters. Instructor in Art Students' League of NY. Address in 1926, 42 Washington Square, New York. Died in 1934.

SMITH, (EDWARD) GREGORY.
Painter. Born Grand Rapids, MI, May 2, 1880. Member: CT AFA; Allied AA; New Soc. Amer. A. Work: "Winter Nocturne," Grand Rapids Art Museum; "Summer," Lincoln, NE, Art Museum. Address in 1929, Old Lyme, CT.

SMITH, E(DWARD) HERNDON.
Painter and sculptor. Born Mobile, July 9, 1891. Pupil of Weir, Tack and Yale School of Fine Arts. Member: Brooklyn S. Modern A. Address in 1929, 111 Government St., Mobile, AL.

SMITH, E(LMER) BOYD.
Illustrator. Born St. John., N.B., Canada, May 31, 1860. Member: Boston AC. Author and illustrator: "The Story of Noah's Ark;" "The Chicken World;" "Pocahontas and Captain John Smith;" "The Story of Our Country," etc. Died in 1943. Address in 1929, 140 West 57th St., Wilton, CT.

SMITH, ELIZA LLOYD.
Painter. Born Urbana, OH, July 21, 1872. Pupil of Corcoran Art School, Washington, DC. Member: Wash. WCC. Address in 1929, 3511 Porter St.; 3702 Macomb St., Washington, DC; Bluemont, MD.

SMITH, ELIZABETH.
Painter. Member: Baltimore, WCC. Address in 1929, 1702 Bolton St., Baltimore, MD.

SMITH, ELLAS B.
Painter, who exhibited "The Long Wharf" at the PAFA, Philadelphia, 1915. Address in 1926, 307 Fenway Studios, Boston, MA.

SMITH, EMMA J.
Painter. Member: Wash. WCC. Address in 1929, The Wyoming, Washington, DC.

SMITH, ERNEST BROWNING.
Painter. Born Brimfield, MA, Nov. 30, 1866. Self-taught. Member: Calif. AC; Laguna Beach AA. Awards: Prize, Sacramento State Fair, 1925; hon. mention, Pomona, CA, 1925 and 1928. Work: "Sycamores in Spring," Los Angeles Museum; "The Sentinel," San Francisco Museum. Address in 1929, 2416 Loma Vista Pl., Los Angeles, CA.

SMITH, ESTHER.
Portrait painter. Born in Connecticut. She studied under Edwin White in NY. She resided in Hartford, CT, and there painted portraits of Theo. D. Judah, Col. G. T. Davis, Judge T. B. Butler and many others. Her specialty was the portraiture of children.

SMITH, F. BERKELY.
Illustrator. Born in Astoria, LI, NY, in 1868; son of F. Hopkinson Smith. Studied architecture at Columbia U., and practiced until 1896. Author and illustrator, "The Real Latin Quarter," "Budapest, the City of the Magyars," etc. Address in 1926, 16 Place de la Madeleine, Paris, France.

SMITH, F. CARL.
Portrait painter. Born Cincinnati, OH, Sept. 7, 1868. Pupil of Bouguereau, Ferrier and Constant in Paris. Member: S. Wash. A.; Wash. WCC; Paris AAA; Calif. AC; Pasadena Fine Arts C; Laguna Beach AA (life). Awards: Hon. mention for water color, AAS, 1902; second figure prize, Southwest Museum, 1921. Work: "Mrs. Charles W. Fairbanks" and "Mrs. John Ewing Walker," D. A. R. Continental Hall, Wash.; Former speaker "Joseph Cannon," Public Lib., MN; "Samuel P. Langley," Allegheny (PA) Observatory; "Governor Shafroth," The Capitol, Denver; portraits of Governor Willis of Ohio in Capitol, Columbus; and Speaker Clark, The Capitol, Washington, DC. Address in 1929, 217 Oakland Ave., Pasadena, CA; summer, Laguna Beach, CA.

SMITH, F. STANLEY.
Painter. Member: Phila. WCC. Address in 1929, R. F. D. North Shirley, MA.

SMITH, F(RANCIS) BERKELEY.
Illustrator and writer. Born Astoria, LI, NY, Aug. 24, 1868; son of F. Hopkinson Smith. Studied Architecture at Columbia University, and practiced until 1896. Author and illustrator of "The Real Latin Quarter," and "Budapest, the City of the Magyars." Address in 1929, 16 Place de la Madeleine, Paris, France.

SMITH, FRANCIS DREXEL.
Painter. Born Chicago, IL, June 11, 1874. Pupil of John Vanderpoel, John F. Carlson, Everett L. Warner. Member: NAC; Denver AA; Buffalo SA; Broadmoor Art Acad. (pres.); Brooklyn SA; Mississippi AA; Wash. AC; CT AFA; New Haven PCC; AFA. Awards: Hon. mention, Seattle Fine Arts Soc., 1923; purchase prize, Kansas City Art Inst., 1924; hon. mention,

Denver Art Mus., 1925; hon. mention, Colo. Springs, 1929. Represented in Kansas City, CO, Art Inst.; Broadmoor Art Acad., Colorado Springs, CO; Vanderpoel Collection, Chicago. Died in 1956. Address in 1929, Broadmoor Art Academy; 531 North Cascade Ave., Colorado Springs, CO.

SMITH, FRANCIS HOPKINSON.
Painter and author. Born in Baltimore, Oct. 23, 1838. Has done much landscape work in water colors, also charcoal work and illustrations. Represented in Walter's Gallery, Baltimore; Marquand collection, etc. Lecturer on art subjects. Awarded bronze medal, Buffalo Expo., 1901; silver medal, Charleston Expo., 1902; gold medal, Phila. Art Club, 1902; gold medal, American Art Society, 1902; Commander Order of the Mejidieh, 1898, and of the Order of Osmanieh by Sultan of Turkey, 1900. Member of the Am. Acad. of Arts and letters, American Society, Civil Engineers, American Water Color Society, Philadelphia Art Club and the Cincinnati Art Club. Address in 1926, 16 Exchange Place, New York, NY. Died April 17, 1915, in NYC.

SMITH, FRANK HILL.
Painter. Born in Boston in 1841. He studied in Boston and later in Paris under Bonnat. He has painted portraits, figure pieces, landscapes, and mural paintings. He died in 1904.

SMITH, G.
This name is signed to well executed script billheads, etc., published in 1790-1800. The work was done in NY.

SMITH, GEORGE GIRDLER.
Born Sept. 8, 1795, in Danvers, MA. He was probably a pupil of Abel Bowen, the Boston engraver, as he was in Bowen's employ in 1815 as an engraver. Little is known about G. G. Smith until 1830, when, in connection with William B. Annin, he was in the general engraving business in Boston, working under the firm name of Annin & Smith. Mr. Smith was early interested in lithography, and visited Paris for

instruction and materials, but for some reason he failed in his efforts to establish himself in that business. Later, he was engaged in the bank note engraving business with Terry and Pelton, and when that firm was absorbed by another company, Smith resumed the general engraving business with two of his former pupils, Knight and Tappan. G. G. Smith engraved portraits chiefly, in both line and stipple, and he did some good work. Died in 1878, in Boston.

SMITH, GEORGE ROBERT JR.
Painter. Born New York City, Sept. 1889. Pupil of ASL of NY, and West End School of Art; George Elmer Browne. Member: Provincetown AA; S. IN. A.; Bronx AG. Address in 1929, 340 East 198th St., Bronx, New York, NY.

SMITH, GEORGE W(ASHINGTON).
Painter and architect. Born East Liberty, PA, Feb. 22, 1879. Studied in Paris and Rome; Architectural School, Harvard Univ. Member: Paris AAA; NAC; Calif. AC; AIA. Address in 1929, 17 Mesa Road, Santa Barbara, CA.

SMITH, GERTRUDE ROBERTS.
Painter, craftsman, and teacher. Born Cambridge, MA, May 11, 1869. Pupil of MA Normal Art School; Chase School; Colarossi Acad., Paris. Member: SSAL; Boston ACS; NOAA; NOACC; Needle and Bobbin C. Award: gold medal, NOAA ($150), Delgado Art Museum. Address in 1929, H. Sophie Newcomb College, New Orleans, LA.

SMITH, GLADYS K.
Painter, sculptor, and teacher. Born Philadelphia, PA, April 30, 1888. Pupil of Phila. School of Design; PAFA. Member: Fellowship PAFA; Plastic C.; Alumni, Phila. School of Design; Eastern AA. Instructor in art, Shaw Junior High School, West Philadelphia. Address in 1929, 5108 Springfield Ave., Philadelphia, PA; summer, Locust Valley, LI, NY.

SMITH, GRACE P.
Painter and illustrator. Born Schenectady, NY. Member: GFLA.

868

Address in 1929, 144 West 11th St.,
New York, NY.

SMITH, HARRIET F(RANCES).
Painter. Born Worcester, July 28,
1873. Pupil of MA Normal Art
School, Denman W. Ross, E. W. D.
Hamilton, Henry B. Snell, C. H.
Woodbury, Philip Hale. Member:
Worcester Art Students' C.; Copley
S.; Eastern Art Assoc.; NYWCC; AFA.
Art Supervisor, Boston Public
Schools. Died in 1935. Address in
1929, 120 Glenville Ave., Allston,
MA.

SMITH, HARRY KNOX.
Painter. Born in Philadelphia, in
1879. Pupil of Penna. Acad. of
Fine Arts; Art Students' League of
NY. Member of NY Architectural
League, 1910. Address in 1926, 601
West 151st Street, New York, NY.

SMITH, HASSEL.
Painter. Born April 24, 1915, in
Sturgis, MI. Earned BS from
Northwestern, taught there and at
SF State, U. of Oregon and
Berkeley. Award Abraham Rosenberg
fellowship, 1941. Exhibited at
Cal. Palce (SF); SF Art Inst.; New
Arts (Houston); S. F. State
College; Whitney; S. F. Mus. of Art
(1976). In collections of Wash.
U.; Tate; Albright Knox; Baltimore;
Pasadena Art Mus.; Whitney;
SUNY/New Paltz and Corcoran.

SMITH, HELEN L.
Painter, craftsman, and teacher.
Born Frederick, Jan. 21, 1894.
Pupil of Maryland Inst. Member:
Frederick AC. Work: "Justice,"
owned by Frederick County, MD.
Address in 1929, 311 North Market
St.; h. McCardell Apts., Frederick,
MD.

SMITH, HENRY PEMBER.
Landscape painter. Born in
Waterford, CT, on Feb. 20, 1854.
He painted New England scenes and
views of Venice; these were his
most frequent subjects. He was a
member of the American Water Color
Society and the Artists Fund
Society of NY. He died Oct. 16,
1907, in Asbury Park, NJ.

SMITH, HENRY T.
A portrait and genre painter of
Phila. He was a member of the
Artists Fund Society and chairman
of its Ex. Committee in 1867. Was
regular exhibitor at the Phila.
Acad., 1861-67. Painted portraits
of Henry C. Carey at the Penna.
Historical Society, and of Jos.
Harrison, Philadelphia.

SMITH, HEZEKIAH WRIGHT.
Engraver. Born in Edinburgh,
SC, in 1828. He disappeared from
Phila. in 1879 and was never heard
of afterward. Smith was brought to
NY when about 5 yrs. old, and was
later apprenticed to an engraver
there. He continued his studies
under Thomas Doney and became a
most meritorious engraver of
portraits, in line and in stipple.
In 1850 he was associated with Jos.
Andrews in Boston, and employed in
NY, 1870-77. In 1877 Smith
established himself in Phila. and
did work there; in April, 1879, he
suddenly abandoned engraving, sold
all his effects, and left that city
and was never heard of again. His
more important plates are a full
length portrait of Dan Webster,
after the painting by Chester
Harding; a three quarter length of
Edward Everet; and his head of
"Washington" after the Athenaeum
head, by Stuart; this latter is
said to be the best engraving of
this famous portrait ever made.

SMITH, HOLMES.
Painter, teacher, writer, and
lecturer. Born Keighley, England,
May 9, 1863. Member: St. Louis
AG; Coll. AA; 2x4 S; AFA.
Professor of drawing and history of
art, Washington Univ., St. Louis.
Specialty, water colors. Died
before 1940. Address in 1929,
Washington Univ.; h. 5440 Maple
Ace, St. Louis, MO.

SMITH, HOPE.
Painter. Born Providence, RI, May
10, 1879. Pupil of Woodbury,
Chase, RI School of Design and
studied in Paris. Member: Prov.
AC. Specialty, landscapes in oil
and water color. Address in 1929,
165 Hope St., Providence, RI.

SMITH, HOWARD EVERETT.
Painter and teacher. Born West
Windham, NH, April 27, 1885. Pupil
of Howard Pyle and E. C.Tarbell;
ASL of NY. Member: ANA, 1921;
Boston GA; Boston AC; Rockport AA;
North Shore AA. Awards: Paige
Traveling Scholarship, School of
the Museum of Fine Arts, Boston;
bronze medal for painting, P.-P.
Exp., San F., 1915; first
Hallgarten prize, NAD, 1917; Isidor
Medal, NAD, 1921; Peabody prize,
AIC, 1923. Work: "Portrait of
Col. W. H. Osborn," Treasury Bldg.,
Washington; "Portrait of Ex-Gov.
Eugene Foss," State House, Boston,
MA. Address in 1929, Art Studio
Bldg., 31 Newbury St.; h. 186
Commonwealth Ave., Boston, MA;
summer, 11 High St., Rockport, MA.

SMITH, ISABEL E.
(Mrs. F. Carl Smith). Miniature
painter. Born Smith's Landing.
near Cincinnati, OH. Pupil of
L'hermitte, Delance and Callot in
Paris. Member: Paris Woman's AC;
Pasadena Fine Arts C. Died in
1938. Address in 1929, 217 Oakland
Ave., Pasadena, CA.

SMITH, ISHMAEL.
Painter, sculptor, and illustrator.
Born Barcelona, Spain, July 16,
1886. Member: Salma. C. Works:
Monument to Pablo Torull, Caja de
Ahorros de Sabadell, Catalunya;
Portrait of Mila Y Fontanals, Inst.
des estudie Catalans; Portrait of
Alphonse Maseras and group in
sculpture, Museum of Barcelona,
Spain. Represented in British
Museum, London; Hispanic Musuem,
New York; Cleveland Museum;
"Blessed Teresa," Carmelite
Fathers, Washington, DC. Address
in 1929, 260 Riverside Drive, New
York, NY.

SMITH, J. ANDRE.
Etcher and painter. Award: Gold
medal for etching, P.-P. Exp., San.
F., 1915. Member: Brooklyn SE.
Address in 1929, Care of Arthur E.
Harlow Co., 712 Fifth Ave., New
York, NY; Pine Orchard, CT.

SMITH, J. FRANCIS.
Painter and teacher. Born in
Chicago. Pupil of Gregori,
Boulanger, Lefebvre, and Constant.

Member: Paris AAA, Chicago SI; CA
AA. Address in 1929, 290 East 72d
St., New York, NY.; summer, Dublin,
NH.

SMITH, JACK W(ILKINSON).
Painter. Born Paterson, NJ, 1873.
Studied at Cincinnati Art Academy
and AIC. Member: CA AC; CA C;
Allied AA; Salma. C.; Laguna Beach
AA. Awards: Silver medal, San
Diego Exp., 1915; bronze medal, San
Diego Exp., 1916; silver medals,
Sacramento Exp., 1917 and 1918;
first prize, Los Angeles Liberty
Exp., 1918; Black prize, CA AC,
1919; gold and bronze medals,
Sacramento Exp., 1919; second
prize, Phoenix, AZ, Exp., 1920;
first prize, Phoenix AZ, 1922.
Represented in Phoenix Municipal
collection. Died in 1949. Address
in 1929, 16 Champion Pl., Alhambra,
CA.

SMITH, JACOB GETLAR.
Painter. Born New York City, Feb.
3, 1898. Pupil of NAD. Award:
Hon. mention, AIC, 1926. Died in
1958. Address in 1929, Care of
Guaranty Trust Co., Paris, France.

SMITH, JAMES CALVERT.
Illustrator. Member: SI; GFLA;
Salma. C. Address in 1929, 114
East 56th St., New York, NY.

SMITH, JAMES P.
Miniature portrait painter. Born
in 1803, and resided in
Philadelphia. He died in
Philadelphia, in 1888.
Comtemporary with Thomas Sully. He
attained great proficiency in his
art. Sully invariably sought his
approval of portraits he painted
before he let them leave his
studio. He painted several
miniatures of Washington, after the
portraits painted by Gilbert
Stuart.

SMITH, JESSIE WILLCOX.
Painter, and illustrator. Born
Philadelphia. Pupil of PAFA;
Drexel Inst. under Howard Pyle.
Member: Plastic C.; Phila. WCC:
Fellowship PAFA; SI 1904 (assoc.);
NY WCC; Phila. Alliance; AFA.
Awards: Bronze medal, Charleston
Exp., 1902; Mary Smith prize, PAFA
1903; silver medal, St. Louis Exp.,

1904; Beck prize, Phila. WCC 1911; silver medal water colors, P.-P. Exp., San F., 1915. Specialty, paintings and illustrations of children. Died in 1935. Address in 1929, "Cogshill," Allen Lane, Philadelphia, PA.

SMITH, JOHN RUBENS.
Engraver. Born Jan. 23, 1775, in London, England. Tuckerman, in his "Book of the Artists," says that John Rubens Smith was the son of the famous English engraver John Raphael Smith (1740-1811). John R. Smith was working as an engraver in Boston in 1811, and in 1816 he was in NY, painting portraits, engraving, and conducting a drawing school. He remained in NY until 1826, and then possibly went to Phila. as he was engraving and teaching drawing in that city in 1835-37. He again appears in NY in 1845 and once more opened his school. Among his known pupils were Sully, Agate, Cummings, Leutze and Swain R. Gifford. In noting his death the Historic Annals of the National Acad. of Design describes Smith as "Short in figure, large head, one sided gait and an expression of countenance." As engraver he worked in stipple, aquatint and mezzotint, chiefly upon portraits, and he was an experienced engraver. Died Aug. 21, 1849, in NYC.

SMITH, JOSEPH LINDON.
Painter, lecturer, and teacher. Born Pawtucket, RI, Oct. 11, 1863. Pupil of Boston Museum School under Crowninshield and Grundmann; Julian Acad., in Paris under Boulanger and Lefebvre. Member: Mural P.; Boston SAC; Copley S. 1882; Century Assoc.; AFA. Award: Beck Prize, Phila. WCC, 1905. Work: Mural paintings in Boston Public Library and Horticultural Hall, Philadelphia. Made studies from sculpture in Italy, Egypt, Turkey, Mexico, Guatemala, Java, India, China, Sudan, Cambodia, Siam, Greece, Honduras, Yucatan and Japan for Museums in US. Represented in Corcoran Gallery and Smithsonian Inst., Wash.; Chicago Art Inst.; Boston Mus.; Harvard Univ.; Rhode Island School of Design; Gardner Collection, Boston; Dartmouth College; Fogg Art Museum, Cambridge, MA, Musee Guimet, Paris; Louvre School, Paris. Died 1950 in Dublin, NH. Address in 1929, 132 East 72d St., New York, NY; summer, Dublin, NH.

SMITH, KATHARINE ENGLISH.
Painter. Born Wichita, KS, March 12, 1899. Pupil of Emma M. Church, Birger Sandzen, Charles Hawthorne, Robert Reid; George B. Bridgman. Member: Wichita AA; Smoky Hill AC. Address in 1929, 520 North Lorraine St., Wichita, KS.

SMITH, MARCELLA.
(Claudia Heber). Painter and teacher. Born East Molesey, Surrey, England, March 6, 1887. Pupil of Delecluse in Paris; Fred Milner at Royal British Acad. in London; Corcoran School of Art, Washington; Phila. School of Design. Member: A. R. B. A.; S. Wash. A. Address in 1929, 1320 New Hampshire Ave., Washington, DC.

SMITH, MARGERY HOFFMAN.
Painter and craftsman. Born Portland, OR, Aug. 30, 1888. Pupil of F. G. Wentz, K. H. Miller, A. B. Dow, Herman Rosse. Member: Port. AA; Port. ACS. Address in 1929, 705 Davis St., Portland, OR.

SMITH, MARSHALL J.
Native of New Orleans. Died in Covington, LA. Studied under R. Clague. Specialty, Lousiana landscapes and portraits. Represented in Louisiana State Museum, New Orleans, LA.

SMITH, MAY MOTT.
See Mott-Smith.

SMITH, MINNA WALKER.
Painter. Born New Haven, March 29, 1883. Pupil of Yale School of Fine Arts. Member: New Haven PCC; New Haven BPC; NYWCC; AFA. Address in 1929, 531 Edgewood Ave., New Haven, CT.

SMITH, OLIVER PHELPS.
Painter. Born Hartford, CT, Dec. 18, 1867. Pupil of NAD. Member: NYWCC. Specialty, stained glass and mural decoration. Died in 1953. Address in 1929, 550 East Lincoln Ave., Mt. Vernon, NY;

summer, CT Valley, Middlesex Co., CT.

SMITH, R. K.
Engraver. A weak stipple portrait of Rev. John Flavel is signed "Engraved by R. K. Smith from an Original." This plate appears as a frontispiece to "The Fountain of Life Opened, Etc.," by Rev. John Flavel, and it was published by Joseph Martin, Richmond, VA, 1824. No other example of the work of the engraver has been found.

SMITH, ROSAMOND L.
See Bouve, Rosamond S.

SMITH, RUSSELL.
Painter. Born April 26, 1812, in Glasgow, Scotland. Came to this Country in 1819 and studied art with Jas. R. Lambdin, and father of Alfred C. Lambdin, the well known local journalist. For 6 yrs. after 1834 he worked at the Chestnut and Walnut St, Theaters as a scene painter, but after his marriage to a fellow artist he took to landscape painting in which he met with great success and became noted as a scientific draughtsman. Later employed by Sir Chas. Lyell and other naturalists, and did similar work for geological surveys of PA and VA. When the Acad. of Mus. was in the process of building the foremost structure of its type in Am. he was engaged to paint scenery, and the drop curtain which he produced, with its handsome landscape, brought him many commissions of the sort from Managers in this and other cities. His "Cave at Chelten Hills" was admired at the Centennial Expo. Died Nov. 8, 1896 in PA.

SMITH, SHARON.
Painter and graphic-artist. Studied: Calif. State Univ. at Long Beach, Calif. Exhibitions: San Luis County Art Show, 1968; Honolulu Academy of Art, 1974; Hallway Gallery, Bishop Museum, Hawaii, 1975. Collections in the City and County of Honolulu.

SMITH, SIDNEY L.
Engraver, painter, and etcher. Born Foxboro, MA in 1845. In 1847 his father moved to Canton, MA. In

1863, Sidney L. Smith was placed with Reuben Carpenter, a commercial engraver, to learn that business; but in the early part of 1864 Mr. Smith enlisted in the Union army and saw some service at the close of the Civil War. Upon returning to peaceful pursuits, he entered the engraving estabishment of Jos. Andrews, in Boston. Smith and Thomas D. Kendricks reproduced on steel the original etchings, and the original woodcuts as well, issued in England for an edition of Dickens' works. As Mr. Andrews was not an etcher and had little liking for this class of work, the young men were left much to their own devices in a task which occupied them for about $2\frac{1}{2}$ yrs. Upon the completion of this work Smith opened an engraving establishment of his own, and for some time was engaged with such work as he could secure. In 1877 Mr. John LaFarge, who had previously tried to induce Mr. Smith to abandon engraving for painting, invited the latter to assist him in the decoration of Trinity Church, in NY, and as an assistant to Mr. LaFarge, Mr. Smith was engaged in this work until 1883; from then on and until 1887 he was chiefly employed in the designing of stained glass windows and in work of decorative character. In 1887 Mr. Smith made some etchings for Mr. Clarence Cook, and finding that other desired work of a similar character he has continued etching and designing for engraver, produced exceptionally good and artistic work as an etcher, his experience along this line was confined to the early part of his professional career, and covers a comparatively brief period.

SMITH, T. HENRY.
A portrait and genre painter of Philadelphia. He was a member of the Artists' Fund Society, and Chairman of its Exhibition Committee in 1867. He was a regular exhibitor in the Penna. Acad. exhibitions from 1861-67.

SMITH, THOMAS HERBERT.
Painter. Born New York City, Oct. 31, 1877. Pupil of George Bellows. Member: NAC; Brooklyn SA;

872

Silvermine GA; S. Indp. A.; Salons of America; AFA; New Rochelle AA. Address in 1929, Wilton, CT.

SMITH, THOMAS LOCHLAN.
Painter. Born Dec. 2, 1835, in Scotland. He came to this country at an early age, and was pupil of George H. Boughton in Albany, NY. He devoted himself chiefly to painting winter scenes. His "Deserted House" and "Eve of St. Agnes" were exhibited at the Centennial in Philadelphia, 1876. He died Nov. 5, 1884 in NYC.

SMITH, THOMAS M.
Painter. A portrait of Maria Catherine Smith was painted by Captain Thomas Smith in 1683. It belongs to the Clapp family of Dorchester, MA.

SMITH, TWIGG.
Painter. Born in Nelson, New Zealand, in 1882. Pupil of Art Inst. of Chicago; also of Harry M. Walcott. Member of Hawaiian Society of Artists; Chicago Art Students' League. Address in 1926, 122 Bates St., Honolulu, Hawaii.

SMITH, VIOLET THOMPSON.
Miniature painter. Born Annapolis, MD, July 28, 1882. Pupil of Archambault. Member: Alliance. Address in 1929, 100 Kings Highway, West Haddonfield, NJ.

SMITH, W. HARRY.
Painter, illustrator, and etcher. Born Brent Devon, England, Dec. 23, 1875. Member: Boston SWCP; Chicago SE; Boston SAC; Whistler AC. Award: Prize, Chicago SE, 1926. Address in 1929, Concord Road, Billerica, MA.

SMITH, W. LINFORD.
Painter. Born in Pittsburgh, PA, in 1869. Pupil of Chris Walters. Member of Pittsburgh Artists Association. Address in 1926, 5029 Amderson Place, Pittsburgh, PA.

SMITH, W(ALTER) GRANVILLE.
Painter, and illustrator. Born S. Granville, NY, Jan. 26, 1870. Pupil of Walter Satterlee, Carrol Beckwith, Willard Metcalf, ASL of NY; studied in Europe. Member: ANA 1908; NA 1915; AWCS; Salma. C.,

1918; SPNY; Allied AA; Greenwich SA; NAC; AFA; Grand Cent. A. Gal. Awards: Third Hallgarten prize, NAD, 1900; bronze medal, Charleston Exp., 1902; Evans prize, AWCS, 1905; first prize, Worcester, 1906; hon. mention, CI Pitts., 1907; Inness gold medal, NAD, 1908; bronze medal, Buenos Aires Exp. 1910; Vezin prize, Salma. C., 1911; Shaw purchase prize ($500), Salma. C., 1913; Hudnut prize ($200), AWCS, 1916; Isidor prize, Salma. C., 1918, Turnbull prize, 1922, Auction exh. prize, 1925; prize ($300) and bronze medal, 1925, NAC; Carnegie prize ($500) NAD, 1927; Purchase prize, ($1,000) Salma. C., 1928; second Altman prize, NAD, 1929. Work: "Grey Day," Smithsonian Inst., Wash., DC, "The Willows," Butler Art Inst., Youngstown, OH; "South Haven Mill," Museum, Toledo, OH; permanent collections, Salmagundi Club, National Arts Club, Lotos Club, Fencers Club of New York, and Art Club of Philadephia. Address in 1929, 96 Fifth Ave., New York, NY; Bellport, LI, NY.

SMITH, WILLIAM.
Engraver. In 1840 William Smith is referred to as a partner of David McClelland, general engravers and copperplate printers, of Washington, DC. No signed work by William Smith is known to the compiler, and it is possible that he was only the printer of the firm.

SMITH, WILLIAM A.
Illustrator. Born in Toledo, OH, in 1918. Studied art in Toledo, Paris, and NY. At the age of 13, he began his career as an illustrator working for the San Francisco Chronicle. His reputation as a print- maker, muralist, and painter began with national advertising assignments in the early 1940's. In 1943 he began working for magazines, especially Cosmopolitan, and later illustrated books by Pearl Buck and Carl Sandburg as well as designing a number of US postage stamps. His works are in the collections of the Metropolitan Museum of Art, LC, and Los Angeles County Museum.

873

SMITH, WILLIAM D.
Engraver. Born c. 1800. In 1829 this capital line engraver was working in Newark, NJ, and he was possibly a pupil of Peter Maverick. From 1835 to 1850 Wm. D. Smith was in business as a general engraver in NYC.

SMITH, WILLIAM GOOD.
Portrait painter in oils and miniatures, who flourished 1844-1846 in NY.

SMITH, WUANITA.
Painter and illustrator. Born Philadelphia, Jan. 1, 1866. Pupil of PAFA; Phila. School of Design for Women and Howard Pyle. Member: Plastic C.; Fellowship PAFA; Alliance; AFA. Award: Hon. mention, Wilmington AA. Illustrated: "The Four Corner Series," "The Admiral's Granddaughter," "Grimm's Fairy Tales," "Gulliver's Travels," "Washington Square Classics," etc. Address in 1929, 1905 Pine St., Philadelphia, PA.

SMITHBURN, FLORENCE BARTLEY.
Painter and teacher. Born New Augusta. Pupil of William Forsyth; John Herron Art School, Indianapolis. Member: Hoosier Salon; IN. AA. Awards: Two second prizes, Indiana State Fair, 1929; water color prize, Hoosier Salon, Chicago, 1929. Address in 1929, New Augusta, IN.

SMITHER, JAMES (3rd).
Engraver. Born in 1772; died in 1793. There is some difficulty in disentangling these 2 names. The evidence of the existence of a "James Smither, 3rd" (signed Jr.), lies in the occurrence of this name among the professional members of the Phila. Assoc. of Artists, organized on Dec. 28, 1794, and plates of birds so signed are among the illustrations in Dobson's edition of Rees' Encyclopedia, published in Phila. in 1794-1803. In the same work, however, plates almost identical in character are signed "James Smither" and "James Smither, Jr." The directories make no distinction between father & son and give no clue. James Smither the 3rd, son of James Smither, died

during the yellow fever epidemic in Phila. in 1793, the father outliving the son for 36 yrs., hence the confusion in the dates of their work.

SMITHER, JAMES.
Engraver. According to data available, this engraver in line, was born in Eng. in 1741; he first appears in this country in Phila. in 1768, when he was engraving for Robt. Bell, a publisher and book seller of that city. He advertised his business as follows in the Penn. Journal of 1768: "James Smither Engraver. At the 1st house in 3rd St., from the Cross Keys, corner of Chestnut St, Phila. Performs all manner of Engraving in gold, silver, copper, and steel and all other medals: coats of arms and seals, done in the neatest manner. Likewise cut stamps, brands and metal cuts for printer, and ornamental tools for book binders. He also ornaments guns and pistols, both engraving & inlaying silver, at the most reasonable rates." This advertisement would seem to justify the tradition that he was originally an ornamenter of guns and a gunsmith, working in the Tower of London previous to his arrival in Phila. He did considerable engraving for Robert Bell, mentioned above; also engraved bookplates and bill heads, and he is credited with having engraved the plates for some of the paper money of the province of PA, and having counterfeited this money for the use of the enemy during the British occupation of Phila. A proclamation was issued by the Supreme Executive Council of PA, on June 25, 1778, accusing Smither and others having "Knowingly and willingly aided and assisted the enemies of this state and the US " and declaring all of them "attainted with high treason." Smither evidently left Phila. with the British troops, as he was working for Hugh Gaine in NY in 1777, and he advertises himself as an engraver, "late of Phila.," in Rivington's Royal Gazette of May, 1779. He returned to Phila., as in 1786 he was engraving for publishers of that city. Died Sept, 1797, in Phila.

SMITHWICK, J. G.
Wood engraver, who worked for Harper's and Scribner's; he afterwards formed a partnership with Frank French.

SMYTH, MARGARITA PUMPELLY.
Painter. Born Newburgh, NY, in 1873. Pupil of Abbott H. Thayer. Address in 1926, Belmont St., Watertown, MA.

SMYTH, S(AMUEL) GORDON.
Landscape painter, mural draftsman, illustrator, and craftsman. Born Holmesburg, Phila., PA, Nov. 21, 1891. Pupil of H. Lachman, W. H. Everett. Work: Series of historical ptgs. in Nat'l. Shawmut Bank, Boston; illustrations for Saturday Evening Post, Collier's. Address in 1929, 2442 Linden Dr., Merwood Park, Upper Darby, PA; summer, Conshohocken, PA.

SNEAD, LOUISE W(ILLIS).
(Mrs. Harry Vairin Snead). Miniature painter, illustrator, writer, and lecturer. Born Charleston S. C. Pupil of Chase; ASL of NY. under Theodora Thayer; studied in Palestine and Egypt. Awards: Hon. mention, Charleston Exp., 1902; prize for seal for a South Carolina city in 1915; first prize for miniatures at Mineola, LI, 1911 and 1912. Work: Portrait of "Capt. Henry M. Shreve," Shreveport (LA) Memorial Library; "Rebecca Mott," D. A. R. Bldg., Charleston, SC. Author and producer of Oriental rugs and Fine Arts. Author and illustrator of "History of Stamford, Conn.;" "Silver and Gold," for Stamford Trust Co. Illustrator of "Suburban Life of Stamford" for Stamford Chamber of Commerce, 1919. Address in 1929, Hotel Brevoort, New York, NY; "Ye Olde King's Highway," Noroton, CT.

SNELGROVE, WALTER H.
Painter. Born in Seattle, Washington, March 22, 1924. Study: Univ. of Washington, 1941-43; Calif. Sch. of Fine Arts, with Hassel Smith, Antonio Sotamayor, James Weeks; Univ. of Calif., Berkeley. BA 1947, MA 1951, with James McCray, M. O'Hagen. Work:

Whitney, NYC; Oakland (CA) Mus.; Calif. Palace of Legion of Honor; others. Exhib.: Carnegie Inst.; Art Inst. of Chicago; Whitney; Albright-Knox, Buffalo, NY; Calif. Palace; others. Awards: Oakland Mus.; San Fran. Mus. of Arts; Calif. Palace of Legion of Honor. Mem.: San Fran. Art Assoc. Address in 1976, Berkeley, CA.

SNELL, FLORENCE FRANCIS.
(Mrs. Henry B. Snell). Painter. Born London, England. Pupil of ASL of NY. Member: NYWCC; AWCS; NA Women PS; NAC. Awards: McMillin landcape prize, NA women PS, 1913; NAC prize, NA Women PS. 1915. Died Jan. 20, 1946. Address in 1929, New Hope, PA.

SNELL, HENRY B(AYLEY).
Marine painter and teacher. Born Richmond, EN, Sept. 29, 1858. Pupil of ASL of NY. Member: ANA 1902; NA 1906; NYWCC; AWCS; SAA 1905; Salma. C., 1903; Lotos C.; Fellowship PAFA 1916; NAC.; Allied AA. Awards: Gold medal, AC Phila., 1896; 1st prize, Nashville Exp., 1897; hon. mention, Paris Exp., 1900; silver medal, Pan Am. Exp., Buffalo, 1901; silver medal, St. Louis Exp., 1904; first prize, Worcester Mus., 1905; Beal prize, NYWCC 1905; silver medal for oil painting and gold medal for water color, P. P. Exp., San F., 1915; hon. men., Phila. AC., 1916; Shaw Purchase Prize, Salma. C., 1918. Assistant dir. of Fine Arts. U.S. Comm., Paris Exp., 1900. Work: "The Citadel at Quebec," Albright Art Gal., Buffalo; "Entrance to the Harbor of Polperro," Worcester Mus.; "Nightfall," Herron Art Inst., Indianpolis; "Lake Como," Metropolitan Mus., NY; "The Windjammer," Harrison Gal., LA, Mus. Died Jan., 1943. Address in 1929, New Hope, PA.

SNOWDEN, ELSIE BROOKE.
Painter. Born Ashton, MD, March 4, 1887. Pupil of Corcoran School of Art, Washington, DC; PAFA. Award: Cresson Traveling Scholarship, PAFA, 1914. Specialty, figure. Address in 1929, 2200 16th St., N.W., Washington, DC; Ashton, MD.

SNVERNIZZI, PROSPER.
Sculptor, who exhibited in the Penna. Acad. of the Fine Arts, Phila., 1926. Address in 1926, 500 West 178th Street, New York City.

SNYDER, CLARENCE W.
Painter. Born Philadelphia, PA, March 10, 1873. Member: PAFA; Drexel Inst.; Fellowship PAFA. Phila. AC. Address in 1929, Barker Bldg., 1520 Chestnut St.; h. 5016 Hazel Ave., Philadelphia, PA.

SNYDER, CORYDON G.
Painter, sculptor, illustrator, etcher, writer, and teacher. Born Atchison, KS, Feb. 24, 1879. Member: Palette and Chisel C. Author of course in fashion illustration published by Federal Schools of Minneapolis; "Modern Advertising Arrangement," "Pen and Ink Technique," pub. by Myer Booth College, Chicago; "Retouching Not Difficult;" "Marriage from the Standpoint of Art." Address in 1929, 1935 South Michigan Ave., h. 245 W. North Ave., Chicago, IL.

SNYDER, HENRY W.
Engraver. Snyder was engraving in NY in 1797-1805, and in 1811 he made some good stipple portraits for the "Polyanthus," of Boston. He usually signed his plates "Snyder," but one plate, published in Boston in 1807, is signed as above. As "H. W. Snyder" he also made a number of the line illustrations in "The American Builder's Companion," published in Boston in 1816.

SOBLE, JACK.
Painter, etcher, and teacher. Born Russia, Jan. 14, 1893. Pupil of Charles C. Curran and Francis C. Jones. Work: Character Studies of Maurice Schwartz, Yiddish Art Theatre Galleries. Address in 1929, Clinton Bldg., 107th West 47th Ave., Bronx, NY; summer, Totem Lodge, Averill Pk., Albany, NY.

SODERBERG, YNGVE EDWARD.
Etcher. Born Chicago, IL, Dec. 21, 1896. Member: Chicago SE. Work: Etching, "Jibbing Around Buoy," AIC. Address in 1929, Mystic, CT.

SODERSTON, HERMAN.
Painter. Born in Sweden, July 12, 1862. Pupil of Royal Acad. of Fine Arts, Stockholm. Member of New Haven Paint and Clay Club; Society of Independent Artists. Represented in Memorial Hall, Hartford; Sheffield Scientific Hall, New Haven, CT. Address in 1926, 840 Chapel St., New Haven, CT. Died July 3, 1926 in New Haven, CT.

SOELLNER, OSCAR D(ANIEL).
Painter, and etcher. Born Chicago, IL, April 8, 1890. Member: Chicago Palette and Chisel C; Chicago PS; Austin, Oak Park and River Forest AL; AFA; Am. APL; IL. AFA; All-IL SA. Work: "River Wharf," public schs. of Oak Park and River Forest; Heroes Mem., Oglesby, IL; "Deserted Farm," State Capitol Bldg., Springfield, IL. Address in 1929, Grand Detour, Dixon, IL; h. 31, Keystone Ave., River Forest, IL.

SOHIER, ALICE RUGGLES.
Painter. Born Quincy, MA, Oct. 21, 1880. Studied in Buffalo; School of Boston Museum of Fine Arts under Tarbell; and in Europe as holder of Paige Traveling Scholarship. Member: Boston GA; Concord AA. Award: Bronze medal, P.-P. Exp., San F., 1915. Address in 1929, Concord, MA.

SOKOLSKY, SULAMITH.
Painter. Born in NY in 1889. Pupil of Cooper Union of the National Academy of Design, New York. Address in 1926, 2103 Vyse Ave., Bronx, New York, NY.

SOLDWEDEL, FREDERIC.
Painter. Born in 1886. Painter of Marine and yachting subjects. His water colors of yachts are considered his best works.

SOLOMON, MAUDE BEATRICE.
(Mrs. Joseph Solomon). Painter, sculptor, and illustrator. Born Seattle, Wash., June 6, 1896. Pupil of Liberty Todd, Hugh Breckenridge. Member: Fellowship PAFA. Illustrated "Aristocrats of the North." Address in 1929, 54 Second Ave., South, Mt. Vernon, NY.

SOLOMON, ROSALIND.
Photographer. Born in Highland Park, IL, in 1930. Studied: Goucher Coll. and with Lisette Model in NYC. Awards: Hunter Mus. of Art, 1974; Atlanta Arts Festival, 1974; AR Fine Arts Center, 1971; Exhibitions: Birmingham Museum of Art, AL, 1975; Neikrug Galleries, NYC, 1975; Slocumb Gallery, Johnson City, TN, 1975. Her one-person show, Israel: Radishes and Roses, toured the eastern US. Collections: Mus. of Mod. Art, NYC; Met. Mus. of Art, NYC; AR Fine Arts Center. She is noted for her photographs of Union Depot, Chattanooga, Tenn. and First Monday, Scottsboro, Alabama.

SOLOMON, SYD.
Painter. Born July 12, 1917 at Uniontown, PA. Studied at L'Ecole des Beaux Arts, Paris (1945), also at Inst. of Chi. (1934). Taught at Ringling School of Art; directed Famous Artists School; taught at U. of Ill. and Fine Arts Inst. at Sarasota. Rec. Ford Found. Purchase Award (1965); Audubon Artists (gold medal, 1957); 1st prize, Fla. State Fair; awards from Am. Inst. of Architects and Silvermine Guild. Exhibited at Lowe Art Gallery, Coral Gables, FL; Stetson Univ.; U. of Fla.; AM. Fed. of Arts, NYC; MMA; Mus. Fine Arts, Houston; U. of IL; Art Inst. of Chi.; NY Coliseum (1959); Boca Raton Center for Arts; Genesis Gallery, NYC and McDowell Gal., Toronto. In collections at Baltimore; Wadsworth Phil. Mus. of Art; Brandeis; Ryder Col., (Trenton, NJ); Whitney; Adelphia U.; Mead Corp. and Butler Inst., Youngstown.

SOLON, HARRY.
Painter. Born San Francisco, June 5, 1873. Pupil of Calif. School of Design, San Francisco; AIC; Julian Acad. in Paris; Henri Royer; Richard Miller. Member: AFA. Work: "Portrait of Dr. Bennett Mitchell," Capitol Building Des Moines; also at Morningside Univ., Sioux City. Address in 1929, 1 West 67th Street, New York, NY.

SOLON, LEON VICTOR.
Portrait and mural painter; also illustrator. Born in England in 1872. Member of National Sculpture Society, and Society of Mural Painters. Address in 1926, 16 East 41st Street, New York.

SOMERBY, J. E.
Engraver. The only record of this man as an engraver is found in the "American Coast Pilot," by Capt. Lawrence Furlong, edited by Edmund M. Blunt, Newburyport, 1804. He engraved two or three maps in this work, the rest being engraved by A. M. Peasley.

SOMMER, EDWIN G.
Painter, illustrator, etcher, and craftsman. Born Roseville, NJ, June 29, 1899. Pupil of William Sommer. Member: Kokoon AC. Awards: First prize for illustration, second prize for water color, 1923, and second prize for illustration, 1924. Cleveland Museum of Art. Work: "The Shower," "The Return" and "The Castle on the Moon," Cleveland Museum of Art; "The Lost Prince," Cleveland Public Schools; mural decoration in the Embassy Club, Cleveland. Address in 1929, 2121 East 21st St.; h. Elderhood Ave., East Cleveland, OH; summer, Route No. 3, Macedonia, OH.

SOMMERS.,
He painted "Westward Ho! or Crossing the Plains." It is now in the Capitol, Washington, DC.

SONN, ALBERT H.
Painter and illustrator. Born Newark, NJ, Feb. 7, 1867. Pupil of NAD. Member: Salma. C., 1900; AWCS; A. Fund S; NYWCC; AFA. Author: "Early American Wrought Iron." Died in 1936. Address in 1929, 282 Parker St., Newark, NJ.

SONNICHSEN, YNGVAR.
Painter, illustrator, etcher, and teacher. Born Christiania, Norway, March 9, 1875. Graduate of Polytechnic School of Christiania, Norway, in mechanical engineering, 1894. Studied in Antwerp, Brussels; at Julian's under Bouguereau and Constant in Paris. Member: Board of Fine Arts, Christiania, Norway; Seattle Art Inst.; AFA. Awards: 1st prize International Exhibition, St. John,

877

N. B., Canada, 1906; gold and silver medals, Alaska-Yukon-Pacific Exp., Seattle, 1909; hon. mention, Northwest Artists Annual Exp., Seattle, 1920. Decorations for Norway Hall, Seattle; portraits in municipal galleries of Christiania, Arendal, and Laurvik, Norway; Free Mason's Lodge, St. John, N. B., Canada; "The Moon, Alaska," Vanderpoel AA, Chicago; Norwegian Club, Brooklyn, NY. Died in 1938. Address in 1929, 520 13th Ave., North, Seattle, Wash.

SONTAG, WILLIAM L.
Landscape painter. Born March 2, 1822 near Pittsburgh, Penna. He was elected an Associate Member of the National Academy in 1860 and an Academician two years later. His principal works are "Morning in the Alleghenies;" "View on Licking River, KY;" "Sunset in the Wilderness;" "Fog rising off Mount Adams" and "Spirit of Solitude." He died Jan. 22, 1900, in NYC.

SOOY, LOUISE PINKNEY.
Painter, writer, lecturer, and teacher. Born Blairstown, IA, Aug. 9, 1889. Pupil of Arthur W. Dow. Member: Calif. PS; The Seven, Honolulu; Arthur Wesley Dow Assoc.; Pacific AA. Author of articles on art education for "Dark and Light." Address in 1929, 855 Vermont Ave., Los Angeles, Calif.; h. 2013 Pelham Road, Sawtelle, CA.

SOPER, J. H. GARDNER.
Painter. Born in Flint, MI, in 1877. Awarded bronze medal, Louisiana Purchase Exposition, St. Louis, 1904. Address in 1926, 12 Gramercy Park, New York, NY.

SOPER, RICHARD F.
Engraver. Born c. 1810 in England. This meritorious engraver of portraits in stipple was employed by NY publishers as early as 1831; he worked largely for J. C. Buttre, of the same city, at a later period. Died c. 1862.

SOREL, EDWARD.
Illustrator. Born in NYC in 1929. Attended Cooper Union and began his career as a founding member of Push Pin Studios in 1953. Five years later he started free-lancing as a political satirist and his work has appeared in Ramparts, Esquire, Atlantic, Time, and New York Magazine, for the last of which he is a contributing editor. He has done several books and illustrates weekly in the Village Voice. In 1973 Cooper Union awarded him their Augustus St. Gaudens Medal for professional achievement.

SORENSON-DIEMAN, CLARA LEONARD.
Sculptor. Born in Indianapolis, IN, in 1877. Pupil of Lorado Taft and Victor Brenner. Member: Chicago Society of Artists; Indiana Society of Artists; Alumnae, Chicago Art Inst. Work: Memorial Tablet, Shortridge High School, Indianapolis; Memorial Tablet YMCA., Cedar Rapids, IA. Address in 1926, 1800 Second Ave., Cedar Rapids, IA.

SOTHERN, E. A.
Painter. "Alpine View" was painted by the elder Sothern (actor), and presented by him to Alfred Sutliffe, editor of the San Francisco Chronicle.

SOTTEK, FRANK.
Painter, illustrator, etcher, and writer. Born Toledo, OH, Oct. 10, 1874. Member: Artklan; Toledo Federation of Art Societies. Award: First prize, Toledo Fed. of Art Societies, 1924. Died in 1939. Address in 1929, 381 South Detroit Ave., Toledo, OH.

SOTTER, GEORGE W.
Painter and craftsman. Born Pittsburgh, Sept. 25, 1879. Pupil of Chase, Anshutz, Redfield, H. G. Keller. Member: Pittsburgh AA.; CT. AFA.; Salma. C; Fellowship PAFA. Awards: Silver medal, P. P. Exp., San. F., 1915; first prize, Pittsburgh Asso. Artists, 1917; art society prize, Pittsburgh Asso. Artists, 1920; hon. mention, CT AFA., 1921; Flagg prize, CT AFA, 1923; hon. mention, CT. AFA, 1926. Works: "The Hill Road," Reading Museum "Pennsylvania Country," State College, State College, PA. Stained glass windows in church of Our Lady of Lourdes, New York; St. Agnes Church, St. Pauls Monastery, Sacred Heart Church, Pittsburgh; Kenrick Seminary, St. Louis; St.

Mark's Church, St. Paul; St. Mary Magadalene Cathedral, Salt Lake City; St. Joseph's Cathedral, Wheeling, W. VA; New Jersey State Museum, Trenton. Died in 1953. Address in 1929, Holicong, Bucks Co., PA.

SOUDEIKINE, S(ERGE) (YURIEVICH).
Painter, illustrator, and teacher. Born Russian in 1886. Pupil of Moscow Art School; St. Petersburg Imp. Academy. Member: Mir Isskustva, Salon D'Automne Union; Russian A. Work: "Les Fiancees de Moscow," Luxembourg Museum, Paris; "Promenade Landscape," Morosoff Gallery, Moscow, etc. Mural decorator and scenic artist. Died in 1946. Address in 1929, 1 W. 67th St., New York, NY.

SOULEN, HENRY J.
Illustrator. Born in Milwaukee, WI, in 1888. Studied at the Chicago Academy of Fine Arts and later with Howard Pyle. He illustrated for most of the major magazines and received the Peabody Award for his magazine cover designs. During World War II he gave free art lessons to veterans at the Valley Forge Military Hospital. His illustrations were known for their strong patterns and rich colors.

SOUTHER, LYNA CHASE.
(Mrs. Latham T. Souther). Painter, sculptor, and writer. Born St. Louis, MO, Oct. 14, 1880. Pupil of Edmund Wuerpel, Boris Lovatt-Lorski, Klasstorner. Member: Springfield AA; Il. AFA. Address in 1929, 1825 South Fifth St., Springfield, IL.

SOUTHWARD, GEORGE.
Landscape, still life, portrait and miniature painter. Born in 1803. Studied in Boston under Ames, and accompanied that artist to Rome. At one time he was a pupil of Thomas Sully. On his return from his studies abroad he settled in Salem, MA, and died there Feb. 19, 1876.

SOUTHWARD, NATHANIEL.
Miniature painter. Born Jan 8, 1806 in Scituate, MA. He worked in Boston 1842-48, visited Europe and

on his return lived in NY and PA. (The name is sometimes spelt "Southworth.") Died April 25, 1858 in Dorchester, MA.

SOUTHWICK, JEANIE LEA.
Painter, teacher, writer, and lecturer. Born Worcester. Pupil of ASL of NY; Boston Museum of Fine Arts School. Member: Alumni, Boston Museum of Fine Arts School; AFA; Corp. memb. Worcester Art Mus. Lecturer on Arts and Crafts of Japan, Java, etc. Specialty, water colors. Address in 1929, 6 Home Street, Worcester, MA.

SOUTHWICK, KATHERINE.
Painter and illustrator. Born Buxton, ME, Jan. 9, 1887. Pupil of Chicago Acad. of FA; AIC; PAFA. Member: Fellowship PAFA. Awards: Cresson traveling scholarship, PAFA, 1911-1913. Address in 1929, 50 Gramatan Ave., Mt. Vernon, NY; summer, 646 Church St., Stevens Point, WI.

SOUTHWORTH, F(RED) W.
Painter. Born Canada, Feb. 7, 1860. Self taught. Member: Tacoma FAA; North West AA.; Chicago Brush and Palette C. Work: "Sunlight on the Sea," Ferry Museum, Tacoma. Died in 1946. Address in 1929, 609 North I St., Tacoma, WA.

SOUTHWORTH, NATHANIEL.
See Southward, Nathanial. Born Jan. 8, 1806 in Scituate, MA. Died April 25, 1858.

SOUTHWORTH, WILLIAM.
An American painter whose name is mentioned by writers on art in this country about 1850.

SOYER, MOSES.
Painter. Born on Dec. 25, 1899, Borisglebsk, South Russia. Emigrated to US with her family in 1913, settling in Phil., PA, then NYC. Studied at Cooper Union, Nat. Acad. of Design Sch. of Art with George W. Maynard; the Ferrer Art Sch. with Robert Henri and George Bellows; Educational Alliance Sch. of Art. Taught at Ed. Alliance Sch. of Art, New Art Sch. and New Sch. for Soc. Res., from 1927-34. Exhibitions were held at Kleenman

Galleries, NY in 1936; Boyer Gallery, Phil., PA, in 1936, 1937; Little Gallery, Wash., DC, in 1939-40; Reading Mus. 1968; Albrech Gallery Mus. of Art, St. Joseph, MO, in 1970; Loch Haven Art Center, Orlando, FL, in 1972. Publ.: Author of Painting the Human Figure, 1964. Died in 1974.

SOYER, RAPHAEL.
Born in Russia, Dec. 25, 1899. Studied at the Art Students' League under Guy Pene du Bois, at Cooper Union and at the National Academy. One-man show was held in 1929. Major retrospectives at the Whitney Museum of American Art and at Associated American Artists, both in 1967, and at the National Collection of Fine Art, 1977. Awards: W. A. Clark Prize from the Corcoran Gallery of Art in Washington, DC, the Temple Gold Medal from the Pennsylvania Academy of Fine Arts, the Kohnstann Prize and the Harris Gold Medal from the Art Institute of Chicago. Taught painting, Art Students' League, Am. Art Sch., New Sch. Soc. Research.

SPACKMAN, CYRIL (SAUNDERS).
Painter, etcher, and architect. Born Cleveland, Ohio, Aug. 15, 1887. Pupil of Henry A. Keller in Cleveland; Kings College Architectural Studio, London. Member: R.S.B.A.; RS. Min. P; R.S. of Antiquaries of Ireland; F.S. of Antiquaries of Scotland; F.R.S.A.; So. Eastern Soc. Arch. Institute of America; Fellow, Member of Council, Art Advisor of the Inc. Association of Architects and Surveyors. Represented in Cleveland Museum; Chicago Art Inst.; Print Room of the British Museum; Permanent collection of the City of Hull. Designed medal of Masonic Million Memorial. Art Editor of "The Parthenon." Address in 1929, 29 Blake Road, East Croydon, Surrey, England.

SPADER, WILLIAM EDGAR.
Painter and illustrator. Born Brooklyn, NY. Pupil of H. Siddons Mowbray, Joseph H. Boston. Member: AWCS; Brooklyn PS; Brooklyn SA. Work: "For the Feast," Museum of Art, Fort Worth, Texas. Address in 1929, 32 Union Square, New York, NY; h. 22 Lake St., Jamaica, NY.

SPAETH, CAROLA HAUSCHKA (MRS.).
Portrait painter. Born Philadelphia, PA, April 29, 1883. Pupil of PAFA; Graphic Sketch C., Phila. Member: Fellowship PAFA; Phila. Alliance. Specialty, children. Died in 1948. Address in 1929, 1819 Green St., Philadelphia, PA.

SPAETH, MARIE HAUGHTON.
(Mrs. J. Duncan Spaeth). Painter. Born Hanover, NH. Pupil of PA FA; PA. School of Design; studied in Spain, France, and Italy. Member: Fellowship PAFA (hon.); NA Women PS; Catherine L. Wolfe AC; AFA. Specialty portraits of children. Work: "Apennine Village," PA Acad. of the Fine Arts; portrait of Dr. Theodore Hunt, Princeton Univ. Died in 1937. Address in 1929, 32 Edgehill Street, Princeton, NJ.

SPAFARD, MYRA B.
Painter and teacher. Born Manchester. Pupil of ASL., Teachers College, and Mrs. E. M. Scott in NY. Member: NA Women PS. Address in 1929, 2181 Hulbert Ave., Detroit, MI; and Manchester, MI.

SPALDING, ELISABETH.
Landscape painter. Born Erie, PA in 1870. Pupil of ASL of NY; PAFA. Member: Wash. WCC; NYWCC; Erie AC; Providence WCC; AFA. Awards: First prize, Erie Art C., 1900; C. E. Kremer prize for water color, AIC, 1921. Work: "Rain," Erie (PA) Art Club; "Twilight Shower, Manoach," Denver Art Association. Died in 1954. Address in 1929, 853 Washington St., Denver, CO.

SPALDING, GRACE.
Painter, who exhibited at the Penn. Acad. of the Fine Arts, Phila., 1924. Address in 1926, New York City.

SPANFELLER, JAMES JOHN.
Illustrator. Born in Phila., PA, in 1930. Studied at the Phila. College of Art and Penn. Academy of Fine Art. His first published illustration appeared in Seventeen in 1956. He has worked for most major magazines and illustrated

over 40 books. He was voted Artist of the Year in 1964 and has received Gold Medals from the ADCs of NY and Wash., and the S of I, where he is a member. He won the New York Herald Tribune Children's Book Award and was also nominated for the National Book Award . He currently teaches at PSD.

SPARHAWK-JONES, ELIZABETH.
Painter. Member: Fellowship PAFA. Awards: Mary Smith prize, PAFA 1908 and 1912; honorable mention, CI Pittsburgh, 1909; Mary Smith prize, PAFA, 1912; Kohnstamm prize ($250), AIC, 1926. Work: "Shop Girls," Art Inst. of Chicago. Address in 1929, 2046 Rittenhouse St., Philadelphia, PA.

SPARK, JOSEPH.
Painter, illustrator, and etcher. Born Jersey City, NJ, Dec. 23, 1896. Pupil of Percy Ives, Paul Honore, Leon Kroll; AIC. Member: Scarab C. Address in 1929, Scarab Club, 217 Farnsworth; h. 8724 Smart Street, Detroit, MI.

SPARKS, ARTHUR WATSON.
Painter. Born in Washington, DC, in 1870. Studied at Julien Academy and Ecole des Beaux Arts, Paris, France, under Laurens, Cormon, Bouguereau, Thaulow, Mucha, Ferrier and Courtois. Exhibited at Paris Salon; Carnegie Inst.; Penna. Acad. of the Fine Arts; National Acad. of Design; Art Institue, Chicago; Corcoran Gallery, etc. Awarded bronze medal, San Francisco Expo., 1915; 2d prize, Associated Artists of Pittsburgh. Principal works: "The Steel Mills;" "Under the Birches;" "Grand View Arizona Canyon;" "Clemance and Cora;" "The Model at Rest;" etc. Professor of painting at Carnegie Inst. Member of Associated Artists of Pittsburgh. Died Aug. 6, 1919 in Phila. PA.

SPARKS, H. L.
Illustrator. Member: SI. Address in 1929, National Park Bank, 214 Broadway, New York, NY.

SPARKS, WILL.
Painter, etcher, writer, and lecturer. Born St. Louis, Mo., Feb. 7, 1862. Pupil of St. Louis

School FA, and Julian Acad. in Paris. Member: Bohemian C., San F.; AFA. Work: Murals: "The Home," Bohemian Club, San F.; "Delores," and "Cypresses," Plaza Hotel, San F.; "Stormy Day," Golden Gate Park Museum, San Francisco; oil paintings: "A Christmas Allegory," Bohemian Club, San. F.; "Soledad Mission," Toledo Art Museum; a portrait in St. Louis Museum. Died in 1937. Address in 1929, 163 Sutter Street, Room 408, San Francicso, CA.

SPARROW, LOUISE KIDDER.
(Mrs. Herbert George Sparrow). Sculptor, and writer. Born Maplewood, Malden, MA, Jan. 1, 1884. Pupil of Eric Pape, Bush Brown, Ulric Dunbar, Frederick Allen, Bela Pratt. Member: S. Wash. A. Work: Bust of Capt. James F. Gilliss, US Government; statue of Col. Archibald Gracie, IV, Museum of the City of NY. Author of "The Last Cruise" of the U.S.S. Tacoma. Address in 1929, 1661 Crescent Place., N.W., Washington, DC.

SPARROW, THOMAS.
Engraver. Born C. 1746. Plates for Maryland paper money, issued in 1770-74, are conspicuously signed "T. Sparrow, Sculp." Sparrow also engraved upon copper the title page to The Deputy Commissary's Guide of Maryland, published by Anne Catherine Green & Son, Annapolis, MD, 1774. Sparrow was chiefly a wood engraver, and thus made book plates, head and tailpieces, bill heads, etc. He was located in Annapolis, MD, and Mr. Charles Dexter Allen, in his "American Book Plates," says that he worked there between 1765-80. This same man was apparently employed in Boston at a possibly earlier date, judging solely from the period of the designer, after whom he engraved a somewhat curious advertisement for the music dealer, John Ashton, of 197 Washinton St., Boston.

SPAULDING, GRACE.
(Mrs. A. M. John). Painter and etcher. Born Battle Creek, MI, Feb. 10, 1890. Member: Tiffany Foundation. Work: "Spring Comes to Bayou," Houston Museum; portrait

of "Miss Aloysius Larchmiller,"
State Capitol, Oklahoma City.
Address in 1929, 1306 Barbee Ave.,
Houston, TX.

SPAULDING, HENRY P(LYMPTON).
Painter. Born Cambridge, MA, Sept.
16, 1868. Pupil of Ross Turner and
Blummers. Member: Boston AC;
Copley S; AFA. Address in 1929, 32
Salisbury Road, Brooklin, MA;
summer, Grapevine Road, East
Gloucester, MA.

SPEAKMAN, ANNA W(EATHERBY PARRY).
(Mrs. T. Henry Speakman).
Illustrator. Born Springfield, IL.
Pupil of PAFA. Member: Fellowship
PAFA; Plastic C.; NA Women PS;
Phila. Alliance. Died in 1937.
Address in 1929, 524 Walnut St.,
Philadelphia, PA.

SPEAKMAN, ESTHER.
A portrait painter of Philadelphia
exhibiting about 1843-61. Daughter
of John Speakman. She painted a
portrait of John Speakman, half
length. He was Treasurer of the
Academy of Natural Sciences,
Philadelphia, PA.

SPEAR, ARTHUR P(RINCE).
Painter. Born Washington, DC,
1879. Pupil of Laurens in Paris.
Member: ANA; St. Botolph C; Allied
AA; Boston GA. Awards: Silver
medal, P. P. Exp.,San F., 1915;
Altman prize, NAD, 1921. Died in
1959. Address in 1929, Fenway
Studios, 30 Ipswich St., Boston,
MA; h. 156 Winchester St.,
Brooklin, MA.

SPEICHER, EUGENE E.
Painter. Born Buffalo, NY, April
5, 1883. Studied in Buffalo, NY,
and Europe. Member: ANA, 1912;
NA, 1927; Portrait painter; NAC;
Comtemporary; Int. S. Painters,
Gravers and Sculptors; New Soc. A.
Awards: Proctor prize, NAD, 1911;
Isidor portrait prize, Salma. C.,
1913; third Hallgarten prize, NAD,
silver medal, P.-P. Exp., San F.,
1915; Beck gold medal, PAFA, 1920
third class medal, 1921; second
class medal, 1922, Carnegie Inst.;
Potter Palmer gold medal ($1,000),
AIC, 1926. Work: "Morning Light,"
Metropolitan Museum, NY; "Mountain

Landscape," Art League, Galveston,
TX; "Portrait of an Old Lady,"
Decatur (IL) Museum; "Mille. Jeanne
Balzac," Cleveland Museum of Art;
"Portrait of a Girl," Phillips
Memorial Gal., Washington, DC;
"Portrait of Katherine Cornell,"
Albright Art Gallery, Buffalo.
Died in 1962. Address in 1929, 165
East 60th St., New York, NY, and
Woodstock, NY.

SPEIGHT, FRANCIS.
Painter. Born in 1896. Exhibited
in Penna. Acad. of the Fine Arts,
Philadelphia, 1926. Address n
1926, The Penna. Acad. of the Fine
Arts, Philadelphia.

SPELLMAN, COREEN MARY.
Lithographer. Born in Forney, TX
in 1909. Studied: Texas State
College for Women; Columbia Univ.;
Art Students League; Univ. for
Women; Columbia Univ.; Art Students
League; Univ. of Iowa; and with
Charles Martin. Awards: West
Texas Art Exhibition, 1940, 1942,
1945, 1946; Univ.of Iowa, 1942;
Texas Printmaker Exhibition, 1942,
1943, 1945; Texas Fine Arts Assoc.,
1943, 1945; Texas General
Exhibition, 1943; Dallas Museum of
Fine Arts, 1951; Southern State Art
League, 1944.

SPELMAN, JOHN A.
Painter. Born Owatonna, MN, Sept.
30, 1880. Pupil of AIC. Member:
Chicago PS; Chicago SA: Palette and
Chisel C; Chicago AG; Oak Park and
River Forest A. Lg.; Chicago Gal.
A.; Duluth AL; All-Ill, SFA; IL.
Acad. FA. Awards: Englewood
Woman's Club prize ($100), AIC,
1926; two prizes ($300) Chicago
Gal. A., 1927, and prize ($250),
1928; gold medal, Ass. Chic. P. and
S., at AIC; first prize, Chicago
Galleries Assn. ($1,000) 1929.
Represented in the collections of
the Springfield Art Asso., the
Chicago Athletic Club, and the
Univ. of Nebraska. Address in
1929, 731 Woodbine Ave., Oak Park,
IL; summer, Spruce Point Lodge,
Hovland, MN.

SPENCELEY, J. WINFRED.
Engraver. Born in Boston, MA, in
1865; living there in 1905. Mr.
Spenceley learned to engrave with

J. A. Lowell & Co., of Boston, and was with that firm in 1882-87, doing lettering, ornamental steel and copper plate engraving with the intention of devoting himself to bank-note work. At the same time he attended the art school of Tomasso Juglaris, in Boston. In 1887 he went into business, and while perfecting himself in freehand drawing he took up etching. In 1901-03 he was with the Western Bank Note Co., of Chicago, and he was later associated with the bank note company of E. Bouligny, of the city of Mexico. While in the employ of J. A. Lowell & Co., Mr. Spenceley worked upon several bookplates, including one for Oliver Wendell Holmes. The freedom of design and the variety incidental to book-plate work appealed to him, and he later made a specialty of this branch of engraving, designing as well as engraving the plates. Among the more important book plates made by Mr. Spenceley may be noted the following: The plate for the Boston Public Library and those for Harvard, Dartmouth, Michigan, Ohio State, and Missouri universities. He has also designed and engraved about 150 plates for other libraries and for private individuals. A descriptive catalogue of Mr. Spenceley's book plates has been published by W. P. Tonesdell, Boston, 1905.

SPENCER, ASA.
Engraver. Born c. 1805 in New England; died in England in 1847. Spencer was a member of the bank-note engraving firm of Murray, Draper, Fairman & Co. of Phila. He invented a process for applying lathe work to bank-note engraving, made improvements in the medal-ruling machine, and introduced other devices connected with the manufacture of bank notes. As mentioned in the note on Gideon Fairman, he accompanied Fairman and Perkins to England in 1817. But Spencer retured to Phila., and later he published a few book illustrations made by his medal-ruling machine.

SPENCER, EDNA ISBESTER.
Painter, sculptor, and lecturer. Born 1883 in St. John, N. B., Canada. Pupil of Bela Pratt, Robert Aitken. Award: Hon. mention, Concord AA., 1919; Paris Salon, 1929. Address in 1929, 17 Park Ave., New York, NY; h. 1454 Beacon St., Brookline, MA.

SPENCER, FREDERICK R.
Painter. Born in Madison County, NY, on the 7th of June, 1806. His parents were from the New England states; his father, General Ischabod S. Spencer from MA, and his mother from CT. Mr. Spencer experienced the usual boy's inclination to imitate prints, and at the age of 15, being with his father in Albany, saw, for the 1st time, a gal. of portraits. In 1825, he came to NY to study, where he drew from the casts of the Am. Acad., and had the favor of the Pres., and received instruction in the methods he was to pursue. In 1827 commenced painting professionally at a village in the neighborhood. He painted for a time in Utica, NY; but finally made the city of NY his heaquarters where he continued painting until his death. Among his portraits, he painted Henry A. Ingalls; Robert Hunter Morris and Frances L. Morris, painted in 1838. Member of Nat. Acad. in 1846. Died April 3, 1875, in Wampoville, NY.

SPENCER, H(ENRY) C(ECIL).
Painter and teacher. Born Mangum, OK, March 5, 1903. Pupil of Ernest Blumenschein; ASL of NY. Member: SSAL; Am. APL. Work: "Blind Beggar," Sociology Dept., Baylor Univ., Waco; "Portrait of Dr. S. P. Brooks," Baylor Univ., Waco; "Portrait of Dr. A. J. Armstrong," Browning collection, Waco. Address in 1929, 1700 South 12th, Waco, TX; summer, College Station, TX.

SPENCER, HOWARD B(ONNELL).
Painter. Born Plainfield, NJ. Pupil of F. V. DuMond, ASL of NY., A. P. Lucas and Walt Kuhn. Member: Barnard C.; Salma. C. Address in 1929, 1292 Madison Ave., New York, NY; summer, Sound Beach, CT.

SPENCER, HUGH.
Illustrator and craftsman. Born
St. Cloud, MN, July 19, 1887.
Pupil of C. S. Chapman, H. Dunn,
A. Covey. Member: Boston SAC;
Phila. ACG. Died in 1975. Address
in 1929, Chester, CT.

SPENCER, JOB B.
Painter of fruit, flowers and
animals. Born in Salisbury, CT, in
1829. He settled in Scranton, PA.

SPENCER, JOSEPH B.
Actually Spencer, Job B. See entry.

SPENCER, MARGARET F(ULTON).
Painter and artist. Born in
Philadelphia, Sept. 26, 1882.
Pupil of Birge Harrison, Robert
Spencer. Work: "Still Life and
Flowers," Alexander Simpson
Collection, Philadelphia, PA.
Address in 1929, New Hope, PA.

SPENCER, MARY
Painter and teacher. Born
Fitchburg, MA. Pupil of Herbert
Adams, Henry B. Snell, Arthur Dow,
and Richard Miller; Pratt Inst.
Member: NA Women PS; Alliance; AFA.
Died in 1923. Address in 1929,
1062A Sterling Palce, Brooklyn, New
York, NY.

SPENCER, MARY.
Painter. Born in Springfield, OH,
in 1835. Pupil of C. T. Webber in
Cincinnati. Member of Cincinnati
Woman's Art Club. Work: "Fruit,"
Cincinnati Museum. Address in
1926, 3612 Woodbridge Place,
Cincinnati, OH.

SPENCER, MRS.
In Tuckerman's "Book of the
American Artists" he notes that a
Mrs. Spencer was painting genre
subjects with decided merit.

SPENCER, NILES.
Painter. Born Pawtucket, RI, May
16, 1893. Pupil of RI School of
Design, also studied in NY and
Paris. Represented in the Newark
Museum; Phillips Memorial Gallery,
Washington, DC; Albright Memorial
Gallery, Buffalo, NY. Died in
1952. Address in 1929, The Daniel
Gal., 600 Madison Ave., New York,
NY.

SPENCER, ROBERT.
Painter. Born Harvard, NE, Dec. 1
1879. Pupil of Chase, DuMond
Henri and Garber. Member: AN
1914; NA 1920; Salma. C.; NA
(life); Century Assoc. Awards
Second Hallgarten prize, NAD 1913
Phila AC; Sesnan medal, PAFA 1914
Inness medal, NAD 1914; Boston A
medal and purchase prize, ($1,000)
1915; P.-P. Exp., San F., 1915
Norman Wait Harris bronze medal
AIC, 1919; hon. mention, Carnegie
Inst., 1920; Altman prize ($500)
NAD, 1920 and 1921; Member
Purchase prize, Salma. C., 1921
Mrs. Wm. K. du Pont prize ($100)
Wilmington SFA, 1921; gold medal
NAD, 1928; gold medal, Phila. AC
1928. Work: MMA; Boston Art Club
Detroit Inst. of Arts; AIC
National Arts Club, NY; Corcoran
Salma. C.; Brooks Memorial
Memphis; NAD; Phila. Art Club
Carnegie Inst.; Brooklyn; Newark
Albright; Society of Fine Arts
Wilimington, DE; and Phillips Mem
Gal., Wash. Died in 1931. Address
in 1929, New Hope, Bucks Co., PA.

SPENCER, W. H.
This engraver of landscapes, i
line, was working in NY in 1825.

SPERRY, REGINALD T.
Landscape painter and designer
Born in Hartford, CT, in 1845. I
1874 he moved to Brooklyn, NY.

SPERRY, THEODORE S.
Landscape painter. Born i
Bozrahville, CT, in 1822. H
painted theatrical scenery, an
lived for years in Hartford, CT
Died c. 1878 in Hartford, CT.

SPICER-SIMSON, THEODORE.
Painter and sculptor. Born Havre
France, June 25, 1871. Studied i
England and Germany and at th
Ecole des Beaux Arts in Paris
Member: Soc. Nationale des Beau
Arts, 1928; Century Association
NSS, 1911. Awards: Highest awar
for medals, Brussels Exp., 1911
and Ghent Exp., 1915; bronze meda
for medals, P.-P. Exp., San F.
1915. Work in: Metropolitan Museur
and Numismatic Museum, NY; Chicag
Art Inst.; Detroit Inst.; MN Mus
of Art; City Mus. of Art, St.
Louis; the Luxembourg, Paris

Victoria and Albert Musem, London; in Holland, Belgium, Germany, Austria, and Czecho-Slovakian Museums. Died in 1959. Address in 1929, 7 West 43rd St., New York, NY; 3 rue Campagen premiere, Paris, France; 3803 Little Ave., Coconut Grove, Florida.

PICUZZA, FRANCESCO J.
Painter. Born in Sicily, July 23, 1883. Member: NYWCC; WI PS. Awards: Bronze medal, St. Paul Inst., 1915; silver medal, St. Paul Inst., 1917; Snyder prize, WI PS., 1919; gold medal ($100), Milwaukee Art Inst., 1922. Represented in St. Paul (MN) Inst.; Milwaukee (WI) Art Inst. Address in 1929, University Bldg.; h. 500 31st Ave., Milwaukee, WI.

SPIERS, HARRY.
Painter. Born Selsea, Sussex, England, Oct. 15, 1869. Pupil of Julian Academie in Paris. Member: Boston SWCP; Boston AC; Dedham ACS. Work: "As the Sunlight Bursts," Boston Museum of Fine Arts; "At the Trough" and "Passing of an Autumn Day," Ontario Government Gallery, Toronto. Address in 1929, 30 Pemberton Sq., Boston, MA; 150 Cedar St., Dedham, MA.

SPINGARN, AMY.
(Mrs. J. E. Spingarn). Painter. Born in NY, Jan. 29, 1883. Pupil of K. H. Miller. Member: S. Indp. A. Address in 1929, 9 West 73rd St., New York, NY; summer, Amenia, NY.

SPITZMILLER, WALTER.
Illustrator. Born in St. Louis, MO, in 1944. Attended Wash. Univ. He began his career there and in 1974 was awarded a gold medal from St. Louis ADC. His editorial work has appeared in McCall's, Redbook, Golf Digest, and Sports Illustrated. Exhibitions of his work have been held in colleges in Quebec City, Atlanta, St. Louis, and in the S of I Annual Exhibition. He presently lives in CT.

SPIZZIRRI, LUIGI.
Painter. Born Spezzano, Grand Prov. of Cosenza, Italy, Oct. 23, 1894. Pupil of Chase, Emil Carlsen,

Vonnoh, Pearson, Daniel Garber, Philip Hale. Member: Fellowship PAFA. Address in 1929, Grand Fraternity Bldg., 1626 Arch St.; h. 825 Wharton St., Philadelphia, PA; summer, Summerdale Park, Camden, NJ.

SPOLLEN, CHRIS JOHN.
Illustrator. Born in NYC, in 1952. Studied at PSD. His first job was an etching for Crawdaddy magazine in 1973. Awards for his work include the Society of Publication Designers Award of Merit, Second Place in the S of I Scholarship Competition and Second Place in the Staten Island Museum Spring Show. Illustrating for Redbook, Viva, Emergency Medicine as well as other major publications, he has shown his work in many galleries in the NY area.

SPRAGUE, FLORENCE.
Sculptor, and teacher. Born Paullina, IA. Pupil of Charles Mulligan, Albin Polasek. Member: IA AC; Des Moines AFA. Work: "Frog Mountain," Des Moines Water Works; bas-relief, "Harvest," Public Library, Des Moines. Head of Art Dept., Drake University. Address in 1929, Department of Fine Arts, Drake University; h. 3200 Pleasant St., Des Moines, IA.

SPRAGUE-SMITH, ISABELLE DWIGHT.
(Mrs. Charles Sprague-Smith). Painter and teacher. Born Clinton, NY, Nov. 11, 1861. Pupil of ASL of NY; studied in Paris. Member: MacD.C.; Archeol. S. of Am. Died in 1951. Address in 1929, 133 East 40 St., New York, NY; h. Anchor to Windward, Seal Harbor, ME.

SPREAD, HENRY FENTON.
Painter. Born in Ireland, in 1844. He studied and travelled in England, Germany and Australia, and in 1870 he came to the United States. He had his studio in Chicago, where he founded "Spread's Art Academy." Among his works are "Chicago Arising from her Ashes" and "Sad News."

SPRINCHORN, CARL.
Painter. Born Broby, Sweden, May 13, 1887. Pupil of Robert Henri. Member: Brooklyn S. Modern S; S.

Indp. A; Salons of America. Represented in Brooklyn Museum. Died in 1971. Address in 1929, 600 Madison Ave., New York, NY.

SPRING, EDWARD ADOLPHUS.
Sculptor. Born in New York City, in 1837. He studied with Henry K. Brown and William Rimmer. He modelled with great success many terra cotta panels. He established the Perth Amboy Terra Cotta Co. and the Eagleswood Art Pottery.

SPRINGER, CARL.
Painter. Born Fultonham, OH, Nov. 4, 1874. Pencil C. of Columbus. Awards: Prize, Scarab C., Detroit, 1916; hon. mention., Ohio State Exp., 1920; first prize, Columbus Art Lg., 1920; second prize, Columbus A. Lg., 1924; Pitts Flateau prize, Columbus A. Lg., 1926. Represented in Gal. of Fine Arts, Columbus, OH. Died in 1935. Address in 1929, Brevort, MI.

SPRINGER, EVA.
Painter. Born in 1882, in Cimarron, NM. Pupil of W. H. Foote, and Kenneth H. Miller in NY; Delecluse and Mem. LaForge and Richard Miller in Paris. Member: Wash. WCC; NA Women PS.; Brooklyn S. Min. P.; PBC; NAC. Died in 1964. Address in 1929, The Dresden, Washington, DC; h. East Las Vegas, NM.

SPRUANCE, BENTON M.
Born in 1904 in Phil., PA. Attended the University of Pennsylvania and the Pennsylvania Academy of Fine Arts. Founding member of the Philadelphia Chapter of Artists Equity. Served on the City of Philadelphia Arts Commission from 1953 until his death. In 1928 and 1929 he was awarded the Cresson Travelling Scholarship by the Pennsylvania Academy of Fine Arts; in 1950 and 1962-63 received grants from the Guggenheim Foundation. Taught at Beaver College and the Philadelphia College of Art. Exhibitions: Pennsylvania Academy of Fine Arts and the Philadelphia Museum of Art shortly following his sudden death.

SPRUNGER, ART(HUR) (L.).
Painter. Born Berne, IN, April 25 1897. Pupil of Wm. Forsyth Member: Hoosier Salon; Northern IN AL. Awards: Hon. mention Artists' League of Northern IN South Bend, 1929; first prize Friends of Art, South Bend, 1929 Address in 1929, 213 Cottage Ave. Goshen, IN.

SQUIRE, JACK.
Sculptor. Born Feb. 27, 1927, i Dixon, IL. Earned B.S. from Indiana U. (1950); MFA from Cornel (1952). Taught at UC/Berkeley, a Cornell since 1952. Exhibited a Alan Gal., NYC (many; 1956-1968) Cornell; Art Inst. of Chicago MOMA; PAFA; Everson Mus. Syracuse Addison Gal (Andover); Carnegie Munson Williams Proctor; Brussel' World's Fair (1958); and Bosto Arts Festival. In collections o Whitney; Cornell; Stanford; MOM and private collections.

SQUIRE, MAUD H(UNT).
Painter, etcher, and illustrator Born Cincinnati, OH. Pupil o Cincinnati AC. Member: NY WCC Chicago SE; Societe du Salo d'Automne, Paris. Work "Concarneau Fisherman" and "At th Well," Herron Art Inst. Indianapolis; South Kensingtor Museum, London; Corcoran Gallery Washington, D.C. Address in 1929 Vence, Alp. Mar., France.

SQUIRES, C. CLYDE.
Illustrator. Born Salt Lake City Aug. 29, 1882. Pupil of Henri Miller, DuMond, Mora and Pyle, N Sch. of Art. Member: GFLA; S 1911. Published first illustr. i 1906 for Life magazine; worked wit Woman's Home Companion, Wester Romances, Western Monthly. Best known for romantic depiction of the West. Died in 1970. Address i 1929, 48 Morton St., New York, NY summer, Little Neck, LI, NY.

ST. CLAIR, GORDON.
Painter, who exhibited "Pavilion o the Moon," Penna. Acad. of the Fine Arts, 1915, Philadelphia. Addres in 1926, 26 Studio Building Chicago, IL.

T. JOHN, J.
Painter and illustrator. Born in Chicago in 1872. Pupil of Art Students' League of NY under Mowbray, Beckwith and Du Mond. Member of Chicago Society of Artists. Address in 1926, Tree Studio Building, Chicago, IL.

T. JOHN, J. ALLEN.
Painter and illustrator. Born Chicago, IL. Pupil of ASL of NY under Mowbray, Chase, Beckwith and DuMond, and Jean Paul Laurens in Paris. Member: Chicago PS; Cliff Dwellers; Chicago Gal. A. Instructor, Art Institute of Chicago, and Business Men's Art Club of Chicago. Address in 1929, Tree Studio Bldg., Chicago, IL.

T. JOHN, LOIA ALBERTA.
Painter. Born in Albany, IN, in 1879. Pupil of H.R. McGinnis; at Cin. Art Acad. under Nowottny and Meakin; under J. O. Adams and Brandt Steele at Indianapolis. Member of Indianapolis Artists Assoc.; Muncie Artists Assoc.; Alliance; Indiana Art Club. Award: Hon. mention, Muncie Artists Assoc. Work: "October Morning," Montpelier, IN, Lib. Address in 1926, Miltanna Garden, Albany, IN.

T. MEMIN, CHAS. BALTHAZAR JULIEN F.
Engraver. Born March 12, 1770, in Dijon, France. At the outbreak of the French Rev. he went to Switzerland; then to Canada in 1793, and soon after he came to NY. As a means of supporting himself in this country he introduced here the engraving of portraits by means of the "Physionotrace," a machine invented by Edme Queneday, of Paris, and intended to exactly reproduce on a reduced scale, the human profile. St. Memin made some improvements upon this device, and with it he made on a tinted paper a profile a little less than life size; this he finished by hand and with crayons directly from the sitter. Drawing as a guide he used a pantograph of special design to still further reduce the profile so that it would go inside a circle of about 2" in diameter, faintly scratching the reduced drawing directly on the copperplate. This copper was now etched and finished in aquatint, with some assistance with the roulette. The result was a soft, pleasing print. For the original crayon, which was ready for framing, for the plate, and for 12 impressions from the plate St. Memin charged $33. These small portraits became very popular, and St. Memin, traveling from North to South over the country, produced about 800 of them. He kept for himself 2 sets of proof impressions; after his death these sets were purchased from his executors and are now in the US, one in the Corcoran Gal. in Wash., DC, and the other was lately in the hands of a Phila. collector. Besides these portraits, St. Memin etched 2 large views of the city of NY, a map of the siege of Savannah, published in The Monthly Military Repository, C. Smith, NY, 1796, and a beautiful etched business card of Peter Mourgeon, "Copperplate printer from Paris," of NY. Died June 23, 1852.

STACEY, ANNA LEE.
(Mrs. John F. Stacey). Painter. Born Glasgow, MO. Pupil of AIC; Delecluse Acad., Paris. Member: Chicago PS; Chicago WCC. Awards: Young Fortnightly prize, AIC 1902; Cahn prize, AIC 1902; $200 prize, Field Exh., 1907; Carr Landscape prize, Chicago SA 1912; Logan bronze medal, AIC, 1921. Work: "A Spanking Breeze," Chicago Woman's Club; "Moonlight in the Guidecca Venice," Kenwood Club, Chicago; "Trophies of the Fields," Union Lg. Club, Chicago; Chicago Art Commission purchase, 1914 and 1924. Address in 1929, 6 East Ohio St.; Studio Bldg., Ohio and State Sts., Chicago, IL.

STACEY, J. GEORGE.
Painter. Born Fayette, NY, Feb. 8, 1863. Pupil of ASL; Charles W. Hawthorne, Susan Ricker Knox. Member: Rochester AC; AFA. Awards: First popular award, 1927, and second popular award, 1928, Rochester, NY. Address in 1929, 112 Jay Street, Geneva, NY.

STACEY, JOHN FRANKLIN.
Painter and teacher. Born Biddeford, ME, 1859. Pupil of MA

Normal School in Boston; Boulanger, Lefebvre and Julian Acad. in Paris. Member: Chicago PS; Cliff Dwellers. Awards: Bronze medal, St. Louis Exp., 1904; $100 prize, Field Exh., 1907; bronze medal, Buenos Aires, 1910; Grower prize, AIC 1911; Logan medal, AIC, 1924; Municipal A. Lg. purchase prize, $500, AIC, 1928. Work: "Church Spires of a New England Village," Museum of Fine Arts, Santiago, Chile; "Across the Hills," Union League Club, Chic.; "Valley of the Darro, Granada, Spain," Herron Art Inst., Indianapolis, IN; purchase, Chicago Art Commission, 1922. Address in 1929, Studio Bldg., Ohio and State Sts., Chicago, IL.

STACKPOLE, RALPH.
Sculptor, etcher, craftsman, and teacher. Born Williams, OR, May 1, 1885. Pupil of Arthur Putnam and G. Piazzoni and Ecole des Beaux Art, Paris. Member: CA SE. Awards: Hon. mention, P.-P. Exp., San. F., 1915; gold medal. San F. AA, 1918; gold medal, San. F. AA., 1920. Work: "Portrait bust of Prof. Hilgard", Univ. of Calif.; "Portrait bust of Prof. Flugel," Stanford Univ., CA; "Portrait busts of Judge Seawell" City Hall, San F. Address in 1929, 50 rue Vercingetorix, Paris, France; 728 Montgomery St., San F., CA.

STADELMAN, HENRYETTE LEECH.
Painter and teacher. Born Brownsville, PA, Dec. 5, 1891. Pupil of Hugh Breckenridge, Hawthorne, and PAFA. Member: Plastic C.; Wilmington SFA; Fellowship PAFA; AFA. Address in 1929, 710 Blackshire Road, Wilmington, DE.

STAFFORD, MARY.
(Mrs. John R. Frazier). Portrait painter. Born Chicago, IL, Feb. 4, 1895. Pupil of AIC; Academy of la Grande Chaumiere; Charles W. Hawthorne. Member: Chicago Gal. A.; Chicago PS; Providence AC. Awards: Hearst prize, 1925, Thompson prize, 1927, AIC. Address in 1929, 74 N Main St.; h. 11 John St., Providence, RI.

STAFFORD, P. SCOTT.
Painter. Born in Brooklyn, NY Pupil of Robert Henri. Member o Pen and Pencil Club of Columbus Ohio. Address in 1926, 194 Broadway, NY.

STAGG, CLARENCE ALFRED.
Painter. Born Nashville, TN, Aug 16, 1902. Pupil of Charles W Hawthorne. Member: SSAL. Awards First prize for still life Nashville, 1927; first prize for self portrait, Nashville, 1928 Address in 1929, Studio 611, 194 Broadway, New York, NY; h. 170 Simkin St., Providencetown, MA.

STAGG, JESSIE A.
Sculptor, craftsman, and teacher Born in England, in 1891. Pupil o ASL of NY; Robert Aitken; C McClure; also in London and Rome Member: NA Women PS.; NY Society Ceramic Arts; AFA. Died in 1958 Address in 1929, 17 East 62nd St. 1160 Fifth Ave., New York, NY summer, Shady, Woodstock, NY.

STAHL, M. LOUIS.
Painter. Born Cincinnati, OH Pupil of Cincinnati Art Acad. under Meakin and Nowottny; ASL of N under Volk, Mowbray and Blum; also of Chase in NY and Spain, an Hawthorne and Webster i Provincetown, MA; Gaspard at Taos NM. Member: Cincinnati Women' AC; Provincetown AA: AFA. Addres in 1929, Ohio Univ. Athens, OH.

STAHR, PAUL C.
Illustrator. Born New York, NY Aug. 8, 1883. Pupil of John War and NAD. Member: SI; GFLA. Work Illustrations for Life, Collier Weekly, American Magazine, Harper Bazaar and Woman's Home Companion. Illustrated "The Hornet," "Th Mask," "The Sear," etc. Address i 1929, 362 Audubon Ave., New York NY; summer, Long Beach, West End LI, NY.

STAIGG, RICHARD MORRELL.
Miniature painter. Born Sept 7 1817, in Leeds, England. He came to the US in 1831 and settled in Newport, RI. He was elected member of the Nat. Acad. of Design in 1861. See Tuckerman's "Book of Artists" for general biographical

details. Died Oct. 11, 1881, in Newport, RI.

STALKER, E.
Well engraved vignettes so signed are found in Philadelphia publications of 1815. There was an E. Stalker engraving in London, in 1801 and again in 1823; it is possible that he was located in Philadelphia for a short time. Several of the plates noted are designed by C. R Leslie.

STAMATO, FRANK.
Sculptor. Born US, Jan. 16, 1897. Pupil of Charles Grafly, Albert Laessle. Member: Fellowship PAFA; Alliance; Graphic Sketch C. Awards: Two Cresson Traveling Scholarships, and Stewardson prize, PAFA. Work: "Pandora," Reading Art Museum; "Head of an Old Man," "Wounded Dog," "Billy Goat," Graphic Sketch C; Painting, "St. Anne France," PAFA, Philadelphia. Died in 1939. Address in 1929, 123 S. 16th St., h. 1316 South Warnock St., Philadelphia, PA.

STAMOS, THEODOROS.
Painter. Born December 31, 1922, in NYC. Has lived in Greece. Studied at American Artists School, NYC. Taught at Art Students' League of NY, Black Mountain Coll., Columbia, Brandeis. Awarded Tiffany Found. Scholarship (1951); Nat. Inst. of Arts and Letters award and Brandeis fellowship (1959); Nat. Arts Found. (1967). Exhibited at Wakefield Gal. (1943); Brandt Gal. (NYC); Whitney (1958 & 1963); in Berlin, Amsterdam, London (the Tate); & Athens Gal. In collections of Wadswortt, Detroit Inst. of Fine Arts, Vassar College, Tel-Aviv, Phillips (Wash., DC), MOMA, Yale, and MMA.

STANCLIFF, J. W.
Marine painter. Born in Chatham, CT, in 1814. Pupil of J. B. Flagg. Later he became Pres. of the Connecticut School of Design.

STANCZAK, JULIAN.
Painter. Born Nov. 5, 1928, in Borownia, Poland. US citizen. Studied in London; earned B. F. A., Cleveland Inst. of Art (1954) and

M. F.A., Yale (1956). Taught at Art Acad. of Cinn.; at Cleveland Inst. of Art since 1964. Rec. awards from Contemp. Arts Center, Cinn.; Dayton Art Inst., and Ohio State on Arts. Exhibited at Dayton Art Inst. (1964); Martha Jackson Gal., NYC; Kent State U.; Corcoran; Dartmouth; Ohio State U.; Butler Inst. (Youngstown); Cleveland Art Inst.; Whitney, MOMA and Brooklyn. In collections of Larry Aldrich Mus.; (Ridgefield, CT); Dayton Art inst.; Baltimore; PAFA; S.F. Mus. Art; Cleveland; Albright Knox and many international collections.

STANFIELD, MARION BAAR.
Painter. Born New York City, Sept. 22, 1895. Pupil of Du Mond, Johansen, Henri. Member: NA Women PS.; American Artists Assn.; North Shore AA. Address in 1929, 310 West 80th St., New York, NY; summer, Westport, CT.

STANGE, EMILIE.
Painter. Born in Jersey City, NJ, in 1863. Member of Salmagundi Club. Address in 1926, North Hackensack, NJ. Died in 1943.

STANKIEWICZ, RICHARD.
Sculptor. Born Dec. 31, 1922 in NYC. Studied at Hans Hoffmann School of Fine Arts (1949); W. Fernand Leger and Ossip Zadkine. Taught at Maryland Inst., Baltimore; U. of Penn.; Skowhegan (Maine); School of Visual Arts, NYC, Syracuse, Princeton; SUNY/Albany. Awards from Ford Foundation, Brnadeis U. and Nat. Council on Arts. Exhibited at MOMA; Carnegie; Stable Gallery, NYC; in San Paulo; and Whitney. In collections of Gugenheim, MOMA, Albright Knox (Buffalo), Whitney, Harvard, MMA, Wash. U. in St. Louis, Stockholm Mus. of Mod Art and private collections.

STANLAWS, PENRYHN.
(Penryhn Stanley Adamson). Illustrator and painter. Pupil of Julian Acad. and of Benjamin Constant and Laurens in Paris. Member: SI 1913. Address in 1929, 1 West 67th St., New York, NY.

STANLEY, IDAHLIA.
Painter. Studied: Brandeis Univ.;
Harvard Univ.; The Art Students'
Lg., NY. Exhibitions: Institute
of Contemporary Art, Boston, 1972;
Phila. Art Alliance, Penn., 1974;
Sketch Club, Phila., 1975.

STANLEY, JANE C. (MAHON).
(Mrs. Louis Crandall Stanley).
Painter. Born Detroit, July 21,
1863. Member: Detroit Soc. of
Women Painters; AWCS; Wash. WCC; NA
Women PS; AFA. Address in 1929,
Care of M. J. Kates, First National
Bank, Detroit, MI.

STANLEY-BROWN, RUDOLPH.
Painter, illustrator, etcher,
artist, and teacher. Born Mentor,
OH, April 9, 1889. Pupil of Col.
School of Arch.; Ecole des Beaux
Arts, Paris. Member: AIA; S. of
Beaux Arts Architects; Cleveland
Print C. represented by etchings
in Cleveland Museum of Art and Yale
University, New Haven. Address in
1929, 1899 E. 87th St., Cleveland,
OH.

STANSON, GEORGE CURTIN.
Painter and sculptor. Born in
Briscut, France, in 1885. Member
of Archaeological Inst., of
America; California Art Club.
Work: 4 murals in the Biological
Museum of the University of
California, La. Jolla, California;
"After the Rain" (mural) in Golden
Gate Park Museum of Archaeology ,
Santa Fe, NM. Address in 1926,
5653 La Mirada Avenue, Los Angeles,
CA.

STANTON, ELIZABETH C(ADY).
(Mrs. Wm. H. Blake). Painter and
teacher. Born New York, NY, Dec.
31, 1894. Pupil of F. Luis Mora,
Geo. Bridgeman, Albert Sterner and
Cecilia Beaux; Barnard C.; Louis
Comfort Tiffany Foundation; AFA.
Address in 1929, 35 Claremont Ave.,
New York, NY; summer, Silver Beach,
North Falmouth, MA; and Grand view
on Hudson, Nyack, NY.

STANTON, GIDEON TOWNSEND.
Painter. Born Morris, MN, July 14,
1885. Member: New Orleans Art
Assoc.; Southern SAL; New Orleans
ACC. Award: Silver medal, New
Orleans Art Assoc., 1911;

President's prize, NOAA., 1925.
Address in 1929, 1314 Jackson Ave.;
601 Hibernia Bldg., New Orleans,
LA.

STANTON, LUCY MAY.
Portrait painter and teacher. Born
Atlanta, GA, May 22, 1875. Pupil
of Colarossi Acad., Lucien Simon,
Emile Blanche, La Gandara and A.
Koopman in Paris. Member: PA S.
Min. P.; Am. S. Min. P.; NA Women
PS; Wash. WCC; G. Boston A.; Copley
S.; Concord AA. Awards: Medal of
honor, PSMP, PAFA, 1917; medal of
honor, Concord AA, 1923; hon.
mention, NA Women PS, 1925.
Represented by oil painting in
Capitol, Washington, DC; miniature,
Lincoln Memorial Museum, Milton,
MA; miniature "Self Portrait,"
Philadelphia Museum. Died in 1931.
Address in 1929, 552 Cobb St.,
Athens, GA; 98 Chestnut St.,
Boston, MA.

STANWOOD, GERTRUDE.
Painter. Born in West Newbury, MA,
in 1874. Pupil of Joseph De Camp,
Ernest Major and Lasar. Member of
Society of Independent Artists.
Address in 1926, 1015 Cathedral
St., Baltimore, MD.

STARK, OTTO.
Painter and illustrator. Born in
Indianpolis in 1859. Pupil of
Lefebvre, Boulanger and Cormon in
Paris. Member: International
Society Art league. Awarded first
Holcomb prize, Herron Art Inst.,
1915. In charge of Art Dept.
Manual Training High School, and
Art Dept, Technical High School,
Indianapolis; instructor, Herron
Art School, Indianapolis, IN. Work:
"Two Boys" and "The Indian Trail,"
Herron Art School, Indianapolis;
"River Valley and Hill," Cincinnati
Art Museum; mural decoration, City
Hospital, Indianapolis, and mural
decorations in the public schools
of Indianapolis; "Portrait of Gen.
George Rogers Clark," Indiana State
House. Address in 1926, 1722 N.
Delaware St., Indianapolis, IN.
Died April 14, 1926, in
Indianapolis.

STARKWEATHER, WILLIAM E. B.
Painter and writer. Born
Edinburgh, Scotland, 1879. Pupil

890

of ASL of NY; Colarossi Acad. in Paris; Sorolla in Madrid, followed by 3 years study in Italy. Member: New Haven PCC; Hispanic S. of America (cor.); AWCS; Salma. A.; NYWCC; Allied AA. Awards: Mrs. William K. Vanderbilt prize, joint water color exhibition, NY, 1925; hon. mention with popular vote for oil painting, New Haven, 1924; Dana gold medal, PAFA, 1925; Jones prize for water color, Baltimore, 1926. Author of "Paintings and Drawings by Francisco Goya in the collection of the Hispanic Society of America, 1916." Represented in the Metropolitan Museum of Art; Brooklyn Museum; San Diego Museum; Univ. of Penna. Collection; Randolph-Macon College, Lynchburg, VA; Institute de Valencia de Don Juan, Madrid. Died in 1969. Address in 1929, 82 State Street, Brooklyn, NY.

STARR, IDA M. H.
Painter and writer. Born Cincinnati, OH, July 11, 1859. Pupil of Myra Edgerly, Lillian Adams and Howard Schultze. Member: S. Indp. A. of NY, Chicago and Buffalo. Address in 1929, Hope House, Easton, MD.

STARR, LORAINE WEBSTER.
(Mrs. William Starr). Painter. Member: Born in 1887. Balto. WCC. Address in 1929, Hope House, Easton, MD.

STARR, MAXWELL B.
Painter, sculptor, and teacher. Born Odessa, Russia, Feb. 6, 1901. Pupil of Kenyon Cox, Charles W. Hawthorne, Ivan G. Olinsky. Member: Tiffany AG. Address in 1929, 54 West 74th St., h. 1150 Anderson Ave., New York, NY.

STARR, SIDNEY.
Painter. Born in Kingston-upon-Hull, Yorkshire, England, in 1857; died in NY in 1925. Pupil of Poynter and of Legros. Awarded bronze medal, Universal Expo., Paris, 1889. Work: Mural decorations, Grace Chapel, New York City; 24 figures in Congressional Library, Washington, DC. Address in 1926, 256 West 85th Street, New York, NY.

STASACK, EDWARD.
Painter. Born Oct. 1, 1929, in Chicago, IL. Also print maker. B.F.A., M.F.A. (1956), Univ. of Illinois. Rec. grad. fellowship; Tiffany found. scholarship; Rockefeller grant McDowell Colony fellow, 1971 & 1975. Taught at U. of Hawaii since 1956. Awards from state of Hawaii and Bicentennial Com. (1976). Exhibited at Fort Sheridan, IL (1954); Cromer & Quint Gallery, Chicago; Honolulu Acad. Arts; Univ. of Illinois; Downtown Gal., NYC; Carnegie; others. In collections of Seattle Art Mus.; Addison Gal.; Butler Inst. (Youngstown); Bradley Univ.; Lib. of Congress; Phil. Museum of Art.

STAUFFER, EDNA (PENNYPACKER).
Painter, illustrator, teacher, and etcher. Born Phoenixville, Chester, Co., PA, Oct. 12, 1887. Pupil of Chase, Beaux, Anshutz, Dow; Andre L'hote, Friesz, Academie Moderne in Paris. Member: Fellowship PAFA. Instructor, Hunter College, NY. Died in 1956. Address in 1929, Whitney Studio Gallery, 10 West 8th St.; 41 West 11th Street, New York, NY; 1900 Rittenhouse Square, Philadelphia, PA.

STEA, CESARE.
Sculptor. Born Bari, Italy, Aug. 17, 1893. Pupil of NAD; Beaux Arts Inst.; Italian Am. AA; Hermon MacNeil, Victor Salvatore, Carl Heber. Member: Italian Amer. AA. Awards: Medal from Beaux Arts for relief in Educational Building, San Francisco, 1915; prize for trophy cup, National Defense Soc.; Barnett prize, NAD, 1926. Died in 1960. Address in 1929, 3 East 14th St., New York, NY.

STEADHAM, TERRY EVAN.
Illustrator. Born in Indianapolis in 1945. Attended the John Herron School of Art and began his career in 1968. He received the Gold Award for Illustration of the Indiana ADC in 1970 and has been represented in the S of I Annual Shows of 1974, 1975, and 1976. Though he started working in advertising, he is currently free-lancing out of NYC, doing

editorial work for children's magazines and other publications.

STEARNS, JUNIUS BRUTUS.
Painter. Born July 2, 1810, in Arlington, VT. Pupil of the NAD. He became an Associate in 1848, and an Academician in the following year. His work is mainly portraiture but he also painted historical subjects; his 5 paintings represented Washington as citizen, farmer, soldier, statesman and Christian are considered his best. His "Millennium" is in the New York Acad. of Design, and several of his portraits hang in the City Hall there. He died in NYC, on Sept. 17, 1885.

STEBBINS, EMMA.
Painter and sculptor, who was born in NYC, Sept. 1, 1815. For yrs. she devoted herself to painting oil and water color. In 1857 she went to Italy and began to model under Italian masters, also with Paul Akers. She produced the figure in Central Park fountain, "Angel of the Waters;" also Statue of Horace Mann, Boston (1860). She was an intimate friend of the actress Charlotte Cushman. She died Oct. 25, 1882, in NYC.

STEBBINS, ROLAND STEWART.
Painter and illustrator. Born in Boston, MA, in 1883. Pupil of DeCamp in Boston; under Hacki in Munich. Member: Boston Art Club. Illustrator of "At the King's Pleasure."

STEDMAN, JEANETTE.
Portrait painter. Born in 1880. She studied in Paris early in her career. Her body was found in Lake Michigan, Chicago, IL on March 8, 1924. She had lived in Chicago, IL, for years.

STEEL, ALFRED B.
This engraver of subject plates was working for Sartain's Magazine in 1850.

STEEL, J.
In 1850 J. Steel was doing very good work for Sartain's Magazine. He was an engraver of buildings, etc.

STEEL, JAMES W.
Engraver. Born in Phila., in 1799. Steel was a pupil of the Phila. engravers Benjamin Tanner and George Murray, and for a time he was engaged in bank note engraving for Tanner, Vallance, Kearney & Co. Later, he became an accomplished line engraver producing a number of portraits, landscape and Annual plates. Steel was working under his own name in 1820; at a later period in his professional life he was employed chiefly upon bank note work. Died June 30, 1879, in Philadelphia.

STEELE, BRANDT (THEODORE).
Painter and architect. Born Battle Creek, MI, Nov. 16, 1870. Pupil of his father, T. C. Steele; Aman-Jean in Paris. Member: Indianapolis Arch. Assoc.; Indiana AC. Instructor, Herron Art Inst. Address in 1929, 811 East Drive, Woodruff Place, Indianapolis, IN.

STEELE, FREDERIC DORR.
Illustrator. Born Marquette, MI, Aug. 6, 1873. Pupil of NAD and ASL in NY. Member: SI 1902. Award: Bronze medal, St. Louis Exp., 1904. Illustrated: "The Return of Sherlock Holmes," and other tales by Doyle; books by R. H. Davis, Mark Twain, Myra Kelly, Gouverneur Morris, Mary Roberts Rinehart, Kipling, Conrad, Bennett, Tarkington, etc. Died in 1944. Address in 1929, Care of The Players, 16 Gramercy Park, New York, NY.

STEELE, THEODORE CLEMENT.
Painter. Born in Owen County, IN, in 1847. Pupil of Royal Acad. in Munich under Benczur and Loefftz. Elected Associate Member of the National Acad., 1914. Awarded honorable mention, Paris Exposition, 1900; Fine Arts Corporation prize, 1910. Work: "Gordon Hill," Cincinnati Museum; "Oaks at Vernon," "Portrait of Rev. N. A. Hyde," "The River," "Winter Sunlight," Herron Art Inst., Indianapolis; "Landscape," St. Louis Museum; "Whitewater Valley," Richmond, IN, Art Association. Address in 1925, Bloomington, IN. Died July 24, 1926 in Bloomington, IN.

STEELE, ZULMA.
(Mrs. Neilson R. Parker). Painter.
Born Appleton, WI, July 7, 1881.
Pupil of Pratt Institute, Brooklyn;
ASL of NY. Member: NA Women PS;
Wash. AC; S. Indp. A. Address in
1929, Woodstock, Ulster Co., NY.

STEENE, WILLIAM.
Painter and sculptor. Born
Syracuse, NY, Aug. 18, 1888. Pupil
of Henri, Jones, Cox, NAD, ASL of
NY, Chase; Beaux Arts, Colarossi
and Julian's, Paris. Member:
Mural P. Work: 3 murals, "History
of Galveston," City Hall,
Galveston, TX; "Commerce," Court
House, Tulsa, OK; "The Coming of
the Traders," Tulsa, OK; War Mem.
to Cherokee Indians, Talequah, OK;
war mem., Wash. County Court House,
AR; portraits of "Pres. Denny,"
U. of AL; "Gov. Whitfield,"
Governor's mansion and "Judge
Cambell," Hist. Soc., Jackson, MS;
"Col. Woodward," GA Military Acad.,
Atlanta; "Melville R. Grant,"
Masonic Hall, Greenville, MS;
"Mayor Wms.," City Auditorium,
Macon, GA; "The Caravan," Macon Art
Assoc.; "Melody," MS Art Assoc.;
"O'Henry Mem.," Asheville, NC; "Dr.
and Mrs. D. B. Johnson," Winthrop
College, Rock Hill, SC; "Dr.
Alexander Graham," Central High
Sch., Charlotte, NC; "Pres. W. M.
Sparks," GSCW, Milledgeville, GA;
"Pres. Angold Shamlee," Tift Coll.,
Forsyth, GA.; "Pres. M. M. Walker,"
A. M. College, Starkville, MS;
"Pres. J. P. Fant," MSCW, Columbus,
MS; "Early Traders," mural, High
School, Tulsa, OK. Died in 1965.
Address in 1929, Tryon, NC.

STEEPER, JOHN.
Engraver. According to an
advertisement in the Pennsylvania
Gazette, in 1762, John Steeper was
engraving "in all its branches" in
Phila. Westcott, in his "Phila.,"
says that the first important
copperplate published in Phila. in
1755 was "A Southeast Prospect of
the Pennsylvania Hospital with the
elevation of the intended plan."
He goes on to say that Montgomery
and Winters drew it. It was
engraved by J. Steeper and H.
Dawkins, and was printed and

sold by Robert Kennedy, of
Philadelphia.

STEERE, LORA WOODHEAD.
Sculptor. Born Los Angeles, CA in
1888. Pupil of Albert Toft in
Berlin; Bela Pratt in Boston;
Lentelli and Ralph Stockpole in San
Francisco; Florence Wyle in
Toronto, Canada. Member: San
Deigo AG; Calif. AC; So. Calif.
Sculptors G; Artland C. Award:
First prize, Clatsop Co. (Oregon)
Exp., 1917. Work: "Ifugao Fire
Dancer," marble bust of Pearl
Keller, and "Dance of Pan," Pearl
Keller School of Dramatic Arts,
Glendale, CA. Represented in Los
Angeles Museum of History, Science
and Art; bronze bas relief, David
Starr Jordan High School, Los
Angeles; bust of Abraham Lincoln,
Lincoln Memorial, University of
Tennesee; bronze of Dr. Geo. F.
Bovard, Bovard Hall, USC. Address
in 1929, 2814 Glendower Ave.,
Hollywood, Calif.; summer,
Idyllwild, CA.

STEES, SEVILLA L.
Painter. Born Philadelphia. Pupil
of PAFA; Woman's School of Design.
Member: Fellowship, PAFA; Plastic
C. Address in 1929, 1806 North
Park, Ave., Philadelphia, PA.

STEICHEN, EDWARD J.
Painter. Born in Milwaukee, WI, in
1879. Represented in Metropolitan
Museum, New York, by "Nocturne,
Temple d'Amour"; Toledo Museum by
"Across the Marshes." His mural
paintings are to be seen at the
Luxembourg, Paris. Address in 1926,
Care of Knoedler & Co., New York
City, NY. Died in 1973.

STEIG, WILLIAM.
Cartoonist and sculptor. Studied
at City College, NY, 1923-25; Nat.
Acad. of Design, 1925-29. Work:
Wood sculpture, RI Mus. of Art and
Smith Col.; paintings, Brooklyn
Mus. Exhibitions: Downtown
Gallery, NY, 1939. Published
several books of his drawings,
incl. "The Lonely Ones," "About
People and Dreams of Glory."
Address in 1982, 1 Box KH2, Kent,
CT.

STEIGER, HARWOOD.
Painter, illustrator, and teacher.
Born Macedon, NY, Jan. 2, 1900.
Pupil of Daniel Garber, Hugh
Breckenridge. Member: Fellowship
PAFA. Awards: Hon. mention, 1928,
and first prize for water color,
1929, Mem. Art Gal., Rochester.
Work: "Trout Stream," "Abandoned
Village" and "Evening," Memorial
Art Gallery, Rochester, NY.
Address in 1929, Rochester Savings
Bank Bldg., Fitzhugh St., South
Rochester, NY; h. 16 West Chruch
St., Fairport, NY; summer, Parker's
Cove, Annapolis Co. Nova Scotia.

STEIN, EVALEEN.
Painter. Born in Lafayette, IN.
Studied art at Art Inst. of
Chicago. Became decorative designer
and illuminator, and exhibited
illuminated manuscripts at the Arts
and Crafts Society in Chicago; also
in Indianapolis, etc. Contributor
of verse to Indianapolis Journal,
1886-1900. Contributor: Society
of Decorative Art, NY and Chicago.
Address in 1926, 708 Hitt St.,
Lafayette, IN.

STEIN.
Dunlap notes that a portrait
painter of that name was born in
Washington, VA, but painted
principally in the region beyond
the Alleghenies. He was said to
have painted a number of portraits
at Steubenville, OH, in 1820.
Stein died when he was a young man.

STEINBERG, N. P.
Painter and illustrator. Born
Palestine, Feb. 15, 1894. Pupil of
AIC; A. Sterba; W. Reynolds;
Seyffert and H. Walcott. Member:
Palette and Chisel C.; Chicago SA.
Address in 1929, Transportation
Bldg., 608 South Dearborn St.; 1231
North Maplewood Ave., Chicago, IL.

STEINKE, WILLIAM (BILL).
Illustrator, cartoonist, writer,
and lecturer. Born Slatington, PA,
Nov. 25, 1887. Pupil of George
McManus; "Vet" Anderson. Member:
Amer. Assoc. of Cartoonists and
Caricaturists. Address in 1929,
Industrial Bldg., 1060 Broad St.,
Newark, NJ; h. 1383 Clinton Ave.,
Irvington, NJ.

STEKETEE, SALLIE HALL.
(Mrs. Paul Frederick Steketee).
Painter. Born Brazil, IN, Sept.
11, 1882. Pupil of Cincinnati Art
Acad. Member: NA Women PS; Hoosier
Salon. Awards: Ball prize,
Hoosier Salon, Chicago, 1926;
Daughters of IN. prize, Hoosier
Salon, 1929. Work: Summer
Flowers," Daughters of Indiana,
Chicago. Address in 1929, 432
Washington St., S. E., Grand
Rapids, MI.

STELLA, FRANK.
Painter. Born in Malden, MA, May
1936. Study: Phillips Acad., with
Patrick Morgan; Princeton Univ.,
with Wm. Seitz, Stephen Greene.
Work: MOMA; Whitney; Pasadena Art
Mus.; Albright - Knox, Buffalo, NY;
Walker Art Un., Minneapolis,
Maryland. Exhibit: Corcoran,
1967, MOMA, 1968-70; Phila. Mus. of
Art, 1968; Whitney, 1969, 71, 72;
Carnegie, 1971; Mus. and Fine Arts,
Houston, 1974; VA Mus. of Fine
Arts, 1974; Walker Art Ctr.
Minneapolis; and many more.
Awarded First Prize, Int'l.
Biennial Exhib. Ptgs., Tokyo.
Rep.: Lawrence Rubin Gal., NYC.
Address in 1982, 29 E. 73rd St.,
NYC.

STELLA, JOSEPH.
Painter, writer, etcher, lecturer,
and teacher. Born in Italy, May
13, 1880. Self-taught. Member:
Societe Anonyme; Modern AA; Salons
of America. Died in 1946. Address
in 1929, 457 West 24th Street; 43
East 57th Street, New York, NY.

STELLAR, HERMINE.
Painter. Born in Austria. Pupil
of AIC; Sorolla in Spain; Bellows.
Member: Chicago SA; Chicago AC.
Award: Traveling scholarship from
Tuesday Art and Travel Club, 1911.
Formerly, Instructor, Art Inst. of
Chicago. Head of Dept. of Drawing
and Painting, Univ. of Nebraska.
Address in 1929, 6732 Oglesby Ave.,
Chicago, IL.

STEMLER, OTTO ADOLPH.
Painter and illustrator. Born in
Cincinnati in 1872. Student of
Cincinnati Art Acad. Specialty,
biblical pictures. Address in
1926, Kennedy Ave., Cincinnati, OH.

STENGEL, G. J.
Painter. Born Newark, NJ, Sept. 26, 1872. Pupil of ASL of NY; Julian Acad., Paris, France. Member: Salma. C.; Yonkers AA.; Allied AA; AFA; Silvermine G; G. Am. P. Died in 1937. Address in 1929, 34 Main St., Ridgefield, CT.

STEPHAN, ELMER A.
Painter and illustrator. Born Pittsburgh, PA, Jan. 31, 1892. Pupil of Joseph Greenwood. Member: Pittsburgh AA.; Pittsburgh Teachers AC. Illustrated "Practical Art Drawing Books," published by Practical Art Co., Dallas, Texas. Director of Art Education, Pittsburgh Public Schools. Died in 1944. Address in 1929, 209 Gladstone Road, Pittsburgh, PA.

STEPHENS, ALICE BARBER.
(Mrs. Charles H. Stephens). Illustrator, wood engraver and teacher. Born near Salem, NJ, July 1, 1858. Pupil of PAFA; Phila. School of Design for Women; Julian and Colarossi academies in Paris. Member: Plastic C.; Fellowship PAFA. Awards: Mary Smith prize, PAFA 1890; bronze medal, Atlanta Exp., 1895; gold medal, London, 1902. Numerous illustrations for Harper's and Century, and wood engravings for Scribner's. Address in 1929, Moylan, PA.

STEPHENS, CHARLES H.
Illustrator. Member: Fellowship PAFA. Address in 1929, Moylan, Delaware Co., PA.

STEPHENS, C(LARA) J(ANE).
Painter and writer. Pupil of Kenyon Cox, W. M. Chase, F. V. DuMond. Member: S. Indp. A.; AFA. Awards: First prize for figure, 1920, and West Seattle prize, Seattle FAS, 1925. Address in 1929, 12 Mulkey Bldg., Portland, OR.

STEPHENS, D(ANIEL) OWEN.
Painter and architect. Born Philadelphia, PA, Aug. 5, 1893. Pupil of William Lathrop and N. C. Wyeth. Member: Phila. Alliance; Fellowship PAFA. Specialty, night landscapes in oil. Died in 1937. Address in 1929, Moylan, PA.

STEPHENS, FRANK L.
Painter. Born in Philadelphia in 1824. He spent most of his professional life in New York City. He was an illustrator and cartoonist and was known for his caricatures; he also painted in water colors. He died in 1882.

STEPHENS, GEORGE FRANK.
Sculptor and craftsman. Born Rahway, NJ, Dec. 28, 1859. Pupil of PAFA. Member: Fellowship PAFA; Phila. Sketch. C.; AC Phila; NAC. Taught modeling in several art schools. Was instructor at Drexel Inst. Created many sculptures for City Hall, Phila. Died in 1935. Address in 1929, Arden, DE.

STERBA, ANTONIN.
Painter and teacher. Born Hermanec, Czechoslovakia, Feb. 11, 1875. Pupil of AIC; Smith Art Acad., Chicago; of Laurens and Constant in Paris. Member: Chicago PS; Cliff Dwellers; Bohemian AC; Chicago Gal. A. Award: Gold medal, Bohemian AC., 1921. Instructor at AIC. Specialty, portraits. Address in 1929, 917 Edgemere Court, Evanston, IL.

STERCHI, EDA (ELISABETH).
Painter. Born Olney, IL. Pupil of AIC: Lucien Simon, Menard and Prinet in Paris; Inst. de Carthage, Tunisie. Member: Chicago SA; Chicago AC. Address in 1929, 214 Fair St., Olney, IL; Hotel de Paris, Tunis, Tunisie.

STERLING, LINDSEY MORRIS (MRS.).
Sculptor. Born Mauch-Chunk, PA, Nov. 8, 1876. Pupil of George Brewster and Jas. Fraser; Bourdelle in Paris. Member: NSS; NA Women PS; New Haven PCC; Allied AA. Awards: Bronze medal, P.-P. Exp., San F., 1915; Prize, NA Women PS, 1916; Joan of Arc medal, NA Women PS, 1923. Address in 1929, Edgewater, NJ; summer, Jay, Essex Co., (Adirondack Mts.), NY.

STERN, MILDRED B.
Painter, who exhibited portrait of "Miss B." at Penna. Acad. of Fine Arts, Philadelphia, 1915. Address in 1926, 4535 Pine St., Philadelphia, PA.

STERNBERG, HARRY.
Etcher. Born NY, July 19, 1904.
Pupil of Harry Wickey. Address in
1929, 20 West 49th St., New York,
NY; h. 106 Arlington Ave.,
Brooklyn, NY.

STERNE, HEDDA.
Painter. Born Aug. 4, 1916, in
Bucharest, Romania. US citizen
since 1944. Studied in Bucharest,
Paris and Vienna. Extensive travel
abroad. Awarded Fulbright (1963);
purchase award from Childe Hassam
Fund (1971). Taught at Carbondale
Col (1964). Exhibited at Wakefield
Gal., (1943); Betty Parsons Gal.
(many 1947-75); Vassar Col.; Sao
Paulo, Brazil; Arts Club of Chi.;
MOMA; Corcoran; Virginia Mus. of
Fine Arts; Roswell (NM) Mus.;
Smithsonian; Carnegie; PAFA; Finch
Col. In collections of Art Inst.
of Chicago; MOMA; Albright Knox;
PAFA; Montclair (NJ); Whitney;
Chase Manhattan Bank; MMA.

STERNE, MAURICE.
Painter, etcher, and sculptor.
Born at Libau, Russia, July 13,
1878. Came to NY at age of 12.
Pupil of NAD and other schools in
NY. Traveled extensively in
Europe; special study of the people
of Bali. Member: New Soc. A.
Award: Logan medal and prize,
$750, AIC, 1928. Work in:
Carnegie Institute, Pittsburgh; RI
School of Design, Providence;
Metropolitan Museum, NY; Boston
Museum of Fine Arts; Detroit
Museum, Harrison Gallery, Los
Angeles Museum; Kaiser Friedrich
Museum, Berlin; Cologne Museum;
Tate Gallery, London. Died in
1957. Address in 1929, care of
Reinhardt Galleries, 730 Fifth
Ave., New York, NY; Villa Strohl,
Fern, Rome, and Italy.

STERNER, ALBERT EDWARD.
Painter, illustr., and teacher.
Born London, EN, March 8, 1863, of
Amer. parents. Studied at
Birmingham, EN; pupil of Julian
Acad., Paris under Boulanger,
Lefebvre and Gerome. Member: ANA,
1910; AWCS; Lotos C.; New SA.
Awards: Hon. mention, Paris Salon,
1891; bronze medal, Paris Exp.,
1900; silver medal for water color
and bronze medal for drawings, Pan

Am Exp., Buffalo, 1901; gold medal,
Munich, 1905. Illus.; "Prue and I,"
by George W. Curtis; "Fenwick's
Career," by Mrs. Ward, etc. Work:
"Portrait of Martin Birnbaum,"
Carnegie Inst., Pittsburgh; "The
Blue Stocking," Met. Mus., NY; "The
Gray Cape," Toronto Mus. of Fine
Arts; "Nude," Brooklyn Museum;
"Amour Mort," South Kensington
Mus., London; drawings and 6
lithographs, K. G. L., Kupferstich
Kabinet Pinakothek, Munich;
drawings and 6 lithographs, K. G.
L., Kupferstich Kabinet, Dresden; 6
lithographs, Royal Print Collecton
of Italy; 6 lithographs, NY Public
Library; "John B. Deaver and His
Clinic," group portrait of 25
figures, for Lankenau Hospital,
Philadelphia, PA. Died in 1946.
Address in 1929, 1 Lexington Ave.,
New York, NY; summer, Richmond, MA,
P.O., RFD. 1, Pittsfield, MA.

STERNGLASS, ARNO.
Illustrator. Born in Berlin, Ger.,
in 1926. Attended PI from 1944 to
1947. His illustrations have
appeared in Esquire, Look, Vogue,
Redbook, Glamour, Seventeen,
Horizon, The New York Times
Magazine, and others. He has won
awards in NY from the ADC, AIGA,
and the S of I.

STERRETT, CLIFF.
Cartoonist. Born Fergus Fall, MN,
Dec. 12, 1883. Pupil of Chase Sch.
of Art. Member: SI. Award: Wm.
Randolph Hearst cash prize for
industrious cartoonists, NY.
Illustrated "Polly and Her Pals"
for Hearst publications. Died in
1964. Address in 1929, 316 W. 72d
St., New York, NY.

STETCHER, KARL.
Painter. Born in Germany in 1832,
he came to NY as a youth and spent
most of his life in that city where
he painted a number of portraits,
besides staining the windows in
Trinity Church, NY. He died in
Wichita, KS, in Jan. 1924.

STETSON, CHARLES WALTER.
Painter. Born on March 25, 1858 in
Tiverton, RI. Exhibited "Twilight,
Pasadena, Cal." His studio was in
Boston, MA. In 1906 he was in

Rome, Italy, and he died there on July 21, 1911.

STETSON, KATHERINE BEECHER.
Painter, sculptor, and teacher. Born Providence, RI, March 23, 1885. Pupil of da Pozzo, Sabate, Noel and Breck in Rome; PAFA under Chase, Kendall and Beaux; landscape under H. D. Murphy and Birge Harrison, Leonard Ochtman and F. Tolles Chamberlin. Member: MacDowell Memorial Assn.; Sculptors Guild of S. Calif.; Calif. AC; Pasadena SA. Awards: Gold medal for sculpture, Calif. AC, 1925; hon. mention, San Diego FAG, 1926; second prize, Los Angeles Co. Fair, 1926. Address in 1929, 223 South Catalina Ave., Pasadena, CA.

STETTHEIMER, FLORINE.
Painter. Born in NY in 1871. Studied in NY, Paris, Rome, Munich. Member: S. Indp. A. Died in 1944. Address in 1929, 80 West 40th St., New York, NY.

STEUART, M. LOUISA.
Painter and teacher. Born Baltimore, MD. Pupil of Hugh Newell, Julius Rolshoven, William Chase, Courtois. Member: Baltimore WCC. Address in 1929, 839 Park Ave., Baltimore, MD; summer, Cascade P. O., MD.

STEVENS, CLARA HATCH (MRS.).
Painter, illustrator, writer, lecturer, and teacher. Born Harrodsburg, KY, April 22, 1854. Pupil of J. Carroll Beckwith, William Chase, P. M. Shurtleff, Puvis de Chavannes. Member: Chicago Municipal A. Lg.; Chicago SA.; North Shore A. Lg. Work: Frieze in Hall of Honor, Women's Bldg., World's Columbian Exp., Chicago, 1893. Address in 1929, 561 Mofferr Raod, Lake Bluff, IL.

STEVENS, DOROTHY.
Etcher and painter. Born in Toronto, in 1888. Pupil of Slade School in London. Member of Chicago Society of Etchers. Awarded silver medal for etching, Panama Pacific Expo., San Francisco, 1915. Address in 1926, 2 Spadina Gardens, 145 West Wellington St., Toronto, Canada. Died in 1966.

STEVENS, EDITH BRISCOE.
Painter. Born Philadelphia, PA. Pupil of A. E. Jones, Harry Leith-Ross, George Elmer Browne. Member: CT. AFA; New Haven PCC; Springfield AL; Gloucester SA; Rockport AA. Work: "Gloucester Wharf," Beach Memorial Collection, Storrs, CT. Address in 1929, 6 Regent St., Hartford, CT.

STEVENS, EDWARD DALTON.
Illustrator. Born Gouchland Co., VA, Dec. 6, 1878. Pupil of Vanderpoel in Chicago; Chase School, NY. Illustrated "Mary Regan," by Leroy Scott; "The Crystal Stopper," by Leblanc; "Peter Rough." Illustrations for Cosmopolitan, Red Book, McCalls, Liberty, etc. Died in 1939. Address in 1929, Tenth St., Studio Bldg., 51 West 10th St., New York, NY; h. 153 Chestnut Ave., Metuchen, NJ.

STEVENS, ESTHER.
(Mrs. Walter T. Barney). Painter. Born in Indianapolis, IN, in 1885. Pupil of Robert Henri; also at Art Students League of NY. Address in 1926, Pt. Loma, San Diego, CA.

STEVENS, GEORGE W.
Miniature painter, who flourished in Boston about 1842.

STEVENS, GEORGE WASHINGTON.
Painter. Born in Utica, NY, in 1866. Pupil of J. Francis Murphy in NY. Member of Salmagundi Club; was Associate of Museum Directors. Director, Toledo Museum of Art since 1903. Address in 1926, Museum of Art, Toledo, OH.

STEVENS, HELEN B.
(Mrs. T. W. Stevens). Etcher. Born Chicago, Feb. 8, 1878. Pupil of AIC; Frank Brangwyn in England. Member: Chicago SE; Pitts. AA. Award: Bronze medal, P.-P. Exp., San F., 1915. Instructor in etching and Assistant Curator of Prints, Art Institute of Chicago, 1909-1912. Address in 1929, care of The Art Institute of Chicago, Chicago, IL.

STEVENS, JOHN CALVIN.
Landscape painter and architect. Born Boston, MA, Oct. 8, 1855.

Member: FAIA; Boston S. Arch.; NY Arch. Lg.; Portland SA; Salma. C.; AFA. Died in 1940. Address in 1929, 711 Chapman Bldg.; h. 31 Craigie St., Portland, ME.

STEVENS, LAWRENCE TENNEY.
Painter, sculptor, etcher, and teacher. Born Brighton, MA, July 16, 1896. Member: NSS. Award: American Prix de Rome, 1922. Work: "Baptism of Christ" (marble), Congregational Church, Brighton, MA, etc. Died in 1972. Address in 1929, 227 West 13th St., New York, NY; summer, Bedford Village, NY.

STEVENS, MARION.
Painter. Member: Wash. SA. Address in 1929, 1332-21st St., N. W., Washington, DC.

STEVENS, THOMAS WOOD.
Mural painter, etcher, and writer. Born Daysville, IL. Pupil of AIC, Armour Inst. of Tech., Chicago; Frank Brangwyn in London; Sorolla y Bastida. Head of Drama Dept. and Director, Goodman Theatre, Art Inst. of Chicago, 1924. Address in 1929, care of the Art Institute of Chicago, Chicago, IL.

STEVENS, VERA.
Painter. Born Hustontown, PA, Aug. 5, 1895. Pupil of George Elmer Brown. Member: Springfield AL; CT AFA; NA Women PS. Address in 1929, 138 West 58th Street, New York, NY; summer, Provincetown, MA.

STEVENS, WILL HENRY.
Landscape painter, draftsman, teacher, and potter. Born Vevay, IN, Nov. 28, 1887. Pupil of Cincinnati Acad. under Caroline Lord; Nowottny, Duveneck and Meakin; Jonas Lie and Van Dearing Perrine in NY. Member: Inter. Soc. AL; Cincinnati AC; New Orleans AA; Southern SAL; New Orleans ACC; NOAA. Award: Foulke prize, Richmond, IN, 1914; hon. mention, SSAL, 1925. Represented in art galleries, Des Moines, IA; Oklahoma Univ. Norman, OK; Shreveport, LA; J. B. Speed Memorial Museum, Louisville, KY. Instructor of painting, Newcomb School of Arts, New Orleans. Decorator at Rookwood Pottery. Director, Natchitoches (LA) Art Colony. Instructor, Texas Artists Camp, San Angelo, TX. Address in 1929, Newcomb School of Art, Tulane University, New Orleans, LA.

STEVENS, WILLIAM CHARLES.
Landscape painter. Born in 1854 in Barre, MA; died in 1917. The Worcester Museum of Fine Arts owns several of his paintings. Address in 1926, 13 West 29th Street, New York, NY.

STEVENS, W(ILLIAM) D(ODGE).
Illustrator. Born Tidioute, PA, Sept. 13, 1870. Pupil of AIC under Vanderpoel and Grover; studied in Paris. Member: GFLA. Address in 1929, 51 West 10th St., New York, NY; h. Metuchen, NJ.

STEVENS, W(ILLIAM) LESTER.
Painter and teacher. Pupil of Parker S. Perkins, Boston Mus. School. Member: NY WCC; North Shore AA; Boston GAS. Awards: fourth Clark prize, Corcoran Gal., Wash., DC, 1921; Gedney Bunce prize, CT AFA, 1924; landscape prize, Springfield, MA, 1925; second Altman prize, NAD, 1927; Wm. A. Delano Purchase prize, AWCS, 1928; Mansfield prize, New Haven PCC, 1929. Works: "Winter Gray Day," Boston City Club; "Winding Road," Boston City Club; Art Mus., Louisville, KY; "Winter Woods," Public Library, Birmingham, AL. Address in 1929, 4 Mercer St., Princeton, NJ.

STEVENSON, BEULAH.
Painter and etcher. Born in Brooklyn. Pupil of John Sloan. Member: NA Women PS; S. Indp. A. Address in 1929, Ovington Bldg., 246 Fulton St.; h. 178 Emerson Place, Brooklyn, New York, NY.

STEVENSON, GORDON.
Painter. Born Chicago, Feb. 28, 1892. Pupil of Sorolla. Member: Salma. C. Address in 1929, 222 West 23rd St., h. 1, Lexington Ave., New York, NY.

STEVENSON, MARGARET PARIS.
Photographer/graphics. Born in Roxboro, NC, in 1937. Studied: Univ. of North Carolina; American Univ., Wash., DC; Corcoran School of Art, Wash., DC. Exhibitions:

898

Ikon Gal., Wash., DC; Martin Luther King Mem. Library, Wash., DC; Smithsonian Institution, Wash., DC.

STEWARDSON, EDMUND A.
Sculptor. Pupil of Penn. Acad. of the Fine Arts. Elected a member of Society of American Artists in 1891. He died in 1892 at Newport, RI.

STEWART, ALBERT T.
Painter, sculptor, and illustrator. Born Kensington, England, April 9, 1900. Member: Animal PS. Works: "Dolphins," Seamen's Church Inst., NY; "Memorial tablet," Amherst College; "Memorial Tablet," Williams College, Williamstown, MA; "Louis Pope Gratacap Memorial," American Museum of Natural History, NY; "Hawk," Metropolitan Museum of Art.

STEWART, CATHERINE T.
Painter, who exhibited water colors at the Penna. Acad. of the Fine Arts, Philadelphia, 1925. Address in 1926, 2206 Locust Street, Philadelphia.

STEWART, CHARLES.
Engraver. In 1841 Stewart engraved a small but exceedingly fine mezzotint portrait of Peter Stuyvesant, printed by A. King, who was the publisher of some of Durand's plates. A pencil memorandum on the print says that it was engraved for the NY Historical Society.

STEWART, GRACE BLISS (MRS.).
Painter and writer. Born Atchison, KS, April 18, 1885. Pupil of ASL of NY; Hawthorne Summer Art School. Member: NAC; NA Women PS; North Shore AA; PBC; AFA. Author of "In and Out of the Jungle," "Jumping into the Jungle," and "The Good Fairy," (Reily-Lee, Chicago). Address in 1929, 50 West 45th St., New York, NY; summer, Spofford, NH.

STEWART, JOSEPH.
Painter, who was born about 1750. He graduated from Dartmouth College in 1780. His portraits of Rev. Eleazer Wheelock, first President of Dartmouth College, and of John Phillips are signed "J. Steward."

He painted a portrait of John Kemble engraved by H. Houston, published in 1796. He became a Congregationalist minister and was said to have been the first instructor of S. L. Waldo.

STEWART, JULIUS L.
Painter. Born in Phila. in 1855. Pupil of J. L. Gerome and R. de Madrazo. Hon. mention, Salon, Paris, 1885; 3d class medal, Salon, 1890; gold medal, Berlin International Art Exhib., 1891; grand gold medal, Berlin, 1895; Munich, 1897. Exhibited at Paris Expo., 1900. Decorated with Order of Leopold of Belgium, Antwerp, 1894; Cross of Legion d'Honneur, 1895. Elected associate member of Societe Nat. des Beaux Arts, 1895; elected member of Societe des Beaux Arts, 1899; member of International Jury, Paris Expo., 1889; member of jury of selection, Chicago Expo., 1893; grand gold medal, Munich, 1901; promoted officer of Legion d'Honneur, 1901; member of advisory and executive committee for St. Louis Expo., 1904. Member: Paris Soc. of Am. Painters; Societe Nationale, Berlin, 1895; Munich, 1897. Exhibited at Paris Club de France; Phila. Club, Phila.; delegate for the fine arts, US sect., to the Liege Exhib., 1905. Died in Paris.

STEWART, LE CONTE.
Painter and illustrator. Born in Glenwood, UT, in 1891. Pupil of Art Students League of NY, and of Carlsen. Awarded second prize, landscape, Utah State Fair, 1914; first prize, landscape, Utah State Fair, 1915. Work: Represented in Utah State collection; mural decorations in the Hawaiian Temple at Laie; Cardston Temple, Cardston, Alta, Canada. Address in 1926, Cardston, Alta, Canada.

STEWART, ROBERT B.
Painter. Member: SI; GFLA. Address in 1929 1947 Broadway, New York, NY; 721 Walnut St., Philadelphia, PA.

STEWART, T. J. (MRS.).
See Horton, Dorothy E.

STICKROTH, HARRY I.
Mural painter. Born in 1844; died in Chicago, 1922. Instructor in mural and decorative painting in AIC. He was associated with Barry Faulkner in the mural work on the Cunard Building, New York.

STILES, SAMUEL.
Born July 15, 1796 in East Windsor, VT. He served his apprenticeship as an engraver with Abner Reed at East Windsor, and in 1824 he removed to Utica, NY, and formed a partnership in the banknote and general engraving business with Vistus Balch. He was also a pupil of Abner Reed. In 1828 he moved to NY as a banknote engraver. He married in 1825 Charlotte Sophia Reed, the daughter of his old preceptor Abner Reed. Died April 3, 1861 in NYC.

STILLSON, BLANCHE.
Painter and teacher. Born in Indianapolis. Pupil of Forsyth, Hawthorne. Member: Indiana Artists C.; Hoosier Salon. Address in 1929, 4245 North Meridian St., Indianapolis, IN.

STILSON, ETHEL M.
Painter. Member: NA Women PS.; Cleveland Woman's AC. Address in 1929, 1962 East 79th St., 2259 Cedar Ave., Cleveland, OH.

STILWELL-WEBER, SARAH S.
Illustrator. Born in 1878. Studied art at Drexel Institute under Howard Pyle from 1894 to 1900 and later attended his summer classes at Chadds Ford, Penn. The Saturday Evening Post covers which she painted in the 1910's and 1920's earned her distinction in the magazine cover field. She is best known for her illustrations of children. Died in 1939.

STIMSON, ANNA K(ATHARINE).
Sculptor. Born New York City, Nov. 14, 1892. Pupil of Charles Grafly. Member: Phila. Alliance; Fellowship PAFA; Phila. WCC. Address in 1929, 3400 Pearl St.; h. 3401 Powelton Ave., Philadelphia, PA; summer, Bolton Landing, NY.

STIMSON, JOHN WARD.
Painter, illustrator, teacher, writer, and lecturer. Born Paterson, NJ, Dec. 16, 1850. Pupil of Ecole des Beaux Arts in Paris under Cabanel and Jacquesson de la Chevreuse. Studied in England, Belgium, Holland, and Italy. Director Met. Mus. School, NY, for 5 yrs. and founder of Artists-Artisan Inst., NY; and of the School of Fine and Industrial Arts, Trenton. Author of "The Gate Beautiful," "The Law of the Three Primaries," "Wandering Chords." Associate Editor of "Arena"; art lecturer at leading universities, etc. Address in 1929, Corona, CA.

STIRNWEISS, SHANNON.
Illustrator. Born in Portland, OR, in 1931. Graduated from ACD in Los Angeles where he studied under John LaGatta, Reynold Brown, and Pruett Carter and shared classes with Jack Potter, Phil Hays, and Chuck McVicker. He received a Gold Medal from the NJ ADC and the Book Writers Award for the best illustrated dog book. He has illustrated 25 books, and many magazines, including Field and Stream, Boys' Life, Reader's Digest, Argosy, and Show, have used his talents. His work has been shown in many galleries, including the S of I, where he was President from 1972 to 1974.

STITT, HOBART D.
Landscape painter. Born Hot Springs, AR, in 1880. Pupil of Howard Pyle, Robert Spencer, and Fred Wagner at PAFA. Member: Salma. C.; Wilmington SFA; SSAL. Work: Wilmington Society of Fine Arts; Art Museum, Little Rock, AR. Address in 1929, Sudbrook, Pikesville, Maryland.

STIVERS, HARLEY ENNIS.
Illustrator and etcher. Born Nokomis, IL, Nov. 25, 1891. Pupil of AIC. Member: SI; GFLA. Illustrates for Saturday Evening Post, Ladies Home Journal, Cosmopolitan, Photoplay, Red Book, etc. Address in 1929, 7 West 42nd St., New York, NY; 20 Edgewood Place, Searsdale, NY.; summer, Belmar, NJ.

STOCKBRIDGE, DANA W.
Painter. Born in Haverhill, MA, on Jan. 29, 1881. Pupil of Sch. of FA at Harvard Univ., Eric Pape Sch. of Arts. Died Nov. 24, 1922.

STOCKMAN, HELEN PARK (MRS.).
Painter, sculptor, and teacher. Born Englewood, NJ, Oct. 16, 1896. Pupil of Jonas Lie, Luis Mora, and Robert Henri. Member: Palisade AA. Address in 1929, Sherwood Place, Englewood, NJ.

STODART, G.
Engraver. A well-engraved portrait of David Stoner, in stipple, is signed "G. Stodart;" apparently published about 1835; but as Stodart also engraved a portrait of Washington, published in London, he may have been an English engraver. David Stoner, however, seems to have been an American.

STODDARD, ALICE KENT.
Painter. Born Watertown, CT, in 1893. Pupil of PAFA. Member: Fellowship PAFA; Plastic C. Awards: Mary Smith prize, PAFA 1911 and 1913; hon. mention, Phila. AC 1913; Fellowship prize, PAFA 1916; Isidor medal, NAD, 1917; Carol Beck medal, PAFA, 1926; Clark prize, 1928. Work: Penn. Acad., Phila.; Delgado Museum, New Orleans, LA; Reading (PA) Mus. Address in 1929, 7930 Crefield St., St. Martin's, Phila. PA.

STODDARD, ELIZABETH M. (MRS.).
Painter. Member: Hartford, AS. Address in 1929, 30 Farmington Ave., Hartford, CT.

STODDARD, FREDERICK L(INCOLN).
Mural painter and illustrator. Born Coaticook, P. Q., Canada, March 7, 1861. Pupil of St. Louis School of Fine Arts; Constant and Laurens in Paris. Member: North Shore AA; St. Louis AG; Salma. C.; NY Arch. League, 1911. Award: Silver medal, St. Louis Expo., 1904. Work: Mural paintings; City Hall, St. Louis; High School, St. Louis; Hebrew Technical School for Girls, NY; "Birth and Development of Education," and War Workers Memorial, Eastern District High School, NY; "The Transfiguration,"

Memorial Church, Baltimore, MD. Died in 1940. Address in 1929, 100 Front St., New York, NY; summer, 107 Mt. Pleasant Ave., Gloucester, MA.

STODDARD, MUSETTE OSLER.
Painter, craftsman, lecturer, and teacher. Born Carson, IA, Pupil of Ralph Johonnot, E. A. Webster, Charles W. Hawthorne and Maud Mason. Member: IN AC; Brown Co. Gal. A.; W.A.A. Award: Silver medal and diploma, Panama Pacific Exp., San Francisco, 1915. Address in 1929, 636 Graham Court, Council Bluffs, Iowa; summer, Nashville, Brown Co., IN.

STOHR, JULIA COLLINS.
(Mrs. Peter C. Stohr). Painter. Born Toledo, OH, Sept. 2, 1866. Pupil of Cooper Union and ASL in NY under Beckwith, Chase, J. Alden Weir, Freer, and W. L. Lathrop, and in Paris. Member: Art Workers Guild of St. Paul; Minnesota State Art Soc.; Chicago WCC; NA Women PS. Address in 1929, "Conifer," Lovell, ME.

STOHR, JULIE.
(Mrs. J. S. Roe). Painter. Born St. Paul, MN, March 19, 1895. Pupil of Simon. Menard in Paris; Henri and Bellows in NY. Member: ASL of NY; S. Indp. A. Address in 1929, 512 Pierce St., Monterey, CA.

STOKES, FRANK W(ILBERT).
Painter and sculptor. Born Nashville, TN. Pupil of PAFA under Thomas Eakins; Ecole des Beaux-Arts in Paris under Gerome; Colarossi Acad. under Collin; Julian Acad. under Boulanger and Lefebvre. Award: Medaille d'Argent, Prix de Montherot de Geographia de Paris. Specialty, arctic and antarctic scenes; Member, Peary Greenland Expedition, 1892 and 1893-94; and Swedish Antarctic Expedition, 1901-02; artists member Amundsen Ellsworth Expedition, 1926. Member: Fellowship PAFA. Work: Mural decorations, Museum of Natural History, NY. Address in 1929, 3 Washington Square, N., New York, NY.

STOLL, FREDERICK H.
Sculptor, who exhibited at the Annual Exhibition, 1923, at PAFA, Phila. Address in 1926, American Museum of Natural History, NY.

STOLL, JOHN (THEODOR) (EDWARD).
Painter, sculptor, illustrator, and etcher. Born Goettingen, Hanover, Germany, Sept. 29, 1889. Chiefly self taught. Member: San Francisco AA; Calif. SE. Represented in Art Museum of Legion of Honor, San Francisco. Address in 1929, 141 San Pablo Ave., St. Francis Wood, San Francisco.

STOLL, R(OLF).
Painter, illustrator, and teacher. Born Heidelberg, Germany, Nov. 11, 1892. Pupil of Academie of Fine Arts in Karlsruhe; Academie of Fine Arts in Stuttgart, Germany. Member: Clev. SA; Kokoon AC. Awards: First prize, Cleveland Museum of Art 1925; first and second prizes, Cleveland Museum of Art, 1926; hon. mention Cleveland Museum of Art, 1927. Represented by decorative panels in the Public Library, Cleveland, OH; oil painting, Gallery of Fine Arts, Columbus, OH. Address in 1929, 1851 Hillside Ave., East Cleveland, OH.

STOLTENBERG, H(ANS) J(OHN).
Painter and teacher. Born Flensburg, Germany, April 8, 1879. Pupil of Dudley Crafts Watson. Member: WI Painters and Sculptors. Award: Hon. mention, Milwaukee Art Inst., 1920. Work: "The Birches," Milwaukee Technical High School; "Winter Landscape," Public Library, and "Morning Shadows," High School, Wauwatosa, WI; "Open Stream in Winter," Milwaukee Art Inst. Address in 1929, Lovers Lane, Wauwatosa, WI.

STONE, ALICE BALCH.
Painter, sculptor, and craftsman. Born Swampscott, MA, July 12, 1876. Pupil of Caroline Rimmer, Wilbur Dean Hamilton, and John Wilson. Member: Copley S; Alliance; Boston SAC. Address in 1929, Pottery Workshop, 79 Chestnut St., Boston, MA; h. Woodland Road, Jamaica Plain, Boston 30, MA; summer, Chocorua, NH.

STONE, ANNA B.
Painter. Born DeWitt, IA, Jan. 8, 1874. Pupil of Edgar Forkner. Member: Seattle AI. Died in 1949. Address in 1929, Olympian, 16th and Madison; h. 1605 East Madison, Seattle, WA.

STONE, DAVID K.
Illustrator. Born in Reedsport, OR, in 1922. Attended the Univ. of Oregon, graduating after serving in World War II. He studied art at the ACD in Los Angeles and also in Mexico. His career began in 1949 in NY with editorial work and he has won several awards since, from the S of I and the ADCs of St. Louis and Richmond. He served as President of the S of I and is a contributor to the USAF Art Program.

STONE, FRANK F(REDERICK).
Sculptor. Born London, England, March 28, 1860. Pupil of Richard Belt. Member: American Numismatic Soc. Awards: First prize for sculpture, San Antonio State Fair; gold medal, Alaska-Yukon-Pacific Exp., 1909. Work: "Gladstone," from life, Treasury Office, London; "Mark Twain Medallion," Sacramento State Library. Address in 1929, 1036 S. Bonnie Brae St., Los Angeles, CA.

STONE, GILBERT LEONARD.
Illustrator. Born in Brooklyn, NY, in 1940. Graduated with honors from PSD after receiving scholarships there and at the Brooklyn Museum. Three years after his first illustration appeared in Seventeen, he was awarded the Prix de Drome. He has been the recipient of four Gold Medals from the S of I for his work in Sports Illustrated, McCall's, Seventeen, and Steelways. His art is part of the permanent collection of the Brooklyn Museum and the Smithsonian Institution.

STONE, HENRY.
Engraver. In 1826 this line engraver was also doing work in Washington, DC. He was doubtless connected with the Mr. and Mrs. W. J. Stone here referred to, possibly a son. Henry Stone drew upon stone

for lithographers of Wash., DC.

STONE, HORATIO.
Sculptor. Born Dec. 25, 1808, in Jackson, NY. At an early age he attempted wood carving, a pursuit which was not encouraged by his father. Leaving home, he did not communicate with his family for many yrs. Instrumental in the organization of the Wash. Union Art Assoc., he was elected its pres. This organization pres. a mem. to Congress requesting recognition of Am. artists in the decoration of the Capitol, and as a result, the Art commission of 1859, consisting of H. K. Brown, Jas R. Lambdin, and John F. Kensett, was appointed by Pres. Buchanan. Stone visited Italy twice in the study of his work as a sculptor. In 1857, he received the medal of the MD Inst. for his busts of Benton and Taney, and exhibited his works in the NAD in 1849 and 1869. He is also credited with models for statues of Prof. Morse, Admiral Farragut, and Dr. Harvey, the discoverer of the circulation of the blood. Died in Italy in 1875.

STONE, J. M.
Painter. Born in Dana, MA, in 1841. He studied in Boston, and later in Munich. He spent his professional life in Boston, where he became an instructor at the School of the Museum of Fine Arts. He painted a number of portraits.

STONE, M. BAINBRIDGE.
Painter. Member: Balto. WCC. Died in 1939. Address in 1929, 223 West Lanvale St., Baltimore, MD.

STONE, SEYMOUR M.
Painter. Born Poland, June 11, 1877. Pupil of the Royal Acad. in Munich under De Loeftz, and of Jank in Munich; Zorn in Sweden; Lefebvre in Paris; John Singer Sargent in London. Member: AFA. Painted royalty and nobility in Europe for 11 years. Knight Commander of Merit of the Constantinian Order of St. George of Italy. Address in 1929, The Withington Apts., 16 East 60th St., New York, NY.

STONE, VIOLA P(RATT).
(Mrs. Joseph H. Stone). Painter and sculptor. Born Omaha, NE. Pupil of J. Laurie Wallace; Kansas City AI; Edna Kelly. Member: Long Beach AA. Address in 1929, 5925 East Seaside Walk, Long Beach, CA.

STONE, WALTER KING.
Illustrator and painter. Born Barnard, NY, March 2, 1875. Pupil of Pratt Inst., Brooklyn, NY, under Arthur Dow. Member: Salma. C. Work: "The Walter Garden," and "Blue Shawdows," Memorial Gal., Rochester, NY; over mantel decorations in many private homes. Assistant professor of painting, Cornell Univ. Died June 21, 1949. Address in 1929, Cornell Univ.; The Byway, Forest Home, Ithaca, NY.

STONE, WILLIAM J.
In 1822 this excellent engraver of portraits in stipple and etcher of buildings, etc., was located in Washington, DC, possibly in Government employ. A map of Washington, published in 1840 by Wm. D. Morrison, is signed "Eng'd by Mrs. W. J. Stone." There is an excellent engraved portrait of Wm. J. Stone.

STONE, WILLIAM OLIVER.
Portrait painter. Born Sept. 26, 1830, at Derby, CT. Studied with Nathaniel Jocelyn at New Haven in 1851, and then moved to NY. In 1856 he was elected an Associate Member of the National Academy, and in 1859 an Academician. He painted portraits of Bishops Williams, Littlejohn and Kip. The NY Historical Society owns his portrait of Thomas J. Bryan and the Metropolitan Museum owns his portrait of Miss Rawle. Died Sept. 15, 1875, in Newport, RI.

STONER, HARRY.
Mural painter, and illustrator. Born Springfield, OH, Jan. 21, 1880. Member: Arch. Lg. of NY; GFLA. Work: Design for glass mosaic curtain, executed by Tiffany Studios for the National Theatre, Mexico City. Address in 1929, 18 West 37th St., New York, NY.

STONER, OLIVE
Painter and teacher. Born Pleasantville, PA. Pupil of Snell, Breckenridge, Garber, Arthur B. Carles, Fred Wagner; Phila. School of Design for Women; PAFA. Member: Fellowship PAFA; Phila. Alliance; AG. of Tiffany Found. Address in 1929, 3408 Baring St., Phila., PA.

STOOPS, HERBERT MORTON.
Illustrator. Born in Idaho, in 1888. Attended Utah State Coll. before joining the staff of the San Francisco Call. He later worked at the Chicago Tribune while attending the AIC. His career as an illustrator of Western scenes began in NY with Bluebook, for which he was a frequent contributor. His illustrations also appeared in Collier's and Cosmopolitan. A member of several professional organizations and President of the AG, he was awarded the Isador Medal from the Salma. Club. Died in 1948.

STOREY, ROSS BARRON.
Illustrator. Born in Dallas, TX, in 1940. Studied at the FAS, SVA under Robert Weaver and the ACD in Los Angeles where he is presently chairman of the illustration department. His career began in 1959 in Dallas and his artwork soon began appearing in Sunday Magazine of The New York Journal American. He has since illustrated for many magazines, including Esquire, Life, This Week, and recently, Time. He has won awards from the S of I and from several ACDs.

STORM, ANNA ALFRIDA.
Painter, craftsman, and teacher. Born Sweden, July 2, 1896. Pupil of Dow. Member: Chicago SA; Chicago NJSA. Award: First prize, Seattle FAS, 1923. Address in 1929, Northwestern University, 1888 Sheridan Road, Evanston, IL; summer, State Teachers College, Greeley, CO.

STORM, G. F.
Engraver. Born in England and came to Philadelphia about 1834. Storm was an admirable engraver of portraits in stipple; he was also a good etcher. Though his stay in the US is said to have been a short one, he engraved a considerable number of American portraits.

STORRS, FRANCES HUDSON.
(Mrs. William M. Storrs). Painter. Born NY. Pupil of Chase, Hawthorne, and Hale. Member: CT AFA; North Shore AA; Springfield AA. Work: "Summer Flowers," Morgan Memorial, Hartford. Address in 1929, 1034 Prospect Ave., Hartford, CT; summer, Hawthorne Inn, East Gloucester, MA.

STORRS, JOHN BRADLEY.
Sculptor and etcher. Born Chicago, June 29, 1885. Pupil of Grafly, Barlett, Rodin. Member: Societe Anonyme; Chic. AC. Died in 1956. Address in 1929, 20 E. Delaware Place, Chicago, IL; summer, 109 rue du Cherche Midi, Paris, France.

STORY, GEORGE HENRY.
Painter. Born Jan. 22, 1835, in New Haven, CT. Studied in NY and Paris. In 1875 he was elected an Assoc. Member of National Academy of Design, and in 1876 he received a medal at the Centennial Expo., Phila. He painted several portraits of Lincoln, and is represented at the Metropolitan Museum by "Self portrait," and "The Young Mother." He died Nov. 24, 1923, in NYC.

STORY, JULIAN.
Portrait painter. Born 1857, in Walton-on-Thames, England. He was the son of W. W. Story (poet and sculptor). Pupil of Frank Duveneck, Boulanger and Lefebvre, Paris. Awards: 3d class medal and honorable mention, Paris Salon, 1889; gold medal, Berlin, 1891; silver medal, Paris Exposition, 1900; made Chevalier Legion d'Honneur, France, 1900. Elected an Assoc. Member of the National Acad. in 1906. He died Feb. 23, 1919, in Phila.

STORY, THOMAS C.
This general engraver of portraits and historical plates was in business in NY during the period 1837-44. The firm of Story & Atwood was engraving in the same city in 1843.

STORY, WALDO.
Sculptor. Son of William Wetmore Story. His studio in now in Rome.

STORY, WILLIAM WETMORE.
Sculptor. Born Feb. 12, 1819, in Salem, MA. Graduated from Harvard College in 1838, he adopted art as a profession and about 1848 went to Italy for study. His statues of Josiah Quincy, Edward Everett, and Colonel Shaw are well known. He died Oct. 7, 1895, in Italy.

STOUFFER, J. EDGAR.
Sculptor. Member: Charcoal C. Award: Rinehart Scholarship to Paris, 1907-1911. Address in 1929, 1230 St. Paul St., Baltimore, MD.

STOUT, GEORGE H.
Engraver. Born 1807, in NYC. The NY directories for 1830-50, inclusive, contain this name as an "engraver of cards, seals and door plates." Died Jan. 26, 1852.

STOUT, IDA McCLELLAND.
Sculptor. Born in Decatur, IL. Pupil of Albin Polasek. Work: "Goose Girl Fountain," Mary W. French School, Decatur, IL; "Princess Badoura," Hillyer Gallery, Smith College. Member of Artist's Guild; Alumni AIC; Chi. Galleries and MacDowell Club. Died Sept. 2, 1927 in Rome, Italy. Address in 1926, Art Institute Chicago, IL.

STOUT, JAMES DEFORREST.
Engraver. Born July 22, 1783, in NYC. This man was a map engraver about 1813, and apparently living in NY. Died July 8, 1868 in NYC.

STOUT, JAMES VARICK.
Engraver. Born in 1809, in NYC. In business in NY in 1834-38, as a general engraver and die sinker. He also engraved some good landscape plates. Son of James D. Stout. Died April 26, 1860, in NYC.

STOVER, ALLAN JAMES.
Painter and illustrator. Born West Point, MI, Oct. 9, 1887. Pupil of Cleveland School of Art. Work: Decoration of Masonic Temple, Corvallis, OR. Illustrated "Oregon's Commercial Forests."

Address in 1929, 429 Silvergate Ave., Point Loma, CA; 2626 Arnold Way, Corvallis, OR.

STOVER, WALLACE.
Painter and illustrator. Born Elkhart, IN, Jan. 5, 1903. Pupil of William Forsyth, Clifton Wheeler, Paul Hadley, and Myra Richards. Member: IN AC; Herron Art School Alumni; Hoosier Salon. Award: first prize, Herron Art, IN, 1925, and third prize, 1927. Specialty, portraits and illustrations. Address in 1929, 230 Riverside Drive, New York, NY; h. 1018 South Second St., Elkhart, IN.

STOWELL, M. LOUISE.
Painter, illustrator, craftsman, and teacher. Born Rochester. Pupil of ASL of NY and Arthur W. Dow. Member: Rochester Soc. of Arts and Crafts; NYWCC. Specialty, water colors. Address in 1929, 714 Ins. Bldg., Main St.; h. 29 Atkinson St., Rochester, NY.

STRAHAN, ALFRED W(INFIELD).
Painter and illustrator. Born Baltimore, MD, June 24, 1886. Pupil of S. Edwin Whiteman and Harper Pennington. Member: Charcoal Club. Address in 1929, 214 Chamber of Commerce Bldg., Baltimore, MD, h. James Road, Woodlawn, P. O., MD.

STRAIN, D. J.
Painter. Born in New Hampshire, he entered Julien's studio in Paris in 1877. In 1883 he opened his studio in Boston. He painted a number of portraits; that of General N. P. Banks is perhaps his greatest achievement. Address in 1926, 278 Boyleston Street, Boston, MA.

STRAIN, FRANCES.
Painter. Born Chicago, Nov. 11, 1898. Pupil of AIC. Member: Indp. A.; Chic. SA; The Ten; Chicago No-Jury Artists; Salons of America. Address in 1929, 5644 Harper Ave.; h. 5200 Dorchester Ave., Chicago, IL.

STRATER, HENRY.
Painter. Born Louisville, KY, Jan. 21, 1896. Pupil of PAFA. Address in 1929, 55 West 8th Street.; h.

905

115 East 86th St., New York, NY; summer, Ogunquit, ME.

STRAUS, MITTELDORFER.
Painter and illustrator. Born Richmond, VA, Jan. 21, 1880. Pupil of ASL of Washington; studied in Europe and Africa. Member: Paris AAA; NYWCC; S. Indp. A.; Alliance; SI. Award: Scholarship, ASL of Wash., to Pratt Inst. Address in 1929, 245 Fifth Ave., New York, NY; and 2025 Monument Ave., Richmond, VA.

STRAWBRIDGE, ANN W(EST).
Painter. Born Philadelphia, PA, March 20, 1883. Pupil of W. M. Chase. Member: Fellowship PAFA; Plastic C.; Phila. Alliance; S. Indp. A.; AFA. Address in 1929, 6711 Wissahickon Ave., Mt. Airy, Philadelphia, PA; summer, care Messrs. Brown Shipley and Co., 123 Pall Mall, London, EN.

STREAN, MARIA JUDSON.
Painter. Born in Washington, PA. Pupil of Art Students' League of NY under Cox and J. Alden Weir; under Prinet and Dauchez in Paris. Member: New York Water Color Club; American Society of Miniature Painters; Allied Artists Assoc.; Nat. Assoc. of Women Painters and Sculptors. Awarded honorable mention, Panama-American Expo., Buffalo, 1901. Address in 1926, 140 West 57th Street, New York, NY.

STREATFIELD, JOSEPHINE.
Portrait painter. Born London, England, May 31, 1882. Pupil of Slade School in London, under Fred Brown. Member: Phila. PC; Soc. Women Artists, London; Alliance. Specialty, pastel and oil portraits and restoring. Address in 1929, 143 West 81st St., New York, NY.

STREATOR, HAROLD A.
Painter. Born in Cleveland, OH. Pupil of Art Students' League of NY, and of the Boston Museum School. Member: Salmagundi Club, 1906. Address in 1926, Box 345, Morristown, NJ.

STREET, FRANK.
Illustrator. Born in Kansas City, MO, in 1893. Attended ASL; studied with Charles Chapman, Harvey Dunn in Leonia, NJ. Editorial illustrations in Saturday Evening Post, Ladies' Home Journal, Cosmopolitan. Active portrait and landscape artist. Member: SI; Salma. C. Died in 1944. Address in 1929, 505 Grand St., Leonia, NJ.

STREET, ROBERT.
Painter of portraits and historical subjects, who was for many yrs. a resident of Phila. He was born Jan. 17, 1796 in Germantown, PA and exhibited in the PA Acad. of the Fine Arts during the period between 1815-1817. In 1824 his portraits were shown in Wash., DC, where he painted several well known men. In 1835 Dunlap records the death of Street and the artist had the most unique experience of calling the author's attention to such a grave error. Dunlap corrects his error with many apologies in the NY Mirror of the issue of Feb. 28, 1835. In 1840, Robert Street held 200 oil paintings of historical subjects, landscapes and portraits. Catalogues of this exhibition are accessible, but unfortunately they give little valuable info. regarding the portraits, as they are frequently recorded as merely "A Portrait of a Lady" or "A Portrait of a Gentleman." This exhibition opened on Nov. 18, 1840, in Phila.

STREETER, JULIA ALLEN.
(Mrs. George L. Streeter). Painter. Born Detroit, MI, June 19, 1877. Pupil of Detroit Art School under Joseph Gies and F. P. Paulus. Member: Baltimore WCC; Arundell C; AFA. Award: Hon. mention, Baltimore Charcoal Club, 1924. Address in 1929, 2022 Eutaw Place, Baltimore, MD; summer, Green Lake P.O., Fulton Co., NY.

STREETER, TAL.
Sculpter. Born in Okla. City, Aug. 1, 1934. Study at Univ. of Kansas, BTA, MFA; Colo. Springs Fine Art Ctr., with Robt. Motherwell; Colo. College; with Seymour Lipton. In Collections of MOMA; S. Fran. Mus. of Art; Wadsworth Atheneum; Smithsonian; Storm King Art Un., NY; others. Commissions in Little Rock, AK; Atlanta, GA; NYC; Trenton, NJ. Exhib. at Aldrich

Mus., Ridgefield, CT; Storm King Art Ctr., Mountainville, NY; Am. Cult. Ctr., Seoul, Korea; Contemp. Arts Mus., Houston; Corcoran (Drawings); MIT; many others. Has taught at numerous institutions; SUNY Purchase from 1973. Address in 1982, Old Verbank School, Millbrook, NY.

STRICKLAND, WILLIAM.
Painter an engraver. Born in Phila., in 1787; died in Nashville, TN, in 1854. Strickland studied architecture under Benjamin H. Latrobe, but in 1809 he took up portrait painting, designing for engravers, and engraving in aquatint. In this manner he produced a few portraits and a number of views illustrating events in the War of 1812. About 1820 Strickland resumed practice as an architect and among the buildings designed by him in Phila. were the Masonic Hall, United States Mint, Bank of the US, the new Chestnut Street, and the Arch. Street theatres and the Merchants Exchange. Died April 6, 1854, in Nashville, TN.

STRINGFIELD, VIVIAN F.
Painter, illustrator, craftsman, and teacher. Born California. Pupil of Mark Hopkins Inst.; Pratt Inst.; Douglas Donaldson and Ralph H. Johonnot. Member: Southern Calif. Art Teachers Assoc.; Boston SAC; Chicago AG. Award: Bronze medal, Panama Calif. Exp., San Diego, 1915. Address in 1929, 229 South Normandie Ave., Los Angeles, CA.

STROHL, CLIFFORD.
Painter. Born in South Bethlehem, PA, in 1893. Pupil of Jules Dieudonne and of Orlando G. Wales; also studied in the Penna. Acad. of the Fine Arts. Member of Salmagundi Club. Address in 1926, 416 Avenue E, Bethlehem, PA.

STRONG, CONSTANCE GILL.
Painter and teacher. Born New York City, May 13, 1900. Pupil of Pratt Inst.; Univ. of PA. Member: Palette and Pencil C. Awards: First and second prizes for water color, Lake County Fair, Crown Point, IN, 1926, 1927, 1928.

Address in 1929, 768 Vermont St., Gary, IN.

STROTHER, COL. DAVID HUNTER.
Portrait painter. Born Sept. 26, 1816, in Martinsburg, VA. Studied in Europe. In 1844, returned to US as illustrator, esp. for Harper's Magazine. Died March 8, 1888 in Charleston, W. VA.

STROTHMANN, FRED.
Painter and illustrator. Born New York, Sept. 23, 1879. Pupil of Carl Hecker; studied in Berlin and Paris. Member: SI. Illustrated books by Mark Twain, Carolyn Wells, Brubacker, Ellis P. Butler, Lucille Gulliver. Died in 1958. Address in 1929, 562 West 190th St., New York, NY; summer, Long Beach, LI, NY.

STROUD, CLARA.
Painter, draftsman, and teacher. Born New Orleans, LA, Nov. 4, 1890. Pupil of Cimiotti, Mary Lantry, Otto W. Beck, Ethel F. Shaurman, Ethel Traphagen and Jay Hambidge. Ralph Johonnot. Member: NA Women PS. Contributor to "Design" and "Every Day Art." Address in 1929, 17 E. 62nd St., New York, NY.

STROUD, IDA WELLS.
Painter and draftsman. Born New Orleans, LA, Oct. 19, 1869. Pupil of Pratt Inst.; ASL of NY. Member: NA Women PS; NYWCC. Instructor, painting, drawing, and design at Newark School of Fine and Industrial Art, Newark, NJ. Address in 1929, 85 North 7th St., Newark, NJ.

STRUBING, LOUISA HAYES.
Painter, sculptor, and craftsman. Born Buffalo, NY, Jan. 15, 1881. Pupil of Buffalo Albright Art School; Robert Reid. Member: Buffalo SA; Buffalo GAA. Address in 1929, 80 Keswick Road, Amherst Estates, Eggertsville, NY.

STRUNK, HERBERT.
Sculptor. Born Shakopee, MN, April 9, 1891. Pupil of St. Paul Inst. School of Art. Member: St. Paul AS. Award: Silver medal, St. Paul Inst., 1915. Work: "Chief Shakopee," model in St. Paul Inst.,

Gal. Died in 1950. Address in 1929, Shakopee, MN.

STRUVEN, GERTRUDE STANWOOD (MRS.).
Painter and etcher. Born West Newbury, MA, March 2, 1874. Pupil of Joseph DeCamp, Charles Lasar in Paris. Member: North Shore AA; Gloucester SA. Address in 1929, Wilmette, IL.

STRYCKER, JACOBUS GERRITSEN.
Artist. Born in 1619. Farmer, trader, magistrate, and "limner." Was born at Ruinen, province of Drenthe, in the Netherlands. His wife was was Ytie Huybrechts, possibly related to the lady of the same surname, whose daughter at about the same time married Titus van Rijn, the son of a greater "limner," Rembrandt. Strycker came to New Netherland in 1651, a gentleman of considerable means and decided culture, and after a successful career died in 1687. We knew something of his office holding; he was Burgher in 1653 and afterwards Alderman of New Amsterdam; also Attorney General Sheriff of the Dutch towns on Long Island up to August, 1673. Very little of his work as an artist is known. Three of his portraits have been identified. He left a son, Gerrit, who became Sheriff of King's County in 1688, and a brother, Jan, who also left descendants.

STUART, F. T.
This good engraver of portraits was working in 1850; at a much later date he was located in Boston.

STUART, GILBERT (CHARLES).
Portrait painter. Born in No. Kingston, RI, Dec. 3, 1755. Considered the greatest American port. painter, and among the great artists of the world. Stuart was educated in Newport and early showed great promise when he painted portraits of the prominent men of Newport. In 1770 Stuart received instruction from Cosimo Alexander, a Scotch gentlemen then residing in Newport. Sailed to England 1775. Painted in the studio of Benjamin West in London for several yrs. Opened own studio in London in 1788 and became one of the most sought after portrait painters in England. There he painted portraits of artists Benjamin West, Sir Joshua Reynolds, Gainsborough, Copley, W. Grant skating in St. James Park (one of his finest works); John Philip Kemble, the actor; the Duke of Northumberland, and Admiral Sir John Jarvis. In 1790 went to Ireland, where he painted important personages including the Duke of Leinster, Lord Fitzgibbon, Hon. John Beresford. Sailed to NY 1792, moved to Phila. 1794 to paint George Washington. There are 124 portraits of Washington listed as painted by Stuart. Moved to Washington in 1803 to paint portrait of President Jefferson. In 1805 moved to Boston. Elected member of American Academy in 1795 and honorary member of Nat. Academy of Design in 1827. Mem. exhib. of portraits held in Boston in 1880. Portraits in collections of many prominent galleries; PAFA owns probably the finest collection of his works. Painted over 1,000 portraits. Died in Boston July 9th, 1828. Biographies include; Life and Works of Stuart for catalogue of other portraits; Pennsylvania Magazine of the Historical Society by Mantle Fielding for list of 200 portraits not noted in Mason.

STUART, JAMES E(VERETT).
Painter. Born near Dover, ME, March 24, 1852. Pupil of Virgil Williams and R. D. Yelland in San Francisco Sch. of Des. Member: San Francisco AA; Am. APL. Work: "Sunset Glow, Mt. Takoma" and "Sacramento River," Kalamazoo (MI) Art Assoc.; "Showers Among the Trees, NJ" and "Sunset Glow, Mt. Jefferson," Omaha Public Library; "Sunset, Sacramento River," Reno Arts and Crafts Club; "Showers, Napa Valley," Oakdale Public Library; "Morning, Mt. Hood," "Mt. Tallac, Lake Tahoe," Los Angeles Museum of History, Science and Art. Originator of a new method of painting on aluminum and wood. Died in 1941. Address in 1929, 684 Commercial St., San Francisco, CA.

STUART, JANE.
Painter. Daughter of Gilbert Stuart. Born about 1812, in Boston, she followed her father's profession for many years. She was a skillful copyist and reproduced many of her father's paintings, especially his portraits of Washington. She died in Newport, RI, April 27, 1888. She published several articles in Scribner's Monthly Magazine of 1877 about her father and his work.

STUART, MICHELLE.
Drawing. Born in Los Angeles, CA, in 1938. Studied: Chouinard Art Institute, Los Angeles, CA; Instituto de Bellas Artes, Mexico; New School for Social Research, NYC. Awards: MacDowell Fellowship, 1974; Tamarind Institute Grant, Albuquerque, NM, 1974. Exhibitions: Westchester Art Soc., 1971; Windham Coll., Putney, VT, 1973; Museum of Modern Art, NYC, 1974. Collections: Int'l Museum, San Fran., CA; Aldrich Museum, Ridgefield, CT.

STUBBS, LU.
Sculptor. Born in NYC in 1925. Studied: Boston Museum of Fine Arts; Academia di Belle Arti, Perugia, Italy. Awards: Providence Art Club, 1972; Art Association of Newport, Rhode Island, 1972. Exhibitions: Milton Academy, Milton, MA, 1968; Thayer Academy, Braintree, MA, 1972; The American Woman, Jordan Marsh, 1975. Collections: Boston Center for Adult Education; Community Systems by Perini, Boston.

STUBBS, MARY H(ELEN).
Painter, illustrator, craftsman, and teacher. Born Greenville, OH, Oct. 31, 1867. Pupil of Cincinnati Art Acad.; Julian Acad. in Paris. Member: Cincinnati Woman's AC; Cincinnati Ceramic C. Award: Hon. mention, Columbian Exp., Chicago, 1893. Address in 1929, 4429 Ellis Ave., Chicago, IL.

STUBER, DEDRICK B(RANDES).
Painter. Born NY, May 4, 1878. Pupil of Bridgman, Julian Onderdonk, Clinton Peters; ASL of NY. Member: Los Angeles PS; Laguna Beach AA; Glendale AA.

Address in 1929, Wilshire Art Galleries, 3309 Wilshire Blvd., Los Angeles; h. Kelton Ave., Westwood, Los Angeles, CA.

STUEVER, CELIA M.
Etcher and painter. Born St. Louis. Pupil of St. Louis School of Fine Arts; Julian Acad. in Paris under Bouguereau and Ferrier; studied in Vienna and Munich. Member: Chicago SE; Calif. SW; NYSE; Calif. P.M. Work in: City Art Museum, St. Louis; Library of Congress, Washington, DC; New York Public Library. Address in 1929, 3444 Russell Ave., St. Louis, MO.

STURDEVANT, S.
A practically unknown American engraver, there being only one example of his work catalogued. It was published in Lexington, KY, in 1822. The portrait is very crude and occurs in a privately printed volume of sermons. It is the earliest known signed portrait engraved west of the Allegheny Mountains.

STURGEON, RUTH B.
Painter and etcher. Born in Sterling, KS, in 1883. Address in 1926, 115 Pearl St., Council Bluffs, IA.

STURGES, DWIGHT CASE.
Painter and etcher. Born Boston, MA, in 1874. Pupil of Cowles Art School in Boston. Member: Chicago SE; Canadian SE; Brooklyn SE; Concord AA; AFA. Awards: Lamont prize, Chicago SE, 1915; silver medal for etching, P.-P. Exp., San Francisco, 1915; Logan medal, AIC, 1924; member's prize. CSE, 1926; Huntington prize, CA. PM, 1927. Work in: Boston Musuem of Fine Arts; Chicago Art Inst.; Oakland (CA) Museum; Library of Congress, Washington; NY Public Library; Toledo Museum of Art. Died in 1940. Address in 1929, Melrose, MA.

STURGES, KATHARINE.
Painter and illustrator. Member: GFLA. Work: Illustrated "Little Pictures of Japan," edited by O. K. Miller (Bookhouse for Children). Address in 1929, 36 East 29th St.,

909

New York, NY; Main St., Roslyn, LI, NY.

STURGES, LEE.
Etcher. Born Chicago, IL, Aug. 13, 1865. Pupil of AIC, PAFA, Chicago SE; Calif. P. M.; Brooklyn SE; AFA; Print Soc. of England. Award: Logan medal, AIC, 1923. Address in 1929, 280 Cottage Hill Ave., Elmhurst, IL.

STURGES, LILLIAN.
Painter, illustrator, writer, and teacher. Born Wilkes-Barre, PA. Member: Pitts. A.A. Author and illustrator of "The Runaway Toys," and several other books for children; illustrated new editions of "Fairy Tales;" "Little Black Sambo;" "Aladdin;" "Eugene Field's Poems," etc. Address in 1929, 2956 Belrose Ave., Pittsburgh, PA.

STURGIS, MABEL R(USSELL).
Painter and craftsman. Born Boston, July 17, 1865. Pupil of Boston Museum of Fine Arts School, Woodbury. Member: Copley S.; AFA; North Shore AA. Address in 1929, 31 Pinckney St.; h. 63 Beacon St., Boston, MA; summer, Manchester, MA.

STURTEVANT, EDITH LOUISE.
Painter and teacher. Born Utica, NY, Dec. 23, 1888. Pupil of PAFA under McCarter, Breckenridge, Garber, and Pearson. Address in 1929, 107 McCartney St., Easton, PA; summer, Masconia Lake, Enfield, NH.

STURTEVANT, HELENA.
Painter. Born Middletown, RI, Aug. 9, 1872. Pupil of Boston Museum School under Tarbell; Colarossi Acad. in Paris under Blanche and Lucien Simons. Member: Int. Soc. AL; Newport AA; AFA; College AAA. Director School of Art Assoc., Newport, RI. Died in 1946. Address in 1929, Second Beach Road, Newport, RI.

STURTEVANT, LOUISA C(LARK).
Landscape painter and draftsman. Born Paris, France, Feb. 2, 1870. Pupil of Boston Museum School under Tarbell; Collin and Simon in Paris. Member: Newport AA; AFA. Award: Silver medal, P.-P. Exp., San Francisco, 1915. Address in 1929, Second Beach Road, Newport, RI.

STUSSY, JAN.
Painter. He was born Aug. 13, 1921, in Benton County, Missouri. Earned BA from UCLA (1944), MFA, U. of So. Cal. (1953). Teaching at UCLA since 1946. Rec. awards from LA County Mus., CA Watercolor Soc.; S.F. Art Assoc.; Critics Award, Best one Man Show (Santiago, Chile, 1968) Exhibited at Ohio State; U. of Nebraska, UCLA; Phoenix Art Mus.; Fresno Arts Center; Santa Barbara Mus.; Mulvane Art Ctr., Topeka, KS; PAFA; Lib. of Congress; MOMA; Stanford U., and others. In private collections, and at S. F. Mus. of Art; MOMA; Santa Barbara and LA County Mus.

STYLES, GEORGE C(HARLES).
Etcher, artist, and craftsman. Born York, England. June 14, 1892. Pupil of Richard Windass, York School of Art. Awards: Kings prize in architecture, 1911; National scholarship in architecture, 1912; Assoc. Royal College of Art, 1914. Address in 1929, 75 Stratfield Road, Bridgeport, CT.

STYLES, GEORGE W(ILLIAM).
Painter and craftsman. Born Sutton, England, Nov. 11, 1887. Pupil of George Elmer Browne; School of Arts and Crafts in London. Member: Scarab C. Award: Walter C. Piper prize ($500), Detroit, 1927. Work: "Low Tide," Dearborn Public Library, Dearborn, MI; "Quiet," High School, Fordson, MI; "Cornish Coast," Scarab Club, Detroit, MI. Designed and executed medal awarded Mrs. Evangeline Lindbergh by the Detroit Board of Education. Died in 1949. Address in 1929, Scarab Club, 217 Farnsworth Ave., h. 37 Marston Ave., Detroit MI.

SUARES, JEAN CLAUDE.
Illustrator. Born in Alexandria, Egypt, in 1942. Attended Sarola Suizzera di Genova and PI. His first published work appeared in The Realist in 1965 and the NY ADC awarded him a Special Gold Medal in 1971. A specialist in pen-and-ink editorial art, he has written

several books on illustration and his works have been shown in the Musee des Beaux Arts in Bordeaux as well as the Musee des Arts Decoratifs in the Louvre.

SUGDEN, THOMAS D.
Wood engraver. Pupil of T. W. Strong. He was connected for years with the engraving department of the Century Co. He wrote a volume on wood engraving, "Remarks on Wood Engraving by One-o'-them," 1904.

SUHR, FREDERIC J.
Illustrator. Born NY, Feb. 15, 1885. Pupil of ASL of NY; Pratt Inst.; Bridgman, Fogarty, and Dufner. Member: Salma C.; SI; Art Directors Club. Died in 1941. Address in 1929, Bayside, LI, NY.

SULLIVAN, ARTHUR B.
Painter. Member: Salma. C.; SI. Address in 1929, care of the Hill Winsten Co., 25 West 44th St., New York, NY.

SULLIVAN, D. FRANK.
Painter, etcher, and teacher. Born Oct. 17, 1892. Pupil of Vesper George, E. L. Major, and Richard Andrew. Member: Pittsburgh AA; AFA. Work: "Olde King Cole," City of Brownsville, PA; "The Keeper of the Garden," the public schools of Pittsburgh. Address in 1929, College of Fine Arts, Carnegie Inst. of Technology; h. 5546 Pocusset St., Pittsburgh, PA; summer, 622 Columbia Road, Dorcester, MA.

SULLIVAN, FRANCES.
Portrait painter. Born in 1861; died in 1925 in NYC. Among his portraits are T. C. DuPont, J. B. McLean and F. W. Woolworth.

SULLIVAN, JAMES AMORY.
Painter. Born in Boston, MA, in 1875. Pupil of Laurens and of Alexander Harrison. Address in 1926, 98 Chestnut Street, Boston, MA.

SULLIVAN, LOUISA KARRER.
(Mrs. William Sullivan). Painter. Born Port Huron, MI, March 15, 1876. Pupil of Phillip L. Hale; Boston Museum of Fine Arts School. Member: Copley S.; AFA. Address in

1929, 9 Claflin Road, Brookline, MA.

SULLIVAN, PAT.
Cartoonist. Born Sydney, Australia, Feb. 2, 1887. Pupil of Pasquin in Sydney. Originator of "Felix the Cat." Address in 1929, 46 West 63rd St.; h. Hotel Alamac, New York, NY.

SULLIVANT, THOMAS S.
Illustrator. Born in Columbus, OH, in 1854. Pupil of Penn. Acad. of Fine Arts. Address in 1926, 1911 Pine Street, Philadelphia, PA.

SULLY, ALFRED.
Painter. Born May 22, 1820, in Phila. Son of Thomas Sully. Graduated from West Point in 1841. He painted in water colors and his views of the western forts where he was stationed are of artistic and historic interest. He died April 27, 1879.

SULLY, JANE.
See Darley, Mrs. Wm. H. W.

SULLY, KATE.
Painter. Member: Rochester AC. Address in 1929, 393 Westminster Road, Rochester, NY.

SULLY, LAWRENCE.
Miniature painter. Born Dec. 28, 1769, in Kilkenny, Ireland. He was the eldest brother of Thomas Sully and came to this country with his father and settled in Charleston, SC, moving later to Virginia where he painted, first in Norfolk and then in Richmond where he died in 1804. His brother Thomas Sully married his widow.

SULLY, ROBERT MATTHEW.
Portrait painter. Born July 17, 1803, in Petersburg, VA. He was a nephew of Thomas Sully and studied with him. He visited London in 1824, painting there till 1828 when he returned to Virginia. He died in Buffalo, NY, on Oct. 16, 1855, as he was enroute to Madison, WI, to execute commissions for portraits. Represented in the Corcoran Art Gallery, Washington, by his portrait of Chief Justice John Marshall.

SULLY, THOMAS W.
Portrait painter. Born in Philadelphia in 1811; died there in 1847. He was the fourth child of the artist Thomas Sully and followed his father's profession. His fondness for the stage caused him to paint a series of portraits of prominent actors of his day, and these were lithographed by Newsam but unfortunately lettered "Thomas Sully." Thomas Wilcocks Sully later changed his signature to "Thomas Sully, Jr."

SULLY, THOMAS.
Portrait painter. Born in England, on June 19, 1783. His parents were actors who came to this country in 1792, bringing their family with them and settling at Charleston, SC. In 1801 he sailed for Norfolk, VA, where he joined his elder brother Lawrence, the miniature painter. In 1801 he began his professional career as a portrait painter, and in 1806 he moved to NYC where he received instructions from the painter Trumbull & Jarvis. Early in 1808 he moved from NY to PA, which he made his permanent home, although making frequent visits to all the principal cities for the practice of his profession, besides making two trips to England. Sully also received a certain amount of criticism and instruction from Gilbert Stuart, whose studio he visited in Boston in 1807 when that artist was at the height of his fame. In 1809 Sully visited London for study, and there he settled down with the Newport artist C. B. King in a course of drawing and painting. He returned to Phila. in 1810 and painted there many of his finest portraits, during the next quarter of the century. In 1837 he revisited London to paint the portrait of Queen Victoria for the St. George Society of Phila. The painting is still owned by the soc. in Phila., replica being presented by the artists to the St. Andrew Society of Charleston, SC; another portrait of the Queen being in the Wallace collection in London. Mr. Sully was a very rapid and industrious painter, and there are over 2,000 listed portraits from his brush besides miniatures, and some 500

subject paintings. He also painted a number of historical subjects, his best known canvas being "Washington Crossing the Delaware." He served for 15 yrs. as a Dir. of the PA Acad. of Fine Arts. His kindness and sympathy to young artists was well known. He died in Phila., loved and respected, on Nov. 5, 1872, in his 89th yr.

SUMICHRAST, JOEZEF.
Illustrator. Born in Hobart, IN, in 1948. Spent two years at the American Academy of Art. He has recently done a number of books, having written as well as illustrated Onomatopoeia. He has many posters to his credit, including those for Graphics, 1975 and 1977. Communication Arts and Art Direction have featured this artist and his work, examples of which are part of the permanent collections of the Library of Congress and the Chicago Historical Society.

SUMMA, E(MILY) B. (MRS.).
Painter. Born Mannheim, Germany, Sept. 20, 1875. Pupil of St. Louis School FA; Bissell; Dawson-Watson. Member: St. Louis AG; St. Louis A. Lg. Award: Frederick Oakes Sylvester, prize for landscape, St. Louis Artists Guild Exh., 1917. Address in 1929, 5059 Raymond Ave., St. Louis, MO.

SUMMERS, DUDLEY GLOYNE.
Painter and illustrator. Born Birmingham, England, Oct. 12, 1892. Studied at New Sch. of Design, Boston; ASL with T. Fogarty, Charles Chapman, F. R. Gruger; also with George Bridgman, D. J. Connoh. Published in MacLean's, Canada; most Am. magazines. Taught at Am. Sch. of Design, NYC, and VanAmburg Sch. of Art, Plainfield, NJ. Member: SI; GFLA. Died in 1975. Address in 1929, 191 West 10th Street, New York, NY; living in NJ at death.

SUMMERS, IVAN F.
Painter and etcher. Born Mt. Vernon, IL. Pupil of ASL of NY; St. Louis School of Fine Arts. Member: Salma C. Award: Ives landscape prize, St. Louis AG, 1916;

landscape prize, ASL of NY, 1916. Address in 1929, Woodstock, NY.

SUMNER, L. W. Y.
Painter. Born Middletown, CT. Pupil of Van Dearing Perrine. Member: PBC; Palisade AA; Silvermine GA. Address in 1929, Round Hill Rd., Greenwich, CT; summer, Watch Point, Raquette Lake, NY.

SUNDBERG, WILDA REGELMAN.
Painter. Born in Erie, PA, in 1930. Studied: Albright Art School, Univ. of Buffalo, NY. Awards: Edinboro Summer Gallery, 1969, 1971; Chautauqua National, 1971. Exhibitions: Ashtabula Winter Show, OH, 1969; Springfield Missouri Art Mus., 1971, 1972; William Penn Mus. Penn., 1971. She is represented in the collection of the Erie Public Library.

SUNDGAARD, ERIK.
Illustrator. Born in New Haven, CT, in 1949. Attended the Paier School of Art, where he studied with Rudolf Zallinger and Ken Davies. In 1970, his first published illustration appeared in Yankee magazine. His work has been hung in John Slade Ely House in New Haven and the S of I Annual Show in 1976.

SUSAN, ROBERT.
Portrait painter. Born in 1888. Student of the Penn. Academy of Fine Arts. Member of Penn. Academy of Fine Arts Fellowship and California Art Club. Address in 1926, 1520 Chestnut Street, Philadelphia, PA.

SUTTON, EILEEN RAUCHER.
Painters. Born in July 28, 1942. Study: Brooklyn, (NY), Mus. Art Sch., 1958-59; ASL NYC, 1961-63; Hunter College NYC, BA Art 1963; Brooklyn Col., MS Art 1971. Exhib.: Women in the Arts, Selected Artists Exhib., Broome St., NYC, Solo, 1978; Cicchinelli Gal., NYC, solo, 1979; Ward-Nasse Gal., NYC, solo, 1982; Azuma Gal., NYC, 1975; Baron's Art Center, Woodbridge, NJ, 1978; Lever House, NYC, 1980; Phoenix Gallery, NYC, 1982; Middlesex Co. Mus.,

Piscataway, NJ, 1982, many other solo, group, museum shows in NY, NJ, FL, PA. Awards: Somerset (NJ) Tri-State Juried Exhib., 1978 (Watercolor Award); Artists Lg. of Central NJ, 1979 (Watercolor Award). Mem.: Artist Equity Assn.; Mensa; Women's Caucus on the Arts; Women in the Arts. Address in 1983, 15 Pleasant Valley Road, Old Bridge, NJ.

SUTTON, GEORGE MIKSCH.
Painter, illustrator, writer, and lecturer. Born Bathany, NE, May 16, 1898. Pupil of Louis Agassiz Fuertes. Illustrated "Birds of Florida" and "Birds of Pennsylvania." Illustrated in Bird Lore, The Wilson Bulletin, Outdoor Life, etc. Died in 1940. Address in 1929, Bethany, W. VA.

SUTTON, HARRY JR.
Painter. Born Salem, MA, April 21, 1897. Pupil of Museum of Fine Arts School, Boston; Julian in Paris. Member: Copley S; Boston SWCP; Boston GA; AFA. Address in 1929, 85 Newbury St., Boston, MA.

SUTTON, RUTH HAVILAND.
Painter. Born Springfield, Sept. 10, 1898. Pupil of Henry B. Snell. Member: Alliance; CT AFA; Springfield AL; Springfield AG; NA Women PS. Awards: Hon. mention, Springfield Art League, 1927; prize, Springfield AL 1928; hon. mention, CT AFA, 1929. Died in 1960. Address in 1929, 142 Thompson St., Springfield, MA.

SUYDAM, E(DWARD) H(OWARD).
Painter, illustrator, and etcher. Born Vineland, NJ, Feb. 22, 1885. Pupil of Thornton Oakley, School of Industrial Art, Phila. Member: Phila. WCC; Phila. Print C.; Phila. Sketch C.; Phila. Soc. Applied Arts; Phila. Alliance. Awards: John Wanamaker prize for illustration, 1916; John Wanamaker prize for water color, 1917. Illustrations for Harper's Monthly, Designer, and Delineator. Died in 1940. Address in 1929, 1430 South Penn Squ.; h. 1305 71st Ave., Oak Lane, Philadephia, PA.

SUYDAM, JAMES AUGUSTUS.
Landscape painter. Born in New Hampshire on March 27, 1819; he studied with Durand and Kensett. He was elected an honorary member of the National School of Design in 1858 and an Academician in 1861. He was most successful with his coast views, his "View on Long Island" and "Hook Mountain on the Hudson" are well known. He died Sept 15, 1865, in North Conway, NH.

SVENDSEN, CHARLES C.
Painter. Born Cin., OH, Dec. 7, 1871. Pupil of Bouguereau, Ferrier, Colarossi Acad. in Paris. Member: Cin. AC. Award: bronze medal, St. Louis Exp., 1904. Specialty, figure and pastoral scenes. Address in 1929, 555 Elberton Ave., Price Hill, Cin., OH.

SVOBODA, J(OSEF) C(ESTMIR).
Illustrator. Born Bohemia, Czechoslovakia, July 28, 1889. Pupil of Antonin Sterba; Ralph Clarkson; Hanz Larwin. Member: AFA; Bohemian AC, Chicago. Awards: First hon. mention, Bohemian AC, 1924; first and second prizes, Arizona State Exhibition, 1926. Address in 1929, 2626 Washington, Blvd.; h. 1931 South Clarence Ave., Berwyn, IL; summer, Taos, NM.

SWAIN, FRANCIS W(ILLIAM).
Painter and etcher. Born Oakland, CA, March 24, 1892. Pupil of Frank Duveneck and F. Van Sloun. Member: Cincinnati AC; CA SE. Work: Decoration in Westwood School, Cincinnati, OH. Died in 1937. Address in 1929, Southern Railway Bldg.; h. 1028 Underwood Place, Cincinnati, OH; summer, 2799 Clay St., San Francisco, CA.

SWAIN, WILLIAM.
Painter. Born Dec. 27, 1803, in NYC. He was elected an Associate Member of the National Academy of Design in 1836. He died in NY, on Feb. 18, 1847. Self-portrait exhibited in Centennial Exhibition on National Academy, NY, 1925-26.

SWALLEY, JOHN F.
Painter and etcher. Born Toledo, Sept. 5, 1887. Member: Dayton SE;

Toledo Art Klan. Address in 1929, 1053 Lincoln Ave., Toledo, OH.

SWAN, FLORENCE (WELLINGTON).
Draftsman and teacher. Born Cambridge, MA, July 13, 1876. Pupil of Amy M. Sacker. Member: Boston SAC (master). Work: Memorial tablets in Beneficent Congregational Church, Providence; St. James Church, Salem. Address in 1929, 6 Rollins Place, Beacon Hill, Boston, MA.

SWAN, PAUL.
Sculptor and painter. Born in Illinois. Studied drawing under John Vanderpoel and sculpture under Taft. Later he studied in NY and Paris. He has exhibited his paintings and sculptures in the National Academy of Design, New York. Address in 1926, Jackson Heights, New York City.

SWANSON, BENNET A.
Painter. Born April 26, 1899. Member: St. Paul AS. Awards; Hon. Mention, State Exhibit. 1920; second award for painting, second award for black and white, MN State Art Soc. Exhibit, 1922; hon. mention for prints and drawings, State Exhibit, 1923; hon. mention for prints and drawings, Minneapolis AI, 1923; second prize for prints and drawings, MN State Art Soc., 1924. Address in 1929, 663 Elfelt St., St. Paul, MN.

SWANSON, JONATHAN M.
Painter, sculptor, and illustrator. Born Chicago, IL, July 21, 1888. Pupil of John Vanderpoel. Member: AIC Alumni; Am. Numis. A.; NY Numis. C. Address in 1929, 15 West 29th St., New York, NY; h. 32 So. 10th St., Newark, NJ.

SWARTZ, HAROLD.
Sculptor, writer, lecturer, and teacher. Born San Marcial, NM, April 7, 1887. Studied in Berlin, Paris. Member: Sculptors G. of South Calif.; CA AC.; CA PS; Municipal Art Comm. Awards: First prize, Arcadia Ex., 1923; first prize, Pomona Exp., 1923. Represented in Los Angeles Museum. Instructor of Sculpture, Chouinard Art School. Address in 1929, 3827 Ronda Vista Place. Los Angeles, CA.

914

SWAYNE, H(UGH) N(ELSON).
Painter, etcher, and teacher. Born Hickman, KY, July 22, 1903. Pupil of Will H. Stevens, C. M. Saz, George Pearse Ennis, John Costigan. Member: Louisville AA; SSAL; Natchitoches Art Colony. Awards: Prize, Louisville AA, 1928; prize, Baton Rouge, LA, 1929. Address in 1929, Hickman, KY.

SWEENEY, NORA.
(Mrs. S. Gordon Smyth). Illustrator. Born Philadephia, PA, June 17, 1897. Pupil of Walter H. Everett. Illustrator of juvenile subjects. Address in 1929, 2442 Linden Dr., Greenwood Park, Upper Darby, PA; summer, Conshohocken, PA.

SWENDEN, GOTTFRIDA.
Painter. Born Sweden, June 19, 1882. Pupil of Knute Heldner and Delecluse, Paris, France. Member: Duluth AS. Award: Hon. mention, and second prize, Duluth AS; popularity prize and third prize, Arrowhead Exhib. Address in 1929, 2001 Jefferson St., Duluth, MN.

SWETT, CYRUS A.
Engraver. As a copperplate engraver this name appears on a "Descent from the Cross," a frontispiece to "Helps to Young Christians," published in Portland in 1839. The plate is signed as "engraved by C. A. Swett, Portland." He later engraved a plan of the city of Boston, published in 1862.

SWETT, WILLIAM OTIS JR.
Landscape painter. Born Worcester, MA. Pupil of Whistler, H. G. Dearth; studied in Munich, Paris, Belgium, and Holland. Member: Salma. C., 1903; Chicago AF; S. Indp. A. Specialty, marines and landscapes. Died in 1939. Address in 1929, 15 West 67th St.; care of Salma. Club, 47th Fifth Ave., New York, NY; and Deerfield, MA.

SWEZEY, AGNES.
Painter. Exhibited at National Academy of Design, New York, 1925. Address in 1926, 39 West 9th Street, New York.

SWIFT, HOMER (MRS.).
See Emma F. MacRae.

SWIFT, IVAN.
Painter, etcher, craftsman, writer, and lecturer. Born Wayne, MI, June 24, 1873. Pupil of AIC; Freer, Von Sulza, Ochtman and Chase. Member: NAC. Work: "A Michigan Home," Detroit Inst. of Arts; "Indian Summer," "Toward the Light," and "In the Shadow of the Hill," Detroit Library; "Lakeland," Michigan Fair Gallery; "The Hooker," Harbor Springs High School; "Lodgers," Michigan State Library. Author of books of verse, "Fagots of Cedar," and "The Blue Crane and Shore Songs." Died in 1945. Address in 1929, Chippewa Cove Woods, Harbor Springs, MI.

SWIFT, S(TEPHEN) (TED).
Illustrator and etcher. Pupil of P. J. Lemos and L. P. Latimer; CA School of Arts and Crafts. Specialty, wood block printing and etching. Staff artist, School Arts Magazine. Address in 1929, Museum Stanford Univ., CA.

SWINDELL, BERTHA.
Miniature painter. Born Baltimore, MD, Dec. 2, 1874. Pupil of Chase, Hawthorne, Bridgman, and Breckenridge; La Forge at Julian Acad. in Paris. Member: Balto. WCC; North Shore AA; PA S. Min. P. Died in 1951. Address in 1929, 200 Fifth Ave., New York, NY.

SWINNERTON, JAMES.
Painter. Born in 1875. Painted Southwestern scenery; his specialty was the American desert lands. He was born in CA, and studied in NY. Among his best known paintings are "Coming Storm, Mojave Desert," "Clouds in Monument Valley, North Arizona," and "Here Ends the Trail."

SWISHER, ALLAN.
Portrait and figure painter. Born Gypsum, KS, Oct. 2, 1888. Pupil of H. M. Walcott, Laurens. Address in 1929, University of Kentucky; h. 119 Bassett Court, Lexington, KY.

SWOPE, H. VANCE.
Painter. Born in southern Indiana, in 1879. Pupil of Julien Acad. in

Paris under Constant. Member: Circle of Am. Painters and Sculptors; Salmagundi Club; NY Architectural League. Work represented in Public Library, Seymout, MN. Address in 1926, Van Dyck Studios, 939 Eighth Ave., New York, NY. Died Aug. 10, 1926.

SWOPE, KATE F. (MRS.).
Painter. Born in Louisville, KY. Pupil of National Academy of Design, NY. Awarded gold medal, Southern Art league, 1895; highest award, Louisville Art League, 1897. Member of Louisville Art League. Address in 1926, 939 Eighth Ave., New York, NY.

SWOPE, VIRGINIA VANCE.
Painter. Born in Louisville, KY. Pupil of DuMond, Mora, Carlson, Penfield, and Bridgman. Address in 1926, 939 Eighth Avenue, New York, NY.

SWORD, JAMES BRADE.
Painter. Born Oct. 11, 1839, in Philadelphia, PA. His early life was spent in Macao, China, and he engaged in art as a profession about 1863. Has served for a number of years as vice president and director of the Art Club of Philadelphia, as president of the Philadelphia Society of Artists, and as president of the Artists Fund Society of Phila. He is represented by portraits and paintings in many public institutions. He was a founder of the Art Club of Phila. He is represented by his Portrait of John W. Jones in the House of Representatives, Washington, DC. Died Dec. 1, 1915, in Philadelphia.

SYKES, CHARLES HENRY.
Painter. Born Brooklin, MA, in 1882. Pupil of Boston Museum School; Cincinnati Art Acad. under Duveneck. Member: Cincinnnati Woman's AC; NA Women PS. Address in 1929, 3007 Vernon Place, Vernonville, Cincinnati, OH.

SYKES, S. D. GILCHRIST.
Painter. Born Cheshire, England. Pupil of Boston Museum Art School. Member: Copley AS.; North Shore AA; Rockport AA. Address in 1929, 100 Winchester St., Brooklin, MA.

SYLVESTER, FREDERICK OAKES.
Mural and landscape painter. Born in Brockton, MA, Oct. 8, 1869. He was a member of the Society of Western Artists. He died March 2, 1915, in St. Louis, MO.

SYMONS, (GEORGE) GARDNER.
Painter. Born Chicago, IL, 1863. Pupil of AIC; studied in Paris, Munich, and London. Member: ANA 1910, NA 1911; Royal Soc. British Artists; Union Inter. des Beaux-Arts et des Lettres; Salma. C. 1900; NAC (life); Chicago SA; Century Assoc.; CA AC; Inst. Arts and Letters; Chic. Gal. A; AFA. Awards: Carnegie prize, NAD, 1909; Evans prize, Salma. C., 1910; bronze medal, Buenos Aires Exp., 1910; NAC prize and gold medal, 1912; third W. A. Clark prize ($1,000) and bronze Corcoran medal, 1912; Saltus medal, NAD, 1913; Altman prize ($500), NAD, 1919. Work: "The Opalescent River," Metropolitan Mus., NY; "Snow Clouds, Corcoran Gal., Wash.; "Sorrow," Cincinnati Mus.; "Snow Clad Fields in Morning Light," Toledo Mus.; "The Top of the Hills and Beyond," and "The Winter Sun," Art Inst. of Chicago; "Through Snow Clad Hills and Valley." City Art Mus., St. Louis; "Through Wooded Hills," Art Assoc., Dallas, TX; "Deerfield River," Brooklyn Inst. Mus.; "River in Winter," Minneapolis Inst. of Arts; "November, Dachau, Germany," Carnegie Inst., Pittsburgh; "Sunlight in the Woods," Fort Worth (TX) Mus.; "Silence and Evening Light," Butler Art Inst., Youngstown, OH; "The Bridge," Harrison Gal., Los Angeles Mus. Also represented in National Arts Club, NY; Des Moines Art Assoc.; Lincoln Art Assoc., NE; Cedar Rapids Art Assoc., IA; Museum of Art, Erie, PA; Rochelle Art Assoc., IN; Union Lg. Club, Chicago; Hyde Park Art Assoc., Chicago. Address in 1929, care of Grand Central Galleries, 15 Vanderbilt Ave.; Arts Club Bldg., 119 East 19th St., New York, NY.

SZAFRAN, GENE.
Illustrator. Born in Detroit in 1941. Trained at the Art School of the Society of Arts and Crafts

916

Receiving his start in studios in Detroit, he produced many auto advertisements in addition to free-lance assignments. Among his many clients since his move to NY in 1967 are Bantam Books, New American Library, Cosmopolitan, Fortune, and Playboy. He has exhibited his works in group shows at the General Electric and Master Eagle Galleries and has held a One-Man Exhibition at the S of I.

TAAKE, DAISY.
Sculptor and teacher. Born St. Louis, MO, March 21, 1886. Pupil of AIC and St. Louis School of Fine Arts; Lorado Taft. Member: St. Louis AL. Winner of St. Louis Art League Fountain Competition. Work: Eight foot decorative figure at Washington University. Address in 1929, Midway Studios, 6016 Ellis Ave., Chicago, IL; h. 1338 North Kingshighway, St. Louis, MO.

TACK, AUGUSTUS VINCENT.
Painter and teacher. Born Pittsburgh, PA, Nov. 9, 1870. Pupil of Mowbray and La Farge in NY; Merson in Paris. Member: ASL of NY (life); CT AFA; New Haven Paint and Clay C.; Century Assoc.; Inter. Soc. AL. Represented in Metropolitan Museum; Phillips Gallery, Washington; Legislative Chamber, New Parliament Buildings, Winnipeg; Cleveland Art Museum; Newark Mus.; Speed Memorial Museum, Louisville, KY; Paulist Church, NY; Chapel of The Cenacle Convent, Newport, RI; St. James Church, South Deerfield, MA; decoration for Governor's Reception Room, Nebraska State Capitol, Lincoln. Died July 21, 1949 in NYC. Address in 1929, 15 Vanderbilt Ave., New York, NY; and Deerfield, MA.

TADAMA, FOKKO.
Painter. Born in 1871 in India. Represented in San Francisco Art Museum. Address in 1926, 2012 Laurelshade Ave., Seattle, Wash.

TADASKY.
See Tadasuke Kuwayama.

TADASUKE, KUWAYAMA.
Painter. Born Aug. 24, 1935 in Nagoya, Japan. Studied at Art Students League. Resides in NYC. Exhibited at Kootz Gal., NYC (1965); MOMA; Albright-Knox; Univ. of Ill.; and in Japan at Nat. Mus. of Mod. Art and Gutai Mus. In collections of MOMA; Albright-Knox; CBS; Brandeis; Houston Mus. of Fine Arts, and in private collections.

TAFFS, C. H.
Illustrator. Member: SI; GFLA. Address in 1929, 29 West 67th St., New York, NY.

TAFLINGER, ELMER E.
Painter. Born Indianapolis, March 3, 1891. Pupil of ASL of NY; George Bridgman. Address in 1929, 46 North Pennsylvania St.; h. 925 North Dearborn St., Indianapolis, IN.

TAFT, LORADO.
Sculptor, teacher, writer, and lecturer. Born Elmwood, IL, April 29, 1860. Pupil of Ecole des Beaux Arts in Paris under Dumont, Bonnassieux and Thomas. Member: NSS 1893; ANA 1909, NA 1911; Nat. Acad. AL; Chicago PS; AFA; AIA (cor.), 1907; IL State Art Com.; National Com. Fine Arts, 1925-1929. Instructor, Chicago Art Inst., 1886-1906; lecturer, Chic. A. Inst., from 1886; lecturer on art, University of Chicago; non-resident professor of art, University of Illinois. Awards: Designers' medal, Columbian Exp., Chicago, 1893; silver medal, Pan-Am. Exp., Buffalo, 1901; gold medal, St. Louis Exp., 1904; Montgomery Ward prize, AIC, 1906; silver medal, P.-P. Exp., San F., 1915. Author: "History of American Sculpture"; "Modern Tendencies in Sculpture." Work: "Solitude of the Soul," Art Inst., Chicago; "Washington Monument," Seattle, Wash.; "Fountain," Paducah, KY; "Trotter Fountain." Bloomington, IL; "Columbus Memorial Fountain," Washington; Ferguson "Fountain of the Great Lakes," Chicago; "Thatcher Memorial Fountain," Denver, Co.; "Blackhawk," Ogle Co. Soldiers Memorial, Oregon, IL; "Fountain of Time," Chicago; Danville (IL) Soldiers Monument; "Lincoln," Urbana, IL; "Pioneers," Elmwood, IL; "Alma Mater," University of Illinois, Urbana, IL. Died Oct. 30, 1946 in Chicago, IL.

TAGGART, EDWIN LYNN.
Painter, sculptor, illustrator, and etcher. Born Richmond, IN, April 23, 1905. Pupil of R. L. Coates, F. F. Brown, B. Waite, CA School of Arts and Crafts. Member: IN AC; Junior AA. Awards: Five prizes at Wayne-County Fair; U. C. T. Art Medal, 1925. Work: Murals in Morton High School, Richmond, IN. Address in 1929, 1 B St., San

918

Mateo, CA; h. 31 South 17th St., Richmond, IN.

TAGGART, GEORGE H(ENRY).
Portrait painter. Born Watertown, NY, March 12, 1865. Pupil of Bouguereau, Ferrier and Lefebvre in Paris. Member: Soc. Inter. des Beaux-Arts et des Lettres; Buffalo SA; S. Indp. A. Awards: Medal of honor and cash prize, Utah State Ex.; hon. mention, Salon d'Antomne, Paris. Represented in private collection of Royal Palace, Berlin, Germany; Palace of Governor, City of Mexico; Mormon Temple, Brigham Young College and City Hall, Salt Lake City; City Hall, Watertown, NY; Tusculum College, Greenville, TN; Chemists Club, NY. Address in 1929, 11 Hillside Ave., Port Washington, LI, NY.

TAGGART, LUCY M.
Painter. Born Indianapolis, IN. Pupil of Forsyth, Chase, and Hawthorne; studied in Europe. Member: NAC (life); Art Workers Club for Women PS; AFA. Represented in the John Herron Art Museum, Indianapolis, IN. Address in 1929, 15 Gramercy Park, New York, NY; h. 1331 North Delaware St., Indianapolis, IN.

TAIRA, FRANK.
Painter and sculptor. Born in San Francisco, CA, Aug. 21, 1913. Study: Calif. Sch. of Fine Arts, 1935-38; Columbia Univ., 1945; ASL, 1956; New Sch. for Soc. Research, 1957. Exhib.: San Fran. Mus. of Art, 1939; Nat'l. Arts Club, 1968; Knickerbocker Artists, 1968; NAD, 1976; Allied Artists of America, 1976; Horizon Galleries, 1982; and others. Awards: First prize, painting, Calif. Sch. of Fine Arts, 1940; first prize, portrait, Cambridge, MA, 1943; Nat'l. Arts Club, 1968; hon. mention, Knickerbocker Artists, 1968; Accademia Italia delle Arti e del Lavoro, 1981. Mem.: Artists Equity Assn. of NY. Media: Oil, watercolor, bronze. Address in 1983, 135 W. 106th St., Apt. 3Y, NYC.

TAIT, ARTHUR FITZWILLIAM.
Painter. Born Aug. 5, 1819 in England. Came to the United States in 1850 and was most successful with paintings of animals. Elected Associate of the National Academy in 1853 and Academician in 1858. Sketched in the Adirondack Mountains. Works: "Duck and Her Young," "Racquette Lake". The "Quail and Young" is in the Corcoran Art Gallery, Washington, DC. Many of his paintings were reproduced in lithograph by Currier & Ives. Died April 28, 1905 in Yonkers, NY.

TAIT, JOHN ROBINSON.
Painter. Born Jan. 14, 1834 in Cincinnati. Studied art abroad. In 1871 he returned to the United States and after 1876 resided in Baltimore, MD. Works: "Lake of Four Cantons," in the Cincinnati Art Museum; his "Landscape and Cattle" was exhibited in the Centennial, in Philadelphia in 1876. Died July 29, 1909, in Baltimore, MD.

TALBOT, CORNELIA BRECKENRIDGE.
Painter. Born in Natrona, Penna., in 1888. Pupil of Penna. Academy of the Fine Arts. She died in 1924. Address in 1924, Talbot Hall, Norfolk County, VA.

TALBOT, GRACE H(ELEN).
Sculptor. Born Billerica, MA, Sept. 3, 1901. Pupil of Harriet W. Frishmuth. Member: NA Women PS; NSS. Awards: Avery prize, Architectural Lg., 1922; Joan of Arc medal, NA Women PS, 1925. Address in 1929, 14 Washington Square, North, New York, NY.

TALBOT, HENRY S.
Painter. Member: Boston Art Club. Work: "Morning in Mid Ocean," Minneapolis Institute of Arts. Address in 1926, 387 Washington St., Boston, Mass.

TALCOTT, ALLEN B.
Landscape painter. He had a studio on the Connecticut River, near Lyme, and painted in water colors. Died in New York City, c. 1925.

TALCOTT, SARAH W(HITING).
Painter. Born West Hartford, CT, April 21, 1852. Pupil of Chase and Cox in NY; Bouguereau and Robert

Fleury in Paris. Member: CT AFA. Address in 1929, Elmwood, CT.

TALLMADGE, THOMAS EDDY.
Etcher. Born Washington, DC, April 24, 1876. Pupil of MA Inst. of Technology, Boston. Member: Cliff Dwellers; Chicago SE; NAC; AIC Alumni; CA SE; F.A.I.A.; Federated Council on Art Education; Art Com., City of Evanston (Pres.); Governing Life Member, AIC. Award: Chicago Arch. Club Traveling scholarship, 1904. Author, "Story of Architecture in America." President, Summer School of Painting, Saugatuck, MI. Hon. Prof. of Architectural History, Armour Inst. of Technology. Address in 1929, 19 East Pearson St.; Burnham Bldg., Chicago, IL.

TALLMAN, M(ARTHA) G(RIFFITH).
Painter. Born Llanidloes, North Wales, Sept. 22, 1859. Pupil of F. S. Church; NAD; ASL of NY; Mrs. Coman; and Jane Peterson. Member: Fellow NAD; Pen and Brush C.; NYWCC (Assoc.); NA Women PS; AFA. Address in 1929, 780 Riverside Drive, New York, NY; studio, Kent, CT.

TAM, REUBEN.
Painter. Born Jan. 17, 1916 in Kapaa, Hawaii. Earned BA in Education, U. of Hawaii, 1937. Studied at Cal. School of Fine Arts; New School for Soc. Research and Columbia, and with Hans Hofmann. Teaching at Brooklyn Mus. Art School since 1948. Rec. awards from Honolulu Acad. of Arts; Brooklyn Mus.; St. Paul Gallery; Nat. Acad. of Design (for landscape) and Guggenheim fellow (1948). Exhibited at Alan Gal., NYC; Whitney; New School for Soc. Reseach; Corcoran; Carnegie; Univ. of IL; Colby Col. (ME); and many others. In collections of Albright-Knox; Newark; Whitney; Brooklyn; Wichita Art Mus.; Temple Univ.; MOMA; MMA and Bowdoin College. Painter and educator. 549 W. 123rd St., NYC.

TAMAYO, RUFINO.
Painter. Born Oxaca, Mexico, 1899. His work is represented at the MOMA, NY; Mus. Art Moderne, Paris, France; Mus. Arte Mod, Rome, Italy; Mus. Royale, Brussels, Belgium;

Phillips Mem. Gal., Wash., DC. Commissions include mural for UNESCO Bldg. in Paris, 1958. Exhibitions: San Fran. Mus. of Art, 1953; Kunsternes Hus, Oslo, Norway, 1959; Biennal Venice. Awarded Oficiel Legion d' Honeur, France; Comendator Repub. Italiana. Member: Inst. and Academy of Arts and Letters; Acad. Arte, Buenos Aires, Arg.; Academy Diseno, Florence, Italy. Mailing address in 1982, Callejon del Santisimo, San Angel, Mexico.

TANBERG, ELLA HOTELLING.
Painter. Born in Janesville, Wisc. Member: West Coast Arts; Janesville Art League; Chicago Art Club; California Art Club; Laguna Beach Artists' Association. Work: "Lily Pond, Lincoln Park," owned by Janesville Art League. Address in 1926, Laguna Beach, Calif.

TANDLER, RUDOLPH (FREDERICK).
Painter and illustrator. Born Grand Rapids, MI, March 22, 1887. Pupil of George Bellows, John Sloan, Andrew Dasburg. Member: S. Indp. S; Scarab C. Address in 1929, 37 West Eighth St., New York, NY; summer, Woodstock, NY.

TANEJI, MOICHIRO TSUCHIYA.
Painter. Born in Ogaki City, Japan, in 1891. Studied in Japan. Member of Penguins. Address in 1926, 61 West 37th St., New York, NY.

TANNAHILL, MARY H.
Painter. Born Warrenton, NC. Pupil of Weir, Twachtman, Cox and Mowbray in NY. Member: PA S. Min. P.; NA Women PS; Provincetown AA; NY Soc. Women S.; Salons of Amer. Award: Prize for best group, NA Women PS, autumn, 1914. Address in 1929, 152 West 57th Street; h. 40C West 118th St., New York, NY; summer, Provincetown, MA.

TANNAHILL, SALLIE B.
Painter, teacher, and draftsman. Born NY, Oct. 25, 1881. Pupil of Arthur W. Dow, V. Preissig. Professor, Art Dept., Teachers College, Columbia Univ. Author of "Ps and Qs" (Doubleday, Doran & Co.). Address in 1929, 400 West

920

118th Street, New York; summer, Lake Mahopac, NY.

TANNER, BENJAMIN.
Engraver. Born March 27, 1775 in New York City. Tanner's master is unknown, but he was engraving in New York in 1792, and was possibly a pupil of Peter R. Maverick. Remained in New York until 1805, and in that year his name appeared in Philadelphia directories. Remained there until 1845, when he moved to Baltimore. In 1811, with his brother Henry S. Tanner, he was a general engraver and map publisher; in 1837 he changed his business to "Stereographer," using steel plates for production of checks, drafts, notes and other mercantile paper. In 1816-24 was member of the engraving firm of Tanner, Vallance, Kearny & Co. Worked in both line and stipple. Produced excellent large plates of portraits and historical subjects, especially views relating to American Revolution and War of 1812. Engraved some plates in connection with W. R. Jones. Died Nov. 14, 1948 in Baltimore, MD.

TANNER, H(ENRY) O(SSAWA).
Painter. Born Pittsburgh, PA, June 21, 1859. Pupil of PAFA under Eakins; Laurens and Constant in Paris. Member: ANA 1901; NA 1927; Paris SAP; Soc. Inter. de Peinture et Sculpture; Fellowship PAFA. Awards: Paris Salon, 1896-97, Lippincott prize, 1900; Silver Medal, Paris Exp., 1900; Pan-Am. Exp. Buffalo, 1901; St. Louis Exp., 1904; Paris Salon, 1906; Harris prize, AIC 1906; P.-P. Exp., San F., 1915. Specialty, biblical subjects. Work: "The Raising of Lazarus," and "The Disciples at Emmaus," Luxembourg Mus., Paris; "Christ at the Home of Mary and Martha," Carnegie; "Nicodemus," PAFA; "The 2 Disciples at the Tomb and "The 3 Marys," AIC; "L'Annonciation," Wilstach Col., Phila.; "Holy Family," Hackley Art Gal., Muskegon, MI; "Christ Walking on the Water," Des Moines AFA; "Daniel in the Lions Den," and "Moonlight, Walls of Tangiers," Harrison Gal., L.A. Mus. Died May 25, 1936. Address in 1929, 15 rue St. Jacques, XIV, Paris, France;

summer, "Edgewood," Trepied, par Etaples, Pas-de-Calais, France.

TANNER, HENRY S.
Engraver. Born 1786 in New York City. In 1811 was in business in Phila. with his brother Benjamin. Engraved outline illustrations for some magazines of that city, though he was chiefly engaged upon map and chart work. The "Port Folio" of 1815 credits him with inventing a process of bank-note engraving to increase the difficulties of counterfeiting. Produced effects by white lines on a black ground, varied in form and intricate in character. In 1843, he moved to New York. Engraved and published maps, charts, etc. Contributed geographical and statistical articles to periodicals, and published guide-books for 6 regions of the United States. Member of the geographical societies of London and Paris, when this distinction was rare among Americans. Died in 1858 in New York City.

TAPPAN, W. H.
An engraver of portraits in mezzotint about 1840; also engraved some line plates, in conjunction with Joseph Andrew, in Boston. Was partner of George C. Smith in the engraving business in Boston.

TARBELL, EDMUND C(HARLES).
Painter and teacher. Born West Groton, MA, April 26, 1862. Pupil of Boston Mus. Sch.; Boulanger and Lefebvre in Paris. Member: Ten Am. P.; ANA 1904; NA 1906; Nat. Inst. AL; Boston GA; AC Phila. Awards: Clarke prize, NAD 1890; Shaw fund, SAA 1893; Columbia Exp., Chic., 1893; 1st Hallgarten prize, NAD 1894; Lippincott prize, PAFA 1895; Temple gold medal, PAFA 1895; AC Phila. 1895; PAFA 1896; Tenn. Exp., Nashville, 1897; Worcester Mus., 1900; Boston Charitable Mechanics Assoc.; Paris Exp., 1900; Worcester Mus., 1904; Harris prize, AIC 1907; medal of honor, PAFA 1908; NAD 1908; 1st prize, Carnegie Inst., Pitts., 1909; 1st W. A. Clark prize, Corcoran AG 1910; Beck gold medal, PAFA 1911; P.-P. Exp., San F., 1915; Carnegie Inst., 1928-29. Work: Corcoran;

Cincinnati; RISD; Boston MFA; Worcester Mus.; PAFA; Wilstach Col., Phila, PA; War Dept., Wash., DC; State House, Boston; Smith Col.; Butler AI; Buffalo AFA. Chairman of Faculty and Chairman of Admin. Council of Sch. of Mus. of FA, Boston. Died 1938. Address in 1929, Fenway Studios, Boston, MA; care Corcoran Gallery of Art, Washington, DC, and New Castle, NH.

TARLETON, MARY LIVINGSTON.
Landscape and miniature painter. Born Stamford, CT. Pupil of Childe Hassam, Charles W. Hawthorne, W. M. Chase, ASL of NY. Member: NA Women PS. Address in 1929, Great Neck, LI, NY.

TATNALL, HENRY LEE.
Painter. Born in Brandywine Village, Del., in 1829. Specialty: Marine and landscape painting. Elected president of the Delaware Artists' Association. Died Sept. 1885 in Wilmington, Del.

TAUCH, WALDINE AMANDA.
Sculptor. Born Schulenburg, Texas, Jan. 28, 1894. Pupil of Pompeo Cappini. Member: SSAL; Soc. Western Sculptors; Am. APL. Work: Oldest inhabitant fountain, San Antonio, Texas; Henderson Memorial, Winchester, KY; Indiana monument to Civil and World War heroes and pioneers, Bedford, IN; "Baptismal Font," Grace Lutheran Church, San Antonio, TX. Address in 1929, 210 West 14th St., New York, NY; h. 4472 Boston Post Road, Pelham Manor, NY.

TAUSZKY, D(AVID) ANTHONY.
Portrait painter. Born Cincinnati, Ohio, Sept. 4, 1878. Pupil of ASL of NY under Blum; Julian Acad. in Paris under Laurens and Constant. Member: Salma. C. 1907; Allied AA; Laguna AA. Awards: Sargent prize, Art Inst., Pasadena, 1928; first prize, Santa Ana, 1928; first hon. mention, Allied AA, 1929; sketch prize, Salma. C, 1929. Work: Portrait of Emp. Franz Josef I, Criminal Court, Vienna; portrait of George W. Wingate, Wingate School, New York, NY. Address in 1929, 47 Fifth Ave., New York, NY; 511 Garfield, S. Pasadena, Calif.

TAVSHANJIAN, ARTEMIS.
(Mrs. Charles A. Karagheusian). Painter and sculptor. Born Englewood, NJ, June 18, 1904. Pupil of Mabel R. Welch, Robert G. Eberhard. Member: NA Women PS. Address in 1929, 91 Central Park West, New York, NY.

TAYLOR.
Miniature painter, who flourished in Philadelphia about 1760. He copied a miniature of Oliver Cromwell, among other works.

TAYLOR, ALEX H.
Portrait painter, who flourished in 1849-50 in New York.

TAYLOR, ANNA HEYWARD.
Painter and craftsman. Born Columbia, SC, Nov. 13, 1879. Pupil of Chase, Lathrop, Hawthorne, Nordfeldt, Meijer. Member: NAC; Wash. AC; Charleston AA; Columbia AA; Columbia Sketch C; SSAL; S. Indp. A; NA Women PS. Address in 1929, 79 Church St., Charleston, SC.

TAYLOR, BEATRICE M.
Painter. Member of Pittsburgh Artists' Association. Address in 1926, 306 South Craig St., Pittsburgh, PA.

TAYLOR, CHARLES JAY.
Painter and illustrator. Born in New York in 1885. Pupil of Art Students' League, National Academy of Design and Eastman Johnson in New York; also studied in London and Paris. Member: SI, 1910; Pittsburgh AA; Pittsburgh Architectural Club; The Players; Philadelphia Art Club. Awards: Honorable mention for drawing, Pan.-Am. Exposition, Buffalo, 1901; bronze medal and hors concours, P.-P. Exposition, San Francisco, 1915. Represented in Carnegie Institute of Technology. Instructor in Carnegie Technical Schools, Pittsburgh, from 1911. Address in 1926, "The Players," 16 Gramercy Park, New York, NY.

TAYLOR, EDGAR J.
Painter and illustrator. Born in Brooklyn, NY, in 1862. Pupil of National Academy of Design; Art Students' League of New York under

922

Beckwith; Brooklyn Art Guild under Eakins. Member: Brooklyn Art Club; Conn. Society of Artists; Society of Independent Artists. Address in 1926, Westbrook, Conn.

TAYLOR, EDWIN C.
Painter and teacher. Born Detroit, MI, March 10, 1874. Pupil of ASL of NY and Kenyon Cox. Member: New Haven PCC. Address in 1929, Yale School of Fine Arts; h. 352 Townsend Ave., New Haven, CT; summer, Liberty, ME.

TAYLOR, ELIZABETH.
Painter. Member: Chicago SA; S. Indp. A.; Provincetown Printers. Work: "Flowers," Detroit Institute. Address in 1929, 1504 East 57th St., Chicago, IL; h. New Berlin, IL; summer, Provincetown, MA.

TAYLOR, EMILY (HEYWARD) DRAYTON.
(Mrs. J. Madison Taylor). Miniature painter and writer. Born Philadelphia, PA, April 14, 1860. Pupil of Cecile Ferrere in Paris; PAFA. Member: PA Soc. Min. P.; Fellowship PAFA; Plastic C; Alliance; AFA. Awards: Gold medal, Earl's Court Exp., London, 1900; gold medal for services on Jury, Charleston Exp., 1902; silver medal, P.-P. Exp., San F., 1915; medal of honor PAFA, 1919; Lea prize ($50), PAFA, 1920; special award of $100, PAFA, 1924, for miniature of Cardinal Mercier. Collaborated with Miss Wharton in writing "Heirlooms in Miniature." Work: Portraits of President and Mrs. William Mc Kinley, Dr. S. Weir Mitchell, George Hamilton and Cardinal Mercier. Died June 19, 1952. Address in 1929, 1504 Pine St., Philadelphia, PA.

TAYLOR, ETHEL C.
Painter. Born Taylor's-on-Schroon, NY. Pupil of Kenneth Hayes Miller. Member: GFLA. Illustrated for Vanity Fair, Vogue, Town and Country, Scribner's, Harper's, etc., and for the "Theatre Magazine," "Times," "Sun" and "Herald Tribune" of NY. Address in 1929, 247 Lexington Ave., New York, NY.

TAYLOR, F. WALTER.
Painter. Born in Philadelphia in 1874. Studied at PAFA, 1869 (awarded traveling scholarship); studied independently in Paris. Established studio in Philadelphia, 1898. Member: Fellowship of PAFA; Society of Illustrators. Illustrator of various books. Received medal of honor, Panama P.I. Exposition, 1915. Contributed numerous short stories to leading magazines. Died in 1921.

TAYLOR, H. WESTON.
Illustrator. Born Chester, PA, May 11, 1881. Pupil of McCarter and Anshutz. Member: Fellowship PAFA. Illustrations for "Saturday Evening Post," "Red Book," "Ladies Home Journal," "Elks Magazine," "American Boy," "MacLean's," etc. Address in 1929, 1012 Walnut St., Philadelphia, PA; h. 2 Seminary Ave., Chester, PA.

TAYLOR, HENRY FITCH.
Painter. Born in Cincinnati, Ohio in 1853. Studied art at Academie Julien, Paris. Exhibited at London, Paris, Rome, New York, Philadelphia, Chicago and San Francisco. Member of Association of American Painters and Sculptors. Inventor of The Taylor System of Organized Color (a device for indicating harmonious color relations). Died in New York in 1925.

TAYLOR, HENRY W(HITE).
Painter and lecturer. Born Otisville, NY, Aug. 22, 1899. Pupil of PAFA; Hugh H. Breckenridge. Member: Fellowship PAFA; Phila. Sketch C.; Phila. Alliance; North Shore AA; East Gloucester SA. Address in 1929, Stonybrook, Ridley Park, PA.

TAYLOR, IDA C.
Painter. Born Le Roy, NY. Pupil of W. M. Hunt; Julian Acad. in Paris. Member: AFA. Portrait, The Rt. Rev. W. D. Walker, Historical Mus. of Buffalo; "Old Trinity College," Alpha Chapter House, Trinity College, Hartford, CT; "Rev. Dr. Pierre Cushing," Episcopal Church, Le Roy, NY; three portraits, Masonic Temple, Le Roy, NY; portrait Rev. N. Barrows, De

Veaux School, Niagara Falls, NY.
Address in 1929, 55 Wolcott St., Le
Roy, NY.

TAYLOR, MARY PERKINS.
(Mrs. William F. Taylor). See Mary
Smyth Perkins.

TAYLOR, RALPH.
Painter. Born in Russia, Jan. 18,
1896. Pupil of PAFA. Member:
Fellowship PAFA; Sketch C; Phila.
Alliance; Am. APL. Award:
European scholarship, PAFA. Work:
"The Studio," PAFA; "Reflections,"
and "The Reading Lessons," Graphic
Sketch Club; "The Clinic,"
Fellowship, Penna. Acad. of the
Fine Arts; "An Outing" and "The
Sculptor," La France Art Inst.,
Phila. Address in 1929, 113 S.
19th St., Phila., PA.

TAYLOR, ROLLA S.
Painter and teacher. Born
Galveston, Texas, Oct. 31, 1874.
Pupil of Jose Arpa. Member: S.
Indp. A.; Chicago NJSA; San Antonio
A. Lg.; San Antonio AG; AFA.
Address in 1929, 100½ East Commerce
St.; h. 503 West Euclid Ave., San
Antonio, Texas.

TAYLOR, T.
Engraver. Good landscape plates,
done in line and published in New
York in 1860, are so signed.
Possibly a bank-note engraver, as
little of his signed work is found.

TAYLOR, WILL S.
Mural painter. Member: Mural P.;
Salma. C.; NY Arch. Lg.; Allied AA.
Work: 16 panels relating to early
life of Alaskan and British
Columbian Indians, Museum of
Natural History, NY; religious
mural for the City Park Chapel,
Brooklyn. Asst. Prof. of Art and
Curator of Art Collection, Brown
University. Address in 1929, Brown
University, Providence, RI.

TAYLOR, WILLIAM FRANCIS.
Painter and illustrator. Born
Hamilton, Ontario, Canada, March
26, 1883. Pupil of W. L. Lathrop,
Albert Sterner. Member: Salma C.
Awards: Hon. mention, Salma. C.,
1924; hon. mention, Phila. AC,
1924. Address in 1929, Lumberville,
Bucks Co., Pa.

TAYLOR, WILLIAM LADD.
Painter and illustrator. Born in
Graftson, Mass., in 1854. Studied
at art schools in Boston and New
York, and under Boulanger and
Lefebvre in Paris, 1884-85. Later
painted and illustrated in the
United States. Works: "Selections
from Longfellow's Poems" (series of
pictures illustrating the 19th
century in New England); series of
pictures of the "Pioneer West;"
"Old Songs Series," 1908-09; "Our
Home and Country," a book of
pictures of American life, 1908;
"Pictures from American
Literature," 1910, "Pictures from
the Old Testament," 1913. Address
in 1926, Wellesley, Mass. Died in
1926.

TAYLOR, WILLIAM N(ICHOLSON).
Painter and artist. Born
Cincinnati, Ohio, Jan. 22, 1882.
Pupil of Louis Bernier. Member:
Mural P.; NSS; Beaux Arts Inst. of
Design; Beaux Arts Architects;
Societe des Architects diplomes par
le Governement Francais; Lyme AA.
Address in 1929, Harvard Club, 127
West 44th St., New York, NY.

TEAGUE, DONALD.
Illustrator. Born Brooklyn, NY,
Nov. 27, 1897. Studied at ASL, and
in England. Member: SI; Am. APL;
GFLA. Address in 1929, 2 Division
St.; h. 38 Locust Ave., New
Rochelle, NY.

TEAGUE, WALTER DORWIN.
Lecturer and draftsman. Born
Decatur, IN, Dec. 18, 1883. Pupil
of George Bridgman. Member: SI;
GFLA. Designer of advertising and
products for Eastman Kodak Co.,
National Carbon and Carbide Co.,
Turner Glass Co., Welte Mignon
Corp., etc. Address in 1929, 210
Madison Ave., New York, NY; h.
Forest Hills, NY.

TEE-VAN, HELEN DAMROSCH.
(Mrs. John Tee-Van). Painter,
illustrator, craftsman, writer, and
teacher. Born New York City, May
26, 1893. Pupil of George de
Forest Brush, Jonas Lie. Work:
Color plates of the Flora and Fauna
of British Guiana, for the Tropical
Research Station of the NY
Zoological Society and for the

Arcturus and Haitian Expeditions under the direction of Wm. Beebe; illustrated "A Birthday Greeting and Other Songs," and other children's books; illustrator and author of stories of South American Indian and animal life; numerous landscapes. Address in 1929, 120 East 75th St., New York, NY.

TEEL, E.
Engraver. Born in the United States about 1830; died in Hoboken, NJ, before 1860. An excellent line-engraver of portraits and landscape. After being employed for some time in NY, he worked for Cincinnati publishers in 1854.

TEESDALE, CHRISTOPHER H.
Painter. Born Eltham, England, April 6, 1886. Member: Ft. Worth PC; SSAL. Work: Portrait of Prof. Emmett Brown, Cleburne Public Schools. Address in 1929, 310 North Walnut; Box 121, Cleburne, Texas.

TEFFT, CARL (or CHARLES) EUGENE.
Sculptor. Born Sept. 22, 1874 in Brewer, Maine. His figure of "Lake Superior" was acclaimed at the Buffalo Exposition. Died Sept. 20, 1951 in Presque Isle, ME.

TELLANDER, FRED.
Painter. Member: Chicago PS; Chicago Gal. A. Award: Fine Arts Bldg. Purchase prize, ($500), AIC, 1927. Address in 1929, 202 South State St.; 7460 Greenview Ave., Chicago, IL.

TELLING, ELISABETH.
Etcher. Born Milwaukee, July 14, 1882. Pupil of W. P. Henderson, George Senseney, H. E. Field, and studied in Munich. Member: Chicago SE; Calif. PM. Work: "Uncle William Creech," California State Library, Pasadena; Associate print for California Print Makers. Address in 1929, 2120 Lincoln Park, West, Chicago, IL.

TEN EYCK, JOHN (ADAMS).
Painter, etcher, and teacher. Born Bridgeport, CT, Oct. 28, 1893. Pupil of NY School of Fine and Appl. Art; ASL of NY under F. Luis Mora, Kenneth Hayes Miller, Joseph Pennell, Charles Hawthorne and Bror

J. O. Nordfeldt. Member: SI, 1922; Salma. C. 1926; Societe des Artistes Indp., Paris; S. Indp.A, 1918; NY Arch. Lg. 1928; Brooklyn S. Modern A. Instructor of landscape and etching, Kihn-Ten Eyck Art School, Stamford, CT. Address in 1929, 51 West 10th Street, New York, NY; h. Shippan Pt., Stamford, CT; summer, P. O. Box 540, Westerly, RI.

TENNEY.
In Tuckerman's "Book of the Artists" he is noted as painting miniatures.

TERRIL, ISRAEL.
Engraver. He arranged the music, engraved the title-page and music, and printed and sold a music-book entitled "Vocal Harmony, No. 1, Calculated for the Use of Singing Schools and Worshipping Assemblies." The imprint is "Newhaven, West Society, Engrav'd Printed and Sold by the Author (Israel Terril)," and the work was copyrighted "21 Aug. in 30th year of Independence" (1806).

TERRILL BROS.
These twin brothers were mezzotint engravers and came from Canada to the United States about 1868. Returned to England about two years later. Pupils of Simmons of London. Engraved large plates of fancy subjects.

TERRY, LUTHER.
Painter. Born July 18, 1813 in Enfield, Conn. Studied in Hartford and in 1838 went to Italy, where he lived for years. Painted portraits and historical compositions. Married the widow of Thos. Crawford, the sculptor, in 1861. His paintings are rarely seen in the U.S. Died in 1869.

TERRY, W. D.
Engraver. In 1836, with Olive Pelton, Terry founded the Bank Note Company of Boston. Terry, Pelton & Co. also did general engraving in Boston. Some of Terry's early vignettes were signed at Providence, RI.

TETLEY, WM. BIRCHALL.
Born in London. Portrait painter in oils and miniatures who flourished in New York about 1774.

TEW, DAVID.
Engraver. The Journals of the Continental Congress record that on Oct. 28th, 1788, they owed him the sum of 213 50/90 dollars, for engraving three copper-plates for bills of exchange, and for repairing two other plates.

TEW, MARGUERITE R.
Sculptor. Born in Magdalena, NM, Jan. 6, 1886. Pupil of PA Museum, School of Independent Artists; PAFA (under Grafly). Member: California Art Club; Fellowship of PAFA; National Association of Women Painters and Sculptors. Awarded Cresson European Scholarship, PAFA, 1913; first sculpture prize, Calif. AC, 1924. Work: Mayan ornament on portal of South West Museum, Los Angeles. Address in 1926, 4122 Pasadena Ave., Los Angeles, Calif.

TEWKSBURY, FANNY W(ALLACE).
Painter and teacher. Born Boston, MA. Pupil of School of Design; MA Inst. of Technology and Ross Turner in Boston. Member: NYWCC. Address in 1929, 11 Maple Ave., Newton, MA.

THACHER, ELIZABETH.
Painter. Born in Brookline, MA, Feb. 13, 1899. Pupil of Leslie Thompson, Philip Hale, William James, Frederick Bosley. Member: Springfield AL. Award: Hon. mention, Jr. League, Boston, 1929. Address in 1929, Fenway Studios, 30 Ipswich St., Boston, MA; h. 21 Dwight St., Brookline, MA; summer, Cohasset, MA.

THACKARA.
This signature as engraver is signed to a crude copperplate frontispiece to "The Instructor, or Young Man's Best Companion, etc," by Geo. Fisher, published by Isaac Collins, Burlington, NJ, 1775. Possibly the plate referred to was engraved by the sailor father of James Thackara.

THACKARA, JAMES.
Engraver. Born in Philadelphia in 1767; died there in 1848. Son of James Thackara, Sr., who settled in Philadelphia in 1764, after having served many years as a seaman in the British navy. Young James was apprenticed to James Trenchard, and later married his daughter. In 1794 Thackara was a partner of John Vallance in the engraving business in Philadelphia, and Thackara's name as engraver appears in directories from 1791 to 1833. Work was done entirely in line and confined to subject plates. For some time after 1826 he was the keeper of the PAFA. A three quarter length, seated, oil portrait of James Thackara was in the possession of his grandson, James Thackara, Lancaster, Penna.

THACKARA, WILLIAM W.
Engraver. Born in Philadelphia in 1791. Son of James Thackara and a pupil of his father. In 1832 they had the firm of Thackara & Son, general engravers in Philadelphia. This firm published, in 1814, "Thackara's Drawing Book, for the Amusement and Instruction of Young Ladies and Gentlemen." Died April 19, 1839.

THAIN, HOWARD A.
Painter. Born Dallas, TX, Nov. 16, 1891. Pupil of Samuel Ostrowsky, Antonin Sterba, F. V. DuMond, Robert Henri, Vivian Anspaugh, F. De F. Schook, Jay Hambidge. Member: S. Indp. A.; Bronx AG; ASL of NY; SSAL. Address in 1929, 327 West 22nd St., New York, NY.

THALINGER, E. OSCAR.
Painter. Born Alsace-Lorraine, France, March 20, 1885. Pupil of St. Louis School of Fine Arts under Wuerpel, Stoddard and Campbell; Gruber in Munich. Member: St. Louis AG; 2 x 4 Soc. Registrar City Art Museum, St. Louis, Mo. Awards: Thumb box group prize, 1926; St. Louis AG. group prize, 1926; Halsey C. Ives landscape prize, 1926, best work prize, 1928; prize, St. Louis Chamber of Commerce, 1927. Address in 1929, 7600 Carondelet Ave., Clayton, Mo.

THAW, FLORENCE.
(Mrs. Alex. Blair Thaw). Painter.
Born NYC, Feb. 17, 1864. Pupil of
Abbott Thayer, Birge Harrison;
Julian in Paris. Member: WA SA; NY
Cosmopolitan C; AFA. Address in
1929, 3255 N. St., WA, DC; summer,
Little River Farm, North Hampton.

THAYER, ABBOTT HENDERSON.
Painter. Born in Boston, August
12, 1849. Went to Paris and
entered the atelier of Gerome, and
from this studio went to Ecole des
Beaux Arts, where his great ability
as a draftsman was recognized. On
his return home from Europe, he
painted cattle and animal studies.
Their backgrounds were indicative
of the mastery he was later to
achieve in his landscapes. After
his return to the US he dedicated
himself to ideal figure pictures.
His painting of a nude is shown in
his great picture "Figure
Half-Draped" which shows well the
command of his technique. Painted
the first of his "Winged Figures in
1889" later owned by Smith College;
then painted the "Caritas" and the
"Virgin", (Freer Gallery,
Smithsonian); "Virgin Enthroned";
and other angel paintings.
Executed mural decoration at
Bowdoin College. The "Winter
Sunrise of Manadnock," in the MMA;
"Sketch of Cornish Headlands" and
"Winter Dawn on Manadnock," (Freer
Gallery) are among the finest
examples of American landscapes.
Died in 1921. In 1922 a Memorial
Exhibition of his work was held at
MMA where 78 paintings and many
drawings and sketches were shown.

THAYER, EMMA B.
(Mrs. Abbott Thayer). Painter.
Born in 1850. Specialty, flower
studies in oil and pastel. Died in
1924.

THAYER, ETHEL R(ANDOLPH).
Painter. Born Boston, Nov. 8,
1904. Pupil of Philip Hale.
Award: First Hallgarten prize, NAD,
NY, 1929. Address in 1929, 77 Bay
State Road, Boston, MA; summer,
Wier River Farm, Hingham, MA.

THAYER, GERALD H.
Painter. Born in
Cornwall-on-Hudson, NY, in 1883.

Pupil of Abbott H. Thayer, his
father. Work: "Partridge,"
Metropolitan Museum of Art;
"Rabbit," Brooklyn Museum of Art.
Author of "Concealing Coloration in
the Animal Kingdom;" "The
Nature-Camouflage Book;" "The Seven
Parsons and the Small Iguanodon."
Address in 1926, Manadnock, NH.

THAYER, GLADYS.
(Mrs. David Reasoner). Painter.
Born in South Woodstock, CT, in
1886. Pupil of her father, Abbott H
Thayer. Address in 1926,
Monadnock, NH.

THAYER, GRACE.
Painter. Born in Boston. Pupil of
Boston Museum School; also of Mme.
Hortense Richard in Paris. Member
of Copley Society, 1885. Address
in 1926, 845 Boylston St., Boston,
MA.

THAYER, RAYMOND L.
Painter. Member: GFLA; SI.
Address in 1929, 139 West 27th St.;
30 West 47th St., New York, NY.

THAYER, SANFORD.
Portrait painter of Syracuse, NY.
Born July 19, 1820 in Coto, NY.
Died Dec., 1880 in Syracuse, NY.

THAYER, THEODORA W.
Miniature painter. Born in Milton,
MA, in 1868. Studied with Joseph
De Camp in Boston. Instructor in
NY School of Art, and at Art
Students Lg. of NY. Her fine
portrait of Bliss Carman is
considered one of the memorable
achievements in American miniature
painting. Died in 1905.

THEISS, J(OHN) W(ILLIAM).
Watercolor P. Born Zelionople, PA,
Sept. 20, 1863. Pupil of Lorenzo
P. Latimer. Address in 1929, 29
Glenwood Ave., Springfield, Ohio.

THEOBALD, ELIZABETH STURTEVANT.
(Mrs. Samuel Theobald, Jr.).
Painter and sculptor. Born
Cleveland, Ohio, July 6, 1876.
Pupil of Chase, Mora, Hawthorne,
F.C. Gottwald, Herman Matzen.
Member: NA Women PS; PS. Address
in 1929, 40 Crescent Ave.,
Arrochar, SI, NY; 430 East 57th
St., New York, NY.

THEOBALD, SAMUEL JR.
Painter. Born Baltimore, MD, Oct. 23, 1872. Pupil of Castaigne and NAD. Address in 1929, 430 East 57th Street, New York, NY; summer, Arrochar, SI, NY.

THERIAT, CHARLES JAMES.
Painter. Born NY in 1860; student of Jules Lefebvre and Boulanger in Paris. Awards: Honorable mention, Paris Exp., 1899; Salon, 1896, and Paris Exp., 1900; bronze medal, Buffalo Exp., 1901. Member of Paris Society of American Painters. Address in 1926, Le Mee, Melum, Seine et Marne, France.

THEUERKAUFF, CARL R.
Painter. Born in Germany in 1875. Member of Rochester Art Club. Address in 1926, Cornwall Bldg., Chicago, IL.

THEUS, JEREMIAH.
Portrait painter. Born c. 1719. One of three brothers who came to South Carolina from Switzerland c. 1736. In the following year he established a studio and painted portraits in Charleston, SC. His work has frequently been attributed to Copley. Died at Charleston, SC, in 1774, after painting for about 35 yrs. in that city.

THEW, (R.) GARRET.
Painter and sculptor. Born Sharon, CT, Oct. 13, 1892. Pupil of Edward Penfield, John Carlson, Walter Biggs. Member: GFLA. Represented in the Newark Museum. Address in 1929, Roseville Road, Westport, CT.

THEW, ROBERT.
Engraver. Born in England. Came to US about 1850, and returned to England about 1865. Worked in NY and in Cincinnati. Engraver of landscapes.

THIEBAUD, WAYNE.
Painter. Born Nov. 15, 1920 in Mesa, Ariz. Earned BA and MA from Sacramento State. Produced many educational films. Rec. awards at Cal. State Fair (1956 art film); Columbia Records Award; Scholastic Art awards. Taught at S. F. Art Inst.; at UC/Davis since 1960. Created mosaic mural (1959) - Sacramento Munic. Utility Bldg.

Exhibited at Crocker Art Gallery, Sacramento (1952); San Jose St. Col.; Allan Stone Gal.; Galleria Schwartz, Milan (1963); Inst. Contemp. Arts, London;Guggenheim; Wadsworth; Brandeis; Art. Inst. of Chicago; the Hague; Diablo Valley, Col.; and the Whitney. In collections of MMA; Albright-Knox; Newark; Stanford U.; MOMA; Bryn Mawr Col.; U. of Miami; Wadsworth and many private collections.

THIEDE, HENRY A.
Illustrator. Born in Germany, Oct. 27, 1871. Member: Palette and Chisel C. Address in 1929, North American Bldg., Chicago, IL; h. 2749 Woodbine Ave., Evanston, IL.

THIEM, HERMAN C.
Painter, architect, and illustrator. Born Rochester, NY, Nov. 21, 1870. Pupil of Mechanic Inst.; Seth Jones, Carl M. Raschen. Member: Rochester AC; Picture Painters C. Address in 1929, 1589 St. Paul St.; summer, Stop 16, Sumerville Blvd., Rochester, NY.

THIEME, A(NTHONY).
Painter and etcher. Born Rotterdam, Holland, Feb. 20, 1888. Pupil of George Hacker; Academie of Fine Arts, The Hague, Holland. Member: Boston AC; Prov. WCC; Boston SAC; North Shore AA; Salma. C; Springfield AL; Rockport AA. Awards: Hon. mention, 1927 and first prize, 1928, Springfield AL; first landscape prize, North Shore AA, Gloucester, 1928. Work: "Gloucester Harbor," Dayton Art Inst., Dayton, Ohio. Address in 1929, 601 Boylston St., Boston, MA; summer, Rockport, MA.

THOBURN, JEAN.
Painter and teacher. Born Calcutta, India, Nov. 27, 1887. Pupil of Frank A. Parsons, H. S. Stevenson, A. W. Dow. Member: Pittsburgh AA. Address in 1929, 4312 Saline St., Squirrel Hill, Pittsburgh, PA.

THOELE, LILLIAN (CAROLINE) (ANNE).
Painter and illustrator. Born St. Louis, Aug. 12, 1894. Pupil of St. Louis School of Fine Arts; PAFA. Member: St. Louis AG; St. Louis AL. Work: "The Vision of Christian

Leadership," Assembly Hall, American Youth Foundation Camp, Shelby, MI. Address in 1929, Purina Mills, 835 South Eighth St.; h. 4025 Shreve Ave., St. Louis, MO.

THOM, JAMES CRAWFORD.
Painter. Born in NY in 1835. He studied at the National Academy in 1859. Went abroad for study and exhibited in London, where he earned several medals. Among his paintings are "By the River-side," "The Monk's Walk," "Forgotten Cares," "The Old Farm House," and a number of landscapes painted along the Hudson River. Died Feb. 16, 1898 in NJ.

THOMAS, ALLAN A. F.
Illustrator. Born in Jackson, MI, Feb. 15, 1902. Pupil of George Harding, PAFA. Award: First Cresson European Scholarship, 1925, second Cresson E. S., 1927; first Lea prize, PAFA, 1926. Member: Phil. PC. Address in 1929, 622 South Washington Sq., Philadelphia, PA.

THOMAS, C. B.
Painter. Member: Mural P. Address in 1929, 132 East 19th St., NYC.

THOMAS, C. H.
Miniature painter, who flourished in NY in 1838-39.

THOMAS, CONRAD ARTHUR.
Painter. Born Dresden, Germany, April 28, 1858. Pupil of Hofmann, Grosse, Schilling. Member: AFA; New Rochelle AA. Work: Allegorical murals, City Hall, St. Louis; Court House, Auburn, IN; Sinton Hotel, Cincinnati, Ohio; historical murals, "La Salle," Court House, South Bend, IN; "Daniel Boone," Seelbach Hotel, Louisville, KY; "Raddison," Raddison Hotel, Louisville, KY; "Adoration of the Magi," Sts. Peter and Paul Cathedral, Philadelphia. Address in 1929, 116 4th St., Pelham, NY.

THOMAS, EMMA W(ARFIELD).
Painter. Born Philadephia, PA. Pupil of Beaux, Chase, Thos. P. Anshutz and Hugh H. Breckenridge. Member: Fellowship PAFA; Phila.

Alliance; Plastic C. Specialty, portraits. Address in 1929, 3409 Hamilton St., Philadelphia, PA.

THOMAS, ESTELLE (L.).
Painter, illustrator, and teacher. Born New York City. Pupil of Martin Borgard, John Sloan, Charles Hawthorne. Member: Pittsburgh AA; Gloucester SA. Address in 1929, 512 North Euclid Ave., Pittsburgh, PA; summer, East Gloucester, MA.

THOMAS, HENRY.
Portrait painter. Pupil of John Neagle. Worked in Philadelphia. His portrait of the actor Junius Brutus Booth was exhibited in the Loan Collection of Historic Portraits, Philadelphia, 1887.

THOMAS, ISAIAH.
Engraver. Born Jan. 19, 1749 in Boston. Served as apprentice to Zachariah Fowle. In 1770, in partnership with Fowle, Thomas published the Massachusetts Spy. About this time he tried engraving on type metal. To this later well-known printer and publisher are credited some very crude cuts signed "I.T.," appearing in "The History of the Holy Jesus, etc., 15th edition, printed by I. Thomas for L. Fowle." Died April 4, 1831 in Worcester, MA.

THOMAS, JOHN.
Painter. Born Feb. 4, 1927 in Bessemer, AL. Earned BA from New School of Soc. Research (1941); studied at U. of Georgia, and earned MA from NYU (1954). Taught at U. of Hawaii in Manoa and Hilo. Awards: Yaddo Foundation; Tuscon Art Center; grant from Nat. Endow. for Arts (1977). Also a printmaker. Exhibited at Birmingham Mus. of Art (many since 1955); Kantor Gal. (Beverly Hills); Alan Gal., NYC; Okla. Art Center; U. of Arizona; Seattle; Denver; State U. of Iowa; Whitney; Wichita Art Mus.; U. of Nebraska; Kootz Gal., NYC; Cal. Palace; Contemp. Art Center, Hawaii. In many private collections and at Smithsonian; Capitol Bldg., Honolulu and Hirshhorn Collection.

THOMAS, MARJORIE.
Painter, who exhibited at the Annual Exhibition of Penna. Acad., Phila., 1924. Address in 1926, Scottsdale, Arizona.

THOMAS, PAUL K(IRK) M(IDDLEBROOK).
Portrait painter. Born Phila., Jan. 31, 1875. Pupil of PAFA under Cecilia Beaux, Chase, and Grafly. Member: Lotos C; New Rochelle AA. Award: Bronze medal, St. Louis Exp., 1904. Work: "Dr. Joseph Taylor," Bryn Mawr College; "Prof. and Mrs. Richard G. Moulton," Chicago University; "A. C. Houghton," Williams College; "Prof. G. T. Ladd," Western Reserve Univ.; "Prof. Dexter," Yale Univ.; "Prof. H. N. Gardiner," Smith College; "Charles Custis Harrison, LL.D.," University of PA, Phila.; "Ambassador Masanao Hanihara," Nippon Club, NY. Address in 1929, 154 Nassau St., New York, NY; 265 Clinton Ave., New Rochelle, NY.

THOMAS, RICHARD.
Sculptor and craftsman. Born Philadelphia, PA, Sept. 4, 1872. Pupil of Charles Grafly, August Zeller, Ed. Maene. Member: Trenton, NJ, AA. Address in 1929, Memorial Art Studio, Crosswick St.; h. Elizabeth St., Bordentown, NJ.

THOMAS, ROLAND.
Painter. Born Kansas City, MO, in 1883. Pupil of William Chase, Robert Henri and Frank Vincent DuMond. Member: Kansas City Arts and Crafts; and American Artists, Munich. Awarded landscape prize, MO State Art Exhibit, 1921. Work: "Autumn," Elverhoj Art Gallery, Milton, NY; "Winter Dachaon," American Artists Club, Munich; mural decoration in Curtiss Bldg., Kansas City, MO. Address in 1929, 409 East 10th St., Kansas City, MO.

THOMAS, RUTH.
Painter. Born Washington, DC, Oct. 10, 1893. Pupil of Albert Sterner, John Elliot, Helena Sturtevant, Cecilia Beaux; Corcoran School of Art. Member: Newport AA. Specialty, portrait drawings. Address in 1929, 62 Ayrault St., Newport, RI.

THOMAS, RUTH F.
See Felker.

THOMAS, S. SEYMOUR.
Painter. Born 1868 in San Augustine, TX. Studied at Art Student's League, NY, 1886-88 and Julien Acad. and Ecole des Beaux Arts, Paris. Work principally portraiture. Awards: Honorable mention, Salon, Paris, 1895; gold medals, Salon, 1901; 2d gold medal, Hors Concours, 1904; bronze medal, Paris Exp., 1900; gold medal, Munich, 1901; Chevalier de la Legion d'Honneur, 1905. Member International Jury of Awards, St. Louis Exp., 1904 and Paris Society of American Painters. Painted Hon. James Bryce, Cardinal William Henry O'Connell, Gen. Lew Wallace; President Woodrow Wilson for the Shire House, and for the State House of NJ; "Portrait of a Lady and Dog," acquired by the Met. Mus., 1915. Address in 1926, 11 Impasse Rousin, Paris, and 80 West 40th St., NYC. Died Feb. 29, 1956.

THOMAS, VERNON. (MRS.).
Painter, illustrator, and etcher. Born Evanston, IL, Sept. 12, 1894. Pupil of Ralph Clarkson, Charles Hawthorne, W. J. Reynolds. Member: Chicago SE; Cordon C. Specialty, painting and etching of children. Address in 1929, Seneca Hotel, 200 East Chestnut St., Chicago, IL.

THOMASON, FRANCIS Q.
Painter, who exhibted at the Penna. Acad. of Fine Arts, Phila., 1914.

THOMPSON.
Some poorly drawn and badly engraved subject plates are thus signed. They were published in NY in 1834.

THOMPSON, ALBERT.
Painter. Born in Woburn, MA in 1853. He became a pupil of Wm. E. Norton in 1880-81; he also studied in Paris. Work was mainly landscapes and cattle. Among his paintings are "After the Shower," "Clearing Up," "Changing Pasture," and "An October Afternoon."

THOMPSON, ALFRED W.
Painter. Born in Baltimore, MD, in 1840. Studied in Paris. His

paintings cover a wide range of subjects. Specialty: Landscapes. Member of National Acad. of Design in 1875. The NY Historical Society owned "The Parting Guests." Died in 1896 in Summit, NJ.

THOMPSON, ARAD.
Painter. Born Dec. 1786 in MA. Graduated from Dartmouth College in 1807. Lived and painted portraits in Middleboro, MA. Died April 23, 1843 in Middleboro, MA.

THOMPSON, CEPHAS G.
Landscape and portrait painter. Born in Middleboro, MA, in 1809. At 18 years he painted portraits in Plymouth, MA, and afterwards in Providence, RI. Had a studio in NY in 1837-47. Resided in Italy 1852-60, and returned to NY. Painted portraits of many American authors. The collection is now owned by the NY Historical Society. Died Jan. 5, 1888.

THOMPSON, D. G.
Engraver. Born in England; died in NY about 1870. He spent a considerable part of his early life in India with a brother who held some official position in that country. Was engraving portraits and landscapes in NYC in 1856. Also a watercolor artist.

THOMPSON, EDITH BLIGHT.
Painter. Born Phila., PA, April 27, 1884. Pupil of F. V. DuMond and Luis Mora. Member: Newport AA. Specialty, interiors. Address in 1929, Westbury, Long Island, NY; summer, Newport, RI.

THOMPSON, ERNEST THORNE.
Painter, etcher, lecturer, and teacher. Born Saint John, N. B., CN, Nov. 8, 1897. Pupil of MA Sch. of Art, under Major, Hamilton and Andrew; Sch. of Boston Mus., under Bosley; European study. Member: Ind. AA; Hoosier Salon; ALA; AFA. Awards: Hoosier Salon, 1927; Cunningham prize, 1929; 50 prints of The Year, 1928. Work: "The Sacred Heart," mural, St. Patrick's Church, McHenry, IL; "Madonna of Sorrows," mural, Holy Cross Seminary, Notre Dame, Ind.; Detroit, MI; "Stations of the Cross," and Football Championship mem., bronze, also world war mem., bronze and mural, Univ. of Notre Dame; "Indiana Snows," Wightman Mem. Gal., Notre Dame; "Adventures of Don Quixote," murals, Oliver Hotel, South Bend, IN; "Net Mender's Yard," Bibliotheque Nationale, Paris. Author, "Technique of the Modern Woodcut," "New England, 12 Woodcuts," works reproduced by principal magazines. Director, Sch. of FA, Univ. of Notre Dame, 1922-28. Address in 1929, School of Art, College of New Rochelle, New Rochelle, NY; summer, 100 Trenton St., East Boston, MA.

THOMPSON, F. LESLIE.
Etcher. Member: Chicago SE; Calif. P.M. Address in 1929, Fenway Studios, Boston, MA; 4700 North Lawndale Ave., Chicago, IL.

THOMPSON, FRED D.
Painter. Member: Providence WCC. Address in 1929, 184 Alabama Ave., Providence, RI.

THOMPSON, FREDERIC LOUIS.
Painter and sculptor. Born Chilmark, MA, in 1868. Pupil of George H. McCord. Member: Salmagundi Club; Societe des Beaux Arts. Address in 1926, 126 East 75th St., New York, NY.

THOMPSON, G(EORGE) A(LBERT).
Painter, teacher, and draftsman. Born New Haven, CT, July 1, 1868. Pupil of Yale School of Fine Arts, Yale Univ.; John La Farge in NY; Merson, Blanc, Courtois and Girardot in Paris. Member: Paint and Clay C. of New Haven; Salma. C. 1909; Mystic AA; Mystic SA. Work: "Nocturne, the Quinnipiack," National Gallery, Uruguay.

THOMPSON, HANNAH.
Painter and etcher. Born in Phila. in 1888. Pupil of Wm. M. Chase. Member of California Art Club and Society of Etchers. Address in 1926, 415 Oakland Ave., Pasadena, CA.

THOMPSON, HARRY IVES.
Painter. Born in West Haven, CT, in 1840. Died there in 1906. First painted under the instruction of Benjamin Coe, a water colorist of New Haven, CT, whom he succeeded

as instructor in the drawing school. While his landscape and figure work was well received, his best work was that of a portrait painter. At the fifty second Annual Exhib. of the NAD he exhibited a portrait of governors of CT, later in library of the State Capitol. Portrait of Jonathan Trumbull was in US Capitol.

THOMPSON, J. D.
In 1860 this capital line engraver of landscapes was working in NY. Probably a bank-note engraver.

THOMPSON, JEROME.
Painter. Born in 1814. Brother of Cephas G. Thompson. Painted portraits at an early age at Cape Cod. Had a studio in NYC and went to Europe in 1852 to study. Painted landscapes and figures. His "Land of Beulah," "Hiawatha's Journey" and "The Voice of the Great Spirit" were well known. Died in 1886.

THOMPSON, JOHN EDWARD.
Painter, draftman, and teacher. Born Buffalo, NY, Jan. 3, 1882. Pupil of ASL of Buffalo and NY; of Laurens, Blanche, Cottet, and Tudor-Hart in Paris. Member: Denver AA; Cactus C. Award: Medal for murals, Denver C., 1929. Represented by decorations in National Bank Buildings, Polo Club, St. Martin's Chapel, and in Art Museum, Denver. Instructor at Chappell School of Arts. Patron at "Atelier" (branch of Beaux Arts). Address in 1929, 515 East Illiff Ave.; h. 421 East Asbury Ave., Denver, CO.

THOMPSON, JULIET.
Portrait painter. Born in NY. Pupil of Corcoran Art School and ASL in Wash.; Kenneth Hayes Miller; Julian Acad. in Paris. Member: NAC; S. Wash. A.; Wash. WCC; S. Indp. A. Award: Medal, Brown Bigelow Competition, 1925. Address in 1929, 48 West 10th St., NYC.

THOMPSON, KATE E.
Painter. Born near Middletown, Orange Co., NY, June 8, 1872. Pupil of Kenneth Hayes Miller,

George Bridgman, ASL of NY. Work: Mural, "Sisterhood," Montclair (NJ) Unitarian Church; "The Law," NJ Dept. of Public Highways. Specialty, small murals for homes. Address in 1929, Pompton Plains, NJ.

THOMPSON, LAUNT.
Sculptor. Born 1883 in Ireland. Came to America in 1847. Pupil of Erastus D. Palmer. Produced several portrait busts and later opened a studio in NY. Elected an Associate Member of National School of Design in 1859 and an Academician in 1862. Work: Statues of Pierson, at Yale College; Bryant, at the Metropolitan Art Museum, NY and Edwin Booth, as Hamlet. Died Sept. 26, 1894 in Middletown, NY.

THOMPSON, LESLIE P(RINCE).
Painter. Born Medford, March 2, 1880. Pupil of Boston Mus. Sch. under Tarbell. Member: ANA; Boston GA; St. Botolph C.; Newport AA. Awards: Bronze medal, St. Louis Exp., 1904; third Hallgarten prize, NAD 1911; H. S. Morris prize, Newport AA 1914; silver medal, P.-P. Exp., San F., 1915; Beck gold medal, PAFA, 1919; silver medal, Sesqui-Centennial Exp., Phila. 1926; Stotesbury prize, PAFA, 1927; purchase prize, Boston AC, 1928. Address in 1929, 308 Fenway Studios, 30 Ipswich St., Boston, MA.

THOMPSON, MARGARET WHITNEY.
(Mrs. Randall Thompson). Sculptor. Born Chicago, IL, Feb. 12, 1900. Pupil of PAFA; Charles Grafly; Schukieff in Paris. Member: Phil. Alliance; Fellowship PAFA. Address in 1929, 124 Forest St., Wellesley Hills, MA.

THOMPSON, MARVIN FRANCIS.
Painter, illustrator, and etcher. Born Rushville, IL, March 14, 1895. Pupil of Chicago AFA; Louis Ritman, Dorothy Viciji. Member: Chicago SA; IL. AFA; Chicago SSAA. Painter, etcher and wood engraver of the American Indian Mythology. Address in 1929, 6933 Stewart Ave., Chicago, IL.

THOMPSON, MILLS.
Mural painter and writer. Born Washington, DC, Feb. 2, 1875. Pupil of Corcoran Art School in Washington; ASL of Washington; ASL of NY. Member: S. Wash. A.; Wash. WCC; AC Phila. Address in 1929, 44 Old Military Road, Saranac Lake, NY.

THOMPSON, NELLIE LOUISE.
Painter and sculptor. Born Jamaica Plain, Boston. Pupil of Sir James Linton and South Kensington School under Alyn Williams and Miss Ball Hughes in London; Cowles Art School in Boston under De Camp; Henry B. Snell. Studied sculpture under Roger Noble Burnham, Bela Pratt, John Wilson, Cyrus Dallin. Member: Copley S. 1893; allied mem. MacD.C.; North Shore AA; Gloucester SA; Boston SS. Address in 1929, Studio, 10 Washington Hall, Trinity Court, Dartmouth St., Boston, MA.

THOMPSON, WALTER W.
Painter and teacher. Born Newton, MA, Jan. 10, 1881. Pupil of W. T. Robinson; John Enneking; C. W. Reed. Member: Darien G. of Seven Arts; AFA. Address in 1929, care of Ainslie Galleries, Inc., 677 Fifth Ave., New York, NY; Marshall Bldg., 22 Wall St., Norwalk, CT.

THOMPSON, WILLIAM JOHN.
Portrait painter. Born 1771 in Savannah, GA. Painted miniatures. In 1812 he moved to Edinburgh, Scotland, and died there in 1845.

THOMPSON, WOODMAN.
Painter and draftsman. Born Pittsburgh, PA, Nov. 19, 1889. Pupil of Arthur W. Sparks, George Sotter, Ralph Holmes. Member: Pitts. AA. Founded Department of Stagecraft at Carnegie Inst. of Technology. Specialty, stage scene designs and mural paintings. Address in 1929, Booth Theater, 222 West 45th St.; h. 684 Riverside Drive, New York, NY.

THOMPSON, WORDSWORTH.
Painter. His picture "Passing the Outpost" was owned by the Union League Club of NY. Elected member of the National Acad. of Design in 1875. Died in 1896.

THOMSON, FRANCES LOUISE.
Painter, lecturer, and teacher. Born Hagerstown, MD, Feb. 22, 1870. Pupil of ASL of NY; MD Inst.; Jean Paul Laurens. Member: Wash. SA; Wash. WCC. Work: "Portrait of Admiral Schley," MD Historical Society, Baltimore.

THOMSON, GEORGE.
Painter. Born Claremont, Ontario, CN, Feb. 10, 1868. Pupil of F. V. DuMond, W. L. Lathrop, H. R. Poore. Member: CT AFA; New Haven Paint and Clay Club. Award: Hon. mention, CT AFA, 1915. Address in 1929, 591 8th St., East, Owen Sound, Ontario, Canada.

THOMSON, H(ENRY) G(RINNELL).
Painter. Born NYC, Nov. 24, 1850. Pupil of NAD, ASL of NY, Chase. Member: S. Indp. A.; Salma. C.; Silvermine GA; AFA. Address in 1929, Wilton, Fairfield Co., CT.

THOMSON, RODNEY.
Illustrator and etcher. Born San Francisco, Calif., Oct. 2, 1878. Pupil of Partington School of Illustrations. Member: SI; GFLA; AFA. Address in 1929, 280 Riverside Drive, New York, NY.

THOMSON, W(ILLIAM) T.
Portrait painter and illustrator. Born Philadelphia, Oct. 5, 1858. Pupil of PAFA. Member: Fellowship PAFA; AC Phila.; Phila. Sketch C.; AAS; Phila. AA. Address in 1929, 1020 Chestnut St.; h. 252 North 16th St., Philadelphia, PA.

THORNDIKE, GEORGE QUINCY.
Painter. Born in 1825; died in 1886. Graduated from Harvard in 1847 and went abroad to study art. On his return he settled in Newport, RI. His work showed the French influences. Elected an Assoc. Member of the National Acad. of Design in 1861. Among his works are "The Wayside Inn," "The Lily Pond," "The Dumplings" and "Newport, RI."

THORNE, ANNA L(OUISE).
Painter, etcher, writer, and lecturer. Born Toledo, Dec. 21, 1878. Pupil of AIC; ASL of NY; Delacluse, M. Castolucio and Andre L'hote in Paris. Member: Detroit

S. Women P; Ohio-Born Women A; Athena Soc. Address in 1929, 405 Lagrange St., Toledo, Ohio.

THORNE, WILLIAM.
Painter. Born Delavan, WI, 1864. Pupil of Constant, Lefebvre and Laurens in Paris. Member: ANA 1902, NA 1913; SAA 1893. Awards: Medal, NAD 1888; hon. mention, Paris Salon, 1891; bronze medal, Pan-Am. Exp., Buffalo, 1901. Work: "The Terrace," Corcoran Gallery, Washington. Address in 1929, Carnegie Hall, 154 West 57th St., New York, NY.

THORNHILL.
He was a music engraver on copper. Located in Charleston, SC, early in the last century.

THORNTON, WILLIAM.
Born May 20, 1759 in Tortola, West Indies. Educated as a physician. Lived in England and Scotland from 1781-83. Came to Phila., and was elected member of Am. Philosophical Soc. of that city in 1787. A skilled architect. Designed the Phila. lib. bldg., completed 1790, and superintended erection of the Capitol in Wash. In 1802 appointed first superintendent of US Patent Office. While in England, made a serious attempt at mezzotint engraving. One of his mezzotints, in the Lib. of Congress, is an enlarged copy of an engraved gem representing Caesar Augustus, fairly well executed, and signed "Thornton" in Greek characters. Assisted Thomas Jefferson with the plans for U. of VA bldg. A collection of his manuscripts, including personal notes, is in the Lib. of Congress. He also copied the profile crayon drawing that Gilbert Stuart made of Jefferson in "Swiss Crayon." Died March, 1828 in Phila.

THORPE, FREEMAN.
Portrait painter. Born in 1844; died in Hubert, MN, in 1922. Painted many portraits of Government officials in Washington, DC.

THORSEN, LARS.
Painter. Born Norway, 1876. Member: Springfield AA. Work:

"Port Jackson," Louise Crombie Beach Memorial Collection, Storrs, CT. Address in 1929, Noank, CT.

THORWARD, CLARA SCHAFER.
Painter and craftsman. Born South Bend, IN, June 14, 1887. Pupil of Cleveland School of Art; AIC; Henry G. Keeler. Member: Hoosier Salon; Artists Lg. of No. Ind.; Boston SAC; Phila. SAC. Award: First prize for Batiks, Cleveland Museum of Art, 1926. Address in 1929, 31 West Mosholu Parkway, New York, NY.

THOURON, HENRY J.
Painter. Studied at the Penna. Acad. of the Fine Arts and later in Paris. On his return to this country he painted a number of altar pictures. Was instructor at the Penna. Acad. of the Fine Arts for several years. Died 1915 in Rome.

THRASHER, LESLIE.
Painter and illustrator. Born Piedmont, West Virginia, Sept. 15, 1889. Pupil of Pyle, Chase and Anshutz. Member: Wilmington SFA; SI; GFLA; Salma. C. Address in 1929, 51 West Tenth St.; h. 11 East 8th St., New York, NY; summer, Center Lovell, ME.

THROCKMORTON, CLEON (FRANCIS).
Painter. Born Atlantic City, NJ, Oct. 3, 1897. Member: Wash. AC. Work: Scenic designs for "Emperor Jones," "Hairy Ape," "Desire Under the Elms," "Rosmersholm," "Romeo and Juliet," "Wings of Chance," "Thrills," "All God's Chilluns Got Wings," etc. Address in 1929, 102 West 3rd St.; h. 133 MacDougal St., New York, NY.

THROOP, DANIEL SCROPE.
Born in Exford, Chenango County, NY, in 1800; died at Elgin, IL. Son of Major Dan Throop (1768-1824) of Norwich, CT. He engraved a good stipple portrait of Lafayette in 1824, evidently made for a Lafayette badge. This plate is signed "D. S. Throop, Sc., Utica, NY."

THROOP, J. V. N.
He was an engraver of portraits, in line and stipple, working in NY and in Baltimore in 1835.

THROOP, JOHN PETER VANNES.
Engraver. Born April 15, 1794 in NYC. Engraver of portraits working in Baltimore, MD, in 1835. Brother of J. V. N. Throop.

THROOP, O. H.
In 1825, O. H. Throop, an engraver of landscape and vignettes, had his office at 172 Broadway, New York City.

THULSTRUP.
See De Thulstrup.

THUM, PATTY PRATHER.
Painter. Born in Louisville, KY. Graduated from Vassar College; studied painting with Henry Van Ingen at Vassar and later at Art Students League of NY. Honorable mention for book illustrations, Chicago Exp., 1893. Member: Louisville Art League; Louisville Artists' League. Contributor to art magazines. Address in 1926, 654 4th St., Louisville, KY.

THURBER, ALICE HAGERMAN.
(Mrs. Thomas L. Thurber). Painter, craftsman, and teacher. Born Birmingham, MI, June 21, 1871. Pupil of Joseph Gies; Detroit Commercial Art School; AIC under St. Pierre; Frederick Fursman; W. W. Kreghbeil. Member: Detroit S. Women P. Awards: First and second prizes for water color, 1915, and first and second prizes for posters, 1916, first miscellaneous water color, 1928 at Michigan Inst. of Art, State Fair. Member: NY Indp. A. Address in 1929, 214 Oak St., Birmingham, MI.

THURBER, CAROLINE.
(Mrs. Dexter Thurber). Portrait painter. Born Oberlin, Ohio. Studied in Italy, Germany, England and Paris. Work: Portraits for Mt. Holyoke College; Western College for Women, Oxford, Ohio; Oberlin College; Boston University; Supreme Courts of Iowa and Rhode Island; portraits of Angelo Patri; Robert Andrews Millikan, Margaret Deland; Dallas Lore Sharp, Dorothy George and other professional people. Address in 1929, 320 Tappan St., Brookline, MA.

THURLOW, HELEN.
Painter. Member: Fellowship PAFA; GFLA. Address in 1929, 143 Gramercy Park, New York, NY.

THURN, ERNEST.
Painter, etcher, writer, lecturer, and teacher. Born Chicago, IL, July 23, 1889. Pupil of Hans Hofmann. Writer and lecturer on "The Modern Movement in Art." Director, Thurn School of Modern Art. Address in 1929, 911 Carnegie Hall, New York, NY.

THURSTON, JANE McDUFFLE.
Painter and sculptor. Born Ripon, WI, Jan. 9, 1887. Pupil of Mannheim, Miller. Member: Calif. AC; Laguna Beach AA; West Coast Arts; Pasadena SA. Awards: Taft prize, West Coast Arts, 1923; hon. mention, Calif. AC, 1925. Address in 1929, 550 West Calif. St., Pasadena, California.

TIEBOUT, CORNELIUS.
Engraver. Born c. 1773. The first American born professional engraver to produce really meritorious work. Apparently died in obscurity in KY about 1830. Some biographers state he was born in NY in 1777, but existing plates show that he was doing creditable work in 1789. Descended from Huguenot family from Holland which held lands on the Delaware as early as 1656 and owned property in Flatbush, Long Island, in 1669. He was apprenticed to John Burger, silversmith of NY, where he learned to engrave on metal. Was engraving maps and subject plates for NY publishers in 1789-90, and line portraits in 1793. Went to London to study and learned to engrave in stipple manner. In 1794 in London a large and well executed stipple plate engraved by Tiebout, after a painting by J. Green, was published. In 1796 Teibout published in London his quarto portrait of John Jay probably the first good portrait engraved by an American born professional engraver (the mezzotint work of the artist Edward Savage not coming under this category). In November, 1796, he was again in NY, engraving and publishing prints with his brother, Andrew Tiebout. His name

disappears from the NY directories in 1799. He went to Phila. about that time as an engraver until 1825.

TIEBOUT, MADEMOISELLE.
French miniature painter, who flourished in NY about 1834.

TIFFANY, LOUIS C(OMFORT).
Painter and craftsman. Born NY, Feb. 18, 1848. Pupil of Geo. Inness and Samuel Colman in NY; Leon Bailey in Paris. Member: ANA 1871; NA 1800; SAA; AWCS; NY Arch. Lg. 1889; Century Assoc.; NAC; NY SFA; NY Municipal AS; AI Graphic A; NSS; AFA; Soc. Nat'l des Beaux Arts; Im. Soc. of Fine Arts, Japan. Awards: Gold medal for applied arts, Paris Exp., 1900; Chevalier of the Legion of Honor of France, 1900; gold medal Dresden Exp., 1901; grand prize, Turin Exp. of Decorative Art, 1901; special diploma of honor, St. Louis Exp., 1904; gold medal, Sesqui Exp., Phila., 1926. In painting, made specialty of oriental scenes; originator of what is known as Favrile glass. Art dir. of Tiffany Studios. In 1918 established the Louis Comfort Tiffany Foundation for art students at Oyster Bay, LI and deeded to it his art collections, Gallery, Chapel and Country estate. Died Jan. 17, 1933 in NYC. Address in 1929, 391 Madison Ave; 46 West 23rd St.; h. 27 E. 72nd St., NY; summer, Laurelton Hall, Oyster Bay, LI, NY.

TIFFANY, MARY A.
Painter in oils and watercolors. Born in Hartford, CT. Pupil of Tryon at Conn. School of Design.

TIFFANY, WILLIAM.
He was from Baltimore, MD. Known as an accomplished draughtsman whose pencil illustrations of Tennyson and Longfellow were remarkable for truth and refined conception. His best known paintings are "Lenore" and "St. Christopher Bearing the Christ Child." Died in NY, 1907.

TILDEN, ALICE F(OSTER).
Portrait painter. Born Brookline, MA. Pupil of Boston Museum School;

Wm. M. Chase in NY; Lucien Simon. Member: Copley S., 1898. Address in 1929, 30 Walnut St., Milton, MA.

TILDEN, ANNA M(EYER).
Sculptor. Born Chicago, IL, Dec. 9, 1895. Pupil of Albin Polasek. Member: Chicago SA; Austin, Oak Park and River Forest AL. Work: World War memorial, River Forest, IL. Address in 1929, 107 Hillcrest Ave., Hinsdale, IL.

TILDEN, DOUGLAS.
Sculptor. Born in Chico, CA, in 1860. Pupil of National Acad. of Design under Ward and Flagg; Gotham Students League under Mowbray; Choppin in Paris. Awarded hon. mention, Paris Salon, 1890; bronze medal, Paris Exp., 1900; gold medal, Alaska Yukon Pacific Expo, Seattle, 1909; commemorative gold medal, St. Louis Exp., 1904. Work: "The Tired Boxer," Art Inst., Chicago; "Baseball Player," Golden Gate Park, San Francisco; memorial monuments at Portland (OR), Los Angeles, San Francisco, etc. Address in 1926, Oakland, CA.

TILDEN, JOHN C(LARK).
Painter and teacher. Born Yonkers, NY, Feb. 10, 1889. Pupil of PAFA. Member: SSAL. Awards: Cresson European Scholarship, PAFA; second Toppan prize, PAFA, 1914. Work: "Autumn, 1918" and 4 portraits, University Club, Houston, Texas; "Portrait of Josiah Jackson," Penn. State University, Philadelphia. Address in 1929, 143 East 62nd St., New York, NY; h 1110 Dennis Ave., Houston, Texas.

TILLER, ROBERT.
There were two engravers of this name in Philadelphia, father and son. The father was an engraver of landscape, working in line in 1818-25. The son engraved portraits in stipple and subject plates in line in 1828-36.

TILLINGHAST, MARY E.
Painter. Born in NY. Pupil of John La Farge in NY, and of Carolus Duran and Henner in Paris. Specialty, designs for stained glass.

TILLOTSON, ALEXANDER.
Painter. Born Waupun, WI, July 9, 1897. Pupil of Frederick Fursman, Maurice Sterne, Max Weber, etc. Member: Wisconsin PS. Award: Gold medal, Milaukee AI, 1926. Director of Art Dept., Boy's Tech. High School, Milwaukee. Address in 1929, 325-25th St., Milwaukee, WI.

TILTON, JOHN ROLLIN.
Painter. Born in Louden, NH, in 1828. Landscape painter, largely self taught. Settled in Rome in 1852. The London Daily News wrote of him, "He was the first American painter since Benjamin West to receive special commendation from the President of the Royal Acad." Recipient of Honorary Degrees of M.A. and Ph.D. from Dartmouth College. Represented by "Venetian Fishing Boats" at the Corcoran. Died March, 1888 in Rome, Italy.

TILTON, OLIVE.
Painter. Born 1886 in Mountain Station, NJ. Pupil of Collin and Delecluse in Paris; also studied in Munich and London. Address in 1926, 24 West 59th St., New York, NY.

TILYARD, PHILLIP.
Portrait painter. Born in 1785 and died in 1830.

TIMMONS, EDWARD J. FINLEY.
Painter. Born Janesville, WI, 1882. Pupil of AIC; Ralph Clarkson, Gari Melchers; Sorolla; also studied in England, Holland, France, Italy and Spain. Member: Chicago SA; Chicago ASL; Association Chicago PS; Il. Acad. FA. Award: Prize, Municipal AL, portrait, AIC, 1929. Work: Portraits in Univ. of Chicago, Univ. of Arkansas, Univ. of IL, Beloit College, State Capitol at Des Moines, Janesville Art League, San Diego Museum of Fine Arts, National Bank of Mattoon, IL; Mt. Clair, IL, Community House; State Capitol, Cheyenne, Wyo.; Municipal Art Collection, Chicago; Polytechnic Inst., Blacksburg, VA; Meyer Memorial, Michael Reese Hospital, Chicago. Instructor AIC. Address in 1929, 317 Webster Ave., Chicago, IL.

TIMOSHENKO, MARINA.
Painter, who exhibited water colors at the PAFA, Philadelphia, 1925. Address in 1926, 1620 Summer St., Philadelphia.

TINDALE, EDWARD H.
Painter. Born Hanson, MA, March 21, 1879. Studied at Munich Acad. under Carl Marr, Hans von Hayeck, Loeftz. Address in 1929, 3 Hampton Road, Brockton, MA; summer, S. Hanover, MA.

TISCHLER, MARIAN CLARA.
Painter. Member: Cincinnati Woman's Art Club. Address in 1926, 453 Riddle Road, Cincinnati, Ohio.

TISDALE, ELKANAH.
Engraver. Born in Lebanon, CT, c. 1771, and was living there in 1834. In 1794-98 Tisdale was in NY as an "Engraver and Miniature Painter," but moved to Hartford and became member of Graphic Co., an association of engravers, though he was the designer rather than engraver. Dunlap says that he remained in Hartford until 1825, designing and engraving plates for Samuel F. Goodrich, of that city, in 1820. Tisdale worked in both line and stipple. The earliest dated plates by Tisdale are full page illustrations to Trumbull's "McFingal," published in NY in 1795. Tisdale was a better designer than engraver. Also a miniature portrait painter.

TITCOMB, M. BRADISH.
Painter and illustrator. Born in NH. Pupil of Boston Museum School under Tarbell, Benson and Hale. Member: Copley Society, 1895; NY Water Color Club; National Assoc. of Women Painters and Sculptors; CT Acad. of Fine Arts. Award: Honorable mention, CT Acad. of Fine Arts, 1917. Represented in the White House, Washington, DC. Address in 1929, Fenway Studios, Ipswich St., Boston, MA.

TITCOMB, VIRGINIA CHANDLER.
Painter and writer. Born in Otterville, IL. Sculptor in bas-relief. Exhibited at NAD. Founder, 1884, and pres. of the Patriotic League of the Revolution. Memorialized 57th Congress for

recognition of services rendered by Theodore R. Timby, the inventor of the revolving turret as used on the "Monitor" and all battleships of US after Civil War. Contributor to Harper's Bazaar, Demorest's Magazine, Brooklyn Eagle, etc. Address in 1926, 101 Lafayette Ave., Brooklyn, NY.

TITLOW, HARRIET W(OODFIN).
Painter. Born Hampton, VA. Pupil of Robert Henri. Member: NA Women PS; PBC; NY Soc. Women A; NAC. Address in 1929, 37 West 10th St., New York, NY.

TITSWORTH, JULIA.
Painter. Born Westfield, MA, 1878. Pupil of AIC; R. Collin in Paris. Member: NA Women PS; AFA. Address in 1929, Bronxville, NY.

TITTLE, WALTER (ERNEST).
Painter and etcher. Born Springfield, Ohio, Oct. 9, 1883. Pupil of Chase, Henri and Mora in NY. Member: Royal Society of Arts, London, England. Author and illustrator, "Colonial Holidays;" "The First Nantucket Tea Party," etc. Etchings in Chicago Art Inst.; Cleveland Art Museum; Library of Congress and National Gallery, Washington; NY Public Library; Brooklyn Museum; Calif. State Library; British Museum; Victoria and Albert Museum, London; Fitzwilliam Mus., Cambridge, England. Address in 1929, 123 E. 77th St., New York, NY; and 135 S. Light St., Springfield, Ohio.

TITUS, AIME BAXTER.
Painter, illustrator, and teacher. He was born Cincinnati, April 5, 1882. Pupil of ASL of NY, Harrison, Mora, Bridgman, DuMond, Chase, San Francisco Inst. Award: silver medal, P.-P. Exp., San F., 1915. Address in 1929, 2924 Juniper St., San Diego, California.

TOBEY, MARK.
Painter. Born Dec. 11, 1890 in Centerville, WI. Studied at the Art Inst. of Chicago; studied with Teng Kwei, Shanghai. His work has been exhibited at Met. Museum of Art, NY; Whitney Museum of Am. Art; Museum of Mod. Art, NY; Seattle Art Museum, Washington. He was awarded the Grant National Prize for Painting, Venice Biennial, 1958; First Prize for painting, Carnegie Inst., Pittsburgh, PA, 1961. Media: Oil and tempera. Address in 1976, 40 Willard Gallery, 29 E. 72nd Street, NYC.

TOBIN, GEORGE T(IMOTHY).
Painter and illustrator. Born Weybridge, VT, July 26, 1864. Pupil of George De Forest Brush. Member: ASL of NY; AFA. Address in 1929, 528 Main St., New Rochelle, NY.

TODD, A.
Engraver. Etched a small bust of Washington for the Washington Benevolent Society, Concord, 1812. The firm of Gray & Todd engraved astronomical plates published in Phila. in 1817. A. Todd may have been a partner.

TODD, CHARLES STEWART.
Painter. Born Owensboro, KY, Dec. 16, 1885. Pupil of Cincinnati Art Academy; Albert Herter in NY. Member: Cinn. AC; Cinn. MacDowell Soc.; Boston SAC. Address in 1929, 2513 Park Ave., Cincinnati, Ohio.

TODD, HENRY STANLEY.
Portrait painter, working in NYC in 1902. Painted the portrait of Judge Emott in that year for the City Hall, NY.

TODHUNTER, FRANCIS.
Painter, illustrator, etcher, and teacher. Born San Francisco, July 29, 1884. Pupil of NAD; Calif. School of Design. Member: Calif. SE; San F. AA; Bohemian C. Address in 1929, 2424 Larkin St., San Francisco; summer, Belmont, Calif.

TOERRING, HELENE.
Miniature painter. Exhibited at the Penna. Acad. of the Fine Arts, Philadelphia, 1925. Address in 1926, 6399 Woodbine Ave., Overbrook, PA.

TOFEL, JENNINGS.
Painter, who exhibited in Phila. in 1921, in "Exhibition of Paintings Showing the Later Tendencies in Art." Address in 1926, 61 Colben St., Newburgh, NY.

TOLLES, SOPHIE MAPES.
Painter. Began studies in Phila. in 1864 with Peter F. Rothermel. Later studied in France and Italy. Her first exhibit in America was a portrait at National Acad. in 1876. In 1878 she exhibited several flower pieces. Among her best known portraits is one of Linda Gilbert of Chicago.

TOLMAN, JOHN.
Portrait painter, lived in Pembroke, MA. Painted in Boston and Salem about 1816. He evidently travelled throughout the country as a portrait painter.

TOLMAN, R(UEL PARDEE).
Painter, restorer, etcher, and teacher. Born Brookfield, CT, March 26, 1878. Pupil of Los Angeles School of Art and Design; Mark Hopkins Inst. of Art; Corcoran School of Art, Washington; ASL of NY; NAD; J. C. Beckwith. Member: S. Wash. A.; Wash. WCC; AFA. Assistant curator in charge, Divison of Graphic Arts, United States National Museum, Washington. Address in 1929, 3451 Mt. Pleasant St., Washington, DC.

TOLMAN, STACY.
Portrait painter and teacher. Born Concord, MA, Jan. 1860. Pupil of Otto Grundmann in Boston; Boulanger, Lefebvre and Cabanel in Paris. Member: Providence AC; Providence WCC; Boston AC. Instructor of anatomy, RI School of Design. Address in 1929, 7 Thomas St., Providence, RI; h. 1182 Mineral Spring Ave., Pawtucket, RI.

TOLSON, MAGDALENA WELTY.
(Mrs. Norman Tolson). Painter, craftsman, and teacher. Born Berne, IN, Feb. 15, 1888. Member: Kansas City SA. Awards: Hon. mention and Sweeney purchase prize, Kansas City Art Inst., 1922. Address in 1929, 1436 Jonquil Terrace, Chicago, IL.

TOLSON, NORMAN.
Painter, illustrator, and etcher. Born Distington, Cumberland, England, March 25, 1883. Pupil of Angelo von Jank, Munich; AIC. Member: Chicago SA; Kansas City SA; Ill. SA. Awards: Edward B.

Butler Art Inst., 1921; hon. mention, Kansas City AI, 1924. Work: Decorative panels in La Salle Hotel, Chicago; murals, Stevens Hotel, Chicago. Address in 1929, 1436 Jonquil Terrace, Chicago, IL.

TOMASO, RICO.
Painter and illustrator. Born Chicago, IL, Feb. 21, 1898. Pupil of Dean Cornwell, Harvey Dunn, J. Wellington Reynolds. Member: SI. Illustrated, "Son of the Gods," by Rex Beach; "The Parrot," by Walter Duranty and "Tagoti," by Cynthia Stockley. Address in 1929, 206 East 33rd St., New York, NY.

TOMKINS, FRANK HECTOR.
Painter. Born in Hector, NY, in 1847; died in Brookline, MA, in 1922. Pupil of Art Students League. Represented at the Penna. Acad. of the Fine Arts by "The Penitent", and in the Boston Mus. by "The Young Mother."

TOMLIN, BRADLEY WALKER.
Painter and illustrator. Born Syracuse, NY, Aug. 19, 1899. Pupil of Jeannette Scott; Academie Colarossi; Le Grand Chaumiere. Member: Louis Comfort Tiffany Foundation. Work: Decorations in Children's Room, Memorial Hospital, Syracuse, NY. Address in 1929, 244 East 48th St., New York, NY; summer, Woodstock, NY.

TOMLINSON, ANNA C.
Painter, who exhibited water colors at the Penna. Acad. of the Fine Arts, Philadelphia, 1925. Address in 1926, 281 Heath St., Boston, MA.

TOMLINSON, HENRY W(ELLING).
Painter. Born Baltimore, MD, Sept. 18, 1875. Pupil of E. S. Whiteman in Baltimore; ASL of NY under Cox and Brush. Address in 1929, Taconic, CT.

TOMPKINS, CLEMENTINA M. G.
Painter. Born in Washington, DC. Lived in Paris, studying with Bonnat. Specialty was portraits and figure pieces. Exhibited in this country in 1876-78.

TONETI, FRANCOIS MICHEL LOUIS.

Sculptor. Born in Paris in 1863. Came to US in 1899. His work at the Chicago Fair in 1893 received an award. Collaborated with Saint Gaudens in work on the Congressional Library in Washington. Died 1920 in NY City.

TOPCHEVSKY, MORRIS.
Painter and etcher. Born Poland, Oct. 17, 1898. Pupil of AIC; Albert Krehbiel, San Carlos Acad., Mex. City. Member: Chicago SA; Il. Acad. FA. Address in 1929, Hull House, 800 South Halsted St., Chicago, IL.

TOPHAM.
Engraver. Well executed landscape plates published in Cincinnati in 1852 are thus signed.

TOPPAN, CHARLES.
Engraver. Born in Newburyport, MA, in 1796. Pupil of Gideon Fairman, engraver. Was with him in Phila. in 1814. After some general engraving on his own, on the death of Fairman in 1827, became partner in bank note company of Draper, Toppan, Long-acre & Co. The firm later became Toppan, Carpenter, Casilear & Co., and in 1854 was Toppan, Carpenter & Co. Having moved to NYC, he became president of the then American Bank Note Co. in 1858-60. Died Nov. 20, 1874 in Florence, Italy.

TOPPING, JAMES.
Landscape painter. Born Cleator Moor, England, in 1879. Studied in England, and at AIC. Member: Palette and Chisel C.; Chicago PS; Oak Park Art Lg.; Chic. Litho. C. Award: Municipal Art Lg. prize, 1923; Robert Rice Jenkins prize, AIC, 1924; Palette and Chisel Club, gold medal, 1924; Cahn prize, AIC, 1926; Perkins prize, Chicago Gal. A., 1926; Bontoux prize, Palette and Chisel C., 1927; prize, Business Men's AC, Chic., 1929. Address in 1929, 541 Forest Ave., Oak Park, IL.

TORRENS, ROSALBA.
Landscape painter, who was practicing her art in Charleston, SC, in 1808.

TORREY, CHARLES CUTLER.
Engraver. According to "The Annals of Salem" (Salem, MA, 1849), Charles Cutler Torrey was brought to Salem by his parents as an infant. Studied engraving in Phila. about 1815 and in 1820 he established himself in business in Salem. Engraved a few portrait plates and some general illustrations for publishers, but his notable work of this period is a large, well executed plate showing a "North East View of the Several Halls of Harvard College," published in Boston, in 1823, by Cummings, Hilliard & Co. A companion plate, "South View of the Several Halls of Harvard College," was engraved by Annin & Smith and published by the same Boston firm. Torey left Salem in 1823 for Nashville, TN, where he died of a fever in 1827. Brother of Manasseh Cutler Torrey, portrait and miniature painter of Salem.

TORREY, ELLIOT (BOUTON).
Painter. Born East Hardwick, VT. Studied in Florence and Paris. Member: Salma. C.; Soc. AA; San Diego FAS; Laguna Beach AA. Award: Guild prize, San Diego, 1929. Represented in Chicago Art Inst., Cleveland Museum of Art; Art Inst., Akron, Ohio; Fine Arts Museum, San Diego, CA. Address in 1929, 4716 Panorama St., San Diego, California.

TORREY, FRED M.
Sculptor. Born Fairmont, W. VA, July 29, 1884. Pupil of Charles J. Mulligan, Lorado Taft. Member: Chicago SA; Western Soc. of Sculptors. Work: Rosenberger medal for the Univ. of Chicago; Susan Colver medal of honor for Brown Univ.; memorial tablet for Theta Delta Chi, Champaign, IL; Hutchinson memorial tablet for Hutchinson Hall, Chicago Univ.; sculpture decorations for Paradise Theatre, Chicago; Esperson portrait bust, Houston, Texas; C. C. Linthicum Foundation medal, Northwestern Univ., Evanston, IL; Beta Sigma Omicron medal, Denver, CO. Address in 1929, 6016 Ellis Ave., Chicago, IL.

TORREY, GEORGE BURROUGHS.
Portrait painter. Born in NY in 1863. Exhibited at Paris Salon, 1900 and after. Painted portraits of William Howard Taft, and Theodore Roosevelt. Decorated by the King of Greece with the Grecian Order of the Savior, 1904. Address in 1926, 27 East 35th St., NYC.

TORREY, MABLE LANDRUM.
Sculptor and teacher. Born Sterling, CO, June 23, 1886. Pupil of Charles J. Mulligan. Member: Alumni AIC; Cordon C. Work: "Wynken, Blynken and Nod Fountain," City and County of Denver; "Buttercup - Poppy and Forget-me-not," South Bend (IN) Library. Address in 1929, 6016 Ellis Ave., Chicago, IL.

TORREY, MANASSEH C.
Portrait and miniature painter. Born 1807 in Salem, MA. Flourished about 1830-37 in NY, Phila. and in Salem. Died Sept. 24, 1837 in Pelham, VT.

TOTTEN, VICKEN VON POST.
(Mrs. George Oakley Totten). Sculptor. Born in Sweden, March 12, 1886. Pupil of the Academie of Beaux Arts, Stockholm. Member: Painters and Sculptors Gal. Assoc.; Soc. of Swedish Women Artists; NA Women PS. Represented in Metropolitan Museum. Address in 1929, 2633 - 16th St., N. W., Washington, DC.

TOWN, HAROLD BARLING.
Painter and writer. 9 Castle Frank Crescent, Toronto, ON M4W 3A2, Canada. Born: Toronto, Canada, June 13, in 1924. Graduated from the Ontario College of Art, Toronto, in 1944, and continued with post graduate study there in 1945. Exhibitions: L'Actuelle Gallery, Montreal, 1957; Loranger Gallery, Ottawa, 1957; Gallery of Contemporary Art, Toronto, 1957; Jordan Gallery, Toronto, 1958; Jerrold Morris International Gallery, Toronto, 1962. Galeria Bonino, Ltd., New York, 1964. Group Exhibitions: Riverside Museum, New York, 1956; Venice Biennale d'arte, 1956; Moderna Galerja, Ljubljana, Yugoslavia, 1957, 1959, 1961, 1963; in Milan,

Italy, 1957; at the Museum of Art, Carnegie Institute, Pittsburgh, 1961; J. B. Speed Art Museum, Louisville, 1962; The Museum of Modern Art, Pratt Graphic Art Center, Pratt Institute, New York, 1962 and many other places.

TOWNSEND, ERNEST N.
Painter and illustrator. Born NY, June 26, 1893. Pupil of Paul Cornoyer, George Maynard, C. Y. Turner, Thomas Fogarty. Member: Salma. C.; Yonkers AA; Allied AA; Am. APL; AWCS. Address in 1929, 41 East 59th St., New York, NY.

TOWNSEND, ETHEL HORE.
Miniature painter. Born Staten Island, NY, Sept. 26, 1876. Pupil of Henry B. Snell and Orlando Rouland in NY. Member: NYWCC. Address in 1929, 63 Hillside Ave., Glen Ridge, NJ.

TOWNSEND, HARRY E(VERETT).
Painter, illustrator, etcher, and craftsman. Born Wyoming, IL, March 10, 1879. Pupil of AIC; Howard Pyle; studied in Paris and London. Member: SI 1911; Allied AA; Brooklyn SE; GFLA; Salma. C.; Silvermine GA. Official artist with the A. E. F. during World War I. Work: Drawings and paintings of the war at War College; and in the Smithonian Inst., Washington, DC; prints in the Metropolitan Museum of Art, NY; paintings and prints in the NY Public Library. Address in 1929, 5 Stevens St., Norwalk, CT.

TOWNSEND, LEE.
Illustrator. Born Wyoming, IL, Aug. 7, 1895. Pupil of Harvey Dunn and AIC. Member: SI. Specialty, magazine illustrations. Address in 1929, Westport, CT.

TOWNSLEY, C. P.
Painter. Born in Sedalia, MO, in 1867. Pupil of Julien and Delecluse Academies in Paris; under Chase in NY. Member: Salmagundi Club; CA Art Club. Director, Chase European classes; London (EN) School of Art, and later, Director Otis Art Inst. Address in 1926, Care of Frank Brangwyn, Temple Lodge, London, England.

TRACY, GLEN.
Painter, illustrator, and teacher.
Born Hudson, MI, Jan. 24, 1883.
Pupil of Nowottny, Meakin,
Duveneck. Member: Cincinnati AC.
Represented in Detroit Art Inst.
Specialty, crayon sketches.
Address in 1929, Mt. Washington,
Cincinnati, Ohio.

TRADER, EFFIE CORWIN.
Miniature painter. Born Xenia,
Ohio, Feb. 18, 1874. Pupil of
Cincinnati Art Academy; T. Dube in
Paris. Member: Cincinnati Woman's
AC; Cincinnati MacD.C. Address in
1929, 3000 Vernon Place,
Cincinnati, Ohio.

TRAIN, H. SCOTT.
Illustrator. Member: SI. Address
in 1929, 352 Singer St., Astoria,
LI, NY.

TRAVER, GEORGE A.
Painter. Member: National Art
Club; Salmagundi Club. Work:
"Intervale," Brooklyn Inst. Museum,
Brooklyn, NY. Address in 1926, 109
West 11th St., New York, NY.

TRAVER, MARION GRAY.
Painter. Born Elmhurst, LI, NY,
June 3, 1896. Pupil of George A.
Traver. Member: NA Women PS; C.
L. Wolfe AC; Allied AA; Three Arts
C. Address in 1929, 109 West 11th
St., New York, NY.

TRAVER, WARDE.
Painter. Born in Ann Arbor, MI, in
1880. Pupil of Royal Academy,
Munich, under Marr; also of Millet
and Snell. Address in 1926,
Central Park Studios, 15 West 67th
St., New York, NY.

TRAVIS, OLIN H(ERMAN).
Painter. Born Dallas, Texas, Nov.
15, 1888. Pupil of AIC; Charles
Francis Browne; Kenyon Cox.
Member: Chicago SA; AFA. Work:
"Ozark Hills," Dallas Public Art
Gallery. Address in 1929, 5641
Monticello Ave., Dallas, Texas.

TRAVIS, PAUL BOUGH.
Painter, etcher, and teacher. Born
Wellsville, Ohio, Jan. 2, 1891.
Pupil of H. G. Keller. Awards:
First prize and Penton medal, 1921;
first prize for etching and for

portraiture, 1922, hon. mention,
water color, 1928, first prize
landscape, hon. mention figure and
water colors, 1929, Cleveland AA.
Work: Seven etchings, two
lithographs, five drawings, two
water colors, Cleveland Museum of
Art; lithograph, NY Public Library.
In 1929 artist member Dr. Geo. W.
Crile, Cleveland Museum of Natural
History, African expedition.
Address in 1929, care of the
Cleveland School of Art; h. 2019
East 115th St., Cleveland, Ohio.

TREASE, SHERMAN.
Painter and illustrator. Born
Galena, KS, March 22, 1889. Pupil
of School of Applied Art; A. H.
Knott. Member: Joplin AG; San
Diego AG. Awards: First landscape
prize, Joplin Spring Ex., 1922;
grand prize, and 1st landscape
prize, Joplin Fall Ex., 1922.
Represented in the Joplin Art
League Gallery, Joplin, MO.
Address in 1929, 303 South Bancroft
St., San Diego, California.

TREBILCOCK, PAUL.
Painter. Born Chicago, Feb. 13,
1902. Pupil of AIC; Seyffert.
Member: Chelsea AC, London; Chicago
PS; Cliff Dwellers. Awards: Cahn
prize, AIC, 1925; Hearst prize, AIC
1926; first prize ($1,000) Chicago
Gal. A., 1926; Logan medal, AIC,
1928. Work: "Old London
Coachman," Albright Art Gal.;
"President David Kinley," Univ. of
Chicago; "Portrait of a Painter,"
AIC; Judge A. A. Bruce,"
Northwestern University. Address
in 1929, 141 East Ontario St.,
Chicago, IL; h. 554 Ashland Ave.,
River Forest, IL.

TREFETHEN, JESSIE B.
Painter, lecturer, and teacher.
Born Peak's Island, ME. Pupil of
Henry McCarter; PAFA. Member:
Fellowship PAFA. Address in 1929,
35 South Professor St., Oberlin,
Ohio; summer, Trefethen, ME.

TREGANZA, RUTH ROBINSON.
Painter, architect, draftsman, and
teacher. Born Elmira, NY, March
30, 1877. Pupil of J. M. Hewlett,
L. C. Tiffany, Arthur W. Dow, H. W.
Corbett. Member: NA Women PS;
AFA. Address in 1929, Teachers

College, Columbia Univ., 230 West 120th St., New York, NY.

TREGO, JONATHAN.
Painter. Born March, 1817 in Penn. Father of William Trego. Painted many of the families of Bucks County, Penna. in a rather stiff and formal manner.

TREGO, WILLIAM T.
Painter. Born in Yardley, Bucks County, Penna., in 1859. Studied with his father Jonathan Trego. In 1879 he entered the schools of the Penna. Acad. of the Fine Arts; he later studied in Paris under Fleury and Bouguereau. Died in North Wales, Penna., in 1909.

TREIMAN, JOYCE.
Sculptor. Born May 29, 1922 in Evanston, IL. Earned B.F.A. from State U. of Iowa (1943), awarded grad. fellowship for Iowa; also Tiffany Scholarship, Tupperware fellow and Ford Found. grant. L.A. Times Woman of the Year for Art, 1965. Rec. L.A. Sculpture Prize (1966 - All City Show); other awards. Taught at UCLA; LA Art Center School and Cal. State U. Exhibited at Paul Theobald Gallery, Chicago (1942); Art Inst. of Chicago; Fair-Weather - Garnett Gal. (IL); Felix Landau Gal; L.A.; Whitney; Stanford U.; MOMA; S. F. Mus. of Art; Watkins Gal., Wash., DC; Milwaukee Art Center; Palos Verdes Art Center; Denver and PAFA. In collections of Ball State Teacher Col.; Pasadena Art Mus.; U. of Oregon; Abbott Lab. Collection; Art Inst. of Chic.; L.A. County Mus.; MOMA; Int. Minerals & Chem. Corp.; Whitney and Denver.

TRENCHARD, E. C.
Engraver. A well executed stipple portrait of Count Rumford is signed "Drawn and Engraved by E. C. Trenchard," as the frontispiece to "The Essays of Count Rumford," published by D. West, Boston, 1798. There is difficulty in locating this E. C. Trenchard who engraved for Boston publishers in 1798. An Edward Trenchard, signed an agreement in Phila. in 1794 to establish a school of architecture, sculpture and painting. The biography of Capt. Edward Trenchard, naval officer in the War of 1812, says that he was born in Salem, NJ., in 1784; studied art with his uncle, James Trenchard, the Phila. engraver, and went to England to complete his education. But in 1800, this Edward Trenchard entered US Navy. He died in Brooklyn, NY, in 1824. The signer of the Phila. Agreement of 1794, and the Edward Trenchard who studied with his uncle before 1793 when James Trenchard left the US might well have been the engraver of the "Count Rumford" in 1798, but the alleged birthdate of the naval officer is 1784, and the engraving is almost too well done for a 14 yr. old. However, the date of 1784 may be an error, and the navel officer may have engraved the portrait in question and his own book plate.

TRENCHARD, EDWARD.
Painter. Born in Philadelphia in 1850. Studied with Peter Moran and at the National Acad. of Design. Work: "The Passing Shower;" "The Old Wreck;" "Sea, Sand and Solitude;" "The Surf." Specialty, marine painting. Died in 1922.

TRENCHARD, JAMES.
Engraver, born 1747. According to Trenchard's grandson, James Thackara, Trenchard came to Phila. from Penns Neck, Salem County, NJ. Was in the city as engraver and seal cutter as early as 1777. In 1787 was artistic member of firm that established Columbian Magazine in Phila. In 1793 he went to England and remained there. Dunlap stated that Trenchard learned to engrave with J. Smither, in Phila. He engraved a few portraits and views in and about Phila. Also a die sinker. Made dies for medal of Agricultural Society of Phila., 1790. Possibly a son or nephew of George Trenchard, Salem, NJ, Attorney General of West NJ in 1776.

TRENHOLM, GEORGE F(RANCIS).
Designer, craftsman, and teacher. Born Cambridge, MA, Oct. 23, 1886. Pupil of Charles E. Heil, Vojtech Preissig. Member: Artists Gld.; Stowaways; AI Graphic A; Boston Soc. P. Work: Designer of

book-type (Trenholm Old Style, Trenholm Italic, Trenholm Bold, Trenholm Ornament) owned by Barnhart Bros. and Spindler, Chicago. Address in 1929, Little Bldg., 80 Boylston St., Boston, MA; h. Ox Bow Road, Weston, MA.

TRENTANOVE, GAETANO.
Sculptor. Born 1858 in Florence, Italy. Educated at the Fine Arts Academies of Florence and Rome. Knighted by the late King Humbert of Italy. Became an American citizen in 1892. Works: Statue of James Marquette, Statuary Hall, United States Capitol; statue of Daniel Webster, Washington, DC; statue of Albert Pike, Washington, DC; Kosciuszko equestrian statue, Milwaukee, WI; "The Last of the Spartans," Layton Art Gallery, Milwaukee, WI; Soldiers Monument, Oshkosh, WI; Chief Oshkosh Statue, Oshkosh, WI; monument to Confederate soldiers, Springfield, MO.; Soldiers Monument, Appleton, WI; and in private collections.

TREVITTS, J.
Painter. Pupil of Penna. Acad. of the Fine Arts. Member of Fellowship, PAFA. Awarded Cresson traveling scholarship, Penna. Acad. of the Fine Arts. Address in 1926, Manistee, MI.

TRICKER, FLORENCE.
Painter, sculptor, and teacher. Born Philadelphia, PA. Pupil of Elliot Daingerfield, Henry B. Snell, Daniel Garber, Charles Grafly, Samuel Murray, Albert Laessle. Member: Phila. Alliance; Plastic C.; Fellowship PAFA; Alumni Phila. School of Design for Women. Awards: Gold medal, Graphic Sketch C; silver medal, first prize, and hon. mention, Plastic C; first prize, Tampa AI; Douglas prize, Tampa AI, 1927. Work: "Across the River" and "Apple Blossoms," Graphic Sketch Club. Instructor, Stage Design, Mary Lyon School, Swarthmore, Penn. Address in 1929, Tricker School of Art, 405 Dartmouth Ave.; h. 112 Park Ave., Swarthmore, Penn.

TRIEBEL, F(REDERIC) E.
Painter. Born United States, Dec. 29, 1863. Pupil of Augusto Rivalta. Member: Academiciare of Merit, Roman Royal Acad., San Luca, Rome, Italy. Awards: Galileo silver medal, Museo Nazionale di Antropologia, Florence, 1889, 1891. Works: Soldier's Monument, Peoria, IL; Iowa State Monument, Shiloh, TN; Miss. State Monument, Vicksburg; Robert G. Ingersoll Statue, Peoria, IL; statues of Senator George L. Shoup and late Senator Henry M. Rice, Statuary Hall, Washington, DC; Otto Pastor Monument, Petrograd, Russia. Address in 1929, North Boulevard, College Point, LI, NY.

TRIPLER, H. E.
About 1850-52 this engraver of portraits and historical plates was working for NY publishers. He engraved for Sartain's Magazine of Philadelphia with John Bannister.

TRISCOTT, SAMUEL PETER ROLT.
Painter. Born in Gosport, England, in 1846. Studied art in England. Came to US in 1871. Represented at Boston Museum of Fine Arts. Died in 1925.

TROBAUGH, ROY (B.).
Painter. Born Delphi, Jan. 21, 1878. Pupil of ASL of NY; J. H. Twachtman. Member: Ind. AC. Address in 1929, 424 Summit St., Delphi, Ind.

TROCCOLI, GIOVANNI BATTISTA.
Painter and craftsman. Born Lauropoli, Italy, Oct. 15, 1882. Pupil of Denman Ross and Julian Acad. Member: Copley S.; Boston SAC; Boston GA; AFA. Awards: Hon. mention, CI Pittsburgh, 1911; Harris silver medal ($500), AIC 1913; gold medal, P.-P. Exp., San F., 1915; Thomas R. Proctor prize ($200), NAD, 1922. Represented in the Detroit Inst. of Arts. Address in 1929, 21 Morseland Ave., Newton Center, MA.

TROMMER, MARIE.
Painter and writer. Born Russia. Pupil of Cooper Union; Wayman Adams, S. Halpert, Barlie. Member: Salons of Amer.; S. Indp. A.; C. L. Wolfe AC. Work: "Still Life" and "Portrait," Corona Mundi, New York, NY. Address in 1929, 1854 - 62nd St., Brooklyn, NY.

TROTT.
A copperplate engraver, who signed his plates "Trott, sp. Boston." The date of publication was 1800 to 1820.

TROTT, BENJAMIN.
Miniature painter. Born in 1770. Considered one of greatest miniaturists of his day. Divided the honors of his profession with Malbone and the Peales. Pupil of Gilbert Stuart. Worked with Thomas Sully in Phila. in 1808. Working in Baltimore in 1796. His miniatures suggest the treatment of Richard Cosway in the use of clouds and blue sky backgrounds. Miniatures by Benjamin Trott were placed in the MMA and RISD and in many collections in the US. Died Nov. 1843 in Wash., DC.

TROTTER, NEWBOLD HOUGH.
Painter. Born in Philadelphia in 1827. Studied at the Academy of the Fine Arts. Painted animals. His most important works include: "The Range of the Bison"; "Grizzly Bears"; "The Last Stand"; "The Young Bull"; "The Barnyard" (signed and dated Phila., 1866). Died at Atlantic City, NJ, in 1898.

TROUBETZKOY, PAUL.
Sculptor. Born Lake Intra, Lake Maggiore, Italy, Feb. 16, 1866. Studied in Italy, Russia, and France. Award: Grand prize, Paris Exp., 1900. Bronzes in the Luxembourg in Paris; National Gallery in Rome; National Gal. in Venice; Museum of Alexander III in Petrograd; Treliakofsky Gal. in Moscow; National Gal. in Berlin; Royal Gallery in Dresden; Leipsig Gallery; Chicago Art Inst.; Detroit Inst.; Toledo Mus.; Buffalo Fine Arts Acad.; Golden Gate Park Mus.; Mus. in Buenos Aires; Brera Mus., Milan. Died Feb. 12, 1938.

TROUBETZKOY, PIERRE.
Painter. Born Milan, Italy, April 19, 1864. Pupil of Ranzoni and Cremona. Works: Portrait of "Gladstone," National Gallery of Edinburgh; "Marquis of Dufferin and Ava as Warden of the Cinq Ports," Town Hall of Dover; "Mr. Archer Huntington," Inst. de Valencia de Don Juan, Madrid; "De Philip Bruce," University of Virginia, Charlottesville. Address in 1929, Hotel Wentworth, 59 West 46th St., New York, NY; summer, Castle Hill, Cobham, Albemarle Co., VA.

TROUT, (ELIZABETH) DOROTHY BURT.
Painter, illustrator, and teacher. Born Fort Robinson, Neb., June 3, 1896. Pupil of E. C. Messer, Bertha Perrie, Catherine Critcher, Howard Giles, C. W. Hawthorne, E. A. Webster. Member: S. Wash. C.; Provincetown AA. Address in 1929, 2713 Ontario Road, Washington, DC.

TROWBRIDGE, VAUGHAN.
Painter. Born in NY in 1869. Abandoned business life in 1897, and took up art studies in Paris with Paul Laurens and Benj. Constant. Exhibited paintings and etching in Paris Salons, 1900-13, and etching printed in color at St. Louis Exp., 1904. Illustrated "Paris and the Social Revolution" (by Alvan F. Sanborn), 1905. Address in 1926, 15 Ave. Libert, Draveil, Seine-et-Oise, France. Died 1945 in Paris, France.

TROYE, EDWARD.
Painter. Born in Switzerland in 1808. Came to US c. 1828. In Phila. he worked on Sartain's Magazine as an animal painter. As a painter of race horses he was most successful, and was styled "The Landseer of America." His equestrian portrait of Genl. Winfield Scott was purchased by the Government. Died in Georgetown, KY, in July, 1874.

TRUAX, SARAH E.
Painter. Born Iowa. Pupil of AIC. Member: ASL of Chicago; Art Guild Members of FAC of San Diego. Awards: Silver and bronze medals, Pan-Pacific Exp., San Diego, CA, 1915; hon. mention, Los Angeles County Fair, Pomona, Calif., 1928. Work: "Cacti," Fine Arts Gallery, San Diego; decoration of table tops, Helping Hand Childrens Home, San Diego; Baptistry Window, First Baptist Church, Breckenridge, MN. Address in 1929, 3620 Fairmount Ave., San Diego, CA.

TRUCKSESS, CLEMENT.
Painter and teacher. Born Brownsburg, IN, Aug. 16, 1895. Pupil of Wm. Forsyth. Award: Second prize for pastel, IN State Fair, 1922. Work: "Woman and Cows," Jefferson School, La Fayette, IN. Address in 1929, Brownsburg, IN.

TRUE, ALLEN TUPPER.
Painter and illustrator. Born Colorado Springs, CO, May 30, 1881. Pupil of Howard Pyle; Corcoran Art Schl. in Wash.; Brangwyn in London. Member: Denver AA; Mural P.; NY Arch. Lg. Assisted Frank Brangwyn with decorations in Wyoming State Capitol; Denver Public Library; Montana National Bank, Billings, Montana; open air Greek Theater, Civic Center, Denver; Voorhees Memorial Arch, Denver, Colorado; pendentives in dome, Mo. State Capitol, Jefferson City, Mo.; "Mother Goose" frieze, Taylor Day Nursery, Colorado Springs; decorations in Colorado Natl. Bank, and in Mountain States Telephone Bldg., Denver. Address in 1929, Box 126 RR 3, Littleton, CO.

TRUE, GRACE H(OPKINS).
(Mrs. E. D. A. True). Painter. Born Frankfort, MI, May 2, 1870. Pupil of John P. Wicker. Member: Detroit S. Women P; Tampa Fed. A. Address in 1929, Melbourne Beach, Melbourne City, Fla.; summer, 5981 Woodward Ave., Detroit, MI.

TRUE, VIRGINIA.
Painter. Born St. Louis, MO, Feb. 7, 1900. Pupil of Wm. Forsyth, Daniel Garber, R. S. Meryman, Hugh Breckenridge, Charles Grafly. Member: IN AC; Hoosier Salon. Award: Prize at IN State Fair. Address in 1929, 167 East 11th St.; 2941 Washington Boulevard, Indianapolis, IN.

TRUESDELL, EDITH P(ARK).
Painter and teacher. Born Derby, CT, Feb. 15, 1888. Pupil of Tarbell, Benson, Hale and Bosley. Member: CA AC; Laguna Beach AA. Awards: First prize, Laguna Beach Anniversary Exhibition, 1924; third prize, Los Angeles Co. Exh., Pomona 1928. Address in 1929, 6310 Franklin Circle, Los Angeles, CA.

TRUESDELL, GAYLORD SANGSTON.
Painter. Born in Waukegan, IL, in 1850; died in NY in 1899. Animal painter. Pupil of Pennsylvania Acad. of the Fine Arts, Phila.; also of A. Morot and Cormon, in Paris. Awards: Bronze medal, Exp. Universelle, 1889; second class medal, Paris Salon, 1892; Hors Concours, Salon des Champs Elysees. His painting "Going to Pasture," painted in 1889, was in the Corcoran.

TRUMBULL, GURDON.
Painter. Born in Stonington, CT, in 1841. Pupil of F. S. Jewett and of James M. Hart in NY. Specialty was painting game fish. Resided for years in Hartford, CT, and died there in 1903.

TRUMBULL, JOHN (COLONEL).
Born in Lebanon, CT, in 1756. Graduated from Harvard in 1773. After college painted "The Death of Paulus Emilius at Cannae," his 1st attempt at composition. Was Rev. War adjutant. His skill as a draftsman attracted the attention of Wash., who made him an aide-de-camp and his military sec. Afterwards joined army of Gen. Gates, as adjutant, but in 1777 he resigned and resumed art studies. In 1778 joined John Sullivan, who volunteered to recover RI from British. In May 1780 he sailed for France, and then to London. After the war, (1784) he again visited London to study under Ben West. Executed hist. paintings of "The Declaration of Independence," "The Battle of Bunker Hill," "The Death of Gen. Montgomery," "The Surrender of Burgoyne," "The Sortie from Gibraltar," and several portraits of Wash. In 1794, went to Eng., as Sec. to John Jay. Returned to US and painted hist. portraits. Not meeting with ready sales, he contracted with Yale to present the collection in return for $1,000. Now an important hist. gal. Work: 4 paintings for the Capitol; "Declaration of Indep.," Surrender of Gen. Burgoyne," "Surrender of Lord Cornwallis," and "Gen. Washington Resigning his Commission." 36 of the figures in "Declaration" were painted from life in 1791. The remaining 9

figures were from memory and from portraits by other artists. Small sizes of the 4 works were hung in the Sch. of FA at Yale. His "Death of Montgomery" is considered one of the most spirited battle-pieces ever painted. His portraits of Gen. Washington are of great interest, and his Alexander Hamilton might be called his best work. Elected Pres. of the Am. Acad. of FA in 1817 and reelected to this office for yrs. Died Nov. 10, 1843 in NYC.

TRUMP, R(ACHEL) B(ULLEY).
(Mrs. Charles C. Trump). Painter. Born Canton, Ohio, May 3, 1890. Pupil of Syracuse University. Member: NA Women PS; Phila. Alliance; Plastic C. Work: "Judge Knapp," United States Circuit Court of Appeals, Richmond, VA. Address in 1929, 503 Baird Road, Merion, PA.

TRYON, BENJAMIN F.
Painter. Born 1824 in New York City. Studied with Richard Bengough and James H. Cafferty. Subjects were chiefly landscapes. Resided for yrs. in Boston, where he exhibited at the Boston Art Club. Among his works are "New England Scenery," "Conway Valley" and "A Quiet Nook."

TRYON, DWIGHT W.
Landscape painter. Born in Hartford, CT, in 1849. Studied in Paris in the atelier of Jacquesson de la Chevreuse; also studied nature out of doors with Daubigny and Harpignies. Returned to U.S. and received immediate recognition and many medals. In 1886 his painting "Daybreak" received gold medal at Prize Fund Exhib., Am. Art Assoc. Other awards include prize at the National Academy in 1895, gold medal at Munich in 1898, and first prize at the Carnegie Institute. In 1891 elected a member of NAD. Member of Society of Am. Artist and the Am. Water Color Society. Represented in Metropolitan Museum of Art by "Moonrise at Sunset," "Early Spring," and "Evening, New Bedford Harbor." Also in principal galleries in America and abroad. (See "American Masters of

Painting," by Charles Caffin.) Died in 1925.

TSCHUDI, RUDOLF.
Painter. Born in Switzerland in 1855. Member of Cincinnati Art Club. Represented by "Surrender of Lee," and portraits of Jefferson and Lincoln. Died in Cincinnati in 1923.

TSCHUDY, H(ERBERT) B(OLIVAR).
Painter and illustrator. Born Plattsburg, Ohio, Dec. 28, 1874. Pupil of NY ASL. Member: Brooklyn Society of Modern Artists; Brooklyn WCC; Phila. WCC; AFA. Work: Decorative panels, four water colors, in Brooklyn Museum; water color, State Museum, Santa Fe, NM. Address in 1929, Brooklyn Museum, Brooklyn, NY.

TSENG, YU-HO.
Painter. She was born Nov. 29, 1923 in Bejing, where she earned degree in art at Fujen U. Also known as Betty Tseng Yu-Ho Ecke. US citizen. Awarded Rockefeller Scholarship (1953), used for study of US collections. Earned MA, U. of Hawaii (1966), PhD., NYU (1972). Taught at Honolulu Acad. of Art (1950-63) where she is consultant on Chinese Art. Now at U. of Hawaii. Exhib. at De Young Mem. Mus., S. F. (1947); Smithsonian; Downtown Gal., NYC; Carnegie; in Paris and in Zurich. In collection of Cornell University; Munson-Williams-Proctor; Art Inst. of Chicago; Walker Art Center; Williams College; Honolulu Acad. of Arts, and others internationally.

TUCKER, ALLEN.
Painter and Architect. Born Brooklyn, NY, June 29, 1866. Pupil of Columbia Univ.; ASL of NY. Member: NY Arch. Lg. 1902; SCUA 1888; Am. PS. Represented in Providence Museum, Brooklyn Museum, Metropolitan Museum of Art, Albright Gallery, Buffalo. Instructor, Art Students League of NY. Died in 1939. Address in 1929, 121 East 79th St.; care of Rehn Gallery, 693 Fifth Ave., New York, NY.

TUCKER, BENJAMIN.
Portrait painter. Born in 1768.
Worked in Newbury, CT.

TUCKER, CORNELIA.
Sculptor. Born Loudonville, NY,
July 21, 1897. Pupil of Grafly;
PAFA. Member: Fellowship PAFA.
Address in 1929, 141 South Lake
Ave., Albany, NY.

TUCKER, WILLIAM E.
Engraver. Born in Phila. in 1801;
died there in 1857. Pupil of
Francis Kearny in Phila. Also was
in England, evidenced by prints
signed "Engraved in London by W. E.
Tucker." Tucker's name as an
engraver appeared continuously in
the directories of Phila. from 1823
to 1845. He was an excellent
engraver in line and stipple, but
his best signed work are small
Annual plates. Later devoted
himself almost entirely to bank
note engraving.

TUCKERMAN, LILIA (McCAULEY).
(Mrs. Wolcott Tuckerman). Painter.
Pupil of Geo. S. Noyes, Chas. H.
Woodbury and DeWitt Parshall.
Member: CA AC; S. Wash. A; San
AA; NAC; Minnesota State AS; San
Diego AG; Santa Barbara AL; AFA.
Work: Background for Elk Group in
Santa Barbara Mus. of National
History. Address in 1929, Foothill
Road, Carpinteria, CA.

TUCKERMAN, STEPHEN SALISBURY.
Painter. Born Boston in Dec. 1830.
Studied in England but returned to
Boston and taught there until 1864.
Noted for his marine views, which
he exhibited in many galleries
abroad. His painting of the "US
Frigate Escaping from the British
Fleet in 1812" was in the Boston
Museum of Fine Arts. Died March
1904, in England.

TUDOR, ROSAMOND.
Painter, sculptor, and etcher.
Born Buzzards Bay, MA, June 20,
1878. Pupil of Boston Mus. Sch.
under Benson and Tarbell; W. H. W.
Bicknell. Mem.: North Shore AA.
Work: "Portrait of Father Zahm,"
Libr. U. of Notre Dame, Notre Dame,
IN. Address in 1929, c/o Port.
Ptr. Gal., 570 5th Ave.; 56 Wash.
Mews, NYC; summer, Redding, CT.

TULLOCH, W(ILLIAM) A(LEXANDER).
Painter and craftsman. Born
Venezuela, Jan. 3, 1887. Pupil of
William Turner. Member: Salons of
Amer.; S Indp. A. Address in 1929,
30 Kalmia Ave., Flushing, NY.

TULLY, CHRISTOPHER.
Engraver. The Pennsylvania
Magazine for 1775 contains a
copperplate of a machine for
spinning wool, which the text said
was "drawn and engraved by
Christopher Tully, who first made
and introduced this machine into
this country." The plate was
evidently made for the Society for
Promoting American Manufactures,
organized in Philadelphia in 1775.
To this society C. Tully and John
Hague submitted models of machines
for spinning wool and cotton goods;
these two machines were so similar
in design, the committee appointed
to examine them decided to divide
the prize of 30 pounds offered by
the society between the 2
inventors.

TUNIS, EDWIN.
Painter, illustrator, and etcher.
Born Cold Spring Harbor, LI, NY,
Dec. 8, 1897. Pupil of Joseph
Lauber, C. Y. Turner, Hugh
Breckenridge. Address in 1929, 10
East Franklin St.; 918 St. Paul
Street, Baltimore, MD.

TUPPER, ALEXANDER G(ARFIELD).
Painter and writer. Born
Gloucester, MA, Oct. 25, 1885.
Pupil of Twachtman. Member:
Gloucester SA; North Shore AA.
Address in 1929, 62 Mt. Pleasant
Ave., East Gloucester, MA.

TURCAS, JULES.
Landscape painter. Born in Cuba in
1854; died in Boston in 1917.
Exhibited in the NY and
Philadelphia galleries.

TURKENTON, NETTA CRAIG.
Painter and teacher. Born
Washington, DC. Pupil of PAFA;
Corcoran School of Art; William M.
Chase. Member: S. Wash. A.
Address in 1929, 1513 33rd St.,
N.W., Washington, DC.

TURLE, SARAH A.
Painter. Exhibited miniatures at the PAFA, Philadelphia, 1925. Address in 1926, 2216 East Superior St., Duluth, MN.

TURMAN, WILLIAM T.
Painter. Born Graysville, IN, June 19, 1867. Pupil of AIC; Chicago AFA; PAFA; J. Francis Smith, A. F. Brooks, Sterba, A. T. Van Laer. Member: Terre Haute Art Assoc.; Indiana AA; Hoosier Salon; AFA. Work in: High School, Columbia City, IN; Public Library, Thorntown, IN; Indiana State Normal School; Turman Township High School, Graysville, IN; Sara Scott and McClain Junior High Schools and Woman's Dept. Club, Terre Haute, IN. Address in 1929, Terre Haute, IN.

TURNBULL, GALE.
Painter and etcher. Born Long Island City, NY, Dec. 19, 1889. Pupil of Guerin, Preissig, Lasar. Member: Paris AAA; Salma. C.; Paris Groupe PSA. Represented in the Luxembourg Museum, Paris; Brooklyn Museum, New York. Address in 1929, 51 Blvd. St. Jacques, Paris, France; summer, Pont Croix, Finistere, France.

TURNBULL, GRACE H.
Painter, sculptor, writer, and lecturer. Born Baltimore, MD. Award: Whitelaw Reid first prize, Paris, 1914. Author, "Tongues of Fire" (Macmillan Co.), 1929. Address in 1929, 223 Chancery Rd., Guilford, Baltimore, MD.

TURNBULL, RUTH.
Sculptor. Born New City, Jan. 25, 1912. Pupil of Ella Buchanan. Address in 1929, 7927 Selma Ave., Hollywood, CA.

TURNER, ALFRED M.
Painter and teacher. Born in England, Aug. 28, 1851. Pupil of his father, Edward Turner. Member: AWCS. Work: "Chancellor McCracken" and "Dean Brush," New York University.

TURNER, CHARLES YARDLEY.
Painter. Born in Baltimore, MD, in 1850. Went to NYC in 1872 and entered school of NAD, where he studied 3 years and rec. awards. Went to Paris and studied under Laurens, Munkacsy and Leon Bonnat. In Holland he found the subject of his famous painting "The Grand Canal at Dordrecht." Was assistant director of decorations at the Columbia Exp. in Chicago in 1893. Elected Assoc. Member of the NAD in 1883, and an Academician in 1886. One of his murals was in the Baltimore Court House, the subject being the incident of the brig "Peggy Stuart" entering the harbor of Annapolis in 1774. Also painted many Puritan subjects. Some of his work was in the Capitol at Madison, WI; also in many bldgs. in NY. Towards the last of his life he concentrated on etching. Died in 1918.

TURNER, FRANCES LEE.
(Mrs. E. K. Turner). Painter and teacher. Born Bridgeport, AL, Nov. 5, 1875. Pupil of Corcoran Art School; ASL of NY; Kenyon Cox; George Elmer Browne; Daniel Garber. Member: SSAL; Atlanta AA. Award: prize, Atlanta AA, 1923. Address in 1929, Emory University, Atlanta, GA.

TURNER, HELEN M.
Painter. Born Louisville, KY. Pupil of ASL NY under Cox. Member: ANA 1913; NA, 1921; NYWCC; Port. P.; NAC; AFA. Awards: Elling prize for landscape, NY Woman's Art Club, 1912; Agar prize, NA Women PS; Shaw memorial prize, NAD, 1913; Altman prize ($500), NAD, 1921; second prize ($400), NAC, 1922; gold medal ($300), NAC, 1927; Maynard prize, NAD, 1927. Work: Miniature, Metropolitan Museum, NY; "Girl with the Lantern," Corcoran Gallery, Washington, and in Detroit Inst.; Delgado Mus., New Orleans, LA.; National Arts Club, New York; Phillips Memorial Gallery, Washington, DC; "Two Women," Houston Art Museum, Texas; "Lilies, Lanterns and Sunshine," Norfolk Museum, Virginia; "Golden Hours," Newark Art Museum; "A Young Girl," Highland Park Society of Arts, Dallas, Texas. Address in 1929, Grand Central Art Galleries; 15 Gramercy Park, NY, NY; summer, Cragsmoor, Ulster Co., NY.

TURNER, JAMES.
Engraver. This name first appears in Boston, MA, signed to a view of Boston which appears in The American Magazine for 1744. In the Boston Evening Post of 1745, he advertised as follows: "James Turner, Silversmith & Engraver, near the Town House in Cornhill Boston. Engraves all sorts of Stamps in Brass or Pewter for the common Printing Press, Coats of Arms, Crests, Cyphers, & c., on Gold, Silver, Steel, Copper, Brass or Pewter. He likewise makes Watch Faces, makes and cuts Seals in Gold, Silver, or Steel: or makes Steel Faces for Seals, and sets them handsomely in Gold or Silver. He cuts all sorts of Steel Stamps, Brass Rolls and Stamps for Sadlers and Bookbinders, and does all sorts of work in Gold and Silver. All after the best and neatest manner and at the most Reasonable Rates." In Boston he engraved the three large folding maps used in "Bill in the Chancery of NJ," published in NY in 1747 by James Parker, and also engraved a fairly good portrait of the Rev. Isaac Watts. About 1758 James Turner was in Phila. as engraver and print-dealer on Arch Street, and he was probably there earlier as he engraved the large map "Province of Pennsyvania," published by Nicholas Scull in Phila. in 1759. Engraved bookplates for residents of Phila., and the Penn coat of arms for the headline of The Pennsylvania Gazette. Died Dec. 1759 in Phila.

TURNER, LESLIE.
Illustrator. Born Cisco, Texas, Dec. 25, 1900. Illustrations for "The Saturday Evening Post," "Ladies Home Journal," "Pictorial Review." Address in 1929, Westport, CT.

TURNER, MATILDA HUTCHINSON.
Painter. Born Jerseyville, IL. Pupil of Hugh Breckenridge, William M. Chase, Cecilia Beaux, Sargeant Kendall, Margaretta Archambault. Exhibited at PAFA. Member: Fellowship PAFA. Address in 1929, 3717 Hamilton St., Philadelphia, PA.

TURNER, ROSS STERLING.
Painter and illustrator. Born in Westport, Essex County, NY, in 1847. Began artistic career after 1873. Studied in Europe, mostly in Germany (Munich) and Italy, 1876-80-82. Among his oils and watercolors are "A Small Court, Mexico;" "El Jardin Modesto;" "A Painted Ship;" "The Flying Dutchman" and "A Bermuda Wedding." Professor at Normal Art School, Boston, in 1909. Author: "Water Colors"; "Art for the Eye" and "School Room Decorations." Published reproduction of the "Golden Galleon" picture, Century Magazine, 1899. Died in 1915.

TURNER, WILLIAM GREEN.
Sculptor. Born in Newport, Rhode Island, in 1833. Went abroad for study and spent much of his life in Italy. Exhibited in Philadelphia in 1876.

TURNEY, AGNES RICHMOND.
See Agnes M. Richmond.

TURNEY, OLIVE.
Painter. Born Pittsburgh, PA, Aug. 4, 1847. Pupil of Pittsburgh School of Design for Women. Member: Am. APL; AFA. Award: Gold medal, 1872. Address in 1929, 322 Amber St., Pittsburgh, PA; summer, Scalp Level, PA.

TURNEY, WINTHROP DUTHIE.
Painter. Born New York, NY. Pupil of Loeb, Du Mond and Brush; ASL of NY. Member: Mural P.; Brooklyn S. Modern A; Fifteen Gal. Represented in the Brooklyn Museum. Address in 1929, 211 Greene Ave., Brooklyn, NY.

TUTHILL, WILLIAM H.
Engraver. In 1825 Tuthill was designing for the early NY lithographer Imbert. In 1830-31 engraved portraits, landscape and book illustrations for NY publishers. The engraving firm of Tuthill & Barnard was working in NY later. His small etching of "Mr. Robert as Wormwood," published in NY, is signed "Tuthill fec't".

TUTTLE, ADRIANNA.
Painter. Born Madison, NJ, Feb. 6, 1870. Pupil of Chase. Member: PA S. Min. P.; NA Women PS; Amer. S.

Min. P. Specialty, portraits on ivory. Address in 1929, 2 Orchard St., Newark, NJ.

TUTTLE, H(ENRY) E(MERSON).
Etcher. Born Lake Forest, IL, Dec. 10, 1890. Member: Brooklyn SE; Chicago SE; AFA. Work: "The Goshawk," Art Inst. of Chicago; "The Goshawk," "Old Raven," "Saw-Whet Owl No. 1," "Great Horned Owl" and "Sharp Shinned Hawk No. 1," British Museum, London; "Afternoon," Memorial Art Gallery, Rochester, NY; "Old Raven," Bibliotheque Nationale, Paris; twenty five prints, Museum of Fine Arts, Yale University, New Haven, CT. Address in 1929, 87 Trumbull St., New Haven, CT.

TUTTLE, MACOWIN.
Painter, illustrator, writer, and lecturer. Born Muncie, IN, Nov. 3, 1861. Pupil of William M. Chase;Duveneck; Laurens and the Acad. Julien, Paris. Member: NAC; Salma C; Paris AAA. Specialty, engravings on wood direct from nature. Address in 1929, 37 West 56th St.; h. 47 Fifth Ave., New York, NY.

TUTTLE, MARY McARTHUR THOMPSON.
Painter and author. Born at Hillsboro, Highland County, Ohio, in 1849. Portrait and landscape painter. In 1895 and after lectured on "Color" in schools and colleges. Painted portrait of her mother exhibited in W.C.T.U. exhibit, St. Louis Exp., 1904, and in Tremont Temple, Boston. Portraits of Prof. Tuttle in Historical Seminary Room, Cornell University, and Billings Library. Author of "Chronological Chart of the Schools of Painting."

TUTTLE, MILDRED JORDAN.
Painter, etcher, and teacher. Born Portland, ME, Feb. 26, 1874. Pupil of Yale School FA; W.M. Chase. Member: New Haven PCC; PA S. Min. P. Work: "Bishop Samuel Senbury," Yale U. Address in 1929, Clinton, CT.

TUTTLE, RUEL CROMPTON.
Portrait and mural painter. Born Windsor, Sept. 24, 1866. Pupil of ASL of NY under Mowbray and J.

Alden Weir. Member: ASL of NY; CT AFA; Wash. WCC; NYWCC; AFA. Lecturer on History of Art, Amherst College. Address in 1929, Greenfield, MA.

TWACHTMAN, JOHN HENRY.
Landscape painter. Born in Cincinnati, Ohio, in 1853. Pupil of School of Design of Cincinnati, under Frank Duveneck; NAD; studied in Munich; in Paris at the Academie Julien under Boulanger and Lefebvre. Awarded Webb prize of the Society of American Artists in 1888; Temple gold medal of 1895. Member of American Art Club of Munich. In 1898 founded organization named "Ten American Painters." Ranks among the greatest American landscape painters. Showed great skill in handling the elements of natural scenery, particularly in representing snow upon tree branches. Probably the first American artist to employ blue shadows. A great master of values. Died 1902 in Gloucester, MA.

TWIBILL, GEORGE W.
Portrait painter. Born in Lancaster County, Penna. in 1806. Pupil of Henry Inman in 1828. Elected an Associate of NA in 1832 and an Academician in 1833. The NY Historical Society has his copy of the portrait of Fitz-Greene Halleck which was painted by his master Henry Inman in 1828. The NAD has his portrait of Colonel John Trumbull in its permanent collection. Died Feb. 1836.

TWIGG-SMITH, W.
Landscape painter. Born Nelson, New Zealand, Nov. 2, 1882. Pupil of AIC; Harry M. Walcott. Member: Hawaiian SA; Chicago ASL. Address in 1929, 122 Bates St., Honolulu, Hawaii.

TWORKOV, JACK.
Painter. Born Aug. 15, 1900 in Biala, Poland. In US since 1913. Studied at Columbia; Nat. Acad. of Design and Art Students League. Taught at Queens College; Pratt; Yale; and Columbia. Awarded Guggenheim (1970); Hon. Doctorates from Maryland Inst.; Columbia; R. I. School of Design. Rec. Corcoran

award, 1963. Exhibited at Charles Egan Gallery, NYC (1947-54); U. of Miss.; Holland Gal., Chicago; Baltimore Mus.; Whitney; Yale; Ohio State; UC/Santa Barbara; PAFA; Seattle World's Fair (1962); Rice U.; many others. In collections of MMA; SUNY/New Paltz; Union Carbide Corp.; MOMA: Owen Corning Corp; RI School of Design; Yale; Kent State U. and Chase Manhatten Bank. Address in 1929, 220 West 17th St., New York, NY; summer, Provincetown, MA.

TYLER, BAYARD H(ENRY).
Portrait painter. Born Oneida, Madison Co., NY, April 22, 1855. Pupil of Syracuse Univ.; ASL and NAD in NY. Member: Lotos C.; Salma. C.; Yonkers AA; NYWCC. Award: Hon. mention, Wash. SA, 1913; first purchase prize, Yonkers AA, 1927. Represented in the Corcoran Gal. of Art, Wash., DC; State Collection, Albany, NY; Banking Dept., Albany; Insurance Underwriters, NY; Aetna Ins. Co., NY; North River Ins. Co., NY; Standard Club, Chicago; Holden Mem., Clinton, MA; Hackley Mem. School, Tarrytown; Albirght Mem. Library, Scranton; Wells College, Aurora; 22nd Regiment Armory, NY; Woman's Coll., New London. Address in 1929, 26 Marshall Road, Yonkers, NY; Hearts Content Camp, R.F.D.1, Catskill, NY.

TYLER, CAROLYN D.
Miniature painter. Born Chicago. Pupil of AIC under Mrs. Virginia Reynolds. Member: Chicago SA; Chicago WCC; Chicago S. Min. P.; Alumni AIC; Chicago AC; Cordon. Address in 1929, 1401 East 53d St., Chicago, IL.

TYLER, ERNEST F(RANKLIN).
Painter and draftsman. Born New Haven, CT, April 13, 1879. Pupil of Yale School of Fine Arts. Member: Society of Beaux-Arts Architects; NY Arch. Lg.; Century A. Work in association with Edgar W. Jenney - decorations in main banking room, Sun Life Assurance Soc., Montreal, Canada; ceilings in State Capitol Bldg., Madison; Union Central Life Bldg., Cincinnati; decorations, Hibernia Bank and Trust Co., New Orleans, LA; Houses of Parliament, Ottawa, CN; Ceiling in Seamen's Bank for Savings, NY; First Nat'l Bank, Jersey City, NJ; hall of standard Oil Co. Bldg., New York; New Palmer House Hotel, Chicago; New Aeolian Co. Bldg., New York; Nat'l Acad. for Sciences Bldg., Wash., DC; War Memorial Bldg., Nashville, TN; Union Planters Bank, Memphis; dining hall, Columbia University, NY; Baptistry, Cathedral of St. John the Divine, NY. Address in 1929, 142 East 30th St.; h. 131 East 66th St., New York, NY.

TYLER, GEORGE WASHINGTON.
Painter. Born in 1803 in NYC. Died in March, 1833 in NYC.

TYLER, HUGH C.
Painter. Exhibited at the Penna. Acad. of the Fine Arts, Phila., 1914. Address in 1926, 115 West Clinch Ave., Knoxville, TN.

TYLER, JAMES G(ALE).
Marine painter, illustrator, and writer. Born Oswego, NY, Feb. 15, 1855. Pupil of A. Cary Smith. Member: Brooklyn AC; Salma. C. 1893; A. Fund S.; Greenwich SA. Some of his prominent works are: "Abandoning the Jeannette" (painted to order for James Gordon Bennett); "The New World;" "Do Not Abandon Me;" "The Constitution;" Contributed illustrations and marine art studies for L. Prang, Harper's, Century, Truth and other magazines. Died in 1931. Address in 1929, Greenwich, CT.

TYLOR, STELLA ELMENDORF MRS.
Sculptor. Member: Wis. PS. Address in 1929, 242½ Maple Ave., Oak Park, IL; 310 North Murray Ave., Madison, Wis.

TYNG, GRISWOLD.
Painter. Member: Boston AC. Address in 1929, 1011 Centre St., Jamaica Plain, MA.

TYNG, MARGARET FULLER.
Painter. Member: Boston GA. Address in 1929, 1011 Centre St., Jamaica Plain, MA.

TYRE, PHILIP S.
 Painter, etcher and architect.
 Born Wilmington, DE, July 14, 1881.
 Pupil of Anshutz, Henry R. Poore.
 Member: Fellowship PAFA; AIA;
 Phila. AC; AFA. Address in 1929,
 Plaza Bldg., 114 South 15th St.,
 Philadelphia, PA; 1100 Oak Lane
 Ave., Oak Lane P. O., Phila., PA.

TYSON, CARROLL S(ARGENT) JR.
 Painter and sculptor. Born
 Philadelphia, Nov. 23, 1878. Pupil
 of PAFA under Chase, Anshutz and
 Beaux; Carl Marr and Walter Thor in
 Munich. Member: AC Phila.;
 Fellowship PAFA; S. Indp. A.
 Awards: Sesnan gold medal, PAFA
 1915; bronze medal, P.-P. Exp., San
 F., 1915. Work in: Art Club of
 Phila.; State College of PA. Died
 March 19, 1956. Address in 1929,
 319 Walnut St.; 8811 Towanda St.,
 Chestnut Hill, Philadelphia, PA.

TYSON, MRS. GEORGE.
 Painter. Member: Boston WCC.
 Address in 1929, 314 Dartmouth St.,
 Boston, MA.

UERKVITZ, HERTA.
Painter. Born in Wisconsin in 1894. Work: "Summer Sunset," Seattle Fine Arts. Address in 1926, 3030 Hoyt Avenue, Everett, Wash.

UEYAMA, TOKIO.
Painter. Born Wakayama, Japan, Sept. 22, 1890. Pupil of PAFA. Represented by portrait in State College, PA. Address in 1929, 214 North Mott Street, Los Angeles, CA.

UFER, WALTER.
Painter. Painted American Indian and Western subjects. Born Louisville, KY, July 22, 1876. Pupil of Royal Applied Art Schools and the Royal Academy in Dresden; AIC; J. Francis Smith Art School, Chicago; Walter Thor in Munich. Member: ANA, 1920; NA, 1926; Chicago SA; Salma. C.; Taos SA; Boston AC (hon.); NAC (life); Allied AA; Fellow Royal SA; Conn. AFA; New Mexico P.; Modern SA, Los Angeles. Awards: Cahn prize, AIC, 1916; first Logan medal ($500), AIC, 1917; Clarke prize, NAD, 1918; hors concours, Ill. P., 1918; third class medal, Int. Exh., Carnegie Inst., Pittsburgh, 1920; first Altman prize ($1,000), NAD, 1921; hon. mention, Conn. AFA., 1922; gold medal, Phila. AC, 1922; Temple gold medal, PAFA, 1923; French gold medal, AIC, 1923; first prize, Kentucky Painters, Nashville, 1925; second Altman prize ($500), NAD, 1926; Isidor gold medal, NAD, 1926. In collections of: Chicago Art Inst.; Springfield, Ill. State House; Brooklyn Inst.; PAFA; Maryland Inst., Baltimore; Mus. of History, Science and Art, LA; Chicago Mun. Coll.; Corcoran; Tulsa, (Okla.) Art Assn.; Rockford, (Ill.) Art Assn.; Joliet, (Ill.) Art Assn.; Met. Mus. A Houston Mus. Died in 1936. Address in 1929, Taos, NM.

UHLE, BERNHARD.
Painter. Born in Chemnitz, Saxony, in 1847. He was brought by his parents to the US in 1851, and received his first instruction in art from his father. He entered the Penna. Academy at fifteen. Between 1867 and 1875, he devoted most of his time to photography. Went to Munich from 1875 to 1877, studying in the Academy there, under Prof. F. Barth (drawing) and Prof. Alex. Wagner (painting); traveled to Italy, visiting the principal art galleries. He opened his studio as a portrait painter in Phila. in 1877. Made a second trip to Europe in 1879, which was exclusively devoted to the study of the Old Masters in Munich and Paris. After his return to Philadelphia in 1880, Uhle was constantly employed in painting portraits.

ULBER, ALTHEA.
Painter, sculptor and teacher. Born Los Angeles, Calif., July 28, 1898. Pupil of Arthur D. Rozaire, F. Tolles Chamberlain, Stanton McDonald Wright. Member: Calif. AC; Art Teachers Assn. of So. Calif. Address in 1929, 1053 South New Hampshire Ave., Los Angeles, CA.

ULBRICHT, ELSA E(MILIE).
Painter, craftsman and teacher. Born Milwaukee, Wis., March 18, 1885. Pupil of Frederick F. Fursman; Wis. School of Art; Alex Mueller; Walter Marshall Clute; George Senseney and Pratt Inst. Member: Wis. PS; Milwaukee Art Inst.; Wis. Society of Applied Arts. Address in 1929, School of Fine and Applied Art, Milwaukee; h. 249 28th St., Milwaukee, Wis.; summer, Summer School of Painting, Saugatuck, Mich.

ULKE, HENRY.
Painter. Born in Frankenstein, Germany, Jan. 29, 1821; died in Washington, DC, Feb. 17, 1910. Pupil of Prof. Wach, court painter in Berlin. He emigrated to the United States and reached New York in 1849, where he found employment as an illustrator and designer. Went to Washington, DC, where he resided for remainder of his life. Among his patrons were many distinguished people, including Charles Sumner, Salmon P. Chase, Chief Justice Taney, James G. Blaine, John Sherman, W. W. Corcoran, Carl Schurz, A. R. Shepherd, Secretary Stanton, Robert G. Ingersoll and Mrs. Jefferson Davis. His portraits of Secretaries of War are in the War

Department, and his portraits of the Secretaries of the Treasury in the Treasury Department. His portrait of Gen. Grant is in the White House. Over 100 portraits were produced by this artist while in Washington. As a naturalist he was very celebrated and is credited with having made the largest known collection of American beetles, now on exhibition in the Museum of Natural History, Carnegie Institute, Pittsburgh.

ULLMAN, ALICE WOODS.
(Mrs. Eugene P.). Painter and illustrator. Born in Goshen, Ind. Member: National Association of Women Painters and Sculptors; National Art Club. Address in 1926, 39 Commercial St., Provincetown, Mass.

ULLMAN, EUGENE PAUL.
Painter. Born New York, March 27, 1877. Pupil of Wm. M. Chase. Member: Salon des Jeunes, Paris; Paris AAA; Salon des Independents, Paris; New Soc. A.; Paris SAP; Salma. C., 1902; Paris Groupe PSA. Awards: Bronze medal, St. Louis Exp., 1904; first class medal, Orleans, France, 1905; second prize, Worcester, 1906; Temple gold medal, PAFA 1906; silver medal, P.-P. Exp., San F., 1915; hon. mention, John Herron Inst. Work: "Portrait of Madam Fisher" and "The Sea," Herron Art Institute, Indianapolis, Ind.; represented French Government Collection, Brooklyn Institute. Died April 20, 1953, in Paris. Address in 1929, 24 rue Denfert Rochereau, Paris, France.

ULLRICH, ALBERT H.
Painter. Born Berlin, Germany, April 24, 1869. Pupil of AIC under Chas. E. Boutwood; Frederick Freer; Gari Melchers and Duveneck, and in Rome, Munich and Paris. Member: Palette and Chisel C., Chicago; Chicago SA; Chicago AC. Address in 1929, 925 Lake Ave., Wilmette, Ill.

ULP, CLIFFORD M(cCORMICK).
Painter, illustrator and teacher. Born Olean, NY, Aug. 23, 1885. Pupil of ASL of NY; William M. Chase and F. Walter Taylor; Mechanics Inst., Rochester.

Member: Board of Directors of the Memorial Art Gallery, Rochester; Rochester AC. Work: "Adoration of the Magi," altar painting, St. Monica's Church, Rochester, NY; mural decorations, Eastman Dental Dispensary, Rochester, NY; "Gen. Allenby in Palestine," National Gallery, Washington. Director, School of Applied Art, Mechanics Inst., Rochester, NY. Address in 1929, 56 South Washington St., Rochester, NY; summer, Saranac, Mich.

ULREICH, EDUARD BUK.
Painter, sculptor, illustrator and craftsman. Born Austria Hungary. Pupil of Mlle. Blumberg. Member: GFLA; Arch. Lg. of NY; Fellowship PAFA; Chicago AC; NY Arch. Lg. Works: Decorations, Denishawn Studios, Calif., and Edgewater Beach Hotel, Chicago; painted wall hangings, Chicago Temple Bldg. Address in 1929, 91 Charles St., New York, NY.

ULRICH, CHARLES FREDERIC.
Painter. Born in New York, Oct. 18, 1858. He studied at the school of the National Academy of Design in New York and later with Loefftz and Lindenschmidt in Munich. In 1884 he was the first recipient of the Clark prize at the National Academy of Design; the prize picture, "In the Land of Promise (Castle Garden); belongs to the Corcoran Art Gallery of Washington, DC. His painting, "The Glass Blowers of Murano," is in the Metropolitan Museum, New York. He resided for many years in Venice, Italy. His pictures are known for their exquisite technique, purity of color and strength of character. Died May 15, 1908, in Berlin, Germany.

UNDERWOOD, CLARENCE F.
Painter. Born in Jamestown, NY, in 1871. Studied at Art Students' League, New York, and in the Julien Academy, Paris, under Constant, Jean Paul Laurens and Bouguereau. Executed illustrations for Century, Studio, McClure's and other publishers in New York and London. Illustrator for Harper's; illustrated London News, Frederick A. Stokes & Co. (New York),

955

Saturday Evening Post, Philadelphia, etc. Address in 1926, 106 West 55th St., New York, NY.

UNDERWOOD, ELISABETH K(ENDALL).
Painter and sculptor. Born Gerrish Island, ME, Sept. 22, 1896. Pupil of Sergeant Kendall; Lee Lawrie. Address in 1929, South Salem, NY.

UNDERWOOD, GEORGE (CLAUDE) LEON.
Painter, sculptor, illustrator, etcher, writer and lecturer. Born London, Dec. 25, 1890. Award: Hon. mention, Carnegie Inst., 1923. Work: "Machine Gunners," Manchester Art Gal., Manchester, Eng.; watercolor drawings, The Whitworth Art Gallery, Manchester; etchings, British Museum and the Victoria and Albert Museum, London. Illustrated: "The Music from Behind the Moon," by James Branch Cabell (John Day Co.); wood engravings and verses for "Animalia" (Payson & Clarke). Address in 1929, care of Brentano's, 225 Fifth Ave., New York, NY; h. 12 Girdler's Rd., London, W. 14, Eng.; summer, care of Brentano's, 2 Portsmouth St., London, W. C. 2, Eng.

UNDERWOOD, THOMAS.
Engraver. Born about 1795; died at Lafayette, Ind., in 1849. Underwood was a good bank note engraver working in Philadelphia in 1829. He was a member of the bank note company of Fairman, Draper, Underwood & Co., and after 1841, of Underwood, Bald, Spencer & Hufty.

UNTHANK, GERTRUDE.
Painter and teacher. Born Economy, Ind., Oct. 26, 1878. Pupil of J. E. Bundy, Martha Walter, C. C. Rosencranz, Knute Heldaner, Pedro J. Lemos. Member: Hoosier Salon, Arrowhead AA. Awards: Second prize, still life, Arrowhead Exhibition, Duluth, Minn., 1928; hon. mention, pastel, landscape, West Duluth, Minn., 1929. Address in 1929, Hotel Androy, Superior, Wisc.

UNVER, GEORGE.
Painter. Award: Bronze medal for portrait, Kansas City AI, 1923. Address in 1929, 5838 East 14 St., Kansas City, MO.

UPJOHN, ANNA MILO.
Painter. Member: NA Women PS. Address in 1929, care of American Red Cross, Washington, DC; care of Credit Lyonnais, Paris, France; 11 Central Ave., Ithaca, NY.

UPTON, FLORENCE K.
Painter and illustrator. Born in NYC. Pupil of Kenyon Cox. Died Oct. 16, 1922, in London, England.

URICH, LOUIS J.
Sculptor and teacher. Born Paterson, NJ, July 4, 1879. Pupil of ASL of NY; Cooper Union; Beaux-Arts Arch. Award: Barnett prize, NAD, 1914. Address in 1929, 79 Gerry Ave., Elmhurst, LI, NY.

USHER, LEILA.
Painter and sculptor. Born Onalaska, La Crosse Co., Wis. Pupil of Geo. T. Brewster in Cambridge, Mass.; ASL in New York under Augustus Saint-Gaudens; H. H. Kitson in Boston; and studied in Paris. Member: Am. APL; AFA. Awards: Bronze medal, Atlanta, Exp., 1895; hon. mention for medal, P.-P. Exp., San F., 1915. Work: Bronze portraits in Harvard University; Johns Hopkins University, Baltimore; Bryn Mawr University; Rochester University; Bowdoin College; Tuskegee and Hampton Universities. Medal in the Royal Danish Mint and Medal Collection, Copenhagen. Bas-relief in Fogg Art Museum, Cambridge, Mass.; bas- relief portrait, National Museum, Washington, DC; "Portrait of John Wesley Powell," Powell Monument, Grand Canyon, Ariz.; portrait in bas-relief, Agassiz Museum, Cambridge, Mass. Address in 1929, 14 East 50th St., New York City.

VAGIS, POLYGNOTIS GEORGE.
Sculptor. Born Island of Thasos, Greece, Jan. 14, 1894. Pupil of Gutzon Borglum, Leo Lentelli, John Gregory. Work: "Greek Soldier," "The Defender," and "The Dreamer." Address in 1929, Beaux Arts Inst. of Design, 126 East 75th St.; h. 75 Allen St., New York, NY.

VAGO, SANDOR.
Painter. Born Hungary, Aug. 8, 1887. Pupil of the Royal Acad. of Budapest and the Royal Acad. of Munich. Member: Founder-Member, Nat. Salon, Royal Art Assoc., and Royal Acad., Budapest; Royal Acad., Munich; Budapest Royal AA; Cleveland SA. Awards: Hon. Mention, 1913, Budapest; 2nd prize, 1924 and 1925, Cleveland Mus. of Art. Work: Nat'l Salon, Budapest; Cleveland Public Lib., Cleveland Hermit C.; Bluffton College (OH); Cleveland Mus. of Art; Union Trust Co. and Cleveland Mid-day Club. Address in 1929, 3920 Euclid Ave., Cleveland, Ohio.

VAIL, MISS ARAMENTA DIANTHE.
Miniature painter, who flourished in New York (1839-41).

VAIL, EUGENE.
Marine and figure painter. Born in Saint-Servan, France, of an American father, September, 1857. Pupil of NY ASL under Beckwith and Chase; Ecole des Beaux- Arts, Paris, under Cabanel, Dagnan-Bouveret and Collin. Awards: Honorable mention, 1886, and third class gold medal, 1888, Paris Salon; first class gold medal, Paris Exposition, 1889; Grand Diploma of Honor, Berlin; second medal, Munich; first class medal, Antwerp; silver medal, St. Louis Exp., 1904; first medal, Liege Exp., 1905; Legion of Honor, 1894. Represented by "Ready About," painted in 1888, at the Corcoran Art Gallery, Washington, D.C. Died in 1934.

VAILLANT, LOUIS D(AVID).
Mural painter. Born Cleveland, OH, Dec. 14, 1875. Pupil of ASL of NY under Mowbray. Member: ASL of NY; NY Arch. Lg., 1902; Mural P.; NY Municipal AS; Century Assoc., Salma. C.; AFA. Award: Second

Hallgarten prize, NAD, 1910. Work: Stained glass windows in Meeting House, Ethical Culture Society, NY; ceiling decoration, First National Bank, Titusville, PA. Address in 1929, 219 East 61st Street, New York, NY; summer, Washington, CT.

VAILLANT, MADAME.
Miniature painter, working in NY in 1825.

VALDENUIT, THOMAS BLUGET DE.
Born in 1763. Some of the portrait plates issued by St. Memin, previous to 1797, are signed "St. Memin & Valdenuit, No. 1 Fair St., N. York." An Aquatint portrait of a man is signed "Drawn by Gimaldi, Engraved by Valdenuit, NY," in Feb. 1797. Died in 1846.

VALENTIEN, ANNA M.
(Mrs. A. R. Valentien). Sculptor, potter, and illustrator. Born Cincinnati, OH, Feb. 27, 1862. Pupil of Cincinnati Art Academy under Rebisso; Rodin, Injalbert and Bourdelle in Paris. Member: San Diego AG; San Diego FAS; La Jolla AA. Awards: Gold medal, Atlanta Exp., 1895; collaborative gold medal, Pan-Calif. Exp., San Diego, 1915; two gold medals, Pan-Calif. Exp., San Diego, 1916; highest award and cash prize, Sacramento State Fair, 1919. Address in 1929, 3903 Georgia St., San Diego, CA.

VALENTINE, ALBERT R.
Painter. Born in Cincinnati, OH, May 11, 1862. Studied in this country, and in Europe with Duveneck. Exhibited in the Paris Salon in 1900. His specialty was the painting of wild flowers, and grasses. Died Aug. 5, 1925.

VALENTINE, DE ALTON.
Illustrator. Born Cleveland, OH, June 6, 1889. Pupil of Ufer, J. Wellington Reynolds. Member: SI; GFLA.; Players. Address in 1929, 32 Union Sq.; h. 135 West 16th Street, New York, NY.

VALENTINE, EDWARD V(IRGINIUS).
Sculptor. Born Richmond, VA, Nov. 12, 1838. Pupil of Couture and Jouffroy in Paris; Bonanti in Italy; Kiss in Berlin. President, Valentine Museum, Richmond, VA.

Work: "Gen. Robert E. Lee," Memorial Chapel, Lexington, VA; "Thomas Jefferson," Richmond; "Gen. Hugh Mercer," Fredericksburg, VA; "I. I. Audubon," New Orleans, LA.; "Jefferson Davis," Richmond, VA; "Gen. R. E. Lee," U.S. Capitol, Washington. Died Oct. 19, 1930. Address in 1929, 809 East Leigh St.; h. 109 North Sixth St., Richmond, VA.

VALENTINE, ELIAS.
Valentine was a copperplate printer and engraver living in NY in 1810-18, according to the directories. As an engraver he seems to have done very little work.

VALENTINE, JANE H.
Painter and etcher. Born Bellefonte, PA. Pupil of William M. Chase. Member: Phila. Alliance; Fellowship PAFA. Died in 1934. Address in 1929, 127 West Springfield Ave., Chestnut Hill, Philadelphia, PA.

VALENTINE, WILLIAM.
Portrait painter. Born in England in 1798; died in 1849. He visited Boston in 1826.

VALK, ELLA SNOWDEN.
Miniature painter. Member of National Association of Women Painters and Sculptors, NY. Address in 1926, 58 West 57th Street, NY.

VALLANCE, JOHN.
Engraver. Born in Scotland, 1770; died in Philadelphia June 14, 1823. Vallance apparently came to Phila. about 1791, as his name as an engraver appears in that city in 1791-99, and in 1811-23. It cannot be stated where he was in the interval 1800-10. In 1794, as a member of the firm of Thackara & Vallance, he was engraving in Philadelphia, and Edwin ascribes to Vallance the portrait of John Howard signed by this firm. The stipple portrait of Hugh Blair, signed by Vallance alone, is an excellent engraving and example of his work. He engraved a large number of encyclopedia plates and other general work. One of the founders of Association of Artists

in America, organized in Phila. in 1794, and in 1810 he became treasurer of the Society of Artists in Phila, Member of the engraving firm of Tanner, Vallance, Kearny & Co., of Phila. An excellent script engraver. Good early bank-notes bear his name.

VALLE, MAUDE RICHMOND FLORENTINO.
Painter, illustrator, writer, and teacher. Pupil of ASL of NY under Cox, Chase, Brush and Beckwith; Julian Academy under Lefebvre, Constant and Beaury-Sorel; Academy Delecluse under Delance and Callot in Paris. Art critic for "Rocky Mountain News." Address in 1929, 1500 Grant St., Denver, CO; summer, "Mt. Falcon," Mt. Morrison, CO.

VALLEE, JEAN FRANCOIS.
Nothing is known of this artist except that he was painting fine miniatures in New Orleans about 1815, when he painted a miniature of General Andrew Jackson which the general pronounced the best portrait of him extant, and then presented to Edward Livingston. Also known for his portrait painting. In 1826 he visited Boston, and in 1828 was painting portraits there.

VAN ALLEN, GERTRUDE E.
Painter. Born Brooklyn, NY, Oct. 15, 1897. Pupil of G. L. Nelson, Anna Fisher, Lewis Skidmore. Address in 1929, 20 Fairview Ave., Port Washington, L.I., NY.

VAN BEEST, ALBERT.
Marine painter and landscapist. His "Engagement between the Constitution and the Guerriere" was sold in New York City. Born June 1820 in Holland. Died in NYC 1860.

VAN BOSKERCK, ROBERT WARD.
Landscape painter. Born Hoboken, NJ, Jan. 15, 1855. Pupil of R. Swain Gifford and A. H. Wyant in NY. Member: ANA 1897, NA 1907; SAA 1887; Lotos C.; A. Aid S. Awards: Silver medal, Pan-Am. Exp., Buffalo, 1901; silver medal, St. Louis Exp., 1904. Represented in Union League and Lotos Club, New York; Layton Art Gallery, Milwaukee; Hamilton Club, Brooklyn. Died April 24, 1932. Address in

1929, 53 West 57th Street, New York, NY.

VAN BUREN, RAEBURN.
Illustrator. Born Pueblo, CO, Jan. 12, 1891. Attended ASL in 1913. Sketch artist for Kansas City Star; illustrated over 350 stories for The Saturday Evening Post; contributed to Redbook, The New Yorker, Esquire, McCalls, McClure's Syndicate, King Features Syndicate; created comic strip, Abbie and Slats. Member: SI; GFLA. Address in 1929, 21 Clover Drive, Great Neck, L.I., NY.

VAN COTT, DEWEY.
Painter, illustrator, craftsman, lecturer, and teacher. Born Salt Lake City, Utah, May 12, 1898. Pupil of Chicago AFA; Julian Acad., Paris; Yale University. Member: Artists Guild, Utah. Work: "Literature" and "History," Washington School, New Britain, CT. Civic Art Director, New Britain, CT. Address in 1929, Walnut Hill Bldg., New Britain, CT.

VAN COTT, FERN H.
(Mrs. Dewey Van Cott). Painter and craftswoman. Born Feb. 6, 1899. Pupil of Dewey Van Cott. Member: Springfield Painters. Work: "Springtime," Art Institute, Springfield. Address in 1929, Walnut Hill; 101 Monroe St., New Britain, CT; h. Salt Lake City, Utah.

VAN DEN HENGEL, WALTER.
Painter, who exhibited water colors at the Penna. Academy of the Fine Arts, Philadelphia, 1925. Address in 1926, 2095 North 63d Street, Philadelphia, PA.

VAN DER VEER, MARY.
Painter. Born Amsterdam, NY, Sept. 9, 1865. Pupil of Chase; PAFA; NAD; Whistler in Paris. Member: NYWCC; NA Women PS. Awards: Bronze medal, St. Louis Exp., 1904; Shaw memorial prize, NAD, 1911. Address in 1929, 1 Arnold Avenue, Amsterdam, NY.

VAN DER VELDE, HANNY.
(Mrs. A. W. Van der Velde). Painter. Born Rotterdam, Holland, Sept. 19, 1883. Pupil of Rotterdam Academy of Fine Arts. Member: NA Women PS; Detroit Soc. Women P. Awards: Rotterdam, 1910; Detroit, 1910, 1924; three first prizes, Michigan State Show, 1926; Arts Club prize for "Best Painting executed in 1926," Detroit IA, 1927. Address in 1929, 1108 East 12 Mile Road, Royal Oak, MI.

VAN DER WEYDEN, HARRY.
Painter. Born Boston, MA, 1868. Pupil of Laurens, Lefebvre and Constant in Paris; Fred Brown in London. Member: Paris SAP; Paris AAA; Inst. of Oil Painters, London. Awards: Third class medal, Paris Salon, 1891; second medal, Inter. Exp., Antwerp, 1894; gold medal, Atlanta Exp., 1895; bronze medal, Paris Exp., 1900; second gold medal, Munich, 1901; gold medal, Vienna, 1902; third medal. Liege Exp., 1905. Work: "Christmas Eve," Art Inst. of Chicago; pictures purchased by French Government, 1906, and 1908. Address in 1929, Rye, Sussex, England.

VAN DRESSER, WILLIAM.
Painter and illustrator. Born Memphis, TN, Oct. 28, 1871. Pupil of F. Luis Mora, George Bridgman and Walter Appleton Clark. Member: SI, 1911; Bronx AG, AM. APL. Specialty, Portraits. Address in 1929, 233 Fourth Ave., New York, NY; h. Palm Beach, Fla.

VAN DUZEE, KATE KEITH.
Painter and craftswoman. Born Dubuque, IA, Sept. 18, 1874. Pupil of Arthur Dow, John Johansen, Adrian J. Dornbush and Charles Woodbury. Member: Dubuque AA. Awards: Medals for water color, Iowa State Fair, 1917. 1918; hon. mention for water color, St. Paul Inst., 1918; Medal for monochromes and water colors, Iowa State Fair, 1919, 1920, 1922, 1923. Work: Oil painting in Dubuque Public Library. Address in 1929, 1471 Main Street, Dubuque, Iowa.

VAN ELTEN, HENDRICK D. K.
Landscape painter. Born in Holland in 1829. He came to NY in 1865. Elected to the National Academy of Design in 1883. Died July 12, 1904 in Paris, France.

VAN EMPEL, JAN.
Painter and writer. Born
Amsterdam, Holland. Pupil of
Robert Henri; Roman Kryzanowsky.
Work: "The Resurrection," St.
Peter's Church, Seward, Alaska;
"The Canadian Rockies," Canadian
National Railroad. Address in 1929,
Profile Farm, Franconia, NH.

VAN EVEREN, JAY.
Painter. Member: Mural P. Died
in 1947. Address in 1929, 509 East
77th Street, New York, NY.

VAN GORDER, L. EMERSON.
Painter and illustrator. Born in
Pittsburgh, PA, 1861. Pupil of
Chase and C. Y. Turner in NY; Ecole
des Beaux Arts in Paris under
Carolus-Duran; also studied in
London. Member: NY Water Color
Club; Toledo Tile Club. Work:
"Quai Aux Fleurs," Museum of Art,
Toledo. Address in 1926, 504
Euclid Ave., Toledo, OH.

VAN INGEN, WILLIAM BRANTLEY.
Mural painter. Born Philadelphia,
PA, Aug. 30, 1858. Pupil of PAFA
under Schuessele and Eakins; La
Farge in NY; Bonnat in Paris.
Member: NY. Arch. Lg. 1889; Mural
P.: Fellowship PAFA; AC Phila.;
NAC; Lotos C.; A. Aid S.; A. Fund
S. Award: Hon. mention, Pan-Am
Exp., Buffalo, 1901. Work: "The
Divine Law," "Signing of the Magna
Charta," "Socrates Discussing the
Nature of Justice." "Cicero
Speaking from the Roman Forum,"
"The Origin of Circuit Courts,"
"The Signing of the Constitution of
the U.S.," Lincoln as a Law
Student" and "Lincoln as
President," eight panels in U.S.
Court House. Chicago; "Justice and
Mercy," "An Appeal to Justice."
U.S. Court House. Indianapolis;
eleven panels representing
"Coinage." four panels. "Gold
Mining," U.S. Mint, Phila.;
fourteen panels representing the
"Early Settlers of PA" State
Capitol Harrisburg, PA." Sixteen
Panels, "Industries of NJ," State
Capitol, Trenton, "The
Departments," six panels in
Congressional Library, Washington;
"Construction of the Canal," five
panels in Administration Bldg.,
Panama Cannal Zone, 1914-15.

Address in 1929, 17 West 10th
Street, New York, NY.

VAN LAER, ALEXANDER THEOBALD.
Painter and lecturer. Born Feb. 9,
1857, in Auburn, NY. Studied art
at NAD, NY and at ASL with R. Swain
Gifford, and with George Poggenbeek
of Holland. Exhibited at the
leading American exhibitions, and
received bronze medal at Charleston
Exp. Lectured on art history at
Chautauqua, NY, for 7 years;
lectured at Brooklyn Inst. and at
schools and colleges. Member:
Jury of Selection and International
Jury of Awards, St. Louis
Exposition, 1904. Elected
Associate Member of National
Academy, 1902, and National
Academy, 1909. Member: American
Water Color Society; New York WCC.
Specialty, landscapes. Died March
12, 1920, in Indianapolis, IN.

VAN LAER, BELLE.
Miniature painter. Born in
Philadelphia in 1862. Pupil of S.
J. Ferris. Address in 1926,
Johnsville, Bucks County, Penna.

VAN LESHOUT, ALEXANDER J.
Etcher and teacher. Born Harvard,
IL, May 16, 1868. Pupil of ASL of
NY; AIC; Carroll Beckwith,
Frederick Freer, John H.
Vanderpoel; studied in Holland and
Paris. Member: SSAL; Chicago SE;
Louisville AA. Director, Louisville
School of Art Dept., Conservatory
of Music. Address in 1929,
Louisville School of Art; h. 1732
Shady Lane, Louisville, KY.

VAN NESS, MRS. BEATRICE WHITNEY.
See Whitney.

VAN PAPPELENDAM, LAURA.
Painter. Born near Donnelson, Lee
Co., IA. Pupil of AIC; Sorolla,
George Bellows, Nicholas Roerich.
Member: Chicago SA; Chicago Gal.
A.; IL. Acad. FA. Represented in
the Vanderpoel AA Collection,
Chicago. Address in 1929, 1418 E.
54th Street; Art Inst., Chicago,
IL.

VAN REUTH, EDWARD C.
Painter. Born in Holland in 1836;
died near Baltimore, MD, in 1924.

VAN ROEKENS, PAULETTE
(Victorine Jeannie). Painter. Born
Chateau-Thierry, France, Jan. 1,
1898. Pupil of Henry B. Snell,
Leopold G. Seyffert, Jos. Pearson
and C. Grafly. Member: Fellowship
PAFA; Alliance; NA Women PS.
Awards: Gold medal, Plastic C.,
1920; Phila. Sketch C. gold medal,
1923; hon. mention, NA Women PS.
Works: "15th St. from Broad St.
Station," PA. State College; "The
New Boulevard," Graphic Sketch
Club; "Treat 'Em Rough," PA Academy
of the Fine Arts; "Gray Towers,"
Reading Museum. Instructor,
School of Design, Philadelphia.
Address in 1929, Sterner Mill Road,
Langhorne, PA.

VAN SCIVER, PEARL A.
Painter, who exhibited water colors
at the Penna. Academy of the Fine
Arts, Philadelphia, 1925. Address
in 1926, 1406 East Willow Grove
Ave., Chestnut Hill, Philadelphia.

VAN SHECK, SIDNEY W. JIROUSEK.
Painter, lecturer, and teacher.
Born Prague. Pupil of Julian
Academy and L'Ecole des Beaux-Arts,
Paris. Member: Boston S. Indp. A.
Work: Mural paintings, H. Burroughs
Newsboy Foundation; Portrait of
President T. G. Masaryk,
Czechoslovakian government, Prague;
portrait of Mrs. T. G. Masaryk,
National Gallery, Prague.
Instructor, Massachusetts School of
Art, Boston. Address in 1929, 322
Broadway, Somerville, MA.

VAN SLOUN, FRANK J.
Painter, etcher, and teacher. Born
St. Paul, MN. Award: Bronze
medal, P.- P. Exp., San F. 1915.
Died in 1938. Address in 1929,
1617 California St.; h. 946 Central
Ave., San Francisco, CA.

VAN SLYCK, LUCILE.
Painter. Born Cincinnati, July 8,
1898. Pupil of H. H. Wessel; J. R.
Hopkins; J. E. Weis; Hawthorne; I.
C. Olinsky. Member: S. Indp. A;
Salons of Amer.; Cincinnati AC.
Address in 1929, Rockdale Ave.,
Cincinnati, OH.

VAN SOELEN, THEODORE.
Painter. Born at St. Paul, MN,
Feb. 15, 1890. Pupil of PAFA.

Member: New Mexico P. Award:
Bronze medal, Sesqui-Centennial
Exp., Phila. PA, 1926. Work:
"Summer Morining," Pennsylvania
Academy of the Fine Arts. Died in
1964. Address in 1929, Tesuque
Valley, Santa Fe, NM.

VAN SOLUN, FRANK J.
Painter and etcher. Born in St.
Paul, MN. Address in 1926, 1617
California St., San Francisco, CA.

VAN TYNE, PETER.
Painter. Born Flemington, NJ, Oct.
24, 1857. Pupil of ASL of NY;
PAFA. Member: Fellowship PAFA;
AFA. Awards: First prize ($50)
for still life, Trenton Fair, 1926.
Address in 1929, Trenton Junction,
NJ.

VAN VEEN, PIETER J. L.
Painter. Born The Hague, Holland,
Oct. 11, 1875. Studied in Holland
and France. Member: Salma. C.;
NAC; NY Municipal AS; Allied AA.
Award: Cross of Legion of Honor by
French Government for series of oil
paintings of Cathedral of France,
1929. Represented in Museum,
Seattle, Washington; Butler Art
Inst., Youngstown, OH; collection
of H. M. Queen of Belgium, with
"The Mission of San Juan
Capistrano, CA"; H. C. Henry
Collection, Washington University,
Seattle. Address in 1929, 58 West
57th Street, New York, NY; summer
care of Equitable Trust Co., Paris,
France.

VAN WART, AMES.
Sculptor. Born in NY. Pupil of
Hiram Powers. Member of Century
Association, New York. Address in
1926, Care of Century Association,
West 43d Street, New York, NY.

VAN WERVEKE, GEORGE.
Illustrator. Member: SI; GFLA.
Address in 1929, 33 West 67th
Street, New York, NY.

VAN WYCK.
See Browne, Matilda.

VAN ZANDT, MRS. HILDA.
Painter and teacher. Born Henry,
IL, June 18, 1892. Member: CA
WCS; CA AC. Address in 1929, 3740
Bluff Place, San Pedro, CA.

VANCE, FRED NELSON.
Mural painter. Born in Crawfordsville, IN, in 1880. Pupil of Art Inst. of Chicago; Smith Academy in Chicago; Julien, Colarossi and Vitti academies in Paris; Max Bohm in Paris; E. Vedder in Rome. Address in 1926, corner Plumb and Jefferson Sts., Crawfordsville, IN. Died Sept. 21, 1926 in Nashville, IN.

VANDERCOOK, MARGARET METZGER.
Sculptor. Born New York City, April 7, 1899. Pupil of Georg Lober in NY; Aristide Rousaud in Paris. Member: NA Women PS. Died in 1936. Address in 1929, 32 Union Sq.; h. 13 Gramercy Park, NYC.

VANDERLYN, JOHN.
Portrait and history painter. Born in Kingston, NY, Oct. 15, 1775. Pupil of Columbian Academy of Archibald Robertson. Employed by Thomas Barrow, the earlist art dealer in the city. Vanderlyn attracted attention of Aaron Burr, who encouraged him to pursue his art studies. About this time Gilbert Stuart returned to his native country and among his first portraits were those of Aaron Burr and Egbert Benson which Vanderlyn was allowed to copy. Vanderlyn studied with Stuart for one year. Returned to NY to begin a career. Painted Citizen Adet, the French Minister, Albert Gallatin and Theodosia Burr, the daughter of his patron. In 1796 Vanderlyn went to France and became pupil of Vincent, exhibiting in the Paris Salon in 1800 several portraits. His self-portrait hangs in the MMA. After 5 years in Paris, he returned to the US, and then returned to Europe in 1803. There he met Washington Allston with whom he travelled to Rome. There he painted his first historical picture, "The Massacre of Miss McCrea" exhibited in the Salon of 1804 and later in the Wadsworth Athenaeum. Exhibited "Caius Marius amidst the Ruins of Carthage," in 1808 which earned medal of honor from Napoleon. In Paris perhaps his greatest painting, "Ariadne Asleep in the Island of Naxos", exhibited in the Paris Salon of 1810 and considered the finest nude yet painted by an American; now at PAFA. Also painted portraits for City Hall, NY, and private commissioners. Portrait of Abraham Hasbrouck is considered one of his finest. Commissioned for one panel in rotunda of Capitol Wash. Also executed paintings and panoramas, that of Versailles being preserved in his home town as a memorial to his honor. His work has frequently been confused with that of Stuart. Died Sept. 23, 1852 in Kingston, NY.

VANDERLYN, JOHN (2d).
Painter. Nephew of the artist and named for him. He was born in 1805; died in 1876.

VANDERLYN, PIETER.
Portrait painter. Member of one of the early Dutch families in New York State. Born in 1687; died in 1778. In 1719, painted portrait of Johannes Van Vechten. About forty of his portraits have been recognized as those of descendants of early Dutch families in this country. He was the grandfather of John Vanderlyn (1775-1852), the noted portrait painter.

VANDERPOEL, EMILY NOYES.
(Mrs. John A. Vanderpoel). Painter and writer. Born New York. Pupil of R. Swain Gifford and Wm. Sartain. Member: NYWCC; NA Women PS; NAC; AFA; Fellow NAD. Award: Bronze medal, Columbian Exp., Chicago, 1893. Author of "Color Problems;" "Chronicles of a Pioneer School;" "More Chronicles of a Pioneer School;" "American Lace and Lace Makers;" "Ypres, 1919," Washington Museum of Army and Navy Relics of the Great War. Died in 1939. Address in 1929, 22 Gramercy Park, New York, NY; summer, Litchfield, CT.

VANDERPOOL, MATILDA.
Painter and teacher. Born Holland. Pupil AIC, David Ericson. Member: Chicago WCC; Chicago SA; Cordon C; Chic. SSAA; IL. Acad. FA. Address in 1929, 9431 Pleasant Avenue, Chicago, IL; summer, Gold Hill, CO.

VANDINE, ELIZABETH.
Engraver. The Journals of the Continental Congress for June 7, 1776, indicate that this women was a counterfeiter, the first on record in the colonies. With her husband, Henry Vandine, of Morris Co., NJ, she was arrested for an attempt to counterfeit bills of credit emitted by Congress. She confessed that "with privity of her said husband she counterfeited several bills of the Continental Currency." For this offense and for passing the same, she and her husband were confined in Morris County Jail.

VANDYCK, JAMES.
Miniature painter, who flourished about 1806-35.

VARIAN, DOROTHY.
Painter. Born New York, April 26, 1895. Member: Salons of Am.; NYS Women A. Address in 1929, 145 West 14th Street; h. 54 Manhattan Ave., Crestwood, New York, NY.

VARIAN, GEORGE EDMUND.
Painter. Born Oct. 16, 1865 in Liverpool, England. Studied at Brooklyn Art Guild and ASL, NY. Illustrated for various magazines and books. Commissioned by McClure's to visit Mont Pelee at time of destruction of St. Pierre. He accompanied Ray Stannard Baker to Europe and made illustrations for his book, Seen in Germany; also illsutrated George Kennan's The Tragedy of Pelee. Exhibited at Paris Salon, 1907. Died April 13, 1923, in Brooklyn, NY.

VARIAN, LESTER E.
Etcher, artist, and teacher. Born Denver, CO, Oct. 20, 1881. Pupil of Donn Barber and Chifflot. Member: Denver AC; AIA. Address in 1929, 565 Gas and Electric Bldg.; h. 464 Williams Parkway, Denver, CO.

VARNUM, WILLIAM HARRISON.
Painter, writer, and teacher. Born Cambridge, MA, Jan. 27, 1878. Pupil of De Camp, Major, Woodbury. Member: Eastern AA; Western AA; Wis. PS. Author of texts: "Industrial Arts Design;" "Pewter Design and Construction;" "Art in

Commemorative Design." Assoc. Professor of applied arts, Univ. of Wis. Address in 1929, Industrial Arts Laboratory, University of Wisconsin; h. 207 Forest St., Madison, WI; summer, Monhegan, ME.

VAUDECHAMP, JEAN JOSEPH.
Painter. Born in France, 1790; died there in 1866. he exhibited in the Salon, Paris, 1817, and afterward. He resided in New Orleans for several years during the 1830s and painted many fine portraits. In 1833 he had a studio as portrait painter at 147 Royal Street, New Orleans, LA.

VAWTER, JOHN WILLIAM.
Painter, illustrator, and etcher. Born Boone Co., VA, April 13, 1871. Member: Hoosier Salon. Award: Prize of $100 for "Our Alley," Exhibition Indiana Artists, Marshall Field Gallery, 1925. Work: Illustrated the Riley Series of books. Address in 1929, Nashville, IN.

VAWTER, MARY H. M(URRAY).
Painter. Born Baltimore, MD, June 30, 1871. Pupil of Edwin S. Whiteman; Irving Wiles; Charcoal Club, Balto.; ASL of NY. Member: IN AC; AFA. Specialty, portraits. Address in 1929, Nashville, IN.

VAYANA, NUNZIO.
Painter, illustrator, and lecturer. Born Castelvetrano, Italy, Aug. 28, 1887. Pupil of Grosso, Morelli and Pisani. Member: Ct. AFA; SCA; SAL; GAS; HAC; VAC; IAS, Rome. Awards: Selective prize, Venice AC, Venice, 1921; popular prize, CT AFA, 1924; hon. mention, I. E., Rome, 1925; William G. Bunce prize, CT AFA, 1926. Address in 1929, P. O. Box 926, Hartford, CT; summer, Ogunquit, ME.

VEDDER, ELIHU.
Painter and illustrator of Omar Khayyam's "Rubaiyat." Born in NY, Feb. 26, 1836. He studied art first under T. H. Mattison at Sherburne, NY; then Paris, in the atelier of Picot. Spent time in Florence and Rome and returned in 1861 to NY, where he remained five years. His murals include five panels in the Library of Congress

in Washington and one in Bowdoin College. His "Greek Actor's Daughter" was shown at the Centennial exhibition in the Metropolitan, Brooklyn, and Boston Museum, and in the Carnegie Inst. Was made a National Academician in 1865. Member of the American Society of Mural Painters, the American Academy of Arts and Letters and The Century Society, NY. Died Jan. 29, 1923 in Rome, Italy.

VELSEY, SETH M.
Sculptor. Born Logansport, IN, Sept. 26, 1903. Pupil of Lorado Taft, Albin Polasek. Award: Mrs. Keith Spalding prize, Hoosier Salon, Chicago, 1928. Address in 1929, 1700 Third Street, N. E., Washington, D.C.; h. 1421 North Delaware Street, Indianapolis, IN.

VER BECK, FRANK.
Illustrator. Born Belmont Co., Ohio, 1858. Illustrator and author of "A Short Little Tale from Bruintown," "Timothy Turtle's Great Day," "The Donkey Child," "The Little Cat Who Journeyed to St. Ives,"; "Ver Beck's Book of Bears:" etc. Designer of the Ver Beck earthenware models. Address in 1929, care of Curtis Brown, Ltd., 6 Henrietta St., Covent Garden, London, England.

VER BRYCK, CORNELIUS.
Landscape and historical painter. Born in NJ on Jan. 1, 1813. He studied under Samuel F. B. Morse, and in 1839 he visited London. In 1833 his portrait was painted by Thomas Sully. He died May 31, 1844, in Brooklyn, NY.

VER STEEG, FLORENCE B(IDDLE).
Painter. Born St. Louis, MO, Oct. 17, 1871. Pupil of St. Louis School of Fine Arts; Richard Miller; Hugh Breckenridge. Member: St. Louis Alliance; St. Louis AG; North Shore AA; AFA; Award: Hon. mention, Kansas City Art Inst., 1923; purchase prize, St. Louis AL, 1928; Mo. Soc. Artists, 1928. Address in 1929, 4646 Lindell Blvd., St. Louis, MO.

VERBEEK, GUSTAVE.
Painter and etcher. Born in Nagasaki, Japan, in 1867. Pupil of Constant, Laurens, Girardot, Blanc and Brush. Died in 1937.

VERGER, P. C.
Engraver. The only known plate of Verger is "The Triumph of Liberty," a folio plate signed "Engraved by T. C. Verger" in 1796. He was an "engraver upon fine stone," an art demanding a very different training and entirely different methods from those required in engraving upon copper. Nagler, in his "Kunstler Lexicon," in speaking of Claude du Verger, a landscape painter of 1780, refers to "a young Verger" who was an engraver on precious stones, working in Paris in 1806.

VERHEYDEN, FRANCOIS (ISIDORE).
Painter, etcher, and teacher. Born Hoeylaert, Belgium, April 8, 1880. Pupil of Royal Academy of Brussels. Address in 1929, Provincetown, MA.

VERMILYE, ANNA JOSEPHINE.
Painter, etcher, craftswoman, writer, lecturer, and teacher. Born Mt. Vernon, NY. Pupil of John F. Carlson, George Bridgman, John C. Johansen, Robert Henri, B. J. Nordfeldt, Allen Lewis. Member: AFA; NA Women PS; ASL of NY; Plainfield AA; Westfield AA; Provincetown AA. Address in 1929, 564 Summit Ave.; h. 428 Lenox Ave., Westfield, NJ.

VERNER, ELIZABETH O'NEILL.
(Mrs. E. Pettigrew Verner). Etcher, writer, and lecturer. Born Charleston, SC, Dec. 21, 1884. Pupil of PAFA. Member: Charleston EC; SSAL; Carolina AA; AFA. Address in 1929, 3 Atlantic St., Charleston, SC; summer, Verner's Lodge, Brevard, NC.

VERNON, THOMAS.
Engraver. Born in England, c. 1824, where he learned to engrave and worked for the London Art Journal, before he came to NY, about 1853. Vernon was chiefly employed here by the bank-note engraving companies, and he returned to England in 1856-57. Died 1872 in London.

VERREES, J. PAUL.
Painter, and illustrator. Born
Turnhout, Belgium, May 24, 1889.
Pupil of Julien de Vriendt, and
Francois Lauwers; Royal Academy of
Fine Arts, Antwerp, and Higher
Inst. of Fine Arts, Belgium.
Member: Brooklyn SE; Chicago SE.
Award: Mr. and Mrs. Frank G. Logan
medal, AIC, 1921. Prints in Art
Institute, Chicago; State Library;
Smithsonian Inst., Washington,
D.C.; Museum of Fine Arts, Boston.
Address in 1929, Scherpenberg,
Westmalle, Belgium.

VERSTILLE, WILLIAM.
Miniature painter. Born about
1755; he died in Boston, MA, Dec.
6, 1803. He painted miniatures in
Philadelphia in 1782 and later in
Boston and Salem, MA. His
miniatures are recognized in nearly
every instance by the piercing
black eyes given to his subjects.

VETTER, CORNELIA C.
Painter and etcher. Born in
Hartford in 1881. Pupil of Robert
Henri; of Andrada in Paris and
Spain. Member of CT Academy of
Fine Arts, Hartford. Address in
1926, 29 Huntington Street,
Hartford, CT.

VEZIN, CHARLES.
Painter. Born Philadelphia, PA,
April 9, 1858. Pupil of ASL of NY
under Du Mond, Chase, George Elmer
Browne, Helen M. Turner, John
Carlson. Member: ASL of NY; Salma.
C. 1902; Municipal AS; Yonkers AA;
Brooklyn SA.; Phila. AC; Brooklyn
PS, NAC; Century Assoc.; Lyme AA;
SPNY; Allied AA; AFA; Springfield
AL. Awards: Hon. mention, S.
Wash. A, 1914; hon. mention, CT
AFA, 1925; popular prize, Lyme AA,
1927. Represented, High Museum,
Atlanta, GA Address in 1929, 169
Columbia Heights, Brooklyn, NY;
summer, Lyme, CT.

VIAVANT, GEORGE.
Painter. Native of New Orleans.
Studied in Southern Art Union under
Parelli. Diploma, New Orleans
Cotton Centennial Exp., 1884.
Specialized in water color sketches
of native birds and animals.
Represented in Louisiana State

Museum. Died in 1925 in New
Orleans, LA.

VIBBERTS, EUNICE WALKER.
Painter. Born New Albany, IN, Aug.
8, 1899. Pupil of Anna Fisher,
Frank V. DuMond. Member:
Louisville AA; NA Women PS.
Address in 1929, 5 Glenwood Rd.,
Scarsdale, NY.

VICE, HERMAN STODDARD.
Painter and illustrator. Born
Jefferson, IN, 1884. Pupil of
Chicago Academy of Fine Arts.
Member: Hoosier Salon; IL Acad.
FA; So. Side AA; Romany Club.
Address in 1929, Dearborn Street,
Chicago, IL.

VICKERS, S. J.
Painter. Born in Middlefield,
Otsego County, NY, in 1872. Among
other things he designed subway
stations and ornamental elevated
structures of the rapid-transit
system of NY. Address in 1929,
Grand-View-on-Hudson, NY.

VICTOR, SOPHIE.
Painter, who exhibited at the
Penna. Academy of the Fine Arts,
Philadelphia, 1924.

VIGNA, GLORIANO.
Painter, sculptor, illustrator,
architect, craftsman, writer and
teacher. Born Paterson, Aug. 20,
1900. Pupil of Bridgman, DuMond,
Fratelli Vigna in Turin, Italy.
Decorator to the King and Queen of
Italy. Address in 1929, 1472
Broadway, New York, NY; h. 30 Ward
St., Paterson, NJ.

VIGNIER, A.
Dunlap recorded him as painting
landscapes in Philadelphia in 1811.

VINCENT, H(ARRY) A(IKEN).
Painter. Born Chicago, IL, Feb.
14, 1864. Self-taught. Member:
ANA; Salma. C., Allied AA; NYWCC;
North Shore AA. Award: Shaw
prize, Salma. C., 1907; Isidor
prize, Salma. C., 1916; Turnbull
prize, Salma. C., 1918; Porter
prize, 1925; Wm. Church Osborne
prize, and Paul L. Hammond prize,
NYWCC. Work: "Rockport Harbor,"
Butler Art Institute, Youngstown,
OH; Illinois State University.

Address in 1929, care Casson Galleries, 575 Boylston St., Boston, MA.

VINTON, FREDERICK PORTER.
Painter. Born Jan. 29, 1846 in Bangor, ME. His specialty was portraiture. Pupil of William Hunt and Dr. Rimmer in Boston, and of Bonnat and Laurens in Paris. Also studied at Royal Academy of Bavaria under Mauger and Dietz. Honorable mention in Paris Salon, 1890. Elected Member of the National Acad. of Design in 1891. A memorial exhibtion of 124 of his paintings, incl. 50 portraits, was held in 1911 at Boston Musuem of Fine Arts. Many statesmen, jurists, authors, and professional men were among his sitters. For life of Frederick P. Vinton, see "New England Artists," by Frank T. Robinson. Died May 19, 1911, in Boston, MA.

VINTON-BROWN, MRS. PAMELA.
Painter. Born Boston, MA, Jan. 28, 1888. Pupil of Collin and Courtois in Paris; Edwin Whiteman in Baltimore. Member: French Miniature Society; Deutscher Werkbund; PA S. Min. P.; Am. Soc. Min. P. Award: Hon. mention, miniature section, Exhibition of American Woman's Work, Paris, 1914; hon. mention, Balto. WCC, 1920. Address in 1929, Woodstock, NY.

VIVASH, RUTH ATHEY.
Painter, illustrator, craftswoman, and teacher. Born St. Louis, MO, March 26, 1892. Pupil of Pratt Inst., Mary Langtry, Ralph Johonnot, O. W. Beck, Ida Haskell, Ethelyn Schaurman, Ethel Traphagen. Member: Alliance; Brooklyn WCC; Am. APL. Address in 1929, 326 St. John's Place, Brooklyn, NY.

VIVIAN, CALTHEA (CAMPBELL).
Painter, etcher, and teacher. Born Fayette, MO. Pupil of Arthur Mathews; Lazar; and Colarossi Academy in Paris. Member: San Francisco AA; San Francisco SE; Laguna Beach AA; Calif. AA; Calif. AC. Represented in Palace of Fine Arts, San Francisco; Arkansas Auditorium Gallery. Address in 1929, Hotel Claremont, Berkeley, Calif.

VOGNILD, EDNA.
Painter. Born Chicago. Pupil of AIC; Hawthorne; J. C. Johansen, H. B. Snell; Colarossi and Delecluse Academies in Paris. Address in 1929, 231 E. Superior St., Chicago, IL.

VOGNILD, ENOCH M.
Painter. Born in Chicago in 1880. Pupil of Art Inst. of Chicago under Johansen and Vanderpoel; in summer under Woodbury; also studied in Julien and Delecluse Academies in Paris. Member: Art Students' League of Chicago; The Round Table; Chicago Art Club; Chicago Arts and Crafts; Chicago Society of Artists. Awarded Municipal Art League prize, 1906. Address in 1926, 22 Tooker Place, Chicago, IL.

VOGT, L. C.
Painter. Born in Cincinnati in 1864. Pupil of H. Siddons Mowbray and Frank Duveneck. Member: Cincinnati Art Club. Represented by three water colors in Cincinnati Museum. Address in 1926, 141 East Fourth Street, Cincinnati, OH.

VOIGHT, CHARLES A.
Illustrator. Member: SI, 1913; New Rochelle AA. Address in 1929, New York Tribune, New York, NY; 514 Rochelle Terrace, Pelham Manor, NY.

VOLK, DOUGLAS.
Painter, teacher, lecturer, and writer. Born Pittsfield, MA, Feb. 23, 1856. Son of the sculptor, Leonard W. Volk. Pupil of Gerome in Paris. Member: ANA 1898, NA 1899; SAA 1880; NAC; A. Fund S.; A. Aid S.; Port. P.; NY Arch. Lg., 1912; Century Assoc.; Inter. Soc. A. L.; Mural P.; SI; Wash. AC; AFA. Awards: Medal, Col. Exp., Chicago, 1893; Shaw Purchase, SAA, 1899; first prize, Colonial Exhibition, Boston, 1899; silver medal, Pan-Am. Exp., Buffalo, 1901; silver medal, Charleston Exp., 1902; Carnegie prize, SAA, 1903; silver medal, St. Louis Exp., 1904; gold medal, Carolina AA 1907; Proctor portrait prize, NAD 1910; Saltus gold medal, NAD, 1910; gold medal, NAC 1915; Maynard portrait prize, NAD 1915; gold medal, P. P. Exp., San. F., 1915; Beck gold medal, PAFA 1916. Cross of officer of the Order of

Leopold II, 1921. Organized handicraft movement at Centre Lovell; director, Minneapolis School of Fine Arts 1886 to 1893; instructor NAD and Cooper Union. Work: "Father Hennepin" and "Battle of Missionary Ridge," mural decorations, St. Paul Capitol, St. Paul, MN; "Puritan Mother and Child," Carnegie Inst., Pittsburgh; "Portrait of Dr. Felix Adler" and "Little Mildred," Met. Mus., NY; "Accused of Witchcraft," Corcoran Gal., Wash.; "Boy with the Arrow," Nat'l Gal., Wash.; "Maiden's Reverie," Pittsfield (MA) Mus.; "Fur Trading Period," mural decoration, 1913, for Court House, Des Moines, IA; "Reverie," Art Mus., Montclair, NJ; "The Artist's Daughter." Memorial Art Gal., Rochester, NY; "Among the Lilies," Nat'l Arts Club, NY; "Adoration," Hackley Art Gal., Muskegon, MI; "By the Pond," Omaha Art Gal.; portraits of King Albert, Lloyd George, Gen. Pershing, Nat. Gal., Wash., DC; "Gov. A. E. Smith," Capitol, Albany; "Lincoln," Albright Gal., Buffalo, NY and Mem. Art Mus., Portland, ME. Address in 1929, 119 E. 19th St., NYC. Died Feb. 7, 1935.

VOLK, LEONARD WELLS.
Sculptor. Born in New York State, Nov. 7, 1828. In 1855 he was sent abroad for study. On returning in 1857 he settled in Chicago. Executed many busts and statues of prominent men. Among his works are the life- size statue of Stephen Douglass in marble, and a portrait bust of Abraham Lincoln. Died Aug. 19, 1895, in Wisconsin.

VOLKERT, EDWARD C(HARLES).
Painter. Born Cincinnati, OH, Sept. 19, 1871. Pupil of Duveneck in Cincinnati; ASL of NY. Member: ANA; NYWCC; AWCS; Allied AA; Salma. C.; Union Inter. des Beaux-Arts et des Lettres; Cincinnati Mac D. S.; Am. Soc. Animal PS; NAC (life); CT, AFA; AFA. Awards: Hudnut prize, NY WCC, 1919; Cooper prize, CT AFA, 1925; Gedney Bunce prize, CT Acad. FA, 1929. Work: Decoration, Woodward and Hughes High School, Cincinnati, OH; Hamilton High School, Hamilton, Montclair, NJ,

Museum. Specialty, cattle. Address in 1929, Lyme, CT.

VOLLMER, GRACE LIBBY.
Painter. Born Hopkinton, MA. Pupil of Martinez, Edward Vysekal, Roscoe Shrader. Member: Pasadena AA; Calif. AC; Laguna Beach AA. Address in 1929, Coast Blvd., Laguna Beach, CA; summer, Equitable Trust Co., 41 Rue Cambon, Paris, France.

VOLLMERING, JOS.
Born in Anhalt, Westphalia, in 1810; died in New York City in 1887. He studied in Amsterdam. In 1847 he moved to NY and opened his studio. Elected an Associate Member of National Academy in 1853. Landscape and Winter-Scene in the Bryan Collection, New York Historical Society.

VOLOZON, DENIS A.
Landscape painter and portrait draftsman in crayons. Volozon was a Frenchman who settled in Philadelphia, exhibited at the Academy and taught drawing there. He also made historical compositions. His crayon of George Washington is in the Penna. Academy of the Fine Arts. He was working in Philadelphia, 1811-20.

VON DER LANCKEN, FRANK.
Painter, sculptor, illustrator, craftsman, and teacher. Born Brooklyn, NY, Sept. 10, 1872. Pupil of Pratt Inst. under Herbert Adams; ASL in New York under Mowbray; Julian Academy in Paris under Constant and Laurens. Member: ASL of NY; Salma. C.; Rochester AC. Awards: Medal, Kentucky Federation of Women's Clubs, 1925; medal of first class. Rochester Exp., 1926. Director of School of Applied and Fine Arts of the Mechanics Inst., Rochester, NY, and lecturer on art at the University of Rochester. Director, Chautauqua School of Arts and Crafts. Address in 1929, 2819 East 4th Street, Tulsa, Okla.; summer, Chautauqua, NY.

VON EISENBARTH, AUGUST.
Painter, and illustrator. Born Hungary, Nov. 15, 1897. Pupil of Royal Hungarian Academy; ASL of NY. Member: National Salon, Budapest;

Alliance; AWCS. Work: "Biedermeyer Doll," National Salon, Budapest, Hungary; "Portrait of a Young Lady," American Water Color Society, NY; Specializing in water colors, commercial advertising and textile designs. Executed series of silk prints: "Tudo-chi," for Corticelli Silk Co., etc. Address in 1929, 66 Leonard St.; 3459 Spuyten Duyvil Road, NY, NY.

VON HOFSTEN, HUGO OLOF.
Painter and illustrator. Born in Sweden, June 20, 1865. Pupil of Royal Academy at Stockholm under M. E. Winge, O. Aborelius and A. Larson. Organizer of the Forestry Painters of Chicago. Award: First water color prize, Swedish American Artists, 1919. Address in 1929, Winnetka, IL.

VON NEUMANN, ROBERT.
Painter and illustrator. Born Rostock, Mecklenburg, Germany, Sept. 10, 1888. Pupil of Emil Topler, Frans Burke. Member: Wisc. PS. Award: Hon. mention, Wisc. PS, Milwaukee, 1926. Address in 1929, 2014 Buffum St., Milwaukee, Wisc.

VON RINGELHEIM, PAUL.
Sculptor. Born in 1938 in Vienna, Austria. Studied at Brooklyn Mus. School, 1952-56 and with Picasso in Cannes, 1958. Taught at Brooklyn and Art Students' League. Work: Farleigh Dickingson U.; MOMA; Art Inst. of Chic; Whitney and many private collections. Exhib.: Felix Landau Gal., NYC; Rose Fried Gal., NYC; Brooklyn; NY World's Fair, 1964; Farleigh Dickinson U., and others.

VON SALTZA, CARL F.
Portrait painter. Born in Sweden in 1858. Studied in Paris. He came to the United States in 1891, and for years was an instructor and teacher. Later he spent some time in Cleveland painting portraits. Died in NY in 1905.

VON SCHMIDT, HAROLD.
Painter, illustrator, lecturer and teacher. Born Alameda, CA, May 19, 1893. Pupil of Worth Ryder; Maynard Dixon; Harvey Dunn. Studied at Calif. College of Arts and Crafts, San Fran. Art Inst. Member: SI; GFLA. Illustrated "Song of Songs;" "Oscar Wilde - Letters and Papers;" illustrated for over 30 major magazines; painted posters during WWI & II; known for beautiful, realistic depiction of the West. Awarded Trustees' Gold Medal, Cowboy Hall of Fame and Western Heritage Ctr. Address in 1929, Evergreen Road, Westport, CT; summer, Taos, N.M.

VON SCHNEIDAU, C.
Painter and teacher. Born Smoland, Sweden, March 24, 1893. Pupil of J. Wellington Reynolds, K. A. Buehr, H. M. Walcott, C. W. Hawthorne, Richard Miller. Member: ASL of Chicago; Chicago Swedish AC; Calif. AC; Laguna Beach AA; Beachcombers Club, Provincetown; CA PS; CA WCS. Awards: First prize AIC, 1915; John Quincy Adams Traveling Scholarship, AIC, 1916; second prize for portrait, MN State Fair, 1916; first prize for portrait Swedish-American Exhibition, Chicago; 1917; gold medal, CA State Fair, 1919 second prize, CA State Fair, 1920; second prize, Swedish Club, Chicago, 1920; first prize for portraits, CA State Fair, 1923; hon. mentions, Exp. Park Museum, 1921, and Pomona, CA, Fair, 1925. Address in 1929, Care of Los Angeles Athletic Club; 920 South St. Andrews Pl., Los Angeles, CA.

VON SCHOLLEY, RUTH.
Painter, who exhibited at the Penna. Academy of the Fine Arts, Philadelphia, 1924. Address in 1926, 132 Riverway Boston, MA.

VON WESTRUM, MRS.
See Baldaugh, Anni.

VONDROUS, JOHN C.
Painter, illustrator, and etcher. Born Bohemia, Europe, Jan. 24, 1884. Pupil of NAD in NY under E. M. Ward, G. Maynard, F. C. Jones and James D. Smillie. Member: S. V. U. Manes and Graphic Arts Soc. "Hollar," of Prague, Czechoslovakia; Chicago SE; Calif. PM. Awards: Bronze medal for etching. P. P. Exp., San F., 1915; Logan prize, Chicago Society of Etchers, 1917, 1918 and 1919;

bronze medal, Sesqui-Centennial Exp. Phila., 1926. Work in: Modern Gallery of Prague; Art Inst., Chicago; NY Public Library; Fogg Museum, Cambridge, MA; Congressional Library, Washington, D.C.; Victoria and Albert Museum, and British Museum, London; Kupferstich Kabinett, Berlin. Address in 1929, Prague-Stresovice, Vorechovka, 486, Czecho-Slovakia; h. East Islip, L.I., NY.

VONNOH, BESSIE (ONAHOTEMA) POTTER. (Mrs. Robert W. Vonnon). Painter and sculptor. Born St. Louis, MO, Aug. 17, 1872. Pupil of AIC under Taft. Member: ANA 1906; NA 1921; NSS 1898; Port. P.; Allied AA. Awards: Second prize, Nashville Exp., 1897; bronze medal, Paris Exp., 1900; hon. mention, Pan-Am. Exp., Buffalo, 1901; gold medal, St. Louis Exp., 1904; silver medal, P.-P. Exp., San F., 1915; Watrous gold medal, NAD, 1921. Specialty, small groups. Work: "The Young Mother," and eleven statuettes, Metropolitan Museum, NY; eleven statuettes, Art Inst. of Chicago; thirteen statuettes, Brooklyn Inst. Museum; "Girl Dancing," Carnegie Inst., Pittsburgh; two statuettes, Corcoran Gal., Washington; two statuettes, Phila. Academy; two statuettes, Newark Museum; two statuettes, Cincinnati Museum; two statuettes, Detroit Inst.; Roosevelt Memorial Bird Fountain, Oyster Bay, L.I., NY. Died in 1955. Address in 1929, 33 West 67th St., NYC; summer, Lyme, CT.

VONNOH, ROBERT. Painter and teacher. Born Hartford, CT, Sept. 17, 1858. Pupil Mass. NAS in Boston; Julian Academy in Paris under Boulanger and Lefebvre. Member: ANA 1900, NA 1906; SAA 1892; NAC; NY. Arch. Lg.; Port. P. (assoc.); Lotos C.; Salma. C., 1904; Fellowship PAFA; Allied AA; Munich Secession (cor.); CT AFA; Gamut C. of Los A. (hon.); Paris AAA.; L. C. Tiffany Foundation; Lyme AA. Awards: Gold medal for portraiture, MA Charitable Mechanics Assn., Boston, 1884; hon. mention, Paris, Salon, 1889; bronze medal, Paris, Exp., 1889 and 1900; medal, Pan-Am. Exp., Buffalo, 1901; gold medal,

Charleston, 1902; Proctor portrait prize, NAD, 1904; gold medal, P.-P. Exp., San F., 1915; Charles Noel Flagg prize, CT. AFA, 1920; Richard S. Greenough prize, Newport. In collections of PAFA; (Phila.) College of Physicians; Buffalo Club, Buffalo, NY; Union Lg. Club, Phila.; Dept. of Justice, Wash., DC; Post Office Dept, Wash.; Brown Univ.; MA Hist. Soc., Boston; White House; MMA; Butler; Brooklyn; L.A. Mus.; Capitol, Hartford, CT; Ft. Worth, Texas, Mus.; Am. Philosophical Soc., Phila.; and Cleveland Mus. Died Dec. 28, 1933. Lived in NYC, CT, France.

VOORHEES, CLARK G(REENWOOD). Painter. Born New York, NY, May 29, 1871. Pupil Julian Academy in Paris. Member: Ct. AFA; Lyme AA; Century C., NY. Awards: Bronze medal, St. Louis Exp., 1904; third Hallgarten prize, NAD, 1906; Eaton purchase prize, Lyme AA, 1923. Address in 1929, Lyme, CT; winter, Somerset, Bermuda.

VORIS, MILLIE ROESGEN. Painter. Born Dudleytown, IN, Aug. 23, 1869. Pupil of L. C. Palmer; Jacob Cox; Chase; Lotta Griffin. Member: IN AA; Columbus AL; Chic. PC. Award: Hon. mention, Columbian Exposition, Chicago, 1893. Work: "Autumn in Brown County" and "Happy Youth," Art Museum, Berlin, Germany. Address in 1929, 737 Lafayette Ave., Columbus, IN.

VOS, HUBERT. Painter. Born Maastricht, Holland, Feb. 17, 1855. Pupil of Academy of Fine Arts in Brussels; Cormon in Paris. Awards: Gold medals Paris, Amsterdam, Munich, Dresden, Brussels, etc. Specialty, types of aboriginal races, portraits and interiors. Address in 1929, 15 West 67th St., NYC; Newport, RI.

VREELAND, ELIZABETH L. W. (Mrs. F. K.). Painter. Born in India, in 1896. Studied in New York, London, Paris and Norway. Address in 1926, 228 Orange Road, Montclair, NJ.

969

VREELAND, FRANCIS WILLIAM.
Painter. Born Seward, NE., March 10, 1879. Pupil of O. W. Beck, Vincent Nowottny, George Bridgman; Julian Academy in Paris. Member: Mural P.; NY. Arch. Lg.; CA AC: Okla. A. Lg.; ACS of So. Calif.; Art and Education Com., Los Angeles Chamber of Commerce; Ch. Art Comm., Hollywood C. of C. Address in 1929, Franmar, 2206 Live Oak Drive, Hollywood, CA.

VUCHINICH, VUK.
Painter, sculptor, and etcher. Born Niksic, Montenegro, Dec. 9, 1901. Pupil of C. C. Curran; Francis Jones; Mestrovic. Member: Kit Kat Club. Address in 1929, 5 West 16th Street, New York, NY.

VUILLEMENOT, FRED A.
Painter, sculptor, and illustrator. Born Ronchamp, France, Dec. 17, 1890. Pupil of Hector Lemaire, E. Deully, David, Benouard. Member: Alliance; Art Decoratif. Awards: Prix wicart de Lille and Prix du Ministre, France. Work: Silver plaquette, Cravereau Museum, France. Address in 1929, 2441 West Brook Drive, Toledo, OH.

VYSEKAL, EDOUARD A(NTONIN).
Painter. Born Kutna Hora, Czechoslovakia, March 17, 1890. Pupil of J. H. Vanderpoel; Harry M Walcott; S. Macdonald Wright. Member: Calif. AC; Chicago Palette and Chisel C.; Calif. WCS. Awards: Harrison prize, CA. PS, 1922; Ackerman prizes, Calif. AC, 1922, 1923, 1924; hon. mention, Western Painters A., 1924; bronze medal, Soc. Western Artists, 1925; gold medal, Calif. AC, 1926; hon. mention, Painters and Sculptors Soc., 1927; first prize, Calif. WCS, 1927; first prize, Pomona WCS, 1927; hon. mention, P and S of the West, 1927; first water color prize, Santa Cruz, 1927. Work: "The Conquest of the Desert," Barbara Worth Hotel, El Centro, California; "Korean," in Mission Inn, Riverside, CA. Instructor, Otis Art Inst., Los Angeles. Address in 1929, 1978 Lucile Ave., Los Angeles, CA.

VYSEKAL, LUVENA BUCHANAN.
(Mrs. E. A. Vysekal). Painter.

Born in Le Mars, IA. Pupil of S. Macdonald Wright, Harry W. Walcott and Ralph Clarkson. Member of California Art Club. Work: Portrait of Christian Hoffman, in State Historical Building, Topeka, Kansas. Address in 1926, 1945 Magnolia Ave., Los Angeles, CA.

WACHTEL, ELMER.
Painter. Born in Baltimore in 1864. Member: "Ten Painters," of Los Angeles, CA. Address in 1926, 315 West Ave., 43, Los Angeles, CA. Died in 1929.

WACHTEL, MARION KAVANAUGH.
(Mrs. Elmer Wachtel). Painter. Born Milwaukee, June 1875. Pupil of AIC and Chase. Member: Ten Painters of Los Angeles; NYWCC.; CA WCS; Pasadena P. Work: "Eucalypus at Evening," California State Building; "San Gabriel Canon," Friday Morning Club, Los Angeles; "San Jacinot Canon," Woman's Club, Hollywood, CA; Cedar Rapids (IA) Museum. Died in 1954. Address in 1929, 1155 Lida St., Pasadena, CA.

WACK, H(ENRY) W(ELLINGTON).
Painter, illustrator, writer and lecturer. Born Baltimore, MD, Dec. 21, 1875. Pupil of Leon Dabo, N. R. Brewer, H. Salem Hubbell, Frank Spenlove. Member: NY Lg. of Painters; Brooklyn SA: Salma C; PS; Salons of Amer.; AFA. Represented in Newark Art Museum; Whistler House, Lowell MA; Vanderpoel Collection, Chicago; Fort Worth (TX) Art Mus. Specialty landscapes. Died in 1954.

WACKERMAN, DOROTHY.
Painter. Born in Cleveland, OH, in 1899. Specialty, landscapes and mural paintings. Address in 1926, 1615 Fourth St., Minneapolis, MN. See Hutton.

WADDELL, MARTHA E.
Painter, writer, and teacher. Born Ontario, Canada, Feb. 27, 1904. Pupil of Butler AI. Member: NA Women PS; Cleveland Art Center; Columbus AL; Youngstown Alliance. Address in 1929, City Club, 5050 Wick Ave., h. 409 Second St., Scienceville, Youngstown, OH.

WADE, CAROLINE D.
Painter. Born Chicago, April 25, 1857. Pupil of AIC; Courtois in Paris. Member: AFA. Address in 1929, Cable Bldg., 57 E. Jackson Blvd., Chicago, IL; h. Elmhurst, IL.

WADE, J. H.
Portrait painter. From 1810 to 1823, he was painting in Cleveland, OH, and throughout the southern states.

WADSWORTH, ADELAIDE E.
Painter. Born in Boston in 1844. Pupil of Wm. M. Hunt, Frank Duveneck, John Twachtman, C. H. Woodbury and Arthur Dow. Member: Copley Society, Boston, 1894.

WADSWORTH, FRANK RUSSELL.
Painter. Born in Chicago, IL, in 1874. Pupil of AIC where he received several prizes. He was a member of the Chicago Society of Artists. Died in Madrid Spain on Oct. 9,1905, where he was painting with William Chase's summer class.

WADSWORTH, WEDWORTH.
Landscape painter and illustrator. Born in Buffalo, NY, in 1846. Member: NY Water Color Club; Salmagundi Club, 1890; Brooklyn Art Club. Author and illustrator of "Leaves from an Artist's Field Book;" illustrated "The Song of the Brook," "A Winter's Walk with Cowper," "Under the Greenwood Tree with Shakespeare," "Through Wood and Field with Tennyson." Address in 1926, Durham, CT. Died in Oct. 22, 1927, in Durham, CT.

WAGENHALS, KATHERINE H.
Painter. Born Ebensburg, PA, in 1883. Pupil of Art Department of Smith College; Art Students' League of New York; Academie Moderne in Paris. Award: Art Assoc. prize, Herron Art Inst., 1916. Work: "The Visitor," Herron Art Inst., Indianpolis. Address in 1926, 2124 Sunset Blvd., San Diego, CA.

WAGER-SMITH, CURTIS.
Portrait painter, illustrator, and writer. She was born in Binghamton, NY. Pupil of Emily Sartain, Alice Barber Stephens and Henry McCarter in Philadelphia. Member: Plastic C.; Soc. of Arts and Letters; City Parks Assoc.; Women's Press Assoc. Award: Silver medal, Dallas Exp., 1890. Illustrated "Rhymes for Wee Sweethearts," "Story Without an End" and other children's books.

971

WAGNER, BLANCHE COLLET.
Painter. Born Grenoble, France, Oct. 26, 1873. Pupil of Clinton Peters in NY; H. Gazan in Paris; Alfonso Grosso in Sevilla, Spain. Member: Carmel AA; Laguna Beach AA; West Coast AA; Springfield AA. Died in 1958.

WAGNER, FRANK HUGH.
Painter, sculptor, and illustrator. Born Milton, Wayne Co., IN, Jan. 4, 1870. Pupil of Freer, Vanderpoel and Von Salza. Member: Indiana AA; Richmond AA; Indiana Traveling AA; Alumni Asso. AIC; Hoosier Salon. Work: "Adoration of the Magi," St. Joseph's Chapel, West Pullman, IL; "Portrait C. W. Hargrave," and "Portrait of A. Kate Huron," Chapel Hall, Danville, IN.

WAGNER, FRED.
Painter and teacher. Born Valley Forge, PA, Dec. 20, 1864. Pupil of PAFA. Member: Phila. Sketch C.; Fellowship PAFA; Phila. WCC. Awards Fellowship prize, PAFA, 1914; hon. mention, Carnegie Inst., 1922. Work: "Addingham Winter," PA Acad; "Along Canal," Phila. Art Club; "Winter Evening," Reading Art Museum; "From the Elevated," Cleveland Mus. Instructor at Addingham Summer School of Outdoor Painting. Died in 1940.

WAGNER, MARY NORTH.
Miniature painter, draftsman, and lecturer. Born Milford, IN, Dec. 24, 1875. Pupil of John Vanderpoel, Charles Francis Browne, Mary S. West, Louis J. Millet, C. J. Mulligan and W. M. Chase. Member: IN. SA; Richmond AA; Hoosier Salon; IN. AA. Work: Four drawings for the "Second Brownie Book," by Mrs. Alpha B. Benson. Address in 1929, 1445 Plaisance Ct., Chicago, IL.

WAGNER, ROB.
Painter, illustrator, and writer. Born Detroit, MI, Aug. 2, 1872. Pupil of Julian Acad. in Paris. Member: CA AC. Awards: Silver medal, Alaska-Yukon Pacific Exp., Seattle, 1909; bronze medal, P.-P. Exp., San F., 1915. Writer and illustrator for Saturday Evening Post, Collier's, etc. Motion Picture director. Died in 1942.

WAGNER, ROSA.
Painter. Member: Wash. WCC. Address in 1929, Rockville, MD.

WAGNER, S. PETER.
Painter. Born in Maryland. Pupil of Corcoran School; ASL of NY and Paul Pascall. Member: Wash. WCC.; Pensacola AC; S. Wash. A; St. Petersburg AC; Wash. AC; AFA. Awards: Hon. mention, Tampa Art Inst., 1928.; first prize, Florida Fed. A.; 1928. Address in 1929, R.F.D. No., 3, Rockville, MD.

WAGNER, WILLIAM.
Seal-engraver residing in York, Penn., in 1820-35. He made a few crude engravings on copper; his plates included a portrait of Rubens and a view of York Springs. He was treasurer of the New York High School in 1835.

WAITE, CHARLES W.
Painter. Studied at Ohio Mechanics Inst. and under Duveneck. Member: Cincinnati AC. Address in 1929, 1355 Locust St., Walnut Hills, Cincinnati, OH.

WAITE, EMILY BURLING.
(Mrs. Arthur Williams Manchester). Painter. Born in Worcester July 12, 1887. Pupil of ASL of NY; Boston Art Museum School; studied in England, France, Belgium, Holland, Germany, Austria, Italy and Spain. Member: Concord AA.; Newport AA; North Shore AA; Wash. WCC; Wash. AC; Brooklyn SE; Chicago SE. Award: Silver medal P.-P. Expo., San Francisco, 1915. Portraits in Tufts College; Clark University; Episcopal Theological School, Cambridge; Worcester Art Mus. School.

WAKEMAN, R(OBERT) C(ARLTON).
Sculptor. Born Norwalk, Oct. 26, 1889. Pupil of Lee Lawrie; Yale School of Fine Arts. Member: NAC; Silvermine GA. Awards: First prize in competition, National Aeronautic Asso., Wash., D.C., first prize in competition, Brown and Bigelow medal. Work: " Dr. W. S. Lively," Southern School of Photography, McMinnville, TN; Dotha Stone Prineo Memorial, Norwalk Public Library; Com. John Rogers Memorial, US. Naval Acad.,

Annapolis, MD. Supervisor of carving, Bok Singing Tower Mountain Lake, Fla. Address in 1929, 1923 Lexington Ave., New York, NY; h. 82 Ward St., Norwalk, CT.

WAKEN, MABEL (J).
Painter. Born Chicago, March 13, 1879. Pupil of Charles Hawthorne, Hugh Breckenridge, Randall Davey. Member: Chicago AC; Wash. AC; AFA.

WALCOTT, BELLE HAVENS.
Painter. Born Havens Corners, Franklin Co., OH, Sept. 21, 1870. Pupil of ASL of NY.; W. M. Chase; Whistler; Colarossi Acad. Award: Third Hallgarten prize, NAD 1903. Represented in St. Louis Club. Address in 1929, 46 The Terrace, Rutherford, NJ; summer, Newark, OH.

WALCOTT, H(ARRY) M(ILLS).
Painter and teacher. Born Torringford, CT, July 16, 1870. Pupil of NAD in NY; Julian Acad. under Constant in Paris. Member: ANA 1903; SAA 1902. Awards: Hon. mention, Paris Salon, 1897; bronze medal, Pan-Am. Exp., Buffalo, 1901; Shaw Fund, SAA 1902; first Hallgarten prize, NAD 1903; Clarke prize, NAD 1904; hon. mention, CI Pittsburgh, 1904; silver medal, P. P. Exp., San F., 1915. Work: "Hare and Hounds," Richmond (IN) Art Assoc.; "The Contest," Erie (PA) Art Assoc.; portrait at Ohio State University, Columbus; portrait at Ohio Wesleyan U., Delaware; "School's Out," H. C. Frick Collection. Died in 1944.

WALDECK, C(ARL) G(USTAVE).
Painter. Born St. Charles, MO, March 13, 1866. Pupil of Constant and Laurens in Paris. Member: St. Louis AG; 2 x 4 Soc. Awards: Bronze medal, St. Louis Exp., 1904; silver medal, Lewis and Clarke Exp., Portland, OR, 1905; gold medal, Missouri State Exp., 1913; Betty Brown prize ($50), St. Louis AG, 1914; Fine Arts Prize, Society of Western Artists, Indianapolis, 1914; first prize, St. Louis AL, 1915; first prize for best group of paintings, St. Louis AG, 1923; second prize, City Art Museum, St. Louis 1923; Officier d'Academie, Paris, 1904. Address in 1929, 103 Edwin Ave., Kirkwood, MO.

WALDECK, NINA V.
Painter, illustrator, etcher, and teacher. Born Cleveland, Jan. 26, 1868. Pupil of Chase; Max Bohm; Julian Acad. in Paris. Member: Orlando AA; Cleveland Womans AC. Work: Portrait of Jane Elliot Snow, Woman's C., Cleveland; portrait of Bishop Schram, Ursaline Acad., Cleveland. Died in 1943. Address in 1929, 2258 Euclid Ave., Cleveland, OH; h. 1364 West Clifton Blvd., Lakewood, OH; winter, 2607 North Dixie Ave., Orlando, FL.

WALDEN, LIONEL.
Marine painter. Born Norwich, CT, May 22, 1861. Pupil of Carolus-Duran in Paris. Member: AFA; Nat. Inst. A.L.; Paris SAP; Societe Inter. de Peinture et Sculpture, Paris. Awards: Second class medal, Crystal Palace Exh., London; Hon. mention, Paris Salon, 1899; silver medal, Paris Exp., 1900; third class medal, Paris Salon, 1903; silver medal, St. Louis Exp., 1904; silver medal, P. P. Exp., San F., 1915. Chevalier of the Legion of Honor, France, 1910. Work: "Fishing in the Roadstead," Wilstach Collection, Phila.; "Cardiff Docks," Luxembourg Gallery, Paris. Represented in Cardiff Museum, Wales; Honolulu Academy of Arts, Honolulu, HI. Address in 1929, P. O. Box 2953 Honolulu, HI.

WALDO, RUTH M(ARTINDALE).
Painter. Born Bridgeport, CT, Jan. 18, 1890. Pupil of Jonas Lie, F. V. DuMond, Charles Hawthorne. Member: Plainfield AA. Address in 1929, 640 West Eighth Street, Plainfield, NJ.

WALDO, SAMUEL LOVETT.
Portrait painter. Born in Windham, CT. April 6, 1783. Studied with Stewart, a portrait painter, at Hartford, CT, and practiced at Charleston, SC. In 1806 he went to London and studied at the Royal Academy and with West and Copley. In 1809 he settled in NY, and, in 1812, William Jewett came to him as a pupil who later formed a partnership with him to paint portraits jointly. Represented at MMA by self portrait; his portrait of his wife Deliverance Mapes

Waldo, painted 1826; and life sketch of general Andrew Jackson, painted in 1817. Also painted George Washington Parke Custis, David C. Colden, William Steele, Joseph M. White and R. G. Livingston De Peyster. Died Feb. 16, 1861, in New York City.

WALDO & JEWETT, SAMUEL L. WALDO.
Born in 1783; died in 1861. Elected Associate Member of the National Academy. William Jewett was born in 1795 and died in 1874. They painted portraits together in NY City for eighteen consecutive years. Work owned by the city of NY, the Metropolitan Museum and a number of prominent Art Galleries in US.

WALDRON, ANNA A.
Painter, who exhibited water colors at the Penna. Acad. of the Fine Arts, Phila., 1925. Address in 1926, Bishop Place, New Brunswick, NJ. Died in 1954.

WALES, GEORGE CANNING.
Etcher and lithographer. Born Boston, Dec. 23, 1868. Pupil of Paxton. Member: Brooklyn SE; Boston GA; AFA. Etchings in Library of Congress and the US National Museum, Wash., DC; New York Public Library; Peabody Museum, Salem; Old Dartmouth Historical Society; British Museum, London; Victoria and Albert Museum, London; Marine Museum, Boston; Museum at Stavanger, Norway. Died in 1940. Address in 1929, 1064 Beacon St., Brookline, MA.

WALES, JAMES ALBERT.
Caricaturist and engraver. Born in 1852; died in 1886. After leaving school he studied with a wood-engraver in Toledo, but being talented at portraiture he began drawing for newspapers; some of his best work appeared in Puck and Judge. He was a founder and chief cartoonist of the latter periodical.

WALES, ORLANDO G.
Painter. Born Philadelphia, PA. Pupil of Wm. M. Chase and Alphonse Mucha. Member: Salma. C., 1908. Address in 1929, 832 Hamilton St., Allentown, PA.

WALES, SUSAN M. L.
Landscape painter. Born in Boston, MA, in 1839. Pupil of Boston Museum School; Vincente Poveda in Rome; under Bloomers in Holland. Member of Boston Water Color Club. Address in 1926, 342 Marlboro St., Boston, MA.

WALKER, A(LANSON) B(URTON).
Illustrator. Born Binghamton, NY, Nov. 19, 1878. Pupil of Kenyon Cox, Bryson Burroughs, Charles Curran, F. V. Du Mond. Member: SI. Illustrations and humorous drawings for Life, Judge, Harper's Weekly, Harpers Bazaar, Scribner's, Century, Harper's Magazine, The American Golfer, St. Nicholas, etc. Died in 1947. Address in 1929, The Playhouse; h. 225 South Main St., New Canaan, CT; summer, Morningside, Milford, CT.

WALKER, CHARLES ALVAH.
Painter, engraver and etcher. Born in 1848, in London, New Hampshire. He engraved on wood and steel, his plate after Daubigny being exhibited at the Paris Salon. Later he turned to painting in water color and oil. He exhibited in the Boston Club, and served as its vice-president. He died April 11, 1920, in Brookline, MA.

WALKER, DUGALD STEWART.
Illustrator, painter, and lecturer. Born Richmond, VA. Studied under Anne Fletcher and Harriotte Taliaferro Montague in Richmond; Graham Cootes at Summer School of University of Virginia; at the NY School of Art; ASL of NY. Work: Illustrated "Hans Anderson's Fairy Tales," "Stories for Pictures," "The Gentlest Giant," etc. Died in 1937. Address in 1929, 304 Carnegie Hall, New York, NY.

WALKER, F. R.
Painter. Member: Cleveland SA. Address in 1929, 1900 Euclid Beach Park, Cleveland, OH.

WALKER, FERDINAND GRAHAM.
Painter. Born in Mitchell, IN, in 1859. Pupil of Dagnan-Bouveret, Puvis de Chavannes, Blanche and Merson in Paris. Member: Society of Indiana Artists; Louisville Artists' Assoc.; Chicago Arts and

Crafts. Portraits in Kentucky at Lexington; Berea College; Agricultural College of Michigan; Lincoln Inst, Simpsonville, KY; Kentucky State Collection at Frankfort; State House, Indianapolis, IN; Public Library, Jefferson Davis Memorial, New Albany, IN, and in other places; also represented by landscapes in the public galleries at New Albany, IN, and Lexington, KY, and by two murals in St. Peter's Church, Louisville, KY. Address in 1926, 308 Commercial Building, Louisville, KY. Died June 1, 1927, in New Albany, IN.

WALKER, GEORGE W.
Painter. Member: Cleveland SA. Address in 1929, Euclid Beach Park, Cleveland, OH.

WALKER, HAROLD E.
Painter. Born Scotch Ridge, OH, Nov. 6, 1890. Pupil of Almon Whiting, Karl Kappes, Frederick Trautman, Wilder M. Darling, Ross Moffett. Member: Toledo Artklan; Beachcombers. Awards: First prize, 1922, and hon. mention, 1923, Toledo Museum of Art. Work: "Overhauling the Nets," permanent Collection, John H. Vanderpoel Art Associaton, Chicago. Address in 1926, Madison Court, Toledo, OH.

WALKER, HENRY OLIVER.
Painter. Born in Boston in 1843. He began in commercial pursuits in that city, but later turned to art, and went to Paris in the early eighties to become pupil of M. Bonnat. Returning to the US he took a studio in Boston, and held a very successful exhibition. A few years later he came to NY and was known to the art public. Member of SSA and NA. At exhibition at NA in 1895 he was awarded Clarke prize for "A Morning Vision." In 1894 at SSA he earned Shaw Fund prize for "The Singers." These compositions, like "The Boy and the Muse," another celebrated work, show graceful, accurate drawing, refined color quality, and beauty of ensemble. Also known for important achievements in mural painting. Executed series of composition and single figures illustrative of lyric poetry for the Congressional

Library at Washington, and an important piece of work for the Appellate Court building, NY. Received medal and diploma for work exhibited at the World's Fair, Chicago, 1893. Studio in NY. Address in 1926, Belmont, MA. Died Jan. 14, 1929 in Belmont.

WALKER, HOBART A(LEXANDER).
Painter and architect. Born Brooklyn, NY, Nov. 1, 1869. Member: AIA; NJ Soc. Arch. Address in 1929, 336 Main St., East Orange, NJ; h. Maplewood, NJ.

WALKER, HORATIO.
Painter. Born Listowel, Ont. Canada, 1858; came to NY in 1885. Member: ANA 1890, NA 1891; SAA 1887; Nat. Inst. AL; Royal Inst. of Painters in Water Colors, England; AWCS; Salma. C.; A. Fund S.; A. Aid S.; Rochester AC.; NAC. Awards: Gold medal, competitive exhibition at American Art Galleries, NY, 1887; Evans prize, AWCS, 1888; bronze medal, Paris Exp., 1889; gold medal and diploma, Columbian Exp., Chicago, 1893; gold medal, Pan Am Exp., Buffalo, 1901; gold medal, Charleston Exp., 1902; gold medal for oil and gold medal for water colors, St. Louis Exp., 1904; gold medal of honor, PAFA 1906; first prize, Worcester, 1907; gold medal, P. P. Exp., San. F. 1915; Hudnut prize, AWCS, 1920. Work: "The Harrower Morning," "The Harrower" and "The Sheepfold," Metropolitan Museum, NY; "Ave Maria," Corcoran Gallery, Washington; "The Wood Cutter" and "Milking Evening" City Mus., St. Louis; "Sheep Shearing," Albright Art Gallery, Buffalo; "Sheepyard Moonlight," National Gallery, Washington; "Moonrise: A Canadian Pastoral," Carnegie Inst., Pittsburgh. Died in 1938. Address in 1929, Ile d'Orleans, Quebec, Canada; care of Montross Gallery, 26 East 56th Street, New York, NY.

WALKER, JAMES.
Painter. Born in England, June 3, 1819. He was brought to NYC as a child, where he resided for most of his life. When young he resided one winter in New Orleans. At the outbreak of the Mexican War he was resident of the city of Mexico,

where he remained hidden for six weeks after the Mexican commander had issued an edict banishing all Americans. Afterwards escaping to the lines of the American Army, he served as an interpreter. Remained during occupation of the Mexican capital by US. After eight years returned to NY (in 1848). Visited South America and established studio in NY in 1850. In 1857-58 he was in Washington, and again for a brief period in 1883. In 1884 he moved to San Francisco, CA, to execute a large French battle picture. Work was principally large battle painting. Most prominent of these are the "Battle of Chapultepec," "Battle of Lookout Mountain" and "Battle of Gettysburg." The commision for the "Battle of Lookout Mountain" was given by Gen. Hooker. His painting "The Battle of Chapultepec" is in the Capitol in Washington, D.C. Died Aug. 29, 1889 in Watsonville, CA.

WALKER, MARIAN D. BAUSMAN.
(Mrs. Otis L. Walker). Sculptor. Born Minneapolis, MN, June 21, 1889. Studied in Minneapolis. Member: Minneapolis SFA. Award: Hon. mention, MN. State Art Soc., 1914. Address in 1929, Casper, WY.

WALKER, NELLIE V(ERNE).
Sculptor. Born Red Oak, IA, Dec. 8, 1874. Pupil of AIC under Lorado Taft. Member: NSS 1911; Chicago SA; Soc. W. Sc.; Chicago PS. Awards: First Chicago Municipal Art League prize, 1907; second Grower prize, AIC 1908; Shaffer prize, AIC 1911. Work: "Stratton Memorial," Colorado Springs, CO; portrait statue of "Senator Harlan," US Capitol, Washington; "Her Son," ideal group, Art Inst. of Chicago; "Chief Keokuk," Keokuk, IA; Sen. Isaac Stephenson, monument, Marmetter, Wisc.; memorial groups at Cadillac, MI; two panels in library, State College, Ames, Iowa. Address in 1929, The Midway Studios, 6016 Ellis Ave., Chicago, IL.

WALKER, SOPHIA A.
Painter, sculptor, and etcher. Born in Rockland, MA, in 1855. Pupil of Lefebvre in Paris; under Mowbray and Chase in NY. Member: of National Art Club. Painted "Portrait of E. B. Woodward," State Normal School, Bridgewater, MA. Address in 1926, 70 West 49th St., New York, NY.

WALKER, WILLIAM H(ENRY).
Cartoonist, portrait and landscape painter. Born Pittston, PA, Feb. 13, 1871. Pupil of ASL of NY. Member: SI 1909; GFLA; AFA. Contributor to Life since 1898. Specialty, political subjects. Died in 1938.

WALKINSHAW, JEANIE WALTER.
Painter. Born Baltimore, MD. Pupil of Charcoal C., Baltimore; Lucien Simon, Rene Menard in Paris; Robert Henri in New York. Member: NA Women PS. Specialty, portraits. Address in 1929, 936 12th Ave., North, Seattle, Wash.; care Miss Valerie Walter, 17 East 59th St., New York, NY.

WALKLEY, DAVID B.
Painter. Born in Rome, OH, in 1849. Pupil of Julien Academy; Penna. Acad. of Fine Arts. Member of Salmagundi Club, 1903, New York. Address in 1926, Rock Creek, OH.

WALKOWITZ, ABRAHAM.
Painter and etcher. Born Tuiemen, Siberia, Russia, March 28, 1880. Pupil of NAD under Ward, Maynard and F. C. Jones in New York; Julian Academy in Paris under Laurens. Member: Paris AAA. Died in 1965.

WALL, A. BRYAN.
Painter. Born Allegheny City, PA. Pupil of his father, A. Wall. Member: AC Phila. Award: Gold medal, AAS 1907. Died in 1937. Address in 1929, 814 Arch St., Pittsburgh, PA.

WALL, WILLIAM ALLEN.
Painter. Born May 19, 1801 in new Bedford, MA. He was apprenticed to a watchmaker, but early turned his attention to painting. Studied with Thomas Sully. Went to Europe in 1831. Returned to New Bedford in 1833. About 1840 copied Stuart's "Landsdowne Washington;" his portrait of N. P. Willis, painted in Italy, is in the New York Historical Society. He died

in New Bedford, MA, Sept 6, 1885. Several of his portraits are owned by Dartmouth College, Hanover, NH.

WALL, WILLIAM G.
Painter. Born in Scotland in 1792. He painted landscapes in NY in 1818 where he began his career as an artist, painting views of the Hudson River. He was elected a member of the National Academy, New York, in 1826. Died after 1864.

WALLACE, FREDERICK E(LLWOOD).
Painter. Born Haverhill, MA, Oct. 19, 1893. Pupil of Joseph DeCamp. Member: Boston GA. Died in 1958. Address in 1929, Fenway Studios, 30 Ipswich St., Boston, MA.

WALLACE, LUCY.
Landscape painter, and craftsman. Born Montclair, NJ, Nov. 13, 1884. Pupil of Kenneth Hayes Miller; J. R. Koopman. Member: NYSC; Boston SAC. Address in 1929, Colonial Studio Apts., 39 West 67th St., New York, NY; summer, Shoreham, LI, NY.

WALLER, FRANK.
Painter. Born in NY, in 1842. Formerly engaged as architect; became a painter after 1903. Fellow of Academy of Design, New York; president of Art Students' League of NY, which he incorporated; honorable sec. Egypt Exploration Society; honorable life fellow, Metropolitan Museum of Art. Wrote: "Report on Art Schools," 1879; also first report Art Students' League, 1886. Died March 9, 1923, in Morristown, NJ.

WALLEY, ABIGAIL B.
Painter. Born Boston. Pupil of Sanderson, Langerfeldt, Bensa and Rice. Member: Copley S; AFA. Specialty, landscapes and gardens in watercolors and pastels. Address in 1929, Hampton Court, 1223 Beacon St., Brookline, MA.

WALSH, ELIZABETH M.
Painter. Born in Lowell, MA. Pupil of Boston Museum of Fine Arts. Member of Concord Art Association. Address in 1926, 419 Andover St., Lowell, MA.

WALTER, ADAM B.
Engraver. Born in Philadelphia, in 1820; died there Oct. 14, 1875. A pupil of Thomas B. Welch, he was associated with Welch in the engraving business until 1848. An excellent engraver of portraits, chiefly executed in mezzotint.

WALTER, CHRISTIAN J.
Landscape painter and craftsman. Born Pittsburgh, PA, Feb. 11, 1872. Member: Associated Artists of Pittsburgh (pres.). Awards: 3rd prize, 1913, Roland prize ($200), 1915, Art Soc. prize ($100), 1921, Drawing and print prize, Associated Artists of Pittsburgh, 1927. Represented in the St. Petersburg, Fla., permanent collection. Specialty, stained glass. Died in 1938. Address in 1929, 5th Ave., Arcade Bldg., Pittsburgh, PA.; summer, Ligonier, PA.

WALTER, EDGAR.
Sculptor. Born in San Francisco, CA, in 1877. Studied at the Mark Hopkins Institute of Art, San Francisco, and later studied in Paris. Address in 1926, 1803 Franklin St., San Francisco, CA. Died in 1938.

WALTER, JEANIE.
See Walkinshaw, Jeanie Walter.

WALTER, JOSEPH.
Painter. Born Galtuer, Austria, July 5, 1865. Pupil of Loefftz, S. Herterich, J. Hackl in Munich; Gripenkerl in Vienna. Work: Murals, Catholic Church, Madison, Nebr.; six murals, Peter and Paul's Church, Petersburg, IA; three murals, St. Joseph's Church, Peoria, IL; mural, St. Patrick Church, Dubuque, Iowa; four paintings in Church, Sherrills, Iowa. Address in 1929, 2625 Carroll St., Dubuque, IA.

WALTER, MARTHA.
Painter. Born Philadelphia, PA. Pupil of PAFA; Julian Acad. in Paris. Member: Fellowship PAFA. Awards: Cresson scholarship, PAFA, 1903; Mary Smith prize, PAFA, 1909; prize, N. A. Women PS., 1915; gold medal, fellowship PAFA, 1923. Work: "Anne," Toledo Museum; "Dorothy Lee Bell," PA Academy of

the Fine Arts; "Umbrellas on the Beach," Norfolk Society of Art; "Baby," Fellowship, PA Acad. of the Fine Arts; "Beach Scene," Art Inst., Milwaukee, Wis.; "La Cape Ecossaise," Luxembourg. Specialty, figures and portraits. Address in 1929, care of Fifth Avenue Bank, New York, NY.

WALTER, VALERIE HARRISSE.
Sculptor. Born Baltimore, MD. Pupil of Ephriam Keyser; Augustus Lukeman; Mrs. Lefebvre's School. Address in 1929, 17 East 59th St., New York, NY; h. and summer, Brightside and Bellona Aves., Woodbrook, Baltimore, MD.

WALTERS, EMILE.
Painter. Born Winnipeg, Canada, Jan. 30, 1893. Pupil of AIC, PAFA, and Tiffany Foundation. Member: Salma. C.; ASL of Chicago; Fellowship PAFA; Pitts. AA; Tiffany Foundation AG; Phila. AC. Awards: Goodwin prize, Chicago Art Inst., 1918, 1919, 1921; municipal prize, Chicago, 1918; Tiffany Foundation Scholarship ($2,000); Murphy Memorial prize, NAD, 1924; first hon. mention, Nat'l Art Exh., Springville, Utah, 1926; second prize, Springville, 1917. Work: "Springtime Blossoms," State College (PA) Museum; "Early Spring," Hundred Friends of Art, Pittsburgh; "Birches in Winter," Houston (TX) Museum of Fine Art; four canvases, Nat. Museum of Iceland; "Harvest Time in the Nittany Valley," Centre Hills Country Club, State College, PA; "Roosevelt's Haunts," Nat'l Gallery of Art, Washington, D.C.; "Blossom Time," Brooklyn Museum; "Spring Blossoms," Los Angeles Mus.; "Late Winter," Fogg Museum, Harvard U., Cambridge; "Winter Haze," Mus. of Rouen, France; "Depth of Winter," Heckscher Park Art Mus., Huntington, LI; "February Thaw," Art Inst., Altoona, PA; "Day in May," Art Club of Philadelphia; "The Passing Storm," Uniontown Friends of Art; "Springfield," Canadian Club of NY; "Morning Light," University of Saskatchewan, Canada; "The Village in Spring," Mus. of Fine Arts, Edmonton, Can.; "Winter-Apple Blossoms," Nutana Collegiate Inst., Saskatoon, CN.

Instructor at summer session of Penn. State College, State College, PA. Address in 1929, 47 Fifth Ave., New York, NY.

WALTERS, JOHN.
Miniature painter and engraver who flourished about 1784, in Philadelphia.

WALTHER, CHARLES H.
Painter and teacher. Born Baltimore, MD, Feb. 10, 1879. Pupil of Maryland Inst.; Blanche, Simon, Cottet and Laurens in Paris. Member: Charcoal C.; Municipal AS. Died in 1937. Address in 1929, 4000 Pimlico Road, Baltimore, MD.

WALTMAN, HARRY FRANKLIN.
Painter. Born in OH, April 16, 1871. Pupil of Constant and Laurens in Paris. Member: ANA, 1917; Salma. C., 1897; Allied AA; NAC. Awards: Isidor prize, Salma. C., 1916; prize, NAC, 1927. Work: "Vermont Woods in Winter," Butler Art Inst., Youngstown, OH. Died in 1951. Address in 1929, Dover Plains, NY.

WALTON, FLORENCE L.
Painter. Born in East Orange, NJ, in 1889. Pupil of George Bellows. Address in 1926, 18 East 8th St., New York, NY.

WAMALINK, H. J.
Painter. Member: Cleveland SA. Address in 1929, 2630 Payne Ave., Cleveland, OH.

WAMSLEY, FRANK C.
Sculptor. Born Locust Hill, MO, Sept. 12, 1879. Pupil of C. J. Mulligan; Albin Polasek; AIC; Beaux Arts Inst. of Design; Salon Borglum; John Gregory; Edward McCarten. Member: Artland C. (life); PS of Los Angeles. Work: "Meditation," Hackley Art Gallery, Muskegon, MI; Urn At Hollywood Crematory; Douglas Memorial Tablet, Covina, CA.

WANDS, ALFRED J(AMES).
Painter, illustrator, and teacher. Born Cleveland, Feb., 19, 1902. Pupil of Cleveland School of Art; F. N. Wilcox; H. G. Keller: John Huntington Inst.; studied in Europe. Member: Clev. SA; Clev.

A. Center; Ohio WCS; Balto. WCC. Awards: Prize for painting, 1923; prize for drawing, 1926, Cleveland Mus.; Chaloner prize, NY, 1926; first prize in lithograph, second prize, figure composition, hon. mention in landscape and in drawing, Clev. Mus. of Art, 1929. Work: "The Last Load," and "Seated Nude," Cleveland Museum of Art; "Alttenha Valley," Cleveland Public School. Address in 1929, 9337 Amesbury Ave., Cleveland, OH.

WARD, EDGAR MELVILLE.
Painter, genre and landscape. Born in Ohio, Feb. 24, 1839. Studied in the National Acad. in 1870 and in Paris, 1872-78. His best known paintings were "Paternal Pride, "Lace Makers," and "Brittany Washer Women," which was shown at the Paris Salon, 1876, and in the Phila. Centennial. His studio was in NY. Elected member of the National Academy in 1915. He died May 15, 1915 in NYC.

WARD, EDMUND F.
Painter and illustrator. Born in White Plains, NY, in 1892. Pupil of Edward Dufner, George Bridgman and Thomas Fogarty. Member of Guild of Free Lance Artists. Made illus. for Saturday Evening Post, Pictorial Review, Red Book, Woman's Home Companion. Address in 1926, 33½ Court St., White Plains, NY.

WARD, ELSIE.
Sculptor. Pupil of Saint Gaudens; practiced her profession in Denver, CO.

WARD, IRVING.
Portrait and landscape painter. Born in 1867. Member of Baltimore Charcoal Club. He died at his home in Baltimore, MD, April 17, 1924.

WARD, J. STEPHEN.
Painter. Born St. Joseph, MO, April, 1876. Pupil of Nicholas Brewer, Maurice Braun. Member: CA AC; Artland C; Los Angeles PS; Glendale AA. Awards: Hon. mention, State Fair, Phoenix, Ariz., 1923; hon, mention, Witte Memorial Museum, San Antonio, Texas., 1929. Work: "Retreating Snow," Fairfax High School,

Hollywood, CA; "Oak Creek Canyon, Arizona" and "Blue Bonnet," Clubb Collection, Kaw City, Okla. Address in 1929, 1364 Garfield, Glendale, CA; summer, June Lake, CA.

WARD, JOHN QUINCY ADAMS.
Sculptor. Born June 29, 1830, near Urbana, OH. Showed great talent. Studied with Henry K. Brown in Brooklyn, NY, remaining in his studio for six years. In 1857 made his first sketch for "The Indian Hunter," now in Central Park, NY. In 1861 opened his studio in NY. Elected Associate Member of NAD in 1862, an Academician the following year, president in 1874. First president of NSS. In 1866 he executed the group of "The Good Samaritan," now in Boston. In the field of portrait statuary one of the masters of his day. His statue of Henry W. Beecher is in Brooklyn; of Commodore Oliver H. Perry in Newport, RI, and of Israel Putnam at Hartford, CT. Other noted statues were of Horace Greeley, Lafayette, President Garfield and the equestrian statue of General Thomas at Washington, D.C. Died May, 1910 in NYC.

WARD, NINA B.
Painter. Born in Rome, GA. Pupil of St. Louis School of Fine Arts; NY School of Art, and Penna. Acad. of Fine Arts. Member of Fellowship, Penna. Acad. of Fine Arts. Awards: Cresson European scholarship, Penna. Academy of Fine Arts, 1908 and 1911; first Toppan prize, Penna. Acad. of Fine Arts, 1912; Mary Smith prize, Penna. Acad. of Fine Arts, 1914. Address in 1926, 1515 Arch. St., Phila. PA.

WARD, WINIFRED.
Sculptor. Born in Clevaland, OH, in 1889. Pupil of Charles Grafly. Member: Fellowship, Penna. Acad. of Fine Arts; Plastic Club; National Association of Women Painters and Sculptors; Society of Independent Artists. Address in 1926, 2006 Mt. Vernon St., Philadelphia, PA.

WARE, EDWARD THOMPSON JR.
Painter. Address in 1926, 127 East
Third St., Cincinnati, OH.

WARE, ELLEN PAINE.
(Mrs. J. W. Ware). Painter. Born
Jacksonport, AR, Nov. 12, 1859.
Pupil of St. Louis School of Art;
Cincinnati School of Design.
Member: Memphis AA. Awards:
Prizes Memphis AA 1920 and 1921.
Address in 1929, Route 4, Station
G. Memphis, TN.

WAREHAM, JOHN HAMILTON DEE.
Painter and craftsman. Born Grand
Ledge, MI. Pupil of Duveneck and
Meakin. Member: Cincinnati
Municipal AS. Award: Bronze
medal, St. Louis Exp., 1904.
Decorations in Fort Pitt Hotel,
Pittsburgh; Seelbach Hotel,
Louisville, Hotel Sinton,
Cincinnati, Poli's Theatre,
Wash., DC. Address in 1929,
Rookwood Pottery Co.; h. 3329
Morrison Ave., Clifton, Cin., OH.

WARHANIK, ELIZABETH C.
(Mrs. C. A. Warhanik). Painter.
Born Philadelphia, PA, Feb. 29,
1880. Pupil of Paul Gustin, Edgar
Forkner. Member: Seattle FAS.
Award: Third prize for oil,
Northwest Artists, Seattle, 1917.
Address in 1929, 6052 Fifth Ave.,
N. W., Seattle, WA.

WARING, LELIA.
Miniature painter. Member: SSAL;
Charleston EC; AFA. Address in
1929, 25 Tradd St., 2 Atlantic St.,
Charleston, SC.

WARNACUT, CREWES.
Painter and etcher. Born Osman,
IL, June 1, 1900. Pupil of William
Forsyth, Charles Hawthorne.
Member: All-Ill. SFA; Hoosier
Salon; Lg. of No. Ind. Awards:
First prizes, All Ill. SFA and
League of Northern Indiana, 1929.
Address in 1929, 1505 Madison St.,
Chicago, IL; h. Inwood, IN.

WARNEKE, HEINZ.
Sculptor. Born Bremen, Germany,
June 30, 1895. Pupil of Acad. of
Fine Arts in Berlin. Awards:
First prize for sculpture, St.
Louis AG, 1924; first prize, St.

Louis AG, 1925. Work: Eagle
facade, Masonic Temple, Fort Scott,
Kansas; memorial tablet, Medical
Society, St. Louis; memorial
tablet, YMCA Building, St. Louis.
Address in 1929, 48 East 78th St.,
New York, NY; h. 9 rue de
Chatillon, Paris XIV, France.

WARNER, C. J.
The only plate of this man known is
a fairly well-executed stipple
portrait of Gen. Anthony Wayne. It
was published by C. Smith, NY,
1796, and probably appeared in "The
Monthly Military Repository,"
published by Smith in the year.

WARNER, EVERETT.
Landscape painter, and etcher.
Born Vinton, IA, July 16, 1877.
Pupil of ASL in Wash. and NY;
Julian Acad. in Paris. Member:
ANA 1913; NY WCC; AWSC; NAC (life);
Wash. WCC; CT AFA; S. Wash. A.;
Salma. C. 1909; Paris AAA. Awards:
First Corcoran prize, Wash. WCC,
1902; Sesnan medal, PAFA, 1908;
silver medal, Buenos Aires Exp.,
1910; second Hallgarten prize, NAD,
1912; Evans prize, Salma C., 1913;
bronze medal, S. Wash. A., 1913;
Vezin prize, Salma C., 1914; silver
medal for painting and bronze medal
for etching, P. P. Exp., San F.,
1915; hon. mention, CT AFA., 1917;
hon. mention, AIC., 1919; Museum
Purchase prize, Lyme AA, 1924.
Work: "Broadway on a Rainy
Evening," Corcoran Gallery,
Washington; "A February Day," PA
Acad. Phila.; "Amsterdam," Erie
(PA) Public Library; "Quebec," PA
Acad. of the Fine Arts; "December
Hillside," Museum of Fine Arts,
Syracuse, NY; "Along the River
Front, NY," and six etchings,
Toledo Art Museum; "The Frozen
Brook," RI. School of Design,
Providence; "A Mountain Village,
Tyrol," City Art Museum, St. Louis;
"The Guardian Elm," National Arts
Club, New York; "Snowfall in the
Woods, Art Inst. of Chicago;
"Falling Snow," Gibbes Art Gallery,
Charleston, SC; "Autumn Afternoon,"
Okalahoma Art League, Oklahoma
City. Died in 1963. Address in
1929, Carnegie Inst. of Tech.,
Pittsburgh, PA.

WARNER, GEORGE D.
Engraver. This name is signed to a botanical plate published in the New York Magazine for Dec., 1791. The book-plate of George Warner is signed "Warner sculpt," and is probably the work of this engraver.

WARNER, LILY G.
Painter and illustrator. Born in Hartford, CT. Painted flower-pieces and illustrated for St. Nicholas Magazine.

WARNER, MARGARET.
Illustrator and writer. Born Mabbettsville, NY, Dec. 5, 1892. Pupil of Corcoran School of Art; Abbott School of Art, Washington, D.C.; NY School of Fine and Applied Art; Berkshire Summer School of Art. Address in 1929, 1624 Eye St., N.W.; h. 3409 Newark St., N. W. Washington, DC.

WARNER, MARY LORING.
Painter. Born Sheffield, MA, Sept. 2, 1860. Pupil of Frank de Haven, Charles Warren Eaton. Member: Ct. AFA.; New Haven PCC. Address in 1929, 344 Washington St., Middletown, CT.

WARNER, NELL WALKER.
Painter. Born Nebraska, April 1, 1891. Pupil of Paul Lauritz; Los Angeles School of Art and Design. Member: Calif. AC; Glendale AA; West Coast A; Laguna Beach AA; Artland C. Awards: Four gold and silver medals, CA. Eisteddfod, 1925; first prize, Southern Calif. Fair, 1925. Address in 1929, 2436 Orange Ave., La Crecenta, CA.

WARNER, OLIN LEVI.
Sculptor. Born in Suffield, CT, in 1844. Studied in Paris. Returned to US and opened his studio in NY. Elected an Associate of the Nat. Acad. in 1888. His portrait busts of Gov. Wm. A. Buckingham and Wm. Lloyd Garrison and his statuettes of "Twilight" and the "Dancing Faun" were well known. Member of the Society of American Artists. Died in 1896.

WARNER, WILLIAM.
Engraver. Born in Phialdelphia about 1813; died there in 1848. Warner was a portrait-painter and a self taught engraver in mezzotint. He made comparatively few plates, but his large plates are fine examples of mezzotint work.

WARNICKE, JOHN G.
Engraver. In 1811-14 and again in 1818 Warnicke was engraving in Philadelphia. The only portrait known is that of Franklin. Died Dec. 29, 1818.

WARR, JOHN.
Engraver. Born c. 1798 in Scotland. There were two men of this name in Philadelphia in 1821-45 working as "general engraver." The older man was seemingly engraving in 1821-28 and the younger man, John Warr, Jr., was engraving in 1825-45. Their work consisted chiefly of vignettes, business-cards, etc., but these were well engraved.

WARR, W. W.
Engraver. This W. W. Warr was a script engraver working in Philadelphia about 1830. He usually signed plates in connection with John Warr as "Engraved by J. & W. W. Warr."

WARREN, A. W.
Marine painter. Born on a farm in Coventry, NY. He studied under T. H. Matteson and in 1863 was elected an Associate Member of the National School of Design. The Brooklyn Institute owns his "Rocky Shore, Mt. Desert." Died in 1873.

WARREN, ASA COOLIDGE.
Engraver. Born March 25, 1819, in Boston, MA. Son of Asa Warren, a portrait and miniature painter. Was apprenticed in 1833 to Bigelow Brothers, jewelers, of Boston. Showing an inclination toward engraving, he was placed with the Boston engraver George G. Smith. At the end of apprenticeship Warren spent another year with Joseph Andrews and he became a reputable line-engraver of vignettes and book illustrations. Employed by New England Bank Note Co. and the Boston publishers, Ticknor & Fields. Abandoned engraving for about five years, and in this interval he drew upon wood for other engravers. In 1863 Mr. Warren moved to NY and engraved for

the Continental Bank Note Co. and book publishers. In June, 1899, he lost the sight of one eye and was compelled to abandon his profession. He occupied his later years in painting. Died Nov. 22, 1904, in NYC.

WARREN, ASA.
Portrait and miniature painter, who flourished about 1846-47 in Boston.

WARREN, ELISABETH B(OARDMAN).
(Mrs. Tod Lindenmuth). Illustrator and etcher. Born Bridgeport, CT, Aug. 28, 1886. Pupil of Vesper L. George, W. H. W. Bicknell. Member: Provincetown AA; Copley S. Illustrated school readers for Ginn & Co., Silver, Burdett & Co.; story books for Lothrop, Lea and Shepard, Bobbs Merrill, and the Pilgrim Press. Specialty, etchings and dry points. Address in 1929, 56 Commericial St., Provincetown, MA.

WARREN, FERDINAND.
Painter. Born, Independence, MO, Aug. 1, 1899. Member: Kansas City SA; L. C. Tiffany AG. Award: Bronze medal, Kansas City AI, 1923; bronze medal for illustrations, Grand Cen. School of Art, 1928. Address in 1929, 10 Hooga Studios, 51 Poplar St., Brooklyn, NY.

WARREN, HAROLD B(ROADFIELD).
Landscape painter, illustrator, and craftsman. Born Manchester, England, Oct. 16, 1859. Pupil of Charles H. Moore and Charels Eliot Norton at Harvard Univ. Member: Copley S. 1891; Boston S. Arch. (Assoc.); Boston SECP; AFA; Boston SAC (Master). Specialty, water color. Work: "The Parthenon," "The Propylaea," "Aegina from the Parthenon" and "Northwest Corner of the Parthenon," Boston Museum of Fine Arts; "The Parathenon," Cleveland Art Mus. Instructor in water color, School of Architecture, Harvard University. Died in 1934. Address in 1929, 8 Craigie Circle, Cambridge, MA.

WARREN, HENRY.
Painter. Born C. 1793. In the exhibition held in 1847 at the Penn. Acad. of the Fine Arts in Philadelphia, "View on the Delaware near Trenton Bridge" is noted as for sale by the artist, "H. Warren." According to an advertisement appearing in the Virginia Gazette for the year 1769, "Henry Warren, Limner who is now at Williamsburg has had the satsifaction of pleasing most gentlemen who have employed him."

WARRICK, META VAUX.
(Mrs. Fuller). Sculptor, illustrator, craftsman, and teacher. Born Philadelphia, June 9, 1877. Pupil of School of Industrial Art; PAFA; Collin, Carl'es; Colarossi Acad. and Rodin in Paris. Member: Alumni Assoc., Philadelphia School of Industrial Art; Fellowship PAFA. Represented in Cleveland Art Museum; New York Public Library. Address in 1929, 31 Warren Road, Framingham, MA.

WARSAW, ALBERT T(AYLOR).
Painter and illustrator. Born New York, Oct. 6, 1899. Pupil of NAD. Address in 1929, 19 North 17th Street, Flushing, LI, NY.

WARSHAWSKY, ABEL GEORGE.
Painter. Born Sharon, PA, Dec. 28, 1883. Pupil of Mowbray and Loeb in NY; Winslow Homer. Member: Paris AAA; Salon d'Automne; Cincinnati AC. Work: Mural decoration, "The Dance," Rorheimer and Brooks Studios, Cleveland, Ohio.; Cleveland Museum of Art; Minneapolis Art Inst. Died in 1962. Address in 1929, Care of Foinet, 19 Rue Vavin, Paris, France; summer, Point de Croix, Bretagne, France.

WARSHAWSKY, XANDER.
Painter. Born in Cleveland, OH, in 1887. Pupil of National Academy of Design. His painting "Overlooking the Mediterranean" is in the Cleveland Museum. Address in 1926, 20 Rue Durantin, Paris, France.

WARWELL.,
"Limner." Died in Charleston SC.

WARWICK, EDWARD.
Painter, craftsman, lecturer, and teacher. Born Philadelphia, Dec. 10, 1881. Pupil of J. Frank Copeland and Charles T. Scott. Member: Phila. Sketch C.; Phila. Alliance; Phila. Print C.; Phila.

WCC. Address in 1929, School of Industrial Art, Broad and Pine Sts.; h. 222 West Hortter St., Germantown, Philadelphia, PA.

WARWICK, ETHEL HERRICK.
Painter. Born New York, NY. Pupil of W. M. Chase, Fred Wagner, Hugh Breckenridge, H. B. Snell. Member: Plastic C.; Phila. Alliance; Fellowship PAFA; Phila. Print C. Address in 1929, 222 West Hortter St., Germantown, Phila., PA.

WASHBURN, CADWALLADER.
Painter, etcher, and writer. Born Minneapolis, MN. Pupil in architecture of MA, Inst. of Technology, Boston; ASL of NY under Mowbray and of Chase; Sorolla in Spain; Besnard in Paris. Member: NAC; Wash. AC; AFA. Awards: Second prize, Paris AAA; gold medal, P. P. Exp., San F., 1915. Died in 1965. Address in 1929, Poste Restante, Mentone, France.

WASHBURN, MARY N(IGHTINGALE).
Painter. Born Greenfield, MA, 1861. Pupil of D. W. Tryon; H. G. Dearth; Smith Col. Art School; ASL of NY. Member: Springfield AL; NA Women PS. Address in 1929, 451 Main St., Greenfield, MA.

WASHBURN, MARY S.
Sculptor. Born Star City, IN. Pupil of AIC Edwin Sawyer in Paris. Awards: Bronze medal, P. P. Exp., San F., 1915. Work: "Statue of Fen. Milroy," Milroy Park, Rennsselaer, IN; medal in Carnegie Inst., Pittsburgh, PA; Memorial to Lt. Joseph Wilson, Logansport, IN, Monument, Waite Memorial, Rock Creek, Wash., D.C.; character sketch medallions, Berkeley Lg. of Fine Arts; bust of Dr. Byron Robinson, Medical Library, Chicago. Address in 1929, 2321 Haite St., Berkeley, CA.

WASHBURN , MRS.
Painter. Daughter of the miniature painter George Munger of New Haven. Produced a few excellent delicate miniature portraits on ivory.

WASHBURN, ROY E(NGLER).
Painter. Born Vandalia, IL, Jan. 10, 1895. Pupil of Duveneck; Meakin; J. R. Hopkins. Member:

Cleveland SA. Address in 1929, Room 1911, The Daily News Plaza, Chicago, IL; 809 Judson St., Evanston, IL.

WASHINGTON, ELIZABETH FISHER.
Landscape and miniature painter. Born Siegfried's Bridge, PA. Pupil PAFA, Hugh Breckenridge, Fred Wagner. Member: Fellowship PAFA; Plastic C.; Phila. Alliance; PA. S. Min. P.; North Shore AA. Awards: Mary Smith prize, PAFA, 1917; Fellowship prize, PAFA, 1917. Represented in Fellowship PAFA Collection, Civic Club, Philadelphia, Pierce Business College, Smith College, Northampton, MA; Municipal Art Gallery, Trenton, NJ; High School Gallery, Springville, Utah. Address in 1929, 1714 Chestnut St.; h. 214 South 43rd St., Philadelphia, PA.

WASSON, GEORGE SAVARY.
Painter and author. Born in Groveland, MA, in 1855. He began his career as a marine artist in Boston and built a house and studio at Kittery Point, Me., 1889, in order to study the sea. Author: "Cap'n Simeon's Store," 1903; "The Green Shay," 1905; "Home from the Sea," 1908. Contributor to leading magazines. Address in 1926, Kittery Point, ME.

WATERMAN, MARCUS.
Painter. Born Sept. 1, 1834 in Providence, RI. Worked in NY 1857-70. Visited Algiers 1879-83. He exhibited at Centennial, Phila., 1876. Principal works: "Foutain, Aligier"; "Arab Girl"; "Roc's Egg" (1886); "Journey to the City of Brass" (1888); also numerous American forest scenes and Arabian subjects. Died April 2, 1914 in Italy.

WATERS, GEORGE FITE.
Sculptor. Born San Francisco, CA, Oct. 6, 1894. Pupil of Elwell of ASL of NY; Rodin in Paris, and studied in Italy and London. Member: Paris AAA; Societe Moderne. Work: Portrait of President Cosgrave, Dublin Art Gallery; "Valdimir Rosing," Eastman School of Music, Rochester, NY; "Dr. Gordon Hewitt," Ottawa National

Gallery; Statue of Abraham Lincoln, Portland, OR; "James K. Hackett," Univ. of NY; "Capt. Sir Bertram Towse, V. C.," St. Dustan's, London. Died in 1961. Address in 1929, 33 rue du Docteur Blanche, Paris, 16e, France.

WATERS, GEORGE W.
Painter. Born in Coventry, Chenango Co., NY, in 1832. He studied art in NY and later in Dresden and Munich. He exhibited a landscape "Franconia Notch" in 1876 at the Centennial Exhibition. His portrait of Joseph Jefferson as "Rip Van Winkle" attracted much attention; he also painted three portraits of Walt Whitman. Art director for many years at Elmira College, NY. He died in Elmira in 1912.

WATERS, R. KINSMAN.
Painter, craftsman, and teacher. Born Columbus, OH, July 21, 1887. Member: NYWCC. Address in 1929, 1241 Lincoln Road, Columbus, OH.

WATKINS, CATHRINE W.
Landscape painter. Born Hamilton, Ontario. Pupil of AIC; Dauchez, Simon, Menard, Miller in Paris; Branzgwyn in London. Member: NA Women PS; Inter. Art Union, and Amer. Women's AA, Paris. Address in 1929, 584 Magellan Ave., San Francisco, CA.

WATKINS, FRANKLIN.
Painter. Born in 1894. Exhibited at Penna. Academy of Fine Arts, Phila., 1924. Address in 1926, 324 South 7th St., Philadelphia. Died in 1972.

WATKINS, SUSAN.
Painter. Born in California in 1875. Pupil of Art Students' League, NY, and of Collin in Paris. She received honorable mention in the Paris Salon of 1889 and third gold medal in the Salon of 1901. Her painting entitled "The Fan" was well known.

WATKINS, WILLIAM REGINALD.
Painter and teacher. Born Manchester, England, Nov. 11, 1890. Pupil of C. Y. Turner; Edward Berge. Member: Char. C; Alumni Asso., MD Inst. Instructor,

Maryland Inst. Address in 1929, 801 William St., Baltimore, MD.

WATROUS, HARRY W(ILLSON).
Painter. Born San Francisco, CA, Sept. 17, 1857. Pupil of Bonnat, Boulanger and Lefebvre in Paris. Member: ANA 1894, NA 1895; SAA 1905; A. Aid S.; Lotos C.; Century Assoc.; NAC; Salma. C.; SPNY; AFA. Awards: Clarke prize, NAD, 1894; bronze medal, Pan Am Exp., Buffalo, 1901; special commemorative gold medal, St. Louis Exp., 1904. Work: "Passing of Summer," Metropolitan Museum, NY; "A Vision of Love," Montpelier (VT) Museum; "A Study in Black." City Art Museum, St. Louis; "An Auto Suggestion," Buffalo Fine Arts Ada.; "The Drop Sinister," and "Moon Lace," Portland (ME) Mus.; "A Couple of Girls," Brooklyn Mus.; "3 Goats," Fort Worth Mus.; "Portrait of My Mother," Corcoran Gal., Wash., DC. Address in 1929, 58 West 57th St.; h. 13 West 90th St., New York, NY; summer, Hague, Warren Co., NY.

WATROUS ELIZABETH, SNOWDEN NICHOLS.
Painter and writer. Wife of the painter Harry W. Watrous. She was born in NY in 1858 and studied with Henner and Carolus-Duran in Paris. She was a member of the NY Woman's Art Club; the Pen and Brush Club; Society of Women Painters and Sculptors; the Professional Women's League. She died on Oct. 4, 1921, in New York City.

WATSON, ADELE.
Painter. Born Toledo, OH, April 30, 1873. Pupil of ASL of NY and Raphael Collin in Paris. Member: PBC; NA Women PS; S. Indp. A. Died in 1947. Address in 1929, 20 West 10th St., New York, NY; summer, 283 South Grand Ave., Pasadena, CA.

WATSON, AMELIA MONTAGUE.
Painter, illustrator, and teacher. Born East Windsor Hill, March 2, 1856. Member: SSAL. Specialty, Southern scenery. Cover and frontispiece in color for "The Carolina Mountains," by Margaret W. Morley; color illustrations for Thoreau's "Cape Cod"; "Thousand Mile Walk to the Gulf," by John Muir. Died in 1934. Address in

1929, "Wild Acres," East Windsor Hill, CT.

WATSON, CHARLES R.
Painter. Born in Balitmore, MD, in 1857. He was a member of the Baltimore Water Color Club and specialized in marine painting. Died in 1923.

WATSON, DUDLEY CRAFTS.
Painter, teacher, writer and lecturer. Born Lake Geneva, WI, April 28, 1885. Pupil of AI Chicago; Sorolla; Sir Alfred East. Member: Cliff Dwellers Club, Chicago; Chicago, AC. Awards: Hon. mention for water colors, AIC, 1911; hon. mention, Wis. PS., 1922; Florence B. Fawcett prize for flower painting, Milwaukee Art Inst., 1923. Work: "Monsalvat and "Hollyhocks," Milwaukee Art Inst.; "Parliament Tower, London," Burlington (IA) Public Library, "Flower Panels," Public High School, Milwaukee, WI, La Mars, IA; "Marines," Milwaukee Yacht Art Club; "Delphinium," Layton Art School, Milwaukee, Lecturer on the fine arts. Art editor, Milwaukee Journal for 5 yrs. Originator of the Music Picture Symphonies; official director of pageantry, City of Milwaukee, 1914-1920; director, Milwaukee Art Inst., 1914-1924; Educational Director of Minneapolis Inst., of Arts, 1922-1923; Rockford, IL, Art Club, 1923-1925; Springfield, IL, Art Assoc.; Director of Art Education since, 1915, Minnesota State Fair; Lecturer on Art, 1920-21, St. Paul Inst. Conductor of art pilgrimages to Europe each year. Extension Lecturer, Art Inst. of Chicago since 1924. Address in 1929, Art Inst. of Chicago; h. Trillium Dell, Ravinia, IL.

WATSON, ELIZABETH H.
Painter. Pupil of PAFA. Member: Fellowship PAFA. Award: Mary Smith prize, PAFA 1896. Address in 1929, 126 South 18th St., Philadelphia, PA.

WATSON, ELIZABETH V. TAYLOR.
Painter. Born in NJ. Pupil of Tarbell, DeCamp, Boston Museum of Fine Arts School. Member: Copley S.; CT. AFA. Awards: Bronze

medal, Tennessee Centennial Exp., Nashville, 1897. Address in 1929, 404 Fenway Studios, Ipswich St., Boston, MA; summer, Clark's Island, Plymouth, MA.

WATSON, ERNEST W.
Illustrator, lecturer, and teacher. Born Conway, MA, Jan. 14, 1884. Pupil of Mass. Art School, Boston; Pratt Inst., Brooklyn. One of the founders and directors of The Berkshire Summer School of Art. Instructor and Supervisor at Pratt Institute. Member: Calif. Print M; Am. Inst. Gr. A.; Boston SAC. Specialty, block prints in color; illustrator. Address in 1929, Pratt Inst., h. 181 Emerson Place, Brooklyn, NY; summer, "Greywold," Monterey, MA.

WATSON, EVA AULD.
Painter, illustrator, and craftsman. Born in Texas, April 4, 1889. Pupil of M. O. Leisser, Pittsburgh School of Design, Pratt Inst., Brooklyn. Member: Boston SAC. Award: Hon. mention, P. P. Exp., San F., 1915. Author: "Coptic Textile Motifs." Address in 1929, 181 Emerson Place, Brooklyn, NY; summer, Monterey, MA.

WATSON, HENRY S(UMNER).
Illustrator. Born Bordentown, NJ, 1868. Pupil of Thomas Eakins in Philadelphia; Laurens in Paris. Member: SI 1904. Specialty, outdoor subjects. Address in 1929, 2 East 12th Street, New York, NY.

WATSON, JESSIE NELSON.
Painter. Born in Pontiac, IL, in 1870. Address in 1926, 1004 Chemical Building, St. Louis, MO.

WATSON, JOHN.
Painter. Born July 28, 1685, in Scotland who came to the Colonies in 1714 from Scotland and set up his easel in the capital of NJ, Perth Amboy. William Dunlap in his "History of the Arts of Design," Vol. 1, devotes four pages to the career of the artist John Watson. In 1731 Watson painted his portrait of Sir Peter Warren who through his marriage into the de Lancey family had relatives living in Perth Amboy, NJ, the home of the artist. This portrait was exhibited at the

Union League Club, NY, in 1925. Died Aug. 22, 1768, in NJ.

WATSON, MINNIE.
Painter. She was a pupil of D. W. Tryon in Hartford, CT, in 1875. Later she studied in NY. Painted excellent still-life subjects true in line and color.

WATT, BARBARA H.
Painter, illustrator, artist, craftsman, and writer. Born Wellesley, MA. Pupil of Albert H. Munsel. V. L. George, J. De Camp and D. J. Connah. Member: Brush and Chisel C.; Alumni Assoc. of MA. Normal Art School; Copley S. Work: Mural decoration, "Pan" MA Art School, Boston. Address in 1929, Grantland Road, Wellesley Hills, MA; summer, The Cape and Wellesley, MA.

WATT, WILLIAM G.
Wood engraver. Born in NY in 1867. Pupil of E. Heinemann, Emile Clement and of the Nat. Acad. of Design. Member of Salmagundi Club in 1903. Work: "The Harvest," after L'Hermitte; "The Pool," after own painting; "A Music Party," after Metsu; "The Trousseau," by C. W. Hawthorne; "Magnolia," by J. J. Shannon. Work represented in NY Public library; Carnegie Inst., Pittsburgh; Public Library, Newark, NJ; Metropolitan Museum Library, NY; Salmagundi Club. Elected an Associate Member of the National Academy in 1922. Died in New York in 1924.

WATTS, JAMES W.
Engraver. Born 1895. About 1850 Watts was a line-engraver of landscape in Boston. He later etched some portraits, and banknotes.

WATTS, WILLIAM CLOTHIER.
Painter. Born Philadelphia, PA. Pupil of PAFA. Member: Fellowship PAFA; Phila. Sketch C.; Phila. WCC; Calif. WCS. Address in 1929, Carmel, Monterey Co., CA.

WAUGH, COULTON.
Painter, illustrator, and etcher. Born St. Ives, England, March 10, 1896. Pupil of George Bridgman, Douglas Volk, Frederick J. Waugh.

Member: Boston SAC; Beachcombers C. Work: Marine drawings and maps reproduced in Country Life, House Beautiful, House and Garden, American Home, American Sketch and Harper's. Died in 1973. Address in 1929, West Vine Street, Provincetown, MA.

WAUGH, ELIZA.
She was a miniature painter, and married the artist Samuel B. Waugh.

WAUGH, FREDERICK J(UDD).
Painter. Born in Bordentown, NJ, in 1861. He was the son of Samuel B. Waugh, portrait painter, and Mary Eliza (Young). Pupil of the PA Academy of the Fine Arts, Phil., and of the Julian Academy in Paris. Was elected an Assoc. Member of the Nat. Acad. in 1909 and an Academician in 1911. He resided at various places in Europe (1892-1907). Illustrated for Graphic and London papers and exhibited in Salons Paris previous to 1892, and later in the Royal Acad. in London. Represented by paintings in the Bristol Acad., Eng.; Walker Art Gallery, Liverpool; Durban Art Gallery (Natal, S. Africa); Nat'l. Gallery, Wash., DC; MOMA, Brooklyn, NY, Inst. Art Club, Phil.; Art Inst. of Chicago; Delgade Art Museum, New Orleans; PA Acad. of FA, Phil., Monclair Arts Club; Mem. of the Natl. Acad., 1909; of the Bristol Acad. of Fine Arts, Royal Acad. of the West of England. His work consists chiefly of marines. Address in 1926, Kent, CT.

WAUGH, IDA.
Painter. Born in Philadelphia. Pupil of PAFA, Philadelphia, and Paris at L'Acadamie Julien and L'Academie Delecluse, 1880 and 1891-92. Principal painting, "Hagar and Ishmael;" received the Norman W. Dodge prize, National Acad. of Design for portrait of Dr. Paul J. Sartain, 1896; has exhibited in Paris Salon; World's Fair (Chicago), 1893; NY; Phila; California; Cincinnati and other places. Member of Historical Society of Penna., and PAFA. Mother of Frederick J. Waugh. Died Jan. 25, 1919 in NYC.

WAUGH, SAMUEL B.
Portrait painter. Born in Mercer, PA, in 1814. Studied drawing while a boy under J. R. Smith, Philadelphia; also studied the works of the old masters in Italy, Paris and England, without a teacher. Lived mainly in Philadelphia, where he was one time President of the Artists Fund Society; honorary member of the Nat. Acad. of Design, NY. Died in 1885, in Wisconsin.

WAXMAN, FRANCIS S.
See Sheafer.

WAY, ANDREW JOHN HENRY.
Painter. Born in Washington, D.C., April 12, 1826. He studied in Baltimore. His work was portraiture and still life, his fruit pieces attracting special attention. Among his works are "A Chirstmas Memory," "Albert Grapes" and "Flora and Pomana." Several of his paintings have been lithographed. He died Feb. 7, 1888, in MA.

WAY, GEORGE BREVITT.
Painter. Son of the artist Andrew John Henry Way. He was born in Baltimore in 1854 and educated at the United States Naval Academy. He later studied in Paris. Among his paintings are "Twilight on the Susquehanna," "On the Upper Potomac" and "Sunset."

WAY, MARY.
Portrait and miniature painter of New London, CT. In the New York Evening Post, in 1811, it notes "Takes Likenesses upon Ivory & Glass, in colors or gold. Also landscapes or views of country Seats. Paintings not approved may be returned without charge at her painting-room No. 95 Greenwich Street, NY."

WEAR, J. F.
Portrait painter. The collection of historic portraits at Independence Hall, Philadelphia, has a portrait of a signer of the Declaration of Independence, painted by J. F. Wear after the portrait painted by John Trumbull.

WEAVER, B. MALE.
Painter, sculptor, and teacher. Born New Hartford, Dec. 12, 1875. Pupil of Ross Turner; Mme. La Forge; George T. Collins; M. Simone. Member: Springfield AL; Holyoke AC. Work: Portraits of Ex-Governors Woodruff, Templeton, Holcomb and Weeks, State of CT. Address in 1929, 533 Pleasant St., Holyoke, MA; summer, Box 204, New Hartford, CT.

WEAVER, BEULAH B(ARNES).
Painter and teacher. Born Wash., DC, July 8, 1886. Pupil of Corcoran Art School.; Pepino Mangravite. Address in 1929, 2433 Wisconsin Ave., Wash., DC; summer, Colonial Beach, VA.

WEAVER, MARGARITA (WRIGLE).
(Mrs. John Weaver). Painter. Born Brandon, VT, Nov. 24, 1889. Pupil of Forsyth in Indianapolis; Lucien Simon and Henri Morriset in Paris. Member: Hoosier Salon; Chicago AC. Awards: Purdue Alumni prize ($100), exhibit Hoosier Artists, Marshall Field's, 1925. Address in 1929, 68 East Goethe St., Chicago, IL; summer, Brandon, VT.

WEAVER, P. T.
Dunlap notes his painting of small portraits in oil, in a hard manner. His portrait of Alexander Hamilton attracted attention by its strong likeness. He often painted portraits in profile on wood panels, and signed several "P. T. Weaver."

WEBB, A. C.
Painter, illustrator, Arch. and etcher. Born Nashville, TN, April 1, 1888. Pupil of AIC, ASL of NY. Member: Beaux Arts Architects; Paris AAA. Award: Municipal Arts prize in Architecture, New York, 1917. Work: Etchings owned by City of Paris, and French Government. Address in 1929, Rue de Alfred Stevens, Montmartre, Paris, France.

WEBB, EDNA DELL.
Painter. Born in Cohoes, NY, in 1891. Pupil of National Academy of Design; Troy School of Arts and Crafts. Address in 1926, Lansing Avenue, Troy, NY.

WEBB, J. LOUIS.
Painter, who was born April 24, 1856. He was elected an Associate Member of National Academy of Design in 1906. Address in 1926, 32 East 42d St., New York, NY.

WEBB, MARGARET ELY.
Illustrator and etcher. Born Urbana, IL, March 27, 1877. Pupil of Twachtman and Cox in New York. Member: Boston AC; Amer. S. Bookplate A. Illustrated "The House of Prayer," by F. C. Converse; "Aldine First Reader," "Under Greek Skies," etc. Address in 1929, 26 West Michiltorena St., Santa Barbara, CA.

WEBB, WARREN.
Marine painter. Specialty in oil paintings.

WEBBER, WESLEY.
Painter. Born in Gardiner, Maine, in 1841. Had a studio in Boston and in NY. Painted landscapes and scenes of the Civil War. Died Nov. 4, 1914, in Boston, MA.

WEBER, AUGUST J(AMES).
Painter. Born Marietta, OH, Oct. 21, 1889. Pupil of Meakin and Duveneck in Cincinnati. Member: Cincinnati AC; Valley of the Moon SP; Ohio WCS. Address in 1929, 131 East 3rd St., Cincinnati, Ohio; h 419-4th Street, Marietta, OH.

WEBER, CARL.
Landscape painter. Born in Philadelphia, in 1850. Son of Paul Weber. Studied in Germany. Represented in many galleries and collections of paintings. Died Jan. 24, 1921, in Ambler, PA.

WEBER, F(REDERICK) (THEODORE).
Painter, sculptor, and etcher. Born Columbia, SC, March 9, 1883. Pupil of Laurens and Ecole des Beaux-Arts in Paris. Member: SSAL; NYWCC; Brooklyn SE (Pres.); Am. APL. Etchings in the Library of Congress, Washington; New York Public Library; Smithsonian Inst., Wash.; Bibliotheque Nationale, Paris. Author, article on "Portrait Painting," Encyclopedia Britannica, 1929. Died in 1956. Address in 1929, 257 West 86th Street, New York, NY.

WEBER, MAX.
Painter, teacher, and lecturer. Born in Russia, April 18, 1881. Pupil of Dow; Laurens and Matisse in Paris, and Pratt Inst. Member: Modern Artists. Award: Potter Palmer gold medal and $1,000, AIC, 1928. Author, "Essays on Art," "Cubist Poems," and "Primitives." Address in 1929, 51 West 10th St., New York, NY. Died in 1961.

WEBER, PAUL.
Landscape and animal painter. Born in Germany, in 1823. Studied in Frankfurt. Came to America in 1848 and settled in Phila. Travelled in Scotland and Germany in 1857, returned to America for a short time; went to Darmstadt in 1858, and was appointed Court painter. His American work was generally pure landscape, of which one of the finest examples is his "Evening," in the permanent collection of the Academy of Fine Arts. The Corcoran Gallery has "Scene in the Catskills," painted in 1858. His later work was of animal life. Died 1916 in Phila.

WEBER, SYBILLA MITTELL.
Painter and etcher. Born NY, May 30, 1892. Pupil of Alfons Purtscher in Munich; Pennell in NY. Member: NA Women PS; NAC; AFA. Work: Painting of "Pointer," Westminster Kennel Club, NY; "Great Dane," Berlin Mus.; "Hackney Pony," "Contented" and "Albert," New Pinakothek, Munich. Died in 1957. Address in 1929, 50 Central Park West, New York, NY.

WEBSTER, AMBROSE E.
Born in 1869. Painter, who exhibited at the Penna. Acad. of the Fine Arts, Philadelphia, 1924. Address in 1926, Provincetown, MA. Died in 1935.

WEBSTER, E. AMBROSE.
Painter and teacher. Born Chelsea, MA, Jan. 31, 1869. Pupil of Boston Museum under Beson and Tarbell; Laurens and Benjamin Constant in Paris. Member: Provincetown AA. Director and instructor, Webster Art School, Provincetown. Died in 1935. Address in 1929, Provincetown, MA.

WEBSTER, H. DANIEL.
Sculptor. Pupil of Banard and Du
Mond in NY. Born at Frankville,
IA. Represented by "Minute Man"
(bronze); Genl. W. H. Beadle
(marble); the bronze doors for
American National Bank Building,
Austin, Texas. Died in 1912.

WEBSTER, HAROLD TUCKER.
Cartoonist. Born Parkersburg, West
VA, Sept. 21, 1885. Member: SI;
Dutch Treat C. Author of "Our
Boyhood Thrills and other
Cartoons"; "Boys and Folks;"
cartoon series entitled "Our
Boyhood Ambitions;" "The Thrill
That Comes Once in a Lifetime;"
"Life's Darkest Moment;" "The
Beginning of a Beautiful
Friendship;" "How to Torture Your
Wife." Died in 1952. Address in
1929, The NY World, NY, NY; h.
"Crest Hill," Shippan Pt.,
Stamford, CT; summer, Meddybemps,
ME.

WEBSTER, HERMAN A(RMOUR).
Painter and etcher. Born New York,
NY, April 6, 1878. Pupil of
Laurens in Paris. Member: R. Soc.
of Painter-Etchers, London; Soc.
Nat. des Beaux Arts, Paris; Paris
AAA; Chelsea AC. Award: Gold
medal, P. P. Exp., San F., 1915;
Chevalier de la Legion d'Honneau,
1927. Work in: Luxembourg, Paris;
South Kensington, London; British
Mus.; Darmstadt; Library of
Congress, Washington; Art Inst.,
Chicago; Metropolitan Museum, New
York; Fogg Museum, Cambridge, etc.
Address in 1929, 39 rue d'Artois,
Paris, France.

WEBSTER, MARY H(ORTENSE).
Painter, sculptor, and teacher.
Born Oberlin, OH. Pupil of
Cincinnati, Art Academy under
Barnhorn and Nowottny; Injalbert,
Verlet, and Waldmann in Paris;
Hitchcock in Holland; Hawthorne in
Provincetown; Lorado Taft in
Chicago. Address in 1929, Midway
Studios, 6012 Ellis Ave., Chicago,
IL.

WEDDERSPOON, R(ICHARD). G(IBSON).
Painter. Born Red Bank, NJ, Oct.
15, 1889. Pupil of Daniel Garber
and Henry McCarter. Member:
Fellowship PAFA; Chicago SA:

Chicago AC. Awards: European
scholarship, PAFA, 1915 and 1916;
first Toppan prize, PAFA, 1917;
Jenkins prize, AIC, 1922.
Represented in Chicago Civic
Committee, De Pauw University.
Professor of fine arts, Syracuae,
University. Address in 1929,
Syracuse Univ., College of Fine
Arts; h. 301 Narshall St.,
Syracuse, NY; summer, New Hope, PA.

WEEDELL, HAZEL.
(Mrs. Gustav F. Goetsch). Painter,
etcher, craftsman, and teacher.
Born Tacoma, Wash., Jan. 26, 1892.
Pupil of Gustave F. Goetsch, Robert
Koehler and Ernest Batchelder.
Member: Alumni, Minneapolis School
of Art; St. Louis AG. Address in
1929, 20 Elm Ave., Glendate, MO.

WEEKS, CAROLINE.
Portrait painter. The collection
of Colonial portraits in
Independence Hall, Philadelphia,
has a copy by Caroline Weeks of
John Trumbull's portrait of Josiah
Barlett of New Hampshire. She
painted most of her pictures from
1860 to 1870.

WEEKS, EDWIN LORD.
Painter. Born in Boston, MA, in
1849. Landscape and figure
painter. Pupil of the Ecole des
Beaux Art; also of Bonnat and
Gerome in Paris. Sketched and
painted in Cairo, Jerusalem,
Damascus, and Tangiers, and is
noted for paintings of Eastern
life. Received hon. mention at the
Paris Salon, 1884, and was awarded
medals at the Salon, 1889; Paris
Exposition, 1889; Art Club,
Philadelphia, 1891; Munich, 1897;
Pan American Exposition, Buffalo,
1901. Chevalier of the Legion of
Honor, 1896; Officer, Order of St.
Michael of Bavaria; member of Paris
Society of American Painters, and
Boston Art Club. Died in 1903.

WEEKS, JAMES.
Painter. Born Dec. 1, 1922, in
Oakland, CA. Studied at S. F. Art
Inst. (1940 and 1946-7); Marian
Hartwell's School of Design, S. F.
and Escuela de Pintura, Mexico
City. Awarded Rosenberg fellowship
(1952) and Nat. Endowment for the
Arts grant (1978); and awards from

989

CA. Palace and Howard U. Taught at S. F. Art Inst.; UCLA; Brandeis; at Boston U. since 1970. Exhibited at Labaudt Gal. S. F. (1951); Cal. Pal., S. F.; Poindexter Gal.; Felix Landau Gal.; Oakland Mus.; Corcoran Standford U.; Art Inst. of Chicago; Boston U.; Scripps Col. and Brown U. In collections of S. F. Mus. of Art; Corcoran; Howard U.; Boston Mus. of Fine Arts; New Eng. Mutual Life and many private collections. Address in 1982, 11 Notre Dame Rd., Bedford, MA.

WEHN, JAMES A.
Sculptor and teacher. Born Indianapolis, IN. Pupil of R. N. Nichols, Will Carson, August Hubert. Member: Seattle AI; Amer. Numismatic Soc. Work: Monument, Seattle, Wash.; Meriwether-Lewis relief, Court House, Chehalis, Wash.; series of historical medalions, Univ. of Wash.; Henry L. Yesler medallion, Yesler Library, Seattle; medal, Garden Club, Seattle; Morgan relief, Northern Life Tower, Seattle. Address in 1929, 710 19th Ave., South Seattle, Wash.; summer, Cresent Beach, Wash.

WEIL, CARRIE H.
Sculptor. Born New York, Aug. 17, 1888. Pupil of P. Hamaan in NY and Paul Landowski in Paris. Member: NA Women PS. Specialty, portrait busts. Address in 1929, 125 East 50th Street, h. Hotel Beverely, New York, NY.

WEILAND, JAMES.
Portrait painter. Born Toledo, OH. Pupil of NAD; Royal Acad. in Munich; Delecluse and Colarossi Acad. in Paris. Member: Salma. C.; Allied AA; Provincetown AA. Represented in the National Museum, Washington, D.C. Address in 1929, 58 West 57th Street, New York, NY; summer, Lyme, CT.

WEILL, EDMOND.
Painter and etcher. Born New York, July 29, 1877. Pupil of NAD under Edgar M. Ward. Member: Brooklyn S. Modern A; Brooklyn WCC; S. Indp. A; Salma. C.; Salons of Amer.; AWCS. Represented in Brooklyn Museum. Address in 1929, 756 East 9th Street, Brooklyn, New York, NY.

WEINBERG, E(MILIE) SIEVERT.
Painter. She was born Chicago, IL. Pupil of AIC and William M. Chase. Member: San F. AA; Calif. AC; Oakland AA; Alumni Asso. AIC.; San F. Soc. Women A. Address in 1929, 1801 California St. San Francisco, CA.

WEINDORF, ARTHUR.
Painter. Born in Long Island City in 1885. Member of Society of Independent Artists. Address in 1926, Woolworth Building, NY.

WEINEDEL, CARL.
Miniature painter. Born in 1795. He was working in New York in 1834; in 1839, he was elected an Associate Member of the Nat. Academy of Design. He died May 11, 1845, in NYC.

WEINERT, ALBERT.
Sculptor. Born in Leipzig, Germany, in 1863. Pupil of Ecole des Beaux Arts in Brussels. Member: National Sculpture Society, 1909; Society of Independent Artists. Work: "Lake George Memorial," Toledo, Ohio; "Statue of Lord Baltimore," Baltimore, MD; marble groups in vestibule of Hall of Records, New York, NY; "Stevens T. Mason Monument," Detroit, Mich.; historical tablets for Sons of the Revolution and Society of Colonial Wars; work at Panama-Pacific Exposition, San Francisco. Calif. Address in 1926, 256 West 55th Street, New York, NY.

WEINMAN, ADOLPH A(LEXANDER).
Sculptor. Born Karlsruhe, Germany, Dec. 11, 1870; came to America in 1880. Pupil of Cooper Union, ASL of NY, Augustus Saint-Gaudens, and Philip Martiny. Assistant to Niehaus, Warner and French. Member: SAA 1903; ANA 1906; NA 1911; NSS 1900 (pres); NY Arch. Lg. 1902; Nat. Inst. A. L.; Century Assoc.; Am. Numismatic Soc.; AFA. Member of Int. Jury for Sculpture, P.-P. Exp., San F., 1915; member Nat'l Commission of Fine Arts, 1929. Awards: Hon. mention, Pan Am Exp., Buffalo, 1901; silver medal Brussels Exp., 1910; gold medal of honor for sculptor, NY. Arch. Lg. 1913; Saltus Medal for

990

medal, American Numismatic Soceity, 1920. Work: Lincoln memorials at Hodgenville, KY, and Madison, WI; "Gen. Macomb Monument," Detroit; "Abraham Lincoln" statuette and "The Rising Sun," Metropolitan Museum, NY; "Chief Black Bird," Brooklyn Inst. Mus.; plaque "Adelaide," Carnegie Inst., Pittsburgh; "Descending Night," Kansas City Museum; "Alexander J. Cassatt," New York, "The Rising Sun" and "Descending Night," Houston Mus., Texas; "Fountain of the Tritons," Missouri State Capitol Grounds; pediment sculpture, Wisconsin State Capitol; pediment sculpture, Missouri State Capitol; frieze and bronze groups, facade of Elks Nat'l Memorial Headquarters Bldg., Chicago; all sculpture on exterior and interior of Pennsylvania Railway Station, NY; sculpture on facade and top of tower, municipal Bldg., New York. Designer of half dollar and dime for US Government, Victory Button for US Army and Navy. Died in 1952. Address in 1929, 234 Greenway South, Forest Hills, NY.

WEIR, CHARLES E.
Painted many cabinet heads as noted in an early Art Union Exhibition. Died June 20, 1845 in NYC.

WEIR, EDITH DEAN.
See Mrs. J. De W Perry.

WEIR, IRENE.
Sculptor and painter. Born in West Point, NY, in 1841. Elected an Associate Member of the National Academy of Design in 1864., and Academician in 1866. He was Director of Yale School of Fine Arts, 1869- 1913. Principal works in scultpure; Statues of Presidents Woosley and Professor Silliman, of Yale. Executed many portraits and other works in paintings, notably "The Gun Foundry," "The Forging of the Shaft," "The Confessional," "An Artist's Studio," "Christmas Eve," "Tapping the Furnace," "Rain and Sunshine," "The Column of St. Mark's, Venice." Author of "John Trumbull and His Works," 1902. Address in 1926, Yale University, New Haven, CT. Died in 1926.

WEIR, JULIAN ALDEN.
Painter and etcher. Born in West Point, NY, in 1852; died in 1919 in NYC. Pupil of his father, Robert W. Weir, at West Point and of Gerome in Paris. Awards: Hon. mention, Paris Salon, 1882; silver medal for painting and bronze medal for drawing, Paris Expo., 1889; AAA NY; medal, Carnegie Inst, Pittsburgh, 1897; bronze medal, Paris Expo., 1900; gold medal for paintings and silver for engravings, Buffalo, 1901; gold medal, NAD, 1906; Lippincott prize, Penna. Acad. of Fine Arts, 1910; Harris silver medal, Chicago Art Inst., 1912; Beck medal, Penna. Acad. of the Fine Arts, 1913; first Wm. A. Clark prize and Corcoran gold medal, the Corcoran Gallery of Art, 1914. Elected Associate, National Academy, 1886, and became its President, 1915- 17. Member: American Water Color Society; Ten American Painters; Nat. Inst. of Arts and Letters. Represented at Corcoran by "Autumn" and portrait of Miss De L. (Awarded the first William A. Clark prize accompanied by the Corcoran gold medal in 1916.) A memorial exhibition was held at the Century Club, NY, of about forty of his best known paintings.

WEIR, ROBERT WALTER.
Painter. Born in New Rochelle, NY, June 18, 1803; died in New York, 1889. Pupil of Jarvis. Studied at Florence, Italy, under Benventi; also in Rome, Italy. Became a professional painter at the age of 20. In 1829 he became a Member of NAD and in 1832 was made professor of drawing at West Point. Among his works are: "The Bourbons Last March;" "Landing of Henry Hudson;" "Indian Captives;" "Christ and Nicodemus;" "Taking the Veil;" "Child's Evening Prayer"; "The Portico of the Palace of Octavia, Rome;" "Our Lord on the Mount of Olives;" and "Last Communion of Henry Clay." His "Embarkation of the Pilgrims," in the rotunda of the Capitol, Washington, was injured during the building of the new dome of the Capitol. Professor Weir repaired this injury in 1861. His portrait of Genral Winfield Scott is owned by MMA.

WEIR, WILLIAM (JOSEPH).
Painter, illustrator, and etcher.
Born Ballina, Ireland, June 8,
1884. Pupil of AIC; Chicago Art
Acad. Member: Chicago Palette and
Chisel C; IL AFA. Work: "The Road
to Lake Ripley," State Museum,
Springfield, IL. Address in 1929,
Palette and Chisel Club, 1012 North
Dearborn St.; h. 1312 Byron St.,
Chicago, IL.

WEIS, JOHN E(LLSWORTH).
Painter, writer, and teacher. Born
Higginsport, OH, Sept. 11, 1892.
Pupil of Duveneck, Meakin, Hopkins,
and Wessel. Member: Cincinnati
AC; Cincinnati MacD. C; Duveneck
Soc. of P. and S. Address in 1929,
Art Acad., Cincinnati, OH; h. 2155
Fulton Ave. W. H. Cincinnati, OH.

WEIS, S(AMUEL) W(ASHINGTON).
Painter. Born Natchez, MI, Aug. 8,
1870. Member: N. O. AA; Salma.
C.; Business Men's AC, Chicago;
Palette and Chisel C, Chicago;
North Shore AL, Winnetka; SSAL.
Address in 1929, Drake Hotel,
Chicago, IL.; summer, Glencoe, IL.

WEISBROOK, FRANK S.
Painter. Award: Bronze medal for
water color, St. Paul Inst., 1918.
Address in 1929, 713 East 13th St.,
Davenport, IA.

WEISEL, DEBORAH D.
Painter, craftsman, lecturer, and
teacher. Born Doylestown, PA.
Pupil of PA. Museum School; PAFA;
Breckenridge, DeVoll. Member:
Fellowship PAFA; Alumni Assoc., PA
Museum School; Friends of Art,
Springfield, MO; AFA. Died in
1951. Address in 1929, Teachers
College; h. 775 East Madison St.,
Springfield, MO; summer, "Gray
Gables," Morrestown, NJ.

WEISENBORN, RUDOLPH.
Painter. Member: Chicago NJSA; Cor
Ardens; Chicago SA. Award: Hon.
mention, AIC 1928. Address in
1929, 1501 North La Salle St.,
Chicago, IL.

WEISENBURG, HELEN M(ILLS).
Painter. Pupil of Phila. School of
Indus. Art; PAFA; Hugh
Breckenridge. Member: Plastic C;
Fellowship PAFA; Phila. Alliance.

Awards: Fellowship prize, PAFA,
1927; gold medal,Plastic Club,
Philadelphia, 1929. Address in
1929, 2129 De Lancey St.,
Philadelphia, PA.

WEISS, MARY L.
Painter, who exhibited at the Penn.
Acad. of Fine Arts, Philadelphia,
1924. Address in 1926, East
Gloucester, MA.

WEISS, WILLIAM L.
Painter, who exhibited at the Penn.
Acad. of Fine Arts, Philadelphia,
1924. Address in 1926, East
Gloucester, MA.

WEISSER, LEONIE.
(Mrs. Fred Weisser). Painter.
Born Guadalupe Country, TX, Oct. 5,
1890. Pupil of Minnie Stanford,
William Jenkins, J. J. Onderdonk.
Member: San Antonio AL; SSAL.
Awards: First prize, Hays County,
Texas Fairs, 1922, 1923, 1924; hon.
mention, Edgar B. Davis competitive
exh., San Antonio, 1929. Address
in 1929, 211 Kennedy Ave., San
Antonio, TX.

WEISZ, EUGEN.
Painter. Member: S. Wash. A.
Died in 1954. Address in 1929, 515
20th St., Washington, D.C.

WELCH, MABEL R.
Painter and teacher. Born New
Haven, CT. Pupil of ASL of NY
under Cox and Reid; Van de Weyden,
Garrido, Lazar and Scott in Paris.
Member: NA Women PS; Am. S. Min.
P.; Pa. S. Min. P. Awards: Silver
medal, P. P. Exp., San F., 1915;
medal of honor, PAFA, 1920. Died in
1959. Address in 1929, Care Van
Dyck Studios, 939 Eighth Ave., New
York, NY.

WELCH, THOMAS B.
Engraver. Born in Charleston, SC,
in 1814. Died in Paris Nov., 1874.
Welch was a pupil of James B.
Longacre in Philadelphia and
apparently soon after his release
from his apprenticeship he formed a
business with A. B. Walter. Over
his own name he produced some good
portraits in stipple and some large
ones in mezzotint. For the Annuals
he engraved some admirable pure

line plates. About 1861 Welch abandoned engraving and went abroad to study art; he remained in Paris for many years. The Philadelphia directories of 1841-45 give his occupation as "portrait painter."

WELDON, C(HARLES) D(ATER).
Illustrator and painter. Born Ohio. Pupil of Walter Shirlaw in NY; Munkacsy in Paris. Member: ANA 1889, NA 1897; AWCS; Century Assoc. Award: Bronze medal, Charleston Exp., 1902. Died in 1935. Address in 1929, 51 Est 10th Street, New York, NY.

WELLIVER, NEIL G.
Painter. Born in Millville, PA, in Dec. 7, 1929. Studied at the Philadelphia College of Art from 1948 to 1952 and at Yale University with Joseph Albers, Burgoyne Diller, and James Brooks, 1953-1954. Taught at Yale University, University of Pennsylvania, and at the University of Santo Thomas, Manila, Republic of the Philippines. Exhibitions: Philadelphia, 1954; Boston, 1959; and in New York at the Stable Gallery, 1962-1964; Whitney Museum of American Art, New York, 1963; The Museum of Modern Art, New York. Address in 1982, RD 2, Lincolnville, ME.

WELLMORE, E.
Portrait painter and engraver in stipple and in line. He was a pupil of James B. Longacre in Phila. and over his own name he engraved some of the portraits in "The National Portrait Gallery" of 1834-35. At a much later period he was engraving book illustrations in NY. He is said to have later become a clergyman. Wellmore was also a miniature painter as we find engravings and lithographs done after portraits painted by E. Wellmore.

WELLS, ALICE RUSHMORE.
Painter. Member: Am. S. Min. P.; Pa. S. Min. P.; NA Women PS. Address in 1929, 226 E. Ninth St., Plainfield, NJ.

WELLS, AMY W(ATSON).
Painter and teacher. Born Lynchburg, VA, Dec. 21, 1899.

Pupil of PAFA. Member: Fellowship PAFA: ASL of Trenton, NJ. Address in 1929, 874 North Pennsylvania Ave., Morrisville, PA.

WELLS, CHARLES S.
Sculptor and teacher. Born Glasgow, Scotland, June 24, 1872. Pupil of Karl Bitter, Augustus Saint-Gaudens, George G. Barnard. Work: Fountain, Gateway Park, City of Minneapolis; Anna T. Lincoln Memorial, Northfield, MN. Address in 1929, Minneapolis School of Art; 5521 Xerxes Ave., South, Minneapolis, MN.

WELLS, ELOISE LONG.
Painter. Born Alton, IL, May 3, 1875. Pupil of St. Louis Art School. Member: St. Louis AG; AFA. Award: Bronze medal for still life painting and gold medal for graphic art, Kansas City Art Inst., 1923. Address in 1929, 936 Lake Shore Drive, Chicago, IL.

WELLS, J.
Engraver. The only information obtainable is that J. Wells was a map engraver working in NY, in 1836.

WELLS, LUCY D.
(Mrs. William A. Wells.). Painter and teacher. Born Chicago, IL, Sept. 4, 1881. Pupil of Vanderpoel, Ralph Clarkson, Randall Davey, Ernest Lawson. Member: Northwest PM; Spokane AA. Address in 1929, 841 Cliff Ave., Spokane, Wash.

WELLS, MARION F.
Sculptor. Born in 1848. Sculptor of the giant figure of "Progress" which crowns the dome of the City Hall, San Fran., CA. Died July 22, 1903, in San Fran.

WELLS, NEWTON ALONZO.
Painter. Born in Lisbon, NY, in 1852. Pupil of Academie Julien, Paris, 1886, 1896. Instructor of drawing and geometry, Union College, NY, in 1877-79; professor of drawing, Syracuse University; professor of art, Univ. of Illinois, 1899. Exhibited at Paris Salon various national and municipal exhibitions; has murals in library of Univ. of Illinois;

Sangamon Co. Court House (Sprinfield, Ill.); Colonial Theatre (Boston); Englewood High School (Chicago); designed Soldiers Monument, Tuscola, IL. Member: Architectural League of America; Architectural League of NY; National Society of Mural Painters. Contributor on art subjects. Series of historical mural paintings in Gayoso Hotel, Memphis, TN. Address in 1926, 1630 Monroe Building, Chicago.

WELLS, RACHEL.
Modeler. Her work was chiefly small profile bas-reliefs in wax; the portraits were well modeled and frequently finished in color. A sister of Patience Wright who married Joseph Wright. He painted portraits of Washington in 1790.

WELLSTOOD, JAMES.
Engraver. Born in Jersey City, NJ, in 1855; died there in 1880. Son and pupil of William Wellstood. He became successful and promising engraver. At the time of his death he was a member of the engraving firm of William Wellstood & Co. His principal plates were "The Pointer" and "Safe in Port;" the latter after a painting by Thomas Moran.

WELLSTOOD, JOHN GEIKIE.
Engraver. Born Edinburgh, Scotland, in 1813; was living in 1889. Wellstood came to NY in 1830. Employed by Rawdon, Wright & Co., where he remained until 1847, when he began business for himself. In 1858 his firm was merged into what became the American Bank Note Company, until 1871. In that year he founded the Columbian Bank Note Company in Washington, D.C., and while president of that company he designed and partially engraved the backs of the US Treasury notes issued at that time. When the printing of US notes passed into the hands of the Treasury Dept., he returned to NY and still employed in 1889 as a Script engraver by the American Bank Note Comp. Made many improvements in the manufacture of bank-notes. Died 1893, in CT.

WELLSTOOD, WILLIAM.
Engraver. Born in Edinburgh, Scotland, in 1819; died in 1900. William was a brother of John G. Wellstood and came to NY with his parents in 1830. Began work there as a letter engraver, but later devoted himself to landscape and pictorial work. From 1846 to 1871 he was employed by the Western Methodist Book Concern in Cinncinati, OH, and by NY firms. A good line engraver. Produced a large amount of work.

WELLWER, NEIL.
Painter. Born July 22, 1929, in Millville, PA. Earned B.F.A. at Phil. Col of Art (1952) and MFA, Yale U. (1954). Taught at Yale; U. of Penn.; Santo Thomas (Univ) Manila; Cooper Union. Nat. Acad. of Design Fellow (1962). Exhibted at Stable Gal., NYC; Am. Fed. of Art, NYC; Whitney; PAFA; Baltimore; MOMA; Bates College; William and Mary G. and U. of Missouri. In collections of Boston Mus. of Fine Arts; Colby College; PAFA; Smith; Vassar; MMA; Brandeis; Whitney, MMA and others.

WELP, GEORGE L.
Art Draftsman. Born Brooklyn, NY, March 30, 1890. Pupil of ASL; Pratt Inst., Walter Biggs. Member: SI; Salma. C.; Art Dir. C. Address in 1929, Chanin Bldg., 122 East 42nd St., New York, NY; h. 157-48 Quince Ave., Flushing, LI, NY.

WELPLEY, CHARLES.
Painter and etcher. Born Washington, D.C., June 11, 1902. Pupil of Burtis Baker, Daniel Garber. Address in 1929, 1912 H. St., N. W., Washington, D.C.

WELSARE, DANIEL.
Painter. Born in 1796. he was a student of Thomas Sully who gave him letters of introduction to many artists in this country and abroad, where he travelled and studied. Later settled in Salem, NC where he painted for years. His son was named Thomas Sully Welsare and Sully painted a self-portrait for his namesake. He died in Salem, NC, in 1841.

994

WELSCH, PAUL.
Painter. Born at Strasbourg, July 26, 1889. Pupil of Maurice Denis, Charles Guerin, Bernhard Naudin in Paris. Represented in: Chicago Art Inst.; Musee de Mulhouse and Musee du Chateau des Rohans in Strasbourg. Address in 1929, 152 rue Broca, Paris 13e, France.

WELSH, B. F.
Engraver. The American engraver William Chapin, in his autobiography, says that in 1824 he worked in a NY office with an engraver by that name. Welsh afterward became a prominent Baptist Clergyman.

WELSH, H. DEVITT.
Painter, illustrator, and etcher. Born Phila., PA, March 2, 1888. Pupil of Thomas Anshutz, William M. Chase Joseph Pennell. Member: Phila. Sketch C.; Fellowship PAFA; SI; Phila. WCC; Art Dir. C.; Phila. Art Week Assoc.; Soc. Allied A. Work: Etching of Rembrandt's "Mill," and "St. Paul," Widener Coll., Phila.; etchings of the White House for President Wilson; etching of "The Lock," by Constable, Elkins Coll., Phila.; eight prints, British Mus. Asnt. Sec'y. of Div. of Pictorial Publ. during World War. Chairman, Executive Committee, Joseph Pennell Memorial Exh., Phila., 1926. Special member, Anglo-American Archaeological Assn. of Mexico D.F. Died in 1942. Address in 1929, 80 West 40th St., NYC.

WELSH, HERBERT.
Painter. Born in Philadelphia in 1851. Pupil of Bonnat in Paris; F. Auguste Ortmanns in Fontainebleau; of Onorato Carlandi in Rome. Member of fellowship, Penna. Acad. of Fine Arts. Address in 1926, 814 Carpenter Lane, Mt. Airy Station, Philadelphia, PA.

WELSH, ROSCOE.
Painter. Born in Laclede, MO, in 1895. Pupil of Eugene, California. Address in 1926, 445 Garfield Ave., Chicago, IL.

WELSH, WILLIAM P.
Painter and illustrator. Born Lexington, KY, Sept. 20, 1889.

Pupil of Mary Kinkead; Delecluse, Baschet and Royer in Paris; Du Mond in NY. Member: GFLA; Chicago SA; Chicago AC. Awards: Third prize, Harry Payne Whitney mural competition, 1910; first prize, First International Water Color Exhibition, 1921; second prize, Tribune mural competition, 1922. Work: "Prisioners of War," Chicago Art Inst.; mural decorations for the Men's Cafe, Palmer House Hotel, Chicago. Address in 1929, 19 East Pearson Street, Chicago, IL.

WENDEL, THEODORE.
Painter. Member: Boston GA. Awards: Sesnan medal, PAFA 1909; silver medal, P.-P. Exp., San F. 1915. Work: "Landscape," Cincinnati Museum; "Winter at Ipswich," Pennsylvania Acad, Philadelphia. Address in Ipswich, MA.

WENDT, JULIA M. BRACKEN.
Painter and sculptor. Born Apple River, IL, June 10, 1871. Pupil of AIC under Taft. Member: Chicago SA; Chicago Municipal A. Lg.; Los Angeles FAA; Calif. AC; NAC; Three Arts C. of Los Angeles; Laguna Beach AA. Awards: Sculpture prize, Chicago, 1898; Chicago Municipal A Lg. prize, 1905; Harrison prize; gold medal, Pan Calif. Exp., San Diego, 1915; Calif. AC., 1918. Work: "Illinois Welcoming the Nations," presented to the State by IL Woman's Bd. Columbian Exp., 1893; group, "Art, Science, and History," Los Angeles Museum. Instructor, Otis Art Inst., Los Angeles. Died in 1942. Address in 1929, 2814 N. Sichel St., Los Angeles, Calif.; Laguna Beach, CA.

WENDT, WILLIAM.
Painter. Born in Germany, Feb. 20, 1865; settled in Chicago 1880. Self-taught. Member: ANA 1912; Chicago SA: NAC; Calif. AC; Ten Painters of Los Angeles; Laguna Beach AA; AFA. Awards: Second Yerkes prize, Chicago, 1893; Young Fortnightly prize, AIC 1897; bronze medal, Pan Am. Exp., Buffalo, 1901; Cahn prize, AIC 1904; silver medal, St. Louis, Exp., 1904; hon. mention, Chicago SA 1905; silver medal, Wednesday Club, St. Louis,

1910; Cahn hon. mention, ACI 1910; Fine Arts Bldg. prize, SWA, 1912; Kirchberger prize, AIC, 1913; silver medal, P. P. Exp., San F., 1915; Black prize, Calif., AC, 1916. Work: "To Join the Brimming River," Cincinnati Mus.; "When All the World is Young." "The Silence of the Night," Art Inst. of Chicago; "Marine," Herron Art Inst., Indianapolis; "Hills in Springtime," Hibbard High School, Richmond, IN; "Montecito," Cliff Dwellers Club Chicago; "Where Peace Abides," Des Moines Assoc. of Fine Arts; "To Mountain Heights and Beyond," Harrison Gallery, Los Angeles Museum. Died in 1946. Address in 1929, care of Gardner Symons, 119 East 19th St., New York, NY; 2814 N. Sichel St., Los Angeles, CA; Laguna Beach, CA.

WENGER, JOHN.
Painter. Born in Russia, June 16, 1887. Pupil of Imperial Art School of Odessa; NAD. Member: Salma C.; Grand Cen. Gal. Award: Bronze medal, Sesqui-Centennial Expo., Phila., 1926. Work: Decorative curtains, Theatre Masque and the Town Hall, NY; designer of moving scenery in "Good Boy," Hammerstein Theatre, NY. Address in 1929, Van Dyke Studios, 939 Eighth Ave.; h. 420 Riverside Drive, New York, NY.

WENIGER, MARIA P.
Sculptor. Born in Germany, in 1880. Studied in Munich. Member of Art Alliance of America. Work: Miniature bronzes, "Dancers." Address in 1926, 442 East 58th Street, New York, NY.

WENTWORTH, ADELAIDE E.
Etcher, craftsman, lecturer and teacher. Born Wakefield, NH. Pupil of D. W. Ross. W. S. Robinson. Arthur Dow. Member: Cincinnati Woman's AC; Crafters Co. Address in 1929, 17 The Somerset, Kittery Depot, ME.

WENTWORTH, CECILE DE.
Painter. Born in New York. Pupil of Alexander Cabanel and Edward Detaille, Paris. Exhibiting every year in the Paris Salon since 1889; medals, Paris; Lyons; Turin; 1st gold medal at the National Exhibition, Tours; exhibited at the

Paris Expo., 1900, receiving a medal for portrait of Pope Leo XIII; represented at Musee du Luxembourg, Paris; Vatican Musee, Rome; Senate Chamber, Paris; Metropolitan Museum of NY and Corcoran Gallery, Washington, D.C., etc.; has made portraits of Thoedore Roosevelt, William H. Taft, Archbishop Corigan and many notable people in Europe. Officier d'Academie, Paris, 1894; Officier de l'instruction Publique; Chevalier Legion d'Honneur, 1901.

WENTWORTH, D(ANIEL) F.
Painter. Studied in Munich, but largely self taught. Member: CT. AFA. (Pres. Emer.). Award: Popular prize, CT. AFA., 1922. Work: "Evening after Snow," Storrs College. Died in 1934. Address in 1929, Whittlesey Ave., New Milford, CT.

WENTWORTH.,
Portrait painter in oils and miniature. He also made profile portraits in pencil. He was working about 1815, in Utica, NY.

WENTZ, HENRY FREDERICK.
Painter, craftsman, lecturer and teacher. Born in The Dalles, OR. Pupil of ASL of NY. Work: "Sand Dune. Neahkahmie," Portland Art Association. Address in 1929, Worcester Bldg., Roof, Portland, OR; summer, Neahkahmie Mt., Nelhalem P. O., OR.

WENZELL, ALBERT BECK.
Illustrator. Born in Detroit 1864; he died in Englewood, NJ on March 4, 1917. He painted the mural panels in the New Amsterdam Theater, NY. Wenzell was a pupil of Strahuber and Loeffitz in Munich.

WENZLER, H. A.
Portrait and landscape painter, also working in miniatures. Was of Danish birth but came to US at an early age and settled in NY. He was elected a Member of the National Acad. in 1860. Died in New York, in 1871.

WERBE, ANNA LAVICK.
Painter and teacher. Born Jan. 2, 1888. Pupil of John H. Vanderpoel,

Frederick Freer, Martha Baker. Member: Alumni AIC; Chicago AC. Address in 1929, 2950 Webb Ave., Detroit, MI.

WERNTZ, CARL N.
Painter, illustrator and teacher. Born Sterling, IL, July 9, 1874. Pupil of J. H. Vanderpoel, Frederick Freer, Lawton Parker, Jeanette Pratt. Orson Lowell. A. Muchas and Robert Reid in America; Richard Miller in Paris; Onorato Carlandi in Rome; Seti Mizuno and Kaho Kawatika in Japan. Member: Western Art Assoc.; Palette and Chisel C.; Illinois Manual Arts Assoc. Formerly cartoonist on "Chicago Record." Illustrated books and magazine articles. Founder, director and instructor, Chicago Acad. of Fine Arts. Died in 1944. Address in 1929, 18 South Michigan Ave., Chicago, IL.

WERTMULLER, ADOLPH ULRIC.
Painter. Born in Stockholm, Sweden, in 1751. Made first studies in art at home; went to Paris where he studied and practiced painting several years. Elected member of the Royal Academies of Sculpture and Painting in Paris and Stockholm; came to Philadelphia in May, 1794. Washington is said to have given him a single sitting for the portrait which was engraved by H. B. Hall for Irving's "Life of Washington," then in possession of Charles Augustus Davis of NY. The artists made several copies of this picture. Remained in this country until Autumn of 1796, when he returned to Stockholm. Came again to Phila. in 1800, and in the following year married a grand-daughter of Hesselius, pastor of the Swedish congregation at Wilmington, Del. Shortly after, he purchased a farm below Marcus Hook on the Delaware, where he died in 1811. After his death his pictures were sold at auction, a small copy of his "Danae," bringing $500.

WESCOTT, SUE MAY.
Miniature painter, who exhibited portrait miniatures at the exhibition at the Penna. Acad. of the Fine Arts, Phila., 1922.

Address in 1926, 5970 Woodbine Ave., Overbrook, PA.

WESSEL, HERMAN H.
Painter, etcher, and teacher. Born Vincennes, IN, 1878. Pupil of Frank Duveneck. Awards: Fine Arts prize, S. Western A., 1915; first portrait prize, Columbus, 1922; first prize, Altanta, 1920. represented in Cincinnati Museum; Engineering College. University of Cincinnati; murals in Scioto Co. (Ohio) Courthouse; Federal Reserve Bank Branch and Holmes Memorial Hospital, Cincinnati. Address in 1929, Art Museum; h. 2152 Alpine Place, Cincinnati, OH.

WESSELHOEFT, MARY FRASER.
Painter, illustrator, and craftsman. Born Boston, MA, Feb. 15, 1873. Pupil of Boston Mus. School; Denman W. Ross. Member: Copley S., 1892; Salons of America; S. Indp. A.; Santa Barbara Com. AA; Santa Barbara AL; Santa Barbara CWA. Specialty, stained glass and water colors. Address in 1929, 914 Santa Barbara St., Santa Barbara, CA.

WEST, BENJAMIN.
Painter. Born Oct. 10, 1738, in PA, on what is now the campus of Swarthmore. Showed great artistic talent in drawing and painting. Said to have been supplied his first colors by an Indian chief. He later received some instruction and materials from Wm. Williams, an Eng. artist then in Phila. West went to Lancaster, and made his first attempt at portraiture, painting a likeness of his friend Wm. Henry, and an historical scene, "The Death of Socrates." Became pupil of Provost Wm. Smith, graduating as a member of the class of 1757 of Univ. of PA. Made study of methods employed by Titian and other Italian painters, while studying in Rome. After 3 yrs. of study went to Eng. and opened a studio in London. Was presented to George III, who ordered a canvas depicting "The Departure of Regulus from Rome." He became a historical painter to the King. In 1765 the King founded the Royal Acad. and Joshua Reynolds became the pres. After his death in 1792 West served

as pres. almost uninterruptedly from 1792 - 1815. He married Elizabeth Shewell, whom he had known in Phila. and had crossed the sea to her artist lover. West painted 4 classes of pictures; portraits, minor historical scenes, great historical scenes and religious subjects. In his painting of the death of Wolfe at Quebec he repudiated traditions of the classical school, clothing his characters in the dress of the time. He said that in 1758 the Indian "Knew nothing about a toga, and it is inappropriate." This painting brought about a revolution in art. Work: "Christ Healing the Sick", British Nat. Gal. artistic expression. Large painting "Death on the Pale Horse," (1817) is 25' Long, 15' high. "Penn's Treaty with the Indian" is at Independece Hall Phila. The Met. Mus. of Mod. Art owns his self-portrait, "Hagar and Ishmael" and "Apollo and Hyacinthus" and others. He taught Charles Willson Pearle, Gilbert Stuart, Thomas Sully, Washington Allston, and Samuel Morse. He was painted by most of them, but the most pleasing portrait is that painted as a young man by his friend Matthew Pratt. Have no very complete life of West. "The Life and Studies of Benjamin West" by John Galt, published in 1816, was written during West's lifetime; its title page states that it is compiled from material furnished by himself. The PA Historical Society, in Phila., have many of West's paintings and drawings besides a large collection of his letters. In 1817, after the death of his wife, West's strength began to fail, though his mental faculties remained unimpaired. Died in London on March 11, 1820, and was buried in St. Paul's Cathedral.

WEST, GEORGE (MRS.) PARSONS.
See Isabell Percy.

WEST, GLADYS (M.G.).
Painter and teacher. Born Philadelphia, Aug. 24, 1897. Pupil of PAFA. Member: Fellowship PAFA; Phila. Alliance. Work: "St. Michael and the Cripples," St. Michael and All Angels,

Philadelphia; altar, pulpit and tabernacle door decorations, Church of the Nativity, Philadelphia; decoration Oak Lane Review Club, Philadelphia. Address in 1929, 5340 Wayner Ave., Philadelphia, PA.

WEST, LEVON.
Painter and etcher. Born Centerville, SD, Feb. 3, 1900. Pupil of Joseph Pennell. Award: Charles M. Lea prize, Philadelphia, 1928. Work: "The Mountain Ranger," Philadelphia Museum, Philadelphia, PA; "Blackfoot Glacier," New York Public Library; "Pine and Sapling," Brooklyn Museum, Brooklyn, NY; "Portrait of Alfonso XIII, Hipsanic Museum, New York City. Died in 1968. Address in 1929, 342 Madison Ave., New York, NY; summer, Mayville, ND.

WEST, PETER.
Animal painter. Born in England in 1833. He came to this country and maintained studios in several cities. In 1878 he was settled in Cleveland, Ohio, where he painted many of the fine horses of that section of the country; he also painted still life and genre subjects.

WEST, WILLIAM EDWARD.
Historical painter and portrait painter in oils and miniature. Born in 1788 in Lexington, KY. West painted miniatures several years before he studied in Philadelphia with Thomas Sully about 1807. In 1819 he went to Natchez. In 1820 he sailed for Europe. At Leghorn he painted a portrait of Shelley from life. In 1824 was in Paris, from 1825 to 1839 in London, then he sailed for Baltimore. In 1840 he was in NY where he lived until 1855, when he moved to Nashville. See: Century Magazine, October, 1905; Putnam's Magazine, September, 1907; Tuckerman, "Book of the Artists." Died Nov., 1857, in Nashville.

WESTFELDT, PATRICK McL.
Painter. Born in New York, NY, died in New Orleans in 1907. Studied with Carl Hecker and William Prettyman. Specialty, landscapes, mostly in water color.

WESTMAN, HARRY JAMES.
Cartoonist, painter, illustrator, teacher, and writer. Born Parkerburg, WV, Aug. 8, 1877. Pupil of Columbus Art School. Member: Columbus Pen and Brush C.; Lg. of Columbus Artists; S. Indp. A; Chicago NJSA; Lg. Amer. A. Cartoonist, McClure Newspaper Syndicate. Died in 1945. Address in 1929, 1661 Franklin Park, South, Columbus, OH.

WESTOBY, M.
Portrait painter. The portrait of Lindley Murray, published in (Longacre and Herring) National Portrait Gallery, is noted as engraved by Gimber after the portrait by Westoby.

WESTON, FRANCES M.
Painter, who exhibited water colors at the PAFA, Phila., 1922. Address in 1926, Haddonfield, NJ.

WESTON, HAROLD.
Painter. Died in 1972. Address in 1929, St. Huberts, Essex Co., NY; care of the Montross Gallery, 26 East 56th St., New York, NY.

WESTON, HARRY ALAN.
Painter and teacher. Born Springfield, IL, Dec. 11, 1885. Pupil of AIC; Grand Central School of Art in NY. Member: Salma C.; AWCS: NYWCC; Am. APL. Awards: Porter prize, Salma C., New York, 1828; hon. mention, AWCS and NYWCC, New York, 1929. Address in 1929, 170 East 78th St., New York, NY.; summer, Idlehour Artist Colony, Oakdale, LI, NY.

WESTON, HENRY W.
Weston was engraving, maps, Bible illustrations, etc. in Philadelphia, in 1803-06, for Mathew Carey, book-publisher of that city.

WESTON, MARY PILLSBURY.
Miniature painter. Born Jan. 1, 1817, in Hebron, NH. Died in 1894, in Lawrence, KS.

WESTON, MORRIS.
Painter, who exhibited at the National Acad. of Design, NY, 1925.

Address in 1926, 127 East 50th St., NY.

WESTWOOD , CHARLES.
Engraver. Born in Birmingham, England. He came to the United States in 1851 with John Rogers, the engraver. Westwood was a talented general engraver.

WETHERALD, HARRY H.
Painter and illustrator. Born Providence, April 3, 1903. Pupil of Frazier; Hawthorne; RI School of Design. Member: Providence, WCC; Prov. AC. Died in 1955. Address in 1929, Fleur de Lis Studios, 7 Thomas St.; H. 91 Pleasant View Ave., Providence, RI; summer, Provincetown, MA.

WETHERBEE, GEORGE.
Painter. Born in Cincinnati, in 1851. Educated in Boston; studied at Royal Acad. of Arts, Anwerp; also in London. Travelled and resided in West Indies, France, Germany, Italy, Belgium; finally settled in London. Member: Royal Inst. of Painters in Water Colors; Royal Society of Oil Painters; Royal British Colonial Society of Artists; New Gallery Society, London. Address in 1926, 18 Redington Road, Hampstead, N.W., London, EN.

WETHERILL, E. KENT K.
Painter, who exhibited at the National Academy of Design, New York, 1925. Address in 1926, 145 East 23d St., New York, NY.

WETHERILL, ROY.
Painter. Born in New Brunswick, NJ, in 1880. Pupil of R. L. Lambdin and of Norman Tolson. Address in 1926, Kansas City Art Inst., Kansas City, MO.

WETMORE, MARY MINERVA.
Painter. Born Canfield, OH. Pupil of Cleveland Art School; ASL of NY; School of Design, Phila.; Art School, San Francisco; Chase in Spain and CA; Julian Acad. and Colarossi Acad. in Paris. Member: Chicago SA; Chicago AC. Address in 1929, 511 West Church St., Champaign, IL.

WETZEL, GEORGE J(ULIUS).
Painter. Born NY, Feb. 8, 1870.
Pupil of ASL of NY under Mowbray,
Beckwith, Cox, and Chase. Member:
ASL of NY (life); Nat. FA Soc.;
AFA. Awards: Hon. mention, AC,
Phila.; Salma. C. Died in 1935.
Address in 1929, East Drive,
Douglas Manor, Douglaston, LI, NY.

WEYAND, MRS. CHARLES L.
See Edith Varian Cockroft.

WEYL, MAX.
Painter. Born Dec. 1, 1837, in
Muhlem Germany. Came to America in
1853. Represented in the Corcoran
and National Art Gallery in Wash.,
and in many private coll. He died
in July 6, 1914, in Wash., DC.

WEYRICK, JOSEPH LEWIS.
Painter. Specialty, water colors.
He died in Baltimore in 1918.

WHALEN, JOHN W.
Painter. Born in Worcester, MA, in
1891. Pupil of Chase and Eric
Pape. Address in 1926, 29 Richards
St., Worcester, MA.

WHALEY, E(DNA) REED.
Painter, writer, and teacher. Born
New Orleans, LA, March 31, 1884.
Pupil of Newcomb School of Art.
Member: Columbia AA (Pres);
Carolina AA; SSAL; Columbia Sketch
C. Awards: First prize for water
color, Columbia AA, 1924; Honorable
mention for Still Life in oil,
SSAL, Feb., 1921. Work:
Illustrated "The Old Types Pass,"
by M. S. Whaley. Address in 1929,
4908 Colonial Drive, College Place,
Columbia, SC.

WHARTON, PHILIP FISHBOURNE.
Painter. Born in Philadelphia in
1841. Studied at the Penn. Acad.
of the Fine Arts and in Paris.
Best known work: "Perdita" which
received a medal at the Centennial
in 1876, "Eventide," "Uncle Jim"
and "Waiting for the Parade." Died
in 1880.

WHARTON, T. H.
According to Dunlap this artist was
painting in NY, in 1834.

WHEELAN, ALBERTINE RANDALL.
Painter, illustrator, and
craftsman. Born San Francisco, CA,
May 17, 1863. Pupil of Virgil
Williams; San Francisco School of
Design. Member: AFA. Designer of
character and costume sketches for
David Belasco; illustrator;
designer of book plates and stained
glass windows; originator of the
newspaper cartoons, "The
Dumbunnies." Address in 1929, care
of American Express, Paris, France.

WHEELER, CLEORA CLARK.
Illustrator and craftsman. Born
Austin, MN. Pupil of Julie
Gauthier. Member: MN State AS; Am.
Bookplate S. Award: First award in
design, MN. State AS., 1913.
Specialty, bookplate designs.
Address in 1929, 1376 Summit Ave.,
St. Paul, MN.

WHEELER, CLIFTON A.
Painter. Born Hadley, IN, Sept. 4,
1883. Pupil of Forsyth in
Indianapolis; Henri, Miller and
Chase in NY; also studied in
Europe. Awards: Richmond (IN)
prize, 1917; Holcomb prize, Herron
Art Inst., 1921, 1923; Art Asso.
prize, 1924; Franklin College
prize, 1926; Rector Memorial prize,
1927; IN Univ., prize, 1828. Work:
Paintings in Herron Art Inst.,
Indianapolis; Thorntown (IN) Public
Library; Morresville (IN) Public
Library; Indiana Univ.,
Bloomington; Purdue Univ.
Lafayette; Rose Polytechnic Inst.,
Terre Haute; Syracuse (IN) Public
Library; mural painting in
Indianapolis City Hospital; St.
Josephs Convent, Tipton IN; Circle
Theatre, Brookside and Whittier
Schools, Indianapolis. Died in
1953. Address in 1929, 5317 Lowell
Ave., Indianapolis, IN.

WHEELER, DORA (MRS. KEITH).
Painter. Born in Jamaica, LI, in
1858. She studied with W. M. Chase
in NY, and with Bouguereau in
Paris. She painted a series of
portraits of English and American
authors, but primarily executed
decorative designs. Address in
1926, 33 West 67th St., NYC.

WHEELER, E. KATHLEEN.
Sculptor. Born in England in 1884;
came to America in 1914.
Specialty, animals. Address in
1926, Hillside, WI.

WHEELER, HELEN C.
Painter. Born in Newark, NJ, in
1877. Pupil of John C. Johansen.
Member of Art Students' League of
New York. Address in 1926, 6 Kirk
Place, Newark, NJ.

WHEELER, JANET D.
Portrait painter. Born in Detroit,
MI. Pupil of PAFA; and of Julien
Academy and Courtois, Paris.
Exhibited at the Salon, Paris, and
the Penna. Acad. of the Fine Arts,
Philadelphia. Address in 1926,
1710 Chestnut St., Philadelphia,
PA. Died Oct. 25, 1945.

WHEELER, KATHLEEN.
Painter. Born Reading, EN, Oct.
15, 1884. Pupil of Esther Moore;
Slade School. Member: Phila.
Alliance. Work: "Death and
Sleep." Hackley Art Gallery,
Muskegon, MI; "The Roundup,"
Canadian Pacific Railway, London.
Address in 1929, 113 West 11th St.;
1526 East 57th St. Chicago, IL.

WHEELER, LAURA B.
Portrait painter, illustrator,
craftsman, and teacher. Born
Hartford, CT. Pupil of W. M. Chase,
Henry McCarter, and Violet Oakley.
Illustrated "The Shadow," "The
Upward Path." Address in 1929,
Brinton Cottage, Cheyney, PA;
summer, 589½ Lafayette Ave.,
Brooklyn, New York, NY.

WHEELER, WILLIAM R.
Portrait painter and miniaturist.
Born in Michigan, in 1832. In 1855
he moved to Hartford, CT. Died c.
1894.

WHEELOCK, MERRILL.
Landscape painter. Born 1822 in
VT. In "Tuckerman's American
Artist Life" the water color
studies of the White Mountain
scenery by Wheelock are noted; died
in 1866.

WHEELOCK, WARREN.
Painter, sculptor, and craftsman.
Born Sutton, MA, Jan. 15, 1880.

Pupil of Pratt Inst., Brooklyn.
Member: S. Indp. A. Award: Hon.
mention, Pan American Exh., Los
Angeles, Calif, 1925. Work: "Old
Man and Child," Los Angeles Museum
of Art. Died in 1960. Address in
1929, 207 West 16th St.; h. 24,
West Eighth St., New York, NY;
summer, Linville Falls, NC.

WHELAND, BLANCHE.
Painter. Born Los Angeles, CA.
Pupil of Los Angeles School of Art
and Design, Boardman Robinson,
Nicholas Haz. Member: Calif. AC;
Laguna Beach AA; West Coast Arts,
Inc.; AFA. Address in 1929, 147
North Norton Ave., Los Angeles, CA.

WHELPLEY, PHILIP M.
Engraver and landscapist, in 1845
located in NY. He engraved
portraits in mezzotint.

WHETSEL, GERTRUDE P.
Painter. Born McCune, KS, Sept.
21, 1886. Pupil of Clyde Leon
Keller. Member: Portland AA.
Awards: First prize for marine,
2nd prize for landscape, Oregon
State Fair, 1922. Address in 1929,
585 east 27th St., North, Portland,
OR.

WHISLER, HOWARD F(RANK).
Painter. Born New Brighton, PA,
Jan. 25, 1886. Pupil of PAFA;
Breckenridge, McCarter. Member:
Fellowship PAFA; Arch. Lg. of NY;
North Shore AA; ASL of NY. Address
in 1929, 55 Tiemann Place, New
York, NY.

WHITE, ALDEN.
Etcher. Born Acushnet, MA, April
11, 1861. Pupil of V. Preissig.
Member: Chicago SE. Address in
1929, R. F. D. No. 1, New Bedford,
MA.

WHITE, BELLE CADY.
Painter. Born Chatham, NY. Pupil
of Pratt Inst. in Brooklyn; Snell,
Woodbury and Hawthorne. Member:
Brooklyn WCC; AWCS (asso.); NA
Women PS.; Brooklyn SA. Director
of the Ashland, Oregon, School of
Art. Instructor at Pratt Inst.
Died in 1945. Address in 1929, 150
Steuben St., Brooklyn, NY; summer,
Old Chatham, NY.

WHITE, C(LARENCE) SCOTT.
Painter. Born Boston, MA, March
14, 1872. Pupil of Charles H.
Woodbury. Member: Boston SWCP;
Copley S; Boston AC. Address in
1929, 97 Somerset St., Belmont, MA;
summer, Cranberry Isles, ME.

WHITE, EDWIN.
Painter. Born in South Hadley, MA,
in 1817. He studied in Paris and
in Dusseldorf. His studio was in
NY. Elected to the Nat. Acad. of
Design in 1849. Best known for his
American historical pictures.
"Washington Resigning His
Commission" was painted for the
State of Maryland. Died at
Saratoga Springs, NY, in 1877.

WHITE, ELIZABETH.
Painter, etcher, and teacher. Born
Sumter, Nov. 22, 1893. Pupil of
PAFA; Alfred Hutty. Member:
Fellow. PAFA; SSAL. Award First
prize for flower painting, SSAL,
Houston, TX, 1926. Address in
1929, 421 N. Main St., Sumter, SC.

WHITE, EMMA L(OCKE) R(IANHARD).
(Mrs. F. Winthrop White). Painter.
Born New Brighton, SI, NY, Nov. 21,
1871. Pupil of Twachtman, Cox,
Mowbray, Brandegee, Chase, etc.
Member: NA Women PS.; Am. APL.
Died in 1953. Address in 1929, 3
Gordon Place, New Brighton, SI, NY;
summer, Kent Kollow, New Preston,
CT.

WHITE, G. I.
This good line-engraver of
portraits was working about 1825-30
in this country, but his prints
give no indication of locality.

WHITE, GEORGE F.
Painter. Born in 1868, in Des
Moines, IA. Exhibited water colors
at the Penna. Acad. of Fine Arts,
Philadelphia, 1922. Address in
1926, 3 S. W. 9th St., Des Moines,
IA.

WHITE, GEORGE H.
Engraver. Some fairly good
portraits, engraved in a mixed
manner about 1870, are thus signed.

WHITE, HELENE MAYNARD.
Painter. Born in Philadelphia.
Pupil of Art Students' League PAFA;
Drexel Institute; studied art in
Paris. Professional portrait
painter since 1895. Exhibited at
all leading art institutions, and
at St. Louis Exposition; painted
portraits of many notable people;
also modeled heroic figure of
"Chingachgook" for Mohican Lodge,
Red Bank, NJ. Awarded gold medals
and silver medal. Member:
Fellowship. Acad. of Fine Arts;
Plastic Club; Harmonic Society of
University of PA; Lyceum Club,
London; Historical Pageant
Associaton. Address in 1926, 1530
Walnut St., Philadelphia.

WHITE, HENRY C(OOKE).
Painter. Born Hartford, Sept. 15,
1861. Pupil of D. W. Tryon and ASL
of NY. Member: CT. AFA; NYWCC;
The Pastellists; ADA. Died Sept.
28, 1952. Address in 1929,
Waterford, CT.

WHITE, J(ACOB) C(AUPEL).
Painter, illustrator, and etcher.
Born New York, NY, Oct. 1, 1895.
Pupil of NAD; Academie Julian,
Paris. Member: AFA. Awards:
Tiffany Foundation Scholarship,
1920. Works: "The Library" and
"The Hall," Tiffany Foundation Art
Gallery. Address in 1929, 352 West
12th St., New York, NY.

WHITE, JOHN BLAKE.
Painter. Born Sept. 2, 1782, in
Charleston, SC. In 1803 he went to
London and studied under Benj.
West. He excelled as a historical
painter. Also an author, practiced
law, and was a member and director
of the South Carolina Acad. of Fine
Arts. Painted "Genl. Marion
Inviting British Officers to
Dinner;" also painted "The Battle
of New Orleans" and "Grave
Robbers." Died Aug. 24, 1859, in
Charleston.

WHITE, MARGARET WOOD.
(Mrs. V. G. White). Painter. Born
Chicago, IL, March 4, 1893. Pupil
of Biloul, Humbert, Richard Miller,
Johansen, Bridgeman. Member: NA
Women PS. Address in 1929,
Woodmere, LI, NY.

WHITE, NELSON C(OOKE).
Painter. Born Waterford, CT, June 11, 1900. Pupil of Henry C. White and NAD. Member: CT. AFA. Address in 1929, Waterford, CT.

WHITE, NONA L.
Painter, writer, lecturer, and teacher. Born in IL, Oct. 4, 1859. Pupil of AIC. Art critic on "L.A. Evening News." Dir. of Art in S. Pasadena Women's Club. Address in 1929, 1134 Wabash St., Pasadena, CA; summer, Laguna Beach. CA.

WHITE, ORRIN A(UGUSTINE).
Painter. Born Hanover, IL, Dec. 5, 1883. Pupil of Phila. School of Applied Art. Member: CA AC. Awards: Silver medal, Panama-CA Exp., San Diego, 1915; Mrs. Henry E. Huntington prize, CA AC, 1921. Work: "Sierra Peaks," Los Angeles Mus. Died in 1969. Address in 1929, 2036 Linda Vista Ave., Pasadena, CA.

WHITE, THOMAS GILBERT.
Portrait and mural painter. Born in Grand Rapids, MI, in 1877. Pupil of Julien Acad. under Constant and Laurens; also student of Whistler and Mac Monnies. Painted mural panels in Pan-American Building, Washington; also painted portrait of Gov. McCreary of Kentucky. Address in 1926, Cowmoney Lodge, Fairfield, CT. Died in 1939.

WHITE, THOMAS STURT.
The New England Weekly Journal, for July 8, 1734, contains the following notice of a possible early engraver and printer of copperplates; "Engraver from London, not having met with such success as he expected since he came to Boston; hereby gives Notice that he intends sailing for London in Fall, unless he meets with sufficient encouragement to oblige him to stay. This therefore is to inform all Gentlemen, Goldsmiths, and others, that they may have all manner of Engraving either on Gold, silver, Copper or Pewter; likewise Rolling Press Printing, as well and cheap as is performed in London. N. B. The said White lives at the Second Door on the Right Hand in Williams Court, in Cornhill."

WHITE, VICTOR GERALD.
Painter and teacher. Born Dublin, Ireland, Feb. 27, 1891. Pupil of Chase, Bellows, Henri Simon, Billoul, etc. Member: Mural P. Died in 1954. Address in 1929, Woodmere, LI, NY.

WHITE, WALTER CHARLES LOUIS.
Landscape painter and teacher. Born Sheffield, Yorkshire, England, Sept. 15, 1876. Pupil of Carlson, Beck, Dow, Hawthorne, Pratt Inst. Member: Brooklyn SA: New Haven PCC; Miss. AA; Brooklyn WCC; Alliance; Springfield AL; NYWCC: AWCS; Nassau Co. AL. Award: Hon. mention, 1925; gold medal, Mississippi AA, 1926. Instructor at the Brooklyn Inst. of Arts and Sciences. Address in 1929, Farmer's and St. Mark's Aves., St. Albans, LI, NY.

WHITE, WILLIAM FLETCHER.
Painter and illustrator. Born Hudson, NY, July 2, 1885. Pupil of Twatchman, Mowbray, Cox, Bridgeman. Member: SI; GFLA. Address in 1929, 66 West 11th Street, New York, NY.

WHITECHURCH, ROBERT.
Engraver. Born in London in 1814. Came to the United States about 1848 and lived in Philadelphia. Worked for the Treasury Dept. of Washington. Engraver of portraits in line, stipple and mezzotint. Died in 1880.

WHITEHAM, EDNA MAY.
Painter and illustrator. Born in Nebraska. Student at Chicago Art Inst. Address in 1926, 9 Westmoreland Ave., Takoma Park, MD.

WHITEHEAD, MARGARET VAN CORTLANDT.
Painter. Member: Pittsburgh A. A.; NA Women PS; AFA. Award: First prize, Pittsburgh AA, 1912. Address in 1929, "The Maples," 80 West Putnam Ave., Greenwich, CT.

WHITEHEAD, WALTER.
Illustrator and teacher. Born Chicago, IL, Sept., 2, 1874. Pupil of AIC and Howard Pyle. Member: SI, 1911; Salma. C.; Art. Dir. C. Instructor of Chicago Acad. of Fine Arts. Died in 1956. Address in 1929, 230 Park Ave., New York, NY.

WHITEHORN, JAMES.
Painter. Born in Rutland Co., VT, in 1787. He was made a member of the National Acad. Specialty was portraiture. His painting of Silas Wright is in the City Hall, New York. Also designed the well known mezzotint engraving of "Henry Clay Addressing the Senate" published about 1846. Died in 1830.

WHITEHURST, CAMELLA.
Painter. Born Baltimore, MD. Pupil of Chase, Beaux. Member: Fellowship PAFA; NA Women PS; Grand Cen. AG. Awards: First prize, All Southern Exhibition, Charleston, SC, 1921; hon. mention, NA Women PS. 1920; 1st prize, Memphis, 1922; Delgado, prize, New Orleans, 1923; 2nd prize, NA Women PS, 1923; bronze medal, Wash. SA, 1925, and first prize, portrait, 1929. Work in Delgado Museum, New Orleans. Died in 1936. Address in 1929, 411 N. Charles St.; h. 1501 Eutaw Place., Baltimore, MD.

WHITEMAN, SAMUEL EDWIN.
Landscape painter. Born in Philadelphia, PA, in 1860. Pupil of Boulanger, Constant and Lefebvre in Paris. Instructor at Johns Hopkins Univeristy. Member of Charcoal Club of Baltimore, MD. Died Oct. 27, 1922.

WHITESIDE, FRANK REED.
Landscape painter. Born in Philadelphia, PA, in 1866. Pupil of PAFA; also Laurens and Constant in Paris. Member: Philadelphia Sketch Club; Fellowship, PAFA; Phila. Water Color Club; Phila. Art Alliance. Address in 1926, 1010 Clinton St., Phila., PA. Died in 1929.

WHITFIELD, EMMA M(OREHEAD).
Painter and teacher. Born Greensboro, NC, Dec. 5, 1874. Pupil of ASL of NY; Raphael Collin in Paris. Work: Portraits in State Library, Richmond, VA.; University of Richmond, Richmond, VA.; Carnegie Library, Greensboro, NC; State Capitols, Raleigh, NC, and Jackson, MI; Guildford Co. Court House, Greensboro, NC; Confederate Battle Abbey, Confederate Memorial Museum and the

Executive Mansion, Richmond, VA; Woman's Club, Raleigh, NC; MI College, Clinton, MI; portrait of "Mrs. R. D. Johnson, Founder," Boys Industrial School, Birmingham, AL. Address in 1929, 1800 Grove Ave., Richmond, VA.

WHITING, ALMON C(LARK).
Painter. Bron Worcester, MA, March 5, 1878. Pupil of MA. Normal Art School in Boston; Constant, Laurens and Whistler in Paris. Member: Paris AA; Salma. C. Director, Toledo Museum, 1901-03. Work: "Notre Dame, Paris," Museum of Art, Toledo. Address in 1929, c/o, The Equitable Trust Co., 41, rue Cambon, Paris, France.

WHITING, JOHN D.
Painter, illustrator, and writer. Born Ridgefield, CT, July 20, 1884. Pupil of John H. Neimeyer, G. A. Thompson, Lucius W. Hitchcock; Yale School of Fine Arts. Member: New Haven Paint and Clay C.; SI; CT. AFA. Address in 1929, 345 Whiney Ave.; h. 291 Edwards ST., New Haven, CT.

WHITLOCK, M(ARY) URSULA.
Painter, craftsman, and teacher. Pupil of J. Alden Weir; Julian Academy in Paris. Member: NA Women PS. Address in 1929, Care of MacDowell Club, 166 East 73d St., New York, NY; summer, Care of Cecilia Beaux, Gloucester, MA.

WHITMAN, PAUL.
Painter and etcher. Born Denver, CO, April 23, 1897. Pupil of Armin Hansen. Award: Prize, International Society of Etchers, Los Angeles, 1928. Address in 1929, San Luis Ave., Carmel CA.

WHITMAN, SARAH WYMAN.
(Mrs. Wiliam Whitman). Born in Baltimore, MD, in 1842. Pupil of William M. Hunt of Boston and of Couture in Paris. Represented in the Boston Museum of Art by "Gloucester Harbor;" "Sunset;" Portrait of Martin Brimmer; "Warm Night;" "Edge of Evening;" "Rhododendrons;" "Roses." Died July, 1904 in Boston, MA.

WHITMER, HELEN C(ROZIER).
Painter and teacher. Born Darby, PA, Jan. 6, 1870. Pupil of Breckenridge, Anshurz, Henri, Thouron, Vonnoh. Member: Pittsburgh AA; S. Indp. A. Address in 1929, 5806 Walnut Street, Pittsburgh, PA.

WHITMORE, ROBERT HOUSTON.
Painter and etcher. Born Dayton, OH, Feb. 22, 1890. Pupil of AIC; Cincinnati Art Academy; H. M. Walcott James R. Hopkins. Member: Dayton Society of Etchers; ASL of Chicago. Awards: Goodman prize, ASL of Chicago, 1920; Bryan prize, Calif. PM, 1924. Represented in Dayton Museum; Steel High School; Normal School, Dayton; Los Angeles Museum of History, Science and Art. Asst. Professor of Fine Arts, Antioch College, Yellow Springs. Address in 1929, R. R. 1, Yellow Springs, OH.

WHITNET, ELIAS.
Wood engraver and painter. Born in 1827. He succeeded Benj. F. Childs as superintendent of engraving for the Tract Society. His engraving of the designs of the Englishman Gilbert are among his best work and can be compared to the engraving of Dalziel. He illustrated largely for Putnam & Co., NY. (See "History of Wood Engraving in America" by W. J. Linton.)

WHITNEY, ANNE.
Sculptor. Born Sept. 2, 1821, Watertown, MA. She studied abroad; on her return to the US established her studio in Boston in 1873. Executed many portraits and ideal groups. Her statue of Harriet Martineau is at Wellesley Coll., and a statue of Charles Sumner is in front of the law school at Harvard. Her statue of Samuel Adams is in the Capitol at Wash. Died Jan. 23, 1915 in Boston, MA.

WHITNEY, BEATRICE.
(Mrs. Van Ness). Painter. Born Chelsea, MA, March 24, 1888. Pupil of Tarbell, Benson, Hale and Pratt. Awards: Julian A. Shaw prize, NAD 1914; silver medal, P. P. Exp., San F., 1915. Address in 1929, 91 Francis St., Brookline, MA.

WHITNEY, CHARLES FREDERICK.
Painter and teacher. Born Pittston, ME, June 18, 1858. Pupil of MA State Normal AS. Author of "Blackboard Sketching," published by Milton Bradley Co., "Blackboard Drawing," published by the Prang Co.; "Indian Designs and Symbols," published by C. F. Whitney, Davers; "Chalk Talks for the Teacher," published by the Practical Drawing Co., Dallas. Address in 1929, The Wheelock School, 100 Riverway; Boston, MA; h. 29 Pine St., Danvers, MA; summer, Camp Vision, Tamworth, NH.

WHITNEY, DANIEL WEBSTER.
Painter. Born Catonsville, MD, May 3, 1895. Pupil of C. Y. Turner, Daniel Garber, Hugh Breckenridge, Joseph Pearson. Address in 1929, Catonsville, MD.

WHITNEY, GERTRUDE V(ANDERBILT).
(Mrs. Harry Payne Whitney). Sculptor. Born April, 1877, New York City. Pupil of James E. Fraser and Andrew O'Connor. Member: NA Women PS; NSS; Port. P.; Newport AA; New Soc. A.; NAC. Awards: Hon. mention, Paris Salon, 1913; NAC prize, NA Women PS, 1914; bronze medal, P. P. Exp., San F. 1915. Founded Whitney Club, forerunner of the Whitney Museum. Died April 18, 1942. Address in 1929, 8 West 8th St., and 19 Macdougal Alley; h. 871 Fifth Ave., New York, NY; summer, Old Westbury, LI, NY.

WHITNEY, HELEN REED.
Painter. Born Brookline, MA, July 1, 1878. Pupil of Boston School of Drawing and Painting under Hale, Benson and Tarbell. Member: Plastic C.; Phila. Alliance; Fellowship PAFA; Phila. WCC. Address in 1929, Moylan, Rose Valley, PA; summer, Nantucket, MA.

WHITNEY, ISABEL L.
Mural painter and craftsman. Born Brooklyn. Pupil of Arthur Dow, Howard Pyle, Hayley Lever. Member: Brooklyn WCC; NAC; S. Indp. A.; Brooklyn Soc. Modern A.; Salons of America. Died in 1962. Address in 1929, 337 Fourth Ave., New York, NY; h. 114 Remsen St., Brooklyn, NY.

WHITNEY, JOSEPHA.
Painter. Born in Washington, DC, in 1872. Pupil of Messer, Perrie and Cherouzet. Address in 1926, 237 Church St., New Haven, CT.

WHITNEY, MARGARET Q.
Sculptor. Born in Chicago, IL, in 1900. Pupil of Charles Graftly. Member: Philadelphia Art Alliance; Fellowship, Penna. Acad. of the Fine Arts. Address in 1926, 147 Gates Ave., Montclair, NJ.

WHITNEY, PHILIP R.
Painter, artist, and teacher. Born Council Bluffs, IA, Dec. 31, 1878. Pupil of Fred Wagner; Dept. of Architecture, MA, Inst. of Technology. Member: Phila. AC.; Phila. Alliance; Phila. WCC. Work: "Winter," in Pennsylvania State College. Professor School of Fine Arts, University of Pennsylvania. Died in 1960. Address in 1929, Moylan, Rose Valley, PA; summer, Nantucket, MA.

WHITTAKER, JOHN BARNARD.
Painter. Born in 1836, in Ireland. A painter of decided merit. He painted several portraits of prominent men for the city of New York. Mr. Whittaker's portrait of John W. Hunter (Mayor of Brooklyn), painted in 1876,hangs in the old City Hall.

WHITTEMORE, C. HELEN SIMPSON.
(Mrs. William J. Whittemore). Painter. Born in England. Pupil of Chase, Collin, Merson, Garrido. Member: NYWCC; NA. Women PS. Address in 1929, 58 West 57th St., New York, NY; summer, East Hampton, LI, NY.

WHITTEMORE, FRANCES D(AVIS).
(Mrs. L. D. Whittemore). Painter, writer, lecturer, and teacher. Born Decatur, IL. Pupil of J. Alden Weir, Kenyon Cox, Ealter Shirlaw, ASL of NY, AIC. Member: AM. College AA.; Wash. AC; Topeka AG. Address in 1929, Director, Mulvane Art Museum, Washburn College; h. 1615 College Ave., Topeka, KS.

WHITTEMORE, GRACE CONNER.
Painter, craftsman, and teacher. Born Columbia, Co., PA, Oct. 29, 1876. Pupil of Daingerfield and Snell. Member: Art Center of the Oranges. Address in 1929, 6 Morse Ave., East Orange, NJ.

WHITTEMORE, WILLIAM J(OHN).
Painter. Born New York, March 26, 1860. Pupil of NY of Wm. Hart, NAD, and ASL under Beckwith; Lefebvre and Constant in Paris. Member: ANA 1897. AWCS; NYWCC; Am. S. Min. P.; Salma. C., 1890; Lotos C.; Allied AA.; SPNY; Century C.; AFA. Awards: Silver medal, Paris Exp., 1889; bronze medal, Atlanta Exp., 1895; bronze medal, Charleston Exp., 1902; Proctor prize, NAD, 1917; Griscom prize, AWCS, 1927; Isidor prise, Salma C, 1927; Weyrich Memorial prize, Balto., 1928. Died in 1955. Address in 1929, 58 West 57th Street, New York, NY.

WHITTREDGE, WORTHINGTON.
Painter. Born in Springfield, OH, May, 1820. Studied landscape and portrait painting in Cincinnati. Going abroad in 1849, he continued his studies in London, Paris and Antwerp, and in Dusseldorf under Andreas Achenbach. He settled in NY, making a specialty of landscapes, and actively participated in art matters. He was elected an Associate Member and, in 1862, an Academician of the National Acad. of Design, of which he was president for the year 1875-76. He received a bronze medal at the Centennial Exhibition, Philadelphia, 1876; honorable mention at the Paris Exposition, 1889; silver medals at the Pan-American Expo., 1901, and the St. Louis Expo., 1904. Died Feb. 25, 1910, in Summit, NJ.

WICKER, MARY.
Painter. Member: Chicago PS; Chicago AC; NAC. Address in 1929, 1510 Title and Trust Bldg. Chicago, IL, 139 West 54th St., New York, NY.

WICKES, WILLIAM JARVIS.
Painter, sculptor, and artist. Born Saginaw, MI, May 26, 1897. Pupil of AIC. Member: Alliance. Address in 1929, 1016 Genesee Ave., Saginaw, MI.

WICKEY, HARRY.
Etcher. Born Stryker, OH, Oct. 14, 1892. Member: Salma C.; Brooklyn SI. Awards: Logan prize, Chicago SE; Shaw prize, Salma. C., 1925; bronze medal, Sesqui-Centennial Expo., Phila., 1926. Work: "Midsummer Night," "Snug Harbor" and "The Park," Met. Mus. of Art, NY; "Midsummer Night," AIC. Address in 1929, 74th St., h. 350 West 21st St., NYC.

WICKEY, HELEN REED.
Painter, who exhibited water colors at the Penn. Acad. of the Fine Arts, Philadephia, 1926. Address in 1926, 139 West 54th St., NYC.

WICKHAM, JULIA M.
Painter. Member: NA Women PS; PBC. Address in 1929, Cuthchogue, LI, NY.

WICKS, HEPPIE EN EARL.
Portrait painter, lecturer, and teacher. Born Le Roy, Genesee Co., NY. Pupil of L. M. Wiles, Iriving R. Wiles, C. Y. Turner, Cecilia Beaux; Julian Academy and Beaux Arts in Paris. Address in 1929, 710 Carnegie Hall, 156 West 57th St., New York, NY; h. 14 Trigon Park, Leroy, NY.

WICKWIRE, JERE R(AYMOND).
Painter. Born Cortland, NY, July 3, 1883. Pupil of W. M. Chase. Member: Salma. C. Address in 1929, 130 West 57th St.; h. 125 East 72nd St., New York, NY; summer, Cortland, NY.

WIDFORSS, G(UNNAR) (MAURITZ).
Painter. Born Stockholm, Sweden, Oct. 21, 1879. Member: Calif. WCS; Scandivian-American A. Award: First prize, Calif. WCS, 1928. Work: "The Three Patriarchs," National Museum, Washington, D.C. Died in 1934. Address in 1929, 3011 Jackson St., San Francisco, CA.

WIEBKING, EDWARD.
Painter. Address in 1926, 104 Mason St., Cincinnati, OH.

WIECHMANN, MARGARET H.
Sculptor. Born in NY in 1886. Pupil of A. Phimister Proctor; Art Students League and National Academy of Design, NY. Specialty, small bronzes of animals. Address in 1926, Wainscott, LI, NY.

WIECZOREK, MAX.
Painter. Born Breslau, Germany, Nov. 22, 1863. Studied in Italy and Germany; pupil of Ferdin and Keller, Max Thedy. Member: CA AC; Laguna Beach AA. (life); CA WCS; NYWCC; Painters of the West; Chic. Gal. A; Artland C. (life). Awards: Silver medal, Pan-CA Exp., San Diego, 1915; Harrison popular prize, Arizona State Fair, 1920, 1922; merit prize, Laguna Beach AA, 1920; Int. Bookplate A., 1926. Work: "Portrait of George Chaffey," Lib. Union Chaffey High Sch., Ont., CA; "The Old Sycamore," Engineers Club, NY, NY; "Foothills," Los Angeles Athletic Club. Died in 1955. Address in 1929: 1007 S. Grand Ave., Los Angeles, CA.

WIEDERSEIM, GRACE GEBBIE.
See Mrs. Drayton.

WIEGAND, GUSTAV. (ADOLPH).
Painter. Born Bremen, Germany, Oct. 2, 1870. Pupil of Dresden Royal Academy under Eugene Bracht; Chase in New York. Member: Salma. C.; Allied AA; NAC. Awards: Bronze medal, St. Louis Exp., 1904; second Hallgarten prize, NAD, 1905. Died Nov. 3, 1957, in Old Chatham, NY. Address in 1929, 44 West 96th St., New York, NY.

WIESSLER, WILLIAM. (Jr.)
Painter and teacher. Born Cincinnati, OH, June 14, 1887. Pupil of Frank Duveneck, L. H. Meakin, Vincent Nowottny. Member: Cincinnati AC.; Valley of the Moon Soc. P.; Duveneck Soc. PS. Address in 1929, 131 East Third St., Cincinnati, OH.

WIGAND, ADELINE ALBRIGHT.
(Mrs. Otto Wigand). Painter. Member: NA Women PS; SPNY. Awards: NY Women's AC prize, 1908; Shaw memorial prize, NAD, 1909. Simpson prize, NY Women's AC, 1909. NAC prize, NY Woman's AC, 1912. Died in 1944. Address in 1929, Woodside Ave., Stapleton, SI., NY.

WIGAND, OTTO CHARLES.
Painter. Born New York. Pupil of
ASL in NY; Boulanger and Lefebvre
in Paris. Member: NYWCC. Died in
1944. Address in 1929, Woodside
Ave., Stapleton, SI., NY.

WIGGIN, J.
This is a fraudulent signature. A
portrait of Benjamin Rush in line
was engraved by J. Akin and
published by him in Philadelphia in
1800. A later impression of this
plate is found with the name of the
engraver and a long dedicatory
address erased; it is relettered
"Engraved by J. Wiggin."

WIGGINS, CARLETON.
Painter. Born Turner's, Orange
Co., NY, March 4, 1848. Pupil of
NAD and George Inness in NY.
Member: ANA 1890, NA 1906; SAA
1887; AWCS; Salma. C., 1898; Lotos
C.; Brooklyn AC; A. Fund S.; A. Aid
S.; Am. Soc. Animal P. and S.; CT
AGA; Lyme AA; AFA. Awards: Gold
medal, Prize Fund Exhibit, NY,
1894; bronze medal, Pan Am, Exp.,
Buffalo, 1901. Work: "A Holstein
Bull," Met. Mus., NY; "The Plow
Horse," Lotos Club, NY; "The
Wanderers." Hamilton Club,
Brooklyn, NY; "October," Corcoran
Gallery, Wash.; "Evening after a
Shower," National Gallery, Wash.;
"Cattle in Pond" and "Sheep and
Landscape," Brooklyn Inst. Museum;
"Lake and Mountains" and "Moonrise
on the Lake," Art Inst. of Chicago;
"Sheep and Landscape," Newark
Mus. Died June 11, 1932. Address
in 1929, Riverwood, Lyme, CT.

WIGGINS, GUY.
Painter. Born Brooklyn, NY, Feb.
23, 1883. Pupil of his father,
Carleton Wiggins and NAD in NY.
Member: ANA, 1916; Salma. C.; CT
AFA; Lotos C.; NAC; Lyme AA.
Awards: Dunham prize, CT. AFA,
1916; Turnbull prize, Salma. C.,
1916; Harris bronze medal and prize
($300), AIC, 1917; hon. mention,
Phila. AC, 1917; Flagg prize, CT
AFA, 1918; Isidor prize, Salma. C.,
1919; J. Francis Murphy Memorial
prize, RI School of Design, 1922;
Cooper prize, CT AFA, 1926; grand
prize, New Rochelle, NY, Soc.,
1929. Work: "The Metropolitan
Tower," Metropolitan Mus., New

York; "Columbus Circle - Winter"
and "Gloucester Harbor;" National
Gal., Wash., "Berkshire Hills -
June," Brooklyn Inst. Mus.; "Old
North Docks," Hackley Art Gallery,
Muskegon, MI; "Snow Crowned Hills"
and "Lightly Falling Snow," Chicago
Art Inst.; "Fifth Avenue, Winter,"
Dallas Art Assoc.; "Opalescent
Days," Lincoln, Neb., AA; "Winter
Morning," Museum, Newark, NJ;
"Through the Storm," Lotos Club;
"Madison Square," Nat. Arts Club;
"On Wintry Hills," Wadsworth
Athenaeum, Hartford, CT; "Winter
Symphony," Beach Memorial Gallery,
Storrs, CT; "Valley and Hills,"
Detroit Athletic Club; "Winter,
NY," Denton College, Texas; "Light
of the Morning," Cincinnati Club,
Cincinnati, Ohio. Represented in
Syracuse Museum and Reading Museum.
Died in 1962. Address in 1929,226
West 59th St., New York, NY; Lyme,
CT.

WIGGINS, MYRA ALBERT.
Painter and teacher. Born Salem,
OR, Dec. 15, 1869. Pupil of
William M. Chase; ASL of NY; NY
School of Art. Member: Seattle
Art Inst.; AFA. Specialty,
pictorial photography and still
life in oils. Died in 1956.
Address in 1929, 214 Pearne St.,
Toppenish, WA.

WIGGINS, SIDNEY M(ILLER).
Painter. Born New Haven, NY, Jan
12, 1883. Pupil of Robert Henri.
Member: Salma. C.; Yonkers AA.
Died in 1940. Address in 1929, 303
Fifth Ave., New York, NY; h. 797
North Broadway, Yonkers, NY.

WIGHT, MOSES.
Painter. Born in Boston, MA, April
2, 1827. Studied in Boston and
later in Paris under Herbert and
Leon Bonnat. He painted a portrait
of Humbolt at the age of 82 in
Berlin, in 1852, now in the
collection of the Boston Museum of
Fine Arts. Died in 1895.

WIGHTMAN, THOMAS.
Engraver. He was in New England
prior to 1806 as "Dean's Analytical
Guide to Penmanship" was published
in Salem in 1802, illustrated by
twenty five copperplates. These
plates were "Collected by Henry

Dean and correctly engraved by Thomas Wightman." Wightman also engraved some of the plates for a mathematical text book published in 1806 by Prof. Webber, of Harvard College. In 1814 he was in the employ of the Boston engraver Able Bowen, and he engraved for "The Naval Monument," published by Bowen that year. The portraits executed by Wightman are fairly well done in stipple. Publication dates indicate he was working until 1820. Wightman engraved some of the plates in "The American Builder's Companion," by A. Benjamin and D. Raynerd, Boston, 1806. Some book plates bear his name as engraver.

WILBUR, DOROTHY THORNTON.
Painter and illustrator. Born Fincastle, CA. Pupil of Frederick F. Fursman, Julius Golz, Alice Schille. Award: Second prize for painting, MN AS., 1924. Illustrated and designed "Stars." Address in 1929, 18 Fourth St., S. E. Washington, DC.

WILCOX, FRANK NELSON.
Painter, etcher, and teacher. Born Cleveland, OH, Oct. 3, 1887. Pupil of H. G. Keller, F. C. Gottwald. Member: Cleveland SA; NYWCC. Award: Penton medal, Cleveland, 1920. Work: "The Old Market," Cleveland Museum of Art. Address in 1929, Cleveland School of Art, Cleveland, OH; h. 2072 Cornell Road, East Cleveland, OH.

WILCOX, JARVIS GEER, JR.
Painter. Born in Houston, TX, July 18, 1942. Study: Yale Univ., BA 1964; with Arthur Stern, 1964-65. Work: Mus. of the City of NY; Chrysler Mus., VA; Academy of Arts, MD. Exhib.: Am. Painters in Paris, 1975; Silvermine Guild Artists, 1978; Audubon Artists Show, NYC, 1978; Am. APL, NYC, 1977-81. Awards: A. Congor Goodyear Prize for Excellence in Art History, Yale Univ., 1964. Mem.: Salmagundi Club, NYC. Media: Oil, conte. Rep.: Audrey Leeds, NYC. Address in 1982, 412 W. 110th St., NYC.

WILCOX, JOHN ANGEL JAMES.
Engraver. Born in Portage, NY, Aug. 21, 1835; living in Boston in 1908. In 1856 Wilcox entered the office of J. C. Kellogg, of Hartford, CT, and there learned to engrave. In 1860 he moved to Boston. Though originally taught engraving in strict line, he worked in stipple, mezzotint and etching with equal facility, engraving in portraits, historical and subject plates and landscapes. Designed book plates and title pages. Also a portrait painter.

WILCOX, LOIS.
Mural painter. Born Pittsburgh, PA. Pupil of Raphael Collin, F. V. DuMond, Philip Hale, Willard L. Metcalf; Charles Hawthorne; recently of Galemberti and Venturini-Papari in Rome. Address in 1929, 335 East 42nd St., New York, NY.

WILCOX, URQUHART.
Painter and teacher. Born New Haven, CT, 1876. Pupil of ASL of Buffalo. Awards: Fellowship prize, Buffalo. Awards: Fellowship prize, Buffalo SA 1906; Hengerer prize (first award), Buffalo SA 1911; Fellowship prize, Buffalo SA 1913. Director School of Fine Arts, Albright Art Gallery, Buffalo, NY. Work: "A Song," Albright Art Gallery, Buffalo. Died in 1941. Address in 1929, 85 North Pearl St., Buffalo, NY.

WILCOX, W. H.
Landscape painter. Born 1831. In 1853 he painted several views of the lakes in New York State, especially of Lake Champlain.

WILDE, HAMILTON G.
Painter. Born in 1827, of Boston, MA. Studied in this country and abroad. Principally a genre painter. Work: "Girl and Doves;" "Sultana" and "Roman Peasant." Died in 1884.

WILDE, IDA M.
Miniature painter, who exhibited at the Penna. Acad. of the Fine Arts, Philadelphia, 1925. Address in 1926, 82 Lafayette Ave., Brooklyn, NY.

WILDE, JENNY.
Painter. Native of New Orleans. She was a member of the Artists'

Association of New Orleans and of the Art League of New York. Did landscape, genre and portrait work, and for many years was engaged in designing tableux and floats for the New Orleans Carnival Organization. Represented in the Louisiana State Museum.

WILDENRATH, JEAN A(LIDA).
Painter and sculptor. Born Denmark, Nov. 3, 1892. Pupil of George Ford Morris, Joshua Dupont; Cooper Union; NAD. Address in 1929, 2707 Sedgwick Ave., NYC.

WILDER, ARTHUR B.
Landscape painter. Born Poultney, VT, April 23, 1857. Pupil of ASL of NY; Brooklyn Art Guild School. Member: Boston AC; AFA. Address in 1929, Woodstock, CT.

WILDER, BERT.
Painter and etcher. Born Taunton, MA, Sept. 17, 1883. Pupil of Cooper Union in NY; Academie Julien in Paris. Address in 1929, 10 East 8th Street, New York, NY; summer, Homer, NY.

WILDER, LOUISE (HIBBARD).
(Mrs. Bert Wilder). Sculptor and etcher. Born Utica, NY, Oct. 15, 1898. Pupil of George T. Brewster. Member: NA Women PS. Award: Hon. mention, National Garden Show, New York, 1929. Address in 1929, 10 East 8th St., New York, NY; summer, Homer, NY.

WILDHACK, ROBERT J.
Illustrator and painter. Born Pekin, IL, Aug. 27, 1881. Pupil of Robert Henri in NY; Otto Stark in Indianapolis. Member: SI, 1910; Salma. C.; GFLA. Specialty, posters and humorous line drawings. Address in 1929: La Crescenta, CA.

WILES, GLADYS (LEE).
Painter. Born New York. Pupil of Cox, Chase, Johansen, Wiles. Member: NA Women PS; MacD. C.; Allied AA; AFA. Award: Medal of French Museum, NA Women PS, 1919. Address in 1929, Care of I. R. Wiles, 130 West 57th Street, New York, NY.

WILES, IRVING R(AMSEY).
Portrait painter. Born Utica, NY, April 8, 1861. Pupil of his father, L. M. Wiles; of Chase and of Beckwith in NY; Carolus-Duran in Paris. Member: ANA 1889, NA 1897; SAA 1887; AWCS; Nat. Inst. AL; Port P.; Allied AA; Century Assoc.; Lotos C.; Paris AAA; NAC; AFA. Awards: 3rd Hallgarten prize, NAD, 1886; Clarke prize, NAD, 1889; hon. mention, Paris Exp., 1889; medal, Col. Exp., Chicago, 1893; Evans prize, AWCS 1897; medal, Tennessee Centennial, Nashville, 1897; Shaw prize, SAA 1900; bronze medal, Paris Exp., 1900; gold medal, Pan Am Exp., Buffalo, 1901; first Corcoran prize, S. Wash. A. 1901; gold medal, St. Louis Exp., 1904; silver medal, Appalachian Exp., Knoxville, 1910; gold medal, Buenos Aires Exp., 1910; Proctor portrait prize, NAD, 1913; gold medal, P.-P. Exp., San. F., 1915; Morris prize, Newport AA, 1917; Maynard portrait prize, NAD, 1919; first prize, Buxbury AA., 1921; Lippincott prize, PAFA, 1922. Work: 4 portrait panels, Hotel Martinique, NY; "Ex-Mayor Schieren," City Hall, Brooklyn, NY; "The Student," Corcoran Gallery, Wash; "The Brown Kimono" and "Russian Tea," Nat. Gal., Wash.; "General Guy V. Henry," "Military Acad., West Point, NY; "L. M. Wiles" and "George A. Hearn," Metropolitan Museum, NY; Portrait of Mrs. Gilbert, "The Sonata," Butler Art Inst., Youngstown, Ohio; "President Roosevelt," University of Berlin, Germany; "William J. Bryan," State Dept., Washington; "Albert H. Wiggin," Chase Bank, and "A. Barton Hepburn," Banker's Club, NY. Died in 1948. Address in 1929, 130 West 57th Street, New York, NY.

WILES, LEMUEL M.
Landscape painter. Born at Perry, NY, in 1826. Pupil of William M. Hart and of J. F. Cropsey. The father of Irving R. Wiles. Died in New York City, Jan. 28, 1905.

WILEY, CATHER.
Painter, who exhibited at the National Acad., NY, 1925. Address in 1926, Knoxville, TN.

WILEY, FREDERICK J.
Painter. Member: Century Assoc.; Lotos C.; Mural P. Award: Bronze medal, St. Louis Exp., 1904. Address in 1929, c/o Paris and Wiley 7 East 48th Street; 139 West 55th Street, NY.

WILEY, HEDWIG.
Painter and teacher. Born Philadelphia, PA. Pupil of Chase, Beaux, Dow and PAFA. Member: Plastic C.; Alliance; Fellowship PAFA; AFA. Address in 1929, 2533 Aspen St., Philadelphia, PA.

WILFORD, LORAN FREDERICK.
Painter and illustrator. Born Wamego, KS, Sept. 13, 1892. Pupil of Kansas City Art Inst. Member: S. Indp. A.; GFLA; Salons of Amer.; NYWCC; AWCS (Assoc.); Salma. C.; NYAG. Awards: Hon. mention, Calif. P. M., 1922; silver medal, Kansas City Art Inst., 1922; Gallatin prize, NYWCC, 1929. Represented in permanent collection of woodcuts, NY Public Library. Address in 1929, R. R. 55, Springdale, CT.

WILGUS, JOHN.
Painter. Born 1819, Buffalo, NY. He was elected an Honorary Member of the NAD in 1839. His painting of an Indian chief was exhibited in the Centennial Exhibition of the Nat. Acad. of Design in 1925. Died in 1853.

WILHELM, ARTHUR L.
Painter. Born in Muscatine, IA, in 1881. Pupil of C. C. Rosenkrantz and of the Art Inst. of Chicago. Award: special mention, MN. State Exhibition, 1916. Address in 1926, 981 Hague Ave., St. Paul, MN.

WILIMOVSKY, CHARLES A.
Painter and etcher. Born Chicago, IL, 1885. Pupil of AIC; J. C. Johansen, and Wm. M. Chase. Member: Chicago ASL; Alumni AIC; Chicago SE; Salif. PM.; Chicago PS.; Chicago Galleries Asso. Awards: Dean prize ($50), Kansas City Fine Arts Inst., 1916; silver medal, Oklahoma Artists, 1917; prize ($100), Kansas City Art Inst., 1920; purchase prize, Kansas City Art Inst., 1923; Rosenwald purchase prize, AIC, 1924 and Clyde

M. Carr prize, 1929. Represented in Lindsborg Univ., Kansas; Kansas City Club; Kansas City Art Inst; City Library, Springfield, MA; collection city of Chicago; Art Inst., Chicago; Art Assoc., Cedar Rapids, IA; Bibliotheque Nationale, Paris. Address in 1929, 1840 Blue Island Ave., Chicago, IL.

WILKE, WILLIAM H(ANCOCK).
Illustrator, etcher, and craftsman. Born at San Francisco. Pupil of A. F. Mathews; Laurens and Blanche in Paris. Member: Calif. SE; Calif. PM. Award: Gold medal, P. P. Exp., San F., 1915. Address in 1929, 447 Sansome St., San Francisco, Calif.; 1130 Shattuck Ave., Berkeley, CA.

WILKINSON, EDWARD.
Painter, illustrator, artist, craftsman, and writer. Born Manchester, England, Jan. 22, 1889. Pupil of James Chillman. Member: Texas FAA; SSAL. Award: Hon. mention, Nashville, TN, 1929. Address in 1929, Box 541, R. 7, Garden Villas, Houston, TX.

WILL, BLANCA.
Sculptor and illustrator. Born Rochester, NY, July 7, 1881. Pupil of Herbert Adams, James Fraser, G. G Barnard, D. W. Tryon, John Alexander; Tyrohn in Karlsruhe; Luhrig in Dresden; Castellucho in Paris. Award: First prize, portrait, Mem. Gal., Rochester. Represented in Memorial Art Gallery, Rochester, NY. Director art instruction, Memorial Art Gallery, Rochester, NY. Address in 1929, 175½ Stonewood Ave., Rochester, NY; summer, Birchlea Studio, Bluehill Falls, ME.

WILLARD, ASAPH.
Engraver. Born 1786 in CT. As early as 1816 A. Willard was in business in Albany, NY, as a member of the firm of Willard & Rawdon, bank-note and general engravers. In 1819-28 he was a member of the Graphic Co., of Hartford, CT. An engraver of maps, portraits, and subject plates. His plates had little merit. Willard is mentioned as having been the first preceptor of John Cheney. Died 1880 in Hartford, CT.

WILLARD, HOWARD W.
Painter and illustrator. Born Danville, IL, Sept. 3, 1894. Pupil of ASL of NY. Member: GFLA. Work: Illustrated "The Silverado Squatters," by Robert Louis Stevenson (Scribner's). Specializing in lithographs of Chinese. Address in 1929, 74 Washington Place, New York, NY.

WILLET, ANNE LEE.
(Mrs. William Willet). Painter, craftsman, and writer. Born at Bristol, PA, Dec. 15, 1866. Pupil of PAFA; studied in France and Eng. Member: Fellowship PAFA; Phila. Alliance; AFA. Author of articles on stained glass. Work: Designer and maker in collaboration with Wm. Willet of all windows, West Point Military Chapel; Great West Window, Post Graduate Col. Princeton; Mather Mem'l. Trinity Cathedral, Cleveland; Guthrie Mem'l. St. John's Church, Locust Valley; St. Paul's Cathedral Medallion, Sanctuary & Lady, Chapel Window, Calvary Church; Harrison Mem., Calvary Church, Germantown; mural paintings in St. Alvernia's Convent; Harrison Mem., Presbyterian Hospital Chapel; Mellon Mem.; Thaw Mem., Third Presbyterian Church; Buchanan Mem'l, St. Nathanael's Church, Phila.; Herbert Hugh Riddle Mem'l, Chicago; all windows in Greenwood cemetary Chapel, NY; Victory Window, Trinity Church, Syracuse; St. Paul's Church, Halifax, NS; Crucifixion Window, Holy Trinity Church, Phila. In collaboration with Henry Lee Willett; Sanctuary and Transept windows, Grace PE Church; the James Mem'l, Doyleston; Ryers Mem'l Baptismal Font, Rose Window and Bronze; The Sanctuary, Jesse Tree Window and entire fenestration, Church of the Most Blessed Sacrament, Detroit; Berry Mem. and entire fenestration, Jefferson Ave. Presbyterian Church; Journeyings of the Pilgrims, Lounge, Hilton Mem., the Chapel, the Library, and all glass. Theological Seminary, Chic.; John B. Murphy Mem., College of Surgeons, Chic.; Sanctuary window, Epiphany Church, Germantown, PA; Colonial Dames, Whitefield Mem., Bethesda at Savannah, GA; all

windows, Grosse Pointe Mem. Church, Grosse Point, MI; Johnson Mem., Prince of Peace Episcopal Church, Phila.; Patton Mem., Lake Vineyard, San Gabriel, CA; Royster Mem., First Presbyterian Church, Norfolk, VA; reredos and transept and McWilliams Chapel, First Presbyterian Church, Chicago. Died in 1943. Address in 1929, 226 South 11th St.; h. 2116 De Lancy St., Phila. PA.

WILLET, WILLIAM.
Mural painter, craftsman, lecturer, and writer. Born in NYC, in 1868. Pupil of Mechanics and Tradesmen's Inst., NY; also of Van Kirk, Chase, John La Farge; studied in FR and EN. Member: Mural Painters; NY Arch. League, 1910; Boston Society of Arts and Crafts; St. Dunstan's Club, Boston; Fellowship of the PA Academy of the Fine Arts; Phila. Art Alliance. His work included; Sanctuary Window, West Point Military Academy; window in Proctor Hall, Princeton; Mather Mem., Trinity Cathedral, Cleveland; Guthrie Memorial, St. John's Church, Locust Valley, LI; St. Paul's Cathedral, Pitts.; Harrison Memorial, Calvary Church, Germantown; mural paintings in St. Alvernia's Convent, Pitts.; Presbyterian Hospital Chapel, Pitts.; Thaw Memorial, Third Presbyterian Church, Pittsburgh; mem'l. in Greenwood Cemetery Chapel, NY; Trinity Church, Syracuse; St. Paul's Church, Halifax, NS. Author of "Stained Glass in Our Churches." Died in Phila. in 1921.

WILLETT, ARTHUR R(EGINALD).
Mural Painter. Born England, Aug. 18, 1868. Member: NY Arch. Lg. 1897; Mural P.; A. Aid S.; AFA. Address in 1929, 15 East 59th St., NYC.

WILLETT, J(ACQUES) (I.).
Painter. Born Petrograd, Russia, June 22, 1882. Pupil of The Imperial Academy of Art, Petrograd. Member: Allied AA; Brooklyn SA; PS; Salons of Am.; S. Indp. A. Work: "Evening Breeze," Newark Museum, Newark, NJ. Address in 1929, 32 Union Sq.; h. 25 Sickles St., New York, NY.

WILLIAMS, ADELE.
Painter. Member: New York Watercolor Club; National Association of Women Painters and Sculptors, New York; Plastic Club. Award: Prize, Pittsburgh Art Association, 1912. Address in 1929, 1009 West Avenue, Richmond, Virginia.

WILLIAMS, ALYN.
Painter, writer, lecturer, and teacher. Born in Wales, England, August 29, 1865. Pupil of Laurens and Courtois in Paris. Member: Royal Society of Miniature Painters (president); Pennsylvania Society of Miniature Painters; Royal Cambrian Academy; Washington Art Club; American Federation of Arts. Work: Miniatures of King Edward VII and Queen Alexandra in Guildhall, London, Art Gallery, Miniatures in Rome of the Pope, Cardinal Garquet, Cardinal Archbishop Bourrie, Premier Mussolini; also Queen Mary, HRH Princess Marie Jose of Belgium, Cardinal Gibbons, President Taft, and President Coolidge. Address in 1929, 1724 Connecticut Avenue, Washington, DC; Barrack's Hill, Plimpton, Sussex, England.

WILLIAMS, BALLARD.
Painter, who exhibited at the Pennsylvania Academy of the Fine Arts, Philadelphia, 1924. Address in 1926, 27 West 67th Street, New York, NY.

WILLIAMS, CAROLINE GREENE.
Painter and etcher. Born in Fulton, New York, May 9, 1855. Pupil of Cleveland School of Art, under Henry Keller; Cullen Yates, Clara McChesney, and Michel Jacobs. Member: Cleveland School of Art Alumni; Cleveland Woman's Art Club. Address in 1929, 1858 Marloes Avenue, East Cleveland, Ohio.

WILLIAMS, CHARLES D.
Illustrator. Born in New York City, Aug. 12, 1880. Member: Society of Illustrators; Artists Guild of the Authors' League of America, New York. Address in 1929, 152 West 42nd Street, New York, NY; h. 10 Stonelea Place, New Rochelle, NY.

WILLIAMS, CHARLES SNEED.
Painter. Born Evansville, IN, May 24, 1882. Studied in Louisville, NY, and London. Member: Union Int'l. des Beaux Arts; Louisville AA (hon. life); Louisville AC; AIC (life) AFA; Hoosier Salon; Chicago Gal. A. Award: 4-yr. resident scholarship at Allan Fraser Art Coll., Scotland, 1902. Portraits in Confederate Mus., Richmond, VA; KY State Capitol, Frankfort; US Capitol, Wash., DC; Speed Mem. Mus., Louisville, KY; Am. Coll. of Surgeons, Chicago. Address in 1929, 408 South Michigan Ave., Chicago, IL; h. 30 Bramham Gardens, London, S. W. 5, England.

WILLIAMS, C(HARLES) WARNER.
Sculptor and lecturer. Born Henderson, KY, April 23, 1903. Pupil of Albin Polasek. Mem.: IN AC; Hoosier Salon. Award: 1st prize, sculpt., Hoosier Salon, Chic., 1928. Work: Sheridan Mem. Tablet, Court House, Frankfort, IN. Herschy mem. portrait, Berea Coll., Berea, KY; plaster, "We Are Three," public schools, Logansport, IN; Seaman memo., Bradwell Sch., Chicago, IL. Address in 1929, 40 East Oak St., Chicago, IL.

WILLIAMS, CLARA ELSENE PARK.
(Mrs. J. Scott). Painter and illustrator. Member: Soc. of Illustrators, 1912; NYWCC; NA Women PS; Fellowship of PAFA. Award: Watrous prize, NY Women's Art Club, 1912. Address in 1926, South Dwight Place, Englewood, NJ.

WILLIAMS, DWIGHT.
Landscape painter and teacher. Born Camillus, Onondaga Co., NY, April 25, 1856. Pupil of John C. Perry. Member: Central NY. Soc. A.; AFA. Work: "Landscape," Hamilton College; "Landscape," Cazenovia Public Lib. Address in 1929, 44 Albany St., Cazenovia, NY.

WILLIAMS, E. G. & BRO.
This engraving firm was producing portraits in New York in 1880.

WILLIAMS, EDWARD K.
Painter. Born Greensburg, PA, June 5, 1870. Pupil of AIC. Member: NYWCC (Assoc.); AWCS (Assoc.); Alumni AIC; Indiana AC. Award:

Business Men's AC purchase prize, $300, AIC, 1928. Died in 1948. Address in 1929, Deerfield, IL; summer, Nashville, IN.

WILLIAMS, ELEANOR PALMER.
Painter. Born Baltimore, MD. Pupil of Maryland Inst. in Baltimore; George H. Smillie, B. West Clinedinst and Hugh Newell in NY; Margaret Lippincott in Phila. Member: Phila. WCC; Plastic C.; Phila. Art Alliance; Print C; PA. Museum and School of Indus. Art; AFA. Address in 1929, 250 South 18th St., Phila. PA.; summer, New Hope, Bucks Co., PA.

WILLIAMS, FLORENCE WHITE.
Painter, illustrator, and writer. Born Putney, VT. Pupil of Henry B. Snell; Frederick Grant; Karl Krafft; AIC; Chicago AFA. Member: South Side AA; Chicago Gal. Asso.; IL. AFA; AFA. Awards: First prize, ASL, 1924; second prize, Boston Line Greeting Card Contest; prize, Chicago Galleries, 1927; Mrs. John B. Hall prize ($350), 1927. Works: "Down on the Coast of Maine," owned by the Commission for Encouragement of Local Art; represented in 3 public Schools, Chicago; illustrations for children's magazines, such as St. Nicholas, Little Folks, Children's Page in the Christian Science Monitor, Child Life. Died in 1953. Address in 1929, 4533 Greenwood Ave., Chicago, IL.

WILLIAMS, FREDERIC A(LLEN).
Sculptor. Born West Newton, MA, April 10, 1898. Pupil of NAD; Beaux Arts Institute of Design. Work: Sundial "The Arrow Maker," Arkell Museum, Canajoharie, NY. Died in 1958. Address in 1929, 1931 Broadway; h. 600 West 113th St., New York, NY; summer, Taos, NM.

WILLIAMS, F(REDERICK) BALLARD.
Painter. Born Brooklyn, NY, Oct. 21, 1871. Pupil of Cooper Union and NAD in New York. Member: ANA 1907, NA 1909; NYWCC; Lotos C.; Salma. C., 1898; NAC; Montclair AA; AFA. Awards: Bronze medal, Pan Amer. Exp., Buffalo, 1901; Inness prize, Salma. C., 1907; Isidor gold medal, NAD, 1909. Work: "A Glade

by the Sea" and "Conway Hills," Nat. Gal. Washington; "Happy Valley" and "L'Allegro," Metropolitan Museum, New York: "Vivacetto," Albright Art Gal., Buffalo; "Chant d'Amour," Brooklyn Inst. Mus.; "Old Viaduct at Little Falls, NJ" and "Sea Echoes," Art Mus., Montclair, NJ; "Grand Canyon," Hackley Art Gal., Muskegon, MI; "Spring," Brooklyn Inst. Mus.; "A Glimpse of the Sea," City Art Mus., St. Louis; "Somewhere in Arcadia," Harrison Gal., Los Angeles Mus. Represented in collections of Dallas Art Association Lotos Club, NY; Nat. Art Club, NY; Quinnipiack Club, New Haven; Milwaukee Art Inst.; Chicago Art Inst.; Grand Rapids AA; Los Angeles Museum; New Britain, CT, Art Assoc.; Engineers Club, NY. Died in 1956. Address in 1929, 27 West 67th St., New York, NY; h. Glen Ridge, NJ.

WILLIAMS, FREDERICK DICKINSON.
Painter. Born 1829 in Boston. He studied in his native city and later in Paris. He devoted his time to landscapes and figure-pieces. He exhibited in 1878. Died Jan. 27, 1915 in Brookline, MA.

WILLIAMS, GEORGE ALFRED.
Painter. Born Newark, NJ, July 8, 1875. Studied under Chase and Cox. Award: Silver medal, P. P. Exp., San F., 1915. Work: "The Drama of Life - The Marginal Way," Art Inst. of Chicago; 6 decorative paintings, "Tristan and Isolde," in Newark Museum. Address in 1929, Beachwood Road, Kennebunkport, ME.

WILLIAMS, GLUYAS.
Illustrator. Born San Francisco, CA, July 23, 1888. Illustrated "Of All Things," "Pluck and Luck" and "The Early Worm," by Robert Benchley. Address in 1929, 194 Boylston St., Boston, MA; h. 14 Sylvan Ave., West Newton, MA; summer, Deer Isle, ME.

WILLIAMS, HENRY.
Engraver and painter. Born in 1787. Stipple portraits are signed as both painted and engraved by H. Williams. In 1814, Williams published in Boston "The Elements

of Drawing," illustrated by twenty six copperplate engravings. As late as 1824, H. Williams advertises as a portrait and miniature painter in the New England Palladium with a studio at No. 6 School Street, Boston. This notice says that "He also continues to paint from the dead in his peculiar manner by Masks, etc." He died Oct. 21, 1830.

WILLIAMS, ISAAC L.
Painter. Born in Phila. June 24, 1817. At 15 he became the pupil in drawing of John R. Smith; he afterwards practiced painting with John Neagle. Lived and followed his profession in Phila. He was pres. and member of Artist Fund Society, in 1860. Until 1844 he devoted himself to portrait painting, but later gave equal or greater attention to landscape. In 1866, at the invitation of an English gentleman, he visited Great Britain to paint his homestead. He travelled in France and Italy, and painted historic pictures. He returned to Phila. and taught drawing in schools and also had private pupils; he was first preceptor of the late Henry E. Hubley. Painted a series of historic mansions of Phila., now in possession of the State Historical Society. He visited Lancaster in 1854 with a commission to paint the portrait of Rev. Bernard Keenan. Died April 23, 1895, in Phila.

WILLIAMS, J(OHN) SCOTT.
Painter, illustrator, etcher, and craftsman. Born Liverpool, England, Aug. 18, 1877. Pupil of AIC. Member: AWCS; NYWCC; Salma. C.; SI.; NY. Arch. Lg.; Phila. Sketch C.; GFLA; Alumni Assoc., AIC. Awards: Shaw black and white prize, Salma. C., 1912; Vezin prize, Salma. C., 1914; Isidor prize, Salma. C., 1919; water color prize, AIC, 1924; Delano purchase prize, combined water color exhibition, AWCS and NYWCC, 1925. Represented by mural and glass work in Bush Terminal Sales Bldg., New York, NY; by water color in permanent collection of the Art Institute of Chicago. Address in 1929, 401 West End Ave.; 6 East 14th St., New York, NY.

WILLIAMS, JOHN A(LONZO).
Painter and illustrator. Born Sheboygan, WI, March 23, 1869. Pupil of ASL of NY and Metropolitan Museum School. Member: SI, 1910; Salma. C; GFLA; NY Arch. Lg.; AWCS; NYWCC; Artists Fund Soc. Awards: Yabriski prize, AWCS NY WCC; prize, water colors, Salma. Club. Address in 1929, 39 West 67th Street, New York, NY.

WILLIAMS, KATE A.
Painter. Member: NA Women PS.; Wash. WCC; AWCS; NAC; Am. APL; Artists branch Am. Pen W; AFA. Died in 1939. Address in 1929, 1264 Boston Road, New York, NY.

WILLIAMS, KEITH SHAW.
Painter, etcher, and teacher. Born Marquette, MI, Oct. 7, 1906. Pupil of Daniel Garber, Ivan G. Olinsky, Charles Hawthorne. Member: NAC; AWCS; Am. APL. Award: Purchase prize, ($100) for water color, NAC, New York, 1928. Died in 1951. Address in 1929, 80 St. James Place, Brooklyn, NY.

WILLIAMS, L(AWRENCE) S.
Painter. Born Columbus, Ohio., July 24, 1878. Pupil of Carroll Beckwith, William M. Chase, F. V. Du Mond. Member: Salma. C. Address in 1929, 121 Engle St., Tenafly, NJ.

WILLIAMS, LOUISE H(OUSTON).
Painter. Born Garnett, KS, April 9, 1883. Pupil of Randall Davey. Member: Seattle AI. Address in 1929, 140 Evergreen St., Mt. Vernon, WA.

WILLIAMS, MAY.
Painter, craftsman, and teacher. Born Pittsburgh, PA. Pupil of Carnegie Coll. of Fine Arts; NY School of Applied Art; Beaux Arts, Fontainebleau, France. Member: Art Association of Pitts.; AFA. Address in 1929, 4860 Ellsworth Ave.; h. 204 North Negley Ave., Pittsburgh, PA.

WILLIAMS, MILDRED EMERSON.
Painter. Born Detroit, MI, Aug. 9, 1892. Pupil of Robert Henri, George Luks, Mahonri Young, and studied in Paris. Member: S. Indp. A.; Detroit S. Women P.

Award for best figure painting, Detroit Inst., 1923. Represented in PAFA and the Detroit Inst. of Arts. Address in 1929, 38 West 10th St., New York, NY; summer, Rockport, MA.

WILLIAMS, PAULINE BLISS.
Painter. Born Springfield, MA, July 12, 1888. Pupil of Du Mond, Bellows, Mora, Henri, Hayes Miller. Member: Springfield AL; Springfield AG; NA Women PS; North Shore AA: Gloucester SA; Brooklyn S. Min. P. Awards: Hon. mention, NA Women PS, 1926. Address in 1929, 128 Mulberry St., Springfield, MA.

WILLIAMS, WALTER REID.
Sculptor. Born Indianapolis, IN, Nov. 23, 1885. Pupil of Charles Mulligan, Bela Pratt; Paul Barlett and Mercie in Paris. Member: Chicago Gal. A; Hoosier Salon. Represented by "Goal," bronze, Woman's Athletic Club, Chicago. Address in 1929, 4544 Greenwood Ave., Chicago, IL.

WILLIAMS, WHEELER.
Sculptor. Born Chicago, IL, Nov. 3, 1897. Pupil of John Wilson in Boston and Jules Coutau in Paris. Member: NY Arch. Lg. Work: Tablet to French Explorers and Pioneers, Michigan Avenue Bridge, Chicago, IL. Died in 1972. Address in 1929, 144 East 66th St., New York, NY.

WILLIAMS, WILLIAM J.
Portrait painter. Born in New York, in 1759. In 1792 he painted in Philadelphia a portrait from life of Washington in Masonic regalia at the request of the Masonic Lodge of Alexandria, VA. The original pastel portrait is in Alexandria, and a copy by Miss Burke is in the Masonic Hall in Philadelphia. Williams died Nov. 30, 1823, and is buried in Cedar Grove near Charleston.

WILLIAMSON, ADA C.
Painter and illustrator. Member: Fellowship Penn. Academy of Fine Arts; Plastic Club. Award: Shillard-Smith gold medal, Plastic Club 1913. Died in 1958. Address in 1929, 1921 Arch St.; care of Art

Alliance, 18th and Walnut Sts., Philadelphia, PA.

WILLIAMSON, J. MAYNARD JR.
Painter and illustrator. Born in Pittsburgh, PA, in 1892. Pupil of F. V. DuMond. Member: Pittsburgh Artists Association. Award: Prize, Pittsburgh Artists Association, 1911. Address in 1926, 514 S. Linden Ave., Pittsburgh, PA.

WILLIAMSON, JOHN.
Painter. Born April 26, 1826, in Scotland. He was brought to this country as a child. He lived in Brooklyn, NY. In 1861, he was elected an Associate Member of the National Academy of Design. Many of his paintings are scenes on the Hudson River or in the Catskill Mountains. Died May 28, 1885, in New York State.

WILLIAMSON, SHIRLEY.
(Mrs. Edward Lincoln Williamson). Painter and craftsman. Born New York. Pupil of Arthur Dow, Art Students' League in NY; Constant and Rodin in Paris. Member: National Association of Women Painters and Sculptors; San Francisco Society of Women Artists; Palo Alto Art Club. Instructor in dramatics, summer school, Stanford University, Calif. Address in 1929, 1344 Tasso Street, Palo Alto, CA.

WILLING, J(OHN) THOMSON.
Painter, craftsman, writer, and lecturer. Born Toronto, Canada, Aug. 5, 1860. Pupil of Ontario School of Art. Member: American Institute of Graphic Arts; Royal Canadian Acad. (assoc.); Art Directors Club; Society of Illustrators. Editor, Gravure Service Corporation. Address in 1929, 25 West 43rd St., New York, NY; h. 5909 Wayne Ave., Germantown, PA; summer, Henryville, Munroe Co., PA.

WILLIS, ALBERT PAUL.
Landscape painter and teacher. Born Philadelphia, Nov. 15, 1867. Pupil of Frank V. DuMond. Member: Philadelphia Watercolor Club; Philadelphia Sketch Club.

1016

Address in 1929, 2332 North Park Ave., Philadelphia, PA; summer, Bailey Island, Casco Bay, ME.

WILLIS, EOLA.
Painter, craftsman, writer, and lecturer. Born Dalton, GA. Pupil of Mrs. J. S. D. Smillie, Chase at ASL of NY; studied in Paris. Member: Carolina AA.; Charleston Sketch C.; Charleston Art Commission; SSAL. Author of "The Charleston Stage in the XVII Century" and "Henrietta Johnston, First Woman Painter in America." Address in 1929, 72 Tradd St., Charleston, SC.

WILLIS, R(ALPH) T(ROTH).
Painter, sculptor, illustrator, etcher. Born Leesylvania, Freestone Point, VA, March 1, 1876. Pupil of Corcoran School of Art; ASL of NY; Academie Julian. Member: Mural P.; CA AC. Works: Murals of 12 naval engagements, Second Battalion Armory and murals in 22nd Regiment Armory, N.Y.N.G., New York City; decoration, Library of Congress, Washington, DC; Murals, Pomona Bldg. Loan Assn.; Pomona CA; and Angeles Temple, Los Angeles, CA; Brock Jewelry Store, Los Angeles. Address in 1929, Gramercy Place, Hollywood; h. Encinitas, CA; summer, Westport, CT.

WILLNER, TOBY S.
Painter and printmaker. Born Sept. 17, 1932. Study: UCLA, Art Center College of Design, Calif. State at Northridge (print and glass). Work: Hospital Corp. of America, Nashville, TN; Disney Found., Burbank, Calif.; Warner Bros. Records, Burbank, Calif.; IBM, San Fran., Los Angles, & NY; Northrup Aviation, Torrance, Calif.; Hilton Hotels, Los Angeles & Baltimore; Capital Hilton, Wash. DC; Columbia Pictures & MGM, Los Angeles; Am. Inst. of Banking, Dallas; Lloyds Bank, Los Angles; many others. Comn.: Davey "C's", Toronto, Canada. Award: Walt Disney Found., 1977. Address in 1983, 6317 Maryland Dr., Los Angeles, CA.

WILLOUGHBY, ALICE ESTELLE.
Painter. Born in Groton, NY. Pupil of Washington Art League;

Corcoran Art School. Member: Washington Water Color Club; Washington Art Club. Address in 1926, The Rockingham, Washington, DC. Died Oct. 28, 1924, in Washington, DC.

WILLSON, EDITH DERRY.
Painter and etcher. Born Denver, CO, Jan. 20, 1899. Pupil of Joseph Pennell; ASL of NY. Member: Chicago SE; NY. Soc. of Women PS. Work: Etchings in Nat. Gal., Munich, Germany; Cincinnati Library, Cincinnati Ohio, Los Angeles Library, Los Angeles, CA., Cleveland Museum of Art, Clevland, Ohio Art Inst., of Chicago, IL, Detroit Museum of Art, Detroit, Mich. Address in 1929, Kleeman Thorman Galleries, 575 Madison Ave., New York, NY; h. 1803 Wilshire Blvd., Los Angeles, CA.

WILLSON, JAMES MALLERY.
Painter and etcher. Born Kissiminee, FL, Dec. 28, 1890. Pupil of Maynard, Henri, Johanson, Fogarty. Member: NYWCC (asso.); ASL (life). Address in 1929, Studio, 17 rue Boissonnade, Paris; h. 267 Barcelona Road, West Palm Beach, FL.

WILLSON, MARTHA B(UTTRICK).
(Mrs. Howard D. Day). Miniature painter. Born Providence, RI, Aug. 16, 1885. Pupil of Lucia Fairchild Fuller; Julian in Paris. Member: Providence AC; AFA. Address in 1929, 88 Congdon St., Providence, RI; summer, Petersham, MA.

WILMARTH, LEMUEL EVERETT.
Painter. Born in Attleboro, MA, in 1835. Studied drawing in Penna. Acad. of Fine Arts, Phila., 1854; went to Europe, 1858; studied at Royal Acad., Munich; also at Ecole des Beaux Arts, Paris. Married Emma B. Barrett, 1872. Professor in charge of schools of NAD, 1870-90. Among his best known pictures are "The Pick of the Orchard;" "Ingratitude;" "Left in Charge;" "Sunny Italy;" "Captain Nathan Hale." Died July 27, 1918 in Brooklyn, NY.

WILMER, WILLIAM A.
Engraver. Wilmer was a pupil of James B. Longacre in Phila., and

engraved some excellent portrait plates in stipple for the "National Portrait Gallery." Died 1855.

WILMES, FRANK.
Painter and craftsman. Born Cincinnati, Oct. 4, 1858. Pupil of L. H. Meakin; Vincent Nowottny; Frank Duveneck. Member: Cincinnati AC. Address in 1929, 1560 Elm St., Cincinnati, OH.

WILMOT, ALTA E.
Painter and teacher. Born Ann Arbor, MI. Pupil of J. Alden Weir; Gustave Courtois, Prinet, etc., in Paris. Member: SPNY.; P. S. Min. P.; AFA. Specialty, miniatures. Address in 1929, 939 Eighth Ave., New York, NY.

WILSHIRE, FLORENCE L.
Painter. Member: New Haven PCC. Address in 1929, 97 Livingston St., New Haven PCC.

WILSON, ALEXANDER.
Engraver. Born in Paisley, Scotland, in 1766; died in Philadelphia, PA, in 1813. In the life of this eminent ornithologist we are told that Wilson was taught to draw, color and etch by his friend Alexander Lawson, the engraver, and he rapidly attained a marked degree of proficiency in delineating birds. For his own great work on "American Ornithology" he later etched 2 plates from his own drawings.

WILSON, ASHTON.
Painter. She was born Charleston, W. VA, April 1, 1880. Pupil of Chase; Hawthorne; Beaux; Twachtman; Borglum; Felicie Howell; Colarossi, Paris. Member: NA Women PS. Address in 1929, 1060 Park Ave., New York, NY; summer, "Fenton," White Sulphur Springs, W. VA.

WILSON, CLAGGETT.
Painter. Born Washington, DC, Aug. 3, 1887. Pupil of ASL of NY; Julian Acad.; F. Luis Mora; Richard Miller, and Laurens in Paris. Member: S. Indp. A.; Salons of Amer.; AFA. Work: "The Corner," "Gypsy Dancer," and "Basque Fishermen," Brooklyn Museum. Represented in Metropolitan Museum,

New York. Died in 1952. Address in 1929, 24 West 56th Street, New York, NY.

WILSON, EDWARD ARTHUR
Illustrator. Born Glasgow, Scotland, March 4, 1886. Studied at AIC, and with Howard Pyle. Began career in NYC in early 1920's. Illustrated advertising campaigns for LaSalle-Cadillac and Victrola; illustrated his Iron Men and Wooden Ships, 1924; illustrated Robinson Crusoe, Treasure Island, Around the World in 80 Days, A Journey to the Center of the Earth. In collections of Met. Mus. of Art, NYC; Lib. of Congress; NY Public Library. Member: SI 1912; Salma. C.; GFLA; Ship Model Soc.; S. Graphic A.; Players C. Address in 1929, 195 24th St., Jackson Heights, Queens, NY. Later moved to Cape Cod. Died in 1970.

WILSON, EMILY L(OYD).
Painter. Born Altoona, PA, Nov. 2, 1868. Pupil of Phila. School of Design for Women; William Sartain. Member: Plastic C. Work: Charcoal portrait of Charles Johnson, Museum of the Historical Society, St. Augustine. Address in 1929, Second St., Beach Haven, NJ; winter, 280 St., George St., St. Augustine, FL.

WILSON, GILBERT B(ROWN).
Painter. Born Terre Haute, March 4, 1907. Pupil of Lucy Arthur Batten, W. T. Turman, E. L. Coe, E. A. Forsberg. Member: Theta Chi Phi Art Fraternity. Award: Culver Military Academy prize, Hoosier Salon, Chicago, 1929. Address in 1929, Art Inst., of Chicago, IL; h. 1201 North 4th St., Terre Haute, IN.

WILSON, HENRIETTA.
Painter and teacher. Born Cincinnati, OH. Pupil of Cincinnati Art Acad. Member: Cincinnati Woman's AC; Ohio Born WA; OWCS. Instructor, Cincinnati Art Academy. Address in 1929, Art Acad., Cincinnati, OH; h. 2215 Monroe Ave., Norwood, OH.

WILSON, JOHN T.
Portrait painter, who flourished about 1844 to 1860 in NY.

WILSON, KATE.
Painter and teacher. Born Cin., OH. Member: Cin. Women's AC. Address in 1929, 2215 Monroe Ave., Norwood, OH.

WILSON, LUCY ADAMS.
Painter. Born Warren, OH, 1855. Pupil of Herron Art Inst., Indianapolis; ASL of NY; William Forsyth and T. C. Steele. Member: Miami Lg. A; Tropical Lg. A; SSAL; AFA. Represented in Herron Art Inst. Address in 1929, 2266 Northwest 33rd St., Miami, FL.

WILSON, MATTHEW.
Portrait painter in oils and miniature. Born in London in 1814. He came to this country as a young man and became a pupil of Henry Inman. First exhibited miniatures in Phila. Elected Asso. Member of the National Academy of Design in 1843. Painted portraits, and drew in pastel from 1861 to 1891. He died in February 1892, in Brooklyn, NY.

WILSON, ROSE CECIL O'NEIL.
Illustrator. Born Wilkes Barre, PA. Member: Soc. des Beaux Arts (assoc.), Paris; SI 1912 (assoc.); GFLA. Address in 1929, 62 Washington Square, New York, NY; Saugatuck, CT.

WILSON, SOLOMON.
Painter and etcher. Born Vilno, Poland, Aug. 23, 1894. Pupil of Ivan G. Olinsky, George Maynard, Robert Henri, George Bellows. Address in 1929, 421 West 141st St., New York, NY.

WILTZ, ARNOLD.
Painter. Born Berlin, Germany, June 18, 1889. Self-taught. Member: Brooklyn S. Modern A; Woodstock AA. Represented in Cincinnati Museum. Died in 1937. Address in 1929; Bearsville, NY.

WILTZ, E. MADELINE SHIFF.
(Mrs. Arnold Wiltz). Painter. Born Denver, CO. Pupil of J. B. Whittaker, F. V. Du Mond, Wm. Chase, H. E. Field. Member: Salons of America; Brooklyn S. Min. P. Award: Charlotte Ritchie Smith Memorial prize, Baltimore WCC.,

1923. Address in 1929, Bearsville, NY; Ardsley studios, 110 Columbia Heights, Brooklyn, NY.

WINCHELL, ELIZABETH BURT.
(Mrs. John Patten Winchell). Painter, lecturer, and teacher. Born Brooklyn, NY, June 20, 1890. Pupil of Elliott Daingerfield, Henry B. Snell, Daniel Garber, W. W. Gilcrist, Jr., Harriet Sartain. Member: Haylofters, Portland, ME; C. L. Wolfe AC. Awards: First prize Wanamaker Exh., Phila., 1910-1911; first prize, Flower Show Exh., Phila., 1911; 2nd and 3rd prizes, Flower Show Exh., Phila., 1928; hon. mention, C. L. Wolfe AC, New York, 1928. Address in 1929, "The Old Cooper Shop," 200 Maine St; h. 3 Green Street, Brunswick, ME; summer, Mere Point, ME.

WINEBRENNER, HARRY F(IELDING).
Sculptor, illustrator, lecturer, and teacher. Born Summersville, W. VA, Jan. 4, 1884. Pupil of Taft, Mulligan, Sciortino. Member: Chicago SA; Calif. AC, Sculptors Guild of So. Calif. Work: "Italian Boy" and "The Passing of the Indian," Oklahoma State Historical Society; "Fountain of Education," "Statue of Welcome," "The Soul of a Dancer," Venice, and head of art dept., Venice Union Polytechnic High School. Address in 1929, 1354 Ashland Ave., Santa Monica, CA.

WINES, JAMES.
Sculptor. Born June 27, 1932, in Chicago. Earned B. A. at Syracuse. Lived in Rome. Taught at School of Vis. Arts, NYC; Cornell; Suny/Buffalo; Jersey School of Arch (Newark, NJ). Awarded Pulitzer (1953); Guggenheim (1964); Ford grant (1964); Nat. End. for Arts (1973 & 1975). Exhibited at Everson Mus. (Syracuse); Baltimore; Art Inst. of Chicago; Carnegie; Walker Art Center; MOMA and Sao Paulo Biennal (1963). In collections of Whitney; Albright-Knox; Curries Gal., NH; Syracuse; Stedelijk (Amsterdam); Tate; Colgate U. and NYC. Address in 1982, 60 Greene St., NYC.

WINGATE, CARL.
Painter and etcher. Born Brooklyn, NY, Dec. 9, 1876. Pupil of Walter Shirlaw; NAD. Specialty, etching. Address in 1929, 22 Curtis Road, P. O. District No. 26, Boston, MA.

WINGERD, LOREEN.
Painter, illustrator, and teacher. Born Delphi, Aug. 2, 1902. Pupil of William Forsyth. Address in 1929, 51 East Market; h. 217 West North St., Delphi, IN.

WINGERT, EDWARD OSWALD.
Painter. Born Philadelphia, Feb. 29, 1864. Pupil of PAFA, Hovenden, Anshutz and Porter in Phila. Member: Fellowship PAFA. Address in 1929, Oak Lane, Phila., PA.

WINKLER, AGNES CLARK.
(Mrs. G. A. M. Winkler). Painter, craftsman, writer, and lecturer. Born Cincinnati, OH, April 8, 1893. Pupil of Leon Lundmark, Watson and Mary Helen Stubbs. Member: Allied AA; ACG of Amer.; Chicago NJSA; All-Ill. SFA; Hoosier Salon. Died in 1945. Address in 1929, 4468 Lake Park Ave., Chicago., IL.

WINKLER, JOHN W.
Painter and etcher. Member: Chicago SI; Brooklyn SE; Societe des Graveurs en Noir, Paris. Awards: Logan prize, Chicago SE, 1918; purchase prize, Calif. SE, 1919; honorable mention, Concord AA, 1920. Work in Chicago Art Inst.; NY Public Library; Library of Congress; Musee du Luxembourg, Paris. Address in 1929, 3026 Benvenue Ave., Berkeley, CA.

WINN, JAMES H(ERBERT).
Painter, sculptor, craftsman, writer, and teacher. Born Newburyport, MA, Sept. 10, 1866. Pupil of AIC. Member: Cliff Dwellers C; Alumni AIC; Asso. of Arts and Industries. Awards: Arthur Heun prize, AIC, 1910; first prize and gold medal, Woman's Conservation Exh., Knoxville, TN, 1913. Instructor, Jewelry and Metal Work, Art Inst., Chicago. Address in 1929, 410 South Michigan Ave., h. 9522 Longwood Drive, Chicago, IL.

WINNER, MARGARET F.
Painter, illustrator, and teacher. Born Philadelphia, Oct. 21, 1866. Pupil of PAFA and Howard Pyle. Member: Plastic C.; Fellowship PAFA; Phila. Alliance. Represented at Dickinson College, Carlisle, PA. Died in 1937. Address in 1929, 1706 North 16th St., Philadelphia, PA.

WINNER, WILLIAM E.
Portrait and genre painter of Phila. Born c. 1815. Member of the Board of Control of the Artists Fund Society from 1843. Exhibitor at the Penna. Acad. of the Fine Arts until 1881. Died 1883.

WINSLOW, EARLE BARTRUM.
Painter. Born Northville, MI, Feb. 21, 1884. Pupil of Detroit Fine Arts School; ASL of NY; AIC; student of George Bellows, Andres Dashburg, John Sloan. First published illustration, Judge magazine, 1919. Illustrated the Gospel of St. Mark for Conde Nast, 1932; originated newspaper cartoon "Bingville Bugle." Member: SI (life); Artists' Guild; Art Dir. Club; GFLA; Woodstock AA; Salma. C. Died in 1969. Address in 1929, Woodstock, NY.

WINSLOW, ELEANOR C. A.
Painter and illustrator. Born Norwich, CT, May, 1877. Pupil of ASL of NY; Whistler in Paris. Award: Third Hallgarten prize, NAD 1907. Member: NA Women PS; CT. AFA; Norwich AA. Address in 1929, 133 East 40th Street, New York, NY.

WINSLOW, HENRY.
Painter, etcher, and engraver. Born Boston, MA, 1874. Pupil of Whistler in Paris. Member: Chicago SE; AI Graphic A. Work in: British Museum, London; Bibliotheque Nationale, Paris; Boston Museum of Fine Arts; New York Public Library. Address in 1929, 24 Marlborough Place., N. W. 8; 10 Fitzroy St., London, W., England.

WINSLOW, LEON LOYAL.
Teacher and writer. Born Brockport, NY. Pupil of Pratt Inst. Member: AFA. Author of Organization and Teaching of Art,

Elementary Industrial Arts and Essentials of Design. Contributor to art and educational journals. Address in 1929 Carrollton and Lafayette Avenues, Baltimore, MD.

WINSTANLEY, WILLIAM.
An English artist who came to America during the last decade of the eighteenth century. He made many good copies of Gilbert Stuart's portraits of George Washington. Returned to England. Exhibited three Virginia landscapes in London at British Institution in 1806.

WINSTANLEY, JOHN BREYFOGLE.
Painter, writer, and illustrator. Born Louisville, KY. Pupil of PAFA. Member: NYWCC. Award: Bronze medal, P. P. Exp., San F., 1915. Died in 1947. Address in 1929, 644 Minneford Ave., City Island, New York, NY.

WINTER, ALICE BEACH.
(Mrs. Charles Allan Winter). Painter, sculptor, and illustrator. Born Green Ridge, MO, March 22, 1877. Pupil of St. Louis School of Fine Arts and ASL of NY. Member: NA Women PS. Specialty, childhood subjects. Address in 1929, 53 East 59th Street, New York, NY; summer, 134 Mt. Pleasant Ave., East Gloucester, MA.

WINTER, ANDREW.
Painter. Born in 1892. Exhibited at National Acad. of Design, New York, 1925. Address in 1926, 136 West 109th Street, New York, NY. Died in 1958.

WINTER, CHARLES A(LLAN).
Painter, and illustrator. Born Cincinnati, OH, Oct. 26, 1869. Pupil of Cincinnati Art Acad., under Noble and Nowottny; Julian Acad. in Paris under Bouguereau and Ferrier. Award: Foreign Scholarship from Cincinnati Art Acad., 1894. Died in 1942. Address in 1929, 53 East 59th St., New York, NY; summer, 134 Mt. Pleasant Ave., East Gloucester, MA.

WINTER, EZRA (AUGUSTUS).
Painter and illustrator. Born Manistee, MI, March 10, 1886. Pupil of Chic. Acad. of Fine Arts;

Am. Acad. in Rome. Member: ANA., Mural P.; NY Arch. Lg. Salma. C.; Players C; AFA. Awards: AM. Acad. at Rome Scholarship, 1911-14; medal of honor, NY. Arch. Lg.; gold medal, NY Society of Arch. Work: Decorations in Great Hall and Vestibule, Cunard Bldg., NY; Kilburn Hall and Eastman Theatre, Rochester, NY; Trading Room, NY Cotton Exchange; Willard Straight Hall, Cornell U., Ithaca, NY; Ceiling decorations, Nat. Chamber of Commerce, Wash., D.C.; Children's Room Frieze and Del. Room frieze, Public Lib., Birmingham, AL; Ceiling and Mosaic panel, Rochester Savings Bank, Rochester, NY; 3 domes, Industrial Trust Bldg., Providence, RI; stained glass window, Straus Bank, Chic.; decorations in the Monroe County Savings Bank, Rochester, NY; Fairy Story decorations NY. Life Bldg. Restaurant, NY; mosaic panel and decorative map, Union Trust Bldg., Detroit, Mich. Died in 1949. Address in 1929, 15 Vanderbilt Ave., New York, NY.

WINTER, GEORGE.
Painter. Born June 10, 1810, in England. Working in NY in 1834. Died Feb. 1876 in IN.

WINTER, MILO.
Illustrator. Born in Princeton, IL, in 1888. Pupil of Art Inst. of Chicago; American Water Color Society; Cliff Dwellers, Chicago. Illustrated "Nights with Uncle Remus," "Aesop's Fables," "Alice in Wonderland," "Bill Pop-Gun," etc. Address in 1926, 621 Sheridan Road, Evanston, IL.

WINTERHALDER, LOUIS A.
Painter and pen and ink artist. Native of New Orleans. He studied at the Art Union and under Molinary, Perrelli and Buck. Exhibited at New Orleans and at the Academy of Fine Arts, Chicago. Specialty, landscapes. Represented in Louisiana State Museum.

WINTRINGHAM, FRANCES M.
Painter. Born Brooklyn, NY, March 15, 1884. Pupil of George Bellows, Kenneth Hayes Miller, Robert Henri, John Sloan, and Charles Hawthorne.

Member: ASL. Address in 1929, 168 Hicks St., Brooklyn, NY.

WIRE, MELVILLE T(HOMAS).
Painter. Born Austin, IL, Sept. 24, 1877. Pupil of Marie Craig and Mrs. Eva Cline-Smith. Member: Ore. SA. Address in 1929, 608 Johnson St., Pendleton, OR.

WIREMAN, EUGENIE M.
Painter and illustrator. Born Philadelphia. Pupil of PAFA; Howard Pyle. Member: Phila. Alliance. Address in 1929, Haworth Bldg., 1020 Chestnut St.; h. 3601 Waltnut St., Philadelphia, PA.

WIRES, MRS. ALDEN CHOATE.
Painter. Born Oswego, NY, Feb. 16, 1903. Member: Tiffany Foundation; Rockport AA. Address in 1929, Winter Park, Florida, summer, Rockport, MA.

WIRTH, ANNA M(ARIA).
Illustrator and writer. Born Johnstown, PA, Nov. 12, 1868. Pupil of PAFA; Phila. School of Design for Women; Phila. School Min. P. Illustrated "Progressive Pennsylvania," by J. M. Swank. Author and illustrator of "The King's Jester." Died in 1939. Address in 1929, 901 North Los Robles Ave., Pasadena, Calif., h. 248 Barron Ave., Johnstown, PA.

WISE, ETHEL BRAND.
(Mrs. L. E. Wise). Sculptor. Born New York City, March 9, 1888. Pupil of James Earle Fraser, Harry Trasher, Arthur Lee. Member: Syracuse Associated A; Syracuse ACG. Work: Plaisted Memorial, Masonic Temple Syracuse, NY; Teachers Mem., Wichita Falls, TX; "Repose," permanent collection, University of Missouri, Columbia. Address in 1929, 201 Clarendon St., Syracuse, NY.

WISE, FLORENCE B(ARAN).
Painter, and lecturer. Born Farmingdale, Long Island, NY, Jan. 27, 1881. Pupil of F. C. Jones, G. W. Maynard, G. Bridgman, RI School of Design. Member: Springfield AL. Work: Copy of Gilbert Stuart's "George Washington," Sherman Hotel, Chicago, IL.

Address in 1929, 90 Sefton Drive, Cranston, RI.

WISE, LOUISE WATERMAN.
(Mrs. Stephen Wise). Portrait painter and writer. Born NY. Pupil of Kenyon Cox, Robert Henri, George Bellows. Member: NA Women PS. Died in 1947. Address in 1929, 27 W. 96th St., New York, NY.

WISELTIER, JOSEPH.
Painter, craftsman, and teacher. Born Paris, France, Oct. 6, 1887. Pupil of Dow, Bement, Snell. Member: Alliance; Eastern Arts Asso. (pres); CT. AA; Hartford ACC; AFA. State Director of Art Education for CT. Address in 1929, 107 Washington Circle, West Hartford, CT.

WISEMAN, ROBERT W.
Painter of animals. Exhibited at the National Academy. His studio was in New Haven, CT.

WISER, GUY BROWN.
Painter and teacher. Born Marion, IN, Feb. 10, 1895. Pupil of Despujols, Gorguet, Hugh H. Breckenridge, Charles Hawthorne, J. R. Hopkins. Member: Hoosier Art Patrons Assoc.; Columbus AL; Ind. AL. Awards: Walter Lippincott prize, PAFA, Phila., 1927; Union Trust prize, Nor. Ind. AL, 1927; George T. Buckingham prize, Hoosier Salon, Chicago, 1927, 1929; first prize, Columbus AL., 1929. Address in 1929, 100 West Duncan Street, Columbus, OH.

WITHERSTINE, DONALD F(REDERICK).
Painter. Born Herkimer, NY, Feb. 9, 1896. Pupil of AIC; PAFA; George Elmer Browne. Member: Salma. C.; Beach Combers; Fellowship PAFA; Boston AC. Works: "Devant le Mosque," Peoria Art Inst.; "The Old Wharf in Moonlight," Bloomington AA; "Andorra Pyrenees," University of IL. Address in 1929, 34 Commercial St., Provincetown, MA.

WITMAN, JOSEPH.
Portrait painter, of Reading, PA. He exhibited portraits at the "Columbianum," Philadelphia, 1795.

WITT, JOHN HARRISON.
Painter. Born in Dublin, Wayne County, IN, in 1840. Machinist and wagon painter in a small agricultural implement factory owned by his uncles. Began portrait painting at an early age; adopted it as a profession c. 1863. Entirely self-taught. Painted portraits of great many governors and other prominent public men of Ohio until about 1879, when he went to NYC. Associate Member of NAD and member of various clubs. Died Sept. 13, 1901 in NYC.

WITTERS, NEIL.
Painter, illustrator, etcher, and craftsman. Born Grand Rapids, MI. Pupil of AIC, PAFA, ASL of NY., John C. Johansen. Member: Alliance; AIC Alumni . Awards: Logan medal for arts and crafts, AIC, 1919; 1st prize for cotton dress goods design, Alliance, 1919; 1st prize wall paper design , Alliance, 1919. Designs for textiles. Address in 1929, 311 Remington St., Saginaw, MI.

WOELFLE, ARTHUR WILLIAM.
Painter. Born Trenton, NJ, Dec. 17, 1873. Pupil of ASL of NY under Mowbray, Beckwith, Cox and Twachtman; NAD under Will Low and C. Y. Turner; Carl Marr and Diez in Munich. Member: ANA, 1929; NAC (life); ASL of NY; Salma. C., 1902; GFLA; Allied AA; AFA. Awards: Hon. mention, Munich; scholarship, Brooklyn Inst.; silver medal, Allied AA, 1928. Work: Murals in Court House at Youngstown, Ohio; Court House of Conshocton, Ohio; also ten portraits of judges in the Court House at Youngstown, Ohio. Died in 1936. Address in 1929, 261 Madison Ave., Fushing, LI, NY.

WOICESKE, RONAU W(ILLIAM).
Painter and craftsman. Born Bloomington, IL. Pupil of John Carlson and St. Louis School FA. Member: New Haven PCC: AFA. Award: Second prize, St. Louis AL. Specialty, etching and stained glass designing. Died in 1953. Address in 1929, Woodstock, NY.

WOISERI, J. I. BOUQUET.
Engraver and painter. As early as 1803 this man was working in New Orleans. Engraved a plan and a view of New Orleans with well-executed aquatint vignette and views of bldgs., and a large aquatint view of Boston. In the General Advertiser in Phila., in 1804 Woiseri advertises his 2 New Orleans pleas "for $10 for both colored." He dedicates his plates "by permission to President Thomas Jefferson." Called himself a "designer, drawer, geographer, and engineer." He worked six years on the New Orleans plates, where he lived for many years.

WOLCHONOK, LOUIS.
Painter. Member: Brooklyn SA; NYWCC. Address in 1929, 258 Riverside Drive, New York, NY; 1068 East 15th Street, Brooklyn, NY.

WOLCOTT, KATHERINE.
Miniature painter. Born in Chicago, IL, in 1880. Pupil of Art Inst. of Chicago. Address in 1926, 5222 Blackstone Ave., Chicago, IL.

WOLF, HAMILTON A(CHILLE).
Painter, illustrator, etcher, writer, lecturer, and teacher. Born New York City, Sept. 11, 1883. Pupil of Robert Henri, William M. Chase, Edward McCartan. Work: Pastel, Huntington Library and Art Gallery, San Marino, CA. Address in 1929, 1627 Walnut St., Berkeley, CA.

WOLF, HENRY.
Painter and wood engraver. Born Aug. 3, 1852, in Eckwershiem, Alsace. Pupil of Jacques Levy, artist-engraver of Strassburg. Exhibited at Paris Salon; Chicago Expo. 1893; Paris Expo., 1889, and in 1900 received the sivler medal, Fine Arts Expo., Rouen, France, 1903; diploma and grand medal of honor for distinguished services in promoting art of engraving, St. Louis Expo., 1904. Member of advisory comm., and later of International Jury of Awards, St. Louis Expo., 1904. elected Asso. Member of the Nat. Acad. in 1905; Nat. Acad., 1908. Member: Am. Federation of Arts; International Soc. of Sculptors, Painters and Gravers; Alliance Francaise; Union Internationale des Beaux Arts et des Lettres, Paris, FR. Principal

works: Engravings illustrating Am. Artist Series, and Gilbert Stuart Series of Men and Women in Century Magazine. Original engravings: "The Morning Star;" "The Evening Star;" "A Duck Pond;" "Morning Mists;" "Lower NY in a Mist;" "The Scattering of the Mists;" "Portrait of Thomas Jefferson;" "Portrait of Thomas Carlyle;" "My Mother;" "Miss Alexander, after Whistler;" "Portrait of Ladies," and "American Artist Series" appeared in Harper's Magazine. Contributor to other magazines. See "History of Wood Engraving in America," by W. J. Linton. Died March 18, 1916, in NYC.

WOLF, MAX (DR.).
Painter and etcher. Born Vienna, Austria, Oct. 22, 1885. Member: Physicians AC; Am. Bookplate S. Address in 1929, 85 East 79th St., New York, NY; summer, Millwood, NY.

WOLFE, NATALIE.
(Mrs. D. D. Michael). Sculptor. Born San Francisco, CA, March 16, 1896. Pupil of Ferrea and Calif. School of FA. Member: NLA Pen W (FA dept.). Work: Bust of M. H. de Young, San Francisco Memorial Museum. Died in 1939. Address in 1929, 75 Hyde St., San Francisco, CA.

WOLFF, GUSTAVE.
Painter. Born in Germany, March 28, 1863. Came to America when three years old. Pupil of St. Louis School of Fine Arts under Paul Cornoyer; studied in Europe. Member: Buffalo SA. Awards: Silver medal, Portland, OR, 1905; first Dolph prize, Competitive Ex., St. Louis, 1906; Wednesday Club silver medal, SWA, 1907. Work: "The Brook," City Art Museum, St. Louis. Died in 1934. Address in 1929, 503 West 175th St., New York, NY.

WOLFF, OTTO.
Painter and illustrator. Born in Cologne, Germany, in 1858. Studied in Paris. Member: Chicago Society of Artists; Chicago Art Club. Award: Honorable mention, Paris Salon, 1888. Address in 1926, 245 West North Ave., Chicago, IL.

WOLFSON, IRVING.
Painter, etcher, and teacher. Born Dec. 10, 1899. Address in 1929, 399 Grand St., New York, NY.

WOLFSON, WILLIAM.
Painter, lithographer, and etcher. Born Pittsburgh, Oct., 26, 1894. Pupil of A. W. Sparks, G. W. Maynard, DuMond. Member: Pitts. AA. Represented in Fifty Print Show, 1928-29; in Bibliotheque Nationale, Paris. Address in 1929, Rochambeau Ave., New York, NY.

WOLINSKI, JOSEPH.
Painter. Born in 1873. Pupil of Royal Art Society of New South Wales; also of Colarossi in Paris. Member: Royal Art Society, New South Wales. Work: "After Life's Fitful Fever He Sleeps Well;" "An Interior," two head studies in charcoal; and "Summer" in Nat. Art Gallery of New South Wales. Address in 1926, 32 Moore Park Road, Sydney, Australia.

WOLLASTON, JOHN.
English portrait painter. He visited the Colonies in the middle of the eighteenth century, and painted many portraits in NY, Phila., and the South from 1750 to 1767. His best portraits seem to have been painted in NY between 1751 and 1757. Among his portraits were those of Martha Dandridge Custis (Mrs. Washington) and the Custis children; Sir Charles Hardy, Gov. of NY, William Allen of Claremont, and Clara Walker Allen.

WOMRATH, A(NDREW) K(AY).
Painter, illustrator, and draftsman. Born Frankford, Phila., PA, Oct. 25, 1869. Pupil of ASL of NY under Twachtman and J. Alden Weir; Grasset and Merson in Paris; Westminster School of Art, London. Member: NY Arch. Lg., 1902; NAC. Address in 1929, 7 Square Port-Royal, Paris (13en), France; h. Kent, CT.

WONNER, PAUL.
Painter. Born April 24, 1920, in Tucson, AZ. Earned B. A. (1942) at Cal. Col. of Arts and Crafts; CIC/Berkeley (BA - 1952 MA; 1953, MLS 1955). Taught at Berkley; UCLA; Otis Art Inst. Exhibited at

DeYoung Mus. SF; SF Art Soc.; Santa Barbara Mus.; Guggenheim; MOMA; Walker; Denver; Carnegie; Art. Inst. of Chicago; Gal. S. D. and Berggruen of Art; U. of Nebraska, Oakland, and many private collections. Address in 1982, 468 Jersey St., San Francisco, CA.

WOOD, E(LLA) MIRIAM.
Painter. Born Birmingham, AL, Feb. 18, 1888. Pupil of Ellsworth Woodward, Henry McCarter, Hawthorne, Chase, Newcomb School of Art, New Orleans; PAFA. Member: NO AG; NO Art and Crafts C. Award: Second prize, Mississippi AA, Jackson. Work: "The Fisherman's Dory," Mississippi Art Assoc. Address in 1929, 7014 St. Charles Ave., New Orleans, LA; summer, Boc 176, Covington, LA.

WOOD, EDITH LONGSTRETH.
Painter. Born Philadelphia. Pupil of PAFA; Scandinavian Art Academy in Paris. Member: Phila. Alliance; Plastic C; Fellowship PAFA; North Shore AA. Address in 1929, 140 North 15th St., Philadelphia, PA.

WOOD, ETHELWYN A.
Painter. Born Germantown, PA, Jan. 10, 1902. Pupil of PA. School of Indust. Art; PAFA. Member: Fellowship PAFA; West Palm Beach AL. Work: Painting, Fellowship of the Pennsylvania Academy of the Fine Arts, Philadelphia, PA. Address in 1929, 903 North N St., Lake Worth, FL.

WOOD, FRANKLIN T.
Etcher. Born Hyde Park, MA, Oct. 9, 1887. Studied at Cowles Art School; ASL of NY; and abroad. Member: Chicago SE. Award: Bronze medal, P. P. Exp., San F., 1915. Represented in Chicago Art Inst. Died May 22, 1945. Address in 1929, Rutland, MA.

WOOD, GEORGE B.
Painter. Born in Phila., in 1832. Studied at the PA Acad. of the Fine Arts. Represented in Wilstach Collection, Fairmount Park, Phila., by landscape "Winter Twilight." The Penna. Acad. of the Fine Arts owns his painting of "Dr. Tyson's Library." Died in MA, in 1910.

WOOD, GRANT.
Painter and sculptor. Born Anamosa, IA, Feb. 13, 1892. Pupil of AIC; Minneapolis Handicraft Guild; Julian Academy in Paris. Work: "Democracy," mural painting, Harrison School, Cedar Rapids; life membership medal, bas-relief and painting, "Doorway at Periguex," for Cedar Rapids Art Assoc.; decoration in National Masonic Research Bldg., Anamosa, Iowa; war memorial window, Memorial Bldg., Cedar Rapids, IA. Died Feb. 12, 1942, in Iowa. Address in 1929, No. 5 Turner Alley, Cedar Rapids, IA; 61 Washington Square, New York, NY.

WOOD, HARRIE (MORGAN).
Painter, and illustrator. Born Rushford, April 28, 1902. Pupil of Pratt Inst.; ASL of NY. Member: NYWCC; WACS; Tiffany Foundation. Illustrated "The Boy Who Was" (Dutton); "Made in America" (Knopf); "Something Perfectly Silly" (Knopf). Address in 1929, 102 Park Avenue, Bronxville, NY; summer, Rushford, NY.

WOOD, JESSIE PORTER.
Painter and illustrator. Born in Syracuse, NY, in 1863. Pupil of J. Carroll Beckwith, George de Forest Brush, Walter Shirlaw, J. Ward Stimson, and others. Address in 1926, 2005 Columbia Road, Washington, DC.

WOOD, JOSEPH.
Miniature painter. Born in Clarkstown, NY, about 1778; died in Washington, DC, in 1830. Largely self-taught, earned his living with his violin in the summer, to study in the winter. In 1804 formed partnership with John Wesley Jarvis, painting miniatures. Dunlap records a visit he made with Malbone to their studio during 1805-06. Both artists received some assistance from Malbone. The partnership was dissolved in 1809. Wood had a studio at 1812-13. Went to Phila. and had a studio at 93 South Third Street. His name occurs in the Phila. directories until 1817. Exhibited at PAFA. Moved later to Washington and in 1827 had a studio on the north side of Penn. Avenue between 9th and

10th Sts. An extended account of the artists appeared in "The Port-Folio," 1811. Died June 15, 1830, in Wash., DC.

WOOD, KATHERYN LEONE.
Painter and writer. Born Kalamazoo, MI. Pupil of Frederick Freer, Lawton Parker and others. Member: AFA. Work: Miniature of Mrs. J. C. Burrows, Continental Memorial Hall, Washington, D.C.; portrait of Judge Severens, US District Court, Cincinnati, Ohio. Died in 1935. Address in 1929, 122 W. Lovell St., Kalamazoo, MI.

WOOD, M LOUISE.
See Mrs. Wright.

WOOD, MARY EARL.
Painter. Born Lowell, MA. Pupil Boston Museum School under Tarbell, Benson and DeCamp. Member: Copley S. Address in 1929, 4040 Fenway Studios, 30 Ipswich St., Boston, MA.

WOOD, NAN.
(Mrs. Charles Morgan Wood). Painter. Born Dayton, OH, Feb. 11, 1872. Pupil of Hugh Breckenridge; ASL of NY. Member: North Shore AA; Tucson PBC. Address in 1929, Northgate Farm, Ipswich, MA, winter, Tucson, AZ.

WOOD, STAN.
Painter. A San Francisco water color artist who exhibited in the New York galleries in 1925.

WOOD, THOMAS WATERMAN.
Painter. Born Nov. 12, 1823, in Montpelier, VT. Studied portrait painting under Chester Harding in Boston, and then established his studio in NY. Wood depicted black americans and their development during the Civil War. Elected Academician in 1871. Painted a number of portraits of prominent men in New York City. He died April 4, 1903, in NYC.

WOOD, VIRGINIA HARGRAVES.
Painter, etcher, and teacher. Born near St. Louis, MO. Pupil of Chase, Du Mond, Hawthorne, and studied abroad. Member: NA Women PS.; Alliance; AFA. Work: Mural decorations in Broadway Cafe;

illustrated several books. Founded Virginia Fine Arts Society. Address in 1929, 601 Madison Ave., New York, NY; h. Ivy Depot, Albermarle, VA.

WOOD, WILLIAM R. C.
Landscape painter. Born April 15, 1875. Pupil of S. E. Whiteman in Baltimore, he was president of the water color club. Died April 30, 1915, in Baltimore, MD.

WOODBURY, CHARLES H(ERBERT).
Marine painter, and etcher. Born Lynn, MA, July 14, 1864. Pupil of MA Inst. of Technology in Boston; Julian Acad. in Paris under Boulanger and Lefebvre. Member: SAA 1899; ANA 1906, NA 1907; AWCS; Boston WCC; NYWCC; St. Botolph C.; Copley S. 1900; Boston GA; North Shore AA; Boston WCC. Awards: Third prize, Boston AC; gold medal, Atlanta Exp., 1895; second prize, Tennessee Centennial, Nashville, 1897; 2 medals, Mechanics fair, Boston; bronze medal, Paris Exp., 1900; bronze medal, Pan Am Exp., Buffalo, 1901; first prize, Worcester Museum, 1903; silver medal, St. Louis Exp., 1904; hon. mention, CI Pittsburgh, 1905; second prize, Worcester, 1907; silver medal, Buenos Aires Exp., 1910; Evans prize, AWCS 1911; second W. A. Clark prize ($1,500) and Corcoran silver medal, 1914; gold medal for oil painting and medal of honor for water colors, P. P. Exp., San., 1915; Dana gold medal, PAFA, 1924. In collections of Carnegie RISD; Boston; Worcester, Herron Art Inst.; St. Louis Corcoran; Detroit; MMA; Gardner Collection, Boston; Fitzgerald Collection, Brookline; State of Utah Collection; Telfair Acad., Savannah, GA. Collection of Queen of Italy. Died in 1940. Address in 1929, 132 Riverway, Boston, MA; and Ogunquit, ME.

WOODBURY, J. C.
Painter. Member: Providence WCC. Address in 1929, 155 Medway St., Providence, RI.

WOODBURY, MARCIA OAKES.
(Mrs. Charles H. Woodbury). Painter. Born June 29, 1865, in So. Berwick, ME. Student of

Woman's Art Club, New York; also with Lassar in Paris. Represented in Boston Museum of Fine Arts by "Tripych," "Mother and Daughter." Died Nov. 7, 1913, in Ogunquit, ME.

WOODCOCK, T. S.
Engraver. Born in Manchester, England. Came to NY about 1830, and in 1836 was working in Philadelphia. A portrait of Andrew Jackson, published in NY in 1834, is engraved with a ruling-machine and is signed by Woodcock. About 1840 Woodcock was located in Brooklyn as an engraver and print publisher, and about this time we find some beautiful plates of butterflies engraved by Woodcock & Harvey, Brooklyn. Woodcock later returned to England.

WOODROFFE, ELEANORE G.
Painter. Member: NA Women PS. Address in 1929, Box 166, Niantic, CT; 9 Jane St., New York, NY.

WOODRUFF, CLAUDE WALLACE.
Illustrator. Member: SI. Address in 1929, 1127 North Dearborn St., Chicago, IL.

WOODRUFF, CORICE.
(Mrs. Henry S. Woodruff). Sculptor and painter. Born Ansonia, CT, Dec. 26, 1878. Pupil of Minneapolis School of Fine Arts under Robert Koehler; Kunte Akerberg; ASL of NY. Member: Artists Guild, Chicago; Attic C., Minneapolis. Awards: First prize for sculpture, Minnesota State Art Society, second prize, 1914; hon. mention for sculpture, St. Paul Inst., 1916. Specialty, small sculpture, bas relief portraits and portrait busts. Address in 1929, 2017 Pleasant Ave.; h. 2431 Pleasant Ave., Minneapolis, MN.

WOODRUFF, JOHN KELLOGG.
Painter, sculptor, and teacher. Born Bridgeport, CT, Sept. 6, 1879. Pupil of Walter Shirlaw; Arthur W. Dow; Charles J. Martin. Member: S. Indp. A; Salons of Amer. Died in 1956. Address in 1929, Grand View on Hudson, NY.

WOODRUFF, WILLIAM.
Engraver of portraits and landscape. He was in business in Philadelphia in 1817-24. He worked quite well in both line and stipple. After 1824 he apparently removed to Cincinnati, as we find prints by him engraved in that city. Died Feb. 26, 1852.

WOODS, LILLA SORRENSON.
(Mrs. E. B. Woods). Painter. Born Portage, WI, April 27, 1872. Pupil of Lydia Ely in Kilburn, WI; AIC; summer class at Delavan, WI; Miss Hawley at Rijsvard in Holland; Laurens in Paris; Corcoran School of Art in Washington; Helen Todd Hammon in Boston. Address in 1929, 30 Occom Ridge, Hanover, NH.

WOODSIDE, JOHN A.
Philadelphia painter. Born 1781. Flourished in the middle of the last century. He painted many portraits, historical and allegorical subjects, and was noted as the decorator of the hose carriages and engines of local fire companies, and the first locomotive. He was painting in Phila. before 1817. Died 1852.

WOODSON, MARIE L.
Painter, craftsman, and teacher. Born Selma, AL, Sept. 9, 1875. Pupil of AIC: Ochtman; NY. School of Fine and Applied Art. Member: Alumni Asso. AIC; Denver AA; AFA; Art Com., City and County of Denver. Award: Prize for "Welcome Arch" for Denver. Work: Mural decoration in Denver Public Library; illustrated "Tunes for Tiny Tots," by Antionette Freneauff. Director of Art Education, Denver Public Schools. Address in 1929, 832 So. Pearl St., Denver, CO.

WOODWARD, DEWING.
Painter, writer, lecturer, and teacher. Born Williamsport, PA, June 6, 1876. Pupil of PAFA; Masters, Robert-Fleury, Jacques Blanche, Raffaelli, Julian Academy in Paris. Member: Femmes Peintres Et Sculpteurs de France; Wash. AC; Blue Dome Fellowship; AFA. Awards: Gold medal, International, Marseilles, 1897; silver medal, Nantes, 1904. Work: "Wings," College of Music of the Univ. of Miami; "Waiting" Museum of the Julian Academy; "Morning Song of

the Pines," Woman's C. of Miami. Director of School of Fine Arts, University of Miami. Address in 1929, Univeristy of Miami, Coral Gables, Fla.; h. 3652 Southwest 23rd St., Miami, FL.

WOODWARD, E. F.
Engraver of maps and small vignettes of events in American history. In a school atlas published in Hartford, CT, in 1839, these engravings are signed "as Engraved by E. F. Woodward."

WOODWARD, ELLSWORTH.
Painter, illustrator, teacher, and craftsman. Born Bristol Co., MA, July 14, 1861. Pupil of RI School of Design in Providence; Carl Marr in Munich. Member: Art Assoc. of New Orleans; Boston SAC; LA. State Art Teachers Assoc.; Southern SAL (pres); Providence AC (hon); Providence WCC; Round Table C. (Pres). Awards: Gold medal, Art Association of New Orleans; gold medal, Miss. AA; bronze medal of honor, Boston SAC. Director of Art Education, Newcomb College, since 1890. Represented in Delgado Museum of Art, New Orleans; Brooklyn Museum of Art. Died in 1939. Address in 1929, Newcomb College; 1316 Pine St., New Orleans, LA.

WOODWARD, HELEN M.
Painter, sculpture, craftsman, and teacher. Born Newton Stewart, IN, July 28, 1902. Pupil of William Forsyth, Charles Hawthorne. Member: Ind. AC. Awards: Prizes, IN State Fair, 1926, 1927, 1928; prize, Hoosier Salon, Chicago, 1928, 1929. Work: Painting, Bedford High School, Bedford High School, Bedford, IN. Address in 1929, 446 Farmers Trust Bldg., h. 3441 College, Indianapolis, IN.

WOODWARD, LELLA GRACE.
Painter and teacher. Born Coldwater, MI, May 2, 1858. Studied in Boston, Chicago, England, Holland, Rome, and Venice, and under Du Mond, Merson, Collin and Whistler in Paris. Address in 1929, National Park Seminary, Forest Glen, MD.

WOODWARD, MABEL MAY.
Painter. Born Providence, RI, Sept. 28, 1877. Pupil of Chase, DuMond, and Cox in NY. Memeber: Providencetown AA. Providence AC; Providence WCC. Died in 1945. Address in 1929, 36 Belvedere Blvd., Providence, RI.

WOODWARD, ROBERT STRONG.
Painter. Born Northampton, MA, May 11, 1885. Mostly self-taught. Member: Salma. C.; AFA. NYWCS. Awards: First Hallgarten prize, NAD, 1919; hon. mention, Concord, AA, 1920; first landscpae prize, Springfield AL, 1927. Represented in Springfield (MA) Art Museum; Forbes Library, Northhampton, MA; Public Library, Stockbridge, MA. Died in 1960. Address in 1929, Shelburne Falls, MA.

WOODWARD, STANLEY W(INGATE).
Painter, illustrator, and etcher. Born Malden, MA, Dec. 11, 1890. Pupil of Eric Paper School of Art; School of the Boston Museum of Fine Arts; PAFA. Member: Chicago SE: Concord AA; Brooklyn SE; Copley S.; Fellowship PAFA; Boston SWCP; Boston AC.; Salma C.; Allied AA; NYWCC; Guild of Boston A; CT. AFA; North Shore AA: Phil. WCC; Springfield AL; AFA. Awards: Hon. men., Concord AA., 1919; second Hallgarten prize, NAD, 1925; Hammond purchase prize ($150). NYWCC and AWCS. 1927; prize ($100) Balto. WCC, 1927; anniversary prize, Springfield AL ($250), 1928. Represented in University of Michigan, Malden Public Library, Concord Art Assoc.; Walker Gallery, Bowdoin College, Brunswick, ME; St. Marks School, Groton, MA; Public Library, Wellesley Hills, MA. Address in 1929, 9 Bonwood St., Newtonville, MA.

WOODWARD, WILLIAM.
Painter, architect, and craftsman. Born Seekonk, MA, May 1, 1859. Pupil of RI School of Design in Providence; MA. Normal Art School in Boston; Boulanger in Paris. Member: Louisiana Chapter AIA; Art Assoc. of New Orleans, AIA, 1897 (hon.); SSAL; Gulf Coast AA; AFA; Laguna Beach AA. Award: Gold medal, Gulf Coast AA, 1927 and 1929. Work: "Rainy Day," New

Orleans Art Asso.; "Orleans Alley," Delgado Art Museum, New Orleans; "Midway Point, Carmel, Calif.,"High Museum of Art, Atlanta, GA; "Hawaiian Landscape," Rogers Art Gallery, Laurel, Miss. Professor of drawing and painting (emeritus), Tulane University, New Orleans. Died in 1939. Address in 1929, Kensington Drive, Biloxi, MI.

WOODWILLOW, RICHARD CATON.
Painter. Born in Baltimore, MD, in 1825. He had access to the pictures of Robert Gilmore, then one of the best collections in the country, and he copied many of the figure pieces among them. He studied at Dusseldorf until his premature death in London on Sept. 30, 1856. His painting "Reading the News" is owned by the National Academy of Design and has been engraved.

WOOLF, S(AMUEL) J(OHNSON).
Portrait painter and writer. Born New York, Feb. 12, 1880. Pupil of ASL of NAD under Cox and Brush. Awards: Third Hallgarten prize, NAD 1904; medal. Appalachian Exp., Knoxville, 1910. Work: "Dr. Finely," College of the City of NY; "Mark Twain," Brook Club; "Dr. Hunter," Normal College; "Cardinal Logue," Catholic Club, NY; also represented in Metropolitan Museum; NY Public Library. Author: "A Short History of Art." As special correspondent with American Expeditionary Force, painted portraits of Joffre, Pershing, and other commanders. Died in 1948. Address in 1929, 253 West 42nd St.; h. 210 West 101st St., New York, NY.

WOOLLEY.
An English painter who divided his time between Philadelphia and NY about 1757. He painted small portraits in oil; also signs and other pictures.

WOOLLEY, VIRGINIA.
Painter, etcher, and teacher. Born Selma, AL, Aug. 27, 1884. Pupil of Jacques Blanche, Lucien Simon, Richard Miller. Member: Atlanta AA; SSAL; Laguna Beach AA. Work: "Provincetown Street," Atlanta Art

Association. Address in 1929, Laguna Beach, CA.

WOOLLEY, WILLIAM.
Engraver in mezzotint and portrait painter. Produced two portraits of George Washington and a companion plate of Mrs. Washington. These plates were published by David Longworth at the Shakespeare Gallery, No. 11 Park Place, New York, probably about 1800. The larger memorial plate bears the inscription "David Longworth Direxit. Woolley-Pinxit et Sculpsit." While this might suggest American origin, it is possible that David Longworth suggested the design, ordered a painting and engraving made in London and then imported both and published the print in NY. No other plates by Woolley are known and the majority of the Washington portraits by Woolley owned by American collectors were purchased in London. They apparently had a very limited sale in this country. The plate was printed later in a reduced, altered state.

WOOLRYCH, BERTHA HEWIT.
(Mrs. F. Humphry Woolrych). Painter and illustator. Born in Ohio in 1868. Pupil of St. Louis School of Fine Arts; Morot, Collin and Courtois in Paris. Member: St. Louis AG; St. Louis Art Students Association. Awards: Medal, Lewis and Clark Exp., Portland, 1905; gold and silver medals, St. Louis School of Fine Art; silver medal, 1908. St. Louis District, General Federation of Women's Clubs. Address in 1929, 3855 Hartford St., St. Louis, MO; summer, Sherman, MO.

WOOLRYCH, E. HUMPHRY W.
Painter and illustrator. Born in Sydney, Australia, 1868. Pupil of Royal Acad., Berlin; Ecole des Beaux Arts, Colarossi Acad., Collin, Courtois and Purvis de Chavannes in Paris. Member: Hellas Art Club, Berlin; St. Louis Arts and Crafts; Brush and Pencil Club; 2 x 4 Society; St. Louis Architectural Club. Awards: Bronze medal, Portland Exposition, 1905; medal for portrait, MO State Fair, Sedalia, 1913. Work: Water color in St. Louis Public Library.

Address in 1926, 1411 International Life Building, St. Louis, MO.

WOOLSEY, C(ARL) E.
Painter. Born Chicago Heights, IL, April 24, 1902. Self-taught. Awards: McCutcheon award for landscape, Hoosier Salon, Chicago, 1928; Butler award for landscape, Hoosier Salon, 1929. Address in 1929, Pueblo Road, Taos, NM.

WOOLSEY, WOOD E.
Painter. Born Danville, IL, June 29, 1899. Self-taught. Work: "El Paseo," High School, Danville, IL; "Part of Taos," Art Association, Kokomo, IN. Address in 1929, Pueblo Road, Taos, NM.

WORCESTER, ALBERT.
Painter and etcher. Born in West Campton, NH, in 1878. Pupil of Luc Olivier Merson and of Jean Paul Laurens in Paris. Address in 1926, 467 West Canfield Avenue, Detroit, MI.

WORDEN, LAICITA WARBURTON.
Painter, sculptor, and illustrator. Born in Philadelphia in 1892. Pupil of Penna. Acad. of the Fine Arts. Member: Fellowship, Penna. Acad. of the Fine Arts. Address in 1926, 4141 North Broad St., Philadelphia, PA.

WORES, THEODORE.
Painter, illustrator, and teacher. Born San Francisco, CA, Aug. 1, 1860. Pupil of Alex. Wagner and Duveneck in Munich. Member: Century Assoc. Award: Gold medal, Alaska Yukon Exp., 1909. Instructor at San Francisco Art Inst., 1907-1912. Died in 1939. Address in 1929, Bohemian Club; h. 1722 Buchanan St., San Francisco, CA.

WORKMAN, DAVID TICE.
Etcher. Born in Wahpeton, ND, in 1884. Pupil of Benson and Hale in Boston; under Pyle in Wilmington; Brangwyn and Swan in London. Member: Chicago Society of Etchers; Attic Club, MN; Minneapolis Society of Artists. Award: First prize, Minnesota State Art Commission, 1914. Work: Mural decorations, Irving School, and East Side High School, Minneapolis, MN; Lincoln High School, Hibbing, MN. Address in 1926, 1210 First Ave., North, Minneapolis, MN.

WORRELL, JAMES.
An early Virginia portrait painter who painted a portrait of Judge John Tyler, who was a Governor of Virginia, 1808-11. The portrait is at the College of William and Mary at Williamsburg, VA.

WORSWICK, LLOYD.
Sculptor, craftsman, and teacher. Born Albany, NY, May 30, 1899. Pupil of Ulrich; Cederstrom, Brewster; Olinsky; Weinman, Bufano. Member: AFA. Address in 1929, 534 East 89th Street, New York, NY.

WORTHINGTON, MARY E.
Painter. Born Holyoke, MA. Studied with Constant, Laurens and F. V. DuMond in Paris, and Henry Read in Denver. Member: Denver Art Museum. Address in 1929, 1455 Humboldt St., Denver, CO.

WORTHLEY, CAROLINE BONSALL.
(Mrs. Irving Tupper Worthley). Painter and craftsman. Born Cincinnati, OH, Dec. 25, 1880. Pupil of Cincinnati Art Academy; Pennsylvannia School of Industrial Art; Fred Wagner; F. G. Copeland. Member: Plastic C.; Phila. Alliance. Died in 1944. Address in 1929, R.F.D. No. 3, Phoenixville, PA.

WRAY, HENRY RUSSELL.
Painter and etcher. Born Dec. 3, 1864, in Philadelphia, PA. Member: Phila. Sketch Club; Colorado Springs Art Society. Address in 1926, 33 West Willamette Ave., Colorado Springs, Co. Died July 29, 1927, in CO.

WRENN, CHARLES L(EWIS).
Painter, and illustrator. Born Cincinnati, OH, Sept. 18, 1880. Pupil of Chase and ASL of NY. Member: SI; Salma. C. Specialty, portraits. Died Oct, 1952. Address in 1929, 18 East 8th Street, New York, NY; Wilson Point, So. Norwalk, CT.

WRENN, ELIZABETH J(ENCKS).
Sculptor. Born Newburgh, NY, Dec. 8, 1892. Pupil of Abastenia

Eberle, George Bridgman, Mahonri Young, Maryland Inst. Member: Norfolk SA; Baltimore Friends of Art. Award: Irene Leach Memorial prize, Norfolk SA, 1922. Address in 1929, 1 West Mount Vernon Place, Baltimore, MD.

WRIGHT, ALICE MORGAN.
Sculptor. Born Albany, NY, Oct. 10, 1881. Pupil of MacNeil, Gutzon Borglum, Fraser, Injalbert. Member: NA Women PS; S. Indp. A.; NSS; Silvermine GA. Award: Helen Foster Bernett prize, NA Women PS, 1920; Agar National Arts Club prize, 1923. Work: Portrait reliefs of Pres. L. Clark Seelye, Prof. Mary A. Jordan and John Doleman, Smith College, Northampton, MA; "Lady Macbeth," Newark Museum; "Faun," Harmanns Bleecker Library, Albany, NY. Address in 1929, 393 State St., Albany, NY.

WRIGHT, ALMA BROCKERMAN.
Painter. He was born Salt Lake City, Nov. 22, 1875. Pupil of Bonnat, Laurens, Ecole des Beaux Arts and Julian and Colarossi academies in Paris. Member: Soc. of Utah Artists; Paris AAA; Salt Lake City Art Commission. awards: State prize, 1904; medal of honor, Utah Art Inst., 1905. Work: mural decorations in L. D. S. Temples at Honolulu; and Cardston, Alberta, Canada; Senate Chamber, Utah State Capitol; terra cotta panels, Mormon Temple, Mesa. Ariz., in collaboration with the sculptor. Head af art department, L. D. S. University, Salt Lake City, UT. Died in 1952. Address in 1929, L.D.S.U., Salt Lake City, UT.

WRIGHT, BERTHA, E. S.
(Mrs. Lawrence Wright). Painter. Born Astoria, LI, NY. Member: S. Indp. A.; Salons of Amer.; Am. APL. Address in 1929, Merrick Road, Merrick, LI, NY.

WRIGHT, CATHARINE MORRIS.
Painter. Born Philadelphia, PA, Jan. 26, 1899. Pupil of Henry B. Snell; Leopold Seyffert; Philadelphia School of Design for Women. Member: NYWCC; AWCS; Phila. WCC; AFA; Balto. WCC; Newport AA. Award: Honorable mention, Phila.,

AC, 1924. Address in 1929, Endsmeet Farm, Glenside, PA.

WRIGHT, CHARLES CUSHING.
Engraver. Born in Damariscota, ME; died in NY on June 7, 1854. Wright orphaned at an early age and adopted by Charles Cushing, whose name he later assumed. After some service as a soldier in the War of 1812, he settled in Utica, NY, and engaged in business as a watchmaker. In 1824 he was associated with A. B. Durand, in NY, doing etching, engraving, and making the dies for a number of medals awarded by the National and State Governments. One of the founders of NAD in NY in 1826. Living in Savannah in 1820, and engraving in Charleston, SC, in 1824. Wright attempted line-engraving without much success; his best work was his etched portraits. Died in 1854.

WRIGHT, CHARLES H.
Painter and illustrator. Born Knightstown, IN, Nov. 20, 1870. Pupil of ASL of NY. Member: SI 1914; Salma. C.; NYWCC; GFLA; New Rochelle AA; Indiana Artists. Died in 1939. Address in 1929, Room 309, 1931 Broadway, New York, NY; 27 Willow Ave., Larchmont, NY.

WRIGHT, CHARLES LENNOX.
Painter and illustrator. Born in Boston, MA, in 1876. Pupil of Art Students' League of NY; under Dagnan-Bouveret in Paris. Address in 1926, Bayside, LI, NY.

WRIGHT, F. E.
Painter. Born in South Weymouth, MA, in 1849. Studied in Paris for some time under Bonnat and Boulanger. His professional life was spent in Boston where many of his portraits are in private collections.

WRIGHT, FRED W.
Portrait painter. Born Crawfordsville, IN, Oct. 12, 1880. Pupil of Julian Academy and P. Marcel Baronneau in Paris; J. Ottis Adams; ASL of NY and Robert Reid in NY. Member: Salma. C.; A. Fund S.; A. Fellowship. Represented in NY State Capitol, Albany; National Democratic Club, Union Club,

Catholic Club, NY; James Jerome Hill Reference Library, St. Paul, MN; College of Industrial Arts, Denton, Texas. Address in 1929, 33 West 67th Street, New York, NY.

WRIGHT, G.
Engraver of vignettes, etc. He was working in Phila. in 1837. About this date the engraving firm of Wright & Balch was producing line portraits in NY. The Wright of this firm was probably G. Wright.

WRIGHT, GEORGE FREDERICK.
Portrait painter. Born in Washington, CT, in 1828. Student at the Nat. Acad., New York, and later spent 2 years abroad. He painted most of his portraits in Hartford and they are remarkable for their natural flesh tints and accuracy of likeness. Died in 1881, in Hartford, CT.

WRIGHT, GEORGE H(AND).
Painter and illustrator. Born Fox Chase, PA, Aug. 6, 1872. Pupil of PAFA and Spring Garden Inst. Member: SI 1901; Salma. C.; GFLA; S. Indp. A. Died in 1951. Address in 1929, Salmagundi Club, 47 Fifth Ave., New York, NY; h. Westport, CT.

WRIGHT, GLADYS YOAKUM.
Painter. Born in Greenville, TX. Pupil of McLeod School of Art in Los Angeles. Address in 1926, 606 West Third St., Fort Worth, TX.

WRIGHT, GRANT.
Painter and illustrator. Born Decatur, MI, Sept. 1, 1865. Pupil of NAD; Ed Ward. Member: Bronx AG. Illustrated "Yazzo Valley Tales," by Ed F. Younger. Died in 1935. Address in 1929, 3 West 29th Street, New York, NY; h. 327 Park Ave., Weehawken, NJ.

WRIGHT, JAMES HENRY.
Portrait and landscape painter, who was born in 1813. His studio was at 835 Broadway, New York City. Died in Brooklyn in 1883. Painted the portrait of Daniel Webster. New York Historical Society owns his view of Donagham Manor.

WRIGHT, JOSEPH.
Portrait painter. Son of Joseph Wright and Patience Lovell, born in Bordentown, NJ, 1756. After the death of his father, his mother took family to London. She became famous as a modeler in wax, and gave her son a good education. Received instruction from West and Hoppner, the latter marrying his sister. Before leaving England, Wright painted portrait of the Prince of Wales, afterward George IV. Went to Paris in 1782. Came to America soon after. Painted the portrait of Washington who gave him several sittings at Rocky Hill, near Princeton, NJ, in 1783. Painted 2 others of Washington about this time and in 1790 drew his profile likeness. In 1787 Wright had a studio in Pearl St., NY, and married Miss Vandervoort. Moved to Phila. and painted portraits, modeled in clay and practiced die sinking. This latter accomplishment gained for him, shortly before his death, the appointment of die sinker to US Mint. Made design for a cent of 1792 though it is not known that this design was ever executed.

WRIGHT, JOSEPHINE M.
Miniature painter, who exhibited miniatures at the PAFA, Phila., 1925. Address in 1926, 1010 North Stoneman Ave., Alhambra, CA.

WRIGHT, M. LOUISE.
(Mrs. John Wright). Painter and illustrator. Born Philadelphia, 1875. Pupil of PAFA; Whistler and Julian Acad. in Paris; F. W. Jackson in England. Member: Phila. WCC; NYWCC; Fellowship, PAFA; Concord AA; AFA. Award: Bronze medal, St. Louis Exp., 1904. Address in 1929, 2 Cheltenham Terrace, London, S.W. England.

WRIGHT, MARGARET HARDON.
(Mrs. James Hayden Wright). Etcher. Born Newton, MA, March 28, 1869. Pupil of Mass. Inst. of Technology in Boston; W. H. W. Bicknell; Merson in Paris. Member: Chicago SE; Copley S; Boston SE. Specialty, bookplates, etchings, Christmas cards. Represented in NY Public Library; Congressional Library, Washington, DC. Died in

1936. Address in 1929, 28 Copley St., Newton, MA.

WRIGHT, MARSHAM E(LWIN).
Painter, illustrator, etcher and craftsman. Born Sidcup, Kent, England, March 27, 1891. Pupil of Leo A. Henkora, Cameron Booth. Address in 1929, 1435 East Franklin Avenue.; h. 4440 Xerxes Ave., South, Minneapolis, IN.

WRIGHT, PATIENCE.
Born in Bordentown, NJ, in 1725, of Quaker parents, Patience and Joseph Wright. After her husband's death she became known by her small portraits in wax, chiefly profile bas-releifs. Her work was well-received in England. Died in London in March, 1786.

WRIGHT, (PHILIP) CAMERON.
Illustrator. Born Philadelphia, June 11, 1901. Pupil of Max Herman; Pratt Inst. Member: GFLA. Illustrated; "Two Fables," by Christopher Morley (Doubleday, Doran & Co.); book jackets (Century Co.); Christmas cover for Country Life, 1925, and full color insert, "Country Life," Christmas, 1926 (Doubleday, Doran & Co.); "Plymouth, 1620," by Walter Prichard Eaton. Address in 1929, 141 25th St., Jackson Heights, NY.

WRIGHT, RUFUS.
Portrait painter. Born in 1832 in Cleveland, OH. He was a pupil of the Nat. Acad. of Design. His portraits include those of Roger B. Taney, Edward M. Stanton and Wm. H. Seward; among his other works are "The Morning Bouquet" and "Feeding the Birds."

WRIGHT, S. MAC DONALD.
Painter, who exhibited at Penn. Acad. of the Fine Arts, 1921 in "Exhibition Showing Later Tendencies in Art." Address in 1926, Los Angeles, CA.

WRIGHT, W. LLOYD.
Painter. Member: SI. Address in 1929, 16 West 67th St.; 146 West 55th St., New York, NY.

WRIGHTSON, J.
Engraver. Born in England. He came to the United States about 1854. A reputable line engraver of landscape and book illustrations. Worked in Boston and in New York. Soon after 1860 he returned to England, and died there in 1865.

WUERMER, CARL.
Painter. Born Munich, Germany, Aug. 3, 1900. Pupil of AIC; Wellington J. Reynolds. Member: AIC Alumni; Allied AA; Springfield AL; IL. Acad. FA; Grand Cent. Gal.; Salons of America. Awards: Hon. mention, AIC, 1926; Eisendrath prize ($250), AIC, 1927; J. Francis Murphy Mem. prize, ($15) NAD; Springfield AL prize, ($50). Address in 1929, 325 West 45th St., Grand Central Art Galleries, 15 Vanderbilt Ave., New York, NY.

WUERPEL, EDMUND H(ENRY).
Painter, teacher, writer, and lecturer. Born St. Louis, May 13, 1866. Pupil of St. Louis Sch. of Fine Arts; Julian Acad. and Ecole des Beaux Arts in Paris under Bouguereau, Robert-Fleury, Ferrier and Aman Jean. Member: St. Louis AG; St. Louis Municipal A. L. (chairman, Art Co.); 2 x 4 Soc.; Paris AAA (hon.). Awards: Bronze medal, Nashville Exp., 1897; hors concours, St. Louis Exp., 1904; silver medal, Missouri Bldg., Lewis and Clarke Exp., OR, 1905; hon. men., Buenos Aires Exp., 1910; St. Louis AG life membership prize, 1914; hors concours, P. P. Exp., San F., 1915. Director, St. Louis School of Fine Arts since 1909. In collections of St. Louis; Herron Art Inst., Indianapolis; H.S. and Public Lib., St. Louis; Buenos Aires Mus.; State Capitol Jefferson City, WO; Church of Unity, St. Louis. Murals in MI Athletic Club and Carpenter Branch Lib. St. Louis, MO. Died in 1958. Address in 1929, 7707 Walinca Terr., Clayton, MO.

WUERTZ, EMIL H.
Painter. Born in Germany. Resided for years in Chicago. Died in 1898.

WULFF, TIMOTHY MILTON.
Painter. Born San Francisco, CA, Oct. 13, 1890. Pupil of Frank Van Sloun. Member: San F. AA. Work: "The Laughing Buffoon," in the Palace of Fine Arts, San Francisco.

Address in 1929, 2245 Turk St., San Francisco, CA.

WUNDER, ADALBERT.
Portrait painter and draughtsman in crayon and ink. Born in Germany in 1827. In 1855 he opened his studio in Hartford, CT.

WYAND, MRS. CHARLES L.
See Cockcroft, Edith Varian.

WYANT, ALEXANDER HELWIG.
Landscape painter. Born in Ohio, in 1836. Devoted himself in early life to painting photographs and portraits in Cincinnati. At 21 he visited George Inness, whose influence is shown in many of his most important works. Later a pupil of Hans Gude in Karlsruhe and a student of the works of Turner and Constable in London. Exhibited first at the Nat. Acad. of Design in NY, in 1865. Elected a Member of Nat. Academy. One of the founders of the American Water Color Society. His studio was in NY. Represented by painting in the Metropolitan Museum; Corcoran Art Gallery; National Gallery, Washington, DC. Died Nov. 29, 1892, in NYC.

WYCKOFF, JOSEPH.
Painter and teacher. Born Ottowa, KS, July 9, 1883. Pupil of AIC., PAFA, Jay Hambidge, Howard Giles. Member: Am. APL. Address in 1929, 248 Sherman Ave., New York, NY.

WYETH, ANDREW.
Painter. Born July 21, 1917, in Chadds Ford, PA. Studied with N.C. Wyeth, his father; received Hon. DFA from Colby & Horrard in 1955; also from Swarthmore, Dickinson, Tufts, Princeton, U. Penn., Amherst, Tufts and others. Awards from Penn. Acad. of Fine Arts (1947), Carnegie, Freedom medal. Numerous exhibits at Macbeth gallery (NYC), Doll and Richards (Boston) and PAFA. Other at Carnegie, Univ. of IL and St. Louis (City Art Mus). In collections of MOMA, Whitney, Carnegie, Univ. of Illinois, St. Louis (City Art), Montclair (NJ) Art Mus. MMA, Joslyn (Omaha) Art Mus., Munson Williams Proctor, Utica,

Addison Gallery (Andover) and Nat. Gallery, Oslo.

WYETH, NEWELL CONVERS.
Painter and illustrator. Born Needham, MA, Oct. 22, 1882. Pupil of Howard Pyle; also studied at Mechanic Art High Sch., Boston; Normal Art High Sch.; Eric Pape Sch. of Art, with Chas. W. Reed. Travelled West and executed many drawings of cowboys, cattle, landscapes; on return, commissioned by all major magazines and book publishers. Illustrated Stevenson's Treasure Island (1911) and Kidnapped (1913); Verne's Mysterious Island (1918); Cooper's Last of the Mohicans. Member: SI 1912; Phila. Sketch C.; Salma. C. 1908; Fellowship PAFA; Wilmington SFA; AFA; NAD. Awards: Beck prize, Phila. WCC, 1910; gold medal, P. P. Expos. San F., 1915. Murals in Missouri State Capitol; Hotel Traymore, Atlantic City; Reading Museum of Fine Arts; Federal Reserve Bank of Boston; NY Public Library; Hotel Utica, Utica, NY. Died in 1945. Address in 1929, Needham, MA; Chadd's Ford, PA.

WYLIE, ROBERT.
Genre painter. Born on the Isle of Man in 1839; died in Pont Aven, Brittany, in 1877. As a child he was brought to America by his parents. Settled in Phila. Pupil of Pennsylvania Acad. of Fine Arts, by the Directors of which he was sent in 1863 to France to study; entered the Ecole des Beaux Arts and worked under Gerome. Awarded second class medal, Paris Salon, 1872.

YATES, ELIZABETH M.
Painter and teacher. Born Stoke-on-Trent, Staffordshire, England, May 13, 1888. Pupil of Pratt Institute. Member: Buffalo GAA. Address in 1929, 374 McKinley Parkway, Buffalo, NY.

YEATS, JOHN BUTLER.
Painter. Born in Ireland in 1839; died in NY City in 1922. Father of the artist, Jack B. Yeats. Painted numerous portraits of well-known people. Member of the Society of Independent Artists.

YELLAND, RAYMOND.
Painter. Born in London, England, in 1848. He came to this country as a youth and studied at the National Academy. Also a pupil of James R. Brevoort and William Page. Among his paintings are: "Half-moon Beach;" "Mount Hood;" "The Columbia River." Died July 27, 1900, in Oakland, CA.

YELLIN, SAMUEL A.
Craftsman. Born Poland, March 2, 1886. Member: AIA; AFA; NY Arch. Lg.; Alliance; Phila. Alliance. Awards: Medal, AIC, Chicago, 1918; medal, Boston SA, 1920; American Institute of Architects medal, 1920; gold medal, Arch. Lg. of NY, 1922; Philadelphia Book Award, 1925. Work: Main entrance, golden door and all other metal work, Bok Carillon Tower, Mountain Lake, Fla.; main entrance, gates and other metal work, Harkness Memorial Quadrangle, Yale Univ.; metal work, Wash., Cathedral, Wash. DC; wrought iron pupil, Mercersburg Academy, Mercersburg, PA; wrought iron pulpit, St. Mary's Church, Detroit, MI; wrought iron work, St. George's Chapel, Newport, RI; wrought iron work, Federal Reserve Bank, Equitable Trust Co. and Central Savings Bank, New York, NY. Died in 1940. Address in 1929, 5520 Arch Street, Philadelphia, PA; h. 331 East Lancaster Pike, Wynnewood, PA.

YENS, KARL (JULIUS HEINRICH).
Mural and portrait painter, illustrator, etcher and teacher. Born Altona, Germany, Jan. 11, 1868. Pupil of Max Koch in Berlin; Constant and Laurens in Paris.

Member: CA AC; Calif. WCS; Laguna Beach AA; Artland C; Los Angeles PSC; Long Beach AA; Int. Bookplate Assoc.; AFA. Awards: Bronze and silver medals, Pan-CA Int. Exp., San Diego, 1915; 2nd Black prize, Calif. AC, 1919; hon. mention, Laguna Beach AA, 1921; 1st Stevens prize, Laguna Beach AA, 1922; 1st Huntington prize, CA WCS 1922; 1st prize, Southern CA Fair, Riverside, 1922; hon. mention, Southwest Museum, 1922; 1st Harrison prize, painters and sculptors exh., Los Angeles, 1923; hon. mention, Arizona State Fair, Phoenix, 1923; third prize, Orange County Fair, Calif., 1923; silver medal, Laguna Beach AA, 1924; grand prize, Laguna Beach AA, 1925; special award, Orange County Fair, Calif., 1925; first prize, Artists of Southern CA, San Diego, 1926; bronze medal, Biltmore Salon, Los Angeles, 1926; first prize, Int. Bookplate Assoc., 1927. Work: Mural decorations in City Hall, Altona, Germany; Country Club House, Brookline, MA; and in Duquesne Club, Pittsburgh, PA. Represented in the Los Angeles Museum of History, Science and Art. Died in 1945. Address in 1929, Laguna Beach, CA.

YEOMANS, WALTER C(URTIS).
Etcher and craftsman. Born Avon, IL, May 17, 1882. Pupil of Fursman, Senseney, Bicknell, AIC. Member: Chicago SE; Palette and Chisel C.; AFA. Address in 1929, Cornwall Bridge, CT.

YERKES, LANE HAMILTON.
(b. 1945). Born in Philadelphia, he attended the Philadelphia College of Art of Art for five years. His first published illustration was for Today Magazine in Pennsylvania in 1962. His work has been shown at the Commercial Museum and he has illustrated for Macmillan, Penthouse, Smithsonian Magazine and The Philadelphia Inquirer.

YEWELL, GEORGE HENRY.
Painter. Born in Havre-de-Grace, MD, Jan 20, 1830. Pupil of Thomas Hicks, NY; student at National Academy of Design, 1851-56. Studied in Paris, 1856-61, in atelier of Thomas Couture. Resided

in Rome, Italy, 1867-78, and for one winter in Cairo, Egypt; after 1878 in NY. Elected member of Nat. Acad., 1880; patron, Metropolitan Museum of Art, NY. Work chiefly portraits. Portraits include Isaac Davis, Alexander Mitchell, Frederick Layton and Robert Lucas. He died Sept. 26, 1923, at Lake George, NY.

YOHN, FREDERICK COFFAY.
Illustrator. Born Indianapolis, IN, Feb. 8, 1875. Pupil of Indianapolis Art School; ASL of NY under Mowbray. Began career in 1894 working for Harper's; illustrated for many book publishers; for Scribner's he did historical and battle scenes, illustrations for Henry Cabot Lodge's The Story of the Revolution. Member: SI 1901; GFLA. Permant collection in Libr. of Congress. Died 1933 in Norwalk. Address in 1929, Norwalk, CT.

YOUNG, ARTHUR (ART).
Cartoonist. Born Stephenson Co., IL, Jan. 14, 1866. Pupil of Julian Academy and Bouguereau in Paris. Cartoons and illustrations in Life, Collier's Weekly, The Masses, The Nation, Saturday Evening Post, etc. Died in 1943. Address in 1929, 9 East 17th Street, New York, NY; summer, Bethel, CT.

YOUNG, ARTHUR R(AYMOND).
Painter, illustrator, etcher, lecturer, and teacher. Born New York, July 10, 1895. Pupil of ASL of NY; NAD. Work: "Athlete" and "Woman Dressing her Hair," British Museum, London. Died 1943. Address in 1929, 154 West 55th Street, h. 417 East 58th Street, New York, NY; summer, Provincetown, MA.

YOUNG, C(HARLES) JAC.
Painter and etcher. Born Bavaria, Dec. 21, 1880. Pupil of E. M. Ward, C. Y. Turner at NAD. Member: Brooklyn SE; Calif. PM; Salma C.; Chicago SE; Yonkers AA; Provincetown AA. Awards: Kate W. Arms Memo. prize, etching, Brooklyn SE, 1928; purchase prize, painting, Yonkers AA, 1929. Represented in Los Angeles Museum; Newark Public Library; Art Gallery, Toronto, Canada; NY Public Library;

etchings, University of Nebraska; Art Inst. of Peoria, IL; Phila. Art Alliance; Art Inst. of Milwaukee; Corcoran Art Gallery, Washington; Hackley Gal. of Art, Muskegon, MI; Library of Congress; Print Club of Phila.; Smithsonian Inst.; painting, Museum of Science and Art, Yonkers, NY. Died in 1940. Address in 1929, 114 Highpoint Ave., Weehawken Heights, NJ.

YOUNG, CHARLES MORRIS.
Landscape painter. Born Gettysburg, PA, Sept. 23, 1869. Pupil of PAFA; Colarossi Acad. in Paris. Member: ANA. Awards: Toppan prize, PAFA; hon. mention, Pan-Am. Exp., Buffalo, 1901; silver medal, St. Louis Exp., 1904; gold medal, AC Phila., 1908; hon. mention, Carnegie Inst., Pittsburgh, 1910; silver medal, Buenos Aires Exp., 1910; gold medal P.- P. Exp., San F., 1915; Sesnan gold medal, PAFA, 1921; Stotesbury prize ($500), PAFA, 1925. Work: "Winter Morning after Snow," PA Acad., Phila. PA; "The North Wind," Corcoran Gallery, Washington, DC. Represented in Boston Art Club; St. Louis Art Club; Budapest National Gallery; Albright Art Gallery, Buffalo; Rochester Art Gallery; National Gallery, Santiago, Chile; Reading Art Museum; Pennsylvania Museum, Philadelphia. Died in 1964. Address in 1929, Radnor, PA.

YOUNG, ELIZA MIDDLETON COXE.
Painter. Born in Philadelphia in 1875. Pupil of Anshutz and Charles Morris Young. Work: "Garden Study," Herron Art Institute, Indianapolis. Address in 1929, Radnor, PA.

YOUNG, ELLSWORTH.
Painter. Member: Chicago SA; Chicago PS; Chicago Gal. A. Address in 1929, 310 Marion Street, Oak Park, IL.

YOUNG, ESTHER CHRISTENSEN.
(Mrs. Charles J. Young). Illustrator, etcher, craftsman, and writer. Born Milwaukee, WI, May 10, 1895. Pupil of Groom, Aiken, Sinclair. Member: WI PS; Clev. PC. Awards: Hon. mention, WI PS, 1924; second prize, Women's Arts and Industries Exp., NY, 1925.

Address in 1929, 1065 Avon Road, Schenectady, NY.

YOUNG, EVA H.
Miniature painter. Exhibited at the Penna. Academy of the Fine Arts, Philadelphia, 1922. Address in 1926, 115 West 16th Street, New York, NY.

YOUNG, GLADYS G.
Painter. Exhibited watercolors at the Penna. Academy of the Fine Arts, Philadelphia, 1925. Address in 1926, 67 Pinckney Street, Boston, MA.

YOUNG, GRACE.
Painter. Member: Cincinnati Woman's AC; AFA. Address in 1929, Art Academy, Cincinnati, OH.

YOUNG, JAMES H.
Engraver. Of Philadelphia, PA, from 1817-45. At times he was a member of the firms of Kneass & Young, and of Young & Delleker, both in business in Philadelphia. The only plates found signed by Young alone are early encyclopedia plates in line.

YOUNG, JAMES HARVEY.
Painter. Born June 14, 1830, in Salem, MA. Moved his studio to Boston in 1848. Worked largely in portraiture. Work: "Wm. Warren" (actor), painted in 1867; "Dr. Peabody" (Exeter Academy); "Mrs. John H. Holmes," "Horace Mann," "Edward Everett." Died 1918 in MA.

YOUNG, MAHONRI M.
Painter, etcher, and sculptor. Born Salt Lake City, Utah, Aug. 9, 1877. Pupil of ASL in NY; Julian Academy in Paris. Member: ANA, 1912; NA, 1923; NSS, 1910; Paris AA; Soc. of Utah Artists; NY Arch. Lg. 1911; Chicago SE; NYWCC; NY SE; New Soc. A.; NAC. Awards: Hon. mention for etching, Paris AAA; Barnett prize, NAD, 1911; silver medal for sculpture, P.- P. Exp., San. F., 1915. Work: Etchings and "Man with Pick," and "Stevedore," Metropolitan Museum, NY; Hopi, Navajo and Apache groups, American Museum of Natural History, NY; bronzes, "A Laborer" and "The Rigger," and etchings, Newark Museum; etchings, NY Public

Library; "Sea Gull Monument," Salt Lake City; bronze, Peabody Inst., Baltimore, MD; Rhode Island School of Design, Providence; painting and sculpture, Art Inst. of Utah, Salt Lake City. Instructor, School of American Sculpture. Died Nov. 2, 1957, in Norwalk, CT. Address in 1929, 143 Prospect Street, Leonia, NJ.

YOUNG, MARY ELIZA.
Miniature painter. Married Samuel B. Waugh. She was the mother of Frederick J. Waugh, the painter.

YOUNG, SUSANNE BOTTOMLEY.
Painter. Born New York, NY, Dec. 28, 1891. Pupil of Alexander, George de Forest Brush. Work: Frieze in Club Royal, New York; ceiling in Le Paradis, Washington, DC. Address in 1929, 73 Hilton Ave., Garden City, LI, NY.

YOUNG, THOMAS.
Painter. Native of Providence, RI, where he produced numerous portraits. The portraits of Thomas Coles and John Matthewson Eddy by Young were in the Providence Athenaeum. Also painted a portrait of Nehemiah Knight, Governor of Rhode Island.

YOUNG, WILLIAM CRAWFORD.
Illustrator. Born Cannonsburg, MI, March 26, 1886. Pupil of AIC and Chicago Art Academy. Member: Silvermine GA. Staff contributor to "Judge" and King Features Syndicate. Address in 1929, Comstock Hill, Norwalk, CT.

YOUNGERMAN, JACK.
Painter and sculptor. Born in Louisville, KY, March 25, 1926. Study: Univ. of NC, 1944-46; Univ. of MO, AB 1947; Ecole des Beaux Arts, Paris, 1947-48. Work: Whitney Mus., MOMA, Guggenheim, all NYC; Hirshhorn Mus., Wash. DC; Art Inst. Chic. Comn.: First PA Bank, Phila., 1966; The Ohio (fiberglass), Pittsburgh Plate Glass, 1977; etc. Exhib.: Guggenheim, Whitney, Jewish Mus., NYU, all NYC; Carnegie Inst., Pittsburgh; Hirshhorn Mus.; Haus der Kunst, Munich. Awards: Nat'l. Counc. Arts & Sci. award, 1966; Nat'l. Endow. Arts award, 1972;

Fellow, Guggenheim Fund., 1976.
Teaching: Yale Univ., 1974-75;
Hunter College, 1981-82; NYU,
1982-83. Rep.: Washburn Gallery,
42 East 57th St., NYC. Address in
1983, 130 W. 3rd St., NYC.

YOUNG-HUNTER, JOHN.
Painter. Born Glasgow, Scotland,
Oct. 29, 1878. Pupil of Royal
Academy Schools under Sargent,
Alma-Tadema and others. Member:
Chelsea AC, London; NAC; Salma. C.;
CT AFA; Allied A. Awards: Hon.
mention, Paris Salon, 1910; silver
medal, Paris Salon, 1914; Dunham
prize, Hartford, 1925. Work: "My
Lady's Garden," the National
Gallery of British Art, London;
"The Dream," Luxembourg, Paris;
"Two Voices," Walker Art Gallery,
Liverpool, England; "Judith
Shakespeare," Art Museum,
Wellington, New Zealand; "Portrait,
Pres. King," Oberlin (OH) Museum;
portrait study, Dayton Museum;
"Raymond Henniker-Heaton,"
Worcester Museum; "Duke of Argyll,"
Government House, Ottawa, Canada.
Died in 1955. Address in 1929, 130
West 57th Street, New York, NY;
summer, Taos, NM.

ZAJAC, JACK.
Sculptor. Born Dec. 13, 1929, in
Youngstown, Ohio. Began as
painter. Studied at Scripps College
in CA; with Millard Sheets, Henry
McFee and Sueo Sarisawa; also at
Am. Acad. in Rome. Taught at
Dartmouth and Pomona. Awards:
From Butler Inst. of Art
(Youngstown); Pasadena Art Museum;
Am. Acad. of Arts and Letters
grant; Guggenheim fellowship;
Limited Editions Club etching
prize; Prix de Rome (3 years).
Exhibited at Felix Landau Gallery
(many times); Pasadena Art Mus.;
Scripps College; Whitney; U. of
Illinois; Whitney Mus.; MOMA;
Guggenheim Mus. (all in NY); UCLA
Mus. of Art, Santa Barbara, CA;
Smithsonian Inst. (drawings by
sculptors); Temple U. in Rome. In
collections of U. of Nebraska at
Lincoln; L. A. Co. Mus.; PAFA;
Calif. Fed. Savings and Loan Assn.;
MOMA.

ZENNER, ROSE.
Painter. Member: Cincinnati
Woman's AC. Address in 1929, 2947
Gilbert Ave., Cincinnati, OH.

ZETTLER, EMIL ROBERT.
Sculptor. Born Chicago. Studied
at AIC; Royal Academy of Berlin;
Julian Academy in Paris. Awards:
Hon. mention, AIC, 1912; medal,
Chicago SA, 1915; bronze medal, P.-
P. Exp., San F., 1915; silver
medal, AIC, 1915; Potter Palmer
gold medal, AIC, 1916; Logan medal
AIC, 1917; Harry A. Frank prize,
AIC, 1921; French memorial gold
medal, AIC, 1925. Work: Municipal
Art Collection, Chicago. Professor
and Head of School of Industrial
Art of The Art Institute of
Chicago; Asst. Professor, Armour
Inst. of Technology. Died Jan. 10,
1946. Address in 1929, 4 East Ohio
Street, Chicago, IL.

ZIEGLER, EUSTACE PAUL.
Painter, illustrator, writer, and
lecturer. Born Detroit, MI, July
24, 1881. Pupil of Ida Marie
Perrault, Yale School of Fine Arts.
Work: Mural decorations in Alaska
Steamship offices, Seattle;
Steamship "Alaska"; mural
decorations in Olympic Hotel,
Seattle, Wash. Died in 1941.

Address in 1929, 5514 White Bldg.,
Seattle, WA.

ZIEGLER, SAMUEL P.
Painter and teacher. Born
Lancaster, PA, Jan. 4, 1882. Pupil
of PAFA under Chase, Anshutz and
Breckenridge. Member: SSAL; Ft.
Worth AA: Fellowship PAFA; Ft.
Worth AA; Fellowship PAFA; Ft.
Worth PC; AFA. Award: Bailey gold
medal, Dallas, 1925; first still
life prize, Nashville, TN., 1927;
first lithograph prize, SSAL, 1929.
Work: "Carnegie Public Library,
Night," Univ. C., Ft. Worth; "A
Texas Acropolis," Burnett Library,
Texas Christian Univ., Ft. Worth;
"Winter Landscape," Ft. Worth
Museum of Art. Died in 1967.
Address in 1929, 2908 Cassell
Blvd.; summer; Texas Christian
Univeristy, Ft. Worth, Texas.

ZILVE, ALIDA.
Sculptor. Born Amsterdam, Holland.
Pupil of Allen G. Newman, Earl
Stetson Crawford. Work:
Bas-reliefs, "Four Master
Schooner," Seaman's Savings Bank,
New York: "Pioneer, " Oil City, PA;
"David H. Burrell," YMCA, Little
Falls, NY; "John A. Collier,"
Canastota Memorial Hospital,
Canastota, NY; "John S. Schofield,"
Macon, GA; "Herman Mahnkin," YWCA,
Bayonne, NJ; "Woodrow Wilson,"
Independent Memorial Bldg., United
Daughters of the Confederacy,
Independence, MO; "Mayor Newman,"
Elks Club, Paterson, NJ; "Edw. V.
Walton," Roselle High School, NJ;
"George Washington," Hempstead, LI;
"Lafayette," Junior High School,
Elizabeth, NJ. Died in 1935.
Address in 1929, 536 West 111th
Street, New York, NY.

ZIM, MARCO.
Painter, etcher,and sculptor. Born
Moscow, Russia, Jan. 9, 1880.
Pupil of ASL of NY under George
Gray Barnard; NAD under Ward and
Maynard; Ecole des Beaux-Arts in
Paris under Bonnat. Member:
Artland Club, Los Angeles; Los
Angeles PSC. Address in 1929, 54
West 74th Street, New York, NY.

ZIMM, BRUNO LOUIS.
Sculptor and artist. Born New
York, Dec. 29, 1876. Pupil of J.

Q. A. Ward, Augustus Saint Gaudens and Karl Bitter. Member: NSS. Award: First mention, collaborative competition, NY Arch. Lg., 1913; silver medal, Paris Exp., 1900. Work: Slocum Memorial and Memorial Fountain, NY; Finnegan Memorial, Houston; Murdoch Memorial, Wichita; sculpture in rotunda of Art Bldg., San Francisco; bust of Robert E. Lee, Baylor College, Belton, Texas; panels of Sergt. York and Paul Revere, Seaboard National Bank, NY; Edward C. Young tablet, 1st Nat. Bank, Jersey City; sculptures, St. Pancras Church and St. Thomas Church, Brooklyn, NY. Died in 1943. Address in 1929, Woodstock, NY.

ZIMMELE, MARGARET.
Painter, sculptor, and illustrator. Born Pittsburgh, PA, Sept. 1, 1872. Pupil of Chase, Shirlaw, Whittemore, Lathrop, Carlson, Hawthorne. Member: S. Wash. A.; Pittsburgh AA; Wash. AC. Address in 1929, 2728-36th Place, Washington, DC; summer, Great Barrington, MA.

ZIMMERMAN, EUGENE ("ZIM").
Caricaturist. Born Basel, Switzerland, May 25, 1862. On staff of "Puck" from 1882; "Judge" from 1884. Author of "This and That About Caricature," "Cartoons and Caricatures," "Home Spun Philosophy." Conducted correspondence school of caricature, cartooning and comic art. Died in 1935. Address in 1929, Horseheads, Chemung Co., NY.

ZIMMERMAN, FREDERICK A(LMOND.).
Painter and sculptor. Born Canton, OH, Oct. 7, 1886. Pupil of University of So. Calif. and Victor D. Brenner. Member: Scarab Club; Calif. AC: Laguna Beach AA; Pasadena SA; So. Calif. SAC; AFA; Am. APL. Address in 1929, 225 South Los Robles Ave., Pasadena, Calif.

ZIMMERMAN, L(ILLIAN) H(ORTENSE.).
Sculptor. Born Milwaukee. Pupil of AIC; ASL of NY. Member: Wis. PS. Award: Medal and prize for sculpture, Milwaukee Art Inst., 1924. Address in 1929, 234 Mason Street, Milwaukee, WI.

ZIMMERMAN, M(ASON) W.
Painter. Born Philadelphia, PA, Aug. 4, 1861. Pupil of Juliar Academy; John Wesley Little. Member: Phila. WCC; Phila. Sketch C.; Salma. C.; Phila. Alliance; AWCS; Wash. WCC; Balt. WCC. Address in 1929, 1518 Waverly Street, Phila., PA; h. Rydal, PA.

ZIROLI, ANGELO.
Sculptor, craftsman, and writer. Born Italy, Aug. 10, 1899. Pupil of Albin Polasek, Antonin Sterba, Vittorio Gigliotti. Member: Chicago Gal. A.; Ill. AFA. Awards: Dunham prize, 1923, Shaffer prize, 1924, AIC, Chicago; first prize for sculpture, Soc. of Wash. Artists, Washington, DC, 1928. Author of "The Life of a Chicago Sculptor." Died in 1948. Address in 1929, Rauen Studios, 245 West North Ave.; h. 717 South Racine Ave., Chicago, IL; summer, Montenero Valcocchiara, Prov. Campobasso, Italy.

ZOLNAY, GEORGE JULIAN.
Sculptor and teacher. Born July 4, 1863. Pupil of Imperial Academy of Fine Arts in Vienna; National Academy of Bucharest. Member: NAC; St. Louis AG; Wash. AC; Union Inter. des Arts et Sciences, Paris; S. Wash. A.; Circolo Artistico, Rome; Tinerimia Romana, Bucharest. Awards: Gold medal, St. Louis Exp., 1904; gold medal, Portland Exp., 1905. Decorated by the King of Romania with the Order "Bene Merenti" first class. Work: "Pierre Laclede Monument," and Confederate monument, St. Louis, MO; "Winnie Davis" and "Jefferson Davis" monuments, Richmond, VA; "Soldiers Monument" and "Sam Davis Monument," Nashville, TN; "Gen. Bartow" and "Gen. McLaws" monument, Savannah, GA; "Soldiers Monument," Owensboro, KY; "Edgar Allan Poe Monument," University of Virginia, Charlottesville, VA; colossal, "Lions," on City Gates, University City, MO; main group, US Customs House, San Francisco, CA; Labor Monument, New Bedford, MA; Sequoyah Statue, US Capitol, Washington; War Memorial, and sculpture of the Parthenon, Nashville, TN. Represented in the Bucharest Royal Inst.; St. Louis Museum; Herron Art Inst., Indianapolis. Address in

1929, 1738 N. St., N. W., Washington, DC; 15 Gramercy Park, New York, NY.

ZORACH, MARGUERITE THOMPSON.
Painter. Born Santa Rosa, CA, Sept. 25, 1888. Member: NY Soc. Women A. Died in 1968. Address in 1929, 123 West 10th Street, New York, NY; summer, Robinhood Farm, Robinhood, ME.

ZORACH, WILLIAM.
Sculptor. Born Feb. 28, 1887, in Eurburg, Lithuania. Lived in NYC and Maine. Studied at Cleveland Inst. of Art, Nat. Acad of Design (NYC) and in Paris. Taught at Des Moines Art Center; Art Students League (NYC) from 1929 to 1966. Awards: MFA (hon.), Bowdoin C.; DFA, Colby C.; Eidener Memorial Medal. Exhibited at Taylor Gal., Downtown Gal., Whitney Mus., Queens College, Brooklyn Mus., Zabriskie Gal. (all in NYC); Art Inst. of Chicago ASL; Contemporary Arts Center, Cincinnati, OH. In collections of Phillips Acad., Andover; Newark Mus.; Webb Gal., VT; Butler Inst., Youngstown, OH; Univ. of Nebraska, Lincoln; Whitney Mus., Columbia U. (both in NYC); IBM. Died Nov. 15, 1966.

ZYLINSKI, ANDREW.
Painter. Born 1869 in Zaile, Lithuania. Pupil of Wojciech, Gerson, and Warsaw (Poland) School of Design. Member: St. Louis Art League. Work: "Early Morning," Delgado Art Museum; "Mark Twain," Commercial Club, Hannibal, MO. Address in 1929, Box 195, Ebenezer, NY.